Contemporary Authors

NEW REVISION SERIES

Contemporary Authors

A Bio-Bibliographical Guide to
Current Writers in Fiction, General Nonfiction,
Poetry, Journalism, Drama, Motion Pictures,
Television, and Other Fields

ANN EVORY
Editor

PETER M. GAREFFA
LINDA METZGER
Associate Editors

NEW REVISION SERIES
volume **6**

GALE RESEARCH COMPANY • THE BOOK TOWER • DETROIT, MICHIGAN 48226

EDITORIAL STAFF

Christine Nasso, *General Editor, Contemporary Authors*

Ann Evory, *Editor, New Revision Series*

Peter M. Gareffa and Linda Metzger, *Associate Editors*

Deborah A. Straub and Thomas Wiloch, *Senior Assistant Editors*

Elaine Guregian, David A. Guy, Stewart R. Hakola, Debra G. Jones, James G. Lesniak,
Margaret Mazurkiewicz, Donna Olendorf, Nancy M. Rusin, Heidi A. Tietjen,
Marian C. Walters, and Michaela Swart Wilson, *Assistant Editors*

Melissa J. Gaiownik, Ellen Koral, and Susan Salter, *Editorial Assistants*

Thomas E. Dasher, Jean W. Ross, and Walter W. Ross, *Interviewers*

Frederick G. Ruffner, *Publisher*   James M. Ethridge, *Editorial Director*

Authors Featured in This Volume

Among the 950 listings in *Contemporary Authors New Revision Series*,
Volume 6, are full-length sketches on these authors and media people.

Chinua Achebe—Nigerian professor of English; considered by many critics to be one of the best contemporary African novelists; author, in English, of novels, short stories, essays, and poems, including *Things Fall Apart*, *Girls at War*, and *Morning Yet on Creation Day*.

Robert S. Allen—Late American journalist; author of the syndicated newspaper columns "Washington Merry-Go-Round," with Drew Pearson, from 1931 to 1942 and "Inside Washington" from 1949 to 1980.

A.R. Ammons—American poet whose work is known for its short lines, sparse punctuation and overall brevity; his *Collected Poems: 1951-1971* received the National Book Award in Poetry in 1973; other works include *Tape for the Turn of the Year*, a long poem composed on adding machine tape, and *A Coast of Trees*.

Jack Anderson—American journalist; co-author with Drew Pearson of the syndicated newspaper column "Washington Merry-Go-Round" from 1965 to 1969 and sole author since 1969; awarded a Pulitzer Prize for national reporting in 1972; he has published several nonfiction books and a novel, *The Cambodia File*.

Herbert Aptheker—American historian and director of the American Institute for Marxist Studies; editor of *The Correspondence of W.E.B. Du Bois* and *The Complete Published Work of W.E.B. Du Bois* and author of numerous nonfiction books. (Sketch includes interview.)

Eric Bentley—British-born American drama critic turned playwright; known not only for his theory of drama, outlined in such books as *In Search of Theater* and *The Life of the Drama*, but also for his work as an editor, translator, and playwright. (Sketch includes interview.)

Gwendoline Williams Butler—British mystery novelist; called one of Britain's best crime writers by a *Times Literary Supplement* reviewer, she is the author of police novels, featuring Detective Inspector John Coffin, and historical mysteries; also author of novels under the pseudonym Jennie Melville.

Victor Canning—Prolific British mystery novelist; *The Satan Sampler* and *Fall from Grace* are among the more than fifty books listed in his sketch.

Barbara Cartland—British writer known as the "Queen of Romance"; the *Guinness Book of World Records* lists her as the world's best-selling author (nearly three hundred million copies of her books have been sold); over three hundred titles are listed in her *CA* bibliography. (Sketch includes interview.)

Roald Dahl—Welsh-born writer of juvenile books, short stories for adults and children, and screenplays; notable titles cited in his bibliography include the screenplays "Chitty Chitty Bang Bang" and "Willy Wonka and the Chocolate Factory."

Gordon R. Dickson—Canadian-born American science fiction writer; his award-winning novels include *Soldier, Ask Not*, *Time Storm*, and *The Far Call*.

Daphne du Maurier—British Gothic novelist and short-story writer whose *Rebecca* is considered a forerunner of the modern romantic novel; also author of *My Cousin Rachel*, *Frenchman's Creek*, and *The Rendez-vous, and Other Stories*.

Ernest J. Gaines—American novelist and short-story writer; author of *Bloodline*, a collection of short stories, and *The Autobiography of Miss Jane Pittman*, a novel later adapted for television.

William Goyen—American short-story writer, novelist, and playwright; author of the novels *The House of Breath* and *In a Farther Country*, among others; many short stories have appeared in prize story collections. (Sketch includes interview.)

Joe Haldeman—American science fiction novelist and short-story writer; his novel *The Forever War* won Hugo, Nebula, and Locus Awards, and *Mindbridge* received the 1978 Galaxy Award. (Sketch includes interview.)

James Jones—Late American novelist; winner of the 1951 National Book Award for *From Here to Eternity*.

Tom Jones—American playwright and lyricist; author of book and/or lyrics for musical comedies, including "The Fantasticks," "I Do! I Do!," and "Colette." (Sketch includes interview.)

Pauline Kael—American film critic for the *New Yorker*; her articles and movie reviews have been published in collections, including *Deeper into Movies*, for which she received the 1974 National Book Award, *Reeling*, and *When the Lights Go Down*. (Sketch includes interview.)

Stanley Kauffmann—American film and theatre critic and playwright; author of fiction and nonfiction works and a recently published book of memoirs, *Albums of Early Life*. (Sketch includes interview.)

Harry Kemelman—American author of the Nicky Welt mystery stories and the popular detective novels *Friday, the Rabbi Slept Late*, *Saturday, the Rabbi Went Hungry*, etc., featuring Rabbi David Small.

Walter Lippmann—Late American political journalist; author of the "Today and Tomorrow" column, syndicated in over 275 papers, and a fortnightly column for *Newsweek*.

Norah Lofts—Popular British historical novelist whose published works include *Jassy, Crown of Aloes,* and *The Old Priory.* (Sketch includes interview.)

Ngaio Marsh—Late New Zealand theatrical producer and mystery writer; her novels, many featuring Inspector Roderick Alleyn, include *A Man Lay Dead, Hand in Glove,* and *Photo Finish;* also author of nonfiction books and an autobiography, *Black Beech and Honeydew.*

Robert Nathan—American novelist whose work is known for its quiet, melancholic mood, precise prose, and satirical fantasy; notable titles include *The Orchid, The Bishop's Wife,* and *Portrait of Jennie.*

John Nichols—American novelist who told *CA* he tries to be both polemical and entertaining in his writings, which include *The Sterile Cuckoo* and *The Nirvana Blues.*

John Jay Osborn, Jr.—American attorney; his novel *The Paper Chase,* has been adapted for film and television.

Andrew Russell Pearson—Late American journalist who wrote under the name Drew Pearson; author (originally with Robert S. Allen and later with Jack Anderson) of the newspaper column "Washington Merry-Go-Round," a mixture of Washington gossip, political commentary, and investigative reporting; also author of nonfiction books and two novels.

Wilferd Arlan Peterson—Former advertising executive; author of "The Art of Living," a series of inspirational essays with topics ranging from the art of success to the art of loafing.

John Crowe Ransom—Late American professor, critic, and poet; founded and edited *Kenyon Review* as a forum for The New Criticism, a method Ransom and others used to analyze works of art.

John Rechy—American novelist and nonfiction writer; author of six novels, including *City of Night, The Fourth Angel,* and *Rushes.* (Sketch includes interview.)

H.A. Rey—Late German-born creator of the "Curious George" series of children's books with his wife, Margret Rey, and author of many other self-illustrated juvenile publications; an amateur astronomer, he also wrote *The Stars* for adults and *Find the Constellations* for children.

John A.T. Robinson—British clergyman; author of popular books on theology including *Honest to God,* a best-selling and controversial work in which he advocated a demythologized and personal God.

Leo C. Rosten—Polish-born American humorist; creator of a series of books featuring the comic character Hyman Kaplan; author of nonfiction, screenplays, and other fiction, including *Captain Newman, M.D., The Joys of Yiddish,* and recently published detective novels *Silky!* and *King Silky!* (Sketch includes interview.)

Francoise Sagan—French writer; best known for her shocking, yet successful, first novel, *Bonjour tristesse,* written when she was eighteen; also author of many other novels (all of which have been translated into English), plays, and nonfiction.

Charles M. Schulz—American cartoonist and illustrator; creator of "Peanuts," one of the most popular comic strips of all time, and author of related books, teleplays, and movies. (Sketch includes interview.)

Khushwant Singh—Indian novelist, short-story writer, historian, journalist, and editor; best known in the Western world for his books *Train to Pakistan* and *I Shall Not Hear the Nightingale.*

Martin Cruz Smith—American free-lance writer; author of the 1981 best-selling novel *Gorky Park* and other books under various pseudonyms.

William Styron—American novelist; winner of the 1968 Pulitzer Prize for *The Confessions of Nat Turner* and the 1980 American Book Award for *Sophie's Choice.* (Sketch includes interview.)

John Toland—American historian and writer; author of many nonfiction books, including *The Rising Sun,* for which he was awarded the Pulitzer Prize in 1970.

Barbara Ward—Late British economist and writer; author of sometimes controversial works promoting international unity, including *Only One Earth* and *Progress for a Small Planet.*

Auberon Waugh—British novelist, political journalist, essayist, and critic whose work is often compared to that of his father, Evelyn Waugh; stopped writing novels in 1973 to protest the British free public library system and has sinced published nonfiction; works include the novels *The Foxglove Saga* and *Consider the Lilies* and the essay collection *In the Lion's Den.*

John A. Williams—American journalist, professor, and writer; author of novels, short stories, and nonfiction, which often explore the black experience in the United States. (Sketch includes interview.)

Herman Wouk—American novelist and playwright; received the Pulitzer Prize in 1952 for *The Caine Mutiny* and has sinced published several other best sellers, including *The Winds of War* and *War and Remembrance.* (Sketch includes interview.)

Preface

The *Contemporary Authors New Revision Series* provides completely updated information on authors listed in previously published volumes of *Contemporary Authors*. Entries for active individual authors from *any* volume of *CA* may be included in a volume of the *New Revision Series*.

As always, the most recent *Contemporary Authors* cumulative index continues to be the user's guide to the location of an individual author's listing.

Compilation Methods

The editors make every effort to secure information directly from the authors. Clippings of all sketches in selected *CA* volumes published several years ago are sent to the authors at their last-known addresses. Authors mark material to be deleted or changed, and insert any new personal data, new affiliations, new books, new work in progress, new sidelights, and new biographical/critical sources. All author returns are assessed, additional research is done, if necessary, and those sketches with significant change are published in the *New Revision Series*.

If, however, authors fail to reply, or if authors are now deceased, biographical dictionaries are checked for new information (a task made easier through the use of Gale's *Biography and Genealogy Master Index*), as are bibliographical sources, such as *Cumulative Book Index, The National Union Catalog*, etc. Using data from such sources, revision editors select and revise nonrespondents' entries which need substantial updating. Sketches not personally reviewed by the authors are marked with a dagger (†) to indicate that these listings have been revised from secondary sources believed to be reliable, but they have not been personally reviewed for this edition by the authors sketched.

In addition, reviews and articles in major periodicals, lists of prestigious awards, and requests from *CA* users are monitored so that authors on whom new information is in demand can be identified and revised listings prepared promptly.

Comprehensive Revision

All listings in this volume have been revised and/or augmented in various ways, though the amount and type of change vary with the author. Revised entries include additions of or changes in such information as degrees, mailing addresses, literary agents, career items, career-related and civic activities, memberships, work in progress, and biographical/critical sources. They may also include the following:

1) Major new awards—Science fiction writer Joe Haldeman's recent efforts have not gone unnoticed by others in his field; his revised entry records the Nebula, Galaxy, two Hugo, and two Locus awards he has received since his sketch last appeared in *CA*. Late British economist Barbara Ward's activities promoting international unity earned her many honors, which, of course, are listed in her revised *CA* sketch. The recipient of numerous honorary degrees, Ward also received three Christopher Book Awards and was named Dame Commander, Order of the British Empire; the year before her death in 1981, Ward also received the Albert Medal of the Royal Society of Arts and the Jawaharlal Nehru Memorial Award for International Understanding.

2) Extensive bibliographical additions—Senior assistant editor Deborah A. Straub corresponded with British novelist Barbara Cartland and the author's American representative and publishers to compile a writings section of over three hundred books; Cartland's *CA* entry now contains one of the most comprehensive bibliographies available for this prolific and popular author.

3) Informative new sidelights—Since its inception in 1931, the syndicated column "Washington Merry-Go-Round" has been published under the by-line of three different journalists—Robert S. Allen, Jack Anderson, and Drew Pearson. Revised entries for each of these columnists conveniently appear in this volume of the *New Revision Series* with sidelights that provide an historical overview of the column and insight into the divergent personalities of its authors. Equally informative sidelights have been prepared for other writers as well, including Chinua Achebe, A.R. Ammons, James Jones, Ngaio Marsh, Robert Nathan, Martin Cruz Smith, and Auberon Waugh.

Writers of Special Interest

CA's editors make every effort to include in each *New Revision Series* volume a substantial number of revised entries on active authors and media people of special interest to *CA*'s readers. Since the *New Revision Series* also includes sketches on deceased authors of special interest, a great deal of effort on the part of *CA*'s editors goes into the revision of entries on important deceased authors. Some of the prominent writers whose sketches are contained in this volume are noted in the list headed "Authors Featured in This Volume" immediately preceding the preface.

Exclusive Interviews

CA provides exclusive, primary information on certain authors in the form of interviews. Prepared specifically for *CA*, the never-before-published conversations presented in the section of the sketch headed *CA INTERVIEW* give *CA* users the opportunity to learn the authors' thoughts, in depth, about their craft. Subjects chosen for interviews are, the editors feel, authors who hold special interest for *CA*'s readers.

Authors and journalists in this volume whose sketches include interviews are Herbert Aptheker, Eric Bentley, Barbara Cartland, William Goyen, Joe Haldeman, Tom Jones, Pauline Kael, Stanley Kauffmann, Norah Lofts, John Rechy, Leo C. Rosten, Charles M. Schulz, William Styron, John A. Williams, and Herman Wouk.

Retaining *CA* Volumes

As the chart on the following page indicates, *CA* users who have all First Revision volumes *and* both *Contemporary Authors Permanent Series* volumes can discard corresponding unrevised volumes 1 through 44.

Since the *New Revision Series* does not supersede any specific volumes of *CA*, all of the following must be retained in order to have information on all authors in the series:

- all revised volumes
- the two *Contemporary Authors Permanent Series* volumes
- *CA* Volumes 45-48 and subsequent original volumes

Cumulative Index Should Always Be Consulted

The *CA* cumulative index published in alternate new volumes of *CA* continues to be the user's guide to the location of an individual author's original and revised entries. Those authors appearing in the *New Revision Series* are listed in the *CA* index with the designation CANR- in front of the specific volume number. For the convenience of those who do not have *New Revision Series* volumes, the index also notes the specific earlier volume of *CA* in which the sketch appeared. Below is a sample *New Revision Series* index citation:

> Vonnegut, Kurt, Jr. 1922- CANR-1
> Earlier sketch in CA 3R
> See also CLC 1, 2, 3, 4, 5, 8, 12
> See also AITN 1

For the most recent information on Vonnegut, users should refer to Volume 1 of the *New Revision Series,* as designated by "CANR-1"; if that volume is unavailable, refer to *CA* 1-4 First Revision, as indicated by "Earlier sketch in CA 3R," for his 1968 listing. (And if *CA* 1-4 First Revision is unavailable, refer to *CA* 3, published in 1963, for Vonnegut's original listing.)

Sketches not eligible for inclusion in a *New Revision Series* volume because the author or a revision editor has verified that no significant change is required will, of course, be available in previously published *CA* volumes. Users should always consult the most recent *CA* cumulative index to determine the location of these authors' entries.

For the convenience of *CA* users, the *CA* cumulative index also includes references to all entries in three

(Preface continues on page following chart)

IF YOU HAVE:	YOU MAY DISCARD:
1-4 First Revision (1967)	1 (1962) 2 (1963) 3 (1963) 4 (1963)
5-8 First Revision (1969)	5-6 (1963) 7-8 (1963)
Both 9-12 First Revision (1974) AND *Contemporary Authors Permanent Series*, Volume 1 (1975)	9-10 (1964) 11-12 (1965)
Both 13-16 First Revision (1975) AND *Contemporary Authors Permanent Series*, Volumes 1 and 2 (1975, 1978)	13-14 (1965) 15-16 (1966)
Both 17-20 First Revision (1976) AND *Contemporary Authors Permanent Series*, Volumes 1 and 2 (1975, 1978)	17-18 (1967) 19-20 (1968)
Both 21-24 First Revision (1977) AND *Contemporary Authors Permanent Series*, Volumes 1 and 2 (1975, 1978)	21-22 (1969) 23-24 (1970)
Both 25-28 First Revision (1977) AND *Contemporary Authors Permanent Series*, Volume 2 (1978)	25-28 (1971)
Both 29-32 First Revision (1978) AND *Contemporary Authors Permanent Series*, Volume 2 (1978)	29-32 (1972)
Both 33-36 First Revision (1978) AND *Contemporary Authors Permanent Series*, Volume 2 (1978)	33-36 (1973)
37-40 First Revision (1979)	37-40 (1973)
41-44 First Revision (1979)	41-44 (1974)
45-48 (1974) 49-52 (1975) 53-56 (1975) 57-60 (1976) ↓ ↓ 104 (1982)	NONE: These volumes will not be super- seded by corresponding revised volumes. Individual entries from these and all other volumes appearing in the left col- umn of this chart will be revised and included in the *New Revision Series*.
Volumes in the *Contemporary Authors New Revision Series*	NONE: The *New Revision Series* does not replace any single volume of *CA*. All volumes appearing in the left column of this chart must be retained to have in- formation on all authors in the series.

related Gale series—*Contemporary Literary Criticism* (CLC), which is devoted entirely to current criticism of the works of today's novelists, poets, playwrights, short story writers, filmmakers, screenwriters, and other creative writers, *Something About the Author* (SATA), a series of heavily illustrated sketches on authors and illustrators of books for young people, and *Authors in the News* (AITN), a compilation of news stories and feature articles from American newspapers and magazines covering writers and other members of the communications media.

As always, suggestions from users about any aspect of *CA* will be welcomed.

CONTEMPORARY
AUTHORS
NEW REVISION SERIES

*† Indicates that a listing has been revised from secondary sources believed to be reliable,
but has not been personally reviewed for this edition by the author sketched.*

ABELSON, Raziel A(lter) 1921-

PERSONAL: Born June 24, 1921, in New York, N.Y.; son of Alter (a rabbi) and Anna (Schwartz) Abelson; married Ulrike Koenigsfeld, August 24, 1947; children: Gabriel. *Education:* Brooklyn College (now Brooklyn College of the City University of New York), student, 1938-40; University of Chicago, M.A., 1950; New York University, Ph.D., 1957. *Politics:* Socialist. *Religion:* Jewish. *Office:* Department of Philosophy, New York University, New York, N.Y.

CAREER: Hunter College (now Hunter College of the City University of New York), New York City, 1950-52; New York University, New York City, 1953—, currently professor of philosophy. Visiting professor at Columbia University, 1962, University of Hawaii, 1965, State University of New York at Buffalo, 1967, and University of California, San Diego, 1970; visiting scholar at Institute of Advanced Studies in Behavioral Sciences, Stanford University, 1965. *Wartime service:* U.S. Maritime Service, radio officer, 1942-46; became lieutenant junior grade. *Member:* American Philosophical Association, American Psychological Association, Mathematical Association of America, American Association of University Professors. *Awards, honors:* Carnegie Foundation fellowship in law and philosophy, 1962; American Council of Learned Societies grant-in-aid, 1968.

WRITINGS—All published by St. Martin's: *Ethics and Metaethics: Readings in Ethical Philosophy,* 1963; *Ethics for Modern Life,* 1975; *Persons: A Study in Philosophical Psychology,* 1977; *The Philosophical Imagination: An Introduction to Philosophy,* 1977. Contributor of articles to encyclopedias and anthologies, and of essays and reviews to philosophy journals.

AVOCATIONAL INTERESTS: Literature, tennis, automobile mechanics, child psychology.†

*   *   *

ABRAMOWITZ, Jack 1918-

PERSONAL: Born October 29, 1918, in Brooklyn, N.Y.; son of Rubin and Bessie (Singer) Abramowitz; married Isabel Lishman, July 22, 1945; children: Alan, Shelley. *Education:* Iowa State Teachers College (now University of Northern Iowa), B.A., 1941; Columbia University, M.A., 1946, Ph.D., 1950. *Home:* 4280 Galt Ocean Dr., Ft. Lauderdale, Fla. 33308.

CAREER: Teacher of social studies in New York, N.Y., 1945-58, and Syosset, Long Island, N.Y., 1958-60; Farmingdale

Public Schools, Farmingdale, Long Island, N.Y., supervisor of social studies, 1960-66; University of London, Goldsmiths College, London, England, visiting professor, 1966-67. Evening lecturer, City College (now City College of the City University of New York), 1953-54. Consultant to boards of education, Portland, Ore., 1962, West Irondequoit, N.Y., 1963, and in New Hampshire, New Jersey, Florida, Georgia, California, and Texas. *Military service:* U.S. Army, 1941-45; became lieutenant. *Member:* National Council for Social Studies, American Historical Association, Organization of American Historians, Southern Historical Association, Florida Council for Social Studies.

WRITINGS—Published by Follett: *World History Study Lessons,* 1962; *American History Study Lessons,* 1963; *Study Lessons on Documents of Freedom,* 1964; *Study Lessons in Our Nation's History,* 1965; *Adult Education American History Study Lessons,* nine books, 1967; *Adult Education Study Lessons in Our Nation's History,* eight books, 1967; *World History,* 1974; *The American Nation,* 1975; *American History,* 1981.

Published by Modern Curriculum Press: *Homelands of the World,* 1977; *Civilizations of the Past,* 1979; *The Earth,* 1981; *United States: People and Leaders,* 1981. Contributor to professional journals.

WORK IN PROGRESS: An economics text, for Globe Book.

*   *   *

ACHEBE, Chinua 1930-

PERSONAL: Born November 16, 1930, in Ogidi, Nigeria; son of Isaiah and Janet Achebe; married Christie Chinwe Okoli, 1961; children: Chinelo (daughter), Ikechukwu (son), Chidi (son), Nwando (daughter). *Education:* Attended Government College, Umuahia, 1944-47; University College, Ibadan, B.A., 1953. *Home:* 305 Marguerite Cartwright Ave., Nsukka, Nigeria. *Office:* Institute of African Studies, University of Nigeria, Nsukka, Nigeria.

CAREER: Nigerian Broadcasting Corp., producer in Lagos, Nigeria, 1954-57, controller in Enugu, 1958-61, director in Lagos, 1961-66; University of Nigeria, Nsukka, senior research fellow, 1966-73, professor of English, 1973—. Visiting professor of English at University of Massachusetts—Amherst, 1972-75, and University of Connecticut, 1975-76. Member of Council, University of Lagos, 1966; chairman, Citadel Books Ltd., 1967; director of Heinemann Educational Books Ltd.

(Nigeria), 1970—, and Nwankwo-Ifejika Ltd. (publisher; Nigeria), 1970—. *Member:* Contemporary Society (Lagos), Mbari Club (Ibadan), Lagos Film Society. *Awards, honors:* Margaret Wrong Memorial Prize, 1959; Nigerian National Trophy, 1960; Rockefeller travel fellowship to East and Central Africa, 1960; UNESCO travel fellowship to United States and Brazil, 1963; Jock Campbell-*New Statesman* award, 1965; D.Litt. from Dartmouth College, 1972, University of Southampton, 1975, and University of Ife (Nigeria), 1978; Commonwealth Poetry Prize, 1974; D.Univ., University of Stirling, 1975; Neil Gunn fellow, Scottish Arts Council, 1975; honorary fellow, Modern Language Association of America, 1975; Lotus Award for Afro-Asian Writers, 1975; LL.D., University of Prince Edward Island, 1976; D.H.L., University of Massachusetts—Amherst, 1977.

WRITINGS: Things Fall Apart (novel), Heinemann, 1958, McDowell, Obolensky, 1959, reprinted, Fawcett, 1977; *No Longer at Ease* (novel), Heinemann, 1960, Obolensky, 1961; *The Sacrificial Egg and Other Stories,* Etudo (Onitsha, Nigeria), 1962; *Arrow of God* (novel), Heinemann, 1964, John Day, 1967; *A Man of the People* (novel), John Day, 1966; *Chike and the River* (juvenile), Cambridge University Press, 1966; *Beware Soul-Brother and Other Poems,* Nwankwo-Ifejika (Nigeria), 1971, Doubleday, 1972, revised edition, Heinemann, 1972; (editor) *The Insider: Stories of War and Peace from Nigeria,* Chatham Bookseller, 1971; (with John Iroaganachi) *How the Leopard Got His Claws* (juvenile), Nwankwo-Ifejika, 1972, bound with *Lament of the Deer,* by Christopher Okigbo, Third Press, 1973; *Girls at War* (short stories), Doubleday, 1973; *Christmas in Biafra and Other Poems,* Doubleday, 1973; *Morning Yet on Creation Day* (essays), Doubleday, 1975. Also author of *The Flute,* 1978, and *The Drum,* 1978. Founding editor, Heinemann "African Writers" series, 1962—; editor, *Okike,* 1971—.

SIDELIGHTS: Chinua Achebe is considered by many critics to be one of the best contemporary African novelists. His writing, as G. D. Killam points out, displays three concerns: "first, with the legacy of colonialism at both the individual and societal level; secondly, with the *fact* of English as a language of national and international exchange; thirdly, with the obligations and responsibilities of the writer both to the society in which he lives and to his art."

Achebe's concern with the impact of colonialism is clearly shown in his novels, which chronicle the experiences of the Ibo, the loosely aligned tribal groups of eastern Nigeria to which he belongs, from before their contact with British missionaries in the 1890's to the present. Abiola Irele asserts that "the immediate subject of Chinua Achebe's novels is the tragic consequence of the African encounter with Europe—this is a theme he has made inimitably his own. His novels deal with the social and psychological conflicts created by the incursion of the white man and his culture into the hitherto self-contained world of African society, and the disarray in the African consciousness that has followed." Similarly, Omolara Leslie finds that "the effects on Nigerian society of the experience of political alienation can be said to be the subject of Achebe's works."

Some critics agree with Killam that it is a mistake to "interpret Achebe's work as mere explication of the Nigerian scene," since, as Killam says, "the novels reveal much more than a study of the traumatic effects of colonialism on a subject people." Killam argues that as a critic of his society, Achebe is "no different than other writers in other places and times"; what makes Achebe's work important is its literary value, not its anthropological or sociological content. Killam quotes Ach-

ebe in support of his contention: "The writer's duty is not to beat this morning's headlines in topicality; it is to explore the depth of the human character."

As David Carroll indicates, Achebe is also concerned with the use of English because, like other African novelists, he faces the problem of writing in a language which embodies the values of the foreign, colonial culture. On the other hand, Achebe comments, "There are not many countries in Africa today where you could abolish the language of the erstwhile colonial powers and still retain the facility for mutual communication. Therefore those African writers who have chosen to write in English or French are not unpatriotic smart alecs with an eye on the main chance—outside their own countries." Thus, Achebe's decision to write in English raises, as he explains, further questions: "My answer to the question, Can an African ever learn English well enough to be able to use it effectively in creative writing?, is certainly yes. If on the other hand you ask: Can he ever learn to use it like a native speaker? I should say: I hope not. It is neither necessary nor desirable for him to be able to do so. . . . The African writer should aim to use English in a way that brings out his message best without altering the language to the extent that its value as a medium of international exchange will be lost. He should aim at fashioning out an English which is at once universal and able to carry his experience."

In another essay, Achebe adds that an African writing in English "often finds himself describing situations or modes of thought which have no direct equivalent in the English way of life. Caught in that situation he can do one of two things. He can try and contain what he wants to say within the limit of conventional English or he can try to push back those limits to accommodate his ideas. . . . The second method can produce something new and valuable to the English language as well as to the material he is trying to put over."

Many critics find that Achebe has been very successful in challenging the boundaries of conventional English without failing to communicate. John Povey observes: "Achebe's style is apparently quite near that of good standard English prose, and yet there is a varient in the density and balance of his writing style which displays a marked originality. . . . It is a good direct English yet it has somehow been colored to reflect the African verbal style; sometimes ponderous, sometimes flippant." More specifically, it is Achebe's use of Ibo proverbs which many critics point to as his writing's most obvious stylistic trait. Ronald Christ condemns their use: "In *Things Fall Apart* . . . Achebe wrote that 'Among the Ibo, the art of conversation is regarded very highly, and proverbs are the palm-oil with which words are eaten.' One must go back to Cervantes and Sancho Panzo to find anyone else as meaninglessly proverbial." In contrast to this, Bernth Lindfors suggests that the proverbs are a central part of Achebe's language and that he uses them to introduce and repeat themes, to differentiate characters, and "to focus on the values of the society he is portraying." Similarly, Donald Weinstock and Cathy Ramadan contend that in *Things Fall Apart* Ibo proverbs and stories foreshadow important plot events and emphasize central themes.

Some reviewers propose that Achebe's use of language involves not only an attempt to portray Ibo society but also more universal themes. Arthur Ravenscroft comments, "Achebe makes [his] language the instrument for analyzing tragic experience and profound human issues of very much more than local Nigerian significance." Margaret Laurence is more specific: "There is one theme which runs through everything [Achebe] has written—human communication and the lack of it. . . . In his novels, we see man as a creature whose means of communication are both infinitely subtle and infinitely clumsy, a prey to invariable misunderstandings. Yet Achebe's writing also conveys the feeling that we must attempt to communicate, however imperfectly, if we are not to succumb to despair or madness. The words which are spoken are rarely the words which are heard, but we must go on speaking.''

According to Killam, Achebe's third concern, his responsibility to his society and art, places him in the role of an educator. Achebe feels he must teach his European audience that Africa's ancestral culture has value, that ''with all its imperfections [it] was not one long night of savagery from which the first Europeans acting on God's behalf delivered them.'' In another essay, Achebe elaborates on his duty as an educator, which includes instructing his African audience: ''As far as I am concerned the fundamental theme of the African writer must first be disposed of. This theme—put quite simply—is that African people did not hear of culture for the first time from Europeans; that their societies were not mindless but frequently had a philosophy of great depth and value and beauty, that they had poetry and, above all, dignity. It is this dignity that many African people all but lost during the colonial period, and it is this that they must now regain. . . . The writer's duty is to help them regain it by showing them in human terms what happened to them, what they lost.''

David Carroll suggests that Achebe's educational goal leaves him vulnerable to aesthetic objections. Ronald Christ, for example, finds both *Things Fall Apart* and *No Longer at Ease* ''long on native customs and idiom, and short on narrative interest.'' Achebe, however, seems untroubled by that type of charge: ''Perhaps what I write is applied art as distinct from pure. But who cares? Art is important but so is education of the kind I have in mind. And I don't see that the two need be mutually exclusive.''

BIOGRAPHICAL/CRITICAL SOURCES: Nigeria Magazine, June 1964; *New Statesman*, January 29, 1965; John Press, editor, *Commonwealth Literature: Unity and Diversity in a Common Culture*, Heinemann, 1965; *Books Abroad*, summer, 1966; *Insight*, October/December, 1966; *Observer*, March 5, 1967; *Canadian Forum*, June, 1967; *Time*, November 10, 1967; *New York Times Book Review*, December 17, 1967; *Negro History Bulletin*, March, 1968; *Critique*, Volume XI, number 1, 1969; G. D. Killam, *The Novels of Chinua Achebe*, Africana Publishing, 1969; David Caroll, *Chinua Achebe*, Twayne, 1970; *Contemporary Literary Criticism*, Gale, Volume I, 1973, Volume III, 1975, Volume V, 1976, Volume VII, 1977, Volume XI, 1979.

—*Sketch by David A. Guy*

*   *   *

ACKLEY, Randall William   1931-

PERSONAL: Born August 9, 1931, in Minneapolis, Minn.; son of Randall Carol (a salesman and machinist) and Katherine (Klym) Ackley; married Rosamartha Morales, May 21, 1956 (divorced); married Brenda Williams, October 30, 1970 (divorced); married Mary Liszak, September 9, 1975; children: (first marriage) Linda Maria, Randall Arthur, Holly Elizabeth; (second marriage) Katherine-Caritas Rainbow. *Education:* University of Minnesota, B.A. (magna cum laude), 1962; Union Graduate School, Yellow Springs, Ohio, Ph.D., 1974. *Politics:* ''Undeclared independent.'' *Religion:* Catholic. *Home:* 3750 Old Glacier Hwy, Juneau, Alaska. *Office:* University of Alaska, 11120 Glacier Hwy., Juneau, Alaska. 99803.

CAREER: University of Texas, Main University (now University of Texas at Austin), instructor in English, 1965-66;

University of Utah, Salt Lake City, assistant professor of English, 1966-67; University of the Americas, Mexico City, Mexico, assistant professor of English, 1967; University of Texas at El Paso, assistant professor of English, 1967-68; St. Mary's College, Notre Dame, Ind., associate professor of English, 1968-69; McMurry College, Abilene, Tex., associate professor of English and chairman of department, 1969-70; Pembroke State University, Pembroke, N.C., associate professor of English and assistant dean, 1970-72; Navajo Community College, Navajo, N.M., coordinator of Arts and Humanities Program and assistant to president, 1973-77; Juneau-Douglas Community College, Juneau, Alaska, director of College of Arts and Sciences, 1977-80; University of Alaska, Juneau, director of development and planning, 1980, director of correctional education, 1980—. Seminar leader, Center for Intercultural Documentation, 1973. *Military service:* U.S. Marine Corps, 1948-50. U.S. Navy, 1950. U.S. Air Force, 1951-52. U.S. Army, 1952-54, 56-60; served in Korea; became first lieutenant.

MEMBER: International Correctional Education Association, Modern Language Association of America, Association for Studies in American Indian Literature (chairman, 1971-74), American Association of University Professors, Association of Departments of English (member of executive committee, 1977-80), National Instructional Administrators Council (member of executive committee, 1980-81), Coordinating Council of Literary Magazines, Southwest Poets Conference (director, 1969-75), Phi Beta Kappa, Sigma Tau Delta. *Awards honors:* Grants from North Carolina Arts Council, 1970-72, and Coordinating Council of Literary Magazines, 1971-74; Litt.D. from Rockdale College, 1971; fellow of International Poetry Society, 1972.

WRITINGS—Poetry: Troll Songs, Tribal Press, 1970; *Lord of All Dreams*, Atlatl Press, 1974; *Troll Erotica*, Solo Press, in press. Poetry represented in anthologies, including *Last Journal of the Tibetan Kite Society* and *Faces of Poetry*. Contributor to over forty journals. Poetry editor of *Conradiana*, 1969-74; editor of *Quetzal*, 1970-73; associate editor of *Pembroke*, 1970-72; consulting editor for *St. Andrews Review*, 1971-72; organizer and editorial writer for *Carolina Indian Voice*, 1972—; guest editor of *Out of Sight*, 1972, and *Cafe Solo*, 1974.

WORK IN PROGRESS: The River; Listen to the Wind; From Socrates to Kohlberg; Introduction to Tribal Indian Literatures.

SIDELIGHTS: Randall William Ackley wrote *CA:* ''I began in dreams, wandered as a quixotic poet and soldier for ten years, found myself again in books, in Eliot, Yeats, Shakespeare, allegory, dream allegory, then found the way again with rivers and the land and Indians, now I am studying the world of glaciers and mountains and the problem of morality and the question of prisons. It seems a life-long task.''

*   *   *

ADKINS, Dorothy C.
See WOOD, Dorothy Adkins

*   *   *

ADLARD, John   1929-

PERSONAL: Born January 15, 1929, in Birmingham, England; son of Herbert Charles Thomas (a distribution manager) and Florence Nell (Sutton) Adlard; married Emiko Saito. *Education:* Merton College, Oxford, B.A., 1952, M.A., 1956, B.Litt., 1956. *Home:* 146 Holland Rd., London W.14, England.

CAREER: Lecturer in English at University of Novi Sad, Novi Sad, Yugoslavia, 1954-56, Catholic University of Lublin, Lublin, Poland, 1957-58, University of Jyvaskyla, Jyvaskyla, Finland, 1958-59, 1960-61, 1962-63, University of Groningen, Groningen, Holland, 1963-64, University of Lodz, Lodz, Poland, 1966-67, University of Antwerp, Antwerp, Belgium, 1969-70, and at various language schools; teacher and writer, 1970—. *Military service:* Royal Army Ordinance Corps, 1947-49. *Member:* Folklore Society of Great Britain, Eighteen-Nineties Society, Black Country Society, Stratford-on-Avon Society.

WRITINGS: Stenbock, Yeats, and the Nineties, Woolf, 1969; (editor) *Blake,* Studio Vista, 1970; *The Sports of Cruelty: Fairies, Folk Songs, Charms, and Other Country Matters in the Work of William Blake,* Woolf, 1972; *The Debt to Pleasure,* Carcanet Press, 1974; *The Fruit of that Forbidden Tree,* Carcanet Press, 1975; (translator) Max Jacob, *Advice to a Young Poet,* Menard, 1976; *Owen Seaman: His Life and Work,* Eighteen-Nineties Society, 1977; *The Softer Paths of Pleasure* (biography of Sally Salisbury), Onny Press, 1980; *Christmas with Count Stenbock,* Enitharmon, 1980; *One Evening of Light Mist in London,* Tragara Press, 1980; *In Sweet St. James's Clerkenwell,* Islington Libraries, in press.

Poetry represented in numerous anthologies. Also translator of French, Italian, Dutch, and Serbo-Croatian poetry which has been printed in magazines and in a series of poetry postcards published by Menard Press. Contributor to *Philological Quarterly, Michigan Quarterly Review, Blake Studies, Blake Newsletter, Folklore, Modern Language Review,* and other journals. Editor with Alan Brownjohn, *Departure,* 1952-54.

WORK IN PROGRESS: Translations of songs by Lorenzo de Medici.

* * *

ALBERS, Henry H. 1919-

PERSONAL: Born November 24, 1919, in Germany; son of Hartwig and Bertha (Lilie) Albers; married Marjorie Klein, 1948; children: Patricia, Elliott. *Education:* University of Iowa, B.A., 1941, M.A., 1946; Yale University, Ph.D., 1951. *Religion:* Congregationalist. *Home:* University of Petroleum and Minerals, No. 307, Dhahran, Saudi Arabia.

CAREER: Iowa State University, Ames, associate professor of economics, 1949-57; University of Iowa, Iowa City, professor of management, 1957-68; University of Nebraska, Lincoln, professor of management, 1968-75, chairman of department, 1968-74, director of advanced program development, 1974-75; University of Petroleum and Minerals, Dhahran, Saudi Arabia, College of Industrial Management, dean, 1975-78, Research Institute, division manager, 1978—. Representative of public and chairman of Great Plains States Regional Manpower Advisory Committee (advisors to secretaries of Labor and Health, Education, and Welfare), 1970-74; consultant to U.S. Army Management Engineering Training Agency, beginning 1961, Trust Territory of Pacific Islands, Government of American Samoa, South Pacific Commission, Strategic Air Command, Mobil Corp., Asian Development Bank, and other governmental and business organizations. *Military service:* U.S. Army, Infantry. *Member:* American Economics Association, American Management Association, American Association of University Professors, Sigma Phi Epsilon, Order of Artus.

WRITINGS: Organized Executive Action: Decision-Making, Communication, and Leadership, Wiley, 1961, 2nd edition published as *Principles of Organization and Management,* 1965,

3rd edition published as *Principles of Management: A Modern Approach,* 1969, 4th edition, 1974; (with Lowell A. Schoer) *Programmed Organization and Management Principles,* Wiley, 1966, reprinted, Robert E. Krieger, 1977; *Cases, Readings and Review Guide for Principles of Management,* compiled by Fred Luthans, Wiley, 1969; *Management: The Basic Concepts,* Wiley, 1972; (with Richard M. Hodgetts) *Cases and Incidents on the Basic Concepts of Management,* Wiley, 1972. Co-author of three television programs on labor-management cooperation, sponsored by the Twentieth Century Fund, New York.

WORK IN PROGRESS: A book on decentralized leadership systems.

* * *

ALCALDE, Miguel
See BURGESS, M(ichael) R(oy)

* * *

ALDRED, Cyril 1914-

PERSONAL: Born February 19, 1914, in London, England; son of Frederick (a civil servant) and Lillian Ethel (Underwood) Aldred; married Jessie Kennedy Morton, 1938; children: one daughter. *Education:* Attended Kings College, London; Courtauld Institute of Art, London, B.A., 1936. *Home:* 4a Polwarth Ter., Edinburgh EH11 1NE, Scotland.

CAREER: Royal Scottish Museum, Edinburgh, Scotland, assistant keeper, 1937; Scottish Education Department, Edinburgh, assistant principal of St. Andrew's House, 1939; Metropolitan Museum of Art, Department of Egyptian Art, New York, N.Y., associate curator, 1955-56; Royal Scottish Museum, keeper of Department of Art and Archaeology, 1961-74. *Military service:* Royal Air Force, Signals, 1942-46. *Member:* Egyptian Exploration Society (member of committee, 1959-76), Society of Antiquaries of Scotland (fellow), Scottish Arts Club (Edinburgh), Royal Society of Edinburgh (fellow).

WRITINGS: Old Kingdom Art in Ancient Egypt, Transatlantic, 1949; *Middle Kingdom Art in Ancient Egypt, 2300 to 1590 B.C.,* Tiranti, 1950; *New Kingdom Art in Ancient Egypt during the Eighteenth Dynasty, 1590 to 1315 B.C.,* Tiranti, 1951, 2nd edition published as *New Kingdom Art in Ancient Egypt during the Eighteenth Dynasty, 1570 to 1320 B.C.,* 1961; *The Development of Ancient Egyptian Art, 3200 to 1315 B.C.,* Tiranti, 1952; *The Egyptians,* Praeger, 1961; *Egypt to the End of the Old Kingdom,* Thames & Hudson, 1965; *Akhenaten, Pharaoh of Egypt: A New Study,* Thames & Hudson, 1968, McGraw, 1969.

Jewels of the Pharaohs: Egyptian Jewelry of the Dynastic Period, Praeger, 1971; *Tutankhamun's Egypt,* British Broadcasting Corp., 1972; *Akhenaten and Nefertiti,* Viking, 1973; (contributor) Denise Schmandt-Besserat, editor, *Immortal Egypt,* Undena, 1978; (contributor) J. Leclant, editor, *Le monde Egyptien,* three volumes, Editions Gallimard, 1978-80; *Tutankhamun: Craftsmanship in Gold in the Reign of the King,* Metropolitan Museum of Art, 1979; *Egyptian Art in the Days of the Pharaohs,* Thames & Hudson, 1980. Contributor to *Cambridge Ancient History, Lexikon der Aegyptologie,* and to *History of Technology.* Author of script, "Tutankhamun's Egypt," British Broadcasting Corp. Contributor to scientific journals.

WORK IN PROGRESS: A study of the art of the Amarna Period; a revision of *The Egyptians.*

AVOCATIONAL INTERESTS: Composing light verse, and gardening.

ALEXANDER, Sidney 1912-

PERSONAL: Born March 6, 1912, in New York, N.Y.; son of David and Sadie (Breslau) Alexander; married Frances Rosenbaum, January 19, 1936. *Education:* Columbia University, B.S., 1934, additional study, 1934-35; New School for Social Research, additional study, 1946-48; University of Florence, Certificate of Merit in Italian Studies, 1949. *Home:* Via Ugo Foscoho 34, Florence, Italy. *Agent:* Roslyn Targ, Roslyn Targ Literary Agency, Inc., 250 West 57th St., New York, N.Y. 10019.

CAREER: Writer. Office of War Information, Washington, D.C., editor on overseas news staff, 1943; *Reporter* magazine, New York, N.Y., consultant, 1947-48, foreign correspondent, 1948-68. Instructor in English at Fairleigh Dickinson University, 1955-56, New School for Social Research, 1955-58, and Hunter College (now Hunter College of the City University of New York), 1957-58; instructor at Syracuse University, 1963-67 and Virginia Commonwealth University, 1978—, and at numerous teaching institutions abroad. Holder of Morton Chair, Ohio University, 1974-75. Guest lecturer at America Italy Society, 1958, Sarah Lawrence College in Florence, 1960-61, Stanford University in Florence, 1960-61, 1962-63, 1965, Syracuse University in Florence, 1961, and Villa Mercede, 1961. Conductor of writing workshops. *Military service:* U.S. Army Air Forces, public relations, 1943-46. *Member:* Authors League, American P.E.N., Royal Society of Arts (fellow), Renaissance Society.

AWARDS, HONORS: Maxwell Anderson Award for dramatic composition in verse from Stanford University, honorable mention, 1938, for "The Third Great Fool," first prize, 1948, for "Salem Story"; *Charm* magazine short story contest, second prize, 1944, first prize, 1945; grants from Ministry of Foreign Affairs, Government of Italy, 1958, 1959, and 1960; grant from Max Ascoli Foundation, 1958-59; Syracuse University faculty research grant, 1965; translation prize, P.E.N., 1970, for *The History of Italy;* D.H.L. from Ohio University, 1977.

WRITINGS: The Man on the Queue (poetry and verse plays), Press of J. A. Decker, 1941; (translator) Valery, *The Marine Cemetery,* [Italy], 1949; *Tightrope in the Dark* (poetry), Press of J. A. Decker, 1949; *The Celluloid Asylum* (novel), Bobbs-Merrill, 1951; *Michelangelo, the Florentine* (novel), Random House, 1957; (translator) *A House in Milan,* Harcourt, 1963; (editor and translator with wife, Frances Alexander) *The Berenson Collection,* Ricordi, 1964; *My Beard to Heaven* (novel), Mario Casalini, c. 1965; *The Hand of Michelangelo* (biographical novel), Mario Casalini, 1966, Twayne, 1967; (editor and translator) Francesco Guicciardini, *The History of Italy,* Macmillan, 1969; *Lions and Foxes,* Macmillan, 1974; *Marc Chagall,* Putnam, 1978.

Plays: "The Great Third Fool," first produced in 1938; "The Hawk and the Flesh" (radio play), first broadcast on WNYC Radio, 1939; "Salem Story" (radio play), first broadcast on WNYC Radio, 1940; "Giles Corey" (based on "Salem Story"), first produced Off-Broadway, 1948.

Work represented in several anthologies, including: *The Poetry of Flight,* edited by Selden Rodman, Duell, Sloan & Pearce, 1941; *Accent Anthology: Selections from Accent, a Quarterly of New Literature, 1940-1945,* edited by Kerker Quinn and Charles Shattuck, Harcourt, 1946; *Best American Short Stories, 1944, 1948,* edited by Martha Foley, Houghton, 1945, 1949; *The Poetry of the Negro, 1746-1949,* edited by Langston Hughes and A. W. Bontemps, Doubleday, 1949; *Modern Po-*

etry, edited by Paul Engle and Warren Carrier, Scott, Foresman, 1955; *The Short Story,* edited by James B. Hall and Joseph Langland, Macmillan, 1956.

Writer for radio and films. Contributor of articles, short stories, and poems to *Collier's Encyclopedia, New Yorker, Virginia Quarterly Review, Accent, Antioch Review, New York Times Book Review,* and other publications in the United States and abroad. English editor, *Journal of the United Nations,* 1952.

SIDELIGHTS: In a review of *The Hand of Michelangelo* for the *New York Times Book Review,* Orville Prescott writes: "Like the mills of the gods, which grind slowly but grind exceeding small, [Sidney] Alexander writes with loving care and a sort of stately grandeur. Steeped in the lore of the time, he is well qualified to write a biography of his hero. He has preferred to write it as fiction, probably because that method allows him to speculate about the gaps in the record, and to interpret the torments and travails of the artist's spirit."

In a review of another Alexander biography, *Los Angeles Times* critic Robert Kirsch explains that for *Marc Chagall* Alexander "interviewed a number of Chagall's contemporaries and relatives. He has obtained a memoir from Virginia Leirens, Chagall's lover for seven years and mother of his son David, on her life and observations of the artist from 1945 to 1952. There are some interesting anecdotes."

BIOGRAPHICAL/CRITICAL SOURCES: Milton Allen Kaplan, *Radio and Poetry,* Columbia University Press, 1949; *Reporter,* May 4, 1967; *New York Times Book Review,* September 9, 1967, August 6, 1978; *Los Angeles Times,* November 11, 1978.

*   *   *

ALLEN, Betsy
See CAVANNA, Betty

*   *   *

ALLEN, Loring
See ALLEN, Robert Loring

*   *   *

ALLEN, Minerva C(rantz) 1935-

PERSONAL: Born April 24, 1935, in Lodgepole, Mont.; daughter of Robert Ernest (a rancher) and Felectius (Chopwood) Allen; married John W. Allen (a tribal chairman), December 13, 1951; children: John, Mike, Donna, Wanda, Dean, Holly, Connie, Lisa. *Education:* Attended Northern Montana College, 1964-73; Central Michigan University, B.S., 1974; Weber State College, additional study, 1975—. *Religion:* Indian. *Home address:* Box 38, Star Rte., Dodson, Mont. 59524. *Agent:* Roxy Gordon, 1216 Lomas N.W., Albuquerque, N.M. 87102.

CAREER: Teacher's aide in public school, Lodgepole, Mont., 1964; Project Headstart, Lodgepole, teacher's aide, 1965-66, teacher, 1966; Montana Legal Service, Havre, legal aide specialist, 1966-70; Ft. Belknap Headstart, Harlem, Mont., director of community education, 1971-79; bilingual director and federal project coordinator for Hays Lodgepole Public Schools, 1980—. Consultant on Indian heritage and performance management to schools and colleges, and to public service organizations.

WRITINGS: Like Spirits of the Past: Trying to Break Out and Walk to the West (Indian poetry and prose), Wowapi Productions (Albuquerque, N.M.), 1974; *Come to Power* (poetry anthology), Crossing Press, 1974; *Women: Portraits,* McGraw, 1976; (contributor) Art Cuelho, editor, *Father Me Home Winds,* Big Timber, 1976; *The Remember Earth,* Red Earth Press, 1979; *Spirits Rest,* Los Angeles Graphic Arts Program, 1981. Contributor to the 1972 edition of *Whole Earth Catalog.*

WORK IN PROGRESS: An article on the Assiniboine tribe (to which Minerva Allen belongs), for inclusion in *Encyclopedia of Indians of the Americas;* working on a school text on tribal government and history concerning the Ft. Belknap Reservation.

* * *

ALLEN, R. Earl 1922-

PERSONAL: Born May 26, 1922, in Fort Worth, Tex.; son of James Roy (a carpenter) and Mary Ellen (Coker) Allen; married Norma Joyce Lovelace, December 25, 1941; children: Norma Alline (deceased), James Todd, Joy Earline. *Education:* Howard Payne College, B.A., 1946; Midwestern University, B.S.; Linda Vista Baptist College, M.A.; additional study, Southwestern Baptist Theological Seminary; Howard Payne College, D.D., 1953. *Home:* 2523 Prairie Ave., Fort Worth, Tex. 76106. *Office:* 2524 Roosevelt St., Fort Worth, Tex. 76106.

CAREER: Ordained to ministry of Southern Baptist Convention, 1940; First Baptist Church, Archer City, Tex., pastor, 1945-47; First Baptist Church, Seagraves, Tex., pastor, 1947-50; First Baptist Church, Floydada, Tex., pastor, 1950-56; Rosen Heights Baptist Church, Fort Worth, Tex., pastor, 1956—. Adjunct instructor, Southwestern Baptist Theological Seminary, 1976—. Member of executive committee of Southern Baptist Convention, 1973—. *Awards, honors:* George Washington Honor Medal award, 1964 and 1968; distinguished alumnus award from Howard Payne College, 1967; Doctor of Laws, Atlanta Law School, 1968; Doctor of Humane Letters, Linda Vista Baptist College, 1968; Doctor of Literature, John Brown University, 1971.

WRITINGS: Bible Paradoxes, Revell, 1963; *Memorial Messages,* Broadman, 1964; (compiler) *Pastor Minister in Time of Death: Bibliography,* 1964; *Trials, Tragedies, and Triumphs,* Revell, 1965; *Christian Comfort: Three Messages of Consolation for the Difficulties of Life,* Broadman, 1965; *Strength from Shadows,* Broadman, 1967; *The Sign of the Star,* Broadman, 1968; *Silent Saturday,* Baker Book, 1968; *The Personal Jesus,* Broadman, 1971; *Speaking in Parables,* Baker Book, 1973; *Persons of the Passion,* Broadman, 1973; *Bible Comparatives,* foreword by Kenneth Chafin, Word Books, 1973; *Divine Dividends: An Inspirational Reading of the Sermon on the Mount,* T. Nelson, 1974; *Days to Remember,* Baker Book, 1974; *Funeral Source Book,* Baker Book, 1974; *Good Morning Lord: Devotions for Hospital Patients,* Baker Book, 1975; *Prayers that Changed History,* Broadman, 1978; *The Hereafter, What Jesus Said about It,* Revell, 1978; *For Those Who Grieve,* Broadman, 1978; *Jesus Loves Me,* Broadman, 1979; *The Words of Christ,* Baker Book, 1981. Also author of *Just When You Need Him.* Anthologized in *Best Sermons of 1966-68.* Contributor of articles to magazines.

* * *

ALLEN, Robert Loring 1921-
(Loring Allen)

PERSONAL: Born July 10, 1921, in Trenton, Mo.; son of Court P. and Alida (Hubbell) Allen; married Jean M. O'Clair, 1941; children: Robert Loring II, Maris Jean. *Education:* University of Redlands, B.A., 1947; Harvard University, M.A., 1950,

Ph.D., 1953. *Home:* 529 Midvale St., St. Louis, Mo. 63130. *Office:* Department of Economics, University of Missouri, St. Louis, Mo. 63121.

CAREER: U.S. Government, Washington, D.C., research economist, 1951-56; University of Virginia, Charlottesville, associate professor of economics, 1956-59; University of Oregon, Eugene, professor, 1959-68; University of Missouri—St. Louis, professor of economics, 1968—. Visiting professor, Universidad de Los Andes, Venezuela, 1963-68, and Simon Bolivar University, 1975-77; Fulbright lecturer, University of Salamanca, Spain, 1966-67. *Military service:* U.S. Army, Infantry, 1941-45; won Bronze Star and Purple Heart.

WRITINGS: Middle Eastern Economic Relations with the Soviet Union, Eastern Europe, and Mainland China, Woodrow Wilson Department of Foreign Affairs, University of Virginia, 1958; *Soviet Influence in Latin America,* Public Affairs Press, 1959; *Soviet Economic Warfare,* Public Affairs Press, 1960; (co-author) *Economic Policies toward Less Developed Countries,* Joint Economic Committee, 1962; (with D. A. Watson) *The Structure of the Oregon Economy,* Bureau of Business and Economic Research, University of Oregon, 1969; *Formation of American Trade Policy,* Institute of Finance, New York University, 1970; *Lecciones de Economia Regional,* Universidad de Los Andes (Venezuela), 1972; (under name Loring Allen) *Venezuelan Economic Development: A Politico-Economic Analysis,* JAI Press, 1977; (under name Loring Allen) *OPEC Oil,* Oelgelschlager, Gunn, & Hain, 1979. Author of economic monographs and contributor of articles to professional journals.

WORK IN PROGRESS: Studies of the economics of energy and the environment; a biography of Joseph Schumpeter.

* * *

ALLEN, Robert S(haron) 1900-1981

PERSONAL: Born July 14, 1900, in Latonia, Ky.; committed suicide, February 23, 1981, in Washington, D.C.; buried in Arlington National Cemetery; son of Harry and Elizabeth (Sharon) Allen; married Ruth Finney (a newspaper correspondent), March 30, 1929 (died, 1979). *Education:* University of Wisconsin, B.A., 1923; graduate study at University of Munich, 1923-24, and George Washington University, 1927-28. *Home:* 1525 28th Street N.W., Washington, D.C. 20007. *Office:* National Press Building, Washington, D.C. 20005.

CAREER: Reporter for *Capital Times, Wisconsin State Journal,* and *Milwaukee Journal* prior to 1923; European correspondent for *Christian Science Monitor,* 1923-24; reporter for United Press Association during mid-1920s; chief of Washington bureau for *Christian Science Monitor* until 1931; author with Drew Pearson of syndicated newspaper column "Washington Merry-Go-Round," 1931-42; author of syndicated newspaper column "Inside Washington," 1949-80. Also worked as reporter for International News Service and as Washington correspondent for *Philadelphia Record. Military service:* U.S. Army, Cavalry; became second lieutenant; served in Mexico, 1916-17, and in France, during World War I. Served in Wisconsin National Guard; became captain. U.S. Army, Intelligence, 1942-45; became colonel; received Silver Star, Bronze Star, Commendation Ribbon with cluster, Purple Heart, Legion of Merit, French Legion of Honor, and Croix de Guerre with palm and gold star. *Member:* White House Correspondents Association, National Press Club, Washington Press Club, Sigma Delta Chi. *Awards, honors:* Sigma Delta Chi Distinguished Service Award, 1942.

WRITINGS: (With Drew Pearson) *The Washington Merry-Go-Round*, Liveright, 1931; (with Pearson) *More Merry-Go-Round*, Liveright, 1932; *Why Hoover Faces Defeat*, Brewer, Warren & Putnam, 1932; (with Pearson) *The Nine Old Men*, Doubleday, Doran, 1936, reprinted, DaCapo Press, 1974; (with Pearson) *Nine Old Men at the Crossroads*, Doubleday, Doran, 1937, reprinted, Da Capo Press, 1974; *Lucky Forward: The History of Patton's Third U.S. Army*, Vanguard, 1947, published as *Lucky Forward: The History of General George Patton's Third U.S. Army*, Macfadden-Bartell, 1965, published under original title, Manor, 1977; (editor) *Our Fair City*, Vanguard, 1947, reprinted, Arno, 1974; (editor) *Our Sovereign State*, Vanguard, 1949; (with William V. Shannon) *The Truman Merry-Go-Round*, Vanguard, 1950.

Also author with Drew Pearson of comic strip "Hap Hazard," 1941, and of radio program "News for the Americas," National Broadcasting Co., Inc., 1941. Regular contributor to *Collier's, Nation,* and *New Republic.*

SIDELIGHTS: In 1932, Robert S. Allen teamed up with fellow newspaperman Drew Pearson to produce one of the decade's most colorful and controversial columns, the "Washington Merry-Go-Round." An offshoot of their gossip-filled book of the same title (the publication of which cost both men their jobs), the "Merry-Go-Round" reported all the inside information on Washington politics that most other newspapers refused to print.

While Pearson developed a reputation for being a charming (but tough) investigator who preferred to chat casually with his informants at parties, restaurants, and other popular gathering spots for diplomats and military officials based in the capital, Allen became known as the emotional, feisty partner who often resorted to blustery confrontation, curses, and insults in his dealings with Congressmen and Supreme Court judges. As Pearson once recalled in a post-World War II tribute to his collaborator: "Bob was always putting burrs under sleepy senators. He would walk into their offices, pound on their desks and demand that they get out on the Senate floor and fight."

Allen's association with the "Washington Merry-Go-Round" ended in 1942 when he re-enlisted in the Army. Assigned to an intelligence unit under the direction of General George S. Patton, he lost an arm during a reconnaissance mission that took place near the end of the war but soon returned to civilian life and wrote a book chronicling the Third Army's push into France and Germany. Allen then decided against rejoining Pearson, choosing instead to pursue a solo writing career until poor health finally forced him to retire the year before his death.

BIOGRAPHICAL/CRITICAL SOURCES: Time, February 13, 1939; *Collier's,* April 22, 1939, September 6, 1947.

OBITUARIES: New York Times, February 25, 1981; *Washington Post,* February 25, 1981.†

*   *   *

ALLSOP, Kenneth   1920-1973

PERSONAL: Born January 29, 1920, in Leeds, Yorkshire, England; died May 23, 1973, in West Milton, England; son of John and Mary Ann (Halliday) Allsop; married Betty Creak, 1942; children: Tristan Andrew Lindley, Amanda Susan, Fabian Halliday. *Education:* Privately educated. *Home:* West Milton, Dorset, England. *Agent:* Sterling Lord Agency, 660 Madison Ave., New York, N.Y. 10021. *Office:* British Broadcasting Corp., Broadcasting House, London W.1., England.

CAREER: Reporter for newspapers in England, including *Slough Observer,* 1938-39, *John Bull,* 1945, *Evening Advertiser*

(Swindon), 1946, and *Sunday Express,* 1946-47; Press Association, England, law courts reporter, 1948-50; *Picture Post,* England, feature writer, 1950-55; Independent Television News, London, England, reporter and commentator, 1955-57; *London Evening Standard,* London, feature writer and columnist, 1955-57; *London Daily Mail,* London, literary editor and book critic, 1957-64; British Broadcasting Corp., London, interviewer and reporter for "Tonight," 1960, anchorman for "This Nation Tomorrow," 1963, "Life," 1968, "Twenty-Four Hours," 1965-72, and "Down to Earth," 1972-73. Presenter of radio programs "The World of Jazz," 1963, "The World of Books," 1966-67, "Wildlife Review," 1967-68, and "Now Read On," 1970. Rector of Edinburgh University, 1968-71. *Military service:* Royal Air Force, 1940-43. *Awards, honors:* John Llewellyn Rhys Memorial Prize, 1950, for *Adventure Lit Their Star;* visiting research fellowship, Merton College, Oxford University, 1968; M.A., Oxford University, 1969.

WRITINGS: Adventure Lit Their Star, Latimer House, 1949, revised edition, Macdonald, 1962, Crown, 1964; *The Sun Himself Must Die* (short stories), Latimer House, 1950; *The Daybreak Edition,* Percival Marshall, 1951; *Silver Flame,* Percival Marshall, 1951; *The Last Voyages of the Mayflower,* Winston, 1955; *The Angry Decade* (criticism), British Book Center, 1958, 3rd edition, P. Owen, 1964; *Rare Bird,* Hutchinson, 1958; (with Robert Pitman) *A Question of Obscenity,* Scorpion Press, 1960; *The Bootleggers and Their Era,* Doubleday, 1961; *Scan* (collected journalism), Hodder & Stoughton, 1965; *Hard Travellin': The Hobo and His History,* New American Library, 1967; *Fit to Live In?,* Penguin, 1970; *In the Country,* Hamish Hamilton, 1972; (with others) *Strip Jack Naked,* Gentry Books, 1972; *Letters to His Daughter,* Hamish Hamilton, 1974. Work included in anthologies. Records columnist for *Nova.* Regular contributor to *The Spectator, Encounter, Twentieth Century, New York Times,* and *Daily Telegraph.*

SIDELIGHTS: Kenneth Allsop's *Hard Travellin',* a study of the American migrant worker, "is a shapeless book, but it is a fascinating and disturbing social document," wrote Joanna Richardson. Allsop "wavers between sympathy for their adventurousness and horror at the costs—lice, jail, pederasts, accidents—of their freedom," reported the *New Yorker.* Allsop noted that his own ambivalence toward hoboes is shared by most Americans. Another popular Allsop book, *The Bootleggers,* explored the history of illegal traffic in alcohol during Prohibition. *Books & Bookmen* said, "We are so used to books debunking legends that perhaps the most surprising thing to emerge from *The Bootleggers* is that the gangster legends are absolutely true."

AVOCATIONAL INTERESTS: Ornithology, jazz.

BIOGRAPHICAL/CRITICAL SOURCES: Observer Review, November 19, 1967; *Listener,* November 30, 1967; *Punch,* December 6, 1967; *Books & Bookmen,* January, 1968, September, 1968; *Spectator,* January 5, 1968; *Christian Science Monitor,* March 19, 1968; *Time,* March 22, 1968; *Newsweek,* March 25, 1968; *New Yorker,* April 20, 1968; *New York Times Book Review,* April 21, 1968.†

*   *   *

ALONSO, William   1933-

PERSONAL: Born January 29, 1933, in Buenos Aires, Argentina; U.S. citizen; son of Amado (a professor) and Joan (Cann-Evans) Alonso; married Mary Ellen Peters (in visual studies), May 9, 1959. *Education:* Harvard University, A.B., 1954, Masters of City Planning, 1956; University of Pennsylvania, Ph.D., 1959. *Home:* 52 Oakvale Ave., Berkeley, Calif.

94705. *Office:* Department of City and Regional Planning, University of California, Berkeley, Calif. 94720.

CAREER: Harvard University, Cambridge, Mass., assistant professor, 1959-64, associate professor of regional planning, 1964-67, acting director of Center for Urban Studies, 1963-66; University of California, Berkeley, professor of regional planning, 1966—, Institute for Urban and Regional Development, member, 1967—, acting chairman, 1967-68. Visiting lecturer at Yale University, 1966; member of Inter-University Committee on Urban Economics, 1969—; adviser and lecturer at Institute of Physical Planning, Cuba, 1972. Private practice as consultant on city and regional planning and development; consultant to Ford Foundation. *Member:* Regional Science Association, Phi Beta Kappa.

WRITINGS: Location and Land Use: Toward a General Theory of Land Rent, Harvard University Press, 1964; (editor with John Friedmann) *Regional Development and Planning: A Reader,* M.I.T. Press, 1964, revised edition published as *Regional Policy: Readings in Theory and Application,* 1975; (contributor) K. S. Lynn, editor, *The Professions in America,* Houghton, 1965; (co-author) *Problems of Theory and Method of Regional Planning,* Marsilio Editori, 1969; (contributor) Mancur Olson and Hans J. Landsberg, *The No-Growth Society,* Norton, 1974.

Monographs: *Location, Primacy and Regional Economic Development,* Harvard University, 1966; *A Reformulation of Classical Location Theory and Its Relation to Rent Theory,* Harvard University, 1967; *Aspects of Regional Planning and Theory in the United States,* Institute of Urban and Regional Development, University of California (Berkeley), 1968; *Beyond the Inter-disciplinary Approach to Planning,* Institute of Urban and Regional Development, University of California, 1968; *Equity and Its Relation to Efficiency in Urbanization,* Institute of Urban and Regional Development, University of California, 1968; *Industrial Location and Regional Policy in Economic Development,* Institute of Urban and Regional Development, University of California, 1968; *National Interregional Demographic Accounts: A Prototype,* Institute of Urban and Regional Development, University of California, 1973.

Contributor of articles on urban topics to scholarly journals. Editor, *Papers and Proceedings of Regional Science Association,* 1957, *Journal of Regional Science,* 1958-59.

WORK IN PROGRESS: Research on national patterns and policies of urbanization.†

*   *   *

ALPERT, Hollis   1916-
(Robert Carroll)

PERSONAL: Born September 24, 1916, in Herkimer, N.Y.; son of Abraham and Myra (Carroll) Alpert; married Joan O'Leary (a teacher), October 1, 1960. *Education:* Attended New School for Social Research, 1947-48. *Address:* Box 142, Shelter Island, N.Y. 11964.

CAREER: Book reviewer for *Saturday Review,* New York City, and *New York Times,* New York City, 1947-59; *New Yorker,* New York City, associate fiction editor, 1950-56; *Saturday Review,* New York City, motion picture critic, 1950-72; *Woman's Day,* Greenwich, Conn., film critic, 1953-60, contributing editor, 1956-69; *World,* New York City, managing editor, beginning 1972, film editor and lively arts editor, beginning 1973; *American Film,* Washington, D.C., editor, 1975-80, consulting editor, 1980—. Writing instructor, Division of General Education, New York University, 1948-53. Past director, Edward MacDowell Association. Judge, representing the United

States, Berlin Film Festival, 1966. *Military service:* U.S. Army, combat historian, 1943-46; became first lieutenant. *Member:* National Society of Film Critics (chairman, 1972-73). *Awards, honors:* Annual award for movie criticism, Screen Directors Guild, 1958.

WRITINGS: The Summer Lovers, Knopf, 1958; *Some Other Time,* Knopf, 1960; (under pseudonym Robert Carroll) *Champagne at Dawn,* Dell, 1961; *The Dreams and the Dreamers,* Macmillan, 1962; (under pseudonym Robert Carroll) *Cruise to the Sun,* Dell, 1962; *For Immediate Release* (novel), Doubleday, 1963; *The Barrymores,* Dial, 1964; *The Claimant,* Dial, 1968; ''The Ski Bum'' (screenplay; based on Romain Gary's book of the same title), Avco, 1968; (editor with Andrew Sarris) *Film 68/69,* Simon & Schuster, 1969; *The People Eaters,* Dial, 1971; (with Arthur Knight) *Playboy's Sex in Cinema, 1970,* Playboy Press, 1971; *Smash,* Dial, 1973; (with Knight) *Playboy's Sex in Cinema 3,* Playboy Press, 1973; (with Ira Mothner and Harold Schonberg) *How to Play Double Bogey Golf,* New York Times Co., 1975; (under pseudonym Robert Carroll) *A Disappearance,* Dial, 1975. Also author of two screenplays, ''The Fun Couple'' and ''Scenes.'' Contributor of short stories and articles on books, movies, and television to numerous magazines, including *New Yorker, Cosmopolitan,* and *Harper's Bazaar.*

SIDELIGHTS: Although best known as a film critic, Hollis Alpert cultivates many literary fields: Novels, biographies, short stories, screenplays, humor, as well as criticism. *The Barrymores,* a biography of the Barrymore family, elicits high praise from several critics, including Charles Dollen who comments in *Best Sellers,* ''All the color and drama of the American Theatre of the early twentieth century is brought to life again in this superb volume by Mr. Hollis Alpert.'' As a novelist, however, Alpert has received some mixed reviews. Clara Siggins finds that *The Claimant* ''attempts seriously to show something of man's capacity to hope in spite of despair; the reader learns about loneliness and companionship, and about the healing effects of time.'' On the other hand, the *New York Times Book Review* critic, James MacBride, comments that ''despite his admirable wish to say something new about the tragedy of the [Holocaust] and its weary aftermath, the author fails to lift his characters above puppet level.''

BIOGRAPHICAL/CRITICAL SOURCES: New York Herald Tribune Book Review, July 20, 1958; *Saturday Review,* August 13, 1960, March 16, 1968, November 20, 1971; *Best Sellers,* December 15, 1964, April 15, 1968, November 15, 1971; *New York Times Book Review,* January 3, 1965, April 28, 1968, November 21, 1971, November 25, 1973; *New York Times,* November 8, 1971.

*   *   *

ALTMAN, Nathaniel   1948-

PERSONAL: Born January 25, 1948, in New York, N.Y.; son of Morris (an electronics engineer) and Sadie (a director of a woman's center; maiden name, Davis) Altman. *Education:* Attended University of Wisconsin, 1966-68, and Universidad de Los Andes, 1968-69; University of Wisconsin, B.A., 1971. *Home:* 169 Prospect Park W., Brooklyn, N.Y. 11215.

CAREER: Theosophical Society in America, Wheaton, Ill., resident staff member, 1971; Krotona Institute of Theosophy, Ojai, Calif., registrar and member of faculty, 1972-74; full-time writer, 1974—. *Member:* Institute for the New Age, Theosophical Society, North American Vegetarian Society.

WRITINGS: Eating for Life: A Book about Vegetarianism, Quest Books, 1973, enlarged edition, 1977; *The Chiropractic Alternative, J. P. Tarcher, 1981; *Nathaniel Altman's Total Vege-tarian Cooking,* Keats Publishing, 1981; *Ahimsa: Dynamic Compassion,* Quest Books, 1981; *Pocket Guide to Vegetarian Restaurants,* Keats Publishing, 1982.

WORK IN PROGRESS: Your Hand, Your Life: Psychological Hand Analysis; a full-length book about Ahimsa.

SIDELIGHTS: Nathaniel Altman writes: "The sense of sepa-rativeness and a general callousness towards human and animal suffering are the obstacles which humanity needs most des-perately to overcome. The practise of Ahimsa and in particular, vegetarianism, can be considered as important first steps to solving these problems."

AVOCATIONAL INTERESTS: Yoga, cycling, healing, hand analysis.

* * *

AMATO, Joseph Anthony 1938-

PERSONAL: Born August 31, 1938, in Detroit, Mich.; son of Joseph (a United Foundation organizer and union secretary) and Ethel May (Linsdeau) Amato; married Catherine Jeanne Bavolack (a nurse), August 6, 1966; children: Felice, Anthony, Adam, Ethel. *Education:* University of Michigan, B.A., 1960; University of Laval, M.A., 1962; graduate study at Indiana University, summer, 1959, and Wayne State University, 1961; University of Rochester, Ph.D., 1970. *Politics:* "Conservative anarchist with socialist leanings." *Religion:* Roman Catholic. *Home:* 202 Park Ave., Marshall, Minn. 56258. *Office:* De-partment of History, Southwest State University, Marshall, Minn. 56258.

CAREER: Public high school teacher of history and Spanish in Michigan, 1960-62; University of Rochester, Rochester, N.Y., instructor in western civilization and Italian Renais-sance, 1963-65; State University of New York at Binghamton, instructor in western civilization and European history, 1965-66; University of California, Riverside, instructor in western civilization and European history, 1966-68; Southwest State University, Marshall, Minn., assistant professor, 1969-72, as-sociate professor, 1972-77, professor of history, 1977—. *Awards, honors:* National Endowment for the Humanities grant, 1975-76, for a study of European culture.

WRITINGS: Emanuel Mounier and Jacques Maritain: A French Catholic Understanding of the Modern World, University of Alabama Press, 1975; *Guilt and Gratitude: A Study of Con-temporary Conscience,* Greenwood Press, 1982; *Ethics, Living or Dead,* Portals Press, 1982. Also author of *Countryside Mir-ror of Ourselves,* a collection of essays. Contributor to the *Annals* of the American Academy of Political and Social Sci-ence. Contributor of articles and reviews to *Worldview, Pro-gressive, Minnesota Teacher, Great Lakes Review,* and *Min-neapolis Tribune.*

WORK IN PROGRESS: Two collections of personal essays on modern life, *Pain, a Suffering Theory* and *Intimacy, Our Good.*

SIDELIGHTS: Joseph Anthony Amato told *CA* that he has two aims in his writings—to seek "understanding and an ethic for our times" and "to discover the personal meaning of self and family." Amato has been a union leader and war protestor, and a concern for social activism is manifested in his writings. Such activism, however, "is counter-balanced by an overall sense of the terrible limits and even destructiveness of public life, both as reality and vocation." *Avocational interests:* Travel, including visits to Mexico, France, England, and Belgium.

AMMONS, A(rchie) R(andolph) 1926-

PERSONAL: Born February 18, 1926, in Whiteville, N.C.; son of Willie M. and Lucy Della (McKee) Ammons; married Phyllis Plumbo, November 26, 1949; children: John Randolph. *Education:* Wake Forest College (now University), B.S., 1949; University of California, Berkeley, studies in English, 1950-52. *Office:* Cornell University, Ithaca, N.Y. 14850.

CAREER: Frederich & Dimmock, Inc., Atlantic City, N.J., executive vice-president, 1952-61; Cornell University, Ithaca, N.Y., teacher of creative writing, 1964—. *Military service:* U.S. Naval Reserve, 1944-46; served in South Pacific. *Awards, honors:* Scholarship in poetry, Bread Loaf Writers' Confer-ence, 1961; John Simon Guggenheim fellowship, 1966; Amer-ican Academy of Arts and Letters traveling fellowship, 1967; Levinson Prize, 1970; D.Litt., Wake Forest University, 1972; National Book Award in Poetry, 1973, for *Collected Poems: 1951-1971;* Bollingen Prize, 1974-75.

WRITINGS—Poetry: *Ommateum,* Dorrance, 1955; *Expres-sions of Sea Level,* Ohio State University Press, 1964; *Corsons Inlet,* Cornell University Press, 1965; *Tape for the Turn of the Year,* Cornell University Press, 1965; *Northfield Poems,* Cor-nell University Press, 1966; *Selected Poems,* Cornell Univer-sity Press, 1968; *Uplands,* Norton, 1970; *Briefings,* Norton, 1971; *Collected Poems, 1951-1971,* Norton, 1972; *Sphere: The Form of a Motion,* Norton, 1973; *Diversifications,* Norton, 1975; *The Snow Poems,* Norton, 1977; *The Selected Poems: 1951-1977,* Norton, 1977; *Selected Longer Poems,* Norton, 1980; *A Coast of Trees,* Norton, 1981. Contributor to *Hudson Review, Poetry, Carleton Miscellany,* and other periodicals. Poetry editor, *Nation,* 1963.

SIDELIGHTS: A. R. Ammons once told the *Winston-Salem Journal & Sentinel:* "I never dreamed of being a Poet poet. I think I always wanted to be an amateur poet." But critics recognized him as more than an amateur, and today he is considered a major American poet. The measure of critics' esteem is implied by the stature of the poets to whom they compare Ammons. Tracing his creative geneology, they are apt to begin with Emerson and Thoreau and work chronolog-ically forward through Whitman, Pound, Frost, Stevens, and Williams. Of those poets, Harold Bloom feels that Emerson and Whitman have influenced Ammons the most. He contends in his book *The Ringers in the Tower: Studies in Romantic Tradition* that "the line of descent from Emerson and Whitman to the early poetry of Ammons is direct, and even the Poundian elements in [Ammons's poem] *Ommateum* derive from that part of Pound that is itself Whitmanian." Bloom also believes that Ammons "illuminates Emerson and all his progeny as much as he needs them for illumination." Daniel Hoffman, writing in the *New York Times Book Review,* agrees that Am-mons's poetry "is founded on an implied Emersonian division of experience into Nature and the Soul," adding that it "some-times consciously echo[es] familiar lines from Emerson, Whit-man and Dickinson."

While they acknowledge Ammons's debt to other writers, re-viewers find that he has forged a style that is distinctly his own. Jascha Kessler writes in *Kayak:* "[Ammons] makes his daily American rounds about lawn and meadow, wood, hill, stream, in an easy, articulate, flat, utterly uneventful expository syntax. Altogether unlike Thoreau's sinewy, exacting, apo-thegmatic prose, and unlike that suavely undulant later Stevens from whom he borrows some of his stanza structures or en-velopes, transmogrifying the Master of Imagination into a freshman-text writer who uses the colon for endless, undigest-ible linkages, never daring Stevens' comma, or venturing Tho-reau's period." Other critics join Kessler in objecting to Ammons's sparse punctuation, but David Kirby defends Ammons, writing in the *Times Literary Supplement* that "his short lines, his overall brevity, his avoidance of punctuation marks other than the occasional comma and that quick stop-and-go colon are hallmarks of his minimalism, his exquisitely unemcumbered technique."

Peter Stevens believes that Ammons's punctuation and form serve his intents well in some cases, poorly in others. Writing in the *Ontario Review*, he argues that the "ongoing flux" in *Tape for the Turn of the Year* (a long poem composed on an adding machine tape) works as "an almost perfect method to allow his notion of organic form to function," but that "no such wedding of form and content" occurs in another long poem, *Sphere: The Form of a Motion*. In the latter work, says Stevens, "the looseness that Ammons believes in derives . . . from the use of a form the poet has tried before. . . . [The poem is] written in three- or four-line stanzas, though there seems to be nothing definite about such paragraphing, running on as they do indiscriminately, often with no periods. Breathing space is provided by commas and colons only. Such a form fits snugly into Ammons' concern with flux and motion, and yet somehow the form seems too arbitrary."

Ammons is concerned with change both in nature and in daily life. William Logan notes in the *Chicago Tribune Book World* that in these interests, Ammons's work is "reminiscent of Frost on one side and Williams on the other, and in the work of both men, as in the [some] dozen books of their heir, intellect copes with its surroundings." According to Robert Shaw in *Poetry*, Ammons does more than describe; he forces the reader to involve himself. "The interest in an Ammons poem," he writes, "is less in the thing perceived than in the imaginative effort of the perceiver." Richard Howard explains further in his *Alone with America: Essays on the Art of Poetry in the United States since 1950* that "Ammons rehearses a marginal, a transitional experience[;] he is a littoralist of the imagination because the shore, the beach, or the coastal creek is not a *place* but an *event*, a transaction where land and water create and destroy each other, where life and death are exchanged, where shape and chaos are won and lost."

M. L. Rosenthal feels that although Ammons shares Wallace Stevens's desire to intellectualize rather than simply describe he falls short of Stevens's success. Rosenthal writes in *Shenandoah*: "Ammons does have certain advantages over Stevens: his knowledge of geological phenomena . . . and his ability to use language informally and to create open rhythms. Everything he writes has the authority of his intelligence, of his humor, and of his plastic control of materials. What he lacks, as compared to Stevens, is a certain passionate confrontation of the implicit issues such as makes Stevens' music a richer, deeper force. There *is* a great deal of feeling in Ammons; but in the interest of ironic self-control he seems afraid of letting the feeling have its way [as Stevens does]." Paul Zweig agrees that "unlike Eliot or Stevens, Ammons does not write well about ideas." He feels that "only when his poem plunges into the moment itself does it gain the exhilarating clarity which is Ammons' best quality." Writing in *Partisan Review*, Zweig asserts that Ammons's strength is in his form. "At first glance," he writes, "Ammons . . . seems to be a maverick, working vigorously against the limitations of the plain style, making a case in his work for a new intricacy of conception. Yet his best poems are closer to the plain style than one might think. It is when one hears William Carlos Williams in the background of his voice that the poems work clearly and solidly, not when one hears Hopkins or Stevens."

Harold Bloom suggests that while readers may indeed hear other voices in the background, Ammons's poems are uniquely valuable because of the personal voice that not only borrows from but also adds to the poetic tradition. Bloom writes: "Ammons's poetry does for me what Stevens's did earlier, and the High Romantics [Bloom's term for Blake, Wordsworth, Coleridge, Shelley, Keats, and Byron] before that; it helps me to live my life. If Ammons is, as I think, the central poet of my generation, because he alone has made a heterocosm, a second nature in his poetry, I deprecate no other poet by this naming. . . . A solitary artist, nurtured by the strength available for him only in extreme isolation, carrying on the Emersonian tradition with a quietness directly contrary to nearly all its other current avatars, he has emerged . . . as an extraordinary master, comparable to the Stevens of *Ideas of Order* and *The Man With the Blue Guitar*. To track him persistently [through his oeuvre] . . . is to be found by not only a complete possibility of imaginative experience, but by a renewed sense of the whole line of Emerson, the vitalizing and much maligned tradition that has accounted for most that matters in American poetry."

BIOGRAPHICAL/CRITICAL SOURCES—Books: Richard Howard, *Alone with America: Essays on the Art of Poetry in the United States since 1950*, Atheneum, 1969; Harold Bloom, *The Ringers in the Tower: Studies in Romantic Tradition*, University of Chicago Press, 1971; *Contemporary Literary Criticism*, Gale, Volume II, 1974, Volume III, 1975, Volume V, 1976, Volume VIII, 1978, Volume IX, 1978; *Authors in the News*, Volume I, Gale, 1976.

Periodicals: *Book Week*, February 20, 1966; *Nation*, April 24, 1967, January 18, 1971; *Hudson Review*, summer, 1967; *Prairie Schooner*, fall, 1967; *Contemporary Literature*, winter, 1968; *Poetry*, April, 1969, November, 1973; *New York Times Book Review*, December 14, 1969, May 10, 1981; *Time*, July 12, 1971; *New York Times*, November 10, 1972; *Shenandoah*, fall, 1972; *Kayak*, summer, 1973; *Partisan Review*, Volume XLI, No. 4, 1974; *Winston-Salem Journal & Sentinel*, December 1, 1974; *Ontario Review*, fall-winter, 1975-76; *Times Literary Supplement*, April 24, 1981; *Chicago Tribune Book World*, July 26, 1981.

—*Sketch by Elaine Guregian*

*   *   *

ANDERSON, Jack(son Northman)   1922-

PERSONAL: Born October 19, 1922, in Long Beach, Calif.; son of Orlando N. (a postal clerk) and Agnes (Mortensen) Anderson; married Olivia Farley, August 10, 1949; children: Cheri, Lance, Lauri, Tina, Kevin, Randy, Tanya, Rodney, Bryan. *Education:* Attended University of Utah, 1940-41, Georgetown University, 1947-48, and George Washington University, 1948. *Religion:* Church of Jesus Christ of Latter-day Saints. *Home:* 7810 Kachina Lane, Bethesda, Md. 20034. *Office:* 1401 16th St. N.W., Washington, D.C. 20036.

CAREER: Part-time reporter for newspapers in Utah, 1934-39; *Salt Lake City Tribune*, Salt Lake City, Utah, reporter, 1939-41; missionary in Georgia, Alabama, and Florida for Church of Jesus Christ of Latter-day Saints, 1941-44; *Deseret News*, Salt Lake City, war correspondent in China, 1945; assistant to Drew Pearson for syndicated newspaper column "Washington Merry-Go-Round," 1947-65, author of column with Pearson, 1965-69, sole author, 1969—. Lecturer; host of "Jack Anderson Radio Report"; television commentator. Part owner, *Annapolis Evening Capital*; publisher, *Investigative Reporter*. Trustee, Chinese Refugee Relief, 1962—. *Military service:* U.S. Merchant Marine, 1944-45. U.S. Army, Quartermaster Corps, 1946-47; staff member of service newspapers and Armed Forces Radio. *Member:* White House Correspondents Association, National Press Club. *Awards, honors:* Pulitzer Prize nomination (with Drew Pearson) for national reporting, 1967, for articles on U.S. Senator Thomas J. Dodd; Pulitzer Prize for national reporting, 1972, for articles on India-Pakistan crisis.

WRITINGS: (With Ronald W. May) *McCarthy: The Man, the Senator, the "ism,"* Beacon Press, 1952; (with Fred Blumenthal) *The Kefauver Story,* Dial, 1956; (with Drew Pearson) *U.S.A.: Second-Class Power?,* Simon & Schuster, 1958; *Washington Expose,* Public Affairs Press, 1967; (with Pearson) *The Case against Congress,* Simon & Schuster, 1968; (with Carl Kalvelage) *American Government . . . Like It Is,* General Learning Press, 1972; (with George Clifford) *The Anderson Papers,* Random House, 1973; (with James Boyd) *Confessions of a Muckraker: The Inside Story of Life in Washington during the Truman, Eisenhower, Kennedy and Johnson Years,* Random House, 1979; (with Bill Pronzini) *The Cambodia File* (novel), Doubleday, 1981. *Parade,* Washington editor, 1954-68, Washington bureau chief, 1968—.

SIDELIGHTS: Jack Anderson, one of America's most widely read newspaper columnists, launched his career as an investigative reporter in the shadow of famed muckraker Drew Pearson. Their association began in 1947 when, on the advice of friends, the then-twenty-five-year-old Anderson approached the Washington-based journalist for a job. Though he arrived in town with (as Anderson himself admits) "little to recommend me but somewhat watered credentials as a 'war correspondent,' a smattering of Chinese slang, and a certain bravado," Pearson hired him as an assistant. According to the *Chicago Tribune Book World*'s Robert Sherrill, it was "the smartest thing Pearson ever did. . . . They made an unbeatable combination—mature Pearson supplying the flair, the high-powered contacts, the boundless ego, the genius for intrigue, the moralistic certitude; youthful Anderson supplying tireless legwork, a gambler's talent for bluffing, and, as he says, a certain bravado."

For ten years Anderson labored in virtual anonymity, despite the fact that, as Sherrill points out, "more often than not, it was he—not Pearson—who got the key document, thawed the crucial witness, made the lucky phone call." In 1957, however, Anderson threatened to quit unless Pearson publicly recognized his contribution to the success of their "Washington Merry-Go-Round" feature. The elder journalist then agreed to give Anderson more bylines and even promised him that he would one day inherit the column. Though Anderson did not officially achieve full partner status until 1965, Sherrill notes that "in Pearson's final years, when he was running out of steam, it was Anderson who kept the column perking along."

Upon Pearson's death in 1969, Anderson became the sole author of "Washington Merry-Go-Round," though he is assisted by several other reporters and investigators (whose contributions he is quick to acknowledge). Since then, the column has developed a reputation for being "a more scrupulous, if somewhat less passionate institution," writes Joe Klein of the *New York Times Book Review*. Anderson, for example, tries to avoid the more blatant propagandizing that was common during Pearson's heyday, and he insists that his reporters go after the "spare, hard expose" regardless of the wrongdoer's political affiliation. (Pearson, a liberal, angered many people with what Anderson calls "his sense of protectiveness" towards those of a similar persuasion.) He also disagrees with Pearson's habit of basing his attacks on instinct rather than on fact; it was not all that unusual for the elder columnist to first make his accusations and then send out his investigators for the proof with which to back them up. Despite this change in philosophy, however, the *Washington Post Book World*'s Godfrey Hodgson

declares that Anderson "has never shrunk from telling [his] readers what they as citizens need to know about what [he] calls 'the gamy pratfalls' of the mighty."

Anderson attributes much of his interest in investigative journalism to his Mormon background. As he once explained to the *Miami Herald*'s Rob Elder, "In the Mormon philosophy the eternal struggle is not only between good and evil but between freedom and force. I was brought up as a youngster to believe that the Constitution of the United States was almost a divine document, in the sense that it was a document of freedom. I was brought up to believe that public office, therefore, was a public trust and that those who abused it were people who should be exposed and removed from office." He makes a point of conducting his investigations without the help of paid informants and without limiting his contacts only to those who have a grudge against the person under scrutiny. Instead, he told Elder, "I seek out the idealistic, . . . those who believe in our system of government, who believe in the public's right to know. I remind them that their salaries aren't paid by [their superiors], but by the American people and that they have an obligation to these people to let them know about wrongdoing, inefficiency, mismanagement and corruption."

As for the charges that his revelations occasionally threaten national security, Anderson insists that is not the point. "I think that is a danger," he says, "but a far greater danger is that the government withholds from the American people what it doesn't want the American people to know. The people own this country, and any time the people in government feel that they are above and beyond the law and that they can make decisions in our behalf without telling us about it, that becomes the great danger. . . . Obviously we can't let them get away with censoring the news by substituting the word 'secret' for 'censored.' . . . We publish [secret information] only when we consider it censored information. . . . The decision is toughest if there's any reason to believe that this story is going to cost a life or endanger a life. I don't want to play God. . . . I think it's my job to report what's going on, not to maneuver behind the scenes."

Even so, he admits, "every success of the investigative reporter means ruin for some human being who is typically weak rather than evil. Most of the time I am militantly convinced that the trade-off is necessary to maintain a free society. But there are seasons when it seems a close call."

Critics of Anderson feel he is not the muckraker Pearson was, citing his lack of major moral and political influence as evidence of his more modest stature. But as the *New Republic*'s Joseph Nocera comments: "During the time the column was in [Pearson's] hands, he was a unique and powerful force in Washington, and undoubtably part of the reason had to do with [his] having cornered the market on muckraking. . . . Jack Anderson hasn't been as lucky. During his term at the helm of the 'Merry-Go-Round' column, journalism has changed dramatically. Now he must compete with dozens of reporters on newspapers all over the country for scoops—and he does not come off well by comparison." For example, Nocera states, "Like Pearson, he still writes too often based more on instinct than fact, still unrelentingly hypes his product, still pounds away at a story, finding a dozen different ways to present the same set of facts. For the sake of the scoop, he can still damage careers with information that is not altogether accurate, or at least not altogether provable."

There are others, however, who feel that in spite of his faults, Anderson performs an invaluable service. "He plays a unique role in American journalism," notes Peter Osnos in the *Washington Post Book World*, "tackling sensitive subjects head on with a permanent sense of indignation at wrongdoing and a determination to get the news that officials might prefer to keep quiet.''

Concludes Anderson in a *Parade* article on why he chooses to ''blow the whistle'': ''[Since 1947] I have tried to break down the walls of secrecy in Washington. But today the walls are thicker than ever. More and more of our policymakers hide behind those walls. Only the press can stand as a true bulwark against an executive branch with a monopoly on foreign policy information. It has all the authority it needs in the first Amendment.''

BIOGRAPHICAL/CRITICAL SOURCES: Parade, February 13, 1972; *Miami Herald,* May 19, 1974; *Authors in the News,* Volume I, Gale, 1976; Jack Anderson, *Confessions of a Muckraker: The Inside Story of Life in Washington during the Truman, Eisenhower, Kennedy and Johnson Years,* Random House, 1979; *Nation,* May 5, 1979; *Chicago Tribune Book World,* May 6, 1979; *New York Times Book Review,* May 20, 1979; *Washington Post Book World,* June 17, 1979, January 18, 1981; *New Republic,* June 30, 1979; *Best Sellers,* August, 1979; *Virginia Quarterly Review,* autumn, 1979; *Los Angeles Times,* March 12, 1981.†

—*Sketch by Deborah A. Straub*

*   *   *

ANDERSON, James E(lliott) 1933-

PERSONAL: Born July 6, 1933, in Galva, Ill.; son of Albin C. (a farmer) and Amy (Nelson) Anderson; married Alberta Hedstrom, June 21, 1953; children: Carrie, Elise, Joel. *Education:* University of Illinois, student, 1950-52; Illinois State Normal University, student, 1952-53; Southwest Texas State College (now Southwest Texas State University), B.S., 1955; University of Texas, Ph.D., 1960. *Politics:* Democrat. *Office:* Department of Political Science, University of Houston, 3801 Cullen Blvd., Houston, Tex. 77004.

CAREER: Wake Forest College (now University), Winston-Salem, N.C., instructor, 1959-60, assistant professor, 1960-64, associate professor of political science, 1964-66; University of Houston, Houston, Tex., associate professor, 1966-69, professor of political science, 1969—. *Member:* American Association of University Professors, American Political Science Association, Policy Studies Organization, Midwest Political Science Association, Southern Political Science Association, Southwestern Political Science Association.

WRITINGS: The Emergence of the Modern Regulatory State, Public Affairs Press, 1962; *Politics and the Economy,* Little, Brown, 1966; (compiler) *Politics and Economic Policy-making: Selected Readings,* Addison-Wesley, 1970; (with Richard Murray and Edward L. Farky) *Texas Politics: An Introduction,* Harper, 1971, 2nd edition, 1975; *Public Policy-making,* Praeger, 1975, 2nd edition, Holt, 1979; (editor) *Cases in Public Policy-making,* Praeger, 1976, 2nd edition, Holt, 1981; (editor) *Economic Regulatory Policies,* Lexington Books, 1976; (with David W. Brady and Charles Bullock III) *Politics and Policy in America,* Duxbury, 1978. Contributor to professional journals.

WORK IN PROGRESS: With Jared Hazleton, *Managing Macroeconomic Institutions: The Johnson Presidency.*

*   *   *

ANDERSON, Mona 1910-

PERSONAL: Born March 11, 1910, in New Brighton, New Zealand; daughter of William and Alice (Holland) Tarling; married Ronald Edward Anderson (a sheep rancher), June 15, 1940. *Education:* Educated in Canterbury, New Zealand. *Religion:* Anglican. *Home:* 15 McMillan St., Darfield, Canterbury, New Zealand.

CAREER: Operator, with husband, of sheep ranch in Rakaia Gorge, Canterbury, New Zealand. Writer. *Awards, honors:* Member of the Order of the British Empire.

WRITINGS—All published by A. H. & A. W. Reed: *A River Rules My Life,* 1963; *Good Logs of Algidus,* 1965; *Over the River,* 1966; *The Wonderful World at My Doorstep,* 1968; *A Letter From James,* 1972; *MaryLou: A High Country Lamb* (children's book), 1975; *The Water-Joey,* 1976; *Old Duke* (children's book), 1977; *Home Is the High Country* (children's book), 1979; *Both Sides of the River,* 1981. Contributor to *Family Doctor, Weekly Press,* and *New Zealand Herald.* Writer of radio scripts.

SIDELIGHTS: Mona Anderson wrote *CA:* ''I began my writing career as a child at school, always scribbling notes and writing little stories. I believe very strongly that young aspiring writers should write about something that comes from the heart.''

*   *   *

ANDERSON, Paul Seward 1913-1975

PERSONAL: Born June 5, 1913, in Yuma, Colo.; died February 4, 1975; son of Albert Victor and Phoebe (Seward) Anderson; married Verna Dieckman (a teacher), February 4, 1954. *Education:* Colorado State College of Agriculture and Mechanic Arts (now Colorado State University), A.B., 1934; University of Wisconsin, M.S., 1952, Ph.D., 1954. *Politics:* Democrat. *Religion:* Presbyterian. *Home:* 3141 Xenophen, San Diego, Calif. *Office:* Department of Education, San Diego State University, San Diego, Calif. 92115.

CAREER: Windsor (Colo.) Public Schools, teacher, 1935-38; chief of textbooks, Seoul, Korea, 1946-49; education officer, Osaka, Japan, 1949-52; U.S. Military Group in Japan, youth affairs officer, 1949-50; Houghton Miflin Co., representative in Wisconsin, 1950-54; San Diego State University, San Diego, Calif., professor of education, 1954-75. Moderator, Kensington Community Church. *Military service:* U.S. Army, Military Police; became major. *Member:* Rotary International.

WRITINGS: Yong Kee of Korea, Scott, 1954; *Resource Materials for Teachers of Spelling,* Burgess, 1959, 2nd edition, 1968; *Red Fox and the Hungry Tiger,* Scott, 1962; *Storytelling with the Flannel Board,* Denison, 1963; *Language Skills in Elementary Education,* Macmillan, 1964, 3rd edition (with Diane Lapp), 1979; *The Boy and the Blind Storyteller,* Scott, 1964; *Readings in the Language Arts,* Macmillan, 1964; (compiler) *Linguistics in the Elementary School Classroom,* Macmillan, 1971; *Young America* (readers; grades 4, 5, 6) Lyons & Carnahan, 1972.†

*   *   *

ANDREANO, Ralph L(ouis) 1929-

PERSONAL: Born April 11, 1929, in Waterbury, Conn.; son of John and Loretta (Creasia) Andreano; married Carol Wessbecher (a teacher), September 5, 1955; children: Maria Carol, Nicholas. *Education:* Drury College, A.B., 1952; Washington University, St. Louis, Mo., M.A., 1955; Northwestern University, Ph.D., 1960. *Home:* 1815 Vilas Ave., Madison, Wis. 53711. *Office:* Department of Economics, University of Wisconsin, 7316 Social Science Bldg., Madison, Wis. 53706.

CAREER: Northwestern University, Evanston, Ill., instructor in economics department, 1959-60; Harvard University, Cambridge, Mass., assistant professor, School of Business Administration, 1960-62; Earlham College, Richmond, Ind., associate professor and chairman of department of economics, 1962-65; University of Wisconsin—Madison, associate professor, 1965-67, professor of economics, 1967—, chairman of department, 1980—, director of undergraduate program, 1965-67, director of graduate program in economic history, 1969-70, director of Health Economics Research Center, 1969-76, 1978—. Delegate of American Economic Association to American Council of Learned Societies, 1964-69; chief economist, Division of Strengthening of Health Services, World Health Organization, 1973-74.

MEMBER: Economic History Association, American Economic Association, Economic History Society (United Kingdom), Organization of American Historians, American Public Health Association, Midwest Economic Association, Midwest Economic History Association, Omicron Delta Kappa, Omicron Delta Gamma. *Awards, honors:* Rotary fellow in Norway, 1951; Fulbright scholar, University of Oslo, 1952-53; National Science Foundation Award, 1963; named Public Servant of the Year, Center for Public Representation, 1977-78; Wisconsin State Legislature citation, 1978, for outstanding public service.

WRITINGS: (Editor) *Economic Impact of American Civil War,* Schenkman, 1963, revised edition, 1967; (with H. F. Williamson) *A History of the American Petroleum Industry,* Volume II: *The Age of Energy,* Northwestern University Press, 1963; *"No Joy in Mudville": The Dilemma of Major League Baseball,* Schenkman, 1965; *New Views on American Economic Development,* Schenkman, 1965; *An Economist's Handbook: A Guide to the Reference Sources,* Schenkman, 1966; (editor) *The New Economic History: Papers on Methodology,* Wiley, 1970; (co-author) *Disease and Economic Development: The Economic Impact of Parasitic Disease in St. Lucia,* University of Wisconsin Press, 1973; (editor) *Super Concentration/Super Corporation,* Warner, 1973; *The Student Economist's Handbook,* Schenckman, 1976; (co-author) *American Health Policy: Perspectives and Choices,* Rand, 1978; (with J. Seigfried) *Economics of Crime,* Wiley, 1981.

Contributor: *Civil War History,* Iowa University Press, 1957; *Oil's First Century,* Harvard School of Business Administration, 1961; *American Government,* Row, Peterson & Co., 1962; *Output, Employment, and Productivity in the U.S. since 1800,* Columbia University Press, 1966; *Business Enterprise and Economic Change,* Kent State University Press, 1973; *Research in Health Economics,* JAI Press, 1979; *Medical Ethics, Regulation and Health Policy,* Bollinger, 1981.

Contributor to National Bureau of Economic Research "Income and Wealth Series," Volume 30, and to history and economics journals in this country and Canada. Editor, *Explorations in Entrepreneurial History,* 2nd series, 1962-70, and *Business History Review,* 1961-62.

*   *   *

ANNIXTER, Jane
See STURTZEL, Jane Levington

*   *   *

ANNIXTER, Paul
See STURTZEL, Howard A(llison)

APPEL, Benjamin 1907-1977

PERSONAL: Born September 13, 1907, in New York, N.Y.; died April 3, 1977, in Princeton, N.J.; son of Louis and Bessie (Mikofsky) Appel; married Sophie Marshak, October 31, 1936; children: Carla, Willa, Marianna Consideration. *Education:* Attended University of Pennsylvania, 1925-26, and New York University, 1926-27; Lafayette College, B.S., 1929. *Politics:* "Utopian." *Residence:* Roosevelt, N.J.

CAREER: Writer, 1929-77, with some short stints during depression years as bank clerk, farmer, lumberjack, tenement house inspector, and other positions. During World War II worked as aviation mechanic; served with various government agencies, including U.S. Office of Civilian Defense, and War Manpower Commission, 1943-45; special assistant to U.S. Commissioner for the Philippines, 1945-46, with simulated rank of colonel in Manila. Visiting author at University of Pennsylvania, spring, 1974. *Member:* Authors Guild, P.E.N.

WRITINGS: Mixed Vintage (poems), Richard G. Badger, 1929; *Brain Guy,* Knopf, 1934; *Four Roads to Death,* Knopf, 1935; *Runaround,* Dutton, 1937; *The Power House,* Dutton, 1939.

The People Talk (nonfiction), Dutton, 1940; *The Dark Stain,* Dial, 1943; *But Not Yet Slain,* Wyn, 1947; *Fortress in Rice,* Bobbs-Merrill, 1951; *Plunder,* Gold Medal, 1952; *Hell's Kitchen* (short stories), Lion Books, 1952; *Dock Walloper* (short stories), Lion Books, 1953; *Sweet Money Girl,* Fawcett, 1954; *Life and Death of a Tough Guy,* Avon, 1955; *We Were There in the Klondike Gold Rush* (juvenile), Grosset, 1956; *We Were There at the Battle for Bataan* (juvenile), Grosset, 1957; *The Raw Edge,* Random House, 1958; *We Were There with Cortes and Montezuma* (juvenile), Grosset, 1959; *The Funhouse,* Ballantine, 1959; *The Death Master,* Popular Library, 1959.

The Illustrated Book about South America, including Mexico and Central America (juvenile), Grosset, 1960; *A Big Man, a Fast Man,* Morrow, 1961; *Shepherd of the Sun,* Obolensky, 1961; *With Many Voices: Europe Talks about America,* Morrow, 1963; *A Time of Fortune,* Morrow, 1963; *Hitler: From Power to Ruin,* Grosset, 1964; *Ben-Gurion's Israel,* Grosset, 1965; *Man and Magic,* Pantheon, 1966; *Why the Russians Are the Way They Are* (juvenile), Little, Brown, 1966; *The Age of Dictators* (juvenile), Crown, 1968; *Why the Chinese Are the Way They Are* (juvenile), Little, Brown, 1968, revised edition, 1973; *The Fantastic Mirror: Science Fiction across the Ages* (juvenile), Pantheon, 1969; *Why the Japanese Are the Way They Are* (juvenile), Little, Brown, 1973; *The Devil and W. Kaspar,* Popular Library, 1977; (adapter) Comte de Caylus, *Heart of Ice,* Pantheon, 1977.

Short stories anthologized in *O. Henry Memorial Award Prize Stories* and O'Brien's *Best Short Stories,* 1934, 1935, and in *Best Short Stories, 1915-39.* Contributor of essays on writers of the 1930s and short stories to magazines, such as *Carleton Miscellany, Literary Review,* and *New Letters.*

SIDELIGHTS: Benjamin Appel first wrote for the "little" literary magazines of the 1930s, reflected on the background of his youth (the "Hell's Kitchen" area of Manhattan) in his first novel, *Brain Guy,* and later developed novels around politics, race relations, and the Philippines, and wrote nonfiction on other contemporary subjects. *Avocational interests:* Fishing.

OBITUARIES: New York Times, April 4, 1977; *Publishers Weekly,* April 25, 1977; *AB Bookman's Weekly,* June 27, 1977.†

*   *   *

APPLEBAUM, William 1906-1979(?)

PERSONAL: Born April 24, 1906, in Pruzana, Russian (now

U.S.S.R.); came to United States in 1920; died c. 1979; son of Lipa (a merchant) and Esther (Volk) Applebaum; married Celia Kiperstein, 1929 (deceased); married Berenice Milgroom, September, 1960 (died March, 1980). *Education:* University of Minnesota, A.B., 1931, graduate study, 1932-33; University of Cincinnati, graduate study, 1931-32. *Religion:* Jewish. *Home:* 2451 Brickell Ave., Miami, Fla. 33129.

CAREER: Kroger Co., Cincinnati, Ohio, market research analyst, 1933-35, chief of market research department, 1935-38; Stop & Shop, Inc., Boston, Mass., director of marketing research department, 1938-42, 1945-47, director of planning and coordination, 1948, assistant general manager, 1949-53, director, 1949-78; Harvard Graduate School of Business Administration, Boston, Mass., visiting consultant on food distribution, 1954-60, lecturer on food distribution and comparative marketing, 1960-68, lecturer emeritus, beginning 1968. Director of Hannaford Brothers Co., Portland, Me., Chatham Super Markets, Inc., Warren, Mich., beginning 1969. Consultant to Research and Development Board, National Security Council, 1948-52; member of advisory committees of U.S. Department of Agriculture and Super Market Institute. Marketing consultant, beginning 1954. Member of committees for various local, state, national, and foreign agencies. *Military service:* U.S. Marine Corps Reserve, on active duty in Office of Strategic Services, 1942-45; became captain; received Bronze Star Medal; inactive service, 1945-57; became major.

MEMBER: American Marketing Association (president, New England chapter, 1946-47; director, 1956-58; chairman of publications policy and review board, 1958-59), American Statistical Association, Association of American Geographers, American Geographical Society, Regional Science Association, American Association for the Advancement of Science (fellow), Food Distribution Research Society, Super Market Institute (honorary), Eta Mu Pi. *Awards, honors:* American Marketing Association National Award, 1950; Association of American Geographers citation of merit, 1959.

WRITINGS: The Secondary Commercial Centers of Cincinnati, two volumes, Institute of Industrial Research, University of Cincinnati, 1932; (with Richard F. Spears) *Shopping Habits of Super Market Customers,* Marketing Research Department, Stop & Shop, 1947; *The Super Market Industry Speaks,* Super Market Institute, 1949; *A Plan for Cooperative Marketing Research in the Food Distribution Industry,* Super Market Institute, 1954; *What Price Success?,* Hannaford Bros. Co., 1955; (with Bernard L. Schapker) *A Quarter Century of Change in Cincinnati Business Centers,* Cincinnati Enquirer, 1956; (with Schapker) *Atlas of Business Centers: Cincinnati-Hamilton County, Ohio, 1955,* American Marketing Association, 1956; (with Richard H. Moulton) *An Exploration into the Reasons Why Super Markets Add and Discontinue Items,* McCall Publishing, 1956.

(With Malcom P. McNair and Walter J. Salmon) *Cases in Food Distribution,* Irwin, 1964; (with Salmon, Robert D. Buzzell, Richard F. Vancil, and John D. Glover) *Product Profitability Measurement and Merchandizing Decisions,* Division of Research, Harvard Business School, 1965; *Patterns of Food Distribution in a Metropolis* (pamphlet), Super Market Institute, 1966; (with Ray Goldberg) *Brand Strategy in United States Food Marketing* [*and*] *Dynamic Brand Strategies,* Division of Research, Graduate School of Business Administration, Harvard University, 1967; *Guide to Store Location Research: With Emphasis on Super Markets,* Addison-Wesley, 1968; *Private Brands: Basic Consideration* (pamphlet), Institute of Food Distribution, 1968; *Store Location Strategy Cases,* Addison-Wesley, 1968; (with Robert Minichello) *Teachers*

Manual: Store Location Strategy Cases, Addison-Wesley, 1968; *Super Marketing: The Past, the Present, a Projection* (pamphlet), Super Market Institute, 1969.

(With Milton P. Brown and Salmon) *Strategy Problems of Mass Retailers and Wholesalers,* Irwin, 1970; *Shopping Center Strategy: A Case Study of the Planning, Location, and Development of the Del Monte Center,* International Council of Shopping Centers, 1970, 3rd edition, 1978; *Hardware Retailing Strategy Cases,* Russell R. Mueller Retail Hardware Research Foundation, 1971; (with S. O. Kaylin) *Case Studies in Shopping Center Development and Operation,* International Council of Shopping Centers, 1974.

Contributor: H. G. Wales and R. Ferber, editors, *Marketing Research: Selected Literature,* W. C. Brown, 1952; *American Geography: Inventory and Prospect,* Syracuse University Press, 1954; *Social Science for Industry,* Stanford Research Institute, 1956; *New Directions in Food Retailing,* University of Pittsburgh Press, 1957; *The Frontiers of Marketing Thought and Science,* American Marketing Association, 1957; *How to Make a Profit in a Highly Competitive Industry,* Super Market Institute, 1957; *Store Location and Development Studies,* Clark University, 1961; *Store Location Research for the Food Industry,* National American Wholesale Grocers Association, 1961; *Guideposts for Decision Makers,* Super Market Institute, 1961; *On the Threshold: Action and Promise in Creative Teamwork,* National American Wholesale Grocer's Association, 1965; Curt Kornblau, editor, *Guide to Store Location Research with Emphasis on Super Markets,* Addison-Wesley, 1968.

Editor of four other Super Market Institute publications, 1947-48. Contributor to *Annals of the Association of American Geographers,* 1961, and to marketing surveys and reports. Author of more than fifty articles published in *Professional Geographer, Chain Store Age, Economic Geography,* and other journals. Member of editorial board, *Journal of Marketing,* 1943-44, *Journal of Retailing,* beginning 1965.†

*   *   *

APPLEMAN, Philip (Dean) 1926-

PERSONAL: Born February 8, 1926, in Kendallville, Ind.; son of William Russell and Gertrude (Keller) Appleman; married Marjorie Haberkorn (a playwright), August 19, 1950. *Education:* Northwestern University, B.S., 1950, Ph.D., 1955; University of Michigan, A.M., 1951. *Office:* Department of English, Indiana University, Bloomington, Ind. 47405.

CAREER: Indiana University at Bloomington, 1955—, began as instructor, professor of English, 1967—. Fulbright scholar, University of Lyon, 1951-52; International School of America, Columbus, Ohio, instructor in world literature and philosophy, 1960-61, instructor and field director, 1962-63, currently member of academic advisory committee; visiting professor, State University of New York College at Purchase, 1973, and Columbia University, 1974. *Military service:* U.S. Army Air Forces, 1944-45. U.S. Merchant Marine, 1946, 1948-49. *Member:* Modern Language Association of America (chairman of English Section II, 1966), National Council of Teachers of English, College English Association, American Association of University Professors (member of National Council, 1969-72), Poetry Society of America (member of National Governing Board, 1981—), Academy of American Poets, P.E.N., Phi Beta Kappa. *Awards, honors:* Fellowship in creative writing for poetry, National Endowment for the Arts, 1975; Castagnola Award, Poetry Society of America, for *Open Doorways.*

WRITINGS: (Editor with William A. Madden and Michael Wolff and contributor) *1859: Entering an Age of Crisis,* Indiana

University Press, 1959; *The Silent Explosion*, Beacon, 1965; *Kites on a Windy Day* (poems), Byron Press, 1967; *Summer Love and Surf* (poems), Vanderbilt University Press, 1968; *In the Twelfth Year of the War* (novel), Putnam, 1970; (editor and contributor) *Darwin* (critical anthology), Norton, 1970; (editor) *An Essay on the Principle of Population* (critical anthology), Norton, 1976; *Open Doorways* (poems), Norton, 1976; *Shame the Devil* (novel), Crown, 1981. Contributor of critical articles and reviews to scholarly periodicals; contributor of poems to *Harper's, Yale Review, Partisan Review, New Republic, Nation, New York Times*, and other periodicals. Founding editor, *Victorian Studies*.

WORK IN PROGRESS: A new volume of poems and a novel.

SIDELIGHTS: Philip Appleman, in his novels, poetry, and nonfiction, has touched upon a wide range of topical issues, including the world population crisis and the theory of evolution. Some reviewers have been critical of Appleman's social conscience and the diversity of his interests. Stanley Plumly in the *American Poetry Review* writes of *Open Doorways:* "When the considering voice in his poems is surrounded by circumstance and reporting directly from the evidence, Appleman's results are impressive. . . . But when the voice begins to lose sight of itself and its individual circumstance, when it begins to sound glibly generalized or socially self-conscious, when subject matter begins to replace the attention paid to specific objects, the poems take on a public, easing-into-profundity posture." Plumly concludes, "A man of his multiple talents should leave his civic conscience to prose."

Reviewing *Open Doorways* for *Poetry*, Jay Parini calls Appleman's poems "clear-eyed, musical, and well-crafted. . . . There is no mistaking the technical competence of this poet, who has a marvelous ear." But, Parini finds, "when he does make a desperate effort to shock us with reality, the result is tragic, [as in one of Appleman's poems about Viet Nam]. . . . Poets rarely make good poems from such inflated subject matter because the emotional overcharge already present before the poet goes to work has to be defused. How do you begin to write about Dachau, Hiroshima, or Viet Nam?" Similarly, Joseph McLellan in the *Washington Post* describes Appleman's writing in the satirical novel *Shame the Devil* as "sometimes brilliant, and the mind that one senses behind the story is a keen one, constantly darting off in a dozen directions at once." But McLellan also comments, "it is when the mind comes wandering back from those dozen directions, bearing all kinds of miscellaneous loot that is poured into the story, that one begins to wonder: Has the author brought the elements of his novel together because they belong together or because they happened to interest and amuse him?"

Other critics admire Appleman's social conscience and his ability to condense a variety of ideas into an organized and literate form. Art Seidenbaum of the *Los Angeles Times* finds *Shame the Devil* entertaining and provocative: "Most of our modern manners are [satirized]. . . . Sex, politics and religion . . . are all examined in Appleman's loony laboratory and found in dubious health. . . . Appleman wants to amuse and drop morals without moralizing; he's smart enough to do it swiftly, knowing the warp of satire soon wears thin." Appleman's first novel, *In the Twelfth Year of the War*, has also been praised for its treatment of social issues. As David F. Sharpe writes in *Best Sellers*, *In the Twelfth Year of the War* combines an "overwhelming and at times devastating plea against war with an equally biting social commentary. . . . Appleman expertly and poetically uses biting satire, black humor, and pathos to tell an excellent story. His characters are as real as the situations and emotions they face." Appleman's social comment is justi-

fied, and the ironies of national policy are expertly and sardonically portrayed. Anyone interested in an ably constructed, well written, realistic novel should enjoy" *In the Twelfth Year of the War.*

Appleman's critical studies have also been praised. Betty Chambers of the *Humanist* applauds the author for lending a "lucid style" to the *Darwin* anthology. T. K. Burch, reviewing *The Silent Explosion* for *Harper's*, commends Appleman for bringing "the intangibles of human problems, including moral values" into the biological and social sciences, and a *New Yorker* critic calls *The Silent Explosion* a "lucid, moving, and convincing discussion. . . . Appleman discusses with great power the absolute need to change . . . attitudes if we are to survive on our meagre planet."

BIOGRAPHICAL/CRITICAL SOURCES: Christian Science Monitor, April 29, 1965; *New Yorker*, June 26, 1965; *Harper's*, August, 1965; *Prairie Schooner*, fall, 1969; *Hudson Review*, spring, 1971; *American Poetry Review*, July-August, 1977; *Poetry*, August, 1977; *Humanist*, July-August, 1980; *Best Sellers*, January 15, 1981; *Los Angeles Times*, April 22, 1981; *Washington Post*, May 15, 1981.

*   *   *

APTHEKER, Bettina 1944-

PERSONAL: Surname is pronounced *ap*-tek-er; born September 2, 1944, in Fort Bragg, N.C.; daughter of Herbert (a writer) and Fay P. (Aptheker) Aptheker; married Jack Kurzweil (a college professor), August 29, 1965; children: Joshua Mark, Jennifer Gloria Lucy. *Education:* University of California, Berkeley, A.B., 1967; San Jose State University, M.A., 1976. *Politics:* Communist. *Home:* 155 South 17th St., San Jose, Calif. 95112. *Office:* Women's Studies Program, San Jose State University, San Jose, Calif. 95114.

CAREER: Free-lance writer and lecturer, 1968—; *People's World*, San Francisco, Calif., editor and writer, 1969—; San Jose State University, San Jose, Calif., assistant instructor in speech, 1974-75, lecturer in Women's Studies Program, 1976—; San Jose City College, San Jose, instructor in speech, 1976—. Member of steering committee, Free Speech Movement, Berkeley, 1964-65; member of national administration committee, Mobilization Committee to End the War in Vietnam, San Francisco and Washington, D.C., 1966-68. Member of board of directors, Pacific Publishing Foundation, Inc. and American Institute for Marxist Studies. Member of Communist Party National Committee, 1966—; member of Angela Davis Defense Committee.

WRITINGS: (With Robert Kaufman and Michael Folsom) *F.S.M.: The Free Speech Movement at Berkeley*, W.E.B. Du Bois Clubs of America, 1965; *Big Business and the American University* (pamphlet), New Outlook Publishers, 1966; *Columbia University, Inc.* (pamphlet), W.E.B. Du Bois Clubs of America, 1968; *Higher Education and the Student Rebellion in the United States, 1966-69: A Bibliography*, American Institute for Marxist Studies, 1969, revised edition, 1970; (with Angela Davis) *If They Come in the Morning, Voices of Resistance*, New American Library, 1971; (with father, Herbert Aptheker) *Racism and Reaction in the United States: Two Marxian Studies* (pamphlet), New Outlook, 1971; *The Academic Rebellion in the United States: A Marxist Appraisal*, Citadel, 1972; *The Morning Breaks: The Trial of Angela Davis*, International Publishers, 1975; (editor and author of introduction) Jane Addams and Ida B. Wells, *Lynching and Rape: An Exchange of Views*, American Institute for Marxist Studies, 1977; (editor) Herbert Aptheker, *The Unfolding Drama: Stud-*

ies in U.S. History, International Publishers, 1979; (with others) *Kent State Ten Years After,* edited by Scott Bills, Kent Popular, 1980; *Women's Legacy: Interpretive Essays in U.S. History,* International Publishers, in press. Contributor of articles and book reviews to *California Law Review, Nation, Guardian, Political Affairs,* and other periodicals.

WORK IN PROGRESS: Research on the history of Afro-American women in the United States; theoretical work in Marxism and feminism.

SIDELIGHTS: One of the leaders of the Free Speech movement at the University of California, Bettina Aptheker has since endeavored to extend her work to various other causes, including the anti-war movement, asserting that "Communists are quite relevant to the peace movement, and play a modest role in it."

She still continues to research and write on the issue of student power in the university. In an article in *Nation* she states: "Many of the worst crises and confrontations on the University of California Campuses have been either provoked by the regents or aggravated by a punitive disciplinary policy. More important, very large numbers of students have been driven into a frustrated fury by the unresponsiveness of the regents, and of higher authorities in general, to their demands, concerns and aspirations."

Aptheker's account of the trial of Angela Davis, *The Morning Breaks,* was labelled "instructive Bicentennial reading" by *Best Seller*'s Cornelia Holbert. The book "is a layman's guide to justice and injustice, to laws pertaining to bail and pre-trial detention, to change of venue, to jury selection, to prisoners' rights and grievous wrongs." Aptheker told *CA* that, as a result of the personal impact of the Angela Davis case, she "switched [her] emphasis from the student movement to Afro-American and women's history." Her thesis ("Mary Church Terrell & Ida B. Wells: A Comparative Rhetorical/Historical Analysis") on the lives of two outstanding black women who lived and worked at the turn of the century led her to explore the lives of other black women. She has delivered several papers on the subject at scholarly conferences and intends to further explore the contributions black women have made to the struggle for women's rights in the United States.

She has traveled to England, Hungary, Czechoslovakia, the U.S.S.R., the German Democratic Republic, Finland, West Germany, Denmark, and France.

AVOCATIONAL INTERESTS: Playing and watching sports, especially baseball and basketball, driving on trips through the U.S., and concerts.

BIOGRAPHICAL/CRITICAL SOURCES: New York Times, November 21, 1965; *Time,* December 3, 1965; *New Republic,* April 29, 1967, June 10, 1967; *Nation,* September 7, 1970, August 16, 1975; *Guardian,* November 7, 1970; *Best Sellers,* June, 1975.†

*   *   *

APTHEKER, Herbert 1915-

PERSONAL: Surname is pronounced *ap*-tek-er; born July 31, 1915, in Brooklyn, N.Y.; son of Benjamin (a manufacturer) and Rebecca (Komar) Aptheker; married Fay P. Aptheker, September 2, 1942; children: Bettina. *Education:* Columbia University, B.S., 1936, A.M., 1937, Ph.D., 1943. *Home:* 211 South 15th St., San Jose, Calif. 95112. *Office:* 480 North First St., San Jose, Calif. 95112.

CAREER: Masses and Mainstream, New York City, associate editor, 1948-53; *Political Affairs,* New York City, editor, 1953-

63; director, American Institute for Marxist Studies, 1964—. Lecturer throughout United States and Europe, 1946—. Member of history department staff, Bryn Mawr College, 1969-73; professor, Hostos Community College of the City University of New York, 1971-77; Du Bois Lecturer, University of Massachusetts—Amherst, 1971-72; visiting lecturer at Yale University, 1976, and University of California at Berkeley Law School, 1978; visiting professor, Humboldt University, Berlin, 1980. *Military service:* U.S. Army, Field Artillery, 1942-46; became major. *Member:* Association for Study of Negro Life and History, American Historical Association, Organization of American Historians, Academy of Political Science.

AWARDS, HONORS: Association for Study of Negro Life and History history award, 1939, heritage award, 1969; Guggenheim fellow, 1946-47; Fund for Social Analysis award, 1960; Social Science Research Council grant, 1961; Rabinowitz Foundation grant, 1965; Ph.D. (H.C.), Martin Luther University, Halle, Germany, 1966; American Council of Learned Societies grant, 1974; Paul Robeson scholar, Rutgers University, 1981.

WRITINGS: The Negro in the Civil War, International Publishers, 1938; *Negro Slave Revolts in the United States, 1526-1860,* International Publishers, 1939; *The Negro in the American Revolution,* International Publishers, 1940; *The Negro in the Abolitionist Movement,* International Publishers, 1941; *American Negro Slave Revolts,* Columbia University Press, 1943, new edition, International Publishers, 1969; *Essays in the History of the American Negro,* International Publishers, 1945; *The Negro People in America,* International Publishers, 1946; *To Be Free: Studies in American Negro History,* International Publishers, 1948.

(Editor) *A Documentary History of the Negro People in the United States,* Citadel, Volume I: *From Colonial Times through the Founding of the National Association for the Advancement of Colored People,* preface by W.E.B. Du Bois, 1951, Volume II: *1910-1932,* preface by Charles H. Wesley, 1973, Volume III: *1933-1945,* preface by William L. Patterson, 1975; *Laureates of Imperialism,* Mainstream, 1954; *History and Reality,* Marzani & Munsell, 1955, 2nd edition published as *The Era of McCarthyism,* 1962; *Toward Negro Freedom,* New Century, 1956; *The Truth about Hungary,* Mainstream, 1957; *A History of the American People,* International Publishers, Volume I: *The Colonial Era,* 1959, 2nd edition, 1966, Volume II: *The American Revolution, 1763-1783,* 1960, Volume III: *Early Years of the Republic: From the End of the Revolution to the First Administration of Washington (1783-1793),* 1976.

(Editor) *Disarmament and the American Economy,* New Century, 1960; *The World of C. Wright Mills,* Marzani & Munsell, 1960; *Dare We Be Free?,* New Century, 1961; (editor) *And Why Not Every Man?: The Story of the Fight against Negro Slavery,* Seven Seas Publishers, 1961, published as *And Why Not Every Man?: Documentary Story of the Fight against Slavery in the United States,* International Publishers, 1971; *American Foreign Policy and the Cold War,* New Century, 1962; *The Negro Today,* Marzani & Munsell, 1962; *Soul of the Republic,* Marzani & Munsell, 1964; *One Continual Cry: David Walker's Appeal to the Colored Citizens of the World, 1829-1830, Its Setting and Its Meaning,* Humanities Press, 1965; (editor) *Marxism and Democracy,* Humanities Press, 1965; (editor) *Marxism and Alienation,* Humanities Press, 1965; *Nat Turner's Slave Rebellion,* Humanities Press, 1966; *Mission to Hanoi,* prefaces by Tom Hayden and Staughton Lynd, International Publishers, 1966; *The Nature of Democracy, Freedom, and Revolution,* International Publishers, 1967, 2nd edition, 1981; (editor) W.E.B. Du Bois, *Autobiography of W.E.*

Burghardt Du Bois: A Soliloquy on Viewing My Life from the Last Decade of its First Century, International Publishers, 1968; (editor) *Marxism and Christianity,* Humanities Press, 1968.

The Urgency of Marxist-Christian Dialogue, Harper, 1970; *Afro-American History: The Modern Era,* Citadel, 1971; (contributor) J. Alan Winter, editor, *The Poor: A Culture of Poverty or a Poverty of Culture,* Eerdmans, 1971; (editor) Du Bois, *The Education of Black People, Ten Critiques, 1906-1960,* University of Massachusetts Press, 1973; *Annotated Bibliography of the Published Writings of W.E.B. Du Bois,* Kraus-Thomson, 1973; (editor) *The Correspondence of W.E.B. Du Bois,* University of Massachusetts Press, Volume I: *1877-1934,* 1973, Volume II: *1934-1944,* 1976, Volume III: *1944-1963,* 1978; (editor) *The Complete Published Work of W.E.B. Du Bois,* forty volumes, Kraus-Thomson, 1973—; *The Unfolding Drama: Studies in U.S. History,* edited by daughter, Bettina Aptheker, International Publishers, 1979; (editor and author of introduction) Du Bois, *Prayers for Dark People,* University of Massachusetts Press, 1980. Also contributor of literary biography of Du Bois to *American Writers,* Scribner, supplement volume, 1981.

Author of numerous monographs and shorter works, including: *The Labor Movement in the South During Slavery,* International Publishers, 1954; *Negro History: Its Lessons for Our Time,* New Century, 1956; *The United States and China: Peace or War?,* New Century, 1958; *Freedom in History,* New Century, 1958; *The Nature of Revolution: The Marxist Theory of Social Change,* New Century, 1959; *Since Sputnik: How Americans View the Soviet Union,* New Century, 1959; *On the Nature of Revolution: The Marxist Theory of Social Change,* New Century, 1959; *On the Nature of Freedom: The Marxist View,* New Century, 1960; *John Brown: American Martyr,* New Century, 1960; *The American Civil War,* International Publishers, 1961; *The New Secession—And How to Smash It,* New Century, 1961; *Reality and Mythology in Today's Japan,* New Century, 1961; *Riding to Freedom,* New Century, 1961; *The Fraud of "Soviet Anti-Semitism,"* New Century, 1962; *Communism: Menace or Promise?,* New Century, 1963; *Dr. Martin Luther King, Vietnam and Civil Rights,* New Outlook, 1967; *Czechoslovakia and Counter-Revolution: Why the Socialist Countries Intervened,* New Outlook, 1969; (with Bettina Aptheker) *Racism and Reaction in the United States: Two Marxian Studies,* New Outlook, 1971; *The Mid-East: Which Way to Peace,* Committee for a Just Peace in the Middle East (New York), c. 1971; *Heavenly Days in Dixie; or, The Time of Their Lives,* Political Affairs (New York), c. 1975.

Contributor to professional journals. Member of editorial board, *Mainstream,* 1955—; editor, *Jewish Affairs,* 1978—.

WORK IN PROGRESS: Additional volumes of *The Complete Published Work of W.E.B. Du Bois,* for Kraus-Thomson; a volume of unpublished essays by Du Bois, for University of Massachusetts Press; *A History of the Abolitionist Movement,* for Twayne; *A History of Anti-Racism in the U.S.,* for Greenwood.

SIDELIGHTS: In 1946 W.E.B. Du Bois asked Herbert Aptheker to edit his correspondence and personal papers. Aptheker agreed and when Du Bois left for Ghana in 1961, two years before his death, he turned over to Aptheker his correspondence (approximately 100,000 letters) and other papers. As Jay Saunders Redding notes in *Phylon,* there were a number of black intellectuals who felt that Du Bois's choice of Aptheker was not a wise decision on two grounds. First, "Aptheker was white, and editing the correspondence of a black American of Dr. Du Bois's stature and international prominence was a job for a Negro American, they said. What could a white man

know about living as a black man in America? How could a white man be expected to understand and respond sympathetically to the Negro American experience?'' Second, Aptheker "was an avowed Marxist, and for Dr. Du Bois to choose someone of that 'political persuasion' to edit his papers gave substance to the allegation (bruited about by McCarthy's gang) that he, Du Bois, was himself a Communist: an 'enemy of the State' and of the American way of life.''

Reviewing the published volumes of Du Bois's correspondence, edited by Aptheker, Redding asserts his belief that Du Bois's choice of Aptheker was "good, and this three-volume collection of correspondence is proof positive. It is an excellent job of editing.'' The reviewer for *Choice* agrees with Redding's assessment, commenting: "The editor has not only been wise in his selections, but has presented succinct and illuminating introductions and notes explaining the circumstances involved in the correspondence and the identities of the correspondents and personalities mentioned. In all, [this is] an excellently edited work of major significance.'' A writer in *The Past Before Us: Contemporary Historical Writing in the U.S.* calls the *Correspondence* "an indispensable resource for scholars in American history and for those general readers who regard Afro-American history as central.''

Eric Foner of the *New York Times Book Review* credits Aptheker's "perseverance'' for making these volumes available at all (for a long time no publisher would even consider the project) and remarks that for Aptheker, "the essentially unassisted task of editing was very much a labor of love.'' Foner calls the editing of the *Correspondence* "able, the footnotes brief but pertinent, and the reasons for the inclusion of the letters compelling. . . . Herbert Aptheker has given us a landmark in Afro-American history.''

One reviewer who is critical of Aptheker's editing of Du Bois's correspondence is Michael Cooke of the *New Republic.* Cooke believes that the published correspondence "manage[s] to devitalize if not to smother Du Bois with an excess of fussy and cryptic attention. . . . This edition of Du Bois's *Correspondence* resembles nothing so much as a loosely concatenated prolegomenon to a biography, without the liability of a formal declaration. Great labor and great learning in bio-politico-historical ranges have gone into the [*Correspondence.*] But a bias has also gone into them.'' Cooke concedes that Aptheker's "effort will increase the appreciation due Aptheker for the way he helped, some decades ago, to raise and establish vital questions in Afro-American history and thought.'' Nonetheless, Cooke concludes, "it also leaves the impression that Aptheker has not substantially enlarged and refined his interests to keep in line with a field that is bursting with new controversy and fruit. Clearly Du Bois could have been more fully and more truly served.''

But Redding, commenting in *Phylon,* a journal founded by Du Bois, remains undaunted in his praise of Aptheker's editing. "Only the editor's diligent research in dozens of private collections and libraries—at Atlanta University, Fisk, Harvard, Howard, Princeton, etc., etc.—and the public archives made possible the identification of the most significant letters to select. There is not an editorial comment nor an editorial footnote that is superfluous. There is not a single letter nor an exchange of letters that does not contribute to the reader's understanding of Du Bois himself or of the history of the times through which Du Bois lived and upon which he had a very considerable effect. . . . *The Correspondence of W.E.B. Du Bois* covers a century of history. What gives a special importance to the letters it contains is the light they shed on the *why* and *how* of this history and on the men and women who made it.''

CA INTERVIEW

CA interviewed Herbert Aptheker at his office in San Jose, California, on May 28, 1981.

CA: You've been a champion of the rights of the Black population for a long time. Did this interest begin with certain experiences you had as a young man?

APTHEKER: It's not easy to convey this briefly because it's been so central a matter in my life. In the United States, people my age—I will be sixty-six this July—are products, in a very fundamental sense, of the Great Depression. During that period, when I was an adolescent, social consciousness was intensified. The most flagrant injustice in the 1930s was the oppression of Black people, which was open, naked, blatant, institutionalized, and in many areas legalized. This naturally attracted my attention.

There were certain specific, personal matters. For example, it happens that a very dear friend of my mother's was a Black woman whose name was Angelina Corbin. I became very attached to her. Later I learned, after she died, that she had been a figure of some consequence in terms of activity among Black people in Brooklyn where I grew up. Then certain things happened. I remember once returning from school—probably high school; I'm not even sure of that—and finding a crowd of people surrounding a truck on the bed of which was a cage. In the cage were men dressed in prisoner outfits of that period, black-and-white-striped suits with a ball and chain on their ankles. Someone was talking out of a kind of megaphone—we didn't have microphones in those days—and some people were handing out leaflets. This concerned the Angelo Herndon case, in which a young labor organizer, a Communist in his twenties, had been arrested and sentenced to death under a slave insurrection law of 1860 because he had organized and initiated a demonstration. He was sentenced to prison at the time and was awaiting death. This was a replica of where he was jailed, that was the idea. I remember I listened for a while—I don't remember what was said but I remember the occasion. I took one of the leaflets home to read and I asked my mother if these things happened, if this were true. Mother, who had been a pioneer organizer for the International Ladies' Garment Workers' Union, said that yes, it was true.

Something else happened soon after. I went on a long automobile trip with my father in the summer. We went down to Alexander City, Alabama, a very long drive in those days. We went through the heart of the South; it was my first visit. We were there for some weeks counting the driving, making a hundred or two hundred miles a day. This was during the depths of the Depression when it was bad in the North and bad for white people, but it was starvation in the South for Black people, absolute starvation. I had never seen this. We weren't rich but we weren't poor; I had never been hungry. Then there was the complete illiteracy and the complete lack of any knowledge. I remember I asked people who was president, and what was the name of the nearest city. Even things of this nature people didn't know. They just didn't know anything and were hungry. Then the open jim crow, that is the signs designating white and black rest rooms and drinking fountains, this kind of thing, was simply appalling.

When I came home from that trip, which lasted about five weeks, I remember I was doing a weekly column in the Erasmus Hall High School newspaper; and I devoted the column to the results of my studies of this matter. I studied the census in order to persuade myself that what I had seen was true, that it existed. I couldn't believe that people knew it existed, that

was the main point—not that it existed, but that people knew it existed, and it went on existing. I found that incredible. By the way, I still do. So I wrote about this, and I'm sure people stopped reading the column because it went on week after week after week. I called it "The Dark Side of the South." I graduated in 1933, so I was doing this probably in 1931 or 1932. I never stopped studying that question after that.

I did many other things, of course. For instance, in college, I wanted to be a historian; I told myself as a boy that I would like to write history, so I had the advantage of knowing what I wanted to do. History in those days was almost unbelievably racist. Here I was a student of history at Columbia. People like U. B. Phillips were the authority on what it meant to be a Black slave. I just knew that these things were not true, could not have been true. So that sort of gave me a lifetime work in history, an effort to investigate this and to find out what really happened. Of course Black writers had done this in part, people like Carter G. Woodson and W.E.B. Du Bois, but when you went to school in those days, you didn't learn that. This represented a great challenge, a great opportunity.

CA: One of your main concerns over the years has been the lack of attention given to the Black in American history textbooks as well as in source readings. Do you think that a lot more space is being given to the Black now?

APTHEKER: It's a great deal more than it was in the period we're talking about, the 1930s. There is the possibility of Black people themselves doing more. For instance, when I went to school at Columbia University in New York, it was a rarity to see a Black person in the classroom, and this is not true any longer. There is a book called *Holders of Doctorates Among American Negroes* by a man named H. W. Greene, which appeared in 1946. It is a book of only three hundred pages. (I'm one of the people in the book—he just assumed that I was Black.) If you had a book now called *Black Holders of the Ph.D.*, it would be the size of the *Columbia Encyclopedia*.

Then there was the outbreak of the great Black struggle of the late 1950s and 1960s, when you had what became a kind of fad of Black studies. This was never welcomed by those who dominate our society; they conceded because of the great pressure. But much of it has been undone, taken back. The fad is gone, publishers are no longer falling over themselves looking for books on Black subjects. The sales of such books have fallen precipitously. So while we're not back to where we were in the 1930s and 1940s, we're a good deal behind where we were in the mid-1960s.

CA: Have Black studies programs fallen off a lot too?

APTHEKER: Oh yes. There have been reports of that. I don't have the exact data but they have fallen off very much and enrollment has gone down. Institution after institution has terminated Black studies departments. At the least they've combined Black studies with other programs. This is a disastrous situation compared to conditions in the 1960s. This is part of the general right-wing drift, the whole campaign against affirmative action. Today affirmative action has been turned into a swearword. This has been accomplished rather deliberately, I think, in the last five years.

CA: Are many Blacks who got degrees in American history in the 1960s and 1970s trying to rewrite the American past?

APTHEKER: I wouldn't say many. Of course, with the Right drift, with the abandonment of Black studies and the closing of the publication market, you get discouraged. All this has an obvious bad effect. But now you have some significant Black-run publications and institutions: the Institute for the Black World, for instance, in Atlanta, and the magazine *The Black Scholar*, the magazine *Freedom Ways*, the Johnson Publishing Company in Chicago, and the Black radio stations. There is this conscious effort, but it is very difficult and it is becoming more difficult; and therefore it is not encouraging to younger men and women to take up this effort.

CA: Do you think, in the course of American history, that there have been any presidents who have really tried to help the cause of the Blacks?

APTHEKER: I'm afraid in a conscious sense, probably no. Perhaps the person with the most sensitivity was Lincoln. This is evident, for instance, in his public speech denouncing lynching in 1837 and his welcoming Harriet Tubman and especially Frederick Douglass to the White House as people from whom he might learn. Douglass had great sensitivity and he reported a lack of racism in Lincoln. I don't think Lincoln was free of it, but the fact that Douglass would say a thing like that is really quite remarkable. I don't know of any other president who had this kind of sensitivity, however limited it was.

Of course there were advances made under Franklin D. Roosevelt. There were some advances forced out of Truman and, for that matter, Johnson during the 1960s. Johnson's speech at Howard University was probably the best speech on the subject made by a president. There is a fairly good book written recently by someone who did a study of presidents and racism. It's a pretty dismal record. There's a recent book also on Theodore Roosevelt, showing his racism and chauvinism toward women. So I'm afraid the record is not good.

CA: You've spent a good deal of your life working on W.E.B. Du Bois's papers. Were they turned over to you?

APTHEKER: In 1946, Dr. Du Bois asked if I would edit his works and his letters, and, of course, I said I would. From that period on, I worked on this and tried to get a publisher and was unable to for more or less obvious reasons. This continued. In 1961, he left for Africa and I took him and his wife to the airport, and he then turned over his correspondence and papers, including about a hundred thousand letters, to Mrs. Aptheker and me for our safekeeping. Files were sent to our house and we set to work on them. They were very disheveled and we spent thousands of hours putting them in order. We had them in our physical possession until 1973, when they were purchased from his widow—of course the legal possession I always considered to be that of Mrs. Du Bois. I visited her soon after he died, in 1964. I urged her to sell the papers and have a university properly take care of them. It was a terrible responsibility. They were in our basement and subject to fire, theft, and so forth. She finally agreed to sell them and it took some time, but the University of Massachusetts bought these papers. When that was completed I helped transfer the shipping of everything to Amherst, and all the papers now are at the University of Massachusetts—Amherst and they finally have been collated and indexed. In fact, the university there published a large book called *The Papers of Du Bois*, and they are now open to scholars.

CA: According to a New Yorker *piece in July, 1973, some of Du Bois's papers and books were still in Africa.*

APTHEKER: Not many. His main library he had taken with him, although he had sold a good many of his books, mainly fiction. Books that he wanted with him he took. The books,

by the way, are still there. After the coup in Ghana they've never been released. They're sealed, as I understand it, in a house, but they're still there. Some of the material Mrs. Du Bois was able to get out when she was forced to leave, and I saw some of it in her apartment in Cairo. Many of the remaining papers were gotten out just recently and are now at Amherst. His autobiography, which I edited in 1968, was posthumously published. I don't know how it reached me, sort of an underground process. The original manuscript is now in the library at Amherst. So that's something of that story.

The three volumes of correspondence have been published. Two more of his manuscripts have been published, one in 1973 called *The Education of Black People: Ten Critiques, 1906-1960*, a marvelous book, and a little while ago a beautiful book called *Prayers for Dark People* (1980), for which I wrote the introduction. I'm editing for Kraus-Thomson the complete published writings of Du Bois. There are to be forty volumes; twenty-five have appeared. That will be all of his books, articles, newspaper columns, studies for the government. There will be a separate volume of his poetry and short stories. There is already a published volume of his book reviews, selections from the magazines he edited like *Crisis, Horizon*, and *Phylon*.

CA: I was astonished to read that his main work, Black Reconstruction, *was never even reviewed in the* American Historical Review.

APTHEKER: That's correct. That gives you a good idea of the state of historiography at that time. And this although the book was published by a leading publisher, Harcourt Brace.

CA: I'm sure that over the years it's been very difficult at times for you, because of your Marxist views, to speak on certain campuses. Is it now easier to obtain speaking engagements?

APTHEKER: I'm not certain about that. It is easier than it was in the 1950s during the McCarthy period. Although even then, I set myself the task of breaking the ban against radical speakers which existed everywhere. I went from university to university and I did it. If I didn't do it the first time, I did it the second time, whether at the University of North Carolina or Buffalo or, for that matter, Berkeley. I broke the ban there in 1963 and now I find myself teaching at its law school. It's hard to believe.

But I want to make the point that although it was difficult, with effort it was possible, you could do it, although sometimes it was at the risk of life and limb. I was assaulted in Chapel Hill, for instance. In Latrobe, Pennsylvania, at Saint Vincent College, a Benedictine college, there was a mob of Ku Klux Klan and other gangsters which prevented me from speaking. They blocked the main highway. State troopers told the people at Saint Vincent's that they could not protect the college. I stayed at a motel, and the president of the college, the monsignor, personally took me to the college the next day, after they had canceled the public lecture. They had closed-circuit television at that college. He canceled all classes, and I was told that I could lecture to the entire student body all day. I did. I spoke for hours on all sorts of subjects, then there was a general questioning period, and then this monsignor drove me himself to the airport so that I could go home safely, something that I will never forget. It reflects the uniquely positive aspects of this country. We do have this kind of resistance and this simple courage. It's needless for me to say that the college authorities were quite opposed to my views. But they were absolutely livid at the attempt to prevent my appearance, which they considered an insult to their institution.

Today I very frequently speak, and often the auspices are quite distinguished. So it's a little different. It is easier, yes.

CA: Is a more positive attitude being taken toward Marxist studies?

APTHEKER: There still persists this necessity to struggle in this area. I am director of the American Institute for Marxist Studies, which has existed now for eighteen years. We established it in order to move from vituperation to conversation about Marxism. To a degree I think we've succeeded. But I still find it astonishing how much ignorance there is in circles where you'd least expect it. I recently reviewed a book on Alexis de Tocqueville in which the professor who wrote the introduction said that one of the great virtues of de Tocqueville was that he was free of "the virus of Marxism." Just think of that in terms of scholarship! This is a professor of some distinction at Yale. And it was absolutely gratuitous. Why bring Marx into a discussion of de Tocqueville at all? I don't think that would occur in any country other than the United States. I don't think it would occur in Turkey, and that a professor would write a thing like that! It is not as bad as in the 1950s, but it's still there, and of course with the present administration I imagine this will intensify.

BIOGRAPHICAL/CRITICAL SOURCES: Journal of Southern History, August, 1973; *Choice,* April, 1974; *Journal of American History,* December, 1974; *American Historical Review,* April, 1975, April, 1977; *New Republic,* February 19, 1977; *Progressive,* October, 1978; *Book Forum,* Volume IV, number 3, 1979; *New York Times Book Review,* January 7, 1979; *Phylon,* June, 1979, March, 1981; Michael Kammen, editor, *The Past Before Us: Contemporary Historical Writing in the U.S.,* Cornell University Press, for American Historical Association, 1980.

—*Interview by Walter W. Ross*

*   *   *

ARCHER, H(orace) Richard   1911-1978

PERSONAL: Born September 13, 1911, in Albuquerque, N.M.; died January 19, 1978, in Boston, Mass.; son of Richard Reece and Martha Julia (Briglieb) Archer; married Margot Hanko, January 26, 1936. *Education:* University of California, Berkeley, B.A., 1940, Certificate of Librarianship, 1941, M.A., 1943; University of Chicago, Ph.D., 1954. *Home:* Sabin Dr., Williamstown, Mass. 01267. *Office:* Chapin Library, Williams College, Williamstown, Mass. 01267.

CAREER: Book shop assistant and manager in Los Angeles, Calif., and order librarian at University of California, Berkeley, while continuing education; University of California, Los Angeles, supervising bibliographer at W. A. Clark Memorial Library, 1944-52, curator of graphic arts, 1952-53; R. R. Donnelley & Sons Co., Chicago, Ill., librarian, 1954-57; Williams College, Chapin Library, Williamstown, Mass., librarian, 1957-77, librarian emeritus, 1977-78, lecturer in graphic arts, 1965-77. Visiting summer instructor, University of Southern California, 1960; visiting lecturer at University of Oklahoma, summer, 1956, University of Michigan, summer, 1962, Simmons College, spring, 1965, State University of New York at Albany, 1968-73, and University of Illinois, summer, 1969. Founder, owner, and operator of private press, Hippogryph Press, beginning 1951.

MEMBER: American Library Association (member of council, 1962-65; chairman of rare books section, 1962-63), Bibliographical Society of America, American Association of University Professors, Society of Private Printers, Private Library Association, William Morris Society, Phi Beta Mu, Society for Italic Writing, Printing Historical Society, Society of Printers (Boston), Typophiles (New York), Library Company of Philadelphia, Faculty Club of Williams College (vice-president, 1962-63), Grolier Club, Zamorano Club, Rounce and Coffin Club. *Awards, honors:* Printing Award of Merit from Society of Typographic Arts, 1956.

WRITINGS: (Contributor) *William A. Clark Memorial Library: Report of the First Decade, 1934-1944,* University of California Press, 1946; (contributor) *Library Trends,* University of Illinois Library School, 1958; (editor) *A Rare Book Manual,* Association of College and Research Libraries, 1959; (editor) *Rare Book Collections: Some Theoretical and Practical Suggestions for Use by Librarians and Students,* American Library Association, 1965; *Modern Fine Printing,* William Andrews Clark Memorial Library, University of California, 1968. Contributor to *Encyclopedia of Library and Information Science.* Contributor of articles and reviews to library journals. Editor, *Hoja Volante,* 1949-53.

WORK IN PROGRESS: Writing on the history of printing, especially in Western Europe and America, on private press and amateur printers, and on problems of curatorship in rare book libraries and special collections; a study of book typography in the field of librarianship.

SIDELIGHTS: H. Richard Archer traveled widely in Europe, lecturing and doing research. He owned a private library of 3,000 volumes, specializing in William Faulkner first editions and other work (300 items), history of private presses and private printing (1,000 items), modern literature, jazz music, and bibliography. His collection of American jazz records ran to 500 platters dating from 1932-1956.

OBITUARIES: AB Bookman's Weekly, February 20, 1978.†

*   *   *

ARCHER, Jules   1915-

PERSONAL: Born January 27, 1915, in New York, N.Y.; married Eleanor McMahon, May 2, 1942; children: Michael, Dane, Kerry. *Education:* College of the City of New York (now City College of the City University of New York), diploma in advertising. *Politics:* Independent. *Agent:* Lenniger Literary Agency, 250 West 57th St., New York, N.Y. 10107.

CAREER: Publicity and advertising copywriter for Universal Pictures and other companies, prior to World War II; freelance writer, 1940—. Consultant to *World Book Encyclopedia. Military service:* U.S. Air Force, World War II; served in Pacific with 5th Air Force, and as war correspondent.

WRITINGS: I Sell What I Write, Fell, 1950; (with Shailer Upton Lawton) *Sexual Conduct of the Teen-Ager,* Greenburg, 1951; (with Abel Green and Joe Laurie) *Show Biz,* Henry Holt, 1951; *What Should Parents Expect from Children* (pamphlet), Public Affairs Committee (New York), 1964; *Achieve Success, Avoid Family Failure,* Grossett, 1969, published as *The Executive Success,* 1970.

All juvenile, except as noted: *Front-Line General: Douglas MacArthur,* Messner, 1963; *Twentieth Century Caesar: Benito Mussolini,* Messner, 1964; *Man of Steel: Joseph Stalin,* Messner, 1965; *Fighting Journalist: Horace Greeley,* Messner, 1966; *Battlefield President: Dwight D. Eisenhower,* Messner, 1967; *The Dictators,* Hawthorn, 1967; *Laws that Changed America,* Criterion, 1967; *World Citizen: Woodrow Wilson,* Messner, 1967; *Red Rebel: Tito of Yugoslavia,* Messner, 1968; *Science Explorer: Roy Chapman Andrews,* Messner, 1968; *The Un-*

popular Ones, Crowell Collier, 1968; *African Firebrand: Kenyatta of Kenya*, Messner, 1969; *Angry Abolitionist: William Lloyd Garrison*, Messner, 1969; *The Extremists: Gadflies of American Society*, Hawthorn, 1969.

Colossus of Europe: Metternich, Messner, 1970; *Congo: The Birth of a New Nation*, Messner, 1970; *Hawks, Doves and the Eagle*, Hawthorn, 1970; *Indian Foe, Indian Friend*, Crowell Collier, 1970; *Philippines' Fight for Freedom*, Crowell Collier, 1970; *Thorn in Our Flesh: Castro's Cuba*, Cowles, 1970; *Ho Chi Minh: Legend of Hanoi*, Crowell Collier, 1971; *1968: Year of Crisis*, Messner, 1971; *Revolution in Our Time*, Messner, 1971; *Treason in America: Disloyalty versus Dissent*, Hawthorn, 1971; *Mao Tse-Tung: Red Emperor*, Hawthorn, 1972; *Uneasy Friendship: France and the United States*, Four Winds, 1972; *Strikes, Bombs and Bullets: Big Bill Haywood and the IWW*, Messner, 1972; *Mexico and the United States*, Hawthorn, 1973; *Chou En-lai*, Hawthorn, 1973; *The Plot to Seize the White House*, Hawthorn, 1973; *Resistance*, Macrae Smith, 1973; *Famous Young Rebels*, Messner, 1973; *They Made a Revolution, 1776*, St. Martin's, 1973; *Trotsky: World Revolutionary*, Messner, 1973; *Riot!: A History of Mob Action in the United States*, Hawthorn, 1974; *China in the Twentieth Century*, Macmillan, 1974; *The Russians and the Americans*, Hawthorn, 1975; *Washington vs. Main Street: The Struggle between Federal and Local Power*, Crowell Collier, 1975; *Watergate: America in Crisis*, Crowell Collier, 1975; *The Chinese and the Americans*, Hawthorn, 1976; *Legacy of the Desert: Understanding the Arabs*, Little, Brown, 1976; *From Whales to Dinosaurs: The Story of Roy Chapman Andrews*, St. Martin's, 1976; *Hunger on Planet Earth*, Crowell Collier, 1977; *Epidemic!: The Story of the Disease Detectives*, Harcourt, 1977; *Police State: Could It Happen Here?*, Harper, 1977; *Superspies: The Secret Side of Government*, Delacorte, 1977; *You and the Law* (young adult), Harcourt, 1978.

You Can't Do That to Me: Famous Fights for Human Rights, Macmillan, 1980. Contributor of short stories and articles to popular periodicals, including *Cosmopolitan*, *Good Housekeeping*, *Playboy*, and *Esquire*.

SIDELIGHTS: Jules Archer states: "I originally became interested in writing books for young people because I have three sons, and I was dismayed at the clap-trap they were given to read in school during their junior high and high school years. The textbooks did not tell the truth about how our government operates, nor about our history at home and abroad. Facts were distorted; only one side of controversial issues was presented. . . . I began writing my books with the premise that I respected the intelligence of youth who would read them, and that if they were given the whole truth about our society, our disgraceful failures as well as our glowing successes, they would be able to make intelligent decisions and value judgments, and as citizens seek to correct our nation's weaknesses, improve our democracy, bring about greater social justice for all."

Critics have praised Archer's impartiality in reporting controversial public figures and events. According to Harvey Dust of *School Library Journal*, Archer exhibits "depth and objectivity" in his account of the Bay of Pigs affair in *Thorn in Our Flesh: Castro's Cuba*. Likewise, Helene Cantarella, in her *Virginia Kirkus' Service* review of *Man of Steel: Joseph Stalin*, commends Archer for writing the "sort of unemotional analysis history's great villains seldom get." In reviewing *Mao Tse-Tung* for *Kirkus Reviews*, Janet G. Polacheck writes that "Archer's value lies in his ability to assess Mao's strengths and weaknesses unemotionally."

In spite of praise from critics, Archer remains concerned about American youth: "I cannot tell how much good my books have done in developing a new awareness of the whole truth about America—and the rest of the world—in the younger generation, although they are fortunately in tune with the thinking of many young people about what is wrong in our society and how to correct it."

Archer's stories, books, and articles have been adapted for television, translated into twelve languages, and reprinted by the U.S. Department of State for distribution overseas.

BIOGRAPHICAL/CRITICAL SOURCES: New York Times Book Review, November 1, 1964, November 3, 1968; *Virginia Kirkus' Service*, September 15, 1965; *Best Sellers*, May 1, 1967, January 1, 1968, December 1, 1968, September 1, 1969, May 1, 1970, June 1, 1970, April 15, 1971; *Young Readers' Review*, May, 1968, October, 1968, December, 1968; *Commonweal*, May 23, 1969; *Book World*, April 12, 1970; *Library Journal*, May 15, 1970, June 15, 1970, September, 1970; *School Library Journal*, September, 1970; *Kirkus Reviews*, March 1, 1972; *Contemporary Literary Criticism*, Volume XII, Gale, 1980.†

*   *   *

ARDEN, William
See LYNDS, Dennis

*   *   *

AREHART-TREICHEL, Joan   1942-

PERSONAL: Born May 19, 1942, in Louisville, Ky.; daughter of Oscar M. (an engineer) and Isabelle (a businesswoman; maiden name, Turner) Arehart; married Horst Klaus Treichel (a shipping company owner), May 13, 1972; children: Tamara, Heidi. *Education:* Attended Institute of European Studies, Sorbonne, University of Paris, 1962, and Oxford University, summer, 1962; Indiana University, A.B., 1964; graduate study at New York University, 1970, and Georgetown University, 1971. *Politics:* "Conservative on economic issues; liberal on social issues (rights of the individual)." *Religion:* Roman Catholic. *Home:* 906 Ravenshead, Sherwood Forest, Annapolis, Md. 21405. *Office: Science News*, 1719 N St. N.W., Washington, D.C. 20036.

CAREER: McCall's, New York City, assistant to senior editor, 1965; Ayerst Laboratories, New York City, magazine editor, 1966-67; free-lance science writer in New York City, 1968-70, in Washington, D.C., 1971—; *Science News*, Washington, D.C., medical editor, 1971—. *Member:* American Society of Journalists and Authors, Washington Independent Writers' Association. *Awards, honors:* Third place award in American Medical Association medical journalism awards contest, 1971, for article "Coral Unexpected Boon to Pharmaceutical Research"; Claude Bernard Science Journalism Award, National Society for Medical Research, honorable mention, 1978, for article "The Science behind the Lactrile Controversy," first place award, 1979, for article "Brain Proteins: Matter over Mind."

WRITINGS: Trace Elements: How They Help and Harm Us (juvenile), Holiday House, 1974; *Immunity: How Our Bodies Resist Disease* (juvenile), Holiday House, 1976; *Poisons and Toxins* (juvenile), Holiday House, 1976; *Biotypes: The Critical Link between Your Personality and Your Health* (adult), Times Books, 1980. Contributor to over twenty popular and science magazines and newspapers, including *Washington Post, Harper's, Boston Globe, Catholic Digest, Oceans*, and *Glamour*.

WORK IN PROGRESS: Magazine articles; a mystery novel with a medical theme.

AVOCATIONAL INTERESTS: Mothering, gardening, biking.

*   *   *

ARNANDEZ, Richard   1912-
(Brother B. Edwin)

PERSONAL: Born January 14, 1912, in New Iberia, La.; son of Jules Gervais (a businessman) and Eugenie (Pellerin) Arnandez. *Education:* Manhattan College, B.A., 1935; University of Lille, Licence es Lettres, 1937. *Home:* 1522 Carmel Ave., Lafayette, La. 70501.

CAREER: Roman Catholic religious; member of Congregation of Brothers of the Christian Schools. Teacher in schools operated by Christian Brothers; Diocesan Tribunal, Lafayette, La., advocate, 1976—.

WRITINGS: (Under name Brother B. Edwin) *Points Worth Pondering,* Bruce, 1961; (under name Brother B. Edwin) *Brother E. Victor,* privately printed, 1963; (under name Brother B. Edwin) *Retreat Conferences for Religious,* Bruce, 1964; (under name Brother B. Edwin) *Examens for Retreat Time,* Bruce, 1964.

(Translator) H. M. Manteau-Bonomy, *Immaculate Conception and the Holy Spirit: The Marian Teachings of Father Kolbe,* Prow Books, 1977; (translator) Alexandre Masseron, *Dante Alighieri: The Poet Who Loved St. Francis So Much,* Franciscan Herald, 1979. Also translator of *Life of St. Margaret Mary,* Prow Books, *Writings of Blessed Maximillian Kolbe,* in press, and *Life of St. Jean Baptiste de La Salle,* by Canon Blain. Contributor of articles to *Key* and *Immaculata.* Editor, *Bulletin des Ecoles Chretiennes* (Rome), 1957-60.

WORK IN PROGRESS: A biography of Aloys Grosde; articles for Catholic periodicals in Europe and America.

AVOCATIONAL INTERESTS: Music, archaeology, mathematical puzzles, swimming.

*   *   *

ARROWAY, Francis M.
See ROSMOND, Babette

*   *   *

ASPREY, Robert B.   1923-

PERSONAL: Born February 16, 1923, in Sioux City, Iowa; son of Peter (a businessman) and Gladys (Brown) Asprey. *Education:* University of Iowa, B.A. (with honors), 1949; studied at New College, Oxford University, 1949-50, University of Vienna, 1955-57, and University of Nice, 1975. *Politics:* Independent. *Religion:* Independent. *Home and office:* Jibsail, Warwick, Bermuda; and Apartado 120, Nueva Andalucia, Malaga, Spain. *Agent:* Georges Borchardt Literary Agency, 136 East 57th St., New York, N.Y. 10022.

CAREER: U.S. Army, Salzburg, Austria, civilian intelligence analyst, 1951-52; free-lance writer, 1955—. *Military service:* U.S. Marine Corps, 1942-46; became first lieutenant; awarded all Pacific ribbons with battle star, Navy Unit Citation with star, Presidential Unit Citation with star, Purple Heart. Also served on active duty, 1952-54; became captain. *Member:* Authors Guild, Oxford University Society, New College Society, Bermuda Bridge Club, Mid-Ocean Golf Club (Bermuda), Frilford Heath Golf Club (England), Nueva Andalucia Golf Club (Spain), Army and Navy Club (Washington, D.C.), Army and Navy Club (London), American Club (Spain). *Awards, honors:* Fulbright scholar, 1949-50.

WRITINGS: The Panther's Feast, Putnam, 1959; *The First Battle of the Marne,* Lippincott, 1962, reprinted, Evergreen Press, 1980; (with A. A. Vandegrift) *Once a Marine,* Norton, 1964; *At Belleau Wood,* Putnam, 1965; *Semper Fidelis: The Story of the Marines in World War II,* Norton, 1967; *War in the Shadows,* Doubleday, 1975; *Operation Prophet,* Doubleday, 1977. Contributor of articles and stories to *Encyclopaedia Britannica, New Yorker, New York Times,* and to American, British, and foreign military publications.

WORK IN PROGRESS: A biography of Frederick the Great of Prussia.

SIDELIGHTS: Robert B. Asprey told *CA* that he began his writing career "at a very young age. I have no idea why, just an inner urge. In 1954 I was invalided out of the U.S. Marines and was given a lump sum severance pay. Instead of getting married and joining the National Security Council as General Graves B. Erskine's deputy, I went to Vienna for three lovely years of researching *The Panther's Feast.* To supplement my income some years later I became contributing editor to the *Marine Corps Gazette* and for some years edited the John A. Lejeune Forum, which was a very popular feature in the *Gazette.* I became very anti-Vietnam (which I covered briefly in 1963 as a military correspondent) and in 1965 resigned from the *Gazette* and began a series of three lengthy articles for the *Encyclopaedia Britannica:* guerilla warfare (still in print), tactics, and jungle warfare. The first article led to further research and to *War in the Shadows.* . . .

"I hope that my important books will be read by generations after me the way I have read important books from the generations before me. In *War in the Shadows,* a two-volume work, I tried to explain the American debacle in Vietnam in the historical terms of guerilla warfare with the overriding theme of 'the arrogance of ignorance' displayed by so many of our civil officials and military officers. I was very impressed that the Military Book Club had the courage to make it their major June selection in 1975. It is their all-time best-seller with over 100,000 copies sold, and it is still selling several thousand copies a year. This means that a lot of people have read what I sincerely believe is the truth behind that awful war that ripped America to shreds."

Asprey comments that when writing his books he tries to "present the subject as best as one can: I try to write for the reader and I try to write as simply as possible. I also try to research as thoroughly as possible. Back in the sixties I had an agent who was burning me out—this was in the period of the Marne, Belleau Wood, Vandegrift, Marine Corps history books. I luckily realized what was happening—you just cannot write a worthy factual book a year, or anyway I can't and really do justice to the subject. So I decided that I don't have all that much longer to live so what I write is going to have to satisfy me—this is why I don't want any contracts with idiotic editors talking about deadlines. . . .

"I think the current literary scene is pretty sick. How can any culture absorb some 40,000 titles a year? Corporate takeover of publishers has been a disaster—books are being produced and marketed like packages of cornflakes or soap. Literary standards have become so incredibly vulgar that even more people than usual are trying to write with one result that agents and publishers are swamped and the few worthy young writers all too often get lost in the mob."

AVOCATIONAL INTERESTS: Travel, foreign languages, reading, golf, and duplicate bridge.

*　　　*　　　*

ASTLEY, Juliet
See LOFTS, Norah (Robinson)

*　　　*　　　*

ATKINS, Thomas (Radcliffe) 1939-

PERSONAL: Born April 5, 1939, in Mobile, Ala.; son of Jack R. (an importer) and Sadie B. (Daves) Atkins; married Mary Ellen O'Brien (an assistant professor of drama), April 14, 1964; children: Shawn, Mark. *Education:* Duke University, B.A., 1961; Yale University, M.F.A., 1964. *Agent:* Joan Fulton, Harold Matson Co., Inc., 22 East 40th St., New York, N.Y. 10016. *Office address:* Department of Theatre Arts, Hollins College, Box 9602, Hollins College, Va. 24020.

CAREER: Vassar College, Poughkeepsie, N.Y., lecturer in drama, 1964-65; Hollins College, Hollins College, Va., instructor, 1965-67, assistant professor, 1967-70, associate professor of drama, 1970-81, professor of theatre arts, 1981—, chairman of department, 1971—. Part-time lecturer in film, City College of the City University of New York, spring, 1971. *Member:* Authors Guild, Dramatists Guild, Mystery Writers of America. *Awards, honors:* Woodrow Wilson fellow, 1961-62; John Golden fellow in playwriting, Yale Drama School, 1963-64.

WRITINGS: Circus Maximus (play), Row, Peterson, 1959; (with John Baxter) *The Fire Came By: The Riddle of the Great Siberian Explosion,* introduction by Isaac Asimov, Doubleday, 1976; *The Blue Man* (novel), Doubleday, 1978; *Pigeons* (play), Haunted Book Shop, in press.

Editor: *Sexuality in the Movies,* Indiana University Press, 1975; *Science Fiction Films,* Simon & Schuster, 1976; *Graphic Violence on the Screen,* Simon & Schuster, 1976; *Frederick Wiseman,* Simon & Schuster, 1976; *Ken Russell,* Simon & Schuster, 1976.

Contributor: Frank N. Magill, editor, *Contemporary Literary Scene, 1973,* Salem Press, 1974; Magill, editor, *Literary Annual, 1973,* Salem Press, 1974; Gerald Peary, editor, *The Classic American Novel and the Movies,* Ungar, 1977; Lewis Jacobs, editor, *The Documentary Tradition,* Norton, 1979.

General editor, "Monarch Film" series, Simon & Schuster, 1974—. Contributor of plays and articles to film and literary journals, including *Cinefantastique, Sight and Sound, Southern Humanities Review, Mill Mountain Review,* and *Kenyon Review.* Founder, editor, and publisher of *Film Journal,* 1971—; editor and publisher with wife, Mary Ellen O'Brien, of *Scripts South,* 1981—.

WORK IN PROGRESS: Two novels, *A Darker Wave* and *Down the Bay;* a play, *Raw Oysters.*

SIDELIGHTS: Thomas Atkins comments in *Library Journal:* "My love of writing goes back at least as far as the fifth grade, when I was pouring through Edgar Rice Burroughs' Martian novels and just beginning to attempt to put my own stories on paper. A teacher happened to see these early efforts and gave me an hour of class time each week to read my work aloud to my fellow students. This got me hooked, I believe, on the pleasure of storytelling."

AVOCATIONAL INTERESTS: Travel, photography, collecting art and books.

BIOGRAPHICAL/CRITICAL SOURCES: Library Journal, June 5, 1978; *Roanoker,* November-December, 1978; *Azalea City News and Review* (Mobile, Ala.), July 30, 1981.

*　　　*　　　*

ATTENBOROUGH, David Frederick 1926-

PERSONAL: Born May 8, 1926, in London, England; son of Frederick Levi and Mary (Clegg) Attenborough; married Jane Elizabeth Oriel, 1950; children: Robert, Susan. *Education:* Clare College, Cambridge, M.A., 1947. *Home:* 5 Park Rd., Richmond, Surrey, England.

CAREER: Editorial assistant in British publishing house, 1949-52; British Broadcasting Corp., Television Service, London, England, producer, 1952-62; controller of programs for BBC-2 television, 1965-68, director of programs and member of board of management, 1969-72; member of Nature Conservancy Council, 1973—. Undertook more than a dozen zoological and ethnographic filming expeditions, including Sierra Leone, 1954, New Guinea, 1957, Zambesi, 1964, Borneo, 1973, and Solomon Islands, 1975. *Military service:* Royal Navy, 1947-49; became lieutenant. *Awards, honors:* Society of Film and Television Arts, special award, 1961, Desmond Davis Award, 1970; Silver Medal, Zoological Society of London, 1966; Silver Medal, Royal Television Society, 1966; D.Litt., University of Leicester, 1970, and City University (London), 1972; Cherry Kearton Award, Royal Geographical Society, 1972; D.Sc., University of Liverpool, 1974, and Heriot-Watt University, 1978; Commander of the Order of the British Empire, 1974; honorary fellow, Manchester Polytechnic, 1976; LL.D., University of Bristol, 1977.

WRITINGS: Zoo Quest to Guiana, Lutterworth, 1956, Crowell, 1957, abridged edition, University of London Press, 1962; *Zoo Quest for a Dragon,* Lutterworth, 1957; *Zoo Quest in Paraguay,* Lutterworth, 1959; *Quest in Paradise,* Lutterworth, 1960; *People of Paradise,* Harper, 1961; *Zoo Quest to Madagascar,* Lutterworth, 1961, published as *Bridge to the Past: Animals and People of Madagascar,* Harper, 1962; *Quest under Capricorn,* Lutterworth, 1963; (editor) *My Favourite Stories of Exploration,* Lutterworth, 1964; (with Molly Cox) *David Attenborough's Fabulous Animals,* BBC Publications, 1975; *The Tribal Eye,* Norton, 1976; *Life on Earth: A Natural History,* BBC Publications, 1979, Little, Brown, 1980.

*　　　*　　　*

AUCHINCLOSS, Louis (Stanton) 1917-
(Andrew Lee)

PERSONAL: Surname is pronounced *Auk*-in-klaus; born September 27, 1917, in New York, N.Y.; son of Joseph Howland and Priscilla (Stanton) Auchincloss; married Adele Lawrence, 1957; children: John Winthrop, Blake Leay, Andrew Sloane. *Education:* Attended Yale University, 1935-39; University of Virginia, LL.B., 1941. *Religion:* Episcopalian. *Home:* 1111 Park Ave., New York, N.Y. 10028. *Agent:* James Brown Associates, Inc., 575 Madison Ave., New York, N.Y. 10022. *Office:* Hawkins, Delafield & Wood, 67 Wall St., New York, N.Y. 10005.

CAREER: Sullivan & Cromwell, New York City, associate, 1941-51; Hawkins, Delafield & Wood, New York City, associate, 1954-58, partner, 1958—. President, Museum of the City of New York; trustee, Josiah Macy, Jr. Foundation, Fellow, Pierpont Morgan Library. *Military service:* U.S. Navy, 1941-45; became lieutenant senior grade. *Member:* American Academy of Arts and Letters, Association of the Bar of the

City of New York (former member of executive committee), Phi Beta Kappa, Century Association. *Awards, honors:* D.Litt., New York University, 1974, Pace University, 1979.

WRITINGS—Novels; published by Houghton, except as indicated: (Under pseudonym Andrew Lee) *The Indifferent Children,* Prentice-Hall, 1947; *Sybil,* 1952; *A Law for the Lion,* 1953; *The Great World and Timothy Colt,* 1956; *Venus in Sparta,* 1958; *Pursuit of the Prodigal,* 1959; *The House of Five Talents,* 1960; *Portrait in Brownstone,* 1962; *The Rector of Justin,* 1964; *The Embezzler,* 1966; *A World of Profit,* 1968; *I Come as a Thief,* 1972; *The Partners,* 1974; *The Dark Lady,* 1977; *The Country Cousin,* 1978; *The House of the Prophet,* 1980; *The Cat and the King,* 1981.

Short stories; all published by Houghton: *The Injustice Collectors,* 1950; *The Romantic Egoists,* 1954; *Powers of Attorney,* 1963; *Tales of Manhattan,* 1967; *Second Chance,* 1970; *The Winthrop Covenant,* 1976.

Criticism; published by University of Minnesota Press, except as indicated: *Edith Wharton* (pamphlet), 1961; *Reflections of a Jacobite* (essays), Houghton, 1961; *Ellen Glasgow* (pamphlet), 1964; *Pioneers and Caretakers: A Study of Nine American Women Novelists,* 1965; *On Sister Carrie,* Merrill, 1968; *Motiveless Malignity* (essays), Houghton, 1969; *Henry Adams* (pamphlet), 1971; *Reading Henry James* (essays), 1975; *Life, Law and Letters* (essays), Houghton, 1979.

Other: (Editor) Edith Wharton, *An Edith Wharton Reader,* Scribner, 1965; "The Club Bedroom" (one-act play; produced on television in 1966 and at Playwrights Unit, 1967), published in *Esquire,* December, 1966; (editor) Anthony Trollope, *The Warden* [and] *Barchester Towers,* Houghton, 1966; (editor) *Fables of Wit and Elegance,* Scribner, 1972; *Richelieu* (biography), Viking, 1972; *A Writer's Capital* (autobiography), University of Minnesota Press, 1974; *Persons of Consequence: Queen Victoria and Her Circle,* Random House, 1979. Also author of four unproduced full-length plays and several one-act plays. Contributor of stories to *New Yorker, Harper's, Good Housekeeping, Town and Country,* and *Atlantic;* contributor of essays to *Partisan Review* and *Nation.*

SIDELIGHTS: Louis Auchincloss is known primarily as an author of novels of manners in the mode of Edith Wharton and C. P. Snow. His novels are peopled by wealthy, well-educated professionals, and critics often note that Auchincloss's personal background—he is a lawyer from a prominent family—makes his writing especially insightful. Robert Kiely contends in the *New York Times Book Review* that Auchincloss describes his characters "with considerable moral tact, sharpness of observation and narrative prudence." In *House of the Prophet,* several critics agree that Auchincloss has modelled his protagonist after columnist Walter Lippmann. For Christopher Lehmann-Haupt, Auchincloss's use of the novel of manners style seems anachronistic: "After all, Felix Leitner, the novel's protagonist, does not really live in a world in which the rules have been made up in advance." But in other stylistic matters, says Lehmann-Haupt, Auchincloss "has not only surpassed the limitations of his technique, he has also turned those limitations to advantage," producing "debatably the most accomplished book he has written to date."

Garrett Epps of the *Washington Post* feels that *The House of the Prophet* is a less-successful derivation of an earlier Auchincloss novel, *The Rector of Justin.* The flaw, says Epps, is in characterization. It is understandable, he argues, for the adolescent protagonist in *Justin* to consider his personal problems more important than those of the world around him, but for an adult character to behave as selfishly when faced with

problems of greater consequence is not nearly as believable. Kiely finds a different weakness in Auchincloss's characterization of Leitner. Although Leitner's "genius is taken for granted by all of the characters and presumably is meant to be accepted by the reader," Kiely is not convinced, since "what [Leitner] has to say about a wide range of topics from the Constitution to Shakespeare's late plays demonstrates neither striking originality nor unusual elegance. He sometimes sounds clever, never profound."

Characterization in *The Cat and the King* presents no such problems to critics. The novel, in the words of a *Newsweek* critic, is patterned after "the Duc de Saint-Simon's 'Historical Memoirs' of life at the court of Versailles during the reign of Louis XIV. Saint-Simon is the narrator of Auchincloss's novel as well, the contrivance being that the duke, having finished his memoirs, cannot let go." Doris Grumbach of the *New York Times Book* Review notes that the memoirs necessarily present much historical detail, and that "fiction that includes so many foreign names, titles and genealogical references inevitably grows dry. But when Mr. Auchincloss creates vignettes of court life . . . he infuses his pale history with blood." According to Grumbach, all characters in this novel "live vigorously in Mr. Auchincloss's elegant prose."

BIOGRAPHICAL/CRITICAL SOURCES: Saturday Review, October 14, 1950, July 14, 1962, April 8, 1967, November 30, 1968, August 26, 1972; *Times Literary Supplement,* September 26, 1958, September 11, 1981; *Commonweal,* December 12, 1958, June 16, 1967; *New Yorker,* August 13, 1960; *New York Times Book Review,* September 11, 1960, March 19, 1967, November 24, 1968, September 14, 1969, November 16, 1978, July 15, 1979, September 23, 1979, March 30, 1980, March 15, 1981; *Christian Science Monitor,* May 25, 1961, March 30, 1967; *Chicago Sunday Tribune,* July 15, 1962; *Atlantic,* August, 1962, September, 1970; Roy Newquist, *Counterpoint,* Rand McNally, 1964; *Critique,* winter, 1964-65; *Harper's,* August, 1965, April, 1967; *Life,* April 15, 1966, December 6, 1968; *Newsweek,* March 27, 1967, April 20, 1981; *Time,* March 31, 1967; *National Observer,* April 3, 1967, December 30, 1968; *Book Week,* April 9, 1967; *Criticism,* spring, 1967; *New York Times,* December 5, 1968, September 13, 1969, August 29, 1970, February 11, 1979, August 30, 1979, March 4, 1980, March 16, 1981; *Book World,* December 29, 1968, August 31, 1969; *Washington Post,* December 31, 1968, September 3, 1969, September 6, 1969, September 10, 1978, August 26, 1979, May 3, 1980; Louis Auchincloss, *A Writer's Capital* (autobiography), University of Minnesota Press, 1974; *New York Review of Books,* July 18, 1974; *Contemporary Literary Criticism,* Gale, Volume IV, 1975, Volume VI, 1976, Volume IX, 1978, Volume XVIII, 1981; Jackson R. Bryer, *Louis Auchincloss and His Critics,* G. K. Hall, 1977; *Detroit Free Press,* October 29, 1978; *Chicago Tribune Book World,* April 5, 1981.

*   *   *

AUER, J(ohn) Jeffery   1913-

PERSONAL: Born May 8, 1913, in Aurora, Ill.; son of John J. (an accountant) and Marie (Jeffery) Auer; married Eleanor R. Richmond, June 25, 1938; children: John J., Jane H., Judy R. *Education:* Wabash College, A.B., 1934; University of Wisconsin, M.A., 1935, Ph.D., 1947. *Politics:* Democrat. *Religion:* Unitarian. *Office:* Department of Speech and Theatre, Indiana University, Bloomington, Ind. 47405.

CAREER: Hanover College, Hanover, Ind., instructor in speech, 1935-37, instructor in political science, 1936-37; Oberlin College, Oberlin, Ohio, professor of public speaking, 1937-52; Indiana University, Bloomington, Ind., professor of speech and chairman of department, 1952-73, professor of speech and theatre and chairman of department, 1973—. *Military service:* U.S. Naval Reserve, 1943-45; became lieutenant junior grade. *Member:* Speech Communication Association of America (president, 1965), American Studies Association.

WRITINGS: (With Henry Lee Ewbank) *Discussion and Debate*, revised edition, Appleton-Century-Crofts, 1951; (with Ewbank) *Handbook for Discussion Leaders*, revised edition, Harper, 1954, reprinted, Greenwood Press, 1974; *Essentials of Parliamentary Procedure*, 3rd edition, Appleton-Century-Crofts, 1959; *An Introduction to Research in Speech*, Harper, 1959, reprinted, Greenwood Press, 1977; (editor) *Anti-Slavery and Disunion, 1858-1861: Studies in the Rhetoric of Compromise and Conflict*, Harper, 1963; (with Jon Eisenson and John V. Irwin) *The Psychology of Communication*, Appleton-Century-Crofts, 1963; (editor) Gaylan Jane Collier, *Assignments in Acting*, Harper, 1966; (editor) *Brigance's Speech Communication*, 3rd edition, Prentice-Hall, 1967; (editor) *The Rhetoric of Our Times*, Appleton-Century-Crofts, 1969; (editor) *Oratory in the Old South, 1828-1860*, Louisiana State University Press, 1970; (editor with Edward B. Jenkinson) *Essays on Teaching Speech in the High School*, Indiana University Press, 1971; (editor) *On Teaching Speech in Elementary and Junior High Schools*, Indiana University Press, 1971. *Speech Monographs*, editor, 1954-56, contributing editor, 1956—.

* * *

AUGSBURGER, Myron S. 1929-

PERSONAL: Born August 20, 1929, in Elida, Ohio; son of Clarence A. (a farmer) and Estella (Shenk) Augsburger; married Esther Kniss, November 28, 1950; children: John Myron, Michael David, Marcia Louise. *Education:* Eastern Mennonite College, A.B., 1955, Th.B., 1958; Goshen College, B.D., 1959; Union Theological Seminary, Richmond, Va., Th.M., 1961, Th.D., 1964. *Home:* 3051 N St. N.W., Washington, D.C. 20007.

CAREER: Minister of Mennonite Church. Inter-Church Evangelism, Inc., Harrisonburg, Va., evangelist, beginning 1956; Eastern Mennonite College, Harrisonburg, Va., professor of theology, 1962-65, president, beginning 1965; currently pastor in Washington, D.C. and professor of theology at Mennonite seminaries. Moderator, Mennonite Church Peace Commission. Member of board of directors, Presbyterian Ministers' Fund. *Member:* Evangelical Theological Association.

WRITINGS: Called to Maturity, Herald, 1960; *Quench Not the Spirit*, Herald, 1962; *Plus Living*, Zondervan, 1963; *Invitation to Discipleship*, Herald, 1964; *Principles of Biblical Interpretation*, Herald, 1967; *Pilgrim Aflame*, Herald, 1967; *Faith for a Secular World*, Word Books, 1968; *The Broken Chalice*, Herald, 1971; *The Expanded Life: The Sermon on the Mount for Today*, Abingdon, 1972; *Walking in the Resurrection*, Herald, 1976; *Faithful unto Death*, Word Books, 1978.

* * *

AVELINE, Claude 1901-

PERSONAL: Born July 19, 1901, in Paris, France; son of Georges (an industrialist) and Cecile (Tchernomordik) Aveline; married Jeanne Barusseaud, 1964; children: Nicolas (adopted), Luce (ward). *Education:* Attended Lycee Hoche, Versailles, and Lycee Janson-de-Sailly, Paris. *Agent:* Hope Leresche & Steele, Jubilee Place 11, London S.W. 3, England.

CAREER: Art editor in Paris, France, 1922-30; writer, 1919—; lecturer, 1928—; painter. Exhibited paintings in Paris, 1972, 1974, 1978, 1980; Ljubljana, 1973; Brussels, 1975; Zagreb, 1976; Belgrade, 1976. *Wartime service:* Enlisted in 1939; member of la Resistance Interieure, 1940-44; made officer of la Legion d'honneur and commandeur des Arts et des Lettres; awarded Medaille de la Resistance avec rosette. *Member:* Societe Anatole France (president d'honneur), Societe Europeenne de Culture (member of executive council), Societe des Gens de Lettres, Societe des Auteurs Dramatiques, P.E.N. *Awards, honors:* Grand prix de la Societe des Gens de Lettres, 1952; Prix Italia (radio), 1955; Prix de la Radio de la Societe des Auteurs Dramatiques, 1976; Grand Prix Poncetton, 1978.

WRITINGS—Novels and short stories: Les Desirs ou le Livre egare, Stols, 1926; *Le Point du jour*, Emile-Paul, 1928, revised edition, Mercure de France, 1960; *L'homme de Phalere*, Emile-Paul, 1935; *Le Prisonnier*, Emile-Paul, 1936, revised edition, Mercure de France, 1971, translation published as *Prisoner Born*, Hutchinson International Authors, 1950, translation by Mervyn Saville, Dobson, 1970, Doubleday, 1971; *Le Temps mort*, Editions de Minuit, 1944, enlarged edition, Mercure de France, 1962; *Pour l'amour de la nuit*, Domat, 1956; *Le Bestiaire inattendu*, Mercure de France, 1959, edited with introduction and notes by Robert Gibson, Harrap, 1964; *Le Poids du feu*, Del Duca, 1959, reprinted, le Livre de poche, 1974; *C'est vrai, mais il ne faut pas le croire*, Mercure de France, 1960; *Hoffmann Canada*, Buchet-Chastel, 1977.

"La Vie de Philippe Denis" trilogy: *Madame Maillart*, Emile-Paul, 1930, revised edition, 1949; *Les Amours et les haines*, Domat, 1952; *Philippe*, Domat, 1955.

Detective stories: *La double Mort de Frederic Belot*, Grasset, 1932, revised edition, Mercure de France, 1962, edited and abridged by R. W. Torrens and J. B. Sanders, Longmans, Green, 1958, translation of original edition by A. K. Shields published as *The Double Death of Frederic Belot*, Holt, 1940, translation by Ann Lindsay published under same title, Dobson, 1949, Doubleday, 1974; *L'Abonne de la ligne U*, Emile-Paul, 1947, revised edition, Mercure de France, 1964, translation by Mervyn Savill published as *The Passenger of the U*, Dobson, 1968, Doubleday, 1969; *Voiture 7, place 15* (also see below), Emile-Paul, 1947, revised edition, Mercure de France, 1970, translation of original edition by David Arkell published as *Carriage 7, Seat 15*, Dobson, 1968, Doubleday, 1969; *Le Jet d'eau*, Roy, 1954, published with preface by Gilbert Sigaux, Circle du Bibliophile, 1970, translation by Peter Green published as *The Fountain at Marlieux*, Dobson, 1954, Doubleday, 1970; *L'oeil-de-chat*, Mercure de France, 1970, translation by Green published as *The Cat's-Eye*, Dobson, 1972, Doubleday, 1973.

Poetry: *Io Hymen, suivi de Chants funebres*, Bernouard, 1925, revised edition, Editions de L'Orycte, 1980; *Portrait de L'Oiseau-Qui-N' Existe-Pas*, [Geneva], 1961, translation by George Buchanan, Jacomet, 1978; *De*, Corti, 1967; (self-illustrated) *Monologue pour un disparu*, Libraire Saint-Germain-de-Pres, 1973.

Theater: *Brouart et le desordre*, edited with an introduction and notes by Robert Gibson, Harrap, 1964, published with preface by Gilbert Figarys, Librairie Theatrale, 1981.

Essays and travel books: *Le Roman d'une ville de France: La Charite-sur-Loire*, Delayance, 1924, revised edition, 1968; *Les Muses melees*, Delpeuch, 1926; *Rodin*, Les Ecrivains Reunis, 1927; *La merveilleuse Legende du Bouddha*, L'Artisan du Livre, 1928; *Routes de la Catalogne; ou, Le Livre de l'amitie*, illustrations by Berthold Mahn, Hartmann, 1932; *La Promenade egyptienne*, Emile-Paul, 1934; *Avec toi-meme*, Emile-Paul, 1944, enlarged edition published as *Avec toi-meme, etc.*, Mercure de France, 1963; *Dans Paris retrouve*, Emile-Paul, 1945; *Les Devoirs de l'esprit*, Grasset, 1945; *Plus vrais que soi*, Savel, 1947; *Pegomancie*, Emile-Paul, 1949; *Et tout le reste n'est rien (La Religieuse portugaise)*, Mercure de France, 1951; *Egypte*, Hachette, 1955, translation published as *Egypt*, Hachette, 1955; *Les Mots de la fin*, Hachette, 1957; *Le Code de jeux*, Hachette, 1961; *Les Reflexions de Monsieur F.A.T.*, Mercure de France, 1963; *Celebration du lit*, Morel, 1966; *Le Haut mal des createurs; ou, Le complexe d'un siecle inexistant*, J. Antoine (Brussels), 1973.

Juvenile: *Baba Diene et Morceau-de-Sucre*, Gallimard, 1937, edited by R. J. Quinault, Harrap, 1939; *De quoi encoire?*, Gallimard, 1946, new edition, La Farandole, 1974, translation by M. Ledesort published as *The Bird That Flew into the Sea and Other Stories*, Harrap, 1961; *L'Arbre Tic-Tac*, Raisons d'Etre, 1950.

Editor: Antoine Bourdelie, *La Sculpture et Rodin*, Emile-Paul, 1937; *Le Line d'or du centenaire d'Anatole France, 1844-1944*, Societe Anatole France, 1949; Anatole France, *Trente ans de vie sociale (1897-1924)*, four volumes, Cercle du Bibliophile, 1971.

Television plays: (With Simone Barde) "Baba Diene et Morceau-de-Sucre," 1953; "C'est vrai, mais il ne faut pas le croire," 1956, translation by Archie Campbell produced in London as "True—But Don't Believe It," 1959; "Voiture 7, place 15," 1958, translation by Mervyn Savill produced in London as "Coach 7, Seat 15," 1962; "L'Abonne de la ligne U," forty episodes, 1964; "L'Entretier," 1968; "De folie et d'amour (une Lyonnoise)," 1968; "Le Jerd'eau," 1973; (with Marianne Oswald) "Le Vol de L'oiseau-Qui-N'Existe-pas," 1968; "L'Hirondelie inattendue" (opera), produced in Poland, 1976.

Radio plays: "La Femme disparue," 1947; "L'Oeil-de-chat," twelve episodes, 1951; "Le Bestiaire inattendu," six parts, 1952, one part translated by Mervyn Savill as "A Visit to the Paradise of Famous Animals, Androcles' Lion," 1963; "Une Histoire de la nuit," 1953; "Le Prisonnier," 1954; "C'Est veai, mais il ne faut pas le croire," 1955; "Le Prodigieux petit Canard," 1957; "Moi, Louis Bertrand (Aloysius Bertrand)," 1957; "L'Abonne de la ligne U," forty episodes, 1958; "La Villa Remiro," 1958; "Les Chiens et la mort," 1959; "Notre pere petrus Borel," 1959; "L'Autre chex les corsaires," 1959; "L'As de coeur," 1961; "Un jeu par jour," twenty parts, 1961; "L'Affaire Magny," 1965; "L'Exception," 1965; "Les Filles blanches d'Amsterdam," 1966; "L'Entretien," 1967; "Hoffmann Canada," 1969; "Coupex les nageoires a l'aide de gros ciseaux," 1970; "Voiture 7, place 15," 1973.

Also author of plays, "Aimez-Vous le theatre? ou la parade de la rengaine" and "Brouart et le desordre"; author of ballet, "L'As de coeur." Contributor to *L'Heure du Choix*, Editions de Minuit, 1947, and *La Voie Libre*, Flammarion, 1951. Author of prefaces and commentaries for many books.

SIDELIGHTS: In the 1950's, Claude Aveline asked painters of all countries and all techniques to paint one "bird which does not exist." In 1963, he made a gift of this collection, numbering 108 paintings, to the Musee National d'Art moderne in Paris. The collection was exhibited in the United States in 1965-66. Now in the Centre National Georges Pompidou in Paris, the collection was re-exhibited during 1978. The great success of the latest exhibition prompted Aveline to undertake a new series which already includes 75 paintings.

BIOGRAPHICAL/CRITICAL SOURCES: Andre Gillois, *Qui etes-vous?*, Gallimard, 1953; *Mercure de France*, May 7, 1960;

F. Mouret, *Les ouvrages de Claude Aveline*, Mercure de France, 1961; *Livres de France*, June-July, 1962; *Listener*, June 27, 1968; *Newsweek*, July 28, 1969; *New York Times Book Review*, October 19, 1969; *Hommage a Claude Aveline, pour les cinquante ans de sa vie litteraire*, Societe Anatole France, 1970; *Observer Review*, August 16, 1970; *Times Literary Supplement*, August 21, 1970; Simone Martin-Chauffier, *A bientot quand meme . . .*, Calmann-Levy, 1976; Martin Blumenson, *The Vilde Affair: Beginnings of the French Resistance*, Houghton, 1977; Alice Mauron, *Ces Fauves domestiques: Vers une psychocritique du genre fantastique*, Mars, 1980; Jean Cassou, *Les Peintures au feutre de Claude Aveline*, Jalons, 1980.

*   *   *

AVI-YONAH, M(ichael)   1904-1974

PERSONAL: Name originally Michael Buchstab; born September 26, 1904, in Lemberg, Austria; died March 26, 1974; son of Solomon Ber and Tamar Ottilie (Weinbaum) Buchstab; married Eva Boyko (a painter and sculptor), August 2, 1955; children: (previous marriage) Miriam Eiyal, Jael; (present marriage) Reuben. *Education:* Attended Hebrew College Gimnasiah Ivrith, Jerusalem; University College, London, B.A. (honors), 1928, M.A., 1941, Ph.D., 1958. *Politics:* Liberal. *Home:* Bialik St., 15, Beth ha-Kerem, Jerusalem, Israel. *Office:* Hebrew University, Jerusalem, Israel.

CAREER: Government of Palestine, Department of Antiquities, archaeological records officer, 1931-48; Government of Israel, Department of Antiquities, research secretary, 1948-53; Hebrew University, Jerusalem, Israel, lecturer, 1953-58, associate professor, 1958-63, professor of archaeology and history of art, beginning 1963. Member, Archaeological Advisory Board of Israel, beginning 1948; trustee, Haifa Museum, beginning 1961; chairman of trustees, Museum of Mediterranean Art. *Military service:* Haganah, 1929-48; Israel Defence Army, 1948-49. *Member:* Israel Exploration Society (member of executive committee, beginning 1949), Israel Numismatic Society (member of executive committee, beginning 1952). *Awards, honors:* Bialik Prize, 1956, for *The Antiquities of Israel*.

WRITINGS: Mosaic Pavements in Palestine, Oxford University Press, 1934; *Map of Roman Palestine*, Oxford University Press, 1936, 2nd edition, 1940; *Abbreviations in Greek Inscriptions*, Oxford University Press, 1940; (contributor) *Syria and Lebanon*, 3rd edition, Steimatzky (Jerusalem), 1942; (contributor) *Jerusalem: The Saga of the Holy City*, Universitas (Jerusalem), 1954; *The Madaba Mosaic Map*, Israel Exploration Society, 1954.

(Editor) *Jerusalem*, Arco, 1960; (with M. Shapiro) *Israel: Ancient Mosaics*, UNESCO, 1960; *Oriental Art in Roman Palestine*, University of Rome Press, 1961; *Massada, Storia di una fortezza*, Marietti, 1961; *The New Testament: A Pictorial Commentary*, McGraw, 1962; (with Emil G. Kraeling) *Our Living Bible*, McGraw, 1962; *Geschichte der Juden im Zeitalter des Talmuds*, Gruyter, 1962; *The Holy Land: A Historical Geography*, Baker Book, 1966; (editor) L. A. Mayer, *A Bibliography of Jewish Numismatics*, Hebrew University, 1966; (with J. Aharoni) *The Macmillan Bible Atlas*, Macmillan, 1968 (revised edition published in England as *The Modern Bible Atlas*, Allen & Unwin, 1979); *The Cities of the Eastern Roman Provinces*, Clarendon Press, 1971; *Ancient Scrolls*, Cassell, 1974; *Introducing Archaeology*, Cassell, 1974; *Archaelogical Encyclopaedia of the Holy Land*, SBS Publishing, 1974 (published in England as *Encyclopedia of Archaeological Excavations in the Holy Land*, Oxford University Press, 1976); *The Jews of Palestine*, Blackwell, 1976; *The World History of the*

Jewish People, W. H. Allen, 1976; *Hellenism and the East,* Hebrew University (Jerusalem), 1978.

In Hebrew: *Bi-yeme Roma u-Bizantiyon,* [Jerusalem], 1946, 3rd edition, 1962; *Geografiyah historit,* [Jerusalem], 1949, 3rd edition, 1962; (with E. Yeivin) *Kadmoniyot artsenu,* Volume 1, [Tel-Aviv], 1955; (editor) *Sefer Yerushalayim,* [Jerusalem], beginning 1956; *Atlas geografi-histori shel Erets-Yisrael,* 195?; (editor) *Yerushalayim,* [Jerusalem], 1960?; *Masot u-mehkarim bi-yedi' at ha-Arets,* 1964; *Atlas Karta li-tekufat Bayit sheni, ha-Mishnah veha-Talmud,* 1966.

Editor, *Israel Exploration Journal,* beginning 1951. Contributor to *Archaeological Encyclopaedia, Hebrew Encyclopaedia, Encyclopaedia Judaica,* and *Atlas of Israel;* author of seventy articles in archaeological journals.

SIDELIGHTS: Michael Avi-Yonah spoke Hebrew, English, German, French, Italian, and Polish. *Avocational interests:* Seventeenth-century painting, eighteenth-century opera.

BIOGRAPHICAL/CRITICAL SOURCES: Bulletin of Israel Exploration Society, Volume XVIII, 1954.†

B

BAGBY, George
See STEIN, Aaron Marc

*   *   *

BAGDIKIAN, Ben Haig   1920-

PERSONAL: Surname is accented on second syllable; born January 30, 1920, in Marash, Turkey; brought to United States in 1920; son of Aram Theodore (a minister) and Daisy (Uvezian) Bagdikian; married Elizabeth S. Ogasapian, October 2, 1942 (divorced May 31, 1974); married Betty Medsger, July 8, 1974; children: (first marriage) Christopher, Frederick. *Education:* Clark University, A.B., 1941. *Politics:* Democrat. *Religion:* Unitarian. *Home and office:* 4410 Albemarle St. N.W., Washington, D.C. 20016. *Agent:* Sterling Lord, 660 Madison Ave., New York, N.Y. 10021.

CAREER: Springfield Morning Union, Springfield, Mass., general reporter, 1941-42; Periodical House, Inc. (magazine publishers), New York City, associate editor, 1946; *Providence Journal,* Providence, R.I., chief Washington correspondent, 1947-61; *Saturday Evening Post,* New York City, contributing editor and writer, 1962-67; director, Rand News Media Study Project, 1967-69; *Washington Post,* Washington, D.C., assistant managing editor of national news, 1970-72; writer and lecturer. Research fellow, American University, 1975-76. President, Mellett Fund for a Free and Responsible Press. Trustee, Clark University, 1964—. *Military service:* U.S. Air Force, navigator, 1942-45; became first lieutenant. *Member:* Overseas Writers, Authors League of America, National Press Club, American Civil Liberties Union, Urban League, Washington Independent Writers, Phi Beta Kappa, Sigma Delta Chi, Fortune Society.

AWARDS, HONORS: George Foster Peabody Award, 1951, for articles analyzing American commentators; Ogden Reid Foundation fellow, 1956; Sydney Hillman Foundation Award, 1956, for study of internal security system; Brotherhood Award, National Conference of Christians and Jews, 1958, for articles on race relations; Guggenheim fellow, 1961; L.H.D., Brown University, 1961; D.Litt., Clark University, 1963.

WRITINGS: (Editor) *Man's Contracting World in an Expanding Universe,* Brown University Bookstore, 1960; (contributor) Lester Tanzer, editor, *The Kennedy Circle,* Luce, 1961; *In the Midst of Plenty: The Poor in America,* Beacon Press, 1964; (contributor) Frederick T.C. Yu, editor, *Behavioral Sciences and the Mass Media,* Russell Sage, 1968; (contributor) Charles V. Daly, editor, *The Media and the Cities,* Center for Policy Study, University of Chicago, 1968; *The Information Machines: Their Impact on Men and the Media,* Harper, 1971; *The Effete Conspiracy: And Other Crimes by the Press,* Harper, 1972; (with Leon Dash) *The Shame of the Prisons,* Pocket Books, 1972; *Caged: Eight Prisoners and Their Keepers,* Harper, 1976; *Bagdikian On: Political Reporting, Newspaper Economics, Law and Ethics,* Texas Christian University, 1977.

Also author of numerous pamphlets, including: *Pitchmen of the Press: The Newsmagazines,* Promotion Department, Providence Journal Co., 1958; *The Principal Instrument of Freedom,* Phi Beta Kappa Society, 1961; *Whose Press Is It?,* International Labor Press Association, 1965; (with Kathleen Archibald) *Televised Ombudsman,* Rand Corporation, 1968; *The Newsman's Scope,* Ford Foundation, 1972; (with James Rhea) *We Went South: What Price Security?; Atomic Age, 1945—?.* Also contributor to *Evaluating the Press: The New England Daily Newspaper Survey,* 1973. Contributor to *Atlantic, New Republic, New York Times Magazine, Coronet, Columbia Journalism Review,* and numerous other periodicals.

SIDELIGHTS: Ben Haig Bagdikian wrote *CA:* "My two main interests in writing are major social problems and analysis and criticism of the news media. A career in journalism sensitized me to these and it is my belief that analysis of society's ways of learning through its mass media cannot be done well without continual immersion, thorough research and writing, into the most compelling substantive social problems of our time."

BIOGRAPHICAL/CRITICAL SOURCES: Washington Post, February 24, 1971; *New York Times,* February 26, 1971; *Saturday Review,* March 13, 1971; *New Republic,* May 1, 1971.†

*   *   *

BAILEY, Paul Dayton   1906-

PERSONAL: Born 1906, in American Fork, Utah (a Mormon community); son of Eli Hawkins and Olive Edith (Forbes) Bailey; married Evelyn Robison, 1927; children: David Paul, Lynn Robison. *Education:* Attended University of Utah, one year.

CAREER: Eagle Rock Press-Advertiser, Eagle Rock, Calif., publisher, 1938-45; Westernlore Press (publishers of books), Los Angeles, Calif., publisher and editor, beginning 1941. *Member:* Authors Club, Printing Industry of America, Western

Writers of America, Death Valley '49ers (director of the board), Los Angeles Press Club, Los Angeles Corral of Westerners (sheriff, 1950), E Clampus Vitus, Zamorano.

WRITINGS—Published by Westernlore, except as indicated: *Type-High*, Suttonhouse, 1937; *For This My Glory: A Story of a Mormon Life*, Lyman House, 1940; *The Gay Saint*, Murray & Gee, 1944; *Deliver Me from Eva*, Murray & Gee, 1946; *Song Everlasting*, 1946; *For Time and All Eternity*, Doubleday, 1964; *The Armies of God*, Doubleday, 1968; *Ghost Dance Messiah*, 1970; *City in the Sun*, 1971; *Polygamy Was Better than Monotony*, 1972; *Concentration Camp U.S.A.*, Tower, 1972; *Those Kings and Queens of Old Hawaii: A Mele to Their Memory*, 1975; *Holy Smoke: A Dissertation on the Utah War*, 1977; *An Unnatural History of Death Valley: With Reflections on the Valley's Varmints, Virgins, Vandals and Visionaries*, Chalfant Press, 1978.

Biographies; published by Westernlore, except as indicated: *Sam Brannan and the California Mormons*, 1943, 3rd edition, 1959; *Jacob Hamblin. A Buckskin Apostle*, 1948; *Walkara: Hawk of the Mountains*, 1954; (with Roger Holmes) *Fabulous Farmer: The Story of Walter Knott and His Berry Farm*, 1956; *Wovoka: The Indian Messiah*, 1957; *Grandpa Was a Polygamist*, 1960; *The Claws of the Hawk: The Incredible Life of Wahker the Ute*, 1966; *Hawaii's Royal Prime Minister: The Life and Times of Walter Murray Gibson*, Hasting House, 1980.

Editor and compiler of *The Mormons in California*. Editor, *Branding Iron*. Book reviewer for various publications.†

*   *   *

BAILY, Nathan A(riel) 1920-

PERSONAL: Born July 19, 1920, in New York, N.Y.; son of Saul (a rabbi and cantor) and Eleanor (Mintz) Baily; married Judith Bernstein, June 20, 1946; children: Alan Eric, Lawrence Joel. *Education:* City College (now City College of the City University of New York), B.S., 1940; Columbia University, M.A., 1941, Ph.D., 1946. *Religion:* Hebrew. *Home:* 5516 Greystone St., Chevy Chase, Md. 20015. *Office:* Department of Management, Nova University, 3301 College Ave., Fort Lauderdale, Fla. 33314.

CAREER: Teacher at City College (now City College of the City University of New York), New York, N.Y., 1942-46; senior editor and economic analyst, Research Institute of America, 1944-45; Office of Price Administration, Washington, D.C., price economist, 1946-47; American University, Washington, D.C., 1947-70, began as assistant professor, became professor of business administration, chairman of department, and founding dean of School of Business Administration, 1955-70; Postal Rate Commission, Washington, D.C., commissioner, 1970-74, chief economist, 1974-75. Distinguished visiting professor of management, Nova University, 1980—; visiting professor of business and government relations, George Washington University, 1980—. Former instructor in economics, Fashion Institute of Technology; instructor and dean of faculty, American Institute of Banking. Management consultant to government agencies, business firms, and professional associations. Director of Washington Mutual Investors Fund, Carrols Development Corp., Carl M. Freeman Associates, Pioneer Foundation, and Homer Hoyt Institute. Trustee, Council on Opportunities in Selling. Member of board of advisors, Federal Realty Investment Trust and Columbia Realty Trust.

MEMBER: American Economic Association, American Society of Association Executives, American Institute of Management (honorary member), American Wholesalers (member of

board of directors; director), National Advisory Council on Economic Education, American Association of University Professors, Chamber of Commerce of the United States (member of board of directors; director) Middle Atlantic Association of Colleges of Business Administration (secretary-treasurer, 1963-64; president, 1964-65), Friends of United States of Latin America (member of board of directors; director), Washington Society of Investment Analysts (charter member), Washington Sales Executives Club (member of board of directors, 1962-63), Phi Beta Kappa, Rho Epsilon, Pi Sigma Epsilon. *Awards, honors:* Awarded fellowships from numerous organizations including Educators' Round Table, General Electric Co., Danforth Foundation, Volker Fund, E.I. Dupont de Nemours, Swift & Co.; Distinguished Salesman's Award, Washington Sales Executives Club; Distinguished Service Award, Society for Religious Organization Management; Pell Gold Medal.

WRITINGS: (Editor) *Marketing Profitably under the Robinson-Patman Act*, Public Affairs Press, 1963; *Marketing Handbook*, Institute of Industrial Launderers, 1972, 2nd edition, 1973; *Guide to Establishing a Company Marketing Program*, Institute of Industrial Launderers, 1973. Contributor to *Business Perspectives* and other professional journals. Contributing editor, *Modern Securities Services*.

*   *   *

BAKER, Betty D(oreen Flook) 1916-
(Elizabeth Renier)

PERSONAL: Born November 22, 1916, in Bristol, England; daughter of Leonard Joseph and Edith (Bath) Flook; married Frank Edward Baker (deceased). *Education:* Attended Merchant Venturers College, Bristol, England. *Religion:* Church of England. *Home:* Inchcoulter Cottage, 15 Douglas Ave., Exmouth, Devonshire, England.

CAREER: Writer. Doctor's secretary. Volunteer helper, Family Planning Association, 1958-62. *Wartime service:* Red Cross, Voluntary Aid Detachment, 1940-42; attached to Royal Army Medical Corps. *Member:* Royal Society for the Protection of Birds, National Trust, Devon Trust for Nature Conservation, West Sussex Writers Club. *Awards, honors:* Pauline Warwick Award from Romantic Novelists' Association, and scholarship to Writers Summer School, both for *The Generous Vine*, 1961.

WRITINGS—Novels; all under pseudonym Elizabeth Renier; published by Hurst & Blackett, except as indicated: *The Generous Vine*, 1962, Ace Books, 1972; *The House of Water*, 1963, Ace Books, 1972; *Blade of Justice*, 1965, Ace Books, 1972; *If This Be Treason*, 1965, published as *If This Be Love*, Ace Books, 1971; *Valley of Nightingales*, Ace Books, 1966; *A Singing in the Woods*, 1966, Ace Books, 1972; *Prelude to Freedom*, 1967, published as *Prelude to Love*, Ace Books, 1972; *The House of Granite*, 1968, Ace Books, 1971; *By Sun and Candlelight*, 1968, Ace Books, 1973; *Tomorrow Comes the Sun*, 1969, Ace Books, 1971.

The Spanish Doll, 1970, Ace Books, 1972; *Valley of Secrets*, 1970, Ace Books, 1972; *Woman From the Sea*, Ace Books, 1972; *Renshawe Inheritance*, 1972, Arrow Books, 1978; *A Time for Rejoicing*, Ace Books, 1973; *Ravenstor*, 1974, Arrow Books, 1979; *The Moving Dream*, Fawcett, 1978; *Landscape of the Heart*, 1978, Fawcett, 1979. Also author of *Yesterday's Mischief*, published by Ace Books.

Children's books; all published by Hamish Hamilton: *The Lightkeepers*, 1977; *The Stone People*, 1978; *The Dangerous Journey*, 1979; *The Post Rider*, 1980.

Contributor of short stories to *Woman's Story, Sincerely, John O'London's,* British Broadcasting Corp. radio and of serials to *Woman's Realm.*

AVOCATIONAL INTERESTS: Natural history, gardening, music, and conservation.

*   *   *

BAKER, Denys Val   1917-

PERSONAL: Born October 24, 1917, in Poppleton, Yorkshire, England; son of Valentine Henry and Dilys (Eames) Baker; married Jess Margaret Bryan (a self-employed potter), January 28, 1948; children: Martin, Gillian, Jane, Stephen, Demelza, Genevieve. *Politics:* Pacifist. *Home:* Mill House, St. Burydn, Cornwall, England.

CAREER: Writer on British daily and trade newspapers, 1935-41; free-lance writer, 1941—.

WRITINGS: Worlds without End (short stories), Sylvan Press, 1945; *The White Rock* (novel), Sylvan Press, 1945, Appleton, 1947; *The More We Are Together* (novel), Low, 1947; *The Return of Uncle Walter, and Other Stories,* Low, 1948; *The Widening Mirror* (novel), Low, 1949.

(Author of introduction) *Paintings from Cornwall,* Cornish Library, 1950; *Britain Discovers Herself,* Christopher Johnson, 1950; *How to Be an Author,* Harvill Press, 1952; *The Title's My Own* (novel), Bles, 1955; *A Journey with Love* (novel), Brideshead, 1955; *Strange Fulfillment* (short stories), Pyramid Press, 1958; (with wife, Jess Baker) *The Pottery Book: An Introduction to an Individual Art and Craft,* Cassell, 1959; *Britain's Art Colony by Sea,* George Ronald, 1959.

The Minack Theatre, George Ronald, 1960; *How to Be a Parent,* Boardman & Co., 1960; *Pottery Today,* Oxford University Press, 1961; *The Sea's in the Kitchen,* Phoenix House, 1962; *The Door Is Always Open,* Phoenix House, 1963; *The Young Potter: A How-It-Is-Done Book of Pottery,* Warne, 1963; *The Flameswallower, and Other Stories from Cornwall,* J. H. Locke, 1963; *Cornwall for the Cornish,* Porthmoor Press, 1964; (contributor) James E. Turner, editor, *Thy Neighbor's Wife: Twelve Original Variations on a Theme,* Cassell, 1964; *The Strange and the Damned* (short stories), Pyramid Press, 1964; *We'll Go around the World Tomorrow,* Baker Publishers, 1965; *To Sea with Sam,* Baker Publishers, 1967; *Adventures before Fifty,* Baker Publishers, 1969.

The Face in the Mirror, Arkham House, 1971; *Woman and the Engine Driver,* United Writers Publications, 1972; *Timeless Land: Creative Spirit in Cornwall,* Adams, 1973; *An Old Mill by the Stream,* Kimber, 1973; *Company of Three,* Milton House, 1974; *As the River Flows,* Milton House, 1974; *Spring at Lake's End,* Kimber, 1974; *Don't Lose Your Cool, Dad,* Milton House, 1975; *A Summer to Remember: Cornish Stories,* Kimber, 1975; *Sunset over the Scillies,* Kimber, 1975; *Fun with Pottery,* Kaye & Ward, 1975; *A View from the Valley,* Kimber, 1976; *A Long Way to Land's End,* Kimber, 1977; *The Secret Place and Other Cornish Stories,* Kimber, 1977; *Wind Blows from the West,* Kimber, 1977; *All This and Cornwall Too,* Kimber, 1978; *Passenger to Penzance and Other Stories from Cornwall,* Kimber, 1978; *Tales of Mystery,* Kimber, 1978; *At the Sea's Edge and Other Stories,* Kimber, 1979; *Barbican's End: A Novel of Cornwall,* Kimber, 1979; *Family for All Seasons,* Kimber, 1979.

Rose: A Novel of Cornwall, Kimber, 1980; *Karenya: A Novel of Cornwall,* Kimber, 1980; *As the Stream Flows By,* Kimber, 1980; *The Spirit of Cornwall,* W. H. Allen, 1980. Also author of *Echoes from the Cornish Cliffs.*

Editor: *Little Reviews, 1914-1943,* Allen & Unwin, 1943; *Little Reviews Anthology,* Volume I, Allen & Unwin, 1943, Volume II-IV, Eyre & Spottiswoode, 1945, 1946, 1948, Volume V, Methuen, 1949; *Writing Today,* Staples, Volume I (with Peter Ratazzi), 1943, Volumes II-IV, 1944-46; *International Short Stories,* two volumes, W. H. Allen, 1944-45; *Modern Short Stories,* Staples, 1944; *Voyage: An Anthology of Selected Stories,* Sylvan Press, 1945; *Writers of Today,* two volumes, Sidgwick & Jackson, 1946-48; *Modern British Writing,* Vanguard, 1947; *One and All: A Selection of Stories from Cornwall,* Museum Press, 1951.

Haunted Cornwall: A Book of Supernatural Stories, Kimber, 1973; *Cornish Harvest: An Anthology,* Kimber, 1974; *Stories of the Sea,* Kimber, 1974; *Cornish Short Stories,* Penguin, 1976; *Stories of the Macabre,* Kimber, 1976; *My Favorite Story: An Anthology,* Kimber, 1977; *Twelve Stories by Famous Women Writers,* W. H. Allen, 1977; *Stories of Horror and Suspense: An Anthology,* Kimber, 1977; *Stories of the Occult and Other Tales of Mystery,* Kimber, 1978; *Sea Survivors,* W. H. Allen, 1979; *Stories of the Supernatural,* Kimber, 1979; *Women Writing: An Anthology,* W. H. Allen, 1979.

Contributor of short stories to *Argosy, Pick of Todays Stories, Esquire, Town and Country, Chicago Review, Western Review, Good Housekeeping, Home, Evening News, Evening Standard, Punch,* and other publications; author of nearly one hundred stories broadcast on British Broadcasting Corp. programs.

WORK IN PROGRESS: Short stories; continuing autobiographical books; novels.

AVOCATIONAL INTERESTS: Surfing and boating.

BIOGRAPHICAL/CRITICAL SOURCES: Times Literary Supplement, March 28, 1980, January 2, 1981.

*   *   *

BAKER, Margaret   1890-

PERSONAL: Born April 8, 1890, in Langley Green, Oldbury, Birmingham, England; daughter of Harry (a head chemist) and Mary (Eccles) Baker. *Education:* Privately educated. *Politics:* Liberal. *Religion:* Society of Friends. *Home:* Tarver's Orchard, Sutton-under-Brailes, near Banbury, Oxfordshire, England.

CAREER: Writer of books for children, most of them illustrated (largely in silhouette) by her sister, Mary Baker. Honorary superintendent of local and county work, National British Women's Total Abstinence Union, 1910-28; lecturer throughout England on total abstinence, prior to 1939. During World War I did volunteer work at Runcorn Cottage Hospital; during World War II assisted local Quakers in repair and furnishing of abandoned homes for use in housing evacuees from London. Chairman of Sutton-under-Brailes Parish Meeting, for twenty years. *Member:* Society of Authors.

WRITINGS: The Black Cats and the Tinker's Wife, Duffield & Co., 1923; *The Dog, the Brownie and the Bramble-Patch,* Duffield & Co., 1924; *The Little Girl Who Curtsied to the Owl,* Duffield & Co., 1925; *Pedlar's Ware,* Duffield & Co., 1925; *Four Times Once Upon a Time,* Duffield & Co., 1926; *The Lost Merbaby,* Duffield & Co., 1927, reprinted, Puffin, 1980; *The Pixies and the Silver Crown,* Duffield & Co., 1927; *The Story of St. Paul,* Oxford University Press, 1927, revised edition published as *St. Paul,* 1947; *The Water Elf and the Miller's Child,* Duffield & Co., 1928; *Tomson's Hallowe'en,* Duffield & Co., 1929.

Favorite Fables, Oxford University Press, 1930; *Noddy Goes A-Plowing,* Duffield & Co., 1930; *Peacock Eggs,* Basil Blackwell, 1931, Duffield & Green, 1932; *Cat's-Cradles for His Majesty*, Duffield & Green, 1933; *Patsy and the Leprechauns*, Basil Blackwell, 1932, Duffield & Green, 1933; *The Button Who Had a Sense of Humour*, Basil Blackwell, 1933, Artists and Writers Guild, 1935; *Pollie Who Did as She Was Told*, Dodd, 1934; *Nick and the Diccon*, Oxford University Press, 1935; *Three for an Acorn*, Dodd, 1935; *A Wife for the Mayor of Buncastle*, Basil Blackwell, 1935; *What Does It Matter?, and Other Tales*, R. J. James, 1935; *Diccon, the Pedlar*, Basil Blackwell, 1936; *Victoria Josephine*, Dodd, 1936 (published in England as *The Roaming Doll*, Basil Blackwell, 1936); *Tales of All the World*, Oxford University Press, 1936; *A Matter of Time*, Basil Blackwell, 1937; *Mrs. Bobbity's Crust*, Dodd, 1937; *The Very Little Dragon, and Other Stories*, Oxford University Press, 1938; *The Witch's Broom, and Other Stories*, Oxford University Press, 1938; *Dunderpate*, Dodd, 1938; *Fifteen Tales for Lively Children*, University of London Press, 1938, Dodd, 1939; *The Margaret and Mary Baker Story Book*, Laurie, 1939; *The Puppy Called Spinach*, Dodd, 1939.

Lady Arabella's Birthday Party, Dodd, 1940; *The Bakers' Big Book*, Dodd, 1941; *Tinker, Tailor and Other Nonsense Tales*, University of London Press, 1941, Dodd, 1942; *The Wishing-Nut Tree*, Basil Blackwell, 1942; *The Weathercock, and Other Stories*, University of London Press, 1943; *The Nightingale*, Shakespeare Head Press, 1944; *The Wind's Adopted Daughter, and Other Stories*, University of London Press, 1944; *Trotters*, Basil Blackwell, 1946; *The Men of Peace*, Friends Peace Committee, 1947; *Seven Times Once Upon a Time*, Carwal, 1948; *A Book of Happy Tales*, University of London Press, 1948.

The Wishing Well, and Other Stories, University of London Press, 1955; *The Key of Rose Cottage*, Collins, 1964; *Juby*, Hutchinson, 1970; *Tell-Them-Again Tales*, Hodder & Stoughton, 1980; *Black Cats and the Silver Crown*, Kestrel Books, 1981.

Author of books and booklets for World Women's Christian Temperance Union, National British Women's Total Abstinence Union, and Temperance Collegiate Association, including *Here's Health to You!*, 1927, 7th revised edition, 1937, *Fit as a Fiddle*, 1937, *The Joy of Living*, 1940, *Temperance Tales to Tell with a Blackboard*, 1952, and "Plain Tales Series." Contributor of stories to "Children's Hour," British Broadcasting Corp.

Editor and illustrator of children's page in *White Ribbon* (periodical of British Women's Total Abstinence Union), 1923-62, and of a monthly leaflet for Hope Union, 1940-61. Also editor of country books for Aubrey Seymour, 1968-72.

SIDELIGHTS: Margaret Baker told *CA:* "My sister Mary and I have lived together all our lives, following the now vanished career of 'daughters at home,' first in Runcorn, Cheshire, then in Leominster, Herefordshire, and, since 1939, in the minute village of Sutton-under-Brailes on the north edge of the Cotswolds.

"It was a great disappointment when the disasterous change in children's reading ended our partnership as author and artist and closed down 'Children's Hour' on the B.B.C. and the Christmas Annuals for which I, in particular, had done a great deal of work. The years of our 'redundancy' were not spent unprofitably, however. We both find much pleasure in the roles of Aunt and Great-Aunt and I am much interested in watching the emergence of family characteristics in the younger generations, such as the irresistible urge to make 'collections', my own interesting achievement being the compilation of a family 'Who's Who,' which, with the aid of numerous cousins of varying degrees, I manage to keep up-to-date.

"The unavoidable restrictions imposed by advancing age have curtailed many of our activities, gardening, for one, and long holidays, when Mary and I, she with her paint-box and brushes and I with a camera, explored the wild and beautiful western areas from Land's End to Orkney and Kerry to Donegal.

"But now—who knows?—being 'in print again' may encourage me to think I have still more tales to tell!"

*   *   *

BAKER, Robert B(ernard)   1937-

PERSONAL: Born December 5, 1937, in New York, N.Y.; stepson of Hal Murray (a podiatrist) and Freda (a puppeteer; maiden name, Ginsburg) Baker; married Arlene S. Bernstein (an artist), November 28, 1958; children: Nathaniel, Meredith. *Education:* City College (now City College of the City University of New York), B.A., 1959; University of Minnesota, Ph.D., 1967; postdoctoral study at Haverford College, summer, 1974, and Albany Medical College, 1977-78. *Politics:* Libertarian. *Religion:* Agnostic. *Residence:* Schenectady, N.Y. *Office:* Department of Philosophy, Humanities Center, Union College, Schenectady, N.Y. 12308.

CAREER: University of Minnesota, Minneapolis, instructor in philosophy, 1964-65; University of Iowa, Iowa City, instructor, 1965-67, assistant professor of philosophy, 1967-69; Wayne State University, Detroit, Mich., visiting professor, 1969-70, assistant professor of philosophy, 1970-73; Union College, Schenectady, N.Y., assistant professor, 1973-80, associate professor of philosophy, 1980—, coordinator-conductor of field study of socialized medicine in Britain, Poland, and Sweden, summers, 1977, 1979, academic coordinator, 1977—. Coordinator of medical ethics and philosophy of medicine at Albany Medical College, 1974-77. Member of Michigan governor's task force on victimless crime, 1972-73; consultant to Michigan Institute for the Study of Non-Violence and Medical Behavioral Research Group.

MEMBER: Society of Philosophy and Public Affairs, Society for the Social History of Medicine (United Kingdom), American Philosophical Association, Hastings Institute of Society, Ethics, and the Life Sciences, Iowa Philosophical Society (president, 1969-70), Schenectady County Mental Health Council. *Awards, honors:* Old Gold research fellowship, 1969; National Endowment for the Humanities, junior research fellowship, 1969, field fellowship, 1975; summer grant from Council of Philosophical Studies, 1974; faculty development grant from Ford Foundation, autumn, 1974; Mellon fellowships, 1976-77, 1977-78; Institute of Health and Human Values fellowship, 1977-78.

WRITINGS: (With D. B. Terrell) *A Workbook in Logic*, Holt, 1967; (editor with others and contributor) *The Report of the Governor's Task Force on Victimless Crime*, Office of Substance Abuse (Lansing, Mich.), 1973; (contributor) Richard Wasserstrom, editor, *Today's Moral Problems*, Macmillan, 1974; (editor and contributor with Frederick Elliston) *Philosophy and Sex*, Prometheus Books, 1975; (contributor) E. Bandman and B. Bandman, editors, *Bioethics and Human Rights: A Reader for Health Care Professionals*, Little, Brown, 1978; (contributor) John Buckley, editor, *Genetics Now: Ethical Issues in Genetic Research*, University Press of America, 1978; (contributor) John Davis and others, editors, *Contemporary Issues in Biomedical Ethics*, Humana Press, 1978; (contributor) W. Reich, editor, *Encyclopedia of Bioethics*, Free Press, 1978; (contributor) S. Spicker and S. Gadow, editors, *Nursing: Images and Ideals*, Springer, 1980; (with Paul Lowinger) *Psychosurgery on Trial*, Humana Press, in press. Contributor to

Moving Out, Nous, Review of Metaphysics, and *Journal of Psychedelic Drugs.*

SIDELIGHTS: Prior to the social ferment of the 1960's, Robert B. Baker's primary interests were logic and metaphysics. During the 1960's, he wrote for the underground press and worked closely with the "resistance" and later with various feminist groups. Since 1970, his work has been in social and political philosophy and the philosophy of medicine.

*   *   *

BALD, R(obert) C(ecil)   1901-1965

PERSONAL: Born January 25, 1901, in Melbourne, Australia; died August 23, 1965; son of George Robert and Rebecca (Grieve) Bald; married Beatrice Harvey Hale, August 13, 1928; children: Margaret J. F. *Education:* University of Melbourne, B.A., 1922; Cambridge University, Ph.D., 1929; University of Adelaide, M.A., 1930, LL.B., 1930. *Home:* 6019 Ingleside Ave., Chicago, Ill. *Office:* 1050 East 59th St., Chicago, Ill.

CAREER: Lecturer in English at University of Western Australia, Perth, 1922, University of Adelaide, Adelaide, South Australia, 1923-24, 1927-33, University of Exeter, Exeter, England, 1933-35; professor of English at University of Stellenbosch, Stellenbosch, South Africa, 1935-37, Cornell University, Ithaca, N.Y., 1937-52, University of Chicago, Chicago, Ill., 1952-65. Alexander Lecturer, University of Toronto, 1960-61; visiting member, Institute for Advanced Study, 1960-61; visiting professor, Princeton University, 1963. *Member:* Modern Language Association of America (member of executive council, 1958-61), International Association of University Professors of English, Bibliographical Society, Malone Society, Phi Beta Kappa. *Awards, honors:* Research fellow, Folger Shakespeare Library, 1936-37 and Huntington Library, 1951-52; D.Litt. from University of Adelaide, 1945; Guggenheim fellow, 1946-47 and 1960-61; Foyle fellow, Shakespeare Institute, 1955-56.

WRITINGS: Donne's Influence in English Literature, St. John's College Press, 1932, reprinted, Peter Smith, 1965; *Bibliographical Studies in the Beaumont and Fletcher Folio of 1647,* Bibliographical Society, 1938, reprinted, Richard West, 1978; *Donne and the Drurys,* Cambridge University Press, 1959; *John Donne: A Life,* edited by Wesley Milgate, Oxford University Press, 1970.

Editor: *A Game at Chesse,* Cambridge University Press, 1929; *Literary Friendships in the Age of Wordsworth,* Cambridge University Press, 1932, reprinted, Octagon, 1968; *Hengist: King of Kent,* Scribner, 1938; (with Herbert John Davis) *Nineteenth Century Studies,* Norwood, 1940, reprinted, Greenwood Press, 1976; *Opium Eater in America,* Victor Hammer, 1941; *Hamlet,* Appleton, 1946; *Henry IV: Part I,* Appleton, 1946; *King Lear,* Appleton, 1949; *Humble Supplication,* Cambridge University Press, 1953; *Honourable Entertainments,* Malone Society, 1953; *Measure for Measure,* Penguin, 1956, revised edition, 1970; *Selected Poems of Samuel Taylor Coleridge,* Appleton, 1956; *Seventeenth Century English Poetry,* Harper, 1959; *Knave in Grain,* Malone Society, 1961; *Six Elizabethan Plays,* Houghton, 1963. Contributor of numerous articles to learned journals. Member of editorial board of Crofts Classics and Golden Tree Books.

SIDELIGHTS: A reviewer for *Christian Century* writes that R. C. Bald's *John Donne: A Life* "is the big one on Donne—a biography worked on for years by . . . Bald, then completed by Wesley Milgate. Though the Donne fad may have long since peaked, Donne is durable; for years people will measure

the biographical aspect of research concerning this poet against Bald's major work."

Also impressed by Bald's work, Paul Delany of *New York Times Book Review* believes that "the book is a monument of painstaking research and judicious handling of evidence; we must regret that the author did not live to enjoy the praise his industry deserves. . . . As a standard life of Donne, based on meticulous documentation, this will certainly supersede previous attempts, and correct the earlier biographers' many mistakes."

BIOGRAPHICAL/CRITICAL SOURCES: Newsweek, April 27, 1970; *Christian Century,* April 29, 1970; *New York Times,* May 16, 1970; *Christian Science Monitor,* May 16, 1970; *New Yorker,* May 23, 1970; *Library Journal,* June 15, 1970; *New York Times Book Review,* June 28, 1970.†

*   *   *

BALFOUR, Michael (Leonard) Graham   1908-

PERSONAL: Born November 22, 1908, in Oxford, England; son of Sir Graham (a writer and administrator) and Rhoda (Brooke) Balfour; married Grizel Wilson, June 28, 1934; children: Alison (Mrs. Francis Holmes A. Court), Rosanne, Corinna. *Education:* Balliol College, Oxford, 1927-32. *Politics:* Independent. *Religion:* Church of England. *Home:* 17 Redington Rd., London N.W.3, England.

CAREER: Oxford University, Magdalen College, Oxford, England, lecturer in politics, 1932-36; Royal Institute of International Affairs, London, England, research secretary, 1936-39; British government, London, principal minister, Ministry of Information, 1939-42, with Foreign Office, 1942-44; Allied Expeditionary Forces, Supreme Headquarters, Paris, France, deputy chief of intelligence in Psychological Warfare Division (as civilian), 1944-46; British Control Commission for Germany, Berlin, director of Information Services Branch, 1945-47; Board of Trade, London, chief information officer, 1947-64. *Awards, honors:* Commander, Order of the British Empire, 1963.

WRITINGS: (Contributor as secretary and drafter to research group) *Nationalism,* Royal Institute of International Affairs, 1939; *States and Mind: Reflections on Their Interaction in History,* Cresset, 1953; (with John Mair) *Four-Power Control in Germany and Austria, 1945-46,* Oxford University Press, 1956, reprinted, Johnson Reprint, 1972; *The Kaiser and His Times,* Houghton, 1964; *West Germany,* Praeger, 1968; *Helmuth von Moltke: A Leader against Hitler,* St. Martin's, 1972; *Propaganda in War, 1939-1945: Organisations, Policies and Publics in Britain and Germany,* Routledge & Kegan Paul, 1979; *The Adversaries: America, Russia and the Open World, 1941-1962,* Routledge & Kegan Paul, 1981. Contributor of articles to *Times* (London).

WORK IN PROGRESS: Research on British history.†

*   *   *

BALFOUR, (John) Patrick Douglas   1904-1976
(Lord Kinross)

PERSONAL: Born June 25, 1904 (inheriting title of 3rd Baron of Glasclune), in Edinburgh, Scotland; died June 5, 1976, in London, England; son of Patrick (Sheriff of Dumfries and Galloway) and Caroline Elsie (Johnstone-Douglas) Balfour; married Angela Mary Culme-Seymour, 1938 (divorced, 1942). *Education:* Balliol College, Oxford, B.A., 1925. *Home:* 4 Warwick Ave., London W.2, England. *Agent:* Harold Matson Co., Inc., 22 East 40th St., New York, N.Y. 10016.

CAREER: Worked for various newspapers in England, 1926-40; free-lance journalist, writer, and broadcaster, 1947-76. *Military service:* Royal Air Force, 1940-47; became squadron leader; detailed to duty in H. M. Diplomatic Service, 1944-47. *Member:* Travellers' Club, Beefsteak Club.

WRITINGS: Society Racket: A Critical Survey of Modern Social Life, John Long, 1933; *Grand Tour: Diary of an Eastward Journey,* John Long, 1934, Harcourt, 1935; (contributor) Ladislas Farago, editor, *Abyssinian Stop Press,* R. Hale, 1936; *Lords of the Equator: An African Journey,* Hutchinson, 1937; *The Ruthless Innocent* (novel), Hamish Hamilton, 1949; *The Orphaned Realm: Journeys in Cyprus,* Percival Marshall, 1951.

Under name Lord Kinross: *The Century of the Common Peer* (essays), Putnam, 1954; *Within the Taurus: A Journey in Asiatic Turkey,* J. Murray, 1954, Morrow, 1955, reprinted, J. Murray, 1970; *Europa Minor: Journeys in Coastal Turkey,* Morrow, 1956; *Portrait of Greece,* Parrish, 1956, Dufour, 1959; *The Candid Eye,* foreword by Malcolm Muggeridge, Richards Press, 1958; *The Innocents at Home,* J. Murray, 1959, Morrow, 1960; *The Kindred Spirit: A History of Gin and of the House of Booth,* Newman Neame, 1959; *Ataturk: The Rebirth of a Nation,* Weidenfeld & Nicolson, 1964, published as *Ataturk: A Biography of Mustafa Kemel, Father of Modern Turkey,* Morrow, 1965; *Portrait of Egypt,* Morrow, 1966; *The Windsor Years: The Life of Edward, as Prince of Wales, King, and Duke of Windsor,* Viking, 1967; *Between Two Seas: The Creation of the Suez Canal,* J. Murray, 1968, Morrow, 1969; (with Dorothy H. Gary) *Morocco,* Viking, 1971; (with others) *Hagia Sophia,* Newsweek, 1972; *The Ottoman Centuries: The Rise and Fall of the Turkish Empire,* Morrow, 1977. Contributor to periodicals, including *Vogue, New Yorker,* and *Punch.*

SIDELIGHTS: Paul Johnson wrote in the *New York Times Book Review* that when Patrick Balfour (who wrote most of his works under his inherited title, Lord Kinross) died, "he left a great many friends and admirers in the Middle East as well as in Britain—and especially in Turkey. There, his biography of Kemal Ataturk was regarded as a masterly and sympathetic presentation of Turkey's greatest modern hero. The affection for Kinross was all the warmer, in that gifted interpreters of Turkish culture and civilization are comparatively rare in the West." Both John Leonard in the *New York Times* and Derek Patmore in the *New York Times Book Review* called Kinross's *Ataturk* the definitive biography of the Turkish soldier-states-man, Mustafa Kemel. A reviewer for the *Times Literary Supplement* also believed that "the life of Ataturk has never been so completely, circumstantially and readably presented."

BIOGRAPHICAL/CRITICAL SOURCES: New Statesman, November 27, 1964; *Times Literary Supplement,* December 24, 1964, January 5, 1967; *New York Times Book Review,* March 21, 1965, December 3, 1967, March 2, 1969, April 10, 1977; *Newsweek,* April 5, 1965; *Time,* April 9, 1965; *Nation,* May 10, 1965; *New York Review of Books,* June 3, 1965; *Harper's,* November, 1967; *Christian Science Monitor,* November 30, 1967; *Best Sellers,* April 15, 1969; *New York Times,* March 22, 1977; *New Republic,* May 7, 1977.†

*   *   *

BALLARD, K. G.
   See ROTH, Holly

*   *   *

BAMBERGER, Bernard J(acob)   1904-1980

PERSONAL: Born May 30, 1904, in Baltimore, Md.; died June 14, 1980, in New York, N.Y.; son of William B. (an attorney) and Gussie (Erlanger) Bamberger; married Ethel R. Kraus, June 14, 1932; children: Henry, David. *Education:* Johns Hopkins University, A.B., 1923; Hebrew Union College, Cincinnati, Ohio, Rabbi, 1926, D.D., 1929. *Politics:* Independent. *Home:* 225 West 86th St., New York, N.Y. 10024. *Office:* Temple Shaaray Tefila, 250 East 79th St., New York, N.Y. 10021.

CAREER: Temple Israel, Lafayette, Ind., rabbi, 1926-29; Congregation Beth Emeth, Albany, N.Y., rabbi, 1929-44; Temple Shaaray Tefila, New York, N.Y., rabbi, 1944-70, rabbi emeritus, 1970-80. President of Synagogue Council of America, 1950-51, Central Conference of American Rabbis, 1959-61, and World Union for Progressive Judaism, 1970-72. *Member:* American Academy for Jewish Research, Society of Biblical Literature and Exegesis. *Awards, honors:* D.H.L., Hebrew Union College, Cincinnati, Ohio, 1950.

WRITINGS: Proselytism in the Talmudic Period, Hebrew Union College Press, 1939, second edition, Ktav, 1968; (editor) *Reform Judaism,* Hebrew Union College Press, 1949; *Fallen Angels,* Jewish Publication Society, 1952; *The Bible: A Modern Jewish Approach,* Hillel Little Books, 1955, 2nd edition, Schocken, 1963; *The Story of Judaism,* Union of American Hebrew Congregations, 1957, 3rd edition, Schocken, 1964; (contributor) David Max Eichhorn, editor, *Conversion to Judaism: A History and Analysis,* Ktav, 1966; (editor) Jacob Z. Leuterbach, *Studies in Jewish Law, Custom, and Folklore,* Ktav, 1970; *The Search for Jewish Theology,* Behrman House, 1978; *Commentary on Leviticus,* edited by W. Gunther Plaut, Union of American Hebrew Congregations, 1979. Contributor of articles, reviews, and sermons to scholarly and popular periodicals. Member of editorial committee preparing new Jewish translation of Bible, Jewish Publication Society.

WORK IN PROGRESS: Further work on American Jewish translation of Bible; research in Talmudic Judaism and in contemporary religious problems.

SIDELIGHTS: Bernard J. Bamberger was competent in French, German, Hebrew, and Aramaic, and had some ability in Latin, Greek, and Italian.

OBITUARIES: New York Times, June 16, 1980; *Chicago Tribune,* June 17, 1980.†

*   *   *

BARBER, James David   1930-

PERSONAL: Born July 31, 1930, in Charleston, W.Va.; son of Daniel Newman (a physician) and Edith Margaret (Naismith) Barber; married former wife, Ann Goodridge Sale (a research assistant), December 27, 1951; married Amanda Joan MacKay-Smith, November 21, 1972; children: Sara Naismith, Jane Lewis, Luke David, Silas Higginson. *Education:* University of Chicago, B.A., 1950, M.A., 1955; Yale University, Ph.D., 1960. *Home:* Cullowhee Spring, Route 2, Box 371, Durham, N.C. 27712. *Office:* Department of Political Science, Duke University, Durham, N.C. 27706.

CAREER: Stetson University, De Land, Fla., assistant professor of political science, 1955-57; Yale University, New Haven, Conn., assistant professor, 1961-65, associate professor, 1965-68, professor of political science, 1968-72, director of graduate studies in political science, 1965-67, director of Office for Advanced Political Studies, 1967-68; Duke University, Durham, N.C., professor of political science and chairman of department, 1972-75, James B. Duke Professor of Political Science, 1979—. Research associate at University of

Chicago Industrial Relations Center, 1951-53, 1955; guest scholar at Brookings Institution, 1964-65; director of Harvard-Yale-Columbia Intensive Summer Studies Program, 1966-67. Member of Wallingford (Conn.) Charter Commission, 1959-61, Board of Finance, 1960-61, and Connecticut Commission on Municipal Employees, 1963-64. *Military service:* U.S. Army, Counter-Intelligence Corps, 1953-55; became sergeant. *Member:* American Political Science Association, American Association of University Professors. *Awards, honors:* Fellow, National Science Foundation, 1961-63, and Center for Advanced Study in Behavioral Sciences, 1968-69.

WRITINGS: (With R. E. Lane and F. I. Greenstein) *An Introduction to Political Analysis,* Prentice-Hall, 1962; (compiler) *Political Leadership in American Government,* Little, Brown, 1964; (editor) Alan Barth, *Heritage of Liberty,* Part II, McGraw, 1964; *The Lawmakers: Recruitment and Adaptation to Legislative Life,* Yale University Press, 1965; *Power in Committees: An Experiment in the Governmental Process,* Rand McNally, 1966; *Citizen Politics: An Introduction to Political Behavior,* Markham, 1969, 2nd edition, 1972; (compiler) *Readings in Citizen Politics: Studies of Political Behavior,* Markham, 1969, 2nd edition published as *Power to the Citizen: Introductory Readings,* 1972; *The Presidential Character: Predicting Performance in the White House,* Prentice-Hall, 1972, 2nd edition, 1977; (editor) *Choosing the President,* Prentice-Hall, 1974; *Race for the Presidency,* Prentice-Hall, 1977; *The Pulse of Politics: Electing Presidents in the Media Age,* Norton, 1980; *Erasmus: A Play on Words,* University Press of America, 1981. Editor of series for Harcourt, 1970—. Contributor to professional journals. Chairman of editorial board, *Political Science,* 1969-71.

SIDELIGHTS: According to the *Washington Post Book World*'s Harry McPherson, James David Barber "is the kind of man who classifies everything. He sees individuals as types and events as part of recurring trends." In *The Pulse of Politics,* it is American presidential elections that Barber classifies, proposing the thesis "that each quadrennial campaign has a theme," reports John Whale in the *Times Literary Supplement,* "and these themes recur on a simple three-point cycle. By chance, too, the themes are alliterative: conflict, conscience, conciliation. It works like this. In the conflict phase, the campaign is a straightforward battle for power, in which the need for surprise is the driving force. Next, as a result of reaction over the following four years, the call is for uplift, high purpose, social conscience. Then, third, because simple trust in American values has proved ineffective, and indeed threatens to polarize the nation into good guys and bad guys, the cry goes up for domestic tranquility and conciliation. And so round again."

McPherson considers Barber's formula to be "overly neat. He has tried to lay a grid on the protean sea, and as in the case of other theorists before him, the sea will not cooperate." Although Whale agrees that the book's formula does not really fit recent history, he adds: "Still, as something to read on the campaign bus, or to feed into the dialogue at a Washington party, the book will do very well."

BIOGRAPHICAL/CRITICAL SOURCES: Washington Post Book World, May 4, 1980; *New York Times Book Review,* May 11, 1980; *Times Literary Supplement,* April 3, 1981.

*   *   *

BARNETT, L. David
    See LASCHEVER, Barnett D.

BARNETT, S(amuel) A(nthony) 1915-

PERSONAL: Born July 16, 1915, in Middlesex, England. *Education:* Attended Oxford University, 1934-37. *Office:* Research School of Biological Sciences, Australian National University, Canberra, Australian Capital Territory 2600, Australia.

CAREER: Ministry of Agriculture, head of pest control research unit, 1946-50; University of Glasgow, Glasgow, Scotland, senior lecturer in zoology, 1951-71; Australian National University, Canberra, Australia, professor and head of zoology department, 1971-80, professor emeritus, 1981—.

WRITINGS: The Human Species: A Biology of Man, Norton, 1950, 5th revised edition, Harper, 1971; (editor and contributor) *A Century of Darwin,* Harvard University Press, 1958.

The Rat: A Study in Behavior, Aldine, 1963 (published in England as *A Study in Behavior: Principles of Ethology and Behavioral Physiology, Displayed Mainly in the Rat,* Methuen, 1963), 2nd revised edition, University of Chicago Press, 1975; *Instinct and Intelligence: Behavior of Animals and Man,* Prentice-Hall, 1967, revised edition, Penguin, 1970.

(Editor) *Ethology and Development,* Heinemann Medical, 1973; (contributor) Ashley Montagu, editor, *Man and Aggression,* 2nd edition (Barnett was not associated with first edition), Oxford University Press, 1973; (with I. Prakash) *Rodents of Economic Importance in India,* Heinemann Educational, 1975.

(Contributor) Montagu, editor, *Sociobiology Examined,* Oxford University Press, 1980; (contributor) P. F. Brain and D. Benton, editors, *Multidisciplinary Approaches to Aggression Research,* Elsevier, 1981; *Modern Ethology: The Science of Animal Behavior,* Oxford University Press, 1981. Contributor to *New Statesman, New Society,* and other publications.

WORK IN PROGRESS: The Skeptical Ethologist: An Essay on Biological Images of Man, for Oxford University Press.

SIDELIGHTS: S. A. Barnett told *CA:* "A constant theme in my writing has been 'science in the service of man.' This does not imply any doubt about the importance of 'pure' or academic research. I have been fortunate in having much experience of economic zoology, in the intervals of a lifetime of university research and teaching. As an ethologist, recently, I have been dismayed by the use of my specialty to do the human species a *dis*service. On the foundation of biological and logical errors, prominent writers have seemed to represent human beings (including, presumably, themselves) as inherently violent, selfish, greedy, and mindless. My current work is especially concerned with this group of myths."

The Human Species has been translated into Spanish, Dutch, Finnish, and Polish, *Instinct and Intelligence* into Italian, German, Japanese, and Rumanian, and *The Rat* into Italian.

*   *   *

BARR, Gladys Hutchison 1904-1976

PERSONAL: Born December 19, 1904, in Butte, Mont.; died December 31, 1976; daughter of David and Laura (Mooney) Hutchison; married Thomas Calhoun Barr, October 27, 1928; children: Thomas C., Jr., Ann Barr Weems, Jane Barr Stump, William H. *Education:* Attended State University of New York, 1923-26; Union University, Albany, LL.B., 1929. *Politics:* Democrat. *Religion:* Presbyterian. *Home:* B 110 Jefferson Sq., 5039 Hillsboro Rd., Nashville, Tenn. 37215.

CAREER: Admitted to New York State Bar, 1927; practiced law in New York, N.Y., 1926-29; David Hutchison Publishing Co., Nashville, Tenn., editor and writer, 1969-76; free-lance writer and lecturer. Vice-chairman of the board, Public Libraries of the Metropolitan Government of Nashville and Davidson County. *Member:* National League of American Pen Women (president, Nashville branch, 1960-62), Authors Guild, Authors League of America, American Library Association, Women's National Book Association, English-Speaking Union of the United States, Ladies Hermitage Association, Southeastern Library Association, New York State Bar Association, Tennessee Library Association, Tennessee Federation of Garden Clubs (member of executive committee), Tennessee Historical Society, Nashville Press and Authors Club (past president), Centennial Club, Richland Country Club. *Awards, honors:* American Legion Woman of the Year, 1950; cited as outstanding Tennessee member of National League of American Pen Women, 1964; Tennessee Library Association top honor award, 1975.

WRITINGS: Monk in Armour, Abingdon, 1950; *Cross, Sword, and Arrow*, Abingdon, 1955; *The Tinker's Armor: The Story of John Bunyan* (juvenile), Broadman, 1961; *The Master of Geneva: A Novel Based on the Life of John Calvin*, Holt, 1961; *The Pilgrim Prince: A Novel Based on the Life of John Bunyan*, Holt, 1963; *The Bell Witch at Adams*, David Hutchison, 1969; *The Ghost at Epworth Rectory*, David Hutchison, 1970. Contributor of short stories and serials to magazines.

WORK IN PROGRESS: The Singing Saint, for Holt.

SIDELIGHTS: Gladys Hutchison Barr's books involved nine trips to Europe and Africa for research purposes.†

* * *

BARROW, Rhoda
See LEDERER, Rhoda Catharine (Kitto)

* * *

BARRY, Spranger
See KAUFFMANN, Stanley

* * *

BARTRUM, Douglas A(lbert) 1907-

PERSONAL: Born June 28, 1907, in Marlow, Buckinghamshire, England; son of George and Maud Bartrum. *Education:* Attended High Wycombe Technical School. *Home:* Sunnyside, Bovingdon Green, Marlow, Buckinghamshire, England.

CAREER: Author.

WRITINGS: Shrubs and Trees for Your Garden, W. & G. Foyle, 1955; *Climbing Plants for Your Garden*, Dover, 1956; *Rhododendrons and Magnolias*, Gifford, 1957; *Hydrangeas and Viburnums*, Gifford, 1958; *Lilac and Laburnum*, Gifford, 1959; *Climbing Plants and Some Wall Shrubs*, Gifford, 1959, revised edition, Branford, 1968; *Magnolias and Camellias*, W. & G. Foyle, 1959.

Foliage Plants for Your Garden, W. & G. Foyle, 1961, Sportshelf, 1963; *Colour and Contrast in the Garden*, Gifford, 1962; *The Gourmet's Garden*, Faber, 1964, International Publications Service, 1971; *Rhododendrons and Azaleas*, W. & G. Foyle, 1964, Sportshelf, 1965; *Evergreens for Your Garden*, Gifford, 1967; *Water in Your Garden*, Branford, 1968; *From Garden to Kitchen*, Gifford, 1969.

Exotic Plants for the Home, Gifford, 1970; *Deep Freezing at Home*, Gifford, 1971; *Rock Gardens*, Gifford, 1971; *Growing Cacti and Succulents*, Hippocrene, 1973.

WORK IN PROGRESS: A book on the fundamentals of music criticism.†

* * *

BASCOM, Willard N. 1916-

PERSONAL: Born November 7, 1916, in New York, N.Y.; son of Willard N. and Pearl (Boyd) Bascom; married Rhoda Nergaard, April 15, 1946; children: Willard B., Anitra. *Education:* Attended Springfield College, 1933-34, and Colorado School of Mines, 1938-41. *Home:* 1900 Ocean Blvd., Long Beach, Calif. 90802. *Office:* Southern California Coastal Water Research Project, 646 West Pacific Coast Hwy., Long Beach, Calif. 90206.

CAREER: Mining engineer in Colorado, Arizona, Idaho, New York, and Washington, 1942-45; University of California, Berkeley, research engineer, 1945-50; University of California Scripps Institution of Oceanography (now University of California, Scripps Institution of Oceanography, San Diego), La Jolla, research engineer, 1951-54; National Academy of Sciences, Washington, D.C., committee technical director, 1954-62, director of Mohole project, 1960-62; Ocean Science and Engineering, Inc., Washington, D.C., president, 1962-71; president, Seafinders, Inc., 1971-73; Southern California Coastal Water Research Project, Long Beach, director, 1973—. Distinguished lecturer, Society of Exploration Geophysicists, 1959-60; adjunct professor of ocean engineering, California State University, Long Beach, 1974; adjunct professor of marine sciences, Scripps Institution of Oceanography, University of California, 1976. Former member, Plowshare Advisory Committee of the U.S. Atomic Energy Commission and Naval Research Advisory Committee; member, Ocean Science Board and Panel on Oceanography from Satellites. U.S. delegate to International Geophysical Year Conferences on Oceanography, 1957; member of U.S. Army Coastal Engineering Research Board, 1981—. *Member:* American Geophysical Union, American Academy of Arts and Sciences, Marine Technological Society (director, 1969-70), Shipbuilders Council, Explorer's Club (New York), Cosmos Club (Washington, D.C.), Adventurer's Club (Los Angeles). *Awards, honors:* Marine Technological Society Distinguished Service Award, 1970; Explorers Medal, 1980; Distinguished Service Medal, Colorado School of Mines.

WRITINGS: A Hole in the Bottom of the Sea: The Story of the Mohole Project, Doubleday, 1961; *Waves and Beaches: The Dynamics of the Ocean Surface*, Anchor Books, 1963, revised and enlarged edition, 1980; (editor) *Great Sea Poetry*, Compass Publications, 1969; *Deep Water, Ancient Ships: The Treasure Vault of the Mediterranean*, Doubleday, 1976. Also author of film scripts, "Diamonds under the Sea," "The First Deep-Ocean Drilling," and "A New Harbor for Cape Town." Contributor of articles on oceanography to *Scientific American*.

WORK IN PROGRESS: Endangered.

* * *

BASSET, Bernard 1909-

PERSONAL: Born March 21, 1909, in London, England; son of Hugh Fortescue and Bessie Lee (Cooper) Basset. *Education:* Campion Hall, Oxford, M.A. (first class honors), 1937; Heythorp College, theological student, 1931-35, 1938-42. *Home:* The Presbytery, 1 Albert Rd., Bournemouth, Hampshire, England.

CAREER: Roman Catholic priest of Jesuit order; Stonyhurst College, Blackburn, England, and Beaumont College, Windsor, England, lecturer in history, 1937-38, 1942-46; associated with Royal Air Force moral leadership courses, 1945-49; national secretary, Roman Catholic Sodality Organisation, 1950-62; Southwell House, Hampstead, London, England, superior, 1954-62; currently lecturer in history and religion, preacher attached to Jesuit church in Bournemouth, Hampshire, England, and organizer of Catholic youth work. Lecturer on two U.S. tours, 1959, 1961. Attached to Vatican Radio for first session of Vatican Council; represented *Catholic Herald* at Eucharistic Congress in Bombay, India, 1964.

WRITINGS: Blessed Edmund Campion (verses), Burns & Oates, 1936; *Mr. Brice Lets Us Down and Other Stories,* Catholic Truth Society, 1939; *A Secret Service Agent and Other Stories,* Catholic Truth Society, 1940; *O.K. and Other Stories,* Catholic Truth Society, 1941; *Margery and Me* (short stories), David Organ, 1945; *The Seven Deadly Virtues, and Other Stories,* David Organ, 1947; *Farm Street,* David Organ, 1949.

Two Hundred Gospel Questions and Enquiries, Sheed, 1959, new edition published as *Gospel Questions and Inquiries,* 1975; *We Neurotics: A Handbook for the Half-Mad,* Academy Guild Press, 1962; (with Vincent Whelan) *Youth and You: A Guide to Youth Work,* Catholic Social Guild, 1962; *Best of Both Worlds: A Guide to Holiness in the Suburbs,* Burns & Oates, 1963, Academy Guild Press, 1964; *Priest in the Piazza: Goal Line Tribute to a Council,* Academy Guild Press, 1963 (published in England as *Priest in the Piazza: Touchline Tribute to a Council,* Burns & Oates, 1963); *The Noonday Devil: Spiritual Support in Middle Age,* Academy Guild Press, 1964; *Priest in the Presbytery: A Psycho-ecclesiastical Extravaganza,* Burns & Oates, 1964, Herder & Herder, 1966; *Born for Friendship: The Spirit of Sir Thomas More,* Sheed, 1965; *Priest in Paradise: With God to Illinois,* Herder & Herder, 1966; *The English Jesuits from Campion to Martindale,* Burns & Oates, 1967, Herder & Herder, 1968; *We Agnostics: On the Tightrope to Eternity,* Herder & Herder, 1968.

How to Be Really With It: Guide to the Good Life, Doubleday, 1970 (published in England as *The Good Life Guide: Saints, Snobs and Sanity,* Sheed, 1971); *Let's Start Praying Again: Field Work in Meditation,* Herder & Herder, 1972; *Guilty, O Lord: Yes, I Still Go to Confession,* Doubleday, 1974 (published in England as *Guilty, My Lord: Yes, I Still Go to Confession,* Sheed, 1974); *Saint Elizabeth Seton,* Catholic Truth Society, 1975; *And Would You Believe It?: The Story of the Nicene Creed,* Doubleday, 1976. Also author of column for *Catholic Herald.* Contributor to periodicals including *Stella Maris.*

SIDELIGHTS: Bernard Basset was once described in the English press as "the only Catholic priest writer who manages to have his tongue in his cheek and the bit between his teeth."†

*   *   *

BATESON, F(rederick) W(ilse)   1901-1978

PERSONAL: Born December 25, 1901, in Styal, Cheshire, England; died October 16, 1978, in Brill, Aylesbury, Buckinghamshire, England; son of Alfred (a cotton broker) and Helga (Wilse) Bateson; married Jan Chancellor, December 31, 1931; children: Sarah, Nicholas. *Education:* Trinity College, Oxford, B.A., 1924, B.Litt., 1926, M.A., 1927; Harvard University, graduate study, 1927-29. *Politics:* Socialist. *Religion:* Agnostic. *Home:* Temple House, Brill, Aylesbury, Buckinghamshire, England.

CAREER: Cambridge University Press, Cambridge, England, editor, 1928-40; Buckinghamshire War Agricultural Committee, statistical officer, 1940-45; Oxford University, Corpus

Christi College, Oxford, England, university lecturer, 1946-60, special university lecturer, 1960-68, fellow and tutor in English literature, 1946-69, emeritus fellow, 1969-78. Visiting professor at University of Minnesota, 1936, Cornell University, 1955, University of California, Berkeley, 1958, and Pennsylvania State University, 1960, 1962, 1964.

WRITINGS: English Comic Drama, 1700-1750, Oxford University Press, 1929, reprinted, Russell & Russell, 1963; (editor) *The Works of Congreve: Comedies, Incognita, Poems,* Davies, 1930; *English Poetry and the English Language,* Oxford University Press, 1934, 3rd edition, 1973; (editor) *Cambridge Bibliography of English Literature,* Cambridge University Press, Volume I: *600-1660,* 1940, Volume II: *1660-1800,* 1940, Volume III: *1800-1900,* 1940, Volume IV: *Index,* 1940, Volume V: *Supplement, A.D. 600-1900,* 1966, revised edition published as *The New Cambridge Bibliography of English Literature,* 1969-77; *Mixed Farming and Muddled Thinking,* Macdonald & Co., 1946; *Towards a Socialist Agriculture,* Gollancz, 1946.

English Poetry: A Critical Introduction, Longmans, Green, 1950, revised edition, 1966; (editor) Alexander Pope, *Epistles to Several Persons,* Yale University Press, 1951, revised edition, 1961; *Wordsworth: A Re-Interpretation,* Longmans, Green, 1954; (editor) William Blake, *Selected Poems,* Barnes & Noble, 1957; *A Guide to English Literature,* Doubleday, 1964, 3rd edition published as *A Guide to English and American Literature,* Longman, 1976; (editor) Matthew Arnold, *Essays on English Literature,* University of London Press, 1965; *Brill: A Short History,* Brill Society, 1966.

The Languages of Literature: Some Linguistic Contributions to Criticism, Routledge & Kegan Paul, 1971; (editor) *Alexander Pope: A Critical Anthology,* Penguin, 1971; *Essays in Critical Dissent,* Rowman & Littlefield, 1972; *The Scholar-Critic: An Introduction to Literary Research,* Routledge & Kegan Paul, 1972. General editor, "Longman Annotated Poets" series, beginning 1965. Founder and editor, *Essays in Criticism: A Quarterly Journal of Literary Criticism,* beginning 1951.†

*   *   *

BATTIN, R(osabell) Ray   1925-

PERSONAL: Born May 25, 1925, in Rock Creek, Ohio; daughter of Harry Walter (a broker) and Sophia (Boldt) Ray; married Tom C. Battin (a professor), August 27, 1949. *Education:* Attended Kent State University, 1944-45; University of Denver, A.B., 1948; University of Michigan, M.S., 1950; University of Miami, Coral Gables, Fla., postgraduate study, 1957; University of Florida, Ph.D., 1959. *Religion:* Unitarian. *Home:* 3837 Meadow Lake Lane, Houston, Tex. 77027. *Office:* 3931 Essex Lane, Houston, Tex. 77027.

CAREER: Clinical neuropsychologist-audiologist at universities and schools in Denver, Colo., Ann Arbor, Mich., and Gainesville, Fla., 1949-54; Houston Speech and Hearing Center, Houston, Tex., audiologist, 1954-56; Hedgecroft Hospital and Rehabilitation Center, Houston, director of department of communicative disorders, 1955-59; licensed psychologist, State of Texas; private practice as speech pathologist, audiologist, and clinical psychologist, Houston, Tex., 1959—. University of Houston, instructor in speech, 1956-59, adjunct instructor in communication disorders; University of Texas, School of Medicine, clinical instructor in department of surgery, 1963-81. *Member:* International Association of Logopedics and Phoniatrics, American Psychological Association, American Speech and Hearing Association (fellow), Biofeedback Society of America, Texas Psychological Association, Texas Speech and Hearing Association, Biofeedback Society of Harris County, Houston Psychological Association, Sigma Alpha Eta.

WRITINGS: A Study of the Comparative Effectiveness of Two Methods of Presenting to Parents Information Relative to Speech and Language Development in the Preschool Child, University of Florida, 1959; (with C. Olaf Haug) *Speech and Language Delay: A Home Training Program,* C. C Thomas, 1964, 2nd edition, 1968.

Private Practice: Guidelines for Speech Pathology and Audiology, edited by Donna Russell Fox, Interstate, 1971; *Vestibulography,* C. C Thomas, 1974; *Pediatric Screening Tests,* edited by W. K. Frankenburg and B. W. Camp, C. C Thomas, 1975; *Hyperactivity,* edited by Betty Lou Kratoville and Peter David Schweich, Parent Press, 1977; *Private Practice: Audiology and Speech Pathology,* Grune & Stratton, 1978; (contributor) *Auditory Disorders in School Children,* Thieme-Stratton, 1981.

Contributor to professional journals, including *Hearing Aid Journal, Journal of Auditory Research,* and *Clinical Neuropsychology.* Book reviewer in speech and hearing for *Players* and *CEA Critic.* Editor, *Journal of Academy of Private Practice of Speech Pathologists and Audiologists and the Academy of Dispensing Audiologists.*

*　　*　　*

BAUER, Erwin A.   1919-
(Ken Bourbon, Nat Franklin, Tom Hardin, Charles W. North, Barney Peters)

PERSONAL: Born August 22, 1919, in Cincinnati, Ohio; son of Adam John (a safety engineer) and Louise (Volz) Bauer; married Doris Parker, April 26, 1941; children: Parker, Robert. *Education:* Studied at the University of Cincinnati for three years.

CAREER: Free-lance writer specializing in outdoor travel and adventure; illustrates own work (average fifty feature stories annually) with photographs. Public relations consultant for outdoor industries. *Military service:* U.S. Army, World War II and Korean Conflict; became first lieutenant; received Purple Heart and Croix de Guerre. *Member:* Society of Magazine Writers, American Society of Travel Writers, Ohio Outdoor Writers Association (former president). *Awards, honors:* Awards from Ohio Outdoor Writers Association for best magazine articles by an Ohio writer, 1949, 1950, 1962; and for best photos, 1965, 1966, 1968, and 1969.

WRITINGS: Bass in America: The Haunts, Habits, and Other Secrets of One of the World's Finest Fresh-Water Game Fish, includes photographs by Bauer and David Goodnow, Simon & Schuster, 1955; *The Bass Fisherman's Bible,* Doubleday, 1961, revised edition, 1980; *The Salt-Water Fisherman's Bible,* Doubleday, 1962; *Complete Book of Outdoor Photography,* Popular Science, 1964, published as *Outdoor Photography,* Harper, 1965, revised edition, Outdoor Life, 1975; *The Duck Hunter's Bible,* Doubleday, 1965; (with George Laycock) *The New Archery Handbook,* Fawcett, 1965; (with Laycock) *Hunting with Bow and Arrow,* Arco, 1966; *My Adventures with African Animals,* includes photographs by Bauer, Norton, 1968; *The Sportsman on Wheels,* Popular Science, 1969; (illustrator) Charles F. Waterman, *The Hunter's World,* includes photographs by Bauer and others, Random House, 1970; *Treasury of Big Game Animals,* Harper, 1972; (editor) *Hunter's Digest,* Follett, 1973, 2nd edition, 1979; *Hunting with a Camera: A World Guide to Wildlife Photography,* Winchester

Press, 1974; (editor with Peggy Bauer) *Camper's Digest,* 2nd edition (Bauer not associated with first edition), Follett, 1974; (editor) *Outdoor Photographer's Digest,* Follett, 1975, 2nd edition, 1980; *Cross-Country Skiing and Snowshoeing,* Winchester Press, 1975; *The Cross-Country Skier's Bible,* Doubleday, 1977; *The Digest Book of Deer Hunting,* Follett, 1979; *The Digest Book of Cross-Country Skiing,* Follett, 1979.

SIDELIGHTS: Erwin A. Bauer has visited fifty-seven countries in carrying out feature assignments. *Avocational interests:* Camping, climbing, exploration, hunting, nature, boating, dogs, ecology, and environment.†

*　　*　　*

BAUM, Daniel (Jay)   1934-

PERSONAL: Born November 24, 1934, in Cincinnati, Ohio; son of Millard M. (a factory worker) and Ida (Friedman) Baum; children: Aaron Edward, Miriam Brav. *Education:* University of Cincinnati, B.A., 1956, LL.B., 1958; New York University, LL.M., 1959, J.S.D., 1960. *Religion:* Jewish. *Home:* 1 Sutcliffe Dr., Toronto, Ontario, Canada. *Office:* Osgoode Hall School, York University, 4700 Keele St., Downsview, Ontario, Canada.

CAREER: Cincinnati Enquirer, Cincinnati, Ohio, reporter, 1953-56; U.S. Federal Trade Commission, Washington, D.C., trial attorney, 1960-62; Indiana University, Indianapolis Campus (now Indiana University—Purdue University at Indianapolis), professor of law, 1962-68; York University, Downsview, Ontario, professor of law and administrative studies, 1968—. Arbitrator, Indiana Department of Labor. Member of Federal Mediation and Conciliation Service; member of National Labor Panel, American Arbitration Association; member of labor panel, Ontario Labor Arbitration Commission. Member of Department of Communications (Canada). Regent of Canadian Institute of Financial Planning. Consultant to National Law Reform Commission (Canada). *Member:* American Bar Association.

WRITINGS: The Robinson-Patman Act: Summary and Comment, Syracuse University Press, 1964; (with Ned B. Stiles) *The Silent Partners: Institutional Investors and Corporate Control,* Syracuse University Press, 1965; *Toward a Free Housing Market,* University of Miami Press, 1969; *The Investment Function of Canadian Financial Institutions,* Praeger, 1972; *Canadian Banks in the Commonwealth Caribbean,* Praeger, 1973; *The Welfare Family,* Praeger, 1974; *The Final Plateau: The Betrayal of Our Older Citizens,* Burns & MacEachern, 1974; *Let Our Children Go!,* Burns & MacEachern, 1975; *Warehouses for Death,* Burns & MacEachern, 1976; *Discount Justice,* Burns & MacEachern, 1978; *Teenage Pregnancy,* General Publishing, 1981. Contributor to law reviews. Editor-in-chief of *Administrative Law Review* (American Bar Association), and *Transportation Law Journal* (U.S. Motor Carriers Association).

WORK IN PROGRESS: A study on surgery.

*　　*　　*

BAUMBACK, Clifford M(ason)   1915-

PERSONAL: Born January 10, 1915, in Dover, N.J.; son of Harry Louis (a stove molder) and Alice (Mason) Baumback; married Janice Sheldon (a psychiatric social worker), December 21, 1945; children: Rex, Mark, Carol (Mrs. Steven R. Spangler). *Education:* Springfield College, Springfield, Mass., B.S., 1938; Northwestern University, M.B.A., 1945; University of Iowa, Ph.D., 1953. *Politics:* Republican. *Religion:*

Episcopalian. *Home:* 705 Diana Ct., Iowa City, Iowa 52240. *Office:* 624 Phillips Hall, University of Iowa, Iowa City, Iowa 52242.

CAREER: Liberty Vulcanizing Works, Troy, N.Y., proprietor, 1938-43; General Electric Co., Erie, Pa., production aide, 1943-44; University of Oklahoma, Norman, assistant professor, 1945-51, associate professor of business management, 1951-55; University of Iowa, Iowa City, research associate, 1955-62, associate professor, 1962-68, professor of management, 1968-80, professor emeritus, 1980—. Visiting professor at Miami University, Oxford, Ohio, summers, 1948, 1949, Roosevelt University, summer, 1969, and Northern Illinois University, 1971-72; Joseph F. Schoen Visiting Professor, Baylor University, spring, 1982. Consultant to Iowa Development Commission, 1962-66.

MEMBER: International Council for Small Business (senior vice-president for programs, 1980—), American Production and Inventory Control Society (director of research, 1963-66), Pi Gamma Mu, Beta Gamma Sigma, Omicron Delta Epsilon, Sigma Iota Epsilon, Masons.

AWARDS, HONORS: American Production and Inventory Control Society citations, 1961 and 1965, for outstanding contributions; named Wilford L. White fellow, International Council for Small Business, 1978, for contributions to small business and the preservation of free enterprise; citation, Harvard Business School, for *Entrepreneurship and Venture Management.*

WRITINGS: (Contributor) Huxley Madehein and others, editors, *Readings in Organization and Management,* Holt, 1964; (with Kenneth Lawyer and Pearce C. Kelley) *How to Organize and Operate a Small Business,* 4th edition (Baumback was not associated with earlier editions), Prentice-Hall, 1968, 6th edition (sole author), 1978; *Structural Wage Issues in Collective Bargaining,* Heath, 1971; (contributor) James H. Greene, editor, *Production and Inventory Control Handbook,* McGraw, 1972, 2nd edition, 1982; (with Joseph Mancuso) *Entrepreneurship and Venture Management,* Prentice-Hall, 1975; *Baumback's Guide to Entrepreneurship,* Prentice-Hall, 1981.

Monographs; all published by Center for Labor and Management, University of Iowa: *Arbitration of Job Evaluation Disputes,* 1954; *Merit and Seniority as Factors in Promotion and In-Grade Progression,* 1956; *Incentive-Wage Problems in Collective Bargaining and Arbitration,* 1956.

Published by Bureau of Business Research, University of Oklahoma, except as indicated: *Patterns of Production Planning and Control,* 1957; *Systematic Work Simplification,* 1960; *An Analysis of Environmental and Managerial Factors in the Success or Failure of Small Manufacturing Enterprise,* Bureau of Business and Economic Research, University of Iowa, 1963.

Contributor to *Encyclopedia of Management,* Van Nostrand. Contributor of more than thirty articles to business, management, and labor journals. Founding editor, *Journal of Small Business Management,* 1962-68; member of editorial board, *Production and Inventory Management,* 1967—.

WORK IN PROGRESS: Basic Small Business Management, for Prentice-Hall.

SIDELIGHTS: Clifford M. Baumback told *CA:* "Thousands of words have been written and spoken about the importance of the smaller, independent business. Such enterprises account for 96 percent of the total number of firms and 43 percent of our gross national product. They provide over 50 percent of the jobs in the private, non-agricultural sector of our economy, and a livelihood for more than 100 million of our fellow Amer-

icans. They create more new and additional jobs than the firms listed in the 'Fortune 500.'

"Impressive as these statistics are, however, they don't begin to touch the real significance of small business to our country. For as long as there is small business formation, we can be sure that there is economic opportunity in our country—opportunity for employees to become employers, for the person who just can't work under others to become his or her own boss, for the individual who can build a new or better mousetrap to market it. And so long as this opportunity lives, our precious personal freedoms are more secure."

*   *   *

BAX, Roger
  See WINTERTON, Paul

*   *   *

BEACH, Edward L(atimer) 1918-

PERSONAL: Born April 20, 1918, in New York, N.Y.; son of Edward Latimer (a U.S. naval officer and writer of children's books) and Alice (Fouche) Beach; married Ingrid Schenck, June 4, 1944; children: Inga (deceased), Edward L., Jr., Hubert Schenck, Ingrid Alice. *Education:* U.S. Naval Academy, B.S. (second in class), 1939; National War College, graduate, 1963; George Washington University, M.A., 1963. *Religion:* Presbyterian. *Home:* 1622 29th St. N.W., Washington, D.C. 20007.

CAREER: U.S. Navy, 1935-66; commissioned ensign, 1939, became captain, 1956. Served at sea continuously, 1939-45 (except for three-month period at submarine school), aboard cruiser *Chester,* destroyer *Lea,* submarines *Trigger, Tirante, Piper.* Other major assignments: Commanding officer, USS *Amberjack,* 1948-49; naval aide and assistant to chairman, Joint Chiefs of Staff, 1949-51; commanding officer, USS *Trigger,* 1951-53; naval aide to President Eisenhower, 1953-57; commanding officer, USS *Salamonie,* 1957-58; commanding officer, USS *Triton,* 1958-61, making 36,000-mile underwater circumnavigation of world, 1960; commander, Submarine Squadron Eight, 1961-62; assigned to Navy Department, Washington, D.C., 1963-66; U.S. Naval War College, Newport, R.I., Stephen B. Luce Chair of Naval Service, 1967-69; U.S. Senate Republican Policy Committee, Washington, D.C., staff director, 1969-77; administrative assistant to U.S. Senator Jeremiah A. Denton, 1981. Trustee, U.S. Naval Academy Alumni Association, 1965-67.

MEMBER: U.S. Naval Institute (member of board of control), National Geographic Society, Naval Historical Association, Metropolitan Club (New York). *Awards, honors*—Military: Navy Cross; Silver Star, twice, Legion of Merit, Bronze Star, twice; letter of commendation, twice, Presidential Unit citation, three times; Legion of Valor. Civilian: Sc.D., American International University; Magellanic Premium, American Philosophical Society, 1962; LL.D., University of Bridgeport, 1963; Alfred Thayer Mahan Award for literary achievement, U.S. Navy League, 1980.

WRITINGS: Submarine!, Holt, 1952; *Run Silent, Run Deep,* Holt, 1955; *Around the World Submerged,* Holt, 1962; *The Wreck of the Memphis,* Holt, 1966; (co-author) *Naval Terms Dictionary,* U.S. Naval Institute Press, 3rd edition, 1971, 4th edition, 1978; *Dust on the Sea,* Holt, 1972; *Cold Is the Sea,* Holt, 1978; *U.S. Navy Today: A Portrait,* U.S. Naval Institute, 1982; *History of the U.S. Navy,* Holt, in press. Contributor of articles to *Argosy, Bluebook, Saturday Evening Post, U.S. Naval Institute, National Geographic,* and *Esquire.* Author of television script, "Enrico Tazzoli."

SIDELIGHTS: Edward L. Beach and his crew of 183 officers and men took the *Triton* on its submerged trip around the world on much the same route followed by Magellan on his 1519-22 voyage. The *Triton*, world's first submarine to be equipped with twin nuclear reactors, left Groton, Conn., on February 16, 1960, and surfaced off Rehoboth Beach, Del., on May 10, 1960. Beach's third book is based on the trip.

MEDIA ADAPTATIONS: Run, Silent, Run Deep, a war story, was made into the United Artists' film with the same title, 1958.

*   *   *

BECK, Warren Albert 1918-

PERSONAL: Born December 9, 1918, in Minneapolis, Minn.; son of Albert Julius (a farmer) and Beata (Middelstadt) Beck; married Phyllis M. Moore, November 9, 1941; children: Warren Jr., James, Kent. *Education:* Wayne State University, B.A., 1947, M.A., 1948; Ohio State University, Ph.D., 1954. *Politics:* Democrat. *Religion:* Lutheran. *Home:* 537 Lee Place, Placentia, Calif. 92670. *Office:* Department of History, California State University, Fullerton, Calif. 92634.

CAREER: Augustana College, Sioux Falls, S.D., instructor in history, 1948-50; Capital University, Columbus, Ohio, assistant professor of history, 1950-55; Eastern New Mexico University, Portales, assistant professor of history, 1955-58; Santa Ana College, Santa Ana, Calif., chairman of social science division, 1958-61; California State University, Fullerton, assistant professor, 1961-63, associate professor, 1963-66, professor of history, 1966—.

WRITINGS: A History of New Mexico, University of Oklahoma Press, 1962; *Student's Manual to Accompany "A History of the American People,"* two volumes, W. C. Brown, 1962; *Student's Manual to Accompany "The United States to 1865,"* by M. Kraus, University of Michigan Press, 1963; *Student's Manual to Accompany "The United States since 1865,"* by F. R. Dulles, University of Michigan Press, 1963; (with Ynez Haase) *A Historical Atlas of New Mexico,* University of Oklahoma Press, 1968.

(With David Williams) *California: A History of the Golden State,* Doubleday, 1972; (with Haase) *A Historical Atlas of California,* University of Oklahoma Press, 1974; (with Myles Clowers) *Understanding American History through Fiction,* two volumes, McGraw, 1974; *The California Experience: A Literary Odyssey,* Peregrine Smith, 1976.

WORK IN PROGRESS: An Historical Atlas of the American West, for University of Oklahoma Press; *God, Guilt and Sex: The Flagellants.*

*   *   *

BEECHCROFT, William
See HALLSTEAD, William F(inn III)

*   *   *

BELGUM, David 1922-

PERSONAL: Born December 22, 1922, in Glenwood, Minn.; son of Anton H. and Selma (Johnshoy) Belgum; married Katherine Geigenmueller, August 8, 1953; children: Karl, Kurt, Kirsten. *Education:* University of Minnesota, B.A., 1944; Northwestern Lutheran Theological Seminary, B.D., 1946; Boston University, Ph.D., 1952. *Home:* 104 Sunset St., Iowa City, Iowa 52240. *Office:* School of Religion, University of Iowa, Iowa City, Iowa 52242.

CAREER: Ordained to Lutheran ministry, 1946; assistant pastor in Minneapolis, Minn., 1946-47; pastor in Boston, Mass., 1947-52; Ypsilanti State Hospital, Ypsilanti, Mich., child therapist, 1952-53; Wittenberg University, Springfield, Ohio, assistant professor, 1953-55; Northwestern Lutheran Theological Seminary, Minneapolis, Minn., 1955-64, began as associate professor, became professor of pastoral counseling; University of Iowa, Iowa City, associate professor in School of Religion, 1964-69, professor in School of Religion and department of internal medicine, 1969—, director of department of pastoral service, university hospitals and clinics. Chaplain supervisor, Institute of Pastoral Care. *Member:* American Psychological Association.

WRITINGS: Clinical Training for Pastoral Care, Westminster, 1956; *His Death and Ours,* Augsburg, 1958; *Why Did It Happen to Me?,* Augsburg, 1960; *The Church and Its Ministry,* Prentice-Hall, 1963; *Guilt: Where Religion and Psychology Meet,* Prentice-Hall, 1963; *Church Camp Counselor's Manual,* Lutheran Church Press, 1964; *The Cross and the Creed,* Augsburg, 1966; *The Church and Sex Education,* Lutheran Church Press, 1967; (editor) *Religion and Medicine: Essays on Meaning, Values, and Health,* Iowa State University Press, 1967; *Why Marry? Since You Don't Need a License to Love,* Augsburg, 1972; *Alone, Alone, All, All Alone,* Concordia, 1972; *Engagement,* Concordia, 1972; *What Can I Do about the Part of Me I Don't Like?,* Augsburg, 1974; *When It's Your Turn to Decide,* Augsburg, 1978; *Religion and Personality in the Spiral of Life,* University Press (Washington, D.C.), 1979.

*   *   *

BELKIN, Samuel 1911-1976

PERSONAL: Born December 12, 1911, in Swislicz, Poland; came to United States in 1929, naturalized in 1941; died April 18, 1976, in New York, N.Y.; son of Solomon (a teacher) and Minna (Sattir) Belkin; married Selma Ehrlich, November 10, 1935 (divorced); married Abby Polesie, January 3, 1963; children: (first marriage) Linda Schuchalter, Salo Maurice. *Education:* Radin Theological Seminary, rabbinical ordination, 1929; attended Harvard University, 1934; Brown University, Ph.D., 1935. *Home:* 101 Central Park W., New York, N.Y. 10023. *Office:* Yeshiva University, 500 West 185th St., New York, N.Y. 10033.

CAREER: New Haven Rabbinical Seminary, Cleveland, Ohio, lecturer in Talmud, 1929-30; Yeshiva University, New York City, instructor in Greek, 1935-40, professor of Hellenistic literature, 1940-43, president, 1943-75, chancellor, 1975-76. Rabbi Isaac Elchanan Theological Seminary, New York City, instructor in Talmud, 1936-40, dean, 1940-43. Formerly co-chairman, New York Citizens Committee on Housing; member, executive committee, American Jewish Tercentenary.

MEMBER: Union of Orthodox Rabbis of the United States and Canada, Jewish Publication Society (member of publication committee), American Jewish Historical Society (member of executive committee), Jewish Academy of Arts and Sciences, New York Academy of Public Education, Jewish Book Council of America, American Academy of Political and Social Science, Phi Beta Kappa. *Awards, honors:* D.D. from Brown University, 1959; Bronze Medal of the City of New York, 1963, for service to higher education; L.H.D. from Dropsie University, 1964; Gold Medal from Board of Overseers of Albert Einstein College of Medicine and Yeshiva University, 1965.

WRITINGS: Philo and the Oral Law: The Philonic Interpretation of Biblical Law in Relation to the Palestinian Halakah,

Harvard University Press, 1940, reprinted, Johnson Reprint, 1968; *Essays in Traditional Jewish Thought*, Philosophical Library, 1956; *In His Image: The Jewish Philosophy of Man as Expressed in Rabbinic Tradition*, Abelard, 1961, reprinted, Greenwood Press, 1979; (contributor) Leon D. Stitskin, editor, *Studies in Judaica*, Ktav, 1974. Also author of *The Alexandrian Halakhah in Apologetic Literature*, 1936. Author of papers and monographs, including "The Four Dimensions of Higher Education," "What Makes a Good Jew," "Man and His Creator," and "The Philosophy of Purpose." Contributor to scholarly journals, including *Journal of Biblical Literature, Jewish Quarterly Review, Hapardes, Talpioth, Horeb,* and *Sura.* Former associate editor of Rabbinics for *Universal Jewish Encyclopedia.*

SIDELIGHTS: Samuel Belkin, who once described himself as "a rabbi who doesn't preach, a doctor who doesn't cure, and a professor who doesn't teach," began his scholarly career very early in life. His father was his first teacher, and after study at the Yeshivot of Radin and Mir, Poland, he was ordained at the age of 17. When he came to the United States the following year, he could speak Polish, Yiddish, and Hebrew, but no English. Six years later, however, he earned his Ph.D. from Brown University and was elected to Phi Beta Kappa. He joined the staff of Yeshiva College as an instructor, and rose quickly through the academic ranks. On May 25, 1943, when he was not yet thirty-two years old, he was elected president. During his tenure, the school attained university status, the first university under Jewish auspices to do so, and experienced substantial growth. One of Belkin's major achievements as president of Yeshiva was the establishment of the Albert Einstein College of Medicine. He personally visited Albert Einstein and, although Einstein was at first reluctant, Belkin persuaded him to give permission to use his name, leading to the opening of the Albert Einstein College of Medicine of Yeshiva University in 1955.

BIOGRAPHICAL/CRITICAL SOURCES: New York Times, March 27, 1961.

OBITUARIES: New York Times, April 19, 1976; *AB Bookman's Weekly,* June 28, 1976.†

*   *   *

BELL, Jack L. 1904-1975

PERSONAL: Born July 24, 1904, in Yates Center, Kan.; died of a stroke September 15, 1975, in Washington, D.C.; son of John H. and Anna J. (Peterson) Bell; married Helen Morey, August 21, 1926; children: Stratton Morey. *Education:* University of Oklahoma, A.B., 1925. *Home:* 4000 Cathedral Ave. N.W., Washington, D.C. 20016. *Office:* National Press Bldg., Washington, D.C. 20004.

CAREER: Daily Oklahoman and *Oklahoma City Times,* Oklahoma City, Okla., city editor, 1929-37; Associated Press, 1937-69, became chief of U.S. Senate staff and chief political writer; columnist, "Jack Bell Reports," Gannett News Service, 1969-75. Frequent panelist on television program, "Meet the Press." *Member:* National Press Club, Gridiron Club, International Club, and Chevy Chase Club (all Washington, D.C.), Phi Beta Kappa, Pi Kappa Alpha.

WRITINGS: The Splendid Misery, Doubleday, 1960, reprinted, Queens House, 1976; *Mr. Conservative: Barry Goldwater,* Doubleday, 1962; *The Johnson Treatment: How Lyndon B. Johnson Took Over the Presidency and Made It His Own,* Harper, 1965; *The Presidency: Office of Power,* Allyn & Bacon, 1967.

WORK IN PROGRESS: A book on the Senate's great dissenters.

AVOCATIONAL INTERESTS: Golf, antiques.

OBITUARIES: New York Times, September 16, 1975; *Washington Post,* September 16, 1975.†

*   *   *

BENEDICT, Joseph
See DOLLEN, Charles Joseph

*   *   *

BENET, Laura 1884-1979

PERSONAL: Born June 13, 1884, at Fort Hamilton, Brooklyn, N.Y.; died February 17, 1979, in New York, N.Y.; daughter of James Walker (an army officer) and Frances Neill (Rose) Benet. *Education:* Emma Willard School, graduate, 1903; Vassar College, A.B., 1907. *Politics:* Democrat. *Religion:* Protestant Episcopal.

CAREER: Spring Street Settlement, New York City, settlement worker, 1913-16; Children's Aid Society, New York City, placement worker, 1917; Red Cross Sanitary Commission, Augusta, Ga., inspector, 1917-19; St. Bartholomew's Mission, New York City, worker, 1924-25; *New York Evening Post,* New York City, assistant editor of book page, 1926-28; *New York Evening Sun,* New York City, assistant to book page editor, 1928-29; *New York Times,* New York City, substitute review editor, 1930; writer, 1930-79. Air raid warden during World War II. *Member:* Poetry Society of America, P.E.N., Women Poets, Craftsman Group, Pen and Brush Club (honorary). *Awards, honors:* Medal from National Poetry Center, 1936; poetry prizes from *Lyric* and *Voices;* D.Litt, Moravian College, 1967.

WRITINGS: Fairy Bread (poems), Thomas Seltzer, 1921; *Noah's Dove* (poems), Doubleday, 1929; *Goods and Chattels* (fiction), Doubleday, 1930, reprinted, Books for Libraries Press, 1970; *Basket for a Fair* (poems), Doubleday, 1934; *The Boy Shelley* (biography), Dodd, 1937, reprinted, 1964; *The Hidden Valley* (juvenile fiction), Dodd, 1938; *Enchanting Jenny Lind* (biography), Dodd, 1939, reprinted, 1964; *Roxana Rampant* (juvenile fiction), Dodd, 1940; *Young Edgar Allan Poe* (biography), Dodd, 1941, reprinted, 1963; *Caleb's Luck* (juvenile), Grosset, 1942; *Come Slowly, Eden* (novel), Dodd, 1942; *Horseshoe Nails,* illustrations by Harvey Kidder, Holt, 1943, reprinted, 1965; *Washington Irving, Explorer of American Legend,* Dodd, 1944; *Is Morning Sure?* (poems), Odyssey, 1947; *Thackeray, of the Great Heart and Humorous Pen* (biography), Dodd, 1947; *Barnum's First Circus, and Other Stories* (juvenile), 1949.

Famous American Poets, Dodd, 1950; *Coleridge, Poet of Wild Enchantment,* Dodd, 1952; (author of biographical introduction) *Tales by Edgar Allan Poe,* Dodd, 1952; (author of biographical introduction) *Thackeray's Henry Esmond,* Heritage, 1952; *Stanley, Invincible Explorer* (biography), Dodd, 1955; *In Love with Time* (poems), Wake-Brook, 1959; *Famous American Humorists,* Dodd, 1959; *Famous Poets for Young People,* Dodd, 1964; *Famous English and American Essayists,* Dodd, 1966; *Famous Storytellers for Young People,* Dodd, 1968; *Famous New England Authors,* Dodd, 1970; *Bridge of a Single Hair* (poems), Branden, 1974; *The Mystery of Emily Dickinson,* Dodd, 1974; *When William Rose, Stephen Vincent, and I Were Young,* Dodd, 1976.

OBITUARIES: New York Times, February 19, 1979.†

BENJAMIN, Alice
  See BROOKE, Avery (Rogers)

* * *

BENNETT, Jack Arthur Walter 1911-1981

PERSONAL: Born February 28, 1911, in Auckland, New Zealand; died January 29, 1981, in Los Angeles, Calif.; son of Ernest and Alexandra (Corrall) Bennett; married second wife, Gwyneth Mary Nicholas, March 29, 1951 (died March, 1980); children: Edmund Piers, Charles Anslem. *Education:* University College, Auckland, New Zealand, M.A., 1933; Merton College, Oxford University, B.A., 1935, M.A., D.Phil. 1938. *Politics:* Liberal. *Religion:* Roman Catholic. *Home:* 10 Adams Rd., Cambridge, England.

CAREER: Oxford University, Oxford, England, Queen's College, research fellow, 1938-46, Magdalen College, fellow and tutor, 1947-64; Cambridge University, Cambridge, England, professor of mediaeval and Renaissance English, 1964-78, fellow of Magdalene College, 1964-81, keeper of Old Library, 1968-81. Alexander Lecturer at University of Toronto, 1970-71; visiting fellow at Australian National University, 1976; Emeritus Leverhulme fellow, 1978. *Wartime service:* British Information Services, New York, N.Y., head of research department, then director, 1940-45. *Member:* British Academy (fellow), Early English Text Society (member of council), Mediaeval Academy of America (correspondence fellow), American Academy of Arts and Sciences (honorary foreign member).

WRITINGS: (Editor) Geoffrey Chaucer, *The Knight's Tale,* Harrap, 1954, 2nd edition, 1958, revised edition, 1977; (editor with H. R. Trevor-Roper) Richard Corbett, *Poems,* Clarendon Press, 1955; (editor) *Devotional Pieces in Verse and Prose from Ms. Arundel 285 and Ms. Harleian 6919,* Scottish Text Society, 1955; *The Parlement of Foules: An Interpretation,* Clarendon Press, 1957; (editor) Walter Oakeshott and others, *Essays on Malory,* Oxford University Press, 1963; *The Humane Medievalist* (inaugural lecture), Cambridge University Press, 1965; (editor with G. V. Smithers) *Early Middle English Verse and Prose,* Clarendon Press, 1966, 2nd edition, 1968; *Chaucer's 'Book of Fame': An Exposition of 'The House of Fame',* Oxford University Press, 1968; (editor) *Selections from John Gower,* Oxford University Press, 1968; (editor) William Langland, *Piers Plowman: The Prologue and Passus i-vii of the B Text as Found in Bodleian Mr. Laud Misc. 581,* Clarendon Press, 1973; *Chaucer at Oxford and at Cambridge,* University of Toronto Press, 1974. Contributor to *Times Literary Supplement, Listener, Landfall* (New Zealand), and to journals. Editor of "Clarendon Medieval and Tudor Series," and of *Medium Aevum,* beginning 1955.

BIOGRAPHICAL/CRITICAL SOURCES: Times Literary Supplement, January 12, 1967, July 25, 1968; *Virginia Quarterly Review,* spring, 1969

OBITUARIES: London Times, February 5, 1981.†

* * *

BENTLEY, Eric (Russell) 1916-

PERSONAL: Born September 14, 1916, in Bolton, Lancashire, England; came to United States in 1939, naturalized U.S. citizen in 1948; son of Fred and Laura (Evelyn) Bentley; married Maja Tschernjakow (divorced); married Joanne Davis, 1953;

children: Eric and Philip (twins). *Education:* Oxford University, B.A., 1938, Litt.B., 1939; Yale University, Ph.D., 1941. *Politics:* Independent. *Religion:* "A matter of definition." *Home:* 194 Riverside Dr., Apt. 4E, New York, N.Y. 10025. *Agent:* Rick Leed, Hesseltine-Baker Associates, 119 West 57th St., New York, N.Y. 10019.

CAREER: Black Mountain College, Black Mountain, N.C., teacher of history, literature, and drama and director of plays, 1942-44; University of Minnesota, Minneapolis, teacher of history, literature, and drama, 1944-48; Harvard University, Cambridge, Mass., Norton Professor of Poetry, 1960-61; Columbia University, New York, N.Y., Brander Matthews Professor of Dramatic Literature, 1954-69; research and writing, 1969-75; State University of New York at Buffalo, Cornell Professor of Theatre, 1975—. Ford Foundation artist-in-residence, Berlin, Germany, 1964-65; Fulbright professor, Belgrade, Yugoslavia, 1980. Guest director at the Abbey Theatre, Dublin, the Schauspielhaus, Zurich, and Teatro Universitario, Padua; assisted Bertolt Brecht in his own production of "Mother Courage," Munich, 1950. *Member:* P.E.N., American Academy of Arts and Sciences (fellow). *Awards, honors:* Guggenheim fellow, 1948-49 and 1967-68; Rockefeller grant, 1949-50; National Institute of Arts and Letters grant, 1953; Longview Award, 1961; George Jean Nathan award, 1967, for drama criticism for the 1965-66 season; D.F.A., University of Wisconsin—Milwaukee, 1975; CBS playwriting fellow, Yale University, 1976-77; Obie Award, 1978, for services to Off-Broadway; honorary doctorate, University of East Anglia, 1979.

WRITINGS: A Century of Hero Worship: A Study of the Idea of Heroism in Carlyle and Nietzsche, with Notes on Other Hero-Worshipers of Modern Times, Lippincott, 1944 (published in England as *The Cult of the Superman,* R. Hale, 1947), 2nd edition, Beacon Press, 1957, published as *The Cult of the Superman: A Study of Heroism in Carlyle and Nietzsche, with Notes on Other Hero-Worshippers of Modern Times,* Peter Smith, 1969; *The Playwright as Thinker: A Study of Drama in Modern Times,* Reynal & Hitchcock, 1946 (published in England as *The Modern Theatre: A Study of Dramatists and the Drama,* R. Hale, 1948), reprinted, Harcourt, 1967; *Bernard Shaw: A Reconsideration,* New Directions, 1947, reprinted, Norton, 1976, revised edition published as *Bernard Shaw, 1856-1950,* 1957 (published in England as *Bernard Shaw,* Methuen, 1967); *In Search of Theater,* Knopf, 1953, reprinted, Atheneum, 1975; *The Dramatic Event: An American Chronicle* (also see below), Horizon, 1954; *What Is Theatre?: A Query in Chronicle Form* (also see below), Beacon Press, 1956; *The Life of the Drama,* Atheneum, 1964; *The Theatre of Commitment, and Other Essays on Drama in Our Society,* Atheneum, 1967; *What Is Theatre?: Incorporating "The Dramatic Event" and Other Reviews, 1944-1967,* Atheneum, 1968; *Theatre of War: Comments on Thirty-Two Occasions,* Viking, 1972, abridged edition published as *Theatre of War: Modern Drama from Ibsen to Brecht,* 1973; *The Brecht Commentaries,* Grove, 1981.

Plays: "Commitments" (adaptations of plays by Euripides and Sophocles), produced in New York at HB Studio, 1967, published as *A Time to Live* [and] *A Time to Die: Two Short Plays* (produced Off-Broadway at La Mama Experimental Theatre Club, February 24, 1971), Grove, 1970; "DMZ Revue" (sketches), produced in New York, 1968; "The Red White and Black," produced Off-Broadway at La Mama Experimental Theatre Club, 1970; *Are You Now or Have You Ever Been: The Investigation of Show Business by the Un-American Activities Committee, 1947-1958* (also see below; produced in New Haven, Conn., November 11, 1972), Harper, 1972; *The Recantation of Galileo Galilei: Scenes from History Perhaps* (also see below; produced in Detroit, Mich., at Bonstelle Theatre, October 19, 1973), Harper, 1972; "Expletive Deleted," produced in New York at Riverside Church, 1974; "From the Memoirs of Pontius Pilate" (also see below), produced in Buffalo, N.Y., at Courtyard Theatre, 1976, produced in New York, January, 1981; *Rallying Cries: Three Plays* (contains "Are You Now or Have You Ever Been," "The Recantation of Galileo Galilei," and "From the Memoirs of Pontius Pilate"), New Republic Books, 1977, published as *Are You Now and Other Plays*, Grove, 1981; "The Kleist Variations: Wannsee," first produced in Buffalo at Courtyard Theatre, 1978; "The Kleist Variations: The Fall of the Amazons," first produced in Buffalo at Centre Theatre, 1979; *Lord Alfred's Lover* (first produced in Gainesville, Fla., at Hippodrome, 1979), Everest House, 1981; "The Kleist Variations: Concord," first produced in Buffalo at Centre Theatre, 1981.

Editor: *The Importance of Scrutiny: Selections from "Scrutiny," A Quarterly Review, 1932-1948*, Stewart, 1948, reprinted, New York University Press, 1964; G. B. Shaw, *On Music*, Doubleday, 1955; (and part translator) *From the Modern Repertoire*, Indiana University Press, series one, 1949, series two, 1952, series three, 1956; *The Play: A Critical Anthology*, Prentice-Hall, 1951; Luigi Pirandello, *Naked Masks: Five Plays* (contains "It Is So If You Think So," "Henry IV," "Six Characters in Search of an Author," "Each in His Own Way," and "Liola"), Dutton, 1952; (and part translator) *The Modern Theatre*, six volumes, Doubleday, 1955-60; (and translator) *Let's Get a Divorce, and Other Plays*, Hill & Wang, 1958; Anton Chekhov, *Brute, and Other Farces*, Grove, 1958; (and part translator) *The Classic Theatre*, four volumes, Doubleday, 1958-61; (and part translator) *The Works of Bertolt Brecht*, Grove, 1962—; *The Storm over "The Deputy"*, Grove, 1964; (and part translator) *The Genius of the Italian Theatre*, New American Library, 1964; (with E. Robinson) *Songs of Bertolt Brecht and Hanns Eisler*, Oak, 1966; Bertolt Brecht, *Galileo*, Grove, 1966; *The Theory of the Modern Stage: An Introduction to Modern Theatre and Drama*, Penguin, 1968, revised edition published as *The Theory of the Modern Theatre: An Introduction to Modern Theatre and Drama*, 1976; (and part translator) *The Great Playwrights: Twenty-Five Plays with Commentaries by Critics and Scholars*, two volumes, Doubleday, 1970; *Thirty Years of Treason*, Viking, 1971.

Translator of plays by Bertolt Brecht: *The Private Life of the Master Race* (produced in New York at City College Auditorium, June 11, 1945), New Directions, 1944, reprinted, J. Laughlin, 1973; *Parables for the Theater* (contains "The Good Woman of Setzuan" [also see below; produced Off-Broadway at Phoenix Theatre, December 18, 1956] and "The Caucasian Chalk Circle" [also see below]), University of Minnesota Press, 1948, revised edition, 1965; "In the Swamp," published in *Seven Plays*, Grove, 1961; "A Man's a Man" (produced Off-Broadway at Masque Theatre, September 19, 1962), published in *Seven Plays*, Grove, 1961; "Baal" (also see below; produced Off-Broadway at Martinique Theatre, May 6, 1965), published in *Anthology of German Expressionist Drama*, edited by Walter Herbert Sokel, Doubleday, 1963; *Mother Courage and Her Children* (produced on Broadway at Martin Beck Theatre, March 28, 1963), Grove, 1963; *Baal, A Man's a Man*, [and] *The Elephant Calf*, Grove, 1964; (with Desmond Vesey) *Threepenny Opera*, Grove, 1964; *The Jewish Wife and Other Short Plays*, Grove, 1965; "The Exception and the Rule," produced Off-Broadway at Greenwich Mews Playhouse, May 30, 1965; *Manual of Piety*, Grove, 1966; *Edward II: A Chronicle Play* (produced in San Francisco at Marine Memorial Theatre, October 22, 1965), Grove, 1966; (with Maja Apelman)

The Caucasian Chalk Circle, revised edition, Grove, 1967; *Happy End: The Prologue and Songs*, [New York], 1970.

Translator of other works: Luigi Pirandello, *Right You Are* (play), Columbia University Press, 1954; Hector Cremieux and Ludovic Halevy, *Orpheus in the Underworld* (libretto), Program Publishing Co., 1956; Wolf Biermann, *The Wire Harp* (ballads, poems, and songs), Harcourt, 1968. Also translator of "The Emperor," by Pirandello, "These Cornfields," by Georges Courteline, "The Underpants," by Carl Sternheim, and "Marriage," by Nicolai Gogol.

Editor, "Dramabook" series. Drama critic, *New Republic*, 1952-56. Contributor to *Harper's, Theater Arts, Kenyon Review, Partisan Review*, and other periodicals.

SIDELIGHTS: Though he now prefers to write rather than review plays, Eric Bentley was for some twenty-five years one of America's foremost drama critics. His first book of essays on the modern theater, *The Playwright as Thinker*, set the tone for much of his subsequent work, both as a critic and as a playwright. It also established him as a controversial figure in the literary world, for in his study Bentley maintains that no great dramas have been written since the days of Henrik Ibsen (1828-1906) and George Bernard Shaw (1859-1950), and that the state of the art in both New York and Hollywood is dismal at best.

Critical reaction to Bentley's work has often been determined by the extent to which a particular reviewer agrees or disagrees with his condemnation of modern theater. To those who disagree, such as *Cue*'s Marilyn Stasio, Bentley's "abrasive, if not outright churlish, critical voice" suggests an "academic brand of critical exclusivity" that is "condescending and misanthropic." A *Times Literary Supplement* reviewer concurs that Bentley's "characteristic posture is that of an antagonist" and goes on to note, "His is a nagging voice, always dissatisfied, indifferent to entertainment . . . , and aspiring to turn drama criticism into a species of political thought." But to those who agree with Bentley, such as the *New York Times*'s Paul Green, he "is one of the most penetrating and dogmatic critics writing on drama and the theatre today. And by dogmatic I mean no derogation at all. . . . [With] gusto and flailing he tore into many of the idols we had shied around so long and called attention to what he felt were their weaknesses and hollow drumming." Or, as H. M. Robinson of the *Saturday Review of Literature* states: "In *The Playwright as Thinker* Eric Bentley ushers in a new era of dramatic criticism by producing a work of bold originality and unimpeachable excellence. . . . His scholarship is vast but he rides it handily. And his critical *apercus*, though fashioned at the traditional academic forge, have a piercing edge and a furled energy that send them quivering deeply into the vitals of his material."

One of Bentley's major objections to modern drama (and one he has tried to remedy in his own plays) is its lack of concern for political affairs. Although he by no means advocates excusing bad writing merely because it appeals, as Albert Bermel of the *New Leader* notes, "to moral obligation, social unity and Leftist solidarity," he is nevertheless a strong proponent of the "theater of commitment." "By 'commitment,'" Bermel explains, "Bentley means overt political propaganda, a radical thesis that need not be Leftist, but is more broadly radical and independent: an assault on prevailing opinions and establishment behavior. . . . He feels powerless in the face of political events . . . and is looking, like many of us, for some way to make his protest heard. Political crises beget artistic crises. At a time of [crisis], a person whose life is bound up with an art form cannot bear to think of its remaining silent and uninfluential. . . . [To Bentley,] a play is inescapably of its time, even when it is 'escapist'—a dramatist may make a significant or a trivial response to his world; he cannot avoid making *some* response. The better the play, the better the response.''

Walter Kerr, commenting in the *New York Herald Tribune Book Review*, summarizes some of Bentley's other positions on the subject of Broadway and the theater of commitment in a review of *In Search of Theater*, a collection of essays written between 1947 and 1952. Observes Kerr: ''Mr. Bentley does not believe in a popular theater; the audience is incapable of valid judgment in esthetic matters; Shakespeare and Shaw are popular in spite of their greatness, not because of it; Broadway fails precisely because it cannot make the 'necessary' distinction between mass art and minority art; Mr. Bentley is for a minority art, for the 'heroic failure.''' Bentley is especially drawn to the ''heroic failure''—usually the product of a playwright who is committed to relating art to life—because he regards it as an intense personal statement ''composed with one man's passion and intellect'' rather than a ''committee play'' that is ''pieced together . . . by the ingenuity of all who stop by at the hotel bedroom, preferably during rehearsal period.'' In short, the ''heroic failure'' is a play written to evoke emotional response and perhaps some sort of action, not just a hodge-podge combining the most marketable features possible.

In *The Life of the Drama*, Bentley attempts to consolidate all of his ideas and devise a comprehensive theory of drama as well as explain the continuing psychological appeal of its five basic forms—tragedy, comedy, melodrama, farce, and tragicomedy. In this book, the author claims that man, by nature, enjoys ''revel[ing] in [the] mishaps and disasters'' of others as he seeks ways ''to cope with [the] despair, mental suffering, guilt and anxiety'' his own quest for self-knowledge inevitably brings. Bentley also believes that man is inherently fond of violence and aggression, essentially as a source of excitement. Thus, one or another of the various forms of drama, says the critic, force us to reflect on the ''nonsensical life we live'' (tragedy), assure us that happy endings are possible (comedy), purge us of fear (melodrama) and aggression (farce), or present a world ''shot through'' with elements of both tragedy and comedy in an effort to offer us ''the only kind of hope we are in a position to accept'' (tragicomedy).

Many reviewers hail *The Life of the Drama* as Bentley's finest achievement. The *New Republic*'s Clancy Sigal declares it to be ''the best general book on theater I have read bar none,'' while John Gassner of the *New York Times Book Review* observes that ''Mr. Bentley has chosen to be what he has always been at his best—a felicitous, rather than facile, writer.'' Continues the critic: ''[His] treatment of the subject is pragmatic without being opportunistic; instead of dogmatically imposing principles upon the drama, he derives them from human nature and the nature of the dramatic medium.''

''Informal in tone, drawing heavily on analogical and illustrative material from the life outside theater, upsetting conventional ideas at every turn, [*The Life of the Drama*] is a remarkable exploration of the roots and bases of dramatic art, the most far-reaching and revelatory we have had,'' states Richard Gilman in *Book Week*. ''Nowhere does [the author] rely on assumptions he has not tested; everywhere his book reveals that freedom from academic construction on the one hand and populist rhetoric on the other, which is so much rarer in our drama criticism than in the study of any of the other arts.''

Concludes the *Virginia Quarterly Review*'s Gordon Rogoff: ''Everywhere in these pages there is a moment of recognition,

that shock of discovery when what is said appears as if it must have been said and known for centuries before. . . . Bentley doesn't suffer sham gladly. Neither is he obstinate or defensive in his own behalf. . . . [*The Life of the Drama*] should be read for its far-reaching suggestiveness, its ambitious, thorough way of blowing cool winds of sanity into the study of an easily scorned art. It is a book badly needed.''

Time—or perhaps his own struggles with what he admits is the ''harder'' and ''slower'' task of writing a play—has mellowed Bentley the critic somewhat. In an interview for the book *American Writers Today*, he comments: ''When I glance back over my work of the past several decades, I do see that some writers took a beating from me mainly because they were not Brechtian enough: I did not do full justice to the non-Brechtians, to writers of, say, a surreal or subjectivist tendency. Today, I think some of my criteria were over-austere, Puritanic. . . . [I see] a certain prejudice against . . . a theater I too easily dismissed as decadent.''

Bentley regards his switch from reviewing to writing plays as little more than a process of moving on to ''the next phase of my life.'' Despite appearances to the contrary, his decision to abandon drama criticism was not a sudden one. ''I had approached [the idea of writing a play] gingerly, gradually. As a translator, mainly,'' he told the interviewer for *American Writers Today*. ''I always dreamed myself the author when I translated. That was why I translated. . . . Sometimes it was a relief to translate the less sublime authors. Or the less sublime works of the more sublime authors. And touch them up a bit. . . . That is how one injects oneself into the pages of Art. I must have been ambitious to do that, for I was becoming progressively more meddlesome. Translations were becoming adaptations. Next step: my own name under the title and above the phrase 'Based on . . .'! I was now a playwright.''

Though he maintains that ''whatever shows up in a person in later life has been there all along,'' Bentley won't go so far as to claim ''that playwrighting was the culmination of everything I had ever done. [It was] just my attempt, at long last, to try my hand at the work I had long regarded as central in my chosen field.''

MEDIA ADAPTATIONS: Eric Bentley is the editor and author of commentary for ''Brecht Before the House Un-American Activities Committee,'' Folkways Records, 1963, and is the adaptor, lyricist, and narrator for the original cast album of Brecht's ''A Man's a Man,'' Spoken Arts Records, 1963. He is also the editor and performer for ''Bentley on Brecht,'' Riverside Records, 1963, ''Songs of Hans Eisler,'' Folkways Records, 1965, ''The Exception and the Rule,'' Folkways Records, 1967, ''The Elephant Calf'' [and] ''Dear Old Democracy,'' Folkways Records, 1967, ''Bentley on Biermann,'' Folkways Records, 1968, and ''The Queen of 42nd Street,'' Pacifica Records, 1969. There is also a Folkways recording entitled ''Eric Bentley.''

CA INTERVIEW

CA interviewed Eric Bentley by phone May 1, 1981, at his home in New York City.

CA: You are both a drama critic and a playwright. Is either job easier because you've also done the other job?

BENTLEY: That's a hard question because I don't do theater criticism anymore. I think criticism might be easier because I've learned playwriting, but I went in the other order. The playwriting was certainly not easier because it came after the criticism. I think it was more difficult, on the whole, because I was too conscious intellectually of what was going on, and that could be slightly inhibiting; it creates a sort of block at times. I'd begin to criticize my own stuff before it was there, and that stops the baby being born.

CA: How do you feel about directing your own plays?

BENTLEY: It's not ideal. I'd prefer to have a director who, while being a kindred spirit, was mainly a director and could bring to the work something that I don't have. Then two heads would be better than one. On the other hand, since directors *aren't* always kindred spirits, I often prefer to do the job myself.

CA: You taught at Black Mountain College early in your career. Did that experience have any impact on your work?

BENTLEY: I was there about two years, and life there was so intense, it's probably equivalent to five anywhere else. Yes, it was there that my interest really switched as a young scholar from history and languages back again to where it had been when I was a kid: to theater.

CA: In an essay titled "The Unliberated University" you wrote about the 1968 student rebellion at Columbia. From the perspective of 1981, do you think anything positive came from the widespread student rebellion of that period?

BENTLEY: Yes, I think there were both positive and negative results. The negative results, all the world knows, are partly that the student movement went toward a terrorism which I think is not only inhumane but in America politically absurd. There were some positive results in education. I think the universities did respond slowly, but markedly, during the 1970s, and that many of them were better places afterwards than they were before. Among other things, the student-teacher relationship is better.

CA: You've worked in theater in England, Ireland, Germany, and Italy as well as in this country. How did you decide to settle here?

BENTLEY: I came here on a scholarship as a graduate student, and it so happened that all my personal and professional relationships were here. Although I thought I would go back to England, the time came when my life was all here. I still feel England is home in a very basic way, and I love it. Nevertheless I have no relationships there, either professional or personal, so I feel I couldn't begin again there. Becoming an American citizen wasn't a political decision.

CA: What are the greatest problems for you in translating plays from one language to another?

BENTLEY: All translations are wrong somehow. You come in for a lot of criticism when you're a translator, and in a sense you deserve it, because there are no perfect translations of great works. They're all either too literal or not literal enough, so they can always be criticized from one side or the other. Some of my early stuff was too literal and staid: people said it was untheatrical. Later they said I departed from the original too much. Scholars attacked my work as too free and loose. You can't hit the jackpot. You're damned if you do and you're damned if you don't. Robert Frost said that poetry is what doesn't come through in the translation.

CA: Many people feel that the critics have too much power. How do you feel about that?

BENTLEY: I'd put it that New York pays far too much attention to critics. In other words, I'd put the blame on a public that pays that much attention. I don't think any of these critics have *claimed* authority. The public has assigned it to them. I could excuse the public, too, and I'm a member of it now, since I'm not one of the critics, and I think twice or even three times before I put down twenty-five or thirty dollars for an orchestra seat. I take advice, and what advisers are there except the people who have just seen the show and have written about it in the paper? However, I learn who to believe and to what extent. I know the enthusiasm of certain critics isn't something I'm likely to share, therefore I don't immediately buy the ticket. You read shrewdly. You read between the lines.

CA: Do you think good theater criticism is being written?

BENTLEY: Yes. In papers like the *Nation* and the *New Republic,* and to a lesser degree in *Time* and *Newsweek.* Not in the daily papers.

CA: Do you think openings in New York should require a wait of two or three days before the reviews appear in print?

BENTLEY: No, because experience shows those people don't write any better after two or three days. Those who do another article on Sunday are not better on Sunday than they were before. I also know from my own experience that what I write an hour afterwards is the immediate, hot-off-the-griddle response. The only thing about a delayed reaction is that, in the case of a play that happens to be subtle or complex, sometimes a second visit will change your mind. I changed my mind over one of Enid Bagnold's plays, *The Chalk Garden.* The first time I saw it, I hated it. The second time I saw it, I began to like it. I reported both of those responses.

CA: You commented in a Theatre Quarterly *interview (spring, 1976) that "even the theater reviewers today are hopelessly overeducated." What did you mean?*

BENTLEY: As contrasted with thirty years ago, when they used to bring in the football reviewers and have them write about theater, I think we're now in an age of the college educated. Even the actors are college educated: you read in the programs that they've all got a B.A. or M.F.A. from Yale. The university, which previously was an ivory tower, is now just Rotary Club. One result is that drama criticism, instead of glorying in its ignorance as it used to, now glories in a certain erudition. The same is true of movie criticism. My friend and ex-student Andrew Sarris, in the *Village Voice,* is a learned movie historian all the time, sometimes to the extent of forgetting to respond to the film he's reviewing. Writers on the *New York Times* brandish their erudition. They make sure to let you know they've seen every performance of a play for the last thirty years.

CA: Your essays on theater are not only informative, but also highly polished pieces of writing. Do you revise a great deal?

BENTLEY: Yes. Though when you publish weekly reviews, you can't rewrite forever. I would usually spend one day on a review, revise on and off all day, then send it in the following morning with a few further revisions. The revision problem is much bigger in playwriting, where you make a dozen versions of the whole play as the months go by. And even afterwards, you're changing this and changing that.

CA: How did your record albums come about?

BENTLEY: I think it was through the translation of Bertolt Brecht's poetry and finding that a lot of the poems had been songs and had been set to music. To do the right job, you really had to translate them *for the music;* you had to be singing them. I learned so many of the songs that I began to sing them to friends, and the audience got a bit bigger, and I ended up recording. I'm now performing in nightclubs.

CA: Do you go to movies or theater for entertainment?

BENTLEY: In a sense, I wouldn't go for anything *but.* Yet that's using the word *entertainment* in the best sense: a good time. I don't go for a professional reason anymore. I don't go because I'm going to write about it. I go only if I think it would be an evening well spent, and twenty-five dollars well spent too! Why not buy a cheaper seat? Well, I've been spoiled by critics' seats. I like to sit where I can see the actors' faces and hear well: that means the best seats. Fifth row: I don't like to sit any further away.

CA: Is there any experimentation going on now in theater or in any of the arts that you find promising?

BENTLEY: Yes, indeed. I think the whole Off-Off-Broadway scene, which has come into being since I did my reviewing, and really wasn't there in the 1950s, is quite interesting. Of course, you have to allow for the fact that out of a hundred shows, you're lucky if one or two have real merit, but that's a natural state of affairs. I think it's a very healthy phenomenon that you *have* these hundreds of shows from which a few significant things can grow. I don't attach any importance to Broadway nowadays; but then I never did.

CA: Do you think regional theater is giving enough encouragement to new playwrights?

BENTLEY: I suppose there can never be enough, but there's more encouragement than in the past. Hundreds of playwrights do get some sort of a performance. Many of the scripts are barely worth it, so my heart does not bleed for the unperformed playwright. I believe you can get performed if you have both some talent and a certain amount of chutzpah. You have to be a self-publicizer: there's no other way.

CA: Are there any new playwrights that you like particularly?

BENTLEY: Some of the young playwrights who have received recognition, such as Sam Shepard, who won a Pulitzer Prize, are very talented, certainly no less so than the pervious generation of American playwrights. I don't think playwriting is in a bad way.

CA: What are your greatest concerns for theater now?

BENTLEY: Selfish ones. I like to get *my own stuff* performed. That's mainly what I'm concerned with nowadays: writing plays and getting them performed. Having the experience of production.

CA: Are you teaching now also?

BENTLEY: Yes, I'm with the State University of New York, a job that allows me to stage my own works at the Center Theater in Buffalo.

CA: Is there one play you're proudest of?

BENTLEY: The play I had the most public success with was *Are You Now Or Have You Ever Been.* But I didn't feel all that much pride in it because it was a documentary. I take more pride in something that's my own *writing,* not just my own selections, something more creative. The play I wrote about Oscar Wilde, *Lord Alfred's Lover,* has *some* documentary basis, I include some quotes from him in it, but it nevertheless is an original play, not purely documentary. So I take more pride in it.

CA: What are you writing now?

BENTLEY: Since *Lord Alfred's Lover,* I've written three more plays, two of which have already been produced. The three have something in common: they're all based on the work of Heinrich von Kleist. No, they're not translations, they're not even adaptations because they're so free and they depart so far from Kleist that I think you could call them original plays though *based on* something else: the way Brecht's *Threepenny Opera* is based on John Gay's *Beggar's Opera.* Kleist is not very well known in this country, which suits me fine. It means that everything about the three plays can be fresh and new for my audience.

CA: Do the three plays have a collective title?

BENTLEY: Yes, the Kleist Variations.

BIOGRAPHICAL/CRITICAL SOURCES: New York Times, June 16, 1946, March 15, 1953, November 28, 1954, March 31, 1971, November 12, 1972, January 30, 1981; *Saturday Review of Literature,* June 22, 1946; *New Republic,* June 24, 1946, April 6, 1953, September 26, 1964; *Nation,* September 7, 1946, February 20, 1967; *Theatre Arts,* November, 1946, May, 1953, spring, 1976; *Chicago Sunday Tribune,* March 29, 1953; *New York Herald Tribune Book Review,* April 5, 1953; Eric Bentley, *The Life of the Drama,* Atheneum, 1964; *Book Week,* October 4, 1964; *New York Times Book Review,* October 11, 1964, December 10, 1967; *Virginia Quarterly Review,* winter, 1965; *New Leader,* December 4, 1967; *Prompt,* No. 13, 1969; *Cue,* July 26, 1969; *Times Literary Supplement,* August 29, 1969, October 16, 1969, May 25, 1973; *New York,* March 12, 1971; *New Yorker,* December 6, 1971; *Variety,* December 13, 1972; *Theatre Quarterly,* spring, 1976; *American Writers Today,* Voice of America, 1982.

—*Sketch by Deborah A. Straub*

—*Interview by Jean W. Ross*

*   *   *

BERGSTEN, Staffan 1932-

PERSONAL: Born November 12, 1932, in Sweden; son of Nils (a headmaster) and Clara (Wangel) Bergsten; married Gunilla Ulander (a university lecturer), July 30, 1957; children: Cecilia, Andreas, Katja. *Education:* University of Uppsala, Ph.D., 1960. *Home:* Malma Ringvaeg 8, S-752 45 Uppsala, Sweden. *Office:* Department of Literary History, Uppsala University, S-751 03 Uppsala, Sweden.

CAREER: Cambridge University, Cambridge, England, deputy lecturer in Swedish, 1957-58; Uppsala University, Uppsala, Sweden, docent in literary history, 1960—, head of department, 1973—. Speaker on literary subjects for Swedish Broadcasting Co., 1965—. *Military service:* Swedish Army, 1954-55. *Member:* International P.E.N. (Stockholm).

WRITINGS: Time and Eternity: A Study in the Structure and Symbolism of T. S. Eliot's Four Quartets, Svenska Bokfoerlaget, 1960; *Stagnelius Bacchanterna* (critical edition), Gebers Foerlag, 1962; *En Stagneliusbibliografi* (title means "A Stagnelius Bibliography''), Svenska Litteratursaellskapet, 1965; *Erotikern Stagnelius* (title means "Stagnelius, the Erotic Poet''), Svenska Bokfoerlaget, 1966; *Jaget och vaerlden: Kosmiska analogier i svensk 1900-talslyrik* (title means "The Self and the World: Cosmic Analogies in Twentieth-Century Swedish Poetry''), Uppsala University, 1971; (editor with G. Bergsten and contributor) *Lyrik i tid och otid* (essays in poetry criticism), Gleerups, 1971; (contributor) *Litteraturens vaerldshistoria* (title means "History of World Literature''), Volume IX, Norstedts, 1973; *Oesten Sjoestrand* (biography), Twayne, 1974; *Mary Poppins and Myth,* Almqvist & Wiksell, 1978; *Gamle Kant* (novel; title means "Old Kant''), Bonniers, 1979; *Olyckan* (novel; title means "The Accident''), Bonniers, 1982. Contributor to *Encyclopaedia Britannica, Columbia Dictionary of Modern European Literature,* 2nd edition, and to *Samlaren* (a yearbook of Swedish literary history). Contributor to *Artes* (a Swedish literary magazine).

WORK IN PROGRESS: A book featuring "a very resourceful heroine.''

SIDELIGHTS: Staffan Bergsten told *CA:* "Having published several scholarly books in the field of literary history, among them, one on a modern English poet, T. S. Eliot, for a Swedish degree, and another on a modern Swedish poet, [Oesten] Sjoestrand, for an English-speaking public, [I] finally wrote [my] first novel.'' Bergsten's first work of fiction, a self-described "historico-fantastic'' novel, features Immanuel Kant as its hero; his second, also part of the fantasy genre, has a contemporary setting. Bergsten adds: [I am] a latecomer to fiction, currently contemplating [my] opus three.''

*   *   *

BERMANT, Chaim 1929-

PERSONAL: Born February 26, 1929, in Breslev, Poland; son of Azriel (a rabbi) and Feiga Tzirl (Daets) Bermant; married Judith Weil, December 17, 1962; children: Alisa, Eve, Azriel, Daniel. *Education:* Attended Rabbinical College, Glasgow, Scotland, 1948-50; University of Glasgow, M.A., 1955, M.Litt., 1960; London School of Economics and Political Science, M.Sc., 1957. *Politics:* Liberal conservative. *Religion:* Jewish. *Home:* 18 Hill Rise, London N.W.11., England. *Agent:* A. P. Watt, 26 Bedford Row, London W.C.1., England.

CAREER: Teacher in London, England, 1955-56; economist in London, 1956-58; television scriptwriter in Glasgow, Scotland, 1958-59, and in London, 1959-61; features editor, *London Jewish Chronicle,* 1961-66; free-lance writer, 1966—.

WRITINGS: Jericho Sleep Alone, Holt, 1963; *Berl Make Tea,* Holt, 1964; *Ben Preserve Us,* Holt, 1964; *Diary of an Old Man,* Holt, 1966; *Swinging in the Rain,* Hodder & Stoughton, 1967; *Israel,* Walker & Co., 1967; (editor with Murray Mindlin) *Explorations: An Annual on Jewish Themes,* Barrie & Rockliff, 1967; *Troubled Eden: The Anatomy of Anglo-Jewry,* Basic Books, 1969; *Here Endeth the Lesson,* Eyre & Spottiswoode, 1969.

Now Dowager, Eyre & Spottiswoode, 1971; *The Cousinhood,* Macmillan, 1971; *Roses Are Blooming in Picardy,* Eyre & Spottiswoode, 1972; *The Last Supper,* St. Martin's, 1973; *The Walled Garden,* Macmillan, 1975; *Point of Arrival,* Macmillan, 1975; *The Second Mrs. Whitberg,* St. Martin's, 1977; *The Jews,* New York Times Co., 1977; *Now Newman Was Old,* St. Martin's, 1979; (with M. Weitzman) *Ebla,* New York Times Co., 1979; *Belshazzar the Cat* (juvenile), Allen & Unwin, 1979; *The Patriarch,* St. Martin's, 1981.

WORK IN PROGRESS: A novel for St. Martin's.

SIDELIGHTS: Chaim Bermant told *CA:* "I suppose I was driven to write by a sort of hedonism, for it gave me a pleasure offered by no other occupation and, unlike other activities which I need not name, it still does. Yet, I did not think it could offer a livelihood, and I dabbled at many things before taking my life in my hands in 1966 and throwing up a secure and fairly lucrative post to devote myself to full time writing and, somehow, I have survived. I used to be in television and journalism before taking up full-time authorship, and I still turn to both between books because they get me out of the house and keep me in touch with people and events, and because I value them—journalism especially—as a discipline. Writing books can be a form of self-indulgence because one has almost all the time and space in the world, whereas journalism with its deadlines and space limitations concentrates the mind wonderfully.

"As I have a fairly large family and live in a fairly spacious house, I am compelled to approach my work in a thoroughly professional manner and am at my typewriter daily from 9:30 to 1:30, whether I have anything to write or not (for I don't know whether I have until I start). In the afternoon I answer letters, fend off creditors, etc., and return to my desk again after dinner. On most working days I do not rise from my labors till about 10 P.M. I sometimes shudder at the torrents of words I produce—on average about 5,000 a day. I begin my working day by re-reading my previous day's output, and if it yields 1,000 useable words I feel I have done well.''

BIOGRAPHICAL/CRITICAL SOURCES: New York Times Book Review, August 2, 1981; *London Times,* August 6, 1981.

*   *   *

BERRIDGE, Elizabeth 1921-

PERSONAL: Born December 3, 1921, in London, England; daughter of Albert (an estate manager) and Phyllis Cecilia (Drew) Berridge; married Reginald Moore (an author and publisher), 1940; children: Lawrence Gaunt, Karen Veronica (Mrs. Philip Craven). *Education:* Attended Regent Street Polytechnic, London, England; also studied French and German privately in Geneva, Switzerland. *Politics:* Liberal. *Home:* 19 Broad Lane, Hampton-on-Thames, Middlesex, England. *Agent:* David Higham Associates, 5-8 Lower John St., Golden Sq., London W1R 4HA, England.

CAREER: Novelist, short-story writer. Held early positions as secretary and journalist, later as publisher's editor, 1956-60, all in London, England; former book critic for *Daily Telegraph, Books and Bookmen,* and *Country Life.* Appeared on radio program "Woman's Hour,'' 1964-71. Local press officer for Liberal Party, 1963-64. *Member:* National Book League, P.E.N., Browning Society. *Awards, honors:* Yorkshire Post award for best novel of the year, 1964, for *Across the Common.*

WRITINGS—Novels, except as indicated: *House of Defence,* Falcon, 1945; *The Story of Stanley Brent,* Falcon, 1945; *Selected Short Stories,* Maurice Fridberg, 1949; *It Won't Be Flowers,* Simon & Schuster, 1949 (published in England as *Be Clean, Be Tidy,* Heinemann, 1949); *Rose under Glass,* Heinemann, 1962; *Across the Common,* Heinemann, 1964, Coward, 1965; *Sing Me Who You Are,* Heinemann, 1967; (editor and author of introduction) *The Barretts at Hope End: The Early Diary of Elizabeth Barrett Browning,* J. Murray, 1974; *Family Matters* (short stories), Heinemann, 1980; *Run for Home,* Pelham Books, 1981; *Playing House,* Heinemann, 1982.

Also author of plays for television and radio. Contributor of poetry and stories to literary magazines; also contributor to

Cornhill Magazine, London Magazine, Winter's Tales, Punch, and *Harper's Bazaar.*

WORK IN PROGRESS: The Reluctant Squire, a novel based on a Welsh ancestor; a sequel to *Run for Home.*

SIDELIGHTS: Elizabeth Berridge wrote *CA:* "The short story has always been my first love. Probably because my husband started his collection of short stories and poetry when we met, and throughout the war we worked together in a remote cottage in Wales, choosing stories from a host sent in by men and women in the Forces. We reared our children without running water, electricity or an indoor loo. A vivid memory is a pailful of frozen nappies (diapers to Americans) in the porch one freezing winter; another is pushing our bikes through banks of piled up snow to buy bread and jam tarts for our son's third birthday.

"Writing short stories is the best discipline for the beginner. It encapsulates, as does no other form, a time and a place; emotion expressed, a turning point in relationships, a subtle characterisation. I remember correcting the proofs of my first story sitting up in bed with a day-old son in a cottage hospital in Hertfordshire. So, being a writer is a way of life. Nothing can be enjoyed until that experience is down on paper, analysed, lived twice. It is a mixed blessing, because in a way one is *too* aware."

AVOCATIONAL INTERESTS: Browsing through nineteenth-century biographies, watching cricket, exploring out-of-the-way places, walking in London, ESP research.

*   *   *

BESTOR, Arthur (Eugene, Jr.) 1908-

PERSONAL: Born September 20, 1908, in Chautauqua, N.Y.; son of Arthur Eugene (president of Chautauqua Institution, 1915-44) and Jeanette (Lemon) Bestor; married Dorothea Nolte, 1931 (divorced); married Anne Carr, 1939 (died, 1948); married Dorothy Alden Koch, 1949; children: (second marriage) William P., Thomas W.; (third marriage) Theodore C. *Education:* Yale University, Ph.B., 1930, Ph.D., 1938. *Home:* 4553 55th Ave. N.E., Seattle, Wash. 98105. *Office:* Department of History, Smith Hall, University of Washington, Seattle, Wash. 98195.

CAREER: Yale University, New Haven, Conn., instructor, 1930-31, 1934-36; Columbia University, Teachers College, New York, N.Y., associate, 1936-37, assistant professor of history, 1937-42; Stanford University, Stanford, Calif., assistant professor of humanities, 1942-45, associate professor of history, 1945-46; University of Illinois at Urbana-Champaign, associate professor, 1947-51, professor of history, 1951-62; University of Washington, Seattle, professor of history, 1962-76, professor emeritus, 1976—. Summer professor, University of Minnesota, 1946, Northwestern University, 1949, University of Wyoming, 1953, Boston College, 1959, University of Washington, 1961, and State University of New York at Stony Brook, 1965; lecturer, University of Wisconsin—Madison, 1947; Harold Vyvyan Harmsworth Professor of American History, Oxford University, 1956-57; inaugural lecturer, American Studies Research Centre, Osmania University (Hyderabad, India), 1964; Fulbright Visiting Professor, University of Tokyo, Rikkyo University, and Doshisha University (Kyoto, Japan), 1967. Member of board of directors, University Centers for Rational Alternatives, 1970—.

MEMBER: American Historical Association (president of Pacific Coast branch, 1975-76), American Studies Association (vice-president, 1962), Organization of American Historians (member of executive committee, 1964-67), Council for Basic Education (president, 1956-57; member of board of directors, 1956-77), University Centers for Rational Alternatives (member of board of directors, 1970—), American Civil Liberties Union (member of state board of directors, 1964), Southern Historical Association, Washington State Historical Society, Illinois State Historical Society (president, 1954-55), Phi Beta Kappa, Elizabethan Club (Yale University). *Awards, honors:* American Historical Association Albert J. Beveridge Memorial Award, 1946, for *Backwoods Utopias;* Newberry Library fellow, 1946; Guggenheim fellow, 1953-54 and 1961-62; M.A., Oxford University, 1956; Shattuck School Centennial Award, 1958, for the advancement of secondary education; LL.D., Lincoln University, 1959; Illinois State Historical Society Award, 1960, for distinguished service to American history.

WRITINGS: Chautauqua Publications: An Historical and Bibliographical Guide, Chautauqua Press, 1934; *David Jacks of Monterey and Lee L. Jacks, His Daughter,* Stanford University Press, 1945; (editor) *Education and Reform at New Harmony: Correspondence of William Maclure and Marie Duclos Fretageot, 1820-1833,* Indiana Historical Society, 1948, reprinted, Augustus M. Kelley, 1973; *Backwoods Utopias: The Sectarian and Owenite Phases of Communitarian Socialism in America, 1663-1829,* University of Pennsylvania Press, 1950, 2nd enlarged edition published as *Backwoods Utopias: Sectarian Origins and Owenite Phase of Communitarian Socialism in America, 1663-1829,* 1970; *Educational Wastelands: The Retreat from Learning in Our Public Schools,* University of Illinois Press, 1953; *The Restoration of Learning: A Program for Redeeming the Unfulfilled Promise of American Education,* Knopf, 1955; (with others) *Three Presidents and Their Books,* University of Illinois Press, 1963.

Contributor: William J. Doty, editor, *Historic Annals of Southwestern New York,* Lewis Historical Publishing, 1940; Caroline F. Ware, editor, *The Cultural Approach to History,* Columbia University Press, 1940; Richard W. Leopold and Arthur S. Link, editors, *Problems in American History,* Prentice-Hall, 1952, 4th edition, 1972; Pierce Butler, editor, *Librarians, Scholars and Booksellers at Mid-Century,* University of Chicago Press, 1953; John J. Murray, editor, *The Heritage of the Middle West,* University of Oklahoma Press, 1958; Brand Blanshard, editor, *Education in the Age of Science,* Basic Books, 1959.

Hiram Haydn and Betsy Saunders, editors, *The American Scholar Reader,* Atheneum, 1960; William H. Cartwright and Richard Watson, Jr., editors, *Interpreting and Teaching American History,* National Council for the Social Studies, 1961; Philip H. Phenix, editor, *Philosophies of Education,* Wiley, 1961; Russel Nye and W. R. Ebbitt, editors, *Structure in Reading and Writing,* Scott, Foresman, 1961; Abraham S. Eisenstadt, editor, *American History: Recent Interpretations,* Crowell, 1962, 2nd edition, 1969; A. C. Riccio and F. R. Cyphert, editors, *Teaching in America,* C. E. Merrill, 1962; Ronald Gross, editor, *The Teacher and the Taught,* Dell, 1963; Sidney Fine and Gerald S. Brown, editors, *The American Past: Conflicting Interpretations of the Great Issues,* 2nd edition (Bestor was not associated with earlier edition), Macmillan, 1965, 3rd edition, 1970; Eisenstadt, editor, *The Craft of American History,* Harper, 1966; R. E. Brown and J. C. Wahlke, editors, *The American Political System: Notes and Readings,* Dorsey, 1967; S. I. Kutler, editor, *The Dred Scott Decision: Law or Politics?,* Houghton, 1967; S. N. Katz and Kutler, editors, *New Perspectives on the American Past,* Little, Brown, 1969, 2nd edition, 1972; H. N. Scheiber, editor, *The Old Northwest,* University of Nebraska Press, 1969.

Rolland E. Stevens, editor, *Research Methods in Librarianship*, Graduate School of Library Science, University of Illinois, 1971; E. C. Drozdowski, editor, *American Civilization: Readings*, Scott, Foresman, 1972; John Porter Bloom, editor, *The American Territorial System*, Ohio University Press, 1973; Sol Cohen, editor, *Education in the United States: A Documentary History*, Random House, 1974; Sidney Hook, editor, *The Idea of a Modern University*, Promethens Books, 1974; L. M. Friedman and Sheiber, editors, *American Law and the Constitutional Order*, Harvard University Press, 1978.

Editor, *Proceedings* of Middle States Association of History and Social Studies Teachers, 1938-41. Contributor to magazines and professional journals, including the *New Republic, Good Housekeeping, Library Quarterly, Scientific Monthly, American Scholar,* and *American Historical Review.* Editor-in-chief, *Chatauquan Daily,* 1931-33; member of board of editors, *Mississippi Valley Historical Review,* 1951-54, and *American Quarterly,* 1963-64.

WORK IN PROGRESS: The "Right and Power of Determining on Peace and War": Distribution of Authority between Congress and President According to the Original Intent of the American Constitution; Commonwealths or Colonies in the West?: Basic Constitutional Issues in the Creation of the American Territorial System; Habeas Corpus; and Anglo-American Constitutionalism: 1591-1867; The Founding Fathers and the Dogma of Sovereignty; other articles and books on constitutional law and history.

SIDELIGHTS: Arthur Bestor divides his career into three distinct periods. While in graduate school and for several years after receiving his degree, he concentrated on the intellectual history of the United States, "particularly the history of social ideas and movements." This interest led to the writing of his first major book, *Backwoods Utopias,* of which J.F.C. Harrison writes in *Quest for the New Moral World,* "all previous work is largely superseded by Arthur Eugene Bestor's thorough and scholarly study."

In the 1950s, alarmed by declining academic standards in the public schools, Bestor turned his attention to a critical examination of progressive education, resulting in the publication of *Educational Wastelands* and *The Restoration of Learning.* Concerning Bestor's writing on education, Lawrence A. Cremin comments in *The Transformation of the School:* "Taken together, these writings constituted by far the most serious, searching, and influential criticisms of progressive education to appear during the fifties."

In the early 1960s, after his tenure as Harmsworth Professor of American History at Oxford University from 1956 to 1957, Bestor entered the third phase of his career as he began to devote more of his time to an in-depth study of American constitutional history. He cites the Oxford experience as the turning-point, explaining to *CA* that "lecturing to English students on slavery and antislavery, I found it more and more important to explain the way the Constitution itself shaped the course of the mid-nineteenth-century controversy and led to its culmination in civil war. . . . Most recently I have focused my attention on the period from the beginning of the American Revolution to the end of the eighteenth century, seeking to get at the original intention of the framers of the American Constitution."

Bestor has published several influential articles in the field of American constitutional history. On the basis of these and other essays, Henry Steele Commager, in a *New York Review of Books* article, referred to Bestor as "that most learned student of our constitutional system."

Several of Bestor's articles and essays have been reprinted as models of expository prose in nearly a dozen manuals on writing.

BIOGRAPHICAL/CRITICAL SOURCES: Lawrence A. Cremin, *The Transformation of the School: Progressivism in American Education,* Knopf, 1961; J.F.C. Harrison, *Quest for the New Moral World,* Scribner, 1969; *New York Review of Books,* September 30, 1976.

* * *

BETTERIDGE, Anne
   See POTTER, Margaret (Newman)

* * *

BIERNATZKI, William E(ugene)   1931-

PERSONAL: Born December 3, 1931, in Niles, Mich.; son of William Albert (in newspaper advertising) and Gertrude (Steck) Biernatzki. *Education:* St. Louis University, A.B., 1961, Ph.L., 1962, Ph.D., 1967. *Politics:* Independent. *Home:* 1, Sinsu Dong, Mapo Ku, Seoul, Korea. *Office:* Sogang University, CPO Box 1142, Seoul, Korea.

CAREER: Entered Roman Catholic order of Society of Jesus as lay brother, 1957; Sogang University, Seoul, Korea, instructor, 1964-67, assistant professor, 1967-71, associate professor, 1971-76, professor of anthropology, 1976—, chairman of department of sociology, 1981—, director of Social Research Institute, 1970-75, director of library, 1975-76, 1981—, director of Communication Research Institute, 1979-81. Acting research director, Centre for the Study of Communication and Culture (London), 1977. *Military service:* U.S. Army, 1953-57; became staff sergeant. *Member:* American Anthropological Association, Society for the Scientific Study of Religion, Korean Sociological Association, Korean Association for Cultural Anthropology.

WRITINGS: (With Francisco Claver and Vincent Cullen) *Bukidnon Politics and Religion,* Institute of Philippine Culture (Manila), 1973; (with Luke Jinchang Im and Anselm K. Min) *Korean Catholicism in the 1970's,* Orbis Books, 1975; *Catholic Communication Research: Topics and a Rationale* (pamphlet), Centre for the Study of Communication and Culture, 1978; *Media and Message Strategies for Educating Post-Korean War Children on Population and Family Planning,* Sogang University, 1979; (contributor) B. R. Crouch and S. Chamala, editors, *Extension Education and Rural Development,* Wiley, 1981. Columnist, *Hyondae Kyongyong,* 1974-76; Korean editor, *Letters from Asia,* 1972-76. Contributor to journals.

WORK IN PROGRESS: Religious Symbolism in Inter-cultural Communication; bibliography of symbolism in mass communication.

SIDELIGHTS: William Biernatzki writes: "As a Jesuit and social scientist I regard my role as supportive of the intellectual dimension of the Catholic missionary effort in East Asia. However, I understand this in the broad sense: that the sincere, rigorous search for scientific truth will ultimately serve religion as well as science. I have done research in the Philippines and Vietnam, as well as Korea, and have traveled extensively in other Southeast Asian nations. My current research interests center on the use of symbols in cross-cultural communication, particularly their religious uses. I speak Korean and read French."

* * *

BIGGS, John B(urville)   1934-

PERSONAL: Born October 25, 1934, in Hobart, Tasmania;

son of Oscar (a teacher) and Ella (Simeon) Biggs; married Ruth Dienes, January 3, 1960 (divorced, 1966); married Peggy Jack, June 6, 1969; children: (first marriage) Michael, Paul; (second marriage) Gregory, Stephen, Carolyn. *Education:* University of Tasmania, B.A. (with honors), 1956; Birkbeck College, London, Ph.D., 1963. *Home:* 48 Ian St., Eleebana, New South Wales 2280, Australia. *Office:* Department of Education, University of Newcastle, Shortland, New South Wales 2308, Australia.

CAREER: Teacher of mathematics in secondary school in Luton, Bedfordshire, England, 1957-58; National Foundation for Educational Research, London, England, research officer, 1958-62; University of New England, Armidale, Australia, lecturer in psychology, 1962-66; Monash University, Melbourne, Australia, educational research officer, 1966-69; University of Alberta, Edmonton, associate professor, 1969-72, professor of educational psychology, 1972-73; University of Newcastle, Shortland, New South Wales, Australia, professor of education, 1973—. Visiting professor at University of Victoria, 1971, and University of British Columbia, 1972. *Member:* International Society for Philosophical Enquiry, American Educational Research Association, Australian Association for Research into Education, Australian Psychological Society, British Psychological Society.

WRITINGS: Anxiety Motivation and Primary School Mathematics, National Foundation for Educational Research, 1963; *Mathematics and the Conditions of Learning,* National Foundation for Educational Research, 1967; *Information and Human Learning,* Cassell (Australia), 1968, Scott, Foresman, 1972; (with R. Telfer) *The Process of Learning,* Prentice-Hall (Australia), 1981; (with K. Collis) *Evaluating the Quality of Learning: The SOLO Taxonomy,* Academic Press, 1981. Contributor to education and psychology journals.

WORK IN PROGRESS: A science fiction novel, *Project Integrens;* a novel, *A Mess of Life;* research on student motivation, learning strategies, and learning quality.

SIDELIGHTS: John Biggs told *CA:* "Until very recently, nearly all my writing (over twenty years) has been technical, albeit, as an educational psychologist, about people. But a scientist can only go so far in experimenting with people. Change the structure of man's brain: how would he then behave? Science fiction released powerful motivational things in me I never thought existed. Fiction gives me a power over writing about people that psychology never gave. I only wish publishers agreed."

*   *   *

BILLIAS, George Athan   1919-

PERSONAL: Born June 26, 1919, in Lynn, Mass.; son of Athan O. and Grace (Papadakis) Billias; married Joyce Ann Baldwin, December 30, 1948; children: Stephen Woolman, Athan David, Nancy Susan. *Education:* Bates College, A.B. (magna cum laude), 1948; Columbia University, M.A., 1949, Ph.D., 1958. *Politics:* Democrat. *Home:* 50 Midland St., Worcester, Mass. 01602. *Office:* Department of History, Clark University, Worcester, Mass. 01610.

CAREER: University of Maine, Orono, associate professor of history, 1954-62; Clark University, Worcester, Mass., associate professor of history, beginning 1962. *Military service:* U.S. Army, Medical Corps, 1941-45; became first lieutenant, received Combat Medical Badge and Bronze Star. *Member:* Manuscript Society, American Historical Association, Organization of American Historians, Phi Beta Kappa. *Awards,*

honors: Guggenheim fellow, 1961-62; American Council of Learned Societies fellowship, 1968-69; National Endowment for the Humanities award, 1970-71.

WRITINGS: The Massachusetts Land Bankers of 1740, University of Maine, 1959; *General John Glover and His Marblehead Mariners,* Holt, 1960; (editor) *George Washington's Generals,* Morrow, 1964; (editor) *The American Revolution: How Revolutionary Was It?,* Holt, 1965, 3rd edition, 1980; (editor) *Law and Authority in Colonial America: Selected Essays,* Barre, 1965; (editor with Gerald N. Grob) *Interpretations of American History: Patterns and Perspectives,* two volumes, Free Press, 1967, 2nd edition, 1972; (editor) *George Washington's Opponents: British Generals and Admirals in the American Revolution,* Morrow, 1969.

(Editor) *The Federalists: Realists or Ideologues?,* Heath, 1970; (editor with Grob) *American History: Retrospect and Prospect,* Free Press, 1971; (editor with Thomas Balch) *The Examination of Joseph Galloway, Esq., by a Committee of the House of Commons,* Gregg, 1972; (editor with Charles K. Bolton) *Letters of Hugh, Earl of Percy, from Boston and New York, 1774-1776,* Gregg, 1972; (editor with Worthington C. Ford) *General Orders Issued by Major-General Israel Putnam,* Gregg, 1972; (editor with Victor H. Palsits) *Minutes of the Commissioners for Detecting and Defeating Conspiracies in the State of New York,* Gregg, 1972; (editor with William O. Raymond) *The Winslow Papers,* Gregg, 1972; (editor) James Rolfe, *The Naval Biography of Great Britain,* Gregg, 1972; (editor with Alden T. Vaughan) *Perspectives on Early American History: Essays in Honor of Richard B. Morris,* Harper, 1973; *Elbridge Gerry: Founding Father and Republican Statesman,* McGraw, 1976; (editor) *The History of the British Empire, from the Year 1765, to the End of 1783,* two volumes, Irvington, 1979; (editor) *The Revolution of America,* Irvington, 1979.

Also editor of *Manuscripts of Captain H. V. Knox,* Irvington, *Manuscripts of the Earl of Dartmouth,* three volumes, Irvington, *Report of the Manuscripts of Mrs. Stopford-Sackville of Drayton House, Northamptonshire,* Irvington, *Report on American Manuscripts in the Royal Institution of Great Britain,* four volumes, Irvington, and *The Centennial of the Settlement of Upper Canada by the United Empire Loyalists, 1784-1884,* Irvington.

BIOGRAPHICAL/CRITICAL SOURCES: New York Times Book Review, April 6, 1969; *New England Quarterly,* December, 1969.†

*   *   *

BISHOP, Morris   1893-1973
(W. Bolingbroke Johnson)

PERSONAL: Born April 15, 1893, in Willard, N.Y.; died November 20, 1973, in Ithaca, N.Y.; son of Edwin Rubergall and Bessie (Gilbert) Bishop; married Alison Mason Kingsbury, June 14, 1927; children: Alison. *Education:* Cornell University, A.B., 1913, M.A., 1914, Ph.D., 1926. *Religion:* Unitarian Universalist. *Residence:* Ithaca, N.Y.

CAREER: Cornell University, Ithaca, N.Y., instructor, 1921-26, assistant professor, 1926-36, professor of Romance languages and literature, 1936-60, professor emeritus, 1960-73, faculty trustee, 1957-60. Visiting professor, University of Athens, 1951-52. Member, American Relief Administration Mission to Finland, 1919; served with Office of War Information, New York and London, 1942-44, and with Psychological Warfare Division, U.S. Army, 1944-45. *Military service:* U.S. Army, Infantry, 1917-19; became first lieutenant. *Member:*

Modern Language Association of America (vice-president, 1959; president, 1964), American Academy of Arts and Sciences (fellow), National Institute of Arts and Letters, American Association of Teachers of French, P.E.N., Phi Beta Kappa, Century Club (New York). *Awards, honors:* Order of White Rose, Finland, 1919; Officier d'Academie, France, 1937; Chevalier, Legion d'Honneur, France, 1948; Dr. honoris causa, University of Rennes, 1948; D.Litt., Union College, 1953, University of Laval, 1954, Hofstra University, 1956, and Colgate University, 1959; Golden Rose of New England Poetry Club, 1959; Litt.D., Trent University, 1969.

WRITINGS: A Gallery of Eccentrics, Minton, Balch, 1928, reprinted, R. West, 1978; *Paramount Poems,* Minton, Balch, 1929; *Love Rimes of Petrarch,* Dragon Press, 1931; *The Odyssey of Cabeza de Vaca,* Century, 1933, reprinted, Greenwood Press, 1971; *Pascal, The Life of Genius,* Reynal & Hitchcock, 1936, reprinted, Greenwood Press, 1964; *Ronsard, Prince of Poets,* Oxford University Press, 1940, University of Michigan Press, 1959; *Spilt Milk,* Putnam, 1942; (under pseudonym W. Bolingbroke Johnson) *The Widening Stain,* Knopf, 1942; *Champlain: The Life of Fortitude,* Knopf, 1948, McClelland & Stewart, 1963, reprinted, Octagon, 1979; *The Life and Adventures of La Rochefoucauld,* Cornell University Press, 1951; *A Bowl of Bishop,* Dial, 1954; *White Men Came to St. Lawrence: The French and the Land They Found,* McGill University Press, 1961; *A History of Cornell,* Cornell University Press, 1962; *Petrarch and His World,* Indiana University Press, 1963; *Blaise Pascal: Life and Works,* Dell, 1966; *Early Cornell, 1865-1900,* Cornell University Press, 1967; *The Horizon Book of the Middle Ages,* Houghton, 1968, published as *The Middle Ages,* American Heritage Press, 1970; *The Exotics, being a Collection of Unique Personalities and Remarkable Characters,* American Heritage Press, 1969; *Saint Francis of Assisi,* Little, Brown, 1974; *The Best of Bishop: Light Verse from the New Yorker and Elsewhere,* Cornell University Press, 1980.

Editor: *Voltaire: Candide and Other Philosophical Tales,* Scribner, 1929, reprinted, 1957; *Casanova: L'Evasion des Plombs,* Holt, 1933; *A Treasury of British Humor,* Coward, 1942, reprinted, Books for Libraries, 1970; *A Survey of French Literature,* Volume I: *The Middle Ages to 1800,* Volume II: *The Nineteenth and Twentieth Centuries,* Harcourt, 1955, revised edition, 1965; *Letters from Petrarch,* Indiana University Press, 1966; *A Medieval Storybook,* Cornell University Press, 1970; *A Classical Storybook,* Cornell University Press, 1970; *A Renaissance Storybook,* Cornell University Press, 1971; *A Romantic Storybook,* Cornell University Press, 1971.

Translator: *Teodoro the Sage,* Liveright, 1922; Moliere, *The Would-be Invalid,* Appleton, 1950; *Eight Plays of Moliere,* Modern Library, 1957; (with Kenneth Muir) J. Guicharnaud, editor, *Seventeenth-Century French Drama,* Modern Library, 1976.

Contributor to periodicals, including *New Yorker* and *Horizon.*

WORK IN PROGRESS: A biography of Cola de Rienzo.†

*   *   *

BISSELL, Richard (Pike) 1913-1977

PERSONAL: Born June 27, 1913, in Dubuque, Iowa; died May 4, 1977, in Dubuque, Iowa; son of Frederick Ezekiel (an industrialist) and Edith Mary (Pike) Bissell; married Marian Van Patten Grilk (an editor and writer), February 5, 1938; children: Thomas, Nathaniel, Anastasia, Samuel. *Education:* Harvard University, B.S., 1936. *Politics:* Independent. *Residence:* Du-

buque, Iowa. *Agent:* Harold Matson Co., Inc., 22 East 40th St., New York, N.Y. 10016. *Office:* American Trust Building, Dubuque, Iowa 52001.

CAREER: Affiliated with Polarizing Instrument Co., 1937; H. B. Glover Co., Dubuque, Iowa, factory superintendent, 1938-40, superintendent and stylist, 1944-52, vice-president, 1944-60; mate and pilot of tugboats, Central Barge Co., 1940-44; Bissell Towing & Transport Co., Dubuque, president, 1958-77. Held pilot and mate's licenses, all tonnage, for Upper Mississippi and Monongahela Rivers. *Member:* Screen Writers Guild, Dramatists Guild, Authors Guild, Mississippi Valley Association, Sons and Daughters of Pioneer Rivermen, Masters, Mates and Pilots Association, Amalgamated Tugboat Owners, Bowfin Yacht Club, Rockdale Athenaeum, The Lambs and Harvard Club (both New York). *Awards, honors:* Antoinette Perry Award, 1954, and Donaldson Award, 1955, both for "The Pajama Game."

WRITINGS—Published by Little, Brown, except as indicated: *A Stretch on the River* (novel), 1950: *The Monongahela,* Rinehart, 1952; *7½ Cents* (novel; Book-of-the-Month Club selection; also see below), 1953 (published in England as *Gross of Pajamas,* Secker & Warburg, 1954); *High Water* (novel), 1954; *Say Darling* (novel; also see below), 1957; *Goodbye Ava* (novel), 1961; *You Can Always Tell a Harvard Man,* McGraw, 1962; *Still Circling Moose Jaw* (novel), McGraw, 1965; *How Many Miles to Galena?; or, Baked, Hashed Brown, or French Fried?,* 1968; *Julia Harrington, Winnebago, Iowa, 1913* (novel), 1969; *My Life on the Mississippi; or, Why I Am Not Mark Twain,* 1973; *New Light on 1776 and All That,* 1975.

Plays: (With George Abbott) *The Pajama Game* (musical comedy; based on his novel *7½ Cents;* produced on Broadway at St. James Theatre, May 13, 1954), Random House, 1954; (with Abe Burrows and wife, Marian Bissell) *Say Darling* (musical comedy; based on his novel of same title; produced on Broadway at ANTA Theatre, May 3, 1958), Little, Brown, 1958. Assisted George Abbott and Douglas Wallop on book for "Damn Yankees," produced on Broadway at Forty-Sixth Street Theatre, May 5, 1955. Co-author of screen play, "The Pajama Game" (based on his novel and play), produced by Warner Brothers, 1957. Contributor of short stories to national magazines and anthologies.

SIDELIGHTS: Two major influences on the subject matter of Richard Bissell's writing are easily surmised from his career: his experiences as mate and pilot on the inland waterways of America and his connection with his family's pajama factory. His novel, *7½ Cents,* written while he was vice-president of his family's factory, is about a strike at a fictional firm, Sleep Tite Pajama Co. of Junction City. Critics and readers enjoyed its natural dialogue and appealing picture of Midwestern life. Some critics likened Bissell to Ring Lardner or Sinclair Lewis. The play adaptation, produced as "Pajama Game," ran on Broadway for 1063 performances. The subsequent movie starred Doris Day and John Raitt.

Although Bissell lived in the New York City area for many years, he considered the upper Mississippi his real home. He once commented that he "did not like New York and suburbia in which I live," and when he retired from active writing in 1975 he returned to his hometown of Dubuque, Iowa.

AVOCATIONAL INTERESTS: Collecting American antiques, junk, steam engines, and old vehicles; mountaineering, boating, history.

BIOGRAPHICAL/CRITICAL SOURCES: New York Herald Tribune Book Review, July 30, 1950, October 24, 1954; *Business Week,* June 5, 1954; *New York Times Book Review,* September 26, 1954, September 9, 1956, October 23, 1960, November 23, 1969; *Newsweek,* April 14, 1968; *Life,* May 12, 1958.

OBITUARIES: New York Times, May 5, 1977; *Newsweek,* May 16, 1977; *Publishers Weekly,* May 23, 1977.†

* * *

BITTEL, Lester Robert 1918-

PERSONAL: Surname rhymes with "little"; born December 9, 1918, in East Orange, N.J.; son of William Frederick (a tradesman) and Helen (Korte) Bittel; married Muriel Albers Walcutt, May 8, 1972. *Education:* Lehigh University, B.S. in Industrial Engineering, 1940; James Madison University, M.B.A., 1974. *Politics:* Democrat. *Religion:* Unitarian Universalist. *Home:* 106 Breezewood Ter., Bridgewater, Va. 22812. *Office:* James Madison University, Harrisonburg, Va. 22807.

CAREER: Leeds & Northrup Co., Philadelphia, Pa., field engineer, 1940-46; Western Electric Co., Kearny, N.J., industrial engineer, 1947; Koppers Co., Inc., plant superintendent at Kearny, N.J., 1947-52, training director at Pittsburgh, Pa., 1952-54; McGraw-Hill Book Co., Inc., New York, N.Y., editor, *Factory* (business paper), 1954-70, director of information systems, 1971-72; Lord Fairfax Community College, Middletown, Va., instructor in management, 1972-74; James Madison University, Harrisonburg, Va., professor of management, 1975—. Member of public information committee, National Safety Council, 1959—, and of industrial board, national board of Young Men's Christian Association, 1965; vice-president of board of trustees of Chilton Memorial Hospital, 1960—. Technical adviser for six films on supervisory problems produced by McGraw-Hill Book Co. *Military service:* U.S. Army Air Forces, 1942-46; became first lieutenant.

MEMBER: American Society of Mechanical Engineers (fellow), American Society for Training and Development, Overseas Press Club, Phi Kappa Phi. *Awards, honors:* Jesse Neale Award of Merit, American Business Press, 1957, 1959, 1960, 1961, 1969; citation from American Society of Mechanical Engineers, 1967, for outstanding engineering leadership; G. M. Loeb Award, International Management Council, 1968, for distinguished business and financial journalism; William McFeeley Award, International Management Council, 1978, for contributions to management and education; Centennial Award and Frederick W. Taylor Award, American Society of Mechanical Engineers, both 1980.

WRITINGS—Published by McGraw, except as indicated: (With Melden and Rice) *Practical Automation,* 1956; *What Every Supervisor Should Know,* 1959, 4th edition, 1980; *Management by Exception,* 1964; (with Robert Craig) *Training and Development Handbook,* 1967.

The Nine Master Keys of Management, 1972; *Improving Supervisory Performance,* 1976; *Shenandoah Management Games for Supervisors,* 1978; *Encyclopedia of Professional Management,* 1979; *Introduction to Business in Action,* 1980; *Essentials of Supervisory Management,* 1981; (with Ronald Burke) *Introduction to Management Practice,* 1981; *Executive Skills Program,* Alexander Hamilton Institute, 1981. Author of film scenario "The Case of the Snarled Parking Lot," for CRM/McGraw-Hill Films, 1981.

SIDELIGHTS: Lester Robert Bittel told *CA:* "Writing is compulsive to me. My technique is to develop an outline while walking or driving, sketch it out while watching television, then put it together in pieces and bits at every available odd moment. If I'm waiting for breakfast, find a few minutes before

class, or whatever idle time arises, I try to make it productive. My other idea is to try to modularize all my writing, that is, to develop an effective chapter format with from five to ten elements, then use this as a framework for all chapters. It is relatively easy to construct a module, and the need for continuity is lessened by it. I keep an enormous, but not particularly well-organized, file of reference materials. I try to subscribe to everything in or near my field of interest. I rarely read a consumer magazine or a newspaper [without] searching for incidents and examples to include in my writing.

"Writing is easy for people who can articulate an idea. The difference is mainly one of organization, materials, and persistence. I'm continually surprised by talented people who can't get it together."

Bittel's books have been translated into Danish, Dutch, Indian, Japanese, and Spanish. His papers have been placed in the Archive of Contemporary History of the University of Wyoming in Laramie.

* * *

BIXBY, William (Courtney) 1920-

PERSONAL: Born June 15, 1920, in San Diego, Calif.; son of Vernon Chamberlain and Courtney (Rudd) Bixby; married Elizabeth L. Knight, 1944; married Susan Babbitt, November 25, 1972; children: (previous marriage) William, Jr., Barbara Ruth. *Education:* Virginia Polytechnic Institute (now Virginia Polytechnic Institute and State University), B.S., 1942.

CAREER: Cowles Magazines, Inc., New York City, staff writer, 1945-47; Famous Artists School, Westport, Conn., editor and writer, 1947-49; Cowles Magazines, Inc., editor and writer, 1949-51; Time, Inc., New York City, associate editor, 1951-53; free-lance writer, beginning 1953. Museum director, beginning 1968. Secondary school and college teacher. *Military service:* U.S. Army, Signal Corps and Air Corps, European Theater campaign; became first lieutenant; received Air Medal. *Awards, honors:* Thomas Alva Edison Foundation Award, 1964, for *The Universe of Galileo and Newton.*

WRITINGS—Published by McKay, except as indicated: *The Impossible Journey of Sir Ernest Shackleton* (Junior Literary Guild selection), Atlantic-Little, Brown, 1960; *The Race to the South Pole,* Longmans, Green, 1961; *Havoc: The Story of Natural Disasters,* Longmans, Green, 1961; *McMurdo, Antarctica,* 1962; *Skywatchers: The U.S. Weather Bureau in Action* (Junior Literary Guild selection), 1962; *Waves: Pathways of Energy,* 1963; *Great Experimenters,* 1964; *The Universe of Galileo and Newton,* American Heritage Publishing, 1964; *Track of the Bear,* 1965; *The Forgotten Voyage of Charles Wilkes,* 1966; *Seawatchers: Oceanographers in Action,* 1967; *Of Animals and Men: A Comparison of Human and Animal Behavior,* 1968.

Rebel Genius: The Life of Herman Melville, 1970; *Robert Scott, Antarctic Pioneer,* Lippincott, 1970; *A World You Can Live In,* 1971; *South Street: New York's Seaport Museum,* 1972; *Connecticut: A New Guide,* Scribner, 1974; *The Hang Gliding Book,* 1978; *Whitewater Sport,* 1978; *Hurricanes,* 1979; *Skydiving and Parachuting,* 1980.

WORK IN PROGRESS: Modern Experimenters.

AVOCATIONAL INTERESTS: Collecting American first editions; antiques and sailing.†

* * *

BLACK, Ian Stuart 1915-

PERSONAL: Born March 21, 1915, in London, England; son

of Stuart and Hilda (Robertson) Black; married Winifred Williamson, February 2, 1931; children: Isobel Anne, Moray, Alison, Alan. *Education:* University of Manchester, B.A. (with honors). *Politics:* Liberal. *Religion:* Church of Scotland.

CAREER: Rank Organisation, Pinewood Studios, London, England, script writer, 1946-49; Associated Television, London, story editor, 1958-64; Granada Television, London, story editor, 1964-65; writer for British and European films, beginning 1965. Company director of Isby Enterprises Ltd. and Telewriters Ltd. *Military service:* Royal Air Force, intelligence officer, 1941-46; became flying officer. *Member:* British Screenwriters Guild (honorary secretary, 1956-58).

WRITINGS: In the Wake of a Stranger, Dakers, 1953; *The Passionate City,* Viking, 1958; *The Yellow Flag,* Hutchinson, 1959; *Love in Four Countries,* Hutchinson, 1961; *The High Bright Sun* (novel), Hutchinson, 1962; *The Man on the Bridge,* St. Martin's, 1975; *Caribbean Strip,* Constable, 1978; *Journey to a Safe Place,* St. Martin's, 1979.

Plays: *We Must Kill Toni* (three-act comedy), Samuel French, 1952; *Nothing Legal* (one-act play), Evans Brothers, 1959; *Even Less Legal,* Evans Brothers, 1964; "Shooting Party" (three-act comedy), first produced in England, 1966, produced at Devonshire Park, Eastbourne, October 12, 1970.

Also author of several screenplays produced on television, including "The Trial of Mary, Queen of Scots," "Ransom for a Pretty Girl," "Wildcat," "The Dummy Run," and "Sunday Collection." Author of screenplay "The High Bright Sun" (based on novel of same title), Rank Organization, 1965; adaptor of Sir Walter Scott's "Red Gauntlet" for television production. Story editor of about 150 television films and author of about 80 television scripts. Contributor to *Guardian.*

WORK IN PROGRESS: A novel; a television series.

AVOCATIONAL INTERESTS: Literature, criticism, travel, sport, art, and money.†

*   *   *

BLACK, Irma Simonton   1906-1972

PERSONAL: Born June 6, 1906, in Paterson, N.J.; died June 18(?), 1972, of stab wounds, in New York, N.Y.; daughter of John Vandervoort and Lida (Duke) Simonton; married James Hammond Black, 1934; children: Constance K. *Education:* Barnard College, A.B., 1927; Bank Street College of Education, graduate study, 1930-31; attended New York University, 1934-40. *Religion:* Protestant. *Office:* Bank Street College of Education, 69 Bank St., New York, N.Y.

CAREER: Bank Street College of Education, New York, N.Y., nursery school teacher, 1931-36, testing and research, 1936-43, teacher of children's literature, 1945-72, chairman of publications and communications, 1951-72. *Member:* National Association for Nursery Education, Phi Beta Kappa. *Awards, honors:* Honorable mention, *Parents'* Magazine, for book for parents.

WRITINGS—Juveniles; all published by Holiday House, except as indicated: *Hamlet: A Cocker Spaniel,* 1938; *Kip, a Young Rooster,* 1939; *Flipper, a Sea-Lion,* 1940; (author of adaptation) *This Is the Bread That Betsy Ate,* W. R. Scott, 1945; *Barbara's Birthday,* W. R. Scott, 1946; *The Dog Doctor,* W. R. Scott, 1947; *Toby, a Curious Cat,* 1948; *Spoodles, the Puppy Who Learned,* W. R. Scott, 1948; *Maggie, a Mischievous Magpie,* 1949; *Dusty and His Friends,* 1950; *Pudge, a Summertime Mixup,* 1953; *Pete the Parakeet,* 1954; *Night Cat,* 1957; *Busy Water,* 1958; *The Troublemaker,* Knopf, 1959; *Big*

Puppy and Little Puppy, 1960; *Castle, Abbey and Town: How People Lived in the Middle Ages,* 1963; *The Little Old Man Who Could Not Read,* Albert Whitman, 1968; *Busy Winds,* 1968; *Busy Seeds,* 1970; *Little Old Man Who Cooked and Cleaned,* Albert Whitman, 1970; *Doctor Proctor and Mrs. Meriwether,* Albert Whitman, 1971; *Is This My Dinner?,* Albert Whitman, 1972.

Adult books: *Off to a Good Start: A Handbook for Modern Parents,* Harcourt, 1946, revised edition, 1953; *Life and Ways of Seven- to Eight-Year-Olds,* Harcourt, 1952; (editor with Lucy Sprague Mitchell) *Believe and Make Believe,* Dutton, 1956. Columnist, *PM,* 1944-49, *Redbook,* 1950-59, and *Saturday Review,* 1959-61. Contributor of articles or reviews to *Ladies' Home Journal, Art in America, New York Times,* and other periodicals. Senior editor and contributor, "The Bank Street Readers," basic reading series for grades 1-3, Macmillan, 1966-72; senior editor and co-author, "Early Childhood Discovery" materials, Macmillan, 1968-72.

WORK IN PROGRESS: Additional children's books.

AVOCATIONAL INTERESTS: Travel, music, theater, books, swimming.

OBITUARIES: New York Times, June 19, 1972.†

*   *   *

BLAKE, Jonas
See HARDY, C. Colburn

*   *   *

BLOCK, Lawrence   1938-

PERSONAL: Born June 24, 1938, in Buffalo, N.Y.; son of Arthur Jerome and Lenore (Nathan) Block; married Loretta Ann Kallett, 1960; children: Amy Jo, Jill Diana. *Education:* Attended Antioch College, 1955-59.

CAREER: Scott Meredith, Inc., New York, N.Y., editor, 1957-58; full-time writer, beginning 1958. *Member:* American Academy of Political and Social Sciences, American Numismatic Association, Middle Atlantic Numismatic Association. *Awards, honors:* Nero Wolfe Award for Best Mystery of 1979, for *The Burglar Who Liked to Quote Kipling.*

WRITINGS: Mona, Fawcett, 1961; *Death Pulls a Doublecross,* Fawcett, 1961; *Markham, the Case of the Pornographic Photos,* Belmont Books, 1961; *The Girl with the Long Green Heart,* Fawcett, 1965; *A Guide Book of Australian Coins,* Whitman Publishing, 1965; (with Delbert Ray Krause) *Swiss Shooting Talers and Medals,* Whitman Publishing, 1965; *Canceled Czech,* Fawcett, 1967; *Ronald Rabbit Is a Dirty Old Man,* Geis, 1971; *In the Midst of Death,* Dell, 1976; *Burglars Can't Be Choosers,* Random House, 1977; *Time to Murder and Create,* Dell, 1977; *The Burglar in the Closet,* Random House, 1978; *The Burglar Who Liked to Quote Kipling,* Random House, 1979; *Writing the Novel: From Plot to Print,* Writer's Digest, 1979; *Ariel,* Arbor House, 1980; *The Burglar Who Studied Spinoza,* Random House, 1981. Also author of *Manuscripts, 1960-69* (correspondence and reminiscences) and of novels under pseudonyms.

"Cock Robin Mystery" series, published by Macmillan: *Deadly Honeymoon,* 1967; *After the First Death,* 1969; *Me Tanner, You Jane,* 1970. Associate editor, *Whitman Numismatic Journal,* beginning 1964.

WORK IN PROGRESS: Leave a Light for the Burglar.

SIDELIGHTS: Lawrence Block's "Bernie" series of detective novels has won broad critical approval. Protagonist Bernard Grimes Rhodenbarr, better known as Bernie, is a burglar and a bibliophile with expensive tastes. A *Chicago Tribune* critic, reviewing *The Burglar Who Studied Spinoza*, notes that "Bernie's world abounds with New Yorky things—addresses, restaurants, behaviors—and is peopled both by low-lifes and the wine-and-cheese crowd." According to that critic, "clues are sprinkled liberally across Block's breezy, tightly written pages, and you don't have to be a whiz to figure [the plot] out. . . . Block and Bernie play fair, though, and I like that. A nicely soft-boiled read." Jean M. White adds in the *Washington Post Book World* that "mystery writers with the comic touch are rare, and Block is one of the best."

John McAleer agrees with White, writing in the *Chicago Tribune Book World* that "Bernie wins our hearts because Block's keen comic touch envelopes him." But other qualities also contribute to Bernie's persuasiveness, says McAleer; unlike protagonists on the right side of the law, Bernie "is refreshingly forthright. He doesn't pretend to be Robin Hood redistributing the wealth for the common good." Bernie admits that his activities are "morally reprehensible, and there are days when it bothers me. But there's no getting around it, I'm a thief and I love to steal. I just plain love it." At the same time, Bernie wins readers because he does have scruples, claims McAleer: "In an inversion of normalcy that Lewis Carroll could not fault, a man bent on supporting himself by breaking the law finds himself, time and again, compelled by necessity and his own bedrock decency, to restore to society the stability it professes to cherish but which, by its transgressions, it puts in jeopardy."

AVOCATIONAL INTERESTS: Old subway cars.

BIOGRAPHICAL/CRITICAL SOURCES: Washington Post Book World, February 3, 1980, February 15, 1981; *Chicago Tribune Book World,* October 19, 1980; *New York Times,* January 14, 1981; *Chicago Tribune,* March 4, 1981.†

* * *

BLOCK, Walter (Edward) 1941-

PERSONAL: Born August 21, 1941, in New York, N.Y.; son of Abraham (an accountant) and Ruth (Peps) Block. *Education:* Brooklyn College of the City University of New York, B.A., 1964; Columbia University, Ph.D., 1972. *Politics:* "Libertarian." *Religion:* None. *Residence:* Vancouver, British Columbia, Canada.

CAREER: National Bureau of Economic Research, Washington, D.C., research analyst, 1967; Bronx Community College of the City University of New York, Bronx, N.Y., instructor in economics, 1967-68; State University of New York at Stony Brook, instructor in economics, 1968; Rutgers University, New Brunswick, N.J., assistant professor of economics, 1968-71; Bernard M. Baruch College of the City University of New York, New York, N.Y., assistant professor of economics, 1971-74; *Business Week* (magazine), New York, N.Y., assistant editor, 1974-75; free-lance writer, 1975—; Fraser Institute, Vancouver, British Columbia, Canada, currently senior economist. Instructor at New York University, 1970, and City College of the City University of New York, 1972.

MEMBER: American Economic Association, Canadian Economic Association, Canadian Association for Business Economists, British Columbia Association of Professional Economists. *Awards, honors:* Earhart fellowship, 1966-68; Cato Institute research fellow, 1977-78; Fraser Institute visiting fellow, 1979.

WRITINGS: Defending the Undefendable: Pimps, Prostitutes, Libelers, Slanderers, Blackmailers, and Other Heroes in the Rogues Gallery of American Society, Fleet Press, 1975; (editor) *Zoning: Its Costs and Perspectives for the 1980s,* Fraser Institute, 1980; (editor with Edgar Olsen and contributor) *Rent Control: Myths and Realities,* Fraser Institute, 1981; (editor) *Minority Rights and Wrongs: An Economic and Social Perspective on Discrimination and Equal Opportunity,* Fraser Institute, 1981. Columnist, *Financial Post.* Contributor to *Journal of Libertarian Studies, American Economist,* and *International Journal for Housing Science.*

* * *

BLOOM, Lynn Marie Zimmerman 1934-

PERSONAL: Born July 11, 1934, in Ann Arbor, Mich.; daughter of Oswald Theodore (a professor of chemical engineering) and Mildred (Kisling) Zimmerman; married Martin Bloom (a social psychologist), July 11, 1958; children: Bard, Laird. *Education:* University of Michigan, B.A., 1956, M.A., 1957, Ph.D., 1963; Ohio State University, graduate study, 1957-58. *Politics:* Liberal. *Home:* 302 Mill Neck Rd., Williamsburg, Va. 23185. *Office:* Department of English, Virginia Commonwealth University, Richmond, Va. 23220.

CAREER: Western Reserve University (now Case Western Reserve University), Cleveland, Ohio, lecturer, 1962-63, instructor, 1963-65, associate in English, 1965-67; full-time writer, 1967-70; Butler University, Indianapolis, Ind., assistant professor, 1970-73, associate professor of English, 1973-74; University of New Mexico, Albuquerque, associate professor of English and director of freshman English, 1975-78; College of William and Mary, Williamsburg, Va., associate professor of English and director of writing program, 1978-81; Virginia Commonwealth University, Richmond, professor of English and chairman of department, 1982—. Judge of various writing contests, 1973—; conductor of writers' workshops, 1978—. Advisor to Indiana Commission on the Humanities project on Indiana racial history, 1973—; consultant in writing research, 1978—. *Member:* Modern Language Association of America, National Council of Teachers of English, American Association of University Professors, College Conference on Composition and Communication (member of executive council, 1980-82), Popular Culture Association, South Atlantic Modern Language Association, Phi Beta Kappa, Phi Kappa Phi, Alpha Lambda Delta, Omicron Delta Kappa. *Awards, honors:* National fiction award, *Mademoiselle* College Board Contest, 1955; Outstanding Educator, Butler University, 1972-73, 1973-74; faculty fellowship, Butler University, 1974; faculty research grants, University of New Mexico, 1976, 1977, 1978; National Endowment for the Humanities grant, 1979-81; U.S. Office of Education grant, Eastern Virginia Writing Project, 1979-81; writing research grant, George Mason University, 1981.

WRITINGS: (Editor with Francis L. Utley and Arthur F. Kinney) *Bear, Man, and God: Seven Approaches to William Faulkner's "The Bear,"* Random House, 1964, revised edition, 1971; (editor with Kinney and Kenneth W. Kuiper) *Symposium,* Houghton, 1969; (editor with Kinney and Kuiper) *Symposium on Love,* Houghton, 1970; *Doctor Spock: Biography of a Conservative Radical,* Bobbs-Merrill, 1972; (with Karen Coburn and Joan Pearlman) *The New Assertive Woman,* Delacorte, 1975; (editor) Natalie Crouter, *Forbidden Diary: A Record of Wartime Internment, 1941-1945,* B. Franklin, 1980; *Strategies for Composition,* Random House, 1981; (with Mary Briscoe) *Bibliography of American Autobiography, 1945-1980,* University of Wisconsin Press, 1982; *Writing Nonfiction,* Heath, in press. Regular contributor to *Abstracts of English Studies,* 1961-68. Regular contributor of book reviews to *St. Louis Post-Dispatch* and *Cleveland Plain Dealer;* contributor of articles on biography, world literature, popular culture, and the teaching and learning of writing (several with husband, Martin Bloom) to scholarly journals; contributor of poetry and reviews to magazines and journals. Member of editorial board, *Journal of English Teaching Techniques,* 1976—, and *Writing Program Administrators,* 1981—.

WORK IN PROGRESS: A book on autobiographical theory and practice; *I Hate/Love to Write: Overcoming Writing Anxiety,* with husband, Martin Bloom.

SIDELIGHTS: Lynn Marie Bloom writes: "To write is to live. To write uncomfortably—with excessive procrastination, fear of known or unknown readers' reactions, or at such a slow rate that deadlines and the writer suffer—is to live unhappily. The research and writing that my husband and I are currently doing with anxious writers is intended to help all writers and would-be writers write more happily than they might otherwise do."

Forbidden Diary has been optioned to CBS-TV for production as a two-hour special.

AVOCATIONAL INTERESTS: Cooking, swimming, travel.

*   *   *

BLUM, Henrik L(eo)   1915-

PERSONAL: Born November 11, 1915, in San Francisco, Calif.; son of Haiman and Pauline Blum; married Marian Haas Ehrich, December 24, 1938. *Education:* University of California, Berkeley, B.S., 1937; University of California, San Francisco, M.D., 1942; postdoctoral study at Johns Hopkins University, 1945, and Stanford University, 1947; Harvard University, M.P.H., 1948. *Home:* 1148 Grizzly Bear Blvd., Berkeley, Calif. 94708. *Office:* Department of City Planning, University of California, Berkeley, Calif. 94720.

CAREER: Chief of preventive medical services, San Diego County Health Department, 1948-50; health officer, Contra Costa County, 1950-66; Stanford University, Stanford, Calif., associate in medicine, beginning 1962; University of California, Berkeley, clinical professor of public health, 1963-68, professor of community health planning, 1968—. Senior assistant surgeon, U.S. Public Health Service. Member of Committee on Social and Physical Environment Variables as Determinants of Mental Health and of Special Grants Review Committee, National Institute of Mental Health. Member of California Advisory Hospital Council, 1961-65, and Governor of California's Committee on Children and Youth, 1964-67.

MEMBER: American Public Health Association (chairman of chronic disease and rehabilitation committee; member of technical development board; member of governing council, 1967—), American Medical Association, American College of Preventive Medicine, California Medical Association, Northern California Public Health Association, Alameda-Contra Costa Medical Association. *Awards, honors:* Western States Tuberculosis award, 1961; World Health Organization fellowship grant, 1962, to study multipurpose workers in four countries.

WRITINGS: (With Henry B. Peters and Jerome W. Bettman) *Vision for Elementary Schools: The Orinda Study,* University of California Press, 1959; (with Alvin R. Leonard) *Public Administration—A Public Health Viewpoint,* Macmillan, 1963; *Control of Chronic Diseases in Man,* American Public Health Association, 1966; *Notes on Comprehensive Planning for Health,* American Public Health Association, 1968, 2nd edition, 1969;

Planning for Health: Development and Application of Social Change Theory, Human Sciences, 1974; *Expanding Health Care Horizons: From a General Systems Concept of Health to a National Health Policy,* Third Party Associates, 1976.

WORK IN PROGRESS: Multipurpose home visitor research project.†

*   *   *

BLUMBERG, Rhoda L(ois Goldstein)   1926-
(Rhoda L. Goldstein)

PERSONAL: Born February 3, 1926, in Brooklyn, N.Y.; divorced; children: Leah, Meyer Harold, Helena Jo. *Education:* Brooklyn College (now Brooklyn College of the City University of New York), B.A., 1946; New School for Social Research, M.A., 1948; University of Chicago, Ph.D., 1954. *Residence:* New York, N.Y. *Office:* Department of Sociology, Douglass College, Rutgers University, New Brunswick, N.J. 08903.

CAREER: Part-time teacher in Chicago, Ill., 1947-48, and Brooklyn, N.Y., 1948-56; consultant on special project for Rockefeller Foundation, University of Chicago, Chicago, 1956; Rutgers University, Douglass College, New Brunswick, N.J., part-time instructor, 1957-61, lecturer, 1962-68, assistant professor, 1968-71, associate professor, 1971-80, professor of sociology, 1980—. Chairman of Franklin Township Civil Rights Commission, 1961-62. Member of executive board of Committee to End Discrimination in Chicago Medical Institutions, 1953-55, Central Jersey Civil Rights Council, 1960-62, Parents' League for Educational Advancement, 1963-65, Highland Park Fair Housing Committee, 1965-66, Special Emergency Legal Force, 1970-72, and Greater New Brunswick Urban League, 1972-74. Organizer and first president of Pine Grove Manor Cooperative Nursery School, 1957-59. Consultant to Heritage Foundation.

MEMBER: American Sociological Association, Society for the Study of Social Problems (member of board of directors), Sociologists for Women in Society, Eastern Sociological Association. *Awards, honors:* Fulbright-Hays scholarship, 1966-67; award from New Jersey Teachers of English, for *Life and Culture of Black People in the United States.*

WRITINGS—All under name Rhoda L. Goldstein, except as indicated: (Contributor) Clifton O. Dummett, editor, *The Growth and Development of the Negro in Dentistry in the United States,* National Dental Association, 1952; (contributor) Arthur B. Shostak, editor, *Sociology in Action,* Dorsey, 1966; (with Bernard Goldstein) *Doctors and Nurses in Industry: Social Aspects of In-Plant Medical Programs* (monograph), Institute of Management and Labor Relations, Rutgers University, 1967; (contributor) F. Baker, P.J.M. McEwan, and A. Sheldon, editors, *Industrial Organizations and Health: Selected Readings,* Tavistock Publications, 1969.

(Editor and author of introduction) *Life and Culture of Black People in the United States,* Crowell, 1971; *Indian Women in Transition: A Bangalore Case Study,* Scarecrow, 1972; (with June T. Albert) *Black Studies Programs at American Colleges and Universities: A Preliminary Report* (pamphlet), Rutgers University, 1973; (contributor) J. V. Gordon and J. M. Rosser, editors, *The Black Studies Debate,* University Press of Kansas, 1974; (contributor) Dhirendra Narain, editor, *Explorations in the Family and Other Essays: Professor K. M. Kapadia Commemoration Volume,* Thacker & Co., 1975; (co-editor under name Rhoda L. Blumberg) *Interracial Bonds,* General Hall, 1979; (under name Rhoda L. Blumberg, with Lee Dwaraki)

India's Educated Women: Options and Constraints, Hindustan Publishing, 1980.

Contributor of more than twenty articles and reviews to sociology journals. Book review editor of *Journal of Asian and African Studies,* 1969-71.

WORK IN PROGRESS: The Civil Rights Movement, for G. K. Hall.

*   *   *

BODEN, Hilda
    See BODENHAM, Hilda Morris

*   *   *

BODENHAM, Hilda Morris   1901-
    (Hilda Boden, Pauline Welch)

PERSONAL: Born September 17, 1901, in Staffordshire, England; daughter of Thomas (a master tinsmith) and Mary (Draper) Morris; married Robert John William Bodenham (a former justice of peace, headmaster, and borough councillor), September 2, 1922 (died, 1968); children: Gillian Bredon Newton, Patricia Clee Dussek, Roger Mynd. *Education:* Educated in Birmingham, England. *Politics:* Conservative. *Religion:* Society of Friends.

CAREER: Writer. *Member:* Haverfordwest Soroptimist Club (secretary), Girl Guides.

WRITINGS—All under pseudonym Hilda Boden: *Pony Trek* (juvenile), Macmillan, 1948; *Family Affair: A Midland Chronicle,* Blue Book, 1948.

Bridge Club, Ronald, 1952; *One More Pony,* A. & C. Black, 1952, Macmillan, 1953; *Caravan Holiday,* Lutterworth, 1953; *Treasure Trove,* Lutterworth, 1955; *Marlows at Newgale,* Brockhampton Press, 1956; *Marlow Wins a Prize,* Brockhampton Press, 1957; *Marlow Digs for Treasure,* Brockhampton Press, 1958; *Two Lost Emeralds,* Abelard, 1958; *Pony Boy,* Lutterworth, 1958; *Marlows into Danger,* Brockhampton, 1959; *Pony Girl,* Lutterworth, 1959; *Two White Tents,* Thomas Nelson, 1959.

Joanna's Special Pony, Burke Publishing, 1960; *Marlows at Castle Cliff,* McKay, 1960; *Noel and the Donkey,* Burke Publishing, 1960; *The New Roof,* Thomas Nelson, 1960; *Little Grey Pony,* Lutterworth, 1960; *Marlows and the Regatta,* Brockhampton Press, 1961; *Faraway Farm* (Junior Literary Guild selection), McKay, 1961; *Joanna Rides the Hills,* Burke Publishing, 1961; *Noel's Happy Day,* Burke Publishing, 1961; *The House by the Sea,* McKay, 1962; *Marlow's Irish Holiday,* Brockhampton Press, 1962; *Noel's Christmas Holiday,* Burke Publishing, 1962; *Foxes in the Valley,* McKay, 1963; *Noel, the Brave,* Burke Publishing, 1963; *Marlow's Pigeon Post,* Brockhampton Press, 1963; *Water Wheel, Turn!,* McKay, 1964; *Noel, the Explorer,* Burke Publishing, 1965; (with Sheila Chapman) *Pony Adventure,* Burke Publishing, 1965; *Highland Holiday,* McKay, 1965; *Job for Noel,* Burke Publishing, 1966; *Peter and Pippin,* Wheaton, 1966; *The Mystery of Castle Croome,* McKay, 1966; *Wonderful Penny Stamp,* Burke Publishing, 1968; *The Mystery of Island Keep,* McKay, 1968; *Canal House,* Burke Publishing, 1969; *Storm over Wales,* McKay, 1969.

Ward of the King, Collins, 1970; *The Severnside Mystery,* McKay, 1970; *Pedro Visits the Country,* Burke Publishing, 1970; *Boomerang,* Burke Publishing, 1973. Contributor to *Punch, Times* (London), *Homes and Gardens, Spectator,* and other magazines.

WORK IN PROGRESS: Marlows in Town, for Brockhampton Press; a book of illustrated rhymes for children.

SIDELIGHTS: Hilda Morris Bodenham wrote *CA:* "As I married very young, and had a family of three, it was some years before I found time to write. Certainly I told stories for my own children, often sitting by an open fire toasting crumpets, in what seem far-off days when there WERE open fires. I have always written poetry, and much of it has been published, but it was not until I was fortyish that I started writing for the press. These were mainly articles—'short stuff'—that dealt with the routine things that happened to me. I remember that my lack of success with a potter's wheel led to some financial success with our monthly humorous magazine *Punch.* My children's experiences with dogs and ponies were turned into adult articles for the 'Home' magazines. Ultimately, of course, I wrote my first children's book, and, equally, of course, it was about ponies—this was *Pony Trek.*

"I think I had written about six books in the Marlow series when I grew bored with the same family, that never grew up, so I wrote another book, and called it *Faraway Farm.* It is still my favourite book for children. I was indeed fortunate, because it was chosen as Junior Literary Guild selection, and I believe at that time Eleanor Roosevelt headed the committee—this still pleases me very much. *Faraway Farm* has been used as a school book, and must have found its way to many parts of the world—I've had letters about it from Africa, Holland, and Australia, as well, of course, as from readers in this country. Which reminds me to add that I have learned a lot, myself, from these letters from American readers. Living in so small a country as England, it is sometimes easy to overlook the vastness of the United States and that even such things as sunset and sunrise can vary so greatly within one country. I also realised this when I visited my son in Australia . . . and, as a result of the visit, wrote a book about school life 'down-under.' I think it is more like life in your schools than in our English ones. This book is called *Boomerang.*

"I do not think I shall write more children's books—at my age, I might be a little out of touch with very junior readers!—but I write more poetry, and am very interested in things of a future so distant that these readers might not be interested in them—spiritual matters. These are important, and I hope you will all grow to recognise this some day."

AVOCATIONAL INTERESTS: Watercolor sketching, gardening, local archaeology.†

*   *   *

BOISSEVAIN, Jeremy   1928-

PERSONAL: Born August 5, 1928, in London, England; son of Cornelis Alfred (a businessman) and Mildred (Goerwitz) Boissevain; married Inga Otterstrand, March 29, 1952; children: Ieneke, Liet, Maria, Anna. *Education:* Sorbonne, University of Paris, Diplome, 1951; Haverford College, B.A., 1952; London School of Economics and Political Science, Ph.D., 1962. *Office:* Department of European and Mediterranean Studies, University of Amsterdam, Sarphatiestraat 106, 1018 GV Amsterdam, Holland.

CAREER: CARE (Cooperative for American Relief Everywhere), New York, N.Y., chief of mission in the Philippines, Japan, India, and Malta, 1953-58; Centro Regionale per lo Sviluppo di Comunita, Sicily, research director, 1962-63; University of Montreal, Montreal, Quebec, assistant professor of social anthropology, 1963-65; University of Sussex, Brighton, England, lecturer in sociology, 1965-66; University of Amsterdam, Amsterdam, Holland, professor of social anthropology, 1966—. Visiting professor at University of Malta and University of Sussex. Consultant to Prime Minister of Malta, British Broadcasting Corp., and UNESCO. *Military service:* U.S. Army, 1946-48.

MEMBER: American Anthropological Association, Royal Anthropological Institute of Great Britain, Commonwealth Association of Social Anthropologists, Association of Sociologists and Anthropologists of the Netherlands, Netherlands Association of Europeanist Anthropologists, Malta Union Club.

AWARDS, HONORS: Research grants from Colonial Social Research Council, 1960-61, American Philosophical Society, 1963—, Canadian Social Science Research Council, 1964—, U.S. Social Science Research Council, 1965—, Wenner-Gren Foundation for Anthropological Research, 1967—, and Netherlands Association for Pure Scientific Research, 1968—; University of Amsterdam research fellowship, 1973-74, 1980.

WRITINGS: Saints and Fireworks: Religion and Politics in Rural Malta, Humanities Press, 1965, revised edition, 1969; *Hal-Farrug: A Village in Malta,* Holt, 1969; *The Italians of Montreal: Social Adjustment in a Plural Society,* Information Canada, 1970; (editor with J. Clyde Mitchell) *Network Analysis: Studies in Human Interaction,* Mouton & Co., 1973; *Friends of Friends: Networks, Manipulators, and Coalitions,* St. Martin's, 1974; (editor with John Friedl) *Beyond the Community: Social Process in Europe,* Netherlands Ministry of Education and Science, 1975; (with Anton Blok) *Two Essays on Mediterranean Societies,* University of Amsterdam Press, 1975; *A Village in Malta,* Holt, 1980.

Contributor: John Davis, editor, *Choice and Change: Essays in Honour of Lucy Mair,* Athlone Press (London), 1974; K. Ishwaran, editor, *The Canadian Family,* Holt, 1976; J. G. Peristiany, editor, *Kinship and Modernization in Mediterranean Society,* Center for Mediterranean Studies, 1976; E. Gellner and J. Waterbury, editors, *Patrons and Clients in Mediterranean Societies,* Duckworth, 1977; Sandra Wallman, editor, *Perceptions of Development,* Cambridge University Press, 1977; *Friends, Followers, and Factions: A Reader in Political Clientelism,* University of California Press, 1977; Ann Sutherland, editor, *Face Value,* BBC Publications, 1978; M. Silverman and R. F. Salisbury, editors, *A House Divided?: Anthropological Studies of Factionalism,* Memorial University of Newfoundland, 1978; *Underdeveloped Europe: Studies in Core-Periphery Relations,* Harvester Press, 1979; Emanuel de Kadt, editor, *Tourism: Passport to Development?,* Oxford University Press, 1979. Contributor to *Journal of Commonwealth Political Studies, New Society, American Anthropologist, Man,* and other anthropological journals. Member of editorial board, *Ethnologia Europea.*

WORK IN PROGRESS: Research into the activities and problems of small entrepreneurs in Western Europe.

AVOCATIONAL INTERESTS: Sailing, wine making, hiking.

*   *   *

BOLGER, Philip C(unningham)   1927-
(Corporal Trim)

PERSONAL: Born December 3, 1927, in Gloucester, Mass. *Education:* Educated in public schools in Gloucester, Mass., and private school in North Andover, Mass. *Politics:* "Libertarian." *Religion:* "Olympian." *Home and office:* 250 Washington St., Gloucester, Mass. 01930.

CAREER: Self-employed boat designer. *Military service:* U.S. Army, 1946-47.

WRITINGS: Small Boats, International Marine Publishing, 1973; *The Folding Schooner and Other Adventures in Boat Design,* International Marine Publishing, 1976; *Different Boats,* International Marine Publishing, 1980; *Thirty-odd Boats,* International Marine Publishing, 1982. Also author of fantasy novels published in abridged serial form, *The Liberation of Tasman's Beatrix* and *The Sea Jockeys.* Contributor, sometimes under pseudonym Corporal Trim, of about 100 articles and essays to various periodicals.

WORK IN PROGRESS: The North Shore War.

*   *   *

BOLT, David (Michael) Langstone   1927-

PERSONAL: Born November 30, 1927, in Harrow, England; son of Richard Percy William and Ruby (Richardson) Bolt; married Sally Hall, 1970; children: (previous marriage) Julian, Vanessa, Stephen, Lucinda, Piers; (current marriage) Clare. *Education:* Attended Dulwich College, 1939-45. *Religion:* Church of England. *Home:* Cedar House, Ripley, Surrey, England. *Office:* Bolt & Watson Ltd., 8-12 Old Queen St., London SW1, England.

CAREER: Assistant superintendent, Malayan Police, 1948-50; Stuttafords, Durban, South Africa, buyer-manager, book department, 1950-53; currently authors' agent, Bolt & Watson Ltd., London, England. *Military service:* Indian Army, 10th Gurkha Rifles, 1945-48; became lieutenant.

WRITINGS: The Albatross, P. Davies, 1954; *A Cry Ascending,* P. Davies, 1955; *Adam,* John Day, 1961, reprinted, Shaw, 1980; *The Man Who Did,* John Day, 1964; *Of Heaven and Hope,* John Day, 1965; *Gurkhas,* Delacorte, 1967; *The Moon Princess,* Hamlyn, 1969; *Samson,* St. Martin's, 1980. Contributor of short stories to periodicals.

AVOCATIONAL INTERESTS: Fencing and riding.

*   *   *

BOND, Brian   1936-

PERSONAL: Born April 17, 1936, in Marlow, Buckinghamshire, England. *Education:* Worcester College, Oxford, B.A. (honors), 1959; King's College, University of London, M.A., 1962. *Office:* Department of War Studies, King's College, University of London, Strand, London WC2R 2LS, England.

CAREER: University of Exeter, Exeter, England, lecturer in history, 1961-62; University of Liverpool, Liverpool, England, lecturer in history, 1962-66; University of London, King's College, London, England, lecturer in war studies, 1966-78, reader in war studies, 1978—. Visiting professor at University of Western Ontario, 1972-73; visiting lecturer at U.S. Naval War College, 1972-74. *Military service:* British Army, Royal Artillery, 1952-54; became second lieutenant. *Member:* Society for Army Historical Research (member of council), Royal United Services Institute (member of council).

WRITINGS: (Editor) *Victorian Military Campaigns,* Hutchinson, 1967; *The Victorian Army and the Staff College,* Eyre Methuen, 1972; (editor) *Chief of Staff,* Leo Cooper, Volume I, 1973, Volume II, 1974; *France and Belgium: 1939-1940,* David-Poynter, 1975; *Liddell Hart: A Study of His Military Thought,* Rutgers University Press, 1977; *British Military Policy between the Two World Wars,* Oxford University Press, 1980; *War and Society in Europe, 1860-1960,* Collins, in press.

Author of television film "The Conduct of War in the Twentieth Century," for Open University. Editor of *War and Society*

Yearbook, 1975-77. Member of editorial panel, *Journal of Strategic Studies.*

BIOGRAPHICAL/CRITICAL SOURCES: Books and Bookmen, July, 1967; *Times Literary Supplement,* February 20, 1981.

* * *

BOORER, Wendy 1931-

PERSONAL: Born November 14, 1931, in St. Albans, England; daughter of William (a clerk) and Winifred (Brookson) Rowan; married Michael Keith Boorer (a zoologist), March 27, 1953; children: James, Matthew, Samantha. *Education:* Attended University College of Leicester (now University of Leicester), 1949-52; University of London, B.A. (with honors in English literature), 1952. *Home:* 34 Milton Park, London N6 5QA, England.

CAREER: Has worked as an aerodynamics technician, teacher, library indexer, market researcher, and magazine editor; currently writer, dog breeder and exhibitor. Advisor on dogs to Elsevier Publishing Co. *Member:* Avicultural Society, Bearded Collie Club of Great Britain (secretary, 1969-73), Griffon Club, Newfoundland Club.

WRITINGS: World of Dogs, Hamlyn, 1969; *Dogs,* Hamlyn, 1970, published as *Dogs: Selection, Care, Training,* Grosset, 1971, revised edition, 1974; *Dog Care,* Hamlyn, 1970; *Introducing Puppies,* Hamlyn, 1970; *The Book of the Dog,* Hamlyn, 1970; (with others) *Treasury of Dogs,* Octopus, 1972; (with others) *The Love of Dogs,* Octopus, 1974; *The All Colour Book of Dogs,* Octopus, 1975, Crescent, 1980; *In Search of Dogs,* Excalibur Books, 1976; (contributor) Douglas James, editor, *Dogs and Puppies,* Octopus, 1977; *Dogs,* St. Michael, 1979; *Domino Guide to Dogs,* Fontana, 1979; *Know Your Birds* (juvenile), Methuen, 1980; *The Kingfisher Guide to Dogs,* Grisewood & Dempsey, 1981. Also author of shorter juvenile book, *Guide to Dogs,* 1979. Contributor to *Avicultural Magazine, Dog's Life, Animal World,* and other periodicals.

SIDELIGHTS: Wendy Boorer writes: "I am fascinated by the pet/owner relationship, dog psychology, dog training and the historical background to the development of different breeds."

* * *

BORDEN, Neil Hopper 1895-

PERSONAL: Born December 7, 1895, in Boulder, Colo.; son of Edmund James (an accountant) and Irene (Gilbert) Borden; married Esther Page, September 11, 1926; children: Rosanne Borden Marshall, Neil H., Jr., John E. P., Penelope. *Education:* University of Colorado, A.B., 1919; Harvard University, M.B.A., 1922. *Office:* Harvard Business School, Soldiers Field, Boston, Mass.

CAREER: Lafayette High School, Lafayette, Colo., principal, 1919-20; Harvard University, Graduate School of Business Administration, Boston, Mass., assistant dean, 1922-25, 1927-30, assistant professor, 1925-28, associate professor, 1928-38, professor of marketing and advertising, 1938-62, professor emeritus, 1962—. Chairman, Advertising Review Panel for Brewing Industry, 1955—. Director, Young Men's Christian Association, Cambridge, Mass., 1932-47; Lexington, Mass. Planning Board, member, 1934-38, chairman, 1937-38; member of Winchester, Mass. School Committee, 1942-48; member of board of trustees, Winchester Public Library, 1948-58; chairman, Winchester Scholarship Foundation, 1961-64; public trustee, Marketing Science Institute, 1962-65. *Military service:* U.S. Army, 1918.

MEMBER: American Marketing Association (vice-president, 1949; president, 1953-54; president of predecessor organization, 1928), American Economic Association, Phi Beta Kappa, Alpha Tau Omega, Acacia, Harvard Club of New York City, Harvard Club of Boston, Monday Club of Winchester, Mass. *Awards, honors:* Kappa Tau Alpha Society Research Award, 1945-46; American Marketing Association, research award, 1946, Paul D. Converse Award, 1951, for advancing the science of marketing, Cincinnati chapter award, 1961, for outstanding contribution to advertising education; distinguished service medal in advertising, Syracuse University, 1949; Charles Coolidge Parlin Memorial Lecture and Award, 1949; Hall of Fame in Distribution, Boston Conference on Distribution, 1952; Charles G. Nichols Award of Alpha Delta Sigma, 1959, for contribution to advertising education; recipient of advertising gold medal for distinguished service to advertising education, 1964.

WRITINGS: (With Charles A. Glover) *Suggestions on Report Writing,* Division of Research, Harvard Business School, 1927; *Problems in Advertising,* Shaw, 1927, 3rd edition, McGraw, 1937; *Cooperative Advertising by Trade Associations,* McGraw, 1932; *Determination of Confusion in Trade-mark Conflict Cases,* Division of Research, Harvard Business School, 1937, reprinted, Kraus Reprint, 1974; (with Mabel Taylor Gragg) *Merchandise Testing as a Guide to Consumer Buying,* Division of Research, Harvard Business School, 1940, reprinted, Kraus Reprint, 1974; *Economic Effects of Advertising,* Irwin, 1942, reprinted, Arno, 1976; *Advertising in Our Economy,* Irwin, 1945, reprinted, Richard West, 1978; (with M. D. Taylor and H. T. Hovde) *National Advertising in Newspapers,* Harvard University Press, 1946; *Advertising: Text and Cases,* Irwin, 1950, revised edition (with M. V. Marshall) published as *Advertising Management: Text and Cases,* 1959. Author of monographs and contributor to professional journals.

BIOGRAPHICAL/CRITICAL SOURCES: Printers' Ink, December 19, 1958; *Madison Avenue,* September, 1959; *Journal of Marketing,* January, 1963.†

* * *

BORING, Edwin G(arrigues) 1886-1968

PERSONAL: Born October 23, 1886, in Philadelphia, Pa.; died July 1, 1968, in Cambridge, Mass.; son of Edwin McCurdy (a pharmacist) and Elizabeth G. (Truman) Boring; married Lucy May Day, June 18, 1914; children: Edwin G., Frank H., Mollie D., Barbara (died, 1950). *Education:* Cornell University, M.E., 1908, A.M., 1912, Ph.D., 1914. *Residence:* Cambridge, Mass. *Office:* William James Hall, Harvard University, Cambridge, Mass. 02138.

CAREER: Cornell University, Ithaca, N.Y., assistant, 1911-13, instructor in psychology, 1913-18; Clark University, Worcester, Mass., professor of experimental psychology and director of psychology laboratory, 1919-22; Harvard University, Cambridge, Mass., associate professor, 1922-28, professor of psychology, 1928-56, Edgar Pierce Professor of Psychology, 1956-57, Lowell Television Lecturer, 1956-57, Edgar Pierce Professor of Psychology Emeritus, 1957-68, director of psychology laboratory, 1924-49. Visiting scholar, Phi Beta Kappa, 1958-59; special university lecturer, University of London, 1959. Honorary president, XVIIth International Congress of Psychology, 1963. Associate editor, Basic Books, 1961-68. *Military service:* U.S. Army, Medical Department, 1918-19; psychological examiner, became captain.

MEMBER: American Association for the Advancement of Science (fellow), National Academy of Science, American Philosophical Society, American Academy of Arts and Sciences (fellow), American Psychological Association (secretary, 1919-22; member of council, 1922-25; president, 1928), British Psychological Society, Societe Francaise de Psychologie, Sociedad Espanola de Psychologie, Society of Experimental Psychologists (fellow), Societa Italiana di Psicologie Scientifica, Harvard Club of New York City, Harvard Club of Boston. *Awards, honors:* Harvard University, A.M., 1942; University of Pennsylvania, Sc.D., 1946; Clark University, D.Sc., 1956; American Psychological Foundation Gold Medal, 1959.

WRITINGS: History of Experimental Psychology, Appleton, 1929, 2nd edition, 1950; *The Physical Dimensions of Consciousness,* Appleton, 1933, reprinted, Dover Publications, 1963; *Sensation and Perception in the History of Experimental Psychology,* Appleton, 1942, reprinted, Irvington, 1977; (with M. Van de Water) *Psychology for the Fighting Man,* Penguin, 1943; *Psychology for the Armed Services,* Infantry Journal, 1945; (editor with others) *Foundations of Psychology,* Wiley, 1948; *Psychologist at Large* (autobiography), Basic Books, 1961; *History, Psychology, and Science: Selected Papers,* edited by R. I. Watson and D. T. Campbell, Wiley, 1963; (with R. J. Herrnstein) *A Source Book in the History of Psychology,* Harvard University Press, 1965; (editor with Helmut E. Adler, and author of introduction) Gustav Theodor Fechner, *Elements of Psychophysics,* Holt, 1966; (editor with Gardner Lindzey) *A History of Psychology in Autobiography,* Volumes IV and V, Appleton, 1967. Also editor of *Psychology: A Factual Textbook,* 1935, and *Introduction to Psychology,* 1939. Editor, *American Journal of Psychology,* 1925-43, *Contemporary Psychology,* 1957-61.

WORK IN PROGRESS: How Psychology Came About, a history of psychology for young people.

BIOGRAPHICAL/CRITICAL SOURCES: Edwin G. Boring, *Psychologist at Large* (autobiography), Basic Books, 1961.

OBITUARIES: Washington Post, July 3, 1968.†

*   *   *

BORLAND, Hal
  See BORLAND, Harold Glen

*   *   *

BORLAND, Harold Glen   1900-1978
  (Hal Borland; Ward West, a pseudonym)

PERSONAL: Born May 14, 1900, in Sterling, Neb.; died February 22, 1978, in Sharon, Conn.; son of William Arthur (a printer and editor) and Sarah (Clinaburg) Borland; married second wife, Barbara Ross Dodge (an author), 1945; children: (first marriage) H.G., Jr. (deceased), Donal W., Neil F. (deceased); (stepdaughter) Diana (Mrs. J. C. Thomson, Jr.). *Education:* Attended University of Colorado, 1918-20; Columbia University, B.Litt., 1923. *Religion:* Protestant. *Home and office:* Weatogue Rd., Salisbury, Conn. 06068. *Agent:* Curtis Brown, Ltd., 575 Madison Ave., New York, N.Y. 10022.

CAREER: Denver Post, Denver, Colo., reporter, 1918; *Flagler News,* Flagler, Colo., associate editor, 1920-21; *Brooklyn Times,* Brooklyn, N.Y., reporter, 1921; United Press, New York City, reporter, 1921-22; member of staff, King Features Service, New York City, 1922; held various positions with newspapers in Salt Lake City, Utah, Carson City, Nev., Fresno, Calif., San Diego, Calif., and Marshall, Tex., 1923-24; telegraph editor in Asheville, N.C., 1924; publicity writer, Ivy L. Lee, 1924-25; *Stratton Press,* Stratton, Colo., publisher, 1925-26; Curtis Newspapers, Philadelphia, Pa., copyreader, 1926-27,

assistant night editor of *Philadelphia Morning Sun,* 1927-28, editorial writer for *Philadelphia Morning Ledger,* 1929-33, literary editor of both morning and evening *Ledger,* 1934-37; *New York Times Sunday Magazine,* New York City, staff writer, 1937-43; free-lance writer, 1943-78. Director of nonfiction section, Rocky Mountain Writers' Conference, University of Colorado, 1955. Member of board of supervisors, Bartholomew's Cobble Nature Reservation, Ashley Falls, Mass., 1963-78; member of Governor's Commission on Conservation Policy for Connecticut, 1970-71; chairman of board, Berkshire-Litchfield Conservation Council, Inc., 1970-78. *Military service:* U.S. Naval Reserve Force, 1918.

MEMBER: Authors Guild, Authors League of America, Sigma Delta Chi, Phi Gamma Delta, Masons, Century Association (New York). *Awards, honors:* Litt.D., University of Colorado, 1944; Westerners Buffalo Award for best non-fiction, and Secondary Education Board annual book award, both, 1957, for *High, Wide and Lonesome;* Alumni Award, Columbia University School of Journalism, 1962; Meeman Award for conservation writing, 1966; John Burroughs Medal for distinguished nature writing, 1968; Interpretive Naturalists award, 1973; Outstanding Science Books for Children award, 1977, for *The Golden Circle; Congressional Record* tribute and presidential tribute, 1978.

WRITINGS: Heaps of Gold (verse), privately printed, 1922; *Rocky Mountain Tipi Tales,* Doubleday, 1924; *Valor: The Story of a Dog* (juvenile), Farrar & Rinehart, 1934; (under pseudonym Ward West) *Trouble Valley* (novel), Greenberg, 1934; (under pseudonym Ward West) *Halfway to Timberline* (novel), Greenberg, 1935; *Wapiti Pete: The Story of an Elk* (juvenile), Farrar & Rinehart, 1938, revised edition published as *The King of Squaw Mountain,* Lippincott, 1964; *America Is Americans* (verse), Harper, 1942; (with Philip Dunning) *What Is America? Or, America Is Americans: A Patriotic Playlet in One Act,* Samuel French, 1942; *An American Year: Country Life and Landscapes through the Seasons* (essays), Simon & Schuster, 1946.

Published by Lippincott, except as indicated: *How to Write and Sell Non-Fiction,* Ronald, 1956, reprinted, Greenwood Press, 1973; *High, Wide and Lonesome* (autobiography), 1956; *This Hill, This Valley* (autobiography), Simon & Schuster, 1957; *The Amulet* (novel), 1957; *The Enduring Pattern* (essays), Simon & Schuster, 1959; *The Seventh Winter* (novel), 1960; *The Dog Who Came to Stay,* 1961; *Beyond Your Doorstep: A Handbook to the Country,* Knopf, 1962; *The Youngest Shepherd* (juvenile), 1962; *When the Legends Die* (novel; Reader's Digest Book Club selection), 1963; (contributor) *Journalists in Action,* edited by Edward W. Barett, Channel Press, 1963; *Sundial of the Seasons* (essays), 1964; *Countryman: A Summary of Belief,* 1965; (editor) *Our Natural World: The Land and Wildlife of America as Seen and Described by Writers since the Country's Discovery,* Doubleday, 1965; *Hill Country Harvest* (essays), 1967; *Homeland: A Report from the Country,* 1969; *Country Editor's Boy* (autobiography), 1970; *Borland Country* (essays), 1971; *Penny: The Story of a Free-Soul Basset Hound,* 1972; *This World of Wonder* (juvenile), 1973; *Seasons* (essays), 1973; *The History of Wildlife in America,* National Wildlife Federation, 1975; *Hal Borland's Book of Days* (essays), Knopf, 1976; *A Place to Begin: The New England Experience,* Sierra Club Books, 1976; *The Golden Circle: A Book of Months* (essays), Crowell, 1977; *Twelve Moons of the Year,* Knopf, 1979; *A Countryman's Flowers,* Knopf, 1981.

Also author of documentary film scripts and radio scripts. Outdoor editorial writer, *New York Sunday Times,* 1942-78; regular contributor of essays to *Progressive*, 1957-78; columnist, *Berkshire Eagle*, 1958-78, *Pittsburgh Press*, 1966-78, and *Torrington Register*, 1971-78. Contributor of fiction and nonfiction to periodicals in the United States and abroad, often with wife, Barbara Dodge Borland. Contributing editor, *Audubon Magazine*, 1967-78.

WORK IN PROGRESS: Countryman's Trees.

SIDELIGHTS: Hal Borland told *CA:* "I am often called a naturalist because I have written a good deal about the natural world. I have a certain competence in that field, but I think of myself as a natural philosopher; I am interested in life, all kinds of life, and must consider it in the framework of this natural world. A few years ago I was a member of the Governor's Committee to draft a conservation policy for Connecticut. . . . I have been chairman of the Berkshire-Litchfield Conservation Council, a regional organization trying to save our area from despoilation by all kinds of spoilers, especially power companies. But privately I prefer to be a private citizen with a typewriter and a place to say things when and if I think they must be said. And writing is my vocation, my avocation, my life. I set out early to see the United States instead of making the usual trip to Europe. I worked my way all across the country and back, and before I was 30 I had spent some time in every state. I had to write books. Juveniles at first, then adult novels, then essays and longer nonfiction, and more fiction. Barbara and I enjoyed the magazine work we did, but when the markets shrank or disappeared in the 1950s we changed over to books. The columns and editorials have been collected or selected from in seven of the books.

"I prefer to live where we do because of the natural setting and the insulating distance from the big cities, where I find a kind of mass psychology and crowd emotions. We are in constant touch but not constantly surrounded. My purpose is to say a few things that may be remembered a few years after I die."

When the Legends Die has been published in nine foreign languages; the novel was produced as a film by Twentieth Century-Fox in 1972. The Hal and Barbara Borland Collection, containing manuscripts and working papers, has been established at the Beinecke Library of Yale University; personal papers and correspondence are being collected by the Library of Congress. The National Audubon Society has created the Hal Borland Trail at the Sharon (Conn.) Audubon Center; a Hal Borland Nature Trail is also being established connecting the national landmarks of Bartholomew's Cobble (Ashley Falls, Mass.) and the Colonel Ashley House.

BIOGRAPHICAL/CRITICAL SOURCES: Wilson Library Bulletin, March, 1960; *Best Sellers*, July 15, 1967, May 15, 1970; *Newsday*, December 16, 1967; *Publishers Weekly*, November 1, 1976.

OBITUARIES: New York Times, February 24, 1978.†

*   *   *

BOSLEY, Keith 1937-

PERSONAL: Born September 16, 1937, in Bourne End, Buckinghamshire, England; son of William Edward and Grace Emily (Bushnell) Bosley; married Helen Sava (a singer), October 13, 1962; children: Benjamin. *Education:* University of Reading, B.A. (with honors), 1960; also attended University of Caen and Institut Britannique, Paris. *Home:* 108 Upton Rd., Slough SL1 2AW, England.

CAREER: Poet, translator. *Member:* Finnish Literature Society. *Awards, honors:* Finnish State Prize for Translators, 1977, for *Finnish Folk Poetry: Epic*.

WRITINGS: Tales from the Long Lakes: Finnish Legends from the Kalevala, Gollancz, 1966, published as *The Devil's Horse: Tales from the Kalevala*, Pantheon, 1971; *Russia's Other Poets*, Longmans, Green, 1968, published as *Russia's Underground Poets*, Praeger, 1969; *An Idiom of Night* (translations from Pierre Jean Jouve), Rapp & Whiting, 1968; *The Possibility of Angels*, Macmillan, 1969.

And I Dance: Poems Original and Translated (juvenile), Angus & Robertson, 1972; *The War Wife: Vietnamese Poetry*, Allison & Busby, 1972; *The Song of Aino*, Moonbird Publications, 1973; *The Three Houses*, Sceptre Press, 1976; *Dark Summer*, Menard Press, 1976; *The Song of Songs*, Whittington Press, 1976; (translator) *Finnish Folk Poetry: Epic*, McGill-Queen's University Press, 1977; *Mallarme: The Poems*, Penguin, 1977; (translator) *A Round O*, Interim Press, 1977; (translator) Joonas Kokkonen, *The Last Temptations*, Savonlinna Opera Festival, 1977; (translator) Eino Leino, *Whitsongs*, Menard Press, 1978; *Stations*, Anvil Press, 1979; (general editor) *Poetry of Asia*, Weatherhill, 1979 (published in England as *The Elek Book of Oriental Verse*, Elek, 1979); (translator) Jerzy Ficowski, *A Reading of Ashes*, Menard Press, 1981; (translator) *The Great Bear*, Finnish Literature Society, in press; (translator) *From the Theorems of Master Jean de la Ceppede*, Carcanet Press, in press.

Also author of radio scripts for BBC. Work appears in anthologies, including *The Young British Poets*, edited by Jeremy Robson, Chatto & Windus, 1971. Contributor of poems, reviews, and articles to periodicals.

*   *   *

BOURBON, Ken
See BAUER, Erwin A.

*   *   *

BOWETT, Derek William 1927-

PERSONAL: Born April 20, 1927, in Manchester, England; son of Arnold William (a company director) and Marion (Wood) Bowett; married Betty Northall, 1953; children: Richard, Adam, Louise. *Education:* Downing College, Cambridge, M.A., LL.B., 1951; University of Manchester, Ph.D., 1956. *Home:* Queens' College, Cambridge, England.

CAREER: Barrister, Middle Temple, London, England; University of Manchester, Manchester, England, lecturer in law, 1951-60; Cambridge University, Cambridge, England, lecturer in law, 1960—, fellow of Queens' College, 1960-70, president of Queens' College, 1970—. Member of legal office, United Nations, New York, N.Y., 1957-59; member of General Counsel of UNRWA, 1966-68.

WRITINGS: Self-Defence in International Law, Praeger, 1958; *The Law of International Institutions*, Praeger, 1963, 3rd edition, Stevens, 1975; (with G. P. Barton and others) *United Nations Forces: A Legal Study of United Nations Practice*, Stevens, 1964, published as *United Nations Forces: A Legal Study*, Praeger, 1965; *The Law of the Sea*, Oceana, 1967; *The Law of the Area*, Oceana, 1967; (with K. Helveg Petersen) *Proposal for Establishment of an International Council for Research and Information on Conflicts*, S. L. Mollers (Copenhagen), 1971; *The Search for Peace*, Routledge & Kegan Paul, 1972; *The Legal Regime of Islands in International Law*, Oceana, 1978. Contributor to law journals.†

BOWMAN, John Wick 1894-

PERSONAL: Born August 3, 1894, in Brownsville, Pa.; son of Winfield Scott (a clergyman) and Maggie Moore (Wick) Bowman; married Alma Louise Coles, June 2, 1919; children: John Scott, Margaret Louise, Douglas Coles. *Education:* Wooster College, A.B., 1916; Princeton University, A.M., 1919; Princeton Theological Seminary, B.D., 1920; Southern Baptist Theological Seminary, Ph.D., 1930; University of Zurich, postdoctoral study, 1936. *Politics:* Democrat. *Religion:* Presbyterian. *Home:* 7550 North 16th St., Apt. 102-6, Phoenix, Ariz. 85020.

CAREER: United Theological College, Saharanpur. India, professor, 1926-36, principal, 1931-36; Western Theological Seminary, Pittsburgh, Pa., Memorial Professor of New Testament, 1936-44; San Francisco Theological Seminary, San Anselmo, Calif., Robert Dollar Professor of New Testament, 1944-61, professor emeritus, 1961—. Fulbright lecturer at St. Andrews University, Scotland, 1949-50, and International Christian University, Tokyo, Japan, 1957-58; lecturer at seminaries in the United States, Japan, and the Philippines, 1946-64. United Church, Sun City, Ariz., Bible lecturer and member of staff. *Member:* Societas Novi Testamenti Studiorum, Phi Beta Kappa, Chi Alpha. *Awards, honors:* Abingdon-Cokesbury Award, 1947, for *The Religion of Maturity;* D.D. from Wooster College, Waynesburg College, and St. Andrews University.

WRITINGS: Introducing the Bible, Westminster, 1940; *The Intention of Jesus,* Westminster, 1943; *The Religion of Maturity,* Abingdon-Cokesbury, 1948; (co-editor) *Westminster Study Bible,* Westminster, 1948; *Prophetic Realism and the Gospel,* Westminster, 1955; *The Drama of the Book of Revelation,* Westminster, 1955, published as *The First Christian Drama: The Book of Revelation,* 1968; (translator and author of commentary with Roland Tapp) *The Gospel from the Mount,* Westminster, 1957; (co-editor) *New Testament Essays,* Manchester University Press, 1959; *The Letter to the Hebrews; The Letter of James; The First and Second Letters of Peter* (Bible commentary), John Knox, 1962; (contributor) *Peake's Commentary on the Bible,* Thomas Nelson, 1962; (contributor) *Interpreter's Dictionary of the Bible,* Abingdon, 1962; *Jesus' Teaching in Its Environment,* John Knox, 1963; *Which Jesus?,* Westminster, 1970; *Rendezvous with India* (novel), Omega Books, 1976; *Unless I See* (novel), Morgan Press, 1977. Contributor to *Collier's Encyclopedia, Schaff-Hertzog Encyclopedia,* and to theological journals. Editor, *Abr-Nahrain.*

* * *

BOYD, Carse
See STACTON, David (Derek)

* * *

BOYNTON, Lewis Delano 1909-

PERSONAL: Born January 25, 1909, in Millersville, Pa.; son of Emerson and Clara (Groff) Boynton; married Thelma Potter; children: John Emerson. *Education:* New York University, B.S., 1942; Columbia University, M.A., 1946, Ed.D., 1951. *Home:* 35 Crocus Lane, Unionville, Conn. 06085. *Office:* Business Education Department, Central Connecticut State College, New Britain, Conn. 06050.

CAREER: Clerical supervisor, ship's purser, high school and college teacher, 1928-48; Columbia University, Teachers College, New York, N.Y., instructor, 1948-51; Central Connecticut State College, New Britain, professor and chairman of

business education department, 1951—. *Member:* National Education Association, National Association for Business Teacher Education (secretary, 1958-60), Eastern Business Teachers Association, New England Business Education Association, Connecticut Business Education Association (president, 1953), Delta Pi Epsilon.

WRITINGS: Methods of Teaching Bookkeeping, South-Western, 1955, 2nd edition, 1970; (co-author) *20th Century Bookkeeping and Accounting, First Year Course,* South-Western, 1962, 23rd edition, 1967; *20th Century Bookkeeping and Accounting, Advanced Course,* South-Western, 1963; (with R. M. Swanson, R. D. Hanson, and K. E. Ross) *Century 21 Accounting: First Year Course,* South-Western, 1972; (with Swanson, Hanson, and Ross) *Century 21 Accounting: Advanced Course,* South-Western, 1974.

AVOCATIONAL INTERESTS: Salt water fishing, gardening.

* * *

BRACKEN, Peg 1920-

PERSONAL: Born February 25, 1920, in Twin Falls, Idaho; daughter of John Lewis and Ruth (McQuesten) Bracken; married Roderick Allyn Lull (an editor), September 20, 1952 (divorced); married Parker Ferguson Edwards, March 17, 1966; children: (first marriage) Johanna Kathleen. *Education:* Antioch College, A.B. 1940. *Politics:* Independent. *Home:* 66 Kahana Pl., Lahaina, Hawaii 96761. *Agent:* Robert Lescher, 155 East 71st St., New York, N.Y. 10021.

CAREER: Radio continuity writer, 1946-48; free-lance advertising copy writer, principally for Botsford, Constantine Gardner, 1956—. *Member:* American Federation of Television and Radio Artists, Screen Actors Guild, Authors Guild, P.E.N.

WRITINGS—Published by Harcourt, except as indicated: (With Helen Berry Moore) *The 9-Months Wonder,* Prentice-Hall, 1958; *The I Hate to Cook Book,* 1960; *The I Hate to Housekeep Book,* 1962; *I Try to Behave Myself,* 1964; *Peg Bracken's Appendix to the I Hate to Cook Book,* 1966; *I Didn't Come Here to Argue,* 1970; *But I Wouldn't Have Missed It for the World,* 1973; *The I Hate to Cook Almanack: A Book of Days,* 1976; *A Window over the Sink,* 1981. Contributor to *Saturday Evening Post, Ladies' Home Journal, Cosmopolitan, McCall's,* and other periodicals.

AVOCATIONAL INTERESTS: Old furniture, English bulldogs, and the British Isles.

BIOGRAPHICAL/CRITICAL SOURCES: Los Angeles Times, May 14, 1981.

* * *

BRASCH, Walter Milton 1945-

PERSONAL: Born March 2, 1945, in San Diego, Calif.; son of Milton and Helen (Haskin) Brasch; married Ila Wales (a journalist-linguist), September 30, 1970 (divorced, March, 1977); married Vivian Fluck, June 14, 1980. *Education:* Attended University of California, 1962-64, and LaVerne College, 1964; San Diego State College (now University), A.B., 1966; Ball State University, M.A., 1969; Ohio University, Ph.D., 1974. *Politics:* Independent Democrat. *Religion:* Jewish. *Home:* c/o 1707 South Pleasant Ave., Ontario, Calif. 91761.

CAREER: Employed as sports editor, city editor, features writer, and investigative reporter for daily newspapers in California, Indiana, Iowa, and Ohio, 1965-71; MID Productions, Athens, Ohio, writer and executive director, 1971-74; Temple University, Philadelphia, Pa., assistant professor of journalism and mass communications, 1974-76; Brasch and Brasch Publishers, Ontario, Calif., editor-in-chief, 1976-80; writer-producer, United Screen Artists, 1976-80; Bloomsburg State College, Bloomsburg, Pa., director of graduate program in communication, 1980—. Free-lance advertising-publicity writer and consultant, 1964—; member of Iowa Governor's Committee for the Employment of the Handicapped, 1971-73; member of Ohio Governor's Committee for the Dictionary of American Regional English, 1973-74; member of U.S. Coast Guard Auxiliary. *Member:* American Dialect Society, Association for Education in Journalism, Popular Culture Association, Society of Professional Journalists, Phi Kappa Phi, Kappa Tau Alpha, Pi Gamma Mu, Alpha Kappa Delta. *Awards, honors:* Certificate of Outstanding Service from Alpha Phi Omega, 1966; Certificate of Appreciation from U.S. Department of Commerce, 1970; Certificate of Merit from Gordon Wiseman Conference on Interpersonal Communication, 1973.

WRITINGS: (With Ila Wales) *A Comprehensive Annotated Bibliography of American Black English,* Louisiana State University Press, 1974; *Black English and the Mass Media,* University of Massachusetts Press, 1981; *Columbia County Place Names,* Columbia County Historical Society, 1982.

Plays: "Answer Me Not in Mournful Numbers," first produced in Waterloo, Iowa at Theatre Seventies, 1969; "Sand Creek," first produced at Theatre Seventies, 1972. Author of television script, "The Royal Symbols of the Kom," 1973; and, with Ila Wales, a radio script, "The Day Santa Claus Forgot . . . ," 1974.

Multimedia shows: "In the Beginning . . . (the Indian)," 1972; "A Language and Culture Happening," 1972; "Songs of the Battle," 1972; "Songs of the Civil War," 1973; (with Edward J. Duffy) "The Firemark: A Language and Culture Study," 1975.

Contributor of over 250 articles to general interest magazines and academic journals.

WORK IN PROGRESS: Zim; a TV documentary; a multimedia show; a series of short stories.

SIDELIGHTS: Walter Brasch writes: "I'm a journalist, a writer who looks at society and tries to understand, then analyze and explain its many complex parts as they relate to an organic whole. For that reason, my writings—both popular as well as academic—can't really be pigeon-holed; the writings are, in reality, about man and his world; the process is journalism. I became a writer-journalist because I did it better than anything else I ever did, and because I found that writing well, with the ability to understand people and their society, and trying to help people understand their part of the world, is one of the most challenging things a person can do. I write from the gut, and for the heart; I write because I enjoy it, and because it has been good to me. I write about what I'm interested in, and go from topic to topic, and issue to issue, as my needs change."

AVOCATIONAL INTERESTS: Music (especially country, bluegrass, dixieland), theatre, popular culture, "and just about anything that happens to tickle my fancy at the moment."

*   *   *

BREAULT, William 1926-

PERSONAL: Born September 17, 1926, in Saratoga Spa, N.Y.; son of Cyril Felix and Ruth (La Bonte) Breault. *Education:* Gonzaga University, Ph.L., 1956; University of Santa Clara, M.S.T., 1963; Collegium Almanum a Sancto Joseph, S.T.L., 1963; San Francisco State College (now University), M.A.

(drama), 1965; College of Notre Dame, Belmont, Calif., B.A. (art), 1969. *Politics:* Democrat.

CAREER: Loyola High School, Los Angeles, Calif., teacher of English and Latin, 1956-59; St. Ignatius High School, San Francisco, Calif., teacher of religion and drama, 1964-69; Jesuit High School, Sacramento, Calif., teacher of theology and artist-in-residence, 1969-81; currently editorial cartoonist for *Catholic Herald.* Independent producer of television shows for station KXTV, Sacramento, 1969—. *Military service:* U.S. Army Air Forces, 1945-47; served in South Pacific. *Awards, honors:* First prize in St. John's Lutheran annual religious art show, 1969, and second prize, Sacramento Valley Art Academy, 1970, both for metal sculpture.

WRITINGS: Power and Weakness, Daughters of St. Paul, 1973; *The Lord's Way,* Daughters of St. Paul, 1974; *Under the Fig Tree,* Ave Maria Press, 1980.

Media shows: *The Man* (a life of Christ), Ave Maria Press, 1975; *Damien, the Leper Priest,* Ave Maria Press.

Cassette tapes; published by Ave Maria Press: "Talks by the Sea"; "Jonah"; "Psalms by the Sea".

Also author of about two dozen television productions, including "Mission," "Damien: Leper Priest," "The Man," and "Islands in the Sun," and of about 95 one-minute spots on prayer, life, and scripture.

WORK IN PROGRESS: Lady from Dublin, a biography of Catherine McAuley; *Tide Pool,* a sequel to *Under the Fig Tree.*

SIDELIGHTS: William Breault told *CA:* "As a priest, whose first duty is to proclaim the good news, or, the Gospel of Christ, I am constantly challenged to see how I can (utilizing all that is most worthwhile in media and life) convey in convincing terms to the modern mentality just what the good news is! For me it includes entertainment, poetry, beauty and adventure—above all, art, without which man cannot function." Breault specializes in watercolors, metal sculpture, and print-work, for which he has had numerous one-man shows and commissions.

*   *   *

BREIT, Harvey 1909-1968

PERSONAL: Born November 27, 1909, in New York, N.Y.; died April 9, 1968, in New York, N.Y.; son of Jacob and Sarah (Beer) Breit; married Alice S. Morris (divorced); married Patricia Rinehart, May 27, 1954 (divorced); children: (first marriage) Luke, Miranda; (second marriage) Sebastian, Gratia. *Education:* Attended New York University, three years. *Politics:* Social-Democrat.

CAREER: Time, New York City, writer, 1933-34; *New York Times Book Review,* New York City, columnist and assistant editor, 1948-57. Co-chairman, with the late William Faulkner, of writers' committee, People-to-People program; American delegate, with James Baldwin and Henry Miller, to the Prix Formentor, international literary award, Spain, 1962. Lecturer, Sarah Lawrence College; trustee, Saxton Fund. *Member:* P.E.N., National Association for the Advancement of Colored People (member of Legal Defense Fund), Grolier Club.

WRITINGS: There Falls Tom Fool (poems), Capricorn Books, 1940; (editor) *Perspectives of India,* Viking, 1952; (editor with Marc Slonim) *This Thing Called Love,* New American Library, 1955; *The Writer Observed,* World Publishing, 1956; (with Budd Schulberg) *The Disenchanted* (play), Random House, 1959; (adapter with Patricia Rinehart) "The Guide" (play; based on R. K. Narayan's novel; produced on Broadway at

Hudson Theatre, March, 1968), 1961; *A Narrow Action,* World Publishing, 1964; (editor with Marjorie Lowry) *The Selected Letters of Malcolm Lowry,* Lippincott, 1964.

Author of introduction; published by Modern Library: William Faulkner, *Absalom, Absalom!; J. B. Byrne, The Silent Years; The Silver Pilgrimage.* Contributor to *Atlantic, Paris Review, Poetry,* and *New Directions;* also contributor of articles on boxing and baseball to non-literary publications. Member of advisory board, *Partisan Review.*

WORK IN PROGRESS: Screenplay for *A Narrow Action;* a novel.

SIDELIGHTS: Harvey Breit's *The Writer Observed,* a collection of sixty interviews with leading authors was, as James Greene of *Commonweal* wrote, "a fascinating potpourri of literary gossip [and] reflections on the writing craft." The *Atlantic*'s C. J. Rolo found that the book "pays handsome dividends to anyone interested in the literary life. It presents, readably and compactly, a rich miscellany of information about a sizable cross section of the leading American and British writers." Reviewing the book for *Catholic World,* R. B. Dooley thought that "the deft, careful word pictures, in which the subject's appearance and manners are captured along with what seems to be his essential personality, should make this book a veritable treasure trove for future literary historians."

AVOCATIONAL INTERESTS: Horse racing, billiards, boxing, baseball, chess, poker.

BIOGRAPHICAL/CRITICAL SOURCES: Saturday Review, February 18, 1956; *Christian Science Monitor,* February 23, 1956; *Commonweal,* March 9, 1956; *Atlantic,* April, 1956; *Catholic World,* August, 1956; *Newsweek,* June 1, 1964; *New York Times Book Review,* June 14, 1964; *Best Sellers,* June 15, 1964; *Book Week,* July 5, 1964; *New Yorker,* March 16, 1968.

OBITUARIES: New York Times, April 10, 1968; *Antiquarian Bookman,* April 22, 1968; *Publishers Weekly,* April 22, 1968; *Time,* April 22, 1968.†

*   *   *

BRIGHTON, Wesley, Jr.
See LOVIN, Roger Robert

*   *   *

BRINGHURST, Robert 1946-

PERSONAL: Born October 16, 1946, in Los Angeles, Calif.; son of George H. and Marion (Large) Bringhurst; married Miki Cannon Sheffield, June 3, 1974 (divorced, 1981). *Education:* Attended Massachusetts Institute of Technology, 1963-64, 1970-71, and University of Utah, 1964-65; Indiana University, B.A., 1973; University of British Columbia, M.F.A., 1975. *Home:* 3253 Point Grey Rd., Vancouver, British Columbia, Canada V6K 1B3.

CAREER: Worked as journalist in Beirut, Lebanon, 1965-66, and in Boston, Mass., 1970-71; dragoman for U.S. Army in Israel and Palestine, 1967-68; law clerk in Panama Canal Zone, 1968-69; University of British Columbia, Vancouver, British Columbia, fellow of creative writing department, 1973-75. *Awards, honors:* Macmillan Prize for Poetry, 1975.

WRITINGS: The Shipwright's Log, Kanchenjunga Press, 1972; *Cadastre,* Kanchenjunga Press, 1973; *Deuteronomy,* Sono Nis Press, 1974; *Eight Objects,* Kanchenjunga Press, 1975; *Bergschrund,* Sono Nis Press, 1975; *Jacob Singing,* Kanchen-

junga Press, 1977; *The Stonecutter's Horses,* Standard Editions, 1979; *New and Selected Poems,* McClelland & Stewart, 1982.

Contributor of essays, poems, translations, and articles to literary magazines, including *Poetry, Malahat Review, Kayak, Ontario Review, Fiddlehead, Ohio Review, Prism International, Canadian Fiction Magazine,* and *West Coast Poetry Review.* Review editor of *Canadian Fiction Magazine,* 1974-75; member of editorial board, 1973-76, and guest editor of Arabic literature and Greek issues of *Contemporary Literature in Translation.*

SIDELIGHTS: Robert Bringhurst translates from Arabic, Greek, Italian, and French, and has given poetry readings on Canadian Broadcasting Corp. network radio and at universities and other institutions in the United States and Canada. His poems have appeared in Polish, Portuguese, German, and French translations.

*   *   *

BROCK, Gavin
See LINDSAY, (John) Maurice

*   *   *

BROCK, Stuart
See TRIMBLE, Louis P(reston)

*   *   *

BRODER, Patricia Janis 1935-

PERSONAL: Born November 22, 1935, in New York, N.Y.; daughter of Milton W. and Rheba (Mantell) Janis; married Stanley H. Broder (an attorney), January 22, 1959; children: Clifford James, Peter Howard, Helen Anna. *Education:* Attended Smith College, 1953-54; Barnard College and Columbia University, joint B.A., 1957; Rutgers University, graduate study, 1962-64. *Home and office:* 488 Long Hill Dr., Short Hills, N.J. 07078.

CAREER: A. M. Kidder (stock broker), New York, N.Y., trainee, 1958-59; Thomson & McKinnon (stock broker), New York, N.Y., customer's broker, 1962-64; art historian and writer, 1964—. Lecturer on art at Southwest Museum, National Cowboy Hall of Fame, Birmingham Art Museum, and St. John's College. Independent investment adviser, 1962-64. Member of Speaker's Bureau of New York Stock Exchange. *Member:* American Association of University Women, Western History Association, Smith Club, Barnard Club. *Awards, honors:* Herbert Adams Memorial Medal from National Sculpture Society, 1975, and Gold Medal from National Academy of Western Art, 1975, both for *Bronzes of the American West;* Wrangler Award, Western Heritage Center, 1975, for best article on the American West, and 1980, for *Taos: A Painter's Dream.*

WRITINGS: Bronzes of the American West, Abrams, 1974; *Hopi Painting Today: The World of the Hopis,* Dutton, 1978; *Dean Cornwell: Dean of Illustrators,* Watson-Guptill, 1978; *Great Painting of the Old American West,* Abbeville Press, 1979; *Taos: A Painter's Dream,* New York Graphic Society, 1980; *American Indian Painting and Sculpture,* Abbeville Press, 1981. Contributor to *Southwest Art, American Art Review, Arizona Highways,* and *Antiques.*

SIDELIGHTS: Patricia Broder has traveled in Europe and in the United States, especially Colorado, Arizona, New Mexico, and Oklahoma. She writes: "Bronze sculpture of the West glorifies the cowboy and the Indian, the explorer and the hunter, wild life and cattle. . . . This history is meaningful in the light of our present day concern with the preservation of our natural resources and our interest in our past and present relationship with the American Indian. I am concerned with bronze sculpture of both the past and the present. I include the vision of pioneer, cowboy, and Indian artists, traditionalist and abstractionist.'' *Avocational interests:* Fox hunting, painting (ink, acrylic, and oil combinations), skiing, and tennis.

*   *   *

BROOKE, Avery (Rogers) 1923-
(Alice Benjamin)

PERSONAL: Born May 28, 1923, in Providence, R.I.; daughter of Morgan Witter and Lucy (Benjamin) Rogers; married Joel Brooke (a sociologist), September 14, 1946; children: Witter, Lucy, Sarah. *Education:* Rhode Island School of Design, B.F.A., 1945; Union Theological Seminary, graduate study, 1968-71. *Politics:* Democrat. *Religion:* Episcopalian. *Home:* 129 Nearwater Lane, Noroton, Conn. 06820.

CAREER: Teacher of art in Pomfret, Conn., 1945-46; teacher of prayer and meditation in Noroton, Conn., 1961-71; Vineyard Books, Inc., Noroton, president, 1972—; Seabury Press, Inc., New York, N.Y., publisher, 1980—. Founder and director of St. Luke's School for Laymen. *Member:* United World Federalists, League of Women Voters, Darien Democratic Town Committee, Darien-Mercara India Committee (co-founder).

WRITINGS: Youth Talks with God, Scribner, 1959; *Doorway to Meditation,* Vineyard Books (Noroton, Conn.), 1973; *Plain Prayers for a Complicated World,* Reader's Digest Press, 1975; (editor) *Roots of Spring,* Vineyard Books, 1975; *How to Meditate without Leaving the World,* Vineyard Books, 1975; (under pseudonym Alice Benjamin; with Harriett Corrigan) *Cooking with Conscience,* Vineyard Books, 1975; *Hidden in Plain Sight,* Seabury, 1979; *The Vineyard Bible,* Seabury, 1980. Founder and editor of *St. Luke's Quarterly.*

SIDELIGHTS: Avery Brooke writes: ''I like to write simply, but not carelessly. I love to think, but I am not a scholar. I lean to practicality, but not if it's dull.''

*   *   *

BROOKS, John (Nixon) 1920-

PERSONAL: Born December 5, 1920, in New York, N.Y.; son of John Nixon and Bessie (Lyon) Brooks; married Rae Everitt; children: Carolyn, John Alexander. *Education:* Princeton University, A.B., 1942. *Home:* 41 Barrow St., New York, N.Y. 10014. *Agent:* Harold Ober Associates, Inc., 40 East 49th St., New York, N.Y. 10017.

CAREER: Full-time writer, 1945—. Member of staff, *New Yorker. Member:* Authors Guild (treasurer, 1964-69; vice-president, 1969-75; president, 1975-79). *Awards, honors:* Loeb Magazine Award, 1964, 1968, for articles published in *New Yorker* magazine, and 1973, for *The Go-Go Years;* John Hancock Award, 1973.

WRITINGS—Novels; all published by Harper: *The Big Wheel,* 1949; *A Pride of Lions,* 1954; *The Man Who Broke Things,* 1958.

Nonfiction; all published by Harper, except as indicated: *The Seven Fat Years: Chronicles of Wall Street,* 1958; *The Fate of the Edsel and Other Business Adventures,* 1963; *The Great Leap: The Past Twenty-Five Years in America,* 1966; *Business Adventures: Twelve Classic Tales from the Worlds of Wall Street and the Modern American Corporation,* Weybright, 1969; *Once in Golconda: A True Drama of Wall Street, 1930-1938,* 1969; *The Go-Go Years,* Weybright, 1973; *The Autobiography of American Business,* Doubleday, 1974; *Telephone: The First Hundred Years,* 1976; *The Games Players,* Times Books, 1980; *Showing Off in America,* Atlantic Monthly Press, 1981.

Editor: (And contributor) *The One and the Many: The Individual in the Modern World,* Harper, 1962. Contributor of articles and reviews to national magazines. Contributing editor, *Time,* 1945-47.

SIDELIGHTS: Although John Brooks is a respected novelist, he is perhaps better known for his nonfiction. For example, R. W. Apple of the *New York Herald Tribune* writes in his review of *The Fate of the Edsel and Other Business Adventures* that ''for all the commercially successful efforts of *The Wall Street Journal* and other publications to better the quality of fiscal journalism, there is still almost no one who writes about business with either wit or grace. One who does is John Brooks of the *New Yorker.* . . . Brooks' account of the passing of the Edsel seems to me admirable in every respect. The same may be said for his reports on the electrical equipment executives who came afoul of the antitrust laws in 1960, in Walter K. Butman, the Proust of Wall Street, and on Clarence Saunders.''

Saturday Review critic W. G. Flanagan believes that ''Brooks is to financial journalism what John Updike is to sports writing. He probably cannot read a financial statement any more than Updike can recall Ted Williams's batting statistics, but he knows high drama and good farce when he sees it, and he has the wit and style to make it all far more entertaining and informative than any annual report could ever be.''

One reason for his success with his nonfiction works, many critics feel, is Brooks' particular journalist approach to presenting his information. John Chamberlain of the *New York Herald Tribune* writes that ''Mr. Brooks is still the behavioristic novelist even when he is reporting facts. You hear his characters chaffing over the omnipresent telephones, you see them bending over the stock tickers, you follow their good-natured explanation of what they do. And always you sense the excitement which is an inseparable part of men's efforts to make a profit or (at worst) to avoid a loss.'' And F. H. Guidry of the *Christian Science Monitor* explains that Brooks writes ''on a novelistic scale, which keeps in view the broad panorama even as it focuses on microscopic details. . . . Some readers may be put off by Mr. Brooks's measured prose . . . [but others] will savor the precise choice of words, the skilled imagery, and the rewarding overtone of a thoroughly humane observer and skilled writer.''

Nation reviewer D. L. Stevenson reports that ''Brooks's *The Man Who Broke Things* reveals him as an amiable, perceptive commentator, essentially an entertainer who keeps all moments of quiet desperation out of bounds. . . . But it should be noticed that . . . documentary novels speak well of only momentary things. . . . I find it difficult to feel anything stronger . . . than admiration for a job of observation rendered intelligently and in clear prose.''

BIOGRAPHICAL/CRITICAL SOURCES: Saturday Review, May 15, 1954, January 19, 1980; *New York Herald Tribune,* March 16, 1958, November 2, 1958, April 7, 1963; *Newsweek,* September 26, 1966; *Christian Science Monitor,* February 18, 1969, October 10, 1973, April 20, 1976; *New York Times Book Review,* November 10, 1974, February 3, 1980, August 2, 1981; *Library Journal,* January 15, 1980; *New York Times,* July 7, 1981; *Chicago Tribune Book World,* July 26, 1981; *Washington Post Book World,* August 9, 1981.

BROOKS, Van Wyck 1886-1963

PERSONAL: Born February 16, 1886, in Plainfield, N.J.; died May 2, 1963; buried in Bridgewater, Conn.; son of Charles Edward (a stockbroker) and Sarah Bailey (Ames) Brooks; married Eleanor Kenyon Stimson, June 1, 1911 (died, 1946); married Gladys Rice Billings (an author), June 2, 1947; children: (first marriage) Charles Van Wyck, Oliver Kenyon. *Education:* Harvard University, A.B., 1908. *Religion:* Episcopalian. *Residence:* Bridgewater, Conn.

CAREER: Although he is listed with the class of 1908 at Harvard University, Van Wyck Brooks finished his courses earlier and began his writing career in London, England, in 1907. He remained in London for two years, and returned there in 1913 for another interval lasting until the outbreak of World War I. In England he followed a pattern of editing, translating, and writing that was continued in the United States from 1909-13, first in New York City with the *Standard Dictionary, Collier's Encyclopedia,* and *World's Work,* and then in California, where he taught English at Stanford University, 1911-13. After his second stay in England he returned to New York City to translate French literature for Century Co. in 1914. He was associate editor of *Seven Arts,* 1917-18, and of *Freeman,* 1920-24. During the twenties he came to be regarded as the leader of a group of critics and writers tagged "rebels," a label that later faded from Brooks. He lived in Connecticut most of the time from 1920 until his death: in Westport from 1920 to 1946, in Cornwall during 1948-49, and in Bridgewater 1949-63.

MEMBER: American Philosophical Society, American Academy of Arts and Letters, American Academy of Arts and Sciences (fellow; chancellor, 1957), Royal Society of Literature (fellow), Phi Beta Kappa, Century Club and The Players (both New York). *Awards, honors:* Dial Prize for distinguished critical work, 1923; Pulitzer Prize in history and National Book Award, both 1937, for *The Flowering of New England;* Gold Medal of National Institute of Arts and Letters, 1946; Theodore Roosevelt Medal, 1954; Litt. D. from Harvard University, Columbia University, Boston University, Bowdoin College, Dartmouth College, Northwestern University, Union College, Northeastern University, Tufts University, University of Pennsylvania, Fairleigh Dickinson University; L.H.D. from Northwestern University. A wing to the Burnham Public Library, Bridgewater, Conn., was dedicated to him.

WRITINGS: The Wine of the Puritans: A Study of Present-Day America, Sisley, 1908, Kennerley, 1909, reprinted, Folcroft, 1969; *The Malady of the Ideal,* A. C. Fifield, 1913, University of Pennsylvania Press, 1947, reprinted, Norwood, 1976; *John Addington Symonds,* Kennerley, 1914, reprinted, Scholarly Press, 1971; *The World of H. G. Wells,* Kennerley, 1915, reprinted, Haskell House, 1973; *America's Coming-of-Age,* Huebsch, 1915, published as *Three Essays on America,* Dutton, 1934, reprinted, 1970; *Letters and Leadership,* Huebsch, 1918; *The Ordeal of Mark Twain,* Dutton, 1920, 3rd edition, 1933, reprinted, 1976; *The Pilgrimage of Henry James,* Dutton, 1925, reprinted, Octagon, 1972; *Emerson and Others,* Dutton, 1927, reprinted, Octagon, 1973; *The Life of Emerson,* Dutton, 1932, reprinted, AMS Press, 1981; *Sketches in Criticism,* Dutton, 1932, reprinted, Folcroft, 1971.

On Literature Today, Dutton, 1941; *The Opinions of Oliver Allston,* Dutton, 1941; *A Chilmark Miscellany: Essays Old and New,* Dutton, 1948, reprinted, Octagon, 1973; *The Writer in America,* Dutton, 1953; *Scenes and Portraits: Memories of Childhood and Youth* (autobiography), Dutton, 1954; *John Sloan:*

A Painter's Life, Dutton, 1955; *From a Writer's Notebook,* St. Onge, 1955, Dutton, 1958; *Helen Keller: A Sketch for a Portrait,* Dutton, 1956; *Days of the Phoenix: The Nineteen-Twenties I Remember* (autobiography), Dutton, 1957; *The Dream of Arcadia: American Writers and Artists in Italy, 1760-1915,* Dutton, 1958; *Howells: His Life and World,* Dutton, 1959; *From the Shadow of the Mountains: My Post-Meridian Years* (autobiography), Dutton, 1961; *Fenollosa and His Circle; With Other Essays in Biography,* Dutton, 1962; *An Autobiography,* Dutton, 1965; Robert E. Spiller, editor, *The Van Wyck Brooks-Lewis Mumford Letters: The Record of a Literary Friendship, 1921-1963,* Dutton, 1970.

Author of "Makers and Finders: A History of the Writer in America, 1800-1915" series, published by Dutton (contains: *The Flowering of New England, 1815-1865,* 1936, revised edition, 1946; *New England: Indian Summer, 1865-1915,* 1940; *The World of Washington Irving,* 1944; *The Times of Melville and Whitman,* 1947, 2nd edition, 1953; *The Confident Years, 1885-1915,* 1955), an abridgement of this series, edited by Otto Bettmann, published with illustrations as *Our Literary Heritage: A Pictorial History of the Writer in America,* Dutton, 1956, reprinted, Paddington, 1977.

Editor: (And author of introduction) Randolph Silliman Bourne, *History of a Literary Radical and Other Essays,* Viking, 1920, reprinted, Biblo & Tannen, 1969; (and author of introduction) Christopher Columbus, *Journal of First Voyage to America,* Boni, 1924; (with others) *American Caravan,* Macaulay, 1927; Gamaliel Bradford, *Journal, 1883-1932,* Houghton, 1933; Bradford, *Letters, 1918-1931,* Houghton, 1934; (and author of preface) Constance Mayfield Rourke, *Roots of American Culture and Other Essays,* Harcourt, 1942, reprinted, Kennikat, 1965; *New England Reader,* Atheneum, 1962.

Translator: Henri Frederick Amiel, *Jean Jacques Rousseau,* Viking, 1922; (with first wife, Eleanor Stimson Brooks) Georges Berguer, *Some Aspects of the Life of Jesus: From the Psychological and Psychoanalytical Point of View,* Harcourt, 1923; Leon Bazalgette, *Henry Thoreau: Bachelor of Nature,* Harcourt, 1924; Romain Rolland, *Mother and Son,* Holt, 1927; Andre Chamson, *Roux the Bandit,* Scribner, 1929; Chamson, *The Road,* Scribner, 1929; Paul Gauguin, *Intimate Journals,* Heinemann, 1930, Crown, 1936, new edition, Liveright, 1970; Chamson, *Crime of the Just,* Scribner, 1930; Amiel, *Philine: From the Unpublished Journals,* Houghton, 1931; (with son, Charles Van Wyck Brooks) Amiel, *Private Journal,* Macmillan (Toronto), 1936; (and author of introduction) Llewelyn Powys, *Earth Memories,* Norton, 1938.

His work also includes introductions to books by Henry Adams, Hamlin Garland, and other writers.

SIDELIGHTS: In a poll reported in *Best Books of the Decade: 1936-1945,* by Asa Don Dickinson, Van Wyck Brooks led the list of "best authors" with 1711 points; his nearest competitor had 1068. *The Flowering of New England* headed national bestseller lists for fifty-nine consecutive weeks. Several of his books were Book-of-the-Month-Club selections. For a scholarly non-fiction writer to reach such heights in the esteem of a large segment of the general public is a rare accomplishment. In the opinion of many critics, Brooks achieved and maintained his position through a combination of talents, not the least of which was an imagination so vivid that he saw, and made his readers see, the historic events of the past as though they were current events. As Leon Edel suggested, "What mattered for Brooks was the scene, the picture, the memory—and always the love of the past for its pastness." He was respected by the critics as one of the few contemporary men of letters and by his readers as one of the few contemporary optimists concerning the traditional American faith and the fundamental integrity of mankind.

During an interview with Harvey Breit before his death, Brooks spoke of the goals he hoped he achieved through his writings. "Everybody is so isolated in this country," Brooks remarked. "You know, the famous talk of America being lonely. The country is so big, everyone is so scattered, there are so many kinds of people and races, and I wanted to create the feeling that a great deal has been done in a much more unified way than has been thought of. . . . I wanted to bring together all the sections of America. The South hates New England and the West hates the East. Well, I wanted to show there is a much closer relationship between these sections than was realized, that we weren't so provincial, and that we were influenced. Melville and Whitman began as imitators of Irving, just as Farell followed Dreiser. The instinct of emulation is very powerful."

BIOGRAPHICAL/CRITICAL SOURCES—Autobiographies: *Scenes and Portraits: Memories of Childhood and Youth*, Dutton, 1954; *Days of the Phoenix: The Nineteen-Twenties I Remember*, Dutton, 1957; *From the Shadow of the Mountains: My Post-Meridian Years*, Dutton, 1961; *An Autobiography*, Dutton, 1965.

Other books: John Paul Pritchard, *Criticism in America*, University of Oklahoma Press, 1956; Harvey Breit, *The Writer Observed*, World Publishing, 1956; Gladys Rice Brooks, *If Strangers Meet: A Memory*, Harcourt, 1967; Claire Sprague, editor, *Van Wyck Brooks: The Early Years*, Harper, 1968; William Wasserstrom, *Van Wyck Brooks*, University of Minnesota Press, 1968; Robert E. Spiller, editor, *The Van Wyck Brooks-Lewis Mumford Letters: The Record of a Literary Friendship, 1921-1963*, Dutton, 1970; Wasserstrom, *The Legacy of Van Wyck Brooks: A Study of Maladies and Motives*, Southern Illinois University Press, 1971; J. E. Vitelli, *Van Wyck Brooks: A Reference Guide*, G. K. Hall, 1977.

Periodicals: *Time*, October 2, 1944, May 10, 1963; *Saturday Review*, February 18, 1961, May 25, 1963; *New York Times*, May 3, 1963; *Newsweek*, May 13, 1963; *Publishers Weekly*, May 13, 1963; *New York Times Book Review*, May 19, 1963; *New Yorker*, July 13, 1963; *Book Week*, February 21, 1965.†

*   *   *

BROWER, Reuben Arthur 1908-1975

PERSONAL: Born May 5, 1908, in Lanesboro, Pa.; son of Arthur and Hannah (Taylor) Brower; died March 27, 1975, of a heart attack in Boston, Mass.; buried in Lanesboro, Pa.; married Helen Porter, September 12, 1934; children: Jonathan, Richard, Ellen Brightly. *Education:* Amherst College, B.A. (summa cum laude), 1930; Cambridge University, B.A., 1932, M.A., 1936; Harvard University, Ph.D., 1936. *Home:* 1 Hay Rd., Belmont, Mass. *Office:* Adams House C-17, Harvard University, Cambridge, Mass. 02138.

CAREER: Harvard University, Cambridge, Mass., instructor in English, 1936-39; Amherst College, Amherst, Mass., assistant professor, 1939-44, associate professor, 1944-48, Class of 1880 Professor of Greek and English, 1948-53; Harvard University, professor of English, 1953-71, Henry B. and Anne M. Cabot Professor of English, 1971-75, master of Adams House, 1954-68. Instructor, Bread Loaf School of English, 1940, 1941, 1947, 1951; fellow, Center for Advanced Study in the Behavioral Sciences, 1961-62; Fulbright senior scholar, Oxford University, 1968-69; Martin Classical Lecturer, Oberlin College, 1970; Phi Beta Kappa Visiting Scholar, 1971-72; overseas fellow, Churchill College • Cambridge, 1974-75.

MEMBER: Modern Language Association of America, American Association of University Professors, American Academy of Arts and Sciences, Club of Odd Volumes (Boston), Classical Association of New England, Phi Beta Kappa, Century Association (New York). *Awards, honors:* Guggenheim fellowship, 1956-57, 1965-66; National Endowment for the Humanities fellowship, 1974; Harvard University Press Faculty prize, honorable mention, 1959; Christian Gauss Award, Phi Beta Kappa, 1960; Explicator Award, 1964, for *The Poetry of Robert Frost*.

WRITINGS: The Fields of Light: An Experiment in Critical Reading, Oxford University Press, 1951, reprinted, Greenwood Press, 1980; (contributor) *Major British Writers*, Harcourt, 1954; *Alexander Pope: The Poetry of Allusion*, Clarendon Press, 1959; (editor) *On Translation*, Harvard University Press, 1959; (editor) *John Dryden*, Dell, 1962; (editor with Richard Poirier) *In Defense of Reading*, Dutton, 1962; *The Poetry of Robert Frost—Constellations of Intention*, Oxford University Press, 1963; (editor) Jane Austen, *Mansfield Park*, Houghton, 1965; (editor with W. H. Bond and author of introduction) Homer, *The Iliad*, translation by Alexander Pope, Macmillan, 1965; (editor) William Shakespeare, *Coriolanus*, New American Library, 1966; (editor with Anne D. Ferry and David Kalstone) *Beginning with Poems: An Anthology*, Norton, 1966; (editor) *Forms of Lyric: Selected Papers from the English Institute*, Columbia University Press, 1970; *Hero and Saint: Shakespeare and the Graeco-Roman Heroic Tradition*, Oxford University Press, 1971; (editor) *Twentieth-Century Literature in Retrospect*, Harvard University Press, 1971; (editor with Helen Vendler and John Hollander) *I. A. Richards: Essays in His Honor*, Oxford University Press, 1973; *Mirror on Mirror: Translation, Imitation, Parody*, Harvard University Press, 1974. Contributor to professional journals. Editor, *Harvard English Studies*, 1969-75.

BIOGRAPHICAL/CRITICAL SOURCES: Christian Century, November 17, 1971; *Yale Review*, March, 1972; *Times Literary Supplement*, April 7, 1972; *New York Review of Books*, October 5, 1972; *New York Times Book Review*, December 10, 1972.

OBITUARIES: New York Times, March 29, 1975.†

*   *   *

BROWN, Joseph E(dward) 1929-

PERSONAL: Born December 14, 1929, in San Francisco, Calif.; son of LeRoy D. and Ora E. (Ackley) Brown; married Christa Brigitte, August 12, 1967; children: Joseph, Mark, Teri, Erik. *Education:* Attended University of Wisconsin, 1952, and University of Hawaii, 1953. *Residence:* San Diego, Calif.

CAREER: San Diego Union, San Diego, Calif., reporter, 1959-69; *Oceans*, San Diego, editor, 1969-71; free-lance writer, 1971—. *Military service:* U.S. Navy, 1948-52. *Member:* Society of Magazine Writers, Authors Guild, Sigma Delta Chi.

WRITINGS—Published by Dodd, except as indicated: *The Golden Sea* (nonfiction), Playboy Press, 1974; *Wonders of a Kelp Forest* (juvenile), 1974; *The Sea's Harvest* (juvenile), 1975; *Wonders of Seals and Sea Lions* (juvenile), 1976; *Harness the Wind* (juvenile), 1978; *Oil Spills*, 1978; *The Mormon Trek West*, Doubleday, 1980; *Rescue from Extinction* (juvenile), 1981.

WORK IN PROGRESS: Yesterdays Wings, for Doubleday; *Return of the Pelican*, for Louisiana State University Press.

AVOCATIONAL INTERESTS: Oceanography, marine science, marine resources, sailing.

BROWN, Marilyn McMeen Miller 1938-
(Marilyn McMeen Miller)

PERSONAL: Born November 6, 1938, in Denver, Colo.; daughter of William Otho (a civil engineer) and Lola Frances (Murphy) McMeen; married Lloyd Clifton Miller, June 1, 1964 (divorced, 1967); married W. William Brown, Jr., October 4, 1975; children: (first marriage) Simeen; (stepchildren) Wendy Lynn, William Cary, Eva Marie, Andrew Kim, Melissa Ann. *Education:* Brigham Young University, B.A., 1962, M.A., 1964. *Politics:* "Conservative: 'Even artists should earn their own way.'" *Religion:* Church of Jesus Christ of Latter-day Saints (Mormons). *Home:* 3674 Little Rock Dr., Provo, Utah 84601. *Office:* Bill Brown Realty, 555 South State, Orem, Utah 84057.

CAREER: Bureau of Reclamation, Denver, Colo., clerk-typist, 1955-60; teacher of Latin and English in junior high school in Denver, 1960-61; Brigham Young University, Provo, Utah, instructor in English, 1962-70; Prudential Federal Savings, Provo, typist, summer, 1971; Brigham Young University Press, Provo, editor and writer, 1972-75; Bill Brown Realty, Orem, Utah, realtor associate, 1980—. Building contractor, Bill Brown Development Corp., 1978—. Member of board of directors of Utah Repertory Theater. *Member:* Utah League of Writers (president, 1969), Utah Poetry Society. *Awards, honors:* First prizes from Utah League of Writers, 1969, other prizes, 1969-72; Utah State Fine Arts prize, 1970, for light verse, 1971, for poem, and 1972, for unpublished novel.

WRITINGS—Published by Art Publishers (Provo, Utah), except as indicated; under name Marilyn McMeen Miller: *Rainflowers* (poems; self-illustrated), 1969; (with John C. Moffitt) *Provo: A Story of People in Motion,* Brigham Young University Press, 1974; *I Have Lost My Heart Again: I Pray I Will Not Lose My Head, Amen* (poems; self-illustrated), 1974.

Under name Marilyn McMeen Brown: *The Grandmother Tree* (poems; self-illustrated), 1979; *The Earthkeepers* (novel), 1980.

Ghost writer of *Roughing It Easy,* by Dian Thomas, Brigham Young University Press, 1974. Contributor of stories, articles, and poems to *Dialogue, Children's Friend, Era, New Era, Ensign, Relief Society,* and other periodicals.

WORK IN PROGRESS: Stones of Blood.

SIDELIGHTS: Marilyn Brown wrote to *CA:* "I am a Mormon writer—immersed in Mormon tradition and local history—who hopes to speak out for the unique contribution of my subculture—this isolated religious community of the West which is now participating in an influential world religious movement. My unpublished novels are all written on Mormon historical subjects: the handcart movement, the settlement of small outlying towns in Utah and Idaho. I have a deep interest in defining the Mormon experience for a modern audience and in creating a literature acceptable to the scrutiny of the most demanding criticism.

"My first novel—a 500 page piece of Mormon historical fiction about the place where I live, Provo, Utah—has received some very positive critical acceptance by my Mormon literary peers whose judgement is so important to me. And I am working on a second book, *Stones of Blood,* about the Mountain Meadows Massacre, which is to be published by a Utah publisher as soon as I can find the time out of my many other responsibilities to finish it. Since my second marriage to a widower with five children I have done a lot of impromptu mothering, contracting for various construction projects (I built a $600,000 house and

recently a duplex), and I have listed and sold many houses to buoy up my husband's real estate sales. Creating an exemplary life is probably as important to me as creating vivid, living literature which will stand the test of time. I love writing and would rather 'write' than 'live.' But I believe my writing will be enriched by my living—so I reluctantly do both.

"To find my place as a recognized contemporary author is all I want of heaven, so—if I make it—dying will be easy and life after death anti-climactic. I pray they'll place a stack of paper and some pencils in my cold hands."

AVOCATIONAL INTERESTS: Art, music, poetry, drama.

*   *   *

BUCKMASTER, Henrietta
See STEPHENS, Henrietta Henkle

*   *   *

BURCHARD, John Ely 1898-1975

PERSONAL: Born December 8, 1898, in Marshall, Minn.; died December 25, 1975, in Boston, Mass.; son of James Clark and Sidonie (Schupp) Burchard; married Marjorie Walker Gaines, 1926; children: John Ely, Jr., Marshall Gaines. *Education:* Attended University of Minnesota, 1915-17; Massachusetts Institute of Technology, S.B., 1923, S.M., 1925. *Home:* 564 Springs Rd., Bedford, Mass. *Office:* Massachusetts Institute of Technology, Cambridge, Mass.

CAREER: Bemis Industries, Inc. and subsidiary, Housing Co., Boston, Mass., 1925-38, director of research, member of board of directors, and vice-president; Massachusetts Institute of Technology, Cambridge, director of Bemis Foundation, 1938-48, director of libraries, 1944-48, dean of school of humanities and social science, 1948-64, dean emeritus, 1964-75; University of California, Berkeley, visiting professor, 1964-66, acting dean of College of Environmental Design, 1966-67, Mellon Visiting Professor of Environmental Design, 1967-68. War work with National Research Council, National Defense Research Committee, Office of Field Service, 1940-45. Guest professor and lecturer, various universities. Mount Holyoke College, member, board of trustees, 1951-61; U.S. Merchant Marine Academy, member, advisory board, 1953-60; Graham Foundation for Advanced Studies in the Fine Arts, Chicago, principal consultant, 1955-60; Boston Museum of Fine Arts, member of board of trustees, 1957-60; Massachusetts Institute of Technology Press Board, past chairman. Consultant to universities. President's Science Advisory Committee, member of panel on science and engineering education, 1958-59; Aspen Institute for Humanistic Studies, past member of advisory board. One of eight Americans sent to confer in France and Norway on problems of higher education; delegate to conference, "Science in Modern Civilization," Japan, 1960; lecturer in Iran, Pakistan, and India, 1962. *Military service:* U.S. Army Medical Corps, American Expeditionary Forces, 1917-19.

MEMBER: American Academy of Arts and Sciences (president, 1954-57), American Institute of Architects (honorary member), Chi Psi, Tau Beta Pi, Examiner Club, St. Botolph Club (both Boston). *Awards, honors:* Presidential medal for merit, 1948, for war work; Smith-Mundt fellow, Australia, 1951; doctor of human letters, Union College, Schenectady, N.Y., 1953; doctor of architecture, University of Michigan, 1956; University of Minnesota's Outstanding Achievement Award, 1960; Officier de l'Ordre des Arts et des Lettres (France), 1964; Thomas Jefferson Memorial Foundation Medal for excellence in architecture, 1969.

WRITINGS: (With Albert Farwell Bemis) *The Evolving House*, M.I.T. Press, three volumes, 1933-36; *Fundamental Principles of Structural ARP*, National Research Council, 1943; (with Lincoln Thiesmeyer) *Combat Scientists*, Atlantic, Little, Brown, 1947; *Q.E.D.; M.I.T. in World War II*, Wiley, 1948; (co-author and editor) *Rockets, Guns and Targets*, Atlantic-Little, Brown, 1948; (editor) *Planning the University Library Building*, Princeton University Press, 1949; (editor) *Mid-Century: The Social Implications of Scientific Progress*, Wiley and M.I.T. Press, 1950; (with Albert Bush-Brown) *The Architecture of America*, Little, Brown, 1961, abridged edition, 1966; (editor with Oscar Handlin) *The Historian and the City*, M.I.T. Press, 1963; *The Voice of the Phoenix: Post-War Architecture in Germany*, M.I.T. Press, 1966; *Design and Urban Beauty in the Central City*, Joint Center for Urban Studies, c. 1967; (collector and editor) *Thoughts from the Lake of Time: A Group of Essays in Honor of the Villa Serbelloni*, Josiah Macy, Jr. Foundation, 1971; *Bernini Is Dead?: Architecture and the Social Purpose*, McGraw, 1976.

Consulting editor on architecture, *Encyclopaedia Britannica*; member of editorial board, *Daedalus*, 1958-73; consulting editor, *Architectural Record*, 1958-61. Contributor of chapters and articles to books and periodicals, both foreign and domestic, on housing, library planning, architecture, urbanism, and educational and cultural subjects.

SIDELIGHTS: John Ely Burchard was described by the *New York Times* as "a widely known and respected architectural critic and historian . . . whose writings and teachings fought for the joining of science and culture and the combining of technological progress with humanism."

BIOGRAPHICAL/CRITICAL SOURCES: Observer Review, April 30, 1967; *Times Literary Supplement*, November 9, 1967; *America*, October 23, 1976; *New York Times Book Review*, November 21, 1976; *Best Sellers*, December, 1976; *Commonweal*, May 27, 1977.

OBITUARIES: New York Times, December 27, 1975; *AB Bookman's Weekly*, January 26, 1976.†

*   *   *

BURGESS, M(ichael) R(oy)   1948-
(Miguel Alcalde, Boden Clarke, [C.] Everett Cooper, Michael Demotes, G. Forbes Durand, Misha Grazhdanin, Peter Harding, Andrew Kapel, Jacob Lawson, Rex Miletus, Walt Mobley, Jack B. Nimble, Daniel Painter, Nero Rale, Reginald, R[obert] Reginald, Lucretia Sharpe, Tertius Spartacus, Lucas Webb)

PERSONAL: Born February 11, 1948, in Fukuoka, Japan; son of Roy Walter (a director of a school district transportation office) and Betty Jane (Kapel) Burgess; married Mary Alice Wickizer Rogers (co-publisher of Borgo Press), October 15, 1976; stepchildren: Richard Albert Rogers, Mary Louise Rogers. *Education:* Gonzaga University, A.B. (with honors), 1969; University of Southern California, M.S. in L.S., 1970. *Politics:* "Monarchist." *Religion:* "Basically anti-." *Home and office address:* P.O. Box 2845, San Bernardino, Calif. 92406.

CAREER: California State College, San Bernardino, periodicals librarian and chief cataloger, 1970—, on leave, 1981—; Borgo Press, San Bernardino, publisher and editor, 1975—; free-lance writer and editor, 1981—. Editor, Newcastle Publishing Co., Inc., 1971—; publisher, *Science Fiction and Fantasy Book Review*, 1979-80. *Member:* Science Fiction Writers of America, Science Fiction Research Association, Fantasy

Association, Mythopoeic Society, William Morris Society and Kelmscott Fellowship, Kentucky Historical Society, Blue Earth County Historical Society.

WRITINGS—Under pseudonym R. Reginald, except as indicated; published by Borgo, except as indicated: *Stella Nova: The Contemporary Science Fiction Authors*, Unicorn & Son, 1970, revised edition published as *Contemporary Science Fiction Authors*, Arno, 1975; (under pseudonym R. Reginald and real name M. R. Burgess) *Cumulative Paperback Index, 1939-1959*, Gale, 1973; (under pseudonym Lucas Webb) *The Attempted Assassination of John F. Kennedy: A Political Fantasy*, 1976; (under pseudonym C. Everett Cooper) *Up Your Asteroid!: A Science Fiction Farce*, 1977; (with Douglas Menville) *Things to Come: An Illustrated History of the Science Fiction Film*, Times Books, 1977; *Science Fiction and Fantasy Literature*, Gale, 1979, Volume I: *A Checklist, 1700-1974*, Volume II: *Contemporary Science Fiction Authors II*.

(With Kevin B. Hancer) *The Paperback Price Guide*, Overstreet Publications, 1980, 2nd edition, 1982; (with Jeffrey M. Elliot) *If J.F.K. Had Lived: A Political Scenario*, 1981; *Science Fiction and Fantasy Awards*, 1981; (with Dan Lewis) *Science Fiction and Fantasy Statistics*, 1982; (with Elliot) *The Analytical Congressional Directory*, 1982; (under pseudonym Boden Clarke) *Eastern Churches Review: An Index to Volumes I-X, 1966-1978*, 1982; (with wife, Mary A. Burgess) *The Milford Series: Popular Writers of Today—An Index to Volumes I-XXXV*, 1982; *A Guide to Science Fiction and Fantasy in the Library of Congress Classification Scheme*, 1982; (with Lewis) *In His Native Habitat: Characteristics of the Science Fiction Writer*, 1982; (with L. W. Currey) *Science Fiction and Fantasy Reference Guide*, 1982; (under real name) *The House of the Burgesses*, 1982; *By Any Other Name: A Comprehensive Checklist of Science Fiction and Fantasy Pseudonyms*, 1982; (with Currey) *Science Fiction Price Guide*, 1982; *To Be Continued . . . : An Annotated Bibliography of Science Fiction and Fantasy Series and Sequels*, 1982; *X, Y, and Z: A List of Those Books Examined in the Course of Compiling "Science Fiction and Fantasy Literature" Which Were Judged to Fall Outside the Genre of Fantastic Literature—An Anti-Bibliography*, 1982; (with M. A. Burgess) *The Wickizer Annals*, 1982; (under pseudonym Boden Clarke) *Lords Temporal and Lords Spiritual: A Chronological Checklist of the Popes, Patriarchs, Katholikoi, and Independent Archbishops and Metropolitans of the Autocephalous Monarchical Churches of the Christian East and West, Including the Roman Catholic Church and Its Eastern Dependencies, the Independent Eastern Orthodox Churches, the Armenian Churches, the Coptic Churches, the Jacobite Churches of Syria and India, the Ethiopian Church, and the Church of the Sinai*, 1982; (with Elliot) *If Germany Had Won the War: A Political Scenario*, 1982.

Editor with Douglas Menville; all published by Arno: *Ancestral Voices: An Anthology of Early Science Fiction*, 1975; *Phantasmagoria: An Original Anthology*, 1976; *Ancient Hauntings*, 1976; *R.I.P.: Five Stories of the Supernatural*, 1976; *The Spectre Bridegroom and Other Horrors*, 1976; *King Solomon's Children: Some Parodies of H. Rider Haggard*, 1978; *Dreamers of Dreams: An Anthology of Fantasy*, 1978; *They: Three Parodies of H. Rider Haggard's "She,"* 1978; *Worlds of Never: Three Fantastic Novels*, 1978.

Advisory editor, with Menville, of "Forgotten Fantasy Library" series, Newcastle, 1973-80, "Science Fiction" series, Arno, 1975, "Supernatural and Occult Fiction" series, Arno, 1976, and "Lost Race and Adult Fantasy" series, Arno, 1978; advisory editor, "Science Fiction Criticism and Dissertations" series, Arno, in press.

Contributor under various pseudonyms of over 100 articles and reviews to periodicals. Associate editor, *Forgotten Fantasy*, 1970-71.

WORK IN PROGRESS: A history of the monarchies of Malaysia; several literary and historical reference works and directories, including *Cumulative Paperback Index, 1960-1969*, a new edition of *Science Fiction and Fantasy Literature* which contains a checklist from 1975-82 and additional author biographies, the second edition of *The Analytical Congressional Directory*, with Elliot, and *The Light in the Window: A Bibliography of the Modern Gothic Novel*, with M. A. Burgess.

SIDELIGHTS: M. R. Burgess, better known to his readers and others in the publishing world as "R. Reginald" or just "Reginald," first used his pseudonym in connection with an article he wrote for Gonzaga University's literary magazine. "I was rather shy and secretive as a kid," he explains, "and I rather relished the thought of publishing under an assumed name." Reginald expropriated the pseudonym from one of his favorite characters in the work of short story writer Saki (H. H. Munro), who had found *his* pseudonym in Edward FitzGerald's version of *The Rubaiyat of Omar Khayyam*. Continues the author: "At first, it was just 'R. Reginald,' but naturally I started getting questions about the 'R' part of it, so I adopted as my given name 'Robert.' . . . Once started, it's impossible to go back."

As for his writing, Reginald admits that "it's difficult to say much about oneself without seeming pompous or just plain silly. The mystique of the writer has been romanticized far beyond the bounds of reality or good sense; I sometimes wonder if any of us have contributed as much to society as one good licensed plumber. Over the years, I've taught myself to write on demand, usually on first draft; it's the tool of my chosen trade, much as the wrench is to the plumber. And, like the craftsman, I sell what skills I have to the highest bidder; what I get per hour is usually far less than what I pay to the man clearing out my drains. I make no claims of being a 'great writer,' whatever that is: my books are not reviewed in the *New York Review of Books;* I've been given no literary prizes; and my name is not spoken at cocktail parties in high society. Most people have never heard of me and never will.

"But I love my work, I love the independence that goes with it, I love making things that would not have existed without me. Call it conceit or egoism or whatever you will, but I like seeing my name in print. The thought that some of my books might just survive this corporeal presence I call R. Reginald still manages to thrill me. I suffer from no illusions that I have changed or will change the course of human events, but I still feel the necessity to fill as many feet of library shelves as I possibly can. I'll stop when death, ill health, or old age forces me to; until then, I'll fight my own private war with entropy, working towards one hundred, two hundred, three hundred dusty, moldy volumes—my creative children, so to speak. When I do reach the point where I can no longer write, my real life will have ended, whether or not the physical part continues on for a few more empty years.

"I write for many reasons: money to pay the bills, ego, an intense dislike of salaried positions—the list is endless. Mostly, I write for joy: the act of immersing oneself in a large creative project is akin, I think, to a religious experience. There is no better existence that I can imagine: I get paid for doing what I enjoy best in life. I see no point in wasting one's life working at a job that one hates or even tolerates; whatever a person does, he or she must be willing to take the final risk of believing in oneself without deluding oneself. To the self-aware, any other course seems to me madness."

BURNETT, Hallie Southgate (Zeisel)

PERSONAL: Born in St. Louis, Mo.; daughter of John McKnight (a consulting engineer) and Elizabeth (Baker) Southgate; married Whitney Ewing Burnett (a writer and editor under name Whit Burnett), 1942 (died, 1973); married William Zeisel, 1977; children: (first marriage) John Southgate, Whitney. *Politics:* Independent. *Religion:* Episcopal. *Home:* 815 Valley Rd., New Canaan, Conn. 08640.

CAREER: Story magazine, New York, N.Y., co-editor, 1942-70; editor, Story Press Books, 1942-65; reader, Book-of-the-Month Club, 1957-59; Prentice-Hall, Inc., Englewood Cliffs, N.J., senior editor, 1959-60; Sarah Lawrence College, Bronxville, N.Y., associate professor of literature and creative writing, 1960-64. Conductor of fiction workshop at New York City Writer's Conference, Wagner College, 1955-60; instructor in short story writing at Hunter College of the City University of New York, 1959-61; lecturer on creative writing at University of Cincinnati, University of Missouri, and other universities and colleges. *Member:* P.E.N. (director, 1951-71), Woman Pays Club, Overseas Press Club. *Awards, honors:* O. Henry Award (third prize), 1942, for "Eighteenth Summer."

WRITINGS: (Editor with husband, Whit Burnett) *Story: The Fiction of the Forties*, Dutton, 1950; *A Woman in Possession* (novel), Dutton, 1951; (editor with W. Burnett) *Story*, four volumes, McKay, 1951-54; *This Heart, This Hunter* (novel), Henry Holt, 1953; *The Brain Pickers* (novel), Messner, 1957; (editor with W. Burnett) *The Fiction of a Generation*, two volumes, MacGibbon & Kee, 1959; (with W. Burnett) *The Modern Short Story in the Making*, Hawthorn, 1964; (editor with W. Burnett) *Story Jubilee: Thirty-three Years of Story*, Doubleday, 1965; *The Watch on the Wall* (novel), Morrow, 1965.

The Boarders in the Rue Madame: Nine Gallic Tales, Morrow, 1966; (editor) *Story: The Yearbook of Discovery*, Four Winds Press, 1968; *The Daughter-in-law Cookbook*, Hewitt House, 1969; *The Millionaire's Cookbook*, Pyramid Publications, 1973; *Fiction Writer's Handbook*, Harper, 1974; *Short Story Writer's Handbook*, Harper, 1982. Contributor of book reviews to *New York Times, Saturday Review*, and *Book of the Month;* contributor of articles and short stories to *Town and Country* and other magazines. Contributing editor, *Junior League Magazine*, 1937-42; fiction edition, *Yankee*, 1959-60; has held editorial posts on *Reader's Digest* and *Book Club*.

WORK IN PROGRESS: Short stories; a novel.

SIDELIGHTS: Hallie Southgate Burnett told *CA:* "[I] have only one recurring problem: what to put on a passport as occupation. [I] have tried editor, novelist, short story writer, college professor, and housewife and finally settled for the latter, as nobody is very impressed anyway.

"I write hard, look soft, think clear, talk vague, and generally wish I had the exterior of somebody else, preferably thinner. I prefer young people to old, old books to new (although I find young talent the most exciting thing in the world), and I hope I never die—at least until I have made a hundred more trips to Europe and at least one around the world."

Burnett's novel, *The Watch on the Wall*, has been translated into German, Japanese, and Portuguese.

*   *   *

BURROWS, Fredrika Alexander 1908-

PERSONAL: Born August 22, 1908, in Montpelier, Vt.; daughter of Fred Wilmer and Lula (Keir) Alexander; married Ronald Powell Burrows, July 12, 1930; children: Martha Jane (Mrs. James Curtis), Roberta Ann (Mrs. Paul Gray). *Education:* Middlebury College, A.B., 1929. *Home address:* Box 447, West Hyannisport, Mass. 02672.

CAREER: High school teacher in Princeton, Mass., 1929-33, in St. Johnsbury, Vt., 1934-36, and substitute teacher in Scituate, Mass., 1948-60; The Children's Shop, Cohasset, Mass., co-owner, 1962-65; reporter for *National Antiques Review*, 1972-76, *Cape Cod Illustrated*, 1974-75, and *Antique Traders' Weekly*, 1980—. *Member:* National League of American Pen Women, American Historical Print Collectors Society, International Molinological Society, Society for the Preservation of Old Mills, Yesteryear's Museum Association, Twelve O'Clock Scholars, Professional Writers of Cape Cod, Centerville Historical Society. *Awards, honors:* Society of Children's Book Writers honorable mention, 1974.

WRITINGS—Published by William S. Sullwold: (Contributor) *Cape Cod Sampler*, 1971; *The Yankee Scrimshanders*, 1973; (contributor) *A Showing of Scrimshaw—Barcelos*, 1974; (contributor) *The Seven Villages of Barnstable*, Part II: *The Revolution*, 1976; *Cannonballs and Cranberries*, 1976; *Windmills on Cape Cod and the Islands*, 1978; (contributor) *Cape Cod Sampler II*, 1979; (editor) *The Prolific Pencil*, 1980. Contributor of articles and fiction to *Good Housekeeping, Yankee, Child Life, Hobbies, New England Guide*, and other publications.

SIDELIGHTS: Fredrika Burrows has travelled throughout the United States, Canada, Europe, and the Caribbean. *Avocational interests:* Collecting scrimshaw, antique dolls, and books.

BIOGRAPHICAL/CRITICAL SOURCES: National Antiques Review, December, 1973.

*   *   *

BUTLER, Gwendoline Williams   1922-
(Jennie Melville)

PERSONAL: Born August 19, 1922, in London, England; daughter of Alfred Edward and Alice (Lee) Williams; married Lionel Butler (a professor of medieval history at University of St. Andrews), October 16, 1949; children: Lucilla. *Education:* Lady Margaret Hall, Oxford, M.A., 1948. *Home:* The Principal's House, The Royal Holloway College, Egham, Surrey, England. *Agent:* John Farquharson Ltd., Bell House, 8 Bell Yard, London WC2A 2JU, England.

CAREER: Writer. *Awards, honors:* Silver Dagger, Crime Writers Association, 1973, for *A Coffin for Pandora;* Romantic Novelists Association prize, 1980, for *The Red Staircase.*

WRITINGS—Published by Bles, except as indicated: *Receipt for Murder*, 1956; *Dead in a Row*, 1957; *The Dull Dead*, 1958, Walker & Co., 1962; *The Murdering Kind*, 1958, Roy, 1964; *The Interloper*, 1959; *Death Lives Next Door*, 1960, published as *Dine and Be Dead*, Macmillan, 1960; *Make Me a Murderer*, 1961; *Coffin in Oxford*, 1962; *Coffin for Baby*, Walker & Co., 1963; *Coffin Waiting*, 1963, Walker & Co., 1965; *Coffin in Malta*, 1964, Walker & Co., 1965; *A Nameless Coffin*, 1966, Walker & Co., 1967; *Coffin Following*, 1968; *Coffin's Dark Number*, 1969; *A Coffin from the Past*, 1970; *A Coffin for Pandora*, Macmillan (London), 1973, published as *Olivia*, Coward, 1974; *A Coffin for the Canary*, Macmillan (London), 1974, published as *Sarsen Place*, Coward, 1974; *The Vesey Inheritance*, Coward, 1975; *The Brides of Friedberg*, Macmillan (London), 1977, published as *Meadowsweet*, Coward, 1977; *The Red Staircase*, Collins, 1980.

Under pseudonym Jennie Melville: *Come Home and Be Killed*, M. Joseph, 1962, British Book Centre, 1964; *Burning Is a Substitute for Loving*, M. Joseph, 1963, British Book Centre, 1964; *Murderers' Houses*, M. Joseph, 1964; *There Lies Your Love*, M. Joseph, 1965; *Nell Alone* (also see below), M. Joseph, 1966; *A Different Kind of Summer*, Hodder & Stoughton, 1967; *The Hunter in the Shadows*, Hodder & Stoughton, 1969, McKay, 1970; *A New Kind of Killer, An Old Kind of Death*, Hodder & Stoughton, 1970, published as *A New Kind of Killer*, McKay, 1971; *Ironwood*, McKay, 1972; *Nun's Castle*, McKay, 1973; *Raven's Forge*, McKay, 1975; *Dragon's Eye*, Simon & Schuster, 1976; *Axwater*, Macmillan (London), 1978, published as *Tarot's Tower*, Simon & Schuster, 1978; *The Wages of Zen*, Secker & Warburg, 1979; *Murder Has a Pretty Face*, Macmillan, 1981.

Contributor: *Ellery Queen's Murder Menu*, World Publishing, 1969; George Hardinge, editor, *Winter's Crimes 4*, Macmillan (London), 1972; Hardinge, editor, *Winter's Crimes 6*, Macmillan (London), 1974. Also author of radio play "Nell Alone" (based on novel of same title), 1968.

SIDELIGHTS: Gwendoline Butler has focused her attention on two different types of mystery writing: police procedural novels featuring Detective Inspector John Coffin and historical mysteries set in Victorian or Edwardian England. In both areas she has achieved critical acclaim for her work.

Detective Inspector John Coffin, according to a *New York Times Book Review* critic, "is often cryptic and indirect, but still artfully effective." Coffin lives in a manor in south London where he finds himself assigned to especially baffling mysteries, usually involving elderly widows. "In her specialized ambience of Coffin's south London manor," a *Times Literary Supplement* reviewer writes, "[Butler] is now one of our best crime writers."

Speaking of Butler's historical mysteries, Patrick Cosgrave of *Spectator* writes: "Since she took up the Victorian and Edwardian periods Mrs. Butler has not put a foot wrong." Cosgrave elaborates in a review of *The Vesey Inheritance*, "So delectable is Mrs. Butler's writing and characterization, so fine and sure her touch, that she must be dubbed the Jane Austen of the crime story."

Sarsen Place, a historical mystery set in Victorian England, has been praised for its skillful combination of the mystery and Gothic genres and its feminist sensibility. Writing in *Newsweek* about the novel, Walter Clemons believes that "it's fun to watch [Butler] deftly fulfill the expectations of the [Gothic] genre . . . while escorting us upstairs and down through a Victorian house and out to a brothel on the outskirts of town to illuminate class structure and the condition of women a century ago." Bruce Allen of *New Republic* describes the book as "a densely plotted, fiendishly misdirected tale of ugly intrigue, whose elegantly phrased facade conceals both a solid social panorama . . . and a witty employment of feminist sentiment."

In a review of the prize-winning *A Coffin for Pandora*, the *Times Literary Supplement* critic provides an overview of Butler's mystery writing as a whole. He concludes: "In a genre where rather a lot of authors talk rather too much about making crime fiction into Real Novels, Miss Butler quietly achieves it."

BIOGRAPHICAL/CRITICAL SOURCES: New York Times Book Review, January 5, 1964, December 12, 1965, January 27, 1974; *Times Literary Supplement*, October 15, 1964, May 12, 1966, December 11, 1969, December 25, 1970, August 31, 1973, September 6, 1974; *Observer*, November 9, 1969, August 19, 1973, August 4, 1974, July 3, 1977; *Spectator*, August 11, 1973, June 12, 1976, October 29, 1977; *Best Sellers*, February 1, 1974, November 15, 1974; *New Republic*, February 2, 1974; *Washington Post Book World*, February 17, 1974; *Newsweek*, February 18, 1974; *Publishers Weekly*, October 7, 1974, May 21, 1979; *Christian Science Monitor*, January 8, 1975; *Listener*, July 8, 1976.

C

CAHILL, James F(rancis) 1926-

PERSONAL: Born August 13, 1926, in Fort Bragg, Calif.; son of James Francis and Mae (Bond) Cahill; married Dorothy Dunlap, 1951; children: Nicholas, Sarah. *Education:* University of California, Berkeley, B.A., 1950; University of Michigan, M.A., 1952, Ph.D., 1957. *Home:* 2422 Hillside Ave., Berkeley, Calif. 94704. *Office:* Department of History of Art, University of California, Berkeley, Calif. 94720.

CAREER: Smithsonian Institute, Freer Gallery of Art, Washington, D.C., curator of Chinese art, 1957-65; University of California, Berkeley, professor of history of art, 1965—, curator of oriental art, University Art Museum. Charles Eliot Norton Professor of Poetry, Harvard University, 1978-79. *Military service:* U.S. Army, 1945-48; became first lieutenant. *Member:* Association for Asian Studies, College Art Association. *Awards, honors:* Fulbright scholar, 1953-54, and Guggenheim fellow, 1972-73, both at University of Kyoto.

WRITINGS: Chinese Painting, Albert Skira (Geneva), 1960, Rizzoli International, 1977; *The Art of Southern Sung China,* Asia House Gallery, 1962; *Fantastics and Eccentrics in Chinese Painting,* Asia House Gallery, 1967; (editor) *The Art of Tomioka Tessai,* International Exhibition Foundation, 1968; *Scholar Painters of Japan: The Nanga School,* Asia House Gallery, 1972; *Hills beyond a River: Chinese Painting of the Yuan Dynasty, 1279-1368,* Weatherhill, 1976; *Parting at the Shore: Chinese Painting of the Early and Middle Ming Dynasty,* Weatherhill, 1978. Contributor of book reviews and articles to professional journals.

WORK IN PROGRESS: A series of five volumes on later Chinese painting.

SIDELIGHTS: James Cahill supervised the photography of Chinese National Palace Museum Collection, Taiwan, 1963-64. *Avocational interests:* Music.

BIOGRAPHICAL/CRITICAL SOURCES: Evening Star, Washington, D.C., March 19, 1961.

* * *

CALLAS, Theo
See McCARTHY, Shaun (Lloyd)

CALLENBACH, Ernest 1929-

PERSONAL: Born April 3, 1929, in Williamsport, Pa.; married Christine Leefeldt; children: Joanna, Hans. *Education:* University of Chicago, Ph.B., 1949, M.A., 1953. *Agent:* Richard Kahlenberg, 225 Santa Monica Blvd., Santa Monica, Calif. 90401. *Office:* University of California Press, 2223 Fulton St., Berkeley, Calif. 94720.

CAREER: University of California Press, Berkeley, Calif., publicity writer and assistant editor, 1955-58, editor of *Film Quarterly,* 1958—, film book editor, 1960—. Founder of Banyan Tree Books.

WRITINGS: Our Modern Art: The Movies, Center for the Study of Liberal Education for Adults, University of Chicago, 1955; *Living Poor with Style,* Bantam, 1972; *Ecotopia,* Banyan Tree, 1975; (with wife, Christine Leefeldt) *The Art of Friendship,* Pantheon, 1979; *The Ecotopian Encyclopedia for the 80's,* And/Or Press, 1981; *Ecotopia Emerging,* Banyan Tree, 1981.

SIDELIGHTS: After his novel *Ecotopia* had been rejected by 25 publishers, Ernest Callenbach decided in 1975 to publish the book himself. Commercial publishers had insisted that the book's ecological theme was passé but, Callenbach states in the *New York Times,* "I couldn't see that because at that very time people were being elected to office on ecology campaigns." Callenbach founded Banyan Tree Books, published *Ecotopia,* and sold the book through a small press distribution company. The book proved an immediate underground cult favorite, selling well over 35,000 copies in its Banyon Tree edition and appearing in several other U.S. editions and in six foreign translations.

Ecotopia tells the story of a utopian society established in the Pacific Northwest of the near future. Alternative energy systems are widely used, decentralized government is the norm, factories and farms are owned in common, and a more humane lifestyle flourishes. Although Spider Robinson of *Analog* describes the premise of *Ecotopia* as "flat out impossible," he nonetheless admits: "I kinda half-believed Callenbach's Ecotopia. Not that simply or painlessly achieved, . . . but it certainly does seem like something to shoot for. . . . It's not a bad little Utopia." Robinson concludes: "You will like some parts [of *Ecotopia*], hate some other parts—and in the end be enormously stimulated in your thinking."

BIOGRAPHICAL/CRITICAL SOURCES: Life, July 14, 1972; *New Republic,* December 2, 1972; *New York Times Book Re-*

view, December 10, 1972, January 25, 1981; *Futures,* October, 1975; *Science Fiction Review,* May, 1976; *New York Times,* October 2, 1977; *New Statesman,* August 4, 1978; *Analog,* June, 1979; *Washington Post,* November 3, 1979.†

*　　*　　*

CALLOW, Philip Kenneth 1924-

PERSONAL: Born October 26, 1924, in Birmingham, Warwickshire, England; son of Hubert Arthur (a clerk) and Beatrice May (Rady) Callow; married Irene Christian Vallance, March 12, 1952 (divorced, 1973); married Penelope Jane Newman, March 6, 1974; children: (first marriage) Fleur Alyse Harvey (daughter). *Education:* Coventry Technical College, certificate, 1939; St. Luke's College, teaching certificate, 1970. *Home:* Little Thatch, Hasselbury, Crewkerne, Somerset, England. *Agent:* Christopher Busby, 44 Great Russell St., London W21, England.

CAREER: Novelist and poet, 1966—. Writer-in-residence, Sheffield City Polytechnic, 1980-82. Engineer apprentice, then toolmaker for Coventry Gauge and Tool Co., 1940-48; telephonist, civil servant with British Ministry of Works and Ministry of Supply, 1949-51; clerical assistant, South West Electricity Board, Plymouth, England, 1952-66; former autosetter with Tecalemit Ltd., Plymouth. *Member:* P.E.N. (London). *Awards, honors:* Bursaries, Arts Council of Great Britain, 1966, 1970, and 1973; traveling scholarship, Society of Authors, 1973; C. Day Lewis fellowship, Southern Arts Association, 1974; fellowship, Falmouth School of Art.

WRITINGS—Novels: *The Hosanna Man,* J. Cape, 1956; *Common People,* Heinemann, 1958; *A Pledge for the Earth,* Heinemann, 1960; *Clipped Wings,* Gibbs & Phillips, 1965; *Going to the Moon* (first novel in trilogy), MacGibbon & Kee, 1968; *The Bliss Body* (second novel in trilogy), MacGibbon & Kee, 1969; *Flesh of Morning* (third novel in trilogy), Bodley Head, 1971; *Yours,* Bodley Head, 1972; *The Story of My Desire,* Bodley Head, 1976; *Janine,* Bodley Head, 1972; *The Subway to New York,* Martin Brian & O'Keeffe, 1979.

Poems: *Turning Point,* Heinemann, 1964; *The Real Life,* Gibbs & Phillips, 1965; *Bare Wires,* Chatto & Windus, 1971; *Cave Light,* Rivelin Press, 1981.

Other: *Native Ground* (short stories), Heinemann, 1959; (contributor) *New Granada Plays,* Faber, 1961; *In My Own Land* (autobiography), Times Press, 1965; *Son and Lover: The Young D. H. Lawrence* (biography), Stein & Day, 1975. Contributor to *New Statesman, Spectator, Tribune,* and *Listener.*

SIDELIGHTS: Philip Kenneth Callow told *CA:* "My writing began in late adolescence, during a period of pathological shyness, and can be seen now as therapy, overcoming feelings of chronic inadequacy. Now I write in order to discover and tap new sources of energy and power and to be put in touch with those forces in man and nature outside myself. Although supposedly in mid-career, I feel an absolute beginner and hope to remain one for the rest of my life. [I] have always felt this, which would account for the obsession with beginnings in my writings—growing up, new encounters, new relationships."

Manuscripts, work sheets, and proof copies of Callow's first eight books have been collected in the University of Texas Library.

BIOGRAPHICAL/CRITICAL SOURCES: Books and Bookmen, July, 1969, June, 1971, May, 1977; *Times Literary Supplement,* April 30, 1971, September 5, 1975, December 2, 1977, December 14, 1979; *New Statesman,* July 18, 1975, May 21, 1976; *New York Times Book Review,* September 21, 1975.

CAMMACK, Floyd M(cKee) 1933-

PERSONAL: Born February 20, 1933, in Frankfort, Kentucky; son of L. D. (an architect) and Helen (Cox) Cammack. *Education:* University of Kentucky, B.A., 1954; Oxford University, B.A., 1956, M.A., 1960; Columbia University, M.S. in L.S., 1957; Cornell University, Ph.D., 1962; additional study at University of Grenoble, 1955. *Home:* 98-1232 Makipwa St., Aiea, Hawaii 96701.

CAREER: Association of College and Research Libraries, Chicago, Ill., publications officer, 1957-58; University of Hawaii, Honolulu, assistant librarian and assistant professor of anthropology, 1962-64, language coordinator of the University's Peace Corps training program, 1962-63; Oakland University, Rochester, Mich., librarian, 1964-70; Aichi Prefectural University, Nagoya, Japan, associate professor of linguistics, 1970-72; Georgia Southern College, Statesboro, Ga., associate director of libraries, 1972-73; University of Guam, Agana, Guam, dean of library services, 1973-75; University of Hawaii, public service librarian, 1975-81. Anthropological field worker in Fiji, 1961-62. Chairman, Hawaii Governor's Committee on State Library Resources, 1963-64. Fulbright-Hays lecturer in Japan, 1966-67. *Member:* American Library Association, Linguistic Society of America, American Anthropological Association, Association for Machine Translation and Computational Linguistics, American Association of Rhodes Scholars, Phi Beta Kappa, Phi Sigma Iota, Beta Phi Mu. *Awards, honors:* Rhodes Scholar, 1954; grants from American Council of Learned Societies, 1959, National Science Foundation, 1960-62, and Friends of the Library of Hawaii, 1979.

WRITINGS: (With Shiro Saito) *Pacific Island Bibliography,* Scarecrow, 1963; *Discovering American Dialog,* Nippon Columbia (Japan), 1970; *Experiments in Spoken English,* Kenkyusha (Japan), 1974; (editor) *Customs of Written English,* Kendall/Hunt, 1977, 2nd edition, 1978; (with Marri DeCosin and Norman Roberts) *Community College Library Instruction,* Shoe String, 1979. Contributor to *Library Journal, Language Learning, English Teachers' Magazine, Journal of English Teaching,* and other publications. Contributor to *Collier's Encyclopedia Yearbook, World Book Encyclopedia Annual,* and *New International Yearbook.*

*　　*　　*

CAMPBELL, Malcolm J(ames) 1930-

PERSONAL: Born April 11, 1930, in Portsmouth, England; son of Francis James (a ship's fitter) and Dorothy (Hellier) Campbell; married Margaret Heather, June 29, 1957; children: Colin, Sarah. *Education:* Associate of Library Association, 1965. *Religion:* Church of England. *Home:* 98 Agar Grove, London NW1 9TL, England. *Office:* City Business Library, 55 Basinghall St., London EC2V 5BX, England.

CAREER: Holborn Public Library, London, England, assistant librarian, 1946-59; British Employers' Confederation, London, librarian, 1959-64; Confederation of British Industry, London, librarian, 1964-68; City Business Library, London, librarian, 1968—. Lecturer at City University (London). Member of British Library Ad Hoc Working Group on Business Information, 1980. *Military service:* British Army, 1952-54; became sergeant. *Member:* Library Association, Association of Special Libraries and Information Bureaux (member of council, 1975—; chairman of publications committee, 1976—).

WRITINGS: Business Information Services, Shoe String, 1974, 2nd edition, 1981; (editor) *Manual of Business and Library*

Practice, Bingley, 1975; *Directory of Financial Directories,* Francis Hodgson, 1976; (contributor) *Encyclopedie de Marketing,* Editions Techniques, 1977; *Printed Reference Material,* Library Association, 1980. Contributor to library journals.

WORK IN PROGRESS: Directory of Financial Directories, 2nd edition; *Case Studies in Business Information.*

SIDELIGHTS: "I believe the public (free) provision of information to business to be important," Malcolm Campbell wrote, "but in the United Kingdom, United States, and elsewhere inadequate, with a few exceptions. Insufficient stress is laid upon this area in education of librarians."

*   *   *

CAMPBELL, R(obert) Wright   1927-

PERSONAL: Born June 9, 1927, in Newark, N.J.; son of William James and Florence (Clinton) Campbell. *Education:* Attended Pratt Institute, 1944-47. *Home address:* Box 412, Carmel, Calif. 93921. *Agent:* JET Associates, 124 East 84th St., New York, N.Y. 10028; and The Associates, 8961 Sunset Blvd., Los Angeles, Calif. 90069.

CAREER: Artist, novelist, screenwriter. Free-lance illustrator, 1947-50. *Military service:* U.S. Army, 1950-52. *Member:* Alcoholics Anonymous, Writers Guild of America, Authors Guild, Dramatists Guild. *Awards, honors:* Academy Award nomination, 1957, for "Man of a Thousand Faces."

WRITINGS: The Spy Who Sat and Waited (novel), Putnam, 1975; *Circus Couronne,* Putnam, 1977; *Where Pigeons Go to Die,* Rawson-Wade, 1978; *Killer of Kings,* Bobbs-Merrill, 1979; *Malloy's Subway,* Atheneum, 1981.

Screenplays: "Five Guns West," American Releasing, 1955; "Naked Paradise," American-International, 1957; "Gun for a Coward," Universal, 1957; "Quantez," Universal, 1957; "Man of a Thousand Faces," Universal, 1957; "Machine Gun Kelly," American-International, 1958; "A New World," Azteca, 1958; "Teenage Caveman," American-International, 1958 (released in England as "Out of the Darkness"); "The Night Fighters," United Artists, 1960; "The Young Racers," American-International, 1963; "The Masque of the Red Death," American-International, 1964; "The Secret Invasion," United Artists, 1964; "Hells Angels on Wheels," U.S. Films, 1967; "Captain Nemo and the Underwater City," Metro-Goldwyn-Mayer, 1969.

Author of filmscripts for television programs, including: "Medic," "Maverick," "Cheyenne," "Mr. Garland," "Twelve O'Clock High," "Loretta Young," "Star and the Story," "Marcus Welby, M.D.," and "Born Free."

WORK IN PROGRESS: Coffin; The Hawk at Caporetto; a musical comedy; a theatrical drama; two screenplays.

SIDELIGHTS: R. Wright Campbell told *CA:* "I came to writing because, while in the army, I tried to determine what I wanted out of life. A sufficiency of money while I was young enough to enjoy it. The freedom to travel at will. Never to have to punch a time clock. Not very unusual for a boy raised in the neighborhoods of Newark, New Jersey, of working class stock. Even though I was a trained illustrator, I felt I'd lost too much time getting started in the highly competitive world of New York advertising and magazine illustration. My brother, having served his time during World War II instead of Korea, had become an actor and, happening to read a screenplay when we were both at home, I saw that my facility with words might prove profitable.

"It did. It also proved unsatisfying in ways I couldn't explain. I fell victim to ennui and alcohol. I came to believe in the harshly existential view that the world, when not being actively hostile, ignored the individual. When I decided to get sober it was because I felt that, if that were true, the best use of a man's life was still to create something of value for no other reason than joy in the creation. I did not, however, intend to suffer holy poverty in order to do so.

"Since then I've tried to walk a careful line between falling victim to the unbridled lust for money and fame that so marks and maims the lives of otherwise worthy persons, and turning my back on the comforts which an occasional compromise might produce. I see it as the difference between writing pieces intended only for entertainment and writing pieces which are vehicles for ideas and the interpretation of the human comedy.

"I often say that fate laid a trap for me. Upon recapturing my sobriety and zest for living and working I found that I was dedicated to the art and craft of writing, that I considered myself most fortunate for being paid to do what I would do even if I were not being paid, and that I had come to the idea that through writing I could fashion a life, not simply living.

"I've travelled fairly extensively in Europe, but since coming to live beside the sea find myself content, in fact unwilling to venture out unless a voyage is demanded of me. I still paint, create silk screens, have cameras to help me in reaching graphic conclusions, cast small bronzes, and read with an appetite that rarely wanes."

*   *   *

CAMPION, Nardi Reeder   1917-

PERSONAL: Born June 27, 1917, in Honolulu, Hawaii; daughter of Russell Potter (an Army colonel) and Narcissa (Martin) Reeder; married Thomas Baird Campion (production director of the *New York Times*), 1941; children: Thomas, Edward, Toby, Narcissa, Russell. *Education:* Wellesley College, A.B., 1938. *Religion:* Episcopalian. *Home:* 8 Wren Lane, Hanover, N.H. 03755. *Agent:* Curtis Brown Ltd., 575 Madison Ave., New York, N.Y. 10022.

CAREER: Newport News (Va.) High School, teacher of English, 1940-41; writer. Committee member, United Negro College Fund. *Member:* Planned Parenthood Association, Wellesley College Alumnae Association (president, 1976-79).

WRITINGS: (With Marty Maher) *Bringing up the Brass,* foreword by Dwight D. Eisenhower, McKay, 1951; (with brother, Red Reeder) *The West Point Story,* Random House, 1956; *Patrick Henry: Firebrand of the Revolution,* Little, Brown, 1961; *Kit Carson,* Garrard, 1963; (with Rosamund W. Stanton) *Look to This Day!: The Biography of Connie Guion, M.D.,* Little, Brown, 1965; *Casa Means Home,* Holt, 1970; *Ann the Word: The Story of Mother Ann Lee, Founder of the Shakers,* Little, Brown, 1976. Contributor to *Encyclopaedia Britannica* and *World Book Encyclopedia.* Contributor to *Reader's Digest, Look, Collier's, Sports Illustrated, Boston Globe Magazine,* and the *New York Times Magazine.* Editor, Sarah Lawrence College *Alumnae Magazine,* 1953.

SIDELIGHTS: Twenty-five thousand paperback copies of Nardi Reeder Campion's *Patrick Henry: Firebrand of the Revolution* were distributed in Africa, India, and the Middle East by the U.S. Information Agency. *Bringing up the Brass* was filmed as "The Long Grey Line," starring Tyrone Power. Campion made six appearances on Jack Paar's television show.

CAMPION, Rosamond
See ROSMOND, Babette

*   *   *

CANE, Melville (Henry)   1879-1980

PERSONAL: Born April 15, 1879, in Plattsburg, N.Y.; died March 10, 1980, in New York, N.Y.; son of Henry William (a merchant) and Sophia (Goodman) Cane; married Florence Naumburg, December 23, 1909 (deceased); children: Katherine (Mrs. Paul Marcus), Mary (Mrs. Arthur Robinson). *Education:* Columbia University, A.B. 1900, LL.B., 1903. *Office:* Ernst, Cane, Berner & Gitlin, 7 West 51st St., New York, N.Y. 10019.

CAREER: Lawyer in New York, N.Y., 1905-80, primarily with Ernst, Cane, Berner & Gitlin. Former director, Harcourt, Brace & World, Inc. (now Harcourt Brace Jovanovich, Inc.). *Member:* Association of the Bar (New York, N.Y.), Poetry Society of America, Columbia University Club. *Awards, honors:* Columbia University, medal for conspicuous alumni service, 1933, and medal for excellence in law and literature, 1948; Melville Cane Prize created by Poetry Society of America, 1962, to honor new books of poetry and critical studies of poetry; Gold Medal, Poetry Society of America, 1971, for longtime contributions to poetry.

WRITINGS—Poems, except as indicated; published by Harcourt, except as indicated: *January Garden,* 1926; *Behind Dark Spaces,* 1930; *Poems: New and Selected,* 1938; *A Wider Arc,* 1947; *Making a Poem* (prose), 1953; (editor with Harry E. Maul) *The Man from Main Street: A Sinclair Lewis Reader* (anthology), Random House, 1953; *And Pastures New,* 1956; *Bullet-Hunting,* 1960; (editor with John Farrar and Louise Townsend Nicholl) *The Golden Year: The Poetry Society of America Anthology,* Books for Libraries, 1960; *To Build a Fire,* 1964; *So That It Flower,* 1966; *All and Sundry: An Oblique Autobiography,* 1968; *Eloquent April: New Poems and Prose,* 1971; *The First Firefly: New Poems and Prose,* 1974; *Snow toward Evening,* 1974. Contributor of poems, articles, and stories to magazines.

BIOGRAPHICAL/CRITICAL SOURCES: Best Sellers, May 1, 1968; *New York Times,* April 24, 1971.

OBITUARIES: New York Times, March 11, 1980; *Publishers Weekly,* March 21, 1980; *Newsweek,* March 24, 1980.†

*   *   *

CANNING, Victor   1911-
(Alan Gould)

PERSONAL: Born June 16, 1911, in Plymouth, Devonshire, England. *Home:* The Bridge House, Pembridge, Herefordshire, England. *Agent:* John Cushman Associates, 25 West 43rd St., New York, N.Y. 10036; and Curtis Brown Ltd., 1 Craven Hill, London W2 3EW, England.

CAREER: Writer. *Military service:* British Army, Royal Artillery, 1939-45; became major. *Member:* Flyfisher's Club (London).

WRITINGS: Polycarp's Progress, Hodder & Stoughton, 1935; *Mr. Finchley's Holiday,* Reynal & Hitchcock, 1935 (published in England as *Mr. Finchley Discovers His England,* Hodder & Stoughton, 1941); *Everyman's England,* Hodder & Stoughton, 1936; *Fly Away Paul,* Reynal & Hitchcock, 1936; *Matthew Silverman,* Hodder & Stoughton, 1937; *Mr. Finchley Goes to Paris,* Carrick & Evans, 1938; *Fountain Inn,* Hodder &

Stoughton, 1939; *Mr. Finchley Takes the Road,* Hodder & Stoughton, 1940; *Green Battlefield,* Hodder & Stoughton, 1944; *The Chasm,* M. S. Mill, 1947; *Panthers' Moon,* M. S. Mill, 1948, abridged edition, edited by John Webber, Chatto & Windus, 1964; *The Golden Salamander,* Morrow, 1949.

Bird of Prey, Morrow, 1950 (published in England as *Venetian Bird,* Hodder & Stoughton, 1951); *A Forest of Eyes,* M. S. Mill, 1950; *The House of the Seven Flies,* Morrow, 1952; *The Man from the "Turkish Slave,"* Sloane, 1954; *A Handful of Silver,* Sloane, 1954 (published in England as *Castle Minerva,* Hodder & Stoughton, 1955); *Twist of the Knife,* Sloane, 1955 (published in England as *His Bones Are Coral,* Hodder & Stoughton, 1955); *Burden of Proof,* Sloane, 1956 (published in England as *Hidden Face,* Hodder & Stoughton, 1956); *The Manasco Road,* Sloane, 1957, published as *The Forbidden Road,* Permabooks, 1959; *The Dragon Tree,* Sloane, 1958; *Oasis Nine* (four short novels), Sloane, 1958 (published in England as *Young Man on a Bicycle, and Other Stories,* Hodder & Stoughton, 1958); *The Burning Eye,* Sloane, 1960; *A Delivery of Furies,* Sloane, 1961; *Black Flamingo,* Hodder & Stoughton, 1962, Sloane, 1963; *The Limbo Line,* Heinemann, 1963, Sloane, 1964; *The Scorpio Letters,* Sloane, 1964; *The Whip Hand,* Morrow, 1965; *Doubled in Diamonds,* Heinemann, 1966, Morrow, 1967; *The Python Project,* Heinemann, 1967, Morrow, 1968; *The Melting Man,* Heinemann, 1968, Morrow, 1969; *Queen's Pawn,* Heinemann, 1969, Morrow, 1970.

The Great Affair (Collectors Editions Club selection), Heinemann, 1970, Morrow, 1971; *Firecrest,* Heinemann, 1971, Morrow, 1972; *The Runaways,* Heinemann, 1971, Morrow, 1972; *The Rainbird Pattern,* Heinemann, 1972, Morrow, 1973; *Flight of the Grey Goose,* Heinemann, 1972, Morrow, 1973; *The Finger of Saturn,* Heinemann, 1973, Morrow, 1974; *The Painted Tent,* Heinemann, 1973, Morrow, 1974; *The Mask of Memory,* Heinemann, 1974, Morrow, 1975; *The Kingsford Mask,* Heinemann, 1975, Morrow, 1976; *The Doomsday Carrier,* Heinemann, 1976, Morrow, 1977; *The Crimson Chalice,* Heinemann, 1977, Morrow, 1979; *Birdcage,* Heinemann, 1978, Morrow, 1979; *The Satan Sampler,* Heinemann, 1979, Morrow, 1980; *Fall from Grace,* Heinemann, 1980, Morrow, 1981.

Under pseudonym Alan Gould; all published by Hodder & Stoughton: *Two Men Fought,* 1936; *Mercy Lane,* 1936; *Sanctuary from the Dragon,* 1938; *Every Creature of God Is Good,* 1939; *The Viaduct,* 1940; *Atlantic Company,* 1941.

Author of television and film scripts and short stories.

SIDELIGHTS: A mystery novelist who has attracted the praise of many reviewers since the publication of his first novel in 1935, Victor Canning is the author of over fifty novels, many of which have moral conflict as their central theme. His characters live in a confusion of good and evil, their "bright aspirations," as Harry Sumrall writes in the *Washington Post,* "beset by the sinister demands of reality." In his review of *Fall from Grace,* Sumrall comments, "Canning is a resourceful writer, adept at illustrating man's paradoxical nature." The main character of *Fall from Grace,* for example, is John Corbin, a selfish blackmailer whom the author endows with sympathetic qualities. *Fall from Grace,* as its title implies, conveys the "ironic lesson," as Charles M. Coffey points out in *Best Sellers,* "that those who are capable of creating great beauty can sometimes be the 'perpetrators' of ugly deeds as well."

Some reviewers are critical of the timing and plot development of *Fall from Grace* and other Canning novels. T. J. Binyon of the *Times Literary Supplement,* for instance, describes *Fall from Grace* as a "slow moving novel, low on incident." The book's ending, Sumrall believes, arrives rather clumsily, "as if Canning suddenly lost interest and decided to dispense with the proceedings." In the *New York Times Book Review*, Robert Brandreth, despite a general high regard for *The Satan Sampler*, calls it a "shade mechanical." Christine Raux, reviewing the book for *Best Sellers*, feels the "action is not fast paced . . . [and] coincidence plays a much too major role in the plot."

Many reviewers, even those critical of the mechanics of Canning's works, are impressed with his characterization. Peta Fordham in *Books and Bookmen* praises *The Satan Sampler*, emphasizing its "unusually real-life hero." Binyon lauds the author's "subtle creation of character" in *Fall from Grace*, and Sumrall finds the book's figures "droll, urbane and finely sketched." As Brandreth sums up, Canning "never introduces a character in black and white. In his books there are real people."

AVOCATIONAL INTERESTS: Golf, travel, fly fishing.

BIOGRAPHICAL/CRITICAL SOURCES: Washington Post Book World, June 3, 1979, May 4, 1980; *Books and Bookmen*, January, 1980; *Times Literary Supplement*, March 7, 1980, November 14, 1980; *New York Times Book Review*, May 11, 1980, March 1, 1981; *Best Sellers*, July, 1980, March, 1981; *Washington Post*, January 5, 1981.

*   *   *

CARAMAN, Philip 1911-

PERSONAL: Born August 11, 1911, in London, England; son of R. A. Caraman. *Education:* Attended Stonyhurst College, 1923-30; Campion Hall, Oxford, M.A. *Home:* 114 Mount St., London W1, England.

CAREER: Roman Catholic priest, member of Society of Jesus. Editor, *Month*, 1948-63. *Member:* Royal Society of Literature (fellow).

WRITINGS: (Translator) John Gerard, *Autobiography of an Elizabethan*, Longmans, Green, 1951; (editor) J. Keating, *Retreat Notes*, Gill & Sons, 1952; (translator) Gerard, *Autobiography of a Hunted Priest*, Pellegrini & Cudahy, 1952; (editor) *Saints and Ourselves*, Kenedy, Volume I, 1953, Volume II, 1955, Volume III, 1958; (editor and author of introduction) F. C. Devas, *What Law and Letter Kill*, Burns, 1953; (editor and author of introduction) Devas, *Law of Love*, Kenedy, 1954; (translator) William Weston, *Autobiography from the Jesuit Underground*, Farrar, Straus, 1955 (published in Canada as *Autobiography of an Elizabethan*, Longmans, Green, 1955); (editor and author of foreword) R. H. Benson, *Come Rack! Come Rope!*, Kenedy, 1957; *Henry Morse, Priest of the Plague*, Farrar, Straus, 1957; (editor with J. J. Dougherty) *Holy Bible for the Family*, Longmans, Green, 1958.

The Other Face: Catholic Life under Queen Elizabeth I, Longmans, Green, 1960, Sheed, 1961; (editor and author of introduction) Ronald Knox, *Pastoral Occasional Sermons*, Burns, 1960; (editor and author of introduction) Knox, *Pastoral Sermons*, Sheed, 1960; (editor with James Walsh) *The Fulton J. Sheen Sunday Missal*, Hawthorn, 1961; *Saint Angela: The Life of Angela Merici, Foundress of the Ursulines (1474-1540)*, Longmans, Green, 1963, Farrar, Straus, 1964; (editor and author of introduction) Knox, *University and Anglican Sermons: Together with Sermons Preached on Various Occasions*, Burns & Oates, 1963, published as *University Sermons: Together with Sermons Preached on Various Occasions*, Sheed, 1964; *Henry Garnet (1555-1606) and the Gunpowder Plot*, Farrar, Straus, 1964; (editor) *The Years of Siege: Catholic Life from James I to Cromwell*, Longmans, Green, 1966; *C. C. Martin-*

dale: A Biography, Longmans, Green, 1967; *Norway*, Longmans, Green, 1969, Eriksen, 1970; *The Cure d'Ars*, Catholic Truth Society, 1969.

(Contributor) Marina Chavchavadze, editor, *Man's Concern with Holiness*, Hodder & Stoughton, 1970; *The Lost Paradise: An Account of the Jesuits in Paraguay, 1607-1768*, Sidgwick & Jackson, 1975, published as *The Lost Paradise: The Jesuit Republic in South America*, Seabury, 1976; *Praying Together*, Catholic Truth Society, 1976; *Saint Cuthbert Mayne*, Catholic Truth Society, 1978; *The University of the Nations: The Story of the Gregorian University*, Paulist Press, 1981. Contributor to *Tablet, Downside Review, Times Literary Supplement*, and other periodicals.

SIDELIGHTS: In a review of Philip Caraman's *The University of the Nations: The Story of the Gregorian University*, Colman McCarthy of the *Washington Post* writes: "With modesty, Caraman says that he is writing 'popular history.' Which is what is needed. The Gregorian, for too long, has been known only to scholars. It ought to be as known, and appreciated, as Oxford, Harvard and Fribourg. With this fine work, perhaps it will be."

BIOGRAPHICAL/CRITICAL SOURCES: Washington Post, September 1, 1981.†

*   *   *

CAREY, John 1934-

PERSONAL: Born April 5, 1934, in London, England; son of Charles William and Winifred Ethel (Cook) Carey; married Gillian Mary Florence Booth, 1960; children: Leo Jonathan, Thomas Charles. *Education:* Oxford University, B.A. (first honors), 1957, M.A., 1960, D.Phil., 1960. *Home:* Brasenose Cottage, Lyneham, near Churchill, Oxon, England.

CAREER: Oxford University, Oxford, England, lecturer at Christ Church, 1958, Andrew Bradley Research Fellow at Balliol College, 1959, fellow of Keble College, 1960-64, lecturer in English literature and fellow of St. John's College, 1964-75, Merton Professor of English Literature at Merton College, 1975—.

WRITINGS: (Editor with Alastair Fowler) *The Poems of John Milton*, Longmans, Green, 1968, Norton, 1972; (editor) James Hogg, *The Private Memoirs and Confessions of a Justified Sinner*, Oxford University Press, 1969; *Milton*, Evans Brothers, 1969, Arco, 1970; (compiler) *Andrew Marvell: A Critical Anthology*, Penguin, 1969; (contributor) Christopher Ricks, editor, *Sphere History of Literature*, Volume II, Sphere Books, 1970; (editor) John Milton, *Complete Shorter Poems*, Longmans, 1971; *The Violent Effigy: A Study of Dickens' Imagination*, Faber, 1973; (translator) Milton, *Christian Doctrine*, Yale University Press, 1973; *Thackeray: Prodigal Genius*, Faber, 1977; *John Donne: Life, Mind, and Art*, Oxford University Press, 1981. Contributor to *Encyclopaedia Britannica*. Contributor of articles to *Modern Language Review* and *Review of English Studies*. Book reviewer, *London Times*.

SIDELIGHTS: John Carey's book *John Donne: Life, Mind, and Art* is, according to Michael Radcliffe of the *London Times*, an "exhilerating case-history of a great poet's imaginative resourcefulness. It will stretch the mind of the average reader. . . . It is also a speculative journey which displays confidence in reader, poet, and the arguments of the critic himself, and the confidence is catching."

Carey proposes several new interpretations of Donne's poetry that break with previous criticism. He emphasizes Donne's conversion from Catholicism to the Anglican church, his ambitious and egotistical nature, and his preoccupation with change and transformation as being the most important aspects to be considered when analyzing Donne's work. As Radcliffe notes, Carey's "case is made with a commanding intensity and wit, covering a wide area of human experience and behaviour. [Carey] stakes out patterns and an overall structure to sustain the apparent contradictions of Donne's work."

Timothy S. Healy of the *Washington Post Book World* especially admires Carey's analysis of Donne's poetry. "Carey," Healy writes, "spins out a running commentary on Donne's lyrics, with skill and insight. . . . Carey's touch on the poems is sure and delicate. When he can stop arguing theology with Donne, . . . he is a first-class critic and explicator of his poetry." Anatole Broyard of the *New York Times* calls *John Donne: Life, Mind, and Art* "a brilliant book."

BIOGRAPHICAL/CRITICAL SOURCES: Washington Post Book World, May 3, 1981; *London Times,* May 14, 1981; *New York Times,* May 30, 1981.

*   *   *

CARGAS, Harry J(ames) 1932-

PERSONAL: Born June 18, 1932, in Hamtramck, Mich.; son of James H. (a businessman) and Sophia (Kozlowski) Cargas; married Millie Rieder, August 24, 1957; children: Martin de Porres, Joachim James, Siena Catherine, Manon Theresa, Jacinta Teilhard, Sarita Jo. *Education:* Attended Aquinas College, 1955-56; University of Michigan, B.A., 1957, M.A., 1958; St. Louis University, Ph.D., 1968. *Religion:* Roman Catholic. *Home:* 127 Park Ave., Kirkwood, Mo. 63122. *Office:* Department of English, Webster College, St. Louis, Mo. 63119.

CAREER: St. David's School, New York, N.Y., English teacher and athletic director, 1958-61; Montclair Academy, Montclair, N.J., instructor in English and athletic coach, 1962-63; St. Louis University, St. Louis, Mo., instructor in English, 1963-69; Webster College, St. Louis, chairman of department of English, 1969—. Staff editor, Simon & Schuster; free-lance editor, Herder & Herder. Moderator and occasional producer of the television program "The Church Is You"; host of book review program "Booking Ahead" on KWMU for seven years. Presidential appointee, U.S. Holocaust Memorial Council. Consulting editor, Catechetical Guild, National Council of Catholic Men, and National Catholic High School Reading Program. *Awards, honors:* Micah Award, American Jewish Committee, 1980; Human Rights Award, United Nations Association, 1980.

WRITINGS: I Lay down My Life: Biography of Joyce Kilmer, Daughters of St. Paul, 1964; (editor) *Graham Greene,* B. Herder, 1968; (editor with Thomas P. Neill) *Renewing the Face of the Earth: Essays in Contemporary Church-World Relationships,* Bruce, 1968; (editor) *The Continuous Flame: Teilhard in the Great Traditions,* B. Herder, 1969; (editor) *Religious and Cultural Factors in Latin America,* St. Louis University, 1970; (editor with Ed Erazmus) *English as a Second Language: A Reader,* W. C. Brown, 1970; (editor with Ann White) *Death and Hope,* Corpus Books, 1970; (editor with *Daniel Berrigan and Contemporary Protest Poetry,* College & University Press, 1972; *Harry James Cargas in Conversation with Elie Wiesel,* Paulist/Newman, 1976; *The Holocaust: An Annotated Bibliography,* Catholic Library, 1978; *Keeping a Spiritual Journal,* Collins & World, 1980.

Also author of *A Christian Response to the Holocaust,* 1981. General editor, "Christian Critic" series, B. Herder. Author

of book columns for *Way, Friar, Catholic Book Reporter,* and *Catholic Library World.* Contributor of articles and more than 500 book reviews to *Jubilee, America, New York Times, Catholic World, Ave Maria,* and other publications. Editor-in-chief, *Catholic Book Reporter,* 1960-61, and *Queen's Work,* 1963-64.

WORK IN PROGRESS: Research on fatherhood in America; work on Thomas Merton.

*   *   *

CARR, Glyn
See STYLES, (Frank) Showell

*   *   *

CARR, Roberta
See ROBERTS, Irene

*   *   *

CARRANCO, Lynwood 1921-

PERSONAL: Born April 2, 1921, in Samoa, Calif.; son of Filberto (a millworker) and Cecilia (Ysais) Carranco; married Ruth Cannam (a teacher), June 12, 1947; children: Robert, Donald. *Education:* Humboldt State College (now University), A.B., 1949; Columbia University, M.A., 1951; University of Southern California, graduate study, 1959-60, and Ball State University, 1967-68; University of Sarasota, Ph.D., 1973. *Politics:* Democrat. *Religion:* Roman Catholic. *Home:* 2778 Buttermilk Lane, Arcata, Calif. 95521. *Office:* Department of English, College of the Redwoods, Eureka, Calif. 95501.

CAREER: Public high school teacher of languages in Arcata, Calif., 1951-56; Humboldt State College (now University), Arcata, Calif., assistant professor, 1956-59, associate professor of English, 1959-64; College of the Redwoods, Eureka, Calif., associate professor, 1964-68, professor of English, 1968—. *Military service:* U.S. Navy, Air Corps, 1942-45. *Member:* Humboldt County Historical Society (president, 1975), Redwood Council of English Teachers (president, 1964).

WRITINGS: Fundamentals of Modern English, Kendall/Hunt, 1963, revised edition, 1977; *The Redwood Country: History, Language, and Folklore,* Kendall/Hunt, 1971; (with John Labbe) *Logging the Redwoods,* Caxton, 1975; (with Estle Beard) *Genocide and Vendetta: The Round Valley Wars of Northern California,* University of Oklahoma Press, 1981; *The Redwood Lumber Industry of Northwestern California,* Golden West, 1981. Contributor of articles to journals.

WORK IN PROGRESS: Steam in the Redwoods; Forest Terminology: Terms Used in the Lumber Industry.

SIDELIGHTS: Lynwood Carranco told *CA:* "Isolated Humboldt County stretches along the rugged California coast about 200 miles north of San Francisco. It encompasses magnificent stands of the world's tallest trees, a seacoast battered and beaten by mighty waves, and quiet uplands and lakes where few roads reach. Fog hangs in the redwood forests, folding and billowing like a canopy, and the air is pungent with the damp richness of things growing. You watch the giants soar into the fog, knowing they reach beyond into the sun, and you shiver, not only because of the silence and chill.

"This area has a fascinating history, and through historical research I have tried to make the local people, and all who care, aware of their heritage and of this beautiful land which can be made to sustain both lumbering and nature. And I know

I have become a better English teacher by continually putting words down on paper over the years—and teaching others to do the same.''

Carranco played professional baseball for two years.

AVOCATIONAL INTERESTS: Travel, gardening.

* * *

CARROLL, Robert
    See ALPERT, Hollis

* * *

CARRUTH, Gorton Veeder 1925-

PERSONAL: Born April 9, 1925, in Woodbury, Conn.; son of Gorton Veeder and Margery Tracy Barrow (Dibb) Carruth; married Gisele Leliet, December 28, 1955; children: Gorton Veeder III, Hayden III, Christopher Leliet. *Education:* University of Chicago, Ph.B., 1948; Columbia University, B.A., 1950, M.A., 1954. *Address:* Box 168, Pleasantville, N.Y. 10570.

CAREER: Thomas Y. Crowell Co., New York City, reference book editor, 1954-63; McGraw-Hill Book Co., New York City, executive editor, 1963-68; Funk & Wagnalls, New York City, editor-in-chief, 1968-71; Morningside Associates, Pleasantville, N.Y., president, 1971—; The Hudson Group, Pleasantville, N.Y., founding member, 1972—. *Member:* Linnaean Society, Phi Beta Kappa.

WRITINGS: (Editor with others) *Encyclopedia of American Facts and Dates,* Crowell, 1956, 7th edition, with supplement, 1979; (co-author) *Where to Find Business Information,* Wiley, 1979, 2nd edition, 1982; *The VNR Dictionary of Business and Finance,* Van Nostrand, 1980; *Oxford American Dictionary,* Oxford University Press, 1980; (co-author) *Oxford Literary Guide to the United States,* Oxford University Press, 1982. Contributor to dictionaries and encyclopedias. Developer of series, *Our Living World of Nature,* McGraw, fourteen volumes, 1966-72.

WORK IN PROGRESS: Illustrated Encyclopedia of World Dates and Events; Dictionary of Historical Place Names.

AVOCATIONAL INTERESTS: Natural history, particularly ornithology; nature education.

* * *

CARSON, Robert B. 1934-

PERSONAL: Born July 6, 1934, in Greensburg, Pa.; son of Harry Robert and Catherine (Postlewaite) Carson; married Marjorie Ruth Gale (an artist), May 31, 1958; children: James Andrew, Sarah Elizabeth. *Education:* Hamilton College, A.B., 1956; Syracuse University, M.A., 1960, Ph.D., 1967. *Home:* 109 East Street, Oneonta, N.Y. 13820. *Office:* Department of Economics, State University of New York, Oneonta, N.Y. 13820.

CAREER: Cazenovia College, Cazenovia, N.Y., instructor in economics, 1961-62; Millersville State College, Millersville, Pa., assistant professor of economics, 1962-63; State University of New York College at New Paltz, assistant professor of economics, 1963-66; State University of New York College at Oneonta, professor of economics, 1966   , director of Center for Economic Education and Research, 1967-70. Consultant to Hudson Valley Council on Economic Education, 1963-66, Project PROBE, 1968-71, and Institute for Policy Studies,

1975; member of board of directors, New York State Council on Economic Education, 1968-70. *Military service:* U.S. Army, 1957-59. *Member:* Association for Evolutionary Economics, United University Professors, New York State Economics Association (treasurer). *Awards, honors:* State University of New York research grants, 1968, 1971.

WRITINGS: (Compiler and contributor) *The American Economy in Conflict: A Book of Readings,* Heath, 1971; *Main Line to Oblivion: The Disintegration of New York Railroads in the Twentieth Century,* Kennikat, 1971; (contributor) David H. DeGrood, Dale M. Reipe, and John Sommerville, editors, *Radical Currents in Contemporary Philosophy,* Warren H. Green, 1971; (contributor) Edward D'Angelo, Reipe, and DeGrood, editors, *Reflections on Revolution,* Spartacus Press, 1971; (with Jerry Ingles and Douglas McLaud) *Government in the American Economy: Conventional and Radical Studies on the Growth of State Economic Power,* Heath, 1973; *Whatever Happened to the Trolley?,* University Press of America, 1977; *Economic Issues Today,* St. Martin's, 1978, 2nd edition, 1980; *Microeconomic Issues Today,* St. Martin's, 1980; *Macroeconomic Issues Today,* St. Martin's, 1980.

Also author of independent study courses, student workbook, and teacher guide. Contributor of articles to *Socialist Revolution, Historian, Journal of Economic Issues, Social Studies, Telos, Monthly Review, Executive Quarterly,* and other professional periodicals.

WORK IN PROGRESS: A textbook introduction to business, for Harcourt.

SIDELIGHTS: Robert B. Carson told *CA:* ''The current drift of economics writing is discouraging. Economists have increasingly become 'little thinkers,' directing their attention to economic matters very much as a mechanic approaches an automobile. I have always thought the bigger picture to be much more interesting and vastly more important.''

* * *

CARTER, Lief Hastings 1940-

PERSONAL: Born October 9, 1940, in New York, N.Y.; son of Robert Spencer and Cynthia (Root) Carter; married Nancy Saunders Batson, December 22, 1962; children: Stephen, Robert, Laurie. *Education:* Harvard University, A.B., 1962, J.D., 1965; University of California, Berkeley, Ph.D., 1972. *Politics:* ''Discerning.'' *Religion:* ''Also discerning.'' *Home:* 475 Forest Rd., Athens, Ga. 30605. *Office:* Department of Political Science, University of Georgia, Athens, Ga. 30602.

CAREER: University of Tennessee, Chattanooga, assistant professor of political science, law, and government, 1971-73; University of Georgia, Athens, assistant professor, 1973-79, associate professor of political science, 1979—. *Member:* American Political Science Association, Bar of the District of Columbia. *Awards, honors:* Edward Corwin Award from American Political Science Association, 1973, for *The Limits of Order.*

WRITINGS: The Limits of Order, Heath, 1974; (contributor) John A. Gardiner and M. Mulkey, editors, *Crime and Criminal Justice,* Heath, 1975; (contributor) Gardiner, editor, *Public Law and Public Policy,* Praeger, 1977; *Reason in Law,* Little, Brown, 1979. Contributor of articles and reviews to *Georgia Law Review, Journal of Politics, American Political Science Review,* and *Policy Studies Journal.*

WORK IN PROGRESS: Law and Public Administration, a textbook.

SIDELIGHTS: Lief Carter told *CA:* ''Putting *Reason in Law* together increased my conviction that people can and do reason and that 'impartiality' is a useful concept in jurisprudence. In fact, I've a hunch that these concepts, and their cousins 'rationality' and 'objectivity,' are due a philosophical renaissance.'' *Avocational interests:* Playing the harpsichord, growing vegetables, playing squash.

*   *   *

CARTER, Nick
   See **LYNDS, Dennis**
   and **SMITH, Martin Cruz**

*   *   *

CARTLAND, Barbara (Hamilton) 1901-
   (Barbara McCorquodale)

PERSONAL: Born July 9, 1901, in England; daughter of Bertram and Polly (Scobell) Cartland; married Alexander George McCorquodale, 1927 (marriage dissolved, 1933); married Hugh McCorquodale, December 28, 1936 (died December 29, 1963); children: (first marriage) Raine (Countess Spencer); (second marriage) Ian, Glen. *Education:* Attended Malvern Girls' College and Abbey House, Netley Abbey, Hampshire, England. *Politics:* Conservative. *Religion:* Church of England. *Home:* Camfield Pl., Hatfield, Hertfordshire, England. *Agent:* Rupert Crew Ltd., King's Mews, Gray's Inn Rd., London WC1N 2JA, England.

CAREER: Writer. Lecturer, historian, political speaker for the Conservative office, and television personality. County councillor for Hertfordshire, nine years; services welfare officer for Bedfordshire, 1941-45; currently chairman of the St. John Council and deputy president of St. John Ambulance Brigade, Hertfordshire, and president of Hertfordshire branch of Royal College of Midwives. *Member:* Oxfam (vice-president), National Association of Health (deputy president, 1965; president, 1966). *Awards, honors:* Dame of Grace, St. John of Jerusalem, Certificate of Merit, Eastern Command, 1946; National Home Furnishings Association Woman of the Year Award, 1981.

*WRITINGS—*Novels: *Jigsaw,* Duckworth, 1925; *Sawdust,* Duckworth, 1926; *If the Tree Is Saved,* Duckworth, 1929.

For What?, Hutchinson, 1930; *Sweet Punishment,* Hutchinson, 1931, Pyramid Publications, 1973; *A Virgin in Mayfair,* Hutchinson, 1932, published as *An Innocent in Mayfair,* Pyramid Publications, 1976; *Just off Piccadilly,* Hutchinson, 1933, published as *Dance on My Heart,* Pyramid Publications, 1977; *Not Love Alone,* Hutchinson, 1933; *A Beggar Wished . . . ,* Hutchinson, 1934, published as *Rainbow to Heaven,* Pyramid Publications, 1976; *Passionate Attainment,* Hutchinson, 1935; *First Class, Lady?,* Hutchinson, 1935, published as *Love and Linda,* Pyramid Publications, 1976; *Dangerous Experiment,* Hutchinson, 1936, published as *Search for Love,* Greenberg, 1937; *Desperate Defiance,* Hutchinson, 1936, Pyramid Publications, 1977; *The Forgotten City* (also see below), Hutchinson, 1936; *Saga at Forty,* Hutchinson, 1937, published as *Love at Forty,* Pyramid Publications, 1977; *But Never Free,* Hutchinson, 1937, published as *The Adventurer,* Pyramid Publications, 1977; *Broken Barriers,* Hutchinson, 1938, Pyramid Publications, 1976; *Bitter Winds,* Hutchinson, 1938, published as *The Bitter Winds of Love,* Jove, 1978; *The Gods Forget,* Hutchinson, 1939, published as *Love in Pity,* Pyramid Publications, 1976; *The Black Panther,* Rich & Cowan, 1939, published as *Lost Love,* Pyramid Publications, 1970, reprinted under original title, Hutchinson, 1972.

Stolen Halo, Rich & Cowan, 1940, reprinted, Hutchinson, 1970, published as *The Audacious Adventuress,* Pyramid Pub-

lications, 1972, reprinted under original title, 1973; *Now Rough, Now Smooth,* Hutchinson, 1941; *Open Wings, a Twenty-Third Novel,* Hutchinson, 1942, published as *Open Wings,* Pyramid Publications, 1976; *The Leaping Flame,* R. Hale, 1942, Pyramid Publications, 1974; *The Dark Stream,* Hutchinson, 1944, published as *This Time It's Love,* Pyramid Publications, 1977; *After the Night,* Hutchinson, 1944, published as *Towards the Stars,* 1971, Pyramid Publications, 1975; *Yet She Follows,* R. Hale, 1945, published as *A Heart Is Broken,* 1972, Pyramid Publications, 1974; *Escape from Passion,* R. Hale, 1945, Pyramid Publications, 1977; *Armour against Love,* Hutchinson, 1945, Pyramid Publications, 1974; *Out of Reach,* Hutchinson, 1945, reprinted, Hurst & Blackett, 1972; *The Hidden Heart,* Hutchinson, 1946, Pyramid Publications, 1970; *Against the Stream,* Hutchinson, 1946, Pyramid Publications, 1977; *The Dream Within,* Hutchinson, 1947, Pyramid Publications, 1976; *If We Will,* Hutchinson, 1947, published as *Where Is Love?,* 1971, Jove, 1978; *Again This Rapture,* Hutchinson, 1947, Pyramid Publications, 1977; *No Heart Is Free,* Rich & Cowan, 1948, Pyramid Publications, 1975; *A Hazard of Hearts,* Rich & Cowan, 1949, Pyramid Publications, 1969; *The Enchanted Moment,* Rich & Cowan, 1949, Pyramid Publications, 1976; *A Duel of Hearts,* Rich & Cowan, 1949, Pyramid Publications, 1970.

The Knave of Hearts, Rich & Cowan, 1950, Pyramid Publications, 1971; *The Little Pretender,* Rich & Cowan, 1950, Pyramid Publications, 1971; *Love Is an Eagle,* Rich & Cowan, 1951, Pyramid Publications, 1975; *A Ghost in Monte Carlo,* Rich & Cowan, 1951, Pyramid Publications, 1973; *Love Is the Enemy,* Rich & Cowan, 1952, Pyramid Publications, 1970; *Cupid Rides Pillion,* Hutchinson, 1952, reprinted, Hurst & Blackett, 1969, published as *The Secret Heart,* Pyramid Publications, 1970; *Elizabethan Lover,* Hutchinson, 1953, Pyramid Publications, 1971; *Love Me for Ever,* Hutchinson, 1954, published as *Love Me Forever,* Pyramid Publications, 1970; *Desire of the Heart,* Hutchinson, 1954, Pyramid Publications, 1969; *The Enchanted Waltz,* Hutchinson, 1955, Pyramid Publications, 1971; *The Kiss of the Devil,* Hutchinson, 1955, Jove, 1981; *The Captive Heart,* Hutchinson, 1956, Pyramid Publications, 1970, published as *The Royal Pledge,* 1970; *The Coin of Love,* Hutchinson, 1956, Pyramid Publications, 1969; *Sweet Adventure,* Hutchinson, 1957, Pyramid Publications, 1970; *Stars in My Heart,* Hutchinson, 1957, Pyramid Publications, 1971; *The Golden Gondola,* Hutchinson, 1958, Pyramid Publications, 1971; *Love in Hiding,* Hutchinson, 1959, Pyramid Publications, 1969; *The Smuggled Heart,* Hutchinson, 1959, published as *Debt of Honor,* Pyramid Publications, 1970, reprinted under original title, Jove, 1982.

Love under Fire, Hutchinson, 1960, Pyramid Publications, 1972; *Messenger of Love,* Hutchinson, 1961, Pyramid Publications, 1971; *The Wings of Love,* Hutchinson, 1962, Pyramid Publications, 1971; *The Hidden Evil,* Hutchinson, 1963, Pyramid Publications, 1971; *The Fire of Love,* Hutchinson, 1964, Avon, 1970; *The Unpredictable Bride,* Hutchinson, 1964, Pyramid Publications, 1969; *Love Holds the Cards,* Hutchinson, 1965, Pyramid Publications, 1970; *A Virgin in Paris,* Hutchinson, 1966, Pyramid Publications, 1971, published as *An Innocent in Paris,* 1975, reprinted under original title, Jove, 1981; *Love to the Rescue,* Hutchinson, 1967, Pyramid Publications, 1970; *Love Is Contraband,* Hutchinson, 1968, Pyramid Publications, 1970; *The Enchanting Evil,* Hutchinson, 1968, Pyramid Publications, 1969; *The Unknown Heart,* Hutchinson, 1969, Pyramid Publications, 1971.

The Innocent Heiress, Pyramid Publications, 1970; *The Reluctant Bride,* Hutchinson, 1970, Pyramid Publications, 1972; *The Secret Fear,* Hutchinson, 1970, Pyramid Publications, 1971;

The Pretty Horse-Breakers, Hutchinson, 1971, Pyramid Publications, 1975; *The Queen's Messenger*, Pyramid Publications, 1971; *Stars in Her Eyes*, Pyramid Publications, 1971; *Lost Enchantment*, Hutchinson, 1972, Pyramid Publications, 1973; *A Halo for the Devil*, Hutchinson, 1972, Pyramid Publications, 1977; *The Irresistible Buck*, Hutchinson, 1972, Pyramid Publications, 1975; *The Complacent Wife*, Hutchinson, 1972, Jove, 1981; *The Daring Deception*, Bantam, 1973; *The Little Adventure*, Hutchinson, 1973, Bantam, 1974; *The Wicked Marquis*, Hutchinson, 1973, Bantam, 1974; *The Odious Duke*, Hutchinson, 1973, Pyramid Publications, 1975; *Journey to Paradise*, Bantam, 1974; *No Darkness for Love*, Bantam, 1974; *The Bored Bridegroom* (also see below), Bantam, 1974; *The Castle of Fear*, Bantam, 1974; *The Cruel Count*, Pan Books, 1974, Bantam, 1975; *The Dangerous Dandy*, Bantam, 1974; *Lessons in Love*, Bantam, 1974; *The Penniless Peer*, Bantam, 1974; *The Ruthless Rake*, Bantam, 1974; *The Glittering Lights*, Bantam, 1974; *A Sword to the Heart*, Bantam, 1974.

Published in 1975, except as indicated; published by Bantam, except as indicated: *Fire on the Snow*, Hutchinson, 1975, Bantam, 1976; *Bewitched; The Call of the Heart; The Devil in Love* (also see below); *The Flame Is Love; The Frightened Bride; The Impetuous Duchess; The Karma of Love; Love Is Innocent; The Magnificent Marriage* (also see below); *The Mask of Love; Shadow of Sin; The Tears of Love; A Very Naughty Angel; As Eagles Fly; Say Yes, Samantha*.

Published in 1976; published by Bantam, except as indicated: *The Elusive Earl; An Angel in Hell; An Arrow of Love; The Blue-eyed Witch; A Dream from the Night; The Fragrant Flower; A Frame of Dreams; A Gamble with Hearts; The Golden Illusion; The Heart Triumphant; Hungry for Love; The Husband Hunters; The Incredible Honeymoon; A Kiss for the King; Love in Hiding*, Pyramid Publications; *Moon over Eden; Never Laugh at Love; No Time for Love; Passions in the Sand; The Proud Princess* (also see below); *The Secret of the Glen; The Slaves of Love; The Wild Cry of Love; Conquered by Love*.

Published in 1977, except as indicated; published by Duron Books, except as indicated: *Love Locked In*, Dutton; *The Mysterious Maid-servant*, Bantam; *The Wild Unwilling Wife*, Dutton; *The Castle Made for Love; The Curse of the Clan; The Dragon and the Pearl; The Hell-cat and the King; Look, Listen and Love; Love and the Loathsome Leopard; The Love Pirate; The Marquis Who Hated Women; The Naked Battle; No Escape from Love; The Outrageous Lady; Punishment of a Vixen; The Saint and the Sinner; The Sign of Love; The Temptation of Torilla; A Touch of Love; The Dream and the Glory*, Bantam; *A Duel with Destiny*, Bantam; *Kiss the Moonlight* (also see below), Pan Books; *The Magic of Love*, Bantam; *A Rhapsody of Love*, Pan Books; *The Taming of Lady Lorinda*, Bantam; *Vote for Love*, Bantam; *The Disgraceful Duke*, Bantam; *Love at the Helm*, Weidenfeld & Nicolson, 1977, Everest House, 1981.

Published in 1978, except as indicated; published by Duron Books, except as indicated: *The Chieftain without a Heart*, Dutton; *A Fugitive from Love; The Ghost Who Fell in Love*, Dutton; *Love Leaves at Midnight; Love, Lords, and Lady-birds*, Dutton; *The Passion and the Flower*, Dutton; *The Twists and Turns of Love; The Irresistible Force; The Judgment of Love; Lord Ravenscar's Revenge; Lovers in Paradise; A Princess in Distress; The Race for Love; A Runaway Star; Magic or Mirage?; Alone in Paris*, Hutchinson, 1978, Duron Books, 1979; *Flowers for the God of Love*, Pan Books, 1978, Dutton, 1979; *The Problems of Love*.

Published in 1979, except as indicated: *The Best of Barbara Cartland* (contains *The Proud Princess, The Magnificent Mar-*

riage, *The Bored Bridegroom, Kiss the Moonlight*, and *The Devil in Love*), Grosset; *The Drums of Love*, Duron Books; *The Duke and the Preacher's Daughter*, Duron Books; *Imperial Splendor*, Dutton; *Light of the Moon*, Duron Books; *Love in the Clouds*, Dutton; *Love in the Dark*, Duron Books; *The Prince and the Pekingese*, Duron Books; *Love Climbs In*, Duron Books; *The Prisoner of Love*, Duron Books; *A Serpent of Satan*, Duron Books; *The Treasure Is Love*, Duron Books; *The Duchess Disappeared*, Duron Books; *A Nightingale Sang*, Duron Books; *The Dawn of Love*, Corgi, 1979, Dutton, 1980; *A Gentleman in Love*, Pan Books, 1979, Bantam, 1980; *Only Love*, Hutchinson, 1979, Bantam, 1980; *Bride to the King*, Corgi, 1979, Dutton, 1980; *Women Have Hearts*, Pan Books, 1979, Bantam, 1980; *Terror in the Sun*, Bantam; *Who Can Deny Love?*, Bantam, 1979, hardcover edition, Duron Books, 1980; *Love Has His Way*, Bantam, 1979, hardcover edition, Duron Books, 1980; *The Explosion of Love*, Bantam.

Published in 1980; published by Bantam, except as indicated: *A Song of Love*, Jove; *Love for Sale*, Dutton; *Lost Laughter*, Dutton; *Free from Fear; The Goddess and the Gaiety Girl; Little White Doves of Love; Ola and the Sea Wolf; The Perfection of Love; The Prude and the Prodigal; Punished with Love; Heart Is Stolen* (published in *Barbara Cartland's World of Romance* magazine), Corgi; *The Power of the Prince; Lucifer and the Angel; Signpost to Love*.

Published in 1981; published by Bantam, except as indicated: *From Hell to Heaven; Pride and the Poor Princess; Count the Stars*, Jove; *Dollars for the Duke; Dreams Do Come True; The Heart of the Clan*, Jove; *In the Arms of Love*, Jove; *Touch a Star*, Jove; *The Kiss of Life; The Lioness and the Lily; Love in the Moon; A Night of Gaiety; The Waltz of Hearts; The Wings of Ecstasy*, Jove; *For All Eternity*, Jove; *Afraid; Love in the Moon; Enchanted; Winged Magic; A Portrait of Love; The River of Love; Gift of the Gods; An Innocent in Russia; A Shaft of Sunlight; Pure and Untouched*.

Published in 1982; published by Bantam: *Love Wins; Secret Harbor; Looking for Love; The Vibrations of Love; Lies for Love; Love Rules*.

"Camfield Romance" series; published in 1982; published by Jove: *The Poor Governess; Winged Victory; Lucky in Love*.

Novels under name Barbara McCorquodale; all reprinted under name Barbara Cartland: *Sleeping Swords*, R. Hale, 1942; *Love Is Mine*, Rich & Cowan, 1952, Pyramid Publications, 1972; *The Passionate Pilgrim*, Rich & Cowan, 1952, Pyramid Publications, 1976; *Blue Heather*, Rich & Cowan, 1953, Pyramid Publications, 1975; *Wings on My Heart*, Rich & Cowan, 1954, Pyramid Publications, 1975; *The Kiss of Paris*, Rich & Cowan, 1956, Pyramid Publications, 1972; *The Thief of Love*, Jenkins, 1957, Pyramid Publications, 1975; *Love Forbidden*, Rich & Cowan, 1957, Pyramid Publications, 1973; *Lights of Love*, Jenkins, 1958, Pyramid Publications, 1973; *The Sweet Enchantress*, Jenkins, 1958, Pyramid Publications, 1976; *A Kiss of Silk*, Jenkins, 1959, Pyramid Publications, 1974; *The Price Is Love*, Jenkins, 1960, Pyramid Publications, 1973; *The Runaway Heart*, Jenkins, 1961, Pyramid Publications, 1974; *A Light to the Heart*, Ward, Lock, 1962, Pyramid Publications, 1973; *Love Is Dangerous*, Ward, Lock, 1963, Pyramid Publications, 1976; *Danger by the Nile*, Ward, Lock, 1964, Avon, 1975; *Love on the Run*, Ward, Lock, 1965, Pyramid Publications, 1973; *Theft of a Heart*, Ward, Lock, 1966, Pyramid Publications, 1977.

Biography: *Ronald Cartland* (brother), preface by Winston Churchill, Collins, 1942, reprinted with introduction by Arthur Bryant, S.P.C.K., 1980; *Bewitching Women*, Muller, 1955;

Polly: The Story of My Wonderful Mother, Jenkins, 1956, reprinted, Hutchinson, 1971; *The Outrageous Queen: A Biography of Christina of Sweden*, Muller, 1956, Pyramid Publications, 1977; *The Scandalous Life of King Carol*, Muller, 1957, reprinted, Corgi, 1974; *The Private Life of Charles II: The Women He Loved*, Muller, 1958, reprinted, Corgi, 1974; *The Private Life of Elizabeth, Empress of Austria*, Muller, 1959, Pyramid Publications, 1974; *Josephine, Empress of France*, Hutchinson, 1961, Pyramid Publications, 1974; *Diane de Poitiers*, Hutchinson, 1962; *Metternich: The Passionate Diplomat*, Hutchinson, 1964, Pyramid Publications, 1974.

Autobiography; published by Hutchinson, except as indicated: *The Isthmus Years: Reminiscences of the Years 1919-1939*, 1943; *The Years of Opportunity: 1939-1945*, 1948; *I Search for Rainbows: 1946-1966*, 1967; *We Danced All Night: 1919-1929*, 1970, Pyramid Publications, 1972; *I Seek the Miraculous*, Dutton, 1978.

Other nonfiction: *Touch the Stars: A Clue to Happiness*, Rider & Co., 1935; (editor) Ronald Cartland, *The Common Problem*, Hutchinson, 1943; *You—in the Home*, Standard Art Book Co., 1946; *The Fascinating Forties: A Book for the Over-forties*, Jenkins, 1954, revised edition, Corgi, 1973; *Marriage for Moderns*, Jenkins, 1955; *Be Vivid, Be Vital*, Jenkins, 1956; *Love, Life and Sex*, Jenkins, 1957, revised edition, Corgi, 1973; *Look Lovely, Be Lovely*, Jenkins, 1958; *Vitamins for Vitality*, W. & G. Foyle, 1959; *Husbands and Wives*, Arthur Barker, 1961, published as *Love and Marriage*, Thorson's, 1971; *Etiquette Handbook*, Paul Hamlyn, 1962, revised edition published as *Barbara Cartland's Book of Etiquette*, Hutchinson, 1972; *The Many Facets of Love*, W. H. Allen, 1963; *Sex and the Teenager*, Muller, 1964; *Living Together*, Muller, 1965; *The Pan Book of Charm*, Pan Books, 1965; *Woman, the Enigma*, Frewin, 1965, Pyramid Publications, 1974; *The Youth Secret*, Corgi, 1968, Bantam, 1973.

The Magic of Honey, Corgi, 1970, Pyramid Publications, 1973, revised edition, Corgi, 1977; *Barbara Cartland's Health Food Cookery Book*, Hodder & Stoughton, 1972, published as *Barbara Cartland's Health Food Cookery*, Pyramid Publications, 1975; *Barbara Cartland's Book of Beauty and Health*, Hodder & Stoughton, 1972; *Men Are Wonderful*, Corgi, 1973; *Food for Love*, Corgi, 1975; *The Magic of Honey Cookbook*, Corgi, 1976; (with Nigel Gordon) *Recipes for Lovers*, Corgi, 1977, Bantam, 1978; (editor) *Barbara Cartland's Book of Useless Information*, foreword by Earl Mountbatten, Bantam, 1977; *Barbara Cartland's Book of Love and Lovers*, Ballantine, 1978; (editor) *The Light of Love: A Thought for Every Day*, Sheldon Press, 1979, published as *The Light of Love: Lines to Live by Day by Day*, Elsevier/Nelson, 1980; *Romantic Royal Marriages*, Beaufort Book Co., 1981.

Editor; "Barbara Cartland's Library of Love" series; published by Bantam: Edith Maude Hull, *The Sheik*, 1977; Ethel May Dell, *The Hundredth Chance*, 1977; Dell, *The Knave of Diamonds*, 1977; Dell, *The Way of an Eagle*, 1977; Elinor Glyn, *The Reason Why*, 1977; Ian Hay, *A Safety Match*, 1977; Dell, *The Bars of Iron*, 1977; Glyn, *Man and Maid*, 1977; Glyn, *The Vicissitudes of Evangeline*, 1977; Hull, *The Lion Tamer*, 1977; Hull, *The Sons of the Sheik*, 1977; Glyn, *His Hour*, 1977; Pamela Wynne, *Ashes of Desire*, 1978; Berta Ruck, *His Official Fiancee*, 1978; Dell, *Tetherstones*, 1978; Glyn, *The Sequence*, 1978; Glyn, *The Price of Things*, 1978; Jeffrey Farnol, *The Amateur Gentleman*, 1978; Farnol, *The Broad Highway*, 1978; Gene S. Porter, *Freckles*, 1978; Wynne, *Rainbow in the Spray*, 1978; Glyn, *The Great Moment*, 1978; Glyn, *It*, 1978; Glyn, *Six Days*, 1978; Dell, *Greatheart*, 1978; Vere Lockwood, *Ramazan the Rajah*, 1979; Farnol, *The Money Moon*,

1979; Wynne, *Leave It to Love*, 1979; L. Adams Beck, *The Treasure of Ho* (also see below), 1979; Dell, *The Rocks of Valpre*, 1979; Charles Garvice, *Only a Girl's Love*, 1980; Ruck, *The Bridge of Kisses*, 1980; Lockwood, *Son of the Turk*, 1980; Dell, *The Obstacle Race*, 1980.

Editor of books in "Barbara Cartland's Library of Ancient Wisdom" series, published by Bantam and Howard & Wyndham, including *The Forgotten City*, by Cartland, *Black Light*, by Talbot Mundy, *Romance of Two Worlds*, by Marie Corelli, and *House of Fulfillment* and *The Treasure of Ho*, both by L. Adams Beck.

Also author of two plays, "Blood Money," 1925, and, with Bruce Woodhouse, "French Dressing," 1943; author of libretto for radio operetta "The Rose and the Violet," produced 1942; author of radio play "The Caged Bird: An Episode in the Life of Elizabeth, Empress of Austria," 1957. Has also written for television. Author of columns "Here's Health" and "Instant Cookery." Contributor of articles to newspapers and of stories to magazines.

WORK IN PROGRESS: Several novels, including *Kneel for Mercy, Music for the Heart, Caught by Love, The King in Love,* and *The Call of the Highlands,* all for Bantam, and *Money, Magic, and Marriage;* three nonfiction works, *Barbara Cartland's Scrapbook, Barbara Cartland's Book of Celebrities,* and *Written with Love: Passionate Love-Letters.*

SIDELIGHTS: Known throughout the world as the "Queen of Romance," Barbara Cartland is today's most prolific writer of romantic fiction. With nearly 300 million copies of her novels in print (the *Guinness Book of World Records* lists her as the best-selling author in the world), Cartland, observes *People* magazine, is a veritable "one-woman fantasy factory." Her typical fantasy is quite simple—a chaste and beautiful young woman meets a rich and handsome (but charmingly rakish) man in an exotic place, usually some time during the nineteenth century. They then proceed to fall in love and spend much of their time on the verge of giving in to passion. After overcoming an assortment of obstacles, the still-pure heroine finally marries her ideal and together they allow their emotions free rein at the end of the novel, as in this last line from *Dollars for the Duke:* "Then love carried them on the waves of ecstasy into the starlit sky, and they knew that nothing mattered except that as man and woman they were one now and through all eternity."

Cartland admits her plots are similar, but insists that she has never repeated a situation. "Of course," she explained to an interviewer from the *New Yorker,* "as I always write a story with a virgin heroine, we *know* the story is always going to be very much the same, because the girl is pure and the man isn't. The man will go to bed with any woman who takes his fancy, so I've got to keep him from going to bed with the heroine until page two hundred, when she has a wedding ring on her finger. I tried writing modern books, but I found it very difficult to create convincing virgins in modern dress, so my stories are always set between approximately 1790 and 1890. As the plots are always similar, I must vary the situations, and I must have exciting and real backgrounds, absolutely authentic. This is the part that interests me most. I love history, and I love research, and I do an enormous amount of it." She also does an enormous amount of traveling, and it is not at all unusual for her to eventually write about some of the many places she has visited: Bali, Singapore, Nepal, Hong Kong, Senegal, Martinique, Guadeloupe, Grenada, and India, to name just a few.

After Cartland does this research, she needs only seven days to complete a novel. Reclining on a chaise lounge in her library, a rug tucked around her feet and her pet Pekingese cuddled next to her, she dictates a chapter a day to a stenographer who arrives promptly at one o'clock and begins to take down Cartland's 10,000-word, 2¼-hour-long monologue. "Dictation is why my books sell so well," she told a *Maclean's* interviewer. "When you dictate, you tend to tell your story in nice short little paragraphs. My readers detest long paragraphs." Indeed, her paragraphs are rarely over three lines long, and the lack of subplots in her novels virtually eliminates any complications that could necessitate somewhat lengthier explanations or descriptions. "I keep the story about the hero and heroine solid all the way through," she remarked in *Publishers Weekly*. "There's no time for anything else."

Cartland also attributes much of her success to the lack of "pornography" in her novels. "My readers are sick of it," she declared in *Maclean's*. "After all, you can't get more naked than naked and my readers begin to wonder if they're normal when they don't have sex upside down swinging from chandeliers. No, my readers want to read about ladies being made love to gently in the moon light with a frilly nightie on, and that's what I give them." Furthermore, she pointed out in the *New Yorker*, "my books are an escape from the depression and boredom and lack of romance in modern life. And I think I'm the only person who writes what I call straight love—you know, the real Cinderella story—and I think that's the answer. I mean, one has frightfully complicated plots, but they all get unwound in the end and everybody's happy and everything is wonderful. That's what people want."

In addition to its prominent position (above the title and in larger type) on the cover of every one of the books, the Cartland name now adorns a variety of other items. In 1978, for instance, "Barbara Cartland's Album of Love Songs," a recording in which the author was backed by none other than the Royal Philharmonic Orchestra, made its first appearance in the stores. In late 1979, publisher Theodore B. Dolmatch launched *Barbara Cartland's World of Romance*, a monthly magazine featuring a full-length Cartland novel in every issue plus beauty tips, recipes, an astrological column, and profiles with such titles as "Bewitching Women" and "Great Lovers." "Barbara Cartland's Romances," a comic strip based on some of the author's novels, was first offered to newspapers in the United States and abroad by United Features Syndicate in late 1980; a paperback collection of the comics followed a year later.

The spring of 1981 marked the beginning of two more major undertakings bearing the Cartland name, both of which were quite unrelated to publishing: a "Decorating with Love" home furnishings collection, consisting of wallpaper, curtains, table linens, bath accessories, stationery, and other items, all with a pink flowers-and-ribbons design inspired by Cartland's own sketches; and "Barbara Cartland's Romantic Tours," a deluxe seven-day tour of England organized with the typical Cartland reader in mind. As an added attraction, the tour participants lunch with Cartland's daughter and son-in-law, Countess Spencer and Earl Spencer (father of Diana, Princess of Wales), and have tea with the author herself at her country estate. Future Cartland endorsements include a line of perfumes, beauty products, and vitamins.

The novels, however, still reign supreme in the Cartland empire. As Scot Haller of the *Saturday Review* points out, she and other writers of genre fiction have an indisputable talent for satisfying—and reflecting—"the fantasies and desires of vast segments of the book-buying public"; in short, he echoes Cartland's own observation that "that's what people want." Concludes the critic: "For the women who make up 98 percent of Cartland's audience, her novels offer a joy ride through the

time tunnel, a travel to an era of seemingly simpler morality and marriages. Although the history lessons differ from title to title, the plots are interchangeable. Her constancy *is* her appeal. Like her chaste heroines, the author is forever faithful to her fans (and her formula). In that regard, she has earned the title frequently bestowed upon her: the High Priestess of Love."

CA INTERVIEW

CA interviewed Barbara Cartland by phone March 18, 1981, at her estate in Hertfordshire, England.

CA: You write two books a month and have never missed a deadline. Does that discipline come naturally, or did you have to work at establishing it?

CARTLAND: What happened really was that up to a little while ago, they would only let me write four to five books a year. It was only when—I suppose it was about six years ago now—I got fed up with writing only five books a year and I suddenly discovered that all the publishers wanted me. So the first year I discovered that, I wrote ten for Pan and ten for Corgi. Then Hutchinson, who had been publishing my books before, was so angry they brought out twenty-two books. I had fifty-two books out that year. It upset the booksellers, but now everybody has settled down and they keep on saying "more, more, more books." I write every day when I'm at home. Last week I was speaking at a luncheon on Wednesday. Thursday I started filming a show for Australia and we went on doing it on Friday, so last week there were only two chapters. I can't write if I'm doing other things.

CA: When you wrote the first novel, did you have any idea you'd become the success you are today?

CARTLAND: No, of course not. In those days no lady worked. The first novel, I always say, was a success because "a lady had soiled her lily-white hands into work." Girls were brought up before the First World War to get married; that was the only career really open for a girl brought up in my sort of family. "*When* you get married you'll do this" and "*When* you get married you'll do that," my relatives would say. When my father was killed in the war, he left us with very little money and my mother said, "Perhaps you can get something to do." It was optimistic because there were a million men coming out of the forces. "Well, I think I'll write a book," I said just like that. In the meantime, one of my friends who was a gossip writer—in those days every newspaper had a gossip column—on the *Daily Express* said, "While you're out dancing tonight, if you see anything interesting or meet anybody important, ring me up in the morning and I'll give you five shillings a paragraph." "Goodness, I'm rich!" I thought. Five shillings in those days was quite a lot of money. So I did that, and I wrote two or three articles for the *Express*. Then Lord Beaverbrook sent for me and said, "I like the way you write" and taught me *how* to write. It has been the greatest blessing to me in my life, because I write like a journalist: I keep to the point, I make things concise. Sir Arthur Bryant, who is our greatest historian, said the other day, "You may not like what Barbara writes, but I consider her a very good writer because she never uses a superfluous word." I really write like a journalist so that it holds the reader's interest; one has to see what happens in the next chapter.

CA: Are the short paragraphs a journalistic technique?

CARTLAND: The short paragraphs came rather later. I suddenly realized (which nobody had before) that people nowadays only listen to conversation. They listen to the radio and the television, all live conversation. I was writing my book about health, *The Magic of Honey,* which is sold all over the world, and I thought that if I wrote long paragraphs people would skip them, so I decided to write it all in conversation. "He said . . ." and "She said . . .". It has sold and sold because it is so easy to read. After that, I realized that it was very important that everything I write for entertainment look like conversation.

CA: Were you ever discouraged by bad reviews?

CARTLAND: No. When I first started writing I had smashing reviews, because it was such a phenomenon to have a society girl doing any kind of work. I was supposed to be out enjoying myself all the time. Later everybody started to write, open shops, and do various other things. But when I first started writing, I was a pioneer in that field.

CA: What kind of books did you read when you were growing up?

CARTLAND: These County-Council children today are so lucky: they are educated for free and they all have the most wonderful libraries. I went to five schools. The last one was a finishing school and it had no library. I had no books to read and I was starved of them. Therefore, in the holidays I found the lending libraries. For a tuppence I could borrow books and, of course, being sort of dragged up in education (nobody worried about a *girl's* education, though the boys had wonderful ones in the public schools and universities), of course I only chose love stories by Ethel M. Dell, Marie Corelli, Elinor Glyn—instead of reading the classics. Later, when I was much older, my brother said, "Goodness, you're uneducated," and made me read the classics. But earlier I read only love stories, which of course turned out to be very, very useful. But I didn't know that at the time; I read them because I liked them.

CA: Aside from research, what books do you enjoy reading now?

CARTLAND: History, which is also my research. Because I write very quickly, I read about ten to twenty history books for every novel I write. The last novel I've just finished was written on Grenada because I went there this year, and I read the whole history of the island. It's complicated because they never stopped having revolutions between the French and the English. Of course I find it fascinating because I love history.

CA: Does one of your sons still help with the research?

CARTLAND: My eldest son, Ian, is my full-time manager; he does all the contracts and all the arranging. My second son, Glen—they've both got history degrees, one from Oxford and one from Cambridge—listens to my books and tells me what he thinks is wrong. They're both so busy they don't have time to do any research for me, but I love doing my own research and I don't really want anyone to do it for me.

CA: Are there any women writers you particularly like?

CARTLAND: I like a book which has just come out in America called *The Far Pavilions* by M. M. Kaye, and I liked her other book even better, *Shadow of the Moon.* These two books were very, very interesting to me because they were all about India and I adore India, even in novels. Another writer I really enjoy is Joanna Richardson, who is one of our great young historians. I read Christopher Hibbert, who's another very good historian. I buy their books as soon as they are published. As for novels,

I read Jean Plaidy occasionally, who writes historical novels. I used to enjoy Louis Bromfield, an American writer who I thought was wonderful. And I must admit to occasionally reading Harold Robbins, although I don't always approve of his subjects, but he's a very quick, easy-to-follow writer. Otherwise I'm very shocked at the American novelists, that's all I can say. They're so disgusting. I think Danielle Steele, who is one of your new ones, writes well; but I'm so horrified at the situations she describes, the lurid details of love, and also the disgusting language the characters use. I don't meet people in America who use that sort of language. No one talks to me in those disgusting terms they use in such books.

CA: What do you do now for relaxation?

CARTLAND: I wait until I get in the grave. I've got no time now. I'm lying in bed at the moment with two lots of proofs to correct and a chapter that has been retyped—my secretary does one chapter a day. I have an enormous amount of research to do on a book I'm thinking of doing, which I don't want to mention at the moment because it's going to be a surprise, and I've also got two new history books which I want to look at to see if I want to buy them. If I get through all that tonight, I shan't do too badly.

CA: Some people say that, given a formula, anyone can write a romantic novel. What do you think about that?

CARTLAND: Let them try! All I can say is that I don't think there's anybody except me who writes real romance as it ought to be, because I write about physical and spiritual romance at the same time. Most of the romance writers I've had anything to do with or read, especially American authors, are entirely physical, with every detail put in. There's very little of the real romantic spiritualness of love, something which was very present with Dante and Beatrice, Heloise and Abelard. Think of all the poems that have been written on real romance—Byron's poems, Keats's poems—they didn't have to use filthy situations and dirty words to get it over, did they?

CA: Because of a serious illness, you became interested in proper diet and vitamins. Do you attribute your remarkable energy and youthfulness to diet and vitamins?

CARTLAND: Yes, I do. I think it's ultimately due, first of all, to vitamins, which are pure food. It is very difficult to get pure food. And I'm violently against the tranquilizers and sleeping pills which more than half the world takes. I saw the Kennedy Report the other day, and it said what I've been saying for ages: in this country, and the same as in America, one woman in five is taking Valium, and one man in ten! I answer ten thousand letters a year—unpaid and unthanked—on health, and the majority of people who write to me are on tranquilizers of some sort. And what is so terrifying to my mind is that the doctors, when they prescribe it for their patients, never tell them that it upsets their sex lives. People write pathetic letters to me saying that everything has gone wrong in their marriages. It's because these awful tranquilizers upset their sexual life together, so it wrecks a marriage straightaway. Apart from that, the Kennedy Report shows that the withdrawal symptoms from Valium are worse than those from heroin. People are never told this. In this country they give you Valium if you cough; it's absolutely frightening. They just hand it out as though it was confetti or sweets for children. They also give it to children, as well as grownups. People shake when they take tranquilizers. I meet people whose hands shake, and I say, "I'm sure you're on Valium," and they say, "Only one!"

I went to Russia last year and I went to see the scientists: I go meet the health scientists in every country I visit—and I said, "What are you working on?" They answered, "The brain." "So am I," I said. They have women of ninety who are doing a full day's work, and I'm sure in Russia a full day's work is a full day's work. They don't allow their people to take all these ridiculous tranquilizers and sleeping pills. What people don't realize is that even one aspirin slows down your brain. If you keep on taking these things which slow your brain, it ceases to work and you become a complete vegetable. I've seen people younger than I am become morons. Their brains don't work anymore. What do they want to be tranquilized for?

CA: Do you think women are too concerned about their weight?

CARTLAND: I think this weight business is terribly dangerous. We've got so many young girls here who have anorexia, which usually means that you can't have a baby afterwards. They slim and slim until it becomes sort of an obsession. I've always said that over forty, you can keep your face or your figure, and it's much better to keep your face and sit down.

CA: Are you still active in the National Association of Health?

CARTLAND: Oh yes, I'm the president. This is why I answer so many letters. I'm always on the radio and television talking about it because it's so dear to my heart. I started it in this country and we've now become a very large organization. The luncheon I was speaking at on Wednesday was for Gloria Swanson. She is my vis-a-vis in your country. She has done so much good work in America in making people realize how important health is. She is marvelous for eighty-two. She made an excellent speech, she signed books, she seems happy; she's had six husbands and I believe she's thinking of taking a seventh! You can't do better than that, can you?

CA: You once advised your daughter to pay more attention to her looks than to her schoolwork because "no man wants a clever woman." Was that an oversimplification or do you truly believe it?

CARTLAND: It was just really a joke. What men don't want now is *aggressively* clever women. I think they want women who are clever enough not to *show* they are clever. No man wants a woman to beat him all the time at business any more than he really wants her to beat him at games. Clever women of all ages have always let the man think he's clever and got things their own way. I think it makes for happy marriage. No man wants the woman wearing the trousers in his home.

CA: It is a fact of life that, for various reasons, more and more women are having careers outside the home. You've said in the past that a woman can have such a career only at a man's expense. Have your views on that changed at all?

CARTLAND: I didn't mean that exactly. Of course women have careers, but you've got to make up your mind what you want out of life. I think the happiest thing for any woman is to be a wife and mother. Only in certain careers can you have a wonderful marriage and be a wonderful mother. Being a politician is not one of them. When my brother was killed in the war—he'd have been prime minister if he'd lived—I was offered two or three safe seats in Parliament. But unless you're as clever as Margaret Thatcher, you cannot have a political career and keep a husband and children happy; it's impossible because the time you want to be with them you're in the House of Commons. So you've got to make up your mind what sort

of career you want. Writing is easy. When my husband was alive, at five o'clock I stopped writing and never thought about it again. I still don't work on weekends because my sons are home and I'm then a mother. You've got to make up your mind what matters to you most. There's no use pretending you can do both *badly,* because that's a mistake. It's the woman who makes the home, the woman who makes the marriage romantic, the woman who inspires and guides her husband. It's a woman's job, and there's no use pretending all of this sharing business can work. That's rubbish.

CA: You set up the world's first camp for Romany gypsies. How is it working out?

CARTLAND: I still own it. What I did was get the law of England changed, because the gypsy children were not being educated. They hadn't been educated since the reign of Henry VIII, when gypsies first came to this country. I said, "You may not like gypsies, but you cannot have a democracy that says everybody must have education except gypsies." I fought a bitter battle and I started my camp as a sort of token. Now in this county of Hertfordshire they have seven County-Council camps for gypsies. Therefore the children all go to school and the parents are learning to read and write; so we have a whole generation of gypsies who are becoming very good citizens.

CA: In 1978 you made a record, "Album of Love Songs." Are you going to try other new things?

CARTLAND: Yes. I have my merchandise coming out in America; I'm coming over in April to open it. I'm going first of all to Colorado Springs because I've been made the Woman of the Year by the National Home Furnishings Association. Mrs. Reagan is supposed to be there and they're all going to wear Cartland pink! I'm to have a Barbara Cartland department in every Macy's store. In New York they also have a conglomeration of all the things I've designed—wallpaper, carpets, curtains, sheets, towels—it's the biggest conglomeration an individual has ever had. As I'm a foreigner in your country, I think it is a great compliment.

CA: Do you enjoy visiting the United States?

CARTLAND: Oh yes. And I'm so delighted that your new president and Mrs. Reagan believe in home, love, and, of course, in high ideals. I think we've been through a very bad period all over the world, where we've had no ideals, and in a great many countries no religion. I think this has had a depressing and bad effect not only on our children but on everybody else. I think that Mr. Reagan and his wife, whom my daughter knows well and whom I admire very much, are bringing back the real values. It's become smart to laugh at people who want to be good. But we *want* people to be good, we want people to believe in good things, we want people to have high ideals and ambitions, to improve themselves and improve their own country. Once you get everything going downhill, it obviously has a very bad effect on the young people, and that's why they worship pop stars and drop out on drugs and all the things we disapprove of. I think we must get back to real values and real ideals.

I wrote a book of prayer the other day, which I hold in my hand in my statue at Madame Tussaud's. They said, "Which book of the 304 you've written are you going to hold in your hand?" and I said, "I'm going to hold my book of prayer because I think it's terribly important." I believe so tremendously in prayer. What worries me in this country—I don't know what you're doing in America—is that we don't teach children in school to pray and I think that's terrible. You and I have been brought up so that if we were told at this minute that a nuclear bomb is going to fall on our heads, what do we do? Automatically we start praying. As the children are brought up in schools now with no prayers, what are they going to do? Scream? We're taking away the sort of fundamental rocks on which people have always relied in adversity. You've got to have something to lean on, something you know is going to support you in adversity, but what are we giving the young people? They're not being given a fundamental faith—it is something they can throw away if they want to, but we ought to give them the chance of being *able* to throw it away. Even the Catholic countries are not as strong in their teaching as they used to be, and every religion bickers among themselves. Children want to know what is right and what is wrong. What people haven't got today is self-discipline, so when things go wrong they don't know what to do.

I know my books are called light literature, but if you read them carefully, there's a lot of very good common sense and a lot of inspiration in them. My heroines always educate themselves and they read, they mind about the poor and the sick, and they pray. All those things are in almost every one of my novels. It may be a very little thing, but if you can just get it into people's heads that that's the right way to live, it's such a tremendous help.

BIOGRAPHICAL/CRITICAL SOURCES: Books, February 21, 1937; Barbara Cartland, *The Isthmus Years: Reminiscences of the Years 1919-1939,* Hutchinson, 1943; Cartland, *The Years of Opportunity: 1939-1945,* Hutchinson, 1948; Kenneth Ullyett, *My Key to Life,* Skeffington, 1958; Cartland, *I Search for Rainbows: 1946-1966,* Hutchinson, 1967; *New Statesman,* August 4, 1967; *Punch,* August 9, 1967, February 3, 1971; *Times Literary Supplement,* November 2, 1967; *Books and Bookmen,* June, 1968, August, 1968, November, 1968, August, 1969, April, 1971; Cartland, *We Danced All Night: 1919-1929,* Hutchinson, 1970, Pyramid Publications, 1972; *Publishers Weekly,* June 7, 1976, April 17, 1981; *Dublin Evening Press,* July 28, 1976; *New Yorker,* August 9, 1976; Cartland, *I Seek the Miraculous,* Dutton, 1978; *Maclean's,* December 11, 1978; *Los Angeles Times Book Review,* March 25, 1979; Henry Cloud, *Crusader in Pink* (biography), Everest House, 1980; *Saturday Review,* March, 1981; *People,* May 25, 1981.

—*Sketch by Deborah A. Straub*

—*Interview by Jean W. Ross*

*   *   *

CASEWIT, Curtis (Werner) 1922-
(D. Green, D. Vernor, K. Werner)

PERSONAL: Born March 21, 1922, in Mannheim, Germany; came to United States in 1948; son of Theodor and Elsa Casewit; married Charlotte Fischer-Lamberg, February, 1954 (divorced); children: Carla, Stephen, Niccolo. *Education:* Attended Florence Language School, Florence, Italy, 1933-38, University of Denver, and University of Colorado. *Home address:* P.O. Box 19039, Denver, Colo. 80219.

CAREER: Free-lance writer, 1964—. Book buyer in department store in Denver, Colo., 1959-64; Denver Opportunity School, teacher of creative writing, 1961-62; University of Colorado, Denver, instructor in non-credit writing program, 1965—. Translator in German, French, and Italian. Consultant, *Writer's Digest. Military service:* French Army, 1940-43. British Army, interpreter, 1945-47; became sergeant. *Member:* Society of American Travel Writers, Society of Magazine Writers, American Society of Journalists and Authors, Colorado

Authors League, Colorado Mountain Club. *Awards, honors:* Edgar Allan Poe Award ("Edgar"), Mystery Writers of America, 1956, for best book reviewing; short story contest award, *Writer's Digest,* 1955; Dutton Award for articles published in *Best Articles of 1964* and *Best Articles of 1976.*

WRITINGS: Accent on Treason, Popular Library, 1954; *Ski Racing: Advice by the Experts,* Arco, 1963, second edition, 1969; *Adventure in Deepmore Cave,* Doubleday, 1965; *How to Get a Job Overseas,* Arco, 1965, revised edition, Arc Books, 1970; *Ski Fever: How to Master the Fastest-Growing Winter Sport,* Hawthorn Books, 1965; *United Air Lines Guide to Western Skiing,* Doubleday, 1967; (with Richard Pownall) *The Mountaineering Handbook: An Invitation to Climbing,* Lippincott, 1968; *Ski Racer,* Four Winds, 1968; *The Hiking-Climbing Handbook,* Hawthorn, 1969.

The Adventures of Snowshoe Thompson, Putnam, 1970; *The Skier's Handbook: Advice from the Experts,* Winchester, 1971; *Overseas Jobs: The Ten Best Countries,* Paperback Library, 1972; *A Guide to Western Skiing,* Chronicle Books, 1972; *Colorado,* Viking, 1973; (translator) Karl Schranz, *The Karl Schranz Seven-Day Ski System,* Macmillan, 1974; *Freelance Writing: Advice from the Pros,* Macmillan, 1974; *America's Tennis Book,* Scribner, 1975; *Skiing Colorado,* Chatham Press, 1975; *The Mountain World,* Random House, 1976; *The Skier's Handbook,* Arc Books, 1976; *The Complete Book of Mountain Sports,* Messner, 1978; *The Stop Smoking Book for Teens,* Messner, 1980; *Freelance Photography: Advice from the Pros,* Macmillan, 1980; *The Graphology Handbook,* Para-Research, 1980; *Making a Living in the Fine Arts,* Macmillan, 1981. Also author of *The Western Tennis Guide* and *The Complete Skier and Ski Traveler.*

Contributor of short stories and articles to more than fifty newspapers and magazines in seven countries, including *Saga, Catholic Digest, Coronet, Overseas Weekly,* and *Science and Mechanics.*

*   *   *

CASEY, Daniel J(oseph) 1937-
(Donal O'Cathasaigh)

PERSONAL: Born February 11, 1937, in Brooklyn, N.Y.; son of John L. (a salesman) and Frances E. (McNerney) Casey; married Linda M. Brown, April 22, 1958; children: Daniel B., Thomas J., Michael P., Conor. *Education:* St. John's University, Jamaica, N.Y., B.A., 1958, M.S., 1960, M.A., 1963; University of Helsinki, Ph.D., 1968. *Religion:* Roman Catholic. *Home address:* R.D. 1, Wilber Lake Rd., Oneonta, N.Y. 13820. *Office:* Department of English, State University of New York, Oneonta, N.Y. 13820.

CAREER: Universita degli Studi di Cagliari, Cagliari, Italy, Fulbright lecturer in English, 1963-64; University of Delaware, Newark, instructor in English, 1964-66; State University of New York College at Oneonta, associate professor, 1968-72, professor of English, 1972—. Visiting professor, New University of Ulster, 1980-81. *Member:* International Association for the Study of Anglo-Irish Literature, Modern Language Association of America, American Conference on Irish Studies. *Awards, honors:* Fulbright grants, 1963, 1967, 1968; American Philosophical Society grants, 1974, 1980; order of merit from Ancient Order of Hibernians, 1974.

WRITINGS: Benedict Kiely, Bucknell University Press, 1974; (editor with Robert Rhodes) *The Irish Peasant, 1800-1916,* Archon Books, 1977; *Poetry of the Cuchulainn Country,* Dundalgan Press, 1978; (with Rhodes) *Irish-American Fiction: Es-*

says in Criticism, AMS Press, 1979; (contributor) James J. Preston, editor, *Mother Worship: Theme and Variations*, University of North Carolina Press, 1981; (with Rhodes) *Friends and Relations: An Anthology of Irish/American Fiction*, AMS Press, 1982.

Contributor to *Antigonish Review, English Record, Anglo-Irish Studies, Moderna Sprak,* and *Critic.* Editor, *Delaware English Journal*, 1965, *Carleton Newsletter*, 1970-73, and *English Record*, 1970-74. Member of editorial board, *Eire 19, Irish Renaissance Annual,* and *Mankind Quarterly.*

WORK IN PROGRESS: Carleton of Tyrone; Hunger Striker: The Life of Bobby Sands.

*   *   *

CASSELLS, John
See DUNCAN, W(illiam) Murdoch

*   *   *

CAVAIANI, Mabel   1919-

PERSONAL: Born September 12, 1919, in Manley, Iowa; daughter of Bert G. and Ida (Hall) Sniffin; married Charles C. Cavaiani, April 14, 1950. *Education:* Iowa State University, B.Sci., 1940; St. Xavier's College, Chicago, Ill., graduate study. *Religion:* United Methodist. *Home address:* P.O. Box 66, Wadena, Iowa 52169.

CAREER: Registered dietitian; in restaurant management in Chicago, Ill., 1940-61; U.S. Army Research Center, Chicago, dietitian, 1961-63; U.S. Food Service Center, Menu Planning Division, Chicago, dietitian, 1963-71, Army representative on Armed Forces Recipe Service Committee, 1967-71. Member of board of trustees of Oak Lawn Public Library, 1968-71; member of board, Wadena Public Library, 1980—. Consultant to nursing homes and programs for the elderly. *Member:* American Dietetic Association, Consultant Dietitians in Health Care Facilities, American Association of University Women, Iowa State Home Economics Alumni Association, United Methodist Women, Chi Anedow Federated Club.

WRITINGS: The Low Cholesterol Cookbook, Regnery, 1972; (with Audrey Ellis) *Farmhouse Kitchen,* Regnery, 1973; (with Muriel Urbashich) *Simplified Quantity Recipes: Nursing-Convalescent Homes and Hospitals,* National Restaurant Association, 1974; *The High-Fiber Cookbook,* Contemporary Books, 1977; (with Urbashich and Frances Nielsen) *Simplified Quantity Regional Recipes,* Hayden, 1979; (with Urbashich and Nielsen) *Simplified Quantity Ethnic Recipes,* Hayden, 1980; *Low Cholesterol Cuisine,* Contemporary Books, 1981.

SIDELIGHTS: Mabel Cavaiani told *CA:* "My husband retired and I quit working in 1971 when both of our government installations moved to different cities. We bought acreage in beautiful northeastern Iowa with huge walnut trees, acres of timber, a spring in the yard, and a winding driveway which was gorgeous in the spring, lovely in the summer, spectacular in the fall, and pure hell in the winter. After five years of being snowed in for several days at a time we gave up our dreams and built a house in town. Like all retired farmers we regret having to move to town and look back on our years in the country as the best period of our lives, but we must be practical and that driveway was just too much for us.

"I started writing cookbooks as an extension of my own needs. In 1953 when the doctor put my husband on a low cholesterol diet, I was upset because I couldn't find any books with recipes for his diet. I finally decided that since I had a B.Sci. degree

in Foods and Nutrition I should start developing my own recipes which were suitable for his diet. I started testing and developing recipes for our own use and eventually decided to turn my knowledge of the low cholesterol diet and my collection of recipes into the book *The Low Cholesterol Cookbook.* Once hooked on writing cookbooks I couldn't stop and have continued to write books related to my work as a dietitian. I feel very strongly about the low cholesterol diet since I feel that strict adherence to the diet saved my husband's life, and I like to think that I helped save a few other lives also.

"I have continued to write cookbooks which I, as a dietitian, feel are needed. My two books of low cholesterol recipes and one of high-fiber recipes have all been very successful and the books I have written with Muriel Urbashich and Frances Nielsen for use in nursing homes and other small institutions have been, I've been told, very helpful to other dietitians and smaller kitchens without a trained kitchen staff.

"Both my husband and I like small town life and are very happy in our little Iowa town. Neither of us regret our years in Chicago but neither do we long to return to the big city. My husband has a huge garden. We can walk downtown to get the mail, and we attend a church with beautiful stained glass windows, old fashioned pews, and the friendliest congregation that I've ever known. Some of our friends feel sorry for us for being so far away from the city but we love it and intend to stay here as long as we are physically able to do so."

*   *   *

CAVANNA, Betty   1909-
(Betsy Allen, Elizabeth Allen Cavanna, Elizabeth Headley)

PERSONAL: Born June 24, 1909, in Camden, N.J.; daughter of Walter and Emily (Allen) Cavanna; married Edward Headley, August 5, 1940 (died, 1952); married George Russell Harrison (a dean of science emeritus at Massachusetts Institute of Technology), March 9, 1957; children: (first marriage) Stephen. *Education:* Douglass College, A.B., 1929. *Religion:* Protestant.

CAREER: Bayonne Times, Bayonne, N.J., reporter, 1929-31; Westminster Press, Philadelphia, Pa., began as advertising manager, became art director, 1931-41; full-time writer, 1941—. *Member:* Writers Guild, Boston Museum of Fine Arts, Philadelphia Art Alliance, Technology Matrons (program chairman, 1961-62), Phi Beta Kappa, Women's Travel Club of Boston (2nd vice-president, 1972-73), Cosmopolitan Club (New York).

WRITINGS—All juvenile or young adult books: *Puppy Stakes,* Westminster, 1943; *The Black Spaniel Mystery,* Westminster, 1945; *Secret Passage,* John C. Winston, 1946; *Going on Sixteen,* Westminster, 1946; *Spurs for Suzanna,* Westminster, 1947; *A Girl Can Dream,* Westminster, 1948; *Paintbox Summer,* Westminster, 1949; *Spring Comes Riding,* Westminster, 1950; *Two's Company,* Westminster, 1951; (compiler) *Pick of the Litter: Favorite Dog Stories,* Westminster, 1952; *Lasso Your Heart,* Westminster, 1952; *Love, Laurie,* Westminster, 1953; *Six on Easy Street,* Westminster, 1954; *The First Book of Seashells,* F. Watts, 1955; *Passport to Romance,* Morrow, 1955; *The Boy Next Door,* Morrow, 1956; *Angel on Skis,* Morrow, 1957; *Stars in Her Eyes,* Morrow, 1958; *The Scarlet Sail,* Morrow, 1959; *Accent on April,* Morrow, 1960; *A Touch of Magic,* Westminster, 1961; *Fancy Free,* Morrow, 1961; *The First Book of Wildflowers,* F. Watts, 1961; *A Time for Tenderness,* Morrow, 1962; *Almost Like Sisters,* Morrow, 1963; *Jenny Kimura,* Morrow, 1964; *Mystery at Love's Creek,* Morrow, 1965; *A Breath of Fresh Air*, Morrow, 1966; (with husband, George Russell Harrison) *The First Book of Wool*, F. Watts, 1966 (published in England as *Wool*, F. Watts, 1972); *The Country Cousin*, Morrow, 1967; *Mystery in Marrakech*, Morrow, 1968; *Spice Island Mystery*, Morrow, 1969; *The First Book of Fiji*, F. Watts, 1969 (published in England as *Fiji*, F. Watts, 1972); *The First Book of Morocco*, F. Watts, 1970; *Mystery on Safari*, Morrow, 1971; *The Ghost of Ballyhooly*, Morrow, 1971; *Mystery in the Museum*, Morrow, 1972; *Petey*, Westminster, 1973; *Joyride*, Morrow, 1974; *Ruffles and Drums*, Morrow, 1975; *Mystery of the Emerald Buddha*, Morrow, 1976.

"Around the World Today" series, published by F. Watts; *Arne of Norway*, 1960; *Lucho of Peru*, 1961; *Paulo of Brazil*, 1962; *Pepe of Argentina*, 1962; *Lo Chau of Hong Kong*, 1963; *Chico of Guatemala*, 1963; *Noko of Japan*, 1964; *Carlos of Mexico*, 1964; *Tavi of the South Seas*, 1965; *Doug of Australia*, 1965; *Ali of Egypt*, 1966; *Demetrios of Greece*, 1966.

"Connie Blair Mystery" series, published by Grosset: *Puzzle in Purple*, 1948; *The Secret of Black Cat Gulch*, 1948; *The Riddle in Red*, 1948; *The Clue in Blue*, 1948; *The Green Island Mystery*, 1949; *The Ghost Wore White*, 1950; *The Yellow Warning*, 1951; *The Gray Menace*, 1953; *The Brown Satchel Mystery*, 1954; *Peril in Pink*, 1955; *The Silver Secret*, 1956.

Under name Elizabeth Headley; published by Macrae Smith: *A Date for Diane* (also see below), 1946; *Take a Call, Topsy!*, 1947; *She's My Girl!*, 1949; *Catchpenny Street*, 1951; *Diane's New Love* (also see below), 1955; *Toujours Diane* (also see below), 1957; *The Diane Stories: All about America's Favorite Girl Next Door* (contains *A Date for Diane, Diane's New Love*, and *Toujours Diane*), 1964.

Contributor of serials to *American Girl* and other magazines.

SIDELIGHTS: Betty Cavanna's books often concern junior high school girls. She explains this as the result of "an almost total emotional recall for this particular period of my own life, which made it possible for me to identify with a teenage heroine. Fashions in clothes and speech change, but the hopes, dreams, and fears of the young remain fairly constant, and over the years I have explored all sorts of youthful problems— among them loneliness, shyness, jealousy, social maladjustment, and the destructiveness of alcoholism, divorce, race prejudice, and mother-daughter rivalry within family situations."

Dwight L. Burton of *English Journal* writes: "Books by Betty Cavanna have been among the most popular with young high school readers." He cites *Going on Sixteen* as particularly "noteworthy". The novel, Burton explains, "rests upon its genuineness and sincerity rather than upon melodrama. Julie, the heroine, is a somewhat shy, nondescript girl who lives on a farm with her father." Burton notes that as the story follows Julie's progress through three years of high school, Cavanna "avoids the easy assumptions present in many books with a similar theme. . . . There is realistic evolution of character brought about by Julie's own efforts and recognition of her faults and by the sympathetic guidance of a teacher."

Cavanna has travelled to the Caribbean, Mexico, Europe, South America, Australia, Japan, the South Seas, Iran, Nepal, Afghanistan, and Africa.

AVOCATIONAL INTERESTS: Art, gardening, antiques.

BIOGRAPHICAL/CRITICAL SOURCES: New York Herald Tribune Book Review, June 10, 1945, May 5, 1946, April 11, 1948, June 17, 1951; *Atlantic*, December, 1946; *New York Times Book Review*, January 5, 1947, July 20, 1947, May 15, 1949, November 15, 1953, December 15, 1957; *Saturday Review*, August 13, 1949; *English Journal*, September, 1951;

Book Week, November 29, 1964; *Christian Science Monitor*, November 4, 1965; *Times Literary Supplement*, May 19, 1966; Dennis Thomison, editor, *Readings about Adolescent Literature*, Scarecrow, 1970; *Contemporary Literary Criticism*, Volume XII, Gale, 1980.†

*   *   *

CAVANNA, Elizabeth Allen
    See CAVANNA, Betty

*   *   *

CHAMBERLAIN, Neil Wolverton   1915-

PERSONAL: Born May 18, 1915, in Charlotte, N.C.; son of Henry Bryan and Elizabeth (Wolverton) Chamberlain; married Marian Kenosian (an economist), June 27, 1942 (divorced June, 1967); married Harriet Feigenbaum (an artist), August 9, 1968. *Education:* Western Reserve University (now Case Western Reserve University), A.B., 1937, M.A., 1939; Ohio State University, Ph.D., 1942. *Home:* 49 West 24th St., New York, N.Y. 10010. *Office:* Department of Business, Columbia University, New York, N.Y. 10027.

CAREER: Brookings Institution, Washington, D.C., research fellow, 1941-42; Yale University, New Haven, Conn., research director, Labor and Management Center, 1946-49, assistant professor, 1947-49, associate professor of economics, 1949-54; Columbia University, New York, N.Y., professor of economics, 1954-59; Yale University, professor of economics 1959-67; Columbia University, professor of economics, 1967-69, Armand G. Erpf Professor of Modern Corporations, 1969-80, professor emeritus, 1981—. Director, Ford Foundation Program in Economic Development and Administration, 1957-60; member of board of directors, Salzburg Seminar in American Studies, 1957-78. Consulting editor, Basic Books Inc., 1969-78. *Military service:* U.S. Naval Reserve, 1942-46; became lieutenant. *Member:* American Economic Association, Industrial Relations Research Association (member of executive board, 1955-58; president, 1967), Phi Beta Kappa.

WRITINGS: Collective Bargaining Procedures, American Council on Public Affairs, 1944; *The Union Challenge to Management Control*, Harper, 1948, reprinted, Shoe String, 1967; (co-editor) *Cases on Labor Relations*, Foundation Press, 1949; *Management in Motion*, Labor and Management Center, Yale University, 1950; *Collective Bargaining*, McGraw, 1951, 2nd edition (with James W. Kuhn), 1965; *Social Responsibility and Strikes*, Harper, 1953; (with J. M. Schilling) *The Impact of Strike*, Harper, 1954; *A General Theory of Economic Process*, Harper, 1955; (editor with Frank Pierson and Theresa Wolfson) *A Decade of Industrial Relations Research*, Industrial Relations Research Association, 1958; *Labor*, McGraw, 1958; *Sourcebook on Labor*, McGraw, 1958, revised and abridged edition (with Richard Perlman), 1964; *The Firm: Micro-Economic Planning and Action*, McGraw 1962; *The West in a World without War*, McGraw, 1963; *The Labor Sector: An Introduction to Labor in the American Economy*, McGraw, 1965, 3rd edition (with Donald Cullen and David Lewin), 1980; *Private and Public Planning*, McGraw, 1965.

(Co-editor) *Frontiers of Collective Bargaining*, Harper, 1967; *Enterprise and Environment: The Firm in Time and Place*, McGraw, 1968; (editor) *Contemporary Economic Issues*, Irwin, 1969, revised edition, 1973; *Beyond Malthus: Population and Power*, Basic Books, 1970; (compiler) *Business and the Cities: A Book of Relevant Readings*, Basic Books, 1970; *The Place of Business in America's Future: A Study in Social Values*, Basic Books, 1973; *The Limits of Corporate Responsi-*

bility, Basic Books, 1973; *Remaking American Values: Challenge to a Business Society,* Basic Books, 1977; *Forces of Change in Western Europe,* McGraw (London), 1980; *Social Strategy and Corporate Structure,* Macmillan, 1982.

Member of editorial board, *American Economic Review,* 1957-59, *Management International,* 1960-70.

* * *

CHAMBERS, Mortimer Hardin, Jr. 1927-

PERSONAL: Born January 9, 1927, in Saginaw, Mich.; son of Mortimer Hardin (a businessman) and Nell (Bishop) Chambers; married Gail Hamilton, June 11, 1949; children: Pamela, Julia, Blake. *Education:* Harvard University, A.B., 1949, Ph.D., 1954; Wadham College, Oxford, M.A., 1955. *Home:* 2122 Selby Ave., Los Angeles, Calif. 90025. *Office:* Department of History, University of California, Los Angeles, Calif. 90024.

CAREER: Harvard University, Cambridge, Mass., instructor in classics, 1954-55; University of Chicago, Chicago, Ill., assistant professor of ancient history, 1955-58; University of California, Los Angeles, 1958—, began as assistant professor, professor of ancient history, 1969—. *Military service:* U.S. Army, 1945-46; became sergeant. *Member:* American Historical Association, American Philological Association.

WRITINGS: (With James Day) *Aristotle's History of Athenian Democracy,* University of California Press, 1962; (editor) *The Fall of Rome: Can It Be Explained?,* Holt, 1963, 2nd edition, 1970; *Greek and Roman History,* Service Center for Teachers of History (Washington, D.C.), 1965; (translator) Polybius, *The Histories,* edited by E. Badian, Washington Square Press, 1966, revised edition, Twayne, 1967; *Ancient Greece,* American Historical Association, 1973; (with others) *The Western Experience,* two volumes, Knopf, 1974, 2nd edition published in three volumes, 1978, Volume I: *Antiquity to the Middle Ages,* Volume II: *The Early Modern Period,* Volume III: *The Modern Era.* Contributor of articles to journals.†

* * *

CHANDLER, Frank
See HARKNETT, Terry

* * *

CHANG, Dae H(ong) 1928-

PERSONAL: Born January 9, 1928, in Nara, Japan; naturalized U.S. citizen; son of Chun B. (a scholar) and Kim I. (Kim) Chang; married Seung Hi Cho, August 20, 1964; children: Morris B., Richard J. *Education:* Michigan State University, B.A., 1957, M.A., 1958, Ph.D., 1962. *Office:* Department of the Administration of Justice, Wichita State University, Wichita, Kan. 67208.

CAREER: National Police Headquarters, Seoul, Korea, lieutenant of police, 1951-56, secretary for director of national police, 1954-55, liaison officer for United Nations Command Force in Korea, 1952-56; Michigan Secretary of State, Lansing, statistical analyst for Driver and Vehicle Service, 1958-61; Olivet College, Olivet, Mich., assistant professor, 1962-63, associate professor of sociology and chairman of department, 1963-66; Northern Illinois University, DeKalb, assistant professor, 1966-69, associate professor of sociology, 1969; University of Wisconsin, Whitewater, professor of sociology and anthropology, 1969-75, chairman of department, 1969-74; Wichita State University, Wichita, Kan., professor of the administration of justice and chairman of department, 1975—.

President of American Corp. for Penal Research and Reform, 1971—. Host of "Around the World in Thirty Minutes," WMMR-Radio, 1965-66, and "International Interlude," WNIU-Radio, 1968; appeared on "Milwaukee Reports," CBS-Television, 1971. Professor and researcher at University of Wisconsin, 1972-73. Member of Wisconsin Task Force for Higher Education, 1972-73; member of steering committee for Wisconsin Criminal Justice Institute, 1973—.

MEMBER: American Sociological Association, American Society of Criminology (chairman, International Liaison Committee, 1980-81), Academy of Criminal Justice Sciences (chairman, International Section, 1980-81), Midwest Sociological Society, Wisconsin Sociological Association, Michigan Academy of Science, Arts, and Letters (vice-chairman of Asian section, 1968, chairman, 1969). *Awards, honors:* Smith-Mundt fellowship, 1954-55, to study American law enforcement agencies; National Science Foundation grant, 1970-75, to study crime control on and near Lake Michigan; received United Nations Service Medal, Korean War Service Medal, and Wharang War Merit Medal.

WRITINGS: (Contributor) Eugene Kim and Ch'angboh Chee, editors, *Aspects of Social Change in Korea,* Western Michigan University, 1969; *Sociology: A Syllabus and Workbook,* Kendall/Hunt, 1970; (with Warren Armstrong) *The Prison: Voices from the Inside,* Schenkman, 1972; *Sociology: An Applied Approach,* Paladin House, 1973; (with Charles Zastrow) *The Personal Problem Solver,* Random House, 1976; *Crime and Delinquency Prevention: A Universalistic Perspective,* Schenkman, 1977; *Criminology: A Cross-Cultural Perspective,* Carolina Academic, 1977; *The Fundamentals of Criminal Justice,* Paladin House, 1977; (contributor) Man Singh Das, editor, *The Asian Family: Past, Present, and the Future,* Lucknow Publishing House, 1980; (with Ronald Iacovetta) *Critical Issues in Criminal Justice: Theory and Application,* Kendall/Hunt, 1980.

Contributor to journals. Associate editor, *International Review of Sociology* and *International Journal of Sociology of the Family,* 1969—; editor, *International Journal of Comparative and Applied Criminal Justice,* 1977—.

WORK IN PROGRESS: Research on inmates' and security guards' perceptions of themselves and of each other; studying aquatic crime; research on police evaluative perceptions of themselves, the general public, and selected occupational groups, on occupational values and attitudes toward modernization of Korea among Korean youths, and on Korean high school students' occupational prestige ranking with special reference to structuralist and culturalist positions.

* * *

CHANG, Parris (Hsu-Cheng) 1936-

PERSONAL: Born December 30, 1936, in Chiayi, Taiwan; son of Chao and Liu (Ch'en) Chang; married Shirley Hsiu-Chu Lin (a librarian), August 3, 1963; children: Yvette, Elaine, Bohdan. *Education:* National Taiwan University, B.A., 1959; University of Washington, Seattle, M.A., 1963; Pennsylvania State University, graduate study, 1963-64; Columbia University, Ph.D., 1969. *Home:* 1221 Edward St., State College, Pa. 16801. *Office:* Department of Political Science, Pennsylvania State University, University Park, Pa. 16802.

CAREER: University of Michigan, Center for Chinese Studies, Ann Arbor, research political scientist, 1969-70; Pennsylvania State University, University Park, assistant professor, 1970-72, associate professor, 1972-76, professor of political science,

1976—. Visiting scholar, Australian National University, 1978. Consultant to RAND Corp., 1974—. *Member:* American Political Science Association, Association for Asian Studies (president of Mid-Atlantic Region, 1976-77), International Studies Association. *Awards, honors:* Fulbright scholar, 1961-62, 1977-78; Social Science Research Council grant for work in Tokyo, Hong Kong, and Taipei, 1972-73; IREX travel grant to East Europe, 1977.

WRITINGS: Radicals and Radical Ideology in China's Cultural Revolution, School of International Affairs, Columbia University, 1973; *Power and Policy in China,* Pennsylvania State University Press, 1975, revised edition, 1978.

Contributor: Robert A. Scalapino, editor, *Elites in Communist China,* University of Washington Press, 1972; William Whitson, editor, *The Role of the Military in China,* Praeger, 1972; Paul Sih, editor, *Taiwan in Modern Times,* St. John's University Press (New York), 1973; Jan Prybyla, editor, *The Pentagon of Power: U.S.A., U.S.S.R., Western Europe, Japan, China,* Center for Continuing Liberal Education and Slavic and Soviet Languages and Area Center, Pennsylvania State University, 1973; Frank Horton and others, editors, *Comparative Defense Policy,* Johns Hopkins Press, 1974; C. E. Welch, Jr., editor, *Civil Control of the Military,* State University of New York Press, 1976; G. C. Chu and F.L.K. Hsu, editors, *Moving a Curtain,* University Press of Hawaii, 1979; V. V. Aspaturian and others, editors, *Eurocommunism between East and West,* Indiana University Press, 1980; C. Howe, editor, *Shanghai: Revolution and Development in an Asian Metropolis,* Cambridge University Press, 1981. Contributor of 60 articles to *Newsweek, Washington Post, Christian Science Monitor,* and other publications.

WORK IN PROGRESS: A study of military intervention in Chinese politics since the 1960s; a study of China's military-industrial complex and its impact on Chinese foreign policy; research on corruption in China.

SIDELIGHTS: Parris Chang told *CA:* "Writing in English is quite a challenge, a trial, but when you see it published the satisfaction is immense. One of my ambitions is to write a political fiction on relations between the U.S. and Asian countries using my knowledge of international relations to dramatize the interactions of nations as well as of the politicians who act in the name of nations."

Chang visited the People's Republic of China in 1972, 1974, and 1979-80, and had a meeting with the late premier Chou En-lai in 1972.

*   *   *

CHANG-RODRIGUEZ, Eugenio

PERSONAL: Born in Trujillo, Peru; son of Enrique and Peregrina (Rodriguez) Chang. *Education:* University of San Marcos, Ph.B., 1946; William Penn College, B.A., 1949; University of Arizona, M.S., 1950; University of Washington, Seattle, M.A., 1952, Ph.D., 1956. *Home:* 60 Sutton Pl. S., New York, N.Y. 10022. *Office:* Department of Romance Languages, Queens College, City University of New York, Flushing, N.Y. 11367.

CAREER: University of Washington, Seattle, instructor in Spanish and assistant to dean of College of Arts and Sciences, 1950-56; University of Pennsylvania, Philadelphia, assistant professor of Romance languages and literatures, 1956-61; Queens College of the City University of New York, Flushing, N.Y., assistant professor, 1961-64, associate professor, beginning 1964, currently professor of Romance languages and literature

and chairman of Latin American Area Studies. University of Southern California, visiting summer professor, 1950, 1961, 1962; lecturer at Columbia University, Barnard College, and other schools. *Member:* International League for the Rights of Man (council chairman, 1970—), International Linguistic Association (president, 1969-72), Modern Language Association of America, United Nations Correspondents Association, American Association of Teachers of Spanish and Portuguese (chapter president, 1954-56), Hispanic Institute, Instituto Internacional de Literatura Iberoamericana, Academy of Political Science, Foreign Correspondents Association, American Association of University Professors, Overseas Press Club, Linguistic Circle of New York, Phi Sigma Iota, Sigma Delta Pi.

WRITINGS: Literatura Politica de Gonzalez Prada, Mariategui y Haya, Studium, 1957; (editor with H. Kantor) *La America Latina de Hoy* (anthology), Ronald, 1961; (editor with G. MacEoin and M. Luz) *The Hemisphere's Present Crisis,* Overseas Press Club, 1963; (with Alphonse G. Juilland) *Frequency Dictionary of Spanish Words,* Humanities, 1965; (with L. Poston and others) *Continuing Spanish,* five volumes, American Book Co., 1969; *The Lingering Crisis: A Case Study of the Dominican Republic,* Las Americas, 1969; (with C. Smith and M. Bermejo) *Collins Spanish Dictionary,* Collins, 1971. Associate editor, *Hispania,* 1963-65.

AVOCATIONAL INTERESTS: Fencing, swimming, skiing, horseback riding.

BIOGRAPHICAL/CRITICAL SOURCES: Seattle Times, June 12, 1952, October 7, 1952; *Seattle Post-Intelligencer,* August 19, 1953; *La Prensa,* September 11, 1956; *Peruvian Times,* September 28, 1956; *Denver Post,* August 24, 1961; *Transcript* (Norman, Okla.), August 8, 1965; *El Comercio* (Lima, Peru), June 20, 1980.

*   *   *

CHANTILES, Vilma Liacouras 1925-

PERSONAL: Surname is pronounced Chan-*till*-eez; born August 11, 1925, in Philadelphia, Pa.; daughter of James Peter and Stella (Lagakos) Liacouras; married Nicholas G. Chantiles (vice-president of International Book Publishing Group, Times-Mirror Co.), March 2, 1952; children: Dean, James, Maria Nicole. *Education:* Drexel Institute of Technology (now Drexel University), B.S., 1947; New York University, M.A., 1970; private study of music (voice), art, weaving, and foreign languages. *Religion:* Greek Orthodox. *Home:* 13 Circle Rd., Scarsdale, N.Y. 10583.

CAREER: Rosenau Brothers, Philadelphia, Pa., designer of "Cinderella Frocks," 1948-50; reporter for *Women's Wear Daily* Philadelphia bureau, 1950-53; freelance reporter from Germany on leather products, 1954; substitute teacher of home economics and art in public schools in Radnor, Pa., 1965-66, and Westchester County, N.Y., 1967-68; home economics teacher in junior high school in Scarsdale, N.Y., 1969; Herbert H. Lehman College of the City University of New York, Bronx, N.Y., lecturer, 1970, instructor in home economics, 1971, adjunct lecturer, 1977; writer and researcher, 1972-73; New York University, New York, N.Y., part-time lecturer in home economics, 1973-74; freelance writer, 1974—. Lecturer, Deree-Pierce College, 1979. *Member:* American Home Economics Association, Home Economists in Business, Westchester Choral Society, Omicron Nu.

WRITINGS: The Food of Greece, Atheneum, 1975; (contributor) *The Great Cooks,* Random House, 1977; (contributor) *The Good Cook,* Time-Life Books, 1979. Author of column

"Library Sampler," *Needle Arts*. Contributor to magazines. Food editor, *Athenian*, 1975—.

WORK IN PROGRESS: Foodways; Greek Embroidery Designs.

SIDELIGHTS: Vilma Chantiles told *CA:* "Intrigued by culture and arts in everyday life, I feel compelled to research and write about their effects on human experience. My first cookbook developed from food cultural history as it affected my extended family, transplanted from Greece to the U.S. My challenge is to overcome discouraging response to my 'specialized' studies and try to enrich my writing with the arts, and hopefully, link our times with the future."

BIOGRAPHICAL/CRITICAL SOURCES: Washington Post, April 10, 1975.

*   *   *

CHASE, Adam
    See MARLOWE, Stephen

*   *   *

CHATELET, Albert   1928-

PERSONAL: Born June 27, 1928, in Lille, France; son of Albert (a mathematician) and Marguerite (Brey) Chatelet; married Lilian Lange (an art historian), March 25, 1961; children: Madeleine. *Education:* Ecole du Louvre, diplome d'etudes superieures; Faculte des Lettres de Paris, licence es lettres, docteur es lettres. *Home:* 7, rue du Faisan, 67460 Mundolsheim, France. *Office:* Palais Universitaire, 67084 Strasbourg Cedex, France.

CAREER: Musee du Louvre, Departement des Peintures, Paris, France, charge de mission, 1951-55, assistant, 1955-59; Centre National de la Recherche Scientifique, Paris, attache, 1959-62; Musee des Beaux-Arts, Lille, France, directeur, 1962-69; Universite des Sciences Humaines de Strasbourg, Strasbourg, France, professor of art history, 1969—. *Member:* International Association of Art Critics, Comite International d'Histoire de l'Art (secretaire scientifique), Societe Nationale des Antiquaires de France, Societe d'Histoire de l'Art Francais.

WRITINGS: Les Sources du XXe siecle (includes slide films), three volumes, Publications Filmees d'Art et Histoire, 1961; *Impressionist Painting,* McGraw, 1962; (with Jacques Thuillier) *La Peinture francaise,* Skira, Volume I: *De Fouquet a Poussin,* 1963, translation by Stuart Gilbert published as *French Painting: From Fouquet to Poussin,* 1963, Volume II: *De Le Nain a Fragonard,* 1964, translation by James Emmons published as *French Painting: From Le Nain to Fragonard,* 1964; *Titien,* Nouvelles Editions Francaises, 1964; (editor with Nicole Reynaud) *Etudes d'art francais offerts a Charles Sterling,* Presses Universitaires de France, 1975; *Van Eyck,* Capitol (Bologna), 1979, translation published under same title, Barron's, 1980; *Les Primitifs septentrionaux: La Peinture dans l'Europe septentrionale et la peninsule hispanique au XVe siecle,* Famot (Geneva), 1979; *Les Primitifs hollandais,* Office du Livre (Fribourg), 1980, translation published as *Early Dutch Painting,* Rizzoli International, 1981. Also author of and contributor to several exposition catalogs; contributor to periodicals in the field of art.

WORK IN PROGRESS: Research on painting in the Netherlands in the fifteenth century.

CHERINGTON, Paul Whiton   1918-1974

PERSONAL: Born June 16, 1918, in Cambridge, Mass.; died of a heart attack, August 11, 1974, in Boston, Mass.; son of Paul Terry (a consultant) and Marie (Richards) Cherington; married Rita Van Dusen, January 20, 1945 (divorced); married Dorothea B. Edwards, August 26, 1971; children: (first marriage) Charlotte Lund, Alexander Whiton, Paul Van Dusen; (second marriage) Anne ten Cate. *Education:* Harvard University, B.S., 1940, D.B.A., 1956; Columbia University, graduate study, 1940-41. *Home:* 9 Coolidge Hill Rd., Cambridge, Mass. *Office:* Baller Library 133, Soldiers Field, Boston, Mass.

CAREER: Pan American Airways, Africa, Ltd., British West Africa, operations, clerk, 1942; Air Transport Command, Washington, D.C., operations and statistical control officer, 1943-45; U.S. Senate Military Affairs Committee, Washington, D.C., economic analyst, for Surplus Property Sub-Committee, 1946; Civil Aeronautics Board, Washington, D.C., Air Coordinating Committee, liaison representative, 1947-48, executive assistant to chairman, 1948-50; Harvard University, School of Business, Cambridge, Mass., assistant professor, 1950-53, associate professor, 1953-58, professor, 1958-63, James J. Hill Professor of Transportation, 1963-74; U.S. Department of Transportation, Washington, D.C., assistant secretary of policy and international affairs, 1969-70; Boston & Maine Railroad, trustee, 1970-71, president and chief executive, 1973-74. Director of research, Aeronautical Research Foundation, 1956-58; founder, director, and consultant, United Research, Inc., 1958-67; president, Transportation Research Foundation, 1965-67; member, Massachusetts Board of Economic Advisors, 1965-67; co-founder and chairman of board, Temple, Barker & Sloane, 1970-74; consultant to numerous private firms and government agencies and institutions, including Department of Defense and Brookings Institution. *Member:* American Economic Association, American Statistical Association, Signet Society, Harvard Club, Cosmos Club and Aviation Club (both Washington, D.C.), Aero Club (Boston). *Awards, honors:* Salzburg Medallion from Syracase University, 1972.

WRITINGS: Airline Price Policy: A Study of Airline Passenger Fares, Division of Research, Harvard Business School, 1958; (with Ralph Gillen) *The Business Representative in Washington,* Brookings Institution, 1962; (with Lewis M. Schneider) *Transportation and Logistics Education in Graduate Schools of Business Administration,* Harvard University Graduate School of Business Administration, 1967; (editor with Leon V. Hirsch and Robert Brandwein) *Television Station Ownership: A Case Study of Federal Agency Regulation,* Hastings House, 1971. Also author of pamphlets and articles pertaining to his professional interests.

WORK IN PROGRESS: Cases in Advanced Systems Development and *The Management of Weapons Acquistitions,* second and fourth volumes of "Weapons Acquisition" series.

SIDELIGHTS: An expert on public transportation, Paul Cherington served as assistant secretary of transportation under then-President Nixon from 1969 to 1970. While in office Cherington was instrumental in drafting legislation to provide a trust fund for the nation's airways and airports. He is also given some credit for revamping the departmental policies which were left over from the previous administration.

Cherington was known for his informality, openness, and quick wit. After becoming assistant secretary he told a reporter: "I'm willing to talk to anyone as long as I can fit them in. The only limitation is the length of the queue."

OBITUARIES: New York Times, August 13, 1974; *Washington Post,* August 13, 1974.†

*   *   *

CHERVIN, Ronda 1937-

PERSONAL: Born April 24, 1937, in Los Angeles, Calif.; daughter of Ralph and Helen (Winner) DeSola; married Martin Chervin (a writer), July 9, 1962; children: Carla, Diana, Charles. *Education:* University of Rochester, B.A., 1957; Fordham University, M.A., 1959, Ph.D., 1967. *Religion:* Roman Catholic. *Home:* 7612 Cowan Ave., Los Angeles, Calif. 90045. *Office:* Department of Philosophy, Loyola Marymount University, Los Angeles, Calif. 90045.

CAREER: Lecturer at Fordham University Extension, University of California, Irvine Extension, Chapman College, and St. Joseph's College, 1967-69; Loyola Marymount University, Los Angeles, Calif., assistant professor, 1969-73, associate professor of philosophy, 1973—.

WRITINGS—Published by Liguori Publications, except as indicated: *Church of Love,* 1973; *The Art of Choosing,* 1975; *Prayer and Your Everyday Life,* 1976; *The Spirit and Your Everyday Life,* 1976; *Love and Your Everyday Life,* 1976; *The Way and the Truth and the Life,* Dove, 1976; *Why I Am a Catholic Charismatic,* 1977; *Christian Ethics and Your Everyday Life,* S.C.R.C. Publications, 1979; (with Mary Neill) *The Woman's Tale,* Seabury, 1980; (with Neill) *Bringing the Mother with You,* Seabury, 1982.

SIDELIGHTS: Ronda Chervin writes that she is a convert from atheism to the Roman Catholic Church.

*   *   *

CHILSON, Richard William 1943-

PERSONAL: Born April 20, 1943, in Grosse Pointe Farms, Mich.; son of Julius Wells (a store manager) and Jean (Bell) Chilson. *Education:* Wayne State University, B.A. (with honors), 1965; University of Illinois, M.A., 1966; St. Paul's College, Washington, D.C., M.A., 1969; Episcopal Theological School, graduate study, 1970-71. *Home and office:* Holy Spirit Parish, 2700 Dwight Way, Berkeley, Calif. 94704.

CAREER: Entered Paulist Community, 1967, ordained Roman Catholic priest of Paulist Order (C.S.P.), 1972; University of Connecticut, Storrs, chaplain, 1972-76; University of California at Berkeley, chaplain, 1976-79; missionary and Catechumenate director, 1979—.

WRITINGS: The Faith of Catholics, Paulist/Newman, 1972, revised edition, 1975; *A Believing People,* Paulist/Newman, 1974; *The Way to Christianity,* Winston Press, 1979; *Creed for a Young Catholic,* Doubleday, 1980; *Prayer Making,* Winston Press, 1981. Contributor to *Thought.*

WORK IN PROGRESS: A work on contemporary American secular spirituality; a full catechumenate program for people becoming Christians.

SIDELIGHTS: Richard Chilson told *CA:* "My main interest is spiritual growth and transformation both in modern disciplines and in ancient traditions. This interest has helped me to rediscover the vitality of Christianity as a Way rather than simply a religion and my work tries to present it as such. Outside of Christianity I am very interested in the Tibetan Buddhist traditions as well as Yoga, Zen, psychological therapies, and the various modern liberation movements." *Avocational interests:* Classical music, rock, opera, films, literature, hiking, nature.

CHIPPERFIELD, Joseph Eugene 1912-1980(?) (John Eland Craig)

PERSONAL: Born April 20, 1912, in St. Austell, Cornwall, England; deceased; son of Edward and Lavinia (White) Chipperfield; married Mary Anne Tully, April 26, 1936. *Education:* Educated privately. *Politics:* Conservative.

CAREER: Author's Literary Service, Cheapside, England, editor, 1930-34; editor and writer of scripts for documentary films, 1934-40; free-lance writer, beginning 1940. *Member:* Auto Club (Great Britain), German Shepherd Dog Club (Ireland).

WRITINGS: Two Dartmoor Interludes, Boswell Press, 1935; *An Irish Mountain Tragedy,* Boswell Press, 1936; *Three Stories* (contains *An Irish Mountain Tragedy, Two Dartmoor Interludes,* and *The Ghosts from Baylough*), Boswell Press, 1936; *This Earth My Home: A Tale of Irish Troubles,* Padraic O'Follain, 1937; *Storm of Dancerwood,* Hutchinson, 1948, Longmans, Green (New York), 1949, revised edition, Hutchinson, 1967.

Greatheart, the Salvation Hunter: The Epic of a Shepherd Dog, Hutchinson, 1950, Roy, 1953; *Beyond the Timberland Trail,* Hutchinson, 1951, Longmans, Green (New York), 1953; *Windruff of Links Tor,* Longmans, Green (New York), 1951; *Grey Chieftain,* Hutchinson, 1952, Roy, 1954; (under pseudonym John Eland Craig) *The Dog from Castle Crag,* Thomas Nelson, 1952; *Greeka, Eagle of the Hebrides,* Hutchinson, 1953, Longmans, Green (New York), 1954, revised edition, Hutchinson, 1962; *Silver Star, Stallion of the Echoing Mountain,* Hutchinson, 1953, Longmans, Green (New York), 1955; *Rooloo, Stag of Dark Water,* Hutchinson, 1955, Roy, 1962, revised edition, Hutchinson, 1962, Roy, 1963; *Dark Fury, Stallion of Lost River Valley,* Hutchinson, 1956, Roy, 1958; *The Story of a Great Ship: The Birth and Death of the Steamship Titanic,* Hutchinson, 1957, Roy, 1959; *Wolf of Badenoch: Dog of the Grampian Hills,* Hutchinson, 1958, Longmans, Green (New York), 1959; *Ghost Horse: Stallion of the Oregon Trail,* Hutchinson, 1959, Roy, 1962.

Grasson, Golden Eagle of the North, Hutchinson, 1960; *Petrus, Dog of the Hill Country,* Heinemann, 1960; *Seokoo of the Black Wind,* Hutchinson, 1961, McKay, 1962; *The Grey Dog from Galtymore,* Heinemann, 1961, McKay, 1962; *Sabre of Storm Valley,* Hutchinson, 1962, Roy, 1965; *A Dog against Darkness,* Heinemann, 1963, published as *A Dog to Trust: The Saga of a Seeing-eye Dog,* McKay, 1964; *Checoba, Stallion of the Comanche,* Hutchinson, 1964, Roy, 1966; *Boru, Dog of the O'Malley,* Hutchinson, 1965, McKay, 1966; *The Two Fugitives,* Heinemann, 1966; *Lone Stands the Glen,* Hutchinson, 1966; *The Watcher on the Hills,* Heinemann, 1968; *Rex of Larkbarrow,* Hutchinson, 1969.

Storm Island, Hutchinson, 1970, *Banner, the Pacing White Stallion,* Hutchinson, 1971; *Lobo, Wolf of the Wind River Range,* Hutchinson, 1974; *Hunter of Harter Fell,* Hutchinson, 1976. Also author of two short story collections and of film scripts. Contributor of short stories, serials, and articles to periodicals.

WORK IN PROGRESS: My Pal Wolf; Glen; Rafferty's Mare; a novel about the troubles in Ireland, tentatively titled, *No More the Green Isle.*

BIOGRAPHICAL/CRITICAL SOURCES: Kathleen Lines, *Four to Fourteen,* National Book League, 1946; *Young Readers' Review,* December, 1966; *Books and Bookmen,* November, 1970.†

CHOLERIC, Brother
  See van ZELLER, Claud

*   *   *

CHUBB, Thomas Caldecot   1899-1972

PERSONAL: Born November 1, 1899, in East Orange, N.J.; died March 22, 1972, after a long illness, in Thomasville, Ga.; son of Hendon (an insurance executive) and Alice (Lee) Chubb; married Edith Onions, July 1, 1938; children: Russell Parsons, Mary Alice Victoria (Mrs. Gerald Wolsfelt), Rosamond Caldecot (Mrs. Hillyer McD. Young). *Education:* Yale University, B.A., 1922. *Politics:* Democrat. *Religion:* Protestant. *Home and office:* Porchuck Rd., Greenwich, Conn.; and Springwood Plantation, Thomasville, Ga. (winter).

CAREER: Popular Radio, New York City, managing editor, 1923; *Time,* New York City, book reviewer, 1924; *New York Times,* New York City and Paris, France, ship news reporter and correspondent, 1925-29; self-employed as a writer, 1929-72. Active in politics; served as delegate to Democratic state conventions, 1954-62, and to national conventions, 1956, 1960; member of Democratic National Finance Committee, 1960. Worked for numerous charities; member of board of trustees, Chubb Foundation, 1953-63, and Rosemary Hall Foundation; vice-president, Victoria Foundation, beginning 1960. Active in Greenwich, Conn., civic affairs, serving on a number of boards and committees; director, Greenwich Chamber of Commerce, 1949-51. *Military service:* U.S. Naval Reserve, 1918; Office of Strategic Services, World War II, chief of port section, 1944, consultant, 1944-45. *Member:* Poetry Society of America (member of governing board, 1956, 1959-62), Dante Society of America, Renaissance Society of America, Mediaeval Academy of America (member of council, beginning 1965), Alpha Delta Phi, Florida-Georgia Field Trial Club, New York Yacht Club, Royal Bermuda Yacht Club, Indian Harbor Yacht Club, Elizabethan Club, Belle Haven Club, Glen Arven Country Club. *Awards, honors:* John Masefield Prize, 1920, Albert S. Cook Prize, 1921, both for poetry; Boys' Clubs of America Junior Book Medal, 1960.

WRITINGS: The White God and Other Poems, Yale University Press, 1920, reprinted, AMS Press, 1971; *Kyrdoon* (poetry), Yale University Press, 1921; *The Life of Giovanni Boccaccio,* Boni, 1930, reprinted, Kennikat, 1969; *Ships and Lovers,* Boni, 1933; *Cliff Pace and Other Poems,* Boni, 1937; *Aretino: Scourge of Princes,* Reynal, 1940; *My Daughter's World,* Rogers, Kellog, Stillson, 1941; *A Time to Speak* (poetry), Fine Editions, 1943; *Cornucopia* (poetry), Fine Editions, 1953; *If There Were No Losses,* Chubb, 1957; *The Byzantines* (juvenile history), World Publishing, 1959; (translator) Folgore da San Gimignano, *The Months of the Year* (poetry), Wake-Brook House, 1960; *Slavic Peoples,* World Publishing, 1962; *The Northmen,* World Publishing, 1964; *Dante and His World,* Little, Brown, 1967; (translator) *The Letters of Pietro Aretino,* Shoe String, 1967; *The Venetians: Merchant Princes,* Viking, 1968; *Prince Henry the Navigator and the Highways of the Sea,* Viking, 1970; (translator) Cecco Angiolieri, *The Sonnets of a Handsome and Well-Mannered Rogue,* Archon Books, 1970. Contributor to *Scribner's, Harper's, Poetry Review* (England), *New York Times Book Review, Saturday Review,* and others. Contributor to *Collier's Encyclopedia;* special consultant to *New Century Cyclopedia of Names.*

AVOCATIONAL INTERESTS: Yachting, quail shooting, and bird dog training (Chubb raced in intersectional and interna-

tional sailing competition; was owner of the yawl *Victoria,* which in 1961 won an important series for yachts of its size).

OBITUARIES: New York Times, March 22, 1972; *Washington Post,* March 23, 1972.†

*   *   *

CLAGETT, John (Henry)   1916-

PERSONAL: Born April 6, 1916, in Bowling Green, Ky.; son of William Argo (a farmer) and Sena (Ballard) Clagett; married Marjorie Douglas; children: Marjorie Douglas, Randi Anne. *Education:* U.S. Naval Academy, B.S., 1940; Yale University, Ph.D., 1954. *Politics:* Independent. *Religion:* Episcopalian. *Address:* Box 16, Middlebury, Vt. *Agent:* Sterling Lord Agency, 660 Madison Ave., New York, N.Y. 10021.

CAREER: U.S. Navy, 1936-46; commissioned ensign in 1940, became lieutenant commander, World War II; received Purple Heart. U.S. Department of State, career foreign service officer, 1946-49; Middlebury College, Middlebury, Vt., 1955—, began as instructor, became associate professor of English, currently professor emeritus.

WRITINGS: Cradle of the Sun, Crown, 1952; *Buckskin Cavalier,* Crown, 1954; *Captain Whitecap,* Crown, 1955; *The Slot,* Crown, 1957; *Run the River Gauntlet,* Ace Books, 1957; *U.S. Navy in Action,* Monarch, 1963; *Jack Darby, Able Seaman,* Bobbs-Merrill, 1963; *The Rebel,* Avon, 1964; *Gunpowder for Boonesborough,* Bobbs-Merrill, 1965; *Island of Dragons,* Putnam, 1967; *Surprise Attack!,* Messner, 1968; *These Hallowed Grounds,* Hawthorn, 1969; *Typhoon,* Messner, 1970; *Papa Tango,* Crown, 1982. Also author of *A World Unknown,* 1976, and *The Orange R,* 1978. Contributor of short stories to *Saturday Evening Post, Collier's,* and *Blue Book.*

WORK IN PROGRESS: Career: The Biography of Admiral H. Kent Hewitt, U.S.N.; Cooper and the Sea; Lee's Youngest General; Midnight Telephone; Houseboat.

AVOCATIONAL INTERESTS: Skiing, trout fishing.

*   *   *

CLARKE, Boden
  See BURGESS, M(ichael) R(oy)

*   *   *

CLEMENS, Rodgers
  See LOVIN, Roger Robert

*   *   *

CLEMO, Jack
  See CLEMO, Reginald John

*   *   *

CLEMO, Reginald John   1916-
  (Jack Clemo)

PERSONAL: Born March 11, 1916, in St. Austell, Cornwall, England; son of Reginald (a kiln laborer) and Eveline (Polmounter) Clemo; married Ruth Grace Peaty, 1968. *Education:* Received elementary education in Trethosa Council School. *Politics:* "No fixed political allegiance." *Religion:* Evangelical Christian. *Home:* Goonamarris, St. Stephen's, St. Austell, Cornwall, England.

CAREER: Writer and poet. *Member:* West Country Writers' Association (honorary member). *Awards, honors:* Atlantic Award in Literature, University of Birmingham, for *Wilding Graft*, 1948; Arts Council Festival Poetry Prize for "The Wintry Priesthood," 1951; Civil List pension from Queen Elizabeth, 1961; Litt.D., University of Exeter, 1981.

WRITINGS—Under name Jack Clemo: *Wilding Graft* (novel), Macmillan, 1948; *Confession of a Rebel* (autobiography), Chatto & Windus, 1949; *The Clay Verge* (poetry), Chatto & Windus, 1951; *The Invading Gospel* (theology), Bles, 1958; *The Map of Clay* (poetry), Methuen, 1961; *Cactus on Carmel* (poetry), Methuen, 1967; *The Echoing Tip* (poetry), Methuen, 1971; *Broad Autumn* (poetry), Methuen, 1975; *The Marriage of a Rebel* (autobiography), Gollancz, 1980. Also contributor of twenty poems to *Penguin Modern Poets 6*, 1964. Contributor of poems to *London Magazine, Poetry Review*, and other periodicals.

WORK IN PROGRESS: Poetry.

SIDELIGHTS: Jack Clemo told *CA:* "[My] interests [have been] limited in recent years by attacks of blindness and partial deafness. I found most of my literary stimulus in theology, evangelism, and erotic mysticism. My early work was pervaded by a deep love for the Cornish clay landscape with its artificial mountains. Since my marriage the range of my work has broadened, many of my later poems being set in foreign countries. I had previously lived a lonely hermit life with a widowed mother. Her death in 1977 released a flood of memories which impelled me to write my second volume of autobiography, *The Marriage of a Rebel*. Since then I have spent long periods at my wife's old home [in] Dorset, which may become my permanent [residence] when I retire. The Dorset coast and countryside appear more often in my work.

"My Cornish life was presented to the British public at Easter, 1980, in a one hour B.B.C. television film called 'A Different Drummer,' based on my first autobiography. The emphasis was on my religious conversion, which supplied the driving force of most of my work after I was twenty years of age. I dislike the humanism, materialism, and cynicism of the modern literary world. I would advise young writers to accept the discipline of a positive Christian faith as a safeguard against bitterness and disillusion. I have tried to bridge the gulf between art and evangelism by conveying Christian truth through symbols and situations, or theological expositions written in a individual style so that I can create and preach at the same time. I have been most deeply influenced by the poet Robert Browning, who gave me the key to realistic optimism and the spiritual basis of happy marriage. I also responded deeply to John Donne and C. S. Lewis. In my portrayal of village life I owe much to Thomas Hardy and T. F. Powys, though I reject their pessimism."

BIOGRAPHICAL/CRITICAL SOURCES: Jack Clemo, *Confession of a Rebel*, Chatto & Windus, 1949; *Western Review*, winter, 1956; *London Magazine*, October, 1960; *Sunday Times Colour Supplement* (London), August 19, 1962; Clemo, *The Marriage of a Rebel*, Gollancz, 1980; *Observer Colour Magazine*, February 17, 1980.

*   *   *

CLEMONS, Walter, Jr.   1929-

PERSONAL: Born November 14, 1929, in Houston, Tex.; son of Walter C. and Margaret (Ewing) Clemons. *Education:* Princeton University, B.A., 1951; Magdalen College, Oxford, B.A., 1953. *Agent:* Curtis Brown Ltd., 575 Madison Ave., New York, N.Y. 10022. *Office: Newsweek*, 444 Madison Ave., New York, N.Y. 10022.

CAREER: Princeton University, Princeton, N.J., Hodder fellow, 1959-60; American Academy of Rome, Rome, Italy, Prix de Rome fellow and writer-in-residence, 1960-62; Alley Theatre, Houston, Tex., member of Ford Foundation Program for Poets and Fiction Writers, 1962-63; McGraw-Hill Book Co., New York City, American history editor, 1966-67, senior editor, 1968; *New York Times Book Review*, New York City, member of history and poetry staff, 1968-71; *Newsweek*, New York City, book reviewer and general editor, 1971-77, senior writer, 1977—. *Awards, honors:* Rhodes Scholar, Oxford University; Benjamin Franklin Magazine Award, University of Illinois, 1957, for short story, "The Poison Tree," published in *Harper's Bazaar;* Jesse Jones Award for best Texas book of fiction, Texas Institute of Letters, 1960, for *The Poison Tree*.

WRITINGS: The Poison Tree, and Other Stories, Houghton, 1959; *"A Separate Peace": A Critical Commentary*, American R.D.M. Corp., 1965; *The Credibility of Harper Lee's Southern Vision*, American R.D.M. Corp., 1965; *Graham Greene's "The Power and the Glory": A Critical Commentary*, American R.D.M. Corp., 1966; *"Tristram Shandy": Chapter Notes and Criticism*, American R.D.M. Corp., 1966. Also author of short story, "The Dark Roots of the Rose," included in Martha Foley's *Best Short Stories of 1957*, and adapted by the author as a screeplay for Hal Wallis, 1959.

WORK IN PROGRESS: A collection of stories.

*   *   *

CLEW, Jeffrey Robert   1928-

PERSONAL: Born January 26, 1928, in London, England; son of Christopher Bertram and Edith Mary (Barnes) Clew; married Audrey Claire Kendrick, May 9, 1953; children: Alison Jane, Philippa Anne. *Education:* Educated in England. *Politics:* None. *Religion:* Church of England. *Home:* "Sulby," Sparkford Hill Lane, Sparkford, Somerset BA22 7JF, England. *Office:* J. H. Haynes & Co. Ltd., Sparkford, near Yeovil, Somerset, England.

CAREER: Distillers Plastics Group, London, England, group information officer, 1955-65; Chevron Oil Europe Ltd., London, information/market research officer, 1966-68; Electricity Council, London, industrial information engineer, 1969-70; Gulton Europe Ltd., Brighton, England, publicity and advertising manager, 1970-72; J. H. Haynes & Co. and G. T. Foulis & Co., Sparkford, England, motorcycle book editor, 1972-77, editorial director, 1977-79, executive editorial director, 1979—. Has appeared on British television and radio programs. *Member:* Institute of Information Scientists, Guild of Motoring Writers.

WRITINGS—Published by G. T. Foulis, except as indicated: (With Bob Burgess) *Always in the Picture: A History of the Velocette Motorcycle*, Goose & Son, 1972, revised edition, G. T. Foulis, 1980; *The Best Twin: A History of the Douglas Motorcycle*, Goose & Son, 1974, revised edition, G. T. Foulis, 1981; *The Scott Motorcycle: The Yowling Two-Stroke*, 1975; *New Castrol Book of Motorcycle Care*, 1975; *Sammy Miller: The Will to Win*, 1976; *British Racing Motorcycles*, 1976; *The Restoration of Vintage and Thoroughbred Motorcycles*, 1976; *Francis Beart: A Single Purpose*, 1978; *Lucky All My Life*, 1979; *Suzuki*, 1980; *The Way to Win Motorcycle Trials*, 1981.

Workshop manuals: "BSA A7 and A10 Twin Cylinder Models," "BSA Bantam," "Honda 50 Motor Cycles," "Honda XL250/ 350 Trail Bikes," "Honda 65, 70, and 90 Motor Cycles," "Honda 750 Fours," "Norton Commando," "Puch Maxi

Mopeds," "Suzuki 250 and 350 Twins," "Triumph 650 and 750 Unit-Construction Twins," "Triumph 500 and 650 Pre-Unit Twins," "Velocette Singles," "Vespa Scooters," "Yamaha 250 and 350 Twins," "Honda 125, 160, 175, and 200 Twins," "Honda 250 Elsinore," "Bultaco Competition Bikes," "Harley-Davidson Sportsters," and "Yamaha 500 Twins."

Contributor to magazines, including *Motor Cycle, Motor Cycle Sport, Cycle,* and *Motor Cycle Mechanics.*

WORK IN PROGRESS: History of the JAP Engine (J. A. Prestwich & Co.).

*   *   *

CLIFFORD, James L(owry)   1901-1978

PERSONAL: Born February 24, 1901, in Evansville, Ind.; died April 7, 1978, of a heart attack, in New York, N.Y.; son of George S. and Emily (Orr) Clifford; married Virginia Iglehart, 1940; children: Emily Orr, James Townley, Joseph Holt. *Education:* Wabash College, A.B., 1923; Massachusetts Institute of Technology, B.S., 1925; Columbia University, M.A., 1932, Ph.D., 1941. *Home:* 25 Claremont Ave., New York, N.Y. 10027. *Office:* English Department, Columbia University, New York, N.Y. 10027.

CAREER: Young Car Co., Evansville, Ind., manager, 1926-28; Evans School, Tucson, Ariz., English master, 1929-32; Lehigh University, Bethlehem, Pa., 1937-44, began as instructor, became associate professor; Barnard College, New York City, associate professor, 1945-46; Columbia University, New York City, professor of English, 1946-69, professor emeritus, 1969-78, William Peterfield Trent Professor of English, 1964. *Member:* Modern Language Association of America, American Association of University Professors, P.E.N., Royal Society of Literature (fellow), Johnson Society of London, The Johnsonians, Phi Beta Kappa, Phi Gamma Delta. *Awards, honors:* Cutting traveling fellowship, Columbia University, 1935; Guggenheim fellowship, 1952-53, 1965-66; Litt.D., Evansville College, 1955; L.H.D., Wabash College, 1956; L.H.D., Indiana University, 1963.

WRITINGS: Hester Lynch Piozzi (Mrs. Thrale), Oxford University Press, 1941, revised edition, 1968; (editor) *Dr. Campbell's Diary,* Cambridge University Press, 1947; (editor with Louis A. Landa) *Pope and His Contemporaries,* Oxford University Press, 1949, reprinted, Octagon, 1978; (compiler) *Johnsonian Studies, 1887-1950,* University of Minnesota Press, 1951; *Young Sam Johnson,* McGraw, 1955, reprinted, 1981; (editor) *Early Eighteenth-Century English Literature,* Oxford University Press, 1959; (editor) *Biography as an Art,* Oxford University Press, 1962; (editor and author of introduction) Tobias Smollett, *The Adventures of Peregrine Pickle,* Oxford University Press, 1964; (editor) *Man Versus Society in Eighteenth-Century Britain,* Cambridge University Press, 1968, Norton, 1972; (compiler) *Twentieth-Century Interpretations of Boswell's "Life of Johnson": A Collection of Critical Essays,* Prentice-Hall, 1970; *From Puzzles to Portraits: Problems of a Literary Biography,* University of North Carolina Press, 1970; (with Donald J. Greene) *Samuel Johnson: A Survey and Bibliography of Critical Studies,* University of Minnesota Press, 1970; *Dictionary Johnson: The Middle Years of Samuel Johnson,* McGraw, 1979. Editor, *Johnsonian News Letter,* 1940-78.

AVOCATIONAL INTERESTS: Book collecting, music, baseball.

BIOGRAPHICAL/CRITICAL SOURCES: New York Times Book Review, October 14, 1979, March 8, 1981; *Washington Post Book World,* November 4, 1979.

OBITUARIES: New York Times, April 8, 1978.†

*   *   *

CLIFTON, Bud
See STACTON, David (Derek)

*   *   *

COCHRAN, Hamilton   1898-1977

PERSONAL: Born September 9, 1898, in Philadelphia, Pa.; died July 27, 1977; son of Joseph Wilson (a clergyman) and Helen (Scudder) Cochran; married Enid Clare Doreen Slee, April 18, 1925; children: Enid Clare Cochran Taylor, Susan Hamilton Cochran Swanson, Margaret Ellen Cochran Miller. *Education:* University of Michigan, B.A., 1922. *Home:* 109 Stratford Rd., Wallingford, Pa.

CAREER: Ronald Press, New York City, salesman, 1922-29; Diamond Wax Paper Co., Rochester, N.Y., vice-president, 1930-32; Government of the Virgin Islands, St. Thomas, commissioner of public welfare, 1932-34; Standard Oil Co. of New Jersey, New York City, advertising executive, 1935-43; *Saturday Evening Post,* Philadelphia, Pa., automotive marketing manager, 1944-60; Curtis Circulation Co., Philadelphia, director of advertising, 1960-62; vice-president, Stanley Publishing Co., 1962-64. Port warden, Philadelphia Maritime Museum, 1962; president, Scudder Association of America, 1962-64. *Military service:* U.S. Coast Guard, 1917-19. U.S. Coast Guard Reserve, 1942-44.

MEMBER: Centro Studi e Scambi Internazionale (Rome), Sons of the American Revolution (member of board of management, 1962; president, 1963-64), American Legion, Boy Scouts of America, Delaware County (Pa.) Historical Society, Monmouth Battlefield Association (vice-president, 1962), Poor Richard Club. *Awards, honors:* Bronze medal, Centro Studi e Scambi Internazionale.

WRITINGS: These Are the Virgin Islands, Prentice-Hall, 1937; *Buccaneer Islands,* Thomas Nelson, 1941; *Windward Passage,* Bobbs-Merrill, 1942; *Captain Ebony,* Bobbs-Merrill, 1943; *Silver Shoals,* Bobbs-Merrill, 1945; *Rogue's Holiday,* Bobbs-Merrill, 1947; *Blockade Runners of the Confederacy,* Bobbs-Merrill, 1958, reprinted, Greenwood Press, 1973; (with others) *Pirates of the Spanish Main,* American Heritage Publishing, 1961; *The Dream Tree,* Bobbs-Merrill, 1961; *Noted American Duels and Hostile Encounters,* Chilton, 1963; *Freebooters of the Red Sea: Pirates, Politicians and Pieces of Eight,* Bobbs-Merrill, 1965; *Scudders in the American Revolution,* Scudder Association, 1976; *Pirate Wench: The Voyages and Adventures of Ann O'Shea,* R. Hale, 1978. Poems have been included in three anthologies. Contributor to *Saturday Evening Post, Esquire, Chambers' Magazine,* and *Shooting Times.*

AVOCATIONAL INTERESTS: Historical archeology, foreign travel, collecting antique weapons.

OBITUARIES: New York Times, August 2, 1977.†

*   *   *

COHEN, John   1911-

PERSONAL: Born January 20, 1911, in England; son of Joseph (a merchant) and Rebecca (Kahn) Cohen; married second wife, Rosemarie Loss, July 20, 1955; children: (first marriage) Katherine, Geoffrey; (second marriage) Nicholas, Oliver, James. *Education:* University College, London, B.S. and M.A., 1936, Ph.D., 1940. *Home:* 15 Didsbury Park, Manchester M2O 0LH,

England. *Agent:* Curtis Brown Ltd., 1 Craven Hill, London W2 3EW, England.

CAREER: British government, London, England, technical adviser to Offices of the War Cabinet, 1941-45, and to Cabinet Office, 1945-48; University of Leeds, Leeds, England, lecturer in psychology, 1948-49; University of Jerusalem, Jerusalem, Israel, professor of psychology, 1949-51; University of London, Birkbeck College, London, lecturer in psychology, 1951-52; University of Manchester, Manchester, England, professor of psychology, 1952-78. Member of interprofessional advisory committee, World Federation of Mental Health, 1949-52; consultant to UNESCO, 1948, 1950, 1962, and 1967; consultant to Open University, 1977-80. *Military service:* British Army, Royal Armoured Corps, 1941. *Member:* World Academy of Art and Science (fellow), International Association of Semiotics (member of executive committee), International Society for the Study of Time, Centre de Recherches de Psychologie Comparative (foreign member), British Psychological Society (fellow). *Awards, honors:* M.A. from University of Manchester.

WRITINGS: (Editor with Robert M. W. Travers and Raymond B. Cattell) *Human Affairs,* Macmillan, 1937, reprinted, Books for Libraries, 1970; (editor with Travers) *Educating for Democracy,* Macmillan, 1939, reprinted, Books for Libraries, 1970; *Human Nature, War and Society,* C. A. Watts, 1946.

(With Mark Hansel) *Risk and Gambling,* Philosophical Library, 1956; (translator) H. E. Hammerschlag, *Hypnotism and Crime,* Rider & Co., 1956; *Humanistic Psychology,* Collier, 1958, 2nd edition, 1962; (translator) Geza Revesz, *The Human Hand,* Routledge & Kegan Paul, 1958; *Chance, Skill and Luck,* Penguin, 1960; *Behaviour in Uncertainty and Its Social Implications,* Basic Books, 1964; (editor) *Readings in Psychology,* Allen & Unwin, 1964; *Human Robots in Myth and Science,* A. S. Barnes, 1966; *A New Introduction to Psychology,* Allen & Unwin, 1966; *Psychological Time in Health and Disease,* C. C Thomas, 1967; (editor) *Psychology: An Outline for the Intending Student,* Routledge & Kegan Paul, 1968; (with Barbara Preston) *Causes and Prevention of Road Accidents,* Faber, 1968.

(With Ian Christensen) *Information and Choice,* Oliver & Boyd, 1970; *Elements of Child Psychology for Student Teachers,* Morten, 1970; *Homo Psychologicus,* Allen & Unwin, 1970; *Psychological Probability,* Allen & Unwin, 1972; *Everyman's Psychology,* Morten, 1973; (with J. H. Clark) *Medicine, Mind, and Man,* W. H. Freeman, 1979; *The Lineaments of Mind,* W. H. Freeman, 1980; *Risk and Religion,* Open University Press, 1980.

Contributor to literary, psychiatric, medical, psychological, and other scientific and learned journals. British editor, *Acta Psychologica* and *Medikon.*

SIDELIGHTS: John Cohen is interested in popular exposition of psychology and allied topics on television and radio, believing that this can be made "both entertaining and dramatic."

"As a member since 1961 of the Pugwash Conferences on Science and International Affairs," Cohen writes, "[I am] profoundly concerned with present trends in the military strategy of the superpowers and their satellites, in the links between such strategy and socio-economic policies of the affluent countries, in the inherent threat in nuclear, chemical, and biological weapons, and hence in cultivating an atmosphere conducive to world peace and plenty."

AVOCATIONAL INTERESTS: Music.

COHON, Beryl David 1898-

PERSONAL: Born February 12, 1898, in Lithuania (now U.S.S.R.); brought to United States in 1905; son of Solomon and Rachel (Kushner) Cohon; married Sally Kivelson, June 30, 1929; children: Albert. *Education:* University of Illinois, B.A., 1921; Hebrew Union College (now Hebrew Union College—Jewish Institute of Religion), Rabbi, 1925. *Home:* 65 Babcock, Brookline, Mass. *Office:* Temple Sinai, 50 Sewall Ave., Brookline, Mass.

CAREER: Temple Beth-El, Pensacola, Fla., rabbi, 1925-27; Temple B'er Chayim, Cumberland, Md., rabbi, 1927-29; Temple Israel, Boston, Mass., associate rabbi, 1929-39; Temple Sinai, Brookline, Mass., founding rabbi, 1939—. Lecturer in Jewish history and culture, Tufts University, 1940-59; former faculty member, Boston University School of Religion and Social Services; lecturer on college campuses. *Member:* Central Conference of American Rabbis (member of executive board, beginning 1953), American Civil Liberties Union (member of executive board), American Jewish Committee. *Awards, honors:* D.D., Hebrew Union College, 1950.

WRITINGS—Published by Bloch Publishing, except as indicated: *Introduction to Judaism: A Book for Jewish Youth,* 1929, 3rd edition, 1964; *The Prophets: Their Personalities and Teachings,* Scribner, 1939, reprinted, Bloch Publishing, 1960; *Feasts of the Lord* (sacred pageant), 1944; *Judaism in Theory and Practice,* 1948, 3rd edition, 1969; *From Generation to Generation,* Bruce Humphries, 1951; *Jacob's Well: Some Jewish Sources and Parallels to the Sermon on the Mount,* A. B. Bookman, 1956; *Out of the Heart: Some Intimate Talks from a Jewish Pulpit on the Personal Issues of Life,* Vantage, 1957; *God's Angry Men: A Student's Introduction to the Hebrew Prophets,* 1961; *My King and My God: Intimate Talks on the Devotions of Life,* 1963; *Vision and Faith: Confirmation Services for Jewish Congregations,* 1968; *Men at the Crossroads between Jerusalem and Rome: The Lives, Times, and Doctrines of the Founders of Talmudic Judaism and New Testament Christianity,* Yoseloff, 1970; *Shielding the Flame: A Personal and Spiritual Inventory of a Liberal Rabbi,* 1972; *Come, Let Us Reason Together: Sermons Presented in Days of Crisis,* 1977.

Contributor to *Classics of Religious Devotion,* Beacon Press, *Reform Judaism,* Hebrew Union College Press, and to *Best Sermons of 1947-48.* Member of editorial board, Central Conference of American Rabbis *Journal.*†

*   *   *

COKER, Jerry 1932-

PERSONAL: Born November 28, 1932, in South Bend, Ind.; son of Curtis (a musician) and Mildred Ruth (Collier) Coker; married Patricia Fitz-Patrick (a journalist and jazz singer), September 23, 1955; children: David Curtis. *Education:* Attended Indiana University, 1950-53, and Yale University, 1957-58; Sam Houston State Teachers College (now Sam Houston State University), B.M.E., 1959, M.A., 1960. *Office:* Department of Music, Monterey Peninsula College, Monterey, Calif. 93940.

CAREER: Jazz composer-arranger and tenor sax soloist with Woody Herman, Stan Kenton, Claude Thornhill, Les Elgart, Ralph Marterie, and Clare Fischer orchestras, on tour and for recordings, 1953-57; Sam Houston State Teachers College (now Sam Houston State University), Huntsville, Tex., instructor in music, 1958-62; Monterey Peninsula College, Monterey, Calif., instructor in music, 1962—. Clinician, lecturer, and jazz festival coordinator. Clarinettist, Monterey Symphony Orchestra,

1963-64. *Member:* American Federation of Musicians, California Teachers Association.

WRITINGS: Improvising Jazz, forewords by Stan Kenton and Gunther Schuller, Prentice-Hall, 1964; (with Jimmy Casale and others) *Patterns for Jazz*, Studio Publications/Recordings, 1970; *The Jazz Idiom*, Prentice-Hall, 1975; *Listening to Jazz*, Prentice-Hall, 1978.

WORK IN PROGRESS: A saxophone method book; a collection of original jazz instructive etudes.†

*　　*　　*

COLBY, C(arroll) B(urleigh)   1904-1977

PERSONAL: Born September 7, 1904, in Claremont, N.H.; died October 31, 1977; son of Melvin Forrest and Stella (Whitcomb) Colby; married Lila Margaret Thoday, November 29, 1928; children: Susan, Fred Melvin. *Education:* School of Practical Art (Boston, Mass.), graduated 1925. *Politics:* Republican. *Religion:* Congregationalist. *Home:* 304 Pine Rd., Briarcliff Manor, N.Y.

CAREER: Free-lance artist, San Juan, Puerto Rico, 1925-26, Boston, Mass., 1926-28; free-lance artist and writer, New York City, 1928-37; *Air Trails, Air Progress*, New York City, editor, 1937-43; *Popular Science*, New York City, aviation editor, 1943-46; free-lance writer, 1946-77. Baircliff Manor village government, village trustee, 1954-58, president of library board, village planning board, fire commissioner and volunteer fireman and member of auxiliary police. *Military service:* U.S. Air Force Auxiliary (Civil Air Patrol), 1946-77; became lieutenant colonel. *Member:* Aviation/Space Writers Association (founder member), Outdoor Writers Association of America, The Company of Military Historians, Sons of the American Revolution, American Ordnance Association, National Rifle Association, Campfire Club of America, Adventurers Club of New York. *Awards, honors:* Several books cited on Bowker's "Best Books for Children" annual list; Pacific Area Travel Association grand award, 1972; Outdoor Writers Association of America award, 1973; Freedom Foundation award, 1973.

WRITINGS—All published by Coward, except as indicated: *Gabbit: The Magic Rabbit*, 1951; *Arms of Our Fighting Men*, 1952, revised, 1972; *Jets of the World*, 1952, revised, 1966; *Wings of Our Air Force*, 1952; *Wings of Our Navy*, 1952; *First Fish*, 1953; *Air Drop*, 1953; *Danger Fighters*, 1953; *Ships of Our Navy*, 1953; *Who Went There?*, Dutton, 1953; *Who Lives There?*, Dutton, 1953; *Submarine*, 1953; *First Rifle*, 1954; *F.B.I.*, 1954, revised, 1970; *Frogmen*, 1954; *Police*, 1954, revised, 1971; *Smoke Eaters*, 1954; *First Bow and Arrow*, 1955; *First Camping Trip*, 1955; *Earthmovers*, 1955; *Fish and Wildlife*, 1955; *Park Ranger*, 1955, revised, 1971; *Tall Timber*, 1955; *First Boat*, 1956; *America's Natural Wonders*, 1956; *Military Vehicles*, 1956; *Operation Watchdog*, 1956; *Six Shooters*, 1956; *First Hunt*, 1957; *Firearms by Winchester*, 1957; *Firing Line*, 1957; *Leatherneck*, 1957; *Soil Savers*, 1957; *Aluminum*, 1958; *Army Engineers*, 1958; *Helicopters to the Rescue*, 1958; *This Your Civil Air Patrol*, 1958; *Mapping the World*, 1959; *Our Space Age Navy*, 1959; *Plastic Magic*, 1959; *Strangely Enough!*, Sterling, 1959, revised, 1972; *Snow Surveyors*, 1959.

Bomber Parade, 1960; *Count Down*, 1960, revised, 1970; *Fighter Parade*, 1960; *Musket to M-14*, 1960; *Night People*, 1961, revised, 1971; *Colby's Nature Adventures*, Dial, 1961; *Better Homes and Gardens Family Camping*, Meredith, 1961; *Fighting Gear of World War I*, 1961; *Fighting Gear of World War II*, 1961; *Our Space Age Army*, 1961; *S A C*, 1961; *Air Force Academy*, 1962; *Aircraft of World War I*, 1962; *Civil War Weapons*, 1962; *Our Space Age Navy*, 1962; *Fur and Fury*, Duell, Sloan & Pearce, 1963; *Ships of Commerce*, 1963; *West Point*, 1963; *Historic American Forts*, 1963; *Revolutionary War Weapons*, 1963; *Wild Cats*, Duell, Sloan & Pearce, 1964; *Trucks on the Highway*, 1964; *Communications*, 1964; *Special Forces*, 1964; *Annapolis: Cadets, Training, and Equipment*, 1964; *Wild Dogs*, Duell, Sloan & Pearce, 1965; *The Weirdest People in the World*, Popular Library, 1965, revised, 1973; *U.S. Coast Guard Academy*, 1965; *Wildlife in Our National Parks: Birds, Reptiles, and Mammals*, 1965; *America's Cliff Dwellings*, 1965; *Survival: Training in our Armed Services*, 1965; *Secret Service*, 1966; *Signal Corps Today*, 1966; *Underwater World*, 1966; *Wild Deer*, Duell, Sloan & Pearce, 1966; *First Book of Animal Signs*, F. Watts, 1966; *Wild Rodents*, Meredith, 1967; *Modern Light*, 1967; *Early American Crafts*, 1967; *Submarine Warfare*, 1967; *Big Game*, 1967; *Historical American Landmarks*, 1968; *Small Game*, 1968; *The Atom at Work*, 1968; *The National Guard*, 1968; *North American Air Defense Command*, 1969; *Astronauts in Training*, 1969.

Moon Exploration, 1970; *Railroads U.S.A.*, 1970; *Sailing Ships*, 1970; *Wild Bird World*, F. Watts, 1970; *The Art and Science of Taking to the Woods*, Stackpole, 1970; *Beyond the Moon*, 1971; *Space Age Spinoffs*, 1972; *Chute*, 1973; *Today's Camping*, 1973; *Space Age Fire Fighters*, 1973; *Border Patrol*, 1974; *Hidden Treasure*, 1975; *Two Centuries of Weapons, 1776-1976*, 1975; *Two Centuries of Seapower, 1776-1976*, 1976; *Underseas Frontiers*, 1977; (editor) *Camper's and Backpacker's Bible*, Stoeger Publishing, 1977. Contributor to magazines. Camping editor, *Outdoor Life*.

SIDELIGHTS: C. B. Colby was an editor, writer, and illustrator all his life, but it was not until he was well past forty that he wrote his first book, *Gabbit: The Magic Rabbit*. That manuscript made the rounds of New York publishers for many months until, finally, Coward saw its possibilities and published it in 1951. Until 1977, Colby turned out more than one hundred books—mostly for Coward—and as many as seven in one year. The millionth copy of the "Colby Books," as they are known to librarians and boys alike, was sold by Coward in December, 1962.

Colby once told *CA* that writing was relatively easy for him but he did extensive preliminary research for each of his books, often involving considerable travel. "I believe completely in *doing first hand* as much as possible the things I write about, whether it is chasing smugglers in the Caribbean or chasing white whales in Hudson Bay."

His books were usually based on his wide range of personal interest, which included aviation ("I learned to fly on gliders in 1931"); hunting with bows and arrows; camping ("we have camped all over the country from Cape Breton to the West Coast and written about it"); travel ("I've been to Alaska and Labrador and Newfoundland and Mexico for stories and research"); archaeology; firearms ("especially old ones"); and wildlife ("our home is in a wooded area, where we have deer, raccoons—of which I feed three every night—opossum, skunks, fox, mink, and other critters, and so I get to know many of them first hand").

A lake in Mont Tremblant Park, in Quebec, was named Lac Colibi after Colby in 1964. He was also the only American to be appointed "Surveillant auxiliaire" (auxiliary warden) of this 1200-mile Canadian provincial park.

BIOGRAPHICAL/CRITICAL SOURCES: Publishers' Weekly, February 18, 1963, March 11, 1963; *Christian Science Monitor*, January 19, 1967; *Christian Century*, April 28, 1971.†

COLE, Margaret Alice
(Rosemary Manning, Julia Renton, Ione Saunders)

PERSONAL: Born in Meerut, India; daughter of Edward (a regular officer in the British Army) and Frances (Hampton) Cole. *Education:* Attended Residential Training College and Hartley University, both Southampton, England. *Politics:* Conservative. *Religion:* Roman Catholic. *Agent:* Robert Sommerville Ltd., Mowbray House, Norfolk St., London W.C.2, England.

CAREER: Employed as teacher in Government Educational Service, London, England, and teacher of English and music for London County Council Evening Institute; full-time writer, 1957—. Pianist. *Member:* Royal Society of Arts (fellow), Royal Overseas League (fellow), Royal Commonwealth Society, Romantic Novelists Association (founder member; literary reader), Society of Women Journalists, London Writers Circle, John O'London Literary Circle.

WRITINGS—Published by R. Hale, except as indicated: *Romance at Butlin's,* 1958; *Passport to Paradise,* 1959; *Holiday Camp Mystery* (juvenile), 1959; *Love for a Doctor,* 1960; *Across the World to Love,* Gresham, 1961; *The Doctor Takes a Wife,* 1961; *Give Me Back Yesterday,* Gresham, 1961; *Love in Venice,* Gresham, 1962; *Love on the Long Walk,* 1962; *Thrilling Holiday* (juvenile), 1962; *Rainbow Beyond,* Gresham, 1963; *Romance in the Tyrol,* Gresham, 1964; *Doctor Verner's Romance,* 1964; *Another Thrilling Holiday* (juvenile), 1964; *Romance in Capri,* 1965; *Two Hearts Bid,* 1965; *The Doctor Decides,* Gresham, 1966; *The Doctor's Fiancee,* Gresham, 1966; *Scottish Rhapsody,* 1966; *Another Holiday Camp Mystery,* 1967; *Flying to Happiness,* Gresham, 1967. Also author of *Jill and Joe on Holiday,* 1961, and *Jill and Joe's Return Holiday,* 1962.

Under pseudonym Rosemary Manning: *Shadowed Starlight,* Gresham, 1961; *Green Smoke,* Penguin, 1967; *Dragon in Danger,* Longman, 1972; *Dragon's Quest,* Kestrel Books, 1973.

Under pseudonym Julia Renton: *Romance in Chelsea,* Gresham, 1961; *Connemara Colleen,* Gresham, 1962; *Starlight for Sheila,* Gresham, 1962; *Life's a Mirror,* Gresham, 1963.

Under pseudonym Ione Saunders: *Rhapsody in Paris,* Gresham, 1963.

Contributor of stories to magazines and newspapers.†

*   *   *

COLLINS, Barbara J(ane)   1929-

PERSONAL: Born April 29, 1929, in Passaic, N.J.; daughter of Cornelius F. (an engineer) and Gladys (Holt) Schenck; married Lorence G. Collins (a professor), February 26, 1955; children: Glenn, Elizabeth, Gregory, Kevin, Rachel. *Education:* Bates College, B.S., 1951; Smith College, M.S., 1953; University of Illinois, Ph.D., 1955, M.S., 1959. *Religion:* Methodist. *Home:* 139 Prentiss St., Thousand Oaks, Calif. 91360. *Office:* California Lutheran College, Thousand Oaks, Calif. 91360.

CAREER: California Lutheran College, Thousand Oaks, professor of biology, 1963—. *Member:* American Society for Microbiology, Phi Beta Kappa, Sigma Xi, Phi Kappa Phi, Sigma Delta Epsilon.

WRITINGS: The Story of Our Earth, Franklin Publications, 1965; *California Plant and Animal Communities,* Franklin Pub-

lications, 1966; *Wildflowers, Trees and Shrubs of Holden Village,* Matador Press, 1970.

"Exploring and Understanding Science" juvenile series; published by Benefic Press: *Exploring and Understanding Insects,* 1970; (with husband, Lorence G. Collins) *Exploring and Understanding beyond the Universe,* 1970; *Exploring and Understanding the Human Body,* 1971.

"Keys" series; published by California State University Foundation: *Key to Coastal and Chaparral Flowering Plants of Southern California,* 1972; *Key to Trees and Wildflowers of the Mountains of Southern California,* 1974; *Key to Trees and Shrubs of the Deserts of Southern California,* 1976; *Key to Wildflowers of the Deserts of Southern California,* 1978.

WORK IN PROGRESS: Key to Trees, Shrubs and Wildflowers of the North Coast Ranges of California.

SIDELIGHTS: Barbara Collins told *CA:* "I started writing the ["Keys" series] as an aid to my freshmen students in botany, because the available books for plant identification in California were either too brief with only a few plants mentioned or too technical for the beginner. Since that time I have enlarged the books and have written them for both students and the layman, hoping to make plant identification simpler and to open a new road of discovery and enjoyment in the out-of-doors. California has a rich flora and I hope that through my books more people can enjoy it to the fullest.

"Each book takes about eight years to write. Most of the time is spent in collecting plants. The actual writing takes me two years and this is done mostly during the summers when my teaching load is light."

AVOCATIONAL INTERESTS: Playing flute and piano, painting, drawing, arts and crafts, tennis, swimming, bicycling, and mountain climbing.

*   *   *

COLLINS, Michael
See LYNDS, Dennis

*   *   *

COMFORT, Iris Tracy

PERSONAL: Born in Racine, Wis.; daughter of A. T. and Iva Tracy; married James Dustin Comfort (an installation supervisor for Southern Bell Telephone Co.), April 19, 1941; children: Alain James. *Home:* 2902 Oxford St., Orlando, Fla. 32803. *Agent:* Larry Sternig Literary Agency, 742 Robertson St., Milwaukee, Wis. 53213.

CAREER: Free-lance writer, mainly for magazines and trade journals, 1945—. Former reporter for *St. Paul Dispatch,* St. Paul, Minn.; member of public relations staff, Allis-Chalmers Manufacturing Co., Milwaukee, Wis.; owner and operator of public relations agency in Milwaukee, Wis., and Chicago, Ill.; editor-in-chief of Chicago edition of *Where* (entertainment magazine); owner and director of wildlife sanctuary, Lake Helen, Fla., 1969—. *Member:* National League of American Pen Women (founder of Orlando branch; branch president, 1974-76), Mystery Writers of America, National Speleological Society, Audubon Society, Spiritual Frontiers.

WRITINGS: Earth Treasures: Rocks and Minerals, Prentice-Hall, 1964; *Let's Grow Things,* Rand McNally, 1968; *Rock Riddles,* Rand McNally, 1968; *Let's Read about Rocks,* Rand McNally, 1969; *Joey Tigertail* (children's book), Ginn, 1973; *Echoes of Evil* (novel; Suspense Book Club selection), Doubleday, 1977; *Shadow Masque* (novel; Suspense Book Club selection), Doubleday, 1980. Contributor of fiction to *New York Daily News*, 1958-64; contributor of stories and articles to *Parents' Magazine, McCall's, Industrial Relations, Etude, Children's Activities, Better Homes and Gardens,* and other periodicals.

WORK IN PROGRESS: Research and writing on the Everglades, the Seminoles, the use and propagation of plants, specific psychic phenomena, and caves; a work of fiction, *Snow Fire,* based on historical research.

SIDELIGHTS: Iris Comfort writes: "Primary research has always been extremely important to me in backgrounding my books—actually collecting rocks and minerals, collecting and growing plants, prowling caves, investigating psychic phenomenon, traveling, [and] learning. One of the exquisite blessings of getting authentic background for whatever I am working on is the delight of packing my suitcases and discovering firsthand what I need to know." Comfort, in an interview with Ruth Barsten in *Central Florida Scene,* advises aspiring writers to "have enough confidence in yourself to write whether or not you sell. Write what you want to write regardless of its immediate commercial value."

AVOCATIONAL INTERESTS: Spelunking, photography, politics.

BIOGRAPHICAL/CRITICAL SOURCES: Central Florida Scene, February, 1980.

*   *   *

COMFORT, Jane Levington
   See STURTZEL, Jane Levington

*   *   *

CONGER, John (Janeway)   1921-

PERSONAL: Born February 27, 1921, in New Brunswick, N.J.; son of John C. and Katharine (Janeway) Conger; married Mayo Trist Kline (a teacher), January 1, 1944; children: Steven Janeway, David Trist. *Education:* Amherst College, B.A. (magna cum laude), 1943; Yale University, M.S., 1947, Ph.D., 1949. *Home:* 130 South Birch, Denver, Colo.

CAREER: Indiana University, Indianapolis Campus (now Indiana University-Purdue University at Indianapolis), assistant professor of psychology, 1949-53; University of Colorado, School of Medicine, Denver, associate professor, 1953-57, professor of psychology, 1957—, head of Division of Clinical Psychology, 1953-57, associate dean, 1961-63, dean, 1963-68, vice-president for medical affairs, 1963-70. Chairman of research committee, President's Committee for Traffic Safety, 1960-63; member of committee on road-user characteristics, Highway Research Board, National Research Council, 1960—; vice-chairman, Colorado State Board of Psychologists, 1961-64; member, President's Commission on Mental Health, 1977-78, vice-president and director of health program, John D. and Catherine T. MacArthur Foundation, 1980—. Consultant to Veterans Administration, 1953—, Division of Research Grants, National Institute of Mental Health, 1959-61, Community Services Branch, U.S. Public Health Service, 1959—, Health Facilities Branch, National Institutes of Health, 1964—, Division of Hospital and Medical Facilities, U.S. Public Health Service, 1964—; member of National Advisory Mental Health Council, U.S. Public Health Service, 1965-69; John F. Kennedy Center for Research on Education and Human Development, National Advisory Committee, member, 1965-77, chairman, 1971-74. *Military service:* U.S. Naval Reserve; ac-

tive duty, 1944-46, 1951-52; served as commanding officer of a destroyer escort, 1945-46, and as chief staff psychologist at U.S. Naval Academy, 1951-52; became lieutenant. *Member:* American Psychological Association (president, 1981-82), American Association for the Advancement of Science (fellow).

WRITINGS: (With P. H. Mussen and J. Kagan) *Child Development and Personality,* Harper, 1956, 5th revised edition, 1979; (contributor) *Alcoholism: Theory, Problem, and Challenge,* Yale Alcohol Studies Press, 1956; (contributor) G. F. Reed, I. D. Alexander, and S. S. Tomkins, editors, *Psychopathology: A Source Book,* Harvard University Press, 1958; (with W. C. Miller) *Personality, Social Class and Juvenile Delinquency,* Wiley, 1966.

(With Mussen and Kagan) *Readings in Child Development,* Harper, 2nd edition, 1970; *Adolescence and Youth: Psychological Development in a Changing World,* Harper, 1973, 2nd edition, 1977; *Adolescence: Generation under Pressure,* Harper, 1979; (with Mussen, Kagan, and J. Geiwitz) *Psychological Development: A Life-Span Approach,* Harper, 1979; (with Mussen and Kagan) *Essentials of Child Development and Personality,* Harper, 1980; (with Mussen and Kagan) *Readings in Child and Adolescence Psychology: Contemporary Perspectives,* Harper, 1980.

Contributor to *The Encyclopedia of Mental Health,* 1963. Contributor of more than twenty articles and reviews to medical, psychological, and highway safety journals.

*   *   *

CONN, Charles Paul   1945-

PERSONAL: Born December 23, 1945, in Leadwood, Mo.; son of Charles W. (a minister) and Edna (Minor) Conn; married Darlia McLuhan, August 15, 1967; children: Vanessa, Heather, Brian. *Education:* Lee College, B.A., 1967; Emory University, M.A., 1970, Ph.D., 1973. *Religion:* Pentecostal. *Home:* 1515 Hillmont Pl., Cleveland, Tenn. 37311.

CAREER: Lee College, Cleveland, Tenn., associate professor of psychology, 1971-81. *Member:* American Psychological Association. *Awards, honors:* Enterprise Award, Associated Press, 1972, for news article; *Kathy* named Book of the Year by *Campus Life* magazine, 1980.

WRITINGS—Published by Revell, except as indicated: *The Music Makers,* Pathway Press, 1971; (with Sammy Hall) *Hooked on a Good Thing,* 1972; *The New Johnny Cash,* 1973; (with Terry Bradshaw) *No Easy Game,* 1973; (with Nicky Cruz) *The Magnificent Three,* 1973; (with Rich De Vos) *Believe!,* 1975; *Julian Carroll of Kentucky,* 1976; *The Possible Dream,* 1977; *The Winner's Circle,* 1979; (with Barbara Miller) *Kathy,* 1980.

*   *   *

CONRAD, Barnaby (Jr.)   1922-

PERSONAL: Born March 27, 1922, in San Francisco, Calif.; son of Barnaby and Helen (Hunt) Conrad; married Dale Cowgill, March 19, 1941; married second wife, Mary Slater, May 18, 1962; children: (first marriage) Barnaby III, Tani, Winston; (second marriage) Kendall (daughter). *Education:* Yale University, B.A., 1944; studied painting at University of Mexico. *Politics:* Republican. *Religion:* Protestant. *Home:* 8132 Puesta del Sol, Carpinteria, Calif. 93013.

CAREER: Author and artist. American vice consul to Vigo, Malaga, Seville, and Barcelona, Spain, 1943-46; student bullfighter with Juan Belmonte, and bullfighter in Spain, Mexico, and Peru, 1943-46; portrait painter and night club pianist in Lima, Peru, 1946; secretary to Sinclair Lewis, 1949; founder and owner of night club, El Matador during the 1950s and 1960s. Teacher of painting, San Francisco College of Art. Exhibited artwork at one-man show in Palm Beach, Fla. Former collector of exotic birds, fish, and monkeys.

WRITINGS: The Innocent Villa (novel), Random House, 1948; (self-illustrated) *Matador* (Book-of-the-Month Club selection), Houghton, 1952; *La Fiesta Brava: The Art of the Bull Ring,* Houghton, 1953; (translator) Carlos Arruza, *My Life as a Matador,* Houghton, 1954; (translator) Luis Spota, *Wounds of Hunger,* Houghton, 1957; *Gates of Fear,* Crowell, 1957; *The Death of Manolete,* Houghton, 1958; *San Francisco: A Profile with Pictures,* Studio Books, 1959; (editor and translator) Torcuato Luca de Tena, *Second Life of Captain Contreras,* Houghton, 1960; *Dangerfield,* Harper, 1961; *Encyclopedia of Bullfighting,* Houghton, 1961; (compiler) *Famous Last Words,* foreword by Clifton Fadiman, Doubleday, 1961; *Tahiti,* Viking, 1962; *How to Fight a Bull,* Doubleday, 1968; (self-illustrated) *Fun While It Lasted* (autobiography), Random House, 1969; *Zorro: A Fox in the City,* Doubleday, 1971; (with Niels Mortensen) *Endangered,* Putnam, 1978. Also author of short story, "Cayetano the Perfect," anthologized in *O. Henry Collection of Prize Stories,* 1949.

WORK IN PROGRESS: With Nico Mastorakis, a novel, *Fire Below Zero;* another novel, *She, Jesus.*

SIDELIGHTS: On publication of Barnaby Conrad's autobiography, a writer for *National Observer* noted the appropriateness of the "epitaph he has suggested for himself, 'Gored but never bored.'" Because of two fight injuries to the same knee, Conrad decided in his mid-twenties not to become a professional bullfighter, although, according to *San Francisco Chronicle*'s William Hogan, "Conrad is an international authority on the sport."

Conrad's background would not ordinarily suggest the makings of a bullfighter. Although he grew up during the Depression, it had little effect on his family. His father was a wealthy investment banker who provided a very secure and comfortable life for Conrad and his older brother. Many of his ancestors were influential and important Americans: his maternal grandfather was a Montana supreme court justice, who later became governor of Puerto Rico; his great grandfather was secretary of state; and his great-great-great-great grandmother was Martha Washington.

While studying painting at the University of Mexico, Conrad was a frequent visitor to the bullfights. He became fascinated by the sport. One day, while swept up in the excitement, he jumped into the arena and began waving his Brooks Brothers' raincoat at the bull. The bull charged three times before Conrad fled the ring unharmed.

Matador Feliz Guzman then took Conrad under his wing and instructed him in the fine art of bullfighting. Several months later, he was severely gored during a practice session. He returned home to California, underwent an operation to repair his badly damaged leg, and completed his university studies.

While working for the State Department in Spain, Conrad met Juan Belmonte, often considered one of the best matadors who ever lived. Conrad's love for bullfighting was rekindled, and he began training with Belmonte. After three years, he appeared on the same bullfighting program with Belmonte. Weeks later, in 1958, Conrad suffered another serious injury which forced him to give up any aspirations of turning professional. After the accident, Conrad spent most of his time painting and writing.

As unique as Conrad's life has been, the subjects of his writings are equally as interesting. He is the author of books on bullfighting, several novels, an autobiography, over eight works of nonfiction (including one on Tahiti and one on San Francisco), and the translator of several more books.

Fun While It Lasted reminds *New York Times Book Review* critic David Dempsey that Conrad "is one of those modern Renaissance men whose multiple talents are peculiarly attuned to the twentieth century and its diversions, without reflecting its real concerns. A romantic at heart, he searched for a personal mystique at a time when his contemporaries were looking for an ideology. As a result, [this autobiography] has a pleasantly anachronistic air about it, as though the author had been set apart, or set back, in an era when it was possible to live a legendary life without being a legend."

BIOGRAPHICAL/CRITICAL SOURCES: New York Times Book Review, July 6, 1952, May 26, 1968, August 24, 1969; *San Francisco Chronicle,* October 9, 1961; *New York Times,* August 9, 1969; *National Observer,* August 25, 1969; Conrad, *Fun While It Lasted,* Random House, 1969; *Writer,* April, 1972.

*   *   *

CONVERSE, Philip E. 1928-

PERSONAL: Born November 17, 1928, in Concord, N.H.; son of Ernest Luther (a minister) and Evelyn (Eaton) Converse; married Jean G. McDonnell, August 25, 1951; children: Peter Everett, Timothy McDonnell. *Education:* Denison University, B.A., 1949; University of Iowa, M.A. in English literature, 1950; University of Paris, Certificat des Etudes Francaises, 1954; University of Michigan, M.A. in sociology, 1956, Ph.D., 1958. *Home:* 1312 Cambridge Rd., Ann Arbor, Mich. 48104. *Office:* Center for Political Studies, University of Michigan, Ann Arbor, Mich. 48104.

CAREER: University of Michigan, Ann Arbor, assistant professor of sociology, 1960-63, associate professor of political science and sociology, 1963-65, professor, 1965-75, Robert C. Angell Professor of Political Science and Sociology, 1975—, study director, Survey Research Center, 1960-65, program director, 1965—. Lecturer in France, Norway, and Sweden; teacher at first UNESCO European Seminar, Cologne, Germany, 1964. Associate director, Inter-university Consortium for Political Research, 1962—; Social Science Research Council, member of Committee on Governmental and Legal Processes, 1964-67, Committee on Comparative Politics, 1967-72, Committee on Social Indicators, 1972-78, and Committee on Mass Media and Political Behavior, 1974-76, chairman of Committee on Social Indicators, 1975-78, and Presidential Search Committee, 1978-79; National Research Council, member of executive committee of Division of Behavioral Sciences, 1970-74, member of Committee on Manpower Sharing Evaluation, 1974-79; Center for Advanced Study in the Behavioral Sciences, fellow, 1979, member of board of trustees, 1980-86. Member of advisory committee on social science, National Science Foundation, 1970-74. *Military service:* U.S. Army, 1950-52.

MEMBER: International Society of Political Psychology (president, 1980-81), American Sociological Association (member of social psychology council, 1966-70; secretary-treasurer, 1970-71), American Political Science Association (member of council, 1970-72; vice-president, 1975), American Association for Public Opinion Research, American Association for the Advancement of Science (fellow), National Academy of Sciences, American Academy of Arts and Sciences, Phi Beta Kappa. *Awards, honors:* Horace H. Rackham fellow, 1955-56; Fulbright research fellow in France, 1959-60; National Science Foundation postdoctoral fellow, 1967-68; Distinguished Faculty Achievement Award, University of Michigan, 1973; D.H.L., Denison University, 1974, and University of Chicago, 1979; Guggenheim fellow, 1975-76.

WRITINGS: (Contributor) Maccoby, T. M. Newcomb and Hartley, editors, *Readings in Social Psychology,* 3rd edition (Converse was not associated with earlier editions), Holt, 1958; (contributor with Angus Campbell) Dorwin Cartwright and Alvin Zander, editors, *Group Dynamics: Research and Theory,* 2nd edition (Converse was not associated with earlier edition), Row, Peterson & Co., 1960; (with Campbell, Warren E. Miller, and Donald E. Stokes) *The American Voter,* Wiley, 1960; (with Newcomb and Ralph Turner) *Social Psychology: The Study of Human Interaction,* Holt, 1965; (with Campbell, Miller, and Stokes) *Elections and the Political Order,* Wiley, 1966; *Some Priority Variables in Comparable Electoral Research,* University of Strathclyde (Glasgow), 1968; (with Milton J. Rosenberg and Verba) *Vietnam and the Silent Majority,* Harper, 1970; (editor with Campbell) *The Human Meaning of Social Change,* Russell Sage, 1972; (co-editor and contributor) *The Use of Time,* Mouton (the Hague), 1972; (with Campbell and Willard Rogers) *The Quality of American Life,* Russell Sage, 1976; *The Dynamics of Party Support: Cohort-Analyzing Party Identification,* Sage Publications, 1976; (editor with Dotson, Hoag, and McGee) *American Social Attitudes Data Sourcebook,* Harvard University Press, 1979. Contributor of articles to journals of political science, sociology, and psychology. Member of editorial board, *Sociometry,* 1966-69.

*   *   *

COOK, Chris(topher) 1945-

PERSONAL: Born June 20, 1945, in Leicester, England; son of William and Kathleen (Chatterton) Cook. *Education:* St. Catharine's College, Cambridge, B.A., 1967, M.A., 1970; Oriel College and Nuffield College, Oxford, D.Phil., 1970. *Politics:* Labor. *Religion:* Anglican. *Residence:* Wimbledon, England. *Agent:* Hilary Rubinstein, A. P. Watt and Co., 26-28 Bedford Row, London WC1R 4HL, England. *Office:* Department of History, Polytechnic of North London, Prince of Wales Rd., Kentish Town, London N.W.5, England.

CAREER: Oxford University, Magdalen College, Oxford, England, lecturer in politics, 1969-70; University of London, London School of Economics and Political Science, London, England, senior research officer, 1970-80; Polytechnic of North London, London, head of department of history, 1980—.

WRITINGS—Published by Macmillan, except as indicated: (Editor with David McKie) *The Decade of Disillusion,* 1972; (editor with John Ramsden) *By-Elections in British Politics,* 1973; (with John Paxton) *European Political Facts: 1918-1973,* 1975; (editor with Gillian Peele) *The Politics of Reappraisal: 1918-1939,* 1975; (with Brendan Keith) *British Historical Facts: 1830-1900,* 1975; (with Philip Jones) *Sources in British Political History,* five volumes, 1975—; *The Age of Alignment: Electoral Politics in Britain, 1922-1929,* 1975; *The Liberal Party: 1900-1975,* 1975; (with John Stevenson) *Atlas of Modern British History,* Longman, 1976; *The Slump: Society and Politics during the Depression,* J. Cape, 1976; (with Stevenson) *British Historical Facts, 1485-1603,* 1980. Editor of *Pears Cyclopaedia,* 1974—.

*   *   *

COOPER, (C.) Everett
See BURGESS, M(ichael) R(oy)

COOPER, Wendy (Lowe) 1919-

PERSONAL: Born December 6, 1919, in Sutton Coldfield, Warwickshire, England; daughter of Walter Edward and Edith (Samworth) Lowe; married Alfred Hebert Jack (in electroplating business), November 14, 1942; children: Jacqueline Ann. *Education:* Attended Sutton Grammar School. *Politics:* Liberal. *Religion:* Humanist. *Home:* 32 Vesey Rd., Sutton Coldfield, Warwickshire B73 5PB, England.

CAREER: Freelance writer and journalist; television and radio writer, interviewer, and panelist. Formerly employed as secretary for British Broadcasting Corp. and Aeronautical Inspection Directorate. *Member:* Society of Authors, Screenwriters Guild. *Awards, honors:* Hannen Swaffer Award, 1966, for British Woman Journalist of the Year.

WRITINGS—Children's books; all published by Brockhampton Press: *The Laughing Lady,* 1957; *Alibi Children,* 1958; *The Cat Strikes at Night,* 1959; *Disappearing Diamonds,* 1960.

Other: *Hair: Sex, Society, and Symbolism,* Stein & Day, 1971; *Don't Change: A Biological Revolution for Women,* Stein & Day, 1975 (published in England as *No Change,* Hutchinson, 1975); *The Fertile Years,* Hutchinson, 1978; (with T.C.G. Smith) *Human Potential: The Limits and Beyond,* David & Charles, 1981.

Also author of play "The Burning Question" and of television and radio plays and serials for adults and children. Contributor of articles on social and medical subjects to *Observer Magazine, Good Housekeeping, Cosmopolitan, Nova, Modern Medicine, World Medicine,* and other journals and periodicals.

SIDELIGHTS: Wendy Cooper told *CA:* "I am currently campaigning in print, on television, and radio for biological lib for the older woman in the form of hormone replacement therapy at menopause. Researching for this and the book involved visiting the United States in 1972 and 1974, with nationwide tours of medical centres.

"I am totally involved in medical campaigning and lecturing at postgraduate conferences. The campaign for availability of hormone replacement therapy and for appropriate treatment of pre-menstrual syndrome is now won in the U.K. The new battle is to get lasers in every main medical centre for outpatient treatment of early cancer of the cervix. The first was installed in 1977, and the story is told in my book *The Fertile Years.* We now have about fifteen lasers in action in the U.K., saving lives and fertility."

Cooper's latest work, *Human Potential: The Limits and Beyond,* is one of fifty books selected by Sotheby's for preservation in a special posterity vault.

AVOCATIONAL INTERESTS: Travel, people, sunbathing, surfing; "tennis, once played for Warwickshire and at Wimbledon, has given way to undistinguished golf."

*   *   *

COOVER, James B(urrell) 1925-
(C. B. James)

PERSONAL: Born June 3, 1925, in Jacksonville, Ill.; son of James V. (a printer) and F. Elizabeth (Burrell) Coover; married Georgena Walker (a childhood specialist), September 28, 1945; children: Christopher, Mauri, Regan. *Education:* Northern Colorado University, B.A., 1949, M.A., 1950; University of Denver, M.A., 1953. *Home:* 111 Marjann Ter., Tonawanda,

N.Y. 14223. *Office:* Department of Music, State University of New York, Buffalo, N.Y. 14214.

CAREER: Bibliographical Center for Research, Denver, Colo., assistant director, 1950-53; Vassar College, George Sherman Dickinson Library, director, 1953-67; State University of New York at Buffalo, professor of music, 1967—, Ziegele Professor, 1981—. Manager and player with Hudson Valley Philharmonic Orchestra, 1959-67. New York State Council on the Arts, member, 1964-65, consultant, 1965-68; member of Mayor's Commission on the Arts, Poughkeepsie, N.Y., 1965-67. *Military service:* U.S. Army, 1943-45; served in European theater. *Member:* Association Internationale des bibliotheques musicales, American Association of University Professors, Music Library Association (president, 1959-60).

WRITINGS: Photoduplication Services: A Survey, 1951, Bibliographical Center for Research, 1951; *A Bibliography of Music Dictionaries,* Bibliographical Center for Research, 1952, 3rd edition published as *Music Lexicography,* Carlisle Books, 1971; *Provisional Checklist of Medieval and Renaissance Music on Long-Playing Records* (pamphlet), Vassar College, 1957; (compiler) *'Festschriften': A Provisional Checklist of Those Proposed for Indexing* (pamphlet), Vassar College, 1958; *Music Lexicography Including a Study of Lacunae: 1500-1700,* Bibliographical Center for Research, 1958; (editor) *The 'Rainbeau' Catalog,* Distant Press, 1962; (author of appendix) Johannes Tinctoris, *Terminorum musicae diffinitorium* (title means "Dictionary of Musical Terms"), Free Press, 1963; (with Richard Colvig) *Medieval and Renaissance Music on Long-Playing Records,* Information Service, 1964; (contributor) C. J. Bradley, editor, *Manual of Music Librarianship,* Music Library Association, 1966; *Gesamtausgaben: A Checklist,* Distant Press, 1970; (with Colvig) *Medieval and Renaissance Music on Long-Playing Records: Supplement, 1962-1971,* Information Coordinators, 1973; (contributor) Bradley, editor, *Reader in Music Librarianship,* Microcard Editions, 1974; (author of preface) Guy A. Marco, *Information on Music,* Kent State University Press, 1974; (under pseudonym C. B. James) *Up to the Hilt!: An Index to an Unwritten Chronicle of the Hardcore,* Leftover Press, 1975; (contributor) *New Grove Dictionary of Music and Musicians,* 6th edition, Macmillan, 1980; *Musical Instrument Collections,* Information Coordinators, 1981; *Puttick and Simpson: Auctioneers of Music, 1794-1971,* Information Coordinators, 1982. Contributor of articles and reviews to music and library journals.

SIDELIGHTS: James B. Coover told *CA:* "The appellation 'author' is probably a bit exalted for a person whose work has been mostly bibliographic. But it's heady, and I like it!"

*   *   *

CORDASCO, Francesco 1920-

PERSONAL: Born November 2, 1920, in West New York, N.J.; son of Giovanni and Carmela (Madorma) Cordasco; married Edna Vaughn, October 22, 1942; children: Michael, Carmela. *Education:* Columbia University, A.B., 1944; New York University, M.A., 1945, Ph.D., 1959; additional study, University of Salamanca, 1946-48, and London School of Economics and Political Science, 1952-53. *Home:* 6606 Jackson St., West New York, N.J. 07093. *Office:* Department of Education, Montclair State College, Upper Montclair, N.J. 07043.

CAREER: Long Island University, Brooklyn, N.Y., 1946-53, began as instructor, became associate professor of English; New Jersey Public Schools, teacher of English and social studies, 1953-63, assistant director of adult education, 1960-62, assistant principal, 1961-63; Montclair State College, Upper

Montclair, N.J., associate professor of education, 1963-65; Jersey City State College, Jersey City, N.J., professor of education and assistant to the president, 1965-66; Montclair State College, professor of education, 1966—, assistant to the president, 1967-72. Adjunct professor, Fairleigh Dickinson University, 1953-58, Seton Hall University, 1958-63; visiting professor, City University of New York, various terms, 1959-73, New York University, summer, 1962, University of Puerto Rico, summer, 1969. Director or staff member of federally funded programs. Archdiocesan Board of Education, Newark, N.J., vice president, 1968-71, president, 1971-73, member, 1973-80; member of board of trustees, Christ Hospital, Jersey City, N.J., 1978-81. Consultant to numerous organizations, including Commonwealth of Puerto Rico, 1961-71, Consumers Union, 1969—, and U.S. government committees; member of New Jersey Advisory Council for Vocational Education, 1968—. *Military service:* U.S. Army, 1941-43.

MEMBER: History of Education Society, National Education Association, National Society for the Study of Education, American Educational Research Association, Society for the Advancement of Education, American Association of University Professors, Bibliographical Society of America, Oxford Bibliographical Society, American Sociological Association (fellow), British Sociological Association (fellow). *Awards, honors:* Founder's Day award, New York University, 1959, for academic excellence; citation from Commonwealth of Puerto Rico, 1967; Brotherhood Award, National Conference of Christians and Jews (New Jersey Region), 1967; Order of Merit, Republic of Italy, 1976.

WRITINGS: (With Elliott Gatner) *University Handbook for Research and Report Writing,* Edwards Brothers, 1946, 15th edition published as *Research and Report Writing,* Barnes & Noble, 1974; (with Gatner) *Study Guides to English Literature,* two volumes, Lamb's Book Exchange, 1947; *A Junius Bibliography, With a Preliminary Essay on the Political Background, Text, and Identity: A Contribution to 18th Century Constitutional and Social History,* B. Franklin, 1949, revised edition, 1974.

(Author of introduction) *A Bibliography of Robert Watt, M.D.,* Kelleher, 1950, reprinted edition edited by Cordasco, Gale, 1968; *A Register of 18th Century Bibliographies and References,* B. Franklin, 1950, reprinted, Gale, 1968; (with Burt Franklin) *Adam Smith: A Bibliographical Checklist,* B. Franklin, 1950; (editor) *Letters of Tobias George Smollett,* Harvard University Press, 1950; (compiler with Kenneth W. Scott) *A Brief Shakespeare Bibliography for the Use of Students,* Phoenix Press, 1950; *The Bohn Libraries: A History and Checklist,* B. Franklin, 1951; (editor) *Works of Spinoza,* Dover, 1955.

Daniel Coit Gilman and the Protean Ph.D.: The Shaping of American Graduate Education, E. J. Brill, 1960, published as *The Shaping of American Graduate Education: Daniel Coit Gilman and the Protean Ph.D.,* Rowman & Littlefield, 1973; *A Brief History of Education: A Handbook of Information on Greek, Roman, Medieval, Renaissance and Modern Educational Practice,* Littlefield, 1963, 2nd edition, 1970; (editor) *Educational Essays of Herbert Spencer* Littlefield, 1963; (contributor) *American Portrait Gallery,* Dover, 1965; (compiler with Leonard Covello) *Educational Sociology: A Subject Index of Doctoral Dissertations Completed at American Universities, 1941-1963,* Scarecrow, 1965; (editor with F. N. Reister) *Readings in American Secondary Education: Reform and Challenge,* Selected Academic Readings, 1966; (editor with Covello) *The Social Background of the Italo-American School Child,* E. J. Brill, 1967; (editor) *Jacob Riis Revisited: Poverty and the Slum in Another Era,* Doubleday, 1968; (editor with Eugene Bucchioni) *Puerto Rican Children in Mainland Schools: A Source Book for Teachers,* Scarecrow, 1968, revised edition published as *The Puerto Rican Community and Its Children on the Mainland: A Source Book for Teachers, Social Workers, and Other Professionals,* 1972; (author of introduction with others) Paul Monroe, *A Cyclopedia of Education,* five volumes, reprinted (Cordasco was not associated with earlier editions), Gale, 1968; (author of introduction) Will Seymour Monroe, *Bibliography of Education,* reprinted (Cordasco was not associated with earlier editions), Gale, 1968; (author of introduction) William Swan Sonnenscheim, *The Best Books,* six volumes, reprinted (Cordasco was not associated with earlier editions), Gale, 1968; (editor with Maurie Hillson) *Education and the Urban Community: Schools and the Crisis of the Cities,* American Book Co., 1969; (with David Alloway) *The Agony of the Cities: Urban Problems in Contemporary America,* Montclair State College Press, 1969; (editor) Covello, *Teacher in the Urban Community,* Littlefield, 1969.

Eighteenth Century Bibliographies: Handlists of Critical Studies . . . (originally published separately as "Eighteenth Century Bibliographical Pamphlets" series, 1947-50), Scarecrow, 1970; (with Alloway) *Minorities in the American City: A Sociological Primer for Educators,* McKay, 1970; (compiler with Hillson and Henry Bullock) *The School in the Social Order: A Sociological Introduction to Educational Understanding,* International Textbook Co., 1970; (editor) Samuel Chester Parker, *A History of Elementary Education,* Littlefield, 1970; (editor) Robert Quick, *Educational Reformers,* Littlefield, 1970; (editor) Elmer Ellsworth Brown, *The Making of Our Middle Schools,* Rowman & Littlefield, 1970; *Teacher Education in the United States: A Guide for Foreign Students,* Institute for International Education, 1971; (with Bucchioni and Diego Castellanos) *Puerto Ricans on the United States Mainland: A Bibliography . . . ,* Rowman & Littlefield, 1972; (with Salvatore LaGumina) *Italians in the United States: A Bibliography . . . ,* Oriole Editions, 1972; (editor) Alice Crow, *Educational Psychology,* revised edition (Cordasco was not associated with earlier editions), Littlefield, 1972; (author of foreword) G. Stanley Hall and J. M. Mansfield, *Hints toward a Select and Descriptive Bibliography of Education,* reprinted (Cordasco was not associated with earlier editions), Gale, 1972; (with Bucchioni) *The Puerto Rican Experience: A Sociological Sourcebook,* Rowman & Littlefield, 1973; *The Italian in America: A Bibliographical Guide,* B. Franklin, 1974; *The Italians: Social Backgrounds of an American Group,* Augustus Kelley, 1974; (editor) *Bibliography of Research Studies in Education, 1926-1940,* four volumes, reprinted (Cordasco was not associated with earlier editions), Gale, 1974; *Studies in Italian American Social History,* Rowman & Littlefield, 1975; (with William W. Brickman) *A Bibliography of American Educational History,* AMS Press, 1975; *Immigrant Children in American Schools,* Augustus Kelley, 1976; (with Thomas Pitken) *The Black Hand: A Chapter in Ethnic Crime,* Littlefield, 1977; *Tobias George Smollett: A Bibliographical Guide,* AMS Press, 1977; *Useful Spanish for Hospital and Medical Personnel,* Blaine Ethridge, 1977; *Italian Americans: A Guide to Information Sources,* Gale, 1978; (with George Bernstein) *Bilingual Education in American Schools,* Gale, 1979; (with Alloway and M. S. Friedman) *The History of American Education,* Gale, 1979; (with Alloway) *Sociology of Education,* Gale, 1979; (with V. Briani) *Italian Immigrants Abroad: A Bibliography,* Blaine Ethridge, 1979.

Italian Mass Immigration: The Exodus of a Latin People, Rowman & Littlefield, 1980; (with Alloway) *Medical Education in the United States,* Gale, 1980; (with Alloway) *American Ethnic Groups; the European Heritage: An Annotated Bibliography of Doctoral Dissertations,* Scarecrow, 1981; (with Pitken) *The White Slave Trade and the Immigrants,* Blaine Ethridge, 1981; *Italians in the United States: An Annotated Bibliography of Doctoral Dissertations Completed at American Universities,* Junius Press, 1981.

Editor: The Social History of Poverty: The Urban Experience, fifteen volumes, Garrett Press, 1969-70; *The Children of Immigrants in Schools,* five volumes, Scarecrow, 1970; *Annual Reports, 1867-1917,* 144 volumes, Rowman & Littlefield, 1970—; *The Puerto Rican Experience,* 33 volumes, Arno, 1975; *The Italian Experience,* 39 volumes, Arno, 1978; "Education Information Guide" series, ten volumes, Gale, 1978-80; *American Ethnic Groups: The European Heritage,* 47 volumes, Arno, 1980.

Contributor of numerous articles and over 200 reviews to professional journals. Contributing editor, *Journal of Human Relations,* 1967-69; education editor, *USA Today,* 1975—.

*   *   *

CORNWALL, E(spie) Judson 1924-

PERSONAL: Born August 15, 1924, in San Jose, Calif.; son of Espie James (a clergyman) and Beulah V. (Stiles) Cornwall; married Eleanor L. Eaton, June 20, 1943; children: Dorothy Darlene Cornwall, Eleanor Jean (Mrs. Robert Miller), Justine (Mrs. Nobert Senftleben). *Education:* Attended Southern California College, 1942-44. *Home and office:* 2501 Custer Rd., Plano, Tex. 75075.

CAREER: Ordained Assembly of God minister, 1948; associate pastor in Bell Gardens, Calif., 1943-44; pastor in Stirling City, Calif., 1945, Kennewick, Wash., 1946-52, Yakima, Wash., 1952-57, and Eugene, Ore., 1957-72; Charles Church, Tabb, Va., minister, beginning 1973; Fountain Gate Church, Plano, Tex., associate, 1980—. Instructor at School of the Bible, 1954-57, and at Fountain Gate Bible College, 1980—.

*WRITINGS—*Published by Logos International: *Let Us Praise,* 1973; *Let Us Draw Near,* 1975; *Let Us Be Holy,* 1977; *Please Accept Me,* 1978; *Profiles of a Leader,* 1979.

Published by Revell: *Let Us Abide,* 1975; *Let Us Enjoy Forgiveness,* 1978; *Let Us See Jesus,* 1979; *Unfeigned Faith,* 1980; *Let God Arise,* 1981.

Published by Omega Publications: *Heaven,* 1977. Contributor to periodicals.

WORK IN PROGRESS: Let Us Worship; Women in Ministry.

SIDELIGHTS: E. Judson Cornwall has traveled to twenty-two countries. He has a private pilot's license and owned his own plane when he was on the West coast. He built his own house in Eugene, Oregon. *Let Us Praise* has had Indonesian, Spanish, Korean, and Danish editions. *Avocational interests:* Gardening.

*   *   *

CORPORAL TRIM
See BOLGER, Philip C(unningham)

*   *   *

CORRIGAN, Robert W(illoughby) 1927-

PERSONAL: Born September 23, 1927, in Portage, Wis.; son of Daniel (an Episcopal bishop) and Elizabeth (Waters) Corrigan; married Elizabeth Seneff (a singer), June 15, 1963; married JoAnn Johnson; children: Michael, Timothy. *Education:*

Cornell University, A.B., 1950; Johns Hopkins University, M.A., 1962; University of Minnesota, Ph.D., 1955. *Politics:* Democrat. *Religion:* Episcopalian. *Home:* 1037 East Ogden Ave., Milwaukee, Wis. 53202. *Office:* School of Fine Arts, University of Wisconsin, Milwaukee, Wis. 53201.

CAREER: Taught at Johns Hopkins University, Baltimore, Md., University of Minnesota, Minneapolis, Carleton College, Northfield, Minn., and Tulane University of Louisiana, New Orleans; Carnegie Institute of Technology, College of Fine Arts, Pittsburgh, Pa., former Andrew Mellon Professor of Drama and head of department of drama; New York University, New York, N.Y., former dean of School of the Arts and professor of dramatic literature; University of Wisconsin—Milwaukee, currently dean of School of Fine Arts.

WRITINGS: The Theatre in Search of a Fix, Delacorte, 1972; *The World of the Theatre,* Scott, Foresman, 1979; *The Making of Theatre: From Drama to Performance,* Scott, Foresman, 1981.

Editor, except as indicated: *The Theatre in the Twentieth Century,* Grove, 1962; (translator) *Six Plays of Chekhov,* Holt, 1962; *New Theatre in Europe,* Dell, Volume I, 1962, Volume II, 1964, Volume III, 1968; (translator with Mary Douglas Dirks) Adolphe Appia, *Music and the Art of the Theatre,* University of Miami Press, 1962; *The Modern Theatre,* Macmillan, 1964, revised edition, 1968; (with James L. Rosenberg) *The Art of the Theatre,* Chandler, 1964, revised edition, 1968; (with Rosenberg) *The Context and Craft of Drama,* Chandler, 1964; *Masterpieces of Classical Drama* (five volumes, including *Sophocles, Euripides,* and *Aeschylus*), Dell, 1964-65; *Comedy: Meaning and Form,* Chandler, 1965, 2nd edition, Harper, 1981; *Tragedy: Vision and Form,* Chandler, 1965, new edition, Harper, 1981; *New American Plays,* Hill & Wang, 1965; *Masterpieces of British Drama: 20th Century,* Dell, 1965; *Four Modern Plays,* Series I, revised edition, Holt, 1965; *Masterpieces of the Modern English Theatre,* Collier, 1965; *Masterpieces of the Modern French Theatre,* Collier, 1965; *Masterpieces of the Modern German Theatre,* Collier, 1965; *Masterpieces of the Modern Irish Theatre,* Collier, 1965; *Masterpieces of the Modern Italian Theatre,* Collier, 1965; *Masterpieces of the Modern Russian Theatre,* Collins, 1965; *Masterpieces of the Modern Scandinavian Theatre,* Collier, 1965; *Masterpieces of the Modern Spanish Theatre,* Collier, 1965.

Greek Comedy, Dell, 1966; *Roman Drama,* Dell, 1966; *Masterpieces of British Drama: 19th Century,* Dell, 1967; *Arthur Miller: 20th-Century Views,* Prentice-Hall, 1968.

Comedy: A Critical Anthology, Houghton, 1971; *Tragedy: A Critical Anthology,* Houghton, 1971; *The Forms of Drama,* Houghton, 1972; *The Transformation of the Avant-Garde,* Delacorte, 1974. General editor, "Chandler Editions in Drama," thirty volumes, Chandler. Founder and former editor, *Tulane Drama Review* (now *Drama Review*).

SIDELIGHTS: Robert Corrigan told *CA:* "The real challenge facing each of us as individuals and all of us as a nation in the world's community is one of imagination. The need to stretch the limits of the human imagination is greater now than it has ever been in history. It is for this reason that the arts are valuable, not just in the broad cultural sense that they enhance and shape the quality of life, but they are also essential to the survival of the human race."

BIOGRAPHICAL/CRITICAL SOURCES: Books, May, 1967.

*   *   *

CORY, Desmond
 See McCARTHY, Shaun (Lloyd)

COSGROVE, Margaret (Leota) 1926-

PERSONAL: Born June 3, 1926, in Sylvania, Ohio; daughter of Maynard Giles (an engineer) and Leota (Holt) Cosgrove. *Education:* Attended Chicago Art Institute and American Academy of Art. *Religion:* Protestant. *Home:* 175 East 93rd St., New York, N.Y. 10028.

CAREER: Cornell University Medical College, New York City, medical artist, 1950; Roosevelt Hospital, New York City, medical artist, 1953-56; free-lance book and medical illustrator. Former afternoon program director, Good Neighbor Community Center, New York City.

WRITINGS—All self-illustrated; all published by Dodd: *Wonders of the Tree World,* 1953, revised edition, 1970; *The Wonders inside You,* 1955; *Wonders of Your Senses,* 1958; *Wonders under a Microscope,* 1959; *Wonders at Your Feet: A New World for Explorers,* 1960; *The Strange World of Animal Senses,* 1961, revised edition, edited by J.C.W. Houghton, Phoenix House, 1963; *Your Hospital, a Modern Miracle,* 1962; *Strange Worlds under a Microscope,* 1962; *A Is for Anatomy,* 1965; *Eggs, and What Happens inside Them,* 1966; *Plants in Time: Their History and Mystery,* 1967; *Bone for Bone,* 1968; *Seeds, Embryos, and Sex,* 1970; *Messages and Voices: The Communication of Animals,* 1974; *Wintertime for Animals,* 1975; *Animals Alone and Together: Their Solitary and Social Lives,* 1978; *It's Snowing!,* 1980; *Your Muscles and Ways to Exercise Them,* 1980.

Illustrator: Sigmund A. Lavine, *Wonders of Animal Disguises,* Dodd, 1962; Sheila L. Burns, *Allergies and You,* Messner, 1980.

WORK IN PROGRESS: Illustrating medical publications, including a book on chest injuries and thoracic surgery; adult fiction.

BIOGRAPHICAL/CRITICAL SOURCES: Christian Science Monitor, May 4, 1967; *Books and Bookmen,* June, 1967, July, 1968; *Young Readers' Review,* October, 1968.†

*   *   *

COTTER, Edward F(rancis) 1917-

PERSONAL: Born January 17, 1917, in New Rochelle, N.Y.; son of William Edward and Elsie M. (Tattler) Cotter; married Ann M. Gilligan, June 20, 1942; children: Brian, Jeffrey, Pamela, Edward Jr., Thomas. *Education:* Columbia University, B.S., 1941, M.S., 1957. *Home:* 851 Amiford Dr., San Diego, Calif. 92107.

CAREER: Commissioned officer in U.S. Coast Guard, 1942-66; retired as captain. U.S. Coast Guard Auxiliary, assistant national director, working in motorboat safety field, 1954-56; captain of the port, Philadelphia, Pa. area, 1965-66; Delaware River Port Authority, Camden, N.J., manager of port planning, 1966-68, director of administrative services, 1968-78; free-lance photojournalist, 1978—. *Member:* U.S. Naval Institute, Lightning Class Association (vice-president, 1951), Penguin Class Association (vice-president, 1956), President's Cup Regatta Association (vice-president, 1959-61), Potomac River Sailing Association (commodore, 1960-61), Cougar Catamaran Association (commodore, 1961-66; honorary commodore, 1966—), Explorers Club, Storm Trysail Club, Southwestern Yacht Club, South Jersey Yacht Racing Association (commodore, 1974—), Alpha Kappa Psi.

WRITINGS: *Sailing and Racing Catamarans*, Chilton, 1963; (editor and contributor) *The International Book of Catamarans and Trimarans*, Crown, 1966; *Multihull Sailboats*, Crown, 1971; *The Offshore Game: Today's Ocean Racing*, Crown, 1977. Contributor of articles to *Yachting, Soundings*, and *Waterfront*. Contributing editor, *Yacht Racing*, 1971-81.

WORK IN PROGRESS: Research on new developments in boating.

SIDELIGHTS: Edward Cotter told *CA:* "My writing and photography blend well with my hobby of yacht racing. As a result, most of my journalistic efforts have been in the boating field. My books have developed from ideas or articles produced for magazines. Books are more satisfying to produce, in that one's own style can be given freer expression and the subject matter can be covered in greater detail. The approach I use is designed to be understandable to the casual reader yet be informative to the person who is familiar with the subject."

Cotter's books have been translated into French, German, and Spanish and have been published in British, Canadian, and Australian editions.

AVOCATIONAL INTERESTS: Racing sailboats; color photography.

BIOGRAPHICAL/CRITICAL SOURCES: *Washington Sunday Star*, May 22, 1960; *Washington Evening Star*, June 9, 1961; *Philadelphia Inquirer*, July 4, 1965; *Cherry Hill News*, October 7, 1965; *Camden Courier Post*, July 7, 1966; *Sports Illustrated*, July, 1973, March, 1974; *San Diego Union*, January 8, 1979; *San Diego Tribune*, November 9, 1979.

*   *   *

COURTLAND, Roberta
See DERN, Erolie Pearl Gaddis

*   *   *

COURTNEY, John
See JUDD, Frederick Charles

*   *   *

COX, William R(obert)   1901-
(Joel Reeve)

PERSONAL: Born 1901, in Peapack, N.J.; son of William and Marion Grace (Wenz) Cox; married Lee Frederic.

CAREER: Professional writer. *Member:* Writers Guild of America, West, Western Writers of America, Academy of Magical Arts, Kansas State Historical Society.

WRITINGS: *Make My Coffin Strong*, Fawcett, 1954; *The Lusty Men*, Pyramid Books, 1957; *The Tycoon and the Tigress*, Fawcett, 1957; *Hell to Pay*, New American Library, 1958; *Comanche Moon: A Novel of the West*, McGraw, 1959; *Death Comes Early*, Dell, 1959; *The Duke*, New American Library, 1959; *Murder in Vegas*, New American Library, 1960; *Luke Short and His Era*, Doubleday, 1961 (published in England as *Luke Short, Famous Gambler of the Old West*, Fireside Press, 1962); *The Outlawed*, New American Library, 1961; *Death on Location*, New American Library, 1962; *Bigger than Texas*, Fawcett, 1962; *The Mets Will Win the Pennant* (nonfiction), Putnam, 1964; (editor) *Rivers to Cross* (collection of stories by members of Western Writers of America), Dodd, 1966; *Moon of Cobre*, Bantam, 1969; *Chicano Cruz*, Bantam, 1972; *The Sixth Horseman*, Ballantine, 1972.

Young adult books; published by Dodd, except as indicated: *Five Were Chosen: A Basket Ball Story*, 1956; *Gridiron Duel*, 1959; *The Wild Pitch*, 1963; *Tall on the Court*, 1964; *Third and Eight to Go*, 1964; *Big League Rookie*, 1965; *Trouble at Second Base*, 1966; *The Valley Eleven*, 1967; (under pseudonym Joel Reeve) *Goal Ahead*, S. G. Phillips, 1967; *Jump Shot Joe*, 1968; *Rookie in the Backcourt*, 1970; *Big League Sandlotters*, 1971; *Third and Goal*, 1971; *Playoff*, Bantam, 1972; *Gunner on the Court*, 1972; *The Backyard Five*, 1973; *The Unbeatable Five*, 1974; *Game, Set, and Match*, 1977; *Battery Mates*, 1978; *Home Court Is Where You Find It*, 1980.

Contributor of more than one thousand stories to magazines, including *Saturday Evening Post, Collier's, This Week, Argosy, American, Pic, Blue Book,* and *Cosmopolitan.*

Author of several screenplays and of more than one hundred television shows for "Fireside Theater," "Broken Arrow," "Bonanza," "Zane Grey Theater," "The Virginian," "The Grey Ghost," "Alcoa Theater," "Wells Fargo," "Route 66," and other programs.

WORK IN PROGRESS: One novel; several untitled juveniles; screenplays and television scripts.†

*   *   *

COX-GEORGE, Noah Arthur William   1915-

PERSONAL: Born June 15, 1915, in Degema, Nigeria; son of Noah Obedial Collingwood (a civil servant) and Rosabel Abigail Regina (Cox) George; married Rachel Ademike Biola Wright, November 14, 1953; children: Luba Bonita (daughter), Siegfried Amadeus Maynard, Beryl Effuah Zorah (daughter), Christabel Isadora Richenda (daughter). *Education:* London School of Economics and Political Science, B.Sc. (with second class honors), 1946, M.Sc., 1951, Ph.D., 1954; Oxford University, graduate study, 1952-53. *Home and office:* 6 College Rd., Kortright-Leicester, Freetown, Sierra Leone.

CAREER: University of Sierra Leone, Fourah Bay College, Freetown, lecturer-in-charge, department of economics, 1946-51, senior lecturer and dean of faculty of economic studies, 1955-61; University of Nigeria, Nsukka, professor of economics and head of department, 1960-64; University of Sierra Leone, professor of political economy, 1964-65; United Nations, director of Trade, Fiscal, and Monetary Division, Economic Commission for Africa, 1965-67, chief of Trade Policies Problem Section, Conference on Trade and Development, 1967-69; University of Sierra Leone, professor of economics, head of department of economics and social studies, and dean of faculty, 1969-79; currently economic consultant in Freetown. Guest lecturer, St. Gallen Graduate School of Economics, Business, and Public Administration (Switzerland), 1967-68; Phelps-Stokes visiting professor, African lecture program, 1973; external examiner in economics in African Studies Programme, University of Delhi and University of Ghana; external examiner, University of Nigeria and University of Ghana Legon. Government of Sierra Leone, chairman, Price Control Advisory Board, 1957-61, Commission of Inquiry into Price Structure of Motor Vehicles, 1960-61, National Commission on Africanisation of Commerce and Industry, 1969-73; chairman of board of directors, Road Transport Corporation, 1969-73; member of Commission of Inquiry into the Civil Services, 1970-71; chairman of Central Bank of Sierra Leone Working Party on Capital Availability and Entrepreneurship, 1970-71. *Member:* West African Economic Association (vice-president), Royal Economic Society (England), Royal Commonwealth Society, Nigerian Economic Society (vice-president, 1962-65), London School of Economics Society (life member), London House Club.

WRITINGS: *Crucifixion of Sierra Leone?*, New Era Press (Freetown, Sierra Leone), 1948; *Finance and Development in West Africa*, Dobson, 1961, Humanities, 1962; *Studies in Finance and Development—The Gold Coast Experience, 1914-1960*, Dobson, 1973. Also author of government publications and political pamphlets; contributor to *Lectures on Export Marketing.* Contributor of articles and reviews to *West African Review, New Commonwealth, West Africa, International Quarterly,* and other journals and newspapers.

WORK IN PROGRESS: An autobiography.

AVOCATIONAL INTERESTS: Political theory, shooting, travel.

* * *

CRAIG, Georgia
See DERN, Erolie Pearl Gaddis

* * *

CRAIG, John Eland
See CHIPPERFIELD, Joseph Eugene

* * *

CREIGHTON, Thomas H(awk)   1904-

PERSONAL: Born May 19, 1904, in Philadelphia, Pa.; son of Frank W. (a clergyman) and Maude (Hawk) Creighton; married Gwen Lux (a sculptor), December 23, 1959; children: Thomas H., Jr., Ann Creighton Fortunato. *Education:* Harvard University, B.A., 1926; attended Beaux Arts Institute of Design, New York, N.Y., 1926-29, and Ecole des Beaux Arts, Paris, France. *Home and office:* 4340 Pahoa Ave., Honolulu, Hawaii 96816.

CAREER: Architect, practising in New York and Vermont, 1927-46; *Progressive Architecture,* New York, N.Y., editor-in-chief, 1946-63; John Carl Warnecke & Associates (architects), San Francisco, Calif., partner, 1963-66; architect in private practice, Honolulu, Hawaii, 1966—. Instructor at several educational institutions. Planning commissioner, Honolulu, 1968-71. *Member:* American Institute of Architects (fellow), Construction Specifications Institute, Citizens for Hawaii (president, 1970-72), San Francisco Planning and Urban Renewal Association (vice-president, 1963-65), Outrigger Canoe Club.

WRITINGS: *Planning to Build,* Doubleday, 1946; (editor) *Building for Modern Man,* Princeton University Press, 1948, reprinted, Books for Libraries, 1969; (with Katherine Morrow Ford) *The American House Today,* Reinhold, 1950; (editor) *Houses: Selected from Progressive Architecture,* Reinhold, 1950; (with Ford) *Designs for Living,* Reinhold, 1952; *Quality Budget Houses,* Reinhold, 1954; *Contemporary Houses,* Reinhold, 1960; *The Architecture of Monuments,* Reinhold, 1962; *American Architecture,* Luce, 1964; *From the Ground Up,* Popular Library, 1967; *The Lands of Hawaii: Their Use and Misuse,* University Press of Hawaii, 1978. Also author of monthly column in *San Francisco Magazine,* 1963-65, and of weekly column in *Honolulu Advertiser,* 1968—. Contributor of articles on architecture and planning to magazines. Architectural consultant to *San Francisco Magazine.*

SIDELIGHTS: Thomas H. Creighton wrote *CA:* "The concerns that have motivated [my] writing [are] the need for a reasonable contemporary architecture, and the need for well-planned, well-managed treatment of land as an irreplaceable resource."

CRESSEY, Donald R(ay)   1919-

PERSONAL: Surname rhymes with "messy"; born April 27, 1919, in Fergus Falls, Minn.; son of Raymond Wilbert (an electrician) and Myrtle (Prentiss) Cressey; married Elaine M. Smythe (a medical technologist), December 16, 1943; children: Martha Jean, Ann Kathleen, Mary Dee. *Education:* Iowa State University of Science and Technology, B.S., 1943; Indiana University, Ph.D., 1950. *Politics:* Democrat. *Religion:* Unitarian Universalist. *Home:* 4310 Via Esperanza, Santa Barbara, Calif. 93110. *Office:* Department of Sociology, University of California, Santa Barbara, Calif. 93106.

CAREER: Illinois State Penitentiary, Joliet, sociologist, 1949; University of California, Los Angeles, 1949-61, began as instructor, professor of sociology, 1959-61, chairman of department of anthropology and sociology, 1957-58, acting dean of Division of Social Science, 1960-61; University of California, Santa Barbara, professor of sociology, 1962—, dean of College of Letters and Science, 1962-67. Research associate at California Institution for Men, 1950-51, and at U.S. Penitentiary, Terre Haute, Ind., 1951; visiting professor at University of Chicago, 1955-56, Institute of Criminal Law and Criminology, Cambridge University, 1961-62, 1970-71, University of Oslo, 1965, University of Washington, 1968, University of Minnesota, 1969, and Australian National University, 1973; faculty research lecturer, University of California, 1978. Member, California Council on Criminal Justice, 1969—. Consultant, President's Commission on Law Enforcement and Administration of Justice, 1966-67, National Commission on Causes and Prevention of Violence, 1968. *Military service:* U.S. Army Air Forces, 1943-46; became sergeant; received five battle stars.

MEMBER: International Society of Criminology, American Sociological Association (member of national council, 1960-63; visiting scientist, 1963—), American Correctional Association, Law and Order Association, Pacific Sociological Association (vice-president, 1957-58; president, 1959-60; member of council, 1960-61). *Awards, honors:* Research grants from Russell Sage Foundation, 1955-56, Ford Foundation, 1960, American Council of Learned Societies, 1960, and Social Science Research Council; citation from Illinois Academy of Criminology, 1964, for contributions to research and the theory and practice of corrections; Edwin H. Sutherland Research Citation, American Society of Criminology, 1967; Distinguished Alumni Service Award, Indiana University, 1974; citation of merit, Iowa State University of Science and Technology, 1978.

WRITINGS: *Other Peoples' Money: A Study in the Social Psychology of Embezzlement,* Free Press of Glencoe, 1953, published with a new introduction, Wadsworth, 1971; (with Edwin H. Sutherland) *Principles of Criminology,* Lippincott, 5th edition (Cressey was not associated with earlier editions), 1955, 10th edition, 1981; (with Richard A. Cloward and others) *Theoretical Studies in Social Organization of the Prison,* Russell Sage, 1960; (editor) *The Prison: Studies in Institutional Organization and Change,* Holt, 1961; *Delinquency, Crime and Differential Association,* Nijhoff, 1964; *The Functions and Structure of Criminal Syndicates,* U.S. Government Printing Office, 1967; *Theft of the Nation: The Structure and Operations of Organized Crime in America,* Harper, 1969; (with David A. Ward) *Delinquency, Crime and Social Process,* Harper, 1969; (editor and author of introduction) *Crime and Criminal Justice,* Quadrangle, 1971; *Criminal Organization: Its Elementary Forms,* Harper, 1972; (with Arthur I. Rosett) *Justice by Consent: Plea Bargains in the American Courthouse,* Lippincott, 1976; (with James W. Coleman) *Social Problems,* Harper, 1980.

Also author of a volume of poetry, *Turkeys in the Peach Garden*, 1977; co-author with Henry Hathaway of motion picture script "Theft of a Nation," based on his book of the same title, 1971. Editor, "Social Problems" series, Harper; chairman of editorial board, "Culture and Society" series, University of California Press, 1953-55, 1956-58. Contributor of chapters to books. Contributor to professional journals. Associate editor, *American Sociological Review*, 1953-56; advisory editor, *American Journal of Sociology*, 1959-62, 1981-83, of *Transactions: Social Science and the Community*, 1963-67, and of *Social Problems*, 1970-76.

WORK IN PROGRESS: A book on business ethics; a study of white-collar crime and corruption in government.

SIDELIGHTS: Donald R. Cressey speaks Norwegian and French, and reads German, French, and Scandinavian languages. He has appeared on numerous television programs in the United States and Europe, and is convinced "that no TV viewer ever bought a book as a result."

*   *   *

CROUSE, William H(arry)   1907-

PERSONAL: Born December 19, 1907, in Anderson, Ind.; son of Jess H. and Beulah (Decker) Crouse; married Ruth E. Briggs (an editorial assistant), September 15, 1933. *Education:* Attended Purdue University, 1926-31.

CAREER: General Motors Corp., Delco-Remy Division, Anderson, Ind., director of field service education, 1937-46; McGraw-Hill Book Co., New York, N.Y., editor of technical books, 1946-51; worked as independent technical and scientific writer, 1951-56; McGraw-Hill Book Co., Charlottesville, Va., editor-in-chief of *McGraw-Hill Encyclopedia of Science and Technology*, 1956—. Member of board of trustees, McIntire Library. *Member:* Society of Automotive Engineers, American Society for Engineering Education, New York Academy of Sciences.

WRITINGS—All published by McGraw: *Automotive Electrical Equipment*, 1941, 8th edition, 1976; (with Donald L. Anglin) *Automotive Mechanics*, 1946, 8th edition, 1980; *Everyday Automobile Repairs*, 1946; *Home Guide to Repair, Upkeep, and Remodeling*, 1947; *Understanding Science*, 1948, 4th edition, 1973; *Electrical Appliance Servicing*, 1950; *Workbook for Automotive Electricity*, 1950, 4th edition, 1971; *Workbook for Automotive Chassis*, 1951, 3rd edition, 1966; *Workbook for Automotive Engines*, 1951, 3rd edition, 1966; *Workbook for Automotive Service and Trouble-Shooting*, 1951, 3rd edition, 1966; *Workbook for Automotive Tools*, 1951, 3rd edition, 1966; *Everyday Household Appliance Repairs*, 1952; (with Anglin) *Automotive Chassis and Body*, 1955, 5th edition, 1976; *Automotive Engines*, 1955, 6th edition, in press; (with Anglin) *Automotive Fuel, Lubricating, and Cooling Systems*, 1955, 6th edition, in press; *Automotive Transmissions and Power Trains*, 1955, 5th edition, 1976; *Science Marvels of Tomorrow*, 1963; *Testbook for Automotive Mechanics*, 1965; (with Anglin) *Automotive Engine Design*, 1970; *Automotive Emission Control*, 1971, 2nd edition, 1977; *Automotive Service Business: Operation and Management*, 1973; *Small Engines: Operation and Maintenance*, 1973, 2nd edition published as *Small Engine Mechanics*, 1980; (with Anglin) *The Auto Book*, 1974, 2nd edition, 1979; *Pocket Automotive Dictionary*, 1976; (with Anglin) *Automotive Air Conditioning*, 1977; (with Anglin) *Automotive Tools, Fasteners, and Measurements*, 1977; *Automotive Tune-up*, 1977; *Motor Vehicle Inspection*, 1978; *Automotive Technician's Handbook*, 1979; (with Anglin) *Automotive Body Repair and Refinishing*, 1980. Consulting editor on automotive books for McGraw.

SIDELIGHTS: Understanding Science has been published in twenty-three languages.

*   *   *

CROWE, John
See LYNDS, Dennis

*   *   *

CUNNINGHAM, Bob
See MAY, Julian

*   *   *

CURRAN, Dolores   1932-

PERSONAL: Surname is pronounced Kern; born February 11, 1932, in Edgerton, Wis.; daughter of William Edward (a farmer) and Lillian (Spohn) Fox; married James Curran (an educator), June 28, 1958; children: Teresa, Patrick, Daniel. *Education:* University of Wisconsin—Whitewater, B.Ed., 1953. *Religion:* Roman Catholic. *Home:* 336 West Peakview, Littleton, Colo. 80120. *Agent:* James Alt, 300 Dauphin, Green Bay, Wis.

CAREER: English teacher in public schools in Beloit, Wis., 1953-55, and Englewood, Colo., 1955-61; free-lance writer, 1961-70; Arapahoe Community College, Littleton, Colo., lecturer in writing, 1970; full-time writer and lecturer, 1970—. Has lectured and conducted workshops in the United States, Canada, and Germany. *Member:* Catholic Press Association, Colorado Author's League. *Awards, honors:* Awards from Colorado Author's League, 1974, for best philosophy and best humor articles, and 1975, for best short-short story; award for best regular column, Catholic Press Association, 1979, 1980; honorary doctor of humanities, Regis College, 1981.

WRITINGS: Who, Me Teach My Child Religion?, Winston Press, 1970, 4th edition, 1981; *Do Not Fold, Staple, or Mutilate*, Ave Maria Press, 1970; *Today's Catholic Woman*, Ave Maria Press, 1971; *What Are Parents for, Anyway?*, Abbey Press, 1972; *And Then God Made Families*, Alt, 1978; *In the Beginning There Were the Parents*, Winston Press, 1978, discussion guide, 1980; *I'm Telling: Confessions of a Middle-Age, Middle-Class Parent*, Paulist/Newman, 1978; *Family Prayer*, Twenty-third Publications, 1979; *Family: A Church Challenge for the Eighties*, Winston Press, 1980; *Traits of the Healthy Family*, Winston Press, 1982.

Author of columns, "From One End of the Log," in *Colorado Education Association Journal*, 1967-69, "Showcase," in *Parent Educator*, 1967-72, "On the Other Hand," syndicated by National Catholic News Service, 1967-74, "Teacher Talking," in *Today's Catholic Teacher*, 1969-71, "Between Parish and Parent," in *Religion Teacher's Journal*, 1972-73, and "Talks with Parents," distributed by Alt-Curran Associates, 1974—. Contributor to more than fifty magazines. Editor-at-large of *Parent Educator*, 1967-72.

WORK IN PROGRESS: A book on home-school relationships.

SIDELIGHTS: Dolores Curran writes: "I have three goals: to touch the forgotten reader's needs, to inject humor in lives, and to write a novel like *To Kill a Mockingbird*.

"My writing has generated a heavy speaking career. Most of my focus is on the health of the family, but now that my own children are beginning to peel away for college and lives of their own, I hope to get at my novel."

*   *   *

CURTIS, Peter
  See LOFTS, Norah (Robinson)

D

DAHL, Roald 1916-

PERSONAL: Given name is pronounced "Roo-aal"; born September 13, 1916, in Llandaff, South Wales; son of Harald (a shipbroker, painter, and horticulturist) and Sofie (Hesselberg) Dahl; married Patricia Neal (an actress), July 2, 1953; children: Olivia (deceased), Tessa, Theo, Ophelia, Lucy. *Education:* Graduate of British public schools, 1932. *Agent:* A. Watkins, Inc., 77 Park Ave., New York, N.Y. 10016.

CAREER: Shell Oil Co., London, England, member of eastern staff, 1933-37, member of staff in Dar-es-Salaam, Tanzania, 1937-39; free-lance writer. *Military service:* Royal Air Force, fighter pilot, 1939-45; became wing commander. *Awards, honors:* Mystery Writers of America Edgar Allan Poe Award, 1954 and 1959.

WRITINGS—Juvenile: *The Gremlins,* Random House, 1943; *James and the Giant Peach,* Knopf, 1961; *Charlie and the Chocolate Factory* (also see below), Knopf, 1964, revised edition, 1973; *The Magic Finger,* Harper, 1966; *Fantastic Mr. Fox,* Knopf, 1970; *Charlie and the Great Glass Elevator: The Further Adventures of Charlie Bucket and Willy Wonka, Chocolate-Maker Extraordinary,* Knopf, 1972; *Danny: The Champion of the World,* Knopf, 1975; *The Enormous Crocodile,* Knopf, 1976; *The Wonderful Story of Henry Sugar and Six More,* Knopf, 1977; *Complete Adventures of Charlie and Mr. Willy Wonka,* Allen & Unwin, 1978; *The Twits,* J. Cape, 1980, Knopf, 1981; *George's Marvellous Medicine,* J. Cape, 1981.

Short story collections, except as indicated: *Over to You: Ten Stories of Flyers and Flying,* Reynal, 1946; *Sometime Never: A Fable for Supermen* (novel), Scribner, 1948; *Someone Like You* (Book-of-the-Month Club alternate selection; also see below), Knopf, 1953, revised edition, M. Joseph, 1961; *Kiss, Kiss* (also see below), Knopf, 1960; *Twenty-Nine Kisses* (contains contents of *Someone Like You* and *Kiss, Kiss*), M. Joseph, 1969; *Selected Stories,* Random House, 1970; *Switch Bitch,* Knopf, 1974; *The Best of Roald Dahl,* Random House, 1978; *Tales of the Unexpected,* Vintage, 1979; *Taste and Other Tales,* Longman, 1979; *My Uncle Oswald* (novel), M. Joseph, 1979, Knopf, 1980; *More Tales of the Unexpected,* Penguin, 1980.

Screenplays: "Oh Death, Where Is Thy Sting-a-Ling-a-Ling?," United Artists; "You Only Live Twice," United Artists, 1967; (with Ken Hughes) "Chitty Chitty Bang Bang," United Artists, 1968; "The Night-digger" (based on "Nest in a Falling Tree" by Joy Crowley), Metro-Goldwyn-Mayer, 1970; "Willy Wonka and the Chocolate Factory" (based on *Charlie and the Chocolate Factory*), Paramount, 1971; "The Lightning Bug," 1971; "The Road Builder." Also author of a play, "The Honeys" produced in New York, N.Y. 1955.

Work is represented in anthologies. Contributor to the *New Yorker, Harper's, Atlantic, Saturday Evening Post, Collier's, Playboy, Esquire, Town and Country,* and other magazines.

SIDELIGHTS: Though he is now recognized as a "master of the macabre and the surprise denouement" as well as a successful author of children's books, Roald Dahl freely admits that making a career out of writing was one of the last things on his mind as he worked in Washington, D.C. during World War II. As Dahl himself remembers: "One day in 1941, I was sitting in my office staring out the window when the door opened. In came C. S. Forester, creator of Captain Hornblower. He asked if he could interview me for a piece he was writing for the *Saturday Evening Post.* . . . He wanted to write up my most exciting war experience. He invited me to a first-class lunch. At lunch he took out a notebook but found he couldn't eat and make notes at the same time, so I offered to scribble some notes and send them round to him later. Well, when I'd finished scribbling the notes I found I'd actually written a story. . . . Forester sent it to the *Saturday Evening Post* under my name, and they paid me $1,000 for it. I lost most of that money playing poker with Senator Harry Truman at the University Club in Washington."

This first story and eleven subsequent wartime stories that first appeared in the *Saturday Evening Post* were eventually published in a collection called *Over to You.* By that time, Dahl was hooked on writing. "As I went on, the stories became less and less realistic and more fantastic. But becoming a writer was pure fluke. Without being asked to, I doubt if I'd ever have thought of it." Dahl has worked full-time at his craft ever since. "If you find your metier," he explains, "you should stick to it."

Dahl's stories have been compared to those of James Thurber as well as to the cartoons of Charles Addams, with most critics agreeing that his ability to "incarnate men's grotesque fantasies" is unrivaled. "Roald Dahl is a master of horror—an intellectual Hitchcock of the writing world," states a *Books and Bookmen* reviewer. "He has left technique a very long way behind him. One is not conscious of *reading,* only of something awful *happening.* . . . He knows the terror of helplessness. He knows the cliffs of fall—*and* what lies over the edge. . . . Mr. Dahl is incapable of the pornographic, the second-rate. What he *is* capable of is so shattering that I cannot find a word for it, but it is always in excessively good taste—which makes it worse!''

Someone Like You and *Kiss, Kiss,* two short story collections, were both well-received by the critics. For example, a *New York Herald Tribune Book Review* critic writes: ''Because Mr. Dahl's style is terse and vivid and his range wide, and because the people inhabiting his tales are alive and stubbornly convincing, he emerges triumphant from the test of being read over and over again. *Someone Like You* is a fascinating book, and deserves the wide audience most collections of short stories never reach.'' A *Saturday Review* critic notes that his ''smoothly-spun tales of the macabre and the fantastic'' will appeal greatly to those readers who have been disappointed by the typical short story of recent years. And the *New York Times* reviewer feels that the contents of *Someone Like You* are so entertaining that ''Mr. Dahl could be a cult without half trying, and he deserves the warm welcome he'll get.''

The stories in *Kiss, Kiss,* comments a *Chicago Sunday Tribune* reviewer, ''are written in a fine tradition.'' Though he feels that ''there is a certain monotony about a group of stories in which each has an ending which is almost a trick,'' in Dahl's case, ''the trick is always a good one; the incidents along the way to it are always lively and pathetic and gay and original. . . . It is pleasant to see a manner of telling a tale so skillfully done.'' A *New York Herald Tribune Book Review* critic notes that ''the writing is crisp but anonymous, and there are certainly no serious implications anywhere. But stripped as they are to this anecdotal minimum, they also have one modest, but uncommon virtue: they lend themselves as aptly to re-telling as anything being written today.'' Malcolm Bradbury of the *New York Times Book Review* also has great praise for Dahl's abilities. ''I don't want to suggest that Roald Dahl's latest collection, *Kiss, Kiss,* has nothing more than good construction; it has. . . . [But] on this score alone he gets straight A's in my creative writing class. He builds his situations beautifully, and his punch-lines have so much punch that I was reeling for several days. . . . His poorer stories . . . are weaknesses in idea—not in treatment. He is also funny. No moralist, no profound seer—but a true craftsman.'' Granville Hicks of the *Saturday Review,* even though he criticizes Dahl's occasional tendency to overelaborate and to turn his plot trickiness ''into mere formula,'' feels that the stories in *Kiss, Kiss* contain ''many of the touches that make Dahl an uncommonly entertaining writer.''

Though both the *New York Herald Tribune Book Review* critic and Bradbury of the *New York Times Book Review* do not regard Dahl as a moralist, there are at least three of their counterparts who do. Naomi Lewis of *New Statesman* writes: ''Mr. Roald Dahl has a considerable narrative gift. . . . [His] approach is calm and mild; he always gives the worst of his characters the benefit of the doubt; still, these really are moral tales. Go wrong and you get some very peculiar deserts.'' A *Times Literary Supplement* reviewer states: ''Where Mr. Dahl differs from the common run of spine-chillers is in the verisimilitude of his cariacature of human weakness, showing this to the edge of extravagance, revealing a social satirist and a moralist at work behind the entertaining fantast.'' A *Spectator* critic concludes simply that ''Dahl exhibits a conscience without being sanctimonious about it.''

The same traits that characterize his adult short stories are evident in his books for children, which are often written on two levels—one for adults to appreciate and one to appeal to children. *James and the Giant Peach* and *Charlie and the Chocolate Factory* are two of his most popular works of this

type, but reviewers are divided as to their suitability for children. Commenting on *James and the Giant Peach,* a *Chicago Sunday Tribune* critic calls it ''a stunning book, to be cherished for its story, a superb fantasy, . . . and for its beautiful illustrations.'' *Commonweal* notes that it is ''a 'juicy' fantasy, 'dripping' with humor and imagination.'' A *Times Literary Supplement* reviewer writes: ''Children's books by sophisticated adult writers are to be dreaded normally; not this one though. . . . The violence is the 'Fee fi fo fum, grind your bones to make my bread' variety, much liked by children, no worse than Alice, Lear, and most fairy tales; harmless anyway. It is vivid, robust, entertaining and funny. There's some splendid verse thrown in as well and that's rare enough.'' A *San Francisco Chronicle* reviewer concludes that *James and the Giant Peach* is ''the most original fantasy that has been published in a long time. . . . [It] may well become a classic.''

Others, however, do not seem to be quite as impressed. ''Some children may find it an exciting and rambunctious fantasy,'' writes a *Saturday Review* critic. ''However, one thing children are not tough-minded about is losing parents suddenly, and at the beginning of this story James's parents are eaten by a large rhinoceros escaped from the zoo, 'their troubles over in thirty-five seconds flat.''' *Library Journal* also notes that the book contains ''some interesting and original elements,'' but that in general, ''the violent exaggeration of language and almost grotesque characterizations of the child's aunts impair the story-telling and destroy the illusion of reality and plausibility which any good fantasy must achieve.''

Reactions to *Charlie and the Chocolate Factory* were also mixed. An *Atlantic* reviewer writes that it is ''full of magical nonsense and uproarious situations, with a tiny germ of a moral artfully inserted in each chapter.'' Alice Dagliesh of *Saturday Review* calls it ''an offbeat fantasy that may be many things to many readers. On the surface it recounts a fascinating visit by Charlie and 'four nasty children' to a chocolate factory. . . . It is also a somewhat sadistic cautionary tale, for unpleasant adventures befall the 'four nasty children.''' John Gillespie and Diana Lembo note that ''younger readers will enjoy [*Charlie and the Chocolate Factory*], with its infectious fun and outlandish episodes, while the more mature ones will discover overtones of a religious nature, as well as the moral precept of good behavior rewarded.''

Eleanor Cameron, herself a noted author of children's books, is sharply critical of several elements in the story. Citing its overall ''tastelessness'' as a major source of her displeasure, she reports that ''what I object to in [*Charlie and the Chocolate Factory*] is its phony presentation of poverty and its phony humor, which is based on punishment with overtones of sadism; [and] its hypocrisy which is epitomized in its moral . . . that TV is horrible and hateful and time-wasting and that children should read good books instead, when in fact the book itself is like nothing so much as one of the more specious television shows.'' Furthermore, as she and several other critics point out, the story has racist overtones (black characters from Africa, known as ''Oompa-Loompas,'' serve as slave laborers in the chocolate factory; revisions included in a 1973 printing of the book eliminated their resemblance to any known racial group and assigned a fictional place of origin for them). In a second review of the book, Cameron concludes that ''[*Charlie and the Chocolate Factory*] is wish-fulfillment in caricature, and as caricature, it is removed from reality. . . . But the situation of the Oompa-Loompas *is* real; it could not be more so, and it is anything but funny.''

Ellen Chamberlain responds to this criticism by pointing out that ''[*Charlie and the Chocolate Factory*] is fantasy . . . [and]

should not be exhorted to weigh itself down with the woes of the real world. . . . We need not spend any more time agonizing over the exploitation of the Oompa-Loompas than we do over that of the poor peasantry in fairy tales. The only valid objection Mrs. Cameron raises is the one concerning the origins and characteristics of the Oompa-Loompas.''

Anne Merrick, writing in *Children's Literature in Education*, finds other faults in *Charlie and the Chocolate Factory*. ''[The] plot develops in a linear, almost picaresque fashion, in that event is added to event in the straightforward structuring of Charlie's adventures. It does not grow from qualities in the characters or from the initial situation. . . . Charlie himself is a cipher, his appeal lying in his poverty and in his politeness. . . . In the end [he] wins all, not because of any positive good of noble qualities, but because he is poor, quiet, and polite.'' Merrick further criticizes the ''exaggerated'' characters of the other children in the story, whom she considers to be more comic strip ''archetypes'' and ''physical and social misfits''; Willy Wonka fares little better, for she labels him a ''larger than life 'character' '' who is a ''loud, boisterous, [and] loquacious'' representative of the ''conservative, traditional attitude of adults to children.'' She concludes: ''Although exaggeration is of the essence of the book, there are times when it seems to me that Dahl's use of language degenerates into carelessness and even coarseness. . . . The pace of *Charlie* is fast, even hectic; it is entirely unsubtle; its humour is fairly crude. . . . [The story] appeals to all . . . children, who recognize in it much that they have met before, especially its most obvious (if, to adult eyes, distorted) moral, that good triumphs over evil.''

Responding to the criticism concerning the violence and exaggeration that typify his work, Dahl insists that ''children love to be spooked, to be made to giggle. They like a touch of the macabre as long as it's funny too. They don't relate it to life. They enjoy the fantasy. And my nastiness is never gratuitous. It's retribution. Beastly people must be punished.'' Furthermore, Dahl explains, his books have an even more important function—to get children to read. A successful children's book writer, he says, must be able to devise a story ''that is so absorbing, exciting, funny, fast and beautiful that the child will fall in love with it. And that first love affair between the young child and the young book will lead hopefully to other loves for other books and when this happens the battle is probably won. The child will have found a crock of gold.''

MEDIA ADAPTATIONS: Twenty-two of Dahl's short stories have been dramatized for television and presented under the series title ''Tales of the Unexpected.''

AVOCATIONAL INTERESTS: Gambling, cultivating orchids, drinking fine wine, collecting antiques, cleaning and restoring old paintings.

BIOGRAPHICAL/CRITICAL SOURCES: New York Times, November 8, 1953, April 29, 1980; *New York Herald Tribune Book Review*, November 8, 1953, February 7, 1960; *Saturday Review*, December 26, 1953, February 20, 1960, February 17, 1962, November 7, 1964; *New York Times Book Review*, February 7, 1960, November 12, 1961, November 8, 1970, September 17, 1972, October 27, 1974, December 25, 1977, September 30, 1979, April 20, 1980, March 29, 1981; *San Francisco Chronicle*, February 15, 1960, December 10, 1961; *Chicago Sunday Tribune*, February 21, 1960, November 12, 1961; *Springfield Republican*, March 13, 1960; *Christian Century*, August 31, 1960; *Times Literary Supplement*, October 28, 1960, December 14, 1967, November 15, 1974, November 23, 1979, November 21, 1980, July 24, 1981; *New Statesman*, October 29, 1960, March 5, 1971, November 4, 1977; *Commonweal*,

November 15, 1961; *Library Journal*, November 15, 1961; *Christian Science Monitor*, November 16, 1961; *Wilson Library Bulletin*, February, 1962; *Atlantic*, December, 1964; *Books and Bookmen*, January, 1969, May, 1970; *Kenyon Review*, Volume XXXI, number 2, 1969; Barry Farrell, *Pat and Roald*, Random House, 1969; *Horn Book*, October, 1972, April, 1973, June, 1973; *Contemporary Literary Criticism*, Gale, Volume I, 1973, Volume VI, 1976, Volume XVIII, 1981; *Children's Literature in Education*, spring, 1975; *Sewanee Review*, winter, 1975; *Children's Literature Review*, Volume I, Gale, 1976; *Writer*, August, 1976; *Washington Post Book World*, November 13, 1977, April 20, 1980; *Spectator*, December, 1977; *Best Sellers*, January, 1978; *Publishers Weekly*, June 6, 1980; *Chicago Tribune Book World*, August 10, 1980, May 17, 1981.

—*Sketch by Deborah A. Straub*

*   *   *

DALLAS, John
    See DUNCAN, W(illiam) Murdoch

*   *   *

DALRYMPLE, Byron W(illiam)   1910-

PERSONAL: Born August 7, 1910, in Fostoria, Mich.; son of Charles E. (a teacher) and Hattie (Church) Dalrymple; married Ellen F. Christoffers (a secretary), April 30, 1949; children: Michael C., Terence A. *Education:* University of Michigan, B.A., 1932. *Home address:* P.O. Box 709, Kerrville, Tex. 78028. *Agent:* August Lenniger, 437 Fifth Ave., New York, N.Y. 10016.

CAREER: Free-lance magazine writer, 1940—; War-Dal Productions (outdoor television filming), Kerrville, Tex., producer, scriptwriter, and actor, 1962—. *Awards, honors:* Sunset Travel Film Festival Award, 1971, for ''Wildlife Cameraman''; citation of merit from National Outdoor Travel Film Festival, 1971, for ''Discovering Wildlife Refuges,'' and 1975, for ''What Is a Living Stream Worth''; Texas Tourist Development Award, 1973, for magazine writings.

WRITINGS: Light Tackle Fishing, McGraw, 1947; *Ice Fishing for Everybody*, Lantern Press, 1948; *Doves and Dove Shooting*, Putnam, 1949; *Fishing, Hunting, Camping*, Pocket Books, 1950, revised edition published as *Fundamentals of Fishing and Hunting*, 1959; *Sportsman's Guide to Game Fish*, World Publishing, 1968, revised edition published as *Complete Guide to Game Fish*, Van Nostrand, 1981; *Hunting Across North America*, Harper, 1970; *Modern Book of the Black Bass*, Winchester Press, 1972; *Survival in the Outdoors*, Dutton, 1972; *Complete Book of Deer Hunting*, Winchester Press, 1973; *North American Big Game Hunting*, Winchester Press, 1974; *How To Call Wildlife*, Outdoor Life Book Club, 1975; *Fishing for Fun with Byron Dalrymple*, Winchester Press, 1975; *How to Rig and Fish Natural Baits*, Funk, 1976; *North American Game Animals*, Crown, 1978; *Deer Hunting with Dalrymple*, McKay, 1978; *Hunting for the Pot, Fishing for the Pan*, Outdoor Life Book Club, 1981.

Contributor: Brian Vesey-Fitzgerald and Francesca LaMonte, editors, *Game Fish of the World*, Harper, 1949; Bill Bueno, editor, *American Fisherman's Guide*, Prentice-Hall, 1952; Chet Fish, editor, *The Outdoor Life Deer Hunting Book*, Outdoor Life Book Club, 1974; Robert Elman, editor, *Hunting America's Game Birds and Animals*, Winchester Press, 1975.

Also author and producer of twenty-four television film scripts. Columnist for *Sports Afield*, *Argosy*, and *Outdoor Life*. Contributor to *Encyclopaedia Britannica*, *Outdoor Encyclopedia*, and *American Oxford Encyclopedia*. Contributor of over two thousand-five hundred articles to magazines, including *Field & Stream, True, Cosmopolitan, Sports Illustrated, Holiday,* and *Better Homes and Gardens.*

SIDELIGHTS: Byron W. Dalrymple travels approximately 30,000 miles annually to gather material for articles and to shoot illustrative photographs. He assisted in the production of and starred in a series of fourteen outdoor films for the Truck and Coach Division of General Motors Corporation. Distributed nationally, each of these films were viewed by fourteen to twenty million people. Dalrymple has also written scripts for and starred in films made for such firms as Custom Coach, Apache Trailer, and Redfield Scope.

*   *   *

D'ANCONA, Mirella Levi   1919-

PERSONAL: Surname sometimes appears as Levi D'Ancona; born June 7, 1919, in Florence, Italy; naturalized American citizen, 1952; daughter of Ezio and Flora (Aghib) D'Ancona. *Education:* University of Florence, Dottore in Lettere e Filosofia, 1941, additional study, 1945-46; New York University, graduate study at Institute of Fine Arts, 1946-48, 1949-51; Bryn Mawr College, M.A., 1949. *Home:* 360 East 72nd St., Apt. C2405, New York, N.Y. 10021. *Office:* Hunter College of the City University of New York, 695 Park Ave., New York, N.Y. 10021.

CAREER: Research assistant at Wildenstein & Co., New York City, 1948, 1950-51, and Frick Art Reference Library, New York City, 1952-54; Wildenstein & Co., researcher, working on catalogue of Italian illuminations, 1954-60; State University of New York College of Science and Engineering on Long Island (now State University of New York at Stony Brook), Oyster Bay, assistant professor of art, 1950-60; Hunter College of the City University of New York, New York City, lecturer, 1960-61, assistant professor, 1961-66, associate professor, 1967-72, professor of art, 1972—. Adjunct associate professor at Institute of Fine Arts, New York, 1967. Consultant (collaboratrice) of Vatican Library, 1968—. *Member:* Istituto d'Arte Lombarda. *Awards, honors:* Grants from American Philosophical Society, 1955, 1956, Bollingen Foundation, 1960, and American Council of Learned Societies, 1960, 1964, 1965, 1966.

WRITINGS: (With others) *The Frick Collections: An Illustrated Catalogue,* Thistle Press, Volume V: *Sculpture,* 1953, Volume VI: *Sculpture,* 1954, Volume XII: *Italian Paintings,* 1955; *The Iconography of the Immaculate Conception in the Middle Ages and the Early Renaissance* (monograph), New York University Press, for Archaeological Institute of America and College Art Association of America, 1957; *Miniatura e Miniatori a Firenze dal XIV al XVI secolo,* Olschki (Florence), 1962; *The Wildenstein Collection of Illuminations: The Lombard School,* Olschki, 1970; *The Garden of the Renaissance,* Olschki, 1977; *Borricelli's Primavera: A Botanical Interpretation Including Astrology, Alchemy and the Medici,* Olschki, in press.

Contributor: *Scritti di Storia dell'Arte in Onore di Mario Selmi, Roma,* De Luca, 1962; *Studi di Bibliografia e di Storia in Onore di Tammaro de Marinis,* Giovanni Mardersteig (Verona), 1964; L. F. Sandler, editor, *Essays in Memory of Karl Lehmann,* J. J. Augustin, 1964; *Contributi alla Storia del libro italiano: Miscellanea in Onore di Lamberto Donati,* Olschki, 1969; *Miscellanea di Studi in Onore di Roberto Ridolfi,* Olschki, for British Musueum, 1973; *Miscellanea Marciana di Studi Bessarionei,* Editrice Antenore, 1976; *Studies in Late Medieval and Renaissance Painting in Honor of Millard Meiss,*

New York University Press, 1977; *Miscellanea di Studi in Memoria di Anna Saitta Revignas,* Olschki, 1978; *Atti del Primo Congresso di Studia della Miniatura Italiana,* Olschki, 1979. Contributor to *Dizionario Biografico degli Italiani* and *Victoria and Albert Museum Yearbook;* contributor of about sixty articles and reviews to journals, including *Commentari, Art Bulletin, Gazette des Beaux-Arts, Bibliofilia, Arte Veneta, Arte Lombarda,* and *Artibus Asiae.*

WORK IN PROGRESS: Venetian Illuminations in the Vatican, a monograph; *History of Venetian Book-illumination; History of Italian Illumination,* with Angela Daneu Lettanzi; *Florentine Book Illumination of the Renaissance.*

*   *   *

DANIEL, Norman (Alexander)   1919-

PERSONAL: Born May 8, 1919, in Manchester, England; son of Frederick George (a building inspector) and Winifred (a writer; maiden name, Jones) Daniel; married Marion Ruth Pethybridge (a teacher at time of marriage), August 23, 1941; children: David Richard Gerald Patrick (deceased). *Education:* Oxford University, B.A., 1940; University of Edinburgh, Ph.D., 1956. *Politics:* "Uncommitted." *Religion:* Roman Catholic. *Home:* Landmark, Flimwell, Wadhurst TN5 7PA, England; and 1, Sh. Masna at Tarabiche, Abbasiah, Cairo, Egypt.

CAREER: Civil Defence, St. Pancras, London, England, light rescue worker, 1941-44; Save the Children Fund, relief worker in Greece, 1944-45; British Council, London, assistant representative in Basra, Iraq, 1947-48, Baghdad, 1948-52, 1957-60, Beirut, Lebanon, 1952-53, Edinburgh, Scotland, 1953-57, 1960-62, and representative in Khartoum, Sudan, 1962-69; Cambridge University, University College, Cambridge, England, visiting fellow, 1969-70; British Council representative counselor and cultural attache at British Embassy in Cairo, Egypt, 1971-79; advisor to Hassan Khalifa group of companies, Cairo, 1979—. *Member:* Coptic Archeological Society (secretary-general). *Awards, honors:* Commander of Order of the British Empire; Egyptian Order of Merit, 1977.

WRITINGS: Islam and the West: The Making of an Image, Aldine, 1960, revised edition, 1966, reprinted, 1980; *Islam, Europe, and Empire,* Aldine, 1966; *The Arabs and Mediaeval Europe,* Longmans, Green, 1975, revised edition, 1979; *The Cultural Barrier,* Edinburgh University Press, 1975; (with others) *Islam: Past Influence and Present Challenge,* Edinburgh University Press, 1979. Contributor to learned journals.

WORK IN PROGRESS: A study of the attitude toward Islam in the chansons de geste.

SIDELIGHTS: Norman Daniel writes that he is primarily a medievalist, also interested in the application of remoter history to modern imperialist and post-imperialist history. He maintains a strong belief in the need for cultures to retain their differences. *Avocational interests:* Gardening.

*   *   *

DANILOV, Victor J(oseph)   1924-

PERSONAL: Born December 30, 1924, in Farrell, Pa.; son of Joseph M. and Ella (Tominovich) Danilov; married Toni Dewey, 1980; children: (previous marriage) Duane, Denise, Thomas. *Education:* Pennsylvania State University, B.A., 1945; Northwestern University, M.S., 1946; University of Colorado, Ed.D., 1964. *Home:* 219 East Lake Shore Dr., Chicago, Ill. 60611. *Office:* Museum of Science and Industry, 57th St. and Lake Shore Dr., Chicago, Ill. 60637.

CAREER: Worked for newspapers in Sharon, Pa., Youngstown, Ohio, and Pittsburgh, Pa., 1943-47; *Chicago Daily News,* Chicago, Ill., reporter, rewriteman, 1947-50; University of Colorado, Boulder, instructor in journalism, 1950-51; University of Kansas, Lawrence, assistant professor of journalism, 1951-53; *Star,* Kansas City, Mo., copyreader, 1953; Illinois Institute of Technology and Armour Research Foundation, Chicago, public relations manager, 1953-57; University of Colorado, director of public information and university relations, 1957-60; Profile Co., Boulder, Colo., president, 1960-62; *Industrial Research,* Beverly Shores, Ind., executive editor and executive vice-president, 1962-71; Museum of Science and Industry, Chicago, director and vice-president, 1971-77, director and president, 1978—.

WRITINGS: Public Affairs Reporting, Macmillan, 1955; (editor) *Crucial Issues in Public Relations,* Colorado Chapter of Public Relations Society of America, 1960; (editor) *Corporate Research and Profitability,* Industrial Research, 1966; (editor) *Innovation and Profitability,* Industrial Research, 1967; (editor) *Research Decision-Making in New Product Development,* Industrial Research, 1968; (editor) *New Products—and Profits,* Industrial Research, 1969; (editor) *Applying Emerging Technologies,* Industrial Research, 1970; (editor) *Nuclear Power in the South,* Southern Governors' Conference, 1970; (editor) *The Future of Science and Technology,* Museum of Science and Industry, 1975; (editor) *Museum Accounting Guidelines,* Association of Science-Technology Centers, 1976; *Starting a Science Center?,* Association of Science-Technology Centers, 1977; (editor) *Traveling Exhibitions,* Association of Science-Technology Centers, 1978; *Science and Technology Centers,* MIT Press, 1982. Contributor of more than one hundred articles to professional journals.

* * *

DARVILL, Fred T(homas), Jr. 1927-

PERSONAL: Born August 16, 1927, in Salt Lake City, Utah; son of Fred Thomas and Ruth (Scholes) Darvill; married Virginia Turner, 1976; children: (previous marriage) Fred Thomas III, Kari Duna. *Education:* University of Washington, Seattle, B.S. (magna cum laude), 1948, M.D. (with honors), 1951. *Office:* 809 South 15th, Mount Vernon, Wash. 98273.

CAREER: King County Hospital, Seattle, Wash., intern, 1951-52; Herman Kiefer Hospital, Detroit, Mich., resident, 1953; Veterans Administration Hospital, Seattle, resident, 1954-55, chief resident, 1955-56; physician in private practice in internal medicine in Mount Vernon, Wash., 1956—. Licensed to practice medicine in states of Washington, 1952, and California, 1965; diplomate of American Board of Internal Medicine, 1959. Member of hospital staff at Veterans Administration Hospital (Seattle), Skagit Valley Hospital (chief of staff, 1968), Swedish Hospital, and University Hospital (Seattle). Assistant in medicine at University of Washington (Seattle), 1954-56, associate, 1956-60, clinical instructor, 1960-69, clinical assistant professor, 1969—. Member of board of directors of North Cascade Conservation Council, 1961-67, Skagit Mountain Rescue Unit, 1964-66 (president, 1967), and Washington Environmental Council, 1972-74; president of Skagit Environmental Council, 1974.

MEMBER: American College of Physicians (fellow), American Society of Internal Medicine, American Federation for Clinical Research, Federation of Western Outdoor Clubs (Washington vice-president, 1964-66), Northwest Society for Clinical Research, Washington State Society of Internal Medicine (fellow), Washington State Heart Association, Washing-

ton Wilderness Society (president, 1969-70), Skagit County Medical Society, Skagit Alpine Club (founder and first president; vice-president, 1969), Phi Beta Kappa, Alpha Omega Alpha.

WRITINGS: (Contributor) James Wilkerson, editor, *Medicine for Mountaineering,* Seattle Mountaineers, 1967, 2nd edition, 1976; *Forty by Fred* (poems), privately printed, 1968; *A Pocket Guide to Selected Trails of the North Cascades National Park and Associated Recreational Complex,* privately printed, 1968; (with Louise B. Marshall) *Winter Hikes: A Pocket Guide to the Lowland Trails in Northwestern Washington,* privately printed, 1970; *A Pocket Guide to the North Cascades National Park and Associated Recreational Complex,* privately printed, 1970; (with Marshall) *Winter Walks: A Pocket Guide to Lowland Trails in Whatcom, Skagit, San Juan, and Island Counties,* Signpost, 1970; *Mountaineering Medicine* (booklet), Skagit Mountain Rescue Unit, 1965, 9th edition, 1980; *Darvill's Guide to the North Cascades National Park and Associated Areas,* Part I: *Western Section,* Part II: *Eastern Section,* privately printed, 1973; *North Cascades Highway Guide,* privately printed, 1973; *Stehekin: The Enchanted Valley,* Signpost, 1981; *Hiking the North Cascades,* Sierra Books, 1982. Also author of *Fifty More by Fred,* privately printed. Contributor to medical journals and mountaineering publications.

SIDELIGHTS: From 1956 to 1958, Fred T. Darvill coached his local Young Men's Christian Association (YMCA) swimming team. *Avocational interests:* Color photography, mountain climbing, travel.

* * *

DAS, Jagannath Prasad 1931-

PERSONAL: Born January 20, 1931, in Puri, Orissa, India; son of Biswanath (in postal service) and Nilomoni (Mohanty) Das; married Gita Dasmohapatra (a psychologist), 1955; children: Satya, Sheela. *Education:* Utkal University, B.A. (with honors), 1951; Patna University, M.A., 1953; University of London, Ph.D., 1957. *Religion:* Hindu. *Home:* 11724—38A Ave., Edmonton, Alberta, Canada. *Office:* Centre for the Study of Mental Retardation, University of Alberta, Edmonton, Alberta, Canada T6G 2E1.

CAREER: Utkal University, Rhubaneswar, India, lecturer, 1953-55, reader in psychology, 1958-63; George Peabody College for Teachers (now George Peabody College for Teachers of Vanderbilt University), Nashville, Tenn., Kennedy Foundation Professor of Psychology, 1963-64; University of California, Los Angeles, associate professor of psychology, 1964-65; Utkal University, reader in psychology, 1965-67; University of Alberta, Centre for the Study of Mental Retardation, Edmonton, Alberta, research professor, 1968-71, director, 1972—. *Member:* Canadian Psychological Association (fellow), American Psychological Association (fellow), American Association for the Advancement of Science. *Awards, honors:* Nuffield Foundation fellow at Institute of Psychiatry, University of London, 1972; Harris Award, International Reading Association, 1979.

WRITINGS: Verbal Conditioning and Behavior, Pergamon, 1969; *Asustha Mana* (title means "Mental Illness"), Orissa Textbook Bureau, 1974; (editor with D. Baine) *Mental Retardation for Special Educators,* C. C Thomas, 1978; (with J. Kirby and R. Jarman) *Simultaneous and Successive Cognitive Processes,* Academic Press, 1979; (editor with Jarman) *Issues in Developmental Disabilities,* University Microfilms, 1980; (editor with M. Friedman and N. O'Connor) *Intelligence and Learning,* Plenum, 1981; (editor with R. Mulcahy and A. E.

Wall) *Theory and Research in Learning Disabilities*, Plenum, 1982. Contributor to *International Review of Research in Mental Retardation*, Volumes III, VI, VIII, edited by N. R. Ellis, published by Academic Press. Contributor of over 100 articles to *Journal of Experimental Psychology, British Journal of Psychology*, and other professional journals. Founding editor, *Indian Journal of Mental Retardation*, 1967-68.

WORK IN PROGRESS: Longitudinal project on reading disability.

*   *   *

DAUW, Dean C(harles) 1933-

PERSONAL: Surname is pronounced Dow; born July 31, 1933, in Rock Island, Ill.; son of Charles J. and Frances (Heffran) Dauw; married Nancy Rettinger, December 16, 1967 (divorced April 1, 1975). *Education:* Spring Hill College, B.S., 1960; St. Thomas College, M.A., 1961; University of Minnesota, Ph.D., 1965. *Home:* 1212 Lake Shore Dr., Chicago, Ill. 60610. *Agent:* Dominick Abel Literary Agency, 498 West End Ave., New York, N.Y. 10024. *Office:* Human Resource Developers, Inc., 112 West Oak St., Chicago, Ill. 60610.

CAREER: Human Resource Developers, Inc., Chicago, Ill., president, 1968—; DePaul University, Chicago, professor of management, 1969—. Consulting psychologist. Director of Three C's Medical Center and six companies. *Member:* International Psychoanalytical Association, American Psychological Association, Association for Humanistic Psychology, American Personnel and Guidance Association, National Vocational Guidance Association, American Association of Sex Educators, Counselors, and Therapists, Society for the Scientific Study of Sex, American Association of University Professors, Industrial Psychologists Association (former president).

WRITINGS: (With A. J. Fredian) *Dynamics of Black Employee Relations*, Simon & Schuster, 1971; *Creativity and Innovation in Organizations*, Kendall/Hunt, 1971, 4th edition, Waveland, 1980; *Up Your Career*, Waveland, 1975, 3rd edition, 1980; *Stranger in Your Bed*, Nelson-Hall, 1979; *Increasing Your Self-Esteem*, Waveland, 1980. Contributor to journals and periodicals, including *Washington Post, Gifted Child Quarterly, Insight, Religious Education, Personnel, Hospital Topics, Management Review, Business World*, and *Journal of Creative Behavior*.

*   *   *

DAVID, Henry P. 1923-

PERSONAL: Born May 28, 1923, in Germany; now U.S. citizen; son of Ferdinand (a lawyer) and Ilse David; married Tema Seidman, March 28, 1953; children: Jonathan V., Gail Ann. *Education:* University of Cincinnati, B.A. (with high honors in psychology), 1948, M.A., 1949; Columbia University, Ph.D., 1951. *Office:* Transnational Family Research Institute, 8307 Whitman Dr., Bethesda, Md. 20034.

CAREER: Diplomate in clinical psychology, American Board of Examiners in Professional Psychology, 1956. Topeka State Hospital, Topeka, Kan., senior clinical psychologist, 1951-52; Western Psychiatric Institute, University of Pittsburgh School of Medicine, Pittsburgh, Pa., instructor in psychology, 1952-55; Wayne State University, Detroit, Mich., assistant professor of psychology and head of division of psychology at Lafayette Clinic, 1955-56; New Jersey State Department of Institutions and Agencies, Trenton, chief psychologist and psychology consultant, 1956-63; World Federation for Mental Health, Geneva,

Switzerland, associate director, 1963-65; American Institutes for Research, Silver Spring, Md., associate director of International Research Institute, 1966-70; director of Transnational Family Research Institute, 1971—. Adjunct lecturer, Rutgers University, 1960-63; lecturer, Princeton University, 1962; associate clinical professor of psychology in department of psychiatry, University of Maryland School of Medicine, 1970—. Research advisor, Preterm Institute, 1971—. Secretary-treasurer, New Jersey Mental Health Research and Development Fund, 1958-63. Occasional consultant to American Psychiatric Association, 1971—; consultant to World Health Organization, 1971—, and Institute of Social Medicine, Copenhagen, 1977—. *Military service:* U.S. Army Air Forces, 1943-46.

MEMBER: International Council of Psychologists (president, 1967-71), International Association of Applied Psychology, International Union for Scientific Study of Population, International Association for Cross-Cultural Psychology, World Federation for Mental Health (member of executive board, 1968-73), Society for International Development, National Council on Family Relations, Inter-American Society for Psychology, American Psychological Association (fellow), American Public Health Association, American Association for the Advancement of Science, Population Association of America, Society for Projective Techniques, District of Columbia Psychological Association, Maryland Psychological Association, Phi Beta Kappa, Sigma Xi.

AWARDS, HONORS: Ford Foundation travel grant to western Europe and Israel, 1957; Social Science Research Council travel grants to western Europe and South Africa, 1961; Human Ecology Fund grant for projects on international resources in clinical psychology and international trends in mental health, 1962; Harold M. Hildreth Memorial Award, American Psychological Association, 1974, for distinguished public service.

WRITINGS: Family Planning and Abortion in the Socialist Countries of Central and Eastern Europe, Population Council (New York), 1970; (with Siegfried Katsch) *Sousa, verheissenes Land*, Sozial Forschungsstelle, University of Muenster, 1970; *Child Mental Health in International Perspective*, Harper, 1972; (with others) *Abortion in Psychosocial Perspective: Trends in Transnational Research*, Springer Publishing Co., 1978; (with R. J. McIntyre) *Reproductive Behavior: Central and Eastern European Experience*, Springer Publishing Co., in press.

Editor: (With H. von Braclaen) *Perspectives in Personality Theory*, Basic Books, 1956; (with J. C. Brengelmann) *Perspectives in Personality Research*, Springer Publishing Co., 1960; *International Resources in Clinical Psychology*, McGraw, 1964; (with Leonard Blank) *Sourcebook for Training in Clinical Psychology*, Springer Publishing Co., 1964; *Population and Mental Health*, Springer Publishing Co., 1964; *International Trends in Mental Health*, McGraw, 1966; *Migration, Mental Health, and Community Services*, Joint Distribution Committee (Geneva), 1968; *Abortion Research: International Experience*, Lexington Books, 1974.

Contributor: L. Miller, editor, *Mental Health in Rapid Changing Society*, Jerusalem Academic Press, 1971; C. F. Westoff and R. Parke, Jr., editors, *Demographic and Social Aspects of Population Growth*, U.S. Government Printing Office, 1972; J. T. Fawcett, editor, *Psychological Perspectives on Population*, Basic Books, 1973; H. J. Osofsky and J. D. Osofsky, editors, *The Abortion Experience: Psychological and Medical Impact*, Harper, 1973; P. A. van Keep and P. Freebody, editors, *The Menstrual Cycles and Menses Regulation*, International Health Foundation (Geneva), 1973; H. J. Osofsky and J. D. Osofsky, editors, *Abortion Experience in the United States*, Harper, 1973; *Epidemiology of Abortion and Fertility-*

Regulating Practices in Latin America: Selected Reports, Pan American Health Organization, 1975; S. H. Newman and V. D. Thompson, editors, *Population Psychology: Research and Educational Issues,* Center for Population Research, 1976.

B. B. Wolman, editor, *International Encyclopedia of Psychiatry, Psychology, Psychoanalysis, and Neurology,* Volume VI, Aesculapius Publishers, 1977; Y. H. Poortinga, editor, *Basic Problems in Cross-Cultural Psychology,* Swets & Zeitlinger (Amsterdam), 1977; J. Money and H. Musaph, *Textbook of Sexology,* Excerpta Medica/Elsevier (Amsterdam), 1977; S. H. Newman and Z. E. Klein, editors, *Behavioral-Social Aspects of Contraceptive Sterilization,* Lexington Books, 1978; P. Ahmed and C. Coelho, editors, *Toward a New Definition of Health: Psychosocial Dimensions,* Plenum, 1979.

L. A. Bond and J. C. Rosen, editors, *Competence and Coping during Adulthood,* University Press of New England, 1980; J. T. Burtchaell, editor, *Abortion Parley,* Andrews & McMeel, 1980; Ahmed, editor, *Coping with Medical Issues: Pregnancy, Children, and Parenthood,* Elsevier-North Holland, in press; G. S. Berger, W. E. Brenner, and L. Keith, editors, *Second Trimester Abortion: Perspectives after a Decade of Experience,* PSG Publishing, in press; J. E. Hodgson, editor, *Techniques of Abortion and Sterilization,* Academic Press, in press; P. Sachdev, editor, *Abortion in Canada: A Sourcebook,* Butterworth, in press; J. J. Sciarra, editor, *Gynecology and Obstetrics,* Volume VI, Harper, in press.

Also editor of and contributor to proceedings. Contributor of articles to professional journals, including *Family Planning Perspectives, Studies in Family Planning, American Journal of Orthopsychiatry, Journal of Biosocial Science, Preventive Medicine,* and *Academic Psychology Bulletin.* Consultant to *Contemporary Psychology,* 1963—, *Journal of Psychiatric Nursing,* 1966-78, *Community Mental Health Journal,* 1966-80, *Studies in Family Planning,* 1977—, and *Population,* 1977—.

*   *   *

DAVIDSON, Paul   1930-

PERSONAL: Born October 23, 1930, in Brooklyn, N.Y.; son of Charles and Lillian (Janow) Davidson; married Louise Tattenbaum, 1952; children: Robert Alan, Diane Carol, Greg Stuart. *Education:* Brooklyn College (now Brooklyn College of the City University of New York), B.S., 1950; City College (now City College of the City University of New York), M.B.A., 1955; University of Pennsylvania, Ph.D., 1959. *Home:* 18 Turner Ct., Princeton, N.J. 08540. *Office:* Department of Economics, Rutgers University, New Brunswick, N.J. 08903.

CAREER: University of Pennsylvania, Philadelphia, instructor in physiological chemistry, 1951-52, instructor in economics, 1955-58; Rutgers University, New Brunswick, N.J., assistant professor of economics, 1958-60; Continental Oil Co., Houston, Tex., assistant director of Economics Division, 1960-61; University of Pennsylvania, assistant professor, 1961-63, associate professor of economics, 1963-66; Rutgers University, professor of economics, 1966—, associate director of Bureau of Economic Research, 1966-75, chairman of New Brunswick Department of Economics and Allied Sciences and director of Bureau of Economic Research, 1975-78. Visiting lecturer, University of Bristol, 1964-65; senior visiting lecturer, Cambridge University, 1970-71; George Miller Distinguished Lecturer, University of Illinois, 1972; Bernardin Distinguished Visiting Lecturer, University of Missouri, 1979; visiting professor, Institute for Advanced Studies, Vienna, 1980. Member, Brookings Economic Panel, 1974; senior visitor, Bank of England,

1979. Participant in government conferences and witness before numerous Congressional committees. Consultant, Resources for the Future, 1964-66, Ford Foundation energy policy project, 1973, International Communications Agency, U.S. Department of State, 1980, and to numerous public and private organizations, including Western Union, Federal Trade Commission, and the State of Alabama; member of national board of advisors, Public Interest Economics Center, 1972—. *Military service:* U.S. Army, 1953-55. *Member:* American Economic Association, Econometric Society, National Association of Business Economists, Royal Economic Society, Epsilon Phi Alpha. *Awards, honors:* Fulbright fellow, 1964-65; Rutgers faculty research fellow, 1970-71; Lindbeck Award for Research, 1975.

WRITINGS: Theories of Aggregate Income Distribution, Rutgers University Press, 1960; (with Eugene Smolensky) *Aggregate Supply and Demand Analysis,* Harper, 1964; (with C. J. Chiccetti and J. J. Seneca) *The Demand and Supply of Outdoor Recreation: An Econometric Study,* Bureau of Economic Research, Rutgers University, 1968; *Money and the Real World,* Macmillan, 1972, 2nd edition, 1978; (with Milton Friedman and others) *Milton Friedman's Monetary Theory: A Debate with His Critics,* University of Chicago Press, 1974; *International Money and the Real World,* Macmillan, 1981.

Contributor: (With F. G. Adams and Seneca) A. V. Kneese and S. C. Smith, editors, *Water Research,* Johns Hopkins Press, 1966; M. G. Garnsney and J. Hibbs, editors, *Social Sciences and the Environment,* University of Colorado Press, 1968; A. Utton, editor, *Towards a National Petroleum Policy,* University of New Mexico Press, 1970; D. R. Croome and H. G. Johnson, editors, *Money in Britain, 1959-1969,* Oxford University Press, 1970; R. Dorfman and N. S. Dorfman, editors, *Economics of the Environment,* Norton, 1972; G. M. Brannon, editor, *Studies in Energy Tax Policy,* Ballinger, 1975; S. Weintraub, editor, *Modern Economic Thought,* University of Pennsylvania Press, 1977; G. Harcourt, editor, *Microfoundations of Macroeconomics,* Cambridge University Press, 1977; V. L. Smith, editor, *Economics of Natural and Environmental Resources,* Gordon & Breach, 1977; D. J. Teece, editor, *R & D in Energy: Implications of Petroleum Industry Reorganization,* Institute for Energy Studies (Stanford, Calif.), 1977; Vicens-Vives, editor, *Desquilibrio, Inflacion y Desempleo,* [Madrid], 1978; (with J. A. Kregal) E. J. Nell, editor, *Growth, Property, and Profits,* Cambridge University Press, 1980; *Stagflation: The Causes, Effects and Solutions,* Joint Economic Committee (Washington, D.C.), 1980. Contributor to economic and public finance journals. Editor, *Journal of Post Keynesian Economics;* member of editorial board, *Energy Journal.*

*   *   *

DAVIES, Thomas M(ockett), Jr.   1940-

PERSONAL: Born May 25, 1940, in Lincoln, Neb.; son of Thomas Mockett (a lawyer) and Faith (Arnold) Davies; married Eloisa Carmela Monzon, June 10, 1968; children: Jennifer Elena. *Education:* University of Nebraska, B.A., 1962, M.A., 1964; University of New Mexico, Ph.D., 1966; also attended Universidad Nacional Autonoma de Mexico, 1961. *Home:* 4617 Edenvale Ave., La Mesa, Calif. 92041. *Office:* Department of History, San Diego State University, San Diego, Calif. 92182.

CAREER: San Diego State University, San Diego, Calif., assistant professor, 1968-72, associate professor, 1972-75, professor of Latin American, Andean, and American history, 1975—, director of Center for Latin American Studies, 1979—, chairman of Latin American studies, 1981-84. Has conducted research in U.S. National Archives and in Peru and Bolivia. Editorial consultant to Longman-Green Publishing House, London, and University of Nebraska Press. Consultant to National Endowment for the Humanities and Canadian Council for the Social Sciences.

MEMBER: Latin American Studies Association, Organization of American Historians, American Historical Association (member of Conference on Latin American History), Organization of Andean Historians, Pacific Coast Council on Latin American Studies, Rocky Mountain Council on Latin American Studies, Baja California-San Diego County Organization of Latin Americanists (president, 1978-79).

AWARDS, HONORS: Fellowship from Henry L. and Grace Doherty Foundation, 1966-68, for research in Peru; postdoctoral fellowship from University of Texas, 1969-70; Hubert Herring Memorial Award from Pacific Coast Council on Latin American Studies, 1973, for a manuscript on Latin America; summer research grants, San Diego State University, 1971-73, 1975, 1980, 1981; Outstanding Faculty award from San Diego State University Alumni and Associates, 1981; grant from National Endowment for the Humanities.

WRITINGS: Indian Integration in Peru: A Half Century of Experience, 1900-1948, University of Nebraska Press, 1974; (contributor) John J. TePaske, editor, *Field Research Guide to the Andean Area,* Duke University Press, 1975; (with Brian Loveman) *The Politics of Anti-Politics: The Military in Latin America,* University of Nebraska Press, 1978; (with Victor Villanueva) *300 documentos para la historia del APRA: Conspiraciones apristas de 1935 a 1939,* Editorial Horizonte (Lima), 1979; (contributor) Franklin Pease G.T., editor, *Homenaje a Jorge Basadre,* Editorial P.L. (Lima), 1979; (with Villanueva) *Los elecciones de 1939: Una historia documental,* Editorial Horizonte, in press; (contributor) Mark Falcoff and Fredrick B. Pike, editors, *The Spanish Civil War: American Hemisphere Perspectives,* University of Nebraska Press, in press. Contributor of articles and reviews to journals, including *New Mexico Historical Review, Choice, American Historical Review, American Anthropologist, New Scholar,* and *The Americas.* Member of editorial advisory board of *New Scholar.* Editorial consultant for Latin American Monograph series of University of Texas Press; editorial consultant for *Hispanic American Historical Review, Societas, Journal of Developing Areas,* and *The Americas.*

WORK IN PROGRESS: The Decade of Violence: A Socio-Political History of Peru in the 1930s; A History of the Peruvian Military.

AVOCATIONAL INTERESTS: Latin American travel, playing stringed instruments, American folk music.

*   *   *

DAVIS, Creath   1939-

PERSONAL: Born November 13, 1939, in Comanche, Tex.; son of Vernon (a telephone lineman and dairyman) and Treva (Johnston) Davis; married Verdell Watson (a teacher and consultant on learning disabilities in children), February 26, 1960; children: David Creath, Shawna Lee, Stephen Mark. *Education:* Howard Payne University, B.A., 1962, graduate study, 1962-65; Southwestern Baptist Theological Seminary, M.Div., 1968; Parkland Hospital, Dallas, Tex., chaplain training, 1968. *Residence:* Dallas, Tex. *Office address:* Christian Concern Foundation, P.O. Box 8049, Dallas, Tex. 75205.

CAREER: Ordained Baptist minister, 1958; minister in Gorman, Tex., 1958-61, and Deleon, Tex., 1961-66; Christian

Concern Foundation, Dallas, Tex., founder, 1965, executive director, 1965—. Personal, marriage and family counselor, 1965—; developed retreat and conference ministry, 1969—, and spiritual growth group materials for small group participants, 1970—; clinical work with the American Association of Marriage and Family Therapists, 1973-76; chaplain of Slaughter Industries, 1973-79. Leader of a World Civilization study tour of Western Europe, the Middle East and Far East during the summer of 1968; teacher of Psycho Cybernetics, 1971-73.

WRITINGS: Beyond This God Cannot Go, Zondervan, 1971, revised edition, Ronald Haynes, 1981; *Sent to Be Vulnerable,* Zondervan, 1973; *How to Win in a Crisis,* Zondervan, 1976; *Lord, If I Ever Needed You, It's Now!,* Ronald Haynes, 1981.

AVOCATIONAL INTERESTS: Ranching, raising wheat, oil and gas exploration.

*   *   *

DAVIS, Curtis Carroll   1916-

PERSONAL: Born February 18, 1916, in Baltimore, Md.; son of Hoagland Cook (a medical doctor) and Katharine (Carroll) Davis; married G. Margarete Wenderoth, October 11, 1969. *Education:* Yale University, A.B., 1938; Columbia University, M.A., 1939; Duke University, Ph.D., 1947. *Politics:* Independent. *Religion:* Roman Catholic. *Home and office:* 16-R, The Carlyle, 500 West University Parkway, Baltimore, Md. 21210.

CAREER: U.S. Central Intelligence Agency, Washington, D.C., desk chief, 1947-49. Free-lance writer. Star-Spangled Banner Flag House Association, Baltimore, Md., member of directorate, 1962—. *Military service:* U.S. Army Air Corps, 1942-46; became captain; received Bronze Star and Presidential Unit Citation. U.S. Army Reserve, Intelligence, 1946-76; now lieutenant colonel (retired). *Member:* American Association of State and Local History, American Historical Association, United States Commission on Military History, Authors Guild, Authors League of America, National Book Critics Circle, Maryland Historical Society (life member; library committee, member, 1965—, chairman, 1973-77), Society for the Preservation of Maryland Antiquities, North Carolina Historical and Literary Association, Virginia Historical Society, Baltimore Bibliophiles, St. George's Society of Baltimore (life member), Manuscript Society, Edgar Allan Poe Society (member of executive committee), Association of Former Intelligence Officers (life member), Council on Abandoned Military Posts, Reserve Officers Association (life member), Circumnavigators Club. *Awards, honors:* Awarded Sterling Trophy by North Carolina Society of the Cincinnati, for *Revolution's Godchild: The Birth, Death, and Regeneration of the Society of the Cincinnati in North Carolina.*

WRITINGS: Chronicler of the Cavaliers: A Life of the Virginia Novelist, Dr. William A. Caruthers, Dietz, 1953; *The King's Chevalier: A Biography of Lewis Littlepage,* Bobbs-Merrill, 1961; (editor) John S. Wise, *The End of an Era,* Thomas Yoseloff, 1965; (editor) *Belle Boyd in Camp and Prison,* revised edition, A. S. Barnes, 1968; (contributor) Louis D. Rubin, Jr., editor, *A Bibliographical Guide to the Study of Southern Literature,* Louisiana State University Press, 1969; (editor) William A. Caruthers, *The Knights of the Golden Horse-Shoe,* revised edition, University of North Carolina Press, 1970; *That Ambitious Mr. Legare: The Life of James M. Legare of South Carolina, Including a Collected Edition of His Verse,* University of South Carolina Press, 1971; (contributor) James S. Presgraves, editor, *Wythe County Chapters,* privately printed,

1972; *Revolution's Godchild: The Birth, Death, and Regeneration of the Society of the Cincinnati in North Carolina,* University of North Carolina Press, 1976.

Contributor to *Proceedings of the American Philosophical Society.* Contributor to *Biographical Dictionary of Southern Literature, Concise Dictionary of American Biography, Dictionary of North Carolina Biography, New-York Historical Society's Dictionary of Artists in America, Dictionary of Literary Biography,* and *World Book Encyclopedia.* Contributor of more than sixty articles on historical topics to periodicals, including *American Heritage, Virginia Cavalcade, William & Mary Quarterly,* and *Civil War History.* Editor, annual brochure, "Society of the War of 1812 in the State of Maryland"; member of editorial board, *Maryland Historical Magazine.*

WORK IN PROGRESS: Damsels of Derring-Do, an anthology of earliest writings by or about women in the American Revolution who performed such non-traditional services as espionage, informing, courier work, soldiering in the field; a biography of William P. Wood, first chief of the secret service.

AVOCATIONAL INTERESTS: Collecting rare beer mugs and military miniatures, travel (has gone "'round the world").

BIOGRAPHICAL/CRITICAL SOURCES: News & Courier (Charleston, S.C.), June 6, 1971; *Baltimore Sun,* January 15, 1979.

* * *

DAVIS, Donald Gordon, Jr. 1939-

PERSONAL: Born August 15, 1939, in San Marcos, Tex.; son of Donald Gordon (a clergyman) and Ethel (Henning) Davis; married Avis Jane Higdon, December 6, 1969; children: Lucinda Ellen, Samuel Higdon, Caroline Louise. *Education:* University of California, Los Angeles, B.A., 1961; University of California, Berkeley, M.A., 1963, M.L.S., 1964; University of Illinois, Ph.D., 1972. *Politics:* "Reform, regardless of party." *Religion:* Presbyterian. *Home:* 3900 Avenue C, Austin, Tex. 78751. *Office:* Graduate School of Library and Information Science, University of Texas, P.O. Box 7576, Austin, Tex. 78712.

CAREER: Fresno State College (now California State University, Fresno), senior reference librarian, 1964-68, head of department of special collections, 1966-68, instructor in library resources, 1967-68; University of Texas at Austin, Graduate School of Library Science, assistant professor, 1971-77, associate professor of library science, 1977—. Part-time senior library assistant, University of California, Berkeley, 1961-64; member of board, Fresno Community Chorus, 1966-68. Visiting principal lecturer, Birmingham Polytechnic, England, 1980-81. *Member:* American Library Association, American Historical Association, American Scientific Affiliation, Association of American Library Schools, Association for the Bibliography of History, Association of Christian Librarians, Hymn Society of America, Conference on Faith and History, Organization of American Historians, Texas Library Association, Texas Association of College Teachers, Beta Phi Mu. *Awards, honors:* Newberry Library fellowship, 1974.

WRITINGS: The American Medical Association and the American Library Association: A Study of Developing Organizational Structure, Graduate School of Library Science, University of Illinois, 1972; *The Association of American Library Schools, 1915-1968: An Analytical History,* Scarecrow, 1974; *Comparative Historical Analysis of Three Associations of Professional Schools,* Graduate School of Library Science, University of Illinois, 1974; (with R. E. Stevens) *Reference*

Books in the Social Sciences and Humanities, Stipes Publishing, 1977; (with M. H. Harris) *American Library History: A Bibliography,* University of Texas Press, 1978; (editor) *Libraries and Culture: Proceedings of Library History Seminar VI,* University of Texas Press, 1981. Abstractor, *Historical Abstracts and America: History and Life,* 1965—; regular reviewer, *American Reference Books Annual, Booklist, Choice,* and *HIS;* referee, *Journal of Library History.* Member of advisory board, *American History and Life,* 1979—, and *Dictionary of American Library Biography* supplements, 1980—.

WORK IN PROGRESS: The Austin Lyceum, with Louise Jarrell.

AVOCATIONAL INTERESTS: Working with Inter-Varsity Christian Fellowship, serious choral music, collecting private press fine printing, visiting local historical and landmark sites, handball, backpacking, bicycling.

* * *

DAVIS, R(alph) H(enry) C(arless) 1918-

PERSONAL: Born October 7, 1918, in Oxford, England; son of Henry William Carless (a historian) and Rosa Jennie (Lindup) Davis; married Eleanor Maud Megaw, November 19, 1949; children: Christopher, Timothy. *Education:* Balliol College, Oxford, B.A., 1945, M.A., 1947. *Religion:* Church of England. *Home:* 56 Fitzroy Ave., Birmingham 17, England. *Office:* University of Birmingham, Birmingham 15, England.

CAREER: Christ's Hospital, Horsham, England, assistant master, 1947-48; University College, London, England, lecturer, 1948-56; Merton College, Oxford, England, fellow and tutor, 1956-70; University of Birmingham, Birmingham, England, professor of medieval history and head of department, 1970—. *Military service:* Friends Ambulance Unit, 1939-45. *Member:* Society of Antiquaries (fellow), Historical Association (member of council, 1952-61; president, 1979-82), Royal Historical Society (fellow; member of council, 1957-60, 1964-66).

WRITINGS: The Mosques of Cairo, Eady, 1943; *The Kalendar of Abbot Samson of Bury St. Edmunds,* Royal Historical Society, 1954; *A History of Medieval Europe,* Longmans, Green, 1957; *King Stephen,* University of California Press, 1967; (editor with H. A. Cronne) *Regesta Regum Anglo-Normannoram,* Oxford University Press, Volume III, 1968; *The Normans and Their Myths,* Thames & Hudson, 1976; (editor with J. M. Wallace-Hadrill) *The Writing of History in the Middle Ages: Essays Presented to R. W. Southern,* Clarendon Press, 1981. Contributor of articles to professional journals. Assistant editor, *History,* 1957-62, editor, 1968-79.

* * *

DAVIS, Roy Eugene 1931-

PERSONAL: Born March 9, 1931, in Levittsburg, Ohio; son of DeWitt Talmage (a farmer and trucker) and Eva Lee (Carter) Davis; married Patricia A. Neeley, November 15, 1959; married second wife, Carolyn Crosby, June, 1965; children: (first marriage) Jeannette Frances, Clark Edward. *Education:* Attended schools in Ohio. *Politics:* Republican. *Religion:* New Thought. *Residence:* St. Petersburg, Fla.

CAREER: Minister of Self-Realization Fellowship Church, Phoenix, Ariz., 1952-53; ordained minister of Divine Science Church, 1960; currently guest lecturer and teacher for Unity, Science of Mind, and other groups in the United States, Japan, and Canada. *Military service:* U.S. Army, 1953-55.

WRITINGS—Published by CSA Press, except as indicated: *Time, Space, and Circumstance,* privately printed, 1960, revised edition, Fell, 1973; *How You Can Use the Technique of Creative Imagination,* privately printed, 1961, revised edition, CSA Press, 1974; *Secrets of Inner Power,* Fell, 1964; *This Is Reality,* 1967, 2nd edition, 1970; *The Hidden Teachings of Jesus Revealed: A Mystical Explanation of the Teachings of Jesus Based on the Gospel According to St. John,* 1968; *Studies in Truth,* 1969; *God's Revealing Word,* 1969.

The Way of the Initiate, 1970; *Miracle Man of Japan: The Life and Work of Masaharu Taniguchi,* 1970; *Finding Your Place in Life,* 1971; *How to Have a Personal Experience with God,* 1971; *Reincarnation and Your Life,* 1971; *Sex and the Spiritual Life,* 1971; *Third Eye,* 1971; *Darshan: The Vision of Light,* 1971; *Success through Superconscious Power,* two volumes, 1971; *The Bhagavad-Gita,* 1972; *Reincarnation and Your Destiny,* 1972; (editor) Sathya Sai Baba, *The Teachings of Sri Satya Baba,* Book Center (Tustin, Calif.), 1974.

The Path of Soul Liberation, 1975; *Yoga Darsana: The Philosophy and Light of Yoga,* 1976; *Health, Healing, and Total Living,* 1977; *Conscious Immortality,* 1978; *An Easy Guide to Meditation,* 1978; *With God We Can!,* 1978; *The Teachings of the Masters of Perfection,* 1979; *Freedom Is New,* 1980. Contributor of articles to religion and metaphysics journals.†

*   *   *

DAWSON, Christopher (Henry) 1889-1970

PERSONAL: Born October 12, 1889, in Hay Castle, Wales; died May 25, 1970, in Budleigh Salterton, England; son of Henry Philip and Mary (Bevan) Dawson; married Valery Mills, 1916; children: Juliana, Christina (Mrs. Rivers Scott), Philip. *Education:* Trinity College, Oxford, B.A., M.A. *Home and office:* Fountain Hill House, Budleigh Salterton, Devonshire, England.

CAREER: University College, Exeter, England, lecturer in history of culture, 1926-33; University of Liverpool, Liverpool, England, Forwood Lecturer in the Philosophy of Religion, 1934; University of Edinburgh, Edinburgh, Scotland, Gifford Lecturer, 1947, 1948; Harvard University, Cambridge, Mass., Stillman Chair of Roman Catholic Studies, 1958-62. *Member:* British Academy (fellow).

WRITINGS—All published by Sheed, except as indicated: *The Age of the Gods,* Murray, 1928, reprinted, F. Hertig, 1970; *Progress and Religion,* 1929, reprinted, Greenwood, 1970; *Christianity and Sex,* Faber, 1930; *Christianity and the New Age,* 1931; *The Modern Dilemma,* 1932; *The Making of Europe,* 1932, reprinted, World Publishing, 1970; *The Spirit of the Oxford Movement,* 1933, reprinted, AMS Press, 1976; *Enquiries into Religion and Culture,* 1933, reprinted, Books for Libraries, 1968; *Medieval Religion,* 1934; *Edward Gibbon,* Oxford University Press, 1934; *Religion and the Modern State,* 1935, reprinted, Norwood, 1977; *Beyond Politics,* 1939, reprinted, Books for Libraries, 1970; *The Judgement of the Nations,* 1942, reprinted, Norwood, 1977; (with Malcolm Spencer) *Democracy and Peace,* National Peace Council, 1946; *Religion and Culture,* 1948, reprinted, AMS Press, 1978; *Religion and the Rise of Western Culture,* 1950, reprinted, AMS Press, 1978; *Understanding Europe,* 1952; *Medieval Essays* (including six essays published as *Medieval Religion*), 1953; (contributor) Phillip Caraman, editor, *Saints and Ourselves,* Hollis & Carter, 1955; (editor) *Mongol Mission,* 1955, published as *Mission to Asia,* Harper, 1966; *Dynamics of World History,* edited by John L. Mulloy, 1957; *Movement of World Revolution,* 1959; *The Historic Reality of Christian Culture,*

Harper, 1960, reprinted, Greenwood, 1976; *The Crisis of Western Education,* 1961; *The Dividing of Christendom,* 1965; *The Formation of Christendom,* 1967; *The Gods of Revolution,* introduction by Arnold Toynbee, New York University Press, 1972; *Religion and World History: A Selection from the Works of Christopher Dawson,* edited by James Oliver and Christina Scott, Image Books, 1975. Contributor of articles to British periodicals and to *Commonweal.*

SIDELIGHTS: Commonweal reviewer William Storey writes that Christopher Dawson may be saved from the "debilitating fate" of datedness and irrelevance "by the quality of his historical research, the craft of his writing and the durability of his central thesis as to the make-up of European history and culture."

BIOGRAPHICAL/CRITICAL SOURCES: Bruno Schlesinger, *Christopher Dawson and the Modern Political Crisis,* University of Notre Dame Library, 1949; *Commonweal,* September 8, 1967.

OBITUARIES: Christian Century, June 10, 1970.†

*   *   *

DAYTON, Irene 1922-

PERSONAL: Born August 6, 1922, in Lake Ariel, Pa.; daughter of F. B. and Effie (Wargo) Glossenger; married Benjamin B. Dayton (a physicist), October 16, 1943; children: David B., Glenn C. *Education:* Roberts Wesleyan College, A.A., 1942. *Politics:* Republican. *Religion:* Protestant. *Home:* Pine Stone, 209 South Hillandale Dr., East Flat Rock, N.C. 28726.

CAREER: Poet. Blue Ridge Technical College, Flat Rock, N.C., instructor in poetry and creative writing, 1978—. Poet-in-residence in high school and college. *Member:* International Academy of Poets (fellow), Poetry Society of America, North Carolina Poetry Society, Rochester Poetry Society (honorary member; president, 1960-62, 1970-72), Marquis Library Society.

AWARDS, HONORS: Finalist in Yale Series of Younger Poets, 1958; first prize, Rochester Festival of Religious Arts, 1959 and 1960; Poetry Guinness Award, Festival of Literature, Cheltenham, England, 1963; honorable mention, Sandburg Contest, 1974; Distinguished Submissions award, Dellbrook Writer's Conference, 1979.

WRITINGS—Poetry; all published by Windy Row Press: *The Sixth Sense Quivers,* 1970; *The Panther's Eye,* 1974; *Seven Times the Wind,* 1977; *In Ox Bow of Time's River,* 1978.

Poems anthologized in *Golden Year Anthology,* edited by Melville Care, John Farrar, and Louise Nicholl, Poetry Society of America, 1960; *Editions Moderne Review,* edited by Jacques Cardonnet, [Paris], 1962, 1964; *The Various Light,* edited by Leah B. Drake and Charles Muses, [Switzerland], 1964; *The Diamond Anthology,* edited by Charles Angoff and others, Poetry Society of America, 1971; *Adam among the Television Trees,* edited by Virginia Mollenkot, Word Books, 1971; *The Writer's Choice: Poetry and Fiction by North Carolina Authors,* Trans Verse Press, 1981; *North Carolina Poetry Society Anthology,* San Ragan Press, 1981; *Parthenon Poetry Anthology,* edited by Angelo Schmuller, Parthenon, 1982. Contributor to numerous poetry journals and literary magazines, including *Poetry-Australia, Literary Review, St. Andrew's Review, South and West, Poet Lore,* and *Roanoke Review.* Editor of *Rochester Poetry Society Anthology,* 1958-59 and 1969-70.

WORK IN PROGRESS: Tale of the Vercors, an epic drama of the French Resistance in novel form.

SIDELIGHTS: Irene Dayton told *CA:* "I am a working poet writing in free verse cadence who truly believes a poet must stay in the stream of life trying to understand the joys and sufferings of mankind. The poet sees the world with heightened awareness that is both the penalty and glory of poets—and follows unmarked paths in imagery, rhythm, meaning through the disciplines of the creative faculty where memory is a winged angel. The poet needs energy and great reserves to draw upon."

*　　*　　*

DEAN, Roy 1925-

PERSONAL: Born August 2, 1925, in London, England; son of Henry Charles (a signwriter) and Alice (Hopkins) Dean. *Education:* Privately educated in Reading, England. *Religion:* Christian. *Residence:* Los Angeles, Calif. *Office:* Rho-Delta Press, 8831 Sunset Blvd., No. 203, Los Angeles, Calif. 90069.

CAREER: Actor and photographer. Has exhibited work at galleries and museums in Los Angeles, New York, and San Francisco, 1968—.

WRITINGS—All published by Rho-Delta Press: *A Time in Eden,* 1969; *Before the Hand of Man,* 1972; *The Naked Image,* 1974; *A World of Nudes,* 1975; *The Ecstasy of Eden,* 1975; *In Search of Adam,* 1975; *Man of Moods,* 1978; *Roy Dean Nudes,* 1978; *Exposures,* 1979; *The Dean's List,* 1980. Also author of scripts for documentary films "The Virgin Islands" and "The October Trees."

WORK IN PROGRESS: Outside of Eden.

SIDELIGHTS: Roy Dean was British hurdling champion for two years.

*　　*　　*

DeCONDE, Alexander 1920-

PERSONAL: Born November 13, 1920, in Utica, N.Y.; son of James and Mary (Tufani) DeConde; married Jeanne Doris Seeger, September 13, 1945 (divorced February 3, 1969); married Glace F. Baeza, May 24, 1973; children: (first marriage) Alexander C., Keith T., Kenneth P., Stephen F. *Education:* San Francisco State College (now University), B.A., 1943; Stanford University, M.A., 1947, Ph.D., 1949. *Politics:* Democrat. *Home:* 5115 Camino Floral, Santa Barbara, Calif. 93111. *Office:* Department of History, University of California, Santa Barbara, Calif. 93106.

CAREER: Stanford University, Stanford, Calif., instructor in history, 1947-48; Whittier College, Whittier, Calif., 1948-52, appointed assistant professor, became associate professor; Duke University, Durham, N.C., assistant professor, 1952-57; University of Michigan, Ann Arbor, associate professor, 1957-61; University of California, Santa Barbara, professor, 1961—, chairman of department, 1964-67. Lecturer in many countries, including India, Thailand, Indonesia, Malaysia, Philippines, all 1971; Germany, Austria, Italy, all 1974; also lecturer at East-West Center, Honolulu, 1979. *Military service:* U.S. Naval Reserve, 1943-46; became lieutenant; received Pacific Theatre, Victory, Philippine Liberation, and American Theatre Medals. *Member:* American Historical Association (consultant, service center for teachers of history, 1960-63), Organization of American Historians, Society for Historians of American Foreign Relations (president, 1969), Society of American Historians, Phi Alpha Theta.

AWARDS, HONORS: Co-winner, award in American history, Pacific Coast branch of American Historical Association, 1949, for *Herbert Hoover's Latin American Policy;* Social Science Research Council grants, 1951-56; Guggenheim fellowship, 1959-60; Rackham grant, University of Michigan, 1958-61; American Philosophical Society grant, 1963; Fulbright fellowship, Council on American Studies, Rome, 1965.

WRITINGS: Herbert Hoover's Latin American Policy, Stanford University Press, 1951; *New Interpretations in American Foreign Policy,* American Historical Association, 1957, new edition published as *American Diplomatic History in Transformation,* 1976; (editor) *Isolation and Security: Ideas and Interests in Twentieth-Century American Foreign Policy,* Duke University Press, 1957; (editor) *Entangling Alliance: Politics and Diplomacy under George Washington,* Duke University Press, 1958.

(Contributor) Norman A. Graebner, editor, *An Uncertain Tradition: American Secretaries of State in the Twentieth-Century,* McGraw, 1961; (contributor) William H. Cartwright and Richard L. Watson, editors, *Interpreting and Teaching American History,* National Council for the Social Studies, 1961; *The American Secretary of State: An Interpretation,* Praeger, 1962; *A History of American Foreign Policy,* Scribner, 1963, 3rd edition, 1978; (author and editor with Armin Rappaport and William R. Steckel) *Patterns in American History* (also see below), two volumes, Wadsworth, 1965, 2nd edition, 1970; (with Robinson, O'Conner, and Travis) *Powers of the President in Foreign Affairs, 1945-1965,* Commonwealth Club of California, 1966; *The Quasi-War: The Politics and Diplomacy of the Undeclared War with France, 1797-1801,* Scribner, 1966; (with Richard N. Current and Harris L. Dante) *United States History,* Scott, Foresman, 1967; (editor) *Patterns in American History* (based on previous book of same title), Wadsworth, 1969; (with Rappaport) *Essays Diplomatic and Undiplomatic of Thomas A. Bailey,* Appleton-Century-Crofts, 1969.

Decisions for Peace: The Federalist Era, Putnam, 1970; *Half-Bitter, Half-Sweet: An Excursion into Italian-American History,* Scribner, 1972; *Student Activism: Town and Gown in Historical Perspective,* Scribner, 1972; *This Affair of Louisiana,* Scribner, 1976; (editor) *Encyclopedia of American Foreign Policy: Studies of Principal Movements and Ideas,* three volumes, Scribner, 1978.

Contributor to *Proceedings of the Institute of World Affairs,* 1952, and *United States Naval Institute Proceedings,* 1953. Contributor to *Encyclopaedia Britannica,* 1959-61 and 1971, *Collier's Encyclopedia,* 1960-61, and *Encyclopedia Americana,* 1971. Contributor to periodicals, including *William & Mary Quarterly, Social Education, Nation, Journal of Southern History, Maryland Historical Magazine,* and *Mississippi Valley Historical Review.* Member of editorial boards of numerous scholarly journals and *Papers of Albert Gallatin.*

WORK IN PROGRESS: A study of ethnic conflict in wars, rebellion, and imperialism in a broad historical context; essays related to American foreign relations.

SIDELIGHTS: Alexander DeConde told *CA:* "In recent years I have acquired an interest in the interaction of history and sociology. In particular, I am concerned with the influence of race and ethnic factors on national and foreign policy. I hope eventually to explore the importance of sociological ideas in the shaping of historical analysis."

AVOCATIONAL INTERESTS: Tennis, gardening, and reading.

*　　*　　*

DEKKER, Carl
See LYNDS, Dennis

DELANEY, Robert Finley 1925-

PERSONAL: Born August 2, 1925, in Fall River, Mass.; son of Joseph Patrick and Mary (Finigan) Delaney; married Mary Elizabeth Flynn, 1950; children: Flynn, Nancy, Peter, Carol, Deirdhre, Sarah. *Education:* Attended Dartmouth College, 1943-44; College of the Holy Cross, B.N.S., 1946; Harvard University, graduate study, 1946; Boston University, A.M., 1948; Catholic University of America, B.S.L.S., 1950, Ph.D., 1959; University of Vienna, graduate study, 1956; attended Naval War College, 1965. *Politics:* Democrat. *Religion:* Roman Catholic. *Home:* Cotuit Rd., West Barnstable, Mass. *Office:* U.S. Naval War College, Newport, R.I.

CAREER: Boston Public Library, Boston, Mass., professional assistant, 1947-48; U.S. Naval Academy Post Graduate School, Washington, D.C., instructor, 1949-50; U.S. Foreign Service, foreign service posts with Department of State and U.S. Information Agency in Rome, Italy, Vienna, Austria, Budapest, Hungary, San Salvador, and Saigon, Vietnam, 1950-63; Esso Standard Oil (Latin America), public relations manager, 1963-65; assistant director of international public opinion, U.S. Information Agency, 1966-68; Tufts University, Fletcher School of Law and Diplomacy, Edward R. Murrow Center, Medford, Mass., professor of public diplomacy and director, 1968-70; American Graduate School of International Management, Glendale, Ariz., president, 1970-71; U.S. Naval War College, Newport, R.I., Milton Miles Professor of International Relations, 1971—. Lecturer, Boston University, 1969-70. Member of Chief Naval Operations Executive Panel, 1970—; consultant, U.S. Department of State, 1971—; advisor, Micronesian Status Negotiations Delegation, beginning 1972. *Military service:* U.S. Navy, 1943-47, 1949; became captain; currently in Naval Reserve. *Member:* American Sociological Association, American Library Association, American Catholic Sociological Society, American Catholic Library Association, Foreign Service Association, Overseas Press Club, Metropolitan Club (Washington), Diplomats and Consular Officers Retired, Dartmouth Club (New York), Holy Cross Alumni Association, Reading Room (Newport, R.I.). *Awards, honors:* Volker Foundation research grant for book on Communism; superior service award, U.S. Government, 1963; 75th anniversary award, Organization of American States, 1965.

WRITINGS: This Is Communist Hungary, Regnery, 1958; *Your Future in the Foreign Service,* Richards Rosen, 1961; *The Literature of Communism in America,* Catholic University of America Press, 1962; *Studies in Guerrilla Warfare,* U.S. Naval Institute, 1963; (co-author) *American Public Diplomacy: The First Years,* Tufts University Press, 1967; (contributor) *International Communication and the New Diplomacy,* Indiana University Press, 1968; *Foreign Policy and U.S. National Security,* Praeger, 1976; *The Art and Science of Psychological Operations,* Johns Hopkins Press, 1976. Also author of *Unconventional Warfare* (Navy training text), 1959. Book reviewer for *Library Journal* and Catholic magazines.

WORK IN PROGRESS: Terrorism, for Ohio University Press.

SIDELIGHTS: Robert Delaney told *CA:* "I write mainly when I am angry or involved. The juices are up and the words flow. I then let it sit for a day and return to edit the venom out. It's fun and filled with therapy to do it this way. Otherwise, for me it would be boring and wooden."

*   *   *

De LIMA, Clara Rosa 1922-
(Penelope Driftwood)

PERSONAL: Born July 27, 1922, in Trinidad, West Indies; daughter of Yldefonso (a merchant) and Rosario (Hernandez) De Lima. *Education:* Attended Long Island University, 1945-48. *Politics:* "Left of center." *Religion:* "None though christened Catholic." *Home:* Aldegonda Flats, 7 St. Anns Rd., Port of Spain, Trinidad, West Indies. *Agent:* Anita Diamant, 51 East 42nd St., New York, N.Y. 10017.

CAREER: Clara De Lima Holdings, Port of Spain, Trinidad, director, 1952-54; during the years 1954-68 traveled as a private executive secretary to a bank vice-president who later became Venezuelan ambassador to Brazil, an economic advisor in the Dominican Republic, and a vice-president of General Electric in England; Yldefonso De Lima and Co., Port of Spain, Trinidad, director, beginning 1968; owner and manager of Art Creators (art gallery), 1979—. Vice-president of City Playhouse; chairman and producer, Trinidad and Tobago Opera Company, 1977; public relations manager for Music Festivals, 1978—; producer with Derek Wolcott of "Marie La Veau," 1980.

WRITINGS—Novels, except as indicated; published by Stockwell, except as indicated: *Tomorrow Will Always Come,* Obolensky, 1965; *Thoughts and Dreams* (poems), 1973; *Dreams Non Stop* (poems), 1974; *Reminiscing* (poems), 1975; *Not Bad Just a Little Mad,* 1975; *Currents of the Yuna,* 1978; *Countdown to Carnival,* 1978; *Kilometre Nineteen,* 1980. Also author of poems, occasionally under pseudonym Penelope Driftwood. Contributor of short stories and articles to periodicals, including *Trinidad Guardian;* contributor to Radio Trinidad. Contributing editor, *People Magazine* and *Inprint Caribbean.*

WORK IN PROGRESS: Memoirs; a murder story.

SIDELIGHTS: Clara Rosa De Lima told *CA:* "I am very disappointed in the new publishing trend. All appears to be profit sharing among the shareholders, hence the standard of writing is on the decline. Less valuable contributions are being discarded. The conglomerates who own the publishers are destroying the contemporary literary scene. You conclude more so when you hear an agent's advice of murders being out and romance in. Keep in mind devils know not because they are devils, but because they are old."

*   *   *

de MARE, Eric S. 1910-

PERSONAL: Born September 10, 1910, in Enfield, Middlesex, England; son of Bror (a timber broker) and Ingrid (Tellander) de Mare; married Marjorie Vanessa Vallance, December 12, 1936 (died, 1972); married Enid Verity, 1974. *Education:* St. Paul's School, London, England, graduate, 1927; Architectural Association School of Architecture, A.A. diploma, 1934, S.R.I.B.A., 1935. *Politics:* Social Crediter. *Home and office:* The Old House Studio, Henley-on-Thames, Oxfordshire R99 4HB, England.

CAREER: Architectural Press, London, England, editor, 1944-48; free-lance writer and photographer on architectural, topographical, and related subjects, 1948—. *Military service:* British Army, Home Guard, 1940-45. *Member:* National Trust, Inland Waterways Association, Victorian Society.

WRITINGS: (Translator with I. R. de Mare) Brynjolf Bjoerset, *Distribute or Destroy!: A Survey of the World's Glut of Goods with a Description of Various Proposals and Practical Experiments for Its Distribution,* Stanley Nott, 1936; *Britain Rebuilt,*

Sidgwick & Jackson, 1942; (editor) *New Ways of Building,* Architectural Press, 1948, 3rd edition, 1958.

The Canals of England, Architectural Press, 1950, British Book Centre, 1951, revised edition, Architectural Press, 1961; *Time on the Thames,* Architectural Press, 1952, British Book Centre, 1953; *Scandinavia: Sweden, Denmark and Norway,* Batsford, 1952; (editor) *New Ways of Servicing Buildings,* Architectural Press, 1954; *The Bridges of Britain,* Batsford, 1954; *Gunnar Asplund, a Great Modern Architect,* Art & Technics, 1955; *Photography,* Penguin, 1957, 7th edition, 1980; (illustrator with photographs) J. M. Richards, *The Functional Tradition in Early Industrial Buildings,* Architectural Press, 1958; *London's Riverside: Past, Present and Future,* Reinhardt, 1958.

Photography and Architecture, Praeger, 1961; (illustrator with photographs) William Gaunt, *London,* Batsford, 1961; (illustrator with photographs) Michael de la Bedoyere, *Francis of Assisi,* Collins, 1962; *Your Book of Bridges,* Faber, 1963; *Swedish Cross Cut: A Book on the Goeta Canal,* Allhems, 1964; *London's River: The Story of a City,* Bodley Head, 1964, McGraw, 1965, new edition, Bodley Head, 1972; (illustrator with photographs) F. A. Reeve, *Cambridge,* Batsford, 1964; (illustrator with photographs) William Gaunt, *Oxford,* Batsford, 1965; *Your Book of Waterways,* Faber, 1965; *The City of Westminster: Heart of London,* Batsford, 1968, Hastings House, 1969; (with wife, Vanessa de Mare) *Your Book of Paper Folding,* Faber, 1968.

London 1851: The Year of the Great Exhibition, Folio Society, 1972; *The London Dore Saw: A Victorian Evocation,* Allen Lane, 1973; *Wren's London,* Folio Society, 1975; *The Victorian Woodblock Illustrators,* Gordon Fraser, 1980. Contributor to journals and newspapers in England and United States, including *Times Literary Supplement, House and Garden, Guardian, Architectural Review, Illustrated London News, Daily Telegraph* (London), and architectural periodicals. Editor, *Architects' Journal,* 1944-48; founder and editor, *The Sun: The Social Credit World Review,* 1950-57.

SIDELIGHTS: Eric S. de Mare writes of his "inherited fanaticism" (from Huguenot ancestors) which he now applies to a private war against the tyranny of banksterdom and debt." He believes in the need to establish a leisure culture through mechanization. He also believes that solutions to architectural and town-planning problems are primarily philosophical and then financial. His beliefs have been recorded in a book which, he says, "so far no one has dared to publish."

*   *   *

DeMILLE, Nelson 1943-
(Ellen Kay, Kurt Ladner, Brad Matthews)

PERSONAL: Born August 23, 1943, in New York, N.Y.; son of Huron (a builder) and Antonia (Panzera) DeMille; married Ellen Wasserman (a medical technologist), July 17, 1971; children: Lauren, Alex. *Education:* Hofstra University, B.A., 1970. *Politics:* Republican. *Religion:* Roman Catholic. *Office:* 55 Hilton Ave., Suite 201, Garden City, N.Y. 11530. *Agent:* Nick Ellison, Edward J. Acton Agency, 17 Grove St., New York, N.Y. 10014.

CAREER: Carpenter, electrician's apprentice, house painter, men's clothing salesman, art dealer, stable boy, deck hand, and insurance investigator; National Learning Corp., Plainview, N.Y., editorial assistant, 1972-73; novelist. *Military service:* U.S. Army, Infantry, 1966-69; became first lieutenant; received Bronze Star Medal, Air Medal, combat infantryman's badge, and Vietnamese Cross of Gallantry. *Member:* Mensa, Authors Guild.

WRITINGS—Published by Manor, except as indicated; under name Nelson DeMille, except as indicated: *The Sniper* (police novel), Leisure Books, 1974; *The Hammer of God* (police novel), Leisure Books, 1974; *The Agent of Death* (police novel), Leisure Books, 1974; *The Smack Man* (police novel), 1975; *The Cannibal* (police novel), 1975; *Night of the Phoenix* (police novel), 1975; *Death Squad* (police novel), 1975; *The Quest* (novel), 1975; (under pseudonym Ellen Kay) *The Five Million Dollar Woman: Barbara Walters* (biography), 1976; (under pseudonym Kurt Ladner) *Hitler's Children* (World War II novel), 1976; (under pseudonym Brad Matthews) *Killer Sharks: The Real Story,* 1976; *By the Rivers of Babylon* (novel; Book-of-the-Month Club selection), Harcourt, 1978; (with Thomas H. Block) *Mayday,* Richard Marek, 1979; *Cathedral* (Literary Guild selection), Delacorte, 1981. Contributor of short stories to *Alfred Hitchcock Magazine* and *Mystery Monthly.* Editor, *Law Officer* (magazine), 1975-76.

WORK IN PROGRESS: An espionage novel, for Delacorte; a screenplay for *Mayday,* for Laurel Productions.

SIDELIGHTS: Nelson DeMille's *By the Rivers of Babylon* received mixed critical response. Christopher Lehmann-Haupt of the *New York Times* notes the author's attempts to incorporate historical fact into the novel, but writes, "Unfortunately, the action in the present is so crammed with stock characters, cliched action, movie-cartoon violence, and a sort of suspense that exhausts instead of entertains, that any historical resonance gets drowned out."

Robert J. Serling of the *Washington Post,* however, lauds *By the Rivers of Babylon,* commenting, "The strength of DeMille's novel lies in his ability to make the most implausible situation appear totally feasible, and frighteningly so." Serling admires the author's research and "stunning" execution. The reviewer does point out one flaw, stating, "My sole criticism of the book is that it tends to drag out at the end," yet he concludes, "This criticism aside, DeMille has written a classic of suspense, as modern as the Concorde itself and as timely as tomorrow's headlines."

About his career as a writer, DeMille told *CA:* "Having tried other forms of writing, I always return to the novel. The novel is the ultimate test of a writer's skills, the most arduous of writing tasks, and the medium most open to criticism. The novelist reveals a good deal of himself in his story and has the final responsibility for every word written. Neither editors nor publicity people, cover artists nor advertising people should be made to share the responsibility for an unsuccessful novel, nor should they share in the triumph of a successful one. A novel is a long-term commitment with little ego reinforcement along the way, a brief flash of the limelight at publication, then back to the typewriter. It takes a great deal of tenacity to stick with a project for so long a period with no guarantee of anything at the end. Yet, the novelist, who by nature must be an optimist, goes on, year after year. I know very few ex-novelists; I know many working novelists and many aspiring novelists. It must be a good job."

BIOGRAPHICAL/CRITICAL SOURCES: New York Times, July 26, 1978; *Washington Post,* August 7, 1978; *Chicago Tribune Book World,* May 24, 1981.

*   *   *

DEMOTES, Michael
See BURGESS, M(ichael) R(oy)

de REGNIERS, Beatrice Schenk (Freedman) 1914-

PERSONAL: Surname is pronounced "drain-yay"; born August 16, 1914, in Lafayette, Ind.; daughter of Harry and Sophia Freedman; married Francis de Regniers (an airline shipping manager), 1953. *Education:* Attended University of Illinois, 1931-33; University of Chicago, Ph.B., 1935, graduate study, 1936-37; Winnetka Graduate Teachers College, M.Ed., 1941. *Agent:* Lynn Nesbit, Sterling Lord Agency, 660 Madison Ave., New York, N.Y. 10021. *Office:* Scholastic Book Services, 50 West 44th St., New York, N.Y. 10036.

CAREER: Writer of juvenile books. Eloise Moore Dance Group, Chicago, Ill., member, 1942-43; Scott, Foresman & Co., Chicago, copywriter, 1943-44; United Nations Relief and Rehabilitation Administration, Egypt, welfare officer, 1944-46; American Book Co., New York City, copywriter, 1948-49; American Heart Association, New York City, director of educational materials, 1949-61; Scholastic Book Services, New York City, editor of Lucky Book Club, 1961—. *Member:* Author's Guild, P.E.N., Loose-enders. *Awards, honors:* Children's Spring Book Festival honor book, *New York Herald Tribune*, 1958, for *Cats Cats Cats Cats Cats;* Boys' Clubs Junior Book Award, 1960, for *The Snow Party;* Indiana Authors Day Awards, honorable mention, 1961, for *The Shadow Book;* Caldecott Award, 1965, for *May I Bring a Friend?;* certificate of excellence, American Institute of Graphic Arts, for communicating with children; Brooklyn Art Books for Children citation, 1973, for *Red Riding Hood: Retold in Verse for Boys and Girls to Read Themselves.*

WRITINGS—All juveniles: *The Giant Story,* Harper, 1953; *A Little House of Your Own,* Harcourt, 1954; *What Can You Do with a Shoe?,* Harper, 1955; *Was It a Good Trade?* (poems), Harcourt, 1956; *A Child's Book of Dreams,* Harcourt, 1957; *Something Special* (poems), Harcourt, 1958; *Cats Cats Cats Cats Cats,* Pantheon, 1958; *The Snow Party,* Pantheon, 1959; *What Happens Next?: Adventures of a Hero,* Macmillan, 1959; *The Shadow Book,* Harcourt, 1960; *Who Likes the Sun?,* Harcourt, 1961; (self-illustrated) *The Little Book,* Walck, 1961; *The Little Girl and Her Mother,* Vanguard, 1963; *May I Bring a Friend?,* Atheneum, 1964; *How Joe the Bear and Sam the Mouse Got Together,* Parents, 1965; *The Abraham Lincoln Joke Book,* Random House, 1965; *David and Goliath,* Viking, 1965; *Penny,* Viking, 1966; *Circus,* Viking, 1966; *The Giant Book,* Atheneum, 1966; *The Day Everybody Cried,* Viking, 1967; *Willy O'Dwyer Jumped in the Fire: Variations on a Folk Rhyme,* Atheneum, 1968; (compiler with Eva Moore and Mary M. White) *Poems Children Will Sit Still For: A Selection For the Primary Grades,* Citation, 1969.

Catch a Little Fox: Variations on a Folk Rhyme, Seabury, 1970; *The Boy, the Rat, and the Butterfly,* Atheneum, 1971; *Red Riding Hood: Retold in Verse for Boys and Girls to Read Themselves,* Atheneum, 1972; *It Does Not Say Meow and Other Animal Riddle Rhymes,* Seabury, 1972; *The Enchanted Forest,* Atheneum, 1974; *Little Sister and the Month Brothers,* Houghton, 1976; *A Bunch of Poems and Verses,* Houghton, 1977; *Laura's Story,* Atheneum, 1979; *Everyone Is Good for Something,* Houghton, 1980; *The Magic Spell* (plays), Houghton, 1982.

WORK IN PROGRESS: I'm Not Laura; Looking for Christmas: A Musical, Magical Christmas Pageant.

SIDELIGHTS: Beatrice Schenk de Regniers writes: "I think of writing—particularly of writing picture books—as a kind of choreography. A picture book must have pace and movement and pattern. Pictures and text should, together, create the pattern, rather than simply run parallel."

De Regniers' books have been translated into French, German, Japanese, and Swedish.

BIOGRAPHICAL/CRITICAL SOURCES: May Hill Arbuthnot, *Children and Books,* 3rd edition, Scott, Foresman, 1964; Lee Bennett Hopkins, *Books Are by People,* Citation Press, 1969.

* * *

DEREKSEN, David
See STACTON, David (Derek)

* * *

DERN, Erolie Pearl Gaddis 1895-1966
(Peggy Dern, Peggy Gaddis; pseudonyms: Roberta Courtland, Georgia Craig, Gail Jordan, Carolina Lee, Perry Lindsay, Joan Sherman)

PERSONAL: Born March 5, 1895, in Gaddistown, Ga.; died June 14, 1966; daughter of Charles William (an engineer) and Carrie Lee (Smith) Gaddis; married John Sherman Dern (a minstrel with the Al G. Field troupe), March 13, 1931 (died November 29, 1950). *Education:* Attended Reinhardt College. *Politics:* Democrat. *Religion:* Unity School of Christianity. *Home and office:* 6093 Lawrenceville Rd. (Route 1, Box 91), Tucker, Ga. *Agent:* Donald MacCampbell, Inc., 12 East 41st St., New York, N.Y. 10017.

CAREER: Writer. In earlier years of career worked on motion picture trade papers and fan magazines. Former editor of *Motion Picture Magazine* and *Motion Picture Classics,* as well as an Atlanta, Ga., trade paper and a fiction magazine, *Love Romances,* published in New York. Also worked as an actress in films and on stage.

WRITINGS—Under name Peggy Dern; all published by Arcadia House, except as indicated: *Dr. Hugh's Two Nurses,* Foulsham, 1960; *Leona Gregory, R.N.,* 1961, reprinted as *Florida Nurse,* Lancer, 1968; *Persistent Suitor,* 1961; *Palm Beach Girl,* 1961; *Orchids for a Nurse,* 1962; *Holiday Nurse,* 1963; *Nurse with a Dream,* 1963; *A Nurse for Apple Valley,* 1964; *Betsy Moran, R.N.,* 1964; *Nurse in the Shadows,* 1965; *Nurse Angela,* 1965; *Nurse Felicity,* 1966; *Nurse's Dilemma,* 1966.

Under name Peggy Gaddis; all published by Godwin, except as indicated: *Shameless,* 1935; *Unfaithful?,* 1935; *Wedding Night,* 1935; *Respectable?,* 1935; *Eve in the Garden,* 1935; *One More Woman,* 1935; *Yaller Gal,* 1936; *Courtesan,* 1936, *Two Women,* 1936; *Overnight Cabins,* 1936; *Harlot's Return,* 1936; *Love in the Springtime,* Arcadia, 1936; *Cottage Colony,* Arcadia, 1936; *Magic of the Mistletoe,* Arcadia, 1936; *Beauty to Burn,* 1937; *Heart's Retreat,* Arcadia, 1937; *Return to Love,* Arcadia, 1937; *Love Is Always New,* Arcadia, 1938; *Tomorrow's Roses,* Arcadia, 1938; *Thirty Days in Eden,* Arcadia, 1938; *Their Hearts to Keep,* Arcadia, 1939. Also author of *Wives in Scarlet.*

All published by Arcadia House: *Midnight in Arcady,* 1940; *Love at Second Sight,* 1940; *Mortgage on the Moon,* 1940; *Feather Brain,* 1940; *Peddler of Dreams,* 1940; *Spring Harvest,* 1941; *Coast Guard Girl,* 1941; *Good-Bye My Heart,* 1941; *Kiss Love Good-Bye,* 1942; *Homemade Heaven,* 1942; *Shabby Glory,* 1942; *Brave Heritage,* 1942; *The Fighting Terhunes,* 1942; *Christmas Hill,* 1942; *Song in Her Heart,* 1943; *Gallant Harvest,* 1943; *Happy Landing,* 1943; *Flight from Yesterday,* 1943; *First Love,* 1944; *Sing for Your Supper,* 1944; *Those Crazy Bartletts,* 1944; *The Old Doctor,* 1944; *Dr. Jerry,* 1944; *Tent Show,* 1945, *County Seat,* 1945; *Frost in April,*

1945; *Dr. Merry's Husband*, 1945; *Heart's Haven*, 1945; *Cadet Nurse*, 1945; *Loving You Always*, 1946, published with *The Girl Next Door*, New American Library, 1975; *Flight Nurse*, 1946, *Stranger Husband*, 1946; *Orchids for Mother*, 1947; *Someone to Love*, 1947; *Mountain Interlude*, 1948; *Suddenly It's Love*, 1949; *Heart's Home*, 1949; *Dr. Christopher*, 1949; *The Girl Next Door*, 1949, published with *Loving You Always*, New American Library, 1975.

All published by Latzen, except as indicated: *Come into My Heart*, Arcadia House, 1950; *Perry Kimbro, R.N.*, Arcadia House, 1950; *Back Home*, Arcadia House, 1950; *Flight from Love*, Arcadia House, 1950; *Her Lover, the Devil*, Quinn; 1950; *Love in the Dark*, 1950; *Two Kinds of Love*, 1950; *Dangerous Females*, 1950; *Rapture for Two*, 1950; *Woman Trap*, 1950; *Maid for Love*, 1950; *Lovely but Damned*, 1950; *Blonde Honey*, 1950; *Maid without Honor*, 1950; *Sin Preferred*, 1950; *Woman Alone*, 1951; *Occasionally Yours*, 1951; *Without Shame*, 1951; *Bride on the Loose*, 1951; *Brass Bound Hussy*, 1951; *Georgia Tramp*, 1951; *Triflin' Woman*, 1951, *Too Many Husbands*, Cramer, 1951; *Country Girl*, 1951; *Hotel Girl*, 1951; *Lovers in the Sun*, 1951; *Unknown Lover*, Cramer, 1952; *Lovers Not*, 1952; *Girl Alone*, Cramer, 1952; *Island Girl*, 1952; *Lovers in Terror*, 1952; *Mountain Woman*, 1952; *Lovers Again*, 1952; *At Ruby's Place*, 1952; *Student Nurse*, 1952.

Kisses Are Petty Cash, Cramer, 1952; *Office Mistress*, Cramer, 1952; *Nora Was a Nurse*, Arcadia House, 1953; *Boss' Mistress*, Cramer, 1953; *Farm Wife*, Latzen, 1953; *Woman of Fire*, Latzen, 1953; *Man Hungry Widow*, Cramer, 1953; *Shanty Girl*, Latzen, 1953; *Female*, Cramer, 1953; *Young Virgin*, Cramer, 1953; *Mountain Girl*, Latzen, 1953; *Guest in Paradise*, Arcadia House, 1954; *Oleander Cove*, Arcadia, 1954; *Lost Girl*, Cramer, 1954; *Scandalous Nurse*, Cramer, 1954; *Man-Hatin' Woman*, Latzen, 1954; *The Non-Virgin Club*, Cramer, 1954; *Roses in December*, Arcadia House, 1955; *The Homesick Heart*, Arcadia House, 1955; *The Joyous Hills*, Arcadia House, 1955; *Night Nurse*, Cramer, 1955.

All published by Arcadia House: *County Nurse*, 1956; *Lady Doctor*, 1956; *Make-Believe Mother*, 1956; *City Nurse*, 1956; *Magic in May*, 1956 (reprinted as *Luxury Nurse*, Macfadden); *Nurse in the Tropics*, 1957; *Beloved Intruder*, 1958; *Nurse at Sundown*, 1958; *Nurse Gerry*, 1958; *Nurse Hilary*, 1958; *Grass Roots Nurse*, 1958; *This Is Tomorrow*, 1958; *A Little Love*, 1958; *This, Too, Is Love*, 1959; *Moon of Enchantment*, 1959; *Kerry Middleton, Career Girl*, 1959; *Mountain Nurse*, 1959; *The April Heart*, 1959; *At Granada Court*, 1959; *Love Is Enough*, 1959; *Settlement Nurse*, 1959, reprinted as *Heiress Nurse*, Lancer, 1968.

All published by Arcadia House, except as indicated: *Nurse Melinda*, 1960, reprinted as *A Nurse's Secret*, Lancer, 1968; *Nurse Polly's Mistake*, Foulsham, 1960; *Shadows on the Moon*, 1960; *The Girl Outside*, 1960; *Peacock Hill*, 1960; *Wedding Song*, 1960; *The Enchanted Summer*, 1960; *Reach for Tomorrow*, 1960; *Island Nurse*, 1960, *Intruder in Eden*, 1960; *Her Day in Court*, 1960; *Rozalinda*, 1960; *This Is Happy*, (c.) 1960; *Wild Orchids*, 1961; *Piney Woods Nurse*, 1961; *Dr. Talbot's Return*, 1961, *Nurse and the Pirate*, 1961; *Hurricane Nurse*, Berkeley Publishing, 1961; *Future Nurse*, 1961; *Leota Foreman, R.N.*, MacFadden, 1962; *Nurse Christine*, 1962; *Robin*, 1962; *Substitute Nurse*, 1962; *Nurse at the Cedars*, 1962, *Clinic Nurse*, 1963; *Nurse and the Star*, 1963; *A Nurse Called Happy*, 1963; *Everglades Nurse*, 1964; *Bayou Nurse*, 1964; *Hill Top Nurse*, 1964; *Nurse Angela*, 1964; *Nurse in Flight*, 1965; *The Listening Nurse*, 1965; *Carolina Love Song*, 1966.

Under pseudonym Roberta Courtland; all published by Gramercy House: *This Can't Be Love*, 1940; *Plane Jane*, 1941; *Furlough Bride*, 1942; *Wings on Her Heart*, 1942; *Fairest of All*, 1942; *Till You Come Back*, 1942; *The Marryin' Kind*, 1945; *The Other Dear Charmer*, 1948. Also author of *Show Boat Girl*.

Under pseudonym Georgia Craig; all published by Arcadia House, except as indicated: *Deadline for Love*, 1944; *Girl in Khaki*, 1944; *Four in Paradise*, 1946; *Secret Honeymoon*, 1947, condensed edition, New American Library, 1968, published with Marion Naismith's *A Handful of Miracles*, New American Library, 1975; *The Heart Remembers*, Gramercy House, 1948; *A Husband for Jennie*, 1951; *Sandy*, 1958; *A Husband for Janice*, 1958; *There's Always Hope*, 1959; *Dr. Grant's Desire*, Foulsham, 1960; *Junior Prom Girl*, 1962; *Rehearsal for a Wedding*, 1962; *A Nurse Comes Home*, 1963; *Nurse Lucie*, 1963; *Emergency Nurse*, 1963; *The Nurse Was Juliet*, 1964; *Love Is Here to Stay*, 1966.

Under pseudonym Gail Jordan; all published by Phoenix: *Sinner in Gingham*, 1940; *Private Office*, 1940; *Love and Forget*, 1941; *The Love Slave*, 1943; *Week-End Husband*, 1943; *Gabrielle's Girls*, 1943; *Love on the Run*, 1944; *Palm Beach Apartment*, 1945; *The Lost Virgin*, 1945; *What Every Widow Knows*, 1945; *Gambling on Love*, 1947; *Godiva Girl*, 1948; *Blonde and Beautiful*, 1948; *Once a Sinner*, 1949; *Lush Lady*, 1949; *Innocent Wanton*, 1950.

Under pseudonym Perry Lindsay; all published by Phoenix: *Passion in the Pantry*, 1941; *The Burning Desire*, 1941; *This Day's Joy*, 1942; *Impatient Lovers*, 1943; *Young and Dangerous*, 1943; *Dark Passion*, 1944; *Six Times a Bride*, 1944; *As Good as Married*, 1945; *Unashamed*, 1945; *No Nice Girl*, 1946; *Shady Lady* (date uncertain); *Blondes Shouldn't Marry*, 1947; *Overnight Cabins*, 1947; *Desire under the Rose*, 1948; *Sin Cinderella*, 1948; *Brief Pleasure*, 1949.

Under pseudonym Joan Sherman: *Wife or Mistress*, Godwin, 1936; *The Earth His Mistress*, Godwin, 1936.

Also author of *Nurse Ellen*, Arcadia House, *Nurse at Burford's Landing*, Arcadia House, 1966, and *Return to Love* [and] *Enchanted Spring*, New American Library, 1976.

SIDELIGHTS: Peggy Dern attributed her prodigious output to a strict writing schedule, six days a week, from "nine until???, when I've finished a minimum of 3,000 words. I am strictly a 'working writer,' not a socializer, and I have never joined any writers club or taken part in self-promotion of my books—feel it's my job to write them and the publisher's job to sell them."

Continuing her comments to *CA*, Dern said: "You ask my purposes in writing. I'd like to say something 'highfalutin' like 'to give pleasure to people'—truth is, I do it to earn my living! But I admit that I love it and wouldn't want ever to do anything else; if suddenly I inherited a million, I'd still go on writing; it's a sort of drug for me, for which I hope no one ever finds a cure. I have no patience with writers who complain that they hate writing, and I always wonder why they do it, in that case. And they complain that it's terribly hard work—which I admit it is, but after all, isn't earning a living at any job work? I can't remember when I 'happened' to begin writing; my parents used to say that when I was no more than ten or eleven years old I used to say 'Some day when I'm a rich-and-famous writer I'll do thus-and-so.' It did not, of course, occur to me that I could ever be a failure at writing, or that I could be famous without being rich! Which is just as well, since that got me through six years of struggling before my first sale, which was in 1928—a short story for *Young's Magazine* called 'Glimpses of the Moon.'''

Despite the amount of writing she did and despite the fact that her books have been published on every continent except Africa and made into motion pictures, Peggy Dern remained a modest person, and devoted a considerable portion of one of her letters to *CA* to the praise of a fellow-writer who had just published her second book, a historical novel, and whom Dern felt was "far more worthy of a place in *Contemporary Authors* than a small-time writer like me!" Of one of her own books, which had recently been reprinted for the fifth time, with several foreign editions, she commented, "I *can't* think *why*, honest!"

AVOCATIONAL INTERESTS: Reading, gardening, and nature.

OBITUARIES: Publishers Weekly, July 11, 1966; *AB Bookman's Weekly*, July 18, 1966.†

*   *   *

DERN, Peggy
  See DERN, Erolie Pearl Gaddis

*   *   *

DERRETT, J(ohn) Duncan M(artin)   1922-

PERSONAL: Surname is accented on second syllable; born August 30, 1922, in London, England; son of John West and Fay (Martin) Derrett; married Margaret Griffiths, September, 1950; children: Elizabeth, Paul, Christopher, Robin, Jonathan. *Eduation:* Jesus College, Oxford, B.A., 1945, M.A., 1947; School of Oriental and African Studies, London, Ph.D., 1949. *Home:* Half Way House, High St., Blockley, Gloucestershire, England. *Office:* School of Oriental and African Studies, University of London, London WC1E 7HP, England.

CAREER: University of London, School of Oriental and African Studies, London, England, lecturer in Hindu law, 1949-56, reader in Oriental laws, 1956-65, professor of Oriental laws, 1965—. Tagore Professor of Law, University of Calcutta, 1953; visiting professor of Indian law, University of Chicago, spring, 1963; lecturer in Hindu law, Council of Legal Education, London, England, 1967—; visiting professor, University of Michigan, summer, 1970; Wilde Lecturer in Natural and Comparative Religion, Oxford University, 1978-81. *Military service:* British Army, 1942-45; served in India. *Member:* Royal Asiatic Society, Studiorum Novi Testamenti Societas, Gray's Inn. *Awards, honors:* D.C.L., Oxford University, 1966; LL.D., University of London, 1971; Naresh Chandra Sen-Gupta Gold Medal, Asiatic Society of Calcutta, 1977.

WRITINGS: The Hoysalas, Oxford University Press, 1957; *Hindu Law, Past and Present*, A. Mukherjee (Calcutta), 1957; *Introduction to Modern Hindu Law*, Oxford Univeristy Press, 1963; (editor) *Studies in the Laws of Succession in Nigeria*, Oxford University Press, 1965; *Religion, Law and the State in India*, Faber, 1968; (editor and contributor) *Introduction to Legal Systems*, Praeger, 1968; *Critique of Modern Hindu Law*, Tripathi (Bombay, India), 1970; *Law in the New Testament*, Darton, 1970; (editor and translator) R. Lingat, *Classical Law of India*, University of California Press, 1973; *Jesus's Audience*, Darton, 1973; *Dharmasastra and Juridical Literature*, Harrassowitz (Wiesbaden), 1973; *Bharuci's Commentary on the Manusmrti*, two volumes (text and translation), Steiner Verlag, 1975; *Essays in Classical and Modern Hindu Law*, four volumes, E. J. Brill (Leiden), 1976-78; *Studies in the New Testament*, two volumes, E. J. Brill, 1977-78; *Death of a Marriage Law*, Vikas (Delhi), 1978. Contributor to journals and festschrifts in England and abroad. Member of editorial

board, *Zeitschrift fuer vergleichende Rechtweissenschaft* and *Kerala Law Times*.

WORK IN PROGRESS: Research studies in New Testament problems; research on early Indian legal procedure and juridical concepts, including Buddhist jurisprudence; a commentary on St. Mark.

SIDELIGHTS: J. Duncan M. Derrett writes: "It seems that literary mystery has never been tackled adequately by an Orientalist. The New Testament still has a future to it and discoveries can be made continually. The results fascinate me. In spite of the introspective circular dance performed by the specialists there is still room for a non-specialist and for interdisciplinary approaches. My reviewers complain that I am not subservient to their heroes who practice 'reduction criticism.' I find this a purely literary and inward-looking technique to study the gospels. They also complain that my 'discoveries' are far-fetched. But their aim is to keep in with each other, for 'faith' is a component of the dictionary definition of 'theology,' and I pay no attention. The wheel keeps turning and my kind of discoveries become less uncommon. The Oriental background to the gospels and epistles improve our focus on what those mighty compositions were trying to achieve, and I shall not give to trying to illuminate them.''

*   *   *

DESCHAMPSNEUFS, Henry Pierre Bernard   1911-

PERSONAL: Born April 7, 1911, in St. Agnes, Cornwall, England; son of Pierre Bernard and Mary (Douglass) Deschampsneufs; married Nora Frances Rowan, June 7, 1946; children: Frances, Alice, Rose. *Education:* Pembroke College, Oxford, B.A. (with honours). *Politics:* Liberal. *Religion:* Church of England. *Home:* 1315 Minster House, St. James Court, Buckingham Gate, London S.W.1, England.

CAREER: Beecham Export Corp., London, England, export manager, 1933-36; Erwin Wasey Co. Ltd., London, account executive, 1936-37; J. Walter Thompson Co. Ltd., London, account executive, 1937-40; Pritchard Wood & Partners Ltd., London, export director, 1947-62; currently self-employed as export marketing and advertising consultant. Director, Practitioners in Marketing Ltd., London. Lecturer; presenter of British Broadcasting Corp. (BBC) series, "A Language in Your Briefcase," 1971-72. *Military service:* British Army, Royal Artillery, 1940-45; became captain. *Member:* Sales Promotion Association, Institute of Export (corporate member; vice-chairman; member of executive and education committees; chairman of council, 1970-71).

WRITINGS: Selling Overseas, Business Publications, 1960; *Selling in Africa*, Business Publications, 1961; *Selling in Europe: An Introduction to the European Markets*, Business Publications, 1963; *Marketing Overseas*, Pergamon, 1967; (with Robin Neillands) *Exporting: A Basic Guide to Selling Abroad*, Pan Books, 1969; *Marketing in the Common Market: A Guide to Selling in the E.E.C.*, Pan Books, 1973; *Export Made Simple*, W. H. Allen, 1977; *Export Is Fun*, Royal Automobile Club, 1979. Also author of "The Principles of Export Marketing," a film. Contributor of articles to *Daily Mail, Director, New Commonwealth, Christian Science Monitor*, and other newspapers, magazines, and business journals.†

*   *   *

de VINCK, Catherine   1922-

PERSONAL: Born February 20, 1922, in Brussels, Belgium; came to United States in 1948; daughter of Joseph (a general in Belgian Army) and Julie Prudence (Oeyen) Kestens; married Jose de Vinck (a writer, publisher, and editor), February 1, 1945; children: Bruno, Oliver, Anne-Catherine (Mrs. John B. Ochs), Christopher, Jose, Jr., Maria-Gloria. *Education:* Attended schools in Brussels. *Religion:* Roman Catholic. *Home:* 672 Franklin Turnpike, Allendale, N.J. 07401; and Domus Aurea, Combermere, Ontario, Canada K0J 1L0. *Office address:* Box 103, Allendale, N.J. 07401.

CAREER: Writer. *Awards, honors:* Keats Society (London) prize, 1975, for poem "Mothering"; New Jersey Council on the Arts fellowship, 1980-81.

WRITINGS—Published by Alleluia Press, except as indicated: *A Time to Gather: Selected Poems,* 1967; *Ikon: Ode to the Virgin Mary,* 1972; *A Liturgy,* Cross Currents, 1974; (contributor) Michele Murray, editor, *A House of Good Proportion: Women in Literature,* Simon & Schuster, 1974; *A Passion Play,* 1975; *A Book of Uncommon Prayers,* 1976; *Readings: John at Patmos and Book of Hours,* 1978; *A Book of Eve* (includes text and long-playing record), 1979; *A Garland of Straw,* 1981.

WORK IN PROGRESS: The Prodigal Son; a book of selected poems.

* * *

DEYERMOND, Alan D(avid)   1932-

PERSONAL: Born February 24, 1932, in Cairo, Egypt; son of Henry (a wholesaler) and Margaret (Lawson) Deyermond; married Ann Marie Bracken (a history teacher), March 30, 1957; children: Ruth Margaret. *Education:* Pembroke College, Oxford, B.A., 1953, M.A. and B.Litt., 1957. *Politics:* Liberal. *Religion:* Church of England. *Home:* 20 Lancaster Rd., St. Albans, Hertfordshire AL1 4ET, England. *Office:* Westfield College, University of London, Hampstead, London NW3 7ST, England.

CAREER: University of London, Westfield College, London, England, assistant lecturer, 1955-58, lecturer, 1958-66, reader, 1966-69, professor of Spanish, 1969—, dean of faculty of arts, 1972-74. Visiting professor, University of Wisconsin, 1972, University of California, Los Angeles, 1977, and Princeton University, 1978-81. *Member:* Asociacion Internacional de Hispanistas, International Arthurian Society, International Courtly Literature Society (president of British branch, 1974-77; international president, 1977—), Societe Rencesvals, Modern Humanities Research Association, Association of Hispanists of Great Britain (committee member, 1970-73), Hispanic Society of America (corresponding member), Mediaeval Academy of America (fellow), Anglo-Catalan Society (member of executive committee, 1964-70), Association of University Teachers (member of central council, 1957-62; local president, 1968-70), London Medieval Society (president, 1970-74).

WRITINGS: The Petrarchan Sources of La Celestina, Oxford University Press, 1961; *Epic Poetry and the Clergy: Studies on the Mocedades de Rodrigo,* Tamesis, 1969; *A Literary History of Spain,* Barnes & Noble, Volume I: *The Middle Ages,* 1971; *Apollonius of Tyre: Two Fifteenth Century Spanish Prose Romances,* University of Exeter, 1973; (with David Blamires and others) *Medieval Comic Tales,* D. S. Brewer, 1973; (editor) Felix Lecoy, *Recherches sur le Libro de buen amor de Juan Ruiz,* 2nd edition, Gregg, 1974; *Lazarillo de Tormes: A Critical Guide,* Grant & Cutler, 1975; *Medieval Hispanic Studies Presented to Rita Hamilton,* Tamesis, 1976; "*Mio Cid*" *Studies,* Tamesis, 1977; *Historia y critica de la literatura espanola,* edited by Francisco Rico, Volume I: *La Edad Media,* Critica, 1979. Also joint general editor, *Critical Guides to*

Spanish Texts and *Research Bibliographies and Checklists;* editor of "Medieval" series, Tamesis Texts. Contributor to *The Oxford Companion to the Theatre* and *Cassell's Encyclopedia of World Literature.* Contributor of articles, notes, and reviews to learned journals in Spanish and English. Member of editorial committee of *Coleccion Tamesis, Romance Philology, Bulletin of Hispanic Studies, Hispanic Review, Journal of Hispanic Philology, Celestinesca,* and *Iberoromania.*

WORK IN PROGRESS: An edition of *Libro de Apolonio,* for Clasicos Castellanos; a critical bibliography of medieval Spanish literature, for Grant & Cutler; *Approaches to Medieval Spanish Literature,* for Juan de la Cuesta Hispanic Monographs; *Ensayos celestinescos,* for Ediciones El Albir.

* * *

DICKINSON, W(illiam) Croft   1897-1963

PERSONAL: Born August 28, 1897, in Leicester, England; died May 22, 1963; son of William (a minister) and Elizabeth (Croft) Dickinson; married Florence Margery Tomlinson, 1930; children: Susan Margery Gibson, Jane Elizabeth. *Education:* University of St. Andrews, M.A., 1921; University of London, D.Lit., 1928.

CAREER: University of London, London School of Economics and Political Science, London, England, librarian, British Library of Political and Economic Science, 1933-34; University of Edinburgh, Edinburgh, Scotland, Sir William Fraser Professor of Scottish History and Paleography, 1944-63. Rhind Lecturer in Archeology, Society of Antiquaries of Scotland, 1942; Andrew Land Lecturer, University of St. Andrews, 1951. Member of Royal Commission on Ancient and Historical Monuments, Scotland, and Scottish Records Advisory Council; member of board of trustees, National Library of Scotland, 1944-60. *Military service:* British Army, Machine Gun Corps, 1916-19; became lieutenant; received Military Cross. *Awards, honors:* Commander, Order of the British Empire, 1963.

WRITINGS: (Editor and author of introduction, notes, and appendices) *The Sheriff Court Book of Fife, 1515-1522,* Scottish History Society, 1928; (author of index) *The Chronicle of Melrose,* Percy Lund Humphries & Co., 1936; (editor and author of introduction) *The Court Book of the Barony of Carnwath, 1923-1542,* Scottish History Society, 1937; *The Study of Scottish History,* Oliver & Boyd, 1944; *Borrobil* (juvenile), Cape, 1944, published with illustrations by John Morton-Sale, Penguin, 1964; *The Eildon Tree* (juvenile), J. Cape, 1947; (editor and author of introduction and notes) *John Knox's History of the Reformation in Scotland,* two volumes, Thomas Nelson, 1949; *The Flag from the Isles,* J. Cape, 1951; (editor and author of introduction) *Two Students at St. Andrews, 1711-1716,* Oliver & Boyd, 1952; *Andrew Lang, John Knox, and Scottish Presbyterianism,* Thomas Nelson, 1952; (editor with others) *A Source Book of Scottish History,* three volumes, Thomas Nelson, 1952-54; *The Sweet Singers,* Oliver & Boyd, 1953; (editor) *Early Records of the Burgh of Aberdeen, 1317, 1398-1407,* Scottish History Society, 1957; *Robert Bruce: Scottish Hero and King,* Thomas Nelson, 1960; *The Scottish Reformation and Its Influence upon Scottish Life and Character,* Saint Andrews Press, 1960; (with George S. Pyle) *A New History of Scotland from the Earliest Times to 1603,* two volumes, Thomas Nelson, 1961, 3rd edition (edited by Archibald A. M. Duncan) published as *Scotland from the Earliest Times to 1603,* Oxford University Press, 1977; *Dark Encounters: A Collection of Ghost Stories,* Harvill, 1963. Editor of *Scottish Historical Review,* 1947-63.†

DICKSON, Gordon R(upert) 1923-

PERSONAL: Born November 1, 1923, in Edmonton, Alberta, Canada; came to United States in 1936; naturalized citizen; son of Gordon Fraser (a mining engineer) and Maude Leola (a teacher; maiden name, Ford) Dickson. *Education:* University of Minnesota, B.A., 1948, graduate study, 1948-50. *Home:* 7400 10th Ave. S., Minneapolis, Minn. 55423. *Agent:* Kirby McCauley Ltd., 60 East 42nd St., New York, N.Y. 10017.

CAREER: Writer. *Military service:* U.S. Army, 1943-46. *Member:* Authors Guild, Authors League of America, Mystery Writers of America, Science Fiction Writers of America (president, 1969-71), Science Fiction Research Association, Minnesota Science Fiction Society.

AWARDS, HONORS: Hugo Award, 1965, for *Soldier, Ask Not;* Nebula Award, Science-Fiction Writers of America, 1966, for short story "Call Him Lord"; E. E. Smith Memorial Award for imaginative fiction, 1975; August Derleth Award, British Fantasy Society, 1976, for *The Dragon and the George;* Jupiter Award, 1978, for *Time Storm;* Hugo Award nomination, 1978, for *Time Storm,* and 1979, for *The Far Call.*

WRITINGS—Science fiction novels: *Alien from Arcturus* (bound with *The Atom Curtain,* by Nick Boddie Williams), Ace Books, 1956, revised edition published as *Arcturus Landing,* 1979; *Mankind on the Run* (bound with *The Crossroads of Time,* by Andre Norton), Ace Books, 1956, published as *On the Run,* 1979; *Time to Teleport* [and] *The Genetic General,* Ace Books, 1960, expanded edition of the latter published as *Dorsai!* (also see below), DAW Books, 1976; *Delusion World* [and] *Spacial Delivery,* Ace Books, 1961, reprinted, 1978; *Naked to the Stars,* Pyramid Publications, 1961, reprinted, Ace Books, 1980; *Necromancer* (also see below), Doubleday, 1962, published as *No Room for Man,* Macfadden, 1963, reprinted under original title, DAW Books, 1978; *The Alien Way,* Bantam, 1965; *Mission to Universe,* Berkley Publishing, 1965; (with Keith Laumer) *Planet Run,* Doubleday, 1967; *Soldier, Ask Not,* Dell, 1967; *The Space Swimmers,* Berkley Publishing, 1967; *None But Man,* Doubleday, 1969; *Spacepaw,* Putnam, 1969; *Wolfing,* Dell, 1969.

Hour of the Horde, Putnam, 1970; *Sleepwalker's World,* Lippincott, 1971; *Tactics of Mistake* (also see below), Doubleday, 1971; *The Outposter,* Lippincott, 1972; *The Pritcher Mass,* Doubleday, 1972; *The R-Master,* Lippincott, 1973; *Three to Dorsai!* (contains *Necromancer, Dorsai!,* and *Tactics of Mistake*), Science Fiction Book Club, 1975; (with Harry Harrison) *The Lifeship,* Harper, 1976 (published in England as *Lifeboat,* Futura, 1978); *The Dragon and the George,* Ballantine, 1976; *Time Storm,* St. Martin's, 1977; *The Far Call,* Dial, 1978; *Pro,* Ace Books, 1978; *Home from the Shore,* Ace Books, 1978; *Spirit of Dorsai,* Ace Books, 1979; *Masters of Everon,* Ace Books, 1980; *Lost Dorsai,* Ace Books, 1980.

Young adult science fiction novels: *Secret under the Sea,* Holt, 1960; *Secret under Antarctica,* Holt, 1963; *Secret under the Caribbean,* Holt, 1964; *Space Winners,* Holt, 1965; *Alien Art,* Dutton, 1973; (with Ben Bova) *Gremlins, Go Home!,* St. Martin's, 1974; (with Poul Anderson) *Star Prince Charlie,* Putnam, 1975.

Collections of short science fiction: (With Anderson) *Earthman's Burden,* Gnome Press, 1957, reprinted, Avon, 1979; (with others) *Five Fates,* Doubleday, 1970; *Danger—Human,* Doubleday, 1970, published as *The Book of Gordon R. Dickson,* DAW Books, 1973; *Mutants: A Science Fiction Adventure,* Macmillan, 1970; (with Anderson and Robert Silverberg) *The Day the Sun Stood Still: Three Original Novellas of Science*

Fiction (contains "A Chapter of Revelation" by Anderson, "Thomas the Proclaimer" by Silverberg, and "Things Which Are Caesar's" by Dickson), T. Nelson (Nashville), 1972; *The Star Road,* Doubleday, 1973; *Ancient, My Enemy,* Doubleday, 1974; *Gordon R. Dickson's SF Best,* Dell, 1977; *In Iron Years,* Doubleday, 1980.

Editor: *1975 Annual World's Best Science Fiction,* DAW Books, 1975; *Combat SF,* Doubleday, 1975; *Nebula Award Winners Twelve,* Harper, 1979.

Author of about 200 short stories and novelettes, some of which appear in anthologies. Also author of radio plays.

WORK IN PROGRESS: The Final Encyclopedia and *Way of a Pilgrim,* both for Ace Books; *The Dragon Knight,* for Ballantine; *Hawkwood,* a historical novel, and *Childe,* both to be, respectively, the first and the final novels of the Childe Cycle.

SIDELIGHTS: Gordon R. Dickson's major work is the ongoing Childe Cycle, a twelve-volume epic which spans a period of time from the early fourteenth century to the late twenty-fourth century. Begun in 1956, the cycle ultimately will consist of three historical, three contemporary, and six futuristic novels which will present Dickson's vision of humanity's evolutionary potential.

In an interview with *Science Fiction Review*'s Clifford McMurray, Dickson states, "I'm making the argument that a type of characteral, moral—spiritual, if you like—evolution began with the Renaissance, is presently continuing unnoticed, and will culminate 500 years from now in what I call the Responsible Man." In Dickson's vision, three successful lines, which he calls Splinter Cultures, have evolved: the warrior (the Dorsai), the philosopher (the Exotics of Mara and Kultis), and the faith-holder (the Friendlies of Harmony and Association). Dickson continues: "My assumption is that the Splinter Cultures have only one character-facet, instead of being full spectrum in character like you and me and the people of old Earth. Concentrated in this way, they are nonviable. If all the rest of the human race was killed off and they were left alone they would eventually die off, too, because they don't have the full spectrum of humanity in them—yet."

So far, four of the futuristic novels have been published: *Dorsai* (originally published as *The Genetic General*), *Necromancer, Soldier, Ask Not,* and *Tactics of Mistake.* Dickson told *CA,* "All twelve books, when completed, will connect to form a single 'novel of thematic argument,' a literary form conceived and demonstrated by me, which will find its best example in the completed cycle. Popularly, the novels of the future segment of the cycle are also often referred to as the 'Dorsai Cycle,' although this is incorrect."

BIOGRAPHICAL/CRITICAL SOURCES: Times Literary Supplement, May 25, 1967; *Science Fiction Review,* July, 1978; *Bulletin of the Science Fiction Writers of America,* fall, 1979; *Extrapolation,* fall, 1979; *Destinies,* February-March, 1980; *Dictionary of Literary Biography,* Volume VIII, Gale, 1981.

* * *

DIEBOLD, William, Jr. 1918-

PERSONAL: Born March 23, 1918, in New York, N.Y.; son of William (a lawyer) and Rose (Theurer) Diebold; married second wife, Ruth Brody Corcoran (a librarian), August 28, 1953; children: (first marriage) Barbara H. (Mrs. Thomas A. Wick), John B., Beatrice A.; (second marriage) William J.; stepchildren: David Corcoran, John Corcoran. *Education:* Swarthmore College, B.A., 1937; graduate study at Yale University and at London School of Economics and Political Science, 1937-39. *Home:* 311 North Broadway, Upper Nyack, N.Y. 10960. *Office:* Council on Foreign Relations, 58 East 68th St., New York, N.Y. 10021.

CAREER: Council on Foreign Relations, New York, N.Y., Rockefeller research fellow, 1939-40, research associate, War and Peace Studies, 1940-43; U.S. Department of State, Division of Commercial Policy, Washington, D.C., staff member, 1945-47; Council on Foreign Relations, director of economic studies, 1947-62, senior research fellow, 1962—. Consultant, U.S. Department of State, 1941-43. *Military service:* Office of Strategic Services, 1943-45; served first as a civilian, later in U.S. Army; became sergeant. *Member:* American Economic Association, Century Association, Phi Beta Kappa.

WRITINGS: New Directions in Our Trade Policy, Council on Foreign Relations, 1941; *Trade and Payments in Western Europe: A Study in Economic Cooperation, 1947-1951,* Harper, 1952; *The Schuman Plan: A Study in Economic Cooperation, 1950-1959,* Praeger, 1959; *The United States and the Industrial World: American Foreign Economic Policy in the Seventies,* Praeger, 1972; *International Policy as an International Issue,* McGraw, 1980. Author of pamphlets. Contributor of articles and reviews to periodicals.

WORK IN PROGRESS: A book on U.S. economic policy towards the U.S.S.R. and Eastern Europe; studies of American industrial policy, the international economic system, and U.S. foreign economic policy.

SIDELIGHTS: William Diebold, Jr. told *CA:* "The reason I write is to tell people what I have found out by research and analysis, and what conclusions I draw as to how the world works and how things can be changed (or kept from changing). Often the focus is national policy and always the economic issues on which I concentrate have to be seen in a 'real world' setting that includes politics and human nature and aspirations as well as things normally thought of as belonging to the 'dismal science.' Political economy is a blend of ingredients that is hard to put together. To find words that will convey the meaning you intend to a highly mixed audience (if there is one at all) can be even more difficult. That is why writing is hard; I do it slowly and revise a great deal.

"Why I like to have written is not that I am always pleased with the product, but that a well thought-out, decently-expressed piece of writing seems to me the only good form in which these subjects can be adequately dealt with and made available 'to whom it may concern,' now or in the future. And one never knows what future a piece of writing may have. My recent studies of contemporary problems have benefited greatly from work that other people did several decades ago. Good writing is worth more than many pictures, and those who understand better by ear can read the words aloud."

*   *   *

DIKTY, Julian May
   See MAY, Julian

*   *   *

DIRINGER, David   1900-1975

PERSONAL: Born June 16, 1900, in Tlumacz, East Galicia; died February 13, 1975, in Cambridge, England; son of Jacob (a town clerk) and Mina Diringer; married, December 1, 1927; children: Kedma. *Education:* University of Florence, D.Litt., 1927, diploma, 1929. *Religion:* Jewish. *Office:* Cambridge

University, Cambridge, England; and University of Florence, Florence, Italy.

CAREER: University of Florence, Florence, Italy, lector, 1931-34, assistant professor, 1934-38; Cambridge University, Cambridge, England, 1948-75, began as lecturer in Semitic epigraphy, became professor emeritus; University of Florence, assistant professor, beginning 1952. Scientific secretary of Conference on Etruscan Studies, 1926, International Congress on Etruscan Studies, 1928, and Congresses of Colonial Studies, 1931, 1934, and 1937, all held in Florence, Italy. Founder of Alphabet Museum, Cambridge, 1959. *Member:* Society of Old Testament Studies, Royal Institute of Anthropology, Institute of Archaeology, Association of University Teachers, Palestine Exploration Society, Anglo-Israel Archaeological Society, Near Eastern Society (president). *Awards, honors:* Awards for oriental studies from Royal Academy of Italy, Royal Geographical Society of Italy, University of Florence, and Bollingen Foundation; M.A. from University of Cambridge, 1948.

WRITINGS: Le Iscrizioni antico-ebraiche palestinesi, Le Monnier Felice, 1934; *L'Alfabeto nella storia della civilta,* G. Barbera Editore, 1937, published as *The Alphabet: A Key to the History of Mankind,* two volumes, Philosophical Library, 1948, 3rd edition (with Reinhold Regensburger), Funk & Wagnalls, 1968; *The Hand-Produced Book,* Philosophical Library, 1953; (with N. Freeman) *The Staples Alphabet Exhibition,* Staples Press, 1953; *The Illuminated Book: Its History and Production,* Philosophical Library, 1958, 3rd edition (with Regensburger), Praeger, 1967; *The Story of the Aleph Beth,* Philosophical Library, 1958; *Writing,* Praeger, 1962; (with H. Freeman) *A History of the Alphabet throughout the Ages and in All Lands,* Unwin Brothers, 1977.

Contributor of over 450 articles in fields of archaeology, philology, epigraphy, Biblical studies, ancient history, and allied fields to encyclopedias, magazines, and learned journals.

WORK IN PROGRESS: Continually enlarging the Alphabet Museum; research on the history of writing and civilization.

SIDELIGHTS: David Diringer has been called "the most prestigious authority in the field" of the alphabet. According to Cyrus Gordon, Diringer's book *The Alphabet* "is destined to remain the leading book on writing for some years to come. It covers a wealth of material, and no matter how learned the reader may be, he will become aware of new facets of a significant subject."

BIOGRAPHICAL/CRITICAL SOURCES: Book World, February 9, 1969.†

*   *   *

DOAK, Wade Thomas   1940-

PERSONAL: Born February 23, 1940, in North Canterbury, New Zealand; son of Deryck Steads and Lorna Evelyn Doak; married Janet Mary Turpin, December 15, 1962; children: Brady, Karla. *Education:* Canterbury University, B.A., 1962. *Home address:* Box 20, Whangarei, New Zealand.

CAREER: Writer. Taught French and English in secondary schools in New Zealand, 1963-81. Publisher of *Dive South Pacific Magazine.*

WRITINGS—Published by Hodder & Stoughton, except as indicated: The Elingamite and Its Treasure, 1969; *Beneath New Zealand Seas,* A. H. Reed, 1971; *Fishes of the New Zealand Region,* 1972, British Book Centre, 1974; *Sharks and Other Ancestors,* 1975; *Islands of Survival,* 1976; *The Cliff Dwellers,* 1979; *Dolphin, Dolphin,* 1981. Contributor to periodicals, including *Mondo Sommerso, American Skindiver, New Zealand Listener, New Zealand Weekly News, Oceans,* and *Sea.*

WORK IN PROGRESS: Research on dolphins and whales.

SIDELIGHTS: Wade Thomas Doak told *CA:* "When I consider the list of books I have written since 1963 a strange pattern emerges, almost as if some wiser, deeper influence beyond my consciousness were leading me on. From the discovery of a horde of treasure coins in an historic shipwreck, I came to a study of marine invertebrates. The treasure gave me the means to full-time devotion to the sea. This led on to a study of fish behaviour and thence to the overall ecology of reef dwellers, including Polynesian and Melanesian peoples, who live in symbiosis with the coral reef.

"Then wild dolphins came into my life, quite unexpectedly, teaching things that demanded a field study, now in its sixth year. This expanded to include whales and extended globally through Project Interlock, founded with my wife, Jan. Why all this? Because, what we are now learning about cetaceans suggests strongly they are the most extraordinary creatures this planet has evolved. And I wonder now how I came to find that treasure. At the time I was afraid to admit to my companions that I visualized those coins before I saw them. *I knew they were there.*"

AVOCATIONAL INTERESTS: Skindiving, underwater photography, marine biology, European literature, and anthropology.

*   *   *

DOANE, Pelagie   1906-1966

PERSONAL: Born April 11, 1906, in Palmyra, N.J.; died December 9, 1966, in Neptune, N.J.; daughter of Warren F(inney) and Pelagie (Plasschaert) Doane; married Warren E. Hoffner, March 26, 1934 (deceased). *Education:* Attended Moore Institute, 1924-28. *Home and office:* 1513 Hamilton Rd., Belmar, N.J.

CAREER: Free-lance writer and illustrator, 1928-66. Designer of book jackets and of covers and illustrations for children's magazines. Illustrator of over one hundred books, including all of her own.

WRITINGS: A Small Child's Bible, Oxford University Press, 1944, Walck 1946; *One Rainy Night,* Walck, 1946; *A Book of Nature,* Oxford University Press, 1952; *The Boy Jesus,* Oxford University Press, 1953, Walck, 1954; *Bible Children,* Lippincott, 1954; *The First Day,* Lippincott, 1956; *The Big Trip,* Walck, 1958; *The Story of Moses,* Lippincott, 1958; *St. Francis,* Walck, 1960; *God Made the World,* Lippincott, 1960; *Understanding Kim,* Lippincott, 1962; *Animals in the Bible,* Golden Press, 1963; *The Twenty-Third Psalm,* Lippincott, 1963; (with Robin Palmer) *Fairy Elves: A Dictionary of the Little People,* Walck, 1964; *Wings of the Morning,* Walck, 1967.

Editor: *Brother, Baby and I,* Grosset, 1947; *A Small Child's Book of Verse,* Oxford University Press, 1948; *Poems of Praise,* Lippincott 1955; *Littlest Ones,* Oxford University Press, 1956.

Illustrator: Laura Oftedahl and Nina Jacobs, *My First Dictionary: The Beginner's Picture Word Book,* Grosset, 1948; Val Teal, *Angel Child,* Rand McNally, 1965.†

*   *   *

DOBIE, J(ames) Frank   1888-1964

PERSONAL: Born September 26, 1888, in Live Oak County, Tex.; died September 18, 1964, in Austin, Texas.; buried in Texas State Cemetary, Austin; son of Richard Jonathan and Ella (Byler) Dobie; married Bertha McKee, 1916. *Education:* Southwestern University, B.A., 1910; Columbia University, M.A., 1914. *Home:* 702 Park Pl., Austin, Tex.

CAREER: Started writing as summer reporter on Texas newspapers; high school and preparatory school teacher, 1910-13; University of Texas, Main University (now University of Texas at Austin), instructor in English, 1914-17, 1919-20; manager of half-million-acre ranch, Texas, 1920-21; University of Texas, Main University (now University of Texas at Austin), instructor in English, 1921-23; Oklahoma A & M College (now Oklahoma State University), Stillwater, head of English department, 1923-25; University of Texas, Main University (now University of Texas at Austin), assistant professor, 1925-26, associate professor, 1926-33, professor of English, 1933-47. Visiting professor of American history, Cambridge University, 1943-44. *Military service:* U.S. Army, Field Artillery, 1917-19; became first lieutenant. U.S. Army, Information and Education, 1945-46; lecturer at Shrivenham American University and to troops in Austria and Germany.

MEMBER: Texas Folklore Society (secretary, 1922-43), Texas Institute of Letters, Town and Gown Club (Austin). *Awards, honors:* Rockefeller Foundation grants, 1930-31, 1934-35; Guggenheim fellowship in literature, 1932-33; Huntington Library research grant, 1948-49; Boys' Club of America Junior Book Award, 1951, for *The Ben Lilly Legend;* Carr P. Collins Award of Texas Institute of Letters, 1952, for *The Mustangs;* Presidential Medal of Freedom, 1964; M.A. from Cambridge University, 1944; D.Litt. from Southern Methodist University, Texas Christian University, and Southwestern University.

WRITINGS: A Vaquero of the Brush Country, Southwest Press, 1929, reprinted, Little, Brown, 1960; *Coronado's Children,* Southwest Press, 1930, reprinted, University of Texas Press, 1978 (published in England as *Lost Mines of the Old West,* Hammond, 1960); (author of introduction) N. A. Jennings, *A Texas Ranger,* Southwest Press, 1930, reprinted, Turner, 1965; *On the Open Range,* Southwest Press, 1931; *Tongues of the Monte,* Doubleday, 1935, published as *The Mexico I Like,* Southern Methodist University Press, 1942; *The Flavor of Texas,* Dealey & Lowe, 1936; *Tales of the Mustang,* Book Club of Texas, 1936; *John C. Duval: First Texas Man of Letters,* Southwest Review, 1939, 2nd edition, Southern Methodist University Press, 1965; *Apache Gold and Yaqui Silver,* Little, Brown, 1939, reprinted, University of New Mexico Press, 1976; *The Longhorns,* Little, Brown, 1941, reprinted, 1972; *Guide to Life and Literature of the Southwest,* University of Texas Press, 1943, revised edition, Southern Methodist University Press, 1952; *A Texan in England,* Little, Brown, 1945; *The Voice of the Coyote,* Little, Brown, 1949; *The Ben Lilly Legend,* Little, Brown, 1950; (contributor) Charles Russell, *Seven Drawings,* Hertzog, 1950; *Sancho and Other Returners: John Latham's Lonesome Longhorn,* Westminster, 1951; *The Mustangs,* Little, Brown, 1952; (author of introduction) Tom Lea, *A Portfolio of Six Paintings,* University of Texas Press, 1953; *Stories of Christmas* [and] *The Bowie Knife,* Steck, 1953; *Up the Trail from Texas,* Random House, 1955; *I'll Tell You a Tale,* Little, Brown, 1960; *Cow People,* Little, Brown, 1964; *Rattlesnakes,* Little, Brown, 1965; *Some Part of Myself,* edited by wife, Bertha M. Dobie, Little, Brown, 1967; *Out of the Old Rock* (character sketches), Little, Brown, 1972; (with Ruth Goddard) *Ralph Ogden* [and] *The Seven Mustangs,* Jenkins, 1973; *Prefaces,* Little, Brown, 1975.

Editor; all originally published by Texas Folklore Society; all reprinted by Southern Methodist University Press: *Coffee in the Gourd,* 1923, reprinted, 1969; *Legends of Texas,* 1924, reprinted, 1976; *Rainbow in the Morning,* 1926, reprinted,

1975; *Texas and Southwestern Lore*, 1927, reprinted, 1967; *Follow de Drinkin' Gou'd*, 1928, reprinted, 1965; *Man, Bird, and Beast*, 1930, reprinted, 1965; *Southwestern Lore*, 1931, reprinted, 1965; *Tone the Bell Easy*, 1932, reprinted, 1965; *Spur-of-the-Cock*, 1933, reprinted, 1965; *Puro Mexicano*, 1935, reprinted, 1969; (with Mody C. Boatwright) *Straight Texas*, 1937, reprinted, 1966; (with Boatright and Harry H. Ransom) *Coyote Wisdom*, 1938, reprinted, 1965; (with Boatwright and Ransom) *In the Shadow of History*, 1939, reprinted, 1971; (with Boatwright and Ransom) *Mustangs and Cow Horses*, 1940, reprinted, 1965; (with Boatwright and Ransom) *Texian Stomping Grounds*, 1941, reprinted, 1967.

Editor: *Happy Hunting Ground*, Texas Folklore Society, 1926, published with L. W. Payne's *When the Woods Were Burnt*, Folklore Associates, 1964; Solomon Wright, *My Rambles as East Texas Cowboy, Hunter, Fisherman, Tie-Cutter*, Texas Folklore Society, 1942; Charles Siringo, *Texas Cowboy*, Sloane, 1950; *Tales of Old-Time Texas*, Little, Brown, 1955. Contributor to *Atlantic Monthly*, *Harper's*, *Saturday Evening Post*, *Holiday*, *Yale Review*, and other magazines.

SIDELIGHTS: J. Frank Dobie once commented on his work: "I've been called a folklorist; I'm not one in a scientific way but have put hundreds of folk tales into books, writing them in my own style. I've been called a historian; I'm not one in a strict sense, but I suppose I can be called a historian of the longhorns, the mustangs, the coyote, and other characters of the West."

Publishers Weekly called him "a controversial figure in his native state of Texas, an individualist who spoke freely in books, articles, and out loud against the 'fascist-minded,' who he had reason to think were becoming more numerous in the country he loved. . . . When a group known as Texans for America were conducting a loud and absurdly effective campaign to remove 'anti-American' textbooks from the Texas school system, [Dobie] testified: 'Censorship is never to let people know but always to darken. It is and for thousands of years has been a main force used by dictators and all manner of tyrannical governments. . . . The more censoring of textbooks, the weaker they become.'"

The Virginia Quarterly Review once lamented that "master commentator that he was of other men's lives, the late Frank Dobie never completed his own projected autobiography," but added, "He did, however, compose a number of initial chapters for such a work, and these [his wife] . . . has happily combined with various published pieces to produce [*Some Part of Myself*], a narrative that covers her husband's [life from his] childhood years in his beloved Brush Country of Southwestern Texas . . . [to] the commencement of his lifelong career collecting the traditional tales and folklore of the Texas-Mexican borderlands. The result is 'straight Texas,' that is, Old Texas: a delightful account of family, ranch, and academic life around the turn of the century, full of the memorable anecdotes, vivid personality sketches, and lively good humor that are the special charm of Dobie's many unique books."

AVOCATIONAL INTERESTS: Book collecting, hunting, swimming, riding.

BIOGRAPHICAL/CRITICAL SOURCES: John William Rogers, *Finding Literature on the Texas Plain*, Southwest Press, 1931; *Time*, September 25, 1964; *Publishers Weekly*, September 28, 1964; *Newsweek*, September 28, 1964; Winston Bode, *Portrait of Pancho*, Pemberton, 1965; *Christian Science Monitor*, December 14, 1967; F. E. Abernethy, *J. Frank Dobie*, Steck-Vaughn, 1967; Mary Louise McVicker, *The Writings of J. Frank Dobie: A Bibliography*, Museum of the Great Plains,

1968; *Virginia Quarterly Review*, Spring, 1968; William A. Owens, *Three Friends*, Doubleday, 1969.†

* * *

DODD, Donald B(radford) 1940-

PERSONAL: Born February 6, 1940, in Manchester, Ala.; son of Ben G. (a businessman and local politician) and Alta (Weaver) Dodd; married Sandra Whitten, June 18, 1961; children: Donna Ellen, Donald Bradford, Jr. *Education:* University of North Alabama, B.S., 1961; Auburn University, M.A., 1966; University of Georgia, Ph.D., 1969. *Religion:* Applied Christianity. *Home:* 6012 Pinebrook Dr., Montgomery, Ala. 36109. *Office:* Department of History, Auburn University, Montgomery, Ala. 36193.

CAREER: Troy State University, Troy, Ala., assistant professor of history, 1968-69; Auburn University, Montgomery, Ala., assistant professor, 1969-72, associate professor, 1972-78, professor of history, 1978—. *Military service:* U.S. Army, 1963-65. U.S. Air Force Reserve, 1972—; now major. *Member:* Organization of American Historians (life member), Southern Historical Association (life member), Phi Alpha Theta, Phi Kappa Phi.

WRITINGS: (With Wynelle Dodd) *Winston: An Antebellum and Civil War History of a Hill County of North Alabama*, Annals of Northwest Alabama, 1972; (with W. Dodd) *Historical Statistics of the South*, University of Alabama Press, 1973; *Historical Atlas of Alabama*, University of Alabama Press, 1974; (with W. Dodd) *Historical Statistics of the Midwest*, University of Alabama Press, 1976; (with Jack Rabin and Wiley Boyles) *Simulations in Government and Contemporary Affairs*, CESCO Press, 1977; (with Ben Williams, Forest Dowdy, and Alfred Goldwaithe) *USAF Credits for the Destruction of Enemy Aircraft*, World War II, Office of Air Force History, 1978; (with Tom Sangster and Dess Sangster) *Alabama Hill Sketches*, Coffeetable, 1980; (author of introduction) Tom Sangster and Dess Sangster, *Alabama's Covered Bridges*, Coffeetable, 1980. Also compiler, with Lynda Brown and Alma Steading, of six bibliographies of Alabama history, published by Vance, 1979-80. Abstractor for *American History and Life* and *Historical Abstracts*, 1971-76. Contributor of articles to *Northwest Alabamian* and *Daily Mountain Eagle* (newspapers), 1971-76; contributor to *American History Illustrated*.

WORK IN PROGRESS: Bibliography of and workbook in Alabama history; *Judging Criteria for History Fairs*; *American Participation in Twentieth Century Wars*; *Unionism in the Confederacy*.

SIDELIGHTS: Donald B. Dodd told *CA:* "My historical research is focused on the history of the people as a whole rather than just the elite. My two statistical compilations and historical atlas use the U.S. Census reports extensively, as the census includes data on all groups and thus is less elitist than traditional sources such as diaries, memoirs, travel accounts, and newspapers. Similarly, popular work on the hill country of Alabama emphasizes the typical, everyday lives of the hill people. Summer educational grants to the ICPSR at the University of Michigan, the Family and Community History Center at Newberry Library in Chicago, and a NEH seminar with the late Bell Wiley at Emory University encouraged my work.

"From a teaching perspective I like the historiographical/multi-disciplinary approach and more classroom participation of students through debating and group problem-solving (techniques of coalition-formation and compromise) which yielded a publication on simulation gaming. I am convinced all undergraduate history students need training in the latest research techniques in the social sciences, interdisciplinary study, and an in-depth probe into an area of interest, e.g. one's own geographical setting, and I am in the process of preparing reference materials and teaching aids to facilitate this training.

"My Air Force Reserve historical research assignment complements my diplomatic history teaching field as does recent work for the Air War College. The latter has given me the opportunity to address a new audience (senior officers in the Air Force) and to reflect on the utility of history. Planned publications will combine military/diplomatic and Southern history."

*   *   *

DOLLEN, Charles Joseph 1926-
(Joseph Benedict)

PERSONAL: Born April 14, 1926; son of Charles Joseph and Cecilia Margaret (Pfeiffer) Dollen. *Education:* St. Bernard's Seminary and College, Rochester, N.Y., B.A., 1948; New Melleray Abbey, advanced study; University of Southern California, Los Angeles, M.S. in Library Science. *Politics:* Democrat. *Home:* 13134 Twin Peaks Rd., P.O. Box 887, Poway, Calif. 92064. *Office:* St. Gabriel's Church, Poway, Calif. 92064.

CAREER: Employee of Eastman Kodak Co., Rochester, N.Y., before entering seminary to study for Roman Catholic priesthood; ordained May 5, 1954; University of San Diego, San Diego, Calif., library director, 1954-65; parish assistant in San Diego, 1954-65, and acting chaplain to Sisters of Social Service, 1957-65; St. Louise de Marillac Parish, El Cajon, Calif., pastor, 1965-68; St. Gabriel's Church, Poway, Calif., founding pastor, 1973—. Acting librarian, St. Francis College, 1965-73, and Immaculate Heart Seminary, 1966-73. Member of board of trustees, Poway Unified School District, 1977-81. *Military service:* U.S. Naval Reserve, chaplain, 1957-64. *Member:* Catholic Library Association (chairman of college section, 1964-65), California Library Association, Knights of Columbus, Legion of Mary.

WRITINGS—Published by Daughters of St. Paul, except as indicated: *Bibliography of the United States Marine Corps,* Scarecrow, 1963; (editor and translator) *A Voice Said Ave!,* 1963; *Jesus Lord,* 1964; *Civil Rights: A Source Book,* 1964, revised edition, 1966; *John F. Kennedy, American,* 1964; *Toward Responsible Parenthood,* Mercy-Guadalupe Clinic, 1964; (editor) C. Marmion, *Fire of Love,* B. Herder, 1964; (editor) St. Augustine, *The Trinity,* 1965; *Index to Sixteen Documents of Vatican II,* 1966; *Mademoiselle Louise: The Life of Louise de Marillac,* 1967; *African Triumph,* 1967; *Ready or Not,* 1968; *Vatican II: A Bibliography,* Scarecrow, 1969; *Messengers to the Americas,* Liturgical Press, 1975; (co-editor) *The Catholic Tradition,* fourteen volumes, Consortium, 1979; *The Catholic Church in the West,* Custombook, 1981. Contributor of articles and book reviews to magazines. Contributing editor, *The Priest,* 1968—.

AVOCATIONAL INTERESTS: Stamp collecting, Marine Corps history.

*   *   *

DONALDS, Gordon
See SHIRREFFS, Gordon D(onald)

*   *   *

DONNA, Natalie 1934-1979

PERSONAL: Born December 25, 1934; died February 9, 1979;

daughter of Patrick B. and Maryanne (Tritto) Donna. *Education:* New York University, B.A. *Home:* 320 East 73rd St., New York, N.Y. 10021.

CAREER: Free-lance writer. Variously worked as advertising agency copywriter in New York, N.Y., and Boston, Mass.; package and product design consultant and copywriter; designer of three historically-based games for children; creator of history, science, math, literature, and geography quizzes for children.

WRITINGS: Boy of the Masai, Dodd, 1964; (self-illustrated) *Bead Craft,* Lothrop, 1972; (self-illustrated) *Peanut Craft,* Lothrop, 1974; *The Peanut Cookbook,* Lothrop, 1976.

WORK IN PROGRESS: Two adult plays; a fact-fiction book on pygmies of the Congo, and the Masai of East Africa; a musical.

SIDELIGHTS: Natalie Donna once told *CA:* "I cannot remember a time when I did not write. As soon as I was technically able to manage a pencil I scribbled poetry and stories. Later I delved into scripts, films and communications. Encouraged to enter the field professionally, I did so as an advertising copywriter."†

*   *   *

DONOVAN, Frank (Robert) 1906-1975

PERSONAL: Born June 6, 1906, in New York, N.Y.; died September 26, 1975, in Norwalk, Conn.; son of Francis Timothy and Lottie (O'Dorell) Donovan; married former wife, Muriel Fischer, 1925; married Joan Douglas, 1947; children: (first marriage) Robert, Muriel Nicholas, Mara Lang; (second marriage) Michael, Kevin. *Religion:* Episcopalian. *Home:* 15 Glory Rd., Weston, Conn.

CAREER: Wildman Advertising Agency, New York City, copywriter, 1922-26; *Magazine of Wall Street,* New York City, business manager, 1929-35; Pathe News, New York City, executive vice-president, 1935-41; Frank Donovan Associates, Inc., New York City, president, 1942-58; writer, 1958-68; instructor, Institute of Children's Literature, 1968-75. *Military service:* U.S. Marine Corps, two years. *Member:* Naval Historical Society, Weston Historical Society. *Awards, honors:* Boys' Clubs of America Junior Book Award, 1963, for *The Early Eagles.*

WRITINGS—All published by Dodd, except as indicated: *The Ironclads* (juvenile), A. S. Barnes, 1961; *The Brave Traitors* (juvenile), A. S. Barnes, 1961; *The Cutters* (juvenile), A. S. Barnes, 1961; *The Medal: The Story of the Medal of Honor,* 1962, revised edition, 1971; *The Tall Frigates,* 1962; (editor) *The Benjamin Franklin Papers,* 1962; *The Early Eagles,* 1962; *Mr. Monroe's Message: The Story of the Monroe Doctrine,* 1963; *The Unlucky Hero,* Duell, Sloan & Pearce, 1963; (editor) *The Thomas Jefferson Papers,* 1963; (editor) *The Autobiography of Benjamin Franklin, and Other Writings,* 1963; (with Whitfield J. Bell) *The Many Worlds of Benjamin Franklin,* 1963; (with Bruce Catton) *Ironclads of the Civil War* (juvenile), American Heritage Publishing, 1964; (with Thomas D. Kendrick) *The Vikings* (juvenile), American Heritage Publishing, 1964; *Famous Twentieth-Century Leaders,* 1964; *Mr. Lincoln's Proclamation: The Story of the Emancipation Proclamation,* 1964; (editor) *The George Washington Papers,* 1964; *The Americanism of Barry Goldwater,* Macfadden, 1964.

Mr. Madison's Constitution: The Story behind the Constitutional Convention, 1965; (editor) *The John Adams Papers,* 1965; *Wheels for a Nation,* Crowell, 1965; *Mr. Roosevelt's Four Freedoms: The Story behind the United Nations Charter,*

1966; *The Women in Their Lives: The Distaff Side of the Founding Fathers,* 1966; *River Boats of America,* Crowell, 1966; *Wild Kids: How Youth Has Shocked Its Elders—Then and Now,* Stackpole, 1967; *Bridge in the Sky,* McKay, 1968; *Dickens and Youth,* 1968 (published in Egland as *The Children of Charles Dickens,* Frewin, 1969); *The Mayflower Compact,* Grosset, 1968; *Mr. Jefferson's Declaration: The Story behind the Declaration of Independence,* 1968; *Raising Your Children: What Behavioral Scientists Have Discovered,* Crowell, 1968; *The Odyssey of the "Essex,"* McKay, 1969.

Prepare Now for a Metric Future, Weybright, 1970; *Never on a Broomstick,* Stackpole, 1971; *Let's Go Metric,* Weybright, 1974.†

* * *

DOSS, Helen (Grigsby)   1918-

PERSONAL: Born August 9, 1918, in Sanderstead, Surrey, England; daughter of Owen Eugene and Maude (Menely) Grigsby; married Carl M. Doss (a Methodist minister), June 20, 1937 (died, 1963); children: Donald, Richard, Dorothy, Elaine, Ted, Laura, Susan, Rita, Diane, Tim, Alex, Gregory. *Education:* Attended Eureka College, 1934-35; Santa Ana Junior College, A.A., 1936; University of Redlands, B.A., 1954; graduate study at University of California, Los Angeles, and Graduate School of Theology, Claremont, Calif. *Religion:* Protestant. *Home:* 6710 East Calle La Paz, No. D, Tucson, Ariz. 85715.

CAREER: Free-lance writer. *Member:* Society of Southwestern Authors.

WRITINGS: The Family Nobody Wanted, Little, Brown, 1954; *A Brother the Size of Me,* Little, Brown, 1957; (with husband, Carl Doss) *If You Adopt a Child,* Holt, 1957; *All the Children of the World,* Abingdon, 1958; *The Really Real Family,* Little, Brown, 1959; *Friends around the World,* Abingdon, 1959; *Jonah,* Abingdon, 1964; *King David,* Abingdon, 1967; *Where Can I Find God?,* Abingdon, 1968; *Young Readers Book of Bible Stories,* Abingdon, 1970; *All the Better to Bite With,* Messner, 1976; *Your Skin Holds You In,* Messner, 1978; *The U.S. Air Force: From Balloons to Spaceships,* Messner, 1981. Contributor of articles to magazines, including *American Girl, McCall's,* and *Readers Digest.*

WORK IN PROGRESS: An adult novel on King David; a British historical novel.

SIDELIGHTS: Helen Doss and her late husband were the parents of twelve adopted children—six boys and six girls—of minority and mixed racial backgrounds. The ancestries of the children include strains of Japanese, Chinese, Filipino, Hawaiian, Mexican, American Indian, East Indian, and various European nationalities. The story of this unusual family is told in *The Family Nobody Wanted, A Brother the Size of Me,* and *The Really Real Family.* This story has twice been adapted for television. In 1956 it was a "Playhouse-90" special on CBS-TV; in 1976 it was an ABC-TV "Movie of the Week" with Shirley Jones playing the part of Helen Doss. The children are now grown and scattered, with homes of their own. So far, Mrs. Doss has twenty-nine grandchildren.

* * *

DOUGLAS, J(ames) D(ixon)   1922-

PERSONAL: Born December 23, 1922, in Glasgow, Scotland; son of James Dickson (a shipyard laborer) and Margaret (Simpson) Douglas. *Education:* Attended University of Glasgow;

University of St. Andrews, M.A., 1949, B.D., 1952; Hartford Theological Seminary (now Hartford Seminary Foundation), Hartford, Conn., S.T.M., 1954, Ph.D., 1955. *Home:* 2 Doocot Rd., St. Andrews, Fife, Scotland. *Office:* c/o *Christianity Today,* 465 Gundersen Dr., Carol Stream, Ill. 60187.

CAREER: Ordained in Church of Scotland, 1953. University of St. Andrews, St. Andrews, Scotland, lecturer in ecclesiastical history, 1955-56; Tyndale House, Cambridge, England, librarian, 1958-61; *Christianity Today,* Carol Stream, Ill., British editorial director and editor-at-large, 1961—. *Military service:* Royal Air Force, 1941-46.

WRITINGS: (Editor) *The New Bible Dictionary,* Eerdmans, 1962; *Light in the North: The Story of the Scottish Covenanters,* Eerdmans, 1964; (editor) *Evangelicals and Unity,* Marcham Manor Press, 1964; (contributor) Carl F.H. Henry, editor, *Baker's Dictionary of Christian Ethics,* Baker Book, 1973; (editor) *The New International Dictionary of the Christian Church,* Zondervan, 1974; (editor) *Let the Earth Hear His Voice,* World Wide Publications, 1975; *Completing the Course: The Story of Lindsay Glegg,* Pickering & Inglis, 1976; *Kingsway Dictionary of the Christian Church,* Kingsway, 1981. Also contributor to *Encyclopedia International.* Author of regular column for *Christianity Today, Church of England Newspaper,* and *Southern Cross.*

SIDELIGHTS: J. D. Douglas writes, "I became a dictionary editor *faute de mieux:* older and wiser scholars rightly recoiled from the task. The sheer logistics are frightening before you even plunge into the morass of minutiae. The trick is to get specialists to do the work while you get your name on the title page. The trouble is, it gives you a reputation for learning which is totally bogus. Said one army colonel to whom I was introduced after my first dictionary was published, 'It's just like meeting the man who built the pyramids.'"

* * *

DOUGLAS-SCOTT-MONTAGU, Edward
See MONTAGU of BEAULIEU, Edward John Barrington

* * *

DREIKURS, Rudolf   1897-1972

PERSONAL: Born February 8, 1897, in Vienna, Austria; came to United States in 1937, naturalized citizen; died May 25, 1972, in Chicago, Ill.; son of Sigmund and Fanny (Cohn) Dreikurs; married Sadie June Ellis, 1943; children: Eric, Eva Ferguson. *Education:* University of Vienna, M.D., 1923.

CAREER: Began practice of medicine in Vienna, Austria, in 1923; Hull House, Chicago, Ill., consulting psychiatrist, 1940-43; Alfred Adler Institute, Chicago, director, 1941-72; Chicago Medical School, Chicago, professor of psychiatry, 1942-66, professor emeritus, 1966-72; Loyola University, Chicago, lecturer in psychiatry, beginning 1957. Founder and medical director, Community Child Guidance Centers of Chicago. Visiting professor, University of Rio de Janeiro, 1946, Northwestern University School of Education, 1947-51, Indiana University, 1951-55, Roosevelt University, 1954-56, University of Oregon, 1957, Southern Illinois University, 1963-64, Bar-Ilan University, Ramat-Gan, Israel, and University of Tel Aviv, Tel Aviv, Israel, 1964-65, Texas Tech University, beginning 1966, and University of Vermont, beginning 1968. Lecturer and speaker at workshops and seminars in Europe, Israel, Brazil and Jamaica.

MEMBER: International Association of Individual Psychology (vice-president, 1957-63), American Psychiatric Association (fellow), Group Psychotherapy Association (fellow), Academy of Psychosomatic Medicine (fellow), American Society of Adlerian Psychology (president, 1954-56), American Society of Group Therapy and Psychodrama (president, 1954-55), American Humanist Association (vice-president, 1950-56), American Academy of Psychotherapists (vice-president, 1959-61), Illinois Society of Personality Study (president, 1945-46).

WRITINGS: Seelische Importenz, S. Hirzel, 1931; *Einfuehrung in die Individual-Psychologie,* [Germany], 1933, translation by Edna G. Fenning published as *An Introduction to Individual Psychology,* K. Paul, Trench & Trubner, 1935, published as *Fundamentals of Adlerian Psychology,* Greenberg, 1950; *The Challenge of Marriage,* Duell, Sloan & Pearce, 1946, revised edition, Hawthorn, 1959, reprinted, Dutton, 1978; *The Challenge of Parenthood,* Duell, Sloan & Pearce, 1948, abridged editions published as *The Challenge of Child Training: A Parents' Guide* and *Coping with Children's Misbehavior: A Parents' Guide,* both Hawthorn, 1972; *Character Education and Spiritual Values in an Anxious Age,* Beacon Press, 1952, reprinted, Alfred Adler Institute, 1971; *Psychology in the Classroom,* Harper, 1957, 2nd edition, 1968; *Adlerian Family Counseling,* University of Oregon Press, 1959; *Group Approaches: Collected Papers of Rudolf Dreikurs,* Alfred Adler Institute, 1960; *Adult-Child Relations,* University of Oregon Press, 1961; *Prevention and Correction of Juvenile Delinquency,* Alfred Adler Institute, 1962; *Psychodynamics, Psychotherapy and Counseling: Collected Papers,* University of Oregon Press, 1963, revised edition, Alfred Adler Institute, 1973; (with Don C. Dinkmeyer) *Encouraging Children to Learn,* Prentice-Hall, 1963; *Child Guidance and Education: Collected Papers,* Alfred Adler Institute, 1964, enlarged edition, 1974; (with Vicki Soltz) *Children: The Challenge,* Duell, Sloan & Pearce, 1964; (with Loren Grey) *Logical Consequences: A New Approach to Discipline,* Hawthorn, 1968, published as *Logical Consequences: A Handbook of Discipline,* Meredith Press, 1968, revised edition published as *A Parents' Guide to Child Discipline,* Hawthorn, 1970; *Grundbegriffe der Individualpsychologie,* E. Klett, 1969.

Social Equality: The Challenge of Today, Regnery, 1971; (with Bernice Bronia Grunwald and Floy C. Pepper) *Maintaining Sanity in the Classroom,* Harper, 1971; (with Pearl Cassel) *Discipline without Tears,* Alfred Adler Institute of Toronto, 1972, 2nd edition, Hawthorn, 1974; (with Erik Blumenthal) *Eltern und Kinder: Freunde oder Feinde?* (based on *The Challenge of Parenthood*), E. Klett, 1973; (with Shirley Gould and Raymond J. Corsini) *Family Council: The Dreikurs Technique for Putting an End to War between Parents and Children (and between Children and Children),* Regnery, 1974, published as *How to Stop Fighting with Your Kids,* Ace Books, 1975. Contributor of articles to scientific journals. Founder, *Journal of Individual Psychology.*

AVOCATIONAL INTERESTS: Chamber music, photography, stamp collecting.

BIOGRAPHICAL/CRITICAL SOURCES: J. Terner and W. L. Pew, *The Courage to Be Imperfect: The Life and Work of Rudolf Dreikurs,* Hawthorn, 1978.†

*   *   *

DRIAL, J. E.
  See LAIRD, Jean E(louise)

DRIFTWOOD, Penelope
  See De LIMA, Clara Rosa

*   *   *

DRINNON, Richard   1925-

PERSONAL: Born January 4, 1925, in Portland, Ore.; son of John Henry (a farmer) and Emma (Tweed) Drinnon; married Anna Maria Faulise, October 20, 1945; children: Donna Elizabeth, Jon Tweed. *Education:* Willamette University, B.A. (summa cum laude), 1950; University of Minnesota, M.A., 1951, Ph.D., 1957. *Politics:* Anarchist. *Office:* Department of History, Bucknell University, Lewisburg, Pa. 17837.

CAREER: University of Minnesota, Minneapolis, instructor in department of interdisciplinary studies, 1953, 1955-57; University of California, Berkeley, instructor, 1957-58, assistant professor of history, 1958-61; University of Leeds, Leeds, England, Bruern Fellow in American Studies, 1961-63; Hobart and William Smith Colleges, Geneva, N.Y., associate professor of history, 1964-66; Bucknell University, Lewisburg, Pa., professor of history, 1966—, chairman of department, 1966-74. Visiting professor, University of Paris, 1975. *Military service:* U.S. Navy, Air Corps, aviation radioman, 1942-46. *Awards, honors:* Fulbright grant to Netherlands, 1953-54; Social Science Research Council faculty research fellowship, 1963-64; National Endowment for the Humanities senior fellowship, 1980-81; American Book Award nomination, 1981, for *Facing West: The Metaphysics of Indian-Hating and Empire-Building.*

WRITINGS: Rebel in Paradise: A Biography of Emma Goldman, University of Chicago Press, 1961; *White Savage: The Case of John Dunn Hunter,* Schocken, 1972; (editor and author of introduction) John D. Hunter, *Memoirs of a Captivity among the Indians of North America,* Schocken, 1973; (editor with wife, Anna M. Drinnon) *Nowhere at Home: Letters from Exile of Emma Goldman and Alexander Berkman,* Schocken, 1974; (editor with A. M. Drinnon) Emma Goldman, *Living My Life,* New American Library, 1977; *Facing West: The Metaphysics of Indian-Hating and Empire-Building,* New American Library, 1980. Contributor to *Nation, Inquiry, New York Times Book Review, Psychoanalytic Review, Twentieth Century, Anarchy,* and *Massachusetts Review.*

WORK IN PROGRESS: Kindly Keeper: Dillon S. Myer and America's Concentration Camps; Charles Erskine Scott Wood: A Biography.

SIDELIGHTS: Richard Drinnon writes to *CA:* " 'What are you? What am I?' asks a shadowy figure in Melville's *Confidence-Man.* 'Nobody knows who anybody is.' I write attempts to find out, to find out what I am and where I might fit into the larger mystery called American history. The books I have written and edited are thus an ongoing series of vision quests that peer (or squint) for answers to two haunting, interrelated questions: How have we become so alienated from [first] ourselves and [second] from the land? Through these writings I seek to liberate myself and sympathetic readers from the strictly *internal* perspective of Western 'civilization' so that we can commence, at long last, to break the national habit of seeing nonwhites as nonpersons. Like Thoreau, whom I revere along with Melville, I too am still looking for the bay horse and the turtledove I lost a long time ago."

*   *   *

DRIVER, Cynthia C.
  See LOVIN, Roger Robert

DRIVER, Harold Edson 1907-

PERSONAL: Born November 17, 1907, in Berkeley, Calif.; son of John Rush and Florence (Flook) Driver; married Wilhelmine Schaeffer, 1950. *Education:* University of California, Berkeley, A.B., 1930, M.A., 1934, Ph.D., 1936; graduate study at University of Chicago, 1930, and Columbia University, 1931. *Home:* 2300 Ptarmigan, Apt. 2, Walnut Creek, Calif. 94595.

CAREER: University of California, Berkeley, research fellow, 1936-37, research associate, 1948-49; Indiana University at Bloomington, assistant professor, 1949-53, associate professor, 1953-58, professor of anthropology, 1958-73. *Member:* American Anthropological Association, American Ethnological Society, Central States Anthropological Society, Indiana Academy of Science (member of committee to choose fellows, 1959-62), Human Relations Area Files (secretary, 1962-63), Sigma Xi (member of committee to select new members), University Club and Anthropology Club (both of Indiana University).

WRITINGS: (With William C. Massey) *Comparative Studies of North American Indians*, American Philosphical Society, 1957; *Indians of North America*, University of Chicago Press, 1961, 2nd edition, 1969; (with wife, Wilhelmine Driver) *Ethnography and Acculturation of the Chichimeca-Jonaz of Northeast Mexico*, Indiana University, 1963; (editor) *The Americas on the Eve of Discovery*, Prentice-Hall, 1964, reprinted, Greenwood Press, 1979; (with W. Driver) *Indian Farmers of North America*, Rand McNally, 1966; (with James L. Coffin) *Classification and Development of North American Indian Cultures: A Statistical Analysis of the Driver-Massey Sample*, American Philosophical Society, 1975; *Culture Groups and Language Groups in Native North America*, Humanities, 1975.

Consultant, ''California Indians'' series, Garland Publishing, beginning 1974. Contributor of articles and monographs to two University of California series, ''American Archeology and Ethnology'' and ''Anthropological Records.'' Contributor to *Encyclopaedia Britannica, International Encyclopedia of the Social Sciences, Encyclopedia Americana, Collier's Encyclopedia,* and to Indiana University's publications of the Research Center in Anthropology, Folklore, and Linguistics. Contributor to professional journals.

AVOCATIONAL INTERESTS: Gardening, photography.

BIOGRAPHICAL/CRITICAL SOURCES: Comparative Studies by Harold E. Driver and Essays in His Honor, Human Relations Area Files, 1974.

* * *

DUBAY, Thomas Edward 1921-

PERSONAL: Born December 30, 1921, in Minneapolis, Minn.; son of Elie Albert and Leah (Caron) Dubay. *Education:* Catholic University of America, M.A., 1951, Ph.D., 1957; University of Ottawa, post-doctoral study, 1957. *Home and office:* Marist Center, 4408 Eighth St. N.E., Washington, D.C. 20017.

CAREER: Ordained Roman Catholic priest, Society of Mary. Notre Dame Seminary, New Orleans, La., teacher, 1952-54, and 1956-67; Marycrest College, Davenport, Iowa, teacher, 1967-68; Russell College, Burlingame, Calif., researcher, 1968-70; Chestnut Hill College, Philadelphia, Pa., teacher, 1970-73. Lecturer for priests and the religious. *Member:* Catholic Theological Society of America, Fellowship of Catholic Scholars.

WRITINGS: The Seminary Rule, Newman, 1954; *The Marist Ideal,* Wickersham, 1959; *The Philosophy of the State as Ed-*

ucator, Bruce Publishers, 1959; *Sisters' Retreats,* Newman, 1963; *Dawn of a Consecration,* Daughters of St. Paul, 1964; *Ecclesial Women: Towards a Theology of the Religious State,* Alba, 1970; *God Dwells within Us,* Dimension Press, 1971; *Caring: A Biblical Theology of Community,* Dimension Press, 1975; *Pilgrims Pray,* Alba, 1975; *Authenticity,* Dimension Press, 1976; *A Call to Virginity,* Visitor Press, 1977; *Religious Commitment,* Dominican Monastery, 1977; *Happy Are You Poor,* Dimension Press, 1981. Also author of *Religious Formation.* Contributor to scholastic and religious journals.

* * *

DUCASSE, C(urt) J(ohn) 1881-1969

PERSONAL: Born July 7, 1881, in Angouleme, France; came to United States in 1900, naturalized in 1910; died September 3, 1969; son of Jean Louis and Clementine Theoda (Grolig) Ducasse; married Mabel Lisle, June 22, 1921 (died, 1976). *Education:* University of Washington, A.B., 1908, A.M., 1909; Harvard University, Ph.D., 1912. *Office:* Brown University, Providence, R.I.

CAREER: University of Washington, Seattle, instructor in philosophy and psychology, 1912-16, assistant professor, 1916-24, associate professor of philosophy, 1924-26; Brown University, Providence, R.I., associate professor, 1926-29, professor, 1929-58, chairman of department of philosophy, 1930-51, acting dean of Graduate School, 1947-49, professor emeritus, 1958-69. Part-time lecturer at New York University, Radcliffe College, and Boston University, visiting summer professor at University of California, University of Michigan, Cornell University, University of Chicago, and Columbia University; University of California, Howison Lecturer, 1944, Foerster Lecturer, 1947; Flint Visiting Professor, University of Washington, 1946, University of California, Los Angeles, spring, 1947; Walker-Ames Visiting Professor, University of Washington, 1946; Prall Memorial Lecturer, 1947; Paul Carus Lecturer, American Philosophical Association, 1949; J. W. Graham Lecturer, Swarthmore College, 1951.

MEMBER: Association for Symbolic Logic (president, 1936-38), American Philosophical Association (president, 1939), American Society for Aesthetics (president, 1945-46; trustee, 1946-49), Philosophy of Science Association (president, 1958-61), American Academy of Arts and Sciences (fellow), American Association for the Advancement of Science (fellow), American Council of Learned Societies (member of executive committee, 1939-41), American Society for Psychical Research (first vice-president, beginning 1966), American Association of University Professors (member of council, 1954-57), British Society for Psychical Research (corresponding member), Phi Beta Kappa. *Awards, honors:* Brown University, A.M. (ad eundem), 1943, D.Litt., 1961.

WRITINGS: Causation and the Types of Necessity, University of Washington Press, 1924, reprinted, Dover, 1969; *The Philosophy of Art,* Dial, 1930, revised edition, Dover, 1966; (contributor) G. P. Adams and W. P. Montague, editors, *Contemporary American Philosophy,* two volumes, Macmillan, 1930; *The Relation of Philosophy to General Education,* Rockefeller Foundation, 1932; *Philosophy as a Science: Its Matter and Its Method,* Oskar Piest, 1941, reprinted, Greenwood Press, 1974; (contributor) P. A. Schlipp, editor, *The Philosophy of G. E. Moore,* Northwestern University, 1943; *Art, the Critics and You,* Oskar Piest, 1944; (with others) *Philosophy in American Education: Its Tasks and Opportunities,* Harper, 1945, reprinted, AMS Press, 1975; *Nature, Mind and Death* (Carus Lectures), Open Court, 1951; *A Philosophical Scrutiny of Re-*

ligion, Ronald, 1953; (with R. M. Blake and E. H. Madden) *Theories of Scientific Method: The Renaissance through the Nineteenth Century*, University of Washington Press, 1960; *A Critical Examination of the Belief in a Life after Death*, C. C Thomas, 1961; *Paranormal Phenomena, Science, and Life after Death* (monograph), Parapsychology Foundation, 1969; *Truth, Knowledge and Causation*, Humanities Press, 1969.

Contributor to ten other books on philosophy, 1930-61. Contributor of more than a hundred articles and eighty reviews to periodicals, mainly professional journals.

WORK IN PROGRESS: Several books in the field of philosophy.

BIOGRAPHICAL/CRITICAL SOURCES: Frederick C. Dommeyer, editor, *Current Philosophical Issues: Essays in Honor of Curt John Ducasse*, C. C Thomas, 1966.†

*   *   *

DUDLEY, Geoffrey A(rthur) 1917-

PERSONAL: Born January 8, 1917, in Grantham, Lincolnshire, England; son of Arthur Edwin and Ethel Florence (Bland) Dudley; married Eva Senescall, January 24, 1942; children: Susan Mary, Carol Frances Mary. *Education:* University of Nottingham, B.A., 1938. *Home:* 1 Thornton Dr., Handforth, Wilmslow, Cheshire SK9 3DA, England. *Office:* R. & W. Heap Publishing Co. Ltd., Bowden Hall, Marple, Cheshire SK6 6NE, England.

CAREER: Psychology Publishing Co. Ltd. (educational publishers), Marple, Cheshire, England, director of studies, beginning 1942; currently director of studies, R. & W. Heap Publishing Co. Ltd., Marple. Director of *Successful Living* magazine, 1952-68. *Military service:* British Army, Royal Artillery, gunner, 1939-41.

WRITINGS: Dreams: Their Meaning and Significance, Thorsons Publishers, 1956, published as *How to Understand Your Dreams*, Wilshire, 1957; (translator from the French) Louis Frederic, *Yoga Asanas*, Thorsons Publishers, 1959; (translator from the German) Otto H. F. Buchinger, *About Fasting*, Thorsons Publishers, 1961; *The Right Way to Interpret Your Dreams*, Elliot Right Way Books, 1961; *Self-Help for Self-Mastery*, Fowler, 1962; *Your Personality and How to Use It*, Emerson, 1962; (editor) Hartrampf, *Vocabulary-Builder*, Psychology Publishing Co., 1963; *Rapid Reading*, Psychology Publishing Co., 1964, revised edition, Thorsons Publishers, 1977; (contributor) *Course in Practical English*, Practical English Programme, 1965; *Use Your Imagination*, Thorsons Publishers, 1965.

Increase Your Learning Power, Thorsons Publishers, 1966; *Budget Accounts*, Lewis's, 1966; (editor) Bergen Evans, *Vocabulary Studies*, Psychology Publishing Co., 1967; (translator from the German) Maria Vogel, *Home Nursing*, Thorsons Publishers, 1967; (translator from the German) Lisa Mar, *Overweight Do's, Don'ts and Diet*, Thorsons Publishers, 1967; *Dreams: Their Mysteries Revealed*, Aquarian Press, 1969; (with Elizabeth Pugh) *How to Be a Good Talker*, Psychology Publishing Co., 1971; *How to Interpret Dreams Correctly*, A. N. Efstratiadis, 1973; (with Georg Fischhof) *Psychogenes Training*, Forum Verlag, 1974; (contributor) *New Course in Practical English*, Practical English Programme, 1975; (contributor) *Effective Speaking and Writing*, Effective Speaking Programme, 1979. Contributor to *International Journal of Sexology*, *Freethinker*, *The Psychologist Magazine*, and *Memo*.

SIDELIGHTS: Geoffrey A. Dudley writes to *CA:* "My writings fall into a category which I call 'self-improvement.' If a reader learns from one of my books just a single point that will benefit him in some way, I feel amply rewarded for writing the book. I regard the writer-reader relationship as a two-way one; [I] try not only to teach something but also to learn what I can from readers' letters. Such letters often contain amusing and surprising comments. For example, one reader who relied on help from a book of mine while preparing for an examination said that she was so surprised when she passed with distinction that she could hardly believe it. She thought the examiner had made a mistake!

"*How to Be a Good Talker* differs from my other books in that it is not arranged in traditional form to be read from one page to the next. It is a programmed book on conversation divided into 'frames,' each containing a unit of instruction followed by a question. The page that a reader goes to next is determined by the the answer he gives to the question. Although this method strikes some readers as unfamiliar, comments on it generally have been favorable."

AVOCATIONAL INTERESTS: Cinema, philately, home wine-making.

*   *   *

du MAURIER, Daphne 1907-

PERSONAL: Born May 13, 1907, in London, England; daughter of Gerald (an actor and manager) and Muriel (an actress; maiden name, Beaumont) du Maurier; married Frederick Arthur Montague Browning (a lieutenant-general and former treasurer to the Duke of Edinburgh), July 19, 1932 (died, 1965); children: Tessa (Mrs. David Montgomery), Flavia Browning Tower, Christian. *Education:* Educated in London, England, Meudon, France, and Paris, France. *Politics:* "Center." *Home:* Kilmarth, Par, Cornwall, England. *Agent:* Mollie Waters, Frith Cottage, Aldington, Kent, England.

CAREER: Writer, 1931—. *Member:* Bronte Society, Royal Society of Literature (fellow). *Awards, honors:* National Book Award, 1938, for *Rebecca;* Dame Commander, Order of the British Empire, 1969.

WRITINGS—Novels: The Loving Spirit, Doubleday, 1931, reprinted, Pan Books, 1976; *I'll Never Be Young Again*, Doubleday, 1932, reprinted, Pan Books, 1975; *The Progress of Julius*, Doubleday, 1933, reprinted, Avon, 1973; *Jamaica Inn* (also see below), Doubleday, 1936, reprinted, Avon, 1977, abridged edition, edited by Jay E. Greene, bound with *The Thirty Nine Steps* by John Buchan, Globe Publications, 1951; *Rebecca* (also see below), Doubleday, 1938, reprinted, Avon, 1978; *Frenchman's Creek* (also see below), Gollancz, 1941, Doubleday, 1942, reprinted, Pan Books, 1976; *Hungry Hill* (also see below), Doubleday, 1943, reprinted, Avon, 1974; *The King's General*, Doubleday, 1946, reprinted, Avon, 1978, abridged edition, edited by Lee Wyndham, Garden City Books, 1954; *The Parasites*, Gollancz, 1949, Doubleday, 1950, reprinted, Avon, 1974.

My Cousin Rachel (also see below), Gollancz, 1951, Doubleday, 1952, reprinted, Bentley, 1971; *Mary Anne* (fictionalized biography of author's great-great grandmother), Doubleday, 1954, reprinted, Avon, 1973; *The Scapegoat*, Doubleday, 1957, reprinted, Queen's House, 1977; *Three Romantic Novels: Rebecca, Frenchman's Creek, Jamaica Inn*, Doubleday, 1961; (with Arthur Quiller-Couch) *Castle d'Or*, Doubleday, 1962; *The Glass-Blowers*, Doubleday, 1963; *The Flight of the Falcon*, Doubleday, 1965; *The House on the Strand* (Literary Guild selection), Doubleday, 1969; *Rule Britannia*, Gollancz, 1972, Doubleday, 1973; *Four Great Cornish Novels* (contains *Ja-*

maica Inn, Rebecca, Frenchman's Creek, and *My Cousin Rachel*), Gollancz, 1978.

Short story collections: *Come Wind, Come Weather*, Heinemann, 1940, Doubleday, 1941; *The Apple Tree: A Short Novel and Some Stories*, Gollancz, 1952, published as *Kiss Me Again, Stranger: A Collection of Eight Stories, Long and Short*, Doubleday, 1953, reprinted, Avon, 1972 (published in England as *The Birds, and Other Stories*, Pan Books, 1977); *The Breaking Point*, Doubleday, 1959 (published in England as *The Blue Lenses, and Other Stories*, Penguin, 1970); *Early Stories*, Todd, 1959; *The Treasury of du Maurier Short Stories*, Gollancz, 1960; *Don't Look Now*, Doubleday, 1971 (published in England as *Not after Midnight*, Gollancz, 1971); *Echoes from the Macabre: Selected Stories*, Gollancz, 1976; Doubleday, 1977; *The Rendez-vous, and Other Stories*, Gollancz, 1980.

Plays: *Rebecca* (three-act; based on author's novel of same title; produced on the West End at Queen's Theatre, April 5, 1940, produced on Broadway at Ethel Barrymore Theatre, January 18, 1945), Gollancz, 1940, Dramatists Play Service, 1943; *The Years Between* (two-act; first produced in Manchester, England, 1944, produced on the West End at Wyndham's Theatre, January 10, 1945), Gollancz, 1945, Doubleday, 1946; *September Tide* (three-act; produced on the West End at Aldwych Theatre, December 15, 1948), Gollancz, 1949, Doubleday, 1950.

Other works: *Gerald: A Portrait* (biography of author's father), Gollancz, 1934, Doubleday, 1935, reprinted, Richard West, 1978; *The du Mauriers* (family history and biography), Doubleday, 1937; *Happy Christmas*, Doubleday, 1940; *Spring Picture*, Todd, 1944; (editor) *The Young George du Maurier: A Selection of His Letters, 1860-1867*, P. Davies, 1951, Doubleday, 1952; *The Infernal World of Branwell Bronte* (biography), Gollancz, 1960, Doubleday, 1961; (editor) Phyllis Bottome, *Best Stories*, Faber, 1963; *Vanishing Cornwall* (history and travel), Doubleday, 1967; *Golden Lads: Sir Francis Bacon, Anthony Bacon and Their Friends*, Doubleday, 1975; *The Winding Stair: Francis Bacon, His Rise and Fall*, Gollancz, 1976, Doubleday, 1977; *Myself When Young: The Shaping of a Writer* (autobiography), Doubleday, 1977 (published in England as *Growing Pains: The Shaping of a Writer*, Gollancz, 1977); *The "Rebecca" Notebook, and Other Memories*, Doubleday, 1980. Also co-author of a screenplay, "Hungry Hill" (based on author's novel of same title), Universal Pictures, 1947.

SIDELIGHTS: "Last night I dreamt I went to Manderley again. . . ." With these words, some of the most recognizable in twentieth-century fiction, Daphne du Maurier began her classic Gothic novel *Rebecca*. Described by the *Spectator*'s Kate O'Brien as "a Charlotte Bronte story *minus* Charlotte Bronte," *Rebecca* takes a familiar situation (the arrival of a second wife in her new husband's home) and turns it into an occasion for mystery, suspense, and violence. Its primary features—an enigmatic heroine in a cold and hostile environment, a brooding hero tormented by a guilty secret, and a rugged seacoast setting—are now virtual staples of modern romantic novels. Though reviewers point out (and du Maurier agrees) that she cannot take credit for inventing this formula, many of them believe that her personal gift for story-telling places her novels a cut above most other Gothic fiction.

Daughter of renowned actor Gerald du Maurier and granddaughter of artist and author George du Maurier (*Trilby*), young Daphne first turned to writing as a means of escape. Despite a happy and financially secure childhood, she always felt "inadequate" and desperately in need of solitude. She delighted in the imaginary world of books and play-acting and stubbornly

resisted "growing up" until her late teens. After shunning the debutante scene and a chance at an acting career, du Maurier determined to succeed on her own terms—as a writer. During one ten-week stay at her parents' country home on the Cornish coast, the twenty-four-year-old Englishwoman wrote her first novel, *The Loving Spirit*, a romantic family chronicle. A bestseller that achieved a fair share of critical acclaim as well, *The Loving Spirit* so impressed a thirty-five-year-old major in the Grenadier Guards that he piloted his motor launch past the du Maurier home in the hope of meeting the author. Major Frederick "Boy" Browning eventually introduced himself as the son of a man who had known Gerald du Maurier at the Garrick Club in London. Daphne and Major Browning married a few months later, setting off by boat on a honeymoon "just like the couple in *The Loving Spirit*," as Nicholas Wade points out in the *Times Literary Supplement*.

Perhaps because of the fairy-tale quality in her own life, du Maurier has displayed a fondness for romance and intrigue throughout her entire writing career. While some critics feel her short stories ("The Birds" and "Don't Look Now" are probably two of the best-known ones) represent her best work in a *literary* sense, few dispute the fact that her novels form the basis of her immense popular success. As V.S. Pritchett remarks in a review of *Rebecca*: "Many a better novelist would give his eyes to be able to tell a story as Miss Du Maurier does, to make it move at such a pace and to go with such mastery from surprise to surprise. . . . From the first sinister rumors to the final conflagration the melodrama is excellent."

The *New York Times*'s M.F. Brown also comments on du Maurier's "ability to tell a good story and people it with twinkling reality," while John Patton of *Books* writes: "[Rebecca] is first and last and always a thrilling story. . . . Du Maurier's style in telling her story is exactly suited to her plot and her background, and creates the exact spirit and atmosphere of the novel. The rhythm quickens with the story, is always in measure with the story's beat. And the writing has an intensity, a heady beauty, which is itself the utterance of the story's mood." The *Manchester Guardian*'s J.D. Beresford agrees, stating that "the actual writing of [Rebecca] has the compelling quality that holds the attention in thrall, keeping our interest unintermittently rapt in the story."

Among those who are less impressed by du Maurier's work (other than *Rebecca*) are critics who feel her novels exhibit too much melodrama, too many plot similarities, and too little character development and analysis. O'Brien describes *Frenchman's Creek*, for example, as "eighteenth century, flashy, wordy, and full of 'sunset and dark water' effects." The *New Yorker*'s Clifton Fadiman terms it "lushly nonsensical," and Edward Weeks of the *Atlantic* believes the "drag in the dialogue," the "flatness in the characters," and the lack of an "inner spark" make this novel an inadequate follow-up to "the overpowering illusion in *Rebecca*." Notes a *Springfield Republican* reviewer: "[Frenchman's Creek] lacks a proper tempo of excitement. Its plot seems artificial. . . . We see [the heroine] only as she is influenced by [her] strange adventurous love affair. . . . One who likes an exceedingly romantic love affair will read this story. . . with pleasure, but it has not the sort of stuff that made readers of *Rebecca* cling to that book until they had read the last page."

With the exception of *My Cousin Rachel*, a book several critics hail as another *Rebecca*, most of du Maurier's later novels seem to suffer in comparison to the work some view as a minor classic. The *Spectator*'s Paul Ableman, for instance, declares that her "plots creak and depend on either outrageous coincidence or shamelessly contrived mood," that her prose is "both sloppy and chaotic," and that her dialog consists of "rent-a-line, prefabricated units for the nobs or weird demotic for the yokels." L.A.G. Strong, another *Spectator* critic, also notes the "facile, out-of-character lines that disfigure the often excellent dialogue," as well as a certain "laziness over detail" and a "mixture of careful with perfunctory work." In addition, insists Beatus T. Lucey of *Best Sellers,* "nowhere does the reader become engaged and involved in the action." Lucey also points out that du Maurier's people are mere "types," a view shared by the *Los Angeles Times*'s Marilyn Murray Willison, who says her male characters are all "creatures who bully—physically or psychologically."

Du Maurier herself admits that she is "not so much interested in people as in types—types who represent great forces of good or evil. I don't care very much whether John Smith likes Mary Robinson, goes to bed with Jane Brown and then refuses to pay the hotel bill. But I *am* passionately interested in human cruelty, human lust and human avarice—and, of course, their counterparts in the scale of virtue."

Despite the views of critics who complain about plot similarities and stereotyped characters, Jean Stubbs of *Books and Bookman* remains convinced that a writer like du Maurier should "seek out his or her personal Wilderness or Eden and stay in it." "Daphne Du Maurier has the deserved reputation of being an outstanding storyteller," Stubbs writes. "She has the gift of conveying mystery and holding suspense, above all of suggesting the grip of the unknown on ordinary lives. . . . She is passionately devoted to Cornwall, and insists on our participation. Her sense of theatre creates some characters a little larger than life, and her commonsense surrounds them with people we have met and known, so that the eccentric and dramatic is enhanced."

Furthermore, as a writer for the *Times Literary Supplement* points out in a review of *Rebecca,* it may not be to anyone's benefit to approach du Maurier's work as one would approach great literature. He states: "If one chooses to read the book in a critical fashion—but only a tiresome reviewer is likely to do that—it becomes an obligation to take off one's hat to Miss du Maurier for the skill and assurance with which she sustains a highly improbable fiction. Whatever else she may lack, it is not the story-teller's flow of fancy. All thing considered, [hers] is an ingenious, exciting and engagingly romantic tale."

Concludes the *Chicago Tribune Book World*'s Anstiss Drake: "There is no doubt that Du Maurier, right at the start of her career, hit on a brilliant combination of ingredients that will continue to hold readers spellbound for a long time. . . . [Her characters] are as real to us as any of Dickens' creations. . . . She sweeps dust away and brings her stories alive. It is a rare talent. . . . In this century few English-speaking authors seem to keep that particular magic. Somerset Maugham was one, and Du Maurier is most definitely another."

MEDIA ADAPTATIONS: Several of Daphne du Maurier's novels and short stories have been adapted for film and television. Alfred Hitchcock directed *Jamaica Inn* for Paramount Pictures Corp. in 1939, *Rebecca* for United Artists Corp. in 1940 (it won an Academy Award for best motion picture as well as a citation by the Film Daily Poll as one of the ten best pictures of the year), and "The Birds" for Universal Pictures in 1963. *Frenchman's Creek* was filmed by Paramount in 1944, *Hungry Hill* by J. Arthur Rank in 1947, *My Cousin Rachel* by Metro-Goldwyn-Mayer, Inc., in 1953, *The Scapegoat* by Metro-Goldwyn-Mayer in 1959, and "Don't Look Now" by Paramount in 1973. In 1979, the British Broadcasting Corp. televised a new adaptation of *Rebecca.*

AVOCATIONAL INTERESTS: Walking, sailing, gardening, country life.

BIOGRAPHICAL/CRITICAL SOURCES: Saturday Review, February 28, 1931, April 24, 1937, September 24, 1938, June 19, 1943, January 12, 1946, February 7, 1948, January 7, 1950, February 9, 1952, July 19, 1952, March 14, 1953, February 23, 1957, October 11, 1969; *Spectator,* February 28, 1931, January 24, 1936, August 12, 1938, September 19, 1941, August 10, 1951, May 14, 1977, November 15, 1980; *Times Literary Supplement,* March 5, 1931, January 11, 1936, August 6, 1938, September 13, 1941, June 3, 1977, December 26, 1980; *New Statesman and Nation,* March 14, 1931, August 11, 1951; *Books,* August 2, 1931, September 25, 1938, February 1, 1942; *New York Times,* August 2, 1931, April 26, 1936, September 25, 1938, February 1, 1942, February 10, 1952; *Outlook,* August 5, 1931; *Nation,* November 11, 1931; *Saturday Review of Literature,* December 12, 1931, April 25, 1936, September 24, 1938, February 14, 1942; *Manchester Guardian,* January 10, 1936, August 5, 1938, September 19, 1941, August 3, 1951; *Christian Science Monitor,* September 14, 1938, October 2, 1969, September 21, 1977; *Newsweek,* September 26, 1938, January 9, 1950, June 24, 1954; *Canadian Forum,* October, 1938; *Publishers Weekly,* February 18, 1939, January 31, 1948.

Springfield Republican, January 11, 1942; *New Yorker,* February 7, 1942, February 9, 1952, September 23, 1967; *Atlantic,* April, 1942; *Commonweal,* April 10, 1942; *Life,* September 11, 1944, February 6, 1970; *Theatre Arts,* March, 1945; *Time,* November 3, 1947, January 16, 1950, February 11, 1952, June 21, 1954, February 25, 1957, February 23, 1962; *New York Herald Tribune Book Review,* February 10, 1952; *Ladies' Home Journal,* November, 1956; *Best Sellers,* May 1, 1963, October 15, 1969; *Observer,* July 16, 1967; *New York Times Book Review,* October 26, 1969, November 6, 1977, September 21, 1980; *Books and Bookmen,* January, 1973; *Contemporary Literary Criticism,* Gale, Volume VI, 1976, Volume XI, 1979; Daphne du Maurier, *Myself When Young: The Shaping of a Writer,* Doubleday, 1977 (published in England as *Growing Pains: The Shaping of a Writer,* Gollancz, 1977); *Listener,* June 9, 1977; *Detroit News,* November 13, 1977; *Critic,* September, 1978; *Chicago Tribune Book World,* September 21, 1980; *Los Angeles Times,* October 3, 1980.

—*Sketch by Deborah A. Straub*

*   *   *

DUNBAR, Janet 1901-

PERSONAL: Surname is accented on second syllable; born May 15, 1901, in Glasgow, Scotland; married Clifford Ernest Webb (a scientist), June 30, 1923; children: Lysbeth (Mrs. Ralph Merrifield), Philip (deceased), Frances (Mrs. Ronald Presley). *Education:* Attended University of London, 1920-23. *Religion:* Non-denominational. *Agent:* John Cushman Associates, 24 East 38th St., New York, N.Y. 10016; and Curtis Brown Ltd., 1 Craven Hill, London W2 3EW, England.

CAREER: Free-lance writer, 1920—. Lecturer on travel and literary subjects. British Broadcasting Corp., London, England, broadcaster on Overseas Services, and on other services, 1942—. *Member:* Society of Authors, Guild of Travel Writers.

WRITINGS: The Early Victorian Woman: Some Aspects of Her Life, 1837-57, Harrap, 1953; *Golden Interlude: The Edens in India, 1936-42* (*Daily Mail* Book-of-the-Month choice in England), J. Murray, 1955; *The Radio Talk,* Harrap, 1957; *Five Festival Plays,* Harrap, 1958; *Flora Robson,* Harrap, 1960; *A Job in Television,* Museum Press, 1961; *Mrs. G.B.S.: A Por-*

trait, Harper, 1963 (published in England as *Mrs. G.B.S.: A Biographical Portrait of Charlotte Shaw*, Harrap, 1963); *A Prospect of Richmond*, Houghton, 1966, revised edition, White Lion Publishers, 1973; *Script-Writing for Television*, Sportshelf, 1966; *Peg Woffington and Her World*, Houghton, 1968; *J. M. Barrie: The Man Behind the Image*, Houghton, 1970; *Laura Knight*, Collins, 1975; *Into Retirement: The Bonus Years*, Arrow Books, 1976; *New Larousse Gastronomique: The World's Greatest Cookery Reference Book*, Hamlyn, 1978; *Richmond-upon-Thames: A Short Guide*, privately printed, 1978. Also author of a play, *Countess in Family*. Writer of radio scripts and two documentary films. Travel adviser, *Woman's Journal*.

WORK IN PROGRESS: Laura Knight: A Biography, for Collins.

AVOCATIONAL INTERESTS: Theatre, music, and travel.

BIOGRAPHICAL/CRITICAL SOURCES: Punch, September 11, 1968; *Times Literary Supplement*, September 19, 1968; *Christian Science Monitor*, September 26, 1968; *Drama*, winter, 1968; *New York Times*, August 28, 1970; *Atlantic*, September, 1970; *Listener*, September 24, 1970; *Books and Bookmen*, October, 1970, June, 1979; *New Statesman*, October 9, 1970, May 16, 1975; *Esquire*, January, 1971.

*   *   *

DUNCAN, Otis Dudley   1921-

PERSONAL: Born December 2, 1921, in Nocona, Tex.; son of Otis Durant and Ola (Johnson) Duncan; married Beverly Davis (a writer), January 16, 1954. *Education:* Attended Oklahoma Agricultural and Mechanical College (now Oklahoma State University), 1938-40; Louisiana State University, B.A., 1941; University of Minnesota, M.A., 1942; University of Iowa, graduate study, 1943; University of Chicago, Ph.D., 1949. *Home:* 626 North Norton Ave., Tucson, Ariz. 85719. *Office:* Department of Sociology, University of Arizona, Tucson, Ariz. 85721.

CAREER: Pennsylvania State College (now University), University Park, assistant professor of sociology, 1948-50; University of Wisconsin—Madison, assistant professor of sociology, 1950-51; University of Chicago, Chicago, Ill., assistant professor of sociology, 1951-56, associate professor of human ecology, 1957-60, professor of human ecology, 1960-62, associate director of Chicago Community Inventory, 1951-56, associate director of Population Research and Training Center, 1953-56; University of Michigan, Ann Arbor, professor of sociology, 1962-69, Charles Horton Cooley University Professor of Sociology, 1969-73, associate director, Population Studies Center, 1962-67, director, 1967-68; University of Arizona, Tucson, professor of sociology, 1973—. Visiting professor, University of Michigan, 1955, University of Southern California, 1960, Institute for Advanced Studies (Vienna), 1973; visitor, Nuffield College, Oxford University, 1968. Member of Human Ecology Study Section of National Institutes of Health, 1959-62, Research Grants Panel, Social Security Administration, 1964-67, Commission on Population Growth and the American Future, 1970-72, and Citizens Committee on Population Growth and the American Future, 1972-73. National Research Council, co-chairman of Committee on the Survey of the Behavioral and Social Sciences, 1967-68, member of Committee on Nuclear and Alternative Energy Systems, 1975-79. Advisor, at various times, to U.S. Department of Health, Education, and Welfare, U.S. Department of Commerce, U.S. Census Bureau, Social Science Research Council, and Institute of Social Research. *Military service:* U.S. Army, 1942-46.

MEMBER: Population Association of America (member of board of directors, 1954-57; vice-president, 1965-66; president, 1968-69), American Statistical Association (fellow; chairman of Social Statistics Section, 1971), American Sociological Association (associate member), American Academy of Arts and Sciences (fellow; member of Western Center executive committee, 1978-79), National Academy of Sciences, American Philosophical Association.

AWARDS, HONORS: Sorokin Award, American Sociological Association, 1968, for *The American Occupational Structure*; Samual A. Stouffler Award, American Sociological Association, 1977, for contributions to the advancement of sociological research; D.H.L., University of Chicago, 1979; Commonwealth Award, 1980, for distinguished service in the field of sociology.

WRITINGS: (With Albert J. Reiss, Jr.) *Social Characteristics of Urban and Rural Communities, 1950*, Wiley, 1956; (editor with Joseph J. Spengler) *Population Theory and Policy: Selected Readings*, Free Press of Glencoe, 1956; (editor with Spengler) *Demographic Analysis: Selected Readings*, Free Press of Glencoe, 1956; (with wife, Beverly Duncan) *The Negro Population of Chicago*, University of Chicago Press, 1957; (editor with Philip M. Hauser and contributor) *The Study of Population: An Inventory and Appraisal*, University of Chicago Press, 1959; (author of foreword) G. Franklin Edwards, *The Negro Professional Class*, Free Press of Glencoe, 1959.

(With W. Richard Scott, Stanley Lieberson, Hal H. Winsborough, and B. Duncan) *Metropolis and Region*, Johns Hopkins Press, 1960; (translator with Harold W. Pfautz) Maurice Halbwachs, *Population and Society: Introduction to Social Morphology*, Free Press of Glencoe, 1960; (with Ray P. Cuzzort and B. Duncan) *Statistical Geography: Problems in Analyzing Areal Data*, Free Press of Glencoe, 1961; (with Reiss, Paul K. Hatt, and Cecil C. North) *Occupations and Social Status*, Free Press of Glencoe, 1961; (editor and author of introduction) William F. Ogburn, *On Culture and Social Change: Selected Writings*, University of Chicago Press, 1964; (with Peter M. Blau) *The American Occupational Structure*, Wiley, 1967; *Toward Social Reporting: Next Steps*, Russell Sage, 1969.

(With David L. Featherman and B. Duncan) *Socioeconomic Background and Achievement*, Seminar Press, 1972; (editor with Arthur S. Goldberger and contributor) *Structural Equation Models in the Social Sciences*, Seminar Press, 1973; (with Howard Schuman and B. Duncan) *Social Change in a Metropolitan Community*, Russell Sage, 1973; *Introduction to Structural Equation Models*, Academic Press, 1975; (with B. Duncan) *Sex Typing and Social Roles: A Research Report*, Academic Press, 1978.

Contributor: Hatt and Reiss, editors, *A Reader in Urban Sociology*, Free Press of Glencoe, 1951; Hatt and Reiss, editors, *Cities and Society*, Free Press of Glencoe, 1957; D. V. Glass, editor, *Teaching of Social Sciences: Demography*, UNESCO, 1957; William Dobriner, editor, *The Suburban Community*, Putnam, 1958.

George A. Theodorson, editor, *Studies in Human Ecology*, Row, Peterson, 1961; Ernest W. Burgess and Donald J. Bogue, editors, *Contributions to Urban Sociology*, University of Chicago Press, 1964; R. E. L. Faris, editor, *Handbook of Modern Sociology*, Rand McNally, 1964; N. J. Smelser and S. M. Lipset, editors, *Social Structure and Social Mobility in Economic Development*, Aldine, 1966; Eleanor B. Sheldon and Wilbert E. Moore, editors, *Indicators of Social Change*, Russell Sage, 1968; Daniel P. Moynihan, editor, *On Understanding Poverty*, Basic Books, 1969.

H. M. Blalock, Jr., editor, *Causal Models in the Social Sciences*, Aldine, 1971; J. M. Ridge, editor, *Mobility in Britain Reconsidered*, Clarendon Press, 1974; T. W. Schultz, editor, *Economics of the Family*, University of Chicago Press, 1974; Roxann A. Van Dusen, editor, *Social Indicators, 1973: A Review Symposium*, Social Science Research Council, 1974; Kenneth C. Land and Seymour Spilerman, editors, *Social Indicator Models*, Russell Sage, 1975; Blalock and others, editors, *Quantitative Sociology*, Academic Press, 1975; (with Blau) A.P.M. Coxon and C. L. Jones, editors, *Social Mobility*, Penguin (Hammondsworth, England), 1975; Hans J. Hummell and Rolf Ziegler, editors, *Korrelation und Kausalitaet*, Ferdinand Enke Verlag, Volume II, 1976, Volume III (with A. O. Haller and A. Portes), 1976; Y. Elkana and others, editors, *Toward a Metric of Science: The Advent of Science Indicators*, Wiley, 1978.

Author of eleven monographs, most with wife, Beverly Davis Duncan, for "Urban Analysis" series, Chicago Community Inventory, University of Chicago, 1951-53; also author of government bulletins. Regular contributor to yearbook, *Sociological Methodology;* contributor to proceedings and to *Encyclopaedia Britannica*, *Collier's Encyclopedia*, and *Woerterbuch der Soziologie*. Contributor of more than sixty articles on population, human ecology, and social stratification, and about fifty reviews to journals.

Associate editor, *American Sociological Review*, 1955-57; member of editorial board, *American Journal of Sociology*, 1955-61, *Journal of Human Ecology*, 1971—, and *Social Science Research*, 1971—; *Sociological Methodology*, advisory editor, 1969-70, member of editorial board, 1970-72; book review editor, *Social Biology*, 1969-71.

*   *   *

DUNCAN, W(illiam) Murdoch 1909-1976
(John Cassells, John Dallas, Neill Graham, Martin Locke, Peter Malloch, Lovat Marshall)

PERSONAL: Born November 18, 1909, in Glasgow, Scotland; died April 19, 1976; son of William Kelly (an engineer) and Mary (Murdoch) Duncan; married Marion Hughes; children: Neil Murdoch, Rosemary Hughes. *Education:* Attended Windsor and Walkerville Collegiate Institutes; University of Glasgow, M.A. (with honors in history), 1934. *Politics:* Conservative. *Religion:* Presbyterian. *Home:* Loup, Clachan, Tarbert, Argyll, Scotland. *Agent:* A. P. Watt & Son, 26/28 Bedford Row, London WC1R 4HL, England.

CAREER: Full-time writer of detective novels. *Military service:* British Army, 1940-41.

WRITINGS—Published by Melrose, except an indicated: *Doctor Deals with Murder*, 1944; *Death Wears a Silk Stocking*, 1945; *Mystery on the Clyde*, 1945; *Murder at Marks Caris*, 1945; *Death Beckons Quietly*, 1946; *Killer Keep*, 1946; *Straight Ahead for Danger*, 1946; *Tiled House Mystery*, 1947; *The Blackbird Sings of Murder*, 1948; *The Puppets of Father Bouvard*, 1948; *The Cult of the Queer People*, 1949; *The Brothers of Judgement*, 1950; *The Black Mitre*, 1951; *The Company of Sinners*, 1951; *The Blood Red Leaf*, 1952; *Death Comes to Lady's Steps*, 1952; *Deathmaster*, Hutchinson, 1954; *Death Stands Round the Corner*, Rich & Cowan, 1955; *Knife in the Night*, Rich & Cowan, 1955; *Pennies for His Eyes*, Rich & Cowan, 1956.

All published by John Long: *Murder Calls the Tune*, 1957; *The Joker Deals with Death*, 1958; *The Murder Man*, 1959; *The Whispering Man*, 1959; *The Hooded Man*, 1960; *The House*

in Spite Street, 1961; *The Nighthawk*, 1962; *Redfingers*, 1962; *The Crime Master*, 1963; *Meet the Dreamer*, 1963; *The Green Knight*, 1964; *The Hour of the Bishop*, 1964; *The House of Wailing Winds*, 1965; *Again the Dreamer*, 1965; *Presenting the Dreamer*, 1966; *Case for the Dreamer*, 1966; *The Council of Comforters*, 1967; *Problem for the Dreamer*, 1967; *Salute the Dreamer*, 1968; *The Dreamer Intervenes*, 1968; *Cord for a Killer*, 1969; *Challenge for the Dreamer*, 1969; *The Green Triangle*, 1969; *The Dreamer Deals with Murder*, 1970; *The Whisperer*, 1970; *Detail for the Dreamer*, 1971; *The Breath of Murder*, 1972; *The Dreamer at Large*, 1972; *The Big Timer*, 1973; *Prey for the Dreamer*, 1974; *Death and Mr. Gilly*, 1974; *Laurels for the Dreamer*, 1975; *Murder of a Cop*, 1976.

Under pseudonym John Cassells; all published by Melrose: *The Sons of Morning*, 1946; *The Bastion of the Damned*, 1946; *Murder Comes to Rothesay*, 1946; *The Mark of the Leech*, 1947; *Master of the Dark*, 1948; *The League of Nameless Men*, 1948; *The Castle of Sin*, 1949; *The Clue of the Purple Asters*, 1949; *The Waters of Sadness*, 1950; *The Circle of Dust*, 1950; *The Grey Ghost*, 1951; *Exit Mr. Shane*, 1951; *The Second Mrs. Locke*, 1952; *The Rattler*, 1952.

All published by Muller: *Salute Inspector Flagg*, 1953; *Case for Inspector Flagg*, 1954; *Enter the Picaroon*, 1954; *Inspector Flagg and the Scarlet Skeleton*, 1955; *Beware! The Picaroon*, 1956; *The Avenging Picaroon*, 1956; *Again, Inspector Flagg*, 1956; *Presenting Inspector Flagg*, 1957.

Published by John Long, except as indicated: *Meet the Picaroon*, 1957; *Case 29*, 1958; *The Engaging Picaroon*, 1958; *Enter Superintendent Flagg*, 1959; *The Enterprising Picaroon*, 1959; *Score for Superintendent Flagg*, 1960; *Salute the Picaroon*, 1960; *Problem for Superintendent Flagg*, 1961; *The Brothers of Benevolence*, 1962; *The Picaroon Goes West*, 1962; *Prey for the Picaroon*, 1963; *The Council of the Rat*, 1963; *Blue Mask*, Hutchinson, 1964; *Challenge for the Picaroon*, 1964; *The Benevolent Picaroon*, 1965; *Grey Face*, 1965; *Plunder for the Picaroon*, 1966; *Blackfingers*, 1966; *The Audacious Picaroon*, 1967; *The Room in Quiver Court*, 1967; *The Elusive Picaroon*, 1968; *Call for Superintendent Flagg*, 1968; *The Night of the Picaroon*, 1969; *The Double-Crosser*, 1969; *Quest for the Picaroon*, 1970; *The Grafter*, 1970; *The Picaroon Collects*, 1970; *The Hatchet Man*, 1971; *Profit for the Picaroon*, 1972; *The Enforcer*, 1973; *The Picaroon Laughs Last*, 1973; *Killer's Rope*, 1974; *Action for the Picaroon*, 1975; *Quest for Superintendent Flagg*, 1975; *The Picaroon Gets the Run-Around*, 1976.

Under pseudonym John Dallas: *The Night of the Storm*, Jenkins, 1962; *Red Ice*, R. Hale, 1973.

Under pseudonym Neill Graham; published by Jarrold's, except as indicated: *The Symbol of the Cat*, Melrose, 1948; *Passport to Murder*, Melrose, 1949; *The Temple of Slumber*, Melrose, 1950; *The Quest of Mr. Sandyman*, 1951; *Murder Walks on Tiptoe,* Melrose, 1951; *Again, Mr. Sandyman*, 1952; *Amazing Mr. Sandyman*, 1952; *Salute Mr. Sandyman*, 1953; *Play It Solo*, 1955; *Murder Makes a Date*, 1955, Roy, 1956; *Say It with Murder*, 1956; *You Can't Call It Murder*, 1957; *Murder Rings the Bell*, 1959.

All published by John Long: *Salute to Murder*, 1958; *Hit Me Hard*, 1958; *Killers Are on Velvet*, 1960; *Murder Is My Weakness*, 1961; *Murder on the "Duchess,"* 1961; *Make Mine Murder*, 1962; *Label It Murder*, 1963; *Graft Town*, 1963; *Murder Makes It Certain*, 1963; *Murder Made Easy*, 1964; *Murder of a Black Cat*, 1964; *Murder on My Hands*, 1965; *Murder's Always Final*, 1965; *Money for Murder*, 1966; *Murder on Demand*, 1966; *Murder Makes the News*, 1967; *Murder Has*

Been Done, 1967; *Pay Off,* 1968; *Candidate for a Coffin,* 1968; *Death of a Canary,* 1969; *Murder Lies in Waiting,* 1969; *Blood on the Pavement,* 1970; *One for the Book,* 1970; *A Matter of Murder,* 1971; *Murder, Double Murder,* 1971; *Frame-Up,* 1972; *Cop in a Tight Frame,* 1973; *Murder in a Dark Room,* 1973; *Assignment Murder,* 1974; *Murder on the List,* 1975.

Under pseudonym Martin Locke: *The Vengeance of Mortimer Daly,* Ward, Lock, 1962.

Under pseudonym Peter Malloch; published by John Long, except as indicated: *11:20 Glasgow Central,* Rich & Cowan, 1955; *Sweet Lady Death,* Rich & Cowan, 1956; *Tread Softly, Death,* Rich & Cowan, 1957; *Walk In, Death,* 1957; *Fly Away, Death,* 1958; *My Shadow, Death,* 1959; *Hardiman's Landing,* 1960; *Anchor Island,* 1962; *Blood Money,* 1962; *Break-Through,* 1963; *Fugitive's Road,* 1963; *Cop-Lover,* 1964; *The Nicholas Snatch,* 1964; *The Sniper,* 1965; *Lady of No Compassion,* 1966; *The Big Steal,* 1966; *Murder of the Man Next Door,* 1966; *Die, My Beloved,* 1967; *Johnny Blood,* 1967; *Murder of a Student,* 1968; *Death Whispers Softly,* 1968; *Backwash,* 1969; *Blood on Pale Fingers,* 1969; *The Adjustor,* 1970; *The Grab,* 1970; *The Slugger,* 1971; *Two with a Gun,* 1971; *Write-Off,* 1972; *Kickback,* 1973; *The Delinquents,* 1974; *The Big Killing,* 1974; *Killer's Blade,* 1975; *The Big Deal,* 1977.

Under pseudonym Lovat Marshall; published by R. Hale, except as indicated: *Sugar for the Lady,* Hurst & Blackett, 1955; *Sugar on the Carpet,* Hurst & Blackett, 1956; *Sugar Cuts the Corners,* John Long, 1957; *Sugar on the Target,* 1958; *Sugar on the Cuff,* 1960; *Sugar on the Kill,* 1961; *Sugar on the Loose,* 1962; *Sugar on the Prowl,* 1962; *Murder in Triplicate,* 1963; *Murder Is the Reason,* 1964; *Ladies Can Be Dangerous,* 1964; *Death Strikes in Darkness,* 1965; *The Dead Are Silent,* 1966; *The Dead Are Dangerous,* 1966; *Murder of a Lady,* 1967; *Blood on the Blotter,* 1968; *Money Means Murder,* 1968; *Death Is For Ever,* 1969; *Murder's Out of Season,* 1970; *Murder's Just for Cops,* 1971; *Death Casts a Shadow,* 1972; *Moment for Murder,* 1972; *Loose Lady Death,* 1973; *Date with Murder,* 1973; *Murder Town,* 1974; *The Strangler,* 1974; *Key to Murder,* 1975; *Murder Mission,* 1975; *Murder to Order,* 1975.

Contributor of short stories to *Detective, Thriller,* and *Tit-Bits.*

SIDELIGHTS: W. Murdoch Duncan used three distinct approaches in writing his mystery novels. Under the name Duncan and the pseudonym Cassells he wrote detective stories in which murder is incidental to the plot. The Graham-Marshall stories feature private detectives, while his Malloch-Dallas books are thrillers of the "true to life" type.

Duncan gave character and plot equal attention. His strong characterizations provided him the opportunity to create several series characters, such as Solo Malcolm (in the Graham novels), Sugar Kane (in the Marshall novels), and Superintendent Flagg and the Picaroon (in the Cassells novels).

Full of intrigue, action, and unexpected solutions, Duncan's books have been translated into several languages, including German, French, Norwegian, Dutch, Portuguese, Italian, and Spanish.†

* * *

DUNLEAVY, Janet Egleson 1928-
(Janet F. Egleson, Janet Frank)

PERSONAL: Born December 16, 1928, in New York, N.Y.; married Gareth W. Dunleavy (a professor), July 25, 1971. *Education:* Hunter College (now Hunter College of the City University of New York), B.A., 1951; New York University,

M.A., 1962, Ph.D., 1966; Dublin Institute for Advanced Studies, post doctoral study, 1978 and 1981. *Home:* 2723 East Bradford, Milwaukee, Wis. 53211. *Office:* Department of English, University of Wisconsin, Milwaukee, Wis. 53201.

CAREER: Hunter College of the City University of New York, New York, N.Y., lecturer in English, 1964-66; State University of New York at Stony Brook, assistant professor of English, 1966-70; University of Wisconsin—Milwaukee, assistant professor, 1970-71, associate professor, 1971-76, professor of English, 1976—. Visiting professor, University of Illinois at Urbana-Champaign, fall, 1978.

MEMBER: International Association for the Study of Anglo-Irish Literature (member of executive committee, 1970-76), Modern Language Association of America, American Committee for Irish Studies (secretary, 1972-75), American Association of University Professors, Wisconsin Academy of Science, Arts and Letters (vice-president for Letters, 1977), Wisconsin Coordinating Council of Women in Higher Education, English Graduate Association of New York University.

AWARDS, HONORS: State University of New York, summer research grants, 1967, 1969, Graduate School faculty summer research grant, 1968; University of Wisconsin—Milwaukee, summer research grants, 1970, 1972, 1977; American Council of Learned Societies grant, 1971; American Irish Foundation grants, 1973, 1974; Fromkin Memorial lecturship and research grant, 1976; elected to Hunter College Hall of Fame, 1978; American Philosophical Society grant, 1980.

WRITINGS: (Under name Janet F. Egleson; with Jim Egleson) *Parents Without Partners,* Dutton, 1961; (under name Janet F. Egleson) *Design for Writing,* Glencoe Press, 1970; *George Moore: The Artist's Vision, the Storyteller's Art,* Bucknell University Press, 1973; (with husband, Gareth W. Dunleavy) *The O'Conor Papers,* University of Wisconsin Press, 1977; (contributor) Herbert Fackler, editor, *The Irish Novel since James Joyce,* Louisiana Southwestern University, 1980; (contributor) John Halperin, editor, *Trollope Centenary Essays,* Macmillan, 1981; (editor) Anthony Trollope, *Castle Richmond,* Arno, in press; (contributor) *Fromkin Memorial Essays,* University of Wisconsin, in press.

Under name Janet Frank; children's books: *Daddies,* Simon & Schuster, 1954; *Davy Crocket and the Indians,* J. C. Winston, 1955; *Happy Days: What Children Do the Whole Day Through,* Simon & Schuster, 1955. Also author of two additional books for children. Contributor to *Treasury of Little Golden Books,* Western Printing & Publishing.

Contributor to professional journals, including *Victorian Studies, Irish University Review, Canadian Journal of Irish Studies, Ireland of the Welcomes, Journal of American Culture,* and *Studies in the Novel.* Editor, *American Committee for Irish Studies Newsletter,* 1971-78; consulting editor, *Transactions of the Wisconsin Academy,* 1976-78. Editorial consultant to encyclopedia firms, university presses, and scholarly journals.

WORK IN PROGRESS: Study of manuscript drafts of fiction by Mary Lavin; *Anthony Trollope's Ireland;* with husband, G. W. Dunleavy, a biography of Douglas Hyde; editing a collection of essays on women's studies.

SIDELIGHTS: Janet Egleson Dunleavy told CA: "Writing is my first love. I am continually fascinated by the way ideas, observations, and impressions of which I have been but half aware shape themselves on the page in my typewriter, as if some other intelligence is making me press the keys. Editing is an engrossing game in which my object is to enhance what someone else has written by making minimal changes in punctuation and phrasing for the sake of clarity or style while preserving the author's voice and convictions.

"Literary criticism is another engrossing game in which I study the techniques used by authors, especially those authors who, with Gauthier, believe that the correction of form is virtue, or with Mary Lavin and Virginia Woolf, practice the art of compression, using a disciplined imagination informed by intuition, perception, and observation. Teaching is a challenge, for it involves trying to help students develop a disciplined imagination informed by intuition, perception, and observation, use that imagination to develop a critical faculty, and apply that critical faculty to enjoy literature and the other arts."

* * *

DUPREY, Richard A(llen) 1929-
(Alan Fields)

PERSONAL: Born September 20, 1929, in Nashua, N.H.; son of Robert Albert (a woodworker) and Theresa (de Montigny) Duprey; married Dorothy Joan Barry, June 26, 1954; children: Stephen Paul, Robert Vincent, Martha Joan, Elizabeth Ann, Marie Paula, Andrew Richard, John Joseph. *Education:* St. Anselm College, B.A. (with honors), 1952; Fordham University, graduate study, 1952-53; Tufts University, A.M., 1958; New York University, Ph.D., 1969. *Politics:* Democrat. *Religion:* Roman Catholic. *Home and office:* 509 Owen Rd., Wynnewood, Pa. 19096. *Agent:* Paul Reynolds Inc., 12 East 41st St., New York, N.Y. 10017.

CAREER: Radio Voice of New Hampshire, Inc., Manchester, N.H., announcer, 1952-53; Nashua Corporation, Nashua, N.H., assistant purchasing agent, 1954-56; Villanova University, Villanova, Pa., 1956-69, began as instructor, became associate professor of theatre; St. Joseph's University, Philadelphia, Pa., assistant to the president, 1970-72; Walnut Street Theatre, Philadelphia, general manager/artistic director, 1972-75; free-lance writer and consultant, 1975—. *Military service:* U.S. Air Force, 1948-49; U.S. Air Force Reserve, six years; became sergeant. *Member:* Association of Theatre Publicists and Managers. *Awards, honors:* Margo Jones Award, 1965, for work in theatre.

WRITINGS: Just off the Aisle, Newman, 1962; *A House Full of Angels,* Lippincott, 1964; *Duel on the Wind,* St. Martin's, 1976; *Revolutionary Playbook,* Pennsylvania Bicentennial Commission, 1976; (under pseudonym Alan Fields) *VJ-Day,* Dell, 1978; "Francis" (showcase), produced Off-Broadway in 1978. Also author of television scripts for CBS and NET. Contributor of articles and short stories to magazines.

WORK IN PROGRESS: Three novels and a play.

SIDELIGHTS: Richard A. Duprey told *CA* that his primary concern as a writer is to impart a reverence for mystery, believing as he does that man has a right to be amazed and baffled. He says he is happiest while writing or teaching. *Avocational interests:* Reading American history, collecting folk music.

* * *

DUPUY, R(ichard) Ernest 1887-1975

PERSONAL: Born March 24, 1887, in New York, N.Y.; died April 25, 1975, of heart failure, at Walter Reed Army Hospital; son of Georges Marie (an artist) and Katharine Pauline (Chute) Dupuy; married Laura Elizabeth Nevitt (an artist), June 1, 1915; children: Trevor Nevitt. *Education:* Field Artillery and Command School, graduate, 1924; Command and General Staff College, graduate, 1933. *Politics:* Independent. *Religion:* Roman Catholic.

CAREER: New York Herald, New York, N.Y., worked as reporter, feature writer, and ship news editor, 1908-17; New York National Guard, 1909-17; U.S. Army, 1917-46, retired as colonel; full-time writer, 1946-75. Assigned during large part of service to public relations duty; served in France during World War I, participating in St. Mihiel and Meuse-Argonne campaigns; served during World War II with General Staff of War Department, 1941-43, 1945-46, and with General Staff of SHAEF, 1943-45. Part-time writer during military career.

MEMBER: Academy of Political Science, American Historical Association, Historical Evaluation and Research Organization (member of board of governors, 1962-75), Association of the United States Army, Naval Institute, Infantry Association, American Military Institute Constitution Island Association (president, 1961-63); Cosmos Club, National Press Club, and Army and Navy Club (all Washington, D.C.); West Point Society (Washington, D.C., and New York); Army-Navy Club and Silurians (both New York). *Awards, honors—*Military: Legion of Merit with oak leaf cluster, Order of British Empire (brigadier), Croix de Guerre with palms. Civilian: *Current History* Magazine citation, 1937, for one of ten best books of the year; co-winner of Fletcher Pratt Memorial Award, Civil War Round Table of New York, 1960, for *Compact History of the Civil War.*

WRITINGS: In France with the Fifty-Seventh, U.S. Army, 1928; *Governors Island 1637-1937,* privately printed by Governors Island Club, 1937; (with G. F. Eliot) *If War Comes,* Macmillan, 1937; *World in Arms,* Military Services Publications, 1939; *Perish by the Sword,* Military Services Publications, 1939; *Where They Have Trod,* Stokes, 1940; (with Hodding Carter) *Civilian Defense of the United States,* Rinehart, 1942; (with son, Trevor Nevitt Dupuy) *To the Colors,* Row, Peterson & Co., 1942; *Lion in the Way,* U.S. Infantry Journal, 1948; *Men of West Point,* Sloane, 1952; *Compact History of the U.S. Army,* Hawthorn, 1956, 2nd revised edition, 1973; (with T. N. Dupuy) *Military Heritage of America,* McGraw, 1956; (with T. N. Dupuy) *Brave Men and Great Captains,* Harper, 1959.

(With T. N. Dupuy) *Compact History of the Civil War,* Hawthorn, 1960; *Battle of Hubbardton* (monograph), State of Vermont, 1960; (with T. N. Dupuy) *Compact History of the Revolutionary War,* Hawthorn, 1963; *Five Days to War: April 2-6, 1917,* Stackpole, 1967; (with William H. Baumer) *The Little Wars of the United States,* Hawthorn, 1968; *World War II: A Compact History,* Hawthorn, 1969; (with T. N. Dupuy) *Encyclopedia of Military History: From 3500 B.C. to the Present,* Harper, 1970, revised edition, 1977; *The National Guard: A Compact History,* Hawthorn, 1971; (with T. N. Dupuy) *An Outline History of the American Revolution,* Harper, 1975; (with Gay Hammerman and Grace P. Hayes) *The American Revolution: A Global War,* McKay, 1977.

General editor of Hawthorn series, "Military History of the United States," 1963-75. Contributor of fiction and feature articles to military and national magazines. Associate editor of *Army, Navy, Air Force Journal-Register,* 1957-61.

SIDELIGHTS: As head of the Public Relations Division at SHAEF, R. Ernest Dupuy made the D-Day announcement of the Normandy invasion to the world.†

* * *

DURAND, G. Forbes
See BURGESS, M(ichael) R(oy)

DVORNIK

DURBRIDGE, Francis (Henry) 1912-
(Paul Temple, a joint pseudonym)

PERSONAL: Born November 25, 1912, in Hull, England; son of Francis and Gertrude Durbridge; married Norah Elizabeth Lawly, 1940; children: two sons. *Education:* Attended Birmingham University. *Agent:* Harvey Unna and Stephen Durbridge Ltd., 24 Pottery Lane, Holland Park, London W11 4LZ, England.

CAREER: Playwright and novelist. Writer and executive producer of television series, 1952—.

WRITINGS—All novels: Send for Paul Temple, John Long, 1938; (with Charles Hatton) *Paul Temple and the Front Page Men,* John Long, 1939; *News of Paul Temple,* John Long, 1940; *Paul Temple Intervenes,* John Long, 1944; *Send for Paul Temple Again!,* John Long, 1948; *Back Room Girl,* John Long, 1950; *Design for Murder,* John Long, 1951; *Beware of Johnny Washington,* John Long, 1951; *The Other Man,* Hodder & Stoughton, 1958; *A Time of Day,* Hodder & Stoughton, 1959.

The Scarf, Hodder & Stoughton, 1960, published as *The Case of the Twisted Scarf,* Dodd, 1961; *Portrait of Alison,* Dodd, Mead, 1962; *The World of Tim Frazer,* Dodd, Mead, 1962; *My Friend Charles,* Hodder & Stoughton, 1963; *Tim Frazer Again,* Hodder & Stoughton, 1964; *Another Woman's Shoes,* Hodder & Stoughton, 1965; *The Desperate People,* Hodder & Stoughton, 1966; *Dead to the World,* Hodder & Stoughton, 1967; *My Wife Melissa,* Hodder & Stoughton, 1967; *The Geneva Mystery: A Paul Temple Novel,* Hodder Paperbacks, 1971; *The Curzon Case: A Paul Temple Novel,* Coronet, 1972; *Paul Temple and the Kelby Affair,* White Lion, 1973; *Paul Temple and the Harkdale Robbery,* White Lion, 1976.

With James Douglas Rutherford McConnell; all published by Hodder & Stoughton: (Under joint pseudonym Paul Temple) *The Tyler Mystery,* 1957; (under joint pseudonym Paul Temple) *East of Algiers,* 1959; *The Pig-Tail Murder,* 1969; *A Man Called Harry Brent,* 1970; *Bat out of Hell,* 1972; *A Game of Murder,* 1975; *The Passenger,* 1977; *Tim Frazer Gets the Message,* 1980; *Breakaway,* 1981.

Plays; all published by Samuel French: *Suddenly at Home,* 1973; *The Gentle Hook,* 1976; *Murder with Love,* 1977.

Screenplays: (With John Argyle) "Send for Paul Temple," 1946; (with A. R. Rawlinson) "Calling Paul Temple," 1948; "Paul Temple Returns," 1952; (with James Matthews) "The Teckman Mystery," 1954; "The Vicious Circle," 1957.

Author of numerous television serials, 1952—, including "The Scarf," "The Desperate People," "A Game of Murder," "The World of Tim Frazer," "A Man Called Harry Brent," "The Other Man," "Melissa," and "Bat out of Hell." Also author of radio plays, 1937-1968, and of play, "House Guest," produced at Savoy Theatre, London. Contributor of articles to periodicals, including *London Daily Mail, Birmingham Post, London Evening News,* and *Radio Times.*

SIDELIGHTS: Francis Durbridge is recognized as a successful writer of television serials, many of which he has turned into novels. His serials, which have one of the largest television audiences in Europe, have been broadcast in over sixteen countries, including Germany, France, Italy, and the United States. In the German-speaking countries alone, they regularly reach an audience of over 25 million viewers.

Apart from his work for television, Durbridge is also well known for his BBC radio plays featuring Paul Temple, a character who also appears in some of his novels. In collaboration with James Douglas Rutherford McConnell, Durbridge further gave life to this character by writing two books "by Paul Temple."

Durbridge told *CA:* "I believe in the Arnold Bennett and Anthony Trollope approach to writing: regular hours, nose to the grindstone technique. I like traveling, getting local colour for my stories, and attending rehearsals of my plays."

AVOCATIONAL INTERESTS: Reading and travel (has visited most countries in Europe and has traveled extensively in the United States).

*   *   *

DVORNIK, Francis 1893-1975

PERSONAL: Born August 14, 1893, in Chomyz, Czechoslovakia; died November 4, 1975, in Kromeriz, Czechoslovakia; came to United States in 1948, naturalized in 1954; son of Francis and Frances (Tomeckova) Dvornik. *Education:* Faculty of Theology, Olomouce, D.D., 1920; Ecole des Sciences Politiques, Paris, diploma, 1923; Sorbonne, University of Paris, Docteur es Lettrès, 1926. *Office:* Dumbarton Oaks, 1703 32nd St., Washington, D.C.

CAREER: Ordained Roman Catholic priest, 1916; Charles University, Prague, Czechoslovakia, lecturer, 1926-28, professor of church history, 1928-49, dean of faculty of theology, 1935; Harvard University, Dumbarton Oaks, Washington, D.C., professor of Byzantine history, 1949-64, professor emeritus, 1964-75. Schlumberger Lecturer, College of France, 1940; Birkbeck Lecturer, Trinity College, Cambridge University, 1946. *Member:* Royal Belgian Academy (associate member), British Academy (corresponding member), American Academy of Arts and Sciences, Mediaeval Academy of America, Royal Historical Society. *Awards, honors:* French Academy prize, 1927, for *Les Slaves, Byzance et Rome au IXieme siecle;* Haskins Gold Medal from Mediaeval Academy of America; French Legion of Honor; D.Litt. from University of London, St. Procopius College, and Fairleigh Dickinson University.

WRITINGS: Les Slaves, Byzance et Rome au IXieme siecle, [Paris], 1926, reprinted, Academic International, 1970; *Vie de St. Gregoire le Decapolite,* [Paris], 1926; *St. Wenceslas: Duke of Bohemia,* [Prague], 1929; *Les Legendes de Constantin et de Methode vues de Byzance,* [Prague], 1933, 2nd edition, Academic International, 1969; *National Churches and the Church Universal,* Westminster, 1944, *The Photian Schism: History and Legend,* Cambridge University Press, 1949, reprinted, 1970; *The Making of Central and Eastern Europe,* Polish Research Center, 1949, 2nd edition, Academic International, 1974; *The Slavs: Their Early History and Civilization,* American Academy of Arts and Sciences, 1956; *The Idea of Apostolicity in Byzantium and the Legend of the Apostle Andrew,* Harvard University Press, 1958; *The Ecumenical Councils,* Hawthorn, 1961 (published in England as *The General Councils of the Church,* Burns & Oates, 1961); (author of commentary with others) *De Administrando imperio,* Athlone Press, 1962; *Czech Contributions to the Growth of the United States,* Benedictine Abbey Press, 1962; *The Slavs in European History and Civilization,* Rutgers University Press, 1962; *Byzance et la primaute romaine,* Editions du Cerf, 1964, published as *Byzantium and the Roman Primacy,* Fordham University Press, 1966, revised edition, 1979; *Early Christian and Byzantine Political Philosophy: Origins and Background,* two volumes, Dumbarton Oaks Center for Byzantine Studies, Harvard University, 1966; *Byzantine Missions among the Slavs,* Rutgers University Press, 1970; *Origins of Intelligence Services,* Rutgers University Press, 1974.†

DYNES, Russell R(owe) 1923-

PERSONAL: Born October 2, 1923, in Dundalk, Ontario, Canada; son of Oliver Wesley (a college professor) and Carlotta (Rowe) Dynes; married Susan M. Swan, July 25, 1947; children: Russell, Jr., Patrick, Gregory, Jon. *Education:* University of Tennessee, B.A., 1948, M.A., 1950; Ohio State University, Ph.D., 1954. *Politics:* Independent Democrat. *Religion:* Methodist. *Home:* 1621 19th St. N.W., Washington, D.C. 20009. *Office:* American Sociological Association, 1722 N St. N.W., Washington, D.C. 20036.

CAREER: University of Tennessee, Knoxville, instructor, 1948-50; Ohio State University, Columbus, associate professor, 1951-65, professor of sociology, 1965-77, chairman of department, 1974-77, co-director of Disaster Research Center, 1964-77; American Sociological Association, Washington, D.C., executive officer, 1977—. Senior Fulbright lecturer, Ain Shams University, United Arab Republic, 1964-65; Fulbright lecturer, Center for Advanced Study in Sociology, University of Delhi, 1972; honorary faculty member, Defense Civil Preparedness Staff College, 1973. President, Disaster Research Services, Inc., 1972-77. Wesley Foundation, trustee, 1958—, treasurer, 1961-63; member of staff, Arab State Centre for Education in Community Development, United Arab Republic, 1964-65; member of Mayor's Faculty Commission, Columbus, 1967-68; chairman of Committee on International Disaster Assistance, 1976-79; director of emergency preparedness task force, President's Commission on the Accident at Three Mile Island, 1979. Member of advisory committee, Committee on International Exchange of Persons, 1970-71; member of special advisory committee on emergency housing, National Research Council-National Academy of Sciences, 1972; consultant to Federal Disaster Assistance Agency, 1978—. *Military service:* U.S. Army, Corps of Engineers, 1942-46; became sergeant.

MEMBER: International Sociological Association, American Sociological Association, American Association for the Advancement of Science, Society for the Scientific Study of Religion (treasurer, 1976-79), Religious Research Association (fellow), American Association of University Professors (member of board of directors, Ohio State University chapter, 1970-71), North Central Sociological Society, Ohio Valley Sociological Society (journal editor, 1958-63; vice-president, 1970-71), Ohio Council of Family Relations (journal editor, 1960-63).

WRITINGS: (With A. Clarke, S. Dinitz, and I. Ishino) *Social Problems: Dissensus and Deviation in an Industrial Society,* Oxford University Press, 1964; *The Functioning of Expanding Organizations in Community Disasters,* Office of Civil Defense, 1968; (editor with Dinitz and Clarke) *Deviance: Studies in the Process of Stigmatization and Societal Reaction,* Oxford University Press, 1969, 2nd edition, 1975; *Organized Behavior in a Disaster,* Heath, 1970; (with E. L. Quarantelli) *Disruption on the Campuses of Ohio Colleges and Universities, Spring, 1970,* Ohio Council of Churches and Ohio Board, United Ministries in Higher Education, 1970; (with Dennis E. Wenger) *Environment Crises,* Water Resources Center, Ohio State University, 1971; (with Wenger) *A Model of Community Problem Solving and Selected Empirical Applications,* Water Resources Center, Ohio State University, 1971; (with Quarantelli and Gary A. Kreps) *A Perspective on Disaster Planning,* Disaster Research Center, Ohio State University, 1972; (with Quarantelli and James L. Ross) *Police Perspectives and Behavior in a Campus Disturbance,* Ohio State University Research Foundation, 1972; (with William A. Anderson) *Social Movements, Violence, and Change: The May Movement in Curacao,* Ohio State University Press, 1975. Also author of *Deviance: Definition, Management, Treatment,* 1975, and of a number of shorter works. Associate editor, *Review of Religious Research,* 1968-76.

WORK IN PROGRESS: Research on organizational reactions in disasters and in various types of crises.

E

EBENSTEIN, William 1910-1976
(William Elwin)

PERSONAL: Born May 11, 1910, in Austria; came to United States in 1936, naturalized in 1942; died April 28, 1976, in Santa Barbara, Calif.; son of Samuel and Gittel (Goldapper) Ebenstein; married Ruth B. Jaburek, December 17, 1938; children: Philip J., Robert S., Andrew J., Alan O. *Education:* University of Vienna, LL.D., 1934; attended University of London, 1934-36; University of Wisconsin, Ph.D., 1938. *Office:* Department of Political Science, University of California, Santa Barbara, Calif.

CAREER: University of Wisconsin—Madison, instructor, 1938-40, assistant professor, 1940-43, associate professor of political science, 1943-46; Princeton University, Princeton, N.J., associate professor, 1946-49, professor of politics, 1949-62; University of California, Santa Barbara, professor of political science, 1962-76. Director of survey methods in political science project for UNESCO, Paris, France, 1948-49; member of advisory committee on political science, Fulbright Commission, 1955-56; Haynes Foundation Lecturer, Occidental College, 1961; director of summer workshops on democracy and totalitarianism, East Carolina University, 1964-66. *Member:* American Political Science Association, Western Political Science Association. *Awards, honors:* Social Science Research Council postdoctoral fellowships.

WRITINGS: (Under pseudonym William Elwin) *Fascism at Work,* M. Hopkinson, 1934, reprinted under real name, AMS Press, 1972, published under real name as *Fascist Italy,* American Book, 1939, reprinted, Russell, 1973; *Die rechtsphilosophische Schule der reinen Rechtslehre,* Taussig & Taussig, 1938, reprinted, Sauer & Auvermann, 1969, translation published as *The Pure Theory of Law,* University of Wisconsin Press, 1945, revised edition, Augustus Kelley, 1969; *The Law of Public Housing,* University of Wisconsin Press, 1940; *The Nazi State,* Farrar & Rinehart, 1943, reprinted, Octagon, 1975; *The German Record: A Political Portrait,* Farrar & Rinehart, 1945; (editor) *Man and the State: Modern Political Ideas,* Rinehart, 1947; (editor) *Great Political Thinkers: Plato to the Present,* Holt, 1951, 4th edition, 1969, excerpts published as *Introduction to Political Philosophy,* Kennikat, 1972; *Modern Political Thought,* Holt, 1954, 2nd edition, 1960; *Today's Isms,* Prentice-Hall, 1954, 7th edition, 1973; *Two Ways of Life: The Communist Challenge to Democracy,* Holt, 1962, 2nd edition, 1965; *Totalitarianism: New Perspectives,* Holt, 1962; *Political*

Thought in Perspective, McGraw, 1963; *Communism in Theory and Practice,* Holt, 1964; (with others) *American Democracy in World Perspective,* with instructor's manual and student's guide, Harper, 1967, 5th edition, 1980; (with Edward W. Mill) *American Government in the Twentieth Century: A Process Approach,* Silver Burdett, 1971. Contributor to *Encyclopedia Americana, Encyclopaedia Britannica,* and *World Book Encyclopedia.*†

*   *   *

ECKE, Betty Tseng Yu-ho 1924-
(Tseng Yu-ho)

PERSONAL: Born November 29, 1924, in Peking, China; daughter of Kuang-ch'in Tseng and Pao-cheng Chang; married Gustav Ecke (a professor and curator). *Education:* Fu-jen University, B.A., 1942; graduate study at three universities in Peking, China, 1942-48, and at University of Hawaii, 1951-56. *Home:* 3460 Kaohinani Dr., Honolulu, Hawaii.

CAREER: Honolulu Academy of Art, Honolulu, Hawaii, instructor in art, 1950-62; University of Hawaii, Honolulu, associate professor of art, 1963—; professional painter whose work has been exhibited at a number of galleries. Summer instructor in art at University of California, Berkeley, 1958. Consultant on Chinese art at Honolulu Academy of Arts. Member of Governor's Culture Committee. *Member:* Painter and Sculptors of Hawaii, Downtown Gallery Painters (New York). *Awards, honors:* Rockefeller Foundation grant, jointly with husband, Gustav Ecke, 1953; American Oriental Society grant, 1960-61.

WRITINGS—Under name Tseng Yu-ho: *Some Contemporary Elements in Classical Chinese Art,* University of Hawaii Press, 1963; *Chinese Calligraphy,* Philadelphia Museum of Art, 1971; *Chinese Folk Art,* University of Hawaii Press, 1977; *Poetry on the Wind: The Art of Chinese Folding Fan,* Honolulu Academy of Arts, 1981. Contributor of articles on Chinese painters of the sixteenth and seventeenth centuries to *Archives* of Chinese Art Society of America, *Arts Asiatiques,* other art periodicals.

WORK IN PROGRESS: Contributions to Ming biographical history project of Columbia University; further studies of Chinese painters of sixteenth and seventeenth centuries; *A History of Chinese Calligraphy,* for University of Hawaii Press.

ECKHOLM, Erik P(eter) 1949-

PERSONAL: Born May 23, 1949, in Tucson, Ariz.; son of Wendell (a public school administrator) and Margaret (Head) Eckholm; married Kathleen Courrier (a writer and editor), September 5, 1972. *Education:* Occidental College, B.A., 1971; Johns Hopkins University, M.A., 1974. *Office:* International Institute for Environment and Development, 1319 F St. N.W., Washington, D.C. 20004.

CAREER: Associate fellow, Overseas Development Council, 1973-74; Worldwatch Institute, Washington, D.C., senior researcher, 1975-79; member of policy planning staff, U.S. Department of State, 1979-80; International Institute for Environment and Development, Washington, D.C., visiting fellow, 1981—. Instructor at Occidental College, summers, 1972-74.

WRITINGS: (With Lester R. Brown) *By Bread Alone*, Praeger, 1974; *Losing Ground: Environmental Stress and World Food Prospects*, Norton, 1976; *The Picture of Health: Environmental Sources of Disease*, Norton, 1977. Also author of a book on global environment and development trends, published by Norton, 1982. Contributor to professional journals, magazines, and newspapers.

*   *   *

ECKSTEIN, Alexander 1915-1976

PERSONAL: Born December 9, 1915, in Novisad, Yugoslavia; died December 5, 1976, in Ann Arbor, Mich.; son of Simon and Erna (Weber) Eckstein; married Ruth Rubinstein, February 21, 1947; children: Robert. *Education:* University of California, B.S., 1939, M.S., 1941, Ph.D., 1952. *Home:* 15 Harvard Place, Ann Arbor, Mich. *Office:* Department of Economics, University of Michigan, Ann Arbor, Mich.

CAREER: University of California, Berkeley, teaching fellow, 1941-42; United Nations, Food and Agriculture Organization, Washington, D.C., economist, 1946-49, 1950-51; Social Science Research Council, New York, N.Y., fellow in Geneva, Switzerland, 1949-50; U.S. Department of State, Washington, D.C., senior economist, 1951-53; Harvard University, East Asian Research Center, Cambridge, Mass., research associate, 1953-56, lecturer in economics and honorary research associate, 1956-59; University of Rochester, Rochester, N.Y., Xerox Professor of International Economics, 1959-61; University of Michigan, Ann Arbor, professor of economics, 1961-76, director of Center for Chinese Studies, 1967-69. Policy advisor to secretary of state, 1966-68. Rockefeller Visiting Research Professor, Brookings Institution, 1974-75. Member, International Committee for Chinese Studies, 1963-64. *Military service:* U.S. Army, 1943-46, became technical sergeant; received Bronze Star.

MEMBER: American Economic Association, Association for the Study of Soviet-Type Economics, Association for the Study of Comparative Economics, American Association for the Advancement of Slavic Studies, Council on Foreign Relations, Association for Asian Studies (member of governing board, 1961-64), Joint Social Science Research Council-American Council of Learned Societies Committee for the Study of Contemporary China, Committee on Scholarly Communication with Mainland China, National Committee on United States-China Relations (member of board, 1966-76; vice-chairman, 1968-69; chairman, 1970-72), Economic History Association, British Economic History Association. *Awards, honors:* Fellowship for advanced field training in Chinese, 1958-59; research grants from American Council of Learned Societies, 1959-60, National Science Foundation and Rockefeller Foundation, 1960-

62, Social Science Research Council, 1963-64, 1966-67, 1972-73, and Arms Control and Disarmament Agency, 1966-68.

WRITINGS: (Contributor) *Prospects for Communist China*, Wiley, 1954; (contributor) *Income and Wealth*, Cambridge University Press, 1955; (contributor) *Moscow-Peking Axis*, Harper, 1957; *The National Income of Communist China*, Free Press of Glencoe, 1962; (contributor) *Economic Development of China and Japan*, Allen & Unwin, 1964; *Communist China's Economic Growth and Foreign Trade: Implications for U.S. Policy*, McGraw, 1966; *Economic Developments in India and China: A Study in Comparative Patterns*, Institute of Constitutional and Parliamentary Studies, 1967; (editor with Walter Galenson and Ta-chung Liu) *Economic Trends in Communist China*, Aldine, 1968; (editor) *Comparison of Economic Systems: Theoretical and Methodological Approaches*, University of California Press, 1971; (editor and author of introduction) Jerome Alan Cohen, Robert F. Dernberger, and John R. Garson, *China Trade Prospects and U.S. Policy*, Praeger, 1971; *China's Economic Development: The Interplay of Scarcity and Ideology*, University of Michigan Press, 1975; *China's Economic Revolution*, Cambridge University, 1977.†

*   *   *

EDEY, Maitland A(rmstrong) 1910-

PERSONAL: Born February 13, 1910, in New York, N.Y.; son of Alfred (a stockbroker) and Marion (a writer; maiden name, Armstrong) Edey; married Helen Winthrop Kellogg (a physician), April 24, 1934; children: Maitland A., Jr., Winthrop K., Beatrice Edey Phear, Marion. *Education:* Princeton University, A.B., 1932. *Politics:* Independent. *Religion:* None. *Home:* Seven Gates Farm, Vineyard Haven, Mass. 02568.

CAREER: Messenger on Wall Street, 1932-33; clerk for book publishers in New York, 1933-41; *Life*, New York City, 1941-55, began as editor of "Speaking of Pictures" section, became assistant managing editor; free-lance writer, 1955-60; Time-Life Books, New York City, 1960-70, began as series editor, became editor-in-chief; free-lance writer, 1972—. Incorporated Village of Upper Brookville, N.Y., trustee, 1946-62, mayor, 1958-62; director of New York Philharmonic Symphony Society, 1950-75; chairman of advisory council of Old Westbury College, 1967-72; member of corporation of Woods Hole Oceanographic Institution, 1968-73; director of Conservation Foundation, Washington, D.C., 1969—; trustee of Putney School, 1958-74, Scudder Special Fund (mutual fund), 1961—, Felix Neck Wildlife Trust, 1973—, and Sheriff's Meadow Foundation, 1978—. *Military service:* U.S. Army Air Forces, Intelligence, 1942-46; became major; received Legion of Merit and presidential citation. *Member:* Century Club (New York), Coffee House Club (New York). *Awards, honors:* American Book Award nomination, 1982, for *Lucy: The Beginnings of Humankind*.

WRITINGS—Published by Time-Life, except as indicated: *American Songbirds*, Random House, 1940; *American Waterbirds*, Random House, 1941; (with F. Clark Howell) *Early Man*, 1965; *The Cats of Africa*, 1968; *The Northeast Coast*, 1972; *The Missing Link*, 1973; *The Sea Traders*, 1974; *The Lost World of the Aegean*, 1975; *Great Photographic Essays*, New York Graphic Society, 1978; (with Donald C. Johanson) *Lucy: The Beginnings of Humankind*, Simon & Schuster, 1981.

WORK IN PROGRESS: A novel; a book on evolution.

SIDELIGHTS: Maitland A. Edey told *CA*: "Never confident in my ability to earn a living as a writer, I went into the book publishing business instead, nearly starved there, and didn't really manage any kind of respectable career in the writing or publishing world until I went to work for *Life* magazine in 1941. There I found myself writing short articles to go with picture stories every week, and occasionally longer ones. I enjoyed this and gained more confidence as a writer, but was escalated into managerial duties, so I resigned in 1955 to devote myself full time to fiction. That was a disaster. I have several completed and partly completed novels in the back of my desk, plus a number of short stories. Some I wrote at that time, some later. None have been published.

"In 1960 I returned to Time Inc., this time as an editor of its newly-formed book division. Again I had opportunities to write, this time book-length works. I learned that any talent I had was for nonfiction, for explaining to others, in as interesting ways as I could, things that interested me. My fields of choice are natural history, archeology, and lately the emergence and evolution of man. I find that subject utterly fascinating, and its complexities a great challenge.

"Having dealt for many years now, both as an editor and a writer, with subjects that are monitored by career professionals, I have learned that too often the professionals—particularly in the field of art—take an elitist view of their domains and are scornful of efforts to make them accessible to the layman. There are notable exceptions, of course. One who comes to mind is the late Harlow Shapley, whose popular explanations of the cosmos are magnificent. Another is George Gaylor Simpson, whose writings about evolution, while not aimed at the layman, are accessible to him. Others are less cooperative with the public; some are downright hostile to it, and I find this shocking.

"I think that it is of critical importance, in a world increasingly dominated by the sciences, that public knowledge about it be made as readily available and as palatable as is possible. I am happy that I have been able to find a congenial niche there. I believe that clarity is the writer's first responsibility and take the position that anything I can comprehend I should be able to make comprehensible to the reader. The art—with which I struggle endlessly—comes in making interesting what you have made comprehensible."

AVOCATIONAL INTERESTS: Ornithology, photography.

*   *   *

EDGAR, Josephine
See MUSSI, Mary

*   *   *

EDMAN, Victor Raymond   1900-1967

PERSONAL: Born May 9, 1900, in Chicago, Ill.; died September 22, 1967; buried in Wheaton Cemetery, Wheaton, Ill.; son of Anders Victor and Alma (Tolf) Edman; married Edith M. Olson, June 18, 1924; children: Charles R., V. Roland, David A., Norman E. *Education:* Boston University, A.B., 1923; Clark University, A.M., 1930, Ph.D., 1933. *Office:* Wheaton College, Wheaton, Ill.

CAREER: El Instituto Biblico del Ecuador, Guayaquil, director, 1923-28; Gospel Tabernacle, Worcester, Mass., pastor, 1929-35; Gospel Tabernacle, New York, N.Y., pastor, 1935-36; Wheaton College, Wheaton, Ill., associate professor, 1936-39, professor of political science and department chairman, 1939-40, president, 1940-65, chancellor, 1965-67. Instructor in history, Nyack Missionary College, 1935-36. Chairman of educational committee, Taxpayers' Federation of Illinois. Member of board of trustees, LeTourneau College and Billy

Graham Evangelistic Association. Frequent speaker at churches, colleges, and conferences. *Military service:* U.S. Army, Infantry, 1918-19. *Member:* American Historical Association, American Academy of Political and Social Science, American Geographic Society, American Political Science Association, American Legion, Christian and Missionary Alliance. *Awards, honors:* Freedom Foundation Award, 1951; LL.D., Houghton College, 1941; D.D., Taylor University, 1948.

WRITINGS: The Disciplines of Life, Van Kampen Press, 1948; *The Light in Dark Ages,* Van Kampen Press, 1949; *Storms and Starlight,* Van Kampen Press, 1951; *Finney Lives On,* Revell, 1951, reprinted, Bethany Fellowship, 1971; (compiler) *In Quietness and Confidence,* Scripture Press, 1953, reprinted, Victor, 1976; *The Delights of Life,* Van Kampen Press, 1954; *Great Is Thy Faithfulness,* Scripture Press, 1954; *Not Ashamed,* Scripture Press, 1955; *Sweeter Than Honey,* Scripture Press, 1956; *Just Why?,* Scripture Press, 1956; *Fear Not,* Scripture Press, 1957; *He Leadeth Me,* Scripture Press, 1959; *They Found the Secret,* Zondervan, 1960; *Wiser Than They Thought,* Scripture Press, 1960; *Out of My Life,* Zondervan, 1961; *But God!,* Zondervan, 1962, reprinted, 1980; *Then and There!,* Zondervan, 1964; *Not Somehow, But Triumphantly!,* Zondervan, 1965; *Windows in Heaven,* Moody, 1967; *Crisis Experiences in the Lives of Noted Christians,* Bethany Fellowship, 1970. Also author of *Swords and Ploughshares,* 1947. Contributor to religious periodicals.†

*   *   *

EDWARDS, Edgar O(wen)   1919-

PERSONAL: Born December 20, 1919, in Foxborough, Mass.; son of John Owen and Winifred (Roberts) Edwards; married Jean Elizabeth Lotz, April 27, 1946; children: Kathryn, Carolyn, Douglas. *Education:* Washington and Jefferson College, B.A., 1947; Johns Hopkins University, M.A., 1949, Ph.D., 1951. *Home:* B26M, 2600 Bellefontaine, Houston, Tex. 77025. *Office:* Department of Economics, Rice University, 6100 Main, Houston, Tex.

CAREER: Telescope Folding Furniture Co., Granville, N.Y., production controller, 1939-41; Princeton University, Princeton, N.J., instructor, 1950-51, lecturer, 1951-52, assistant professor, 1952-56, associate professor, 1956-59; Rice University, Houston, Tex., Hargrove Professor of Economics, 1959-69, chairman of department, 1959-64; economic advisor, Asia and Pacific Program of Ford Foundation, 1969-74; economic advisor, Republic of Kenya, 1974-77; Rice University, Henry Gardiner Symonds Professor of Administrative Science and Economics, 1977—. Visiting scholar, Yale University, 1968-69. Program specialist, Ford Foundation, 1963-65 and 1966-68. *Military service:* U.S. Army, Infantry, 1942-46; became captain. *Member:* American Economic Association, American Accounting Association, Southern Economic Association, Phi Beta Kappa. *Awards, honors:* Stockton Preceptor, Princeton University, 1953-56; Guggenheim fellow, 1954-55; Washington and Jefferson College Citation for Distinguished Service, 1962.

WRITINGS: (Contributor) *Depreciation and Replacement Policy,* North-Holland Publishing, 1961; (co-author) *The Theory and Measurement of Business Income,* University of California Press, 1961; (editor) *The Nation's Economic Objectives,* University of Chicago Press, 1964; (editor) *Employment in Developing Nations,* Columbia University Press, 1974; (co-author) *Accounting for Economic Events,* Scholars Book Co., 1980. Also contributor to Kenya Development Plans. Contributor of articles to professional journals.

WORK IN PROGRESS: Planning and development; income theory.

*   *   *

EDWIN, Brother B.
   See ARNANDEZ, Richard

*   *   *

EGLESON, Janet F.
   See DUNLEAVY, Janet Egleson

*   *   *

EICHENBERG, Fritz   1901-

PERSONAL: Born October 24, 1901, in Cologne, Germany; came to United States in 1933, naturalized in 1940; son of Siegfried and Ida (Marcus) Eichenberg; married Mary Altmann, 1926 (died, 1937); married Margaret Ladenburg, 1941 (divorced, 1965); married Antonie Ida Schulze-Forster (a graphic designer), January 7, 1975; children: (first marriage) Suzanne Eichenberg Jensen; (second marriage) Timothy. *Education:* Attended School of Applied Arts, Cologne, 1916-20; State Academy of Graphic Arts, Leipzig, M.F.A., 1923. *Religion:* Society of Friends (Quakers). *Home and studio:* 142 Oakwood Dr., Peace Dale, R.I. 02883.

CAREER: Graphic artist and illustrator of classics and other books. Started as newspaper artist in Germany, 1923, and worked as artist and traveling correspondent for Ullstein Publications, Berlin, before settling in United States; New School for Social Research, New York, N.Y., member of art faculty, 1935-45; Pratt Institute, Brooklyn, N.Y., professor of art, 1947-72, chairman of department of graphic arts, 1956-63, founder-director of Graphic Arts Center, 1956-72; University of Rhode Island, Kingston, professor of art, 1966-71, chairman of department, 1966-69; Albertus Magnus College, New Haven, Conn., professor of art, 1972-73. Had one-man shows at New School for Social Research, 1939, 1949, Associated American Artists Gallery, 1967, 1977, Pratt Manhattan Center Gallery, 1972, and Klingspor Museum (Offenbach, Germany), 1974. Work has been shown in Xylon international exhibitions in Switzerland, Yugoslavia, and other countries, in U.S. Information Agency traveling exhibits, and in Society of American Graphic Artists shows. Work represented in collections of National Gallery of Art, Hermitage Museum (Leningrad), Metropolitan Museum of Art, Philadelphia Museum of Art, and other museums. Member of Pennell Committee, Library of Congress, 1959-65, and Yale University Library, 1979. *Member:* National Academy of Design, Royal Society of Arts (London; fellow), Society of American Graphic Artists.

AWARDS, HONORS: Joseph Pennell Medal from Pennsylvania Academy of Fine Arts, 1944; first prize for print from National Academy of Design, 1946; Silver Medal from Limited Editions Club, 1954; grant from John D. Rockefeller III Fund, 1968; D.F.A. from Southeastern Massachusetts University, 1972, University of Rhode Island, 1974, and California College of Arts and Crafts, 1976; S.F.B. Morse Medal from National Academy of Design, 1973; National Book Award nomination, 1979, for *Endangered Species, and Other Fables with a Twist.*

WRITINGS: (Self-illustrated) *Ape in a Cape: An Alphabet of Odd Animals* (juvenile), Harcourt, 1952; (self-illustrated) *Art and Faith* (booklet), Pendle Hill, 1952; (self-illustrated) *Dancing in the Moon: Counting Rhymes* (juvenile), Harcourt, 1955, reprinted, Harcourt, 1975; (translator with William Hubben) Helmut A.P. Grieshaber, *H.A.P. Grieshaber,* Arts, 1965; (au-

thor of text) Naoko Matsubara, *Nantucket Woodcuts,* Barre Publishers, 1967; (editor) *Artist's Proof: A Collector's Edition of the First Eight Issues of the Distinguished Journal of Print and Printmaking,* New York Graphic Society, 1971; (translator and illustrator) Desiderius Erasmus, *In Praise of Folly,* Aquarius, 1972; *The Print: Art, Masterpiece, History, Technics,* Abrahams, 1975; *The Wood and the Graver,* C. N. Potter, 1977; *Endangered Species, and Other Fables with a Twist,* Stemmer House, 1979.

Illustrator: Puss in Boots, Holiday House, 1936; Joel Chandler Harris, *Uncle Remus Stories,* limited edition, Peter Pauper Press, 1937; Moritz A. Jagendorf, *Tyll Ulenspiegel's Merry Pranks,* Vanguard, 1938; Therese Lenotre, *Mystery of Dog Flip,* translation from the French by Simone Chamoud, Stokes, 1939; Robert Davis, *Padre: The Gentlemanly Pig,* Holiday House, 1939, enlarged edition, 1948; Rosalys Hall, *Animals to Africa,* Holiday House, 1939.

Stewart Schackne, *Rowena, the Skating Cow,* Scribner, 1940; Eula Griffin Duncan, *Big Road Walker,* Stokes, 1940; Babette Deutsch, *Heroes of the Kalevala: Finland's Saga,* Messner, 1940; Jonathan Swift, *Gulliver's Travels,* Heritage Press, 1940, junior text edition, 1947, new edition, 1961; Richard A.W. Hughes, *Don't Blame Me* (short stories), Harper, 1940; William Shakespeare, *Tragedy of Richard the Third,* Limited Editions Club, 1940; Henry Beston, *The Tree That Ran Away,* Macmillan, 1941; Marjorie Fischer, *All on a Summer's Day,* Random House, 1941; Irmengarde Eberle, *Phoebe-Bell,* Greystone Press, 1941; Ivan S. Turgenev, *Fathers and Sons,* translation from the Russian by Constance Garnett, Heritage Press, 1941; Mabel Leigh Hunt, *"Have You Seen Tom Thumb?,"* Stokes, 1942; Charlotte Bronte, *Jane Eyre* [and] Emily Bronte, *Wuthering Heights* (companion volumes), Random House, 1943; Henrik Ibsen, *Story of Peer Gynt,* retold by E. V. Sandys, Crowell, 1943; Eberle, *Wide Fields: The Story of Henry Fabre,* Crowell, 1943; Eleanor Hoffmann, *Mischief in Fez,* Holiday House, 1943; Leo N. Tolstoi, *Anna Karenina,* translation from the Russian by Constance Garnett, two volumes, Doubleday, 1944; Edgar Allen Poe, *Tales,* Random House, 1944; Mark Keats, *Sancho and His Stubborn Mule,* W. R. Scott, 1944; Rose Dobbs, *No Room: An Old Story Retold,* Coward, 1944; Feodor M. Dostoevski, *Crime and Punishment,* translation from the Russian by Garnett, Heritage Press, 1944.

Stephen Vincent Benet, *The Devil and Daniel Webster,* Kingsport, 1945; Dostoevski, *The Grand Inquisitor,* Haddam House, 1945; Glanville W. Smith, *Adventures of Sir Ignatius Tippitolio,* Harper, 1945; Anna Sewell, *Black Beauty,* Grosset, 1945; Terence H. White, *Mistress Masham's Repose,* Putnam, 1946; Emily Bronte, *Wuthering Heights,* Random House, 1946; Maurice Dolbier, *The Magic Shop,* Random House, 1946; Felix Salten, compiler, *Favorite Animal Stories,* Messner, 1948; Dostoevski, *The Brothers Karamazov,* translation from the Russian by Garnett revised with introduction by Avrahm Yarmolinsky, Limited Editions Club, 1949; Ruth Stiles Gannett, *Wonderful House-Boat-Train,* Random House, 1949.

Rudyard Kipling, *Jungle Book,* Grosset, 1950; Mark van Doren, *The Witch of Ramoth,* Maple Press, 1950; Wilkie Collins, *Short Stories,* Rodale Books, 1950; (with Vassily Verestchagin) Tolstoi, *War and Peace,* translation from the Russian by Louise and Aylmer Maude, two volumes in one, Heritage Press, 1951; Margaret Cousins, *Ben Franklin of Old Philadelphia,* Random House, 1952; Dorothy Day, *Long Loneliness* (autobiography), Harper, 1952; Nathaniel Hawthorne, *Tale of King Midas and the Golden Touch,* Limited Editions Club, 1952; Johann Wolfgang von Goethe, *Story of Reynard the Fox,* translation by Thomas J. Arnold from original German poem, Heritage Press, 1954; Dostoevski, *The Idiot,* translation from the Russian by Garnett revised with introduction by Yarmolinsky, Heritage Press, 1956; Elizabeth J. Coatsworth, *The Peaceable Kingdom and Other Poems,* Pantheon, 1958; Edna Johnson and others, compilers, *Anthology of Children's Literature,* 3rd edition (Eichenberg did not illustrate earlier editions), Houghton, 1959, 4th edition, 1970.

Dostoevski, *The Possessed,* translation from the Russian by Garnett, Heritage Press, 1960; Tolstoi, *Resurrection,* translation by Leo Wiener revised and edited by F. D. Reeve, Heritage Press, 1963; Jean Charlot, *Posada's Dance of Death,* Graphic Arts Center, Pratt Institute, 1965; Etienne Decroux, *Mime: The Art of Etienne Decroux,* Pratt Adlib Press, 1965; Dylan Thomas, *A Child's Christmas in Wales,* limited edition, New Directions, 1969.

Tolstoi, *Childhood, Boyhood, Youth,* translation by Wiener, Press of A. Colish, 1972; John M. Langstaff, *The Two Magicians,* Atheneum, 1973; Dostoevski, *A Raw Youth,* Limited Editions Club, 1974; J. C. Grimmelshausen, *The Adventurous Simplicissimus,* Limited Editions Club, 1981.

Contributor to *American Artist* and other journals. Founder and chief editor, *Artist's Proof: An Annual of Prints and Printmaking,* Pratt Institute, 1960-72.

SIDELIGHTS: Fritz Eichenberg's favorite mediums are lithographs, wood engravings, and woodcuts. Many of the classics he has illustrated have been reissued several times, and there have been British and Japanese editions of some of the classics and children's books. In 1979-1981, an exhibition of six decades of Eichenberg's prints was circulated by the International Exhibition Foundation.

BIOGRAPHICAL/CRITICAL SOURCES: American Artist, December, 1944, May, 1964, October, 1975; *Graphis,* Volume XIII, number 43, 1952; *Library of Congress Quarterly,* April, 1965; *Rhode Islander,* August 12, 1973; *Idea* (Tokyo), January, 1974.

*   *   *

EIGNER, Larry
See EIGNER, Laurence (Joel)

*   *   *

EIGNER, Laurence (Joel) 1927-
(Larry Eigner)

PERSONAL: Born August 7, 1927, in Swampscott, Mass.; son of Israel and Bessie (Polansky) Eigner. *Education:* Correspondence courses from University of Chicago. *Politics:* "Safety is no more than a by-product of well-being." *Residence:* Berkeley, Calif.

CAREER: Poet.

WRITINGS—Under name Larry Eigner; poetry, except as indicated: *From the Sustaining Air,* Divers Press (Mallorca), 1953, Toad Press, 1967; *Look at the Park,* privately printed, 1958; *On My Eyes,* foreword by Denise Levertov, Jargon, 1960; *Murder Talk. The Reception. Suggestions for a Play. Five Poems. Bed Never Self Made,* Duende Press, 1964; *The Music, the Rooms,* Desert Review Press, 1965; *The Memory of Yeats, Blake, DHL,* Circle Press, 1965; (contributor) *Free Poems among Friends,* Detroit Artist's Workshop, 1966; *The-/Towards Autumn,* Black Sparrow Press, 1967; *Another Time in Fragments,* Fulcrum Press, 1967; *Six Poems,* Wine Press, 1967; *Air; the Trees,* Black Sparrow Press, 1968; *The*

Breath of Once Live Things/In the Field with Poe, Black Sparrow Press, 1968; *A Line that May Be Cut: Poems from 1965,* Circle Press, 1968; *Clouding* (short stories), Samuel Charters, 1968; *Farther North* (short stories), Samuel Charters, 1969; *Valleys, Branches,* Big Venus, 1969; *Flat and Round,* Pierrepont Press, 1969; (contributor) *Panama Gold,* Zero Publications, 1969.

Over and Over, ends; or, As the Wind May Sound, Restau Press, 1970; *Poem Nov. 1968,* Tetrad Press, 1970; *Circuits: "A Microbook, A Microbook,"* Athanor Press, 1971; *Looks Like Nothing/the Shadow/through Air,* Circle Press, 1972; *What You Hear,* Edible Magazine, 1972; *Selected Poems,* edited by Samuel Charters and Andrea Wyatt, Oyez, 1972; *Words Touching/Ground Under,* Hellric Publications, 1972; *Shape/Shadow/Elements/Move,* Black Sparrow Press, 1973; *Things Stirring/Together/or Far Away* (poetry and prose), Black Sparrow Press, 1974; *Anything on It's Side,* Elizabeth Press, 1974; *No Radio,* Lodestar Press, 1974; *My God the Proverbial* (poetry and prose), L Publications, 1975; *Suddenly/It Gets Light/and Dark in the Streets,* Green Horse Press, 1975; *The Music Variety,* Roxbury Poetry Enterprises, 1976; *The World and Its Streets, Places,* Black Sparrow Press, 1977; *Watching/How or Why,* Elizabeth Press, 1977; *Cloud, Invisible Air,* Station Hill Press, 1978; *Heat Simmers Cold,* Orange Export, 1978; *Flagpole Riding,* Stingy Artist, 1978; *Running Around,* Burning Deck, 1978; *Country/Harbor/Quiet/Act/Around* (prose), edited by Garrett Whatten, This Press, 1978; *Time/Details/of a Tree,* Elizabeth Press, 1979; *Lined Up Bulk Senses,* Burning Deck, 1979; *Earth Birds,* Circle Press, 1980; *There's a/Morning/Enormous Hulk of the Sky,* Elizabeth Press, 1981; *Waters/Places/a Time,* Black Sparrow Press, 1981.

Work is represented in several anthologies, including: *A New Folder, Americans,* Folder Editions, 1959; *New American Poetry,* Grove, 1960, new edition, 1981; *A Controversy of Poets,* Doubleday, 1965; *Poems Now,* Kulchur Press, 1966; *Inside Outer Space,* Anchor Press, 1970; *The Voice That Is Great Within Us,* Bantam, 1970; *America: A Prophecy,* Random House, 1973; *Shake the Kaliedoscope,* Simon & Schuster, 1973; *A Gist of Origins,* Grossman, 1975; *A Big Jewish Book,* Anchor Press, 1978.

Contributor to periodicals, including *Origin, Black Mountain Review, Poetry, Paris Review,* and *Chicago Review.*

SIDELIGHTS: Larry Eigner, palsied as a result of injury at birth, has spent all his life confined to a bed or a wheelchair. His poetry reflects what he has seen of the world through the windows of houses, cars, and planes. *Dictionary of Literary Biography* writer Idris McElveen comments that Eigner's "perception of reality, what can be seen from his windows, is a vision of the world as it is, stripped of artifice and implication, spare and direct." According to Samuel Charters in *Some Poems/Poets: Studies in American Underground Poetry since 1945,* Eigner writes "with an emotional suddeness. The poem is conceived and written at almost the same moment. He writes many poems, and most of them have the abrupt, gesturing feel of the way they were written. The term he uses himself is 'hot'—and the writing process he has described in letters is of immediate excitement in his perception."

Discussing his writing, Eigner told *CA:* "A poem can be like walking down the street and noticing things. It can extend itself at times, more or less, without obscurity or too much effort. Though the more scarce things around you are, the less spontaneity; creation may even be impossible. Trying too hard gets you nowhere. You can only do the best you can. Robert Frost, saying a poem takes its own course, remarked how 'Step by step the wonder of unexpected supply keeps growing' and it's a wonder to me how dense meter and rhyme, which has almost always been beyond me, must've been at the tip of his head, his tongue. And though the future is inescapable, near or in the background or over the horizon, maybe the most a poem can be is a realization of things that come together. Or moments. (Nothing lasts forever or for ages, and it's a question how much can or should anything last or occupy attention.)

"There doesn't have to be anything like padding anywhere at all when there's no meter or regular thyme. A piece of language in verse, measured, deliberated, can be really a stretch thinking, process of thought—one thought really attained, in a second or longer time, leading to another, a math of everyday life, penetrating or, anyway, evaluative. The line or stanza break provides the means of assessment, the stress it can give in the absence of obscuring meter. The line is a typographical device as much as A or Z, comma or colon, indentation or lacuna. A thing can be overemphasized, made too much of, yet it seems that, ultimately, one is as important as any other. There's no hierarchy, so evaluation or assessment amounts to realization.

"Also, though, there might be too much to realize as well as too little. The atmosphere might get or be too thick. Things live, go too fast, whirl past. A few years back, I could feel in things a lot more than I've been able to since I moved to Berkeley (from Massachusetts Bay). It seems I feel the world as a neighborhood, or two dozen square miles of it anyway. Fairly still waters run deep. But slowing or winding down isn't a problem, or hardly so, for me at least. My eyes [are] still big for my head; most things were always tantalizingly beyond or almost beyond sight and hearing, out of reach. I've had quite an impression of this anyway, and often enough I guess of barely managing to reach/grasp things when I have, no doubt due to inability to explore much on my own from babyhood on, my curiosity exacerbated.

"As a kid I took to heart all songs, slogans—a good number anyway—proverbs and admonitions (not only the Ten Commandments). The warning against too much candy, for instance, has never been far from my mind. And then too there's the matter of over-excitement. Every hour or two is a new day around the world, but by now I opine you can have overkill in anything; for example, there's no shortage of any kind of writing that I can see. Nor is work any longer a very great good—life or living is its purpose. Career or profession seem obsolete in enough ways by now, and I think of a return to amateurism (as much as that's feasible for anyone)."

Andrew Hoyem, in an article in *Poetry,* notes: "Many poets have been fascinated by the apparently disjointed random notations scattered over the page in the poems of Eigner. Some have hoped that his palsy enabled him to *see* as others have not. This notion links to the romantic aura of the madman, the privileged state of the psychedelic. . . . Eigner *in toto* is neither invalid nor superior because of his confinement to a wheelchair. . . . He has, as Robert Duncan says, come into the full of his poetic voice."

BIOGRAPHICAL/CRITICAL SOURCES: Listener, February 1, 1968; *Poetry,* March, 1969, July, 1969, June, 1975; Samuel Charters, *Some Poems/Poets: Studies in American Underground Poetry since 1945,* Oyez, 1971; (under name Larry Eigner) *Contemporary Literary Criticism,* Volume IX, Gale, 1978; (under name Larry Eigner) *Dictionary of Literary Biography,* Volume V, Gale, 1980.

*   *   *

EISELEY, Loren Corey 1907-1977

PERSONAL: Born September 3, 1907, in Lincoln, Neb.; died July 9, 1977, of cancer, in Philadelphia, Pa.; son of Clyde Edwin and Daisy (Corey) Eiseley; married Mabel Langdon, August 29, 1938. *Education:* University of Nebraska, B.A., 1933; University of Pennsylvania, A.M., 1935, Ph.D., 1937. *Religion:* Protestant. *Office:* Department of Anthropology, University Museum, University of Pennsylvania, Philadelphia, Pa. 19174.

CAREER: University of Kansas, Lawrence, assistant professor, 1937-42, associate professor of sociology and anthropology, 1942-44; Oberlin College, Oberlin, Ohio, professor of sociology and anthropology and chairman of department, 1944-47; University of Pennsylvania, Philadelphia, professor and chairman of the department of anthropology, 1947-59, provost, 1959-61, professor of anthropology and history of science, 1961-63, chairman of department of history of science, 1961-63, Benjamin Franklin and University Professor of Anthropology and History of Science, 1961-77, curator of early man, University of Pennsylvania Museum, 1948-77, chairman of department of history and philosophy of science, Graduate School of Arts and Sciences, 1961-64. Visiting professor of anthropology, Columbia University, summers, 1946, 1950, University of California at Berkeley, summer, 1949, Harvard University, summer, 1952, and University of Kansas. Hosted television program, "Animal Secrets," 1966-68. Member of presidential task force on preservation of natural beauty, 1964-65. Member of board of directors, Samuel S. Fels Foundation; National Parks Division, Department of the Interior, member of advisory board, 1966-72, member of council, 1972-77.

MEMBER: American Anthropological Association (fellow; vice-president, 1948-49), American Institute of Human Paleontology (president, 1949-52), American Association for the Advancement of Science (fellow; vice-president, 1969), National Academy of Arts and Sciences (fellow), National Institute of Arts and Letters (fellow), American Philosophical Society (fellow), American Academy of Political and Social Science (member of board of directors), American Association of University Professors, American Association of Physical Anthropologists, Society for American Archaeology, New York Academy of Sciences (fellow), Philadelphia Anthropological Society (vice-president, 1947; president, 1948), Phi Beta Kappa, Sigma Xi, Century Club (New York).

AWARDS, HONORS: Athenaeum of Philadelphia Award for nonfiction, 1958, for *Darwin's Century;* first Phi Beta Kappa award in science, 1959; Page One Award of the Philadelphia Newspaper Guild, 1960; John Burroughs Medal and Pierre Lecomte du Nouy Foundation Award, both 1961, for *Firmament of Time;* Philadelphia Arts Festival Award for literature, 1962; Bradford Washburn Award from Boston Museum of Science, 1976, for his "outstanding contribution to the public understanding of science"; Joseph Wood Krutch Medal from Humane Society of the United States, 1976, for his "significant contribution to the improvement of life and the environment in this country"; Social Science Research Council postdoctoral fellow, 1940-41; Wenner-Gren Foundation of Anthropology, research grant, 1952-53; Center for Advanced Study in the Behavioral Sciences fellowship, Stanford, Calif., 1961-62; Citation for Outstanding Service to Education, Department of Public Instruction, Commonwealth of Pennsylvania, 1962; Guggenheim fellow, 1964-65. Recipient of over 35 honorary degrees.

WRITINGS: (Editor) John Moss and others, *Early Man in the Eden Valley,* University of Pennsylvania Museum, 1951; (editor) *An Appraisal of Anthropology Today,* University of Chicago Press, 1953; *The Immense Journey,* Random House, 1957; *Darwin's Century: Evolution and the Men Who Discovered It,*

Doubleday, 1958; (with others) *Social Control in a Free Society,* University of Pennsylvania Press, 1958, reprinted, Greenwood Press, 1975; *Firmament of Time,* Atheneum, 1960; *The Mind as Nature,* Harper, 1962; *Francis Bacon and the Modern Dilemma,* University of Nebraska Press, 1963, revised and expanded edition published as *The Man Who Saw through Time,* Scribner, 1973; *The Unexpected Universe,* Harcourt, 1969; *The Invisible Pyramid,* Scribner, 1970; *The Night Country,* Scribner, 1971; (author of introduction) *The Shape of Likelihood: Relevance and the University,* University of Alabama Press, 1971; *Notes of an Alchemist* (poems), Scribner, 1972; *The Innocent Assassins* (poems), Scribner, 1973; *All the Strange Hours: The Excavation of a Life* (autobiography), Scribner, 1975; *Another Kind of Autumn* (poems), Scribner, 1977; *The Star Thrower,* Times Books, 1978; *Darwin and the Mysterious Mr. X: New Light on the Evolutionists* (essays), edited by Kenneth Heuer, Dutton, 1979; *All the Night Wings* (poems), Times Books, 1979.

Contributor of verse and prose to literary anthologies. Contributor to scientific journals, including *Science* and *American Anthropologist,* and to newspapers and national magazines, including *Saturday Evening Post, Harper's, Saturday Review of Literature, Scientific American, Horizon, New York Herald Tribune,* and *New York Times.* Member of editorial board, *American Scholar* and *Expedition.*

SIDELIGHTS: Melvin Maddocks noted in *Life* that "the market is becoming a little crowded with latter-day Thoreaus—writers who try to combine the walk along the beach with Big Thoughts About Life. . . . Among these nature pundits Loren Eiseley remains supreme and rather majestically different. . . . Evolution, as Eiseley treats it, is a kind of tragicomic fairy tale: The wistful, once-upon-a-time story of how mankind madly questing . . . went astray." Eiseley was described as a scientist "who can also write with poetic sensibility and with a fine sense of wonder and of reverence before the mysteries of life and nature." Edward Hoagland, also of *Life,* supported this view, commenting that Eiseley's "command of the language is that of a literary man. He is one of those transcendent imaginative thinkers who are not limited to one branch of science, nor to science itself. . . . He's a writer so good he can stop you dead in your tracks for a day or a week."

There are those, however, who felt that Eiseley shirked his responsibilities as a scientist in producing his books. The *Nation*'s Harold Fruchtbaum granted that "perhaps it is unfair to ask more of Eiseley than that which he usually gives the large audiences who have enjoyed . . . his books—a vivid blend of anthropology, archaeology, natural history and the history of science written in dramatic and at times sentimental, somewhat mystical prose. He is a stimulating teacher for the layman, and that is by no means a small accomplishment. Yet one hopes for more from a man with Eiseley's background as a professional anthropologist and student of the history of science. The serious reader expects the penetrating anthropological and historical insights which our era needs. Instead, Eiseley gives but a superficial sketch of man and nature in society, some clever metaphors, and the warning that something must be done to save the natural world. . . . He has avoided what may be one of the intellectual's primary functions—to place responsibility for the failures of society on the people and the institutions that control the society. . . . [His book] gives the reader a false sense of understanding a major problem and its solution. At the moment we do not need such illusions."

Jascha Kessler, commenting in *Parnassus,* called more than Eiseley's approach into question. "I am sorry to say that I am mortified for him," he wrote of *Notes of an Alchemist.* "He

doesn't really have any more sense of what a poem is than do most undergraduates. . . . It's his prose that's poetical, densely flowing with meditative and rich passions and rhythm, while his verse is notebook phrases, anecdotes, and reflections. . . . For such a man poetry is too trivial a pursuit. But poetry is also too important a calling and event to be piddled about like this."

Ray Bradbury defended Eiseley in his *Detroit News* review of *The Night Country,* noting that the book "can be read . . . in about three hours. The vibrations from those three hours, however, might well last the rest of your life, because to read Eiseley is to fall instantly in love. . . . [This book] comes just in time, for we are starved for ideas and language. The gift of tongues is absent among most modern writers. . . . If all the people ran as beautifully as Eiseley writes, the world would be full of gazelles." He continued, "This book [and others by him] . . . will have more substance, warm breath and good blood in them in the year 2001 than 99 out of 100 writers who say they are alive today."

One can see why the *New York Times*'s Alden Whitman might have felt that "criticizing Eiseley is akin to finding fault with pumpkin pie." Nevertheless, one particular complaint stands, even among those who sincerely appreciated his writing. Marston Bates wrote in the *Washington Post Book World,* "Loren Eiseley . . . seems always to have looked at the world with wonder," but added, "I am not sure that I always understand what Eiseley is saying. [In *The Unexpected Universe*] he has written a book that needs to be savored and pondered, and that I found best to read a little at a time." Bates conceded, "I am not sure I need to understand—the rich imagery of the language may be reward enough."

W. H. Auden noted in the *New Yorker* that Eiseley "can at times write sentences which [are] . . . too dependent upon some private symbolism of his own to be altogether comprehensible to others," but also pointed out that this criticism never bothered Eiseley one bit. "I suspect Dr. Eiseley of being a melancholic," he added. "He recognizes that man is the only creature who speaks personally, works, and prays, but nowhere does he overtly say that man is the only creature who laughs."

BIOGRAPHICAL/CRITICAL SOURCES: Christian Science Monitor, October 16, 1969; *Washington Post Book World,* November 26, 1969, July 22, 1979; *Best Sellers,* December 15, 1969, December 1, 1970; *Life,* February 6, 1970, November 19, 1971; *New Yorker,* February 21, 1970; *Nation,* March 8, 1971; *New York Times,* November 10, 1971, December 18, 1975; *Detroit News,* December 26, 1971; *Parnassus: Poetry in Review,* fall/winter, 1973; Loren Corey Eiseley, *All the Strange Hours: The Excavation of a Life* (autobiography), Scribner, 1975; *Contempory Literary Criticism,* Volume VII, Gale, 1977; *Washington Post,* July 8, 1978; *New York Times Book Review,* July 22, 1979.†

*   *   *

EISENBERG, Daniel Bruce 1946-

PERSONAL: Born October 4, 1946, in Long Island City, N.Y.; son of Louis (a physician) and Marcia (a librarian; maiden name, Jesiek) Eisenberg; married Lynn Rimmer, May 31, 1968 (divorced, 1974); married Irene Ferreira de Sousa, June 15, 1974 (separated, 1980). *Education:* University of Madrid, Diploma de estudios hispanicos, 1966; Johns Hopkins University, B.A., 1967; Brown University, M.A., 1968, Ph.D., 1971. *Religion:* "Jewish Atheist." *Residence:* Tallahassee, Fla. *Office:* Department of Modern Languages, Florida State University, Tallahassee, Fla. 32306.

CAREER: University of North Carolina at Chapel Hill, assistant professor of Spanish, 1970-73; City College of the City University of New York, New York City, assistant professor of Spanish, 1973-74; Florida State University, Tallahassee, associate professor, 1974-78, professor of Spanish, 1978—. *Member:* Asociacion Internacional de Hispanistas, Modern Language Association of America, Cervantes Society of America, South Atlantic Modern Language Association. *Awards, honors:* National Endowment for the Humanities fellowship, 1972; research award from American Philosophical Society, 1975.

WRITINGS: Textos y documentos lorquianos (title means "Lorca Texts and Documents"), privately printed, 1975; (editor) Diego Ortunez de Calahorra, *Espejo de principes y caballeros* (title means "The Mirror of Princely Deeds and Knighthood"), six volumes, Espasa-Calpe (Madrid), 1975; (editor) Federico Garcia Lorca, *Songs,* translation by Philip Cummings, Duquesne University Press, 1976; *"Poeta en Nueva York": Historia y problemas de un texto de Lorca* (title means "'Poet in New York': History and Problems of a Lorca Text"), Ariel (Barcelona), 1976; *Castilian Romances of Chivalry in the Sixteenth Century: A Bibliography,* Grant & Cutler (London), 1979; *Romances of Chivalry in the Spanish Golden Age,* Juan de la Cuesta (Newark, Delaware), 1981; (editor) Alejo Venegas del Busto, *Primera parte de las diferencias de libros que ay en el universo* (title means "First Part of the Types of Books which There Are in the Universe"), Puvill (Barcelona), 1981. Contributor to professional journals. Founder and editor, *Journal of Hispanic Philology,* 1976—.

WORK IN PROGRESS: Editing a critical edition of Feliciano de Silva's *Amadis de Grecia;* research on sexuality in Spain and in Spanish literature.

SIDELIGHTS: Daniel Eisenberg writes: "My research has been in several quite diverse areas within the field of Spanish literature; my work on Lorca, for example, began as a hobby and has turned into a major interest. Much of my work has been focused on correcting errors of perspective held by many writers on Spanish literature; I think of myself more as a literary historian, biographer, and textual critic than as a literary critic."

*   *   *

ELIAS, Taslim Olawale   1914-

PERSONAL: Born November 11, 1914, in Lagos, Nigeria; son of Momolesho and Ibidun (Balogun) Elias; married Ganiat Yetunde Fowosere (a lawyer), January 12, 1932; children: Olubunkola Gbolahan, Olusoji Adeola. *Education:* Attended Igbobi College, Lagos, Nigeria; University College and Institute of Advanced Legal Studies, London, B.A., 1944, LL.B. (with honors), 1946, LL.M., 1947, Ph.D., 1949. *Home:* 20 Ozumba Mbadiwe, Victoria Island, Lagos, Nigeria. *Office:* c/o International Court of Justice, Peace Palace, The Hague, Netherlands.

CAREER: Government Audit Department, Lagos, Nigeria, assistant, 1934-35; Nigerian Railway, Lagos, Nigeria, with chief accountant's office, 1935-44; called to Bar at Inner Temple, London, England, 1947; University of Manchester, Manchester, England, Simon Research Fellow, instructor in law and social anthropology, 1951-53; Oxford University, Queen Elizabeth House, Oxford, England, Oppenheimer Research Fellow, 1954-60; University of London, London, governor of School of Oriental and African studies, 1957-60; Nigerian Government, Lagos Federal Attorney-General, 1960-72, Minister of Justice, 1960-66, Commissioner for Justice, 1967, chief justice, 1972-75; University of Lagos, Lagos, Nigeria, pro-

fessor of law and dean of faculty of law, 1966-72; currently affiliated with International Court of Justice, The Hague, Netherlands. Visiting professor, University of Delhi, 1956. Member, then chairman, International Law Commission of the United Nations, 1961-75. *Member:* World Association of Judges (president, 1975—), International Commission of Jurists (member of executive council, 1975—), Institute of International Law (associate member), The Hague Academy of International Law (member of curatorium, 1975—), American Society of International Law (honorary member), Society of Public Teachers of Law (honorary member). *Awards, honors:* Queen's Counsel, 1961; Commander of the Federal Republic, Nigeria, 1962; LL.D., University of Dakar, 1962, University of London, 1962, Howard University, University of Hull, University of Jodhpur, University of Ife; D.Litt., University of Lagos, University of Ibadan, University of Nsukka; National Merit Award, Republic of Nigeria, 1979.

WRITINGS: Nigerian Land Law and Custom, Routledge & Kegan Paul, 1951, 4th edition published as *Nigerian Land Law,* Sweet & Maxwell, 1971; *Groundwork of Nigerian Law,* Routledge & Kegan Paul, 1954, second edition published as *The Nigerian Legal System,* 1963; *Nature of African Customary Law,* Manchester University Press, 1956, Humanities, 1962; *Government and Politics in Africa,* Asia Publishing House, 1961, second edition, 1963; *Ghana and Sierra Leone: Development of Their Laws and Constitutions,* Stevens, 1962; *British Colonial Law,* Stevens, 1962; *Nigeria: The Development of Its Law and Constitution,* Stevens, 1967; (editor) *The Prison System in Nigeria,* University of Lagos, 1969; (editor) *Nigerian Press Law,* Evans Brothers, 1969; *Africa and the Development of International Law,* Oceana, 1972; (editor) *The Nigerian Magistrate and the Offender,* Ethiope Publishing (Nigeria), 1972; (editor) *Law and Social Change in Nigeria,* University of Lagos, 1972; *Law in a Developing Society,* Ethiope Publishing, 1973; *New Horizons in International Law,* Oceana, 1974; *The Modern Law of Treaties,* Oceana, 1974. Also author of *Judicial Process in Commonwealth Africa,* 1976.

*   *   *

ELLIOT, Elisabeth (Howard)   1926-

PERSONAL: Born December 21, 1926, in Brussels, Belgium; daughter of Philip Eugene (an editor) and Katharine (Gillingham) Howard; married Philip James Elliot, October 8, 1953 (died, 1956); married Addison H. Leitch, January 1, 1969 (died, 1973); married E. Lars Gren, 1977; children: (first marriage) Valerie. *Education:* Wheaton College, Wheaton, Ill., B.A., 1948. *Home:* 746 Bay Rd., Hamilton, Mass. 01936.

CAREER: Missionary in eastern jungle of Ecuador, 1952-63; Gordon-Conwell Theological Seminary, Hamilton, Mass., adjunct professor, 1974-80; Gordon College, Wenham, Mass., writer-in-residence, 1981—.

WRITINGS: Through Gates of Splendor, Harper, 1957; *Shadow of the Almighty,* Harper, 1958; *The Savage My Kinsman,* Harper, 1960; *No Graven Image,* Harper, 1966; *Who Shall Ascend?,* Harper, 1968; *The Liberty of Obedience,* Word, Inc., 1968; *A Slow and Certain Light,* Word, Inc., 1973; *These Strange Ashes,* Harper, 1975; *Twelve Baskets of Crumbs,* Christian Herald, 1976; *Let Me Be a Woman,* Tyndale House, 1976; *The Journals of Jim Elliot,* Revell, 1979; *Love Has a Price Tag,* Christian Herald, 1980; *The Mark of a Man,* Revell, 1981.

WORK IN PROGRESS: A book on discipline, for Revell.

BIOGRAPHICAL/CRITICAL SOURCES: Life, January 20, 1956; *Reader's Digest,* April, 1962.

ELLISON, Craig W(illiam) 1944-

PERSONAL: Born August 21, 1944, in Springfield, Mass.; son of William C. (a school district administrator) and Marilyn (Otto) Ellison; married Sharon Andre (a registered nurse), September 20, 1969; children: Scott, Timothy. *Education:* King's College, Briarcliff Manor, N.Y., B.A. (magna cum laude), 1966; Wayne State University, M.A., 1969, Ph.D., 1972. *Religion:* Protestant. *Office:* Department of Psychology, Westmont College, 955 La Paz Rd., Santa Barbara, Calif. 93108.

CAREER: Westmont College, Santa Barbara, Calif., assistant professor of psychology, 1971—. Community organizer for Metropolitan Action Center (Detroit, Mich.), summer, 1968; visiting professor at State University of New York at Binghamton, summer, 1973; director of International Conference on Human Engineering and the Future of Man, 1975. Director of Central City Conference of Evangelicals (Detroit), 1969-71. *Member:* American Psychological Association (western regional director, 1978; member-at-large of governing council, Division 36), American Scientific Affiliation, Christian Association for Psychological Studies (member of board of directors, 1974-80), Society for the Psychological Study of Social Issues, World Future Society, Western Psychological Association, Western Association of Christians for Psychological Studies (executive director, 1974-78), Psi Chi.

WRITINGS: (Editor) *The Urban Mission,* Eerdmans, 1974; (editor) *Self-Esteem,* Christian Association for Psychological Services/Southwestern Press, 1976; (editor) *Modifying Man: Implications and Ethics,* University Press of America, 1977; *Loneliness: The Search for Intimacy,* Christian Herald, 1980; *Self-Esteem: A New Look,* Harper, 1982. Contributor to psychology and religion journals.

SIDELIGHTS: Craig Ellison told *CA:* "I feel that it is important to help bridge the gap of understanding and communication between the religious and behavioral science communities and fields of inquiry. My activity and writing are devoted in large part to that goal."

*   *   *

ELLISON, H(enry) L(eopold) 1903-

PERSONAL: Original surname, Zeckhausen; assumed mother's maiden surname in 1925; born July 10, 1903, in Cracow, Austria; son of Leopold (a clergyman) and Sarah Jane (Ellison) Zeckhausen; married Adeline Mary Todd, August 21, 1937; married second wife, Patrica Jean Worrall, June 30, 1981; children: (first marriage) Nancy Dorothea Ellison Urwin, Ruth Christine, Elisabeth Mary. *Education:* University of London, B.A. (King's College), 1925, B.D. (London College of Divinity), 1927. *Religion:* Christian. *Home:* 14 Rosyl Ave., Holcombe, Dawlish, Devon EX7 0LE, England.

CAREER: London College of Divinity, London, England, tutor, 1927-30; church missions to Jews and Mildmay Mission to Jews, missionary in Poland and Rumania, 1930-39; Mildmay Mission to Jews, London, England, assistant director, 1939-49; London Bible College, London, England, tutor for Old Testament studies, 1949-55; numerous visiting lectureships, 1957-63; Moorlands Bible College, Dawlish, England, senior tutor, 1963-68. *Member:* Society for Old Testament Studies, Victoria Institute (member of council, 1953-60), International Hebrew Christian Alliance (executive, 1939—; vice-president, 1947-50), Hebrew Christian Alliance of Great Britain (secretary, 1942-49; treasurer, 1950-63; vice-president, 1961—), Churches' Committee on the Jewish People.

WRITINGS: Roumanian Self-Taught, Marlborough, 1939; (editor) James Neil, *Peeps into Palestine,* Walter, 1944; (editor) John Wilkinson, *God's Plan for the Jews,* Paternoster Press, 1946.

Men Spake from God: Studies in the Hebrew Prophets, Paternoster Press, 1952, Eerdmans, 1958, published as *The Old Testament Prophets: A Study Guide,* Zondervan, 1966, 3rd edition, 1971; *The Servant of Jehovah,* International Hebrew Christian Alliance, 1953; *The Centrality of the Messianic Idea for the Old Testament,* Inter-Varsity Fellowship, 1953; *Ezekiel: The Man and His Message,* Paternoster Press, 1956; *The Christian Approach to the Jew,* Edinburgh House, 1958; *From Tragedy to Triumph: The Message of the Book of Job,* Eerdmans, 1958, published as *A Study of Job: From Tragedy to Triumph,* Zondervan, 1972; *The Household Church,* Paternoster Press, 1963, 2nd edition published as *The Household Church: Apostolic Practice in a Modern Setting,* 1979; *The Mystery of Israel: An Exposition of Romans 9-11,* Eerdmans, 1966; *Joshua, Judges, Ruth, I and II Samuel,* Scripture Union, 1966, Eerdmans, 1968; *The Psalms,* Scripture Union, 1967, Eerdmans, 1968; *I and II Peter, I, II and III John, Jude, Revelation,* Eerdmans, 1969; *The Message of the Old Testament,* Eerdmans, 1969; *The Prophets of Israel: From Ahijah to Hosea,* Eerdmans, 1969; (editor; author with George Cecil Douglas Howley) *A New Testament Commentary,* Zondervan, 1969.

Understanding a Jew, Olive Press, 1972; (with Edward Musgrave Blaiklock) *The Life of Christ,* Scripture Union, 1973, published as *Jesus' Earthly Life,* 1978; *From Babylon to Bethlehem: The Jewish People from the Exile to the Messiah,* Paternoster Press, 1976; *Jesus as Man,* Scripture Union, 1978; *Fathers of the Covenant: Some Great Chapters in Genesis and Exodus,* Paternoster Press, 1978. Also editor and contributor to *A Bible Commentary for Today,* 1979; also translator of *Sauer: The King of the Earth,* 1962. Contributor to *New Bible Commentary,* 1953, *The Church and the Jewish People,* 1954, *Baker Dictionary of Theology,* 1960, *New Bible Dictionary,* 1962, and *The Illustrated Bible Dictionary,* 1980. Editor, *I.H.C.A. Theological Bulletin.*

*   *   *

ELWIN, William
See EBENSTEIN, William

*   *   *

ENDORE, (Samuel) Guy 1900-1970
(Harry Relis)

PERSONAL: Born July 4, 1900, in New York, N.Y.; died February 12, 1970, in Los Angeles, Calif.; married Henrietta Portugal, 1927; children: Marcia, Gita. *Education:* Attended Carnegie Institute of Technology (now Carnegie-Mellon University); Columbia University, A.B., 1923, M.A., 1925. *Home:* 211 First Anita Dr., Los Angeles, Calif. *Agent:* Barthold Fles Literary Agency, 507 Fifth Avenue, New York, N.Y. 10017.

CAREER: Self-employed writer and novelist. *Member:* Academy of Motion Picture Arts and Sciences, Screen Writers Guild, Authors League of America. *Awards, honors:* Oscar nomination, 1945, for screenplay, "G.I. Joe."

WRITINGS: Casanova: His Known and Unknown Life, John Day, 1929; (translator) Julien Viand, *An Iceland Fisherman,* P. A. Norstedt, 1931; *The Werewolf of Paris,* Farrar & Rinehart, 1933, reprinted, Pocket Books, 1976; *The Sword of God: Joan of Arc,* Garden City Publishing Co., 1933; *Babouk,* Vanguard, 1934; *The Crime at Scottsboro,* Hollywood Scottsboro

Committee, 1938; *The Sleepy Lagoon Mystery,* Sleepy Lagoon Defense Committee, 1944, reprinted, R & E Research Associates, 1972; *Methinks the Lady,* Duell, 1946; *King of Paris* (Book-of-the-Month Club selection), Simon & Schuster, 1956; *Detour at Night,* Simon & Schuster, 1958; *Voltaire! Voltaire!,* Simon & Schuster, 1961 (published in England as *The Heart and the Mind,* W. H. Allen, 1962); *Satan's Saint,* Crown, 1965; *Call Me Shakespeare: A Play in Two Acts,* Dramatists Play Service, 1966; *Synanon,* Doubleday, 1968; (translator) Hanns H. Ewers, *Alraune,* edited by R. Reginald and Douglas Menville, Arno, 1976. Also author of *Man from Limbo,* Farrar & Rinehart.

Screenplays; some in collaboration with others; some under pseudonym Harry Relis: "The Devil Doll," Metro-Goldwyn-Mayer, 1936; "The League of Frightened Men," Columbia, 1937; "Carefree," RKO, 1938; "Song of Russia," Metro-Goldwyn-Mayer, 1944; "G.I. Joe," United Artists, 1945; "The Vicious Circle," United Artists, 1948; "Johnny Allegro," Columbia, 1949; "Tomorrow Is Another Day," Warner Brothers, 1951; "He Ran All the Way," United Artists, 1951; "Captain Sinbad," Metro-Goldwyn-Mayer, 1963.

Author of several published speeches. Contributor to magazines.

SIDELIGHTS: In the late forties, Guy Endore, long active in liberal causes, came to the attention of the House Committee on Un-American Activities which was investigating alleged Communist infiltration of the film industry. He was reputedly blacklisted by some film studios because of this investigation and was forced to use the pseudonym Harry Relis for a time in order to sell his screenplays. Despite the restrictions put upon his writing career, Endore stood by his beliefs. "I feel I failed to make the grade as a human being and as a writer," he said at the time, "if I am not known as subversive to everything the investigating committee stands for."

BIOGRAPHICAL/CRITICAL SOURCES: New Statesman, February 11, 1966; *Christian Science Monitor,* August 10, 1968; *New York Times,* February 21, 1970; *Rolling Stone,* October 7, 1976; *Washington Post Book World,* November 28, 1976.†

* * *

ENGELS, John David 1931-

PERSONAL: Born January 19, 1931, in South Bend, Ind.; son of Norbert Anthony (a teacher) and Eleanor (a teacher; maiden name, Perry) Engels; married Gail Jochimsen (a social worker), February 1, 1957; children: Jessica, David, John, Jr., Laura, Matthew, Philip (died, 1965). *Education:* University of Notre Dame, A.B., 1952; University of Dublin, graduate study, 1955; University of Iowa, M.F.A., 1957. *Politics:* Democrat. *Religion:* Roman Catholic. *Home address:* R.F.D. 1, Box 247, North Williston, Vt. 05495. *Office:* Department of English, St. Michael's College, Winooski, Vt. 05404.

CAREER: St. Norbert College, West De Pere, Wis., instructor in English, 1957-62; St. Michael's College, Winooski, Vt., 1962—, began as assistant professor, professor of English, 1970—. Visiting lecturer, University of Vermont, 1974, 1975, 1976; Sue Reid Slaughter Lecturer in English, Sweet Briar College, winter, 1976. Vermont Council on the Arts, secretary to the board of trustees, 1971-72, trustee, 1971-75. *Military service:* U.S. Navy, 1952-55; became lieutenant. *Member:* Winooski/Central Vermont Trout Unlimited (president, 1972-73). *Awards, honors:* Bread Loaf scholarship in poetry, 1960; Robert Frost fellow in poetry, Bread Loaf, 1976.

WRITINGS: (With father, Norbert Engels) *Writing Techniques,* McKay, 1962; (with N. Engels) *Experience and Imagination,*

McKay, 1965; *The Homer Mitchell Place* (poems), University of Pittsburgh Press, 1968; (editor) *The Merrill Guide to William Carlos Williams,* C. E. Merrill, 1969; (editor) *The Merrill Checklist of William Carlos Williams,* C. E. Merrill, 1969; (editor) *The Merrill Studies in Paterson,* C. E. Merrill, 1971; *Signals from the Safety Coffin,* University of Pittsburgh Press, 1975; *Blood Mountain,* University of Pittsburgh Press, 1977; *Vivaldi in Early Fall* (poems), University of Georgia Press, 1981. Contributor of poetry and reviews to *Poetry, Antaeus, Hudson Review, Nation, New Yorker,* and other journals and periodicals.

WORK IN PROGRESS: A book of selected poems, *The Seasons of Vermont.*

* * *

ENRICK, Norbert Lloyd 1920-

PERSONAL: Born April 11, 1920, in Berlin, Germany; son of Max M. (a medical doctor) and Elfe (Wilkiser) Enrick; married Mary Lynch, May 17, 1952; children: Ellen Marguerite, Robert Neal. *Education:* City College (now City College of the City University of New York), New York, N.Y., B.A., 1941; Columbia University, M.S., 1945, additional study, 1948-50; University of Virginia, Ph.D., 1963. *Home:* 1577 Morris Rd., Kent, Ohio 44240. *Office:* Administrative Sciences Department, Kent State University, Kent, Ohio 44242.

CAREER: Werner Management Consultants, New York, N.Y., management consulting engineer, 1948-53; Institute of Textile Technology, Charlottesville, Va., director of operations research and computer laboratory, 1953-60; University of Virginia, Charlottesville, associate professor of management, 1960-65; Stevens Institute of Technology, Hoboken, N.J., professor of management science, 1965-66; Kent State University, Kent, Ohio, professor of administrative sciences, 1966—. Consultant to National Aeronautics and Space Administration and to business firms. *Member:* American Society for Quality Control (fellow), American Statistical Association (president of Virginia section, 1956-58), Operations Research Society of America, American Society for Testing and Materials, Fiber Society, Academy of Marketing Science, Scientific Society, Sigma Xi.

WRITINGS: Quality Control, Industrial Press, 1948, 7th edition published as *Quality Control and Reliability,* 1977; *Cases in Management Statistics,* Holt, 1963; *Management Control Manual,* Rayon Publishing, 1964; *Sales and Production Management Manual,* Wiley, 1964; *Management Operations Research,* Holt, 1965; *Management Planning,* McGraw, 1967; *Market and Sales Forecasting,* Intext, 1969; *Decision Oriented Statistics,* Mason & Lipscomb, 1970; *Statistical Functions,* Kent State University Press, 1970; *Effective Graphic Communication,* Mason & Lipscomb, 1972; *Quality Control for Profit,* Industrial Press, 1978; *Market and Sales Forecasting,* Robert E. Kreiger, 1979; *Management Control Manual,* Robert E. Krieger, 1980; *Industrial Engineering Manual,* Robert E. Krieger, 1980; *Handbook of Effective Graphic and Tabular Communication,* Robert E. Krieger, 1980; *Management Handbook of Decision-Oriented Statistics,* Robert E. Krieger, 1980; *Statistical Functions and Formulas,* Robert E. Krieger, 1981. Editor, *Journal of the Academy of Marketing Science;* assistant editor, *Journal of Neurologic and Orthopedic Surgery.*

* * *

EVANOFF, Vlad 1916-

PERSONAL: Born December 12, 1916, in New York, N.Y.; son of Thomas and Lucy (Zwirka) Evanoff. *Education:* Attended Cooper Union, 1932-35. *Office:* Box 9032, Coral Springs, Fla. 33065.

CAREER: Worked as commercial artist for five years after high school; free-lance writer and illustrator, 1945—. *Military service:* U.S. Army, 1941-45. *Member:* Outdoors Writers Association of America.

WRITINGS: Surf Fishing, Ronald, 1948, new edition, Harper, 1974; *How to Make Fishing Lures,* Ronald, 1959; *Natural Baits for Fishermen,* A. S. Barnes, 1959, published as *Fishing with Natural Baits,* Prentice-Hall, 1975; *A Complete Guide to Fishing,* Crowell, 1961; *Modern Fishing Tackle,* A. S. Barnes, 1961; *How to Fish in Salt-Water,* A. S. Barnes, 1962; (editor) *Fishing Secrets of the Experts,* Doubleday, 1962; *Spin Fishing,* A. S. Barnes, 1963; *Fresh-Water Fishermen's Bible,* Doubleday, 1964, revised edition, 1980; *Hunting Secrets of the Experts,* Doubleday, 1964; *1001 Fishing Tips and Tricks,* Harper, 1966; *Another 1001 Fishing Tips and Tricks,* Harper, 1970; *Best Ways to Catch More Fish in Fresh and Salt Water,* Doubleday, 1975; *Make Your Own Fishing Lures,* A. S. Barnes, 1975; (compiler) *The Fisherman's Catalog,* Dolphin Books, 1977; *Fishing Rigs for Fresh and Salt Water,* Harper, 1977; *Five Hundred Fishing Experts and How They Catch Fish,* Doubleday, 1978. Contributor to periodicals, including *Salt-Water Sportsman, Motor Boating, True Fishing Yearbook, Sports Afield, Field and Stream,* and *Outdoor Life.*

SIDELIGHTS: Vlad Evanoff writes: "I have been fishing since I was 14 years old. I have derived so many benefits from it in the study of nature, scenery, making new friends and relaxing and having a lot of fun that I have felt a constant compulsion to pass these feelings on to others through my writings. If even one or two readers have taken up fishing because of my writings, I feel I have accomplished my mission in this world."

BIOGRAPHICAL/CRITICAL SOURCES: Life, April 7, 1961.

*   *   *

EVANS, Howard Ensign   1919-

PERSONAL: Born February 23, 1919, in East Hartford, Conn.; son of Archie J. and Adella (Ensign) Evans; married Mary Alice Dietrich, June 6, 1954; children: Barbara, Dorothy, Timothy. *Education:* University of Connecticut, B.A., 1940; Cornell University, M.S., 1941, Ph.D., 1949. *Home:* 304 Off Shore Rd., Fort Collins, Colo. 80524. *Office:* Department of Zoology and Entomology, Colorado State University, Fort Collins, Colo. 80523.

CAREER: Kansas State College (now Kansas State University of Agriculture and Applied Science), Manhattan, assistant professor, 1949-52; Cornell University, Ithaca, N.Y., assistant professor of entomology, 1954-59; Harvard University, Cambridge, Mass., associate curator, Museum of Comparative Zoology, 1959-64, curator, 1964-70, Alexander Agassiz Professor of Zoology, 1970-73; Colorado State University, Fort Collins, professor of entomology, 1973—. *Military service:* U.S. Army, 1942-45; became second lieutenant. *Member:* National Academy of Sciences, Society for the Study of Evolution. *Awards, honors:* National Book Award nomination, 1964, for *Wasp Farm.*

WRITINGS: Song I Sing (verses), Humphries, 1952; *Studies on the Comparative Ethology of Digger Wasps of the Genus Bembix,* Cornell University Press, 1957; *Wasp Farm,* Natural History Press-Doubleday, 1963; *The Comparative Ethology and Evolution of the Sand Wasps,* Harvard University Press, 1966; *Life on a Little-Known Planet,* Dutton, 1968; (with Mary Jane West Eberhard) *The Wasps,* University of Michigan Press,

1970; (with wife, Mary Alice Evans) *William Morton Wheeler, Biologist,* Harvard University Press, 1970. Contributor to scientific journals.

SIDELIGHTS: Howard Ensign Evans' *Life on a Little-Known Planet* describes the life histories and mating habits of several common insects. *New York Times Book Review* writer Robert W. Stock comments: "Evans, a skilled writer in the unlikely guise of a Harvard University entomologist, has the wit and charm to make us care about the life-styles of locusts and bedbugs. . . . The 'little-known planet' of the title is earth; and Evans is pleading for a greater understanding of earth life— even unto the smallest bug. Seldom, if ever, has the case for the natural sciences—and for conservation—been presented with such reasoned, convincing eloquence."

AVOCATIONAL INTERESTS: Photography, backpacking, fishing.

BIOGRAPHICAL/CRITICAL SOURCES: New York Times Book Review, November 17, 1968; *Times Literary Supplement,* May 28, 1970; *Christian Century,* March 3, 1971.

*   *   *

EVELYN, (John) Michael   1916- (Michael Underwood)

PERSONAL: Born June 2, 1916, in Worthing, Sussex, England; the son of Edward Ernest and Kate Rosa (Underwood) Evelyn. *Education:* Christ Church, Oxford, M.A., 1938. *Home:* 7 Southlea Rd. Datchet, Berkshire SL3 9BY, England. *Agent:* A. M. Heath Ltd., 40/42 William IV St., London WC2N 4DD, England; Harriet Wasserman Literary Agency, 230 East 48th St., New York, N.Y.

CAREER: Called to the Bar, Grays Inn, London, England, 1939; Department of Public Prosecutions, London, member of British Government legal service, 1946-76, assistant director, 1969-76. *Military service:* British Army, 1939-46; became major. *Member:* Crime Writers Association, Mystery Writers of America, Detection Club, Garrick Club (London).

WRITINGS: All under pseudonym Michael Underwood: *Murder on Trial,* Hammond, 1954, Washburn, 1958; *Murder Made Absolute,* Hammond, 1955, Washburn, 1957; *Death on Remand,* Hammond, 1956; *False Witness,* Hammond, 1957, Walker 1961; *Lawful Pursuit,* Doubleday, 1958; *Arm of the Law,* Hammond, 1959; *Death by Misadventure,* Hammond, 1960; *Cause of Death,* Hammond, 1960; *Adam's Case,* Doubleday, 1961; *The Case against Philip Quest,* Macdonald, 1962; *Girl Found Dead,* Macdonald, 1963; *The Crime of Colin Wise,* Doubleday, 1964; *The Unprofessional Spy,* Doubleday, 1964; *The Anxious Conspirator,* Doubleday, 1965; *A Crime Apart,* Macdonald, 1966; *The Man Who Died on Friday,* Macdonald, 1967; *The Man Who Killed Too Soon,* Macdonald, 1968; *The Shadow Game,* Macdonald, 1969.

The Silent Liars, Doubleday, 1970; *Shem's Demise,* Macmillan, 1970; *A Trout in the Milk,* Macmillan, 1971, Walker, 1972; *Reward for a Defector,* Macmillan, 1973, St. Martin's, 1974; *A Pinch of Snuff,* St. Martin's, 1974; *The Juror,* St. Martin's, 1975; *Menaces, Menaces,* St. Martin's, 1976; *Murder with Malice,* St. Martin's, 1977; *The Fatal Trip,* St. Martin's, 1977; *Crooked Wood,* St. Martin's, 1978; *Anthing But the Truth,* St. Martin's, 1979; *Smooth Justice,* St. Martin's, 1979; *Victim of Circumstance,* St. Martin's, 1980; *A Clear Case of Suicide,* St. Martin's, 1980; *Crime upon Crime,* St. Martin's, 1981; *Double Jeopardy,* St. Martin's, 1981. Contributor to *Winter's Crimes Four,* edited by George Hardinge,

Macmillan, 1972, and *Verdict of Thirteen: A Detection Club Anthology,* edited by Julian Symons, Harper, 1979.

SIDELIGHTS: Punch critic Leo Harris praises Michael Evelyn as a writer who can be relied on for "a painstakingly constructed crime novel, particularly strong on the legal side." In each of his books, Evelyn draws from his legal knowledge to describe the police investigations, legal procedures and court scenes which invariably follow a criminal act. Although factually correct, Evelyn's books are always fictional rather than based on an actual crime. *Times Literary Supplement* writer Kate Flint comments that all of Evelyn's books are "well-written and unassuming, with a solid background and satisfying plot."

Some of Eveyln's books have been dramatized for French radio, and they have been translated into French, Dutch, Spanish, German, Norwegian, Portuguese, Italian, Japanese, Swedish, Danish, and Serbo-Croatian.

BIOGRAPHICAL/CRITICAL SOURCES: Punch, May 28, 1969; *Times Literary Supplement,* May 9, 1980.

*   *   *

EVERY, George 1909-

PERSONAL: Born February 3, 1909, in Tipton, Devonshire, England; son of George (a clergyman) and Frances Rebecca (Branson) Every. *Education:* Attended University College of the South West (now University of Exeter), 1926-29; University of London, B.A. (external degree; with first class honors in history), 1929; Kelham Theological College, student-tutor, 1929-32. *Religion:* Roman Catholic. *Home:* 7 Lenton Ave., The Park, Nottingham, England.

CAREER: Kelham Theological College, Kelham, Newark, England, lecturer in church history, 1934-72, lecturer in comparative religion and liturgics, 1950-72, librarian, 1953-73;

Oscott College, Sutton Coldfield, Birmingham, England, assistant lecturer, 1973—. Lay brother, Society of the Sacred Mission (Church of England), 1933-73. Lecturer, Centre for Indian and Inter-Religious Studies, Pontifical Oriental Institute (Rome), 1977. Library consultant, visiting Kenya, Uganda, and Tanganyika for East African Association of Theological Colleges, 1963.

WRITINGS: (Contributor) K. Mackenzie, editor, *The Union of Christendom,* S.P.C.K., 1936; *Christian Discrimination,* S.P.C.K., 1940; (with S. L. Bethell and J.D.C. Pellow) *Selected Poems,* Staples Press, 1943; *The Byzantine Patriarchate,* S.P.C.K., 1947, 2nd edition, Allenson, 1962, reprinted, AMS Press, 1980; *Poetry and Personal Responsibility,* S.C.M. Press, 1952; *The High Church Party, 1688-1718,* S.P.C.K., 1956; *Lamb to the Slaughter,* J. Clarke, 1957; *Light under a Door* (Christmas poems), Faith Press, 1958; *The Baptismal Sacrifice,* S.C.M. Press, 1959.

Basic Liturgy, Faith Press, 1961; (contributor) A. H. Armstrong and E.J.B. Fry, editors, *Rediscovering Eastern Christendom,* Darton, Longman & Todd, 1963; *Misunderstandings between East and West,* John Knox, 1966; *Christian Mythology,* Paul Hamlyn, 1970; (contributor) M. Basil Pennington, editor, *One Yet Two, Christian Studies 29,* Cistercian Publications, 1976; (with Simon Tugwell, John Mills, and Peter Hocken) *New Heaven? New Earth?,* Darton, Longman & Todd, 1976, Templegate, 1977; *The Mass,* Our Sunday Visitor, 1978; *Understanding Eastern Christianity,* Dharamaram (Bangalore, India), 1978, 2nd edition, S.C.M. Press, 1980. Contributor to *Encyclopaedia Britannica.* Contributor to *New English Weekly, Time and Tide, Theology, Heythrop Journal, New Blackfriars, Christian Parapsychologist,* and other periodicals. Editor, *Eastern Churches Review,* 1968-80.

WORK IN PROGRESS: An English translation of *Protevangelion of James and Related Texts.*

F

FACKLAM, Margery Metz 1927-

PERSONAL: Born September 6, 1927, in Buffalo, N.Y.; daughter of Eduard Frederick (a civil engineer) and Ruth (Schauss) Metz; married Howard F. Facklam, Jr. (a teacher), July 9, 1949; children: Thomas, David, John, Paul, Margaret. *Education:* University of Buffalo, B.A., 1947; State University of New York College at Buffalo, M.S., 1976. *Home:* 9690 Clarence Center Rd., Clarence Center, N.Y. 14032.

CAREER: Erie Country Department of Social Welfare, Buffalo, N.Y., caseworker, 1948; high school teacher of science in Snyder, N.Y., 1949-50; Buffalo Museum of Science, Buffalo, assistant administrator of education, 1970-74; Aquarium of Niagra Falls, Niagra Falls, N.Y., curator of education and public relations, 1974-77; Buffalo Zoo, Buffalo, director of education, 1977-79; free-lance writer and manager of book store. *Member:* National League of American Pen Women, Authors Guild, Authors League of America, Chi Omega.

WRITINGS: Whistle for Danger, Rand McNally, 1962; *Behind These Doors: Science Museum Makers,* Rand McNally, 1968; (with Patricia Phibbs) *Corn Husk Crafts,* Sterling, 1973; *Frozen Snakes and Dinosaur Bones* (Junior Literary Guild selection), Harcourt, 1976; *Wild Animals, Gentle Women* (Junior Literary Guild selection), Harcourt, 1978; (with husband, Howard Facklam) *From Cell to Clone* (Book-of-the-Month Club selection), Harcourt, 1979. Also author of *The Brain, Magnificent Mind Machine,* 1982. Contributor to periodicals, including *Redbook* and *Guideposts.*

SIDELIGHTS: Margery Metz Facklam told *CA:* ''I write because I love ideas; I hate to be bored, and a writer is never bored, moving from idea to idea. I particularly like to write for children, even though it seems to be a more disciplined job requiring much rewriting for me, because I love children. They are never boring; they, too, love to go to new things, asking why, wondering, and seeing things we skim over as adults. They are so full of what Rachel Carson called a sense of wonder, and writing for children helps me hang onto some of the wonder, too.''

AVOCATIONAL INTERESTS: Nature in general, animals in particular, reading, writing, ''my grandson, family, and anything new and exciting in the world.''

BIOGRAPHICAL/CRITICAL SOURCES: Buffalo Courier Express, September 16, 1962.

FAIRBANK, Alfred John 1895-

PERSONAL: Born July 12, 1895, in Great Grimsby, England; son of Alfred John (an engineer) and Emma (Greetham) Fairbank; married Elsie Kneeshaw, April 2, 1919; children: John Richard. *Education:* Central School of Arts and Crafts (London, England), Diploma of Fellowship, 1933. *Politics:* Independent. *Home:* 27 Granville Rd., Hove, Sussex BN3 1TG, England.

CAREER: British Admiralty, London and Bath, England, 1917-55, began as civil servant, became senior executive officer. Free-lance calligrapher, letterer, palaeographer, writing-master, type-designer, judge of handwriting competitions, and lecturer. *Member:* Society of Scribes and Illuminators (founder member; president, 1951-63), Society for Italic Handwriting (founder member; vice-president, 1953—), Society of Designer Craftsmen (honorary member), Royal Society of Arts, Double Crown Club (honorary member). *Awards, honors:* Commander, Order of the British Empire, for services to calligraphy, 1951; Leverhulme research awards, 1956, 1957; honored on seventieth birthday with a festschrift, *Calligraphy and Palaeography,* published in England by Faber, 1965, and in America by October House, 1966.

WRITINGS: A Handwriting Manual, Dryad, 1932, 9th edition, Watson-Guptill, 1975; *A Book of Scripts,* Penguin, 1949, new edition, Faber, 1977; (with Charlotte Stone and Winifred Hooper) *The Beacon Writing Books* (series of eight copybooks), Ginn (London, England), 1957-59; (with B. L. Wolpe) *Renaissance Handwriting: An Anthology of Italic Scripts,* World Publishing, 1960; (with R. W. Hunt) *Humanistic Scripts,* Bodleian Library, 1960; *A Roman Script for Schools,* Ginn, 1961; (with Bruce Dickins) *The Italic Hand in Tudor Cambridge,* Bowes, 1962; (author of preface) Hermann Degering, *Lettering: Modes of Writing in Western Europe from Antiquity to the Eighteenth Century,* 2nd edition, Benn, 1965; *The Story of Handwriting: Origins and Development,* Watson-Guptill, 1970; (author of introduction) *Augustino da Siena: The 1568 Edition of His Writing Book in Facsimile,* Merrion Press, 1975. Contributor of numerous articles on handwriting to *Journal of the Society for Italic Handwriting* and other publications.

SIDELIGHTS: Alfred John Fairbank told *CA,* ''My published books are counterparts to unique illuminated manuscript books, written on vellum, which I made with Louise Powell ('Ecclesiasticus,' 'Horace,' 'Virgil,' etc.) during the period 1925 to 1939.''

Commenting on his work as a whole, he continues: "We all need creative outlets. For me, the study, the practice, and the teaching of calligraphy, and particularly of italic handwriting (whether of the Renaissance or of today), have provided the outlets. By raising the standards of such a commonplace activity as handwriting, one helps, however little, to raise the standards of civilization."†

*   *   *

FALCONER, Lee N.
   See MAY, Julian

*   *   *

FALL, Bernard B.   1926-1967

PERSONAL: Born November 11, 1926, in Vienna, Austria; died February 21, 1967, in a land mine explosion near Hue, Vietnam; buried in Rock Creek Cemetery, Washington, D.C.; son of Leon and Anne (Selignan) Fall; married Dorothy Winer (an art designer), February 20, 1954; children: Nicole Francoise, Elisabeth Anne. *Education:* Attended University of Paris, 1948-49, University of Munich, 1950, and University of Maryland (Overseas Program), 1951; Syracuse University, M.A., 1952, Ph.D., 1955. *Politics:* Liberal. *Home:* 4535 31st St. N.W., Washington, D.C. 20008.

CAREER: War Crimes Trials, Nuremberg, Germany, war crimes investigator, 1946-48; International Tracing Service, Munich, Germany, tracing officer, 1949-50; *The Stars and Stripes*, Nuremberg, assistant district manager, 1950-51; Cornell University, Ithaca, N.Y., instructor in Asian studies, 1954-55; American University, Washington, D.C., assistant professor, 1955-56; Howard University, Washington, D.C., professor of international relations, 1956-67. Consultant on Southeast Asian affairs and guerrilla warfare to several government agencies. *Military service:* French Underground, 1942-44; Fourth Moroccan Mountain Division, 1944-46; received Medal of Liberated France for guerrilla operations in occupied France. *Member:* Association for Asian Studies, French War Veterans (president, Washington, D.C. chapter, 1966), American Association of University Professors, American Political Science Association, International Political Science Association, Centre d'Etudes de Politique Etrangere. *Awards, honors:* Fulbright, Rockefeller, and Southeast Asia Treaty Organization fellowships; Guggenheim fellowship, 1966-67; George Polk Memorial Award of Long Island University for achievement in journalism, 1966.

WRITINGS: The Viet-Minh Regime, Department of Far Eastern Studies, Cornell University, 1954, 2nd revised edition, Cornell University and Institute of Pacific Relations, 1956, reprinted, Greenwood Press, 1975; *Street without Joy: Indochina at War, 1946-54*, Stackpole, 1961, 4th revised edition, 1964; *Two Viet-Nams: A Political and Military History*, Praeger, 1963, 4th revised edition, 1966; (editor with Marcus G. Raskin) *The Viet-Nam Reader*, Random House, 1965, revised edition, 1967; *Viet-Nam Witness, 1953-66*, Praeger, 1966; (author of introduction) *Victor Charlie: Viet Cong der Unheimliche Feind*, Molden, 1966, published in the United States as *Victor Charlie: The Faces of the War in Vietnam*, Praeger, 1967; *Hell in a Very Small Place*, Lippincott, 1967; (editor and author of introduction) *Ho Chi Minh on Revolution: Selected Writings, 1920-66*, Praeger, 1967; (author of preface) Ho Chi Minh, *Prison Diary*, Swan Publishing (Toronto), 1968; *Last Reflections on a War*, preface by wife, Dorothy Fall, Doubleday, 1968; *Anatomy of a Crisis: The Laotian Crisis of 1960-1961*, edited by Roger M. Smith, Doubleday, 1969.

Contributor of more than two hundred articles on politics, military affairs, and Indochinese problems to *Foreign Affairs*, *Military Review*, *Saturday Evening Post*, and other publications.

SIDELIGHTS: Bernard B. Fall was an authority on the Vietnam War and Communist guerrilla warfare throughout the world. For fourteen years, he wrote books and articles about the military struggles of the French and Americans in Vietnam. His book *Hell in a Very Small Place*, which concerns the bloody battle of Dienbienphu, the last major battle of the French stay in Vietnam, was well-received by the critics. Both hawks and doves quoted his work since his own view of the war lay somewhere between what he called their "two extremes." "Vietnam is simply a test case," he once wrote, "on our side of 'credibility' in resisting Communist penetration; on the Viet Cong side of the possibility of changing the world balance by leap-frogging (or burrowing under) the nuclear stalemate of the big powers." He saw American chances of victory in Vietnam as small because, although the Americans had superior military equipment, they did not have the "militant doctrine" and determination of the Viet Cong.

Last Reflections on a War, a collection of his articles and talks published posthumously, covers a number of different aspects of the war in both scholarly articles and personal remembrances. Included is his article "This Isn't Munich, It's Spain!," an eyewitness account of an American bombing of a Vietnamese fishing village. Napalm was exploded in the air, Fall relates, so the intense heat would drive the villagers out of their huts and into the open; fragmentation bombs and 20 mm. cannons were then employed. Fall notes that it was "not known" how many of those killed may have been Viet Cong.

It was while accompanying a Marine patrol just north of Hue, Vietnam, along a muddy strip of road called "The Street without Joy" (a name he used for one of his book titles), that Fall met his death. He and a Marine sergeant tripped off a Viet Cong booby trap and died instantly in the resulting explosion. His last words, preserved by a tape recorder into which he was speaking while he walked, were "It smells bad. . . .[It] could be an amb. . . ."

Fall's writing has been translated into French, German, and Spanish.

BIOGRAPHICAL/CRITICAL SOURCES: New York Times, February 22, 1967; *Newsweek*, March 6, 1967; *Publishers Weekly*, March 6, 1967; *New York Times Book Review*, July 23, 1967, September 17, 1967, December 10, 1967; *Times Literary Supplement*, August 3, 1967; *New Statesman*, August 4, 1967; *Time*, November 17, 1967; *Commonweal*, December 1, 1967; *Book World*, December 31, 1967; *Christian Science Monitor*, January 18, 1968; *Commentary*, March, 1968; *Nation*, May 19, 1969.†

*   *   *

FANE, Julian Charles   1927-

PERSONAL: Born May 25, 1927, in London, England; son of Vere Anthony Francis St. Clair (the fourteenth Earl of Westmorland; deceased) and Diana (Lister) Fane; married Gillian Swire, 1976. *Education:* Attended Harrow School. *Home:* 63 Eccleston Sq., London SW1V 1PH, England.

CAREER: Novelist.

WRITINGS—Published by Hamish Hamilton, except as noted: *Morning*, John Murray, 1956; *A Letter*, John Murray, 1960; *Memoir in the Middle of the Journey*, 1971; *Gabriel Young*, 1973; *Tug-of-War*, 1975; *Hounds of Spring*, 1976; *Happy End-*

ings, 1979; *Revolution Island,* 1979; *Gentleman's Gentleman,* 1981.

SIDELIGHTS: Julian Fane brings a privileged background to his writings. Members of British nobility, his parents experienced some financial setbacks, but they managed to maintain a comfortable way of life for their children. Much of Fane's writing has received favorable reviews, although critics of some of his books have commented that his upper-class upbringing and values pervade his writing, occasionally to its detriment.

Morning, an account of boyhood and Fane's first novel, was met with critical acclaim with only a few reviewers expressing any strong reservations. Richard Sullivan comments in the *New York Times:* "Because the 30-year-old author is the second son of the fourteenth Earl of Westmorland, some readers may approach this book with the faint, intrusive hope that it will proffer autobiographical revelations of life as lived by ancient noble families of this century. The novel itself will soon set them straight. Whatever autobiography is here has been transfigured into prose fiction of rare, memorable, almost incomparable beauty." *Manchester Guardian's* Anne Duchene calls the novel "an extraordinarily good, calm re-creation of childhood." N. S. Nelson of the *Christian Science Monitor* concurs wih the opinions of the previously cited critics: "Mr. Fane's style is carefully simple, his dialogue vivid. There is no sentimentality, only fresh emotions from a very real boy." Not all critics, however, found the novel to be a realistic evocation of childhood. Isabel Quigly admits that Fane "does manage to hit off certain aspects [of childhood] rather well," but she complains in the *Spectator* that "his attitude is sugary, complaisant: tenderness towards childhood one can accept; nostalgic gush, and from so young a writer, one cannot."

Many of Fane's later novels and short story collections received positive reviews. Reviewing *Tug-of-War,* Elaine Feinstein of the *New Statesman* calls Fane "an accomplished writer. . . . He is a master of single, telling images . . . [and] the dialogue is always sharply written." A *Books and Bookmen* critic calls the same novel "an exquisite book which lodges in the memory." However, some reviewers of the short story collection *Happy Endings* expressed dissatisfaction with the vestiges of Fane's upper-class sensibility. *Spectator's* Mary Hope thinks the book contains "much exhaustive middle-class detail and a great deal of quiet conservatism." A reviewer for *Books and Bookmen* writes of the short stories: "There's a whiff of late-Victorian smugness about the message advanced; a dated Panglossian assurance that, whatever damning evidence to the contrary, we really *do* live in the best of all possible worlds. . . . Fane's characters are almost exclusively upper middle-class, with private incomes and impeccable backgrounds. This makes it hard to agonize over [their lots]. . . . But happiness is easy, Fane confidently avers. . . . Admittedly, it's certainly a lot easier for a well-heeled few but for the remainder of us a good laugh is the best pesticide, if not the only one."

BIOGRAPHICAL/CRITICAL SOURCES: Manchester Guardian, September 4, 1956; *Times Literary Supplement,* September 7, 1956, February 12, 1971, November 23, 1979; *Spectator,* September 7, 1956, January 27, 1979; *New York Times,* August 25, 1957; *Christian Science Monitor,* August 29, 1957; *New Statesman,* January 17, 1975, January 26, 1979; *Books and Bookmen,* April, 1975, May, 1979, December, 1979.

*   *   *

FAYER, Mischa Harry 1902-1977

PERSONAL: Born June 6, 1902, in New York, N.Y.; died April 14, 1977, in Lexington, Ky.; son of Max and Sonia Fayer; married Margaret L. Wilson, 1938 (died, 1964); married Florence Lewis Kleinman, May 18, 1968; stepchildren: Ellen J. Kleinman, Jill T. Kleinman. *Education:* University of Minnesota, A.B., 1926, M.A., 1928; Columbia University, Ph.D., 1945; additional study at Sorbonne and Claremont College. *Home:* 2121 Nicholasville Rd., Lexington, Ky. 40503.

CAREER: North Dakota State Teachers College, Dickinson, member of faculty, 1929-41; Michigan State College of Agriculture and Applied Science (now Michigan State University), East Lansing, member of faculty, 1941-43; Middlebury College, Middlebury, Vt., professor of Russian, 1943-67, professor emeritus, 1967-77, head of department, 1943-67, director of Institute of Soviet Studies, 1958-67; University of Kentucky, Lexington, professor of Russian and chairman of Slavic and Oriental languages department, 1967-72. Public lecturer on the Soviet Union. *Member:* American Association of Teachers of Slavic and East European Languages, Modern Language Association of America, American Association of University Professors, Lambda Alpha Psi.

WRITINGS: Gide, Freedom and Dostoevsky, Lane, 1946; *Simplified Russian Grammar,* Pitman, 1949, 3rd edition, National Textbook Corp., 1977; *Basic Russian,* Book 1, Pitman, 1959, revised edition, National Textbook Corp., 1977, workbook, Pitman, 1960, Book 2, Pitman, 1961.†

*   *   *

FEILEN, John
See MAY, Julian

*   *   *

FELL, Joseph P(hineas) III 1931-

PERSONAL: Born May 22, 1931, in Troy, N.Y.; son of Joseph Phineas, Jr. (a business executive) and Mabel (Hunt) Fell; married Cynthia Ross (associate director of Bucknell University Press), June 12, 1958; children: John Whittum, Caroline. *Education:* Williams College, B.A., 1953; Union Theological Seminary, New York, N.Y., graduate study, 1953-54; Columbia University, M.A., 1960, Ph.D., 1963. *Politics:* Democrat. *Home:* 315 Stein Lane, Lewisburg, Pa. 17837. *Office:* Department of Philosophy, Bucknell University, Lewisburg, Pa. 17837.

CAREER: Pennsylvania State University, University Park, instructor, 1962-63; Bucknell University, Lewisburg, Pa., assistant professor, 1963-67, associate professor, 1967-71, professor of philosophy, 1971—, chairman of department, 1977—. Visiting assistant professor, Columbia University, summer, 1966. Consultant to numerous publishing houses, including Macmillan, University of Chicago Press, and Fortress Press. *Military service:* U.S. Army, 1954-56. *Member:* American Philosophical Association, Society for Phenomenology and Existential Philosophy, Phi Beta Kappa (honorary member). *Awards, honors:* Clarke F. Ansley Award, Columbia University, 1963, for manuscript of *Emotion in the Thought of Sartre;* Bucknell University summer fellowship, 1965, 1967, and 1973; Lindbeck Award, Bucknell University, 1968-69, for distinguished teaching; National Endowment for the Humanities Younger Scholars fellowship, 1969-70, for research in West Germany; National Endowment for the Humanities publication grant, 1978.

WRITINGS: Emotion in the Thought of Sartre, Columbia Univeristy Press, 1965; (contributor of translation) Ernest Keen, editor, *Three Faces of Being: Toward an Existential Clinical Psychology,* Appleton-Century-Crofts, 1970; (contributor) U.

Guzzoni, B. Rang, and L. Siep, editors, *Der Idealisms und seine Gegenwart: Festschrift fuer Werner Marx zum 65. Geburtstag,* Felix Meiner Verlag (Hamburg), 1976; (contributor) D. K. Candland and others, editors, *Emotion,* Brooks/Cole, 1977; *Heidigger and Sartre: An Essay on Being and Place,* Columbia University Press, 1979; (contributor) P. A. Schipp, editor, *The Philosophy of Jean-Paul Sartre,* Open Court, in press. Author of a number of papers presented to professional organizations. Contributor of articles and reviews to numerous journals, including *Bucknell Review, Psychoanalytic Review, Philsophical Quarterly, School and Society, Journal of British Society for Phenomenology,* and *Review of Metaphysics.*

WORK IN PROGRESS: A study of the later philosphy of Martin Heidigger.

SIDELIGHTS: Joseph P. Fell is competent in Greek, Latin, French, and German. *Avocational interests:* Music, literature (especially D. H. Lawrence).

*   *   *

FELLOWES, Anne
See MANTLE, Winifred (Langford)

*   *   *

FENTON, Carroll Lane   1900-1969

PERSONAL: Born February 12, 1900, near Parkersburg, Iowa; died November 16, 1969, in New Brunswick, N.J.; son of William Alexander and Maude (Lana) Fenton; married Mildred Adams (an author), 1921. *Education:* University of Chicago, S.B., 1921, Ph.D., 1926. *Home and office:* 404 Livingston Ave., New Brunswick, N.J.

CAREER: University of Michigan, Ann Arbor, geology instructor, 1922-23; University of Cincinnati, Cincinnati, Ohio, curator and national research fellow, 1926-29; University of Buffalo (now State University of New York at Buffalo), assistant professor of physical science, 1929-31; Rutgers University, New Brunswick, N.J., editorial consultant, 1944-46; author. *Military service:* U.S. Army, Infantry, 1918. *Member:* Sigma Xi.

WRITINGS: The World of Fossils, Appleton, 1933; *Our Amazing Earth,* Doubleday, 1938; *Our Living World,* Doubleday, 1942; *Tales Told by Fossils,* Doubleday, 1966.

Adult books; originally published by Doubleday, except as indicated; with wife, Mildred Adams Fenton: *Records of Evolution,* Haldeman-Julius, 1924; *The Rock Book,* 1940, reprinted, 1970; *The Story of the Great Geologists,* 1945, reprinted, Books for Libraries Press, 1969, revised and enlarged edition published as *Giants of Geology,* Doubleday, 1952; *Rocks and Their Stories,* 1951; *The Fossil Book: A Record of Prehistoric Life,* 1958.

Juvenile books; published by John Day: *Along the Hill,* 1935; *Life Long Ago: The Story of Fossils,* 1937, reprinted, 1965; *Earth's Adventures,* 1942; *Along Nature's Highway,* 1943; *Weejack and His Neighbors,* 1944; *Wild Folk in the Woods,* 1952; *Prehistoric World,* 1954; *Wild Folk in the Mountains,* 1958; *Wild Folk at the Seashore,* 1959; *Goldie Is a Fish,* 1961; *Animals and Plants,* 1962; *The Moon for Young Explorers,* 1963.

Juvenile books; with Mildred Adams Fenton: *Mountains,* Doubleday, 1942, reprinted, Books for Libraries Press, 1969; *The Land We Live On,* Doubleday, 1944, revised edition, 1966; *Worlds in the Sky,* John Day, 1950, revised edition, 1963; *Riches from the Earth,* John Day, 1953, reprinted, 1970; *Our*

Changing Weather, Doubleday, 1954; *Prehistoric Zoo,* Doubleday, 1959; *In Prehistoric Seas,* Doubleday, 1963.

Juvenile books; published by Macmillan; with Edith M. Patch: *Holiday Shore,* 1935; *Mountain Neighbors,* 1936; *Desert Neighbors,* 1937; *Forest Neighbors,* 1938; *Prairie Neighbors,* 1938.

Juvenile books; published by John Day; with Dorothy C. Pallas: *Birds and Their World,* 1954; *Trees and Their World,* 1954; *Insects and Their World,* 1956; *Oliver Pete Is a Bird,* 1959; *Reptiles and Their World,* 1961.

Juvenile books; published by John Day; with Herminie B. Kitchen: *Plants That Feed Us,* 1956, revised edition published as *Plants We Live On: The Story of Grains and Vegetables,* 1971; *Animals That Help Us,* 1959, revised edition, 1973; *Fruits We Eat,* 1961; *Birds We Live With,* 1963.

Other: (With Paul E. Kambly) *Basic Biology* (textbook), Macmillan, 1947, revised edition, 1953; (with Evelyn Carswell) *Wild Folk in the Desert* (juvenile), John Day, 1958; (with Alice Epstein) *Cliff Dwellers of Walnut Canyon* (juvenile), John Day, 1960; (with Eloise Turner) *Inside You and Me: A Child's Introduction to the Human Body* (juvenile), John Day, 1961; (with Louis Zara) *Rocks, Minerals, and Gems,* Doubleday, 1965; (with Vivian Fuchs) *Larousse Encyclopedia of the Earth,* Crown, 1972. Also author of over a dozen natural science booklets.

AVOCATIONAL INTERESTS: Travel, photography.†

*   *   *

FERGUSON, Alfred R(iggs)   1915-1974

PERSONAL: Born August 15, 1915, in Franklin, Ind.; died May 5, 1974, in Scituate, Mass.; son of John B. and Margaret (Williams) Ferguson; married Mary Anne Heyward (a professor of English), May 23, 1948; children: Margaret W., Jean Ferguson Carr, Lucy Ferguson Allen. *Education:* College of Wooster, B.A., 1937; Yale University, M.A., 1942, Ph.D., 1948. *Politics:* Democrat. *Religion:* Episcopalian. *Office:* Department of English, University of Massachusetts, Boston, Mass. 02116.

CAREER: Yale University, New Haven, Conn., reader, 1938-41; Middlebury College, Middlebury, Vt., instructor, 1941-42; Ohio State University, Columbus, instructor, 1942; Ohio Wesleyan University, Delaware, 1947-65, began as instructor, became professor of English; University of Massachusetts—Boston, professor of English, 1965-74, chairman of department. Visiting professor, University of Hamburg, 1957-58. *Military service:* U.S. Navy, 1942-46, became lieutenant. *Member:* American Association of University Professors, Modern Language Association of America, Phi Beta Kappa.

WRITINGS: Edward Rowland Sill: The Twilight Poet, Martinus Nijhoff, 1955; (co-editor) *The Journals and Miscellaneous Notebooks, of Ralph Waldo Emerson,* Harvard University Press, 1960-74; (editor with Merton M. Sealts, Jr.) *Emerson's "Nature": Origin, Growth, Meaning,* Dodd, Mead, 1969; (compiler) *The Merrill Checklist of Ralph Waldo Emerson,* C. E. Merrill, 1970. Editor-in-chief, "The Works of Ralph Waldo Emerson," Harvard University Press, 1960-74. Contributor of articles on American literature to professional journals.

AVOCATIONAL INTERESTS: Sports, music.†

*   *   *

FERGUSON, Clarence Clyde, Jr.   1924-

PERSONAL: Born November 4, 1924, in Wilmington, N.C.;

son of Clarence Clyde (a minister) and Georgena (Owens) Ferguson; married Dolores Zimmerman, February 14, 1954 (deceased); children: Claire Oberon, Hope Elizabeth, Eve Marie. *Education:* Ohio State University, A.B. (cum laude), 1948; Harvard University, LL.B. (cum laude), 1951. *Religion:* Unitarian Universalist. *Home:* Soldiers Field Park, Harvard University, Cambridge, Mass. *Office:* Griswold Hall 400, Harvard Law School, Cambridge, Mass. 02138.

CAREER: Admitted to Massachusetts bar, 1951, New York State bar, 1953, and New Jersey bar. Baltimore, Paulson and Canudo, New York, N.Y., counsel, 1951-54; State of New York, Moreland Act Commission to Investigate Harness Racing, assistant counsel, 1953-54; Department of Justice, Southern District of New York, assistant U.S. attorney, 1954-55; Rutgers University Law School, Newark, N.J., professor of law, 1955-63; U.S. Commission on Civil Rights, Washington, D.C., general counsel, 1962-63; Howard University School of Law, Washington, D.C., dean and professor of law, 1964-69; U.S. Ambassador to Uganda, 1970-72; U.S. Deputy Assistant Secretary of State for African Affairs, 1972-73; U.S. Representative, Economic and Social Council of the United Nations, 1973-75; Harvard University, Cambridge, Mass., Stimson Professor of Law, 1975—. Lecturer-in-law, School of Law, Catholic University of America; lecturer at Institute for Continuing Legal Education of New Jersey, Bankers Association of New Jersey, and at universities in London, Oxford, Paris, Louvain, Geneva, Africa, and Asia. U.S. representative to western hemisphere UNESCO Conference, Havana, Cuba, 1952, and to UNESCO-Oxford Roundtable on Human Rights, 1965. General Counsel to U.S. Commission on Civil Rights, 1960-64; special legal advisor, U.S. Mission to the United Nations, 1963-64; U.S. expert to the United Nations Sub-Commission on Discrimination, 1965. Secretary and research director of New Jersey State Commission to Study and Report on the Uniform Commercial Code; chairman, New Jersey Committee on Housing for the Aged; treasurer, East Orange Housing Authority (New Jersey). Consultant to Governor Nelson Rockefeller, New York, 1958-64; consultant to federal and international agencies. *Military service:* U.S. Army, 1943-46; received Bronze Star.

MEMBER: National Association for the Advancement of Colored People (chairman, Newark branch, legal defense committee), American Society of International Law (president), American Association of University Professors (president, Rutgers Newark chapter), American Association of Law Schools (member, committee on racial discrimination), Essex County Bar Association, New York County Lawyers Association, Boston Bar Association, Harvard Law School Alumni Association, Phi Beta Kappa, Alpha Phi Alpha. *Awards, honors:* LL.D. from Rutgers University, 1966, and Williams College, 1976.

WRITINGS: (With Albert P. Blaustein) *Desegregation and the Law: The Meaning and Effect of the School Segregation Cases,* Rutgers University Press, 1957, 2nd edition, 1960; *Materials on Trial Presentations,* Rutgers University, 1957; *Enforcement and Collection of Judgments and Liens,* Institute for Continuing Legal Education, Rutgers University, 1961; *Secured Transactions: Article IX Uniform Commerical Code in New Jersey,* Sooney & Sage, 1961; (with others) *Racism in American Education,* Random House, 1970; (contributor) Lillich, editor, *U.S. Ratification of the Human Rights Treaties,* University of Virginia Press, 1981. Contributor to *Proceedings of American Society of International Law,* 1968, and *Proceedings of the Academy of Political Science,* 1977. Contributor to professional journals, including *Rutgers Law Review, Buffalo Law Review, Law Library Journal, Harvard Law School Bulletin, Denver Law Journal,* and *Foreign Affairs.*

SIDELIGHTS: Clarence Clyde Ferguson was one of the founders of the concept of affirmative action in 1963 and the principal draftsman of the 1967 UNESCO Statement on Race. In 1969 he negotiated the "Protocol on Relief to Nigeria Civilian Victims of the Civil War."

*   *   *

FERGUSON, Helen
See KAVAN, Anna

*   *   *

FERGUSSON HANNAY, Doris
(Doris Leslie)

PERSONAL: Born in London, England; married John Leslie (an actor) while in her teens (deceased); married Sir Walter Fergusson Hannay (a physician; knighted in 1951), 1936 (died, 1961). *Education:* Attended private schools in London, England, and Brussels, Belgium; studied art and drama in London and Florence. *Religion:* Roman Catholic convert, 1961. *Address:* c/o A. P. Watt & Son, 26-28 Bedford Row, London WC1R 4HL, England.

CAREER: Novelist and historian. *Wartime service:* London's Civil Defence, 1941-45; wounded on duty. *Member:* Society of Authors, P.E.N., United Hunts Club (London). *Awards, honors: As the Tree Falls* selected as best historical novel of the year by *Books and Bookmen,* 1958; named Woman of the Year for Literature by the Catholic Women's League, 1970.

WRITINGS—All under name Doris Leslie; novels: *The Starling,* Century Press, 1927; *Fools in Mortar,* Century Press, 1928; *The Echoing Green,* Hurst & Blackett, 1929; *Terminus,* Hurst & Blackett, 1931; *Puppet's Parade,* John Lane, 1932; *Full Flavor,* Macmillan, 1934; *Fair Company,* Macmillan, 1936, reprinted, Heinemann, 1967; *Concord in Jeopardy,* Macmillan, 1938, reprinted, Heinemann, 1969; *Another Cynthia: The Adventures of Cynthia, Lady Ffulkes (1780-1850) Reconstructed from Her Hitherto Unpublished Memoirs* (also see below), Macmillan, 1939; *House in the Dust,* Macmillan, 1942, reprinted, Heinemann, 1969; *Folly's End* (also see below), Hutchinson, 1944; *The Peverills* (also see below), Hutchinson, 1946; *Tales of Grace and Favour* (contains *Folly's End, The Peverills,* and *Another Cynthia*), Hutchinson, 1956; *As the Tree Falls,* Hodder & Stoughton, 1958; *A Young Wives' Tale,* Heinemann, 1971; *The Dragon's Head,* Heinemann, 1973; *Call Back Yesterday,* Heinemann, 1975.

Biographical studies: *Royal William: The Story of a Democrat,* Hutchinson, 1940, Macmillan, 1941, reprinted, Heinemann, 1966; *Polonaise,* Hutchinson, 1943, reprinted, Heineman, 1971; *Wreath for Arabella,* Hutchinson, 1948, Roy, 1949, reprinted, Popular Library, 1973; *That Enchantress,* Hutchinson, 1950, reprinted, Popular Library, 1973; *The Great Corinthian: A Portrait of the Prince Regent,* Eyre & Spottiswoode, 1952, Oxford University Press, 1953, new edition, Heinemann, 1967; *A Toast to Lady Mary,* Hutchinson, 1954, reprinted, Popular Library, 1973; *Peridot Flight: A Novel Reconstructed from the Memoirs of Peridot, Lady Mulvarnie, 1872-1955,* Hutchinson, 1956; *The Perfect Wife,* Hodder & Stoughton, 1960, published as *The Prime Minister's Wife,* Doubleday, 1961; *Vagabond's Way: The Story of Francois Villon,* Doubleday, 1962 (published in England as *I Return: The Story of Francois Villon,* Hodder & Stoughton, 1962); *This for Caroline,* Popular Library, 1964; *Paragon Street,* Heinemann, 1965; *The Sceptre and the Rose,* Heinemann, 1967; *The Marriage of Martha Todd,* Heinemann, 1968; *The Rebel Princess,* Heinemann, 1970, Popular Library, 1973; *The Desert Queen,* Heinemann, 1972;

The Incredible Duchess: The Life and Times of Elizabeth Chudleigh, Heinemann, 1974; *Notorious Lady: The Life and Times of the Countess Blessington,* Heinemann, 1976; *The Warrior King: The Reign of Richard the Lion Heart,* Heinemann, 1977; *Crown of Thorns: The Life of Richard II,* Heinemann, 1979.

SIDELIGHTS: Doris Leslie began to write after she finished her first year as an art student in Florence. After publishing her first book, Leslie then wrote three books which she later considered to be "incredibly bad." She believes that her literary career did not begin until after she acknowledged the inferiority of her early efforts. Her first big success was *Full Flavor,* an English family chronicle covering 1848-1914. The book, dramatized and translated into ten languages, became an international best-seller.

In a nationwide poll conducted several years ago, Leslie was named the second most popular historical novelist of Britain, an honor that also took into account the fictional aspects of her historical biographies.

MEDIA ADAPTATIONS: Peridot Flight was televised in ten weekly episodes by the British Broadcasting Corp. in 1960.

AVOCATIONAL INTERESTS: Exhibiting prize bulldogs.

*   *   *

FERMI, Laura   1907-1977

PERSONAL: Born June 16, 1907, in Rome, Italy; came to United States in 1939, naturalized in 1944; died December 26, 1977, in Chicago, Ill.; daughter of Augusto (an officer in Italian navy) and Costanza (Romanelli) Capon; married Enrico Fermi (a nuclear physicist), July 19, 1928 (died, 1954); children: Nella Fermi Weiner, Giulio. *Education:* Attended University of Rome, 1926-28. *Home:* 5532 South Shore Dr., Chicago, Ill. 60637.

CAREER: Atomic Energy Commission, Washington, D.C., historian, 1955-56; Massachusetts Institute of Technology, Cambridge, member of staff of physical Science Study Committee, 1957. Member of Air Pollution Control Committee, Chicago, beginning 1960, Northeastern Illinois Metropolitan Area Air Pollution Control Board, 1962-63, and women's board of University of Chicago. Member of board of governors, International House, Chicago. Co-founder of Cleaner Air Committee of Hyde Park and Kenwood, and Civil Disarmament Committee. Lecturer. *Member:* Authors Guild, League of Women Voters. *Awards, honors:* Guggenheim fellowship, 1957; Friends of Literature prize, 1968, for *Illustrious Immigrants.*

WRITINGS: (With Ginestra Amaldi) *Alchimia del Tempo Nostro,* Hoepli-Torino, 1936; *Atoms in the Family: My Life with Enrico Fermi,* University of Chicago Press, 1954, Italian translation by the author published as *Atomi in famiglia,* A. Mondadori, 1965; *Atoms for the World,* University of Chicago Press, 1957, reprinted, 1974; *The Story of Atomic Energy,* Random House, 1961; (with Gilberto Bernardini) *Galileo and the Scientific Revolution,* Basic Books, 1961; *Mussolini,* University of Chicago Press, 1961; *Illustrious Immigrants: The Intellectual Migration from Europe, 1930-41,* University of Chicago Press, 1968, 2nd edition, 1971.

SIDELIGHTS: In his *Washington Post Book World* review of *Illustrious Immigrants,* Hans Sahl writes that Laura Fermi "has rendered a unique service. With her ability to convert scientific data into living experience, she has written an adventure story of the human spirit." Peter Gay of the *New York Times Book Review* calls it "an honest and informative book; it is well-organized, well-informed, well-balanced. . . . If [*Illustrious Immigrants*] is, finally, not wholly satisfactory, that must be because it is not wholly adequate to its great and often tragic theme."

Fermi's book *Atoms in the Family* has been translated into ten languages; *Mussolini* has been translated into five. *The Story of Atomic Energy* has been translated into eight languages and is used extensively by the United States Information Agency.

BIOGRAPHICAL/CRITICAL SOURCES: Laura Fermi, *Atoms in the Family: My Life with Enrico Fermi,* University of Chicago Press, 1954; *Washington Post Book World,* March 24, 1967; *New York Times Book Review,* April 7, 1968; *Bulletin of Atomic Science,* May, 1978.†

*   *   *

FERRELL, Robert H(ugh)   1921-

PERSONAL: Born May 8, 1921, in Cleveland, Ohio; son of Ernest Henry and Edna Lulu Ferrell; married Lila E. Sprout, September 8, 1956; children: Carolyn Irene. *Education:* Bowling Green State University, B.S. in Ed., 1946, B.A., 1947; Yale University, M.A., 1948, Ph.D., 1951. *Religion:* Protestant. *Home:* 512 South Hawthorne, Bloomington, Ind. *Office:* Department of History, Indiana University, Bloomington, Ind. 47401.

CAREER: Michigan State University, East Lansing, Mich., 1952-61, began as instructor, became associate professor of history; Indiana University at Bloomington, professor of history, 1961—. *Member:* American Historical Association, Organization of American Historians. *Awards, honors:* Grants from Carnegie Foundation, 1955-56, Social Science Research Council, 1956 and 1961-62, Smith-Mundt Act, 1958-59, and Fulbright Act, 1969-70; LL.D., Bowling Green State University, 1971.

WRITINGS: Peace in Their Time, Yale University Press, 1952; *American Diplomacy in the Great Depression,* Yale University Press, 1957; *American Diplomacy: A History,* Norton, 1959, 3rd edition, 1975; (with Richard B. Morris and William Greenleaf) *America: A History of the People,* Rand McNally, 1971; (with Samuel F. Wells and David F. Trask) *The Ordeal of World Power: American Diplomacy since 1909,* Little, Brown, 1975.

Editor: (With Howard H. Quint) *The Talkative President: The Off-the-Record Press Conferences of Calvin Coolidge,* University of Massachusetts Press, 1964; (and compiler) *History of American Diplomacy,* University of South Carolina Press, Volume I: *Foundations of American Diplomacy, 1775-1872,* 1968, Volume II: *America as a World Power, 1872-1945,* 1971, Volume III: *America in a Divided World, 1945-1972,* 1975; *Off the Record: The Private Papers of Harry S. Truman,* Harper, 1980; *The Autobiography of Harry S. Truman,* Colorado Associated University Press, 1980; *The Eisenhower Diaries,* Norton, 1981. Also editor of "American Secretaries of State and Their Diplomacy" series, Volume XI—, Cooper Square, 1963—.

WORK IN PROGRESS: World War I, 1917-1921, for Harper.

*   *   *

FIELDS, Alan
See DUPREY, Richard A(llen)

*   *   *

FISHER, C(harles) William   1916-

PERSONAL: Born December 23, 1916, in Blackwell, Okla.;

son of Charles Webster (a realtor) and Sarah Rose (McCrady) Fisher; married Marjorie Crooks, December 23, 1940; children: Byron Ray, Billy. *Education:* Bethany Nazarene College, Th.B. *Politics:* Republican. *Home:* 1 Antigua Ct., Coronado, Calif. 92118. *Office address:* Box 527, Kansas City, Mo.

CAREER: Evangelist; has conducted more than one thousand crusades in the United States and abroad, including Europe and South Africa, 1941—. *Awards, honors:* D.D., Bethany Nazarene College, 1962.

WRITINGS—Published by Nazarene Publishing, except as indicated: *Time Is Now,* 1950; *Second Hand Religion,* 1952; *Wake Up and Lift,* 1954; *Our Heritage and Our Hope,* 1957; *Why I Am a Nazarene,* 1958; *This Uncommitted Generation,* 1960; *Don't Park Here,* Abingdon, 1962; *It's Revival We Need,* 1967; *Evangelistic Moods, Messages and Methods,* 1970; *You'll Like Being a Christian,* 1974. Contributor to religious periodicals.

WORK IN PROGRESS: The Place of Revival in Evangelism.

AVOCATIONAL INTERESTS: Music.

*   *   *

FISHWICK, Marshall William   1923-

PERSONAL: Born July 5, 1923, in Roanoke, Va.; son of William and Nellie (Cross) Fishwick; married Lucy Farley, July 12, 1945; children: Jeffrey, Ellen, Susan, Lucy Cross. *Education:* University of Virginia, B.A., 1943; University of Wisconsin, M.A., 1946; Yale University, Ph.D., 1949; additional studies at International People's College, Denmark, Union Theological Seminary, Mainz Universitat. *Politics:* Democrat. *Religion:* Episcopalian. *Home:* 113 Cohee Rd., Blacksburg, Va. 24060. *Office:* Agnew Hall, Virginia Polytechnic Institute and State University, Blacksburg, Va. 24061.

CAREER: Washington and Lee University, Lexington, Va., assistant professor, 1950-54, associate professor, 1955-58, professor of American studies, 1959-67; Lincoln University, Lincoln University, Pa., professor of art and history, 1968-70; Temple University, Philadelphia, Pa., professor of history, 1970-76; Virginia Polytechnic Institute and State University, Blacksburg, Va., professor of communication, 1976—. Fulbright professor, Denmark, 1959, Germany, 1962, India, 1968; member of summer faculty, University of Milan, 1969-73; lecturer or summer instructor at numerous universities, including Oxford University, Warsaw University, University of Minnesota, University of Wyoming, and Yale University. Director of American history studies and research project, Wemyss Foundation, beginning 1962; director of Delaware State Arts Committee, 1967-68; director of American Studies Institute, 1968-70; research associate, Winterthur Museum. State Department specialist on eastern European tours, 1962, 1964, 1965. Historiographer for Diocese of Southwestern Virginia, National Committee for College Work, Episcopal Church. Consultant to *Life,* National Lexicographic Board Ltd., and Seabury Press. *Military service:* U.S. Navy, 1943-45; became lieutenant. *Member:* American Studies Association, American Historical Association, Fellows in American Studies (president), Phi Beta Kappa. *Awards, honors:* Sterling, Carnegie, Fulbright, Rockefeller, and Glenn grants for research and travel.

WRITINGS: The Face of Jang, Hobson, 1945; *Isle of Shoals,* Hobson, 1946; *Virginians on Olympus,* Richmond, Whittet & Shepperson, 1950; *American Heroes,* Public Affairs, 1954, reprinted, Greenwood Press, 1975; *General Lee's Photographer,* University of North Carolina Press, 1954; *The Virginia Tradition,* Public Affairs, 1955; *Virginia: A New Look at the*

Old Dominion, Harper, 1959; *Gentlemen of Virginia,* Dodd, 1961; *The South in the Sixties,* Wesleyan University Press, 1962; *Lee after the War,* Dodd, 1962; *Faust Revisited: Some Thoughts on Satan,* Seabury, 1963; *Great Silver Crowns,* Golden Quill, 1963; (with others) *Jamestown: First English Colony,* American Heritage, 1965; (with others) *Clara Barton,* Silver Burdett, 1966; *Jane Addams,* Silver Burdett, 1968; *The Hero: American Style,* McKay, 1969; *Parameters of Popular Culture,* Bowling Green University, 1974; *Springlore in Virginia,* Bowling Green University, 1980; *Common Culture and the Great Tradition,* Greenwood Press, 1982. Also author, with Richard T. Feller, of *For Thy Great Glory,* Community Press.

Editor: R. L. Durham, *Since I Was Born,* Richmond, Whittet & Shepperson, 1952; *American Studies in Transition,* University of Pennsylvania Press, 1965, Houghton, 1969; *Icons of Popular Culture,* Bowling Green University, 1970; *Remus, Rastus, Revolution,* Bowling Green University, 1971; Ray Broadus Browne, compiler, *Heroes of Popular Culture,* Bowling Green University, 1972; (with J. Meredith Neil) *Popular Architecture,* Bowling Green University, 1974; (with Browne) *Icons of America,* Bowling Green University, 1978.

Contributor to historical and literary magazines and journals, including *American Historical Review, American Heritage, Yale Review,* and *Saturday Review.* Editor, *Shenandoah;* contributing editor, *Commonwealth.*

WORK IN PROGRESS: American Studies: Methods, Models, Prospects; Middle Atlantic States: The New Frontier.

AVOCATIONAL INTERESTS: Linguistics, international education.

*   *   *

FITZHARDINGE, Joan Margaret   1912-
(Joan Phipson)

PERSONAL: Born November 16, 1912, in Warrawee, New South Wales, Australia; married Colin Hardinge Fitzhardinge; children: one son, one daughter. *Education:* Frensham School, Mittagong, New South Wales, Australia. *Home:* Wongalong, Mandurama, New South Wales 2792, Australia. *Agent:* A. P. Watt & Son, 10 Norfolk St., Strand, London W.C.2, England.

CAREER: Author of children's books. *Member:* Australian Society of Authors. *Awards, honors:* Children's Book Council of Australia Book of the Year Award, 1953, for *Good Luck to the Rider,* and 1963, for *The Family Conspiracy;* Boys' Clubs of America Junior Book Award, 1963, for *The Boundary Riders; New York Herald Tribune* Children's Spring Book Festival Award, 1964, for *The Family Conspiracy.*

WRITINGS—All under pseudonym Joan Phipson: *Good Luck to the Rider,* Angus & Robertson, 1952, Harcourt, 1968; *Six and Silver,* Angus & Robertson, 1954; *It Happened One Summer,* Angus & Robertson, 1957; *The Boundary Riders,* Harcourt, 1962; *The Family Conspiracy,* Harcourt, 1962; *Threat to the Barkers,* Harcourt, 1963; *Birkin,* Lothian, 1965, Harcourt, 1966; *A Lamb in the Family,* Hamish Hamilton, 1966; *The Crew of the Merlin,* Constable, 1966, published as *Cross Currents,* Harcourt, 1967; *Peter and Butch,* Harcourt, 1969; *The Haunted Night,* Harcourt, 1970; *Bass and Billy Martin,* Macmillan, 1972; *The Way Home,* Atheneum, 1973; *Horse With Eight Hands,* Atheneum, 1974; *Polly's Tiger,* Dutton, 1974; *The Cats,* Macmillan, 1976; *Fly Into Danger,* Atheneum, 1976, published as *The Bird Smugglers,* Methuen, 1979; *When the City Stopped,* Atheneum, 1978, published as *Keep Calm,* Macmillan, 1978; *Fly Free,* Atheneum, 1979, published as *No*

Escape, Macmillan, 1979; *Mr. Pringle and the Prince,* Hamish Hamilton, 1979; *A Tide Flowing,* Atheneum, 1981.

* * *

FLACK, Dora D(utson)   1919-

PERSONAL: Born July 9, 1919, in Kimberly, Idaho; daughter of Alonzo Edmund and Iona (James) Dutson; married A. LeGrand Flack (an accountant), January 7, 1946; children: Marc Douglas, Lane LeGrand, Kent Dutson, Marlane (Mrs. Alan T. Smith), Karen (Mrs. Ronald B. Hall), Marie (Mrs. Leonard Hardle). *Education:* Attended University of Utah, Brigham Young University, Utah State University, and Latter-day Saints Business College. *Religion:* Church of Jesus Christ of Latter-day Saints. *Home and office:* 448 East 775 North, Bountiful, Utah 84010.

CAREER: Secretary to bank executive, Salt Lake City, Utah, 1938-46. Writer; lecturer on the drying, preservation, and storage of food. Professional entertainer and singer. *Member:* National League of American Pen Women, Soroptimists International, League of Utah Writers (board member; chapter president, 1972-74, state president, 1975-76). *Awards, honors:* Writing awards from Utah State Institute of Fine Arts, League of Utah Writers, National League of American Pen Women; *Dry and Save* was selected by U.S. Information Agency for showcase of American books at International Book Fair, Cairo, Egypt, 1978.

WRITINGS: (With Vernice G. Rosenvall and Mabel H. Miller) *Wheat for Man: Why and How,* Bookcraft, 1952, 3rd edition, Woodbridge Press, 1974; (with Ida Watt Stringham) *England's First Mormon Convert,* Utah Printing, 1956; (with Louise Nielsen) *The Dutson Family History,* Utah Printing, 1957; *What about Christmas?,* Horizon, 1971; (contributor) Duane S. Crowther and Jean D. Crowther, editors, *The Joy of Being a Woman,* Horizon, 1972; *Fun with Fruit Preservation,* Horizon, 1973, revised edition, 1980; (with Lula Parker Betenson) *Butch Cassidy, My Brother,* Brigham Young University Press, 1975; *Dry and Save,* Bookcraft, 1976; (with Janice T. Dixon) *Preserving Your Past,* Doubleday, 1977; *Christmas Magic,* Bookcraft, 1977; *Testimony in Bronze,* Olympus, 1980. Contributor of articles and short stories to periodicals, including *Utah Historical Quarterly, American West, Organic Gardening, Guideposts, Friend,* and *New Era.*

WORK IN PROGRESS: A "Mormon" cookbook; a book on motivations for writing personal and family history; a drying manual to accompany a specific food dehydrator; a book-length "history of my parents"; ancestral, personal, and family histories.

SIDELIGHTS: Dora D. Flack writes: "Expressed pleas for me to share with others my ideas and expertise, particularly in the homemaking fields, has pushed me into writing several books and many published articles. I lecture frequently on writing personal and family history and this has led to sharing my ideas in other books and articles. I am a Christmas 'nut' so it has been only natural to share in books and stories what many people feel is the true spirit of Christmas. These have been pleasurable writings.

"Always I have experienced a fascination to preserve in writing the lives and modes of living of past generations. Hence writing biography has been intensely absorbing. Unless someone writes these down, the lives of our ancestors and other fascinating people are lost to posterity. Never will I have enough time to write all that I wish. Indeed it is an addiction—but where could I find a more rewarding and serving addiction? Service to others is the thrust of all I do."

FLYNN, Jackson
See SHIRREFFS, Gordon D(onald)

* * *

FORD, David
See HARKNETT, Terry

* * *

FORMAN, Brenda   1936-

PERSONAL: Born August 1, 1936, in Hollywood, Calif.; daughter of Harrison (a writer) and Sandra (Carlyle) Forman. *Education:* Barnard College, B.A., 1956; City University of New York, Ph.D., 1969. *Home:* 2401 Elba Ct., Alexandria, Va. 22306. *Office:* Office of Export Administration, Division of Policy Planning, Room 1634, Department of Commerce, Washington, D.C. 20301.

CAREER: Free-lance writer, 1956-64; Mitre Corp., McLean, Va., began as analyst, became systems analyst, 1969-73; Office of Assistant Secretary for International Security Affairs, Washington, D.C., foreign affairs analyst, 1973-78; Office of Export Administration, Department of Commerce, Washington, D.C., director of Division of Policy Planning, 1978—. Lecturer to various community groups. *Member:* Phi Beta Kappa.

WRITINGS: (With father, Harrison Forman) *The Land and People of Nigeria,* Lippincott, 1964, revised edition, 1972; *The Story of Thailand,* McCormick-Mathers, 1965; *America's Place in the World Economy,* Harcourt, 1969; (with Thomas Kiernan) *B-Fifteen: The Miracle Vitamin,* Grosset, 1979.

"Famous First Name" series for children, published by Frommer-Pasmantier: *Is Your Name James?,* 1965; . . . *John?,* 1965; . . . *Richard?,* 1965; . . . *Robert?,* 1965; . . . *William?,* 1965; . . . *Michael?,* 1965.

SIDELIGHTS: Brenda Forman told *CA:* "My writing aim is to make historical and political subjects interesting and stimulating to young readers, particularly the teen-age groups."

In the introduction to *The Land and People of Nigeria,* Forman and her father write: "This book will try to give you a picture of Nigeria, one of these new nations—its history, its problems, its strengths, its weaknesses, and its people. Youth is usually a painful time, whether it is the youth of an individual or a nation. But then it is also a vigorous and exciting time too." A *Best Sellers* reviewer calls this "an informative book" in which "everything is uncovered and considered about this small but interesting country."

In *America's Place in the World Economy,* Forman explains the United States' economic condition and international economic relations for younger readers. *Saturday Review* writer Zena Sutherland comments, "Crystal-clear and meticulously detailed, this survey of the intricacies of the role of the United States in the world economy is an excellent example of a complicated subject made lucid and interesting."

BIOGRAPHICAL/CRITICAL SOURCES: Best Sellers, December 15, 1964; *Saturday Review,* August 16, 1969.

* * *

FORREST, Felix C.
See LINEBARGER, Paul M(yron) A(nthony)

FORREST, Julian
   See WAGENKNECHT, Edward (Charles)

*   *   *

FRANK, Janet
   See DUNLEAVY, Janet Egleson

*   *   *

FRANKENBERG, Lloyd   1907-1975

PERSONAL: Born September 3, 1907, in Mt. Vernon, N.Y.; died March 12, 1975, in New York, N.Y.; son of Henry and Helen (Conklin) Frankenberg; married Loren MacIver (an artist), 1929. *Education:* Attended Columbia University, 1924-29. *Home:* 61 Perry St., New York, N.Y.

CAREER: Writer, with intermittent jobs as newspaper rewrite man, outside reader, free-lance editor, and lecturer at various institutions, including New School for Social Research, New York, N.Y.; Fulbright visiting lecturer at Universities of Caen and Lyon, France. Member of Commission on Awards in the Arts, Brandeis University; member of poetry jury, Second National Book Awards. *Wartime service:* Conscientious objector; worked in a civilian public service camp and as an attendant in a psychiatric hospital, 1943-45. *Member:* P.E.N. *Awards, honors:* Spenser Award, 1938; Guggenheim fellowship, 1940; Carnegie grant, 1942; Academy of American Letters grant, 1947; Rockefeller Foundation fellowships, 1952, 1954.

WRITINGS: The Red Kite (poems), Farrar & Rinehart, 1939; *Pleasure Dome: On Reading Modern Poetry,* Houghton, 1949, reprinted, Doubleday, 1968; (editor) *Invitation to Poetry: A Round of Poems from John Skelton to Dylan Thomas* (Book Find Club selection), Doubleday, 1956; (editor) *A James Stephens Reader,* Macmillan (New York), 1962 (published in England as *James Stephens: A Selection,* Macmillan [London], 1962); (editor) *James, Seumas & Jacques: Unpublished Writings of James Stephens,* Macmillan, 1964; (editor) William Shakespeare, *Poems,* Crowell, 1966; (editor) *Poems by Robert Burns,* Crowell, 1967; (editor) *Wings of Rhyme,* Funk & Wagnalls, 1967; *The Stain of Circumstance: Selected Poems,* Ohio University Press, 1974. Contributor of poems, stories, articles, and reviews to *Harper's, Nation, New Yorker, Saturday Review, New York Times, New York Herald Tribune,* and other magazines and newspapers. Member of editorial board, *Decision,* 1942, and *Tiger's Eye,* 1947-48.

WORK IN PROGRESS: A collection of autobiographical poems, tentatively entitled *Those Years.*

AVOCATIONAL INTERESTS: Painting, sculpture, and music.†

*   *   *

FRANKLIN, Nat
   See BAUER, Erwin A.

*   *   *

FRAZER, Andrew
   See MARLOWE, Stephen

*   *   *

FREDERICKS, Frohm
   See KERNER, Fred

FREEDMAN, Ronald   1917-

PERSONAL: Born August 8, 1917, in Winnipeg, Manitoba, Canada; son of Issador (a merchant) and Ada (Greenstone) Freedman; married Deborah G. Selin (an economist), December 4, 1941; children: Joseph Selin, Jane Ilene. *Education:* University of Michigan, B.A., 1939, M.A., 1940; University of Chicago, Ph.D., 1947. *Religion:* Jewish. *Home:* 1404 Beechwood Rd., Ann Arbor, Mich. 48103. *Office:* Department of Sociology, University of Michigan, Ann Arbor, Mich. 48104.

CAREER: University of Michigan, Ann Arbor, 1946—, began as instructor, now professor of sociology, director of Population Studies Center, and research associate of Survey Research Center. *Military service:* U.S. Army Air Forces, 1942-45; became warrant officer junior grade. *Member:* Population Association of America (president, 1964-65), American Sociological Association, American Statistical Association, Phi Beta Kappa. *Awards, honors:* Award for Excellence in Teaching, University of Michigan, 1952; Guggenheim fellow and Fulbright fellow, 1957; Distinguished Faculty Service Award, 1970.

WRITINGS: Recent Migration to Chicago, University of Chicago Press, 1950; (with others) *Principles of Sociology: A Text with Readings,* Holt, 1952, revised edition, 1956; *Future School and College Enrollments in Michigan: 1955 to 1970,* J. W. Edwards, 1955; (with Samuel J. Eldersvald) *Political Affiliation in Metropolitan Detroit,* Michigan Governmental Studies, 1957; (with Pascal K. Whelpton and Arthur A. Campbell) *Family Planning, Sterility, and Population Growth,* McGraw, 1959.

The Sociology of Human Fertility, Basil Blackwell, 1963; (editor) *Population: The Vital Revolution,* Doubleday, 1964; (with Lolagene C. Coombs) *Use of Telephone Interviews in a Longitudinal Fertility Study,* University of Michigan Population Studies Center, 1964; *The Accelerating Fertility Decline in Taiwan,* University of Michigan Population Studies Center, 1965; (with David Goldberg and Doris Slesinger) *Current Fertility Expectations of Married Couples in the United States,* University of Michigan Population Studies Center, 1965, revised edition (with Goldberg and Larry Bumpass), 1965; (editor) *Fertility and Family Planning: A World View,* University of Michigan Press, 1969; (with John Y. Takeshita and others) *Family Planning in Taiwan: An Experiment in Social Change,* Princeton University Press, 1969.

(With Coombs) *Cross-Cultural Comparisons: Data on Two Factors in Fertility Behavior* (monograph), Population Council (New York), 1974; *Community-Level Data in Fertility Surveys* (monograph), International Statistical Institute (Voorburg, the Netherlands), 1974; *Examples of Community-Level Questionnaires* (monograph), International Statistical Institute, 1974; *The Sociology of Human Fertility: An Annotated Bibliography,* Irvington, 1975; (contributor) *Social Science Research on Population and Development,* Ford Foundation, 1975; (contributor) *Population and Development: Status and Trends of Family Planning/Population Programs in Developing Countries,* U.S. Government Printing Office, 1978; (contributor) P. M. Hauser, editor, *World Population and Development: Challenges and Prospects,* Syracuse University Press, 1979.

(Contributor) R. A. Easterlin, editor, *Population and Economic Change in Developing Countries,* University of Chicago Press, 1980. Contributor of articles to professional journals, including *Social Forces, Demography, Studies in Family Planning, Population Studies,* and *Scientific American.*

FREEMAN, Howard E(dgar) 1929-

PERSONAL: Born May 28, 1929, in New York, N.Y.; son of Herbert M. (a business executive) and Rose (Herman) Freeman; married Sharon Kleban, August 7, 1953 (divorced, 1973); married Marian A. Solomon, 1978; children: (first marriage) Seth Richard, Lisa Jill. *Education:* New York University, B.A., 1948, M.A., 1950, Ph.D., 1956. *Home:* 11260 Overland Ave., Culver City, Calif. *Office:* Department of Sociology, University of California, Los Angeles, Calif.

CAREER: Brandeis University, Waltham, Mass., associate professor, 1960-63, professor of social research, 1964-69, Morse Professor of Urban Studies, 1969-72, director of research center, 1960-66; Ford Foundation, social science advisor for Mexico, Central America, and the Caribbean, 1972-74; University of California, Los Angeles, professor of sociology, 1974—, director of Institute for Social Science Research, 1974-81. Lecturer and research consultant, Boston College, 1957-65; visiting professor of sociology, University of Wisconsin, 1966-67, University of Colorado, summer, 1967. Russell Sage Foundation, sociologist, 1967-72, consulting sociologist, 1974-77. Director, Task Force of Sociology, National Library of Medicine Project, 1966-67. Research advisor, Demonstration and Grant Program, Social Security Administration, 1961-65, Institute of Nutrition of Central America and Panama of Pan American Health Organization, 1965—; senior research advisor, Robert Wood Johnson Foundation, 1976—. Member of professional advisory committee, Massachusetts Association for Mental Health, Inc., 1962-65; member of administrative committee, Massachusetts Health Research Institute, 1963-66; member of Panel on Social Indicators, Office of the Secretary, Department of Health, Education and Welfare, 1966-69; member of review committee, State Comprehensive Health Planning Program for Massachusetts, 1968-72. Consultant or research consultant to numerous organizations, including V.A. Hospitals in Boston, Bedford, and Brockton, 1956-65, National Institute of Nutrition, Bogota, Columbia, 1968-79, National Status Offender Program, 1976—, and National Science Foundation, 1977-79. *Military service:* U.S. Air Force Reserve, 1953-62; became captain.

MEMBER: American Sociological Association, American Psychological Association, American Association for Public Opinion Research, National Conference on Social Welfare, U.S.-Mexico Border Health Association, Eastern Sociological Society, Society for the Study of Social Problems, Sociological Research Association. *Awards, honors:* Hofheimer Prize, American Psychiatric Association, 1963, for *The Mental Patient Comes Home.*

WRITINGS: (With Ozzie G. Simmons) *The Mental Patient Comes Home,* Wiley, 1963; (editor with Sol Levine and Leo G. Reeder) *Handbook of Medical Sociology,* Prentice-Hall, 1963, 3rd edition, 1979; (with others) *The Middle-Income Negro Family Faces Urban Renewal,* Housing and Home Finance Agency, 1965; (with Camille Lambert) *The Clinic Habit,* College and University Press, 1967; (with Norman R. Kurtz) *America's Troubles: A Casebook on Social Conflict,* Prentice-Hall, 1969, 2nd edition, 1973; (editor with others) *The Dying Patient,* Russell Sage, 1970; (with Clarence Sherwood) *Social Policy and Social Research,* Prentice-Hall, 1970; (with Wyatt C. Jones) *Social Problems: Causes and Controls,* Rand McNally, 1970, 3rd edition (with Jones and Lynne G. Zucker), 1979; (author of foreword and contributor) Francis G. Caro, editor, *Readings in Evaluation Research,* Russell Sage, 1971, 2nd edition, 1977; (editor with others) *The Social Scene,* Winthrop Publishing, 1972; (with Ilene N. Bernstein) *Academic and Entrepreneurial Research,* Russell Sage, 1975; (author of fore-

word) Thomas Cook, *Sesame Street Revisited,* Russell Sage, 1975; (author of foreword) Stephen M. Shortell and William C. Richardson, *Health Program Evaluation,* C. V. Mosley, 1978; (editor) *Policy Studies Review Annual II,* Sage Publications, 1978; (with Peter H. Rossi and Sonia R. Wright) *Evaluation: A Systematic Approach,* Sage Publications, 1979; (editor with wife, Marian A. Solomon) *Evaluation Studies Review Annual VI,* Sage Publications, 1981.

Contributor: E. Gartley Jaco, editor, *Patients, Physicians, and Illness,* Free Press, 1958; Dorrian Apple, editor, *Sociological Studies of Health and Sickness,* McGraw, 1959; Theodore R. Saprin, editor, *Studies in Behavior Pathology,* Reinhart & Winston, 1961; William McPhee and William A. Glaser, editors, *Public Opinion and Congressional Elections,* Free Press, 1962; William T. Smelser and Neil J. Smelser, editors, *Personality and Social Systems,* Wiley, 1963, reprinted, 1977; *The Social Welfare Forum,* Columbia University Press, 1963; William Gomberg and Arthur Shostak, editors, *Blue Collar World,* Prentice-Hall, 1964; Stanton Wheeler, editor, *Controlling Delinquents,* Wiley, 1967; Leigh M. Roberts and others, editors, *Comprehensive Mental Health: The Challenge of Evaluation,* University of Wisconsin Press, 1968; S. Kirson Weinberg, editor, *The Sociology of Mental Disorders,* Aldine, 1968; E. Borgatta and R. Evans, editors, *Smoking, Health and Behavior,* Aldine, 1968; Stephen P. Spitzer and Norman K. Denzin, editors, *The Mental Patient: Studies in the Sociology of Deviance,* McGraw, 1968; Alvin Winder, editor, *Adolescence: Contemporary Studies,* American Book Co., 1968; W. A. Many and Frank W. Lanning, editors, *Basic Education for the Adult Learner,* Houghton, 1968; G. Lindzey and E. Aronson, editors, *Handbook of Social Psychology,* Volume V, 2nd edition, Addison-Wesley, 1969.

William S. Sahakian, editor, *Psychopathology Today,* F. E. Peacock, 1970; Herbert Schulberg and others, editors, *Program Evaluation in the Health Fields,* Behavioral Publications, 1970; Morton Levitt and Ben Rubenstein, editors, *The Mental Health Field: A Critical Appraisal,* Wayne State University Press, 1971; Richard O'Toole, editor, *The Organization, Management and Tactics of Social Research,* Schenckman, 1971; Carol H. Weiss, editor, *Evaluating Action Programs: Readings in Social Action and Education,* Allyn & Bacon, 1972; James E. Albert and Murry Komioss, editors, *Social Experiments and Social Program Evaluation,* Bollinger Publishing, 1974; Frank R. Scarpitti and Paul T. McFarland, editors, *Deviance: Action, Reaction, Interaction,* Addison-Wesley, 1975; Nicholas J. Demerath and others, editors, *Social Policy and Sociology,* Academic Press, 1975; Gene M. Lyons, editor, *Social Research and Public Policies,* Dartmouth College, 1975; Stuart S. Nagel, editor, *Policy Studies and the Social Sciences,* Heath, 1975; Gerald T. Horton, editor, *Readings on Human Services Planning,* Human Services Institute for Children and Families, 1975; Jack Meslin, editor, *Rehabilitation Medicine and Psychiatry,* C. C Thomas, 1976; Robert W. Binstock and Ethel Shanas, editors, *Handbook of Aging and the Social Sciences,* Van Nostrand, 1976; Marcia Guttentag, editor, *Evaluation Studies Review Annual II,* Sage Publications, 1977.

Clark C. Abt, editor, *Problems in American Social Policy Research,* Abt Books, 1980; Erwin S. Solomon, editor, *Evaluating Social Action Projects,* UNESCO, 1980; Robert A. Levine and others, editors, *Evaluation Research and Practice,* Sage Publications, 1981; Richard O. Mason and E. Burton Swanson, *Measurement for Management Decision,* Addison-Wesley, 1981; Allan W. Johnson and others, editors, *Contemporary Health Services: Social Science Perspectives,* Auburn House, 1981; John W. Reich, editor, *Experimenting in Society:*

Issues and Examples in Applied Psychology, Scott, Foresman, 1982.

Editor of Prentice-Hall series in social policy, 1970-76. Contributor to proceedings of Institute on Health Care Needs of the Elderly Patient, 1961, Conference of New England Gerontological Society, 1963, American Statistical Association, 1964, Council of University Institutes for Urban Affairs, 1970. Contributor to numerous journals, including *American Journal of Sociology, American Sociological Review, American Sociologist, Contemporary Sociology, Journal of Psychology, Public Opinion Quarterly.* Co-editor, *Evaluation Review,* 1976—; associate editor, *American Sociological Review,* 1962-66, *Social Problems,* 1962-66, *Sociological Methods and Research,* 1971-76, *Journal of Health and Social Behavior,* 1966-69, editor, 1969-72; consulting editor, *Community Mental Health Journal,* 1964-80. Member of editorial advisory board, *New Directions for Program Evaluation,* 1981—; member of editorial board, *Values and Ethics in Health Care,* 1977, *Annals of Public Administration,* 1979—; referee, *American Journal of Public Health,* 1974—.

*   *   *

FRIEDMAN, Myles I(van)   1924-

PERSONAL: Born April 5, 1924, in Chicago, Ill.; son of Max and Ethel Friedman. *Education:* University of Chicago, M.A., 1957, Ph.D., 1959. *Office:* College of Education, University of South Carolina, Columbia, S.C. 29208.

CAREER: Corporate executive, 1946-57; Northwestern University, Evanston, Ill., assistant professor, 1958-60, associate professor of education, 1960-63; University of South Carolina, Columbia, professor of education, 1964-75, E. Smythe Gambrell Distinguished Professor, 1975—. Director of Head Start Evaluation and Research Center, 1966-70; director of research at Regional Education Laboratory for the Carolinas and Virginia, 1966-70; professor at University of California, Berkeley, summer, 1968. *Military service:* U.S. Army Air Forces, meteorologist, 1942-46. *Member:* American Psychological Association, American Educational Research Association.

WRITINGS: Rational Behavior, University of South Carolina Press, 1975; (with Patricia Brinlee and Patricia Dennis Hayes) *Improving Teacher Education,* Longman, 1979; (with Michael D. Rowls) *Teaching Reading and Thinking Skills,* Longman, 1979; (with Martha Willis) *Human Nature and Predictability,* Lexington Books, 1981. Author of ''Pre-Primary Profile,'' a test, Science Research Associates, 1963.

*   *   *

FRIEDMANN, Wolfgang (Gaston)   1907-1972

PERSONAL: Born January 25, 1907, in Berlin, Germany; killed by robbers September 20, 1972, in New York, N.Y.; buried in North Salem, N.Y.; son of Leonhard and Anna (Kapferer) Friedmann; married Leah May Lewis, January 9, 1937; children: Anthony, John Peter, Martin. *Education:* University of Berlin, Dr. jur., 1930; University of London, LL.M., 1936, LL.D., 1947; University of Melbourne, LL.M., 1948. *Residence:* North Salem, N.Y. *Office:* Law School, Columbia University, New York, N.Y. 10027.

CAREER: Barrister-at-law, Middle Temple, London, England, 1944; University of London, London, reader in law, 1938-47; Allied Military Government of Germany, held posts with SHEAF

and British Control Commission, 1944-47; University of Melbourne, Parkville, Victoria, Australia, professor of public law, 1947-50; University of Toronto, Toronto, Ontario, professor of law, 1950-55; Columbia University, New York, N.Y., professor of international law and director of international legal research, 1955-72. Visiting professor at University of Paris, 1968-69, and The Hague Academy of International Law, 1969-72. United Nations consultant, Rangoon Conference on Public Industrial Enterprise, 1954; consultant, Food and Agricultural Organization, United Nations, 1971. *Member:* American Society of International Law (member of executive council, 1958-61), American Academy of Arts and Sciences (fellow).

WRITINGS: Die Bereicherungshaftung, Walter de Gruyter, 1930; *English Equity and International Equity Tribunals,* Constable, 1935; *World Revolution and the Future of the West,* C. A. Watts, 1939; *The Crisis of the National State,* Macmillan, 1943; *The Allied Military Government of Germany,* Stevens & Sons, 1947.

Principles of Australian Administrative Law, Melbourne University Press, 1950, 2nd edition (with D. G. Benjafield), Law Book Company of Australasia, 1962, 4th edition (with Benjafield), 1971; *Law and Social Change in Contemporary Britain,* Stevens & Sons, 1951; *Law in a Changing Society,* University of California Press, 1959, 2nd edition, Columbia University Press, 1972, abridged edition, Penguin Books, 1964; *Legal Theory,* 4th edition, Stevens & Sons, 1960, 5th edition, Columbia University Press, 1967; *An Introduction to World Politics,* St. Martin's, 1961, 5th edition, 1965; *The Changing Structure of International Law,* Columbia University Press, 1964; (with George Kalmanoff and Robert F. Meagher) *International Financial Aid,* Columbia University Press, 1966; (project director) R. K. Hazari and S. D. Mehta, *Public International Development Financing in India: A Research Project of the Columbia University School of Law,* Asian Studies Press, 1968; (with Oliver J. Lissitzyn and Richard Crawford Pugh) *Cases and Materials on International Law,* West Publishing, 1969, supplement, 1972.

The State and the Rule of Law in a Mixed Economy, Stevens & Sons, 1971; *The Future of the Oceans,* Braziller, 1971; (with Jean-Pierre Beguin) *Joint International Business Ventures in Developing Countries: Case Studies and Analysis of Recent Trends,* Columbia University Press, 1971; *Governmental Enterprises,* J.C.B. Mohr, 1972; (contributor) Philip C. Jessup, *The United States and the World Court,* Garland Publishing, 1972; (collaborator) John Norton Moore, editor, *Law and Civil War in the Modern World,* Johns Hopkins Press, 1974.

Editor: *The Public Corporation,* Carswell, 1954; *Matrimonial Property Law,* Carswell, 1955; *Anti-Trust Laws: A Comparative Symposium,* Carswell, 1956; (with Pugh) *Legal Aspects of Foreign Investments,* Stevens & Sons, 1959; (with Kalmanoff) *Joint International Business Ventures,* Columbia University Press, 1961; (with Leo Mates) *Joint Business Ventures of Yugoslav Enterprises and Foreign Firms,* Rothman, 1968; (with J. F. Garner) *Government Enterprise: A Comparative Study,* Columbia University Press, 1971; (with Louis Henkin and Lissitzyn, and contributor) *Transnational Law in a Changing Society: Essays in Honor of Philip C. Jessup,* Columbia University Press, 1972; *Public and Private Enterprise in Mixed Economies,* Columbia University Press, 1974.

BIOGRAPHICAL/CRITICAL SOURCES: University Bookman, spring, 1967; *Washington Post,* June 23, 1971; *New York Times,* September 21, 1972.†

G

GABRIEL, A(strik) L. 1907-

PERSONAL: Born December 10, 1907, in Pecs, Hungary; came to United States in 1948, naturalized in 1953; son of Alois and Marie (Boross) Gabriel. *Education:* University of Budapest, M.A., 1934, Ph.D., 1936; attended Sorbonne, University of Paris, 1932-33, and Ecole des Chartres, 1935-36. *Religion:* Roman Catholic. *Home and office address:* Box 578, University of Notre Dame, Notre Dame, Ind. 46556.

CAREER: French College Canons of Premontre, Hungary, director, 1938-47; Royal Pazmany University, Budapest, Hungary, privat dozent, 1941-47; University of Notre Dame, Notre Dame, Ind., professor of mediaeval civilization, 1948-74, director of Mediaeval Institute, 1953-74, professor emeritus, 1974—. Pontifical Institute of Mediaeval Studies, Toronto, Ontario, visiting professor, 1947-48, honorary fellow, 1977; Institute for Advanced Study, Princeton, N.J., member, 1950-51 and 1980; Fulbright Scholar, Luxembourg, 1959, and Germany, 1972. Harvard University, Cambridge, Mass., Charles Chauncey Stillman Guest Professor, 1963-64. Ambrosiana Micro-filming Project, director.

MEMBER: International Academy of Arts and Letters (fellow), International Commission for Historical Sciences (president, 1970—), Societe de l'Histoire de France (fellow), Royal Historical Society (fellow), Institute de France (corresponding fellow), Bavarian Academy of Science (corresponding fellow), Mediaeval Academy of America (fellow), American Catholic Historical Association (president, 1973), Historical Committee on Canons of Premontre.

AWARDS, HONORS: Prix Thorlet, 1956, and Prix Dourlans, 1965, both from French Academie des Inscriptions; honorary doctorate, Ambrosiana Library, Milan, 1967; presented with festschrift entitled *Studium Generale: Studies Offered to Astrik L. Gabriel by His Former Students at the Mediaeval Institute, University of Notre Dame,* published by Mediaeval Institute, University of Notre Dame in 1967; Officier, Legion d'Honneur; Officier, Palmes Academiques, France; Commander, Order of Merit, Italy; Golden Medal, Pro Ecclesia et Pontifice, Paul VI (Vatican).

WRITINGS: Index romain et litterature francaise a l'epoque romantique, University of Budapest Press, 1936; *Les rapports dynastiques franco-hongrois au moyen-age,* University of Budapest Press, 1944; *Sainte Marguerite de Hongrie,* Posner, 1944; *Student Life in Ave Maria College, Mediaeval Paris,* Mediaeval Institute, University of Notre Dame, 1955; *The Ed-*

ucational Ideas of Vincent of Beauvais, Mediaeval Institute, University of Notre Dame, 1956; (contributor) *Middle Ages-Reformation Volkskunde: Festschrift for John G. Kunstmann,* University of North Carolina Press, 1959.

Skara House at the Mediaeval University of Paris, Mediaeval Institute, University of Notre Dame, 1960; (contributor) Francis Lee Utley, editor, *The Forward Movement of the Fourteenth Century,* Ohio State University Press, 1961; *Motivation of the Founders at Mediaeval Colleges,* Walter de Gruyter, 1964; (co-editor) *Auctarium Chartularii Universitatis Parisiensis VI, Liber receptorum,* Volume VI, Didier, 1964; *Res quaedam notatu dignae Nationem Anglicanam (Alemanniae) Parisiensem saeculo xv spectantes,* Didier (Paris), 1965; *A Summary Catalogue of Microfilms of One Thousand Scientific Manuscripts in the Ambrosiana Library, Milan,* Mediaeval Institute, University of Notre Dame, 1968; *Garlandia: Studies in the History of the Mediaeval University,* Mediaeval Institute, University of Notre Dame, 1969; *The Mediaeval Universities of Pecs and Pozsony,* Mediaeval Institute, University of Notre Dame, 1969.

Les origines de la Faculte de Decret de l'ancienne Universite de Paris, [Paris], 1973; *Summary Bibliography of the History of the Universities of Great Britain and Ireland up to 1800, Covering Publications between 1900 and 1968,* Mediaeval Institute, University of Notre Dame, 1974; *The Ambrosiana Collection at the University of Notre Dame,* Sears Bank and Trust Co., 1976; *The Conflict between the Chancellor and the University of Masters and Students at Paris during the Middle Ages,* Walter de Gruyter, 1976; (editor) *The Economic and Material Frame of the Mediaeval University,* International Commission for the History of Universities, 1977; *Petrus Cesaris Wagner and Johannes Stoll: Fifteenth Century Printers at the University of Paris,* University of Notre Dame Press, 1979; (contributor) Pierre Cockshaw and others, editors, *Miscellanea F. Masai,* Gand, 1979.

Contributor of papers, articles, and reviews on historical and religious subjects to English, French, German, Hungarian, and Spanish scholarly journals. Co-editor, "Texts and Studies in the History of Mediaeval Education," "Publications in Mediaeval Studies," and *Folio Ambrosiana.*

WORK IN PROGRESS: Chartularium Universitatis Parisiensis II; Pars Posterior; Collegia Parisiana; Iconographical Index of the Illuminated Manuscripts in the Ambrosiana Library.

GADDIS, Peggy
See DERN, Erolie Pearl Gaddis

*   *   *

GAFFNEY, James 1931-

PERSONAL: Born February 21, 1931, in New York, N.Y.; son of James George (a banker and lawyer) and Lucille (a secretary; maiden name, Lynch) Gaffney; married Kathleen McGovern (a teacher), June 20, 1970; children: Elizabeth, Margaret. Education: Spring Hill College, B.S., 1956; Fordham University, M.A., 1965; Gregorian University of Rome, Ph.D., 1968; Texas Southern University, M.Ed., 1971. Politics: "More socialist than otherwise." Religion: Christian. Home: 4420 Fontainebleau Dr., New Orleans, La. 70125. Office: Department of Religious Studies, Loyola University, New Orleans, La. 70118.

CAREER: High school teacher of languages in New York, N.Y., 1956-59; University of Gonzaga, Florence, Italy, assistant professor of philosophy and theology, 1968-70; University of Liberia, Monrovia, lecturer in foreign languages, 1970-72; Illinois Benedictine College, Lisle, associate professor of religious studies and chairman of department, 1973-76; Loyola University, New Orleans, La., professor of religious studies, 1976—. Member: American Academy of Religion, American Society of Christian Ethics, American Society for Religion in Public Education, Catholic Theological Society of America, College Theology Society, Dante Society.

WRITINGS—Published by Paulist/Newman, except as indicated: (Contributor) A. D. Lee, editor, Vatican II: The Theological Dimension, Thomist Press, 1963; Focus on Doctrine, 1975; Moral Questions, 1975; (contributor) Thomas McFadden, editor, Revolution, Liberation, and Freedom, Seabury, 1975; Biblical Notes on the Sunday Lectionary, 1977; Newness of Life, 1979. Contributor to philosophy and theology journals and to other publications, including Commonweal, America, Chicago Studies, and New Catholic World.

WORK IN PROGRESS: A book on the changing conceptions of sin.

*   *   *

GAGE, Wilson
See STEELE, Mary Q(uintard Govan)

*   *   *

GAINES, Ernest J. 1933-

PERSONAL: Born January 15, 1933, in Oscar, La.; son of Manuel (a laborer) and Adrienne J. (Colar) Gaines. Education: San Francisco State College (now University), B.A., 1957; Stanford University, graduate study, 1958-59. Home: 932 Divisadero St., San Francisco, Calif. 94115. Agent: Dorothea Oppenheimer, 866 United Nations Plaza, Room 4029, New York, N.Y. 10017.

CAREER: "Writing, five hours a day, five days a week." Awards, honors: Joseph Henry Jackson Award, 1959, for "Comeback" (short story); National Endowment for the Arts award, 1967; Rockefeller grant-in-aid, 1970; Guggenheim award, 1971; Black Academy of Arts and Letters award, 1972; California Commonwealth Gold Medal, 1972; Louisiana Library Association award, 1972; honorary doctorate of letters, Denison University, 1980.

WRITINGS—Novels, except as indicated: Catherine Carmier, Atheneum, 1964; Of Love and Dust, Dial, 1967; Bloodline (short stories; also see below), Dial, 1968; A Long Day in November (originally published in Bloodline), Dial, 1971; The Autobiography of Miss Jane Pittman, Dial, 1971; In My Father's House, Knopf, 1978.

WORK IN PROGRESS: A novel, A Gathering of Old Men.

SIDELIGHTS: Ernest J. Gaines told CA that his ambition is "to learn as well as I can the art of writing (which I'm sure will take the rest of my life)." In a Time review Melvin Maddocks writes: "Ernest J. Gaines has not received anything like the attention he deserves, for he may just be the best black writer in America. He is so good, in fact, that he makes the category seem meaningless, though one of his principal subjects has been slavery—past and present. Born on a Louisiana plantation . . . , Gaines is first and last a country-boy writer. He sets down a story as if he were planting, spreading the roots deep, wide and firm. His stories grow organically, at their own rhythm. When they ripen at last, they do so inevitably, arriving at a climax with the absolute rightness of a folk tale."

Although he moved to Vallejo, California, when he was fifteen and has spent his adult life elsewhere, Gaines regularly visits the region where he grew up. This region appears in Gaines' work as the imaginary Bayonne, Louisiana, and it has been compared to Faulkner's Yoknapatawpha County. In an interview with Gaines, Jerome Tarshis of the San Francisco comments that "[Gaines] went to predominantly white colleges in the 1950s, when Hemingway and Faulkner were enormously admired in creative writing classes." Gaines readily acknowledges the influence Faulkner and Hemingway have had on his work, telling Tarshis that he reads "the two old men" all the time.

In a Washington Post interview with Joseph McLellan, Gaines explains how he began writing: "After we moved to California, I used to hang around on the corner with the boys, and my father, who was in the merchant marine, told me, 'Get off the block or you're going to get into trouble.' I had a choice of two places to spend my time—the YMCA or the library. I had never been in a library in Louisiana, so I went there looking for books about my people—blacks, especially southern blacks—and I didn't find much. Eventually, I started to write about my old home; if the book you want doesn't exist, you try to make it exist."

William E. Grant, writing in the Dictionary of Literary Biography, calls Gaines' first novel, Catherine Carmier, "an apprentice work more interesting for what it anticipates than for its accomplishments." The novel chronicles the story of Jackson Bradley who returns to the Bayonne area after completing his education in California. He falls in love with Catherine, the daughter of a Creole sharecropper who refuses to let his family associate with anyone darker than themselves. After a violent confrontation with Catherine's father, Jackson finally realizes that Catherine will always remain loyal to her father and his beliefs.

Gaines sets this novel in the time of the Civil Rights movement, yet he deliberately avoids making the movement a primary force in the novel. Grant comments: "In divorcing his tale from contemporary events, Gaines declares his independence from the political and social purposes of much contemporary black writing. Instead, he elects to concentrate upon those fundamental human passions and conflicts which transcend the merely social level of human existence." Grant finds Gaines "admirable" for doing this, but he also believes that Jackson's credibility is marred because he remains aloof from contemporary events. For Grant, the novel "seems to float outside time and place rather than being solidly anchored in the real world of the modern South."

Of Love and Dust, the narrative of Marcus Payne, a young, rebellious Negro serving time on a Louisiana plantation, also involves forbidden romance. The overseer, Sidney Bonbon, unsuccessfully tries to break Marcus' rebellious spirit. Attempting to get back at Bonbon, Marcus pays attention to the overseer's wife, Louise; the two of them fall in love and plan to run away. The novel ends in a violent confrontation during which Marcus is killed. Throughout the novel is the sense that the characters' actions are limited by the social system in which they live. Grant remarks that "in Gaines' early fiction even the strongest are but victims of forces which control them."

Punch critic Joy Melville praises *Of Love and Dust,* calling it "spellbinding. . . . The atmosphere is timeless; gradually one realises that the date is postwar and a point has been unobtrusively made. . . . Beautifully organised, the novel has the virtues of traditional fiction. Its impact, apart from the skill of the narration, is due to the deadly quietness of tone." In reviewing the book for *Nation,* Sara Blackburn says that Gaines is "a writer of terrific energy. . . . It takes a lot of nerve to write a novel like this today, and a lot of skill to bring it off. Mr. Gaines has plenty of both."

The protagonist of *The Autobiography of Miss Jane Pittman* is a woman who refuses to be limited by the forces of fate. Miss Jane Pittman's personal history spans the time from slavery up through the Civil Rights movement of the 1960s, and her story is also the story of rural Louisiana blacks. For this novel Gaines has adapted the oral narrative to fiction. He presumably obtained the material for the book from tape-recorded interviews with Miss Jane, who is well over one hundred years old when she relates her history. In a *Life* review, Josh Greenfield writes: "Never mind that Miss Jane Pittman is fictitious, and that her 'autobiography,' offered up in the form of taped reminiscences, is artifice. The effect is stunning." Gaines told *San Francisco*'s Tarshis that he had originally planned to have Miss Jane and a group of her friends tell this story, but later decided that Miss Jane should be the sole narrator.

The Autobiography of Miss Jane Pittman could be called the embodiment of the black experience in America. Martin Amis, writing in the *New Statesman,* remarks: "In Thomas Berger's *Little Big Man* the 111-year-old-narrator told the story of his highly eventful life. . . . The story evoked, and elegised, the spirit of the American Indian. In *The Autobiography of Miss Jane Pittman* Ernest Gaines does the same for the black American." *Nation* reviewer Jerry H. Bryant states: "Jane's story is an epic poem. Literally, it is an account of Jane's life. Figuratively, it is a metaphor of the collective black experience. . . . The length of Jane's life is itself an expression of the race's longevity." A critic for the *Times Literary Supplement* says that the narrative is "cheerfully free of self-pity or dramatics, taking for granted unspeakable persecutions and endurances, faded into matter-of-factness by the suggestion of old age remembering."

According to Bryant, "No American novelist, either white or black, has been able to harmonize these discordant notes [of black political and artistic expression]. No novelist, that is, before Gaines. The secret of his success in *The Autobiography of Miss Jane Pittman* is the character of Miss Jane." Greenfield notes: "I know of no black novel about the South that exudes quite the same refreshing mix of wit and wrath, imagination, misery and poetry. And I can recall no more memorable female character in Southern fiction since Lena of Faulkner's *Light in August* than Miss Jane Pittman herself."

Gaines' fourth novel, *In My Father's House,* utilizes the same setting and the same types of characters found in his previous books. *New York Times* critic Mel Watkins explains: "The

setting is Southeastern Louisiana, near Baton Rouge and the Mississippi River. The characters too are familiar; they are the staunch rural types . . . whom Mr. Gaines has portrayed with such authenticity in his previous works. All are familiar—all, that is, except Robert X, who emerges in this tale as a gaunt Giacomettilike figure amid a landscape peopled by stalwart, Old South provincials."

Robert X arrives in St. Adrienne, Louisiana, from Chicago, and for several days his unexplained presence is a puzzle to the townspeople. Eventually Robert X's identity is revealed; he is one of the offspring from a relationship the Reverend Phillip Martin had in his younger, more wild years. Robert X has come to confront the father who never claimed him. This confrontation forces the Reverend Martin to examine his past and re-evaluate his priorities.

In a *New York Times Book Review* interview with Paul Desruisseaux, Gaines says: "In my books there always seem to be fathers and sons searching for each other. . . . Even when the father was not in the story, I've dealt with his absence and its effect on his children." Watkins calls *In My Father's House* a "deeply layered, resonant tale. Its themes of alienation between parents and offspring, and the irrevocable unity of past and present, are certainly large enough to command attention."

Gaines believes that many young black writers have been influenced disproportionately by Richard Wright's *Native Son.* In an interview in the *San Francisco* Gaines says: "So many of our writers have not read any farther back than *Native Son.* Too many of our novels deal only with the great city ghettos; that's all we write about, as if there's nothing else." Gaines continues: "We've only been living in these ghettos for 75 years or so, but the other 300 years—I think this is worth writing about."

MEDIA ADAPTATIONS: The Autobiography of Miss Jane Pittman was filmed for television in 1974; "The Sky Is Gray," a short story which originally appeared in *Bloodline,* was adapted for public television in 1980.

BIOGRAPHICAL/CRITICAL SOURCES: Times Literary Supplement, February 10, 1966, March 16, 1973; *Negro Digest,* November, 1967, January, 1968, January, 1969; *New York Times Book Review,* November 19, 1967, June 11, 1978; *Nation,* February 5, 1968, April 5, 1971; *Punch,* June 12, 1968; *Best Sellers,* August 15, 1968; *Newsweek,* June 16, 1969; *Life,* April 30, 1971; *Time,* May 10, 1971, December 27, 1971; *New Statesman,* September 2, 1973; *San Francisco,* July, 1974; *Contemporary Literary Criticism,* Gale, Volume III, 1975, Volume XI, 1979, Volume XVIII, 1981; *Authors in the News,* Volume I, Gale, 1976; *Dictionary of Literary Biography,* Volume II, Gale, 1978; *New York Times,* July 20, 1978.

—Sketch by Debra G. Jones

*   *   *

GALBRAITH, John S. 1916-

PERSONAL: Born November 10, 1916, in Glasgow, Scotland; son of James M. and Mary (Marshall) Galbraith; married Laura E. Huddleston, August 22, 1940; children: James, John H., Mary. *Education:* Miami University, Oxford, Ohio, B.S., 1938; University of Iowa, M.A., 1939, Ph.D., 1943. *Home:* 654 Thayer Ave., Los Angeles, Calif. 90024. *Office:* Department of History, University of California, Los Angeles, Calif. 90024.

CAREER: Ohio University, Athens, Ohio, assistant professor, 1947-48; University of California, Los Angeles, professor of history, 1948-64; University of California, San Diego, vice-chancellor, 1964, chancellor, 1964-68; University of California, Los Angeles, professor of history, 1968—. Culver City (Calif.) Board of Education, member, 1953-55. *Military service:* U.S. Army, historical officer, Third Air Force, 1943-46; became lieutenant. *Member:* American Historical Association, Royal Historical Society, African Studies Association, Society of American Historians, Canadian Historical Association, Phi Beta Kappa.

WRITINGS: The Establishment of Canadian Diplomatic Status at Washington, University of California Press, 1951; *The Hudson's Bay Company as an Imperial Factor,* University of California Press, 1957; *Reluctant Empire,* University of California Press, 1963; *MacKinnon and East Africa,* Cambridge University Press, 1972; *Crown and Charter,* University of California Press, 1974; *The Little Emperor,* Macmillan, 1976.

*   *   *

GALL, Meredith D(amien) 1942-

PERSONAL: Born February 18, 1942, in New Britain, Conn.; son of Theodore Albert (a procurement specialist) and Ray (Ehrlich) Gall; married Joyce Pershing (a psychologist), June 15, 1968. *Education:* Harvard University, A.B. and Ed. M., 1963; University of California, Berkeley, Ph.D., 1968. *Residence:* Eugene, Ore. *Office:* College of Education, University of Oregon, Eugene, Ore. 97403.

CAREER: San Francisco Veterans Administration Hospital, San Francisco, Calif., clinical psychologist, 1965-66; University of California, Counseling Center, Berkeley, counseling psychologist, 1966-67; Far West Laboratory for Educational Research and Development, San Francisco, psychologist in Program for Effective Teacher Education, 1968-74; University of Oregon, Eugene, professor of education, 1975—. *Member:* American Psychological Association, American Educational Research Association, Phi Delta Kappa. *Awards, honors:* Golden Eagle Award from International Film Committee for Non-Theatrical Events, 1972, for instructional films in "Higher Cognitive Questioning" training program; Phi Delta Kappa Award, 1978, for contributions to education in evaluation, development, and research, 1978.

WRITINGS: (With W. R. Borg and others) *The Mini-course: A Microteaching Approach to Teacher Education,* Macmillan Educational Services, 1970; (with Borg) *Educational Research: An Introduction,* 2nd edition (Gall was not associated with earlier edition), McKay, 1971, 3rd edition, Longman, 1979; (contributor) J. K. Hemphill and F. S. Rosenau, editors, *Educational Development,* Center for Advanced Study in Educational Administration, 1972; (contributor) Amelia Melnik and John Merritt, editors, *The Reading Curriculum,* University of London Press, 1972, General Learning Press, 1973; (contributor) B. C. Mills and R. A. Mills, editors, *Designing Instructional Strategies for Young Children,* W. C. Brown, 1972; (contributor) Morton Bloomberg, editor, *Creativity: Theory and Research,* College & University Press, 1973; (with Borg and N. T. Bell) *Student Workbook in Educational Research,* McKay, 1974; (editor with B. A. Ward) *Critical Issues in Educational Psychology,* Little, Brown, 1974; (with K. A. Acheson) *Techniques in the Clinical Supervision of Teachers,* Longman, 1980; *Handbook for Evaluating and Selecting Curriculum Materials,* Allyn & Bacon, 1981.

Training materials; films or audio tapes with accompanying handbooks for students and manuals for teachers: (With B. B. Dunning and J. Galassi) *Individualizing Instruction in Mathematics,* Macmillan, 1970; (with Dunning and R. Weathersby) *Higher Cognitive Questioning,* Macmillan, 1971; (with Acheson and J. H. Hansen) *Teacher Supervision: A Brief Training*

Program in Observation and Conference Techniques, University of Oregon, 1973; (with Weathersby, M. K. Lai, and R. A. Elder) *Discussing Controversial Issues,* Far West Laboratory for Educational Research and Development, 1973.

Contributor to journals in his field.

*   *   *

GALLAGHER, Richard (Farrington) 1926-

PERSONAL: Born January 22, 1926, in New York, N.Y.; son of William Harrison and Flora (MacMaster) Gallagher; divorced; married Dorothy White, December, 1962; children: (first marriage) Cynthia, Catherine. *Education:* Attended Adelphi College (now University), two years; Syracuse University, B.A.

CAREER: Nassau Daily Review Star, Rockville Centre, N.Y., reporter and desk man, 1950-53; *Long Island Daily Press,* Jamaica, N.Y., reporter and desk man, 1953; Adelphi College (now University), Garden City, N.Y., publicity director, 1953-54; *Long Island Independent,* Long Beach, N.Y., editor, 1954; Magazine Management Co., New York, N.Y., executive editor, 1954-61; free-lance writer, 1961—. *Military service:* U.S. Army Air Forces, two years.

WRITINGS: Nuremberg—The Third Reich on Trial, Avon, 1961; *Women without Morals,* Avon, 1962; *Malmedy Massacre,* Paperback Library, 1963; *Diseases That Plague Modern Man: A History of Ten Communicable Diseases,* Oceana, 1969; *The Doomsday Committee,* Award Books, 1970; (with Forrest Perrin) *A Surprising Election-Year Almanac,* Benjamin Co., 1972. Contributor to national magazines.†

*   *   *

GALTON, Lawrence 1913-

PERSONAL: Born October 30, 1913, in Bayonne, N.J.; son of Arthur (a businessman) and Frieda (Globe) Galton; married Barbara Brandt, 1945; children: Christopher, Gillian, Jeremy. *Education:* Attended Columbia University, 1930-32; Rutgers University, B.S., 1936. *Home and office:* 1140 Fifth Ave., New York, N.Y. 10028.

CAREER: Automatic Electric Co., New York, N.Y., sales promotion manager, 1937-42; free-lance writer, 1946—. Visiting professor and consultant to dean of engineering, Purdue University, 1961-72. *Military service:* U.S. Army, Signal Corps, 1943-46; became first lieutenant. *Member:* National Association of Science Writers, American Association for the Advancement of Science, American Medical Writers Association, Society of Magazine Writers. *Awards, honors:* Cecil Award, Arthritis Foundation, 1956 and 1965; American Dental Association Science Writers' Award, 1970; Blakeslee Award, American Heart Association, 1979.

WRITINGS: Outdoorsman's Fitness and Medical Guide, Outdoor Life, 1967; (with Benjamin Frank Miller) *The Family Book of Preventative Medicine: How to Stay Well All the Time,* Simon & Schuster, 1971; *The Laboratory of the Body: Dental Research, Science's Newest Frontier,* Pyramid House, 1972; (with Miller) *Freedom from Heart Attacks,* Simon & Schuster, 1972; (with William Likoff and Bernard Segal) *Your Heart: Complete Information for the Family,* Lippincott, 1972; (with Lawrence W. Friedmann) *Freedom from Backaches,* Simon & Schuster, 1973; *The Silent Disease: Hypertension,* Crown, 1973; (with W. Hugh Missildine) *Your Inner Conflicts: How to Solve Them,* Simon & Schuster, 1974; *The Disguised Disease: Anemia,* Crown, 1975; *Don't Give Up on An Aging Parent,* Crown, 1975.

How Long Will I Live?: And 434 Other Questions Your Doctor Doesn't Have Time to Answer and You Can't Afford to Ask, Macmillan, 1976; *The Truth about Fiber in Your Food,* Crown, 1976; (with Broda Otto Barnes) *Hypothyroidism: The Unsuspected Illness,* Crowell, 1976; *Medical Advances,* Crown, 1977; *Save Your Stomach: The Answers to Every Question about the Stomach; How It Works, How to Keep It Healthy, How to Overcome Any of Its Problems,* Crown, 1977; *The Patient's Guide to Surgery: How to Make the Best of Your Operation,* Avon, 1977; (with Oscar Roth) *Heart Attack! A Question and Answer Book,* Lippincott, 1978; *The Complete Book of Symptoms and What They Can Mean,* Simon & Schuster, 1978; (with Miller) *The Complete Medical Guide,* 4th edition, Simon & Schuster, 1978; *The Complete Medical, Fitness, and Health Guide for Men,* Simon & Schuster, 1979; *The Truth about Senility—And How to Avoid It,* Crowell, 1979; *You May Not Need a Psychiatrist: How Your Body May Control Your Mind,* Simon & Schuster, 1979; *Your Child in Sports,* F. Watts, 1980. Columnist for Washington Star Syndicate and for *Parade* and *Family Circle* magazines. Contributor to *New York Times Magazine* and *Reader's Digest.*

WORK IN PROGRESS: Nonfiction books.

SIDELIGHTS: Lawrence Galton told *CA:* "Quite likely, inability because of the Great Depression to go on to medical school after completing pre-medical training has fostered an intense interest in science in general and medicine in particular. I have written more than 500 articles for major magazines over the last 25 years, many of them concerned with medicine and health. Virtually all my books as well have been health-related."

*   *   *

GANS, Herbert J. 1927-

PERSONAL: Born May 7, 1927, in Cologne, Germany; emigrated to the United States in 1940, naturalized in 1945; son of Carl M. (a businessman) and Elise (Plaut) Gans; married Louise Gruner (a lawyer), March 19, 1967; children: David. *Education:* University of Chicago, Ph.B., 1947, M.A., 1950; University of Pennsylvania, Ph.D., 1957. *Home:* 435 Riverside Dr., Apt. 112, New York, N.Y. 10025. *Office:* Department of Sociology, 404 Fayerweather Hall, Columbia University, New York, N.Y. 10027.

CAREER: American Society of Planning Officials, Chicago, Ill., research assistant, 1950; Chicago Housing Authority, Chicago, assistant planner, 1950-51; P.A.C.E. Associates (planners), Chicago, chief research planner, 1951-52; U.S. Housing and Home Finance Agency, Division of Slum Clearance, Washington, D.C., field representative, 1952-53; University of Pennsylvania, Philadelphia, Institute for Urban Studies and department of city planning, research associate, 1953-57, assistant professor, 1958-61, research associate professor of city planning and urban studies, 1961-64, department of sociology, lecturer, 1958-59; Columbia University, New York City, Teachers College, associate professor of sociology and education, 1964-66, adjunct professor of sociology and education, 1966-69, Institute for Urban Studies, research associate, 1964-65; Center for Urban Education, New York City, research associate, 1965-66, senior staff sociologist, 1966-69; Massachusetts Institute of Technology, Cambridge, professor of sociology and planning, 1969-71, Massachusetts Institute of Technology-Harvard University Joint Center for Urban Studies, faculty associate, 1969-71; Center for Policy Research, New York City, senior research associate, 1971-80; Columbia University, professor of sociology, 1971—. Visiting professor,

Columbia University, spring, 1969. Consultant to numerous planning agencies, including the Ford Foundation, U.S. Department of Health, Education, and Welfare, and U.S. Department of Housing and Urban Development. *Military service:* U.S. Army, 1945-46.

MEMBER: American Sociological Association (member of council, 1968-71), Society for the Study of Social Problems (member of executive committee, 1968-71), Sociological Research Association, Eastern Sociological Society (president, 1972-73), Phi Beta Kappa. *Awards, honors:* Research grants from Center for the Study of Leisure, University of Chicago, 1957, National Institute of Mental Health, 1959-60, 1973-76, Annenberg School of Communication, University of Pennsylvania, 1960, American Philosophical Society, 1961, Social Science Research Council, 1962, Pennsylvania-New Jersey-Delaware Metropolitan Project, 1962-63, Urban Studies Center, Rutgers University, 1963, Bullitt Foundation, 1964-68, Ford Foundation, 1969-73, and National Endowment for the Humanities, 1973; Guggenheim fellow, 1977-78; Theatre Library Association Award, 1979, and National Association of Educational Broadcasters Book Award, 1980, both for *Deciding What's News.*

WRITINGS: *The Urban Villagers: Groups and Class in the Life of Italian-Americans,* Free Press, 1962; *The Levittowners: Ways of Life and Politics in a New Suburban Community,* Pantheon, 1967; *People and Plans: Essays on Urban Problems and Solutions,* Basic Books, 1968; *The Uses of Television and Their Educational Implications,* Center for Urban Education, 1968; *More Equality,* Pantheon, 1973; *Popular Culture and High Culture,* Basic Books, 1974; *Deciding What's News: A Study of CBS Evening News, NBC Nightly News, Newsweek and Time,* Pantheon, 1979; (editor with Nathan Glazer, Joseph R. Gusfield, and Christopher Jencks) *On the Making of Americans: Essays in Honor of David Riesman,* University of Pennsylvania Press, 1979.

Contributor of chapters to over fifty books, including Howard S. Becker, editor, *Social Problems: A Modern Approach,* Wiley, 1966; P. Lazarsfeld, W. Sewell, and H. Wilensky, editors, *Uses of Sociology,* Basic Books, 1966; S. Withey and T. Abeles, *Television and Social Behavior,* Erlbaum, 1980; contributor to the "Kerner Report," 1968. Author of monographs and of column, "Gans on Films," *Social Policy,* 1971-78. Contributor of articles to magazines and scholarly journals, including *Commonweal, Nation, New York Times Magazine, Saturday Review,* and *American Sociological Review.* Advisory editor of *Journal of the American Institute of Planners,* 1965-75, *Urban Life,* 1971—, *Society,* 1971-76, *Social Policy,* 1971—, *Public Opinion Quarterly,* 1972—, *American Journal of Sociology,* 1972-73, *Journal of Communication,* 1974—, and *Ethnic and Racial Studies.*

WORK IN PROGRESS: A revised edition of *The Urban Villagers;* a book on social theory.

SIDELIGHTS: Herbert J. Gans is known for his participant-observation sociological studies in which he immerses himself in the life of the community under consideration. John Goldthorpe finds that Gans's studies generally expose social myths. *The Urban Villagers,* Gans's study of Boston's West End, is, Goldthorpe feels, "in effect an excellent piece debunking the whole idea of the happy urban peasant." *The Levittowners,* an analysis of a New Jersey suburb, attacks the myth of the suburb, which holds, according to Goldthorpe's summary, that suburbanites are anxious, bored, cultureless social climbers without communal roots. Gans discovers, remarks Goldthorpe, that "most of the charges made against suburbia simply do not stick. . . . There are no good reasons for believing that the residents of Levittown are any more conformist, insecure, anxious, status-conscious, bored, etc. than otherwise comparable Americans who are not suburbanites.''

On the other hand, Richard Kluger comments, ''Mr. Gans is so zealous a champion of the Levittown brand of suburb that one suggests . . . he has overstated its virtues and understated its drawbacks to about the same extent that suburbia's critics have overstated the drawbacks and understated the virtues.'' Kluger argues that Gans ignores the fact that ''Levittown lacked a number of features that would seem to be universally desirable in a community, . . . [such as] 'visual interest, cultural diversity, entertainment, esthetic pleasure, variety, and emotional stimulation.'''

Gans continues to contradict common social beliefs in *Popular Culture and High Culture,* in which, remarks Richard Todd in *Atlantic,* he argues that ''American culture includes several levels of taste—Gans calls them 'taste cultures'—and that any one of them is as good as any other, because each serves the needs and wants of a particular public.'' Gans also opposes policies which would urge that these ''taste cultures'' be improved and, as Christopher Lehmann-Haupt summarizes, ''instead encourages 'more cultural pluralism' by means of 'subcultural programming' (or cultural programs that would appeal to groups that are now excluded by mass culture, like the poor, the old, and the ethnic).'' Lehmann-Haupt agrees with the latter position, noting that ''anyone who has ever tried to force 'high art' down the throats of intelligent people whose tastes run to what Professor Gans identifies as the 'lower-middle' cultural range will recognize all too well what he means when he argues that 'high art' isn't necessarily 'better' and that exposure to such levels of culture doesn't automatically 'improve.'''

In writing *Deciding What's News,* a study of news organizations, Gans returned to a participant-observer role, spending a few months each at NBC, CBS, *Newsweek,* and *Time.* Deirdre Carmody, who sees the study as suffering a few serious limitations, considers Gans ''at his best when he analyzes the relationship between the journalists he has observed and their sources,'' for Gans found that journalists contact a limited number of people who are mostly like themselves. Frank Mankiewicz makes a similar point and concludes: ''*Deciding What's News* is a good study. It tells us that our colleagues who set much of the nation's agenda have solid, bourgeois, mildly reformist views, respect authority, want to be liked and probably see the unfamiliar as vaguely threatening. The result is that tomorrow's news is going to look very much like today's, even if the world does not.''

BIOGRAPHICAL/CRITICAL SOURCES: Book Week, May 14, 1967; *Christian Science Monitor,* June 8, 1967; *Nation,* July 17, 1967; *New Statesman,* November 10, 1967; *Times Literary Supplement,* December 7, 1967, December 5, 1980; *New York Review of Books,* May 23, 1968; *Partisan Review,* summer, 1968; *Commonweal,* April 25, 1969; *New York Times,* December 2, 1974, July 13, 1979; *New Yorker,* March 10, 1975; *Atlantic,* March, 1975; *Washington Post Book World,* April 28, 1979; *Chicago Tribune,* May 6, 1979; *New York Times Book Review,* June 24, 1979.

*   *   *

GARBER, Eugene K. 1932-

PERSONAL: Born October 5, 1932, in Birmingham, Ala.; son of Eugene Keenan (in real estate) and Margaret (Reid) Garber; married Barbara Morrow, November 27, 1954; children: Anne Morrow, William Keenan. *Education:* Tulane University, B.A., 1954; University of Iowa, M.A., Ph.D. *Politics:* Democrat.

Religion: Episcopalian. *Home:* 49A Dove St., Albany, N.Y. 12210. *Office:* Department of English, State University of New York, Albany, N.Y. 12222.

CAREER: University of Iowa, Iowa City, instructor, 1958-61, assistant professor of English, 1962-68; Western Washington State College (now Western Washington University), Bellingham, associate professor, 1968-74, professor of English, 1974-77; State University of New York at Albany, professor of English and director of writing, 1977—. Member of the national advisory panel of the National Writing Project, 1979-81. *Military service:* U.S. Navy, 1954-57; became lieutenant. *Member:* Modern Language Association of America, National Council of Teachers of English, Phi Beta Kappa, Eta Sigma Phi. *Awards, honors:* National Endowment for the Arts creative writing fellow, 1979-80; Associated Writing Programs award for short fiction, 1981, for *Metaphysical Tales.*

WRITINGS: (With Walter Blair and John Gerber) *Better Reading I,* Scott, Foresman, 1963; (with Blair and Gerber) *Better Reading II,* Scott, Foresman, 1966; (with John Crossett) *Liberal and Conservative,* Scott, Foresman, 1968; *Metaphysical Tales,* preface by Joyce Carol Oates, University of Missouri Press, 1981. Contributor of short stories to journals.

WORK IN PROGRESS: A second collection of tales; a novel.

SIDELIGHTS: Eugene Garber told *CA:* ''Readers may be interested in my passionate and perhaps curious fascination with the tale (as opposed to the realistic short story) and especially with tales that make metaphysical probes. The crux of the matter is, I suppose, that I am more interested in myth than history, more arrested by archetype than individual—an aesthetic position fraught with terrible dangers.'' *Avocational interests:* Fly-fishing.

*   *   *

GARDNER, Ralph D(avid) 1923-

PERSONAL: Born April 16, 1923, in New York, N.Y.; son of Benjamin and Myra (Berman) Gardner; married Nellie Jaglom, April 9, 1952; children: Ralph D., Jr., John Jaglom, Peter Jaglom, James Jaglom. *Education:* New York University, certificate in journalism, 1942; Colorado State College (now University), certificate in military administration, 1943. *Home:* 135 Central Park W., New York, N.Y. 10023. *Office:* Ralph D. Gardner Advertising, 745 Fifth Ave., New York, N.Y. 10022.

CAREER: New York Times, New York City, staff member and foreign correspondent, 1942-55, started International Edition, Paris, France, 1949, bureau manager for Germany and Austria, Frankfurt, Germany, 1950; Ralph D. Gardner Advertising, New York City, president, 1955—. Mary C. Richardson Lecturer, State University of New York at Geneseo, 1974; faculty member, Georgetown University Writers Conference, 1976, 1980; Hess Research Fellow, University of Minnesota, 1979; visiting lecturer at colleges and universities, including University of Wyoming. Host and producer, ''Ralph Gardner's Bookshelf'' (literary interview and talk show), WVNJ-NY. Member of board, Fresh Air Council, 1964-66. *Military service:* U.S. Army, 1943-46; served as newswriter in Europe. *Member:* Overseas Press Club of America, Bibliographical Society of America, National Book Critics Circle, P.E.N., Manuscript Society, Children's Literature Association, Society of Silurians, Brandeis University Bibliophiles (honorary member), Syracuse University Library Associates (honorary member), Friends of Princeton University Library, Frankfurt Press Club, Grolier Club, Alpha Epsilon Pi. *Awards, honors:* Horatio Alger Society of America Prize for Literature, 1964, for *Horatio Alger; or, The American Hero Era,* and 1972, for *Road to Success: The Bibliography of the Works of Horatio Alger;* special citation scroll, Horatio Alger Awards Committee, 1978.

WRITINGS: Horatio Alger; or, The American Hero Era, Wayside Press, 1964, revised edition published as *Road to Success: The Bibliography of the Works of Horatio Alger,* 1971; (author of introduction) Horatio Alger, *Silas Snobden's Office Boy,* Doubleday, 1973; (author of introduction) Horatio Alger, *Cast upon the Breakers,* Doubleday, 1974; (contributor) Madeleine B. Stern, editor, *Publishers for Mass Entertainment in the Nineteenth Century,* G. K. Hall, 1980; (editor and author of introduction) *A Fancy of Hers,* Van Nostrand, 1981; (editor and author of introduction) *The Disagreeable Woman,* Van Nostrand, 1981.

Author of column, "Ralph Gardner's Celebrity Collector," in *Acquire.* Contributor of articles and reviews on military subjects, foreign travel, and nineteenth-century American literature and bibliography to newspapers and magazines, including *New York Times Book Review, Saturday Evening Post, Book Critic,* and *Chicago Daily News.*

SIDELIGHTS: Ralph D. Gardner says he wrote the biography of Horatio Alger to set the record straight on a writer who "had meager literary quality, but was, nevertheless, America's most influential and all-time best-selling author." *Road to Success* is the most complete bibliography of Horatio Alger's novels, articles, short stories, and poems. Gardner speaks French and German.

AVOCATIONAL INTERESTS: Foreign travel, collecting nineteenth-century American first editions and manuscripts.

*   *   *

GARDONS, S. S.
   See SNODGRASS, W(illiam) D(e Witt)

*   *   *

GARFIELD, Brian (Wynne) 1939-
   (Bennett Garland, Alex Hawk, Frank O'Brian,
   Jonas Ward, Brian Wynne, Frank Wynne)

PERSONAL: Born January 26, 1939, in New York, N.Y.; son of George (a lawyer and architect) and Frances (O'Brien) Garfield; married Virve Sein, August 16, 1962 (divorced December, 1965); married Shan Willson (an actress), July 16, 1969. *Education:* University of Arizona, B.A., 1959, M.A., 1963. *Home address:* P.O. Box 376, Alpine, N.J. 07620. *Agent:* Henry Morrison, Inc., 58 West Tenth St., New York, N.Y. 10011.

CAREER: "The Casuals" (dance band), Tucson, Ariz., musician, 1958-59; "The Palisades" (dance band), on tour, musician, 1959-60; University of Arizona, Tucson, instructor in English, 1962-63; Shan Productions Co., New York, N.Y., president, 1974—. Free-lance writer. *Military service:* U.S. Army and Army Reserve, 1957-65. *Member:* Mystery Writers of America (member of board of directors, 1974-78), Writers Guild of America, Authors Guild, Western Writers of America (vice-president, 1966-67), Tucson Federation of Musicians. *Awards, honors:* Edgar Award, Mystery Writers of America, 1976, for *Hopscotch;* American Book Award nomination, 1980, for *Wild Times.*

WRITINGS: (Editor) *War Whoop and Battle Cry,* Scholastic Book Services, 1968; *The Thousand Mile War: World War II in Alaska and the Aleutians* (history), Doubleday, 1969; *The*

Villiers Touch (novel), Delacorte, 1970; (with Donald E. Westlake) *Gangway!* (novel), M. Evans, 1973; (under pseudonym Frank O'Brian) *Act of Piracy* (novel), Dell, 1975; (editor and author of introduction) *I, Witness: True Personal Encounters with Crime by Members of the Mystery Writers of America,* Times Books, 1978; (author of introduction) Charles King, *The Colonel's Daughter,* Gregg, 1978; *Wild Times* (novel), Simon & Schuster, 1978; *Complete Guide to Western Films,* Dutton, 1980.

Mystery and suspense fiction: (Under pseudonym Frank O'Brian) *The Rimfire Murders,* Boureguy, 1962; *The Last Bridge,* McKay, 1966; *The Hit,* Macmillan, 1970; *What of Terry Conniston?,* World Publishing, 1971; *Deep Cover,* Delacorte, 1971; *Relentless* (Detective Book Club selection), World Publishing, 1972; *Death Wish* (Detective Book Club selection), McKay, 1972; *The Three-persons Hunt* (Detective Book Club selection), M. Evans, 1974; *Kolchak's Gold,* McKay, 1974; *The Romanov Succession* (Detective Book Club selection), M. Evans, 1974; *Hopscotch* (Detective Book Club selection), M. Evans, 1975; *Death Sentence* (Detective Book Club selection), M. Evans, 1975; *Recoil* (Book-of-the-Month Club selection; Detective Book Club selection), Morrow, 1977; *The Paladin,* Simon & Schuster, 1980.

Westerns: *Range Justice,* Avalon, 1960; *The Arizonans,* Avalon, 1961; *The Lawbringers,* Macmillan, 1962; *Trail Drive,* Avalon, 1962; *Vultures in the Sun,* Macmillan, 1963; *Apache Canyon,* Avalon, 1963; *The Vanquished,* Doubleday, 1964; (under pseudonym Frank O'Brian) *Bugle and Spur,* Ballantine, 1966, published under name Brian Garfield, 1975; (under pseudonym Jonas Ward) *Buchanan's Gun,* Fawcett, 1968; (under house pseudonym Alex Hawk) *Savage Guns,* Paperback Library, 1968; *Valley of the Shadow,* Doubleday, 1970; *Sliphammer,* Dell, 1970; *Sweeny's Honor,* Dell, 1971 (published in England under pseudonym Frank Wynne, Coronet, 1974;) *Gun Down,* Dell, 1971, published as *The Last Hard Men,* Fawcett, 1976; *Tripwire,* McKay, 1973.

Westerns; under pseudonym Frank Wynne: *Massacre Basin,* Avalon, 1961; *The Big Snow,* Avalon, 1962; *Arizona Rider,* Avalon, 1962; *Dragoon Pass,* Avalon, 1963; *Rio Concho,* Avalon, 1964; *Rails West,* Avalon, 1964; *Lynch Law Canyon,* Ace, 1965; *The Wolf Pack,* Ace, 1966; *Call Me Hazard,* Ace, 1966; *The Lusty Breed,* Avalon, 1966; *Letter to a Gunfighter,* Monarch, 1966.

Westerns; under pseudonym Bennett Garland: *Seven Brave Men,* Monarch, 1962, published under name Brian Garfield, Lancer, 1969; (with Theodore V. Olson under joint pseudonym Bennett Garland) *High Storm,* Monarch, 1963, published under name Brian Garfield, Lancer, 1970; *The Last Outlaw,* Monarch, 1964, published under name Brian Garfield, Lancer, 1970; *Rio Chama,* Universal Publishing, 1968.

Westerns; under pseudonym Brian Wynne; all published by Ace: *Mr. Sixgun,* 1964; *The Night It Rained Bullets,* 1965; *The Bravos,* 1966; *The Proud Riders,* 1967; *A Badge for a Badman,* 1967; *Brand of the Gun,* 1968; *Gundown,* 1969; *Big Country, Big Men,* 1969.

Work appears in anthologies, including: *Rivers to Cross,* edited by William R. Cox, Dodd, 1966; *They Opened the West,* edited by Thomas W. Blackburn, Doubleday, 1967; *Iron Men and Silver Stars,* edited by Donald Hamilton, Fawcett, 1967; *Best Detective Stories of 1978,* edited by Edward D. Hoch, Dutton, 1978; and *Best Detective Stories of 1979,* edited by Hoch, Dutton, 1979.

Also author of books under undisclosed pseudonyms. Author of column, *Roundup* (magazine), 1965-66. Contributor of short stories and articles to *Ellery Queen's Mystery Magazine, Alfred Hitchcock's Mystery Magazine, Saturday Review, Bookswest, Writer's Digest, New York Times Book Review,* and other publications.

SIDELIGHTS: Brian Garfield told *CA:* "Since about 1970 I've written one or two books each year and these have been categorized mainly (and clumsily) as 'suspense fiction'—that awkward catch-all description by which we attempt to define novels that are not quite mysteries, not quite adventure tales and not quite romances.

"Most of my stories have been set against backgrounds of menace on the international scene . . . or backgrounds of survival and pursuit in the contemporary or historical American Southwest. . . . In that respect, *Death Wish,* an urban crime story, was a departure from my usual subjects. My strongest literary proclivities vector toward history, both for its own sake and for its applicability to current questions; many of my novels have been Westerns and quite a few of my more recent books deal with historical subjects—the Russian Civil War, for example (in *Kolchak's Gold*).

"The 'thriller', or suspense entertainment, provides unlimited space in which the writer can explore history and character; there are no formulas or conventions. And, ever since I reacted with revulsion to the Hollywood film version of my novel *Death Wish,* I've found great stimulus in the challenge of writing novels like *Hopscotch* [and] *Recoil . . .* in each of which there is little or no overt violence. (Suspense is a matter of menace, not violence). The judges who conferred the 1976 [Mystery Writers of America] Edgar Award on *Hopscotch* as best novel of the year confirmed that they did so partly because the book delivered suspense without brutality. Recently, in interviews and broadcast appearances and before audiences at . . . colleges, I've been soapboxing for the consideration of alternatives to overt violence in dramatic entertainments. The writer's cleverness can only be stimulated if he refuses himself the use of lazy contrivances of mayhem and gore. We've seen much recent evidence that the depiction of violence in entertainments has terrible effects on the attitudes and behavior of audiences. The writer of such entertainments may not feel an obligation toward the fringe crazies in his audience; but I do feel he must acknowledge his responsibility toward those who may become their victims. To an extent, popular novels and movies help to set moral standards and the writer, whether he likes it or not, serves *in loco parentis* to his audience. I've made no call for censorship of any kind; but I've tried to encourage writers of popular entertainments to explore alternatives to the use of constant violence as a melodramatic crutch.

"As a novelist I see myself as the first audience for my work; I try (usually without success) to write a book that I would love to read if someone else had written it; and I feel compelled never to write the same book twice—life isn't long enough to be wasted on pointless repetitions. Once past my apprenticeship in Westerns and potboilers, I resolved not only to avoid repetition of specifics but also to avoid, as much as possible, writing the same *kind* of book twice. When a writer behaves in such a fashion he makes it difficult for the world to identify him; we tend to be most comfortable with that which we can pigeonhole, and a writer who refuses to be type-cast does so at his commercial peril. Nevertheless, it's the only way I can justify my toil in the profession."

Garfield's books have sold over twelve million copies and have been translated into seventeen languages.

MEDIA ADAPTATIONS: Garfield's novel *Death Wish* was filmed by Paramount in 1974, *Gun Down* was filmed by Twen-

tieth Century-Fox Corp. as "The Last Hard Men" in 1976, *Relentless* was filmed for television by Columbia Broadcasting System in 1977, *Wild Times* was presented as a television mini-series in 1980, and *Hopscotch* was filmed in 1980.

BIOGRAPHICAL/CRITICAL SOURCES: New York Times Book Review, February 8, 1970, May 14, 1972, June 8, 1975, March 18, 1979, February 8, 1981; *America,* May 2, 1970; *Book World,* November 8, 1970, April 14, 1974, February 1, 1981; *New Republic,* October 16, 1971; Dean R. Koontz, *Writing Popular Fiction,* Writer's Digest, 1972; *New York Times,* July 14, 1972; *Observer,* October 15, 1972; *Books & Bookmen,* July, 1973, April, 1979; *Times Literary Supplement,* September 6, 1974; *Contemporary Review,* October, 1974; *Publishers Weekly,* September 29, 1975; *Spectator,* April 17, 1976; *Bookswest,* October, 1977; *Chicago Tribune Book World,* April 8, 1979; *Washington Post Book World,* March 2, 1980.

*   *   *

GARLAND, Bennett
See GARFIELD, Brian (Wynne)

*   *   *

GARRISON, Winfred Ernest   1874-1969

PERSONAL: Born October 1, 1874, in St. Louis, Mo.; died February, 1969; son of James Harvey and Judith E. (Garrett) Garrison; married Annie Gaines Dye, October 1, 1900; children: Frederic Garrett, Elisabeth Jean Crawford. *Education:* Eureka College, A.B., 1892; Yale University, A.B., 1894; University of Chicago, B.D., Ph.D., 1897. *Religion:* Disciples of Christ. *Office:* Department of Philosophy, University of Houston, Houston, Tex. 77004.

CAREER: University of Chicago, Chicago, Ill., assistant in history and instructor in Disciples' Divinity House, 1897-98; Butler College (now University), Indianapolis, Ind., professor of Hebrew and church history, 1898-1900, president, 1904-06; assistant editor, *Christian-Evangelist,* 1900-04; New Mexico Normal University (now New Mexico Highlands University), Las Vegas, president, 1907-08; New Mexico A. & M. College (now New Mexico State University), Las Cruces, president, 1908-13; Claremont School for Boys (now Claremont Men's College), Claremont, Calif., founder and headmaster, 1913-20; University of Chicago, associate professor, 1921-35, professor of church history, 1935-43, professor emeritus, 1943-69; University of Houston, Houston, Tex., professor of philosophy and religion, 1951-64, M. D. Anderson Professor, 1957-64, professor emeritus of philosophy, 1964-69, chairman of department, 1955-59. Peter Ainslie Lecturer at Rhodes University, South Africa, 1961. Sculptor in bronze, with works in colleges, churches, and other institutions. Delegate to New Mexico Constitutional Convention, 1910; director of National Groups Division, Illinois War Finance Committee, 1943-45.

MEMBER: American Society of Church History (president, 1928), Southwestern Philosophical Society, Phi Beta Kappa, Phi Kappa Phi, Beta Theta Pi; Cliff Dwellers (president, 1944-46) and Quadrangle Club (both Chicago). *Awards, honors:* Litt.D. from Eureka College, 1935; LL.D. from Bethany College, 1950; D.D. from Butler University, 1955, and Yale University, 1964; the Winfred Ernest Garrison Lectureship was established at Yale University Divinity School in 1959.

WRITINGS: Alexander Campbell's Theology, Christian Publishing Co., 1900; *Catholicism and the American Mind,* Willett, 1928; *Affirmative Religion,* Harper, 1928.

Religion Follows the Frontier, Harper, 1931; *The March of Faith: The Story of Religion in America since 1865,* Harper, 1933, reprinted, Greenwood Press, 1971; *Intolerance,* Round Table, 1934; (compiler with Thomas Clark) *One Hundred Poems of Peace,* Willett, 1934, reprinted, Books for Libraries Press, 1971; (compiler with Clark) *One Hundred Poems of Immortality,* Willett, 1935; (editor) *Faith of the Free,* Willett, 1940; *An American Religious Movement,* Christian Board of Publications, 1945; *The Disciples of Christ,* Christian Board of Publication, 1948, revised edition, Bethany Press, 1958.

A Protestant Manifesto, Abingdon-Cokesbury, 1952; *Christian Unity and the Disciples of Christ,* Bethany Press, 1955; *The Quest and Character of a United Church,* Abingdon, 1957; (with Paul Hutchinson) *Twenty Centuries of Christianity,* Harcourt, 1959; *Heritage and Destiny,* Bethany Press, 1961; *Variations on a Theme: "God Saw That It Was Good,"* Bethany Press, 1964; *Thy Sea So Great* (verse), Bethany Press, 1965; (compiler) *Singing Sages: An Anthology of Poems as Aids to Reflection,* Bethany Press, 1966; *Invitation to Philosophy,* edited by C. Dwight Dorough, University of Houston, 1970.

Contributor of chapters to fourteen other books. Also contributor to *Encyclopaedia Britannica, Dictionary of American Biography,* and other encyclopedias. Literary editor, *Christian Century,* 1923-55.

BIOGRAPHICAL/CRITICAL SOURCES: Christian Century, December 30, 1964, February 26, 1969; *New York Times,* February 8, 1969.†

*   *   *

GARVE, Andrew
See WINTERTON, Paul

*   *   *

GARVIN, Charles D.   1929-

PERSONAL: Born June 17, 1929, in Chicago, Ill.; son of Hyman and Etta (Raphaelson) Garvin; married Janet Tuft (a social worker), January 27, 1957; children: David, Amy, Anthony. *Education:* Attended Wright Junior College, 1946-48; University of Chicago, A.M., 1951, Ph.D., 1968. *Religion:* Jewish. *Home:* 2925 Park Ridge, Ann Arbor, Mich. 48103. *Office:* Department of Social Work, Frieze Building, University of Michigan, Ann Arbor, Mich. 48109.

CAREER: Henry Booth House, Chicago, Ill., director of social service, 1954-56; Jewish Community Centers of Chicago, Chicago, program director, 1957-64; University of Michigan, Ann Arbor, professor of social work, 1965—. Consultant to Chapin Hall for Children (Chicago), and to Family Group Homes of Ann Arbor. *Military service:* U.S. Army, 1952-54. *Member:* National Association of Social Workers, American Sociological Association, American Orthopsychiatric Association, Academy of Certified Social Workers, Council on Social Work Education, British Association of Social Workers.

WRITINGS: (With Harvey Bertcher) *Staff Development in Social Welfare Agencies,* Campus Publishers, 1968; (contributor) *Social Work Practice,* Columbia University Press, 1969; (contributor) Fred M. Cox and others, editors, *Strategies of Community Organization,* Peacock Press, 1970, 3rd edition, 1979; (contributor) Paul Glasser, Rosemary Sarri and Robert Vinter, editors, *Individual Change through Small Groups,* Free Press, 1974; (editor and contributor) *Incentives and Disincentives to Participation in the Work Incentive Program,* School of Social Work, University of Michigan, 1974; (editor with William Reid and Audrey Smith) *The Work Incentive Experience,* Al-

lanheld, Osmun, 1978; *Contemporary Group Work,* Prentice-Hall, 1981; *Social Work Treatment Text,* Prentice-Hall, 1982. Also author of social science training materials for Michigan Department of Social Services, 1967-69. Contributor to *Social Work Encyclopedia.* Also contributor of articles to *Social Welfare Forum, Journal of Jewish Communal Service, Social Service Review, Public Welfare* and other professional publications.

WORK IN PROGRESS: Research on child abuse and family stress.

*   *   *

GAUNT, William   1900-1980

PERSONAL: Born July 5, 1900, in Hull, Yorkshire, England; died May 24, 1980; son of William (a designer and lithographer) and Harriet (Spence) Gaunt; married Mary Catherine Connolly, April 5, 1935 (died, 1980). *Education:* Worcester College, Oxford, B.A. (with honors), 1922, M.A., 1926. *Home:* 35B Lansdowne Rd., London W. 11, England. *Agent:* A. P. Watt & Son, 26-28 Bedford Row, London WC1R 4HL, England.

CAREER: Art historian, painter, and critic. Studio Publications, London, England, editorial director, 1926-39; Odhams Press Ltd., London, editor of documentary war-time publications, 1939-45; *Evening Standard,* London, art critic, 1945-47; museums correspondent to *Times,* London, 1963-71. *Military service:* British Army, Durham Light Infantry, 1918. *Member:* International Association of Art Critics, Association of Art Historians.

WRITINGS: English Rural Life in the Eighteenth Century, Connoisseur, 1925; (editor) *The Etchings of Frank Brangwyn* (catalog), Studio, 1926; *Rome, Past and Present,* edited by C. Geoffrey Holme, Studio, 1926; (author of introduction) *Etchings of Today,* edited by Holme, Studio, 1929; (self-illustrated) *London Promenade,* Harcourt, 1930; *Touring the Ancient World with a Camera,* photographs by Holme, W. E. Rudge, 1932; *Bandits in a Landscape: A Study of Romantic Painting from Caravaggio to Delacroix,* Studio Publications, 1937; (editor with Frank A. Mercer) *Poster Progress,* Studio Publications, 1939.

The Pre-Raphaelite Tragedy, Harcourt, 1942, revised edition, J. Cape, 1975, published as *The Pre-Raphaelite Dream,* Schocken, 1966; (with Frederic Gordon Roe) *Etty and the Nude: The Art and Life of William Etty,* F. Lewis, 1943; *The Aesthetic Adventure,* Harcourt, 1945, revised edition, J. Cape, 1975; *British Painting from Hogarth's Day to Ours,* Avalon and Central Institute of Art and Design, 1945, revised edition, 1946; (author of introduction and notes) *Hogarth, 1697-1764,* Faber, 1947; (editor and author of introduction) *Selected Writings of William Morris,* Falcon Press, 1948; *The March of the Moderns,* J. Cape, 1949, reprinted, Hyperion Press, 1979; *Victorian Olympus* (a study of the works of Lord Leighton and other artists of late Victorian times), Oxford University Press, 1952, revised edition, J. Cape, 1975; (editor and author of introduction) *Renoir,* Phaidon, 1952, 3rd edition, 1976; *Chelsea,* Batsford, 1954, revised edition bound with *Kensington,* 1975; (editor) Henri Schmidt-Degener, *The Teach Yourself History of Painting,* English Universities Press, 1954; (author of introduction and notes on illustrations) *London in Colour: A Collection of Colour Photographs by James Riddell,* Batsford, 1955, Studio Publications, 1956; *Arrows of Desire: A Study of William Blake and His Romantic World,* Fernhill, 1956, reprinted, Folcroft, 1978; (editor) Schmidt-Degener, *The Dutch School,* Roy, 1956; (editor) Schmidt-Degener, *The*

Flemish School, Roy, 1956; *The Lady in the Castle*, W. H. Allen, 1956; *Teach Yourself to Study Sculpture*, English Universities Press, 1957; (contributor) *Eugene Boudin, 1824-1898* (catalog of exhibition held in London, November-December, 1958), Marlborough Fine Art Ltd., 1958; *Kensington*, Batsford, 1958, revised edition bound with *Chelsea*, 1975; *The Observer's Book of Painting and Graphic Art*, Warne, 1958; (author of introduction and notes on illustrations) *Old Inns of England in Colour: A Collection of Colour Photographs*, Batsford, 1958.

(Author of introduction) Benvenuto Cellini, *The Life of Benvenuto Cellini*, translated by Anne Macdonell, Dent, 1960; *London*, Viking, 1961; (compiler) *Everyman's Dictionary of Pictorial Art*, two volumes, Dutton, 1962; (editor and author of introduction) Giorgio Vasari, *The Lives of the Painters, Sculptors and Architects* (revision of translation by A. B. Hinds), four volumes, Dutton, 1963; *A Concise History of English Painting*, Praeger, 1964, reprinted, Thames & Hudson, 1978; *The Observer's Book of Modern Art: From Impressionism to the Present Day*, Warne, 1964; *Oxford*, Batsford, 1965, Hastings House, 1966; *The Observer's Book of Sculpture*, Warne, 1966; *A Companion to Painting*, Thames & Hudson, 1967; *Dante Gabriel Rossetti*, Purnell, 1967; *A Guide to the Understanding of Painting*, Abrams, 1968; *Flemish Cities—Bruges, Ghent, Antwerp, Brussels: Their History and Art*, Putnam, 1969; *Impressionism: A Visual History*, Praeger, 1970; *The Impressionists*, Thames & Hudson, 1970; *Great Century of British Painting: From Hogarth to Turner*, Phaidon, 1971, 2nd edition, 1978; *Turner*, Phaidon, 1971; (with M.D.E. Clayton-Stamm) *William De Morgan*, New York Graphic Society, 1971; *The Restless Century: Painting in Britain, 1800-1900*, Phaidon, 1972, 2nd edition, 1978; *The Surrealists*, Putnam, 1972; (author of introduction) *Painters of Fantasy: From Hieronymus Bosch to Salvador Dali*, Phaidon, 1974; *Marine Painting: An Historical Survey*, Secker & Warburg, 1975, Viking, 1976; (editor) *Stubbs*, Phaidon, 1977; *Treasury of Painting through Five Centuries*, Phaidon, 1978; *The World of William Hogarth*, J. Cape, 1978. Contributor to *Times Literary Supplement* and to art magazines.

SIDELIGHTS: William Gaunt told *CA* that he "has a general appetite for books in English and French. My writing about art is more concerned with making its history intelligible to the wider public than with specialization." His travels included countries of Europe and the Mediterranean, and longer journeys ranging from Lapland to Yucatan. He was an "assiduous explorer of the vast chaos of London, especially along the river."

BIOGRAPHICAL/CRITICAL SOURCES: Times Literary Supplement, April 23, 1970; *Best Sellers*, November 1, 1970; *Time*, December 14, 1970.

OBITUARIES: London Times, May 26, 1980.†

*   *   *

GEIS, Gilbert 1925-

PERSONAL: Born January 10, 1925, in Brooklyn, N.Y.; son of Joseph (a salesman) and Ida (List) Geis; married Ruth Steinberg (a teacher), April 4, 1948; married second wife, Robley Huston (a psychologist), December 17, 1966; children: (first marriage) Ellen, Jean. *Education:* Colgate University, A.B., 1947; Brigham Young University, M.S., 1949; University of Wisconsin, Ph.D., 1953. *Politics:* Democrat. *Home:* 31461 Alta Loma Dr., South Laguna, Calif. 92677. *Agent:* Paul R. Reynolds, Inc., 12 East 41st St., New York, N.Y. 10017. *Office:* Program in Social Ecology, University of California, Irvine, Calif. 92717.

CAREER: University of Oklahoma, Norman, instructor, 1952-55, assistant professor, 1955-57; California State College (now University), Los Angeles, assistant professor 1957-60, associate professor, 1960-63, professor of sociology, 1963-72; University of California, Irvine, professor of social ecology, 1972—, acting director of program in social ecology, 1974-75. Member of training faculty, National Council of Juvenile Court Judges, 1963-65; visiting professor, State University of New York at Albany, 1969-70, University of California, Irvine, 1971-72, and University of Sydney, 1979; member of faculty National College of the State Judiciary, 1972-74; visiting fellow, Institute of Criminology and Wolfson College, 1976-77. Member of Narcotics Addiction and Drug Abuse Review Committee, National Institute of Mental Health, 1970-74, and Criminal Justice Advisory Board, 1976-77. Principal investigator, research director, or project director for a number of studies and projects, including Evaluation of Aftercare Program of Narcotic Addict Rehabilitation Act, Public Compensation for Victims of Crime, and Explorations in Deterrence and Criminal Justice. Consultant, President's Committee on Narcotic and Drug Abuse, 1963-64, Jobs Corps, Office of Economic Opportunity, 1964-66, President's Commission on Law Enforcement and Administration of Justice, 1966, Joint Commission on Correctional Manpower and Training, 1967-69, National Commission on Causes and Prevention of Violence, 1968-70. *Military service:* U.S. Navy, 1942-45.

MEMBER: British Institute of Securities Laws (honorary member, 1977—), National Council on Crime and Delinquency, American Society of Criminology (president, 1975-76), American Sociological Association, Pacific Sociological Society, Association for Criminal Justice Research, Society for the Study of Social Problems. *Awards, honors:* Fulbright fellowship, Oslo, Norway, 1951-52; liberal arts fellowship in law and sociology, Harvard Law School, 1964-65; senior scholar grant for Australia, Council for International Exchange of Scholars, 1979.

WRITINGS: (With Herbert A. Bloch) *Man, Crime, and Society: The Forms of Criminal Behavior*, Random House, 1962, 2nd edition, 1970; (with Houshang Poorkaj and Ronald Honnard) *The Role of the Institutional Teacher*, Youth Studies Center, University of Southern California, 1964; (with William E. Bittle) *The Longest Way Home: Chief Alfred C. Sam's Back-to-Africa Movement*, Wayne State University Press, 1964; *Juvenile Gangs*, President's Committee on Juvenile Delinquency and Youth Crime, 1965; *The East Los Angeles Halfway House for Narcotic Addicts*, Institute for the Study of Crime and Delinquency, 1966; (editor and contributor) *White-Collar Criminal: The Offender in Business and the Professions*, Atherton, 1968, revised edition (with Robert F. Meier) published as *White-Collar Crime: Offenses in Business, Politics, and the Professions*, Free Press, 1977; *Crime and Delinquency in a Changing Society*, Joint Commission on Correctional Manpower and Training, 1969; (with others) *Addicts in the Classroom: The Impact of an Experimental Narcotics Educational Program on Junior High School Pupils*, Economic and Youth Opportunities Agency, 1969; (with Bruce Bullington and John G. Munns) *Ex-Addicts as Streetworkers: The Boyle Heights Narcotics Prevention Project*, Economic and Youth Opportunities Agency, 1969.

(Author of introduction) Jerome Michael and Mortimer J. Adler, *Crime Law and Social Science*, Patterson Smith, 1971; (with Leonard W. Seagren) *A Model for Criminal Justice System Planning and Control: School Survey*, Digital Resources Corp., 1971; (with Virginia Munns and Seymour Pollack) *The NARA Title-II Program in Los Angeles: September 1969-July 1971*, Public Systems Research Institute, University of Southern California, 1971; (author of introduction) Eugene Smith,

Criminal Law in the United States, Brown Reprints, 1971; *Not the Law's Business?: An Examination of Homosexuality, Abortion, Prostitution, Narcotics and Gambling in the United States*, U.S. Government Printing Office, 1972, published as *One Eyed Justice: An Examination of Homosexuality, Abortion, Prostitution, Narcotics and Gambling in the U.S.*, Drake, 1974; (with Herbert Edelhertz) *Public Compensation to Victims of Crime*, Praeger, 1974; (with Vincent H. Myers and Bill D. Miller) *The Value of Drug Diversion in the County of Orange, California*, Drug Program Coordination Office, 1974; (with C. Ronald Huff and Ross F. Conner) *Planning Correctional Reform: An Assessment of the American Bar Association's BASICS Program*, American Bar Association, 1975; (author of foreword) Daniel Katkin, Drew Hyman, and John Kramer, *Juvenile Delinquency and the Juvenile Justice System*, Duxbury, 1976; (author of introduction) Stephen Schafer, editor, *Readings in Contemporary Criminology*, Reston, 1976; (author of foreword) Bruce Bullington, *Heroin Use in the Barrio*, Heath, 1977; (editor with Duncan Chappell and with wife, Robley Geis, author of introduction, and contributor) *Forcible Rape: The Crime, the Victim, and the Offender*, Columbia University Press, 1977; (editor with Ezra Stotland) *White-Collar Crime: Theory and Research*, Sage Publications, 1980.

Contributor: Herman Mannheim, editor, *Pioneers in Criminology*, Stevens, 1960, 2nd edition, Patterson Smith, 1972; Joseph C. Roucek, editor, *The Sociology of Crime*, Philosophical Library, 1960; Lee O. Garber, editor, *The Yearbook of School Law*, Interstate, 1962; Carol Spencer, editor, *Experiments in Culture Expansion*, Institute for the Study of Crime and Delinquency, 1964; John R. Mulcahy, Jr., editor, *Perspectives on Narcotic Addiction*, Massachusetts Health Research Institute, 1964; Charles W. Tenney, Jr., editor, *Current Readings in the Juvenile Court*, National Council of Juvenile Court Judges, 1964.

Robert Fulton, editor, *Death and Identity*, Wiley, 1965; Robert Schasre and Jo Wallach, editors, *Readings in Delinquency and Treatment*, Volume VII, Youth Studies Center, University of Southern California, 1965; *Report of the Conference on Undergraduate Education for the Social Services*, California State Colleges, 1965; *The Offender: An Answer to the Correction of Manpower Crisis*, Institute for the Study of Crime and Delinquency, 1966; Walter C. Reckless, *The Crime Problem*, 4th edition, Appleton-Century-Crofts, 1967; John H. Gagnon and William Simon, editors, *Sexual Deviance*, Harper, 1967; Orman W. Ketcham and Monrad G. Paulsen, *Cases and Materials Relating to Juvenile Courts*, Foundation Press, 1967; Ronald Steel, editor, *New Light on Juvenile Delinquency*, H. W. Wilson, 1967; S. B. Sells, editor, *Rehabilitating the Narcotic Addict*, Vocational Rehabilitation Administration, 1967; *Crime and Its Impact: An Assessment*, President's Commission on Law Enforcement and Administration of Justice, 1967; Marshall B. Clinard and Richard Quinney, editors, *Criminal Behavior Systems: A Typology*, Holt, 1967; Roma K. McNickle, editor, *Research in Correctional Rehabilitation*, Joint Commission on Correctional Manpower and Training, 1967; Earl Rubington and Martin S. Weinberg, editors, *Deviance: The Interactionist Perspective*, Macmillan, 1968; Mhyra S. Minnis and Walter J. Cartwright, editors, *Sociological Perspectives: Readings in Deviant Behavior and Social Problems*, W. C. Brown, 1968; Simon Dinitz and Reckless, editors, *Critical Issues in the Study of Crime: A Book of Readings*, Little, Brown, 1968; Shalom Endleman, editor, *Violence in the Streets*, Quadrangle Books, 1968; Joan Grant, editor, *The Arts, Youth, and Social Change*, National Council on Crime and Delinquency, 1968; McNickle, editor, *Offenders as a Correctional Manpower Resource*, Joint Commission on Correctional Man-

power and Training, 1968; August Meier and Elliott Rudwick, editors, *The Making of Black America*, Volume II, Atheneum, 1969; Dinitz, Russell R. Dynes, and Alfred C. Clarke, editors, *Deviance: Studies in the Process of Stigmatization and Societal Reaction*, Oxford University Press, 1969; *Crimes of Violence*, Volume XIII, National Commission on the Causes and Prevention of Violence, 1969.

Richard D. Knudten, editor, *Crime, Criminology, and Contemporary Society*, Dorsey, 1970; Knudten and Stephen Schafer, editors, *Juvenile Delinquency: A Reader*, Random House, 1970; Bruce J. Cohen, editor, *Crime in America: Perspectives on Criminal and Delinquent Behavior*, F. E. Peacock, 1970, 2nd edition, 1977; Robert M. Carter and Leslie T. Wilkins, editors, *Probation and Parole: Selected Readings*, Wiley, 1970; Carl A. Bersani, editor, *Crime and Delinquency: A Reader*, Macmillan, 1970; David E. Smith, editor, *The New Social Drug: Cultural, Medical, and Legal Perspectives on Marijuana*, Prentice-Hall, 1970; Robert C. Twombly, editor, *Blacks in White America since 1865*, McKay, 1971; Ronald M. Holmes, editor, *Sexual Behavior: Prostitution, Homosexuality, Swinging*, McCutchan, 1971; Cecil E. Johnson and Malcolm M. MacDonald, *Society and the Environment: Contemporary Readings*, Van Nostrand, 1971; Stanley E. Grupp, editor, *Marihuana*, C. E. Merrill, 1971; Carol Whalen, editor, *Survey of Social Ecology*, Volume I, Simon & Schuster, 1971; James M. Henslin, editor, *Studies in the Sociology of Sex*, Appleton-Century-Crofts, 1971; Clifton D. Bryant, editor, *The Social Dimensions of Work*, Prentice-Hall, 1972; Charles E. Reasons and Jack L. Kuykendall, editors, *Race, Crime, and Justice*, Goodyear Publishing, 1972; Karl K. Taylor and Fred W. Soady, Jr., editors, *Violence: An Element of American Life*, Holbrook, 1972; Peter Worsley, editor, *Problems Of Modern Society*, Penguin, 1972; Robert M. Carter, Daniel Glaser, and Leslie T. Wilkins, editors, *Correctional Institutions*, Lippincott, 1972; John P. Reed and Fuad Baali, editors, *Faces of Delinquency*, Prentice-Hall, 1972; Leon Brill and Louis Lieberman, editors, *Major Modalities in the Treatment of Drug Abuse*, Behavioral Publications, 1972.

Reckless, *American Criminology: New Directions*, Appleton-Century-Crofts, 1973; Benjamin Frank, editor, *Contemporary Corrections: A Concept in Search of Content*, Reston, 1973; Donald R. McQueen, editor, *Understanding Sociology through Research*, Addison-Wesley, 1973; Ralph Nader and Mark J. Green, editors, *Corporate Power in America*, Grossman, 1973; Nader, editor, *The Consumer and Corporate Accountability*, Harcourt, 1973; Herbert H. Liebowitz, William O. Johnson, and Adele Pilsk, editors, *Vocational Rehabilitation of the Drug Abuser*, Volume III, U.S. Department of Health, Education, and Welfare, 1973; Edward Eldefonso, editor, *Issues in Corrections: A Book of Readings*, Glencoe, 1974; James McIntosh, editor, *Perspectives on Marginality: Understanding Deviance*, Allyn & Bacon, 1974; Martin R. Haskell and Lewis Yablonsky, *Criminology: Crime and Criminality*, Rand McNally, 1974; Haskell and Yablonsky, *Crime and Delinquency*, 2nd edition, Rand McNally, 1974; Jackwell Sussman, editor, *Crime and Justice, 1971-1972*, AMS Press, 1974; Alan Casty and Donald J. Tighe, editors, *Staircase to Writing and Reading: A Rhetoric and Anthology*, 2nd edition, Prentice-Hall, 1974; Charles E. Reason, editor, *The Criminologist: Crime and the Criminal*, Goodyear Publishing, 1974; Gerald F. Uelmen and Victor G. Haddox, editors, *Drug Abuse and the Law: Cases, Texts and Materials*, West Publishing, 1974; Abraham S. Blumberg, editor, *Current Perspectives on Criminal Behavior: Original Essays on Criminology*, Knopf, 1974; Israel Drapkin and Emilio Viano, editors, *Victimology*, Heath, 1974; Terence P. Thornberry and Edward Sagarin, editors, *Images of Crime: Offenders and Victims*, Praeger, 1974; Glaser, editor, *Handbook of Criminology*, Rand McNally, 1974; Leonard Gross, editor, *Sexual Behavior: Current Issues*, Spectrum, 1974; Charles Winick, editor, *Sociological Aspects of Drug Dependence*, CRC Press, 1974.

Dinitz, Dynes, and Clarke, editors, *Deviance: Studies in Definition, Management, and Treatment*, 2nd edition, Oxford University Press, 1975; Karsten J. Stuhl and Paula Rothenberg Stuhl, editors, *Ethics in Perspective: A Reader*, Random House, 1975; Sanford H. Kadish and Monrad G. Paulsen, *Criminal Law and Its Processes: Cases and Materials*, 3rd edition, Little, Brown, 1975; Drapkin and Viano, editors, *Victimology: A New Focus*, Volume V, Heath, 1975; Duncan Chappell and John Monahan, editors, *Violence and Criminal Justice*, Heath, 1975; Viano, editor, *Criminal Justice Research*, Heath, 1975; David A. Jones and Catherine M. Jones, editors, *The Sociology of Correctional Management*, Mss Information, 1976; James A. Inciardi and Harvey A. Siegal, editors, *Crime: Emerging Issues*, Praeger, 1976; Burt Galaway, Joe Hudson, and C. David Hollister, editors, *Community Corrections: A Reader*, C.C Thomas, 1976; Don G. Dutton, editor, *Social Psychology: A Book of Readings*, Centre for Continuing Education, University of British Columbia, 1976; Thomas Lickona, editor, *Moral Development and Behavior: Theory, Research, and Social Issues*, Holt, 1976; Rudolph J. Gerber, editor, *Contemporary Issues in Criminal Justice: Some Problems and Suggested Reforms*, Kennikat, 1976; Viano, editor, *Victims and Society*, Visage Press, 1976; William F. McDonald, editor, *Criminal Justice and the Victim*, Sage Publications, 1976; Jack Goldsmith and Sharon S. Goldsmith, editors, *Crimes and the Elderly*, Heath, 1976; Daniel M. Carrier, editor, *Perspectives in Criminology*, Kendall/Hunt, 1977; *Readings in Social Psychology 77/78*, Dushkin, 1977; Hudson and Galaway, editors, *Restitution in Criminal Justice: A Critical Assessment of Sanctions*, Heath, 1977; Peter Wickman, editor, *Readings in Social Problems: Contemporary Perspectives*, Harper, 1977; Marlene A. Young Rifai, editor, *Justice and Older Americans*, Heath, 1977.

M. David Ermann and Richard J. Lundman, editors, *Corporate and Governmental Deviance: Problems of Organizational Behavior in Contemporary Society*, Oxford University Press, 1978; Peter Wickman and Phillip Whitten, editors, *Readings in Criminology*, Heath, 1978; Norman Johnston and Leonard D. Savitz, editors, *Justice and Corrections*, Wiley, 1978; Peter W. Lewis and Kenneth D. Peoples, editors, *The Supreme Court and the Criminal Process: Cases and Comments*, Saunders, 1978; George G. Killinger and Paul F. Cromwell, Jr., *Introduction to Corrections: Selected Readings*, West Publishing, 1978; Henslin and Sagarin, editors, *The Sociology of Sex: An Introductory Reader*, revised edition, Schocken, 1978; Ermann and Lundman, editors, *Corporate and Governmental Deviance: Problems of Organizational Behavior in Contemporary Society*, Oxford University Press, 1978; John R. Snortum and Ilana Hader, *Criminal Justice: Allies and Adversaries*, Pacific Publishing, 1978; Winick, editor, *Deviance and Mass Media*, Sage Publications, 1978; Lewis and Peoples, editors, *Constitutional Rights of the Accused: Cases and Comments*, Saunders, 1979; Sagarin, editor, *Criminology, New Concerns: Essays in Honor of Hans W. Mattick*, Sage Publications, 1979; Hans Toch, editor, *Crime and Criminal Justice*, Holt, 1979; Marvin E. Wolfgang, editor, *Prisons: Present and Possible*, Heath, 1979.

Contributor to annals and proceedings and to *Encyclopedia Americana*. Contributor of articles to journals, including *Education*, *Prison Journal*, *Criminologica*, *Community Mental Health Journal*, *Vital Issues*, and *Journal of Drug Issues*. As-

sociate editor, *Pacific Sociological Review*, 1967-70, *Victimology: An International Journal*, 1976—, and *Criminology Review Yearbook*, 1979—; assistant editor, *Criminology*, 1974-79; consulting editor, *Journal of Research in Crime and Delinquency*, 1976—, and *The Company Lawyer*, 1979. Member of editorial board, *Journal of Criminal Justice*, 1972—, *Addictive Diseases*, 1974—, *Sage Annual Reviews of Alcohol and Drug Abuse*, 1977-80, *Law and Human Behavior*, 1977—, and *Journal of Criminal Justice Contemporary Issues*, 1979—.

*   *   *

GETLEIN, Frank 1921-

PERSONAL: Surname is pronounced *Get*-line; born March 6, 1921, in Ansonia, Conn.; son of Frank (an economic supervisor) and Katherine (Sheehan) Getlein; married Dorothy Woollen (a writer), May 26, 1943; children: Christine, Steve, Mary, Bill, Karl. *Education:* College of the Holy Cross, B.S., 1942; Catholic University of America, M.A., 1947. *Politics:* Independent. *Religion:* Catholic.

CAREER: English instructor at St. Ambrose College, Davenport, Iowa, and lecturer at Fairfield University, Fairfield, Conn., 1947-51; Otto and Eloise Spaeth Foundation, Milwaukee, Wis., executive secretary, 1951-53; affiliated with Barkin & Herman (public relations firm), Milwaukee, 1953-56; *Milwaukee Journal*, Milwaukee, art critic, 1956-59; *New Republic*, Washington, D.C., art critic, beginning 1957; *Washington Evening Star*, Washington, D.C., art critic, beginning 1961, editorial writer, beginning 1963. Lecturer at Marquette University, 1964-65, and at other colleges, universities, and art groups. Member of Fulbright Committee, 1961-64; chairman of advisory committee of Department of Agricultural Graduate School Lectures on Design, 1964-65. *Military service:* U.S. Army, 1942-45; served in Italy. *Member:* National Press Club.

WRITINGS: (With wife, Dorothy Getlein) *Christianity in Art*, Bruce, 1959.

(Author of commentaries) H. W. Janson and Dora Jane Janson, *Standard Treasury of World's Great Paintings*, Abrams, 1960; *Abraham Rattner*, American Federation of Arts, Ford Foundation, 1960; (with Dorothy Getlein) *Christianity in Modern Art*, Bruce, 1961; *A Modern Demonology: Being Social Criticism in the Form of a Scholarly Dissertation, Complete with Sociological Findings Collected by the Latest Approved Methods, on the Need for a Rehabilitation of the Ancient Science of Demonology, the Discovery and Destruction of Demons Inhabiting Various Individuals and Groups in the Social Order, the Body Politic and the Economic Milieu*, C. N. Potter, 1961; (with Harold C. Gardiner) *Movies, Morals and Art*, Sheed, 1961; (with Dorothy Getlein and Anne Peck) *Wings of an Eagle: The Story of Michelangelo*, Hawthorn, 1963; (with Dorothy Getlein) *The Bite of the Print: Satire and Irony in Woodcuts, Engravings, Etchings, Lithographs and Serigraphs*, C. N. Potter, 1964; (with Dorothy Getlein) *Georges Rouault's Miserere*, Bruce, 1964; *The Trouble with Catholics*, Helicon, 1964.

(Author of text) *Jack Levine*, Abrams, 1966; (author of introductory text) *Walter Kuhn, 1877-1949* (catalogue of exhibition), Kennedy Galleries, 1967; (compiler and author of commentaries) *Ten French Impressionists: A Portfolio of Color Prints*, Abrams, 1967; (author of introduction) *Herman Maril: A Monograph*, Baltimore Museum of Art, 1967; *Art Treasures of the World: One Hundred Most Precious Masterpieces of All Time in Full Color*, C. N. Potter, 1968; (author of introductory text) *The Silver Sculpture of Earl Krentzen* (catalogue of exhibition), Kennedy Galleries, 1968; (author of introductory text) *Peter Blume* (catalogue of exhibition), Kennedy Galleries, 1968; (author of introductory text) *Ben Shahn* (catalogue of exhibition), Kennedy Galleries, 1968; *The Politics of Paranoia* (collection of articles), Funk, 1969; *Harry Jackson: Monograph—Catalogue*, Kennedy Galleries, 1969; (author of introductory text) *Colleen Browning* (catalogue of exhibition), Kennedy Galleries, 1969; (author of introductory text) *Abraham Rattner* (catalogue of exhibition), Kennedy Galleries, 1969.

(Author of introduction) Bruce Harris and Seena Harris, editors, *The Complete Etchings of Rembrandt*, Bounty Books, 1970; *Milton Hebald*, Viking, 1971; *Playing Soldier: A Diatribe*, Holt, 1971; (with others) *The Lure of the Great West*, Country Beautiful Corp., 1973; *Chaim Gross*, Abrams, 1974; *Mary Cassatt: Paintings and Prints*, Abbeville Press, 1980; *Twenty-five Impressionist Masterpieces*, Abrams, 1981.

Washington correspondent for *Art in America* and *Burlington*. Contributor to *Country Beautiful, Horizon, Commonweal, Jubilee, Sign, American Scholar, Time*, and other publications.

SIDELIGHTS: Although most of Frank Getlein's books are concerned with the art world, he is also the author of articles and books dealing with political topics and social criticism. In one such book, *The Trouble with Catholics,* Jean Holzhauer of *Commonweal* writes that she believes Getlein "presents his best effort to date, having simultaneously hit his stride and found his length. . . . Doubtless some of his readers will be more annoyed than amused by all this levity. Even our more advanced thinkers take their religious views very solemnly indeed. . . . Hypersensitive readers, therefore, should keep in mind that Mr. Getlein is himself a Catholic and has suffered with the rest of us the ludicrous defects and pretensions that he here so urbanely attacks."

Another of Getlein's political ventures is described by R. B. Wathen of *Best Sellers*. He writes that *Playing Soldier: A Diatribe* "is rough all the way around on any of us who have had anything to do with a war or a uniform. . . . But Mr. Getlein tells us in his title that he is writing a diatribe, and a diatribe is not supposed to be playing patsy with the subject. And if the squares are bothered, Mr. Getlein will win the affection of the growing segment of our society that is tired of war and the men who make war. Indeed *Playing Soldier* is a book of our time, catching the anti-military spirit that is running through our land. . . . [It is] both captivating and amusing. Mr. Getlein is far more devastating when he is making fun of the military than when he is engaging in a frontal attack with merely his prejudice as a weapon."

BIOGRAPHICAL/CRITICAL SOURCES: Commonweal, November 20, 1964; *Best Sellers,* August 15, 1971; *Washington Post,* December 21, 1980.†

*   *   *

GIBB, Hamilton (Alexander Rosskeen) 1895-1971

PERSONAL: Born January 2, 1895, in Alexandria, Egypt; died October 22, 1971, in England; son of Alexander Crawford and Jane (Gardner) Gibb; married Helen Jessie Stark, July 12, 1922; children: John Alexander Crawford, Dorothy Sim (Mrs. Edward J. Greenslade). *Education:* University of Edinburgh, M.A., 1919; University of London, M.A., 1922; Oxford University, M.A. 1937.

CAREER: University of London, London, England, lecturer in School of Oriental Studies, 1921-30, professor of Arabic, 1930-37; Oxford University, Oxford, England, Laudian Professor of Arabic, 1937-55; Harvard University, Cambridge, Mass., James Richard Jewett Professor of Arabic, 1955-64, professor

emeritus, 1964-71. Haskell Lecturer, University of Chicago, 1945. Chairman, Permanent Committee on Geographical Names (England), 1947-55. *Military service:* Royal Field Artillery, 1914-19; became captain. *Member:* British Academy (fellow), Fuad I Academy of Arabic Languages (founding member), American Academy of Arts and Sciences (honorary member), American Philosophical Society, Institut d'Egypte (associate member), Danish Academy (fellow). *Awards, honors:* Knight Bachelor (Great Britain), 1954; Chevalier, Legion d'Honneur (France); Commander of Order of Orange-Nassau (the Netherlands). Honorary doctorate, University of Algiers, 1943; LL.D., University of Edinburgh, 1952; A.M., 1955, and D.Litt., 1963, both from Harvard University.

WRITINGS: The Arab Conquests in Central Asia, Royal Asiatic Society, 1923, reprinted, AMS Press, 1970; *Arabic Literature: An Introduction,* Oxford University Press, 1926, 2nd revised edition, 1974; (editor) *Whither Islam?: A Survey of Modern Movements in the Moslem World,* Golancz, 1932, reprinted, AMS Press, 1973; *Modern Trends in Islam,* University of Chicago Press, 1947, reprinted, Octagon Books, 1972; *Mohammedanism: An Historical Survey,* Oxford University Press, 1949, 2nd revised edition, 1962; (with Harold Bowen) *Islamic Society and the West,* Oxford University Press, 1950, 2nd edition, 1957; (editor with J. H. Kramers) *Shorter Encyclopedia of Islam,* Cornell University Press, 1953; *An Interpretation of Islamic History,* Orientalia Publishers (Lahore), 1957; (contributor) Walter Ze'ev Laqueur, editor, *The Middle East in Transition: Studies in Contemporary History,* Routledge & Kegan Paul, 1958, reprinted, Books for Libraries Press, 1971; (editor with others) *Encyclopedia of Islam,* Volume I, Humanities, 1960; *Studies on the Civilization of Islam,* edited by Stanford J. Shaw and William R. Polk, Routledge & Kegan Paul, 1962; *The Life of Saladin: From the Works of Imad ad-Din and Baha' ad-Din,* Clarendon Press, 1973; *Saladin: Studies in Islamic History,* Arab Institute for Research and Publication, 1974.

Translator: Ibn Batuta, *Travels in Asia and Africa, 1325-1354,* Routledge & Kegan Paul, 1929, reprinted, A. M. Kelley, 1969; Ibn al-Qualanisi, *The Damascus Chronicle of the Crusades,* Luzac, 1932, reprinted, 1967; C. Defremery and B. R. Sanguinetti, editors, *The Travels of Ibn Battuta,* Cambridge University Press, for the Hakluyt Society, 1971. Also translator of *Turkestan at Time of Mongolian Invasion,* Luzac.

OBITUARIES: Washington Post, October 30, 1971.†

*   *   *

GILBERT, Sara (Dulaney) 1943-

PERSONAL: Born October 5, 1943, in Washington, D.C.; daughter of Ben Bane (a journalist) and Jean (an editor; maiden name, Brownell) Dulaney; married Ian R. Gilbert (a lawyer), August 31, 1963; children: Sean Dulaney. *Education:* Attended Brown University, 1961-63; Barnard College, B.A. (with honors), 1966. *Residence:* New York, N.Y. *Agent:* Marilyn Marlowe, Curtis Brown Ltd., 575 Madison Ave., New York, N.Y. 10022.

CAREER: Author. Staff aide, "ABC News" for American Broadcasting Corp., Washington, D.C., 1963-64; editor, writer, and researcher, *Cowles Encyclopedia,* New York, N.Y., 1966-68. *Member:* American Society of Journalists and Authors, Authors Guild. *Awards, honors:* Mr. Freedom Award from Religious Liberty Association, 1972.

WRITINGS: Three Years to Grow: Guidance for Your Child's First Three Years, Parents' Magazine Press, 1972; *What's a*

Father For?, Parents' Magazine Press, 1975; *Fat Free*, Macmillan, 1975; *You Are What You Eat*, Macmillan, 1977; *Feeling Good: A Book about You and Your Body*, Four Winds, 1978; *Ready, Set, Go*, Four Winds, 1979; *Trouble at Home*, Lothrop, 1981; *How to Live with a Single Parent*, Lothrop, 1982; *Talk It Out: What Happens in Therapy*, Lothrop, 1982; *By Yourself: A Kid's Book on Coping*, Lothrop, 1982.

Also author of filmstrips, newsletters, speeches, and pamphlets. Contributor to *Baby Care*, *Ms.*, *Good Housekeeping*, *Travel*, *Campfire Girl*, *Negro Digest*, *Liberty*, *Metrolines*, *National Businesswoman* and other periodicals.

WORK IN PROGRESS: Research for publication on several topics including adolescence, family life, personal development, and physical and psychological health.

SIDELIGHTS: Sara Gilbert told *CA*: "I find that the major interest in my life is the 'why' of people, and that the qualities I value most in other people, no matter what their superficial characteristics, are the ability to and interest in exploring and understanding the motivations for behavior and the underlying emotional forces in themselves and in others. In a sense, it is through my writing that I've become aware of this interest, and in my writing, past, present and future, I pursue it."

AVOCATIONAL INTERESTS: Travel.

* * *

GILLELAN, G(eorge) Howard 1917-
(Captain Jim Purdy)

PERSONAL: Born January 25, 1917, in Baltimore, Md.; son of Joshua Thomas and Mary E. (MacDowell) Gillelan; married Ann Marie Stinson, 1945; children: Joshua T., Ann Eden, Ian MacDowell, Mary Elizabeth, Harriet Stinson. *Education:* Attended Johns Hopkins University, 1936-38, and Cornell University, summers, 1938, 1939. *Residence:* Royal Oak, Md. 21662.

CAREER: Hilbert Optical Co., Baltimore, Md., vice-president, 1945-56; *Archery World* (formerly *Bowhunting*), Baltimore, co-editor, 1956-60, roving editor, 1960-64; *Outdoor Life*, New York, N.Y., archery editor, 1959-77, Washington, D.C., editor, 1964-69; *News American*, Baltimore, regional correspondent, 1976-78; outdoor editor (under pseudonym Captain Jim Purdy), *Talbot Banner*, 1978-80. *Military service:* U.S. Army, one year; became second lieutenant. *Member:* Outdoor Writers' Association of America, National Press Club, National Field Archery Association, Izaak Walton League of America, Mason-Dixon Outdoor Writers' Association, Maryland Sportsmen's Luncheon Club (vice-president, 1959-60), St. Andrews Society of the Eastern Shore (president, 1974-75).

WRITINGS: (With William Stump) *Archery Handbook*, Trend Books, 1958; *Young Sportsman's Guide to Archery*, Thomas Nelson, 1962; *Young Sportsman's Guide to Photography*, Thomas Nelson, 1964; *Archery for Boys and Girls*, Follett, 1965; *ABC's of the Bow and Arrow*, Stackpole, 1967; *Complete Book of Archery*, Stackpole, 1971; *Archery at Home*, McKay, 1980. Contributor to *Hunter's Encyclopedia*, 1966. Contributor to *Washington Post*, *Baltimore*, *Maryland*, and to archery publications.

SIDELIGHTS: G. Howard Gillelan is experienced in travel, hunting, fishing, camping, and photography. He has visited Europe, Canada, Cuba, the Caribbean, Mexico, and Alaska.

GILLMER, Thomas C(harles) 1911-
(Tom Gillmer)

PERSONAL: Born July 17, 1911, in Warren, Ohio; son of Derr Oscar (an investment broker) and Hazel (Voit) Gillmer; married Anna May Derge, June 5, 1937; children: Christina (Mrs. Richard Erdmann), Charles Voit. *Education:* Attended Western Reserve University (now Case Western Reserve University), 1930-31; U.S. Naval Academy, B.S., 1935; Johns Hopkins University, graduate study, 1947. *Politics:* Independent. *Religion:* Protestant. *Home:* 1 Shipwright Harbor, Annapolis, Md. 21401. *Office:* Thomas Gillmer Naval Architects, 300 State St., Annapolis, Md. 21403.

CAREER: U.S. Navy, career officer, 1935-45, retiring as lieutenant commander; U.S. Naval Academy, Annapolis, Md., assistant professor, 1946-49, associate professor, 1949-63, professor of marine engineering, 1963-67, director of Model Towing Basin, 1955-67, director of Ship Hydrodynamics Laboratory, 1956-67, chairman of department of naval architecture, 1961-67, chairman of department of naval engineering, 1964-67; Thomas Gillmer Naval Architects, Annapolis, Md., owner and director, 1967—. Editor, Weems System of Navigation, 1939; member of board of directors, Historic Annapolis, Inc., 1968-72; member of panel of experts for fishing craft, Food and Agriculture Organization of United Nations; former delegate to International and American Tank Towing Conferences. During military service, served in Atlantic and Mediterranean theaters on cruisers and destroyers. *Member:* Society of Naval Architects and Marine Engineers, American Society of Naval Engineers, Boating Industry Association (member of yacht engineering committee), American Association of University Professors, Annapolis Yacht Club, Club de Voile (Villefranche, France; honorary life member).

WRITINGS: (With Erich Neitch) *Simplified Theory of Flight*, Van Nostrand, 1941; (with Neitch) *Clouds, Weather, and Flight*, Van Nostrand, 1945; (with J. Adair) *Naval Construction and Damage Control*, U.S. Naval Institute, 1950; *Fundamentals of Construction and Stability of Naval Ships*, U.S. Naval Institute, 1956, revised edition, 1959; *Modern Ship Design*, U.S. Naval Institute, 1970, revised edition, 1975; *Working Watercraft: A Survey of Surviving Local Boats of America and Europe* (with own photographs), International Marine Publishing Co., 1972; *Ships of the American Revolution*, Admiralty, 1973; *Brigs and Sloops of the American Navy*, Admiralty, 1973; *Gillmer's Cruising Designs: Sail and Power*, McKay, 1980. Contributor, occasionally under name Tom Gillmer, to boating magazines, including *American Neptune*, *Yachting*, *Rudder*, and *Sail*.

WORK IN PROGRESS: *The Ancient Boat*, a history of oceanic craft; *The Chesapeake Sloop*, a history of an expired American sailing craft, for Chesapeake Bay Maritime Museum; *Introduction to Naval Architecture*, with Bruce Johnson.

SIDELIGHTS: Thomas C. Gillmer writes to *CA*: "My career has developed in the field of theoretical ship design with the specialty of hydrodynamic research in ship model testing tanks. During the quarter-century of my activity I was privileged to teach my specialty to many students who were in a position to become influential in naval engineering. This is a great privilege to any man, whatever his profession. In my retirement I have found more work than many men who are employed. I know that the vital thing is useful productivity."

Gillmer has concerned himself mainly with the design of small vessels and yachts. Among his designs are the ketch *Apogee*, the first fiberglass boat to circumnavigate the world, and *Pride of Baltimore*, a schooner built in the tradition of the old line of Baltimore Clippers.

GILLMER, Tom
See GILLMER, Thomas C(harles)

*   *   *

GILMAN, George G.
See HARKNETT, Terry

*   *   *

GLASER, William A(rnold)   1925-

PERSONAL: Born December 4, 1925, in New York, N.Y.; son of Lewis and Evelyn (Wiener) Glaser; married Mary Todd Daniels, 1958; married Gilberte Van sintejan, 1981; children: James Todd, Andrew Rollins, Gillian Elisabeth. *Education:* New York University, B.A., 1948; Harvard University, M.A., 1949, Ph.D., 1952. *Home:* 56 Morningside Dr., New York, N.Y. 10027. *Office:* Center for the Social Sciences, Columbia University, 420 West 118th St., New York, N.Y. 10027.

CAREER: Michigan State University of Agriculture and Applied Science (now Michigan State University), East Lansing, instructor, 1952-55, assistant professor of social science, 1955-56; Columbia University, New York, N.Y., research assistant, 1956-58, senior research associate in sociology and political science, 1958—. Consultant to various health and rehabilitation organizations. *Military service:* U.S. Army Medical Corps, 1944-46; became staff sergeant. *Member:* International Political Science Association, International Sociological Association, International Studies Association, Policy Studies Organization, American Sociological Association, American Political Science Association.

WRITINGS: Three Papers on the Integrated Bar, Bureau of Applied Social Research, Columbia University 1960; *Public Opinion and Congressional Elections,* Free Press of Glencoe, 1962; *The Government of Associations,* Bedminster, 1966; *An International Survey of Sheltered Employment,* National Labour Market Board (Stockholm), 1966; *Pretrial Discovery and the Adversary System,* Russell Sage, 1968; *Social Settings and Medical Organization,* Atherton, 1970; *Paying the Doctor,* Johns Hopkins Press, 1970; *The Brain Drain,* Pergamon, 1978; *Health Insurance Bargaining,* Gardner Press, 1978.

WORK IN PROGRESS: Federalism in Canada and Germany: Lessons for the United States; Paying the Hospital: Foreign Lessons for the United States.

*   *   *

GOLDBARTH, Albert   1948-

PERSONAL: Born January 31, 1948, in Chicago, Ill.; son of Irving (a life underwriter) and Fannie (a secretary; maiden name, Seligman) Goldbarth. *Education:* University of Illinois, Chicago Circle, B.A., 1969; University of Iowa, M.F.A., 1971; University of Utah, further graduate study, 1973-74. *Religion:* "Non-observant Jew." *Office:* Department of English, University of Texas, Austin, Tex. 78712.

CAREER: Elgin Community College, Elgin, Ill., instructor in English, 1971-72; University of Utah, Salt Lake City, instructor in creative writing, 1973-74; Cornell University, Ithaca, N.Y., visiting assistant professor of creative writing, 1974-76; Syracuse University, Syracuse, N.Y., writer-in-residence, 1976; University of Texas at Austin, professor of creative writing, 1977—. Member of advisory panel to literature committee on National Endowment for the Arts. *Awards, honors:* Theodore

Roethke Prize from *Poetry Northwest,* 1972; first prize in poetry from *Northwest Review,* 1973; annual poetry award from *Ark River Review,* 1973, 1975; creative writing fellowship from National Endowment for the Arts, 1974, 1979; creative writing award from Illinois Arts Council, 1974; National Book Award in Poetry nomination, 1975; Texas Institute of Letters Poetry Award, 1980.

WRITINGS—Books of poems: *Under Cover,* Best Cellar Press, 1973; *Coprolites,* New Rivers Press, 1974; *Opticks: A Poem in Seven Sections,* Seven Woods Press, 1974; *Jan. 31,* Doubleday, 1974; *Keeping,* Ithaca House, 1975; *Comings Back: A Sequence of Poems,* Doubleday, 1976; *A Year of Happy,* North Carolina Review Press, 1976; *Curve: Overlapping Narratives,* New Rivers Press, 1976; *Different Fleshes,* Hobart & William Smith Colleges Press, 1979; (editor) *Every Pleasure: The "Seneca Review" Long Poem Anthology,* Seneca Review Press, 1979; *Ink Blood Semen,* Bits Press, 1980; *Smugglers Handbook,* Chowder Chapbooks, 1980; *Eurekas,* St. Luke's Press, 1981; *Who Gathered and Whispered behind Me,* L'Epervier Press, 1981.

WORK IN PROGRESS: Several long poems.

SIDELIGHTS: Unlike some post-World War II poets, Albert Goldbarth delights in verbosity. Goldbarth "is a compulsive poet, a born show-off and gabber who has, fortunately, the gift of gab," writes Peter Schjeldahl in the *New York Times Book Review.* Schjeldahl also credits Goldbarth with "a sprawling, crazy-quilt erudition." A *Choice* reviewer presents a similar opinion, saying that "it is obvious that [Goldbarth] loves language, and his poetry, or prose-poetry, is witty and learned."

In a *Midwest Quarterly* review of *Opticks,* Dave Smith comments that Goldbarth's "poetic blitz overwhelms us with fresh images, thought, imaginative scope, but also . . . buries us with the unfinished detritus of a mind (and an ego) whose accelerator is frozen." Smith continues: "I must, however, applaud Goldbarth's energy, his willingness to challenge big tasks, his refusal to accomplish the easy. Even the worst of his poems demonstrate his marvelous equipment, his intelligence, his straining for vision."

Michael Heffernan, also writing in the *Midwest Quarterly,* states that *Coprolites* "reveals Goldbarth's uncanny gifts at their most playful. . . . Goldbarth has extended his range perhaps broader than any other poet of the mid-seventies and, in so doing, has taught himself more tricks than most mature poets could use by the end of the century."

BIOGRAPHICAL/CRITICAL SOURCES: Midwest Quarterly, winter, 1975; *West Coast Poetry Review,* winter/spring, 1975; *Choice,* June, 1975, June, 1977, September, 1980; *Contemporary Literary Criticism,* Volume V, Gale, 1976; *New York Times Book Review,* November 21, 1976; *American Poetry Review,* March/April, 1980.

*   *   *

GOLDSTEIN, Rhoda L.
See BLUMBERG, Rhoda L(ois Goldstein)

*   *   *

GOLEMBIEWSKI, Robert T(homas)   1932-

PERSONAL: Born July 2, 1932, in Trenton, N.J.; son of John (an engineer) and Pauline (Pelka) Golembiewski; married Margaret H. Hughes, September 1, 1956; children: Alice, Hope, Geoffrey. *Education:* Princeton University, A.B., 1954; Johns

Hopkins University, additional study, 1954-55; Yale University, M.A., 1956, Ph.D., 1958. *Politics:* Independent. *Religion:* Roman Catholic. *Home:* 145 Highland Dr., Athens, Ga. 30601. *Office:* 211 Baldwin Hall, University of Georgia, Athens, Ga. 30602.

CAREER: Princeton University, Princeton, N.J., instructor in political science, 1958-60; University of Illinois at Urbana-Champaign, Urbana, assistant professor, 1960-64; University of Georgia, Athens, associate professor, 1964-66, professor, 1966-67, research professor of political science and management, 1967—. Lecturer, City College (now City College of the City University of New York), fall, 1959. Visiting lecturer, Yale University, 1963-64. Sensitivity trainer. Consultant for various business and government agencies.

MEMBER: International Association of Applied Social Scientists (regional coordinator, 1977—), American Political Science Association, American Society for Public Administration, Academy of Management, Southern Political Science Association (vice-president, 1974-76; president, 1976-78), Southern Management Association.

AWARDS, HONORS: Ford summer fellowship in mathematical applications to business, 1961-62; summer faculty fellowship from University of Illinois, 1962-64; grant from Lilly Foundation for one year's research, 1962-64; James A. Hamilton Hospital Administrator's Book Award, 1967, for *Men, Management, and Morality;* award from American Society for Training and Development, 1968; named Social Scientist of the Year by Eastern Academy of Management, 1972; Douglas McGregor Memorial Award, 1976, for "excellence in applications of behavioral sciences"; Chester I. Barnard Memorial Award, 1980.

WRITINGS: The Small Group: An Analysis of Research Concepts and Operations, University of Chicago Press, 1962; *Behavior and Organization,* Rand McNally, 1962; *Men, Management, and Morality: Toward a New Organizational Ethic,* McGraw-Hill, 1965; (editor with Frank Gibson and Geoffrey Y. Cornog) *Public Administration: Readings in Institutions, Processes and Behavior,* Rand McNally, 1966, 3rd edition, 1976; (co-editor) *Managerial Behavior and Organization Demands: Management As a Linking of Levels of Interaction,* Rand McNally, 1967, 2nd edition, 1978; *Organizing Men and Power,* Rand McNally, 1967; *Perspectives on Public Management,* F. E. Peacock, 1967, 2nd edition, 1976; (editor with Jack Rabin) *Public Budgeting and Finance: Readings in Theory and Practice,* F. E. Peacock, 1968, 2nd edition, 1975; (with William Welsh and William Crotty) *A Methodological Primer for Political Scientists,* Rand McNally, 1969.

(Editor with Michael Cohen) *People in Public Service: A Reader in Public Personnel Administration,* F. E. Peacock, 1970, 2nd edition, 1976; (editor with Arthur Blumberg) *Sensitivity Training and the Laboratory Approach,* F. E. Peacock, 1970, 3rd edition, 1977; (editor with Charles Bullock and Harrell Rodgers) *The New Politics: Polarization or Utopia?,* McGraw, 1970; *Renewing Organizations: The Laboratory Approach to Planned Change for Individuals and Groups,* F. E. Peacock, 1972, 2nd edition published in two volumes as *Approaches to Planned Change,* Dekker, 1978; (editor with Malcolm Moore and Rabin) *Dilemmas of Political Participation: Issues for Thought and Simulations for Action,* Prentice-Hall, 1973; (editor with Michael White) *Cases in Public Management,* Rand McNally, 1973, 3rd edition, 1979.

(With others) *The Policy Vacuum: Toward a More Professional Political Science,* Lexington Books, 1975; (with Arthur Blumberg) *Learning and Change in Groups: Processes, Problems,*

and Applications of Laboratory Education, Penguin, 1976; *The Small Group in Political Science: The Last Two Decades of Development,* University of Georgia Press, 1978; *Public Administration As a Developing Discipline,* two volumes, Dekker, 1977; (editor with William B. Eddy) *Organization Development in Public Administration,* two volumes, Dekker, 1978; (co-author) *Toward the Responsive Organization: The Theory and Practice of Survey/Feedback,* Brighton, 1979.

Editor of Rand McNally series on organizations. Contributor of chapters to numerous books. Also contributor to handbooks and encyclopedias, and contributor to many professional journals, including *Public Administration Review, American Political Science Review, Personnel, Administrative Science Quarterly,* and *Journal of Applied Behavioral Science.* Member of editorial board of *Journal of Politics,* 1968-75, *Academy of Management Journal,* 1972-75, *Academy of Management Review,* 1975—, *Administration and Society,* 1976—, *Southern Review of Public Administration,* 1977—, *Journal of Health and Human Resources Administration,* 1978—, and *Journal of Management,* 1978—.

AVOCATIONAL INTERESTS: Hunting, fishing, and elementary gunsmithing.

BIOGRAPHICAL/CRITICAL SOURCES: Trenton Times, April 10, 1962.

*   *   *

GOODERS, John 1937-

PERSONAL: Born January 10, 1937, in London, England; son of Edwin and Winifred Alice Gooders; children: Timothy, Sophie. *Education:* Southampton University, B.Sc.; Institute of Education, London, post-graduate certificate of education and diploma in philosophy of education. *Home:* 52 Colmer Rd., London S.W.16, England.

CAREER: Teacher at a comprehensive school in London, England, 1959-65, and at Avery Mill Teachers College, London, 1967-69; International Publishing Co., London, editor of "Birds of the World" series, 1969-71; founded monthly magazine, *World of Birds,* 1971, leaving shortly thereafter to write scripts and commentaries for "Survival," a television wildlife series; full-time writer. *Member:* British Ornithologists Union, British Trust for Ornithology. *Awards, honors:* Churchill fellowship, 1970, for study and travel in North Africa.

WRITINGS: Where to Watch Birds, Deutsch, 1967, revised edition, 1974; (editor) *Birds of the World,* nine volumes, International Publishing, 1969-71; (with Jeremy Brock) *Where to Watch Birds in Britain and Europe,* Deutsch, 1970, British Book Center, 1971, revised edition, Deutsch, 1974; (with Eric Hosking) *Wildlife Photography,* Hutchinson, 1973, Praeger, 1974; (editor) *The Bird-Watcher's Book,* David & Charles, 1974; *The Second Bird-Watcher's Book,* David & Charles, 1975; *Birds: A Survey of the Bird Families of the World,* Dial, 1975; *Wildlife Paradises,* Praeger, 1975; *How to Watch Birds,* Deutsch, 1975; *Bird Seeker's Guide,* Deutsch, 1979; (editor) *The Encyclopedia of Birds,* seven volumes, Orbis, 1979-80; *A Day in the Country,* Deutsch, 1980; (with Peter Alden) *Finding Birds around the World,* Houghton, 1981; *Birds That Come Back,* Deutsch, 1981.

Children's books: *How and Why Book of Birds,* Transworld, 1972; *How and Why Book of the Spoilt Earth,* Transworld, 1973.

Author of scripts for film series "Wild, Wild World of Animals," Time-Life, 1974-75, and for "The World about Us," BBC-TV, 1975. Contributor to Reader's Digest *Book of the*

British Countryside and to numerous periodicals, including *Country Life, Animals, Observer, Teachers World,* and *Birds*.

WORK IN PROGRESS: All the Birds of the World, ten volumes.

SIDELIGHTS: John Gooders told *CA:* "Travel to see wildlife particularly in India and Nepal, in which a keen interest is conservation, [is] now a primary aim in any articles that I write. The effects of wildlife conservation on the people that live alongside animals is a key in my approach." Gooders has traveled widely in pursuit of birds and other wildlife.

*   *   *

GORDON, Myron J(ules)   1920-

PERSONAL: Born October 15, 1920, in New York, N.Y.; son of Joseph M. and Eva (Goodman) Gordon; married Helen E. Taylor, March 14, 1945; children: Joseph R., David A. *Education:* University of Wisconsin, B.A., 1941; Harvard University, M.A., 1947, Ph.D., 1952. *Home:* 33 Elmhurst Ave., Apt. 1009, Willowdale, Ontario, Canada M2N 6E8. *Office:* Department of Management, University of Toronto, 246 Bloor St. W., Toronto, Ontario, Canada M5S 1V4.

CAREER: Carnegie Institute of Technology (now Carnegie-Mellon University), Pittsburgh, Pa., 1947-52, began as instructor, became assistant professor; Massachusetts Institute of Technology, Cambridge, assistant professor, 1952-55, associate professor, 1955-62; University of Rochester, Rochester, N.Y., professor, beginning 1962; currently member of faculty of management studies, University of Toronto, Ontario. Member of faculty of Advanced Management Program, Kashmir, India, 1961; visiting professor, University of California, Berkeley, 1966-67, Hebrew University, Jerusalem, 1973, and University of Pennsylvania, 1977. Consultant to National Science Foundation and to Ford Foundation, 1960-62. *Military service:* U.S. Army; became lieutenant.

MEMBER: Institute of Management Sciences (member of executive committee, College of Measurements in Management, 1959-62, chairman, 1963-65; president of Boston area chapter, 1950-60), American Accounting Association (member of committee on accounting theory, 1957-59; member of committee on management accounting, 1959-60; chairman, 1964-66), American Economic Association, American Finance Association (president, 1975), Operations Research Society. *Awards, honors:* Ford Foundation faculty research fellowship in business administration and economics, 1962-63.

WRITINGS: (With T. M. Hill) *Accounting: A Management Approach,* Irwin, 1959, 6th edition (with Gordon Shillinglaw and Joshua Ronen), 1979; *The Investment, Financing and Valuation of the Corporation,* Irwin, 1962; *The Cost of Capital to a Public Utility,* Michigan State University Press, 1974.

Contributor: William W. Cooper and Yuji Ijiri, editors, *Eric Louis Kohler, Accounting's Man of Principles,* Reston, 1976; Andrew B. Whinston and Ijiri, editors, *Quantitative Planning and Control,* Academic Press, 1979; Haim Levy, editor, *Research in Finance,* Volume III, Jai Press, 1981. Contributor to professional journals.

*   *   *

GORDON, Stewart
See SHIRREFFS, Gordon D(onald)

GORHAM, Charles Orson   1911-1975

PERSONAL: Born 1911, in Philadelphia, Pa.; died October 17, 1975, in New Haven, Conn.; son of Wilson and Dessa (Durand) Gorham; married Ethel Bloom, 1936; children: Deborah Sara, Keith, Abigail, John Howland. *Education:* Attended Columbia University, 1934. *Agent:* William Morris, 1350 Avenue of the Americas, New York, N.Y. 10019.

CAREER: Doubleday Publishing Company, New York, N.Y., publicity director, 1936-42; novelist, beginning 1948. *Military service:* U.S. Army Air Forces, 1942-47; became lieutenant; awarded Distinguished Flying Cross, five Air Medals. *Member:* International Association of Poets, Playwrights, Editors, Essayists, and Novelists, Authors Guild (council member), The Players (New York).

WRITINGS: The Gilded Hearse, Creative Age, 1948; *The Future Mr. Dolan,* Dial, 1949; *Trial by Darkness,* Dial, 1951; *Martha Crane,* Farrar, Straus, 1953; *The Gold of Their Bodies,* Dial, 1954; *Wine of Life,* Dial, 1958; *Carlotta McBride,* Dial, 1959; *McCaffery,* Dial, 1961; *The Lion of Judah: A Life of Haile Selassie I, Emperor of Ethiopia,* Farrar, Straus, 1966; *Leader at Large: The Long and Fighting Life of Norman Thomas,* Farrar, Straus, 1970.

AVOCATIONAL INTERESTS: Painting, politics, conversation.

OBITUARIES: New York Times, October 19, 1975.†

*   *   *

GOTSHALK, D(ilman) W(alter)   1901-1973

PERSONAL: Born September 11, 1901, in Trenton, N.J.; died February 19, 1973, in Olney, Ill.; son of William Calvin and Josephine (Walters) Gotshalk; married Naomi Irene Smith, October 17, 1930; children: Richard A., Mary (Mrs. Joseph Kinney). *Education:* Princeton University, A.B., 1922; Cornell University, Ph.D., 1927. *Residence:* Olney, Ill.

CAREER: Mohegan Lake School, Mohegan Lake, N.Y., instructor in English language and literature, 1922-24; Colgate University, Hamilton, N.Y., acting professor of philosophy, 1927; University of Illinois at Urbana-Champaign, instructor, 1927-30, assistant professor, 1930-36, associate professor, 1936-43, professor of philosophy, 1943-65, professor emeritus, 1965-73, chairman of department, 1951-61. *Member:* American Philosophical Association (vice-president of Western division, 1947-48, 1949-50, president, 1950-51; chairman, national board of officers, 1951-52; chairman of Carus lecture committee, 1953-65), American Society for Aesthetics (trustee, 1952-55, 1959-61; vice-president, 1955-57; president, 1957-59; representative to American Council of Learned Societies, 1959-61), American Association of University Professors (president, University of Illinois chapter, 1955-56), American Association for the Advancement of Science (fellow).

WRITINGS: Structure and Reality: A Study of First Principles, Dial, 1937, reprinted, Greenwood Press, 1968; *Metaphysics in Modern Times,* University of Chicago Press, 1940; *Art and the Social Order,* University of Chicago Press, 1947, 2nd edition, Dover, 1962; *The Promise of Modern Life: An Interrelational View,* Antioch Press, 1958; *Patterns of Good and Evil: A Value Analysis,* University of Illinois Press, 1963; *Human Aims in Modern Perspective: Outlines of a General Theory of Value with Special Reference to Contemporary Social Life and Politics,* Antioch Press, 1966; *The Structure of Awareness: Introduction to a Situational Theory of Truth and Knowledge,* University of Illinois Press, 1969; *Twentieth Century Theme: A Philosophical Study,* Coronado Press, 1971.

Contributor: *Heritage of Kant*, Princeton University Press, 1939; R. W. Stallman, editor, *The Critic's Notebook*, University of Minnesota Press, 1950; *Perspectives on a Troubled Decade: Science, Philosophy and Religion, 1939-49*, Harper, 1950; M. M. Rader, editor, *A Modern Book of Esthetics*, Holt, 1952, 3rd edition, 1960; E. Vivas and M. Krieger, editors, *The Problems of Aesthetics*, Rinehart, 1953. Contributor to *Dictionary of World Literature, Encyclopedia of the Arts,* and *P. F. Collier's General Encyclopedia.* Contributor of articles on social philosophy, aesthetics, and values to periodicals.

AVOCATIONAL INTERESTS: Golf.†

*   *   *

GOULD, Alan
See CANNING, Victor

*   *   *

GOYEN, (Charles) William   1915-

PERSONAL: Born April 24, 1915, in Trinity, Tex.; son of Charles Provine (a lumber dealer) and Mary Inez (Trow) Goyen; married Doris Roberts (an actress), November 10, 1963; children: Michael (stepson). *Education:* Rice University, B.A., 1932, M.A., 1939. *Religion:* Protestant. *Home:* 6225 Quebec Dr., Los Angeles, Calif. 90068; and New York, N.Y. *Agent:* International Creative Management, 40 West 57th St., New York, N.Y. 10019.

CAREER: Writer. New School for Social Research, New York City, instructor in the novel, drama, and short story, 1955-60; Columbia University, New York City, lecturer in the novel, short story, and playwriting, and participant in the Columbia University Writing Program, 1963-65; McGraw-Hill Book Co., New York City, senior editor in trade division, 1966-71; Brown University, Providence, R.I., visiting professor of English, 1972-73; Princeton University, Princeton, N.J., writer-in-residence, 1976-78. Visiting writer at Hollins College, 1978, Stephens College, 1979, and University of Houston, 1981; instructor at University of Southern California, 1981-82. Associated with the American Place Theatre, New York City. *Military service:* U.S. Navy, 1940-45; became lieutenant. *Member:* P.E.N., American Society of Composers, Authors, and Publishers, Authors Guild, Authors League of America, Dramatists Guild, Texas Institute of Arts and Letters, Actors Studio.

AWARDS, HONORS: McMurray Award, 1950, for *The House of Breath;* Guggenheim fellow in creative writing, 1952, 1954; Texas Institute of Arts and Letters award for best comic novel, 1962, for *The Fair Sister;* Ford Foundation grant to novelists writing for the theater, Lincoln Center Repertory Co., New York, N.Y., 1963-64; American Society of Composers, Authors, and Publishers award for musical composition, 1965, 1966, 1968-70; Distinguished Alumni Award, Rice University, 1977.

WRITINGS: Ghost and Flesh (stories and tales), Random House, 1952; (translator) Albert Cossery, *The Lazy Ones*, New Directions, 1952; *The Faces of Blood Kindred* (novella and stories), Random House, 1960; *A Book of Jesus* (biography), Doubleday, 1973; *Selected Writings of William Goyen*, Random House, 1975; *The Collected Stories of William Goyen*, Doubleday, 1975; *Nine Poems*, Albondocani Press, 1976; *Wonderful Plant* (novella), Palaemon Press, 1979; *Arthur Bond*, Palaemon Press, 1980.

Novels: *The House of Breath*, Random House, 1950, reprinted, 1975; *In a Farther Country*, Random House, 1955; *The Fair Sister*, Doubleday, 1963 (published in England as *Savata, My*

Fair Sister, P. Owen, 1963); *Come, the Restorer*, Doubleday, 1974.

Plays: "The House of Breath" (based on his novel of the same title), first produced in New York at Circle in the Square Theatre, April, 1957, produced as "House of Breath, Black/White" in Providence, R.I., at Trinity Square Playhouse, November, 1969; "The Diamond Rattler," first produced in Boston at Charles Playhouse, May, 1960; "Christy," first produced in New York at American Place Theatre, March, 1964; "Aimee," first produced in Providence at Trinity Square Theatre, December, 1973. Also author of two television plays, "A Possibility of Oil" for "Four Star Theatre," CBS-TV, 1958, and "The Mind" (based on unused material from his story "The Horse and the Day Moth") for "Directions '62," ABC-TV, 1961. Author of lyrics for "The Left-Handed Gun," Warner Bros., 1958.

Criticism: *Ralph Ellison's "Invisible Man": A Critical Commentary*, American R.D.M. Corp., 1966; *My Antonia: A Critical Commentary*, American R.D.M. Corp., 1966. Contributor of critical articles to *New York Times Book Review*, 1950-70.

Stories have been published in prize story collections, including *Best American Short Stories, 1951*, edited by Martha Foley, Houghton, 1951, *Best American Short Stories, 1964*, edited by Foley and David Burnett, Houghton, 1964, and *The Bicentennial Collection of Texas Short Stories*, edited by James P. White, Texas Center for Writers Press, 1974. Contributor of short stories to periodicals, including *Southwest Review, Mademoiselle, Harper's, Transatlantic Review, Redbook,* and *Saturday Evening Post.*

WORK IN PROGRESS: Arcadio, a novel; *Precious Door,* a collection of seven stories and a novella; biographies of St. Paul and St. Francis; *Six Women,* an autobiography-memoir.

SIDELIGHTS: Already well-known in Europe, short-story writer and novelist William Goyen is becoming increasingly popular in America. His short stories have appeared in major magazines since 1949 and have been included in prize story collections since 1951. In the *Dictionary of Literary Biography,* Thomas E. Dasher comments that while Goyen's short stories have always received critical acclaim, his novels have just begun to receive the attention they deserve. He continues: "Goyen, of course, seeks neither unpopularity nor obscurity. Rather he seeks an audience that comes to each of his works with only the expectation of being challenged and stimulated."

In the preface to his *Collected Stories,* Goyen writes: "I've been mainly interested in the teller-listener situation. . . . I've not been interested in simply reproducing a big section of life off the streets or from the Stock Exchange or Congress. I've cared most about the world in one person's head. Mostly, then, I've cared about the buried song in somebody, and sought it passionately; or the music in what happened." Jay S. Paul, in *Critique: Studies in Modern Fiction,* considers Goyen's stories to be "a testament to the essentiality of telling. He regards such communication as a force of love, a process including seeing and saying."

Joyce Carol Oates remarks in the *New York Times Book Review* that *The Collected Stories of William Goyen* makes "an excellent introduction to [Goyen's] haunting, intensely poetic fictional world." *Southern Review* writer Robert Phillips states: "In the past, some critics have dismissed Goyen's work as too 'poetic' or too 'regional'. . . . Yet the surprise of his *Collected Stories* is the extraordinary range of his work. . . . Goyen dives down deeper and stays down longer in the human psyche than most American writers practicing fiction today. In these twenty-seven stories he depicts the timeless conflicts between the past and the present, the visible and the invisible.''

Goyen began writing short stories while he was serving in the United States Navy. During this time he also wrote his first novel, *The House of Breath*. In a 1950 *New York Times Book Review* article, Goyen told Harvey Breit: ''The war had a great deal to do with the writing of the novel. The war necessitated this kind of novel, which I would have written, but perhaps much later on. But all of it boiled up in me—this search for a place and an identity.''

The young man who narrates *The House of Breath* speaks for himself in the present and in the past as he tells the history of various members of his family. In a *New York Times* review of the novel when it was first published, Katherine Anne Porter called it ''a sustained evocation of the past, a long search for place and identity, and the meaning of an intense personal experience. . . . The writing as a whole is disciplined on a high plane, and there are long passages of the best writing, the fullest and richest and most expressive, that I have read in a very long time.''

Other reviewers also expressed praise for the writer and his first novel. ''Coming as it does from a very young writer,'' commented C. J. Rolo in the *Atlantic*, ''it announces a notable talent which already has great verbal resources at its command.'' *Christian Science Monitor* reviewer Ruth Chapin echoed Rolo's opinion, calling the novel ''a major achievement and William Goyen a young writer to be reckoned with.'' Twenty-five years later, the anniversary edition of the novel received the same favorable response from reviewers.

Goyen's second novel, *In a Farther Country*, met with ''indifference and incomprehension'' explains Robert Phillips in the *Southwest Review*. The novel focusses on the dehumanization that results from living in an industrialized and mechanized world. Phillips writes: ''Part of the reason Goyen's message fell on deaf ears was, perhaps, a matter of technique. He treated these problems, his themes, not in a naturalistic or realistic manner at all. Goyen did not aspire to become the Upton Sinclair of the ecological or urban crisis. Instead, he attacked the problems within the elusive framework of a romance.'' A *Nation* critic voices a similar opinion: ''Occasionally a book appears which is called a novel because all things, including books, must be given a name. These mavericks of literature, because of their structural eccentricity, often irritate and confuse readers. When a work is as lovely as *In a Farther Country*, however, the question of what sort of a book it is hardly matters.''

Goyen's fourth novel has also generated strong reaction. *Houston Post* writer Elizabeth Bennett remarks: ''Television interviewers won't talk about its contents on the air. Rex Reed, that intrepid critic who seems shocked by nothing, found it extremely sexy. One recent reviewer called it, among other things, 'bawdy and outrageous.' '' Goyen told Bennett that he could not understand ''all the hubbub'' about *Come, the Restorer*. Goyen says that he ''had a ball'' writing the book which he considers ''my biggest accomplishment, my richest.''

Set in the fictional Texas town of Rose, the novel is a lament for a past gone forever. The once pristine Rose has been polluted by greedy oil magnates and fouled by the presence of a chemical factory. Yearning to save some fragment of their past, the people of Rose turn to Mr. de Persia, the restorer of old photographs. For them, he becomes a sort of savior. Thomas E. Dasher contends that *Come, the Restorer* ''finally suggests that man's very quest for a savior, for a restorer, is futile if he looks only outside himself.'' Dasher believes that this ''mes-

sianic yearning'' runs throughout Goyen's work and that Goyen wants to make the point that ''the messiah lies within man himself.''

CA INTERVIEW

CA interviewed William Goyen by phone May 18, 1981, at his New York City apartment. It was a special day for Mr. Goyen; he had been up since five o'clock that morning putting the last touches on his new book of short stories before it went off to the publisher.

CA: The ''true music'' of the people you grew up among, their distinctive speech, figures largely in your writing. How early did you perceive speech as music?

GOYEN: I did very early on. By that I mean early teens. It was music for me. Actually, I wanted to write music, words and songs. It took a lot of people to keep me from doing that, mainly a good strong family that I guess I let get in my way. I've said a lot of times that I finally decided I'd just write words instead of words and music because it was quieter, nobody could hear me. I got by with that.

CA: When you began to travel to other areas, would you immediately listen for distinctive speech patterns?

GOYEN: Yes. It's almost painful for me to this day, the way people talk. I'm immediately perceptive of it and keen on it. I feel like I know people when I can hear them speak a little while, though maybe that's presumptuous. Speech so often does tell personality and landscape. It's amazing how landscape can lie in speech, and character, of course.

CA: Does music figure in the actual writing process in any way?

GOYEN: I very rarely listen to music when I'm writing because music is so powerful, I would listen to the music instead. It takes over. Only once, when I wrote the novel *Come, the Restorer* (my favorite novel), I played over and over a symphony that I bought quite blindly that I'd never heard before, Schubert's First Symphony; I just started playing that early in the morning. This novel came out of the very early morning, and I played that music until the tape was worn. I literally wrote the novel around hearing the music. It's the only time I've ever done that. It truly expressed the people in that novel for some reason, and it all came together. But generally I don't. I really hear speech when I write, like the song of speech. I hear the voice, the lyric voice, more than the music itself.

CA: You have described your earliest work as ''above all . . . homesick, and written at home.'' What was the homesickness?

GOYEN: All my life I've tried to find that out. As I've grown older, some people have said, ''Don't you know it was God?'' and other people have said, ''It really was your mother,'' and it truly *was* home in many other explanations. It was a yearning, really a profound one, and I still feel it. It's a perplexing thing. One can write a lot about that. My home is in New York, and I come here and then I immediately feel that, well, maybe my home is in New Mexico, and were I to go there it would not be there. It's a deeper place. Maybe it's really the Garden, you know? But it was a deeper yearning that I've come to see as I've grown older. It's kind of *no place*, and thank God. I'm relieved, because I looked for a place for so many years. I really think it's *no place*, it's probably within me, within us, that home. But it was a homesickness that came to me very early as a *yearning,* that's the word, and not for a specific place, finally.

CA: You spoke of yourself as an indifferent student of the humanities until, around your junior year of college, the "thunderstrike" occurred and you discovered the good writers. What was the immediate impact of that discovery on your own work?

GOYEN: It was immense. I immediately began to write like the people I discovered. For a little while I had to go through that. The range was wide. It did not include people I've been compared to, because they were not contemporary writers. I had to read Faulkner and D. H. Lawrence and Whitman very late, way after college, because I was caught in the nineteenth century and the eighteenth century and the seventeenth century. I read Hawthorne and Balzac and de Maupassant and Dante. I read a lot of French writers. I was studying comparative literature, trying to learn those languages so that I could read the literature in them. And Chaucer. Chaucer was another language too. I was truly caught in the whole tradition of literature. And thank God (although I fought it then) I got that foundation and a sense of continuity. I try to tell young writers about it. They need to get off the surface of current writing, to stop reading all of us and go back into the mainstream—earlier than Joyce and Proust, I mean: begin with Chaucer and Shakespeare. That gave me such a sense of the "line" of literature, and it helped me to see my own people, whom I was sure to write about, in terms of the world. It really saved me from being a regional writer—which is not a bad thing, but I know that I am not, that I escaped that.

CA: Your friendship with Frieda Lawrence was an early influence on your writing. How was she most influential on your work?

GOYEN: After I got that foundation I've just described, I went into the war, where I found a whole physical life which again saved me. We get little jumps like a battery does from a jumper cable. All my life I've gotten jumped like that; those were saving things for me. I might have been a scholar, I might have just hung back there in reading, if the war hadn't physically jumped me into that phase and refreshed everything and made me fight for my life.

Then I was jumped into the life in New Mexico where this woman [Frieda Lawrence] was who brought me a sense of the great world, of European life which I knew nothing about—the simplest kind of life was what it was. I learned about simplicity of life and, again, a tradition beyond my own of the Southwest, one I had only read about. Here was a woman who spoke of Goethe and Heine and Moricke and read them to me. And German folk literature came alive for me through her. She sang in a booming voice of fox and geese, and she sang farewell songs and lovers' parting songs from old eighteenth-century songbooks. I don't know about influence, but they're alive in my life. I do know that the fable of *Tatzlewurm* got into *The House of Breath,* which I was writing during our friendship, and she became Granny Ganchion's (my Alabama-born grandmother) interrogator in the root cellar. Frieda brought me a sense of the richness of the great world, and that, together with what I had come through—college, Texas, the war—got me ready to move into the real world that I had never been in.

I left there and lived in Europe for quite some while as I continued to write *The House of Breath.* That youthful novel about a simple family in a small Texas town had some roots in and was nourished by a German peasant baroness and her sense of life and by the splendor of Europe that followed my initiation. The Sistine Chapel and the Parthenon are the dom-

inant images—and set down on the first two pages of *The House of Breath.*

CA: Is the adobe house you built in New Mexico still there?

GOYEN: It's a villa now, a kind of small palazzo. It's truly one of the beautiful places in that valley. Some people bought that little crude thing a friend and I and the two Indians built and used it as a nucleus for a really lovely adobe villa. They respected it and kept it as the matrix, the central room. I've stayed there again over the years a few times with the owners, in the old original room. It's still alive and wonderful and mysterious and has been regenerating for me each time.

CA: In some instances you've published parts of novels before the novels were actually published. In those cases, has the response to the excerpts influenced the further shaping of the books?

GOYEN: No, not at all. So far, when excerpts have been published, I was already through with the book and I felt that I had done the best I could with it. I've always reworked my books so carefully and so long—I'm slow, slow, slow—that by the time I'm through I've literally kind of abandoned it, and I really *couldn't* do any more, even if there were adverse comments to excerpts. Mostly the reaction to those early things was praise, and that did nothing more than really scare the hell out of me. I knew there was more to come that they hadn't seen.

CA: How do you deal with writing that's hit a snag?

GOYEN: Writing for me is totally physical; the whole process and life of writing is like my body. I see that more and more. If the work has reached a point where it won't let me touch it—you know how we are sometimes rejected by people who are not ready for us even to shake their hand, in that sense of touching—then I have to respect that. If somebody doesn't want me to shake his hand, then I think, the hell with him, I just won't be around him for a while. So I wait. I find that by letting the writing go, when it's like that, something obviously happens to me; it's I who was not ready to really shake hands. The physical thing, of course, always resides in me. I've been waiting a long, long time for some pieces of work. I don't know enough, it may be, or I won't let myself. But when I come back to those pieces, sooner or later, there is more life there than there was before—I suppose *I've* brought it. Waiting is writing for me, or writing is waiting—it truly is most of the time. If I push it, if I demand prematurely that it shake my hand, I will find that I've overwritten it.

CA: You've adapted some of your books to the stage. Is it difficult to take material you've put together so painstakingly in one form and reshape it into quite a different form?

GOYEN: It's really difficult. I've learned not to do it. In doing the adaptation, I went right back through the whole slow and painful process that was required to write the book originally, so here I was doubling that pain. I just went deeper into the characters. I suppose sometimes dramatization must have something to do with simplifying characters and making them fairly superficial in order to get them accessible, moving around on the stage. The depth of characters in dramatic writing is revealed through relationships on the stage, through events that happen on the stage. Well, my relationships were not on the stage because not much happened there; and my large concern—a fiction-writer's instinct—was with further exploration of the characters, which further depressed my director and brought more problems to the actors. Once again, my characters had caught me. Those characters that had haunted me and that I had finally freed myself from in a story had gotten me again, and they were going to lead me down. So I can't begin to tell you what that process of writing plays was like. I ended up with five acts and a thickened novel. I had to write a lot of plays to learn that. The way I got through that, really, was to write a couple of musicals. That was terrific fun; my songs came through and I was able to play on the surface.

CA: You've written some for television, too. How do you think television and the other electronic media have influenced the writer's imagination?

GOYEN: This one hasn't been influenced any, I can tell you that. Serious writers? I find that they just don't look at television. But so many of my friends and people that I know about want to write for film seriously, so they see a lot of films. Right now there seems to be a whole wave of serious novelists and story writers wanting to write screenplays. It's never interested me at all, but it does interest them. I heard Larry McMurtry say that the short story was now probably being replaced by the screenplay. It fascinates a lot of writers. But not me.

CA: You've indicated that your teaching has actually been helpful to beginning writers because you "believe everybody can write." What kind of help does an aspiring writer usually need most?

GOYEN: So many of them don't feel that they have anything to say. These are the students that interest me the most and that I most enjoy working with, to help them discover that they do. We all have lives. A lot of beginning writers have an urge to imitate; surely they want to write, but it's very hard for them to be in touch with the material of their lives. I've helped many of them to see that they too have stories in their lives, to search and find what's worthy of writing about, and then to get out and do it as well as they can. It's also fun working with people who have to learn the basic skills of telling a story for themselves, their way, in their voice. We can all do that; I feel it's a gift, a universal gift. Some have a sort of genius for it, but we're all storytellers. Have you ever met anybody who was not a potential storyteller if he could find the voice for it? I suppose "teaching"—or helping others to write—is helping them find their voice.

CA: Rather than resenting your critics, you've tended to welcome whatever insights the best of them might have brought to your work. Have any of them actually revealed things to you about your work?

GOYEN: Oh yes, they have, particularly when I feel that they're really reading me and not hostile to me. It took me a while to learn that those with hostility had nothing to give anybody. Until then I got hurt a little bit. But those people who have shown me my work, well, they're really all I have *beyond* my work. When I lose them, it's a great loss to me, and some of them are going. We need each other. That doesn't mean we have to be praising each other to the skies, but we need to share deeply in each other's work and be honest about it and to care and to let each other know.

CA: Have the French critics been especially helpful to you?

GOYEN: They have been. They have tended to describe my work as being surreal or sexual, mainly those two things. I don't know that I'm a surrealist at all. It doesn't amuse me,

but it really does enlighten things for me. I'm impressed that people take that much time to see what they see, and in the end I don't know what I am. I really don't know what my work means; I guess I'd be in a fix if I did.

CA: How do you feel about the recent Delta *issue dedicated to your life and work?*

GOYEN: I thought a few things in it were just dazzling; they got me right on the nose. Overall it was good. I guess I wanted more; I think I wanted it to be more comprehensive than it was. The editors couldn't get some people to finish what they had been writing—Stephen Spender had been writing an essay, and Joyce Carol Oates, and Katherine Anne Porter—so it missed that kind of balance that I would have liked. But naturally it pleased me.

CA: Has any recent writing provided insight into why the Europeans have responded so strongly to your work?

GOYEN: No. My stories seem to change, but they go right on publishing them; they seem to care and understand and to really want to publish me, particularly in France and Germany. The French and the Germans are very different people, but both still welcome my work and are my real friends. Whatever they know about American writing is something I don't know, I guess. Maybe they feel it's very contemporary and they're concerned with life as it is right now. It could be that they're a little tired of *New Yorker* interpretations, a kind of writing that no longer serves their own perceptions, their interests, even their curiosity maybe.

CA: Is there anything you'd like to do that you haven't done yet?

GOYEN: I want to go on writing stories; short fiction is what I most care about. I do want to write about the lives of Paul and Francis. I've written a little life of Jesus, and it's part of a trilogy that I want to finish so that I can get something said about those three men I admire and whose lives are curious and compelling. But otherwise, I just want to deepen what I know about writing American fiction. I have so much in my head—and so much started, too—that I want to do. I don't care about experimenting. I just want to go on where I am and do it better; and if I have the time, I'll do it, God willing. I have a strong feeling about art as the only way of life, and that includes a very strong sense of God as well. More and more I see that it's the only . . . I don't want to say *salvation* or anything like that, but I'm talking about that—the one *freeing* way for the human being. I want to make art, I want to make beautiful and true stories, just to be able to do that, and so far I am. I think all the time about having enough silence and solitariness to be able to see clearly what I can do. That takes silence and solitariness. It also takes some other things, like a bit of money, but somehow the material things always seem to be provided if I stay honestly and persistently with my deep need of wanting to make the best stories I can and being alone and quiet to do so.

BIOGRAPHICAL/CRITICAL SOURCES: New York Times Book Review, August 20, 1950, August 7, 1960, November 3, 1974, November 16, 1975; *New York Times,* August 20, 1950, July 24, 1955; *Atlantic,* September, 1950; *New York Herald Tribune Book Review,* September 10, 1950, February 10, 1952, July 10, 1955, August 21, 1960; *Christian Science Monitor,* September 16, 1950; Orville Prescott, *In My Opinion,* Bobbs, 1952; *Saturday Review,* March 22, 1952, July 23, 1955, October 5, 1963; *Time,* July 25, 1955; *New Yorker,* August 6, 1955; *Nation,* October 22, 1955, November 19, 1960.

Times Literary Supplement, July 12, 1963; Louise Y. Gossett, *Violence in Recent Southern Fiction,* Duke University Press, 1965; *Southwest Review,* summer, 1971, winter, 1975, autumn, 1976; *Houston Post,* December 27, 1974; *Dallas News,* April 30, 1975; *Chicago Tribune Book World,* November 9, 1975; *The Collected Stories of William Goyen,* Doubleday, 1975; *Authors in the News,* Volume II, Gale, 1976; *Contemporary Literary Criticism,* Gale, Volume V, 1976, Volume VIII, 1978, Volume XIV, 1980; *Critique: Studies in Modern Fiction,* Volume XIX, number 2, 1977; *Dictionary of Literary Biography,* Volume II, Gale, 1978; *Bulletin of Bibliography,* July/September, 1978; *Southern Review,* January, 1979.

—Sketch by Debra G. Jones

—Interview by Thomas E. Dasher
and Jean W. Ross

*   *   *

GRAHAM, Neill
See DUNCAN, W(illiam) Murdoch

*   *   *

GRAHAM, Robert
See HALDEMAN, Joe (William)

*   *   *

GRANGER, Darius John
See MARLOWE, Stephen

*   *   *

GRANT, Bruce   1893-1977

PERSONAL: Born April 17, 1893, in Wichita Falls, Tex.; died April 9, 1977, in Winnetka, Ill. of a self-inflicted gunshot wound; son of James Erskine and Daisy Dean (Nolen) Walker; married Catharine Bauer, 1931; children: Gordon, Ginger Grant LaFaire. *Education:* Attended University of Kentucky, 1911-12. *Home and office:* 439 Maple Ave., Winnetka, Ill. 60093.

CAREER: Reporter or rewrite man on newspapers in Louisville, Ky., Dallas, Tex., Buenos Aires, Argentina, Chicago, Ill., and New York City, 1913-28; King Features Syndicate, New York City, writer, 1929-33; *Chicago Times,* Chicago, rewrite man, city editor, and war correspondent, 1933-45; freelance writer, 1946-77. *Military service:* U.S. Army, Field Artillery, 1917-19; became lieutenant. *Member:* Authors Guild, Midland Authors (director), Nautical Research Guild (chairman of board of governors), Children's Reading Roundtable, Chicago Literary Society, Chicago Yacht Club. *Awards, honors:* Honorable mention, O'Brien's *Best Short Stories,* 1922, 1923.

WRITINGS: (With Eng Ying Gong) *Tong War!: A History of the Chinese Tongs in America,* Nicholas Brown, 1930; *Isaac Hull, Captain of Old Ironsides,* Pelligrini & Cudahy, 1947; *Eagle of the Sea,* Rand McNally, 1949.

Leather Braiding, Cornell Maritime, 1950; *Cowboy Encyclopedia,* Rand McNally, 1951; *Boy Scout Encyclopedia,* Rand McNally, 1952, revised edition, 1965; *How to Make Cowboy Horse Gear,* Cornell Maritime, 1953, revised and enlarged edition (with Lee M. Rice) published as *How to Make Cowboy Horse Gear* [and] *How to Make a Western Saddle,* 1956; *Warpath: A Story of the Plains Indians,* World Publishing, 1954; *Fight for a City: The History of the Union League Club of Chicago,* Rand McNally, 1955; *Davy Crockett, American Hero,*

Rand McNally, 1955; *Six-Gun: A Story of the Texas Rangers,* World Publishing, 1955; *Longhorn: A Story of the Chisholm Trail,* World Publishing, 1956; *The Adventures of Robin Hood,* Rand McNally, 1956; *Pony Express,* Rand McNally, 1956; *Leopard Horse Canyon: The Story of the Lost Appaloosas,* World Publishing, 1957; *Pancho, A Dog of the Plains,* World Publishing, 1958; *American Indians Yesterday and Today,* Dutton, 1958; *Cyclone,* World Publishing, 1959.

Thomas Truxtun, Captain of the Constellation, Putnam, 1960; *Zachary, the Governor's Pig,* World Publishing, 1960; *The Star-Spangled Rooster,* World Publishing, 1961; *Know Your Car and How to Drive,* Rand McNally, 1962; *Northwest Campaign: The George Rogers Clark Expedition,* Putnam, 1963; *American Forts Yesterday and Today,* Dutton, 1965; *My Cowboy Book,* Rand McNally, 1967; *How Chicks Are Born,* Rand McNally, 1967; *A Trip in Space,* Rand McNally, 1968; *My Indian Book,* Rand McNally, 1968; *Ride, Gaucho,* World Publishing, 1969; *Fire Fighters,* Rand McNally, 1971; *Famous American Trails,* Rand McNally, 1971; *Encyclopedia of Rawhide and Leather Braiding,* Cornell Maritime, 1972. Contributor to magazines.

AVOCATIONAL INTERESTS: Swimming, sailing, rawhide and leather braiding, model ship building.

OBITUARIES: New York Times, April 10, 1977; *AB Bookman's Weekly,* May 9, 1977.†

*   *   *

GRANT, J(ohn) B(arnard)   1940-
(Jack Grant)

PERSONAL: Born March 23, 1940, in Hartford, Conn.; son of Ellsworth S. (a historical writer and maker of documentary films) and Marion (a historical writer; maiden name, Hepburn) Grant; married Ann Halterman, May 28, 1965; children: Jason, Schuyler. *Education:* University of California, Berkeley, B.A., 1965. *Residence:* Sebastopol, Calif.

CAREER: High school teacher during 1960's; skipper of a charter sailing boat for a private school located in Florida, 1968-70; writer and editor, 1970—. *Military service:* U.S. Marine Corps, 1960-64.

WRITINGS: The Geocentric Experience, Lamplighters Roadway Press, 1972; (with Katharine Houghton) *Two Beastly Tales,* Lamplighters Roadway Press, 1975.

Under name Jack Grant, published by Celestial Arts, except as indicated: (With Stanley Keleman) *Your Body Speaks Its Mind,* Simon & Schuster, 1975; *Skateboarding: A Complete Guide to the Sport,* 1976; (with Jim Gault) *The World of Women's Gymnastics,* 1976; *Soccer: A Personal Guide for Players, Coaches and Parents,* 1978.

Also author of three novels and a volume of short stories, all unpublished. Contributor of numerous stories and poems to magazines; contributor of essays to *San Francisco Review of Books.*

WORK IN PROGRESS: Joan Rainbow, a two-act play centering on the life of Joan of Arc; with Laeh Garfield, *You Are Never Alone,* a practical introduction to working with spirit guides; *Jack Possum's Time,* a novel about a man, a woman, and their mutual friend in the California of the early 1970's.

SIDELIGHTS: J. B. Grant told *CA:* "Writing is my principal means for exploring and celebrating life's ups and downs. What interests me is anything whose whole is greater than the sum of its parts: from sonnets to atoms to apple trees to marriages.

In nonfiction as well as fiction and poetry, I'm most satisfied when able to convey an inside view along with the descriptive one.'' *Avocational interests:* Playing and coaching soccer, rollerskating, caring for an orchard, working on his house, playing piano and singing for Old Delicious, a rhythm-and-blues band.

*   *   *

GRANT, Jack
  See GRANT, J(ohn) B(arnard)

*   *   *

GRANT, John Webster 1919-

PERSONAL: Born June 27, 1919, in Truro, Nova Scotia; son of William P. and M. Dorothy (Waddell) Grant; married Gwendolen M. Irwin, June 3, 1944. *Education:* Dalhousie University, B.A., 1938, M.A., 1941; Princeton University, graduate study, 1938-39; Oxford University, D.Phil., 1948. *Home:* 86 Gloucester St., Apt. 1002, Toronto, Ontario, Canada M4Y 2S2. *Office:* Emmanuel College, Queen's Park Crescent, Toronto, Ontario, Canada M5S 1K7.

CAREER: Clergyman, United Church of Canada. Wartime Information Board, Ottawa, Ontario, director of religious information, 1942-43; Union College of British Columbia, Vancouver, professor of church history, 1949-59; Ryerson Press, Toronto, Ontario, editor-in-chief, 1959-63; Victoria University, Emmanuel College, Toronto, professor of church history, 1963—. Visiting professor of church history, United Theological College of South India and Ceylon, Bangalore, India, 1957-58. *Military service:* Royal Canadian Navy, chaplain, 1943. Royal Canadian Navy (reserve), 1952-57. *Member:* Canadian Historical Association, Canadian Society of Church History. *Awards, honors:* D.D., Union College of British Columbia, 1961, Pine Hill Divinity Hall, Halifax, Nova Scotia, 1962, and University of Toronto, 1981.

WRITINGS: Free Churchmanship in England, Independent Press (London), 1955; *World Church: Achievement or Hope?,* Ryerson, 1956; *God's People in India,* Highway Press, 1960; *The Ship under the Cross,* Ryerson, 1960; *George Pidgeon: A Biography,* Ryerson, 1962; *God Speaks . . . We Answer,* Ryerson, 1965; *The Canadian Experience of Church Union,* John Knox, 1967; *The Church in the Canadian Era,* McGraw, 1972.

Editor: *The Churches and the Canadian Experience,* Ryerson, 1963; (associate editor) *The Cross in Canada,* Ryerson, 1966; *Salvation! O the Joyful Sound: The Selected Writings of John Carroll,* Oxford University Press, 1967; *Die unierten Kirchen,* Evangelisches Verlagswerk (Stuttgart), 1973.

WORK IN PROGRESS: A history of Christian-native encounters in Canada.

*   *   *

GRANT, Matthew G.
  See MAY, Julian

*   *   *

GRANT, Maxwell
  See LYNDS, Dennis

*   *   *

GRAY, Betsy
  See POOLE, Gray Johnson

GRAZHDANIN, Misha
  See BURGESS, M(ichael) R(oy)

*   *   *

GREEN, D.
  See CASEWIT, Curtis (Werner)

*   *   *

GREEN, Fletcher Melvin 1895-1978

PERSONAL: Born July 12, 1895, in Gainesville, Ga.; died February 28, 1978; buried in Chapel Hill Memorial Cemetery, Chapel Hill, N.C.; son of Robert Chambers and Mary Mahalia (Haynes) Green; married Mary Frances Black, 1930; children: Fletcher Melvin II, Mary Carolyn Green Hughes, Robert Ramsey, Elizabeth Haynes. *Education:* Emory University, B.Ph., 1921; University of North Carolina, M.A., 1922, Ph.D., 1927. *Politics:* Democrat. *Religion:* Methodist Episcopal Church. *Home:* 401 Laurel Hill Rd., Chapel Hill, N.C. *Office:* Department of History, University of North Carolina, Chapel Hill, N.C.

CAREER: University of North Carolina at Chapel Hill, instructor, 1922-23; Sparks College, Shelbyville, Ill., professor of history, 1923-24; Vanderbilt University, Nashville, Tenn., assistant professor of history, 1924-25; University of North Carolina at Chapel Hill, Institute for Research in the Social Sciences, fellow, 1925-27, assistant professor, 1927-30, associate professor of history, 1930-33; Emory University, Atlanta, Ga., professor of history, 1933-36; University of North Carolina at Chapel Hill, professor of history, 1936-78, Kenan Professor of History, 1945-78, chairman of department, 1953-60. Visiting professor at Harvard University, 1944-45, and at other universities and colleges. Member of executive board, North Carolina State Department of Archives and History, 1955. *Military service:* U.S. Army, Medical Corps, 1918-19.

MEMBER: Organization of American Historians (president, 1961), American Historical Association, Southern Historical Association (president, 1945), Historical Society of North Carolina (president, 1953), North Carolina Literary and Historical Association (president, 1955), Phi Beta Kappa, Alpha Tau Omega, Chapel Hill Golf Club. *Awards, honors:* Litt.D. from Emory University, 1957, Washington and Lee University, 1960.

WRITINGS: Constitutional Development in the South Atlantic States, 1776-1860: A Study in the Evolution of Democracy, University of North Carolina Press, 1930, reprinted, Da Capo Press, 1971; *Heroes of the American Revolution,* University of North Carolina Press, 1931; *Romance of the Western Frontier,* University of North Carolina Press, 1932, reprinted, Folcroft, 1977; *The Lides Go South and West,* University of South Carolina Press, 1952; *The Role of the Yankee in the Old South,* University of Georgia Press, 1968; *Democracy in the Old South and Other Essays,* Vanderbilt University Press, 1969.

Editor: Henry Kyd Douglas, *I Rode with Stonewall,* University of North Carolina Press, 1940; *Essays in Southern History,* University of North Carolina Press, 1949, reprinted, Greenwood Press, 1977; (with Thomas F. Hahn and Nathalie W. Hahn) John Blackford, *Ferry Hill Plantation Journal,* University of North Carolina Press, 1961, reprinted, American Canal and Transportation Center, 1975; *Travels in the South, 1865-1880,* University of Oklahoma Press, 1962; William Watson Davis, *Civil War and Reconstruction in Florida,* University of Florida Press, 1964; Susan Dabney Smedes, *Memorials of a Southern Planter*, Knopf, 1965, reprinted, University Press of Mississippi, 1981; T. P. Kettell, *Southern Wealth and Northern Profits*, University of Alabama Press, 1966; (with J. Isaac Copeland) *The Old South*, AHM Publishing, 1980.

Contributor to *Collier's Encyclopedia, Dictionary of American Biography*, and *Dictionary of American History*. Contributor to historical journals. Member of editorial board, *Journal of Southern History*, 1935-36.

BIOGRAPHICAL/CRITICAL SOURCES: Arthur S. Link and Rembert W. Patrick, editors, *Writing Southern History: Essays in Historiography in Honor of Fletcher M. Green*, Louisiana State University Press, 1965.†

* * *

GREENBLATT, Augusta 1912-

PERSONAL: Born August 13, 1912, in New York; daughter of Raful and Rissi (Hendelman) Pecker; married I. J. Greenblatt (a professor of clinical pathology at Long Island University), March 28, 1940; children: Richard, Laurence. *Education:* Cornell University, B.A., 1933; graduate study at Brooklyn College (now Brooklyn College of the City University of New York), 1938-40; Hofstra University, M.S., 1956. *Religion:* Jewish. *Home:* 511 Allen Rd., Woodmere, N.Y. 11598.

CAREER: New York City Department of Hospitals, New York, N.Y., supervisor of clinical chemistry and microbiology, 1935-42; U.S. Army, Medical Department, Camp Stoneman, Calif., civilian supervisor of clinical laboratories, 1942-45; Clinical Diagnostic Laboratory, Woodmere, N.Y., director, 1950-64; Hewlett-Woodmere Continuing Education, Hewlett, N.Y., lecturer, 1964-74; writer and lecturer on science and health topics for the general public, 1964—. Lecturer at School of Continuing Education, New York University, 1965, 1967; conductor of weekly lecture series, "What's behind the Headlines in Science and Medicine." Writer and editor, U.S. Public Health Service, 1968. *Member:* National Association of Science Writers, American Medical Writers Association, American Public Health Association, Authors Guild, Authors League of America, American Society of Journalists and Authors. *Awards, honors:* Certificate of Commendation, Army Service Forces, 1944; Blakeslee Book Award, American Heart Association, 1979, for *Your Genes and Your Destiny*.

WRITINGS: Teenage Medicine: Questions Young People Ask about Their Health, Cowles, 1970, published as *Why Do I Feel This Way*, Pyramid, 1974; *Heredity and You: How You Can Protect Your Family's Future*, Coward, 1974; (with husband, I. J. Greenblatt) *Your Genes and Your Destiny: A New Look at a Longer Life when Heart Disease, High Blood Pressure, Diabetes or Obesity Is a Family Affair*, Bobbs-Merrill, 1979. Contributor to *Grolier's Encyclopedia*. Contributor to professional journals, including *Journal of Biochemistry* and *American Journal of Medical Sciences*, and popular magazines, including *Family Circle, Woman's Day, National Forum*, and *McCall's*.

SIDELIGHTS: Augusta Greenblatt writes to *CA:* "Having dealt with genetic counseling and the most familar genetic disorders in *Heredity and You*, I felt as if I were waiting for the other shoe to drop. While most of us will never know a family with Tay Sachs disease, cystic fibrosis, sickle cell disease, hemophilia, Down's Syndrome, Wilson's disease, PKU, and other inborn errors, families touched by coronary heart disease, high blood pressure and diabetes may be our own or our neighbors'. Contrary to the popular belief that genetic diseases are rare, the fact is that heredity plays a role in 15-30 percent of the 30 million Americans with high blood pressure, in the majority of America's 10 million diabetics, and one in every five coronary heart disease victims under the age of sixty. The good news is that with early identification of who is at risk, the not-so-rare hereditary disorders are often preventable, sometimes reversible, and always controllable.

"*Your Genes and Your Destiny* took two-and-a-half years to research and write. Given my husband's pioneering work in atherosclerosis (forerunner of coronary heart disease), our collaboration was a natural and marked our first joint writing venture since several research publications in the early days of our marriage when we worked in the same laboratory.

"Since 1964—when I switched careers from the laboratory to the typewriter and lectern—I have been constantly reinforced in my early belief (and hope) that there are women who would rather talk DNA than diapers; teenagers who are willing to open their minds on touchy subjects when they are not preached at or talked down to; and persons of all ages who welcome the translation of the technical jargon of the scientist to everyday language. There is a growing trend (more of a trickle so far than a torrent) to adopt science books for educational use that have not only substance but style as well.

"Finally, a special dimension is added to my enjoyment in communicating new advances through my ongoing lecture series for non-scientists. A face-to-face weekly encounter with 100 women and men on topics ranging from genetic engineering to longevity, nutrition, immunology, etc., [the series] not only keeps me on track, but also makes writing a less 'lonely' endeavor."

* * *

GREENE, Bert 1923-

PERSONAL: Born October 16, 1923, in Flushing, N.Y.; son of Samuel Michael (an electrical contractor) and Paula (a pianist; maiden name, Cohn) Greene. *Education:* Attended College of William and Mary, Richmond Professional Institute, Pratt Institute, and Yale University. *Politics:* "Independent, with Democrat bias." *Religion:* None. *Home:* 240 West 12th St., New York, N.Y. 10014; and Main St. Amagansett, Long Island, N.Y. 11930. *Agent:* Nat Sobel Associates, 128 East 56th St., New York, N.Y. 10022.

CAREER: Helena Rubenstein, Inc. (beauty preparations), New York City, art director, 1950-53; I. Miller & Sons (shoe firm), New York City, art director, 1954-60; *Esquire* magazine, New York City, art director in promotion, beginning 1970; food editor, *Gentleman's Quarterly* magazine, 1977—. Founder and co-owner of The Store in Amagansett, 1966-76.

WRITINGS: (With Denis Vaughan) *The Store Cookbook*, Regnery, 1974; (with Phillip Stephen Schulz) *Pity the Poor Rich*, Contemporary Books, 1978; *Bert Greene's Kitchen Bouquets*, Contemporary Books, 1979; *Honest American Fare*, Contemporary Books, 1981; *Greene on Greens*, Workman Publishing, 1982.

Plays: (Adaptor with Aaron Fine) Franz Kafka, "The Trial" (two-act), first produced Off-Broadway at Provincetown Playhouse, June 19, 1955; (adaptor) Frank Wedekind, "Spring's Awakening" (three-act), first produced Off-Broadway at Provincetown Playhouse, November 1, 1956; "The Summer of Daisy Miller" (two-act), first produced Off-Broadway at Phoenix Theatre, May 17, 1964.

Television plays: (Adaptor) Colette, "My Mother's House" (three-act), produced on WNET-TV, New York, 1969; "Colette,'' produced on National Educational Television's "Playhouse,'' February, 1971.

Author of weekly column, "Bert Greene's Kitchen,'' syndicated in numerous newspapers, including *New York Daily News*. Contributor to periodicals, including *Vogue, Esquire, Cuisine, Cosmopolitan, Self,* and *International Review of Food and Wine*.

WORK IN PROGRESS: Several books about food.

SIDELIGHTS: Bert Greene told *CA*: "I began to write early on, but the conflict of a double talent waylaid me into graphics where I strayed too long. My formal career as a wage-earning writer began in 1976. My single greatest influence has always been women writers. I love Elizabeth Bowen, Rosamond Lehmann and Colette dearly and have an ongoing friendship with M.F.K. Fisher—who inducted me into the mysteries of taste and smell. I am a gourmand who loves to cook and eat well and takes enormous pleasure in writing about food." *Avocational interests:* Travel, especially to England, France, and Haiti.

*   *   *

GREENE, Felix   1909-

PERSONAL: Born May 21, 1909, in Berkhamsted, England; son of Edward and Eva (Stutzer) Greene; married Elena Lindeman; children: Anne. *Education:* Attended Cambridge University, two years. *Home and office:* 8 York House, Upper Montagu St., London W.1, England.

CAREER: Office of the Prime Minister, London, England, political worker, 1931-33; senior official for British Broadcasting Corp. (BBC) in London and the United States, 1932-40, head of offices in New York, N.Y., five years; free-lance radio and television commentator, filmmaker, and lecturer on international affairs, 1940—. *Member:* Royal Institute of International Affairs, Society for Anglo-Chinese Understanding (vice-president), P.E.N. *Awards, honors:* First prize, Melbourne International Film Festival, for "China!"; British Film Academy nomination for best feature-length documentary, 1968, for "Inside North Vietnam"; received honorary doctorate for his work towards creating understanding between the people of America and the Far East.

WRITINGS: What's Really Happening in China?, City Lights, 1960; *Awakened China: The Country Americans Don't Know*, Doubleday, 1961, published as *China: The Country Americans Are Not Allowed to Know*, Ballantine, 1962 (published in England as *The Wall Has Two Sides: A Portrait of China Today*, J. Cape, 1962); *Let There Be a World*, Fulton, 1963; *A Curtain of Ignorance: How the American Public Has Been Misinformed about China*, Doubleday, 1964; *Viet Nam! Viet Nam!*, Fulton, 1966; *The Enemy: Notes on Imperialism and Revolution*, J. Cape, 1970, published as *The Enemy: What Every American Should Know about Imperialism and Revolution*, Random House, 1971; *Peking*, Mayflower Books, 1978.

Films include interviews with Chou En-lai, 1960, 1963, and 1972, Ho Chi Minh, 1965, Chairman Hua Guofeng, 1979, and Vice-chairman Deng Xiaoping, 1979, as well as the documentaries "China!," 1963, "Peking Symphony Orchestra," 1963, "Inside North Vietnam," 1967, and "One Man's China" (series of eight films on different aspects of modern China), broadcast by the BBC and distributed in the United States by Time-Life Films, 1972.

SIDELIGHTS: Felix Greene's work, first as a correspondent for the BBC and later as a free-lance writer and filmmaker, has taken him to virtually every country in the world. One of his favorite destinations is China; he has visited there some sixteen times, occasionally for periods as long as six months. Accompanied by a film crew consisting only of his wife (the sound recorder) and his daughter (the production assistant), Greene (the cameraman) begins each new China film project with one major goal in mind: to provide the West with what he believes is a more realistic and positive view of modern-day China than has been portrayed in the past.

In 1960, for example, Greene obtained a filmed interview with Premier Chou En-lai, the first such interview ever granted by a Chinese leader. A subsequent project, the 1963 film "China!," was the first full-length documentary on that country made by a Westerner since the Communist revolution; another extended visit in 1972 furnished Greene with enough material for eight more films, each on a different aspect of contemporary life in China.

Despite these and many other films to his credit, Greene told *CA* that he considers himself "more of an author than a filmmaker." In many cases, though, reviewers (especially American reviewers) have criticized his written work for what they consider to be a one-sided approach to the subject matter. Greene attributes their negative reaction to the overall political climate of the 1960s and early 1970s. He explains: "When my books *Awakened China* and *A Curtain of Ignorance* were written, the prevailing attitude towards China was one of extreme hostility—at least in the United States. Almost nothing even remotely positive about China could be written without being challenged as subversive. A Gallup poll of that period indicated that the public considered China as a far more dangerous enemy than even the Soviet Union. It is a strange fact that virtually nothing that these books contained would today be challenged either in fact or in spirit. . . . [As for *Viet Nam! Viet Nam!,*] this again was published before the full enormity of that war had become apparent to world opinion. . . . Nothing written in that book would today be questioned."

In discussions on *Awakened China* dating back to 1961, for example, many reviewers praised Greene's attempt to report on such a long-neglected topic, but they also criticized him for glossing over or entirely omitting facts unfavorable to his thesis. As Tillman Durdin of the *New York Times Book Review* wrote: "[Greene] has produced a book that consistently errs, by commission and omission, in favor of the Communist regime but which, on the other hand, effectively portrays successful, dynamic aspects of the New China that Americans should acknowledge and know better. . . . [But] *Awakened China*, though well-written and bright with perceptive passages, is simply not a balanced and objective work."

Takashi Oka of the *Christian Science Monitor* believed that "many . . . conversations, notably about restrictions on criticism in a Communist society, show that Mr. Greene was by no means one-sidedly impressed by all he saw. Nevertheless the total impact of the book is disturbing, for one feels that beside the many things which Mr. Greene did see and record there were others which he passed by. And there is misinformation as well."

The *Guardian*'s Frank Edmead remarked: "Travellers to China, particularly if they know anything of the anarchy and wickedness of Kuomintang rule, must find infuriating the more lurid stories printed in Western newspapers. But often their burning desire to counteract these stories betrays them into partisanship equally unacceptable in the opposite way, and their purpose is defeated. So it is with [*Awakened China*]."

Though the *Saturday Review*'s Gerald Clark admitted to a few reservations about Greene's personal convictions, he decided that the author's main purpose in writing *Awakened China* was "to get the 'feel' of the land in the big sense, its feverish sense of strength and possibility, the dedication of the young people, the patriotic pride and hopes for the future. And this he has done admirably well." *New York Herald Tribune Books* critic J. Tuzo Wilson felt that regardless of any bias present in *Awakened China*, "those who most hate communism and who most fear China should logically be those to study this and other first hand accounts most carefully." And the *Spectator's* Nicholas Wollaston simply stated: "The facts of China's prodigious advance cannot be drummed too often into the ears of a complacent West, and Mr. Greene has several notable qualifications which make [*Awakened China*] the most valuable account since Edgar Snow exploded his *Red Star over China* twenty-five years ago."

Greene's subsequent works encountered objections quite similar to those raised in connection with *Awakened China*. Commenting on *A Curtain of Ignorance*, an examination of media coverage of China, a critic in *Book Week* wrote: "It is not possible, without matching his research, to refute Greene as he picks and chooses his way through mountains of old newspapers and magazines, but one wonders how representative his selection of quotations is. The press is not fettered or monolithic. It has its wild men, and the author quotes some of them at length. . . . [But] despite its lopsidedness, there is truth in the small hard core of Greene's argument. The press has never reported China well. Greene could have demonstrated this convincingly with a less biased and partisan approach."

H. L. Boorman of the *New York Times Book Review* felt that "many of the points made by Mr. Greene are both valid and worthy of emphasis. Yet the net effect of this book is as misleading as the type of writing on China that its author condemns. . . . Unfortunately, Mr. Greene has laced his negative case on China reporting with more impatience than perspective. Had he taken the time to produce a shorter and less polemical book, the purposes which stimulated his writing might have been better served."

But *Best Sellers* critic W. M. Moses noted: "[Greene] points out that our news media have apparently relied to a great extent on the reports of refugees who probably have an axe to grind, on press releases and reports emanating from Chiang Kai-shek's headquarters on Formosa and on information furnished by the 'China Lobby' which has had almost unlimited funds with which to attempt to mold American public opinion. . . . [*A Curtain of Ignorance*] presents a severe indictment of our Federal administration. . . . [It also] presents an even more severe indictment of all of our news media. . . . It is a thought provoking book in which the author's conclusions are well documented."

The *New Republic's* James Gilbert described *The Enemy*, Greene's study of revolution and the link between capitalism and imperialism (written from a Marxist-Leninist point of view), as "a statement of faith and the documentation of what must have been the reason for the author's decision to join the revolutionary struggle." But, said Gilbert, the book ultimately fails "because the author, as he admits, sees no need to present the good as well as the bad aspects of capitalism. In one stroke he thus tosses out the complexities and converts his indictment to rhetoric." Another critic wrote in *New Statesman*: "This book is a piece of wartime propaganda, and hence it can perhaps be forgiven for containing a fair proportion of rhetorical exaggeration. . . . What is lacking in Greene's whole analysis of imperialism is any sense of the complexities of this subject. . . . [He] has chosen a subject of first importance; but he has written a second-rate book."

A *Times Literary Supplement* reviewer agreed that the author's "moral indictment is not in the least assisted by the simplistic Marxism with which Mr. Greene feels obliged to back it. For what he gets from Marx is not science but demonology." Nevertheless, the reviewer concludes, "Mr. Greene is a reporter of immense reputation, and the reputation is wholly justified; here [in *The Enemy*] he builds up a crescendo of invective on the basis of official statistics and some terrifying, self-destructive quotations. . . . Almost everything Mr. Greene has to say is true and important."

AVOCATIONAL INTERESTS: Reading, walking.

BIOGRAPHICAL/CRITICAL SOURCES: Saturday Review, September 9, 1961; *New York Times Book Review,* September 10, 1961, August 23, 1964; *Christian Science Monitor,* September 20, 1961; *Chicago Sunday Tribune,* September 24, 1961; *New York Herald Tribune Books,* October 1, 1961; *Spectator,* January 12, 1962; *New Statesman,* February 2, 1962, December 11, 1970; *Guardian,* February 2, 1962; *Book Week,* September 6, 1964; *Best Sellers,* September 15, 1964; *New York Times,* May 26, 1965; *Times Literary Supplement,* May 25, 1967, March 19, 1971; *New Republic,* May 29, 1971.

—*Sketch by Deborah A. Straub*

* * *

GREENWOOD, Marianne (Hederstrom) 1926-

PERSONAL: Born April 5, 1926, in Lapland, Sweden; daughter of Sune (president of state forests) and Elin (Pettersson) Hederstrom; children: Christer K. Hederstrom, Allan Greenwood. *Education:* Studied at art academy in Stockholm, Sweden, for three years; also studied in Switzerland, one year. *Agent:* Bertha Klausner, International Literary Agency, Inc., 71 Park Ave., New York, N.Y. 10016.

CAREER: Photographer and self-described "bird and gypsy," who adds that "being on a perpetual journey I sometimes find the time to write about what I feel and see, but I think that living in itself is a profession, taking up all time."

WRITINGS: Det tatuerade hjaertat (autobiography; includes photographs by Greenwood), Raben & Sjoegren, 1964, translation by Greenwood published as *The Tattooed Heart of Livingston,* Stein & Day, 1965; *Indianerna kallar det soett salt,* Seelig, 1975; *Mein indianerna Sommer: ein Reisebuch,* C. Bertelsmann, 1975.

Photographic illustrator: Jacques Prevert, *Vignette pour les vignerons,* Falaize, 1950; Andre Verdet, *Picasso in Musee d'Antibes,* Falaize, 1951; Evert Taube, *Svarta Tjurar,* Raben & Sjoegren, 1958; Taube, *Aterkomst,* Raben & Sjoegren, 1958; Dor de la Souchere, *Picasso in Antibes,* Pantheon, 1961; Carleton Beals, *Land of the Mayas: Yesterday and Today,* Abelard, 1967; Beals, *The Incredible Incas: Yesterday and Today,* Abelard, 1973; *Mexico,* Universe Books, 1973.

Also illustrator of small art books published in France. Contributor of photographs to accompany various articles in *Mankind;* contributor of articles to *VI* (weekly magazine, Stockholm), and short stories to *Cad, Adam, Knight,* and other periodicals.

WORK IN PROGRESS: A picture book about the Navajo Indians, to be published by Mankind; second part of autobiography.†

* * *

GREER, Georgeanna H(errmann) 1922-

PERSONAL: Born March 11, 1922, in Ann Arbor, Mich.;

daughter of George R. (a physician) and Anna (Williams) Herrmann; married Sam J. Greer (a surgeon), August 5, 1943; children: Cassandra (Mrs. Mark P. Gainey), Walter M., Margret S. (Mrs. J. D. Whisenant). *Education:* University of Texas, Main University (now University of Texas at Austin), B.A., 1940; University of Texas Medical Branch at Galveston, M.D., 1943; San Antonio Art Institute, postgraduate study, 1958-65. *Religion:* Episcopalian. *Home and office:* 213 Black Hawk, San Antonio, Tex. 78232.

CAREER: University of Michigan Hospital, Ann Arbor, intern, 1943-44, assistant resident, 1944-45, resident in pediatrics, 1946; Texas State Health Department, Austin, pediatric clinician, 1946; private practice of medicine in Ann Arbor, 1947-51; San Antonio City Health Department, San Antonio, Tex., part-time physician, 1954—. Consultant to Texas State Historical Commission, 1972-75; volunteer assistant at Witte Museum. *Member:* Historic Site Archeology Conference, Society for Historical Archeology, American Ceramic Circle, Texas Historical Association.

WRITINGS: (With Harding Black) *The Meyer Family,* Trinity University Press, 1971; *Made by Hand: Mississippi Folk Art,* Mississippi State Museum, 1980; *Potters of the Catawba Valley,* Mint Museum, Charlotte, N.C., 1980; *American Stonewares: The Art and Craft of Utilitarian Potters,* Schiffer, 1981. Contributor to *Historic Site Archeology Forum Paper, Ceramics Monthly, Antiques,* and other publications.

SIDELIGHTS: Georgeanna Greer writes: "I have always had an interest in ceramics, and after we had lived in San Antonio a few years, I found that excellent classes were given here in making of stoneware on the potter's wheel and glazing and firing. After about eight years of this study I found by accident that much utilitarian pottery had been made in Texas, but that no history or material was available on the subject. This started me on an investigation of early potteries and collecting of early wares which has not waned. It is entirely an avocation, but quite consuming in the past few years."

*   *   *

GREET, Kenneth (Gerald) 1918-

PERSONAL: Born November 17, 1918, in Bristol, England; son of Walter Henry and Renee (Muir) Greet; married Mary Eileen Edbrooke, July 26, 1947; children: Susan, John, Elizabeth. *Education:* Attended Handsworth College, 1945-47. *Home:* 16, Orchard Ave., Shirley, Croydon, Surrey, England. *Office:* Methodist Conference Office, 1 Central Buildings, London S.W.1, England.

CAREER: Bristol Corp., Bristol, England, clerk, 1935-40; Methodist minister in Rhondda Valley, South Wales, 1947-54; Methodist Department of Christian Citizenship, London, England, secretary, 1954-71; Methodist Conference, London, secretary of conference, 1971—, president, 1980-81.

WRITINGS—Published by Epworth, except as indicated: *Man and Wife Together,* 1958; *Large Petitions,* 1958; *The Mutual Society,* 1962; *Guide to Loving,* Hutchinson, 1964; *The Art of Moral Judgement,* 1970; *When the Spirit Moves,* 1975; *A Lion from a Thicket,* 1978; *The Big Sin,* Marshalls Educational, 1982. Contributor to religious journals.

*   *   *

GREGORY, J. Dennis
See WILLIAMS, John A(lfred)

GRIFFITH, Richard (Edward) 1912-1969

PERSONAL: Born October 6, 1912, in Winchester, Va.; died October 17, 1969, near Winchester, Va., in an automobile accident; buried in Mt. Hebron Cemetery, Winchester, Va.; married Ann Warren, November 26, 1947. *Education:* Haverford College, B.A., 1935. *Home:* 42-24 208th St., Bayside 61, New York, N.Y. *Office:* Museum of Modern Art, 11 West 53rd St., New York, N.Y.

CAREER: Northern Virginia Daily, Winchester, Va., reporter, 1935-37; Museum of Modern Art Film Library, New York City, curatorial assistant, 1937-38, 1940-42, curator, 1951-65; National Board of Review of Motion Pictures, New York City, executive director, 1945-49. Lecturer, Wesleyan University, 1967. *Military service:* U.S. Army Signal Corps, Army Pictorial Service, 1942-45; became sergeant. *Member:* New York Film Council (president, 1946), Society of Cinematologists (president, 1963-64). *Awards, honors:* Rockefeller Foundation fellowship, 1937-38.

WRITINGS: (With Paul Rotha) *The Film Till Now,* Funk, 1950; (with Rotha and Sinclair Road) *Documentary Film,* new edition, Faber, 1951; *The World of Robert Flaherty,* Duell, 1953, reprinted, Greenwood Press, 1970; (with Arthur Mayer) *The Movies,* Simon & Schuster, 1957, revised edition, 1970; *Anatomy of a Motion Picture,* Hutchinson, 1959; *The Movie Stars,* Doubleday, 1970; (editor) Benjamin B. Hampton, *History of the American Film Industry to 1931,* Dover, 1970; (editor) *The Talkies: Articles and Illustrations from "Photoplay" Magazine, 1928-1940,* Dover, 1971.

Author of monographs on Frank Capra, Samuel Goldwyn, Fred Zinnemann, Marlene Dietrich, and Gene Kelly.

OBITUARIES: New York Times, October 19, 1969; *Variety,* October 22, 1969.†

*   *   *

GRISEZ, Germain G. 1929-

PERSONAL: Surname is pronounced "Gree-zay"; born September 30, 1929, in University Heights, Ohio; son of William J. and Mary C. (Lindesmith) Grisez; married Jeannette Eunice Selby, June 9, 1951; children: Thomas, James, Joseph (deceased), Paul. *Education:* John Carroll University, B.A. (magna cum laude), 1951; Dominican College of St. Thomas Aquinas, River Forest, Ill., M.A. and Ph.L. (summa cum laude), 1951; University of Chicago, Ph.D., 1959. *Politics:* Independent. *Religion:* Catholic. *Office:* Department of Philosophy, Mount St. Mary's College, Emmitsburg, Md. 21727.

CAREER: Federal Reserve Bank, Chicago, Ill., clerical worker, 1951-56; Georgetown University, Washington, D.C., 1957-72, began as assistant professor, became professor of philosophy; University of Regina, Campion College, Regina, Saskatchewan, professor of philosophy, 1972-79; Mount St. Mary's College, Emmitsburg, Md., Reverend Harry J. Flynn Professor of Christian Ethics, 1979—. Lecturer at University of Virginia, 1961-62; Archdiocese of Washington, D.C., special assistant, 1968-69, consultant, 1969-72. *Member:* American Philosophical Association, Metaphysical Society of America, American Catholic Philosophical Association (member of executive council, 1968-70), Fellowship of Catholic Scholars (founding member). *Awards, honors:* Lilly postdoctoral fellowship in religion, 1963-64; summer research grants, Georgetown University, 1962 and 1968; research grants, Medora A. Feehan Charitable and Educational Trust, 1967, 1973, 1975, and 1979; Pro Ecclesia et Pontifice Medal, 1972; international travel grant, Canada Council, 1974; research grants, University of Regina, 1974-78, Canada Council, 1977, and De Rance, Inc., 1980; special award, Fellowship of Catholic Scholars, 1981, for scholarly work.

WRITINGS: Contraception and the Natural Law, Bruce, 1965; *Abortion: The Myths, the Realities, and the Arguments,* Corpus Publications, 1971; (with Russell Shaw) *Beyond the New Morality: The Responsibilities of Freedom,* University of Notre Dame Press, 1974, 2nd edition, 1981; *Beyond the New Theism: A Philosophy of Religion,* University of Notre Dame Press, 1975; (with Joseph M. Boyle, Jr. and Olaf Tollefsen) *Free Choice: A Self Referential Argument,* University of Notre Dame Press, 1976; (with Boyle) *Life and Death with Liberty and Justice: A Contribution to the Euthanasia Debate,* University of Notre Dame Press, 1979. Contributor to philosophy and theology journals, including *Natural Law Forum.*

WORK IN PROGRESS: Christian Moral Principles.

*   *   *

GROSSACK, Martin Myer   1928-

PERSONAL: Born June 11, 1928, in Boston, Mass.; son of Albert L. (a salesman) and Rose Grossack; married Judith Tractenberg, June 29, 1952; children: David, Richard. *Education:* Northeastern University, B.A., 1948; Boston University, M.A., 1949, Ph.D., 1952. *Religion:* Jewish. *Home and office:* 99 Revere St., Hull, Mass. 02045.

CAREER: Clinical and social psychologist, in private practice; Grossack Research Co., Hull, Mass., president, 1957—. *Military service:* U.S. Air Force, 1952-55; became captain. *Member:* American Psychological Association.

WRITINGS: (Editor) *Mental Health and Segregation: A Selection of Papers and Some Book Chapters,* Springer Publishing Co., 1963; (editor) *Understanding Consumer Behavior,* Christopher, 1964, 2nd edition, 1966; *You Are Not Alone: A Guide for Mental Health in Our Times,* Christopher, 1965; (with Howard Gardner) *Man and Men: Social Psychology as a Social Science,* International Textbook Co., 1970; *Consumer Psychology: Theory and Practice,* Branden Press, 1971; *Consumer Psychology for Humanized Bank Marketing,* Schenkman, 1971; (with Barbara Levin) *Love and Reason,* Institute for Rational Living, 1976; *Love, Sex and Self-Fulfillment: Keys to Successful Living,* New American Library, 1978.

*   *   *

GRUBER, Joseph John, Jr.   1930-

PERSONAL: Born February 11, 1930, in Chicago, Ill.; son of Joseph John (a dock foreman) and Olive Marie (Schommer) Gruber; married Patricia Lorene Caylor, August 3, 1952; children: Cathy Louise, Jodyne Patricia, Michael Joseph, Jay Leslie. *Education:* Purdue University, B.P.E., 1952, M.P.E., 1953, Ph.D., 1959. *Politics:* Republican. *Religion:* Baptist. *Home:* 3419 Woodstock Circle, Lexington, Ky. 40506. *Office:* Department of Health and Physical Education, Seaton Bldg., University of Kentucky, Lexington, Ky. 40506.

CAREER: West Lafayette (Ind.) High School, teacher of physical education and coach, 1952-53; Utah State Industrial School, Ogden, teacher of physical education and biology, 1953; Purdue University, West Lafayette, Ind., graduate counselor, 1955-57, associate professor of physical education, 1957-67; University of Kentucky, Lexington, professor of physical education and chairman of department of health and physical education, 1967—. Young Men's Christian Association, Lafayette, Ind., assistant physical director, 1955-57, member of physical

education committee, 1955-63; president, Lafayette Church Recreation Council, 1958. *Military service:* U. S. Army, Ordnance Corps, served in Korea, 1953-55. *Member:* North American Society for the Psychology of Sport and Physical Activity, American Association for Health, Physical Education and Recreation, American Academy of Physical Education (fellow), American College of Sports Medicine, College Physical Education Association, Indiana Association for Health, Physical Education and Recreation, Alpha Kappa Delta.

WRITINGS: Physical Education: An Interpretation for Parents, Indiana State Board of Health, 1962; (with H. D. Edgren) *Teachers Handbook of Indoor and Outdoor Games,* Prentice-Hall, 1963; (with A. H. Ismail) *Integrated Development,* C. E. Merrill, 1967; (with D. R. Kirkendall and R. E. Johnson) *Measurement and Evaluation for Physical Educators,* W. C. Brown, 1980. Contributor to proceedings of national and international physical education conferences. Contributor of 40 articles to professional journals, including *International Journal of Sport Psychology, International Review of Sport Sociology, Journal of Motor Behavior, Behavioral Disorders, Education,* and *Research Quarterly for Exercise and Sport.*

*   *   *

GULLEY, Halbert E(dison)   1919-

PERSONAL: Born November 21, 1919, in Sesser, Ill.; son of Roy A. (a legislator and real estate agent) and Mary (Martel) Gulley; married Nadine Ellen Dauderman (a public school teacher), June 28, 1941; children: Gerald Baird, Ellen Elizabeth, William Bruce. *Education:* Southern Illinois University, B.Ed., 1940; State University of Iowa (now University of Iowa), M.A., 1941, Ph.D., 1948. *Politics:* Republican. *Religion:* Congregational, United Church of Christ. *Home:* 1103 Shore Dr., Twin Lakes, Wis.

CAREER: Hannibal High School, Hannibal, Mo., teacher of speech, 1941-42; Shrivenham American University, Shrivenham, England, teacher of speech and head of speech department, 1945; State University of Iowa (now University of Iowa), Iowa City, instructor in communication, 1946-48; University of Illinois at Urbana-Champaign, Urbana, professor of speech, 1948-67, head of division of general studies, 1963-67; Colorado State University, Fort Collins, professor of speech, 1967-68; University of Kentucky, Lexington, professor and chairman of department of speech, 1968-70; Northern Illinois University, DeKalb, chairman of department of communication studies, 1970-78, professor, 1978-79, professor emeritus, 1979—. Lecturer on communication for communication seminars, U.S. Air Force Chaplains in Japan and Hawaii, 1963, Britain and West Germany, 1964, and Agency for International Development, Cacapon Lodge, W.Va., and Boyne Mountain, Mich. University of Illinois Y.M.C.A., member of board, 1956-59, 1962—, chairman of board, 1963-65; member of board, Illinois Disciples Foundation, 1956-62. *Military service:* U.S. Army, Infantry, served in German campaign during World War II; received Purple Heart. *Member:* Speech Communication Association, Central States Speech Association (executive secretary, 1957-58), Illinois Speech Association (president, 1955-56).

WRITINGS: (Contributor) *Speech Education in America,* Appleton, 1954; *Essentials of Discussion and Debate,* Henry Holt, 1955; *Discussion, Conference, and Group Process,* Holt, 1960; (contributor) *American Public Addresses,* University of Missouri Press, 1961; (contributor) *Anti-Slavery and Disunion,* Harper, 1963; (with Phillips R. Biddle) *Essentials of Debate,* Holt, 1969; (with Biddle) *Essentials of Discussion,* Holt, 1971;

(with Dale Leathers) *Communication and Group Process,* Holt, 1977; (with wife, Nadine Gulley) *I Tell You Truly: Communication for Marrieds,* Interperson Press, 1981.

AVOCATIONAL INTERESTS: Printing; collecting and polishing rocks.

*   *   *

GUNDREY, Elizabeth 1924-

PERSONAL: Born June 11, 1924, in London, England; daughter of Victor Gareth and Mabel (Carey) Gundrey; married; children: one son. *Education:* University of London, B.A. (with honors in history), 1946. *Home:* 19 Fitzjohns Ave., London NW3 5JY, England.

CAREER: Writer and editor. *Shopper's Guide,* London, England, founder and editor, 1957-64; former feature writer for *News Chronicle;* former home editor of *House and Garden* and *Housewife. Member:* Society of Authors, Guild of Travel Writers.

WRITINGS—Adult books: *Your Money's Worth,* Penguin, 1962; *At Your Service,* Penguin, 1954; *A Foot in Your Door,* Muller, 1965; *Value for Money,* Hodder & Stoughton, 1966; *Jobs for Mothers,* Hodder & Stoughton, 1967; (with Jean Carper) *Stay Alive!: How to Prevent Accidents in the Home,* MacGibbon & Kee, 1967; (editor) *The Book of Egg Cookery,* Spectator Publications, 1969.

Juvenile: *Fun Foods,* Galt & Co., 1971; *Then—1745, 1815, 1832, 1848, 1901, 1920,* Way, 1972; *Making Decorations,* Pan Books, 1973; *Sewing Things,* Pan Books, 1973; *Fun with Flowers,* Galt & Co., 1973; *Fun Dressing-Up,* Galt & Co., 1973; *Growing Things,* Pan Books, 1973; *Make Your Own Monster,* Pan Books, 1973; (with Martin Mayhew and Cherille Mayhew) *Fun with Art,* Galt & Co., 1973; *Collecting Things,* Pan Books, 1974; *The Summer Book,* Methuen, 1974; *You and Your Money,* Evans Brothers, 1976; *All Your Own,* Hamlyn, 1977; *Kings and Queens,* Pan Books, 1977; *Send Off for It,* Hamlyn, 1978; *Joining Things,* Severn House, 1978; *The Winter Book,* Methuen, 1978; *Fun in the Garden,* Pan Books, 1978; *Exploring England by Bus,* Hamlyn, 1981; *Sparing Time: Guide to Helping Others,* Allen & Unwin, 1981; *200 More Things to Send For,* Hamlyn, 1981; *Helping Hands,* Allen & Unwin, 1981; *England by the Sea,* Severn House, 1982; *Staying off the Beaten Track,* Hamlyn, 1982.

Also author and editor of numerous books for adults on consumer economics, industrial hygiene, careers, cookery, and interior decoration. Contributor to television programs of the British Broadcasting Corp. and other networks. Regular contributor to British newspapers, including the *Observer.*

AVOCATIONAL INTERESTS: British history and architectural heritage, enjoying the English countryside and wildlife, painting.

*   *   *

GUPPY, Nicholas (Gareth Lechmere) 1925-

PERSONAL: Born December 22, 1925, in Trinidad, British West Indies; son of Gareth Everard Lechmere (in Colonial Service) and Marjorie A. Glass (Hooper) Guppy; married Shusha Assar (an actress and singer), April 4, 1961 (divorced); married Sarah Grenney, February 14, 1980; children: (first marriage) Darius, Constantine. *Education:* Attended Kelly College; Trinity College, Cambridge, B.A. (honors), 1947, M.A., 1951; additional study at Magdalen College, Oxford. *Politics:* Progressive conservative. *Religion:* Christian. *Home:*

21a Shawfield St., London SW3 4BD, England; and The Pond, Haddenham, Cambridgeshire, England. *Agent:* A.M. Heath & Co., Ltd., 40-42 William IV St., London WC2N 4DD, England.

CAREER: British Colonial Forestry Service, assistant conservator of forests in British Guiana, 1948-53; New York Botanical Garden, Bronx Park, N.Y., research associate, 1953-55. Critic and adviser on investment in art alongside ecological work. Leader or member of eight expeditions in northern South America. Scientific adviser on nature films, Granada Television Network, 1959. Chairman, Sovereign American Arts Corp., 1969-70; founder and chairman, Survival International, 1970. *Member:* Zoological Society of London (scientific fellow), Royal Geographical Society (fellow), Royal Horticultural Society (fellow), Society of Authors.

WRITINGS: Wai-Wai: Through the Forests North of the Amazon, J. Murray, 1958; (contributor) *Nature,* Macdonald & Evans, 1960; (contributor) *Mountains,* Putnam, 1962; (contributor) *Oceans and Islands,* Weidenfeld & Nicolson, 1962; *Calder Gouaches,* Lincoln House, 1962; (co-author) *The Amazon,* Time-Life, 1970; *A Young Man's Journey,* J. Murray, 1974; (author with Yseult Bridges) *Child of the Tropics,* Collins, 1980; (contributor) N. Polunin, editor, *Growth without Ecodisaster,* Macmillan, 1980. Also author of reports on South American vegetation and on interpretation of aerial photographs of tropical forest country. Contributor to *House and Garden, Vogue, Queen, Natural History, Harper's Bazaar, Saturday Review, Observer,* and other periodicals.

Consultant for "The World We Live In" series, published in *Life,* 1954. Advisory editor to Rathbone's *Keys to Understanding,* 1958, and *Wildlife* (formerly *Animals*), 1963-81.

WORK IN PROGRESS: Schomburgk, a book about the nineteenth-century explorer and botanist; a book on the structure of symbols and concepts; "a book on 'frontiers,' physical, geographical, social, and mental."

SIDELIGHTS: Nicholas Guppy wrote *CA:* "I first wrote when I was eight years old. It was an article about three pages long and described the life and adventures of a water spider I had been reading about in one of the Rev. J. G. Wood's books. When I was thirteen I wrote my first article to be published. It was about the tiny Guppy fish (named after my grandfather). . . . I reread it recently and was surprised: It is quite remarkably informative and shows how keen an observer I was as a child in Trinidad, West Indies, where I lived until twelve years old.

"From 1940 to 1942 I lived with my mother in Strathyre, a then remote village in Perthshire, Scotland. I did not attend school, but educated myself by reading secondhand books, mostly on natural history, which I purchased on visits to Glasgow and Edinburgh. It was at this time that I decided to be a writer. This decision stayed firm during my subsequent school and university days and thereafter.

"My two books, *Wai-Wai* and *A Young Man's Journey,* were motivated by the desire to combine both the external and the internal worlds: the objective accuracy of a scientist, with the subjective feelings and emotions experienced by that same individual. Each book describes an expedition—an event that naturally and genuinely possesses a beginning, a developmental middle section, and an end. Within this structure I have shaped events to form an arch—like a rainbow, whose ends touch earth on either side; and within that arch are colours, interruptions, digressions, and details.

"I hoped that my books would be easy to read and would convey new and sometimes difficult ideas to a large audience and change their view of the world. My style was intended to be so transparent that the reader would forget the words and just grasp the meaning.

"I enjoy the contemporary literary scene but do not always admire what I see. I once felt it sad that the greatest writers of today, like Solzhenitsyn, concerned themselves with questions that the more evolved nations solved 100 years ago, like that of personal freedom. But now I feel they are right to warn us of the threats to all civilized values that are posed worldwide by ruthless and greedy seekers of political power.

"Besides the works of these great moralists I delight in all forms of literary exploration into hitherto unknown aspects of human behaviour, and am particularly drawn to experiments in maximizing the expressiveness of the language such as those of John Lennon. Such important work must continue—and it can only continue in the remaining free parts of the world."

Guppy has travelled extensively, especially from 1960 to 1969, to South America, the Near and Far East, Eastern Archipelagos, the Pacific, and Antarctica.

AVOCATIONAL INTERESTS: Listening to music, walking, swimming.

*   *   *

GUTTMACHER, Alan F(rank)   1898-1974

PERSONAL: Born May 19, 1898, in Baltimore, Md.; died March 18, 1974, of leukemia, at Mount Sinai Hospital in New York, N.Y.; son of Adolf and Laura (Oppenheimer) Guttmacher; married Leonore Gidding, July 22, 1925; children: Ann (Mrs. Robert Loeb), Sally (Mrs. Eric Holtzman), Susan (Mrs. Ben Green). *Education:* Johns Hopkins University, A.B., 1919, M.D., 1923. *Home:* 1185 Park Ave., New York, N.Y. *Office:* 515 Madison Ave., New York, N.Y.

CAREER: Johns Hopkins University, Medical School, Baltimore, Md., assistant in anatomy, 1923-24; University of Rochester, Rochester, N.Y., assistant in anatomy, 1924-25; Johns Hopkins Hospital, Baltimore, internship, 1925-26; Johns Hopkins University, Medical School, 1926-52, became associate professor of obstetrics; Mount Sinai Medical School, New York City, professor of obstetrics and gynecology, 1952-62, professor emeritus, 1962-74, chief of obstetrics and gynecology, Mount Sinai Hospital; president, Planned Parenthood Federation of America, 1962-74. Columbia University, College of Physicians and Surgeons, clinical professor, 1952-63, lecturer, 1963-74; lecturer in maternal and child health, Harvard School of Public Health, beginning 1963; visiting professor, Einstein Medical School. Private practice of medicine, Baltimore, 1929-52, New York City, 1952-74. Diplomate, American Board of Obstetrics and Gynecology. Member of board of directors, Margaret Sanger Research Bureau. *Military service:* U.S. Army Infantry, 1918. *Member:* American Association of Obstetricians and Gynecologists (fellow), American College of Obstetricians and Gynecologists, International Planned Parenthood Federation (chairman of medical committee, 1964-68), American Society for Study of Sterility (fellow), American Eugenics Society (vice-president, 1956), New York Academy of Medicine, New York Obstetrical Society. *Awards, honors:* Lasker Award, 1947; Broniman Award, 1970.

WRITINGS: Life in the Making, Viking, 1933, 2nd edition published as *Human Sex Life,* Sun Dial, 1940; *Into This Universe,* Viking, 1937; *Having a Baby,* New American Library, 1950; (with Harold Speert) *Obstetric Practice,* McGraw, 1956; *Pregnancy and Birth: A Book for Expectant Parents,* Viking, 1957, 3rd edition published as *Pregnancy, Birth, and Family*

Planning: A Guide for Expectant Parents in the 1970's, 1973; *Babies by Choice or by Chance,* Doubleday, 1959; (editor with Joseph J. Rovinsky) *Medical, Surgical and Gynecological Complications of Pregnancy,* Williams & Wilkins, 1960, revised edition published as *Medical, Surgical, and Gynecologic Complications of Pregnancy,* 1965; (with Winfield Best and Frederick S. Jaffe) *The Complete Book of Birth Control,* Ballantine, 1961, 3rd edition published as *Planning Your Family,* Macmillan, 1964, published as *Birth Control and Love: The Complete Guide to Contraception,* 1969; *Conception Control, Its Implications for the Individual and the World,* Alpha Kappa Kappa Medical Fraternity Lecture, 1961; (with others) *The Consumers Union Report on Family Planning,* Consumers Union, 1962, 2nd edition, 1966; (editor with Stephan A. Richardson) Elaine Grimm and others, *Childbearing: Its Social and Psychological Aspects,* Williams & Wilkins, 1967; (editor) *The Case for Legalized Abortion Now,* Diablo Press, 1967; *Understanding Sex: A Young Person's Guide,* Harper, 1970. Contributor of numerous articles to professional and popular periodicals.

SIDELIGHTS: Alan Guttmacher was a staunch supporter of family planning both on a national and international basis. During his years as president of Planned Parenthood, he fought for widespread dissemination of birth control information, national programs based on voluntary family planning, and legalized abortions. He lectured throughout the world and testified before numerous legislative bodies in support of birth control and was considered one of the movement's elder statesmen.

BIOGRAPHICAL/CRITICAL SOURCES: New York Times Magazine, February 9, 1969.

OBITUARIES: New York Times, March 19, 1974; *Washington Post,* March 20, 1974.†

*   *   *

GYLDENVAND, Lily M.   1917-

PERSONAL: Born May 26, 1917, in La Moure, N.D.; daughter of Ole C. (a merchant) and Karen G. (Myhr) Gyldenvand. *Education:* Concordia College, Moorhead, Minn., B.A., 1939. *Religion:* Lutheran. *Home:* 2545 Fry St., Roseville, Minn. 55113.

CAREER: Evangelical Lutheran Church, Department of Christian Education, Minneapolis, Minn., secretary, 1939-41; U.S. Department of Agriculture, Commodity Credit Corporation, Minneapolis, secretary, 1941-52; American Lutheran Church, Minneapolis, administrative and editorial assistant, 1953-60; American Lutheran Church Women, Minneapolis, editor of *Scope* magazine, 1960-79; writer and lecturer, 1979—. Formerly employed in Publication Development Division, Augsburg Publishing House. *Member:* Associated Church Press, Lutheran Daughters of the Reformation (international president, 1948-54). *Awards, honors:* L.H.D., Concordia College (Moorhead, Minn.), 1975.

WRITINGS—All published by Augsburg: Beyond All Doubt, 1949; *What Am I Saying?,* 1952; *Of All Things,* 1956; *So You're Only Human,* 1957; *What Am I Praying?,* 1964; *Call Her Blessed: Every Woman Who Discovers the Gifts of God,* 1967; *Invitation to Joy,* 1969; *Prayer Scrapbook,* 1974; *Martin Luther, Giant of Faith,* 1980; *Joy in His Presence,* 1981.

Co-author of Bible study manuals for American Lutheran Church Women, 1964, 1965. Author of tracts and radio scripts. Contributor of articles and book reviews to periodicals. Editor, *Yearbook of the Evangelical Lutheran Church,* 1953-60; editorial assistant, *Annual Report of the Evangelical Lutheran Church,* 1953-60.

BIOGRAPHICAL/CRITICAL SOURCES: Minneapolis Sunday Tribune, December 27, 1964.

H

HAAS, Kenneth B(rooks), Sr.   1898-

PERSONAL: Surname is pronounced "Haws"; born January 24, 1898, in Pennsylvania; son of John Louis (a businessman) and Mary (a seamstress; maiden name, Brooks) Haas; married Verna Hoffman, December 24, 1921; children: Kenneth B., Jr., Noel L. *Education:* University of Pittsburgh, B.S., 1924, M.A., 1931; New York University, Ed.D., 1935. *Politics:* Republican. *Religion:* Protestant. *Home:* 3747 Atlantic Ave., Long Beach, Calif. 90807.

CAREER: Proprietor of small wholesale business in Pittsburgh, Pa., 1924-28; high school teacher of commerce in the public schools of Pennsylvania and New Jersey, 1928-35; College of Commerce, Bowling Green, Ky., professor of marketing, 1935-38; U.S. Office of Education, Washington, D.C., specialist in business education, 1938-46; Montgomery Ward, Chicago, Ill., national retail training director, 1946-48; training consultant in Chicago and New York, N.Y., 1948-58; Hofstra University, Hempstead, N.Y., professor of marketing, 1958-63; University of Washington, Seattle, lecturer in marketing, 1963-67. *Military service:* U.S. Navy, 1915-19. U.S. Naval Fleet Reserve, 1919-23. U.S. Army, Chemical Warfare Service, 1942-43; became major. *Member:* Veterans of World War I, California Genealogical Society, Historical Society of Western Pennsylvania, Masons.

WRITINGS: *Studies in Problems of the Consumer,* College of Commerce, 1936; *Adventure in Buymanship,* College of Commerce, 1937; *Distributive Education,* Gregg, 1941; *Better Retailing,* National Cash Register, 1941; *Military Instructor's Manual,* U.S. Army, Washington, D.C., 1942; *How to Coordinate School-Work Experience,* Gregg, 1944; (with O. P. Robinson) *How to Establish and Operate a Retail Store,* Prentice-Hall, 1946; (with H. Q. Packard) *Preparation and Use of Audio-Visual Aids,* Prentice-Hall, 1946; (with C. H. Ewing) *Tested Training Techniques,* Prentice-Hall, 1949; (with W. H. Wilson) *The Film Book,* Prentice-Hall, 1949; (author and editor) *Handbook of Sales Training,* Prentice-Hall, 1949.

Creative Salesmanship, Prentice-Hall, 1950; (with son, Kenneth B. Haas, Jr.) *Business Practices in Veterinary Medicine,* Veterinary Medicine Publishing, 1953; (with E. C. Perry) *Sales Horizons,* Prentice-Hall, 1957, 3rd edition, 1968; *How to Develop Successful Salesmen,* McGraw, 1959; *Opportunities in Selling,* Vocational Guidance Manuals, 1960; *Professional Salesmanship,* Holt, 1962; (with John W. Ernest) *Creative Salesmanship,* Free Press, 1969, 3rd edition, 1978.

Opportunities in Sales-Marketing, National Textbook Co., 1980; *The Haas Family of Western Pennsylvania,* privately printed, 1980. Author of more than two hundred manuals, monographs, and magazine articles for professional and scientific publications. Author of film scripts and scenarios for sales training purposes.

WORK IN PROGRESS: *Our Scotch-Irish Heritage,* to be privately printed.

SIDELIGHTS: "I was a grade school dropout and never attended secondary school," Kenneth B. Haas once told *CA.* "I worked on farms, drove a team of horses, worked in retail stores, and served in the U.S. Navy. My absence from formal schooling gained me an enormous advantage; I taught myself during those years, and what I learned was practical and thorough, even if sketchy. Thus I got into my bones the essentials of a secondary education and more, which enabled me to pass college entrance exams with ease. One principle I learned was 'never give in; never yield to adversity.' That rage to succeed is the quality which carried me through my low points, for fortune never smiled on me except when I applied this principle."

                    *   *   *

HADAS, Moses   1900-1966

PERSONAL: Born June 25, 1900, in Atlanta, Ga.; died August 17, 1966, in Aspen, Colo.; son of David and Gertrude (Draizen) Hadas; married Ethel Elkus, April 7, 1926 (divorced); married Elizabeth Chamberlayne, 1945; children: (first marriage) Jane Streusand, David; (second marriage) Elizabeth, Rachel. *Education:* Emory University, A.B., 1922; attended Jewish Theological Seminary, 1922-26; Columbia University, A.M., 1925, Ph.D., 1930. *Home:* 460 Riverside Dr., New York, N.Y. 10027. *Office:* Columbia University, New York, N.Y. 10027.

CAREER: Columbia University, New York, N.Y., 1925-66, began as instructor, associate professor, 1946-53, professor, 1953-56, Jay Professor of Greek, 1956-66. Instructor in classics, University of Cincinnati, 1928-30. *Military service:* Office of Strategic Services, 1943-46. *Member:* American Philological Association, International Society for the History of Ideas, Phi Beta Kappa. *Awards, honors:* Litt.D. from Emory University, 1956; D.H.L. from Kenyon College, 1958, and Lehigh University, 1962.

WRITINGS: Sextus Pompey, Columbia University Press, 1930, reprinted, AMS Press, 1966; *A History of Greek Literature*, Columbia University Press, 1950; *A History of Latin Literature*, Columbia University Press, 1952; *Ancila to Classical Reading*, Columbia University Press, 1954; *Hellenistic Culture: Fusion and Diffusion*, Columbia University Press, 1959; *Humanism: The Greek Ideal and Its Survival*, Harper, 1960, published as *The Greek Ideal and Its Survival*, 1966; *Old Wine, New Bottles*, Simon & Schuster, 1962; *Imperial Rome*, Time Inc., 1965; (with Morton Smith) *Heroes and Gods: Spiritual Biographies in Antiquity*, Harper, 1965; (author of introduction) Suetonius Tranquillus, *The Lives of the Twelve Caesars*, translation by Philemon Holland, Heritage Press, 1965; *Introduction to Classical Drama*, Bantam, 1966; *The Living Tradition*, New American Library, 1967.

Translator: (With Jacob Hammer) *Hellenistic Poetry*, Columbia University Press, 1929; (with J. H. McLean) Euripedes, *Plays*, Dial, 1936; Hermann Vogelstein, *Rome*, Jewish Publication Society of America, 1941; Ismar A. Elbogen, *A Century of Jewish Life*, Jewish Publication Society of America, 1944; Elias Bickerman, *The Maccabees*, Schocken, 1947; Ferdinand Gregorovius, *The Ghetto and the Jews of Rome*, Schocken, 1948; Karl Vietor, *Goethe, the Poet*, Harvard University Press, 1949, reprinted, Russell, 1970; Jakob Burckhardt, *Age of Constantine the Great*, Pantheon, 1949; Walter Otto, *The Homeric Gods: The Spiritual Significance of Greek Religion*, Pantheon, 1954, reprinted, Thames & Hudson, 1979; Seneca, *Oedipus*, Liberal Arts Press, 1955; Seneca, *Medea*, Liberal Arts Press, 1956; Seneca, *Thyestes*, Liberal Arts Press, 1957; Joseph be Meir ibn Zabara, *Book of Delight*, Columbia University Press, 1960; (with Joe P. Poe) Titus Livius, *A History of Rome: Selections*, Modern Library, 1962; (with James Willis) Hermann Frankel, *Early Greek Poetry and Philosophy*, Harcourt, 1975.

Editor: Tacitus, *Complete Works*, Modern Library, 1942, reprinted, 1964; Solomon Maimon, *Solomon Maimon: An Autobiography*, Schocken, 1947; *The Greek Poets*, Modern Library, 1953; Plato, *Euthyphro, Apology, Crito, and Symposium*, Regnery, 1953; Cicero, *Basic Works*, Modern Library, 1961; *Essential Works of Stoicism*, Bantam, 1961; Aristophanes, *Complete Plays*, Bantam, 1962; Edward Gibbon, *The Decline and Fall of the Roman Empire*, abridged edition, Putnam, 1962; Tacitus, *Complete Works*, Modern Library, 1964; Sophocles, *The Complete Plays of Sophocles*, translation by Richard Claverhouse Jebb, Bantam, 1967; *Greek Drama*, Bantam, 1968. Also editor, author of introductions and commentaries, and reader of two recordings, "The Story of Virgil's Aeneid" and "The Latin Language," both for Folkways Records, 1955.

Editor and translator: Euripedes, *Electra*, Bobbs-Merrill, c. 1950; *Aristeas to Philocrates*, Harper, 1951, reprinted, Ktav, 1974; *Three Greek Romances*, Doubleday, 1953; *Third and Fourth Book of Maccabees*, Harper, 1953; *Heinrich Heine* (autobiography), Jewish Publication Society of America, 1956; *A History of Rome from Its Origins to 529 A.D., as Told by the Roman Historians*, Doubleday, 1956; Julius Caesar, *The Gallic War*, Modern Library, 1957; Plutarchus, *On Love, the Family, and the Good Life*, New American Library, 1957; Heliodorus, *Ethiopian Romance*, University of Michigan Press, 1957, reprinted, Greenwood Press, 1976; *The Stoic Philosophy of Seneca*, Doubleday, 1958; *Latin Selections*, Bantam, 1961; Seneca, *The Plays of Seneca*, Bobbs-Merrill, 1965; *Fables of a Jewish Aesop* (from "Fox Fables of Berechiah ha-Nakdan"), Columbia University Press, 1967.

OBITUARIES: New York Times, August 18, 1966.†

HALDEMAN, Joe (William) 1943-
(Robert Graham)

PERSONAL: Born June 9, 1943, in Oklahoma City, Okla.; son of Jack Carroll (a hospital administrator) and Lorena (Spivey) Haldeman; married Mary Gay Potter (a teacher), August 21, 1965. *Education:* University of Maryland, B.S., 1967; University of Iowa, M.F.A., 1975; also attended American University and University of Oklahoma. *Politics:* "Skeptic." *Religion:* "Skeptic." *Home and office:* 345 Grove St., Ormond Beach, Fla. 32074. *Agent:* Kirby McCauley, 425 Park Ave. S., New York, N.Y. 10016.

CAREER: Writer. Former editor of *Astronomy;* has taught writing at University of North Florida and other schools. *Military service:* U.S. Army, 1967-69; became combat engineer; served in Vietnam; wounded in combat; received Purple Heart and other medals. *Member:* Science Fiction Writers of America (treasurer, 1970-72; chairman of Grievance Committee, 1979-80), Authors Guild, National Space Institute, Writers Guild, L-5 Society, Poets and Writers. *Awards, honors:* Hugo Award, World Science Fiction Convention, 1975, Nebula Award, Science Fiction Writers of America, 1975, and Locus Award, *Locus* magazine, 1975, all for *The Forever War;* Hugo Award, World Science Fiction Convention, 1976, and Locus Award, *Locus* magazine, 1976, both for best short story, for "Tricentennial"; Galaxy Award, 1978, for *Mindbridge*.

WRITINGS—Novels, except as indicated: *War Year*, Holt, 1972; (editor) *Cosmic Laughter*, Holt, 1974; *The Forever War*, St. Martin's, 1974; *Mindbridge*, St. Martin's, 1976; *All My Sins Remembered*, St. Martin's, 1977; *Planet of Judgment*, Bantam, 1977; (editor) *Study War No More*, St. Martin's, 1977; (contributor) *Close Up: New Worlds*, St. Martin's, 1977; (author of introduction) Robert A. Heinlein, *Double Star*, Gregg, 1978; *Infinite Dreams*, (short story collection), St. Martin's, 1978; *World without End*, Bantam, 1979; *Worlds*, Viking, 1981. Also author of play, "The Devil His Due," produced at the University of Iowa Film Workshop.

Under pseudonym Robert Graham: *Attar's Revenge*, Pocket Books, 1975; *War of Nerves*, Pocket Books, 1975.

Work has appeared in anthologies, including: *Orbit Eleven*, edited by Damon Knight, Putnam, 1971; *The Best from Galaxy*, edited by Ejler Jakobbsen, Universal-Award, 1972; *Showcase*, edited by Roger Elwood, Harper, 1973; *Best SF: 1972*, edited by Harry Harrison and Brian Aldiss, Putnam, 1973; *The Best Science Fiction of the Year—1972*, edited by Terry Carr, Ballantine, 1973; *Analog 9*, edited by Ben Bova, Doubleday, 1973; *Best SF: 1973*, edited by Harrison and Aldiss, Putnam, 1974; *Combat SF*, edited by Gordon Dickson, Doubleday, 1975; *The Best from Galaxy*, Volume III, Award, 1975; *Nebula Award Stories II*, Harper, 1975; *Frights*, edited by Kirby McCauley, St. Martin's, 1976; *Best Science Fiction Stories*, Dutton, 1977; *Nebula Award Stories XII*, Harper, 1977; *Annual World's Best SF*, DAW, 1978; *Time of Passage*, Taplinger, 1978; *The Endless Frontier*, Ace Books, 1979; *The Road to SF 3*, Mentor, 1979; *Thieve's World*, edited by Robert Asprin, Ace Books, 1979; *The Future at War*, Ace Books, 1980; *Dark Forces*, edited by McCauley, Viking, 1980.

Contributor of forty short stories and articles to *Analog, Galaxy, Omni, Playboy, Isaac Asimov's SF Adventures, Magazine of Fantasy and Science Fiction*, and other publications.

WORK IN PROGRESS: There Is No Darkness, with his brother, Jack C. Haldeman II; short stories and nonfiction; *Stars*, a sequel to *Worlds*.

SIDELIGHTS: In his award-winning science fiction novel *The Forever War*, Joe Haldeman combines his experiences as a soldier during the Vietnam War, in which he was severely wounded, with a realistic, scientifically-accurate presentation. The novel tells of a war that stretches across intergalactic distances and long periods of time, the soldiers involved travelling to remote battlefields via black holes. Because the soldiers travel at faster-than-light speeds, they age far slower than the civilians for whom they fight. This difference in relative age—the soldiers a few years older, their society centuries older—results in an alienation between the soldiers and the people they defend.

"Haldeman exercises his literary license," James Scott Hicks writes in the *Dictionary of Literary Biography*, "to comment on, and ultimately to expunge from his memory, America's last ground war [Vietnam]." Hicks points out that Haldeman's first novel, *War Year*, based on his army diaries, deals with the Vietnam fighting directly. "But the demon of Vietnam," Hicks writes, "was not exorcised from Haldeman's soul by writing [*War Year*], and frontline combat became the subject of . . . *The Forever War*." Haldeman, Hicks believes, is particularly adept at presenting his "theme of quiet resentment felt by those waging war."

Because of his scientific training in physics and astronomy, Haldeman is particularly careful to present *The Forever War* as realistically and accurately as possible. "The technology involved in this interplanetary campaign," Martin Levin of the *New York Times Book Review* notes in his review of *The Forever War*, "is so sophisticated that the book might well have been accompanied by an operator's manual. But then, all the futuristic mayhem is plugged into human situations that help keep the extraterrestrial activity on a warm and even witty plane."

Among newer novelists in the field, Haldeman, Richard Geis of *Science Fiction Review* believes, "is one of the best realistic science fiction writers going; maybe *the* best." Hicks finds that "Haldeman confronts his readers with painful questions, but he asks them with no small literary skill and with careful attention to scientific credibility." "It's comforting to know,'" writes Algis Budrys of the *Magazine of Fantasy and Science Fiction*, "that the cadre of impressive talent among younger writers is not diminishing, and to think that people like Haldeman will be around for a long time to set high standards."

Haldeman's novels have been translated into French, Italian, German, Dutch, Japanese, Hebrew, Spanish, and Swedish.

AVOCATIONAL INTERESTS: Classical guitar, bicycling, woolgathering, strong drink, travel, gardening.

CA INTERVIEW

CA interviewed Joe Haldeman by phone May 28, 1981, at his home in Ormond Beach, Florida.

CA: Your undergraduate work was in physics and astronomy. What were your career plans at that point?

HALDEMAN: I had an outside chance of being an astronaut, because at that time NASA was running a program they called "Scientist as Astronaut." You had to get a Ph.D. in certain sciences, and physics and astronomy were two of them. They'd teach you how to be a test pilot. In fact, only one person got out of that program and on to the moon, and that was Harrison Schmitt. But I was drafted after I got my B.A., and by the time I got out of the army, the program was pretty much done for.

CA: Although you've done other kinds of writing, most of your work has been science fiction. Do you, like some science-fiction

writers, resent having a distinction made between science fiction and so-called mainstream fiction?

HALDEMAN: No, I don't really resent the distinction. They are two different kinds of activity. A good science-fiction novel can be approached as a good work of literature. But it's odd that a book can be good science fiction and very bad literature. There can be a quality of thought to it that isn't literary at all, but just interesting in other ways. I don't think anybody would argue that Orwell's *1984* was great literature, but it's certainly an interesting book anyhow.

CA: You have described Damon Knight's Milford Conference, at which in 1970 you got the encouragement that led you into full-time writing. Is that conference still held annually?

HALDEMAN: It is, but Damon Knight isn't holding it anymore. He did twenty and decided that was plenty and passed it on to younger folks. Now it's being run out in Colorado by a bunch of younger writers.

CA: When Damon Knight was running the conference, how did he select aspiring writers for invitation?

HALDEMAN: He asked you to send a selection of your best work. At first there would only be four or five new writers, and perhaps fifteen to twenty established ones. Slowly, in the last few years, that proportion was almost reversed. I think Damon felt that it was becoming more and more of a social event and that everybody knew what everybody else was going to say about their manuscripts.

CA: Do you attend the large science-fiction conventions?

HALDEMAN: I try to get to the World Convention every year and I even go to it when it's outside the country. It's not so much a social event anymore as a professional necessity. It's one place where all the editors and critics are all together. A lot of deals are made and you get to catch up with friends who are there more or less on business. Also it is an opportunity to see people you only see once a year. It's gotten very hectic, with as many as five or six thousand people there, perhaps a thousand writers and editors and critics and so forth. You can go all four days and not find somebody. It's sort of like the annual meeting of the American Booksellers Association; it's hard to find somebody there.

CA: You have an M.F.A. from the University of Iowa. In what ways were the academic work and atmosphere most helpful to you in your writing?

HALDEMAN: The Writers' Workshop in Iowa ideally tries to give an aspiring writer a couple of years of relief from financial stress. It's not enough for most people to live on, but it is enough that you don't have to go out and hold a job. That was the main reason I went there, and I guess that was the main benefit I got from it—not to downgrade the academic experience. You see, I had written a couple of books by the time I arrived there and my literary style was getting about as set as it ever does get. I also got a lot out of meeting people who have been writing for years and seeing how they adjust to a rather odd life.

CA: You dedicated Mindbridge *(1976) to your teachers at the Iowa Writers' Workshop. Are you still in touch with any of them regularly?*

HALDEMAN: I'm in touch with Stephen Becker and we send mash notes back and forth to John Leggett every now and then.

We get into Iowa City once a year and renew acquaintances at the Workshop. I guess about five or six of the people who were there when I was are still there now.

CA: You've named John Dos Passos as an influence on your work. Are there other major influences that you can identify?

HALDEMAN: Critics usually drag out Hemingway and Crane and Robert Heinlein. I regard them, especially Heinlein, as precursors to my writing. I hesitate to name any writer as an influence, especially in science fiction. What I have is the reading experience of literally thousands of books in the genre; both the good ones and the bad ones have had an effect on me. If I found that my style was very much like some established writer, I would probably work hard to change it.

CA: Do you carefully structure your novels before you begin writing?

HALDEMAN: Yes, normally I do, but I always feel free to change the structure. I don't work up the plot ahead of time; that's something I like to surprise myself with. But I do work out the formal structure, as to how the time and viewpoint are going to be handled. I think it's sort of like a crossword puzzle.

CA: You've written about using the short story to try out a new technique before experimenting with it in a novel. Is there a novel that resulted from such a tryout?

HALDEMAN: *Mindbridge* did, and so did *Worlds*. With *Mindbridge*, it was an experiment with structure, and in *Worlds* it was trying out a character. The *Mindbridge* story was "To Howard Hughes: A Modest Proposal." *Worlds* was "Tricentennial." The main character there was a woman in her sixties going on seventy, and I thought I would write a trilogy, starting with her in her early twenties and going on through her life.

CA: Among your other editing credits, you were senior editor of Astronomy *for "one long month," as you put it. What did you mean by that?*

HALDEMAN: They were having management problems, and in essence they hired me to do the work of two people. I was really juggling that job around. They were falling about six weeks behind, and for a monthly that's pretty bad. I just went in there with a great amount of energy and expended it all in a month, and did get them back on their track. I wound up, however, in total disagreement with the publisher about the editorial thrust of the magazine, and before they could fire me, I quit.

CA: You were also, in 1979-1980, chairman of the Grievance Committee of the Science Fiction Writers of America. What does that job entail?

HALDEMAN: It's mostly being a shoulder for people to cry on. In terms of the day-to-day job, it's getting letters from authors, usually inexperienced, who feel they've been done poorly by publishers. Normally you either explain to them that publishers do that to everybody or, if there's a legitimate grievance, pull out your letterhead and write to the publisher or editor concerned. We've had a very good record of success because I wrote a long, detailed report every month that went out to all the members, and if an editor or publisher had not responded well to a complaint, I just explained in that report why not. Almost everybody in science fiction belongs to the Science Fiction Writers of America; it's almost a total-involvement guild. If the Grievance Committee chairman tells people

to stay away from somebody, that person is going to find he's not getting any manuscripts until the black mark is expunged.

CA: Science-fiction writers seem to have a special closeness. Do you get a lot of cries for help from aspiring writers?

HALDEMAN: I do, and I'm quite willing to talk to them and help them along, anything short of reading manuscripts. I get two or three or four manuscripts a week, literally. I have to send them back unopened. If I did read a manuscript and then ten years later wrote a similar book, I could be hauled into court and probably the other person would win.

CA: Discussing the writer's problem of getting started, you quoted Gordon R. Dickson's advice to "start typing"—anything rather than nothing. Is that one of the biggest problems you observe in other writers?

HALDEMAN: Only in the beginning, I think. If you do it for a living, you usually have several projects on the burner and if one of them doesn't get you enthusiastic, there's another one that will. After you've had several years of getting up every morning and working, no matter how you feel, then you'll always be able to produce something. I've found that I do have off-days when what I'm producing is so obviously bad I might as well go work in my garden or something, but I can keep typing.

CA: The Vietnam War has provided firsthand material for much of your writing. Why do you think more good writing hasn't come out of that war?

HALDEMAN: I suspect it's because of the demographics of the war. There were very few people educated beyond high school or even to high school who actually wound up in combat positions. This was unlike the two world wars and Korea, where it was a more evenly spread thing. Anyone who had a college degree in Vietnam instantly had the nickname "professor." If you could read and write without difficulty you were a very valuable person, because things did come down with printed directions. There were college graduates around, but they didn't seem to be where the shooting was.

CA: Your work is read in England, Europe, Japan, and other countries. Do you get a stronger response from any one country?

HALDEMAN: The response from readers is strongest from England and Australia; because of the language, they can write me directly. In terms of critical response, it seems that I'm stronger in France and the Low Countries than I am in English-speaking countries. My work translates better than I write it!

CA: How does your traveling relate to your writing?

HALDEMAN: We have social contacts with science–fiction editorial communities all over Europe. In fact, we can travel all over Europe without ever having to stay in a hotel. It's lovely. Science fiction is as friendly over there as it is here. Last year we spent a month in Europe and only spent two days in hotels, and that was only because we had to escape; we didn't want to be guests anymore. I go out there and have autograph parties and get interviewed and that sort of thing, but it's mostly keeping in contact with editors, the same reason we go to New York every now and then.

CA: Do you often write while you're on a trip?

HALDEMAN: I find it difficult. I can write nonfiction and occasional stuff, and I can do rewriting and editing, but I find it difficult to create original fiction when I'm not in my own little pit here.

CA: How do you feel about the reviewing and critical writing that is done on science fiction?

HALDEMAN: Most of it is pretty silly. There are some good critics: Algis Budrys is a remarkably able critic, and Baird Searles. The problem is when mainstream people review science fiction, they come from the direction of both ignorance and contempt. They lack the background in science as well as in science fiction to be able to tell the difference between good work and bad work. So often if somebody with some reputation in mainstream literature writes science fiction, the reviewers think it's wonderful when it's really second-rate.

CA: Like Timothy Leary and Frank Herbert, you're concerned with the colonization of space. Do you think it's possible at this point to predict when that might begin in earnest?

HALDEMAN: There are so many political and economic factors that you can't make a simple prediction. The technology, the simple engineering of it, is not that difficult to predict. If we started now, we could have a useful habitat in space in perhaps thirty years—that is, if it weren't a crash project, if we just went ahead and did it doggedly. But the thing is that no politician is going to be for it; no industrial entity is after something that won't pay for itself for twenty years or more. I think that's the stumbling block more than the technology.

CA: Are there ways that you would like to see science fiction improved or changed?

HALDEMAN: No. I just sit back bemused and watch what happens. As a practical matter, I'd like to see science fiction be a little more remunerative than it is. But I have no reason to complain; I'm making a living. It would be nice if we got more respect, but if we did get more respect from conventional critics, then it might change the direction of science fiction into sort of a satellite of the mainstream, which it definitely is not now. So there are plusses and minuses.

CA: Are you teaching now?

HALDEMAN: Yes. I'm teaching a workshop at the University of North Florida. It's fun. I like to do that every few years.

CA: Do you find that you're often able to get someone started writing seriously?

HALDEMAN: It's difficult. It depends on the workshop situation. This one is meeting once a week, and it's difficult to motivate anybody. I have a few students who are turning into real typing machines; they really want to write. I told them that the only way you can do it is to write an awful lot, write a thousand words a day, and every weekend I'll go through their seven thousand words and make some changes. A few of them are willing to do that, but it would be better if I could be there every day and glare around the room and say, "Well, where's your thousand words?"

BIOGRAPHICAL/CRITICAL SOURCES: New York Times Book Review, May 21, 1972, March 23, 1975, February 27, 1977; *Commonweal,* October 27, 1972; *Magazine of Fantasy and Science Fiction,* May, 1975, October, 1975, April, 1977, September, 1979; *Futures,* June, 1975; *Booklist,* June 1, 1975;

Science Fiction Review, August, 1976, February, 1977, February, 1978; *Chicago Tribune,* September 26, 1976; *Galaxy,* December, 1976, March, 1978; *Best Sellers,* December, 1976, February, 1978; *Observer,* May 8, 1977; *Algol,* summer-fall, 1977, summer-fall, 1978; *Times Literary Supplement,* July 8, 1977; *New Republic,* November 26, 1977; *Analog,* March, 1978, September, 1978, July, 1979; *Foundation,* May, 1978; *Destinies,* November/December, 1978; *Starlog,* 17, 1978; *Thrust,* summer, 1979; *Dictionary of Literary Biography,* Volume VIII, Gale, 1981; *Washington Post Book World,* April 26, 1981; *Chicago Tribune Book World,* June 14, 1981.

—*Interview by Jean W. Ross*

*   *   *

HALL, J. Tillman 1916-

PERSONAL: Born January 16, 1916, in Big Sandy, Tenn.; son of Travis M. and Sophia (Akers) Hall; married Louise Babb, 1940; children: Nancy, Joanne. *Education:* George Pepperdine College (now Pepperdine University), B.A., 1940; University of Southern California, M.A., 1947, D.Ed., 1951. *Home:* 8065 Kentwood Ave., Los Angeles, Calif. *Office:* Department of Physical Education, University of Southern California, Los Angeles, Calif. 90007.

CAREER: Big Sandy High School, Big Sandy, Tenn., coach, 1940-42; George Pepperdine College (now Pepperdine University), Los Angeles, Calif., department head, 1946-50; University of Southern California, Los Angeles, teacher, 1951—, chairman of physical education department, 1965—. Organizer of Westchester Lariats, nationally-known dance troupe. *Military service:* U.S. Navy, four years. *Member:* National Recreation Association, American Association for Health, Physical Education, and Recreation (president of southwest district, 1965-66), California Association for Health, Physical Education, and Recreation, California Recreation Society.

WRITINGS: Recreational Dance, Wadsworth, 1963; *Organization, Supervision, and Administration of School Recreation,* W. C. Brown, 1965; *Administration Principles, Theory and Practice,* Goodyear Publishing, 1973; *Until the Whistle Blows,* Goodyear Publishing, Volume I, 1977, Volume II, 1978; *Physical Fitness,* Goodyear Publishing, 1979; *Total Fitness for Men,* Goodyear Publishing, 1980; *Physical Education in the Elementary Schools,* Goodyear Publishing, 1980.

WORK IN PROGRESS: The Philosophy of Leisure in the American Culture.

*   *   *

HALL, Wade H. 1934-

PERSONAL: Born February 2, 1934, in Union Springs, Ala.; son of Wade (a farmer) and Sarah (Waters) Hall. *Education:* Troy State College (now University), B.S., 1953; University of Alabama, M.A., 1957; University of Illinois, Ph.D., 1961. *Politics:* Democrat. *Religion:* Baptist. *Home:* 1568 Cherokee Rd., Louisville, Ky. 40205. *Office:* Department of English, Bellarmine College, Louisville, Ky. 40205.

CAREER: High school teacher of English and social studies in Opp, Ala., 1953-54; University of Illinois at Urbana-Champaign, instructor in English, 1957-61; University of Florida, Gainesville, assistant professor of English, 1961-62; Kentucky Southern College, Louisville, associate professor and head of department of English, 1962-69, chairman of the Division of Humanities, 1965-69; Bellarmine College, Louisville, chairman of department of English and Division of Humanities,

1969—. *Military service:* U.S. Army, 1954-56; became sergeant. *Member:* American Studies Association, National Council of Teachers of English, English-Speaking Union, South Atlantic Modern Language Association, Kentucky Historical Society, Kappa Delta Pi, Phi Kappa Phi, Filson Club.

WRITINGS: Reflections of the Civil War in Southern Humor, University of Florida Press, 1962; *The Smiling Phoenix: Reflections of Southern Life in Southern Humor,* University of Florida Press, 1965; *The Truth Is Funny: A Study of Jesse Stuart's Humor,* Indiana Council of Teachers of English, 1972; *This Place Kentucky,* Data Courier, 1975; *The Kentucky Book,* Data Courier, 1979. Contributor to professional journals, including *Southern Folklore Quarterly.*

WORK IN PROGRESS: An oral autobiography of Lyman Johnson; a play based on the career of actress Mary Anderson.

* * *

HALLSTEAD, William F(inn III)   1924-
(William Beechcroft)

PERSONAL: Born April 20, 1924, in Scranton, Pa.; son of William F. II (a publisher) and Winifred (Mott) Hallstead; married Jean Little, October 9, 1948; children: William F. IV, Alyssa Jean. *Education:* Educated in Pottstown, Pa. *Politics:* Republican. *Religion:* Episcopalian. *Home:* 2027 Skyline Rd., Ruxton, Md. 21204. *Office:* Maryland Center for Public Broadcasting, Owings Mills, Md. 21117. *Agent:* Evelyn Singer Agency, Inc., Box 1600, Briarcliff Manor, N.Y. 10510.

CAREER: Scranton Municipal Airport Corp., Scranton, Pa., flight instructor, 1947-49; Pennsylvania Department of Highways, Scranton, draftsman, 1950-52; Whitman, Requardt & Associates (consulting engineers), Baltimore, Md., senior highway designer, 1952-58; Colony Publishing Corp., Baltimore, president, 1958-64; The Rouse Co. (real estate developers), Baltimore, director of information services, 1965-68; Maryland Center for Public Broadcasting, Owings Mills, director of development and information services, 1968—. *Military service:* U.S. Army Air Forces, 1942-45; radio operator-gunner on B-24 with 15th Air Force in Italy; became sergeant. *Member:* National Association of Educational Broadcasters, Associated Business Writers of America, American Aviation Historical Society, Authors Guild. *Awards, honors:* Book of the Year Award from Child Study Association, 1980, for *Conqueror of the Clouds.*

WRITINGS: Eve Kris: Aviation Detective, John Day, 1961; *Dirigible Scout,* McKay, 1967; *Sky Carnival* (Junior Literary Guild selection), McKay, 1969; *The Missiles of Zajecar,* Chilton, 1969; *Ghost Plane of Blackwater,* Harcourt, 1974; *How to Make Money Writing Articles,* Kirkley Press, 1976; *The Man Downstairs* (Young Adult Literary Guild selection), Elsevier/Nelson, 1980; *Conqueror of the Clouds* (Young Adult Literary Guild selection), Elsevier/Nelson, 1980; *The Launching of Linda Bell,* Harcourt, 1981; (under pseudonym William Beechcroft) *Position of Ultimate Trust,* Dodd, 1981. Also author of the thirty-first book in the "Hardy Boys" series, *The Secret of Wildcat Swamp,* Grosset, 1952.

Youth stories have been anthologized in several junior high school readers and textbooks. Contributor of short stories to *Boy's Life* and other juvenile magazines and of articles to engineering trade journals and other periodicals. Managing editor, *Architects' Report,* 1960-64, and *Maryland Engineer,* 1963-64. Editor, *Baltimore Scene* (bi-monthly magazine), 1963-64, and *Journal of the Maryland Center for Public Broadcasting,* 1969—.

WORK IN PROGRESS: A book on careers in broadcasting, for Dutton.

SIDELIGHTS: William F. Hallstead told *CA:* "I have spent almost a decade in public television which is an audio and visual way of learning, but my great regret is that so many young people have turned toward television and away from books.

"If you get the chance, listen to a good radio drama. Notice how just a few simple sound effects—plus a good script—come to life even though radio is no more than sound: no fancy sets, no colors, no light or shadow. Why does radio work so well? Because it takes place in the greatest theater in the world: your own imagination.

"And books are a lot like radio. There is only the printed word, but the story is formed and lives in that great theater of your mind. Through no more than paper and an alphabet of twenty-six shapes, you can travel to the Florida Everglades, the Alaskan wilderness, Africa or Tibet. You can meet some of the most fascinating people, live through the most exciting adventures. You can journey to the stars on the wings of these twenty-six symbols. What a miracle is the understanding of print! What an incredible adventure is the ability to read.

"It began for me when I was very young and my father became one of the first suburbanites. We lived on a converted farm two miles from a small town which was thirteen miles from the nearest city of any size. There were no local children, aside from my brother and sister. Reading—and radio—were big entertainments in those days—the 1930's. I discovered high adventure with the grand old pulp magazines: *Doc Savage, The Lone Eagle, The Spider, G-8 and His Battle Aces.* . . . I actually knew the date each new magazine would be delivered to Fred Erb's variety store in nearby Dalton."

The Launching of Linda Bell has been optioned by Marble Arch Productions as a possible television movie.

* * *

HALPERIN, John   1941-

PERSONAL: Born September 15, 1941, in Chicago, Ill.; son of S. William (a historian) and Elaine (a translator; maiden name, Philipsborn) Halperin. *Education:* Bowdoin College, A.B., 1963; University of New Hampshire, M.A., 1966; Johns Hopkins University, M.A., 1968, Ph.D., 1969. *Office:* Department of English, University of Southern California, Los Angeles, Calif. 90007.

CAREER: Wall Street Journal, New York, N.Y., reporter, 1963; Associated Press, Albany, N.Y., editor, 1963-64; State University of New York at Stony Brook, assistant professor of English, director of summer school, and assistant to academic vice-president, 1969-72; University of Southern California, Los Angeles, associate professor, 1972-77, professor of English, 1977—, director of graduate studies, 1973-75. Honorary fellow, Wolfson College, Oxford University, 1976. *Military service:* U.S. Army Reserve, 1963-69; became staff sergeant. *Member:* Modern Language Association of America, American Philosophical Society (fellow). *Awards, honors:* Rockefeller Foundation fellow, 1976; Guggenheim Foundation fellow, 1978-79.

WRITINGS: The Language of Meditation, Stockwell, 1973; (editor) Henry James, *The Golden Bowl,* Popular Library, 1973; (editor) *The Theory of the Novel,* Oxford University Press, 1974; *Egoism and Self-Discovery in the Victorian Novel,* B. Franklin, 1974; *Jane Austen,* Cambridge University Press, 1975; (co-author) *Plots and Characters in the Fiction of Jane Austen,* the Brontes, and George Eliot, Archon Books, 1976; Trollope and Politics, Barnes & Noble, 1977; Gissing: A Life in Books, Oxford University Press, 1982; (editor) Trollope Centenary Essays, Macmillan, 1982. Also author of Conversations with Snow: An Oral Biography and The Life of Jane Austen. Contributor of articles about Jane Austen and Trollope to academic journals.

WORK IN PROGRESS: Eminent Moderns.

*   *   *

HAMILL, Ethel
See WEBB, Jean Francis (III)

*   *   *

HANEY, David P. 1938-

PERSONAL: Born January 11, 1938, in Dayton, Ohio; son of George G. (a clergyman) and Lucille (Bales) Haney; married Aileen Faulkner (a teacher), November 9, 1957; children: Karen, Steven, Philip. Education: Attended Harrison-Chilhouse Baptist Academy, 1955-57; Georgetown College, B.A., 1961; Southeastern Baptist Theological Seminary, graduate study, 1961-62; Earlham School of Religion, M.A., 1966; Luther Rice Seminary, Th.D., 1969. Office: Baptist Brotherhood, 1548 Poplar, Memphis, Tenn. 38104.

CAREER: Ordained to Baptist ministry, 1958; pastor of Baptist churches in Sadieville, Ky., 1958-61, New Lebanon, Ohio, 1961-67, and Annapolis, Md., 1967-74; Southern Baptist Convention, Memphis, Tenn., director of lay ministries, 1974-80, director of Baptist Men's Division, 1980—.

WRITINGS: Renew My Church, Zondervan, 1972; The Idea of the Laity, Zondervan, 1973; Breakthrough into Renewal, Broadman, 1974; Journey into Life, Brotherhood Commission, 1974; Renewed Reminders, Broadman, 1976; The Lord and His Laity, Broadman, 1978; Couples on Mission, Brotherhood Commission, 1979.

*   *   *

HANLEY, Gerald (Anthony) 1916-

PERSONAL: Born February 17, 1916; son of Edward Michael and Bridget (Roche) Hanly. Address: c/o Gillon Aitken, 17 Belgrave Pl., London SW2X 8B5, England.

CAREER: Author. Military service: Royal Irish Fusiliers, seven years; became major. Member: Irish Academy of Letters, India Club (London), Srinagar Club (Kashmir, India).

WRITINGS—All published by Collins, except as indicated: Monsoon Victory, 1946, reprinted, White Lion, 1974; The Consul at Sunset, 1951; The Year of the Lion, 1953, reprinted, 1974; Drinkers of Darkness, 1955, reprinted, Chivers, 1973; Without Love (Book Society choice), 1957, reprinted, Chivers, 1973; The Journey Homeward (Book Society choice), 1961; Gilligan's Last Elephant, 1962; See You in Yasukuni, 1969; Warriors and Strangers, Harper, 1972.

SIDELIGHTS: "[Many] years ago," a New York Times Book Review critic comments, "Gerald Hanley began writing beautifully engineered novels that examined the impact of war on culture and character. The Consul at Sunset, an early triumph, orchestrated some of the cross-purposes set in motion in East Africa by British military victory and imperial decline. [See You in Yasukuni], as fine [a novel] as any Hanley has written, anatomizes the Japanese military mind with the author's characteristic subtlety and understanding."

MEDIA ADAPTATIONS: Hanley's novel Gilligan's Last Elephant was made into a motion picture entitled "The Last Safari" by Paramount in 1967.

AVOCATIONAL INTERESTS: Folk music of India and the Balkans.

BIOGRAPHICAL/CRITICAL SOURCES: Books, October, 1969; New York Times Book Review, May 3, 1970.

*   *   *

HANNA, David 1917-
(Anthony James, Gloria Laine)

PERSONAL: Born September 11, 1917, in Philadelphia, Pa.; son of Hugh J. (a writer) and Lenore (an actress; maiden name, Torriani) Hanna. Education: Attended Pepperdine College. Home: 49 West 44th St., New York, N.Y. Office: Tower Publications, 2 Park Ave., New York, N.Y. 10016.

CAREER: Los Angeles Daily News, Los Angeles, Calif., feature writer, 1940-46; Hollywood Reporter, Los Angeles, feature writer, 1947-52; free-lance journalist in Europe and the United States, 1952-62; editor of Confidential and Whisper, 1963-65; editor of Uncensored and Inside Story, 1965-72; Tower Publications, New York, N.Y., writer and editor, 1972—.

WRITINGS: Ava: Portrait of a Star, Putnam, 1960; Virginia Hill: Queen of the Underworld, Belmont-Tower, 1974; Murder, Inc., Leisure Books, 1974; Frank Costello: The Gangster with a Thousand Faces, Belmont-Tower, 1974; Vito Genovese, Belmont-Tower, 1974; Bugsy Siegel: The Man Who Invented Murder, Inc., Belmont-Tower, 1974; Harvest of Horror: Mass Murder in Houston, Belmont-Tower, 1974; King of the Mafia: Carlo Gambino, Belmont-Tower, 1975; Henry Kissinger: His Rise and ?, Manor, 1975; The Lucky Luciano Connection, Belmont-Tower, 1975; Robert Redford: The Superstar Nobody Knows, Belmont-Tower, 1975; The World of Jacqueline Susann, Manor, 1975.

Second Chance, Belmont-Tower, 1976; Bogart, Belmont-Tower, 1976; Angel, Leisure Books, 1976; Hollywood Confidential, Leisure Books, 1976; Come Up and See Me Sometime, Belmont-Tower, 1976; Four Giants of the West, Belmont-Tower, 1976; When the Clock Strikes Thirteen, Leisure Books, 1976; The Love Goddess, Belmont-Tower, 1977; Elvis: Lonely Star at the Top, Leisure Books, 1977; The Vacant Throne, Belmont-Tower, 1979; The Mafia: Two Hundred Years of Terror, Manor, 1979.

The Capri Affair, Tower, 1980; Flying Sand, Belmont-Tower, 1981; Mafia over Hollywood, Manor, 1981.

Under pseudonym Anthony James: A New Look at Capital Punishment, Belmont-Tower, 1977; Presley: Entertainer of the Century, Belmont-Tower, 1977; The Grabbers, Leisure Books, 1977; Hot on the Trail, Belmont-Tower, 1981.

Under pseudonym Gloria Laine: Looking, Leisure Books, 1981.

*   *   *

HARBERGER, Arnold C. 1924-

PERSONAL: Born July 27, 1924, in Newark, N.J.; son of Ferdinand C. (an accountant) and Martha (Bucher) Harberger; married Ana Valjalo, March 15, 1958; children: Paul, Carl. Education: Attended Johns Hopkins University, 1941-43; University of Chicago, M.A., 1947, Ph.D. 1950. Office: Department of Economics, University of Chicago, Chicago, Ill.

CAREER: Johns Hopkins University, Baltimore, Md., assistant professor of political economy, 1949-53; University of Chicago, Chicago, Ill., associate professor, 1953-59, professor of economics, 1959-77, Gustavas F. and Ann M. Swift Distinguished Service Professor of Economics, 1977—, chairman of department, 1964-71, 1975-80. Visiting professor, Harvard University, 1971, and Princeton University, 1973-74. Economist, International Monetary Fund, 1950, and Massachusetts Institute of Technology Center for International Studies and Indian Planning Commission (New Delhi), 1961-62. Consultant to Committee for Economic Development, 1955, U.S. Department of Agriculture, 1955, U.S. Treasury Department, 1962—, U.S. Department of State, 1963-77, International Bank for Reconstruction and Development, 1963—, U.S. Department of Commerce, 1965, U.S. Council of Economic Advisers, 1969-74, Indonesian Ministry of Finance, 1974, 1981, Bolivian Ministry of Finance, 1976, Canadian Department of Regional Economic Expansion, 1975-78, and Canadian Department of Employment and Immigration, 1980—; member of research advisory committee, Office of Scientific Personnel, National Academy of Sciences, 1961-65. *Military service:* U.S. Army, 1943-46. *Member:* American Economic Association (member of executive committe), Econometric Society (fellow), American Academy of Arts and Sciences (fellow), Phi Beta Kappa. *Awards, honors:* Social Science Research Council faculty research fellow, 1951-53; 1954-55; Guggenheim fellow in England, 1958; Ford Foundation faculty research fellow, 1967-68.

WRITINGS: (Editor and author of introduction) *The Demand for Durable Goods,* University of Chicago Press, 1960; *Project Evaluation,* Rand McNally, 1973; *Taxation and Welfare,* Little, Brown, 1974.

Contributor: *Resources for Freedom,* U.S. Government Printing Office, 1952; *Federal Expenditure Policy for Economic Growth and Stability,* U.S. Government Printing Office, 1957; Roy G. Francis, editor, *The Population Ahead,* University of Minnesota Press, 1958; Carl F. Christ and others, editors, *Measurement in Economics,* Stanford University Press, 1963; Werner Baer and Isaac Kerstenetsky, editors, *Inflation and Growth in Latin America,* Irwin, 1964; Paul N. Rosenstein-Rodan, editor, *Pricing and Fiscal Policies,* M.I.T. Press, 1964; *The Role of Direct and Indirect Taxes in the Federal Revenue System,* Princeton University Press, 1964; Charles A. Anderson and Mary J. Bowman, editors, *Education and Economic Development,* Aldine, 1965; Marion Krzyzaniak, editor, *Effects of Corporation Income Tax,* Wayne State University Press, 1966; *Evaluation of Industrial Projects,* United Nations Industrial Development Organization, 1968.

Estudios Sobre Politica Arancelaria, Incentivos y Comerico Exterior, Direccion General de Planificacion y Administacion (Panama), 1970; *Estudios Sobre el Sistema Monetario y Bancario de Panama,* Direccion General de Planificacion y Administracion, 1970; Gary Fromm, editor, *Tax Incentives and Investment Spending,* Brookings Institution, 1970; Willy Sellekaertz, editor, *Economic Development and Planning,* Macmillan, 1974; Karl Wohlmuth, editor, *Employment Creation in Emerging Societies,* Praeger, 1975; Charles R. Frank, Jr. and Richard C. Webb, editors, *Income Distribution and Growth in the Less-Developed Countries,* Brookings Institution, 1977; H. Schwarts and R. Berney, editors, *Social and Economic Dimensions of Project Evaluation,* Inter-American Development Bank, 1977; Michael J. Artis and A. R. Nobay, editors, *Contemporary Economic Analysis,* Croom Helm Ltd. (London), 1978; Norman Walbek and Sidney Weintraub, editors, *Conflict, Order, and Peace in the Americas,* Volume I: *Dialogues on the Central Issues,* Lyndon B. Johnson School of Public Affairs, 1978; Henry J. Aaron and Michael J. Boskin, editors, *The Economics of Taxation,* Brookings Institution, 1980;

M. J. Flanders and Assaf Razin, editors, *Development in an Inflationary World,* Academic Press. 1981.

Also contributor to *Federal Tax Policy for Economic Growth and Stability,* 1955.

Contributor of more than thirty articles to economics journals. Member of board of editors, *American Economic Review,* 1959-61.

*   *   *

HARDIN, Tom
See BAUER, Erwin A.

*   *   *

HARDING, Peter
See BURGESS, M(ichael) R(oy)

*   *   *

HARDISON, O(sborne) B(ennett, Jr.)   1928-

PERSONAL: Born October 22, 1928, in San Diego, Calif.; son of Osborne Bennett (a naval officer) and Ruth (Morgan) Hardison; married Marifrances Fitzgibbon, December 23, 1950; children: Charity Ruth, Sarah Frances, Laura Fitzgibbon, Agnes Margaret, Osborne Bennett, Matthew. *Education:* University of North Carolina, A.B., 1949, M.A., 1950; University of Wisconsin, Ph.D., 1956. *Politics:* Democrat. *Home:* 18 Third St. S.E., Washington, D.C. 20003. *Office:* Folger Shakespeare Library, 201 East Capital St., Washington, D.C. 20003.

CAREER: University of Tennessee, Knoxville, instructor in English, 1954-56; Princeton University, Princeton, N.J., instructor in English, 1956-57; University of North Carolina, Chapel Hill, assistant professor, 1957-60, associate professor, 1960-63, professor of English, 1963-69; Folger Shakespeare Library, Washington, D.C., director, 1969—. Co-chairman, Duke University-University of North Carolina Program in Humanities. *Member:* Modern Language Association of America, South Atlantic Modern Language Association, Southeastern Institute of Medieval and Renaissance Studies (chairman), Renaissance Society of America, Phi Beta Kappa. *Awards, honors:* Fulbright Fellow, Italy, 1953-54; Folger Library Fellow, summer, 1958; Guggenheim Fellow, 1963-64; Haskins Medal of Mediaeval Academy of America, 1967, for *Christian Rite and Christian Drama in the Middle Ages.*

WRITINGS: (Contributor) *Poets of Today,* Volume V, Scribner, 1958; *Modern Continental Literary Criticism,* Appleton, 1962; *The Enduring Monument,* University of North Carolina Press, 1962; *Renaissance Literary Criticism,* Appleton, 1963; (contributor) *Poets of North Carolina,* Garrett, 1963; (with Alex Preminger and Frank Warnke) *Encyclopedia of Poetry and Poetics,* Princeton University Press, 1965; *Christian Rite and Christian Drama in the Middle Ages,* Johns Hopkins Press, 1965; *Practical Rhetoric,* Appleton, 1966; *The Renaissance,* P. Owen, 1968; (author of commentary) Aristotle, *Poetics,* Prentice-Hall, 1968; *Toward Freedom and Dignity: The Humanities and the Idea of Humanity,* Johns Hopkins Press, 1974; *Pro Musica Antiqua* (poems), Louisiana State University Press, 1978; *Entering the Maze: Identity and Change in Modern Culture,* Oxford University Press, 1982. Contributor to professional journals, and to *Raleigh News and Observer.*

WORK IN PROGRESS: The second and third volumes of a trilogy on identity in modern culture.

HARDY, C. Colburn 1910-
(Jonas Blake, Hart Munn, Leonard Peck)

PERSONAL: Born January 13, 1910, in Boston, Mass.; son of Charles A. (a corporate executive) and Gladys M. (an engineer; maiden name, Blake) Hardy; married Ruth E. Hart (a public relations director), June 27, 1942; children: Dorcas Ruth. *Education:* Yale University, A.B., 1931; Columbia University, additional study, 1934. *Religion:* Unitarian-Universalist. *Office:* C. Colburn Hardy & Associates, 2542 Canterbury Dr. S., West Palm Beach, Fla. 33407.

CAREER: Republican representative in New Jersey Assembly, 1943; Carl Byoir & Associates (public relations firm), New York City, 1948-59, began as staffer, became vice-president; Jones Brakeley & Rockwell (public relations firm), New York City, executive vice-president, 1960-64; Federal Pacific Electric Co., Newark, N.J., director of public relations, 1965-67; General Dynamics Co., New York City, director of public relations, 1967-72; C. Colburn Hardy & Associates (public relations firm), West Palm Beach, Fla., president, 1972—. President of Social Welfare Council and Community Service Council (both N.J.), 1967-69; member of board of directors, United Way, 1967-70, and JET Corp., 1971—; president of board of directors, Help Aid Youth (H.A.Y.), 1969-72. Director, Orange Mountain Council of Boy Scouts of America. *Military service:* U.S. Naval Reserve, 1943-46; became lieutenant commander; received seven battle stars. *Member:* Public Relations Society of America, Phi Beta Kappa.

WRITINGS: (With John Winthrop Wright) *Q-V-T: The Three Keys to Stock Market Profits*, Prentice-Hall, 1970; *Personal Money Management*, Funk, 1976; *ABC's of Investing Your Retirement Funds*, Medical Economics, 1978, 2nd edition, 1982; *Investor's Guide to Technical Analysis*, McGraw, 1978; *Your Money and Your Life*, American Management Association, 1979, 2nd edition, 1982; *Safe in Retirement*, Bantam, 1980; *Financing Retirement*, Harper, 1982.

Editor of Dunn & Bradstreet's annual publication, *Guide to Your Investments*, 1974—. Contributor, sometimes under pseudonyms, to *Physician's Management, Dental Management, Banking, Money,* and others.

WORK IN PROGRESS: Q-V-T: Quality-Value-Timing—Three Keys to Stock Market Success, with Wright.

*   *   *

HARKNESS, Georgia (Elma) 1891-1974

PERSONAL: Born 1891 in Harkness, N.Y.; died August 21, 1974, of a heart attack, in Claremont, Calif.; daughter of Joseph Warren and Lillie (Merrill) Harkness. *Education:* Cornell University, A.B., 1912; Boston University, M.A., M.R.E., 1920, Ph.D., 1923; attended Yale University, 1928-29, and Union Theological Seminary, 1935-36. *Office:* Pacific School of Religion, 1798 Scenic Ave., Berkeley, Calif.

CAREER: High school teacher in Schuylerville, N.Y., 1912-14, and in Scotia, N.Y., 1915-18; Boston University, School of Religious Education, Boston, Mass., instructor in English Bible, 1919-20; Elmira College, Elmira, N.Y., assistant professor of religious education, 1922, associate professor of philosophy, 1923, professor of religious education and philosophy, 1926-37; Mount Holyoke College, South Hadley, Mass., associate professor of religion, 1937-39; Garrett Theological Seminary (now Garrett-Evangelical Theological Seminary), Evanston, Ill., professor of applied theology, 1940-50; Pacific School of Religion, Berkeley, Calif., professor of applied theology, 1950-61, professor emeritus, 1961-74. Visiting profes-

sor of Christianity, International Christian University, Japan, 1956-57. Active in ecumenical movement; delegate to Oxford, Madras, Amsterdam, Lund, and Evanston conferences of the World Council of Churches and related bodies. *Member:* American Philosophical Association, National Association of Biblical Instructors, Phi Beta Kappa. *Awards, honors:* General Federation of Women's Clubs Award, 1941, for pioneer work in religion; Abingdon-Cokesbury Award, 1948, for *Prayer and Common Life;* named churchwoman of the year, 1958, by Religious Heritage of America, Inc. Litt.D. from Boston University, 1939, MacMurray College, 1943, and Elmira College, 1962; D.D. from Wilson College, 1943, and Pacific School of Religion, 1961; LL.D. from Mills College, 1958.

WRITINGS—All published by Abingdon, except as indicated: *The Church and the Immigrant*, Doran, 1921; *Conflicts in Religious Thought*, Holt, 1929, revised edition, 1949; *John Calvin: The Man and His Ethics*, Holt, 1931, reprinted, Gordon Press, 1977; *Holy Flame*, Humphries, 1935; *The Resources of Religion*, Holt, 1936; *The Recovery of Ideals*, Scribner, 1937; *Religious Living*, Association Press, 1937; *The Faith by Which the Church Lives*, 1940; *The Glory of God*, 1943; *The Dark Night of the Soul*, 1945; *Understanding the Christian Faith*, 1947, reprinted, 1981; *Prayer and the Common Life*, 1948; *The Gospel and Our World*, 1949.

Through Christ Our Lord, 1950; *The Modern Rival of Christian Faith: An Analysis of Secularism*, 1952, reprinted, Greenwood Press, 1978; *Toward Understanding the Bible*, 1952; *Be Still and Know*, 1953; *The Religious Life*, Association Press, 1953; *The Sources of Western Morality*, Scribner, 1954, reprinted, AMS Press, 1976 (published in England as *Sources of Western Culture*, Skeffington, 1955); *Foundations of Christian Knowledge*, 1955; *Christian Ethics*, 1957; *Religious Living*, Association Press, 1957; *The Bible Speaks to Daily Needs, 1959*.

The Providence of God, 1960; *Beliefs That Count*, 1961; *The Church and Its Laity*, 1962; (compiler) *The Glory of God: Poems and Prayers for Devotional Use*, 1963; *The Methodist Church in Social Thought and Action*, 1964; *Our Christian Hope*, 1964; (with D. Waitzmann) *A Special Way to Victory* (autobiography), John Knox, 1964; *What Christians Believe*, 1965; *The Fellowship of the Holy Spirit*, 1966; *Disciplines of the Christian Life*, John Knox, 1967; (compiler) *A Devotional Treasury from the Early Church*, 1968; *Grace Abounding*, 1969; *Stability amid Change*, 1969; *The Ministry of Reconciliation*, 1971; *Women in Church and Society: A Historical and Theological Inquiry*, 1971; *Mysticism: Its Meaning and Message*, 1973; *Understanding the Kingdom of God*, 1974; (with Charles F. Kraft) *Biblical Backgrounds of the Middle East Conflict*, 1976.

AVOCATIONAL INTERESTS: Church activities, cooking, and gardening.

BIOGRAPHICAL/CRITICAL SOURCES: A Special Way to Victory, John Knox, 1964; *Grace Abounding*, Abingdon, 1969.

OBITUARIES: New York Times, August 22, 1974; *Washington Post*, August 23, 1974.†

*   *   *

HARKNETT, Terry 1936-
(Frank Chandler, David Ford, George G. Gilman, Jane Harman, Joseph Hedges, Charles R. Pike, William Pine, James Russell, Thomas H. Stone, William Terry; William M. James, a joint pseudonym)

PERSONAL: Born December 14, 1936, in Rainham, Essex,

England; son of Frederick Thomas (a truck driver) and Louisa (a waitress; maiden name, Jaggs) Harknett; married Jane Harman (a secretary), January 16, 1960. *Education:* Attended secondary school in England. *Politics:* "Depends, but Rightism." *Religion:* Church of England. *Home:* Mill Gate House, Annings Lane, Burton Bradstock, Bridport, Dorset DT6 4QN, England.

CAREER: Reuters News Agency, London, England, copyboy, 1951-52; Newspapers Features Ltd., London, feature writer, 1952-55; Twentieth Century-Fox, London, exploitation assistant, 1957-58; *National Newsagent* (trade magazine), London, features editor, 1958-71; professional writer and novelist, 1971—. *Military service:* Royal Air Force, 1955-57.

WRITINGS—All novels, except as indicated: *The Benevolent Blackmailer*, R. Hale, 1962; *The Scratch on the Surface*, R. Hale, 1962; *Invitation to a Funeral*, R. Hale, 1963; *Dead Little Rich Girl*, R. Hale, 1963; *The Evil Money*, R. Hale, 1964; *The Man Who Did Not Die*, R. Hale, 1964; (under pseudonym William Pine) *The Protectors*, Constable, 1967; *Death of an Aunt*, Hammond, Hammond, 1967; *The Softcover Kill*, R. Hale, 1971; (under pseudonym Jane Harman) *W.I.T.C.H.*, New English Library, 1971; (under pseudonym James Russell) *The Balearics* (guide book), New English Library, 1972; *The Caribbean* (guide book), New English Library, 1972; *Promotion Tour*, New English Library, 1972; (under pseudonym Frank Chandler) *A Fistful of Dollars*, Tandem Books, 1972; (under pseudonym David Ford) *Cyprus* (guide book), New English Library, 1973; *The Upmarket Affair*, R. Hale, 1973; *Sweet and Sour Kill*, Futura, 1974; *Macao Mayhem*, Futura, 1974; *Bamboo Shoot-Out*, Futura, 1975.

Under pseudonym George G. Gilman; all published by New English Library: *The Loner*, 1972; *Ten Thousand Dollars American*, 1972; *Apache Death*, 1972; *Killer's Breed*, 1972; *Blood on Silver*, 1972; *The Blue the Grey and the Red*, 1973; *California Killing*, 1973; *Seven Out of Hell*, 1973; *Bloody Summer*, 1973; *Vengeance Is Black*, 1973; *The Violent Peace*, 1974; *The Bounty Hunter*, 1974; *Hell's Junction*, 1974; *Sioux Uprising*, 1974; *The Biggest Bounty*, 1974; *A Town Called Hate*, 1974; *The Big Gold*, 1974; *Blood Run*, 1975; *The Final Shot*, 1975; *Ten Tombstones to Texas*, 1975; *Valley of Blood*, 1975; *Gun Run*, 1975; *The Killing Art*, 1975; *Crossfire*, 1975; *Comanche Carnage*, 1976; *Badge in the Dust*, 1976; *The Losers*, 1976; *Lynch Town*, 1976; *Ashes and Dust*, 1976; *Sullivan's Law*, 1976; *Rhapsody in Red*, 1977; *Slaughter Road*, 1977; *Echoes of War*, 1977; *The Day Democracy Died*, 1977; *Death Trail*, 1977; *Bloody Border*, 1977; *Delta Duel*, 1977; *River of Death*, 1977; *Nightmare at Noon*, 1978; *Satan's Daughter*, 1978; *Violence Trail*, 1978; *Savage Dawn*, 1978; *Eve of Evil*, 1978; *The Living, the Dying and the Dead*, 1978; *The Hard Way*, 1978; *The Tarnished Star*, 1979; *Wanted for Murder*, 1979; *Wagons East*, 1979; *Fort Despair*, 1979; *Waiting for a Train*, 1979; *The Guilty Ones*, 1979; *The Frightened Gun*, 1979; *The Hated*, 1979; *A Ride in the Sun*, 1980; *Death Deal*, 1980; *Manhunt*, 1980; *Steele's War: The Woman*, 1980; *Edge Meets Steele: Two of a Kind*, 1980; *Steele's War: The Preacher*, 1981; *Steele's War: The Storekeeper*, 1981; *Steele's War: The Stranger*, 1981; *Town on Trial*, 1981; *Vengeance at Ventura*, 1981; *Massacre Mission*, 1981; *Black as Death*, 1981; *Destined to Die*, 1981; *Funeral by the Sea*, 1981.

Under pseudonym Joseph Hedges; all published by Sphere Books: *Funeral Rites*, 1973; *Arms for Oblivion*, 1973; *The Chinese Coffin*, 1974; *The Gold-Plated Hearse*, 1974; *The Rainbow-Coloured Shroud*, 1974; *Corpse on Ice*, 1975; *The Mile-Deep Grave*, 1975.

Under pseudonym Charles R. Pike; all published by Mayflower Books: *The Killing Trail*, 1974; *Double-Cross*, 1974; *The Hungry Gun*, 1975.

Under pseudonym Thomas H. Stone; all published by New English Library: *Dead Set*, 1972; *One Horse Race*, 1972; *Stopover for Murder*, 1973; *Black Death*, 1973; *Squeeze Play*, 1973.

Under psuedonym William Terry; published by New English Library, except as indicated: *Once a Copper*, Hammond, Hammond, 1965; *A Town Called Bastard*, 1971; *Hannie Caulder*, 1971; *The Weekend Game*, 1971; *Red Sun*, 1972.

With Laurence James under pseudonym William M. James; all published by Pinnacle Books: *The First Death*, 1974; *Knife in the Night*, 1974; *Duel to the Death*, 1975.

WORK IN PROGRESS: "One new book each month."

*   *   *

HARLE, Elizabeth
See ROBERTS, Irene

*   *   *

HARMAN, Jane
See HARKNETT, Terry

*   *   *

HARRINGTON, Geri

PERSONAL: Born in New Haven, Conn.; daughter of Frederick A. and Evelyn (Richey) Spolane; married Don Harrington (in advertising); children: Peter Tyrus, John Jeffrey. *Education:* Smith College, B.A. *Home:* Merwin Lane, Wilton, Conn. 06897.

CAREER: Good Housekeeping magazine, New York City, market research analyst, 1949-50; U.S. Department of Commerce, Washington, D.C., writer/analyst, 1950-52; Columbia University, Bureau of Applied Social Research, New York City, writer and analyst, 1953-55; Ted Bates, Inc., New York City, copywriter, 1955-57; Grey Advertising, New York City, copywriter, 1957-59; Don Harrington Associates (advertising firm), Wilton, Conn., partner, 1960—. *Member:* Northeast Archeological Researchers. *Awards, honors:* Book club selections, *Better Homes and Gardens* and *Popular Mechanics*, for *The Wood-Burning Stove Book.*

WRITINGS: The College Cookbook, Scribner, 1975, revised edition, 1977; *Summer Garden, Winter Kitchen*, Atheneum, 1976; *The Salad Book*, Atheneum, 1977; *The Wood-Burning Stove Book*, Macmillan, 1977, revised edition, 1979; *Fireplace Stoves, Hearths and Inserts*, Harper, 1980; *Never Too Old: A Complete Guide for the Over-Fifty Adult*, Times Books, 1981; *Total Warmth* (cookbook for wood- and coal-burning stoves), Macmillan, 1981. Contributor of articles and poems to magazines.

*   *   *

HARRIS, Andrea
See WALKER, Irma Ruth (Roden)

*   *   *

HARRIS, Christie (Lucy) Irwin   1907-

PERSONAL: Born November 21, 1907, in Newark, N.J.; emigrated to Canada in 1908; daughter of Edward (a farmer) and Matilda (Christie) Irwin; married Thomas Arthur Harris (a Canadian immigration officer), February 13, 1932; children: Michael, Moira (Mrs. Donald Johnston), Sheilagh (Mrs. Jack Simpson), Brian, Gerald. *Education:* Attended University of British Columbia, 1925. *Religion:* Church of England. *Home:* 302-975 Chilco St., Vancouver, British Columbia, Canada V6G 2R5.

CAREER: Novelist, author of historical fiction, short stories, and plays especially for young people. Teacher in British Columbia, 1926-32; free-lance writer for Canadian Broadcasting Corp. Radio, beginning 1936. *Member:* Writers' Union of Canada. *Awards, honors:* First award in educational radio and television competitions in Columbus, Ohio, for school radio series, "Laws for Liberty"; Book of the Year for Children Medal from Canadian Association of Children's Librarians, 1967 and 1977; Children's Literature Prize from Canada Council, 1981; member of the Order of Canada, 1981; Vickie Metcalf Award, 1982.

WRITINGS—Published by Atheneum, except as indicated: *Cariboo Trail,* Longmans, Green, 1957; *Once upon a Totem,* 1963; *You Have to Draw the Line Somewhere,* illustrations by daughter, Moira Johnston, 1964; *West with the White Chiefs,* 1965; *Raven's Cry,* 1966; *Confessions of a Toe Hanger,* 1967; *Forbidden Frontier,* 1968; *Let X Be Excitement,* 1969; (with Johnston) *Figleafing through History: The Dynamics of Dress,* 1971; *Secret in the Stlalakum Wild,* 1972; (with husband, Thomas Arthur Harris) *Mule Lib,* McClelland & Stewart, 1972; *Once More upon a Totem,* 1973; *Sky Man on the Totem Pole?,* 1975; *Mystery at the Edge of Two Worlds,* 1979; *The Trouble with Princesses,* 1980; *The Trouble with Adventures,* 1982.

"Mouse Woman" series; published by Atheneum: *Mouse Woman and the Vanished Princesses,* 1976; *. . . and the Mischief-Makers,* 1977; *. . . and the Muddleheads,* 1979.

Also author of twelve adult plays, juvenile stories, and radio scripts, including several hundred school programs. Women's editor, *A S & M News.*

SIDELIGHTS: Although a diversified writer with over nineteen books to her credit, Christie Irwin Harris is noted and respected most for her works depicting Indian legends and the Canadian West. As a child, Harris grew up in a log cabin in British Columbia, and this region of western Canada is the chief source of Harris's material.

Kenneth Radu explains in *Canadian Children's Literature: A Journal of Criticism and Review:* "Indian folk-lore and mythology have quite clearly made their imprint upon Mrs. Harris's imagination. Her finest work is directly concerned with the Indian life and legends of the Northwest. *Raven's Cry . . .* remains a singularly moving paean to the now extinct Haida civilization of the Queen Charlotte Islands. Fully and accurately researched, *Raven's Cry* portrays the complexities and uniqueness of the Haida culture with insight, wonder, and compassion. Mrs. Harris's view is neither sentimental, romantic, nor patronizing. She reports Haida life as it was lived on the islands with the clear eye and honesty of the sympathetic chronicler."

The Republic of Childhood: A Critical Guide to Canadian Children's Literature in English author Sheila Egoff also recognizes Harris's talent for interpreting Indian legends. "The potential for children's literature inherent in the Indian legends is most fully realized by Christie Harris in *Once upon a Totem,*" Egoff writes. "Other collections may have more charm, or a more fluid style, but the legends chosen by Harris and her interpretation of them are outstanding in that they seek quietly to illuminate universal values. The stories are very much a part of early Indian life and very much a part of today."

Priscilla L. Moulton notes in *Horn Book Magazine* that Harris has "rediscovered and reproduced a dignified and inspiring picture of [Haida] culture in a work of epic proportions [*Raven's Cry*]. Painstaking research and intense absorption in anthropological details have enabled the author to write with rare commitment and involvement from the Haida point of view. . . . Dealing as it does in a highly artistic and complicated manner with the whole range of human emotion and character, it makes demands of the reader but rewards him with new understanding of the forces that shape civilizations. . . . This distinguished work, probably classified as fiction, will occupy a respected position in historical, anthropological, and story collections."

Critics often cite Harris's sensitivity in portraying Indian tales as one reason for her large and loyal readership. It has been said that she makes the myths or legends come alive, and many of the young readers, in turn, better understand the ways of their Indian brothers. For example, S. Yvonne MacDonald of *In Review* believes that *Raven's Cry* and *Forbidden Frontier* "combine the author's knowledge of Indian folklore and custom with historical fact to describe the collision between European white man's civilization and Indian culture. Harris writes with sympathy for the Indians, apparently determined to tell their side of the story. . . . This knowledge of legend and folklore seems to me to be the author's main strength, whether in her collections of myths or in her novels."

While it has been written that Harris writes all her books with sensitivity, realism, and a strong respect for history, it also has been suggested that it is her sense of humor that makes her books an enjoyable learning experience for her readers. Kenneth Radu contends that "the hallmark of [Harris's] style is good-humored briskness which carries the story along in an uncomplicated, well-placed narrative." Critic Priscilla L. Moulton writes in another review published in *Horn Book Magazine* that she feels that Harris usually writes with "an abundance of humor—a rare quality in exploration accounts." And in her *Washington Post* review of *You Have to Draw the Line Somewhere,* Margaret Sherwood Libby notes that "Harris has achieved a minor miracle, a romance-career story that is sparkling and well written, filled with humor that springs naturally from character and situation."

Readers and critics alike have also delighted in Harris's books for the sometimes unusual, often comical, and almost always life-like characters she creates. A perfect example of her use of a strong, dominant character to carry her message is offered by S. Yvonne MacDonald. She writes that *Mouse Woman and the Vanished Princesses,* a "collection of legends from the mythology of the Northwest Coast Indians of Canada, is uniquely linked through the character of Mouse Woman, a Narnauk or Supernatural Being. . . . The stories are clearly and lyrically told, with perhaps the most distinctive quality being the characterizations of the Narnauks. Harris manages to evoke the magical and essentially alien World of the Supernaturals and also its familiarity to the Indians, for these spirits were a daily part of their lives."

New York Times Book Review critic Benjamin Capps explains in a review of *West with the White Chiefs* that "the journal of two Englishmen . . . who crossed western Canada in 1863 is the basis for this fictionalized account of a perilous trip through little-known, difficult land. . . . Comic relief is supplied by a roguish Irishman, a ridiculous, helpless freeloader who intrudes into the party and makes the journey with the explorers. He quotes Latin aphorisms, is generally unavailable for any work, always makes outrageous demands on the others. He is a wonderful creation, a delightful contrast to the hard-working, serious Indians and Englishmen.'' And Sriani Fernando of *In Review* writes in an article about *The Trouble with Princesses* that ''within each story, the characters are distinctive and adequately developed. The difference in impetus—depending on whether the protagonists resort to wit, cunning or magic to achieve their ends—lends variety to the stories.''

Besides tales of Indian lore and adventures in western Canada, Harris is also the author of other books for young people. Several of her books are based on the experiences of her own family. For example, *Let X Be Excitement* is based on the life of her oldest son, Michael (Ralph to Harris's readers). Julie Losinski writes that in *Let X Be Excitement* ''for Ralph, discovering his life's occupation meant finding a job that offered intellectual challenge and satisfied his love of excitement and the outdoors. . . . Ralph's satisfaction in doing what comes naturally, combined with a sense of humor, results in a appealing zest for living. Readers (boys particularly) facing career decisions will empathize with Ralph, and enjoy, even though they may not be able to equal, his adventures.'' In *Confessions of a Tow Hanger*, comments Shirley Ellison of *Profile*, ''Mrs. Harris ventured once more into family collaboration to tell the story of her younger daughter, Sheilagh. . . . The humorous but poignant account of the 'ordinary' middle child in a talented family is now the favourite reading of Sheilagh's own daughters.'' Ellison continues to explain that Harris's *You Have to Draw the Line Somewhere* ''recreates the story of her older daughter, Moira, a fashion artist. It was undertaken at Moira's suggestion.'' Helen M. Kovar of *School Library Journal* notes that *You Have to Draw the Line Somewhere* ''is the story of a young Canadian girl who aspires to become a *Vogue* fashion artist. The British Columbia setting is refreshing and the style is humorous. . . . It is a frank picture of the non-glamorous side of fashion art and modeling and the amount of work necessary to become first-rate in either profession. With a light touch the story offers depth and mature values. . . . This has much more to offer than most girls' fiction.''

BIOGRAPHICAL/CRITICAL SOURCES: Horn Book Magazine, April, 1963, June, 1964, June, 1965, October, 1966, April, 1968, April, 1975; *New York Times Book Review*, May 12, 1963, April 4, l965; *School Library Journal*, April, 1964, September, 1969; *Washington Post*, May 17, 1964; *Scientific American*, December, 1966; *American Museum of Natural History*, November, 1967; *Profile*, 1971; *Kirkus Review*, March 1, 1973, March 15, 1975, April 15, ·1976; Sheila Egoff, *The Republic of Childhood: A Critical Guide to Canadian Children's Literature in English*, 2nd edition, Oxford University Press, 1975; *Canadian Children's Literature: A Journal of Criticism and Review*, Number 2, 1975, Number 5, 1976, Number 6, 1976; *In Review*, autumn, 1975, autumn, 1976, August, 1980; *Contemporary Literary Criticism*, Volume XII, Gale, 1980.

—*Sketch by Margaret Mazurkiewicz*

*   *   *

HARRIS, Miles F(itzgerald)   1913-

PERSONAL: Born February 2, 1913, in Brunswick, Ga.; son of James Madison (a lumberman) and Louise (Fitzgerald) Harris; married Marguerite Leonard (a kindergarten teacher), May 13, 1938; children: Ann Harris Zuniga, Theresa Geraldine Harris Scarano, Emily Leland Harris Feudo. *Education:* Attended Mercer University, 1932-34, George Washington University, 1939-40, 1942, 1953-55, and University of Chattanooga (now University of Tennessee at Chattanooga), 1940-41; New York University, B.S., 1944, M.S., 1957. *Politics:* Liberal. *Reli-*

gion: Congregationalist. *Home:* 40 Lothrop St., Beverly, Mass. 01915. *Office:* American Meteorological Society, 45 Beacon St., Boston, Mass. 02108.

CAREER: U.S. Weather Bureau, Macon, Ga., assistant weather observer, 1932-35; South Atlantic Steamship Line, Savannah, Ga., deck cadet-clerk, 1935-37; U.S. Weather Bureau, 1937-66, began as weather observer, analyst, forecaster, research meteorologist, at stations in Savannah, Macon, Chattanooga, Tenn., New York, N.Y., San Juan, Puerto Rico, became chief of editing and publishing branch, Washington, D.C.; member of staff, Scientific Information and Documentation Division, Environmental Science Services Administration, Rockville, Md., 1966-70; American Meteorological Society, Boston, Mass., editor of *Monthly Weather Review*, 1968-70, general editor of society publications, 1970—, technical editor of *Bulletin of American Meteorological Society*, 1970-74 and *Monthly Weather Review*, 1974-75. Part-time consultant, 1975—. *Member:* American Meteorological Society, American Geophysical Union. *Awards, honors:* Superior accomplishment award, U.S. Weather Bureau, 1963; Bronze Medal, Department of Commerce, 1970, for contributions to science through research, writing, and editing.

WRITINGS: Man against Storm: The Challenge of Weather, Coward, 1962; *Getting to Know the World Meteorological Organization*, Coward, 1966; (contributor) *Investigating the Earth* (secondary school text), Houghton, 1967, revised edition, 1978; *Opportunities in Meteorology*, Universal Publishing, 1972; (contributor) Cornelius S. Hurlbut, Jr., editor, *The Planet We Live On*, Abrams, 1976. Contributor to *Encyclopedia Americana*, and to professional journals.

WORK IN PROGRESS: Revised editions of *Opportunities in Meteorology* and *Investigating the Earth;* writing poetry and fiction.

*   *   *

HARRISON, Allan E(ugene)   1925-

PERSONAL: Born September 13, 1925, in Tucson, Ariz.; son of Frank and Evelyn (Gower) Harrison; married Marjorie Sultzbaugh (a bank teller), June 22, 1945; children: Dian, Frank, Allan A., James. *Education:* San Jose State College (now University), B.A., 1949; graduate study at University of Santa Clara, 1950. *Religion:* Protestant. *Home:* 21863 Brill Rd., Riverside, Calif. 92508.

CAREER: Elementary school teacher in Moreno Valley Unified School District, 1959-74. Owner of private elementary school, 1971. *Military service:* U.S. Air Force, 1943; became captain. U.S. Air Force Reserve, 1959.

WRITINGS: How to Teach Children Twice As Much, Arlington House, 1973; *Discipline at Home Made Simple*, Harrison Educational Motivation Enterprises (Riverside, Calif.), 1979; *Discipline at School Made Easy*, Harrison Educational Motivation Enterprises, 1979. Author of 38 syndicated articles for Freedom Newspapers, Inc., 1979-80.

WORK IN PROGRESS: Self-responsibility Training for Children.

SIDELIGHTS: Allan E. Harrison writes to *CA:* ''Until adults realize that children must be trained through self-accountability methods which produce a desire for self-responsibility, true freedom for the resultant society is unthinkable. This means youngsters must be allowed to make their own decisions and mistakes and reap their own rewards, with adult advice sought (and readily available) rather than being forced upon them as it is now with the tremendous time-consuming effort that accomplishes so little. The method of accomplishment is known to every self-reliant adult in a free society: It's merely an instructional method that will teach life as we adults live it but scaled down to a level youngsters can understand and use in the classroom and home. I call such a program the 'Harrison system,' but perhaps a better name might be 'self-motivation and self-discipline training.' The secret of such instruction involves utilizing a scorekeeper (such as our money or a point system) to make children truly self-accountable rather than responsible to some adult. To do otherwise (as we are doing now), merely produces citizens who are perfectly equipped to live in China or Russia and a steadily increasing burden on the fewer and fewer taxpaying individuals who manage to escape present authoritarian training and struggle to support those who haven't.''

*   *   *

HART, Alexandra   1939-
(Alexandra Jacopetti)

PERSONAL: Born August 1, 1939, in Preston, Idaho; daughter of Newell Scheib (a musician, carpenter, and writer) and Ruth (a store manager; maiden name, Cutler) Hart; married Gregory L. Williams, May, 1957 (divorced November, 1958); married Roland Jacopetti (a radio producer), October 8, 1960; children: Hobert, Lucas, Natalia. *Education:* Attended University of Utah, 1956-57. *Politics:* Feminist. *Religion:* Subud. *Home and office address:* P.O. Box 414, Cazadero, Calif. 95421.

CAREER: Alexandra Hart Fibre Arts (weaving), Cazadero, Calif., fibre artist, 1967—. Member of board of directors and gallery director of Berkeley Experimental Arts Foundation, 1965-66; director of apprentices in weaving for Baulines Craftsman's Guild, Marin Co., Calif., 1972-75, member of board of directors, 1972-74; co-founder and partner of Folkwear Ethnic Patterns, 1976-79. Participating artist in numerous group shows and traveling exhibits; designer and weaver of tapestries for various public and private organizations; organizer of non-profits arts foundations and guilds. *Awards, honors:* Book award for graphic design, *Publisher's Weekly,* and young adult book award, American Library Association, both for *Native Funk and Flash.*

WRITINGS—Under name Alexandra Jacopetti, except as indicated: (With collaborator and photographer, Jerry Wainwright) *Native Funk and Flash: An Emerging Folk Art,* Scrimshaw Press (California), 1974.

Contributor: Gail Ellison, *Play Structures,* Pacific Oaks Press, 1974; *California Design X,* California Design, 1976; Roland Jacopetti, *Rescued Buildings,* Capra, 1977; *Craftsman Lifestyle,* California Design, 1977; Menagh and Meilach, *Exotic Needlework,* Van Nostrand, 1978; (under name Alexandra Hart) *The Fiber Arts Design Book,* Fiberarts Hasting House, 1980.

WORK IN PROGRESS: Organizing an exhibit of local historical quilts.

SIDELIGHTS: ''I am mainly a visual artist and craftswoman working in textile fibres,'' Alexandra Hart writes to *CA.* ''I have found that those who are most productive and satisfied with their lives are people who are actively involved with making inner states through an art or craft.''

An exhibit of material from *Native Funk and Flash* toured several western states in 1974-75. Another traveling exhibit, ''The Art and Romance of Peasant Clothes,'' was curated by Hart in 1978-79. Hart has also helped make a film, ''Saga of Macrame Park,'' detailing her construction of a play structure for the town of Bolinas, California.

BIOGRAPHICAL/CRITICAL SOURCES: Saturday Review of Education, May, 1973; Ben Van Meter, ''Saga of Macrame Park'' (film), Eccentric Circle Films, 1973; *Sunset,* June, 1974; *Art Week,* September 28, 1974; *Fibrearts,* September-October, 1976; *Shuttle, Spindle & Dyepot,* spring, 1977.

*   *   *

HARVEY, John Hooper   1911-

PERSONAL: Born May 25, 1911, in London, England; son of William (an architect) and Alice Mabel (Wilcox) Harvey; married Sarah Cordelia Story, February 24, 1934; children: Richard, Charles, Eleanour. *Education:* Regent Street Polytechnic, Registered Architect, 1940. *Politics:* Royalist. *Religion:* Pagan. *Home:* Half Moon Cottage, Bookham, Surrey, England.

CAREER: Architects' assistant in London, England, 1928-33, and Jerusalem, Palestine, 1933-35; His Majesty's Office of Works, London, assistant in ancient monuments branch, 1936-42; William Harvey (architect), Bookham, Surrey, England, assistant, 1943-46; Winchester College, Winchester, Hampshire, England, consultant architect, beginning 1947, archivist, 1949-64. Lecturer on repair of medieval buildings, University College, University of London, 1950-60. Member of records and antiquities committee, Surrey County Council, 1948-63; secretary, Archbishop's Commission on Redundant Churches in the City of York; member, York Diocesan Advisory Committee on the Care of Churches. *Member:* British Archaeological Association (member of council), Society of Antiquaries (fellow), Royal Society of Literature (fellow), Society of Genealogists (fellow), British Records Association, Canterbury and York Society. *Awards, honors:* Leverhulme Research fellowship, 1958-59, for work on *Itineraries of William Worcestre;* honorary doctorate, University of York, 1976.

WRITINGS: Henry Yevele, c.1320-1400: The Life of an English Architect, Batsford, 1944; *Gothic England: A Survey of National Culture, 1300-1550,* Batsford, 1947; *The Plantagenets, 1154-1485,* Batsford, 1948, 3rd edition, Severn House, 1976; *Dublin: A Study in Environment,* Batsford, 1949, enlarged edition, S. R. Publishers, 1972, Charles River, 1977; *An Introduction to Tudor Architecture,* Art & Technics, 1949; *The Gothic World: A Survey of Architecture and Art, 1100-1600,* Batsford, 1950, Harper, 1969; (with Herbert Felton) *The English Cathedrals,* Batsford, 1950, 2nd edition (sole author), 1956; *English Cathedrals: A Reader's Guide,* National Book League, 1951; *English Mediaeval Architects: A Biographical Dictionary to 1550,* Batsford, 1954; *The Cathedrals of Spain,* Batsford, 1957; (reviser) Muirhead, *Northern Spain,* Benn, 1958.

(Contributor) E. M. Jope, editor, *Studies in Building History,* Odhams, 1962; (reviser) Muirhead, *Southern Spain,* Benn, 1964; (contributor) Joan Evans, editor, *The Flowering of the Middle Ages,* Thames & Hudson, 1966; (editor and translator) *Itineraries of William Worcestre,* Oxford University Press, 1969; *Catherine Swynford's Chantry,* Lincoln Minster, 1971; *The Master Builders,* Thames & Hudson, 1971, McGraw, 1972; *Early Gardening Catalogues,* Phillimore, 1972; *Mediaeval Architect,* St. Martin's, 1972; *Conservation of Buildings,* University of Toronto Press, 1973; *Man the Builder,* Priory Press, 1973; *Early Horticultural Catalogues: A Checklist,* University of Bath, 1973; *Sources for the History of Houses,* British Records Association, 1974; *Early Nurserymen,* Phillimore, 1974; *Cathedrals of England and Wales,* Hastings House, 1974; *Mediaeval Craftsmen,* David & Charles, 1975; *York,* Batsford, 1975; *The Black Prince and His Age,* Rowman & Littlefield, 1976; *The Perpendicular Style,* Batsford, 1978; *Mediaeval Gardens,* Batsford, in press.

Also author of monographs published by Ancient Monuments Society: *Old Buildings: Problem and Challenge*, 1955; *Conservation of Old Buildings: A Select Bibliography*, 1959; *Mediaeval Design*, 1959. Contributor to archaeological and historical journals. Editor of York City volumes, Royal Commission on Historical Monuments, 1963-70.

* * *

HASKELL, Francis (James Herbert) 1928-

PERSONAL: Born April 7, 1928, in London, England; son of Arnold (a writer) and Vera (Saitroff) Haskell; married Larissa Salmina, August 10, 1965. *Education:* King's College, Cambridge, M.A. (first class honors), 1951. *Residence:* Oxford, England. *Office:* Trinity College, Oxford University, Oxford, England.

CAREER: House of Commons, London, England, junior library clerk, 1953-54; Cambridge University, Cambridge, England, fellow, 1954-67, librarian of Faculty of Fine Arts, 1961-67; Oxford University, Trinity College, Oxford, England, professor of art history, 1967— . Lecturer at universities and art galleries in Europe and United States.

WRITINGS: (Translator) Franco Venturi, *Roots of Revolution: A History of the Populist and Socialist Movements in Nineteenth Century Russia*, Knopf, 1960; *Patrons and Painters: A Study of the Relations between Italian Art and Society in the Age of the Baroque*, Knopf, 1963, revised edition, Yale University Press, 1980; *Gericault*, Purnell & Sons, 1966; (with Anthony Burgess) *The Age of the Grand Tour*, Merrimack Book Service, 1967; (editor with others) *The Artist and the Writer in France: Essays in Honour of Jean Seznec*, Oxford University Press, 1974; *Rediscovered in Art: Some Aspects of Taste, Fashion and Collecting in England and France*, Cornell University Press, 1975, revised edition, 1979; (with Nicholas Penny) *Taste and the Antique: The Lure of Classical Sculpture 1500-1900*, Yale University Press, 1980. Contributor of articles and reviews to *Burlington Magazine, Art Bulletin, New Statesman, Nation*, and other publications.

WORK IN PROGRESS: Research into the reception of modern art in England and France during the nineteenth century.

SIDELIGHTS: In a review of *Patrons and Painters*, a critic from the *Washington Post Book World* notes that Francis Haskell "has illuminated some of the most persistent issues in the history of culture. How much control should a patron exercise over an artist? Should an artist seek private aid or government sponsorship? How does the marketplace influence artistic production and quality? What is the importance of exhibitions? Why does one artist become popular and another, equally good, languish in neglect? Such perennial questions are addressed in this book, using 17th-century Italy as an example of how one society answered them."

Haskell turned his attention to another topic—the effect of past art on present work—in *Taste and the Antique*. Specifically, this book deals with "'The Lure of Classical Sculpture' between 1500 and 1900." J. Mordaunt Cook writes: "The catalogue is superb. The bibliography is admirable. The illustrations are lavish—there is even a glorious Panini on the dust jacket. But the explanatory chapters are far too brief. The nineteenth century section, in particular the shift in taste from Roman to Greek, remains curiously thin."

BIOGRAPHICAL/CRITICAL SOURCES: Washington Post Book World, February 15, 1981; *London Times*, April 2, 1981; *Times Literary Supplement*, April 3, 1981; *New York Times Book Review*, September 20, 1981.

HAWK, Alex
See GARFIELD, Brian (Wynne)

* * *

HAYSTEAD, Wesley 1942-

PERSONAL: Born April 11, 1942, in New York, N.Y.; son of Kenneth Mark (a minister) and Gladys (Brown) Haystead; married Judy DeVries, July 24, 1964 (divorced, 1973); married Sheryl Hamstod, July 31, 1976; children: (first marriage) Karen; (second marriage) Andrew. *Education:* Cascade College, B.A., 1964; University of Southern California, M.S.Ed., 1974. *Religion:* Christian. *Home:* 1366 Rubicon, Ventura, Calif. 93003. *Office:* Gospel Light Publications, 2300 Knoll Dr., Ventura, Calif. 93003.

CAREER: Truck driver in Portland, Ore., 1960-62; elevator operator in Portland, 1962-63; minister of education for Assembly of God churches in Portland, 1964-65, and Alhambra, Calif., 1965-72; Gospel Light Publications, Ventura, Calif., writer and editor, 1973-75, senior editor of Education Division, 1980— ; early childhood coordinator, International Center for Learning, 1970-80. Conductor of seminars on Christian education.

WRITINGS—Published by Gospel Light Publications, except as indicated: *Ways to Plan and Organize Your Sunday School: Early Childhood*, 1971; *You Can't Begin Too Soon: Guiding Little Ones to God*, 1974, published as *Teaching Your Child about God*, 1981; (with Donna Harrel) *Creative Bible Learning for Young Children*, 1977; (with Ron Stone) *Helping Babies and Toddlers Learn*, 1978; *Planbook—Early Childhood*, Regal Books, 1978. Contributor to education and religion journals.

SIDELIGHTS: Wesley Haystead writes to *CA:* "The major concern of my work is to help upgrade the quality of Christian education, particularly as it is conducted within the structure of local congregations. This work includes writing and conducting seminars for lay teachers." *Avocational interests:* Bicycling, gardening.

* * *

HAYWARD, Jack 1931-

PERSONAL: Born August 18, 1931, in Shanghai, China; son of Menahem (a businessman) and Stella (Isaac) Hayward; married Margaret Glenn, December 14, 1965; children: Clare, Alan. *Education:* London School of Economics and Political Science, B.Sc., 1952, Ph.D., 1958; graduate study at Institute of Political Studies, Paris, 1952-53, and Sorbonne, University of Paris, 1955-56. *Politics:* Liberal socialist. *Religion:* Agnostic. *Home:* "Hurstwood," Church Lane, Kirkella, Humberside, England. *Agent:* A. P. Watt & Sons, 26-28 Bedford Row, London WC1R 4HL, England. *Office:* Department of Politics, University of Hull, Cottingham Rd., Hull HU6 7RX, England.

CAREER: University of Sheffield, Sheffield, England, lecturer in politics, 1959-63; University of Keele, Staffordshire, England, lecturer, 1963-68, senior lecturer in politics, 1969-73; University of Hull, Hull, England, professor of politics, 1973— . Senior research fellow at Nuffield College, Oxford University, 1968-69; visiting professor at University of Paris, 1979-80. *Military service:* Royal Air Force, 1956-58; became flying officer. *Member:* Association for Franco-British Political Studies (chairman, 1974—), Political Studies Association of the

United Kingdom (chairman, 1975-77; president, 1979-81; vice-president, 1981—).

WRITINGS: *Private Interests and Public Policy*, Longmans, Green, 1966; *The One and Indivisible French Republic*, Weidenfeld & Nicolson, 1973; (editor with Michael Watson) *Planning Politics and Public Policy: The British, French, and Italian Experience*, Cambridge University Press, 1975; (editor with O. Narkiewicz) *Planning in Europe*, Croom Helm, 1978; (editor with R. N. Berki) *State and Society in Contemporary Europe*, Martin Robertson, 1979; (editor) *Trade Unions and Politics in Western Europe*, Cass, 1980. Contributor to *Parliamentary Affairs*, *Political Studies*, *Government and Opposition*, and *Comparative Politics*. Member of editorial board of *West European Politics*, *Journal of Public Policy*, and *British Journal of Political Science*.

WORK IN PROGRESS: A study of the French left in the Fifth Republic.

AVOCATIONAL INTERESTS: Listening to classical and preclassical music, gardening, walking.

*   *   *

HEADLEY, Elizabeth
See CAVANNA, Betty

*   *   *

HEATER, Derek (Benjamin) 1931-

PERSONAL: Born November 28, 1931, in London, England; son of Benjamin Lawrence (a shop manager) and Enid (Nunn) Heater; married Joyce Dean (a teacher), March 31, 1956; children: Jane Elizabeth, Michael John Benjamin. *Education:* University of London, B.A. (with honors), 1953, postgraduate certificate in education, 1954. *Home:* 5 Queen Mary Ave., Hove, Sussex BN3 6X9, England. *Office:* Department of Humanities, Brighton Polytechnic, Falmer, Brighton BN1 9PH, England.

CAREER: Assistant teacher in boys' schools in Leyton, England, 1957-59, and Buckhurst Hill, England, 1959-62; Brighton Polytechnic, Brighton, England, lecturer in history, 1962-76, head of department, 1966-76, dean of the faculty of social and cultural studies, 1976-79, head of the department of humanities, 1976—. *Military service:* Royal Air Force, education officer at Joint Air Reconnaissance Intelligence Center, 1954-57; became flight lieutenant. *Member:* Royal Society of Arts (fellow, 1981—), Historical Association, Politics Association (founder and chairman, 1969-73).

WRITINGS: *Political Ideas in the Modern World*, Barnes & Noble, 1960, 4th edition, 1971; *Order and Rebellion: A History of Europe in the Eighteenth Century*, Harrap, 1964; *The Cold War*, Oxford University Press, 1965, 2nd edition, 1969; (editor and contributor) *The Teaching of Politics*, Barnes & Noble, 1969; (with Gwyneth Owen) *World Affairs*, Harrap, 1972, 3rd edition, two volumes, 1978; *Contemporary Political Ideas*, Longman, 1974, 2nd edition, 1982; *History Teaching and Political Education* (pamphlet), Politics Association, 1974.

Britain and the Outside World, Longman, 1976; (with Bernard Crick) *Essays on Political Education*, Falmer Press, 1977; (with Owen) *Health and Wealth*, Harrap, 1977; *Peace and War since 1945*, Harrap, 1979; *Essays on Contemporary Studies*, Hesketh, 1979; *World Studies: Education for International Understanding in Britain*, Harrap, 1980; (editor with Judith A. Gillespie) *Political Education in Flux*, Sage Publications, 1981; *The Concepts, Attitudes and Skills Related to Human Rights Education* (pamphlet), Council of Europe, 1981.

Contributor: J. L. Henderson, editor, *Since 1945*, Methuen, 1966, 2nd edition, 1971; Martin Ballard, editor, *New Movements in the Study and Teaching of History*, Indiana University Press, 1970; Michael Raggett and Malcolm Clarkson, editors, *The Middle Years Curriculum*, Ward Lock, 1974; Tom Brennan, editor, *Schools Council General Studies Report Collection: Politics*, Longman, 1974; Jonathan Brown and Brennan, editors, *Teaching Politics: Problems and Perspectives*, BBC Publications, 1975; Bernard Crick and A. Porter, editors, *Political Education and Political Liberty*, Longman, 1978.

General editor, with Bernard Crick, of "Political Realities" series, Longman, 1974—. Contributor to history, politics, and education journals, including *Teaching History*, *History*, *Political Quarterly*, *Times Educational Supplement*, *New Era*, and *British Journal of International Studies*. Editor of *Teaching Politics* (journal of the Politics Association), 1973-79; member of editorial board, *International Journal of Political Education*.

WORK IN PROGRESS: A school-level book on twentieth-century world history, for Oxford University Press; a history of the Council for Education in World Citizenship; articles for the *International Encyclopedia of Education*.

*   *   *

HECHT, Anthony (Evan) 1923-

PERSONAL: Born January 16, 1923, in New York, N.Y.; son of Melvyn Hahlo (a businessman) and Dorothea (Holzman) Hecht; married Patricia Harris (divorced); married Helen D'Alessandro, June 12, 1971; children: (first marriage) Jason, Adam; (second marriage) Evan Alexander. *Education:* Bard College, B.A., 1944; Columbia University, M.A., 1950. *Home:* 19 East Boulevard, Rochester, N.Y. 14610. *Office:* Department of English, University of Rochester, Rochester, N.Y. 14627.

CAREER: Has taught at Kenyon College, State University of Iowa, New York University, and Smith College; Bard College, Annandale-on-Hudson, N.Y., associate professor of English, 1962-67; University of Rochester, Rochester, N.Y., John H. Deane Professor of Poetry and Rhetoric, 1967—. Visiting professor, Harvard University, 1973, and Yale University, 1977. *Military service:* U.S. Army, three years; served in Europe and Japan; temporary duty with Counter-Intelligence Corps. *Member:* National Institute of Arts and Letters, American Academy of Arts and Sciences (fellow), Academy of American Poets (chancellor). *Awards, honors:* Prix de Rome fellowship, 1951; Guggenheim fellowships, 1954, 1959; *Hudson Review* fellowship, 1958; Ford Foundation fellowships, 1960, 1968; Brandeis Univeristy Creative Arts Award in poetry, 1965; Russell Loines Award, 1968; Miles Poetry Prize, 1968; Pulitzer Prize in poetry, 1968, for *The Hard Hours;* Academy of American Poets fellowship, 1969; recipient of honorary doctorates from Bard College and Georgetown University.

WRITINGS—All poetry: *A Summoning of Stones*, Macmillan, 1954; *The Seven Deadly Sins* (pamphlet; includes wood engravings by Leonard Baskin), Gehenna Press, 1958; *Struwwelpeter, a Poem*, Gehenna Press, 1958; (editor with John Hollander) *Jiggery-Pokery: A Compendium of Double Dactyls*, Atheneum, 1967; *The Hard Hours*, Atheneum, 1967; *Aesopic* (couplets; includes wood engravings by Thomas Bewick), Gehenna Press, 1968; (translator with Helen Bacon) Aeschylus, *Seven against Thebes*, Oxford University Press, 1973; *Millions of Strange Shadows*, Atheneum, 1977; *The Venetian Vespers*, Atheneum, 1977.

Poems included in *New Pocket Anthology of American Verse*, edited by Oscar Williams, World Publishing, 1955, *Contem-*

porary American Poetry, edited by Donald Hall, Penguin, 1962, *Poet's Choice,* edited by Paul Engle and Joseph Langland, Dial, 1962, *A Controversy of Poets,* edited by Paris Leary and Robert Kelly, Doubleday-Anchor, 1965, *Poems of Our Moment,* edited by John Hollander, Pegasus, 1968, and in other anthologies. Has done translations from French and German. Contributor to *Hudson Review, New York Review of Books, Quarterly Review of Literature, Transatlantic Review,* and *Voices.*

WORK IN PROGRESS: A translation, with William Arrowsmith, of Sophocles' *Oedipus at Colossus.*

SIDELIGHTS: For a contemporary poet, Anthony Hecht is unusually absorbed by old forms and language. "If there is a genteel tradition in American poetry, Mr. Hecht is commonly supposed to belong to it," notes Denis Donoghue in the *New York Times Book Review,* and George P. Elliott contends in the *Times Literary Supplement* that "Hecht's voice is his own, but his language, more amply than that of any living poet writing in English, derives from, adds to, is part of the great tradition." According to Michael Dirda in the *Washington Post Book World,* Hecht's stylistic progenitors, "subtly acknowledged" in his work, "are those reflective and witty poets of the compressed and sensual, chief among whom are Horace, La Fontaine, Pope, Byron, Baudelaire, the early Eliot and Stevens."

Reviewing his first collection of poetry, *A Summoning of Stones,* critics often comment on Hecht's ornate style. Joseph Bennett writes in the *Hudson Review:* "A Baroque exuberance in the medium characterizes Hecht's poetry; the words whirl and perform their curves. . . . This sets the dominant tone, the individual note of Hecht's writing. Echoes of Stevens at the beginning of the poem give way to language considered purely for itself." R. W. Flint also notes the influence of poets from another age, suggesting in *Partisan Review* that "Hecht belongs to the courtly tradition." For some critics, Hecht's style seems mannered and dated. Donald Davie writes in *Shenandoah* that "the poems are full of erudite and cosmopolitan references, epigraphs from Moliere and so on; and the diction is recherche, opulent, laced with the sort of wit that costs nothing. Here and there too the poet knowingly invites what some reviewers have duly responded with, the modish epithet 'Baroque.' But . . . the right word [to describe his style] is the much less fashionable 'Victorian.'"

Hecht's style changes strikingly in his collection *The Hard Hours,* according to Laurence Lieberman in the *Yale Review.* "In contrast with the ornate style of many of Hecht's earlier poems," writes Lieberman, "the new work is characterized by starkly undecorative—and unpretentious—writing." Elliott feels that the change in Hecht's approach signals new depth in his work. "One measure of Hecht's maturing as a poet," writes Elliott, "is in his skill at handling the ornaments of poetry. His youthful verse, in *A Summoning of Stones,* [was less successful: it] fed off poetry, skilfully and even handsomely, far more than off experience or felt thought."

Donaghue feels that Hecht continues retrenching in *Millions of Strange Shadows.* "Effects of diction no longer call attention to themselves," he asserts. Steven Madoff, writing in *Nation,* disagrees. He concedes that *The Hard Hours* "carries within it a stylistic progression from an early adjectival overabundance to a highly wrought simplicity of tone and directness of vision." But he points out evidence of Hecht's rekindled interest in complexity in *Millions of Strange Shadows.* According to Madoff, Hecht is much like Wallace Stevens in his interest in music "as a medium and transcendent force" and he is especially influenced by "the melodic intricacy of expression,

and the expansive discourse that is propelled through its argument as much by the perfection of the words' sounds as by the thesis that they construct" in Stevens's writing. Unfortunately, says Madoff, "the complexity of this marriage [of sound and meaning] makes for a certain inscrutability."

In the collection *The Venetian Vespers,* too, Christopher Ricks notes an obliqueness in Hecht's approach. He writes in the *New York Times Book Review:* "Hecht's latest work . . . returns to a language that is not directly transparent (and that repeatedly speaks explicitly of brilliance, polish and scintillation) but that draws attention to itself." Still, Ricks feels that the collection succeeds because Hecht has genius in his command of rhythms, above all, where an imagined self-command falters and yet does not break. One would need his powers of economy to get far enough in praise." Michael Dirda adds his recommendation to Ricks's: "To my mind and ear, Hecht's . . . *The Venetian Vespers* . . . demonstrates again that he may be the most accomplished master of technique since Auden. The verse is musical, the diction precisely nuanced, the syntax smooth and conversational. There is never a jarring line, never a word out of place; everything fits together with the inevitable rightness of the classical poet."

BIOGRAPHICAL/CRITICAL SOURCES: Perspective, spring, 1962; *Atlantic,* February, 1967; *New Yorker,* February 25, 1967; *Listener,* October 19, 1967; *Observer,* November 12, 1967; *Times Literary Supplement,* November 23, 1967, May 6, 1977, May 30, 1980; *Christian Science Monitor,* February 1, 1968; *Reporter,* February 22, 1968; *London Magazine,* Volume VII, number 12, 1968; *Shenandoah,* spring, 1968; *Carleton Miscellany,* Volume IX, number 3, 1968; *New York Review of Books,* August 1, 1968, August 17, 1978; *Harper's,* August, 1968; *Poetry,* September, 1968; *Yale Review,* spring, 1969; *Contemporary Literature,* spring, 1969; *Nation,* September 3, 1977; *Contemporary Literary Criticism,* Gale, Volume VIII, 1978, Volume XIII, 1980, Volume XIX, 1981; *Washington Post Book World,* December 30, 1970.

*   *   *

HEDGES, Joseph
See HARKNETT, Terry

*   *   *

HEGEL, Richard   1927-

PERSONAL: Born April 26, 1927, in Philadelphia, Pa.; son of Henry John and Clara (Lehr) Hegel; married Linda Pratt, June 29, 1968. *Education:* U.S. Merchant Marine Academy, graduate, 1948; Yale University, B.S., 1950; Southern Connecticut State College, M.L.S., 1969, M.A., 1972, M.S., 1976, M.S., 1981. *Home:* 29 Loomis Pl., New Haven, Conn. 06511. *Office:* Library, Southern Connecticut State College, 501 Crescent St., New Haven, Conn. 06515.

CAREER: Industrial power engineer, Connecticut Light & Power Co., 1953-67; New Haven Colony Historical Society, New Haven, Conn., executive director, 1968-70; Southern Connecticut State College, New Haven, assistant director of library services, 1971-75, director, 1975—. Member of New Haven Historic District Commission, 1970—; member of executive committee of New Haven Bicentennial Commission, 1973-76; member of New Haven Library Board, 1981—; former vice-president of New Haven Festival of Arts. *Military service:* U.S. Naval Reserve, active duty; served in Korea; became lieutenant junior grade.

MEMBER: New Haven Colony Historical Society (member of board of directors, 1974—), New Haven Preservation Trust (secretary, 1970—), Friends of the New Haven Free Public Library (co-chairman, 1973-81), Woman's Seaman's Friend Society (member of board of managers, 1969—), Yale Club (New Haven; member of board of directors, 1974—), Graduates Club, Mory's, New Haven Lawn Club, Quinnipiack Club, Ronan-Edgehill Neighborhood Association (vice-president and secretary, 1971—).

WRITINGS: Nineteenth-Century Historians of New Haven, Archon, 1972; *Carriages from New Haven: A History of New Haven's Nineteenth-Century Carriage Industry,* Archon, 1974; (co-compiler) *New Haven: A Portfolio for the Bicentennial,* New Haven Bicentennial Commission, 1975; (co-compiler) *New Haven Celebrates the Bicentennial: A Commemorative Book,* New Haven Bicentennial Commission, 1976; (co-editor) *New Haven: An Illustrated History,* Windsor Publications, 1981.

*   *   *

HEILMAN, Joan Rattner

PERSONAL: Daughter of Louis and Erna (Schneider) Rattner; married Morton Heilman (an engineer), August 12, 1956; children: Katherine, Julia, David. *Education:* Smith College, B.A. *Home and office:* 812 Stuart Ave., Mamaroneck, N.Y. 10543. *Agent:* Anita Diamant, 51 East 42nd St., New York, N.Y. 10017.

CAREER: This Week (magazine), New York, N.Y., women's editor, 1954-69; free-lance writer, 1969—. *Member:* American Society of Journalists and Authors, Authors League.

WRITINGS: The Official Knit-a-Dress-a-Day Knitting Book, Grosset, 1968; (with Jean Nidetch) *The Story of Weight Watchers,* World Publications, 1970; *Large-Type Knitting Book of Babies and Children's Clothes,* Crowell, 1971; (editor) *Kenneth's Complete Book on Hair,* Doubleday, 1972; (with Alvin Eden) *Growing Up Thin,* McKay, 1975; (editor) *The Lila Nachtigall Report on Menopause,* Putnam, 1977; *The Complete Book of Midwifery,* Dutton, 1977; *Having A Cesarean Baby,* Dutton, 1978; *Diabetes: Controlling It the Easy Way,* Random House, 1982.

Contributor of non-fiction articles to numerous periodicals, including *Ladies' Home Journal, Family Circle, Parade, Family Health,* and *Good Housekeeping.*

*   *   *

HEIMAN, Grover G(eorge, Jr.)   1920-

PERSONAL: Born July 26, 1920, in Galveston, Tex.; son of Grover George (an oil refining supervisor) and Rose Mary (Ulch) Heiman; married Virginia Deene Williamson, February 14, 1942; children: Virginia Dean Myers, Grover III, Deborah Suzanne, Richard V. S. *Education:* Attended Lee College, Baytown, Tex., 1937-39, and University of Texas, 1940-41; University of Southern California, B.S., 1959. *Politics:* Democrat. *Religion:* Roman Catholic. *Home:* 2881 Glenvale Dr., Fairfax, Va.

CAREER: Sun-Light Publishing Co., Corsicana, Tex., reporter, 1945-47; U.S. Air Force, member of combat crew, operations staff, and public relations staff, 1947-68, retired as colonel. *Military service:* U.S. Army Air Forces, 1941-45. *Member:* Beta Gamma Sigma, Alpha Psi Omega. *Awards, honors:* Winner of U.S. Air Force international short story contest, 1953; George Washington Honor Medal, Freedoms Foundation, 1955; Los Angeles National Office Management Award, 1959.

WRITINGS: (With W. Rutherford Montgomery) *Jet Navigator,* Dodd, 1959; *Jet Tanker,* Holt, 1961; *Jet Pioneers,* Duell, 1963; (with daughter, Virginia Myers) *Careers for Women in Uniform,* Lippincott, 1971; *Aerial Photography,* Macmillan, 1973. Author of numerous ghost-written articles and speeches. Contributor of articles to *Air Force Magazine, U.S. Lady, Man Hunt, Pace,* and *Airline Pilot.* Managing editor, *Armed Forces Management,* 1968-70; *Nation's Business,* associate editor, 1970, managing editor, 1978-80, editor, 1980—.

WORK IN PROGRESS: A novel.

AVOCATIONAL INTERESTS: Amateur radio.

*   *   *

HENREY, Madeleine   1906-
(Mrs. Robert Henrey; Robert Henrey, a pseudonym)

PERSONAL: Born August 13, 1906, in Paris, France; emigrated to England in 1920; naturalized British subject; daughter of Emile (a bricklayer) and Mathilde (a seamstress and worker of fine lace; maiden name, Bernhard) Gal; married Robert Selby Henrey (a journalist), December 1, 1928; children: Robert John Edward. *Education:* Attended school in Paris, France, and Convent of the Sacred Heart, London, England. *Home:* Villers-sur-Mer, Calvados I4 640, France.

CAREER: Writer. Formerly employed as a secretary, shop girl, manicurist; columnist for *London Evening News,* 1928-38; owner of farm in Normandy, France, 1936—. *Member:* Women's Press Club (London).

WRITINGS—Under name Mrs. Robert Henrey; published by Dent, except as indicated: *A Journey to Vienna,* 1950; *Matilda and the Chickens,* 1950; *The Little Madeleine,* 1951, published as *The Little Madeleine: The Autobiography of a Young Girl in Montmartre,* Dutton, 1953; *Paloma,* 1951, Dutton, 1955; *Madeleine Grown Up,* 1952, published as *Madeleine Grown Up: The Autobiography of a French Girl,* Dutton, 1953; *An Exile in Soho,* 1952; *Madeleine's Journal,* 1953; *Madeleine, Young Wife: The Autobiography of a French Girl,* Dutton, 1954 (published in England as *Madeleine, Young Wife,* 1960); *A Month in Paris,* 1954; *Milou's Daughter, Madeleine: A Sentimental Journey to the South of France,* Dutton, 1955 (published in England as *Milou's Daughter,* 1955); *Bloomsbury Fair,* 1955; *This Feminine World,* 1956; *A Daughter for a Fortnight,* 1957; *The Virgin of Aldermanbury: Rebirth of the City of London,* 1958; *Mistress of Myself,* 1959; *The Dream Makers,* 1961; *Spring in a Soho Street,* 1962; *Her April Days,* 1963; *Wednesday at Four,* 1964; *Winter Wild,* 1966; *London under Fire, 1940-1945,* 1969; *She Who Pays,* 1969; *Julia: Reminiscences of a Year in Madeleine's Life as a London Shop Girl,* 1971; *A Girl at Twenty: Six Months in the Life of the Young Madeleine,* 1974; *Green Leaves,* 1976; *The Golden Visit,* 1979.

Under pseudonym Robert Henrey; published by Dent, except as indicated: *A Farm in Normandy* (also see below), 1941; *A Journey to Gibraltar,* 1943; *A Village in Piccadilly,* 1943; *The Incredible City,* 1944; *The Foolish Decade,* 1945; *The King of Brentford,* P. Davies, 1946; *The Seige of London,* 1946; *The Return to the Farm* (also see below), P. Davies, 1947; *London,* 1948, Dutton, 1949; *A Film Star in Belgrave Square,* P. Davies, 1948; *A Farm in Normandy* [and] *The Return to the Farm,* 1952.

SIDELIGHTS: In order to form a chronological narrative, Madeleine Henrey suggests that a group of her books be read in the following order: *The Little Madeleine, An Exile in Soho,*

Julia, A Girl at Twenty, Madeleine Grown Up, Green Leaves, Madeleine, Young Wife, London under Fire, 1940-1945, Her April Days, Wednesday at Four, She Who Pays, and *The Golden Visit.*

Henrey writes to *CA:* "My aim in the twenty or more volumes in this long, female autobiographical sequence (the narrative runs from 1906 until 1981) has been to recount in detail the successive phases in the life of a sensitive girl living in Western Europe." Each book describes one phase—girlhood, work, love, marriage, mother, grandmother, etc. She calls it, "an attempt at a complete confession of a female mind against such a turbulent canvas [which] has probably never been attempted before—perhaps the nearest being Dorothy Richardson's *Pilgrimage.*" Some of these books have been in print, continuously, for as long as thirty-five years.

AVOCATIONAL INTERESTS: Gardening, sewing, knitting, reading.

*   *   *

HENREY, Mrs. Robert
See HENREY, Madeleine

*   *   *

HENREY, Robert
See HENREY, Madeleine

*   *   *

HENRY, Carl F(erdinand) H(oward)   1913-

PERSONAL: Born January 22, 1913, in New York, N.Y.; son of Karl F.E. and Johanna (Vaethroeder) Henry; married Helga Bender, August 17, 1940; children: Paul Brentwood, Carol Jennifer. *Education:* Wheaton College, B.A., 1938, M.A., 1940; Northern Baptist Theological Seminary, B.D., 1941, Th.D., 1942; Boston University, Ph.D., 1949; postdoctoral study at Loyola University, Chicago, Ill., 1941, Indiana University, 1944, New College, University of Edinburgh, 1953, and Cambridge University, 1968. *Home:* 3824 North 37th St., Arlington, Va. 22207.

CAREER: Ordained Baptist minister, 1941. Former editor of weekly newspapers in Smithtown and Port Jefferson, N.Y., and correspondent for *New York Times, New York Herald Tribune,* and *Chicago Tribune;* Northern Baptist Theological Seminary, Chicago, Ill., assistant professor, 1940-42, professor and chairman of department of philosophy of religion, 1942-47; Fuller Theological Seminary, Pasadena, Calif., professor of theology and Christian philosophy, 1947-56; *Christianity Today,* Washington, D.C., editor, 1956-68, editor-at-large, 1968—; Eastern Baptist Theological Seminary, Philadelphia, Pa., visiting professor, 1969-70, professor of theology, 1970-71, professor-at-large, 1971-74; World Vision, Monrovia, Calif., lecturer-at-large, 1974—. Lecturer at various times since 1959 in Latin America, Korea, Taiwan, Japan, the Philippines, and Yugoslavia; lecturer with World Vision team in Burma, Thailand, Malaya, Columbia, India, Ceylon, and Singapore; lecturer with Billy Graham in Germany and Switzerland. Co-chairman of Rose Bowl Sunrise Service, 1948-56; broadcaster on radio and television, including daily program on KPOL, Los Angeles, 1952-53. Chairman of World Congress on Evangelism, Berlin, 1966; program chairman of Jerusalem Conference on Biblical Prophecy, 1971; program chairman of Conference on Christianity and the Counterculture, 1971; board of directors of Institute for Advanced Christian Studies, president, 1971-73, member, 1975-79, 1981—; mem-

ber of board, Ethics and Public Policy Center. Member of advisory board, Evangelical Book Club, "Catalyst" (a taped digest for ministers), and Institute on Religion and Democracy; member of advisory council, World Evangelical Fellowship Theological Commission, Commission on Christian Ethics, Baptist World Alliance.

MEMBER: American Philosophical Society, American Theological Society (president, 1980-81), Evangelical Theological Society (president, 1969-70), Society of Biblical Literature, National Association of Biblical Instructors, Society for the Scientific Study of Religion, Society of Christian Philosophers, American Association for the Advancement of Science, American Society of Church History, American Schools of Oriental Research, American Society for Christian Social Ethics, Evangelical Press Association (honorary life member), Asian Theological Association (member of reference board), Victoria Institute (Great Britain), Cosmos Club (Washington D.C.). *Awards, honors:* Freedoms Foundation Medal for article, "Christianity and the American Heritage"; D.Litt., Seattle Pacific College, 1959, Wheaton College, 1968; L.H.D., Houghton College, 1973; Religious Heritage of America award, 1975; D.D., Northwestern College, 1979.

WRITINGS: A Doorway to Heaven, Zondervan, 1941; *Successful Church Publicity,* Zondervan, 1942; *Remaking the Modern Mind,* Eerdmans, 1948; *The Uneasy Conscience of Modern Fundamentalism,* Eerdmans, 1948; *Giving a Reason for Our Hope,* W. A. Wilde, 1949; *The Protestant Dilemma,* Eerdmans, 1949; *Note on the Doctrine of God,* W. A. Wilde, 1949; *Fifty Years of Protestant Theology,* W. A. Wilde, 1950; *The Drift of Western Thought,* Eerdmans, 1951; *Personal Idealism and Strong's Theology,* Van Kampen, 1951; *Glimpses of a Sacred Land,* W. A. Wilde, 1953; *Christian Personal Ethics,* Eerdmans, 1957; *Evangelical Responsibility in Contemporary Theology,* Eerdmans, 1957.

Aspects of Christian Social Ethics, Eerdmans, 1964; *Frontiers in Modern Theology,* Moody, 1966; *The God Who Shows Himself,* Word Books, 1966; *Evangelicals at the Brink of Crisis,* Word Books, 1967; *Faith at the Frontiers,* Moody, 1969; *A Plea for Evangelical Demonstration,* Baker Book, 1971; *New Strides of Faith,* Moody, 1972; *Evangelicals in Search of Identity,* Word Books, 1976; *God, Revelation and Authority,* Volumes I and II, 1976, Volumes III and IV, 1979.

Editor: *Contemporary Evangelical Thought,* Channel, 1957; *Revelation and the Bible: Contemporary Evangelical Thought,* Baker Book, 1959, 3rd edition, 1967; *The Biblical Expositor,* Holman, 1960; (consulting editor) *Baker's Dictionary of Theology,* Baker Book, 1960; *Basic Christian Doctrines,* Holt, 1962; *Christian Faith and Modern Theology,* Meredith, 1964; *Jesus of Nazareth: Saviour and Lord,* Eerdmans, 1966; (with W. Stanley Mooneyham) *One Race, One Gospel, One Task,* two volumes, World Wide Publications, 1967; *Fundamentals of the Faith,* Zondervan, 1969; *Baker's Dictionary of Christian Ethics,* Baker Book, 1973; *Horizons of Science,* Harper, 1978. Contributor to religious journals and magazines. Literary editor, *United Evangelical Action,* 1945-52.

WORK IN PROGRESS: Volumes V and VI of *God, Revelation and Authority,* for Word Books.

SIDELIGHTS: Carl F.H. Henry has traveled more than a million miles on religious missions and lectured on every continent. His books have been translated into numerous languages, including Korean and Mandarin.

BIOGRAPHICAL/CRITICAL SOURCES: Time, July 13, 1962, February 14, 1977.

HESS, Margaret Johnston 1915-

PERSONAL: Born February 22, 1915, in Ames, Iowa; daughter of Howard Wright (a clergyman) and Jane (Stevenson) Johnston; married Bartlett Leonard Hess (senior pastor of a Presbyterian church), July 31, 1937; children: Daniel Bartlett, Deborah (Mrs. Hans Morsink), John Howard and Janet Elizabeth (twins). Education: Coe College, B.A., 1937. Religion: Presbyterian. Home: 16845 Riverside Dr., Livonia, Mich. 48154.

CAREER: Writer. Teacher of Bible classes in the Philippines and in India, 1961; teacher of community Bible classes at Ward Presbyterian Church, Livonia, Mich., and Christ Church Cranbook, Bloomfield Hills, Mich. Tour conductor, primarily to the Bible lands.

WRITINGS: (With husband, Bartlett Leonard Hess) How to Have a Giving Church, Abingdon, 1974; (with B. L. Hess) The Power of a Loving Church, Regal Books, 1977; Love Knows No Barriers, Victor Books, 1978; Esther: Courage in Crisis, Victor Books, 1980; Unconventional Women, Victor Books, 1981. Contributor to church publications.

WORK IN PROGRESS: A book on marriage.

SIDELIGHTS: Margaret Hess comments: "I have tried various forms of writing, even a novel, but find that what people really want to read about is what I teach—the Bible. Their interest in learning what the Bible has to say to today's world constantly amazes me. For me, digging into the history, geography, and everyday customs of Bible times through contemporary literature and archeological findings has been a life-long passion. To write about the Bible all I have to do is review my facts, then popularize. I seek to make Bible characters and times come alive for today's reader. I show how the Bible can help us with the practical problems of everyday living."

*   *   *

HEWITT, James 1928-

PERSONAL: Born April 9, 1928, in Belfast, Northern Ireland; married Kathleen Ellen Casselden, September 13, 1969; children: Bryan James, Amanda Susan. Education: Educated in Belfast, Northern Ireland. Politics: "No label." Religion: "No label." Home: 11 Howard Rd., Dorking, Surrey, England.

CAREER: Daily Express, London, England, reporter in Belfast, 1946-52; free-lance reporter and writer in Belfast, 1953-62; employed with Thorsons Publishers Ltd., London, 1963; British Foreign Office, London, member of staff in research department, 1964-68; Royal National Institute for the Blind, London, joint-warden of residential hostel in Bayswater, 1969-72; free-lance writer and photographer, 1972—.

WRITINGS: Relax and Be Successful, Thorsons, 1951; The Art of Relaxed Living, Thorsons, 1955; Teach Yourself Yoga, English Universities Press, 1960; About Sea Foods, Thorsons, 1964; Yoga and You, Anthony Gibbs, 1966; New Faces, Books for You, 1966; Isometrics and You, Books for You, 1967; Techniques of Sex Fitness, Universal Publishing, 1969; A Practical Guide to Yoga, Funk, 1969.

Eye-Witness to Nelson's Battles, Osprey, 1972; Eye-Witnesses to the Indian Mutiny, Osprey, 1972; Eye-Witnesses to Wagon Trains West, Scribner, 1973; Eye-Witnesses to Ireland in Revolt, Osprey, 1974; Yoga and Vitality, Yoga and Meditation, Yoga Postures, Barrie & Jenkins, 1977, published as The Complete Yoga Book: Yoga and Vitality, Yoga and Meditation, Yoga Postures, Schocken, 1978; Teach Yourself Meditation, Hodder & Stoughton, 1978; Famous Names in World Exploration, Wayland, 1979; Talking about Northern Ireland, Wayland, 1980; Isometrics, Thorsons, 1980; Foods for Health, Hodder & Stoughton, 1981; Relaxation East and West, Roder, 1982. Contributor of short stories and features on historical events to British Broadcasting Corp. radio.

*   *   *

HICK, John (Harwood) 1922-

PERSONAL: Born January 20, 1922, in Scarborough, England; son of Mark D. (a lawyer) and Aileen (Hirst) Hick; married Hazel Bowers, August 30, 1953; children: Eleanor, Mark, Peter, Michael. Education: University of Edinburgh, M.A. (first class honors), 1948; Oxford University, D.Phil., 1950; Westminster Theological College, Cambridge, theological study, 1950-53. Office: Department of Theology, University of Birmingham, Birmingham B15 2TT, England.

CAREER: Presbyterian minister in Northumberland, England, 1953-56; Cornell University, Ithaca, N.Y., assistant professor of philosophy, 1956-59; Princeton Theological Seminary, Princeton, N.J., Stuart Professor of Christian Philosophy, 1959-64; Cambridge University, Cambridge, England, lecturer in divinity, 1964-67; University of Birmingham, Birmingham, England, H. G. Wood Professor of Theology, 1967—. Wartime service: Served with Friends' Ambulance Unit, 1942-45. Member: Royal Institute of Philosophy, American Philosophical Association, American Theological Society, Society of Psychical Research, Mind Association. Awards, honors: Guggenheim fellowship, 1963-64.

WRITINGS: Faith and Knowledge: A Modern Introduction to the Problem of Religious Knowledge, Cornell University Press, 1957, 2nd edition, 1966; Philosophy of Religion, Prentice-Hall, 1963, 2nd edition, 1973; (editor) Classical and Contemporary Readings in the Philosophy of Religion, Prentice-Hall, 1964, 2nd edition, 1970; (editor) Faith and the Philosophers, St. Martin's, 1964; (editor and author of introduction) The Existence of God, Macmillan, 1964; Evil and the Love of God, Harper, 1966, revised edition, 1977; (compiler with Arthur C. McGill) The Many-Faced Argument: Recent Studies on the Ontological Argument for the Existence of God, Macmillan, 1967; Christianity at the Centre, Macmillan, 1968, Herder & Herder, 1970, 2nd edition published as The Center of Christianity, 1978.

Arguments for the Existence of God, Herder & Herder, 1971; Biology and the Soul, Cambridge University Press, 1972; (editor) M. J. Charlesworth, Philosophy of Religion: The Historic Approaches, Herder & Herder, 1972, 2nd edition, Prentice-Hall, 1973; (editor) William A. Christian, Oppositions of Religious Doctrine, Herder & Herder, 1972; (editor) Kai Neilsen, Contemporary Critiques of Religion, Herder & Herder, 1972; God and the Universe of Faiths, St. Martin's, 1973, revised edition, Collins, 1977; Death and Eternal Life, Harper, 1977; (editor) The Myth of God Incarnate, Westminster, 1978; Christianity and Other Religions, edited by Brian Hebblethwaite, Collins, 1980; God Has Many Names: Britain's New Pluralism, Macmillan, 1980. Also author of Truth and Dialogue, 1974. Member of editorial board, Encyclopedia of Philosophy; member of editorial council, Theology Today.

SIDELIGHTS: John Hick has long been recognized as one of England's more respected philosophers and writers on religion. Readers often cite the clarity of his writing style and his gentle persuasive ability as qualities that endear his books to his many followers. For example, R. E. Willis of Christian Century writes that "Hick presents his views with clarity, moving with assurance toward a contemporary statement of the 'essence' of Christianity. That one comes away feeling that the latter presents, for the most part, a resume of the liberal theological arsenal is not necessarily a bad thing, unless one's inclinations lie elsewhere." In another issue of *Christian Century*, Frederick Sontag explains that in *Christianity at the Centre* "Hick makes Christianity as doctrine seem easy and obvious and natural, and he ends his examination of God with a reaffirmation of resurrection belief. His mode of argument is essentially to show that things we accept in everyday life make belief reasonable." And a reviewer for *Choice* writes, in an article on *God and the Universe*, that "Hick is a truly fine philosopher of religion. Not only does he think clearly, but he also writes well, so well that the reader is hardly aware that he is exploring difficult ideas. Hick is a modern thinker, completely liberated from subservience to theological orthodoxy. But his conclusions, while fresh and appealing, have a remarkable continuity with and appreciation for the Christian tradition. . . . Anyone who is intrigued by the title . . . can understand and profit from this book."

BIOGRAPHICAL/CRITICAL SOURCES: Christian Century, March 22, 1967, November 18, 1970, November 15, 1978; *Encounter,* autumn, 1967; *Choice,* September, 1974; *Library Journal,* November 15, 1976; *America,* March 19, 1977; *Critic,* June, 1979.†

*   *   *

HIDORE, John J. 1932-

PERSONAL: Born July 6, 1932, in Cedar Falls, Iowa; son of John Henry (a factory foreman) and Vearle (Thomas) Hidore; married Ruth Norton (a teacher), June 6, 1954 (divorced June 6, 1979); children: Jill Helen, John Warren. *Education:* Iowa State Teachers College (now University of Northern Iowa), B.A., 1954; University of Iowa, M.A., 1958, Ph.D., 1960. *Home:* 6 West Oak Ct., Greensboro, N.C. 27407. *Office:* Department of Geography, University of North Carolina at Greensboro, Greensboro, N.C. 27412.

CAREER: Illinois Central Railroad, Waterloo, Iowa, rodman and member of field survey crew, summers, 1952-54; mathematics teacher in public schools in Esterville, Iowa, spring, 1957; University of Wisconsin—Madison, instructor in geography, 1960-62; Oklahoma State University, Stillwater, assistant professor, 1962-64, associate professor of geography, 1964-66; Indiana University at Bloomington, associate professor, 1966-72, professor of geography, beginning 1972; University of North Carolina at Greensboro, professor of geography and head of department, 1980—. Visiting professor at State College of Iowa (now University of Northern Iowa), summers, 1960-61, Wisconsin State University—Eau Claire (now University of Wisconsin—Eau Claire), summer, 1965, University of Ife, 1971-72, University of Khartoum, 1974-75, and Ben Gurion University of the Negev, 1978. Member of conference on water resources at New Mexico State University, summers, 1963, 1969; director of National Defense Education Act (NDEA) Institute in Geography at Oklahoma State University, summer, 1966. *Military service:* U.S. Army, topographic computor, 1955-56; served in France.

MEMBER: American Geographical Society, American Meteorological Society, American Water Resources Association, Association of American Geographers, National Council for Geographic Education.

WRITINGS: The Undergraduate Curriculum in Geography, Iowa Department of Public Instruction, 1966; *Introduction to Physical Geography: Laboratory Exercises,* W. C. Brown,

1967; *A Workbook of Weather Maps,* W. C. Brown, 1968, 2nd edition, 1971; *A Geography of the Atmosphere,* W. C. Brown, 1969, 2nd edition, 1972; (with Michael C. Roberts) *Physical Geography: A Laboratory Manual,* Burgess, 1974, 2nd edition, 1978; *Physical Geography: Earth Systems,* Scott, Foresman, 1974.

Contributor: *Reading Wisconsin's Landscape,* State of Wisconsin Department of Public Instruction, 1962; John W. Alexander, editor, *Economic Geography,* Prentice-Hall, 1963; Peter Haggett, editor, *Locational Analysis in Human Geography,* Edward Arnold, 1965; Robert E. Gabler, editor, *Handbook for Secondary Teachers,* National Council for Geographic Education, 1966; Howard G. Roepke, editor, *Readings in Economic Geography,* Wiley, 1967; Maurice H. Yeates, editor, *An Introduction to Quantitative Analysis in Economic Geography,* McGraw, 1968; G. J. Fielding, R. E. Hure, and K. W. Rumage, editors, *Computer Assisted Instruction in Geography,* Commission on College Geography, Association of American Geographers, 1969; Peter E. Lloyd and Peter Dicken, editors, *Location in Space: A Theoretical Approach to Economic Geography,* Harper, 1972; L. Lloyd Haring and Marilyn Haring, editors, *Problem Solving in World Geography,* Education Associates, 1973; Paul Richards, editor, *African Environment: Problems and Perspectives,* International African Institute (London), 1975; J. Odland and R. Taaffe, editors, *Geographical Horizons,* Kendall-Hunt, 1977. Contributor to professional journals.

*   *   *

HIGHAM, John 1920-

PERSONAL: Born October 26, 1920, in Jamaica, N.Y.; son of Lloyd Stuart and Margaret (Windred) Higham; married Eileen Moss, August 26, 1948; children: Constance, Margaret, Jay, Daniel. *Education:* Johns Hopkins University, B.A., 1941; University of Wisconsin, M.A., 1942, Ph.D., 1949. *Home:* 309 Tuscany Rd., Baltimore, Md. 21218. *Office:* Department of History, Johns Hopkins University, Baltimore, Md. 21218.

CAREER: American Mercury, New York, N.Y., editorial assistant, 1945-46; University of California, Los Angeles, instructor, 1948-50, assistant professor, 1950-54; Rutgers University, New Brunswick, N.J., associate professor, 1954-58, professor, 1958-60; University of Michigan, Ann Arbor, professor of history, 1960-68, Moses Coit Tyler Professor of History, 1968-71, 1972-73; Johns Hopkins University, Baltimore, Md., John Martin Vincent Professor of History, 1971-72, 1973—. Visiting associate professor, Columbia University, 1958-59; Commonwealth Fund Lecturer, University College, University of London, 1968; Phi Beta Kappa visiting scholar, 1972-73; Fulbright lecturer, Kyoto American Studies Seminar, 1974. Member of board of directors, American Immigration Conference, 1956-60. Member, Institute for Advanced Study, 1973-74. *Military service:* U.S. Army Air Forces, 1943-45; served in Italy as historian for Twelfth Air Force; became staff sergeant.

MEMBER: American Studies Association (president of Middle Atlantic States chapter, 1956-57), Organization of American Historians (member of executive committee, 1964-67, 1974-77; president, 1973-74), American Historical Association (member of council and executive committee, 1971-74), American Antiquarian Society, Society of American Historians, American Academy of Arts and Sciences, Immigration History Society (vice-president, 1976-79; president, 1979—), New Society Letters Lund (Sweden), Michigan Society of Fellows. *Awards, honors:* American Historical Association John H.

Dunning Prize, 1956, for *Strangers in the Land: Patterns of American Nativism;* Princeton University Council for the Humanities fellow, 1960-61; Center for Advanced Studies in the Behavioral Sciences fellow, 1965-66; Woodrow Wilson International Center for Scholars fellow, 1976-77.

WRITINGS: Strangers in the Land: Patterns of American Nativism, Rutgers University Press, 1955, 2nd edition, Atheneum, 1963; (editor and co-author) *The Reconstruction of American History,* Harper, 1962; (with others) *History,* Prentice-Hall, 1965; (contributor) John Weiss, editor, *The Origins of Modern Consciousness,* Wayne State University Press, 1965; *From Boundlessness to Consolidation: The Transformation of American Culture, 1848-1860,* Clements Library, University of Michigan, 1969; *Writing American History: Essays on Modern Scholarship,* Indiana University Press, 1970; *Send These to Me: Jews and Other Immigrants in Urban America,* Atheneum, 1975; (editor) *Ethnic Leadership in America,* Johns Hopkins Press, 1978. Also editor, with Paul Conkin, of *New Directions in American Intellectual History,* 1979. Editor, "The Meaning of American History" series, Harper. Contributor to professional journals. Member of editorial board, *American Quarterly,* 1964-67; consulting editor, *Comparative Studies in Society and History,* 1972—.

*   *   *

HIGHET, Gilbert (Arthur)   1906-1978

PERSONAL: Born June 22, 1906 in Glasgow, Scotland; came to the United States in 1937, naturalized in 1951; died January 20, 1978, of cancer, in New York, N.Y.; son of Gilbert (a post office official) and Elizabeth Gertrude (Boyle) Highet; married Helen MacInnes (a writer), September 22, 1932; children: Gilbert Keith MacInnes. *Education:* Glasgow University, M.A., 1929; Oxford University, B.A., 1932, M.A., 1936. *Home:* 535 Park Ave., New York, N.Y. *Agent:* Curtis Brown Ltd., 575 Madison Ave., New York, N.Y. 10022. *Office:* Philosophy Hall, Columbia University, New York, N.Y.

CAREER: Oxford University, Oxford, England, fellow of St. John's College, 1932-38; Columbia University, New York, N.Y., professor of Greek and Latin, 1938-50, Anthon Professor of Latin Language and Literature, 1950-72, professor emeritus, 1972-78, chairman of the department of Greek and Latin, 1965-72. Book-of-the-Month Club judge, beginning 1954; commentator on weekly radio program, "People, Places, and Books," originating from WQXR, New York, and broadcast by more than 300 stations in United States and Canada, 1952-59. Member of British mission in United States, Canada, 1941-43. *Military service:* British Army, 1943-46, became lieutenant colonel; served in Allied Military Government in Germany, 1945-46. *Member:* Royal Society of Literature (England; fellow), American Philological Association, Classical Association of New England (honorary member), Century Club (New York), Maidstone (East Hampton). *Awards, honors:* Guggenheim fellowship, 1951; Litt.D., Glasgow University, 1951, Oxford University, 1954, Syracuse University, 1960, Adelphi University, 1964; L.H.D., Case Institute, 1951; award of merit from American Philological Association, 1963, for *The Anatomy of Satire.*

WRITINGS—All originally published by Oxford University Press, except as indicated: *The Classical Tradition: Greek and Roman Influences on Western Literature,* 1949, reprinted, 1967; *The Art of Teaching,* Knopf, 1950, reprinted, 1968; *People, Places, and Books,* 1953; *Man's Unconquerable Mind,* Columbia University Press, 1954; *The Migration of Ideas,* 1954; *Juvenal the Satirist,* 1954; *A Clerk of Oxenford,* 1954; *Poets*

in a Landscape, Knopf, 1957, reprinted, Greenwood Press, 1979; *Talents and Geniuses,* 1957; *The Powers of Poetry,* 1960; *The Anatomy of Satire,* Princeton University Press, 1962; *Explorations,* 1971; *The Speeches in Vergil's Aeneid,* Princeton University Press, 1972; *The Immortal Profession: The Joy of Teaching and Learning,* Weybright & Talley, 1976.

Translator: (With wife, Helen MacInnes) Otto Kiefer, *Sexual Life in Ancient Rome,* Dutton, 1935, reprinted, AMS Press, 1972; Werner Jaeger, *Paideia: The Ideals of Greek Culture,* Volume I: *Archaic Greece: The Mind of Athens,* 1939, 2nd edition, 1945, reprinted, 1965, Volume II: *In Search of the Divine Center,* 1939, Volume III: *The Conflict of Cultural Ideals in the Age of Plato,* 1939. Also translator of poems for *Oxford Book of Greek Verse.* Contributor to *Oxford Classical Dictionary.* Chief literary critic, *Harper's,* 1952-54; chairman, editorial advisory board, *Horizon,* 1958-78.

SIDELIGHTS: As a popularizer of intellectual topics, Gilbert Highet was surprisingly successful. He often preferred to be entertaining rather than profound and, for this reason, he was severely criticized by those preferring scholarly treatment of poetry, satire, literary history, criticism, and classicism. Highet wrote "the English language with affectionate ease" and, though he was at times patronizing, his approach was generally personal, enthusiastic, and anecdotal.

Although Highet's purpose was often the instruction of the lay reader, the initiated will find no lack of erudition in his work. For example, *Juvenal the Satirist,* a work requiring eighteen years for production, was the "first exhaustive analysis of the Roman poet." It has been said that Highet took "all literature for his province" but few would assert that he was incapable of definitive handling of the field.

AVOCATIONAL INTERESTS: Playing piano duets with his wife, mountain climbing, painting, and architecture.

BIOGRAPHICAL/CRITICAL SOURCES: Chicago Sunday Tribune, May 22, 1960; *Library Journal,* June 1, 1960; *Christian Science Monitor,* November 1, 1962; *Publishers Weekly,* April 12, 1976.

OBITUARIES: New York Times, January 21, 1978; *AB Bookman's Weekly,* April 3, 1978.†

*   *   *

HILL, Mary Raymond   1923-
(Lee Raymond)

PERSONAL: Born September 2, 1923, in Great Falls, Mont.; daughter of Raymond Ernest Hill (a salesman) and Mary Caroline (a teacher; maiden name, Brantly) Hill; divorced. *Education:* University of Colorado, B.A., 1944, graduate study, 1946-48; graduate study at University of Illinois, 1945-46; San Francisco State University, M.A., 1970. *Home:* 6069 Contra Costa Rd., Oakland, Calif. 94618; and P.O. Box 183, Arroyo Seco, N.M. 87514.

CAREER: Phillips Petroleum Co., Bartlesville, Okla., geologist, 1944-45; Illinois Geological Survey, Urbana, Ill., geologist, 1945-46; State of California, Division of Mines and Geology, Sacramento, Calif., geologist, 1949-75; U.S. Geological Survey, Western Region, Menlo Park, Calif., information officer, 1975-80; San Francisco State University, San Francisco, Calif., adjunct professor, 1979—. *Member:* Geological Society of America, Earth Science Editors Association (founding member; president, 1973-74), Sierra Club, Audubon Society.

WRITINGS: Guide to Virginia City, Nevada, and the Comstock Lode Area, Including Book and Map which Locate and Describe Points of Interest in the History of Mining the Lode: A Self-Guided Tour for the Serious Tourist, Pages of History, 1959; *Diamonds in California,* Pages of History, 1959, revised edition published as *Hunting Diamonds in California,* Naturegraph, 1972; *Diving and Digging for Gold,* Pages of History, 1960, 2nd edition, Naturegraph, 1974; *California Public Outdoor Recreation Plan,* Parts I and II, State of California, 1960; *Haight Ashbury—San Francisco Hippieville,* W. T. Samhill, 1967; (with others) *The Status of California's Heritage: A Report to the Governor and Legislature of California,* State of California, 1973; (editor with Wendell Cochran and Peter Fenner) *Geowriting: A Guide to Writing, Editing, and Printing in Earth Science,* American Geological Institute, 1973, 3rd edition, 1980; *Geology of the Sierra Nevada,* University of California Press, 1975; (with Cochran) *Into Print: A Practical Guide to Writing, Illustrating, and Publishing,* William Kaufmann, 1976; *Landforms of California,* University of California Press, in press; *Volcanic Eruptions of 1980 at Mount St. Helens,* U.S. Geological Survey, in press; *Geologic Guide to the Sierran Gold Country,* California Division of Mines and Geology, in press.

Also author of monographs, including one under pseudonym Lee Raymond, on Indian and Californian history. Author of weekly earth science column, "On Earth." Author and photographer of "Barrier Beach," a 16mm film distributed by ACI Films, New York. Contributor to *California Almanac;* contributor to geology journals. Editor of *California Geology* (formerly *Mineral Information Service*), 1952-73, and *Sausalito Pictorial Quarterly,* 1960-62.

WORK IN PROGRESS: An Almanac of Gold, for William Kaufmann; a study of dune and beach sand that makes noises; *Rocks and Mountains; Mountains of the World;* co-authoring *Sacred Mountains.*

AVOCATIONAL INTERESTS: Hiking, music.

BIOGRAPHICAL/CRITICAL SOURCES: Independent Journal (San Rafael, Calif.), July 30, 1969; *California Geology,* September, 1974.

*   *   *

HILL, Polly
See HUMPHREYS, Mary Eglantyne Hill

*   *   *

HITTI, Philip K(huri)   1886-1978

PERSONAL: Born June 24, 1886, in Shimlan, Lebanon; died December 24, 1978, in Princeton, N.J.; son of Iskandar and Sa'da (Nawfal) Hitti; married Mary George, May 22, 1918 (deceased); children: Viola (Mrs. R. Bayly Winder). *Education:* American University of Beirut, B.A., 1908; Columbia University, Ph.D., 1915. *Home:* 144 Prospect Ave., Princeton, N.J. 08540. *Office:* Department of Near Eastern Studies, Princeton University, Princeton, N.J.

CAREER: Columbia University, New York, N.Y., lecturer, 1915-20; American University of Beirut, Beirut, Lebanon, professor of Oriental history, 1920-26; Princeton University, Princeton, N.J., assistant professor, 1926-28, associate professor, 1929-36, professor of Semitic literature, 1936-54, professor emeritus, 1954-78, chairman of department of Oriental languages and literatures, 1944-54, founder and director, program in Near Eastern studies, 1947-54. Visiting professor, University of Sao Paulo, Brazil, 1954, and Harvard University,

1954-55. Director, Army specialized training program (Arabic, Turkish, and Persian), Princeton University, during World War II. Member of national board, American University of Beirut, and American Friends of the Near East; former president, American Middle East Rehabilitation.

MEMBER: American Oriental Society, American Historical Association, Mediaeval Academy of America (fellow), Arab Academy of Damascus (fellow), Middle East Studies Association (honorary fellow). *Awards, honors:* Recipient of Lebanese Republic Médaille d'Honneur du Mérite en Vermeil, L'Ordre du Cédre (Officier, Commandeur), Syrian Republic Order of Merit, First Degree, and Republic of Egypt Order of Merit, First Degree; name inscribed at New York World's Fair, 1940, among American citizens of foreign birth "who have made notable contributions to our living ever-growing democracy"; Litt.D., Princeton University, 1966.

WRITINGS: (Editor and translator) A. Y. al-Baladhuri, *The Origins of the Islamic State,* Volume I, Columbia University, 1916, reprinted, Khayats (Beirut), 1966; *The Origins of the Druze People and Religion,* Columbia University, 1928, reprinted, AMS Press, 1966; *History of the Arabs, from the Earliest Times to the Present,* Macmillan, 1937, 10th edition, St. Martin's, 1970, condensed version published as *Arabs: A Short History,* Princeton University Press, 1943, 2nd revised edition, Regnery, 1970; (with others) *The Arab Heritage,* Princeton University Press, 1944, reprinted, Russell & Russell, 1963; *History of Syria including Lebanon and Palestine,* Macmillan, 1951, condensed version published as *Syria: A Short History,* Macmillan, 1959; *Lebanon in History,* St. Martin's, 1957, 3rd edition, 1967; *The Near East in History,* Van Nostrand, 1961; *Islam and the West: A Historical Cultural Survey,* Van Nostrand, 1962; (translator) U. ibn-Munqidh, *Memoirs of an Arab-Syrian Gentleman,* Khayats (Beirut), 1964; *A Short History of Lebanon,* St. Martin's, 1965; *A Short History of the Near East,* Van Nostrand, 1966; *Makers of Arab History,* St. Martin's, 1968; *Islam: A Way of Life,* University of Minnesota Press, 1970; *Capital Cities of Arab Islam,* University of Minnesota Press, 1973. Contributor to *Encyclopaedia Britannica, Encyclopedia of Islam, New Catholic Encyclopedia,* and *Encyclopedia of Social Sciences;* editorial consultant, *Encyclopedia Americana;* consultant, *The Middle East,* Scholastic Book Services, 1972; member of advisory board, *Speculum.*

OBITUARIES: New York Times, December 28, 1978; *Washington Post,* December 30, 1978.†

*   *   *

HOARE, Robert J(ohn)   1921-1975
(Adam King)

PERSONAL: Born November 5, 1921, in Manchester, England; died August 30, 1975; son of John William (a journalist) and Margaret (Giles) Hoare; married Eileen Mary Hodgkinson, July, 1952; children: Clare Susan, Zoe Therese, Lois Joanne. *Education:* Alsager Training College, Cheshire, England, Ministry of Education teaching certificate; University of Reading, diploma in advanced study of education. *Politics:* "Undecided." *Religion:* Catholic. *Home:* "Karina," Wells Lane, Ascot, Berkshire, England.

CAREER: Allied Newspapers (later Kemsley Newspapers), Manchester, England, sub-editor, 1937-41, 1946-48; St. Cuthbert's Senior Mixed School, Manchester, assistant master, 1949-56; St. Peter's Primary School, Marlow, Buckinghamshire, England, assistant master, 1956-59; St. Mary's College, Twickenham, Middlesex, England, tutor and librarian, 1959-75. Author of juveniles and texts. *Military service:* Royal Air

Force, 1941-46; became leading aircraftsman. *Member:* Association of Training Colleges and Departments of Education, Society of Authors, Simmarian Athletic Club.

WRITINGS—Juveniles: *Wings over the Atlantic*, Phoenix House, 1956, Branford, 1957; *The Sinister Hoard*, Parrish, 1958; *The First Book of Aviation*, Cassell, 1958; *The Second Book of Aviation*, Cassell, 1958; *Desperate Venture*, Parrish, 1958; *The Story of Aircraft and Travel by Air*, A. & C. Black, 1958, 4th edition, 1968; (with Jim Peters) *Spiked Shoes*, Cassell, 1959; *Rangi to the Rescue*, Hamish Hamilton, 1960; *Secret in the Sahara*, Parrish, 1960; *Temba Becomes a Tiger*, Hamish Hamilton, 1960; (compiler) *True Stories of Capture and Rescue* (anthology), Hamish Hamilton, 1960, new edition, 1961; *Travel by Sea*, A. & C. Black, 1961, Dufour, 1965, 2nd edition, A. & C. Black, 1967; (editor) Margaret Hyde, *Flight Today and Tomorrow*, Brockhampton Press, 1961; *First Person: An Anthology of Achievement*, Odhams, 1963; *Deep Waters*, Ginn, 1966; *The High Peaks*, Ginn, 1966; *Southwards*, Ginn, 1966; *Christianity Comes to Britian*, Geoffrey Chapman, 1968; *The Old West*, Muller, 1969; *Messages*, Muller, 1969; *Cowboys and Cattle Trails*, Hulton Educational, 1971; *True Mysteries*, Carousel, 1971; *Men of the Old West*, Chatto & Windus, 1972; *Saints*, Chatto & Windus, 1972; *Sporting Giants*, Heinemann, 1973; *More True Mysteries*, Carousel, 1974; (under pseudonym Adam King) *Who Wants to Be a Dead Hero?*, Macmillan, 1974; *At the Bottom of the Deep Blue Sea*, Heinemann, 1975; *Gold*, Muller, 1975; *Underwater*, Muller, 1975; *Great Escapes of World War II*, Carousel, 1976; *When the West Was Wild*, A. & C. Black, 1976.

''Champion Library'' series, published by Macmillan: *Four-Minute Miler and the Boy from Bowral*, 1962; *The Fighting Marine and the Boy Who Loved Horses*, 1962; *Queen of Tennis and She Jumped to Fame*, 1962.

Textbooks: ''Planned Composition,'' series, five books, Odhams, 1957-61; ''Understanding'' series, four books, Longmans, Green, 1961; ''Modern Age Readers,'' Books 1-4, Odhams, 1962, Books 5-8, Ginn, 1966; (co-author) ''Catholic Workbooks,'' four books, Macmillan, 1963-64; *From the Earliest Times to the Assyrian Empire*, Macmillan, 1963; *From the New Babylon to the Time of Christ*, Macmillan, 1964; (with Sean D. Healy) *From the Roman Empire to the Crowning of Harold*, Macmillan, 1964; (with A. M. Dyer) *From the Norman Conquest to the Flight of James II*, Burns & Oates, 1964; (with F. C. Price) *From William and Mary to the Mechanical Age*, Burns & Oates, 1965; ''Planned English'' series, four books, Ginn, 1966; (with Adolf Heuser) *Christ through the Ages: A Church History for Secondary Schools*, Geoffrey Chapman, Volume I: *From the Beginning to the Fifteenth Century*, 1966, Volume II: *From the Reformation to Second Vatican Council*, 1966; ''Our Saints'' series, eight books, Longmans, Green, 1967; ''Write Away'' series, four books, Longmans, Green, 1969; ''Words in Action'' series, four books, Philograph Publications, 1970; *Topic Work with Books*, Geoffrey Chapman, 1971; *World War I: An Illustrated History in Colour*, William Macdonald, 1973; *World War II: An Illustrated History in Colour*, William Macdonald, 1973; *Turn of the Century: An Illustrated History in Colour, 1899-1913*, Macdonald Educational, 1975; ''Beginning Write Away'' series, two books, Longman, 1976; *A Dictionary of People*, Longman, 1976.

Contributor to *Times Educational Supplement, Teachers World, Teacher, School Librarian, Books for Your Children, Bookseller*.

SIDELIGHTS: The Sinister Hoard was broadcast in installments on British Broadcasting Corp. ''Children's Hour,'' 1960.

True Mysteries and *Great Escapes of World War II* were published in German; *At the Bottom of the Deep Blue Sea* was published in Africaans. *Avocational interests:* Running, swimming.†

*   *   *

HODGES, Donald Clark   1923-

PERSONAL: Born October 22, 1923, in Fort Worth, Tex.; son of Count Hal and Elinor (Clark) Hodges; married Gabrielle Baptiste, November 14, 1949 (divorced, 1963); married Margaret Helen Deutsch, January 3, 1963 (divorced, 1980); children: (first marriage) Justin Blake, Peter Robin; (second marriage) MacIntyre Hardy, John Oliver, Ernest Van Every. *Education:* Attended Swarthmore College, 1942-43; New York University, B.A. (summa cum laude), 1947; Columbia University, M.A., 1948, Ph.D., 1954. *Home:* 1600 Pullen Rd., Tallahassee, Fla. 32303. *Office:* Department of Philosophy, Florida State University, Tallahassee, Fla. 32306.

CAREER: Hobart and William Smith Colleges, Geneva, N.Y., instructor in philosophy, 1949-52; University of Missouri—Columbia, instructor, 1952-54, assistant professor, 1954-57, associate professor of philosophy, 1957-63, chairman of humanities department; University of South Florida, Tampa, professor of philosophy, 1963-64; Florida State University, Tallahassee, professor of philosophy, 1964—, head of department, 1964-69, director of Center for Graduate and Postgraduate Studies in Social Philosophy, 1967-71. Visiting professor at University of Nebraska, 1963, and University of Hawaii, 1965-66. Associate member, Institute for Social Philosophy, Pennsylvania State University. *Member:* American Philosophical Association, Society for the Philosophical Study of Dialectical Materialism (secretary-treasurer, 1963-73), Society for the Philosophical Study of Marxism (secretary-treasurer, 1973—).

WRITINGS: (Editor with Kuang T. Fann) *Readings in U.S. Imperialism*, Sargent, 1971; (editor with Abu Shanab) *National Liberation Fronts*, Morrow, 1973; (editor and translator) *Philosophy of the Urban Guerilla: The Revolutionary Writings of Abraham Guillen*, Morrow, 1973; *Socialist Humanism: The Outcome of Classical European Morality*, Warren Green, 1974; *The Latin American Revolution*, Morrow, 1974; *Argentina 1941-1976: The National Revolution and Resistance*, University of New Mexico, Press, 1976; *The Legacy of Che Guevara*, Thames & Hudson, 1977; (with Abraham Guillen) *Revaloracion de la guerrilla urbana*, El Caballito, 1977; (with Ross Gandy) *El destino de la revolucion Mexicana*, El Caballito, 1977; *Marxismo y revolucion en el siglo XX*, El Caballito, 1978; (with Gandy) *Mexico 1910-1976: Reform or Revolution?*, Zed Press, 1979; *The Bureaucratization of Socialism*, University of Massachusetts, 1981.

Work represented in numerous anthologies. Contributor of articles to many periodicals, including *Journal of Philosophy, Modern Schoolman, Archives of Criminal Psychodynamics, Science and Society, Inquiry,* and *Il Politico.* Consulting editor, *Indian Sociological Bulletin,* 1963—; member of editorial board, *Philosophy and Phenomenological Research,* 1969—; co-editor, *Social Theory and Practice,* 1971—, and *Latin American Perspectives,* 1978—.

SIDELIGHTS: Although Donald Hodges was born in Texas, he grew up in Argentina. He returned to the United States to attend college.

*   *   *

HOFFMAN, Frederick J(ohn)   1909-1967

PERSONAL: Born September 21, 1909, in Port Washington,

Wis.; died December 24, 1967, at his home; son of Henry G(eorge) and Christina (Goldammer) Hoffman; married former wife, Eleanor C. Thompson, October 10, 1936; married Mary Charlotte Holm, August 19, 1967; children: (first marriage) Caroline. *Education:* Stanford University, B.A., 1934; University of Minnesota, M.A., 1936; Ohio State University, Ph.D., 1942.

CAREER: Ohio State University, Columbus, instructor, 1942-45, assistant professor, 1945-47; University of Oklahoma, Norman, associate professor, 1947-48; University of Wisconsin—Madison, 1948-60, began as associate professor, became professor; University of California, Riverside, professor of modern literature, 1960-65; University of Wisconsin—Milwaukee, Distinguished Professor of English, 1965-67. Visiting professor, Harvard University, 1953, Sorbonne, University of Paris, 1954, University of Washington, summer, 1957, Duke University, summer, 1958, University of Minnesota, 1960, University of California, Riverside, 1963, Washington State University, 1965, University of California, Los Angeles, 1966, and University of Notre Dame, 1966; Fulbright professor, France, Italy, 1953-54. *Member:* Modern Language Association of America, American Studies Association, Phi Beta Kappa. *Awards, honors:* Rockefeller fellowship, 1945.

WRITINGS: Freudianism and the Literary Mind, Louisiana State University Press, 1945, 2nd edition, 1957, reprinted, Greenwood Press, 1977; (with Charles Allen and Carolyn F. Ulrich) *The Little Magazine: A History and a Bibliography,* Princeton University Press, 1946, 2nd edition, 1947, reprinted, Kraus Reprints, 1967; (editor with Milton Ellis, Louise Pound, and G. W. Spohn) *A College Book of American Literature,* American Book, 1949, 3rd edition, 1965.

The Modern Novel in America, Regnery, 1951, revised edition, 1963; (editor with Olga Vickery) *William Faulkner: Two Decades of Criticism,* Michigan State University Press, 1951; (editor with Harry T. Moore) *The Achievement of D. H. Lawrence,* University of Oklahoma Press, 1953; *The Twenties: American Writing in the Postwar Decade,* Viking, 1955, revised paperback edition, Collier, 1962; (editor with E. H. Cady and R. H. Pearce) *The Growth of American Literature* (two volumes), American Book Co., 1956.

(Editor with Vickery) *William Faulkner: Three Decades of Criticism,* Michigan State University Press, 1960; *William Faulkner,* Twayne, 1961, revised edition, 1964; *Samuel Beckett: The Language of Self,* Southern Illinois University Press, 1962; (editor) *The Great Gatsby: A Study,* Scribner, 1962; *Conrad Aiken,* Twayne, 1962; (editor) *Perspectives on Modern Literature,* Row, Peterson, 1962; (editor) *Marginal Manners: The Variants of Bohemia,* Row, Peterson, 1962; *The Mortal No: Death and the Modern Imagination,* Princeton University Press, 1963; (author of revisions) Milton Ellis and others, editors, *A College Book of American Literature,* 3rd edition, American Book Co., 1965; *The Art of Southern Fiction: A Study of Some Modern Novelists,* Southern Illinois University Press, 1967; *The Imagination's New Beginning: Theology and Modern Literature,* University of Notre Dame Press, 1967; (author of introduction) *The Achievement of Randall Jarrell,* Scott, Foresman, 1970. Editor, *PMLA,* beginning 1954; advisory editor, *College English,* 1961-62.

OBITUARIES: New York Times, December 26, 1967; *Poetry,* March, 1968.†

*   *   *

HOHENBERG, John 1906-

PERSONAL: Born February 17, 1906, in New York, N.Y.;

son of Louis and Jettchen (Scheuermann) Hohenberg; married Dorothy Lannuier, October 16, 1928 (died, 1977); married JoAnn Fogarty, March 9, 1979; children: Pamela Jo, Eric Wayne. *Education:* Attended University of Washington, Seattle, 1922-24; Columbia University, B.Litt., 1927; University of Vienna, graduate study, 1928. *Home:* 7700 Gleason Rd., Apt. 31C, Knoxville, Tenn. 37919; and Aquebogue, N.Y.

CAREER: Reporter for newspapers in Seattle, Wash., and New York City, 1923-25; foreign correspondent for United Press and *New York Evening Post,* 1927-28; *New York Post,* New York City, assistant city editor, 1928-33; *New York Journal-American,* New York City, political writer and military affairs editor, 1933-42; *New York Post,* United Nations and foreign correspondent, 1946-50; Columbia University, New York City, lecturer in English, 1948, associate in journalism, 1949-50, professor of journalism, 1950-74, professor emeritus, 1974—, special lecturer, 1974-76; University of Tennessee at Knoxville, Meeman Distinguished Professor of Journalism, 1976-77; University of Kansas, Lawrence, Gannett Professional-in-Residence, 1977-78; University of Florida, Gainesville, Gannett Distinguished Professor of Journalism, 1981-82. Visiting fellow, Council on Foreign Relations, 1964-65; visiting professor, Chinese University of Hong Kong, 1970-71; Nieman Foundation Lecturer, Harvard University, 1981. Traveling specialist in Asia, U.S. State Department, 1963-64; senior specialist, East-West Center, 1967; member of Japanese-American Assembly in Japan, 1967. Special consultant, Office of the Secretary of the U.S. Air Force, 1953-63; secretary of advisory board on the Pulitzer Prizes, 1954-76; special consultant, German Marshall Fund of the U.S., 1980. *Military service:* U.S. Army, 1943-45.

AWARDS, HONORS: Pulitzer traveling scholar, 1927-28; distinguished service awards, Society of Professional Journalists, Sigma Delta Chi, 1964, for *Foreign Correspondence,* 1967, for *Between Two Worlds,* and 1978, for *A Crisis for the American Press;* Knight Foundation in Europe grant, 1968-69; Ford Foundation in Asia grant, 1970-71; L.H.D., Wilkes College, 1971; outstanding teacher of journalism national award, Society of Professional Journalists, Sigma Delta Chi, 1974; Gold Key Award, Columbia Scholastic Press Association, 1974; Pulitzer Prize Special Award, 1976, for services to American journalism; Gannett Foundation grant for first amendment study, 1976-77; inducted into Journalism Hall of Fame, 1981.

WRITINGS: The Pulitzer Prize Story, Columbia University Press, 1959; *The Professional Journalist,* Holt, 1960, 5th edition, 1982; *Foreign Correspondence: The Great Reporters and Their Times,* Columbia University Press, 1964; *The New Front Page,* Columbia University Press, 1965; *Between Two Worlds: Policy, Press, and Public Opinion in Asian-American Relations,* Praeger, 1967; *The News Media: A Journalist Looks at His Profession,* Holt, 1968; *Free Press/Free People: The Best Cause,* Columbia University Press, 1971; *New Era in the Pacific,* Simon & Schuster, 1973; *A History of the Pulitzer Prizes,* Columbia University Press, 1975; *A Crisis for the American Press,* Columbia University Press, 1978; *The Pulitzer Prize Story II,* Columbia University Press, 1980.

*   *   *

HOLLEY, Edward Gailon 1927-

PERSONAL: Born November 26, 1927, in Pulaski, Tenn.; son of Abe Brown and Maxie (Bass) Holley; married Robbie Lee Gault, June 19, 1954; children: Gailon Boyd, Edward Jens, Amy Lin, Beth Alison. *Education:* David Lipscomb College, B.A., 1949; George Peabody College for Teachers (now George

Peabody College for Teachers of Vanderbilt University), M.A., 1951; University of Illinois, Ph.D., 1961. *Politics:* Democrat. *Religion:* Church of Christ. *Home:* 1508 Ephesus Church Rd., Chapel Hill, N.C. 27514. *Office:* Manning Hall, 026-A, University of North Carolina, Chapel Hill, N.C. 27514.

CAREER: David Lipscomb College, Nashville, Tenn., assistant librarian, 1949-51; University of Illinois at Urbana-Champaign, Urbana, librarian in photographic reproduction laboratory, 1951-52, assistant in Library Science Library, 1956-57, librarian in Education, Philosophy and Psychology Library, 1957-62; University of Houston, Houston, Tex., director of libraries, 1962-71; University of North Carolina at Chapel Hill, dean of School of Library Science, 1972—. *Military service:* U.S. Naval Reserve, 1951—; active duty, 1953-56; became lieutenant (senior grade). *Member:* American Library Association (president, 1974-75), Texas Library Association (president, 1971), Kappa Delta Pi, Beta Phi Mu. *Awards, honors:* Scarecrow Award of American Library Association, 1964, for *Charles Evans: American Bibliographer,* as an outstanding contribution to library literature.

WRITINGS: Charles Evans: American Bibliographer, University of Illinois Press, 1963; *Raking the Historic Coals,* Beta Phi Mu, University of Illinois, 1967; *Resources of Texas Libraries,* Texas State Library, 1968; *Resources of South Carolina Libraries,* South Carolina Committee on Higher Education, 1976; *American Library Association at 100,* American Library Association, 1976. Editor of *1876 Scrapbook* of American Library Association. Contributor to *Library Journal, College and Research Libraries, Library Trends, Journal of Academic Librarianship, American Libraries,* and other journals.

WORK IN PROGRESS: Biography of Charles Harvey Brown, 1875-1960.

SIDELIGHTS: Edward Gailon Holley wrote *CA:* ''My continuing interest in the biography of librarians stems from my fascination with how people think, act, and behave. Even in the corporate society individuals still make a difference, and my own research is aimed at finding out why.''

*   *   *

HOLLY, J(ohn) Fred   1915-

PERSONAL: Born December 29, 1915, in Elizabethton, Tenn.; son of Earl H. and Rada (Jordan) Holly; married Sarah Wilma Dickenson, June 2, 1941; children: William Frederick (deceased), John Fred, Jr. (deceased). *Education:* Milligan College, A.B., 1937; University of Tennessee, M.A., 1938; Clark University, Ph.D., 1949. *Politics:* Democrat. *Religion:* Methodist. *Home:* 1029 Cherokee Blvd., Knoxville, Tenn. 37919.

CAREER: Educator and arbitrator. Milligan College, Milligan, Tenn., professor of economics, 1940-45; Bristol, Va., industrial consultant, 1945-47; University of Tennessee, Knoxville, professor of labor relations, 1947-51, professor and head of department of economics, 1951-68; Tennessee Council on Education, executive director, 1965-68. Consultant, Tennessee Valley Authority, 1953-54, Tennessee State Department of Labor, 1954-58; labor arbitrator, 1947—. Tennessee Council on Economic Education, treasurer, 1950-65; Joint Council on Economic Education, trustee, 1954-56. *Member:* National Academy of Arbitrators (board of governors, 1960-63), American Economic Association, Southern Economic Association (vice-president), Industrial Relations Research Association, American Arbitration Association (national panel of arbitrators), Phi Kappa Phi, Beta Gamma Sigma, Omicron Delta Kappa, Phi Sigma Kappa.

WRITINGS: The Economy of Greeneville, Tennessee, University of Tennessee Press, 1950; (with B. D. Mabry) *Protective Labor Legislation and Its Administration in Tennessee,* University of Tennessee Press, 1955; *Critical Issues in Arbitration,* Bureau of National Affairs, 1957; (with H. S. Dye and J. R. Moore) *Economics: Principles, Problems and Perspectives,* Allyn & Bacon, 1962, 3rd edition, 1966; *Inflation: 1970 Study,* Southern Newspaper Publishers Association, 1970; *Current Status of Employee-Employer Relations in the Public Service,* Tennessee Survey of Business, 1972; *The Cooperative Town Company of Tennessee: A Case Study of Planned Economic Development,* Eastern Tennessee Historical Society, 1974.†

*   *   *

HOLT, Edgar Crawshaw   1900-1975

PERSONAL: Born November 2, 1900, in Burnley, Lancashire, England; died October 29, 1975; son of Richard Crawshaw and Maggie Florence (Parkinson) Holt; married Doris Evelyn Bailey, 1942 (died, 1959); children: Pauline, Waveney. *Education:* Oxford University, B.A., 1923. *Office:* Church Information Office, Church House, Westminster, London, England.

CAREER: Daily Dispatch, Manchester, England, reporter, 1924-27, assistant editor, 1947-55; *Yorkshire Post,* Leeds, England, assistant editor, 1928-30; British Broadcasting Corp., London, England, assistant editor, 1930-37; *Liverpool Daily Post,* Liverpool, England, deputy editor, 1937-47; Church Information Office, London, chief press officer, beginning 1960. *Member:* National Liberal Club (London).

WRITINGS: Quick Work (novel), Eldon Press, 1933; *It's All Arranged* (novel), Metrose, 1936; *The World at War, 1939-45,* Putnam, 1956; *The Boer War,* Putnam, 1960; *Protest in Arms,* Coward, 1961; *The Strangest War,* Putnam, 1962; *The Opium Wars in China,* Putnam, 1964; *The Carlist Wars in Spain,* Dufour, 1967; *Giuseppe Mazzini: The Great Conspirator,* Dobson, 1967; *Politics Is People: The Men of the Menzies Era,* Verry, 1969; *The Making of Italy, 1815-1870,* Atheneum, 1970 (published in England as *Risorgimento: The Making of Italy, 1815-1870,* Macmillan, 1970); *Plon-Plon: The Life of Prince Napoleon,* M. Joseph, 1973; *The Tiger: The Life of Georges Clemenceau, 1841-1929,* Hamish Hamilton, 1976.

BIOGRAPHICAL/CRITICAL SOURCES: New York Times, March 26, 1971.

OBITUARIES: AB Bookman's Weekly, December 22-29, 1975.†

*   *   *

HOPPER, Vincent Foster   1906-1976

PERSONAL: Born April 19, 1906, in West New York, N.J.; died January 19, 1976, of cancer in New York, N.Y.; son of Abram Whittaker and Isabel (Timmons) Hopper; married Grace Brewster Murray, June 12, 1930; married Mabel Sterling Lewis, May 6, 1945; children: (second marriage) David Whittaker. *Education:* Princeton University, A.B., 1927, M.A., 1928; Columbia University, Ph.D., 1938. *Home:* 203 River Edge Rd., Tenafly, N.J.

CAREER: New York University, New York, N.Y., School of Commerce, Accounts, and Finance, instructor, 1928-32, assistant professor, 1932-41, associate professor, 1941-48, professor of general literature, 1948-63, Washington Square College, professor of English, 1963-73, professor emeritus, 1973-76. Secretary, Tenafly Boys Activities Committee, 1959-60. *Military service:* U.S. Army, 1943-45. *Member:* College English Association, National Council of Teachers of English, American Association of University Professors, Phi Beta Kappa.

WRITINGS—All published by Barron's, except as indicated: *Medieval Number Symbolism: Its Sources, Meaning, and Influence on Thought and Expression*, Columbia University Press, 1939, reprinted, Folcroft, 1976; (editor) Geoffrey Chaucer, *Canterbury Tales: An Interlinear Translation*, 1948, revised edition, 1970; (with B.D.M. Grebanier) *Essentials of European Literature*, Volume I: *Early Middle Ages to Romantic Movement*, 1952, Volume II: *Romantic Movement to Present*, 1952; (with Grebanier) *World Literature*, two volumes, 1952; (with William Rod Horton) *Backgrounds of European Literature*, Appleton, 1954, 2nd edition, Prentice-Hall, 1975; (with Grebanier) *Bibliography of European Literature*, 1954; (with Cedric Gale) *Practice for Effective Writing*, 1961, revised edition, 1971; (with Gale) *Essentials of Effective Writing*, 1961, 2nd edition published as *Essentials of English*, 1967, revised and enlarged edition (with Gale and Ronald Foote), 1973; *A Simplified Approach to Dante*, 1964; *A Simplified Approach to Goethe's "Faust," Part I and Part II, and His Other Major Works*, 1964; *1001 Pitfalls in English Grammar, Spelling and Usage*, 1969, revised edition, 1970, published as *English Verb Conjugations: 123 Irregular Verbs Fully Conjugated*, 1975; *Card Guide to English Grammar, Punctuation and Usage*, 1970.

Editor with Gerald B. Lahey: William Congreve, *Way of the World*, 1958; William Goldsmith, *She Stoops to Conquer*, 1958; Richard B. Sheridan, *School for Scandal*, 1958; Sheridan, *Rivals*, 1959; Ben Jonson, *Valpone*, 1959; Oscar Wilde, *The Importance of Being Earnest*, 1959; John Webster, *The Duchess of Malfi*, 1960; Wilde, *Lady Windermere's Fan*, 1960; *Medieval Mystery Plays*, 1962; George Farquhar, *The Beaux Strategem*, 1963; *Classic American Short Stories*, 1964.

OBITUARIES: *New York Times*, January 21, 1976.†

*   *   *

HORN, D(avid) B(ayne) 1901-1969

PERSONAL: Born July 9, 1901, in Edinburgh, Scotland; died August 7, 1969; son of James Adam Bayne and Lilias (Mossman) Horn; married Barbara Mary Scott, 1929; children: Hazel, Alison Horn Cairns. *Education:* University of Edinburgh, M.A. (first class honors), 1922, D.Litt., 1929. *Home:* 8 Pentland Ave., Edinburgh 13, Scotland. *Office:* Department of History, Old College, South Bridge, Edinburgh 8, Scotland.

CAREER: University of Edinburgh, Edinburgh, Scotland, lecturer in history, 1927-36; Hull University College, Hull, England, professor of history, 1935-36; University of Edinburgh, lecturer in history, 1937-54, professor of modern history, 1954-69. Member, Edinburgh Corporation Education Committee, 1959-64. *Military service:* Royal Air Force, 1941-44; became flight lieutenant. *Member:* Historical Association of Scotland, (president, 1956-59), Royal Historical Society (fellow), Edinburgh Workers Educational Association (honorary president).

WRITINGS: *A History of Europe, 1871-1920*, J. Murray, 1927; *Sir Charles Hanbury Williams and European Diplomacy*, Harrap, 1930; *A History of Europe*, Harrap, Volume III: (with Andrew Browning) *Modern Europe, 1648-1815*, 1931, Volume IV: *Modern Europe, 1789-1930*, 1931; (editor) *British Diplomatic Representatives, 1689-1789*, Royal Historical Society, 1932; *British Public Opinion and the First Partition of Poland*, Oliver & Boyd, 1945; (editor with Mary Ransome) *English Historical Documents, 1714-83*, Eyre & Spottiswoode, 1958; *The British Diplomatic Service, 1689-1789*, Clarendon Press, 1961; (editor) *English Historical Documents, 1815-70*, Methuen, 1964; *Frederick the Great and the Rise of Prussia*, English Universities Press, 1964, Harper, 1969; *Short History*

of the University of Edinburgh, 1556-1889*, Aldine, 1967; (editor) *English Historical Documents, 1714-1815*, Methuen, 1967; *Great Britain and Europe in the Eighteenth Century*, Oxford University Press, 1967.

BIOGRAPHICAL/CRITICAL SOURCES: Ragnhild Hatton and M. S. Anderson, editors, *Studies in Diplomatic History: Essays in Memory of David Bayne Horn*, Archon Books, 1970.

OBITUARIES: *Times* (London), August 9, 1969.†

*   *   *

HORTON, Stanley M(onroe) 1916-

PERSONAL: Born May 6, 1916, in Huntington Park, Calif.; son of Harry Samuel (a minister) and Myrle May (a librarian; maiden name, Fisher) Horton; married Evelyn Gertrude Parsons (an organist), September 11, 1945; children: Stanley, Jr., Edward, Faith. *Education:* University of California, Berkeley, B.S., 1937; Gordon-Conwell Theological Seminary, M.Div., 1944; Harvard University, S.T.M., 1945; Central Baptist Theological Seminary, Th.D., 1959. *Politics:* Republican. *Home:* 615 West Williams St., Springfield, Mo. 65803. *Office:* Assemblies of God Graduate School, 1445 Boonville Ave., Springfield, Mo. 65802.

CAREER: Ordained minister of Assemblies of God Church, 1946; Metropolitan Bible Institute, North Bergen, N.J., instructor in Bible, 1945-48; Central Bible College, Springfield, Mo., assistant professor, 1948-56, associate professor, 1956-60, professor of Bible, 1960-75; Assemblies of God Graduate School, Springfield, professor of Bible, 1973—. Guest professor at Near East School of Bible and Archaeology, Jerusalem, 1962, and Southern Asia Bible College, Bangalore, India, 1981. *Member:* Society of Biblical Literature, Evangelical Theological Society, American Scientific Affiliation, Society for Pentecostal Studies, American Association of Professors of Hebrew, National Association of Evangelicals, Phi Alpha Chi.

WRITINGS—All published by Gospel Publishing: *Into All Truth*, 1955; *Panorama of the Bible* (manual), 1961; *Great Psalms* (manual), 1962; *Bible Prophecy* (manual), 1963; *Gospel of John* (manual), 1965; *The Promise of His Coming*, 1967; *Ready Always*, 1974; *It's Getting Late*, 1975; *Welcome Back Jesus*, 1975; *What the Bible Says about the Holy Spirit*, 1976; *Book of Acts: A Radiant Commentary on the New Testament*, 1981. Also author of *Adult Teacher*, an annual, 1952—. Contributor to *Encyclopedia Americana*. Contributor to *Pentecostal Evangel* and *Advance*. Consulting editor to *Paraclete*, 1967-75.

WORK IN PROGRESS: Greek and Hebrew word studies; an eschatology textbook; a commentary on the Book of Revelation.

SIDELIGHTS: Stanley Horton has reading competence in French, German, Hebrew, Aramaic, and New Testament Greek.

*   *   *

HOSKEN, Fran(ziska) P(orges) 1919-

PERSONAL: Born July 12, 1919, in Vienna, Austria; came to United States, 1938; naturalized U.S. citizen, 1944; daughter of Otto (a physician and educator) and Mary (an artist; maiden name, Low) Porges; married James C. Hosken (an engineer), 1947 (divorced, 1962); children: John, Caroline, Andrew. *Education:* Attended University of Vienna and University of Zurich, 1937-38; Smith College, B.A., 1940; Harvard University, M.Arch., 1944; Massachusetts Institute of Technology, special studies in urban planning, 1964-67. *Politics:* "My own/feminist.'' *Religion:* None. *Home and office:* 187 Grant St., Lexington, Mass. 02173.

CAREER: Skidmore, Owings & Merrill, Chicago, Ill., architectural designer, 1946-47; Hosken, Inc. (design and manufacture of contemporary furniture), Boston, Mass., owner, manager, and designer-in-chief, 1948-54; Architectural Color Slides (educational slides and slide programs with text, by mail order), owner and photographer, 1948—; founder of Women's International Network, 1975. Teacher of interior design, Garland College, Boston, and Cambridge Adult Education Center, 1958-61; technical editor, Bertram Goldberg & Associates, 1968-69; professor of urban design, Experimental College, Tufts University, 1970; teacher and developer of urban teaching programs, Education for Urban Living project of Harvard University and Community Projects Laboratory of Massachusetts Institute of Technology, 1970-71; associate professor of urban studies, University without Walls, 1971-74. Witness before Congressional committees on foreign relations and foreign aid. Has developed multi-media presentations on architecture and urban affairs; has shown photography at Lexington Library, 1969-70, and paintings at Boston City Hall Concourse Gallery, 1973, 1974. Member of board, University without Walls. Interior design consultant, M. Brown, 1959-61; consultant in housing. *Military service:* U.S. Coast Guard Women's Reserve, Communication Intelligence, 1944-45.

MEMBER: National Urban League, American Institute of Architecture, American Society of Planning Officials, American Institute of Planners (associate member), National Housing Conference, Society for International Development, National Organization for Women, Women's Equity Action League, National Women's Political Caucus, Federation of Professional Women's Organizations, Boston Society of Architects (associate member). *Awards, honors:* Awards from Museum of Modern Art, New York, 1948, 1949, for furniture design.

WRITINGS: The Language of Cities, Macmillan, 1968, 2nd edition, Schenkman, 1972; (self-illustrated with photographs) *The Functions of Cities,* Schenkman, 1972; *The Kathmandu Valley Towns,* Weatherhill, 1974; (compiler) *Directory of Women's International Development Organizations,* Agency for International Development, 1977; *The Hosken Report: Genital and Sexual Mutilations of Females,* Women's International Network, 1979; *Female Sexual Mutilations: The Facts and Proposals for Action,* Women's International Network, 1980; *The Childbirth Picture Book: International Prototype,* Women's International Network, 1981.

Designer of media packages, including ''The Changing Form and Functions of Cities'' (twenty-one tapes), McGraw, 1970, and ''The Visual City'' (filmstrip and text), Warren Schloat Productions, 1972. Developed twelve newsletters for National Urban League, 1968-70. Weekly columnist on urban affairs, *Boston Globe,* 1964-65. Contributor to professional journals and *Christian Science Monitor, St. Louis Post, Boston Herald,* and other newspapers and magazines. Correspondent-at-large, *Architectural Forum,* 1972-74; founder and editor, *WIN News* (of Women's International Network), 1975—.

WORK IN PROGRESS: Women and the Urban Environment; a cross-cultural study, *Commitment for Change: The Status of Women around the World;* organizing the Women's International Network.

SIDELIGHTS: Fran Hosken has made urban study and photography trips to Europe, the Near East, Africa (East, West, and South), South and Central America, Japan, India, and Asia, and has visited Australia, New Zealand, and the U.S.S.R. She is bilingual in German and English, fluent in French, and knows Latin, Spanish, and Italian.

HOWARD, Mary
See MUSSI, Mary

*   *   *

HOWELL, S.
See STYLES, (Frank) Showell

*   *   *

HOYLE, Geoffrey 1942-

PERSONAL: Born January 12, 1942, in Scunthorpe, Lancashire, England; son of Fred (a scientist and author) and Barbara (Clark) Hoyle; married Valerie Jane Coope (an accountant), April 21, 1971. *Education:* Attended St. John's College, Cambridge, 1961-62. *Home:* Laytus Hall Farm, Inskip, Preston PR40TJ, England.

CAREER: Worked in documentary film production, 1963-67; novelist, 1967—.

WRITINGS—Novels; with father, Fred Hoyle; published by Harper, except as indicated: *Fifth Planet,* 1963; *Rockets in Ursa Major,* 1969; *Seven Steps to the Sun,* 1970; *The Molecule Men,* 1971; *Inferno,* 1973; *Into Deepest Space,* 1974; *The Incandescent Ones,* 1977; *The Westminster Diaster,* 1978; *Commonsense in Nuclear Energy,* Freeman, 1980.

For children: *2010: Living in the Future,* Parents Magazine Press, 1972; *Disaster,* Heinemann Educational, 1975; (with Janice Robertson) *Ask Me Why,* PAN, 1976.

AVOCATIONAL INTERESTS: Skiing, target-shooting.

*   *   *

HUBER, Leonard Victor 1903-

PERSONAL: Born May 25, 1903, in New Orleans, La.; son of Victor (a contractor) and Eleonora (Reisig) Huber; married Audrey Wells, September 27, 1928; children: Leonard V., Jr., Lloyd Wells. *Education:* Attended Tulane University, 1926-35. *Politics:* ''Democrat who generally votes Republican.'' *Religion:* Presbyterian. *Home:* 204 Fairway Dr., New Orleans, La. 70124. *Office:* 4841 Canal St., New Orleans, La. 70119.

CAREER: Victor Huber & Sons, Inc. (contractors), New Orleans, La., president, 1938—. President of St. John Cemetery Association, Inc., 1941—, and of Orleans Parish Landmarks Commission, 1956—; member of Vieux Carre Commission, 1957-61; chairman of board of trustees of Keyes Foundation, 1961-78. *Member:* Louisiana Historical Association (president, 1978-79), Friends of the Cabildo (president, 1972-73), Orleans Philharmonic Symphony Society, Friends of the Tulane University Library (president of board of directors, 1976-80). *Awards, honors:* M.H.L. from Tulane University, 1974; award of merit from American Association of State and Local History, 1980, for ''preserving and publishing Louisiana and New Orleans history.''

WRITINGS: (With Clarence A. Wagner) *The Great Mail: A Postal History of New Orleans,* American Philatelic Society, 1949.

Impressions of Girod Street Cemetery and a Plan to Rescue Some of Its Monuments (booklet), Louisiana Landsmarks Society, 1951; (with Samuel Wilson, Jr. and Garland F. Taylor) *Louisiana Purchase* (booklet), Louisiana Landmarks Society, 1953; (with Ray Samuel and Warren C. Ogden) *Tales of the*

Mississippi, Hastings House, 1955; (with Albert R. Huber) *The New Orleans Tomb*, Design Hints, 1956; *Advertisements of Lower Mississippi River Steamboats: 1812-1920*, Steamship Historical Society, 1959.

Beginnings of Steamboat Mail on Lower Mississippi (booklet), American Philatelic Society, 1960; (with Guy F. Bernard) *To Glorious Immortality: The Rise and Fall of the Girod Street Cemetery*, Alblen Books, 1961; (with Wilson and Abbye A. Gorin) *The St. Louis Cemeteries of New Orleans* (booklet), St. Louis Cathedral, 1963; (with Wilson) *Baroness Pontalba's Buildings*, Louisiana Landmarks Society, 1964; (with John C. Chase, Hermann B. Deutsch, and Charles L. Dufour) *Citoyens, Progres et Politique de la Nouvelle Orleans: 1889-1964* (title means "Citizens, Progress, and Politics of New Orleans"), E. S. Upton, 1964; (with Wilson) *The Basilica on Jackson Square and Its Predecessors: 1727-1965*, Basilica of St. Louis, 1965; *New Orleans as It Was in 1814-1815* (booklet), Battle of New Orleans One Hundred and Fiftieth Anniversary Committee, 1965.

(With Wilson) *The Cabildo on Jackson Square*, Friends of the Cabildo, 1970; (with Dufour) *If Ever I Cease to Love: One Hundred Years of Rex, 1872-1971*, School of Design, Rex Organization, 1971; *New Orleans: A Pictorial History from the Earliest Times to the Present Day*, Crown, 1971; *Lakeview Lore* (booklet), First National Bank of Commerce, 1972; *Mardi Gras Invitations of the Gilded Age*, Upton Printing, 1972; (with Peggy McDowell and Mary Lou Christovich) *New Orleans Architecture: The Cemeteries*, Friends of the Cabildo, 1974; *Notable New Orleans Landmarks*, Orleans Parish Landmarks Commission, 1974; *Louisiana: A Pictorial History*, Scribner, 1975; *The Church that Would Not Die*, Our Lady of Guadalupe Church, 1976; *Mardi Gras: A Pictorial History*, Pelican, 1977.

Creole Collage, Center for Louisiana Studies, 1980; (with Wilson) *The Presbytere on Jackson Square*, Friends of the Cabildo, 1981.

Contributor to magazines, including *Waterways Journal, Louisiana History, Dixie, New Orleans, American Heritage,* and *Civil War History.*

WORK IN PROGRESS: Clasped Hands and Other Gravestone Symbols, for the Center for Louisiana Studies; with Wilson, *Jackson Square, 1721-1981.*

SIDELIGHTS: Leonard Victor Huber told *CA:* "I might be called an iconographic historian since all my published works are copiously illustrated. I believe that pictures, particularly those contemporary with the subject or action, are of great help to the reader."

Huber spent forty years assembling a collection of more than ten thousand pictures, prints, and other items chronicling the history of New Orleans and Louisiana. His archives were acquired by the Kemper and Leila Williams Foundation for inclusion in the Historic New Orleans Collection, housed in the Vieux Carre.

BIOGRAPHICAL/CRITICAL SOURCES: New Orleans Times-Picayune, May 19, 1974.

*   *   *

HUFF, Robert   1924-

PERSONAL: Born April 3, 1924, in Evanston, Ill.; son of Robert E. (a dentist) and Elaine (Fontaine) Huff; married Sally Ann Sener, March, 1959 (divorced, 1973); children: Ursula, Michele, Dylan. *Education:* Wayne University (now Wayne State University), A.B., 1949, A.M., 1952. *Office:* English

Department, Western Washington University, Bellingham, Wash. 98225.

CAREER: Wayne University (now Wayne State University), Detroit, Mich., assistant part-time instructor in humanities and counselor for College of Liberal Arts, 1950-52; University of Oregon, Eugene, instructor in English, 1952-53; Fresno State College (now California State University, Fresno), Fresno, Calif., instructor in English, 1953-55; Oregon State College (now University), Corvallis, instructor in English, 1955-57, 1958-60; Wayne State University, instructor in English, 1957-58; University of Delaware, Newark, assistant professor and poet-in-residence, 1960-64; Western Washington University, Bellingham, assistant professor of English, 1964—. *Military service:* U.S. Army Air Forces, 1943-46. *Awards, honors:* Indiana University School of Letters fellowship, 1957; Bread Loaf Writers' Conference fellowship, 1961; MacDowell Colony fellowship, 1963; poetry prize, Virginia Commonwealth University, 1977, for *The Ventriloquist.*

WRITINGS—Poems: *Colonel Johnson's Ride, and Other Poems*, Wayne State University Press, 1959; *Poems*, Portland (Ore.) Art Museum, 1959; *The Course: One, Two, Three, Now!*, Wayne State University Press, 1966; *The Ventriloquist: New and Selected Poems*, University Press of Virginia, 1977.

Contributor to anthologies: Mark Strand, editor, *The Contemporary American Poets*, World Publishing, 1969; R. F. Dietrich, editor, *The Realities of Literature*, Blasidell Publishing, 1970; Miller Williams, editor, *Contemporary Poetry in America*, Random House, 1973; Williams and John Ciardi, editors, *How Does a Poem Mean?*, Houghton, 1975.

Contributor of poems to numerous periodicals, including *Harper's, Prairie Schooner, Poetry, Atlantic Monthly, Saturday Review,* and *Paris Review.* Poetry editor, *Concerning Poetry*, 1968—.

WORK IN PROGRESS: Shore Guide to Flocking Names, a book for young people; *Taking Her Sides on Immortality*, a volume of poems.

SIDELIGHTS: Much of the imagery in Robert Huff's poetry is drawn from the shores of Lake Michigan, the forests of the Northwest, and the inland waters of upper Puget Sound. He writes to *CA:* "I believe that place (not regionalism) is important to poetry. I am often stimulated by specific reactions to individual detail to recall similarities of appearance from an earlier experience in a different place. I'm frequently moved to make a poem out of comparing this past memory to immediate occurences. Once in a while I'm led by my natural environment to think about what I have read by gifted writers whose response to the natural world I feel I share. At one time, after losing a big salmon, I sat down on a river bank and began a poem by talking to a wild flower about animals, fish, myself, and D. H. Lawrence. When it was completed I called it, fairly, 'To a Violet.' But it was about time and place, something very important to writers like Flannery O'Connor and Eudora Welty, whose short stories I find far more poetical than most contemporary poems I run across in magazines these days. Prosaic poetry seems to be in fashion. With rock music and its lyrics in mind, pray that fashions are always temporary. Amen."

Huff's poetry has been recorded for the Library of Congress.

AVOCATIONAL INTERESTS: Hunting and fishing, "both of which seem to be turning into bird watching and sitting by the sea."

HUGHES, James Quentin   1920-

PERSONAL: Born February 28, 1920, in Liverpool, England; son of James Stanley (an estate agent) and Marjorie (Edwards) Hughes; married Margaret Evans, April 27, 1947 (divorced); married Josephine Radcliff; children: Ceridwen Ann, Deborah Sian, Alice Jane Semantha. *Education:* University of Liverpool, Bachelor of Architecture (with honors), 1945, Diploma in Civic Design, 1948; University of Leeds, Ph.D., 1954. *Home:* 10A Fulwood Park, Liverpool L17 5AH, England. *Office:* School of Architecture, University of Liverpool, Liverpool, England.

CAREER: Practicing architect, 1948—. University of Leeds, School of Architecture, Leeds, England, senior lecturer, 1950-56; University of Liverpool, School of Architecture, Liverpool, England, lecturer and studio instructor, 1954-61, senior lecturer, 1961—, reader, 1972—, sub-dean, 1964. Professor of architecture and dean of faculty of engineering, Royal University of Malta, 1968. Chairman, Chester Civic Trust. *Military service:* British Army, Second Special Air Service Regiment, 1940-45; became captain; received Military Cross and bar. *Member:* Royal Institute of British Architects, Royal Society of Arts (fellow), Royal Historical Society (fellow).

WRITINGS: The Buildings of Malta during the Period of the Knights of St. John of Jerusalem, 1530-1795, Tiranti, 1956; (with Norbert Lynton) *Renaissance Architecture,* Longmans, Green, 1962; *Seaport—Architecture and Townscape of Liverpool,* Lund, Humphries, 1964; *Fortress—Architecture and Military History in Malta,* Lund, Humphries, 1966.

Liverpool, Studio Vista, 1970; *Malta,* Prestel Verlag, 1972; *Military Architecture,* Evelyn, 1974; (translator) Rudolf Huber and Renate Rieth, editors, *Festungen, Forteresses, Fortresses, Glossarium Artis,* 1979; *A Chronology of Events in Fortification from 1800 to 1914 and an Illustrated English Glossary of Terms Used in Military Architecture,* Farrar, Straus, 1980; *Britain in the Mediterranean,* Farrar, Straus, 1981. Editor of *Fort.*

*   *   *

HUGHES, R(ichard) E(dward)   1927-

PERSONAL: Born July 11, 1927, in Amsterdam, N.Y.; son of Harold Joseph (an attorney) and Mildred (Vunk) Hughes; married Gay Beichert, July 15, 1950; children: Richard, Elizabeth, Noel, Jocelyn, Melissa. *Education:* Siena College, A.B., 1949; Boston College, M.A., 1950; University of Wisconsin, Ph.D., 1954. *Politics:* Democrat. *Religion:* Roman Catholic. *Home:* 65 Hitty Tom Rd., Duxbury, Mass. *Agent:* Wendy Lipkind Agency, 225 East 57th St., New York, N.Y. 10022.

CAREER: Ohio State University, Columbus, instructor in English, 1953-55, assistant professor, 1955-58; Boston College, Chestnut Hill, Mass., associate professor, 1958-63, professor of English, 1963—, dean of College of Arts and Science, 1969-72. Visiting professor, Nijmegen University, 1979-80. Library trustee, Ashland, Mass., 1960—. *Member:* College English Association.

WRITINGS: (Editor) John Joyne, *Journal,* Augustan Reprint Society, 1959; (with P. A. Duhamel) *Rhetoric: Principles and Usage,* Prentice-Hall, 1962; (with Duhamel) *Persuasive Prose,* Prentice-Hall, 1964; (with Duhamel) *Literature: Form and Function,* Prentice-Hall, 1965; *The Progress of the Soul: The Interior Career of John Donne,* Morrow, 1968; *The Lively Image,* Winthrop Publishing, 1974; *Unholy Communion,* Doubleday, 1982. Contributor of articles to literature and language journals.

SIDELIGHTS: In a review of R. E. Hughes's book, *The Progress of the Soul: The Interior Career of John Donne,* Robert F. Capon writes in the *New York Times Book Review* that "Hughes's great merit is that he tries to recapture the whole Donne whole. Such a man for all seasons, he argues—especially in this our season of alienation and quest—must not be left to the deadly mercies of the paradox splitters. . . . For Hughes . . . there is a progress from one Donne to another, but there is no room for antithetical divisions. They fit neither the man nor the facts of his life. Not the man, for Donne is all one palpable delight no matter where you take him: His love poems continually vault into theology, his sermons into wooing and winning; and not the facts of his life, because everything overlaps."

Hughes was a participant in and, at times, host of an educational television panel program broadcast on WGBH-TV, Boston, 1955-59.

BIOGRAPHICAL/CRITICAL SOURCES: New York Times Book Review, December 8, 1968.

*   *   *

HUMPHREYS, Mary Eglantyne Hill   1914-
(Polly Hill)

PERSONAL: Born June 10, 1914, in Cambridge, England; daughter of A. V. (a professor) and M. N. Hill; children: Susannah Maynard Humphreys. *Education:* Newnham College, Cambridge, B.A., 1936. *Address:* 28 Lawn Rd. Flats, London N.W.3, England.

CAREER: University of Ghana, Legon, research fellow in economics department, 1955-63, senior research fellow, Institute of African Studies, 1963-65; University of Michigan, Ann Arbor, research associate, Center for Research on Economic Development, 1965—. Visiting senior research fellow, Nigerian Institute of Social and Economic Research, Ibadan; research fellow, Clare College, Cambridge University.

WRITINGS—Under name Polly Hill: *The Unemployment Services,* Routledge & Kegan Paul, 1940; *Through the Dark Wood,* Chatto & Windus, 1945; *The Gold Coast Cocoa Farmer,* Oxford University Press, 1956; *The Migrant Cocoa Farmers of Southern Ghana,* Cambridge University Press, 1963; (with others) *Children's Creative Centre: Methods and Objectives,* Canadian Government Pavilion, 1967; *Hidden Trade in Hausaland,* Center for Research on Economic Development, University of Michigan, 1969; *Studies in Rural Capitalism in West Africa,* Cambridge University Press, 1970; *The Occupations of Migrants in Ghana,* University of Michigan, 1970; *Rural Hausa: A Village and a Setting,* Cambridge University Press, 1972; *Population, Prosperity, and Poverty: Rural Kano, 1900 and 1970,* Cambridge University Press, 1977. Contributor to professional journals.†

*   *   *

HUNTER, A(rchibald) M(acbride)   1906-

PERSONAL: Born January 16, 1906, in Kilwinning, Ayrshire, Scotland; son of Archibald (a minister) and Crissie (MacNeish) Hunter; married Margaret Wylie Swanson, March 14, 1934; children: Archibald Stewart, Fiona Mary (Mrs. John L. Harper). *Education:* University of Glasgow, M.A. (first class honors), B.D. (with distinction), Ph.D.; University of Marburg, advanced study; Oxford University, D.Phil. *Home:* 3 Carwinshoch View, Ayr County, Scotland. *Agent:* S.C.M. Press, London, England.

CAREER: Clergyman, Church of Scotland. Minister at Comrie, Perthshire, Scotland, 1934-37; Oxford University, Mansfield College, Oxford, England, professor of New Testament, 1937-42; minister at Kinnoull, Perthshire, Scotland, 1942-45; University of Aberdeen, Aberdeen, Scotland, professor of New Testament, 1945-71, professor emeritus, 1971—, master of Christ's College, 1957-71, master emeritus, 1971—. Sprunt Lecturer at Richmond, Va., 1954; Sir D. Owen Evans Lecturer, 1962. *Awards, honors:* D.D., University of Glasgow, 1950.

WRITINGS: Paul and His Predecessors, Nicholson & Watson, 1940, revised edition, Westminster, 1961; *The Unity of the New Testament,* S.C.M. Press, 1943, published as *The Message of the New Testament,* Westminster, 1944; *Introducing the New Testament,* S.C.M. Press, 1945, Westminster, 1946, 3rd edition, 1973; *The Gospel According to St. Mark,* S.C.M. Press, 1948, Macmillan, 1949.

The Work and the Words of Jesus, S.C.M. Press, 1950, Westminster, 1951; *Interpreting the New Testament, 1900-1950,* S.C.M. Press, 1951, Westminster, 1952; *A Pattern for Life: An Exposition of the Sermon on the Mount,* Westminster, 1953, revised edition, 1965 (published in England as *Design for Life: An Exposition of the Sermon on the Mount,* S.C.M. Press, 1953, revised edition, 1965); *Interpreting Paul's Gospel,* S.C.M. Press, 1954, Westminster, 1955, revised edition published as *The Gospel According to St. Paul,* S.C.M. Press, 1966, Westminster, 1967; *The Epistle to the Romans,* Macmillan, 1955, published as *The Epistle to the Romans: The Law of Love,* 1968; *Introducing New Testament Theology,* S.C.M. Press, 1957, Westminster, 1958; *The First Epistle of Peter,* Abingdon, 1959; *The Letter of Paul to the Galatians, The Letter of Paul to the Ephesians, The Letter of Paul to the Philippians* [and] *The Letter of Paul to the Colossians,* John Knox, 1959 (published in England as *Galatians, Ephesians, Philippians, Colossians,* S.C.M. Press, 1960).

Interpreting the Parables, S.C.M. Press, 1960, Westminster, 1961, 2nd edition, S.C.M. Press, 1964; *Teaching and Preaching the New Testament,* Westminster, 1963; *Commentary on St. John's Gospel,* Cambridge University Press, 1964; *The Gospel According to John,* Cambridge University Press, 1965, published as *According to John: A New Look at the Fourth Gospel,* Westminster, 1968; (editor) Thomas Murray Taylor, *Speaking to Graduates,* Oliver & Boyd, 1965; *Bible and Gospel,* Westminster, 1969.

The Parables Then and Now, S.C.M. Press, 1971, Westminster, 1972; *Exploring the New Testament,* Saint Andrew Press, 1971, published as *Probing the New Testament,* John Knox, 1972; *Taking the Christian View,* John Knox, 1974; *P. T. Forsyth* (biography), Westminster, 1974; *The New Testament Today,* Saint Andrews Press, 1974; *Gospel and Apostle,* S.C.M. Press, 1975; *Jesus Lord and Saviour,* Eerdmans, 1976; *The Fifth Evangelist,* S.C.M. Press, 1980; *Christ and the Kingdom,* Saint Andrews Press, 1980.

*   *   *

HUNTER, Jack D(ayton)   1921-

PERSONAL: Born June 4, 1921, in Hamilton, Ohio; son of Whitney Guy (a business executive) and Mary Irene (Dayton) Hunter; married Shirley Thompson, October 31, 1944; children: Lee and Lyn (twin daughters), Jill, Jack Dayton, Jr. *Education:* Pennsylvania State University, B.A., 1943. *Politics:* Independent. *Religion:* Presbyterian. *Home:* 20 Hypolita St., St. Augustine, Fla. 32084; and 5043 Turkey Point Rd., North East, Md. 21901. *Agent:* Blassingame, McCauley & Wood, 60 East 42nd St., New York, N.Y. 10017. *Office:* Flagler College, St. Augustine, Fla. 32084.

CAREER: Chester Times, Chester, Pa., news reporter, 1939-40; Station WILM, Wilmington, Del., newscaster, 1946-47; *Evening Journal,* Wilmington, news reporter, 1947-50; U.S. House of Representatives, Washington, D.C., executive secretary to member from Delaware, 1950-52; E. I. du Pont de Nemours & Co., Wilmington, affiliated with public relations and advertising department, 1952-75; *Sunday Journal,* Wilmington, columnist, 1975-77; U.S. Senate, Washington, D.C., special counsel to member from Delaware, 1977-79; Flagler College, St. Augustine, Fla., adjunct professor, 1980—. Writing coach, *Florida Times-Union and Journal,* 1981—. Public relations consultant to small firms. *Military service:* U.S. Army, 1943-46; special agent in Counter Intelligence Corps; received Bronze Star and six campaign ribbons. U.S. Air Force Reserve; retired as major. *Member:* Authors Guild, Sigma Delta Chi, Sigma Alpha Epsilon. *Awards, honors:* Edgar Allan Poe Award from Mystery Writers of America, for *The Expendable Spy.*

WRITINGS—Novels: *The Blue Max,* Dutton, 1964; *The Expendable Spy,* Dutton, 1965; *One of Us Works for Them,* Dutton, 1967; *Spies Incorporated,* Dutton, 1969; *Word of Life,* Simon & Schuster, 1976; *The Blood Order,* Times Books, 1979; *The Terror Alliance,* Leisure Books, 1980; *The Tin Cravat,* Harper, 1981; *Florida Is Closed Today,* Tower, 1982.

SIDELIGHTS: Jack Hunter told *CA:* "I play jazz piano. As a water colorist, I've turned out vast numbers of paintings—the only one of which to meet the public eye being that on the jacket of my first novel. As a major hobby I pursue every shred of information to be found on aircraft of the 1914-18 period. I am thoroughly addicted to the restoration of historic homes."

MEDIA ADAPTATIONS: The Blue Max was produced as a film by Twentieth Century-Fox Film Corp. in 1965; the film rights to *The Expendable Spy* were under option to International Film Traders; the film rights to *One of Us Works for Them* were acquired by Bristol Productions.

*   *   *

HURSTFIELD, Joel   1911-1980

PERSONAL: Born November 4, 1911, in London, England; died November 29, 1980, in California; married Elizabeth Valmai Walters; children: one daughter, one son. *Education:* University College, London, B.A. (first class honors), 1934. *Office:* Department of History, University College, University of London, Gower St., London WC1E 6BT, England.

CAREER: University of Southampton, University College, Southampton, England, lecturer in history, 1937-40; National Savings Committee, London, England, assistant commissioner, 1940-42; Officers of War Cabinet, London, official historian, 1942-46; University of London, London, England, lecturer in history at Queen Mary College, 1946-51, University College, lecturer, 1951-53, reader, 1953-59, professor of history, 1959-62, Astor Professor of English History, 1962-79, fellow, beginning 1967, Public Orator, 1967-71; senior research associate, Huntington Library, 1979-80. Visiting professor at Northwestern University, 1967; Shakespeare Birthday Lecturer, Washington, D.C., 1969; first Leverton Lecturer, Fairleigh Dickinson University, 1971; James Ford Special Lecturer in History, Oxford University, 1972; senior research fellow at Folger Shakespeare Library, 1973. *Member:* Royal Historical Society, Athenaeum Club. *Awards, honors:* Pollard Prize; Gladstone Prize; D.Litt. from University of London, 1964.

WRITINGS: Control of Raw Materials, H.M.S.O., 1953; *The Queen's Wards: Wardship and Marriage under Elizabeth I,* Harvard University Press, 1958, 2nd edition, International School

Book Service, 1973; *Elizabeth I and the Unity of England*, Macmillan, 1960, Harper, 1969; *The Elizabethan Nation*, British Broadcasting Corp., 1964, Harper, 1967; *Freedom, Corruption and Government in Elizabethan England*, Harvard University Press, 1973; *The Historian as Moralist: Reflections on the Study of Tudor England*, Athlone Press, 1975; *The Illusion of Power in Tudor Politics*, Humanities, 1979; *The English Commonwealth, 1547-1640*, Leicester University Press, 1979.

Editor: (With S. T. Bindoff and C. H. Williams) *Elizabethan Government and Society: Essays Presented to Sir John Neale*, Oxford University Press, 1961; *Tudor Times*, Routledge & Kegan Paul, 1964; (with James R. Sutherland) *Shakespeare's World*, St. Martin's, 1964; *The Reformation Crisis*, Edward Arnold, 1965, Barnes & Noble, 1966; (with Alan G. R. Smith) *Elizabethan People: State and Society*, St. Martin's, 1972; (with K.H.D. Haley) *The Historical Association Books of the Tudors and the Stuarts*, St. Martin's, 1973; *The Great Reform Act*, Humanities, 1974.

Contributor to *Transactions of the Royal Historical Society;* also contributor of articles and reviews to journals and periodicals, including *American Historical Review, English History Review, Economic History Review, London Times, Telegraph, Guardian* and *Spectator*.

OBITUARIES: London Times, December 1, 1980; *AB Bookman's Weekly*, January 19, 1981.†

*   *   *

HUTCHINGS, Arthur (James Bramwell)   1906-

PERSONAL: Born July 14, 1906, in Sunbury-on-Thames, England; married Marie Constance Haverson, May 7, 1940; children: Josephine. *Education:* University of London, B.A., 1929, B.Mus., 1939, Ph.D., 1950. *Home:* 8 Rosemary Lane, Coylton, Devon EX13 6NL, England.

CAREER: Musician (organist, violinist), and schoolmaster, 1928-39; University of Durham, Durham, England, professor of music, 1947-68; University of Exeter, Exeter, England, professor of music, 1968-74. Composer; organizer of concerts and operas. Member of governing board and chairman of corporation, Trinity College of Music; advisory panelist for the British Broadcasting Corporation. *Military service:* Royal Air Force, 1940-46; awarded Burma Star. *Member:* Royal Academy of Music (honorary). *Awards, honors:* Fellow of Trinity School of Music, London; fellow of Royal School of Church Music; Associate of the Royal College of Organists.

WRITINGS: Schubert, Dent, 1940, revised edition, 1978; *Delius*, Macmillan, 1948, reprinted, Greenwood Press, 1970; *A Companion to Mozart's Piano Concertos*, Oxford University Press, 1949, second edition, 1950; *The Invention and Composition of Music*, Novello, 1952; *The Baroque Concerto*, Faber, 1962, reprinted, Scribner, 1979; *Church Music in the 19th Century*, Chapman & Hall, 1966; *Mozart: The Man, the Music*, foreword by Kingsley Amis, Schirmer, 1976.

Contributor: *The Mozart Companion*, Rockcliff, 1954; *A Chopin Symposium*, Chapman & Hall, 1961; *New Oxford History of Music*, Oxford University Press, 1963; *The Pelican History of Music*, Volume III, Pelican, 1964; *Church Music in the Nineteenth Century*, Oxford University Press, 1967, reprinted, Greenwood Press, 1977.

Editor, Charles Henry Phillips, *The Singing Church* (Hutchings was not associated with earlier editions), Faber, 1968, Archon, 1969. Composer of a comic opera, ''The Plumber's Arms'' and of ''O quanta qualia, or Heart's Desire,'' for orchestra and double chorus. Also composer of motets and other church music, and of works for string orchestra. Contributor to *Listener, Musical Quarterly, Music and Letters, Musical Times, Times* (London) and *Times Literary Supplement*. Member of board of editors, *The English Hymnal*, 1952—.

SIDELIGHTS: Arthur Hutchings's *Mozart: The Man, the Music* contains 170 color pictures grouped into essays on various aspects of Mozart's musical and personal life. One hundred fifty black and white photographs also accompany the text, which investigates questions from performance practice of the era to Mozart's character and societal role. Hans Keller believes that Hutchings avoids the common biographer's pitfall of projecting his own feelings onto those of his subject. In this clear-headed presentation, writes Keller in *Books and Bookmen*, ''the mythological man Mozart as we think we know him is not so much brought down to earth as up to reality.'' Denis Matthews points to the difficulties of such independent thinking: ''Accepted images of great composers and traditional attitudes to accepted works are hard to challenge,'' he notes in the *Times Literary Supplement*. But in Matthews's opinion, Hutchings's name ''promises [and delivers] lively and fluent prose, scrupulous scholarship, stimulation—and if needs be, provocation.'' He agrees with Kingsley Amis, who writes in a foreword to the book that within a single volume Hutchings, without any recourse to musical example, has achieved ''a triumphant mastery of his subject and his task.''

BIOGRAPHICAL/CRITICAL SOURCES: Arthur Hutchings, *Mozart: The Man, the Music*, foreword by Kingsley Amis, Schirmer, 1976; *Times Literary Supplement*, November 2, 1967, June 10, 1977; *Books and Bookmen*, August, 1977.

I

IMMEL, Mary Blair 1930-

PERSONAL: Born December 8, 1930, in Wichita, Kan.; daughter of Clinton C. and Hope (de Vore) Blair; married Daniel M. Immel (a minister), September 7, 1950; children: Daniel C., Michael, Douglas. *Education:* Chapman College, B.A., 1952; Purdue University, M.A., 1967. *Religion:* Disciples of Christ. *Home:* 911 Thomasson Lane, Paradise, Calif. 95969.

CAREER: Former primary teacher and substitute teacher; former assistant to the director, Tippecanoe County Historical Association and Museums, Lafayette, Ind.; instructor at Butte Community College; lecturer; consultant. *Awards, honors:* Indiana University Writers' Conference scholarship for short story; Hoosier Authors Award, Indiana University, for *Two Way Street;* Knights of Pythias Award for creative writing; Teen-age Book Club selection, 1974, for *Two Way Street.*

WRITINGS: Men of God, Christian Board of Publication, 1958; (with Bertie Lane) *Keys to Many Doors,* Christian Board of Publication, 1963; *Two Way Street* (teen-age novel), Bethany, 1965; *Call up the Thunder* (young adult novel), Bethany, 1967; *River of Wind* (historical novel for children), Aurora, 1977; *Come to the Table* (religious drama), privately printed, 1981. Writer of church school curriculum materials. Contributor of more than 100 poems, articles, and stories to religious and secular periodicals.

WORK IN PROGRESS: A novel, *A Taste of Aloes;* an historical novel for children, *No Longer Sings the Brown Thrush.*

SIDELIGHTS: Mary Blair Immel told *CA:* "Writing is as much a part of my life as any of my senses. It heightens my enjoyment of everyday life and my appreciation of persons. Transferring the words in my head onto paper helps me to synthesize my thinking and makes me vitally aware of the nuances of life. Sharing all this with others energizes me." *Avocational interests:* Travel (has visited forty states and fourteen countries), sketching, painting, quilt-making, gardening, tennis, canoeing, genealogy, back-packing, hiking, swimming.

*   *   *

IREMONGER, Lucille (d'Oyen)

PERSONAL: Married T. L. Iremonger (a member of Parliament, and Lloyd's underwriter); children: Pennant (daughter). *Education:* St. Hugh's College, Oxford, M.A. *Politics:* Conservative. *Religion:* Church of England. *Home:* 34 Cheyne Row, Chelsea, London S.W.3, England.

CAREER: Author and political journalist. Participant in British Broadcasting Corp. programs, 1948—. Member, London County Council. President King George's Hospital Patients League. *Member:* Royal Society of Literature (fellow), Authors Society, Forum Club, Ilford Conservative Association (vice-president), Norwood Conservative Association.

AWARDS, HONORS: Society of Women Journalists' Lady Brittain trophy for best book of the year, 1948, for *It's a Bigger Life,* and Lady Violet Astor trophy for best article of the year, 1948; Silver Musgrave Medal (Jamaica) for contributions to literature in connection with the West Indies, 1962; Centenary Medal from Institute of Jamaica, for "sustained and outstanding contribution to cultural development in Jamaica in the field of creative writing."

WRITINGS: It's a Bigger Life, Hutchinson, 1948; *Creole* (novel), Hutchinson, 1950; *The Cannibals* (novel), Hammond Hammond, 1952; *The Young Traveller in the South Seas,* Phoenix House, 1952; *The Young Traveller in the West Indies,* Phoenix House, 1952, Dutton, 1955; *West Indian Folk Tales: Anansi Stories* (retold for English children), Harrap, 1956; *The Ghosts of Versailles: Miss Moberly and Miss Jourdain and Their Adventure—A Critical Study,* Faber, 1957; *Love and the Princess* (biography of Princess Sophia, daughter of George III), Crowell, 1958, published as *Love and the Princesses,* 1960.

And His Charming Lady, Secker & Warburg, 1961; *Yes, My Darling Daughter* (autobiographical), Secker & Warburg, 1964; *The Fiery Chariot: A Study of British Prime Ministers and the Search for Love,* Secker & Warburg, 1970; *How Do I Love Thee* (fictionalized biography of Robert and Elizabeth Browning), Morrow, 1976; *Lord Aberdeen,* Collins, 1978; *My Sister, My Love,* Morrow, 1981; *The Daughters of Queen Victoria,* Hodder & Stoughton, 1982.

Contributor: *Adventure and Discovery* (anthology), J. Cape, 1949—; *On the Air: An Anthology of the Spoken Word,* Oxford University Press, 1951; *Caribbean Anthology of Short Stories,* Pioneer Press (Jamaica), 1953; *Independence Anthology,* Pioneer Press, 1962. Contributor to *The Radio Listener's Week End Book,* published by Odhams, and to *Magazine Digest,* 1950; contributor to *Times* (London), *Sunday Times* (London), *Daily Telegraph, Observer, Evening Standard,* and other newspapers and journals.

WORK IN PROGRESS: Sequel to *The Fiery Chariot.*

SIDELIGHTS: *The Young Traveller in the West Indies* and *The Young Traveller in the South Seas* have been translated for a number of foreign-language editions.

BIOGRAPHICAL/CRITICAL SOURCES: Lucille Iremonger, *Yes, My Darling Daughter*, Secker & Warburg, 1964; *Punch*, December 2, 1970; *New Statesman*, December 4, 1970; *Books and Bookmen*, April, 1971.

*   *   *

ITALIAANDER, Rolf (Bruno Maximilian) 1913-

PERSONAL: Born February 20, 1913, in Leipzig, Germany; son of Kurt and Charlotte Italiaander; *Education:* Studied in Leipzig, Berlin, Paris, London, Oxford, and Rome. *Home:* St. Benedictstrasse 29, Hamburg 13, Federal Republic of Germany. *Agent:* Joan Daves, 145 East 49th St., New York, N.Y. 10017.

CAREER: Writer, ethnologist, and explorer in Africa and Asia. Visiting professor of African history and civilization at colleges and universities, including Michigan State University, Kalamazoo College, schools of the United Negro College Fund, and Hope College. Co-founder and honorary secretary of Free Academy of Art, Hamburg, 1948-69; founder of Museum of Naive Art in Hamburg-Rade. German Translator's Union, founder, 1954, currently honorary president. Consul to Senegal 1964.

MEMBER: International Africa Institut (London), Frobenius Institut (Frankfurt), Societe des Africanistes (Paris), Michigan Academy of Science, Arts, and Letters, American Academy of Political and Social Science, American Committee on Africa, New York Academy of Sciences, Austrian Explorers Society, Rissho kosei-kai (honorary), Brighter Society Movement, Heinrich Bart Society, Gesellschaft zur Erforschung der Naturvoelker, Islam Institute, Phi Alpha Theta. *Awards, honors:* Hans Henny Jahnn Prize for literary work and efforts toward the betterment of race relations; officer, Order of the Senegal; Distinguished Achievement Award from Hope College, 1976.

WRITINGS: *So Lernte ich Segelfliegen*, Orell Fuessli, 1931; *Hallo! Boys!*, Haupt, 1932; *Mein Fahrrad und Ich*, Weiss, 1935; *Lennart und Faber*, Weiss, 1935; *Segelflug in Aller Welt*, Reclam, 1936; *Erlebnisse Beim Segelflug*, Reclam, 1936; *Gebrueder Lenz auf Tippelfahrt*, Oxford University Press, 1937; *Manfred Freiherr von Richthofen*, Weichart, 1938; *Goetz von Berlichingen*, Weichert, 1939; *Spiel und Lebensziel*, G. Weise, 1939; *Wegbereiter Deutscher Luftgeltung*, Gutenburg, 1941; *Werkpilot Steffens*, Franckh, 1942; *Italo Balbo*, Knorr & Hirth, 1942; *Banzai!*, [Riga], 1943; *Besiegeltes Leben*, Volksbuecherei-Verlag, 1949.

Nordafrika Heute, Zsolnay, 1952; *Land der Kontraste*, Broschek, 1953; *Wann reist du ab, Weisser Mann?*, Broschek, 1954; *Door Het Oerwoud Naar de Woestijn*, Donker, 1955; *Vom Urwald in die Wueste*, Broschek, 1955; *In het Land van Albert Schweitzer*, Donker, 1955; *Geliebte Tiere*, Westermann, 1957; *De Blanke Oganga: Albert Schweitzer*, Donker, 1957; *Neue Kunst in Afrika*, Bibliographisches Institut, 1957; *Menschen in Africa*, Bibliographisches Institut, 1957; *Mubange: Der Junge aus dem Urwald*, C. Ueberreuter, 1957; *Hedendaagse Negerkunst uit Centraal-Afrika* [Amsterdam], 1957, translation published as *Contemporary Negro Painting and Graphic Art from Central Africa: The Collection of Rolf Italiaander*, Hope College, 1962; *Der Ruhelose Kontinent*, Econ-Verlag, 1958; *Im Lande Albert Schweitzers*, Broschek, 1958.

Taenzer, Tiere und Daemonen, Wancura, 1960; *Tanz in Afrika: Ein Phaenomen in Leben der Neger*, Rembrandt-Verlag, 1960;

Die Neuen Maenner Afrikas: Ihr Leben, ihre Taten, ihre Ziele, Econ-Verlag, 1960, translation published as *The New Leaders of Africa*, Prentice-Hall, 1961; *Moebange, de Jongen mit het Oerwould*, Broekman & DeMeris, 1961; *1,001 Tausenhundeine Weisheit*, Wancura, 1961; *Africana: Selected Bibliography of Readings in African History and Civilization*, History Department, Hope College, 1961; *Schwarze Haut im roten Griff*, Econ-Verlag, 1962; *Hans and Jean: A Reader for Colleges and Universities*, Hope College Press, 1962; *Afrika in Opkomst: Geschiedenis en economische ontwikkeling van alle staten*, Broekman & DeMeris, 1962; *Immer wenn ich unterwegs bin: Verse und kleine Prosa*, Mundusverlag, 1962; *Der Buhnenbildner Karl Groening* [Hamburg], 1962; *Brueder der Verdammten: Menschliche Entwicklungshilfe in Afrika, Amerika, Asien*, Signum, 1963, published as *Neue Hoffnung fuer Aussaetzige*, Mission, 1971; *Die neuen Maenner Asiens*, Econ-Verlag, 1964; *Die Friedensmacher: Drei Neger erhielten den Friedens-Nobelpreis (R. Bunche, Martin Luther King, Albert John Luthuli)*, Oncken, 1965; *Im Namen des Herrn im Kongo: Geschnisse, Erlegnisse, Ergebnisse* (foreword by St. C. Neill), Oncken, 1965; *Burg Pyrmont in des Eifel*, Pillig/Eifel, 1965.

Bingo und Bongo vom Kongo, illustrations by Stefan Lemke and Marie-Luise Pricken, Agentur des Rauhen Hauses, 1967; *Karl May*, Editions Quebec, 1967; *Lebensentscheidung fuer Israel*, foreword by Asher Ben-Natan, J. Fink, 1967; *Gedanken ueber Albert Schweitzer*, Freie Akademie der Kuenste, 1968; *Richard N. Coudenhove-Kalergi: Begruender der Pancuropa-Bewegung*, afterword by Pierre Gregoire, Eurobuch-Verlag, 1969; *Terra dolorosa: Wandlungen in Lateinamerika*, introduction by Rudolf Grossmann, afterword by Gilberto Freyre, Brockhaus, 1969.

Hallelujas, Christians, 1970; *Denn man beruehrt uns nicht*, Mission, 1971; *Profile und Perspektiven*, Evangelisch-Lutheranischen Mission, 1971; *Wird Europa untergehen?*, Industrie und Handelskammer 1971; *Juden in Latein-America*, Olamenu (Tel-Aviv), 1971; *Die neuen Herren der alten Welt*, Econ-Verlag, 1972; *Das Elefanten-Maedchen*, Bitter, 1972; *Partisanen und Profeten*, Evangelisch-Lutheranischen Mission, 1972; *Sokagakkai: Japans neue Buddhisten*, Evangelisch-Lutheranische Mission, 1973; *Spass an der Freund: Laienmaler und naive Maler an 99 Beispielen Dargestellt*, Christians, 1974.

Kiri, Geister der Suedsee: Phantastiche Geschichten, E. Klopp, 1975; (with Klaus Gundermann and Joachim Buechner) *Geld in der Kunst: Geld und Geldeswert in Skulptur, Graphik und Malerei*, Steinbock-Verlag, 1976; (with others) *Buecherrevision: Zwischen Erfolgen und Niederlagen*, Christians, 1977; *Naive Kunst und Folklore*, Edition Museum Rade, 1977; (with Neiz Pentzlin) *Bei Wempe gehn die Uhren anders: Chronik ein mittelstaend*, Christians, 1978; *Jack London*, Colloquium-Verlag, 1978; *Wer Seinen Bruder nicht liebt . . . : Begegnungen und Erfahrungen in Asien*, Evangelisch-Lutheranischen Mission, 1978; *Harmonie mit dem Universum: Zweigespraech zwischen Europa und Japan*, foreword by Werner Kohler, Aurum-Verlag, 1978; *Afrika hat viele Gesichter: Ein humanist Lesebuch* (afterword by Mobyem M. K. Mikanza), Droste-Verlag, 1979; *Die Suedsee, auch eine Herausforderung: Tagebuecher ein Individualisten aus Indonesien und Papua-Nigeria*, Droste-Verlag, 1979; (with Arnold Bauer and Herbert Krafft) *Berlins Stunde Null: 1945*, Droste-Verlag, 1979; (with Martin Gosebruch and Reinhardt Guldager) *Afrikanische Impressionen: Kunst, Kult, Architektur*, Droste-Verlag, 1980.

Editor: Joachim Christian Nettelbeck, *Mein Leben*, Sporn, 1938; *Englische Perspektiven*, Laatzen, 1948; *Frank Theiss*, Krueger, 1950; *Henry Benrath in Memoriam*, Deutsche Verlags-Anstalt, 1954; *Nordafrika: Marokko, Algerien, Tunesien, Libyen*, Reich, 1956; *Herrliches Hamburg*, Broschek, 1957; (with

Willy Haas) *Berliner Cocktail,* Zsolnay, 1957; *Ivo Hauptmann,* Freie Akademie der Kuenste, 1957; *Schwarze Weisheiten: Negersprichwoerter,* Klemm, 1958, published as *Schwarze Weisheiten: Sprichwoerter, Anekdoten und Meditationen aus Afrika,* Droste-Verlag, 1978; *Hans Leip: Leben und Werk,* Freie Akademie der Kuenst, 1958; *Teenagers,* Broschek, 1958; *Hans Henny Jahnn, Aufzeichnungen eines Einzelgaengers,* List, 1959; *Kongo: Bilder und Verse,* Bertelsmann, 1959.

Fritz Kronenberg, Frein Akademie der Kuenste, 1960; *Jahnn, Buck der Freunde,* Freie Akademie der Kuenste, 1960; *Herder-Blaetter: Faksimile-Ausgabe zum 70. Geburtstag von Willy Haas,* Freie Akademie der Kuenst, 1962; *Der Buehenbilden Karl Groening,* Freie Akademie der Kuenst, 1962; *Pariser Cocktail* (foreword by Andre Maurois), Zsolnay, 1963; *Koenig Leopolds Kongo: Dokumente und Pamphlete von Mark Twain, Edmund D. Morel, Roger Casement,* Ruetten & Loening, 1964; *Umbestaendliche und Eigentliche Beschreibung von Africa 1668,* Steingrueben (Stuttgart), 1964; *Peter Martin Lampel,* Freie Akademie der Kuenste, 1964; *Gleise und Nebengleise des O. H. Strohmeyer,* Freie Akademie der Kuenste, 1964; *Internationaler Kongress Literarischer Uebersetzer,* Athenaeum-Verlag, 1965; *Die Herausforderung des Islam,* Musterschmidt-Verlag, 1965; *Mutter Courage und ihr Theater: Ida Ehre und die Hamburger Kammerspiele,* Freie Akademie der Kuenst, 1965.

In der Palmweinschenke, Erdmann, 1966; *Frieden in der Welt, aber wie? Gedanken des Friedens-Nobelpreistraeger* (foreword by Carl Friedrich von Weizsaecker), J. Fink, 1967; *Heinrich Barth, Im Sattel durch Nord-und Zentralafrika: Reisen und Entdeckung in den Jahren 1849-1855,* Brockhaus, 1967; *Weder Krankheit noch Verbrechen,* Gala-Verlag, 1969; *Kultur ohne Wirtschaftswunder,* Delp, 1970; *Akzente eines Lebens* (afterword by Peter Jokostra), C. Schuenemann, 1970; *Ade, Madame Muh! Bauersleute dichten heute* (afterwords by Karl Krolow and Heinz Haushofer), Pandion, 1970; *Albanien: Vorposten China,* Delp, 1970; *Er schloss uns einen Welteil auf,* Pandion, 1970.

Diktaturen im Nacken, Delp, 1971; *Argumente kritischer Christen: Warum wir nicht aus der Kirche austreten,* Echter-Verlag, 1971; *Moral—wozu? Ein Symposium,* Delp, 1972; *Eine Religion fuer den Frieden: Die Rissho Kose-Kai: Japanische Buddhisten fuer die Oekumene der Religionen* (foreword by Werner Kohler), Evangelisch-Lutheranischen Mission, 1973; *Heisses Land Neugini,* Evangelische-Lutheranische Mission, 1974; *Indonesiens verantwortliche Gelleschaft,* Evangelische-Lutheranische Mission, 1974; *Hugo Eckener, Im Luftschiff ueber Laender und Meere: Erlebnisse und Erinnerungen,* Heyne, 1979; *Schleswig-Holstein: 2 Meere, Ein Land,* Weidling, 1979; *Hugo Eckener: Ein Moderner Columbus,* Stadler, 1979.

Hugo Eckener: Weltschau eines Luft schiffers, Husum, 1980; *Ferdinand Graft von Zeppelin,* Stadler, 1980; *Ich bin ein Berliner,* Weidling, 1980; *Jenseits der Deutsch-Deutschen Grenze,* Weidling, 1981; *Ein Deutscher Namens Eckener,* Stadler, 1981; *Die Grobe Zeit der Deutschen Hanse,* Husum, 1981; *Wir Erlebten das Ende der Weimarer Republik,* Droste, 1982; *Ein Mann Kaempft fuer den Frieden,* Aurum, 1982; *Mehr als Schwarze Magie,* Aurum, 1982; *De Fall Oscar Wilde,* Eremillen, 1982.

*   *   *

IYER, Raghavan (Narasimhan)   1930-

PERSONAL: Born March 10, 1930, in Madras, India; son of Lakshmi Narasimhan (an accountant) and Laxmi (Aiyer) Iyer; married Nandini Mehta (a professor of philosophy), November 17, 1955; children: Siddharth Pico. *Education:* University of

Bombay, B.A., 1948, M.A., 1950; Magdalen College, Oxford, B.A., 1953, M.A., 1956; Nuffield College, Oxford, D.Phil., 1962. *Politics:* "Beyond isms." *Religion:* "Theosophist (beyond isms)." *Home:* 1975 Old San Marcos Rd., Santa Barbara, Calif. 93111. *Office:* Department of Political Science, University of California, Santa Barbara, Calif. 93106.

CAREER: Indian Institute of World Culture, Bangalore, India, director, 1954-55; Government of India, New Delhi, chief research officer of Planning Commission, 1955-56; Oxford University, St. Antony's College, Oxford, England, fellow and lecturer in politics, 1956-63; University of Chicago, Chicago, Ill., visiting professor, 1963; University of Ghana, Legon, visiting professor, 1964; University of California, Santa Barbara, professor of political science, 1966—. President, Institute of World Culture, Santa Barbara, 1976—. Visiting professor, Oslo University, 1958. Consultant to Fund for the Republic, 1966-69. *Member:* World Association of World Federalists, United Nations Association, American Society for Legal and Political Philosophy, Club of Rome, Oxford University Socratic Club, Reform Club. *Awards, honors:* Rhodes scholar at Oxford University, 1950-53; grants from Ford Foundation, 1960, Humanities Institute, 1967.

WRITINGS: (Editor and contributor) *South Asian Affairs,* Chatto & Windus, 1960; (editor and contributor) *The Glass Curtain,* Oxford University Press, 1965; *Looking Forward: The Abundant Society,* Fund for the Republic, 1966; (contributor) Thomas C. Greening, editor, *Existential Humanist Psychology,* Brooks-Cole, 1971; (contributor) *The Future Is Tomorrow,* Mouton, 1972; *The Moral and Political Thought of Mahatma Gandhi,* Oxford University Press, 1973; *Parapolitics: Toward the City of Man,* Oxford University Press, 1979; *Novus Ordo Seclorum,* Concord Grove Press, 1980; (editor) *The Descent of the Gods,* Smythe, 1981. Associate editor of *Aryan Path,* 1954-55; editor of *Hermes,* 1975—.

SIDELIGHTS: Alan Ryan writes of Raghavan Iyer's *Parapolitics* in the *Times Literary Supplement:* "[It] is a work of large-scale political theory, not a piece of autobiography. . . . The book is a very fluent and readable piece of work, and it is written with some rhetorical flair. . . . The one thing which one might complain of, however, is the lack of a more extended discussion of the relations between political thought and political practice." A *Times Literary Supplement* reviewer describes *The Moral and Political Thought of Mahatma Gandhi* as an "important contribution. . . . This is a book demanding and deserving close and patient study. . . . [It] will assist many readers to understand [the Gandhian ethic] and therefore be in a position to attempt their own personal evaluation" of Gandhi's work. And James Cameron of the *New Statesman* calls Iyer's study of Gandhi "a very important book, an immensely thorough and not wholly idolatrous appraisal of its unique subject. . . . Professor Iyer very properly does not treat of the dead martyr but of the living leader who was a saint among politicians and a politician among saints. . . . Iyer brings great dedication and scholarship to his examination of the Mahatma's concepts of non-violence, freedom, obligation, means and ends."

Iyer has traveled and lectured in Europe, Africa, and Japan. He writes that he is a practitioner of three rules—Einstein's maxim that "fulfillment equals work plus relaxation plus silence," Unamuno's motto "if you wish to achieve the impossible, attempt the absurd," and Lamartine's axiom that "the ideal is only truth at a distance."

BIOGRAPHICAL/CRITICAL SOURCES: Times Literary Supplement, April 19, 1974, October 17, 1980; *Nation,* May 18, 1974; *American Historical Review,* February, 1979; *Journal of Politics,* February, 1981.

J

JACKENDOFF, Ray S. 1945-

PERSONAL: Born January 23, 1945, in Chicago, Ill.; son of Nathaniel (a professor) and Elaine (a guidance counselor; maiden name, Flanders) Jackendoff; married Elise Feingold, 1976; children: Amy, Beth. *Education:* Swarthmore College, B.A., 1965; Massachusetts Institute of Technology, Ph.D., 1969. *Politics:* Anarchist. *Religion:* Jewish. *Office:* Department of Linguistics, Brandeis University, Waltham, Mass. 02154.

CAREER: University of California, Los Angeles, lecturer in English, 1969-70; Brandeis University, Waltham, Mass., assistant professor, 1971-73, associate professor, 1973-78, professor of linguistics, 1978—. Clarinet soloist with the Boston Pops Orchestra, 1980. *Member:* Linguistic Society of America, North East Linguistic Society. *Awards, honors:* Gustave O. Arlt Award from Council of Graduate Schools, 1974, for *Semantic Interpretation in Generative Grammar;* National Endowment for the Humanities fellowship, 1978.

WRITINGS—Published by MIT Press: *Semantic Interpretation in Generative Grammar,* 1972; *X-Bar Syntax: A Theory of Phrase Structure,* 1977; (with Fred Lerdahl) *A Generative Theory of Tonal Music,* 1982; *Semantics and Cognition,* in press. Contributor to journals in his field.

*   *   *

JACKSON, Barbara (Ward) 1914-1981
(Barbara Ward)

PERSONAL: Born May 23, 1914, in York, England; died of cancer, May 31, 1981, in Lodsworth, England; daughter of Walter (a lawyer) and Teresa (Burge) Ward; married Robert Gillman Allen Jackson (a senior consultant to the United Nations Development Program), November 16, 1950; children: Robert. *Education:* Attended Lycee Moliere and Sorbonne, University of Paris, 1929-31; Somerville College, Oxford, B.A. (with first class honors), 1935. *Home:* The Pound House, Lodsworth near Petworth, Sussex, England.

CAREER: Cambridge University, Cambridge, England, extension course lecturer, 1936-39; *Economist,* London, England, assistant editor, 1939-40, foreign editor, 1940-50, contributing editor, beginning 1950; Harvard University, Cambridge, Mass., visiting scholar, 1958-68; Columbia University, New York City, Albert Schweitzer Professor of International Economic Development, 1968-73; International Institute of Environment and Development, London, president, 1973-80. British Broadcasting Corp., London, panelist on discussion program "Brains Trust," 1943-46, member of board of governors, 1946-50; member of council, Royal Institute of International Affairs, 1943-44 and 1973-81; member of board of governors, Old Vic and Sadler's Wells Theatres, 1944-53, and International Development Research Centre, 1970-73; member of board of directors, Adlai Stevenson Institute of International Affairs, beginning 1968. Adviser on international economics to United Nations Secretary-General U Thant and to U.S. Presidents John F. Kennedy and Lyndon B. Johnson. Member of Pontifical Commission for Justice and Peace, beginning 1967. Frequent speaker and lecturer. *Wartime service:* Worked for British Ministry of Information in Washington, D.C., during World War II. *Member:* American Academy of Arts and Sciences (honorary member), Catholic Women's League (national president, 1948-50).

AWARDS, HONORS: L.H.D. from Fordham University, 1949, Columbia University, 1954, Kenyon College, 1957, and Harvard University, 1957; LL.D. from Smith College, 1949, and Brandeis University, 1961; recipient of numerous other honorary degrees. Christopher Book Awards, 1955, for *Faith and Freedom,* 1959, for *Five Ideas That Change the World,* and 1973, for *Only One Earth;* Carnegie fellowship, 1958-66; Campion Award, Catholic Book Club, 1964; Dame Commander, Order of the British Empire, 1974; made a life peeress of the House of Lords with title Baroness Jackson of Lodsworth, 1976; Albert Medal, Royal Society of the Arts, 1980; Jawarharlal Nehru Memorial Award for International Understanding, 1980.

WRITINGS—Under name Barbara Ward: *The International Share-Out,* Thomas Nelson, 1938; (with others) *Hitler's Route to Bagdad,* Allen & Unwin, 1939, reprinted, Books for Libraries, 1971; (contributor) A. E. Baker, editor, *A Christian Basis for the Post-War World,* Morehouse, 1941; *Turkey,* Oxford University Press, 1942; *Democracy, East and West,* Bureau of Current Affairs (London), 1947, revised edition, 1949; *Are Today's Basic Problems Religious?* [and] *Moral Order in an Uncertain World* (Mott Foundation lectures), University of Michigan Press, 1953; *Herbert Lehman at 80: Young Elder Statesman* (originally published in *New York Times Magazine,* March 23, 1958), Overbrook Press, 1958.

(With others) *The Legacy of Imperialism: Essays,* Chatham College, 1960; *The Rich Nations and the Poor Nations* (Massey lectures), Canadian Broadcasting Corp., 1961, Norton, 1962; *The Plan under Pressure: An Observer's View,* Asia Publishing

House (New York), 1963; (with Maurice Zinkin) *Why Help India?*, Macmillan, 1963; *Towards a World of Plenty* (Sir Robert Falconer lectures), University of Toronto Press, 1964; (with P. T. Bauer) *Two Views on Aid to Developing Countries*, Institute of Economic Affairs (London), 1966; *Spaceship Earth* (George B. Pegram lectures), Columbia University Press, 1966; *World Poverty—Can It Be Solved?*, Franciscan Herald, 1966; (author of commentary) Pope Paul VI, *Populorum Progressio* (encyclical letter on the development of peoples), Paulist Press, 1967; (editor with Lenore d'Anjou and J. D. Runnalls) *The Widening Gap: Development in the 1970's*, Columbia University Press, 1971; *An Urban Planet*, Girard Bank, 1971; *Angry Seventies: Second Development Decade—A Call to the Church*, Pontifical Commission on Justice and Peace, 1972; *A New Creation?: Reflections on the Environmental Issue*, Pontifical Commission on Justice and Peace, 1973; *The Age of Leisure*, International Union of Local Authorities (The Hague), 1973; *Human Settlements: Crisis and Opportunity*, Information Canada, 1974; (with Gerald Ward) *The John Ward House*, Essex Institute, 1976; (with W. R. Ward) *The Andrew-Safford House*, Essex Institute, 1976; (with G. Ward) *Silver in American Life*, David R. Godine, 1979.

Published by Norton, except as indicated: *The West at Bay*, 1948; *Policy for the West*, 1951, reprinted, Greenwood Press, 1970; *Faith and Freedom*, 1954, reprinted, Greenwood Press, 1974; *The Interplay of East and West: Points of Conflict and Co-operation* (Beatty Memorial lectures), 1957 (published in England as *The Interplay of East and West: Elements of Contrast and Co-operation*, Allen & Unwin, 1957), published with a new epilogue, 1962; *Five Ideas That Change the World* (Aggrey-Fraser-Guggisberg lectures), 1959; *India and the West*, 1961, revised edition, 1964; *Nationalism and Ideology* (Alan P. Plaunt lectures), 1966; *The Lopsided World* (Christian A. Herter lectures), 1968; (with Rene Dubos) *Only One Earth: The Care and Maintenance of a Small Planet*, 1972; (with others) *Who Speaks for Earth?*, edited by Maurice F. Strong, 1973; *The Home of Man*, introduction by Enrique Penalosa, 1976; *Progress for a Small Planet*, 1979.

Also author of pamphlets, essays, and reports on politics, economics, labor, and religion. Contributor of articles to numerous publications, including *America*, *Dublin Review*, *Blackfriars*, *Atlantic*, *Harper's*, *Foreign Affairs*, and *New York Times*.

WORK IN PROGRESS: A book on global environment and social justice.

SIDELIGHTS: A writer, lecturer, and adviser and friend of statesmen, Barbara Ward Jackson, known professionally as Barbara Ward, was "an eloquent evangelist for the needs of the developing countries and for the interdependence of nations," wrote Paul Lewis in the *New York Times*. According to Lewis, most of the industrial world has accepted her fundamental conviction that the growing division between rich and poor nations "presents a threat to international peace and the security of the West." But Ward's optimistic strategies for promoting international unity, expressed in works written for the layman as well as the professional economist, have sometimes sparked controversy. "At the bottom of all her pleas," said Richard Pearson of the *Washington Post*, "was the theory that foreign aid, 'direct transfers of wealth from rich nations to poor nations,' is the solution to many world problems." Lewis believed that Ward, "not truly a scholar, [but] clearly more than a journalist," was best described as "a synthesizer and a propagandist who was not afraid to search through history and across many academic disciplines to find support for the causes she espoused."

In *Five Ideas That Change the World*, Ward discussed nationalism, industrialism, colonialism, communism, and internationalism as dominating forces of world history. H. J. Muller noted in the *New York Times* that Ward's analysis of the changing world is "consistently reasonable and just, as well as lucid and humane." In the *New Republic*, however, D. M. Friendenberg stated that "an air of unreality hangs thick over her words. . . . Examples of this unreality abound and seem to have their root in a refusal to see the economic interest underlying attitudes." Kenneth Colegrove of the *Chicago Sunday Tribune* claimed that Ward "failed to emphasize the truth that industrial development takes time, that capital is acquired from savings, [and] that the importance of foreign capital must be preceded by political stability and firm adherence to international law." Writing in *Spectator*, Harry Johnson also saw Ward's description of the process of economic development as being too simplistic but concluded that she was nevertheless "worth reading: she [had] her heart in the right place and her head screwed tight on her shoulders, and she [wrote] with a fluent command of history."

The lectures collectively published as *Spaceship Earth* focused on three disproportions that divide the world community—power, wealth, and ideology—and how they can be overcome through foreign aid programs. A *Choice* reviewer claimed that although the brevity of the book "results in over-generalization and simplification of historical developments, the theme is convincingly treated . . . with scholarly objectivity and international realism." Calling the diagnosis "painfully realistic" and the conclusions highly optimistic, a *Times Literary Supplement* critic added: "Since more than once Ward takes refuge in faith rather than reasoned crystal-gazing, it is relevant to mention that [she] is a devout Roman Catholic as well as a distinguished economic journalist. . . . Her vision, although necessarily speculative, is compelling."

Ward advocated in *Nationalism and Ideology* the formation of a world order—with federations and organizations on a level below the United Nations and above the nation-state—to better distribute the fruits of the world's economy. The book prompted R. L. Heilbroner to comment in *Book Week:* "It is easy to see why Ward's vision will win support and admiration. When she . . . paints a picture of the modern world she is vivid and convincing. . . . [But] it is when she turns to the future that I find the sharp sense of realism giving way to a kind of wishful, not to say pietistic, thinking. For instance, [she] urges us not to lose faith in the prospects of the underdeveloped nations. But she avoids telling us candidly of the terrible actualities facing these countries, so that our faith is hardly likely to measure up to the trials it will be called on to endure."

In *Only One Earth*, written with Rene Dubos, Ward extended the base of her appeal for international cooperation to include environmental as well as economic concerns. P. J. Henriot wrote in *America* that "Ward's sensitive hand is evident in the pages which describe the dilemma of the poor nations—called to modernization and industrialization in order to raise their people from misery, yet hindered by the rich nations' traditional exercise of power and now by a new concern for pollution and ecological balance." R. F. Dasmann of *Natural History*, however, considered the treatment culturally insensitive: "Relatively little attention is given in the book to the diversity and complexity of the natural world and its significance to man's welfare. . . . The rights of those who . . . do not hold political power and who may not seek to participate in an urbanized world of high technology, but rather to find different paths to happiness, are certainly not examined. Instead, economic development in its traditional Western sense is considered to be essential for the United Nations family. All men must be caught in the technological net.''

John Kenneth Galbraith, writing in the *Washington Post Book World*, claimed that in her last book, *Progress for a Small Planet*, Ward spoke ''competently'' over a wide range of knowledge, wrote ''on deeply technical matters in clear English without jargon,'' and above all, ''retain[ed] an absolute conviction that by social and cooperative effort and by intelligent resort to government, people can solve in a reasonably prompt way most of the problems by which, in fear or reality, they are oppressed, including those of energy supply, air pollution, urban living, adequate nutrition, and economic development.'' In the *Christian Science Monitor*, Kenneth Boulding called the book ''decent, humane, and civilized . . . in the best sense of the word'' but ultimately considered the analysis ''deficient in many points.'' J. W. Dyer, reviewing the book for *Best Sellers*, believed the discussions on energy, growth, pollution, urban decay, and the third world ''all suffer from the same faulty lack of realism'' and that Ward needed to ''start suggesting what would be economically feasible to change the way we live.'' However, a reviewer for the *New Yorker* maintained that ''on almost every subject Ward tells us what can be done . . . [to] support life on [Earth] in decency and comfort.'' And Galbraith found ''both her information and her faith quite wonderful.'' He concluded: ''Though I'm not as optimistic as Ward, I would be ashamed, after reading her book, to think that I am more cynical. I hope that thousands of others will read it and be similarly improved.''

BIOGRAPHICAL/CRITICAL SOURCES: Saturday Review, November 20, 1954; *Catholic World*, January, 1955; *Commonweal*, January 14, 1955; *New York Times*, March 1, 1959, June 1, 1981; *Newsweek*, March 2, 1959; *Christian Science Monitor*, March 12, 1959, June 7, 1972, June 1, 1976, November 7, 1979; *Chicago Sunday Tribune*, March 15, 1959; *Spectator*, March 20, 1959; *Atlantic*, April, 1959, August, 1972; *New Republic*, April 13, 1959, October 27, 1979; *Book Week*, June 5, 1966; *Times Literary Supplement*, June 30, 1966; *Choice*, November, 1966; *McCall's*, June, 1967; *New Statesman*, May 26, 1972; *America*, June 17, 1972; *Commentary*, October, 1972; *Natural History*, October, 1972; *Best Sellers*, August, 1976, November, 1979; *Washington Post Book World*, September 2, 1979; *New Yorker*, October 29, 1979; *Washington Post*, June 1, 1981.†

—*Sketch by James G. Lesniak*

*   *   *

JACKSON, C(aary) Paul 1902-
(Caary Jackson; pseudonyms: O. B. Jackson, Colin Lochlons, Jack Paulson)

PERSONAL: Born 1902, in Urbana, Ill., son of Caary and Goldie (Harding) Jackson; married Orpha Cook, 1922; children: Betty Jackson Soudek, Paul L., William L., Mae L. *Education:* Western Michigan University, A.B., 1929; University of Michigan, M.A., 1943.

CAREER: Teacher in public schools in Van Buren County, Mich., 1922-27 and Kalamazoo, Mich., 1929-51; full-time writer of books for young people, 1951—.

WRITINGS—All published by Crowell: *All-Conference Tackle*, 1947; *Tournament Forward*, 1948; *Rose Bowl All-American*, 1949; *Rookie First Baseman*, 1950; *Rose Bowl Line Backer*, 1951; *Clown at Second Base*, 1952; *Dub Halfback*, 1952; *Little Leaguer's First Uniform*, 1952; *Giant in the Midget League*, 1953; *Spice's Football*, 1955; *How to Play Better Baseball*,

1963; *How to Play Better Basketball*, 1968; *How to Play Better Football*, 1972; *How to Play Better Soccer*, 1978.

All published by Hastings House: *Bud Plays Junior High Football*, 1957; *Two Boys and a Soap Box Derby*, 1958; *Little League Tournament*, 1959; *Bud Plays Junior High Basketball*, 1959; *Bud Baker: T-Quarterback*, 1960; *World Series Rookie*, 1960; *Bullpen Bargain*, 1961; *Pro Hockey Comeback*, 1961; *Bud Baker: Racing Swimmer*, 1962; *Pro Football Rookie*, 1962; *Tommy: Soap Box Derby Champion*, 1963; *Little Major Leaguer*, 1963; *Chris Plays Small Fry Football*, 1963; *Pee Wee Cook of the Midget League*, 1964; *Super Modified Driver*, 1964; *Bud Plays Senior High Basketball*, 1964; *Fullback in the Large Fry League*, 1965; *Minor League Shortstop*, 1965; *Junior High Freestyle Swimmer*, 1965; *Rookie Catcher with the Atlanta Braves*, 1966; *Bantam Bowl Football*, 1967; *Bud Baker: High School Pitcher*, 1967; *Tim: The Football Nut*, 1967; *Hall of Fame Flankerback*, 1968; *Second Time Around Rookie*, 1968; *Big Play in the Small League*, 1968; *Pennant Stretch Drive*, 1969; *Baseball's Shrine: The National Baseball Hall of Fame and Museum*, 1969; *Stepladder Steve Plays Basketball*, 1969; *Pass Receiver*, 1970; *Rose Bowl Pro*, 1970; *Bud Baker: College Pitcher*, 1970; *Tom Mosely: Midget Leaguer*, 1971; *Halfback!*, 1971; *Fifth Inning Fadeout*, 1972; *Eric and Dud's Football Bargain*, 1972; *Beginner Under the Backboards*, 1974.

Under name Caary Jackson; all published by Follett, except as indicated: ''Shorty'' series: *Shorty Makes the First Team*, 1950; *. . . at Shortstop*, 1951; *. . . Carries the Ball*, 1952; *. . . at the State Tournament*, 1955; *Buzzy Plays Midget League Football*, 1956; *Stock Car Racer*, 1957; *The Jamesville Jets*, 1959; *A Uniform for Harry*, 1962; *Seashores and Seashore Creatures*, Putnam, 1964; *Midget League Catcher*, 1966; *Haunted Halfback*, 1969.

Under name Caary Jackson; with wife, Orpha B. Jackson; all published by McGraw: *Star Kicker*, 1955; *Hillbilly Pitcher*, 1956; *Basketball Clown*, 1956; *Puck Grabber*, 1957; *Freshman Forward*, 1959; *The Short Guard*, 1961; *High School Backstop*, 1963; *No Talent Letterman*, 1966.

Under pseudonym O. B. Jackson; all published by McGraw: *Basketball Comes to North Island*, 1963; *Southpaw in the Mighty League*, 1965.

Under pseudonym Colin Lochlons; all published by Crowell: *Three and Two Pitcher*, Crowell, 1951; *Triple Play*, Crowell, 1952; *Barney of the Babe Ruth League*, Crowell, 1954.

Under pseudonym Jack Paulson: *Fourth Down Pass*, John C. Winston, 1950; *Match Point*, Westminster, 1956; *Side Line Victory*, Westminster, 1957.

Also author of short stories; contributor to magazines.

WORK IN PROGRESS: ''Always books in progress; try to do four a year but rarely make it and settle for three, or two.''

SIDELIGHTS: C. Paul Jackson once wrote *CA*: ''Lots of people think of a writer as somebody different, I suppose. All the writers I know, including myself, do not think we are different than run-of-the-mill people. Certainly there is nothing 'highbrow' or aloof about Jackson.

''I wrote short stories for pulp magazines before I wrote books, chiefly because I always enjoyed reading sports stories. My first book was written more because an editor wrote that 'while Jackson writes on-field action well done enough to create an illusion of the reader being there, I doubt that he can motivate a book-length manuscript.' Such a challenge has always been like waving a red cloth in front of a bull. I vowed that I would write a book, get it published and send the first copy to that so-and-so. I wrote the book—*All-Conference Tackle*—and have had more than seventy others published since, but I never sent so-and-so a copy.

"I enjoy writing and I especially enjoy knowing through fan letters and librarians and teachers that a certain amount of entertainment is brought to young readers by books I write. I hope the Man Upstairs continues to grant me the privilege of writing for a long, long time yet."†

*   *   *

JACKSON, Caary
   See JACKSON, C(aary) Paul

*   *   *

JACKSON, O. B.
   See JACKSON, C(aary) Paul

*   *   *

JACKSON, Robert B(lake)   **1926-**

PERSONAL: Born November 11, 1926, in Hartford, Conn.; son of Blake Smith (a merchant) and Frieda (Welz) Jackson; married Marcella F. Goral (a teacher), June 29, 1970. *Education:* Amherst College, A.B., 1950; Columbia University, M.S., 1953. *Home:* 31 Parkland Dr., Woodbury, Conn. 06798.

CAREER: Johnson's Bookstore, Springfield, Mass., clerk and book buyer, 1950-52; East Orange Public Library, East Orange, N.J., began as intern, became coordinator of readers' service, 1953-66. Trustee, Woodbury Public Library, 1973. *Military service:* U.S. Army, 1945-46; became sergeant. *Member:* International Brotherhood of Magicians, Authors League of America, Authors Guild, Society of American Magicians. *Awards, honors:* Book awards, Boys Club of America, 1964, for *Sports Cars*, and 1968, for *The Remarkable Ride of the Abernathy Boys.*

WRITINGS: (With Harold L. Roth) *New Jersey Public Libraries and Adult Education*, New Jersey Association for Adult Education, 1961; (with John F. Moran) *Services to Community Agencies and Organizations*, American Library Association, 1961.

Published by Walck: *Sports Cars*, 1963, revised edition, 1972; *Road Racing, USA*, 1964, revised edition, 1972; *Road Race Round the World: The 1908 New York to Paris Race*, 1965, revised edition, 1977; *Grand Prix at the Glen*, 1965, revised edition, 1974; *The Remarkable Ride of the Abernathy Boys*, 1967; *Gasoline Buggy of the Duryea Brothers*, 1968; *Joe Namath, Superstar*, 1968, revised edition, 1974; *Let's Go Yaz: The Story of Carl Yastrzemski*, 1968; *Stock Car Racing: Grand National Competition*, 1968, revised edition, 1973; *Blue and White Abroad: The United States in International Automobile Racing*, 1969; *Thirty-one and Six: The Story of Denny McLain*, 1969; *Earl the Pearl: The Story of Earl Monroe*, 1969, 2nd revised edition, 1974; *Steam Cars of the Stanley Twins*, 1969.

Bradley of the Knicks, 1970; *Championship Trail: The Story of Indianapolis Racing*, 1970; *Racing Cars*, 1970; *Here Comes Bobby Orr*, 1971; *Johnny Bench*, 1971; *Behind the Wheel: Great Road Racing Drivers*, 1971; *Cars against the Clock: The World Land Speed Record*, 1971; *Jabbar: Giant of the NBA*, 1972; *Can-Am Competition: World's Fastest Sports Racing Cars*, 1972; *Supermex: The Lee Trevino Story*, 1973; *Classic Cars*, 1974; *Waves, Wheels and Wings: Museums of Transportation*, 1974; *Antique Cars*, 1975; *Quarter-Mile Combat: The Explosive World of Drag Racing*, 1975; *Bicycle Racing*,

1976; *Fisk of Fenway Park*, 1976; *Road Racers: Today's Exciting Driving Stars*, 1977; *Soccer: The International Sport*, 1978; *Swift Sport: Car Racing Up Close*, 1978; *Robert B. Jackson's Big Book of Old Cars*, 1978. Book reviewer, *Library Journal*, 1955-65.

WORK IN PROGRESS: Steam Locomotives; The Great Magic Show Mystery; Road Racing: Cars and Drivers.

AVOCATIONAL INTERESTS: Magic, reading contemporary English and American literature.

*   *   *

JACOBS, Frank   **1929-**

PERSONAL: Born May 30, 1929, in Lincoln, Neb.; son of David (a businessman) and Miriam (Frosh) Jacobs; married Barbara Stellman, September 1, 1964 (divorced, 1976); children: Alexander. *Education:* University of Nebraska, B.A., 1951. *Home:* 315 East 65th St., New York, N.Y. 10021.

CAREER: Freelance writer, 1957—. *Military service:* U.S. Army, correspondent and editor for *Pacific Stars and Stripes*, 1952-54.

WRITINGS: (With Sy Reit) *Canvas Confidential*, Dial, 1963; (with Alfred Gescheidt) *30 Ways to Stop Smoking*, Pocket Books, 1964; *The Highly Unlikely Celebrity Cookbook*, New American Library, 1964; *Alvin Steadfast on Vernacular Island*, Dial, 1965; *Mad for Better or Verse*, New American Library, 1968, new edition (with Paul Coker), Warner Books, 1975; *Sing Along with Mad*, New American Library, 1970; (with Jack Rickard) *Mad about Sports*, Warner Books, 1972; *The Mad World of William M. Gaines*, Lyle Stuart, 1972; *Mad's Talking Stamps*, Warner Books, 1974; (with Bob Clarke) *Mad Jumble Book*, Warner Books, 1975; (with Clarke) *More Mad about Sports*, Warner Books, 1977; *Mad around the World*, Warner Books, 1979; *Mad Goes Wild*, Warner Books, 1981. Also contributor of verse to an *Almanac of Words at Play*. Contributor of articles to *Mad, Oui, Playboy, Punch, Town and Country, New York*, and *Signature.*

*   *   *

JACOBSON, Helen S(altz)   **1921-**

PERSONAL: Born November 30, 1921, in New York, N.Y.; daughter of Arthur (a businessman) and Minnie (Blumenkrantz) Saltz; married Eugene Jacobson (a professor of physics), June 25, 1943; children: Peter, Janet. *Education:* Brooklyn College (now of the City University of New York), B.A., 1943; graduate study at University of Chicago and University of Wisconsin; New York University, M.A., 1966. *Home and office:* 55 Thompson Hay Path, Setauket, N.Y. 11733; and R.F.D. 3, Box 98, Putney, Vt. 05346.

CAREER: State University of New York, Agricultural and Technical Institute, Alfred, instructor in Russian, 1959-60; high school Russian teacher in Lincoln, Neb., 1960-61; Suffolk College, Selden, N.Y., instructor in Russian, 1961-64; Adelphi College—Suffolk (now Dowling College), Oakdale, N.Y., instructor in Russian, 1964-65; State University of New York at Stony Brook, instructor in Russian, 1967-70; free-lance translator from Russian to English, 1970—. *Military service:* Women's Army Corps, psychiatric social worker, 1944-45. *Member:* American Translators Association. *Awards, honors:* State University of New York grant, 1969, to speak at an international conference in Moscow.

WRITINGS: Have Diet, Will Travel, Rodale Press, 1982. Also author of Russian textbooks for correspondence courses at the University of Nebraska.

Translator: Robert Magidoff, editor, *Russian Science Fiction, 1968*, New York University Press, 1968; (and editor) *Diary of a Russian Censor: Aleksandr Nikitenko*, University of Massachusetts Press, 1975; A. Strugatsky and B. Strugatsky, *Prisoners of Power*, Macmillan, 1977; K. Bulychev, *Half a Life*, Macmillan, 1977; *New Soviet Science Fiction*, Macmillan, 1979; *Hermit's Swing*, Macmillan, 1980.

WORK IN PROGRESS: A science fiction novel, *Prisoner of Time.*

AVOCATIONAL INTERESTS: Hiking, bicycling, cross-country skiing, tennis.

*   *   *

JACOPETTI, Alexandra
See HART, Alexandra

*   *   *

JAMES, Anthony
See HANNA, David

*   *   *

JAMES, C. B.
See COOVER, James B(urrell)

*   *   *

JAMES, (William) Louis (Gabriel)

PERSONAL: Born in Shrewsbury, England; son of Henry Gerard (a clergyman) and Grace (Dunham) James; married Jill Alison Hemmings, July 29, 1961; children: Nicola, Michele, Hilary, Adrian. *Education:* Jesus College, Oxford, A.M. and D.Phil., both 1961. *Politics:* Liberal. *Religion:* Christian. *Home and office:* Keynes College, University of Kent at Canterbury, Canterbury, Kent CT2 7NZ, England.

CAREER: University of Hull, Hull, England, staff tutor in English, 1958-63; University of the West Indies, Kingston, Jamaica, lecturer in English, 1963-66; University of South Carolina, Columbia, assistant professor, 1969-70; University of Ibadan, Ibadan, Nigeria, fellow, 1973-74; University of Colorado, Boulder, professor, 1978-80; University of Kent at Canterbury, Keynes College, Canterbury, England, reader in Victorian and modern literature, 1981—.

WRITINGS: Fiction for the Working Man, Oxford University Press, 1963; (editor and author of introduction) *The Islands in Between: Essays on West Indian Literature*, Oxford University Press, 1968; *Print and the People*, Allen Lane, 1976, published as *English Popular Literature*, Columbia University Press, 1976; *Jean Rhys*, Longman, 1978; (editor with David Bradby and Bernard Sharratt) *Performance and Politics in Popular Theatre*, Cambridge University Press, 1980. Author of television scripts on Victorian popular culture for British broadcasts. Contributor to *Encyclopaedia Britannica*. Contributor to journals.

WORK IN PROGRESS: A social history of the English novel, 1820-1850, for Routledge & Kegan Paul; research into drama and third world literature.

SIDELIGHTS: Louis James writes to *CA:* "Our whole assessment of cultural values is undergoing a radical change. I hope that my work on popular drama and popular fiction is making some small contribution to a view of society in which the vital values of the common people have their proper place." *Avocational interests:* Conjuring, cycling, sleeping.

JAMES, William M.
See HARKNETT, Terry

*   *   *

JAQUES, Elliott   1917-

PERSONAL: Surname is pronounced "Jacks"; born January 18, 1917, in Toronto, Ontario, Canada. *Education:* University of Toronto, B.A., 1936, M.A., 1937; Johns Hopkins University, M.D., 1940; Harvard University, Ph.D., 1942. *Home:* 147 Gloucester Terr., London W.2., England. *Office:* Brunel University, Uxbridge, Middlesex, England.

CAREER: Tavistock Institute of Human Relations, London, England, founding member and senior project officer, 1946-51, director of Glacier Project (industrial social research), 1952; certified as psychoanalyst, British Psycho-Analytical Society, 1951; private practice as psychoanalyst and as industrial social consultant, London, England, 1952—; Brunel University, London, England, professor and director of Institute of Organization and Social Studies, 1965—. Honorary secretary, Melanie Klein Trust. *Military service:* Royal Canadian Army, Medical Corps, 1941-45; became major. *Member:* British Medical Association, British Psycho-Analytical Society (honorary scientific secretary, 1961-64; member of council), Royal College of Psychiatry (founding fellow).

WRITINGS: The Changing Culture of a Factory, Dryden, 1951; (contributor) M. Klein and others, editors, *New Directions in Psycho-Analysis*, Tavistock Publications, 1955, Basic Books, 1956; *Measurement of Responsibility: A Study of Work, Payment and Individual Capacity*, Harvard University Press, 1956; (contributor) J. D. Sutherland, editor, *Psycho-Analysis and Contemporary Thought*, Hogarth Press, 1958; *Equitable Payment: A General Theory of Work, Differential Payment, and Individual Progress*, Wiley, 1961; (with Wilfred Brown) *Product Analysis Pricing*, Basic Books, 1965; *Time-Span Handbook*, Basic Books, 1965; (with Brown) *Glacier Project Papers*, Basic Books, 1965; *Work, Creativity, and Social Justice*, International Universities Press, 1970; *A General Theory of Bureaucracy*, Heinemann Educational, 1976; *Levels of Abstraction in Logic and Human Actions*, Heinemann Educational, 1978; (editor) *Health Services*, Heinemann Educational, 1978. Contributor of some thirty articles to periodicals.

WORK IN PROGRESS: An assessment of human capability; studies of the organization of the National Health Service, the Church of England, and other institutions.

SIDELIGHTS: Elliott Jaques writes to *CA:* "My overall objective is to understand human capability and behavior in its full social context. Our present political and economic theories and arrangements are grossly lacking in such understanding."

*   *   *

JARRELL, Randall   1914-1965

PERSONAL: Surname accented on second syllable; born May 6, 1914, in Nashville, Tenn.; died October 14, 1965; buried in New Garden Friends Cemetery, Greensboro, North Carolina; son of Owen and Anna (Campbell) Jarrell; married Mary Eloise von Schrader, November 8, 1952. *Education:* Vanderbilt University, A.B., 1935, A.M., 1938. *Address:* 5706 South Lake Dr., Greensboro, N.C.

CAREER: Kenyon College, Gambier, Ohio, instructor, 1937-39; University of Texas Main University (now University of Texas at Austin), instructor in English, 1939-42; Sarah Lawrence College, Bronxville, N.Y., instructor in English, 1946-

47; Princeton University, Princeton, N.J., visiting fellow in creative writing, 1951-52; Woman's College of the University of North Carolina (now University of North Carolina at Greensboro), associate professor, 1947-51, 1953-54, professor of English, 1958-65. Taught at the Salzburg Seminar in American Civilization, Salzburg, Austria, 1948; visiting professor, Princeton University, 1951-52, and University of Illinois, 1953; George Elliston Lecturer, University of Cincinnati, 1958-65; Phi Beta Kappa visiting scholar, 1964-65. Consultant in poetry to the Library of Congress, 1956-58. *Military service:* U.S. Army Air Forces, 1942-46; became celestial navigation tower operator. *Member:* Academy of American Poets (chancellor), National Institute of Arts and Letters, Phi Beta Kappa. *Awards, honors:* Guggenheim fellowship in poetry, 1946; Levinson prize, 1948; Oscar Blumenthal prize, 1951; National Institute of Arts and Letters grant, 1951; National Book Award, 1961, for *The Woman at the Washington Zoo;* O. Max Gardner award, 1962; D.H.L., Bard College, 1962; Ingram-Merrill Literary award, 1965; fellow, Indiana University School of Letters.

WRITINGS: (Contributor) *Five Young American Poets,* New Directions, 1940; *Blood for a Stranger* (poems), Harcourt, 1942; *Little Friend, Little Friend* (poems), Dial, 1945; *Losses* (poems), Harcourt, 1948; (translator) Ferdinand Gregorovius, *The Ghetto and the Jews of Rome,* Schocken, 1948; *The Seven-League Crutches* (poems), Harcourt, 1951; *Poetry and the Age* (criticism), Knopf, 1953, reprinted, Noonday, 1972; *Pictures from an Institution: A Comedy* (novel), Knopf, 1954; *Selected Poems,* Knopf, 1955; (editor) *The Anchor Book of Stories,* Doubleday-Anchor, 1958; *Uncollected Poems,* [Cincinnati], 1958.

The Woman at the Washington Zoo (poems and translations), Atheneum, 1960; (editor) *The Best Short Stories of Rudyard Kipling,* Doubleday, 1961; *A Sad Heart at the Supermarket* (essays and fables), Atheneum, 1962; (translator) Ludwig Bechstein, *The Rabbit Catcher,* Macmillan, 1962; (translator) Jakob Grimm, *The Golden Bird,* Macmillan, 1962; (editor) Rudyard Kipling, *The English in England,* Doubleday, 1963; (editor) R. Kipling, *In the Vernacular: The English in India,* Doubleday, 1963; (editor) *Six Russian Short Novels,* Doubleday, 1963; *The Gingerbread Rabbit* (juvenile), illustrations by Garth Williams, Macmillan, 1963; *The Bat Poet* (juvenile), illustrations by Maurice Sendak, Macmillan, 1964; (translator) Anton Chekhov, "The Three Sisters," produced at Morosco Theatre, 1964; *The Lost World* (new poems), Macmillan, 1965, published with an appreciation by Robert Lowell, Collier Books, 1966; *The Animal Family,* illustrations by Sendak, Pantheon, 1965; *Randall Jarrell, 1914-1965,* edited by Lowell, Peter Taylor, and Robert Penn Warren, Farrar, Straus, 1968; *Complete Poems,* Farrar, Straus, 1968, reprinted, 1980; *The Death of the Ball Turret Gunner,* illustrations by Robert Andrew Parker, David Lewis, 1969; *The Third Book of Criticism,* Farrar, Straus, 1969; *Jerome: The Biography of a Poem,* illustrations by Albrecht Duerer, Grossman, 1971; *Fly by Night* (juvenile), illustrations by Sendak, Farrar, Straus, 1976; *Goethe's Faust, Part I,* Farrar, Straus, 1976; *A Bat Is Born,* illustrations by John Schoenherr, Doubleday, 1978; *Kipling, Auden & Co.: Essays and Reviews 1935-1964,* Farrar, Straus, 1979.

Was acting literary editor of *Nation;* poetry critic, *Partisan Review,* 1949-51, and *Yale Review,* 1955-57; member of editorial board, *American Scholar,* 1957-65. Contributor to *New Republic, New York Times Book Review,* and other publications.

SIDELIGHTS: Best known as a literary critic but also respected as a poet, Randall Jarrell was noted for his acerbic, witty, and

erudite criticism. In a volume of essays about Jarrell titled *Randall Jarrell, 1914-1965,* nearly all of the writers praised his critical faculties. They also noted, commented Stephen Spender in the *New York Review of Books,* "a cruel streak in Jarrell when he attacked poets he didn't like." Elizabeth Bishop, a poet and contributor to the volume, wrote that "Jarrell's reviews did go beyond the limit; they were unbelievably cruel, that's true. . . . He hated bad poetry with such vehemence and so vigorously that it didn't occur to him that in the course of taking apart—where he'd take a book of poems and squeeze, like that, twist—that in the course of doing that, there was a human being also being squeezed."

Jarrell could be harsh, critics agreed, but his vehemence was a barometer of his love for literature. Robert Lowell wrote in the *New York Times Book Review* that Jarrell was "almost brutally serious about literature." Lowell conceded that he was famed for his "murderous intuitive phrases," but defended Jarrell by asserting that he took "as much joy in rescuing the reputation of a sleeping good writer as in chloroforming a mediocre one." Helen Vendler also felt that Jarrell's commitment to promoting good writers was the source of his vitriolic reviews. She wrote in the *New York Times Book Review* that "nobody loved poets more or better than Randall Jarrell—and irony, indifference or superciliousness in the presence of the remarkable seemed to him capital sins." Michael Dirda of the *Washington Post Book World* agreed that Jarrell had the best interests of literature in mind when he used invective. According to Dirda, Jarrell defended his willingness to "bury" (Jarrell's word) a work that did not meet his standards by saying that "taste has to be maintained (or elevated if it's at too low a level to make maintenance bearable) and there is no other way of doing it." John K. Roth noted similarly in the *Los Angeles Times* that Jarrell believed "artistic worth is not a relative, let alone a financial matter. There are such traits as trained and scrupulous taste, [and] reasoned critical judgement."

Christopher Lehmann-Haupt attributed a gradual change in Jarrell's approach to his concern for writers. He wrote in the *New York Times:* "Randall Jarrell was in his early years a harsh and witty disparager. . . . Even [later in his career] when he has praise for a poet, he often begins by knocking a work down, and then floors the reader by pronouncing the poet worth reading. Yet somewhere along the way the zingers and twisteroos die out. . . . [Perhaps] part of the reason Jarrell eases up on his fellow poets is simply because he is worried about their extinction." And although he softened his blows, Jarrell maintained his traditionally-based standards. Suzanne Ferguson wrote in her *Poetry of Randall Jarrell* that his criticism, with standards based on "broad, deep reading in *all* kinds of writing," would "ask always, both explicitly and implicitly, whether the poem tells truth about the world; whether it helps the reader see a little farther, a little more clearly the dark and light of his situation."

Jarrell tried to guide the reader not just by the content but also the style of his writing. A straightforward approach was as important to Jarrell in his own writing as in that of the writers he reviewed, noted D. J. Enright in *Listener:* "Just as common feeling informs his best poetry, so what underlies Randall Jarrell's criticism is common sense—that quality derided by frothy phonies who have failed to notice how uncommon it is—strengthened and clarified by exactly remembered reading, considerable knowledge of what is essential to know, and his own experience in the art of writing." Jarrell's insistence on clarity and accessibility in writing alienated him from some academicians; his denouncement of the New Criticism set him even further afield. According to Hilton Kramer in *New Leader,* the advent of the New Criticism "induced a profound despair over the very nature of the critical vocation, and his response to that despair was to adopt a tone and a method markedly different from the despised weightiness and solemnity he saw overtaking the whole literary enterprise. This change in his critical outlook had the unfortunate effect of depriving Jarrell of a certain seriousness." Michael Dirda interpreted Jarrell's stance in a more positive way: "In a time when criticism was already turning professional and academic, Jarrell spoke as a reader, one who tried to convey his enthusiasm or his disappointment in a book as sharply as he could manage."

Jarrell's passion for clarity extended from his criticism to his poetry. Julian Moynahan asserted in the *New York Times Book Review* that "Jarrell was a master of the modern plain style, the style which in poets like Frost, Hardy and Philip Larkin (Jarrell's favorite younger English poet) is used to connect the vicissitudes of ordinary experience with modes of primary feeling which move deep down within, and between, all of us." A *Time* reviewer suggested that in forming his style, Jarrell "rejected what Poet [Karl] Shapiro calls 'Eliot's High Church voice' in favor of 'plain American, which dogs and cats can read.' He demanded plain American speech and uttered it." Other critics have commented on the "colloquial, intimate mode of speech" that James Atlas of the *American Poetry Review* identified with Jarrell; for Karl Shapiro, writing in *Book World*, it seemed that "what Jarrell did was to locate the tone of voice of his time and of his *class* (the voice of the poet-professor-critic who refuses to surrender his intelligence and his education to the undergraduate mentality)."

While Jarrell retained his colloquial voice with no "discernable 'development'" over the years, he did branch out thematically, according to Hugh B. Staples, who asserted in *Contemporary Literature* that his "diversity is reflected in the considerable canon of his work." Suzanne Ferguson, writing in her *The Poetry of Randall Jarrell*, identified Jarrell's themes as "relatively few and closely related as they evolve through his thirty-year writing career: in the poems of the thirties, the 'great Necessity' of the natural world and the evils of power politics; in the poems of the early forties, the dehumanizing forces of war and ways to escape or recover from these through dreams, mythologizing, or Christian faith; in the poems of the fifties, and continuing into the sixties, loneliness and fear of aging and death, again opposed by the imagination in dreams and works of art; and in some of the last poems, the defeat of Necessity and time through imaginative recovery of one's own past."

One of Jarrell's favorite themes was war. Hayden Carruth wrote in *Nation* that out of "a considerable bulk of poetry . . . the war poems make a distinct, superior unit." According to Carruth, World War II (in which Jarrell, too old to serve as a combat pilot, served as a pilot instructor) left a dark psychological imprint on his poetry. Carruth noted the stylistic progression: "His early poems are sometimes mannered or imitative, and often artificially opaque; but from the first, he wrote with ease, and suffered none of the verbal embarrassment customary among young poets. When the war came he already possessed a developed poetic vocabulary and a mastery of forms. Under the shock of war his mannerisms fell away. He began to write with stark, compressed lucidity."

Helen Vendler also believed that the war inspired Jarrell to find a new focus for his writing. She wrote in the *New York Times Book Review* that "his first steady poems date from his experience in the Air Force, when the pity that was his tutelary emotion, the pity that was to link him so irrevocably to Rilke, found a universal scope." Although "ordinarily he resisted

any obvious political rhetoric," according to M. L. Rosenthal in his *Randall Jarrell,* the subject of war elicited a fervent emotional response from Jarrell, and his impassioned treatment won him an appreciative audience. Robert Weisberg echoed many critics when he wrote in the *New York Times Book Review* that Jarrell's poems "entered the spirit of the American soldier with . . . subtle empathy," noting that "perhaps his most famous piece of writing is a stark five-line lyric ['The Death of the Ball Turret Gunner'], the ultimate poem of war."

Vernon Scannell asserted that the war poem "Mail Call" was another example of a work in which Jarrell identified the military's "inescapable reduction of man to either animal or instrument by the calculated process of military training and by the uniformed civilian's enforced acceptance of the murderer's role, the cruel larceny of all sense of personal identity." To make his point on this subject about which he felt so strongly, Jarrell used powerful language. Jonathan Galassi noted in *Poetry Nation* that "the grisly irony reminds one of Auden, an inevitable influence on Jarrell's work of this period, but there is a horrible closeness to the event which Auden would not have ventured. Jarrell's best war poems . . . are . . . rich in dramatic tension, and grounded, as his best work always is, in vivid detail. His ubiquitous generalizations earn their significance from gorgeously terrible descriptions of carnage and fear."

Despite the impact of his images, some critics suggested that Jarrell lost force by making specific incidents serve a general rhetoric, in the kind of "ubiquitous generalizations" cited above. A *Times Literary Supplement* reviewer noted that in his war poetry Jarrell "seldom dealt with the carefully shaped, irreplaceable persons the world had lost. Instead, he wrote about the possible life the men had missed. This vanished futurity could hardly be concrete or particular, and the soldier therefore was too often a case rather than a person." J. C. Levenson agreed in the *Virginia Quarterly Review* that "The Death of the Ball Turret Gunner" "establishes the matter-of-factness of flak and fight more successfully than it establishes its big generalization about airmen—and boys—as creatures of the State." Helen Vendler defended Jarrell, writing in the *New York Times Book Review* that "it has been charged that Jarrell's poetry of the war shows no friends, only, in James Dickey's words, 'killable puppets'—but, Jarrell's soldiers are of course not his friends because they are his babies, his lambs to the slaughter— he broods over them." Scannell concluded that "there are moments in [Jarrell's] war poetry when the force of his passion results in confusion and overstatement but far more frequently it is directed and controlled through a technical assurance that has produced some of the most relentless indictments of the evil of war since [Siegfried] Sassoon and [Wilfred] Owen."

Even when he was not writing on war themes, Jarrell often viewed his characters with pity. Jerome Mazzaro noted the insecurity of his characters, writing in *Salmagundi* that "Jarrell's personae are always involved with efforts to escape engulfment, implosion, and petrification, by demanding that they somehow be miraculously changed by life and art into people whose ontologies are psychically secure." The passivity Mazzaro alludes to was frequently cited by other critics, often in reference to Jarrell's portrayals of women. Some critics felt that Jarrell held a particular compassion for women because he viewed them as being trapped by society; the poem "The Woman at the Washington Zoo" represents one often-cited example of this view. Jonathan Galassi wrote in *Poetry Nation* that "Jarrell's women, though conscious there is something wrong in their lives, are unable to define precisely or to respond creatively to their predicaments; they are merely witnesses to their victimization." Some critics objected to Jarrell's tone when he wrote about women. M. L. Rosenthal, writing in his *Randall Jarrell* asserted that "there is at times a false current of sentimental condescension toward his subjects, especially when they are female." But more often than not, critics valued Jarrell's perspective, appreciating it for its uncommon compassion.

Jarrell's acute sense of involvement with other people permeated both his poetry and his criticism, according to J. C. Levenson in the *Virginia Quarterly Review.* "Though his heart might go out to people as they are and things as they are, he had an ingrained drive to make them better. He could not help telling them to change a word, change a line, change their lives, but the demands he made came out of concern and not out of overbearing authority. No one doubted that. 'To Randall's friends,' writes Peter Taylor [in *Randall Jarrell, 1914-1965*], 'there was always the feeling that he was their teacher. To Randall's students, there was always the feeling that he was their friend.'"

BIOGRAPHICAL/CRITICAL SOURCES—Books: Edward Hungerford, editor, *Poets in Progress,* Northwestern University Press, 1962, new edition, 1967; Howard Nemerov, *Poetry and Fiction,* Rutgers University Press, 1963; Stephen Stepanchev, *American Poetry since 1945,* Harper, 1965; Robert Lowell, Peter Taylor, and Robert Penn Warren, editors, *Randall Jarrell: 1914-1965,* Farrar, Straus, 1967; Karl Shapiro, *Randall Jarrell,* Gertrude Clark Whittall Poetry and Literature Fund, Library of Congress, 1967; Suzanne Ferguson, *The Poetry of Randall Jarrell,* Louisiana State University Press, 1971; M. L. Rosenthal, *Randall Jarrell,* University of Minnesota Press, 1972; *Contemporary Literary Criticism,* Gale, Volume I, 1973, Volume II, 1974, Volume VI, 1976, Volume IX, 1978, Volume XIII, 1980; Vernon Scannell, *Not Without Glory: Poets of the Second World War,* Woburn Press Ltd., 1976; Sister Bernetta Quinn, *Randall Jarrell,* Twayne, 1981.

Periodicals: *New York Times Book Review,* October 7, 1961, September 3, 1967, February 2, 1969, September 17, 1972; *New York Times,* October 16, 1965, March 2, 1966, July 30, 1980; *New York Review of Books,* November 25, 1965, November 23, 1967; *Commentary,* February, 1966; *Reporter,* September 8, 1966; *Harper's,* April, 1967; *Time,* September 15, 1967; *Carleton Miscellany,* winter, 1967; *Partisan Review,* winter, 1967; *Virginia Quarterly Review,* spring, 1968; *Book World,* January 26, 1969; *Commonweal,* April 18, 1969; *Nation,* July 7, 1969; *New Leader,* December 8, 1969; *Salmagundi,* fall, 1971; *Books Abroad,* winter, 1971; *Listener,* January 23, 1975; *American Poetry Review,* January/February, 1975; *Poetry Nation,* Number 4, 1975; *Washington Post Book World,* July 20, 1980; *Los Angeles Times,* August 4, 1980; *Times Literary Supplement,* June 19, 1981.†

—*Sketch by Elaine Guregian*

*　　*　　*

JENKINS, Alan 1914-

PERSONAL: Born September 5, 1914, in London, England; son of Donald James (an insurance underwriter) and Mabel (Witcomb) Jenkins; married Margaret Elizabeth Hoskin (a teacher), December 15, 1956; children: Annabel. *Education:* St. Edmund Hall, Oxford, B.A. (with honors), 1935, M.A., 1948. *Politics:* "Vaguely Conservative." *Religion:* "Vaguely Church of England." *Home:* Stars Wood, High Barn Lane, Effingham, Surrey, England. *Agent:* David Higham Associates Ltd., 5-8 Lower John St., Golden Square, London W1R 4HA, England.

CAREER: Nash's Magazine, London, England, fiction editor, 1936-37; *Argosy,* London, assistant editor, 1938-39; Hulton Press Ltd., London, assistant editor of *World Review* and *Lilliput,* 1940, 1946-51; *John Bull,* London, fiction editor, 1952-54; Ogilvy, Benson & Mather, London, public relations director, 1954-70; full-time writer, 1970—. *Military service:* British Army, Intelligence Corps, 1941-46; became major. *Member:* Savage Club.

WRITINGS: Castle Avalon (novel), Cassell, 1941; *Absent without Leave* (novel), Heinemann, 1949; *The Swimming Pool* (novel), Heinemann, 1951; *The Young Mozart* (children's book), Parrish, 1961; *Drinka Pinta,* Heinemann, 1970; *On Site,* Heinemann, 1971; *The Stock Exchange Story,* Heinemann, 1973; *London's City,* Heinemann, 1973; *The Twenties,* Universe Books, 1974; *The Thirties,* Heinemann, 1976; *The Forties,* Heinemann, 1977; *The Rich Rich: The Story of the Big Spenders,* Weidenfeld & Nicolson, 1978; *The Social Theory of Claude Levi-Strauss,* Macmillan, 1979; *Stephen Potter: Inventor of Gamesmanship* (biography), Weidenfeld & Nicolson, 1980. Also author of radio and television plays. Contributor to popular magazines.

WORK IN PROGRESS: Order to View, a history of an international property firm.

SIDELIGHTS: Alan Jenkins's *Stephen Potter: Inventor of Gamesmanship,* John Stewart Collis writes in the *Times Literary Supplement,* "is well-shaped, witty, and full of surprises. The portrait of Stephen Potter which eventually emerges is thoroughly alive. But Mr. Jenkins takes Gamesmanship too seriously. None of it can possibly be applied to real life." Referring to gamesmanship, Potter's method of "how to win without actually cheating," Russell Davies of the *Times Literary Supplement* notes: "Potter was a man trapped in his own joke. It would be too much to say that the life and the joke grew to be identical, but they certainly became inextricable, one from the other; so Alan Jenkins, in chronicling Potter's life, is to some extent caught up in the unenviable business of furnishing jokes with explanations. His method of avoiding embarrassment is to keep his head down, and his nose pressed into the cuttings book. His judgments of Potter are fleeting and circumstantial, and the way the narrative hurries on gives the book a melancholy air, as though the sense of gradual waste amid the jocularity were a little too painful to be spoken of. But the story remains an interesting one: it deserves to be teased forth from its minutiae."

The Rich Rich, Jenkins's account of the lives of the "very rich" during the years 1850 to 1930, has also drawn critical attention. Ruth Brandon of the *Times Literary Supplement* comments on the book: "Mr. Jenkins appeals successfully and unashamedly to the voyeur in all of us. I suspect there is more fun to be got out of this book than out of actually living among the rich." And Auberon Waugh writes in *Books and Bookmen:* "Mr. Jenkins takes us on a racy, vulgar trot. . . . As a work of scholarship, the book is deplorable. As a contribution towards the philosophy of wealth, it is laughable. . . . But for all that, Mr. Jenkins takes us on quite an enjoyable romp." As Jenkins once told *CA:* "I regard myself as an entertainer rather than as an artist. I am not unhappy enough to be a true artist."

AVOCATIONAL INTERESTS: Travel, including visits to eight oriental countries, Europe, and the United States.

BIOGRAPHICAL/CRITICAL SOURCES: Times Literary Supplement, August 27, 1971, April 21, 1978, October 17, 1980; *Best Sellers,* February 1, 1975; *Economist,* October 16, 1976, October 1, 1977; *Books and Bookmen,* January, 1977; *London Times,* October 9, 1980.

JENKINS, Ferrell 1936-

PERSONAL: Born January 3, 1936, in Huntsville, Ala.; son of B. M. (a grocer) and Vera (Mann) Jenkins; married Elizabeth A. Williams (a member of the business faculty at Florida College), December 16, 1954; children: Ferrell, Jr., Stanley. *Education:* Florida College, A.A., 1957; Harding Graduate School of Religion, M.A., 1971. *Home:* 9211 Hollyridge Pl., Temple Terrace, Fla. 33617. *Office:* Department of Religion, Florida College, Temple Terrace, Fla. 33617-5578.

CAREER: Minister at Spring & Blaine Church of Christ, St. Louis, Mo., 1958-62, West End Church of Christ, Bowling Green, Ky., 1962-64, Emerson Church of Christ, Indianapolis, Ind., 1965-66, and at Brown St. Church of Christ, Akron, Ohio, 1966-67; Florida College, Temple Terrace, professor of Bible, 1969—. Cogdill Foundation (publishing company), Marion, Ind., editor, 1968-75. Leader of study groups to the Middle East, Europe, Scandinavia, and British Isles, 1967—; participant in archaeological excavation at Lachish, Israel, 1980. *Member:* Evangelical Theological Society, American Schools of Oriental Research, Near East Archaeological Society.

WRITINGS: (Contributor) W. Smith, editor, *The New Smith's Bible Dictionary,* Doubleday, 1966; *The Theme of the Bible,* Cogdill Foundation, 1969; *The Old Testament in the Book of Revelation,* Cogdill Foundation, 1973; (contributor) *Resurrection,* C.E.I. Publishing, 1974; (contributor) *The Restoration Heritage in America,* Cogdill Foundation, 1976; *Introduction to Christian Evidences,* Guardian of Truth, 1981. Editor, *Evidence Quarterly,* 1960-62; associate editor, *Truth in Life* (Bible class series), 1969-75.

WORK IN PROGRESS: A book on Christian apologetics; a photo book on Bible lands.

AVOCATIONAL INTERESTS: Photography (several of his photos have been published in *Truth in Life* literature).

*   *   *

JOHNS, Albert Cameron 1914-

PERSONAL: Born December 28, 1914, in Rockford, Ill.; son of Robert Alexander (a contractor) and Jane Scott (Anderson) Johns; married Edna Gale (a teacher), August 23, 1941; children: Ronald Cameron, Janene Laurie, Pamela Gayle. *Education:* Los Angeles City College, A.A., 1942; Chapman College, B.A., 1948; Claremont Graduate School, M.A., 1963, Ph.D., 1965. *Religion:* Methodist. *Home:* 5433 Longridge Ave., Las Vegas, Nev. 89102. *Office:* Department of Political Science, University of Nevada, 4505 Maryland Pkwy., Las Vegas, Nev. 89109.

CAREER: Pasadena Star News, Pasadena, Calif., reporter, 1950-52; Tournament of Roses Association, Pasadena, director of public relations, 1952-59; *Los Angeles Times,* Los Angeles, Calif., real estate editor and columnist, 1959-62; University of Redlands, Redlands, Calif., instructor in government, 1963-64; Chapman College, Orange, Calif., assistant professor, 1964, associate professor of political science and chairman of department, 1965-66; Pennsylvania State University, University Park, associate professor of political science, 1967; University of Nevada, Las Vegas, associate professor, 1967-72, professor of political science, 1972—, chairman of department, 1967-72. President, Al Johns Co. (public relations), Pasadena, 1950-67, and Las Vegas, 1967—; director of public relations for Miss Universe Pageant, Long Beach, Calif., 1955-58, for political campaigns, and for organizations. Vice-president, Southern Nevada Community Concert Association. *Military service:* U.S. Army, 1942-46; became first lieutenant. Medical Service Corps Reserve, 1946-56.

MEMBER: American Political Science Association, American Society for Public Administration, National Education Association, American Association of University Professors, Western Political Science Association, Rocky Mountain Social Science Association. *Awards, honors:* National Association of Real Estate Editors Award for Excellence, 1960; Alumnus of the Year Award, Chapman College, 1960.

WRITINGS—Published by Kendall/Hunt, except as indicated: *Rocky Mountain Urban Politics,* Utah State University Press, 1971; *Nevada Government and Politics,* 1971, revised edition, 1973; *Nevada Politics,* 1973, 3rd edition, 1978; *Governing Our Silver State,* 1973; (with Andrew C. Tuttle and Robert M. Bigler) *American Politics in Transition,* 1977. Author of weekly column "Down to Earth," *Los Angeles Times,* 1959-61.

WORK IN PROGRESS: Nevada, a book on the legislature, budgets, and local government.†

*   *   *

JOHNSON, Albert (Franklin) 1904-

PERSONAL: Born August 14, 1904, in Arkansas; son of George Webster and Lena (Keep) Johnson; married Bertha French (a writer, teacher, and drama director), January 30, 1932; children: Christina, Anne. *Education:* University of Redlands, A.B., 1930; additional study at Yale University, 1930-32 and State University of Iowa, 1937-38. *Politics:* Democrat. *Religion:* United Church of Christ. *Home:* 33551 Capstan Dr., South Laguna, Calif. 92677.

CAREER: Cornell College, Mount Vernon, Iowa, director of department of drama, 1932-47, and founder of first summer theatre west of the Mississippi; La Jolla Players, La Jolla, Calif., director, 1948-50; University of Redlands, Redlands, Calif., director of department of drama, 1951-70; writer. Co-director with wife of more than four hundred plays produced for stage and air, of Redlands Bowl summer productions, 1952-58, of residence company at National Christian Writers Center, Green Lake, Wis., 1959-62, and of Drama Trio on cross-country tours. Adapter of "Hamlet" and "Romeo and Juliet" for National Broadcasting Co. television spectaculars, 1961, 1962. Member of theatre for victory committee, National Theatre Conference, 1942-45; national president, American Communal Theatre, 1943-45; National Council of Churches, member of religious drama committee, 1957-62, and of broadcasting and film commission, 1962-70.

MEMBER: International Christian Writers Conference, American Educational Theatre Association, National Writers Conference, American Association of University Professors. *Awards, honors:* Freedoms Foundation award, 1957; citation from National Christian Writers Conference, 1961; Grail Award from Knights of the Round Table, 1966; citation for distinguished service from the trustees of the University of Redlands, 1970.

WRITINGS: Drama Technique and Philosophy, Judson, 1963; *Psalms for the New Millenium* (verse), Wake-Book, 1964; *Church Plays and How to Stage Them,* United Church Press, 1966; *Best Church Plays: A Bibliography of Religious Drama,* Pilgrim Press, 1968; (with wife, Bertha Johnson) *Drama for Classroom and Stage,* A. S. Barnes, 1969; (with Bertha Johnson) *Directing Methods,* A. S. Barnes, 1970; *Shakespeare Vignettes: Adaptations for Acting,* A. S. Barnes, 1970; (with Bertha Johnson) *Drama for Junior High with Selected Scenes,* A. S. Barnes, 1971; (with Bertha Johnson) *Oral Reading: Creative and Interpretive,* A. S. Barnes, 1971; (with Bertha

Johnson) *To See a Play: A Primer for Playgoers,* A. S. Barnes, 1972; (with Bertha Johnson) *Shakespeare at My Shoulder,* A. S. Barnes, 1972; (with Bertha Johnson) *Plays for Readers' Theatre,* Baker's Plays, 1972.

Plays: *Leave to Marry* (three-act comedy), Row, Peterson, 1943; *Days without Daddy* (three-act comedy), Row, Peterson, 1944; *Go Ye to Bethlehem* (spoken cantata), Row, Peterson, 1944; *Parents Are Like That* (three-act comedy), Iowa Art Craft Play Co., 1948; *Westward from Eden: A Choric Drama for Churches,* Row, Peterson, 1944; *Love Your Neighbor* (three-act comedy), Row, Peterson, 1945; *So Help Me!* (three-act comedy), Heuer, 1946; *Maybe It's Love* (three-act comedy-drama), Heuer, 1947; *If This Be Bliss* (three-act comedy), Heuer, 1947; *Boys About Babbette* (three-act comedy-drama), Heuer, 1947; *People Are Talking* (three-act comedy), Heuer, 1948; *Glory to Goldy* (three-act comedy), Heuer, 1948; *We're in the Money* (three-act comedy), Baker's Plays, 1949.

Dear Dexter (three-act comedy), Heuer, c.1950; *Head Over Heels* (three-act comedy), Heuer, c.1950; *Out on a Limb* (three-act comedy), Art Craft, c.1950; *Sweet Sue* (three-act comedy), Heuer, c.1950; *Roger Williams and Mary: A Drama for Three Players,* Friendship, 1957.

Adam and Eve Meet the Atom, Baker's Plays, 1961; *Conquest in Burma,* Friendship, 1962; *The People Versus Christ: A Drama Trio Play,* Baker's Plays, 1962; *Except John Leland,* Pioneer Drama Service, 1964; *The Innocent,* Baker's Plays, 1966; *Even the Hater: A Drama Trio Play,* Baker's Plays, 1967.

We Give You Gilbert and Sullivan, Baker's Plays, 1970; *Adrift with a Myth,* Baker's Plays, 1972; *Devil and Saint,* Baker's Plays, 1972; *Adam, Up and At 'Em,* Baker's Plays, 1974; *Flight of Fancy,* Baker's Plays, 1976; *Look Who's Playing God,* Baker's Plays, 1976; *Beloved Betrayer,* Baker's Plays, 1977; *Oh Rose of Sharon,* Baker's Plays, 1978; (adaptor) *The Cherry Orchard,* Baker's Plays, 1978.

WORK IN PROGRESS: In Eyes of Eric, "a novel spanning the first three decades of this century, to be part one of a trilogy."

SIDELIGHTS: Albert Johnson told *CA* that since retiring from academe, he and his wife, Bertha French Johnson are enjoying full time writing. *Avocational interests:* "Next to writing I like best our swims, walks, study sessions, time with friends and keeping active in church and community."

*   *   *

JOHNSON, Carol Virginia   1928-

PERSONAL: Born September 7, 1928, in Rockford, Ill.; daughter of Harry Ernest (a pharmacist) and Pearl (Ryburn) Johnson. *Education:* College of St. Catherine, B.A., 1950; Marquette University, M.A., 1958; Indiana University, postgraduate study, 1958; State University of Iowa, M.F.A., 1959; University of Bristol, postgraduate study, 1961-63. *Politics:* Socialist. *Religion:* Agnostic humanist. *Office:* Department of English, University of Victoria, Victoria, British Columbia, Canada.

CAREER: University of North Carolina, Greensboro, university lecturer in English, 1959-60, 1963-65; University of Victoria, Victoria, British Columbia, associate professor of English, 1968—. *Awards, honors:* Academy of American Poets prize, 1959, for "Threnode."

WRITINGS: Figure for Scamander: Poems and Translations, Martinsville High School, 1960, published as *Figures for Scamander and Others* (poems, 1950-1963), Swallow Press, 1964; *Reason's Double Agents,* University of North Carolina Press,

1966; *The Disappearance of Literature,* Rodopi, 1980. Contributor of poetry, articles, essays, criticism, and reviews to periodicals, including *Sewanee Review, Shenandoah, Commonweal, Poetry, Spectator.*

SIDELIGHTS: Carol Virginia Johnson told *CA:* 'I've now become interested in the life and achievements of the People's Republic of China. My spiritual commitment is to Chinese-Marxist humanism. I spend part of my time teaching in and touring China.''*Avocational interests:* Theater, painting, music.

BIOGRAPHICAL/CRITICAL SOURCES: The Seminars at Martinsville, T. H. Carter, 1960.

*   *   *

JOHNSON, Chalmers A(shby)   1931-

PERSONAL: Born August 6, 1931, in Phoenix, Ariz.; son of David F., Jr. and Katherine (Ashby) Johnson; married Sheila Knipscheer, May 25, 1957. *Education:* University of California, Berkeley, A.B., 1953, M.A., 1957, internship to United Nations, 1958, Ph.D., 1961. *Home:* 679 Creston Rd., Berkeley, Calif. *Office:* Department of Political Science, University of California, Berkeley, Calif. 94720.

CAREER: University of California, Berkeley, associate professor of political science, 1962—. *Military service:* U.S. Navy, 1953-55; became lieutenant junior grade. *Member:* Association for Asian Studies, American Political Science Association. *Awards, honors:* Ford Foundation fellowship to Japan, 1961-62; Social Science Research Council fellowship to Hong Kong, 1965-66.

WRITINGS: Freedom of Thought and Expression in China: Communist Policies toward the Intellectual Class, Union Research Institute (Hong Kong), 1959; *Peasant Nationalism and Communist Power: The Emergence of Revolutionary China, 1937-1945,* Stanford University Press, 1962; *An Instance of Treason: Ozaki Hotsumi and the Sorge Spy Ring,* Stanford University Press, 1964; *Revolution and the Social System,* Hoover Institution on War, Revolution and Peace, 1964; (contributor) Robert A. Scalapino, editor, *The Communist Revolution in Asia,* Prentice-Hall, 1965; *Revolutionary Change,* Little, Brown, 1966.

(Editor and contributor) *Change in Communist Systems,* Stanford University Press, 1970; *Conspiracy at Matsukawa,* University of California Press, 1972; *Autopsy on People's War,* University of California Press, 1973; (editor) *Ideology and Politics in Contemporary China,* University of Washington Press, 1973; *Japan's Public Policy Companies,* American Enterprise Institute for Public Policy Research, 1978; *MITI and the Japanese Miracle: The Growth of Industrial Policy, 1925-1975,* Stanford University Press, 1982. Contributor to professional journals.

*   *   *

JOHNSON, Dorothy M(arie)   1905-

PERSONAL: Born December 19, 1905, in McGregor, Iowa; daughter of Lester Eugene and Louisa (Barlow) Johnson. *Education:* Montana State University (now University of Montana), B.A., 1928. *Home:* 2309 Duncan Dr., Missoula, Mont. *Agent:* McIntosh & Otis, Inc., 475 Fifth Ave., New York, N.Y. 10017.

CAREER: Gregg Publishing Co., New York City, magazine editor, 1935-44; Farrell Publishing Corp., New York City, magazine editor, 1944-50; *Whitefish Pilot,* Whitefish, Mont., news editor, 1950-52; University of Montana, Missoula, assistant professor of journalism, 1952-67. Secretary-manager, Montana State Press Association, 1952-67. *Awards, honors:* Spur Award, Western Writers of America, 1956; Distinguished Service Award, University of Montana Alumni Association, 1961; Litt.D., University of Montana, 1973; Levi Strauss Golden Saddleman Award, 1976; Western Heritage Wrangler Award, 1978; runner-up, best western historical novel of 1977, Western Writers of America, 1978, for *Buffalo Woman.*

WRITINGS: Beulah Bunny Tells All, Morrow, 1942; *Indian Country,* Ballantine, 1953; *The Hanging Tree,* Ballantine, 1957; *Flame on the Frontier* (short stories), Dodd, 1967; *Witch Princess,* Houghton, 1967; *Warrior for a Lost Nation: A Biography of Sitting Bull,* Westminster, 1969; *The Bloody Bozeman,* McGraw, 1971; (with R. T. Turner) *The Bedside Book of Bastards,* McGraw, 1973; *Buffalo Woman,* Dodd, 1977; *All the Buffalo Returning,* Dodd, 1979.

Juvenile: *Famous Lawmen of the Old West,* Dodd, 1964; *Greece: Wonderland of the Past and Present,* Dodd, 1964; *Farewell to Troy,* Houghton, 1964; *Some Went West,* Dodd, 1965; *Montana,* Coward, 1970; *Western Badmen,* Dodd, 1970.

Contributor of short stories to anthologies. Contributor of stories and articles to magazines.

SIDELIGHTS: Dorothy M. Johnson, an honorary member of the Blackfeet tribe in Montana, is well-known for her western stories. Johnson, a former professor of journalism, tries to recapture the reality of the Western past in her tales. As Frederick J. Stefon points out in a review of *All the Buffalo Returning* for *Best Sellers,* Johnson "has provided the reader with a sensitive portrayal of a period of American history often distorted by historians and sensationalized by novelists who offer a mere stereotypical image of the Indian." In the *New York Times Book Review,* Doris Faber writes of *Warrior for a Lost Nation:* "Johnson . . . is admirably fair to Sitting Bull without in the least glamorizing the famous Sioux chieftain. Despite her easy, conversational style, she avoids the pitfall of shallowness by using interesting quotes from contemporary sources." Finally, Oscar A. Bouise praises Johnson's award-winning novel *Buffalo Woman* in *Best Sellers:* "While relating this beautiful story, the author provides the reader with vivid accounts of Indian customs and practices. . . . Dorothy Johnson depicts the Indians as humans, with human sufferings and problems, with human joys and happinesses, with births and deaths and celebrations and ceremonial sorrowings."

Johnson's stories have been translated into German, Spanish, Indonesian, Urdu, Polish, and Russian.

MEDIA ADAPTATIONS: The Hanging Tree was produced as a motion picture by Warner Brothers in 1959. The movies "The Man Who Shot Liberty Valence," Paramount, 1962, and "A Man Called Horse," Cinema Center Films, 1972, are based on Johnson's stories.

BIOGRAPHICAL/CRITICAL SOURCES: New York Times Book Review, September 21, 1969; *Saturday Review,* October 31, 1970; *American Historical Review,* October, 1973; *Best Sellers,* August, 1977, August, 1979.

*   *   *

JOHNSON, Douglas W(ayne)   1934-

PERSONAL: Born August 21, 1934, in Clinton County, Ill.; son of Noel Douglas and Laura Margaret (Crocker) Johnson; married Phyllis A. Heinzmann, June 8, 1956; children: Kirk Wayne, Heather Renee, Kirsten Joy, Tara Carlynne. *Education:* McKendree College, B.A., 1956; Boston University,

S.T.B., 1959, M.A., 1963; Northwestern University, Ph.D., 1968. *Home and office:* 420 Cambridge Rd., Ridgewood, N.J. 07450.

CAREER: Ordained Methodist minister, 1959; pastor in Chicago, Ill., 1960-64; Rock River Conference of the Methodist Church, Chicago, director of research for Chicago Home Missionary and Church Extension Society, 1964-66; Garrett Theological Seminary, Evanston, Ill., research assistant in Bureau of Social and Religious Research, 1966-68, teaching fellow, 1967-68; National Council of Churches, New York, N.Y., director of research services in Office of Planning and Program, 1968-73, associate in Office of Research, Evaluation and Planning, 1973-76; Institute for Church Development, Ridgewood, N.J., executive director, 1976—. Teacher at Western Connecticut State College, 1969-73. *Member:* American Sociological Association, Religious Research Association (member of board of directors, 1970-76), Society for the Scientific Study of Religion, Rural Sociological Society, Religious Education Association.

WRITINGS: (Editor) *Information and Research Needs of the Churches in the 1970s,* National Council of Churches, 1970; (with Paul Picard and Bernard Quinn) *Churches and Church Membership in the United States: 1971,* Glenmary Research Center, 1971; (with George W. Cornell) *Punctured Preconceptions: What North American Christians Think about the Church,* Friendship Press, 1972; *Managing Change in the Church,* Friendship Press, 1974; (contributor) Jackson W. Carroll, editor, *Small Churches Are Beautiful,* Harper, 1977; *The Care and Feeding of Volunteers,* Abingdon, 1978; (with Carroll and Martin Manty) *Religion in America,* Harper, 1978; *The Challenge of Single Adult Living,* Judson, 1982. Contributor to religion journals.

WORK IN PROGRESS: The Destiny, a novel; papers.

*   *   *

JOHNSON, Lois Walfrid   1936-

PERSONAL: Born November 23, 1936, in Starbuck, Minn.; daughter of A. B. (a clergyman) and Lydia (Christiansen) Walfrid; married Roy A. Johnson (an elementary school teacher), June 26, 1959; children: Gail, Jeffrey, Kevin. *Education:* Gustavus Adolphus College, B.A. (magna cum laude), 1958; additional study at University of Oklahoma, 1968-72, and Northwestern-Lutheran Theological Seminary, 1976-78. *Politics:* Independent. *Religion:* Lutheran. *Home:* 8117 35th Ave. N., Minneapolis, Minn. 55427.

CAREER: High school English teacher in Wayzata, Minn., 1958-59, and lay reader in Edina, Minn., 1962-63, 1964-65; free-lance writer and speaker, 1971—. Has taught at *Decision* magazine's School of Christian Writing, 1973-75, 1979-80, Midwest Writer's Conference, 1974-75, 1978, Wartburg Seminary Writer's Conference, 1977, and Brite Christian Writer's Conference, 1980. Editorial associate, *Writer's Digest* School (correspondence school), 1974-77. *Member:* Society of Children's Book Writers, Authors League of America, Minnesota Guild of Christian Writers (vice-president, 1970-71; president, 1971-72), Iota Delta Gamma. *Awards, honors:* Dwight L. Moody Award for Excellence in Christian Literature from *Decision* magazine's School of Christian Writing, 1969, for short story "Spaces in the Heart."

WRITINGS—Juvenile; all published by Augsburg: Just a Minute, Lord (prayers for girls), 1973; *Aaron's Christmas Donkey* (picture book), 1974; *Hello, God! Prayers for Small Children* (picture book), 1975; *You're My Best Friend, Lord,* 1976; *Come As You Are: Devotions for Young Teens,* 1982.

Adult books; all published by Augsburg: *Gift in My Arms: Thoughts for New Mothers,* 1977; *Either Way, I Win: A Guide to Growth in the Power of Prayer,* 1979; *Songs for Silent Moments: Prayers for Daily Living,* 1980.

Work has been anthologized in: *Complete Christmas Programs,* edited by Grace Ramquist, Zondervan, 1972; *Children of Light* (juvenile), edited by Wilson G. Egbert, Augsburg, 1973; *Jesus Stood by Us,* by Helen Reagan Smith, Broadman, 1970; *Family Prayers,* edited by Ron and Lyn Klug, Augsburg, 1979.

Also author of lyrics for hymns, including "Father, Lead Us to Your Table," Augsburg, 1974, and "Come to Us, Living Spirit," Augsburg, 1975. Contributor of over eighty articles, poems, short stories, and reviews to religious and general magazines, including *Decision, Scope, Moody Monthly, A.D., The Lutheran, Joy, The Episcopalian,* and *Newstime.*

WORK IN PROGRESS: Articles; an adult book.

SIDELIGHTS: Lois Walfrid Johnson wrote *CA:* "In our nation of instants we find self-gratification a part of the package. Yet my writing efforts can be compared to an experienced baker setting out on a trip into unknown territory. I want to take along what is most needed, and in the way of food that means hearty, homemade bread.

"As I travel, I can keep for myself that bread I've baked from stone-ground grain, or I can divide my bounty with others. With the first, there's the chance it will become moldy because I cannot eat it fast enough. With the second there's the possibility that someone won't like my bread as much as I do. But if my loaves are not crumbly nor too heavy, and if I slice them in an appealing way, they become a meal enjoyed, a food shared in love.

"Most of us who write desire to shape thought, and I am no different. But what is my responsibility to shape thought for good? It takes time, and effort, and the desire to produce loaves of the right texture. To bring forth whole grain bread—honest, nutritious, yet also mouth-watering. To bake loaves that satisfy a real hunger, bringing people together around a kitchen table. In the kneading process I as a breadmaker and my bread become one, because it is something into which I pour my best.

"When faced with the demands of writing, I sometimes feel overwhelmed. But always there is One to whom I can turn. Having given himself as bread and poured out wine, Jesus Christ calls me to do the same. In the midst of a world standing on the edge of a variety of possible disasters, I cannot do otherwise."

AVOCATIONAL INTERESTS: Biking, swimming, gardening, cross-country skiing, playing piano and flute, traveling, photography, reading.

*   *   *

JOHNSON, W. Bolingbroke
See BISHOP, Morris

*   *   *

JONES, Daniel   1881-1967

PERSONAL: Born September 12, 1881, in London, England; died December 4, 1967; son of Daniel (barrister) and Viola (Carte) Jones; married Cyrille Motte, August 23, 1911; children: Olivier Daniel, Michelle Constance. *Education:* King's College, Cambridge, M.A., 1907. *Home:* 3 Marsham Way, Gerrards Cross, County of Bucks, England.

CAREER: University of London, University College, London, England, lecturer in phonetics, 1907-14, reader, 1914-21, professor, 1921-49, professor emeritus of phonetics, 1949-67. *Awards honors:* Doctor of Philosophy from University of Zurich, 1936; LL.D. from University of Edinburgh, 1957; corresponding member of German Academy of Sciences, Berlin, 1951; honorary member of Royal Irish Academy, 1957.

WRITINGS: The Pronunciation of English, Cambridge University Press, 1907, 4th edition, 1962; *Phonetic Readings in English,* Winter, 1912, revised edition, 1956; (with Woo Kwing Tong) *A Cantonese Phonetic Reader,* University of London Press, 1912; (with S. T. Plaatje) *A Sechuana Reader,* University of London Press, 1916, reprinted, Gregg, 1970; *An English Pronouncing Dictionary,* Dent, 1917, 12th edition published as *Everyman's English Pronouncing Dictionary,* Dutton, 1963, 14th edition, 1977; *An Outline of English Phonetics,* Teubner, 1918, 9th edition, Heffer, 1960; (with H. S. Perera) *A Colloquial Sinhalese Reader,* Manchester University Press, 1919; (with M. V. Trofimov) *The Pronunciation of Russian,* Cambridge University Press, 1923; *The Phoneme: Its Nature and Use,* Heffer, 1950, 3rd edition, 1967; *The History and the Meaning of the Term "Phoneme"* (monograph), International Phonetic Association, 1964; (with Dennis Ward) *Phonetics of Russian,* Cambridge University Press, 1969.

Editor; all published by University of London Press: *A German Phonetic Reader,* 1913; *A Panjabi Phonetic Reader,* 1914; *Conversations francaises,* 1920, 2nd edition, 1960; *An Italian Phonetic Reader,* 1921; *An English Phonetic Reader,* 1923; *A French Phonetic Reader,* 1923; *A Polish Phonetic Reader,* 1924; *A Burmese Phonetic Reader,* 1925; *A Czech Phonetic Reader,* 1925; *A Bengali Phonetic Reader,* 1925; *A Welsh Phonetic Reader,* 1926; *A Dutch Phonetic Reader,* 1930; *A Danish Phonetic Reader,* 1933; *A Serbo-Croat Phonetic Reader,* 1939.

SIDELIGHTS: A writer for the *London Times* reports that Daniel Jones's "influence as an authority on the pronunciation of English was world wide. . . . He was one of the first phoneticians to make practical use of the concept of the phoneme and it was in 1950 that he published *The Phoneme: Its Nature and Use."* *Avocational interests:* Music, especially Bach.

BIOGRAPHICAL/CRITICAL SOURCES: English Language Teaching, July-September, 1961; *London Times,* December 6, 1967.†

*   *   *

JONES, Evan   1915-

PERSONAL: Born May 6, 1915, in Le Sueur, Minn.; son of Lewis R. and Elizabeth (McLeod) Jones; married Judith Bailey (an editor); children: Bronwyn Jones Dunne, Pamela (Mrs. John Knopp). *Education:* Educated in Minneapolis and Le Sueur, Minn. *Home and office:* 139 East 66th St., New York, N.Y. 10021. *Agent:* Robert Lescher, 155 East 71st St., New York, N.Y. 10021.

CAREER: Free-lance writer. Editor, *Weekend Magazine,* Paris, France, 1947-49.

WRITINGS: (With Roland Wells Robbins) *Hidden America,* Knopf, 1959; (editor) *The Father: Letters to Sons and Daughters,* Holt, 1960; *Trappers and Mountain Men,* American Heritage Publishing Co., 1961; *The Minnesota: Forgotten River,* Holt, 1962; (contributor) *American Heritage Cook Book and Illustrated History of American Eating and Drinking,* American Heritage Publishing Co., 1964; *Citadel in the Wilderness: The Story of Fort Snelling and the Old Northwest Frontier,* Coward,

1966; (with others) *The Plains States: Iowa, Kansas, Minnesota, Missouri, Nebraska, North Dakota, and South Dakota,* Time-Life, 1968.

(Editor and author of notes) Jane Grigson, *Good Things,* Knopf, 1971; *American Food: The Gastronomic Story,* Dutton, 1975, revised edition, Random House, 1981; *The World of Cheese,* Knopf, 1976; *A Food Lover's Companion,* Harper, 1979; (with wife, Judith B. Jones) *Knead It, Punch It, Bake It,* Crowell, 1981; (with J. B. Jones) *The Bread Book,* Harper, 1982.

SIDELIGHTS: In a review of one of Evan Jones's books on and about food, Lawrence Van Gelder of the *New York Times* writes that *A Food Lover's Companion* "is an easy book to put down. Which is not to say that it isn't a thoroughgoing delight. But after all, this new collection of brief articles, excerpts, reminiscences, fiction, poems and whatnot is about food. And while reading about food is fun, it can't quite compare to eating.... So making one's way through this 389-page work," Van Gelder continues, "is likely to be a process interrupted at frequent intervals by trips to the refrigerator, cupboard and stove.... *The Food Lover's Companion* is a good companion. It offers much pleasure and knowledge and whets the appetite for more."

Jones explains to *CA* why he chose food as the topic of several of his recent books. "Gathering material for my books about the American frontier," he remarks, "I realized anew how important it is for the historian to know about food as a part of any given culture. And so I was led to examine the culinary influences brought to this continent in *American Food: The Gastronomic Story.* Research for *The World of Cheese* also emphasized the ways in which food often sways the deeds of historic figures, and *A Food Lover's Companion* helps to make a similar point by gathering thoughts about food, some frivolous, some serious, of men and women of the present as well as of the past. I like to think that if there is a theme running through my work it is a deep interest in people."

BIOGRAPHICAL/CRITICAL SOURCES: New York Times, October 17, 1979.

*   *   *

JONES, James   1921-1977

PERSONAL: Born November 6, 1921, in Robinson, Ill.; died May 9, 1977 of congestive heart failure in Southampton, N.Y.; son of Ramon (a dentist) and Ada (Blessing) Jones; married Gloria Mosolino, 1957; children: Kaylie Ann, Jamie Anthony. *Education:* Attended University of Hawaii, 1942, and New York University, 1945. *Residence:* Sagaponack, N.Y.

CAREER: Writer. Writer-in-residence, Florida International University, 1974-77. *Military service:* U.S. Army, 1939-44; became sergeant; received Purple Heart and Bronze Star. *Awards, honors:* National Book Award, 1951, for *From Here to Eternity.*

WRITINGS—Novels: From Here to Eternity, Scribner, 1951, reprinted, Delacorte, 1980; *Some Came Running,* Scribner, 1957, reprinted, Dell, 1979; *The Pistol,* Scribner, 1959, reprinted, Dell, 1979; *The Thin Red Line,* Scribner, 1962; *Go to the Widow-Maker,* Delacorte, 1967; *The Merry Month of May,* Delacorte, 1971; *A Touch of Danger,* Doubleday, 1973; *Whistle,* edited by Willie Morris, Delacorte, 1978.

Others: *The Ice-Cream Headache and Other Stories,* Delacorte, 1968; (with Art Weithas) *Viet Journal,* Delacorte, 1974; *World War II,* Grosset, 1975.

SIDELIGHTS: By most people's standards James Jones's first novel *From Here to Eternity* was an enormous success. It won the National Book Award in 1951 and sold more than four million copies. Although Jones's later books have been on the best seller's list, most critics feel that *From Here to Eternity* was his finest novel and that he never achieved that same level of success in his other novels.

David Sanders wrote that "James Jones was victimized by the success of his novel.... He was termed the 'great natural talent' among contemporaries whose talents were presumably more refined. He was compared to Dreiser and Thomas Wolfe. Worse, he was made a celebrity.... He was peculiarly vulnerable to adverse criticism as six years passed before the appearance of his second novel."

When asked once about the fact that most readers continued to associate him with *From Here to Eternity,* Jones replied: "I used to say that damn book has become the bane of my life. I've written at least three novels that are better than that, but everything gets compared to it, adversely, usually, because it was such a huge best seller and such a big film. It's being compared by the notoriety it got, rather than as a work of art."

Gene Baro wrote of the book: "James Jones has taken no less than life itself for his theme, and he has written of it in the strongest tradition of realism, seeking truth, sparing nothing. He has transcended the graphic and explicit; he has permitted himself neither ornament nor nicety; he has produced a book entirely adult." And Charles Rolo was impressed with *From Here to Eternity*'s "tremendous vitality and driving power and graphic authenticity."

Critics have argued about the merit of Jones's writing, with a few critics suggesting that Jones's success was limited to a particular milieu. Milton Viorst felt that Jones "acquired the reputation of being a man's writer, preoccupied with men's urges, men's morality, men's hang-ups. Almost obsessively, Jones explores the nature of virility. His measure of a man seems all but primordial: The ability to withstand pain, the response to danger, the capacity to manage women.... Jones's people move in a world of violence, where life tends to be a brutalizing experience. Yet Jones denies that he is an artless admirer of the elemental male, crude and insensitive. He insists that such an interpretation is a profound misreading of what he is trying to convey in his writings. His feelings are mixed and, in fact, tend toward contempt, he says, for the man who is, for instance, merely brave."

Edmond L. Volpe also noticed this recurring theme weaving through Jones's novels. "James Jones's fictional terrain is limited to that peculiar all-male world governed by strictly masculine interests, attitudes, and values," Volpe wrote. "Into this world, no female can step without immediately altering its character.... In this atmosphere, men strip themselves of the refinements of sensibility and language that they adopt in their life with women. Not intellect, nor manners, nor moral and aesthetic sensitivity, but technical skill and knowledge, physical strength and endurance, boldness and courage are the coveted virtues of this exclusively male world.... Jones's vision of human existence is brutal and unsentimental, and he conveys it with superb artistry.... Jones's fictional terrain is limited, but within that limited area he has presented a frightening twentieth-century view of individual man's insignificance in society and in the universe."

Assessing Jones's work, Wilfred Sheed commented: "With most writers, once you've said the book is bad you've said all there is to say; but with James Jones, you have barely begun at that point. For Jones is the king of the good-bad writers, those writers who seem to be interesting by mistake and in spite of themselves.... Yet the body of his work amounts to something, and this very fact thrusts him ahead of his betters and earns him at least some of his money. . . . His vulnerability included a vulnerability to experience, which many of his tight-faced competitors lack, but that by itself would not be enough—we have had our fill of absorbent writers over the years. What Jones adds to it (besides impressive and easy-to-miss gifts for construction and process descriptions) is that rarest of blessings or curses, a private obsession that picks up echoes elsewhere, an obsession of public value.''

In answer to some of the negative criticism of his books, Jones remarked: ''Naturally these writers object to my writing style. You think I don't know that it's not elegant? But there's a certain method in that. In my view, a well-turned phrase communicates itself as such and not the thought it contains. It becomes an end in itself. I prefer an inelegant sentence with meaning to an elegant one at the price of meaning. . . . I'm the common man's novelist. I'm not writing for Ph.D.'s at Harvard. I'd like to be read and understood by the rank and file of the United States, by the private in the Army and not just by some professor of English. I'm the last of the proletarian novelists.''

An *Esquire* reviewer noted that ''Jones is not an observer of humanity but a prober of the soul—principally his own. . . . He writes not of man's current foibles but of his elementary passions and his eternal concerns: Jealousy, integrity, fidelity, honor. On every page of his prose, Jones spreads himself out unselfconsciously in all his wisdom and his foolishness, his cynicism and his romanticism, his dedication to the most conventional values and his insistence on the daring and the risque. Throughout his work, the pain of personal revelation is etched in every line.''

The point Jones felt compelled to inject into his novels is that ''everybody suffers. . . . That's the lesson I try to hold to in my own writing. Even the worst SOB in the world has suffered. If you can tag on to where and how and why, then you can create empathy for him while you're writing. It's that that makes him a real person rather than a stereotype. If a person is a creep, he's a creep for certain reasons.''

As Jones once explained to Harvey Breit: ''I'm no intellectual radical. But I'd always been a rebel. . . . A writer should be everything. He should be able to be everybody.''

MEDIA ADAPTATIONS: From Here to Eternity was filmed by Columbia in 1953, and received three Academy Awards, one for best picture, and two for the best male and female supporting actors. In 1979, a remake of the original movie ''From Here to Eternity'' was broadcast on national television. *Some Came Running* was filmed by Metro-Goldwyn-Mayer, in 1958, and *The Thin Red Line* was filmed by Allied Artists in 1964.

AVOCATIONAL INTERESTS: Reading, photography, classical ballet, jazz, boxing, skin diving, and collecting Indian carvings, pewter knives, and guns.

BIOGRAPHICAL/CRITICAL SOURCES: New York Herald Tribune Book Review, February 25, 1951, September 9, 1962; *Atlantic Monthly,* March, 1951, June, 1967, June, 1978; *Phylon,* Number 4, 1953; Harvey Breit, *The Writer Observed,* World Publishing, 1956; *New York Times Book Review,* September 8, 1957, January 12, 1962; Maxwell Geismar, *American Moderns,* Hill & Wang, 1958; *Saturday Review,* January 11, 1958, September 15, 1962; *Time,* January 13, 1958, September 14, 1962; *New Yorker,* January 18, 1958, November 17, 1962; *Commonweal,* September 21, 1962; Nona Balakian and Charles Simmons, editors, *The Creative Present,* Doubleday, 1963; Harry T. Moore, editor, *Contemporary American*

Novelists, Southern Illinois University Press, 1964; *Books,* March, 1964; *New York Times,* January 29, 1965, February 28, 1978; *Esquire,* February, 1967; *Life,* August 4, 1967; *Contemporary Literary Criticism,* Gale, Volume I, 1973, Volume III, 1975, Volume X, 1979; John R. Hopkins, *A Checklist—James Jones,* Bruccoli-Clark, 1974; *Miami Herald,* January 5, 1975; *Pittsburgh Press,* December 14, 1975; *Authors in the News,* Gale, Volume I, 1976, Volume II, 1976. Willie Morris, *James Jones: A Friendship,* Doubleday, 1978; *Detroit News,* December 3, 1978.

OBITUARIES: New York Times, May 10, 1977, May 16, 1977; *National Review,* May 23, 1977; *Publishers Weekly,* May 23, 1977; *Time,* May 23, 1977; *Newsweek,* May 23, 1977.†

—*Sketch by Margaret Mazurkiewicz*

*   *   *

JONES, Tom 1928-

PERSONAL: Born February 17, 1928, in Littlefield, Tex.; son of William T. (a hatcheryman) and Jessie (Bellomy) Jones; married Elinor Wright (a writer), June 1, 1963. *Education:* University of Texas, B.F.A., 1949, M.F.A., 1951. *Residence:* West Cornwall, Conn. *Office:* 7 West 96th St., New York, N.Y. 10025.

CAREER: Playwright, lyricist. Began writing for theatre while in college, in collaboration with Harvey Schmidt; came to New York in 1955, writing material for supper club revues, for entertainers, and other free-lance material; began writing musicals in late 1950's, first production being ''The Fantasticks,'' 1960; established, with Schmidt, Portfolio (a studio-workshop), New York, N.Y. *Military service:* U.S. Army, Counter-Intelligence Corps, 1951-53. *Member:* American Society of Composers, Authors and Publishers. *Awards, honors:* First prize in San Francisco Film Festival for ''A Texas Romance, 1909''; Vernon Rice Drama Desk Award, 1961, and Swedish Theatre Award of Merit, 1963, both for ''The Fantasticks''; Antoinette Perry (''Tony'') Awards, winner for ''I Do! I Do!,'' nominee for best lyricist, both 1967; Outer Critics' Circle Award, 1975, for ''Philemon.''

WRITINGS—Musical comedies; book and lyrics by Jones, except as indicated; music by Harvey Schmidt: *The Fantasticks* (also see below; two-act; based on Edmond Rostand's ''Les Romanesques''; first produced Off-Broadway at Sullivan Street Playhouse, May 3, 1960), Drama Book Shop, 1964; (author of lyrics) ''110 in the Shade'' (based on Richard Nash's ''The Rainmaker''), book by Nash, first produced on Broadway at Broadhurst Theatre, October 24, 1963; ''I Do! I Do!'' (two-act; based on Jan de Hartog's ''The Fourposter''), first produced on Broadway at 46th Street Theatre, December 5, 1966; ''Celebration'' (two-act; first produced on Broadway at Ambassador Theatre, January 22, 1969), published in *The Fantasticks* [and] *Celebration,* Drama Book Shop, 1973; ''Portfolio Revue'' (two-act), first produced in New York at Portfolio Studio, December 6, 1974; ''Philemon'' (two-act), first produced at Portfolio Studio, January 3, 1975; ''Colette'' (based on the life of Colette), first produced in Seattle, Wash., February 9, 1982.

Drama: (Author of lyrics) ''Colette'' (selections from the words of Colette), compiled by Elinor Jones, music by Harvey Schmidt, first produced in New York at Ellen Stewart Theatre, May 6, 1970; ''The Bone Room'' (one-act), first produced at Portfolio Studio, February 28, 1975.

Author of film script for ''A Texas Romance, 1909,'' privately produced. Author of book and lyrics for television revue, ''New

York Scrapbook." Contributor of lyrics to New York revues, including: "Shoestring '57," 1956; "Four Below," 1956; "Kaleidoscope," 1957; "Demi-Dozen," 1958; "Pick a Number XV," 1965.

SIDELIGHTS: Although it opened to lukewarm reviews in 1960, "The Fantasticks" became the longest-running New York stage production in American theatre history in 1968 as it passed its 3,224th performance. It continues to play to capacity houses more than twenty years after its opening and has gone into over a thousand other productions in the United States and abroad. In accounting for the play's wide popularity, Jones once remarked that "the simpler you do something, the better off it's going to be. . . . The proper words and music can evoke a spectacle in the mind that's so much more satisfying than anything the most skillful designer could possibly devise. . . . The thing to do is to take something that is around us every day, that we see and touch, and put it in terms that are poetic."

"I have written only for the musical theatre," Jones told *CA*. "I will write only for the musical theatre. Within this form, there lies the possibility of re-establishing the greatness of the theatre. (Besides, it is all I know.) My partner and I hope someday to have a theatre of our own."

Jones played a role, incognito, in the original production of "The Fantasticks" and directed "Celebration" and "Philemon." "The Fantasticks" was produced for television by Hallmark Hall of Fame and broadcast by NBC in 1964. Chappel Music has published the scores of "The Fantasticks," "110 in the Shade," "I Do! I Do!," and "Celebration."

CA INTERVIEW

CA interviewed Tom Jones by phone May 27, 1981, at his home in West Cornwall, Connecticut.

CA: You are best known for "The Fantasticks." What were your wildest hopes for it when the show opened in 1960?

JONES: My wildest hopes, I suppose, were that the show have a respectable run and that I would get out of the book shop where I was working. As it turned out, we got tepid notices and had a long run and I did get out of the book shop.

CA: You studied theater and were writing songs in college. When did you first know that you wanted to have a career in theater, or to be a songwriter?

JONES: I'm really not a songwriter; I don't *think* of myself as a songwriter. I do write the lyrics to songs we do and I write the books too, the librettos, but I don't even think of myself really as a writer. I'm a theater person. As far as I can remember, I've always wanted to be involved in the theater, originally as an actor, I thought. When I went to school at the University of Texas in Austin, I started off wanting to be an actor. Then I studied directing and got a bachelor's degree and a master's degree in what UT calls production, which in effect means directing. While I was there, I did a couple of college shows with Harvey Schmidt, who was studying art there; he wrote the music. Then I came to New York still hoping to be a director, and while waiting for that miraculous thing to take place, I met some people in nightclubs, supper clubs, revues, that sort of thing, where there was at least an immediate market. It didn't pay very much, but it allowed one to make a modest living in some kind of theatrical activity by writing comedy material and songs. I did that until we did "The Fantasticks." I've never ever thought of myself as a songwriter, although of

course that's what I do. It's one of the things that I really think I know *how* to do. It's harder to know how to write the book than it is to write lyrics, in a way.

My influences were not particularly from the world of musical comedy. Relating to my training, my influences were very much from the world of classical theater; I would say Shakespeare is clearly the most important influence. There's a certain kind of theater, a presentational theater which involves, in addition to music and dance, nonrealistic scenery and linguistic magic, using the language in more than a realistic way: a soliloquy addressing the audience, a narrator, open admission of theatricality, and with that the potential to do things in more than a realistic way. It also involves the potential to compress. All of these influences were very clearly evident in "The Fantasticks." We took, in fact, every theatrical convention that we could possibly think of and put them all together, including commedia and rhymed verse and Chinese prop man—everything that seemed theatrical.

CA: Compression seems to be a major characteristic of your work. Isn't it difficult to do sometimes, especially in adaptations?

JONES: It's always difficult to do. Of course, writing lyrics is the ultimate compression; in a sense, it's the most restricted and compressed form of all. Musicals are very elusive in form. Not many people know that much about them, and the people who do know the most are uncertain in their knowledge. The form isn't clear-cut, particularly in our time. What was earlier an established, conventional form was no longer particularly accepted by the critics by the late 1950s and the early 1960s, although it was by the public—like the Rogers and Hammerstein musicals. And there's never been a very clear indication of what should replace that. There is a kind of sixth sense that comes from practice, and maybe it's inbred to a certain extent, about what makes a musical. Not many people know about it that certainly. Compression is a part of it, but it's only a part. Almost all the techniques that one learns as a dramatist or as a director are not applicable to the musical. In fact, they're just the opposite. That isn't true of Shakespeare, however; I think Shakespeare is as good a guide for anybody writing musicals as you can go to.

CA: What's been the hardest part of the shows you've done?

JONES: The hardest is when we try to do originals. Traditionally, that's been hard for everybody, I think. I don't have a native gift for storytelling that way. I have a good gift for adapting a story, but I'm not a natural storyteller, a dramatist. The sense of form does not come; I get tripped up on my own ideas. So it's very hard for me to do originals, but I'm very drawn to *try* to do them.

CA: "The Fantasticks" has played in a number of other countries. Has there ever been any problem with translation?

JONES: It's hard for me to say since I'm not really conversant in other languages. I'd assume that there are problems. Once I was submitted a script for a French production which I'd had translated so that I could check it out. I was so horrified by it that we denied the production, because they not only translated, they had changed everything around. Instead of a sword fight they had switchblade fights. "West Side Story" had been a success there, so they were trying to put "West Side Story" into "The Fantasticks." They opened it with the two old actors as emissaries from God. All of this might be wonderfully entertaining and provocative, but it wasn't this show.

CA: Has it been especially popular in certain countries?

JONES: In the Scandinavian countries. They're very theatrical. All of our shows are more popular in Scandinavia—maybe everybody's shows are, I don't know. Our shows are probably least popular in England; we have a hard time there with all of them. Most of our shows here were hits, but we did one called "Celebration," in workshop and later on Broadway, that was definitely not a hit in New York. That show is quite a success in Scandinavia. It's still being done there and around this country, too.

CA: So you have several shows with long runs still going outside New York?

JONES: Aside from "The Fantasticks," we have had another show called "I Do! I Do!," which Mary Martin and Robert Preston did in New York. It has been going for ten years in a theater in Minneapolis; I went there recently for the anniversary. It's a two-character musical, and the same two people have been playing in it for ten years! They have gotten married and have two children. After they had played in the show for a couple of years they got divorced from their other spouses and married each other.

CA: Was it particularly difficult making those two characters strong enough to carry the show?

JONES: It wasn't just making them strong enough, although God knows what they really needed was physical strength, because they do all the songs, all the scenes, and they practically never get offstage. She has eight costume and wig changes, so she gets off, but never for more than about two minutes. And while they're getting those changes, they have to continue talking from offstage. They have to move all the scenery, all the props—it has two hundred props, really a very heavy prop show. They have to do aging makeup. It's a real workout. What was hard was to make it seem like a big Broadway musical with only two people, and it does seem like that. If the production is done properly (of course, frequently it isn't), it seems like a very big show, much bigger than "The Fantasticks."

CA: You had some early offers to move "The Fantasticks" from the Sullivan Street Playhouse to larger theaters uptown. Was it intuition that kept you from doing that, or did you know that the show would lose something in the move?

JONES: Probably both, really. We didn't want to go to the Sullivan Street Playhouse initially, we wanted a larger theater; the show plays better in a larger theater than that. Sullivan Street is a little too close, too intimate, and it has no backstage, it has no crossover, it has lots of things that just seemed impossible, but it was the only theater that we could get to open in that season. We did a lot of rewriting and a lot of restaging to fit it into that space. The show has often played in large theaters, sometimes very large theaters, one time to three thousand people. But those Broadway offers came at the end of six months, and it just seemed that things were going well enough. It seemed silly to risk a move.

CA: Does the collaborative process between you and Harvey Schmidt always work in a specific way or does it vary from show to show?

JONES: It has changed slightly over the years. We've been working together for thirty years. In the beginning, for example, I always did the lyrics first. Then I became aware of the fact that Harvey was writing lots of melodies without the lyrics. He's one of those people that melodies come out of, which is not true of all composers. Many composers need a lyric to work from, but not Harvey. So I began to write some songs to melodies that were already done. As time went on we would often agree upon a title for a song, or I would do a key phrase or maybe even three or four lines, and then Harvey would set that to a complete melody and I would do the rest of the lines after that. It works in all of these ways, and they vary with no specific reason. It may change from show to show to a certain extent.

CA: What led you to found Portfolio Studio?

JONES: It's very easy for me to put noble motives on it, and at the time I certainly told myself all of these noble motives, but if I look at it with absolute honesty, I think I just wanted more power, more control. It seemed like a logical progression in our megalomania. We had come to New York, we had written revue material for nightclubs, then we did an Off-Broadway show, "The Fantasticks," which was vaguely based on another play—not an original, but we did the book and the lyrics. Then we next did a Broadway show, "110 in the Shade," based on a play, "The Rainmaker," and Richard Nash wrote the libretto. It's the only show we've done that I didn't do the book for. It was the first Broadway show, but we just did the score. Then for the next Broadway show, "I Do! I Do!," we did book and score, but it was based on another piece, "The Fourposter." So the logical next step was to do an original, we felt. There was an element of expansion to all of this.

So we thought we would get the studio, and it was a perfectly sound idea except that we were not ready for it. What we secretly hoped was that we'd have the success that later on went to "A Chorus Line," which did the same kind of thing: they went into a workshop and experimented and came up with a show which was a smash hit. At the bottom line, this was what we really hoped for, a smash hit. With the Broadway shows there was not much opportunity for risk, and we wanted to try originals that dealt with strange or taboo subject matter that was challenging, like mixing low clown theater with religious theater, that sort of thing. We weren't so crazy that we thought they were easy to do. I didn't know how hard they were then, but I know now.

CA: What hand did you have in the movie "A Texas Romance, 1909?"

JONES: That was a very strange, personal, family-album type of thing. It was the brainstorm of one of our roommates from Texas (we all went to New York), Bob Benton, who later went on to fame and fortune in movies, directing as well as writing. His most recent success was "Kramer vs. Kramer." At that time Bob was art director of *Esquire.* He found in a shoebox in an attic some love letters that belonged to his great-uncle in Texas, love letters back and forth between the uncle and the woman he married. As it turned out, the woman died from a ruptured appendix a year or so after they were married. Bob decided he wanted to make a short film out of this, and so we did it in the most difficult way it could be done, all with paintings. Bob did a section and Harvey Schmidt did a section. It was illustrated by Robert Weaver and another illustrator named Elaine Mortogen; each of them took one section of the story and they did thirty paintings or so. We did it not as animation or anything, but as a study of the paintings. Pat Hingle did the narration and Harvey did the music and we told the story. It won a few prizes. Some people love it very much and some people absolutely hate it because, for one thing, they view it as sentimental. It is and it isn't; it's a little of both. But it's very, very slow. It takes its own sweet time, and with the fast film images going around now, it's just amazing that anybody would dare—and it was only from ignorance, I guess— to take such a long time. It was a kind of little side trip; it certainly was not connected to anything before or since in any of our careers, including Bob Benton's.

CA: Are you planning anything for television now?

JONES: At the moment, just as of today—just as of the past two hours—we've been in negotiations for doing "I Do! I Do!" on cable, and we just got word that Carol Burnett is going to do it. She did a tour of it a couple of years ago which was very successful, a summer tour with Rock Hudson back when Gower Champion was still alive. But this will be, I think, with Steve Lawrence. The only other thing we did for television was during the first year of "The Fantasticks," when we did a revue called "New York Scrapbook" for WNET. It was impressions of New York, comedy routines, song and dance, paintings, photographs, poems, just a scrapbook of things about New York City.

CA: What are you happiest about in your career so far?

JONES: I'm happy to have survived; that's always hard. But beyond that, we've had an extraordinary thing for this business in that we've had this success—with "The Fantasticks" and "110 in the Shade" and "I Do! I Do!"—without ever having a SUCCESS, that kind of big, smashing thing where your life suddenly changes. "The Fantasticks" opened on a Thursday, and there was a strong doubt that we would run past Sunday night because of the early reviews. Suddenly we realized we were struggling along and had survived from May till Christmas, and then we kind of struggled along and it was the end of one year and it got a little better. After a couple of years, Hallmark did a one-hour version on television. After the third or fourth year, "Try to Remember" began to be recorded, and suddenly, in the fourth year, we began to sell out and sold out for a number of years. Likewise, "I Do! I Do!" opened to wonderful notices for Mary Martin and Robert Preston and quite poor notices for Harvey and myself.

We've been able to live well. We have a very good, solid income from productions around the country, and yet we've never been through the tortures of success in a way. It's been quite possible for us to live like human beings, and we've never had to do the kind of thing that, as an extreme example, Michael Bennett did after "A Chorus Line." How can you follow "A Chorus Line"? In effect, we have yet to be great. And that's a great incentive. While not really having won recognition, we've been able to support ourselves.

CA: Besides the cable production of "I Do! I Do!," what are your plans for the immediate future?

JONES: We're very involved in a new Broadway show based on the life of Colette, which we've been working on for four years.

BIOGRAPHICAL/CRITICAL SOURCES: New York, December 5, 1966; Martin Gottfried, *A Theatre Divided: The Post-War American Stage*, Little, Brown, 1968; *Life*, March 14, 1969; Stanley Green, *The World of Musical Comedy*, revised edition, A. S. Barnes, 1969; David Ewen, *New Complete Book of the American Musical Theatre*, Holt, 1970.

—*Interview by Jean W. Ross*

JORDAN, Gail
See DERN, Erolie Pearl Gaddis

*   *   *

JOSEPH, Bertram L(eon)   1915-1981

PERSONAL: Born July 1, 1915, in Maesteg, South Wales; came to United States, 1965; naturalized U.S. citizen, 1979; died September 3, 1981, of a heart attack in Glen Cove, New York; son of Barnett and Ella (Levy) Joseph; married Ada E. Goldschmidt (a cancer researcher), July 10, 1939; children: Hilary Margaret, Anthony. *Education:* University College of South Wales and Monmouthshire, B.A., 1936; Magdalen College, Oxford, D.Phil., 1946, B.A., 1947, M.A., 1947. *Office:* Department of Drama and Theatre, Queens College of the City University of New York, Flushing, N.Y.

CAREER: University of Wales, Cardiff, fellow in English, 1946-49; University of Bristol, Bristol, England, lecturer, 1949-61; reader in Renaissance English literature, 1961-64; University of Western Ontario, London, visiting senior professor, 1964-65; University of Washington, Seattle, professor of drama, 1965-70; Queens College of the City University of New York, Flushing, N.Y., professor of drama and chairman of department of drama and theater, 1970-81. Tutor to various colleges of Oxford University, 1946-49. Director of Shakespeare studies, East Fifteen Acting School, London, England; teacher of Shakespearean acting, London Academy of Music and Dramatic Art. Director of Shakespearean productions at Mermaid Theatre, 1951-53, and at Bristol Old Vic. Director of Globe Shakespeare Company performances for recordings by Macdonald & Evans; also director of Drama 1600 Company performances recorded by Teaching Programmes Ltd. *Military service:* British Army, Intelligence Corps, 1940-44. *Member:* Society for Theatre Research.

WRITINGS: Elizabethan Acting, Oxford University Press, 1951, 2nd edition, 1964; *Conscience and the King: A Study of Hamlet,* Chatto & Windus, 1953, Richard West, 1978; *The Tragic Actor,* Routledge & Kegan Paul, 1959; *Acting Shakespeare,* Routledge & Kegan Paul, 1960, 2nd edition, Theatre Arts, 1969; (editor and author of introduction and notes) Kyd, *The Spanish Tragedy,* Benn, 1964; (contributor) *Classical Drama and Its Influence,* Methuen, 1965; (editor and author of introduction and notes) Shakespeare, *King Lear,* University of London Press, 1966; *Shakespeare's Eden: The Commonwealth of England, 1558-1629,* Barnes & Noble, 1971; *A Shakespeare Workbook,* two volumes, Theatre Arts, 1980. Also author of teaching machine courses on *Macbeth* and *Hamlet.* Wrote and recorded three audio-visual courses on Shakespeare for 3-M Co. Contributor to *Cassell's Encyclopaedia of Literature, Encyclopaedia Britannica, Pelican Guide to English Literature, Drama Survey.*

SIDELIGHTS: The gap between Shakespeare in education and in the theater occupied Bertram L. Joseph for many years. He once told *CA* of his findings: "Experience suggests that English school teachers are likely to be less averse than university teachers to the imaginative effort required (in the teaching of plays). I find the singleminded concentration given by actors delightfully refreshing in contrast to the flabby self-indulgence of what too often passes for Shakespeare criticism as written by academics and repeated by students." Joseph modified this viewpoint, however, after coming to the United States. In a 1967 postscript he wrote: "[Now] I find it possible to teach drama to graduate students in a way which combines academic discipline with an experience of practical theatre."

AVOCATIONAL INTERESTS: Gardening, swimming (almost daily).

OBITUARIES: New York Times, September 5, 1981.†

*   *   *

JOSEPH, M(ichael) K(ennedy)   1914-1981

PERSONAL: Born July 9, 1914, in Chingford, Essex, England; died October 4, 1981, in Auckland, New Zealand; son of George Frederick (a company director), and Ernestine (Kennedy) Joseph; married, August 23, 1947; children: Anthony, Charles, Barbara, Peter, Nicholas. *Education:* Auckland University College, B.A., 1933, M.A., 1934; Merton College, Oxford, B.A., 1938, B.Litt., 1939, M.A., 1946. *Politics:* Tory Radical. *Religion:* Catholic. *Home:* 185 Victoria Ave., Remuera, Auckland S.E.2, New Zealand.

CAREER: University of Auckland, Auckland, New Zealand, junior lecturer in English, 1935-36, lecturer, 1946-49, senior lecturer, 1950-59, associate professor, 1960-69, professor of English literature, 1970-79. *Military service:* British Army, Royal Artillery, 1940-46; became bombardier. *Member:* English Association, British Film Institute, Oxford Society, Merton Society. *Awards, honors:* Hubert Church Prose Award, 1958, for *I'll Soldier No More;* Jessie Mackay Poetry Award, 1959, for *The Living Countries;* other New Zealand national awards.

WRITINGS: Imaginary Islands (verse), privately printed, 1950; *Charles Aders,* Auckland University College, 1953; *The New Zealand Short Story,* R. E. Owen, c. 1956; *I'll Soldier No More* (novel), Gollancz, 1958; *The Living Countries* (verse), Paul's Book Arcade, 1959; *A Pound of Saffron* (novel), Gollancz, 1962; *Byron, the Poet* (criticism), Gollancz, 1964, Humanities, 1966; *The Hole in the Zero* (novel), Gollancz, 1967, Dutton, 1968; (editor and author of introduction) Mary W.G. Shelley, *Frankenstein; or, The Modern Prometheus,* Oxford University Press, 1969; *Inscription on a Paper Dart* (verse), Oxford University Press, 1974; *A Soldier's Tale* (novel), Collins, 1976; *The Time of Achamoth* (novel), Collins, 1977. Contributor of articles to *New Zealand Listener, Islands,* and numerous other periodicals.

SIDELIGHTS: M. K. Joseph traveled in the Mediterranean countries of Europe whenever circumstances permitted; he once told *CA* that he was not wholly at home either in Europe or New Zealand but wouldn't want to be without either. He was a part-time author who wrote when he could, and he wished he could write more often.

BIOGRAPHICAL/CRITICAL SOURCES: Times Literary Supplement, September 21, 1967; *New York Times Book Review,* February 11, 1968.

OBITUARIES: London Times, October 23, 1981.

*   *   *

JOSEPH, Richard   1910-1976

PERSONAL: Born April 24, 1910, in New York, N.Y.; died September 30, 1976, on a plane returning to New York from the Virgin Islands; son of Isaac (a manufacturer) and Harriet (Isaacson) Joseph; married Morgan Howard, September 5, 1954; children: Jamieson Anne, Richard Matthew. *Education:* Ohio State University, B.Sc. in Journalism, 1932; Alliance Francaise, Paris, graduate study, 1937-38. *Home:* 303 East 33rd St., New York, N.Y.; and Route 63, Goshen, Conn. *Office: Esquire,* 488 Madison Ave., New York, N.Y. 10022.

CAREER: Columbus Citizen, Columbus, Ohio, reporter, 1932; *New York Evening Journal,* New York City, reporter, 1933-37; Walt Disney—Mickey Mouse S.A., Paris, France, com-

pany director, 1937-39; *New York Post,* New York City, reporter, 1939-40; New Haven Railroad, Boston, Mass. and New York City, public relations representative, 1940-42; *Esquire,* New York City, travel editor, 1946-76. Author of syndicated weekly newspaper travel column; television and radio travel programs on Columbia Broadcasting System, National Broadcasting Co., and Mutual Network; lecturer. *Military service:* U.S. Army, 1942-45; became staff sergeant; received the Croix de Guerre. *Member:* New York Travel Writers Association (president, 1950-53), Society of American Travel Writers (director, 1961), Overseas Press Club. *Awards, honors:* Officer, French Ordre de Merite Touristique, 1962; Italian Star of Solidarity; nineteen travel industry journalism awards.

WRITINGS—All published by Doubleday, except as indicated: *Your Trip Abroad,* 1950; *Your Trip to Britain,* 1952; *Richard Joseph's World Wide Money Converter and Tipping Guide,* 1953; *Richard Joseph's World Wide Travel Guide,* 1953; *Richard Joseph's Guide to Europe and the Mediterranean,* 1956, revised edition published as *Guide to Europe, 1960 to 1961,* 1960; *A Letter to the Man Who Killed My Dog,* Fell, 1956; *Esquire's Europe in Style,* Harper, 1960; *Hilton Hotels Around-the-World Travel Guide,* 1966; *Haiti,* 1964; *Hawaii,* 1966; *America's Favorite Vacation Spots,* 1966; *Bermuda,* 1967; *Florida,* 1967; *New England,* 1967; *Around the World with the Experts: An Anthology of the Society of American Travel Writers,* 1970.

SIDELIGHTS: In the course of his career, Richard Joseph visited 115 countries and traveled an average of 100,000 miles a year. Thomas Ennis described him in the *New York Times* as "an authority on world cruises, tropical islands, restaurants, and grand and not so grand hotels just about anywhere."

OBITUARIES: New York Times, October 2, 1976.†

*   *   *

JOURARD, Sidney M(arshall)   1926-1974

PERSONAL: Born January 21, 1926, in Toronto, Ontario, Canada; died December 2, 1974, in Gainesville, Fla.; son of Albert Lewis (a store owner) and Anna (Rubinoff) Jourard; married Antoinette Ruth Hertz (a kindergarten teacher), June 20, 1948; children: Jeffrey, Martin, Leonard. *Education:* University of Toronto, B.A., 1947, M.A., 1948; University of Buffalo, Ph.D., 1953; *Office:* Department of Psychology, University of Florida, Gainesville, Fla.

CAREER: Emory University, Atlanta, Ga., assistant professor of psychology, 1951-56; University of Alabama Medical School, Birmingham, chief of clinical psychology, 1956-57; private practice of psychology, Birmingham, Ala., 1957-58; University of Florida, Gainesville, associate research professor in College of Nursing, 1958-62, associate professor, 1962-64, professor of psychology, 1964-74. Part-time private practice of psychotherapy in Gainesville, 1958-74. Member of board of directors, National Institute of Humanistic Psychology. Consultant to National Office of Vital Statistics, 1959-61, U.S. Peace Corps, 1963, and Milledgeville (Ga.) State Hospital, 1963-74.

MEMBER: American Psychological Association, American Academy of Psychotherapists, American Association for Humanistic Psychology (president, 1963-64), American Association of University Professors, Southeastern Psychological Association, Florida Psychological Association, Sigma Xi. *Awards, honors:* Fellowship to Tavistock Clinic, London, England, 1964-65.

WRITINGS: Personal Adjustment: An Approach through the Study of Healthy Personality, Macmillan, 1958, 2nd edition,

1963, 3rd edition published as *Healthy Personality: An Approach from the Viewpoint of Humanistic Psychology,* 1974, 4th edition, 1980; *The Transparent Self: Self-Disclosure and Well-Being,* Van Nostrand, 1964, revised edition, 1971; (editor with Dan Overlade) Franklin J. Shaw, *Reconciliation: A Theory of Man Transcending,* Van Nostrand, 1966; (editor) *To Be or Not to Be: Existential Psychological Perspectives on the Self,* University of Florida Press, 1967; *Disclosing Man to Himself,* Van Nostrand, 1968; (contributor) Herbert Otto and John Mann, editors, *Ways of Growth,* Grossman, 1968; *Self-Disclosure: An Experimental Analysis of the Transparent Self,* Wiley, 1971. Also author of scripts for sound recordings, "Human Uses for Behavioral Research," Big Sur, 1966, and "Humanistic Psychology: Its Implications for Psychotherapy," Big Sur, 1970. Contributor to professional and popular journals.

WORK IN PROGRESS: Research in self-disclosure, psychotherapy, factors in mental health.

AVOCATIONAL INTERESTS: Playing classic guitar, handball.†

*   *   *

JUDD, Frederick Charles 1914-
(John Courtney, A. Lester-Rands, G. R. Miller)

PERSONAL: Born June 5, 1914, in England; son of Charles Alfred (a cordwainer) and Hilda Judd; married (wife's name, Freda Lilian); children: Jean Lilian (Mrs. Antony White), Terrence Frederick Charles, Trevor Victor, Peter Andrew. *Home and studio:* 174 Maybank Rd., South Woodford, London E. 18, England.

CAREER: Electronics and radar researcher for various companies, 1950-58; currently director of F. C. Judd Ltd. (sound recording studio), and of Recorded Tuition Ltd. (recordings under label of Castle). Chartered member of Institute of Electronics. Has lectured on electronic music at Oxford and Cambridge Universities, other schools, and to learned societies. Amateur radio operator with call letters, G2BCX, 1934—. *Military service:* Royal Air Force, radar technician, 1939-45. *Member:* Radio Society of Great Britain. *Awards, honors:* Norman Keith Adams Prize, Radio Society of Great Britain, for research and papers on ground wave propagation and radio aerials; winner of professional section of British Tape Recording Contest, 1965, with electronic music.

WRITINGS: Radio Controlled Models, Data Publications, 1950, published as *Radio Control for Model Ships, Boats and Aircraft,* Gilfer Associates, 1954, revised edition (with Raymond R. Stock) published as *Radio Control for Models: Ships, Boats and Aircraft,* Data Publications, 1962, Leader Enterprises, 1966; *Electronic Music and Musique Concrete,* Spearman, 1958; *Tape Recording for Everyone,* Blackie & Son, 1961; *Radio and Electronic Hobbies,* Museum Press, 1963; *Audio and Tape Recording Circuit Book,* Haymarket Press, 1965; *Circuits for Audio and Tape Recording,* Haymarket Press, 1966; *Electronics in Music,* Spearman, 1972; *Two-Metre Antenna Handbook,* Newnes Technical Books, 1979. Co-editor of *Amateur Radio Handbook.* Contributor of more than three hundred articles on electronics to British technical journals; occasional contributor to Australian, Canadian, and U.S. periodicals. Editor, *Amateur Tape Recording Magazine.*

WORK IN PROGRESS: A film on the techniques of electronic music.

SIDELIGHTS: Frederick Charles Judd produces FX and electronic music sound tracks for television and films. He has also produced ten records under his own name.†

K

KAEL, Pauline   1919-

PERSONAL: Born June 19, 1919, in Sonoma County, Calif.; daughter of Issac Paul (a farmer) and Judith (Friedman) Kael; children: Gina James. *Education:* Attended University of California, Berkeley, 1936-40. *Office: New Yorker,* 25 West 43rd St., New York, N.Y. 10036.

CAREER: Free-lance writer, 1953—; film critic in New York City for *Life* magazine, 1965, *McCall's* magazine, 1965-66, and *New Republic,* 1966-67; *New Yorker,* New York City, film critic, 1968-79, 1980—. Executive consultant on film projects to Paramount Pictures Corp., 1979-80. Lecturer on films to colleges and universities. *Member:* National Society of Film Critics (chairman, 1970), New York Film Critics.

AWARDS, HONORS: Guggenheim fellowship, 1964; George Polk Memorial Award for Criticism, 1970; National Institute of Arts and Letters Award, 1970; National Book Award, 1974, for *Deeper into Movies;* Front Page Award from Newswomen's Club of New York, 1974. Academic: L.L.D. from Georgetown University, 1972; D.Litt. from Columbia College (Chicago), 1972, Smith College, 1973, and Allegheny College, 1979; D.H.L. from Kalamazoo College, 1973, Reed College, 1975, and Haverford College, 1975.

WRITINGS—All published by Little, Brown, except as indicated: *I Lost It at the Movies,* 1965; *Kiss Kiss Bang Bang* (collection of author's articles and movie reviews), 1968; *Going Steady,* 1970; *The Citizen Kane Book* (includes shooting script and cutting continuity from the film), 1971; *Deeper into Movies* (collection of author's movie reviews), 1973; *Reeling* (collection of author's movie reviews), 1976; *When the Lights Go Down* (collection of author's movie reviews and profile of Cary Grant), Holt, 1980. Contributor to *Partisan Review, Vogue, McCall's, Atlantic, Film Quarterly, Massachusetts Review, Sight and Sound, Modern Writing, New Republic, Second Coming, Harper's, Movie Goer, New York Times Book Review,* and other publications.

SIDELIGHTS: Pauline Kael has long been regarded as one of the most nurturing, enthusiastic, and knowledgeable reviewers of films today. Many of her readers feel that by sharing her positive attitude toward films through her writing, she has strengthened the concept of films as a viable art form. For example, *Saturday Review* critic Hollis Alpert feels that "a good deal of the currently intense interest in film criticism is due to this same dedicated lady, who feels that movies are worth as much time and attention 'as any art form that involves the emotions and minds of people, and affects their lives.'"

Kael reviews have become almost a collaboration between herself and the reader. She provokes feeling about films—whether you agree or disagree is not important. Gary Carey observes in *Library Journal* that "Kael's reviews are a total turn-on— a combination of uncanny perceptions and an idiosyncratic prose style that takes its rhythms and patterns from the movies themselves. She packs in everything and sometimes she's so deep inside her own responses, so far beneath the surface of the film, that the reader is momentarily befuddled. But this seeming failure may be Kael's greatest strength. . . . She allows us to share her excitement and confusion in coming to terms with the movies; and she not only makes us defend our opinions and sharpen our perceptions, she also deepens our enthusiasm."

Christian Science Monitor reviewer, David Sterritt agrees with Carey's assessment of Kael's gift and explains that he feels she "is not so much a film critic as she is a movie reviewer . . . who is at least as interested in the psychology of watching films and the sociology of response to films as she is in the works themselves." And Jack Kroll seems to sum up the opinion of a number of people when he writes in *Newsweek* that "Kael has been the literary intellectuals' favorite movie critic, a liaison woman between the sacred groves of academe and the plebeian, popcorn-redolent movie houses."

Mordecai Richler believes that Kael fills this liaison role well. In a review in *Book World* he explains she has the talent or "merciless ability to cut through modish hyperbole and see movies plain. . . . [Kael] sees through the pretensions of the new trendy films . . . which do no more than flirt with contemporary concerns. . . . Almost everywhere, I find [her] judgments wonderfully apt." And in agreement, *Commonweal* critic F. A. Macklin believes that Kael's "strength (and it is a valuable one) is her insight into popular culture—the mass media aspects of film. She is a brilliant exposer of cant and hypocrisy."

One aspect of Kael's writing style that endears her to many is the element of humor she introduces in her writings. In his review of *I Lost It at the Movies,* in the *New York Times Book Review,* Richard Schickel writes: "I am not certain just what Miss Kael thinks she lost at the movies, but it was assuredly neither her wit nor her wits. Her collected essays confirm what those of us who have encountered them separately over the last few years, mostly in rather small journals, have suspected—that she is the sanest, saltiest, most resourceful and least attitudinizing movie critic currently in practice in the United States.''

C. T. Samuels attributes much of Kael's popularity to still another aspect of her writing style. He writes in the *New York Times Book Review* that Kael's ''style is attractively personal: Casual yet tart. She is a splendid critic of acting and fully understands the category 'movie star.' On film lore in general, she is always informative, because of her unique grasp of movies both as business and as social institutions.''

Although an avid moviegoer as a child (she saw her first movie at the age of four), teenager, and college student, Kael happened upon her career as a movie critic by chance. A philosophy major at the University of California, Berkeley, she had a passion for literature and the arts. After she left school, she tried her hand at writing (plays, film scripts, and literary essays) while working at various odd jobs in order to support herself and her daughter, Gina. According to Hollis Alpert: ''Kael's first published writing in San Francisco's *City Lights* was, as it happened, an essay on movies. She also began doing [radio] broadcasts on movies for KPFA, the Pacifica Foundation station in Berkeley, and soon developed a following.'' Kael moved to New York City and in 1965 started working for *Life* magazine. Several magazines and three years later, she began writing for the *New Yorker*.

Reviewing movies for the *New Yorker* for well over a decade, Kael shared the critic duties with Penelope Gilliatt. Alpert explains that ''with no stipulations on the length of what she writes for the *New Yorker*, she has been able to go into the kind of careful analysis she feels is her forte as a writer on film.'' An example of one of Kael's unusually long articles is an in-depth exploration of the movie ''Citizen Kane.'' According to *Saturday Review* it was a 50,000 word essay, entitled ''Raising Kane,'' and it ''took up most of two successive issues of the *New Yorker*.'' J. A. Avant remarks in *Library Journal* that ''Raising Kane'' ''is probably the best thing Kael has written, a mixture of journalism, biography, autobiography, gossip, and criticism, carried along by a style so exhilarating that one seems to be reading a new, loose kind of critical biography.''

Reflecting the feeling of a number of other critics, David Lubin writes in an article in the *Christian Science Monitor* that ''regardless of our personal reaction to how seriously Pauline Kael takes herself, we ourselves cannot escape taking her seriously. There's just too much truth in what she says. For every perception of hers that we reject, there are two or three that strike home, sometimes making such a direct hit that we look up from the page amazed at how close to that truth we've lived all these years without knowing it.''

Kael describes her philosophy of film reviewing in her introduction to *Deeper into Movies*. Kael writes that she views her collection of reviews as ''a record of the interaction of movies and our national life during a frantic time when three decades seem to have been compressed into three years and I wrote happily—like a maniac—to keep up with what I thought was going on in movies—which is to say, in our national theatre.'' She continues: ''I try to use my initial responses (which I think are probably my deepest and most honest ones) to explore not only what a movie means to me, but what it may mean to others: to get at the many ways in which movies, by affecting us on sensual and primitive levels, are a supremely pleasurable—and dangerous—art form.''

In the middle of 1979, Kael left the *New Yorker* and returned to her native California to work for the movie industry. Although she was originally hired to assist Warren Beatty with the production duties of a James Toback film, Kael became an executive consultant of film projects for Paramount Pictures. Richard Christiansen of the *Chicago Tribune* explains that ''her consulting job consisted of initiating some projects, discouraging others, evaluating scripts, contacting writers whom [Kael] thought might be interested in working in the movies.''

When it was time to renew her contract, she decided against renewal. She explains her reason to *Village Voice* writer Arthur Bell this way: ''The real truth is I decided it wasn't for me. In order to be effective, I would have had to spend too many years of my life there. It's too late to take that on. . . . The fact is, I missed writing.'' And Kael told *Chicago Tribune*'s Richard Christiansen: ''It killed me when I couldn't write about some movies. And when I read in a review that 'The Black Stallion' probably wasn't a movie for kids, my jaw dropped. How could anyone say that about one of the classic children's films of all time?''

In 1980, after preparing her book *When the Light Go Down* for publication, Kael returned to the *New Yorker* to become the magazine's year-round ''Cinema'' columnist. ''With the *New Yorker* now,'' Kael told Arthur Bell, ''I'll be on all year, but filing every two weeks, though not necessarily running every other week. There'll be the occasional thematic piece and I'll want to discuss the industry more. I learned a lot in L.A.''

CA INTERVIEW

CA interviewed Pauline Kael by phone May 12, 1981, at her home in the Massachusetts Berkshires.

CA: In your preface to Deeper into Movies, *you explained, ''I try to use my initial responses . . . to explore not only what a movie means to me, but what it may mean to others. . . .'' Has your initial response ever seemed wrong in retrospect?*

KAEL: I know I would get credit for humility if I said yes, but the fact is I don't go back to the movie. There's so much, it's impossible to keep up with everything. So I see a movie once and write about it and that's it. If I have been unjust, surely other critics will balance it out. A movie review isn't brain surgery.

CA: In putting the individual articles together for your books, you don't reevaluate any of the original writing?

KAEL: No. I never revise opinions. That would mean really writing a separate new article. And the date is always attached to them, so that's the review from the time.

CA: How much time do you usually have between seeing a film and then turning in a finished piece?

KAEL: Sometimes very little. People think if you're writing for a weekly, that means you have lots of time. It doesn't work that way. I see a lot of movies, but I don't know which ones I want to write about until I've seen everything that's available in that time period. Very often it's a matter of seeing the movie you're most interested in the night before your copy is due, and so sometimes I sit up all that night to get it done. I try, these days, since I've become older and can't count on the physical energy I used to have, to allow myself a few days. But it all depends on the season. When the New York Film

Festival is on and the American companies are having their showings, you may have to see fifteen movies in a week and store them up in the back of your head. You'll be writing about them in the months to come. So it's highly variable. Luckily, I'm a very fast writer.

CA: You often write as if your own thoughts were taking shape in the process.

KAEL: Sure. That's the fun of writing. If it were all formulated in advance, if I didn't learn something while I was writing, there wouldn't be any point to doing the writing.

CA: It gives the reader a sense of involvement in your building to a conclusion.

KAEL: You are in on it all right, because although I know whether I like something or don't like it when I see it, I really discover *why* when I'm doing the writing.

CA: Is this a writing approach that comes naturally to you?

KAEL: It's natural, but I'm also very conscious of it. I don't do much as a writer that I'm not conscious of. I'm always amused when reviewers cite my book titles as if I were unaware of the overtones, because of course they are quite deliberate in terms of what movies are about and what their appeal is.

CA: One hears and reads that many movie critics have little or no technical understanding of filmmaking. Is this true?

KAEL: Sometimes the people who have the most technical knowledge have the worst judgment. I have a fair amount in some areas, but movies involve so many technical things that there are often effects achieved by means I couldn't pretend to understand. I might not be able to explain to you how a particular kind of animation was done. But what really counts for a critic is being able to evaluate the results. You need to know a certain amount about who does what on a movie so you don't give the wrong people credit. But even that varies a great deal from movie to movie, and the credits on a movie really don't tell you too clearly who did what. But if you go to a lot of movies, and if you're really interested, you develop a better sense of how much the individual cinematographer or editor contributes because you know his previous work and you begin to recognize his hand.

CA: When did you first know you wanted to be a movie critic?

KAEL: I think these things are fairly accidental. I'd always been interested in movies and talked about them from childhood on. At a certain point I did an article on movies, and the various kinds of knowledge I had all seemed to fuse. It's a very difficult thing to do, if you want to go about it with any seriousness, because it does require a knowledge of most of the other arts. I happen to have been interested in literature and painting and music and opera and the theater—all those things which come together in movies. It was just fun; right from the first I seemed to write about them very easily.

CA: Do you get a lot of letters in response to the column?

KAEL: Yes, an incredible number. I have my desk piled high at the office. My office is so tiny that there isn't room to work on my galleys because of the mail that piles up. And I've got stacks of it on the tables and chairs here at home.

CA: Do you try to respond to it?

KAEL: I try to respond when there is a direct question. Lots of the mail comes from young critics or even older ones who want me to evaluate their work for them or want an opinion of something they've done or want help on something. I had a package this week from Africa, from a young movie critic who wanted me to give him an opinion of his work. That's a delicate matter, too. People sometimes get offended, even though they've asked for an opinion. So sometimes I'm slow; sometimes it's months before I will answer an inquiry. People don't understand; they think you have a staff of secretaries or something. There wouldn't even be room for anybody in my dinky *New Yorker* office. There's something else that makes the answering slow: I don't type—I work by hand. Sometimes sprawling off letters by hand takes a while, and they're so badly written that I wonder if people can read them. I *don't* answer hate mail.

CA: You once wrote that Sandy Dennis had made an acting style out of postnasal drip. Do you ever get responses from people that you've said such things about?

KAEL: Sometimes you encounter them, and the *look* they give you—it's terrible! I made that comment about Sandy Dennis at a certain period, and I think it was valid then. Later on, she didn't use so many mannerisms and affectations. I really loved her in "Nasty Habits." There was also a movie that I didn't get a chance to write up that she was in called "The Out-of-Towners," in which I thought she was very funny. But sometimes people remember the awful things you've said about them and not the praise. If I've been very harsh on a performer or a director, I try not to be again. I don't want to kick somebody twice. I hate it when I read critics who hammer away at the same people over and over again. On the other hand, sometimes I find myself doing it because there's no way out. What do you do if you hate Neil Simon's work, and you keep seeing Neil Simon movies? They come out two or three times a year, and a black cloud descends on you. You can't always ignore them; you've got to review them—and there it is.

CA: When you are writing the column, do you think consciously of your readers and what kind of response you'd like from them?

KAEL: I think in terms of making my responses as clear as possible, and then it's up to the readers. If I started worrying too much about the readers, the fun and the excitement would go out of writing. I get a lot of mail from very young kids who seem not to have any difficulty at all. I mean eleven-year-olds and twelve-year-olds in small Southern towns, and a lot of teenagers. They sometimes say that they had begun to think they were crazy because they disagreed with people they saw the movie with, or with the local critic, and then when they read me, I agreed with them and they felt really happy about it. That's something that you wouldn't expect from the *New Yorker* readership. People often think of it in terms of the elegant ads. They don't realize that since it is a wonderful magazine, it's the magazine that a lot of literate kids in small towns turn to.

I think sometimes the young readers who are really interested in the arts understand what I'm saying much better than professional people, who often write me angry letters on the basis of a complete misinterpretation. I get a lot of mail from analysts and architects, from professors, and especially from scientists—physicists seem to be very interested in movies. Quite a lot from people in advertising. Less than you would imagine from high-school teachers, and more incomprehension from them than you might imagine. And there's a steady amount from kids who are writing movie columns in their school papers or college papers.

Sometimes readers will call my attention to a particular thing in a movie and will want to know why I didn't deal with it, and I can only reply that it's because I didn't think of it. Sometimes people come up with marvelous bits of interpretation that simply didn't occur to me, and then they seem so obvious and so right that I feel like a fool.

CA: You get along well with college students. Do you get some intelligent questions from college lecture audiences?

KAEL: Sure. I do less college lecturing now because it's just too difficult physically—it takes too much time and energy. But when I do, the questions are generally very intelligent. Sometimes a question is couched in a silly way, but yet you realize there's a basic problem underlying it if you can penetrate the wording. So if the question doesn't seem a very sensible one, I generally try to probe to find out what is behind it, and sometimes it is something quite remarkable. Often students put it in false terms because they are embarrassed; they don't know how to say what really is bugging them.

CA: You've received several awards, including a 1974 National Book Award, and some honorary degrees. Is there a single honor that has been most special or most encouraging to you?

KAEL: The National Book Award, I'd say, and of course the Guggenheim very early when I really needed it, back in the mid-1960s. That made a lot of difference for me because I was earning my living in other ways while I was writing, and that enabled me to put a book together and then to get a job in the field. Up until the mid-1960s, I always had to make my living in other ways. Now it seems like bliss to be able to write what you enjoy writing and to make a living out of it.

CA: In the mid-1970s you wrote about how people were going "for the obvious, the broad, the movies that didn't ask them to feel anything." Do you think that has changed at all?

KAEL: No, I think that is still true. Right now it's linked to the marketing of films. Movie companies want movies they can market very easily, via television commercials, and that they can also finance in advance of production by sales to television, Home Box Office, cable, and cassettes. The most obvious subjects and star-ridden projects—I suppose I should say star-*laden* projects—are the ones that they can finance the most easily and can sell to the public most easily. I think the worst thing that has happened to movies in the last few years is that the companies no longer know how to sell an unusual movie—pictures such as "The Stunt Man," "Melvin and Howard," "Atlantic City."

CA: You don't think it's likely to change?

KAEL: No, I don't. I think it may get worse. They're now afraid to finance anything that's unusual; they will point to the record of other unusual films, which they actually have failed to sell, as if the public didn't want them. When they don't know how to market a film, they always say, "You can't force the public to buy a ticket," and that really means they have not worked out a strategy for selling it.

CA: What experiences of value came out of your recent work in Hollywood?

KAEL: It was really a very good experience because I was able to see the obstacles more clearly. You have more sympathy for bad pictures when you see what people have to go through before they can get *any* picture under way. Also, everybody screams, "Why aren't there better scripts?" But I read many very fine scripts out there that are not going to be filmed. So I realized that the problem is not really with the writers. Pictures only get made if they have a certain obviousness and if a studio or producer can interest a big director or big stars in them. If they can't interest a star in a project, it may get rewritten to interest him; it may go through five or six drafts until everything that was good in it is gone. A lot of the best work gets rewritten, and by the time it arrives on the screen it's a mess.

There have been some good movies this year, but only a few of them actually did well at the box office. "The Empire Strikes Back" and "Dressed to Kill" both did quite well. But "The Chant of Jimmie Blacksmith," a marvelous Australian film, and "Christ Stopped at Eboli," the wonderful Italian film, and a lot of other movies didn't do nearly as well as they should have. "Used Cars" is a little American movie that didn't do as well as it should have. "Honeysuckle Rose" did almost nothing. "The Black Stallion" and "The Elephant Man," blessedly, did quite well. But there are good movies that people don't go to see because they haven't heard of them. And they haven't heard of them because the marketing people didn't believe in them and didn't devise methods for publicizing them.

CA: Robert Brustein commented in reviewing Reeling *that, after twenty years of reviewing, you still "sustain the same keen appetite for celluloid fantasy, the same intense interest in movie stars, as the most avid Hollywood fan." Do you still find it very exciting to sit and watch a movie?*

KAEL: Oh yes. Of course I've always walked out when something becomes intolerable; that saves my sanity. When I see a movie that does something new, I know I'll have an opportunity to write about something exciting. If a movie is dull or if there's nothing fresh in it, then it's no fun writing about it. But as long as there's something new—for example, Peter O'Toole's performance in "The Stunt Man"—I have the pleasure of experiencing it and then the pleasure of trying to evoke it in words. It's always a test of yourself—trying to do justice to the experience.

BIOGRAPHICAL/CRITICAL SOURCES: New York Times Book Review, March 14, 1965, February 22, 1970, April 4, 1976, April 6, 1980; *Best Sellers,* April 1, 1965; *Book Week,* April 4, 1965; *Commonweal,* April 9, 1965, June 28, 1968; *Book World,* April 28, 1968; *Christian Science Monitor,* May 4, 1968, May 21, 1970, July 19, 1976; *Newsweek,* May 20, 1968, June 21, 1976, May 21, 1979; *Harper's,* March, 1971; *Saturday Review,* April 24, 1971, April, 1973; *Publishers Weekly,* May 24, 1971; *Library Journal,* August, 1971, February 15, 1976; *Esquire,* October, 1972; *National Review,* March 30, 1973; *Vogue,* September, 1973; Pauline Kael, *Deeper into Movies,* Little, Brown, 1973; *New Yorker,* August 5, 1974; *Choice,* October, 1976; *Chicago Tribune,* April 22, 1980; *New Republic,* April 26, 1980; *Village Voice,* June 9, 1980.

—*Sketch by Margaret Mazurkiewicz*

—*Interview by Jean W. Ross*

*   *   *

KAHN, Gilbert   1912-1971

PERSONAL: Born November 28, 1912, in West New York, N.J.; died July 17, 1971; son of Nathan (a businessman) and

Amelia (Kafig) Kahn; married Olga Poraske, July 4, 1936; children: Gilbert, Jr., Gregory. *Education:* Rider College, B.C.S., 1931; New York University, B.S., 1936, M.A., 1941, Ed.D., 1955. *Home:* 7 Randolph Pl., Verona, N.J. *Office:* Montclair State College, Upper Montclair, N.J. 07043.

CAREER: Teacher at various high schools, 1931-46; East Side High School, Newark, N.J., chairman of business department, 1947-65; teacher at Montclair State College, Upper Montclair, N.J. Visiting summer professor at Stanford University, Northwestern University, Virginia Polytechnic Institute, and other colleges. Lecturer for professional and business groups in United States and Canada. *Member:* National Office Management Association (member of board of directors, 1957-58), New Jersey Business Education Association (president, 1952-53), New Jersey Education Association, New Jersey Department Heads Association, New York City Gregg Shorthand Teachers Association (president, 1957-58), Delta Pi Epsilon. *Awards, honors:* National Business Teacher of the Year Award from National Office Management Association, 1956; Secondary School Distinguished Teaching Award from Princeton University, 1963.

WRITINGS: (With Goodfellow) *Projects in Clerical Training,* South-Western Co., 1941; (with J. Marshall Hanna and M. Herbert Freeman) *Bookkeeping and Accounting Simplified,* McGraw, 1953; (with Theodore Yerian and Jeffrey R. Stewart, Jr.) *Progressive Filing,* 6th edition (Kahn was not associated with earlier editions), McGraw, 1955, 8th edition, 1969; (with Meehan) *How to Use Ten-Key Adding Machines,* McGraw, 1955; (with Hanna and Freeman) *Bookkeeping and Accounting Simplified, Advanced Course,* McGraw, 1958; (with Yerian and Stewart) *Progressive Filing and Records Management,* McGraw, 1962, 2nd edition published as *Filing Systems and Records Management,* 1971; (with Donald J. D. Mulkerne) *The Term Paper, Step by Step,* Doubleday, 1964, 2nd edition (by Mulkerne), Anchor Press, 1977; (with Mulkerne) *How Do You Spell It?,* Doubleday, 1964; (with others) *Gregg Quick Filing Practice,* McGraw, 1965, 2nd edition (by Stewart), 1979; *Business Data Processing: Basic Principles and Applications,* McGraw, 1966; (with Freeman and Hanna) *Accounting 10/12,* McGraw, 1968; (with Mulkerne) *The Word Book,* Glencoe Press, 1975. Contributor to professional journals.†

*   *   *

KAPEL, Andrew
  See BURGESS, M(ichael) R(oy)

*   *   *

KARP, Stephen A(rnold) 1928-

PERSONAL: Born August 28, 1928, in Brooklyn, N.Y.; son of James and Ruth (Bagully) Karp; married Elaine Gelernter, 1952; children: Henry, Abby, Julie. *Education:* Brooklyn College (now Brooklyn College of the City University of New York), B.A., 1949; New School for Social Research, M.A., 1952; New York University, Ph.D., 1962. *Home:* 2207 Rogene Dr., Baltimore, Md. 21209. *Office:* Department of Psychology, George Washington University, Washington, D.C. 20052.

CAREER: State University of New York Downstate Medical Center, Brooklyn, instructor, 1954-64; Sinai Hospital of Baltimore, Baltimore, Md., chief psychologist, 1964-69; George Washington University, Washington, D.C., associate professor of psychology, 1969—. Assistant professor of pyschology, John Hopkins University School of Medicine, Baltimore, 1964-69. *Military service:* U.S. Army, 1952-54. *Member:* American Psychological Association, American Association of Univer-

sity Professors, Eastern Psychological Association, Maryland Psychological Association.

WRITINGS: (With Witkin and others) *Psychological Differentiation,* Wiley, 1962; (with Witkin and others) *Manual for the Embedded Figures Tests,* Consulting Psychologists Press, 1971; (with Williams and others) *Environmental Pollution and Mental Health,* Information Resources Press, 1973. Also author of a kit of selected distraction and cognitive tests, 1962, and, with Konstadt, a manual for children's embedded figures and cognitive tests, 1963.

*   *   *

KAUFFMANN, Stanley 1916-
  (Spranger Barry)

PERSONAL: Born April 24, 1916, in New York, N.Y.; son of Joseph H. (a dentist) and Jeannette (Steiner) Kauffmann; married Laura Cohen, February 5, 1943. *Education:* New York University, B.F.A., 1935. *Home:* 10 West 15th St., New York, N.Y. 10011. *Agent:* Brandt & Brandt Literary Agents, Inc., 1501 Broadway, New York, N.Y. 10036.

CAREER: Writer, editor, actor, director, theater and film critic. Washington Square Players, New York City, actor and stage manager, 1931-41; Bantam Books, New York City, associate editor, 1949-52; Ballantine Books, New York City, editor-in-chief, 1952-56, consulting editor, 1957-58; Alfred A. Knopf, Inc., New York City, editor, 1959-60; *New Republic,* Washington, D.C., contributing editor and film critic, 1958-65, 1968—, associate literary editor, 1966-67, theater critic, 1969-79; *New York Times,* New York City, drama critic, 1966; *Saturday Review,* New York City, theater critic, 1979—. Visiting professor, Yale School of Drama, 1967-73, 1977—; City University of New York, distinguished professor, 1973-76, visiting professor in Graduate School and University Center, 1977—. Conductor of weekly program "The Art of Film," for WNDT-TV, 1963-67. *Awards, honors:* Honorary fellow of Morse College of Yale University, 1964; Ford Foundation fellow; visiting fellow in humanities at the University of Colorado; recipient of George Jean Nathan Award for dramatic criticism, 1972-73.

WRITINGS—Plays: *The Red-Handkerchief Man* (three-act), Samuel French, 1933; *How She Managed Her Marriage* (one-act), Samuel French, 1935; *The Singer in Search of a King* (one-act), Samuel French, 1935; *The True Adventure* (three-act comedy), Samuel French, 1935; *Altogether Reformed* (three-act comedy), Samuel French, 1936; *Father Spills the Beans* (three-act comedy), Walter H. Baker Co., 1936; *A Word from the Wise, for Three Women,* Eldridge Entertainment House, 1937; *Come Again: A South Seas Vignette in One Act,* Dramatists Play Service, 1937; *Coming of Age* (one-act comedy), Samuel French, 1937; *Eleanor on the Hill: A One-Act Fantasia on Comic Themes,* Samuel French, 1937; *The Cow Was in the Parlor* (one-act comedy), Denison, 1938; *Mr. Flemington Sits Down* (one-act comedy), Samuel French, 1938; *Right under Her Nose* (one-act comedy), Penn Publishing Co., 1938; (under pseudonym Spranger Barry) *Play Ball!,* Samuel French, 1940; (under pseudonym Spranger Barry) *Close Courting* (one-act comedy), Willis N. Bugbee Co., 1940; *Prince Who Shouldn't Have Shaved: A Frolic in One Act,* Ingram, c. 1940; *Salvation of Mr. Song,* Ingram, c. 1940; *Bobino, his Adventures* (two-act; juvenile), Row, Peterson, 1941; (under pseudonym Spranger Barry) *Pig of My Dreams* (one-act comedy), Dramatic Publishing Co., 1942; *Food for Freedom: A United Nations Play for Elementary School Children in One Act,* Food for Freedom, Inc., 1944.

Other: *The King of Proxy Street* (fiction), John Day, 1941; *The Bad Samaritan*, Cassell, 1943; *This Time Forever: A Romance*, Doubleday, Doran, 1945; *The Hidden Hero* (fiction), Rinehart, 1949; *The Tightrope*, Simon & Schuster, 1952, published in England as *The Philanderer* (fiction), Secker & Warburg, 1953, 2nd edition, 1956, published with *The Summing-Up by Justice Stable in the Trial for an Alleged Obscene Libel*, Secker & Warburg, 1954; *A Change of Climate*, Rinehart, 1954; *Man of the World*, Rinehart, 1956, published in England as *The Very Man*, Secker & Warburg, 1956; *If It Be Love*, M. Joseph, 1960; *A World on Film: Criticism and Comment*, Harper, 1966; *Figures of Light: Film Criticism and Comment*, Harper, 1971; (editor with Bruce Henstell) *American Film Criticism: From the Beginnings to Citizen Kane*, Liveright, 1972; *Living Images: Film Comment and Criticism*, Harper, 1975; *Persons of the Drama: Theater Criticism and Comment*, Harper, 1976; *Before My Eyes: Film Criticism and Comment*, Harper, 1980; *Albums of Early Life* (memoirs), Ticknor & Fields, 1980.

Contributor to *Theatre Arts, Show, Reporter, Commentary, New York Times Book Review, Saturday Review,* and *Punch.*

SIDELIGHTS: Stanley Kauffmann is one of the most well-known contemporary film and theater critics. A *Choice* reviewer feels that he "is so intelligent, argues, writes, chastises, and corrects so well and so thoroughly that one is tempted to vote him the best film critic writing today." S. Schoenbaum of *Book World* feels that Kauffmann succeeds because he "writes precisely, not confusing parameters with perimeters; and while knowledgeable about art directors, editors, cinematographers and the like, he also knows books and plays." Kauffmann's wide-ranging knowledge is valuable, agrees Robert Asahina in the *New York Times Book Review.* "Mr. Kauffmann continues to see films in the broad cultural and historical context that eludes the tunnel-vision reviewers whose only reference points are Hollywood and old movies," he writes. "In this epoch of fake profundity it is a pleasure to read Mr. Kauffmann's sensible and discriminating reviews and essays."

Joan Didion dissents with Kauffmann's admirers. She writes in the *New York Review of Books:* "Some people who write about film seem so temperamentally at odds with what both Fellini and Truffaut have called the 'circus' aspect of making film that there is flatly no question of their ever apprehending the social or emotional reality of the process. In this connection I think particularly of Kauffmann, whose idea of a nasty disclosure about the circus is to reveal that the aerialist is up there to get our attention." Similarly, Jack Richardson, writing in the *New York Times Book Review,* notes in Kauffmann's theater criticism an "atmosphere of academic primness in which authorities are cited in support of an opinion without regard to their appropriateness and with a faith in their cultural status that in anyone except a critic would, nowadays, be quaintly touching."

In his memoirs, *Albums of Early Life,* Kauffmann takes the model of a photograph album to organize his reminiscences. According to Sam Birkrant in the *Los Angeles Times,* Kauffmann creates "finely honed" and "sharply focused" images in the ten chapters of the book, but generally critics express reservations about Kauffmann's presentation. Birkrant, for example, finds Kauffmann's "emotional detachment" disturbing, and Paul Zweig, writing in the *New York Times Book Review* asserts that Kauffmann's tone is egocentric. "The portraits, especially of women, are powerful," writes Zweig, "but they are miniaturized by the figure parading in the foreground, the 'I' who is always on stage, always stealing the scene with 'I thought . . . I felt . . . I did.'"

Christopher Lehmann-Haupt of the *New York Times* is also put off by Kauffmann's perspective. He wonders: "Is the highly artful obliqueness of these memoirs meant to be an invitation on Mr. Kauffmann's part to look beneath the crystal plates of his life? Or is it simply a way of covering up what he would prefer not to write about?" Lehmann-Haupt concludes that despite his feeling that each of the albums is "skillfully and economically crafted and each has its decisive impact," Kauffmann's approach makes it "hard to assess the results of his experiment."

CA INTERVIEW

CA interviewed Stanley Kauffmann by phone February 17, 1981, at work in New York City.

CA: In your memoirs Albums of Early Life *(1980) you write about the "series of alternative lives" your life has encompassed. As your careers as actor, director, editor, writer, and critic have overlapped, have you ever felt torn between jobs?*

KAUFFMANN: Constantly. I'm never satisfied with what I'm doing. I feel that about every four or five years I ought to be changing my life, but I'm running out of chunks of five years. I love what I'm doing just now, teaching and writing criticism, but I keep thinking of other things I *might* be doing and that makes me a little discontented. Maybe that's good for the thing I'm doing.

CA: You wrote also in that book, "I graduated in 1935 with a good warped education. I had learned a lot about what interested me, much less about most other subjects." In view of how that education has served you, would you do it differently in retrospect?

KAUFFMANN: Very differently. I would, first of all, ground myself in at least one, preferably two foreign languages. If there's one signal, salient, depressing gap in my education, it's in languages. I'm not really competent in any foreign language. I can struggle along with a couple, but I've missed very much the fluency that I wish I had in at least two other languages. And I wish I had some formal training in philosophy, in which I read a lot as an amateur. I have no real grip in any serious sense on science, and I wish I had at least some grip on the philosophy of science. This could go on endlessly; who isn't dissatisfied with himself? I do know something about music, and if I had my life to live over again, really from scratch, I think I would be a musician. I think I'd like to have been a pianist and a conductor.

CA: Do you use music to relax from your writing?

KAUFFMANN: No, I use music to tauten my writing. Music infiltrates my whole life, and I flatter myself—I hope not too foolishly—that things I hear in music affect my writing beneficially, in a rhythmic sense—even, one might say, in a melic sense.

CA: You were writing successfully as a very young man. Where did the ambition come from?

KAUFFMANN: That's difficult to say. Probably these things begin with emulation. My father wasn't a writer, he was a dentist, but he did a lot of writing for professional journals, so I was around a sort of writing all the time. I began to read very early, thanks to my mother, who taught me some reading before I went to school. I was in the atmosphere of words very early on.

CA: Was the writing encouraged at home?

KAUFFMANN: Very much so. Not professionally, of course, because no one thought of that in the beginning, but certainly to do it, to write, yes.

CA: Back in the 1960s you wrote, "The Film Generation can help make the foreseeable future of film interesting and important. Let us see." Do you think that's happening?

KAUFFMANN: No, I think at the present moment the film situation in this country, and in a relative degree throughout the world, is quite shadowy. One of the strong reasons is that the economics of film is always closely tied to large sums of money, and the costs are increasing. *Profits* are increasing, but the very fact that profits are increasing on the successes makes the chances more difficult for films that may not have huge success. Money is a strangulating factor for the present film situation in this country, because of both the great losses and the great successes.

There's also the fact that, in my view, film education in this country has been misguided, has been partial instead of holistic. I'm making broad statements here, speaking in generalities, but American film education has tended to turn out technological experts with nothing much in themselves to make films *about*. The difference between this country and Europe is not black and white, not by any means, but the film schools of Europe tend to turn out more generally cultivated graduates.

CA: You observed filmmaking abroad for several months in 1964. Did you observe anything on that trip that has since had some significant effect on movies?

KAUFFMANN: I saw the beginnings of some young talents, and some that were coming along were pointed out to me in various countries that I visited. I learned something about intrinsic conditions of filmmaking in a number of countries in both Eastern Europe and Western Europe, and I got some smell of the universality of problems—that was one of the most interesting things I learned in those months. For example, I had assumed that the difference between Eastern European filmmaking and Western filmmaking was the difference between capitalism and communism. That was not true. The difference between them is more a matter of detail—both sectors are interested primarily in success and operate to that end, generally. There's not the blitheness about profits in the East that I thought there would be.

That's the gloomy side of it. The other side of it is that I saw in Eastern Europe and in Western Europe a kind of film education that was really marvelous. The best-integrated film schools are in Europe, and there is more connection between those schools and the profession there than there is here. One sees the fruit of this: there are still European films by new people coming along to some degree even in this strangulating economy. I've just had a notice from the French film office in New York that there's going to be a showing at the Museum of Modern Art in New York of a dozen films by new people which can't get commercial release for here.

CA: Is that quite a problem?

KAUFFMANN: Yes, that's a problem for all filmmakers throughout the world. It's roughly equivalent with writing a symphony and not being able to get it performed. There is, I ought to add—I get angry letters about this every once in a while—a whole other terrain of filmmaking in this country and

elsewhere: the independent filmmakers who usually work in nonfiction, documentary form. It's a highly active field, and those filmmakers are not looking, for the most part, for conventional theater release. But they have a very difficult time getting their films shown. There are filmmakers who make films and then pack them in suitcases and travel around the country from campus to campus and show them, or have to find specialized means of distribution. Occasionally one such film will break through to national attention. You may have seen a film called *Best Boy* that won an Academy Award last year. A year or two before that there was one called *Harlan County, U.S.A.* That was made by Barbara Kopple, a young woman who was determined to make her film. There was a fiction film by a young woman named Claudia Weill called *Girlfriends* that was made the same way. It's a whole large area that the public at large doesn't know much about. Just as the public assumes that if you write a book it gets published, so they assume that if you make a film it gets shown.

CA: Do you think there should be subsidies for this kind of filmmaking?

KAUFFMANN: It's very easy for me to say yes, I think so, but it's ridiculous to talk about it in the atmosphere today. This is the only country in the world that provides no kind of subsidy or financial encouragement for filmmaking. Every other country has some way of assisting films. Either they do it through direct grants or through tax remissions or by contributions to the industry or by prizes that are given by the government a year or two after the film has been released if it has not made its cost back. In any case, there is some way of helping the filmmaker substantially.

There's a day-and-night difference in this country, and it cuts down through all the arts. For four years I was on the theater advisory panel of the National Endowment of the Arts. We met five or six times a year and debated how to allot throughout the United States of America a total budget of—at its highest—almost three million dollars. At the same time the city of Hamburg, Germany, was giving its opera house six and a half million dollars a year. That is only one of many examples of the difference in government attitudes toward the arts, here and abroad. To talk about American subsidy for films in any useful way is a joke at the present moment because films have become so expensive that if we asked for help in any way that really made a difference, Congress would just faint.

CA: As film critic for a magazine such as the New Republic, *does one have time to mull over a film in his mind before writing a review, or is there more pressure?*

KAUFFMANN: There's usually plenty of time. For me, plenty of time is a couple of days, though often it's longer; it depends on when I see the film in relation to when I'm going to write about it. Sometimes I have a week or two weeks. I don't like to wait too long because then details become fuzzy. Anyway, when I see a film that is of some texture and depth, I almost always try to see it again before I write about it. I wouldn't dream of reviewing, let us say, an Ingmar Bergman film on one viewing. You've only got to see a really interesting film a second time to be scared by the thought that you might have written about it on one viewing. It frightens you to see what you've missed.

CA: Do you ever see a film or play you find difficult to write about?

KAUFFMANN: Yes. That's particularly true in the theater, where there is a kind of art growing called "performance art," which doesn't deal with plays and scripts in the conventional sense. They do theater pieces, more than plays, which really don't deal much in traditional structures or characters, that are really, one could say roughly, attempts to incorporate the modes of ballet and painting into the theater. Some of the people who work that way are Richard Foreman and Robert Wilson. Their work is extremely difficult for me to write about with any helpfulness because the vocabulary of dramatic criticism doesn't really accommodate it in a useful way. One has, if one can, almost to evolve a separate aesthetic for each one of these art forms.

There's a production in New York now, for example, by Richard Foreman, called *Penguin Touquet*. I don't think I'm going to review it because the *Saturday Review* has given me limited space and there are other things I must write about. But if I had to review it I would really have my work cut out for me. Most of the reviewing of such a piece, for me, turns out to be description with some pretense at comment thereafter. The reader has no way of telling what you're talking about, no reference points, unless you describe the thing in considerable detail.

CA: What do you consider the weaknesses in film and drama criticism?

KAUFFMANN: The chief thing that's wrong, I think, is that it's still generally thought that anyone who can write can do film or theater criticism. We have plenty of instances in both fields of people who write reasonably well who are doing such criticism and who are really betraying to me—and I'm glad to say to a few others—that they have neither the informational foundation nor the quality of perception the critic needs; and more, if I may put it this way, the moral rigor—a commitment to the art, a passion to see it improve, a disregard for any kind of popularity.

CA: What is your current opinion on film festivals?

KAUFFMANN: Unchanged. I wrote my first piece on the subject in 1965, and nothing in the last sixteen years has changed my opinion. What I've seen is mainly the New York Film Festival—though I have been to three or four others. I have no wish to travel to film festivals any more. I've seen through the years at the New York Film Festival a number of films that I would not have seen otherwise, and I'm very grateful for that. On the other hand, my opinion on the form of film festivals and the hoopla about them is unchanged. They give the false impression that they are dealing adequately with international production, and they do it in a jam-packed way that makes seeing film a marathon instead of a pleasure. I said then and I say again that there should be—as I believe there still is in Sweden—a way of importing foreign films under bond so they don't have to pass customs and no import duty has to be paid, which is possible if they're going to be shown only in selected club situations to members. It would take some time, but it wouldn't be hard to set up around this country a thousand such cinema clubs at universities. Films could be imported to be shown all year long at those places. There could be in the course of a year more than a hundred films from abroad shown in that way, and it wouldn't impair the commercial possibilities of those films, if they had any, because they would not have been reviewed and would not have been shown for profit.

CA: In your years of writing criticism you've followed a number of actors whose early work you thought promising. Have any of them notably fulfilled that promise?

KAUFFMANN: Not yet, no. The trouble with both film and the theater is that almost all the ingrained factors militate against seriously pursuing an acting career. I can think of one exception to that, Meryl Streep, who comes from the Yale School of Drama, where I teach (though I was not her teacher). She seems to be holding to a fairly rigorous line, doing good films when she can get them and trying to do good things in the theater. There are other people whose efforts I admire, like Christopher Walken and James Earl Jones, but nothing has yet come to a point where I can feel that anyone of that generation is fulfilling his promise. Jane Fonda—I was one of the first ones to take her seriously and was hooted at for it—seems to me to be fiddling around.

CA: In Albums of Early Life *you wrote about your work as an editor of comic books and about the brief period in 1954 when you became "Terry Kirk" long enough to write a Western. Is there anything different from your present life that you'd like to try?*

KAUFFMANN: If I had the chance, I'd like to direct a play or two again. I occasionally get an offer to do a little acting, but I haven't been able to do so because of the pressures of my work. As it happens, I did a reading last night from *Albums of Early Life* at a theater club in New York, and someone there suggested I do a part in a play there, which I would like to do but don't have time. And—this is pure fantasy—I think that in the right circumstances and with the right material, I wouldn't be a bad film director—but there's no point in thinking about that. I'm not a frustrated film director. I'm not abnormally frustrated in my present life; I'm doing a lot of things that I really enjoy and that are worthwhile. I have five jobs. I teach at the Yale School of Drama two days a week; I go up on Thursday and come back on Friday. I teach on Monday afternoons in the theater department of the City University Graduate Center in New York. I write a weekly film article for the *New Republic* and a monthly theater article for *Saturday Review*, and I do a bimonthly article, usually on television actors, for the *Dial*, a good new magazine sponsored by public-television stations.

CA: Do you feel at all optimistic about the future of the arts?

KAUFFMANN: Having said so many gloomy things about the prospects of film and having *not* said some almost equally gloomy things that I might have said about the current state of playwriting, I ought to say that I think some art in this country is thriving. Poetry in this country is very good, there's some good fiction being written, and, as far as I can tell, some good painting. My wife, who is a ballet enthusiast, tells me there's some wonderful dancing. So it's not a philistine desert.

BIOGRAPHICAL/CRITICAL SOURCES: New York Times Book Review, February 25, 1945, September 12, 1954, May 15, 1966, December 17, 1972, June 20, 1976, July 6, 1980, November 16, 1980; *Harper's,* November, 1965; *Newsweek,* December 20, 1965; *Prompt,* Number 12, 1968; *New York Review of Books,* March 22, 1973; *Books and Bookmen,* April, 1973; *Book World,* April 27, 1980; *Los Angeles Times Book Review,* August 3, 1980; *Los Angeles Times,* September 23, 1980; *New York Times,* October 9, 1980; Stanley Kauffmann, *Albums of Early Life,* Ticknor & Fields, 1980.

—Interview by Jean W. Ross

*   *   *

KAUPER, Paul Gerhardt   1907-1974

PERSONAL: Born November 9, 1907, in Richmond, Ind.; died

May 22, 1974, in Ann Arbor, Mich.; son of Frederick John (a cabinetmaker) and Mary (Tubesing) Kauper; married Anna Nicklas, September 22, 1934; children: Thomas Eugene, Carolyn Ann. *Education:* Earlham College, A.B., 1929; University of Michigan, J.D., 1932. *Religion:* Lutheran. *Home:* 1702 Shadford Rd., Ann Arbor, Mich. *Office:* Law School, University of Michigan, Ann Arbor, Mich. 48104.

CAREER: Admitted to Bar of New York State, 1936; White & Case, New York, N.Y., attorney, 1934-36; University of Michigan, Law School, Ann Arbor, assistant professor, 1936-39, associate professor, 1939-46, professor of law, 1946-65, Henry M. Butzel Professor of Law, 1965-74, Henry Russell Lecturer, 1971. Member of legal department, Pan American Petroleum & Transport Co., 1942-45. Visiting professor, Max Planck Institute, Heidelberg, Germany, 1959, 1966; Rosenstiel Distinguished Visiting Professor, University of Arizona, 1971. Member of Ann Arbor Charter Revision Commission, 1953, Ann Arbor Planning Commission, 1956-59, and Board of College Education, American Lutheran Church, 1960-66. *Member:* American Bar Association, Michigan Bar Association, Order of the Coif (president, 1965-67; member of executive committee, 1968-70), Tau Kappa Alpha. *Awards, honors:* Ross Essay Prize from American Bar Association, 1951; LL.D. from Capital University, 1956, Earlham College, 1958, Valparaiso University, 1959, and Texas Lutheran College, 1965; University of Michigan faculty achievement award, 1959; J.D. honoris causa from Heidelberg University, 1970.

WRITINGS: (Editor) *Constitutional Law: Cases and Materials,* Prentice-Hall, 1954, 5th edition (with Francis Beytagh), Little, Brown, 1980; *Frontiers of Constitutional Liberty,* Law School, University of Michigan, 1956, reprinted, Da Capo Press, 1971; (contributor) E. Walter, editor, *Religion and the State University,* University of Michigan Press, 1958; (with E. B. Stason) *Cases on Municipal Corporations,* West Publishing, 1959; *Civil Liberties and the Constitution,* University of Michigan Press, 1962, reprinted, Greenwood Press, 1980; *Religion and the Constitution,* Louisiana State University Press, 1964; (with Everett McKinley Dirksen and others) *The Article V Convention Process: A Symposium,* Da Capo Press, 1971.

Author of monographs, including: *The State Constitution: Its Nature and Purpose,* Citizens Research Council of Michigan (Detroit), 1961; *Comparative Constitutional Law Seminar,* Law School, University of Michigan, 1961; (compiler) *Tests of Constitutions,* Law School, University of Michigan, 1964; *The Supreme Court: Hybrid Organ of State* (Robert G. Storey Lecture), School of Law, Southern Methodist University, 1967; *Government and Religion: The Search for Absolutes* (Henry Russell Lecture), University of Michigan, 1971; *The Higher Law and the Rights of Man in a Revolutionary Society,* American Enterprise Institute for Public Policy Research, 1974. Contributor to law reviews and other journals.

AVOCATIONAL INTERESTS: Gardening, reading.

OBITUARIES: New York Times, May 23, 1974.†

*   *   *

KAVAN, Anna   1901-1968
(Helen Ferguson)

PERSONAL: Original name, Helen Woods; name changed by deed poll; born 1901, in Cannes, A-M, France; died December 5, 1968, in London, England; daughter of C.C.E. and Helen (Bright) Woods; first husband, Donald Ferguson; second husband, Stuart Edmonds; children: (first marriage) one son (deceased). *Education:* Attended church school (Church of En-

gland); privately educated. *Home:* 19a Hillsleigh Rd., London W.8, England.

CAREER: Writer.

WRITINGS—Novels; under name Helen Ferguson, except as indicated: *A Charmed Circle,* J. Cape, 1929; *The Dark Sisters,* J. Cape, 1930; *Let Me Alone,* J. Cape, 1930, reprinted under name Anna Kavan, P. Owen, 1979; *A Stranger Still,* John Lane, 1935; *Goose Cross,* John Lane, 1936; *Rich Get Rich,* John Lane, 1937.

Under name Anna Kavan: *Change the Name,* J. Cape, 1941; *The House of Sleep,* Doubleday, 1947 (published in England as *Sleep Has His House,* Cassell, 1948, reprinted, Michael Kesend, 1980); *A Scarcity of Love,* Angus Downie, 1956, reprinted, McGraw, 1974; *Eagles' Nest,* P. Owen, 1957; *Who Are You?,* Scorpion Press, 1963, P. Owen, 1975; *Ice,* P. Owen, 1967, Doubleday, 1970.

Short stories: *Asylum Piece and Other Stories,* J. Cape, 1940, Doubleday, 1946, reprinted, Michael Kesend, 1980; *I Am Lazarus,* J. Cape, 1945, reprinted, P. Owen, 1978; *A Bright Green Field and Other Stories,* P. Owen, 1958; *Julia and the Bazooka and Other Stories,* P. Owen, 1970, Knopf, 1975; *My Soul in China: A Novella and Stories,* P. Owen, 1975.

Also author, with K. T. Bluth, of *The Horse's Tale,* Gaberbocchus, 1949. Contributor of short stories to periodicals.

SIDELIGHTS: Anna Kavan took her name from the fictional heroine of her novel *Let Me Alone.* In the *New Statesman,* Stanley Reynolds comments that this renaming was "rather as if Dickens had changed his name by deed poll to David Copperfield." Reynolds points out that the decision to adopt this particular name "is even more interesting when you consider that Kavan is not the heroine's original surname but the name of the hated and despised husband of the novel."

In the 1920s and 1930s Kavan wrote conventional romantic novels under her first married name, Helen Ferguson. These novels reflect the comfort she felt in her Chilterns home, where she took great satisfaction in breeding bulldogs. Her marriage to her second husband, a moderately rich painter, was also surrounded in comfort. Nothing about her life at this point indicated what was to come: mental breakdowns, drugs, compulsions to suicide, and desperate attempts at withdrawal from drug addiction.

As a child Kavan traveled extensively with her wealthy, emotionally cold mother, with whom she maintained a love-hate relationship all her life. This relationship generated a rage which frequently surfaced in her writings. In a short story, "A World of Heroes," she wrote: "What could have been done to make me afraid to grow up out of such a childhood? Later on, I saw things in proportion, I was always afraid of falling back into that ghastly black isolation of an uncomprehending, solitary, oversensitive child."

After her second marriage failed and ended, like the first, in divorce, Kavan entered a Swiss clinic where she received treatment for mental disorders. She recorded her experiences at the clinic and published them as a series of sketches entitled *Asylum Piece,* her first book to bear the name Anna Kavan. In an article in *Books and Bookmen,* Rhys Davies calls *Asylum Piece* "extraordinarily moving and original." He also notes that Kavan's next novel, *Change the Name,* contains traces of the Ferguson style, indicating that "the metamorphosis [of Ferguson to Kavan] was not yet complete."

Davies's friendship with Kavan began when she was Helen Ferguson. They had lost touch with each other for three or four years, so Davies knew nothing of Kavan's stay in two mental hospitals or of her drug addiction. At their first meeting after these years, he failed to recognize his friend: ''This spectral woman, attenuated of body and face, a former abundance of auburn hair shorn and changed to metallic gold, thinned hands restless, was so different that my own need to readjust to her was a strain.''

Like Davies, several of Kavan's friends, familiar only with the affable Helen Ferguson, found it difficult to accept this transformed woman. Her drug addiction created a capriciousness that was unpleasant to experience. She wanted isolation yet at the same time expected attention from a select few. In shunning her past identity, Kavan callously rejected many people connected to it. This need for isolation and retreat from a threatening world appears consistently as a theme in much of Kavan's work.

A registered addict for nearly thirty years, Kavan found escape through heroin. She suffered from acute depression and attempted suicide twice. Davies believes that the heroin acted as a preservative of both sanity and physical energy for Kavan. In addition to writing novels and numerous short stories, she purchased and renovated old houses on Campden Hill and did editorial work for a literary magazine. She also designed and presided over the building of the modernistic house in which she spent the last twelve years of her life.

When British authorities imposed new and tighter regulations on drug addicts, Kavan was forced to attend regularly scheduled sessions which she considered to be disciplinary punishment, but she attended them out of fear that the National Health Service workers would hold back her drug supply. This reinforced her idea of the inimical world she often described in her novels. Davies remarks that in spite of this, Kavan always returned to the ''valid discipline'' of her stories and that ''their clarity of style, their spurning of sensationalism, and their own code of logic were another justification of her vision.''

Kavan died with a loaded syringe in her hand. Her usual shot of heroin had not obliterated the final moments. Jill Robinson, in an article in the *New York Times Book Review*, comments: ''The facts of one's difficult existence do not guarantee literature. Anna Kavan is not interesting because she was a woman, an addict or had silver blond hair. She is interesting because her work comes through with a powerful androgynous individuality and because the stories are luminous and rich with a fresh kind of peril. She knows how to pull us into her world, her dreams and nightmares—how to have all of it become ours.''

BIOGRAPHICAL/CRITICAL SOURCES: Times Literary Supplement, September 14, 1967, March 12, 1970, February 5, 1971, June 14, 1974; Anna Kavan, *Ice*, introduction by Brian W. Aldiss, Doubleday, 1970; *Listener*, March 12, 1970; *Observer Review*, January 17, 1971; *Books and Bookmen*, March, 1971, June, 1978; *New Statesman*, January 11, 1974, March 28, 1975; Kavan, *Julia and the Bazooka*, edited and with an introduction by Rhys Davies, Knopf, 1975; *New York Times Book Review*, May 11, 1975; *Spectator*, January 31, 1976.

OBITUARIES: London Times, December 6, 1968; *New York Times*, December 7, 1968.†

—*Sketch by Debra G. Jones*

*   *   *

KAY, Ellen
See DeMILLE, Nelson

KAY, Ernest 1915-
(George Ludlow, Alan Random)

PERSONAL: Born June 21, 1915, in Darwen, Lancashire, England; son of Harold (a mill manager) and Florence (Woodall) Kay; married Marjorie Peover (a journalist), August 11, 1942; children: John Michael, Richard Andrew, Belinda Jean. *Politics:* Labour. *Religion:* Quaker. *Home:* 11 Madingley Rd., Cambridge CB3 OEG, England. *Agent:* David Higham Associates Ltd., 5-8 Lower John St., London W1R 4HA, England. *Office:* International Biographical Center, Cambridge CB2 3QP, England.

CAREER: Journalist, 1933-66; *Evening News*, London, England, managing editor, 1955-58; *John O'London's* (weekly), London, editor, 1959-62; *Time and Tide* (news magazine), London, managing editor, 1962-66; International Biographical Center, Cambridge, England, and New York, N.Y., founder and director general, 1967— . *Member:* Royal Society of Arts, Royal Geographical Society, Community of European Writers.

WRITINGS: Great Men of Yorkshire, Bodley Head, 1956; *Isles of Flowers: The Story of the Isles of Scilly*, Redman, 1956, 2nd edition, 1963; *Pragmatic Premier: An Intimate Portrait of Harold Wilson*, Frewin, 1967; (compiler) *The Wit of Harold Wilson*, Frewin, 1967; (editor) *Two Thousand Women of Achievement*, Dartmouth, 1969; (editor) *International Who's Who in Poetry*, 2nd edition, Melrose Press, 1970, 5th edition, 1978; (editor) *Dictionary of Latin American and Caribbean Biography*, 2nd edition, Melrose Press, 1971; (editor) *Dictionary of Scandinavian Biography*, Melrose Press, 1972; (editor) *Two Thousand Men of Achievement*, Melrose Press, 1972; (editor) *International Who's Who in Music and Musician's Directory*, 7th edition, Melrose Press, 1975; (with Katherine Kay) *Walk Along Offa's Dyke*, Spurbooks, 1977. Also editor of other biographical reference books. Contributor of articles to newspapers and magazines.

WORK IN PROGRESS: A humorous book, *A Limey in Manhattan*.

*   *   *

KAY, Kenneth (Edmond) 1915-

PERSONAL: Born February 12, 1915, in Atlanta, Ga.; son of Kenneth Edmond and Dorothy (Bennett) Kay; married Phyllis Charline Bockhold, March 31, 1953; children: Nancy, Elizabeth, Alice, Ariane, Kenneth. *Education:* Attended Young Harris Junior College, 1932-34, and Northwestern University, 1938-39; University of Denver, B.A., 1952; graduate study at Old Dominion University and University of South Florida. *Address:* 10238 Valle Dr., Tampa, Fla. 33612. *Agent:* Clyde Taylor, Curtis Brown Ltd., 575 Madison Ave., New York, N.Y. 10022. *Office:* Department of English, University of South Florida, Tampa, Fla. 33620.

CAREER: Great American Insurance Co., 1934-41, 1946-47, began as mail clerk, became special agent in Chicago, Ill., then in Nashville, Tenn.; U.S. Army, 1941-45, became major; U.S. Air Force, career officer, 1947-66, became lieutenant colonel; University of South Florida, Tampa, adjunct professor of English, 1969— . During World War II served in India and China; later served as exchange officer with Royal Air Force in England and as staff officer of U.S. European Command in Paris, France. *Member:* Toastmasters International (chapter president, 1963), Authors League of America. *Awards, honors*—Military: Distinguished Unit Emblem, Commendation

Ribbon, Asiatic-Pacific Campaign Medal with two battle stars; winner of annual U.S. Air Force short story contest, 1954 and 1956. Civilian: *Porgie* bronze medal, 1980, for *Disposable People.*

WRITINGS: *Trouble in the Air* (novel), Eyre & Spottiswoode, 1959; (with Marshall Goldberg) *The Chengtu Strain* (novel), Pinnacle Books, 1976; (with wife, Phyllis Charline Bockhold Kay) *The Magic Dolls* (novel), Valkyrie Press, 1977. Also author, with Goldberg, of *Disposable People.* Contributor of articles and short stories to periodicals, including *Writer, Saturday Evening Post, Country Gentlemen, Argosy, Jing Bao Journal,* and *Floridian.*

WORK IN PROGRESS: *The Man Who Must Not Die,* with Marshall Goldberg, for Tower.

MEDIA ADAPTATIONS: Kenneth Kay's stories "Ballad of Jubal Pickett," "Mechanical Cook," and "Fair Young Ghost" were adapted for television.

*   *   *

KEESING, Nancy (Florence) 1923-

PERSONAL: Born September 7, 1923, in Sydney, New South Wales, Australia; daughter of Gordon Samuel (an architect) and Margery Louise (Hart) Keesing; married A. M. Hertzberg, February 2, 1955; children: Margery, John. *Education:* University of Sydney, Diploma of Social Studies. *Religion:* Jewish. *Home:* 3 Garrick Ave., Hunter's Hill, New South Wales NSW 2110, Australia.

CAREER: Writer. Clerk for Department of Navy, Sydney, Australia, 1942-45; social worker, Royal Alexandra Hospital for Children, Sydney, 1947-51. Member of literature board of Australia Council, 1973-74; member of board of governors of Winifred West Schools Ltd., 1973—. Member of council, Kuring-gai College of Advanced Education. *Member:* English Association (vice-president of Sydney branch, 1979—), Australian Society of Authors (executive member; member of management committee, 1969-73). *Awards, honors:* Order of Australia.

WRITINGS—Published by Angus & Robertson, except as indicated: *Imminent Summer* (poetry), Lyre-Bird Writers, 1951; *Three Men and Sydney* (poetry), 1955; (editor with Douglas Stewart) *Australian Bush Ballads,* 1955; (editor with Stewart) *Old Bush Songs and Rhymes of Colonial Times,* 1957; (editor) *Australian Poetry, 1959,* 1959.

By Gravel and Gum: The Story of a Pioneer Family (juvenile), Macmillan, 1963; *Douglas Stewart,* Lansdowne Press, 1965, revised edition, Oxford University Press, 1969; (author of commentary) *Elsie Carew: Australian Primitive Poet,* Wentworth, 1965; (editor with Stewart) *The Pacific Book of Bush Ballads,* 1967, published as *Bush Songs, Ballads and Other Verses,* Discovery Books, 1968, revised edition published as *Favourite Bush Ballads,* 1977; (editor and author of introduction, notes, and commentary) *Gold Fever: The Australian Goldfields 1851 to 1890s* (anthology), 1967, published as *A History of the Australian Gold Rushes,* 1976; *Showground Sketchbook and Other Poems,* 1968.

(Editor) *Transition* (anthology), 1971; *The Golden Dream* (juvenile), Collins, 1974; *The Kelly Gang,* Ure Smith, 1975; (editor) *Australian Post-War Novelists,* Jacaranda, 1975; *Garden Island People,* Wentworth, 1975; *The White Chrysanthemum,* 1977; (editor) *Henry Lawson: Favourite Verse,* Thomas Nelson, 1978; (editor) *Shalom,* Collins, 1978; *John Lang and 'The Forger's Wife,'* John Ferguson, 1970.

Work represented in numerous anthologies, including: *Australia Writes,* F. W. Cheshire, 1953; *Australian Signpost,* F. W. Cheshire, 1956; *A Book of Australian Verse,* Oxford University Press, 1956; *Australian Poets Speak,* Adelaide, 1961; *Poetry in Australia II,* Angus & Robertson, 1964; *Songs for All Seasons,* Angus & Robertson 1967; *A Map of Australian Verse,* Oxford University Press, 1975; *Australian Verse from 1805,* Rigby, 1976. Contributor to *Bulletin, Southerly, Bridge, Overland,* and other periodicals, and to Australian Broadcasting Commission programs. Editor, *Australian Author,* 1971-73.

WORK IN PROGRESS: A series of short stories; a collection of poems.

SIDELIGHTS: Nancy Keesing told *CA:* "My main interest is poetry. More or less by accident I seem to find myself writing mostly criticism and 'popular' history." *Avocational interests:* Reading, gardening, walking.

*   *   *

KEFFERSTAN, Jean
See PEDRICK, Jean

*   *   *

KELLEY, William 1929-

PERSONAL: Born May 27, 1929, in Staten Island, N.Y.; son of Edward Thomas (a lawyer) and Alethea (a lawyer; maiden name Waldegrave) Kelley; married Cornelia Ann Chamberlin (an artist), September 18, 1954; children: Maura, Shaun. *Education:* Brown University, B.A., 1955; Harvard University, M.A., 1957. *Home address:* P.O. Box 18, Mammoth Lakes, Calif. 93546. *Agent:* Ned Brown, 407 North Maple Dr., Suite 228, Beverly Hills, Calif. 90210. *Office:* 501 South Fuller Ave., Los Angeles, Calif. 90036.

CAREER: Writer. Doubleday & Co., editor in New York City, 1957-58, West Coast editor in San Francisco, Calif., 1958-61; McGraw-Hill Book Co., New York City, editor, 1961-62. *Military service:* U.S. Air Force, 1947-50; became sergeant. *Member:* Phi Beta Kappa, E Clampus Vitus, Harvard Club, Brown Club, California Yacht Club, Mammoth Bucket Brigade, Riviera Country Club (Los Angeles), Los Angeles Athletic Club. *Awards, honors:* Spur Award for best western television script, Western Writers of America, 1975, for "Gunsmoke," and 1978, for "How the West Was Won."

WRITINGS: *Gemini* (novel), Doubleday, 1959; *Miracle in the Evening* (biography of Norman Bel Geddes), Doubleday, 1961; *The God Hunters* (novel), Simon & Schuster, 1964; "The Winds of Kitty Hawk" (screenplay), produced by National Broadcasting Co., 1978; *The Tyree Legend* (novel), Simon & Schuster, 1979. Also author of screenplay "Sitka"; author of scripts for television programs, including "Gunsmoke," "Kung Fu," "How the West Was Won," "Judd for the Defense," and "The McCrackens."

WORK IN PROGRESS: *Bodie,* a novel.

SIDELIGHTS: William Kelley told *CA:* "I've spent the last ten years learning to be a screenwriter because it got impossible to live on what I was making (or figured to make) as a novelist. But the novel is still my central business. I have *Bodie* underway, the next one in rough outline, and at least three more in mind. I live in the mountains in Northern California—Mammoth Lakes, in the high Sierras—and visit Hollywood as infrequently as possible."

KEMELMAN, Harry 1908-

PERSONAL: Born November 24, 1908, in Boston, Mass.; son of Isaac and Dora (Prizer) Kemelman; married Anne Kessin (a medical secretary-technician), March 29, 1936; children: Ruth (Mrs. George Rooks), Arthur Frederick, Diane (Mrs. Murray Rossant). *Education:* Boston University, A.B., 1930; Harvard University, M.A., 1931, additional study, 1932-33. *Politics:* Independent. *Religion:* Jewish. *Home:* 47 Humphrey St., Marblehead, Mass. 01947. *Agent:* Scott Meredith Literary Agency, Inc., 845 Third Ave., New York, N.Y. 10022.

CAREER: Substitute high school teacher, 1935-37; full-time English teacher in Boston and Cambridge, Mass., 1937-41; Northeastern University, Boston, English instructor in evening division, 1938-41; U.S. Army Transportation Corps, Boston Port of Embarkation, Boston, chief wage administrator (civilian), 1942-46; chief job analyst and wage administrator, New England Division, War Assets Administration, 1948-49; operated own business, and did free-lance writing, 1949-63; Franklin Technical Institute, Boston, assistant professor of English, 1963-64; Boston State College, Boston, associate professor of English, 1964-70; full-time writer. *Member:* Authors League of America, Mystery Writers of America. *Awards, honors:* Edgar Award for best first novel, 1965, for *Friday, the Rabbi Slept Late;* Faith and Freedom Communications Award, 1967.

WRITINGS—Novels, except as indicated: *Friday, the Rabbi Slept Late*, Crown, 1964; *Saturday, the Rabbi Went Hungry*, Crown, 1966; *The Nine Mile Walk: The Nicky Welt Stories of Harry Kemelman* (contains "The Nine Mile Walk," "The Straw Man," "The Ten O'Clock Scholar," "End Play," "Time and Time Again," "The Whistling Tea Kettle," "The Bread and Butter Case," and "The Man on the Ladder"), Putnam, 1967; *Sunday, the Rabbi Stayed Home*, Putnam, 1969; *Weekend with the Rabbi*, Doubleday, 1969; *Common Sense in Education* (nonfiction), Crown, 1970; *Monday, the Rabbi Took Off*, Putnam, 1972; *Tuesday, the Rabbi Saw Red*, Author Fields' Books, 1973; *Wednesday, The Rabbi Got Wet*, Morrow, 1976; *Thursday, the Rabbi Walked Out*, Morrow, 1978; *Conversations with Rabbi Small: A Rational Interpretation of Judaism* (nonfiction), Morrow, 1981. Also author of "Nicky Welt" series in *Ellery Queen's Mystery Magazine;* contributor to *Bookman.*

SIDELIGHTS: Harry Kemelman's popular mystery novels had their beginning in the Nicky Welt stories he has long written for *Ellery Queen's Mystery Magazine.* According to a reviewer for the *New York Times Book Review,* Kemelman, who is Jewish, wrote *The Building of the Temple,* a novel about a Jewish community in suburbia, as a change of pace from his usual mystery stories. However, after reading the manuscript, an editor with Crown Publishers suggested that *The Building of the Temple* would appeal to the book buying public only if there were a mystery story involved within the plot. This suggestion resulted in *Friday, the Rabbi Slept Late,* the first in a series of best sellers combining suburban American Judaism, social commentary, and amateur sleuthing.

Anthony Boucher describes *Saturday, the Rabbi Went Hungry* as a perfect example of the novels in the series. He illustrates in a *New York Times Book Review* article that this book is "an excellent formal puzzle; a joyous novel of people and their problems; and a richly illuminating picture of Jewish liturgy and theology which merits a special award for painless ecumenical communication." Boucher explains further in another review also published in the *New York Times Book Review* that Kemelman's "delightful novels . . . are among the very top

best sellers in hard covers in the history of the formal detective story. Their phenomenal sales are probably due less to their excellence as essays in detection than to their warm portrayal of suburban, all-but-assimilated Jewish life." And M. J. Bandor writes in the *Christian Science Monitor* that "Kemelman is quite aware of the issues of the day, and is an avid student of the contemporary scene among youth and in religious circles."

The main character in these detective novels is Rabbi David Small. *New York Times Book Review* critic Newgate Callendar suggests that "Kemelman has created a real character in Rabbi Small. Scholarly stubborn, activated by conscience and the demands of his religion, not warm but definitely an understanding man, David Small is a Talmudic teacher in the best sense of the word. . . . There is nothing namby-pamby about Kemelman's cast. His Jews are presented with warts and all; they are a segment of American society, and some are good, some bad. But their speech patterns are most definitely not those of middle America, and Kemelman's good ear and vivid writing style catches the typical intonations of the middle-class Jew."

In the opinion of several critics, including *Book World*'s Judith Crist, *The Nine Mile Walk* (a collection of Nicky Welt stories) exemplifies some of the best "armchair detection" fiction being written today. She also cautions the reader not to read all eight stories at once, as "you might become attuned to the Professor's brand of logic and find yourself outracing his armchair toward a logical solution. This last is an indirect compliment to Mr. Kemelman, who gives the reader his fair share in facts and clues. For this we honor him—and even more for providing us with the classic cool of a cerebral sleuth." A reviewer for the *New York Times Book Review* agrees with Crist and believes that these stories "are among the brightest gems in the literature of pure armchair detection. Here are all eight of them from the earliest to the latest, longest and most intricate. . . . They reveal that their creator has as nice a perception of New England academic life as he has of suburban Judaism."

MEDIA ADAPTATIONS: The film rights to *Friday, the Rabbi Slept Late* have been purchased, and the novel was the basis of a television series entitled "Lanigan's Rabbi."

BIOGRAPHICAL/CRITICAL SOURCES: New York Times Book Review, July 24, 1966, November 26, 1967, March 19, 1972, September 12, 1976; *New Statesman,* March 24, 1967; *Books and Bookmen,* May, 1967; *Book World,* November 12, 1967, May 25, 1969; *Christian Science Monitor,* January 6, 1968, March 27, 1969; *Show Business,* February 1, 1969; *New York Times,* February 21, 1969; *Best Sellers,* September 1, 1970, March 1, 1972; *Library Journal,* January 1, 1974; *Contemporary Literary Criticism,* Volume I, Gale, 1974; *Fort Lauderdale Sun-Sentinel,* January 20, 1975; *Authors in the News,* Volume I, Gale, 1976.

* * *

KENDALL, Robert 1934-

PERSONAL: Born June 26, 1934; son of William Austin and Valla Eunice (Bentley) Kendall. *Education:* Attended Emanuel Missionary College, Berrien Springs, Mich., 1952, La Sierra College, 1953-54, and University of Southern California, 1956; Los Angeles State College (now California State University, Los Angeles), B.A., 1959, and graduate study; University of California, Los Angeles, graduate study.

CAREER: Actor and writer. Made film debut at thirteen as elephant boy in "Song of Scheherazade," 1947; other motion picture appearances include "Casbah" (Universal International), 1949, "Benny Goodman Story," 1953, "The Ten Commandments," 1956, "Women of Pitcairn," 1958, "Guns Don't Argue," 1959, "Ma Barker's Killer Brood," 1960, and "Boy from Thailand," 1961. Has made television appearances on "Ford Hour," "Twentieth Century-Fox Hour," "Gangbusters" series, and "Casablanca" series. Lecturer on juvenile delinquency at more than one hundred churches in forty cities, using Gospel Films picture, "Betrayed," in which he plays the lead. *Member:* Screen Actors Guild, Writers Guild, Young Men's Christian Association, Desert Highlands Club.

WRITINGS: White Teacher in a Black School, Devin-Adair, 1964 (published in England as *Never Say Nigger,* Universal-Tandem Publishing Co., 1960); *The Girl from Panama,* Venice Poetry (Beverly Hills), 1973; *Her Dream Came True,* Dove-Hill Press, 1977; *The Golden Locket,* Dove-Hill Press, 1977; *Castles in the Sand,* Carousel, 1981.

WORK IN PROGRESS: A screenplay for Dimitrios Films, "UFOs around the World," and a book, *The Last Rites,* both with William Hare.

*   *   *

KENDALL, Willmoore 1909-1967
(Alan Monk)

PERSONAL: Born March 5, 1909, in Konawa, Okla.; died, 1967; son of Willmoore (minister) and Pearl A. (Garlick) Kendall. *Education:* University of Oklahoma, B.A., 1927; Northwestern University, M.A., 1928; Oxford University, B.A., 1935, M.A., 1938; University of Illinois, Ph.D., 1941. *Religion:* Catholic. *Home:* 2119 West Irving Blvd., Irving, Tex.

CAREER: United Press, Madrid, Spain, foreign correspondent, 1935-36; Louisiana State University, Baton Rouge, instructor in government, 1937-40; Hobart College, Geneva, N.Y., assistant professor of political science, 1940-41; Yale University, New Haven, Conn., associate professor of political science, 1947-60; Johns Hopkins University, Operations Research Office, Bethesa, Md., project chairman, psychological warfare, 1950-54; *National Review,* New York, N.Y., senior editor, beginning 1955. Visiting professor of government, Stanford University, 1958-59, Georgetown University, 1961-62, Los Angeles State College of Applied Arts and Sciences (now California State University, Los Angeles), 1962-63; chairman of the department of politics and economics, University of Dallas, beginning 1963. *Military service:* U.S. Air Force; became lieutenant colonel. *Member:* American Political Science Association, Southern Political Science Association, Greater Los Angeles Press Club. *Awards, honors:* Rhodes scholarship; Guggenheim fellowship.

WRITINGS: John Locke and the Doctrine of Majority-Rule, University of Illinois Press, 1941; (with Austin Ranney) *Democracy and the American Party System,* Harcourt, 1955, reprinted, Greenwood Press, 1974; (with the editors of *National Review) The Committee and Its Critics,* Putnam, 1962; *The Conservative Affirmation,* Regnery, 1963; (with George W. Carey) *Liberalism versus Conservatism,* Van Nostrand, 1966; (with Carey) *The Basic Symbols of the American Political Tradition,* Louisiana State University Press, 1970; *Willmoore Kendall Contra Mundum* (addresses, essays, and lectures), edited by Nellie D. Kendall, Arlington House, 1971; (translator) Jean-Jacques Rousseau, *The Government of Poland,* Bobbs-Merrill, 1977; (translator) Rousseau, *The Social Contract,* Regnery, 1977. Also author, with Frederick D. Wilhelmsen, of *Cicero and the Politics of the Public Orthodoxy,* 1965.

WORK IN PROGRESS: Doctrine and Strategy for an American Conservative Movement; The Bill of Rights.†

*   *   *

KENNAMER, Lorrin, Jr. 1924-

PERSONAL: Born December 20, 1924, in Abilene, Tex.; son of L. G. (a professor) and Ruie (Hart) Kennamer; married Laura Durham (an administrative secretary), December 22, 1948. *Education:* Attended University of Notre Dame and George Pepperdine College (now Pepperdine University); Eastern Kentucky State College (now Eastern Kentucky University), A.B., 1947; University of Tennessee, M.S., 1948; George Peabody College (now George Peabody College for Teachers of Vanderbilt University), Ph.D., 1952. *Religion:* Unitarian Universalist. *Home:* 2704 San Pedro No. 9, Austin, Tex. 78705. *Office:* Department of Geography, University of Texas at Austin, Austin, Tex. 78712.

CAREER: Oak Ridge High School, Oak Ridge, Tenn., social studies and mathematics teacher, 1947-49; East Texas State College (now University), Commerce, instructor, 1952-53, assistant professor, 1953-54, associate professor of geography and geology and chairman of department, 1954-56; University of Texas at Austin, assistant professor, 1956-58, associate professor, 1958-63, professor of geography and chairman of department, 1963-67, associate dean of College of Arts and Sciences, 1960-67; Texas Tech University, Lubbock, professor of geography and dean of College of Arts and Sciences, 1967-70; University of Texas at Austin, professor of geography and dean of College of Education, 1970—. Visiting professor, summers, George Peabody College (now George Peabody College for Teachers of Vanderbilt University), 1956, University of Vermont, 1958, Michigan State University, 1960, and University of Washington, 1967; visiting geographical scientist under the auspices of National Science Foundation and Association of American Geographers, spring, 1968, 1969, and 1970. College Entrance Examination Board, chairman of committee on examinations, 1964-72, member of college-level examination program committee, 1966-72, member of board of trustees, 1970-78, vice-chairman, 1972-74, chairman, 1974-76; chairman, Commission on Cooperation in Higher Education, Association of Texas Colleges and Universities, 1969-74; member of Texas Commission on the Arts and Humanities, 1971-78. Member of social science panel, *World Book Encyclopedia,* 1966-70, and educational advisory board, Hammond Corp., 1967-71; consultant to Texas Education Agency, U.S. Office of Education, Coronet Instructional Films, Computer Image Corp., Kuwait Ministry of Education, and local school boards. *Military service:* U.S. Naval Reserve, 1943-46; served in Pacific Theater; became lieutenant (junior grade).

MEMBER: National Council for Geographic Education (secretary, 1959-64; president, 1967), National Council for the Social Studies, National Association of Deans of Education of State Universities and Land-Grant Universities, Association of American Geographers (chairman of committee on careers in geography, 1961-62), Southwestern Social Science Association (president, 1972-73), Texas Council for Social Studies, Texas Academy of Science (secretary and treasurer, 1958-60), Pi Gamma Mu, Sigma Xi, Phi Kappa Phi, Phi Delta Kappa, Gamma Theta Upsilon, Kappa Delta Pi, Omicron Delta Kappa. *Awards, honors:* Teaching Excellence Award, University of Texas at Austin, 1964; Distinguished Service Award, George Peabody College, 1971, and National Council for Geographic Education, 1972; Distinguished Alumni Award, Eastern Kentucky University, 1974.

WRITINGS: (Coauthor) *Texas Resources and Industries,* Bureau of Business Research, University of Texas, 1958; (with Hoffman and Bowden) *Geography Worktext Series* (four paperbacks), Steck, 1960, revised edition, 1965; (with Paul Wishart) *Geography,* Steck, 1962; (with S. A. Arbingast) *Atlas of Texas,* Bureau of Business Research, University of Texas, 1963, revised edition, 1976; *Texans and Their Land,* Steck, 1963; (coauthor) *Life Near and Far,* revised edition, 1965, 4th edition, 1980; (coauthor) *Life in Different Lands,* revised edition, 1965, 4th edition, 1980; (coauthor) *Life in the Americas,* revised edition, 1965, 4th edition, 1980; (coauthor) *Life in Lands Overseas,* revised edition, 1965, 4th edition, 1980; (co-editor) *Geography as a Professional Field,* U.S. Office of Education, 1966; (author of introduction) E. W. Meinig, *Imperial Texas,* University of Texas Press, 1969; (editor) *Lands and Peoples of the World,* Aldus Books, 1969; (editor) *The Planet We Live On,* Aldus Books, 1970; (with James V. Reese) *Texas, Land of Contrast: Its History and Geography,* Benson, 1972; (contributor with Gene Hall) H. Freiberg and R. Olivarez, editors, *Dimensions of Inservice Education,* Teacher Corps., 1978; (author of introduction) *Government and the Humanities,* Lyndon Baines Johnson Library, 1979; (contributor) *Credit by Examination Comes of Age,* College Board, 1980.

Co-editor of "Foundations of World Regional Geography" series, published by Prentice-Hall: *Australia's Corner of the World,* 1970; *Geography of Europe,* 1971; *Geography of Latin America,* 1972; *Oriental Asia,* 1973.

Also author or editor of teaching manuals and maps. Contributor to periodicals, including *Journal of Geography, Southwestern Social Science Quarterly, Social Education, Instructor, Journal of Individual Psychology,* and *Ecumene. Journal of Geography,* associate editor, 1956-67, editorial consultant, 1967-70; member of editorial advisory board, *Social Education,* 1960-64, 1980-83, and *Ecumene,* 1968—; member of editorial policies committee, *Southwestern Social Science Quarterly,* 1976—.

*   *   *

KENNEDY, Gerald (Hamilton) 1907-
(G. Hobab Kish)

PERSONAL: Born August 30, 1907, in Benzonia, Mich.; son of Herbert Grant and Marian (Phelps) Kennedy; married Mary Leeper, June 2, 1928. *Education:* University of the Pacific, B.A., 1929; Pacific School of Religion, M.A., 1931, B.D., 1932; Hartford Theological Seminary, S.T.M., 1933, Ph.D., 1934. *Politics:* Republican. *Home:* 624-C Avenida Sevilla, Laguna Hills, Calif. 92653.

CAREER: Ordained elder in Methodist Church, 1932; pastor in Collinsville, Conn., 1932-36, San Jose, Calif., 1936-40, Palo Alto, Calif., 1940-42, and Lincoln, Neb., 1942-48; elected bishop, Western Jurisdictional Conference of Methodist Church, 1948, assigned to Portland area, 1948-52, and Los Angeles area, beginning 1952. Acting professor of homiletics, Pacific School of Religion, 1938-42, and Southern California School of Theology, beginning 1957; lecturer in religion, Nebraska Wesleyan University, 1942-43; special lecturer at universities and divinity schools, 1946-68, including Peyton Lecturer at Southern Methodist University, 1949, Lyman Beecher Lecturer at Yale University, 1954, Auburn Lecturer at Union Theological Seminary, 1957, and Grey Lecturer at Duke University, 1957. Member of general board, National Council of Churches, beginning 1957; Methodist Church, president of council of bishops, 1960-61, president of General Board of Evangelism, 1964-68. Radio preacher on KFAB and KFRO, Lincoln, Neb.,

1945-58, and KEX, Portland, Ore., 1949; moderator of ABC radio program "Pilgrimage in World of Books," 1954. Member of board of directors, Wesley Foundation, Stanford University, 1940-42, Africultural Aids Foundation, California Western University, Pasadena Playhouse, and Goodwill Industries of Southern California; trustee, Pacific School of Religion, University of the Pacific, and Southern California School of Theology. *Member:* University Club (Pasadena, Calif.). *Awards, honors:* LL.D., College of Puget Sound, 1949, and Ohio Wesleyan University, 1952; Litt.D., Nebraska Wesleyan University, 1950; L.H.D., Beloit College, 1952, and California Western University, 1960; D.D., Pacific School of Religion, 1952, Redlands University, 1954, and Bucknell University, 1959; H.H.D., Bradley University, 1956.

WRITINGS: The Lion and the Lamb, Abingdon, 1950; *If They Be Prophets,* Tidings, 1952; *Heritage and Destiny,* Board of Missions of Methodist Church, 1953; *Who Speaks for God?,* Abingdon, 1954; *God Is Our Strength,* Tidings, 1954; *I Believe,* Abingdon, 1958; *The Methodist Way of Life,* Prentice-Hall, 1958; *The Marks of a Methodist,* Methodist Evangelistic Materials, 1960; *David the King,* Doubleday, 1961; *While I'm on My Feet* (autobiography), Abingdon, 1963; *The Preacher and the New English Bible,* Oxford University Press, 1972; (compiler) *My Third Reader's Notebook,* Abingdon, 1974.

Published by Harper: *His Word through Preaching,* 1947; *Have This Mind,* 1948; (editor) *The Best of Henry Jowett,* 1948; *With Singleness of Heart,* 1951; *Go Inquire of the Lord,* 1952; (compiler) *A Reader's Notebook,* 1953; *God's Good News,* 1955; *The Christian and His America,* 1956; (compiler) *A Second Reader's Notebook,* 1959; *The Parables,* 1960; *For Preachers and Other Sinners,* 1964; *Fresh Every Morning,* 1966; *Seven Worlds of the Minister,* 1968; *For Laymen and Other Martyrs,* 1969.

Also author of script for sound recording "Living in the Faith," Word, Inc., 1973. Contributor to periodicals, including *Pulpit Digest, Pulpit, Together,* and *Christian Century.*

AVOCATIONAL INTERESTS: Sports cars, horseback riding, swimming, golf, professional football and baseball.

BIOGRAPHICAL/CRITICAL SOURCES: Newsweek, March 29, 1955; *Time,* April 11, 1960, May 24, 1964.†

*   *   *

KERN, E. R.
See KERNER, Fred

*   *   *

KERNER, Fred 1921-
(Frohm Fredericks, E. R. Kern, Frederick Kerr, M. N. Thaler)

PERSONAL: Born February 15, 1921, in Montreal, Quebec, Canada; son of Sam and Vera (Goldman) Kerner; married second wife, Sally Dee Stouten, May 18, 1959; children: (first marriage) Jon; (second marriage) David, Diane. *Education:* Sir George Williams University, B.A., 1942. *Home:* 25 Farmview Crescent, Willowdale, Ontario, Canada M2J 1G5. *Office:* 225 Duncan Mill Rd., Don Mills, Ontario, Canada M3B 1Z3.

CAREER: Montreal Gazette, Montreal, Quebec, assistant sports editor, 1942-44; Canadian Press, variously newsman, editor, news executive, in Montreal, Toronto, Ontario, and New York City, 1944-50; Associated Press, New York City, assistant night city editor, 1950-56; Hawthorn Books, Inc., New York

City, editor, 1957-58, president and editor-in-chief, 1965-67; Fawcett Publications, Inc., New York City, editor-in-chief of Crest and Premier Books, 1958-64; Hall House, Inc., Greenwich, Conn., editor, 1963-64; Centaur House Publishers, Inc., New York City, president and editor-in-chief, 1964-75; Fred Kerner Publishing Projects, New York City, managing director, 1968—; Harlequin Books Ltd., Don Mills, Ontario, vice-president and publishing director, 1975—. Publishing director, Book and Educational Division, Reader's Digest Association (Canada), 1969-75. Lecturer at Long Island University, 1968; editor-in-residence at many writers' conferences. Judge, Cobalt National Poetry Contest; trustee, Canadian Authors Association Literary Awards, Benson & Hedges Awards, and Gibson Awards. Chairman, International Affairs Conference for College Editors, 1965; panelist at various conferences. Director, Publitex International Corp., Peter Kent, Inc., Pennorama Crafts, Inc., Diasque Design, Inc., National Mint, Inc., and Personalized Services, Inc. Member of board of governors, Concordia University, Montreal, 1973-77, and Canadian Copyright Institute, 1975—; member of local school boards.

MEMBER: International Platform Association, Canadian Authors Association (founding chairman; president of Montreal branch, 1972-75; vice-president, 1973-80), Organization of Canadian Authors and Publishers (founding member; member of board of governors, 1977—), Canadian Association for the Restoration of Lost Positives (president, 1969—), Mystery Writers of America, Overseas Press Club (chairman of election committee, 1960-64; chairman of library and book-night committee, 1961), Canadian Society of Professional Journalists, Authors Guild, Authors League of America, American Academy of Political and Social Science, American Management Association, Edward R. Murrow Fund (chairman of publisher's committee), Advertising Club of New York, Association of Alumni of Sir George Williams University (president of New York branch, 1959-64; president, 1973-75), Authors' Club (London, England), Toronto Men's Press Club (founding director), Canadian Society (New York), Dutch Treat Club (New York), Deadline Club (New York), Sigma Delta Chi.

WRITINGS—Published by Hawthorn, except as indicated: (With Leonid Kotkin) *Eat, Think, and Be Slender,* 1954, new edition, Wilshire, 1960; (with Walter Germain) *The Magic Power of Your Mind,* 1956; (with Joyce Brothers) *Ten Days to a Successful Memory,* Prentice-Hall, 1957; (editor) *Love Is a Man's Affair,* Fell, 1958; (contributor) Larston Farrar, editor, *Successful Writers and How They Work,* 1958; (contributor) Roy Copperud, editor, *Words on Paper,* 1960; *Stress and Your Heart,* 1961; (contributor) Sigrid Schultz, editor, *The Overseas Press Club Cookbook,* Doubleday, 1962; (under pseudonym Frederick Kerr) *Watch Your Weight Go Down,* Pyramid Publications, 1963; (editor) *A Treasury of Lincoln Quotations,* Doubleday, 1965; (with Germain) *Secrets of Your Supraconscious,* 1965; (with David Goodman) *What's Best for Your Child—and You,* 1966; (with Jesse Reid) *Buy High, Sell Higher!,* 1966; (under pseudonym M. N. Thaler) *It's Fun to Fondue,* Centaur Press, 1968; (with Ion Grumeza) *Nadia,* 1977.

Contributor to *Chambers's Encyclopedia.* Contributor to periodicals, including *Coronet, American, American Weekly, Reporter, Today's Health, Science Digest, Sports Digest, Reader's Digest, Liberty, Best Years, Weight Watchers, Byline, Weekend,* and *True.* Also author of television scripts for Joyce Brothers' program for two years; author of Anita Colby column, and of Enid Haupt column. Editor, *Third Degree.*

WORK IN PROGRESS: Canadian-English usage.

KERR, D(onald) G(ordon) G(rady)   1913-1976

PERSONAL: Born March 29, 1913, in Prince Rupert, British Columbia, Canada; died October 22, 1976; son of Frederick William and Mary Elizabeth (Grady) Kerr; married Roberta Briggs, 1938 (died, 1958); married Martha Elaine Williams, August 26, 1961. *Education:* Attended University of Manitoba, 1930-32; McGill University, B.A. (with honors), 1935; School of International Studies (Geneva), graduate study, 1936-37; University of London, Ph.D., 1937. *Home:* 29 Benson Cres., London, Ontario, Canada N5X 2B1. *Office:* Department of History, University of Western Ontario, London, Ontario, Canada N6A 3K7.

CAREER: Protestant School Board, Montreal, Quebec, teacher at West Hill High School, 1937-43; Mount Alison University, Sackville, New Brunswick, Stiles-Bennett Professor of History and head of department, 1947-58, director of department of extension, 1953-58; University of Western Ontario, London, professor of history, 1958-76, dean of Talbot College, beginning 1965, senior professor of history, Middlesex College, beginning 1966. Member of advisory board of Canadian History Section, New Brunswick Museum, 1948-58, Canadian Social Science Research Council, 1952-55, New Brunswick Historical Site Board, 1954-58, and Nuffield Foundation Selection Committee, beginning 1959. Chairman of Humanities and Social Science Research Council Selection Committee in connection with Canada Council Scholarship, 1958-61, and special advisory committee on the social sciences, Commonwealth Scholarship Committee, 1961-63. *Military service:* Royal Canadian Navy, 1943-47, serving as director of Historical Section, 1944-46, participating in writing *The Naval Service of Canada;* became lieutenant commander. *Member:* Canadian Historical Association (member of council, 1947-51, 1955-58), American Historical Association, Association for Adult Education (member of national council, 1955-58). *Awards, honors:* Sir William Macdonald Scholarship in English and History, 1933; Lieutenant Governor's Silver Medal in History, 1935; Nuffield fellowship, 1952-53; Canada Council grant, 1966-73.

WRITINGS: (With J. A. Gibson) *Sir Edmund Head, a Scholarly Governor,* University of Toronto Press, 1954; (editor) *A Historical Atlas of Canada,* Thomas Nelson, 1961, 3rd revised edition, 1975; (with J. Lewis Robinson and Edgar B. Wesley) *Canadian History in Maps,* Geographical Research Institute (Chicago), 1965; (with Jacob Spel) *The Changing Face of Toronto: A Study in Urban Geography,* Department of Mines and Technical Surveys (Ottawa), 1965; (with R.I.K. Davidson) *Canada: A Visual History,* Thomas Nelson, 1966. Editor of "Canadian History" series (maps), Denoyer Geppert, 1964. Member of advisory board, *Canadian Historical Review,* 1950-52.†

*   *   *

KERR, Frederick
See KERNER, Fred

*   *   *

KETTLE, Arnold   1916-

PERSONAL: Born March 17, 1916, in London, England; son of Charles and Ethel (Barry) Kettle; married Marguerite Gale, January 30, 1946; children: Martin James, Nicholas David. *Education:* Attended Merchant Taylor's School, 1928-34; Pembroke College, Cambridge, B.A., Ph.D. *Politics:* Communist Party of Great Britain. *Home:* Berry Lane Corner, Aspley Guise, Milton Keynes, England. *Office:* Walton Hall, Open University, Milton Keynes MK7 6AA, England.

CAREER: University of Leeds, Leeds, England, senior lecturer in English literature, 1947-67; University of Dar es Salaam, Dar es Salaam, Tanzania, professor of literature, 1967-70; Open University, Milton Keynes, England, professor of literature, 1970—, academic vice-chancellor, beginning 1973. *Military service:* British Army, 1942-46; became captain.

WRITINGS: *An Introduction to the English Novel*, Longmans, Green, Volume I: *To George Eliot*, 1951, published as *Defoe to George Eliot*, Harper, 1960, Volume II: *Henry James to the Present*, 1953, 2nd edition of both volumes, Hutchinson, 1967, Harper, 1968; (contributor) Boris Ford, editor, *The Pelican Guide to English Literature*, Penguin, Volume VI, 1958, Volume VII, 1961; (contributor) D. W. Jefferson, editor, *The Morality of Art: Essays Presented to G. Wilson Knight by His Colleagues and Friends*, Routledge & Kegan Paul, 1959; *Karl Marx, Founder of Modern Communism*, Weidenfeld & Nicolson, 1963, Roy, 1964, revised edition, Weidenfeld & Nicolson, 1968; (editor and contributor) *Shakespeare in a Changing World: Essays*, International Publishers, 1964, reprinted, Folcroft, 1978; *Communism and the Intellectuals*, Lawrence & Wishart, 1965; (editor and author of introduction) Thomas Hardy, *Tess of the d'Urbervilles: A Pure Woman Faithfully Presented*, Harper, 1966; *Hardy the Novelist: A Reconsideration* (W. D. Thomas memorial lecture, given at University College of Swansea, November 28, 1966), University College of Swansea, 1967; (with V. G. Hanes) *Man and the Arts: A Marxist Approach* (articles originally published in *Horizons* [Toronto]; includes "Man and the Arts," by Kettle, and "Frye's Theory of Literature and Marxism," by Hanes), American Institute for Marxist Studies, 1968; (editor) *The Nineteenth-Century Novel: Critical Essays and Documents*, Heinemann, 1972. Contributor to *Encyclopaedia Britannica* and to journals, including *Review of English Studies* and *Marxism Today*.

WORK IN PROGRESS: Research on the nineteenth- and twentieth-century English novel.

* * *

KEVE, Paul W(illard) 1913-

PERSONAL: Born October 5, 1913, in Omaha, Neb.; son of Oliver and Vera (Moore) Keve; married Constance Conway, 1936; children: Anne B., Paula M. *Education:* George Washington University, B.A., 1943; College of William and Mary, M.S., 1947. *Religion:* Presbyterian. *Home:* 3347 Sherbrook Rd., Richmond, Va. 23255. *Office:* Department of Administration of Justice, Virginia Commonwealth University, Richmond, Va. 23284.

CAREER: National Training School for Boys, Washington, D.C., shop instructor, 1941-42; Virginia State Probation and Parole System, Arlington, probation and parole officer, 1942-45; Virginia Department of Welfare and Institutions, Richmond, various positions in juvenile corrections, 1945-52; Hennepin County District Court, Minneapolis, Minn., director of court services, 1952-67; State of Minnesota, Minneapolis, commissioner of corrections, 1967-71; Research Analysis Corp., McLean, Va., director of department of public communications and safety, 1971-73; State of Delaware, Dover, director of corrections, 1973-76; Virginia Commonwealth University, Richmond, professor of administration of justice, 1977—. *Member:* National Association of Social Workers, National Council on Social Work Education, National Council on Crime and Delinquency, American Correctional Association (board member).

WRITINGS: *Prison, Probation or Parole?: A Parole Officer Reports*, University of Minnesota Press, 1954; *The Probation*

Officer Investigates: A Guide to the Presentence Report, University of Minnesota Press, 1960; *Imaginative Programming in Probation and Parole*, University of Minnesota Press, 1967; *Prison Life and Human Worth*, University of Minnesota Press, 1974; *Corrections*, Wiley, 1981. Contributor of articles to professional journals.

WORK IN PROGRESS: *The Macneil Century;* a book on the history of corrections in Virginia.

AVOCATIONAL INTERESTS: Woodworking.

* * *

KEY, Alexander (Hill) 1904-1979

PERSONAL: Born September 21, 1904, in La Plata, Md.; died July 25, 1979; son of Alexander Hill (a cotton dealer) and Charlotte (Ryder) Key; married Alice Towle, December 21, 1945; children: Zan. *Education:* Attended Chicago Art Institute, 1921-23. *Religion:* "Freethinker." *Home:* Summerhill Rd., Eufaula, Ala. 36027. *Agent:* McIntosh and Otis, Inc., 475 Fifth Ave., New York, N.Y. 10017.

CAREER: Painter, illustrator, and free-lance writer. Began as book illustrator in Chicago, Ill., illustrating first book at 19, while still a student. Later taught art in Chicago at Studio School of Art. Began writing juvenile books and stories in 1929; then adult fiction and magazine article writing followed. *Military service:* U.S. Navy, 1942-45; became lieutenant commander. *Member:* Authors Guild. *Awards, honors:* American Association of University Women Award, 1965, for *The Forgotten Door;* Lewis Carroll Shelf Award, 1972.

WRITINGS—Juveniles; published by Westminster, except as indicated: *Red Eagle*, Volland, 1930; *Liberty or Death*, Harper, 1931; *Caroliny Trail*, Holt, 1941; *Cherokee Boy*, 1957; *Sprockets: A Little Robot*, 1963; *Rivets and Sprockets*, 1964; *The Forgotten Door*, 1965; *Bolts: A Robot Dog*, 1966; *Mystery of the Sassafras Chair*, 1967; *Escape to Witch Mountain*, 1968; *Golden Enemy*, 1969; *The Incredible Tide*, 1970; *Flight to the Lonesome Place*, 1971; *The Strange White Doves*, 1972; *The Preposterous Adventures of Swimmer*, 1973; *The Magic Meadow*, 1975; *Jagger: The Dog from Elsewhere*, 1976; *The Sword of Aradel*, 1977; *Return from Witch Mountain*, 1978; *The Case of the Vanishing Boy*, Archway, 1979.

Adult novels: *The Wrath and the Wind*, Bobbs-Merrill, 1949; *Island Light*, Bobbs-Merrill, 1950. Contributor to *Saturday Evening Post, Argosy, Elks, Cosmopolitan, American Mercury,* and many other periodicals.

SIDELIGHTS: Alexander Key once wrote *CA:* "I've always called my Maryland birth a bio-geographical accident, for I'm almost a native Floridian. I say almost, for at this point I can hardly call any state my own. The first Keys settled in Virginia, circa 1670—the old place in Sussex County is still standing—but about a century-and-a-half ago thirteen members of the family died of yellow fever in thirteen days, so the three remaining members fled over the mountains to Muscle Shoals and were doing very nicely until that rascally Sherman came along, followed by the carpetbaggers. So the tattered Keys fled once more, this time to a log cabin in Florida.

"Anyway, after the Maryland incident, my first six years were spent on the Suwannee River, where my father had one of the first sawmills and cotton gins in the region—both burned by 'night-riders' just before his death. Night-riders were bands of plundering rascals who killed and burned if they didn't like someone's politics or economics. (The Suwannee was really wild in those days, and I could write a book about it.) My mother was killed in an accident soon after, and I spent an erratic youth with various relatives, attending no less than fourteen schools until, at seventeen, I took something or other by the horns and headed for Chicago to study at the Chicago Art Institute.

"A bank failure put me out on the street at nineteen, trying to make art pay. It did, in the nick of time, but only after I'd grown a mustache and put on a pair of horn-rimmed glasses to make me look older, and attired myself in a borrowed suit to give the impression of prosperity. I owed three months rent and was downright hungry the day I sold my first drawing to a publisher."

MEDIA ADAPTATIONS: Escape to Witch Mountain was the basis of a motion picture of the same title produced by Buena Vista in 1975; *Return to Witch Mountain* was also the basis of a motion picture of the same title produced by Walt Disney Productions. The film rights to *The Forgotton Door* have been sold.

BIOGRAPHICAL/CRITICAL SOURCES: Helen Ferris, *Writing Books for Boys and Girls*, Doubleday, 1952; *Book World*, May 4, 1969; *Library Journal*, July, 1970.†

*   *   *

KIMBROUGH, Robert (Alexander III) 1929-

PERSONAL: Born June 26, 1929, in Philadelphia, Pa.; son of Robert Alexander, Jr. (a physician) and Agnes (McComb) Kimbrough; married Gertrude Bolling Alfriend, July 11, 1953 (divorced, April 9, 1976); children: Elizabeth, Robert, John. *Education:* Williams College, B.A., 1951; Stanford University, M.A., 1955; Harvard University, Ph.D., 1959. *Home:* 3206 Gregory, Madison, Wis. 53711. *Office:* Department of English, H. C. White Hall, University of Wisconsin—Madison, Madison, Wis. 53706.

CAREER: University of Wisconsin—Madison, instructor, 1959-60, assistant professor, 1960-64, associate professor, 1964-68, professor of English, 1968—. *Military service:* U.S. Marine Corps, 1951-54; served in Korea; received Purple Heart and Bronze Star. U.S. Marine Corps Reserve, 1948-76; retired as colonel. *Member:* Modern Language Association of America, Shakespeare Association, American Federation of Teachers, Renaissance Society.

WRITINGS: (Editor) Joseph Conrad, *Heart of Darkness: An Authoritative Text, Backgrounds and Sources, Essays in Criticism*, Norton, 1963, revised edition, 1972; *Shakespeare's Troilus and Cressida and Its Setting*, Harvard University Press, 1964; *Trolius and Cressida: A Scene-by-Scene Analysis with Critical Commentary*, American R.D.M., 1966; (editor) Henry James, *The Turn of the Screw: An Authoritative Text, Backgrounds and Sources, Essays in Criticism*, Norton, 1967; (contributor) Shiv K. Kumar, editor, *Victorian Literature: Recent Reevaluations*, New York University Press, 1969; (editor) Sir Philip Sidney, *Selected Prose and Poetry*, Holt, 1969; *Sir Philip Sidney*, Twayne, 1971; (contributor) *The Predecessors of Shakespeare*, University of Nebraska Press, 1972; (editor) *English Renaissance Drama: Essays in Honor of Madeleine Doran and Mark Beckes*, University of Illinois Press, 1976; (editor) Conrad, *The Nigger of the "Narcissus": An Authoritative Text, Backgrounds and Sources, Reviews and Criticism*, Norton, 1979. Contributor of articles and reviews to learned journals.

WORK IN PROGRESS: Shakespeare and the Art of Human Kindness.

KING, Adam
See HOARE, Robert J(ohn)

*   *   *

KINGSBURY, John M(erriam) 1928-

PERSONAL: Born July 4, 1928, in Boston, Mass. *Education:* University of Massachusetts, B.S., 1950; Harvard University, M.A., 1952, Ph.D., 1954. *Office:* 204C Plant Science Building, Cornell University, Ithaca, N.Y. 14853.

CAREER: Brandeis University, Waltham, Mass., laboratory instructor in biology, 1952-54; Cornell University, New York State College of Agriculture and Life Science, Ithaca, assistant professor, 1954-60, associate professor, 1960-70, professor of botany, 1970—, New York State Veterinary College, lecturer in phytotoxicology, 1963-78, professor of clinical science, 1978—. Shoals Marine Laboratory, founder, 1966, director, 1966-79; adjunct professor of botany, University of New Hampshire, 1976—. *Member:* American College of Veterinary Toxicologists (fellow). *Awards, honors:* National Science Foundation fellow, 1957; Fulbright senior fellow, 1980.

WRITINGS: Poisonous Plants of the United States and Canada, Prentice-Hall, 1964; *Deadly Harvest: Common Poisonous Plants*, Holt, 1965; *Seaweeds of Cape Cod and the Islands*, Chatham-Viking, 1969; *The Rocky Shore*, Chatham-Viking, 1970; (contributor) L. J. Casarett and J. Doull, editors, *Toxicology, the Basic Science of Poisons*, Macmillan, 1975; *Oil and Water: The New Hampshire Story*, Shoals Marine Laboratory (Ithaca, N.Y.), 1975; *Transect Study of the Intertidal Biota of Star Island, Isle of Shoals*, Shoals Marine Laboratory, 1976; (contributor) R. F. Keeler, K. R. Van Kampen, and L. F. James, editors, *Effects of Poisonous Plants on Livestock*, Academic Press, 1978; (author of introduction) C. Thaxter, *An Island Garden*, Heritage Books (Bowie, Md.), 1978; (contributor) R. F. Duncan and J. P. Ware, editors, *A Cruising Guide to the New England Coast*, 8th edition (Kingsbury was not associated with earlier editions), Dodd, 1979; (contributor) A. D. Kinghorn, editor, *Toxic Plants*, Columbia University Press, 1979. Contributor to *Collier's Encyclopedia*, 1970, and *Funk & Wagnalls New Encyclopedia*, 1972. Contributor of articles to scientific journals, including *American Journal of Botany, Journal of Animal Science, Biology Bulletin*, and *Journal of Phycology*.

*   *   *

KINROSS, Lord
See BALFOUR, (John) Patrick Douglas

*   *   *

KINTNER, William R(oscoe) 1915-

PERSONAL: Born April 21, 1915, in Lock Haven, Pa.; son of Joseph J. (a lawyer) and Florence (Kendig) Kintner; married Xandree Hyatt, June 15, 1940; children: Kay (Mrs. Mord Bogie), Jane (Mrs. Michael Hogan), Gail (Mrs. George Markou), Carl H. *Education:* U.S. Military Academy, B.S., 1940; Georgetown University, M.A., Ph.D. *Home:* 2470 Woodland Rd., Bryn Athyn, Pa. 19009. *Office:* 3508 Market St., Philadelphia, Pa. 19104.

CAREER: U.S. Army, career officer, 1940-61, retired as colonel with last assignment as chief of long-range plans in Strategic Analysis Section, Coordination Group, Chief of Staff; University of Pennsylvania, Foreign Policy Research Institute, Philadelphia, professor of political science, 1961—, deputy director, 1961-69, director, 1969-73, president, 1976; U.S. Ambassador to Thailand, 1973-75. Served as commander of an infantry battalion in the Korean War; member of senior staff, Central Intelligence Agency, 1950-52, planning staff, National Security Council, 1954, and staff of special assistant to the President, 1955. Senior adviser to Operations Research Office, Johns Hopkins University, 1956-57; member of academic board, Inter-American Defense College, 1962-72, Board of Foreign Scholarships, 1970-73, and civilian faculty advisory committee, National War College, 1970-72. Consultant to President's Committee to study the U.S. Assistance Program, 1959, U.S. Department of Defense, National Security Council, and Stanford Research Institute. Has appeared on television programs, including "This Is Strategy" network series, Philadelphia, Pa., 1961-62. *Member:* Council on Foreign Relations, National Planning Association, American Political Science Association, American Academy of Political and Social Science. *Awards, honors*—Military: Legion of Merit with oak leaf cluster; Bronze Star with oak leaf cluster. Civilian: Fellow, Hudson Institute.

WRITINGS: The Front Is Everywhere, University of Oklahoma Press, 1950; (with George C. Reinhardt) *Atomic Weapons in Land Combat*, Stackpole, 1953; (with Joseph I. Coffey and Raymond J. Albright) *Forging a New Sword*, Harper, 1958; (with Robert Strausz-Hupe, James E. Dougherty and Alvin J. Cottrell) *Protracted Conflict*, Harper, 1959; (with Strausz-Hupe) *The Haphazard Years*, Doubleday, 1960; (with Strausz-Hupe and Stefan T. Possony) *A Forward Strategy for America*, Harper, 1961; (with Joseph Z. Kornfeder) *The New Frontier of War: Political Warfare, Present and Future*, Regnery, 1962; (with Strausz-Hupe and Dougherty) *Building the Atlantic World*, Harper, 1963; *Peace and the Strategy Conflict*, Praeger, 1967; (translator and editor with Harriet Fast Scott) *The Nuclear Revolution in Soviet Military Affairs*, University of Oklahoma Press, 1968; (editor) *Safeguard: Why the ABM Makes Sense*, Hawthorn, 1969.

(With Wolfgang Klaiber) *Eastern Europe and European Security*, Dunellen, 1971; (with Robert L. Pfaltzgraff, Jr.) *Soviet Military Trends: Implications for U.S. Security*, American Enterprise Institute, 1971; *The Impact of President Nixon's Visit to Peking on International Politics*, Foreign Policy Research Institute, University of Pennsylvania, 1972; (with Pfaltzgraff) *SALT: Implications for Arms Control in the 1970s*, University of Pittsburgh Press, 1973; (with Harvey Sicherman) *Technology and International Politics: The Crisis of Wishing*, Lexington Books, 1975; (with John F. Copper) *A Matter of Two Chinas: The China-Taiwan Issue in U.S. Foreign Policy*, Foreign Policy Research Institute, University of Pennsylvania, 1979. Contributor of articles and reviews to periodicals, including *Reporter, Esquire, Reader's Digest*, and *Yale Review*. Editor, *Orbis*, 1969-73, 1976—.

BIOGRAPHICAL/CRITICAL SOURCES: New York Times, October 22, 1967; *American Political Science Review*, June, 1969.†

* * *

KIRK, Irene 1926-
(Irina Kirk)

PERSONAL: Born September 28, 1926, in Harbin, Manchuria; children: Michael, Mark, Kathryn. *Education:* University of Hawaii, B.A., 1961; Indiana University, Ph.D., 1968. *Politics:* Democrat. *Home:* 49 River Rd., Mansfield Center, Conn. 06250; and 323 Lahaina Shores, Lahaina, Maui, Hawaii 96791 (summer). *Agent:* Jean Naggar, 420 East 72nd St., New York, N.Y. 10021. *Office:* Department of Germanic and Slavic Languages, University of Connecticut, Storrs, Conn. 06268.

CAREER: Registered nurse at hospitals in Shanghai, China, and Los Angeles, Calif., 1945-50; *Honolulu Star Bulletin*, Honolulu, Hawaii, book reviewer, 1957-60; Indiana University at Bloomington, lecturer in Russian literature, 1965-67; University of Connecticut, Storrs, assistant professor, 1967-70, associate professor, 1970-77, professor of Germanic and Slavic languages, 1977—. Instructor at International Russian Studies Seminar, Unterweissenbach, Austria, 1964, 1965, and 1968, and at University of Kansas Slavic Workshop in Russian Literature, 1967; visiting lecturer at colleges and universities, including Queens College, 1968, University of California, Berkeley, 1968, University of Colorado, 1969, Colorado College, 1969, University of Hawaii, 1970, Indiana University, 1972, Annapolis Naval Academy, 1972, Massachusetts Institute of Technology, 1975, University of Hartford, 1975, Brown University, 1975, and Harvard University, 1976. Panelist or writer-in-residence at professional conferences. Guide at American National Exhibit, Moscow, U.S.S.R., summer, 1959; leader of Indiana University educational tours of Soviet Union, summer, 1962 and 1966. *Member:* International Association of Dostoevsky Scholars, Modern Language Association of America (member of board of directors, Northeast Conference, 1973), American Association of Comparative Literature Scholars, Phi Beta Kappa. *Awards, honors:* Eugene Banks Memorial Award for best short story, 1960; grant to visit Finland, 1964-65; Best Teacher Award, University of Connecticut, 1971.

WRITINGS—Under name Irina Kirk: *Born with the Dead*, Houghton, 1963; *Dostoevsky and Camus*, Fink (Munich), 1975; *Profiles in Russian Resistance*, Times Books, 1975; *Anton Chekhov*, Twayne, 1981. Contributor to periodicals, including *St. Andrews Review, Bucknell Review, New Zealand Slavonic*, and *Studia Slavic* (Budapest).

* * *

KIRK, Irina
See KIRK, Irene

* * *

KIRKLAND, Edward Chase 1894-1975

PERSONAL: Born May 24, 1894, in Bellows Falls, Vt.; died May 24, 1975, in Hanover, N.H.; son of Edward and Mary (Chase) Kirkland; married Ruth Babson, September 4, 1924; children: Edward S. *Education:* Dartmouth College, B.A., 1916; Harvard University, M.A., 1921, Ph.D., 1924. *Residence:* Thetford Center, Vt.

CAREER: Dartmouth College, Hanover, N.H., instructor, 1920-21; Massachusetts Institute of Technology, Cambridge, instructor, 1922-24; Brown University, Providence, R.I., assistant professor, 1924-30; Bowdoin College, Brunswick, Me., associate professor, 1930-31, professor of history, 1931-55, professor emeritus, 1955-75. Commonwealth Lecturer, University College, University of London, 1952; Pitt Professor of American History, Cambridge University, 1956-57. *Military service:* U.S. Army, Ambulance Corps, 1917-19; awarded French Croix de Guerre. *Member:* American Antiquarian Society, American Historical Association (member of council, 1953-56), Mississippi Valley Historical Association (president, 1955-56), American Academy of Arts and Sciences, American Economic History Association (president, 1953-54), American Association of University Professors (president, 1946-48), Massachusetts Historical Society, Colonial Society of Massachusetts, Phi Beta Kappa (senator, 1951-70). *Awards, honors:* Litt.D. from Dartmouth College, 1949, Princeton University, 1957, and Bowdoin College, 1961; Guggenheim scholar, 1955-56; M.A., Cambridge University, 1956.

WRITINGS: The Peacemakers of 1864, Macmillan, 1926, reprinted, AMS Press, 1969; *A History of American Economic Life,* Appleton, 1932, 4th edition, 1969; *Men, Cities and Transportation: A Study in New England History,* two volumes, Harvard University Press, 1948, reprinted, Russell & Russell, 1968; *Business in the Gilded Age: The Conservative's Balance Sheet,* University of Wisconsin Press, 1953; *Dream and Thought in the Business Community,* Cornell University Press, 1956; *Industry Comes of Age: Business, Labor and Public Policy, 1860-1900,* Holt, 1961; (editor) *Andrew Carnegie: Gospel of Wealth,* Harvard University Press, 1962; *Charles Francis Adams, Jr., 1835-1915: The Patrician at Bay,* Harvard University Press, 1965; *Rhetoric and Rage over the Division of Wealth in the Eighteen Nineties,* American Antiquarian Society, 1970; (compiler) *American Economic History since 1860,* Appleton-Century-Crofts, 1971. Contributor to scholarly journals.

OBITUARIES: New York Times, May 25, 1975; *AB Bookman's Weekly,* August 25, 1975.†

*   *   *

KIRKWOOD, James 1930-
(Jim Kirkwood)

PERSONAL: Born August 22, 1930, in Los Angeles, Calif.; son of James and Lila (Lee) Kirkwood (both silent film stars). *Education:* Studied acting for three years with Sandy Meisner Professional Classes, New York, N.Y.; studied writing at New York University and University of California, Los Angeles. *Religion:* Catholic. *Home:* 58 Oyster Shores Rd., East Hampton, N.Y. 11937. *Agent:* (Novels) Jed Mattes, International Creative Management, 40 West 57th St., New York, N.Y. 10019; (screenplays) Ron Mardigan, William Morris Agency, 151 El Camino Real, Beverly Hills, Calif. *Office:* No. 45R, 484 West 44th St., New York, N.Y. 10036.

CAREER: Principal career most of adult life has been acting; currently combining acting and writing. Appeared on Broadway in "Junior Miss," "Small Wonder," "Dance Me a Song," and on tour in "Joan of Lorraine," "Call Me Madam," "Wonderful Town," "Welcome Darling," and in "Mary, Mary," summer, 1966; made South Africa tour in cast of "Never Too Late"; featured on television in "Garry Moore Show," "Ed Sullivan Show," "Alfred Hitchcock Presents," and "Kraft Theatre"; nightclub appearances with Lee Goodman as comedy-satire team include the Bon Soir, Le Ruban Bleu, the Blue Angel, and the Mocambo (Hollywood); radio work includes a week-day program with Goodman, running for two years over WOR, New York, a twenty-six week series, "Teenagers Unlimited," on Mutual network, other appearances on "Henry Aldrich," "Theatre Guild of the Air." *Member:* Actor's Equity Association, American Federation of Television and Radio Artists, Screen Actors Guild, American Guild of Variety Artists, Dramatists Guild, Authors League. *Awards, honors:* Pulitzer Prize in drama, 1976, Tony Award, 1976, Drama Desk Award, Drama Critics Circle Award, and Theatre World Award, all for "A Chorus Line."

WRITINGS: There Must Be a Pony! (novel), Little, Brown, 1960; *U.T.B.U.* (Unhealthy to Be Unpleasant; play; produced on Broadway, 1965), Samuel French, 1966; *Good Times/Bad Times* (novel), Simon & Schuster, 1968; *American Grotesque* (nonfiction), Simon & Schuster, 1970; *P.S. Your Cat Is Dead* (novel), Stein & Day, 1972; *Some Kind of Hero* (novel), Crowell, 1975; (author of book with Nicholas Dante) "A Chorus

Line" (musical), first produced by New York Shakespeare Festival, May 21, 1975, produced on Broadway at Shubert Theater, July 5, 1975; *P.S. Your Cat Is Dead* (play; based on his novel of the same title; first produced on Broadway, 1975), Samuel French, 1976; *Hit Me with a Rainbow* (novel), Delacorte, 1980; "Surprise" (one-act play), first produced at John Drew Theatre, summer, 1981. Also author of play, "There Must Be a Pony," 1962, and screenplay, "Some Kind of Hero," 1981, both based on his novels of the same titles.

WORK IN PROGRESS: Screenplays based on his novels, "Good Times/Bad Times," for United Artists, and "There Must Be a Pony!," for Columbia Pictures Television; original screenplay, "Witch Story," for United Artists; an original musical, "Murder at the Vanities"; a novel, *I Teach Flying.*

SIDELIGHTS: James Kirkwood's best known work is the highly acclaimed musical "A Chorus Line." The musical, presented in the form of an audition in which the dancers are asked to tell something about themselves, was conceived by director Michael Bennett, who had tape recorded some all night talk sessions with a group of dancers. Bennett and Kirkwood's co-author Nicholas Dante edited the tapes and then developed the play in Joseph Papp's Theater Workshop. They found, however, that the musical needed much more work, so they brought in Kirkwood. Kirkwood's appearance marked the beginning of a great deal of rewriting, for as Bennett told Robert Berkvist, "We reworked the material so often, I think we must have discarded six versions of the show."

Walter Kerr of the *New York Times* praises the final result, calling it a "brilliant" accomplishment. At the same time, Kerr finds that "rather too many [of the dancers' life stories] are familiar and thin: the girl who was born just to keep a marriage together (no dice); the girl who compensated for a dreary life by dancing because 'everyone is beautiful in ballet. . . .'" On the other hand, Kerr recognizes that the ordinariness of their everyday lives strengthens the contrast with their professional lives, with the magic they feel when dancing. As Kerr comments, "[Bennett] wants us to feel the happiness that overtakes these nonentities so long as toes slap the ground or fly in air—at the same time that we recognize the essential hopelessness of their lot."

The movie rights to "A Chorus Line" were sold to Universal Pictures.

BIOGRAPHICAL/CRITICAL SOURCES: New York Times, June 1, 1975, June 15, 1975, October 26, 1975, May 4, 1976; *Authors in the News,* Volume II, Gale, 1976; *Contemporary Literary Criticism,* Volume IX, Gale, 1978.

*   *   *

KIRKWOOD, Jim
See KIRKWOOD, James

*   *   *

KISH, G. Hobab
See KENNEDY, Gerald (Hamilton)

*   *   *

KLUGER, Richard 1934-

PERSONAL: Born September 18, 1934, in Paterson, N.J.; son of David (a business executive) and Ida (Abramson) Kluger; married Phyllis Schlain, March 23, 1957; children: Matthew, Theodore. *Education:* Princeton University, B.A. (cum laude),

1956. *Home:* 12 Edgehill Rd., New Haven, Conn. 06511. *Agent:* Georges Borchardt, Inc., 136 East 57th St., New York, N.Y. 10022.

CAREER: Wall Street Journal, New York City, city editor, 1956-57; *Country Citizen,* New City, N.Y., editor and publisher, 1958-60; *New York Post,* New York City, staff writer, 1960-61; *Forbes* magazine, New York City, associate editor, 1962; *New York Herald Tribune,* New York City, general books editor, 1962-63, book editor, 1963-66; *Book Week,* New York City, editor, 1963-66; Simon & Schuster, New York City, managing editor, 1966-68, executive editor, 1968-70; Atheneum Publishers, New York City, editor-in-chief, 1970-71; Charterhouse Books, New York City, president and publisher, 1972-73. *Member:* Princeton Club of New York. *Awards, honors:* National Book Award nomination, 1976, for *Simple Justice: A History of Brown v. Board of Education.*

WRITINGS: When the Bough Breaks (novel), Doubleday, 1964; *National Anthem* (novel), Harper, 1969; *Simple Justice: A History of Brown v. Board of Education,* Knopf, 1976; *Members of the Tribe* (novel), Doubleday, 1977; *Star Witness* (novel), Doubleday 1979; *Un-American Activities,* Doubleday, 1982. Contributor to *Partisan Review, New Republic, Harper's, Nation, New York Times Book Review,* and other periodicals.

WORK IN PROGRESS: A history of the *New York Herald Tribune,* for Knopf.

SIDELIGHTS: A *New York Times* writer reports that Richard Kluger's third book, *Simple Justice: A History of Brown v. Board of Education,* "documents the school desegregation campaign from its beginning through the landmark decision in Brown v. Board of Education. A principal figure in the book is Justice Thurgood Marshall. . . . Justice Marshall, as the chief lawyer for the NAACP, Legal Defense and Educational Fund Inc., represented black parents before the court."

A legal theme also runs through another of Kluger's books, *Star Witness.* This novel is called "daring" and "ambitious" by Jonathan Yardley of the *New York Times Book Review.* He writes: "Daring because Mr. Kluger's narrator, Tabor Hill, is a woman, and ambitious because the novel presents something of a *tour de horizon* of present-day legal issues. Miss Hill . . . comes to work for a prominent firm in the Connecticut city of Amity. . . . She is the firm's first woman member, and soon enough becomes its self-appointed social conscience. . . . Both of which, needless to say, get her in trouble."

Washington Post reviewer Laura B. Hoguet explains that "the first half of [*Star Witness*] poses a classic feminist question: Assuming that certain qualities are required for success in the law (brains, and aggressiveness, Kluger seems to think), can a woman endowed with these qualities as fully as any man achieve a man's success? The answer seems to be a resounding 'yes'." In the second half of the book, Hoguet writes, "Kluger's focus now shifts to the question of whether any very bright and ambitious professional can afford to release some energy from the care of his or her own all-important career to pay some unselfish attention to another person."

The television rights to *Simple Justice* have been purchased by the Children's Television Workshop.

BIOGRAPHICAL/CRITICAL SOURCES: Newsweek, July 13, 1964; *Best Sellers,* May 1, 1969; *Observer Review,* October 26, 1969; *Virginia Quarterly Review,* autumn, 1969; *New York Times,* February 22, 1977, September 23, 1977, February 28, 1979; *New York Times Book Review,* February 25, 1979; *Washington Post,* March 1, 1979; *Chicago Tribune,* March 4, 1979.

KNAPP, Bettina (Liebowitz)

PERSONAL: Born in New York, N.Y.; daughter of David and Emily (Gresser) Liebowitz; married Russell S. Knapp (a lawyer); children: Albert, Charles. *Education:* Barnard College, B.A., 1947; Columbia University, M.A., 1949, Ph.D., 1955; also attended Sorbonne, University of Paris. *Residence:* New York, N.Y. *Office:* Hunter College of the City University of New York, 68th St. and Park Ave., New York, N.Y. 10021.

CAREER: Columbia University, New York City, lecturer, 1952-61; Hunter College and Graduate Center of the City University of New York, New York City, assistant professor, beginning 1961, currently professor of French and comparative literature. Lecturer, C. G. Jung Foundation. *Member:* Northeast Modern Language Association (president). *Awards honors:* Guggenheim fellow; Palmes Academiques; American Philosophical Association award.

WRITINGS: Louis Jouvet: Man of the Theatre, Columbia University Press, 1957; (co-author) *That Was Yvette,* Holt, 1964; *Louise Labe,* Lettres Modernes, 1964; *Cymbalum Mundi,* Twayne, 1965; *Aristide Bruant: A Biography,* Nouvelles Editions Debresse, 1968; *Jean Genet: A Critical Study,* Twayne, 1968; *Antonin Artaud: Man of Vision,* David Lewis, 1969; *Jean Cocteau: A Critical Study,* Twayne, 1970; *Jean Racine: Mythos and Renewal in Modern Theatre,* University of Alabama Press, 1971; *Georges Duhamel: A Critical Study,* Twayne, 1972; *Celine: Man of Hate,* University of Alabama Press, 1974; *Off-Stage Voices,* Whitston Publishing, 1974; *Maurice Maeterlinck,* Twayne, 1975; *French Novelists Speak Out,* Whitston Publishing, 1976; *Dream and Image,* Whitston Publishing, 1977; *Fernand Crommelynck,* G. K. Hall, 1978; *Anais Nin,* Ungar, 1978; *The Prometheus Syndrome,* Whitston Publishing, 1979; *Emile Zola,* Ungar, 1980; *Theatre and Alchemy,* Wayne State University Press, 1980.

Contributor of articles on the French theater to *Columbia Encyclopedia* and *Grolier Encyclopedia.* Contributor to periodicals, including *Tulane Drama Review, Yale French Studies, Horizon, French Review, Revue d'Histoire du Theatre,* and *Modern Drama.*

*   *   *

KNIGHT, James A(llen)   1918-

PERSONAL: Born October 20, 1918, in St. George, S.C.; son of Thomas S. and Carolyn Knight; married Sally Templeman; children: Steven Allen. *Education:* Wofford College, A.B., 1941; Duke University Divinity School, B.D., 1944; Vanderbilt University, M.D., 1952; Tulane University, M.P.H., 1962; additional study at C. G. Jung Institute, Zurich, 1961, and University of California, Berkeley, 1962. *Office:* School of Medicine, Louisiana State University, 1542 Tulane Ave., New Orleans, La. 70112.

CAREER: Ordained minister of Methodist church, 1944; licensed to practice medicine in Tennessee, Florida, Louisiana, Texas, and New York; certified psychiatrist, American Board of Psychiatry and Neurology, 1960. Grady Memorial Hospital, Atlanta, Ga., intern, 1952-53; Duke University Hospital, Durham, N.C., assistant resident in pediatrics, 1953-54; American Cyanamid Co., Fortier Plant, New Orleans, La., medical director, 1954-55; Tulane University, School of Medicine, New Orleans, assistant, 1955-57, instructor in psychiatry, 1957-58; Baylor University, College of Medicine, Houston, Tex., assistant professor of psychiatry, 1958-61, assistant dean, 1960-

61; Tulane University, School of Medicine and School of Public Health, associate professor of psychiatry and preventive medicine and director of Section on Community Psychiatry, 1961-63; Union Theological Seminary, New York, N.Y., director of program in psychiatry and religion, 1963-64; Tulane University, School of Medicine, associate dean and director of admissions, School of Medicine and School of Public Health, professor of psychiatry, 1964-74; Texas A & M University, College of Medicine, College Station, professor of psychiatry and dean, 1974-77; Louisiana State University, School of Medicine, New Orleans, professor of psychiatry, 1977—. Advisor to International Educational Futures, Foundation for Thantology, Institute for the Medical Humanities, and Institutes for Religion and Health. *Military service:* U.S. Navy, 1944-46; served as chaplain in Pacific Theater; became lieutenant.

MEMBER: American Academy of Psychoanalysis, Institutes of Religion and Health, American Psychiatric Association, Group for the Advancement of Psychiatry, Society for the Study of Religion, American Osler Society, Blue Key, Phi Beta Kappa, Delta Omega. *Awards, honors:* Named most outstanding clinical professor, School of Medicine, Louisiana State University, 1979.

WRITINGS: A Psychiatrist Looks at Religion and Health, Abingdon, 1964; (with Winborn E. Davis) *A Manual for the Comprehensive Community Mental Health Clinic,* C. C Thomas, 1964; (with Margaretta Bowers, Edgar Jackson, and Lawrence LeShan) *Counseling the Dying,* Nelson, 1964; (with John P. McGovern) *Allergy and Human Emotions,* C. C Thomas, 1967; (editor with Ralph Slovenko) *Motivations in Play, Games and Sports,* C. C Thomas, 1967; *For the Love of Money: Human Behavior and Money,* Lippincott, 1968; *Conscience and Guilt,* Appleton-Century-Crofts, 1969; *Medical Student: Doctor in the Making,* Appleton-Century-Crofts, 1973; (author of prologue with George C. Sullivan) L. B. McCullogh and J. P. Morris III, editors, *Implications of History and Ethics—Veterinary and Human,* Texas A & M University Press, 1978; *Doctor-to-Be: Coping with the Trials and Triumphs of Medical School,* Appleton-Century-Crofts, 1981.

Contributor: Harold I. Lief and others, editors, *The Psychological Basis of Medical Practice,* Harper, 1963; Gene L. Usdin, editor, *Adolescence: Care and Counseling,* Lippincott, 1967; H.L.P. Resnik, editor, *Suicidal Behaviors: Diagnosis and Management,* Little, Brown, 1968; Austin H. Kutscher, editor, *Death and Bereavement,* C. C Thomas, 1969; Jeremiah W. Canning, editor, *Values in an Age of Confrontation,* C. E. Merrill, 1970; Nordan C. Murphy, editor, *Stewardship 70,* National Council of the Churches of Christ, 1970; Howard J. Clinebell, Jr., editor, *Community Mental Health: The Role of Church and Temple,* Abingdon, 1970; Jack L. Leedy, editor, *Compensation in Psychiatric Disability and Rehabilitation,* C. C Thomas, 1971; Paul E. Johnson, editor, *Healer of the Mind,* Abingdon, 1972; McGovern and C. E. Burns, editors, *Humanism in Medicine,* C. C Thomas, 1973; Kutscher and others, editors, *Death and Ministry,* Seabury, 1975; H. T. Engelhardt, Jr. and S. F. Spicker, editors, *Mental Health: Philosophical Perspectives,* D. Reidel (Dordrecht, Netherlands), 1978; Elliott M. Goldwag, editor, *Inner Balance: The Power of Holistic Healing,* Prentice-Hall, 1979; Stanley E. Gitlow and Herbert Peyser, editors, *Alcoholism: A Practical Treatment Guide,* Grune, 1980.

Contributor of more than seventy articles to psychiatric and other medical journals, including *Medical Times, Psychiatric Quarterly, American Journal of Psychiatry, Pastoral Psychology, Journal of Existential Psychiatry,* and *American Journal of Medical Education.* Member of editorial board, *Current

Concepts in Psychiatry, Journal of Clinical Psychiatry,* and *Pastoral Psychology.*

*   *   *

KNOWLTON, Derrick 1921-

PERSONAL: Born April 4, 1921, in Hampshire, England; son of James (a master baker) and Laura Letitia (Snook) Knowlton; married Gladys May Shelley (a writer), May 2, 1945 (died, 1978); children: Heather. *Education:* Attended school in Hampshire, England. *Religion:* Christianity. *Home and office:* 66 Stoke Common Rd., Eastleigh, Hampshire, England.

CAREER: Apprentice joiner in building industry in Hampshire, England, 1935-39; clerk in Hampshire, 1940-41; fireman, 1941-46; administrative assistant in local government, 1946-69; freelance writer, 1969—. *Member:* Royal Society for the Protection of Birds, British Naturalists Association, Hampshire Ornithological Society, Hampshire Naturalists Trust, Southampton Natural History Society (chairman, 1965).

WRITINGS: The Naturalist in Central Southern England, David & Charles, 1973; *The Naturalist in Scotland,* David & Charles, 1974; *Discovering Walks in the New Forest,* Shire Publications, 1976, 2nd edition, 1980; *The Naturalist in the Hebrides,* David & Charles, 1977; *Walks in Hampshire,* Spurbooks, 1978; *Discovering Central Southern England,* Faber, 1979. Contributor to country life magazines, including *Hampshire* and *Scottish Gardener.*

WORK IN PROGRESS: A Christian biography, *The Vijay Menon Story.*

SIDELIGHTS: Derrick Knowlton writes that "experiencing frustration in local government career and believing physical and mental health coupled with job satisfaction more important than money [I] gave up pensionable post for fulltime writing on countryside subjects." *Avocational interests:* Christian activities, observing nature, gardening, walking.

*   *   *

KOCH, Kenneth 1925-

PERSONAL: Surname is pronounced "coke"; born February 27, 1925, in Cincinnati, Ohio; son of Stuart and Lillian (Loth) Koch; married Mary Janice Elwood, June 12, 1954; children: Katherine. *Education:* Harvard University, A.B., 1948; Columbia University, M.A., 1953, Ph.D., 1959. *Home:* 25 Claremont Ave., New York, N.Y. 10027. *Office:* 414 Hamilton Hall, Columbia University, New York, N.Y. 10027.

CAREER: Rutgers University, Newark, N.J., lecturer, 1953-58; Brooklyn College (now Brooklyn College of the City University of New York), Brooklyn, N.Y., lecturer, 1957-59; Columbia University, New York, N.Y., assistant professor, 1959-66, associate professor, 1966-71, professor of English and comparative literature, 1971—. Director of Poetry Workshop, New School for Social Research, 1958-66. *Military service:* U.S. Army, 1943-46. *Awards, honors:* Fulbright grants to France and Italy; Guggenheim fellow, 1960-61; National Endowment for the Arts grant, 1966; Ingram Merrill Foundation fellowship, 1969; Harbison Award, 1970, for teaching; Frank O'Hara Prize, *Poetry,* 1973; National Institute of Arts and Letters award, 1976.

WRITINGS—Poetry, except as indicated: Poems, Tibor de Nagy Gallery, 1953; *Ko, Or a Season on Earth,* Grove, 1959; *Permanently,* Tiber Press, 1960; *Thank You and Other Poems,* Grove, 1962; *Poems from 1952 and 1953* (limited edition),

Black Sparrow Press, 1968; *The Pleasures of Peace,* Grove, 1969; *When the Sun Tries to Go On,* Black Sparrow Press, 1969; *Sleeping with Women* (limited edition), Black Sparrow Press, 1969; *Wishes, Lies and Dreams: Teaching Children to Write Poetry* (nonfiction), Chelsea House, 1970; (with Alex Katz) *Interlocking Lives* (fiction), Kulchur Foundation, 1970; *Rose, Where Did You Get That Red? Teaching Great Poetry to Children* (nonfiction), Random House, 1973; (contributor) *Penguin Modern Poets 24,* Penguin, 1974; *The Art of Love,* Random House, 1975; *The Red Robins* (novel; also see below), Random House, 1975; *The Duplications,* Random House, 1977; *I Never Told Anybody: Teaching Poetry Writing in a Nursing Home* (nonfiction), Random House, 1977; *Les Couleurs des Voyelles* (nonfiction), Casterman (Paris), 1978; (with Ted Berrigan) *ZZZZZZ,* Z Press, 1978; *The Burning Mystery of Anna in Nineteen Fifty-One,* Random House, 1979; (with Kate Farrell) *Sleeping on the Wing,* Random House, 1981.

Plays: "Little Red Riding Hood," first produced Off-Broadway at Theatre De Lys, 1953; *Bertha and Other Plays* (also see below; contains "Bertha" [opera; music by Ned Rorem], first produced in New York City at Living Theatre, 1959, produced Off-Broadway at Cherry Lane Theatre, 1962; "Pericles," produced Off-Broadway at Cherry Lane Theatre, 1960; "George Washington Crossing the Delaware," produced Off-Broadway at Maidman Playhouse, 1962; "The Construction of Boston," produced Off-Broadway at Maidman Playhouse, 1962; "Guinevere, or the Death of the Kangaroo," produced in New York City at New York Theatre for Poets, 1964; "The Gold Standard," produced in New York City, 1975; "The Return of Yellowmay"; "The Revolt of the Giant Animals"; "The Building of Florence"; "Angelica"; "The Merry Stones"; "The Academic Murders"; "Easter"; "The Lost Feed"; "Mexico"; "Coil Supreme"), Grove, 1966.

"The Artist" (opera based on poem of the same title; music by Paul Reif), produced in New York City at Whitney Museum, 1972; "A Little Light," produced in Amagansett, N.Y., 1972; *A Change of Hearts: Plays, Films, and Other Dramatic Works, 1951-1971* (contains the contents of *Bertha and Other Plays* and "E. Kology"; "The Election," produced in New York City at Living Theatre, 1960; "The Tinguely Machine Mystery, or the Love Suicides at Kaluka," produced in New York City at the Jewish Museum, 1965; "The Moon Balloon," produced in New York City in Central Park, 1969; "Without Kinship"; ten filmscripts: "Because," "The Color Game," "Mountains and Electricity," "Sheep Harbor," "Oval Gold," "Moby Dick," "L'Ecole Normale," "The Cemetery," "The Scotty Dog," and "The Apple"; "Youth"; "The Enchantment"), Random House, 1973; "Rooster Redivivus," produced in Garnerville, N.Y., 1975; *The Red Robins: A Play* (based on novel of the same title; first produced in New York City at Theater at St. Clement's, January 17, 1978), Theatre Arts, 1979.

Contributor of fiction, poetry, and plays to magazines, including *Art and Literature, Locus Solus, Poetry,* and *Partisan Review.* Member of editorial board, *Locus Solus,* 1960-62.

SIDELIGHTS: Kenneth Koch, one of the founders of the "New York School of Poetry" and whom John Gardner termed "a superb poet," began an experiment in teaching poetry to children at P.S. 61, a New York City elementary school, in 1968. Lisa Hammel of the *New York Times* describes the reception Koch received from his students: "The fifth grade class stood up and cheered so wildly when the tall man with a mop of wavy hair came into the room, he might have been a baseball player. Or an astronaut. But he wasn't. The man . . . who seemed to invade rather than come into the room was their

poetry teacher." How writing poetry became exciting for these students is described in *Wishes, Lies and Dreams,* which Herbert Kohl considers "perhaps the best book I have read portraying the joy and excitement young people experience when writing in a happy place where people care about their works."

Why did the children delight in writing poetry? Hammel quotes Koch's explanation: "They get to talk about their secret feelings . . . and somebody is taking their feelings seriously. It's nice to find out that these feelings you have really mean something. As one little girl said, 'When you write, you feel as if it's really happening.' And you're using your whole self to make something." In addition, Kohl emphasizes the environment Koch was able to create: "Koch's classes were obviously fun. There was noise, movement, life. In a deathly quiet and clean environment, the most interesting ideas are immediately sterilized."

Koch found that his students borrowed from each other's work, creating their own poetic tradition, but, Gardner writes, "the children themselves felt a need for something more. Koch's response was to shift the experiment to 'teaching great poetry to children,' thus broadening the tradition available to them. And the record of this experiment and its startling results is *Rose, Where Did You Get That Red?*" Rather than worry about all the details, Koch discussed a poem such as Blake's "The Tyger" until the children understood the central idea of it. Then, he had them work on their own writing. Gardner finds some of the resulting poetry "brilliant" and "terrific." In concluding, Gardner remarks that although not everyone will be as successful a teacher as Koch, his methods "will work for everyone at least some of the time. His two books could—*should*—be the beginning of a great [educational] revolution."

Koch also worked with another group of seemingly unlikely poets, the residents of Manhattan's American Nursing Home. *I Never Told Anybody* "is a collection of the patients' poems and Koch's highly readable account of how he coaxed his students along," comments a *Time* writer. At first unresponsive, the residents eventually wrote poems that Koch called "wonderful." Moreover, notes the *Time* reviewer, Koch "hopes that his book will prompt other workshops in other homes—and not just as therapeutic busywork. Argues Koch: 'As therapy it may help someone to be a busy old person, but as art and accomplishment it can help him to be fully alive. It was cheering to find such a lot of life and strength in the nursing home. I hadn't known there was so much passion and wit.'"

Mike Nussbaum dramatized *The Art of Love,* which was produced in Chicago, Ill. in 1976.

BIOGRAPHICAL/CRITICAL SOURCES: Poetry, May, 1967, September, 1969; *New York Times Book Review,* February 11, 1968, December 23, 1973; *New Republic,* August 2, 1969, July 11, 1970; *New York Times,* November 21, 1970, January 19, 1978, January 12, 1979; *New Leader,* January 25, 1971; *Saturday Review,* March 20, 1971; *Contemporary Literary Criticism,* Gale, Volume V, 1976, Volume VIII, 1978; *Time,* April 4, 1977.

* * *

KOLLER, Larry
  See KOLLER, Lawrence Robert

* * *

KOLLER, Lawrence Robert 1912-1967
  (Larry Koller)

PERSONAL: Born September 6, 1912, in Brooklyn, N.Y.; died

August 16, 1967, at his home in Monroe, N.Y.; son of John Joseph (an accountant) and Elizabeth (Wilson) Koller; married Alma Drake; children: Ann (Mrs. John Van Sant), Lawrence, Jr., Paul William. *Religion:* Catholic. *Office:* Maco Magazines, 757 Third Ave., New York, N.Y.

CAREER: Winchester Repeating Arms Co., New Haven, Conn., stock maker; High Standard Manufacturing Co., New Haven, barrel maker; Marlin Firearms Co., New Haven, tool room foreman; Uslan Rod Co., Spring Valley, N.Y., plant manager; Daystrom Electronics, Poughkeepsie, N.Y., chief model maker; also hunting guide, camp cook, professional photographer, writer, and editor. Panel member, "Rod and Gun Club of the Air," Mutual Network, 1949-51. *Awards, honors:* Fishing Hall of Fame, 1953; Montana Distinguished Service award, 1959; Carling Conservation award, 1959; "Outdoorsman of the Year" nominee, 1964, 1966.

WRITINGS: Shots at Whitetails, Little, Brown, 1948, revised edition, Knopf, 1970; *Taking Larger Trout,* Little, Brown, 1950; *Fireside Book of Guns,* Simon & Schuster, 1959; *The Golden Guide to Guns,* Golden Press, 1961, revised edition, 1966; *Larry Koller's Complete Guide to Handguns,* G. H. Levy, 1962; *Treasury of Angling,* Golden Press, 1963; *How to Shoot,* Doubleday, 1964, revised edition, 1976; *The Treasury of Hunting,* Odyssey, 1965. Author of ten gun annuals, six fishing annuals, a camping book, sportsman's workshop book, two books on hand guns, all published by Maco Magazines, 1953-62, ten of them reprinted by Bobbs-Merrill and Random House. Contributor of articles to *Field and Stream, Outdoor Life, Gentry, Life, American Gun,* and other magazines. Outdoors editor, *Argosy,* 1950-60; supervising editor, *Guns and Hunting* magazine, 1958-67.

WORK IN PROGRESS: Sportsman's Cook Book, for Doubleday; *Hunter's Field Guide,* for Knopf.

OBITUARIES: New York Times, August 19, 1967.†

* * *

KOPPMAN, Lionel   1920-

PERSONAL: Born November 24, 1920, in Waco, Tex.; son of Meyer and Ethel (Siegel) Koppman; married Mae Zuckerman (a free-lance proofreader and copy editor), December 5, 1948; children: Stephen, Debra. *Education:* Baylor University, B.A., 1942; Hebrew Union College, New York, N.Y., M.A., 1969. *Religion:* Jewish. *Office:* National Jewish Welfare Board, 15 East 26th St., New York, N.Y. 10010.

CAREER: National Jewish Welfare Board, New York, N.Y., public relations consultant; Temple Isaiah, Forest Hills, N.Y., teacher of Jewish history. *Member:* Health and Welfare Public Relations Association (treasurer), American Jewish Public Relations Society (vice-president). *Awards, honors:* Jewish Book Council award, 1954, for *A Jewish Tourist's Guide to the U.S.*

WRITINGS: (With Bernard Postal) *A Jewish Tourist's Guide to the U.S.,* Jewish Publication Society, 1954; (with Postal) *Jewish Landmarks in New York: An Informal History and Guide,* Hill & Wang, 1964, revised edition published as *Jewish Landmarks of New York: A Travel Guide and History,* Fleet Press, 1978; (with Postal) *American Jewish Landmarks: A Travel Guide and History,* Fleet Press, Volume I, 1977, Volume II: *The South and Southwest,* 1979; (with Postal) *Guess Who's Jewish in American History: From Wyatt Earp's Wife to Sandy Koufax,* New American Library, 1978. Also author of one-act play, "Francis Salvador, Patriot." Contributor of more than one hundred articles to magazines and newspapers. Contributing editor, *Jewish Digest.*

WORK IN PROGRESS: A book on American Jewish folklore; *Judaism for Christians.*

BIOGRAPHICAL/CRITICAL SOURCES: New York Times, November 14, 1978.

* * *

KOSLOW, Jules   1916-

PERSONAL: Born December 22, 1916, in Philadelphia, Pa.; married; wife's name, Sue; children: Julian, Jon, Evan. *Education:* Temple University, bachelor's degree, 1937; University of Southern California, M.A., 1948. *Home:* 5 Town Crier Lane, Westport, Conn. 06880. *Agent:* Bertha Klausner, International Literary Agency, Inc., 71 Park Ave., New York, N.Y. 10016.

CAREER: New Yorker, New York City, member of editorial staff, 1950-57; Ford Foundation, New York City, writer-editor, 1957-60; RCA Corp., New York City, director of publications and public affairs, 1960—.

WRITINGS: The Green and the Red: Sean O'Casey, the Man and His Plays, Arts, 1950, revised edition published as *Sean O'Casey: The Man and His Plays,* Citadel, 1966; *The Bohemian,* Pyramid, 1953; *The Kremlin,* Thomas Nelson, 1958; *Ivan the Terrible,* Hill & Wang, 1962; *The Despised and the Damned: The Russian Peasant through the Ages,* Macmillan, 1972; (editor) Tobia Frankel, *The Russian Artist,* Macmillan, 1972; (editor) Irving R. Levine, *The New Worker in Soviet Russia,* Macmillan, 1973; (editor) Albert Parry, *The Russian Scientist,* Macmillan, 1973.

SIDELIGHTS: Most of Jules Koslow's books have been translated into European languages.

* * *

KRISTELLER, Paul Oskar   1905-

PERSONAL: Born May 22, 1905, in Berlin, Germany; came to United States in 1939, naturalized in 1945; son of Heinrich and Alice (Magnus) Kristeller; married Edith Lewinnek (a physician), 1940. *Education:* University of Heidelberg, Dr.phil. 1928; postdoctoral study at University of Berlin, 1928-31, and University of Freiburg, 1931-33; University of Pisa, Dott. in Filosofia, 1937. *Home:* 423 West 120th St., New York, N.Y. 10027. *Office:* 1161 Amsterdam Ave., New York, N.Y. 10027.

CAREER: Istituto Superiore di Magistero, Florence, Italy, lecturer in German, 1934-35; Scuola Normale Superiore and University of Pisa, Pisa, Italy, lecturer in German, 1935-38; Yale University, New Haven, Conn., lecturer in philosophy, 1939; Columbia University, New York, N.Y., associate, 1939-48, associate professor, 1948-56, professor of philosophy, 1956-68, F.J.E. Woodbridge Professor of Philosophy, 1968-73, F.J.E. Woodbridge Professor of Philosophy Emeritus, 1973—. Scuola Normale Superiore, visiting professor, 1949 and 1952, Lincei professor, 1974; lecturer at other institutions in Europe and the United States. Member, Institute for Advanced Study, Princeton, N.J., 1954-55, 1961, and 1968-69. Secretary of cooperative research project, Mediaeval and Renaissance Latin Translations and Commentaries, sponsored by learned societies, including Union Academique Internationale.

MEMBER: American Philosophical Association, American Philosophical Society, Mediaeval Academy of America (fellow; vice-president, 1965-68, 1974-75; president, 1975-76), American Association of Teachers of Italian, American Academy of Arts and Sciences (fellow), American Society of Church

History, Renaissance Society of America (president, 1957-59), Medieval Club of New York (president, 1959-60), Phi Beta Kappa; corresponding fellow of Accademia dei Sepolti (Volterra), British Academy, Arcadia (Rome), Monumenta Germaniae Historica (Munich), Academie des Inscriptions (Paris), Istituto Veneto (Venice), Accademia degli Instronati (Siena), Accademia Toscana La Colombaria (Florence), and Accademia Patavina (Padua).

AWARDS, HONORS: Research grants from Oberlander Trust, 1939-41, and American Philosophical Society, 1949, 1952, 1955, and 1958; Fulbright fellowship to Italy, 1952; Guggenheim fellowship, 1958, 1968-69; Serena Medal for Italian Studies, British Academy, 1958; honorary degrees from University of Padua, 1962, Middlebury College, 1972, Columbia University, 1974, Catholic University of America, 1976, University of Rochester, 1977, and Duke University, 1979; Premio, Internazionale Forte dei Marmi, 1968; decorated commendatore dell'Ordine al Merito della Repubblica Italiana, 1971.

WRITINGS: Der Begriff der Seele in der Ethik des Plotin, Mohr (Tubingen), 1929; *Supplementum Ficinianum: Marsilii Ficini Florentini Opuscula,* two volumes, Olschki, 1937, published in one volume as *Supplementum Ficinianum: Opuscala Inedita et Dispersa,* 1973; *The Philosophy of Marsilio Ficino,* translation by Virginia Conant, Columbia University Press, 1943, reprinted, Peter Smith, 1964, original Italian edition published as *Il pensiero filosofico di Marsilio Ficino,* Sansoni, 1953; (editor with E. Cassirer and J. H. Randall, Jr. and author of introduction with Randall) *The Renaissance Philosophy of Man,* University of Chicago Press, 1948, reprinted, 1967; *Latin Manuscript Books Before 1600: A Bibliography of the Printed Catalogues of Extant Collections,* Cosmopolitan Science & Art Service, 1948, 3rd edition, Fordham University Press, 1965; *Die Italienischen Universitaten der Renaissance,* Scherpe-Verlag, 1953; *The Classics and Renaissance Thought* (Martin Lectures), Harvard University Press, 1955, revised and enlarged edition published as *Renaissance Thought: The Classic, Scholastic, and Humanist Strains,* Harper, 1961; *Studies in Renaissance Thought and Letters,* Edizioni di Storia e Letteratura, 1956; *Nuove fonti per la medicina salernitana,* [Salerno], 1958.

(Editor-in-chief) *Catalogus Translationum et Commentariorum: Mediaeval and Renaissance Latin Translations and Commentaries,* Catholic University of America Press, Volume I, 1960, Volume II, 1971, (with F. Edward Cranz) Volume III, 1976, (with Cranz) Volume IV, 1980; *Iter Italicum: A Finding List of Uncatalogued or Incompletely Catalogued Humanistic Manuscripts of the Renaissance in Italian and Other Libraries,* Brill, Volume I, 1963, Volume II, 1967; *Eight Philosophers of the Italian Renaissance,* Stanford University Press, 1964; *Renaissance Thought II: Papers on Humanism and the Arts* (sequel to *Renaissance Thought*), Harper, 1965, published as *Renaissance Thought and the Arts: Collected Essays,* Princeton University Press, 1980; *Renaissance Philosophy and the Mediaeval Tradition* (Wimmer Lecture), Archabbey Press, 1966; (editor) Cassirer, *Dall'Umanesimo all'Illuminismo,* La Nuova Italia, 1967; *Le Thomisme et la pensee Italienne de la Renaissance* (Conference Albert-le-Grand), J. Vrin (Paris), 1967; (compiler with Philip P. Wiener) *Renaissance Essays,* Harper, 1968; (author of introduction) Siegfried Kracauer, *History: The Last Things before the Last,* Oxford University Press, 1969; *Der Italienische Humanismus und seine Bedeutung,* Helbing & Lichtenhahn, 1969; *Renaissance Concepts of Man and Other Essays,* Harper, 1973; *Humanismus und Renaissance,* two volumes, Fink, 1974-76; *Medieval Aspects of Renaissance Learning: Three Essays,* edited and translated by Edward P. Mahoney, Duke University Press, 1974; *Renaissance Thought and*

Its Sources, Columbia University Press, 1979; *Studien zur Geschichte der Rhetorik und zum Begriff des Menschen in der Renaissance,* Stephan Fuessel, 1981.

Contributor: *Miscellanea Giovanni Mercati,* [Vatican City], 1946; Vergilius Ferm, editor, *A History of Philosophical Systems,* Philosophical Library, 1950; *Miscellanea Giovanni Galbiati,* [Milan], 1951; *Medioevo e rinascimento: Studi in onore di Bruno Nardi,* Volume I, [Florence], 1955; *Studi e memorie per la storia dell'universita de Balogna,* University of Bologna, 1956; *Studi letterari: Miscellanea in onore di Emilio Santini,* U. Manfredi, 1956; *Artes liberales von der Antiken Bildung zur Wissenschaft des Mittelalters,* Leiden-Koeln, 1959; Karl H. Dannenfeldt, editor, *The Renaissance: Medieval or Modern?,* Heath, 1959; *Facets of the Renaissance* (Arensberg Lectures), University of Southern California Press, 1959.

Medium Aevum Vivum: Festschrift fuer Walther Bulst, University of Heidelberg, 1960; Tinsley Helton, editor, *The Renaissance: A Reconsideration of the Theories and Interpretations of the Age,* University of Wisconsin Press, 1961; *Chapters in Western Civilization,* Volume I, 3rd edition, Columbia University Press, 1961; S. Prete, editor, *Didascaliae: Studies in Honor of Anselm M. Albareda,* Bernard M. Rosenthal, 1961; *Wort und Text: Festschrift fuer Fritz Schalk,* Klostermann, 1963; *Melanges Eugene Tisserant,* [Vatican City], 1964; *Classical, Medieval and Renaissance Studies in Honor of Berthold Louis Ullman,* Volume II, Edizioni de Storia e Letteratura, 1964; *Studi di bibliografia e di storia in onore di Tammaro de Marinis,* Mardersteig, 1964; Charles H. Carter, editor, *From the Renaissance to the Counter-Reformation: Essays in Honor of Garrett Mattingly,* Random House, 1965; *Harry Austryn Wolfson Jubilee Volume,* Volume I, [Jerusalem], 1965; Bernard O'Kelly, editor, *The Renaissance Image of Man and the World,* Ohio State University Press, 1966; L. Wallach, editor, *The Classical Tradition: Literary and Historical Studies in Honor of Harry Caplan,* Cornell University Press, 1966; John P. Anton, editor, *Naturalism and Historical Understanding: Essays on the Philosophy of John Herman Randall, Jr.,* State University of New York Press, 1967; John M. Headley, editor, *Medieval and Renaissance Studies: Proceedings of the Southeastern Institute of Medieval and Renaissance Studies,* University of North Carolina Press, 1968.

J. G. Rowe and W. H. Stockdale, editors, *Florilegium Historiale: Essays Presented to Wallace K. Ferguson,* University of Toronto Press, 1971; Bernard S. Levy, editor, *Developments in the Early Renaissance,* State University of New York Press, 1972; John J. O'Meara and B. Naumann, editors, *Latin Script and Letters A.D. 400-900: Festschrift Presented to Ludwig Bieler on the Occasion of His Seventieth Birthday,* Brill, 1976; Stuart F. Spicker, editor, *Organism, Medicine, and Metaphysics: Essays in Honor of Hans Jonas,* Reidel, 1978; *Science and History: Studies in Honor of Edward Rosen,* Wroclaw, 1978; *Il Rinascimento: Interpretazioni e Problemi,* Laterza, 1979.

Also author of sound recording, "Humanism, Platonism and Aristotelianism." Contributor of more than one hundred articles on Renaissance and philosophical subjects to professional journals in the United States, Italy, and other countries; contributor of book reviews to *American Historical Review, Hispanic Review, Art Bulletin, Speculum, Renaissance Quarterly,* and philosophy journals. Member of editorial board, *Journal of the History of Ideas,* 1943—; book editor, *Journal of Philosophy,* 1940-51; editor, *Manuscripta.*

SIDELIGHTS: C. B. Schmitt writes in the *Times Literary Supplement* that Paul Oskar Kristeller "is responsible for establishing Renaissance philosophy as a particular field of enquiry, at least among English-speaking scholars. . . . Indeed, one can say without fear of contradiction that the influence exerted by Kristeller on the philosophico-intellectual side of Renaissance studies has been greater than that of any of his contemporaries. Though he has had fewer direct students than many lesser scholars, his teaching through indirect means has been remarkably broad and pervasive for two generations. There are few working in medieval and Renaissance philosophy or intellectual history who have not benefited from his erudition and generosity.''

BIOGRAPHICAL/CRITICAL SOURCES: Times Literary Supplement, July 25, 1980.

* * *

KRONHAUSEN, Eberhard W(ilhelm) 1915-

PERSONAL: Born September 12, 1915, in Berlin, Germany; married Phyllis Ulrickson (a psychologist and writer), September 12, 1954. *Education:* University of Minnesota, B.S., 1947, M.A., 1951; Columbia University, Ed.D., 1956.

CAREER: Group Community Guidance Center, New York, N.Y., consulting psychologist, 1953-58; a program director, National Institute for Mental Health Research Grant, 1956-57; in private practice of psychology, 1953—. Producer with wife, Phyllis C. Kronhausen, of experimental films, and of a sound film-short, ''Psychomontage No. 1,'' distributed by Cinema 16, a full-length documentary, ''Why Are They Doing It?,'' produced by Palladium Film (Denmark), 1971, and a full-length erotic feature film, ''The Hottest Show in Town,'' produced by Europa Film (Sweden), 1972. *Member:* American Psychological Association.

WRITINGS—All with wife, Phyllis C. Kronhausen: *Pornography and the Law: The Psychology of Erotic Realism and Pornography,* Ballantine, 1959, 2nd edition, revised and enlarged, 1964.

Sex Histories of American College Men, Ballantine, 1960; *The Sexually Responsive Woman,* preface by Simone de Beauvoir, Grove, 1964 (published in England as *Sexual Response in Women,* J. Calder, 1965); *Walter: The English Casanova,* Ballantine, 1967 (published in England as *Walter, the English Casanova: A Presentation of His Unique Memoirs, ''My Secret Life,''* Polybooks, 1967); *The First International Exhibition of Erotic Art,* Kronhausen Books, 1968; (compiler) *Erotic Art: A Survey of Erotic Fact and Fancy in the Fine Arts,* Grove, 1968.

(Compiler) *Erotic Fantasies: A Study of the Sexual Imagination,* Grove, 1970; *Drs. Eberhard and Phyllis Kronhausen Present the Second International Exhibition of Erotic Art* (at Liljevalchs Konsthall, Stockholm, April 2-May 18, 1969), Societe d'Etudes Financieres (Stockholm), 1970; (compiler) *Erotische Exlibris* (erotic book-plates), Gala Verlag (Hamburg), 1970; (compiler) *Erotic Art 2,* Grove, 1970; *More Walter: Being A Further Examination of ''My Secret Life,''* Morntide, 1970; *Freedom to Love,* Grove, 1970; *The Sex People: Erotic Performers and Their Bold New Worlds,* Playboy Press, 1974. Also author of numerous articles and monographs on psychological topics.

WORK IN PROGRESS: Exploration of alternate life styles; research in ''tropical survival farming in Costa Rica, Central America, health, nutrition, and spiritual growth.''

SIDELIGHTS: Eberhard W. Kronhausen wrote *CA:* ''We (my wife and I) have always defended the undefendable, from por-

nography to 'sex as entertainment' (live shows, porno movies, etc.), and all the way to such non-monogamous sexual arrangements as group sex, group marriage, and the like. Why? Because, for one, we felt that fundamental issues concerning freedom of personal choice and freedom of expression are involved in these matters; and, secondly, because it is not beyond reasonable doubt that even the most distasteful pornography may have some redeeming social value (e.g., cathartic)—to say nothing of the (to us) rather obvious possible merits of even the most unorthodox sexual arrangement between 'consenting adults,' at least for those who seem to have decided personal preferences along these lines (and aren't bothering anybody else in so doing).

''We still believe strongly, in this later part of our lives, that—for most people—to liberate themselves from whatever sexual hangups, false shame, and groundless inhibitions they might be subject to, is a 'jolly good thing.' However, as we (my wife and I) have by now well entered the tranquil—we like to call it 'post-tantric'—phase of our lives, we also feel that it is of paramount importance for human beings to feel connected with something greater than themselves and to nurture and develop their own higher selves.

''Living, these days, most of the time with our three German shepards on a small, experimental 'survival' farm in sunny Costa Rica, we have come closer to 'Mother Nature' than ever. As previously, in our psychotherapeutic work we had deliberately trained ourselves to become extremely sensitive to the emotional needs and subtle—can we say extra-sensory?—vibes of other people, so we are now happily engaged in another kind of voluntary sensitivity training with the plants and animals all around us. And through them, we feel, we are also getting into closer contact with that mysterious source of energy, that great cosmic dynamo which is the life of all living things.

''And when the plants and the dogs and the ducks and the chickens and everything and everybody else are going to be in good enough shape, and if our health stands up, we still hope to finish the unfinished books (and, no, they are only tangentially sex related, if at all!) that had to be put on the back burner in favor of this, our latest and, perhaps, somewhat overly ambitious 'living experiment.'''

Kronhausen and his wife are collectors of erotic art. Their collection has been exhibited at the Museum of Erotic Art, San Francisco, Calif., 1970-73, and at numerous private and public exhibitions in Europe, 1968-77.

MEDIA ADAPTATIONS: Freedom to Love was made into a documentary feature produced by Reginald Puhl in West Germany in 1970.

AVOCATIONAL INTERESTS: ''Cross-cultural studies, sexual liberation, and mental health remain abiding interests.''

BIOGRAPHICAL/CRITICAL SOURCES: Washington Post, December 13, 1965; *New Statesman,* December 1, 1967; *Commonweal,* November 7, 1969; *Variety,* February 25, 1970.

* * *

KRONHAUSEN, Phyllis C(armen) 1929-

PERSONAL: Born January 26, 1929, in Minnesota; daughter of Fred J. and Ruby (Hagen) Ulrickson; married Eberhard W. Kronhausen (a psychologist and writer), September 12, 1954. *Education:* University of Minnesota, B.B.A. (summa cum laude), 1951; Columbia University, Ed.D., 1958.

CAREER: University of Minnesota, Minneapolis, administrative assistant and foreign student adviser, 1951; U.S. Government, Department of State, assistant vice-counsel, 1951-53; Columbia University, New York, N.Y., lecturer, 1956-58; research grant program director, National Institute for Mental Health, 1956-57; in private practice of psychology, 1957—. Producer, with husband, Eberhard W. Kronhausen, of experimental films, and of a sound film-short, "Psychomontage No. 1," distributed by Cinema 16, a full-length documentary, "Why Are They Doing It?," produced by Palladium Film (Denmark), 1971, and a full-length erotic feature film, "The Hottest Show in Town," produced by Europa Film (Sweden), 1972. *Member:* American Psychological Association.

WRITINGS—All with husband, Eberhard W. Kronhausen: *Pornography and the Law: The Psychology of Erotic Realism and Pornography,* Ballantine, 1959, 2nd edition, revised and enlarged, 1964.

Sex Histories of American College Men, Ballantine, 1960; *The Sexually Responsive Woman,* preface by Simone de Beauvoir, Grove, 1964 (published in England as *Sexual Response in Women,* J. Calder, 1965); *Walter: The English Casanova,* Ballantine, 1967 (published in England as *Walter, the English Casanova: A Presentation of His Unique Memoirs, "My Secret Life,"* Polybooks, 1967); *The First International Exhibition of Erotic Art,* Kronhausen Books, 1968; (compiler) *Erotic Art: A Survey of Erotic Fact and Fancy in the Fine Arts,* Grove, 1968.

(Compiler) *Erotic Fantasies: A Study of the Sexual Imagination,* Grove, 1970; *Drs. Eberhard and Phyllis Kronhausen Present the Second International Exhibition of Erotic Art* (at Liljevalchs Konsthall, Stockholm, April 2-May 18, 1969), Societe d'Etudes Financieres (Stockholm), 1970; (compiler) *Erotische Exlibris* (erotic book-plates), Gala Verlag (Hamburg), 1970; (compiler) *Erotic Art 2,* Grove, 1970; *More Walter: Being a Further Examination of "My Secret Life,"* Morntide, 1970; *Freedom to Love,* Grove, 1970; *The Sex People: Erotic Performers and Their Bold New Worlds,* Playboy Press, 1974. Also author of numerous articles and monographs on psychological topics.

WORK IN PROGRESS: Exploration of alternate life styles; research in "tropical survival farming in Costa Rica, Central America, health, nutrition, and spiritual growth."

SIDELIGHTS: Phyllis C. Kronhausen and her husband are collectors of erotic art. Their collection has been exhibited at the Museum of Erotic Art, San Francisco, Calif., 1970-73, and at numerous private and public exhibitions in Europe, 1968-77. *Media adaptations: Freedom to Love* was made into a documentary feature produced by Reginald Puhl in West Germany in 1970.

AVOCATIONAL INTERESTS: Experimental films.

BIOGRAPHICAL/CRITICAL SOURCES: Washington Post, December 13, 1965; *New Statesman,* December 1, 1967; *Commonweal,* November 7, 1969; *Variety,* February 25, 1970.†

*   *   *

KRULL, Felix
See WHITE, Stanley

*   *   *

KURIHARA, Kenneth Kenkichi   1910-1972

PERSONAL: Born January 8, 1910, in Kutchan, Japan; came to United States in 1930, naturalized in 1963; died June 12, 1972, in Binghamton, N.Y.; son of Kichzo and Natsu (Koshida) Kurihara; married; wife's name Kyo (an artist); married second wife, Tina Yoshiko Fukimbara, November 2, 1971. *Education:* Ohio Wesleyan University, B.A., 1935; Oberlin College, M.A., 1936; University of Iowa, Ph.D., 1942.

CAREER: Princeton University, Princeton, N.J., instructor in economics, 1946-47; Rutgers University, New Brunswick, N.J., lecturer, 1947-50, assistant professor, 1950-56, associate professor, 1956-60, professor of economics, 1960-68; State University of New York at Binghamton, Distinguished Professor of Economic Theory, 1968-72. Visiting professor of economics, University of Washington, spring, 1958; visiting research professor, Institute of Statistics, Oxford University, spring, 1961; guest lecturer, Cambridge University, 1961; Fulbright visiting professor of economics, Tokyo Metropolitan University, spring, 1965. *Member:* American Economic Association, Royal Economic Society (life member), Metropolitan Economics Association of New York (vice-president, 1954-55), Order of Artus. *Awards, honors:* Dr. Econ., Hitotsubashi University, 1958; Distinguished Teaching Award from Christian R. and Mary Lindbark Foundation, 1963.

WRITINGS: Labor in the Philippine Economy, Stanford University Press, 1945, reprinted, AMS Press, 1973; *Monetary Theory and Public Policy,* Norton, 1950; (editor) *Post-Keynesian Economics,* Rutgers University Press, 1954; *Introduction to Keynesian Dynamics,* Columbia University Press, 1956; *Keynesian Theory of Economic Development,* Columbia University Press, 1959; *National Income and Economic Growth,* Rand McNally, 1961; *Applied Dynamic Economics,* Allen & Unwin, 1963; *Macroeconomics and Programming,* Allen & Unwin, 1964; *The Growth Potential of the Japanese Economy,* Johns Hopkins Press, 1971; *Essays in Macrodynamic Economics,* State University of New York Press, 1972. Contributor to professional journals. Editor, *Indian Journal of Economics,* beginning 1960.

AVOCATIONAL INTERESTS: Modern painting.

OBITUARIES: New York Times, June 14, 1972.†

*   *   *

KURZ, Artur R.
See SCORTIA, Thomas N(icholas)

*   *   *

KUSAN, Ivan   1933-

PERSONAL: Born August 30, 1933, in Sarajevo, Yugoslavia; son of Jaksa and Marija (Murko) Kusan. *Education:* Studied painting at Academy of Fine Arts, Zagreb, Yugoslavia. *Home:* Draskoviceva 13, 41000 Zagreb, Yugoslavia.

CAREER: Free-lance writer. Former editor at Zagreb-Radio, Zagreb, Yugoslavia, and manager of story department at Zagreb Cartoon Motion Picture Studio. *Member:* Writers' Union of Yugoslavia. *Awards honors:* Zagreb Literary Prize, 1961, for juvenile book, *Domaca zadaca,* and 1971; Andersen Prize, 1974.

WRITINGS: Uzbuna na Zelenom vrhu (juvenile), Matica Hrvatska (Zagreb), 1956, 2nd edition, Mladost (Zagreb), 1973, translation by Michael B. Petrovich published as *The Mystery of Green Hill,* Harcourt, 1962; *Trenutak unaprijed* (short stories; title means "A Moment in Advance"), Naklada Drustva Knjizevnika Hrvatske (Zagreb), 1957; *Koko i duhovi* (juvenile), Kadok (Belgrade), 1958, translation by Drenka Willen published as *Koko and the Ghosts,* Harcourt, 1966; *Razapet izmedu* (novel; title means "The Crucified"), Nolit (Belgrade), 1958.

Zidom zazidani (novel; title means "The Walled"), Znanje (Zagreb), 1960; *Domaca zadaca* (juvenile; title means "The Homework"), Matica Hrvatska, 1960; *Tajanstveni djecak* (juvenile; title means "The Mysterious Boy"), Kadok, 1962; *Zagonetni djecak,* Prosveta (Belgrade), 1963; (with Slobodan Novak and Cedo Prica) *Dvadeset godina jugoslavenske proze,* Naprijed (Zagreb), 1966.

Toranj: Ljetopis za razbibrigu, Kolo Matice Hrvatske (Zagreb), 1970; *Veliki dan: Pripovijetke,* Matica Hrvatska, 1970;

U selu i gradu, u radu i igri, Skolska Knjiga (Zagreb), 1970; *Koko u Parizu,* Mladost (Zagreb), 1972, translation by Willen published as *The Mystery of the Stolen Painting,* Harcourt, 1975; *Naivci,* Znanje, 1975; *Zapisi o vlastitom umiranju: Proza,* Znanje, 1979. Editor of *Moji pronalasci,* 1977. Translator of several books from English, French, and Russian into Yugoslav, including Mark Twain's *Tom Sawyer.* Author of radio plays and a television script.

WORK IN PROGRESS: An adult novel; a book of short stories for children; a book of essays.

SIDELIGHTS: Ivan Kusan's children's books, all self-illustrated in Yugoslav editions, have been translated into five languages. *Avocational interests:* Painting.

L

LABAREE, Benjamin Woods 1927-

PERSONAL: Born July 21, 1927, in New Haven, Conn.; son of Leonard Woods (a professor) and Elizabeth (Calkins) Labaree; married Linda Carol Prichard, June 27, 1959; children: Benjamin Woods, Jr., Jonathan Martin, Sarah Calkins. *Education:* Yale University, B.A., 1950; Harvard University, A.M., 1953, Ph.D., 1957. *Politics:* Democrat. *Religion:* Congregationalist. *Home:* 205 High St., Mystic, Conn. 06355. *Office:* Williams-Mystic Seaport Program in American Maritime Studies, Mystic, Conn. 06355.

CAREER: Phillips Exeter Academy, Exeter, N.H., instructor in history, 1950-52; Connecticut College, New London, instructor in history, 1957-58; Harvard University, Cambridge, Mass., 1958-63, began as instructor, became assistant professor of history, Allston Burr Senior Tutor, Winthrop House, 1958-62; Williams College, Williamstown, Mass., associate professor, 1963-67, professor of history, 1968-77, dean of college, 1963-77, director of Williams–Mystic Seaport Program in American Maritime Studies, 1977—. Chairman of board of editors, American Maritime Library. *Military service:* U.S. Navy, 1945-46. *Member:* American Historical Association, American Antiquarian Society, Colonial Society of Massachusetts, Massachusetts Historical Society.

WRITINGS: (Editor) *Samuel McIntire: A Bicentennial Symposium, 1757-1957,* Essex Institute, 1957; *Patriots and Partisans: The Merchants of Newburyport, 1764-1815,* Harvard University Press, 1962; *The Road to Independence, 1763-1776,* Macmillan, 1963; *The Boston Tea Party,* Oxford University Press, 1964; (with Joseph Huthmacher and Vincent P. De Santis) *American Past and Present,* Allyn & Bacon, 1968; *New England and the Sea,* Wesleyan University Press, 1971; *America's Nation-Time 1607-1789,* Allyn & Bacon, 1973; (editor) *The Atlantic World of Robert G. Albion,* Wesleyan University Press, 1975; (with Ian R. Christie) *Empire or Independence, 1760-1776,* Phaidon, 1976. Essex Institute's *Historical Collections,* member of board of editors, 1956—, editor, 1956-60.

*   *   *

LADNER, Kurt
See DeMILLE, Nelson

LAFFERTY, Perry (Francis) 1917-

PERSONAL: Born October 3, 1917, in Davenport, Iowa; son of Herbert Ray and Elizabeth (Perry) Lafferty; married Mary Frances Carden, January 16, 1943; children: Marcy, Steven. *Education:* Yale University, certificate in music, 1938. *Home:* 335 South Bristol Ave., Los Angeles, Calif. 90049.

CAREER: Television producer and director, beginning 1947; became vice-president of programs, Columbia Broadcasting System, Hollywood, Calif.; currently senior vice-president of programs and talent, National Broadcasting Co., Burbank, Calif. Shows he produced include "Robert Montgomery Presents," "Studio One," "Your Hit Parade," "The Andy Williams Show," "Person to Person," "The Danny Kaye Show," "Frankie Laine," "Dream World," and "The Mary Tyler Moore Hour." Conducted seminar on radio and television production at Sarah Lawrence College, 1952. *Military service:* U.S. Army Air Forces, 1944-45; became captain. *Member:* Directors Guild of America, Screen Producers Guild, Authors League of America.

WRITINGS: Birdies Sing and Everything, Dodd, 1964; *How Come the Pilot's Not Afraid?,* Price, Stern, 1980; *How to Lose Your Fear of Flying,* Price, Stern, 1980.

*   *   *

LAINE, Gloria
See HANNA, David

*   *   *

LAIRD, Jean E(louise) 1930-
(J. E. Drial, Marcia McKeever, Jean L. Wakefield)

PERSONAL: Born January 18, 1930, in Wakefield, Mich.; daughter of Chester A. and Agnes (Petranek) Rydeski; married Jack E. Laird (owner of retail lumberyards and investment companies), June 9, 1951; children: John E., Jayne E., Joan-An P., Jerilyn S., Jacquelyn T. *Education:* Duluth Business University, graduate, 1948; additional study at University of Minnesota, 1949-50, and Michigan State University, 1951. *Religion:* Roman Catholic. *Home:* 10540 South Lockwood Ave., Oak Lawn, Ill. 60453; and Wildwood Ave., Grand Beach, Mich. 49118.

CAREER: Former secretary for seven years for firms and schools in Minnesota and Michigan; free-lance writer, mostly of nonfiction for magazines; Oak Lawn High School, Adult Evening School, Oak Lawn, Ill., journalism teacher, 1964-72; St. Xavier College, Chicago, Ill., instructor in journalism, 1974—. *Member:* Canterbury Writer's Club (Chicago; president, 1961; member of governing board, 1962-64), Oak Lawn Business and Professional Women's Club; St. Linus Guild, Mt. Assisi Academy, Marist, Queen of Peace (parents' clubs).

WRITINGS: Lost in the Department Store (juvenile), Denison, 1964; *Around the House Like Magic* (Book-of-the-Month Club selection), Harper, 1967; *Around the Kitchen Like Magic,* Harper, 1969; *The Plump Ballerina* (juvenile), Denison, 1970; *The Alphabet Zoo* (juvenile), Oddo Press, 1972; *The Porcupine Story Book* (juvenile), Concordia Press, 1974; *Fried Marbles and Other Fun Things to Do* (juvenile), Scholastic Books, 1975; *The Homemaker's Book of Time and Money Savers,* Stephen Greene, 1979; *The Homemaker's Book of Energy Savers,* Stephen Greene, 1981.

Also author of *How to Get the Most from Your Appliances,* 1967, *Hundreds of Hints for Harrassed Homemakers,* 1971, *The Book of Dollar Savers and Budget Stretchers,* and about 200 National Research Bureau booklets. Travel editor, *Travel/ Leisure* (magazine) and, under pseudonym Marcia McKeever, *Oldsmobile's Magazine;* author of hobby columns in *Modern Maturity* and *Vacations Unlimited;* author under pseudonym Jean L. Wakefield of beauty column "Ladylikes," *Ladycom* (magazine); author of columns "Around the House with Jean" and "A Woman's Work," 1965-70, "The World as I See It," *Chicagotown News,* 1969, and "Time and Money Savers," *Lady's Circle Magazine,* 1973—. Contributor of over 900 articles to periodicals, including *Popular Medicine, Good Housekeeping, Parents' Magazine, Coronet, Pageant, Modern Bride, Better Homes and Gardens, American Home, Family Digest, Chicago Tribune Magazine, Catholic Digest, Chicago Sun-Times Magazine, Reader's Digest,* and *Parade.*

SIDELIGHTS: Lost in the Department Store has been read on children's television shows, including "Tree Top House," "Ray Raynor Show," and "Sesame Street."

BIOGRAPHICAL/CRITICAL SOURCES: Life and Health, March, 1964.

*   *   *

LAMBRICK, Hugh Trevor 1904-

PERSONAL: Born April 20, 1904, in Breaston, Derby, England; son of Charles Menzies (a clergyman) and Jessie (Trevor) Lambrick; married Gabrielle Jennings, October 8, 1948 (died, 1968); children: Charles Trevor, George Henry. *Education:* Oriel College, Oxford University, B.A. (with first class honors), 1926, M.A., 1947. *Home:* Picketts Heath, Boars Hill, Oxford, England.

CAREER: Indian Civil Service, 1927-47, posts in Bombay and Sind provinces, India, include assistant commissioner in Sind, 1931, secretary to governor, 1941, civil adviser to commander of Upper Sind Force, 1942-43, and special commissioner for Sind, 1943-46; Oxford University, Oxford, England, fellow of Oriel College, 1947-71, fellow emeritus, 1971—. *Member:* Sind Historical Society (president, 1940-43), Society of Antiquaries (fellow, 1971), East India and Sports Club. *Awards, honors:* Companion, Order of the Indian Empire, 1944; D.Litt., Oxford University, 1971.

WRITINGS: Sir Charles Napier and Sind, Clarendon Press, 1952; *John Jacob of Jacobabad,* Cassell, 1960, 2nd edition, Oxford University Press, 1975; *History of Sind,* Volume I:

Sind: A General Introduction, Sindhi Adabi Board (Pakistan), 1964, 2nd edition, Oxford University Press, 1975, Volume II: *Sind: Before the Muslim Conquest,* Oxford University Press, 1973; (contributor) C. H. Philips and Mary D. Wainwright, editors, *The Partition of India: Policies and Perspectives, 1935-1947,* Allen & Unwin, 1970; (editor and translator) *The Terrorist,* Benn, 1972. Also author of Sind Tables, Volume 12 of Census of India, 1942. Contributor of articles on archeology and history to *Collier's Encyclopedia.* Contributor of articles and book reviews to periodicals, including *Sind Historical Society,* 1935-46, and *Listener.*

WORK IN PROGRESS: Henry Viscount Hardinge; Franz Schubert's Annus Mirabilis.

AVOCATIONAL INTERESTS: Composing music (has written a sonata for violin and piano, cycle of songs without words for oboe and piano, and "Duo Sonatina," "Adagio for Organ," and other piano pieces).†

*   *   *

LANE, Robert E(dwards) 1917-

PERSONAL: Born August 19, 1917, in Philadelphia, Pa.; son of Robert Porter and Bess (Edwards) Lane; married Helen Sobol, 1944; children: R. Lawrence, Thomas E. *Education:* Harvard University, B.S., 1939, Ph.D., 1950. *Home:* 558 Chapel St., New Haven, Conn. 06511. *Office:* 3532 Yale Station, New Haven, Conn. 06520.

CAREER: Yale University, New Haven, Conn., 1948—, began as instructor, currently professor of political science. *Military service:* U.S. Army, Infantry and Air Forces, 1942-46; became captain. *Member:* International Society of Political Psychology (president, 1978-79), American Political Science Association (president, 1970-71), American Sociological Association, Society for the Psychological Study of Social Issues. *Awards, honors:* Center for Advanced Study in the Behavioral Sciences fellow, 1956-57; Social Science Research Council fellow, 1957-59; Woodrow Wilson International Center for Scholars fellow, 1970-71; Fulbright-Hayes senior fellowship, 1972-73; National Endowment for the Humanities fellowship, 1976-77.

WRITINGS: Problems in American Government, Prentice-Hall, 1952, 3rd edition (with others) published as *An Introduction to Political Analysis,* 1962, 4th edition, 1967; *The Regulation of Businessmen: Social Conditions of Government Economic Control,* Yale University Press, 1954; *Political Life: Why People Get Involved in Politics,* Free Press of Glencoe, 1959; *The Liberties of Wit, Humanism, Criticism and the Civic Mind,* Yale University Press, 1961; *Political Ideology: Why the American Common Man Believes What He Does,* Free Press of Glencoe, 1962; (with David Sears) *Public Opinion,* Prentice-Hall, 1964; *Political Thinking and Consciousness: The Private Life of the Political Mind,* Markham, 1969; *Political Man,* Free Press, 1972.

*   *   *

LANG, Frances
See MANTLE, Winifred (Langford)

*   *   *

LANGFORD, Jane
See MANTLE, Winifred (Langford)

LANHAM, Frank W(esley) 1914-

PERSONAL: Born May 4, 1914, in Bloomington, Ill.; married Cathryn Parker. *Education:* Illinois State University, B.Ed., 1937; University of Michigan, M.A., 1947, Ph.D., 1956. *Home:* 65 Annapolis Lane, Rotonda West, Fla. 33947. *Office:* College of Education, Wayne State University, Detroit, Mich. 48202.

CAREER: Teacher at Stambaugh Community High School, Mt. Morris Community High School, and Northern (Flint) High School (all in Michigan); General Motors Institute, Flint, Mich., instructor, 1943; Illinois Wesleyan University, Bloomington, instructor, 1946; University of Michigan, Ann Arbor, 1947-69, became professor of education; Wayne State University, Detroit, Mich., professor of education, 1969-79, professor emeritus, 1979—. *Military service:* U.S. Army, Infantry, 1943-46; served in European Theater; became technical sergeant. *Member:* Association of School Business Officials, American Business Writers Association, National Business Education Association (research division president), National Education Association, Eastern Business Teachers Association, Michigan School Business Officials Association, Michigan Business Education Association, Michigan Education Association, Pi Omega Pi, Phi Delta Kappa (chapter president), Delta Pi Epsilon (chapter president), Phi Kappa Phi. *Awards, honors:* Distinguished service award, Michigan Business Education Association, 1963.

WRITINGS: (With Marie M. Stewart and others) *Business English and Communication,* McGraw, 1961, 5th edition, 1977; *The Meaning of School Accounts,* Ann Arbor Publishers, 1961, 2nd edition, University Council for Education Administration (Columbus, Ohio), 1964; (with others) *English and College Communication,* McGraw, 1964; (with Stewart and Kenneth Zimmer) *College English and Communication,* McGraw, 1964, 3rd edition, 1975; (with Fred S. Cook) *Opportunities and Requirements for Initial Employment of School Leavers,* College of Education, Wayne State University, 1966; (with J. M. Trytten) *Review and Synthesis of Research in Business and Office Education,* Center for Research and Leadership Development in Vocational and Technical Education, Ohio State University, 1966; (editor) *Business Education Meets the Challenges of Change,* National Business Education Association, 1966; (with Stewart and Zimmer) *English for Business,* McGraw, 1968; *Development of Performance Goals for a New Office and Business Education Learnings System, NOBELS: Final Project Report,* Center for Research and Leadership Development in Vocational and Technical Education, Ohio State University, 1970; (with others) *Development of Task Performance Statements for a New Office and Business Education Learnings System (NOBELS),* Center for Research and Leadership Development in Vocational and Technical Education, Ohio State University, 1972.

* * *

La PALOMBARA, Joseph 1925-

PERSONAL: Born May 18, 1925, in Chicago, Ill.; son of Louis (a tailor) and Helen (Teutonico) La Palombara; married Lyda Mae Ecke, June 22, 1947 (divorced); married Constance Ada Bezer, June, 1971; children: (first marriage) Richard Dean, David D., Susan Dee. *Education:* University of Illinois, A.B., 1947, M.A., 1950; Princeton University, M.A., 1952, Ph.D., 1954; University of Rome, graduate study, 1952-53. *Politics:* Democrat. *Home:* 8 Reservoir St., New Haven, Conn. 06511. *Office:* Department of Political Science, Yale University, New Haven, Conn. 06520.

CAREER: Oregon State College (now University), Corvallis, 1949-50, began as instructor, became assistant professor of political science; Princeton University, Princeton, N.J., instructor in politics, 1952; Michigan State University, East Lansing, assistant professor, 1953-56, associate professor, 1956-58, professor of political science and chairman of department, 1958-64; Yale University, New Haven, Conn., professor of political science, 1964-65, Arnold Wolfers Professor of Political Science, 1965—, chairman of department, 1974-78. Visiting professor of political science, University of Florence, Italy, 1957-58, University of California, Berkeley, 1962, and Columbia University, 1965-66. Director of Michigan Citizenship Clearing House, 1955; member of staff, Social Science Research Council, 1966-73; member of executive committee, Inter-University Consortium on Political Research, 1968-70; chairman of Western European foreign area fellowship program, Social Science Research Council-American Council of Learned Societies, 1972—; senior research associate, Conference Board of New York, 1975—; cultural attache, U.S. Embassy, Rome, Italy, 1980-81. Consultant to Federal Civil Defense Agency, 1956, Carnegie Corp., 1959, Brookings Institution, 1962, Ford Foundation, 1965—, Twentieth Century Fund, 1965-69, Agency for International Development, 1967-68, Foreign Service Institute, 1968-72, Educational Testing Service, 1970—, and to several major U.S. corporations, 1975—.

MEMBER: International Political Science Association, American Political Science Association, American Political Science Association (vice-president, 1977-78), American Society for Public Administration, Society for Italian Historical Studies, Italian Social Science Association, Societa Italiana di Studi Elettori, Midwest Conference of Political Scientists, Phi Beta Kappa, Phi Kappa Phi, Phi Eta Sigma. *Awards, honors:* Center for Advanced Study in the Behavioral Sciences fellow, 1961-62; Rockefeller fellow, 1963-64; Order of Merit, Republic of Italy, 1964; M.A., Yale University, 1964; Ford Foundation faculty fellow, 1969; Guggenheim fellow, 1971-72; named Knight Commander, Order of Merit, Republic of Italy, 1974.

WRITINGS: The Initiative and Referendum in Oregon, Oregon State College Press, 1950; *The Italian Labor Movement: Problems and Prospects,* Cornell University Press, 1957; *Guide to Michigan Politics,* Michigan State University, 1960; (co-editor) *Elezioni e comportamento politico in Italia,* Communita, 1962; *Bureaucracy and Political Development,* Princeton University Press, 1963; *Interest Groups in Italian Politics,* Princeton University Press, 1964.

Italy: The Politics of Planning, Syracuse University Press, 1966; (editor with Myron Weiner) *Political Parties and Political Development,* Princeton University Press, 1966; (with others) *Crises and Sequences in Political Development,* Princeton University Press, 1971; *Politics within Nations,* Prentice-Hall, 1974; (with Stephen Blank) *Multinational Corporations and National Elites,* Conference Board of New York, 1976; (with Blank) *Multinational Corporations in Comparative Perspective,* Conference Board of New York, 1977; (with Blank) *Multinational Corporations and Developing Countries,* Conference Board of New York, 1979.

Contributor: D. S. Piper and R. T. Cole, editors, *Post-Primary Education and Political and Economic Development,* Duke University Press, 1964; L. Pyle and S. Verba, editors, *Political Culture and Political Development,* Princeton University Press, 1965; H. Penniman, editor, *Italy at the Polls,* American Enterprise Institute for Public Policy Research, 1976; A. Ranney and G. Sartori, editors, *Eurocommunisn: The Italian Case,* American Enterprise Institute for Public Policy Research, 1978; Pyle and Verba, editors, *The Citizen and Politics,* Greylock Press, 1978; Penniman, editor, *Italy at the Polls: 1979,* American Enterprise Institute for Public Policy Research, 1981. Contributor to *Nation, World Politics, Pacific Spectator, Mediterranean Observer,* and to professional journals in the United States, Italy, Spain, and Germany.

SIDELIGHTS: Joseph La Palombara has visited all of Europe, Japan, Vietnam, the Philippines, India, Pakistan, Israel, Mexico, and Brazil. *Avocational interests:* Photography, book collecting, fishing.

*   *   *

LASCHEVER, Barnett D.   1924-
(L. David Barnett)

PERSONAL: Born March 13, 1924, in Hartford, Conn.; son of Abraham and Ida Laschever; married Dolores S. Palanker, 1949; children: Jonathan, Sara, Adam, Ann-Rebecca. *Education:* University of Michigan, B.S. *Religion:* Jewish. *Office:* Director of Tourism, Connecticut Department of Economic Development, 210 Washington St., Hartford, Conn. 06106.

CAREER: Detroit Free Press, Detroit, Mich., reporter, 1945; United Press, Detroit, reporter, 1945-46; *Hartford Times,* Hartford, Conn., travel editor, 1950-56; *New York Herald-Tribune,* New York, N.Y., travel editor, beginning 1956; currently affiliated with Connecticut Department of Economic Development, Hartford. *Military service:* U.S. Army, Signal Corps, twenty months; reporter and feature writer for army newspaper, *Stars and Stripes. Member:* Society of American Travel Writers (first vice-president, 1957; northeast regional vice-president, 1962), American Society of Travel Agents (allied member), Overseas Press Club, New York Travel Writers (president, 1959-60). *Awards, honors:* New England Managing Editor's Associated Press award, 1953, for best big city feature story.

WRITINGS: (Associate editor with Robert C. Fisher) Eugene Fodor, editor, *Fodor's Guide to South America,* McKay, 1967; (contributing editor) Fodor, editor, *Fodor's Guide to New England,* McKay, 1974.

"Getting to Know" series; published by Coward: *Getting to Know Hawaii,* 1959; . . . *India,* 1960; . . . *Pakistan,* 1961; . . . *Cuba,* 1962; . . . *Venezuela,* 1962.

Author of garden column, *Sunday Hartford Courant.* Contributor to *Travel, Cosmopolitan, McCall's, Saturday Review,* and other magazines.

WORK IN PROGRESS: A novel; two cookbooks.

AVOCATIONAL INTERESTS: Tennis, swimming, and gardening.

*   *   *

LATTIMORE, Eleanor Frances   1904-

PERSONAL: Born June 30, 1904, in Shanghai, China; daughter of American nationals, David (a professor at Chinese universities, later at Dartmouth College) and Margaret (Barnes) Lattimore; married Robert Armstrong Andrews (a free-lance writer and designer), November 29, 1934 (died, 1963); children: Peter van Etten, Michael Cameron. *Education:* Educated at home by father; studied art at California School of Arts and Crafts, 1920-22, at Art Students League and Grand Central School of Art, New York, N.Y., 1924.

CAREER: Grew up in China, spent a year in Switzerland as a child, and came to United States with parents in 1920; after art school worked as a free-lance artist until 1930; writer and illustrator of children's stories, beginning 1930. Work exhibited in group shows at galleries in Boston, New York, and

Charleston, S.C., and represented in permanent collections of libraries throughout the United States.

WRITINGS—Juveniles; self-illustrated, except as indicated; published by Harcourt: *Little Pear: The Story of a Little Chinese Boy,* 1931, reprinted, 1968; *Jerry and the Pusa,* 1932; *The Seven Crowns,* 1933; *Little Pear and His Friends,* 1934; *The Lost Leopard,* 1935; *The Clever Cat,* 1936; *Junior, a Colored Boy of Charleston,* 1938; *Jonny,* 1939; *The Story of Lee Ling,* 1940; *The Questions of Lifu: A Story of China,* 1942; *Storm on the Island,* 1942; *Peachblossom,* 1943; *First Grade,* 1944.

Published by Morrow, except as indicated: *Turkestan Reunion,* Day, 1934; *Bayou Boy,* 1946; *Jeremy's Isle,* 1947; *Three Little Chinese Girls,* 1948; *Davy of the Everglades,* 1949; *Deborah's White Winter,* 1949; *Christopher and His Turtle,* 1950; *Indigo Hill,* 1950; *Bells for a Chinese Donkey,* 1951; *The Fig Tree,* 1951; *Lively Victoria,* 1952; *Jasper,* 1953; *Wu, the Gatekeeper's Son,* 1953; *Holly in the Snow,* 1954; *Diana in the China Shop,* 1955; *Willow Tree Village,* 1955; *Molly in the Middle,* 1956; *Little Pear and the Rabbits,* 1956; *The Journey of Ching Lai,* 1957; *The Monkey of Crofton,* 1957; *Fair Bay,* 1958; *Happiness for Kimi,* 1958; *The Fisherman's Son,* 1959; *The Youngest Artist,* 1959.

Beachcomber Boy, 1960; *The Chinese Daughter,* 1960; *Cousin Melinda,* 1961; *The Wonderful Glass House,* 1961; *The Bittern's Nest,* 1962; *Laurie and Company,* 1962; *Janetta's Magnet,* 1963; *The Little Tumbler,* 1963; *Felicia,* 1964; *The Mexican Bird,* 1965; *The Bus Trip,* 1965; *The Search for Christina,* 1966; *The Two Helens,* 1967; *Bird Song,* 1968; *The Girl on the Deer,* 1969; *The Three Firecrackers,* 1970; *More About Little Pear,* 1971; *A Smiling Face,* 1973; *The Taming of Tiger,* 1975; *Adam's Key,* illustrated by Alan Tiegreen, 1976; *Proudfoot's Way,* illustrated by Beatrice Darwin, 1978.

Illustrator: Bertha Metzger, *Picture Tales from the Chinese,* Stokes, 1934; Florence Crannell Means, *Rainbow Bridge,* Missionary Education Movement, 1934; E. Freivogel, *All Around the City,* Missionary Education Movement, 1938.

Contributor of short stories to *Jack and Jill, Story Parade, Trailways, American Junior Red Cross Magazine,* and *Christian Science Monitor.*

SIDELIGHTS: Eleanor Frances Lattimore's books have been translated into several foreign languages and transcribed into Braille.

BIOGRAPHICAL/CRITICAL SOURCES: Bertha E. Miller, *Illustrators of Children's Books 1946-56,* Horn Book, 1958; *New York Times,* February 2, 1958.†

*   *   *

LAUBER, Patricia (Grace)   1924-

PERSONAL: Born February 5, 1924, in New York, N.Y.; daughter of Hubert Crow (an engineer) and Florence (Walker) Lauber; married Russell Frost III, 1981. *Education:* Wellesley College, B.A., 1945. *Agent:* McIntosh & Otis, Inc., 475 Fifth Ave., New York, N.Y. 10017.

CAREER: Writer of children's books, 1954—. *Look,* New York City, writer, 1945-46; Scholastic Magazines, New York City, writer and editor, 1946-55; Street & Smith, New York City, editor-in-chief of *Science World,* 1956-59; Grolier, Inc., New York City, chief editor, science and mathematics, *The New Book of Knowledge,* 1961-66.

WRITINGS—Juvenile nonfiction: *Magic Up Your Sleeve,* Teen-Age Book Club, 1954; *Battle against the Sea: How the Dutch*

Made Holland, Coward, 1956 (published in England as *Battle against the Sea: The Challenge of the Dutch and the Dikes,* Chatto & Windus, 1963), revised edition, 1971; *The Quest of Galileo,* Doubleday, 1959; *Our Friend the Forest: A Conservation Story,* Doubleday, 1959; *The Quest of Louis Pasteur,* Doubleday, 1960; *Famous Mysteries of the Sea,* Thomas Nelson, 1962; *Big Dreams and Small Rockets: A Short History of Space Travel,* Crowell, 1965; *Of Man and Mouse: How House Mice Became Laboratory Mice,* Viking, 1971; *Everglades: A Question of Life or Death,* Viking, 1973; *Cowboys and Cattle Ranching,* Crowell, 1973; *What's Hatching Out of That Egg?,* Crown, 1979; *Seeds Pop, Stick, Glide,* Crown, 1981.

Published by Coward: *Highway to Adventure: The River Rhone of France,* 1956; *Valiant Scots: People of the Highlands Today,* 1957; *Penguins on Parade,* 1958; *Dust Bowl: The Story of Man on the Great Plains,* 1958; *Rufus, the Red-Necked Hornbill,* 1958; *Changing the Face of North America: The Challenge of the St. Lawrence Seaway,* 1959, revised edition, 1968; *Getting to Know Switzerland,* 1960.

Published by Random House: *All about the Ice Age,* 1959; *All about the Planets,* 1960; *The Story of Numbers,* 1961; *All about the Planet Earth,* 1962; *Your Body and How It Works,* 1962; *The Friendly Dolphins,* 1963; *The Surprising Kangaroos and Other Pouched Mammals,* 1965; *The Story of Dogs,* 1966; *The Look-It-Up Book of Mammals,* 1967; *The Look-It-Up Book of Stars and Planets,* 1967; *The Look-It-Up Book of the Fifty States,* 1967; *Bats: Wings in the Night,* 1968; *The Planets,* 1968; *This Restless Earth,* 1970; *Who Discovered America?: Settlers and Explorers of the New World before the Time of Columbus,* 1970; *Earthquakes: New Scientific Ideas about Why the Earth Shakes,* 1972.

Published by Garrard: *Junior Science Book of Icebergs and Glaciers,* 1961; *The Mississippi: Giant at Work,* 1961; *Junior Science Book of Penguins,* 1963; *The Congo: River into Central Africa,* 1964; *Junior Science Book of Volcanoes,* 1965; *Who Needs Alligators?,* 1974; *Life on a Giant Cactus,* 1974; *Too Much Garbage,* 1974; *Great Whales,* 1975; *Earthworms: Underground Farmers,* 1976; *Sea Otters and Seaweed,* 1976; *Mystery Monsters of Loch Ness,* 1978; *Tapping Earth's Heat,* 1978.

Juvenile fiction: *Clarence, the TV Dog,* Coward, 1955; *Clarence Goes to Town,* Coward, 1957; *Found: One Orange-Brown Horse,* Random House, 1957; *The Runaway Flea Circus,* Random House, 1958; *Clarence Turns Sea Dog,* Coward, 1959; *Adventure at Black Rock Cave,* Random House, 1959; *Champ, Gallant Collie,* Random House, 1960; *Curious Critters,* Garrard, 1969; *Home at Last,* Coward, 1980.

Contributor of adult short stories and light essays to magazines. Former editor of Coward's ''Challenge Books'' and Garrard's ''Good Earth'' series; free-lance editor, *Scientific American Illustrated Library.*

WORK IN PROGRESS: A book on planetary exploration; a work of fiction ''presumably written by two cats.''

AVOCATIONAL INTERESTS: The theatre, music, animals, sailing, and travel.

*   *   *

LAWSON, Jacob
      See BURGESS, M(ichael) R(oy)

*   *   *

LECLERC, Victor
      See PARRY, Albert

LEDERER, Rhoda Catharine (Kitto)   1910-
      (Rhoda Barrow)

PERSONAL: Born August 23, 1910, in St. Mawgan, Cornwall, England; daughter of John Vivian (librarian of the House of Commons) and Nettie Catherine (Ryves) Kitto; married Tony Lederer. *Education:* Attended St. Albans High School, Hertfordshire, and Kerr Saunders College, London, England. *Home:* April Cottage, Chalfont Heights, Chalfont St. Peter, Buckinghamshire, England.

CAREER: Bridge teacher and writer. *Member:* International Bridge Press Association, English Bridge Union Teachers' Association (secretary), American Bridge Teachers' Association, and other bridge organizations.

WRITINGS: Acol-ite's Quiz: Including the Basic Rules of the Acol System, Quiz Exercises and Competition Quizzes, Allen & Unwin, 1970; (with Eric Jannersten) *Cards on the Table: The Art of Guessing Right,* Allen & Unwin, 1971; (with Jannersten) *Precision Bridge,* Allen & Unwin, 1972, Scribner, 1973; (with husband, Tony Lederer) *Learn Bridge with the Lederers,* Cassell, 1977.

With Ben Cohen; under name Rhoda Barrow, except as indicated: *Acol Without Tears: Being the Basic Principles of the Acol System of Contract Bridge,* Allen & Unwin, 1962, published as *Bidding Better Bridge: Acol for Americans,* A. S. Barnes, 1965, 2nd edition, 1967; *Basic Acol,* Allen & Unwin, 1962, 3rd revised edition (under name Rhoda Lederer), 1979; *Your Lead, Partner,* Allen & Unwin, 1963, published as *Opening Leads to Better Bridge,* A. S. Barnes, 1964, 3rd revised edition (under name Rhoda Lederer), Allen & Unwin, 1979; *Acol Quiz,* Allen & Unwin, 1963; *The ABC of Contract Bridge: Being a Complete Outline of the Acol Bidding System and the Card Play of Contract Bridge Especially Prepared for Beginners,* Anthony Blond, 1964, A. S. Barnes, 1965, 4th edition (under name Rhoda Lederer), Allen & Unwin, 1979; *Contract Bridge,* Collins, 1965, revised edition (under name Rhoda Lederer) published as *Contract Bridge for Beginners,* 1974; *Calling a Spade a Spade; or, Acol in Action,* Anthony Blond, 1965, A. S. Barnes, 1966; *Conventions Made Clear: A Handbook for Contract Bridge Players,* Anthony Blond, 1966, revised edition (under name Rhoda Lederer) published as *Current Conventions Made Clear,* Allen & Unwin, 1970; *All about Acol,* Allen & Unwin, 1969, 4th edition (under name Rhoda Lederer), 1979.

Editor, with Cohen, of *The Bridge Players' Encyclopedia,* international edition, Hamlyn, 1966. Compiler and distributor of the annual *Bridge Player's Acol Diary.* Contributor of regular columns to periodicals, including *Buckinghamshire Advertiser, Windsor, Slough & Eton Express, Bridge Magazine,* and *Northwestern Evening Mail.*

*   *   *

LEE, Andrew
      See AUCHINCLOSS, Louis (Stanton)

*   *   *

LEE, Carolina
      See DERN, Erolie Pearl Gaddis

*   *   *

LEE, John Michael   1932-

PERSONAL: Born March 29, 1932, in Sheffield, Yorkshire,

England; son of John Ewart (a bank manager) and May (Humber) Lee; married Mary Joy Bowman, June 23, 1962; children: Matthew, Helen. *Education:* Attended Christ Church, Oxford, 1950-54. *Office:* Department of Politics, University of Bristol, 77-79 Woodland Rd., Bristol BS8 1US, England.

CAREER: Schoolmaster and part-time research student, Oxford, England, 1954-57; University of Manchester, Manchester, England, lecturer, 1958-66, senior lecturer in government, 1966-68; Her Majesty's Treasury, temporary principal, 1968-69; University of London, London, England, Institute of Commonwealth Studies, senior lecturer, 1969-72, Birkbeck College, senior lecturer, 1972-75, reader in politics, 1981; University of Bristol, Bristol, England, professor of politics, 1981—. Lecturer, Makerere College, Uganda, 1962-63; visiting summer lecturer, University of Ghana, 1963.

WRITINGS: Social Leaders and Public Persons, Oxford University Press, 1963; (co-editor) *Victoria County History of Leicestershire,* Volume V, Oxford University Press, 1964; (contributor) A. Rogers, editor, *The Making of Stamford,* Leicester University Press, 1965; *Colonial Development and Good Government,* Clarendon Press, 1967; *African Armies and Civil Order,* Praeger, 1969; (with Bruce Wood) *The Scope of Local Initiative: A Study of Cheshire County Council, 1961-1974,* Martin Robertson, 1974; *The Historical Approach to Public Administration,* Open University Press, 1974; *Reviewing the Machinery of Government, 1942-1952,* Civil Service Department, 1977; *The Churchill Coalition,* Batsford, 1980; (with Martin Petter) *The Colonial Office, War and Development Policy,* Temple Smith, 1982.

*   *   *

LEISHMAN, J(ames) Blair 1902-1963

PERSONAL: Born May 8, 1902, in Cumberland, England; died, August 14, 1963; son of Matthew Shaw and Sarah (Crossfield) Leishman. *Education:* St. John's College, Oxford, M.A. and B.Litt. *Home:* 10B Bandwell Rd., Oxford, England. *Office:* St. John's College, Oxford, England.

CAREER: University of Southampton, Southampton, England, lecturer in English literature, 1928-46; Oxford University, Oxford, England, senior lecturer in English literature, 1946-63, senior research fellow at St. John's College. *Member:* Association of University Teachers.

WRITINGS: The Metaphysical Poets, Clarendon Press, 1934, reprinted, Russell, 1963; (editor) *The Three Parnassus Plays,* Nicholson & Watson, 1949; *The Monarch of Wit: An Analytical and Comparative Study of the Poetry of John Donne,* Hutchinson, 1951, 7th edition, 1967; (author of introduction) Rainer Maria Rilke, *Letters to Merline, 1919-1922,* translated by Violet M. Macdonald, Methuen, 1951; (author of introduction) Rilke, *Correspondence in Verse with Erika Mitterer,* translated by N. K. Cruikshank, Hogarth, 1953; (author of introduction) Rilke, *Selected Works,* translated by G. Craig Houston, Hogarth, 1954; *Translating Horace,* Cassirer, 1956; *Some Themes and Variations in the Poetry of Andrew Marvell,* British Academy, 1961; *Themes and Variations in Shakespeare's Sonnets,* Hillary House, 1961, 2nd edition, Harper, 1966; *The Art of Marvell's Poetry,* Hutchinson, 1966, Funk, 1968; *Milton's Minor Poems,* Hutchinson, 1969, University of Pittsburgh Press, 1971.

Translator: Rainer Maria Rilke, *Poems,* Hogarth, 1934; Rilke, *Requiem, and Other Poems,* Hogarth, 1935, 2nd edition, 1957; Rilke, *Sonnets to Orpheus,* Hogarth, 1936, 2nd edition, 1946; Rilke, *Later Poems,* Hogarth, 1938; (and author of introduction

with Stephen Spender) Rilke, *Duino Elegies,* Norton, 1939, 4th edition, Chatto & Windus, 1978; Rilke, *Selected Poems,* Hogarth, 1941, 2nd edition, 1946, reprinted, Penguin, 1978; Rilke, *From the Ramains of Count C.W.,* Hogarth, 1952; Friedrich Hoelderlin, *Selected Poems,* Hogarth, 1954, 2nd edition, Grove, 1956, reprinted, Hyperion Press, 1978; (and author of introduction) Rilke, *Poems 1906-1926,* New Directions, 1957; Rilke, *New Poems,* New Directions, 1964; Rilke, *Possibility of Being: A Selection of Poems,* New Directions, 1977.

AVOCATIONAL INTERESTS: Walking, cycling, travel.†

*   *   *

LERNER, Daniel 1917-1980

PERSONAL: Born October 30, 1917, in New York, N.Y.; died of cancer, May 1, 1980, in Santa Cruz, Calif.; son of Louis and Louetta (Swiger) Lerner; married Jean Weinstein, 1947; children: Louise, Thomas, Amy Muguette. *Education:* Attended Johns Hopkins University, 1934-36; New York University, A.B., 1938, M.A., 1939, Ph.D., 1948. *Home:* 232 Northrop Pl., Santa Cruz, Calif. 95060.

CAREER: New York University, New York, N.Y., instructor, 1939-41; Stanford University, Stanford, Calif., 1946-53, began as associate professor, became professor; Massachusetts Institute of Technology, Cambridge, beginning 1953, Ford Professor of Sociology and International Communications, beginning 1958. Visiting professor at universities in Europe, Middle East, Asia, and Latin America. *Military service:* U.S. Army, 1941-45; became captain; awarded Purple Heart, Bronze Star. *Member:* American Sociological Association, World Association for Public Opinion Research, American Psychological Association, American Political Science Association, Reform Club (London). *Awards, honors:* Officier de l'Academie (France); Palmes Academique (France).

WRITINGS: Sykewar: Psychological Warfare against Germany, George W. Stewart, 1949, published as *Psychological Warfare against Nazi Germany: The Sykewar Campaign D-Day to VE-Day,* MIT Press, 1971; *Propaganda in War and Crisis,* George W. Stewart, 1951, reprinted, Arno, 1972; (with Harold D. Lasswell) *The Policy Sciences: Recent Developments in Scope and Methods,* Stanford University Press, 1951; *The Nazi Elite,* Stanford University Press, 1952; *Comparative Study of Symbols,* Stanford University Press, 1952; (with Raymond Aron) *France Defeats E.D.C.,* Praeger, 1957; *The Passing of Traditional Society: Modernizing the Middle East,* Free Press, 1958; (editor) *The Human Meaning of the Social Sciences,* Meridian, 1959; *Evidence and Inference,* Free Press, 1959; *Quantity and Quality,* Free Press, 1961; *Parts and Wholes,* Free Press, 1963; *Cause and Effect,* Free Press, 1965; *World Revolutionary Elites: Studies in Coercive Ideological Movements,* M.I.T. Press, 1965, reprinted, Greenwood Press, 1980; *Communication and Change in the Developing Countries,* University Press of Hawaii, 1967; (with Morton Gorden) *Euratlantica: Changing Perspectives of the European Elite,* MIT Press, 1969; (editor with Wilbur Schramm) *Communication and Change: The Last Ten Years and the Next,* University Press of Hawaii, 1976; (editor with Lyle M. Nelson) *Communication Research: A Half-Century Appraisal,* University Press of Hawaii, 1977; *Propaganda and Communication in World History,* three volumes, University Press of Hawaii, 1979. Contributor to *Esprit* (Paris), *Rias* (Berlin), *Harper's, Commentary, New Leader, Encounter* (London), *American Scholar,* and to sociology journals.

SIDELIGHTS: Daniel Lerner told *CA,* "My main purpose has been to make the scientific study of man in society accessible to the educated general reader.'' Most of Lerner's books have been translated into several languages.

* * *

LESLIE, Doris
See FERGUSSON HANNAY, Doris

* * *

LESSER, Milton
See MARLOWE, Stephen

* * *

LESTER-RANDS, A.
See JUDD, Frederick Charles

* * *

LEVENSON, Joseph Richmond   1920-1969

PERSONAL: Born June 10, 1920, in Boston, Mass.; died April 6, 1969 in a boating accident near Guerneville, Calif.; buried in Oakland, Calif.; son of Max Lionel and Eva (Richmond) Levenson; married Rosemary Sebag-Montefiore, October 5, 1950; children: Richard Montefiore, Irene Anne, Thomas Montefiore, Leo Montefiore. *Education:* Harvard University, A.B., 1941, A.M., 1946, Ph.D., 1949. *Religion:* Jewish. *Home:* 261 Stonewall Rd., Berkeley, Calif. *Office:* Department of History, University of California, Berkeley, Calif.

CAREER: Harvard University, Cambridge, Mass., teaching fellow, 1946-48, junior fellow in Society of Fellows, 1948-51; University of California, Berkeley, assistant professor, 1951-56, associate professor, 1956-60, professor of history, 1960-65, Sather Professor of History, 1965-69. *Military service:* U.S. Naval Reserve, 1942-46; became lieutenant. *Member:* American Historical Association, Association for Asian Studies (member of board of directors, 1965-68), Association for Asian Art, Phi Beta Kappa. *Awards, honors:* Fulbright fellow, School of Oriental and African Studies, University of London, 1954-55; Center for Advanced Study in the Behavioral Sciences fellow, 1958-59; Guggenheim fellow, 1962-63; American Council of Learned Societies fellow, 1966-67.

WRITINGS: Liang Ch'i-ch'ao and the Mind of Modern China, Harvard University Press, 1953, 2nd revised edition, University of California Press, 1967; *Confucian China and Its Modern Fate,* University of California Press, Volume I: *The Problem of Intellectual Continuity,* 1958, published as *Modern China and Its Confucian Past: The Problem of Intellectual Continuity,* 1958, published as *Modern China and Its Confucian Past: The Problem of Intellectual Continuity,* Doubleday, 1964, Volume II: *The Problem of Monarchical Decay,* 1964, Volume III: *The Problem of Historical Significance,* 1965, combined edition published as *Confucian China and Its Modern Fate: A Trilogy,* 1968; (compiler) *European Expansion and the Counter-Example of Asia, 1300-1600,* Prentice-Hall, 1967; (with Franz Schurmann) *China: An Interpretive History from the Beginnings to the Fall of Han,* University of California Press, 1969; (compiler) *Modern China: An Interpretive Anthology,* Macmillan, 1970; *Revolution and Cosmopolitanism: The Western Stage and the Chinese Stages,* University of California Press, 1971. Member of board of editors, *Journal of Asian Studies* and *Pacific Historical Review.*

WORK IN PROGRESS: Research in Chinese history.

OBITUARIES: New York Times, April 8, 1969; *Washington Post,* April 9, 1969.†

LEVI D'ANCONA, Mirella
See D'ANCONA, Mirella Levi

* * *

LEVI-STRAUSS, Claude   1908-

PERSONAL: Born November 28, 1908, in Brussels, Belgium; son of Raymond (a painter) and Emma (Levy) Levi-Strauss; married Dina Dreyfus (divorced); married Rosemarie Ullmo (divorced); married Monique Roman, April 5, 1954; children: (second marriage) Laurent; (third marriage) Matthieu. *Education:* Universite de Paris, licence, 1929, Agregation, 1932, Doctorat es Lettres, 1948. *Home:* 2 rue des Marronniers, Paris 75016, France. *Office:* College de France, Place Marcelin-Berthelot 11, Paris 75005, France.

CAREER: Universidade de Sao Paulo, Sao Paulo, Brazil, professor, 1935-39; New School for Social Research, New York, N.Y., visiting professor, 1942-45; Sorbonne, Ecole Pratique des Hautes Etudes, Paris, France, director of research, 1950—, College de France, Paris, professor of social anthropology, 1959—. Cultural counselor, French Embassy, Washington, D.C., 1946-47. *Member:* Academie francaise, National Academy of Sciences, American Academy and Institute of Arts and Letters, British Academy, Royal Academy of the Netherlands (foreign member), Academy of Norway (foreign member), Royal Anthropological Institute of Great Britain (honorary fellow), American Museum of Natural History (fellow), American Academy of Arts and Sciences, American Philosophical Society, Norwegian Academy of Letters and Sciences, New York Academy of Sciences. *Awards, honors:* Honorary doctorate, University of Brussels, Oxford University, Yale University, University of Chicago, Columbia University, Sterling University, Universite Nationale du Zaire, University of Uppsala, University Laval, Universidad Nacional Autonoma de Mexico, and Johns Hopkins University; Viking Fund medal, Wenner-Gren Foundation, 1966; Erasmus Prize, 1975; Commandeur de la Legion d'Honneur; Commandeur de l'Ordre nationale du Merite; Commandeur de l'Ordre des Palmes Academiques; Commandeur des Arts et des Lettres; Commandeur de la Coronne de Belgique.

WRITINGS—All published by Plon, except as indicated: *La Vie familiale et sociale des Indiens Nambikwara,* Societe de Americanistes, 1948; *Les Structures elementaires de la parente,* Presses Universitaires de France, 1949, translation by J. H. Bell and J. R. von Strumer published as *The Elementary Structures of Kinship,* Beacon, 1969; *Race et histoire,* Gonthier, 1952; *Tristes Tropiques,* 1955, revised edition, Adler, 1968, partial translation by John Russell, Criterion, 1961 (published in England as *A World on the Wane,* Hutchinson, 1961), complete translation by John Weightman and Doreen Weightman, J. Cape, 1973, Atheneum, 1974; *Anthropologie structurale,* Volume I, 1958, translation by Claire Jacobson and Brooke Grundfest Schoepf published as *Structural Anthropology,* Basic Books, 1964, Volume II, 1973, translation by Monica Layton, Basic Books, 1977; *La Pensee sauvage,* 1962, revised edition, 1968, translation published as *The Savage Mind,* University of Chicago Press, 1966; *Le Totemisme aujourd'hui,* Presses Universitaires de France, 1962, translation by Rodney Needham published as *Totemism,* Beacon, 1963, revised edition, Penguin, 1969; *Mythologiques,* Volume I: *Le Cru et le cuit,* 1964, Volume II: *Du Miel aux cendres,* 1967, Volume III: *L'Origine des manieres de table,* 1968, Volume IV: *L'Homme nu,* 1971, translation by J. Weightman and D. Weightman published as *Introduction to a Science of Mythology,* Volume

I: *The Raw and the Cooked,* Harper, 1969, Volume II: *From Honey to Ashes,* J. Cape, 1973, Harper, 1974, Volume III: *The Origin of Table Manners,* Harper, 1978, Volume IV: *The Naked Man,* Harper, 1981; *La Voie des masques,* two volumes, Skira, 1975.

SIDELIGHTS: Ranked with Sartre and Malraux as one of France's greatest contemporary intellectuals, Claude Levi-Strauss has baffled anthropologists and provoked heated discussions. Articles dealing with his ideas have appeared frequently in learned journals. Marshall D. Sahlins, an anthropologist, believes the professional attention accorded Levi-Strauss is almost "unparalleled in the history of anthropology."

John B. Hess explains: "Over the last two decades, Levi-Strauss has become a world figure not only by his findings in social anthropology but in his philosophical approach to it. This approach, known as structuralism, seeks objectivity—a pragmatic effort to learn how things work, what they are, rather than to fit them into patterns shaped by such value judgments as the notion that modern civilization marks a step forward from savagery." Robert Sklar, who calls him "the most original and influential of living anthropologists," adds that Levi-Strauss "is opposed not so much to either the relativism or the evolutionary concern of his predecessors as he is to their common assumption that primitive life is more instinctive, more simple, more natural than life in modern civilization." In *The Savage Mind,* he demonstrates "that the savage brings the same qualities of observation, intellectual application, and abstract thinking to his universe as does a modern scientist to ours," writes J. H. Plumb.

"But there is more to understanding Levi-Strauss than knowing what he himself has written," adds Godfrey Lienhardt. "Perhaps beyond any other living anthropologist he has established a dialogue with part of the intellectual public, appearing to speak personally to educated general readers and engaging them in his own processes of analysis and reflection." Lienhardt continues: "Yet there is a deeper appeal, and one which probably moves those who have not worked as social anthropologists more than those who have. It is an exhortation to wonder at the complex creativity of mankind, to revere it and finally to see through it. . . . From his most cerebral excursions into the intricacies of myth or kinship structures, Levi-Strauss always returns to a reasoned nostalgia for a primitive integrity now lost, and a reasoned optimism that some substitute for it on a rational plane may be produced by taking the right kind of thought." The reviewer concludes, "Levi-Strauss should be seen not only as a social anthropologist, but as a significant element in an intellectual and moral pattern which connects other features of our culture at this time." Similar observations led David Maybury-Lewis to write in 1967, "Levi-Strauss has . . . become an institution."

In contrast, Terence Turner comments: "The central problem of structuralism in its Levi-Straussian form is the failure to develop an adequate concept of structure. . . . Levi-Strauss's elimination of the subjective factor leaves him with no basis for distinguishing between the structure of thought (or of language) and the structure of what is thought (or spoken), namely the mental and linguistic images and constructs that cultures or individuals employ to 'say something of something.'"

Levi-Strauss cheerfully admits that his books "are hard to understand" and that he "stands outside of the anthropological mainstream," notes a writer for *Newsweek.* "'I think,' he says, 'I'm a school by myself.'" As Joan Bamberger writes: "No one can deny the persuasiveness of his technique, but one can question the value of it as scientific method. . . . But whatever

the future impact of his work, certainly the anthropological study of myth will never be the same."

BIOGRAPHICAL/CRITICAL SOURCES: Times Literary Supplement, May 12, 1961, June 15, 1967, September 12, 1968; *Spectator,* May 12, 1961, March 21, 1969; *Book Week,* February 9, 1964; *Saturday Review,* December 31, 1966, May 17, 1969; *Newsweek,* February 23, 1967; *Kenyon Review,* March, 1967; *Reporter,* April 6, 1967; *Time,* June 30, 1967; *New York Review,* October 12, 1967; *Hudson Review,* winter, 1967; *Commentary,* May, 1968; *Listener,* May 23, 1968; *Atlantic,* July, 1969; *New Republic,* July 22, 1969, May 18, 1974; *Book World,* November 9, 1969; *New York Times,* December 31, 1969; *Nation,* March 16, 1970; *L'Express,* March 15-21, 1971; *New York Times Book Review,* June 3, 1973; *Natural History,* June/July, 1973.

* * *

LEVY, Alan 1932-

PERSONAL: Born February 10, 1932, in New York, N.Y.; son of Meyer and Frances (Shield) Levy; married Valerie Wladaver, August 7, 1956; children: Monica, Erika. *Education:* Brown University, A.B., 1952; Columbia University, M.S. in Journalism, 1953. *Home and office:* Bennogasse 8, Apt. 7, A-1080 Vienna, Austria. *Agent:* Alexandria Hatcher, 150 West 55th St., New York, N.Y. 10019.

CAREER: Louisville Courier-Journal, Louisville, Ky., reporter, 1953-60; free-lance writer, New York, N.Y., 1960-67; investigator for President Johnson's Carnegie Commission on Educational Television, 1966-67; free-lance writer and accredited foreign correspondent in Prague, Czechoslovakia, 1967-71, and in Vienna, Austria, 1971—. Dramaturg (script and film consultant), Vienna's English Theatre Ltd., 1977-81. Lecturer on contemporary theater, Salzburg Seminar in American Studies, 1981. Trustee, Thomas Nast Foundation, Landau, Germany, 1977—. *Military service:* U.S. Army, 1953-55. *Member:* Authors Guild, Authors League of America, American Society of Journalists and Authors, P.E.N., Foreign Press Association of Vienna, Overseas Press Club.

AWARDS, HONORS: New Republic Younger Writer Award, 1957; Sigma Delta Chi regional award for newspaper coverage of Cuban revolution, 1959; Bernard DeVoto Fellowship in Prose to Bread Loaf Writers' Conference, Middlebury, Vt., 1963; Pacific Area Travel Association award, 1978, for best newspaper article; Golden Johann Strauss Medal of City of Vienna, 1981, for services to culture and tourism.

WRITINGS: (With Bernard Krisher and James Cox) *Draftee's Confidential Guide: How to Get Along in the Army,* Indiana University Press, 1957, revised edition, (with Richard Flaste) New American Library, 1966; *Operation Elvis,* Holt, 1960; *The Elizabeth Taylor Story,* Hillman Books, 1961; *Wanted: Nazis Criminals at Large,* Berkley Publishing, 1962; *Interpret Your Dreams,* Pyramid Publications, 1962, 7th edition, 1975; (contributor) Leonard Lief and David Hawke, editors, *American Colloquy,* Bobbs-Merrill, 1963; (with Gilbert Stuart) *Kind-Hearted Tiger,* Little, Brown, 1964; (contributor) *Casebook on Godot,* Grove, 1967; (contributor) *College Reading and Writing,* Macmillan, 1968; *The Culture Vultures; or, Whatever Became of the Emperor's New Clothes?,* Putnam, 1968; *God Bless You Real Good: My Crusade with Billy Graham,* Essandess, 1969; (contributor) *Marilyn Monroe: A Composite View,* Chilton, 1969; *Rowboat to Prague,* Grossman, 1972, 2nd edition published as *So Many Heroes,* Second Chance, 1980; *Good Men Still Live!: ("I Am the Other Karel Capek)—The Odyssey of a Professional Prisoner,* J. Philip O'Hara, 1974; *The Blue-*

bird of Happiness: The Memoirs of Jan Peerce, Harper, 1976; Forever, Sophia (Biography Book Club selection), Baronet, 1979; "Ruth Brinkmann as Ruth Draper" (play), first produced at Vienna's English Theatre in 1982.

Contributor to numerous periodicals, including Life, Harper's, Saturday Evening Post, Atlantic, Cosmopolitan, and Saturday Review. Book reviewer for New York Post, 1962-64, and Los Angeles Times, 1977. Vienna correspondent for ARTnews.

WORK IN PROGRESS: Book based on experience at Vatican Museums; college textbooks on Ezra Pound, W. H. Auden, and Vladimir Nabokov, for Permanent Press.

SIDELIGHTS: Alan Levy writes: "In 1967, having achieved enough success in New York to work anywhere in the world and still have publishing outlets, I moved with my wife and two daughters to Prague, Czechoslovakia—to cut down on my journalism and try my hand as a playwright, adapting a Semafor Theatre satire for director Milos Forman, who had staged it in Prague and wanted to do it in America. This plunged me into the hot center of what erupted as the Prague Spring and, by early 1968, I found myself writing history as well as journalism. My family and I lived through the downfall of Antonin Novotny's Stalinism, the rise of Alexander Dubcek, the Soviet invasion of August 21, 1968, the dismemberment of Prague Spring by August Winter, and our expulsion in 1971 for my writing Rowboat to Prague (later titled So Many Heroes).

"'How many beginnings can a man afford?' is one of the themes of my book, Good Men Still Live! In Vienna, where we live now, my family and I picked up the pieces of our lives and our love affair with Prague. Denied access to the east for several years, I functioned as a free-lance foreign correspondent with a cultural emphasis. And when my first play, 'Ruth Brinkmann as Ruth Draper,' has its world premiere in 1982 at Vienna's English Theatre, then the first reason why we went to Europe fifteen years earlier will be fulfilled at last."

In 1980-81, Levy became the first outside journalist ever admitted behind the scenes of the Vatican Museums. He met with Pope John Paul II, scaled six scaffolds to stand at the ceiling of the Sistine Chapel with the latest restorer of Michelangelo's painting, and went behind St. Peter's bulletproof glass with two of the sculpture restorers who retrieved Michelangelo's "Pieta" from a madman's hammer attack.

BIOGRAPHICAL/CRITICAL SOURCES: Redbook, February, 1960; Life, January 20, 1967; Christian Science Monitor, September 12, 1968; Harper's September, 1969; New York Times Magazine, May 16, 1971; ARTnews, October, 1981.

*   *   *

LEVY, Wilbert J.   1917-

PERSONAL: Born March 20, 1917, in Brooklyn, N.Y.; son of Benjamin (a fire chief) and Minnie (Wolfe) Levy; married Jeanne Hassberg, March 20, 1941; children: Nora Elizabeth (Mrs. William Johnston), Jonathan Benjamin. Education: City College (now City College of the City University of New York), B.S., 1936; Columbia University, M.A., 1938; Brooklyn College (now Brooklyn College of the City University of New York), graduate study, 1941-42; New York University, graduate study, 1944, 1949. Home: 123-60 83rd Ave., Kew Gardens, N.Y. 11415. Office: AMSCO School Publications, Inc., 315 Hudson St., New York, N.Y. 10013.

CAREER: New York City Civil Service Commission, New York City, examiner, 1942-45; Midwood High School, Brooklyn, N.Y., teacher of English, 1945-54; Newton High School, Queens, N.Y., chairman of department of English, 1954-74;

AMSCO School Publications, Inc., New York City, consultant, 1968—. Member, East Norwich-Oyster Bay Board of Education, 1962-66. Military service: U.S. Navy, 1945. Member: National Council of Teachers of English.

WRITINGS—All published by AMSCO School Publications: Patterns of Meaning: A Program towards More Powerful Reading, 1969; (with Samuel F. Zimbal) Reading Comprehension, 1972; Man Studies Himself, 1973; Man Studies His Past, 1973; Man Studies the World around Him, 1973; Reading and Growing, 1975; Sense of Sentences, 1975; Paragraph Power, 1977; Poems: American Themes, 1979; Writing English: Forty-four Short Lessons, 1982; Composition, 1982. General editor, "AMSCO Literature Program" series, twenty-one volumes, 1971-75.

AVOCATIONAL INTERESTS: "Reading, ceramics and glasswork, reading, alpine gardening, reading, European travel, reading, golf, reading."

*   *   *

LEWELLEN, T(ed) C(harles)   1940-

PERSONAL: Born June 26, 1940, in Redding, Calif.; son of Lowell F. (a structural steel worker) and Dianne (Carmen) Lewellen. Education: Attended San Jose State College (now University), 1959-60; Alaska Methodist University, B.A. (magna cum laude), 1963; New York University, M.A., 1973; University of Colorado, Ph.D., 1977. Politics: Independent. Religion: Independent. Office: Department of Sociology, University of Richmond, Richmond, Va. 23173.

CAREER: Formerly employed as fire fighter for U.S. Forest Service, assemblyman for Ford Motor Co. in California, gandy dancer and game warden in Alaska, construction worker, advertising copywriter for various New York publishers, and teacher at Texas Tech University, Lubbock; currently teaching in department of sociology, University of Richmond, Richmond, Va. Founder and faculty advisor, University of Richmond chapter of Amnesty International. Military service: U.S. Army, 1963-65.

WRITINGS: The Ruthless Gun (novel), Gold Medal Books, 1964; The Billikin Courier (novel), Random House, 1968; Peasants in Transition: The Changing Economy of the Peruvian Aymara, Westview, 1978; (contributor) Sam Long, editor, The Handbook of Political Behavior, Plenum, 1981.

WORK IN PROGRESS: The High Plain, a novel about missionaries in Peru; a book on political anthropology.

SIDELIGHTS: T. C. Lewellen told CA that he has moved from novels to nonfiction writing in the field of anthropology, but he adds: "During long nights of field work, living with an Aymara family in a remote community near Lake Titicaca, I could not help but write a novel about Peru. The novel is not very good as it stands, but I keep hoping to find time from teaching and research to revise it.

"Peasants in Transition is, like most of my recent writing, directed toward an audience of professional anthropologists. In the long run, I hope to combine my anthropological training with my experience with the novel to write nonfiction for a general audience."

AVOCATIONAL INTERESTS: Human rights and U.S. policy in Latin America, hiking and backpacking.

*   *   *

LEWIS, Claudia (Louise)   1907-

PERSONAL: Born October 14, 1907, in Corvallis, Ore.; daughter of Claude I. and Marie (Berry) Lewis. *Education:* Reed College, B.A., 1930; University of Minnesota, M.A., 1943; Columbia University, Ph.D., 1959. *Home:* 259 West 11th St., New York, N.Y. 10014.

CAREER: Highlander Folk School Nursery School, Monteagle, Tenn., organizer, 1938-41; Bank Street College of Education, New York, N.Y., teacher of language arts, children's literature, and writing for children, beginning 1943; writer on social anthropology, and of poetry and fiction for children. Summer instructor at Indiana University, 1953, Pacific Oaks College, 1962, and general extension division, Oregon State System of Higher Education, 1962—; member of Doukhobor Research Committee, University of British Columbia, summers, 1950 and 1951. *Member:* American Anthropological Association, National Council of Teachers of English.

WRITINGS: Children of the Cumberland, Columbia University Press, 1946; *Writing for Young Children,* Simon & Schuster, 1954, reprinted, Doubleday, 1981; (co-author) *Know Your Children in School,* edited by Lucy Sprague Mitchell, Macmillan, 1954; (co-author) *The Doukhobors of British Columbia,* edited by H. B. Hawthorn, University of British Columbia Press, 1955; *Straps the Cat,* W. R. Scott, 1957; *When I Go to the Moon,* Macmillan, 1961; *The Strange Room,* Albert Whitman, 1964; *Poems of Earth and Space,* Dutton, 1967; *Indian Families of the Northwest Coast: The Impact of Change,* University of Chicago Press, 1970; *Up and Down the River: Boat Poems,* Harper, 1979; *A Big Bite of the World: Children's Creative Writing,* Prentice-Hall, 1979.

Contributor of children's verse: *Another Here and Now Story Book,* Dutton, 1937; *Believe and Make Believe,* Dutton, 1956; *Let's Read More Stories,* Garden City, 1960. Also contributor of annual review of young people's books to *Book of Knowledge Annual,* of monographs to *Journal of Experimental Education* and *Genetic Psychology,* and of articles to other education journals.

WORK IN PROGRESS: Books for and about children.

AVOCATIONAL INTERESTS: Music (plays piano and harpsichord with amateur chamber music groups), painting, traveling.†

*   *   *

LEWIS, John E(arl)   1931-

PERSONAL: Born December 23, 1931, in Provo, Utah; son of Walter E. and Marie (Burt) Lewis; married Carolyn Coles, September 24, 1953; children: Lynn Anne, John R., Jeannine. *Education:* Brigham Young University, B.S., 1953; graduate study at Brigham Young University, 1957-59, and at University of Utah, 1960-61. *Religion:* Church of Jesus Christ of Latter-day Saints (Mormon). *Home:* 682 West 40 North, Orem, Utah 84057. *Office:* Utah State Department of Employment Security, 190 West 800 North, Provo, Utah 84601.

CAREER: Utah State Department of Employment Security, 1954—, began as assistant personnel director in Salt Lake City, currently assistant personnel director and lead interviewer in Provo. *Military service:* U.S. Army Reserve, 1950—; currently colonel. *Member:* International Association of Personnel in Employment Security (vice-president of Utah chapter, 1965), Reserve Officers Association (president of central Utah chapter, 1975—). *Awards, honors:* Freedoms Foundation essay awards, 1970, 1972.

WRITINGS—Novels: *Vengence Is Mine,* Lenox Hill Press, 1975; *The Man Called Sam,* Lenox Hill Press, 1975; *The Silver Mine Trail,* Avalon, 1979; *Escape to Fort Bridger,* Avalon, 1980;

The Guns of Tombstone, Avalon, 1980; *Utah Vengeance,* Avalon, 1981; *The Valiant Die but Once,* Avalon, 1981. Contributor of more than fifty articles to *National Guardsman, Christian Science Monitor, Family Weekly,* and *Supervision.*

WORK IN PROGRESS: A western novel concerned with law enforcement in El Paso, Texas, during the 1890s, entitled *The Fallen Star.*

AVOCATIONAL INTERESTS: Travel, skiing, tennis, reading.

*   *   *

LEY, Alice Chetwynd   1915-

PERSONAL: Surname rhymes with "day"; born October 12, 1915, in Halifax, Yorkshire, England; daughter of Frederick George (a journalist) and Alice Mary (Chetwynd) Humphrey; married Kenneth James Ley (a journalist), February 3, 1945; children: Richard James Humphrey, Graham Kenneth Hugh. *Education:* University of London, Diploma in Sociology, 1962. *Politics:* Liberal. *Religion:* Church of England. *Home:* 42 Cannonbury Ave., Pinner, Middlesex, England. *Agent:* Curtis Brown Ltd., 1 Craven Hill, London W2 3EW, England.

CAREER: Novelist. *Member:* Romantic Novelists Association, Society of Women Writers and Journalists, Jane Austen Society.

WRITINGS—Novels; published by R. Hale, except as indicated: *The Jewelled Snuff Box,* 1959; *The Georgian Rake,* 1960; *The Guinea Stamp,* 1961, published as *The Courting of Joanna,* Ballantine, 1976; *Master of Liversedge,* 1966, published as *The Master and the Maiden,* Ballantine, 1977; *Clandestine Betrothal,* 1967, Ballantine, 1975; *Toast of the Town,* 1969, Ballantine, 1976; *Letters for a Spy,* 1970, published as *The Sentimental Spy,* Ballantine, 1977; *A Season at Brighton,* 1972, Ballantine, 1976; *Tenant of Chesdene Manor,* 1974, published as *Beloved Diana,* Ballantine, 1977; *Beau and the Bluestocking,* 1975, Ballantine, 1977; *At Dark of the Moon,* 1977, Ballantine, 1978; *An Advantageous Marriage,* 1977, Ballantine, 1978; *A Regency Scandal,* Ballantine, 1979; *A Conformable Wife,* Ballantine, 1981.

WORK IN PROGRESS: Another historical romance set in France and Sussex, for Ballantine.

AVOCATIONAL INTERESTS: History, literature, sociology, gardening.

BIOGRAPHICAL/CRITICAL SOURCES: Birmingham Post, Birmingham, England, July 10, 1961.

*   *   *

LIEBMAN, Arthur   1926-

PERSONAL: Born September 22, 1926, in Brooklyn, N.Y.; son of Louis (a furrier) and Yetta (Schneider) Liebman; married Joyce Ann Braufman (a concert pianist and teacher), December 19, 1954; children: Robert. *Education:* Brooklyn College (now Brooklyn College of the City University of New York), B.A., 1954, M.A., 1959; New York University, Ph.D. (with honors), 1971. *Politics:* Democrat. *Religion:* Jewish. *Home:* 18 Meadow Lane, Roslyn Heights, N.Y. 11577.

CAREER: High school English teacher in Roslyn, N.Y., 1965—; Hofstra University, Hempstead, N.Y., lecturer in English, 1969-74; State University of New York at Stony Brook, adjunct assistant professor of English, 1975—. Lecturer on science fiction and mystery characters, including Dracula, Frankenstein, Sherlock Holmes, and Dr. Watson. Consultant to Human

Resources School. *Military service:* U.S. Navy, radioman, 1944-46. *Member:* Broadcast Music Inc., Song Writers Association.

WRITINGS—Published by Rosen Press, except as indicated: *Macbeth: A Student's Workbook*, Educator's Publishing, 1970; *Thirteen Classic Detective Stories: A Critical History of Detective Fiction*, 1973; (editor) *Tales of Horror and the Supernatural*, 1974; (editor) *Classic Crime Stories*, 1975; (editor) *The Book of Quickie Thrillers*, Simon & Schuster, 1975; *Tales of Espionage and Intrigue*, 1977; (editor) *Science Fiction: Creators and Pioneers*, 1979; *Science Fiction: The Best of Yesterday*, 1980; *Science Fiction: Masters of Today*, 1981.

WORK IN PROGRESS: Everything You Wanted to Know about Sherlock Holmes.

SIDELIGHTS: Arthur Liebman, who has devised a dramatics program for the handicapped students at the Human Resources School, is also the creator of several computer question-and-answer games. His "1,001 Questions from Sherlock Holmes and Other Famous Mysteries," "1,001 Questions on Words," and "1,001 Questions on Monsters, Vampires, Witches and Ghosts" are marketed by Coleco Industries.

AVOCATIONAL INTERESTS: Chamber music, astronomy.

*   *   *

LINDSAY, (John) Maurice 1918-
(Gavin Brock)

PERSONAL: Born July 21, 1918, in Glasgow, Scotland; son of Matthew (an insurance manager) and Eileen Frances (Brock) Lindsay; married Aileen Joyce Gordon (a teacher), August 3, 1946; children: Seona Morag (Mrs. David Barr), Kirsteen Ann, Niall Gordon Brock, Morven Morag Joyce. *Education:* Attended Glasgow Academy, 1926-36, Scottish National Academy of Music, 1936-39. *Politics:* Liberal. *Home:* 7, Milton Hill, Milton, Dumbarton, Scotland. *Office:* The Scottish Civic Trust, 24, George Square, Glasgow C. 2, Scotland.

CAREER: Scottish Daily Mail, Edinburgh, Scotland, drama critic, 1946-47; *Bulletin*, Glasgow, Scotland, music critic, 1946-60; British Broadcasting Corp., Glasgow, free-lance broadcaster, 1946-61; Border Television, Carlisle, England, program controller, 1961-62, production controller, 1962-64, features executive and senior interviewer, 1964-67; Scottish Civic Trust, Glasgow, director, 1967—. *Military service:* British Army, World War II; became captain. *Member:* Saltire Society (honorary publications secretary, 1948-52). *Awards, honors:* Rockefeller Atlantic Award for *The Enemies of Love*, 1946; holder of Territorial Decoration; Commander, Order of the British Empire, 1979.

WRITINGS: A Pocket Guide to Scottish Culture, Maclellan, 1947, Universal Distributors, 1947; *The Scottish Renaissance*, Serif Books, 1948; *The Lowlands of Scotland*, R. Hale, Volume I: *Glasgow and the North*, 1953, Volume II: *Edinburgh and the South*, 1956, both volumes, International Publications Service, 1956, reprinted, R. Hale, 1973; *Robert Burns: The Man, His Work, the Legend*, MacGibbon & Kee, 1954, Dufour, 1963, revised edition, St. Martin's, 1979; *Dunoon: The Gem of the Clyde Coast* (guidebook), Town Council of Dunoon, 1954; *Clyde Waters: Variations and Diversions on a Theme of Pleasure*, R. Hale, 1958; *The Burns Encyclopaedia*, Hutchinson, 1959, 3rd edition, St. Martin's, 1980; (with David Somervell) *Killochan Castle, Ayrshire* (guidebook), Pilgrim Press, 1960, reprinted, 1974; *By Yon Bonnie Banks: A Gallimaufry*, Hutchinson, 1961; *The Discovery of Scotland, Based on Accounts of Foreign Travellers from the Thirteenth to the Eighteenth Centuries*, R. Hale, 1964, Roy, 1965, reprinted, R.

Hale, 1979; (author of introduction) Robert Laird Mackie, compiler, *A Book of Scottish Verse*, 2nd edition, Oxford University Press, 1967; *The Eye Is Delighted: Some Romantic Travellers in Scotland*, Muller, 1971, Transatlantic, 1972; *Portrait of Glasgow*, R. Hale, 1972, revised edition, 1981; *Robin Philipson*, Edinburgh University Press, 1977; *History of Scottish Literature*, R. Hale, 1977; *Francis George Scott and the Scottish Renaissance*, Paul Harris Publishing, 1980.

Poetry: *The Advancing Day*, privately printed, 1940; *Perhaps To-morrow*, privately printed, 1941; *Predicament*, Alden Press, 1942; *No Crown for Laughter*, Fortune Press, 1943; *The Enemies of Love: Poems, 1941-1945*, Maclellan, 1946; *Selected Poems*, Oliver & Boyd, 1947; *Hurlygush: Poems in Scots*, introduction by Hugh MacDiarmid, Serif Books, 1948; *At the Woods Edge*, Serif Books, 1950; *Ode for St. Andrew's Night, and Other Poems*, New Alliance Press, 1951; *The Exiled Heart: Poems, 1941-1956*, edited and introduced by George Bruce, R. Hale, 1957; *Snow Warning, and Other Poems*, Linden Press, 1962; *One Later Day, and Other Poems*, Brookside Press, 1964; *This Business of Living*, Akros Publications, 1969; *Comings and Goings*, Akros Publications, 1971; *Selected Poems, 1942-1972*, R. Hale, 1973; *The Run from Life: More Poems, 1942-1972*, Cygnet Press, 1975; *Walking without an Overcoat: Poems, 1972-76*, R. Hale, 1977; *Collected Poems*, Paul Harris Publishing, 1979.

Editor: *Sailing To-morrow's Seas: An Anthology of New Poems*, introduction by Tambimuttu, Fortune Press, 1944; *Poetry-Scotland*, Volume I, Maclellan, 1944, Volume II, Maclellan, 1945, Volume III, Maclellan, 1947, Volume IV (with Hugh MacDiarmid) Serif Books, 1949; (and contributor) *Modern Scottish Poetry: An Anthology of Scottish Renaissance, 1920-1945*, Faber, 1946, 3rd edition, Carcanet Press, 1976; (and contributor, with Fred Urquhart) *No Scottish Twilight: New Scottish Short Stories* (includes "Boxing Match," by Lindsay), Maclellan, 1947; *Selected Poems of Alexander Gray*, Maclellan, 1948; *Poems by Sir David Lyndsay of the Mount*, Oliver & Boyd, 1948; (with Helen B. Cruickshank and author of introduction) *Selected Poems by Marion Angus*, Serif Books, 1950; (and author of introduction) *John Davidson: A Selection of His Poems* (includes essay by MacDiarmid), preface by T. S. Eliot, Hutchinson, 1961; (with Edwin Morgan and George Bruce) *Scottish Poetry*, Aldine, Volume I, 1966, Volume II, 1966, Volume III, 1968, Volume IV, 1969, Volume V, 1970, Volume VI, 1972, Volume VII, 1974, Volume VIII, 1976, Volume IX, 1977; (consultant editor) *Voices of Our Kind: An Anthology of Contemporary Scottish Verse for Schools*, Saltire Society, 1971; (and contributor) *Scotland: An Anthology*, R. Hale, 1974, St. Martin's, 1975; *As I Remember: Ten Scottish Writers Reflect How Writing for Them Began*, R. Hale, 1979; *Scottish Comic Verse 1425-1980*, R. Hale, 1981. Also editor, with Douglas Young, of Oliver & Boyd's "Saltire Modern Poets" series, 1947.

Author of librettos for two operas, "The Abbot of Drimmock," 1957, and "The Decision," music by Thea Musgrave, J. & W. Chester, 1967. Author of commentaries for two films. Contributor to *Grove's Dictionary of Music and Musicians*. Editor, *Scots Review*, 1949-50, and *Scottish Review*, 1975—.

SIDELIGHTS: Maurice Lindsay told *CA* that although he is the author of more than a dozen prose books about Scotland, his main preoccupation has always been with poetry. He writes, "Strongly visual selections of my work include vivid impressions of present-day Glasgow as well as poems which deal with the wider human situation."

BIOGRAPHICAL/CRITICAL SOURCES: James Kinsley, editor, *Scottish Poetry: A Critical Survey*, Cassell, 1955; *Observer*

Review, July, 1968; *Scottish Review,* Number 16, 1979; *Scottish Literary Journal Supplement,* summer, 1980; *Times Literary Supplement,* June 26, 1981.

* * *

LINDSAY, Perry
See DERN, Erolie Pearl Gaddis

* * *

LINEBARGER, Paul M(yron) A(nthony)   1913-1966
(Felix C. Forrest, Carmichael Smith, Cordwainer Smith)

PERSONAL: Born July 11, 1913, in Milwaukee, Wis.; died August 6, 1966, in Baltimore, Md.; buried in Arlington National Cemetery; son of Paul Myron Wentworth and Lillian (Bearden) Linebarger; married Margaret Snow, September 7, 1936 (divorced, 1949); married Genevieve Cecilia Collins, March 20, 1950; children: (first marriage) Johanna Lesley, Marcia Christine. *Education:* Attended University of Nanking, 1930, North China Union Language School, 1931; George Washington University, A.B., 1933; graduate study at Oxford University, 1933, American University, 1934, University of Chicago, 1935; Johns Hopkins University, M.A., 1935, Ph.D., 1936; post-doctoral study at University of Michigan, 1937, 1939; Washington School of Psychiatry, certificate in psychiatry, 1955; attended Universidad Interamericana, 1955, 1960. *Religion:* Episcopalian. *Home:* 2831 29th St. N.W., Washington, D.C. 20008. *Agent:* Harry Altshuler, 225 West 86th St., New York 24, New York.

CAREER: Private secretary to legal advisor of National Government of China, Nanking and Washington, 1930-36; Harvard University, Cambridge, Mass., instructor, 1936-37; Duke University, Durham, N.C., began as instructor, became associate professor, 1937-46; School of Advanced International Studies of the Johns Hopkins University, Washington, D.C., professor of Asiatic politics, 1946-66. University of Pennsylvania, Philadelphia, visiting professor, 1955-56; Australian National University, Canberra, visiting professor, 1957. Helped found Office of War Information, World War II, as member, Operations Planning and Intelligence Board; U.S. Army consultant to British land forces, Malaya, 1950, and to 8th Army, Korea, 1950-52. Lecturer at service colleges, academies. *Military service:* U.S. Army, intelligence service, 1942-66; became lieutenant-colonel; awarded Bronze Star; served in Washington, D.C., and China-Burma-India Theater Headquarters, Chungking, 1942-46. *Member:* American Peace Society (president), American Political Science Association, American Society of International Law, Council on Foreign Relations, American Association for Asian Studies, American Philatelic Society, Psywar Society (England), American Legion, Reserve Officers Association, Association of the U.S. Army, Southern Political Science Association, D.C. Political Science Association, Phi Beta Kappa, Pi Gamma Mu, Masonic Order, Cosmos Club (Washington). *Awards, honors:* Litt.D., Universidad Interamericana, 1964; D.C.L., National Chengchi University, 1965.

WRITINGS: The Political Doctrines of Sun Yat-sen, Johns Hopkins Press, 1937, reprinted, Greenwood Press, 1973; (editor) *Ocean Men,* privately printed, 1937; *Government in Republican China,* McGraw, 1938, reprinted, Hyperion Press, 1973; *The China of K'ai-shek,* World Peace Foundation, 1941, reprinted, Greenwood Press, 1973; *Psychological Warfare,* Infantry Journal Press, 1948, 2nd edition, Duell, 1954, reprinted, Arno, 1972; (with Djang Chu and Ardath W. Burks) *Far East-*

ern Governments and Politics: China and Japan, Van Nostrand, 1954, 2nd edition, 1956.

Novels; all published by Duell: (Under pseudonym Felix C. Forrest) *Ria,* 1947; (under pseudonym Felix C. Forrest) *Carola,* 1948; (under pseudonym Carmichael Smith) *Atomsk,* 1949.

Science fiction; short story collections, except as indicated; under pseudonym Cordwainer Smith: *You Will Never Be the Same,* Regency, 1963; *The Planet Buyer* (novel; also see below), Pyramid, 1964; *Space Lords,* Pyramid, 1965; *Quest of the Three Worlds,* Ace Books, 1966; *The Underpeople* (novel; also see below), Pyramid, 1968; *Under Old Earth and Other Explorations,* edited by Anthony Cheetham, Panther Books, 1970; *Stardreamer,* Beagle Books, 1971; *Norstrilia* (novel; includes parts of *The Planet Buyer* and *The Underpeople*), Ballantine, 1975; *The Best of Cordwainer Smith,* edited by J. J. Pierce, Doubleday, 1975; *The Instrumentality of Mankind,* Ballantine, 1979.

Contributor to encyclopedias. Contributor of short stories to science fiction magazines, including *Galaxy* and *Fantasy Book.*

SIDELIGHTS: Paul M.A. Linebarger wrote his first science-fiction story, "War No. 81-Q" (collected in *The Instrumentality of Mankind*), when he was fifteen. He began publishing science fiction in the 1950s under what has become his best-known pseudonym, Cordwainer Smith. Because he was so successful in keeping his name from being linked to his pseudonym, few readers knew anything about Linebarger's multi-cultural background which colors his science fiction. As a child, he traveled extensively with his parents and received his early schooling in Honolulu, Shanghai, and Baden Baden. At age seventeen he became secretary to his father, who was then a legal advisor to Sun Yat Sen, and he negotiated a silver loan to China.

For many years his work, full of departures from traditional science-fiction themes and ideas, was considered to be a curiosity. Gary K. Wolfe and Carol T. Williams, *Dictionary of Literary Biography* writers, comment: "As distance gives us added critical perspective on the mass of science fiction produced during the 1950s and 1960s, certain authors emerge as unusual shaping forces. One such author is certainly Paul Myron Anthony Linebarger." Wolfe and Williams believe that the 1975 publication of *The Best of Cordwainer Smith* established Linebarger "as a seminal force in contemporary science fiction. . . . He cannot be easily pigeonholed. His stories reveal not only a science-fiction writer, but also a historian, a dialectical philosopher, a stylist imbued with the values and conventions of myth and oral narrative, a Christian, and ultimately a Romantic."

BIOGRAPHICAL/CRITICAL SOURCES: New York Times, August 8, 1966; *Dictionary of Literary Biography,* Volume VIII, Gale, 1981.

* * *

LIPPMANN, Walter   1889-1974

PERSONAL: Born September 23, 1889, in New York, N.Y.; died December 14, 1974; son of Jacob (a clothing manufacturer) and Daisy (Baum) Lippmann; married Faye Albertson, May 24, 1917 (divorced, 1938); married Helen Byrne Armstrong, March 26, 1938. *Education:* Harvard University, A.B. (cum laude), 1909, graduate study, 1909-10. *Politics:* Independent. *Home:* Hotel Lowell, 28 East 63rd St., New York, N.Y. 10021; and Southwest Harbor, Mount Desert, Me.

CAREER: Worked for *Everybody's Magazine* as Lincoln Steffens's secretary, 1910, became associate editor within a year;

executive secretary to George R. Lunn, Socialist mayor of Schenectady, N.Y., during four months in 1912; with Herbert Croly, founded the *New Republic,* 1914, served as associate editor until 1917, returned to it in 1919; assistant to Secretary of War Newton D. Baker, 1917; secretary to a governmental organization, 1917, was one of the authors of President Woodrow Wilson's Fourteen Points; *The Inquiry,* secretary, 1917-18; editorial staff member of *New York World,* 1921-29, editor, 1929-31; columnist ("Today and Tomorrow") for *New York Herald Tribune,* 1931-62, column syndicated by *Washington Post* and *Los Angeles Times* syndicates, 1963-67; also syndicated in over 275 papers around the world; fortnightly columnist, *Newsweek,* beginning 1962. Member of board of overseers, Harvard University, 1933-39; member of board of directors, Fund for the Advancement of Education, beginning 1951. *Military service:* U.S. Army Military Intelligence, 1918-19; commissioned a captain; attached to General Pershing's headquarters.

MEMBER: National Institute of Arts and Letters, American Academy of Arts and Letters (fellow), National Press Club, Phi Beta Kappa (senator, 1934-40), Sigma Delta Chi (fellow, 1950); Cosmos Club, Metropolitan Club, Army-Navy Country Club (all Washington, D.C.); Century Club, River Club, Harvard Club, Coffee House Club (all New York); Harvard Club, Tavern Club (both Boston).

AWARDS, HONORS: Commander, Legion of Honor (France), 1946; Commander, Legion of Honor, Officer of Order of Leopold (Belgium), 1947; Knight's Cross of Order of St. Olav (Norway), 1950; Commander, Order of Orange Nassau (Netherlands), 1952; Overseas Press Club Award, 1953, 1955, and 1959; Pulitzer Prizes, 1958 and 1962; George Foster Peabody Award, 1962; Presidential Medal of Freedom, 1964, for "profound interpretation of his country and the affairs of the world"; Gold Medal, National Academy of Arts and Letters, 1965. LL.D., Wake Forest College, 1926, University of Wisconsin, 1927, University of California and Union College, 1933, Wesleyan University and University of Michigan, 1934, George Washington University and Amherst College, 1935, University of Rochester, 1936, College of William and Mary and Drake University, 1937, University of Chicago, 1955, New School for Social Research, 1959; Litt.D. from Dartmouth College and Columbia University, 1932, Oglethorpe College, 1934, Harvard University, 1944.

WRITINGS: A Preface to Politics, Mitchell Kennerly, 1913; *Drift and Mastery: An Attempt to Diagnose the Current Unrest,* Mitchell Kennerly, 1914, new edition with an introduction and notes by William E. Leuchtenberg, Prentice-Hall, 1961, reprinted, Greenwood Press, 1977; *The Stakes of Diplomacy,* Holt, 1915, 2nd edition, 1917; *The World Conflict in Its Relation to American Democracy* (originally published in *Annals of the American Academy of Political Science,* July, 1917), U.S. Government Printing Office, 1917; *The Political Scene: An Essay on the Victory of 1918,* Holt, 1919; *Liberty and the News* (portion originally published in *Atlantic*), Harcourt, 1920; *France and the European Settlement* (pamphlet), Foreign Policy Association, 1922; *Public Opinion,* Harcourt, 1922, reprinted, Free Press, 1965; *Mr. Kahn Would Like to Know* (pamphlet; originally published in *New Republic,* July 4, 1923), Foreign Policy Association, 1923; *The Phantom Public,* Harcourt, 1925, published as *The Phantom Public: A Sequel to "Public Opinion,"* Macmillan, 1930; *H. L. Mencken* (pamphlet; originally published in *Saturday Review,* December 11, 1926), Knopf, 1926; *Men of Destiny,* drawings by Rollin Kirby, Macmillan, 1927, reprinted with an introduction by Richard Lowitt, University of Washington Press, 1969; *American Inquisitors: A Commentary on Dayton and Chicago,* Macmillan,

1928; *A Preface to Morals,* Macmillan, 1929, published with a new introduction by Sidney Hook, Time, Inc., 1964.

Notes on the Crisis (pamphlet; originally published in *New York Herald Tribune,* September, 1931), John Day, 1931; (with W. O. Scroggs and others) *The United States in World Affairs: An Account of American Foreign Relations, 1931,* Harper, Volume I, 1932, Volume II, 1933; *Interpretations, 1931-1932,* edited by Allan Nevins, Macmillan, 1932; *A New Social Order* (pamphlet), John Day, 1933; *The Method of Freedom,* Macmillan, 1934; (with G.D.H. Cole) *Self-Sufficiency: Some Random Reflections* [and] *Planning International Trade* (the former by Lippmann; the latter by Cole), Carnegie Endowment for International Peace, 1934; *The New Imperative* (portions originally published in *Yale Review,* June, 1935), Macmillan, 1935; *Interpretations, 1933-1935,* edited by Nevins, Macmillan, 1936; (editor with Nevins) *A Modern Reader: Essays on Present-day Life and Culture,* Heath, 1936, 2nd edition, 1946; *An Inquiry into the Principles of the Good Society,* Little, Brown, 1937, new edition, 1943 (published in England as *The Good Society,* Allen & Unwin, 1938), reprinted, Greenwood Press, 1973; *The Supreme Court: Independent or Controlled?,* Harper, 1937; *Some Notes on War and Peace,* Macmillan, 1940; *American Trade Policy* (originally published in [London] *Sunday Times*), 1943; *U.S. Foreign Policy: Shield of the Republic,* Little, Brown, 1943, reprinted, Johnson Reprint, 1972; *U.S. War Aims,* Little, Brown, 1944, reprinted, Da Capo Press, 1976; *In the Service of Freedom* (pamphlet), Freedom House, c.1945; *The Cold War: A Study in U.S. Foreign Policy,* Harper, 1947, reprinted, 1972.

Commentaries on American Far Eastern Policy (pamphlet), American Institute of Pacific Relations, 1950; *Isolation and Alliances: An American Speaks to the British,* Little, Brown, 1952; *Public Opinion and Foreign Policy in the United States* (lectures), Allen & Unwin, 1952; *Essays in the Public Philosophy,* Little, Brown, 1955 (published in England as *The Public Philosophy,* Hamish Hamilton, 1955); *America in the World Today* (lecture), University of Minnesota Press, 1957; *The Communist World and Ours,* Little, Brown, 1959; *The Confrontation* (originally published in column "Today and Tomorrow," September 17, 1959), Overbrook Press, 1959; (with Clarence C. Little) *Speeches of Walter Lippmann and Clarence C. Little,* [Cambridge], 1960; *The Coming Tests with Russia,* Little, Brown, 1961; *The Nuclear Era: A Profound Struggle* (pamphlet), University of Chicago Press, 1962; *Western Unity and the Common Market,* Little, Brown, 1962; *The Essential Lippmann: A Political Philosophy for Liberal Democracy,* edited by Clinton Rossiter and James Lare, Random House, 1963; (author of introduction) *Fulbright of Arkansas: The Public Positions of a Private Thinker,* edited by Karl E. Meyer, Luce, 1963; *A Free Press* (pamphlet), Berlingske Bogtrykkeri (Copenhagen), c. 1965; *Conversations with Walter Lippmann* (CBS Reports television program), introduction by Edward Weeks, Little, Brown, 1965; (author of introduction) Carl Sandburg, *The Chicago Race Riots, July, 1919,* Harcourt, 1969; *Early Writings,* introduction by Arthur Schlesinger, Jr., Liveright, 1971; *Public Persons,* edited by Gilbert A. Harrison, Liveright, 1976. Also editor of *The Poems of Paul Mariett,* 1913.

Contributor: Arno Lehman Bader, Theodore Hornberger, Sigmund K. Proctor, and Carlton Wells, editors, *Prose Patterns,* Harcourt, 1933; Edward Simpson Noyes, editor, *Readings in the Modern Essay,* Houghton, 1933; Albert Craig Baird, editor, *Essays and Addresses toward a Liberal Education,* Ginn, 1934; Joseph Bradley Hubbard and others, editors, *Current Economic Policies: Selected Discussions,* Holt, 1934; Frank Howland McCloskey and Robert B. Dow, editors, *Pageant of Prose,* Harper, 1935; Frank Luther Mott and Ralph D. Casey, editors,

Interpretations of Journalism: A Book of Readings, F. S. Crofts, 1937; Hillman M. Bishop and Samuel Hendel, editors, *Basic Issues of American Democracy: A Book of Readings,* Appleton, 1948, 6th edition, 1969; William Ebenstein, editor, *Modern Political Thought: The Great Issues,* Rinehart, 1954, 2nd edition, 1960; Robert U. Jamison, editor, *Essays Old and New,* Harcourt, 1955; H. J. Rockel, editor, *Reflective Reader: Essays for Writing,* Holt, 1956; Alan P. Grimes and Robert Horwitz, editors, *Modern Political Ideologues,* Oxford University Press, 1959; C. Wright Mills, editor, *Images of Man,* Braziller, 1960; Harry K. Girvetz, editor, *Contemporary Moral Issues,* Wadsworth, 1963; Arthur A. Ekirch, editor, *Voices in Dissent: An Anthology of Individualistic Thought in the U.S.,* Citadel, 1964; D. L. Larson, editor, *The Puritan Ethic in United States Foreign Policy,* Van Nostrand, 1966.

Anthologized in numerous volumes, including *Roots of Political Behavior,* edited by Richard Carlton Snyder and H. Herbert Wilson, American Book Co., 1949, *State of the Social Sciences,* edited by L. D. White, University of Chicago Press, 1956, *Conflict and Cooperation among the Nations,* edited by Ivo D. Duchacek and K. W. Thompson, Holt, 1960, and *Power and Civilization: Political Thought in the Twentieth Century,* edited by David Cooperman and E. V. Walter, Crowell, 1962.

Contributor to many periodicals, including *Atlantic, Yale Review, New Republic, Life,* and *Harper's.*

SIDELIGHTS: "Anything that makes the world more humane and more rational is progress," Walter Lippmann once said. "That's the only measuring stick we can apply to it." This statement exemplifies the attitude that characterized Lippmann's career. Although he was always fully cognizant of the occurrences of the day, he also attempted to place these events in a larger perspective in his effort to make reason out of the chaos of political events. He once stated: "I have led two lives. One of books and one of newspapers. Each helps the other. The philosophy is the context in which I write my columns. The column is the laboratory or clinic in which I test the philosophy and keep it from becoming too abstract."

This objective viewing of current events as though they were already part of history made Lippmann unique. Norman Podhoretz, in *Doings and Undoings: The Fifties and After in American Writing,* recognized this quality in Lippmann, although he believed that it had its disadvantages. Podhoretz wrote in 1964: "His main fault, I think, is a tendency toward pomposity which showed itself even in his most youthful efforts and which, if anything, has been encouraged by the veneration that his advancing years . . . have brought upon him. Presidents come and go; Congressmen and Senators come, and even they eventually go; but Walter Lippmann stays on in Washington forever—the last articulate representative of the political ambience of an older America, our last remaining link to the ethos of the Federalist Papers. He is, apparently, heeded and feared in Washington in a way that no other writer is, for his judgment of a government official, or of a policy, or of a bill seems to carry with it all the authority of the basic intentions of the American political system. When he speaks, it is as though the true Constitution were speaking, or as though Jefferson and Madison and Hamilton were communicating a mystical consensus through him—so thoroughly has he steeped himself in their spirit, and with such authenticity is he capable of recapturing the accents of their intellectual style. This, I suspect, is the secret source of his unique power to make the mighty listen: Walter Lippmann's opinion is the closest they can ever come to the judgment of history upon them. Under these circumstances, it is no wonder that Lippmann should occasionally be given to delivering himself of portentous platitudes without being aware that platitudes are what they are. The wonder is that he should be capable of anything else at all."

Podhoretz's comparison of Lippmann to the founding fathers is characteristic of many other analyses of Lippmann's philosophy and writing. In *A Continuing Journey,* Archibald MacLeish described Lippmann's attitude toward freedom in a democracy as one which closely paralleled the idealism of the leaders of the American Revolution: "True freedom, to Mr. Lippmann, is not the freedom of the liberal democracies. True freedom was founded on the postulate that there was a universal order on which all reasonable men were agreed: *within that public agreement* on the fundamentals and on the ultimates, it was sage to permit, and it would be desirable to encourage, dissent and dispute. True freedom for Mr. Lippmann, in other words, is freedom to think as you please and say as you think provided what you say and think falls within the periphery of what all reasonable men agree to be fundamentally and ultimately true." For Lippmann rationality was not only the highest ideal, but the possible savior of modern society. He once said: "The world will go on somehow, and more crises will follow. It will go on best, however, if among us there are men who have stood apart, who refused to be anxious or too much concerned, who were cool and inquiring, and had their eyes on a longer past and longer future."

It was in the field of foreign affairs that Lippmann revealed the principles central to his view of man and the modern world. In a *New York Times Magazine* interview, Lippmann stated that U.S. foreign policy was most responsible for the political unrest and social crises of the 1960s: "I ascribe the essence of the failure [of the United States to solve its internal problems] to miscalculation, to misunderstanding our post-World War II position in the world. That has turned our energies away from our real problems. The error is not merely the trouble in Vietnam, but the error lies in the illusion that the position occupied in the world by the United States at the end of the war was a permanent arrangement of power in the world. It wasn't. The United States was victorious; but by then all the imperial structures which set the bounds of American power had been destroyed: the German Reich, the Japanese empire. The result is that we flowed forward beyond our natural limits and the cold war is the result of our meeting the Russians with no buffers between us. That miscalculation, which was made by my generation, has falsified all our other calculations—what our power was, what we could afford to do, what influence we had to exert in the world."

One of Lippmann's chief concerns was that lack of reasonable attitudes toward other nations and domestic dissenters would continue to lead to an illogical disregard for the truly significant issues with which U.S. leaders must deal. "You have only to look at the Senate of the United States," Lippmann wrote in 1912, "to see how that body is capable of turning itself into a court of preliminary hearings for the Last Judgment, wasting its time and our time and absorbing public enthusiasm and newspaper scareheads. For a hundred needs of the nation it has no thought, but about the precise morality of an historical transaction eight years old there is a meticulous interest . . . enough to start the Senate on a protracted man-hunt. Now if one half of the people is bent upon proving how wicked a man is and the other half is determined to show how good he is, neither half will think very much about the nation." Lippmann also applied this disparagement of emotional politics to the passionate anti-Communists: "The reactionary radicals, who would like to repeal the twentieth century, are, so they tell us, violently opposed to Communism. But Communism also belongs to the twentieth century and these reactionary radicals do not understand it and do not know how to resist it."

Lippmann believed that it was his ultimate role as a journalist to reveal the absurdity of these emotional diversions. With this goal he hoped to influence the people to accept his creed; he objectified events so that the populace could comprehend them. "If the country is to be governed with the consent of the governed, then the governed must arrive at opinions about what their governors want them to consent to. How do they do this? They do it by hearing on the radio and reading in the newspapers what the corps of correspondents tells them is going on in Washington and in the country at large and in the world. Here we perform an essential service . . . we do what every sovereign citizen is supposed to do, but has not the time or the interest to do for himself. This is our job. It is no mean calling, and we have a right to be proud of it."

Some of Lippmann's books have been translated into French, German, Italian, Spanish, and Chinese.

BIOGRAPHICAL/CRITICAL SOURCES: David E. Weingast, *Walter Lippmann: A Study in Personal Journalism,* Rutgers University Press, 1949, reprinted, Greenwood Press, 1970; Max Lerner, *Actions and Passions: Notes on the Multiple Revolution of Our Time,* Simon & Schuster, 1949; Henry Steele Commager, *The American Mind,* Yale University Press, 1950; Kenneth Norman Stewart and John Tibbel, *Makers of Modern Journalism,* Prentice-Hall, 1952; John Mason Brown, *Through These Men: Some Aspects of Our Passing History,* Harper, 1956; Marquis Childs and James Reston, editors, *Walter Lippmann and His Times,* Harcourt, 1959; Felix S. Cohen, *The Legal Conscience,* Yale University Press, 1960; Charles B. Forcey, *The Crossroads of Liberalism: Croly, Weyl, Lippmann, and the Progressive Era 1900-1925,* Oxford University Press, 1961; Hans J. Morgenthau, *The Restoration of American Politics,* University of Chicago Press, 1962; Arthur Schlesinger, Jr., *The Politics of Hope,* Houghton, 1963; Norman Podhoretz, *Doings and Undoings: The Fifties and After in American Writing,* Farrar, Straus, 1964; Anwar H. Syed, *Walter Lippmann's Philosophy of International Politics,* University of Pennsylvania Press, 1964; Aylesa Forsee, *Headliners: Famous American Journalists,* Macrae, 1967; Archibald MacLeish, *A Continuing Journey,* Houghton, 1967; F. C. Cary, *The Influence of Walter Lippmann, 1914-1944,* State Historical Society of Wisconsin, 1967; Edward L. Schapsmeier and Frederick H. Schapsmeier, *Walter Lippmann: Philosopher, Journalist,* Public Affairs Press, 1969; Charles Wellborn, *Twentieth Century Pilgrimage: Walter Lippmann and the Public Philosophy,* Louisiana State University Press, 1969; *New York Times Magazine,* September 14, 1969; Eric Sevareid, *Conversations with Eric Sevareid,* Public Affairs Press, 1976; *Authors in the News,* Volume I, Gale, 1976; Ronald Steel, *Walter Lippmann and the American Century,* Atlantic/Little, Brown, 1980.†

*   *   *

LIVERANI, Giuseppe   1903-

PERSONAL: Born September 17, 1903, in Faenza, Italy; son of Cesare (a worker) and Maria (Fagnocchi) Liverani; married Sella Bice, July 18, 1934; children: Carlo, Giovanna. *Education:* Istituto d'Arte per la Ceramica, Faenza, Italy, Perito ceramista, 1922. *Home:* Via Martiri Ungheresi 4, Faenza, Italy. *Office:* Museo Internazionale delle Ceramiche, Faenza, Italy.

CAREER: Museo Internazionale delle Ceramiche, Faenza, Italy, keeper, 1924-53, director, 1953—; Istituto d'Arte per la Ceramica, Faenza, teacher, 1931—. Member of Faenza building committee, 1949—. *Military service:* Italian Army, antiaircraft artillery, 1940-45; awarded War Cross. *Member:* De-

putazione di Storia Patria (Bologna), Accademia Pietro Vannucci (Perugia), Accademia Clementina (Bologna), Amis de Sevres, English Ceramic Circle, Rotary International. *Awards, honors:* Knight of the Order Al Merito della Repubblica Italiana.

WRITINGS: Catalogo delle Porcellane dei Medici, Lega, 1936; *Itinerario del Museo Internazionale delle Ceramiche Faenza,* Istituto Poligrafico dello Stato, 1937, reprinted, 1975; *Il Regio Istituto d'arte per la ceramica di Faenza,* F. Le Monnier, 1941; *La Maiolica Italiana,* Electa Edition, 1957; *Italiensk Majolika,* Allhems Forlag, 1958; *Five Centuries of Italian Majolika,* McGraw, 1960; *A Giuseppe Liverani nel settantesimo Compleanno,* Museo Internazionale della Ceramiche, 1973; *Italian Ceramics,* Kodansha, 1981. *Selazione di Opere* (bulletin of the Museo Internazionale delle Ceramiche), editor, 1924—, director, 1953—.

BIOGRAPHICAL/CRITICAL SOURCES: Il Mattino, Napoli, Italy, June 28, 1961; *Il Piccolo,* Trieste, July 1, 1961; *L'Italia Turistica,* Rome, Italy, September 10, 1961.†

*   *   *

LOCHLONS, Colin
See JACKSON, C(aary) Paul

*   *   *

LOCKE, Martin
See DUNCAN, W(illiam) Murdoch

*   *   *

LOCKSPEISER, Edward   1905-1973

PERSONAL: Born May 21, 1905, in London, England; died February 3, 1973, in London; son of Leon (a jeweler) and Rose (Gleitzman) Lockspeiser; married Eleanore Weinstein, May 16, 1927 (divorced); children: Mary (Mrs. Robert Frank). *Education:* Attended Royal College of Music, London, England. *Home:* 70 Harley St., London W.1, England. *Agent:* Curtis Brown Ltd., 1 Craven Hill, London W2 3EW, England.

CAREER: British Broadcasting Corp., London, England, member of music department, 1940-49, later musical adviser and broadcaster; *Encyclopaedia Britannica,* musical adviser, 1958-66; *Listener,* music critic, beginning 1961; King's College, University of London, lecturer in music, 1966-70. Lecturer at Harvard, Yale, and Columbia, 1961. *Member:* P.E.N., Society of Authors. *Awards, honors:* Officer d'Academie Paris, 1949, for services to French music; Leverhulme fellowship to complete Volume II on Debussy, 1963.

WRITINGS: Debussy, Dent, 1936, 5th edition, 1980; *Debussy: His Life and Mind,* Macmillan, Volume I: *1862-1902,* 1962, Volume II: *1902-1918,* 1965, both volumes reprinted, Cambridge University Press, 1978; *Getting to Know the Orchestra,* Encyclopaedia Britannica International, 1965; *Music and Painting: A Study in Comparative Ideas from Turner to Schoenberg,* Harper, 1973; (with Anthony Blunt) *French Art and Music since 1500,* Methuen, 1974.

Editor: (And translator) Henry Prunieres, *A New History of Music,* Macmillan, 1943, reprinted, Vienna House, 1972; *Claude Debussy: Lettres inedites a Andre Caplet,* Editions du Rocher, 1957; *The Literary Clef,* J. Calder, 1958; *Debussy et Edgar Poe,* Editions du Rocher, 1962.†

LOFTON, John (Marion) 1919-

PERSONAL: Born April 11, 1919, in McClellanville, S.C.; son of John Marion (a farmer) and Harriett (Lucas) Lofton; married Anne Watson, December 27, 1954 (died, 1968); married Priscilla Alvarado, 1969; children: (first marriage) John M., Jr., Charles Lewis; (second marriage) Cathy. *Education:* College of Charleston, B.S., 1940; Duke University, J.D., 1942; University of Pittsburgh, M.A., 1956; Stanford University, graduate study, 1960-61. *Politics:* Democrat. *Religion:* Unitarian. *Home:* 9 Bon Price Lane, St. Louis, Mo. 63132. *Office: St. Louis Post-Dispatch,* 900 North Tucker Blvd., St. Louis, Mo. 63101.

CAREER: Admitted to South Carolina Bar, 1942, but most of career has been spent in newspaper field; member of editorial staff of *Spartanburg Herald,* Spartanburg, S.C., 1945-47, *Seattle Star,* Seattle, Wash., 1947, *Times and Democrat,* Orangeburg, S.C., 1947-48, *Arkansas Gazette,* Little Rock, Ark., 1948-52; *Pittsburgh Post-Gazette,* Pittsburgh, Pa., associate editor, 1952-66; editor of editorial page, 1966-70; University of Pittsburgh, Pittsburgh, Pa., associate professor of speech, 1970-71; *St. Louis Post-Dispatch,* St. Louis, Mo., member of editorial board, 1971—. Conference director, Association of Scientists for Atomic Education, 1947. *Military service:* U.S. Army, 1942-45. *Member:* National Conference of Editorial Writers, American Bar Association, American Judicature Society, American Civil Liberties Union (member of board of directors, Pittsburgh branch). *Awards, honors:* American Bar Association Gavel Award for distinguished series of articles and editorials on the roles of judges and lawyers in the American judicial process, 1960; mass media fellowship, Fund for Adult Education, 1960-61.

WRITINGS: (With George Swetnam, William M. Schutte, and Donald M. Goodfellow) *Pittsburgh's First Unitarian Church,* Boxwood Press, 1961; *Insurrection in South Carolina: The Turbulent World of Denmark Vesey,* Antioch Press, 1964; *Justice and the Press,* Beacon Press, 1966; *The Press as Guardian of the First Amendment,* University of South Carolina Press, 1980. Contributor to numerous periodicals, including *New Republic, Nation, Christian Science Monitor, Bulletin of the Atomic Scientists, Current History,* and *American Psychologist.*

SIDELIGHTS: In *The Press as Guardian of the First Amendment,* John Lofton reveals that historically the press has not always defended the freedom of speech and of the press. He examines what America's early leaders thought about a free press and concludes that the new nation had a tenuous commitment to the First Amendment. "By the time the Bill of Rights was 25 years old," writes Lofton, "the First Amendment guarantee of press freedom had already been undermined by all three branches of government."

New York Times writer Linda Greenhouse states that the book is "refreshing" to read in this age where "the press indeed sees itself as the embattled defender of the constitutional guarantees of free speech and freedom of the press." Greenhouse continues: "Somehow, from a rather unpromising start, First Amendment values gradually became central to the country's image of itself as a democracy. That this development took place with little assistance from the established press is fascinating. . . . This is a worthwhile and provocative book."

AVOCATIONAL INTERESTS: Civil liberties and rights, conservation, and international relations.

BIOGRAPHICAL/CRITICAL SOURCES: New York Times, July 4, 1981; *Columbia Journalism Review,* September/October, 1981.

LOFTS, Norah (Robinson) 1904-
(Juliet Astley, Peter Curtis)

PERSONAL: Born August 27, 1904, in Shipdham, Norfolk, England; daughter of Isaac and Ethel (Garner) Robinson; married Geoffrey Lofts, December 29, 1933 (died, 1948); married Robert Jorisch, 1949; children: Geoffrey St. Edmund Clive Lofts. *Education:* Norwich Training College, Teaching Diploma, 1925. *Politics:* Conservative. *Home:* North-Gate House, Bury St. Edmund's, Suffolk IP33 1HQ, England. *Agent:* Curtis Brown, 575 Madison Ave., New York, N.Y. 10022.

CAREER: Writer. Guildhall Feoffment Girls' School, taught English and history, 1925-36. Member of Bury St. Edmund's Borough Council, 1957-62; member of Board of Managers for two schools. *Member:* Family Planning Association (president). *Awards, honors:* American Booksellers' Association award, 1935, for *I Met a Gypsy;* Georgette Heyer Award, 1979, for *The Day of the Butterfly.*

WRITINGS—Novels: I Met a Gypsy, Knopf, 1935, reprinted, Hodder & Stoughton, 1979; *Here Was a Man: A Romantic History of Sir Walter, His Voyages, His Discoveries, and His Queen,* Knopf, 1936, reprinted, Hodder & Stoughton, 1976; *White Hell of Pity,* Knopf, 1937, reprinted, Manor, 1975; *Requiem for Idols* (also see below), Knopf, 1938, reprinted, Corgi Books, 1972; *Out of This Nettle,* Gollancz, 1938, published as *Colin Lowrie,* Knopf, 1939, reprinted under original title, Manor, 1976; *Blossom Like the Rose,* Knopf, 1939, reprinted, Manor, 1976.

Hester Roon, Knopf, 1940, reprinted, Corgi Books, 1978; *The Road to Revelation,* P. Davies, 1941, reprinted, Corgi Books, 1976; *The Brittle Glass,* M. Joseph, 1942, Knopf, 1943, reprinted, Fawcett, 1977; *Michael and All Angels,* M. Joseph, 1943, published as *The Golden Fleece,* Knopf, 1944, reprinted, Fawcett, 1977; *Jassy* (also see below), M. Joseph, 1944, Knopf, 1945, reprinted, Fawcett, 1979; *To See a Fine Lady,* Knopf, 1946, reprinted, Fawcett, 1976; *Silver Nutmeg,* Doubleday, 1947, reprinted, Corgi Books, 1974; *A Calf for Venus,* Doubleday, 1949, published as *Letty,* Pyramid Publications, 1968, reprinted under original title, Corgi Books, 1974.

Esther, Macmillan, 1950, reprinted, Corgi Books, 1973; *The Lute Player,* Doubleday, 1951, reprinted, Fawcett, 1976; *Bless This House* (Literary Guild selection; also see below), Doubleday, 1954, reprinted, Queens House, 1977; *Winter Harvest,* Doubleday, 1955, reprinted, Fawcett, 1976; *Eleanor the Queen: The Story of the Most Famous Woman of the Middle Ages,* Doubleday, 1955 (published in England as *Queen in Waiting,* M. Joseph, 1955), published as *Queen in Waiting,* Doubleday, 1958, reprinted under original title, Fawcett, 1977; *Afternoon of an Autocrat,* Doubleday, 1956, published as *The Deadly Gift,* Pyramid Publications, 1967 (published in England as *The Devil in Clevely,* Morley Baker, 1968), published under original title, Hodder & Stoughton, 1978; *Scent of Cloves* (also see below), Doubleday, 1957, reprinted, Queens House, 1977; *The Town House,* Doubleday, 1959, reprinted, Fawcett, 1976.

The House at Old Vine, Doubleday, 1961, reprinted, Queens House, 1977; *The House at Sunset,* Doubleday, 1962, reprinted, Fawcett, 1978; *The Concubine: A Novel Based Upon the Life of Anne Boleyn, Henry VIII's Second Wife,* Doubleday, 1963 (published in England as *Concubine,* Arrow Books, 1965); *How Far to Bethlehem?* (also see below), Doubleday, 1965; *The Lost Queen,* Doubleday, 1969 (published in England as *The Lost Ones,* Hutchinson, 1969); *Madeslin,* Corgi Books, 1969; *The King's Pleasure,* Doubleday, 1969.

Lovers All Untrue, Doubleday, 1970; *A Rose for Virtue: The Very Private Life of Hortense, Stepdaughter of Napoleon I, Mother of Napoleon III,* Doubleday, 1971; *Out of the Dark,* Doubleday, 1972 (published in England as *Charlotte,* Hodder & Stoughton, 1972); *Nethergate,* Doubleday, 1973; *Crown of Aloes,* Doubleday, 1974; *Checkmate,* Corgi Books, 1975, Fawcett, 1978; *Walk into My Parlour,* Corgi Books, 1975; *Knight's Acre* (first novel in trilogy; also see below), Doubleday, 1975; *The Homecoming* (second novel in trilogy; also see below), Hodder & Stoughton, 1975, Doubleday, 1976; *The Lonely Furrow* (third novel in trilogy), Hodder & Stoughton, 1976, Doubleday, 1977; *Gad's Hall,* Hodder & Stoughton, 1977, Doubleday, 1978; *Haunted House,* Hodder & Stoughton, 1978, published as *The Haunting of Gad's Hall,* Doubleday, 1979; *The Day of the Butterfly,* Bodley Head, 1979, Doubleday, 1980; *Selected Works* (contains *Jassy, Bless This House, Scent of Cloves,* and *How Far to Bethlehem?*), Octopus Books, 1979.

A Wayside Tavern, Doubleday, 1980; *Two by Norah Lofts* (contains *Requiem for Idols* and *You're Best Alone*), Doubleday, 1981; *The Claw,* Hodder & Stoughton, 1981; *The Old Priory,* Bodley Head, 1981.

Short story collections: *Heaven in Your Hand and Other Stories,* Doubleday, 1958, reprinted, Fawcett, 1975; *Is There Anybody There?,* Corgi Books, 1974, published as *Hauntings: Is There Anybody There?,* Doubleday, 1975.

Other: *Women in the Old Testament: Twenty Psychological Portraits,* Macmillan, 1949; (with Margery Weiner) *Eternal France: A History of France, 1789-1944,* Doubleday, 1968; *The Story of Maude Reed* (juvenile), Transworld Publications, 1971, published as *The Maude Reed Tale,* T. Nelson, 1972; *Rupert Hatton's Tale* (juvenile), Carousel Books, 1972, published as *Rupert Hatton's Story* (Junior Literary Guild selection), T. Nelson, 1973; *Domestic Life in England,* Weidenfeld & Nicholson, 1976, Doubleday, 1977; *Queens of England,* Doubleday, 1977 (published in England as *Queens of Britain,* Hodder & Stoughton, 1977); *Emma Hamilton,* Coward, 1978; *Anne Boleyn,* Coward, 1979. Also author of *Uneasy Paradise,* 1965 (published in England as *Her Own Special Island,* Corgi Books, 1973).

Under pseudonym Juliet Astley: *The Fall of Midas,* Coward, 1975; *Copsi Castle,* Coward, 1978.

Under pseudonym Peter Curtis, except as indicated: *Dead March in Three Keys,* P. Davis, 1940, published as *No Question of Murder,* Doubleday, 1959, published under name Norah Lofts as *Bride of Moat House,* Fawcett, 1975; *You're Best Alone,* Macdonald, 1943, reprinted, Corgi Books, 1971; *Lady Living Alone,* Macdonald, 1945; *The Devil's Own,* Doubleday, 1960 (published in England as *The Witches,* Pan Books, 1966), published as *The Little Wax Doll,* Doubleday, 1970.

Contributor to *Ladies' Home Journal, Woman's Journal, Reader's Digest, Cosmopolitan,* and *Writer.*

WORK IN PROGRESS: A collection of contemporary stories.

SIDELIGHTS: "The past can be reached only by a willing imagination," states Norah Lofts in the *Writer.* "It takes more imagination to write about the past than about the future, for the future is being shaped by the present; the seed is already planted."

For her historical novels, Lofts chooses figures she believes will be relevant to her and to her readers: Anne Boleyn in *The Concubine,* Catherine of Aragon in *The King's Pleasure,* Isabella of Spain in *Crown of Aloes.* She has not made one particular period her specialty; instead, she prefers to select an interesting character and then research the era in which that

person lived. Learning what she can from such sources as books, old newspapers, letters, and diaries, Lofts then "colors her fictionalized account of her central characters' lives with vivid descriptions of the eras in which they lived," states a *Detroit News* writer. However, she concentrates more on the psychology of her characters than on the setting of the novel. "All these are merely *things;* a novel deals with *people,*" she explains in the *Writer.*

Imagination is a necessary element of writing historical fiction. Documents and records will supply the facts, but then the imagination must step in to present the facts in a logical, unified, and captivating manner. Lofts, who is considered a skillful master of blending fact and fancy, writes in a chapter heading of *The Concubine,* "I do not say that this is how it happened: I only say that this is how it could have happened."

Lofts cites an example of her technique in another article for the *Writer:* "Fact stated that some Ursuline nuns arrived in Loudun in 1636. That statement calls up no picture in the mind and evokes no emotion. . . . What kind of weather that day? Since the story was to be tragic as well as horrific, I chose a day of dull rain. I made the nuns arrive toward evening, bone-weary; but weariest of all was the narrator, who was almost a dwarf and positively a hunchback. I saw her . . . struggling to keep up with the able-bodied, now and again compelled to take a few running steps, like a child." A *Washington Post Book World* writer, praising Lofts's ability to create a readable story from unadorned fact, states, "[She] evokes history with such vigor that the reader irresistibly thinks: If this isn't the way it was, it's the way it should have been."

Because it is almost impossible to know exactly what was said by people from the past, much of the conversation in a historical novel must be invented. Lofts contends this is permissible provided that the conversation is consistent with the character of the speaker and does not conflict with anything known to be said. "Fact supplies a few scraps of dialogue, . . . mainly in indirect speech, which never makes quite the same impact as direct speech," she says in the *Writer.*

The question of whether to use period language is a persistent one for many writers of historical novels. Lofts is against it for reasons she describes in the *Writer:* "It comes between the reader and the story. (Anyone who craves to read ye olde Englishe can always reach for Chaucer.) Not enough is known about period language. We know how people wrote, but not how they spoke. If every record of twentieth-century speech were completely lost and a thousand years from now the would-be writer of a historical novel had nothing to go on but a few plays, a popular song or two, and the written record of a Parliamentary debate, and if he tried to use these as the basis for conversation in his twentieth-century novel, the result would be very odd and misleading. . . . Characters [should] talk as people always have—to communicate with one another."

Along with obsolete language, Lofts also avoids what she calls "obviously modern words and expressions." Her purpose is to relay a story that will attract readers and not alienate them because of the language. "I like decent, basic English," explains Lofts in the *Writer.* "I'm no pedant, and for 'precious' writing I have no use at all."

Many critics believe that Lofts has certainly achieved her goal. James Doyle, in a *Best Sellers* article, calls Lofts's style "concise, direct, witty, penetrating and easily readable." Caroline Thompson of the *Los Angeles Times* notes how Lofts "adeptly melds details of the era in the telling of the tale itself." Another *Best Sellers* reviewer remarks, "It has been well said that Miss Lofts can make fiction sound like veritable history; and recorded history she brings to light as though it were the most fantastic of tales.''

Lofts has received many letters from readers who hated history lessons but enjoy reading her historical novels. This has led her to suspect that history is being taught badly in the schools. Part of the problem, Lofts believes, is the emphasis on dates and battles. With her novels, Norah Lofts has proven again and again that what makes history interesting is the people. *Christian Science Monitor* critic Carolyn Hall comments, ''Lofts makes history come alive on the page as she paints her characters, warts and all.''

MEDIA ADAPTATIONS: Jassy was filmed by General Film Distributors in 1947; *You're Best Alone* was filmed as ''Guilt Is My Shadow'' by Associated British and Pathe Film Distributors in 1950; *The Devil's Own* was filmed as ''The Witches'' by Twentieth Century-Fox in 1966.

CA INTERVIEW

CA interviewed Norah Lofts by phone April 21, 1981, at Northgate House, her home in Bury St. Edmund's, England.

CA: You've said you always wanted to write. Was teaching planned as a stopgap, a means of support until you got established as a writer?

LOFTS: Yes. I had to do something to earn a living. You see, I like to eat.

CA: Did you expect to be successful at the writing all along?

LOFTS: Hoped. It took me five years to peddle my first manuscript.

CA: During the five years your first book, your ''homing pigeon,'' was making the rounds of publishers, did you continue to write fiction?

LOFTS: No. I couldn't bear to. I was too despairing, and I thought if that wasn't good enough, I should never do anything that would be.

CA: So you had faith in the book, even though it wasn't sold at once?

LOFTS: Well, it took five years to peddle, but it's taken longer to die. It was published in 1935 and is still in print today. That's not bad, is it?

CA: Did you write anything during those years?

LOFTS: I wrote poetry and voluminous letters.

CA: You wrote several books under the pseudonym Peter Curtis. Was it easier to sell books with a male pseudonym?

LOFTS: No, it was for the sake of my faithful readers—of whom at the time I had about two—and I thought they would both be disappointed if I suddenly landed a crime story on them.

CA: How did you pick that name?

LOFTS: Peter for my publisher, Peter Davis, and *Curtis* for my agent, Curtis Brown.

CA: How were you discovered to be Peter Curtis?

LOFTS: I don't really know. I gave up using that as a pseudonym, and then suddenly I found books were coming out ''by Norah Lofts'' writing ''as Peter Curtis.'' But how that came about I never did discover.

CA: You've pointed out that people who hated history in school will avidly read your historical novels. Do you think history could be made more interesting to students?

LOFTS: I know it could because I taught history for twelve years. My girls were all mad on it.

CA: Why do you think it's mostly made so dull?

LOFTS: Because if you concentrate on the Seven Years' War and the War of the Spanish Succession and the War of the Austrian Succession, that *is* dull. It's the people who matter.

CA: Are you still doing most of your research at home, having books sent to you?

LOFTS: Yes, but I had an accident and I'm now chairbound. I broke my hip last August and it hasn't mended up, so I've had to employ somebody to go around for me a bit.

CA: Before that, you commented that you didn't like to go into London too much. Was it because of the big-city atmosphere?

LOFTS: I hate it. I'm absolutely overcome by it. I made up my mind long ago not to go anymore. Now, of course, I never shall.

CA: Do you recall any one book that's been the most difficult to research?

LOFTS: Yes. I had to have help with that, too. *Crown of Aloes,* the one about Isabella of Spain. Most of the things I wanted to know were in Spanish and had never been in English.

CA: Were they hard to find as well as hard to get translated?

LOFTS: No. The girl who does my research work is extremely clever. She knew exactly what I wanted, and she knew almost enough Spanish to do the translation, and she knew a Spaniard who would help her. That was very fortunate.

CA: Did she actually go to Spain to get the material?

LOFTS: Some of it, yes.

CA: Does she work for you full-time as a researcher?

LOFTS: No, just part-time.

CA: Have you ever had to give up a book you'd planned or started because of research problems?

LOFTS: No.

CA: Is there one book that you've most enjoyed writing?

LOFTS: Let's just say that I enjoy it all so much. I'm just one of those people who are really only happy knocking off some story on the typewriter. That's why those five years were times of such frustration to me. I quite enjoyed teaching and I liked my girls, and I think I did something to help the teaching of history in a way, but that wasn't what I wanted to do. All the other things I've done with my life, I would really rather have been on the typewriter.

CA: So many writers say that writing is the world's worst work, they hate every minute of it, it's miserable and lonely. But you don't feel any of that?

LOFTS: I don't feel that, no. Indeed, when I'm very, very miserable—and I've had so many blows in my life, quite enough to be miserable about—when things are at a crisis, I think, oh, let me get away to wherever it is I'm writing about.

CA: You get a lot of mail. Do people ever write offering you unsolicited ideas for books?

LOFTS: Oh yes, many times. I've never had one that clicked yet. I'm open to suggestions, but my writing self likes to go its own way.

CA: Do you respond to them in any way?

LOFTS: I say I'll think about it and thank you very much.

CA: Do you have many aspiring writers asking for advice?

LOFTS: Endless.

CA: Do you try to help them in any way?

LOFTS: I try sometimes. It's very difficult now because one's agent won't take anybody who isn't established already. I will read the stuff sometimes, and I suggest where it could be improved. I do try.

CA: Several of your books have been filmed. Have you taken any active part in the screenwriting or the production of those films?

LOFTS: No, none.

CA: Have you ever been interested in doing that?

LOFTS: I would have been, had I been consulted, but I never was. Well, actually, the script was being written for *Scent of Cloves,* and the man who was writing it consulted me day and night. Then he died and the whole project was dropped, which was a pity.

CA: Have you been happy with the films?

LOFTS: Not very, no. I could bear "Jassy," but I thought "The Witches" was so badly overacted and overdone. Evil, to me, shouldn't show its face quite so openly. I like evil behind the corner, as it were. It's much worse then.

CA: Do you have time to read anything beyond research for your books?

LOFTS: Oh yes, I read two books a day, often old ones. I reread my favorites because that's like going home again. I like MacDonald Fraser and Paul Scott, who is marvelous. He wrote one of the best books in the English language, I think. I have just read a good thriller by a woman whose work I hadn't met before called Palma Harcourt. I'm going around now beating the gong for Palma Harcourt.

CA: You like thrillers a lot?

LOFTS: If they're good, yes.

CA: Do you have much contact with other writers?

LOFTS: Hardly any. Rebecca West once wrote me a fan letter, believe it or not. And Elizabeth Jenkins is a friend.

CA: Have you in the past tried to maintain contact with them?

LOFTS: Not much, really.

CA: Is historical romance reviewed more in England than in this country?

LOFTS: I always contend that I'm not a historical romantic writer. I'm a realist. If it's history, they get very little space in England. About once every two months, four inches called "Historical Novels," and they will review, say, eight, with one sentence each, which isn't very helpful. America gives more space. They still have more paper, I suppose.

CA: Have you made many trips to the United States?

LOFTS: I've been three times.

CA: Have you found publishers in the United States generally easy to deal with?

LOFTS: Marvelous. I've been at it since 1935, and I've only changed my publisher once.

CA: Have you found publishers in the United States good about promoting the books?

LOFTS: Very good.

CA: How did you come to live in Northgate House?

LOFTS: I was living in Bury at the time, and I needed rather more room. This was for sale. I came and looked at it, and it is a charming old house. Having seen it, I fell in love with it one June afternoon—that was in 1955, I think—and it's been a lasting love affair. It's an expensive mistress; the best ones always are, of course. It's kept me very poor—it always needs something new—but I still like it very much.

CA: Did you do a lot of research on the history of the house?

LOFTS: We can't find out anything about it prior to 1745. There is a gutter spout which is stamped 1713. And even that is an addition because the house itself consists of two Tudor houses. Somebody who knows these things came and looked at the timbers in the roof and assured me of that. And then somebody put the back on in Queen Anne's reign, and somebody put the front on about 1776.

CA: If you had it to do over, is there anything you'd change about your life or your career?

LOFTS: It sounds a trivial thing: I would have some typing lessons. I never did learn. I've acquired a certain amount of skill. I must have done millions of words, if you think of the rewriting, the articles, the short stories, the letters. But I still couldn't pick my own name out without looking at the keyboard. And if I'm absent from it, as I was when I was in the hospital, I lose that skill and I have to begin all over again.

CA: Other than that, you're happy with what you've done?

LOFTS: I think I've been very blessed. I've had a sitting-down job, an indoor job—because I don't like being out-of-doors—and I've had a certain amount of financial reward, a certain amount of friendly letters of appreciation and love. I consider

I'm badly neglected, but that's an occupational disease, isn't it?

BIOGRAPHICAL/CRITICAL SOURCES: Best Sellers, March 15, 1969, October 1, 1969, October, 1977; Times Literary Supplement, May 14, 1970, May 27, 1977; Writer, November, 1970, March, 1974, July, 1976, September, 1979, August, 1981; Detroit News, April 2, 1972; Milwaukee Journal, October 19, 1975; Authors in the News, Volume II, Gale, 1976; Christian Science Monitor, December 19, 1979; Los Angeles Times, February 14, 1980; London Times, May 8, 1980; Washington Post Book World, November 2, 1980.

—Sketch by Debra G. Jones

—Interview by Jean W. Ross

* * *

LOGAN, Jake
    See SMITH, Martin Cruz

* * *

LOGSDON, Thomas S(tanley)   1937-
    (Tom Logsdon)

PERSONAL: Born September 27, 1937, in Springfield, Ky.; son of George Stanley (a miller) and Margaret (a nurse; maiden name, Buckman) Logsdon; married Fae Shobe (a teacher), August 21, 1960 (divorced, 1977); children: Donna Lorraine. Education: Eastern Kentucky University, B.S., 1959; University of Kentucky, M.S., 1961; graduate study at University of California, Los Angeles, 1961-81. Home: 235 Clipper Way, Seal Beach, Calif. 90740. Office: Rockwell International, Seal Beach Blvd., Seal Beach, Calif. 90740.

CAREER: Naval Ordnance Laboratory, Silver Spring, Md., student trainee, 1958; Douglas Aircraft, Santa Monica, Calif., senior engineer, 1959-63; Rockwell International, Seal Beach, Calif., flight mechanics engineer, 1963—; University of Southern California, Los Angeles, adjunct professor of computer science, 1978—. Member: North American Mathematical and Statistical Community, American Institute of Aeronautics and Astronautics, American Astronautical Society, American Mathematical Society, National Aerospace Education Council, American Institute for the Advancement of Science, American Platform Speakers Association, Institute of Navigation, Thursday Exchange Club. Awards, honors: Radio Corp. of America science scholarship, 1957-58; National Defense fellow, 1959; Sustained Superior Performance Award, National Aeronautics and Space Administration, 1968; Rockwell Presidential Award, 1973; inducted into Hall of Distinguished Alumni at Eastern Kentucky University, 1974.

WRITINGS: The Rush toward the Stars, W. C. Brown, 1969; (under name Tom Logsdon) An Introduction to Computer Science and Technology, Franklin Publishing (Palisade, N.J.), 1974; (under name Tom Logsdon; with Fae Logsdon) The Computers in Our Society, Anaheim Publishing, 1974, workbook, 1975; (under name Tom Logsdon) Programming in BASIC: With Applications, Anaheim Publishing, 1977; (with F. Logsdon) Our Computerized Society with BASIC Programming, Anaheim Publishing, 1978; Computers and Social Controversy, Computer Science Press, 1980; How to Cope with Computers, Hayden, 1981. Author of columns "Grouches by Groucho" and "The Spice of Life" in Eastern Progress.

WORK IN PROGRESS: The Sex Life of American Blurbles, a joke book; Project Skyhook, on the ultimate solution to the energy crisis; Soft Landings, a how-to book on single living;

Data Processing; Ready or Not . . . Here Comes the Robot Revolution!, on the use of mechanical workers in offices and factories.

SIDELIGHTS: Thomas Logsdon told CA that he first became interested in writing when he "was forced into doing punishment papers for filling the waste paper baskets with water and setting off firecrackers in Prof. Robert Robertson's American history class at Springfield High School in the bluegrass region of Kentucky. Now that I have become a professional writer and engineer, I have, of course, begun to specialize in more sophisticated and esoteric enterprises. This year my specialty consists of shooting rubber bands into co-workers coffee cups and constructing enormous strings of paper clips which I drape over the desks and file cabinets of company executives."

* * *

LOGSDON, Tom
    See LOGSDON, Thomas S(tanley)

* * *

LONDON, Kurt L(udwig)   1900-

PERSONAL: Born September 12, 1900, in Berlin, Germany; came to United States, 1936, naturalized, 1942; son of Maurice and Betty (Conn) London; married Jean Louise Fraser, May 12, 1951. Education: Attended Universities of Berlin and Heidelberg; University of Wuerzburg, Ph.D., 1928. Religion: Unitarian Universalist. Home: 710 Christine Dr., Palo Alto, Calif. 94303.

CAREER: Foreign correspondent in Berlin, Germany, Paris, France, London, England, Moscow, U.S.S.R., 1929-38; research at Sorbonne, University of Paris, Paris, and University of London, London, 1933-35; member of political science faculty, City College (now City College of the City University of New York), New York, N.Y., 1938-39, and Brooklyn College (now Brooklyn College of the City University of New York), Brooklyn, N.Y., 1940-42; U.S. Government, Washington, D.C., specialist in Soviet and Eastern European affairs and Sino-Soviet relations for Office of War Information, 1942-45, Department of State, 1945-47, and Central Intelligence Agency, 1947-62; George Washington University, Washington, D.C., professor of international affairs and founder-director of Institute for Sino-Soviet Studies, 1962-70, professor emeritus, 1970—. Visiting professor, University of Denver, 1940; adjunct professor of Soviet foreign affairs, Naval Postgraduate School, 1976. Military service: U.S. Air Force Reserve, 1950-60; became lieutenant colonel. Member: International Studies Association, American Political Science Association, American Association for the Advancement of Slavic Studies, American Association of University Professors, Washington Institute for Foreign Affairs, Cosmos Club (Washington, D.C.). Awards, honors: U.S. Government Certificate of Merit with Distinction, 1962.

WRITINGS: Film Music, Faber, 1963, reprinted, Arno, 1970; The Seven Soviet Arts, Yale University Press, 1938, reprinted, Greenwood Press, 1970; Backgrounds of Conflict: Ideas and Forms of World Politics, Macmillan, 1945; How Foreign Policy Is Made, Van Nostrand, 1949, 2nd edition, 1950; (editor) Unity and Contradiction: Major Aspects of Sino-Soviet Relations, Praeger, 1962; The Permanent Crisis: Communism in World Politics, Walker, 1962, 2nd edition, Blaisdell, 1968; (editor) New Nations in a Divided World: The International Relations of the Afro-Asian States, Praeger, 1963; The Making of Foreign Policy: East and West, Lippincott, 1965; (editor) Eastern Europe in Transition, Johns Hopkins Press, 1966; (editor) *The Soviet Union: A Half Century of Communism*, Johns Hopkins Press,1968; (editor) *The Soviet Impact on World Politics*, Hawthorn, 1974; (editor) *The Soviet Union in World Politics*, Westview Press, 1980. Contributor to professional journals.

AVOCATIONAL INTERESTS: Classical music, legitimate theater.

BIOGRAPHICAL/CRITICAL SOURCES: New Leader, April 24, 1967.

*   *   *

LONGMATE, Norman Richard   1925-

PERSONAL: Born December 15, 1925, in Newbury, Berkshire, England; son of Ernest (a photographer) and Margaret (Rowden) Longmate; married Elizabeth Taylor (a teacher), August 8, 1953; children: Jill. *Education:* Attended Christ's Hospital, Horsham, England, 1936-43; Worcester College, Oxford, B.A. (with honors), 1950, M.A., 1954. *Religion:* Anglican. *Address:* c/o Hutchinson Ltd., 3 Fitzroy Square, London W.1, England. *Agent:* Bolt & Watson Ltd., 8-12 Old Queen St., London S.W. 1, England. *Office:* British Broadcasting Corp., Broadcasting House, London W. 1, England.

CAREER: Daily Mirror, London, England, feature writer, 1953-57; Electricity Council, London, administrator in industrial relations department, 1957-63; British Broadcasting Corp., London, radio producer, 1963-65, administrator in secretariat, 1965—. Historical consultant to television and film companies and to Imperial War Museum, London. *Military service:* British Army, 1944-47. *Member:* Association of Broadcasting Staff, Oxford Society, Society of Sussex Downsmen, Worcester College Society, Authors' Society.

WRITINGS—History: King Cholera: The Biography of a Disease, Hamish Hamilton, 1966; *The Waterdrinkers: A History of Temperance*, Hamish Hamilton, 1968; *Alive and Well: Medicine and Public Health, 1830 to the Present Day*, Penguin, 1970; *How We Lived Then: A History of Everyday Life during the Second World War*, Hutchinson, 1971; *If Britain Had Fallen*, Hutchinson, 1972, Stein & Day, 1974; *The Real Dad's Army: The Story of the Home Guard*, Arrow Books, 1974; *The Workhouse*, St. Martin's, 1974; *Milestones in Working Class History*, BBC Publications, 1975; *The G.I.s: The Americans in Britain 1942-5*, Hutchinson, 1975, Scribner, 1976; (author of historical postscript) Jimmy Perry and David Croft, *Dad's Army*, Elm Tree Books, 1975; *Air Raid: The Bombing of Coventry*, Hutchinson, 1976, McKay, 1978; *When We Won the War: The Story of Victory in Europe, 1945*, Hutchinson, 1977; *The Hungry Mills: The Story of the Lancashire Cotton Famine 1861-5*, Temple Smith, 1978; *The Doodlebugs: The Story of the Flying-Bombs*, Hutchinson, 1981; (editor) *The Home Front, 1938-1945: An Anthology of Personal Experience*, Chatto & Windus, 1981; *The Bombers: The Story of the British Strategic Air Offensive against Germany*, Hutchinson, 1982.

Detective stories; published by Cassell, except as indicated: *Death Won't Wash*, 1957; *A Head for Death*, 1958; *Strip Death Naked*, 1959; *Vote for Death*, 1960; *Death in Office*, R. Hale, 1961.

Other: (Editor and author of historical introduction) *A Socialist Anthology*, Phoenix House, 1953; *Oxford Triumphant* (documentary about university life), Phoenix House, 1954; *Keith in Electricity* (juvenile career book), Chatto & Windus, 1961; *Electricity Supply* (juvenile career book), Sunday Times Publications, 1961; *Electricity as a Career* (juvenile career book),

Batsford, 1964; (editor and author of introduction) *Writing for the BBC*, BBC Publications, 1966.

Contributor of articles to periodicals, including *Observer, Spectator, Listener, New Society, Sunday Mirror*, and *Daily Telegraph*. Contributor to British Broadcasting Corp. radio and television.

SIDELIGHTS: Norman Richard Longmate told *CA:* "My special field of interest is relating major events (e.g. a cholera epidemic or a war) to the individual human experience. I have tried to find unexplored aspects of important subjects, e.g. civilian experience during World War II or the human story of workhouse inmates, not merely the legal and administrative facts about the setting up of the institution. The book which best illustrates my distinctive technique is *How We Lived Then*."

For *How We Lived Then*, Longmate queried hundreds of people about their World War II reminiscences. "For me, as for so many people," states Longmate, "the war is still far more vivid in my recollection than anything which has happened since." Focusing on the "everyday life" of people on the homefront, the book brings together a myriad of personal war experiences. In a *Spectator* review, Angus Maude praises the book as being "minutely detailed, accurate, skilfully marshalled and engagingly written." Maude recommends the book for both social historians and general readers: "Its compilation is a real *tour-de-force*, most brilliantly done. For the young, it will provide a new slant on what their parents went through. For the parents themselves, it will provide a total and nostalgic recall."

AVOCATIONAL INTERESTS: Reading and country walking.

BIOGRAPHICAL/CRITICAL SOURCES: Times (London), November 17, 1966; *Listener*, November 24, 1966, March 25, 1971, August 22, 1974, November 27, 1975; *Observer*, December 10, 1966; *Times Literary Supplement*, December 11, 1966, April 9, 1971, August 30, 1974, June 3, 1977, June 9, 1978, July 3, 1981; *British Medical Journal*, January 28, 1967; *Church Times*, February 3, 1967; *Punch*, October 2, 1968; *Guardian*, October 4, 1968; *Observer Review*, October 6, 1968, March 21, 1971; *Spectator*, April 10, 1971, June 29, 1974.

*   *   *

LORIMER, Lawrence T(heodore)   1941-

PERSONAL: Born March 26, 1941, in Denver, Colo.; son of Robert L. and Norma (Gustafson) Lorimer; married Janice McClintic, June 5, 1964; children: Paul, Judith. *Education:* Attended University of St. Andrews, 1962-63; Augustana College, Rock Island, Ill., B.A., 1964; Columbia University, M.A., 1967. *Residence:* New York, N.Y.

CAREER: Prentice-Hall, Inc., New York City, assistant editor of professional books, 1964-65; Random House, Inc., New York City, assistant editor of juvenile books, 1965-66; Cowles Book Co., New York City, associate editor of reference books, 1968; Random House, Inc., editor of juvenile books, 1970-76; free-lance writer and editor, 1976—. Member of Hudson Group, Inc., 1979—.

WRITINGS: (Editor and compiler) *Breaking In: Nine First-Person Accounts about Becoming an Athlete*, Random House, 1974; (co-author) *The Football Book*, Random House, 1977; *The Tennis Book*, Random House, 1979; *Secrets* (novel), Holt, 1981.

AVOCATIONAL INTERESTS: Music, books.

LOVELL, (Alfred Charles) Bernard 1913-

PERSONAL: Born August 31, 1913, in Oldland Common, Gloucestershire, England; son of G. Lovell; married Mary Joyce Chesterman, 1937; children: three daughters, two sons. *Education:* University of Bristol, B.Sc., and Ph.D. *Home:* The Quinta, Swettenham, near Congleton, Cheshire, England. *Office:* Nuffield Radio Astronomy Laboratories, Jodrell Bank, Macclesfield, Cheshire, England.

CAREER: University of Manchester, Manchester, England, assistant lecturer in physics, 1936-39, lecturer in physics at Physical Laboratories and at Jodrell Bank Experimental Station, Cheshire, 1945-47, senior lecturer, 1947-49, reader in physics at Physical Laboratories and Jodrell Bank Experimental Station, 1949-51, university professor of radio astronomy, and director of Nuffield Radio Astronomy Laboratories, Jodrell Bank, Cheshire, 1951—. Member of staff, Telecommunications Research Establishment, 1939-45; Reith Lecturer, 1958; Condon Lecturer and Guthrie Lecturer, both 1962; Halley Lecturer, 1964; Queen's Lecturer in Berlin, 1970; Brockington Lecturer in Kingston, Ontario, 1970; visiting Montague Burton Professor of International Relations, University of Edinburgh, 1973; Bickley Lecturer at Oxford University, 1977; Angel Memorial Lecturer in Newfoundland, 1977.

MEMBER: International Astronomical Union (vice-president, 1970-76), Royal Astronomical Society (president, 1969-71), Royal Society (fellow), Institute of Physics (fellow), American Academy of Sciences (honorary foreign member), New York Academy of Science (honorary life member), Royal Swedish Academy (honorary member), Institute of Electrical Engineers (fellow), Society of Engineers (honorary fellow), American Philosophical Society, Athenaeum Club. *Awards, honors:* Order of the British Empire, 1946; Duddell Medal from Physical Society, 1954; Royal Medal from Royal Society, 1960; knighted, 1961; LL.D. from University of Edinburgh, 1961, and University of Calgary, 1966; D.Sc. from University of Leicester, 1961, University of Leeds, 1966, University of London, 1967, University of Bath, 1967, and University of Bristol, 1970; Daniel and Florence Guggenheim International Astronautics Award, 1961; L'Ordre du Merite pour la Recherche et l'Invention, 1962; Churchill Gold Medal of Society of Engineers, 1964; D.Univ. from University of Stirling, 1974, and University of Surrey, 1975; Commander's Order of Merit from Polish People's Republic, 1975; Benjamin Franklin Medal from Royal Society of Arts, 1980; gold medal from Royal Astronomical Society, 1981.

WRITINGS: Science and Civilization, Nelson, 1939; *World Power Resources and Social Development,* Pilot Press, 1945; *Electronics and Their Application in Industry and Research,* Pilot Press, 1947; (with J. A. Clegg) *Radio Astronomy,* Wiley, 1952; *Meteor Astronomy,* Clarendon Press, 1954; (with Robert Hanbury Brown) *The Exploration of Space by Radio,* Wiley, 1958; *The Individual and the Universe* (Reith lectures), Harper, 1959; *The Exploration of Outer Space* (Gregyog lectures), Harper, 1962; (with Joyce Lovell) *Discovering the Universe,* Harper, 1963; (with Tom Margerison) *The Explosion of Science: The Physical Universe,* Meredith Press, 1967; *Our Present Knowledge of the Universe,* Harvard University Press, 1967; *The Story of Jodrell Bank,* Harper, 1968; *The Origins and International Economics of Space Exploration,* Edinburgh University Press, 1973; *Out of the Zenith: Jodrell Bank, 1957-70,* Oxford University Press, 1973, Harper, 1974; *Man's Relation to the Universe,* Freeman, 1975; *P.M.S. Blackett: A Biographical Memoir,* Royal Society, 1976; *In the Center of Immensities,* Harper, 1978; *Emerging Cosmology,* Columbia University Press, 1981.

SIDELIGHTS: Bernard Lovell is the creator of a 250-foot radio telescope at Jodrell Bank. Originally Lovell had not intended the telescope to be so large, but he soon noticed that this spot was perfect for the study of ionized trails left by meteors. So began the ten year struggle for the building and finally the completion of the telescope. Public sentiment was not always with Lovell, and missing also was the expected funding for the project. Lovell faced a prison term (he could not give the chairman of the University Council a writ for one million pounds) and was subjected to social ostracism before the telescope was completed.

The Story of Jodrell Bank chronicles "the difficulties which Bernard Lovell had to overcome in building the great 250-foot steerable radio telescope," according to a *Times Literary Supplement* reviewer. *Out of the Zenith,* the sequel to *The Story of Jodrell Bank,* "deals with the major astronomical work of this instrument since it began operations," writes the same critic. John Taylor of *Encounter* calls *Out of the Zenith* "a very personal account of the political intrigues and machinations needed to create large radio-telescopes and keep them in operation." A *Choice* critic labels the volume "unique" and "so filled with the author's wide knowledge that it is virtually a textbook on this important area of astronomy."

Lovell has also written a number of books which explain various aspects of his field to the lay person. One such book is *In the Center of Immensities,* in which Lovell relates the history of the development of astronomy as a science, tracing its earlier connection to religious and ethical systems through an increasing reliance on scientific theory and observable data. Martin Gardner of the *New York Review of Books* believes the book was "written with wisdom and grace [and] with a sound knowledge of the history of science and philosophy." Patrick Moore remarks in *Books and Bookmen:* "The whole of the text is accessible to the reader with no previous knowledge of science, but it is anything but superficial. . . . There can be no doubt that *In the Center of Immensities* is a first-class book—but one would not expect Sir Bernard Lovell to produce anything else."

AVOCATIONAL INTERESTS: Cricket, gardening, and music.

BIOGRAPHICAL/CRITICAL SOURCES: Times Literary Supplement, February 27, 1959, February 22, 1974, May 31, 1974; *New Statesman,* March 7, 1959; *Christian Science Monitor,* May 7, 1959; *New York Times,* May 24, 1959; *Saturday Review,* January 26, 1963, March 5, 1966; *New York Times Book Review,* April 7, 1963; *Time,* April 15, 1966; *Encounter,* January, 1974; *Choice,* July/August, 1974; *New York Review of Books,* November 23, 1978; *Books and Bookmen,* March, 1979.

*   *   *

LOVIN, Roger Robert 1941-
(Wesley Brighton, Jr., Rodgers Clemens, Cynthia C. Driver)

PERSONAL: Surname rhymes with "oven"; born May 11, 1941, in Knoxville, Tenn.; son of Chet E. (an engineer) and Molly (Rogers) Lovin; married Sandra Dale Trahan (a philosopher), November 7, 1963 (divorced). *Education:* Attended Louisiana State University, 1964. *Politics:* "Intense dislike of politics and politicians. If cornered, I'd probably call myself a Technocratic Royalist." *Religion:* "Discordian." *Agent:* Virginia Kidd, Box 278, Milford, Pa. 18337.

CAREER: Painter and owner of La Boheme (gallery), New Orleans, La., 1963-65; musician and bandleader, 1965-68; *The Ungarbled Word* (weekly newspaper), New Orleans, publisher, 1968-69; *Los Angeles Free Press,* Los Angeles, Calif., columnist and environment editor, 1969-73; free-lance writer, 1973—. Creative writing instructor, University of New Orleans, 1979. *Military service:* U.S. Navy, 1959-63. *Member:* Science Fiction Writers of America, Authors Guild, Authors League of America, Luckner Writers Circle, Rainbow Bridge International.

WRITINGS: The Complete Motorcycle Nomad, Little, Brown, 1974; (under pseudonym Rodgers Clemens) *The Presence,* Fawcett, 1977; *The Apostle,* Donning, 1978; *The Roger Robert Lovin Science Fiction Hornbook,* Stardragon Press, 1980. Contributor, under own name and pseudonyms, of articles, essays, short fiction, and book reviews to periodicals.

WORK IN PROGRESS: Anamampas, a trilogy in the "alternate worlds/high fantasy tradition."

SIDELIGHTS: Roger Robert Lovin writes: "The past decade has taken a bit of the shine off my idealism, but has left me more deeply committed than ever to idealism *per se.* I still find it essential that the individual strive for excellence, and I attempt to make this point with my writings. The pursuit of excellence produces taste, which is the ability to tell best from second best. This ability is in decline today, and in an increasingly complex and technological world the lack of taste can be, ultimately, fatal.

"It has been said that from the stones we cast at them, poets build new roads for us to walk. Too frequently, we miss the turn-off to the new road simply because we've lost the 'taste' necessary to recognise it. Or, more usually, we pass it by because we've lost the determination to excellence, since new roads, like those who build them, are rocky, ill-lit, and without the comfort of signposts to tell us their destinations."

*   *   *

LOWELL, C. Stanley 1909-

PERSONAL: Born June 9, 1909, in Hastings, Minn.; son of Charles Stanley and Dora May (Parker) Lowell; married Arianne Hadley, December 31, 1953; children: Eric Hadley, Cadance Ann, Arianne Parker. *Education:* Asbury College, A.B., 1930; Duke University, M.A., 1932; Yale Divinity School, B.D., 1933. *Home:* 3505 Woodbine St., Chevy Chase, Md. 20015. *Office:* Americans United for Separation of Church and State, 8120 Fenton St., Silver Spring, Md. 20910.

CAREER: Ordained minister of Methodist Church, 1935; pastor of various churches, 1934-56; Americans United for Separation of Church and State, Silver Spring, Md., editor of *Church and State,* 1956—, associate director, 1956-74, executive director of Americans United Research Foundation, 1974—. Trustee, Matthews Trust and Cherl Ormond Williams Foundation.

WRITINGS: Federal Aid to Parochial Schools: Testimony Presented to Congressional Committees, Americans United for Separation of Church and State, 1961; *Protestant-Catholic Marriage,* Broadman, 1962; *Embattled Wall; Americans United: An Idea and a Man,* Americans United for Separation of Church and State, 1966; *The Ecumenical Mirage,* Baker Book, 1967; (with Martin Alfred Larson) *The Churches: Their Riches, Revenues, and Immunities,* Luce, 1969; *The Great Church-State Fraud,* Luce, 1973; (with Larson) *The Religious Empire,* Luce, 1976. Also author of shorter works, including *The Hidden Wealth of the Roman Catholic Church,* 1967, *The Changing Climate in Church and State,* 1968, and *The Last Best Hope: Insurance against Holocaust.* Contributor to religious publications.

AVOCATIONAL INTERESTS: Mountain-climbing, tennis, gardening.†

*   *   *

LUDLOW, George
See KAY, Ernest

*   *   *

LUDWIGSON, Kathryn Romaine 1921-

PERSONAL: Born July 30, 1921, in York, Pa.; daughter of Norman Henry (a pattern maker) and Verna (Gohn) Miller; married Carl Raymond Ludwigson, 1947; children: Carl Raymond, Jr. *Education:* Columbia College, B.A. (cum laude), 1944; Wheaton College, Wheaton, Ill., M.A., 1946; Northern Illinois University, M.S., 1957; Northwestern University, Ph.D., 1963. *Residence:* Toccoa Falls, Georgia. *Office:* Division of General Studies, Toccoa Falls College, Toccoa Falls, Ga. 30598.

CAREER: Wheaton College, Wheaton, Ill., instructor in Greek, 1945-47; Trinity College, Deerfield, Ill., assistant professor of English, 1955-56; Wheaton College, instructor in English, 1957-58, 1959-62; high school teacher in West Chicago, Ill., 1958-59; Northern Illinois University, DeKalb, assistant professor of English, 1963-65; Trinity College, professor of English, 1965-70, chairman of department, 1965-69, chairman of Division of Humanities, 1965-70; King' College, Briarcliff Manor, N.Y., professor of English, 1970-75, chairman of Division of Humanities, 1970-74, director of Learning Center for Adults, 1974-75, founder of Community Speakers Bureau, 1970; Toccoa Falls College, Toccoa Falls, Ga., professor of English, 1977—. *Member:* Modern Language Association of America, College English Association, National Education Association, Conference on Christianity and Literature.

WRITINGS: (With husband C. R. Ludwigson) *A Survey of Bible Prophecy,* Zondervan, 1973; *Edward Dowden,* Twayne, 1973; *The Structure of the Revelation,* Ludwigson Press, 1975; *The Gospel in the Old Testament,* Ludwigson Press, 1975. Ghost writer of a book on achievement motivation for college students, 1969. Author of text for "Christianity and Literature Cassettes," produced by King's College, Briarcliff Manor, N.Y., 1973. Author of multi-media travel films, "Great Lakes Country," "Florida Fantasy," and "Of Olde New England," all 1968; author of multimedia documentary, "Kelly Barnes: Toccoa Falls College Pioneer Extraordinary," 1980. Translation editor, *New International Bible,* 1970-76.

WORK IN PROGRESS: A Study of the English Sentence; An Approach to Meaning in Literature.

SIDELIGHTS: Kathryn Ludwigson has traveled in the British Isles, Europe, and the Mideast. She has also conducted a literary tour of the British Isles for college students.

*   *   *

LYNDS, Dennis 1924-
(William Arden, Nick Carter, Michael Collins, John Crowe, Carl Dekker, Maxwell Grant, Mark Sadler)

PERSONAL: Born January 15, 1924, in St. Louis, Mo.; son of John Douglas and Gertrude (Hyem) Lynds; married Doris Flood, 1949 (divorced, 1956); married Sheila McErlean, 1961; children: Katherine, Deirdre. *Education:* Hofstra College (now University), B.A., 1949; Syracuse University, M.A., 1951. *Home:* 633 Chelham Way, Santa Barbara, Calif. 93108. *Agent:*

Harold Ober Associates, 40 East 49th St., New York, N.Y. 10017.

CAREER: Chemical Week, New York City, assistant editor, 1951-52; *Chemical Engineering Progress,* New York City, managing editor, 1958-61; *Chemical Equipment,* Morristown, N.J., editor, 1962-65, 1973-75; *International Instrumentation,* Great Neck, N.Y., editor, 1975—. *Military service:* U.S. Army, Infantry, 1943-46; served in European Theater; received Purple Heart and three battle stars. *Member:* Authors Guild, Authors League of America, Mystery Writers of America, Crime Writers Association of Great Britain. *Awards, honors:* Mystery Writers of America Edgar Allan Poe Award for best first mystery novel, 1967, for *Act of Fear,* and Special Award, 1968, for short story "Success of a Mission" in *Argosy.*

WRITINGS: Combat Soldier, New American Library, 1962; *Uptown, Downtown,* New American Library, 1963; *Charlie Chan Returns,* (novelization of a television play), Bantam, 1974; *S.W.A.T.—Crossfire* (novelization of a television play), Pocket Books, 1975; *Why Girls Ride Sidesaddle* (short stories), December Press, 1980.

Under pseudonym William Arden; published by Dodd, except as indicated: *A Dark Power,* 1968; *Deal in Violence,* 1969; *The Goliath Scheme,* 1971; *Die to a Distant Drum,* 1972; *Deadly Legacy,* 1973; *Mystery of the Blue Condor* (juvenile), Ginn, 1973.

Under pseudonym William Arden; author of books in "Alfred Hitchcock and the Three Investigators" series; all published by Random House: *Alfred Hitchcock and the Three Investigators in the Mystery of the Moaning Cave,* 1968; . . . *the Mystery of the Laughing Shadow,* 1969; . . . *the Secret of the Crooked Cat,* 1970; . . . *the Mystery of the Shrinking House,* 1972; . . . *the Secret of Phantom Lake,* 1973; . . . *the Mystery of the Dead Man's Riddle,* 1974; . . . *the Mystery of the Dancing Devil,* 1976; . . . *the Mystery of the Headless Horse,* 1977; . . . *the Mystery of the Deadly Double,* 1978; . . . *the Secret of Shark Reef,* 1979.

Under pseudonym Nick Carter; all published by Award: *The N3 Conspiracy,* 1974; *The Green Wolf Connection,* 1976; *Triple Cross,* 1976.

Under pseudonym Michael Collins; published by Dodd, except as indicated: *Act of Fear,* 1967; *The Brass Rainbow,* 1969; *Lukan War,* Belmont-Tower, 1969; *Night of the Toads,* 1970; *The Planets of Death,* Berkley Publishing, 1970; *Walk a Black Wind,* 1971; *Shadow of a Tiger,* 1972; *The Silent Scream,* 1973; *Blue Death,* 1975; *The Blood-Red Dream,* 1976; *The Nightrunners,* 1978; *The Slasher,* 1980.

Under pseudonym John Crowe: *Another Way to Die,* Random House, 1972; *A Touch of Darkness,* Random House, 1973; *Bloodwater,* Dodd, 1974; *Crooked Shadows,* Dodd, 1975; *When They Kill Your Wife,* Dodd, 1977; *Close to Death,* Dodd, 1979.

Under pseudonym Carl Dekker: *Woman in Marble,* Bobbs-Merrill, 1973.

Under pseudonym Maxwell Grant; all published by Belmont-Tower: *The Shadow Strikes,* 1964; *Shadow Beware,* 1965; *Cry Shadow,* 1965; *The Shadow's Revenge,* 1965; *Mark of the Shadow,* 1966.

Under pseudonym Mark Sadler; all published by Random House, except as indicated: *The Falling Man,* 1970; *Here to Die,* 1971; *Mirror Image,* 1972; *Circle of Fire,* 1973; *Touch of Death,* Raven House, 1982.

Work represented in anthologies, including *New Voices 2: American Writing Today,* Farrar, Straus, 1955, *New World*

Writing, Number 11, New American Library, 1957, *Best American Short Stories 1965,* Houghton, 1965, *Best Detective Stories of the Year,* Dutton, 1965, *Beyond the Angry Black,* Cooper Square, 1966, *The Short Story: Fiction in Transition,* Scribner, 1969, *Crime without Murder,* Scribner, 1970, and *Short Stories from the Literary Magazines,* Scott, Foresman, 1970.

Contributor of poems and short stories to magazines and literary journals, including *Mike Shayne Mystery Magazine, Alfred Hitchcock Mystery Magazine, Ellery Queen's Mystery Magazine, Argosy, Literary Review, Hudson Review,* and *Minnesota Review.*

WORK IN PROGRESS: Novels and short stories.

SIDELIGHTS: Dennis Lynds told *CA:* "I write because I can. I write because I have to try to understand this world I live in, and, perhaps, the people who live in it with me. I probably never will, but, as Henze has said, it's the only folly worth living for—the attempt to find out what I see, what I feel, what is.

"I write about people driven to certain actions by forces from inside and outside. The forces of the world in which they, and I, live. I write about the people *and* the forces as best I can see them—as they really are, I hope.

"I write in the same way and for the same reasons whether I am writing under my own name or one of my pseudonyms, whether I am writing short stories, novels, suspense novels or sci-fi. A novel is a novel, and 'genre' novels are no less novels than sonnets or ballads or sestinas are poems. The only 'difference' in a crime novel is that it centers on an overt crime, an actual specific act of violence that is anti-social at the moment. I like to write 'crime' novels because a society and its people, its pressures and its codes, its horrors and its hopes, can be seen in sharp outline at such moments.

"I hope my books 'entertain' the reader, excite the reader, but it is the entertainment of truth I want to give, the excitement of seeing, understanding, experiencing what we all know but have, perhaps, not quite understood or seen clearly. All my books and stories are attempts to deal with Man in his relation with himself, other people, and his world—irrational and indifferent though it may be."

AVOCATIONAL INTERESTS: The theater, fishing, wine, music, poker.

BIOGRAPHICAL/CRITICAL SOURCES: Book World, January 14, 1968; *New York Times Book Review,* October 22, 1967, March 2, 1969, April 20, 1975, September 11, 1977, July 9, 1978.; *Xenophile,* March/April, 1978; *Unicorn,* October, 1979, February, 1980; *Megavore,* June, 1980.

*   *   *

LYSAUGHT, Jerome Paul 1930-

PERSONAL: Born March 4, 1930, in Kansas City, Kan.; son of Michael Clarence (a manufacturer) and Minnie (Hill) Lysaught; married Dolores Marie Gergick, June 6, 1953; children: Jan Marie, Paula Marie, Clare Marie, Eileen Marie. *Education:* University of Kansas, A.B. and M.A., 1954; University of Rochester, Ed.S., 1963, Ed.D., 1964. *Politics:* Democrat. *Religion:* Roman Catholic. *Home:* 17 Bretton Woods Dr., Rochester, N.Y. 14618. *Office:* University of Rochester, Rochester, N.Y. 14618.

CAREER: Eastman Kodak Co., Rochester, N.Y., training specialist, 1954-60; Recordak Corp., Rochester, assistant product manager, 1960-62; University of Rochester, Rochester, associate lecturer in education, 1962-63, assistant professor, 1963-66, associate professor, 1966-69, professor of education, 1969—, research associate in medical education, 1964—. Visiting professor and guest lecturer at numerous colleges and universities; Eberhardt fellow, University of Kansas, 1953. Coordinator, Rochester Clearinghouse for Information on Self-Instruction, 1964—; past director, National Commission for the Study of Nursing and Nursing Education. Director, Rochester Junior Chamber of Commerce, 1957; member of board of directors, Genesee Settlement House, 1963-65, Phi Kappa Theta Foundation, 1969-1974, Comprenetics, Inc., 1970—; member of board of trustees, Rochester Chamber of Commerce, 1957-59; member of advisory board, Community College of the Air Force, 1973—; member of board of visitors, University of Pittsburgh, School of Nursing, 1974—. Editorial consultant, John Wiley & Sons, Inc., and McGraw-Hill Book Co. Consultant to organizations and universities, including American Hospital Association, American Society of Clinical Pathologists, National Committee for Careers in Medical Technology, Harvard University School of Public Health, and Rush University of the Health Sciences. *Military service:* U.S. Marine Corps, 1947-48, 1950-52; served in Korea; became captain; awarded Korean service ribbon with star, Korean Presidential Unit Citation, and U.S. Presidential Unit Citation.

MEMBER: National Society for Programmed Instruction (member of board of directors, 1965-66), American Academy of Political and Social Science, American Association for Higher Education, American Association of University Professors, American Educational Research Association, Association of Medical Colleges, Health Sciences Communication Association, Phi Beta Kappa, Phi Delta Kappa, Pi Sigma Alpha, Pi Gamma Mu, Pi Kappa Delta, Omicron Delta Kappa, Phi Kappa Theta. *Awards, honors:* Outstanding Long Term Contribution Award from National Society of Programmed Instruction, 1968; *Action in Nursing: Progress in Professional Purpose* was named Book of the Year in Nursing by *American Journal of Nursing;* commendation from Secretary of the Air Force, 1977.

WRITINGS: (With Clarence M. Williams) *A Guide to Programmed Instruction,* Wiley, 1963; *An Abstract for Action: Report of the National Commission for the Study of Nursing and Nursing Education,* McGraw, 1970; *An Abstract for Action: Appendices to the Report of the National Commission for the Study of Nursing and Nursing Education,* McGraw, 1971; *From Abstract into Action: Implementation of the Recommendations of the National Commission for the Study of Nursing and Nursing Education,* McGraw, 1973; *Trends and Issues in American Nursing: An Independent View,* McGraw, 1979; *Action in Affirmation: Towards an Unambiguous Profession of Nursing,* McGraw, 1981.

Editor: (And contributor) *Programmed Learning: Evolving Principles and Industrial Applications,* Foundation for Research on Human Behavior, 1961; (and contributor) *Programmed Instruction in Medical Education,* Rochester Clearinghouse, 1965; (with Hilliard Jason and contributor) *Self-Instruction in Medical Education,* Rochester Clearinghouse, 1968; (and contributor) *Individualized Instruction in Medical Education,* Rochester Clearinghouse, 1968; *Instructional Systems for Medical Education,* Rochester Clearinghouse, 1971; *Instructional Technology in Medical Education,* Rochester

Clearinghouse, 1973; *Action in Nursing: Progress in Professional Purpose,* McGraw, 1974; *A Luther Christman Anthology,* Nursing Resources, 1978.

Contributor: S. Margulies and L. D. Eigen, editors, *Applied Programmed Instruction,* Wiley, 1962; G. Teal, editor, *Programmed Instruction in Industry and Education,* Public Service Research, 1963; W. A. Fullagar and others, editors, *Readings for Educational Psychology,* 2nd edition, Crowell, 1964; G. D. Oflesh, editor, *Programmed Instruction: A Guide to Management,* American Management Association, 1965; J. S. Roucek, editor, *Programmed Teaching: A Symposium of Automation in Education,* Philosophical Library, 1965; D. N. Nunney, editor, *New Approaches in Training and Educational Systems,* Wayne State University, 1965; W. O. Russell and R. A. Kolvoord, editors, *Education for Tomorrow: Developments in Educational Technology,* American Society of Clinical Pathologists, 1966; J. Leedham and D. Unwin, editors, *Aspects of Educational Technology,* Methuen, 1967; D. J. Fox and R. L. Kelly, editors, *The Research Process in Nursing,* Appleton-Century-Crofts, 1967; *Programmed Instruction and the Hospital,* Hospital Research and Educational Trust, 1967; R. G. Pierleoni, editor, *Perspectives in Programming,* University of Rochester, 1967; L. J. Issing, editor, *Der programmierte Unterricht in den USA heute,* Verlag Julius Beltz, 1967; *Toward Improved Learning,* Communicable Disease Center, Public Health Service, 1967; *Aspects of Educational Technology, II,* Methuen, 1969.

D. W. Allen and E. Seifman, *The Teacher's Handbook,* Scott, Foresman, 1971; M. L. Berman, editor, *Motivation and Learning: Applying Contingency Managment Techniques,* Educational Technology Publications, 1971; I. J. Patel and others, editors, *A Handbook of Programmed Learning,* Indian Association for Programmed Learning, 1973; Daniel S. Schechter, *Agenda for Hospital Continuing Education,* Hospital Research and Educational Trust, 1974; *Motivating Personnel and Managing Conflict,* Contemporary Publishing, 1974, 2nd edition, 1976; *Nursing Digest 1975: Focus on the Work Environment,* Contemporary Publishing, 1975; *Nursing Digest 1975: Focus on Professional Issues,* Contemporary Publishing, 1975; B. Bullough and V. Bullough, *Expanding Horizons for Nurses,* Springer Publishing Co., 1977.

Contributor to numerous professional journals, including *New Physician, Teaching Aids News, Personnel Journal, Medical Times, Educational Technology,* and *Nursing Outlook.* Editor, *Bulletin of the Clearinghouse on Self-Instructional Materials for Health Care Facilities,* 1966-71; contributing editor, *Educational Technology,* 1967-72. Member of editorial board, *Journal of the National Society for Programmed Instruction,* 1966-72, *Erfurschung und Veranderung der Schule,* 1967-74, *Journal of the Association for Programmed Learning and Educational Technology,* 1972—, *Journal of Biocommunication,* 1973-78, *Evaluation and the Health Professions,* 1977—. Member of correspondent board, *Journal of the Indian Association for Programmed Learning and Educational Innovations,* 1976—.

WORK IN PROGRESS: Research on selection of individuals to serve as programmers for auto-instructional materials, on the effectiveness of programmed instruction, and on health professionals and changing settings for care.

M

MacCLINTOCK, Dorcas 1932-

PERSONAL: Born July 16, 1932, in New York, N.Y.; daughter of James T. (a businessman) and Helen (Kay) Eason; married Copeland MacClintock (an invertebrate paleontologist), June 30, 1956; children: Margaret, Pamela. *Education:* Smith College, A.B., 1954; University of Wyoming, A.M., 1957. *Politics:* Independent. *Religion:* Episcopalian. *Home:* 33 Rogers Rd., Hamden, Conn. 06517.

CAREER: American Museum of Natural History, New York, N.Y., student assistant, 1947-53; Yale University, Peabody Museum of Natural History, New Haven, Conn., curator of osteology collection, 1965-67. Research associate, California Academy of Sciences, San Francisco, 1958—. *Member:* American Society of Mammalogists, Society of Vertebrate Paleontology, Society of Animal Artists, Sigma Xi. *Awards, honors:* *A Natural History of Giraffes* received New York Academy of Sciences award for outstanding science book, 1973, and was selected by Children's Book Council as one of the outstanding books of the year.

WRITINGS—Published by Scribner, except as indicated: *Squirrels of North America,* Van Nostrand, 1970; (with Ugo Mochi) *A Natural History of Giraffes* (juvenile), 1973; *A Natural History of Zebras,* 1976; *Horses As I See Them,* 1980; *A Natural History of Raccoons,* 1981; *A Raccoon's First Year,* 1982.

SIDELIGHTS: Dorcas MacClintock told *CA:* "Interest in natural history, especially mammals, stems from childhood." Reviewing *A Natural History of Giraffes, Scientific American* writers Philip and Phylis Morrison comment, "The text is brief, rich and clear, the work of mammalogist who can write and who has seen giraffes in the savanna."

BIOGRAPHICAL/CRITICAL SOURCES: Scientific American, December, 1973.

*   *   *

MacDONALD, Charles B(rown) 1922-

PERSONAL: Born November 23, 1922, in Little Rock, S.C.; son of K. L. and Mary (MacQueen) MacDonald. *Education:* Presbyterian College, A.B., 1942; graduate study at Columbia University, 1946, McGill University, 1947, University of Missouri, 1947, and George Washington University, 1948. *Home:* 5300 Columbia Pike, Arlington, Va. 22204. *Agent:* Brant & Brant Literary Agents, Inc., 1501 Broadway, New York, N.Y. 10036.

CAREER: Presbyterian College, Clinton, S.C., instructor in English, 1946-47; Department of the Army, Office of Chief of Military History, Washington, D.C., historian, 1948-52, chief of European section, 1952-56, chief of general history branch, 1956-67, deputy chief historian, 1967-80. *Military service:* U.S. Army, 1942-46; became captain; received Purple Heart, Bronze Star, Silver Star. U.S. Army Reserve, 1946-76; retired as colonel. *Awards, honors:* Secretary of the Army research and study fellowship in military history, 1957-58; Litt.D., Presbyterian College, 1967.

WRITINGS: Company Commander, Infantry Journal Press, 1947, revised edition, Ballantine, 1961; (with Sidney T. Mathews) *Three Battles: Arnaville, Altuzzo, and Schmidt,* U.S. Government Printing Office, 1952; (contributor) Kent R. Greenfield, editor, *Command Decisions,* Harcourt, 1961; *The Siegfried Line Campaign,* Office of Chief of Military History, Department of the Army, 1963; *The Battle of the Huertgen Forest,* Lippincott, 1963; (contributor) *History of the Second World War,* Purnell Books, 1966; *The Mighty Endeavor: American Armed Forces in the European Theater in World War II,* Oxford University Press, 1969; (contributor) Maurice Matloff, editor, *American Military History,* U.S. Government Printing Office, 1969; *Airborne,* Ballantine, 1970 (published in England as *By Air to Battle,* Macdonald & Co., 1970); *The Last Offensive,* U.S. Government Printing Office, 1973; (contributor) Ray Bonds, editor, *The Encyclopedia of Land Warfare,* Salamander, 1976; (editor with Anthony Cave Brown) *The Secret History of the Atomic Bomb,* Dial, 1977; (contributor) Thomas Parrish, editor, *The Encyclopedia of World War II,* Simon & Schuster, 1978; (contributor) Bonds, editor, *The Vietnam War: The Illustrated History of the Conflict in Southeast Asia,* Salamander, 1979; (with Brown) *On a Field of Red: The Communist International and the Coming of World War II,* Putnam, 1981. Contributor of articles on military subjects to *Encyclopedia Americana, Encyclopaedia Britannica, Grolier Encyclopedia, World Book Encyclopaedia, New York Times Magazine,* and various Army publications.

SIDELIGHTS: Charles B. MacDonald told *CA:* "The account of my experience as a rifle company commander in Europe in World War II, *Company Commander,* which has been called 'the infantry classic of World War II' and is still in print after first publication in 1947, brought me into the business of military history. I find it an intriguing field, for however deplorable war is, we must admit that mankind spends a considerable amount of time and endeavor at it, and it behooves an enlightened public to understand it.''

When *Company Commander* appeared in 1947, *New York Times* reviewer H. A. DeWeerd called it ''an impressive first book.'' In the *Saturday Review of Literature,* A. C. Fields praised the book: ''This is a simple story, told in simple language, of a tough war, and of all the zany and horrible things that went into making it the greatest war in history. There will probably be books which will do a more craftsmanlike literary job in describing World War II; there may even be more lucid explanations of the strategies employed and the problems confronted in this last global battle; but nowhere, I venture to say, will there be a more honest, unassuming portrayal of the hopes and dreams and fears of a young infantry captain than is found here.''

In *The Mighty Endeavor* MacDonald describes American involvement in World War II from 1939 to 1945. *National Observer* writer T. R. Temple calls the book ''a surprisingly rare achievement'' which presents ''critical but detached judgments of personalities and events.'' A *National Review* critic offers a similar opinion: ''The great accomplishment of this book is that it brings within the covers of a single volume a clear, understandable and competent account of the American contribution to decisive Allied victory in Europe in World War II. . . . MacDonald's warm and sympathetic understanding of the American Army is . . . the very essence of this book.''

AVOCATIONAL INTERESTS: Skiing.

BIOGRAPHICAL/CRITICAL SOURCES: Saturday Review of Literature, November 1, 1947; *New York Times,* November 16, 1947; *Christian Science Monitor,* November 29, 1969; *National Review,* December 2, 1969; *National Observer,* January 12, 1970; *Washington Post Book World,* May 24, 1981.

*   *   *

MacDOWELL, Douglas M(aurice) 1931-

PERSONAL: Born March 8, 1931, in London, England; son of Maurice A. and Dorothy J. (Allan) MacDowell. *Education:* Balliol College, Oxford, B.A., 1954, M.A., 1958. *Office:* Department of Greek, University of Glasgow, Glasgow G12 8QQ, Scotland.

CAREER: University of Manchester, Manchester, England, assistant lecturer, 1958-61, lecturer, 1961-68, senior lecturer, 1968-70, reader in Greek and Latin, 1970-71; University of Glasgow, Glasgow, Scotland, professor of Greek, 1971—.

WRITINGS: (Editor) Andokides, *On the Mysteries,* Oxford University Press, 1962; *Athenian Homicide Law,* Manchester University Press, 1963; (editor) Aristophanes, *Wasps,* Oxford University Press, 1971; *The Law in Classical Athens,* Cornell University Press, 1978. Contributor to classical journals.

*   *   *

MACHLUP, Fritz 1902-

PERSONAL: Born 1902, in Wiener-Neustadt, Austria; son of Berthold and Cecile (Haymann) Machlup; married Mitzi Herzog, 1925; children: Stefan, Hanna Machlup Hastings. *Education:* University of Vienna, Dr.rer.pol., 1923. *Home:* 279 Ridgeview Rd., Princeton, N.J. 08540. *Office:* Department of Economics, New York University, New York, N.Y. 10003.

CAREER: Ybbstaler Pappenfabriken Adolf Leitner und Bruder, Vienna, Austria, partner and managing director, 1924-33; Harvard University, Cambridge, Mass., visiting lecturer, 1934-

35, 1938-39; University of Buffalo (now State University of New York at Buffalo), Buffalo, N.Y., Goodyear Professor of Economics, 1935-47; Johns Hopkins University, Baltimore, Md., Hutzler Professor of Political Economy, 1947-60; Princeton University, Princeton, N.J., Walker Professor of Economics and International Finance, 1960-71; New York University, New York, N.Y., professor of economics, 1971—. Visiting professor, American University, 1943-46, Kyoto University, 1955, Doshisha University, 1955, University of Melbourne, 1970, University of Osaka, 1970, and University of Vienna, 1973. Research director, U.S. Office of Alien Property Custodian, Washington, D.C., 1943-46.

MEMBER: American Economic Association (member of board of editors, 1938-41; acting managing editor, 1944-45; vice-president, 1956; president, 1966), American Association of University Professors (first vice-president, 1960-62; president, 1962-64), International Economic Association (president, 1971-74), Royal Economic Society, List Gessellschaft, Mont Pelerin Society (treasurer, 1954-59), Southern Economic Association (president, 1959-60), Phi Beta Kappa. *Awards, honors:* Received two Rockefeller fellowships; Ford Foundation fellowship; named honorary senator, University of Vienna, 1971. LL.D., Lawrence College, 1956, Lehigh University, 1967, and La Salle College, 1968; Dr.Sc. Pol., University of Kiel, 1965; L.H.D., Case Western Reserve University, 1967; Dr.oecon., University of St. Gall, 1972.

WRITINGS: Die Goldkernwaehrung, Meyer (Halberstadt), 1925; (translator) *Vorschlaege fuer eine wirtschaftliche und sichere Waehrung von David Ricardo,* Meyer, 1927; *Die neuen Waehrungen in Europa,* Enke (Stuttgart), 1927; *Boersenkredit, Industriekredit und Kapitalbildung,* Springer (Vienna), 1931; *Fuehrer durch die Krisenpolitik,* Springer, 1934; *Guide a travers les panacees economiques,* Librairie de Medicis (Paris), 1939; *The Stock Market: Credit and Capital Formation,* Macmillan, 1940; *International Trade and the National Income Multiplier,* Blakiston, 1943, reprinted, Kelley, 1965; (with others) *Financing American Prosperity,* Twentieth Century Fund, 1945; (with others) *A Cartel Policy for the United Nations,* Columbia University Press, 1945; *The Basing-Point System,* Blakiston, 1949.

The Political Economy of Monopoly, Johns Hopkins Press, 1952; *The Economics of Sellers' Competition,* Johns Hopkins Press, 1952; *An Economic Review of the Patent System,* U.S. Government Printing Office, 1958; *Plans for Reform of the International Monetary System,* International Finance Section, Princeton University, 1962, 2nd edition, 1964; *The Production and Distribution of Knowledge in the United States,* Princeton University Press, 1962; *Essays on Economic Semantics,* edited by Merton H. Miller, Prentice-Hall, 1963, published as *Essays in Economic Semantics,* New York University Press, 1975; (editor with Burton G. Malkiel) *International Monetary Arrangements: The Problem of Choice,* Princeton University, 1964; *International Payments, Debts, and Gold,* Scribner, 1964 (published in England as *International Monetary Economics: Collected Essays,* Allen & Unwin, 1966), revised and enlarged edition, New York University Press, 1976; *Involuntary Foreign Lending,* Almquist & Wiksell, 1965; (with others) *Maintaining and Restoring Balance in International Payments,* Princeton University Press, 1966; *Remaking the International Monetary System: The Rio Agreement and Beyond,* Johns Hopkins Press, 1968; (contributor) Robert L. Heilbroner, editor, *Economic Means and Social Ends: Essays in Political Economics,* Prentice-Hall, 1969.

(Contributor) George N. Halm, editor, *Approaches to Greater Flexibility of Exchange Rates,* Princeton University Press, 1970;

Education and Economic Growth, University of Nebraska Press, 1970; *The Alignment of Foreign-Exchange Rates*, Praeger, 1972; (contributor) *Reshaping the International Economic Order: A Tripartite Report by Twelve Economists*, Brookings Institution, 1972; (with others) *International Monetary Problems*, American Enterprise Institute for Public Policy Research, 1972; *International Monetary Systems*, General Learning Press, 1975; *Selected Economic Writings of Fritz Machlup*, edited by George Bitros, New York University Press, 1976; *A History of Thought on Economic Integration*, Columbia University Press, 1977; *Methodology of Economics and Other Social Sciences*, Academic Press, 1978; (with Kenneth Leeson) *Information through the Printed Word: The Dissemination of Scholarly, Scientific, and Intellectual Knowledge*, Praeger, Volume I: *Book Publishing*, 1978, Volume II: *Journals*, 1978, Volume III: *Libraries*, 1978, Volume IV: *Books, Journals, and Bibliographic Services*, 1980; *Knowledge: Its Creation, Distribution, and Economic Significance*, Volume I: *Knowledge and Knowledge Production*, Princeton University Press, 1980. Contributor to professional journals and to newspapers.

WORK IN PROGRESS: A second volume of *Knowledge: Its Creation, Distribution, and Economic Significance*, entitled *The Branches of Learning, Information Sciences, and Human Capital.*

BIOGRAPHICAL/CRITICAL SOURCES: Los Angeles Times, April 13, 1981.

*   *   *

MACLACHLAN, Lewis   1894-1980

PERSONAL: Born November 7, 1894, in Blackford, Perthshire, Scotland; died November 10, 1980; son of David Stevenson and Margaret (Scrimgeour) Maclachlan; married Mary Hally, August 11, 1921; children: Jean (Mrs. Wilfred A. Kerr), David, Eric Hally. *Education:* University of Glasgow, M.A., 1915; additional study at Westminster College, Cambridge, England. *Home:* 30 Cliff Dr., Canford Cliffs, Poole, Dorsetshire BH13 7JG, England.

CAREER: Ordained minister of Presbyterian Church of England; served in China at Changpu, Amoy, 1921-27, in England, at Southend-on-Sea, Essex, 1928-33, Byker, Newcastle-upon-Tyne, 1933-39, Haverstock Hill and Kentish Town, 1942-48, Crouch Hill, London, 1948-57, and Gravesend, Kent, 1957-68. Exchange preacher for National Council of Churches in United States, 1960; lecturer in United States and Canada, 1964. *Member:* Churches Council of Healing, Guild of Health (chaplain), Fellowship of Reconciliation (vice-president).

WRITINGS—Published by James Clarke, except as indicated: *Religion for the Non-Religious*, 1931; *Prayers of World Fellowship*, 1941; *The Faith of Friendship*, Fellowship of Reconciliation, 1942; *Intelligent Prayer*, 1946, reprinted, Attic Press, 1968; *Defeat Triumphant*, Fellowship of Reconciliation, 1947; *The Teaching of Jesus on Prayer*, 1952; *Christian Pacifist Forestry Units*, Fellowship of Reconciliation, 1952; *How to Pray for Healing*, 1956; *Commonsense about Prayer*, 1962; *21 Steps to Positive Prayer*, Arthur James, 1965, reprinted, Judson, 1978; *God Face to Face: A Statement of Some Aspects of the Christian Faith*, 1968; *Miracles of Healing: Studies of the Healing Miracles in the New Testament*, Arthur James, 1968; *Triumphant Living*, Arthur James, 1977. Editor, *Presbyterian Messenger*, 1954-63; former editor, *Reconciliation.*

WORK IN PROGRESS: The Kingdom of God.†

MADARIAGA (Y ROJO), Salvador de   1886-1978

PERSONAL: Born July 23, 1886, in La Coruna, Spain; died December 14, 1978, in Locarno, Switzerland; son of Jose (a colonel) and Ascension (Rojo) de Madariaga; married Constance Helen Margaret Archibald, October 10, 1912 (died, 1970); married Emilie Szekely Rauman, November 18, 1970; children: (first marriage) Nieves and Isabel (daughters). *Education:* Educated in Paris, France, 1900-11, graduating from College Chaptal, 1906, attending Ecole Polytechnique, 1906-08, and graduating from Ecole Nationale Superieure des Mines, 1911. *Politics:* Liberal. *Home:* L'Esplanade, 6600 Locarno, Switzerland.

CAREER: Employed by Railway Company of Northern Spain, Madrid, 1911-16, simultaneously writing political articles for newspapers under a pseudonym; decided to become a writer, and spent 1916-21 in London, doing research and working as a journalist and critic; entered Secretariat of League of Nations, Geneva, Switzerland, 1921, member of press section, 1921-22, head of disarmament section, 1922-27; first occupant of King Alfonso XIII Chair of Spanish Studies at Oxford University, Oxford, England, 1927-30, during which time he also lectured in North America on extended leaves; Spanish Ambassador to United States, 1931, to France, 1932-34, and Spain's permanent delegate to League of Nations Assembly, 1931-36; served briefly as Spain's Minister of Education, 1934, then as Minister of Justice; declined to take sides in Spanish Civil War and returned to Oxford to live in 1936. Broadcaster to Latin America for British Broadcasting Corp. during war; broadcaster in Spanish, French, and German to European countries. Associated with various international organizations in postwar years, serving as first president of Liberal International (became president of honor) and honorary president of Congress for Cultural Freedom. Honorary co-chairman of Spanish Refugee Aid, Inc. Emory L. Ford Professor of Spanish at Princeton University, 1954; lecturer and speaker in many countries. *Member:* Spanish Academy of Letters and of Moral and Political Sciences, French Academy of Moral and Political Sciences, Academy of History of Caracas, and many other Spanish-American learned societies; Reform Club (London), Ateneo (Madrid).

AWARDS, HONORS: M.A., Oxford University, 1928; gold medalist, Yale University; fellow, Exeter College, University of Pavia; honorary doctor of the Universities of Arequipa, Lima, Poitiers, Liege, and Lille, and of Oxford and Princeton Universities; Ere Nouvelle Prize, for *Englishmen, Frenchmen, Spaniards;* Knight Grand Cross of Order of the Republic (Spain), White Lion (Czechoslovakia), Order of Merit (Chile), Order of Jade in Gold (China), Order of Merit (Hungary), Boyaca (Colombia), Order of the White Rose (Finland), Grand Cross of Legion d'Honneur (France), Aztec Eagle (Mexico), and Order of the Sun (Peru); Europa Prize, Hans Deutsch Foundation, Bern University, 1963; Hanseatic Goethe Prize, 1967.

WRITINGS—Biography and history: *Quatre Espangnols a Londres*, Plon, 1928; *Spain* (also see below), Scribner, 1930, 3rd edition, J. Cape, 1942, Creative Age, 1943; *Christopher Columbus: Being the Life of the Very Magnificent Lord Don Cristobal Colon* (first of the "New World" trilogy), Hodder & Stoughton, 1939, Macmillan, 1940, new edition, Hollis & Carter, 1949, Ungar, 1967; *Hernan Cortez: Conqueror of Mexico* (second in the trilogy), Macmillan, 1941, 2nd edition, Regnery, 1955, reprinted, Greenwood Press, 1979; *Spain*, two volumes (first volume based on previous book of same title), J. Cape, 1942, Creative Age, 1943; *Cuadro historico de las Indias*, Editorial Sudamericana, Volume I: *El auge del Imperio Espanol en America*, 1945, 2nd edition, 1959, reprinted, Espasa-Calpe, 1977, translation published as *The Rise of the Spanish-American Empire*, Macmillan, 1947, reprinted, Greenwood Press, 1975, Volume II: *El ocaso del Imperio Espanol en America*, 1945, 2nd edition, 1959, translation published as *The Fall of the Spanish-American Empire*, Hollis & Carter, 1947, Macmillan, 1948, revised edition, Collier, 1963, reprinted, Greenwood Press, 1975; *Bolivar* (third in the trilogy), two volumes, Editorial Hermes (Mexico), 1951, 3rd edition, Editorial Sudamericana, 1959, translation by the author published in abridged edition with the same title, Hollis & Carter, 1951, reprinted, Greenwood Press, 1979; *De Colon a Bolivar*, E.D.H.A.S.A. (Editorial y Distribuidora Hispano Americana, S.A.; Barcelona), 1956; *El ciclo hispanico*, two volumes, Editorial Sudamericana, 1958; *Spain: A Modern History*, Praeger, 1958; *Espanoles de mi tiempo*, Editorial Planeta, 1974, 5th edition, 1976; *Memorias, 1921-1936: Amanecer sin mediodia*, Espasa-Calpe, 1974.

Political books: *La guerra desde Londres*, Editorial Monclus (Tortosa), 1918; *Disarmament*, Coward, 1929, reprinted, Kennikat Press, 1967; *Discursos internacionales*, M. Aguilar (Madrid), 1934; *Anarquia o jerarquia*, M. Aguilar, 1935, 3rd edition, 1970, translation by the author published as *Anarchy or Hierarchy*, Allen & Unwin, 1937, reprinted, 1970; *Theory and Practice in International Relations: William J. Cooper Foundation Lectures, 1937*, Swarthmore College, University of Pennsylvania Press, 1937; *The World's Design*, Allen & Unwin, 1938; (with Edward Hallett Carr) *Future of International Government*, Universal Distributors, 1941; (with others) *The British Commonwealth and the U.S.A. in the Postwar World*, National Peace Council, 1942; *Ojo, vencedores!*, Editorial Sudamericana, 1945, translation by the author published as *Victors, Beware*, J. Cape, 1946; *De l'Angoisse a la liberte*, Calmann-Levy (Paris), 1954, translation of second part by M. Marx published in England as *Democracy Versus Liberty?*, Pall Mall Press, 1958; *Rettet die Freiheit!* (selected articles originally published in *Neue Zuercher Zeitung*, 1948-57), Francke (Bern), 1958; *General, marchese usted!* (collection of lectures broadcast for the Spanish Service of the Radiodiffusion Francaise, 1954-57), Ediciones Iberica, 1959; *The Blowing Up of the Parthenon; or, How to Lose the Cold War*, Praeger, 1960, revised edition, 1961; *Latin America between the Eagle and the Bear*, Praeger, 1962; *Weltpolitisches Kaleidoskop* (second collection of articles originally published in *Neue Zuercher Zeitung*), Fretz & Wasmuth Verlag (Zurich), 1965.

Essays: *Shelley and Calderon, and Other Essays on English and Spanish Poetry*, Constable, 1920, reprinted, Kennikat Press, 1965; *The Genius of Spain, and Other Essays on Spanish Contemporary Literature*, Clarendon Press, 1923, reprinted, Books for Libraries, 1968; *Arceval y los ingleses*, Espasa-Calpe (Madrid), 1925, reprinted, 1973; *Guia del lector del "Quijote,"* Espasa-Calpe, 1926, reprinted, 1976, translation by the author published as *Don Quixote: An Introductory Essay in Psychology*, Gregynogg Press (Wales), 1934, revised edition, Oxford University Press, 1961; *Englishmen, Frenchmen, Spaniards: An Essay in Comparative Psychology*, Oxford University Press, 1928, 2nd edition, Hill & Wang, 1969; *Americans*, Oxford University Press, 1930, reprinted, Books for Libraries, 1968; *On Hamlet*, Hollis & Carter, 1948, 2nd edition, Barnes & Noble, 1964; *Bosquejo de Europa* (also see below), Editorial Hermes, 1951, reprinted, Editorial Sudamericana, 1969, translation by the author published as *Portrait of Europe*, Hollis & Carter, 1952, Roy, 1955, revised edition, University of Alabama Press, 1967; *Essays with a Purpose*, Hollis & Carter, 1954; *Presente y porvenir de Hispanoamerica, y otros ensayos*, Editorial Sudamericana, 1959, 2nd edition, 1974; *De Galdos a Lorca*, Editorial Sudamericana, 1960; *El Quijote de Cer-*

vantes, Editorial Sudamericana, 1962; *Retrato de un hombre de pie*, E.D.H.A.S.A., 1965, translation by the author published as *Portrait of a Man Standing*, University of Alabama Press, 1968; *Memorias de un federalista*, Editorial Sudamericana, 1967; (contributor) Ivar Ivask and Juan Marichal, editors, *Luminous Reality: The Poetry of Jorge Guillen*, University of Oklahoma Press, 1969; *Selecciones de Madariaga* (includes selections from *Bosquejo de Europa* [and] *El enemigo de Dios*), edited by Frank Sedwick and Elizabeth Van Orman, Prentice-Hall, 1969; *Mujeres espanolas*, Espasa-Calpe, 1972; *Obras escogidas: Ensayos*, Editorial Sudamericana, 1972.

Novels: *The Sacred Giraffe: Being the Second Volume of the Posthumous Works of Julio Arceval* (satire), Hopkinson, 1925; *Sir Bob* (juvenile), Harcourt, 1930; *El enemigo de Dios* (also see above), M. Aguilar, 1926, 2nd edition, Editorial Sudamericana, 1965; *Ramo de errores*, Editorial Hermes, 1952, translation by the author published as *A Bunch of Errors*, J. Cape, 1954; *La camarada Ana*, Editorial Hermes, 1954, 2nd edition, Editorial Sudamericana, 1956; *Sanco Panco*, Latino-Americana (Mexico), 1963.

Poetry: *Romances de ciego*, Publicaciones Atenea (Madrid), 1922; *La fuente serena*, Editorial Cervantes, 1927; *Elegia en la muerte de Unamuno*, Oxford University Press, 1937; *Elegia en la muerte de Federico Garcia Lorca*, Oxford University Press, 1938; *The Home of Man* (18 sonnets), privately printed, 1938; *Rosa de cieno y ceniza*, Editorial Sudamericana, 1942; *El sol, la luna y las estrellas: Romances a Beatriz*, Editorial Juventud (Barcelona), 1954, 3rd edition, 1974; *La que huele a tomillo y a romero*, Editorial Sudamericana, 1959; *Poppy*, bilingual Spanish and English edition, Imprenta Bernasconi (Lugano), 1965; *Obra poetica*, Plaza & Janes (Barcelona), 1977.

Dramatic works: *Elysian Fields*, Allen & Unwin, 1937; *El toison de oro, y tres obras mas: La Muerte de Carmen, Don Carlos* [y] *Mio Cid* (the first a lyrical fantasy in three acts; the following three dramatic poems), Editorial Sudamericana, 1940, 2nd edition, 1945; *Don Juan y la Don-Juania* (one-act verse play), Editorial Sudamericana, 1950; *Los tres estudiantes de Salamanca* (includes "Los tres estudiantes de Salamanca," a three-act tragicomedy; "Viva la muerte," a three-act modern tragedy, produced in the Piccola Scala, Milan, Italy, 1966; and "El doce de octubre de Cervantes," a one-act historical fantasy), Editorial Sudamericana, 1962; *La Mappe-monde et le Pape-monde* (three-act French verse play; broadcast by Radiodiffusion Francaise, 1948), Editions d'Art Jacques O'Hana (London), 1966; *La cruz y la bandera* [y] *Las tres carabelas* (romances), Editorial Sudamericana, 1966; *Numance: Tragedie lyrique en un acte* (opera; first produced in Paris, 1954), libretto by Henri Barraud, Boosey & Hawkes, 1970; *Dialogos famosos: Campos eliseos—Adan y Eva*, Editorial Sudamericana, 1970.

Radio plays: "Campos eliseos" (Spanish version of "Elysian Fields"), broadcast by the British Broadcasting Corp. (BBC) for Spain, Radio Varsovia, updated version broadcast in German by Radio Berna, 1966; "Cristobal Colon," BBC, 1941; "Las tres carabelas," BBC, 1942; "Numancia" (English verse translation of Cervantes' tragedy), BBC, 1947; "Christophe Colomb" (dramatization of the discovery of America in French), Radiodiffusion Francaise, 1954.

Other: (Author of introduction) Miguel de Unamuno, *The Tragic Sense of Life*, Macmillan, 1921; (contributor) *A League of Minds* (letters), International Institute of Intellectual Cooperation, League of Nations, 1933; *Europe: A Unit of Human Culture*, European Movement (Brussels), 1952; *Sobre mi Bolivar*, Editorial Sudamericana, 1953; *Critique de l'Europe* (originally published as preface to *European Annual*), Council of Europe, 1959; (author of introduction) *Echo de monde*, Metz Verlag (Zurich), 1960; (contributor) *Dauer im Wandel*, Verlag Georg D.W. Callwey (Munich), 1961; (editor) Miguel de Cervantes, *El ingenioso hidalgo don Quijote de la Mancha*, Editorial Sudamericana, 1962; (contributor) *Die Kraft zu leben*, Bertelsmann Verlag (Guetersloh), 1963; *Yo-yo y yo-el*, Editorial Sudamericana, 1967; (compiler) *Charles Quint*, A. Michel, 1969; (with others) *Freiheitliche Politik fuer eine freie Welt*, M. Hoch (Ludwigsburg), 1969; (with others) *Ist die Marktwirtschaft noch gesichert?*, M. Hoch, 1971; *Morgen ohne Mittag* (memoirs), Ullstein (Berlin), 1973, translation published as *Morning without Noon*, Saxon House, 1974; *A la orilla del rio de los sucesos*, Ediciones Destino, 1975; *Dios y los espanoles*, Editorial Planeta, 1975.

"Esquiveles y Manriques" series; published by Editorial Sudamericana, except as indicated: *El corazon de piedra verde*, 1943, reprinted, Espasa-Calpe, 1975, translation by the author published as *The Heart of Jade*, Creative Age, 1944, reprinted, Hamilton, 1964, published in Spanish in three volumes, 1952, Volume I: *Los fantasmas*, Volume II: *Los dioses sanguinarios*, Volume III: *Fe sin blasfemia; Guerra en la sangre*, 1956, 4th edition, 1971, bound with *Una gota de tiempo*, Espasa-Calpe, 1977, translation by the author published as *War in the Blood*, Collins, 1957; *Una gota de tiempo*, 1958, 3rd edition, 1971, bound with *Guerra en la sangre*, Espasa-Calpe, 1977; *El semental negro*, 1961, 2nd edition, 1967, bound with *Satanael*, Espasa-Calpe, 1977; *Satanael*, 1966, bound with *El semental negro*, Espasa-Calpe, 1977.

Translator: *Manojo de poesias ingleses puestas en verso castellano*, William Lewis (Cardiff), 1919; (and compiler) *Spanish Folk Songs*, Constable, 1922; (and editor) William Shakespeare, *Hamlet*, bilingual edition, Editorial Sudamericana, 1949. Assisted L. Araquistain in translating Rudyard Kipling's "The Fringes of the Fleet" and "Tales of 'The Trade'" (stories) into Spanish.

Also author of numerous essays, studies, and commentaries on current affairs. Contributor to periodicals.

SIDELIGHTS: A great European liberal, citizen of the world, scholar, and statesman, Salvador de Madariaga was one of Spain's outstanding intellectuals. Aristide Briand described him as one of the ten best conversationalists in Europe. "Man's most precious possession is the gift of thinking freely," Madariaga once stated, "of adventuring in the realms of the mind and of nature, thus to discover his own existence and remain master of his fate."

In addition to his native Spanish, Madariaga wrote in English, German, and French. He occasionally prepared some of his books in all four languages. Many of Madariaga's writings, of both literary and political content, have stimulated heated discussion. The third book in the "New World" trilogy, *Bolivar*, proved to be "a literary bombshell that caused Spain and Latin America to go to war again, with plenty of ink spilled on both sides," said Marcelle Michelin of *Books Abroad*. Highly revered in Latin America as a key figure in the struggle for independence, Bolivar, according to Madariaga, was "nothing but a vulgar imitator of Napoleon with dreams of reigning over a South American empire." Although very well received in North America and England, the book generated shock and outrage in Latin America and was banned in Argentina.

A severe critic of Francisco Franco's regime, Madariaga traveled to England in self-imposed exile at the outbreak of the Spanish Civil War in 1936 and did not return to Spain until after Franco died in 1975. Although he bore a passionate love for his homeland, he believed that Spain was caught in the grip of a totally destructive dictatorship. "Fascism hardly counts in Spain," he wrote. "It is the Army that keeps its boot on the neck of the Spanish people." In an August, 1969, article in the *New York Times*, he made the statement that Franco, "once an intelligent colonel, . . . [has] turned insane by decades of unchecked power. . . . We are told by his friends that he gave Spain thirty years of peace and ten of prosperity. Neither of these assertions is true. Outward quiet is not peace. Before it explodes, a bomb is quiet enough."

BIOGRAPHICAL/CRITICAL SOURCES: New York Herald Tribune Book Review, October 12, 1952; *Books Abroad*, autumn, 1953; *Newsweek*, June 9, 1958; *Saturday Review*, July 2, 1960; *Washington Post*, May 26, 1961; *Times Literary Supplement*, February 22, 1968; *New York Times*, August 9, 1969.

OBITUARIES: Chicago Tribune, December 15, 1978; *Washington Post*, December 15, 1978; *Time*, December 25, 1978.†

* * *

MAGILL, Frank N(orthen) 1907-

PERSONAL: Born November 21, 1907, in Atlanta, Ga.; son of James William (a newspaperman) and Sarah (Carter) Magill; married Elizabeth Love Brown, October 11, 1947; children: James Lawrence, Peter Scott, Holly Elizabeth. *Education:* Georgia Institute of Technology, B.S., 1931; Columbia University, M.S., 1934; University of Southern California, Ed.D.; Pepperdine University, LL.D., 1964. *Politics:* Republican. *Religion:* Protestant. *Home:* 607 Foxwood Rd., La Canada Flintridge, Calif. 91011.

CAREER: Bostwick & Magill, New York, N.Y., partner, 1935-38; freelance writer, 1938-41; freelance editor, 1947—. University of Southern California, Los Angeles, president of support group, School of Library Science, 1967-71, adjunct professor of library science, 1968—. Director of Salem Press, 1949—, and Salem Audiovisual, 1966—; founder of Magill Publications. Local chairman, American Bureau for Medical Aid to Free China, 1962—; founding member and treasurer, Foundation for Human Resources Development, 1967. Member of consumer issues advisory panel, Secretary's Commission on Medical Malpractice, U.S. Department of Health, Education, and Welfare, 1972; member of Citizen's Advisory Committee on Curriculum, La Canada School District, 1975-76. *Military service:* U.S. Army Air Forces, 1942-46; became major. *Member:* Pi Kappa Alpha, University Club (New York, N.Y.), Los Angeles Athletic Club, La Canada Country Club. *Awards, honors:* Literary Achievement Award, Christian Freedom Foundation, 1971; Golden Scroll Award, Academy of Science Fiction, Fantasy, and Horror Films, 1981.

WRITINGS—Editor: (With Dayton Kohler) *Masterplots*, four series, Salem Press, 1949-68, published as *Masterpieces of World Literature in Digest Form*, Harper, 1952-63, revised edition published as *Masterplots: 2010 Plot Stories and Essay Reviews from the World's Fine Literature*, Salem Press, 1976; *Masterplots Annual* (also see below), Salem Press, 1954—; (with Kohler) *Cyclopedia of World Authors*, Harper, 1958-63, published as *Masterplots Cyclopedia of World Authors*, Salem Press, 1963, revised edition published under original title, Salem Press, 1974; (with Ian McGreal) *Masterpieces of World Philosophy in Summary Form*, Harper, 1961-63; (with McGreal) *Masterpieces of Christian Literature in Summary Form*, Harper, 1963; *Best Masterplots, 1954-62*, Salem Press, 1963; *Cyclopedia of Literary Characters*, Harper, 1963, published as *Masterplots Cyclopedia of Literary Characters*, Salem Press, 1963; *Masterpieces of Catholic Literature in Summary Form*,

Harper, 1965; *Magill's Quotations in Context,* Harper, Series I, 1965, Series II, 1969.

Survey of Contemporary Literature: Updated Reprints of 1500 Essay-Reviews from Masterplots Annuals, 1954-1969, Salem Press, 1971, revised edition published as *Survey of Contemporary Literature: Updated Reprints of 2300 Essay-Reviews from Masterplots Annuals, 1954-1976,* 1977; *Great Events from History,* Salem Press, Series I: *Ancient and Medieval Series,* 1972, Series II: *Modern European Series,* 1973, Series III: *American Series,* 1975, Series IV: *Worldwide Twentieth Century Series,* 1980; *Magill's Literary Annual,* Salem Press, 1977—; *1,300 Critical Evaluations of Selected Novels and Plays,* Salem Press, 1978; *Magill's Bibliography of Literary Criticism: Selected Sources for the Study of More than 2500 Outstanding Works of Western Literature,* Salem Press, 1979; *Contemporary Literary Scene II,* Salem Press, 1979; *Survey of Science Fiction Literature,* Salem Press, 1979; *Magill's Survey of Cinema,* Salem Press, Series I, 1980, Series II, 1981; *Magill Books Index,* Salem Press, 1980; *Critical Survey of Short Fiction,* Salem Press, 1981.

*   *   *

MALIN, Irving   1934-

PERSONAL: Born March 18, 1934, in New York, N.Y.; son of Morris and Bertha (Silverman) Malin; married Ruth Lief; children: Mark Charles. *Education:* Queens College (now Queens College of the City University of New York), B.A., 1955; Stanford University, Ph.D., 1958. *Home:* 96-13 68th Ave., Forest Hills, N.Y. 11375. *Office:* Department of English, City College of the City University of New York, New York, N.Y. 10021.

CAREER: Stanford University, Stanford, Calif., acting instructor in English, 1955-56, 1957-58; Indiana University at Bloomington, instructor in English, 1958-60; City College of the City University of New York, New York, N.Y., assistant professor, 1960-69, associate professor, 1969-72, professor of English, 1972—. Consultant to Jewish Publication Society, 1964, National Endowment for the Humanities, 1972, 1979-81, B'nai B'rith, 1974-75, Yaddo, 1975-77, Jewish Book Council, 1976, 1979, P.E.N., 1977-82, International Exchange for Scholars, 1981, and numerous university presses.

MEMBER: Modern Language Association of America, Society for the Study of Southern Literature, English Institute, English-Speaking Union, Henry James Society, Nathaniel Hawthorne Society, Sherwood Anderson Society, Poe Studies Association, Melville Society, P.E.N., Authors Guild, Authors League of America, National Book Critics Circle, American Jewish Historical Society, American Jewish Congress, American Studies Association, American Association of University Professors, New York Academy of Sciences, Phi Beta Kappa. *Awards, honors:* Yaddo fellowship, 1963; National Foundation for Jewish Culture fellowship, 1963-64; Huntington Library fellowship, 1978.

WRITINGS: William Faulkner: An Interpretation, Stanford University Press, 1957; *New American Gothic,* Southern Illinois University Press, 1962; (co-editor) *Breakthrough: A Treasury of Contemporary American Jewish Literature,* McGraw, 1964; *Jews and Americans,* Southern Illinois University Press, 1965; (editor) *Psychoanalysis and American Fiction,* Dutton, 1965; (editor) *Saul Bellow and the Critics,* New York University Press, 1967; (editor) *Truman Capote's "In Cold Blood": A Critical Handbook,* Wadsworth, 1968; (editor) *Critical Views of Isaac Bashevis Singer,* New York University Press, 1969; *Saul Bellow's Fiction,* Southern Illinois University

Press, 1969; (editor with Melvin J. Friedman) *William Styron's "The Confessions of Nat Turner": A Critical Handbook,* Wadsworth, 1970; *Nathanael West's Novels,* Southern Illinois University Press, 1972; *Isaac Bashevis Singer,* Ungar, 1972; (editor) *Contemporary American Jewish Literature: Critical Essays,* Indiana University Press, 1973; (editor with Robert K. Morris) *The Achievement of William Styron,* University of Georgia Press, 1975; (co-editor) *The Achievement of Carson McCullers,* University of Georgia Press, 1982.

Contributor: Neil D. Isaacs and Louis Leiter, editors, *Approaches to the Short Story,* Chandler Publishing, 1963; Frederick Utley, Lynn Bloom, and Arthur Kinney, editors, *Bear, Man, and God: Eight Approaches to Faulkner's "The Bear,"* Random House, 1963; Lily Edelman, editor, *Jewish Heritage Reader,* Taplinger, 1965; Charles Shapiro, editor, *Contemporary British Novelists,* Southern Illinois University Press, 1965; Friedman and Lewis A. Lawson, editors, *The Added Dimension,* Fordham University Press, 1966; David Madden, editor, *Tough Guy Writers of the Thirties,* Southern Illinois University Press, 1968.

M. T. Inge, editor, *William Faulkner: "A Rose for Emily,"* Bobbs-Merrill, 1970; Madden, editor, *American Dreams, American Nightmares,* Southern Illinois University Press, 1970; Friedman, editor, *The Vision Obscured,* Fordham University Press, 1970; *Contemporary Novelists of the English Language,* St. Martin's, 1972; J. C. Pratt, editor, *Ken Kesey: One Flew over the Cuckoo's Nest,* Viking, 1973; Abraham Chapman, editor, *Jewish American Literature,* New American Library, 1974; Earl Rovit, editor, *Saul Bellow,* Prentice-Hall, 1975; Morris, editor, *Old Lines, New Forces: Essays on the Contemporary British Novel,* Fairleigh Dickinson University Press, 1976; Rosette Lamont and Friedman, editors, *The Two Faces of Eugene Ionesco,* Whitston Publishing, 1978; Linda Wagner, editor, *Critical Essays on Joyce Carol Oates,* G. K. Hall, 1979; James L. W. West III, editor, *Critical Essays on William Styron,* G. K. Hall, 1982; Jackson R. Bryer, editor, *The Stories of F. Scott Fitzgerald,* University of Wisconsin Press, 1982; Friedman, editor, *Critical Essays on Flannery O'Connor,* G. K. Hall, 1982.

Contributor to *Encyclopedia Judaica.* Contributor to numerous periodicals, including *London Magazine, Kenyon Review, Saturday Review, Nation, New Republic,* and *Commonweal.* Consultant, *American Quarterly,* 1964; advisory editor, *Studies in American-Jewish Literature,* 1976—, and *Southern Quarterly,* 1982; book review editor, *Jewish Daily Forward,* 1981—.

WORK IN PROGRESS: A book on Bernard Malamud and one on Conrad Aiken's prose writings.

*   *   *

MALLINSON, Jeremy (John Crosby)   1937-

PERSONAL: Born March 16, 1937, in Ilkley, Yorkshire, England; son of Harold Crosby and Kay (Parkinson) Mallinson; married Odette Louise Guiton, October 26, 1963; children: Julian Justin Crosby, Sophie Jayne. *Education:* Educated in England. *Home:* Clos Tranquil, Rue de Croquet, St. Aubin, Jersey, Channel Islands. *Agent:* Curtis Brown Ltd., 1 Craven Hill, London W2 3EW, England. *Office:* Jersey Wildlife Preservation Trust, Trinity, Jersey, Channel Islands.

CAREER: Member of staff, H. Crosby Mallinson's (vintners), Jersey, Channel Islands, 1954-56, and Rhodesia & Nyasaland Staff Corps., 1956-58; Jersey Zoological Park, Trinity, Jersey, keeper, 1959-62; Jersey Wildlife Preservation Trust, Jersey, deputy director, 1963-72, zoological director, 1972—. *Member:* Royal Geographical Society (fellow), Institute of Biology.

WRITINGS: Okavango Adventure, David & Charles, 1973, Norton, 1974; *Earning Your Living with Animals,* David & Charles, 1975; (compiler and author of preface) *Modern Classic Animal Stories,* David & Charles, 1977, published as *Such Agreeable Friends,* Universe Books, 1978; *The Shadow of Extinction: Europe's Threatened Wild Mammals,* Macmillan (London), 1978; *The Facts about a Zoo,* G. Whizzard/Deutsch, 1980. Contributor to *International Zoo Yearbook* and to zoological journals.

SIDELIGHTS: Jeremy Mallinson has made expeditions to Southern Rhodesia and Bechuanaland, Bolivia, Brazil, Guiana, Madagascar, Assam, India, and the Zaire River to collect and study animals.

*   *   *

MALLOCH, Peter
   See DUNCAN, W(illiam) Murdoch

*   *   *

MANDEL, Morris   1911-

PERSONAL: Born July 15, 1911, in Poland; son of Max and Rebecca (Eisen) Mandel; married Shirley Roth (a teacher), December 24, 1938; children: Allen. *Education:* St. John's University, Jamaica, N.Y., B.B.A., 1933, M.B.A., 1935; Brooklyn College and Columbia University, graduate study, 1955-60; Alfred Adler Institute of Individual Psychology, diplomate, 1957.

CAREER: George W. Wingate High School, Brooklyn, N.Y., guidance counselor, twenty years; Academy Toras Emes, Brooklyn, principal for thirty years. Lecturer. Jewish Fellowship Foundation, executive secretary. *Member:* Commerical Teachers Association, American Personnel Guidance Association, Delta Mu Delta.

WRITINGS—Published by Jonathan David, except as indicated: (With A. L. Lavine) *Business Law for Everyday Use,* Holt, 1947, 4th edition, 1956; *The Pilot,* Holt, 1947; *The Counselor,* Holt, 1947; *As the Twig Is Bent,* 1959.

Thirteen: A Teenage Guide to Judaism, 1961; *Heaven, Man and a Carrot,* 1962; (compiler and editor) *Stories for Speakers,* 1964; *Take Time to Live: A Happy Guide to Healthy Living,* 1965; (compiler and editor) *Story Anthology for Public Speakers,* 1966; (with Leo Gartenberg) *Israel through Eight Eyes: An Orthodox View of the Holy Land,* 1967; *How to Be Married and Happy,* 1968; (with Gartenberg) *Israel: The Story of a Miracle,* 1969.

(With Gartenberg) *Sidra by Sidra,* 1970; *Advice to the Lonely, Frustrated, and Confused,* 1972; (compiler and editor) *A Complete Treasury of Stories for Public Speakers,* 1974; (compiler) *Affronts, Insults and Indignities,* 1975; *Secret Love Affairs,* 1975; (with Gartenberg) *Tomorrow Is Today,* Pen Quill Press, 1977.

AVOCATIONAL INTERESTS: Tennis, reading.†

*   *   *

MANHEIM, Jarol B(ruce)   1946-

PERSONAL: Born April 17, 1946, in Cleveland, Ohio; son of Harvey (a salesman) and Norma (Blaugrund) Manheim; married Amy Lowen, September 6, 1969. *Education:* Rice University, B.A., 1968; Northwestern University, M.A., 1969, Ph.D., 1971. *Home:* 709 Circle Dr. N.W., Blacksburg, Va.

24060. *Office:* Department of Political Science, Virginia Polytechnic Institute and State University, Blacksburg, Va. 24061.

CAREER: City College of the City University of New York, New York, N.Y., assistant professor of political science, 1971-75; Virginia Polytechnic Institute and State University, Blacksburg, assistant professor, 1975-77, associate professor of political science, 1977—. Advisory editor in political communication, Longman, Inc. *Member:* American Political Science Association, Policy Studies Organization, Center for the Study of the Presidency, Southern Political Science Association. *Awards, honors:* Woodrow Wilson fellow, 1970-71.

WRITINGS: The Politics Within: A Primer in Political Attitudes and Behavior, Prentice-Hall, 1975, 2nd edition, Longman, 1982; (with Melanie Wallace) *Political Violence in the United States, 1875-1974: A Bibliography,* Garland, 1975; *Deja Vu: American Political Problems in Historical Perspective,* St. Martin's, 1976; (with Richard C. Rich) *Empirical Political Analysis: Research Methods in Political Science,* Prentice-Hall, 1981. Editor of "Annual Editions: Readings in American Government" series, Dushkin, 1974-76; editor of "Professional Studies in Political Communication and Policy" series (monographs), Longman. Contributor of articles and reviews to professional journals. Associate editor, *Journal of Politics,* 1978-79; literature review editor and member of editorial board, *Policy Studies Journal,* 1980—.

WORK IN PROGRESS: American Politics Yearbook for Longman; research on mass media and politics and on telecommunications policy.

*   *   *

MANNING, Rosemary
   See COLE, Margaret Alice

*   *   *

MANTLE, Winifred (Langford)
   (Anne Fellowes, Frances Lang, Jane Langford)

PERSONAL: Born in Merry Hill, Staffordshire, England; daughter of Joseph Langford and Florence (Fellows) Mantle. *Education:* Lady Margaret Hall, Oxford, B.A. (with first class honors), and M.A.; additional study at University of Strasbourg. *Religion:* Church of England. *Home:* 7 The Parklands, Finchfield, Wolverhampton, England.

CAREER: Novelist and short story writer, 1954—. St. Katharine's Training College, Liverpool, England, lecturer in French, 1938-41; University of St. Andrews, St. Andrews, Scotland, assistant lecturer in French, 1941-46. *Member:* Society of Authors, Romantic Novelists Association. *Awards, honors:* Award for best historical novel, Romantic Novelists Association, 1961, for *A Pride of Princesses.*

WRITINGS: Happy Is the House, Chatto & Windus, 1951; *Country Cousin,* Chatto & Windus, 1953; *Five Farthings,* Hurst & Blackett, 1958; *Kingsbarns,* Hurst & Blackett, 1959; *Lords and Ladies,* Hurst & Blackett, 1959; *The Hiding-Place* (juvenile), Gollancz, 1962, Holt, 1963; *Griffin Lane,* Hurst & Blackett, 1962; *Sandy Smith* (juvenile), Benn, 1963; *Bennet's Hill,* Hurst & Blackett, 1963; *Tinker's Castle* (juvenile), Gollancz, 1963, Holt, 1964; *The Chateau Holiday* (juvenile), Gollancz, 1964, Holt, 1965; *The River Runs,* Hurst & Blackett, 1964; *A View of Christowe,* Collins, 1965; *The Painted Cave,* Gollancz, 1965, Holt, 1966; *The Same Way Home,* Collins, 1966; *The Penderel House* (juvenile), Holt, 1966; *Summer at Temple Quentin,* Collins, 1967; *The Admiral's Wood* (juvenile), Gollancz, 1967; *Winter at Wycliffe,* Collins, 1968; *Pip-*

er's Row (juvenile), Gollancz, 1968; *The May Tree,* Collins, 1969; *A Fair Exchange,* Collins, 1970; *The House in the Lane,* R. Hale, 1972; *Jonnesty* (juvenile), Chatto & Windus, 1973; *The Inconvenient Marriage,* R. Hale, 1974; *Jonnesty in Winter* (juvenile), Chatto & Windus, 1975; *The Beckoning Maiden,* R. Hale, 1976.

Under pseudonym Anne Fellowes; all published by Mills & Boon: *The Morning Dew,* 1957; *Green Willow,* 1958; *The Keys of Heaven,* 1958.

Under pseudonym Frances Lang: *Marriage of Masks,* Hurst & Blackett, 1960; *A Pride of Princesses,* Hurst & Blackett, 1961; *The Sun in Splendour,* Hurst & Blackett, 1962; *The Leaping Lords,* Hurst & Blackett, 1963; *Blind Man's Buff,* Collins, 1965; *The Marrying Month,* Collins, 1965; *The Well-Wisher,* Collins, 1967; *The Duke's Daughter,* Collins, 1967; *The Malcontent,* Collins, 1968; *Double Dowry,* Collins, 1970; *The Tower of Remicourt,* R. Hale, 1971; *Milord Macdonald,* R. Hale, 1973; *The Prince's Pleasure,* R. Hale, 1974; *The Marquis's Marriage,* R. Hale, 1975; *Stranger at the Gate,* R. Hale, 1975; *The Baron's Bride,* R. Hale, 1978; *The Vanishing Bridegroom,* R. Hale, 1980; *The Filigree Bird,* R. Hale, 1981; *Fortune's Favorite,* R. Hale, 1981.

Under pseudonym Jane Langford; all published by Mills & Boon: *Haste to the Wedding,* 1955; *The Secret Fairing,* 1956; *King of the Castle,* 1956; *Half-Way House,* 1957; *Promise of Marriage,* 1957; *One Small Flower,* 1958; *Strange Adventure,* 1958; *Weather House,* 1958; *Change of Tune,* 1959; *Happy Return,* 1960.

Author of short stories under pseudonyms Anne Fellowes and Jane Langford.

WORK IN PROGRESS: To Be a Fine Lady, under pseudonym Frances Lang; *A Maiden Transplanted;* two children's books, *Poppy Poppyhead* and *Merrifield Lane; a family biography.*

SIDELIGHTS: Winifred Mantle's books have been serialized in many countries, including England, South Africa, Italy, Netherlands, Norway, Greece, Australia, France, Sweden, Canada, and Denmark.

* * *

MANUEL, Frank Edward 1910-

PERSONAL: Born September 12, 1910, in Boston, Mass.; married October 6, 1936. *Education:* Harvard University, A.B., 1930, M.A., 1931, Ph.D., 1933. *Home:* 85 East India Row, Boston, Mass. 02110. *Office:* Brandeis University, Waltham, Mass. 02254.

CAREER: Harvard University, Cambridge, Mass., teacher of history, government, and economics, 1935-37; research and administrative positions with National Defense Commission and Office of Price Administration, 1940-43, 1945-47; Western Reserve University (now Case Western Reserve University), Cleveland, Ohio, professor of history, 1947; Brandeis University, Waltham, Mass., professor of history and moral psychology, 1949-65; New York University, New York, N.Y., professor, 1965-76, Kenan Professor of History, 1970-76; Brandeis University, Alfred and Viola Hart University Professor, 1977—. Visiting professor at Harvard University, 1960, Hebrew University of Jerusalem, 1972, University of Chicago, 1975, and University of California, Los Angeles, 1976. Eastman Visiting Professor, Oxford University, 1972-73. Visiting research fellow, Australian National University, 1974. Member of Institute for Advanced Study, 1976-77. Phi Beta Kappa visiting scholar, 1978. *Military service:* U.S. Army, 1943-45; served as combat intelligence officer with Twenty-First Corps;

received Bronze Star. *Member:* American Historical Association, Authors League, Phi Beta Kappa. *Awards, honors:* Guggenheim fellow, 1957-58; Center for Advanced Study in the Behavioral Sciences fellow, 1962-63; American Academy of Arts and Sciences fellow; Melcher prize; Emerson Award from Phi Beta Kappa, for *Utopian Thought in the Western World;* Litt.D. from Jewish Theological Seminary, 1979; American Book Award nomination, 1980, for *Utopian Thought in the Western World.*

WRITINGS: The Politics of Modern Spain, McGraw, 1938; *The Realities of American-Palestine Relations,* Public Affairs Press, 1949; *The Age of Reason,* Cornell University Press, 1951; *The New World of Henri Saint-Simon,* Harvard University Press, 1956; *The Eighteenth Century Confronts the Gods,* Harvard University Press, 1959.

The Prophets of Paris, Harvard University Press, 1962; *Isaac Newton: Historian,* Harvard University Press, 1963; *Shapes of Philosophical History,* Stanford University Press, 1965; (editor) *The Enlightenment,* Prentice-Hall, 1965; (editor) *Utopias and Utopian Thought,* Houghton, 1966; (editor, translator, and author of introduction with Fritzie P. Manuel) *French Utopias: An Anthology of Ideal Societies,* Free Press, 1966; *A Portrait of Isaac Newton,* Harvard University Press, 1968; (editor) Johann Gottfried von Herder, *Reflections on the Philosophy of the History of Mankind,* University of Chicago Press, 1968.

Freedom from History, and Other Untimely Essays, New York University Press, 1971; *The Religion of Isaac Newton,* Clarendon Press, 1974; (with Fritzie P. Manuel) *Utopian Thought in the Western World,* Harvard University Press, 1979. Member of board of editors, *Dictionary of the History of Ideas,* 1969-71; consulting editor, *Psychoanalysis and Contemporary Science,* 1970—; advisory editor, *Clio,* 1971—.

SIDELIGHTS: New York Times Book Review critic Leo Marx writes that Frank Edward Manuel's *Utopian Thought in the Western World* "is a work of monumental scope, written with authority, wit and unfailing lucidity. . . . Psychological insight is yielded by a series of indepth studies of individual utopian writers. . . . The book's essence lies in these audacious character studies in which a particular life and work and cultural milieu is connected to the overall history of the mode."

Robert Nisbet of *New Republic* also praised Manuel's treatment of utopianism from ancient and medieval times to the present. He writes that it "is without any doubt the finest single historical study of Western utopias to be found anywhere. It is comprehensive, covering the last 2500 years, from early Hebrew and Greek texts, richly detailed, and written with verve and unerring eye for the illuminating essence of whatever the authors happen to be dealing with."

BIOGRAPHICAL/CRITICAL SOURCES: Virginia Quarterly Review, spring, 1967, autumn, 1969; *New York Times Book Review,* February 25, 1968, October 21, 1979; *Saturday Review,* February 1, 1969; *New York Review of Books,* April 10, 1969; *New Republic,* March 1, 1975, November 10, 1979; *New York Times,* December 1, 1979.

* * *

MANVELL, (Arnold) Roger 1909-

PERSONAL: Born October 10, 1909, in Leicester, England; son of Arnold and Gertrude (Baines) Manvell. *Education:* Attended University of Leicester; University of London, B.A. (first class honours in English language and literature), 1930, Ph.D., 1936. *Home:* 15 Above Town, Dartmouth, Devonshire, England. *Agent:* John and Charlotte Wolfers, 3 Regent Square,

London WC1, England. *Office:* School of Public Communication, Boston University, 640 Commonwealth Ave., Boston, Mass. 02215.

CAREER: University of Bristol, Department of Extra-Mural Studies, Bristol, England, lecturer in literature and drama, 1937-40; wartime officer, Government of Great Britain, Ministry of Information, Films Department, 1940-45; research officer and lecturer, British Film Institute, 1945-47; British Film Academy, London, England, director, 1947-59; consultant to Society of Film and Television Arts, 1959-75; Boston University, Boston, Mass., visiting professor of film, 1975-81, professor of film, 1981—. Visiting fellow, University of Sussex; Bingham Professor of Humanities, University of Louisville, 1973. Governor, London Film School, 1966-74; vice-chairman, National Panel for Film Festivals, 1974-78. Author. Has served on juries of international film festivals, appeared on television in many countries, and lectured widely. *Member:* Radio-writers' Association (chairman, 1962-64), Society of Authors (member of committee of management, 1954-57, 1965-68), Society of Lecturers (chairman, 1959-61), Screen and Television Writers Association. *Awards, honors:* Commander of Order of Merit of the Italian Republic, 1970; Order of Merit (First Class) of Federal Republic of Germany, 1971; D.Litt. from University of Sussex, 1971, and University of Louisville, 1979; D.F.A., New England College, 1974.

WRITINGS: Film, Pelican, 1944; (contributor) *Twenty Years of British Film,* Grey Walls Press, 1947; (editor) *Experiment in the Film,* Grey Walls Press, 1948, reprinted, Arno, 1970; (with Rachael Low) *The History of the British Film,* Volume I: *1896-1906,* Allen & Unwin, 1948; (with Paul Rotha) *Movie Parade, 1888-1949,* Studio Publications, 1950; (editor) *Three British Screenplays,* Methuen, 1950; *A Seat at the Cinema,* Evans Brothers, 1951; (editor with R.K.N. Baxter) *Cinema,* Penguin, 1952, reprinted, Arno, 1978; *On the Air,* Deutsch, 1953; *The Animated Film,* Sylvan, 1954; *The Film and the Public,* Pelican, 1955; (with John Huntley) *The Technique of Film Music,* Focal Press, 1957, 2nd edition, 1976; *The Dreamers* (novel), Simon & Schuster, 1957; (with John Halas) *The Technique of Film Animation,* Focal Press, 1959, 4th edition, 1976.

The Passion (novel), Heinemann, 1960; (with Heinrich Fraenkel) *Doctor Goebbels: His Life and Death,* Simon & Schuster, 1960, revised edition published as *Dr. Goebbels,* New English Library, 1968; *The Living Screen,* Harrap, 1961; (with Halas) *Design in Motion,* Studio Publications, 1962; (with Fraenkel) *Goering,* Simon & Schuster, 1962 (published in England as *Hermann Goering,* Heinemann, 1962); (with Fraenkel) *The Man Who Tried to Kill Hitler,* Coward, 1964 (published in England as *The July Plot: The Attempt in 1944 on Hitler's Life and the Men Behind It,* Bodley Head, 1964); (with Fraenkel) *Himmler,* Putnam, 1965 (published in England as *Heinrich Himmler,* Heinemann, 1965); *What Is a Film?,* William Macdonald, 1965; *New Cinema in Europe,* Dutton, 1966; *This Age of Communication,* Blackie & Son, 1966; (editor with A. William Bluem) *Television: The Creative Experience,* Hastings House, 1967 (published in England as *The Progress of Television,* Focal Press, 1967); (with Fraenkel) *The Incomparable Crime: Mass Extermination in the Twentieth Century: The Legacy of Guilt,* Putnam, 1967; *New Cinema in the USA,* Dutton, 1968; *Ellen Terry,* Putnam, 1968; *New Cinema in Britain,* Dutton, 1969; (with Fraenkel) *The Canaris Conspiracy: The Secret Resistance to Hitler in the German Army,* McKay, 1969.

S.S. and Gestapo: Rule by Terror, Ballantine, 1970; *Sarah Siddons,* Putnam, 1970; (with Halas) *Art in Movement,* Hastings House, 1970; (with Fraenkel) *The German Cinema,* Prae-

ger, 1971; *The Conspirators: 20 July 1944,* Ballantine, 1971; *Shakespeare and the Film,* Praeger, 1971, revised edition, A. S. Barnes, 1979; (with Fraenkel) *Hess: A Biography,* MacGibbon & Kee, 1971; (editor) *International Encyclopedia of Film,* Crown, 1972; *Goering,* Ballantine, 1972; (author of introduction) *Masterworks of the German Cinema,* Harper, 1974; *Charles Chaplin,* Little, Brown, 1974; (with Fraenkel) *The Hundred Days to Hitler,* St. Martin's, 1974 (published in England as *Seizure of Power: One Hundred Days to Hitler,* Dent, 1974); *Films and the Second World War,* A. S. Barnes, 1975; *The Trial of Annie Besant and Charles Bradlaugh,* Horizon Press, 1976; *Love Goddesses of the Movies,* Crescent, 1975; (with Fraenkel) *Inside Adolph Hitler,* Pinnacle Books, 1975, revised edition published as *Hitler: The Man and the Myth,* 1977; *Theater and Film: A Comparative Study of the Two Forms of Dramatic Art, and of the Problems of Adaptation of Stage Plays into Films,* Farleigh Dickinson University Press, 1979; *Ingmar Bergman,* Arno, 1980; *Art and Animation: The Story of Halas and Batchelor Animation Studio, 1940-1980,* Hastings House, 1980.

Also author with Louise Manvell of commentary to *The Country Life Book of Sailing Boats,* Country Life, 1962; author of "The July Plot," a television play based on his book of the same title, 1966. Editor, "National Cinema" series, Grey Walls Press, 1948-53. Contributor of articles to *Encyclopaedia Britannica* and film journals. Editor, *Penguin Film Review,* 1946-49, and Society of Film and Television Arts *Journal,* 1959-75; associate editor, *New Humanist,* 1967-75.

WORK IN PROGRESS: Image of Madness, a study, with Michael Fleming, of the portrayal of insanity in feature films.

SIDELIGHTS: Roger Manvell's work encompasses two distinct fields: film and theater and the history of the Third Reich. In both areas, Manvell receives critical praise. A *Times Literary Supplement* critic finds that *Ellen Terry,* a biography of the Victorian actress, "will probably be the standard work on Ellen Terry for a long time. . . . [Manvell] has made a useful contribution to the history of the English theatre and to our understanding of one of the greatest of our actresses." *The Canaris Conspiracy,* a study of German opposition to Nazi rule, "is a competent and admirably-written account, historical journalism of the best kind," comments another *Times Literary Supplement* reviewer.

BIOGRAPHICAL/CRITICAL SOURCES: Times Literary Supplement, April 13, 1967, August 10, 1967, May 9, 1968, July 17, 1969; *Best Sellers,* July 1, 1968, July 15, 1969, February 15, 1971; *New York Times Book Review,* May 26, 1968; *National Observer,* May 27, 1968; *Newsweek,* May 27, 1968.

*   *   *

MAPLE, Eric William 1915-

PERSONAL: Born January 22, 1915, in London, England; son of William Alfred and Edith Anne (Baker) Maple; married Dora Savage (a teacher), December 22, 1951; children: Alan. *Education:* Attended schools in Southend, England; primarily self-educated. *Politics:* Liberal. *Religion:* "Pantheist." *Home:* 52 Buckingham Rd., Wanstead, London E11 2EB, England.

CAREER: Employed in gas industry as accounts supervisor in Southend-on-Sea and London, England, 1929-66; writer. Witchcraft consultant; folklorist; lecturer; free-lance broadcaster, 1960—. *Military service:* British Army, 1940-46. *Member:* Folklore Society.

WRITINGS: The Dark World of Witches, R. Hale, 1962, A. S. Barnes, 1964; *The Realm of Ghosts,* A. S. Barnes, 1964; *The*

Domain of Devils, A. S. Barnes, 1966; *Magic, Medicine and Quackery*, A. S. Barnes, 1968; *Superstition and the Superstitious*, W. H. Allen, 1971, A. S. Barnes, 1972; *The Magic of Perfume: Aromatics and Their Esoteric Significance*, Samuel Weiser, 1973; *Incantations and Words of Power*, Samuel Weiser, 1974; *The Ancient Art of Occult Healing*, Samuel Weiser, 1974; *Witchcraft*, Octopus, 1974; *Deadly Magic*, Samuel Weiser, 1976; *Supernatural England*, R. Hale, 1977; *Monsters* (juvenile), Scimitar Books, 1978; *Ghosts* (juvenile), Scimitar Books, 1978; (with Lyn Myring) *Haunted Houses: Ghosts and Spectres*, Usborne, 1979; (with Eliot Humberstone) *Mysterious Powers and Strange Forces*, Usborne, 1979; *The Secret Lore of Plants and Flowers*, R. Hale, 1980; *Devils and Demons*, Pan Piccolo Books, 1981; *Old Wives Tales*, R. Hale, 1981.

Editorial consultant for seven children's books published by Usborne, 1977-80. Major contributor and consultant to *Man, Myth and Magic*, *Guide to Britain*, *Folklore Myths and Legends of Britain*, and *Strange Stories, Amazing Facts*, and to several Readers' Digest books. Contributor to numerous periodicals, including *Folklore Society Journal*, *Prediction*, and *Journal of the British Tourist Authority*.

WORK IN PROGRESS: A study of witchcraft links between New England and old England; *The Folklore of Shakespeare's England*; *Pagan Survivals*.

SIDELIGHTS: Eric William Maple wrote *CA:* "I have always been fascinated by the magical beliefs of the men and women I met—even the children are repositories of supernatural lore. This magic is a common bond uniting all races and creeds and therefore, possibly, the most democratic principle in the world.

"From gathering these beliefs I graduated to broadcasting them on radio and television and later to authorship. After fourteen years I find my interest undiminished for it is constantly renewed from the well of superstition in the minds of the folk.

"As a folklorist I am not consciously aware of having been unduly influenced by the writings of others for so much that is published in this field is a rehash of other books. (Incidentally in exploring the depths of black magic I have found a sense of humour invaluable.) Everything about people is important but most significant of all is the magic in their minds."

In 1979, Maple "toured the United States for the British Tourist Authority with presentations of haunted Britain."

BIOGRAPHICAL/CRITICAL SOURCES: Washington Post, October 25, 1979.

*   *   *

MARCOMBE, Edith Marion
See SHIFFERT, Edith (Marcombe)

*   *   *

MARKS, Mickey Klar

PERSONAL: Born in Brooklyn, N.Y.; daughter of Barnet J. and Pauline (Finklestein) Klar; married Nathan Harold Marks, 1935; children: Andrew Roger. *Education:* Attended New York University, three and a half years, and Columbia University, two years. *Home:* North Greenwich Rd., Armonk, N.Y. 10504.

CAREER: Writer. Has lectured in many schools and libraries. *Awards, honors:* Petry Prize, American Sonnets and Lyrics; Parents Book Club award.

WRITINGS: Hucklebones, Albert Whitman, 1950; *Let's Go to the Fair*, Albert Whitman, 1951; *Little Peter What's My Name,*

Book Creators, 1953; *Over the Shoulder Book*, Albert Whitman, 1953; *Fish on the Tide*, Childrens Press, 1956; *Fine Eggs and Fancy Chickens*, Holt, 1956; *The Holiday Shop*, Holt, 1958; *Strawhat Theater*, Knopf, 1960; *What Can I Buy?*, Dial, 1962; *Sand Sculpturing*, Dial, 1962; *Slate Sculpturing*, Dial, 1963; *Wax Sculpturing*, Dial, 1964; *Painting Free*, Dial, 1965; *Collage*, Dial, 1968; (with Edith Alberts) *Op-Tricks*, Lippincott, 1972; (with Stan Werner) *The Adventures of Edam Stilton* (musical play), Pioneer Drama, 1973; *The Spell of Malatesta* (play), Pioneer Drama, 1975; *Is It Soup Yet?* (play), Contemporary Drama, 1976; (with Werner) *Theatre in Education* (textbook), DOK Publishers, 1979. Also author of *Oh Susanna!*, Mattel. Author of cartoon movies, "Little Cut-Up," and "Flip Flap," both produced by Paramount. Contributor of over 500 short stories and articles to periodicals, including *Good Housekeeping*, *Woman's Day*, *Child Life*, *Calling All Girls*, and *Young Miss.*

SIDELIGHTS: A collection of Mickey Klar Marks's papers is housed in the McCain Library of the University of Southern Mississippi. *Avocational interests:* Sculpture, tennis, swimming, gardening, and dancing.

*   *   *

MARLOWE, Stephen   1928-
(Milton Lesser; pseudonyms: Adam Chase, Andrew Frazer, Darius John Granger, Jason Ridgeway, C. H. Thames, Stephen Wilder)

PERSONAL: Original name Milton Lesser; name legally changed in 1958; born August 7, 1928, in Brooklyn, N.Y.; son of Norman (a real estate broker) and Sylvia (Price) Lesser; married Leigh Lang, June 20, 1950 (divorced June, 1962); married Ann Humbert (a novelist), November 29, 1964; children: Deirdre, Robin (daughters). *Education:* College of William and Mary, B.A., 1949.

CAREER: Science fiction and crime novelist, 1954—. Scott Meredith Literary Agency, Inc., New York, N.Y., executive editor, 1949-50; College of William and Mary, Williamsburg, Va., writer-in-residence, 1974-75, 1980-81. *Military service:* U.S. Army, 1952-54. *Member:* Mystery Writers of America (vice-president of New York region, 1961-64; former member of board of directors), Crime Writers of America.

WRITINGS: Catch the Brass Ring, Ace Books, 1952; *Model for Murder*, Graphic, 1954; *Dead on Arrival*, Ace Books, 1954; *Turn Left for Murder*, Ace Books, 1955; (under pseudonym C. H. Thames) *Violence Is Golden*, Bouregy, 1956; *Blond Bait*, Avon, 1959; (under pseudonym Adam Chase) *The Golden Ape*, Bouregy, 1959; (under pseudonym Andrew Frazer) *Find Eileen Hardin—Alive*, Avon, 1960; (under pseudonym Jason Ridgeway) *Adam's Fall*, Pocket Books, 1960; (under pseudonym Andrew Frazer) *The Fall of Marty Moon*, Avon, 1961; (under pseudonym Jason Ridgeway) *People in Glass Houses*, Pocket Books, 1961; (under pseudonym Jason Ridgeway) *Hardly a Man Is Now Alive*, Pocket Books, 1961; *Passport to Peril*, Crest, 1961; *The Shining*, Trident, 1963; *The Search for Bruno Heidler*, Macmillan, 1966; *Come Over Red Rover*, Macmillan, 1968; *The Summit*, Geis, 1970; *Colossus*, Macmillan, 1972; *The Man with No Shadow*, Prentice-Hall, 1974; *The Cawthorn Journals*, Prentice-Hall, 1975; *Translation*, Prentice-Hall, 1976; *The Valkyrie Encounter*, Putnam, 1978.

"Chester Drum" series; all published by Gold Medal: *The Second Longest Night*, 1955; *Mecca for Murder*, 1956; *Trouble Is My Name*, 1956; *Murder Is My Dish*, 1957; *Killers Are My Meat*, 1957; *Terror Is My Trade*, 1958; *Violence Is My Business*, 1958; *Homicide Is My Game*, 1959; *Double in Trouble,*

1960; (with Richard S. Prather) *Danger Is My Line*, 1960; *Peril Is My Pay*, 1960; *Jeopardy Is My Job*, 1961; *Death Is My Comrade*, 1961; *Manhunt Is My Mission*, 1963; *Francesca*, 1963; *Drumbeat—Berlin*, 1964; *Drumbeat—Dominique*, 1965; *Drumbeat—Madrid*, 1966; *Drumbeat—Erica*, 1967; *Drumbeat—Marianne*, 1968.

Under name Milton Lesser: *Earthbound*, Winston, 1952; (editor) *Looking Forward* (science fiction anthology), Beechhurst Press, 1953; *The Star Seekers*, Winston, 1953; *Stadium beyond the Stars*, Holt, 1961; *Lost Worlds and Men Who Found Them*, Whitman Publishing, 1962; *Walt Disney's Strange Animals of Australia*, Whitman Publishing, 1963; *Secret of the Black Planet*, Belmont Books, 1965.

WORK IN PROGRESS: A novel, *1956*, for Arbor House.

SIDELIGHTS: Stephen Marlowe told *CA:* "Traveling is essential to my writing. The view of an outsider is one among several valid views in fiction, and it is the one I feel comfortable with. I've wandered on four continents over the past twenty years, not specifically researching any given novel but researching everything in range of my senses. I love high mountains and wide oceans. To become a ski-bum is often tempting, but I've never given in—although I do ski a great deal, usually in the Alps.

"I do not believe that 'creative writing'—whatever creative writing is—can be taught. But a reasonably successful commercial novelist brings a certain aura with him, an approach, a way of life, that shows students that writing is possible, not a mere dream. A writer who cares can also help talented students more quickly discover the talent and skills they have. Since the future of the novel as an art form always seems to be in jeopardy, and since I'm all for it lasting, I feel it an obligation to be a writer-in-residence from time to time.

"My wife Ann has published two novels and is working on a third. A married couple, both writers of novels, is, I guess, a rarity. We serve as each other's first-look editors and still manage to remain on far more than speaking terms. This may or may not be considered amazing. One day we'll do a novel together, but not yet.

"I'll continue to live, more or less, as an outsider to society, a state that Thomas Mann understood so well. It is one font of creativity. There are others, but I will leave them to other writers."

Marlowe's books have been published in 14 languages, including Finnish, Japanese, and Turkish.

AVOCATIONAL INTERESTS: Skiing, sailing, mountain hiking, cooking, history.

* * *

MARSH, (Edith) Ngaio 1899-1982

PERSONAL: First name is pronounced *Nye-o;* born April 23, 1899, in Christchurch, New Zealand; died February 18, 1982, in Christchurch; daughter of Henry Edmund and Rose Elizabeth (Seager) Marsh. *Education:* Attended St. Margaret's College, New Zealand, 1910-14, and Canterbury University College School of Art, 1915-20. *Religion:* Church of England. *Home:* 37 Valley Rd., Christchurch S.2, New Zealand. *Agent:* Harold Ober Associates, Inc., 40 East 49th St., New York, N.Y. 10017; and Hughes Massie Ltd., 69 Great Russell St., London WC1B 3DH, England.

CAREER: Actress with touring Shakespearean company in Australia and New Zealand, 1920-23; theatrical producer, 1923-

27; interior decorator in London, England, 1928-32; returned to New Zealand and lived there and in London, writing detective novels, 1933-82; D. D. O'Connor Theatre Management, producer, 1944-52; directed ten Shakespearean productions and many modern plays; director of first all-New Zealand Shakespearean company, Canterbury University College Student Players, 1946; also directed at Embassy Theatre, London, England, and on a professional tour of Australasia. Honorary lecturer in drama, Canterbury University College, 1948. Head section leader, Red Cross Transport Unit in New Zealand, 1939. *Member:* Royal Society of Arts (fellow), British Authors, Playwrights and Composers Society, P.E.N., Queen's Club (Christchurch). *Awards, honors:* Officer, Order of the British Empire, 1948; D.Litt., University of Canterbury, 1963; Dame Commander, Order of the British Empire, 1966; Grand Master Award, Mystery Writers of America, 1977.

WRITINGS—Detective novels; published by Little, Brown, except as indicated; reprinted by Aeonian Press: *A Man Lay Dead*, Bles, 1934, Sheridan, 1942, reprinted, 1976; *Enter a Murderer*, Bles, 1935, Sheridan, 1942, reprinted, 1976; (with Henry Jellett) *The Nursing-Home Murder*, Bles, 1935, Sheridan, 1941, reprinted, 1976; *Death in Ecstasy*, Bles, 1936, Sheridan, 1941, reprinted, 1976; *Vintage Murder*, Bles, 1937, Sheridan, 1940, reprinted, 1976; *Artists in Crime*, Furman, 1938, reprinted, 1976; *Death in a White Tie*, Furman, 1938, reprinted, 1976; *Overture to Death*, Furman, 1939, reprinted, 1976.

Death of a Peer, 1940, reprinted, 1976 (published in England as *Surfeit of Lampreys* [also see below], Collins, 1941); *Death at the Bar*, 1940, reprinted, 1976; *Death and the Dancing Footman*, 1941, reprinted, 1976; *Colour Scheme*, 1943, reprinted, 1976; *Died in the Wool*, 1945, reprinted, 1976; *Final Curtain* (originally published as serial in *Saturday Evening Post*, March 8-April 12, 1947), 1947, reprinted, 1976; *A Wreath for Rivera* (also see below), 1949, reprinted, 1976 (published in England as *Swing, Brother, Swing*, Collins, 1949).

Night at the Vulcan (also see below), 1951, reprinted, 1976 (published in England as *Opening Night*, Collins, 1951); *Spinsters in Jeopardy* (also see below), 1953, reprinted, 1976; *Scales of Justice* (also see below), 1955, reprinted, 1976; *Death of a Fool*, 1956, reprinted, 1976 (published in England as *Off with His Head*, Collins, 1957); *Singing in the Shrouds* (also see below), 1958, reprinted, 1976 (bound with *A Stir of Echoes*, by Richard Matheson, and *The Malignant Heart*, by Celestine Sibley, Walter J. Black, 1958); *False Scent* (also see below), 1959, reprinted, 1976 (bound with *The Man Who Followed Women*, by Bert and Dolores Hitchens, and *Tiger on My Back*, by Gordon and Mildred Nixon Gordon, Walter J. Black, 1960).

Three-Act Special (contains *A Wreath for Rivera*, *Spinsters in Jeopardy*, and *Night at the Vulcan*), 1960; *Another Three-Act Special* (contains *False Scent*, *Scales of Justice*, and *Singing in the Shrouds*), 1962; *Hand in Glove*, 1962, reprinted, 1976; *Dead Water*, 1963, reprinted, 1976; *Killer Dolphin*, 1966 (published in England as *Death at the Dolphin*, Collins, 1967); *Clutch of Constables*, Collins, 1968, Little, Brown, 1969.

When in Rome, Collins, 1970, Little, Brown, 1971; *Tied Up in Tinsel*, 1972; *Black as He's Painted*, 1975; *Last Ditch*, 1978; *Grave Mistake*, 1978; *Photo Finish*, 1980.

Nonfiction: (With Randal Matthew Burdon) *New Zealand*, Collins, 1942, reprinted, Aeonian Press, 1976; (contributor) Walter J. Turner, editor, *The British Commonwealth and Empire*, Collins, 1943; *A Play Toward: A Note on Play Production*, Caxton Press, 1946; *Perspectives: The New Zealander and the Visual Arts*, Auckland Gallery Associates, 1960; *Play Production*, R. E. Owen, Government Printer (New Zealand),

1960; *New Zealand* (juvenile), Macmillan, 1964; *Black Beech and Honeydew* (autobiography), Little, Brown, 1965.

Plays: (With Owen B. Howell) "Surfeit of Lampreys" (based on Marsh's novel of same title), produced in London in 1950; (with Eileen MacKay) "False Scent" (based on Marsh's novel of same title), produced in England in 1961; *The Christmas Tree* (juvenile), Religious Drama Society of Great Britain, 1962; "A Unicorn for Christmas," music by David Farquhar, produced in Australia in 1965; "Murder Sails at Midnight" (based on *Singing in the Shrouds*), produced in England in 1972. Also author of television play, "Evil Liver."

Contributor to anthologies, including *Queen's Awards 1946*, edited by Ellery Queen, Little, Brown, 1946, *Anthology 1969*, edited by Queen, Davis Publications, 1968, *Ellery Queen's Murdercade*, Random House, 1975, *Ellery Queen's Crime Wave*, Putnam, 1976. Contributor of short stories, travel articles, and reviews to periodicals.

WORK IN PROGRESS: Another detective novel.

SIDELIGHTS: Ngaio Marsh, a well-traveled mystery writer and theatrical producer, wrote detective stories which have been called the best of their kind. Her theatrical background and the wide variety of people and scenery she encountered in her travels provided a rich source of material for her novels, which have received world-wide recognition. A *Spectator* critic praised Marsh's "extraordinary gift for the drawing of characters just this side of eccentricity" as well as her "amazing sense of the visual: her atmospheres and scenic set pieces are always pure magic."

In her first novel, *A Man Lay Dead,* Marsh created Inspector Roderick Alleyn, a practical, charming detective who has captured readers' imaginations and contributed to Marsh's enduring popularity. A tall, lean man with dark hair, Alleyn belongs to the ranks of the socially privileged, yet he possesses little social snobbery. According to *New York Times* writer Thomas Lask, Alleyn has a "keen eye" and an "unflappable, cool style" which always uncovers the guilty person. Although Alleyn appears in a majority of her novels, Marsh once stated that she never grew tired of him: "It would be an affectation to say I'm sick of him. I'm not. I'm completely crazy about him."

Some of Marsh's novels are set in the theatre, and most of them make reference to Shakespeare's plays. *Killer Dolphin* (the title refers to a crumbling nineteenth-century London theatre where a murder is committed) contains a stage presentation of Shakespeare's life. In the *New York Times Book Review,* Anthony Boucher stated that Marsh "writes about the London theatrical scene delightfully, vividly and inimitably. . . . [*Killer Dolphin*] is a joy absolute."

The 1980 publication of *Photo Finish* prompted *Washington Post Book World*'s Jean M. White to write: "It is good news, indeed, to report that . . . the 81-year-old queen dowager of British mystery is the same stylish, witty and lively writer that she has been over a span of nearly five decades and some 30 novels. . . . She hasn't lost her touch." Newgate Callendar of the *New York Times Book Review* echoed White's opinion: "Marsh . . . has been writing mystery stories since 1934, but you wouldn't know it from her prose. By some kind of miracle she has retained stylistic freshness. . . . Characterizations are, as always, sharply drawn, and there is a great deal of quiet humor. *Photo Finish* is a book that should make all readers happy."

AVOCATIONAL INTERESTS: Art, Shakespeareana.

BIOGRAPHICAL/CRITICAL SOURCES: Wilson Library Bulletin, September, 1940; *Saturday Evening Post,* March 8, 1947; *New York Times Book Review,* June 5, 1960, September 25, 1966, April 7, 1971, January 18, 1981; *Newsweek,* June 13, 1960; *Christian Science Monitor,* November 2, 1965, December 4, 1978; *Times Literary Supplement,* June 29, 1967; *Spectator,* December 12, 1970, May 4, 1974; *Saturday Review,* April 24, 1971; *Detroit News,* June 4, 1972; *National Observer,* July 15, 1972; *New York Times,* July 22, 1972, January 26, 1979; *Contemporary Literary Criticism,* Volume VII, Gale, 1977; *Washington Post Book World,* November 16, 1980.

OBITUARIES: New York Times, February 19, 1982; *Chicago Tribune,* February 19, 1982; *Washington Post,* February 19, 1982.

*   *   *

MARSHALL, Lovat
See DUNCAN, W(illiam) Murdoch

*   *   *

MARTIN, Dorothy   1921-

PERSONAL: Born March 19, 1921, in Chisholm, Minn.; daughter of John Cameron and Aimee (Sanborn) McKay; married Alfred Martin (vice-president and dean of education at Moody Bible Institute), October 9, 1945; children: Dorothy (Mrs. Timothy Sumners), John, Sarah (Mrs. James Ibison). *Education:* Macalester College, A.B., 1943; New York Theological Seminary, M.R.E., 1945. *Politics:* Republican. *Religion:* Evangelical Protestant. *Home:* 1502 Cherrycrest Lane, Dallas, Tex. 75228.

CAREER: Writer. Editor and proofreader for Moody Press and Moody Correspondence School.

WRITINGS—Published by Moody, except as indicated: *Christian Etiquette for Everyday Living,* 1969, published as *Etiquette for Everyday Living,* 1974; *No Place to Hide,* 1971; *Creative Family Worship,* 1976; *Moody Bible Institute: God's Power in Action,* 1977.

Personal Bible study guides; with husband, Alfred Martin: *The Bible,* 1971; *The Lord Jesus Christ,* 1973; *The Holy Spirit,* 1974.

Adolescent fiction: *A Shining Tomorrow,* Zondervan, 1963; *Edge of Belonging,* 1963; *Light at the Top of the Stairs,* 1974; *The Other Side of Yesterday,* 1978.

"Peggy" series: *New Life for Peggy,* 1957; *Open Doors for Peggy,* 1958; *More Answers for Peggy,* 1959; *Mystery Solved for Peggy,* 1962; *Hopes Fulfilled for Peggy,* 1963; *Wider Horizons for Peggy,* 1964; *Chapter Closed for Peggy,* 1966; *Faith at Work for Peggy,* 1970; *Prayers Answered for Peggy,* 1976.

"Vickie" series: *Mystery of the Missing Bracelets,* 1980; *Mystery on the Fourteenth Floor,* 1980; *Mystery of the Jade Earring,* 1980; *The Mystery of the Empty House,* 1981; *Mystery in the Neighbor's Apartment,* 1982.

Contributor to church publications.

WORK IN PROGRESS: A biography; two novels; the sixth and final book in the "Vickie" series.

SIDELIGHTS: "Fiction is my first love, both to read and to write," Dorothy Martin told *CA.* "I am never bored or lonely or at loose ends with characters—people—living with me, some of whom are as real as my own children. One of the best ways to give guidance to young people seeking to establish values is a well-written novel about people.''

* * *

MARTIN, L(eslie) John 1921-

PERSONAL: Born January 5, 1921, in Budapest, Hungary; U.S. citizen; son of Joseph (an accountant) and Elizabeth (Kiss) Martin; married Lois A. Henze (an associate school superintendent), March 22, 1951; children: Keith D., Brian J. *Education:* American University, Cairo, Egypt, B.A., 1947; University of Oregon, graduate study, 1948-49; University of Minnesota, M.A., 1951, Ph.D., 1955. *Politics:* Democrat. *Religion:* Episcopalian. *Home:* 5313 Iroquois Rd., Bethesda, Md. 20816. *Office:* College of Journalism, University of Maryland, College Park, Md. 20742.

CAREER: Newspaperman and foreign correspondent in the Near East, 1941-47; University of Minnesota, Minneapolis, assistant director of International Relations Center, 1952-53; University of Nebraska, Lincoln, assistant professor of journalism, 1954-57; *Detroit Free Press,* Detroit, Mich., copy editor, 1957-58; University of Florida, Gainesville, professor of journalism and director of research and graduate studies in journalism and communication, 1958-61; U.S. Information Agency, Washington, D.C., chief of Near East and South Asia Division Office of Research, 1961-66, coordinator of overseas research, 1966-67, chief of Program Analysis Division, 1967-69; University of Maryland, College Park, professor of journalism, 1969—, acting dean, 1975, 1979-80. Research associate with legislative council of Nebraska Legislature, summer, 1955; adjunct professor at American University, 1966-67; lecturer at U.S. Veterans Administration hospitals, 1972. *Military service:* British Army, 1944-45.

MEMBER: International Communication Association, Association for Education in Journalism (member of executive committee of International Communication Division, 1973-74), Society for Professional Journalists, American Association for Public Opinion Research (president of Washington-Baltimore chapter, 1979-80), Kappa Tau Alpha. *Awards, honors:* Distinguished service award from Sigma Delta Chi, 1958, for *International Propaganda;* Pearl Prize from British Council.

WRITINGS: (With Harold L. Nelson and Thomas Copeland) *Analysis of TIME's Performance in Reporting the News,* three volumes, Communications Research Center, University of Minnesota, 1954; *International Propaganda: Its Legal and Diplomatic Control,* University of Minnesota Press, 1958; (editor) *Propaganda in International Affairs* (annals), American Academy of Political and Social Science, 1971; *Radio Listening and Other Media Habits in the Soviet Union of Ethnic German Emigrants,* U.S. Information Agency, 1975; (editor) *Role of the Mass Media in American Politics* (annals), American Academy of Political and Social Science, 1976; *Assessment of ICA Arabic Language Wireless File,* U.S. Information Agency, 1978.

Contributor: Heinz-Dietrich Fischer and John C. Merrill, editors, *International Communication,* Hastings House, 1970; Fischer and Merrill, editors, *International and Intercultural Communication,* Hastings House, 1976; *The Art and Science of Psychological Operations: Case Studies of Military Application,* Volume II, Department of the Army, 1976; Everette Dennis, Arnold Ismach, and Donald Gillmor, editors, *Enduring Issues in Mass Communication,* West Publishing, 1977; Joseph S. Roucek, editor, *Social Control for the 1980s,* Greenwood Press, 1978; Harold D. Lasswell, Daniel Lerner, and Hans Speier, editors, *Propaganda and Communication in World*

History, Volume III, University of Hawaii Press, 1980; *Science Indicators, 1980,* National Science Foundation, 1981; *Handbook of Political Communication,* Sage Publications, 1981; *The Twelfth Board Report: National Science Board,* National Science Foundation, in press.

Contributor to *Encyclopaedia Britannica* and *Worldmark Encyclopedia of the Nations.* Contributor of articles and reviews to periodicals, including *Journalism Quarterly, Gazette, Journalism Educator, Annals of the American Academy of Political and Social Science, Public Opinion,* and *Journal of Politics.* Copy editor, *Rochester Democrat and Chronicle,* summers, 1956-57; member of editorial staff, *St. Paul Pioneer-Press,* 1959, and *Louisville Courier-Journal,* 1960. *Journalism Quarterly,* editor of "Annotated Foreign Bibliography," 1953-64, member of editorial advisory board, 1972—, associate editor, 1977—; *International Communication Bulletin,* member of editorial advisory board, 1966-74, editor, 1974—. Member of editorial advisory board, *Journalism Monographs,* 1973—; contributing editor, *Communication Yearbook,* Volumes III and IV, 1978-80.

WORK IN PROGRESS: International Communication, for Wiley; editing, with Anju Chaudhary, *Comparative Mass Media Systems,* for Longman; with John C. Merrill, *Global Journalism,* for Longman.

SIDELIGHTS: L. John Martin writes: "My major interest is in international and cross-cultural communication. I also have a lifelong interest in the Near East, where I grew up.''

* * *

MARTIN, Tony 1942-

PERSONAL: Born February 21, 1942, in Trinidad; son of Claude G. and Vida (Scope) Martin. *Education:* Honourable Society of Gray's Inn, Barrister-at-Law, 1965; University of Hull, B.Sc. (with honors), 1968; Michigan State University, M.A., 1970, Ph.D., 1973. *Office:* Department of Black Studies, Wellesley College, Wellesley, Mass. 02181.

CAREER: Called to English Bar, 1966, and to Trinidad Bar, 1969; accounts clerk in Water Department, Trinidad Public service, 1961; accounts clerk, Office of the Prime Minister, Federal Government of the West Indies, Trinidad, 1961-62; master of Latin, French, Spanish, English, history, and geography, St. Mary's College, Trinidad, 1962-63; lecturer in economics and politics, Cipriani Labour College, Trinidad, 1968-69; Michigan State University, East Lansing, instructor in history, 1970-71; University of Michigan—Flint, assistant professor of history and coordinator of African-Afro-American studies program, 1971-73; Wellesley College, Wellesley, Mass., associate professor, 1973-79, professor of black studies, 1979—, chairman of department, 1976-78 and 1981—. Visiting associate professor at Brandeis University, fall, 1974, and at University of Minnesota, fall, 1975. *Member:* Association for the Study of Afro-American Life and History, African Heritage Studies Association, Association of Caribbean Historians, African Studies Association of the West Indies.

WRITINGS: (Contributor) John Henrik Clarke, editor, *Marcus Garvey and the Vision of Africa,* Random House, 1974; *Race First: The Ideological and Organizational Struggles of Marcus Garvey and the Universal Negro Improvement Association,* Greenwood Press, 1976; (co-author) *Rare Afro-Americana: A Reconstruction of the Adger Library,* G. K. Hall, 1981; *The Caribbean and Africa,* Caribbean Research Unit, 1981; *Literary Garveyism: The Political Works and Literary Influence of Marcus Garvey,* G. K. Hall, 1982.

Also author of pamphlets. Contributor of more than twenty articles and reviews to professional journals, including *Negro History Bulletin, American Historical Review, Journal of Modern African Studies, African Studies Review, Journal of Negro History, Mazungumzo, Race,* and *Journal of Human Relations.* Guest editor, *Pan-African Journal,* 1974.

WORK IN PROGRESS: Amy Ashwood Garvey: Pan-Africanist, Feminist and Wife Number One, for Fairleigh Dickinson University; *Black American Voluntary Organizations: A Historical Dictionary,* for Greenwood Press.

*   *   *

MARTINDALE, Don (Albert) 1915-

PERSONAL: Born February 9, 1915, in Marinette, Wis.; son of Don Lucian and Elsie Caroline (Tetzloff) Martindale; married Edith Plotkin (a social worker), February 2, 1943. *Education:* University of Wisconsin, B.A. (summa cum laude), 1939, M.A., 1940, Ph.D., 1948. *Religion:* Methodist. *Home:* 2900 West Owasso Blvd., St. Paul, Minn. 55112. *Office:* Department of Sociology, University of Minnesota, Minneapolis, Minn. 55455.

CAREER: University of Wisconsin—Madison, instrutor in sociology, 1946-48; University of Minnesota, Minneapolis, assistant professor, 1948-52, associate professor, 1952-54, professor of sociology, 1954—. *Military service:* U.S. Army, 1942-46; became captain. *Member:* American Sociological Association, American Academy of Political and Social Science, American Association of University Professors, Phi Beta Kappa. *Awards, honors:* D.L., Memorial University of Newfoundland.

WRITINGS: (With Elio D. Monachesi) *Elements of Sociology,* Harper, 1951; *The Nature and Types of Sociological Theory,* Houghton, 1960, 2nd edition, 1981; *American Social Structure,* Appleton-Century-Crofts, 1960; *American Society,* Van Nostrand, 1960; *Social Life and Cultural Change,* Van Nostrand, 1962; *Community, Character and Civilization,* Free Press of Glencoe, 1963; (editor and contributor) *Functionalism in the Social Sciences,* (monograph), American Academy of Political and Social Science, 1965; *Institutions, Organizations and Mass Society,* Houghton, 1966; (editor) *National Character in the Perspective of the Social Sciences,* American Academy of Political and Social Science, 1967; (with R. Galen Hanson) *Small Town and the Nation: The Conflict of Local and Translocal Forces,* Greenwood Press, 1969.

(Author of preface) Franklin Giddings, *Principles of Sociology,* Johnson Reprint, 1970; (with wife, Edith Martindale) *The Social Dimensions of Mental Illness, Alcoholism and Drug Dependence,* Greenwood Press, 1972; (with E. Martindale) *Social Psychiatry in Minnesota: Coping with Mental Illness, Alcoholism, and Drug Dependence,* Windflower, 1972; *American Society,* Robert E. Krieger, 1972; (with E. Martindale) *Psychiatry and the Law: The Crusade against Involuntary Hospitalization,* Windflower, 1973; *Sociological Theory and the Problem of Values,* C. E. Merrill, 1974; *Prominent Sociologists since World War II,* C. E. Merrill, 1975; (editor with Raj P. Mohan) *Handbook of Contemporary Developments in World Sociology,* Greenwood Press, 1975; *The Romance of a Profession,* Windflower, 1976; (with Mohan) *Ideals and Realities: Some Problems of Contemporary Social Science,* Intercontinental Press, 1980; *Ideals and Realities of Ph.D. Advising,* Intercontinental Press, 1980.

Editor and translator: (With Hans Gerth) Max Weber, *Ancient Judaism,* Free Press of Glencoe, 1952; (with Gerth) Max Weber, *Religions of India,* Free Press of Glencoe, 1958; (with Gerald Neuwirth; and contributor) Max Weber, *The City,* Free Press of Glencoe, 1958; (with Neuwirth and Johannes Riedel; and contributor) Max Weber, *The Rational and Social Foundations of Music,* Southern Illinois University Press, 1958.

Contributor: Howard P. Becker and Reuben Hill, editors, *Family, Marriage and Parenthood,* Heath, 1955; Alvin Boskoff and Becker, editors, *Modern Sociological Theory,* Holt, 1957; *Mathematics and the Social Sciences* (monograph), American Academy of Political and Social Science, 1963; George Zollschan and Walter Hirsch, editors, *Explorations in Social Change,* Houghton, 1964; Herbert A. Otto, editor, *Explorations in Human Potentialities,* C. C Thomas, 1966; A. Chakravorti, editor, *India since 1946,* Allied Publishers (Bombay), 1967; Gerald Theilbar and Saul Feldman, editors, *Issues in Social Inequality,* Little, Brown, 1972; Zollschan and Hirsch, editors, *Social Change,* Wiley, 1976.

Editor of sociology monograph series for Greenwood Press. Contributor to the *Annals* of American Academy of Political and Social Science. Contributor to scholarly journals, including *Alpha Kappa Deltan, Indian Journal of Social Research,* and *International Journal of Contemporary Sociology.*

WORK IN PROGRESS: The Monologue: Hans Gerth (1908-1978), a Memoir.

SIDELIGHTS: "Writing is an agonizing business," Don Martindale told *CA,* "but it is the only way I know to find out what one thinks." Martindale's writings have been translated into Italian, Japanese, and Spanish.

BIOGRAPHICAL/CRITICAL SOURCES: International Journal of Contemporary Sociology, April-July, 1974.

*   *   *

MARX, Herbert L(ewis), Jr. 192-

PERSONAL: Born February 1, 1922, in Albany, N.Y.; son of Herbert Lewis and Ruth (Naumburg) Marx; married Hilda Fisher, January 1, 1948 (divorced, 1973); married Dorothy Sachs (a personnel administrator), June 12, 1973; children: (first marriage) Jonathan B., Timothy S., Alison L. *Education:* Dartmouth College, A.B., 1943; New York University, M.B.A., 1955. *Home and office:* 20 Waterside Plaza, New York, N.Y. 10010.

CAREER: Albany Times-Union, Albany, N.Y., reporter, 1941; U.S. Office of Strategic Services, assignments in Washington, D.C., London, England, and Paris, France, 1942-45; Scholastic Magazines, New York, N.Y., associate editor and national affairs editor, 1945-51; General Cable Corp., Greenwich, Conn., assistant to the director of personnel relations, 1951-52, personnel manager, 1952-56, assistant plant manager, 1956-58, assistant director of personnel relations, 1958-68, director of personnel relations, 1968-69, director of industrial relations, 1969-71, vice president of industrial relations, 1971-74; labor-management arbitrator and fact-finder, 1975—. Permanent arbitrator for U.S. Postal Service and Postal Unions (Northeast Region) and National Railroad Adjustment Board; member of arbitration panels and fact-finding and mediation panels. Instructor, New York State School of Industrial and Labor Relations Credit and Certification Program; adjunct professor of labor-management relations, Pace University Graduate School of Business. *Member:* International Industrial Relations Association, National Academy of Arbitrators, Industrial Relations Research Association (president of New York chapter, 1972-73), Society of Professionals in Dispute Resolution, Society of Silurians, Veterans of the Office of Strategic Services, Phi Beta Kappa, Beta Gamma Delta.

WRITINGS: Facing Military Service (pamphlet), Oxford Book Co., 1953; (contributor) Bargaining Today, Bureau of National Affairs, 1971.

Editor; all published by H. W. Wilson: The Welfare State, 1950; American Labor Unions: Organization, Aims, and Power, 1950; Universal Conscription for Essential Service, 1951; Gambling in America, 1952; Television and Radio in American Life, 1953; Defense and National Security, 1955; Community Planning, 1956; State and Local Government, 1962; American Labor Today, 1965; Collective Bargaining for Public Employees, 1969; The American Indian: A Rising Ethnic Force, 1973; The World Food Crisis, 1975; Religions in America, 1977.

Contributor of articles to periodicals, including Factory, Business Week, New York Herald Tribune, Nation, Foreman's Letter, and Mill & Factory.

WORK IN PROGRESS: Preparing the arbitration section of Handbook of Health Care Personnel Management, for Aspen Systems Corp.

*   *   *

MARX, Melvin H(erman)   1919-

PERSONAL: Born June 8, 1919, in Brooklyn, N.Y.; married September 5, 1948; children: Diana, Christine, Ellen, James. Education: Washington University, St. Louis, Mo., A.B., 1940, M.A., 1941, Ph.D., 1943. Home: 604 Scott Blvd., Columbia, Mo. 65201. Office: University of Missouri, Columbia, Mo. 65211.

CAREER: University of Missouri—Columbia, member of psychology department, 1944—. Member: American Psychological Association, Midwestern Psychological Association, Psychonomic Society, American Association of University Professors, Phi Beta Kappa, Sigma Xi. Awards, honors: Research Career Award, National Institute of Mental Health, 1964.

WRITINGS: (Editor) Psychological Theory, Macmillan, 1951, published as Theories in Contemporary Psychology, 1963, 2nd edition (with Felix E. Goodson), 1976; (with W. A. Hillix) Systems and Theories in Psychology, McGraw, 1963, 3rd edition, 1979; (with Tom M. Tombaugh) Motivation: Psychological Principles and Educational Implications, Chandler, 1967; Learning, three volumes, Macmillan, 1969-70; Introduction to Psychology, Macmillan, 1976; (editor with M. E. Bunch) Fundamentals and Applications of Learning, Macmillan, 1977.

*   *   *

MARX, Robert F(rank)   1936-

PERSONAL: Born December 8, 1936, in Pittsburgh, Pa.; son of Frank J. and Mary Ann (Salopeck) Marx; married Mary Stanford (an actress and dancer); married second wife, Jenifer Grant (a writer), 1970; children: (first marriage) Cheryl; (second marriage) Hilary. Education: Attended Los Angeles City College, 1951-53, and University of Maryland. Politics: Democrat. Religion: Roman Catholic. Home and office: 330 Thyme St., Satellite Beach, Fla. 32937.

CAREER: Marine archaeologist and naval historian. Leader of underwater and land archaeological expeditions in Mexico, South America, Spain, France, United States, the Caribbean, Bahamas, Indian Ocean, Australia, and Nova Scotia. In 1955, discovered off Cape Hatteras, the USS Monitor of the Civil

War; in 1962 was navigator of the Columbus replica, Nina II, following the route of Columbus to America; in 1964 attempted in replica of 10th century Viking ship to reach America from Yugoslavia, but a gale broke up the ship off Tunisia; in 1968 discovered two shipwrecks of Columbus which were lost in St. Anne's Bay, Jamaica in 1504; in 1969 was organizer and captain of a voyage of replica of 10th century Gokstad Viking ship, from Limerick, Ireland to Gibraltar. Visiting lecturer in underwater archaeology to Scripps Institution of Oceanography, 1974, and University of California at San Diego, 1974-75. Director of research and salvage, Real Eight Co., Inc., 1968-71; vice-president, Seafinders, Inc., 1971-74; president, Sea World Enterprises, Inc., 1974-76; expedition leader, L.O.S.T., Inc., 1978; director of operations, Phoenician Explorations, 1979—. Consultant to International Minerals and Chemicals Corp., 1959-60, Ocean Industry Insurers, Ltd., 1971, and International Oceanographic Foundation, 1974. Military service: U.S. Marine Corps, 1953-56; ran diving school; became sergeant.

MEMBER: American Institute of Nautical Archaeology, National Maritime Historical Society, Council of Underwater Archaeology, American Littoral Society, Underwater Society of America, Society for Historical Archaeology, Sea Research Society, Society for Nautical Research, American Scandinavian Foundation, Escuela de Estudios Hispano-Americano, Academia Real de la Historia, Club de Exploraciones Deportivas Acuaticas de Mexico, Caribbean Research Institute, Jamaican Historical Society, Underwater Exploration Society of Israel, Explorer's Club, Adventurer's Club, Save the Dolphin Foundation.

WRITINGS—Published by World Publishing, except as indicated: Historia de Isla de Cozumel, [Merida, Yucatan], 1959; Following Columbus: The Voyage of the Nina II, 1964; The Battle of the Spanish Armada, 1588, 1965; The Battle of Lepanto, 1571, 1966; They Dared the Deep: A History of Diving, 1967; Always Another Adventure, 1967; Pirate Port: The Story of the Sunken City of Port Royal, 1967; The Treasure Fleets of the Spanish Main, 1968; Clay Smoking Pipes Recovered from the Sunken City of Port Royal: October 1, 1967-March 31, 1968, Jamaica National Trust Commission, 1968; Reports on the Sunken City of Port Royal, Jamaica National Trust Commission, 1968; Wine Glasses Recovered from the Sunken City of Port Royal: May 1, 1966-March 31, 1968, Jamaica National Trust Commission, 1968; Shipwrecks in Florida Waters, Scott Publishing, 1969; (compiler) E. L. Towle, editor, Shipwrecks of the Virgin Islands, 1523-1825, Caribbean Research Institute, 1969.

Shipwrecks of the Western Hemisphere, 1492-1825, 1971, 2nd edition, McKay, 1975; Sea Fever, Doubleday, 1972; Fort Royal Rediscovered, Doubleday, 1973; The Lure of Sunken Treasure, McKay, 1973; Underwater Dig: Manual of Underwater Archaeology, McKay, 1975; Secrets Beneath the Sea, Belmont-Tower, 1975; Capture of the Spanish Plate Fleet: 1628, McKay, 1976; Still More Adventures, Mason Charter, 1976; Buried Treasures of the United States, McKay, 1978; Into the Deep: A History of Man's Underwater Explorations, Van Nostrand, 1978; Spanish Treasures in Florida Waters, Mariner Press, 1978; Diving for Adventure, McKay, 1979; (with wife, Jenifer Marx) Pre-Columbian Voyages to America, Stein & Day, 1979; (with J. Marx) Gold: From the Dawn of Time to the Fall of Rome, McKay, 1980; Buried Treasures of the Spanish Main, McKay, 1980; (with J. Marx) Gold: From the Fall of the Roman Empire to the Present, McKay, 1982; (with J. Marx) Pirates, Privateers and Bucaneers of the Spanish Main, Van Nostrand, 1982. Also author of The Discovery and Excavation of the Treasure Galleon Maravilla, 1980.

Contributor of over 500 articles to numerous periodicals including *Saturday Evening Post, Travel, Skin Diver, Cavalier, Paris Match, Stern,* and *Epoca.* Adventure editor, *Saturday Evening Post,* 1963; archaeology editor, *Argosy,* 1967-78; contributing editor, *Dive,* 1965-74, and *Aquarius,* 1972-76.

BIOGRAPHICAL/CRITICAL SOURCES: Clay Blair, Jr., *Diving for Pleasure and Treasure,* World Publishing, 1960; *Saturday Evening Post,* December 14, 1964; *New York Times Book Review,* August 6, 1967.

*   *   *

MASON, Herbert Molloy, Jr.   1927-

PERSONAL: Born October 24, 1927, in Lockney, Tex.; son of Herbert Molloy (a colonel in the U.S. Air Force) and Maude (Cheney) Mason; married Rigmor Aase Hansen (a painter); children: Berit Lynne. *Education:* Studied at American University of Beirut, 1947-48, L'Alliance Francaise, Paris, France, 1949; Trinity University, San Antonio, Tex., A.B. in Journalism, 1951. *Agent:* Paul R. Reynolds, Inc., 12 East 41st St., New York, N.Y. 10017.

CAREER: Radio Station KONO, San Antonio, Tex., news department, 1951-52; *True* (magazine), New York, N.Y., aviation editor, 1953-62; free-lance writer, 1962—. *Military service:* U.S. Marine Corps, 1944-46.

WRITINGS: The Lafayette Escadrille, Random House, 1964; *High Flew the Falcons,* Lippincott, 1965; *The Commandos,* Duell, Sloan & Pearce, 1966; *Bold Men, Far Horizons,* Lippincott, 1966; *The Texas Rangers,* Meredith, 1967; *Famous Firsts in Explorations,* Putnam, 1967; *The New Tigers,* McKay, 1967; *The Great Pursuit,* Random House, 1970; *Duel for the Sky,* Grosset, 1970; *Death from the Sea,* Dial, 1972; *The Rise of the Luftwaffe,* Dial, 1973; *Missions of Texas,* Oxmoor House, 1974; *The U.S. Air Force,* Charter, 1975; *Secrets of the Supernatural,* Four Winds, 1976; *The Fantastic World of Ants,* McKay, 1977; *To Kill the Devil,* Norton, 1979; *War in the Desert,* Viking, 1982.

SIDELIGHTS: Herbert Mason has flown in numerous types of historical aircraft, from World War I vintage to 1000-miles-per-hour Air Force jets. He has lived and traveled in thirty countries and wrote his first two books while spending two years in Norway. He is proficient in Spanish, Norwegian, and basic Arabic.

*   *   *

MASTERMAN, John Cecil   1891-1977

PERSONAL: Born January 12, 1891, in Kingston Hill, Surrey, England; died June 6, 1977; son of John (a captain, Royal Navy) and Edith Margaret (Hughes) Masterman. *Education:* Attended Royal Navy Colleges at Osborne and Dartmouth; Worcester College, Oxford, B.A., 1913, M.A., 1914. *Religion:* Church of England. *Agent:* Curtis Brown Ltd., 1 Craven Hill, London W2 3EW, England.

CAREER: Oxford University, Oxford, England, lecturer and tutor at Christ Church, 1913-47, provost of Worcester College, 1947-61, vice-chancellor of university, 1957-58. Adviser on personnel matters, Birfield Ltd., London, England, beginning 1961. Fellow, Eton College; governor, Wellington College. *Military service:* British Navy, World War I; prisoner of war in Germany, 1914-18. Intelligence Corps, 1940-45; directed British and Allied counterintelligence units; became major. *Awards, honors:* Order of British Empire, 1944, Knight Bachelor, 1959; LL.D., University of Toronto; D.C.L., University of King's College.

WRITINGS: An Oxford Tragedy, Gollancz, 1933; *Fate Cannot Harm Me,* Gollancz, 1935, Penguin (New York), 1940; *Marshall Ney* (five-act play), Cobden-Sanderson, 1937; *To Teach the Senators Wisdom; or, An Oxford Guide Book,* Oxford University Press, 1952; *The Case of the Four Friends: A Diversion in Pre-Detection,* Hodder & Stoughton, 1957, British Book Centre, 1959; *Bits and Pieces,* Hodder & Stoughton, 1961; *The Double-Cross System in the War of 1939-1945,* Yale University Press, 1971; *On the Chariot Wheel* (autobiography), Oxford University Press, 1975.

SIDELIGHTS: During World War II, John Cecil Masterman was, a *Newsweek* writer reports, "a master spy in the British counterespionage unit that foiled German spy efforts. . . . [He was head of the Twenty Committee (from the Roman numeral XX, symbolizing double-cross) that] caught German spies in England and converted them into double agents who succeeded in misleading the Nazis consistently without rousing their suspicions." A *New York Times* reporter further explains Masterman's wartime activities: "As deputy chief of British Intelligence, known as MI5, [Masterman] ran a network of double agents that infiltrated the German system. Their crowning achievement . . . was to lead the Germans into thinking that the 1944 Allied invasion of Europe would take place near Calais and not in Normandy. As a result many German troops were retained near Calais."

In August of 1941, Masterman's group also uncovered clues that Pearl Harbor might be attacked by the Japanese if the United States became involved in World War II. Unfortunately, the significance of this information was not fully grasped at the time it was received.

Masterman recounted his World War II activities in *The Double-Cross System in the War of 1939-1945.* Although he wrote the manuscript in 1945, at the request of several British security chiefs it was not released for general publication until 1971. While Masterman had originally agreed that for security reasons the manuscript's publication should be delayed, he "became convinced," according to a *Publishers Weekly* writer, that "as time went on, the need for secrecy . . . steadily receded, and the need to show the security services' genuine record of achievement became urgent. In the 1950s and early 1960s, the services' reputation was terribly damaged by a series of defections and scandals. The very existence of intelligence services came under attack. Sir John found many people, in and out of government, who agreed with him that the story of how the double-agent aspect of intelligence had contributed to saving Britain and defeating Hitler should be told."

Beginning in 1961, Masterman tried to obtain clearance from the British government for the publication of his manuscript. But the British authorities blocked his every move in that direction. He then began to consider the possibility of publishing his book outside of England. He showed his manuscript to the Yale University Press's Chester Kerr who did not know at the time that it was a classified, top-secret document protected under Crown copyright protection. When Yale University Press agreed to publish Masterman's report, Kerr went to England to arrange the details. There he was confronted by British authorities who pointed out the legal problems involved in the publication of this work.

Kerr enlisted the help of several distinguished lawyers who negotiated with, and finally persuaded, the British Government to allow publication. According to the *Publishers Weekly* writer: "The government people suggested several dozen small exclusions; Sir John and Yale agreed to about a third of these. At every point possible, the government people accepted Sir John's wishes. Their respect for him as 'our distinguished former public servant' was evident. It was clear, too, that they readily found common ground with the Yale representatives and were sensitive to Yale's efforts to handle a delicate matter with the dignity it deserved.'' Finally all sides agreed with the completed version and the presses started.

BIOGRAPHICAL/CRITICAL SOURCES: Publishers Weekly, February 7, 1972; *New York Times,* June 7, 1977; *Newsweek,* June 20, 1977; *Time,* June 20, 1977.†

*   *   *

MATEJKO, Alexander J.   1924-

PERSONAL: Born July 21, 1924, in Warsaw, Poland; son of Peter (an engineer) and Maria (a lawyer; maiden name, Wroblewska) Matejko; married Joanna Grzeskowiak (a historian), April 4, 1952; children: Agnieszka. *Education:* Jagiellonian University, M.A. (economics) and M.A. (sociology), 1949; University of Michigan, graduate study, 1957-59; University of Warsaw, Ph.D., 1960, docent in sociology, 1962. *Politics:* "No political activity." *Religion:* Roman Catholic. *Home:* 7623 119th St., Edmonton, Alberta T6G 1W4, Canada. *Office:* Department of Sociology, University of Alberta, Edmonton, Alberta, Canada T6G 2H4.

CAREER: University of Warsaw, Warsaw, Poland, associate professor of sociology, 1959-68; University of Alberta, Edmonton, professor of sociology, 1970—. Visiting professor, University of Leningrad, 1962, University of Moscow, 1962-63, University of North Carolina, 1966, University of Zambia, 1968-69, Carleton University, 1974-75, and St. Anthony College, Oxford University, 1975-76. Guest lecturer at numerous universities and institutions in Europe, United States, and Canada. *Member:* International Sociological Association, Canadian Sociology and Anthropology Association, American Sociological Association, Amnesty International.

WRITINGS: Socjologia zakladu pracy (title means "Sociology of a Work Place"), Wiedza Powszechna, 1961, 2nd edition, 1969; *Sacjologia przemyslu w Stanach Zjednoczonych Ameryki Polnocnej* (title means "Industrial Sociology in the U.S.''), PWN (Warsaw), 1962; *Kultura pracy zbiorowej* (title means "Culture of Work"), Wydawnictwo Zwlazkowe, 1962; *Praca i kolezenstwo* (title means "Work and Companionship"), Wiedza Powszechna, 1962; *Postawy zawodowe dziennikarzy na tle systemu spolecznego redakcji* (title means "Professional Attitudes of Journalists within the Social System of a Newsroom"), KOBP (Krakow), 1963; *Spoleczne warunki pracy tworczej* (title means "Social Conditions of Creative Work"), PWN, 1963; *Hutnicy na tle ich srodowiska pracy* (title means "Steelworkers and Their Work Environment"), SIN (Katowice, Poland), 1964; *Czlowiek i technika wspolczesna* (title means "Man and Modern Technology"), Wydawnictwo Zwiazkowe, 1964; *System spoleczny zespolu naukowego* (title means "Social System of Research Teams"), PWN, 1965; *Kierowanie kadrami pracowniczymi* (title means "Personnel Administration"), PWE (Warsaw), 1966; *Nastin sociologie prace* (title means "Outline of Sociology of Work"), Nakladatelstvi Prace (Prague), 1967; *System spoleczny instytutu* (title means "Social System of Research Institutes"), PWN, 1967; *Socjologia pracy* (title means "Sociology of Work"), PWE, 1968; *System spoleczny katedry* (title means "Social System of College Departments"), PWN, 1969; *Wiez i konflikt w zakladzie pracy* (title means "Integration and Conflict at Work Place"), KIW (Warsaw), 1969; *Socjologia kierownictwa* (title means "Sociology of Management"), PWE, 1969.

Uslovia tworczeskogo truda (title means "Conditions of Creative Work''), Mir (Moscow), 1970; *Sociology of Work and*

Leisure, European Centre for Leisure and Education (Prague), 1972; *Social Change and Stratification in Eastern Europe: An Interpretive Analysis of Poland and Her Neighbours,* Praeger, 1974; *Social Dimensions of Industrialism,* Sadhna Prakashan (Meerut, India), 1974; *The Social Technology of Applied Research,* Sadhna Prakashan, 1975; *The Upgrading of Zambians,* Sadhna Prakashan, 1976; *Overcoming Alienation in Work,* Sadhna Prakashan, 1976; *The Polish Blue Collar Worker,* North American Study Center of Polish Affairs, 1977.

Contributor: Wanda Litterer and Adam Andrzejewski, editors, *Zaludnierie i uzytkowanie mieszkan w nowych osiedlach* (title means "Population of New Towns and Utilization of Public Housing"), Arkady, 1959; Adam Sarapata, editor, *Socjologiczne problemy przedsiebiorstwa socjalistycznego* (title means "Sociological Problems of the Socialist Enterprises"), PWE, 1966.

Adam Podgorecki, editor, *Socjotechnika* (title means "Sociotechnique"), KIW, 1970; S.M.A. Hameed and D. Tullen, editors, *Work and Leisure in Alberta,* University of Alberta, 1971; J. Tunstall, editor, *Media Sociology,* Constable, 1971; K. Krotki and G. Nettler, editors, *Social Science and Social Policy,* Alberta Human Resources Research Council, 1971; Adam Bromke and John W. Strong, editors, *Gierek's Poland,* Praeger, 1973; Benedykt Heydenkorn, editor, *Past and Present,* Canadian Polish Research Institute, 1974; Heydenkorn, editor, *From Prairies to Cities,* Canadian Polish Research Institute, 1975; Zbigniew Fallenbuchl, editor, *Economic Development in the Soviet Union and Eastern Europe,* Praeger, 1975.

B. L. Faber, editor, *The Social Structure of Eastern Europe,* Praeger, 1976; A. H. Turrittin, editor, *Proceedings of the Workshop on Blue Collar Workers and Their Communities,* York University, 1976; Albert B. Cherns, editor, *Sociotechnics,* Malaby Press, 1976; Robert Dubin, editor, *Handbook of Work, Organization and Societies,* Rand McNally, 1976; J. P. Shapiro and W. Potichnyj, editors, *Change and Adaptation in Soviet and East European Politics,* Praeger, 1976; *Selected Papers from the Social Indicators Conference,* Alberta Bureau of Statistics, 1977; Tom M.S. Priestly, editor, *Proceedings of the First Banff Conference on Central and East European Studies,* Central and East European Studies Association, 1977; *Poland of Tomorrow,* Canadian Polish Congress, 1977; W. Isajiw, editor, *Identities,* Peter Martin Press, 1977; J. Rose, editor, *Current Topics in Cybernetics and Systems,* Springer Verlag, 1978; *Proceedings of the Second Banff Conference on Central and East European Studies,* Central and East European Studies Association, 1978; Jean Leonard Elliott, editor, *Two Nations, Many Cultures: Ethnic Groups in Canada,* Prentice-Hall (Toronto), 1979; Raj P. Mohan, editor, *Management and Complex Organizations in Comparative Perspective,* Greenwood Press, 1979; Cherns, editor, *Quality of Working Life and the Kibbutz Experience,* Norwood, 1980; H. Niemeyer, editor, *Soziale Beziehungsgeflechte,* Duncker & Humblot (Berlin), 1980.

Contributor to newspapers and journals. Co-editor, *Przeglad Zagadnien Socjalnych,* 1950-51; member of editorial board, *International Journal of Contemporary Sociology,* 1971—, and *Canadian Slovonic Papers,* 1971-73.

WORK IN PROGRESS: Dilemmas of Industrial Democracy.

SIDELIGHTS: Alexander Matejko is fluent in Polish, Russian, Czech, and German, and he knows some French.

*   *   *

MATLOFF, Maurice   1915-

PERSONAL: Born June 18, 1915, in New York, N.Y.; son of

Joseph and Ida (Glickhouse) Matloff; married Gertrude Glickler (a teacher), October 25, 1942; children: Howard Bruce, Jeffrey Lewis, Jody Matloff Dove. *Education:* Columbia University, B.A., 1936; Harvard University, M.A., 1937, Ph.D., 1956; Yale University, Certificate in Russian Area and Language, 1944. *Home:* 4109 Dewmar Ct., Kensington, Md. 20795. *Office:* Center of Military History, Department of the Army, 20 Massachusetts Ave. N.W., Washington, D.C. 20314.

CAREER: Brooklyn College (now Brooklyn College of the City University of New York), Brooklyn, N.Y., instructor, 1939-42, associate professor of history, 1946; U.S. Department of the Army, Center of Military History, Washington, D.C., senior historian in Historical Section, Operations Division, 1946-49, chief of Strategic Plans Section, 1949-60, deputy and acting chief of Post-World War II Branch, 1960-62, senior historical adviser and chief of Current History Branch, 1962-66, senior historical adviser and chief of General History Branch, 1966-68, deputy chief historian, 1969-70, chief historian, 1970—. Professorial lecturer at University of Maryland, 1957-71; Harmon Memorial Lecturer, U.S. Air Force Academy, 1964; visiting professor, University of California, Davis, 1968-69, Dartmouth College, spring, 1977, University of Maryland, fall, 1981, and San Francisco State College (now University); Distinguished Visiting Professor, University of Georgia, spring, 1974; Regents' Professor, University of California, Berkeley, spring, 1980; adjunct professor, American University; lecturer at Columbia University, National Defense University, and numerous other universities and war colleges. Lecturer for adult education classes, Young Women's Christian Association, 1948-51. Moderator of foreign policy conferences, U.S. Naval Academy, 1964, 1967, and 1970; fellow, Woodrow Wilson International Center for Scholars, 1981-82; charter member, Senior Executive Service of the Federal Government. Member of advisory council, George C. Marshall Research Foundation; historical consultant to numerous governmental committees and non-profit research organizations. *Military service:* U.S. Army Air Forces, 1942-46; served as historian and intelligence instructor.

MEMBER: International Institute of Strategic Studies (London), American Historical Association (member of first books program committee), Organization of American Historians, American Military Institute (trustee), American Committee on the History of the Second World War (member of executive board), Society for Historians of American Foreign Relations, Society for History in the Federal Government, Inter-University Seminar on Armed Forces and Society, Phi Beta Kappa. *Awards, honors:* Outstanding Service Award, Department of the Army, 1958, 1972, 1974, 1976, 1978, and 1980; Secretary of the Army fellowship for study in Europe, 1959-60; Meritorious Civilian Service Medal, Department of the Army, 1965.

WRITINGS: (With E. M. Snell) *Strategic Planning for Coalition Warfare, 1941-42,* U.S. Government Printing Office, 1953; *Strategic Planning for Coalition Warfare, 1943-44,* U.S. Government Printing Office, 1959; (general editor) *American Military History,* U.S. Government Printing Office, 1969, revised edition, 1973; (editor) *The Civil War: A Concise History of the War between the States,* McKay, 1978; (editor) *World War I,* McKay, 1979; *World War II,* McKay, 1980.

Contributor: *Washington Command Post,* U.S. Government Printing Office, 1951; (and member of editorial panel) *Command Decisions,* revised edition (Matloff was not associated with earlier edition), U.S. Government Printing Office, 1961; Harry Coles, editor, *Total War and Cold War,* Ohio State University Press, 1962; Abraham S. Eisenstadt, editor, *Recent Interpretations of U.S. History,* Crowell, 1962, 2nd edition

published as *American History: Recent Interpretations,* 1969; S. Harcave, editor, *Readings in Russian History,* Crowell, 1962; Michael Howard, editor, *Theory and Practice of War,* Cassell, 1965; *D-Day: The Normandy Invasion in Retrospect,* University Press of Kansas, 1971; *Soldiers and Statesmen,* U.S. Government Printing Office, 1973; *New Dimensions in Military History,* Presidio Press, 1975; *A Guide to the Study and Use of Military History,* U.S. Government Printing Office, 1979.

General editor of eight series for U.S. Army Center of Military History. Member of editorial staff, *Dictionary of Everyday Usage, German-English, English-German,* Army Information and Education Division and American Council of Learned Societies, 1945; member of editorial advisory board, *Marshall Papers,* George C. Marshall Research Foundation. Contributor to *Encyclopaedia Britannica* and *U.S. Naval Institute Proceedings.* Contributor of articles and reviews to *School and Society, Military Affairs, Air University Review, Journal of Modern History,* and *American Historical Review.* Member of editorial advisory board, *The Public Historian.*

WORK IN PROGRESS: Development of Modern Strategic Thought.

SIDELIGHTS: Maurice Matloff told *CA:* "Writing contemporary history is a demanding and challenging art. My writings have focused on problems of national security, coalition warfare, and international relations confronting the United States in the global arena since World War II. My aim has been to understand and try to illuminate the great issues of war and peace that trouble contemporary society. To search for the truth in these complex, often controversial areas, and to incorporate the findings, conclusions, and interpretations in clear, readable prose is a difficult but rewarding enterprise."

Matloff speaks French, German, and Russian. His books have been translated and are used in universities and war colleges in the United States and abroad.

*   *   *

MATTHEWS, Brad
See DeMILLE, Nelson

*   *   *

MAY, Ernest Richard 1928-

PERSONAL: Born November 19, 1928, in Fort Worth, Tex.; son of Ernest and Rachel (Garza) May; married Nancy Caughey, 1950; children: John Ernest, Susan Rachel, Donna La Ree. *Education:* University of California, A.B., 1948, M.A., 1949, Ph.D., 1951. *Politics:* Democrat. *Religion:* Episcopalian. *Home:* 320A Harvard St., Cambridge, Mass. 02138. *Office:* Department of History, Harvard University, Cambridge, Mass. 02138.

CAREER: Los Angeles State College of Applied Arts and Sciences (now California State University, Los Angeles), lecturer, 1950-51; Harvard University, Cambridge, Mass., instructor, 1954-56, assistant professor, 1956-59, associate professor and Allston Burr Senior Tutor in Kirkland House, 1959-63, professor of history, 1963-81, Charles Warren Professor of History, 1981—, dean of Harvard College, 1969-72, director of Institute of Politics, 1971-74. *Military service:* U.S. Naval Reserve, 1951-54; became lieutenant junior grade. *Member:* American Historical Association, Organization of American Historians, Council on Foreign Relations, American Academy of Arts and Sciences, American Association of University Professors, Massachusetts Historical Society. *Awards, honors:* Guggenheim fellow, 1958-59; Social Science Research Council faculty research fellow, 1959-61; American Historical Association George Louis Beer Prize, 1959, for *The World War and American Isolation, 1914-1917;* Center for Advanced Study in the Behavioral Sciences fellow, 1963-64; Robert H. Lord Award for excellence in historical studies, 1981.

WRITINGS: The World War and American Isolation, 1914-1917, Harvard University Press, 1959; *The Ultimate Decision: The President as Commander-in-Chief,* Braziller, 1960; *Imperial Democracy: The Emergence of America as a Great Power,* Harcourt, 1961; *The American Foreign Policy,* Braziller, 1963; (with John Walton Caughey) *A History of the United States,* Rand McNally, 1964; (with the editors of *Life*) *The Progressive Era: 1901-1917,* Time, Inc., 1964; (with the editors of *Life*) *War, Boom and Bust: 1917-1932,* Time, Inc., 1964; (with Caughey and John Hope Franklin) *Land of the Free: A History of the United States,* Ritchie, 1965, revised edition, Benziger, 1966; (editor) *Anxiety and Affluence: 1945-1965,* McGraw-Hill, 1966; *American Imperialism: A Speculative Essay,* Atheneum, 1968.

(Editor with James C. Thomson, Jr.) *American-East Asian Relations: A Survey,* Harvard University Press, 1972; *"Lessons" of the Past: The Use and Misuse of History in American Foreign Policy,* Oxford University Press, 1973; *The Truman Administration and China: 1945-1949,* Lippincott, 1975; *The Making of the Monroe Doctrine,* Harvard University Press, 1975; (with Dorothy G. Blaney) *Careers for Humanists,* Academic Press, 1981. Also author, with Charles S. Maier, of a taped discussion, "America's Role in Europe in the Twentieth Century," BFA Educational Media, 1974. Contributor to professional journals and to *Foreign Affairs, New Republic,* and *Saturday Review.*

BIOGRAPHICAL/CRITICAL SOURCES: New York Times, July 4, 1968; *Book World,* September 8, 1968, December 23, 1973; *Virginia Quarterly Review,* winter, 1969.

*   *   *

MAY, Georges Claude 1920-

PERSONAL: Born October 7, 1920, in Paris, France; came to United States, 1942; naturalized citizen, 1943; son of Lucien (a businessman) and Germaine (Samuel) May; married Martha Corkery, February 19, 1949; children: Anne Charlotte, Catherine Ellen. *Education:* University of Paris, B.A. and B.S., 1937; Licence-es-Lettres, 1941; University of Montpellier, Diplome d'Etudes Superieures, 1941; University of Illinois, Ph.D., 1947. *Home:* 177 Everit St., New Haven, Conn. 06511. *Office:* Department of French, Yale University, New Haven, Conn. 06520.

CAREER: Yale University, New Haven, Conn., 1946—, began as instructor, professor of French, 1956-71, Sterling Professor of French, 1971—, dean of Yale College, 1963-71, university provost, 1979-81. Visiting summer professor, University of Illinois, 1946, University of Minnesota, 1948, Middlebury College, 1951 and 1954, University of Michigan, 1952, and University of California, Berkeley, 1959. *Military service:* French Army, 1939-40. U.S. Army, 1943-45. *Member:* Association Internationale des Etudes Francaises, Association of American Teachers of French, Societe d'Histoire Litteraire de la France, Societe d'Etudes du XVIIe Siecle, American Society for Eighteenth-Century Studies (president, 1974-75), Modern Language Association of America, American Philosophical Association, American Academy of Arts and Sciences, Academy of Literary Studies, Phi Beta Kappa. *Awards, honors:* Guggenheim fellow, 1950-51; Chevalier, French Legion d'Honneur, 1971.

WRITINGS: Tragedie cornelienne, tragedie racinienne, University of Illinois Press, 1948; *D'Ovide a Racine,* Yale University Press, 1949; *Quatre Visages de Denis Diderot,* Boivin-Hatier, 1951; *Diderot et La Religieuse,* Yale University Press, 1954; *Rousseau par lui-meme,* Editions du Seuil, 1961; *Le Dilemme du roman au XVIIIe siecle: Etude sur les rapports du roman et de la critique, 1715-1761,* Yale University Press, 1963; (editor and author of introduction and notes) Pierre Corneille, *Polyeucte and Le Menteur,* Dell, 1964; (editor, annotator, and author of introduction) Franciscus Hemsterhuis, *Lettre sur l'homme et ses rapports: Avec le commentaire inedit de Diderot,* Yale University Press, 1964; (editor) Denis Diderot, *Oeuvres Completes,* French and European Publications, Volume XI: *La Religieuse,* 1975, Volume XIII: *Sur Terence,* 1980; *L'Autobiographie,* Presses Universitaires de France, 1979. Contributor of articles on French literature to professional journals.

WORK IN PROGRESS: Research in French literature of the seventeenth and eighteenth centuries, especially fiction and drama.

*   *   *

MAY, Herbert Gordon 1904-1977

PERSONAL: Born December 26, 1904, in Fair Haven, Vt.; died October 8, 1977, in Jacksonville, Fla.; son of Charles Leon and Mabel Marie (Cottrill) May; married Helen Isabel Porter, February 11, 1927; children: Gola Joyce Kina Deem, Helen Emily. *Education:* Wesleyan University, B.A., 1927; University of Chicago, M.A., 1929, Ph.D., 1932; Chicago Theological Seminary, B.D., 1930. *Religion:* United Church of Christ. *Home:* 5754 Jim Tom Dr., Jacksonville, Fla. 32211.

CAREER: First Congregational Church, Melvin, Ill., minister, 1928-29; University of Chicago, Oriental Institute, Chicago, Ill., fellow, 1930-31, epigrapher in Megiddo, Palestine, 1931-34; Oberlin College, Graduate School of Theology, Oberlin, Ohio, professor of Old Testament language and literature, 1934-70, professor emeritus, 1970-77; Vanderbilt University, Divinity School, Nashville, Tenn., professor of Old Testament language and literature, 1967-70. Union Theological Seminary, New York, N.Y., visiting professor, summers of 1952, 1956, 1959; American School of Oriental Research, Jerusalem, Jordan, honorary lecturer, 1960. Trustee, American Schools of Oriental Research. *Member:* Society of Biblical Literature (president, 1962), American Oriental Society, American Archaeological Institute, National Association of Bible Instructors, American Society for the Study of Religion, Standard Bible Committee, Phi Beta Kappa, Rotary International. *Awards, honors:* D.D., Wesleyan University, 1952; L.H.D., Oberlin College, 1976.

WRITINGS: Material Remains of the Megiddo Cult, University of Chicago Press, 1935; (with W. C. Graham) *Culture and Conscience,* University of Chicago Press, 1936; (editor with Chester C. Crown) *A Remapping of the Bible World,* Nelson, 1949; *Our English Bible in the Making,* Westminster, 1952, revised edition, 1965; *Introduction to Ezekiel: Interpreter's Bible,* Abingdon, 1956; (editor) *Oxford Bible Atlas,* Oxford University Press, 1962, 2nd edition, 1974; (associate editor) *Interpreter's Dictionary of the Bible,* Abingdon, 1962; (editor with Bruce M. Metzger) *Oxford Annotated Bible, Revised Standard Version,* Oxford University Press, 1962, revised edition published as *New Oxford Annotated Bible, Revised Standard Version,* 1973; (editor with Metzger) *The Oxford Annotated Bible with the Apocrypha,* Oxford University Press, 1965, revised edition published as *The New Oxford Annotated Bible* with the Apocrypha, 1977; (editor) *Abingdon Bible Maps*, Abingdon, 1966. Regular contributor to religious and Biblical journals. Member of editorial board, *Vetus Testamentum;* member of translation committee, *Holy Bible, Revised Standard Version.*

OBITUARIES: *New York Times*, October 11, 1977; *AB Bookman's Weekly*, February 6, 1978.†

*   *   *

MAY, J. C.
See MAY, Julian

*   *   *

MAY, Julian 1931-
(Julian May Dikty; pseudonyms: Bob Cunningham, Lee N. Falconer, John Feilen, Matthew G. Grant, J. C. May, Ian Thorne, Jean Wright Thorne, George Zanderbergen)

PERSONAL: Born July 10, 1931, in Chicago, Ill.; daughter of Matthew M. and Julia (Feilen) May; married T. E. Dikty, 1953; children: Alan Sam, David, Barbara. *Education:* Attended Rosary College, 1949-52.

CAREER: Free-lance writer and editor; co-owner with husband, T. E. Dikty, of a book production and design service, 1957—.

WRITINGS—Published by Popular Mechanics Press, except as indicated: *There's Adventure in Atomic Energy*, 1957; *There's Adventure in Chemistry*, 1957; *There's Adventure in Electronics*, 1957; *There's Adventure in Rockets*, 1958; *You and the Earth Beneath Us*, Childrens Press, 1958; *There's Adventure in Geology*, 1958; *There's Adventure in Marine Science*, 1959; *There's Adventure in Jet Aircraft*, 1959; *Show Me the World of Astronomy*, Pennington Press, 1959; *Show Me the World of Modern Airplanes*, Pennington Press, 1959; *Show Me the World of Electronics*, Pennington Press, 1959; *Show Me the World of Space Travel*, Pennington Press, 1959.

Published by Follett, except as indicated: *There's Adventure in Automobiles*, Hawthorn, 1961; *There's Adventure in Astronautics*, Hawthorn, 1961; *The Real Book about Robots and Thinking Machines*, Doubleday, 1961; *Motion*, Accelerated Instruction Methods, 1962; (with husband, T. E. Dikty) *Every Boy's Book of American Heroes*, Fell, 1963; *They Turned to Stone*, Holiday House, 1965; *Weather*, 1966; *Rockets*, 1967; *They Lived in the Ice Age*, Holiday House, 1967; *Astronautics*, 1968; *The Big Island*, 1968; *The First Men*, Holiday House, 1968; *Horses: How They Came to Be*, Holiday House, 1968; *Climate*, 1969; *Living Things and Their Young*, 1969; *How We Are Born*, 1969; *Man and Woman*, 1969; *Alligator Hole*, 1969; *Moving Hills of Sand*, Hawthorn, 1969; *Before the Indians*, Holiday House, 1969; *Why the Earth Quakes*, Holiday House, 1969.

Published by Creative Educational Society, except as indicated: *The First Living Things*, Holiday House, 1970; *Why Birds Migrate*, Holiday House, 1970; *Millions of Years of Eggs*, 1970; *Do You Have Your Father's Nose?*, 1970; *A New Baby Comes*, 1970; *How to Build a Body*, 1970; *Dodos and Dinosaurs Are Extinct*, 1970; *Tiger Stripes and Zebra Stripes*, 1970; *Wildlife in the City*, 1970; (with others) *The Ecology of North America*, 1970; *Why Plants Are Green Instead of Pink*, 1970; *These Islands Are Alive*, Hawthorn, 1971; *Why People Are Different Colors*, Holiday House, 1971; *Blue River: The Land Beneath the Sea*, Holiday House, 1971; *Cactus Fox*, 1971.

Plankton: Drifting Life of the Waters, Holiday House, 1972; *Islands of the Tiny Deer*, Young Scott Books, 1972; *The Mysterious Evergreen Forest*, 1972; *Forests That Change Color*, 1972; *Deserts: Hot and Cold*, 1972; *The Cloud Book*, 1972; *Rainbows, Clouds and Foggy Dew*, 1972; *The Land Is Disappearing*, 1972; *Living Blanket on the Land*, 1972; *What Will the Weather Be?*, 1972; *The Prairie Has an Endless Sky*, 1972; *Snowfall!*, 1972; *The Arctic: Top of the World*, 1972; *The Antarctic: Bottom of the World*, 1972; *Cascade Cougar*, 1972; *Prairie Pronghorn*, 1972; *Sea Lion Island*, 1972; *Glacier Grizzly*, 1972; *Giant Condor of California*, 1972; *Sea Otter*, 1972; *Eagles of the Valley*, 1972; *Captain Cousteau: Undersea Explorer*, 1972; *Matthew Henson: Co-Discoverer of the North Pole*, 1972; *Sojourner Truth: Freedom Fighter*, 1972; *Sitting Bull: Chief of the Sioux*, 1972; *Willie Mays: Most Valuable Player*, Crestwood, 1972; *Hank Aaron Clinches the Pennant*, Crestwood, 1972; *Mickey Mantle Slugs It Out*, Crestwood, 1972; *Jim Brown Runs with the Ball*, Crestwood, 1972; *Johnny Unitas and the Long Pass*, Crestwood, 1972.

Wild Turkeys, Holiday House, 1973; *The Life Cycle of an Opposum*, 1973; *The Life Cycle of a Red Fox*, 1973; *The Life Cycle of a Cottontail Rabbit*, 1973; *The Life Cycle of a Raccoon*, 1973; *The Life Cycle of a Snapping Turtle*, 1973; *The Life Cycle of a Bullfrog*, 1973; *The Life Cycle of a Polyphemus Moth*, 1973; *The Life Cycle of a Monarch Butterfly*, 1973; *Mammals We Know*, 1973; *Birds We Know*, 1973; *Reptiles We Know*, 1973; *Fishes We Know*, 1973; *Insects We Know*, 1973; *Quanah: Leader of the Comanche*, 1973; *Hillary and Tenzing: Conquerers of Mount Everest*, 1973; *Thor Heyerdahl: Modern Viking Adventurer*, 1973; *Amelia Earhart: Pioneer of Aviation*, 1973; *Ernie Banks: Home Run Slugger*, Crestwood, 1973; *Gale Sayers: Star Running Back*, Crestwood, 1973; *Kareem Abdul Jabbar: Cage Superstar*, Crestwood, 1973; *Fran Tarkenton: Scrambling Quarterback*, Crestwood, 1973; *Roberto Clemente and the World Series Upset*, Crestwood, 1973; *Bobby Orr: Star on Ice*, Crestwood, 1973.

How the Animals Came to North America, Holiday House, 1974; *The Baltimore Colts*, 1974; *The Kansas City Chiefs*, 1974; *The Dallas Cowboys*, 1974; *The Green Bay Packers*, 1974; *The New York Jets*, 1974; *The Miami Dolphins*, 1974; *O. J. Simpson: Juice on the Gridiron*, Crestwood, 1974; *Bobby Hull: Hockey's Golden Jet*, Crestwood, 1974; *Lee Trevino: The Golf Explosion*, Crestwood, 1974; *Roy Campanella: Brave Man of Baseball*, Crestwood, 1974; *Billie Jean King: Tennis Champion*, Crestwood, 1974.

The World Series, 1975; *The U.S. Open Golf Championship*, 1975; *Wimbledon: World Tennis Focus*, 1975; *The Kentucky Derby*, 1975; *The Indianapolis 500*, 1975; *The Olympic Games*, 1975; *The Super Bowl*, 1975; *The Masters Tournament of Golf*, 1975; *The Stanley Cup*, 1975; *The NBA Playoffs: Basketball's Classic*, 1975; *Phil Esposito: The Big Bruin*, Crestwood, 1975; *Evonne Goolagong: Smasher from Australia*, Crestwood, 1975; *Evel Knievel: Daredevil Stuntman*, Crestwood, 1975; *Vince Lombardi: The Immortal Coach*, Crestwood, 1975; *Frank Robinson: Slugging toward Glory*, Crestwood, 1975; *Joe Namath: High Flying Quarterback*, Crestwood, 1975; *Muhammad Ali: Boxing Superstar*, Crestwood, 1975; *Pele: World Soccer Star*, Crestwood, 1975; *Chris Evert: Princess of Tennis*, Crestwood, 1975; *Janet Lynn: Figure Skating Star*, Crestwood, 1975; *A. J. Foyt: Championship Auto Racer*, Crestwood, 1975; *Arthur Ashe: Dark Star of Tennis*, Crestwood, 1975; *Bobby Clarke: Hockey with a Grin*, Crestwood, 1975.

The Triple Crown, 1976; *America's Cup Yacht Race*, 1976; *The Winter Olympics*, 1976; *Forest Hills and the American Tennis Championship*, 1976; *The Grand Prix*, 1976; *Boxing's*

Heavyweight Championship Fight, 1976; *The Daytona 500*, 1976; *The Rose Bowl*, 1976; *The PGA Championship*, 1976; *The Pittsburgh Steelers*, 1976; (under pseudonym Jean Wright Thorne) *Horse and Rider*, Crestwood, 1976; (under pseudonym Jean Wright Thorne) *Rodeo*, Crestwood, 1976.

The New York Giants, 1977; *The Los Angeles Rams*, 1977; *The Minnesota Vikings*, 1977; *The San Francisco 49ers*, 1977; *The Washington Redskins*, 1977; *The Oakland Raiders*, 1977; (under pseudonym Lee N. Falconer) *A Gazeteer of the Hyborian World of Conan*, Starmont House, 1977.

The Oakland Raiders: Superbowl Champions, 1978; *The Warm-Blooded Dinosaurs*, Holiday House, 1978; *Cars and Cycles*, Bowmar-Noble, 1978; *The Cincinnati Bengals*, 1980; *The Denver Broncos*, 1980; *The San Diego Chargers*, 1980; *The Dallas Cowboys* (different from previous publication of same title), 1980; *The Pittsburgh Steelers* (different from previous publication of same title), 1980; *The Baltimore Colts* (different from previous publication of same title), 1980; *The Green Bay Packers* (different from previous publication of same title), 1980; *The Kansas City Chiefs* (different from previous publication of same title), 1980; *The Miami Dolphins* (different from previous publication of same title), 1980; *The New York Jets* (different from previous publication of same title), 1980; *The Many-Colored Land*, Houghton, 1981.

Under pseudonym Bob Cunningham; all published by Crestwood: *Ten-Five: Alaska Skip*, 1977; *Ten-Seven for Good Sam*, 1977; *Ten-Seventy: Range Fire*, 1977; *Ten-Thirty-Three: Emergency*, 1977; *Ten-Two Hundred: Come on Smokey!*, 1977.

Under pseudonym John Feilen: *Air*, Follett, 1965; *Squirrels*, Follett, 1967; *Deer*, Follett, 1967; *Dirt Track Speedsters*, Crestwood, 1976; *Winter Sports*, Crestwood, 1976; *Racing on the Water*, Crestwood, 1976; *Motocross Racing*, Crestwood, 1978; *Four-Wheel Racing*, Crestwood, 1978.

Under pseudonym Matthew G. Grant; published by Creative Educational Society, except as indicated: *A Walk in the Mountains*, Reilly & Lee, 1971; *Geronimo: Apache Warrior*, 1974; *Crazy Horse: War Chief of the Oglala*, 1974; *Chief Joseph of the Nez Perce*, 1974; *Pontiac: Indian General and Statesman*, 1974; *Squanto: The Indian Who Saved the Pilgrims*, 1974; *Osceola and the Seminole War*, 1974; *Columbus: Discoverer of the New World*, 1974; *Leif Ericson: Explorer of Vinland*, 1974; *DeSoto: Explorer of the Southeast*, 1974; *Lewis and Clark: Western Trailblazers*, 1974; *Champlain: Explorer of New France*, 1974; *Coronado: Explorer of the Southwest*, 1974; *Daniel Boone in the Wilderness*, 1974; *Buffalo Bill of the Wild West*, 1974; *Jim Bridger: The Mountain Man*, 1974; *Francis Marion: Swamp Fox*, 1974; *Davy Crockett: Frontier Adventurer*, 1974; *Kit Carson: Trailblazer of the West*, 1974; *John Paul Jones: Naval Hero*, 1974; *Paul Revere: Patriot and Craftsman*, 1974; *Robert E. Lee: The South's Great General*, 1974; *Ulysses S. Grant: General and President*, 1974; *Sam Houston of Texas*, 1974; *Lafayette: Freedom's General*, 1974; *Clara Barton: Red Cross Pioneer*, 1974; *Jane Addams: Helper of the Poor*, 1974; *Elizabeth Blackwell: Pioneer Doctor*, 1974; *Harriet Tubman: Black Liberator*, 1974; *Susan B. Anthony: Crusader for Women's Rights*, 1974; *Dolly Madison: First Lady of the Land*, 1974.

Under pseudonym Ian Thorne; published by Creative Educational Society, except as indicated: *Meet the Running Backs*, 1975; *Meet the Quarterbacks*, 1975; *Meet the Coaches*, 1975; *Meet the Linebackers*, 1975; *Meet the Receivers*, 1975; *Meet the Defensive Linemen*, 1975; *The Great Defensemen*, 1976; *The Great Goalies*, 1976; *The Great Centers*, 1976; *The Great Wingmen*, 1976; *King Kong*, Crestwood, 1977; *Godzilla*,

Crestwood, 1977; *Frankenstein*, Crestwood, 1977; *Dracula*, Crestwood, 1977; *Mad Scientists*, Crestwood, 1977; *The Wolf Man*, Crestwood, 1977; *Ancient Astronauts*, Crestwood, 1978; *The Bermuda Triangle*, Crestwood, 1978; *Bigfoot*, Crestwood, 1978; *The Loch Ness Monster*, Crestwood, 1978; *Monster Tales of Native Americans*, Crestwood, 1978; *UFO's*, edited by Howard Schroeder, Crestwood, 1978.

Under pseudonym George Zanderbergen; all published by Crestwood: *The Beatles*, 1976; *Laugh It Up: Carol Burnett, Bill Cosby, Mary Tyler Moore*, 1976; *Made for Music: Elton John, Stevie Wonder, John Denver*, 1976; *Nashville Music: Loretta Lynn, Mac Davis, Charley Pride*, 1976; *Singing Sweetly: Cher, Roberta Flack, Olivia Newton John*, 1976; *Stay Tuned: Henry Winkler, Lee Majors, Valerie Harper*, 1976.

Also author of *Dune Roller*. Editor, "Life in God's Love" series, Franciscan Herald, 1963.

WORK IN PROGRESS: The Exiles, an adult science-fiction novel.

SIDELIGHTS: Julian May told *CA:* "Voluminous reading, especially in the field of science, eventually led me to science-fiction—which remains my first love. My first published novelette, *Dune Roller*, became a minor classic in the field; but in the early 1950's it was not possible to earn a living writing sf, and so I turned to non-fiction. As an encyclopedia editor I wrote some 7,000 articles on science and natural history, and then did my first science juveniles for Popular Mechanics Press, beginning in 1957. My avalanche of books for young people includes many science titles, as well as biographies and sports books. I do the book design and art direction for many of my books, as well as write them. Because I am an experienced researcher and a fast writer, I am able to do non-fiction books very quickly. This leaves time for hobbies such as canoeing and backpacking, making costumes, and gardening. From the beginning, my husband and I shared the care of house and children and pursued overlapping careers. Now that our children are grown and the pace of life has slowed a bit, I have returned to science-fiction writing for adults, a genre that has always been close to my heart.

"Because my juvenile writing has been a job rather than a sideline, I have never been anxious to talk about my work. I have little emotional involvement in my juvenile books, and this tends to disappoint young readers and librarians who have romantic ideas of authorhood. I did not write my long list of books because of a creative itch, but because I was good at it and it paid the bills. The professional writer is at an economic disadvantage in this country unless he or she produces a Best Seller. Since juvenile books rarely attain such heights, the ambitious writer has no other recourse but to keep on truckin'—which, for better or worse, I have done. The result is manifest."

A *Young Reader's Review* critic comments: "Julian May's books on scientific subjects are quite distinctive because of the unusual manner of presentation. She limits herself to one small but important aspect of a subject. The important fact or basic premise is amazingly simplified without distortion. And that clear and accurate simplification is given an elaborate presentation that the readers will remember."

Julian May told *CA* that contrary to information published in certain bibliographies, she has never used the pseudonym "Julian Chain."

BIOGRAPHICAL/CRITICAL SOURCES: Young Reader's Review, May, 1968, November, 1968; *Book World*, November 10, 1968, November 9, 1969; *Times Literary Supplement*, October 16, 1969.

MAYER, Charles Leopold 1881-
(Reyam)

PERSONAL: Born June 22, 1881, in Paris, France; son of Leopold and Eugenie (Pasquier) Mayer; married Helen Colin-Lefrancq, 1926. *Education:* Lycee Hoche, Bachelor; Ecole Superieure de Chimie Industrielle de Lyon, Chemical Engineer, 1904; Sorbonne, University of Paris, Dr. of Sciences.

CAREER: Scientist. Societe Europienne de Gestion et de Participations, Paris, France, president, 1928-62; Holding Economique et Financiere, Paris, director, 1959-62. *Member:* American Chemical Society, Societe Chimique de France, American Association for the Advancement of Science, Foundation Charles Leopold Mayer of the Academie des Sciences, Societe de Chimie Biologique, Cercle Republican, Comite France Amerique. *Awards, honors:* Laureat de l'Academie des Sciences Morales et Politiques, Paris.

WRITINGS: Condensation des imines avec les cetones et application a l'obtention de composes cycliques, Gauthier-Villars (Paris), 1939; *Les Principles de Machiavel et la politique de la France,* Editions de la Maison Francaise, 1943; *L'Homme ne vaut que par le progres,* Editions de la Maison Francaise, 1945; *Materialisme progressite,* Societe Francais de Presse (Paris), 1947; *L'Economie au service du progres,* Marcel Riviere, 1948; *Man: Mind or Matter?,* translation by Harold A. Larrabee, Beacon, 1951; *La Morale de l'avenir,* Marcel Riviere, 1953, translation by Larrabee published as *In Quest of a New Ethics,* Beacon, 1954; *Ma vie d'abeille,* Productions de Paris, 1959; *Memoires de la terre,* Productions de Paris, 1959; *La Sensation: Cree la vie,* Marcel Riviere, 1960, 2nd edition, 1961, translation published as *Sensation: The Origin of Life,* Antioch, 1961; *L'Homme face a son destin,* Marcel Riviere, 1964, 2nd edition, 1969, translation by Heloise Norwell, J. S. Norwell, and D. C. Fox published as *Man Faces His Destiny,* Johnson Reprint, 1968. Founder, *Revue Liberale,* 1953.†

*   *   *

MAYNE, Richard (John) 1926-

PERSONAL: Born April 2, 1926, in London, England; son of John William and K. H. (Angus) Mayne. *Education:* Trinity College, Cambridge, B.A. (first class honors, with distinction), 1950, M.A., 1953, Ph.D., 1955. *Home:* 67 Harley St., London W.1, England.

CAREER: New Statesman, London, England, Rome correspondent, 1953-54; Cambridge Institute of Education, Cambridge, England, assistant tutor, 1954-56; European Coal and Steel Community, Luxembourg, staff member of High Authority, 1956-58; Commission of European Economic Community, Brussels, Belgium, staff member, 1958-68; Action Committee for United States of Europe, Paris, France, director of Documentation Center, 1963-66; Federal Trust for Education and Research, London, director, 1970-73; Commission of the European Communities, London, head of United Kingdom offices, 1973-79, special adviser, 1979—. *Military service:* British Army Royal Signals, 1944-47; became lieutenant. Army Officers' Emergency Reserve, 1947—. *Awards, honors:* Scott-Moneriff Prize for translation, *The Memoirs of Jean Monnet.*

WRITINGS: The Community of Europe, Gollancz, 1962, Norton, 1963; *The Institutions of the European Community,* Political & Economic Planning (London), 1968; *The Recovery of Europe,* Harper, 1970; *The Europeans,* Weidenfeld & Nicolson, 1972; (editor) *Europe Tomorrow,* Fontana Books, 1972; (editor) *The New Atlantic Challenge,* Charles Knight, 1975; (translator) *The Memoirs of Jean Monnet,* Doubleday, 1978.

WORK IN PROGRESS: Postwar: A Study of Europe, 1945-1960.

SIDELIGHTS: Richard Mayne's *The Recovery of Europe* is a narrative of the growth of unity and economic stability in Europe following the devastation of the Second World War. Brian Walden of the *Observer Review* writes that Mayne's book "is so deeply researched, so logically assembled, full of so many acute insights, that there is no danger that it will be neglected by historians." In *New Statesman,* Christopher Serpell describes *The Recovery of Europe* as "inspirational reading" and notes that Mayne "writes elegantly and with a minimum of cliche: his style is imaginative and at times poetic. . . . His skill in narrative is demonstrated particularly by his handling of such episodes ,of human futility as the muddles over the German surrender, or the haphazard way in which the face of post-war Europe was drawn by so-called statesmen." Serpell states, "I should make Richard Mayne's book required reading for any young man or woman who does not approach history from an academic point of view but does want to know why things are the way they are."

Richard Mayne's works have been translated into six languages.

BIOGRAPHICAL/CRITICAL SOURCES: Observer Review, August 30, 1970; *Times Literary Supplement,* September 18, 1970; *New Statesman,* October 1, 1970.

*   *   *

McBRIDE, Alfred 1928-

PERSONAL: Born December 12, 1928, in Philadephia, Pa.; son of Charles and Mary (Shannon) McBride. *Education:* St. Norbert College, B.A., 1950; Lumen Vitae, Brussels, Belgium, diploma, 1963; Catholic University of America, Ph.D.; postdoctoral study at Oxford University. *Address:* St. Norbert Abbey, De Pere, Wis. 54115.

CAREER: Ordained Roman Catholic priest, 1953; member of Norbertine Fathers. Worked as high school Latin and religion teacher; parish priest in De Pere, Wis., 1953-59; St. Norbert Abbey, De Pere, master of novices, beginning 1959, currently community planner. Former director of National Forum for Religious Education, National Catholic Education Association; lecturer on the teaching of religion to educators in the midwest; conductor of seminars on religious education in the United States and Canada. *Member:* Society for American Archaeology, Catholic Homiletic Society. *Awards, honors:* Honorary doctorate, Belmont Abbey College.

WRITINGS: Bible Themes for Modern Man, St. Norbert Abbey, 1964; *Homilies for the New Liturgy,* Bruce, 1965; *Catechetics: A Theology of Proclamation,* Bruce, 1966; *The Human Dimensions of Catechetics,* Bruce, 1967; *Growing in Grace* (Bible stories), Gastonia Press, 1969; *The Pearl and the Seed* (church history), Allyn & Bacon, 1971; *Heschel: Religious Educator,* Dimension Press, 1973; *The Gospel of the Holy Spirit,* Arena Lettres, 1974; *The Kingdom and the Glory,* Arena Lettres, 1976; *Creative Teaching in Christian Education,* Allyn & Bacon, 1978; *Death Shall Have No Dominion,* W. C. Brown, 1979; *Faithful God, Faithful People,* St. Anthony Messenger Press, 1980; *Saints Are People: Church History through the Lives of the Saints,* W. C. Brown, 1981. Also author of *Fulfillment of the Promise,* 1980. Contributor of more than 500 columns and articles to newspapers and periodicals, including

Worship, Today, Ave Maria, American Ecclesiastical Review, America, and *Pastoral Life.*

WORK IN PROGRESS: Two books; a sermon series.

*   *   *

McBRIDE, William Leon 1938-

PERSONAL: Born January 19, 1938, in New York, N.Y.; son of William J. (a pharmacist) and Irene (a high school teacher; maiden name, Choffin) McBride; married M. Angela Barron (a writer and college teacher), June 12, 1965; children: Catherine Alexandra, Kara Angela. *Education:* Georgetown University, A.B., 1959; University of Lille, additional study, 1959-60; Yale University, M.A., 1962, Ph.D., 1964. *Home:* 744 Cherokee Ave., Lafayette, Ind. 47905. *Office:* Department of Philosophy, Purdue University, West Lafayette, Ind. 47907.

CAREER: Yale University, New Haven, Conn., instructor, 1964-66, assistant professor, 1966-71, associate professor of philosophy, 1971-73; Purdue University, West Lafayette, Ind., associate professor, 1973-76, professor of philosophy, 1976—. Lecturer at Korcula (Yugoslavia) Summer School, summers, 1971, 1973, and at Northwestern University, summer, 1972. Member of Center for Humanistic Studies, Purdue University, 1981. *Member:* Association des Amis de Romain Rolland (secretary of United States chapter, 1963-75), American Association of University Professors, American Civil Liberties Union, American Philosophical Association, American Society for Political and Legal Philosophy, Society for Phenomenology and Existential Philosophy (co-secretary, 1977-80). *Awards, honors:* Fulbright scholar, 1959-60; Woodrow Wilson fellow, 1960-61; Social Science Research Council fellow, 1963-64; Morse fellow at Yale University, 1968-69.

WRITINGS: Fundamental Change in Law and Society: Hart and Sartre on Revolution, Mouton, 1970; *The Philosophy of Mary,* St. Martin's, 1977; *Social Theory at a Crossroads,* Duquesne University Press, 1980; (with Robert Dahl) *Demokrati og Autoritet,* Dreyers, 1980.

Contributor: George A. Schrader, Jr., editor, *Existential Philosophers,* McGraw, 1967; Graham Hughes, editor, *Law, Reason and Justice,* New York University Press, 1969; James Edie, editor, *New Essays in Phenomenology,* Quadrangle, 1969; James R. Pennock and John W. Chapman, editors, *Voluntary Associations,* Atherton, 1969; Edie and others, editors, *Patterns of the Life-World,* Northwestern University Press, 1970; Hwa-Yol Jung, editor, *Existential Phenomenology and Political Theory,* Regnery, 1972; Pennock and Chapman, editors, *Coercion,* Aldine-Atherton, 1972; Pennock and Chapman, editors, *The Limits of the Law,* Lieber-Atherton, 1974; Bandman and Bandman, editors, *Bioethics and Human Rights: A Reader for Health Professionals,* Little, Brown, 1978; Paul A. Schilpp, editor, *The Living Philosophy of Jean-Paul Sartre,* Open Court, 1981. Contributor to professional journals.

WORK IN PROGRESS: A book on "institutional injustices."

SIDELIGHTS: William Leon McBride wrote *CA:* "I see my writing (whether fatuously or not is for others to judge) as primarily aimed at providing rational and scholarly support for progressive social and intellectual ideals. To undertake this during a period of political reaction and cultural retrogression is often a discouraging, lonely enterprise. But, as a Norwegian friend recently wrote to me concerning his own, similar endeavors, 'It is an indication of being alive.'"

AVOCATIONAL INTERESTS: Travel.

McCARTHY, Shaun (Lloyd) 1928-
(Theo Callas, Desmond Cory)

PERSONAL: Born February 16, 1928, in Lancing, Sussex, England; son of William Henry Lloyd and Iris Mary (Chatfield) McCarthy; married Blanca Rosa Poyatos, February 16, 1956; children: John Francis, Alexander Justin Lloyd, Richard Charles, Dewi Anthony. *Education:* St. Peter's College, Oxford, B.A., 1951, M.A., 1960; University of Wales, Ph.D., 1976. *Politics:* Liberal. *Religion:* Anglican. *Home:* "Los Arqueros," Torreblanca, Fuengirola, Spain. *Agent:* John Farquharson Ltd., Bell House, 8 Bell Yd., London WC2A 2JU, England.

CAREER: Cenemesa (electrical engineering), Cordoba, Spain, technical translator, 1953; Academia Britanica (language school), Cordoba, teacher, 1953-60; University of Wales, Institute of Science and Technology, Cardiff, lecturer in English, 1960-77; University of Qatar, associate professor of English, 1977-80; University College, Bahrain, associate professor of English, beginning 1980. *Military service:* Royal Marines, 45 Commando, 1945-48. *Member:* Institut des Arts et des Lettres (Geneva; fellow), Institute of Linguists (fellow), Society of Authors, Radiowriters' Association, Mystery Writers of America, Press Club (London).

WRITINGS: Lucky Ham, Macmillan, 1977; *The Modes of Comedy* (nonfiction), Volturna, 1980.

Under pseudonym Theo Callas: *The City of Kites,* Muller, 1955, Walker, 1964; *Ann and Peter in Southern Spain,* Muller, 1959.

Under pseudonym Desmond Cory: *Secret Ministry,* Muller, 1951; *Begin, Murderer!,* Muller, 1951; *This Traitor, Death,* Muller, 1952; *This Is Jezebel,* Muller, 1952; *Dead Man Falling,* Muller, 1953; *Lady Lost,* Muller, 1953; *Intrigue,* Muller, 1954; *The Shaken Leaf,* Muller, 1955; *The Height of Day,* Muller, 1955; *The Phoenix Sings,* Muller, 1955; *High Requiem,* Muller, 1956; *Johnny Goes North,* Muller, 1956; *Pilgrim at the Gate,* Muller, 1957, Ives Washburn, 1958; *Johnny Goes East,* Muller, 1958; *Johnny Goes West,* Muller, 1958, Walker, 1967; *Johnny Goes South,* Muller, 1959, Walker, 1964; *Pilgrim on the Island,* Muller, 1959, Walker, 1961.

The Head, Muller, 1960; *Jones on the Belgrade Express,* Muller, 1960; *Stranglehold,* Muller, 1961; *Undertow,* Muller, 1962, Walker, 1963; *Hammerhead,* Muller, 1963, published as *Shockwave,* Walker, 1964; *The Name of the Game,* Muller, 1964; *Deadfall,* Walker, 1965; *Feramontov,* Walker, 1966; *Timelock,* Walker, 1967; *The Night Hawk,* Walker, 1969; *Sunburst,* Walker, 1971; *Take My Drum to England,* Hodder & Stoughton, 1971; *Even If You Run,* Doubleday, 1972; *A Bit of a Shunt Up the River,* Doubleday, 1974; *The Circe Complex,* Macmillan, 1975; *Bennett,* Macmillan, 1977.

Also author of radio play, "Orbit One" for British Broadcasting Corp., 1961, and of a film adaptation of Graham Greene's *England Made Me.* Contributor of fiction to mystery anthologies, and contributor of articles, stories, and translations to periodicals, including *Western Mail, London Magazine, London Mystery Magazine, Observer,* and *Truth.*

WORK IN PROGRESS: The Tides of Tradition, with A. M. Kinghorn; *Snow;* a study of Lawrence Durrell's work; two novels, *The Caligula Conspiracy* and *The Eye of Shiva.*

SIDELIGHTS: Shaun McCarthy is well-known in the United Kingdom for his mystery-thrillers written under the pseudonym Desmond Cory. A number of critics feel that McCarthy's books offer his readers a bit more than merely a good mystery with some exciting moments. One such reviewer, M. R. Grant of

Library Journal, offers *Deadfall* as a perfect example of this point. He explains that the novel "is a serious psychological study of crime, and of the crime mind, its motivations, and its aspirations, combined with all the tension, fast action, and suspense expected from Mr. Cory's adventures."

However, Newgate Callendar sees a slight problem with McCarthy's writing. In his review of *Sunburst* in the *New York Times Book Review,* Callendar writes that "in some respects, this is a thoughtful and even brilliant book with an apocalyptic ending; in others, it is conventional secret-agent derring-do. . . . If Cory can rid himself of his Ian Fleming syndrome, he can develop into quite a writer. As it is, most readers should have a good time with the play and counterplay."

Often asked why he writes thrillers, McCarthy once told *CA:* "It may be because I had in some ways what the British call a Victorian childhood, while at the same time my school days coincided exactly with the last war. The war shaped me so much that there's a sense in which I've never got used to peace. Most of the thriller writers I've met are very mild, unassuming people—Chandler, Fleming and Coles were that way, almost out of touch, you'd say, with the post-war world. The real tough eggs don't have that inner conflict to resolve and don't, as a rule, write thrillers.

"Two things have influenced me particularly, Oxford University and Spain—semi-private worlds which enable you to sit back and look at what is happening to your own generation from a certain distance. Rather like what Europe was to Malcolm Cowley's exiles.

"My wife is Spanish and my sons are bilingual. I try to be interested in as many things as possible and hence have rather a ragbag of a mind. On the whole I don't feel it matters."

MEDIA ADAPTATIONS: Deadfall was adapted to film by Bryan Forbes for Twentieth Century-Fox Film Corp. in 1965; *The Circe Complex* was presented as a four-part serial on Thames Television, London, in 1980.

BIOGRAPHICAL/CRITICAL SOURCES: Library Journal, September 1, 1965; *Times Literary Supplement,* June 1, 1967; *New York Times Book Review,* August 6, 1967, May 16, 1971; *Book World,* August 17, 1969; *Best Sellers,* April 15, 1971.

*   *   *

McCARTHY, William E(dward) J(ohn)   1925-

PERSONAL: Born July 30, 1925, in London, England; son of Edward (a clerk) and Hyland McCarthy; married January 18, 1956; wife's name, Margaret. *Education:* Ruskin College, student, 1953-55; Merton College, Oxford, B.A. (first class honors), 1957; Nuffield College, Oxford, Ph.D., 1959. *Politics:* Labour Party. *Religion:* Agnostic. *Home:* 4 William Orchard Close, Old Headington, Oxford, England. *Office:* Nuffield College and Centre for Management Studies, Oxford University, Oxford, England.

CAREER: Oxford University, Oxford, England, research fellow of Nuffield College, 1959-63, staff lecturer and tutor in industrial relations, 1964-65; Royal Commission on Trade Unions and Employers' Association, London, England, director of research, 1965-68; Oxford University, fellow of Nuffield College and Centre for Management Studies, 1968—. Special adviser for European Economic Commission, 1974-75. University examiner and academic adviser to management schools and technical colleges. *Member:* Consumer's Association, University Industrial Relations Association, Fabian Society.

WRITINGS: The Future of the Unions, Fabian Society, 1962; *The Closed Shop in Britain,* University of California Press,

1964; *The Role of Shop Stewards in British Industrial Relations: A Survey of Existing Information and Research,* H.M.S.O., 1966; (with Arthur Ivor Marsh) *Disputes Procedures in Britain,* H.M.S.O., 1967; (with V. G. Munns) *Employer's Associations: The Results of Two Studies* (contains *The Functions and Organisation of Employers' Associations in Selected Industries,* by Munn, and *A Survey of Employers' Association Officials,* by McCarthy), H.M.S.O., 1967; (contributor) *Three Studies in Collective Bargaining,* H.M.S.O., 1968; *The Role of Government in Industrial Relations,* Ditchley Foundations, 1968; *Shop Stewards and Workshop Relations: The Results of a Study,* H.M.S.O., 1968; (editor) *Industrial Relations in Britain: Guide for Management and Unions,* Lyon, Grant & Green, 1969; *The Reform of Collective Bargaining: A Series of Case Studies,* H.M.S.O., 1971; *Trade Unions: Selected Readings,* Penguin, 1972; (with A. S. Collier) *Coming to Terms with Trade Unions: Six Case Studies in Collective Bargaining Strategy,* Institute of Personnel Management (London), 1973; (with N. D. Ellis) *Management by Agreement: An Alternative to the Industrial Relations Act,* Hutchinson, 1973; (with J. F. O'Brien and V. G. Dowd) *Wage Inflation and Wage Leadership: A Study of the Role of Key Wage Bargains in the Irish System of Collective Bargaining,* Economic and Social Science Research Institute (Dublin), 1975.

AVOCATIONAL INTERESTS: The Labour Party and the state of the English theatre.

*   *   *

McCLANE, Kenneth Anderson, Jr.   1951-

PERSONAL: Born February 19, 1951, in New York, N.Y.; son of Kenneth Anderson (a physician) and Genevieve (a painter; maiden name, Greene) McClane. *Education:* Cornell University, A.B. (with distinction), 1973, M.A., 1974, M.F.A., 1976. *Politics:* "Believe strongly in non-violence." *Home:* 114 Glenside Rd., Ithaca, N.Y. 14850. *Office:* Department of English, Cornell University, Ithaca, N.Y. 14850.

CAREER: Cornell University, Ithaca, N.Y., assistant professor of English, 1976—. Assistant director of writing center, City College of City University of New York, 1978-79. Consultant to educational television station in Elmira, N.Y., 1977-78. *Member:* Phi Beta Kappa. *Awards, honors:* Corson Morrison Poetry Prize, 1973; George Harmon Coxe Award in creative writing, Cornell University, 1973.

*WRITINGS—*Poetry: *Out Beyond the Bay,* Ithaca House, 1975; *Moons and Low Times,* Ithaca House, 1978; (contributor) Roseann P. Bell and others, editors, *Sturdy Black Bridges: Vision of Black Women in Literature,* Anchor Books, 1979; *To Hear the River,* West End Press, 1981. Contributor of poems to numerous periodicals, including *Vineyard Gazette, Beloit Poetry Journal, Wind, Texas Review, Black Scholar,* and *Thoreau Journal Quarterly.* Member of editorial staff of *Rainy Day, Epoch,* and *Dam* magazines; advisory editor of *Watu: A Journal of Black Thought.*

WORK IN PROGRESS: At Winter's End, a book of poems.

SIDELIGHTS: Kenneth Anderson McClane told *CA:* "Writing poetry is, I guess, my highest and most fragile pleasure. Words, and you learn to love them, seem to bring everything into question: heaven and hell, the monumental and the commonplace—all want the rigors and excitements of language to occasion them. And I guess that is what I am about, the occasion and its occasion, the world and its greater worlds. And there is a lot that is scary in this: the world does not terribly like one's sense of order—she has her own—and the paths to ruination are most clear. I think (and this is most obvious in my longer poems) that I am losing touch with it all, losing sight of the hill for the valley and yet both exist. The images are most distinct, but the meaning is difficult. And it is in these tough places, these difficult ones, that good writing is found. Other areas are most painful.''

*   *   *

McCLUNG, Robert M. 1916-

PERSONAL: Born September 10, 1916; son of Frank A. (a banker) and Mary A. (Goehring) McClung; married Gale Stubbs (editor of *Mount Holyoke Alumnae Quarterly*), July 23, 1949; children: William Marshall, Thomas Cooper. *Education:* Princeton University, A.B., 1939; Cornell University, M.S., 1948. *Religion:* Protestant. *Home:* 91 Sunset Ave., Amherst, Mass. 01002.

CAREER: McCann, Erickson, Inc. (advertising agency), New York City, copywriter, 1940-41, 1946-47; New York Zoological Park, New York City, assistant in animal departments, 1948-52, curator of mammals and birds, 1952-55; National Geographic Society, Washington, D.C., editor, 1958-62; freelance writer and illustrator of children's books, 1955-58, 1962—. *Military service:* U.S. Naval Reserve, active duty as deck officer and naval aviator, 1941-46; became lieutenant commander.

WRITINGS—Self-illustrated, except as noted; published by Morrow, except as noted: *Wings in the Woods*, 1948; *Sphinx: The Story of a Caterpillar*, 1949.

Ruby Throat: The Story of a Hummingbird, 1950; *Stripe: The Story of a Chipmunk*, 1951; *Spike: The Story of a Whitetail Deer*, 1952; *Tiger: The Story of a Swallowtail Butterfly*, 1953; *Bufo: The Story of a Toad*, 1954; *Vulcan: The Story of a Bald Eagle*, illustrated by Lloyd Sandford, 1955; *Major: The Story of a Black Bear*, 1956; *Green Darner: The Story of a Dragonfly*, 1956; *Leaper: The Story of an Atlantic Salmon*, 1957; *Luna: The Story of a Moth*, 1957; *Little Burma*, illustrated by Hord Stubblefield, 1958; *All about Animals and Their Young*, Random House, 1958; *Buzztail:The Story of a Rattlesnake*, 1958; *Whooping Crane*, illustrated by Sandford, 1959; *Otus: The Story of a Screech Owl*, illustrated by Sandford, 1959.

Shag: Last of the Plains Buffalo, illustrated by Louis Darling, 1960; *Whitefoot: The Story of a Woodmouse*, 1961; *Mammals and How They Live* (illustrated with photographs), Random House, 1963; *Possum*, 1963; *Screamer: Last of the Eastern Panthers*, illustrated by Sandford, 1964; *Spotted Salamander*, 1964; *Honker: The Story of a Wild Goose*, illustrated by Bob Hines, 1965; *Caterpillars and How They Live*, 1965; *The Swift Deer* (illustrated with photographs), Random House, 1966; *Ladybug*, 1966; *Moths and Butterflies and How They Live*, 1966; *The Mighty Bears* (illustrated with photographs), Random House, 1967; *Horseshoe Crab*, 1967; *Black Jack: Last of the Big Alligators*, illustrated by Sandford, 1967; *Redbird: The Story of a Cardinal*, 1968; *Lost Wild America: The Story of Our Extinct and Vanishing Wildlife*, illustrated by Hines, 1969; *Blaze: The Story of a Striped Skunk*, 1969.

Aquatic Insects and How They Live, 1970; *Thor: Last of the Sperm Whales*, illustrated by Hines, 1971; *Bees, Wasps, and Hornets, and How They Live*, 1971; *Scoop: Last of the Brown Pelicans*, illustrated by McClung and Sandford, 1972; *Treasures in the Sea* (illustrated with photographs), National Geographic Society, 1972; *Samson: Last of the California Grizzlies*, illustrated by Hines, 1973; *Mice, Moose, and Men: How Their Populations Rise and Fall*, 1973; *How Animals Hide*

(illustrated with photographs), National Geographic Society, 1973; *Gypsy Moth: Its History in America*, 1974; *Creepy Crawly Things: Reptiles and Amphibians* (illustrated with photographs), National Geographic Society, 1974; *Sea Star*, 1975; *Lost Wild Worlds: The Story of Extinct and Vanishing Wildlife of the Eastern Hemisphere*, 1976; *Animals that Build Their Homes* (illustrated with photographs), National Geographic Society, 1976; *Peeper, First Voice of Spring*, illustrated by Carol Lerner, 1977; *Hunted Mammals of the Sea*, illustrated by William Downey, 1978; *America's Endangered Birds: Programs and People Working to Save Them*, illustrated by George Founds, 1979; *Snakes: Their Place in the Sun* (illustrated with photographs), Garrard, 1979.

The Amazing Egg, Dutton, 1980; *Vanishing Wildlife of Latin America*, illustrated by Founds, 1981.

Editor and contributor, all published by National Geographic Society: *Wild Animals of North America*, *Song and Garden Birds of North America*, *Water, Prey, and Game Birds of North America*, and *Vacationland U.S.A.* Contributor to Grolier's *New Book of Knowledge*, and to magazines.

SIDELIGHTS: Robert McClung writes: ''Practically all of my books deal with wild animals and the natural environment. Unfortunately, more and more of the vital habitat that wildlife needs for survival is being polluted or destroyed by the actions of *Homo sapiens*. Through the years I have increasingly stressed in my writings the importance of a healthy environment and the conservation and wise use of all earth's resources. My aim in all of my books is to heighten the reader's awareness and appreciation of nature, and to develop his or her interest in and sympathy for all living things. The sooner a child develops an appreciation of the world he lives in, and realizes that it could be destroyed, the better prepared he will be to make sane and wise choices when he becomes an adult.''

*   *   *

McCONNELL, James Douglas Rutherford 1915-
(Douglas Rutherford; Paul Temple, a joint pseudonym)

PERSONAL: Born October 14, 1915, in Kilkenny, Ireland; son of James and Edith (Cooney) McConnell; married Margaret Laura Goodwin (an author's consultant), 1953; children: Mike. *Education:* Attended Sedburgh School; Clare College, Cambridge, M.A., 1937; University of Reading, M.Phil., 1977. *Home and office:* Hal's Croft, Monxton, Andover, Hampshire SP11 8AS, England. *Agent:* Richard Scott Simon, 32 College Cross, London M11 PR, England.

CAREER: Eton College, Windsor, England, language teacher and housemaster, 1946-73. *Military service:* British Army, Intelligence Corps, 1940-46; served in North Africa and Italy; mentioned in dispatches, 1944. *Member:* Crime Writers Association, Detection Club, Tidworth Golf Club.

WRITINGS: Learn Italian Quickly, MacGibbon & Kee, 1960; *Learn Spanish Quickly*, MacGibbon & Kee, 1961, Citadel, 1963; *Learn French Quickly*, MacGibbon & Kee, 1966; *Eton: How It Works*, Faber, 1967, Humanities, 1968; *Eton Repointed: The New Structures of an Ancient Foundation*, Faber, 1970; (editor) *Treasures of Eton*, Chatto & Windus, 1976; *Early Learning Foundation*, Four Seasons Publications, 1979; *The Benedictine Commando*, Hamish Hamilton, 1981.

With Francis Durbridge; all published by Hodder & Stoughton: (Under joint pseudonym Paul Temple) *The Tyler Mystery*, 1957; (under joint pseudonym Paul Temple) *East of Algiers*, 1959; *The Pig-Tail Murder*, 1969; *A Man Called Harry Brent*, 1970;

Bat out of Hell, 1972; *A Game of Murder,* 1975; *The Passenger,* 1977; *Tim Frazer Gets the Message,* 1980; *Breakaway,* 1981.

Under name Douglas Rutherford; published by Collins, except as indicated: *Comes the Blind Fury,* Faber, 1950; *Meet a Body,* Faber, 1951; *Flight into Peril,* Dodd, 1952 (published in England as *Telling of Murder,* Faber, 1952); *Grand Prix Murder,* 1955; *The Perilous Sky,* 1955; *The Chequered Flag,* 1956; *The Long Echo,* 1957, Abelard, 1958; *A Shriek of Tyres,* 1958, published as *On the Track of Death,* Abelard, 1959.

Murder Is Incidental, 1961; *The Creeping Flesh,* 1963, Walker & Co., 1965; (editor) *Best Motor Racing Stories,* Faber, 1965; *The Black Leather Murders,* Walker & Co., 1966; *Skin for Skin,* Walker & Co., 1968; (editor and author of introduction) *Best Underworld Stories,* Faber, 1969; *The Gilt-Edged Cockpit,* 1969, Doubleday, 1971.

Clear the Fast Lane, 1971, Holt, 1972; *Gunshot Grand Prix,* 1972; *Killer on the Track,* 1973; *Kick Start,* 1973, Walker & Co., 1974; *Rally to the Death,* 1974; *Mystery Tour,* 1975, Walker & Co., 1976; *Race against the Sun,* 1975; *Return Load,* Walker & Co., 1977; *Collision Course,* Macmillan, 1978; *Turbo,* 1980; *Porcupine Basin,* 1981.

WORK IN PROGRESS: Research for a book on motor racing or fast cars; plans for a nonfiction book on Eton College.

SIDELIGHTS: James Douglas Rutherford McConnell told *CA:* "I wanted to be a writer from boyhood. Intelligence work in World War II gave me a background. During two decades as a master at Eton College, writing suspense stories provided the diversity I needed. Writing was and remains a pastime as much as work. I like to be diversified. Now a full time writer, I have been writing serious theses on education, novels for young teenagers, learning systems for the under five-year-olds, suspense novels, and a serious historical novel. I am approaching my half-century in published works.

"I now live in a thatched cottage in a Hampshire village, have a London pied-a-terre, and travel Europe often. When on a book, I work four hours mornings and sometimes two hours evenings. My books have been translated into many languages. I reckon they have been read by a number equal to the population of greater London. I want to live long enough to write another fifty books.

"My advice to aspiring authors? The first and final requirement is to want to see your work in print ardently enough to endure the labour and torment of writing and submitting a book."

AVOCATIONAL INTERESTS: Golf, music, glamorous cars, travel.

BIOGRAPHICAL/CRITICAL SOURCES: New Statesman, March 10, 1967; *Times Literary Supplement,* April 13, 1967; *New York Times Book Review,* February 9, 1969, January 4, 1981; *Spectator,* November 22, 1969; *Best Sellers,* April 1, 1971.

*   *   *

McCORQUODALE, Barbara
See CARTLAND, Barbara (Hamilton)

*   *   *

McCOY, J(oseph) J(erome) 1917-

PERSONAL: Born January 4, 1917, in Philadelphia, Pa.; son of Joseph J. (a civil engineer) and Clara (Tinaro) McCoy; married Josephine Barbara Kocyan (an actress and teacher),

April 13, 1948; children: Tara Irene, Liza Marie. *Education:* Pennsylvania State University, Associate degree in Agriculture. *Agent:* Bertha Klausner, International Literary Agency, 71 Park Ave., New York, N.Y. 10016.

CAREER: Author. Radio producer-director in Philadelphia, Pa., 1946-47; Children's Aid Society, New York City, instructor in agriculture and nature, 1947-48; farm manager in Connecticut, 1948-50; Bide-A-Wee Home For Animals, New York City, manager, 1951-56; Gaines Dog Research Center, New York City, assistant to director, 1956-60; author of syndicated column "All about Pets," for General Features Corp. and Los Angeles Times Syndicate, 1965-68; Board of Animal Regulation, Fort Washington, Pa., chairman, 1965-70; chairman of Frenchtown (N.J.) Board of Health, 1974-76, and Shade Tree Commission, 1977-81. *Military service:* U.S. Army, Veterinary Service, 1942-46; became technical sergeant. *Member:* Authors Guild, American Horse Protection Association, Hawk Mountain Sanctuary Association.

AWARDS, HONORS: New York Herald Tribune Spring Book Festival, Honor Book, 1966, and National Association of Independent Schools Award, 1967, for *The Hunt for the Whooping Cranes;* National Science Teachers Association and the Childrens Book Council, outstanding science book for children, 1973, for *Our Captive Animals,* and 1975, for *A Sea of Troubles;* New Jersey Council on the Arts writer fellowships, 1976 and 1980; Environmental Protection Award from New Jersey Soil Conservation Service, 1980.

*WRITINGS—*Adult: (With H. J. Deutsch) *How to Care for Your Cat,* Cornerstone, 1961; *The Complete Book of Dog Training and Care,* Coward, 1962; *The Complete Book of Cat Health and Care,* Putnam, 1966; *Saving Our Wildlife,* Macmillan, 1970; *The Cancer Lady: Maud Slye and Her Heredity Studies,* Thomas Nelson, 1977; *In Defense of Animals,* Seabury, 1978.

Juvenile: *Lords of the Sky,* Bobbs-Merrill, 1963; *Animal Servants of Man,* Lothrop, 1963; *The World of the Veterinarian,* Lothrop, 1964; *The Hunt for the Whooping Cranes,* Lothrop, 1966; *Swans,* Lothrop, 1967; *House Sparrows: Ragamuffins of the City,* Seabury, 1968; *The Nature Sleuths: Protectors of Our Wildlife,* Lothrop, 1969; *Shadows over the Land,* Seabury, 1970; *To Feed a Nation,* Thomas Nelson, 1971; *Our Captive Animals,* Seabury, 1972; *Wild Enemies,* Hawthorn Books, 1974; *A Sea of Troubles,* Seabury, 1975; *Pet Safety,* F. Watts, 1979.

WORK IN PROGRESS: A memoir, *The Great Professor: Louis Agassiz in America;* a novella, *All God's Creatures Have Rights.*

SIDELIGHTS: J. J. McCoy writes: "Writing good nonfiction is an exacting task, whether one's readers are adults or children. The successful juvenile author does not write down to children; indeed, one is lucky to keep up with them. In my experience, based on letters from juvenile readers and questions asked me when I visit schools and libraries as a guest speaker, children want their intelligence and sensitivities to be respected. And they demand accuracy, clarity, and interesting books. Apropos visits to schools and libraries: I think it is very important for juvenile writers, fiction or nonfiction, to get out and talk with the potential readers of their books. A juvenile writer should find out what children think and what they want to read—one should avoid writing books based too much on the writer's recollections of childhood or early experiences."

*   *   *

McCRACKEN, Paul Winston 1915-

PERSONAL: Born December 29, 1915, in Richland, Iowa; son

of Charles Sumner (a farmer) and Mary (Coffin) McCracken; married Emily Ruth Siler, May 28, 1942; children: Linda Jo, Paula Jeanne. *Education:* William Penn College, B.A., 1937; Harvard University, M.A., 1942, Ph.D., 1948. *Politics:* Republican. *Religion:* Presbyterian. *Home:* 2564 Hawthorn, Ann Arbor, Mich. 48104. *Office:* School of Business Administration, University of Michigan, Ann Arbor, Mich. 48104.

CAREER: Berea College, Berea, Ky., member of faculty, 1937-40; U.S. Department of Commerce, Washington, D.C., economist, 1942-43; Federal Reserve Bank of Minneapolis, Minneapolis, Minn., director of research, 1945-48; University of Michigan, School of Business Administration, Ann Arbor, associate professor, 1948-50, professor of business administration, 1950-66, Edmund Ezra Day University Professor of Business Administration, 1966—. Council of Economic Advisers, Washington, D.C., member, 1956-59, chairman, 1969-71. Director of Consolidated Foods, Dow Chemical Corp., Kmart Corp., Texas Instruments, Inc. *Member:* American Economic Association, Royal Economic Society, American Statistical Association (fellow), American Finance Association, Econometric Society, Cosmos Club (Washington, D.C.), Harvard Club (New York). *Awards, honors:* L.H.D. from William Penn College.

WRITINGS: Taxes and Economic Growth in Michigan, Upjohn, 1960; (with Emile Benoit) *The Balance of Payments and Domestic Prosperity,* School of Business Administration, University of Michigan, 1963; (with others) *Consumer Installment Credit and Public Policy,* School of Business Administration, University of Michigan, 1965; (with others) *Fiscal Policy and Business Capital Formation,* American Enterprise Institute for Public Policy Research, 1967; (with Murray L. Weidonbaum) *Fiscal Responsibility: Tax Increases or Spending Cuts?,* New York University Press, 1973; *The Energy Crisis,* American Enterprise Institute for Public Policy Research, 1974; *Towards Full Employment and Price Stability,* Organization for Economic Cooperation and Development (Paris), 1977. Also author of numerous shorter works and monographs. Contributor to professional journals.

*   *   *

McDERMOTT, John Francis (III)   1902-1981

PERSONAL: Born April 18, 1902, in St. Louis, Mo.; died April 23, 1981; son of John F. and Mary Elizabeth (Steber) McDermott; married Mary Stephanie Kendrick, December 20, 1924; children: John Francis IV. *Education:* Washington University, St. Louis, Mo., A.B., 1923, A.M., 1924. *Politics:* Republican. *Home:* 6345 Westminster Pl., St. Louis, Mo. 63130. *Office:* Southern Illinois University, Edwardsville, Ill. 62025.

CAREER: Washington University, St. Louis, Mo., instructor, 1924-36, assistant professor, 1936-49, associate professor of English, 1949-61, associate professor of American cultural history, 1961-63; Southern Illinois University at Edwardsville, research professor of humanities, 1963-71, adjunct research professor, 1971-81. Consultant on early Western American history and nineteenth century American painting. Chairman of conference on research opportunities in American cultural history, Washington University, 1959, and conference on the Frontier re-examined, Southern Illinois University, 1965; chairman and participant in numerous other conferences on American history. *Military service:* U.S. Army Air Forces, 1942-45; became captain.

MEMBER: Modern Language Association of America (cochairman of Comparative Literature V, 1939; chairman of Comparative Literature V, 1940; member of bibliographical committee and co-editor, Anglo-French and Franco-American Studies, 1938-39, 1948-54), Modern Humanities Research Association (life member), Bibliographical Society of America, American Antiquarian Society, Institut Francais de Washington (trustee, beginning 1958), Academie de Macon (associe membre perpetuel), Society of American Historians, American Name Society, American Studies Association, American Folklore Society (member of council, 1958-60), American Association of University Professors, National Folk Festival Association (first vice-president, 1952-53; president, 1952-62; chairman of folklore conferences, 1953, 1955), Organization of American Historians, American Historical Association, State Historical Society of Missouri, Illinois State Historical Society, Indiana Historical Society, Kansas Historical Society, Minnesota Historical Society, New York Historical Society, Missouri Historical Society (member of board of trustees, 1950-59; secretary of board, 1951-54), William Clark Society (president, 1952, 1953, 1961-62), St. Louis Westerners (vice-president, 1946-61; president, 1962), St. Louis Historical Documents Foundation (secretary, 1946-48; president and editor, beginning 1948).

AWARDS, HONORS: Newberry Library fellow in Midwestern Studies, 1947-48; research grants from Washington University, 1950, 1957, 1960, American Philosophical Society, 1939, 1940, 1954, 1957, 1958-59, 1963, 1964, Michigan State University, 1950-51, American Council of Learned Societies, 1960, Pro-Helvetia Foundation, Zurich, 1961, Henry E. Hunington Library and Art Gallery, 1965, and Southern Illinois University, 1963, 1964, 1965; Guggenheim Memorial fellow, 1954-55; award of merit from Missouri Historical Society, 1961; Palmes Academiques, 1966; chevalier, Ordre National du Merit, 1970; D.H.L. from University of Missouri, 1977, and Southern Illinois University, 1980.

WRITINGS: (Editor) *The Collected Verse of Lewis Carroll,* Dutton, 1929; (editor with K. B. Taft and D. O. Jensen) *Contemporary Thought,* Houghton, 1929; (with Taft and Jensen) *The Technique of Composition,* Richard R. Smith, 1931, 5th edition, Rinehart, 1960; (editor) *Modern Plays,* Harcourt, 1932; (editor with Taft and Jensen) *Contemporary Opinion,* Houghton, 1933; (editor) *The Russian Journal and Other Selections from the Work of Lewis Carroll,* Dutton, 1935, reprinted, Dover, 1977; *Private Libraries in Creole Saint Louis,* Johns Hopkins Press, 1938.

(Editor) *Tixier's Travels on the Osage Prairies,* University of Oklahoma Press, 1940; *A Glossary of Mississippi Valley French, 1673-1850,* Washington University Press, 1941; (with Taft, Jensen, and W. H. Yeager) *English Communication,* Farrar & Rinehart, 1943; (editor) *The Western Journals of Washington Irving,* University of Oklahoma Press, 1944, 2nd edition, 1966; (editor with J. P. Donnelly, R. J. Boylan, B. R. Gieseker, C. van Ravenswaay, and I. Dilliard) *Old Cahokia: A Narrative and Documents Illustrating the First Century of Its History,* St. Louis Historical Documents Foundation, 1949.

(Editor) *Travels in Search of the Elephant: The Wanderings of Alfred S. Waugh, Artist, 1845-46,* Missouri Historical Society, 1951; (editor) *Up the Missouri with Audubon: The Journal of Edward Harris,* University of Oklahoma Press, 1951; (editor) *The Early Histories of St. Louis,* St. Louis Historical Documents Foundation, 1952; (editor) Thaddeus A. Culbertson, *Journal of an Expedition to the Mauvaises Terres and the Upper Missouri in 1850,* Smithsonian Institution, 1952; (editor) John Treat Irving, Jr., *Indian Sketches Taken during an Expedition to the Pawnee Tribes, 1833,* University of Oklahoma Press, 1955; (editor) *A Tour on the Prairies by Washington Irving,* University of Oklahoma Press, 1956; (editor)

Louis LeClerc de Milford, *Memoir or a Cursory Glance at My Different Travels and My Sojourn in the Creek Nation*, Lakeside Press, 1956; (editor) *Prairie and Mountain Sketches*, University of Oklahoma Press, 1957; *A Frontier Library: The Books of Isaac McCoy*, Bibliographical Society of America, 1958; *The Lost Panoramas of the Mississippi*, University of Chicago Press, 1958; *The Art of Seth Eastman*, Smithsonian Institution, 1959; *George Caleb Bingham: River Portraitist*, University of Oklahoma Press, 1959.

Seth Eastman: Pictorial Historian of the Indian, University of Oklahoma Press, 1961; (editor) *Research Opportunities in American Cultural History*, University of Kentucky Press, 1961; (editor) John S. Robb, *Streaks of Squatter Life*, Scholars' Facsimiles & Reprints, 1962; (editor) *The Western Journals of Dr. George Hunter, 1795-1804*, American Philosophical Society, 1963; (editor) *Audubon in the West*, University of Oklahoma Press, 1965; (editor) *The World of Washington Irving*, Dell, 1965; (editor) *The French in the Mississippi Valley*, University of Illinois Press, 1965; *The American Angle of Vision*, Cross Currents, 1966; (editor) Henry Marie Brackenridge, *Modern Chivalry and Louis-Philippe*, Historical Society of Western Pennsylvania, 1967; (editor) *The Frontier Re-examined*, University of Illinois Press, 1967; (editor) *An Artist on the Overland Trail: The 1849 Diary of James F. Wikins*, Huntington Library, 1967; (editor) *Before Mark Twain: A Sampler of Old, Old Times on the Mississippi*, Southern Illinois University Press, 1968; *Frenchmen and French Ways in the Mississippi Valley*, University of Illinois Press, 1969; *Lost Manuscripts of Western Travel*, University of Arizona Press, 1967.

Travelers on the Western Frontier, University of Illinois Press, 1970; *Seth Eastmans's Mississippi: A Lost Portfolio Recovered*, University of Illinois Press, 1973; *The Spanish in the Mississippi Valley: 1762-1804*, University of Illinois Press, 1974; (editor) Philip Pittman, *The Present State of the European Settlements on the Mississippi*, Memphis State University Press, 1977. General editor, "Travels on the Western Waters" series, published by Southern Illinois University Press, 1965-81. Contributor of more than 160 articles and reviews to encyclopedias, professional publications, and magazines. Associate editor, *French American Review*, 1950; member of advisory board, *Papers on Language and Literature*, beginning 1965.

WORK IN PROGRESS: A biography of Pierre Laclede, founder of St. Louis, to be published by University of Oklahoma Press; a biography of Auguste Pierre Chouteau; editing journal of R. F. Kurz, a Swiss artist, on the Upper Missouri, 1851-52; editing the diary of J. B. Truteau, a fur trader, 1794-96.†

* * *

McDONALD, Eva (Rose)

PERSONAL: Born in London, England; daughter of Edgar William Jary and Louisa Harriet (Roberts) McDonald. *Education:* Attended South London Commercial College. *Religion:* Christian. *Home:* Wyldwynds, 105 Bathurst Walk, Iver, Buckinghamshire SL0 9EF, England.

CAREER: Novelist. *Member:* Society of Authors.

WRITINGS—All published by R. Hale: *Lazare the Leopard*, 1959; *Dark Enchantment*, 1960; *The Rebel Bride*, 1960; *The Prettiest Jacobite*, 1961; *The Captive Lady*, 1962; *The Maids of Taunton*, 1963, reprinted, 1980; *The Black Glove*, 1964; *The Reluctant Bridegroom*, 1965; *The Runaway Countess*, 1966; *The Gretna Wedding*, 1967; *The Austrian Bride*, 1968; *Lord Byron's First Love*, 1968; *The Lost Lady*, 1969.

The Wicked Squire, 1970; *The French Mademoiselle*, 1970; *Shelley's Springtime Bride*, 1970; *The White Petticoat*, 1971; *The Spanish Wedding*, 1971; *The Lady from Yorktown*, 1972; *Regency Rake*, 1973; *The Revengeful Husband*, 1974; *Lament for Lady Flora*, 1974; *Lord Rochester's Daughters*, 1974; *Roman Conqueror*, 1975; *November Nocturne*, 1975; *Cromwell's Spy*, 1976; *King in Jeopardy*, 1976; *Dearest Ba*, 1976; *Norman Knight*, 1977; *The Road to Glencoe*, 1977; *Cry Treason Thrice*, 1977; *The Deadly Dagger*, 1978; *Candlemas Courtship*, 1978; *Queen Victoria's Prince*, 1978; *Napolean's Captain*, 1979; *John Ruskin's Wife*, 1979; *Chateau of Nightingales*, 1979; *House of Secrets*, 1980.

SIDELIGHTS: Eva McDonald writes to *CA:* "I adore traveling, having been to Scandinavia and Europe, . . . in Switzerland, France, Italy, Germany, and Yugoslavia. I also adore cats but, alas, lost two, Smokey and Pinto, both dear little creatures. One followed me like a dog, and Pinto used to meet me when I came off my train in the evening—he was so clever that he knew at what time I would come.

"As to my writing, my first book, *Lazare the Leopard*, was written when I was 21, but it was published many years later. I always meant to be a writer, but I must confess to great despondency. Both my mother and grandmother . . . encouraged me tremendously; to them both I owe a tremendous debt. It was my Grandmother who arranged for me to be taught the piano and, when I was in my twenties and thirties, it was my darling mother who so encouraged me, although, alas, neither she nor my grandmother lived to see my first book published.

"I have always regarded myself a 'natural' writer, and, because of that perhaps, I do not feel that creative writing can be taught."

AVOCATIONAL INTERESTS: Playing the piano, travel.

*   *   *

McDOUGAL, Myres Smith 1906-

PERSONAL: Born November 23, 1906, in Burton, Miss.; son of Luther Love (a physician) and Lulu B. (Smith) McDougal; married Frances McDannold Lee, December 27, 1933; children: John Lee. *Education:* University of Mississippi, B.A., 1926, M.A., 1927, LL.B., 1935; Oxford University, B.A. in Jurisprudence, 1929, B.C.L., 1930; Yale University, J.S.D., 1931. *Politics:* Democrat. *Home:* 427 Saint Ronan St., New Haven, Conn. *Office:* Yale Law School, 401A Yale Station, New Haven, Conn. 06520.

CAREER: University of Illinois at Urbana-Champaign, assistant professor of law, 1931-34; Yale University, Law School, New Haven, Conn., associate professor, 1934-39, professor, 1939-44, William K. Townsend Professor of Law, 1944-58, Sterling Professor of Law, 1958-75, Emeritus Sterling Professor of Law, 1975—. Visiting professor of law, Cairo University, 1959-60. Assistant general counsel, U.S. Lend Lease Administration, 1942; general counsel, Office of Foreign Relief and Rehabilitation Operations, U.S. State Department, 1943. Member, U.S. panel, Permanent Court of Arbitration, 1963-69. *Member:* American Bar Association, American Society of International Law (president, 1958), Association of American Law Schools (president, 1966); Graduate Club, Lawn Club, Morey's Club (all New Haven); Yale Club (New York). *Awards, honors:* L.H.D. from Columbia University, 1954 and Temple University, 1975; L.L.D. from Northwestern University, 1966, York University, 1970, and University of New Haven, 1975; Hudson Medal, American Society of International Law, 1976.

WRITINGS: (With David Hober) *Property, Wealth, Land*, Michie Co., 1947; (with M.E.H. Rotival) *The Case for Regional*

Planning, Yale University Press, 1947; *Municipal Land Policy and Control,* Practising Law Institute, 1946; *The World Constitutive Process of Authoritative Decision,* Yale University Law School, 1959; (co-author) *Studies in World Public Order,* Yale University Press, 1960; (with F. P. Feleciono) *Law and Minimum World Public Order,* Yale University Press, 1961; (with W. T. Barke) *The Public Order of the Oceans,* Yale University Press, 1962; (with Harold D. Lasswell and Ivan Vlosic) *Law and Public Order in Space,* Yale University Press, 1964; (with Lasswell and James C. Miller) *Interpretation of Agreements and World Public Order Principles of Content and Procedure,* Yale University Press, 1967; (with Lasswell and Chen) *Human Rights and World Public Order: The Basic Policies of an International Law of Human Dignity,* Yale University Press, 1979; (with W. M. Reisman) *International Law in Contemporary Perspective: The Public Order of the World Community,* Foundation Press, 1981; (contributor) *International Law Essays,* Foundation Press, 1981.

*   *   *

McDOW, Gerald
See SCORTIA, Thomas N(icholas)

*   *   *

McGOEY, John Heck 1915-

PERSONAL: Born February 16, 1915, in Toronto, Ontario, Canada; son of Joseph J. and Josephine (Heck) McGoey. *Education:* Attended St. Michael's College School, Toronto, Ontario, 1926-32, and St. Augustine's Seminary, Toronto, 1932-38. *Home:* Scarboro Foreign Missions Society, 2685 Kingston Rd., Scarboro, Ontario, Canada M1M 1M4.

CAREER: Roman Catholic priest, member of Scarboro Foreign Mission Society; missionary to China, 1939-49; Scarboro Foreign Mission Society, Scarboro, Ontario, director of promotion work, 1949-53, superior of Scarboro Missions in Bahamas, 1954-62; Blessed Sacrament Church, Harbour Island, Bahamas, pastor, 1954-68; teacher, preacher, writer, lecturer, personal and marriage counselor, family life and sex education consultant, 1968—. Director, Catholic Welfare Committee of China, 1946-49; executive secretary, American Aid to China Committee on Health and Welfare, 1948-49. Handled medical and welfare phases of Marshall Plan for China under auspices of Joint Catholic-Protestant Voluntary Agency Committee. Civilian chaplain, U.S. Navy, Shanghai, 1946-49. Family life consultant, St. Petersburg, Florida, Diocese.

WRITINGS: Fathering Forth, Bruce, 1958 (published in Ireland as *The Priest and the Priesthood,* Clonmore & Reynolds, 1961); *Nor Scrip, Nor Shoes* (autobiography), Little, Brown, 1958; *The Sins of the Just,* Bruce, 1963; *Speak, Lord!* (poems), Bruce, 1966; *The Uncertain Sound,* Bruce, 1967; *Dare I Love?,* Gall, 1971, Our Sunday Visitor, 1974; *Through Sex to Love,* Gall, 1971; *Sex, Love and the Believing Boy,* Gall, 1980; *Sex, Love and the Believing Girl,* Gall, 1980. Also author of the "McGoey Series" of sex education films. Columnist, "If You Ask Me," Catholic Register (Toronto). Contributor of articles to *Homiletic and Pastoral Review* and *Sponsa Regis.* Editor, *Scarboro Missions.*

SIDELIGHTS: John Heck McGoey told *CA* that he wrote his sex education books as a "revolt against the current obsession with sex as selfish self-indulgence not love." He hopes his books will "work to show the difference between sex and love as well as explain and promote emotional maturity." McGoey comments, "I want to inspire people to a more thoughtful, loving personal life."

McGoey's books have been translated into French, Spanish, and Chinese.

*   *   *

McGRATH, Thomas 1916-

PERSONAL: Born November 20, 1916, near Sheldon, N.D.; son of James Lang and Catherine (Shea) McGrath; married Eugenia Johnson, February 13, 1960; children: Thomas Samuel Koan. *Education:* University of North Dakota, B.A., 1939; Louisiana State University, M.A., 1940; New College, Oxford, additional study, 1947-48. *Politics:* "Unaffiliated far left." *Office:* Department of English, Moorhead State University, Moorhead, Minn. 56560.

CAREER: Poet. Colby College, Waterville, Me., instructor in English, 1940-41; Los Angeles State College of Applied Arts and Sciences (now California State University, Los Angeles), assistant professor of English, 1950-54; C. W. Post College, Long Island, N.Y., assistant professor of English, 1960-61; North Dakota State University, Fargo, N.D., associate professor of English, 1962-67; Moorhead State University, Moorhead, Minn., associate professor of English, 1969—. *Military service:* U.S. Army Air Forces, 1942-45. *Member:* Phi Beta Kappa. *Awards, honors:* Rhodes Scholar, Oxford University, 1947-48; Alan Swallow Poetry Book Award, 1954, for *Figures from a Double World;* Amy Lowell travelling poetry scholarship, 1965-66; Guggenheim fellowship, 1968; Minnesota State Arts Council grant, 1973; National Foundation for the Arts grant, 1974; Bush Foundation fellowship, 1976; Minnesota Arts Board grant, 1979.

WRITINGS—Poetry, except as indicated: *First Manifesto,* Swallow & Critchlow, 1940; (contributor) *The Dialectics of Love in Three Young Poets: Thomas McGrath, William Peterson, James Franklin Lewis,* Press of James A. Decker, 1942; *To Walk a Crooked Mile,* Alan Swallow, 1947; *Longshot O'Leary's Garland of Practical Poesie,* International Publishers, 1949; *Witness to the Times,* privately printed, 1954; *Figures from a Double World,* Alan Swallow, 1955; *The Gates of Ivory, The Gates of Horn* (novel), Mainstream Publishers, 1957; *About Clouds* (juvenile), Melmont, 1959; *The Beautiful Things* (juvenile), Vanguard, 1960; *Letter to an Imaginary Friend,* Volume I, Alan Swallow, 1962, Volume II, Swallow Press, 1970; *New and Selected Poems,* Alan Swallow, 1964; *The Movie at the End of the World: Selected Poems,* Alan Swallow, 1972; *Voyages to the Inland Sea #3,* Center for Contemporary Poetry, 1973; *Voices from beyond the Wall,* Territorial Press, 1974; *A Sound of One Hand,* Minnesota Writers Publishing House, 1975; *Open Songs,* Uzzano, 1977; *Letter to Tomasito,* Holy Cow!, 1977; *Trinc: Praises II,* Copper Canyon Press, 1979; *Waiting for the Angel,* Uzzano, 1979.

Also author of about twenty film scripts. Poetry anthologized in *Poetry for Pleasure,* edited by Ian M. Parsons, Doubleday, 1960, *New Poets of England and America,* edited by Donald Hall, Meridian, 1962, *Poets of Today,* edited by Walter Lowenfels, International Publishers, 1964, *Heartland,* edited by Lucien Stryk, Northern Illinois University Press, 1967, and *Where Is Vietnam?,* edited by Lowenfels, Doubleday, 1967. Contributor of poetry, criticism, and short stories to magazines, including *Kayak, Sixties,* and *Poetry.* Founder and editor, with wife, Eugenia McGrath, *Crazy Horse;* former assistant editor of *California Quarterly* and other literary magazines.

WORK IN PROGRESS: Volume III of *Letter to an Imaginary Friend;* a book of lyric poems.

SIDELIGHTS: Some critics believe that Thomas McGrath's leftist political views have kept him from the recognition his work warrants. *New York Times Book Review* critic Kenneth Rexroth comments, "It is the other peoples' opinions which have kept him from being as well known as he deserves, for he is a most accomplished and committed poet." A *New Republic* reviewer believes that "McGrath is one of the best American poets extant, but he is of the wrong political and esthetic camp, and therefore consistently neglected by our literary power brokers." Other critics, however, do not believe that McGrath's polemics interfere with his art. Hugh Gibb, writing in the *New York Times*, describes McGrath: "In the first place, when contemplating a harsh and chaotic world, he never allows his genuine pity for the oppressed to degenerate into self-pity; and secondly, he is never forced to retreat into a world of private fantasy and introspection. In consequence he has been able not only to sustain the tradition which would otherwise appear to be almost extinct, but has brought to it a new and vigorous honesty."

McGrath told *CA:* "I've gone on teaching—with years off when I had money to pay for writing time—and writing films. My main energies in recent years have gone to my son Thomasito and my continuing long poem *Letter to an Imaginary Friend*, which is apparently my main work. Looking forward to a life of poverty (but *leisure*) in a few years. I expect to continue to give readings of my poems—which I do more and more these years—and summer workshops. This may still keep the wolf at the door, but I should be able to feed him from time to time, maybe domesticate him. It's time to invent the dog."

McGrath has wandered around Europe and Mexico, covered America by car, freight car, and hitchhiking, worked at odd ("some very odd") jobs to finance an interlude of writing poetry. He says his dream is to find a place where he could teach one semester at a time and a film producer for whom he could do a few documentaries at intervals—thus clearing the way for working several months at a stretch at poetry.

BIOGRAPHICAL/CRITICAL SOURCES: New York Times, March 7, 1948; *Saturday Review,* April 17, 1948; *New York Times Book Review,* February 21, 1965; *Antioch Review,* fall-winter, 1970-71; *New Republic,* April 21, 1973.

*   *   *

McILHANY, William H(erbert) II   1951-

PERSONAL: Surname is pronounced mack-el-hay-nee; born March 10, 1951, in Roanoke, Va.; son of H. Hoge (an executive and distributor of construction equipment) and Zirleta (Kent) McIlhany; married Mary Lee Merrill (a high school teacher of English), June 29, 1974. *Education:* Washington and Lee University, B.A., 1973. *Politics:* "Libertarian: Non-party affiliated." *Religion:* Anglican Orthodox. *Home:* 416 Vista Trucha, Newport Beach, Calif. 92660. *Agent:* Cherry Weiner Literary Agency, 1734 Church St., Rahway, N.J. 07065.

CAREER: McIlhany Equipment Co., Roanoke, Va., director and consultant, 1973-75; full-time writer in Newport Beach, Calif., 1973—. Instructor at Santa Ana College, 1974—; lecturer, American Opinion Speakers Bureau, 1975—. Editor, researcher, and video documentary writer, American Media, 1979—. *Member:* International Brotherhood of Magicians (vice-president of Roanoke chapter, 1972-73), Society of American Magicians, Academy of Magical Arts, John Birch Society.

WRITINGS: Klandestine: The Untold Story of Delmar Dennis and His Role in the F.B.I.'s War against the Ku Klux Klan, Arlington House, 1975; *The A.C.L.U. on Trial,* Arlington House, 1976; *The Tax-Exempt Scandal: America's Leftist Founda-*

tions, Arlington House, 1980. Contributor to *Libertarian Review, Review of the News,* and *Commerce Review.* Associate editor, *Commerce Review,* 1973.

WORK IN PROGRESS: A multi-volume world history, starting with the year 1776, from the viewpoint of the John Birch Society, *History of the Master Conspiracy; No Civil War at All: Eighty Years of Conspiracy to Destroy the United States; Father Did Know Best: The Story of Lauren Chapin; An Eye for An Eye: The Suppressed Story of Cell Therapy;* ghost-writing a book for a major investment newsletter writer.

SIDELIGHTS: William McIlhany told *CA* that he is "not interested in writing just to be writing, but rather writing only in areas where [my] principles and convictions can be thoroughly upheld. The goal of my writing presently, in nonfiction, is to expose the efforts of those in and out of government who are trying to impose tyranny across the world. As an alternative for the future, I am proposing a very limited constitutional republic and a free market economy. I hope to carry some of these themes into fictional form in the future. Another interest is the broad range of unorthodox views which receive little or no attention in all fields of academia."

AVOCATIONAL INTERESTS: Magic, cinematography, collecting rare books, science fiction and horror feature films and serials.

*   *   *

McKEEVER, Marcia
See LAIRD, Jean E(louise)

*   *   *

McKIE, Ronald (Cecil Hamlyn)   1909-

PERSONAL: Surname is pronounced mick-*kee;* born December 11, 1909, in Toowoomba, Queensland, Australia; son of Allan (a banker) and Nesta (Brown) McKie; married Anne Lindsay, January 5, 1940; children: Iain. *Education:* Attended University of Queensland. *Home:* 147 Sutherland St., Paddington, Sydney, Australia 2021. *Agent:* Sanford J. Greenburger Associates, Inc., 825 Third Ave., New York, N.Y. 10022.

CAREER: Reporter and feature writer of newspapers in Australia, Singapore, and China, 1937-60; war correspondent for *Sydney Daily Telegraph* and *London Evening Standard* in Burma, 1943-44, in Europe, 1944-45; Eric White Associates, Sydney, Australia, consultant, beginning 1960. *Military service:* Australian Imperial Forces, 1942-43. *Member:* P.E.N., Australian Society of Authors. *Awards, honors:* Smith-Mundt fellowship, 1952; grants from Commonwealth Literature Fund, 1970, and Australian Council for the Arts, 1974; Miles Franklin Award for Literature, 1974.

WRITINGS: This Was Singapore, Angus & Robertson, 1942; *The Survivors,* Bobbs-Merrill, 1953 (published in Australia as *Proud Echo,* Angus & Robertson, 1953); (contributor) *With the Australians in Korea,* Australian War Memorial, 1954; (contributor) *Australia at Arms,* Australian War Memorial, 1955; *The Heroes,* Angus & Robertson, 1960, Harcourt, 1961; *The Emergence of Malaysia,* Harcourt, 1963 (published in Australia as *Malaysia in Focus,* Angus & Robertson, 1963); *The Company of Animals,* Angus & Robertson, 1965, Harcourt, 1966; *Bali,* Angus & Robertson, 1969; *Singapore,* Angus & Robertson, 1972; *The Onango Tree,* Collins, 1974; *The Crushing,* Collins, 1977, Scribner, 1979; *Bitter Bread,* Collins, 1978.†

McLEAN, George F(rancis) 1929-

PERSONAL: Born June 29, 1929, in Lowell, Mass.; son of Arthur William and Agnes Veronica (McHugh) McLean. *Education:* Attended Oblate College, Newburgh, N.Y., 1946-48; Gregorian University, Rome, Italy, Ph.B., 1951, Ph.L., 1952, S.T.B., 1954, S.T.L., 1956; Catholic University of America, Ph.D., 1958. *Politics:* Democrat. *Home:* 391 Michigan Ave. N.E., Washington, D.C. 20017. *Office:* Department of Philosophy, Catholic University of America, Washington, D.C. 20017.

CAREER: Ordained Roman Catholic priest; member of Oblate Fathers of Mary Immaculate. Oblate College, Washington, D.C., professor of philosophy, 1956—; Catholic University of America, Washington, D.C., instructor, 1958-61, assistant professor, 1961-64, associate professor, 1964-67, professor of philosophy, 1967—, director of philosophy workshop, 1961—. Secretary of Joint Committee of Catholic Learned Societies and Scholars, 1975-77, and Inter-University Committee on Research and Policy Studies, 1975—. *Member:* World Union of Catholic Philosophical Societies (secretary general; treasurer, 1972—), International Society for Metaphysics (secretary-treasurer, 1975—), American Catholic Philosophical Association (secretary, 1963-80), American Philosophical Association, American Catholic Theological Society, Metaphysical Society of America.

WRITINGS: Man's Knowledge of God According to Paul Tillich: A Thomist Critique, Catholic University of America Press, 1958; (with Patrick J. Aspell) *Ancient Western Philosophy: The Hellenic Emergence,* Appleton-Century-Crofts, 1971; *Plentitude and Participation,* University of Madras (India), 1978.

Editor: (With Leo A. Foley) *Philosophy in a Pluralistic Society,* Catholic University of America Press, 1963; *The History and Philosophy of Science,* Catholic University of America Press, 1964; *Philosophy and the Arts,* Catholic University of America Press, 1965; *Index of the Proceedings of the American Catholic Philosophical Association,* American Catholic Philosophical Association, 1966; (and compiler) *Philosophy in the Twentieth Century: Catholic and Christian,* Ungar, Volume I: *An Annotated Bibliography of Philosophy in Catholic Thought, 1900-1964,* 1967, Volume II: *A Bibliography of Christian Philosophy and Contemporary Issues,* 1967; (with Aspell) *Readings in Ancient Western Philosophy,* Appleton-Century-Crofts, 1970; *Religion in Contemporary Thought,* Alba House, 1973; *Traces of God in a Secular Culture,* Alba House, 1973; *The Role of Reason in Belief,* Concorde Publishing, 1974; *The Impact of Belief: The New Dialogue of Philosophy and Theology,* Concorde Publishing, 1974; *New Dynamics in Ethical Thinking,* Concorde Publishing, 1974; *Inter-University Cooperation in Research,* Concorde Publishing, 1975; *Moral Values,* CLS (Washington, D.C.), 1975; *Man and Nature,* Oxford University Press, 1978.

Editor of proceedings of Catholic University of America workshops, all published by Catholic University of America: *Philosophy and the Integration of Contemporary Catholic Education,* 1962; *Philosophy in a Technological Culture,* 1963; *Teaching Thomism Today,* 1964; *Christian Philosophy and Religious Renewal,* 1966; *Christian Philosophy in the College and Seminary,* 1966; *Philosophy and Contemporary Man,* 1968; *Current Issues in Modern Philosophy: New Departures in Colleges and Seminaries,* 1969.

Editor of proceedings of American Catholic Philosophical Association, all published by American Catholic Philosophical Association: *Scholasticism in the Modern World,* 1966; (with

Valerie Voorhies) *The Nature of Philosophical Inquiry,* 1967; *Philosophy and the Future of Man,* 1968; *Truth and the Historicity of Man,* 1969; (with Jude P. Dougherty) *Philosophy and Christian Theology,* 1970; *Myth and Philosophy,* 1971; *The Existence of God,* 1972; *The Philosopher as Teacher,* 1973; *Thomas and Bonaventure: A Septicentenary Commemoration,* 1974; *Philosophy and Civil Law,* 1975; *Freedom,* 1976; *Ethical Wisdom: East and/or West,* 1977; *Immateriality,* 1978; *The Human Person,* 1979.

Also editor of *Perspectives on Reality: Readings on Metaphysics from Classical Philosophy to Existentialism,* 1966, and *Man and Society,* proceedings of the International Society for Metaphysics, 1977. Area editor, *New Catholic Encyclopedia,* 1960—. Compiler of index to Volumes I-XL of *New Scholasticism.* Contributor of quarterly report to *New Scholasticism,* 1963-79.

*   *   *

McLEAVE, Hugh George 1923-

PERSONAL: Born July 28, 1923, in Kilwinning, Scotland; son of Nathaniel and Letitia (Johnstone) McLeave; married December 19, 1956. *Education:* University of Glasgow, M.A., 1949. *Religion:* Church of Scotland. *Home:* 36, Cours Gambetta, Aix-en-Provence, France. *Agent:* Harold Ober Associates, 40 East 49th St., New York, N.Y. 10017.

CAREER: Journalist in London, England, 1950–67, served as science correspondent for *News Chronicle* and *Daily Mail,* 1954–67, and as editor of *Stethoscope* (medical journal); full-time writer, 1967—. *Military service:* British Army, more than five years in World War II, with service in Far East most of that time; became captain. *Member:* Savage Club. *Awards, honors: The Risk Takers* was chosen by American Heart Association as one of the best medical books of 1963; *The Damned Die Hard* was chosen by Military Book Club as its book of 1973.

WRITINGS: Chesney: The Fabulous Murderer, W. H. Allen, 1954; *McIndoe: Plastic Surgeon,* Muller, 1961; *The Risk Takers,* Muller, 1962, Holt, 1963; *A Time to Heal: The Life of Ian Aird,* Heinemann, 1964; *The Last Pharaoh: Farouk of Egypt,* M. Joseph, 1969, McCall, 1970; *The Damned Die Hard* (Playboy Book Club and Literary Guild selection), Saturday Review Press, 1973; *A Man and His Mountain* (biography of Cezanne), Macmillan, 1977; *Rogues in the Gallery,* David R. Godine, 1981.

Fiction: *The Steel Balloon,* Muller, 1964; *The Sword and the Scales,* Harcourt, 1968; *Vodka on Ice,* Harcourt, 1969; *A Question of Negligence,* Harcourt, 1970; *Only Gentlemen Can Play,* Harcourt, 1974; *A Borderline Case,* Scribner, 1979; *Double Exposure,* Scribner, 1979; *No Face in the Mirror,* Macmillan, 1980.

SIDELIGHTS: Hugh George McLeave told *CA:* "For me, writing is like breathing—a compulsive activity. I like to think creative writing is really holding a dialogue with the subconscious mind and allowing humanity to eavesdrop on the result."

McLeave's books have been translated into several languages, including German, Dutch, French, and Danish.

AVOCATIONAL INTERESTS: Travel, music, golf, swimming, chess, languages (speaks French, Spanish, and German).

*   *   *

McLOUGHLIN, William G. 1922-

PERSONAL: Born June 11, 1922, in Maplewood, N.J.; son

of William G. (a lawyer and teacher) and Florence M. (Quinn) McLoughlin; married Virginia Ward Duffy; children: Helen, Gail, Martha. *Education:* Princeton University, A.B., 1947; Harvard University, A.M., 1948, Ph.D., 1953. *Home:* 204 Bowen St., Providence 6, R.I. *Office:* Department of History, Brown University, Providence, R.I. 02912.

CAREER: Harvard University, Graduate School of Arts and Sciences, Cambridge, Mass., assistant dean, 1950-53; Brown University, Providence, R.I., assistant professor, 1954-60, associate professor, 1960-63, professor of history, 1963—, co-chairman of American Civilization Program, 1973—. *Member:* American Historical Association, American Studies Association, American Association of University Professors, Institute of Early American History and Culture (member of executive committee, 1973—), Phi Beta Kappa.

AWARDS, HONORS: Fulbright scholarship to England, 1953-54; Guggenheim fellow, 1960-61; Harvard Center for the Study of the History of Liberty fellow, 1960-62; National Endowment for the Humanities senior fellow, 1968-69, 1979-80; Frederick G. Melcher Book Award, 1972, for *New England Dissent, 1630-1833: The Baptists and the Separation of Church and State;* American Council of Learned Societies fellow, 1972-73; John Nicholas Brown Award, Rhode Island Association for Local History, 1980, for distinguished service to local history.

WRITINGS: Billy Sunday Was His Real Name, University of Chicago Press, 1955; *Modern Revivalism: Charles Grandison Finney to Billy Graham,* Ronald, 1958; *Billy Graham: Revivalist in a Secular Age,* Ronald, 1960; (editor) Charles Grandison Finney, *Lectures on Revivals of Religion,* Harvard University Press, 1961; (contributor) Daniel Boorstin, editor, *An American Primer,* University of Chicago Press, 1966; *Isaac Backus,* Little, Brown, 1967; *The Meaning of Henry Ward Beecher,* Knopf, 1967; (contributor) Henning Cohen, editor, *The American Experience,* Houghton, 1968; (editor) *The American Evangelicals,* Harper, 1968; (editor with Robert N. Bellah) *Religion in America,* Beacon, 1968; (editor) Isaac Backus, *Pamphlets on Church, State and Calvinism,* Harvard University Press, 1968; (contributor) D. R. Cutler, editor, *The Religious Situation,* Beacon, 1969.

New England Dissent, 1630-1833: The Baptists and the Separation of Church and State, two volumes, Harvard University Press, 1971; (contributor) S. G. Kurtz and J. H. Hutson, editors, *Essays on the American Revolution,* Norton, 1973; (contributor) *Dictionary of Notable American Women,* Harvard University Press, 1973; *Rhode Island: A Bicentennial History,* Norton, 1978; *Revivals, Awakenings and Reform,* University of Chicago Press, 1978; (editor) *The Diaries of Isaac Backus,* three volumes, Brown University Press, 1979; (editor and author of introduction) *Lyman Abbott, Henry Ward Beecher,* Chelsea Press, 1980. Editor, *American Quarterly,* 1962-64; member of editorial board, *William and Mary Quarterly,* 1972-73.

WORK IN PROGRESS: A history of the slaveholding Indians in the South, 1790-1870, with special reference to missionary activities.

*   *   *

McMULLIN, Ernan 1924-

PERSONAL: Born October 13, 1924, in Donegal, Ireland; son of Vincent (a lawyer) and Carmel (a doctor; maiden name, Farrell) McMullin. *Education:* Maynooth College, Ireland, B.Sc., 1945, B.D., 1948; Institute of Advanced Studies, Dub-

lin, Ireland, graduate study, 1949-50; University of Louvain, Ph.D., 1954. *Home address:* P.O. Box 36, Notre Dame, Ind. *Office:* Department of Philosophy, University of Notre Dame, Notre Dame, Ind. 46556.

CAREER: Ordained Roman Catholic priest. University of Notre Dame, Notre Dame, Ind., instructor, 1954-59, assistant professor, 1959-64, associate professor, 1964-67, professor of logic and philosophy of science, 1967—, chairman of department of philosophy, 1965-72. Research fellow, Yale University, 1957-59, 1973-74, Cambridge University, 1968-69, and University of Pittsburgh, 1979; visiting lecturer and research associate, Center for the Philosophy of Science, University of Minnesota, 1964-65; visiting professor, Georgetown University, summer, 1963, College of Science, University of Cape Town, summers, 1972 and 1973, University of California, Los Angeles, 1977, and Immaculate Heart College. U.S. delegate to International Congress for Logic and Methodology, Amsterdam, 1967, Bucharest, 1977; president of Philosophy of Science Division, International Congress of Philosophy, Vienna, 1968, Varna, 1973. Member of editorial board, University of Notre Dame Press, 1974-78. Member of advisory panel on the philosophy of science, National Science Foundation, 1963-65.

MEMBER: International Federation of Philosophical Societies (member of Congress Commission, 1979—), International Philosophy of Science Association (member of executive council, 1970-73), American Philosophical Association (member of Western Division executive council, 1979—), Council for Philosophical Studies (member of executive committee, 1970-75), American Association for the Advancement of Science (fellow; chairman of section on the history and philosophy of science, 1977-78), American Catholic Philosophical Association (president, 1966-67), Philosophy of Science Association (member of executive council, 1970-73; president, 1980), Metaphysical Society of America (member of executive council, 1968-70; president, 1973-74), Society for Religion in Higher Education (fellow), Sigma Xi. *Awards, honors:* Fellowships or research grants from Yale University, 1957-59, Cambridge University, 1968-69, 1973-74, and University of Pittsburgh, 1979; D.HL., Loyola University, Chicago, 1969; faculty award, University of Notre Dame, 1973, for distinguished service.

WRITINGS: (Translator) A. Dondeyne, *Contemporary European Thought and Christian Faith,* Duquesne University Press, 1958; (editor and author of introduction) *The Concept of Matter,* University of Notre Dame Press, 1963, revised edition published as *The Concept of Matter in Modern Philosophy,* 1978; (editor and author of introduction and bibliography) *Galileo: Man of Science,* Basic Books, 1967; (author of introduction) J. Roslansky, editor, *The Uniqueness of Man,* North-Holland Publishing, 1968; *Newton on Matter and Activity,* University of Notre Dame Press, 1978; (editor and author of introduction) *Death and Decision,* Westview, 1978.

Contributor: J. C. Steinhardt, editor, *Science and the Modern World,* Plenum, 1966; C. Singleton, editor, *Art, Science and History in the Renaissance,* Johns Hopkins Press, 1968; P. Kuntz, editor, *The Concept of Order,* University of Washington Press, 1968; I. Barbour, editor, *Science and Religion,* Harper, 1968; B. van Rootselaar, editor, *Logic, Methodology and Philosophy of Science,* Volume III, [Amsterdam], 1968; A. Fisher and G. Murray, editors, *Philosophy and Science As Modes of Knowing,* Appleton-Century-Crofts, 1969; R. Stuewer, editor, *Historical and Philosophical Perspectives of Science,* University of Minnesota Press, 1969; A. G. Karczmar and J. C. Eccles, editors, *Brain and Human Behavior,* Springer Verlag (Berlin), 1972; *Marxism, Communism and Western Society: A*

Comparative Encyclopedia, Herder (Friedburg), 1973; O. Gingerich, editor, *The Nature of Scientific Inquiry,* [Washington, D.C.], 1975; R. Butts and J. Hintikka, editors, *Historical and Philosophical Dimensions of Logic, Methodology and Philosophy of Science,* Reidel (Dordrecht, Netherlands), 1977; Butts and J. Pitt, editors, *New Perspectives on Galileo,* Reidel, 1978; G. Radnitzky and G. Andersson, editors, *Progress and Rationality in Science,* Reidel, 1978; P. Asquith and H. Kyburg, editors, *Current Research in Philosophy of Science,* [East Lansing, Mich.], 1979; T. Englehardt and others, editors, *Clinical Judgement: A Critical Appraisal,* Reidel, 1979; F. E. Mosedale, editor, *Philosophy and Science,* [Englewood Cliffs, N.J.], 1979; G. Tagliacozzo and others, editors, *Vico and Contemporary Thought,* Humanities, 1979; J. Speck and others, editors, *Handbuch wissenschratstheoretischer Begriffe,* [Goettingen], 1979.

Editor, "Fundamentals of Logic" series, Prentice-Hall, 1963-66. Contributor to *Dictionary of Scientific Biography,* Volume I, 1970, and *New Catholic Encyclopedia* (supplemental volume), 1974; also contributor to proceedings of the International Congress of Philosophy, Vienna, 1969, Fourth International Conference on the Unity of the Sciences, 1976, and International Congress on Logic, Methodology and Philosophy of Science, 1979. Contributor to journals, including *New Blackfriars, Boston Studies in the Philosophy of Science, Centaurus, American Philosophical Quarterly, Philosophy of Science,* and *Review of Metaphysics.*

Editorial consultant, *New Catholic Encyclopedia,* 1967, and *Encyclopaedia Britannica,* 1974; member of board of referees, *Philosophy Research Archives,* 1974—. Member of editorial board, *Notre Dame Journal of Formal Logic,* 1968—, *Philosophy of Science,* 1975—, and *Nature and System,* 1978—. Editorial consultant, *American Philosophical Quarterly,* 1964-73, and *New Scholasticism,* 1964—; consulting editor, *Studies in History and Philosophy of Science,* 1970-75; advisory editor, *Isis,* 1976-80; member of advisory board, *Journal of Medicine and Philosophy,* 1977—.

WORK IN PROGRESS: Studies of the nature of explanation in the natural sciences, the realism of science, and the relations of science and religion.

*   *   *

McNAIL, Eddie Gathings 1905-

PERSONAL: Born November 28, 1905, in Prairie, Miss.; daughter of James Covington (a physician) and Lavinia (Prewett) Gathings; married John Leonard McNail, April 5, 1928; children: Joseph Covington (deceased), Mary Gathings (Mrs. Grover Williams). *Education:* University of Mississippi, B.A., 1927; University of Texas, additional study, 1945; Agricultural and Industrial University, M.A., 1948. *Home:* 204 West, La Feria, Tex. 78559.

CAREER: La Feria Independent School District, La Feria, Tex., English teacher, 1927-37; Mercedes Independent School District, Mercedes, Tex., English teacher, 1950-60; La Feria Independent School District, English teacher, 1960-69. Caretaker of Our Lady of Visitation Catholic Church, Santa Maria, Tex. Member of La Feria Bicentennial Committee, 1974-76. District governor for Beautify Texas Council, 1974—. *Member:* Daughters of the American Colonists, Daughters of the American Revolution, Order of the Eastern Star, American Legion Auxiliary, Texas State Teachers Association, Cameron County Historical Commission, Rio Grande Valley Poetry Society (president, 1969-71), Cultura Club (president, 1964-65), Rio Grande Valley Federation of Women's Clubs (president,

1973-75), Delta Kappa Gamma (president of Zeta Rho chapter, 1964-66). *Awards, honors:* Daughters of the American Revolution State Leadership Award, 1974-75, and award for television coverage at state level, 1974-75; American Cancer Society, outstanding service plaque, 1978, certificate of exemplary service, 1980, and certificate of merit, 1980; special certificate of appreciation, Texas State Teachers Association, 1980.

WRITINGS: The Silver Cord (poems), Dorrance, 1971; *The Bicentennial History of La Feria,* privately printed, 1975; *The History and Development of Irrigation in the Lower Rio Grande Valley,* privately printed, 1977; *Scrapbook and History of Local Teachers Association,* Texas State Teachers Association, 1980. Also author of *The History of the La Feria Methodist,* 1981.

WORK IN PROGRESS: A book of poetry.

SIDELIGHTS: Eddie Gathings McNail told *CA* she was instrumental in securing historical markers for five buildings in Texas, including the Longoria House (the oldest house in La Feria), the Cameron County Bank (the first bank in La Feria), and Our Lady of Visitation Catholic Church in Santa Maria.

*   *   *

McWHINEY, Grady 1928-

PERSONAL: Born July 15, 1928, in Shreveport, La.; son of Henry Grady and Mayme (Holland) McWhiney; married Sue Baca (a free-lance writer), December, 1947. *Education:* Centenary College, Shreveport, La., B.S., 1950; Louisiana State University, M.A., 1951; Columbia University, Ph.D., 1960. *Residence:* Hurricane Hills, Tuscaloosa County, Alabama. *Office:* Center for the Study of Southern History and Culture, Box CS, University of Alabama, University, Alabama 35486.

CAREER: Troy State Teachers College (now Troy State University), Troy, Ala., assistant professor of history, 1952-54; Millsaps College, Jackson, Miss., assistant professor of history, 1956-59; Northwestern University, Evanston, Ill., assistant professor of history, 1960-65; University of British Columbia, Vancouver, associate professor, 1965-68, professor of history, 1968-70; Wayne State University, Detroit, Mich., professor of history, 1970-75; University of Alabama, University, professor of history, 1975—, chairman of department, 1975-79, director and distinguished senior fellow, Center for the Study of Southern History and Culture, 1976—. University California, Berkeley, visiting instructor, 1959-60, visiting associate professor of history, 1967-68; visiting professor of history, Tulane University, summer, 1970, and University of Michigan, 1972-73. *Military service:* U.S. Marine Corps, 1946-47. *Member:* American Civil War Round Table of the United Kingdom (honorary member), Southern Historical Association (member of executive council, 1976-79), Alabama Historical Association (member of executive committee, 1975-79; president, 1978-79), Chicago Civil War Round Table, Ulysses S. Grant Association, Confederate Historical Institute (honorary first fellow). *Awards, honors:* Gallant Service Award from Chicago Civil War Round Table.

WRITINGS: (Editor with Douglas S. Freeman) *Lee's Dispatches to Jefferson Davis,* Putnam, 1957; (co-author) *The Southerner as American,* University of North Carolina Press, 1960; (editor) *Reconstruction and the Freedmen,* Rand McNally, 1963; (editor with Robert Wiebe) *Historical Vistas: Readings in United States History,* Allyn & Bacon, Volume I, 1963, Volume II, 1964; (editor) *Grant, Lee, Lincoln and the Radicals,* Northwestern University Press, 1964; (editor with wife, Sue McWhiney) *To Mexico with Taylor and Scott 1845-1847,* Blaisdell, 1969; *Braxton Bragg and Confederate Defeat,* Columbia University Press, 1969; *Southerners and Other Americans,* Basic Books, 1973; (with Perry D. Jamieson) *Attack and Die: Civil War Military Tactics and the Southern Heritage,* University of Alabama Press, 1982. Contributor to *Encyclopedia Americana* and *Encyclopedia of American Biography.* Contributor of articles and reviews to *Washington Post* and to professional journals. Member of editorial board, Ulysses S. Grant Association, 1972—.

WORK IN PROGRESS: Life and Leisure in the Old South, for University Press of Kentucky; *Jefferson Davis and His Generals,* for Columbia University Press; with Forrest McDonald, *The Celtic South.*

* * *

MEEK, Ronald L(indley)   1917-1978

PERSONAL: Born July 27, 1917, in Wellington, New Zealand; died August 18, 1978; son of Ernest William (a merchant) and Isabel Matilda (Williams) Meek; married Dorothea Luise Schulz, October 20, 1951; children: Roger Duncan, Alison Fiona. *Education:* Victoria University College, LL.B., 1938, LL.M., 1939, B.A., 1945, M.A., 1946; St. John's College, Cambridge, Ph.D., 1949. *Home:* 27 The Fairway, Oadby, Leicestershire LE2 2HN, England. *Office:* Department of Economics, University of Leicester, Leicester, England.

CAREER: University of Glasgow, Glasgow, Scotland, lecturer, 1948-61, senior lecturer in political economy, 1961-63; University of Leicester, Leicester, England, professor of economics, beginning 1963. Member of East Midlands Regional Economic Planning Council, beginning 1967; member of board of directors, Leicester Theatre Trust, beginning 1974.

WRITINGS: Maori Problems Today: A Short Survey, Progressive Publishing Co., 1943; (editor, translator, and author of introduction) *Marx and Engels on Malthus,* Lawrence & Wishart, 1953, International Publishers, 1954, published as *Marx and Engels on the Population Bomb,* Ramparts Press, 1970, 2nd edition, 1971; *Studies in the Labour Theory of Value,* International Publishers, 1956, 2nd edition, Monthly Review Press, 1976; *The Economics of Physiocracy: Essays and Translations,* Allen & Unwin, 1962, Harvard University Press, 1963; *Hill-Walking in Arran,* W. & R. Chambers, 1963; *The Rise and Fall of the Concept of the Economic Machine,* Humanities, 1965; *Economics and Ideology and Other Essays: Studies in the Development of Economic Thought,* Barnes & Noble, 1967; (editor with M. Kuczynski) *Quesnay's Tableau Economique,* Macmillan, 1971; *Figuring Out Society,* Fontana, 1971; (editor and author of introduction) *Precursors of Adam Smith,* Rowman & Littlefield, 1973; (editor and translator) Anne Robert Jacques Turgot, *Progress, Sociology, and Economics,* Cambridge University Press, 1973; *Social Science and the Ignoble Savage,* Cambridge University Press, 1976; *Smith, Marx, After: Ten Essays in the Development of Economic Thought,* Wiley, 1977; (editor and translator with D. D. Raphael) Adam Smith, *Lectures on Jurisprudence,* Claredon Press, 1978; *Maurice Herbert Dobb, 1900-76,* British Academy, 1979.

Contributor to *Science and Society, Soviet Studies,* and other professional journals. Member of editorial board, *Adam Smith's Works and Correspondence,* beginning 1958.

WORK IN PROGRESS: The Economics of Electricity Supply.

BIOGRAPHICAL/CRITICAL SOURCES: Times Literary Supplement, July 17, 1969.†

MEHL, Roger   1912-

PERSONAL: Born May 10, 1912, in Relanges, France; son of Adolphe and Louise (Wasser) Mehl; married Herrade Koehnlein (a professor of religion), July 16, 1938; children: Idelette, Jean-Michel, Claire-Lise. *Education:* Universite de Strasbourg, Licence en Philosophie, 1934, Agregation de Philosophie, 1935, Licence en Theologie, 1945, Doctorat en Theologie, 1956. *Religion:* Reformee. *Home:* Rue Blessig 6, Strasbourg, France.

CAREER: Gymnase Protestant, Strasbourg, France, professeur, 1936-39; Lycee Thiers, Marseille, France, professeur, 1940-44; Eglise Reformee de France, Ales, pasteur, 1944-45; Universite de Strasbourg, Faculte de Theologie Protestante, maitre de conferences, 1945-56, professeur titulaire (ethique), 1956—, doyen de la faculte, 1967-69, 1976-79, doyen honoraire. Participant at World Council of Churches assemblies, Evanston, Ill., 1954, New Delhi, India, 1961, Upsala, 1968, and at Conference de Foi et Constitution, Montreal, Quebec, 1963. *Member:* Federation Protestante de France, World Council of Churches (member of central committee, 1968-75; Commission on Faith and Order, 1961-75), Commission des Etudes Oecumeniques (president). *Awards, honors:* Commandeur des palmes academiques; chevalier de la Legion d'Honneur; Officier de l'Ordre National du Merite; D.H.L., University of Glasgow and University of Basel; membre correspondant de l'Academie des Sciences Morales et Politiques.

WRITINGS: La Condition du philosophe chretien, Delachaux & Niestle, 1947, translation by Eva Kushner published as *The Condition of the Christian Philosopher,* James Clarke, 1963, Fortress, 1964; (with Jacques Bois and Jean Boisset) *La Probleme de la morale chretienne,* Presses Universitaires de France, 1948; *Images de l'homme,* Labor & Fides, 1953, translation by James H. Farley published as *Images of Man,* John Knox, 1965; *La Recontre d'Autrui,* Delachaux & Niestle, 1955; *La Vieillisement et la mort,* Presses Universitaires de France, 1956; *De L'Autorite des valeurs: Essai d'ethique chretienne,* Presses Universitaires de France, 1957; *Du Catholicisme romain: Approche et interpretation,* Delachaux & Niestle, 1957; *Explication de la confession de foi de la Rochelle,* Collection "Les Bergers et Les Mages," 1959; *Societe et amour: Problemes ethiques de la vie familiale,* Labor & Fides, 1961, translation by Farley published as *Society and Love: Ethical Problems of Family Life,* Westminster, 1964; *Decolonisation et missions protestantes,* Societe des Missions Evangeliques de Paris, 1964; *Traite de sociologie de protestantisme,* Delachaux & Niestle, 1965, translation by Farley published as *The Sociology of Protestantism,* Westminster, 1970; *La Theologie protestante,* Presses Universitaires de France, 1966; *Pour une ethique sociale chretienne,* Delachaux & Niestle, 1967; *Notre Vie et Notre Mort,* S.C.E., 2nd edition, 1967.

Ethique Catholique et ethique protestante, Delachaux & Niestle, 1970, translation by Farley published as *Catholic Ethics and Protestant Ethics,* Westminster, 1971; *Les Attitudes Morales,* Presses Universitaires de France, 1971; *Les Pouvoirs de l'homme,* L'Age d'Homme, 1975; *Le Catholicisme francais dans la societe actuelle,* Le Centurion, 1977; *Vie Interieuve et transcendance de Dieu,* CERF, 1980. Editor-in-chief, *Revue de'Histoire et de Philosophie Religieuses,* 1947-69.

WORK IN PROGRESS: Le Protestantisme francais de 1945 a 1980; Essai sur la fidelite.

BIOGRAPHICAL/CRITICAL SOURCES: Times Literary Supplement, October 2, 1970.

MEHLINGER, Howard D(ean) 1931-

PERSONAL: Born August 22, 1931, in Hillsboro, Kan.; son of Alex (a businessman) and Alice (Skibbee) Mehlinger; married Carolee Ann Case, December 28, 1952; children: Bradley Case, Barbara Ann, Susan Kay. *Education:* McPherson College, B.A., 1953; University of Kansas, M.S., 1959, Ph.D., 1964. *Home:* 3606 Park Lane, Bloomington, Ind. 47401. *Office:* Third and Jordan, Bloomington, Ind. 47405.

CAREER: Lawrence High School, Lawrence, Kan., history teacher, 1953-63, chairman of social studies department, 1961-63; Pittsburgh public schools, Pittsburgh, Pa., co-director of Project Social Studies, 1963-64; North Central Association, Chicago, Ill., assistant director of Foreign Relations Project, 1964-65; Indiana University, Bloomington, assistant professor of history, 1965-70, associate professor, 1970-74, professor of education and history, 1974—, director of high school curriculum center in government, 1966-71, director of Social Studies Development Center, 1968-71, coordinator of doctoral program in social studies education, 1971-74, director of Center for Global Studies, 1979-81, dean of school of education, 1981—. Co-director of summer workshops for world history teachers, Northwestern University, 1961, 1963. President, Mid-America Center, Inc. Member of board of directors, Indiana Consumer and Economic Education Project; member of education activities advisory board, *New York Times;* editorial advisor to Houghton Mifflin Co. Consultant to universities, government agencies, and public-service foundations, including Northwestern University, U.S. Department of State, and Ford Foundation.

MEMBER: International Political Science Association, International Studies Association, World Council for Curriculum and Instruction, American Educational Research Association, American Political Science Association, American Historical Association, American Association for Advancement of Slavic Studies, American Bar Association, National Education Association, Social Science Education Consortium (member of board of directors), Association for Supervision and Curriculum Development, Indiana Council for the Social Studies, Phi Beta Kappa, Phi Alpha Theta, Phi Delta Kappa, Pi Sigma Alpha.

AWARDS, HONORS: Travel grants from Federal Republic of Germany, 1966, 1971; recipient of numerous grants from the U.S. Office of Education, 1966-76, Ford Foundation, 1970-81, Population Council, 1970-71, National Science Foundation, 1972-81, UNESCO, 1976-80, and Danforth Foundation, 1979-80; U.S. Department of State short-term lecturer grant for Africa, 1975; study grant from the Deutscher Akademischer Austauschdienst, 1978; visiting scholar grant from Japan Society for the Promotion of Science, 1979.

WRITINGS: (Editor) *Communism in Theory and Practice: A Book of Readings for High School Students,* Chandler Publishing, 1964; (editor) *The Study of Totalitarianism: An Inductive Approach,* National Council for the Social Studies, 1965; *The Study of American Political Behavior,* High School Curriculum Center in Government, Indiana University, 1967; (editor with James M. Becker) *International Dimensions in Social Studies,* National Council for the Social Studies, 1968; (with John M. Thompson) *Count Witte and the Tsarist Government in the 1905 Revolution,* Indiana University Press, 1971; (with John J. Patrick) *American Political Behavior,* Ginn, 1972; (with others) *Toward Effective Instruction in the Social Studies,* Houghton, 1974; (with others) *Global Studies for American Schools,* National Education Association, 1979; (co-editor) *Social Studies in Other Nations,* National Council for the Social Studies, 1979; (co-editor) *The Social Studies,* National Society

for the Study of Education, 1981; (co-author) *Citizenship Education,* National School Boards Association, 1981.

Contributor: *The School and the Democratic Environment,* Columbia University Press, 1970; *The Encyclopedia of Education,* Volume IX, Macmillan, 1971; *Strategies for Curriculum Development,* McCutchan, 1975; *The Report of the National Task Force on Citizenship Education: Education for Responsible Citizenship,* McGraw, 1977; *Teaching Social Studies in Other Nations,* National Council for the Social Studies, 1979; *Education in the 1980s,* National Education Association, 1981.

Principal designer of nine films for use in high school world history classes, produced by McGraw in 1970; co-designer of four films for use in high school American government classes, produced by Ginn, 1972-73. Contributor to periodicals, including *Educational Record, Kansas Studies in Education, Social Education, Today's Education, New York Times,* and *Indiana Social Studies Quarterly.* Member of editorial board, *DEA News;* member of advisory board, *The History Teacher.*

*   *   *

MELTZER, David 1937-

PERSONAL: Born February 17, 1937, in Rochester, N.Y.; son of Louis (a musician and writer) and Rosemunde (a musician; maiden name Lovelace) Meltzer; married Christina Meyer (an artist and teacher) April 1, 1959; children: Jennifer Love, Margaret Joy, Amanda Rose, Adam Benjamin. *Education:* Attended Los Angeles City College and University of California, Los Angeles. *Home address:* P.O. Box 129, Bolinas, Calif. 94924.

CAREER: Discovery Book Shop, San Francisco, Calif., manager, 1959-67; has read poetry to jazz accompaniment at The Cellar, San Francisco; member of various musical groups in the late 1960s, including Snopes Country Camp Followers and Serpent Power; Urban School, San Francisco, teacher of poetry and jazz history and head of dream workshop, 1975-76; Vacaville State Prison, Vacaville, Calif., writing workshop teacher, 1979-81; New College, San Francisco, currently teacher of poetics in M.A. program. Owner, Tree Books. *Member:* Science Fiction Writers of America. *Awards, honors:* Grants from Coordinating Council of Literary Magazines, National Endowment for the Arts, and the California Arts Council.

WRITINGS: (With Donald Schenker) *Poems,* privately printed, 1957; *Ragas,* Discovery Books (San Francisco), 1959; *The Clown: A Poem,* Semina (Larkspur), 1960; (editor with Lawrence Ferlinghetti and Michael McLure) *Journal for the Protection of All Beings #1: A Visionary and Revolutionary Review,* City Lights, 1960; *We All Have Something to Say to Each Other: Being an Essay Entitled "Patchen" and Four Poems,* Auerhahn Press (San Francisco), 1962; (author of introduction) *The Outsiders,* Rodale (Fort Lauderdale, Fla.), 1962; *Bazascope Mother,* Drekfesser Press (Los Angeles), 1964; *Station,* [San Francisco], 1964; *The Blackest Rose,* Oyez, 1964; (contributor) *Notes from the Underground Press,* Underground Press, 1964; *In Hope I Offer a Fire-wheel: A Poem,* Oyez, 1965; *Oyez!,* Oyez, 1965; *The Process,* Oyez, 1965; *The Dark Continent,* Oyez, 1967; *Nature Poem,* Unicorn Press, 1967; *Journal of the Birth,* Oyez, 1967; *The Agent,* Essex House, 1968; *How Many Blocks in the Pile?,* Essex House, 1968; *Round the Poem Box: Rustic and Domestic Home Movies for Stan and Jane Brakhage,* Black Sparrow Press, 1969; *Healer,* Essex House, 1969; *Agency,* Essex House, 1969; *Lovely,* Essex House, 1969; *The Martyr,* Essex House, 1969; *ORF,* Essex House, 1969; *Poem for My Wife,* Maya, 1969; *Yesod,* Trigram Press, 1969; *From Eden Book,* Maya, 1969; *Abulafia,* Unicorn Press, 1969.

Letters and Numbers, Oyez, 1970; *Bronx Lil/Head of Lillin S.A.C.,* Capra, 1970; *32 Beams of Light,* Capra, 1970; *The Brain-Plant Tetralogy: Lovely, Healer, Out, and Glue Factory,* Essex House, 1970; *Star,* Essex House, 1970; *Greenspeech,* Christopher Books, 1970; *Isle Vista Notes,* Christopher Books, 1970; *Luna,* Black Sparrow Press, 1970; (editor) *The San Francisco Poets,* Ballantine, 1971; *Hero,* Unicorn Press, 1971; *Knots,* Tree Books, 1971; *Hero-Lil,* Black Sparrow Press, 1972; *Tens: Selected Poems, 1961-1971,* McGraw, 1973; *The Eyes, the Blood,* Mudra, 1973; (editor) *Birth: An Anthology,* Ballantine, 1973; *French Broom,* Oyez, 1974; *Blue Rags,* Oyez, 1974; *Harps,* Oyez, 1975; *Six,* Black Sparrow Press, 1976; (editor) *Golden Gate: Interviews with Five San Francisco Poets,* Wingbow Press, 1976; *Bolero,* Oyez, 1976; (editor) *The Secret Garden: Anthology of Kabbalistic Texts,* Continuum Books, 1976; *Abra* (juvenile), Hipparchia, 1976; (translator with Allen Say) Shiga Naoya, *Morning Glories,* Oyez, 1977; *Two-Way Mirror: A Poetry Note-Book,* Oyez, 1977; (editor) *Birth: Hymns, Prayers, Documents, Myths, Amulets,* North Point Press, 1981; *The Art, the Veil,* Membrane Press, 1981.

Work appears in anthologies, including: *The New American Poetry: 1945-1960,* edited by Donald M. Allen, Grove, 1960; *Beatitude Anthology,* edited by Lawrence Ferlinghetti, City Lights, 1960; *Junge Amerikanische Lyrik,* edited by Carl Hanser, [Munich], 1961; *The Real Bohemia,* edited by Francis J. Regney and L. Douglas Smith, Basic Books, 1961; *On the Mesa: Anthology of Bolinas Writers,* edited by Joel Weishaus, City Lights, 1971; *Mark in Time: Portraits & Poetry—San Francisco,* edited by Nick Harvey, Glide, 1971; *A Caterpillar Anthology: A Selection of Poetry and Prose from Caterpillar Magazine,* edited by Clayton Eshleman, Doubleday, 1971; *Visions of America,* edited by David Kherdian, Macmillan, 1973; *John Keats's Porridge: Favorite Recipes of American Poets,* edited by Victoria McCabe, University of Iowa Press, 1975; *A Big Jewish Book,* edited by Jerome Rothenberg, Doubleday, 1978; *Calafia: The California Poetry,* edited by Ishmael Reed, Y'bird, 1979.

Recordings: "Serpent Power," Vanguard, 1968; "Poet Song," Vanguard, 1969; "Re-Runs," S-Tapes, 1980.

Editor with Jack Shoemaker, Maya Quarto Series, Maya, 1966-71. Author of column "Green Atom," *Los Angeles Free Press,* 1969. Contributor to *Caterpillar, Co-Evolution Quarterly, American Book Review, Yale Review, Oyez, New World Journal, Haight-Ashbury Literary Journal,* and many other publications. Editor, *Tree* (annual), 1970—.

SIDELIGHTS: In 1960, David Meltzer described his relationship to his work in the following way: "At 14 I left for the West and stayed in L.A. for 6 formative years in which I met Wallace Berman and Robert Alexander, who were instrumental in turning me on to the fantastic possibilities of art and the self. Moved to San Francisco in 1957. Spent many months reading at The Cellar with jazz. I no longer believe in the poet as a public target. I have decided to work my way thru poetry and find my voice and the stance I must take in order to continue my journey. Poetry is NOT my life. It is an essential PART of my life."

Commenting on his earlier remarks, Meltzer told *CA:* "In 1960 I was 23, an age for making STATEMENTS and not statements. Everything I wrote down wanted to outdistance the page, had to be final with a capital F. In 1960 I arrived at the simple-minded fact that art and life were inseparable. In 1981 I remain doggedly simple-minded and devoted to such revelations. IT assumes equal power to 'it' or It or it. It's constant. And what the it is is what the art is and what they are or aren't is really also up to you."

BIOGRAPHICAL/CRITICAL SOURCES: David Kherdian, *Six Poets of the San Francisco Renaissance,* Giligia Press, 1965; Kherdian, *David Meltzer: A Sketch from Memory and Descriptive Checklist,* Oyez, 1965; *Poetry,* August, 1973; *Village Voice,* May 16, 1977; *Books West,* June, 1977.

*   *   *

MELVILLE, Anne
   See POTTER, Margaret (Newman)

*   *   *

MELVILLE, Jennie
   See BUTLER, Gwendoline Williams

*   *   *

MEREDITH, William (Morris)   1919-

PERSONAL: Born January 9, 1919, in New York, N.Y.; son of William Morris and Nelley Atkin (Keyser) Meredith. *Education:* Princeton University, A.B. (magna cum laude), 1940. *Politics:* Democrat. *Home:* Kitemaug Rd., Uncasville, Conn. 06382. *Office:* Department of English, Connecticut College, New London, Conn. 06320.

CAREER: New York Times, New York, N.Y., 1940-41, began as copy boy, became reporter; Princeton University, Princeton, N.J., instructor in English and Woodrow Wilson fellow in writing, 1946-50; University of Hawaii, Honolulu, associate professor of English, 1950-51; Connecticut College, New London, associate professor, 1955-65, professor of English, 1965—. Middlebury College, Middlebury, Vt., instructor at Bread Loaf School of English, 1958-62. Member of Connecticut Commission on the Arts, 1963. Poetry consultant, Library of Congress, 1978-80. *Military service:* U.S. Army Air Forces, 1941-42; U.S. Navy, Naval Aviation, 1942-46; served in Pacific Theater; became lieutenant. U.S. Naval Reserve, active duty in Korean War as naval aviator, 1952-54; became lieutenant commander; received two Air Medals. *Member:* National Institute of Arts and Letters, Academy of American Poets (chancellor), American Choral Society (second vice-president).

AWARDS, HONORS: Yale Series of Younger Poets award for *Love Letter from an Impossible Land,* 1943; Harriet Monroe Memorial Prize, 1944, and Oscar Blumenthal Prize, 1953, for poems published in *Poetry;* National Institute of Arts and Letters grant in literature, 1958; Ford Foundation fellowship for drama, 1959-60; Loines Prize from National Institute of Arts and Letters, 1966; Van Wyck Brooks Award, 1971; Guggenheim fellow, 1975-76; International VAPTSAROV Prize for Literature, 1979.

*WRITINGS—*Poetry, except as indicated: *Love Letter from an Impossible Land,* Yale University Press, 1944; *Ships and Other Figures,* Princeton University Press, 1948; *The Open Sea and Other Poems,* Knopf, 1958; (librettist) "The Bottle Imp" (opera), music by Peter Whiton, produced in Wilton, Conn. in 1958; (editor and author of introduction) *Shelley: Poems,* Dell, 1962; (translator) Guillaume Apollinaire, *Alcools: Poems, 1898-1913,* Doubleday, 1964; *The Wreck of the Thresher and Other Poems,* Knopf, 1964; *Earth Walk: New and Selected Poems,* Knopf, 1970; *Hazard, the Painter,* Knopf, 1975; *The Cheer,* Knopf, 1980. Contributor to poetry magazines. Opera critic for *Hudson Review,* 1955-56.

SIDELIGHTS: A former Air Force pilot, William Meredith frequently incorporates images of sky and ocean as seen from vast heights into his poems, especially the earlier ones. His first book of poetry, *Love Letter from an Impossible Land,* was selected by Archibald MacLeish for the "Yale Series of Younger Poets." At that time MacLeish commented about the "way in which the literary vehicle (for it is nothing else) of the Princeton undergraduate turns into the live idiom of a poet's speech reading for poetry."

This criticism encouraged Meredith to concentrate on developing his own poetic voice. In the *Hollins Critic,* Henry Taylor states: "[Meredith's] earlier poems show us a young poet diligently studying his craft. In the brief lyrics which acknowledge various masters, there is little room for the voice of Meredith, but there is in them a serious and intelligent setting-forth after the tools that will give the voice, when it speaks, the distinctiveness and force of the later poems."

Content to work slowly, Meredith produces approximately six poems a year. In *Corgi Modern Poets in Focus 2* he explains, "Chiefly I think my poverty of output stems from the conviction that an unnecessary poem is an offense to the art." Meredith defines a "necessary" poem as one in which he confronts something he does not understand: "Maybe that is the likeliest prescription for a work of art: a puzzle about which one has a glimmering." *Dictionary of Literary Biography* writer Keith Moul does not believe that Meredith's output constitutes a "poverty": "Instead [it is] a rare thing among poets, a discriminating taste."

Critics such as Robert Mazzocco in the *New York Review of Books* refer to Meredith as a "durable" poet who possesses a "conservative sense of people and place." Peter Meinke writes in the *New Republic,* "Moving gracefully with the years, William Meredith's poetry has modified its former formal elegance to a point where it can absorb casual conversation; observations of nature, human and otherwise; and meditations on art and society." Mazzocco concludes, "If he is really too disciplined and adjusted an individual, too genial, too much the hero of the buried life . . . he is, nevertheless, a poet who knows . . . that the dispassionate, domestic, monogamous world has its dramas and sorrows, that rectitude itself can be an adventure, a moral adventure almost as Kierkegaard dreamed."

BIOGRAPHICAL/CRITICAL SOURCES: Jeremy Robson, *Corgi Modern Poets in Focus 2,* Transworld Publishers, 1971; *New York Review of Books,* June 15, 1972; *Contemporary Literary Criticism,* Gale, Volume IV, 1975, Volume XIII, 1980; *New Republic,* June 14, 1975; *Washington Post,* October 11, 1978; *Hollins Critic,* February, 1979; *Dictionary of Literary Biography,* Volume V: *American Poets since World War II,* Gale, 1980; *Los Angeles Times Book Review,* November 30, 1980; *New York Times Book Review,* March 22, 1981.

*   *   *

MERRELL, Karen Dixon 1936-

PERSONAL: Born December 19, 1936, in Payson, Utah; daughter of Jack V. (a steel worker) and Jean Dixon; married V. Dallas Merrell (a management consultant), June 8, 1959; children: Ann, Kay, Joan, Paul Dixon, Mary (deceased), Mark Jensen, John Carter, Ilene, David Porter. *Education:* Brigham Young University, B.S., 1959. *Religion:* Mormon. *Home:* 13917 Crest Hill Lane, Silver Spring, Md. 20904.

CAREER: Writer. Elementary school teacher in Provo, Utah, 1959-60. Summer lecturer at Brigham Young University. *Member:* White Key.

WRITINGS: Prayer (juvenile), Brigham Young University Press, 1964; *Tithing,* Extension Publications (Brigham Young Uni-

versity), 1966; *Baptism,* Deseret, 1968; *Joseph Smith,* Deseret, 1970.

SIDELIGHTS: Karen Merrell told *CA:* "I began writing children's books out of need. We had three small children in 1962, and faced with a long trip we stopped to buy some religious-oriented books for the three to five year olds. To our dismay there were only five or six to choose from and none really conveyed the Mormon concepts accurately. We wrote the first book on the road and then took months to convince a publisher that a picture book with only a line or two of script would really sell. We take great pride in starting a 'trend' among Mormon writers. If you go into that same store and look for books for the younger child today, you will literally find walls covered with them.

"As adults we must not underestimate the learning ability of the very young. They absorb much more than most of us realize. My books were written to teach as well as to entertain."

*   *   *

MERRILL, P. J.
See ROTH, Holly

*   *   *

MERTENS, Thomas R(obert) 1930-

PERSONAL: Born May 22, 1930, in Fort Wayne, Ind.; son of Herbert F. and Hulda (Burg) Mertens; married Beatrice Abair (a secretary), April 1, 1953; children: Julia Ann, David Gerhard. *Education:* Ball State University, B.S., 1952; Purdue University, M.S., 1954, Ph.D., 1956; post-doctoral study at Stanford University, 1963-64. *Politics:* Independent. *Religion:* Lutheran. *Home:* 2506 Johnson Rd., Muncie, Ind. 47304. *Office:* Department of Biology, Ball State University, Muncie, Ind. 47306.

CAREER: Ball State University, Muncie, Ind., assistant professor, 1957-62, associate professor, 1962-66, professor of biology, 1966—, director of doctoral programs in biology, 1974—. *Member:* American Association for the Advancement of Science, Genetics Society of America, American Genetic Association, National Association of Biology Teachers, National Science Teachers Association, Indiana College Biology Teachers (president, 1968-69), Indiana Academy of Science (fellow), Sigma Xi, Sigma Zeta (national president, 1966-67). *Awards, honors:* National Science Foundation faculty fellow at Stanford University, 1963-64; Ball State University outstanding faculty service award, 1981.

WRITINGS: (With J. C. Malayer) *Laboratory Exercises in the Principles of Biology,* Burgess, 1966, 2nd edition, with A. S. Bennett, published as *Laboratory Investigations in the Principles of Biology,* 1968, 3rd edition, 1973; (with S. F. Cooper) *Probability and Chi-Square for Biology Students: A Programmed Text,* Educational Methods, 1969, 2nd edition, 1974; (with E. J. Gardner) *Genetics Laboratory Investigations,* Burgess, 1970, 3rd edition, 1980; (with J. L. Lines) *Principles of Biosystematics,* Educational Methods, 1970, 2nd edition, 1978; (with Michael Geary) *Animal Development,* Educational Methods, 1970, 2nd edition, 1977; (with Gary E. Parker) *Life's Basis: Biomolecules,* Wiley, 1973; (editor with S. K. Robinson) *Human Genetics and Social Problems: A Book of Readings,* MSS Information Corp., 1973; (with Rex Reynolds) *The Microscope: A Programmed Text,* Allied Education Council, 1973; (with Thomas Mangum) *Ecology: The Environmental Crisis,* Educational Methods, 1973; (with F. F. Stevenson) *Plant Life Cycles,* Wiley, 1975; (editor) *Human Genetics:*

Readings on the Implications of Genetic Engineering, Wiley, 1975; (with Stevenson) *Plant Anatomy,* Wiley, 1976; (with B. D. Allamong) *Energy for Life: Photosynthesis and Respiration,* Wiley, 1976; (with A. M. Winchester) *Human Genetics,* C. E. Merrill, 1982. Contributor to proceedings. Contributor of reviews and articles to journals.

SIDELIGHTS: Thomas R. Mertens told *CA:* "The many recent and significant advances in human genetic engineering must be made understandable to the nonscientist. Achieving this objective has increasingly become the goal of my journal articles and books. As individuals and as a society, we are increasingly confronted with the need for making decisions about controversial issues growing out of advances in genetics. Wise decisions can only be made by informed citizens; I hope that my writing can help individuals make such decisions."

*   *   *

METRESS, James F(rancis)
   See METRESS, Seamus P.

*   *   *

METRESS, Seamus P.   1933-
   (James F[rancis] Metress)

PERSONAL: Born September 25, 1933, in Southampton, N.Y.; son of James F. (a machinist) and Hilda (Gugel) Metress; married Eileen Ryan (a professor of community health education), October 31, 1974. *Education:* University of Notre Dame, B.S., 1955; Columbia University, M.A., 1957; Indiana University, Ph.D., 1971. *Religion:* Roman Catholic. *Home:* 4625 Paisley Rd., Toledo, Ohio 43615. *Office:* Center for Studies in Aging, University of Toledo, Toledo, Ohio 43606.

CAREER: High school teacher of biology and coach in the public schools of Spring Valley, N.Y., 1955-57, and Saginaw and Fennville, Mich., 1957-64; Aquinas College, Grand Rapids, Mich., instructor in biology, 1964-65; Clarion State College, Clarion, Pa., assistant professor, 1966-68, associate professor of anthropology, beginning 1968; University of Toledo, Toledo, Ohio, associate professor, 1969-76, professor of anthropology, 1976—. *Member:* American Association of Physical Anthropologists, American Anthropological Association, Society for the Study of Social Biology, Society for Medical Anthropology, Catholic Historical Society, Immigration History Society, Clan na Gael, Irish Labor History Society, Celtic League International, Irish-American Cultural Institute. *Awards, honors:* Outstanding Teacher Award, University of Toledo, 1972.

WRITINGS—Under name James F. Metress: (Editor) *Man in Ecological Perspective,* MSS Educational Publishing, 1971; (editor with C. L. Brace) *Man in Evolutionary Perspective,* Wiley, 1973; (with Thor A. Conway) *A Guide to the Literature on the Dental Anthropology of Post Pleistocene Man* (monograph), Toledo Area Aboriginal Research Club, 1974.

Under name Seamus P. Metress: (With Cary S. Kart and wife, Eileen Metress) *Aging and Health,* Addison-Wesley, 1978; (with Kart) *Nutrition and Aging: A Bibliographic Survey,* Vance, 1979; *Listen, Irish People* (poems), Todd & Honeywell, 1979; *The Irish-American Experience,* University Press of America, 1981; (with Kart) *Society, Nutrition, and Old Age,* Prentice-Hall, in press.

Co-editor of *Toledo Area Aboriginal Research Club Bulletin,* 1972-75.

WORK IN PROGRESS: The Irish in the Great Lakes Region; The Irish-American Role in the Struggle for Irish Freedom.

AVOCATIONAL INTERESTS: Irish folk music, Irish Nationalist politics.

*   *   *

METZLER, Paul   1914-

PERSONAL: Born June 9, 1914, in Sydney, Australia; son of Paul Gerhardt (a wool buyer) and Veryl (Buss) Metzler; married Iris Louise French, November 1, 1941; children: July (Mrs. Richard Lawrence Hargrave), Geoffrey Richard. *Education:* Attended Barker College, Sydney, Australia. *Politics:* Liberal. *Religion:* Church of England. *Home:* Airlie, 12 Buena Vista Ave., Mosman, New South Wales 2088, Australia.

CAREER: Royal Australian Air Force, regular officer, beginning 1938, retired as group captain. *Member:* Commonwealth Club, Catalina Club.

WRITINGS: Advanced Tennis, Angus & Robertson, 1967, Sterling, 1968, revised edition, 1971; *Tennis Styles and Stylists,* Angus & Robertson, 1969, Macmillan, 1970; *Getting Started in Tennis,* Sterling, 1971; *Tennis Weaknesses and Remedies,* Sterling, 1973; *Tennis Doubles: Tactics and Formations,* Sterling, 1975; *Fine Points of Tennis,* Sterling, 1978; *A Foreign Father* (juvenile fiction), Hodder & Stoughton (Australia), 1978; *Great Players of Australian Tennis,* Harper, 1979. Contributor of short stories to magazines.

*   *   *

MEYERS, Walter E(arl)   1939-

PERSONAL: Born July 1, 1939, in Pittsburgh, Pa.; son of Walter F. (a truck driver) and Margaret (Bentz) Meyers; married Julia Reed (a music teacher), February 11, 1961; children: Matthew, Michael, Julia Margaret. *Education:* Duquesne University, A.B., 1964; University of Florida, Ph.D., 1967. *Politics:* Democrat. *Religion:* Roman Catholic. *Home:* 403 Carriage Lane, Cary, N.C. 27511. *Office:* Department of English, North Carolina State University, Raleigh, N.C. 27650.

CAREER: North Carolina State University at Raleigh, assistant professor, 1967-72, associate professor, 1972-78, professor of English, 1978—. *Military service:* U.S. Army, 1956-59. *Member:* Modern Language Association of America, American Dialect Society, Science Fiction Writers of America, Science Fiction Research Association, South Atlantic Modern Language Association, Phi Beta Kappa, Phi Kappa Phi. *Awards, honors:* Danforth fellowship, 1964; South Atlantic Modern Language Association Studies Award, 1978.

WRITINGS: A Figure Given: Typology in the Wakefield Plays, Duquesne University Press, 1970; *Handbook of Contemporary English,* Harcourt, 1974; (consulting editor) *Survey of Science Fiction Literature,* Salem Press, 1979; (with Michelle Rippon) *Combining Sentences,* Harcourt, 1979; *Aliens and Linguists: Language Study and Science Fiction,* University of Georgia Press, 1980. Contributor to *College English, PMLA, College Composition and Communication, American Speech, Science Fiction Studies,* and other periodicals.

WORK IN PROGRESS: A collection of essays on the monster in literature; investigation of attitudes toward fantasy in nineteenth and twentieth century culture.

SIDELIGHTS: A reviewer for the Science Fiction Research Association's *Newsletter* explains that Walter E. Meyers' *Aliens and Linguists: Language Study and Science Fiction* is "a well-documented study which is concerned with the uses to which science fiction writers put linguistics. Meyers sees communication as 'centrally important to an enormous portion of science fiction, and crucial to its understanding.' He notes the 'striking contrast between the wealth of language problems in science fiction and the relative poverty of linguistic explanation' in recent critical studies.''

Paul Granahan of *Best Sellers* writes: ''Communication has always been a primary theme and concern of science fiction. Whether it involves men, aliens or time-travelers, the urge to overcome the barriers prohibiting understanding is constantly expressed in the genre. The chief mode of communication is language, and it is with SF's multifarious handling of this integral factor of existence that this volume deals quite effectively. This rather ambitious undertaking is carried off in a very impressive fashion. Meyers . . . has published several books on linguistics and in this layman's opinion seems more than competent in the field.''

AVOCATIONAL INTERESTS: Simulation gaming.

BIOGRAPHICAL/CRITICAL SOURCES: Best Sellers, June, 1980; Science Fiction Research Association *Newsletter,* September, 1980; *Times Literary Supplement,* November 7, 1980.

* * *

MIGDAL, Joel S(amuel) 1945-

PERSONAL: Born April 1, 1945, in Roosevelt, N.J.; son of Benjamin (a storekeeper) and Rebecca (Marshak) Migdal; married R. Marcia Alexander (a developer of curriculum in education), July 4, 1968; children: Ariela, Tamar. *Education:* Rutgers University, B.A., 1967; Harvard University, M.A., 1968, Ph.D., 1972. *Religion:* Jewish. *Office:* School of International Studies, University of Washington, Seattle, Wash. 98195.

CAREER: Tel-Aviv University, Tel-Aviv, Israel, lecturer in political science, 1972-75; Harvard University, Cambridge, Mass., associate professor of government, 1975-80; University of Washington, Seattle, associate professor of international studies, 1980—. *Member:* American Political Science Association, Phi Beta Kappa. *Awards, honors:* Woodrow Wilson fellowship, 1967-68.

WRITINGS: Peasants, Politics, and Revolution: Pressures toward Political and Social Change in the Third World, Princeton University Press, 1974; (editor with others) *Patterns of Policy,* Transaction Books, 1979; (with others) *Palestinian Society and Politics,* Princeton University Press, 1980. Contributor to international studies journals.

WORK IN PROGRESS: A book on U.S. training of police in the Third World; *Strong Societies and Weak States.*

SIDELIGHTS: Joel S. Migdal has traveled and studied in Mexico, Spain, Portugal, India, and Israel. *Avocational interests:* Photography.

BIOGRAPHICAL/CRITICAL SOURCES: Times Literary Supplement, May 23, 1980.

* * *

MIKES, George 1912-

PERSONAL: Born February 15, 1912, in Siklos, Hungary; son of Alfred (a lawyer) and Margit Alice (Gal) Mikes; married Lea Hanak, January 2, 1948; children: Martin Alfred, Judith Pamela. *Education:* University of Budapest, LL.D., 1933. *Religion:* Roman Catholic. *Home:* 1B Dorncliffe Rd., London S.W.6, England. *Agent:* Russell & Volkening, Inc., 551 Fifth Ave., New York, N.Y. 10017.

CAREER: Writer; governor of London Oratory School. *Member:* P.E.N. in Exile (president, 1973-80); Garrick Club and Hurlingham Club (both London).

WRITINGS: The Epic of Lofoten, Hutchinson, 1941; *Darlan: A Study,* Constable, 1943; *We Were There to Escape: The True Story of a Jugoslav Officer,* Nicholson & Watson, 1945; *Pont ugye mint az angolok* (songs and verses), Londoni Podium, 1945; *How to Be an Alien: A Handbook for Beginners and More Advanced Pupils,* Deutsch, 1946, British Book Centre, 1950; *How to Scrape Skies: The United States Explored, Rediscovered, and Explained,* Deutsch, 1948, published as *How to Be a Swell Guy: The United States Explored, Rediscovered, and Explained,* Doubleday, 1959.

Wisdom for Others, Deutsch, 1950; *Milk and Honey: Israel Explored,* Deutsch, 1950, Transatlantic, 1965; *Talicska: Humoreszkek, esszek, sohajtasok,* Big Ben Kiadasa, c. 1950; *Down With Everybody!: A Cautionary Tale for Children over Twenty-One, and Other Stories,* Deutsch, 1951, British Book Centre, 1952; *Shakespeare and Myself,* Deutsch, 1952, British Book Centre, 1953; *Uber Alles: Germany Explored,* Deutsch, 1953; *Eight Humorists,* Deutsch, 1954; *Leap through the Curtain: The Story of Nora Kovach and Istvan Rabovsky,* Weidenfeld & Nicolson, 1955, Dutton, 1956; *Little Cabbages,* Deutsch, 1955; *Italy for Beginners,* Deutsch, 1956, Transatlantic, 1965; *The Hungarian Revolution,* Deutsch, 1957; *East Is East,* Deutsch, 1958; *A Study in Infamy: The Operations of the Hungarian Secret Police,* Deutsch, 1959.

How to Be Inimitable: Coming of Age in England, Deutsch, 1961, Transatlantic, 1966; *As Others See You,* Newman Neame, 1961; *Tango: A Solo across South America,* Deutsch, 1961, Transatlantic, 1965; *The Best of Mikes,* Pan Books, 1962; *Switzerland for Beginners,* Deutsch, 1962, Transatlantic, 1965; *Mortal Passion,* Deutsch, 1963, Transatlantic, 1966; *How to Unite Nations,* Deutsch, 1963, Transatlantic, 1965; (editor) *Prison: A Symposium,* Routledge & Kegan Paul, 1963, Horizon Press, 1964; *How to Be an Alien: In Britain, France, Italy, Germany, Switzerland, Israel, Japan,* Basic Books, 1964; (with John R.R. Bedford) *The Duke of Bedford's Book of Snobs,* P. Owen, 1965, published as *The Book of Snobs,* Coward, 1966; *Eureka!: Rummaging in Greece,* Deutsch, 1965; (editor) *Germany Laughs at Herself: German Cartoons since 1848,* Bassermann (Stuttgart), 1965; *How to Be Affluent,* Deutsch, 1966, James Heineman, 1967; *Not By Sun Alone,* Deutsch, 1967; *Boomerang: Australia Rediscovered,* Deutsch, 1968; *Coat of Many Colors: Israel,* Gambit, 1969 (published in England as *The Prophet Motive: Israel Today and Tomorrow,* Deutsch, 1969).

Humour in Memoriam, Routledge & Kegan Paul, 1970; *The Land of the Rising Yen: Japan,* Gambit, 1970; *Laughing Matter,* Library Press, 1971; *Any Souvenirs?,* Gambit, 1972; (with Bedford) *How to Run a Stately Home,* Transatlantic, 1972; *The Spy Who Died of Boredom,* Deutsch, 1973, Harper, 1974; *Charlie,* Deutsch, 1976; *How to Be Decadent,* Deutsch, 1977; *Tsi-Tsa, the Biography of a Cat,* Deutsch, 1978; *English Humour for Beginners,* Deutsch, 1980.

Contributor to *Observer, Encounter, Times Literary Supplement,* and other periodicals.

SIDELIGHTS: A *Times Literary Supplement* reviewer states: ''[George] Mikes has made a profession of the paradox, and some twenty books reflect his special gift of observing human behaviour—especially when the humans are English—from the acute angle of the adopted Englishman. Cynical, amused, determined not to be taken in, he is that man with the heavy accent in the corner taking notes: for him face values are no values at all.''

Mikes' books have been translated into twenty-one languages.

AVOCATIONAL INTERESTS: Tennis.

BIOGRAPHICAL/CRITICAL SOURCES: New Statesman, March 17, 1967; *Times Literary Supplement,* April 27, 1967; *Christian Science Monitor,* January 18, 1968; *Observer Review,* October 20, 1968; *Books and Bookmen,* December, 1968; *Punch,* March 18, 1970; *Listener,* December 31, 1970.

*   *   *

MILETUS, Rex
    See BURGESS, M(ichael) R(oy)

*   *   *

MILLER, Donald C(urtis)   1933-

PERSONAL: Born July 15, 1933, in Carthage, S.D.; son of Carl Louis and Elsie (Anderson) Miller; married Sue C. MacKenzie, November 24, 1961 (divorced March, 1974); children: Shari Lynne. *Education:* University of South Dakota, B.A., 1955, M.A., 1960; Columbia University, further graduate study, 1963-64. *Home:* 1031 Lexington, Butte, Mont. 59701. *Office:* Humanities and Social Science Department, Montana College of Mineral Science and Technology, Butte, Mont. 59701.

CAREER: Has worked as recording engineer, studio engineer, and remote engineer; KOTA-Radio and Television, Rapid City, S.D., announcer and newsman, summer, 1955; University of South Dakota, Vermillion, instructor in radio, television, and film, 1957-63; KUSD-Radio and Television, Vermillion, S.D., acting production director, 1957-58, film director, 1958-60, program director, 1960-63; WDSE-Television, Duluth, Minn., program director, 1964-66; University of Minnesota, St. Paul, writer and photographer, summer, 1966; University of Montana, Missoula, assistant professor, 1966-71, associate professor of radio news, cinematography, elementary photography, news photography, and public affairs, 1971-78; free-lance writer and photographer, 1978-81; Montana College of Mineral Science and Technology, Butte, associate professor, 1981—. Director and cinematographer for Vermont Educational Television Series, 1968. *Military service:* U.S. Army, Writers Branch, 1955-57; served in Germany; became first lieutenant. *Member:* Western Montana Ghost Town Preservation Society (president, 1971-74). *Awards, honors:* Columbia Broadcasting System (CBS) news and public affairs fellowship, 1963-64; grants from National Endowment for the Humanities, 1971, to photograph Western ghost towns, and from American Philosophical Society, 1973.

WRITINGS: (With Stan Cohen) *The Big Burn,* Pictorial Histories Publishing, 1978; *Ghosts of the Black Hills,* Pictorial Histories Publishing, 1979; (with Cohen) *The University of Montana,* Pictorial Histories Publishing, 1980.

"Ghost Towns" series; published by Pruett: *Ghost Towns of Montana,* 1974; *. . . of Idaho,* 1976; *. . . of Washington and Oregon,* 1977; *. . . of Wyoming,* 1977; *. . . of California,* 1978; *. . . of Nevada,* 1979; *. . . of the Southwest,* 1980.

Also author of film, "Gary Schildt: A Self Portrait," National Endowment for the Arts, 1970. Author of documentary films for the U.S. Army. Contributor of about 70 articles to magazines and newspapers.

WORK IN PROGRESS: Research, with photography, on ghost towns of Colorado; researching a pictorial history of Missoula, Montana.

SIDELIGHTS: Donald Miller told *CA:* "I research, write about, and photograph Western ghost towns and mining camps because these 'playthings of the wind' are fast disappearing. If these remnants aren't captured on film now, we'll lose a significant part of our past."

*   *   *

MILLER, G. R.
    See JUDD, Frederick Charles

*   *   *

MILLER, Lyle L.   1919-

PERSONAL: Born August 20, 1919, in Deer Lodge, Mont.; son of Birl O. and Anna E. (Oakley) Miller; married Grace E. Moore (a professional consultant), September 12, 1942; children: Thomas O., Patricia Ann. *Education:* Montana State College, B.S., 1940; University of Southern California, M.S., 1944; Ohio State University, Ph.D., 1949. *Religion:* Presbyterian. *Home:* 1944 Sheridan, Laramie, Wyo. *Office:* Room 35, Education Hall, University of Wyoming, Laramie, Wyo. 82070.

CAREER: Gallatin County High School, Bozeman, Mont., teacher, 1940-42; Douglas Aircraft & California Flyers, Los Angeles, Calif., industrial personnel worker, 1942-44; Flathead County High School, Kalispell, Mont., teacher, 1944-46; Ohio State University, College of Education, Columbus, assistant junior dean, 1946-49; University of Wyoming, Laramie, professor of education, 1949—, supervisor of student employment and study skills center, 1949-53, chairman of guidance and special education, 1953-65, head of department of guidance and counselor education, 1964-72, director of reading research center, 1971—. Member of national executive board, Boy Scouts of America. Consultant to Wyoming State Department of Education, U.S. Office of Education, and U.S. Social Security Administration.

MEMBER: International Council for Exceptional Children, International Reading Association, National Education Association (life member), American School Counselors Association, American College Personnel Association, American Psychological Association, Association for Group Psychodrama and Psychotherapy, American Personnel and Guidance Association (life member), Association for Counselor Education and Supervision (president, 1963-64), National Vocational Guidance Association, American Association of University Professors (chapter president, 1965-67), Wyoming Personnel and Guidance Association, Wyoming Mental Health Association (member of executive board, 1963-68), Wyoming Education Association, Laramie Chamber of Commerce, Phi Delta Kappa. *Awards, honors:* Educational Service Award, Wyoming Personnel and Guidance Association, 1964, 1972; National Service Award, Association for Counselor Education and Supervision, 1968.

WRITINGS: (With Alice Z. Seeman) *Guidebook for Prospective Teachers,* Ohio State University Press, 1948; *Increasing Reading Efficiency,* Holt, 1956, 4th edition, 1978; *Maintaining Reading Efficiency,* Holt, 1959, 4th edition, Developmental Reading Distributors, 1980; *Developing Reading Efficiency,* Pruett, 1963, 4th edition, Burgess, 1980; (compiler) *Counseling Leads,* Pruett, 1962, 3rd edition, Developmental Reading Distributors, 1980; (editor) *Teaching Reading Efficiency,* Pruett, 1963, 2nd edition published as *Accelerating Growth in Reading Efficiency,* Burgess, 1967, revised edition published as *Teaching Efficient Reading Skills,* Burgess, 1972; (editor) *Challenge for Change in Counselor Education,* Burgess, 1969; *Person-*

alizing Reading Efficiency, Burgess, 1975, 2nd edition, 1981; *A Half-Century of Guidance in Wyoming,* Developmental Reading Distributors, 1981. Contributor of articles to professional journals, including *Journal of Developmental Reading, Journal for Counselor Education and Supervision,* and *School Counselor.* Associate editor, *Journal of Secondary and Adult Reading;* former editor of *Wyoming Personnel and Guidance Newsletter.*

WORK IN PROGRESS: Continued research on developmental reading material.

SIDELIGHTS: "My basic concern in writing," Lyle Miller told *CA,* "has always been to recognize individual differences and help all individuals understand and achieve their own potential through a better understanding of the society in which they live. In all of my reading books I emphasize speed *with* comprehension. My motto is 'seek the ideas behind the words.'"

*   *   *

MILLER, Marilyn McMeen
   See BROWN, Marilyn McMeen Miller

*   *   *

MILLER, William McElwee   1892-

PERSONAL: Born December 12, 1892, in Middlesboro, Ky.; son of Henry (a minister) and Flora (McElwee) Miller; married Isabelle Haines Nicholson, November 12, 1924 (died December 11, 1980); children: William, Flora, Elsie (Mrs. David Sprunt), Margaret (Mrs. Alan Weir). *Education:* Washington and Lee University, B.A., 1912, M.A., 1913; Princeton Theological Seminary, B.D., 1919. *Politics:* Democrat. *Home:* c/o William M. Miller, Jr., Box 22, Princeton, N.J. 08540.

CAREER: Ordained minister of Presbyterian Church in the United States, 1916; missionary in Iran, 1919-62. *Member:* Committee of Fellowship of Faith for Muslims, Bible and Medical Missionary Fellowship (member of board, 1965—), Phi Beta Kappa. *Awards, honors:* D.D., Washington and Lee University, 1932.

WRITINGS: (Translator) *Al-Babu'l-Hadi 'Ashar* (Shi'ite creed), Royal Asiatic Society, 1928, reprinted, 1958; *Baha'ism: Its Origin, History, and Teachings,* Revell, 1931; (translator with E. E. Elder) *Al-Kitab Al-Aqdas,* Royal Asiatic Society, 1961; (contributor) Howard F. Vos, editor, *Religions in a Changing World,* Moody, 1959; *Ten Muslims Meet Christ,* Eerdmans, 1969; *Beliefs and Practices of Christians,* Masihi Isha'at Khana (Lahore, Pakistan), 1973; *The Baha'i Faith: Its History and Teachings,* William Carey Library (Pasadena, Calif.), 1974; *A Christian's Response to Islam,* Presbyterian and Reformed Publishing, 1976; *What Is the Baha'i Faith?,* Eerdmans, 1977; *Tales of Persia: A Book for Children,* Dorrance, 1979.

Creator of Bible correspondence courses for Pakistan Bible Correspondence School. Also author of *The Way of Evangelism* and *The Way of Salvation,* both published in Teheran by Inter-Mission Literature Committee, of *A History of the Ancient Church in the Roman and Persian Empires,* published in Germany in 1931, and of commentaries on several books of the New Testament, all in Persian. Also author of works in English published by Christian publishing houses in Pakistan, Bangladesh, Indonesia, and other countries. Contributor of articles to publications.

SIDELIGHTS: William Miller told *CA:* "When I was a young man I believed that God had called me to go overseas as a missionary, to help make the truth and love of Christ known

to people who had not had the opportunity of knowing him. Later when I was a student in Seminary I came to know Dr. Samuel S. Zwemer, a pioneer missionary to Moslems in Arabia and an authority on Islam. As a result I decided to become a missionary to Moslems, and volunteered to go to Meshed in Iran under the Presbyterian Church. This I did in 1919, and had the privilege of serving Christ in different parts of Iran until I retired in 1962.

"In Iran my contacts were chiefly with Moslems, and I wanted to understand their beliefs as well as I could, so I studied Arabic as well as Persian, the national language, and came to know many Moslems and to understand their Shi'ite religion. Also in Iran, people came to see me who told me they were Baha'is, and I found it necessary to study this religion also. As I did so I learned that this faith, which was an offshoot of Shi'ite Islam, claimed to be the true religion of the world for the next thousand years, and that Baha'i missionaries were carrying this message to Europe and America, and to all the world. Since there were at that time no books in print in English which dealt with this movement, except the publications of Baha'is which too often were marred by serious historical errors, I was urged by friends to write a book, which I did. I became quite unpopular with the followers of this faith for so doing. My purpose was to tell the story of this movement as accurately as possible, to help those interested in understanding it correctly."

*   *   *

MILTON, Hilary (Herbert)   1920-

PERSONAL: Born April 2, 1920, in Jasper, Ala.; son of Hilary Herbert and Erline (Moore) Milton; married Patty Sanders (a writer), September 26, 1952; children: Michelle, David Rodgers. *Education:* Attended Alabama Polytechnic Institute (now Auburn University), 1938, and Birmingham-Southern College, 1939-40; University of Alabama, A.B., 1948, M.A., 1949. *Politics:* Independent. *Religion:* Methodist. *Home:* 3540 Oakdale Dr., Birmingham, Ala. 35223. *Office:* Department of English, Samford University, 800 Lakeshore Dr., Birmingham, Ala.

CAREER: University of Alabama, Tuscaloosa, instructor in business writing, 1948-51; U.S. Department of the Air Force, civilian educational specialist in Montgomery, Ala., 1951-52, informational specialist in St. Louis, Mo., 1952-55, editorial director in Washington, D.C., 1955-56, speech writer in Washington, D.C., 1956-62; National Aeronautics & Space Administration (NASA), Washington, D.C., report writer, 1962-70; full-time researcher and writer, 1970-71; Samford University, Birmingham, Ala., writer-in-residence, 1971—. Special lecturer at George Washington University, 1960. *Military service:* U.S. Army Air Forces, 1942-45.

WRITINGS—Novels, except as indicated: *Steps to Better Writing* (instruction book), Spartan, 1962; *The Gitaway Box,* Luce, 1968; *The House of God and Minnie May,* Luce, 1969; *The Tipple Bell,* Luce, 1970; *November's Wheel,* Abelard, 1976; *Nowhere to Run,* F. Watts, 1977; *Emergency! 10-33 on Channel 11!,* F. Watts, 1978; *Mayday! Mayday!,* F. Watts, 1979; *The Longest Highway,* David Cook, 1979; *Blind Flight,* F. Watts, 1980; *The Brats and Mr. Jack,* Beaufort Books, 1980; *Shutterbugs and Car Thieves,* Wanderer Books, 1980; *Dognappers,* Wanderer Books, 1982. Author of writing instruction manuals. Contributor of articles on U.S. space activities to encyclopedias; contributor of articles to educational and government publications.

WORK IN PROGRESS: Escape from Pelham's Ridge; Two from the Dead; The Kingdom of Koom; Siege!

SIDELIGHTS: Hilary Milton told *CA:* "Most of my recent novels have been what might be termed 'family novels' or novels for young readers. I prefer to write about situations which allow me to set the stories in the South. I particularly like to write books for young readers because they demand a story that holds them—and I must discipline myself to avoid fillers. As a by-product of these efforts, I often speak to school-age youngsters and receive letters from readers across the nation. The questions which they ask convince me that the wrong young people are getting all the media attention. I have a lot of confidence in the youth of today—a confidence that makes me believe this nation will be in good hands in the years to come. I've said it before and I'll say it again: When young people are faced with a challenge, they respond with courage, enthusiasm, self-reliance, and a willingness to act. In addition to my interest in young people, I try in my writings to picture the South as it is now—a region that has kept its traditions of family ties, of faith in God, of independence and self-reliance—while effectively meeting the challenges of modern America."

AVOCATIONAL INTERESTS: Family, photography, target shooting, the CB radio.

* * *

MITCHELL, Pamela Holsclaw   1940-

PERSONAL: Born June 27, 1940, in Denver, Colo.; daughter of Harold L. and Maurine (Boatman) Holsclaw; married Donald W. Mitchell (a physician), September 17, 1966; children: Robert, Kenneth, Andrew. *Education:* University of Washington, Seattle, B.S.N., 1962; University of California, San Francisco, M.S., 1965. *Politics:* Democrat. *Religion:* Protestant. *Residence:* Seattle, Wash. *Office:* Department of Physiological Nursing, University of Washington, Seattle, Wash. 98195.

CAREER: Massachusetts General Hospital, Boston, staff nurse, 1962-63, head nurse in neurology, 1963-64; Dane County Health Department, Madison, Wis., public health nurse, 1966-67; Emory University, Atlanta, Ga., instructor in nursing, 1967-68; University of Washington, Seattle, assistant professor of nursing, 1971-77, associate professor of physiological nursing and research affiliate of Regional Primate Research Center, 1977—. *Member:* American Association of University Professors, American Association for the Advancement of Science, American Nurses Association, American Academy of Nursing, American Association of Neurosurgical Nurses, Sierra Club, Common Cause, Washington State Heart Association, Sigma Theta Tau, Alpha Gamma Delta.

WRITINGS: (Contributor) H. C. Moidel and others, editors, *Nursing Care of Patients with Medical Surgical Disorders,* McGraw, 1971, 2nd edition, 1976; (editor and principal author) *Concepts Basic to Nursing,* McGraw, 1973, 3rd edition, 1981; (contributor) Judith Bloom, Geraldene Pardee, and Doris Molbo, editors, *The Dynamics of the Problem-Oriented Approach to Patient Care,* Lippincott, 1976; (contributor) M. Kinney and others, editors, *AACN Clinical Reference for Critical Care Nursing,* McGraw, 1980; (contributor) M. Van Meter, editor, *Learning Needs in Neurological Dysfunction,* Appleton-Century-Crofts, 1981; (contributor) G. Hongladarom, R. McCorkle, and Nancy F. Woods, editors, *The Complete Book of Women's Health,* Prentice-Hall, 1981; (with Doris Carnevali and Nancy F. Woods) *Clinical Decision-Making in Nursing,* Lippincott, 1982; (with Margarethe Cammermeyer, Judith Ozuna, and Nancy F. Woods) *Neurologic Assessment and Nursing Practice,* Reston, 1982. Contributor to *Nursing Forum, Nursing Research,* and *Nursing Clinics of North America.*

WORK IN PROGRESS: Psychobiology of stress response; sex differences in stress response; research on the effects of nursing care on intracranial pressure and on increased intracranial pressure.

SIDELIGHTS: Pamela Mitchell writes: "My interest in problems of neurologically-handicapped persons has been maintained since my first staff nursing position and is the focus of my current teaching and research." Her work has been published in Norway, Mexico, and Denmark.

* * *

MOBLEY, Walt
See BURGESS, M(ichael) R(oy)

* * *

MONCURE, Jane Belk   1926-
(Bruce Wannamaker)

PERSONAL: Born December 16, 1926, in Orlando, Fla.; daughter of J. Blanton (a Presbyterian minister) and Jennie (Wannamaker) Belk; married James Ashby Moncure (a vice-president of Elon College), June 14, 1952; children: James Ashby, Jr. *Education:* Virginia Commonwealth University, B.S., 1952; Columbia University, M.A., 1954. *Religion:* Christian. *Home:* 1046 Briarcliff Rd., Burlington, N.C. 27215.

CAREER: Woodward School, New York, N.Y., teacher, 1952-53; First Presbyterian Church Nursery School, New York, N.Y., teacher-director, 1953-54; Richmond Professional Institute, Richmond, Va., instructor in early childhood education, 1955-57; Southside Day Nursery, Richmond, director, 1957-59; Town and Garden School, Richmond, director, 1960-64; Richmond Public Schools, Richmond, junior primary teacher, 1964-66; Virginia Commonwealth University, Richmond, instructor in early childhood education, 1966-71; Virginia Union University, Richmond, staff member of language arts project, 1972-73; University of Richmond, Westhampton College, Richmond, instructor in early childhood education, 1973-74; Burlington Day School, Burlington, N.C., kindergarten teacher, 1974-78; consultant in early childhood education, 1978—. Part-time consultant on day care for children under six, Department of Welfare and Institutions, Richmond, Va., 1964. Conductor with husband of University of Richmond Summer School Abroad, 1963-70; lecturer, summer session, Adelphi College (now Adelphi University), Garden City, N.Y. *Member:* International Council of Richmond. *Member:* National Association for the Education of Young Children, Virginia Association for Early Childhood Education (first president, 1956), Southern Association for Children Under Six, Delta Kappa Gamma, University of Richmond Faculty Wives Club (president, 1964). *Awards, honors:* Research grant from Stanford University, 1971; Virginia Association for Early Childhood Education award, 1979, "for outstanding service to young children in Virginia."

WRITINGS—Published by Child's World (Elgin, Ill.), except as indicated: *Pinny's Day at Play School,* Lothrop, 1955; *Bunny Finds a Home,* Orion, 1962; *Flip: The True Story of a Dairy Farm Goat,* Farrar, Straus, 1964; *"Wait," Says His Father,* 1975; *All by Myself,* 1976; *A New Boy in Kindergarten,* 1976; *What Does a Koala Bear Need?,* 1976; *Where Things Belong,* 1976; *When I'm Afraid* (based on Sylvia Root Tester's *Sometimes I'm Afraid*), 1979; *Christmas Is a Happy Time,* 1980; *The Talking Tabby Cat,* 1980; *The Lad Who Made the Princess Laugh,* 1980; (with Tessa Colina) *You and Me: A Handbook about Needs,* 1980.

"Science and Social Science" series: *Try on a Shoe*, 1973; *Animal, Animal, Where Do You Live?*, 1975; *The Bunny Who Knew All about Plants*, 1975; *Fall Is Here!*, 1975; *One Little World*, 1975; *People Who Help People*, 1975; *Pets Are Smart*, 1975; *Plants Give Us Many Kinds of Food*, 1975; *Spring Is Here!*, 1975; *Summer Is Here!*, 1975; *Thank You, Animal Friends*, 1975; *Winter Is Here!*, 1975; *People Who Come to My House*, 1975; *Jobs People Do*, 1976; *Just the Right Place*, 1976; *See My Garden Grow*, 1976; *What do the Animals do in the Zoo?*, 1976; *What Will It Be?*, 1976; *Barbara's Pony, Buttercup*, 1977; *What Causes It?: A Beginning Book about Weather*, 1977; *What Will It Rain?*, 1977.

"Creative Expression Books" series: *How Do You Feel?*, 1973; *About Me*, 1976; *A Rabbit Has a Habit*, 1976; *Rhyme Me a Rhyme*, 1976; *Riddle Me a Riddle*, 1977; *Wishes, Whispers, and Secrets*, 1979.

"A Special Day" series: *Our Thanksgiving Book*, 1976; *Our Valentine Book*, 1976; *Our Easter Book*, 1976; *Our Birthday Book*, 1977; *Our Christmas Book*, 1977; *Our Halloween Book*, 1977; *Our Mother's Day Book*, 1977.

"Creative Dramatics" series: *If a Dinosaur Came to Dinner*, 1978; *The Four Magic Boxes*, 1978; *Tick, Tock, the Popcorn Clock*, 1978; *Skip aboard a Space Ship*, 1978; *Birds, Baboons and Bearfoot Bears*, 1978; *A Beach in my Bedroom*, 1978.

"Religious Education" series: *The Gift of Christmas*, 1979; *The Boy Samuel*, 1979; *But I'm Thankful, I Really Am*, 1979; *I Never Say I'm Thankful, But I Am*, 1979; *My Baby Brother Needs a Friend*, 1979; *My Baby Brother Needs Me*, 1979.

"Magic Monsters" series: *Magic Monsters Look for Colors*, 1979; *. . . Look for Shapes*, 1979; *. . . Count to Ten*, 1979; *. . . Learn about Manners*, 1980; *. . . Act the Alphabet*, 1980; *. . . Learn about Health*, 1980; *. . . Learn about Space*, 1980. Also author of *Magic Monsters Robot School*.

"Values to Live By" series: *Love*, 1980; *Caring*, 1980; *Honesty*, 1980; *Courage*, 1980; *Kindness*, 1981.

"Early Bird Reader" series: *Word Bird's Circus Surprise*, 1981; *Stop! Go! Word Bird*, 1981; *No, No, Word Bird: Word Birds for Early Birds*, 1981.

"Going Places" series; under pseudonym Bruce Wannamaker: *We Visit the Zoo*, 1976; *We Visit the Farm*, 1976.

Author of "Sound Box" series, nineteen books, 1977-79; also author of "Alphabet Books" series, ten books, of *The Christmas Elves*, and of materials for early childhood education, including fold out picture charts, teaching picture sets, table games, and time line sequence stories.

BIOGRAPHICAL/CRITICAL SOURCES: Sanford Herald (Sanford, N.C.), November 21, 1980.

*   *   *

MONK, Alan
   See KENDALL, Willmoore

*   *   *

MONTAGU of BEAULIEU, Edward John Barrington 1926-
   (Edward Douglas-Scott-Montagu)

PERSONAL: Family name, Douglas-Scott-Montagu; born October 20, 1920, in London, England; son of John Walker Edward (2nd Baron of Beaulieu) and Pearl (Crake) Douglas-Scott-Montagu; married Elizabeth Belinda Crossley, April 11, 1959

(marriage dissolved, 1974); married Fiona Margaret Herbert, September 26, 1974; children: (first marriage) Ralph, Mary Rachel; (second marriage) Jonathan. *Education:* Attended New College, Oxford, 1948-49. *Politics:* Independent Conservative. *Religion:* Church of England. *Home:* Palace House, Beaulieu, Hampshire, England; and Flat 11, 3 Wyndham Pl., London W.1, England. *Agent:* Curtis Brown Ltd., 1 Craven Hill, London W.2, England.

CAREER: Voice and Vision Ltd. (public relations firm), London, England, director, 1950-53; *Veteran and Vintage Magazine*, London, editor, 1956-79; Pioneer Publications Ltd., London, chairman, 1956—. Founder and director of National Motor Museum (formerly Montagu Museum), 1952—, and founder and chairman of National Motor Museum Trust. Lecturer on tours in South Africa, Australia, New Zealand, and the United States. *Military service:* British Army, Grenadier Guards, 1945-48; became lieutenant.

WRITINGS: The Motoring Montagus: The Story of the Montagu Motoring Museum, Cassell, 1959; *Lost Causes of Motoring*, Cassell, 1960, 2nd edition, 1966, Sportshelf, 1967; *Jaguar: A Biography*, Cassell, 1961, Norton, 1962, 3rd edition, Cassell, 1967, A. S. Barnes, 1969; *The Gordon Bennett Races*, Cassell, 1963; *Rolls of Rolls Royce: A Biography of Hon. C. S. Rolls*, Cassell, 1966, A. S. Barnes, 1967; *Gilt and the Gingerbread; or, How to Live in a Stately Home and Make Money*, M. Joseph, 1967; *Lost Causes of Motoring: Europe*, two volumes, A. S. Barnes, 1969; *More Equal Than Others: The Changing Fortunes of British and European Aristocracies*, M. Joseph, 1970; (with Anthony Bird) *Steam Cars*, Cassell, 1971; (with G. N. Georgano) *Early Days on the Road*, M. Joseph, 1976; (with F. Wilson McComb) *Behind the Wheel*, Paddington Press, 1977; (with Michael Frostick) *Royalty on the Road*, Collins, 1980. Consulting editor, *Collector's Car*, 1979—.

AVOCATIONAL INTERESTS: Shooting, water sports, skiing, photography, music.

*   *   *

MOONEYHAM, W(alter) Stanley 1926-

PERSONAL: Born January 14, 1926, in Houston, Miss.; son of Walter Scott and Mary (Sullivan) Mooneyham; married La Verda M. Green, December 13, 1946; children: Carol Gwen, Eric Scott, Robin Anne, Mark Randall. *Education:* Oklahoma Baptist University, B.S., 1950. *Home:* 2227 Canyon Dr., Arcadia, Calif. 91006. *Office:* World Vision International, 919 West Huntington Dr., Monrovia, Calif. 91016.

CAREER: Ordained Baptist minister, 1947. *News-Star*, Shawnee, Okla., reporter, 1949; First Free Will Baptist Church, Sulphur, Okla., pastor, 1949-53; National Association of Free Will Baptists, Nashville, Tenn., executive secretary, 1953-59; National Association of Evangelicals, Wheaton, Ill., director of information, 1959-64, interim executive director, 1964; Billy Graham Evangelistic Association, Atlanta, Ga., special assistant to Billy Graham, 1964-67, vice-president of international relations, 1967-69, coordinating director, World Congress on Evangelism, Berlin, 1966, and Asia-South Pacific Congress on Evangelism, Singapore, 1968; World Vision International, Monrovia, Calif., president, 1969—. Interim director, Coordinating Office for Asian Evangelism, 1969. Member of advisory board, Family Concern, Inc., 1974; member of advisory council, International Congress of Chinese Evangelicals, 1975; consulting editor, Word Books, Inc. *Military service:* U.S. Navy, 1943-45; became petty officer second class.

MEMBER: International Congress on World Evangelization (member of continuation committee, 1975—), National Association of Evangelicals (member of administrative board, 1964), National Association of Free Will Baptists (moderator, 1959-62), Evangelical Foreign Missions Association (member of board of directors), Evangelical Press Association (vice-president, 1962-64; president, 1964-65), National Sunday School Association (secretary, 1958-60; vice-president, 1960-61), Jesus People. *Awards, honors:* Litt.D., Houghton College, 1964; Order of Civil Merit (highest award given to a non-Korean), Republic of Korea, 1973; Alumni Achievement Award, Oklahoma Baptist University, 1975; D.H.L., Taylor University, 1977; LL.D., Seattle Pacific University, 1978.

WRITINGS: (Editor) *The Dynamics of Christian Unity: A Symposium on the Ecumenical Movement,* Zondervan, 1963; (co-editor) *One Race, One Gospel, One Task,* Worldwide Books, 1967; (editor) *Christ Seeks Asia,* Rock House (Hong Kong), 1969; *What Do You Say to a Hungry World?,* Word Books, 1978; *Come Walk the World,* Word Books, 1978; *China: A New Day,* Logos International, 1979; *Sea of Heartbreak,* Logos International, 1980. Also author of *China: The Puzzle,* 1971. Editor, *Contact,* 1953-59, *United Evangelical Action,* 1959-64; consulting editor, *Decision,* 1964-69.

WORK IN PROGRESS: Research in the field of communication, especially as it relates to the Christian message.

* * *

MOORE, Russell Franklin 1920-

PERSONAL: Born July 28, 1920, in Woodward, Iowa; son of Lawrence Alva (a businessman) and Sadie (Minger) Moore; married Ruth Emily Moller, May 29, 1946; children: Shelby Lynn. *Education:* State University of Iowa, student, 1937-40; New York Law School, LL.B., 1959.

CAREER: Ronald Press Co., New York City, assistant to the president, 1947-57; Simmons-Boardman Publishing Corp., New York City, vice-president, 1957-65; private practice of law, 1965-67; American Management Association, New York City, editor, 1967-70; Counsel Press, Inc., New York City, vice-president, beginning 1970. *Military service:* U.S. Army, served in European theater, World War II; became captain; received Bronze Star. *Member:* Classical Association (life), American Bar Association, Maison des Ailes (Brussels).

WRITINGS: Mentality and Consciousness, Franklin Publishing, 1937; *Oriental Philosophies,* R. F. Moore Co., 1937, 3rd edition (with William D. Gould and George B. Arbaugh), 1951.

(Editor) *Ramayana,* R. F. Moore Co., c.1950; (editor) *Readings in Oriental Philosophy,* R. F. Moore Co., 1951; *Bibliography for "Oriental Philosophies,"* R. F. Moore Co., 1951; (editor) *Modern Constitutions: With Brief Commentaries,* Littlefield, 1957; *Stare Decisis: Some Trends in British and American Application of the Doctrine,* Simmons-Boardman, 1958.

Letter from Bern, Whittier Books, 1960; *Principality of Liechtenstein: A Brief History,* Simmons-Boardman, 1960; *The Family History Book: A Genealogical Record,* Simmons-Boardman, 1961; *Selected Ancestral Lines: Moore-Minger Genealogical Record,* [New York], 1962; (with Max J. Wasserman and Charles W. Hultman) *The Common Market and American Business,* Simmons-Boardman, 1964; (editor) *Compensating Executive Worth,* American Management Association, 1968; (editor) *Law for Executives,* American Management Association, 1968.

(Editor) *The American Management Association Management Handbook,* American Management Association, 1970; *Selling to Southeast Asia (Indonesia, Malaysia, Singapore, Thailand): A Marketing Guide for U.S. Businessmen,* Thai-American Pub-

lishers, 1975; *Thailand-Malaysia-Singapore: People, Places, History,* Thai-American Publishers, 1975; *Selling to the Arab World, Middle East and North Africa,* Thai-American Publishers, 1976. Editor, *Who's Who in Railroading in North America,* Simmons-Boardman, 14th edition, 1959, 15th edition, 1964.†

* * *

MOORE, Ruth

PERSONAL: Born in St. Louis, Mo.; daughter of William D. (a lawyer) and Ethel (Sledd) Moore; married Raymond W. Garbe. *Education:* Washington University, A.B., M.A. *Home:* 860 Lake Shore Dr., Chicago, Ill. 60611.

CAREER: Chicago Sun-Times, Chicago, Ill., reporter, 1943-70, correspondent in Washington D.C., 1943-50. President of women's board, University of Chicago, 1973-77; chairman of Prairie Avenue Historic District, 1973—; commissioner of Commission on Chicago Historical and Architectural Landmarks, 1976—; president of Chicago Architecture Foundation, 1978. *Member:* Women's National Press Club (Washington, D.C.), Press Club (Chicago), Phi Beta Kappa. *Awards, honors:* D.Litt. from McMurray College, 1955; Friends of Literature annual award, 1955; alumni citation, Washington University, 1963; Champion Fighter for a Better Chicago award, Metropolitan Housing and Planning Council; national awards from National Municipal League and American Association of Planning Officials; named Chicago Preservationist of the Year, 1981.

WRITINGS—Published by Knopf, except as indicated: *Man, Time, Fossils,* 1953; *Charles Darwin: A Great Life in Brief,* 1955; *The Earth We Live On,* 1956, 2nd edition, 1971; *The Coil of Life,* 1960; *Evolution,* Time, Inc., 1962; *Niels Bohr: The Man, His Science and the World They Changed,* 1966; *Man in the Environment,* 1974; (with Sherwood L. Washburn) *Ape into Man,* Little, Brown, 1975, 2nd edition published as *Ape into Human,* 1980.

BIOGRAPHICAL/CRITICAL SOURCES: Times Literary Supplement, October 5, 1967; *Observer Review,* October 29, 1967; *New Statesman,* December 8, 1967.

* * *

MOORE, Sally Falk 1924-

PERSONAL: Born 1924, in New York, N.Y.; daughter of Henry Charles (a surgeon) and Mildred (a painter; maiden name, Hymanson) Falk; married Cresap Moore (a professor of history), July 14, 1951; children: two. *Education:* Barnard College, B.A., 1943; Columbia University, LL.B., 1945, Ph.D., 1957. *Residence:* Cambridge, Mass. *Office:* 320 William James Hall, Harvard University, Cambridge, Mass. 02138.

CAREER: Spence, Hotchkiss, Parker & Duryea, New York, N.Y., associate attorney, 1945-46; staff attorney for U.S. Department of War at Nuremburg Trials in Germany, 1946; University of Southern California, Los Angeles, assistant professor, 1963-65, associate professor, 1965-67, 1969-70, professor of anthropology, 1970-77, part-time lecturer in Law School, 1970-77, chairman of anthropology section, department of sociology and anthropology, 1972-77; University of California, Los Angeles, professor, 1977-81; Harvard University, Cambridge, Mass., professor, 1981—. Research associate, University College, University of East Africa, 1968-69, and University of Dar es Salaam, 1973-74, 1979-80; visiting professor, Yale University, 1975-76, and Harvard University, 1978. Morgan Lecturer, Rochester University, 1981. Social Science Research Council, member of board, 1974-76, member of committee on law and social science, 1975—. *Member:* International African Institute, American Anthropological Association (fellow), Law and Society Association, Royal Anthropological Institute (Great Britain; fellow), Association of Social Anthropologists (United Kingdom), New York State Bar. *Awards, honors:* Postdoctoral research grant, African Studies Center, University of California, Los Angeles, 1967-68; Social Science Research Council grant, 1968-69; National Science Foundation grant, 1972-75, 1979-80; honorary research fellow, University College, London, 1973-77.

WRITINGS: Power and Property in Inca Peru, Columbia University Press, 1958; (editor and contributor with B. Myerhoff) *Symbol and Politics in Communal Ideology,* Cornell University Press, 1975; (editor and contributor with Myerhoff) *Secular Rituals,* Royal Van Gorum, 1977; (with P. Puritt) *The Chagga and Meru of Tanzania,* International African Institute (London), 1977; *Law as Process,* Routledge & Kegan Paul, 1978.

Contributor: *A History of the Faculty of Political Science: The Bicentennial History of Columbia University,* Columbia University Press, 1955; J. Middleton, editor, *Myth and Cosmos,* Natural History Press, 1967; L. Nader, editor, *Law in Culture and Society,* Aldine, 1969; B. Siegel, editor, *Biennial Review of Anthropology,* Stanford University Press, 1969; M. Gluckman, editor, *The Allocation of Responsibility,* Manchester University Press, 1972; I. Hamnett, editor, *Social Anthropology and Law,* Academic Press, 1977; Myerhoff and A. Simic, editors, *Life's Career: Aging,* Sage Publications, 1978; P. Gulliver, editor, *Cross-Examinations,* E. J. Brill, 1979.

Contributor to *American Anthropologist, Law and Society Review, Africa, Current Anthropology,* and other publications.

WORK IN PROGRESS: Process and Sequence: Essays Theoretical and Ethnographic on the Chagga of Kilimanjaro, Tanzania.

* * *

MOOREHEAD, Alan (McCrae) 1910-

PERSONAL: Born July 22, 1910, in Melbourne, Australia; son of Richard (a journalist) and Louise (Edgerton) Moorehead; married Lucy Milner, October 29, 1939; children: John, Caroline, Richard. *Education:* Melbourne University, B.A., 1931. *Office:* National Bank of Australasia, Australia House, Strand, London WC2, England. *Agent:* Laurence Pollinger Ltd., 18 Maddox St., London W.1, England.

CAREER: Journalist for newspapers in Australia and England, mostly as war correspondent, 1930-46; free-lance writer, 1946—; currently affiliated with National Bank of Australasia, London, England. *Member:* Garrick Club (London). *Awards, honors:* Mentioned in dispatches, 1939 and 1945 (while war correspondent); Order of the British Empire, 1946; *Sunday Times* Gold Medal and Duff Cooper Memorial Award, both for *Gallipoli,* 1956; Royal Society of Literature Award, 1964.

WRITINGS: Mediterranean Front (also see below), Hamilton, 1941, McGraw, 1942; *Don't Blame the Generals* (also see below), Harper, 1943 (published in England as *A Year of Battle,* Hamilton, 1943); *The End in Africa* (also see below), Harper, 1943; *African Trilogy* (contains *Mediterranean Front, A Year of Battle,* and *The End in Africa*), Hamilton, 1945, Harper, 1965, abridged edition published as *The Desert War,* Hamilton, 1965, published as *The March to Tunis: The North African War, 1940-1943,* Harper, 1967; *Eclipse,* Coward, 1946, abridged edition, Hamilton, 1967; *Montgomery: A Biography,* Coward, 1946; *The Rage of the Vulture,* Scribner, 1948; *The*

Villa Diana, Scribner, 1951; *The Traitors: The Double Life of Fuchs, Pontecorvo, and Nunn May,* Scribner, 1952, revised edition, Harper, 1963; *Rum Jungle,* Hamilton, 1953, Scribner, 1954; *A Summer Night,* Harper, 1954; *Winston Churchill in Trial and Triumph,* Houghton, 1955; *Gallipoli,* Harper, 1956, new edition, Hamilton, 1967; *The Russian Revolution,* Harper, 1958; *No Room in the Ark,* Hamilton, 1959, Harper, 1960.

The White Nile, Hamilton, 1960, Harper, 1961, abridged edition, with wife, Lucy Moorehead, published as *The Story of the White Nile,* Harper, 1967; *Churchill: A Pictorial Biography,* Viking, 1960, revised edition published as *Churchill and His World: A Pictorial Biography,* Thames & Hudson, 1965; *The Blue Nile,* Harper, 1962, abridged edition by L. Moorehead published as *The Story of the Blue Nile,* Harper, 1966; *Cooper's Creek,* Hamilton, 1963, Harper, 1964; *The Fatal Impact: An Account of the Invasion of the South Pacific, 1767-1840,* Harper, 1966; *Darwin and the Beagle,* Harper, 1969; *A Late Education: Episodes in a Life* (autobiography), Hamilton, 1970, Harper, 1971. Contributor to *New Yorker, Harper's,* and other magazines.

SIDELIGHTS: Alan Moorehead began his writing career as a correspondent during the Second World War. As Edward Weeks of the *Atlantic* writes, however, "Moorehead is one of the few distinguished war correspondents who have gone on to write better and better books." Moorehead's books include travelogues, histories, and biographies.

Moorehead's first books were based on his own experiences as a correspondent in Africa and the Mediterranean and dealt with the military battles which he reported. These books gained Moorehead recognition as one of the most talented of the war correspondents. V. S. Pritchett of the *New Statesman & Nation,* in a review of *The End in Africa,* judges Moorehead to be "the most brilliant [and] the most imaginative" of the war correspondents. Moorehead has "a fine control of language, a constant curiosity . . . , and a stimulating judgement." *Don't Blame the Generals,* according to Walter Millis of the *Weekly Book Review,* is "the best book on the desert war" in North Africa. Speaking of the same work, Frank Gervasi of the *New York Times* states that it "is indispensable to a fuller understanding of the war in the Mediterranean and for that reason to a wider comprehension of the war as a whole." Leigh White of *Books* finds *Mediterranean Front* "the best example of military reporting yet to come out of the war."

In *Gallipoli,* Moorehead turned his attention to the First World War and the history of the unfortunate Gallipoli military campaign. The book was praised for its combination of historical accuracy and fine writing. "It is masterly," G. A. Craig writes in the *New York Herald Tribune Book Review,* "in its reconstruction of the development of the strategical situation on both sides of the fighting lines, impartial in its handling of the bitter controversies which raged during and after the campaign, and sympathetic in its treatment of the individuals [involved]." Craig ranks the history "among the very best books on the subject." Raymond Postgate of *Nation* believes *Gallipoli* to be "the first really satisfactory history of [the campaign] to be published." Weeks calls the book "a classic of that ill-fated campaign." Drew Middleton of the *New York Times* states: "I have read no better piece of descriptive writing about either world war than Mr. Moorehead's [*Gallipoli*]," while a *Kirkus* reviewer judges it to come "as near being a literary-historical masterpiece as anything published in our time."

In his books *The White Nile* and *The Blue Nile,* Moorehead recounts the history of the exploration of the Nile River in Africa. *The Blue Nile* presents the explorations of the first half of the nineteenth century, while *The White Nile* details those of the latter half of the century.

William Mulvihill of the *Chicago Tribune* finds *The White Nile* "an important book because it is more than surface deep. [Moorehead's] book is a masterpiece of research and writing." Pritchett admires Moorehead's "mastery of panorama [and] his power of bringing clear detail and physical life to a large and confusing subject." "Moorehead is an historian of great skill," a critic for the *Times Literary Supplement* remarks, and "his scholarship [is] worn with deceptive lightness. He is a travel writer of charm and perception. But above all he is a teller of tales." Reviewing *The White Nile* some years after its original publication, Byron Farwell of the *Washington Post Book World* finds that it "has stood the test of time" and is "a book which has become a classic." Farwell goes on to state that "with *The White Nile* [Moorehead] entered that category of writers who use history as sculptors use clay; history can provide the raw material with which good writers can create good literature."

The Blue Nile recounts four expeditions on the Nile River of the early nineteenth century. The *Times Literary Supplement* reviewer, although believing *The Blue Nile* "is less perfect" than *The White Nile*, nonetheless concludes that "Moorehead's failures are other men's triumphs, and it need hardly be said that *The Blue Nile* is packed with good things." Basil Davidson of the *New York Times Book Review* is of the opinion that "Moorehead sometimes obscures more than he illuminates" in *The Blue Nile* but still finds that he "greatly enjoyed [this] exciting and unusual book." Peter Fleming of *Spectator* writes that "Moorehead is a splendid chronicler" and *The Blue Nile* is "an extremely enjoyable, instructive, and stylish book." In *The Blue Nile*, Harold Nicolson writes in the *New York Herald Tribune Book Review*, "Moorehead enjoys adventure, is amused by human vanity, relishes the unfamiliar, and is careful to be both accurate and fair."

A more recent book that has garnered critical attention is *Darwin and the Beagle*, the story of biologist Charles Darwin and his five year round-the-world research voyage on the H.M.S. Beagle. It was during this journey that Darwin first formulated his theory of evolution, based upon his observations of animal and plant life around the world. Weeks considers the book to be "the most engaging biography" of Darwin. Alfred Friendly of the *Washington Post Book World* calls it "the kind of story in which Moorehead is unrivalled; he could not tell it badly if he tried." A reviewer for the *Times Literary Supplement* writes: "Moorehead's admirable prose style, his entrancing narrative of Darwin's activities during those years, and his geographical and biological picture of the countries Darwin visited are beyond praise."

Moorehead's books have been translated into French, German, Italian, Spanish, and Arabic.

BIOGRAPHICAL/CRITICAL SOURCES: Books, March 15, 1942; *Atlantic*, May, 1942, November, 1969, April, 1971; *New York Times*, April 23, 1943, June 1, 1947, March 14, 1954, September 16, 1956, August 24, 1958, December 7, 1971; *Weekly Book Review*, April 25, 1943; *Saturday Review*, May 15, 1943, December 18, 1943, May 8, 1954, September 22, 1956, February 25, 1961, January 24, 1970; *Christian Science Monitor*, May 29, 1943, December 27, 1943, August 21, 1958, July 12, 1968, May 27, 1971; *New Statesman & Nation*, November 6, 1943; *New Yorker*, November 27, 1943, August 23, 1958, April 24, 1971; *Manchester Guardian*, November 29, 1946, May 4, 1956; *Times Literary Supplement*, December 7, 1946, October 16, 1953, December 30, 1960, July 13, 1962, September 25, 1969, October 16, 1969; *New Statesman*, Jan-

uary 6, 1951, October 18, 1958, January 6, 1961, December 25, 1970; *New York Herald Tribune Book Review*, March 21, 1954, September 16, 1956, January 15, 1961, August 5, 1962; *San Francisco Chronicle*, March 26, 1954, August 20, 1958, January 9, 1961; *Kirkus*, July 15, 1956, June 15, 1958; *New York Times Book Review*, September 16, 1956, August 12, 1962, November 9, 1969; *Nation*, September 29, 1956; *Commonweal*, November 9, 1956; *Chicago Tribune*, August 24, 1958, January 22, 1961; *Springfield Republican*, October 5, 1958.

Spectator, December 9, 1960, July 13, 1962, September 27, 1969; *Time*, January 20, 1961, August 31, 1962, December 29, 1969, December 20, 1971; *Punch*, October 23, 1968, November 25, 1970; *Washington Post*, October 16, 1969; *Washington Post Book World*, October 19, 1969, November 28, 1971, June 22, 1980; *Newsweek*, October 20, 1969; *Listener*, October 30, 1969; *Esquire*, December, 1969, August, 1971; *America*, December 6, 1969; *National Observer*, December 22, 1969; *Observer*, November 15, 1970; *Audience*, March-April, 1971; *New Leader*, May 31, 1971; *Books & Bookmen*, December, 1972; *Christian Century*, May 14, 1975; *New York Review of Books*, February 7, 1980.†

—*Sketch by Thomas Wiloch*

*   *   *

MOREHEAD, Joe
 See MOREHEAD, Joseph H., Jr.

*   *   *

MOREHEAD, Joseph H., Jr. 1931-
 (Joe Morehead)

PERSONAL: Born January 30, 1931, in New York, N.Y.; son of Joseph H. and Irma (Gray) Morehead; married Bebe Ann Behnke, September 4, 1966; children: Adam Gray. *Education:* Trinity College, Hartford, Conn., B.A., 1952; Columbia University, M.A., 1955; University of Kentucky, M.L.S., 1964; University of California, Berkeley, Ph.D., 1973. *Office:* School of Library and Information Science, State University of New York at Albany, Albany, N.Y. 12222.

CAREER: Orlando Junior College, Orlando, Fla., instructor in English, 1954-56; U.S. Department of the Air Force, education director in London, England, 1957-62; San Francisco Public Library, San Francisco, Calif., documents librarian, 1964-70; State University of New York at Albany, 1970—, began as assistant professor, currently associate professor of library and information science. *Military service:* U.S. Air Force, 1952-54; became first lieutenant. *Member:* American Library Association, Government Documents Round Table, New York Library Association, Phi Beta Kappa (charter member of Alpha Alpha chapter).

WRITINGS—Under name Joe Morehead: (Contributor) Bill Katz, editor, *Magazines for Libraries*, Bowker, 2nd edition (Morehead was not associated with first edition), 1972; (editor) *Albany Municipal Documents: A Directory of Sources* (booklet), School of Library and Information Science, State University of New York at Albany, 1974; *Introduction to United States Public Documents*, Libraries Unlimited, 1975, 2nd edition, 1978; *Theory and Practice in Library Education: The Teaching-Learning Process*, Libraries Unlimited, 1980.

Author of columns "Into the Hopper" for *Serials Librarian* and "Quorum of One" for *Documents to the People*. Contributor of articles and reviews to *Synergy, Bulletin of Bibliography, Reference Quarterly, Journal of Education for Li-*

brarianship, *College Student Journal, Library Journal, Government Publications Review,* and *American Reference Books Annual.*

SIDELIGHTS: Joe Morehead told *CA:* "My teaching and writing are largely concerned with the impact of public policy decisions on the production and distribution of government publications. In the present climate of less government and budgetary retrenchment, there is a real danger that access to public documents will be abridged under the guise of saving taxpayer dollars. People in my profession have an obligation to exercise vigilance in the face of that threat."

*　　*　　*

MORENO, Martin
　See SWARTZ, Harry (Felix)

*　　*　　*

MORRIS, John W(esley) 1907-

PERSONAL: Born November 14, 1907, in Billings, Okla.; son of Henry L. and Lillian M. (Knowles) Morris; married Mary Elizabeth Russell, February 19, 1932; children: Carroll June (Mrs. Harvey Wilson), Russell A. *Education:* University of Oklahoma, B.S., 1930; Oklahoma State University, M.S., 1934; George Peabody College for Teachers (now George Peabody College for Teachers of Vanderbilt University), Ph.D., 1941. *Home:* 833 McCall Dr., Norman, Okla. 73069.

CAREER: Seminole Junior College, Seminole, Okla., instructor in geography, 1931-38; Southeastern State College, Durant, Okla., associate professor, 1939-42, professor of geography, 1946-48; University of Oklahoma, Norman, associate professor, 1948-50, 1952-54, professor of geography and head of department, 1954-73. Visiting summer professor at University of Florida, 1949, George Peabody College for Teachers (now George Peabody College for Teachers of Vanderbilt University), 1957, 1958, Western Washington College, 1962, Michigan State University, 1964, Moorhead State College, 1969, University of British Columbia, 1971, and University of Wyoming, 1973. Consultant to National Park Service, 1952-53, and Southern Appalachian Studies Program, 1958-60; consulting editor, Harlow Publishing Corp., 1940-68. *Military service:* U.S. Navy, 1942-46, 1950-51; became commander; received Commendation Ribbon and Pacific Ribbon with five battle stars.

MEMBER: National Council for Geographic Education (fellow; secretary, 1955-58; president, 1960; director of publications, 1961-63), Association of American Geographers (chairman of Southwestern division, 1955-56, 1961-63), American Geographical Society (fellow), Southwestern Social Science Association (president, 1964), Oklahoma Education Association (chairman of geography section, 1940, 1947, 1949, 1954; member of board of directors, 1963), Oklahoma Academy of Science (fellow; chairman of geography section, 1953), Sigma Xi, Phi Beta Sigma, Phi Delta Kappa, Pi Gamma Mu, Phi Alpha Theta, Gamma Theta Upsilon, Lions Club. *Awards, honors:* Grants from U.S. Office of Naval Research, 1952-54, National Park Service, 1954, Ford Foundation, 1959, and University of Oklahoma Faculty Research Fund; Distinguished Former Student Award, Central Oklahoma State College; Distinguished Service Award, National Council for Geographic Education, 1966; Outstanding Scientist of Oklahoma Award, Oklahoma Academy of Science, 1978.

WRITINGS: A Preliminary Index to the Source Materials of Oklahoma Geography, Oklahoma Council of Geography

Teachers, 1929; *Comprehensive Guidebook for Commercial and Industrial Geography,* Harlow Publishing, 1931; *Population Projections for Oklahoma Towns and Cities of 2500 or More,* Arkansas-White-Red River Basin Authority, 1951; *Oklahoma Geography,* Harlow Publishing, 1952, 3rd edition, 1962; *An Analysis of the Tourist Industry in Selected Counties of the Ozark Area,* National Park Service, 1952; *Boreal Fringe Areas of Marsh and Swampland: A General Background Study,* Office of Naval Research, 1954; *Boreal Fringe Areas of Marsh and Swampland: Photoidentification Key for the Summer (Foliage) Season,* Office of Naval Research, 1954; *Boreal Fringe Areas of Marsh and Swampland: Photoidentification Key for the Winter (Non-Foliage) Season,* Office of Naval Research, 1954.

(Editor with Otis Freeman) *World Geography,* with study guide and instructor's manual, McGraw, 1958, 3rd edition, 1972; (with Harry E. Hoy) *Know Your America—Oklahoma,* American Geographical Society, 1965; (with Edwin C. McReynolds) *Historical Atlas of Oklahoma,* University of Oklahoma Press, 1965, 2nd edition, 1976; (editor) *Methods of Geographic Instruction,* Blaisdell, 1968; *Southwestern United States,* Van Nostrand, 1970; *Geography of Oklahoma,* Oklahoma Historical Society, 1977; *Ghost Towns of Oklahoma,* University of Oklahoma Press, 1977; (editor) *Cities of Oklahoma,* Oklahoma Historical Society, 1979; (editor) *Boundaries of Oklahoma,* Oklahoma Historical Society, 1980; (with Charles R. Goins) *Oklahoma Homes: Past and Present,* University of Oklahoma Press, 1980; (editor) *Development of Mineral Resources in Oklahoma,* Oklahoma Historical Society, 1981.

Contributor: Kent Ruth, editor, *Oklahoma: A Guide to the Sooner State,* University of Oklahoma Press, 1957; William H. Cartwright, editor, *Teaching American History in High School,* National Council for the Social Studies, 1961; Thomas R. Ford, editor, *The Southern Appalachian Region: A Survey,* University of Kentucky Press, 1962.

Author of thirty workbooks and laboratory manuals on geography of the United States, Canada, Latin America, and other parts of the world for use in elementary, junior high, and high schools. Co-compiler of "Oklahoma History Maps" series of ten wall maps. Contributor to *World Book Encyclopedia* and *Student Merit Encyclopedia.* Contributor to professional journals.

WORK IN PROGRESS: Two books, *Historical Atlas of American Indians,* for University of Oklahoma Press, and, with Louise Welsh, *The Greater Seminole Area,* for Oklahoma Heritage Association.

AVOCATIONAL INTERESTS: Foreign travel, photography, cartography.

*　　*　　*

MORRISON, Denton E(dward) 1932-

PERSONAL: Born in 1932. *Education:* South Dakota State University, B.S., 1954, M.S., 1958; University of Wisconsin, Ph.D., 1962. *Office:* Department of Sociology, Michigan State University, East Lansing, Mich. 48824.

CAREER: University of California, Berkeley, assistant professor of sociology, 1962-64; Michigan State University, East Lansing, assistant professor, 1964-67, associate professor, 1967-71, professor of sociology, 1971—. Researcher at Michigan Agricultural Experiment Station, 1964—. Visiting professor, University of Wisconsin, 1967, 1971. Member, Sociopolitical Risk/Impact Resource Group, National Academy of Sciences, 1976-80; member, Integration of Socioeconomic Criteria Panel,

National Academy of Sciences, 1980; member, Conservation Panel, U.S. Department of Energy, 1980. *Member:* American Sociological Association, Rural Sociological Society, International Association for the Advancement of Appropriate Technology in Developing Countries, World Future Society.

WRITINGS: (With G. A. Kristjanson) *Personal Adjustment among Older Persons,* Agricultural Experiment Station, South Dakota State University, 1958; (editor with Dale Hathaway, James Shaffer, and Richard Feltner, and contributor) *Michigan Farmers in the Mid-Sixties: A Survey of Their Views of Marketing Problems and Organizations,* Agricultural Experiment Station, Michigan State University, 1966; (with Patricia Phillips) *A Silent Minority: A Research Feasibility Probe of Discontent among the Rural Poor* (pamphlet), Rural Manpower Center, Michigan State University, 1970; (editor) *Farmers' Organizations and Farmers' Movements: Research Needs and a Bibliography of the United States and Canada,* Agricultural Experiment Station, Michigan State University, 1970; (editor with Ramon E. Henkel) *The Significance Test Controversy,* Aldine, 1970; *A Directory of Environmental Organizations,* Environmental Resources, 1971; (compiler with Kenneth E. Hornback and W. Keith Warner) *Environment: A Bibliography of Social Science and Related Literature,* U.S. Government Printing Office, 1974; (editor) *Energy: A Bibliography of Social Science and Related Literature,* Garland Publishing, 1975; (editor with Hornback) *Collective Behavior: A Draft Bibliography,* Gardland Publishing, 1976; (editor with Virginia Bemis and others) *Energy II: A Bibliography of 1975-1976 Social Science and Related Literature,* Garland Publishing, 1977; (with Frederick H. Buttel) *The Environmental Movement: A Research Bibliography with Some State-of-the-Arts Comments,* Council of Planning Libraries, 1977; (editor with Charles Unseld, David Sills, and Charles P. Wolf) *The Social Effects of Energy Use and Policy,* National Academy of Sciences, 1980.

Contributor: James Copp, editor, *Projection Papers: Orientations for Rural Sociological Research and Action,* Rural Sociological Society, 1964; William Burch, Neil Cheek, and Lee Taylor, editors, *Social Behavior, Natural Resources, and the Environment,* Harper, 1972; Robert Evans, editor, *Readings in Social Movements,* Rand McNally, 1973; Zaltman and other editors, *Processes and Phenomena of Social Change,* Wiley, 1973; Evans, editor, *Social Movements,* Rand McNally, 1973; A. Murch, editor, *Environmental Concern,* MSS Educational Publishing, 1974; Marcello Truzzi, editor, *Sociology for Pleasure,* Prentice-Hall, 1974; *Perspectives on the Land,* Program on Lifelong Education, Michigan State University, 1976; *The Energy Problem Continues: Impacts and Implications for Urban and Industrial Centers,* Center for Urban Affairs, Michigan State University, 1976; *Energy Guide: A Directory of Information Resources,* Garland Publishing, 1977; *Energy Policy in the United States: Social and Behavioral Dimensions,* Praeger, 1978; *Research in Social Movements, Conflict, and Change,* Volume II, Jai Press, 1979; *Collective Decision Making: Applications from Public Choice Theory,* Johns Hopkins University Press, 1979; *Energy in Transition: 1985-2010,* National Academy of Sciences, 1979; *Rural Society: Issues for the 1980s,* Westview Press, 1981; *Annual Review of Energy,* Volume VI, Annual Reviews, 1981.

Contributor to proceedings. Contributor of articles to journals, including *Journal of Voluntary Action Research, Rural Sociology, Natural Resources Journal,* and *Journal of Cooperative Extension.*

*   *   *

MORRISON, Roberta
See WEBB, Jean Francis (III)

MUDGE, Jean McClure 1933-

PERSONAL: Born December 4, 1933, at Fort Benning, Ga.; daughter of Robert Battey (a general, U.S. Army) and Eva Eugenia (Colby) McClure; married Lewis Seymour Mudge (dean of McCormick Theological Seminary), June 15, 1957; children: Robert Seymour, William McClure, Anne Evelyn. *Education:* Stanford University, B.A., 1955; University of Delaware, M.A., 1957; Yale University, Ph.D., 1973. *Religion:* Presbyterian. *Home:* 1218 East Madison Park, Chicago, Ill. 60615.

WRITINGS: Chinese Export Porcelain for the American Trade, 1785-1835, University Publishers, 1962, 2nd edition, Associated University Presses, 1981; *Emily Dickinson and the Image of Home,* University of Massachusetts Press, 1975.

Films: "Emily Dickinson: A Certain Slant of Light," 1978; "Herman Melville: Consider the Sea," 1981.

WORK IN PROGRESS: A book on Chinese export porcelain in North America; films on Edgar Allan Poe, Nathaniel Hawthorne, and Walt Whitman.

AVOCATIONAL INTERESTS: Photography, reading, tennis, and writing poetry.

*   *   *

MULISCH, Harry 1927-

PERSONAL: Born July 29, 1927, in Haarlem, Netherlands; son of Kurt and Alice (Schwarz) Mulisch. *Home:* 103 Leidsekade, Amsterdam, Netherlands. *Agent:* De Bezige Bij, Van Miereveldstract 1, Amsterdam, Netherlands.

CAREER: Writer. Participant in writer's congresses in Finland, Scotland, Romania, and Germany. *Awards, honors:* Reina Prinsen Geerligs Prize, 1951, for *Archibald Strohalm;* Bijenkorf Literatuur Prize, 1957, for *Het Zwarte licht;* Anne Frank Prize, 1957; Visser Neerlandia Prize, 1960, for *Tanchelijn, kvoniek van een ketter;* Athos Prize, 1961.

WRITINGS—Published by De Bezige Bij (Amsterdam), except as indicated: *Archibald Strohalm* (novel), 1952; *Chantage op het leven* (two stories), 1953; *Di Diamant* (novel), 1954; *Het Mirakel: Episodes van troost en liederlijkheid uit het leven van der heer Tiennoppen,* De Arbeiderspers, 1956; *Het Zwarte licht* (novel), 1956; *De Versierde mens* (stories), 1957; *Manifesten* (aphorisms), Heinisz, 1958; *Het Stenen bruidsbed* (novel), 1959, translation by Adrienne Dixon published as *The Stone Bridal Bed,* Abelard, 1962.

Tanchelijn, kroniek van een ketter (play), 1960; *De Knop* (one-act play), 1960; *Voer voor psychologen* (autobiographical), 1961; *Wenken voor de bescherming van uiw gezin en uzelf, tijdens de jongste dag,* 1961; *De Zaak 40/61: Een Reportage* (about Eichmann Trial), 1962; *The Discovery of Moscou,* 1964; *De Sprong der paarden en de zoete zee,* Meulenhoff, 1964; *Nol Gregoor in gesprek met Harry Mulisch,* 1965; *Bericht aan de rattenkoning* (about Provo), 1966; *Wenken voor de jongste dag* (political), 1967; *Het Woord bij de daad: Getuigenis van de revolutie op Cuba,* 1968; *Israel is zelf een mens: Onzukelijke notities uit de zaak 40/61,* Bakker, 1969.

Paralipomena orphica (autobiographical), 1970; *De Verteller* (novel), 1970; *Oidipous, Oidipous, naar Sofokles,* 1972; *Soep lepelen met een vork,* 1972; *De Toekomst van gisteren,* 1972; *Wat gebeurde er met sergeant Massuro?,* 1972; *Woorden, woorden, woorden,* 1973; *Het seksuele bokwerk,* 1973; *Be-*

zoekuur, 1974; *De Vogels*, Polak & Van Gennep, 1974; *Volk en vaderliefde*, 1975; *Twee vrouwen: roman*, 1975, translation by Els Early published as *Two Women*, Riverrun Press, 1980; *Tegenlicht* (poetry), Polak & Van Gennep, 1975; *Mijn getijdenboek*, 1975; *Het ironische van de ironie: over het geval G. K. van het Reve*, Manteau, 1976; *De wijn in drinkbaar dank zij het glas*, 1976; *Vergrote raadsels: verklaringen, paradoxen, mulischesken*, Orion, 1976; *Verzamelde verhalen, 1947-1977*, Athenaeum-Polak & Van Gennep, 1977. Founding editor, *Randstad*.

SIDELIGHTS: In a review of *Two Women*, Tom Clark of the *Los Angeles Times* admires Harry Mulisch's "spare, detached prose." "His use of images and themes in the writing," Clark continues, "engages us primarily on a symbolic, psychological level that makes the severe plot acceptable in intuitive terms— as a real story, not as a thesis." Clark concludes that "we ought to be hearing more about [Mulisch] soon."

BIOGRAPHICAL/CRITICAL SOURCES: Times Literary Supplement, October 3, 1980; *Los Angeles Times*, December 22, 1980.†

*   *   *

MUNN, Hart
See HARDY, C. Colburn

*   *   *

MURDICK, Robert Gordon   1920-

PERSONAL: Born August 26, 1920, in Philadelphia, Pa.; son of Philip Pierce (a chemist) and Mary (Heath) Murdick; married Emily Beckstedt, January 1, 1942; children: William Maxwell, Kent Gordon. *Education:* Duke University, A.B. (magna cum laude), 1941; attended University of Maryland, 1941-42, and Union College, 1948-49; Rensselaer Polytechnic Institute, M.S., 1960; University of Florida, Ph.D., 1962. *Home:* 4189 Northwest Forth Ave., Boca Raton, Fla. *Office:* Department of Business, Florida Atlantic University, Boca Raton, Fla. 33432.

CAREER: Scott Field Radio School, Scott Field, Ill., teacher of radio theory, 1942-43; worked as an engineer and patent coordinator, 1946-51; General Electric Co., supervisor of technical reports and instruction books, 1951-55, engineer-administrator, 1955-60; manager in marketing research, Randac Systems, 1961; University of Louisville, Louisville, Ky., professor of management, 1962-63; State University of New York, Albany, professor of management, 1963-68; Florida Atlantic University, Boca Raton, professor of management, 1968—. Consultant to University of Santiago, summer, 1963. *Member:* Academy of Management.

WRITINGS: (With D. W. Karger) *Managing Engineering and Research*, Industrial Press, 1963, 2nd edition, 1969; (with A. E. Schaefer) *Sales Forecasting for Lower Costs and Higher Profits*, Prentice-Hall, 1967; (with D. D. Deming) *Management of Capital Expenditures*, McGraw, 1968; *Business Research: Concepts and Practices*, Intext Press Paperbacks, 1969; *Mathematical Models in Marketing*, Intext Press Paperbacks, 1971; (co-author) *New Product Venture Management*, Gordon & Breach, 1972; (co-author) *Management Update*, AMACOM, 1973; (co-editor) *MIS in Action*, West Publishing, 1975; (co-author) *Introduction to Management Information Systems*, Prentice-Hall, 1977; (co-author) *Human Resources Management*, Irwin, 1978; (co-author) *Accounting Information Systems*, Prentice-Hall, 1978; *MIS: Concepts and Design*, Prentice-Hall, 1980. Also co-author of *Information Systems for Modern Management, Business Policy: A Framework for Anal-*

ysis, and *Production/Operations Management for Small Businesses*.

*   *   *

MURPHEY, Murray Griffin   1928-

PERSONAL: Born February 22, 1928, in Colorado Springs, Colo.; son of Bradford James (a physician) and Margaret (Griffin) Murphey; married Allene Arnholter, March 28, 1964 (divorced, 1973); children: Kathleen Rachel, Christopher Bradford, Jessica Lenoir. *Education:* Harvard University, A.B., 1949; Yale University, Ph.D., 1954. *Home:* 200 Rhyl Lane, Bala-Cynwyd, Pa.

CAREER: Cambridge University, Cambridge, England, Fulbright fellow, 1953-54; University of Pennsylvania, Philadelphia, Rockefeller fellow, 1954-56, assistant professor, 1956-61, associate professor, 1961-66, professor, 1966—.

WRITINGS: The Development of Peirce's Philosophy, Harvard University Press, 1961; *Our Knowledge of the Historical Past*, Bobbs-Merrill, 1973; *Science and Technology in Philadelphia* (pamphlet), [Philadelphia], 1976; (with Elizabeth Flower) *A History of Philosophy in America*, Putnam, 1977.

Contributor: J. A. Hague, editor, *American Character and Culture*, Everett/Edwards, 1964; H. Cohen, editor, *Landmarks of American Writing*, Basic Books, 1969; *New Directions in American Intellectual History*, Johns Hopkins University Press, 1979.

Contributor to *Collier's Encyclopedia* and *Encyclopedia of Philosophy*. Contributor of articles and reviews to *Saturday Review, Emory Quarterly, American Quarterly*, and *Massachusetts Review*.

*   *   *

MURPHY, Roland Edmund   1917-

PERSONAL: Born July 19, 1917, in Chicago, Ill.; son of John Michael and Marian (Haugh) Murphy. *Education:* Catholic University of America, M.A., 1943, M.A., 1949, S.T.D., 1948; Pontifical Biblical Institute (Rome, Italy), S.S.L., 1958. *Home:* 211 McCauley St., Chapel Hill, N.C. *Office:* Divinity School, Duke University, Durham, N.C. 27706.

CAREER: Entered Carmelite Order, 1935; ordained to priesthood, 1942. Catholic University of America, Washington, D.C., instructor, associate professor of Semitic languages, 1948-56, professor of theology, 1956-70; Duke University, Durham, N.C., professor of the Old Testament, 1971—. Visiting professor, Pittsburgh Theological Seminary, 1964-65, Yale University Divinity School, 1965, Duke University, 1967-68, and Princeton Theological Seminary, 1970-71. *Member:* Catholic Biblical Association of America, Society of Biblical Literature, American Schools of Oriental Research. *Awards, honors:* American Schools of Oriental Research fellowship to Jerusalem, 1950-51; D.Litt., St. Francis College.

WRITINGS: The Dead Sea Scrolls and the Bible, Newman, 1956; *Seven Books of Wisdom*, Bruce, 1960; (co-editor) *Jerome Biblical Commentary*, Prentice-Hall, 1968; *Psalms Job*, Fortress, 1977; *Wisdom Literature*, Eerdmans, 1981. Editor-in-chief, *Catholic Biblical Quarterly*, 1958-65; scripture editor of *Concilium;* member of editorial council, *Interpretation Old Testament Abstracts*, and *Vetus Testamentum*.

WORK IN PROGRESS: A commentary on the *Song of Songs* and *Ecclesiastes* for Fortress.

MUSGROVE, Frank 1922-

PERSONAL: Born December 16, 1922, in Nottingham, England; son of Thomas (a mining engineer) and Fanny (Swain) Musgrove; married Dorothy Nicholls, September 12, 1948; children: Gail. *Education:* Magdalen College, Oxford, B.A., 1947; University of Nottingham, Ph.D., 1958. *Home:* 11 Ookwood Dr., Prestbury, Cheshire, England.

CAREER: Colonial Education Service, Uganda, education officer, 1950-53; University of Leicester, Leicester, England, lecturer, 1957-62; University of Leeds, Leeds, England, senior lecturer, 1963-65; University of Bradford, Bradford, England, professor of research in education, 1965-70; University of Manchester, Manchester, England, Sarah Fielden Professor of Education, 1971—. Visiting professor, University of British Columbia, 1965, University of California, 1969; Chancellor's Lecturer, University of Wellington, 1970. *Military service:* Royal Air Force, Bomber Command, 1941-45; served as navigator; became flying officer. *Member:* Royal Society of Arts (fellow).

WRITINGS: The Migratory Elite, Heinemann, 1963; *Youth and the Social Order,* Routledge & Kegan Paul, 1964, University of Indiana Press, 1965; *The Family, Education, and Society,* Routledge & Kegan Paul, 1966; (with Philip Taylor) *Society and the Teacher's Role,* Routledge & Kegan Paul, 1969; *Patterns of Power and Authority in English Education,* Methuen, 1971; *Ecstasy and Holiness: Counter Culture and the Open Society,* Indiana University Press, 1974; *Margins of the Mind,* Methuen, 1977; *School and the Social Order,* Wiley, 1979.

WORK IN PROGRESS: A book on anthropology and education, entitled *Other Cultures and the Teacher.*

SIDELIGHTS: Frank Musgrove told *CA:* "I write because I think I have something to say. It is an addition to knowledge and understanding of human behavior, especially of the conditions under which behavior can be changed. When I have nothing to say I shall stop writing. I like constructing sentences. I enjoy reconstructing long sentences into short ones. I also like removing abstract nouns and putting in concrete ones. I like national and international recognition. That is really an incredible privilege, and I remain astonished that I have achieved any."

* * *

MUSSI, Mary 1907-
(Josephine Edgar, Mary Howard)

PERSONAL: Born December 27, 1907, in London, England; daughter of George (an author) and Jenny (Howard) Edgar; married Rudolph F. Mussi, March 6, 1934; children: Max Edgar, Susan Jane (Mrs. F. Renaga Sykes). *Education:* "Private and brief." *Home:* 27 Woodfield Ave., London SW16 1LQ, England. *Agent:* Irene Josephy, 35 Craven St., Strand, London WC2N 5NG, England.

CAREER: Writer. *Member:* P.E.N., Crime Writers Association (London), Society of Women Writers and Journalists (London; former chairman). *Awards, honors:* Romantic Novelists Association, Major Award, 1960, for *More Than Friendship,* and Elinor Glynn Award, 1961, for *Surgeon's Dilemma.*

WRITINGS—Novels; under pseudonym Josephine Edgar: My Sister Sophie, Collins, 1964, Pocket Books, 1974; *The Dark Tower,* Collins, 1966; *The Dancer's Daughter,* Collins, 1969, Dell, 1970; *The Devil's Innocents,* Collins, 1972; *The Stranger at the Gate,* Collins, 1973; *Time of Dreaming,* Collins, 1968, Pocket Books, 1974; *The Lady of Wildersley,* Macdonald &

Jane's, 1975, Pocket Books, 1977; *Countess,* St. Martin's, 1976; *Duchess,* Macdonald & Jane's, 1976, Warner Books, 1979.

Under pseudonym Mary Howard: *Windier Skies,* John Long, 1930; *Dark Morality,* John Lane, 1932; *Partners for Playtime,* Collins, 1938; *Strangers in Love,* Collins, 1939, Doubleday, 1941; *It Was a Romance,* Collins, 1939.

The Untamed Heart, Collins, 1940; *Far Blue Horizons,* Collins, 1940, Doubleday, 1942; *Uncharted Romance,* Doubleday, 1941; *Devil in My Heart,* Doubleday, 1941; *Tomorrow's Hero,* Collins, 1941, Doubleday, 1942; *Reef of Dreams,* Collins, 1942, reprinted, White Lion, 1975; *Gay Is Life,* Doubleday, 1943, reprinted, White Lion, 1976; *Have Courage, My Heart,* Collins, 1943, reprinted, Severn House, 1976; *Anna Heritage,* Collins, 1944, Arcadia House, 1945; *The Wise Forget,* Collins, 1944, Arcadia House, 1945; *Family Orchestra,* Arcadia House, 1945; *Return to Love,* Arcadia House, 1946; *The Man from Singapore,* Collins, 1946; *Weave Me Some Wings,* Collins, 1947, reprinted, Severn House, 1976; *The Clouded Moon,* Arcadia House, 1948; *Strange Paths,* Collins, 1948; *Star-Crossed,* Collins, 1949; *First Star,* Arcadia House, 1949; *There Will I Follow,* Collins, 1949, reprinted, White Lion, 1973.

The Young Lady, Arcadia House, 1950 (published in England as *Bow to the Storm,* Collins, 1950); *Mist on the Hills,* Arcadia House, 1950; *Sixpence in Her Shoe,* Collins, 1950, Arcadia House, 1954; *Two Loves Have I,* Collins, 1950, reprinted, Severn House, 1977; *Promise of Delight,* Arcadia House, 1952; *The Gate Leads Nowhere,* Collins, 1953; *Fool's Haven,* Collins, 1954, Arcadia House, 1955; *Sew a Fine Seam,* R. Hale, 1954, reprinted, F. A. Thorpe, 1973; *Before I Kissed,* Collins, 1955; *The Grafton Girls,* Collins, 1956; *A Lady Fell in Love,* R. Hale, 1956, reprinted, F. A. Thorpe, 1973; *Shadows in the Sun,* Collins, 1957; *Man of Stone,* Collins, 1958; *The Intruder,* Collins, 1959, reprinted, White Lion, 1973.

The House of Lies, Collins, 1960, published as *The Crystal Villa,* Lenox Hill, 1970; *More Than Friendship,* Collins, 1960; *Surgeon's Dilemma,* Collins, 1961; *The Pretenders,* Collins, 1962; *The Big Man,* Collins, 1965; *The Interlopers,* Collins, 1967; *The Repeating Pattern,* Collins, 1968; *The Bachelor Girls,* Collins, 1968.

The Pleasure Seekers, Collins, 1970; *Home to My Country,* Collins, 1971; *A Right Grand Girl,* Collins, 1972; *The Cottager's Daughter,* Dell, 1972; *Soldiers and Lovers,* Collins, 1973; *Who Knows Sammy Halliday,* Collins, 1974; *The Young Ones,* Collins, 1975; *Spanish Summer,* Collins, 1977; *Mr. Rodriguez,* Collins, 1979.

SIDELIGHTS: Mary Mussi told *CA* that she considers herself purely a "popular" writer, with "no axe to grind apart from writing a 'good read' for entertainment and relaxation." Her work falls into two categories: novels with a contemporary setting written under the pseudonym Mary Howard, and novels set in the nineteenth century, under the pseudonym Josephine Edgar. The author notes that the Josephine Edgar novels have been the more popular of the two in the United States.

* * *

MYERS, Robert J(ulius) 1912-

PERSONAL: Born October 31, 1912, in Lancaster, Pa.; son of Laurence B. (a civil engineer) and Edith (Hirsh) Myers; married Ruth McCoy (a program specialist), December 20, 1938; children: Jonathan K., Eric L. *Education:* Lehigh University, B.S., 1933; University of Iowa, M.S., 1934. *Religion:*

Lutheran. *Home:* 9610 Wire Ave., Silver Spring, Md. 20901. *Office:* University of Connecticut, Storrs, Conn. 06268.

CAREER: U.S. Social Security Administration, Washington, D.C., various actuarial positions, 1934-47, chief actuary, 1947-70; Temple University, Philadelphia, Pa., professor of actuarial science, 1970-79; University of Connecticut, Storrs, Conn., lecturer in actuarial science, 1973—. Professor of insurance, Howard University, 1981. Member of Committee of Social Security Experts, International Labour Office, 1947-72; member of board of pensions, Lutheran Church in America, 1956-68 and 1970—; member of Pensions Committee, National Council of the Churches of Christ, 1957—; member of Pension Research Council, Wharton School of Finance and Commerce, University of Pennsylvania, 1957—; United Nations, member of Pension Review Group, 1958-60, member of Committee of Actuaries, Joint Staff Pension Fund, 1961—; member of Private Pension-Social Security Committee, U.S. Chamber of Commerce, 1971; president, International Fisheries Commissions Pension Society. Member of board of trustees, Group Health Association, 1962-65; member of board of directors, Aid Association for Lutherans, 1973-75. Member of social security technical assistance missions to thirty-five countries, including Bolivia, Ethiopia, West Germany, Israel, Japan, and Viet Nam. Actuarial consultant to various Congressional committees and to the Federal Judiciary, 1949—, and to the Organization of American States; member of Actuarial Advisory Committee on Railroad Retirement, 1974—; consultant on social security matters to Financial Executives Institute, National Association of Life Underwriters, American Life Insurance Association, and Edward H. Friend & Co. *Military service:* U.S. Army, Medical Statistics Division, Office of the Surgeon General, 1942-45; became captain.

MEMBER: International Social Security Association (vice-chairman of committee of social security actuaries and chairman of regional committee, 1956-70), International Actuarial Association (vice-president, 1975—), International Association of Consulting Actuaries, International Congresses of Actuaries (member of permanent committee), International Union for the Scientific Study of Population, Inter-American Association of Social Security Actuaries (president, 1961—), Conference of Actuaries in Public Practice (fellow), Society of Actuaries (fellow; president, 1971-72), American Academy of Actuaries (president, 1971-72), Fraternal Actuarial Association (fellow), Casualty Actuarial Society (fellow), National Health and Welfare Retirement Association (member of board of trustees, 1972—), Population Association of America (first vice-president, 1962), American Association for the Advancement of Science (fellow), French Institute of Actuaries (corresponding member), Spanish Institute of Actuaries (corresponding member), Institute of Actuaries (England; associate member), Royal Statistical Society (fellow).

AWARDS, HONORS: Distinguished Service Award, U.S. Department of Health, Education, and Welfare, 1956; Career Service Award, National Civil Service League, 1959; LL.D., Muhlenberg College, 1964, and Lehigh University, 1970; Award of Merit, International Social Security Association, 1975; Dis-

tinguished Alumni Achievement Award, University of Iowa, 1980.

WRITINGS: Social Insurance and Allied Government Programs, Irwin, 1965; *Medicare,* Irwin, 1970; *Social Security,* Irwin, 1975, 2nd edition, 1981; *Indexation of Pension and Other Employee Benefits,* Irwin, 1978; *Social Insurance: A Guide to Information Sources,* Gale, 1979. Contributor of more than 400 articles to technical and scientific journals.

SIDELIGHTS: In addition to his travels on technical assistance missions, Robert J. Myers has visited ten other countries, including the Soviet Union, England, and the Philippines, to study their social security systems.

*   *   *

MYRICK, David F.

PERSONAL: Born in Santa Barbara, Calif.; son of Donald and Charlotte W. (Porter) Myrick. *Education:* Attended University of California, Santa Barbara, and Babson College. *Home address:* P.O. Box 5237, Santa Barbara, Calif. 93108.

CAREER: Southern Pacific Transportation Co., San Francisco, Calif., 1944-77, special assistant to vice-president and treasurer, 1962-73, assistant to vice-president, 1973-77. Editor and publisher, *Telegraph Hill Bulletin,* 1956-60; vice-president and director, *The Dakota Farmer Co.,* 1961-67. Chairman of advisory board, Josephine D. Randall Junior Museum, 1971-73. *Member:* American Association for State and Local History, Railway and Locomotive Historical Society, Arizona Historical Society, Book Club of California, Eastern California Museum Association, Nevada Historical Society, Santa Barbara Historical Society, San Francisco Museum of Art, Roxburghe Club of San Francisco, Bohemian Club. *Awards, honors:* Merit award, American Association for State and Local History, 1964, for *Railroads of Nevada and Eastern California.*

WRITINGS: Railroads of Nevada and Eastern California, Howell-North Books, Volume I, 1962, Volume II, 1963; *New Mexico's Railroads: An Historical Survey,* Colorado Railroad Museum, 1970; *San Francisco's Telegraph Hill,* Howell-North Books, 1972; *Rails along the Bohemian Grove,* Lawton Kennedy, 1973; (contributor) David E. Miller, editor, *The Golden Spike,* University of Utah Press, 1973; *Railroads of Arizona,* Howell-North Books, Volume I, 1975, Volume II, 1980. Also author of *Potosi, An Empire of Silver,* 1980, and of historical monographs.

Author of introduction: Thompson and West, *History of Nevada,* Howell-North Books, 1958; Lord, *Comstock Mining and Miners,* Howell-North Books, 1959; Richard E. Lingenfelter, *The Newspapers of Nevada, 1858-1958,* John Howell, 1964; G. Chappell, *Rails to Carry Copper,* Pruett, 1973. Contributor of articles to magazines and historical society publications.

WORK IN PROGRESS: Volume III of *Railroads of Arizona; Rails and Mines of Sonora and Baja California;* a book of local history, *Santa Barbara and Montecito.*

N

NAISAWALD, L. Van Loan 1920-

PERSONAL: Born June 11, 1920, in Garden City, N.Y.; son of H. Louis and Louise (Van Loan) Naisawald; married Mary Lou Rust, 1949; children: Gretchen, Christian, Robin. *Education:* Virginia Military Institute, B.A., 1942; University of North Carolina, M.A., 1948. *Religion:* Episcopalian. *Home:* 9108 Main St., Manassas, Va. *Office:* Department of the Army, HQ DARCOM, Washington, D.C.

CAREER: Office of the Chief of Military History, Washington, D.C., historian, 1949-50; Operations Research Office, Washington, D.C., historian, 1950-55; L. C. Naisawald & Sons, New York, N.Y., broker, 1955-58; National Park Service, Manassas, Va., historian, 1958-60; Department of the Army, Washington, D.C., writer-editor, 1960-77, editor-in-chief, *Army Research, Development and Acquisition Magazine,* 1977—. *Military service:* U.S. Army, 1942-46; became captain; U.S. Army Reserve, retired as colonel.

WRITINGS: Grape and Canister, Oxford University Press, 1960; *In Some Foreign Field,* Blair, 1972; *Manassas Junction and the Doctor,* A. V. Lake, 1981. Contributor of articles to military journals, historical magazines, and travel magazines.

SIDELIGHTS: L. Van Loan Naisawald told *CA:* "I got into the writing game thanks to my graduate school advisor who, upon reading the first chapter of my academically written thesis, asked the question: 'Do you want someone to read this, or do you just intend to complete the requirement and have this filed?' I replied that I was hopeful *someone* would read it. 'Well, write as you talk,' he answered. 'Most people can talk in an interesting manner. Write the same way.' That has been the single most beneficial piece of advice I've ever received."

AVOCATIONAL INTERESTS: Hunting, fishing, travel.

*   *   *

NATHAN, Robert (Gruntal) 1894-

PERSONAL: Born January 2, 1894, in New York, N.Y.; son of Harold and Sarah (Gruntal) Nathan; married Dorothy Michaels, 1915 (divorced, 1922); married Nancy Wilson, 1930 (divorced, 1936); married Lucy Lee Hall Skelding, 1936 (divorced, 1939); married Janet McMillen Bingham, 1940 (divorced); married Clara May Blum Burns, 1951 (divorced); married Shirley Keeland, December 14, 1955 (died, 1969);

married Joan Boniface Winnifrith, 1970; children: (first marriage) Joan (Mrs. M. Bergstrom). *Education:* Attended Harvard University, 1912-15. *Home:* 1240 North Doheny Dr., Los Angeles, Calif. 90069. *Agent:* Swanson Agency, 8523 Sunset Blvd., Los Angeles, Calif. 90069.

CAREER: Novelist, playwright, and poet. New York University School of Journalism, New York, N.Y., lecturer, 1924-25; Metro-Goldwyn-Mayer, Hollywood, Calif., screen writer, 1943-49. Member of literary committee, Huntington Hartford Foundation. *Member:* National Institute of Arts and Letters (vice-president, 1939), Academy of American Poets (chancellor; fellow), Dramatists Guild, Writers Guild of America (West), Academy of Motion Picture Arts and Sciences, American Society of Composers, Authors, and Publishers (ASCAP), P.E.N. (charter member; president, 1940-43), Screen Writers Guild. *Awards, honors:* U.S. Treasury Department Silver Medal, World War II; California Writer's Guild Award of Honor.

WRITINGS—Novels, except as indicated; published by Knopf, except as indicated: *Peter Kindred,* Duffield, 1919; *Autumn,* McBride, 1921; *The Puppet Master,* McBride, 1925; *Jonah,* McBride, 1925 (published in England as *Son of Amittai,* Heinemann, 1925), 2nd edition, 1934; *The Fiddler in Barly* (also see below), McBride, 1926; *The Woodcutter's House* (also see below), Bobbs-Merrill, 1927; *The Bishop's Wife* (also see below), Bobbs-Merrill, 1928; *There Is Another Heaven* (also see below), Bobbs-Merrill, 1929.

The Orchid (also see below), Bobbs-Merrill, 1931; *One More Spring,* 1933; *Road of Ages,* 1935; *The Enchanted Voyage,* 1936; *The Barly Fields: A Collection of Five Novels* (contains *The Fiddler in Barly, The Woodcutter's House, The Bishop's Wife, The Orchid,* and *There Is Another Heaven*), 1938; *Winter in April,* 1938; *Journey of Tapiola,* 1938.

Portrait of Jennie, 1940, reprinted, Dell, 1977; *They Went On Together,* 1941; *Tapiola's Brave Regiment,* 1941; *The Sea-Gull Cry* (also see below), 1942; *But Gently Day,* 1943; *Journal for Josephine* (memoirs), 1943; *Mr. Whittle and the Morning Star,* 1947; *Long after Summer,* 1948; *The River Journey* (also see below), 1949.

The Married Look, 1950 (published in England as *His Wife's Young Face,* Staples Press, 1951); *The Innocent Eye* (also see below), 1951; *Nathan 3* (contains *The Sea-Gull Cry, The Innocent Eye,* and *The River Journey*), Staples Press, 1952; *The Train in the Meadow,* 1953; *Sir Henry,* 1955, reprinted, Borgo

Press, 1979; *The Rancho of the Little Loves,* 1956; *So Love Returns,* 1958; *The Snowflake and the Starfish* (juvenile), 1959.

The Weans, 1960; *The Color of Evening,* 1960; *The Wilderness-Stone,* 1961; *A Star in the Wind,* 1962; *The Devil with Love,* 1963; *The Fair,* 1964; *The Mallot Diaries,* 1965; *Stonecliffe,* 1967; *Tappy* (juvenile), 1968; *Mia,* 1970; *The Elixer,* 1971; *The Summer Meadows,* Delàcorte, 1973; *Heaven and Hell and the Megas Factor,* Delacorte, 1975.

Poetry: *Youth Grows Old,* McBride, 1922; *The Cedar Box,* Bobbs-Merrill, 1929; *Selected Poems,* Knopf, 1935; *A Winter Tide: Sonnets and Poems,* Knopf, 1940; *Dunkirk: A Ballad,* Knopf, 1942; *Morning in Iowa,* Knopf, 1944; *The Darkening Meadows,* Knopf, 1945; *The Green Leaf: Collected Poems,* Knopf, 1950; *The Married Man,* Knopf, 1962; *Evening Song: Selected Poems, 1950-1973,* Capra, 1973.

Plays: "Music at Evening," first produced in White Plains, N.Y., 1937; *Jezebel's Husband* [and] *The Sleeping Beauty* ("Jezebel's Husband" first produced in Germany, 1955), Knopf, 1953; *Juliet in Mantua,* Knopf, 1966; "Susan and the Stranger," first produced in Los Angeles, Calif., 1978.

Screenplays: "The White Cliffs of Dover," Metro-Goldwyn-Mayer, 1944; "The Clock," Metro-Goldwyn-Mayer, 1945; "Pagan Love Song," Metro-Goldwyn-Mayer, 1950.

Contributor: A. S. Dashiell, editor, *Editor's Choice,* Putnam, 1934; Frances Brentano, editor, *The Word Lives On,* Doubleday, 1951; Edward L. Ferman, editor, *The Best from "Fantasy and Science Fiction": 17th Series,* Doubleday, 1968.

Contributor to *New Yorker, Atlantic, Harper's, Scribner's, Century, Red Book, Cosmopolitan,* and other publications.

SIDELIGHTS: Robert Nathan's novels are known for their quiet, melancholic mood, their precise and delicate prose, and their gently satirical fantasy. Several critics have noted that because of these characteristics Nathan's work occupies a place of its own in modern literature. He is, as a reviewer for *Time* states, "a lineal descendant of James Branch Cabell. Their type of gently spoofing, satirical fantasy is not much in vogue these days, but author Nathan is an expert practitioner of the genre." B. R. Redman of *Saturday Review* sees Nathan "steadily cultivating his garden in his unique way . . . and he has had the pleasure of knowing that the fruits and flowers of this garden have been valued by a group of admirers, not large but faithful."

The tranquil, delicate feeling of Nathan's novels has been particularly admired. A *Springfield Republican* critic, for example, states that "one always feels after reading a book by Robert Nathan that he has been given a delicate, lovely miniature with soft colors, beauty of texture, and all sharp outlines softened." Referring to *The Devil with Love,* Aileen Pippett of *Saturday Review* comments that it is "as light as a feather, as soft as a sigh, as sweet as a cream bun, as tinged with gentle melancholy as a calm evening, as predictable as the phases of the moon." In a review of *The Orchid,* the *Boston Transcript* critic sadly notes: "Closing the book we sigh slightly and return to the world of realities with a strange regretfulness."

It is Nathan's prose style which creates this special mood. Nathan's prose, Herschel Brickell writes in *Books,* is "full of emotional echoes and admirably suited to the evocation of moods or the creation of atmosphere." A reviewer for the *Boston Transcript* agrees, noting "the charm with which [Nathan] imbues his prose [and] the combination of subtlety and simplicity which makes his style at once so clear and yet so expressive of deep mutations." Patricia Stiles of *Library Journal* describes Nathan's writing as "prose that sings and images

that shimmer in fresh, clear beauty. Mr. Nathan is a subtle master of the seafoam world of half illusion."

Fantasy is an integral part of Nathan's novels and, although he has written of ghosts, angels, and lost tribes, one of his favorite themes is, as a reviewer for *Booklist* notes, "the power of love to transcend time and place." In such books as *Portrait of Jennie,* which concerns a pair of young lovers who visit each other across time and space, and *The Wilderness-Stone,* in which a woman goes back in time to join a poet she loves, Nathan has explored this theme. Jay Don Coppersmith writes in the *Dictionary of Literary Biography* that *Portrait of Jennie* "reflects the ideas that love has the power to surmount any obstacle, that destiny is operative in human affairs, and that time is a mental frame of reference rather than an actual fact. This idea of time as a subjective phenomenon runs through most of Nathan's fiction, as does the theme of love and faith as the cure for human ills."

It is Nathan's concern with such themes that elevate his fantasies to a more serious level. "Mr. Nathan," writes Virgilia Peterson of the *New York Times Book Review,* "is the least pretentious philosopher, but that he has a philosophy—and, however ironic, a seriousness [is] clear." Nathan writes fantasies, J. H. Jackson of the *San Francisco Chronicle* believes, "in which he has something to say to every reader, disguising his moral behind the fantasy." In a review of *Journey of Tapiola* the *Saturday Review's* R. C. Benet agrees: "It is the subtle, underlying implications that count in [Nathan's] fantasy."

Nathan most often employs a subtle irony and a satirical eye to express his thematic concerns. "I know," Roberts Tapley of *Bookman* writes, "of no other contemporary writer who, without raising his voice and with no more apparent emphasis than inheres in a rueful smile, is capable of being as devastating as Mr. Nathan." Lucy Tompkins of the *New York Times* believes that Nathan's irony "is the kind of irony, it sometimes seems, that God must exercise when contemplating us." Another *New York Times* reviewer writes: "Nathan mingles the gently sublime with the gently ridiculous, and understanding always follows his satire."

Called by Stephen Vincent Benet of *Saturday Review* "one of our most individual and scrupulous artists," Nathan has garnered considerable attention and praise during his more than fifty years as a writer. "About every phase of his work," writes Brickell, "there is evidence of the most painstaking care; his brief novels are from the hand of a stonecutter and jewel polisher." *Christian Century's* Raymond Kresensky calls Nathan "a good writer . . . scrupulous in the use of words—and one who respects our tastes and intelligence and isn't afraid to put in a little valuable philosophy for our own good." "If Robert Nathan," Peterson writes in the *New York Herald Tribune Book Review,* "still insists upon speaking in a small voice, audible only to the sharp-eared, intended for those who confer in murmurs, he has none the less one of the best modulated and tenderest voices of our day."

MEDIA ADAPTATIONS: *The Enchanted Voyage* was filmed as "Wake Up and Dream" by Twentieth Century-Fox, 1946; *The Bishop's Wife* was filmed by RKO, 1947; *Portrait of Jennie* was filmed by David O. Selznick, 1948, and has been adapted for a musical by Enid Futterman and Dennis Rosa; *One More Spring* was filmed by Twentieth Century-Fox, 1950.

BIOGRAPHICAL/CRITICAL SOURCES—Periodicals: *New York World,* November 14, 1926; *Saturday Review,* November 27, 1926, November 5, 1927, September 28, 1929, October 29, 1938, February 5, 1955, July 9, 1960, August 24, 1963, April 11, 1964, September 11, 1965, August 22, 1970; *New York*

Evening Post, October 22, 1927; *Books,* September 29, 1929, April 12, 1931, January 9, 1938, October 30, 1938; *New York Times,* October 6, 1929, March 22, 1931, February 5, 1933, August 30, 1936, January 9, 1938, October 30, 1938, January 7, 1940, January 29, 1982; *Boston Transcript,* October 30, 1929, May 29, 1931, September 5, 1936, January 13, 1940; *New Republic,* November 6, 1929; *Christian Century,* August 5, 1931; *Bookman,* October, 1932, February, 1933; *Atlantic Bookshelf,* March, 1933; *Sewanee Review,* spring, 1933; *Chicago Tribune,* September 5, 1936; *Springfield Republican,* January 14, 1940; *Modern Language Studies,* May, 1941; *New York Times Book Review,* May 7, 1950, June 24, 1962, August 22, 1965, May 17, 1970, August 22, 1971, October 21, 1973, August 31, 1975; *Time,* January 17, 1955; *New York Herald Tribune Book Review,* January 23, 1955, November 1, 1959; *San Francisco Chronicle,* January 28, 1955; *Atlantic,* March, 1955; *Christian Science Monitor,* November 5, 1959, June 27, 1970.

Booklist, July 1, 1961; *Catholic World,* January, 1962; *Yale University Library Gazette,* #37, 1962; *Best Sellers,* May 1, 1963, May 15, 1970; *Prairie Schooner,* winter, 1966; *Library Journal,* February 15, 1967; *Spectator,* December 19, 1970; *Detroit News,* September 5, 1971; *Publishers Weekly,* October 8, 1973; *American Book Collector,* Volume 23, number 4, 1973; *Books and Bookmen,* April, 1974.

Books: L. Bromfield, *The Work of Robert Nathan,* Bobbs-Merrill, c.1930; Russell Blankenship, *American Literature,* Holt, 1931; Robert Van Gelden, *Writers and Writing,* Scribner, 1946; Harvey Breit, *The Writer Observed,* World Publishing, 1956; Dan H. Lawrence, *Robert Nathan: A Bibliography,* Yale University Library, 1960; Clarence Kenneth Sandelin, *Robert Nathan,* Twayne, 1968; *The Dictionary of Literary Biography,* Volume IX, Gale, 1981.

—Sketch by Thomas Wiloch

*   *   *

NEIL, William   1909-1979

PERSONAL: Born June 13, 1909, in Glasgow, Scotland; died November 10, 1979; son of William MacLaren and Jean C. (Hutchison) Neil; married Effie L. Park, December 18, 1936; children: Graham MacLaren, Lindsay Douglas. *Education:* University of Glasgow, M.A., 1929, B.D., 1932, Ph.D., 1936; University of Heidelberg, postgraduate study, 1932-33. *Home:* 590 Derby Rd., Adams Hill, Nottingham, England.

CAREER: Clergyman, Church of Scotland (Presbyterian). Minister at Bridge of Allan, Scotland, 1937-46; University of Aberdeen, Aberdeen, Scotland, head of department of biblical studies, 1946-53; University of Nottingham, Nottingham, England, warden of Hugh Stewart Hall, 1953-75, and reader in biblical studies, 1965-75. *Military service:* British Army, chaplain, 1940-45; mentioned in dispatches. *Member:* Societas Novi Testamenti Studiorum, Association of University Teachers (chairman of Nottingham branch, 1961-62), University Wardens Conference (chairman, 1962-65), Nottingham Scottish Association (president, 1964-65), Rotary International. *Awards, honors:* D.D. from University of Glasgow, 1961.

WRITINGS: The Epistle of Paul to the Thessalonians (Moffat New Testament commentary), Harper, 1950, published as *Thessalonians,* Hodder & Stoughton, 1950; *The Rediscovery of the Bible,* Hodder & Stoughton, 1954, Harper, 1955; *The Epistle to the Hebrews: Introduction and Commentary,* Macmillan, 1955, published as *The Epistle to the Hebrews: Ritual and Reality,* S.C.M. Press, 1968; (translator) Werner Keller, *The Bible as History: A Confirmation of the Book of Books,*

Morrow, 1956, revised edition, 1964 (published in England as *The Bible as History: Archaeology Confirms the Book of Books,* Hodder & Stoughton, 1956, revised edition, 1975); *The Plain Man Looks at the Bible,* Collins, 1956, reprinted, 1976, revised edition published as *Modern Man Looks at the Bible,* Association Press, 1958; *St. Paul's Epistles to the Thessalonians: Introduction and Commentary* (Torch Bible commentary), Allenson, 1957; (translator) Paul Bruin, *Jesus Lived Here,* photographs by Philipp Geigel, Morrow, 1958.

(Editor) *The Bible Companion: A Complete Pictorial and Reference Guide to the People, Places, Events, Background, and Faith of the Bible,* McGraw, 1960; *One Volume Bible Commentary,* Hodder & Stoughton, 1962, published as *Harper's Bible Commentary,* Harper, 1963; (translator) Keller, *The Bible as History in Pictures,* Morrow, 1964; *Prophets of Israel,* Abingdon, 1964; (editor) Robert Davidson, *Old Testament,* Hodder & Stoughton, 1964; (editor) F. W. Dillistone, *Christian Faith,* Hodder & Stoughton, 1964; *The Life and Teaching of Jesus,* Lippincott, 1965; *The Bible Today* ("Lift Up Your Hearts" series), B.B.C. Publications, 1965; *Apostle Extraordinary: The Life and Letters of Saint Paul,* Religious Education Press, 1966; (with Eric Newton) *2000 Years of Christian Art,* Harper, 1966; (with Newton) *The Christian Faith in Art,* Hodder & Stoughton, 1966; *The Letter of Paul to the Galatians,* Cambridge University Press, 1967; *The Truth About Jesus,* Hodder & Stoughton, 1968; (editor) F. R. Barry, *The Atonement,* Hodder & Stoughton, 1968.

The Truth About the Early Church, Hodder & Stoughton, 1970; *The Bible Story,* Collins, 1970, Abingdon, 1971; *The Truth About the Bible,* Hodder & Stoughton, 1972; *Acts,* Attic Press, 1973 (published in England as *The Acts of the Apostles,* Oliphants, 1973); (editor and compiler) *Concise Dictionary of Religious Quotations,* Eerdmans, 1974; *The Importance of the Bible,* Denholm House, 1975; *The Difficult Sayings of Jesus,* Eerdmans, 1975 (published in England as *What Jesus Really Meant: New Light on the "Hard" Sayings of Jesus,* Mowbray, 1975); *Can We Trust the Old Testament?,* Seabury, 1979; *The Message of the Bible: A Concise Introduction to the Old and New Testament,* Mowbray, 1979, Harper, 1980.

Contributor to *Cambridge History of the Bible, Interpreter's Dictionary of the Bible,* and *Peake's Commentary.* General editor of "Knowing Christianity" series, Lippincott, beginning 1964.†

*   *   *

NELSON, Ethel Florence   1913-
(Nina Nelson)

PERSONAL: Born March 20, 1913, in St. Johns, Newfoundland, Canada; daughter of Claude (a director) and Florence Noonan; married Anthony D. Nelson (a colonel in the British Army), June 25, 1938. *Education:* Attended Bishop Spencer College, St. Johns, Newfoundland. *Home:* The Knowle, Crown Lane, Virginia Water, Surrey GU25 4HW, England. *Agent:* Laurence Pollinger Ltd., 18 Maddox St., London W1R 0EU, England.

CAREER: Writer. Occasional broadcaster for BBC. *Member:* Guild of Travel Writers.

WRITINGS—Under name Nina Nelson; published by Batsford, except as indicated: *Shepheards Hotel,* Barrie & Rockliff, 1960, reprinted, Chivers, 1974; *Holland,* 1970; *Mena House,* Upper Egypt Hotels, 1970; *Denmark,* 1973; *Tunisia,* 1974; *Belgium and Luxembourg,* 1975; *Egypt,* 1978; *Malta,* 1979; *Canada,* 1980; *Hong Kong,* in press.

Author of "Your Guide" series, published by Redman: *Your Guide to Egypt*, 1964; . . . *to Lebanon*, 1965; . . . *to Jordan*, 1966; . . . *to Syria*, 1966; . . . *to Czechoslovakia*, 1968; . . . *to Malta*, 1969.

Contributor to newspapers. Belgium, Malta, and Gibraltar editor for Fodor, 1974—.

SIDELIGHTS: Ethel Florence Nelson wrote *CA:* "I trained as a singer and was beginning to achieve some professional success but I found it difficult, moving round the world with my husband, to build a reputation in any one place. Reckoning that the typewriter is more portable than the piano, I decided to try writing and give up singing if I was successful. Travel writing seemed a good idea though I had no inkling then that it would take off as it has done. While it will never be in the best seller league it opens doors to many interesting places and a great deal of fun.

"I find it best not to stay in a place too long or I lose my 'tourist eye' and become enmeshed in detail. I prefer writing the 'armchair travel' type of book where I am free to tell stories and describe the things which interest me rather than get into a mass of detailed information. There are plenty of the latter type of books. I believe that it was Henry James who said: 'The world exists so we can write about it' and I agree with him wholeheartedly."

AVOCATIONAL INTERESTS: Photography, singing, music, growing flowers.

*　　*　　*

NELSON, Nina
See NELSON, Ethel Florence

*　　*　　*

NEWMAN, Charles L.   1923-

PERSONAL: Born September 22, 1923, in New York, N.Y.; son of Harry and Rosetta (Nareff) Newman; married Della Scott, February 11, 1961; children: Mark, Scott, Lowell. *Education:* New York University, B.A., 1949, M.P.A., 1950, D.P.A., 1970; graduate study at University of North Dakota Law School, 1953, and University of Minnesota, summers, 1954-56. *Politics:* Republican. *Religion:* Methodist. *Home:* 5939 Copperwood Lane, Dallas, Tex. 75248. *Office:* Center for Criminal Justice Research and Planning, University of Texas at Arlington, Arlington, Tex. 76019.

CAREER: Youth House, New York City, shift supervisor, 1949-50; Welfare Department, Fraud Investigation Unit, New York City, investigator, 1950-51; Fairleigh Dickinson University, Rutherford, N.J., instructor in sociology, 1950-51; American Red Cross, Services to Military Installations, Fort Knox, Ky., field director and liaison to military stockade, 1951-52; University of North Dakota, Grand Forks, instructor in sociology, 1952-55; Florida State University, School of Social Welfare, Tallahassee, assistant professor of criminology and corrections and liaison to governmental human services agencies, 1955-59; University of Louisville, Kent School of Social Work, Louisville, Ky., associate professor, director of Program of Correctional Training, and director of Graduate Program in Criminal Justice, 1959-66; Pennsylvania State University, University Park, professor of law enforcement and corrections and coordinator of law enforcement and corrections services, 1966-76, professor emeritus, 1977—; University of Texas at Arlington, Institute of Urban Studies, professor of criminal justice and director of Center for Criminal Justice Research and Planning, 1976-79, 1981—; director, Dallas County Jail System,

Dallas Sheriff's Department, 1979-81. Research director and case consultant, Leon County (Fla.) Juvenile Court, 1956-59; director, Institute on Probation and Parole Supervision, 1959-66; founder and member of board of directors, Kentucky Citizens for Correctional Research, 1961-66; member, Kentucky Governor's Task Force on Criminal Justice, 1965-66, and Joint Commission on Correctional Manpower and Training, 1965-70; member of board of directors, Pennsylvania Program for Women and Girl Offenders, Inc., 1968-75; Central Region Planning Council, Pennsylvania Governor's Justice Commission, member of board, 1969-76, vice-chairman, 1973-76; Pennsylvania Traffic Commission, member, 1972-75, vice-chairman, 1974-75; director, National Jail Resources Study, 1974-79. Lecturer to professional and community organizations in the United States and Canada. Consultant to numerous universities, corrections systems, and organizations, including Jefferson County (Ky.) Juvenile Court, 1959-64, Ohio Youth Commission, 1969-70, Corrections Training Program, Ohio State University, 1971-73, Drug Enforcement Agency, 1973-73, National Institute of Corrections, 1976-79, and National Institute on Drug Abuse, 1979—. *Military service:* U.S. Army, 1943-46. New York National Guard, Medical Services Corps, 1946-48; became second lieutenant.

MEMBER: International Society of Criminology, Interamerican Society of Criminology (honorary member), American Society of Criminology (executive secretary, 1962-66; fellow, 1965 and 1977; member of executive board, 1973—), American Correctional Association, American Association for the Advancement of Science (fellow), National Council on Crime and Delinquency (co-founder of Kentucky council; president of Kentucky council, 1963-64; member of board of directors of Pennsylvania council, 1970-73), National Sheriff's Association, Western Society of Criminology (fellow, 1978), Southwestern Academy of Crisis Interveners (honorary member). *Awards, honors:* State award, Florida Federation of Social Workers, 1958; Herbert Block Memorial Award, American Society of Criminology, 1966; named honorary parole officer, Kentucky Department of Parole and Probation, 1966; Founder's Day Award for Scholarship, New York University, 1970; distinguished service awards, Kentucky Council on Crime and Delinquency and Pennsylvania Board of Probation and Parole, both 1975.

WRITINGS: (Co-author) *Indiana Probation Survey*, three volumes, National Probation and Parole Association, 1957; *Educational Aspects of Delinquency, Illegitimacy, and Crime among Negroes in Florida*, State of Florida, 1957; *Sourcebook on Probation, Parole, and Pardons*, C. C Thomas, 1958, 3rd edition, 1977; (editor with Walter Reckless) *Interdisciplinary Problems in Criminology*, Ohio State University Press, 1965; (senior editor with William H. Parsonage and Barbara Price) *Training Modules in the Administration of Criminal Justice*, thirteen volumes, Pennsylvania State University Press, 1969; *Interviewing in Corrections*, Virginia Commonwealth University Press, 1969; (with William Hewitt) *Police-Community Relations*, Foundation Press, 1970; (with Price) *Probation, Parole and Pardons* (study manual), Pennsylvania State University Press, 1970; *Personnel Practices in Adult Parole Systems*, C. C Thomas, 1971; (editor with William Amos) *Parole: Legal Issues, Decision-Making, Research*, Aberdeen Press, 1975; (with Stanley Goehring and Ellen Pierce) *Training Modules for Trainers of Personnel in the Administration of Justice*, five volumes, Pennsylvania State University Press, 1975; (with Price) *Jails and Drug Treatment*, Sage Publications, 1977.

Contributor: Vedder and Kay, editors, *Penology*, C. C Thomas, 1964; Dale B. Harris and John A. Sample, editors, *Violence in Contemporary American Society*, Pennsylvania State University Press, 1969; S. I. Cohn, editor, *Law Enforcement Science and Technology II*, International Telephone & Telegraph Corp. Research Institute, 1969; R. M. Carter and L. T. Wilkins, editors, *Probation and Parole*, Wiley, 1970; Paul F. Cromwell and George Keefer, editors, *Police-Community Relations*, West Publishing, 1973; Mustafa T. Yucek, editor, *Suc ve Ceza Anatomisi* (title means "Anatomy of Crime and Punishment"), [Ankara, Turkey], 1973; McLean, editor, *Education for Crime Prevention and Control*, C. C Thomas, 1974; MacNamara and Montanino, editors, *Incarceration: The Sociology of Imprisonment*, Sage Publications, 1978; (with Price) Wickman and Whitten, editors, *Readings in Criminology*, Heath, 1978; Sagarin, editor, *Criminology: New Concerns*, Sage Publications, 1979.

Author of more than twenty research reports sponsored by various governmenal organizations. Editor of proceedings of Institute of Probation Parole and Institute on Correctional Administration; contributor, with Barbara Price, to the proceedings of the Congress on Corrections, American Correctional Association, 1975. Contributor to professional journals, including *International Journal of Comparative and Applied Criminal Justice*, *International Review of Criminology*, *Journal of Criminal Law*, *Criminology*, *Federal Probation*, and *North Dakota Law Review*. Editor of *Criminologica* (journal of the American Society of Criminology), 1962-65; *Criminology*, founding editor, 1962-66, editor-in-chief, 1973-76, member of executive board, 1973—; member of editorial board, *Police*, 1967-73.

*   *   *

NEWMAN, Ralph Abraham   1892-

PERSONAL: Born March 30, 1892, in Pittsfield, Mass.; son of Abraham Joseph and Caroline (Goldstone) Newman; married Clarice Henle, 1920; children: John, Betty C., Guillois. *Education:* Harvard University, A.B., 1914, Js.D., 1916. *Home:* 1390 Market St., No. 1411, San Francisco, Calif. 94102.

CAREER: St. John's University, Jamaica, Long Island, N.Y., professor of law, 1937-56; American University, Washington, D.C., professor of law, 1956-64, professor emeritus, 1964—; University of California, Hastings College of the Law, San Francisco, professor of law, 1964-72, professor emeritus, 1972—. Lecturer at International University of Comparative Sciences, Luxembourg, 1960 and 1962, and at Conference on American Jurisprudence, Curatiba, Brazil, 1961. *Military service:* U.S. Army, 1917-19, 1943-46; became major; received Croix de Guerre. *Member:* American Society for Legal History (president, 1962-63; director, 1964—). *Awards, honors:* Evening Star Award, American University, 1958.

WRITINGS: Law of Trusts, Foundation Press, 1949, 2nd edition published as *Newman on Trusts*, 1955; *Law of Labor Relations*, Dennis, 1953; (with wife, Clarice H. Newman) *Role of Law in Society*, Lerner Law Book Co., 1957; *Equity and Law: A Comparative Study*, Oceana, 1961; (editor) *Essays in Jurisprudence in Honor of Roscoe Pound*, Bobbs-Merrill, 1962; (contributor) *Perspectives of Law: Essays for A. W. Scott*, Little, Brown, 1964; (editor) Giorgio Del Vecchio, *Man and Nature: Selected Essays*, University of Notre Dame Press, 1969; (editor) *Equity in the World's Legal Systems: A Comparative Study Dedicated to Rene Cassin*, Emile Bruylant (Brussels), 1973; (editor) *The Unity of Strict Law*, Emile Bruylant, 1978.

*   *   *

NICHOLS, Charles H(arold)   1919-

PERSONAL: Born July 6, 1919, in New York; son of Charles

F. (a clergyman) and Julia (King) Nichols; married Mildred Thompson (a career counselor), August 19, 1950; children: David, Keith, Brian. *Education:* Brooklyn College (now Brooklyn College of the City University of New York), B.A. (with honors), 1942; Brown University, Ph.D., 1948. *Politics:* Independent. *Religion:* Society of Friends (Quakers). *Residence:* Providence, R. I. *Office:* Department of English, Brown University, Providence, R.I. 02912.

CAREER: Morgan State College, Baltimore, Md., associate professor of English, 1948-49; Hampton Institute, Hampton, Va., professor of English, 1949-59; Free University of Berlin, Berlin, Germany, professor of North American literature, 1959-69; Brown University, Providence, R.I., professor of English, 1969—. Visiting professor at Grinnell College, 1969, and Stanford University, 1973. *Member:* Modern Language Association of America, American Studies Association, American Association of University Professors. *Awards, honors:* Fulbright lecturer at Aarhaus University, 1954-55; senior fellowship from National Endowment for the Humanities, 1973-74; Fulbright grant for research in Germany, 1973-74.

WRITINGS: Many Thousand Gone: The Ex-Slaves' Account of Their Bondage and Freedom, E. J. Brill, 1963; *Instructor's Guide to Accompany "Cavalcade: Negro American Writing from 1760 to the Present,"* Houghton, 1970; (editor) *African Nights: Black Erotic Folk Tales*, Herder & Herder, 1971; (editor) *Black Men in Chains: An Anthology of Slave Narratives*, Lawrence Hill, 1972; (contributor) *Comic Relief*, University of Illinois Press, 1978; (editor and author of introduction) *Arna Bontemps and Langston Hughes Letters, 1925-1967*, Dodd, 1980; (contributor) *The Dilemma of the New Black Middle Class*, University of Pennsylvania Press, 1980.

Contributor of more than sixty articles and reviews to education, literature, and literary journals in the United States and abroad, including *William and Mary Quarterly*, *America in the Twentieth Century*, *Nation*, *Modern Language Journal*, *Phylon*, *American-Scandinavian Review*, *School and Society*, and *Jahrbuch fuer Amerikastudien*. Member of editorial boards of *Studies in Black Literature* and of *Novel: A Forum in Fiction*.

SIDELIGHTS: Los Angeles Times reviewer Robert Kirsch writes in his review of *Arna Bontemps and Langston Hughes Letters, 1925-1967* that "the letters here, admirably edited by Professor Charles H. Nichols, along with an introduction and epilogue . . . are above all professional. They are vocational in the sense of mutual assistance marketing ideas, shop talk, awards, itineraries, publication, criticism, job offers."

Kirsch continues to explain that the letters selected and edited by Nichols show Bontemps and Hughes as "artists each in their own right, they became deep good friends, collaborators on a few books, testers of each other's ideas, sharers of experiences when it was almost as arduous to be a black writer as a black baseball player in the South. They had dignity but it was hard to achieve, scuffling to make a living, doing a review here, an article there, lecture tours by running a Ford along potted highways to remote colleges, driving in their tuxedos, facing out the slings and barbs of restaurant waitresses and motel keepers."

BIOGRAPHICAL/CRITICAL SOURCES: Ernest Dunbar, *The Black Expatriates*, Dutton, 1968; *Chicago Tribune*, April 13, 1980; *Los Angeles Times*, June 2, 1980; *Times Literary Supplement*, December 5, 1980.

*   *   *

NICHOLS, John (Treadwell)   1940-

PERSONAL: Born July 23, 1940, in Berkeley, Calif.; son of

David G. (a psycho-linguist) and Monique (Robert) Nichols; divorced; children: Luke, Tania. *Education:* Hamilton College, B.A., 1962. *Home address:* Box 1165, Taos, N.M. 87571. *Agent:* Curtis Brown Ltd., 575 Madison Ave., New York, N.Y. 10022.

CAREER: Writer. Has held various jobs, including that of blues singer in a Greenwich Village cafe, firefighter in the Chiricuahua Mountains of Arizona, and dishwasher in Hartford, Conn.; partner and artist in "Jest-No" greeting card business, 1962; English teacher in Barcelona, Spain, three months.

WRITINGS—Novels, except as indicated: *The Sterile Cuckoo,* McKay, 1965; *The Wizard of Loneliness,* Putnam, 1966; *If Mountains Die* (nonfiction), photographs by William Davis, Knopf, 1979; *A Ghost in the Music* (Quality Paperback Book Club selection), Holt, 1979.

New Mexico Trilogy: *The Milagro Beanfield War,* Holt, 1974; *The Magic Journey* (Quality Paperback Book Club selection), Holt, 1978; *The Nirvana Blues,* Holt, 1981.

WORK IN PROGRESS: The Last Beautiful Days of Autumn, a nonfiction photo essay.

SIDELIGHTS: John Nichols' New Mexico Trilogy traces the four-decade transformation of a small New Mexico town from a quiet, traditional society to its modern, commercial lifestyle. In the trilogy, Nichols is concerned with the destruction of traditional communities and cultures in the name of progress and, in particular, with the economic system that fosters such destruction.

"At the beginning of the trilogy," John McLellan writes in the *Washington Post,* "New Mexico was still a relatively unspoiled land, the possession of Indians and Mexicans who lived off the land. It was ripe for spoiling, and the story of that spoiling is a major concern of the trilogy." As Jeffrey Burke of *Harper's* explains the story: "Speculators, developers, politicians—the usual crowd of cashers-in—have weaned the locals away from a land-based economy to the almighty greenback and introduced them to the marvels of installment plans, menial labor, and debt. By the time the older Pueblo get around to actively protesting, they've lost their children, their culture, [and] their farms to the maw of red-blooded, white-skinned capitalism."

In *The Magic Journey,* the second novel of the trilogy, Nichols underlines his theme by quoting the words of President Woodrow Wilson: "We are all caught in a great economic system which is heartless." "Nichols proposes," Bruce Cook of the *Washington Post* writes, ". . . to change that system." Norbert Blei of the *Chicago Tribune Book World* holds that "there used to be writers that cared about people. . . . Proletarian writers they were called. . . . Nichols, now, seems almost alone upon this inherited terrain." Blei believes that Nichols' work "reminds us of the love and laughter, the courage it takes to be honest, caring human beings in an age when greed and self-fulfillment seem synonymous."

Many critics have admired the versatility of Nichols' prose. McLellan notes Nichols' "virtuoso style, the profusion of strange but believable characters, the skill with which small incidents are developed and the curious blend of humor and pathos, which are often found fighting for supremacy in a single phrase." In a *Book Week* review of *The Sterile Cuckoo,* Patricia MacManus lists "an effervescent wit, a remarkable ear for dialogue, . . . a feeling for off-beat characterizations, and—oh, yes—the saving grace . . . of a rueful sense of the ludicrous" as being some of Nichols' writing assets. Nichols "has all of Steinbeck's gifts," Blei states, "the same overwhelming compas-

sion for people, plus an even finer sense of humor, and the need to celebrate the cause and dignity of man."

Nichols' use of humor has been particularly successful. Blei calls Nichols "a satirist of the first rank as he takes apart our society today." Burke, in his review of *The Magic Journey,* finds Nichols' talent for humor to be too strong for the good of the book. "This work asks to be taken seriously," he maintains, ". . . yet Nichols' creative energy runs so often to comic invention, to caricature instead of character, to spates of bathos and discursive high jinks, that he entertains far more than he instructs." Speaking of his use of humor, Nichols told *CA:* "I am a great believer in humor as a weapon and feel that while some of my work may be polemical, it's important that it is also funny and entertaining, and above all compassionate."

Blei concludes his evaluation of the New Mexico Trilogy with high praise. "It will be," he states, "one of the most significant contributions to American literature in some time. . . . Nichols has left us with a classic American trilogy."

Nichols explained to *CA* his motivations for writing and how they underwent a change beginning with his third novel: "Basically, my life, my literary focus, my ambitions, changed radically during the mid-Sixties when I was active in the anti-Vietnam War movement. I came to view the world, and how it functions, from a mostly Marxist perspective, and most of what I've written since 1966 reflects this perspective. During the Sixties and early Seventies I wrote nearly a dozen novels, motivated by this new point of view, none of which saw the light of publishing day. Yet eventually I began to learn how to create an art that is both polemical and entertaining, and have managed in the past five years to guide a handful of new books into print.

"I am strongly committed, in my life and in my work, to bringing about changes in the nature of our society which I believe absolutely necessary to the well-being of us all. I'm tired of our destruction of human, spiritual, and natural resources, particularly among minorities and working class and third world peoples—both in our country and abroad. I hope some day to see a more equal distribution of wealth and opportunity in our nation and around the world, and an end to American imperialism. I have a great faith in the energy of our people, in the vitality of our myriad cultures. I have a tendency to believe that the survival or the destruction of our planet is in the hands of the U.S.A. That makes our nation one of the scariest and most exciting countries on earth. I just wish that more of our artists and writers would accept social responsibility as an integral part of their credos, instead of wallowing in the cynical, self-centered nihilism that characterizes too much of what is popular and successful nowadays."

MEDIA ADAPTATIONS: The Sterile Cuckoo was filmed by Paramount in 1969. Film options to *The Milagro Beanfield War, The Nirvana Blues,* and *The Wizard of Loneliness* have been sold.

BIOGRAPHICAL/CRITICAL SOURCES: Best Sellers, January 15, 1965, November, 1979; *New York Times Book Review,* January 17, 1965, March 6, 1966, April 16, 1978, June 10, 1979, October 28, 1979; *Book Week,* January 24, 1965, February 20, 1966; *Saturday Review,* January 30, 1965, February 26, 1966; *Christian Science Monitor,* February 4, 1965; *America,* February 26, 1966; *Atlantic,* March, 1965; *Harper's,* April, 1965, March, 1966, August, 1978; *National Observer,* November 16, 1974; *Observer,* May 15, 1977; *Washington Post,* June 17, 1978, August 28, 1981; *La Confluencia,* October, 1978; *New America,* spring, 1979; *Village Voice,* June 30, 1979; *Washington Post Book World,* September 9, 1979, August 28, 1981; *Chicago Tribune Book World*, October 7, 1979, August 16, 1981.

*   *   *

NICHOLS, Scott
    See SCORTIA, Thomas N(icholas)

*   *   *

NICOLSON, (Lionel) Benedict   1914-1978

PERSONAL: Born August 6, 1914, in Sevenoaks, England; died May 22, 1978; son of Harold George and Victoria (Sackville-West) Nicolson; married Luisa Vertova (an art historian), August 8, 1955 (marriage dissolved, 1962); children: Vanessa. *Education:* Attended Balliol College, Oxford, 1933-36. *Home:* 45 B Holland Park, London W. 11, England. *Office:* Elm House, 10-16 Elm St., London W.C. 1, England.

CAREER: Deputy surveyor of the King's Pictures, 1939-47; editor of *Burlington Magazine*, London, England, 1947-78. Honorary director of Royal College of Art, 1971; member of executive committee, National Art Collections Fund, beginning 1972. *Military service:* British Army, Intelligence, 1939-45; served in Italy and Middle East; became captain. *Member:* British Academy (fellow), Beefsteak Club, Brooks's Club. *Awards, honors:* Member of the Royal Victorian Order, 1947; Commander of the Order of the British Empire, 1971.

WRITINGS: The Painters of Ferrara, Elek, 1950; *Hendrick Terbrugghen*, Lund, Humphries, 1958; *Joseph Wright of Derby: Painter of Light*, two volumes, Pantheon, 1968; *John Hamilton Mortimer ARA, 1740-1779*, Paul Mellon Foundation for British Art, 1968; *The Treasures of the Foundling Hospital*, Clarendon Press, 1972; *Courbet: The Studio of the Painter*, Viking, 1973; *Saved for the Nation: The Achievement of the National Art-Collections Fund, 1903-1973*, Victoria and Albert Museum, 1974; (with Christopher Wright) *Georges de la Tour*, Phaidon, 1974; *The International Carvaggesque Movement: Lists of Pictures by Caravaggio and His Followers throughout Europe from 1590 to 1650*, Phaidon, 1979. Contributor to *New Statesman, Observer, Listener*, and *Art de France*.†

*   *   *

NIMBLE, Jack B.
    See BURGESS, M(ichael) R(oy)

*   *   *

NIMS, John Frederick   1913-

PERSONAL: Born November 20, 1913, in Muskegon, Mich.; son of Frank McReynolds and Anne (McDonald) Nims; married Bonnie Larkin, September 11, 1947; children: John, Frank, George (deceased), Sarah, Emily. *Education:* Attended DePaul University for two years; University of Notre Dame, A.B., 1937, A.M., 1939; University of Chicago, Ph.D., 1945. *Politics:* Democrat. *Religion:* Roman Catholic. *Office:* Department of English, University of Illinois at Chicago Circle, Chicago, Ill. 60680.

CAREER: Teacher of English and Latin in a preparatory school in Portland, Ore., 1936; University of Notre Dame, Notre Dame, Ind., 1939-45, 1946-62, began as instructor, professor of English, 1955-62; University of Illinois at Urbana-Champaign, professor of English, 1962-65; University of Illinois at Chicago Circle, professor of English, 1965-73, 1977—; University of Florida, Gainesville, professor of English, 1973-77. Visiting professor, University of Toronto, 1945-46, Bocconi

University, 1952-53, University of Florence, 1953-54, University of Madrid, 1958-60, Harvard University, 1964, 1968-69, summer, 1974, and Breadloaf School of English, 1965-69; visiting writer, University of Illinois of Urbana-Champaign, 1961-62, and University of Chicago, spring, 1982. Poetry judge, National Book Awards, 1969, and American Book Awards, 1970 and 1971. *Awards, honors:* Harriet Monroe Memorial Prize, 1942; Friends of Literature award, 1947, for *The Iron Pastoral;* National Book Award nomination, 1960, for *Knowledge of the Evening;* National Foundation for the Arts and Humanities grant, 1967-68; American Academy of Arts and Letters award, 1968; Brandeis University citation for poetry, 1974.

WRITINGS: (Contributor) *Five Young American Poets: Third Series*, New Dirctions, 1944; *The Iron Pastoral* (poems), Sloane, 1947; *A Fountain in Kentucky* (poems), Sloane, 1950; (translator) *Poems of St. John of the Cross*, Grove, 1959, 3rd edition, University of Chicago Press, 1979; (contributor of translations) *Complete Greek Tragedies*, University of Chicago Press, 1959; *Knowledge of the Evening* (poems), Rutgers University Press, 1960; (associate editor and contributor) *The Poem Itself*, Holt, 1960; (editor) Ovid, *Metamorphoses*, Macmillan, 1965; *Of Flesh and Bone* (poems), Rutgers University Press, 1967; (translator) *Sappho to Valery: Poems in Translation*, Rutgers University Press, 1971, 2nd edition, Princeton University Press, 1980; *Western Wind: An Introduction to Poetry*, Random House, 1974; (editor) *The Harper Anthology of Poetry*, Harper, 1981; *The Kiss* (poems), Houghton, 1982; *Selected Poems*, University of Chicago Press, 1982.

Contributor to periodicals, including *Poetry, Accent, Partisan Review, Saturday Review, Harper's*, and *Kenyon Review*. *Poetry*, member of editorial board, 1945-48, visiting editor, 1960-61, editor, 1978—.

WORK IN PROGRESS: Poems.

SIDELIGHTS: Since John Frederick Nims's first book appeared in 1947, many reviewers have praised the intelligence and wit exhibited in his poems and translations. M. L. Rosenthal, reviewing *The Iron Pastoral* for the *New York Herald Tribune*, writes: "Nims's first book of poems reveals sprightly wit combined with social and moral integrity, sensuous responsiveness combined with an inquisitive intellect. He is capable of being very light and playful." Horace Gregory in the *New York Times* lauds Nims for writing *The Iron Pastoral* in "a new language—often witty and brilliant," while William Rose Benet, reviewing the book for the *Saturday Review of Literature*, says: "The work of John Frederick Nims seems to me to rank high among modern verse. . . . Ordinarily his sense of balance and sense of humor do not fail him." J. P. Clancy, in a review of *Knowledge of the Evening* for *Commonweal*, observes that Nims has "a very real gift for irony, for colloquial wit," and Walker Gibson of *Nation* attributes the author's success to his "craftmanship and wit and educated sensibility."

Other critics have found Nims's style to be, at times, overly intellectual and disruptive of the emotional impact of his verse. "Sharp-sighted and keen-witted though he is, Nims does not release us, as he should, into the world of imagination," writes Louise Bogan in a *New Yorker* review of *The Iron Pastoral*. "He continually hampers that escape not only with his artfulness, his involutions, and his studied grotesquerie but by a fundamental lack of humility of motive." A *Times Literary Supplement* reviewer calls *Of Flesh and Bone* "an uneasy mixture of neat antiquarianism and roguish modernity," but Chad Walsh, writing in *Book World*, admires Nims's ability to blend traditional style with a modern perspective, concluding, "This is verse that should be carved in simple but elegant lettering on small blocks of marble.'' Finally, John Holmes in the *New York Times Book Review*, noting that Nims's style in *Knowledge of the Evening* ''combines a colloquial and contemporary voice with wide-ranging classical reference,'' describes the book as a ''substantial addition to today's poetry.''

Nims's work as a translator, specifically in *Sappho to Valery*, a collection of poems translated from six languages and three dialects, has been widely acclaimed. Nims's renditions, according to Philip Murray in *Poetry*, are ''absolute miracles . . . [and his] introductory remarks on Sappho are particularly sensible. He cuts through jungles of nonsense with a sharp and witty pen. . . . Rarely in the translator's art have such knowledge, skill, sensitivity and breadth of interest coincided so felicitously in a single hand.'' Vernon Young calls *Sappho to Valery* ''one of those books I would not willingly live without, once having made its acquaintance.'' In the *Hudson Review*, Young expresses ''pure delight with Nims's craftmanship; his wit, his common sense and his resolve to convey a poem's form as accurately as possible or, where accuracy is plainly impossible to render, to invent, with spectacular result, an incredible paraphrase which you feel must be more inspired than the original.'' Brewster Ghiselin finds that ''in reading the translation, it is as if the scene and mood of the original were re-experienced under almost identical conditions of place and time.'' Writing in the *Sewanee Review*, Ghiselin cites one reason for the success of Nims's translations: ''He constantly feels the allurement and excitement of the original poetry, and answers it as a poet, with poetry.''

BIOGRAPHICAL/CRITICAL SOURCES: Saturday Review of Literature, March 22, 1947; *New Yorker*, April 5, 1947; *New York Times*, May 25, 1947; *New York Herald Tribune Weekly Book Review*, June 29, 1947; *Library Journal*, November 1, 1960; *Commonweal*, November 11, 1960; *New York Times Book Review*, November 13, 1960; *Nation*, November 26, 1960; *Christian Century*, February 28, 1961; *Prarie Schooner*, winter, 1961-62; *Book World*, September 10, 1967; *Times Literary Supplement*, September 14, 1967; *Kenyon Review*, November, 1967; *Poetry*, August, 1968, January, 1969, August, 1972; *Sewanee Review*, spring, 1973; *Hudson Review*, winter, 1974-75; *Dictionary of Literary Biography*, Volume V: *American Poets since World War II*, Gale, 1980.

*   *   *

NOCHLIN, Linda Weinberg 1931-

PERSONAL: Born January 30, 1931, in Brooklyn, N.Y.; daughter of Jules and Elka (Heller) Weinberg; married Philip Nochlin, December 20, 1953 (deceased); children: Jessica. *Education:* Vassar College, B.A., 1951; Columbia University, M.A., 1952; New York University, Ph.D., 1963. *Politics:* Democrat. *Religion:* Jewish.

CAREER: Vassar College, Poughkeepsie, N.Y., beginning 1952, began as assistant professor of art history, became Mary Conover Mellon Professor of Art. *Member:* College Art Association, Phi Beta Kappa. *Awards, honors:* Kingsley Porter Prize, 1967; E. Harris Harbison Award for gifted teaching, 1972; American Council of Learned Societies fellowship, 1972-73; Fulbright fellow; Fels fellow.

WRITINGS: Mathis at Colmar: A Visual Confrontation, Red Dust, 1963; (editor) *Impressionism and Post-Impressionism, 1874-1904: Sources and Documents*, Prentice-Hall, 1966; *Realism and Tradition in Art, 1848-1900: Sources and Documents*, Prentice-Hall, 1966; *Realism*, Penguin, 1971; (editor with Thomas B. Hess) *Woman As Sex Object: Studies in Erotic Art, 1730-1970*, Newsweek, 1972; (contributor) Abram Lerner

and others, editors, *The Hirschhorn Museum and Sculpture Garden, Smithsonian Institution*, Abrams, 1974; *Gustave Courbert: A Study of Style and Society*, Garland Publishing, 1976; (with Ann Harris) *Women Artists, 1550-1950*, Knopf, 1977; (editor with Henry Millon) *Art and Architecture in the Service of Politics*, M.I.T. Press, 1978.†

*   *   *

NORMAN, Frank 1930-1980

PERSONAL: Born June 9, 1930, in London, England; died December 23, 1980; illegitimate son of a cockney costermonger; married Geraldine Keene, July 16, 1971. *Education:* Attended state schools in England. *Home:* 5 Seaford Ct., 222 Great Portland St., London W. 1, England. *Agent:* Gillon Aitken, 17 Belgrave Pl., London S.W. 1, England.

CAREER: Writer. Had been in jail for burglary four times; worked as a van driver after being released. *Military service:* British Army, two years. *Member:* P.E.N. *Awards, honors:* Drama award, *London Evening Standard*, 1960.

WRITINGS—Published by Secker & Warburg, except as indicated: *Bang to Rights*, 1958; *Stand on Me: A True Story of Soho, with a Glossary of Slang for Those Who Need It* (autobiography), 1960, Simon & Schuster, 1961; *Fings Ain't Wot They Used T'Be* (play; first produced at Garrick Theatre, February, 1960), Grove, 1962; *The Guntz* (autobiography), 1963; *Soho Day and Night*, 1966; *The Monkey Pulled His Hair*, 1967, published as *Only the Rich*, Avon, 1969; *Barney Snip—Artist*, 1968; *Banana Boy* (autobiography), 1969; *Norman's London*, 1969; ''Insideout'' (play), first produced in London at Royal Court Theatre, December 1, 1969.

Dodgem-Greaser, Hodder & Stoughton, 1971; *Lock 'Em Up and Count 'Em*, Charles Knight, 1971; ''Costa Packet'' (musical), first produced in London at Theatre Royal, October 5, 1972; *The Lives of Frank Norman* (anthology), Penguin, 1972; *One of Our Own*, Hodder & Stoughton, 1973; *Down and Out in High Society*, Hodder & Stoughton, 1975; *Why Fings Went West*, Lemon Tree Press, 1975; (with Tom Keating and wife, Geraldine Norman) *The Fake's Progress*, Hutchinson, 1977; *The Dead Butler Caper*, Macdonald & Jane's, 1978, St. Martin's, 1979; *Too Many Crooks Spoil the Caper*, Macdonald & Jane's, 1979, St. Martin's, 1980.

Also author of several television plays and filmscripts, including ''A Kayf up West,'' ''Just Call Me Lucky,'' and ''The Incorrigible Rogue.''

SIDELIGHTS: Although Frank Norman was best known for his play, *Fings Ain't Wot They Used T'Be*, his other books, such as *Stand on Me*, were also well received. V. S. Pritchett wrote in the *New Statesman*, ''Norman is a born comic and a late self-education has not on the whole damaged the gift.'' *Springfield Republican* critic Richard McLaughlin believes that Norman ''reveals a natural skill in bringing everything alive, so that one does not hesitate to mention him in the same breath with such intrepid literary Gullivers as Damon Runyon and Nelson Algren. And he, too, writes in a lingo which gives the reader the odd feeling he's traveling in a strange land.''

BIOGRAPHICAL/CRITICAL SOURCES: New Statesman, January 9, 1960, December 2, 1966; *Newsweek*, January 9, 1961; *Springfield Republican*, January 15, 1961; *Spectator*, March 21, 1969; *New York Times Book Review*, November 23, 1980.

*   *   *

NORTH, Charles W.
See BAUER, Erwin A.

NYE, F(rancis) Ivan   1918-

PERSONAL: Born April 27, 1918, in Prospect, Ore.; son of Nelson M. and Clarice (Paul) Nye; married Esther Miller (a teacher); children: Beverly Irene, Lloyd Nathan, Betty Jean (Mrs. Clyde Morrison). *Education:* Willamette University, A.B., 1946; Washington State University, M.A., 1947; Michigan State University, Ph.D., 1952. *Politics:* Democrat. *Religion:* Congregational. *Home:* Southwest 165 Skyline Dr., Pullman, Wash. 99163. *Office:* Department of Rural Sociology, Washington State University, Pullman, Wash. 99163.

CAREER: Ohio State University, Columbus, assistant professor of rural sociology, 1948-50; University of Missouri, Columbia, assistant professor of rural sociology, 1950-52; Bucknell University, Lewisburg, Pa., associate professor of sociology, 1952-54; Florida State University, Tallahassee, professor of sociology, 1960-63; Washington State University, Pullman, 1954-60, began as assistant professor, professor of sociology,

1963—, chairman of department of rural sociology and director of interdivisional doctoral program in marriage and family living, director of sociology research lab, 1954-60. *Member:* American Sociological Association, American Association for the Advancement of Science, Rural Sociological Society, National Council on Family Relations, Pacific Sociological Association.

WRITINGS: Family Relationships and Delinquent Behavior, Wiley, 1958, reprinted, Greenwood Press, 1973; (editor with Lois Wladis Hoffman) *The Employed Mother in America,* Rand McNally, 1963; (editor with Felix M. Berardo) *Emerging Conceptual Frameworks in Family Analysis,* Macmillan, 1966; (with Berardo) *The Family: Its Structure and Interaction,* Macmillan, 1973; (with Hoffman) *Working Mothers: An Evaluative Review of the Consequences for Wife, Husband, and Child,* Jossey-Bass, 1974; *Role Structure and Analysis of the Family,* Sage Publications, 1976. Editor, *Marriage and Family Living,* 1960-64.†

O

OAKLEY, Ann 1944-

PERSONAL: Born January 17, 1944, in London, England; daughter of Richard Morris (a university professor) and Kathleen (a social worker; maiden name, Miller) Titmuss; children: three. *Education:* Somerville College, Oxford, M.A. (honors), 1965; Bedford College, London, Ph.D., 1974. *Politics:* Feminist. *Agent:* Deborah Rogers Ltd., 5-11 Mortimer St., London W1N 7RH, England. *Office:* National Perinatal Epidemology Unit, Radcliffe Infirmary, Oxford OX2 6HE, England.

CAREER: University of London, Bedford College, London, England, research officer in Social Research Unit, 1974-79; Radcliffe Infirmary, National Perinatal Epidemology Unit, Oxford, England, Wellcome Research Fellow, 1980—.

WRITINGS: Sex, Gender & Society, Maurice Temple Smith, 1972, Harper, 1973; *The Sociology of Housework,* Martin Robertson, 1974, Pantheon, 1975; *Housewife,* Allen Lane, 1974, published as *Woman's Work: A History of the Housewife,* Pantheon, 1975; (contributor) David Tuckett, editor, *Medical Sociology,* Tavistock, 1975; (editor with Juliet Mitchell) *The Rights and Wrongs of Women,* Penguin, 1976; *Becoming a Mother,* Martin Robertson, 1979, Schocken, 1980; *Women Confined,* Schocken, 1980; *Subject Women,* Pantheon, 1981.

WORK IN PROGRESS: The Captured Womb: A History of Prenatal Care; Unsolved Problems: The Personal History of a Feminist.

*   *   *

OBOLER, Eli M(artin) 1915-

PERSONAL: Surname is pronounced *Ob*-o-ler; born September 26, 1915, in Chicago, Ill.; son of Leo (an optometrist) and Clara (Obeler) Oboler; married Marcia Lois Wolf (an art teacher), December 25, 1938; children: Leon David, Carol Judy. *Education:* University of Chicago, B.A., 1941, graduate study, 1946-49; Columbia University, B.S. in L.S., 1942. *Politics:* Independent. *Religion:* Jewish. *Home:* 1397 Jane St., Pocatello, Idaho 83201. *Office:* Idaho State University Library, Pocatello, Idaho 83209.

CAREER: U.S. War Production Board, Washington, D.C., assistant chief of lend-lease expediting bureau, 1942-43; University of Chicago, Chicago, Ill., head of reserve room, 1946-49, University College, librarian, 1947-49; Idaho State University, Pocatello, librarian, 1949-80, university librarian

emeritus, 1981—. Great Books Foundation, consultant, 1947-49, lecturer, 1948-49. Lecturer at Utah State University, 1960, 1966, and University of Washington, Seattle, 1975. National Advisory Committee on Library Training and Research Projects of U.S. Office of Education, member, 1966-69, chairman, 1968-69. Member of Pocatello Chamber of Commerce, 1966-68; member of advisory committee of Pacific Northwest Regional Health Sciences Library, 1968-77, and Idaho Health Information Retrieval Center, 1974-76; Freedom to Read Foundation, member of board of trustees, 1971-75, vice-president, 1979-80. Commentator on weekly radio program, "Books and You," KEYY, 1949-50, KSEI, 1950-76; participant on television program, "You're Invited," KID, 1959-60, "It Seems to Me," KBGL, 1965-66, and "Idaho Looks at the World," KBGL, 1972-76. *Military service:* U.S. Army, 1943-46; served in Canal Zone.

MEMBER: American Library Association (councilor, 1954-59, 1977-81; chairman, Intellectual Freedom Round Table, 1980-81), Association of College and Research Libraries (chairman of college section, 1963-64), American Association of University Professors, Pacific Northwest Library Association (honorary life member; president, 1955-56), Idaho State Library Association (president, 1950-53), Idaho Council of State Academic Librarians (chairman, 1968-69, 1973-74), B'nai B'rith (president of Pocatello chapter, 1951-53), Kiwanis (member of local board of directors, 1972-74). *Awards, honors:* American Library Association-H. W. Wilson Co. library periodical award, 1964, for editorship of *PNLA Quarterly;* commendation by Pocatello Mayor's Committee on Employment of Handicapped, 1968; selected as Idaho Librarian of the Year by Idaho Library Association, 1974; Robert B. Downs Award for Intellectual Freedom, 1976.

WRITINGS: (Editor) *College and University Library Accreditation Standards: 1957,* Association of College and Research Libraries, 1958; (contributor) Eric Moon, editor, *Book Selection and Censorship in the Sixties,* Bowker, 1969; (contributor) Alan Angoff, editor, *Public Relations for Libraries,* Greenwood Press, 1973; *The Fear of the Word: Censorship and Sex,* Scarecrow, 1974; *Ideas and the University Library,* Greenwood Press, 1977; *Defending Intellectual Freedom,* Greenwood Press, 1980; *Education and Censorship,* H. W. Wilson, 1981.

Author of regular column for *Intermountain,* 1952-60, *Idaho State Journal,* 1960-65, 1980—, *Intermountain Observer,* 1967-73, and *Western Critic,* 1973-75. Contributor of more than 200 articles and reviews to journals. Editor of *Idaho Librarian,* 1950-54, 1957-58, *PNLA Quarterly,* 1958-67, and *Temple Topics,* 1969-73; *Library Periodicals Round Table Newsletter,* assistant editor, 1953-54, editor, 1961-62; member of editorial board, *College and Research Libraries,* 1962-63.

WORK IN PROGRESS: To Free the Mind: Libraries, Technology, and Intellectual Freedom.

SIDELIGHTS: Eli Oboler has become known for his writings about censorship and freedom of expression. Jerold Nelson of the *Newsletter on Intellectual Freedom* claims that Oboler "has few peers when it comes to providing regular and persistent commentary concerning censorship related issues." Richard Rubin writes in the *Ohio Library Association Bulletin* that "Oboler is a restless and eloquent spokesman for the free dissemination of ideas. . . . He never lets us forget that mere condemnation of censorship is not enough."

BIOGRAPHICAL/CRITICAL SOURCES: Ohio Library Association Bulletin, July, 1981; *Newsletter on Intellectual Freedom,* July, 1981.

*   *   *

O'BRIAN, Frank
See GARFIELD, Brian (Wynne)

*   *   *

O'BRIEN, Edna 1936-

PERSONAL: Born December 15, 1936, in Tuamgraney, Ireland; daughter of Michael and Lena (Cleary) O'Brien; married Ernest Gebler (an author), 1952 (divorced, 1967); children: Sasha, Carlos (sons). *Education:* Attended Pharmaceutical College of Ireland. *Residence:* England. *Agent:* Robert Lescher, 155 East 71st St., New York, N.Y. 10021.

CAREER: Novelist, playwright, and screenwriter. *Awards, honors:* Kingsley Amis Award, 1962; *Yorkshire Post* novel award, 1971.

WRITINGS—Novels, except as indicated: *The Country Girls,* Knopf, 1960; *The Lonely Girl,* Random House, 1962, published as *The Girl with Green Eyes,* Penguin, 1970; *Girls in Their Married Bliss,* J. Cape, 1964, Houghton, 1968; *August Is a Wicked Month,* Simon & Schuster, 1965; *Casualties of Peace,* J. Cape, 1966, Simon & Schuster, 1967; *Zee and Company,* Weidenfeld, 1970; *Night,* Knopf, 1972; *Mother Ireland* (nonfiction), photographs by Fergus Bourke, Harcourt, 1976; *Arabian Days* (nonfiction), Quartet Books, 1977; *Johnny I Hardly Knew You,* Weidenfeld, 1977, published as *I Hardly Knew You,* Doubleday, 1978; (editor) *Some Irish Loving* (anthology), Harper, 1979; *James and Nora: A Portrait of Joyce's Marriage* (nonfiction), Lord John Publishers, 1981.

Short stories: *The Love Object,* J. Cape, 1968, Knopf, 1969; *A Scandalous Woman and Other Stories,* Harcourt, 1974; *A Rose in the Heart,* Doubleday, 1979.

Plays: *A Cheap Bunch of Nice Flowers* (produced in London, England, 1962), Elek, 1963; *A Pagan Place* (produced on the West End at Royal Court Theatre, October, 1972), Knopf, 1970; "The Gathering," first produced in Dublin, Ireland, 1974, produced in New York, N.Y., at Manhattan Theatre Club, 1977. Also author of play, "The Keys of the Cafe."

Screenplays: "The Girl with Green Eyes" (based on O'Brien's novel *The Lonely Girl;* also see above), Lopert, 1964; "I Was Happy Here," 1968; "Three into Two Won't Go," Universal, 1969; "X Y and Zee" (based on O'Brien's novel *Zee and Company;* also see above), Columbia, 1972. Also author of screenplay, "A Woman at the Seaside."

Television plays: "The Wedding Dress," 1963; "The Keys of the Cafe," 1965; "Give My Love to the Pilchards," 1965; "Which of These Two Ladies Is He Married To?" 1967; "Nothing's Ever Over," 1968.

Contributor to *Oh! Calcutta!,* compiled by Kenneth Tynan, Grove, 1969. Also contributor to *New Yorker* and various English journals.

SIDELIGHTS: Edna O'Brien has been hailed by many critics as a champion of "the condition of women, especially their sexual repression." As James R. Frakes writes: "O'Brien thoroughly convinces me that she knows the mazed caverns of the mind and emotions of women driven by desperate love—the blind alleys, the slimy stalagmites and phallic formations, the harmless bats and deadly butterflies, the noxious wisps of nonsense songs, the smells of smoke."

One reason for this insightful portrayal of her characters is that O'Brien patterns the characters after herself. Vivien Raynor points out: "The women Edna O'Brien writes about have led lives similar to her own. They were born in Ireland around 1930 and left early to live among the foe. The Brits, the painted people. A land where the king has piles. Usually they have married disastrously and have only a son or two to show for it." Agreeing with this assessment, Julia O'Faolian comments in her review for the *New York Times Book Review:* "Miss O'Brien's range is narrow and obsessional. The larger world does not interest her. Her social settings are perfunctory. . . . Her sex and self-absorbed women are undisturbed by the day-to-day. Nothing intervenes to prevent their passion reaching boiling point. However, theirs never boils over. There is no explosion. No climax. This slice of life is chopped off more or less neatly and a few sentences of melanchology Stoicism tie it up."

But some people take offense at this typical character that O'Brien uses in her novels. They see the heroines as failures, chained to an inadequate man, "once fallen unable to rise, if they do totter to their feet, it is only to fall again." A reviewer for *Book World* described the usual O'Brien heroines as "women getting a kind of higher education at the hands of men. Jobs and professions notwithstanding, they are descendants of Byron's ladies, for whom love was their whole existence. . . . Her protagonists move gamely from one unsatisfactory man to the next, taking notes as they go. They have divested themselves of illusions and have assumed a bachelor bravado, letting the sexual chips fall where they may." Bernard Bergonzi agrees with these descriptions and feels: "If I were a woman I would be pretty disturbed by the way in which Miss O'Brien implicitly accepts and even reinforces traditional male prejudicies about women, of the kind advanced by the ideologues of European reaction and most available in English in the writings of Wyndham Lewis. This view of woman sees her as certainly biologically different from man and, in most respects, inferior; a creature rooted in matter, whose main function is reproductive and who is correspondingly mindless; quite incapable of rationality, judgment, or any form of intellectual activity."

However, Julia O'Faolian sees more to O'Brien's writings: "Although a feminist republic of free, responsible women might be tempted to ban Miss O'Brien's defeatist writings, they should rather, I think, be grateful to her. Her stories are bulletins from a front on which they will not care to engage, field reports on the feminine condition at its most acute. Only a woman fiction writer can safely and authentically explore feminine passivity to the full. She can experience it totally in her characters while protected from its virus by the fact that she is, qua writer, simultaneously active. Miss O'Brien explores with persuasive thoroughness.''

''That O'Brien has been called a feminist develops not so much from an ideal or from a philosophical cause but from a realistic appraisal of the female condition and of the male-female relationship,'' Grace Eckley explains. ''In the final analysis, loneliness and independence must be acknowledged as dominant themes in Edna O'Brien's fiction. Stresses, especially those of loneliness, most dramatically take the form of a quest for someone to love, and that person not only has a body but also reflects the protagonist's state of mind. . . . Still a second factor exposed by Miss O'Brien's literary stethoscope should cause more discomfort than this exclusive submergence in the love theme, and that is the thoroughness with which one's choice of someone to love defines the entire range of one's personality; it exposes a streak of masochism, describes one's pathetic ideals, or reflects conditions of loneliness.''

BIOGRAPHICAL/CRITICAL SOURCES: Books and Bookmen, December, 1964; *Books,* June, 1965; *New York Review of Books,* June 3, 1965, August 24, 1967; *Saturday Review,* June 5, 1965, March 25, 1967; *National Observer,* June 21, 1965; *Atlantic Monthly,* July, 1965; *New York Times Book Review,* March 26, 1967, February 9, 1969. September 22, 1974, June 27, 1978, February 11, 1979; *Vogue,* September 1, 1971; *Washington Post-Book World,* January 7, 1973; Grace Eckley, *Edna O'Brien,* Bucknell University Press, 1974; *Contemporary Literary Criticism,* Gale, Volume III, 1975, Volume V, 1976, Volume VIII, 1978, Volume XIII, 1980; *People,* April 17, 1978; *Los Angeles Times,* April 3, 1979.

*   *   *

O'CATHASAIGH, Donal
See CASEY, Daniel J(oseph)

*   *   *

O'DONNELL, James Kevin   1951-
(Jim O'Donnell)

PERSONAL: Born May 14, 1951, in Jersey City, N.J.; son of Amos Louis (an electrical engineer) and Vera (a teacher; maiden name, Horan) O'Donnell. *Education:* St. Peter's College, B.A., 1973. *Home:* 822 Pavonia Ave., Jersey City, N.J. 07306.

CAREER: Writer. Teacher of ''Rock 'n' Roll for Your Mind,'' at St. Peter's College, 1975; teacher of English and journalism at Hudson Catholic High School, 1978—. *Awards, honors:* Most Valuable Staffer Award from *Jersey Journal,* 1969; North Jersey Press scholarship, 1972; New Jersey Press scholarship, 1972.

WRITINGS—All under name Jim O'Donnell: *The Young Estate,* Centennial Books, 1972; *The Rock Book,* Pinnacle Books, 1975; *Born to Rock,* Peacock Books, 1981. Sportswriter for *Jersey Journal,* 1969-70; correspondent for *New York Times,* 1971-72.

*   *   *

O'DONNELL, Jim
See O'DONNELL, James Kevin

*   *   *

O'FLAHERTY, Louise   1920-

PERSONAL: Born September 27, 1920, in Indianapolis, Ind.,

daughter of Carl (a lawyer) and Helen (Akin) Wilde; married Joseph S. O'Flaherty (an executive and historian), December 15, 1944; children: Joseph, Michael, Mary (Mrs. Darwin Horn). *Education:* Wellesley College, B.A., 1942. *Religion:* Roman Catholic. *Residence:* Rolling Hills, Calif. 90274. *Agent:* Curtis Brown, Ltd., 60 East 56th St., New York, N.Y. 10022.

WRITINGS—All novels: *House of the Lost Woman,* Pyramid Publications, 1974; *A Tear in the Silk,* Pyramid Publications, 1976; *The Farthest Eden,* Ballantine, 1979; *Gospel Swamp,* Ballantine, 1980; *Poppies in the Wind,* Ballantine, 1981; *The Golden Land,* Ballantine, in press.

WORK IN PROGRESS: A sequel to *The Golden Land.*

SIDELIGHTS: Louise O'Flaherty told *CA:* ''One hears a lot of ridicule these days about the work ethic. Myself, peering out across the far boundary of middle age, a time of life which for too many women lacks purpose or fulfillment, I feel incredibly lucky. To be a professional writer, to find a place in today's market which fairly bristles with formidable competition, requires long hours, complete dedication, and giving the best that one has. What greater privilege could anyone— man or woman—ask than to love his work?''

*   *   *

OGILVIE, Robert Maxwell   1932-

PERSONAL: Born June 5, 1932, in Edinburgh, Scotland; son of Sir Frederick and Lady Mary (Macaulay) Ogilvie; married Jennifer Roberts, July 4, 1959; children: Isobel, Alexander, Charles. *Education:* Attended Balliol College, Oxford, 1950-54. *Home:* Errachd, Fort William, Scotland. *Office:* St. Salvator's College, University of St. Andrews, Fife, Scotland.

CAREER: Cambridge University, Clare College, Cambridge, England, fellow in classics, 1955-57; Oxford University, Balliol College, Oxford, England, fellow in classics, 1957-70; Tonbridge School, Kent, England, headmaster, 1970-75; University of St. Andrews, St. Salvatore's College, Fife, Scotland, professor of humanities, 1975—. Visiting professor, University of Toronto, 1965-66; chairman of board of governors, Trinity College, Glenalmond. *Member:* British Academy (fellow), Royal and Ancient Golf Club (St. Andrews), Royal Society of Edinburgh (fellow). *Awards, honors:* D.Litt., Oxford University, 1967.

WRITINGS: Latin and Greek, Shoe String, 1964; *Commentary on Livy Books, 1-5,* Oxford University Press, 1965; (editor with Sir Ian Richmond) Cornelius Tacitus, *De Vita Agricolae,* Oxford University Press, 1967; *The Romans and Their Gods,* Chatto & Windus, 1970; *Early Rome and the Etruscans,* John M. Fontana, 1972; *Roman Literature and Society,* Penguin, 1975; *The Library of Lanctantius,* Oxford University Press, 1975. Contributor to *Journal of Roman Studies, Journal of Hellenic Studies, Classical Quarterly,* and *Listener.*

WORK IN PROGRESS: A new text of Livy's ''Fragments,'' for Oxford Classical Texts.

SIDELIGHTS: Oliver Nicholson writes of *The Library of Lanctantius* in the *Times Literary Supplement:* ''[It] is a skilful and meticulous examination of [Lanctantius'] citations and their sources. . . . Scholars will find concentrated in Professor Ogilvie's book much valuable material. . . . They will anticipate with pleasure the work he promises us'' in the future.

AVOCATIONAL INTERESTS: Mountaineering in Scotland, field archaeology in Italy.

BIOGRAPHICAL/CRITICAL SOURCES: Times Literary Supplement, April 19, 1980; *Washington Post Book World,* August 31, 1980.

OGLESBY, Richard E(dward) 1931-

PERSONAL: Born March 27, 1931, in Waukegan, Ill.; son of Harold W. and Hedwig (Staranowicz) Oglesby; married Eugenia Basquin, May 11, 1957; children: Susan Deborah. *Education:* Northwestern University, B.S., 1953, M.A., 1957, Ph.D., 1962. *Home:* 925 Calle Cortita Rd., Santa Barbara, Calif. 93109. *Office:* Department of History, University of California, Santa Barbara, Calif. 93106.

CAREER: Eastern Illinois University, Charleston, assistant professor of history, 1961-65; University of California, Santa Barbara, assistant professor, 1965-69, associate professor of history, 1969—, chairman of department, 1973-76. *Military service:* U.S. Army Counter-Intelligence Corps, 1953-55; became sergeant. *Member:* American Historical Association, Organization of American Historians, Western History Association, Missouri Historical Society, Montana Historical Society.

WRITINGS: Manuel Lisa and the Opening of the Missouri Fur Trade, University of Oklahoma Press, 1963; (editor) Manuel Lisa, *The American West, an Appraisal,* Museum of New Mexico Press, 1963; (contributor) *The Frontier Re-examined,* University of Illinois Press, 1967; (contributor) *The Fur Trade and the Mountain Men,* Arthur H. Clark, 1967; (co-author) *American Profile,* Heath, 1969; (co-author) *Portrait of a Nation,* Volume II, Heath, 1972.

WORK IN PROGRESS: A history of the modern West.

AVOCATIONAL INTERESTS: Travel.†

* * *

OLSON, Elder (James) 1909-

PERSONAL: Born March 9, 1909, in Chicago, Ill.; son of Elder James and Hilda (Schroeder) Olson; married Ann Elisabeth Jones, 1937 (divorced, 1948); married Geraldine Louise Hays, 1948; children: (first marriage) Ann, Elder; (second marriage) Olivia, Shelley. *Education:* University of Chicago, B.A., 1934, M.A., 1935, Ph.D., 1938. *Home:* 1501 Los Alamos Ave., Albuquerque, N.M. 87104.

CAREER: Armour Institute of Technology, Chicago, Ill., 1935-42, began as instructor, became assistant professor; University of Chicago, Chicago, assistant professor, 1942-48, associate professor, 1948-53, professor of English, 1953-71, distinguished service professor, 1971-77, professor emeritus, 1977—. Patten Lecturer, Indiana University, 1965; Rockefeller visiting professor, University of the Philippines, 1966-67; visiting professor and lecturer at other universities and colleges in the United States and abroad. *Member:* Societe Europeenne de Culture, International P.E.N. *Awards, honors:* Witter Bynner Award, 1927; Guarantor's Award, *Poetry,* 1931; Friends of Literature Award, 1935, for *Thing of Sorrow;* Eunice Tietjens Memorial Award for poetry, 1953; Poetry Society of America Chap-Book Award for a notable work dealing with poetry, 1955, for *The Poetry of Dylan Thomas;* Longview Foundation Award for poetry, 1958; Emily Clark Balch Award, *Virginia Quarterly Review,* 1965; Quantrell Award, University of Chicago, 1966; Academy of American Poets award, 1966; University of the Philippines distinguished service award, 1967; Society of Midland Authors award, 1976.

WRITINGS: General Prosody: Rhythmic, Metric, Harmonics, University of Chicago Press, 1938; (contributor) R. S. Crane, editor, *Critics and Criticism,* University of Chicago Press, 1952; *The Poetry of Dylan Thomas,* University of Chicago Press, 1954, 2nd edition, 1961; *Tragedy and the Theory of Drama,* Wayne State University Press, 1961; *The Theory of Comedy,* Indiana University Press, 1968; *On Value Judgements in the Arts, and Other Essays,* University of Chicago Press, 1976.

Poetry: *Thing of Sorrow,* Macmillan, 1934; *The Cock of Heaven,* Macmillan, 1940; *The Scarecrow Christ,* Noonday Press, 1954; *Plays and Poems: 1948-1958,* University of Chicago Press, 1958, reprinted, 1975; *Collected Poems,* University of Chicago Press, 1963; *Olson's Penny Arcade,* University of Chicago Press, 1975.

Editor: *American Lyric Poems: From Colonial Times to the Present,* Appleton, 1964; *Aristotle's Poetics and English Literature: A Collection of Critical Essays,* University of Chicago Press, 1965; *Major Voices: 20 British and American Poets,* McGraw, 1973.

Contributor to *Encyclopaedia Britannica.* Contributor of articles, plays, and poems to *New Yorker, Poetry, First Stage,* and other publications.

SIDELIGHTS: As a prominent member of the neo-Aristotelian school which emerged at the University of Chicago in the 1940s, Elder Olson has expressed, in both his criticism and his poetry, the group's belief that the principles set down by Aristotle in the *Poetics* should be applied to contemporary literature.

Olson's *Poetry of Dylan Thomas,* "the first considerable attempt to evaluate the whole body of [Thomas's] verse" as Dudley Fitts of *Saturday Review* describes it, was widely praised for its critical insights. Paul Engle of the *Chicago Tribune* finds the book "always helpful and often brilliant, making discoveries in the poetry of Thomas which not only illuminate the poems under discussion, but throw a revealing light on poetry in general." Nicholas Joost of *Commonweal* considers the study a "just and intelligent and dignified appraisal." "Olson," Jacob Korg of *Nation* writes, "leaves little doubt that he has discovered the key to an understanding of these poems."

In *The Theory of Comedy,* Olson applies Aristotelian theory to a study of comedy in literature and drama. A reviewer for *Yale Review* notes that with this book, Olson continues "a career of resolute neo-Aristotelianism that stretches back more than twenty years." He finds the study "Aristotelian in rigor and intended exclusiveness . . . yet freely expansive and liberally applied over a wide panorama of comic examples." Unfortunately, he concludes that the result is often "one obvious statement after another [and] a repeated pedagogic buttonholing and patronage of the reader." In contrast to this view, Kenneth Burke of the *New Republic* calls *The Theory of Comedy* "an unusually able and superior work." Burke also finds that Olson's analysis "abounds in gratifyingly acute comments on particular texts." He concludes, "I greatly admire this book and hope it gets the attention it deserves."

Olson's poetry, written in "strict and formal lyric forms" as Louise Bogan of the *New Yorker* states, is particularly noted for its superb craftsmanship and intelligence. Olson has avoided many of the current literary trends in favor of traditional poetic concerns. M. E. Rosenthal of the *New York Times Book Review,* in an evaluation of *Collected Poems,* writes that Olson "gives us some exquisitely sculptured, intense poems, and some others that are . . . robust. . . . Taken all together, Mr. Olson's poems are not quite a continuum, not quite in concentrated focus. Taken one at a time, they yield not only hard gems but plain human revelations." Speaking of the same collection, George Garrett of *Virginia Quarterly Review* believes that Olson's work is a "considerable achievement over a sustained period of time, and this is the sign of a true poet." Although Gilbert Sorrentino of *Book Week* finds some of the poems in the collection "hopelessly marred by archaic syntax and verbiage," he thinks that Olson's "moods and interests are varied and rich, and his intelligence is remarkable."

Olson's Penny Arcade, containing a verse play and poems, was well-received by the critics. A reviewer for *Choice* describes the play as "strong, sententious, and filled with vigor, intensity, and keen insight, characteristics usually present in all of Olson's work. The poetry, however, is not such consequence." The critic for *Hudson Review,* after calling the book "a rather oddly assorted volume ([but] some very good books of verse are oddly assorted)," writes that "many of the poems are excellent." He judges Olson's comic verse "Four Immensely Moral Tales" as "delightfully told." "*Olson's Penny Arcade,*" Paul Ramsey states in the *Sewanee Review,* "is a fine book, not with the fineness of gossamer, or sighs, but of ivory, of steel, of the true scholar's eyes focusing on the page. It is a privilege to be in the presence of so much intelligence, integrity, and fully controlled poetic skill."

Speaking of Olson's stature as a poet, Joost writes in the *Chicago Tribune:* "Olson is one of those American poets who never receives publicity and the adulation awarded to flashier talents among us. But his kind of poet keeps doggedly on, developing what he has to say until we recognize it immediately as the expression of a real person and not a literary fashion."

BIOGRAPHICAL/CRITICAL SOURCES: Nation, April 24, 1954; *Saturday Review,* May 1, 1954, June 18, 1955; *Chicago Tribune,* May 2, 1954, May 27, 1955, January 4, 1959; *Christian Science Monitor,* May 6, 1954; *Commonweal,* May 14, 1954, May 21, 1976; *New York Herald Tribune Book Review,* May 23, 1954; *San Francisco Chronicle,* June 13, 1954; *Spectator,* August 20, 1954; *Canadian Forum,* September, 1954; *Catholic World,* November, 1954; John Crowe Ransom, *Poems and Essays,* Knopf, 1955; *New Yorker,* April 30, 1955; *New York Times,* May 22, 1955; *Poetry,* June, 1955, August, 1959, June, 1964; *Yale Review,* summer, 1955, summer, 1969; *Comparative Literature,* spring, 1963, summer, 1970; *Book Week,* March 1, 1964; *New York Times Book Review,* March 8, 1964; *Virginia Quarterly Review,* spring, 1964, summer, 1976; *Times Literary Supplement,* May 7, 1964; *New Republic,* March 15, 1969; *Quarterly Journal of Speech,* October, 1969; Thomas E. Lucas, *Elder Olson,* Twayne, 1972; *Choice,* March, 1976; *Hudson Review,* spring, 1976; *Sewanee Review,* July, 1976.†

*   *   *

ORLICK, Terrance D(ouglas) 1945-

PERSONAL: Born May 21, 1945, in Montreal, Quebec, Canada; son of Emanuel (a small business consultant) and Agnes (a special education teacher; maiden name, Whalen) Orlick; married Catharine Payne (a high school teacher), August 17, 1968 (divorced August, 1977); married Sylvie Lavoie (a dancer), 1978; children: (second marriage) Anouk Lavoie Orlick (daughter). *Education:* Syracuse University, B.A., 1967; College of William and Mary, M.Ed., 1968; University of Alberta, Ph.D., 1972. *Home:* Chelsea, Quebec, Quebec, Canada J0X 2N0. *Office:* School of Human Kinetics and Leisure Studies, University of Ottawa, Ottawa, Ontario, Canada.

CAREER: Montclair State College, Montclair, N.J., assistant professor of physical education, 1968-70; University of Western Ontario, London, Ontario, assistant professor of physical education, 1972-73; University of Ottawa, Ottawa, Ontario, associate professor, 1973-79, professor of kinanthropology, 1979—. Consultant to Canadian National Coaching Devel-

opment Program, 1973-80. Co-chairman, 5th World Sport Psychology Congress, 1981; co-founder, Sport in Perspective, Inc. *Member:* International Society for Sport Psychology, Canadian Sport Psychology Society (member of executive committee, 1973-75).

WRITINGS: (With Cal Botterill) *Every Kid Can Win,* Nelson-Hall, 1975; *The Cooperative Sports and Games Book,* Pantheon, 1978; *Winning through Cooperation,* Acropolis, 1978; *In Pursuit of Excellence,* Human Kinetics, 1980; *The Second Cooperative Sports and Games Book,* Pantheon, 1982.

Contributor: B. S. Rushall, editor, *The Status of Psychomotor Learning and Sport Psychology Research,* Sport Science Association, 1975; T. Craig, editor, *The Humanistic and Mental Health Aspects of Sports, Exercise, and Recreation,* American Medical Association, 1976; J. S. Salmela, editor, *The Advanced Study of Gymnastics,* C. C Thomas, 1976; G. Roberts and K. Newell, editors, *Psychology of Motor Behavior and Sport,* Human Kinetics, 1978; R. Martens, editor, *Joy and Sadness in Children's Sports,* Human Kinetics, 1978; F. Smoll and R. Smith, editors, *Psychological Perspectives in Youth Sports,* Hemisphere Publishing, 1978; D. S. Eitzen, editor, *Sport in Contemporary Society,* St. Martin's, 1979; M. J. Melnick, editor, *Sport Sociology: Contemporary Themes,* Kendall/Hunt, 1979; L. Sinclair, editor, *Gymnastics: Everything You Wanted to Know,* Canadian Gymnastics Federation, 1980; J. Knight, editor, *All about Play: A Handbook of Resources on Children's Play,* Canadian Council on Children and Youth, 1980; P. Klavora and K. Wipper, editors, *Psychological and Sociological Factors in Sport,* School of Physical Education, University of Toronto, 1980.

Contributor to proceedings. Contributor of articles to *Canadian Runner, Coaching Review, Cooperative Games Newsletter, CAHPER Journal, Recreation Research Review,* and *Mouvement.*

WORK IN PROGRESS: Cross cultural work on playstyles and lifestyles; writings for and about young people; work on stress control and personal growth for those "living in the fast lane of life."

SIDELIGHTS: Terrance Orlick told *CA:* "Some of my greatest reflections and insights about my own culture have come about as a result of visiting and living with such peoples as the Inuit (Eskimo) from the Arctic Circle, the Australian Aborigines, and the Konga people from Papua New Guinea. I write primarily to reach people in hopes of touching the world in which I live in a constructive way." *The Cooperative Sports and Games Book* has been translated into Swedish, Finnish, German, and Russian.

AVOCATIONAL INTERESTS: Travel, outdoor sports ("especially cross country ski touring, canoeing, playing and loving").

*   *   *

OSBORN, John Jay, Jr. 1945-

PERSONAL: Born August 5, 1945; son of John Jay and Anne (Kidder) Osborn; married Emilie H. S., 1968. *Education:* Harvard University, B.A., 1967, J.D., 1970. *Religion:* Episcopal. *Home:* 4695 Independence Ave., Riverdale, New York, N.Y. 10471.

CAREER: Admitted to Bar of State of New York, 1974; practicing attorney, 1974—.

WRITINGS: The Paper Chase, Houghton, 1971; *The Only Thing I've Done Wrong,* Houghton, 1977; *The Associates,* Houghton,

1979; *The Man Who Owned New York,* Houghton, 1981. Contributor to *Yachting.*

SIDELIGHTS: John Jay Osborn's novels deal with characters in the legal profession and are based on his own experiences as a lawyer. "We may normally think of contracts and corporate law as lying just a little beyond our ken," Christopher Lehmann-Haupt writes in the *New York Times,* "but in Mr. Osborn's hands such legal arcana seem as accessible as the rules for Parcheesi."

Osborn's first novel, *The Paper Chase,* tells of a young law student at Harvard University. Written while Osborn was himself attending Harvard Law School, the novel has been cited for its accurate portrayal of university life. "Seldom has the bleakness and despair of American college life been portrayed with such immediacy and truth," writes L. J. Davis of *Book World.* A. L. Fessler of *Library Journal* calls it a "terse, dramatic novel . . . about what takes place behind the scenes at Harvard."

In subsequent novels, Osborn continued to explore the legal world. *The Associates,* for example, a novel about a young lawyer at a large New York law firm, earned praise for its realism. "The novel captures well," writes Diana Vincent-Davis of *Library Journal,* "the insularity of a high-powered firm, and has some extremely funny incidents." With *The Man Who Owned New York,* however, Osborn expanded his horizons. Although the novel concerns another lawyer and his problems in settling an estate, it is also, as Carol Eisen Rinzler of the *Washington Post* states, an "attempt to reach beyond entertainment. . . . With *The Man Who Owned New York* [Osborn] has determined to leave his comfortable niche as a clever chronicler of fledgling counselors. . . . He appears to have cast his lot with literature. At its worst, his novel is better than most, and one wishes him the best."

MEDIA ADAPTATIONS: The Paper Chase was filmed by Twentieth Century-Fox in 1974 and was adapted as a television series.

BIOGRAPHICAL/CRITICAL SOURCES: Library Journal, June 15, 1971, September 1, 1971, April 15, 1979; *Best Sellers,* August 15, 1971; *Book World,* September 12, 1971; *Publishers Weekly,* January 10, 1977; *New York Times,* February 22, 1979; *Washington Post,* February 22, 1979, June 13, 1981; *New York Times Book Review,* February 25, 1979; *Time,* March 26, 1979; *New Yorker,* April 16, 1979; *Virginia Quarterly Review,* summer, 1979; *Chicago Tribune Book World,* May 24, 1981.

*   *   *

OSBORNE, Harold 1905-

PERSONAL: Born in 1905, in London, England; son of Owen John (a teacher) and Dulcibella Eden (Greville) Osborne. *Education:* Cambridge University, M.A. *Home:* Kreuzstrasse 12, 8640 Rapperswil, S. G., Switzerland.

CAREER: Former British civil servant; attached to staff of British Embassy in La Paz, Bolivia, 1947-52. *Member:* International Committee for Aesthetics (vice-president), British Society of Aesthetics (president), Mind Association, Aristotelian Society.

WRITINGS: Foundations of the Philosophy of Value, Cambridge University Press, 1933; *A Mirror of Charactery,* University Tutorial Press, 1935; *Indians of the Andes,* Routledge & Kegan Paul, 1952; *Theory of Beauty,* Routledge & Kegan Paul, 1952; *Bolivia: A Land Divided,* Oxford University Press, 1954, 3rd edition, 1964; *Aesthetics and Criticism,* Routledge & Kegan Paul, 1955; *Aesthetics and Art Theory,* Longmans,

Green, 1968, Dutton, 1970; *Aesthetics in the Modern World,* Thames & Hudson, 1968; *South American Mythology,* Hamlyn, 1968; (editor) Francis Bacon, *New Atlantis,* University Tutorial Press, 1969; *The Art of Appreciation,* Oxford University Press, 1970; (editor) *The Oxford Companion to Art,* Clarendon Press, 1970; *Aesthetics,* Oxford University Press, 1972; (editor) *The Oxford Companion to the Decorative Arts,* Oxford University Press, 1975; *Abstraction and Artifice in Twentieth-Century Art,* Oxford University Press, 1979; (editor) *The Oxford Companion to Twentieth-Century Art,* Oxford University Press, 1981. Former editor, *British Journal of Aesthetics.*

SIDELIGHTS: Harold Osborne is competent in French, Spanish, German, and Polish and knows ancient Greek and Latin. *Avocational interests:* South American art and culture, aesthetics and philosophy.

*   *   *

OST, David H(arry) 1940-

PERSONAL: Born February 1, 1940, in Parkers Prairie, Minn.; son of Harry and Adele (Ostgarrd) Ost; married Belva J. Massie, September 24, 1960 (divorced May 30, 1975); married Linda Jean Clay, December 31, 1975; children: (first marriage) Dee Ann Carol, Phillip Douglas, John Mathew. *Education:* Augsburg College, B.A., 1961; University of Michigan, M.A., 1965; University of Iowa, Ph.D., 1970. *Home:* 6430 Dena Ct., Bakersfield, Calif. 93308 *Office:* Department of Biology, California State College, 9001 Stockdale Hwy., Bakersfield, Calif. 93309.

CAREER: Biology teacher in public schools of Owatonna, Minn., 1961-64; Wisconsin State University—Platteville, instructor in biology, 1965-66; Carthage College, Kenosha, Wis., assistant professor of biology, 1966-67; University of Iowa, Iowa City, instructor in science education, 1967-70; California State College at Bakersfield, associate professor, 1971-74, professor of education and biology, 1974-77, professor of biology and chairman of department, 1977—. Coordinator of teacher education program in science and mathematics, American Association for the Advancement of Science, 1970. Director of Center for Professional Development, 1975-77; director of numerous projects or programs for Education Development Center, 1971-72, and National Science Foundation, 1972-76 and 1980-81. Member of advisory boards, Unified Science and Mathematics for Elementary School, 1972-74, National Consortium for Interdisciplinary Real Problem Solving, 1974-75, National Assessment of Educational Progress, 1974-76, and Energy Consortium Advisory Council, 1978-80. Consultant for elementary science study implementation, Webster Division, McGraw-Hill Book Co., 1973—, and Harcourt Brace Jovanovich, Inc., 1977-81.

MEMBER: Association for the Education of Teachers in Science (member of board of directors, 1974-76; president, 1977-78; member of executive committee, 1976-79), National Association of Biology Teachers (life member; vice-president, 1975; member of board of directors, 1975-77), National Education Association (life member), American Association for the Advancement of Science, National Association for Research in Science Teaching, National Science Teachers Association (life member; member of board of directors, 1977-78), School Science and Mathematics Association (life member; chairman of publications committee, 1972-75), American Association for Higher Education (life member), American Association of University Professors (chapter president, 1972-73). *Awards, honors:* Outstanding Young Science Educator's

Award nominee, Association for the Education of Teachers in Science, 1971 and 1973.

WRITINGS: A Laboratory Manual for a Survey of Science, University of Iowa Press, 1968; *Evolution,* Educational Methods, 1970, 2nd edition, 1977; (editor) *Guidelines for the Education of Secondary School Teachers of Science,* American Association for the Advancement of Science, 1971; *The Chemical Basis of Life,* Educational Methods, 1974; *Guide for Inservice Training in Elementary School Science,* Los Angeles County Schools, 1974; *Explorations in Professional Development: The First Three Years,* California State University and College System, 1977. Also author of series of three programmed texts, *DNA, Energy Relationships,* and *Human Reproduction.*

Contributor; all published by Education Development Center: *Protecting Property,* 1975; *Describing People,* 1975; *Ways to Learn,* 1976; *Growing Plants,* 1976. Contributor of numerous articles and reviews to journals, including *American Biology Teacher, Science Education News, Arithmetic Teacher,* and *Journal of Research in Science.* Chairman of editorial board, *Yearbook* of Association for the Education of Teachers in Science, 1973—.

*   *   *

OSTENDORF, (Arthur) Lloyd (Jr.) 1921-

PERSONAL: Born June 23, 1921, in Dayton, Ohio; son of Arthur Lloyd (an architect) and Edith C. (Stomps) Ostendorf; married Rita Mary Hoefler (a dancing teacher), December 30, 1941; children: Daniel Lee, Thomas Lloyd, Roxanne Louise. *Education:* Attended School of the Dayton Art Institute, 1939-42. *Home:* 225 Lookout Dr., Dayton, Ohio 45419. *Office:* Ostendorf Art Academy, 504 East Dorothy Lane, Kettering, Ohio 45419.

CAREER: Dayton Journal-Herald, Dayton, Ohio, newspaper artist, 1936-39; free-lance artist for periodical and book publishers, 1939—; Milton Caniff & Associates, New York, N.Y., cartoonist assistant, 1940; artist and illustrator, U.S. Government, Wright Field, 1941; Ostendorf Art Academy, Kettering, Ohio, director and teacher, 1969—. *Military service:* U.S. Army Air Forces, 1941-45; became technical sergeant. *Member:* Royal Society of Arts (London; fellow), Illinois State Historical Society, Dayton Society of Painters and Sculptors, Montgomery County Historical Society (vice-president, Dayton, 1957-59), Manuscript Society, Civil War Round Table of Dayton, Ohio (president, 1959, 1965). *Awards, honors:* Prize for design, for "Chicago Lincoln statue"; honorary member, Lincoln National Sesquicentennial Commission, 1959; Lincoln Memorial University, Diploma of Honor, 1966, Doctor of Arts, 1974; Doctor of Letters, Lincoln College, 1968.

WRITINGS: Mr. Lincoln Came to Dayton, Otterbein Press, 1959; *A Picture Story of Abraham Lincoln,* Lothrop, 1962; (with Charles Hamilton) *Lincoln in Photographs: An Album of Every Known Pose,* University of Oklahoma Press, 1963; *The Magnetism of Lincoln, the Faces of Lincoln,* Lincoln College (Lincoln, Ill.), 1968; *The Photographs of Mary Todd Lincoln,* Illinois State Historical Society, 1969; (with Adin Baber) *Sarah and Abe in Indiana,* Moore Publishing, 1970; *Abraham Lincoln: The Boy, the Man,* Lamplight, 1977; (with David W. Balsinger) *Mister Abe,* Celestial Arts, 1980.

Illustrator: *Illustrated Catechism,* Bruce Publishing, 1941; Sister Margaret Patrice, *The Keeper of the Gate,* Bruce Publishing, 1941; Gerald T. Brennan, *The Man Who Dared a King,* Bruce Publishing, 1941; Albert Paul Schimberg, *The Larks of Um-*

bria, Bruce Publishing, 1942; Arthur R. McGratty, *I'd Gladly Go Back,* Newman Press, 1951; *A Nation United,* Sadlier, 1952; Floyd Anderson, *The Bishop's Boy,* Bruce Publishing, 1957; Howard E. Crouch, *Brother Dutton of Molokai,* Bruce Publishing, 1958; Frank Dell'Isola, *The God-Man Jesus,* Bruce Publishing, 1959; *Our Faith, God's Great Gift,* Bruce Publishing, 1959; Charles J. Carmody, *Learning to Serve,* Bruce Publishing, 1961; Anamae Martin, *Columbus: The Buckeye Capital,* C. E. Merrill, 1962; Eva M. Betz, *The Quiet Flame: Mother Marianne of Molokai,* Bruce Publishing, 1963; V. H. Cassidy, *Long Ago in the Old World,* C. E. Merrill, 1964; *Chemistry: A Modern Course,* C. E. Merrill, 1965; Gladys E. Deck, *Meet the Holy Family,* Prow Books, 1978; Helen B. Walters, *No Luck for Lincoln . . . ,* Abingdon, 1981. Contributor to periodicals.

SIDELIGHTS: Lloyd Ostendorf owns the world's largest collection of photographs of Abraham Lincoln. He has spoken about Lincoln in lectures and during television appearances.

*   *   *

OXENHANDLER, Neal 1926-

PERSONAL: Born February 3, 1926, in St. Louis, Mo.; son of Joseph (an insurance broker) and Billie (Lutsky) Oxenhandler; married Jean Romano, June 23, 1951 (divorced, November, 1975); married Judith I. Menza, December, 1979; children: (first marriage) Noel, Daniel, Alica. *Education:* University of Chicago, A.B., 1948; University of Paris, graduate study, 1948-49; Columbia University, M.A., 1950; University of Florence, graduate study, 1953-54; Yale University, Ph.D., 1955. *Religion:* Roman Catholic. *Home:* Sawnee Bean Rd., Thetford Center, Vt. 05075. *Agent:* Gunther Stuhlmann, Author's Representative, P.O. Box 276, Becket, Mass. 01223. *Office:* Department of Languages and Literature, Dartmouth College, Hanover, N.H. 03755.

CAREER: St. Louis University, St. Louis, Mo., lecturer in French, 1950-51; Yale University, New Haven, Conn., assistant instructor, 1951-53, instructor in French, 1954-57; University of California, Los Angeles, assistant professor, 1957-60, associate professor of French, 1960-65; University of California, Santa Cruz, associate professor, 1965-66; professor of French, 1966-69; Dartmouth College, Hanover, N.H., professor of French, 1969—. Director of summer seminar on postmodern fiction, National Endowment for the Humanities, 1980. Consultant to French-American Foundation, 1980. *Member:* Society for Religion in Higher Education, Modern Language Association of America. *Awards, honors:* Fulbright fellow, 1953-54; Guggenheim fellow, 1961-62; disciplinary fellowship, Society for Religion in Higher Education, 1966-67.

WRITINGS: Scandal and Parade: The Theatre of Jean Cocteau, Rutgers University Press, 1957; (with Robert J. Nelson) *Aspects of French Literature: An Anthology along Critical Lines,* Appleton-Century-Crofts, 1961; *A Change of Gods* (novel), Harcourt, 1962; *Max Jacob and Les Feux de Paris* (monograph), University of California Press, 1964; (editor and author of introduction) *French Literary Criticism* (anthology in French), Prentice-Hall, 1966; (contributor) *The Quest for Imagination,* Press of Case Western Reserve University, 1971; (contributor) *French Literary Criticism,* University of Chicago Press, 1972; (contributor) Stanley J. Soloman, editor, *The Classic Cinema: Essays in Criticism,* Harcourt, 1973; (contributor) Mary A. Caws, editor, *About French Poetry from Dada to 'Tel Quel,'* Wayne State University Press, 1974. Also contributor of prose poem to *New Directions Anthology,* 1953, and essay on seven authors to *Lexikon Weltliterateur.* Contributor of more than twenty articles, poems, and reviews to journals, including *Perspective, Yale Review, French Review, Contemporary Literature, Chicago Review,* and *L'Esprit createur.* Advisory editor, *Film Quarterly.*

WORK IN PROGRESS: A study of literary narcissism; a book of personal essays.

SIDELIGHTS: Neal Oxenhandler told *CA:* "I write to solve the riddle of my own personality and, as a teacher, to help my students understand the great books of our culture. Today I work to combat a kind of literary criticism that has become dehumanizing and destructive of value. In my essays I am trying to capture some simple truths about being a father, about anger, about love and about the future of our civilization—if it has one."

*   *   *

OYLE, Irving 1925-

PERSONAL: Born September 12, 1925, in New York, N.Y.; son of Harry (a grocer) and Ethel (Ackiron) Oyle; married Pearl Ann Adler, February 11, 1951 (divorced, 1975); married Susan Jean Gordon, April 23, 1980; children: (first marriage) Julie, Frederick, Abby and Ben (twins). *Education:* City College (now City College of the City University of New York),

B.S., 1947; New York University, graduate study, 1947-49; Philadelphia College of Osteopathic Medicine and Surgery, D.O., 1953. *Politics:* Independent. *Religion:* "Alchemist." *Residence:* Hawaii.

CAREER: Physician and psychiatrist in private practice in New York, N.Y., 1955-70, in West Marin, Calif., 1970-75, and in Hawaii, 1975—. Associate clinical professor, University of Hawaii. Director, Spencer Church Health Service, 1968-70, and Headlands Healing Service, 1970-75. Lecturer at New York University, 1948-49.

WRITINGS: Magic, Mysticism & Modern Medicine, privately printed, 1973, Celestial Arts, 1976; *The Healing Mind,* Celestial Arts, 1975; *Time, Space, and Mind,* Celestial Arts, 1976; *The New American Medicine Show: Discovering the Healing Connection,* Unity Press, 1979. Contributor to *American Journal of Acupuncture.*

WORK IN PROGRESS: On Life and Living.

SIDELIGHTS: Irving Oyle was a hand puppeteer with the Bread & Puppet Theatre in New York City, 1960-66.

BIOGRAPHICAL/CRITICAL SOURCES: Marin Independent Journal, February 15, 1975; *San Francisco Examiner & Chronicle,* March 23, 1975; *Harpers' Weekly,* June, 1975.

P

PAINTER, Daniel
See BURGESS, M(ichael) R(oy)

*   *   *

PALMER, Alan Warwick 1926-

PERSONAL: Born September 28, 1926, in Ilford, Essex, England; son of Warwick Lindley and Edith (Perriam) Palmer; married Veronica Mary Cordell, September 1, 1951. *Education:* Oriel College, Oxford, M.A. and M.Litt., 1951. *Home:* 4 Farm End, Woodstock, Oxford, England. *Agent:* Campbell Thomson & McLaughlin Ltd., 31 Newington Green, London N16 9PU, England.

CAREER: Writer. Highgate School, London, England, assistant master, 1951-53, senior history master, 1953-69. *Military service:* Royal Navy, 1944-47. *Member:* Royal Society of Literature (fellow).

WRITINGS: Dictionary of Modern History, 1789-1945, Cresset, 1962; (with C. A. Macartney) *Independent Eastern Europe: A History,* Macmillan, 1962; *Yugoslavia,* Oxford University Press, 1964; *The Gardeners of Salonika,* Simon & Schuster, 1965; *Napoleon in Russia,* Simon & Schuster, 1967; *The Lands Between,* Weidenfeld & Nicolson, 1970; *Metternich,* Harper, 1972; *The Life and Times of George IV,* Weidenfeld & Nicolson, 1972; *Russia in War and Peace,* Macmillan, 1972; *Alexander I,* Harper, 1974; *Frederick the Great,* Weidenfeld & Nicolson, 1974; *Bismarck,* Scribner, 1976; (with wife, Veronica Palmer) *Quotations in History,* Harvester Press, 1976; *The Kaiser,* Scribner, 1978; *Princes of Wales,* Weidenfeld & Nicolson, 1979; *Dictionary of 20th Century History,* Facts on File, 1979; *Who's Who in Modern History,* Holt, 1980; (with Veronica Palmer) *Who's Who in Shakespeare's England,* St. Martin's, 1981.

WORK IN PROGRESS: The Chancelleries of Europe, 1814-1919; with wife, Veronica Palmer, a royal gazetteer of Great Britain.

AVOCATIONAL INTERESTS: Travel.

*   *   *

PANKHURST, Richard (Keir Pethick) 1927-

PERSONAL: Born December 3, 1927, in London, England; son of Sylvia Pankhurst; married. *Education:* London School of Economics and Political Science, B.Sc., 1949, Ph.D., 1952. *Home:* 22 Lawn Rd., London N.W.3, England.

CAREER: Addis Ababa University, Addis Ababa, Ethiopia, professor, beginning 1957, director of Institute of Ethiopian Studies, 1963-76; Royal Asiatic Society, London, England, currently librarian.

WRITINGS: (With mother, Sylvia Pankhurst) *Ethiopia and Eritrea: The Last Phase of the Reunion Struggle, 1941-1952,* Lalibela House Press, 1954; *William Thompson: Britain's Pioneer Socialist, Feminist, and Cooperator,* C. A. Watts, 1954; *Kenya: The History of Two Nations,* Independent Publishing Co., 1954; *The Saint Simonians, Mill and Carlyle: A Preface to Modern Thought,* Humanities, 1957, reprinted, Norwood, 1976.

An Introduction to the Economic History of Ethiopia from Early Times to 1800, Humanities, 1961; (editor with S. Chojnacki and William A. Shack) *Register of Current Research on Ethiopia and the Horn of Africa,* Haile Sellassie I University, 1963; *Some Historic Journeys in Ethiopia,* Oxford University Press, 1964; *The Great Ethiopian Famine of 1888-1892: A New Assessment,* Haile Sellassie I University, 1964.

Some Factors Depressing the Standard of Living of Peasants in Traditional Ethiopia, Faculty of Arts, University College, 1965; (editor) *Travellers in Ethiopia,* Oxford University Press, 1965; *State and Land in Ethiopian History,* Institute of Ethiopian Studies and Faculty of Law, Haile Sellassie I University, 1966; (editor) *The Ethiopian Royal Chronicles,* Oxford University Press, 1967; *An Introduction to the History of the Ethiopian Army,* Imperial Ethiopian Air Force, 1967; *Primitive Money, Money and Banking in Ethiopia,* [Addis Ababa], 1967; *A Brief Note on the Economic History of Ethiopia from 1800 to 1935,* Haile Sellassie I University, 1967; *Economic History of Ethiopia, 1800-1935,* Haile Sellassie I University Press, 1968; *The Penetration and Implications of Fire-Arms in Ethiopia Prior to the Nineteenth Century,* Haile Sellassie I University, 1968; (with Geoffrey Last) *A History of Ethiopia in Pictures,* Oxford University Press, 1969; *Language and Education in Ethiopia: Historical Background to the Post-War Period,* Haile Sellassie I University, 1969.

(Editor with Michael Belaynesh and S. Chojnacki) *The Dictionary of Ethiopian Biography,* Institute of Ethiopian Studies, Addis Ababa University, 1975; *Sylvia Pankhurst, Artist and Crusader: An Intimate Portrait,* Paddington, 1979; (editor and translator with Germa-Selassie Asfaw) *Tax Records and In-*

ventories of Emperor Tewodros of Ethiopia, 1855-1868, School of Oriental and African Studies, University of London, 1979.

* * *

PARKER, Don(ald) H(enry) 1912-

PERSONAL: Born April 18, 1912, in Syracuse, N.Y.; son of Henry Melvin and Ethel (Madden) Parker; married third wife, Lahoma Stull; children: (first marriage) Dona Jean (Mrs. Roger Sell). *Education:* Attended Jacksonville Junior College, 1946-48; University of Florida, B.A. (with honors), 1950, M.A., 1952; Columbia University, Ed.D., 1957. *Home address:* Heartsong House, P.O. Box 4855, Carmel, Calif., 93921. *Office:* Institute for Multilevel Learning International, 215 West Franklin, Monterey, Calif. 93940.

CAREER: Sears Roebuck & Co., all phases of retail department store work in southeastern United States, 1930-43, assistant store manager, 1943-46; Personnel Research Counselors (psychological testing and guidance service), Jacksonville, Fla., director, 1946-50; consultant in reading and psychology, Bradford County (Fla.) Public Schools, 1950-51; University of North Carolina at Chapel Hill, lecturer and director of Reading Laboratory, 1952-54; director of reading centers, Charlotte College, Charlotte, N.C., and Charlotte Public Schools, 1954-55; Columbia University, New York, N.Y., instructor in reading, 1955-57; University of Bridgeport, Bridgeport, Conn., professor of education and director of Reading Laboratory, 1957-58; Science Research Associates, Chicago, Ill., multilevel consultant in reading and general education, 1957-64; Institute for Multilevel Learning International, Monterey, Calif., co-founder, director, 1964—; Biofeedback Counseling Center, Monterey, Calif., director, 1976—. Psychologist, Childrens Home Society of Florida, 1948-50. Lecturer on multilevel philosophy, 1950—; has lectured in Europe, 1960, 1963, 1971, and 1978, in Southeast Asia, Australia, and New Zealand, 1969, and in Africa, India, Thailand, Hong Kong, and the Philippines, 1971; participant and lecturer, World Congress on Parapsychology and Psychotronics, Prague, 1973, and Monte Carlo, 1975. Consultant to U.S. Agency for International Development, Venezuela, 1965-67. *Military service:* U.S. Navy, 1943-45.

MEMBER: International Reading Association, International Association for Psychotronics Research, American Psychological Association, Science Teachers Association, American Personnel and Guidance Association, Association for Supervision and Curriculum Development, American Association for the Advancement of Science, National Council of Teachers of English, National Science Teachers Association, National Education Association, National Society for the Study of Education, Council for Basic Education, Phi Delta Kappa.

WRITINGS: Schooling for Individual Excellence, Thomas Nelson, 1963; (contributor) Albert Harris, editor, *Readings on Reading Instruction*, McKay, 1963; *Vocabulab Three*, Science Research Associates, 1968; *Schooling for What?*, McGraw, 1970; (with others) *The Metric System: Syllabus* (with cassette recordings), National Book Co., 1974. Also author of *Science Research Associates Reading Laboratories*, 1955—, *Science Research Associates Spelling Word Power Laboratories* (with Frederic Walker), 1960-63, and *Science Research Associates Learnings in Science Laboratories* (with Donald Stotler), 1963. Contributor to education journals in the United States, Canada, Australia, Argentina, and Venezuela.

WORK IN PROGRESS: Computerizing the *Science Research Associates Reading Laboratories;* research on "opening up the subconscious for better learning."

AVOCATIONAL INTERESTS: Reading, music, painting, sailing.

BIOGRAPHICAL/CRITICAL SOURCES: Clearing House, October, 1962.

* * *

PARKER, T(homas) H(enry) L(ouis) 1916-

PERSONAL: Born September 28, 1916, in Hampshire, England; son of Henry Frederick William and Louisa Pinyon (Sell) Parker; married Mary Angwin, 1940; children: Anne Elisabeth, Paul Thomas Angwin, David Charles. *Education:* Emmanuel College, Cambridge, B.A., 1935, M.A., 1942, B.D., 1950, D.D., 1961. *Home:* 72 Windsor Rd., Cambridge, England.

CAREER: Ordained deacon, Church of England, 1939, priest, 1940; curate in Chesham, England, 1939-42, Cambridge, England, 1942-45, and Cobham, England, 1945-48; vicar of country parishes in Lincolnshire and Cambridgeshire, England, 1948-71; University of Durham, Durham, England, lecturer, 1971-75, reader in theology, 1975-81, dean of Faculty of Divinity, 1979-81. Air raid warden, 1940-45. *Member:* International Calvin Congress (member of presidium), Renaissance Society, Cambridge Union Society.

WRITINGS: The Oracles of God, Lutterworth, 1947; *The Doctrine of the Knowledge of God*, Oliver & Boyd, 1952, Eerdmans, 1959, revised edition published as *Calvin's Doctrine of the Knowledge of God*, Oliver & Boyd, 1969; *Portrait of Calvin*, S.C.M. Press, 1954, Westminster, 1955; (editor and translator) *Calvin's Sermons on Isaiah 53*, James Clarke, 1956; (editor) *Essays in Christology for Karl Barth*, Lutterworth, 1956; (editor with J. I. McCord) *Service in Christ*, Epworth, 1966; (editor) *English Reformers*, Westminster, 1966; *Karl Barth*, Eerdmans, 1970; *Calvin's New Testament Commentaries*, S.C.M. Press, 1971; *John Calvin: A Biography*, Dent, 1975, Westminster, 1976; (editor) *Iohannis Calvini Commentarius in Epistolam Pauli ad Romanos*, E. J. Brill, 1981.

Translator: *Calvin's Commentary on John*, two volumes, Oliver & Boyd, 1959; (with David Cairns and E. Brunner) *Dogmatics*, Volume III, Lutterworth, 1962; *Calvin's Commentary on Galatians*, Oliver & Boyd, 1965; *Calvin's Commentary on Psalms*, Volume I, James Clarke, 1965; Calvin, *The Epistles of Paul the Apostle to the Galatians, Ephesians, Phillippians, and the Colossians*, Oliver & Boyd, 1965, Eerdmans, 1966; *Calvin's Commentary on the Harmony of the Gospels*, Volume II, Oliver & Boyd, 1972. Also co-translator and assistant editor of volumes in the "Church Dogmatics" series by Karl Barth, T. & T. Clark, 1956-69.

Contributor to *Encyclopaedia Britannica* and *Chambers's Encyclopaedia* and to various theology journals in Great Britain and Europe.

WORK IN PROGRESS: Research on sixteenth-century Roman Catholic and Reformed commentaries on *Romans;* an edition of *Sermons de Jean Calvin sur Isaie 30-42*, for *Supplementa Calviniana.*

AVOCATIONAL INTERESTS: Literature, music, cricket, bookbinding, gardening.

* * *

PARRY, Albert 1901-
(Victor Leclerc)

PERSONAL: Born February 24, 1901, in Rostov on-the-Don, Russia; naturalized citizen, 1926; son of Joseph and Elizabeth

(Blass) Parry; married Louise Emily Goodman, October 25, 1941 (divorced, 1971); children: James Donald, Thomas Hugh. *Education:* Attended Columbia University, 1921, 1925-26, University of California, Los Angeles, 1927; University of Chicago, A.B., 1935, Ph.D., 1938. *Politics:* Independent. *Home:* 6919 Place de la Paix, South Pasadena, St. Petersburg, Fla. 33707.

CAREER: Newspaper writing, magazine free-lancing, New York, N.Y., and Chicago, Ill., 1921-37; Consolidated Book Publishers, Inc., Chicago, editor, 1937-41; *Chicago Sun*, Chicago, research director, air edition (radio broadcasts), 1941-42; Northwestern University, Evanston, Ill., associate professor of political science, 1946-47; Colgate University, Hamilton, N.Y., associate professor, 1947-49, professor of Russian civilization and language, 1947-69, chairman of department of Russian Studies, 1949-69, director of Russian Area and Language Institutes, 1961-66; Case Western Reserve University, Cleveland, Ohio, professor of Russian civilization and language and chairman of department of Slavic and Eastern European languages, 1969-71. Assistant, Division of Social Sciences, University of Chicago, 1939; executive officer, Committee to Defend America by Aiding Allies, 1940-41, and Fight for Freedom Committee, 1941; program consultant, Radio Free Europe, 1950-52; visiting scholar, Radio Liberty (Munich), 1967-68. Visiting lecturer, U.S. Army War College, 1958-72, and Inter-American Defense College, 1962-68. Consultant, Special Operations Research Office, Department of the Army, 1960. *Military service:* Office of Strategic Services, information officer, 1942-45. *Member:* American Association of Teachers of Slavic and East European Languages (president, 1961), American Association for the Advancement of Slavic Studies, Phi Beta Kappa. *Awards, honors:* American Council of Learned Societies grant, 1961; Humanities Fund, Inc. grant, 1961; Human Ecology Fund grant, 1962; U.S. Office of Education grant and Modern Language Association of America grant, both 1965-66.

WRITINGS: Tattoo, Simon & Schuster, 1933, reprinted, Collier, 1971; *Garrets and Pretenders: A History of Bohemianism in America*, Covici-Friede, 1933, revised edition, Dover, 1960; *Whistler's Father*, Bobbs-Merrill, 1939; (with Williams) *Riddle of the Reich*, Prentice-Hall, 1941; *Russian Cavalcade: A Military Record*, I. Washburn, 1944; (contributor) Bernadotte E. Schmitt, *Some Historians of Modern Europe*, University of Chicago Press, 1942; (translator and editor) Simon Liberman, *Building Lenin's Russia*, University of Chicago Press, 1945, reprinted, Hyperion Press, 1978; (with others) *Korea, an Annotated Bibliography*, Library of Congress, 1950; (with Harnett T. Kane, under pseudonym Victor Leclerc) *Scandalous Mrs. Blackford*, Messner, 1957; *Russia's Rockets and Missiles*, Doubleday, 1960; *The New Class Divided: Science and Technology versus Communism*, Macmillan, 1966; *America Learns Russian*, Syracuse University Press, 1967; (editor and translator) *Peter Kapitsa on Life and Science*, Macmillan, 1968; (translator) Boris A. Kordemsky, *Moscow Puzzles*, Scribner, 1972; *The Russian Scientist*, Macmillan, 1973; (with Harry T. Moore) *Twentieth Century Russian Literature*, Southern Illinois University Press, 1974; *Terrorism: From Robespierre to Arafat*, Vanguard, 1976. Regular columnist, "Soviet Affairs," *Missiles and Rockets*, 1957-63.

SIDELIGHTS: Albert Parry's articles about Russian rocketry met with something less than enthusiasm from publishers until 1954 when *The Reporter* published his "Will the Russians Beat Us to the Moon?" In 1957, he forecast Russia's first satellite, less than three weeks before the launching of Sputnik I. His periodic appearances on television since then have dealt largely with problems of Soviet science and politics.

BIOGRAPHICAL/CRITICAL SOURCES: Book Week, August 7, 1966; *New York Times Book Review*, December 22, 1968.

* * *

PARRY, J(ohn) H(orace)   1914-

PERSONAL: Born April 26, 1914, in Handsworth, England; came to United States in 1965; son of Walter Austin (a teacher) and Ethel (Piddock) Parry; married Joyce Carter, March 18, 1939; children: Michael, Joanna Garth Dales, Katharine, Elizabeth. *Education:* Clare College, Cambridge, M.A. and Ph.D., 1938; additional studies at Harvard University, 1936-37. *Home:* Pinnacle Rd., Harvard, Mass. 01451. *Office:* Widener Library 45, Cambridge, Mass.

CAREER: Cambridge University, Clare College, Cambridge, England, tutor, 1945-49, senior proctor, 1947-48, university lecturer in history, 1946-49; University College of the West Indies, Kingston, Jamaica, professor of modern history, 1949-56; University College, Ibadan, Nigeria, principal, 1956-60; University College of Swansea, Swansea, Wales, principal, 1960-65; University of Wales, Cardiff, vice-chancellor, 1963-65; Harvard University, Cambridge, Mass., Gardiner Professor of Oceanic History and Affairs, 1965—. Visiting professor, Harvard University, 1954-55. Vice-president, Royal Institution of South Wales, 1960-65; governor, Christ College, Brecon, and Badminton School, Westburyon-Trym, Bristol. Member of executive committee, Swansea Festival of Music and Arts; member of council, Hakluyt Society, 1962-65. *Military service:* Royal Navy, 1940-45; became lieutenant commander.

MEMBER: American Philosophical Society, American Academy of Arts and Sciences (fellow), Royal Historical Society (fellow), Society for Nautical Research, Harvard Club (New York City), Odd Volumes Club (Boston), Oxford Club, Cambridge Club, Athenaeum (London), United University Club. *Awards, honors:* Order of the British Empire, 1942; Companion of the Order of St. Michael and St. George, 1960; L.L.D., University of Ceara, 1964; Commander of the Order of Alfonso X (Spain), 1976.

WRITINGS: The Spanish Theory of Empire in the Sixteenth Century, Cambridge University Press, 1940, reprinted, Richard West, 1978; *The Audiencia of New Galicia in the Sixteenth Century: A Study in Spanish Colonial Government*, Cambridge University Press, 1949, reprinted, 1968; *Europe and a Wider World, 1415-1715*, Hutchinson, 1949, 3rd edition published as *The Establishment of the European Hegemony, 1415-1715: Trade and Exploration in the Age of the Renaissance*, Harper, 1966; *The Sale of Public Office in the Spanish Indies*, University of California Press, 1953; (with P. M. Sherlock) *A Short History of the West Indies*, Macmillan, 1956, 3rd edition, St. Martin's, 1971; *The Age of Reconnaissance*, World Publishing, 1963, 2nd edition, Weidenfeld & Nicolson, 1966; *The Spanish Seaborne Empire*, Knopf, 1966; (editor) *The European Reconnaissance*, Walker & Co., 1968; *Trade and Dominion: The European Overseas Empires in the Eighteenth Century*, Praeger, 1971; *The Discovery of the Sea*, Dial, 1974; *The Discovery of South America*, Taplinger, 1979. Consultant, *Pizarro and the Conquest of Peru*, by Ceil Howard, American Heritage Publishing Co., 1968. Author of reviews for British Broadcasting Corp.; contributor of articles and reviews to professional journals.

AVOCATIONAL INTERESTS: Sailing, fishing, mountain walking, ornithology.†

PASCAL, Roy   1904-1980

PERSONAL: Born February 28, 1904, in Birmingham, England; died August 24, 1980, in Birmingham; son of Colin Sidney (a grocer) and Mary (Edmonds) Pascal; married Feiga Polianovska, June 27, 1931; children: Rachel Mary Pascal Moss, Susan Elizabeth Pascal Turner. *Education:* Pembroke College, Cambridge, B.A. (first class honors), 1927; graduate study at University of Berlin, 1927-28, and University of Munich, 1928. *Home:* 102 Witherford Way, Birmingham 29, England.

CAREER: Cambridge University, Pembroke College, Cambridge, England, fellow, 1929-39, university lecturer in German, 1934-39, director of modern language studies, 1936-39; University of Birmingham, Birmingham, England, professor of German, 1939-69. *Member:* British Academy (fellow), Association of University Teachers of Great Britain (president, 1944-45), Conference of University Teachers of German (chairman, 1959-61), English Goethe Society (member of council), Modern Language Association. *Awards, honors:* Litt.D., Cambridge University, 1953; J. G. Robertson Prize, University of London, 1956, for *The German Sturm und Drang;* Gold Medal, Goethe Institut, 1965; Shakespeare Prize, Hamburg, 1969; LL.D., University of Birmingham, 1974; honorary fellow, Pembroke College, Cambridge University, 1976; D.Litt., University of Warwick, 1979.

WRITINGS: Martin Luther: The Social Basis of the German Reformation, C. A. Watts, 1933, reprinted, Augustus Kelley, 1971; *The Nazi Dictatorship,* Routledge, 1934; *Shakespeare in Germany, 1740-1815,* Cambridge University Press, 1937, reprinted, Norwood, 1976; (editor and author of introduction) Karl Marx and Friedrich Engels, *German Ideology,* Lawrence, 1938, International Publishers, 1939; (contributor) *The German Mind and Outlook,* Chapman, 1945; *The Growth of Modern Germany,* Cobbett Press, 1946, reprinted, Russell, 1969; *The German Sturm und Drang,* University of Manchester Press, 1953, reprinted, 1968; *The German Novel,* University of Manchester Press, 1956; (author of introduction) Friedrich Nietzsche, *Thus Spake Zarathustra,* Dent, 1958; *Design and Truth in Autobiography,* Routledge & Kegan Paul, 1959; (with Hannah Priebsch Closs) *Introduction to German Literature,* Volume II: *German Literature in the Sixteenth and Seventeenth Centuries,* Barnes & Noble, 1968; *From Naturalism to Expressionism: German Literature and Society, 1880-1918,* Basic Books, 1973; *Culture and the Division of Labour: Three Essays on Literary Culture in Germany,* University of Warwick, 1974; *The Dual Voice: Free Indirect Speech and Its Functioning in the Nineteenth-Century European Novel,* Rowman & Littlefield, 1977.

Also author of *The German Revolution: 1848,* 1948. Contributor to books, including *Essays on Goethe,* 1949, *The Third Reich,* edited by Vermeil, 1955, *Stil und Formprobleme in der Literatur,* edited by P. Boeckmann, 1959, and *Spaetzeiten,* edited by Kohlschmidt, 1962, and to presentation volumes in honor of R.L.G. Ritchie, 1949, L. A. Willoughby, 1952, H. A. Korff, 1957, J. Boyd, 1959, W. H. Bruford, 1962, K. Hoppe, 1962, P. Boeckmann, 1964, and F. Martini, 1969. Contributor to *Encyclopaedia Britannica* and to professional journals.

WORK IN PROGRESS: Research on Brecht and Shakespeare.

AVOCATIONAL INTERESTS: Carpentry, fishing.†

*   *   *

PASSMORE, John (Arthur)   1914-

PERSONAL: Born September 9, 1914, in Manly, New South Wales, Australia; son of Frederick Maurice (a pay clerk) and Ruby (Moule) Passmore; married Annie Doris Sumner, December 16, 1936; children: Helen Katherine (Mrs. Paul Hoffmann), Diana Margaret. *Education:* University of Sydney, B.A., 1934, M.A., 1940. *Office:* Australian National University, Canberra, Australian Capital Territory, Australia.

CAREER: University of Sydney, Sydney, New South Wales, Australia, successively tutor, lecturer, and senior lecturer in philosophy, 1935-49; University of Otago, Dunedin, New Zealand, professor of philosophy, 1950-55; Australian National University, Institute of Advanced Studies, Canberra, reader, then professor of philosophy, 1956-79, university fellow, 1980—. Ziskind Visiting Professor at Brandeis University, 1960; visiting fellow at All Souls College, Oxford University, 1970 and 1978, and Clare Hall, Cambridge University, 1973 and 1980. *Member:* Australian Academy of the Humanities (president, 1974-77), Australian Academy of the Social Sciences, American Academy of Arts and Sciences (foreign honorary member), Australian Association of Psychology and Philosophy, British Academy (corresponding fellow), Danish Academy (foreign member), Institut International de Philosophie.

WRITINGS: T. S. Eliot, Sydney University Literary Society, 1934; *Reading and Remembering,* Melbourne University Press, 1942; *Talking Things Over,* Melbourne University Press, 1945, 4th edition, 1969; *Ralph Cudworth,* Cambridge University Press, 1951; *Hume's Intentions,* Cambridge University Press, 1952, 3rd edition, Duckworth, 1980; *A Hundred Years of Philosophy,* Duckworth, 1957, 2nd edition, 1966.

Philosophical Reasoning, Duckworth, 1961, 2nd edition, 1970; (contributor) *The Pattern of Australian Culture,* Cornell University Press, 1963; (contributor) *Princeton Studies,* Prentice-Hall, 1964; (editor and author of introduction) *Joseph Priestley: Writings on Philosophy, Science, and Politics,* Macmillan, 1965; *The Perfectibility of Man,* Duckworth, 1970, Scribner, 1971; *Man's Responsibility for Nature,* Scribner, 1974, 2nd edition, Duckworth, 1980; *Science and Anti-Science,* Rutgers University Press, 1978; *Philosophy of Teaching,* Harvard University Press, 1981. Contributor to collections of essays; author of introductions to various books. Contributor to *Encyclopaedia Britannica, Encyclopedia Americana, Collier's Encyclopedia, Encyclopedia of Philosophy, Encyclopedia of the History of Ideas,* and to philosophical journals. Editor, *Australian Journal of Philosophy,* 1947-49.

WORK IN PROGRESS: Essays on the philosophy of university education; a book on the seriousness of the arts; a book on the limits of government.

SIDELIGHTS: John Passmore states: ''One principal objective has dominated my work: to defend the claims of the critical imagination against, on the one side, the view that thought consists either in pure reason or pure observation and, on the other side, against uncritical fancy. I hope to strengthen the spirit of moderation against any sort of fanaticism, but in the manner which allows for the supreme importance of enthusiastic devotion.''

*   *   *

PATERSON, John Harris   1923-

PERSONAL: Born September 23, 1923, in London, England; son of George (a pastor) and Edith (Chapman) Paterson; married Evangeline Warke, September 13, 1952; children: Ronan, Michael, Carolyn. *Education:* Cambridge University, B.A., 1948; University of Wisconsin, M.A., 1950. *Home:* 2 Stoneygate Ave., Leicester, England. *Office:* Department of Geography, University of Leicester, Leicester, England.

CAREER: Cambridge University, Cambridge, England, assistant lecturer in geography, 1951-56; University of St. Andrews, St. Andrews, Scotland, 1956-74, began as lecturer, became senior lecturer; University of Leicester, Leicester, England, professor of geography, 1975—. *Military service:* British Army, Royal Artillery, 1942-47; became captain. *Member:* Institute of British Geographers.

WRITINGS: North America: A Regional Geography, Oxford University Press, 1960, 3rd edition published as *North America: A Geography of Canada and the United States,* 1965, 6th edition, 1979; *The Greatness of Christ,* Evangelical, 1962, Revell, 1963; *Land, Work and Resources,* Edward Arnold, 1972, 2nd edition, 1976. Contributor to *Chambers's Encyclopaedia, Everyman's Encyclopaedia, Encyclopaedia Britannica,* and *Encyclopedia Americana.*

*   *   *

PAULSON, Jack
See JACKSON, C(aary) Paul

*   *   *

PEARLMAN, Maurice   1911-
(Moshe Pearlman)

PERSONAL: Born March 23, 1911, in London, England; emigrated to Israel in 1948; son of Lipman and Rebecca (Winegarten) Pearlman. *Education:* University of London, B.Sc., 1933. *Religion:* Jewish. *Home:* 16 David Marcus St., Jerusalem, Israel.

CAREER: Government Press Division, Jerusalem, Israel, director, chief government spokesman, and chief army spokesman, 1949-52; Israel Broadcasting Service, Jerusalem, director, 1952-55; director of Information Services and public affairs adviser to Prime Minister, Government of Israel, 1955-60; full-time writer, 1960—. Representative of Government of Israel on various missions, primarily to new states of Africa, 1958-60; special assistant to Minister of Defense during Six Day War, 1967. *Military service:* British Army, Royal Artillery, 1940-46; served in North Africa, Italy, and Greece campaigns; became major. Israel Army, 1948-49; became colonel.

WRITINGS—All under name Moshe Pearlman: Collective Adventure (also see below), Heinemann, 1938; *Mufti of Jerusalem,* Gollancz, 1947; *Adventure in the Sun: An Informal Account of the Communal Settlements of Palestine* (based on *Collective Adventure*), Gollancz, 1948; *The Army of Israel,* Philosophical Library, 1950; (contributor) *Irregulars, Partisans, Guerrillas,* Simon & Schuster, 1954; *The Capture and Trial of Adolf Eichmann,* Simon & Schuster, 1963; (translator) Y. Yadin, *The Art of Warfare in Biblical Lands in the Light of Archaeological Study,* McGraw, 1963; (with Joan Comay) *Israel,* Macmillan, 1964; (with Yaacov Yannai) *Historical Sites in Israel,* W. H. Allen, 1964, Vanguard, 1965, revised edition, Simon & Schuster, 1969; *Ben Gurion Looks Back,* Simon & Schuster, 1965; (translator) Yadin, *Masada: Herod's Fortress and the Zealots' Last Stand,* Random House, 1966; *The Zealots of Masada: Story of a Dig,* Scribner, 1967; (with T. Kollek) *Jerusalem: A History of Forty Centuries,* Random House, 1968 (published in England as *Jerusalem: Sacred City of Mankind,* Weidenfeld & Nicolson, 1968); (with Kollek) *Pilgrims to the Holy Land,* Harper, 1970; *The Maccabees,* Macmillan, 1973; *The First Days of Israel in the Footsteps of Moses* (also see below), World Publishing, 1973 (published in England as *In*

the Footsteps of Moses, Cassell, 1974); *Moses: Where It All Began* (adapatation of *The First Days of Israel in the Footsteps of Moses*), Abelard-Schuman, 1974; *In the Footsteps of the Prophets,* Crowell, 1975; *Digging up the Bible: The Stories behind the Great Archaeological Discoveries in the Holy Land,* Morrow, 1980.

BIOGRAPHICAL/CRITICAL SOURCES: Best Sellers, February 1, 1968, November 1, 1968; *Times Literary Supplement,* October 16, 1969; *Los Angeles Times,* October 9, 1980.

*   *   *

PEARLMAN, Moshe
See PEARLMAN, Maurice

*   *   *

PEARSON, Andrew Russell   1897-1969
(Drew Pearson)

PERSONAL: Born December 13, 1897, in Evanston, Ill.; died September 1, 1969, in Washington, D.C.; son of Paul Martin and Edna (Wolfe) Pearson; married Countess Felicia Gizycka, March 12, 1925 (divorced); married Luvie Moore, November 12, 1936; children: (first marriage) Ellen Pearson Arnold. *Education:* Swarthmore College, A.B., 1919. *Religion:* Quaker.

CAREER: Director of American Friends Service Committee in Serbia, Montenegro, and Albania, 1919-21; University of Pennsylvania, Philadelphia, instructor in industrial geography, 1921-22; Columbia University, New York, N.Y., lecturer in commercial geography, 1924; staff member, *United States Daily,* 1926-33, and *Baltimore Sun,* Baltimore, Md., 1929-32; author with Robert S. Allen of syndicated newspaper column "Washington Merry-Go-Round," 1932-42, sole author of column, beginning 1942, author with Jack Anderson, 1965-69. Occasional correspondent in Far East and Europe, 1922-31 and 1942-59; interviewed "Europe's Twelve Greatest Men" for newspaper syndicate, 1923, and also Premier Khrushchev, 1961 and 1963, President Tito, 1962, the King and Queen of Greece, and Premier Fanfani of Italy; accompanied President Kennedy to Venezuela and Colombia, 1962. Weekly radio commentator, beginning 1935. Organized Friendship Train to Europe, 1947-48; president, Food for Peace Committee, beginning 1961; secretary, America's Conscience Fund, beginning 1963; president of Washington, D.C., chapter, Big Brothers. *Military service:* U.S. Army, 1918.

MEMBER: International Platform Association (president, 1950), Overseas Writers, National Press Club, Circus Fans of America, Phi Beta Kappa, Kappa Sigma, Delta Sigma Rho, Cosmos Club (Washington, D.C.). *Awards, honors:* LL.D., Harding College, 1945, and William Jewell College, 1948; Sigma Delta Chi national award for best Washington journalism, 1942; Father of the Year, 1948; Knights of Columbus International Gold Medal, 1948; French Legion of Honor; First Order Star of Solidarity (Italian Republic); Variety Club Heart of Gold Award, 1963; Pulitzer Prize nomination (with Jack Anderson) for national reporting, 1967, for articles on U.S. Senator Thomas J. Dodd.

WRITINGS—All under name Drew Pearson: (With Robert S. Allen) *Washington Merry-Go-Round,* Liveright, 1931; (with Allen) *More Merry-Go-Round,* Liveright, 1932; (with Constantine Brown) *The American Diplomatic Game,* Doubleday, Doran, 1935; (with Allen) *The Nine Old Men,* Doubleday, Doran, 1937, reprinted, Da Capo Press, 1974; (with Allen) *Nine Old Men at the Crossroads,* Doubleday, Doran, 1937, reprinted, Da Capo Press, 1974; (with Jack Anderson) *U.S.A.:*

Second-Class Power?, Simon & Schuster, 1958; (with Anderson) *The Case against Congress*, Simon & Schuster, 1968; (with Gerald Green) *The Senator* (novel), Doubleday, 1968; (with Green) *The President* (novel), Doubleday, 1970; *Diaries: 1949-1959*, edited by Tyler Abell, Holt, 1974.

Also author with Robert S. Allen of comic strip "Hap Hazard," 1941, and of radio program "News for the Americas," National Broadcasting Co., Inc., 1941; author of television films "Report on the Holy Land," "Report on Alaska," and "The Gentle Persuaders." Editor of weekly newsletter, *Personal from Pearson*, beginning 1953. Contributor to magazines.

SIDELIGHTS: The most widely read columnist of his day, Drew Pearson specialized in reporting what the *New Republic*'s C. W. Gilbert once called "the gossip which the Capital loves to whisper but hates to see in print." At its peak, his "Washington Merry-Go-Round" feature ran in 600 papers seven days a week, reaching an audience of about forty million people. During the course of his long career, Pearson's "aggressive, raucous, and occasionally sensational" exposes (as another *New Republic* writer described them) led some 275 people to file more than $200 million worth of lawsuits against the columnist, only one of which he lost—for $50,000. Vilified by those he attacked (including J. Edgar Hoover, Robert Kennedy, and Joseph McCarthy) and praised by those who escaped his eye for scandal, Pearson regarded himself as a "voice for the voiceless," or, as *Time*'s Michael Demarest stated, "a kind of national ombudsman." But his greatest contribution was not the *amount* of wrongdoing he exposed; more important, noted Demarest, was the fact that Pearson's "impassioned" approach to weeding out corruption in government circles established "a pattern of investigative reporting [that] permanently emboldened American journalism."

Heir to a crusading tradition that made its first appearance in America around the turn of the century, Pearson launched his career in 1931 when he teamed up with fellow reporter Robert S. Allen to produce an anonymous, gossipy account of behind-the-scenes life in Washington, *The Washington Merry-Go-Round*. Pearson, then with the *Baltimore Sun*, and Allen, a *Christian Science Monitor* bureau chief, packed their controversial book with inside material on the Hoover administration their own papers had refused to publish. After they were revealed as the authors of *The Washington Merry-Go-Round*, both men were fired from their respective newspapers. A short time later, however, Pearson and Allen signed up with United Features to write a syndicated column (also called "Washington Merry-Go-Round") modeled after their original collaboration. The two men worked together on the column for the next ten years; when Allen joined the Army in 1942, Pearson began writing alone and continued to do so until the late 1950s when one of his investigators, Jack Anderson, became his associate. Anderson then took over the column after Pearson's death in 1969.

Most observers, even those who felt, such as Demarest, that Pearson "was often unfair, egotistical and quixotic" in his relentless pursuit of government figures, agreed that "for all his vanities and vendettas, [he] was a valuable man." The *Washington Post*, for example, remarked that "he was a moralist who was proud to be a muckraker," a man who exhibited "the conscience of a Quaker and the touch of a stevedore" during "his extraordinary career as the most successful, in many ways the most effective, and certainly the most controversial journalist of his time. . . . Most of the time he had the right targets and the right causes, and he brought to his crusades a powerful, innovative and relentless force." As the *New York Times Book Review*'s C. V. Shannon declared: "[Pearson] had the curiosity, the physical energy, the quickness of mind and

the gritty determination to be on top of every story and to elbow himself to the front of every crowd that mark the journalist in his purest form." To the *Chicago Tribune Book World*'s Robert Sherrill, Pearson was simply "the greatest muckraker of all time. Woodward and Bernstein may have toppled Richard Nixon, but as practitioners of muckraking they are drab apprentices compared to Pearson. . . . [But he] was not merely a muckraker; he was the embodiment of everything in the unregenerate press that politicians and corporate malefactors hate and fear—and grudgingly respect. Reporting was just one gun in his arsenal. He was also [, according to his longtime colleague Jack Anderson,] the 'maximum politico—part intelligence sleuth, part commentator, part lobbyist, part conspirator, part caucus-master.' In his quiet, Quaker fashion he could play dirty as hell."

Not everyone, however, was willing to overlook Pearson's "dirty play" as he set out to demonstrate that the end justifies the means. The *Saturday Review*'s M. W. Childs, for example, once noted that the columnist habitually displayed "an unfortunate self-righteousness, which comes out in his telling of his own propaganda exploits." This self-righteousness often led him to attack someone *before* he had proof of any criminal wrongdoing. While this may, in retrospect, seem unimportant to many in the case of a Senator Joseph McCarthy, there were times, as the *New Republic*'s Joseph Nocera pointed out, when "the vendettas, the politicking, the steady stream of columns were used on dozens of politicians far less evil than McCarthy."

One of these targets was James Forrestal, Roosevelt's secretary of the Navy and Truman's secretary of defense. Explained Joe Klein of the *New York Times Book Review*: "It wasn't that Forrestal had done anything specific or illegal to offend Pearson; it was merely that Pearson disliked his Wall Street, right-wing style, and *sensed* there was corruption somewhere in Forrestal's past." Over a period of several years, Pearson pursued Forrestal in a manner even Jack Anderson characterized as full of "low blows" that occasionally descended to the level of "poison gas." In the end, Nocera recalled, "Forrestal cracked, committed suicide, and a large portion of the blame was placed squarely on Pearson."

Whether they admired or despised him, most observers agree that there will never be another journalist quite like Drew Pearson. To Arthur Cooper of *Newsweek*, he was "that rare combination of showman and newsman, and every day his pungent blend of punditry and titillating gossip would set off quaking shocks on the Washington seismograph. He had the power to enrage presidents and unmake senators. . . . But unlike I. F. Stone, Drew Pearson was not content merely to exorcise the corruptors, grafters and scoundrels from the corridors of power. He demanded entree to those corridors himself in order to effect changes in government policy. Which is why Pearson was something more than a journalist—and something less." Concluded Cooper: "It is unlikely—and this may not be a bad thing—that any newsman will ever again wield as much influence as Pearson."

BIOGRAPHICAL/CRITICAL SOURCES: New York Times, July 26, 1931, January 27, 1935, September 2, 1972; *Outlook*, July 29, 1931; *New Republic*, August 12, 1931, December 23, 1936, October 13, 1958, October 5, 1968, June 30, 1979; *Nation*, August 26, 1931, February 13, 1935, September 23, 1968; *Bookman*, September, 1931; *Forum*, September, 1931, March, 1935; *Saturday Review of Literature*, September 5, 1931, January 19, 1935; *Survey*, December 1, 1931; *Boston Transcript*, January 19, 1935; *Books*, January 20, 1935, November 8, 1936; *Atlantic Bookshelf*, April, 1935; *American*

Political Science Review, June, 1935; *Times Literary Supplement,* August 29, 1935; *Current History,* December, 1936; *Yale Law Journal,* January, 1937; *Time,* December 13, 1948, August 23, 1968, March 4, 1974; *San Francisco Chronicle,* October 13, 1958; *Saturday Review,* October 18, 1958, November 9, 1968; *New York Herald Tribune Book Review,* December 7, 1958.

New York Times Book Review, July 28, 1968, March 17, 1974, May 20, 1979; *Washington Post,* August 8, 1968, October 10, 1968, September 11, 1970; *Life,* August 9, 1968; *Washington Post Book World,* August 11, 1968, June 17, 1979; *Best Sellers,* August 15, 1968, October 1, 1968, September 15, 1970; *New Yorker,* September 28, 1968, February 25, 1974; *New York Review of Books,* February 13, 1969; *Newsweek,* October 21, 1968, February 25, 1974; *National Observer,* October 28, 1968; *National Review,* December 31, 1968; *Spectator,* January 18, 1975; *Listener,* February 6, 1975; Jack Anderson and James Boyd, *Confessions of a Muckraker: The Inside Story of Life in Washington during the Truman, Eisenhower, Kennedy and Johnson Years,* Random House, 1979; *Chicago Tribune Book World,* May 6, 1979.

OBITUARIES: New York Times, September 2, 1969; *London Times,* September 2, 1969; *Variety,* September 3, 1969; *Washington Post,* September 3, 1969.†

—*Sketch by Deborah A. Straub*

* * *

PEARSON, Drew
See PEARSON, Andrew Russell

* * *

PECK, Leonard
See HARDY, C. Colburn

* * *

PEDERSEN, (Thelma) Jean J(orgenson) 1934-

PERSONAL: Born September 17, 1934, in Salt Lake City, Utah; daughter of Ralph Enoch (a physician and eye specialist) and Margaret Thelma (Turpin) Jorgenson; married Kent Alden Pedersen (an electrical engineer), May 31, 1956; children: Christen Kent, Jennifer Jean. *Education:* Brigham Young University, B.S., 1955; University of Utah, M.S., 1958; *Religion:* Church of Jesus Christ of Latter-day Saints (Mormon). *Home address:* P.O. Box 26, New Almaden, Calif. 95042. *Office:* Department of Mathematics, University of Santa Clara, Santa Clara, Calif. 95053.

CAREER: Brigham Young University, Provo, Utah, mathematics teacher at university high school, 1955-56; high school mathematics teacher in Salt Lake City, Utah, 1958-59; University of Utah, Salt Lake City, instructor in mathematics, 1959-65; University of Santa Clara, Santa Clara, Calif., lecturer, 1966-72, assistant professor of mathematics, 1972—. Visiting scientist for National Science Foundation, 1963-65; coordinator, Bay Area Women and Mathematics Lectureship Program, 1975-80; lecturer, Mathematical Association of America, 1980—. *Member:* Mathematical Association of America (governor of Northern California section, 1981-84), American Mathematical Society, National Council of Teachers of Mathematics (president of local chapter, 1976-77), Utah Council of Teachers of Mathematics (member of board of directors, 1963-65), California Mathematics Council, Sigma Xi, Pi Kappa Kappa, Pi Mu Epsilon.

WRITINGS: (With E. Allan Davis) *Essentials of Trigonometry,* Prindle, 1969, 2nd edition, James E. Freel & Associates, 1973; (with husband, Kent A. Pedersen) *Geometric Playthings,* Troubador, 1973; (with Davis) *Trigonometry,* Page-Ficklin, 1975; (with Franz O. Armbruster) *A New Twist: Developing Arithmetic Skills through Problem Solving,* Addison-Wesley, 1979; (contributor) *In the Geometric Vein,* Springer-Verlag, 1981; (with Peter Hilton) *Fear No More: An Adult Guide to Mathematics,* Addison-Wesley, 1982.

Contributor of several articles to *Mathematics Teacher, Fibonacci Quarterly, Utah Newsletter, Mathematical Log, Australian Mathematics Teacher, Two Year College Mathematics Journal, Mathematical Monthly, Matimyas Matematika, Mathematics,* and *Cahiers de Topologie et Geometrie Differentielle.* Associate editor, *Mathematics,* 1981—.

WORK IN PROGRESS: With Peter Hilton, two sequels to *Fear No More,* the first dealing with algebra and geometry and the second with calculus, both for Addison-Wesley.

* * *

PEDRICK, Jean 1922-
(Jean Kefferstan)

PERSONAL: Born August 5, 1922, in Salem, Mass.; daughter of Laurence Davis (a businessman) and Elfrieda (Virchow) Pedrick; married F. J. Kefferstan (a physician), February 8, 1948; children: Laurence, John. *Education:* Wheaton College, Norton, Mass., B.A., 1943. *Home:* 48 Mt. Vernon St., Boston, Mass. 02108.

CAREER: Houghton Mifflin Co., Boston, Mass., secretary and first reader, 1944-47; writer, 1947-68 and 1970-72; Northeastern University, Boston, instructor in poetry at Center for Continuing Education, 1968-70; *Executive Digest,* Boston, editor, 1972-74; volunteer worker, Alice James Poetry Cooperative, Inc., 1974—; poetry workshop instructor, Boston Center for Adult Education, 1975—; president, Rowan Tree Press, Ltd., 1980—. *Member:* P.E.N., New England Poetry Club. *Awards, honors:* Gretchen Warren Award, 1972, for "Making the Skelton," and Melora Hobbs Pond Award, 1973, for "Intensive Care," both from New England Poetry Club.

WRITINGS: The Fascination (novel), Houghton, 1947; *Wolf Moon* (poems), Alice James Books, 1974; *Pride and Splendor* (poems), Alice James Books, 1976; *The Gaudy Book* (poems), Juniper Press, 1978; *Saints* (poems), Rowan Tree Press, 1980; *greenfellow* (poems), New Rivers Press, 1981. Regular contributor of essay features under name Jean Kefferstan to *Beacon Hill News,* 1967—.

WORK IN PROGRESS: Two books of poetry, *The Book of Nines* and *The Glorious Fourth;* a novel, *Journal of Josephine Graves, Spnstr.*

* * *

PENROSE, Harold

PERSONAL: Married Nora Sybil; children: Sybil Anne, Ian. *Education:* University of London, Diploma in Engineering, 1926. *Home:* Nether Compton, Sherborne, Dorsetshire, England.

CAREER: Westland Aircraft Ltd., Yeovil, England, 1925—, employed as designer, production manager, test pilot, group sales manager, and special director. Director of several marine companies. *Military service:* Royal Air Force Reserve, 1927-31. *Member:* Royal Aeronautical Society (fellow), Royal Institute of Naval Architects, Royal Motor Yacht Club. *Awards, honors:* Order of the British Empire.

WRITINGS: I Flew with the Birds, Scribner, 1949; *No Echo in the Sky,* Cassell, 1958; *Airymouse,* Vernon & Yates, 1965; *British Aviation: The Pioneer Years,* Putnam, 1967; *British Aviation: Great War and Armistice,* Putnam, 1969; *British Aviation: The Adventuring Years,* Putnam, 1973; *British Aviation: Widening Horizons,* H.M.S.O., 1979; *British Aviation: Ominous Skies,* H.M.S.O., 1980; *Wings across the World,* Cassell, 1980; *Cloud Cuckooland,* Air Life, 1981. Contributor of marine, aeronautical, historical, and natural history articles and reviews to periodicals.

WORK IN PROGRESS: An autobiography, *Fate, My Friend.*

SIDELIGHTS: Harold Penrose writes that he had a "lifetime interest in literature" and a "devotion to the romance of aviation even before [my] first flight as a schoolboy in 1919." *Avocational interests:* Sailing, flying, archaeology, yacht design, art, music, countryside conservation.

*   *   *

PERRY, John   1914-

PERSONAL: Born February 25, 1914, in Newark, N.J.; son of John Franklin (a manufacturer) and Helen Remsen (Anthony) Perry; married Jane Greverus (an economist and author), January 1, 1944; children: Jefferson, Forest, Gale. *Education:* Attended Lehigh University, 1930-31. *Home:* 6208 Carnegie Dr., Bethesda, Md. 20034. *Agent:* Margot Johnson, 405 East 54th St., New York, N.Y. 10022. *Office:* National Zoological Park, Washington, D.C. 20009.

CAREER: Management consultant, working at intervals as industry and government executive, 1944—; Pritchard, Schaffer & Woodyatt, Stamford, Conn., associate, beginning 1961; National Zoological Park, Washington, D.C., 1966—, currently assistant director. Vice-president, Fred Rudge Associates. Producer with wife, Jane Perry, of educational filmstrips; freelance writer. Trustee, Research Ranch, Inc.; executive secretary, Wild Animal Propagation Trust. *Member:* International Union for the Conservation of Nature (chairman of international zoo group), American Association of Zoological Parks and Aquariums (fellow; member of conservation committee), National Science Teachers Association, Fauna Preservation Society, Audubon Society, American Management Association, Friends of the National Zoo (governor; former president).

WRITINGS: Human Relations in Small Industry, McGraw, 1954, 3rd edition (with Martin M. Bruce) published as *Human Relations in Small Business,* Small Business Administration, 1969; *Our Wonderful Eyes,* Whittlesey House, 1955; *The Story of Standards,* Funk, 1955; *American Ferryboats,* Funk, 1957; *17 Million Jobs,* Whittlesey House, 1958; *Our Polluted World: Can Man Survive?,* F. Watts, 1967, revised edition, 1972; *The World's a Zoo,* Dodd, 1969; *Zoos,* F. Watts, 1971.

With wife, Jane G. Perry: *Exploring the River,* Whittlesey House, 1960; *Exploring the Seacoast,* Whittlesey House, 1961; *Exploring the Forest,* Whittlesey House, 1962; *Foresters and What They Do,* F. Watts, 1963; *Veterinarians and What They Do,* F. Watts, 1964; *The Random House Guide to Natural Areas of the Eastern United States,* Random House, 1980. Contributor to general magazines, business, management, and professional journals.

WORK IN PROGRESS: A book, *Water, Air, and Life,* with wife, Jane G. Perry, and filmstrips on the same subject.†

PETERS, Barney
See BAUER, Erwin A.

*   *   *

PETERSON, Wilferd Arlan   1900-

PERSONAL: Born August 21, 1900, in Whitehall, Mich.; son of Peter Hans and Elsie Marie (Gilbert) Peterson; married Ruth Irene Rector, June 21, 1921 (died July 22, 1979); children: Lilian Grace (Mrs. Gordon Albert Thorpe). *Education:* Attended business college in Muskegon, Mich., and took special courses at Michigan State University and University of Michigan. *Politics:* Republican. *Religion:* Liberal Protestant. *Home:* Pilgrim Manor, 2000 Leonard N.E., Grand Rapids, Mich. 49505.

CAREER: Jaqua Co. (advertising agency), Grand Rapids, Mich., 1928-65, began as copywriter, became vice-president, creative director, and secretary of board of directors; full-time writer and lecturer, 1965—. *Member:* Rotary International (Grand Rapids). *Awards, honors:* Silver Medal Award from *Printers' Ink,* Advertising Federation of America, and Advertising Club of Grand Rapids in honor of being named Advertising Man of the Year, 1963; George Washington Medal, Freedoms Foundation, 1958.

WRITINGS—Published by Simon & Schuster, except as indicated: *The Art of Getting Along: Inspiration for Triumphant Daily Living,* Harmony Press, 1949; *Twenty-three Essays on the Art of Living* (also see below), This Week, 1961, hardcover edition, Simon & Schuster, 1961; *The New Book of the Art of Living: A New Series of Twenty-seven Essays* (also see below), 1963; *More about the Art of Living: A Third Book of Twenty-five New Essays* (also see below), 1966; *Adventures in the Art of Living: A Fourth Book of New Essays,* 1968; *The Art of Living in the World Today: A Search for a Way of Life for These Times,* 1969; *The Art of Living: Day by Day,* 1972; *The Art of Living Treasure Chest* (contains *Twenty-three Essays on the Art of Living, The New Book of the Art of Living,* and *More about the Art of Living*), 1977. Also author of monthly page in *Science of Mind;* contributor to *Reader's Digest* and *Unity.* Former editor of twenty-five industrial house magazines; member of editorial board, *Science of Mind.*

WORK IN PROGRESS: Another book for Simon & Schuster.

SIDELIGHTS: As the author of numerous inspirational essays whose subjects range from "The Art of Success" to "The Art of Loafing," Wilferd Peterson has touched millions of readers through the years with his warmth and his optimistic outlook on life. An advertising executive by profession, Peterson wrote his first essays for promotional magazines his agency compiled for distribution by various companies to their customers. In 1960, the editor of the popular Sunday newspaper supplement *This Week* saw some of these essays and asked Peterson if he would be interested in contributing regularly to the magazine's "Words to Live By" page. Peterson, who had long harbored a wish to see his work reach a wider audience, jumped at the chance to write for *This Week,* and the "Art of Living" series began.

Public response to the essays was so overwhelmingly positive that *This Week* brought out a paperback collection in 1961 and quickly sold nearly 500,000 copies. Simon & Schuster then approached Peterson with the idea of publishing a deluxe, gold-trimmed hardcover edition, projecting sales would reach about 10,000 copies. By the mid-1960s, however, the hardcover edition had sold more than 1,000,000 copies; in 1981, that first collection went into its twenty-fifth printing.

A typical Peterson essay is not at all like the complex philosophical musings of many other writers. According to *Success*

Unlimited's Kevin Shyne, "Peterson does not overwhelm the reader with words. The essence of his style is simplicity. He inspires the reader with a few, carefully chosen words." Relying on "a strain of music, an item in a newspaper or anything else that triggered a chain of thought" for inspiration, Peterson reports that his goal was always "to express the good life as I saw it in miniature essays that people could easily read and absorb. Almost no one will read a 300-page book on friendship or achievement or peace. But they will read 300 words. In writing, I would take a subject such as happiness, then read what philosophers, psychologists, ministers and other thinkers had to say about it. I would clip everything I could find on the subject, make page after page of notes, then sit quietly to think and reflect. I would distill it all into 300 words so that it could be read in two or three minutes. . . . In a way I think I was writing many of my essays to myself. Most of the early ones were written when I was [still in advertising], so I was thinking in terms of my own career and success."

Peterson advises those who are seeking success, be it in the writing field or in any other line of endeavor, to follow the "rules" he has lived by throughout his life: read about and associate with great people. "We inherit all the creativity of the great people who have ever lived," he told Shyne. "It is all waiting for us in the library. You can go to read about geniuses like Leonardo da Vinci and Thomas Edison and absorb their creative spirit. . . . [By associating] with people who have great purposes, great goals and great dreams, . . . you begin to catch their spirit."

Despite the many hours he has spent contemplating the benefits of positive thinking, Peterson insists that he has only "scratched the surface" in his continuing search for the ingredients that make up a productive and happy life. "There is no end to discovering the art of living," he notes. "It goes in so many directions and involves so many things that no one can ever measure or reach the scope of the art."

MEDIA ADAPTATIONS: Twelve essays from Peterson's "Art of Living" series were recorded by *This Week* magazine. Several have also been adapted by Hallmark, Inc., for use in greeting cards, booklets, and, for sixteen years, an annual "Art of Living" calendar.

BIOGRAPHICAL/CRITICAL SOURCES: Good Business, October, 1956; *This Week,* November, 1961; *Wonderland,* May 7, 1978; *Grand Rapids Press,* July 10, 1979; *Success Unlimited,* March, 1980.

*   *   *

PETESCH, Natalie L(evin) M(aines)

PERSONAL: Born in Detroit, Mich.; daughter of Samuel and Anna (Goldman) Levin; married John Maines, December 21, 1945 (divorced January, 1959); married Donald Anthony Petesch (a professor of contemporary literature), August 30, 1959; children: (first marriage) Rachel Maines; (second marriage) Nicholas Donald. *Education:* Attended Wayne State University; Boston University, B.S., 1955; Brandeis University, M.A., 1956; University of Texas at Austin, Ph.D., 1962. *Home and office:* 6320 Crombie St., Pittsburgh, Pa. 15217.

CAREER: University of Texas at Austin, special instructor, 1959-60, instructor in British and American literature, 1963-65; San Francisco State College (now University), San Francisco, Calif., assistant professor of British and American literature, 1961-62; Southwest Texas State College (now University), San Marcos, assistant professor of British and American literature, 1961-62; full-time writer, 1965—. Distinguished

Visiting Professor in Creative Writing, University of Idaho, January, 1982. *Awards, honors:* Iowa School of Letters award for short fiction, 1974, for *After the First Death There Is No Other; Kansas Quarterly* Fiction Award, 1976; First Prize, *Louisville Review* fiction competition, 1978; Pennsylvania Council on the Arts literature fellowship, 1980; Dobie-Paisano fellowship in literature nomination, 1981.

WRITINGS: After the First Death There Is No Other (short story collection), University of Iowa Press, 1974; *The Odyssey of Katinou Kalokovich* (novel), United Sisters, 1974; *Two Novels: The Long Hot Summers of Yasha K.* [and] *The Leprosarium,* University of Missouri—Kansas City Press, 1978, published as *Seasons Such as These,* Ohio University Press, 1979; *Soul Clap Its Hands and Sing* (short story collection), South End Press, 1980; *Duncan's Colony* (novel), Ohio University Press, 1981.

Work is represented in anthologies, including *Different Drummers,* edited by Elizabeth Canar and Cecile Vye, Random House, 1973, *Michigan Hot Apples: An Anthology of Michigan Writers,* edited by Gay Rubin, Hot Apples Press, 1973, *Moving to Antarctica,* edited by Margaret Kaminski, Dustbooks, 1975, *Best American Short Stories of 1978,* edited by Theodore Solotaroff and Shannon Ravenel, Houghton, 1978, and *Fiction Omnibus,* New Letters, 1979. Contributor of short stories to literary journals.

WORK IN PROGRESS: "A triptych representing son, fiancee, and mother-awaiting-the-war"; a novel.

AVOCATIONAL INTERESTS: Travel in Latin America, Third World culture, French culture, Latin American literature and culture.

BIOGRAPHICAL/CRITICAL SOURCES: Los Angeles Times Book Review, March 9, 1980.

*   *   *

PETO
    See WHITE, Stanley

*   *   *

PETO, James
    See WHITE, Stanley

*   *   *

PFLAUM, Melanie L(oewenthal)   1909-

PERSONAL: Born April 12, 1909; daughter of Edward and Judith (Weill) Loewenthal; married Irving Peter Pflaum (a professor of Latin American studies), February 11, 1930; children: John, Peter, Thomas. *Education:* Attended University of Wisconsin, 1927-28; University of Chicago, Ph.B., 1929; other study at Sorbonne, University of Paris. *Home and office:* El Tosalet 323, Javea, (Alicante), Spain.

CAREER: American Medical Association, Chicago, Ill., manuscript editor, 1930-33; Scripps Howard Syndicate, foreign correspondent in Paris, Rome, Budapest, Athens, Warsaw, Madrid, 1933-39; manuscript editor for medical yearbooks, Chicago, 1939; Board of Economic Warfare, Washington, D.C., chief, Iberian Division, 1940-43; affiliated with U.S. Office of Censorship, Chicago, 1943-45; free-lance writer for educational films, radio series, and magazines, 1945-55, novelist, 1955—; Northwestern University, Evanston, Ill., teacher of creative writing, 1958-59; Inter-American University of Puerto Rico, San German, teacher of literature and creative writing,

1960-65. *Member:* Society of Women Geographers, Society of Midland Authors, American Association of University Professors, Theta Sigma Phi, Arts Club (Chicago).

WRITINGS: Bolero, Heinemann, 1956, St. Martin's, 1957; *Windfall,* Cassell, 1962; *The Insiders,* Cassell, 1963; *The Gentle Tyrants,* Carlton, 1965; *Ready by Wednesday,* Carlton, 1970; *Second Conquest,* Univers, 1971; *The Maine Remembered,* Pegasus, 1972; *Costa Brava,* Ediciones Juan Ponce de Leon, 1972; *Lili,* Pegasus, 1974; *Safari,* Pegasus, 1975; *The Old Girls,* Pegasus, 1977; *Shadow of Doubt,* Pegasus, 1979. Contributor of stories and articles to *Vogue, American Mercury, Reporter, Canadian Home Journal,* and *Interamerican Review.* Writer of radio series on science.

WORK IN PROGRESS: A novel with a New Zealand background.

SIDELIGHTS: As the wife of a foreign correspondent, foreign editor, radio and television commentator, and university professor, Melanie Pflaum has lived in several countries of Europe, and in South America, Cuba, and other Latin American lands. She speaks, reads, and writes Spanish, French, and Italian. Several of her recent books have been published in France by Fleuve Noir.

*   *   *

PHILLIPS, E(lmo) Bryant   1905-1975

PERSONAL: Born May 23, 1905, in Lincoln, Neb.; died December 19, 1975; son of Reber Clyde (employed in field of personal relations) and Josie (Bryant) Phillips; married Violet Lee, June 6, 1931; children: Colleen Lee. *Education:* Nebraska Wesleyan University, A.B., 1927; University of Nebraska, M.A., 1931, Ph.D., 1944. *Politics:* Republican. *Religion:* Presbyterian. *Office:* Department of Economics, University of Southern California, Los Angeles, Calif. 90007.

CAREER: Lincoln High School, Lincoln, Neb., teacher, 1932-43; Los Angeles City College, Los Angeles, Calif., instructor in economics, 1947; University of Southern California, Los Angeles, assistant professor, 1947-50, associate professor, 1950-59, professor of economics, beginning 1959, chairman of department, 1961-62. Professor, California State University, Los Angeles, 1971. *Military service:* U.S. Army Air Forces, instructor in cadet school, 1943-44; U.S. Signal Corps, 1944-46; became captain. *Member:* American Marketing Association, American Economic Association, American Finance Association, Western Economic Association, Order of Artus (national secretary-treasurer, 1958-62), Omicron Delta Epsilon (national treasurer, 1963-72, president, beginning 1972). *Awards, honors:* Committee for Economic Development essay prize, 1956.

WRITINGS: Consumer Economic Problems, Henry Holt, 1957; (with Sylvia Lane) *Personal Finance,* Wiley, 1963, 4th edition, 1980; *Nebraska Street and Interurban Railways,* J-B Publishing, 1974; (with Lane) *How to Manage Your Personal Finances: A Short Course for Professionals,* Wiley, 1978. Contributor of articles to state history journals.

WORK IN PROGRESS: Pricing practices and their regulation.†

*   *   *

PHIPSON, Joan
See FITZHARDINGE, Joan Margaret

PICKLE, Hal B(rittain)   1929-

PERSONAL: Born January 16, 1929, in Ennis, Tex.; son of Oren M. (a barber) and Bessie Mae (Beard) Pickle; married Anna Lucille Toupal, June 27, 1953; children: Debra Lyn, Karen Kay, Eric Brian, Lance Oram. *Education:* North Texas State College (now University), B.B.A., 1959, M.B.A., 1960; University of Arkansas, Ph.D., 1964. *Home:* 4905 Saddle Dr., Austin, Tex. 78759. *Office:* St. Edward's University, Austin, Tex. 78704.

CAREER: Southwest Texas State University, San Marcos, associate professor of management, 1962-69; Auburn University, Auburn, Ala., professor of management, 1969-73; Hal B. Pickle (research and consulting firm), Austin, Tex., president, 1973-75; St. Edward's University, Austin, associate professor, 1975-78, professor, 1978—. President, Auburn Business Consultants, Inc., 1972—. *Military service:* U.S. Army, Engineers, 1950-52. *Member:* Academy of Management, National Council of Small Business Management Development. *Awards, honors:* Outstanding Educator of America Award, 1971 and 1972; research grants from National Science Foundation, 1971, Small Business Administration, 1971, and Office of Water Resources, 1971-73.

WRITINGS: Personality and Success: An Evaluation of Personal Characteristics of Successful Small Business Managers, Small Business Administration, 1964; (with Abrahamson) *Introduction to Business: Text and Cases,* Goodyear Publishing, 1972, 4th edition, 1980; (with Abrahamson) *Introduction to Business: Readings* (also see below), Goodyear Publishing, 1972, 2nd edition, 1974; (with Abrahamson) *Introduction to Business: Study Guide,* Goodyear Publishing, 1972, 2nd edition, 1974, 3rd edition published as *Introduction to Business: Study Guide and Readings,* 1977, 4th edition, 1980; (with Abrahamson) *Introduction to Business: Instructor's Manual,* Goodyear Publishing, 1972, 4th edition, 1980; (with Rucks) *The Impact of Water Pollution Abatement on Competition and Pricing in the Alabama Textile Industry,* Water Resources Research Institute, Auburn University, 1973; (with Rowe) *The Impact of Water Pollution Abatement on Competition and Pricing in the Alabama Steel Industry,* Water Resources Research Institute, Auburn University, 1973; (with Rucks and Sisson) *The Economic Benefits of Abating Water Pollution in the Steel, Textile, and Paper Industries in Alabama,* Water Resources Research Institute, Auburn University, 1973; (with Abrahamson) *Small Business Management,* with study guide and instructor's manual, Wiley, 1976, 2nd edition, 1981. Contributor to professional journals.

WORK IN PROGRESS: Fifth editions of the *Introduction to Business* books.

*   *   *

PIKE, Charles R.
See HARKNETT, Terry

*   *   *

PILCH, Judah   1902-

PERSONAL: Born September 8, 1902, in Vachnovka, Russia (now U.S.S.R.); came to United States in 1923; naturalized citizen in 1928; son of Yosef and Baba Sheve (Milstein) Pilch; married Bernice F. Shapery, June 24, 1933; children: Yosef Hayim, Ben Zion. *Education:* Received rabbinical degree; Lewis Institute of Chicago, B.S., 1932; Columbia University, M.A., 1946; Dropsie College (now University), Ph.D., 1952. *Reli-*

gion: Jewish. *Home:* 520 South Burnside Ave., Los Angeles, Calif. 90036.

CAREER: College of Jewish Studies, Chicago, Ill., lecturer, 1929-39; Jewish Education Association, Rochester, N.Y., education director, 1939-45; Bronx Council for Jewish Education, Bronx, N.Y., director, 1945-47; Jewish Education Association of Essex County, Newark, N.J., executive director, 1947-49; American Association for Jewish Education, New York City, executive director, 1949-60, director of National Curriculum Research Institute, 1960-67; Dropsie College (now University), Philadelphia, Pa., lecturer in history of education, 1960-67; Jewish Teachers Seminary and Peoples' University, New York City, dean of Graduate Division, 1965-72; University of Judaism, Los Angeles, Calif., visiting professor of The Holocaust, 1972-76. Associate professor of Judaica, New York University, 1961-64. Chairman of Hadoar Associates, 1959-63, and National Bible Contest Committee, 1959-66.

MEMBER: Religious Education Association of the United States and Canada (vice-president, 1953-59; chairman of executive committee, 1959-68), National Council for Jewish Education, (president, 1948-50), National Conference of Jewish Communal Service (president, 1954-55), Society for the Scientific Study of Religion, American Academy of Religion and Mental Health, Histadrut Ivrith of America (president, 1966-72). *Awards, honors:* Citation for distinguished service to the 300th anniversary of Jewish settlement in America, 1955; citation from Dropsie College for outstanding contribution to Jewish scholarship, 1957; Doctor of Jewish Literature from Jewish Teachers Seminary, 1978; citation from Hebrew Union College for scholarship, teaching ability, and skill, 1978; Certificate of Honor from Jewish Book Council for *The Story of the Jewish Catastrophe in Europe.*

WRITINGS: Jewish Life in Our Times, Behrman, 1943; *The Hedar Metukan,* Dropsie College, 1951; (editor) *Jewish Education Register and Directory,* American Association for Jewish Education, Volume I, 1952, Volume II, 1959, Volume III, 1965; (editor) Horace Meyer Kallem, *Of Them Which Say They Are Jews and Other Essays on the Jewish Struggle for Survival,* Bloch Publishing, 1954; (editor) *Readings in Jewish Educational Philosophy,* American Association for Jewish Education, Volume I, 1961; *Fate and Faith: The Contemporary Jewish Scene,* Bloch Publishing, 1963; *Basic Jewish Concepts,* National Curriculum Research Institute, 1965; (editor with Meir Ben-Horin and author of introduction) *Judaism and the Jewish School: Selected Essays on the Direction and Purpose of Jewish Education,* Bloch Publishing, 1966; *The Story of the Jewish Catastrophe in Europe,* National Curriculum Research Institute, 1967; (editor) *Phillip W. Lown: A Jubilee Volume,* Bloch Publishing, 1967; *A History of Jewish Education in the United States,* National Curriculum Research Institute, 1968; *The Weak against the Strong: Simple Folk in the Grip of Turbulent Times,* Bloch Publishing, 1973; (editor) Samuel M. Blumenfield, *Thou Shalt Teach: Selected Essays of Samuel M. Blumenfield,* Department of Education and Culture, World Zionist Organization, 1973; *Between Two Generations,* Bloch Publishing, 1977. Member of editorial board, *Jewish Education* and *The Reconstructionist.*

Books in Hebrew: *Hakolelim Hayehudim B'America,* Hadoar Associates, 1938; *Sinat Yisrael B'America,* Hadoar Associates, 1953; *Musagim Yehudim,* National Curriculum Research Institute, 1962; *Anashim Pshutim,* Ogen Publishers, 1972; *Yalkut,* Ogen Publishers, 1980.

WORK IN PROGRESS: An autobiography; translating *The Heder Metukan* into Hebrew.

PINE, William
See HARKNETT, Terry

*   *   *

PINNEY, Roy   1911-

PERSONAL: Born August 13, 1911, in New York, N.Y.; son of Max and Sara Pinney; married Doris Bertelsen, July 24, 1944; children: Ria, Roy, Jr., Tor, Sara. *Education:* Attended New York University, Pratt Institute, Syracuse University, and Columbia University.

CAREER: Paramount Newsreel, New York City, cameraman, 1928; *New York Daily News,* New York City, reporter and photographer, 1929-38; *Life,* New York City, photographer, 1938-39; free-lance magazine writer and photographer, 1939—; Photo Library, Inc. (worldwide stock photo agency), New York City, president, 1951—. Photographer on more than seventy scientific trips; war corespondent and photographer during Normandy invasion, 1944. Producer of television series "Secrets of Nature," 1955-59; cameraman and director of television series "Wild Cargo," 1961. Lecturer, Metropolitan Camera Club Council, 1940; instructor, School of Modern Photography, 1943-45. Inventor of underwater photography equipment, 1948. *Member:* Picture Agency Council of America (founder; president, 1954), American Society of Magazine Photographers (founder; trustee). *Awards, honors:* First prize for television commercials, Cannes Film Festival, 1963.

WRITINGS: The Golden Book of Wild Animal Pets (also see below), Golden Press, 1958; *Advertising Photography,* Hastings House, 1960; *Complete Book of Cave Exploration,* Coward, 1961; (with others) *How to Survive Atomic Attack,* Fawcett, 1961; *Cats: A Photo-Book,* U.S. Camera, 1962; *Vanishing Wildlife,* Dodd, 1963; *Young Israel,* Dodd, 1963; *Animals, Inc.,* Doubleday, 1964; *Careers with a Camera,* Lippincott, 1964; *The Animals in the Bible,* Chilton, 1964; *Collecting and Photographing Your Microzoo,* World Publishing, 1965; *Quest for the Unknown: Explorers of Today,* Lippincott, 1965; *Wild Animal Pets* (adaptation of *The Golden Book of Wild Animal Pets*), Golden Press, 1965; *Wildlife in Danger,* Duell, Sloan, & Pearce, 1966; *Vanishing Tribes,* Crowell, 1968; *Pets from Wood,* Golden Press, 1969; *Underwater Archaelogy: Treasures beneath the Sea,* Hawthorn, 1970; *Slavery: Past and Present,* Thomas Nelson, 1972; *The Snake Book,* Doubleday, 1981.

Camera columnist, *Parents' Magazine* and *U.S. Camera,* 1948-52. Contributor of photographically illustrated articles to *Life, Look, Collier's, New York Times,* and other magazines and newspapers; contributor of technical articles to *Encyclopedia of Photography* and to photography and advertising journals.

SIDELIGHTS: Roy Pinney was the photographer on the New York Aquarium Society expedition to the Sargasso Sea and the Oxford University expedition to British Guiana; he has also participated in archaeological expeditions to Guatemala, Honduras, India, Israel, Peru, and Yucatan, volcanic expeditions to Mexico, Japan, and Hawaii, and botanical expeditions throughout the West Indies.†

*   *   *

PITTMAN, David J(oshua)   1927-

PERSONAL: Born September 18, 1927, in Rocky Mount, N.C.; son of Jay W. and Laura (Edwards) Pittman. *Education:* University of North Carolina, B.A., 1949, M.A., 1950; Columbia

University, graduate study, 1952; University of Chicago, Ph.D., 1956. *Religion:* Episcopal. *Home:* 230 South Brentwood, Clayton, Mo. 63105. *Office:* Department of Sociology, Washington University, Lindell & Skinker Sts., St. Louis, Mo. 63130.

CAREER: University of Rochester, Rochester, N.Y., instructor, 1950-53, assistant professor of sociology, 1955-58; Washington University, St. Louis, Mo., assistant professor, 1958-60, associate professor, 1960-64, professor of sociology, 1964—, chairman of department, 1976—, School of Medicine, research assistant professor, 1958-60, research associate professor of sociology in psychiatry, 1960—, Social Science Institute, research associate, 1958-60, director, 1963-76, research director, 1976—. Greater St. Louis Council on Alcoholism, member of board of directors, 1966—, president, 1970-71, vice-president, 1971-76, treasurer, 1976-77; member of board, St. Louis Foundation for Alcoholism and Related Dependencies; honorary director, Harris House Foundation; former member or official of numerous other councils and committees on alcoholism and drug abuse; consultant to private and governmental organizations in the United States and abroad. *Military service:* U.S. Army Air Forces, 1946-48.

MEMBER: International Council on Alcohol and Alcoholism (Lausanne, Switzerland; member of executive committee, 1962—; chairman of 1968 International Congress on Alcohol and Alcoholism), North American Association of Alcoholism Programs (president, 1965-67), Alcohol and Drug Problems Association of North America, Society for the Study of Social Problems (chairman of alcoholism committee, 1957-59), National Council on Alcoholism (member of board of directors, 1966—; member of executive committee, 1978—), American Sociological Association (fellow), Distilled Spirits Council of the U.S. (member of scientific advisory council, 1976—), American Society of Criminology (fellow), American Statistical Society, Phi Beta Kappa, Sigma Xi.

AWARDS, HONORS: National Institute of Mental Health special fellow in the Netherlands and Great Britain, 1966-67; St. Louis Newspaper Guild Page One Award, 1967, for helping to found the first detoxification center for public inebriates in North America; award from University of Alaska Center for the Study of Alcoholism, for contributing most to the field of organizing alcoholism services in the State of Alaska during 1970-73; National Council on Alcoholism Research and Evaluation Advisory Committee Volunteer Service Award, 1974-75; Greater St. Louis Council on Alcoholism Bronze Key Award, 1976; award from Community Alcohol Programs of Kansas City, Inc., 1976, for contributions made in the field of alcoholism in the State of Missouri and nationally; National Council on Alcoholism Silver Key Award, 1978, for excellent and devoted service to the organization.

WRITINGS: (With C. W. Gordon) *Revolving Door: A Study of the Chronic Police Case Inebriate,* Free Press of Glencoe and Rutgers Center of Alcohol Studies, 1958; (editor and contributor) *Alcoholism: An Interdisciplinary Approach,* C. C Thomas, 1959; (editor with C. R. Snyder and contributor) *Society, Culture, and Drinking Patterns,* Wiley, 1962, revised edition, Southern Illinois University Press, 1968; (with Archer Tongue) *Handbook of Organizations for Research on Alcohol and Alcoholism Problems,* International Council on Alcohol and Alcoholism, 1964; (with Muriel W. Sterne) *Alcoholism: Community Agency Attitudes and Their Impact on Treatment Services,* Public Health Service Publications, 1965; (editor and contributor) *Alcoholism,* Harper, 1967, hardcover edition, 1969; (with others) *The Drug Scene in Great Britain: Journey into Loneliness,* Williams & Wilkins, 1967, revised edition, Edward Arnold, 1969; (with Sterne) *Drinking Patterns in the*

Ghetto, two volumes, Social Science Institute, Washington University, 1973; (with M. Dow Lambert) *Alcohol, Alcoholism, and Advertising: A Preliminary Investigation of Asserted Associations,* Social Science Institute, Washington University, 1978; *Primary Prevention of Alcohol Abuse and Alcoholism: An Evaluation of the Control of Consumption Policy,* Social Science Institute, Washington University, 1980; (with Donald E. Strickland) *The Effects of Alcohol Beverage Advertising Practices and Messages on Alcohol Problems and Alcoholism in the U.S.,* Social Science Institute, Washington University, 1981; (author of foreword) David E. Aaronson, C. Thomas Dienes, and Michael C. Musheno, *Decriminalization of Public Drunkenness: Tracing the Implementation of a Public Policy,* U.S. Department of Justice, in press.

Contributor: J. B. Gittler, editor, *Review of Sociology,* Wiley, 1957; Joseph S. Roucek, editor, *Juvenile Delinquency,* Philosophical Library, 1958; Chester J. Eugene, editor, *The Role of the Clergy in Understanding and Counseling the Alcoholic and the Family,* North Dakota Agricultural College, 1960; John C. Glidewell, editor, *Parental Attitudes and Child Behavior,* C. C Thomas, 1961; George Winokur, editor, *Determinants of Human Sexual Behavior,* C. C Thomas, 1963; Mildred B. Kantor, editor, *Mobility and Mental Health,* C. C Thomas, 1965; A. W. Gouldner and S. M. Miller, editors, *Applied Sociology in Action,* Free Press, 1965; Arthur B. Shostak, editor, *Sociology in Action,* Dorsey, 1966; *Manual on Alcoholism,* American Medical Association, 1967; Clinard and Quinney, *Criminal Behavior Systems,* Holt, 1967; Joseph Hirsh, editor, *Opportunities and Limitations in the Treatment of Alcoholics,* C. C Thomas, 1967; Ruth Fox, editor, *Alcoholism: Behavioral Research, Therapeutic Approaches,* Springer Publishing Co., 1967; R. J. Catanzaro, *Alcoholism: The Total Treatment Approach,* C. C Thomas, 1968; Jules H. Masserman, editor, *Current Psychiatric Therapies,* Volume VIII, Grune, 1968; McCall and Simmons, editors, *Issues in Participant Observations,* Addison-Wesley, 1969; T. Cook, D. Gath, and C. Hensman, editors, *The Drunkenness Offense,* Pergamon, 1969.

Elizabeth D. Whitney, *World Dialogue on Alcohol and Drug Dependence,* Beacon Press, 1970; Bruce J. Cohen, editor, *Crime in America: Perspectives in Criminal Delinquent Behavior,* F. E. Peacock, 1970; Marc Pilisuk and Phyllis Pilisuk, *Poor Americans: How the White Poor Live,* Aldine, 1971; Howard E. Freeman and Wyatt C. Jones, *Social Problems: Causes and Controls,* Rand McNally, 1973; Sawyer F. Sylvester, Jr., and Edward Sagarin, editors, *Politics and Crime,* Praeger, 1974; Daniel Glaser, editor, *Handbook of Criminology,* Rand McNally, 1974; *Alcohol, Health and the Research World,* National Institute on Alcohol Abuse and Alcoholism, 1974; F. Harper, editor, *Alcohol Abuse and Black America,* Douglass Publishers, 1976; James M. Henslin, *Deviant Life Styles,* Transaction Books, 1977; Edith Lynn Hornick, *The Drinking Woman,* Association Press, 1977; Irving L. Horowitz and Charles Nanry, editors, *Sociological Realities II: A Guide to the Study of Society,* Harper, 1978; R. Mnookin, *Child, Family, and State,* Little, Brown, 1978; Marc Galanter, editor, *Currents in Alcoholism: Recent Advances in Research and Treatment,* Volume VII, Grune, 1980; Meltzer and Nord, editors, *Making Organizations Human and Productive: A Handbook for Practitioners,* Wiley, 1981; E. Mansell Pattison and Edward Kaufman, *The American Handbook of Alcoholism,* Gardner M. Spungin, in press.

Also author of reports; editor of and contributor to proceedings. Contributor to *International Encyclopedia of the Social Sciences, American Peoples Encyclopedia Yearbook, Encyclopaedia Britannica, Academic American Encyclopedia,* and *Cyclopedia of Policing.* Columnist, *Alcoholism: The National*

Magazine. Contributor of numerous scientific papers and reports to professional journals, including *Journal of Criminology, Social Problems, British Journal of Addiction, Alcoholism: The National Magazine, Transaction,* and *Brewer's Digest.* Associate editor, *Alcoholism;* member of editorial board, *U.S. Journal of Drug and Alcohol Dependence,* 1976-78, and *Addictive Diseases: An International Journal;* member of international editorial board, *Drug and Alcohol Dependence: An International Journal on Biomedical and Psychological Approaches.*

WORK IN PROGRESS: Continued research on the effects of alcoholic beverage advertising practices and messages on alcohol problems and alcoholism in the United States.

BIOGRAPHICAL/CRITICAL SOURCES: St. Louis Globe-Democrat, September 29, 1962.

*   *   *

POAGUE, Leland A(llen) 1948-

PERSONAL: Born December 15, 1948, in San Francisco, Calif.; son of Lloyd Allen (an officer in the U.S. Air Force) and Betty (Prior) Poague; married Susan Aileen Jenson (a weaver), August 24, 1969; children: Amy, Melissa. *Education:* San Jose State College (now University), B.A., 1970; University of Oregon, Ph.D., 1973. *Office:* Department of English, Iowa State University, Ames, Iowa 50011.

CAREER: State University of New York College at Geneseo, assistant professor of English, 1973-78; Iowa State University, Ames, assistant professor, 1978-81, associate professor of English, 1981—. *Member:* Modern Language Association of America, British Film Institute.

WRITINGS: The Cinema of Frank Capra: An Approach to Film Comedy, A. S. Barnes, 1975; *The Cinema of Ernst Lubitsch: The Hollywood Films,* A. S. Barnes, 1978; *The Hollywood Professionals,* Volume VII: *Billy Wilder and Leo McCarey,* A. S. Barnes, 1980; *Howard Hawks,* Twayne, 1982; (with William Cadbury) *Toward a Counter Theory of Film Criticism,* Iowa State University Press, 1982. Contributor to *Modern Drama, Journal of Popular Film, Velvet Lighttrap,* and *Journal of Popular Culture.*

WORK IN PROGRESS: Counter-Practice: Essays in Film Criticism.

SIDELIGHTS: Leland A. Poague writes: "I have come increasingly to see film criticism and literary criticism as aesthetic problems to be solved by reference to the tradition of aesthetic philosophy. For the record, my favorite film is John Ford's 'How Green Was My Valley.'"

*   *   *

POLETTE, Nancy (Jane) 1930-

PERSONAL: Second syllable of surname is pronounced "leat"; born May 18, 1930, in Richmond Heights, Mo.; daughter of Willard A. (a lawyer) and Alice (a librarian; maiden name, Colvin) McCaleb; married Paul L. Polette (an engineering planner), December 23, 1950; children: Pamela (deceased), Paula, Keith, Marsha. *Education:* William Woods College, A.A., 1950; Washington University, St. Louis, Mo., B.S.Ed., 1962; Southern Illinois University, M.S.Ed., 1968; University of Missouri, graduate study, 1972-73. *Politics:* Democrat. *Religion:* Disciples of Christ. *Home:* 203 San Jose Court, O'Fallon, Mo. 63366. *Office:* Department of Education, Lindenwood College, St. Charles, Mo. 63301.

CAREER: Elementary school teacher in Jefferson County, Mo., 1950-51, and in Ritenour, Mo., 1954; Pattonville School District, Maryland Heights, Mo., elementary school teacher, 1955-65, coordinator of elementary school materials, 1965-80; Southern Illinois University at Carbondale, instructor, 1968-72; Lindenwood College, St. Charles, Mo., 1970—, began as instructor, associate professor of education, 1979—. Editor-in-chief, Book Lures, Inc. Lecturer and workshop leader, 1968—. Educational consultant, ECA, Denver, Colo., 1977—. Member of board of directors of Leukemia Guild of Missouri, 1959-70, and of Illinois, 1959-70. *Member:* American Library Association, American Association of School Librarians, National Council of Teachers of English, Association for Supervision and Curriculum Development, Missouri Library Association, Missouri Association of School Librarians (vice-president, 1973-74), Missouri State Teachers Association, Suburban Library Association, Chicago Children's Reading Round Table.

WRITINGS: Basic Library Skills, Milliken Publishing, 1971; *Library Skills for Primary Grades,* Milliken Publishing, 1973; *Developing Methods of Inquiry,* Scarecrow, 1973; *In Service: School Library/Media Workshops and Conferences,* Scarecrow, 1973; *The Vodka in the Punch and Other Notes from a Library Supervisor,* Shoe String, 1975; (with Marjorie Hamlin) *Reading Guidance in a Media Age,* Scarecrow, 1975; (editor) Helen Saunders, *The Modern School Library,* 2nd edition (Polette was not associated with earlier edition), Scarecrow, 1975; *E Is for Everybody,* Scarecrow, 1977; *Celebrating with Books,* Scarecrow, 1978; *Katie Penn,* Concordia, 1978; *Exploring Books with Gifted Children,* Libraries Unlimited, 1980; *Picture Books for Gifted Programs,* Scarecrow, 1981.

Also author of tape and transparencies series for library use. Editor, Miller-Brody Newbery Literary Activities Pack Program, 1974-75. Member of book review staff, *School Library Journal,* 1972-73. Contributor to journals.

WORK IN PROGRESS: The Jonah Room, for Concordia; *Three R's for the Gifted,* for Libraries Unlimited.

SIDELIGHTS: Nancy Polette comments: "In believing that one should practice what one preaches, I spend most of my time travelling around the United States and Canada doing full-day workshops for teachers and librarians with the theme 'To Catch a Reader' or how to bring books into the hands and hearts of children." *Avocational interests:* Theatre, drama.

*   *   *

POLIS, A(lbert) Richard 1937-

PERSONAL: Born March 25, 1937, in Philadelphia, Pa.; son of Louis (a businessman) and Beatrice (Thalheimer) Polis; married Sandra E. Ratner, June 19, 1961; children: Adam Bram, Daniel Lee. *Education:* West Chester State College, B.S., 1959; University of Pennsylvania, M.S., 1965; Temple University, Ed.D., 1974. *Home:* 1917 Palomino Dr., Warrington, Pa. 18976. *Office:* Graduate Studies Office, Beaver College, Glenside, Pa. 19038.

CAREER: Teacher of mathematics in public schools of Folsom, Pa., 1960-65, and Abington, Pa., 1965-66; Camden County College, Blackwood, N.J., assistant professor of mathematics, 1967-68; Beaver College, Glenside, Pa., assistant professor, 1968-75, associate professor, 1975-77, professor of mathematics education, 1977—, dean of graduate studies, 1980—. *Member:* Mathematical Association of America, National Council of Teachers of Mathematics, American Association of University Professors, Pennsylvania Council of Teachers of

Mathematics, Association of Teachers of Mathematics of Philadelphia and Vicinity, Kappa Delta Pi, Phi Delta Kappa. *Awards, honors:* National Science Foundation grant, 1966-67.

WRITINGS: Fundamental Mathematics for Elementary Teachers: A Behavioral Objectives Approach, Harper, 1973; *Fundamental Mathematics: A Cultural Approach,* Harper, 1977; *Motivational Activities for Child Involvement in Mathematics,* FABMATH, 1980; *Magic Squares and Arrays,* FABMATH, 1980; *Problem Solving in Mathematics for Children,* FABMATH, 1982.

AVOCATIONAL INTERESTS: Writing books for children, music, poetry.

*   *   *

POLLARD, William G(rosvenor)   1911-

PERSONAL: Born April 6, 1911, in Batavia, N.Y.; son of Arthur Lewis (a mycologist and sales engineer) and Ethel (Hickox) Pollard; married Marcella Hamilton, December 27, 1932; children: William Grosvenor III, Arthur Lewis II, James H. (deceased), Frank H. *Education:* University of Tennessee, B.A., 1932; Rice Institute (now Rice University), M.A., 1934, Ph.D., 1935. *Politics:* Democrat. *Home:* 222 Virginia Rd., Oak Ridge, Tenn. 37830. *Office:* Oak Ridge Associated Universities, P.O. Box 117, Oak Ridge, Tenn. 37831.

CAREER: University of Tennessee, Knoxville, assistant professor, 1936-41, associate professor, 1941-43, professor of physics, 1943-46; Oak Ridge Associated Universities (formerly Oak Ridge Institute of Nuclear Studies), Oak Ridge, Tenn., incorporator, 1946, and executive director, 1947—. Protestant Episcopal Church, ordained deacon, 1952, priest, 1954; priest associate of St. Stephen's Church, Oak Ridge, Tenn., 1954—; priest in charge of St. Alban's Chapel, Clinton, Tenn., 1959-65. Columbia University, research scientist, 1944-45; University of the South, member of faculty, Graduate School of Theology, 1956, 1960, 1961, trustee, 1955-70.

MEMBER: American Physical Society (fellow; chairman of southeastern section, 1951-52), American Association for the Advancement of Science (fellow), American Nuclear Society (fellow; member of first board of directors, 1955-60), Tennessee Academy of Science, Phi Beta Kappa, Sigma Xi, Phi Kappa Phi, Sigma Pi Sigma, Beta Gamma Sigma. *Awards, honors:* Distinguished Service Award, Southern Association of Science and Industry, 1950; Semicentennial Medal of Honor, Rice University, 1962. Honorary D.Sc. from Ripon College, 1951, University of the South, 1952, Kalamazoo College, 1955; D.D. from Hobart College, 1956, Grinnell College, 1957, Philadelphia College of Pharmacy and Science, 1977; LLD. from University of Chattanooga, 1958, Kenyon College, 1964; L.H.D., Keuka College, 1962, Long Island University, 1965, Seattle Pacific College, 1969, Westminister College, 1969.

WRITINGS: (Author of introductions) *The Hebrew Iliad,* translated by R. H. Pfeiffer, Harper, 1957; *The Christian Idea of Education* (Kent School anniversary seminar) Part I, edited by Edmond Fuller, Yale University Press, 1957; *Chance and Providence,* Scribner, 1958; *Physicist and Christian,* Seabury, 1962; *Atomic Energy and Southern Science,* Oak Ridge Associated Universities, 1966; *Man on a Spaceship,* Claremount University Center, 1967; *Science and Faith: Twin Mysteries,* Nelson, 1970; *Oak Ridge Associated Universities from the Beginning,* Oak Ridge Associated Universities, 1980.

Contributor: James Pike, editor, *Modern Canterbury Pilgrims,* Morehouse, 1956; Edmund Fuller, editor, *Schools and Scholarship,* (Part II of *The Christian Idea of Education*), Yale Uni-

versity Press, 1962; Stephen Bayne, editor, *Space Age Christianity,* Morehouse, 1963; Frank Cellier, editor, *Liturgy Is Mission,* Seabury, 1964; *Religion and the University,* University of Toronto Press, 1964; Michael Hamilton, editor, *This Little Planet,* Scribner, 1970; E. Berkeley Tompkins, editor, *Peaceful Change In Modern Society,* Hoover Institution Press, 1971; Ian G. Barbour, editor, *Earth Might Be Fair,* Prentice-Hall, 1972; Bob E. Patterson, editor, *Science, Faith, and Revelation,* Broadman Press, 1979. Contributor to university centennial publications.

SIDELIGHTS: William G. Pollard writes: "The major portion of my writing has been devoted to the problem of seeing how Christian theology as perfected 1600 years ago is consistent with the view of reality of modern science formulated mainly in the past sixty years. I have come to believe that the key elements in this task are the reality of the transcendent and the reality of many alternative histories determined by chance. The most recent practical application has been an article, 'Theological View of Nuclear Energy,' published originally in *Nuclear News* which has been widely reprinted and translated into French, German, and several other languages."

BIOGRAPHICAL/CRITICAL SOURCES: "A Deacon in Oak Ridge," *New Yorker,* February 7, 1943 (reprinted in Daniel Lang's *The Man in the Thick Lead Suit,* Oxford University Press, 1954, and *From Hiroshima to the Moon,* Simon & Schuster, 1959).

*   *   *

POOLE, Gray Johnson   1906-
(Betsy Gray)

PERSONAL: Born September 26, 1906, in Philadelphia, Pa.; daughter of Oscar Warren and Elisabeth (Shaughnessy) Johnson; married Lynn D. Poole (an educator and writer), January 1, 1941 (died April 14, 1969). *Education:* Attended Johns Hopkins University, 1926-29. *Religion:* Episcopalian. *Home:* 1873 Veteran Ave., Los Angeles, Calif. 90025.

CAREER: Evening Sun, Baltimore, Md., reporter, 1934-37; Hutzler's (department store), Baltimore, fashion copywriter, 1937-42; free-lance writer. *Member:* P.E.N., Society of Children's Book Writers. *Awards, honors:* Robert E. Sherwood Award for television script, 1956, for documentary program on public school desegregation in Baltimore.

WRITINGS: Opportunities Unlimited: The Engineer in IBM, International Business Machines Corp., 1956; *IBM Engineering Opportunities,* International Business Machines Corp., 1957; (with Ted Shawn) *One Thousand and One Night Stands* (biography of Shawn), Doubleday, 1960, reprinted, Da Capo Press, 1979; *Architects and Man's Skyline,* Dodd, 1972; *Nuts from Forest, Orchard, and Field,* Dodd, 1974; *Mistletoe: Fact and Folklore,* Doubleday, 1976.

With husband, Lynn Poole: *Scientists Who Changed the World,* Dodd, 1960; *Weird and Wonderful Ants,* Obolensky, 1961; *Balloons Fly High: 200 Years of Adventure and Science,* Whittlesey House, 1961; *Carbon-14 and Other Science Methods That Date the Past,* Whittlesey House, 1961; *Danger! Icebergs Ahead!,* Random House, 1961; *Volcanoes in Action: Science and Legend,* McGraw, 1962; *Deep in Caves and Caverns,* Dodd, 1962; *Insect-Eating Plants,* Crowell, 1963; *Scientists Who Work Outdoors,* Dodd, 1963; *History of Ancient Olympic Games,* Obolensky, 1963; *Scientists Who Work with Astronauts,* Dodd, 1964; *Electronics in Medicine,* McGraw, 1964; *Fireflies in Nature and the Laboratory,* Crowell, 1965; *Scientists Who Work with Cameras,* Dodd, 1965; *Frontiers of*

Science, McGraw, 1965; *Doctors Who Saved Lives*, Dodd, 1966; *One Passion, Two Loves: The Story of Heinrich and Sophia Schliemann, Discoverers of Troy*, Crowell, 1966 (published in England as *One Passion, Two Loves: The Schliemanns of Troy*, Gollancz, 1967); *The Magnificent Traitor: A Novel of Alcibiades and the Golden Age of Pericles*, Dodd, 1968; *Men Who Dig up History*, Dodd, 1968; *Men Who Pioneered Inventions*, Dodd, 1969.

Contributor to *Encyclopaedia Britannica*. Author of art column, *Pasadena Star News*, 1945; author of column under pseudonym Betsy Gray, *Living for Young Homemakers*, 1952-53. Contributor to magazines, occasionally under pseudonym Betsy Gray.

WORK IN PROGRESS: Articles for magazines.

* * *

POPHAM, Hugh 1920-

PERSONAL: Born May 15, 1920, in Devonshire, England; son of Sir Henry Bradshaw and Irene (Collyer) Popham; married; children: Peter, Amanda. *Education:* Corpus Christi College, Cambridge, B.A. *Politics:* Liberal. *Home:* Napper's Cottage, Lyatts, Hardington, Mandeville, Yeovic, Somerset BA22 9NR, England.

CAREER: Lodge School, Barbados, West Indies, teacher, 1947-48; writer. *Military service:* British Navy, fighter pilot with Royal Naval Volunteer Reserve, 1940-46. *Member:* International P.E.N., Society of Authors.

WRITINGS: Against the Lightning (poems), John Lane, 1944; *The Journey and the Dream* (poems), John Lane, 1945; *To the Unborn: Greetings* (poems), Dropmore Press, 1946; *Beyond the Eagle's Rage* (novel), John Lane, 1951; *Sea Flight* (autobiographical), Kimber, 1954; *Cape of Storms* (documentary), Hart-Davis, 1957; *Monsters and Marlinspokes* (juvenile), Hart-Davis, 1958; *The Fabulous Voyage of the Peagsus*, Criterion, 1959; *The Sea Beggars* (novel), Morrow, 1961; *The Shores of Violence* (novel), Cassell, 1963; *The House at Cane Garden* (novel), Sidgwick & Jackson, 1966; *The Somerset Light Infantry*, Hamish Hamilton, 1968; *Gentleman Peasants*, Deutsch, 1968; *Into Wind: A History of British Naval Flying*, Hamish Hamilton, 1969; *The Dorset Regiment*, Leo Cooper, 1970; (editor with Robin Popham) *A Thirst for the Sea: The Sailing Adventures of Erskine Childers*, Stanford Maritime, 1979.

Also author of television play "Trouble in the Sun," 1953, documentary film "All Square Aft," Martin Films, 1955, and radio play "The Seige of Mocking Hill," 1956. Occasional contributor to *Blackwood's, Time and Tide*, and other magazines.

SIDELIGHTS: Though for many years the sea was his main interest (he once crossed the Atlantic in a fishing boat and spent four years in the West Indies), Hugh Popham reports that he is "now living in rustic tranquillity surrounded by goats, ducks and hens," about which he occasionally writes "with humorous self-deprecation."

* * *

POTTER, Margaret (Newman) 1926-
(Anne Betteridge, Anne Melville)

PERSONAL: Born June 21, 1926, in London, England; daughter of Bernard (an author) and Marjory (a teacher; maiden name, Donald) Newman; married R. Jeremy Potter (a publisher), 1950; children: Jocelyn, Jonathan. *Education:* St. Hugh's College, Oxford, M.A. *Residence:* London, England. *Agent:*

A. D. Peters, 10 Buckingham St., London WC2N 6BU, England.

CAREER: Author. Editor of *King's Magazine* (children's magazine), 1950-55; staff member of Citizens Advice Bureau, London, England, 1960-70. *Member:* Society of Authors. *Awards, honors:* Romantic novel award, 1967, for *The Truth Game*.

WRITINGS—Children's books: *The Touch-and-Go Year*, Dobson, 1968; *The Blow-and-Grow Year*, Dobson, 1970; *Sandy's Safari*, Dobson, 1971; *The Story of the Stolen Necklace*, Dobson, 1974; *Trouble on Sunday*, Methuen, 1974; *The Motorway Mob*, Methuen, 1976; *Tony's Special Place*, Bodley Head, 1977.

Novels; under pseudonym Anne Betteridge; all published by Hurst & Blackett: *The Foreign Girl*, 1960; *The Young Widow*, 1961; *Spring in Morocco*, 1962; *The Long Dance of Love*, 1963; *The Younger Sister*, 1964; *Return to Delphi*, 1964; *Single to New York*, 1965; *The Chains of Love*, 1965; *The Truth Game*, 1966; *A Portuguese Affair*, 1966; *A Little Bit of Luck*, 1967; *Shooting Star*, 1968; *Love in a Rainy Country*, 1969; *Sirocco*, 1970; *The Girl Outside*, 1971; *Journey from a Foreign Land*, 1972; *The Sacrifice*, 1973; *A Time of Their Lives*, 1974; *The Stranger on the Beach*, 1974; *The Temp*, 1976; *A Place for Everyone*, 1977; *The Tiger and the Goat*, 1978.

Under pseudonym Anne Melville: *The Lorimer Line*, Doubleday, 1977; *Alexa*, Doubleday, 1979 (published in England as *The Lorimer Legacy*, Heinemann, 1979); *Lorimers at War*, Heinemann, 1980; *Blaize*, Doubleday, 1981.

WORK IN PROGRESS: Another book in the Lorimer series.

AVOCATIONAL INTERESTS: Tennis, gardening, travel abroad.

* * *

POWELL, Eric F(rederick) W(illiam) 1899-
(Peter Rusholm)

PERSONAL: Born August 28, 1899, in Cinderford, Gloucestershire, England; son of Frederick James (a tradesman) and Frances (Cooper) Powell; married Irene Hilda Sharp (a homoeopath), September 19, 1935; children: Brian Gerald, Christopher Douglas, Michael John, David Francis, Richard Graham. *Education:* British Naturopathic Association, N.D., 1923; St. Andrew's Ecumenical University College, London, England, Ph.D., 1955. *Religion:* Jehovah's Witness. *Home and office:* 21 Bloomfield Rd., Harpenden, Hertfordshire, England.

CAREER: Naturopath and homoeopath, London, England, and Harpenden, Hertfordshire, England; writer and lecturer. Adviser and therapeutics, Ghana Institute of Homeopathy.

WRITINGS: Water Treatments, C. W. Daniel, 1929; *Cell Nutrition*, C. W. Daniel, 1934; *Balance: Spiritual, Physical, Intellectual*, C. W. Daniel, 1934; *Health Secrets of All Ages*, Health Science Press, 1934; *The Biochemic Pocket Book*, Health Science Press, 1954; *The Group Remedy Prescriber*, Health Science Press, 1955, reprinted, Beekman, 1980; *A Simple Way to Successful Living*, World's Work, 1957; *Health from the Kitchen*, Health Science Press, 1958, 2nd revised edition, 1969, Beekman, 1980; *Kelp: The Health Giver*, Health Science Press, 1958, revised edition, 1968, Beekman, 1980; *The Biochemic Prescriber*, Formur International, 1960; *Building a Healthy Heart*, Health Science Press, 1961, 2nd edition, 1964, State Mutual Book, 1980; *The Natural Home Physician*, Health Science Press, 1962, revised edition, 1975, State Mutual Book, 1980; *Biochemistry Up-to-Date*, Formur International, 1963, new edition, Health Science Press, 1972, Beekman, 1980; *Lady Be Beautiful*, Health Science Press, 1964, revised edition, 1972;

The Modern Botanic Prescriber, Fowler, 1965; *Tranquillization with Harmless Herbs*, Health Science Press, 1968, Beekman, 1980; *Health from Earth, Air and Water*, Health Science Press, 1970; *About Dandelions*, Thorsons, 1972; *A Home Course in Nutrition*, Health Science Press, 1978, Beekman, 1980.

Also author of *Life Abundant*, 1943, *Healing by Auto-Induction*, Academic Publications, and, under pseudonym Peter Rusholm, *Air and Water Country Medicines*, 1971; author of booklets. Contributor to health magazines.†

* * *

POWERS, Andy 1896-

PERSONAL: Born May 12, 1896, in Lexington, Tenn.; son of William Clark (a farmer) and Fredonia (Harroll) Powers; married Lena Mae Scott, August 25, 1923; children: Charles Andrew. *Education:* Attended Ardmore Business College, 1932, and University of Oklahoma, 1967-68. *Religion:* Methodist. *Home and office:* 431 North Sunset Dr., Hereford, Tex. 79045.

CAREER: Worked as salesman with Libby, McNeil & Libby, 1921; worked in dry cleaning and laundry business in Texas and Oklahoma, c. 1922; owner of dry cleaning and laundry plant in Ardmore, Okla., 1923-39; employed by Warren Refining and Chemical Co., 1940-50, field sales manager, 1943-50; jewelry store owner and operator, 1950-62; poet and author. *Military service:* U.S. Army, 1918. *Member:* National Writers Club, Writers Association of the Golden Spread, Masons, Shriners, Eastern Star, American Legion (adjutant), Lions Club.

WRITINGS: How I Whipped Arthritis, Jim Hess Press, 1972; *Here Lies Our Heart* (poems), Adams Press, 1974; *The Arkansas John the Baptist* (novel), Branden Press, 1975; *Heavenly Days* (poems), Nortex, 1976; *A Bit of Heaven* (poems), Nortex, 1978.

WORK IN PROGRESS: Buddy, a swampland novel; *El Santo and Pancho Villa*, a novel.

* * *

PRATT, J(oseph) Gaither 1910-1979

PERSONAL: Born August 31, 1910, in Winston-Salem, N.C.; died November 3, 1979; son of Joseph Monroe (a farmer) and Mattie (Hauser) Pratt; married Nellie Ruth Pratt (a nurse administrator), June 14, 1936; children: John Herman, Vernon Gaither, Joseph Marion, Ellen Wilson. *Education:* Duke University, A.B., 1931, M.A., 1933, Ph.D., 1936. *Home:* Route 1, Keswick, Va. 22947.

CAREER: Duke University, Durham, N.C., research associate in Parapsychology Laboratory, 1937-63; University of Virginia, Medical School, Charlottesville, research associate, 1964-65, assistant professor, 1966-70, associate professor of neurology and psychiatry, 1970-73, professor of psychiatry, 1973-79. President, Psychical Research Foundation, Inc. Principal investigator for homing pigeon project, U.S. Office of Naval Research, 1953-58. *Military service:* U.S. Naval Reserve, 1944-46. *Member:* American Association for the Advancement of Science, American Psychological Association, Parapsychological Association (member of council, 1959-62, beginning 1964; president, 1960), Southern Society for Philosophy and Psychology, Phi Beta Kappa, Omicron Delta Kappa, Tau Kappa Alpha, Sigma Xi. *Awards, honors:* McDougall Award, Institute for Parapsychology, 1970.

WRITINGS: Towards a Method of Evaluating Mediumistic Material, Boston Society for Psychic Research, 1936; (editor with

Charles Edward Stuart) *Handbook for Testing Extrasensory Perception*, Farrar & Rinehart, 1937; (with Joseph Banks Rhine, Burke M. Smith, Joseph A. Greenwood and Stuart) *Extrasensory Perception After Sixty Years: A Critical Appraisal on the Research in Extrasensory Perception*, Holt, 1940; (with Rhine) *Parapsychology, Frontier Science of the Mind: A Survey of the Field, the Methods, and the Facts of ESP and PK Research*, C. C Thomas, 1957, revised edition, 1962; *Parapsychology: An Insider's View of ESP*, Doubleday, 1964; *On the Evaluation of Verbal Material in Parapsychology* (monograph), Parapsychology Foundation, 1969; *A Decade of Research with a Selected ESP Subject*, American Society for Psychical Research, 1973; *ESP Today: A Study of Developments in Parapsychology Since 1960*, Scarecrow, 1973; (with Naomi A. Hintze) *The Psychic Realm: What Can You Believe?*, Random House, 1975. Contributor of about one hundred scientific articles and reviews to psychological and biological journals. Editor, *Journal of Parapsychology*, 1942-63.

WORK IN PROGRESS: A book on extrasensory perception research in Russia and around the world.

OBITUARIES: Washington Post, November 8, 1979.†

* * *

PRATT, William C(rouch, Jr.) 1927-

PERSONAL: Born October 5, 1927, in Shawnee, Okla.; son of William Crouch (owner of shoe store) and Irene (Johnston) Pratt; married Anne Cullen Rich, October 2, 1954; children: Catherine Cullen, William Stuart, Randall Johnston. *Education:* University of Oklahoma, B.A., 1949; Vanderbilt University, M.A., 1951, Ph.D., 1957; University of Glasgow, graduate study, 1951-52. *Politics:* Republican. *Religion:* Episcopalian. *Home:* 212 Oakhill Dr., Oxford, Ohio 45056. *Office:* Department of English, Miami University, Oxford, Ohio.

CAREER: Vanderbilt University, Nashville, Tenn., instructor in English, 1955-57; Miami University, Oxford, Ohio, 1957—, began as instructor, associate professor and director of freshman English, 1964-69, professor of English, 1969—. Fulbright professor of American literature at University College, Dublin, Ireland, 1975-76; resident scholar at Miami University European Center, Luxembourg, fall, 1976. *Military service:* U.S. Naval Reserve, active duty, 1945-46, 1953-55; became lieutenant. *Member:* Modern Language Association of America, National Council of Teachers of English, Ohio English Association, Phi Beta Kappa. *Awards, honors:* Rotary fellowship to University of Glasgow.

WRITINGS: (Editor) *The Imagist Poem*, Dutton, 1963; *The Fugitive Poets*, Dutton, 1965; *The College Writer*, Scribner, 1969; (contributor) *Bibliographical Guide to the Study of Southern Literature*, Louisiana State University Press, 1969; *Ezra Pound: The London Years, 1908-1920*, AMS Press, 1978; *Southern Writers: A Biographical Dictionary*, Louisiana State University Press, 1979.

WORK IN PROGRESS: A translation of a book on French origins of modern poetry; a translation of the poetry of Rainer Maria Rilke; a critical biographical study of William Faulkner; a critical history of modern poetry.

SIDELIGHTS: William C. Pratt told *CA:* "Writing, for me, has always been the link between reading literature and teaching it. Reading, writing, and teaching flow so naturally into each other that I tend to think of them not as separate activities, but as connected ways of thinking. Happily, I find that as I grow older, my appetite for reading and writing and teaching increases along with my enjoyment of them. So the literary profession keeps me drinking at the fountain of youth; I read more, write more, teach more with every passing year, and I am more and more satisfied, though my thirst is never filled.''

*   *   *

PRENTICE, Ann E(thelynd)   1933-

PERSONAL: Born July 19, 1933, in Cambridgeport, Vt.; daughter of Homer O. (a logger) and Helen (Cooke) Hurlbut; married Paul Prentice (an engineer), 1954 (divorced); children: David, Melody, Holly, Wayne. *Education:* University of Rochester, B.A., 1954; State University of New York at Albany, M.L.S., 1964; Columbia University, D.L.S., 1972. *Home:* 5000 Oak Ridge Hwy., Knoxville, Tenn. 37921. *Office:* 804 Volunteer Blvd., Knoxville, Tenn. 37916.

CAREER: State University of New York at Albany, assistant professor of library science, beginning 1972; University of Tennessee, Knoxville, director of Graduate School of Library and Information Science, 1978—. Trustee, Hyde Park Free Library, 1973—, and Mid-Hudson Library System. *Member:* American Library Association, American Management Association, American Society for Information Science, Special Library Association, Southeastern Library Association, New York Library Association, Tennessee Library Association. *Awards, honors:* Litt.D., Keuka College, 1979.

WRITINGS: The Public Library Trustee, Scarecrow, 1973; *Suicide,* Scarecrow, 1974; *Public Library Finance,* American Library Association, 1977; *Strategies for Survival: Library Financial Planning,* Bowker, 1979; *Financial Planning for Libraries,* Scarecrow, in press.

AVOCATIONAL INTERESTS: History; historical research; collecting, preparing, and eating natural foods.

*   *   *

PRESS, (Otto) Charles   1922-

PERSONAL: Born September 12, 1922; son of Otto and Laura (Irion) Press; married Nancy Miller, June 10, 1950; children: Edward, William, Thomas, Laura. *Education:* Attended Elmhurst College, 1939-43; University of Missouri, B.J., 1948; University of Minnesota, M.A., 1951, Ph.D., 1953. *Politics:* Independent. *Religion:* Protestant. *Home:* 987 Lautern Hill Dr., East Lansing, Mich. 48823. *Office:* Department of Political Science, Michigan State University, East Lansing, Mich. 48824.

CAREER: North Dakota Agricultural College (now North Dakota State University), Fargo, instructor in political science, 1956-57; University of Wisconsin—Madison, assistant professor, 1957-58; Michigan State University, East Lansing, assistant professor, 1958-62, associate professor, 1962-65, professor of political science, 1965—, department chair, 1965-72. Director, Grand Rapids Metropolitan Area Study, 1956-57. *Military service:* U.S. Army, 1943-45. *Member:* American Political Science Association, National Municipal League, Midwest Political Science Association (president, 1974-75), Michigan Conference of Political Scientists (president, 1972-73).

WRITINGS: (With Oliver Williams) *Democracy in Urban America,* Rand McNally, 1962, 2nd edition, 1970; *Main Street Politics,* Institute for Community Development, Michigan State University, 1962; (with Charles Adrian) *The American Political Process,* McGraw, 1965, 2nd edition, 1969; *Democracy in the Fifty States,* Rand McNally, 1966; (with Alan Arian) *Empathy and Ideology,* Rand McNally, 1966; (with Walter C. Adrian) *Governing Urban America,* 4th edition, McGraw, 1972,

5th edition, 1977; (with Kenneth VerBurg) *States and Communities in the Federal System,* Wiley, 1979; (with VerBurg) *American Policy Studies,* Wiley, 1981.

*   *   *

PRESTON, Ralph C(lausius)   1908-

PERSONAL: Born April 12, 1908, in Philadelphia, Pa.; son of Gilbert Kent and Anna E. (Clausius) Preston; married Debora Steer, November, 1933 (divorced October, 1949); married Madeline Perry, October 18, 1952; children: (first marriage) Kathleen, Elizabeth Ann (Mrs. Arthur U. Ayres, Jr.), John Nicholas. *Education:* Attended Antioch College, 1928-30; Swarthmore College, A.B., 1932; Columbia University, M.A., 1934, Ph.D., 1941. *Religion:* Society of Friends. *Home:* 516 Revere Rd., Drexel Hill, Pa. 19026.

CAREER: Teacher in public and private schools in Pennsylvania, New York, and Connecticut, 1931-41; University of Pennsylvania, Philadelphia, assistant professor, then associate professor, 1941-53, professor of education, 1953-76, professor emeritus, 1976—, director of reading clinic, 1946-76, vice-dean of Graduate School of Education, 1963-67. U.S. Department of State education specialist in Germany, 1952. Consultant to Young America Films, and Cornet Instructional Films. *Member:* American Educational Research Association, American Psychological Association, National Council for the Social Studies, International Reading Association. *Awards, honors:* Fulbright research scholar in Germany, 1959.

WRITINGS: Children's Reactions to a Contemporary War Situation, Teachers College, Columbia University, Bureau of Publications, 1942; *Science: An Approach in the Elementary School,* School District of Philadelphia, 1945; *Teaching Social Studies in the Elementary School,* Rinehart, 1950, 4th edition (with W. Herman), Holt, 1974, 5th edition, 1981; (editor and contributor) *Teaching World Understanding,* Prentice-Hall, 1955; (with Morton Botel) *How to Study,* Science Research Associates, 1956, 4th edition, 1981; *Teaching Study Habits and Skills,* Rinehart, 1959; (with J. Wesley Schneyer and Franc J. Thyng) *Guiding the Social Studies Reading of High School Students,* National Council for the Social Studies, 1963; (with Elizabeth A. Cox and Ardra S. Wavle) *A New Hometown,* Heath, 1964, revised edition, 1969; (with Frances V. Nichols and Wavle) *In School and Out,* Heath, 1964, revised edition, 1969; (with Martha McIntosh and Mildred M. Cameron) *Greenfield, U.S.A.,* Heath, 1964; (with Eleanor Clymer) *Communities at Work,* Heath, 1964, revised edition, 1969; *In These United States,* Heath, 1966, revised edition, 1969; (with Tottle) *In Latin American Lands and Canada,* Heath, 1967, revised edition, 1969; (with McIntosh and Cameron) *Greenfield and Far Away,* Heath, 1969; (with Tottle, Marion Murphy, and James Flannery) *Culture Regions in the Eastern Hemisphere,* Heath, 1971; (with Botel, K. Conner, and J. Willens) *Ways to Read, Write, Study: Social Studies,* Botel/Shepard, 1981; (with Botel) *Ways to Read, Write, Study: Science,* Botel/Shepard, 1981. Contributor to *Mental Hygiene, English Journal, Journal of Educational Research,* and other periodicals.

WORK IN PROGRESS: Additional publications in *Ways to Read, Write, Study* series; a biography of the German educator, Erich Hylla; a book on children's career aspirations and their subsequent careers as adults.

SIDELIGHTS: Ralph C. Preston writes: ''Shortly after I began teaching, I became aware of the plethora of writing for children that was condescending, on the one hand, and that shot over children's heads, on the other. I discovered that children do not like to be talked down to by an author. Furthermore, if reading about how an airplane flies or what the geography of Switzerland is like, they are more often annoyed than not by an author who insists on introducing a narrative setting. Most children welcome information when it is presented in a straight forward manner, provided, of course, that the writing is clear, simple, and graceful.

"My second discovery was the high degree of frustration children experience by an author's presentation of a large number of ideas in a passage. Too few content books for children do a good job of expanding and illustrating a new concept before rushing on to the next.

"I was challenged to try my hand at writing children's school books to avoid these twin pitfalls. Though such books are better than they used to be, much room remains for improving their readability.

"Early in my career I was also motivated to see if I could write books and articles addressed to teachers that they would want to read and would respect. Pedagogical writing has been roundly and justifiably condemned by critics for dealing with trivia, propounding the obvious, and using pretentious jargon. I learned that solid material of help to the teachers can be produced without offending their intelligence, without patronizing them, and without boring them.''

*   *   *

PRYOR, Adel
   See WASSERFALL, Adel

*   *   *

PURCELL, Roy E(verett) 1936-

PERSONAL: Born June 25, 1936, in Los Angeles, Calif.; son of Clifford Loren and Ella Dean (Mace) Purcell; married Florence Kinsey, February 7, 1959; children: Cyntea, Ramiel, Rischele, Loren, Taana, Saronna, Kasyn. *Education:* Utah State University, B.S., 1963, graduate study, 1963-64. *Home and office:* 224 Minor, Henderson, Nev. 89015.

CAREER: Director and exhibits designer, Mohave Museum of History and Arts, Kingman, Ariz., 1967-70, and Southern Nevada Museum, Henderson, 1970-74; poet and artist. Work has been exhibited nationally and is included in many public and private collections. *Military service:* U.S. Army, Infantry, 1954-56. *Awards, honors:* Decade Award, Nevada State Council on the Arts.

WRITINGS—Self-illustrated: *The Wayfarer* (autobiographical), Celestial Arts, 1975; (with Dale Robertson) *The Wells Fargo Legend,* Celestial Arts, 1975; *Chloride: The Murals,* Nevada Publications, 1978; *Wilderness Journey,* Sierra Trails Press, 1979; *On the Banks of the Mother River,* Nevada Publications, 1976; *This Man from Galilee,* Spiritual Arts Publications, 1981.

Also author of *The Journey* (etchings and poetry), *The Wayfarers: Songs of Love, Remnants from Consciousness, The Mountain, Journey Images, The Long Walk,* and *The Eternal Feminine.* Illustrator of numerous magazine articles and books.

WORK IN PROGRESS: Notes from Nazareth; Sinai Speaks; murals for Egypt-Israel peace project.

SIDELIGHTS: Roy E. Purcell writes: "For me art is no end for which I seek—the works do not exist simply for their own sake, but are more truly images reflected from the world within. They are by-products, being merely the record of a journey. . . , a 'movie' of a man in search of himself. There are

moments of pure vision, recognition of obscure aspects of the personality which can only be recorded by use of symbols: the serpent, portraying the creative power, the drive within, around which all other aspects of the personality orbit; there is the woman as symbol, that fascinating, intuitive, alluring side of the psyche which has acted as a soul guide on the journey of discovery; the tree which rises from the center of my world, signifying life-time, around which the journey-dance evolves; and lately, the cross, symbol of the integration of mind and spirit which makes possible the transformation of the personality.

"Within me lives also an old man, one side of myself wiser than the rest—an eternal spirit who dictates much of my poetry and keeps me searching for wisdom and understanding. To him the world is a keyboard of images with which to weave a philosophy. To him everything is in balanced opposition, ordered disunity where death is the necessary prelude to birth—where both are the parents of experience, and where wisdom is the golden sun that casts its aura over all.

"Around these symbols the viewer or reader must weave the record of the journey, an inward search for self. Without them there is no real understanding of the works, therefore no understanding of the personality from which they emerged. And, more importantly, no enrichment within the personality of those who come to share this vision of the world.

"As the artist, I am not separate, a strange individual living in my own world. I am one with all life . . . living in your world. What I have found within myself I have found in all men and in all women, for I am a part of both. In learning to understand myself through the images of art and poetry, I have only come to understand others, and in the recording of this knowledge comes a special responsibility—the recording of the life's journey we all share. The creative, sensitive person must become the eyes and ears of the world. That is his special burden.

"So life has become an endless, if seemingly impossible, search to see, understand and love all—this journey has become my goal. In [my] works, through the images reflected and the words recorded, I strive to break down all walls, open all doors, to stand before you without shame, a soul unveiled. I am no longer mine, but the world's, having exposed myself through art and poetry. I harbor no secrets, therefore no fears—growing in love for all I meet.''

*   *   *

PURDY, Captain Jim
   See GILLELAN, G(eorge) Howard

*   *   *

PUSHKAREV, Boris S. 1929-

PERSONAL: Born October 22, 1929, in Prague, Czechoslovakia; came to United States in 1949, naturalized in 1954; son of Sergei G. (a historian) and Julie (Popov) Pushkarev; married Iraida Vandellos-Legky, 1973. *Education:* Yale University, B.Arch., 1954, Master of City Planning, 1957. *Religion:* Russian Orthodox. *Home:* 300 Winston Dr., Apt. 921, Cliffside Park, N.J. 07010. *Office:* Regional Plan Association, 1040 Avenue of the Americas, New York, N.Y. 10018.

CAREER: Maurice E. H. Rotival & Associates (planning consultants), New York City, planner, 1954-57; Yale University, New Haven, Conn., instructor in city planning, 1957-61; Regional Plan Association, New York City, chief planner, 1961-69, vice-president of research and planning, 1969—. Adjunct assistant professor, Graduate School of Public Administration, New York University, 1967-78. Lecturer and consultant. Member of board of directors, National Alliance of Russian Solidarists, 1979—. *Awards, honors:* National Book Award, 1964, for *Man-Made America.*

WRITINGS: (With Christopher Tunnard) *Man-Made America: Chaos or Control?,* Yale University Press, 1963; (with Jeffrey Zupan) *Urban Space for Pedestrians,* MIT Press, 1975; *Public Transportation and Land Use Policy,* Indiana University Press, 1977; *Urban Rail in America,* Indiana University Press, 1982. Also author, co-author, or editor of more than a dozen studies for the Regional Plan Association on transit financing, subway expansion programs, highway policy, and related topics. Contributor to *New York Affairs, Slavic Review,* and other publications. Contributing editor, *Possev* (Russian-language monthly).

WORK IN PROGRESS: Urban research; Russian area studies in conjunction with *Possev* and the Russian Research Foundation.

*   *   *

PUSHKAREV, Sergei Germanovich 1888-

PERSONAL: Born August 8, 1888, in Kursk Province, Russia (now U.S.S.R.); naturalized U.S. citizen; son of German Iosifovich (a lawyer) and Alexandra (Shatilova) Pushkarev; married Julie Popova, September 2, 1927 (died August 19, 1961); children: Boris. *Education:* University of Kharkov, degree (with distinction), 1917; attended University of Heidelberg and University of Leipzig, 1911-14. *Religion:* Russian Orthodox. *Home:* 300 Winston Dr., Apt. 921, Cliffside Park, N.J. 07010.

CAREER: University of Kharkov, Kharkov, Russia (now U.S.S.R.), assistant in history, 1917-19; Free Russian University, Prague, Czechoslovakia, docent in history, 1924-44; Yale University, New Haven, Conn., instructor in Russian, 1950-55. Lecturer in Russian history, Fordham University, 1951-52. Permanent fellow, Czech Academy of Sciences, 1929-44. *Military service:* Army service as volunteer under Provisional Government of Russia, 1917; White Russian Army, 1919-20. *Member:* American Historical Association, American Association for the Advancement of Slavic Studies. *Awards, honors:* Ford Foundation grant for *Source Book in Russian History* project, 1957-72.

WRITINGS: Proiskhozhdenie krest' ianskoi pozemel' noperediel' noiobshchiny v Rossii (title means "Origins of the Repartitional Peasant Commune"), Svobodne Slovo (Prague), Volume I, 1939, Volume II, 1941, both volumes reprinted and published with Volume III as *Krest' ianskaia pozemel' no-perediel' naia obshchina v Rossii* (title means "The Peasants' Repartitional Land-Commune in Russia"), Oriental Research Partners, 1976; *Obzor Russkoi istorii* (title means "A Survey of Russian History"), East European Fund, 1953; *Rossiia v XIX veke* (title means "Nineteenth-Century Russia"), East European Fund, 1956, published as *Istoriia Rossiia v XIX veke* (title means "Nineteenth-Century Russian History"), [Czechoslovakia], 1956, translation by Robert H. McNeal and Tova Yedlin of a revised edition published as *The Emergence of Modern Russia, 1801-1917,* Holt, 1963; (compiler) *Dictionary of Russian Historical Terms from the Eleventh Century to 1917,* Yale University Press, 1970; (compiler and co-editor) *A Source Book for Russian History from Early Times to 1917,* three volumes, Yale University Press, 1972; *Petr Velikii,* [New York], 1973; *Lenin i Rossiia,* [Frankfurt-am-Main], 1978; (editor) *Russian Historiography,* translated by George Vernadsky, Nordland, 1978.

Also author of booklets, including *Ocherk istorii krest'ianskogo samoupravleniia v Rossii* (title means "An Outline of the History of Peasant Self-Government in Russia"), 1924, *Sviato-troitskaia sergieva lavra* (title means "History of St. Sergei's Monastery"), 1928, *Znachenie pravoslavnoi tserkvi v istorii Rosskoi kul'tury i gosudarstvennosti* (title means "The Role of the Orthodox Church in Russian Cultural and Political History"), 1938, and *Mestsky stav a mestske zrizeni v chechach v 14 a 15 stoletich* (title means "The Urban Class and the Municipal Organization in Bohemia in the Fourteenth and Fifteenth Centuries"), 1938.

*   *   *

PUTT, S(amuel) Gorley 1913-

PERSONAL: Born June 9, 1913, in Brixham, England; son of Poole (a captain in the Royal Naval Reserve) and Ellen (Gorley) Putt. *Education:* Christ College, Cambridge, B.A. (first class honors), 1933, M.A., 1937; Yale University, M.A., 1936. *Politics:* Liberal. *Religion:* Anglican. *Home:* Christ College, Cambridge University, Cambridge, England.

CAREER: Commonwealth Fund of New York, Division of International Fellowships, member of staff, 1949-68, director, 1966-68; Cambridge University, Christ College, Cambridge, England, fellow, 1968—, senior tutor, 1968-78, praelector, 1976-80. Fellow, Yale University, beginning 1968. *Military service:* Royal Naval Volunteer Reserve, 1940-46; became lieutenant commander. *Member:* Royal Society of Literature (fellow), English-Speaking Association (vice-president), Athenaeum (London). *Awards, honors:* Cafe Royal Literary Prize, 1957, for *View from Atlantis;* Officer, Order of the British Empire, 1966; Cavaliere, Order of Merit of Italy, 1980.

WRITINGS: Men Dressed as Seamen, Christophers, 1943; *View from Atlantis,* Constable, 1956; (editor) *Cousins and Strangers,* Harvard University Press, 1957; *Coastline,* Hugh Evelyn, 1959; *Scholars of the Heart,* Faber, 1962, Hillary, 1963; (compiler) *Essays and Studies,* Humanities, 1963; *Henry James: A Reader's Guide,* Cornell University Press, 1966 (published in England as *A Reader's Guide to Henry James,* Thames & Hudson, 1966, published as *The Fiction of Henry James: A Reader's Guide,* Penguin, 1968); (editor) Henry James, *In the Cage and Other Stories,* Penguin, 1974; (editor) James, *The Aspern Papers and Other Stories,* Penguin, 1976; *The Golden Age of English Drama: Enjoyment of Elizabethan/Jacobean Plays,* D. S. Brewer, 1981. Also editor of various works by Henry James, Penguin, 1969—. Contributor of reviews to *Times Literary Supplement.*

WORK IN PROGRESS: Preface to Henry James, for Longman.

*   *   *

PYKE, Magnus 1908-

PERSONAL: Born December 29, 1908, in England; son of Robert and Clara (Lewis) Pyke; married Dorothea Vaughan (a chartered accountant), 1937; children: John, Elizabeth. *Education:* McGill University, Diploma in Agriculture, 1929, B.Sc., 1933; University College, London, Ph.D., 1936. *Home:* 3 St. Peters Villas, London W6 9BQ, England.

CAREER: Vitamins Ltd., London, England, chief chemist, 1934-40; Ministry of Food, Scientific Adviser's Division, London, principal scientific officer (nutrition), 1940-45, 1946-48; Allied Commission for Austria, British Element, Vienna, Austria, nutritional adviser, 1945-46; Distillers Co., Ltd., Glenochil Research Station, Menstrie, Scotland, manager, 1948-

73; British Association for the Advancement of Science, London, secretary and chairman of council, 1973-77.

WRITINGS: Manual of Nutrition, H.M.S.O., 1945, 2nd edition, 1947; *Industrial Nutrition*, Macdonald & Evans, 1950; *Townsman's Food*, Turnstile Press, 1952; *Automation: Its Purpose and Future*, Hutchinson, 1956; *Nothing Like Science*, J. Murray, 1957; *Slaves Unaware*, J. Murray, 1958; *About Chemistry*, Oliver & Boyd, 1959, Macmillan, 1960; *The Boundaries of Science*, Harrap, 1961; *The Science Myth*, Macmillan, 1962; *Nutrition*, English Universities Press, 1962; *Food Science and Technology*, J. Murray, 1964, 3rd edition, 1970; *What Scientists Are Up To*, Zenith, 1966; *The Science Century*, J. Murray, 1967; *The Human Predicament*, Collins, 1967; *Food and Society*, J. Murray, 1968; *Man and Food*, Weidenfeld & Nicolson, 1970; *Synthetic Food*, J. Murray, 1970; *Food Glorious Food*, Ginn, 1971; *Technological Eating*, J. Murray, 1972; *Catoring Science and Technology*, J. Murray, 1974; *Success in Nutrition*, J. Murray, 1975; *Butter-side Up*, J. Murray, 1976; *There and Back*, J. Murray, 1978; *Our Future*, Hamyln, 1980; *Long Life*, Dent, 1980; *Food for All the Family*, J. Murray, 1980; *The Six Lives of Pyle*, Dent, 1981.

Contributor: *Industrial Medicine and Hygiene*, Butterworth & Co., 1954; *Yeasts*, Junk, 1957; *The Chemistry and Biology of Yeast*, Academic Press, 1958; *What the Human Race Is Up To*, Gollancz, 1962; *Protein Food*, Volume III, Academic Press, 1978.

Writer of radio scripts. Contributor to *Listener*.

WORK IN PROGRESS: A book on scientific facts and feats, with Patrick Moore.

Q

QUINN, Martin
See SMITH, Martin Cruz

* * *

QUINN, Simon
See SMITH, Martin Cruz

* * *

QUOIREZ, Francoise 1935-
(Francoise Sagan)

PERSONAL: Born June 21, 1935, in Cajarc, France; daughter of Pierre (an industrialist) and Marie (Laubard) Quoirez; married Guy Schoeller, March 13, 1958 (divorced, 1960); married Robert James Westhoff, January 10, 1962 (divorced, 1963); children: (second marriage) Denis. *Education:* Attended Sorbonne, University of Paris.

CAREER: Writer. Director of film "Les Fougeres bleues," 1976. *Awards, honors:* Prix des Critiques, 1954, for *Bonjour tristesse.*

WRITINGS—Under pseudonym Francoise Sagan; novels, except as indicated: *Bonjour tristesse,* Julliard, 1954, translation by Irene Ash published under same title, Dutton, 1955, reprinted, Popular Library, 1974; *Un Certain Sourire,* Julliard, 1956, translation by Anne Green published as *A Certain Smile,* Dutton, 1956; *Dans un mois, dans un an,* Julliard, 1957, translation by Frances Frenaye published as *Those without Shadows,* Dutton, 1957; *Aimez-vous Brahms?,* Julliard, 1959, translation by Peter Wiles published under same title, Dutton, 1960; *Les Merveilleux Nuages,* Julliard, 1961, translation by Green published as *The Wonderful Clouds,* Murray, 1961, Dutton, 1962; *La Chamade,* Julliard, 1965, translation by Robert Westhoff published under same title, Dutton, 1966; *Le Garde du coeur,* Julliard, 1968, translation by Westhoff published as *The Heart Keeper,* Dutton, 1968; *Un peu de soleil dans l'eau froide,* Flammarion, 1969, translation by Terence Kilmartin published as *A Few Hours of Sunlight,* Harper, 1971 (translation by Joanna Kilmartin published in England as *Sunlight on Cold Water,* Weidenfeld & Nicolson, 1971); *Des bleus a l'ame,* Flammarion, 1972, translation by J. Kilmartin published as *Scars on the Soul,* McGraw, 1974; *Des yeux de soie: Nouvelles* (short stories), Flammarion, 1975, translation by J. Kilmartin published as *Silken Eyes,* Delacorte, 1977; *Un Profil perdu,* Flammarion, 1974, translation by J. Kilmartin published as

Lost Profile, Delacorte, 1976; *Le Lit defait,* Flammarion, 1977, translation by Abigail Israel published as *The Unmade Bed,* Delacorte, 1978. Also author of novel *Le Chien couchant,* 1980.

Plays: *Chateau en Suede* (comedy; title means "Castle in Sweden"; first produced in Paris at Theatre d'Atelier, March, 1960), Julliard, 1960; *Les Violons parfois* (two-act; first produced in Paris at Theatre Gymnase, 1961), Julliard, 1962; *La Robe mauve de Valentine* (first produced at Theatre des Ambassadeurs, 1963), Julliard, 1963; *Bonheur, impair, et passe,* Julliard, 1964; *Le Cheval evanoui* [and] *L'Echarde* (title means "The Fainted Horse" [and] "The Splinter"; first produced together in Paris at Theatre Gymnase, September, 1966), Julliard, 1966; *Un Piano dans l'herbe* (two-act comedy; title means "A Piano in the Grass"; first produced in Paris at Theatre d'Atelier, October 15, 1970), Flammarion, 1970; *Il fait beau jour et nuit* (title means "It's Nice Day and Night"), Flammarion, 1979. Also author of play "Zaphorie," 1973.

Other: *Toxique* (autobiographical fragments), illustrated by Bernard Buffet, Julliard, 1964, translation by Frenaye published under same title, Dutton, 1964; (with Federico Fellini) *Mirror of Venus,* photographs by Wingate Paine, Random House, 1966; (with Guillaume Hanoteau) *Il est des parfums* (nonfiction), J. Dullis, 1973; *Responses: 1954-1974* (interviews), J.-J. Pauvert, 1974, translation published as *Nightbird: Conversations with Francoise Sagan,* Crown, 1980; (author of introduction and commentary) *Brigitte Bardot,* Flammarion, 1975, translation by Judith Sachs published as *Brigitte Bardot: A Close-Up,* Delacorte, 1976.

Filmscripts: "Dans un mois, dans un an" (based on author's novel of same title); (with Claude Chabrol) "Landru"; (with Alain Cavalier) "La Chamade" (based on author's novel of same title), co-produced by Les Films Ariane, Les Productions and Artistes Associes, and P.E.A. (Rome), 1969; (author of dialogue with Philippe Grumbach) "Le Bal du Comte d'Orgel" (based on novel by Raymond Radiguet), produced by Les Films Marceau-Cocinor, 1970; (with Jacques Quoirez and Etienne de Monpezat) *Le Sang dore des Borgia* (television film), Flammarion, 1977.

Also author, with Michael Magne, of scenario for ballet "Le Rendez-vous manque" (title means "The Broken Date"), first produced in Monte Carlo, January, 1958; author of commentary for a volume of photographs of New York City; writer of lyrics for singer Juliette Greco.

SIDELIGHTS: Described by critic Brigid Brophy as "the most under-estimated presence in postwar French writing," Francoise Sagan has tried for more than twenty years to live up to—or live down, depending on one's point of view—the reputation she established in the 1950s as the precocious author of *Bonjour tristesse.* Born into an upper-middle-class family and educated in private and convent schools in France and Switzerland, Sagan was a mere eighteen years old when, having failed the examinations that would have allowed her to continue her studies at the Sorbonne, she sat down one lazy August day in 1953 and began working on a novel. Bored and eager to placate her parents, she completed a manuscript (parts of which she read to friends in order to gauge their reactions) in only three weeks; in it she told the bittersweet story of Cecile, a worldly seventeen-year-old girl who plots to break up her philandering father's sudden engagement to his former mistress by subtly pitting her against his current mistress.

Considered rather shocking in its time (more for its disturbing *amorality* than for its *immorality*), *Bonjour tristesse* ("Hello Sadness") met with immense commercial and critical success after its release in the spring of 1954. Its astonishing reception made Sagan a celebrity virtually overnight; people quickly came to regard her as a spokesperson for a whole generation of bored and blase young adults. This particular assumption, formulated so early in Sagan's career, combined with her well-known fondness for the "good life"—namely gambling, dancing, drinking, and driving fast, expensive sports cars (preferably in her bare feet)—convinced many readers and critics that she was living the aimless, cynical, and ultimately self-destructive type of life she described with such obvious insight and authority. It is a reputation that has plagued her throughout her career, making it impossible for some critics to take her work seriously while others, such as the *Washington Post Book World*'s L. J. Davis, admit to feeling "a persistent, uneasy, and half-baffled sense that she is really up to more than she seems to be, that behind the mask there lurks a shrewd seriousness of intent that defies and perhaps even deliberately mocks analysis."

For the most part, the plots and characters of a typical Sagan novel are interchangeable. Each story depicts a confrontation between young and old, either in the form of a middle-aged man and his much younger mistress or, less often, a middle-aged woman and her young lover. The scene of this confrontation is usually a place frequented by the idle rich, occasionally on the Riviera, even once in the Florida Keys and once in Southern California, but mostly in the nightclubs, salons, and theaters of Paris. Despite the glamorous locales, however, action and physical description are kept to a bare minimum; instead, Sagan focuses on the interrelationships between her characters as each one leads a life seemingly devoid of a past, a future, or a purpose. As the title of her first novel suggests, an atmosphere of sadness, disillusionment, resigned pessimism, loneliness, and cynicism permeates Sagan's stories. Though her characters are constantly in pursuit of pleasure, they are fully aware that true happiness, assuming they ever experience it, is a transitory state at best, liable to vanish at a moment's notice. Furthermore, as *Bonjour tristesse*'s Cecile concludes after her father Raymond's fiancee (Anne) commits suicide (Cecile had led her to believe that Raymond no longer loved her), what a person *thinks* will result in happiness or satisfaction often has precisely the opposite effect. All of these painful discoveries are related in a prose style that critics have compared to that of the great classical French writers: subdued, non-judgmental, precise, and deceptively simple and spare, almost to the point of austerity. Yet in mood, Sagan's stories reflect the feelings of malaise and doubt that were prevalent

among educated, upper-class French youth in the 1950s and 1960s.

As it had the year before in Paris, *Bonjour tristesse* overwhelmed critics when it appeared in an English translation in 1955. A typical reaction was that of Rose Feld, who wrote in the *New York Herald Tribune Book Review* that "some may find it shocking and immoral, but none will gainsay that here is a talent extraordinary not only for its maturity of style but for its adult perceptiveness of human character." A *Saturday Review* critic, noting that the novel was "sensational yes; but skilfully and quietly done," had special praise for Sagan's accurate portrayal of the "confused feelings" of adolescence. The *Atlantic*'s Charles J. Rolo remarked that "the novel has about it such a solid air of reality that I originally suspected a sizable element might be autobiographical," but he was pleased to discover that "in fact, it is a genuine work of the imagination, which makes it all the more impressive." The *Nation*'s Haakon Chevalier felt that it was nothing short of a "miracle" for one so young to have written a novel that "transcends its subject matter, as in classic tragedy."

Even those who found the work flawed in several respects admitted that Sagan was definitely a talented writer. As John Raymond of the *New Statesman and Nation* observed: "It has been suggested that this novel is slick and meretricious. Personally I do not find it so. Setting aside Mlle. Sagan's extraordinary precocity, the book seems to me a considerable achievement, a work of art of much beauty and psychological perception. If the writer alters anywhere, it is, I think, in her melodramatic ending and, perhaps even more, in her portrait of Anne, who never quite comes alive except as a paragon and as a victim. But with the father and daughter Mlle. Sagan excells."

The *New York Times*'s Marcel Arland called *Bonjour tristesse* "a charming story," but declared that "the theme lacks probability. . . . The plot savors of the artificial, the characters are a little too conventional and slightly superficial. All the same, the fact remains that the writer disarms us and that her book is light and fragile and pleasant to read from beginning to end (or almost so)."

V. P. Hass of the *Chicago Sunday Tribune*, however, did not agree. Though he described it as "a brilliant, casually decadent little novel," he reported being "repelled" by the "glossy rottenness" and "carnality" of the story. *Commonweal*'s Nora L. Nagid declared that, in addition to being "as preposterous a book as one is likely to come across," it was "childish and tiresome in its singleminded dedication to decadence." Somewhat less offended, a *Times Literary Supplement* critic dismissed it as "only at one remove from the more banal form of romantic novelette." Finally, John Metcalf of the *Spectator* commented: "[*Bonjour tristesse*] is a clever schoolgirl's version of Colette, pretentious, precocious and—for all its avowed lack of moral fibre—priggish. . . . Mlle. Sagan does not lack for effrontery. It will be interesting to see what comes next."

What came next was *A Certain Smile,* the story of a brief but passionate affair between a twenty-year-old Sorbonne student and a married man who is twice her age. For the most part, reviewers felt that it was a worthy successor to *Bonjour tristesse. Commonweal*'s Anne Fremantle, for example, found Sagan's second novel "as deceptively simple as her first, and written in that quiet, uncluttered prose that she has now perfected at the age of twenty, and with an economy and skill most writers wish they could achieve at three times her age." Peter Quennell of the *Spectator* concluded that the new novel was "decidedly better than the first; and, while [Sagan] has reaffirmed her existing qualities, many of the faults that marred *Bonjour tristesse* have been quietly dropped overboard."

Several critics, however, noted enough similarities between the two novels to suggest that perhaps Sagan was already displaying a tendency to limit herself thematically and stylistically. While granting that staging a "repeat performance" of a book like *Bonjour tristesse* "in itself is quite an achievement," a *Times Literary Supplement* reviewer declared that "one is still inclined to think she has been lucky in the extent of the interest and the excitement she has aroused." Hass, commenting once again in the *Chicago Sunday Tribune,* wrote that "it's all very Gallic, but I found [*A Certain Smile*] unwholesome and rather revolting. . . . One hopes that Miss Sagan, having worked this profitable lode twice, will turn her unquestioned talent to something of greater moment." After praising Sagan's writing for its "exceptional economy and elegance," the *Atlantic*'s Phoebe Adams also expressed a desire to see her branch out artistically, stating: "If there is any cause for concern in *A Certain Smile,* it is the lack of a sign that the author has tried to expand her view, vary her methods, or explore more deeply in the minds of her characters. *A Certain Smile* is a bull's-eye, true enough, but on the same range and the same target [as *Bonjour tristesse*]."

These last few comments more or less sum up the opinions critics have held on Sagan's work since 1956. Almost without exception, they have become progressively more bored and annoyed by her unwillingness or inability to depart from the rigid pattern established in *Bonjour tristesse* and *A Certain Smile.* Though Marjorie Perloff of the *Washington Post Book World* characterizes all of her subsequent work as little more than "pulp fiction," the reaction of the *Atlantic*'s Rolo to *Those without Shadows* is a somewhat more typical one: "After her remarkable first book, which had a core of genuine feeling, Mlle. Sagan has slid into progressive apathy. Her present novelette has nothing to say. . . . For all her literary skills and graces, which are considerable, her juvenile world-weariness has become tiresome."

Aimez-Vous Brahms?, for instance, though hailed by some as the work of a "mature artist," elicited its share of negative comments as well. "There are times when Mlle. Sagan writes so appallingly that one would like to shoot the pen out of her hand," declared Patrick Dennis in the *Saturday Review.* "At other times her perception, her economy, and her utter style leave one speechless with admiration. . . . [But] she is all style with absolutely nothing to say." Praising Sagan's skill at "exploring and defining the territory of sexual attraction and experience," the *New York Herald Tribune Book Review*'s Feld admitted that "this is no small gift but with repetition and without enrichment of other worlds . . . it grows thin with usage. The promise offered by [Sagan's] first book seems to be bogging down in works that are contrived or designed for popular erotic appeal. On that level, they're good but it's not good enough for her."

Some sixteen years later, in 1976, reviewers such as the *Times Literary Supplement*'s Victoria Glendinning were still writing: "Sagan has in her time said some wry things about love; in *Lost Profile,* the insights are thin on the ground. . . . To her contemporaries, her early work was indeed 'sophisticated and erotic.' But now she is still writing for adolescents of the 1950s, hung-up on father figures, mad about puppies." The *Spectator*'s Duncan Fallowell agreed with this assessment of *Lost Profile.* Describing Sagan's fictional world as "a narrow mix of sympathy and arrogance," he stated that "writing *Bonjour tristesse* Miss Sagan had an excuse for such a self-opinionated heart. To find that in her tenth novel . . . she has advanced her profundity not at all, is still playing the cramped teenager trying to escape Daddy, comes as something of a shock." Anatole Broyard of the *New York Times* merely noted: "The

precocious adolescent who burst upon the world murmuring 'hello, sadness,' is now a writer of shamelessly happy love stories. Perhaps French sophistication has outlived its usefulness."

In 1974, the publication of *Scars on the Soul,* an intermingling of fiction, personal reflection, and autobiography, prompted some critics to conclude that Sagan had become nearly as dissatisfied with her own work as they had. While the book's novel portion, in which Sagan resurrects two characters from one of her plays and chronicles their romantic escapades, is judged to be only marginally interesting, its personal revelations surprised many readers, especially in light of Sagan's characteristic reluctance to discuss her private thoughts. In these nonfiction sections, the author self-mockingly describes "the revulsion, the boredom, the distaste I now feel for a way of life that until now, and for very good reasons, had always attracted me." Meditating on paper about her past and her work, she wonders how to write this particular novel, and even whether to write it at all.

Broyard, for one, seems to wish she hadn't. He writes: "Deft, spare, understated, subtle, disciplined, classic—these are the words critics have used to praise the novels of Francoise Sagan. She possessed to an uncommon degree, they said, the typically French flair for nuance. She could sketch in a character in a gesture, immortalize him or her in a line or two of dialogue. Her sentences were as well shaped as a Chanel suit. She dealt in essences, light and sensuous as a perfume. National pride preened itself on her. . . . Now, in *Scars on the Soul,* Miss Sagan has exposed the woman behind the novels and very nearly destroyed her own myth. The book is a very flimsy novella padded out by alternating chapters of 'self-portrait.' . . . [This] nonfiction part of the book paradoxically discards all those qualities for which Miss Sagan was esteemed. . . . [They] are replaced by a coy pomposity and page after page of puerile philosophizing."

Commenting in the *New Yorker,* John Updike observes that the novel portion of *Scars on the Soul* displays "a dainty wit [and] a parody of decadence. . . . The book reads easily; it is *company.* The author's cry of personal crisis . . . feels sincere. . . . However, there is about *Scars on the Soul* an arrogant flimsiness that invites a quarrel. . . . Mlle. Sagan has for fabric only the shreds and scraps of a world she has come to despise." Noting that her defense of the bored and idle rich who people her stories "rings hollow," Updike concludes: "We have indeed come a long, heavy way from *Bonjour tristesse,* with its sparkling sea and secluding woods, its animal quickness, its academically efficient plot, its heroes and heroines given the perfection of Racine personae by the young author's innocent belief in glamor. Her present characters seem—by this retrospect—degenerate forms of the incestuous affection between Cecile and her father in *Bonjour tristesse.* . . . Mlle. Sagan—at this juncture in her career, at least—has ceased to love herself, and has lost with love the impetus to create a fictional world."

In a final comment, a *New York Times Book Review* critic echoes Updike's remarks regarding Sagan's failure to charm and move readers as she once did. Calling attention to the reissue of *Bonjour tristesse* and *A Certain Smile* (timed to coincide with the publication of *Scars on the Soul*), he reports that the passage of time has not altered the fact that they are "effortlessly, economically, elegantly told tales." But time *has* made its mark in other ways, he concludes. "The existentialist overtones, the overlay of 'French decadence' seems *deja vu,*" the reviewer notes. "Since then, Anglo-Saxons, even Americans, have come a long way."

MEDIA ADAPTATIONS: In 1958, *Bonjour tristesse* was filmed by Columbia Pictures Industries, Inc., and *A Certain Smile* was filmed by Twentieth Century-Fox Film Corp. *Aimez-vous Brahms?* was filmed as "Goodbye Again" by United Artists Corp. in 1961.

BIOGRAPHICAL/CRITICAL SOURCES—Books: Georges Hourdin, *Le Cas Francoise Sagan*, Editions du Cerf, 1958; Malcolm Cowley, editor, *Writers at Work*, Viking, 1958; Francoise Sagan, *Toxique* (autobiographical fragments), Julliard, 1964, translation by Francis Frenaye published under same title, Dutton, 1964; Brigid Brophy, *Don't Never Forget: Collected Views and Reviews*, Holt, 1966; Sagan, *Des bleus a l'ame*, Flammarion, 1972, translation by Joanna Kilmartin published as *Scars on the Soul*, McGraw, 1974; *Responses: 1954-1974* (interviews), J.-J. Pauvert, 1974, translation published as *Nightbird: Conversations with Francoise Sagan*, Crown, 1980; (under pseudonym Francoise Sagan) *Contemporary Literary Criticism*, Gale, Volume III, 1975, Volume VI, 1976, Volume IX, 1978, Volume XVII, 1981.

Periodicals: *New York Herald Tribune Book Review*, February 27, 1955, August 19, 1956, October 27, 1957, March 13, 1960; *New York Times*, February 27, 1955, August 19, 1956, October 27, 1957, April 15, 1974, April 22, 1976; *Saturday Review*, March 5, 1955, August 18, 1956, October 26, 1957, March 12, 1960, July 14, 1962; *New Yorker*, March 5, 1955, November 2, 1968, August 12, 1974, May 10, 1976, November 21, 1977, December 25, 1978; *Springfield Republican*, March 13, 1955, April 10, 1960; *Atlantic*, April, 1955, September, 1956, November, 1957, August, 1962, May, 1974; *Chicago Sunday Tribune*, April 24, 1955, August 19, 1956, March 13, 1960; *Commonweal*, May 13, 1955, September 14, 1956, November 29, 1957; *Spectator*, May 20, 1955, August 17, 1956, February 19, 1960, March 27, 1976; *New Statesman and Nation*, May 21, 1955; *Times Literary Supplement*, May 27, 1955, August 24, 1956, February 26, 1960, December 8, 1961, October 27, 1966, March 19, 1976; *Nation*, August 13, 1955; *San Francisco Chronicle*, August 12, 1956, October 28, 1957, March 11, 1960, July 9, 1962; *Manchester Guardian*, August 14, 1956; *New Republic*, August 20, 1956; *Catholic World*, December, 1956; *New Statesman*, October 26, 1957, February 27, 1960, March 19, 1976, October 14, 1977; *Time*, October 28, 1957, March 14, 1960, May 20, 1974, April 27, 1981; *New York Times Book Review*, March 13, 1960, November 13, 1966, November 10, 1968, April 14, 1974, October 30, 1977, December 10, 1978; *Best Sellers*, November 15, 1968, May 1, 1971, February, 1978, April, 1979; *Holiday*, January, 1969; *Washington Post Book World*, April 11, 1971, April 28, 1974, July 6, 1975; *Books and Bookmen*, January, 1975; *Listener*, March 25, 1976; *Los Angeles Times*, November 7, 1980.†

—*Sketch by Deborah A. Straub*

R

RALE, Nero
  See BURGESS, M(ichael) R(oy)

* * *

RANDOM, Alan
  See KAY, Ernest

* * *

RANSOM, John Crowe   1888-1974

PERSONAL: Born April 30, 1888, in Pulaski, Tenn.; died July 3, 1974, in Gambier, Ohio; son of John James (a Methodist minister) and Ella (Crowe) Ransom; married Robb Reavill, December 22, 1920; children: Helen (Mrs. O. D. Forman), David Reavill, John James. *Education:* Vanderbilt University, A.B., 1909; Christ Church College, Oxford, B.A. in Lit.Hum., 1913; attended University of Grenoble, briefly, after World War I. *Residence:* Gambier, Ohio.

CAREER: Taught Latin in a preparatory school for one year; Harvard University, Cambridge, Mass., assistant in English, 1914; Vanderbilt University, Nashville, Tenn., 1914-37, professor of English, 1927-37; Kenyon College, Gambier, Ohio, Carnegie Professor of Poetry, 1937-58, professor emeritus, 1958-74. Summer lecturer, Colorado State Teachers College (now University of Northern Colorado), George Peabody College for Teachers (now George Peabody College for Teachers of Vanderbilt University), University of New Mexico, University of Florida, University of Kentucky, University of Texas, University of Chattanooga, Women's College of the University of North Carolina (now University of North Carolina at Greensboro), West Tennessee Teachers College (now Memphis State University), Harvard University, and Bread Loaf School of English. Honorary consultant in American letters, Library of Congress. *Military service:* U.S. Army, 1917-19; served with 5th Field Artillery; became first lieutenant. *Member:* American Academy of Arts and Letters, American Academy of Arts and Sciences, Phi Beta Kappa, Kappa Sigma. *Awards, honors:* Rhodes scholar, Oxford University; Guggenheim fellow, 1931; Bollingen Prize for poetry, 1951; Russell Loines Prize for poetry, 1951; honored at Chicago Poetry Day, 1957; Brandeis University Creative Arts Award, 1958-59; Academy of American Poets fellow, 1962; National Book Award, 1964, for *Selected Poems;* National Endowment for the Arts award ($10,000), 1967; Emerson-Thoreau Medal, American Academy of Arts

and Sciences, 1968; Gold Medal, National Institute of Arts and Letters, 1973.

WRITINGS: Poems about God, Holt, 1919, reprinted, Folcroft, 1972; *Armageddon* (poem; bound with *A Fragment* by William Alexander Percy and *Avalon* by Donald Davidson), Poetry Society of South Carolina, 1923; *Chills and Fever* (poems), Knopf, 1924, reprinted, Folcroft, 1972; *Grace after Meat* (poems), introduction by Robert Graves, L. & V. Woolf, 1924; *Two Gentlemen in Bonds* (poems), Knopf, 1927; *God without Thunder: An Unorthodox Defense of Orthodoxy* (essays), Harcourt, 1930, reprinted, Shoe String, 1965; (with others) *I'll Take My Stand* (essays), Harper, 1930; (editor) *Topics for Freshman Writing,* Holt, 1935; *The World's Body* (essays), Scribner, 1938, reprinted, Louisiana State University Press, 1968; *The New Criticism* (essays), New Directions, 1941, reprinted, Greenwood Press, 1979; (contributor) Donald A. Stuffer, editor, *The Intent of the Critic,* Princeton University Press, 1941, reprinted, Peter Smith, 1963; *Poetics* (essays), New Directions, 1942; *A College Primer of Writing,* Holt, 1943; *Selected Poems,* Knopf, 1945, reprinted, Richard West, 1977, 3rd revised edition, Knopf, 1969; (editor) *The Kenyon Critics: Studies in Modern Literature from the "Kenyon Review,"* World Publishing, 1951, reprinted, Kennikat, 1967; *Poems and Essays,* Vintage Books, 1955; *Exercises on the Occasion of the Dedication of the New Phi Beta Kappa Memorial Hall, the College of William and Mary in Virginia* (an address), College of William and Mary, 1958; (with Delmore Schwartz and John Hall Wheelock) *American Poetry at Mid-Century* (lectures), Library of Congress, 1958, reprinted, Norwood, 1977; (editor) Thomas Hardy, *Selected Poems,* Macmillan, 1961; (with others) *Symposium on Formalist Criticism,* University of Texas, 1967; *Beating the Bushes: Selected Essays, 1941-1970,* New Directions, 1972.

Also author of an unpublished book on aesthetics, 1926. Cofounder, editor, and publisher, *Fugitive,* 1922-25; *Kenyon Review,* founder and editor, 1939-59, editor emeritus, 1959-71.

SIDELIGHTS: Around the year 1915, a group of fifteen or so Vanderbilt University teachers and students began meeting informally to discuss trends in American life and literature. Led by John Crowe Ransom, a member of the university's English faculty, these young "Fugitives," as they called themselves, opposed both the traditional sentimentality of Southern writing and the increasingly frantic pace of life as the turbulent war years gave way to the Roaring Twenties. They recorded their concerns in a magazine of verse entitled the *Fugitive,* which, though it appeared little more than a dozen times after the first issue was published in 1922, proved to be in the vanguard of a new literary movement—Agrarianism—and a new way of analyzing works of art—the New Criticism. As one of the group's major spokesmen (along with fellow members Allen Tate, Robert Penn Warren, and Donald Davidson), John Crowe Ransom eventually came to be known as the dean of twentieth-century American poets and critics.

Agrarianism was a direct descendent of the Fugitive philosophy; the Agrarians, in fact, were former Fugitives (the original group drifted apart around 1925) who banded together again in the late 1920s to extoll the virtues of the rural South and to promote the establishment of an agrarian as opposed to an industrial economy. As far as Ransom and his fellow Agrarians were concerned, noted John L. Stewart in his study of the poet and critic, "poetry, the arts, ritual, tradition, and the mythic way of looking at nature thrive best in an agrarian culture based on an economy dominated by small subsistence farms. Working directly and closely with nature man finds aesthetic satisfaction and is kept from conceitedness and greed by the many reminders of the limits of his power and understanding. But in an industrial culture he is cut off from nature. He gets into the way of thinking that machinery can give him limitless control over it, and he is denied the little indulgences of the sensibility. His arts and religions wither and he lives miserably in a rectilinear jungle of factories and efficiency apartments." In short, explained Louis D. Rubin, Jr., in *Writers of the Modern South*, "for Ransom the agrarian image is of the kind of life in which leisure, grace, civility can exist in harmony with thought and action, making the individual's life a wholesome, harmonious experience. . . . His agrarianism is of the old Southern plantation, the gentle, mannered life of leisure and refinement without the need or inclination to pioneer."

Though the rustic dream of the Agrarians more or less evaporated with the coming of the Depression, it left its philosophical imprint on Ransom's later work. As Richard Gray observed in his book *The Literature of Memory*, "the thesis that nearly all of [Ranson's] writing sets out to prove, in one way or another, is that only in a traditional and rural society—the kind of society that is epitomized for Ransom by the antebellum South—can the human being achieve the completeness that comes from exercising the sensibility and the reason with equal ease."

Ransom's poems, written primarily between 1915 and 1927 but revised several times during the following years, reflected this preoccupation with regionalism and the struggle between reason and sensibility from a thematic as well as a stylistic standpoint. Ransom's "poetic world," for instance, reported the *Washington Post Book World*'s Chad Walsh, "is mostly the South, not the South as it actually was when cotton and slavery were crowned heads, not the empirical South that the sociologists study today, but a might-have-been South, a vision of gentleness in all senses of that Chaucerian word." Stewart agreed that Ransom was "truly a Southern writer," but he attributed this less to the poet's choice of themes and backgrounds than to "his style and his vision." Explained the critic: "[Regional] qualities, violence coupled with elegance, affinity for unusual diction, concern with the insignia of feudalism and the chevalier as the embodiment of its values, mockery of the man of ideas, and so forth, are transformed by Ransom's double vision and irony into a poetry so conspicuously his own that his individuality rather than any regionalism first impresses the reader. . . . Yet it is difficult to conceive of such poetry being written in twentieth-century American by anyone not from the South."

Besides being unmistakably Southern in character, Ransom's world is a world of fundamental opposites, a world where man is constantly made aware of "the inexhaustible ambiguities, the paradoxes and tensions, the dichotomies and ironies that make up [modern] life," wrote Thomas Daniel Young in a study of the poet. His themes, continued Young, emphasized "man's dual nature and the inevitable misery and disaster that always accompany the failure to recognize and accept this basic truth; mortality and the fleetingness of youthful vigor and grace, the inevitable decay of feminine beauty; the disparity between the world as man would have it and as it actually is, between what people want and need emotionally and what is available for them, between what man desires and what he can get; man's divided sensibilities and the wars constantly raging within him, the inevitable clash between body and mind, between reason and sensibility; the necessity of man's simultaneous apprehension of nature's indifference and mystery and his appreciation of her sensory beauties; the inability of modern man, in his incomplete and fragmentary state, to experience love."

These various dualisms in Ransom's poetry could best be described in terms of a debate between the head and the heart—that is, as Young noted, between reason and aesthetic sensibility. Ransom continually sought a balance between the two, a balance which, however precarious it might have been, tried to give equal time to both logic and sentiment. He detested extremes of either kind and deliberately strived for a certain detachment in his poetry that struck some critics as being rather cold and academic. By establishing such an "aesthetic distance," however, Ransom felt that he could provide the reader with a better view of his subject than those poets who imbued their work with sentimentalism and other distracting personal attitudes. Thus, the typical Ransom poem was never autobiographical or didactic, for, as Wesley Morris pointed out in his book *Towards a New Historicism*, "[Ransom's] dualistic theory demands that in the realm of poetic discourse the artist must never assert his own personality; he must remain as 'nearly anonymous' as possible." As a result, Thorton H. Parsons observed in his critical study, "a proper appreciation of Ransom's poetry calls for a modest cultivation of literary asceticism. The reader must accustom himself to the idea that he will encounter no portrayal of strong personalities, no highly emotional drama, and (except very faintly and indirectly) little sense of a poet's dreadful self-discovery. He must tune himself to register elusive subtleties of perception and elegances of rhyme, wit, and rhetoric. He must be somewhat willing to forgive Ransom for the acute esthetic self-consciousness that made him habitually subordinate passion to tonal control. He must be indulgent of Ransom's addictions to pale or paralyzing irony and to refined whimsicality. In brief, he should accept the limitations inherent in a civilized poetry and try to savor the fragile excellences."

In Ransom's case, as Parsons suggested, these "fragile excellences" had more to do with actual poetic technique than with the creation of a particular mood. Many critics, in fact, felt Ransom was one of the greatest stylists of modern American poetry due to what Stewart described as the "unabashed elegance and artifice [of his work], both carried at times to the edge of affectation and preciousness. This poetry is *made* and proudly exhibits its technical ingenuity." Randall Jarrell, among others, regarded this obsession with what he called "rhetorical machinery" as Ransom's "way of handling sentiment or emotion without ever seeming sentimental or over-emotional; as a way of keeping the poem at the proper aesthetic distance from its subject; and as a way for the poem to extract from its subject, no matter how unpleasant or embarrassing, an unembarrassed pleasure."

Stylistically, Ransom maintained a "proper aesthetic distance" through wit (primarily irony), tone, and diction. His humor, noted Karl F. Knight in *The Poetry of John Crowe Ransom,* is similar to that of Voltaire, Rabelais, Swift, and Twain in that "it is based upon a sense of far-reaching incongruity. The times are out of joint, Ransom seems to say, but we can still take an objective look at things. And a good way to keep one's balance is to look at things through a witty and ironic style."

For the most part, stated Robert Buffington in his book *The Equilibrist,* this irony stemmed from a particular use of the language and "a subtle, and gentle, irony of tone." Rueful, wry, and often whimsical, Ransom's poetry was "detached, mock-pedantic, [and] wittily complicated," according to Jarrell, and displayed, said Parsons, a "peculiar kind of self-indulgence" and a certain "archaism and grandiloquence." His speech, wrote Buffington, "is that of the Gentleman, rather than that of the Common Man. . . . His sentences have the effect of an ease that can indulge itself in the direction of elegance. . . . He is learned enough and assured enough to range in his words from the colloquial to the archaic or pedantic. . . . Or to play a Latinate vocabulary off against an Anglo-Saxon." The *Sewanee Review*'s George Core also identified a certain dualism in Ransom's writing, describing it as "deliberately archaic yet timeless, occasionally eccentric but never obscure, at once quiet and nervous, pedantic and plain, formal and idiomatic, mannered and colloquial." A *Times Literary Supplement* critic once remarked that "the language of Ransom's people suggests the old-fashioned speech of pious Southern farmers in his boyhood; and it is not without a parodical trace of Southern oratory. The words are often Biblical in flavour or otherwise archaic; the phrasing is angular or enigmatically concise. Mixed with rarities are coarse words and slang. Often an obsolete or etymological sense is preferred to the normal meaning." In short, concluded the critic, Ransom "has invented an idiom that both connects him with and separates him from the situations he describes. His language implies a judgment on the people around him, a distance between present and past, speaker and story. But it also implies an ironic depreciation of the poet; for this is only *his* judgment."

Many of these same qualities and attitudes eventually found their way into the new philosophy of criticism developed by Ransom and others in the 1930s. Using the *Kenyon Review* (founded by Ransom in 1939) as their principal forum, he and his fellow proponents of the "New Criticism" rejected the romanticists' commitment to self-expression and perfectability as well as the naturalists' insistence on fact (mostly scientific fact) and inference from fact as the basis of evaluating a work of art. Instead, the New Critics focused their attention on the work of art as an object in and of itself, independent of outside influences (including the circumstances of its composition, the reality it creates, the author's intention, and the effect it has on readers). The New Critics also tended to downplay the study of genre, plot, and character in favor of detailed textual examinations of image, symbol, and meaning. As far as they were concerned, the ultimate value (in both a moral and an artistic sense) of a work of art was a function of its own *inner* qualities. In short, explained James E. Magner, Jr., in the book *John Crowe Ransom: Critical Principles and Preoccupations:* "[Ransom] wishes the world and the poem to be perceived as what they are and not as someone would have them to be. . . . [He] is a critic who wishes to be faithful to the reality of 'the world's body,' who wishes the poem aesthetically to reveal that reality, and wishes criticism to show the poem as revealing or distorting it. . . . [He is] bent on letting the poem be itself and not something else; not, for example, a means of moral propaganda or psychic therapy. . . . Ransom believes that in

knowing this aesthetic being, the poem, we will more surely and deeply know its correlative—the world, in the fullness and realness of its 'body.'"

Ransom's interest in the conflict between reason and aesthetic sensibility, so prominent in his own poetry, was also reflected in his "structure/texture" approach to poetry criticism. As interpreted by Young, this time commenting in the *Georgia Review,* Ransom's theory required a poem "to perform a dual role with words. On the one hand they must be arranged in such a manner as 'to conduct a logical sequence with their meaning,' and on the other they must 'realize an objective pattern with their sounds.'" The actual process of creating a poem, wrote Magner, is therefore "a movement from simple realization in the mind [the structure or theme] to a phrase that textures the realization and stimulates the creative mind into spinning further texture and further poetic suspension, until the original realization has been textured into the web of poetic existence." According to John Paul Pritchard in his book *Criticism in America,* Ransom believed that since this "texture"—sounds, imagery, and other details meant to enhance the poem's basic meaning—overwhelms the structure, "the critic should devote his most careful attention to the texture, realizing that he is analyzing an ontology, an order of existence which cannot be treated by scientific modes of thought."

Ransom's theories were not greeted with universal enthusiasm. Magner, for example, comparing his style to that of T. S. Eliot, pointed out that "neither Ransom nor Eliot is particularly logical in his critical progression. They lack the order which the mind urges when reading them. They do not define, divide, and discuss very systematically. Both critics intimate a part of a definition, make somewhat arbitrary divisions, and then discuss what they are interested in, with a casual unpredictability." Core, echoing the views of those who felt Ransom's own poetry was too cool, subdued, and philosophical, cited Ransom's "neglect of the emotive dimension of the poem" as "the most serious possible deficiency in [his] theoretical formulations about poetry." Despite these and other reservations, however, most critics agreed with Magner that "Ransom has given the world a redirection. . . . He has made the pragmatists clear their vision again and again, and made them focus upon the poem, whose reason for existence, he thinks, is to catch up the world beautifully in the texture of its worded being."

The debate continues as to whether Ransom will be remembered in the years to come primarily as a poet or as a critic. Although Pritchard contended that "of all the American New Critics, Ransom is the most significant figure," Stewart was of the opinion that "inevitably his reputation in criticism will deline. The theories are too insubstantial and the criticism itself (of which there is surprisingly little, considering how much he wrote about it) is too occasional. But his reputation as a poet, which is high, will continue to rise." Stewart based this conclusion on his belief that Ransom's "conception of the mind and fury against abstraction which . . . served his poetry well when qualified by narrative and image . . . served his poetics ill. To the poems they gave a unique vision; to the criticism they brought myopia."

Hyatt H. Waggoner, commenting in his *American Poets from the Puritans to the Present,* concurred with Stewart that "Ransom's poetry will outlast his critical theory. His influence has been enormous, . . . all out of proportion, really, to his actual accomplishments as a critic. He taught a generation how to write poems and how to criticize them. . . . [But] he will be remembered as a distinguished minor poet who, chiefly in his early youth, wrote a small number of perfectly wrought, finely textured poems that are likely to be remembered a long time."

On the other hand, Robert D. Jacobs stated in the *South Atlantic Quarterly* that "John Crowe Ransom may be called a minor poet, and by some an eccentric critic, but within his special province he is unique." Core, impressed by both Ransom the poet *and* Ransom the critic, agreed that his contributions to literature should not be minimized. He concluded: "The present fame of John Crowe Ransom is very great, perhaps greater than it will be in a few decades when the fires are banked down but continuing to throw forth radiant light and steady warmth, but this much is clear: the essential reputation is certain and will endure."

BIOGRAPHICAL/CRITICAL SOURCES—Books: Randall Jarrell, *Poetry and the Age*, Knopf, 1953; John Paul Pritchard, *Criticism in America*, University of Oklahoma Press, 1956; Louis Untermeyer, *Lives of the Poets*, Simon & Schuster, 1959; John L. Stewart, *John Crowe Ransom*, University of Minnesota Press, 1962; Howard Nemerov, *Poetry and Fiction*, Rutgers University Press, 1963; Louis D. Rubin, Jr., *Writers of the Modern South: The Faraway Country*, University of Washington Press, 1963; Karl F. Knight, *The Poetry of John Crowe Ransom: A Study of Diction, Metaphor, and Symbol*, Mouton, 1964; Robert Buffington, *The Equilibrist: A Study of John Crowe Ransom's Poems, 1916-1963*, Vanderbilt University Press, 1967; Hyatt H. Waggoner, *American Poets from the Puritans to the Present*, Houghton, 1968; Thornton H. Parsons, *John Crowe Ransom*, Twayne, 1969; James E. Magner, Jr., *John Crowe Ransom: Critical Principles and Preoccupations*, Mouton, 1971; Thomas Daniel Young, *John Crowe Ransom*, Steck, 1971; Wesley Morris, *Towards a New Historicism*, Princeton University Press, 1972; *Contemporary Literary Criticism*, Gale, Volume II, 1974, Volume IV, 1975, Volume V, 1976, Volume XI, 1979; Richard Gray, *The Literature of Memory: Modern Writers of the American South*, Johns Hopkins Press, 1978.

Periodicals: *Books*, May 8, 1938; *Time*, May 9, 1938; *Saturday Review of Literature*, May 21, 1938, July 5, 1941, July 14, 1945; *New Republic*, August 10, 1938; *Yale Review*, autumn, 1938; *New York Times*, December 18, 1938, July 8, 1945; *Nation*, July 12, 1941; *New Yorker*, July 7, 1945; *Sewanee Review*, summer, 1948, summer, 1968, summer, 1969, fall, 1974; *Christian Science Monitor*, August 1, 1963, December 18, 1969; *Life*, May 10, 1968; *Georgia Review*, summer, 1968, fall, 1968, spring, 1969, spring, 1971, summer, 1973; *Kenyon Review*, Vol. XXX, No. 120, issue 3, 1968; *Poetry*, February, 1969; *Spectator*, February 14, 1970; *South Atlantic Quarterly*, spring, 1969; *Washington Post Book World*, September 7, 1969; *Times Literary Supplement*, April 23, 1970.

OBITUARIES: New York Times, July 4, 1974; *Washington Post*, July 5, 1974; *Newsweek*, July 15, 1974; *Time*, July 15, 1974; *Publishers Weekly*, July 29, 1974; *Antiquarian Bookman*, October 14, 1974.†

—*Sketch by Deborah A. Straub*

*   *   *

RAWSON, Philip Stanley 1924-

PERSONAL: Born, 1924, in Yorkshire, England; son of Stanley Walter and Phyllis (Bargate) Rawson; married, 1949; children: Piers Bartholomew. *Education:* Oxford University, wartime sections in philosophy, 1942; University of London, Courtauld Institute of Art, B.A., 1947, School of Oriental Studies, M.A., 1952. *Home:* Higher Hewood, Hewood, Chard, Somerset, England. *Office:* School of Art and Design, Goldsmiths' College, New Cross, London SE 14, England.

CAREER: Art teacher in public authority schools, England, 1947-49; University of London, London, England, demonstrator in archaeological technology in Institute of Archaeology, 1950-55, lecturer in history of Indian art in School of Oriental and African Studies, 1952-55; Oxford University, Oxford, England, assistant keeper of Ashmolean Museum, 1955-79; Royal College of Art, London, senior tutor, 1979-81; Goldsmiths' College, London, dean of School of Art and Design, 1981—. Curator of Gulbenkian Museum, University of Durham, 1960-79. Instructor in adult education courses. UNESCO museological expert in India, 1964. *Military service:* Royal Fleet Air Arm, 1942-43.

WRITINGS: Indian Painting, Universe Books, 1961; *Early Buddhist Paintings of Japan*, UNESCO, 1963; *Indian Sculpture*, Studio Vista, 1966; *The Arts of South East Asia*, Thames & Hudson, 1967; *The Indian Sword*, Royal Danish Arms and Armour Society, 1967, Arco, 1969; *The Art of Southeast Asia: Cambodia, Vietnam, Thailand, Laos, Burma, Java, Bali*, Praeger, 1967; *Erotic Art of the East: The Sexual Themes in Oriental Painting and Sculpture*, Putnam, 1968; *Drawing*, Oxford University Press, 1969; *Ceramics*, Oxford University Press, 1971; *Tantra*, Arts Council of Great Britain, 1971, 2nd edition, 1972; *Indian Art*, Dutton, 1972; (editor) *Primitive Erotic Art*, Putnam, 1973; (with Laszlo Legeza) *Tao: The Chinese Philosophy of Time and Change*, Avon, 1973; *Introducing Oriental Art*, Hamlyn/American, 1973; *Tantra: The Indian Cult of Ecstasy*, Avon, 1973; *The Art of Tantra*, New York Graphic Society, 1973; (with Ajitcoomar Mookerjee) *Yoga Art*, New York Graphic Society, 1975; *Erotic Art of India*, Universe Books, 1977; *Indian Asia*, Elsevier-Phaidon, 1977; *Seeing through Drawing*, BBC Publications, 1979; *Oriental Erotic Art*, A & W Publishers, 1981.

Contributor: *Pictorial History of Architecture*, Batchworth Press, 1963; *Aesthetics Today*, Thames & Hudson, 1966; *The Body as a Means of Expression*, Allen Lane, 1975; *The Legacy of India*, Oxford University Press, 1974.

Also author of material for television and the British Broadcasting Corp. Contributor to *Encyclopaedia Britannica*. Contributor to *London Times*, *Times Literary Supplement*, *Sunday Telegraph*, *Oriental Art*, *Art News*, *British Journal of Aesthetics*, *Durham University Journal*, and other newspapers and magazines.

SIDELIGHTS: Philip S. Rawson told *CA:* "I cannot remember a time when I did not write creatively. At age thirteen I began to paint and draw, and two years later to compose music, having become a tenor choirman at Winchester College, where I was at school. For several years I was a professional singer, studying with Glyndebourne's Jani Strasser and working at musical composition with two pupils of Arnold Schoenberg. (I was the first person to sing a note of Schoenberg's music in public in Oxford, 1941, accompanied by Egon Wellesz.) When I moved towards making visual art primarily, and studied art history, this study of musical composition gave me the particular insight into artistic structure and meaning which I have since pursued in all my writing.

"I was lucky to be taken as a private pupil by the great German sculptor and scholar Kurt Badt, when he was in England. He gave me a direct and vital link to the art tradition which included Marees, Guggenbichler and Gregor Erhart (then totally unknown in Britain). Philosophy then helped to provide a skeleton of thought around which areas of study crystallised.

"I have always followed my interests looking especially for gaps in accepted knowledge. Prose I hope to make a fairly stern art (not just academic foodstuff) related to my poetry.

Hence most of my books have been 'sleepers' overlooked by reviewers until years after publication. Art and writing have been done in conjunction, fertilising each other. Teaching followed as a natural function.

"Main early influences [in my life] were Heinrich Zimmer and C. G. Jung, plus A. K. Coomaraswamy. But far the most important lifetime influence has been the work of the Kashmiri Tantric colossus, Abhinavagupta, and the semanticist Bhartrihari, both writing in Sanskrit (which I studied). I believe India's achievements have been grossly misrepresented and underrated out of sheer ignorance and lack of translation. The world is still unaware of the productions (including techniques and logics) of a culture more prolific even than the Western. Most of my work has involved some kind of effort genuinely to assimilate Indian creative conceptions into Western codes.

"I was lucky to ride a fairly free academic system. What we have now has laid a dead hand on initiative and freedom of imagination. Private devils: B. F. Skinner and phony 'methodology.' Real methodology is a way of using all the human faculties. If you 'abstract' it you cut off its root.''

AVOCATIONAL INTERESTS: Sculpture, drafting, musicology.

*   *   *

RAYMOND, Lee
See HILL, Mary Raymond

*   *   *

READ, Gardner   1913-

PERSONAL: Born January 2, 1913, in Evanston, Ill.; son of Gardner (an insurance broker) and Letitia (Hebert) Read; married Vail Payne, September 17, 1940; children: Cynthia Anne. *Education:* Eastman School of Music, B.Mus., 1936, M.Mus., 1937; private study of piano, organ, conducting, and orchestration; studied composition with Ildebrando Pizzetti in Italy and Jan Sibelius in Finland, 1939, and with Aaron Copland, summer, 1941. *Politics:* Independent. *Home:* Forster Rd., Manchester, Mass.

CAREER: Composer, conductor, and teacher of music theory and composition. Boy soloist with Episcopal church choir, Evanston, Ill., beginning 1921; head of composition department of St. Louis Institute of Music, St. Louis, Mo., 1941-43, Kansas City Conservatory of Music, Kansas City, Mo., 1943-45, and Cleveland Institute of Music, Cleveland, Ohio, 1945-48; Boston University, School of Fine and Applied Arts, Boston, Mass., professor of composition and music theory and composer-in-residence, 1948-78, professor emeritus, 1978—, chairman of department of theory and composition, 1950-52. Visiting professor, University of California, Los Angeles, 1966. Composer of commissioned orchestral works premiered by Chicago Symphony Orchestra, 1938, Indianapolis Symphony Orchestra, 1943, Cleveland Orchestra, 1946, and Louisville Orchestra, 1954; composer of other commissioned works for music festivals, string quartet, and stage; major works also performed by the Boston, New York Philharmonic, Cincinnati, Philadelphia, Indianapolis, San Francisco, Rochester, St. Louis, and Pittsburgh symphony orchestras, and other orchestras in the United States, Europe, and South America. Guest conductor with Boston Symphony Orchestra, 1943, 1954, St. Louis Philharmonic Orchestra, 1943, 1944, Kansas City Philharmonic Orchestra, 1944, and Philadelphia Orchestra, 1964. Originator and commentator, weekly educational radio series, "Our American Music," Boston, 1953-60. Member of board

of trustees, Boston Arts Festival, 1959-61; special panelist, Conference on New Musical Notation, University of Ghent, 1974. *Member:* American Society of Composers, Authors, and Publishers, MacDowell Colonists.

AWARDS, HONORS: Summer fellowships, MacDowell Colony, 1936, 1937, 1946, 1950, and Berkshire Music Center, 1941; Cromwell traveling fellowship, 1938-39; U.S. Department of State grant to lecture and conduct in Mexico, summers, 1957 and 1964; Huntington Hartford Foundation fellowship, 1960 and 1965; D.Mus., Doane College, 1962. Awards for compositions include first prize for symphonies, New York Philharmonic Symphony Society, 1937, and Paderewski Fund Competition, 1943; co-winner of prize for "Suite for Organ," Pennsylvania College for Women, 1950; also recipient of a number of awards for chamber works.

WRITINGS: Thesaurus of Orchestral Devices, Pitman, 1953, reprinted, Greenwood Press, 1969; *Music Notation: A Manual of Modern Practice*, Allyn & Bacon, 1964, 2nd edition, Crescendo, 1972; *Contemporary Instrumental Techniques*, Schirmer Books, 1976; *Modern Rhythmic Notation*, Indiana University Press, 1978; *Style and Orchestration*, Schirmer Books, 1979. Editor of "Birchard-Boston University Contemporary Music" series, 1950-60. Correspondent for *Musical Leader* (Chicago), 1935-37, and *Musical Courier* (New York). Contributor of articles and reviews to music journals and to *New York Times, Arts in Society, Boston Globe,* and *Christian Science Monitor.*

WORK IN PROGRESS: Twentieth Century Notation; Genesis of an Opera; Instrumental Combinations; musical compositions.

AVOCATIONAL INTERESTS: Chess, photography, wildlife.

*   *   *

RECHY, John (Francisco)   1934-

PERSONAL: Born in 1934, in El Paso, Tex.; son of Roberto Sixto and Guadalupe (Flores) Rechy. *Education:* Texas Western College (now University of Texas at El Paso), B.A.; attended New School for Social Research. *Residence:* Los Angeles, Calif.; and New York, N.Y. *Address:* c/o Grove Press, 196 West Houston St., New York, N.Y. 10016.

CAREER: Writer. Conducted writing seminars at Occidental College and University of California. *Military service:* U.S. Army; served in Germany. *Member:* Authors Guild, Authors League of America, P.E.N. *Awards, honors:* Longview Foundation fiction prize, 1961; National Endowment for the Arts grant, 1976.

WRITINGS—Novels, published by Grove, except as indicated: *City of Night*, 1963; *Numbers*, 1967; *This Day's Death*, 1969; *The Vampires*, 1971; *The Fourth Angel*, Viking, 1973; *The Sexual Outlaw* (nonfiction), 1977; *Rushes*, 1979. Also author of a screenplay based on his novel *City of Night* and a play based on *Rushes*.

Contributor: LeRoi Jones, editor, *The Moderns*, Corinth, 1963; Robert Rubens, editor, *Voices*, M. Joseph, 1963; Bruce Jay Friedman, editor, *Black Humor*, Bantam, 1965; Donald M. Allen and Robert Creeley, editors, *New American Story*, Grove, 1965; *Collision Course*, Random House, 1968. Contributor to periodicals, including *Evergreen Review, Nugget, Big Table, London Magazine, New York Times Book Review, Village Voice,* and *Nation;* contributor of translations from Spanish to periodicals.

SIDELIGHTS: "Broadly speaking, Rechy's work may be said to belong to the self-revelatory school of Romantic Agony," writes Terry Southern in *Contemporary American Novelists.* The school's basic rule is "Feel everything and leave nothing unsaid." And, although Southern feels that Rechy is genuinely creative, he admits that the author's technique "often leads to an embarrassing amount of overstatement, subjectivity, and a complete lack of craftsmanship." Southern believes that Rechy, like Jack Kerouac, writes at great speed, off the top of his head, and that this accounts for the strength of his work, a strength which lies in "the relentless, almost schizoid integrity of self-revelation, the absence of conscious artifice," and the lack of guile. However, Southern's initial supposition may be inaccurate because Rechy reportedly rewrites extensively, often doing more than twelve versions of one chapter. Rechy told *CA* that his novel *Rushes,* for instance, is as "carefully structured as a Catholic Mass" and insisted that "form is essential" to his meaning in all of his works.

Rechy's best known book, *City of Night,* a novel about homosexuality and male prostitution, met with mixed reviews. A typical evaluation, by Peter Buitenhuis of the *New York Times Book Review,* reads: "At first, the book is slightly shocking; soon it becomes irritating, then it begins to get boring. . . . The novel is sloppy, chaotic, repetitious, humorless and sometimes sleep-inducing. And yet, in spite of all this, *City of Night* is a remarkable book, . . . [written] in an authentic jive-like slang; the nightmare existence is explored with a clarity not often clouded by sentimentality and self-pity. The book therefore has the unmistakable ring of candor and truth." Southern expands on this: "The quality of *credibility* is of first importance to a book like *City of Night,* because we are being taken into an unfamiliar world, . . . and we need to feel that we are being told the truth about it. . . . It is the kind of truth . . . which can only obtain after the narrator has convinced us that he has *nothing to gain or lose* by telling it." According to *Saturday Review*'s Granville Hicks, this truth is, for the most part, related without sensationalism. "Rechy's style," notes Hicks, "though it can be tiresomely exclamatory, is usually controlled and quietly forceful. . . . He is more than a good reporter, for he has touched his materials with the imagination and the craft of a writer."

In a review of *Rushes,* Darryl Pinckney of the *Village Voice* calls the novel an "intensely homoerotic work, obsessed with the subject of men wanting men" and makes the point that "Rechy's fiction has always shown an interest in the night side of human feeling." Pinckney finds that Rechy "is indifferent to the psychologies of his characters. In this he is unlike most novelists with homosexual protagonists who are at pains to explain the history of their preoccupation. During the long, long night of drinking, talking, plotting, and watching, Rechy's characters do not think back to unhappy childhoods or to idyllic adolescent affairs. Their memories are rather short and desolate. If they grieve over lost passions, it is last month's. Only the scene matters. The moment is everything." In a *New York Times Book Review* article, Alan Friedman notes that "Sadomasochism is [*Rushes'*] central concern. . . . Yet there's no doubt in my mind that the book's sadism is not just a ritual played out among characters. It's also a literary rite directed at the reader. The language of the text demands that the reader suffer sexually: hurt, submit, and therefore love this book. That's too much to ask. Still, provided one is willing to make the effort, there's a lot to appreciate here, if not love. For one thing, Mr. Rechy is working a difficult vein of fiction, the tragedy of manners. For another, he supplies an abundance of arcane information about the homosexual pecking order. Then there's the book's construction. It's painstaking. . . . But finally it seems to me that almost none of this matters, because the book's sight and speech are hopelessly infected. . . . Clot-

ted with jargon, delirious with repetition and weak with the heavy breathing of pornography, *Rushes* has several close brushes with the Angel of Death."

When *City of Night* was first published in 1963, there was much speculation on the extent to which the book might have been autobiographical. At the time, a book on male prostitution was still something of a novelty, and readers wanted personal information about the author. Rechy, however, carefully guarded his privacy. But as he continued to write about homosexuality, he began to open up a bit, and when *Sexual Outlaw* came out in 1977, according to Eleanor Hoover of *People,* he made "a conscious decision not to hold back" any more. Hoover calls the book "a passionate manifesto for gay rights by an author who openly and unapologetically identifies himself as a participant," and says that Rechy "chose to go public about his own life because of what he fears is a growing climate of 'heterosexual fascism.' Speaking at a Yale University assembly [in 1977], he warned: 'No one concerned with freedom can afford to ignore the impact of Anita Bryant. Historically, repression begins with the persecution of homosexuals.'" Hoover notes that the author "has been arrested twice for prostitution by L.A. undercover police who he says entrapped him," but that he "finds nothing demeaning—let alone sinful or criminal—in the street life. He thinks it pointless to speculate on what creates a homosexual. 'Is it psychological or genetic? Nobody knows,' he says. 'It just is and must be coped with.'"

Rechy told *CA* that he works sporadically, "sometimes not writing for weeks, other times working from eight in the morning until late at night, with only brief interruptions." Literary figures whom he admires include Dostoevsky, Hawthorne, Poe, Faulkner, Nabokov, Proust, Joyce, and Gertrude Stein.

CA INTERVIEW

CA interviewed John Rechy by phone April 23, 1981, at his home in Los Angeles.

CA: Your first novel, City of Night, *was called by Webster Schott "one of the landmarks in the new homosexual fiction" (*New York Times Book Review, *January 14, 1968). Did you accomplish in that novel what you set out to accomplish?*

RECHY: It's difficult to remember what I set out to accomplish; it all has to be retrospective now. At the time, I was simply writing about something that I knew intimately, a world that I was living. It was a great surprise to me when this became, in the words of several critics, a shocker. Did I accomplish what I now think I wanted to accomplish at the time? I would give a rueful yes. Despite the fact that those were very repressive, ugly times no one would ever want to go back to, the hope that was inchoate in those beginnings has certainly not been fulfilled. I feel a dual sadness: that the repressive pressures still exist, and that "homosexual liberation" has developed new problems it doesn't want to deal with. *City of Night,* which in its own time was considered so realistic, has almost become, for me, romantic.

CA: Do you mean that there are new problems within the homosexual community?

RECHY: Yes, I definitely mean that we have problems we won't face, and I don't shy away from saying it, although that's an area of enormous controversy and one which has alienated me from much of what is known as "the movement." I think a great deal of misinterpretation has happened, but this happens, of course, in many revolutions. Revolutions have a way of going wrong, and I have a lot to criticize in what has developed. Emphatically this does not mean that those repressive periods were better—far from it—and it is important to underscore that no criticism of the homosexual world may be made which does not more powerfully indict the heterosexual totalitarianism which pressures and shapes us.

CA: You are concerned, as you told Eleanor Hoover for People *magazine (May 22, 1978), with the increasing climate of "heterosexual fascism." What do you think can be done about that?*

RECHY: We homosexuals are in grave danger in two general areas, from the lingering hatred outside, and inside, by confusing our liberation with what I call heterosexual imitation. We therefore may lose what is special to us, and because of its specialness, enriching to the heterosexual. Positive difference enhances all of us. And there is too the confusion between what is liberating and what is debasing, and that, of course, is one of the inner conflicts, what I call the saboteur in the homosexual—that confusion as to what we should be defending and what we should not be defending. I find us, from my point of view, sometimes defending the wrong things—for example, that we are exactly like everyone else (even as dull!)—and not standing up for the correct ones—our abundant sexuality (judgmentally labeled promiscuity).

CA: That conflict makes it very difficult to withstand the pressure from the general community?

RECHY: Yes. It drains our energies to offset homophobic assaults. I think that some of our rich specialness is being surrendered to conformity; an enormous danger when it restricts experience. You find some homosexuals virtually apologizing for ever having sex, and writers like Masters and Johnson saying we're all the same. Again, you see, it ends up an assault on difference rather than an acceptance of difference. To be different is to be questionable, and so we must all move into that gray limbo where everyone who conforms to a new dull "norm" is acceptable. New outsiders are created. To me, that's not being liberated, that's being erased.

CA: Did City of Night *bring you a heavy response from readers, both in this country and in the other countries where the book was available?*

RECHY: Everywhere. This was one of the thrills of writing *City of Night.* I was not in touch with the literary world. I was traveling around the country, just as in the book, and I wasn't aware that people were reading it so eagerly in the quarterlies where it was appearing in sections—*Evergreen Review* and *Big Table.* Then the book became a huge best-seller, which was totally unexpected. The inundation of letters was enormous. They were really beautiful letters from people who often began with "I've never written to a writer before," and although that's a cliche, I could tell the genuineness. The letters came from all over the world. I answered every letter. When the book came out, I separated myself from the furor; I cherish privacy. I went to the Caribbean, and then returned for several years to the virtual isolation of my hometown, El Paso, Texas. I stayed there until my beautiful mother died in 1970. But people came to El Paso to see me. That was touching, because the critical reception was at first enormously hostile.

CA: Do you think it's difficult to get fair reviews because of the homosexual themes and content of your books?

RECHY: Yes. I think that's one of the unfairest things. I don't pretend to be modest; I think that's usually a pose. I'm an excellent writer. All of my books, from *City of Night* on through my most recent one, *Rushes,* are quite consciously structured. The sexual content that has aroused so much disguised "critical" ire I often use on both a literal and a metaphoric level. *Numbers,* my second novel, delineates more than thirty explicit sexual encounters (numbered by the protagonist); but its subject is really death and dying. Still, I have been called an "accidental writer"! I don't think there's anything that hurts more than that. I don't think I've written one book that has not gone through at least six full versions, and some chapters up to twenty. Yet the sexual content of my books—why sex should be demeaning as a subject for literature I don't know; that is one of the main impediments to suicide, what keeps us going—has blinded many critics to the craft, the structure, the imagery. In *Rushes* I used the structure of the mass. I find a sense of triumph in that my books are now read in literature courses and my work is included in textbooks and anthologies. But with every book the initial critical reaction is primarily critical of the material. I know without doubt that I am as good as any other writer writing today—and much better than most. Critics are still overwhelmed, not only by sexuality, but by homosexuality. A lot of the major journals still exclude any mention of homosexual writing.

CA: Is the structure carefully planned before you begin the actual writing?

RECHY: Very often. I've tried a lot of methods. For example, with *Rushes* (I was raised a Catholic, but I'm not a practicing Catholic anymore), I would read the mass every day before I began writing—not for godly inspiration, believe me, but to saturate myself in its structure, so it would permeate the novel. I knew at which point in the mass, for example, the incense is wafted, and that would be the point in the book at which amyl nitrite would be popped in the "leather bar" in which the book is set. The pornographic drawings on the walls of the bar correspond to the stations of the cross. This is a book about homosexuals in a bar, yes, but it is also an allegory on the destructiveness of Christian rituals.

I think part of the problem of the critical reaction to my work is the difficulty critics have in accepting that I could live in the world I deal with often—especially male hustling and "promiscuity"—and still be able to write about it beyond sociology, into literature. I move intimately in both worlds. That world of the street and that world of the hustlers is obviously one that one had to experience on a primary level; you couldn't write about it otherwise. I think that has become irreconcilable to a lot of people and continues to be, that I can exist on the streets as I still do and also function as a writer; this is where the clash comes for critics.

CA: Have you found it to be generally true that, until recently, most homosexual literature in this country has been written from a moralistic point of view?

RECHY: Until recently, of course, this was true, absolutely. I think that was one of the major impacts that *City of Night* had: here finally was a book that did not moralize. It still remains, for all the romantic elements, probably the only book dealing with homosexuality that is generally known, including the rest of my work, by a whole range of people. The area of the so-called gay novel—that word "gay" is one I detest—has become very restrictive now; we're writing for each other. This of course provides no real illumination. It's very much turned inward.

CA: Did you have any early ambition to write?

RECHY: Yes. When I was a little kid, I wanted very much to write and I wanted to act. I was a professional child actor for a short time; I played Jesus as a little boy, and I was an enormous success. By the time I was seventeen years old, I had written a historical novel called *Time on Wings.* I wrote another one and then I went into the army. *City of Night* began as a letter, I didn't intend to write a book about hustling. It began as a letter to a friend of mine after I had had some experiences in New Orleans. Then I was just drifting around the country.

CA: Was there much early encouragement from anyone?

RECHY: In high school I had one grand teacher—and I do so believe in giving credit—Maude Isaacks, may she rest in peace. She was wonderful and encouraging to me. Then there was Fanny Foster. And then in college there was Mrs. Ball, who predicted that I would do something very creative, although she thought it would be in the area of acting. Yes, I had a lot of encouragement. One of the people who encouraged me most is a top Broadway director now. I met him in El Paso when I was about seventeen; he was in the army. He encouraged me to write what became my first novel (*Pablo!*) though not published. And of course Barney Rosset at Grove and my editors, Don Allen and Kent Carroll. James Baldwin encouraged me and so did Norman Mailer. Norman Mailer, in fact, quoted me at length before I had published other than in the little magazines. We exchanged mutual macho letters. James Baldwin used to call me every time he was in the country and urge me to move on with the book.

CA: D.D.C. Chambers wrote for Contemporary Novelists, *"The 'youngmen' of* City of Night *and* Numbers *are the fallen angels of an eternally inaccessible paradise and their lives are characterized by a search for the* eros *that will at last become* agape.*" As far as it goes, how accurate do you consider this assessment?*

RECHY: "Agape" in the sense of love? I don't put too much stock in "love"; it's usually a lie, a myth—and always linked with pain. There should be another word for the feeling of real closeness, which I do feel. Now it is true that the imagery of angels and fallen angels is rampant throughout my books. Religious themes are very important in my work. The loss of innocence, as much a cliche as it is in literature, still continues to be one of my major themes. As I grow older, it becomes not the loss of innocence, but the regaining of innocence—a paradise-lost, paradise-regained sort of thing, the return to a state of a knowing purity. This, of course, is how my books move almost in a circle. I really consider my first seven books to have completed a cycle. I'm moving into other areas in my writing now.

CA: You've been working on a screenplay based on City of Night *and a play based on* Rushes. *How are they going?*

RECHY: I have several directors interested in the play based on *Rushes.* The screenplay of *City of Night* is out with three interested directors. We'll see. I've dealt in those areas before, and, my God, it's an Alice-in-Wonderland world, one moment you're "the greatest", another moment you're "on-hold" on the telephone.

CA: Can you pinpoint specific influences on your work?

RECHY: A lot of my writing is influenced by my interest in movies. I'm a great movie fan. We're all supposed to say we've been influenced by Shakespeare and Proust and Milton and Joyce, and indeed I was influenced by Shakespeare, Proust, Milton, and Joyce. But I was also influenced by Margaret Mitchell, Kathleen Winsor, King Vidor, and I'm proud of it. The scene in which Scarlett swears never to be hungry again is masterful, a study in effect for any writer. Bette Davis influenced my writing a great deal and Errol Flynn certainly did. "Terry and the Pirates" was a major influence too. We're kind of dishonest when we're asked about influences. We dredge up the books that make us sound very intelligent, citing at least one obscure writer, and some of the primary influences are really left out. There is a litany of writers that are safe to mention, and God knows they have influenced me—Hawthorne is one of my favorite American writers, and Faulkner. But equally so, at that formative time, I was seeing those great Hollywood movies. Remember Pearl Chavez crawling up the hill toward Gregory Peck? Remember they shoot each other and manage to kiss and then die, and a flower blooms? That is a great scene! How could such scenes not influence one's writing? To say otherwise is dishonest. Even bad writing or a bad movie can influence you. You can convert it and make it good.

CA: How are you best able to help students in your writing seminars?

RECHY: I'm proud of that. I've been doing a professional writers' seminar at UCLA for several years and I've done one at Occidental. I'm going to do it at USC, and then I'm going to Columbia next year. Three novels, so far, have come out of those courses, and certain prize-winning stories. I find that the reason I'm so good at it—and I am very, very good at it—is that I don't try to "teach writing." That, of course, is deadly. I try to create a very supportive but highly professional atmosphere. To be supportive at the same time that you give good and honest criticism, that's the balance that has to be achieved.

CA: Do you feel your own writing has become progressively stronger, better?

RECHY: Absolutely. As far as the structure and the writing and the conception, *Rushes* is my very best book. I would not say a favorite because that would be like choosing among your children, but it's my best book in that all the elements come together.

In my books I have moved from the "youngman" in *City of Night* who of course is very young and terribly realistic—he thinks, but now *I* think terribly romantic—on to Johnny Rio in *Numbers,* who is facing the fact that he is not as much a young man as he was before. Then the writing takes a leap in the worst book I ever wrote, which I wish I hadn't written, *This Day's Death.* Yet in it, the protagonist fully accepts his homosexuality. In *The Fourth Angel* I used children to look at my troubled present, at the time, with drugs, and to face my mother's death. *The Vampire* is the inside of me, my soul. In *The Sexual Outlaw* (a "documentary" in which the structure is totally original, a fact not noticed by those who actually sought to ban the book—in 1977!), the main character has already become a mature man, facing survival in a different sort of way. To survive in the "sexual arena" he has developed his muscles to replace "youth." I'm very much involved in bodybuilding. I view the structure of the body as an art form, like the structure of a book. Then finally, in *Rushes,* the narrator of *City of Night* has become Endore, who is looking sadly at what the homosexual world has become as heterosexuals continue to despise us. It is appropriate that *Rushes* ends with a mock crucifixion (homosexual, in an orgy room) and a real "crucifixion" (murder of a homosexual by heterosexuals). Endore's unfinished "benediction" at the last—a gesture which ends as a clenched fist—sums up the religious symbolic structure of my seven books to now.

BIOGRAPHICAL/CRITICAL SOURCES: Richard Gilman, *The Confusion of Realms,* Random House, 1963, 5th edition, 1969; *Library Journal,* February 1, 1963; *Saturday Review,* June 8, 1963; *New York Times Book Review,* June 30, 1963, January 14, 1968, April 3, 1977, July 17, 1977, February 17, 1980; Harry T. Moore, editor, *Contemporary American Novelists,* Southern Illinois University Press, 1964; *New York Times,* December 27, 1967; *London Magazine,* June, 1968; *Times Literary Supplement,* September 11, 1970; *Prairie Schooner,* fall, 1971; *Contemporary Literary Criticism,* Gale, Volume I, 1973, Volume VII, 1977, Volume XIV, 1980, Volume XVIII, 1981; *Washington Post Book World,* August 12, 1973; *Nation,* January 5, 1974; James Vinson, editor, *Contemporary Novelists,* St. Martin's, 1976; *Village Voice,* August 22, 1977, October 3, 1977, March 3, 1980; *People,* May 22, 1978.

—*Interview by Jean W. Ross*

* * *

RECK, Andrew J(oseph) 1927-

PERSONAL: Born October 29, 1927, in New Orleans, La.; son of Andrew Gervais and Katie (Mangiaracina) Reck. *Education:* Tulane University, B.A., 1947, M.A., 1949; Yale University, graduate study, 1949-52, Ph.D., 1954; University of St. Andrews, graduate study, 1952-53; Sorbonne, University of Paris, postdoctoral study, summers, 1962, 1964. *Office:* Department of Philosophy, Tulane University, New Orleans, La. 70118.

CAREER: Yale University, New Haven, Conn., instructor in philosophy, 1955-58; Tulane University, New Orleans, La., 1958—, began as assistant professor, currently professor of philosophy and chairman of department. *Military service:* U.S. Army, 1953-55; served in Berlin, Germany. *Member:* American Philosophical Association, Metaphysical Society of America (member of council, 1971-74; president, 1977-78), American Association of University Professors, Southern Society for Philosophy and Psychology (treasurer, 1969-72; president, 1976-77), Southwestern Philosophical Society (president, 1972-73), Phi Beta Kappa. *Awards, honors:* Fulbright fellowship, 1952-53; American Council of Learned Societies grant, 1961; Howard Foundation fellowship, 1962-63; American Philosophical Society grant, 1972; Huntington Library fellowship, 1973.

WRITINGS: (Contributor) Irwin Lieb, editor, *Experience, Existence and the Good: Essays in Honor of Paul Weiss,* University of Southern Illinois Press, 1961; *Recent American Philosophy,* Pantheon, 1964; (editor) *Selected Writings of George Herbert Mead,* Bobbs-Merrill, 1964, reprinted, University of Chicago Press, 1981; (contributor) Sidney Rome and Beatrice Rome, editors, *Philosophic Interrogations,* Holt, 1964; (contributor) *Spirit as Inquiry: Essays in Honor of Bernard Lonergan,* Continuum, 1964; *Introduction to William James,* Editions Seghers (Paris), 1966, Indiana University Press, 1967; *New American Philosophers,* Louisiana State University Press, 1968.

Speculative Philosophy, University of New Mexico Press, 1972; *Knowledge and Value,* Nijhoff, 1972; (contributor) F. Hetzler and A. Kutscher, editors, *Philosophical Aspects of Thanatology,* Arno, 1978; (contributor) P. Caws, editor, *Two Centuries of American Philosophy,* Basil Blackwell, 1980; *Handbook of World Philosophy,* Greenwood Press, 1980; *The Philosophy of*

Brand Blanshard, Open Court, 1980; *France and North America,* University of Southwestern Louisiana Press, 1980. Contributor of more than 100 articles to professional journals.

WORK IN PROGRESS: Books on the philosophical background of the American Revolution, on metaphysics, and on William James.

* * *

REEVE, Joel
See COX, William R(obert)

* * *

REGINALD
See BURGESS, M(ichael) R(oy)

* * *

REGINALD, R(obert)
See BURGESS, M(ichael) R(oy)

* * *

REID BANKS, Lynne 1929-

PERSONAL: Born July 31, 1929, in London, England; daughter of James (a doctor) and Muriel (an actress; maiden name, Marsh) Reid Banks; married Chaim Stephenson (a sculptor), 1965; children: Adiel, Gillon, Omri (sons). *Politics:* "Marginally right of centre in Britain; decidedly left in Israel." *Religion:* Atheist. *Home:* 16 Rosemont Rd., London W3, England. *Agent:* Sheila Watson, Bolt & Watson, 8-12 Old Queen St., London SW1, England.

CAREER: Actress in English repertory companies, 1949-54; free-lance journalist, 1954-55; Independent Television News, London, England, reporter and scriptwriter, 1955-62; teacher of English in Israeli kibbutz, 1962-71; full-time writer, 1971—. *Awards, honors:* Yorkshire Arts Literary Award, 1976, for *Dark Quartet.*

WRITINGS—Published by Simon & Schuster, except as indicated: *The L-Shaped Room,* 1961, revised edition, Longman, 1977; *House of Hope,* 1962 (published in England as *An End to Running,* Chatto & Windus, 1962); *Children at the Gate,* 1969; *The Backward Shadow,* 1971; *One More River,* 1973; *Two Is Lonely,* 1974; *Sarah and After,* Doubleday, 1975; *The Adventures of King Midas* (juvenile), Dent, 1976; *The Farthest-Away Mountain* (juvenile), Abelard, 1976; *Dark Quartet: The Story of the Brontes,* Delacorte, 1976; *My Darling Villian,* Harper, 1977; *Path to the Silent Country: Charlotte Bronte's Years of Fame,* Harper, 1978; *I, Houdini: The Autobiography of a Self-Educated Hamster* (juvenile), Dent, 1978; *Letters to My Israeli Sons: A Personal View of Jewish Survival for Young Readers,* W. H. Allen, 1979, F. Watts, 1980; *The Indian in the Cupboard* (juvenile), Dent, 1980, Doubleday, 1981; *Writing on the Wall* (juvenile), Chatto & Windus, 1981; *Defy the Wilderness,* Chatto & Windus, 1981.

Plays: (With Victor Madden) *Miss Pringle Plays Portia,* H.W.F. Deane, 1954; *It Never Rains,* H.W.F. Deane, 1954; *All in a Row,* H.W.F. Deane, 1956; *The Killer Dies Twice* (three-act), H.W.F. Deane, 1956; *Already It's Tomorrow,* Samuel French, 1962; "The Gift," first produced in London, England, 1965.

Also author of radio and television plays. Contributor to magazines and newspapers, including *McCall's* and *Ladies' Home Journal.*

WORK IN PROGRESS: A novel; an oral history of the Israeli War of Independence, for F. Watts.

SIDELIGHTS: Lynne Reid Banks told *CA:* "Perhaps it is my age . . . but there are very few things left in this world that I am certain of, be it in the realms of creative writing, politics, domesticity, or personal relationships. Since I have, very foolishly as I now see, built my whole life and personal security on certain convictions, which one by one have been and are being whittled away by experience and observation, let me try to sort out of my muddle just a few random items about which I am, temporarily no doubt, still reasonably sure.

"1. Men and women should not have children unless they have had enough experience of living together, and sufficient knowledge of themselves, to bank on themselves as good and permanent joint parents. Once they've had children, they should stick with them through thick and thin.

"2. Individuals should not be judged, or allotted status by society, or rewarded, according to the type of work they do, but by how well they do it . . . and by the benefits it brings.

"3. Nobody is 'born equal,' and everybody gets more and more unequal as they go through life. This is not just a fact, it is a Good Thing. Next to love (of certain kinds) and goodness (of certain kinds), variety is the next most exciting, important, stimulating, and life-enhancing thing in the world.

"4. Speaking of love, sex is not the whole business (communication is) and being in love is a species of madness. Nobody should do anything final when they're in love, any more than when they're drunk.

"5. Nevertheless, recklessness is better than passivity, interference than apathy, anger than indifference. Commitment is the mark of the contributor, doubt of the intellectual, responsibility of the mature.

"6. Critics and lawyers are among the lowest forms of life. Communism doesn't work. To believe in God because he's been good to Number One is sheer arrogance. Menachem Begin is bad for Israel, and eating people is wrong."

BIOGRAPHICAL/CRITICAL SOURCES: New Yorker, June 8, 1968; *Punch,* August 7, 1968; *Books & Bookmen,* September, 1968, November, 1976; *Observer,* August 9, 1970, April 7, 1974; *Listener,* April 11, 1974; *New Statesman,* April 18, 1975; *Times Literary Supplement,* December 10, 1976; *New York Times Book Review,* October 16, 1977; *Commonweal,* November 11, 1977; *Times Educational Supplement,* November 24, 1978.

*   *   *

RELIS, Harry
    See ENDORE, (Samuel) Guy

*   *   *

RENIER, Elizabeth
    See BAKER, Betty D(oreen Flook)

*   *   *

RENTON, Julia
    See COLE, Margaret Alice

*   *   *

REPS, (Saladin) Paul   1895-

PERSONAL: Born September 15, 1895, in Cedar Rapids, Iowa;

son of August Charles and Nettie (Wakefield) Reps. *Education:* "None." *Religion:* "All." *Address:* 2225 12th Ave. E., Seattle, Wash. 98102; and c/o Tuttle Co., Suido 1, Come 2-6, Bunkyo-ku, Japan.

CAREER: Author, poet, and designer.

WRITINGS: Nature's Brotherhood, Red Rose Press, 1927; (translator with others) Shih Hui-k'ai, *The Gateless Gate,* J. Murrary, 1934; (translator with Nyogen Senzaki) *The Ten Bulls,* Preview Publications, 1935, reprinted, Jasmine Press, 1973; *Exploring Our Name,* Preview Publications, 1938; (compiler) *101 Zen Stories,* McKay, 1940; *Unknotting,* Let's Live Publishers, 1947; (compiler) *Zen Flesh, Zen Bones: A Collection of Zen and Pre-Zen Writings,* Tuttle, 1957, 2nd edition, 1964; *Unknot the World in You,* privately printed, 1955; *Komo Hadaka Zuihitsu* (title means "Naked Essays"), Hayakawa Shobo (Tokyo), 1960; *Big Bath: Poems Reps,* Liu Publishers, 1961; *Zen Telegrams: Seventy-Nine Picture Poems,* Tuttle, 1962; *Gold/Fish Signatures* (poems), Auerhahn Press, 1962; *Picture-Poem Primer,* American Fabrics Publications, 1964; *Unwrinkling Plays,* Tuttle, 1965; *Ask a Potato: The Coming New World of the Young,* 2nd edition, Doric Publishing Co., 1967; *Square Sun, Square Moon: A Collection of Sweet Sour Essays,* Tuttle, 1967; *Ten Ways to Meditate: No Need to Kill,* Weatherhill, 1969; *Be: New Uses for the Human Instrument,* Weatherhill, 1971; *Juicing: Words and Brushwork,* Anchor Books, 1978. Also author of *Ecology: Me.* Contributor to *Mainichi Daily News,* Tokyo, 1952—.

WORK IN PROGRESS: Prose works for Tuttle; a book, *School for Waking.*

SIDELIGHTS: Paul Reps once wrote of his way of life: "Zen spirit has come to mean not only peace and understanding, but devotion to art and to work, the rich unfoldment of contentment, opening the door to insight, the expression of innate beauty, the intangible charm of incompleteness."

To *CA* he wrote: "I have no home outside this world and am ever traveling, three times in Himalayas, ten times in Japan, three times in Scandanavia. I believe whatever we see or hear to be a poem. We feel it, free it, it frees us. My poems are pictures, my pictures poems. Through them I am evoking new beings on earth." He believes fish swim in tears, and affirms that "as our breath of life pauses, we perfect."†

*   *   *

REUSS, Henry S(choellkopf)   1912-

PERSONAL: Surname rhymes with "choice"; born February 22, 1912, in Milwaukee, Wis.; son of Gustav (a banker) and Paula (Schoellkopf) Reuss; married Margaret Magrath, October 24, 1942; children: Christopher, Michael, Jacqueline, Ann. *Education:* Cornell University, B.A., 1933; Harvard University, LL.B., 1936. *Politics:* Democrat. *Religion:* Episcopalian. *Home:* 1301 North Astor, Milwaukee, Wis. 53202. *Office:* 2413 Rayburn Bldg., Washington, D.C. 20515.

CAREER: Admitted to Wisconsin State Bar, 1936; lawyer in Milwaukee, Wis., 1936-55; U.S. House of Representatives, Washington, D.C., congressman for Fifth Wisconsin District, 1955—, chairman of committee on banking, finance, and urban affairs, 1975-81, of joint economic committee, 1981—, and of international economics committee, member of several other economic committees. Assistant corporation counsel, Milwaukee County, 1939-40; assistant general counsel, Office of Price Administration, Washington, D.C., 1941-42; member of advisory committee, National Resources Board, 1948-52; deputy general counsel, Marshall Plan, Paris, France, 1949; special prosecutor, Milwaukee County Grand Jury, 1950; member, Milwaukee School Board, 1953-54. Lecturer, Wisconsin State College (now University of Wisconsin—Milwaukee), 1950. Director, American Youth Hostels. Member of council, Cornell University. *Military service:* U.S. Army, Infantry, 1943-45; became captain; received Bronze Star. U.S. Army Reserve, retired as lieutenant colonel, 1964. *Member:* Children's Service Society (director), Milwaukee County Bar Association (chairman of constitution and citizenship committee), Milwaukee Bar Association, Junior Bar Association of Milwaukee (vice-chairman), Chi Psi Alumni Association (vice-president), Milwaukee City Club.

WRITINGS: The Task for 1962: A Free World Community, U.S. Government Printing Office, 1961; *The Critical Decade: An Economic Policy for America and the Free World,* introduction by Hubert H. Humphrey, McGraw, 1964; (with Robert Ellsworth) *Off Dead Center: Some Proposals to Strengthen Free World Economic Cooperation,* U.S. Government Printing Office, 1965; (with Paul A. Fino) *Food for Progress in Latin America,* U.S. Government Printing Office, 1967; *Revenue-Sharing: Crutch or Catalyst for State and Local Governments?,* Praeger, 1970; (with Humphrey) *Observations on the East-West Economic Relations: U.S.S.R. and Poland,* U.S. Government Printing Office, 1973; (with Charls Edward Walker) *Major Tax Reform: Urgent Necessity or Not?,* American Enterprise Institute for Public Policy Research, 1973; *To Save a City,* U.S. Government Printing Office, 1977, published as *To Save Our Cities: What Needs to Be Done,* Public Affairs Press, 1977. Contributor of articles to magazines. Alumni overseer, *Harvard Law Review,* 1956-60.

*   *   *

REX, John A(rderne) 1925-

PERSONAL: Born March 5, 1925, in Port Elizabeth, South Africa ; son of Frederick Edward George (a postal worker) and Winifred Natalie (Arderne) Rex; married Pamela Margaret Rutherford, July 9, 1949 (divorced, 1963); married Margaret Ellen Biggs, June 5, 1965; children: (first marriage) Catherine Anne, Helen Joan; (second marriage) Frederick John, David Malcolm. *Education:* University of South Africa, B.A., 1948; Leeds University, Ph.D., 1956. *Home:* 33 Arlington Ave., Leamington Spa, England. *Office:* Research Unit on Ethnic Relations, St. Peter's College, University of Aston, College Rd., Birmingham B8 3TE, England.

CAREER: Leeds University, Leeds, England, lecturer in sociology, 1949-62; Birmingham University, Birmingham, England, lecturer, 1962-64; University of Durham, Durham, England, professor of social theory and institutions, 1964-70; University of Warwick, Coventry, England, professor of sociology, 1970-79; University of Aston, Birmingham, visiting professor and director of Research Unit on Ethnic Relations, 1979—. Visiting lecturer, University of Hull, 1960-61; visiting professor, University of Toronto, 1974-75. Member of housing panel, National Committee for Commonwealth Immigrants, 1966-68; member of various United Nations committees on minorities, race, and racial prejudice. *Military service:* South African and Royal Navies, 1963-65; served as able seaman. *Member:* International Sociological Association (president of committee on racial and ethnic minorities, 1974-82), British Sociological Association (chairman, 1969-71), British Association for the Advancement of Science, Association of University Teachers.

WRITINGS—Published by Routledge & Kegan Paul, except as indicated: *Key Problems of Sociological Theory,* 1961; (with

Robert Moore) *Race, Community and Conflict,* Oxford University Press, 1967; *Race Relations in Sociological Theory,* Weidenfeld & Nicolson, 1970; *Race, Colonialism and the City,* 1973; *Discovering Sociology,* 1973; (editor, author of introduction, and contributor) *Approaches to Sociology,* 1974; *Sociology and the Demystification of the Modern World,* 1974; (with Sally Tomlinson) *Colonial Immigrants in a British City: A Class Analysis,* 1979. Also author of *Social Conflict,* 1981.

Contributor: R. Pahl, editor, *Readings in Urban Sociology,* Pergamon, 1968; Burgess, editor, *Matters of Principle,* Penguin, 1968; T. Raison, editor, *The Founding Fathers of Sociology,* Pelican, 1968; S. Zubaida, editor, *Race and Racialism,* Tavistock, 1970; Butterworth and Weir, *The Sociology of Modern Britain,* Fontana, 1970; K. H. Tjaden, *Soziale Systeme,* Gluchterhand (Berlin), 1971; A. Sahey, editor, *Max Weber and Modern Sociology,* Routledge & Kegan Paul, 1971; *Ethnies,* Volume I, Mouton, 1971; Richardson and Spears, editors, *Race, Culture and Intelligence,* Penguin, 1972; *Etniska Minoriteter 1,* Norden (Lund), 1972; Leftwich, editor, *South Africa: Economic Growth and Political Change,* Alison & Busby, 1974; Giddens and Stanworth, editors, *Elites and Power in British Society,* Cambridge University Press, 1974; B. Parekh, editor, *Colour, Consciousness and Culture,* [London], 1974; Leo Kuper, editor, *Race, Science and Society,* UNESCO, 1975; Lambert and Weir, *Cities in Modern Britain,* Fontana, 1975; Bowker and Carrier, *Race and Ethnic Relations,* Hutchinson, 1976.

Editor of sociology series, Granada Books/MacGibbon & Kee, 1970-73; editor, "International Library of Sociology" series, Routledge & Kegan Paul, 1973. Contributor to *Enzyklopadie der Geisteswissenschaftlichen Arbeitsmethoden.* Contributor to professional and popular publications, including *British Journal of Sociology, Sociological Review, Political Quarterly, Population Studies, New Statesman and Nation, New Society, Sunday Times, Times Literary Supplement,* and *Sociology.* Consulting editor, *American Journal of Sociology,* 1974-76.

SIDELIGHTS: Comments John A. Rex: "My object in writing about sociological topics is to demystify them. Too much sociology mystifies social reality through the use of jargon and pretentious scientism. My main political concern, however, is justice for racial minorities, and I have sought to bring together arguments and evidence which will help this cause, particularly in South Africa and Britain. My hope is to live to see the day when a non-racial democracy is established in South Africa, now the most fully racialist state in the modern world."

*   *   *

REY, H(ans) A(ugusto) 1898-1977
(Uncle Gus)

PERSONAL: Name legally changed; born September 16, 1898, in Hamburg, Germany; came to United States in 1940; died August 26, 1977, in Boston, Mass.; son of Alexander and Martha (Windmuller) Reyersbach; married Margret Elizabeth Waldstein (a writer and illustrator), 1935. *Education:* Attended University of Munich, 1919-20, and University of Hamburg, 1920-23. *Home:* 14 Hilliard St., Cambridge, Mass. 02138; and Waterville Valley, N.H. 03223 (summer).

CAREER: Executive in export-import business and owner of an advertising agency in Rio de Janeiro, Brazil, 1924-36; writer and illustrator of children's books in Paris, France, 1937-40, in New York, N.Y., 1940-63, and in Cambridge, Mass., 1963-77. Teacher of astronomy at Cambridge Center for Adult Education. *Military service:* German Army, Infantry and Medical Corps, 1916-19; served in France and Russia. *Member:* American Association for the Advancement of Science, Federation of American Scientists, Amateur Astronomers Association, Astronomical League, Waterville Valley (N.H.) Athletic and Improvement Association.

WRITINGS—Self-illustrated juveniles, except as indicated: *Zebrology*, Chatto & Windus, 1937, reprinted, 1953; *How the Flying Fishes Came into Being*, Chatto & Windus, 1938; *Raffy and the Nine Monkeys*, Chatto & Windus, 1939, published as *Cecily G. and the Nine Monkeys*, Houghton, 1942; (editor) *Au Clair de la Lune and Other French Nursery Songs*, Greystone, 1941; *How Do You Get There?*, Houghton, 1941; *Uncle Gus's Farm*, Houghton, 1942; *Uncle Gus's Circus*, Houghton, 1942; *Tit for Tat*, Harper, 1942; *Elizabite: The Adventures of a Carnivorous Plant*, Harper, 1942, reprinted, 1962; *Anybody at Home?*, Houghton, 1942; (under pseudonym Uncle Gus) *Christmas Manger*, Houghton, 1942; (illustrator) Margaret Wise Brown, *Don't Frighten the Lion*, Harper, 1942; *Tommy Helps, Too*, Houghton, 1943; *Where's My Baby?*, Houghton, 1943; (editor) *Humpty Dumpty and Other Mother Goose Songs*, Harper, 1943; *Feed the Animals*, Houghton, 1944; (editor) *We Three Kings and Other Christmas Carols*, Harper, 1944; (illustrator) Margret Rey (wife), *Pretzel*, Harper, 1944.

Look for the Letters: A Hide and Seek Alphabet, Harper, 1945; (illustrator) M. Rey, *Spotty*, Harper, 1945; (with M. Rey) *Pretzel and the Puppies*, Harper, 1946; (with M. Rey) *Billy's Picture*, Harper, 1948; *Mary Had a Little Lamb*, Penguin, 1951; *The Stars: A New Way to See Them* (adult book), Houghton, 1952 (published in England as *A New Way to See the Stars*, Hamlyn, 1966), enlarged edition, 1976; (illustrator) Emmy Payne, *Katy No-Pocket*, Chatto & Windus, 1953; *Find the Constellations*, Houghton, 1954, revised edition, 1976; *See the Circus*, Houghton, 1956.

(With M. Rey) "Curious George" series (published in England as "Zozo" series); published by Houghton, except as indicated: *Curious George*, 1941, reprinted, 1973 (published in England as *Zozo*, Chatto & Windus, 1942); *Curious George Takes a Job*, 1947, reprinted, 1974 (published in England as *Zozo Takes a Job*, Chatto & Windus, 1954); *Curious George Rides a Bike*, 1952, reprinted, 1973 (published in England as *Zozo Rides a Bike*, Chatto & Windus, 1954); *Curious George Gets a Medal*, 1957, reprinted, 1974 (published in England as *Zozo Gets a Medal*, Chatto & Windus, 1958); *Curious George Flies a Kite*, 1958 (published in England as *Zozo Flies a Kite*, Chatto & Windus, 1961); *Curious George Learns the Alphabet*, 1963 (published in England as *Zozo Learns the Alphabet*, Chatto & Windus, 1963); *Curious George Goes to the Hospital*, 1966 (published in England as *Zozo Goes to the Hospital*, Chatto & Windus, 1967).

WORK IN PROGRESS: Several more children's books.

SIDELIGHTS: H. A. Rey was best known as the creator of Curious George, the impish main character in a series of seven children's books. George made his first appearance as one of a group of monkeys in *Raffy and the Nine Monkeys* (later published as *Cecily G. and the Nine Monkeys*), but the character seemed so outstanding that Rey devoted an entire book to him in 1941. H. A. and Margret Rey, co-authors of the Curious George books, had no intention of doing a whole series, but the mischievous antics of the little monkey proved to be enormously popular with young readers, and the Reys continued to write about him until 1966. These books, according to a *Publishers Weekly* article, have come to be "widely regarded as modern classics in children's literature."

In addition to the "Curious George" series, Rey, an amateur astronomer, was well known for the two books he wrote on

the stars: *The Stars: A New Way to See Them* (for adults) and *Find the Constellations* (for children). Both of them explained a unique system of star identification invented by Rey. The author told Lee Bennett Hopkins in *Books Are by People* that these two books have "created a revolution in practical star recognition."

H. A. Rey's books have been translated into nine languages, including Dutch, Swedish, Portuguese, and Japanese. "Curious George" was recorded by Caedmon in 1972, with actress Julie Harris reading an adaptation of the first four books in the series.

BIOGRAPHICAL/CRITICAL SOURCES: Lee Bennett Hopkins, *Books Are by People*, Citation, 1969.

OBITUARIES: New York Times, August 28, 1977; *Publishers Weekly*, October 3, 1977.†

* * *

REYAM
  See MAYER, Charles Leopold

* * *

REYNOLDS, Ernest (Randolph)   1910-

PERSONAL: Born September 13, 1910, in Northampton, England; son of Alfred and Fanny (Roddis) Reynolds. *Education:* University of Nottingham, B.A. (with first class honors in English language and literature), 1930; Cambridge University, Ph.D., 1934. *Home:* 43 Wantage Rd., Abington Park, Northampton, England. *Agent:* Curtis Brown Ltd., 1 Craven Hill, London W2 3EW, England.

CAREER: Lecturer and writer in London, England, 1934-39; King Faisal College, Baghdad, Iraq, principal, 1940-41; British Council lecturer in Portugal, 1942-44; University of Birmingham, Birmingham, England, lecturer in English, 1946-55; full-time writer, 1955—. Professional actor in English theaters. *Awards, honors:* Kirke White Poetry Prize, 1930, for poem "Tristram and Iseult."

WRITINGS: Early Victorian Drama, 1830-1870, Heffer, 1936, reprinted, R. West, 1975; *Mephistopheles and the Golden Apples* (poetic fantasy), Heffer, 1943; *Modern English Drama, 1900-1950*, Harrap, 1949, University of Oklahoma Press, 1951, reprinted, R. West, 1975; *The Plain Man's Guide to Antique Collecting*, M. Joseph, 1963, published as *Guide to European Antiques*, A. S. Barnes, 1964; *The Plain Man's Guide to Opera*, M. Joseph, 1964; *Collecting Victorian Porcelain*, Arco, 1966, Praeger, 1968; *Northamptonshire Treasures: A Personal Selection*, Ruth Bean, 1972; *Northampton Town Hall*, Northampton Corp., 1974; *Northampton Repertory Theatre*, [Northampton, England], 1976; "Queens of England" (drama in verse), first produced in Northampton at the Royal Theatre, 1980. Author of "The Three Musketeers," a play based on Alexandre Dumas's novel, which premiered in 1951 and has since been produced at various English theatres; also author of five short verse plays published in Lisbon and a verse drama, "Candlemas Night," broadcast on British Broadcasting Corp. "Third Programme." Contributor of articles on theatre, architecture, and railway history to periodicals.

WORK IN PROGRESS: A long poetic drama, in progress for many years (*Mephistopheles and the Golden Apples* is the first part), with working title of "Martinsmoon."

SIDELIGHTS: Ernest Reynolds told *CA:* "I regard myself as primarily a poet, and my poetic work is what I most hope to be able to go on with. In my opinion, the production of one fine poem is worth a dozen books in prose.'' Reynolds advises aspiring writers to ''write poetry for love but always see that you get paid well for prose.''

AVOCATIONAL INTERESTS: Travel, studying railways, collecting antiques, especially porcelain and French clocks.

*   *   *

RICHEY, Dorothy Hilliard

PERSONAL: Born in Norphlet, Ark.; daughter of Albert and Ruth (Gremillion) Hilliard; married Noyes Richey (a chemist), April 12, 1947; children: Noyes, Jr., Dorothy Ruth Rumsey, Kenneth Albert, Jeanne Elizabeth Sanders, William Henry. *Education:* University of Southwestern Louisiana, B.A., 1947; graduate study, McNeese State College (now University), 1948, and University of Oklahoma, summers. *Address:* P.O. Drawer 5328, Beaumont, Tex. 77706.

CAREER: Muller Co., Lake Charles, La., radio director and fashion coordinator, 1948-50; television performer in Lake Charles, 1953-56; staff writer and free-lance columnist in Houston, Tex., and Miami, Fla.; KLVI, Beaumont, Tex., star of daily radio program, 1965-72; currently vice-president, Richey-Bosch International (film and news syndicate). Writer of fiction and nonfiction for network radio and television, 1948—; lecturer, 1953—. Member of press corps accompanying President Nixon to Moscow summit, 1974, and to other presidential meetings as representative of Texas State Radio Network, Sentinel Newspapers, and five television stations; attends briefings for editors and broadcasters at U.S. Department of State. Instructor in creative writing and in writing for television, Evening Division, Lamar State College (now University), 1963. *Member:* American Women in Radio and Television (national director, 1968-71), National Academy of Television Arts and Sciences, American Association of University Women, Women in Communications, Beaumont Symphony Society. *Awards, honors:* American Women in Radio and Television Golden Mike Award, 1968.

WRITINGS: Road to San Jacinto (juvenile), Naylor, 1961; (with Patricia Bosch) *How to Be Rich and Beautiful,* Patrick Press, 1968; *Early Morning Man,* Patrick Press, 1974. Also author of *The Jury Cried* and *Wives' Seminar* and of two books under a pseudonym. Author of syndicated columns ''The Other Side,'' ''Travel Talk,'' and, with Bosch, ''Today's Woman in Today's World.'' Contributor to trade journals and popular magazines, occasionally under a pseudonym.

WORK IN PROGRESS: Revised editions of *How to Be Rich and Beautiful* and *The Jury Cried; Caribbean Love Caper; Madame President; The Spy They Loved;* with Betty Holberg, *The Winning Edge;* script for a television mini-series.

SIDELIGHTS: Dorothy Richey comments: ''Ever since I was ten years old I knew I wanted to be a writer. The fact that as an adult I could combine broadcasting and lecturing and other related fields never daunted my original career direction. Even with all five children at home, I managed most of the time to get my 'hours' in, whether it be early, late or midday, at the typewriter. It was a challenge to combine homemaking, motherhood and being a wife, but it has worked out very well. So many women will attest to the fact that while it isn't easy, it *is* possible.

''From my earliest years, when I talked with Harnett Kane, to my latest visits with writer-producer Ivan Goff, I knew I was in the right field. There's something special about never, absolutely *never,* being bored—not when you can go anywhere and do anything—on paper. And it certainly spices up your own life—the 'real world' as some of us call it—as well.

''To aspiring writers I'd say realize Kane's old truth that it is first and foremost necessary to 'apply the seat of the pants to the seat of the chair.' True, writing *is* a lonely profession, but it is also one that gives you more freedom than any other. Set smaller goals first—they're easier to achieve, and let them be stepping stones to your Big Novel or Big Script or whatever it is you want to do. Seeing your name in print—and on a check—is terrific motivation to continue!

''DON'T talk about your 'in progress' work. It saps it away, often demolishing it. Set a realistic 'writing time' if you can, beginning with just a quarter hour, if that's all you can spare.

''And help others who are beginning, if time allows. From Howard Leveque in Lake Charles, La., to the late Rod Serling in California, I've been helped many times by those who might have been too busy. I try, as Rod said, to 'pass it along.' It's a bit like paying back all the good that has been given you.

''It also helps to have parents like I did, who let me believe that I could achieve anything I wanted! And later, a husband and family who continued the wonderful support!''

*   *   *

RIDGEWAY, Jason
See MARLOWE, Stephen

*   *   *

RIDLEY, Jasper (Godwin)   1920-

PERSONAL: Born May 25, 1920, in West Hoathly, Sussex, England; son of Geoffrey William (an architect) and Ursula (King) Ridley; married Vera Pollakova (a translator), October 1, 1949; children: Barbara Susan (Mrs. David Miler), Benjamin Nicholas, John Simon. *Education:* Studied at Sorbonne, University of Paris, 1937, and Magdalen College, Oxford, 1938-39. *Politics:* Liberal. *Home:* 6 Oakdale Rd., Tunbridge Wells, Kent, England. *Agent:* Curtis Brown Ltd., 1 Craven Hill, London W2 3EW, England.

CAREER: Private practice of law, London, England, 1946-52; full-time writer, 1953—. Parliamentary candidate, 1955, 1959; St. Pancras Borough Council, councillor, 1945-49. *Military service:* British Army, anti-aircraft gunner, 1940-41. *Member:* Royal Society of Literature (fellow), P.E.N. (vice-chairman of English section), Royal Society of International Affairs, Hardwicke Society, Sussex County Cricket Club. *Awards, honors:* James Tait Black Memorial Prize for biography, 1970, for *Lord Palmerston.*

WRITINGS: Nicholas Ridley, Longmans, Green, 1957; *The Law of Carriage of Goods,* Shaw Publishing Co., 1957; *Thomas Cranmer,* Oxford University Press, 1962; *John Knox,* Oxford University Press, 1968; *Lord Palmerston,* Constable, 1970, Dutton, 1971; *Mary Tudor,* Weidenfeld and Nicolson, 1973; *Garibaldi,* Constable, 1974, Viking, 1976; (contributor) *The Prime Ministers,* Allen & Unwin, 1974; *The Roundheads,* Constable, 1976; *Napoleon III and Eugenie,* Constable, 1979, Viking, 1980; *History of England,* Routledge & Kegan Paul, 1981. Writer of radio scripts on historical subjects for British Broadcasting Corp., 1963-74, including the series ''Dear and Honored Lady'', 1973-74.

WORK IN PROGRESS: A joint biography of Cardinal Wolsey and Sir Thomas More, to be published by Constable and Viking; a biography of Henry VIII.

SIDELIGHTS: Jasper Ridley writes: "I began writing historical biographies 28 years ago, when my wife said she would like to read a biography of my distant ancestor Nicholas Ridley, the sixteenth-century bishop and martyr. When I told her that there was no biography of him, she said, 'Why don't you write one?'; so I did. Since then I have written other biographies of sixteenth-century people, and after switching to the nineteenth century with biographies of Lord Palmerston, Garibaldi, and Napoleon III and Eugenie, I am now back in the sixteenth century with Thomas More, Cardinal Wolsey, and Henry VIII.

"For me, the study of history and of the men and women who made it throws a fascinating light on the characters and behavior of individuals and of masses, and on the different types of human beings—the idealists, the power-politicians and the opportunists—who reappear in every century. I am interested in what is the same and what is different in the attitude of people in past and present generations. Though I enjoy research, which has taken me to Italy, Spain and South America as well as all over Britain, it is for me only a prelude to the writing, to attempting to bring alive the events of the past and to interpret the people of earlier centuries to my twentieth-century readers.

"I spend most of my time writing books, but I walk for at least an hour every day, and enjoy meeting my friends, going to parties, playing chess, and food, wine and cigars."

* * *

RIESSMAN, Frank 1924-

PERSONAL: Born April 9, 1924, in New York, N.Y.; son of Frank and Paula (Michaelis) Riessman; married Catherine Kohler, 1960; children: Robin Elizabeth, Janet Mary, Jeffrey Frank. *Education:* City College (now City College of the City University of New York), B.S.S., 1944; Columbia University, M.A., 1951, Ph.D., 1955. *Home:* 7 East 14th St., New York, N.Y. 10003. *Office:* Graduate School and University Center, City University of New York, 33 West 42nd St., New York, N.Y. 10036.

CAREER: Columbia Grammar School, New York City, school psychologist, 1944-45; City College (now City College of the City University of New York), New York City, research associate, 1950-55; Bard College, Annandale-on-Hudson, N.Y., associate professor of psychology and chairman of department, 1955-64; Yeshiva University, Albert Einstein College of Medicine, Bronx, N.Y., associate professor of psychology, 1964-66; New York University, New York City, professor of educational sociology and director of New Careers Development Center, 1966-71; Queens College of the City University of New York, Flushing, N.Y., professor of education, beginning 1971; currently affiliated with Graduate School and University Center of the City University of New York, New York City. Visiting professor, College of Physicians and Surgeons, New York University, 1961-62; director of mental health aide program, Mental Health Services, Lincoln Hospital (Bronx), 1964-66. Consultant, Mobilization for Youth, 1962-64. *Military service:* U.S. Army, 1946. *Member:* American Psychological Association, American Association of University Professors. *Awards, honors:* Columbia University fellow, 1946; Social Science Research Council fellowship, 1946-47; National Institute of Mental Health grant, 1961-62.

WRITINGS: The Culturally Deprived Child, Harper, 1962; (with Jerome Cohen and Arthur Pearl) *Mental Health of the Poor,* Free Press of Glencoe, 1964; (with Pearl) *New Careers for the Poor,* Free Press of Glencoe, 1965; (with Hermine Popper) *Up from Poverty,* Harper, 1968; (with S. M. Miller) *Social Class and Social Policy,* Basic Books, 1968; *Strategies against Pov-*

erty, Random House, 1969; (with Alan Gartner) *The Service Society and the Consumer Vanguard,* Harper, 1974; *The Inner City Child,* Harper, 1976; (with Gartner) *Self-Help in the Human Services,* Jossey-Bass, 1977; *HELP—A Working Guide to Self-Help Groups,* F. Watts, 1979. Contributor to professional journals. Special editor, *Journal of Social Issues,* 1949; editor, *Social Policy.*

* * *

RIEWALD, J(acobus) G(erhardus) 1910-

PERSONAL: Born August 15, 1910, in Doesburg, Netherlands; son of Gerhardus Marie (a coppersmith) and Gerritje (Hendriks) Riewald; married Elisabeth Maria Bergefurt, December 31, 1941; children: Lucia (Mrs. W. Mutsaers), Jacobus, Elisabeth (Mrs. P. H. M. van Genugten), Hildebrand. *Education:* University of Michigan, graduate study, 1951; U.S. Office of Education, diploma, 1951; University of Nijmegen, Ph.D., 1953. *Religion:* Roman Catholic. *Home:* "Froonacker," 35 Westerse Drift, 9752 LB Haren (Gr.), Netherlands. *Agent:* Author Aid Associates, 340 East 52nd St., New York, N.Y. 10022. *Office:* Faculty of Arts Building, 2-1 Grote Kruisstraat, University of Groningen, 9712 TS Groningen, Netherlands.

CAREER: Teacher in elementary and secondary schools in Arnhem, Netherlands, 1929-36, Ede, Netherlands, 1936-41, Doesburg, Netherlands, 1941-46, and Nijmegen, Netherlands, 1946-60; University of Groningen, Groningen, Netherlands, instructor in English, 1960-66, reader, 1966-80, professor of English and American literature, 1980—. Part-time instructor, Katholieke Leergangen, 1956-63, Gelderse Leergangen, 1959-60, and Fryske Akademy, 1963—; examiner, English Language Institute, University of Michigan, 1955-68. *Member:* European Association for American Studies, Netherlands Association for American Studies, Dutch Modern Language Association (chairman of English section and member of general committee, 1955-61; vice-chairman, 1958-59), Maatschappij der Nederlandse Letterkunde, Modern Language Association of America, Netherlands-America Institute, Thijmgenootschap. *Awards, honors:* Fulbright-Hays award, 1951-52; U.S. Government grant, 1972.

WRITINGS: Sir Max Beerbohm, Man and Writer: A Critical Analysis with a Brief Life and a Bibliography, prefatory letter by Max Beerbohm, Nijhoff, 1953, Greene, 1961; (with L. Grooten and T. Zwartkruis) *A Book of English and American Literature,* Paul Brand, Volume I, 1953, 10th edition, 1981, Volume II, 1953, 8th edition, 1976; (with Grooten and Zwartkruis) *The Student's Companion to a Book of English and American Literature,* Paul Brand, Volume I, 1955, 8th edition, 1981, Volume II, 1955, 6th edition, 1970; *Word Study: A Graded English Vocabulary for Dutch Secondary Schools,* Paul Brand, Volume I, 1957, 11th edition, 1981, alternative edition, 1971, revised alternative edition, 1972, Volume II, 1958, 13th edition, 1980, Volume III, 1960, 11th edition, 1981; (with A. J. de Witte, S. G. van der Meer, and J. P. van der Linden) *Moedertaa-automatismen en het Onderwijs in de Levende Talen,* Malmberg, 1960; (compiler) *Max in Verse: Rhymes and Parodies by Max Beerbohm,* Greene, 1963.

Reynier Jansen of Philadelphia, Early American Printer: A Chapter in Seventeenth-Century Nonconformity, Wolters-Noordhoof, 1970; *Nieuw Engels Woordenboek: De Meest voorkomende Engelse woorden en uitdrukkingen in zinsverband,* Paul Brand, 1974; (editor and author of introduction) *The Surprise of Excellence: Modern Essays on Max Beerbohm,* Shoe String, 1974; (with Grooten) *Perspectives in British and American Literature: A Survey for Students,* Paul Brand, 1974; *Beer-*

bohm's *Literary Caricatures: From Homer to Huxley,* Shoe String, 1977; (with J. Bakker) *The Critical Reception of American Literature in the Netherlands, 1824-1900: A Documentary Conspectus from Contemporary Periodicals,* Rodopi, 1981.

Editor of English and American literature section, *De Katholieke Encyclopaedie,* 1949-55. Contributor of numerous articles on English and American literature and on the teaching of English as a foreign language to *English Studies, Neophilologus, Levende Talen,* and other journals.

WORK IN PROGRESS: A Critical Analysis of Max Beerbohm's Literary Caricatures; Dutch Translations of Nineteenth-Century American Literature; The Latin Correspondence of Willem Sewel, 1653-1720.

BIOGRAPHICAL/CRITICAL SOURCES: J. Bakker and D.R.M. Wilkinson, editors, *From Cooper to Philip Roth: Essays on American Literature Presented to J. G. Riewald on the Occasion of His Seventieth Birthday,* Rodopi, 1980.

*   *   *

RIMLAND, Bernard   1928-

PERSONAL: Born November 15, 1928, in Cleveland, Ohio; son of Meyer (a carpenter) and Anna (Lansky) Rimland; married Gloria Belle Alf, August 28, 1951; children: Mark, Helen, Paul. *Education:* San Diego State College (now University), B.A., 1950, M.A., 1952; Pennsylvania State University, Ph.D., 1954. *Home:* 4758 Edgeware Rd., San Diego, Calif. 92116. *Office:* Institute for Child Behavior Research, 4157 Adams Ave., San Diego, Calif. 92116.

CAREER: U.S. Navy Personnel Research Laboratory, San Diego, Calif., project director, branch head, and department director, 1953-73; U.S. Navy Personnel Research and Development Center, San Diego, director of Applied Psychobiology Program, 1973—. Part-time lecturer at San Diego State University, 1955-64; founder and director of Institute for Child Behavior Research, 1967—. Fellow of Center for Advanced Study in the Behavioral Sciences, Stanford University, 1964-65; visiting professor and guest lecturer at more than seventy universities and medical schools, 1964—. Adviser to numerous national organizations and foundations, including National Society for Autistic Children, Huxley Foundation for Biosocial Research, and Cancer Foundation.

MEMBER: International Council of Psychologists, American Psychological Association (fellow), Academy of Orthomolecular Psychiatry (vice-president, 1971—), Orthomolecular Medical Society (vice-president, 1975—), American Association for Educational Research, National Council on Measurement in Education, Association for Advancement of Behavior Therapy, Psychometric Society, Classification Society.

AWARDS, HONORS: Century Award for distinguished contribution to psychology, 1963, for *Infantile Autism;* named Creative Scientist of the Year by San Diego Institute for Creativity, 1968; American Medical Association medical journalism award, 1969; U.S. Air Force and Navy Technology Symposium award, 1978; International Academy of Applied Nutrition achievement award, 1979; Dixie Annette Award for scientific contribution, Huxley Institute, 1981.

WRITINGS: Infantile Autism: The Syndrome and Its Implications for a Neural Theory of Behavior, Appleton-Century-Crofts, 1964; (co-editor) *Modern Therapies,* Prentice-Hall, 1976. Contributor of articles, reports, chapters to books. Member of editorial boards of *Journal of Autism and Developmental Disorders, Journal of Orthomolecular Psychiatry,* and *Journal of Learning Disabilities.*

WORK IN PROGRESS: Three books—on the unfortunate effects of psychoanalysis on contemporary life, on biological approaches to human thought and nature, and on nature and cause of mental illness.

SIDELIGHTS: Bernard Rimland, a noted psychologist and specialist in child autism, believes that good nutrition and vitamins can be linked to mental health. He expanded on the concept of mental health by inventing the term behavioral health. Rimland states, ''By behavioral health I mean positive, constructive behavior characterized by good attitude and morale, and freedom not only from mental illnesses such as schizophrenia and depression but also from behavioral problems such as learning disabilities, hyperactivity, alcohol and drug dependence, delinquency and criminality.''

BIOGRAPHICAL/CRITICAL SOURCES: San Diego Union, February 23, 1979; *San Mateo Times,* March 6, 1979.

*   *   *

RITTERBUSH, Philip C.   1936-

PERSONAL: Born August 9, 1936, in Orange, N.J.; son of Leonard Charles and Anne (Allman) Ritterbush. *Education:* Yale University, B.A., 1958; Oxford University, D.Phil., 1961. *Politics:* Democrat. *Home:* 2913 29th St. N.W., Washington, D.C. 20008.

CAREER: U.S. Senate, Washington, D.C., legislative assistant to Senator Tom McIntyre of New Hampshire, 1962-64; Smithsonian Institution, Washington, D.C., special assistant on scientific matters, 1964-66, staff assistant to the secretary, 1967-68, director of academic programs, 1968-70; Organization Response, Washington, D.C., chairman and director of archives of institutional change, beginning 1970; National Trust for American Culture, Washington, D.C., president and director of commissioned studies in the relations of science, education, and culture, 1971—. Lecturer in history of science and medicine, Yale University, 1962. *Awards, honors:* Rhodes scholar, 1958.

WRITINGS: Overtures to Biology: The Speculations of Eighteenth-Century Naturalists, Yale University Press, 1964; *Education and Federal Science Establishment,* [Washington, D.C.], 1964; *The Art of Organic Forms,* Smithsonian Institution Press, 1968; (contributor) G. S. Rousseau, editor, *Organic Form: The Life of an Idea,* Routledge & Kegan Paul, 1972; *Federal Programs for Popular Education in the Sciences,* Institute for Cultural Programs, 1980; *A Study of Cultural Policies in the United States,* UNESCO (Paris), 1982.

Editor; published by Acropolis Books, except as indicated: *Talent Waste: How Institutions of Learning Misdirect Human Resources,* 1972; (with others) *The Bankruptcy of Academic Policy,* 1972; *Documenting Change in the Institutions of Knowledge,* 1972; *Let the Entire Community Become Our University,* 1972; *Scientific Institutions of the Future,* 1972; *Technology as Institutionally Related to Human Values,* 1974; (with Chauncey Starr) *Science, Technology and the Human Prospect,* Pergamon, 1980.

WORK IN PROGRESS: Research on the cultural influences of science.

*   *   *

ROBE, Stanley L(inn)   1915-

PERSONAL: Born July 26, 1915, in Tangent, Ore.; son of Hermon Linn (a teacher) and Estella (Kirk) Robe; married Alice Rosetta Mueller (a teacher), August 26, 1943; children: Robert

Carl, Margaret Ann. *Education:* University of Oregon, B.A., 1936, M.A., 1939; University of Chicago, graduate study, 1941; University of North Carolina, Ph.D., 1949. *Religion:* Presbyterian. *Home:* 979 South Bundy Dr., Los Angeles, Calif. 90049. *Office:* University of California, 405 Hilgard Ave., Los Angeles, Calif. 90024.

CAREER: University of North Carolina at Chapel Hill, part-time instructor in Spanish and Portuguese, 1940-41 and 1946-49; University of California, Los Angeles, instructor, 1949-51, assistant professor, 1951-57, associate professor, 1957-63, professor of Spanish, 1963—, chairman of department of Spanish and Portuguese, 1962-63 and 1972-75. Fulbright lecturer, Instituto Caro y Cuervo, Bogota, Colombia, 1961. *Military service:* U.S. Army, Counter Intelligence Corps, 1942-46; became technical sergeant; received Army Commendation Ribbon. *Member:* International Society for Folk Narrative Research, Modern Language Association of America, Linguistic Society of America, American Folklore Society (fellow), Folklore Americas. *Awards, honors:* Ford Foundation fellow, Veracruz, Mexico, 1965.

WRITINGS—Published by University of California Press, except as indicated: *The Spanish of Rural Panama: Major Dialectical Features,* 1960; *Index of Mexican Folktales, Including Narrative Texts from Mexico, Central America, and the Hispanic United States,* 1973; *Azuela and the Mexican Underdogs,* 1979.

Editor: *"Coloquios de pastores" from Jalisco, Mexico,* 1954; *Hispanic Riddles from Panama* (monograph), 1963; *Mexican Tales and Legends from Los Altos,* 1970; *Mexican Tales and Legends from Veracruz,* 1971; *Antologia del saber popular,* Chicano Studies Center, University of California, Los Angeles, 1971; *Amapa Storytellers,* 1972; *Hispanic Folktales from New Mexico: Narratives from the R. D. Jameson Collection,* 1977.

Contributor to professional journals. Editor, *Folklore Americas,* 1966—.

WORK IN PROGRESS: A demographic study, *The Colonial Population of Tepatitlan, Jalisco, Mexico; The Literature of Mexico's Cristero War.*

SIDELIGHTS: Stanley L. Robe has recorded on tape or discs some three hundred folktales of Panama and west-central Mexico.†

*   *   *

ROBERTS, Archibald Edward 1915-

PERSONAL: Born March 21, 1915, in Cheboygan, Mich.; son of Archibald Lancaster and Madeline Ruth (Smith) Roberts; married Florence Snure, September 25, 1940 (divorced February, 1950); married Doris Elfriede White, June 23, 1951; children: (first marriage) Michael James, John Douglas; (second marriage) Guy Archer, Charles Lancaster, Christopher Corwin. *Education:* U.S. Army Command and General Staff College, graduate, 1952; attended U.S. Armed Forces Institute, 1953, and University of Maryland, 1958. *Home:* 2218 West Prospect, Fort Collins, Colo. 80521. *Office:* 480 Savings Bldg., Fort Collins, Colo. 80521.

CAREER: U.S. Army, 1939-65; served in Far East and Europe; retired as lieutenant colonel; Committee to Restore the Constitution, Fort Collins, Colo., director, 1970—. Information officer in United States, Japan, and Europe, 1950-58; special projects officer in Germany and United States, 1959-61; participated in U.S. Senate Armed Services Committee hearings, 1962. Co-owner and director, Roberts & Roberts Advertising Agency, 1946-49; president, Foundation for Education, Schol-

arship, and Patriotism, 1975. *Member:* Airborne Association, Reserve Officers Association, Sons of the American Revolution, Sons of the American Colonists. *Awards, honors*—Military: Department of the Army Commendation Ribbon, 1957. Civilian: Award of merit from American Academy of Public Affairs, 1967; Good Citizenship Medal from Sons of the American Revolution, 1968; medal of merit from American Legion, 1972.

WRITINGS: Rakkasan, Benson Printing Co., 1955; (with others) *Screaming Eagles: 101st Airborne,* Benson Printing Co., 1957; *The Marne Division,* Konrad Triltsch (Wuerzburg, Germany), 1957; *Victory Denied,* Hallberg, 1966; (compiler) *Peace: By the Wonderful People Who Brought You Korea and Viet Nam,* Educators Publications, 1972; *The Anatomy of a Revolution* (booklet), Betsy Ross Press, 1973; *The Republic: Decline and Future Promise,* Betsy Ross Press, 1975; *The Crisis of Federal Regionalism: A Solution* (booklet), Betsy Ross Press, 1976; (with others) *Emerging Struggle for State Sovereignty,* Betsy Ross Press, 1979.

Also author of material for cassettes, including "Should the United States Participate in and Encourage the Development of the United Nations Organization?," "Regional Bureaucracy," "Land Control Laws: Do They Cancel Your Private Property Rights?," "U. S. Constitution versus Regionalism," and "Regional Government." Contributor to magazines.

SIDELIGHTS: In 1962, Archibald E. Roberts was suspended from active duty in the U.S. Army when his speech on the United Nations, made before the Daughters of the American Revolution, was deemed improper by the secretary of the army. Roberts took legal action and, in 1964, was restored to his former status with back pay and retroactively promoted to lieutenant colonel.

Following his retirement from the military, Roberts began organizing a national network of county and state affiliates whose purpose is "to enforce provisions of the Constitution within the borders of the respective states." A strong advocate of states' rights and personal freedoms, Roberts often testifies before state legislatures, county commissions, and public meetings on the dangers of what he views as a trend towards a type of "Federal Regionalism" that is reminiscent of the Soviet system. His objective, he reports, is to expose this trend and "void federally imposed regional (socialist) governance and other excesses of federal agencies [in order to] restore control of government to the people."

In his book *Emerging Struggle for State Sovereignty,* Roberts contends that there is "a plot to erect a corporate state upon the ruins of the Republic. A power elite seeks to overthrow the U.S. Constitution, seize control of private property, and reduce Americans to the status of economic serfs on the land which once was theirs." He identifies the members of this "power elite" as scholars at and supporters of the Center for the Study of Democractic Institutions in Santa Barbara, California, who, he says, have already drafted a new constitution which establishes ten federal regions in place of the current fifty states and contains none of the guarantees now in our Constitution. Edwards urges Americans "to halt and reverse the march toward a socialist U.S.A." through active participation in local government, especially at the state level. Failure to do so, he warns, will result in an alternative that is "too depressing to contemplate."

*   *   *

ROBERTS, Bruce (Stuart) 1930-

PERSONAL: Born February 4, 1930, in Mount Vernon, N.Y.;

son of Charles Wesley (a business executive) and Marion (McNally) Roberts; married Nancy Correll (a writer), February 27, 1957 (divorced); married Susan Hemmingway, 1978; children: (first marriage) Nancy Lee, David Correll. *Education:* New York University, B.S., 1951; University of Florida, graduate study, 1954. *Religion:* Presbyterian. *Home:* 5018 Juita Dr., Irondale, Ala. 35210. *Office: Southern Living,* 820 Shades Creek Pky., P.O. Box 523, Birmingham, Ala. 35201.

CAREER: Tampa Tribune, Tampa, Fla., reporter, 1954-55; editor and publisher of weekly newspapers, *Lumberton Post,* Lumberton, N.C., and *Scottish Chief,* Maxton, N.C., 1956-58; *Charlotte Observer,* Charlotte, N.C., staff photographer, 1959-61; director of photography for Wilmington, Del., newspapers, 1962-63; free-lance photographer for magazines and books, 1963-78; *Southern Living* (magazine), Birmingham, Ala., director of photography, 1978—. Director, Carolina Illustrated, Inc. (photographic service). *Military service:* U.S. Air Force, 1951-53. *Member:* American Society of Magazine Photographers, National Press Photographers Association, Sigma Delta Chi. *Awards, honors:* Named Southern Photographer of the Year, 1959 and 1961; first place awards in National Press Photographers Association news pictures competition, 1959, 1960, and 1961; *Where Time Stood Still* chosen by the *New York Times* editorial board as one of the outstanding children's books of 1970.

WRITINGS: (Editor) *The Face of North Carolina,* illustrated with photographs by the author and others, McNally & Loftin, 1962; *The Carolina Gold Rush: America's First,* illustrated with photographs by the author and others, McNally & Loftin, 1971, 2nd edition, 1972.

With Nancy Roberts; self-illustrated with photographs: *Where Time Stood Still: A Portrait of Appalachia,* Crowell-Collier, 1970; *This Haunted Land,* McNally & Loftin, 1970; *Ghosts and Specters: Ten Supernatural Stories from the Deep South,* Doubleday, 1974; *Ghosts of the Wild West,* Doubleday, 1976; *America's Most Haunted Places,* Doubleday, 1976.

Photographer: W. J. McNally, *Harper's Ferry in Pictures,* McNally (Charlotte, N.C.), 1960; David Stick, *The Cape Hatteras Seashore,* McNally & Loftin, 1964, revised edition, 1973; Frances Griffin, *Old Salem in Pictures,* McNally & Loftin, 1966; Malcolm Boyd and Eric Sevareid, *You Can't Kill the Dream* (contains *Reflections* by Boyd and *The American Dream* by Sevareid), John Knox, 1968; Joel Rothman, *At Last to Ocean: The Story of the Endless Cycle of Water,* Crowell-Collier, 1971; John Foster West, *This Proud Land: The Blue Ridge Mountains,* McNally & Loftin, 1974.

Photographer for books by N. Roberts: *An Illustrated Guide to Ghosts and Mysterious Occurrences in the Old North State,* Heritage House, 1959, 2nd edition, McNally & Loftin, 1967; *Ghosts of the Carolinas,* McNally & Loftin, 1962, 2nd edition, 1967; *David,* John Knox, 1968; *Sense of Discovery: The Mountain,* John Knox, 1969; *A Week in Robert's World: The South,* Crowell-Collier, 1969; *The Governor,* McNally & Loftin, 1972; *The Goodliest Land: North Carolina,* Doubleday, 1973; *The Faces of South Carolina,* Doubleday, 1976; *You and Your Retarded Child,* Concordia, 1977; *Appalachian Ghosts,* Doubleday, 1978; *Southern Ghosts,* Doubleday, 1979.

BIOGRAPHICAL/CRITICAL SOURCES: William Powell, *North Carolina Lives,* Historical Record Association, 1962; *U.S. Camera,* May, 1962; *Editor and Publisher,* March 2, 1963.

*　　*　　*

ROBERTS, Daniel (Frank) 1922-

PERSONAL: Born November 14, 1922, in Paris, France; son

of Charles Raoul and Marie-Antoinette (Bonnami) Roberts; married Geraldine Anne MccGwire, 1954; children: one. *Education:* Attended private schools in Paris, France. *Home:* Downgate Lodge, Tidebrook, Wadhurst, Sussex TN5 6PB, England.

CAREER: Went into French Maquis at sixteen, serving for four years; sometime worker on farms, in forestry, and as photographer in London, England; teacher in preparatory schools in England for twelve years before giving up academic career to write full time; currently teacher. *Member:* Society of Assistant Teachers in Preparatory Schools.

WRITINGS: Francois et l'armee secrete, House of Grant, 1957; *La Ligue des chamois,* Cambridge University Press, 1960; *La Chapelle sous la glace,* Cambridge University Press, 1961; (compiler) Romain Rolland, *L'Enfance de Jean Christophe,* Cambridge University Press, 1961; *Marmot Valley,* Oxford University Press, 1962; *Nibbleneat* (juvenile), Oxford University Press, 1963; *Calixte,* Oxford University Press, 1964; *Roller Skate War,* Methuen, 1967; *Histoires comme ci, comme ca,* J. Murray, 1968; *Archery for All,* David & Charles, 1971; *Conversation dirigee* (textbook), Edward Arnold, 1973; *Jetzt Sprechen Wir!* (textbook), Edward Arnold, 1975. Contributor of short stories and articles to French and English magazines and to education journals.

WORK IN PROGRESS: Two children's novels and a humorous book on skiing for adults.

SIDELIGHTS: Daniel Roberts's first adventure story was published in a boy's magazine when he was only sixteen. He told *CA* that in writing books for children, he hopes to show "the necessity for high ideals [and] the fun of risks intelligently taken and to instill or develop a love of nature." He regards success (which he defines as "being published") as the greatest motivating factor in his life, noting that "with it comes the pleasure of readers' appreciation."

AVOCATIONAL INTERESTS: Skiing, photography, wildlife.

*　　*　　*

ROBERTS, I.
See ROBERTS, Irene

*　　*　　*

ROBERTS, I. M.
See ROBERTS, Irene

*　　*　　*

ROBERTS, Irene 1926-
(I. Roberts, I. M. Roberts; pseudonyms: Roberta Carr, Elizabeth Harle, Ivor Roberts, Iris Rowland, Irene Shaw)

PERSONAL: Born September 27, 1926, in London, England; daughter of Charles Harry and Ivy (Carpenter) Williamson; married Terence Granville Leonard Roberts (an artist), December 26, 1947; children: Paul Trevor, Peter John, Tracey Lynn. *Education* Attended schools in London, England. *Religion:* Church of England. *Home:* Alpha House, Higher Toun, Malborough, Kingsbridge, Devon TQ7 3RL, England.

CAREER: Writer. Teacher of creative writing at Kingsbridge College. Variously worked as chain store assistant, seller of plants on market stall, typist "of sorts," saleswoman in clothing stores. *Member:* Writers Club (West Essex branch), Kingsbridge Writers' Group (founder and president), Rosicrucian Order.

WRITINGS: *Squirrel Walk*, Gresham, 1960; *Love Song of the Sea*, Fleetway Publications, 1960; *Beloved Rascals*, Gresham, 1961; *The Shrine of Marigolds*, Gresham, 1961; *Come Back Beloved*, Gresham, 1961; *Only to Part*, Fleetway Publications, 1961; *Sweet Sorrel*, Gresham, 1962; *The Dark Night*, Fleetway Publications, 1962; *Laughing Is for Fun* (girls' book), Micron, 1962; *Tangle of Gold Lace*, Gresham, 1962; *Cry of the Gulls*, Fleetway Publications, 1963; *Holiday for Hanbury* (girls' book), Micron, 1963.

All published by R. Hale: *Whisper of Sea-Bells*, 1964; *Echo of Flutes*, 1965; *The Mountain Sang*, 1965; *Where Flamingoes Fly*, 1965; *Shadows on the Moon*, 1966; *A Handful of Stars*, 1966; *Jungle Nurse*, 1967; *Love Comes to Larkswood*, 1967; *Alpine Nurse*, 1968; *Nurse in the Hills*, 1968; *The Lion and the Sun*, 1968; *Thunder Heights*, 1968; *Surgeon in Tibet*, 1969; *Birds without Bars*, 1969; *The Shrine of Fire*, 1970; *Gull Haven*, 1970; *Sister at Sea*, 1971; *Moon over the Temple*, 1972; *The Golden Pagoda*, 1972; *Desert Nurse*, 1975; *Nurse in Nepal*, 1975; *Stars above Raphael*, 1976; *Hawks Barton*, 1976; *Symphony of Bells*, 1978; *Nurse Moonlight*, 1980; *Sister on Leave*, 1981.

Under name I. Roberts: *Green Hell* (war story), Micron, 1961.

Under name I. M. Roberts: *The Throne of Pharaohs*, R. Hale, 1974; *Hatshepsut, Queen of the Nile*, R. Hale, 1977.

Under pseudonym Roberta Carr: *Red Runs the Sunset*, Gresham, 1962; *Sea Maiden*, Gresham, 1963; *Fire Dragon*, Gresham, 1966; *Golden Interlude*, Gresham, 1970.

Under pseudonym Elizabeth Harle: *Golden Rain*, Gresham, 1963; *Gay Rowan*, Gresham, 1964; *Sandy*, Gresham, 1966; *The Silver Summer*, R. Hale, 1970; *Spray of Red Roses*, Gresham, 1970; *Buy Me a Dream*, Gresham, 1970; *The Burning Flame*, R. Hale, 1978.

Under pseudonym Ivor Roberts: *Jump Into Hell* (war story), Brown, Watson, 1960; *Trial by Water* (war story), Micron, 1960.

Under pseudonym Iris Rowland; published by Gresham, except as noted: *The Tangled Web*, 1961; *Island in the Mist*, 1961; *The Morning Star*, 1962; *With Fire and Flowers*, 1962; *Golden Flowers*, 1964; *A Fountain of Roses*, 1965; *Valley of Bells*, 1965; *Blue Feathers*, 1966; *A Veil of Rushes*, 1966; *To Be Beloved*, 1967; *Rose Island*, 1968; *Cherries and Candlelight*, 1968; *Nurse at Kama Hall*, 1968; *Moon over Moncrieff*, 1968; *The Knave of Hearts*, R. Hale, 1969; *Star Drift*, 1969; *Rainbow River*, 1969; *The Wild Summer*, 1969; *Orange Blossom for Tara*, 1970; *Blossom in the Snow*, 1970; *Sister Julia*, 1971; *To Lisa with Love*, R. Hale, 1974; *Golden Bubbles*, R. Hale, 1975; *The Golden Triangle*, R. Hale, 1976; *Forgotten Dreams*, R. Hale, 1977; *Hunters Dawn*, R. Hale, 1977; *Dance Ballerina Dance*, R. Hale, 1978; *Weave Me a Moonbeam*, R. Hale, 1980; *The Romantic Lady*, R. Hale, 1981.

Under pseudonym Irene Shaw: *The House of Lydia*, Wright & Brown, 1965; *Moonstone Manor*, Wright & Brown, 1967; *The Olive Branch*, Wright & Brown, 1968; *Murderer's Mansion*, Doubleday, 1976.

Contributor of short stories and serials to magazines in England, United States, Belgium, Norway, Denmark, Netherlands, Sweden, and Italy.

WORK IN PROGRESS: *Death of a Pharoah* and *The Achaemian Eagle*, both under name I. M. Roberts.

SIDELIGHTS: Irene Roberts writes: "One of the greatest motivating factors important to my career has been my determination not to accept the word impossible. I was told at great length that I could never become an author because I was not educated (I left school at 13 when my school was evacuated from London during the Second World War) and because I did not know anyone in the writing world.

"I have always loved the works of Emily Bronte, Charlotte Bronte, Henry Ridger Haggard, Charles Dickens, William Shakespeare, H. G. Wells, Agatha Christie, Arnold Bennet, and the writers of the books in the Bible. I must have been influenced by all of them. Jean Plaidy is my favorite contemporary author. She makes history come alive for me in a quite remarkable way.

"I hope that there is going to be a toning down of the explicit sex for effect in women's light fiction. As a reviewer, I read a great number of these works. Sadly, the sexual paragraphs one reads in them are becoming increasingly stereotyped and therefore incredibly boring. It has always been my view that a good story does not need gimmicks of any kind. On the other hand, I accept that sex—well-written—is sometimes necessary to add depth to a straight novel."

Irene Roberts's works have been published in foreign language editions in Norway, Denmark, Italy, Sweden, Holland, Belgium, France, Spain, Germany and Finland.

*   *   *

ROBERTS, Ivor
See ROBERTS, Irene

*   *   *

ROBERTS, Nancy Correll 1924-

PERSONAL: Born May 30, 1924, in South Milwaukee, Wis.; daughter of Milton Lee (a chemist) and Maud (MacRae) Correll; married Bruce Stuart Roberts (a free-lance photographer), February 27, 1957 (divorced); children: Nancy Lee, David Correll. *Education:* Attended Centre College, 1942-44; University of North Carolina, B.A., 1947; University of Miami, graduate study, 1947-48. *Religion:* Presbyterian. *Home:* 3600 Chevington Rd., Charlotte, N.C. 28211.

CAREER: *Scottish Chief*, Maxton, N.C., editor and publisher, 1954-57; free-lance writer. President, Maxton (N.C.) Development Corp., 1954-55. Town commissioner of Maxton, 1952-56. *Awards, honors: Where Time Stood Still* chosen by the *New York Times* editorial board as one of the outstanding children's books of 1970.

WRITINGS: *Help for the Parents of a Handicapped Child*, Concordia, 1981.

Illustrated with photographs by Bruce Roberts: *An Illustrated Guide to Ghosts and Mysterious Occurrences in the Old North State*, Heritage House, 1959, 2nd edition, McNally & Loftin, 1967; *Ghosts of the Carolinas*, McNally & Loftin, 1962, 2nd edition, 1967; *David*, John Knox, 1968; *Sense of Discovery: The Mountain*, John Knox, 1969; *A Week in Robert's World: The South*, Crowell-Collier, 1969; *The Governor*, McNally & Loftin, 1972; *The Goodliest Land: North Carolina*, Doubleday, 1973; *The Faces of South Carolina*, Doubleday, 1976; *You and Your Retarded Child*, Concordia, 1977; *Appalachian Ghosts*, Doubleday, 1978; *Southern Ghosts*, Doubleday, 1979.

With B. Roberts; illustrated with photographs by B. Roberts: *Where Time Stood Still: A Portrait of Appalachia*, Crowell-Collier, 1970; *This Haunted Land*, McNally & Loftin, 1970;

Ghosts and Specters: Ten Supernatural Stories from the Deep South, Doubleday, 1974; *Ghosts of the Wild West,* Doubleday, 1976; *America's Most Haunted Places,* Doubleday, 1976.

BIOGRAPHICAL/CRITICAL SOURCES: New York Times Book Review, November 9, 1969.

* * *

ROBERTSON, James (Irvin), Jr. 1930-

PERSONAL: Born July 18, 1930, in Danville, Va.; son of J. Irvin (a banker) and Mae (Kympton) Robertson; married Elizabeth Green, June 1, 1952; children: Beth Robertson Brown, James I. III, Howard. *Education:* Randolph-Macon College, B.A., 1955; Emory University, M.A., 1956, and Ph.D., 1959. *Religion:* Anglican. *Home:* 405 Stonegate Dr. N.W., Blacksburg, Va. 24060. *Office:* Department of History, Virginia Polytechnic Institute and State University, Blacksburg, Va. 24061.

CAREER: University of Iowa, Iowa City, editor of *Civil War History,* 1959-61; George Washington University, Washington, D.C., associate professorial lecturer, 1962-65; University of Montana, Missoula, associate professor of history, 1965-67; Virginia Polytechnic Institute and State University, Blacksburg, professor of history, 1967-76, C. P. Miles Professor of History, 1976—, chairman of the department, 1969-76. Executive director, U.S. Civil War Centennial Commission, 1961-65. Certified football official, for Atlantic Coast Conference.

MEMBER: American Historical Association, Organization of American Historians, Jefferson Davis Association (member of board of directors), Ulysses S. Grant Association (member of board of directors), Southern Historical Association, Virginia Historical Society (member of board of directors). *Awards, honors:* Harry S Truman Historical award; Mrs. Simon Baruch University award; Bennett Memorial Historical award of Randolph-Macon College; centennial medallion, U.S. Civil War Centennial Commission.

WRITINGS: (Editor and author of foreword) Sarah Dawson, *A Confederate Girl's Diary,* Indiana University Press, 1960; (editor and author of introduction and notes) *From Manassas to Appomattox: Memoirs of the Civil War in America,* Indiana University Press, 1960; *Virginia, 1861-1865: Iron Gate to the Confederacy* (booklet), Virginia Civil War Commission, 1961; (editor and author of introduction and notes) Walter Herron Taylor, *Four Years with General Lee,* Indiana University Press, 1962; (editor) Dolly Sumner Burge, *Diary,* University of Georgia Press, 1962; *The Stonewall Brigade,* Louisiana State University Press, 1963; *The Civil War: A Student Handbook,* U.S. Civil War Centennial Commission, 1963; *The Sack of Lawrence: What Price Glory?,* World Co. (Lawrence, Kan.), 1963; (compiler) *Civil War History: Cumulative Index, 1955-1959,* Volumes I-V, State University of Iowa, 1963; (editor) John H. Worsham, *One of Jackson's Foot Cavalry,* McCowat-Mercer, 1965; (editor) *The Civil War Letters of General Robert McAllister,* Rutgers University Press, 1965; (editor with Allan Nevins and Bell I. Wiley) *Civil War Books: A Critical Bibliography,* two volumes, Louisiana State University Press, 1967-69.

The Concise Illustrated History of the Civil War, Stackpole, 1971; (editor) *Four Years in the Stonewall Brigade,* Morningside Bookshop, 1972; (editor with Richard McMurry) *Rank and File: Civil War Essays in Honor of Bell Irvin Wiley,* Presidio Press, 1977; (compiler) *An Index Guide to the Southern Historical Society Papers, 1876-1959,* two volumes, Kraus International, 1980; *Civil War Sites in Virginia,* University Press of Virginia, 1981. Also editor of *Proceedings of the*

Advisory Council of the State of Virginia, Virginia State Library, 1977. Contributor of more than forty articles on American history to periodicals. Member of board of editors, *Civil War History, Lincoln Herald,* and *American History Illustrated.*

SIDELIGHTS: James Robertson wrote *CA:* "My major field of study is the American Civil War. I am a social historian in a military period, for my interests are not primarily in battles and leaders. Rather, I am more concerned with the feelings of the soldiers and the common folk—how they lived, worshipped, coped with sickness, etc."

* * *

ROBINSON, Joan Violet 1903-

PERSONAL: Born October 31, 1903; daughter of Major General Sir Frederick Maurice; married E.A.G. Robinson, 1926; children: two daughters. *Education:* Girton College, Cambridge, economics tripos, 1925. *Home:* 62 Grange Rd., Cambridge, England.

CAREER: Cambridge University, Cambridge, England, assistant lecturer, 1931-37, university lecturer, 1937-49, reader, 1949-64, professor of economics, 1965-71. Special professor, Stanford University, spring, 1969. *Member:* British Academy (fellow).

WRITINGS: The Economics of Imperfect Competition, Macmillan, 1933, 2nd edition, St. Martin's, 1969; *Essays in the Theory of Employment,* Macmillan, 1937, 2nd edition, Basil Blackwell, 1947, Macmillan, 1948, reprinted, Hyperion Press, 1980, revised edition, Macmillan, 1969; *Introduction to the Theory of Employment,* Macmillan, 1937, 2nd edition, St. Martin's, 1969; *An Essay on Marxian Economics,* Macmillan, 1942, 2nd edition, St. Martin's, 1967; (with others) *Can Planning Be Democratic?: A Collection of Essays Prepared for the Fabian Society,* G. Routledge & Sons, 1944; *Collected Economic Papers,* Volume I, Basil Blackwell, 1951, Volume II, Basil Blackwell, 1960, Volume III, Humanities, 1966, Volume IV, Humanities, 1972, Volume V, Basil Blackwell, 1979, Volumes I-V reprinted, MIT Press, 1980; *The Rate of Interest, and Other Essays,* Macmillan, 1952, reprinted, Hyperion Press, 1980, 2nd edition published as *The Generalisation of the General Theory, and Other Essays,* St. Martin's, 1979; *The Accumulation of Capital,* Irwin, 1956, 3rd edition, Macmillan, 1969.

Exercises in Economic Analysis, Macmillan, 1960, St. Martin's, 1961; *Essays in the Theory of Economic Growth,* Macmillan, 1962, St. Martin's, 1963; *Economic Philosophy,* Aldine, 1962; *Economics: An Awkward Corner,* Allen & Unwin, 1966, Pantheon, 1967; (compiler) *The Cultural Revolution in China,* Penguin, 1969; *Freedom and Necessity: An Introduction to the Study of Society,* Pantheon, 1970; *Economic Heresies: Some Old-Fashioned Questions in Economic Theory,* Basic Books, 1971; (contributor) Rendigs Fels, editor, *The Second Crisis of Economic Theory, and Other Selected Papers,* foreword by John Kenneth Galbraith, General Learning Press, 1972; (editor) *After Keynes,* Barnes & Noble, 1973; (with John Eatwell) *An Introduction to Modern Economics,* McGraw, 1973, revised edition, 1974; (with Michael Kalecki and P. A. Baran) *Aspetti politici della piena occupazione,* Celuc (Milan), 1975; *Joan Robinson Reports from China, 1953-76,* Anglo-Chinese Educational Institute (London), 1977; *Contributions to Modern Economics,* Academic Press, 1978; *Aspects of Development and Underdevelopment,* Cambridge University Press, 1979; *What Are the Questions?, and Other Essays: Further Contributions to Modern Economics,* M. E. Sharpe, 1981 (published in England as *Further Contributions to Modern Economics,* Basil Blackwell, 1981).

Booklets: *Economics Is a Serious Subject,* Heffer, 1932; *Private Enterprise or Public Control,* English Universities Press, 1942; *The Problem of Full Employment: An Outline for Study Circles,* Workers Educational Association, 1943, revised edition, 1949; *The Future of Industry,* Muller, 1943; *Conference Sketch Book: Moscow, April, 1952,* Heffer, 1952; *On Re-Reading Marx,* Students' Bookshops, 1953; *Letters from a Visitor to China,* Students' Bookshops, 1954; *Marx, Marshall, and Keynes,* School of Economics, University of Delhi, 1955; (with Sol Adler) *China: An Economic Perspective,* foreword by Harold Wilson, Fabian International Bureau, 1958; (with R. Frisch) *Draft of a Multilateral Trade Clearing Agency,* Institute of Economics, University of Oslo, 1962; *Notes from China,* Monthly Review Press, 1964; *The New Mercantilism: An Inaugural Lecture,* Cambridge University Press, 1966; *Economics Today,* Polygraphischer Verlag (Zurich), 1970; *Economic Management: China 1972,* Anglo-Chinese Educational Institute, 1973, 2nd edition published as *Economic Management in China,* 1975, 3rd edition, 1976; *Reflections on the Theory of International Trade,* Manchester University Press, 1974. Contributor to economics journals.

* * *

ROBINSON, John A(rthur) T(homas) 1919-

PERSONAL: Born June 15, 1919, in Canterbury, Kent, England; son of Arthur William (a clergyman) and Beatrice (Moore) Robinson; married Ruth Grace, April 10, 1947; children: Stephen, Catherine, Elizabeth, Judith. *Education:* Attended Marlborough College; Jesus College, Westcott House, and Trinity College, all Cambridge, B.A., 1942, M.A., 1945, Ph.D., 1946, B.D., 1962, D.D., 1968. *Home:* Trinity College, Cambridge University, Cambridge CB2 1TQ, England.

CAREER: Church of St. Matthew, Moorfields, Bristol, England, curate, 1945-48; Wells Theological College, Wells, England, chaplain and lecturer, 1948-51; Cambridge University, Cambridge, England, fellow and dean of Clare College, 1951-59, assistant university lecturer, 1953-54, university lecturer in divinity, 1954-59; Church of England, Diocese of Southwark, bishop of Woolwich, 1959-69, assistant bishop, 1969-80; Cambridge University, Trinity College, lecturer in theology, fellow, and dean of chapel, 1969—; Church of England, Bradford, Yorkshire, England, assistant bishop of Bradford, 1981—. Visiting professor and Noble Lecturer, Harvard University, 1955; visiting professor or lecturer at numerous other colleges and universities, including Union Theological Seminary, 1958, Virginia Theological Seminary, 1958, Hartford Seminary, 1964, Cornell University, 1964, Wabash College, 1966, Stanford University, 1966, University of Lancaster, 1971, University College of Aberystwyth, 1971, University of South Africa, 1975, University of Witwatersrand, 1977, and St. John's College, 1979. Examining chaplain to Archbishop of Canterbury, 1953-59; Six Preacher, Canterbury Cathedral, 1958-68; proctor in the convocation of Canterbury, 1960-70. *Member:* Society of New Testament Studies. *Awards, honors:* LL.D., University of Southern California, 1980.

WRITINGS: In the End, God, Allenson, 1950, new edition, New American Library, 1968; *The Body: A Study in Pauline Theology,* Regnery, 1952, reprinted, Westminster, 1977; *Jesus and His Coming,* Abingdon, 1957, 2nd edition, Westminster, 1979; *On Being the Church in the World,* S.C.M. Press, 1960, Westminster, 1962, reprinted, Mowbray, 1977; *Christ Comes In,* Mowbray, 1960; *Liturgy Coming to Life,* Westminster,

1960; *Twelve New Testament Studies,* Allenson, 1962; *Honest to God,* Westminster, 1963; *Christian Morals Today,* Westminster, 1964; *The New Reformation?,* Westminster, 1965; *But That I Can't Believe!,* Collins, 1967; *Exploration into God,* Stanford University Press, 1967; *Christian Freedom in a Permissive Society,* Westminster, 1970; *The Difference in Being a Christian Today,* Westminster, 1972; *The Human Face of God,* Westminster, 1973; *Redating the New Testament,* Westminster, 1976; *Can We Trust the New Testament?,* Eerdmans, 1977; *Wrestling with Romans,* Westminster, 1979; *Truth Is Two-Eyed,* Westminster, 1979; *The Roots of a Radical,* Crossroad Publishing Co., 1981.

Contributor to numerous books, including *Christian Faith and Common Faith,* 1953, *Becoming a Christian,* 1954, *The Historic Episcopate,* 1954, *Jesus Christ: History, Interpretation and Faith,* 1956; *New Ways with the Ministry,* 1960, *Bishops,* 1961, *The Interpreter's Dictionary of the Bible,* Abingdon, 1962, *Layman's Church,* Allenson, 1963, *The Roads Converge,* 1963, *The "Honest to God" Debate,* 1963, *"Honest to God" and "The 'Honest to God' Debate,"* S.C.M. Press, 1964, *The Authorship and Integrity of the New Testament,* 1965, *The Restless Church,* 1966, *Theologians of Our Time,* 1966, *Theological Freedom and Social Responsibility,* 1967, *Sermons from Great St. Mary's,* 1968, *The Christian Priesthood,* 1970, *More Sermons from Great St. Mary's,* 1971, *Theological Crossings,* 1971, *Christ, Faith and History,* 1972, *To God Be the Glory,* 1973, *Christ and Spirit in the New Testament,* 1973, *Face to Face with the Turin Shroud,* 1978, and various symposia and festschriften.

Also translator of *The New English Bible.* Contributor to theology journals, mainly on New Testament subjects.

SIDELIGHTS: Outspoken and unorthodox in his views, John A.T. Robinson created a furor in the mid-1960s with his book *Honest to God.* A rarity of sorts in the publishing world—a best-selling work on modern theology—*Honest to God* not only challenged conventional belief, it also, noted Robert C. Dentan in the *New York Times Book Review,* "made theological discussion for the first time seem interesting and important to the contemporary layman."

Robinson wrote *Honest to God* in 1962 when a back injury required a period of convalescence. "I determined to use the opportunity to allow their head to ideas that had been submerged by pressure of work for some time past," the clergyman remarked in the *Observer.* "Over the years convictions had been gathering—from my reading and experience—which I knew I couldn't with integrity ignore, however disturbing they might seem."

One of these "disturbing convictions," inspired in part by the theories of Rudolf Bultmann, Dietrich Bonhoeffer, and Paul Tillich, holds that the concept of God as an imposing male figure who resides "up there" in some celestial palace is meaningless to most thinking people nowadays and may indeed cause many of them to simply dismiss Christianity entirely. Instead, Robinson argues, religion should be "demythologized" and made more personal; everyone must come to realize that God is inside each and every man, woman, and child and that this presence is the ultimate reality of life. To reject the old idea of God, he explains, is not to reject God himself; it is to acknowledge, as God would wish, that mankind has "grown up" and therefore desires a more sophisticated belief system.

Though the ideas it contained were by no means new, *Honest to God* had an impact that reached far beyond the norm for books on theology. It had, after all, been written not by a member of the academic world, but by a bishop of the Church of England. Furthermore, he had addressed his words not to theologians and fellow churchmen, but to the general public. Some members of both groups—the clergy and the public—denounced the book as heresy or as Robinson's confession of atheism and demanded his resignation. Others welcomed it as the beginning of a reformation in theological thinking that promised some hope to those who had become uncomfortable with the old ways. In any case, Robinson was (and still is) rather surprised at the amount of controversy *Honest to God* generated in the years after its publication. "This was quite apart from my own field [New Testament studies]," he explained to *Publishers Weekly* interviewer Philippa Toomey in 1979. "That book really brought me into an entirely different world—and afterward, everybody was very keen to publish anything I liked to offer them."

Though Toomey describes him as "a man who still relishes a controversial question," Robinson insists that he is really more traditional than trendy. Don Cupitt, reviewing *The Roots of a Radical,* a collection of essays in which the clergyman examines how his beliefs evolved, seems to agree. Concludes the critic: "In the old tradition of the 'middle way' [Robinson] avoids both biblical fundamentalism and ecclesiastical absolutism, holding that one should be firmly rooted in a few central values, commitments and doctrinal themes, while being open and exploratory at the edges. . . . The unhesitating imprudence with which he follows his conscience and takes the side of the scapegoat has nothing to do with [prevailing trends]. . . . He simply throws himself into the fray, with a truly Victorian confidence and disregard of the consequences. . . . He is usually on the side of the angels."

BIOGRAPHICAL/CRITICAL SOURCES: David Lawrence Edwards, editor, *The "Honest to God" Debate,* Westminster, 1963; *Observer,* March 17, 1963; *Punch,* May 20, 1964; *New York Times Book Review,* November 26, 1967; *New Republic,* July 6, 1968; *Encounter,* winter, 1969; *Books,* April, 1970; *Library Journal,* September 1, 1970; *Publishers Weekly,* February 12, 1979; John A.T. Robinson, *The Roots of a Radical,* Crossroad Publishing Co., 1981; *Times Literary Supplement,* August 7, 1981.

* * *

ROBINSON, Robert H(ouston) 1936-

PERSONAL: Born May 5, 1936, in Lewes, Del.; son of Julian Thomas and Mary (Houston) Robinson; married; wife's name Battle. *Education:* University of North Carolina, B.A., 1959. *Residence:* Georgetown, Del. *Office:* Sussex Countian and Sussex Prints, 115 North Race, Georgetown, Del. 19947.

CAREER: Sussex Countian (weekly newspaper), Georgetown, Del., news editor, 1962—; Sussex Prints, Inc., Georgetown, president and publisher. *Military service:* U.S. Navy, 1959-62; became lieutenant junior grade.

WRITINGS: Going the Other Way (novella), bound with *Mister Jack* by Eleanor Widmer and *The Coming of Monsieur Alazay* by Egon Pohoryles and published as *Three, 1964,* Random House, 1964; *Visiting Sussex, Even If You Live Here,* Sussex Prints, 1976; *The Craft of Dismantling a Crab,* Sussex Prints, 1977; *Shellfish Heritage Cookbook,* Part 1, Sussex Prints, 1981. Also author of *Old Country Churches of Sussex County.*

WORK IN PROGRESS: Editing *Shellfish Digest,* a series of publications on catching and cooking shellfish.

SIDELIGHTS: Robert H. Robinson comments: "Because I was not being published by other publishers I decided to start my own publishing company. Of course it's impossible, but it's

too bad more writers can't do this. They would understand what editors and publishers have to go through. The safest and easiest position to be in the publishing and book world is a reader of books. Between writing, editing, publishing and trying to sell books, I don't even have time for that."

BIOGRAPHICAL/CRITICAL SOURCES: New Yorker, May 19, 1980.

* * *

ROCKWOOD, Joyce 1947-

PERSONAL: Born June 1, 1947, in Ames, Iowa; daughter of Frank Bradford (an Episcopalian priest) and Katherine (Graves) Rockwood; married Charles Hudson (a professor of anthropology), May 28, 1968. *Education:* University of Georgia, A.B. (cum laude), 1969; also attended University of Wisconsin. *Residence:* Georgia.

CAREER: Writer. *Member:* Authors Guild, Authors League of America, Southern Anthropological Society, Phi Beta Kappa.

WRITINGS—All novels; all published by Holt: *Long Man's Song,* 1975; *To Spoil the Sun,* 1976; *Groundhog's Horse,* 1978; *Enoch's Place,* 1980. Contributor to *Appalachian Journal.*

WORK IN PROGRESS: Apalachee, a novel about colonial America's early Southern frontier.

SIDELIGHTS: Joyce Rockwood writes: "I consider myself an anthropologist as well as a novelist. In my writing I attempt to draw the reader into the drama of other worlds, real worlds where the characters are as human and as moving and as rational as in our own. I write primarily about the American Indians, setting my stories in the cultures of the past, relying heavily on anthropological and historical research in order to recreate the reality that has since been shattered by the European invasion. Yet I strive above all to entertain. My purpose is not to teach, but to offer a powerful human experience."

* * *

ROEMER, Milton I(rwin) 1916-

PERSONAL: Born in 1916, in Paterson, N.J.; married; children: two. *Education:* Cornell University, B.A., 1936, M.A., 1939; New York University, M.D., 1940; University of Michigan, M.P.H., 1943. *Office:* School of Public Health, University of California, Los Angeles, Calif. 90024.

CAREER: Barnert Memorial Hospital, Paterson, N.J., rotating intern, 1940-41; New Jersey State Department of Health, Trenton, medical officer in Venereal Disease Control Division, 1941-42; Yale University, New Haven, Conn., assistant professor, 1949-50, associate professor of public health, 1950-51; World Health Organization, Geneva, Switzerland, chief of social and occupational health section, 1951-53; Saskatchewan Department of Public Health, Regina, director of medical and hospital services, 1953-56; Yeshiva University, Albert Einstein College of Medicine, New York, N.Y., lecturer in medicine, 1956-57; Cornell University, Ithaca, N.Y., associate research professor, 1957-60, research professor of administrative medicine, 1960-62, director of research at Sloan Institute of Hospital Administration, 1957-62; University of California, Los Angeles, professor of health services and preventive medicine, 1962—, head of Division of Medical Care Organization, 1962-64, head of Division of Medical and Hospital Administration, 1965-67, head of Division of Health Administration, 1967-70. Member, U.S. National Subcommittee on Medical Care Statistics, Institute of Medicine (of National Academy of Sciences), California State Health Department committees on medical care for children, seasonal agricultural workers, and hospital utilization, California Center for Health Services Research (member of policy board, 1968-72), Los Angeles Psychiatric Service (member of board of directors), and Los Angeles County Committee on Affairs of the Aging. Fellow, Institute of European Health Services Research. Diplomate, National Board of Medical Examiners, 1941, and American Board of Preventive Medicine and Public Health. Consultant to state and federal government agencies and to international organizations. *Wartime service:* U.S. Public Health Service, 1943-51; served as assistant to chief medical officer in War Food Administration, 1943-45, associate in medical care administration to chief of the States Relations Division, 1945-47, and director of West Virginia Public Health Training Center and Monongalia County Health Department, 1948-49; became senior surgeon.

MEMBER: International Epidemiological Association, American Public Health Association (fellow; member of governing council, 1967—), American Sociological Association, American College of Preventive Medicine, California Academy of Preventive Medicine (president, 1972—), Phi Beta Kappa, Sigma Xi, Phi Kappa Phi, Alpha Omega Alpha, Delta Omega.

WRITINGS: Social Factors Influencing American Medical Practice, Cornell University, 1939; *A System for Quantitative Appraisal of Voluntary Hospitalization Insurance Plans,* University of Michigan, 1942; (with F. D. Mott) *Rural Health and Medical Care,* McGraw, 1948.

A Health Demonstration Area in El Salvador, World Health Organization, 1951; *A Health Demonstration Area in Ceylon,* World Health Organization, 1951; (with E. A. Wilson) *Organized Health Services in a County of the United States,* U.S. Government Printing Office, 1952; *Medical Care in Relation to Public Health: A Study of Relationships between Preventive and Curative Health Services throughout the World,* World Health Organization, 1956; (with Max Shain) *Hospital Utilization under Insurance,* American Hospital Association, 1959; (editor) *Henry E. Sigerist on the Sociology of Medicine,* M.D. Publications, 1960; *Medical Care Administration: Content, Positions, and Training in the United States,* Western Branch, American Public Health Association, 1963; *Medical Care in Latin America,* Pan American Union, 1963; *Health Services in the Los Angeles Riot Area,* University of California, Los Angeles, 1965; (with Olive Manning) *The Rural Health Services Scheme in Malaysia,* Office for the Western Pacific, World Health Organization, 1969; *The Organization of Medical Care under Social Security: A Study of the Experience of Eight Countries,* International Labour Office, 1969.

(Editor with D. M. Du Bois and S. W. Rich) *Health Insurance Plans: Studies in Organizational Diversity,* School of Public Health, University of California, Los Angeles, 1970; (with J. W. Friedman) *Doctors in Hospitals: Medical Staff Organization and Hospital Performance,* Johns Hopkins Press, 1971; *Evaluation of Community Health Centres,* World Health Organization, 1972; (with R. F. Bridgman) *Hospital Legislation and Hospital Systems,* World Health Organization, 1973; (with R. W. Hetherington, C. E. Hopkins, and others) *Health Insurance Effects,* School of Public Health, University of Michigan, 1973; *Health Care Systems in World Perspective,* University of Michigan Health Administration Press, 1976; *Rural Health Care,* Mosby, 1976; *Comparative National Policies on Health Care,* Dekker, 1977; *Social Medicine: The Advance of Organized Health Service in America,* Springer Publishing Co., 1978; (with Ruth Roemer) *Health Care Systems and Comparative Manpower Policies,* Dekker, 1981; *Ambulatory Health Services in America: Past, Present, and Future,* Aspen Systems Corp., 1981.

Contributor of about two hundred articles on social and organizational aspects of health services to professional journals.

*   *   *

RONAN, Colin A(listair)   1920-

PERSONAL: Born June 4, 1920, London, England; son of Amos Hudson and Aileen (Nathan) Ronan. *Education:* University of London, B.Sc., 1949, M.Sc., 1953. *Home and office:* 13 Acorn Ave., Bar Hill, Cambridge CB3 8DT, England.

CAREER: Royal Society of London, London, England, senior member of secretariat, 1949-60; Oxford University, Oxford, England, extra-mural lecturer in astronomy and history of astronomy, 1956—; Colin Ronan Ltd. (consultants and science writers and broadcasters), Bar Hill, Cambridge, England, director, 1961—. Radio and television lecturer. Consultant to theatrical producers on space travel and history of science. *Military service:* British Army, 1940-46; served as deputy assistant director of artillery; became major. *Member:* Royal Astronomical Society (fellow), British Astronomical Association (editor and publications coordinator), Archaeological Institute, National Film Archive Science Advisory Committee.

WRITINGS: Changing Views of the Universe, Macmillan, 1961; *The Earth from Pole to Pole,* Harrap, 1962; *The Meaning of Light,* Weidenfeld & Nicolson, 1962; *Clocks and Watches,* Doubleday, 1962; *Radio and Radar Astronomy,* Doubleday, 1963; *The Universe,* Parrish, 1963, F. Watts, 1968; *The Astronomers,* Hill & Wang, 1964; *Man Probes the Universe,* Doubleday, 1964.

Optical Astronomy, Roy, 1965; *The Stars,* Bodley Head, 1965, McGraw, 1966; *Ages of Science,* Harrap, 1966; *The Easy Way to Understand Photography,* Parrish, 1966; *Exploring Space,* Odhams, 1966; *The Meaning of Sound,* Weidenfeld & Nicolson, 1967; *Their Majesties' Astronomers,* Bodley Head, 1967, published as *Astronomers Royal,* Doubleday, 1969; *Isaac Newton,* International Textbook Co., 1969; *Invisible Astronomy,* Lippincott, 1969; *Edmund Halley: Genius in Eclipse,* Doubleday, 1969.

A Book of Science (juvenile), Oxford University Press, 1970; *Discovering the Universe,* Basic Books, 1971; *Astronomy,* Barnes & Noble, 1973; *Lost Discoveries: The Forgotten Science of the Ancient World,* McGraw, 1973; *Galileo,* Putnam, 1974; (abridger) Joseph Needham, *The Shorter Science and Civilisation in China,* Cambridge University Press, Volume I, 1978, Volume II, 1981; (contributor) *China,* Crown, 1981; *The Practical Astronomer,* Macmillan, 1981.

Editor, "Survey of Astronomy" series, Macmillan. Contributor to *Encyclopaedia Britannica* and *Dictionary of Scientific Biography;* contributor of articles to *Notes and Records of the Royal Society.* Editor, *Journal of the British Astronomical Association.*

WORK IN PROGRESS: Deep Space, a sequel to *The Practical Astronomer;* a history of world science; preparing an abridged edition of another volume of *The Shorter History of Science and Civilization in China.*

*   *   *

ROSAGE, David E.   1913-

PERSONAL: Born February 19, 1913, in Johnstown, Pa.; son of John V. (a steel worker) and Lena (Sellman) Rosage. *Education:* Pontifical College Josephinum, Worthington, Ohio, B.A., 1937; Pontifical Seminary, M.A., 1943. *Home:* Immaculate Heart Retreat, Route 3, Box 653, Spokane, Wash. 99203.

CAREER: Roman Catholic priest. Diocese of Spokane, Spokane, Wash., former youth director, parish priest and pastor; Immaculate Heart Retreat House, Spokane, retreat director, 1957—.

WRITINGS: Letters to an Altar Boy, Bruce, 1952; *Crumbs from the Master's Table,* Immaculate Heart Retreat, 1961; *At Mass with Mary,* Immaculate Heart Retreat, 1962; *One Way, His Way,* Immaculate Heart Retreat, 1970; *Mary: The Model Charismatic,* Immaculate Heart Retreat, 1971; *Retreats and the Charismatic Renewal,* Dove, 1972; *Speak Lord, Your Servant Is Listening,* Servant Publications, 1974; *Discovering Pathways to Prayer,* Living Flame Press, 1975; *Praying with Scripture in the Holy Land,* Living Flame Press, 1977; *The Bread of Life,* Servant Publications, 1979; *Praying with Mary,* Living Flame Press, 1980; *A Lenten Pilgrimate,* Servant Publications, 1980; *Listen to Him,* Servant Publications, 1981.

*   *   *

ROSELIEP, Raymond 1917-

PERSONAL: Surname is pronounced *Rose*-leap; born August 11, 1917, in Farley, Iowa; son of John Albert (a caterer) and Anna Elizabeth (Anderson) Roseliep. *Education:* Loras College, B.A., 1939; Catholic University of America, M.A., 1948; University of Notre Dame, Ph.D., 1954. *Home and office:* Holy Family Hall, 3340 Windsor Ave., Dubuque, Iowa 52001.

CAREER: Ordained Roman Catholic priest, 1943; assistant pastor of church in Gilbertville, Iowa, 1943-45; *Witness,* Dubuque, Iowa, managing editor, 1945-46; Loras College, Dubuque, instructor, 1946-48, assistant professor, 1948-60, associate professor of English, 1960-66; Holy Family Hall, Dubuque, resident chaplain, 1966—. Poet-in-residence, Georgetown University, summer, 1964. Poet; reader of poetry at colleges and universities.

MEMBER: Poetry Society of America, Academy of American Poets, Modern Language Association of America, National Council of Teachers of English, Catholic Press Association, Haiku Society of America (honorary member), Yuki Teikei Haiku Society, Marquis Biographical Library Society, State Historical Society of Iowa, Notre Dame English Association, Delta Epsilon Sigma. *Awards, honors:* Named to Gallery of Living Catholic Authors, 1957; Kenneth F. Montgomery Poetry Award, Society of Midland Authors, 1968; Harold G. Henderson Haiku Award, Haiku Society of America, 1977; Shugyo Takaha Award, Yuki Teikei Haiku Society, 1980; Poetry in Public Places Award, 1980; other poetry prizes from *Carolina Quarterly, Writer's Digest,* Leigh Hanes Memorial Poetry Contest, *Modern Haiku,* and *Yankee.*

WRITINGS—Poetry, except as indicated: (Editor) *Some Letters of Lionel Johnson* (prose), University Microfilms, 1954; *The Linen Bands,* Newman Press, 1961; *The Small Rain,* Newman Press, 1963; *Love Makes the Air Light,* Norton, 1965; *Voyages to the Inland Sea* (poetry and prose), University of Wisconsin—La Crosse, 1974; *Flute over Walden,* Vagrom Chap Books, 1976; *Walk in Love,* Juniper Press, 1976; *Light Footsteps,* Juniper Press, 1976; *A Beautiful Woman Moves with Grace,* Rook Press, 1976; *Sun in His Belly,* High/Coo Press, 1977; *Step on the Rain,* Rook Press, 1977; *Wake to the Bell,* Rook Press, 1977; (editor) *Into the Round Air,* Rook Press, 1977; *A Day in the Life of Sobi-Shi,* Rook Press, 1978; (editor) David Lloyd, *Snowman,* Pilot Light Editions, 1978; *Sailing Bones,* Rook Press, 1978; *Sky in My Legs,* Juniper Press, 1979; *Firefly*

in My Eyecup, High/Coo Press, 1979; *The Still Point,* Uzzano, 1979; *A Roseliep Retrospective* (collection of poetry and prose), edited by David Dayton, Alembic Press, 1980; *Listen to Light,* Alembic Press, 1980.

Poetry represented in many anthologies, including: *Fire and Sleet and Candlelight: New Poems of the Macabre,* edited by August Derleth, Arkham, 1961; *Of Poetry and Power: Poems Occasioned by the Presidency and by the Death of John F. Kennedy,* edited by Erwin A. Glikes and Paul Schwaber, Basic Books, 1964; *Out of the War Shadow,* edited by Denise Levertov, War Resisters League, 1967; *Inside Outer Space,* edited by Robert Vas Dias, Doubleday, 1970.

Contributor of poems to more than two hundred and twenty-five periodicals and newspapers, including *Transatlantic Review, Tablet* (London), *Poetry, Dubliner, Midwest Quarterly, Critic, Nation, Commonweal, Minnesota Review, College English, New York Times, Sign, America, English Journal, University Bookman, Prairie Schooner,* and *Modern Age.* Poetry editor, *Sponsa Regis* (publication of Benedictine Order), 1959-66.

WORK IN PROGRESS: Two books of poems, *Tip the Earth* and an untitled collection of haiku; preparing a recording of his poems for the Library of Congress.

SIDELIGHTS: Catholic World's Joseph Tusiani writes that Raymond Roseliep's "poetry has the free, large scope of truly human art. It observes man's passions in their rarefied moments of grace and never succumbs to crudities of personal nature. This is achieved through a detachment that seems both innocent and astute—a tongue-in-cheek analysis of men and events in an aura of lyricism."

Roseliep told *CA:* "Every day I meet head-on the shadow and substance of life, and from my attention and reverence for visible and invisible creation I am sometimes moved to attire my thoughts and feelings in words. A poem fulfills my being, justifies my existence, concretizes my gift from on high. I share my poems with others because a new reality deserves the passage from isolation to association. Having people enter my poems and creatively participate in them by responding with their own vibrations is what makes the arduous work of writing one of eventual pure pleasure."

Roseliep recorded his poems for modern poetry collections at Harvard University and Fenn College.

AVOCATIONAL INTERESTS: Reading—the moderns in poetry, criticism, mystical theology, art, fiction, and drama and the comic strips "Peanuts" and "Pogo."

BIOGRAPHICAL/CRITICAL SOURCES: Sister Mary Therese, editor, *I Sing of a Maiden,* Macmillan, 1947; *Mutiny,* spring, 1961, fall-winter, 1961-62; *Catholic World,* November, 1961; *Today,* October, 1963; *Contemporary Literature,* winter, 1968; *New Catholic World,* January/February, 1976; *Poetry,* December, 1980.

*   *   *

ROSENBLOOM, Joseph 1928-

PERSONAL: Born June 28, 1928, in New York, N.Y.; son of Jacob and Annie (Heck) Rosenbloom. *Education:* Attended New York University, 1946-48; University of Chicago, M.A., 1951; Rutgers University, M.S.L.S., 1965. *Religion:* Jewish. *Home:* 58 Middagh St., Brooklyn, N.Y. 11201.

CAREER: Einstein Free Public Library, Pompton Lakes, N.J., library director, 1965-67; Piscataway Township Libraries, Piscataway, N.J., library director, 1967-74; full-time writer, 1974—.

WRITINGS—Adult nonfiction: *Consumer Complaint Guide*, Macmillan, 1972, 8th edition, 1981; *Kits and Plans*, Oliver Press, 1973; *Craft Supplies Supermarket*, Oliver Press, 1974; *Consumer Protection Guide*, Macmillan, 1977, 2nd edition, 1978.

Juvenile; published by Sterling, except as indicated: *Biggest Riddle Book in the World*, 1976; *Dr. Knock-Knock's Official Knock-Knock Dictionary*, 1977; *Daffy Dictionary*, 1978; *The Gigantic Joke Book*, 1978; *Twist These on Your Tongue*, Thomas Nelson, 1978; *Bananas Don't Grow on Trees: A Guide to Popular Misconceptions*, 1979; *Silly Verse and Even Worse*, 1979; *Maximilian You're the Greatest*, Grosset, 1979, hardcover edition, Elsevier/Nelson, 1980; *Polar Bears Like It Hot: A Guide to Popular Misconceptions*, 1979; *How Do You Make an Elephant Laugh?*, 1979; *Monster Madness*, 1980; *Dictionary of Dinosaurs*, Messner, 1980; *Snappy Put-Downs and Funny Insults*, 1981; *Ridiculous Nicholas Riddle Book*, 1981; *Ridiculous Nicholas Pet Riddles*, 1981; *Sports Riddles*, Harcourt, 1982; *Dinosaur Riddles*, Messner, 1982; *The Looniest Limericks in the World*, 1982.

BIOGRAPHICAL/CRITICAL SOURCES: Times Literary Supplement, September 19, 1980.

*   *   *

ROSENTHAL, Eric   1905-

PERSONAL: Born July 10, 1905, in Cape Town, South Africa; son of Richard (a mining agent) and Hedwig (De Beer) Rosenthal; married Jeannette Marguerite Bradley, December 18, 1934; children: Elizabeth (Mrs. Derrick Mills), Richard, Gerald, Alison (Mrs. William Victor Kidd). *Education:* St. John's College, Johannesburg, South Africa, graduate, 1921; University of the Witwatersrand, qualified as attorney, 1926. *Home:* White Horses, 48 Hillside Rd., Fish Hoek, South Africa. *Office address:* P.O. Box 3800, Cape Town, South Africa.

CAREER: Practiced law in Johannesburg, South Africa, 1926-39; participated in special war work, 1939-44; industrial and commercial historian, specializing in research work on South Africa, particularly company and commodity histories for large corporations, Cape Town, South Africa, 1946—. Free-lance journalist for newspapers in South Africa, Great Britain, and United States, 1925—. Publicity manager of Empire Exhibition, Johannesburg, 1935-36, and of South African Jewish War Appeal, 1944-45. Member of South African national and international radio quiz teams, 1947—. *Member:* South African Association for the Advancement of Science, South African P.E.N., Owl Club (Cape Town; president, 1965—), Rotary Club of Cape of Good Hope.

WRITINGS: From Drury Lane to Mecca: Being an Account of the Strange Life and Adventures of Hedley Churchward (Also Known as Mahmoud Mobarek Churchward), an English Convert to Islam, Low, 1931; *Old-Time Survivals in South Africa*, Government Printer (Pretoria), 1936; *Stars and Stripes in Africa: Being a History of American Achievements in Africa*, G. Routledge & Sons, 1938, revised edition, Tri-Ocean, 1968.

The Fall of Italian East Africa, Hutchinson, 1941; *Fortress on Sand: An Account of the Siege of Tobruk*, Hutchinson, 1943; *General Dan Pienaar: His Life and His Battles*, Afrikaanse Pers, 1943, 2nd edition, Unie-Volkspers Beperk (Cape Town), 1943; *Japan's Bid for Africa: Including the Story of the Madagascar Campaign*, Central News Agency (Johannesburg), 1944; *General De Wet: A Biography*, Unie-Volkspers Beperk, 1946,

2nd edition, Simondium Publishers (Cape Town), 1968; *Gold Bricks and Mortar: Sixty Years of Johannesburg History*, Printing House (Johannesburg), 1946; *South Africa's Own: Happy Hours for Boys and Girls*, Newman Art Publishing Co. (Johannesburg), 1946; *Eric Rosenthal's South African Quiz Book*, Howard Timmins, 1948, 2nd edition, 1955; (compiler with Allister Macmillan) *Homes of the Golden City*, Hortors (Cape Town), 1948; (compiler) *The South African Saturday Book: A Treasury of Writing and Pictures of South Africa, Old and New, Homely and Extraordinary*, Hutchinson, 1948; *African Switzerland: Basutoland of To-day*, Hutchinson, 1949; *They Walk by Night: True South African Ghost Stories and Tales of the Supernormal*, Howard Timmins, 1949, enlarged edition published as *They Walk in the Night: True South African Ghost Stories and Tales of the Supernormal*, 1965.

(Editor) *The City of Cape Town Official Guide*, R. Beerman Publishers (Cape Town), 1950; *Shovel and Sieve*, Howard Timmins, 1950; *South African Jews in World War II*, South African Jewish Board of Deputies, 1950; *Here Are Diamonds*, R. Hale, 1950; *The Hinges Creaked: True Stories of South African Treasure Lost and Found*, Howard Timmins, 1951; *Shelter from the Spray*, Allen & Unwin, 1952; *Other Men's Millions*, Howard Timmins, 1953; (author of introduction) *Cave Artists of South Africa*, A. A. Balkema (Cape Town), 1953; *Cutlass and Yardarm*, Howard Timmins, 1955; (compiler) *The Story of Poppe, Schunhoff and Guttery*, Galvin & Sales (Cape Town), 1956; (editor) *The Story of Table Mountain: The Table Mountain Aerial Cableway Official Souvenir Guide*, W. J. Flesch, 1956, 2nd edition, 1961; *Today's News Today: The Story of the Argus Company*, Argus Printing and Publishing Co. (Johannesburg), 1956; *The Changing Years: A History of the Cape Province Municipal Association*, Cape Province Municipal Association, 1957; *River of Diamonds*, Bailey Bros. & Swinfen, 1957; *The Way I Saw It*, Howard Timmins, 1957; *The Cape of Good Hope Triangular Stamp and Its Story*, A. A. Balkema, 1957; (with Albert Jackson) *Trader on the Veld*, A. A. Balkema, 1958; *One Hundred Years of Victoria West, 1859-1959*, [Victoria West], 1959; *Apology Refused*, Bailey Bros. & Swinfen, 1959.

The Taeuber & Corssen Story, privately printed, 1960; (editor, translator, and author of introduction) *The Matabeleland Travel Letters of Marie Lippert, 1891*, Friends of the South African Public Library, 1960; (author of text) Heinrich Egersdoerfer, *An Old-Time Sketch Book: 'N Outydse sketsboek* (in English and Afrikaans), Nasionale Boekhandel (Cape Town), 1960; (editor) *Warne-Juta Rand-Cent Ready Reckoner* (in English and Afrikaans), Warne, 1960; *Tankards and Tradition*, Howard Timmins, 1961; *The Story of the Cape Jewish Orphanage*, [Cape Town], 1961; (editor) *Encyclopedia of Southern Africa*, Warne, 1961, 7th edition, 1978; *Alphabetic Index to the Biographical Notices in South Africa, 1892-1928*, Johannesburg Public Library, 1963; *Schooners and Skyscrapers*, Howard Timmins, 1963; *Manne en maatskappye: Die Geskiedenis van die eerste afrikaanse sakemanne* (in Afrikaans), Human & Rousseau (Cape Town), 1963; *The William Atkinson Story*, Howard Timmins, 1963; *South African Surnames*, Howard Timmins, 1965; (compiler) *South African Dictionary of National Biography*, Warne, 1966; *Three Hundred Years of the Castle at Cape Town*, H. M. Joynt, 1966; *Vesting van die Suide: Bastion of the South* (in English and Afrikaans), H. M. Joynt, 1966; *On 'Change through the Years: A History of Share Dealing in South Africa*, Flesch Financial Publications, 1968; *A History of Fish Hoek, Cape*, Fish Hoek Chamber of Commerce, 1968; *Cape Directory 1800*, Howard Timmins, 1969; (with Eliezer Blum) *Runner and Mailcoach: Postal History and Stamps of Southern Africa,* Purnell (Cape Town), 1969, Tri-Ocean, 1972.

Gold! Gold! Gold!: The Johannesburg Gold Rush, Macmillan, 1970; *South Africa's Oil Search down the Years,* Howard Timmins, 1970; *Meet Me at the Carlton,* Howard Timmins, 1972; (with Ray Ryan) *Cape Town,* Purnell, 1973; *Fifty Years of Healing,* Cape Town City Council, 1974; *The Rand Rush,* A. Donker, 1974; *You Have Been Listening: The Early History of Radio in South Africa,* Purnell, 1974; *The Best of Eric Rosenthal* (collection of addresses, lectures, and essays), Howard Timmins, 1975; *Total Book of South African Records,* Total South Africa, 1975; *Victorian South Africa,* Tafelberg, 1975; *Rolling Years,* Felstar, 1976; *Fish Horns and Hansom Cabs,* A. Donker, 1977; *Rustenburg Romance,* Perskor, 1979; *Memories and Sketches,* A. Donker, 1979; *Milnerton,* Milnerton Municipality, 1980.

Pamphlets: (Editor) *Eclipse Postal District Guide and Pocket Dictionary of Johannesburg,* Central News Agency, 1940; *Life in America,* African Bookman (Cape Town), 1945; *The Gateway to South Africa,* South African Railways, 1947; *South Africa in a Nutshell,* South African Information Department (London), 1948; *South African Diplomats Abroad,* South African Institute of International Affairs (Johannesburg), 1949; *Our Royal Visitors,* Stewart Printing Co. (Cape Town), 1949; *Bantu Journalism in South Africa,* Society of the Friends of Africa (Johannesburg), 1949; (editor) *South African Tables and General Information, Including Weights and Measures in Use in South Africa,* Central News Agency, 1949.

Tea in Our Land through Three Centuries, Tea Bureau of South Africa (Johannesburg), 1950; *How to Look after Your Money,* Longmans, Green, 1950, 2nd edition, 1960; *Royal Automobile Club of South Africa—Golden Jubilee,* Royal Automobile Club (Cape Town), 1952; *Three Hundred Years of Men's Clothing in South Africa,* Monatic Alba Co. (Wynberg), 1952; *History of the Rand Water Board,* privately printed, 1953; *Johannesburg's New Randles,* privately printed, 1953; *G.E.C. in South Africa,* privately printed, 1953; *History of Johannesburg Building Society,* privately printed, 1953; *Fifty Years of Furnishing: The Story of Bradlows,* Hortors, 1953; *History of John Marcus & Co.,* privately printed, 1954; *Sixty Years of Haddon & Sly,* privately printed, 1954; *History of Federal Insurance Corporation of South Africa,* privately printed, 1954; *Insurance City,* privately printed, 1955; *Two Hundred Years of Greatrex,* privately printed, 1955.

Golden Jubilee of the Carlton Hotel, privately printed, 1956; *History of General Estate and Orphan Chambers,* privately printed, 1956; *History of Lamson Paragon over Fifty Years,* privately printed, 1956; *History of Phoenix Assurance Company,* privately printed, 1956; *One Hundred Years of Northern Assurance Company,* privately printed, 1956; (compiler with Hal Nattrass) *1856-1956, a Century of Service: The Story of Henwoods, Their First Hundred Years,* Knox Printing Co. (Durban), 1956; *Fifty Years of Holmes Service,* privately printed, 1957; *History of the Western Province Agricultural Society,* Western Province Agricultural Society (Cape Town), 1958; *History of R. H. Morris (Pty) Ltd.,* privately printed, 1958; (compiler with Ena Cloete) *Index to J. W. Matthews' "Incwadi Yami; or, Twenty Years Personal Experience in South Africa,"* Johannesburg Public Library, 1958; (compiler with Cloete) *Index to John Angove's "In the Early Days: The Reminiscences of Pioneer Life on the South Africa Diamond Field,"* Johannesburg Public Library, 1958; (with Cloete) *Index to Barbara Isabella Buchanan's "Natal Memories,"* Johannesburg Public Library, 1958; (compiler with Cloete) *Index to Barbara Buchanan's "Pioneer Days in Natal,"* Johannesburg Public Li-

brary, 1958; *History of Liverpool, London & Globe Insurance Company,* privately printed, 1959.

History of Industrial Development Corporation of South Africa, privately printed, 1960; (with J. P. Hutchings) *Shopfitters Cavalcade: Being Half-a-Century of the History of Fredk. Sage & Company in Southern Africa,* [Johannesburg], 1960; *One Hundred Sixty Years of Cape Town Printing,* Cape Town Association of Printing House Craftsman, 1960; *History of Duly & Company,* privately printed, 1961; *History of Union Steel Corporation (South Africa) Ltd.,* privately printed, 1961; *As Pioneers Still, 1911-1961: An Appreciation of Lever Brothers Contribution to South Africa,* Hayne & Gibson (Durban), 1961; *Natal Navigation & Estate Company: Golden Jubilee,* privately printed, 1962; *History of Mobil in South Africa,* privately printed, 1962; *History of Goodyear in South Africa,* privately printed, 1963; *British United—Fifty Years in South Africa,* privately printed, 1963; *History of Dunswart Iron & Steel Works,* privately printed, 1963; *Fifty Years of the Cape Town Orchestra, 1914-1964,* [Cape Town], c. 1963; *History of Chemico (Pty) Ltd.,* privately printed, 1964; *From Barter to Barclays,* Barclays National Bank, 1968.

One Hundred Twenty-five Years of Music in South Africa: Darter's Jubilee, privately printed, 1970; *South Africa's Oil Search down the Years,* Howard Timmins, 1970; *The Thesen Centenary,* privately printed, 1970; *Trends in South African Publishing,* English Studies in Africa (Johannesburg), 1970; *The Story of Portland Cement in South Africa,* Portland Cement Institute (Johannesburg), 1971; *One Hundred Years in South Africa,* Norwich Union, 1975; *Rembrandt: An Early Portrait of His Mother,* Keyzer, 1977. Also author of *Daniel Mills History,* 1977.

Contributor to *Encyclopaedia Britannica.* Assistant editor, *South African Mining Journal,* 1936-37; editor, *Guinness Book of Records* (South African edition), 1967-74.

WORK IN PROGRESS: Continuous research on histories of industries and commodities in South Africa.

* * *

ROSENZWEIG, Norman 1924-

PERSONAL: Born February 28, 1924, in New York, N.Y., son of Jacob Arthur and Edna (Braman) Rosenzweig; married Carol Treleaven, September 20, 1945; children: Elizabeth Ann. *Education:* Attended New York University, 1941-44; Chicago Medical School, M.B., 1947, M.D., 1948; University of Michigan, M.S., 1954. *Home:* 1234 Cedarholm Lane, Bloomfield Hills, Mich. 48013. *Office:* Department of Psychiatry, Sinai Hospital of Detroit, 6767 West Outer Dr., Detroit, Mich. 48235.

CAREER: Jamaica Hospital, Jamaica, N.Y., intern, 1947-48; St. John's Long Island City Hospital, Long Island City, N.Y., intern, 1948; Kings Park State Hospital, New York, N.Y., resident, 1949-51; Veterans Administration Hospital, Battle Creek, Mich., resident, 1951-52; University of Michigan Medical School, Ann Arbor, senior clinical instructor, 1952-53, instructor, 1953-55, assistant professor, 1957-61, lecturer in psychiatry, 1961-63; Sinai Hospital of Detroit, Detroit, Mich., head of department of psychiatry, 1961—; Wayne State University, School of Medicine, Detroit, assistant professor, 1961-68, associate professor, 1968-73, professor of psychiatry, 1973—. Visiting lecturer, University of Southern California, 1972, University of California, Los Angeles, 1973, Mercy College, 1974, and University of Ottawa, 1974. Director, University of Michigan-Ypsilanti State Hospital joint research project in schizophrenia and psychopharmacology, 1957-59. Diplomate, American Board of Psychiatry and Neurology, 1954. *Military service:* U.S. Air Force, 1955-57, served in Psychiatric Service; became captain.

MEMBER: Pan American Medical Association, American Association for the Advancement of Science, American Association of Directors of Psychiatric Residency Training, American Association of University Professors, American College of Psychiatrists (fellow), American Medical Association, American Psychiatric Association (fellow), British Society of Clinical Psychiatrists, Michigan Psychiatric Society (president, 1975), Michigan State Medical Society (chairman of section on psychiatry, 1974—), New York Academy of Sciences, Wayne County Medical Society, Beta Lambda Sigma, Tau Kappa Alpha. *Awards, honors:* Certificate from Michigan Society of Psychiatry and Neurology, 1971; American Medical Association Physician's Recognition Award, 1971 and 1975; American Psychiatric Association Rush Gold Medal Award, 1974.

WRITINGS: Community Mental Health Programs in England: An American View, Wayne State University Press, 1975; (editor with H. Griscom) *Psychopharmacology and Psychotherapy: Synthesis or Antithesis?,* Human Sciences, 1978; (editor with F. P. Pearsall) *Sex Education for the Health Professional: A Curriculum Guide,* Grune, 1978.

Contributor: Robert Westlake, editor, *Shaping the Future of Mental Health Care,* Ballinger, 1976; Robert O. Pasnau, editor, *Psychosocial Aspects of Medical Practice,* Volume II, Addison-Wesley, 1981; Jules H. Masserman, editor, *Current Psychiatric Therapies,* Volume XX, Grune, 1981; *Being Sexual: A Reader,* Unitarian Universalist Association, in press.

Contributor to *International Encyclopedia of Psychiatry, Psychology, Psychoanalysis and Neurology.* Contributor of numerous articles to *Journal of Nervous and Mental Disorders, Psychopharmacologia, American Journal of Psychiatry, Mental Health Digest,* and other professional publications.

AVOCATIONAL INTERESTS: Travel, photography, collecting opera and classical music recordings.

*   *   *

ROSKILL, Mark W(entworth) 1933-

PERSONAL: Born November 10, 1933, in London, England; became permanent resident of United States, 1959; son of Stephen Wentworth (a writer and official British Naval historian of World War II) and Elizabeth (van den Bergh) Roskill; married Deirdre Toller, October 24, 1959; married second wife, Nancy Lee Muench, March 9, 1974; children: (first marriage) Jonathan Wentworth, Andrew Wentworth; (second marriage) Damian Mark Wentworth. *Education:* Trinity College, Cambridge, B.A., 1956, M.A., 1961; Harvard University, M.A., 1957; attended Courtauld Institute of Art, London, 1957-59; Princeton University, M.F.A., 1961, Ph.D., 1961. *Religion:* Episcopalian. *Home:* 82 North Prospect St., Amherst, Mass. 01002. *Office:* Department of Art History, Bartlett Hall, University of Massachusetts, Amherst, Mass. 01002.

CAREER: Princeton University, Princeton, N.J., instructor in history of art, 1959-61; Harvard University, Cambridge, Mass., instructor, 1961-63, assistant professor of history of art, 1963-68; University of Massachusetts—Amherst, associate professor, 1968-72, professor of history of modern art, 1972—. Art consultant, Clowes Fund, 1965-69. *Military service:* British Army, Intelligence Corps, 1951-53; became second lieutenant. *Awards, honors:* American Council of Learned Societies fellow, 1965-66 and 1974-75.

WRITINGS: English Painting from 1500 to 1865, Thames & Hudson, 1959; (editor and author of introduction) *The Letters of Vincent van Gogh,* Atheneum, 1963; *Dolce's "Aretino" and Venetian Art Theory of the Cinquecento,* New York University Press, 1968; *Van Gogh, Gaugin and the Impressionist Circle,* New York Graphic Society, 1970; *What Is Art History?,* Harper, 1976.

Poetry is represented in British anthologies. Contributor of articles to *Art News, Victorian Studies, Arts, Burlington Magazine, Critical Inquiry, Philosophy,* and other publications; contributor of poems to British magazines.

WORK IN PROGRESS: Writings on photography, art theory, and the interpretations of Cubism.

AVOCATIONAL INTERESTS: Literary criticism, contemporary philosophy, jigsaw puzzles, tennis.

*   *   *

ROSKILL, Stephen W(entworth) 1903-

PERSONAL: Born August 1, 1903, in London, England; son of John Henry (a barrister) and Sybil (Dilke) Roskill; married Elizabeth van den Bergh, August 12, 1930; children: Nicholas, Mark, Theresa (Mrs. Michael Till), Mary (Mrs. Martin Caroe), Thomas, Clare (Mrs. Malcolm Dean), Christopher. *Education:* Attended Royal Naval College, Osborne, England, and Royal Naval College, Dartmouth; Cambridge University, M.A., 1961, Litt.D., 1970. *Politics:* Independent Liberal. *Religion:* Church of England. *Home:* Frostlake Cottage, Malting Lane, Cambridge CB3 9HF, England. *Office:* Churchill College, Cambridge, England.

CAREER: Royal Navy, career service, 1917-48, invalided out as captain, 1948; Cabinet Office, London, England, official naval historian, 1949-60; Cambridge University, Cambridge, England, Lees-Knowles Lecturer, 1961, fellow of Churchill College, 1961-70, life fellow, 1970—. Served at sea as commander of H.M.S. *Warspite,* 1939, and as commander and captain of H.M.N.Z.S. *Leander,* 1941-44; member of Naval Staff, 1939-41; senior observer, Bikini Atomic Tests, 1946; deputy director, Naval Intelligence, 1946-48. Distinguished Visiting Lecturer, U.S. Naval Academy, 1965; Richmond Lecturer, Cambridge University, 1967; Chesney Memorial Lecturer, 1975. *Member:* Royal Historical Society (fellow), British Academy (fellow), Navy Records Society (vice-president, 1964; honorary vice-president, 1974), Travellers' Club (London). *Awards, honors*—Military: Distinguished Service Cross, 1944; Legion of Merit. Civilian: Commander, Order of the British Empire, 1971; Litt.D., University of Leeds, 1975; honorary degree, Oxford University, 1980.

WRITINGS: The War at Sea, 1939-1945 (official history), H.M.S.O., Volume I: *The Defensive,* 1954, reprinted, 1976, Volume II: *The Period of Balance,* 1957, Volume III: *The Offensive,* Part 1, 1960, Part 2, 1961; *H.M.S. Warspite: The Story of a Famous Battleship,* Collins, 1957, reprinted, Futura Publications, 1975; *The Secret Capture,* Collins, 1959; *White Ensign: The British Navy at War, 1939-1945,* U.S. Naval Institute, 1960 (published in England as *The Navy at War, 1939-1945,* Collins, 1960); *The Strategy of Sea Power,* Collins, 1962, reprinted, Greenwood Press, 1981; *A Merchant Fleet in War: Alfred Holt & Co., 1939-1945,* Collins, 1962; *The Art of Leadership,* Collins, 1964, Archon Books, 1965; *Naval Policy between the Wars,* Volume I: *The Period of Anglo-American Antagonism, 1919-1929,* Collins, 1968, Walker, 1969, Volume II: *The Period of Reluctant Rearmament, 1930-1939,* Walker, 1976; (editor) *Documents Relating to the Naval Air*

Service, 1908-1918, Navy Records Society, 1969; *Hankey: Man of Secrets*, Volume I, Collins, 1970, St. Martin's, 1972, Volume II, Collins, 1972, Naval Institute Press, 1979, Volume III, Collins, 1974; *Churchill and the Admirals*, Collins, 1977, Morrow, 1978; *Admiral of the Fleet Earl Beatty: The Last Naval Hero—An Intimate Biography*, Collins, 1980, Atheneum, 1981.

Contributor to *Proceedings of U.S. Naval Institute*. Regular contributor to *Sunday Times, Sunday Telegraph*, and *Economist*.

WORK IN PROGRESS: Editing the second volume of *Documents Relating to the Naval Air Service, 1908-1918;* naval memoirs, 1917-1948.

AVOCATIONAL INTERESTS: Country life, painting.

* * *

ROSMOND, Babette 1921-
(Francis M. Arroway, Rosamond Campion)

PERSONAL: Born November 4, 1921, in New York, N.Y.; daughter of A. E. and Blanche (Thisler) Rosmond; married Henry Stone (a lawyer), April 2, 1944; children: James Martin, Eugene Robert. *Home:* 230 East 49th St., New York, N.Y. 10017.

CAREER: Street & Smith, New York City, editor, 1941-48; fiction editor, *Today's Family*, New York City, 1952-53, *Better Living*, New York City, 1953-56, and *Seventeen*, New York City, 1957-75.

WRITINGS: The Dewy Dewy Eyes, Dutton, 1946; *A Party for Grown-Ups*, Dutton, 1948; *Lucy; or, The Delaware Dialogues*, Simon & Schuster, 1952; *The Children*, Harcourt, 1956; *The Lawyers*, Walker & Co., 1962; (under pseudonym Francis M. Arroway) *Diary of a Candid Lady*, Doubleday, 1964; *Robert Benchley: His Life and Good Times*, Doubleday, 1970; (under pseudonym Rosamond Campion) *The Invisible Worm*, Macmillan, 1972; *Error Hurled*, Bantam, 1976; *Monarch*, Marek, 1978.

Editor: *Seventeen's Stories*, Lippincott, 1958; (with Henry Morgan) Ring Lardner, *Shut Up, He Explained*, Scribner, 1962; *Seventeen from Seventeen*, Macmillan, 1967; *Seventeen Book of Prize Stories*, Macmillan, 1968; *Today's Stories from Seventeen*, Macmillan, 1971.

Also author of radio scripts. Contributor to *New Yorker, Mademoiselle, McCall's, New York Times, Punch*, and other popular publications.

WORK IN PROGRESS: A novel.

SIDELIGHTS: In the late 1960s, armed with scrapbooks, personal files, and the reminiscences of family members and friends, Babette Rosmond set out to write a biography of noted American humorist, drama critic, and commentator Robert Benchley. Rosmond first met Benchley when she was a teenager and he was a well-established figure on the New York literary and theatrical scene. Like so many others who knew him, a *Best Sellers* critic writes, Rosmond obviously "found him . . . not only affable but memorable." *Newsweek*'s Paul Zimmerman notes that her "casual biography captures [Benchley] with [an] affectionate generosity of spirit."

Louis Kronenberger of the *Atlantic* is bothered somewhat by Rosmond's tone, remarking that it results in a biography in which there is "too unshaded an appreciation and too unperspectived an appraisal" of Benchley's "brightly gilded, rather shallow world." Nevertheless, the reviewer goes on to state,

"Miss Rosmond has written as a true believer of Benchley and his times, and today, when we are even more distant from them in attitudes than in years, her choice of a hero and his stamping grounds is altogether welcome."

Punch's Lewis Bates is pleased to see that "Benchley's life is chronicled systematically and long extracts from his work are woven in at appropriate places, so that one sees the event or the environment and then what he made of it." Concludes the critic: "Entertaining, charming and briskly affectionate, [*Robert Benchley: His Life and Good Times*] makes a more solid memorial than most clowns ever win."

BIOGRAPHICAL/CRITICAL SOURCES: Library Journal, March 15, 1970; *Newsweek*, March 30, 1970; *Atlantic*, April, 1970; *Best Sellers*, May 1, 1970; *Punch*, June 10, 1970.

* * *

ROSS, Alan 1922-

PERSONAL: Born May 6, 1922, in Calcutta, India; married Jennifer Fry, 1949; children: Jonathan. *Education:* Attended Haileybury College and St. John's College, Oxford. *Home:* 4 Elm Park Lane, London SW3, England.

CAREER: Employed by British Council, 1947-50; *Observer*, London, England, member of staff, 1950-71; *London Magazine*, London, editor, 1961—. Managing director, London Magazine Editions (publishers). *Military service:* Royal Navy, Intelligence, 1942-46. *Member:* Royal Society of Literature (fellow), Garrick Club. *Awards, honors:* Atlantic Award for Literature, Rockefeller Foundation, 1947.

WRITINGS: Time Was Away: A Notebook in Corsica, Lehmann, 1948; *The Forties: A Period Piece*, Weidenfeld & Nicolson, 1950; *The Gulf of Pleasure*, Weidenfeld & Nicolson, 1951; *The Bandit on the Billiard Table: A Journey through Sardinia*, Verschoyle, 1954, revised edition published as *South to Sardinia*, Hamish Hamilton, 1960; (self-illustrated with photographs) *Australia 55: A Journal of the M.C.C. Tour*, M. Joseph, 1955; *Cape Summer and the Australians in England*, Hamish Hamilton, 1957; *The Onion Man* (juvenile), Hamish Hamilton, 1959; *Through the Caribbean: The M.C.C. Tour of the West Indies, 1959-1960*, Hamish Hamilton, 1960; *Danger on Glass Island* (juvenile), Hamish Hamilton, 1960; *The West Indies at Lord's*, Eyre & Spottiswoode, 1963; *Australia 63*, Eyre & Spottiswoode, 1963; *The Wreck of Moni* (juvenile), Alan Ross, 1965; *A Castle in Sicily* (juvenile), Alan Ross, 1966; (author of introduction) Hugo Williams, compiler, *London Magazine Poems, 1961-66*, Alan Ross, 1966.

Poetry: *The Derelict Day: Poems in Germany*, Lehmann, 1947; *Poetry, 1945-1950*, Longmans, Green, 1951; *Something of the Sea: Poems, 1942-1952*, Verschoyle, 1954, Houghton, 1955; *To Whom It May Concern: Poems, 1952-57*, Hamish Hamilton, 1958; *African Negatives*, Eyre & Spottiswoode, 1962, Dufour, 1964; *North from Sicily: Poems in Italy, 1961-64*, Eyre & Spottiswoode, 1965; *Poems, 1942-67*, Eyre & Spottiswoode, 1967; *Tropical Ice*, Covent Garden Press, 1972; *The Taj Express*, London Magazine Editions, 1972; *Open Sea*, London Magazine Editions, 1975; *Death Valley and Other Poems in America*, London Magazine Editions, 1980; *Colours of War: War Art, 1939-45*, J. Cape, 1982.

Editor: (And author of introduction) John Gay, *Poems*, Grey Walls Press, 1950; (with wife, Jennifer Ross) F. Scott Fitzgerald, *Borrowed Time* (short stories), Grey Walls Press, 1951; (and author of foreword) *Abroad: Travel Stories*, Faber, 1957; *The Cricketer's Companion*, Eyre & Spottiswoode, 1960; *Stories from the London Magazine*, Volume I, Eyre & Spottiswoode, 1964, Volumes II-XII published as *London Magazine Stories*, London Magazine Editions, 1967-80; *The Turf*, Oxford University Press, 1982.

Translator: Philippe Diole, *The Undersea Adventure*, Messner, 1953; Pierre Gaisseau, *The Sacred Forest*, Weidenfeld & Nicolson, 1954; Diole, *Gates of the Sea*, Messner, 1955 (published in England as *The Seas of Sicily*, Sidgwick & Jackson, 1955).

Work is represented in anthologies, including *Anthology of Contemporary Verse*, edited by Margaret June O'Donnell, Blackie & Son, 1953, *An Anthology of Modern Verse, 1940-1960*, edited by Elizabeth Jannings, Methuen, 1961, *Poetry of the Forties*, edited by Robin Skelton, Penguin, 1968, and *Oxford Book of Twentieth Century Verse*, edited by Philip Larkin, Oxford University Press, 1978. Contributor to *New Statesman, Spectator, New Yorker*, and other periodicals.

WORK IN PROGRESS: Memoirs.

SIDELIGHTS: Reviewing *Poems, 1942-67*, Martin Dodsworth writes that Alan Ross "is largely a descriptive poet. His landscapes are not at all symbolic, but stand for themselves, for the real world we all inhabit. . . . His poetry springs from a need to lay claim to the world, as though he were in fact excluded from it. . . . But the poems work by letting you feel that it is impossible for them to contain all that there is to say, by suggesting a world that is at once substantial and elusive."

Both Julian Symons of the *New Statesman* and a *Times Literary Supplement* critic note a certain distance in Ross's poems, an apparent determination, as Symons writes, "to remain uninvolved in what he describes." Continues the reviewer: "Most of [his] poems are occasional, reflecting the outer life of Alan Ross. . . . All of them make vivid pictures, and the later ones do so in a language admirably spare and firm, but the bright colours show only a surface." The *Times Literary Supplement* critic comments: "Mr. Ross, though not a public poet, is not really a private one either. Most of [his] poems are carefully circumstantial notations of responses to places, things, and persons. . . . What they all share is densely observed detail, a sensuous dwelling on particularities which aren't always properly brought into focus. . . . What seems to be lacking is any firm personal centre to [Ross's] exotic and much-travelled world."

AVOCATIONAL INTERESTS: Cricket, travel, racing, contemporary art.

BIOGRAPHICAL/CRITICAL SOURCES: New Statesman, December 1, 1967; *Punch*, February 7, 1968; *Times Literary Supplement*, January 18, 1968, January 23, 1969, October 17, 1980; *Listener*, February 1, 1968; *Observer*, February 11, 1968.

*   *   *

ROSS, Leonard
    See ROSTEN, Leo C(alvin)

*   *   *

ROSS, Leonard Q.
    See ROSTEN, Leo C(alvin)

*   *   *

ROSSI, Nicholas Louis, Jr. 1924-
    (Nick Rossi)

PERSONAL: Born November 14, 1924, in San Luis Obispo, Calif.; son of Nicholas A. (a public accountant) and Lillian A.

(McCurry) Rossi. *Education:* Glendale College, A.A., 1942; additional study at Muskingum College, 1942-43, and Conservatoire de Musique, Marseille, France, 1946; University of Southern California, B.Mus., 1948, M.Mus., 1951. *Politics:* Republican. *Religion:* Christian Science. *Home:* 16 East 17th St., New York, N.Y. 10003. *Office:* LaGuardia Community College of the City University of New York, 31-10 Thomson Ave., Long Island City, N.Y. 11101.

CAREER: Los Angeles City School Districts, Los Angeles, Calif., music consultant, 1948-70; University of Bridgeport, Bridgeport, Conn., assistant professor, 1970-73; LaGuardia Community College of the City University of New York, Long Island City, N.Y., associate professor of music, 1973—. Music chairman, Glendale Council of Churches, 1959-60; member of executive board, Community Concert Association, 1960-70; associate editor, Keyboard Publications, American Book Co., 1969-79. Composer. *Military service:* U.S. Army, Corps of Engineers, 1942-46; became staff sergeant.

MEMBER: International Castelnuovo-Tedesco Society (founder; president, 1977—), American Musicological Society, Music Educators National Conference (life member), National Association of American Composers and Conductors (member of executive board), Choral Conductors Guild (honorary member), California Music Educators Association, Southern California Vocal Association, Los Angeles Secondary Music Teachers Association, Phi Mu Alpha, Pi Kappa Lambda.

WRITINGS—Under name Nick Rossi: (With Sadie Rafferty) *Music through the Centuries*, Humphries, 1963, reprinted, University Press of America, 1981; (compiler with Robert A. Choate) *Music of Our Time*, Taplinger, 1969; *Pathways to Music*, American Book Co., 1970: *A Musical Pilgrimage*, Branden Press, 1971; *Electronic Music*, American Book Co., 1971; *20th Century Music and Art*, American Book Co., 1972; *The Realm of Music*, Crescendo, 1974; *Hearing Music: An Introduction*, Harcourt, 1981. Also author of *Catalogue of Works by Mario Castelnuovo-Tedesco*, 1977.

Collections of choral arrangements; all published by MCA Music: *Musical Masterpieces for Men's Voices*, 1966; *Musical Masterpieces for Female Voices*, 1967; *Musical Masterpieces for Young Voices*, 1970. Also author of 71 additional choral arrangements.

Composer of librettos for operas: "Liberty?," music by Roy Harris, 1964; "Again, D.J.?," music by Neil Slater, 1973; "Tobias and the Angels," music by Mario Castelnuovo-Tedesco, 1975; "Crazy to Do My Act," music by Nolan Rice, 1980.

Author of monographs on contemporary composers. Author and producer of 68 filmstrips for Bowmar/Noble, American Book Co., and L'Unicorno Productions. Contributor to music and music education journals, including *Keyboard, Music Journal, Musical America, The American Music Teacher, Man and His Music*, and *Journal of Church Music*.

WORK IN PROGRESS: Zephyr, a novel on the mystical world of unicorns; "J. S. Bach: A Life in Pictures," a filmstrip based on new iconographic research in East Germany and West Germany.

SIDELIGHTS: Nick Rossi told *CA:* "I started out to be—or at least try to be—a good classroom music teacher. Because I felt there weren't adequate books available either for music appreciation classes or choral ensembles, I became involved in writing texts and making choral arrangements. Then it dawned on me that words alone didn't really bring the historical picture alive for students, so I started writing and producing filmstrips on the historical epochs of music, the lives of composers, and the origins of various kinds of ethnic music. This was exciting! Besides the research, I had the opportunity to travel, study and visit composers and musicologists all over the world. Then came the requests from music journals to write about all these wonderful, exciting experiences, to describe my discoveries and talk about my reactions. So I guess I gradually turned from being a classroom music teacher into a world traveler, musicologist, writer and college professor.''

Rossi has researched his books in Europe, the Soviet Union, China, Japan, Africa, the Middle East, and South America.

* * *

ROSSI, Nick
See ROSSI, Nicholas Louis, Jr.

* * *

ROSTEN, Leo C(alvin) 1908-
(Leonard Ross, Leonard Q. Ross)

PERSONAL: Born April 11, 1908, in Lodz, Poland; son of Samuel and Ida (Freundlich) Rosten; married Priscilla Mead, 1935 (deceased); married Gertrude Zimmerman, 1960; children: (first marriage) Philip, Madeline, Peggy. *Education:* University of Chicago, Ph.B., 1930, Ph.D., 1937; attended London School of Economics and Political Science, 1937. *Office:* 36 Sutton Pl. S., New York, N.Y. 10022.

CAREER: University of Chicago, Chicago, Ill. research assistant in political science, 1934-35; fellow, Social Science Research Council, 1935-36; member of research staff, President's Committee on Administrative Management, 1936; director, Motion Picture Research Project, 1939-41; National Defense Commission, Washington, D.C., special consultant, 1939-40; National Defense Advisory Commission and Office for Emergency Management (Executive Office of the President), Washington, D.C., consultant, 1941; Office of Facts and Figures, Washington, D.C., chief of Motion Pictures Division, 1942; Office of War Information, Washington, D.C., deputy director, 1942-44; Secretary of War Office, Washington, D.C., special consultant, 1945; *Look* Magazine, New York, N.Y., special editorial advisor, 1950-74. Consultant, President Eisenhower's Commission on National Goals, 1960; faculty associate, Columbia University; Ford Visiting Professor of Political Science, University of California, Berkeley, 1960-61; lecturer at various universities. Member of board, National Book Commitee.

MEMBER: Authors Guild of America (member of national council), Authors League of America (member of national board), National Education Association (member of education polcies commission), American Association for the Advancement of Science, American Political Science Assocation, American Academy of Political and Social Science, Phi Beta Kappa, Author's Club (London), Cosmos Club (Washington, D.C.), Chaos Club (New York). *Awards, honors:* Freedom Foundation award, 1955; George Polk Memorial Award, 1955; University of Chicago Alumni Award, 1969; D.H.L., University of Rochester, 1975, and Hebrew University, 1980; fellow, London School of Economics; Commonwealth Club Silver Medal for Literature.

WRITINGS: The Washington Correspondents, Harcourt, 1937, reprinted, Arno, 1974; *Hollywood: The Movie Colony, the Movie Makers,* Harcourt, 1941; *112 Gripes about the French,* U.S. War Department, 1945; (editor) *A Guide to the Religions of America,* Simon & Schuster, 1955 (published in England

as *Religions of America,* Heinemann, 1957); *The Return of H*Y*M*A*N K*A*P*L*A*N,* Harper, 1959; *The Story behind the Painting,* Doubleday, 1961; *Captain Newman, M.D.,* Harper, 1961; *The Many Worlds of L*E*O R*O*S*T*E*N,* Harper, 1964 (published in England as *The Leo Rosten Bedside Book,* Gollancz, 1965); *A Most Private Intrigue,* Atheneum, 1967; *The Joys of Yiddish,* McGraw, 1968.

A Trumpet for Reason, Doubleday, 1970; *People I Have Loved, Known, or Admired,* McGraw, 1970; *Rome Wasn't Burned in a Day: The Mischief of Language,* Doubleday, 1972; *Leo Rosten's Treasury of Jewish Quotations,* McGraw, 1972; *Dear Herm,* McGraw, 1974; (editor) *The Look Book,* Abrams, 1975; *The 3:10 to Anywhere,* McGraw, 1976; *O K*A*P*L*A*N! My K*A*P*L*A*N!,* Harper, 1976; *The Power of Positive Nonsense,* McGraw, 1977; *Passions and Prejudices; or, Some of My Best Friends Are People,* McGraw, 1978; (editor) *Infinite Riches,* McGraw, 1979; *Silky!: A Detective Story,* Harper 1979; *King Silky!,* Harper, 1980.

Under pseudonym Leonard Q. Ross: *The Education of H*Y*M*A*N K*A*P*L*A*N,* Harcourt, 1937; *The Strangest Places,* with illustrations by George Price, Harcourt, 1939; *Adventure in Washington,* Harcourt, 1940.

Under pseudonym Leonard Ross: *Dateline: Europe,* Harcourt, 1939; *The Dark Corner,* Century, 1945; *Sleep, My Love* (also see below), Triangle Publications, 1946.

Screenplays: ''All through the Night,'' Warner Brothers, 1942; ''The Conspirators,'' Warner Brothers, 1944; ''Lured,'' Universal, 1947 (released in England as ''Personal Column''); ''Sleep, My Love'' (based on the author's novel), United Artists, 1947; ''The Velvet Touch,'' R.K.O., 1948; ''Where Danger Lives,'' R.K.O., 1950; ''Double Dynamite,'' R.K.O., 1952; ''Walk East on Beacon,'' Columbia, 1952 (released in England as ''The Crime of the Century'').

Contributor to *Look, Harper's, New Yorker, Saturday Review, Public Opinion Quarterly,* and other publications.

SIDELIGHTS: Leo Rosten is best-known for creating the character Hyman Kaplan, an immigrant whose fractured attempts at learning the English language are the basis of many humorous stories. A critic for *Booklist* notes the ''unique spellings, mispronunciations, and amazing linguistic logic'' that Kaplan employs while seeking to master the intricacies of English grammar. *Horn Book*'s M.C. Scoggin finds the Kaplan stories suited ''for the reader who enjoys play on words, whose ear is attuned to the variety of accents, and who appreciates the diabolic logic which gives the opposite of 'inhale' as 'dead'.''

Mr. Parkhill's class at the Night Preparatory School for Adults—a class for those who must learn English to become citizens—is the scene of Kaplan's misadventures. In class, Kaplan makes sure he sits front row center where, as Gilbert Millstein writes in the *New York Times Book Review,* he ''rises rooster-like, crowing and undaunted, from the shards of his broken English;. . . he is the scourge (and the life) of Mr. Parkhill's earnest, illiterate brood.'' ''The class's tumultuous proceedings,'' Charles Rolo writes in the *Atlantic,* ''. . .treat us to an entrancing display of the ways in which the English language can be violated. All the characters commit atrocities, but Kaplan towers above them.'' In a *Spectator* review, Evelyn Waugh finds the Kaplan stories ''fresh and original,'' especially ''Kaplan's pride in his new country, his devotion to his teacher, [and] his fierce competition with his fellows in the class.'' Helen MacAfee of the *Yale Review* quotes Kaplan: ''I don't care if I don't pass, I love the class.''

Although the Kaplan stories make extensive use of verbal humor—including puns, dialect, and linguistic illogic—they also have a warm and compassionate side. The *Times Literary Supplement* reviewer notes that Rosten "has a tender eye for small dramatic moments of truth in pathos, and a beautiful knack of individualizing characters." Gerald Gottlieb of the *New York Herald Tribune Book Review* believes that "the humor produced by this remarkable crew [Kaplan's class] does not rest solely on Mr. Rosten's dialect inventions, . . . but comes from something warm and sympathetic and human that he has somehow instilled." R. L. Shebs of the *Chicago Tribune* praises Rosten for "his deep concern with genuine dialect and his affectionate regard for [his characters'] struggles and handicaps." In a review of *The Education of H*Y*M*A*N K*A*P*L*A*N* for *Saturday Review*, Louis Untermeyer admires the book's "gorgeous humor and its ingratiating humanity, its moments of unforced tenderness and its hours of sheer fun."

"More than the Liberty Bell, more than the Declaration of Independence," Rolo writes, "[Rosten's] Night Preparatory School for Adults is a truer symbol of that great, resounding 'Yes' that meant America for my father and yours. America! That dream!"

MEDIA ADAPTATIONS: Dateline: Europe and *The Dark Corner* were both filmed by Twentieth Century-Fox in 1946; *Captain Newman, M.D.* was filmed by Universal in 1963. *The Education of H*Y*M*A*N K*A*P*L*A*N* was adapted as a musical and produced at the Alvin Theatre in New York City in April, 1968.

CA INTERVIEW

CA interviewed Leo Rosten by phone March 28, 1981, at his home in New York City.

CA: In The Return of H*Y*M*A*N K*A*P*L*A*N, *you described humor as "the affectionate communication of insight." Do you, like your admirer Norman Cousins, believe in the therapeutic value of humor?*

ROSTEN: I do indeed. Humor is an indication of a wholeness of character structure. People without humor have no sense of proportion, or take themselves too seriously, or fail to enrich life with those precious moments of amusement or disdain that preserve our sanity. Indeed, I would say that one of the requirements for sanity is a sense of humor—and its absence is crippling. Humor is the secret of mental health.

CA: You've written about the "passion for clarity" that led you to do graduate study in politics, economics, and psychology before you came back to writing. In retrospect, are you happy to have spent so much time in those studies?

ROSTEN: I just can't imagine not having done so, considering the richness they lent to all the rest of my life and work. In a sense, I had no choice. I grew profoundly discontented with what I *knew*. Sooner or later I would have been driven by the need to find out something, at least, about how people act, why they do what they do, how society is organized, why there are wars and depressions, murders and prejudice and fanaticism. These problems troubled many kids of my age, growing up in the Great Depression, and the Nazi horror, and several horrible wars. It wasn't enough to say, "These are things I don't understand." I had to try, at least, to understand them. I was lucky in my graduate work; I found a remarkable group of professors and classmates at the University of Chicago, then at the London School of Economics and Political Science. I was given access to the best brains and the most sophisticated

knowledge. Those years were certainly among the most exciting and rewarding times of my life.

CA: Obviously you wouldn't agree with those who believe that education that can't be directly put to work in a job is a waste.

ROSTEN: I go further than that. The most important education is the kind that is "useless." There's nothing more rewarding than learning how to use the mind. There's nothing more wonderful than poetry or paintings, algebra or music. To the degree that it opens the horizons of thought, of ideas, of values, of philosophy and science—that kind of education endows the learner with the capacity for magic. People who want to learn "useful" things should go to a trade school. (I went to a trade high school.)

I used to be amused by much in the progressive-education movement. I had children who were growing up. I'd be in one or another seminar or PTA group. I used to say, "Why do you want to make learning so 'easy'?" If a child masters the difficult, he or she gains a priceless sense of achievement. He can look back and say, "That was a tough problem. But I solved it." Children are rewarded by challenges which they overcome. We're taking a lot of the pleasure out of learning by making things more visual, cozy, cute, and simple. There isn't much adventure in walking a step at a time. There's a lot of excitement in running, jumping, getting lost in an alleyway, falling down and picking yourself up. I prefer the complex to the banal.

CA: You did your doctoral dissertation on the Washington newspaper correspondents. Do you think the newspapers and other reportorial media do a good job of informing the public?

ROSTEN: The press reports well, on the whole. Never has it been possible to learn so much about events around the world so fast. But that's just the first step. The human race is running into problems that become more complicated as we learn more about them. Answers are temporary—and raise more questions. Take the front page of newspapers. You may see a story on Central America, another on Russia, another on taxes, the UN, atomic energy, inflation. The tips of the icebergs are easy to see. But if you try to report economic dilemmas, for example, you discover very soon how inadequate our knowledge is. The experts disagree, and ordinary men interpret problems in the simplest, and often the most distorted, way, such as, "Why don't they just take the money from the rich and give it to the poor?"

The journalist, as an expositor, need also be a clarifier. But how many reporters have the skill or expertise to do that? It is so difficult to explain so many problems that it's impossible for the media to do the kind of job critical people fully approve of. And our educational system has not given readers the knowledge and the ability to comprehend very difficult problems; it's foolhardy to expect newspapers to become teachers—though I wish they could.

This brings up a related concern. It has always been taken for granted that writers are intelligent people. (In the past, the only people who wrote were certainly unusual and, on the whole, intelligent.) This spread into the idea that people who are *articulate* are intelligent. But a curious thing has happened. With the proliferation of education, with the simplification of complicated subjects into terms that are comprehensible today (that would not have been comprehensible to most people centuries ago), we have gotten into a prolonged series of violent arguments about *technical* problems. You find a hundred people arguing for or against a program in economics, ninety-five of whom could not pass an elementary examination in economics. This is a tough problem because we are obliged to vote, to voice our opinions, to affect public policy, and we are asked to do it on questions increasingly complicated and paradoxical: minimum wages, unemployment, crime, rent control. The technicians are driven into what appear to be political positions, and they are labeled conservative, liberal, reactionary, progressive. But the problems are not affected by those labels. So I despair when writers, those who are part of my fraternity, express such confident opinions, about everything from reforestation to atomic energy, when they just don't *know* enough to know what they're talking about. And they sweep the field, because it's their skill to write and to talk—and to get published. It frightens me that dogmatic opinions are expressed, or confident positions taken, with so little validity.

CA: You became a movie fan as a very little boy, wrote screenplays briefly, and wrote the first sociological study of Hollywood: Hollywood: The Movie Colony, the Movie Makers. *That was published in 1941. Many things have changed in movies since then. Are you still a fan?*

ROSTEN: I think the movies are, par excellence, the magic of the twentieth century. Television, which uses film to record and preserve, is certainly the most important single cultural event of our time. What it does or can do is simply phenomenal. The pictures from Voyager II that we received from Saturn are as miraculous as anything man could have imagined. But as for entertainment, and what has happened, that's a mixed bag. I have yet to see a movie of the last twenty years that compares in durability or in grandeur to two dozen movies I could name which were made during the so-called golden day of Hollywood, when so-called illiterate producers were in charge. There *have* been some amusing, diverting changes, inventions in style, a breaking up of the old forms. It's not unlike what happened in poetry when certain metric forms were broken; in prose with Joyce's *Ulysses* and Proust and Hemingway; in the visual arts with Picasso and so on. We've seen the same thing in film—the use of the frozen shot, the jump cut—it's quite refreshing. But in the final analysis, what you come down to is what is this all *about?*

Most of the films of the last ten years—especially films made by the younger people—aren't about anything much worth seeing. Someone asked me if I had seen a certain film and I said, "No. I don't want to spend two hours with a bum. I wouldn't want to spend two hours with him at my home or his home or on a bus." The point was granted at once: "You're right." I said, "You don't understand what I mean. If you have a great playwright or screenwriter, he can make that bum Falstaff, he can make that bum a character out of Dickens or Dostoevski or Mark Twain." The trouble with the stories we're getting is not just that they're about bums, but they're realized with vapidity or lack of insight or absurd sentimentalization. The subject matter is banal and the treatment is fake. These movies exalt the aberrant; they exalt the kooks. I find little satisfaction in watching empty souls in drug-besotted fantasies; I regard it with dismay. I don't want any part of it. And there, I don't think the critics have done well. Many of them just weren't strong enough or clear enough to realize that a movie like, say *Easy Rider*, which caused such a sensation—the story of two guys who get some marijuana on the Mexican border—was a shameful story. It was a distressing, glorifying, maudlin story about pathetic people. I don't think there was anything interesting or illuminating about it. The ending was fradulent: they had a redneck kill the two boys—why?

CA: In your speech at the 1962 National Book Awards you called the equality of men and women a myth, saying, "Men and women belong to different races, as different as Eskimos and Hottentots." Were you attacked by women's lib for this?

ROSTEN: Oh no. That speech was a relaxed minor excursion into half a dozen subjects. What I was trying to say was that being different has nothing to do with being superior—or inferior. Any man who thinks he completely understands a woman is wrong. And any woman who thinks she really understands a man is wrong. Their experiences, in the deepest sense—their physiological determinants, their anxiety, their expectations—are so different that it's foolhardy to pretend they're not. But those differences have nothing to do with how you *treat* women (or men), or what opportunities you give them, or what rewards. If people thought about it, they'd realize a curious paradox: the more equal the opportunity, the greater will be the inequality of outcome. Why? Because the range of people's talents is so different. Take that beyond IQ to other things—sense about how to use money, or how to invest, or how to build, or whatever you want. The range of the gap between the top ten percent and the lower ten percent would be even greater than it is today.

I've never had any problem with the women's liberation movement: I was raised by a mother who was a pioneer in women's rights. She was one of the earliest suffragettes. She insisted on the right of women to observe the polling booths and the ballot count in Chicago. They were thrown out of the voting places by goons. The political organization in Chicago wasn't going to take any of this nonsense, especially from immigrant women. I heard stories as a little boy about the idea of equal rights. That seemed self-evident to me. I always felt that the human race has so much to gain from what one person *may* contribute that it's absurd not to take advantage of all the people you have. To discriminate against half the human population is insanity.

CA: You've written thrillers, you've said, as an exercise in working out problems. Does this writing function as a kind of vacation from your other writing, or do you write both simultaneously?

ROSTEN: I do write different books simultaneously. It's hard when writing melodrama because the form is all-consuming. It's a nagging, constant problem. The first stories I ever told or wrote as a child were melodramas. That's the form all stories originally were; that is, tales about something dramatic that *happened.* They have a narrative structure and they lend themselves to telling. When I was working in Hollywood, I found that I could write a melodrama a year as "an original," a story structured as a movie, not meant for publication, meant to be acted and photographed. Then I could spend the rest of my time in research and travel, doing whatever I wanted. So I wrote about one "original" a year for about ten years. Most appeared on the screen; a few were published in magazines. They were a form of recreation, in a sense.

My most recent forays into the field were based on my inability to find good melodramas to read. That may seem odd, considering the great number that have been published. There are some first-rate mystery writers. But what I wanted to do myself was to see whether, as a technical problem, I could create an exciting story and load that story with laughs, which very few private-eye stories ever have—a lot of laughter, but laughter that would not diminish the dramatic tension. Secondly, to have a group of characters who hang in the mind, linger in the memory. Most melodramas have characters who don't mean a damn one way or another. You don't *care* about them while the tale is going on, and once it's over you forget them. Third, I wanted a corking love story. All this was not a small aim. I have done two stories about a new kind—I think—of private eye. The first was called *Silky!*, and the second is *King Silky!* To my delight, half a dozen reviewers saw the point and said, "Don't mourn the deaths of Dashiell Hammett and Raymond Chandler; here's a new private eye." Some of them got the point about a kind of private eye who will grip your attention, rock you with laughter, and give you a love story. I've enjoyed doing the Silky books enormously. It's like skiing through the Grand Canyon with caviar and champagne.

CA: You've talked about our great emphasis on having fun and being happy, and how instead we should work hard and try to have it matter *that we've been here at all. Do you think we've largely lost that capacity for unselfishness?*

ROSTEN: I wouldn't know how to measure it. But I do think that we are faced with an entirely different kind of society now, a society of people who believe they have a claim on other people, they have a right to demand from other people all sorts of returns, monetary and otherwise. We certainly never had that before in the United States. I don't say that's bad. I happen to believe that it is proper for our society to make sure people do not starve, that the old are not thrown onto ash-heaps, that people who can't afford doctors or medical bills should have the country provide medical attention, hospitalization. In other words, the blows of fate upon decent, innocent people are so harsh that we can no longer say they must handle those blows themselves, or have their un-rich children saddled with them, often for a lifetime. Some of the welfare-state programs warrant my passionate support. But those aspects which subsidize indolence or incompetence, which give anyone with a grievance the idea that he has a legitimate complaint, are taking an appalling toll on us—not only in money, but in terms of the relationship of groups in our society. We have more special-interest groups than we've ever had before, and each becomes a pressure group.

People think the costs are paid by "someone else." When the president says he wants to cut down on subsidies involving the arts, there is an outcry: "How shocking!" No one asks them, "How much do *you* want to give aspiring, but as yet unproven, ballet designers? How much do you want to contribute each year out of your own money?" The assumption is that someone else will pay. The worse assumption is that government money will solve any and all problems.

To come back to the statement about having fun: the emphasis on television and in other media on just having a good time in your life is appalling. It's understandable. You can't do many dramatic stories about *ideas*. Even if you could, the audience for that is small, and those who don't want doses of philosophy aren't likely to be converted. The stuff that appeals to millions of people is the kind of stuff we're getting on television; the results are sad, to me. I don't blame the producers or the networks for this. Quite the contrary: it's a democratic medium, and people *vote* for programs. The ratings polls are not to be swept under a rug. There are plenty of good things on television, and I love it and watch it. But there is so much narcotic exaltation of *self-indulgence*—that's the only word I can think of. The stuff for the young is pagan, it emphasizes the gratification of the sense, *now*.

CA: Herbert Mitgang, in the New York Times Book Review *(September 20, 1959), told the story of your taking a Rorschach test to find out which of your many facets was dominant, and totally confusing the Viennese psychologist who analyzed the results. Would the same thing happen today?*

ROSTEN: I suppose so, unless they've refined the test. I'm not entirely surprised. I was given unusual genes—by fate, luck, not effort. I deserve credit or blame for how I have *used* my fortunate inheritance. My earliest desires were to be a writer, a painter, an artist of some kind. Then I became interested in science, and rejected the whole area of so-called creative work. I did a great deal of study in the social sciences, in economics, political theory, sociology—scientific method, really. There always was this constant tug-of-war within me, which I resolved in the simplest of ways. It was like being on a seesaw. When I felt like going down, or when the inner plank went down, I didn't fight it. I went down. And when it "wanted" to come up, I went up. I respected the unguided impulse, so I would work on whatever appealed to me at the moment, without thinking of the final or total effect.

I remember a literary agent once scolding me, saying that I was foolish to spread myself over so many fields. He said, "The critics don't know what to call you: a novelist, a social scientist, an essayist, a humorist, a social commentator." I said, "That's *their* problem." In a sense, I write for myself, but I know that there are a certain number of people who share my world and will be interested in my work. So it doesn't worry me if I don't get pigeonholed, if I don't win an award as a novelist or a journalist, a humorist or writer of melodrama or social scientist. I have enjoyed a wonderful degree of independence. I have been very lucky: I've been able to write or research what I most wanted to. There aren't many writers who can say that. I have few regrets. Sure, I haven't solved Fourier's equation, or found the cure for paranoia, or been to China (how I have loved to travel!), or written a passacaglia and fugue, or painted the water lilies as Monet (and God) did. I am reconciled to my limitations, and happy to have written thirty-four books.

BIOGRAPHICAL/CRITICAL SOURCES: Saturday Review, August 21, 1937, September 26, 1959, December 7, 1968; *Books,* August 22, 1937; *Nation,* August 28, 1937, November 27, 1937; *New York Times,* August 29, 1937, December 17, 1968, January 25, 1969; *Yale Review,* autumn, 1937; *Boston Transcript,* October 2, 1937; *Christian Science Monitor,* November 19, 1937, September 17, 1959, December 14, 1968, December 3, 1970; *New Republic,* December 15, 1937; *Atlantic,* February, 1938, November, 1959, November, 1968, April, 1979; *Chicago Tribune,* September 20, 1959; *New York Herald Tribune Book Review,* September 20, 1959; *New York Times Book Review,* September 20, 1959, December 15, 1968, March 24, 1974, March 14, 1976, July 11, 1976, October 30, 1977, June 18, 1978, June 10, 1979, January 25, 1981; *Booklist,* October 15, 1959, March 15, 1971, October 15, 1977, November 1, 1980; *Spectator,* October 16, 1959; *New Statesman,* December 5, 1959, March 13, 1970.

Horn Book, February, 1960; Roy Newquist, *Counterpoint,* Simon & Schuster, 1964; *Best Sellers,* November 1, 1964, December 1, 1968, December 15, 1970, February, 1981; *Book World,* November 3, 1968, May 10, 1970, January 8, 1978; *Commentary,* March, 1969; *Observer,* January 25, 1970; *Catholic World,* September, 1971; *Detroit News,* April 16, 1972; *Time,* January 15, 1973, June 28, 1976, May 8, 1978; *Economist,* June 23, 1973; *Christian Century,* August 20, 1975, January 4, 1978; *Antioch Review,* spring-summer, 1977.

—*Interview by Jean W. Ross*

*   *   *

ROTBERG, Robert I. 1935-

PERSONAL: Born April 11, 1935, in Newark, N.J. *Education:*

Oberlin College, A.B., 1955; Princeton University, M.P.A., 1957; Oxford University, Rhodes Scholar, 1957, D.Phil., 1960. *Office:* Department of Political Science, Massachusetts Institute of Technology, Cambridge, Mass.

CAREER: Harvard University, Cambridge, Mass., instructor, then assistant professor, 1961-68, research associate, Center for International Affairs, 1961—; Massachusetts Institute of Technology, Cambridge, 1968—, began as associate professor, currently professor of political science and history. Research director, Twentieth Century Fund, 1968-70. Member of Lexington (Mass.) School Committee, 1974-77; president of Alumni Association of Oberlin College, 1981. Member of Council on Foreign Relations; trustee of World Peace Foundation. *Member:* African Studies Association, Conference on British Studies, American Historical Association (chairman of nominations committee, 1978), Social Science History Association, Royal Geographical Society (fellow). *Awards, honors:* Rockefeller Foundation grant; Ford Foundation grant; Guggenheim fellow; Hazen Foundation fellow.

WRITINGS: Christian Missionaries and the Creation of Northern Rhodesia, Princeton University Press, 1965; *The Rise of Nationalism in Central Africa,* Harvard University Press, 1965; *A Political History of Africa,* Harcourt, 1965; (editor) *Strike a Blow and Die,* Harvard University Press, 1967; (editor) *Africa and Its Explorers,* Harvard University Press, 1970; (editor with Ali A. Mazrui) *Protest and Power in Black Africa,* Oxford University Press, 1970; (with C. K. Clague) *Haiti: The Politics of Squalor,* Houghton, 1971; (editor) *Rebellion in Black Africa,* Oxford University Press, 1971; *Joseph Thomson and the Exploration of Africa,* Oxford University Press, 1971; (editor with Theodore K. Rabb) *The Family in History: Interdisciplinary Essays,* Harper, 1973; (editor with H. Neville Chittick) *East Africa and the Orient: Cultural Syntheses in Precolonial Times,* Africana Publishers, 1975; (editor with Martin Kilson) *The African Diaspora: Interpretive Essays,* Harvard University Press, 1976; (with Jeffrey Butler and John Adams) *The Black Homelands of South Africa,* University of California Press, 1977; *The Mixing of Peoples: Problems of Identity and Ethnicity,* Greylock Publishers, 1978; *Black Heart: Gore-Browne and the Politics of Multiracial Zambia,* University of California Press, 1978; (editor with John Barratt) *Conflict and Compromise in South Africa,* Lexington Books, 1980; *Suffer the Future: Policy Choices in Southern Africa,* Harvard University Press, 1980; (editor with Robb) *Marriage and Fertility: Studies in Interdisciplinary History,* Princeton University Press, 1981.

Editor of *Journal of Interdisciplinary History,* 1970—; senior consulting editor for Harvard University Press, 1973-74. Regular contributor to the *Christian Science Monitor.*

*   *   *

ROTH, Holly   1916-1964
(K. G. Ballard, P. J. Merrill)

PERSONAL: Born 1916, in Chicago, Ill.; died, 1964, after falling off a small sailing vessel while fishing in the Mediterranean; daughter of B. R. and Ethel (Ballard) Roth; married Josef Franta. *Agent:* McIntosh & Otis, Inc., 475 Fifth Ave., New York, N.Y. 10017.

CAREER: Held various positions with *Cosmopolitan,* Dell Books, *Seventeen, American Journal of Surgery, New York Post. Member:* Mystery Writers of America (former secretary).

WRITINGS: The Content Assignment, Simon & Schuster, 1954; *The Mask of Glass,* Vanguard, 1954; *The Sleeper,* Simon & Schuster, 1955; *Shadow of a Lady,* Simon & Schuster, 1956;

The Crimson in the Purple, Simon & Schuster, 1957; (under pseudonym K. G. Ballard) *The Coast of Fear,* Doubleday, 1957; *The Van Dreisen Affair,* Random House, 1959; (under pseudonym K. G. Ballard) *Trial by Desire,* T. V. Boardman, 1959; (under pseudonym P. J. Merrill) *The Slender Thread,* Harcourt, 1959; (under pseudonym K. G. Ballard) *Bar Sinister,* Doubleday, 1960; *Too Many Doctors,* Random House, 1963; (under pseudonym K. G. Ballard) *Gauge of Deception,* Doubleday, 1963; *Button, Button,* Harcourt, 1966. Contributor to *Saturday Evening Post, Redbook, Collier's,* and other magazines.

AVOCATIONAL INTERESTS: Yachting.†

*   *   *

ROTHBARD, Murray Newton   1926-

PERSONAL: Born March 2, 1926, in New York, N.Y.; son of David (a chemist) and Ray (Babushkin) Rothbard; married Jo Ann Schumacher, January 16, 1953. *Education:* Columbia University, B.A., 1945, M.A., 1946, Ph.D., 1956. *Politics:* Libertarian. *Home:* 215 West 88th St., New York, N.Y. 10024. *Office:* Polytechnic Institute of New York, 333 Jay St., Brooklyn, N.Y. 11201.

CAREER: City College (now City College of the City University of New York), New York, N.Y., instructor in economics, 1948-49; Foundation for Economic Education, Irvington, N.Y., economist, 1956-57; Princeton Panel, Princeton, N.J., economist, 1957-61; William Volker Fund, Burlingame, Calif., senior analyst, 1961-62; Polytechnic Institute of New York, Brooklyn, N.Y., associate professor, 1966-74, professor of economics, 1974—. Associate in seminar in history of legal and political thought, Columbia University, 1964—; senior fellow, Cato Institute, 1977-79. Member of board, Center for Libertarian Studies; member of national executive committee, Libertarian Party, 1977-79. *Member:* Society of Historians of the Early American Republic, Mont Pelerin Society, Phi Beta Kappa. *Awards, honors:* Lilly Endowment research grant, 1963-66.

WRITINGS: (Contributor) *On Freedom and Free Enterprise,* Van Nostrand, 1956; (contributor) *Scientism and Values,* Van Nostrand, 1960; *Man, Economy and State,* two volumes, Van Nostrand, 1962; *The Panic of 1819: Reactions and Policies,* Columbia University Press, 1962; *Moneda: Libre y Controlada,* [Bueno Aires], 1962; (contributor) *In Search of a Monetary Constitution,* Harvard University Press, 1962; *America's Great Depression,* Van Nostrand, 1963, 3rd edition, Sheed, 1975; *What Has Government Done to Our Money?,* Pine Tree Press, 1963, revised edition, Rampart College, 1974; (contributor) *Central Planning and Neo-Mercantalism,* Van Nostrand, 1964; *Monopolio y Competencia,* Centro de Estudios sobre la Libertad (Buenos Aires), 1965; *Depressions: Their Cause and Cure,* Constitutional Alliance, 1969.

Power and Market: Government and the Economy, Institute for Humane Studies, 1970; *Freedom, Inequality, Primitivism, and the Division of Labor,* Institute for Humane Studies, 1971; *Education: Free and Compulsory,* Center for Independent Education, 1972; (editor with R. Radosh) *A New History of Leviathan,* Dutton, 1972; *For a New Liberty,* Macmillan, 1973, 2nd edition, 1978; (with E. Hawley, R. Himmelberg, and G. Nash) *Herbert Hoover and the Crisis of American Capitalism,* Schenkman, 1973; *The Essential Von Mises,* Bramble Minibooks, 1973; *The Case for a 100 Per Cent Gold Dollar,* Libertarian Review Press, 1974; *Egalitarianism as a Revolt against Nature and Other Essays,* Libertarian Review Press, 1974; *Conceived in Liberty,* Arlington House, Volume I: *American*

Colonies in the 17th Century, 1975, Volume II: *"Salutary Neglect,"* 1975, Volume III: *Advance to Revolution, 1760-1775*, 1976, Volume IV: *The Revolutionary War*, 1979; (with I. Kirzner and L. Lachmann) *Foundations of Modern Austrian Economics*, Sheed, 1976; (editor and author of introduction) F. A. Fetter, *Capital, Interest, and Rent*, Sheed, Andrews, 1977; *Toward a Reconstruction of Utility and Welfare Economics*, Center for Libertarian Studies, 1977; *Left and Right: The Prospects for Liberty*, Cato Institute, 1979; *Individualism and the Philosophy of the Social Sciences*, Cato Institute, 1979; *Ethics of Liberty*, Humanities, 1982.

Contributor to numerous scholarly and popular publications, including *New Economic Review, American Historical Review, Political Science Quarterly, Journal of the History of Ideas, American Political Science Review, Journal of Economic History, New York Times, Fortune, National Review, Modern Age,* and *Ramparts.* Contributing editor, *Libertarian Review, Reason, Inquiry, Silver and Gold Newsletter, Personal Finance, Libertarian Vanguard,* and *Literature of Liberty;* co-editor, *Left and Right*, 1965-68; editor, *Libertarian Forum*, 1969—, and *Journal of Libertarian Studies*, 1977—.

WORK IN PROGRESS: A book on the workings of money, banking, and central banking; a book on the history of economic thought; a history of the Progressive period.

SIDELIGHTS: Murray N. Rothbard told *CA:* "All my writing, scholarly and popular, has centered around one theme: the theme of human liberty. I have been a lifelong libertarian, and an advocate of individual liberty against its enemies, particularly the organized oppression of the State. I began in the field of economics, analyzing the benefits of the free market as contrasted to the ills caused by government intervention. I later branched out into political theory and American history, in these areas either exploring the theory of liberty, or the workings of the confrontation of liberty versus power in various eras of American history. Almost all of my community activism is also devoted to advancing the libertarian cause.

"Personally, I am what *Time* would call 'affable and balding,' and am also witty—a trait that often clashes with the robotic types one often finds in any ideological movement. I am fun-loving, a marked night person. Since I am the last one to go to bed at any gathering, this impresses people falsely as being extremely energetic; far fewer people observe my sleeping late in the morning. I am a great fan of 1930s culture: jazz, show tunes (Gershwin, Rodgers and Hart, Porter), and movies. I detest rock and disco. I am pro-martinis and anti-marijuana. My favorite writer—who was also a libertarian—is H. L. Mencken, bless him. I like board games (Risk, Careers), and even more like singing old show tunes. I don't like inarticulate youth with glassy eyes, regardless of their ideology or lack thereof. Born, bred, and living always in New York, I had always been an inveterate New Yorker; after living in California (Bay Area) for over two years on a leave of absence from teaching, however, I am now a Bay Area convert. Not only is the ambience beautiful there, and the climate not humid, but also I learned in California that the Hobbesian model of a war of all against all is not necessarily true for mankind.

"I am optimistic about the future of liberty; I think we are going to win. For one thing, the libertarian movement has grown from a half dozen people thirty years ago to an impressive and vital ideological and political movement today."

AVOCATIONAL INTERESTS: Movies, spy stories, political satire, nostalgia, jazz.

ROTHSTEIN, Arthur 1915-

PERSONAL: Born July 17, 1915, in New York, N.Y.; son of Isidor and Nettie (Perlstein) Rothstein; married Grace Goodman, July 4, 1947; children: Robert, Ann, Eve, Daniel. *Education:* Columbia University, B.A., 1935. *Home:* 122 Sutton Manor, New Rochelle, N.Y. 10805. *Office: Parade* Magazine, 750 Third Ave., New York, N.Y. 10017.

CAREER: U.S. Farm Security Administration, Washington, D.C., photographer, 1935-40; *Look* (magazine), New York City, photographer, 1940-41; U.S. Office of War Information, New York City, picture editor, 1941-43; *Look*, technical director of photography, 1946-49, director of photography, 1949-71; *Infinity* (magazine), New York City, editor, 1971-72; *Parade* (magazine), New York City, director of photography, 1972—. Member of faculty, Graduate School of Journalism, Columbia University, 1961-71. Photographs are in the permanent collections of major museums and have been exhibited at the Smithsonian Institution, Museum of Modern Art, International Museum of Photography, Royal Photographic Society, and Bibliotheque Nationale. Consultant to U.S. Environmental Protection Agency and American Iron and Steel Association. *Military service:* U.S. Army, 1943-46; served in China-Burma-India theater; received Army Commendation Medal.

MEMBER: Photographic History Society, American Society of Magazine Photographers (founding member), Society of Photographers in Communications, National Press Photographers Association, Photographic Administrators (president, 1961-63), Royal Photographic Society (fellow), New York Press Photographers Association, Sigma Delta Chi. *Awards, honors:* Recipient of numerous awards for photography, including First International Photo Exposition award, 1938, New York Art Directors Club award, 1963, Photographic Scientists and Engineers award, 1966, National Press Photographers Association award, 1967, for career work, Professional Photographers of America award, 1967, and the Photographic Society of America International Understanding through Photography award, 1968.

WRITINGS: Photojournalism, Ambassador, 1956, 4th revised edition, Amphoto, 1979; *Creative Color in Photography*, Chilton, 1963; (with William Saroyan) *Look at Us*, Cowles, 1967; *Color Photography Now*, Chilton, 1970; *The Depression Years*, Dover, 1978; *Words and Pictures by Arthur Rothstein*, Amphoto, 1979; *The American West in the Thirties*, Dover, 1981.

WORK IN PROGRESS: Two books, *Beyond My Lens* and *China before Mao.*

SIDELIGHTS: While working for the Farm Security Administration during the late 1930s, Arthur Rothstein was assigned to photograph small towns, rural areas, and general agricultural conditions throughout the United States. In the introduction to his book *The American West in the Thirties*, a collection of some of the photographs he took while with the F.S.A., Rothstein comments: "As a photographer for more than forty-five years, I have had the opportunity to photograph the people and places of this varied and vibrant world. . . . In photographing for the Farm Security Administration, I became conscious of a new concept—that photographs could be used to communicate ideas and emotions, as well as present facts, for the camera captures the decisive moment and records events with greater accuracy than does the human eye.

"My photography is based on the concept of knowing the subject and telling the story as graphically as I can. I use design and composition to enhance the effect and make the message clear. I prefer to portray people with dignity and sympathy and to capture expressions with the greatest meaning. Sometimes I will select a revealing detail or fragment of the whole scene in order to make a more effective statement. My photographs are primarily designed to serve a useful purpose in communication, yet many of them have been considered works of art.

"Because powerful images are fixed in the mind more readily than words, the photographer needs no interpreter. A photograph means the same thing all over the world and no translator is required. Photography is truly a universal language, transcending all boundaries of race, politics and nationality.

"The photographer who uses this universal language has a great social responsibility. Accepting this challenge, I have probed the problems of our times and used my camera to communicate ideas, facts and emotions.

"For those who see my photographs . . . , I hope that these images will be a remembrance of the past, a record of accomplishment and an affirmation of faith in humanity."

BIOGRAPHICAL/CRITICAL SOURCES: Arthur Rothstein, *The Depression Years*, Dover, 1978; Rothstein, *The American West in the Thirties*, Dover, 1981.

*   *   *

ROURKE, Francis E(dward)   1922-

PERSONAL: Born September 11, 1922, in New Haven, Conn.; son of Joseph Francis and Bridget (Malone) Rourke; married Lillian Irene Randall, 1948; children: Katherine, Stephen, Anne. *Education:* Yale University, B.A., 1947, M.A., 1948; University of Minnesota, Ph.D., 1952. *Home:* 7100 Copeleigh Rd., Baltimore, Md. 21212. *Office:* Department of Political Science, Johns Hopkins University, Baltimore, Md. 21218.

CAREER: Yale University, New Haven, Conn., instructor, 1952-54; Johns Hopkins University, Baltimore, Md., 1954—, began as assistant professor, professor of political science, 1961—, chairman of department, 1964-70. Assistant director, Committee on Government and Education, Baltimore, 1957-59; editorial advisor, Outdoor Recreation Resources Review Commission, 1961; director, Commission for the Expansion of Higher Education in Maryland, 1961-62; member, Mayor's Charter Revision Committee, 1963-64. *Military service:* U.S. Army, 1943-46; became technical sergeant. *Member:* American Political Science Association, American Society for Public Administration (president of Maryland chapter, 1960-61), Phi Beta Kappa (honorary member), Johns Hopkins Club.

WRITINGS: Intergovernmental Relations in Employment Security, University of Minnesota Press, 1952; *The Campus and the State*, Johns Hopkins Press, 1959; *Secrecy and Publicity: Dilemmas of Democracy*, Johns Hopkins Press, 1961; *Bureaucratic Power in National Politics*, Little, Brown, 1965, 3rd edition, 1978; *Managerial Revolution in Higher Education*, Johns Hopkins Press, 1966; *Bureaucracy, Politics and Public Policy*, Little, Brown, 1969, 2nd edition, 1976; *Bureaucracy and Foreign Policy*, Johns Hopkins University Press, 1972. Also co-author of *Politics and the Oval Office*, 1981. Contributor to professional journals.

WORK IN PROGRESS: Presidential Leadership and Bureaucratic Autonomy.

AVOCATIONAL INTERESTS: Gardening and golf.

*   *   *

ROWLAND, Arthur Ray   1930-

PERSONAL: Born January 6, 1930, in Hampton, Ga.; son of Arthur and Jennie (Goodman) Rowland; married Jane Thomas, July 5, 1955; children: Dell Ruth, Anna Jane. *Education:* Mercer University, A.B., 1951; Emory University, Master of Librarianship, 1952. *Religion:* Baptist. *Home:* 1339 Winter St., Augusta, Ga. 30904. *Office:* Augusta College Library, 2500 Walton Way, Augusta, Ga. 30904.

CAREER: Georgia State College (now University) Library, Atlanta, circulation assistant, 1952, circulation librarian, 1952-53; Armstrong College of Savannah (now Armstrong State College), Savannah, Ga., librarian, 1954-56; Auburn University Library, Auburn, Ala., head of circulation department, 1956-58; Jacksonville University, Jacksonville, Fla., librarian and associate professor, 1958-61; Augusta College, Augusta, Ga., librarian and associate professor, 1961-76, librarian and professor, 1976—. Business manager of *Florida Libraries*, 1959-61; lecturer, University of Georgia Extension in Augusta, 1962-66; chairman of academic committee on libraries, University System of Georgia, 1969-71; chairman of Governor's Conference on Georgia Libraries and Information Services, 1977; delegate to White House Conference on Libraries and Information Services, 1979; trustee of Historic Augusta, Inc., 1969—, Augusta-Richmond County Public Library, 1980—.

MEMBER: American Library Association, Association of College and Research Libraries, National Trust for Historic Preservation, Southeastern Library Association (executive board member, 1971-72), Georgia Association of Junior Colleges (chairman of library section, 1964), Georgia Library Association (2nd vice-president, 1965-67 and 1971-73; 1st vice-president, 1973-75; president, 1975-77), Georgia Historical Society (member of board of curators, 1981—), Georgia Trust for Historic Preservation, Georgia Baptist Historical Society, Georgia Genealogical Society, Florida Library Association (secretary of reference services division, 1960-61), Central Savannah River Area Library Association (vice-president, 1962-64; president, 1964-65), Richmond County Historical Society (curator, 1964—; director, 1965-67; president, 1967-70), Duval County Library Association (vice-president, 1960-61).

WRITINGS: (Editor) *Reference Services: Contributions to Literary Literature*, Shoe String, 1964; (contributor) Charles Thinker, editor, *Library Services for Junior Colleges*, American Southern Press, 1964; *A Bibliography of the Writings on Georgia History*, Shoe String, 1965, revised edition published as *A Bibliography of the Writings on Georgia History*, 1900-1978, Reprint Co., 1978; (editor) *Historical Markers of Richmond County, Georgia*, Richmond County Historical Society, 1967, revised edition, 1971; *A Guide to the Study of Augusta and Richmond County, Georgia*, Richmond County Historical Society, 1967; (editor) *The Catalog and Cataloging*, Shoe String, 1969; (with Helen Callahan) *Yesterday's Augusta*, E. A. Seemann, 1976; *The Librarian and Reference Service*, Shoe String, 1977. Contributor of articles to literary and historical publications. Founder and editor of *Richmond County History* (journal of Richmond County Historical Society), 1969—.

WORK IN PROGRESS: Early Printing in Augusta, Georgia; Printing in Georgia.

AVOCATIONAL INTERESTS: Antiques and genealogy.

*   *   *

ROWLAND, Iris
See ROBERTS, Irene

*   *   *

ROWLINGSON, Donald T(aggart)   1907-

PERSONAL: Born March 9, 1907, in Syracuse, N.Y.; son of

Clyde Adelbert and Mary (Taggart) Rowlingson; married former wife, Louise J. Kendrick, 1935; married Lilian Mary Edwards, January 16, 1960: children: Ann Louise Rowlingson Austin, Elisabeth Rowlingson Dorman, John Kendrick. *Education:* Allegheny College, A.B., 1929; Boston University, S.T.B., 1932, Ph.D., 1938; attended University of Berlin, 1932-33, and Cambridge University, 1958-59. *Politics:* Democrat. *Home:* 15 Ridge St., Winchester, Mass. 01890. *Office:* First Congregational Church, The Common, Winchester, Mass. 01890.

CAREER: Ordained Methodist minister, 1934. Allegheny College, Meadville, Pa., instructor in religion, 1937-39; Emory University, Atlanta, Ga., professor of New Testament, 1939-49; Boston University, School of Theology, Boston, Mass., professor of New Testament, 1950-72, professor emeritus, 1972—, faculty chairman of Senate Council, 1954-55. Associate pastor, Community Church, Islington, Mass., 1930-37; teacher in adult church schools, Glenn Memorial Church, Atlanta, Ga., 1941-49, and First Congregational Church, Winchester, Mass., 1949—; pastor of Federated Church of Christ, Brookline, N.H., 1954-58. United Methodist Church, member of Central New York Conference, 1934-42, 1949—, and of Virginia Conference, 1942-49. Visiting professor, University of Southern California, summer 1952, and Emory University, summer, 1953. Member of YMCA Camp Committee, Boston, Mass., 1951-58, school board of Brookline, N.H., 1955-58, curriculum committee of Boston Theological Institute, 1967-69, and Winchester Interagency Council, 1976; Mystic Valley Mental Health Center Association, member of board of directors, 1975—, vice president, 1977—. *Member:* Society of Biblical Literature (vice-president, Southern section, 1949-50), American Association of University Professors, American Academy of Religion (member of member council, 1948-49), Phi Delta Theta, Omicron Delta Kappa, Kappa Phi Kappa. *Awards, honors:* Jacob Sleeper fellow, Boston University, 1932-33; exchange fellow, Institute of International Education, 1932-33; American Association of Theological Schools fellow, Cambridge University, 1958-59; D.D., Allegheny College, 1962.

WRITINGS: (Contributor) E. P. Booth, editor, *New Testament Studies,* Abingdon, 1942; (contributor) J. R. Spann, editor, *The Church and Social Responsibility,* Abingdon, 1953; *Introduction to New Testament Study,* Macmillan, 1956; *Jesus the Religious Ultimate* (Religious Book Club selection), Macmillan, 1961; (contributor) *The Interpreter's Dictionary of the Bible,* Abingdon, 1962; *A Bibliographical Outline of New Testament Research and Interpretation,* Boston University Bookstores, 1963, 3rd edition, 1969; *The Gospel-Perspective on Jesus Christ,* Westminster, 1968; (contributor) Barnabis Lindars and Stephen S. Smalley, editors, *Christ and Spirit in the New Testament,* Cambridge University Press, 1973. Contributor of articles to religious journals.

*   *   *

RUBIN, Louis D(ecimus), Jr. 1923-

PERSONAL: Born November 19, 1923, in Charleston, S.C.; son of Louis D. (an electrical contractor) and Janet (Weinstein) Rubin; married Eva Redfield (a professor), June 2, 1951; children: Robert, William. *Education:* Attended College of Charleston, 1940-42; University of Richmond, B.A., 1946; Johns Hopkins University, M.A., 1949, Ph.D., 1954. *Politics:* Democrat. *Religion:* Reformed Jewish. *Home:* 702 Grimghoul Rd., Chapel Hill, N.C. 27514. *Office:* Department of English, University of North Carolina, Chapel Hill, N.C. 27514.

CAREER: Bergen Evening Record, Hackensack, N.J., reporter, 1946-47; *News Leader,* Staunton, Va., city editor, 1947-

48; Associated Press staff writer, 1948; assistant telegraph editor, *Morning News,* Wilmington, Del.; Johns Hopkins University, Baltimore, Md., instructor in English, 1948-54; University of Pennsylvania, Philadelphia, assistant professor of American civilization, 1954-55; *News Leader,* Richmond, Va., associate editor, 1956-57; Hollins College, Hollins College, Va., associate professor, 1957-59, professor of English and chairman of department, 1959-67; University of North Carolina at Chapel Hill, professor of English, 1967-72, University Distinguished Professor of English, 1972—. Visiting professor at Louisiana State University, summer, 1957, University of North Carolina, spring, 1965, University of California, Santa Barbara, summer, 1966, and Harvard University, summer, 1969; Fulbright professor, University of Aix-Marseilles (Nice, France), summer, 1960. Coordinator, U.S. Information Agency Forum, 1973-74, 1976-78. *Member:* American Studies Association (executive secretary, 1954-56; member of executive council, 1959-60, 1960-62; vice-president, 1960-61), Modern Language Association of America, Society for the Study of Southern Literature (member of executive council, 1968—; president, 1974-76), Southern Historical Association, Phi Beta Kappa. *Awards, honors: Sewanee Review* fellowship, 1953; Guggenheim fellowship, 1956; American Council of Learned Societies fellowship, 1964; Jules F. Landry Award, Louisiana State University Press; Distinguished Virginian Award, 1972; Litt.D., University of Richmond, 1974; Mayflower Society award, 1978.

WRITINGS: Thomas Wolfe: The Weather of His Youth, Louisiana State University Press, 1955; *No Place on Earth: Ellen Glasgow, James Branch Cabell, and Richmond-in-Virginia,* University of Texas Press, 1959; *The Golden Weather* (novel), Atheneum, 1961; *The Faraway Country: Writers of the Modern South,* University of Washington Press, 1963, published as *Writers of the Modern South: The Faraway Country,* 1966; *The Curious Death of the Novel: Essays in American Literature,* Louisiana State University Press, 1967; *The Teller in the Tale,* University of Washington Press, 1967; *George W. Cable: The Life and Times of a Southern Heretic,* Pegasus, 1969; *The Writer in the South,* University of Georgia Press, 1972; (with Blyden Jackson) *Black Poetry in America: Two Essays in Interpretation,* Louisiana State University Press, 1974; *William Elliott Shoots a Bear: Essays on the Southern Literary Imagination,* Louisiana State University Press, 1976; *Virginia: A Bicentennial History,* Norton, 1977; *The Wary Fugitives: Four Poets and the South,* Louisiana State University Press, 1978; *The Boll Weevil and the Triple Play* (fiction), Tradd Street Press, 1979; *Surfaces of a Diamond* (novel), Louisiana State University Press, 1981.

Editor: (With R. D. Jacobs) *Southern Renascence: The Literature of the Modern South,* Johns Hopkins Press, 1953; (with J. J. Kilpatrick) *The Lasting South,* Regnery, 1957; *Teach the Freeman: Correspondence of Rutherford B. Hayes and the Slater Fund for Negro Education, 1881-1893,* two volumes, Louisiana State University Press, 1959; (with Jacobs) *South: Modern Southern Literature in Its Cultural Settings,* Doubleday, 1961; (with J. R. Moore) *The Idea of an American Novel,* Crowell, 1961; *The Hollins Poets,* University Press of Virginia, 1967; *A Bibliographical Guide to the Study of Southern Literature,* Louisiana State University Press, 1969; Beatrice Ravenel, *The Yemassee Lands: The Poems of Beatrice Ravenel,* University of North Carolina Press, 1969; (with R.H.W. Dillard) *The Experience of America,* Macmillan, 1969; (with R. B. Davis and C. H. Holman) *Southern Writing, 1585-1920,* Odyssey, 1970; *Thomas Wolfe: A Collection of Critical Essays,* Prentice-Hall, 1973; *The Comic Imagination in American Literature,* Rutgers University Press, 1973; (with Holman) *Southern Literary Study: Prospects and Possibilities,* University of

North Carolina Press, 1975; *The Literary South,* Wiley, 1979; (with others) *Southern Writers: A Biographical Dictionary,* Louisiana State University Press, 1979; *The American South: Portrait of a Culture,* Voice of America, 1979, Louisiana State University Press, 1980.

Editor of "Southern Literary Studies" series, Louisiana State University Press, 1964-73, 1975—. Contributor to newspapers and professional journals. Editor of *Hopkins Review,* 1949-53, *Provincial,* 1956-57, *Hollins Critic,* 1963-69, and *Southern Literary Journal,* 1969—; member of editorial advisory board, *Mississippi Quarterly;* advisory editor, University of North Carolina Press, 1973-75.

AVOCATIONAL INTERESTS: Fishing, sailing, and baseball.

BIOGRAPHICAL/CRITICAL SOURCES: New York Times, March 7, 1968; *Kenyon Review,* Volume XXX, number 4, 1968; *Sewanee Review,* winter, 1969; *New York Times Book Review,* March 25, 1979; *Washington Post,* December 2, 1981.

*   *   *

RUSH, Richard Henry   1915-

PERSONAL: Born March 6, 1915, in New York, N.Y.; son of Henry Frederick and Bessie (Vreeland) Rush; married Julia Ann Halloran, August 15, 1956; children: Sallie Haywood. *Education:* Attended Wesleyan University, 1933-34; Dartmouth College, A.B. (summa cum laude), 1937, Master of Commercial Science, 1938; Harvard University, M.B.A., 1941, Doctor of Commercial Science, 1942. *Religion:* Episcopalian. *Home:* North St., Greenwich, Conn. 06830; and Villa Palladio, Piombino, Dese, Italy. *Agent:* Lurton Blassingame, 60 East 42nd St., New York, N.Y. 10017. *Office address:* Box 62, Glenville Station, Greenwich, Conn. 06830.

CAREER: Allegheny Airlines, Wilmington, Del., chief economist and chairman of planning committee, 1943-45; U.S. Bureau of Foreign and Domestic Commerce, Washington, D.C., director of aviation, 1945-46; National Security Resources Board, Washington, D.C., director of aircraft division, 1948-51; executive assistant in charge of Washington relations for J. Paul Getty, Tulsa, Okla., 1951-52; Rush & Halloran (finance and insurance company), Washington, D.C., partner, 1953-58; North American Acceptance Corp., Washington, D.C., president and chairman of the board, 1956-58; Richard H. Rush Enterprises (financiers), Washington, D.C., president, 1958-77; writer and lecturer. Professor of finance and investments and chairman of department, School of Business Administration, American University, 1967-70 and 1978-79. Contributing editor, Wall Street Reports Publishing Corp., 1973—. Economic expert before the Tax Court of the United States, 1951—; tax consultant to various companies. Trustee and member of executive committee, Finch College, 1968-72. *Member:* International Platform Association, American Marketing Association (chairman of national committee), American Economic Association, American Statistical Association, American Association of University Professors, Phi Beta Kappa, Phi Kappa Phi, Omicron Delta Kappa, Harvard Club. *Awards, honors:* Littauer fellow, Harvard University, 1941-42.

WRITINGS: Opportunities for New Businesses in Aviation, U.S. Government Printing Office, 1947; *Art as an Investment,* Prentice-Hall, 1961; *A Strategy of Investing for Higher Return,* Prentice-Hall, 1962; *The Techniques of Becoming Wealthy,* Prentice-Hall, 1963, 3rd edition, U.S. News and World Report, 1976; *Antiques as an Investment,* Prentice-Hall, 1968; *The Wrecking Operation: Phase One,* Anglo-American Publications, 1972; *Investments You Can Live with and Enjoy,* U.S.

News and World Report, 1974, 3rd edition, 1976; *Selling Your Collectibles,* New York Times, 1981; *Investing in Antique and Classic Cars,* Macmillan, 1981. Also author of a bi-weekly newsletter, *The Art/Antiques Investment Report,* Wall Street Publications. Contributor of articles to popular and professional publications. Contributing editor, *Wall Street Transcript,* 1971—.

SIDELIGHTS: Richard Henry Rush is a leading authority on the purchase of art and antiques as investments. Besides making numerous appearances on television and radio programs, Rush speaks throughout the country on the financial rewards of collecting; his talks on the subject have included a series of sixteen lectures at the Smithsonian Institution in 1979 as well as symposia held on Kiawah Island in 1979 and 1980.

*   *   *

RUSHOLM, Peter
See POWELL, Eric F(rederick) W(illiam)

*   *   *

RUSSELL, James
See HARKNETT, Terry

*   *   *

RUSSELL, Ray   1924-

PERSONAL: Born September 4, 1924, in Chicago, Ill.; son of William James and Margaret (Otto) Russell; married Ada Beth Stevens, September 5, 1950; children: Marc Antony, Amanda. *Education:* Attended Chicago Conservatory of Music, 1947-48, and the Goodman Theatre, Chicago, 1949-51. *Residence:* Beverly Hills, Calif. *Agent:* H. N. Swanson, Inc., 8523 Sunset Blvd., Los Angeles, Calif. 90069.

CAREER: Playboy magazine, Chicago, Ill., associate editor, 1954-55, executive editor, 1955-60; free-lance writer and editor, 1960—. *Military Service:* U.S. Army Air Forces, 1943-46. *Member:* Writers Guild of America West. *Awards, honors:* Received first prize, *Writer's Digest* poetry contest, 1976, and Sri Chinmay poetry contest, 1977.

WRITINGS—Novels: *The Case against Satan,* Obolensky, 1962; *The Colony,* Sherbourne, 1969; *Incubus,* Morrow, 1976; *Princess Pamela,* Houghton, 1979; *The Bishop's Daughter,* Houghton, 1981.

Short story collections: *Sardonicus and Other Stories* (also see below), Ballantine, 1961; *Unholy Trinity,* Bantam, 1967; *Sagittarius,* Playboy Press, 1971; *Prince of Darkness,* Sphere, 1971; *Devil's Mirror,* Sphere, 1980; *The Book of Hell,* Sphere, 1980.

Screenplays: "Mr. Sardonicus" (based on Russell's short story of same title), Columbia, 1961; "Zotz!" (based on novel by Walter Karig), Columbia, 1962; (with Charles Beaumont) "The Premature Burial" (based on short story by Edgar Allan Poe), American International Pictures, 1962; "X" (original title, "X, the Man with the X-ray Eyes"), American International Pictures, 1963; "The Horror of It All," Twentieth Century-Fox, 1964; (with Stephen Kandell) "Chamber of Horrors," Monogram, 1966.

Other: (Editor) *The Permanent Playboy,* Crown, 1959; *Little Lexicon of Love* (satire), Sherbourne, 1966; *Holy Horatio* (chapbook), Capra, 1976. Contributor to over seventy text books and anthologies. Also contributor of over 100 articles, poems, and short stories to many periodicals including *Paris Review, Midatlantic Review, Playboy,* and *Omega.* Contributing editor, *Playboy,* beginning 1968.

WORK IN PROGRESS: A novel, *The Witch and the Wizard;* a collection of seven gothic tales, *Haunted Castles;* a poetry collection, *Apocalypsiad and Other Poems.*

SIDELIGHTS: Ray Russell calls his editorship of *Playboy* during its formative first seven years "a delightful detour from the main highway of my life, writing.

"Although much of my work has been in the realms of the satirical and the fantastic, I feel that even in such material, the writer must draw, consciously or otherwise, from his own deepest and most personal experiences. Writing, if it is any good, should be a form of self-discovery for the author. I agree with Thomas Mann when he wrote, 'It is better to ruin a work and make it useless for the world than not to go to the limit at every point.'"

Russell continues: "Except for poetry, which [I] compose in longhand, [I] write directly on an old Royal manual typewriter manufactured in 1936, the year [Rudyard] Kipling died. An FM radio is usually providing Bach or Stravinsky in the background as [I] work." Russell looks upon himself as "a lapidary craftsman, continuously polishing [my] words through many drafts." He writes that he belongs to what he calls "that small, exclusive brotherhood of non-alcoholic writers." Editions of Russell's books have been published in French, German, Spanish, Italian, Portuguese, Japanese, and the Scandinavian languages.

BIOGRAPHICAL/CRITICAL SOURCES: Playboy, June, 1969; *New York Times Book Review,* June 29, 1969; *Washington Post,* October 23, 1979; *Chicago Tribune Book World,* November 25, 1979; *Washington Post Book World,* September 6, 1981.

* * *

RUTHERFORD, Douglas
See McCONNELL, James Douglas Rutherford

* * *

RUTMAN, Darrett B(ruce) 1929-

PERSONAL: Born March 4, 1929, in New York, N.Y.; son of Laurence (a newspaperman) and Jane (Saville) Rutman; married Anita Helen Greiff, April 30, 1954; children: James Morgan, Elizabeth Whitney. *Education:* University of Illinois, A.B., 1950; University of Virginia, Ph.D., 1959. *Politics:* Republican. *Religion:* Society of Friends. *Home:* Laurel Lane, RFD, Durham, N.H. 03824. *Office:* Department of History, University of New Hampshire, Durham, N.H. 03824.

CAREER: Newsday, Long Island, N.Y., reporter, 1950-51, promotion manager, 1953-55; University of Virginia, Charlottesville, instructor, 1958-59; University of Minnesota, Minneapolis, instructor, 1959-61, assistant professor, 1961-64, associate professor of history, 1964-68, director of graduate studies in history, 1966-68; University of New Hampshire, Durham, professor of history, 1968—, director of graduate studies in history, 1968-73. *Military service:* U.S. Army, Counter-Intelligence Corps, 1951-53.

MEMBER: American Historical Association, Social Science History Association, Institute of Early American History and Culture, Organization of American Historians, Southern Historical Association, New England Historical Association, Hakluyt Society, Phi Beta Kappa, Phi Alpha Theta, Raven Society (University of Virginia).

AWARDS, HONORS: McKnight Foundation Humanities Award in American military history, 1960; American Council of Learned Societies grants, 1961, 1973; grants-in-aid of research from University of Minnesota, 1961, 1962, 1964, and 1965, and from University of New Hampshire, 1969-71, 1975-79; McKnight Foundation Humanities Award in American history and biography for manuscript of *Winthrop's Boston,* 1963; P. D. McMillan travel fellowship, 1965; National Endowment for the Humanities project grants, 1974-77.

WRITINGS: (Editor) *The Old Dominion: Essays for Thomas Perkins Abernethy,* University Press of Virginia, 1964; *Winthrop's Boston: Portrait of a Puritan Town, 1630-1649,* University of North Carolina Press for Institute of Early American History and Culture, 1965; (contributor) George Billias, editor, *Law and Authority in Colonial America,* Barre, 1965; *The Farms and Villages of New Plymouth Colony, 1620-1692,* Plimoth Plantation, Inc., 1966; *Husbandsmen of Plymouth: Farms and Villages in the Old Colony, 1620-1692,* Beacon Press, 1967; (editor) *The Great Awakening,* Wiley, 1970; *American Puritanism: Faith and Practice,* Lippincott, 1970; *The Morning of America, 1603-1789,* Houghton, 1971; (contributor) William L. O'Neill, editor, *Insights and Parallels: Problems and Issues of American Social History,* Burgess, 1973; *John Winthrop's Decision for America,* Lippincott, 1975; *A Militant New World, 1607-1640,* Arno, 1979; (contributor) Thad W. Tate and David L. Ammerman, editors, *The Chesapeake in the Seventeenth Century: Essays on Anglo-American Society,* University of North Carolina Press, 1979.

Contributor to *Collier's Encyclopedia;* also contributor of articles and reviews to *American Heritage, New York Times, William and Mary Quarterly,* and to historical journals.

WORK IN PROGRESS: A study of communal and family life in a Chesapeake county during the late seventeenth and early eighteenth century; a study on the idea and form of community from the England of the late sixteenth century to modern America.

SIDELIGHTS: Darrett B. Rutman writes: "Over the years my interest has grown in near-organic fashion: from the introduction of an English culture into America in the seventeenth century, through the elaboration of that culture in America to about mid-eighteenth century, to the whole complex of changes in life-style between then (England of roughly 1600) and now. To this point it has been a matter of curiosity. Eventually it must come to judgment."

AVOCATIONAL INTERESTS: Water (not to fish or indulge in water-sports, but to be on water), gardening, and tending a New Hampshire woodlot.

* * *

RUTSALA, Vern 1934-

PERSONAL: Born February 5, 1934, in McCall, Idaho; son of Ray Edwin (a salesman) and Virginia (Brady) Rutsala; married Joan Colby, April 6, 1957; children: Matthew, David, Kirsten. *Education:* Reed College, B.A., 1956; State University of Iowa, M.F.A., 1960. *Office:* English Department, Lewis and Clark College, Portland, Ore. 92719.

CAREER: Lewis and Clark College, Portland, Ore., 1961—, currently professor of English. Visiting professor, University of Minnesota, 1968-69, and Bowling Green State University, 1970. *Military service:* U.S. Army, 1956-58.

WRITINGS: The Window: Poems, Wesleyan University Press, 1964; *Small Songs: A Sequence* (poems), Stone Wall Press, 1969; *The Harmful State,* Best Cellar, 1971; (editor) *British Poetry 1972,* Baleen Press, 1972; *Laments,* New Rivers Press, 1975; *The Journey Begins,* University of Georgia Press, 1976;

Paragraphs, Wesleyan University Press, 1978; *The New Life,* Trask House, 1978.

Poetry anthologized in *West of Boston,* edited by G. Stevenson, Qara Press, 1959, *Midland,* edited by Paul Engle and others, Random House, 1961, *Where Is Vietnam?: American Poets Respond,* edited by Walter Lowenfels, Doubleday-Anchor 1967, *Modern Poetry of Western America,* edited by Stafford and Larson, Brigham Young University Press, 1975, and *A Geography of Poets,* edited by Edward Field, Bantam, 1979. Contributor to *Paris Review, Nation, Midland, Poetry, New Yorker, Harper's, American Poetry Review, Poetry Northwest,* and other publications. Poetry editor, *December,* 1959-62.

WORK IN PROGRESS: Poetry and fiction.

SIDELIGHTS: In a review of *The Window, Chicago Review's* Norman Friedman comments: "Vern Rutsala . . . seems to me to have one of the keenest poetic senses of contemporary society that I can remember since Cummings, Auden, the earlier Karl Shapiro, and a few of Simpson's poems, coupled with one of the most natural yet elevated styles of any of the in-between poets discussed so far."

R. D. Spector of the *Saturday Review* writes that "for all the casual language, there is a precision of metaphor: for all the quietness, a moving force, and for all the commonplace experiences, a genuine significance. . . . Rutsala is a poet of the very real world. . . . It is not merely authenticity but understanding and wisdom that speak out."

BIOGRAPHICAL/CRITICAL SOURCES: Saturday Review, February 13, 1965; *Chicago Review,* June, 1967.

*   *   *

RUTT, Richard   1925-
(Ro Tae-yong)

PERSONAL: Born August 27, 1925, in Langford, Bedfordshire, England; son of Cecil (a local government officer) and Mary (Turner) Rutt; married Joan Mary Ford, 1969. *Education:* Attended Kelham Theological College, 1942-51; Pembroke College, Cambridge, B.A., 1954, M.A., 1958. *Home and office:* Bishop's Lodge, 10 Springfield Rd., Leicester LE2 3BD, England.

CAREER: Ordained priest of Church of England, 1952; consecrated bishop, 1966; St. George's Church, Cambridge, England, curate, 1952-54; Anglican Church in Korea, 1954-74, parish priest in Korean village, 1956-59, warden of St. Bede's Student Center, Seoul, 1959-64, rector of Diocesan Seminary, Seoul, 1964-66, bishop of Taejon, 1968-74; bishop of St. Germans, Cornwall, England, 1974-79; bishop of Leicester, Leicester, England, 1979—. Bard of the Gorsedd of Cornwall, 1976. *Military service:* Royal Naval Volunteer Reserve, 1943-46; became sublieutenant. *Member:* Royal Asiatic Society (councilor, Korea branch, 1955-74; president, 1974—). *Awards, honors:* Tasan Award, 1964, for foreign writings on Seoul, Korea; commander of the British Empire, 1973; order of civil merit (Peony class), Republic of Korea, 1974; D.Litt. from Confucian University, 1974.

WRITINGS: The Church Serves Korea, Society for the Propagation of the Gospel in Foreign Parts, 1956; *An Introduction to the Sijo: A Form of Short Korean Poem,* Korean Branch of the Royal Asiatic Society, 1958; *Korea: Answers to Your Questions about the Korean People, Their Customs, Politics and Religion,* Korean Mission, Church of England, 1959; (editor) *Church Music and Hymnbook* (in Korean), Anglican Church (Seoul), 1962; (editor and compiler) *Contribution of Literature*

and the Arts to Korean Modernization, [Seoul], 1963; *Korean Works and Days: Notes from the Diary of a Country Priest,* Tuttle, 1964, revised edition, Royal Asiatic Society, 1978; *P'ungnyu Han' guk* (essays in Korean), Sin T'aeyang Co. (Seoul), 1964; (editor and translator) *An Anthology of Korean Sijo,* Ch'ongja Sijo Society, 1970; *The Bamboo Grove: An Introduction to Sijo,* University of California Press, 1971; (editor and annotator) J. S. Gale, *History of the Korean People,* Royal Asiatic Society, 1971; *Virtuous Women,* UNESCO, 1974. Contributor of articles in both English and Korean to newspapers and periodicals in Korea and elsewhere, including regular articles in daily press on customs, literature, and liturgy.

WORK IN PROGRESS: Translating verse written in Chinese by Korean writers.

*   *   *

RUUTH, Marianne   1933-

PERSONAL: Born April 28, 1933, in Kumla, Sweden; naturalized U.S. citizen in 1964; daughter of Paul and Maria (Steen) Petersson; married Helge O. Bylund, April, 1955 (divorced, 1957); married Patrick J. Daly (an industrial designer), June 23, 1966; children: Joanne. *Education:* Attended University of Stockholm, 1955-56, Los Angeles City College, 1957-58, and University of California, Los Angeles, 1958-59. *Politics:* "The individual has to come first!" *Home:* 3128 Waverly Dr., Los Angeles, Calif. 90027.

CAREER: Actress in Stockholm, Sweden, 1952-57; free-lance writer, 1955—. *Member:* Mensa, Hollywood Foreign Press Association. *Awards, honors:* Bonnier Short Story Award, 1971.

WRITINGS: Droemmen om Hollywood (title means "The Hollywood Dream"), Bonnier, 1970; *Look to the Blue Horse,* Bouregy, 1973; *Game of Shadows,* Ace Books, 1974; *A Question of Love,* Bouregy, 1975; *Tapestry of Terror,* Ace Books, 1975; *Outbreak,* Manor, 1977; *Journey into Fear,* Leisure Books, 1977; *Vem kanner Anna Helm?,* Askild/Karnekull, 1978; *Stevie Wonder,* Holloway, 1980; *Nanna,* Bra Boecker, 1982. Contributor of articles and short stories to journals.

SIDELIGHTS: "Why do I write?" Marianne Ruuth wrote to *CA.* "Because it's one way to discover life? Because I don't believe 'ordinary' human beings exist? (How common is the common man?) Because it is exciting to put a few human beings in a certain situation and say 'imagine it . . . ?' Because I'd like to learn to understand, analyze, categorize, inform, communicate, create meaning in chaos—all at once? Because I've always wished to be Lewis Carroll? Who knows—and does it matter?"

*   *   *

RYAN, Bernard, Jr.   1923-

PERSONAL: Born December 2, 1923, in Albion, N.Y.; son of Bernard (a judge in the New York State Court of Claims) and Harriet (Fitts) Ryan; married Jean Bramwell, September 18, 1948; children: Nora Louise, Barbara Ann. *Education:* Princeton University, A.B., 1945. *Home:* 5 Woodchuck Lane, Wilton, Conn. 06897. *Agent:* Claire Smith, Harold Ober Associates, Inc., 40 East 49th St., New York, N.Y. 10017.

CAREER: Staff announcer at radio stations in New Brunswick, N.J., 1947-48, and Buffalo, N.Y., 1948-49; WHAM and WHAM-TV, Rochester, N.Y., staff announcer and director, 1949-50; Batten, Barton, Durstine & Osborn, Inc. (advertising agency), New York, N.Y., copy supervisor, 1950-65; Wilson, Ryan & Leigh, Inc. (advertising agency), Westport, Conn., chairman of board, 1969-74; director of communications, Economic Development Council of New York City, Inc., 1977-80; director of public information, New York City Partnership, Inc., 1980—. *Member:* Wilton Playshop.

WRITINGS: So You Want to Go into Advertising, Harper, 1961; (with Leonard Eames Ryan) *So You Want to Go into Journalism,* Harper, 1963; *Your Child and the First Year of School,* World Publishing, 1969; *The Poisoned Life of Mrs. Maybrick,* Kimber (London), 1977; *How to Help Your Child Start School,* Soundview Books, 1980.

AVOCATIONAL INTERESTS: Photography, theatre.

S

SACHAR, Howard Morley 1928-

PERSONAL: Born February 10, 1928, in St. Louis, Mo.; son of Abram Leon (a founder and president of Brandeis University) and Thelma (Horwitz) Sachar. *Education:* Swarthmore College, B.A., 1947; Harvard University, M.A., 1950, Ph.D., 1953. *Politics:* Democrat. *Religion:* Jewish. *Office:* Department of History, George Washington University, Washington, D.C. 20052.

CAREER: University of Massachusetts—Amherst, instructor, 1953-54; University of California, Los Angeles, director of Hillel Foundation, 1954-57; Stanford University, Palo Alto, Calif., director of Hillel Foundation, 1959-61; Brandeis University, Jacob Hiatt Institute, Jerusalem, Israel, director, 1961-64; George Washington University, Washington, D.C., associate professor, 1965-66, professor of history, 1966—. *Member:* American Historical Association, Phi Beta Kappa, Delta Sigma Rho.

WRITINGS: The Course of Modern Jewish History, World Publishing, 1959; *Aliyah: The Peoples of Israel,* World Publishing, 1961; *From the Ends of the Earth: The Peoples of Israel,* World Publishing, 1964; *The Emergence of the Middle East, 1914-1924,* Knopf, 1969; *Europe Leaves the Middle East, 1936-1954,* Knopf, 1972; *A History of Israel,* Knopf, 1976; *The Man on the Camel* (novel), Times Books, 1980; *Egypt and Israel,* Putnam, 1981. Contributor to periodicals.

SIDELIGHTS: Howard M. Sachar is the author of several highly-praised historical studies of modern Israel, the Zionist movement, and the Middle East. Unlike the works of many of his fellow academics, Sachar's "encyclopedic" books have consistently been praised for their readability. *Commentary*'s Joseph Shattan, for example, calls *A History of Israel* "an extraordinary work, a triumph of comprehensive scholarship which is also a delight to read," while the *New York Times Book Review*'s Meyer Levin writes: "With masterful control of the extraordinarily complex and profuse accumulation of material, with an underlying universal compassion, and an historical objectivity that nevertheless does not disguise his personal viewpoint, Sachar has provided the overall picture of the Jewish movement to statehood, and since statehood. . . . Though written in the controlled, even tone of the historian, the work, particularly in its accounts of the wars of survival, has enormous tension."

The *Nation*'s Phebe Marr points to *The Emergence of the Middle East* as "the best and most comprehensive account thus far [of the events in that area from 1914 to 1924]. It is also among the most balanced and by far the most fascinating." The same book prompts Lord Kinross to comment in the *New York Times Book Review:* "Historians do not always combine scholarship with narrative style, a dramatic sense, an eye for human personality and a feeling for atmosphere. Churchill, the man of action, had these talents to perfection. They are shared to a distinct if unassuming degree by Howard M. Sachar. . . . In unfolding [his] story . . . , he clothes the bare bones of historical fact with the flesh and blood of living, warring peoples."

In a review of *The Course of Modern Jewish History,* the *Springfield Republican*'s Donald Derby summarizes this skill as the ability to write "with learning and with feeling," a sentiment echoed by Ellis Rivkin in a *New York Herald Tribune Book Review* article on the same work. Concludes Rivkin: "Howard Sachar . . . has gone far towards writing the kind of Jewish history that yields understanding. . . . Although the volume is packed with facts, his presentation is anything but pedantic. He has strong opinions and he expresses them; he never shrinks from candid appraisal. He attempts to explain phenomena, and he holds the reader's interest by the pace, the enthusiasm, and sometimes even the excitement of his writing. . . . [His book] is a work of merit, full of fine insights, written with clarity, enthusiasm, and passion, brimming with data, sweeping in its ambitious scope."

BIOGRAPHICAL/CRITICAL SOURCES: New York Herald Tribune Book Review, May 25, 1958; *Springfield Republican,* July 20, 1958; *Saturday Review,* August 2, 1958; *New York Times Book Review,* November 23, 1969, January 21, 1973, August 7, 1977; *Nation,* January 26, 1970; *Annals of the American Academy of Political and Social Science,* July, 1973; *West Coast Review of Books,* January, 1977; *Washington Post Book World,* January 9, 1977; *Choice,* February, 1977; *Commentary,* February, 1977; *Los Angeles Times Book Review,* November 2, 1980.

*   *   *

SACKETT, S(amuel) J(ohn) 1928-

PERSONAL: Born January 23, 1928, in Redlands, Calif.; son of Eben John and Jeannette (DeWolfe) Sackett; married Marjorie McGrath, 1950 (divorced, 1977); children: Robert Eben, John Samuel. *Education:* University of Redlands, A.B., 1948, M.A., 1949; Stanford University, graduate study, 1950; University of California, Los Angeles, Ph.D., 1956. *Religion:* Unitarian Universalist. *Office:* Salt City Business College, Hutchinson, Kan.

CAREER: Hastings College, Hastings, Neb., instructor in English and journalism, 1949-51; Fort Hays State University, Hays, Kan., assistant professor, 1954-57, associate professor, 1957-65, professor of English, 1965-77, professor emeritus, 1977—; Salt City Business College, Hutchinson, Kan., dean, 1978—. *Member:* Lambda Iota Tau (executive secretary, 1963-73).

WRITINGS: (Editor) Henry Fielding, *The Voyages of Mr. Job Vinegar,* Augustan Reprint Society, 1958; (with W. E. Koch) *Kansas Folklore,* University of Nebraska Press, 1961; *English Literary Criticism, 1726-1750,* Fort Hays Studies, 1962; (translator) Johan Daisne, *The Man Who Had His Hair Cut Short* (novel), Horizon Press, 1965; *Cowboys and the Songs They Sang,* W. R. Scott, 1967; *Edgar Watson Howe,* Twayne, 1972; (contributor) *American Government through Science Fiction,* Rand McNally, 1974. Contributor of articles to folklore and literary journals, poems to *American Weave, Kansas Magazine, Antioch Review, Paris Review,* and other magazines, and fiction to various periodicals.

WORK IN PROGRESS: A novel and a book of poems.

SIDELIGHTS: S. J. Sackett told *CA:* "I can no more stop writing than an oyster can stop secreting a pearl once it gets a grain of sand into its shell." Sackett's current "goal in writing is to get [my] readers to think about social-psychological, political, and ethical issues; earlier most of [my] work was informative."

Sackett feels that "the true literary man writes to ordinary readers. Making literature an object of study in the universities . . . has created a nation-wide coterie. Most of the current writing which appears in the literary quarterlies and is discussed in college classrooms is composed by assistant professors for assistant professors. A writer should be 'a man speaking to other men.'"

AVOCATIONAL INTERESTS: Bicycling, karate, woodcarving.

*   *   *

SADLER, Mark
See LYNDS, Dennis

*   *   *

SAGAN, Francoise
See QUOIREZ, Francoise

*   *   *

SAMUELS, Gertrude

PERSONAL: Born in Manchester, England; daughter of Sam and Sarah (Benjamin) Samuels; children: Paul Oppenheimer. *Education:* Attended Busch Conservatory of Music, 1933, and George Washington University, 1935-37; New York University, B.A. *Home:* 75 Central Park W., New York, N.Y. 10023.

CAREER: Staff member of *New York Post,* 1937-41, *Newsweek* (magazine), 1942, and *Time* (magazine), 1943; *New York Times,* New York, N.Y., staff writer for Sunday magazine, 1943-75, staff writer and photographer, 1947-72, editor of magazine staff, 1972-75; free-lance writer and photographer, 1975—. War correspondent in Korea, 1952. Special United Nations observer for United Nations Children's Fund in eight European countries, 1948. *Member:* Authors Guild, Dramatists

Guild, American Newspaper Guild, U.N. Correspondents Association, Drama Desk, Actors Studio, Playwrights Unit (New York). *Awards, honors:* Front Page Awards, American Newspaper Guild, for articles on Little Rock crisis and drug addiction; George Polk Award, Long Island University, 1955, for articles on school desegregation; Overseas Press Club citation, 1956, for refugee coverage; Page One Award, New York Newspaper Guild, 1959 and 1965; *New York Times* publisher's award, 1959, for article on juvenile delinquency; Spirit of Achievement Award, Yeshiva University, 1960; recipient of various photography awards.

WRITINGS: Report on Israel, Herzl Press, 1960; (self-illustrated with photographs) *B-G, Fighter of Goliaths: The Story of David Ben-Gurion,* Crowell, 1961, revised edition, 1974; *The People vs. Baby: A Documentary Novel,* Doubleday, 1967; (self-illustrated with photographs) *The Secret of Gonen,* Avon, 1969; *Run, Shelley, Run!* (novel), Crowell, 1974; *Mottele: A Partisan Odyssey,* Harper, 1976; *Adam's Daughter* (novel), Crowell, 1977; *Of David and Eva: A Love Story* (nonfiction), New American Library, 1978.

Plays: "The Corrupters" (produced in New York at W.P.A. Theatre), published in *The Best Short Plays: 1969,* edited by Stanley Richards, Chilton, 1969; "The Plant That Talked Back," produced in New York at Lambs Club Theatre, January 26, 1970; "Judah the Maccabee and Me," produced at Lambs Club Theatre, January 26, 1970; "The Assignment," produced in Manchester, England, 1974, broadcast over Radio Oslo, Oslo, Norway, 1976; "Reckonings," 1976; "Of Time and Thomas Wolfe," 1980.

Work is represented in anthologies. Contributor of articles and photographs to newspapers and magazines.

BIOGRAPHICAL/CRITICAL SOURCES: U.S. Camera, January, 1961; *New York Times Book Review,* May 7, 1967; *Variety,* February 14, 1970.

*   *   *

SANDERS, J. Oswald   1902-

PERSONAL: Born October 17, 1902, in Invercargill, New Zealand; son of Alfred (an accountant) and Margaret (Miller) Sanders; married Edith M. Dobson, December 19, 1931 (deceased); children: J. Wilbur. *Education:* Attended University of Otago, 1920-23. *Religion:* Baptist. *Home and office:* 2/281 Hillsborough Rd., Mt. Roskill, Auckland, New Zealand.

CAREER: Onetime solicitor of Supreme Court of New Zealand; New Zealand Bible Training Institute, Auckland, principal, 1933-45; China Inland Mission, home director for Australia and New Zealand, 1946-54, general director of overseas missionary fellowship, 1954-69. Managing director, Keswick Book Depot, Melbourne, Australia, 1950-54; principal, Christian Leaders Training College, New Guinea, 1973-74.

WRITINGS: Divine Art of Soul-Winning, Moody, 1937; *Christ Indwelling and Enthroned,* Marshall, Morgan & Scott, 1939, revised edition published as *The Pursuit of the Holy,* Zondervan, 1972; *Holy Spirit of Promise,* Marshall, Morgan & Scott, 1940, published as *The Holy Spirit and His Gifts,* Zondervan, 1970; *Light on Life's Problems,* Marshall, Morgan & Scott, 1944, revised edition published as *Spiritual Problems,* Moody, 1971; *Heresies Ancient and Modern,* Marshall, Morgan & Scott, 1948, revised edition published as *Heresies and Cults,* 1967; *Christ Incomparable,* Marshall, Morgan & Scott, 1952, revised edition published as *The Incomparable Christ,* Moody, 1971; *A Spiritual Clinic,* Moody, 1958 (published in England as *Problems of Christian Discipleship,* O.M.F. Publishers, 1958).

On to Maturity, Moody, 1962, published as *Spiritual Maturity*, Moody, 1970; *Cultivation of Christian Character*, Moody, 1965 (published in England as *The Best That I Can Be*, O.M.F. Publishers, 1968); *Robust in Faith*, Moody, 1965; *Men from God's School*, Marshall, Morgan & Scott, 1965, published as *Bible Men of Faith*, Moody, 1975; *What of the Unevangelized?*, A.M.F. Publishers, 1966, published as *How Lost Are the Heathen?*, Moody, 1972; *Spiritual Leadership*, Moody, 1967; *Expanding Horizons*, Institute Press (New Zealand), 1971; *World's Greatest Sermon*, Marshall, Morgan & Scott, 1972, published as *For Believers Only*, Bethany, 1976; *Real Discipleship*, Zondervan, 1973; *At Set of Sun*, Marshall, Morgan & Scott, 1973; *One Hundred Days with Matthew*, Marshall, Morgan & Scott, 1974, published as *Bible Studies in Matthew*, Zondervan, 1974; *Satan Is No Myth*, Marshall, Morgan & Scott, 1974, Moody, 1975; *One Hundred and Five Days with John*, O.M.F. Publishers, 1976; *Certainties of Christ's Second Coming*, O.M.F. Publishers, 1977; *Prayer Power Unlimited*, Moody, 1977; *People Just Like Us*, Moody, 1978; *Planting Men in Melanesia*, Christian Leaders Training College, 1978; *Enjoying Intimacy with God*, Moody, 1980; *Enjoying Growing Old*, Moody, in press. Also author of *Just the Same Today*, O.M.F. Publishers. Editor of *Reaper* (New Zealand), 1933-45.

*   *   *

SAUL, George Brandon   1901-

PERSONAL: Born November 1, 1901, in Shoemakersville, Pa.; son of Daniel Brandon and Mary E. (Stamm) Saul; married Dorothy M. Ayers, June 28, 1925 (died, 1937); married Eileen S. Lewis, July 3, 1937; children: (first marriage) George Brandon II; (second marriage) Michael Brandon, Barbara Brigid Brandon (Mrs. Johnson M. C. Townsend, Jr.). *Education:* University of Pennsylvania, A.B., 1923, A.M., 1930, Ph.D., 1932. *Religion:* Lutheran. *Home:* 136 Moulton Rd., Storrs, Conn. 06268.

CAREER: University of Connecticut, Storrs, instructor, 1924-29, assistant professor, 1929-32, associate professor, 1932-42, professor of English, 1942-72, professor emeritus, 1972—. Editorial consultant, Pratt & Whitney Aircraft, 1956-61. *Member:* Poetry Society of America, American Committee for Irish Studies, Modern Language Association of America. *Awards, honors:* Prizes for poetry appearing in *Contemporary Verse*, *Lyric*, and *Poet Lore;* research awards for study in Ireland from University of Connecticut, 1967, 1970.

WRITINGS: The Cup of Sand (poetry), Vinal, 1923; *Bronze Woman* (poetry), Humphries, 1930; *A. E. Coppard: His Life and His Poetry*, [Philadelphia], 1932; (translator, and author of introduction and notes) *The Wedding of Sir Gawain and Dame Ragnell*, Prentice-Hall, 1934; *Major Types in English Literature*, Burgess, 1935; (editor and bibliographer). A. E. Coppard, *Cherry Ripe*, Hawthorn House, 1935; *Unimagined Rose* (poetry), Hawthorn House, 1937.

"*Only Necessity . . .*" (poetry), privately printed, 1941; *King Noggin* (juvenile), privately printed, 1943, revised edition, Walton Press, 1971; *Selected Lyrics*, Decker, 1947; *The Elusive Stallion* (essays), Decker, 1948; *October Sheaf* (poetry), Prairie Press, 1951; *Handbook of English Grammar and Writing Conventions*, Stackpole, 1953; *The Shadow of the Three Queens*, Stackpole, 1953, revised and expanded edition published as *Traditional Irish Literature and Its Backgrounds: A Brief Introduction*, Bucknell University Press, 1970; *Stephens, Yeats, and Other Irish Concerns*, New York Public Library, 1954; *Prolegomena to the Study of Yeats's Poems*, University of Pennsylvania Press, 1957; *Prolegomena to the Study of Yeats's Plays*, University of Pennsylvania Press, 1958.

(Editor) *Age of Yeats* (anthology), Dell, 1964; (editor) *Owls' Watch* (stories), Fawcett, 1965; *In . . . Luminous Wind* (essays on Yeats), Dolmen Press, 1966; *The Wild Queen*, Blair, 1967; *Quintet: Essays on Five American Women Poets*, Mouton & Co., 1967; *Hound and Unicorn: Collected Verse—Lyrical, Narrative, and Dramatic*, Walton, 1969; *Rushlight Heritage* (essays), Walton, 1969; *Carved in Findruine* (short stories), Walton, 1969; *A Little Book of Strange Tales*, Walton, 1969; *Concise Introduction to Types of Literature in English*, Walton, 1969.

Candlelight Rhymes for Early-to-Beds, Walton, 1970; *Withdrawn in Gold* (essays), Mouton & Co. ,1970; *In Mountain Shadow* (novel), Walton, 1970; *Seumas O'Kelly* (monograph), Bucknell University Press, 1971; *The Forgotten Birthday* (juvenile), Walton, 1971; *Liadain and Curithir* (Irish novella and short stories), Walton, 1971; *Postscript to Hound and Unicorn* (poetry), Walton, 1971; *A Touch of Acid* (satiric verse), Walton, 1971; *Advice to the Emotionally Perturbed* (parody), Walton, 1971; *Skeleton's Progress: Being a Second Postscript to Hound and Unicorn*, Walton, 1971; (editor) Seumas O'Kelly, *The Shuiler's Child*, DePaul University, 1971; *Daniel Corkery* (monograph), Bucknell University Press, 1973; (editor) Daniel Corkery, *Fohnam the Sculptor*, Proscenium Press, 1973; *The Stroke of Light* (poetry), Golden Quill, 1974; *In Praise of the Half-Forgotten* (essays), Bucknell University Press, 1976; *Two Plays*, privately printed, 1976; *Adam Unregenerate: Selected Lyrical Poems*, Stemmer House & McCloud, 1977; *In Borrowed Light* (poetry), privately printed, 1979; *Vision of Ghostly Horses* (poetry), Wings Press, 1981. Also author of musical composition, *Four Songs*, published by Brandon Press, 1965.

Contributor to *Collier's Encyclopedia, Encyclopedia of Poetry and Poetics, Encyclopedia of World Literature, Dictionary of Irish Literature, Writers of the English Language,* and other scholarly collections. Contributor of poems, book reviews, and some seventy-five articles to periodicals. Contributing editor, *Journal of Irish Literature,* 1971—.

WORK IN PROGRESS: Verse, fiction, and essays.

AVOCATIONAL INTERESTS: Composing music for piano and songs.

*   *   *

SAUNDERS, Ione
See COLE, Margaret Alice

*   *   *

SAVAGE, Christopher I(vor)   1924-1969

PERSONAL: Born September 3, 1924, in Coventry, England; died June 19, 1969; son of Christopher Joseph and Maria (Bailey) Savage; married Joan Andrews, 1952; children: Brian Keith, Roger David. *Education:* University of Birmingham, B.Com., 1946, M.Com., 1949. *Office:* Faculty of Social Sciences, University of Leicester, Leicester, England.

CAREER: Cabinet Office, Historical Section, London, England, narrator for official war history, 1948-51; University of St. Andrews, St. Andrews, Scotland, lecturer in political economy, 1951-60; University of Edinburgh, Edinburgh, Scotland, lecturer in commerce, beginning 1961; University of Western Australia, Nedlands, professor of economics, 1963-67; University of Leicester, Leicester, England, professor of economics and dean of Faculty of Social Sciences, 1967-69. *Military service:* Royal Air Force, eighteen months. *Member:* Royal Economic Society, Scottish Economic Society.

WRITINGS: Inland Transport, H.M.S.O., 1957; (with G. Walker) *Inland Carriage by Road and Rail,* Cambridge University Press, 1958; *An Economic History of Transport,* Hutchinson, 1959, 3rd revised edition (with Theodore Cardwell Barker) published as *An Economic History of Transport in Britain,* 1974; (with J. R. Small) *An Introduction to Managerial Economics,* Hutchinson, 1967, Hillary, 1968. Advisor and contributor of sections on transport to *Chambers's Encyclopedia.* Contributor of articles and reviews on transport subjects to newspapers and journals.

WORK IN PROGRESS: Further work on economics of transport and on economics and industrial problems.

AVOCATIONAL INTERESTS: Walking, music.†

* * *

SAVORY, Theodore Horace 1896-1980

PERSONAL: Born April 28, 1896, in London, England; died November 27, 1980; son of Horace Reginald and Eveline (Besant) Savory; married Helen Mabel Walch, April 24, 1920; children: Brian Theodore, Helen Patricia Busby. *Education:* St. John's College, Cambridge, B.A., 1918, M.A., 1927. *Religion:* Church of England. *Home:* 11 Orchard Rd., Dorking, Surrey, England.

CAREER: Aldenham School, Hertfordshire, England, assistant master, 1918-19; Malvern College, Worcestershire, England, assistant master, 1920-51; Haberdashers' School, London, England, senior biologist, 1951-58; Stafford House Tutorial College, London, vice-principal, 1958-70. Chairman, Malvern Public Library, 1949-51. *Member:* Zoological Society of London (fellow).

WRITINGS: British Spiders: Their Haunts and Habits, Clarendon Press, 1926; *The Biology of Spiders,* Macmillan, 1928; *Spiders and Allied Orders of the British Isles,* Warne, 1935; *The Arachnida,* Arnold, 1935; *Mechanistic Biology and Animal Behaviour,* C. A. Watts, 1936; (translator) V. A. Kostitzyn, *Mathematical Biology,* Harrap, 1939; *Animals,* Oxford University Press, 1942; (with others) *Seven Biologists,* Oxford University Press, 1943, reprinted, 1965; *Latin and Greek for Biologists,* University of London Press, 1946, new edition, Merrow, 1971; *Browsing among Words of Science,* C. A. Watts, 1951; *The Spider's Web,* Warne, 1952; *The Language of Science,* Deutsch, 1953, 2nd edition, 1967; *The World of Small Animals,* University of London Press, 1954; *The Art of Translation,* J. Cape, 1957, new edition, Writer, Inc., 1968; *The Book of the Body,* Clarke, Irwin, 1959.

Instinctive Living, Pergamon, 1960; *Spiders, Men, and Scorpions,* University of London Press, 1961; *Teach Yourself Zoology,* English Universities Press, 1962; *Naming the Living World: An Introduction to the Principles of Biological Nomenclature,* Wiley, 1962; *Practical Biology at Home,* Dobson, 1963, Roy, 1965; *Arachnida,* Academic Press, 1964, 2nd edition, 1977; *Spiders and Other Arachnids,* English Universities Press, 1964; *The True Book about Spiders,* Muller, 1965; *Introduction to Zoology,* Philosophical Library, 1968; *Animal Taxonomy,* Heinemann Educational, 1970; *Biology of the Cryptozoa* (monograph), Merrow, 1971; *Evolution in the Arachnida* (monograph), Merrow, 1971; *The Principles of Mechanistic Biology* (monograph), Merrow, 1971; *Spiders,* Ginn, 1971; (with John Sankey) *British Harvestmen: Arachnida, Opiliones—Keys and Notes for the Identification of the Species,* Muller, 1974, Crane-Russak, 1975.†

SAWYER, P(eter) H(ayes) 1928-

PERSONAL: Born June 25, 1928, in Oxford, England; son of William and Grace (Woodbridge) Sawyer; married Ruth Howard, 1955; children: Richard, Catherine, Dorothy, John. *Education:* Jesus College, Oxford, B.A., 1951. *Office:* School of History, University of Leeds, Leeds LS2 9JT, England.

CAREER: University of Edinburgh, Edinburgh, Scotland, assistant lecturer in history, 1953-56; University of Leeds, Leeds, England, assistant lecturer in history, 1956-57; University of Birmingham, Birmingham, England, lecturer in history, 1957-64; University of Leeds, lecturer in history, 1964-67, reader, 1967-70, professor of medieval history, 1970—.

WRITINGS: (Editor) *Early English Manuscripts in Facsimile: Textus Roffensis,* Rosenkilde & Bagger, Volume VII, Part 1, 1957, Volume XI, Part 2, 1962; *The Age of the Vikings,* Edward Arnold, 1962, St. Martin's, 1963, 2nd edition, Edward Arnold, 1971, St. Martin's, 1972; *Anglo-Saxon Characters: An Annotated List and Bibliography,* Royal Historical Society, 1968; (editor) *Medieval Settlement: Continuity and Change,* Crane, Russak, 1977; (editor with I. N. Wood) *Early Medieval Kingship,* Rowman & Littlefield, 1977; *From Roman Britain to Norman England,* St. Martin's, 1978; (editor) *Charters of Burton Abbey,* Oxford University Press, 1979; (editor) *English Medieval Settlement,* Edward Arnold, 1979; (editor) *Names, Words and Graves: Early Medieval Settlement,* School of History, University of Leeds, 1979.

WORK IN PROGRESS: A general study of the Vikings.

BIOGRAPHICAL/CRITICAL SOURCES: Times Literary Supplement, May 9, 1968.

* * *

SCAGLIONE, Aldo D(omenico) 1925-

PERSONAL: Born January 10, 1925, in Torino, Italy; son of Teodoro (a bank clerk) and Angela (Grasso) Scaglione; married Jeanne Mathilde Daman, June 28, 1952. *Education:* Ginnasio-Liceo Classico Cavour, Torino, Italy, Maturita Classica, 1944; Universita di Torino, Laurea di Dottore in Lettere Moderne, 1948. *Home address:* Route 4, Box 539, Chapel Hill, N.C. 27514. *Office:* Department of Romance Languages, University of North Carolina, Chapel Hill, N.C.

CAREER: University of Toulouse, Toulouse, France, lecturer, 1949-51; University of Chicago, Chicago, Ill., instructor in Italian, 1951-52; University of California, Berkeley, 1952-68, began as instructor in Italian, became professor of Italian and comparative literature, 1963-68; University of North Carolina at Chapel Hill, W. R. Kenan Professor of Romance Languages and Comparative Literature, 1968—. Visiting professor, Yale University, 1965-66; H. Johnson Research Professor, Institute for Research in the Humanities, University of Wisconsin—Madison, 1981-82. *Military service:* Italian Partisan Army, 1944-45. *Member:* Renaissance Society of America, Modern Language Association of America (member of executive council, 1980-84), American Boccaccio Association (president, 1979-81), American Association of University Professors of Italian (vice-president, 1980-83), Dante Society of America, Medieval Academy of America, Renaissance Society of Northern California (president, 1962). *Awards, honors:* Fulbright fellowship, 1951; Guggenheim fellowship, 1958-59; Newberry Library senior fellowship, 1964-65; senior fellow, Southeastern Institute for Medieval and Renaissance Studies, 1968; senior fellow, Cini Foundation, Venice, Italy, 1973.

WRITINGS: (Editor) M. M. Boiardo, *Orlando Innamorato-Amorum Libri,* two volumes, Utet, 1951, revised edition, 1963; *Nature and Love in the Late Middle Ages,* University of California Press, 1963; *Ars grammatica,* Mouton, 1970; *The Classical Theory of Composition,* University of North Carolina Press, 1972; (editor) *Francis Petrarch, Six Centuries Later,* University of North Carolina Press, 1975; *Ariosto 1974 in America,* Longo, 1976; (editor) H. Weil, *The Order of Words,* John Benjamins, 1978; *Komponierte Prosa von der Antike bis zur Gegenwart,* two volumes, Klett (Stuttgart), 1981; *The Theory of German Word Order,* University of Minnesota Press, 1981. Contributor of fifty articles and one hundred book reviews on Italian and French literature to periodicals.

WORK IN PROGRESS: Research on themes of European Latin humanism, in particular, the development of style theories, language theories, and rhetoric.

SIDELIGHTS: Aldo D. Scaglione is competent in Italian, French, Spanish, Latin, and German.

BIOGRAPHICAL/CRITICAL SOURCES: Yale Review, spring, 1964; *Romance Philology,* May, 1976.

*   *   *

SCAMMELL, William McConnell   1920-

PERSONAL: Born November 20, 1920, in Belfast, Northern Ireland; son of Francis William and Alice (McConnell) Scammell; married Kathleen Pollock (a college lecturer), July 22, 1946. *Education:* Attended Technical College, Belfast, Northern Ireland; Queen's University, Belfast, B. Com. Sc. (first class honors in economics), 1945, Ph.D., 1959. *Home:* 11 Falls View Rd., Greensville, Ontario, Canada. *Office:* Department of Economics, McMaster University, Hamilton, Ontario, Canada L8S 4M4.

CAREER: University College of North Wales, Bangor, lecturer in economics, 1945-56; economic advisor, British Treasury, 1956-58; University College of North Wales, senior lecturer in economics, 1958-65; Simon Fraser University, Vancouver, British Columbia, professor of economics, 1965-69; McMaster University, Hamilton, Ontario, professor of economics, 1969—. *Member:* Royal Economic Society.

WRITINGS: International Monetary Policy, St. Martin's, 1957, 2nd edition, Macmillan (London), 1961, St. Martin's, 1962; *The London Discount Market,* Paul Elek, 1968; *International Trade and Payments,* St. Martin's, 1974; *International Monetary Policy: Bretton Woods and After,* Halsted, 1975; *The International Economy since 1945,* St. Martin's, 1980. Contributor to professional journals and banking magazines in Great Britain, Germany, and the United States.

AVOCATIONAL INTERESTS: Travel, gardening, photography.

*   *   *

SCHALL, James V(incent)   1928-

PERSONAL: Born January 20, 1928, in Pocahontas, Iowa; son of Lawrence Nicholas and Mary (Johnson) Schall. *Education:* Gonzaga University, B.A., 1954, M.A., 1955; Georgetown University, Ph.D., 1960; University of Santa Clara, M.S.T., 1964; Oude Abdij, Drongen, Belgium, Jesuit studies, 1964-65. *Politics:* Democrat. *Office:* Department of Government, Georgetown University, 37th and O Sts. N.W., Washington, D.C. 20057.

CAREER: University of San Francisco, San Francisco, Calif., instructor in political science, 1955-56; ordained Roman Cath-

olic priest, Society of Jesus (Jesuits), 1963; Gregorian University, Istituto Sociale, Rome, Italy, lecturer, 1965-77; Georgetown University, Washington, D.C., associate professor in department of government, 1978—. Associate professor in department of government, University of San Francisco, springs, 1968-77.

WRITINGS: (With Donald J. Wolf) *American Society and Politics,* Allyn & Bacon, 1964; (editor with Wolf) *Current Trends in Theology,* Doubleday, 1965; *Redeeming the Time,* Sheed, 1968; *Human Dignity and Human Numbers,* Alba, 1971; *Play On: From Games to Celebrations,* Fortress Press, 1971; *Far Too Easily Pleased: A Theology of Contemplation, Play, and Festivity,* Benziger/Macmillan, 1976; *Welcome, Number 4,000,000,000!,* Alba, 1977; *The Sixth Paul,* Alba, 1977; *The Praise of "Sons of Bitches": On the Worship of God by Fallen Men,* St. Paul Publications, 1978; *Christianity and Life,* Ignatius Press, 1981; *Christianity and Politics,* St. Paul Editions, 1981; (editor and author of introduction) *The Whole Truth about Man: John Paul II to Students and Faculties,* St. Paul Editions, 1981; *The Social Teaching of John Paul II,* Franciscan Herald, 1982; *Liberation Theology,* Ignatius Press, 1982.

Contributor of articles to *Commonweal, World Justice, New Scholasticism, Catholic World, America, Social Order, Modern Age, Worship, Thomist,* and to political science journals.

BIOGRAPHICAL/CRITICAL SOURCES: Encounter, autumn, 1968.

*   *   *

SCHANCHE, Don A.   1926-

PERSONAL: Born May 16, 1926, in New Brunswick, N.J.; son of Carl and Anne (Shennum) Schanche; married Marybelle Waddington, January 7, 1952; children: Donald Arthur, Didrick Miller, Anne Waddington. *Education:* University of Georgia, B.A., 1949. *Politics:* Democrat. *Religion:* Unitarian Universalist. *Home address:* P.O. Box 1535, Cairo, Egypt.

CAREER: Marietta Daily Journal, Marietta, Ga., city editor, 1947; staff and war correspondent for International News Service in Atlanta, Ga., Raleigh, N.C., Miami, Fla., Japan, and Korea, 1949-52; *Life,* assistant editor in New York City, 1953, military editor in New York City and Washington, D.C., 1955-60; *Sports Illustrated,* New York City, staff writer, 1954; *Saturday Evening Post,* Washington, D.C., and New York City, associate editor, contributing editor, executive editor, 1960-64; *Holiday,* New York City, editor, 1964-67; free-lance writer, 1967-76; Middle East correspondent for *Los Angeles Times,* 1976—. *Military service:* U.S. Naval Reserve, active duty, 1943-46; served as radioman. *Member:* National Press Club, Sigma Delta Chi, Pi Kappa Alpha.

WRITINGS: (With David G. Simons) *Man High,* Doubleday, 1960; *Mister Pop,* McKay, 1970; *The Panther Paradox,* McKay, 1970.

Contributor to periodicals, including *Saturday Evening Post, Life, Sports Illustrated, Reader's Digest,* and *Esquire.*

AVOCATIONAL INTERESTS: Travel, sailing, underwater archeology.

*   *   *

SCHERF, Margaret   1908-1979

PERSONAL: Born April 1, 1908, in Fairmont, W.Va.; died May 12, 1979; daughter of Charles Henry and Miriam (Fisher) Scherf; married Perry E. Beebe, December 9, 1965. *Education:*

Attended Antioch College, 1925-28. *Politics:* Democrat. *Religion:* Episcopalian. *Agent:* Blassingame, McCauley & Wood, 60 East 42nd St., New York, N.Y. 10017.

CAREER: Robert M. McBride & Co. (publishers), New York City, secretary to the editor, 1928-29; Wise Book Co., New York City, secretary and copywriter, 1932-34; reader for publisher in New York City, 1934-39; writer, 1940-79. Member of House of Representatives, Montana State Legislature, 1965. *Member:* Authors Guild.

WRITINGS—Mystery novels, except as indicated; published by Doubleday, except as indicated: *The Corpse Grows a Beard,* Putnam, 1940; *The Case of the Kippered Corpse,* Putnam, 1941; *They Came to Kill,* Putnam, 1942; *The Owl in the Cellar,* 1945; *Always Murder a Friend,* 1948; *Murder Makes Me Nervous,* 1948; *Gilbert's Last Toothache,* 1949; *The Gun in Daniel Webster's Bust,* 1949.

The Curious Custard Pie, 1950; *The Green Plaid Pants,* 1951; *The Elk and the Evidence,* 1952; *Dead: Senate Office Building,* 1953; *Glass on the Stairs,* 1954; *The Cautious Overshoes,* 1956; *Judicial Body,* 1957; *Never Turn Your Back,* 1959.

Wedding Train (historical novel), 1960; *The Diplomat and the Gold Piano,* 1963 (published in England as *Death and the Diplomat,* R. Hale, 1964); *The Mystery of the Velvet Box* (juvenile), F. Watts, 1963; *The Corpse in the Flannel Nightgown,* 1965; *The Mystery of the Shaky Staircase* (juvenile), F. Watts, 1965; *The Mystery of the Empty Trunk* (juvenile), F. Watts, 1966; *The Banker's Bones,* 1968.

The Beautiful Birthday Cake, 1971; *To Cache a Millionaire,* 1972; *If You Want a Murder Well Done,* 1974; *Don't Wake Me up While I'm Driving,* 1977; *The Beaded Banana,* 1978.

AVOCATIONAL INTERESTS: Antiques, travel.†

*   *   *

SCHLECK, Charles A. 1925-

PERSONAL: Born July 5, 1925, in Milwaukee, Wis.; son of Raymond M. (a mechanical engineer) and Lucile (Van Eimeren) Schleck. *Education:* University of Notre Dame, A.B., 1948; Pontifical University of St. Thomas, Rome, Italy, S.T.B., 1950, S.T.L., 1952, S.T.D., 1953. *Address:* Sacred Congregation for the Evangelization of Peoples, Piazza di Spagna 48, Rome 00187, Italy.

CAREER: Roman Catholic priest, Congregation of Holy Cross; University of Notre Dame, Notre Dame, Ind., instructor in theology, 1953-54; Holy Cross College, Washington, D.C., professor, 1954-61; College of Santa Croce, Rome, Italy, director of studies, 1961-62; Holy Cross College, professor of theology, 1962-68; consultant on sister formation planning, Russell College, 1968-72; Sacred Congregation for the Evangelization of Peoples, Rome, member of faculty, 1972—. *Member:* North American Society of Josephology, Catholic Theological Society of America.

WRITINGS: The Nature of Sacramental Grace according to St. Thomas, J. H. Furst, 1956; *The Theology of Vocations,* Bruce, 1963; *The Sacrament of Matrimony: A Dogmatic Study,* Bruce, 1964.

Contributor: Stephen Sullivan, editor, *Readings in Sacramental Theology,* Prentice-Hall, 1965; J. Viall, editor, *The Religious Woman,* Daughters of St. Paul, 1975; D. S. Amalorpavadoss, editor, *Asian Conference of Major Superiors,* [Bangalore, India], 1978.

Contributor to *New Catholic Encyclopedia* and to other encyclopedias and periodicals, including *Review for Religious, Cross and Crown,* and *Sponsa Regis.*

SIDELIGHTS: Charles A. Schleck told *CA:* "[My] career as a writer began with the practical and pragmatic need to publish a dissertation! But the continued study of various aspects of theology and spirituality led to a desire to know the truth at whatever cost and to share insights with others, especially those in the same field or interested in the areas of research and reflections speculation and everyday life. So writing became a true ministry as well as a source of personal pleasure and a desire to stimulate the thought and reflection of others and be stimulated by them in return through their writings and responses on topics of mutual interest.

"Above all, writing became and remains a 'way to God' and a constant search for that Wisdom which is not merely human but ultimately a Divine Person."

*   *   *

SCHLESINGER, Hilde S(tephanie)

PERSONAL: Born in Vienna, Austria; daughter of Edmond Robert and Frida Schlesinger. *Education:* University of Arizona, B.A. (cum laude), 1948; University of Louisville, M.D., 1953. *Office:* Center on Deafness, University of California, 1474 Fifth Ave., San Francisco, Calif. 94143.

CAREER: U.S. Public Health Service Hospital, Boston, Mass., intern, 1953-54, staff member, 1954-55; U.S. Public Health Service Hospital, San Francisco, Calif., senior surgeon, 1960-62; Langley Porter Psychiatric Institute, San Francisco, resident in psychiatry, 1962-64, fellow in child psychiatry, 1964-66; director, Center on Deafness, working with University of California at San Francisco, State Department of Mental Hygiene, and Langley Porter Psychiatric Institute, 1966—. Center for Training in Community Psychiatry and Mental Health Administration, fellow, 1966-68, member of faculty, 1968-70; University of California, San Francisco, assistant clinical professor, 1969-73, associate clinical professor, 1973-79, clinical professor, 1979-80, professor-in-residence, 1980—. Member of guest faculty at San Francisco State College (now University), 1967, University of Rochester, 1969, San Fernando Valley State College (now California State University, Northridge, Los Angeles), 1969, 1970, 1971, Western Maryland College, 1971, and University of Maryland's Institute on Services for the Hearing Handicapped. Member of board of fellows of Gallaudet College, 1974. Lecturer at workshops and conferences for parents, teachers, and vocational counselors for the deaf, and at numerous universities and institutions. *Military service:* U.S. Public Health Service, senior surgeon and medical officer in Foreign Quarantine Station of American Consulate General, 1953-60, active duty, 1955-60; served in Germany; became lieutenant commander.

MEMBER: American Deafness and Rehabilitation Association, American Psychiatric Association (fellow), Society for Research in Child Development, National Association for the Deaf, California Association of the Deaf, California Psychiatric Association, Alpha Omega Alpha. *Awards, honors:* Grants from Social and Rehabilitation Services, 1967-68, and 1968-71, U.S. Department of Health, Education, and Welfare, 1970-75, U.S. Office of Education, 1971-77, San Francisco Foundation, 1971-74, Rosenberg Foundation, 1971-74, Office of Rehabilitation Services, 1973-76, State of California Department of Health, 1975-80, and Rehabilitation Services Administration, 1977-80; Media Award from American Psychological Association, 1973, for *Sound and Sign: Childhood Deafness and Mental Health*, 1973; Dan Cloud Memorial Leadership Award from California State University, Northridge, Los Angeles, 1974; Powrie Doctor Chair Award from Gallaudet College, 1974; Alice Cogswell Award for Valuable Service to Deaf Persons from Gallaudet College, 1980.

WRITINGS: (With Kathryn P. Meadow) *Sound and Sign: Childhood Deafness and Mental Health*, University of California Press, 1972.

Contributor: David Lille, editor, *Parent Programs in Child Development Centers: First Chance for Children*, Volume I, University of North Carolina Press, 1972; A. G. Norris, editor, *Deafness*, Professional Rehabilitation Workers with the Adult Deaf, 1972; Norbert Enzer, editor, *Workbook for Pre-School Teachers*, University of North Carolina, 1978; I. M. Schlesinger and L. Namir, editors, *Sign Language of the Deaf*, Academic Press, 1978; L. S. Liben, editor, *Deaf Children: Developmental Perspectives*, Academic Press, 1978; I. Berlin and J. Noshpitz, editors, *Basic Handbook of Child Psychiatry*, Volume II and Volume IV, Basic Books, 1979; (with S. Margaret Lee) *Annual Review of Rehabilitation*, Springer Publishing Co., 1980.

Contributor to proceedings; contributor of about twenty articles and reviews to professional journals, including *Deaf American, California Medicine, Volta Review, Hearing and Speech News, Community Mental Health Journal*, and others. Member of editorial board of *American Annals of the Deaf*.

WORK IN PROGRESS: Infancy and deafness, longitudinal studies of deaf youths.

BIOGRAPHICAL/CRITICAL SOURCES: American Medical News, June 17, 1974.

*   *   *

SCHOENFELD, Clarence Albert 1918-

PERSONAL: Born December 16, 1918, in Mineral Point, Wis.; son of Albert Henry (a minister) and Leda (Jones) Schoenfeld; married Jane Showe, 1944; married second wife, Sheryl Stateler Smith, 1969; children: (first marriage) Lee, Laurie, Lisbeth. *Education:* University of Wisconsin—Madison, B.A., 1941, M.A., 1949. *Religion:* Congregational. *Home:* 312 South Owen Dr., Madison, Wis. 53705. *Office:* 433 North Murray St., Madison, Wis. 53706.

CAREER: Leader, Lake Mills, Wis., city editor, 1936-38; *Wisconsin State Journal*, Madison, reporter, 1936-40; *Wisconsin Alumnus*, Madison, editor, 1946-48; University of Wisconsin—Madison, associate director of news service, 1949-51, assistant professor, 1953-56, associate professor of journalism, 1956-64, professor of journalism and mass communications, and affiliate professor of wildlife ecology, 1966—, assistant to president, 1949-51, assistant to dean of Extension Division, 1953-56, associate director of summer sessions, 1956-64, director, 1966—, assistant chancellor of University Center System, 1964-66, chairman of Center for Environmental Communications and Education Studies, 1966—, director of Office of Inter-College Programs, 1973—. Past president, North Central Conference of Summer Schools and American Summer Sessions Senate. Consultant to foundations, federal resource management agencies, and environmental science centers. Freelance magazine writer. *Military service:* U.S. Army, 1941-46, 1951-53; became captain. U.S. Army Reserve, 1956-74; retired as colonel. *Member:* Association for Education in Journalism, National Association for Environmental Education (past president), Association of University Summer Sessions (past

president), American Forestry Association, Wildlife Society, Phi Beta Kappa, Phi Kappa Phi, Sigma Nu, Sigma Delta Chi.

WRITINGS: (Contributor) *Outdoors Unlimited*, Barnes & Noble, 1949; *The University and Its Publics*, Harper, 1954; *Effective Feature Writing*, Harper, 1960; *The Shape of Summer Sessions to Come*, University of Wisconsin Press, 1961; *Publicity Media and Methods*, Macmillan, 1963; *Year-Round Education*, Dembar Educational Research Services, 1964; *University Extension*, Center for Applied Research in Education, 1965; *Wisconsin Sideroads to Somewhere*, Dembar Educational Research Services, 1966; *The American University in Summer*, University of Wisconsin Press, 1967; *Cabins, Conservation and Fun*, Barnes & Noble, 1968; *Everybody's Ecology*, Barnes & Noble, 1971; *The Outreach University*, Office of Inter-College Programs, University of Wisconsin, 1977; (with John Hendee) *Wildlife Management in Wilderness*, Boxwood Press, 1978; *Down Wisconsin Sideroads*, Tamarack Press, 1979; *Environmental Communication*, ERIC/SMEAC, 1980; (with Karen Diegmueller) *Self-Help Guide to Effective Feature Writing and Selling*, Holt, 1982.

Editor: (With Ruth Hine) *Canada Goose Management*, Dembar Educational Research Services, 1968; *Outlines of Environmental Education*, Dembar Educational Research Services, 1971; (with Hendee) *Human Dimensions in Wildlife Programs*, Wildlife Management Institute, 1973; *Interpreting Environmental Issues*, Dembar Educational Research Services, 1973; (with John Disinger) *Environmental Education in Action*, Center for Science, Mathematics, and Environmental Education, Volume I, 1977, Volume II, 1978, Volume III, 1979; (with Renee Guellerie) *Environmental Communication Research*, ERIC/SMEAC, 1979. Executive editor and founder, *Journal of Environmental Education*, 1969-75.

WORK IN PROGRESS: Interpreting Public Issues, for Random House.

*   *   *

SCHOENFELD, Hanns Martin W(alter) 1928-

PERSONAL: Born July 12, 1928, in Leipzig, Germany; came to United States in 1962, naturalized in 1968; son of Alwin (a school principal) and Lisbeth (Kirbach) Schoenfeld; married Margit Frese, August, 1956; stepchildren: Gabriele Martina (Mrs. Derek S. Robinson). *Education:* University of Hamburg, Diplom-Kaufmann, 1952, Dr. rer. pol., 1954; Technical University of Braunschweig, Dr. habil., 1966. *Religion:* Episcopalian. *Home:* 1014 Devonshire Dr., Champaign, Ill. 61820. *Office:* Department of Accountancy, University of Illinois, 211 Commerce West, 1206 South Sixth St., Champaign, Ill. 61820.

CAREER: Junior accountant for certified public accounting firm in Hamburg, Germany, 1948-55; University of Hamburg, Hamburg, research assistant, 1955-56; German Productivity Center, Darmstadt, Germany, business consultant, 1957-62; University of Illinois at Urbana-Champaign, assistant professor, 1962-65, associate professor, 1965-68, professor of accountancy and business administration, 1968-76, Weldon Powell Professor of Accountancy, 1976—, director of West European studies, 1980—. Lecturer at European management development institutes in Germany, Austria, France, and Switzerland, 1957-62; visiting professor at Technical University of Braunschweig, 1966, University of Michigan, 1972, Technical University of Berlin, intermittent, 1965-74, Free University of Berlin, 1972-73, and University of Lodz, 1975. *Military service:* German Army, 1944-46; held prisoner of war, 1945-46.

MEMBER: Academy of Accounting Historians (vice-president, 1976-77; president, 1978-79; member of board of trustees),

Academy of International Business, American Accounting Association (chairman of International Accounting section, 1976-77), American Association of University Professors, Verband der Hochschullehrer fuer Betriebswirtschaft, German Association of Work Study. *Awards, honors:* Organization for European Economic Cooperation fellowship to University of Illinois, 1956.

WRITINGS: (With W. Sommer) *Management Dictionary,* Walter DeGruyter, Volume I: *English-German,* 1960, 5th edition, 1979, Volume II: *German-English,* 1961, 4th edition, 1978; *Fuehrungsausbildung im Betrieb* (title means "Management Development within the Firm"), Betriebswirtschaftlicher Verlag Th. Gabler, 1960; *Kostenrechnung* (title means "Cost Accounting"), C. E. Poeschel, 1961, 7th edition published in three volumes, 1974-75; *Planung* (title means "Business Planning"), Betriegswirtschaftlicher Verlag Th. Gabler, 1963; *Finanzwesen mit Case Studies* (title means "The Financing Function"), German Productivity Center, 1963; *Grundlagen des Rechnungswesens* (title means "Introduction to Accounting"), C. E. Poeschel, 1964, 2nd edition, 1969; *Die Fuehrungsausbildung im Betrieblichen Funktionsgefuege* (title means "Management Development as a Function of the Firm"), Betriebswirtschaftlicher Verlag Th. Gabler, 1967.

(With G. M. Scott and others) *An Introduction to Financial Control and Reporting in Multinational Enterprises,* Bureau of Business Research, University of Texas, 1973; *Cost Terminology and Cost Theory: A Study of Its Development and Present State in Central Europe* (monograph), Center for International Education and Research in Accounting, University of Illinois, 1974; (editor) *The Status of Social Reporting in Selected Countries,* Center for International Education and Research in Accounting, 1978; (editor with Jagdish N. Sheth) *Export Marketing: Lessons from Europe,* Bureau of Business and Economic Research, 1981.

Contributor of over eighty articles to professional journals. Member of editorial board of *Management International Review,* 1970, *International Journal of Accounting,* 1975, *Journal of International Business Studies,* 1980—, and *Accounting Historians Journal,* 1980—.

WORK IN PROGRESS: Research interests include international accounting, management accounting, social accounting, corporate social responsibility, and management development.

AVOCATIONAL INTERESTS: Music, literature, foreign affairs, travel.

*   *   *

SCHOOLFIELD, George C(larence) 1925-

PERSONAL: Born August 14, 1925, in Charleston, W.Va.; son of Raymond Roy and Bernice (Stalnaker) Schoolfield; married Gloria Della Selva, 1949; children: Susan Rand, Marguerite Roy. *Education:* University of Cincinnati, A.B., 1946, M.A., 1947; Princeton University, Ph.D., 1949. *Home:* 50 Tokeneke Dr., Hamden, Conn. 06518. *Office:* Department of Germanic Language and Literature, Yale University, New Haven, Conn. 06520.

CAREER: Harvard University, Cambridge, Mass., instructor in German, 1949-52; University of Buffalo (now State University of New York at Buffalo), assistant professor, 1952-55, associate professor of German, 1955-59; Duke University, Durham, N.C., associate professor of German, 1959-61; University of Cincinnati, Cincinnati, Ohio, professor of German and Scandinavian and chairman of department, 1961-64; University of Pennsylvania, Philadelphia, professor of German

language and literature, 1964-69; Yale University, New Haven, Conn., professor of German and Scandinavian literature, 1969—. Visiting professor at University of Florida, 1971, Graduate School and University Center of the City University of New York, 1971-72, and Harvard University, 1980. *Member:* Modern Language Association of America, Society for the Advancement of Scandinavian Studies, American Association of Teachers of German, Swedish Literary Society (Finland; corresponding member). *Awards, honors:* Fulbright research fellowship, 1952-53, 1967-68, and 1972; Guggenheim fellow, 1955-56; American Council of Learned Societies grant, 1960, 1966; Colston Foundation fellow, 1962; grants from German government, 1964, Swedish government, 1975, and Finnish government, 1976; Institute for Advanced Study in the Humanities fellow, University of Einburgh, 1978, 1981.

WRITINGS: The Figure of the Musician in German Literature, University of North Carolina Press, 1956; *The German Lyric of the Baroque in English Translation,* University of North Carolina Press, 1961; (translator) Fredrik Book, *Hans Christian Andersen,* University of Oklahoma Press, 1962; (translator) Hagar Olsson, *The Woodcarver and Death,* University of Wisconsin Press, 1965; *Rilke's Last Year,* University of Kansas Press, 1969; (editor with Donald Crosby) *Studies in the German Drama: A Festschrift in Honor of Walter Silz,* University of North Carolina Press, 1974; *Swedo-Finnish Short Stories,* American-Scandinavian Foundation, 1974; (translator) A. M. Nagler, *The Medieval Religious Stage,* Yale University Press, 1976; (translator) Henning Fenger, *Kierkegaard-Myths and Kierkegaard Sources,* Yale University Press, 1980; *Janus Secundus,* Twayne, 1980. Contributor to professional journals. *Scandinavian Studies,* managing editor, 1969-73, review editor, 1973-76, associate managing editor, 1976—.

*   *   *

SCHUBERT, Glendon 1918-

PERSONAL: Born June 7, 1918, in Oneida, N.Y.; married; five children. *Education:* Syracuse University, A.B. (magna cum laude), 1940, Ph.D., 1948. *Office:* Department of Political Science, University of Hawaii—Manoa, Honolulu, Hawaii 96822.

CAREER: Syracuse University, Syracuse, N.Y., instructor, 1947-48; University of California, Los Angeles, instructor in political science, 1948-49; Howard University, Washington, D.C., visiting assistant professor of government, 1949-50; Rutgers University, New Brunswick, N.J., lecturer, 1950-51; Franklin and Marshall College, Lancaster, Pa., chairman of department of political science, 1951-52; Michigan State University, East Lansing, assistant professor, 1952-55, associate professor, 1955-58, professor of political science, 1958-67; University of North Carolina at Chapel Hill, William Rand Kenan, Jr., Professor, 1967-68; York University, Toronto, Ontario, university professor, 1968-70; University of Hawaii—Manoa, Honolulu, university professor, 1971—. Visiting professor, Syracuse University, 1950, University of Minnesota, 1955, and University of Hawaii, 1966-67; Fulbright lecturer, University of Oslo, 1959-60. Center for Advanced Study in the Behavioral Sciences fellow, 1960-61; senior scholar-in-residence, East-West Center, University of Hawaii, 1963-65; Fulbright research scholar in the Netherlands, 1977; National Science Foundation fellow, University of Groningen, 1977-78; NATO senior fellow in the United Kingdom, 1978; Center for Advanced Study in the Humanities and Social Sciences fellow, 1978-79. *Military service:* U.S. Army, Signal Corps (Intelligence), 1942-46; became first lieutenant; awarded Bronze Star.

MEMBER: International Political Science Association, International Society for Political Psychology, International Society for Human Ethology, International Primatological Society, Animal Behavior Society, Association for Politics and the Life Sciences (member of council, 1980—), American Political Science Association (member of council, 1967-69), American Society of Primatologists, Phi Beta Kappa. *Awards, honors:* American Philosophical Society research grant, 1957; Rockefeller Foundation research grant, 1958; Social Science Research Council grant-in-aid, 1963; Regents' Medal and Award for Excellence in Research, University of Hawaii, 1975.

WRITINGS: The Presidency in the Courts, University of Minnesota Press, 1957; *Quantitative Analysis of Judicial Behavior,* Free Press of Glencoe, 1959; *Constitutional Politics: The Political Behavior of Supreme Court Justices and the Constitutional Policies That They Make,* Holt, 1960; *The Public Interest: A Critique of the Theory of a Political Concept,* Free Press of Glencoe, 1961; (editor) *Judicial Decision-Making,* Free Press of Glencoe, 1963; (editor) *Judicial Behavior: A Reader in Theory and Research,* Rand McNally, 1964; (editor) *Reapportionment,* Scribner, 1965; *Judicial Policy-Making,* Scott, Foresman, 1965; *The Judicial Mind: The Attitudes and Ideologies of Supreme Court Justices,* Northwestern University Press, 1965; (editor) *Dispassionate Justice: A Synthesis of the Judicial Opinions of Robert H. Jackson,* Bobbs-Merrill, 1969; (editor with Takeyoshi Kawashima) *Comparative Judicial Behavior,* Oxford University Press, 1969; *The Constitutional Polity,* Boston University Press, 1970; (co-author) *American National Government: Policy and Politics,* Scott, Foresman, 1971; *The Judicial Mind Revisited,* Oxford University Press, 1974; *Human Jurisprudence,* University Press of Hawaii, 1975; *Political Attitudes and Ideologies: A Cross-Cultural Interdisciplinary Approach,* Sage Publications, 1977; *Comparative Judicial Study: Switzerland and South Africa,* 2nd edition, Interuniversity Consortium for Political and Social Research, 1981.

Also author of monographs. Contributor of more than sixty articles to political science, law, biology, and life science journals. Member of board of editors, *Midwest Journal of Political Science,* 1956-69, *Journal of Social and Biological Structures,* 1978—, and *Behavioral and Brain Sciences,* 1981—.

WORK IN PROGRESS: Editing *The Biology of Primate Social Behavior.*

*   *   *

SCHULZ, Charles M(onroe) 1922-

PERSONAL: Born November 26, 1922, in Minneapolis, Minn.; son of Carl (a barber) and Dena (Halverson) Schulz; married Joyce Halverson, April 18, 1949 (divorced, 1972); married Jean Clyde, 1973; children: (first marriage) Meredith, Charles Monroe, Craig, Amy, Jill. *Education:* Studied cartooning in an art school after graduation in 1940 from public high school in St. Paul, Minn. *Office:* Number One Snoopy Place, Santa Rosa, Calif. 95401.

CAREER: Cartoonist and illustrator. Art instructor at Art Instruction Schools, Inc. (correspondence school), Minneapolis, Minn.; cartoonist, *St. Paul Pioneer Press* and *Saturday Evening Post,* 1948-49; creator of syndicated comic strip, "Peanuts," 1950. *Military service:* U.S. Army, 1943-45, served with Twentieth Armored Division in Europe; became staff sergeant.

AWARDS, HONORS: Reuben Award as outstanding cartoonist of the year, National Cartoonists' Society, 1955 and 1964; Yale

Humor Award as outstanding humorist of the year, 1956; School Bell Award, National Education Association, 1960; L.H.D., Anderson College, 1963; Peabody Award and Emmy Award, both 1966, for CBS cartoon special, "A Charlie Brown Christmas"; D.H.L., St. Mary's College of California, 1969; Charles M. Schulz Award, United Feature Syndicate, 1980, for his contribution in the field of cartooning.

WRITINGS—Cartoon books, many collected from newspaper work: *Peanuts,* Rinehart, 1952; *More Peanuts* (also see below), Rinehart, 1954; *Good Grief, More Peanuts!* (also see below), Rinehart, 1956; *Good Ol' Charlie Brown* (also see below), Rinehart, 1957; *Snoopy* (also see below), Rinehart, 1958; *Young Pillars,* Warner Press, 1958; *But We Love You, Charlie Brown* (also see below), Rinehart, 1959; *Peanuts Revisited: Favorites Old and New,* Rinehart, 1959; *You're Out of Your Mind, Charlie Brown* (also see below), Rinehart, 1959.

"Teenager" Is Not a Disease, Warner Press, 1961; *Happiness Is a Warm Puppy,* Determined Productions, 1962, enlarged edition, 1979; *Security Is a Thumb and a Blanket,* Determined Productions, 1963; *Christmas Is Together-Time,* Determined Productions, 1964; *I Need All the Friends I Can Get,* Determined Productions, 1964, reprinted, 1981; *What Was Bugging Ol' Pharaoh?,* Warner Press, 1964; *A Charlie Brown Christmas* (adapted from the television production; also see below), World Publishing, 1965; *Love Is Walking Hand in Hand,* Determined Productions, 1965; *Charlie Brown's All-Stars* (adapted from the television production; also see below), World Publishing, 1966; *Home Is on Top of a Doghouse,* Determined Productions, 1966; *Charlie Brown's Reflections,* Hallmark, 1967; *Happiness Is a Sad Song,* Determined Productions, 1967; *It's the Great Pumpkin, Charlie Brown* (adapted from the television production; also see below), World Publishing, 1967; *Teenagers, Unite!,* Bantam, 1967; *"He's Your Dog, Charlie Brown!"* (adapted from the television production; also see below), World Publishing, 1968; *Suppertime!,* Determined Productions, 1968; *You're in Love, Charlie Brown* (adapted from the television production; also see below), World Publishing, 1968; *Charlie Brown's Yearbook* (includes *"He's Your Dog, Charlie Brown!," It's the Great Pumpkin, Charlie Brown, You're in Love, Charlie Brown,* and *Charlie Brown's All-Stars*), World Publishing, 1969; *Peanuts School Year Date Book, 1969-1970,* Determined Productions, 1969.

For Five Cents, Determined Productions, 1970; *It Was a Short Summer, Charlie Brown* (adapted from the television production; also see below), World Publishing, 1970; *It Really Doesn't Take Much to Make a Dad Happy,* Determined Productions, 1970; *Peanuts Date Book 1972,* Determined Productions, 1970; *It's Fun to Lie Here and Listen to the Sounds of the Night,* Determined Productions, 1970; *The World According to Lucy,* Hallmark, 1970; *Winning May Not Be Everything, But Losing Isn't Anything!,* Determined Productions, 1970; *Play It Again, Charlie Brown* (adapted from the television production; also see below), World Publishing, 1971; *You're Elected, Charlie Brown* (also see below), World Publishing, 1972; *Snoopy's Secret Life,* Hallmark, 1972; *The Peanuts Philosophers,* Hallmark, 1972; *Love a la Peanuts,* Hallmark, 1972; *It's Good to Have a Friend,* Hallmark, 1972; *A Charlie Brown Thanksgiving,* Random House, 1974; *There's No Time for Love, Charlie Brown* (adapted from the television production; also see below), Random House, 1974; *It's a Mystery, Charlie Brown,* Random House, 1975; *Be My Valentine, Charlie Brown,* Random House, 1976; *It's the Easter Beagle, Charlie Brown* (adapted from the television production; also see below), Random House, 1976; *You're a Good Sport, Charlie Brown,* Random House, 1976; *Hooray for You, Charlie Brown,* Random House, 1977; *It's Another Holiday, Charlie Brown,* Random House, 1977;

Summers Fly, Winters Walk (also see below), Volumes I-II, Holt, 1977, Volume III, Fawcett, 1980; *It's Arbor Day, Charlie Brown* (adapted from the television production; also see below), Random House, 1977; *The Loves of Snoopy*, Hodder & Stoughton, 1978; *Lucy Rules OK?*, Hodder & Stoughton, 1978; *The Misfortunes of Charlie Brown*, Hodder & Stoughton, 1978; *Snoopy and His Friends*, Hodder & Stoughton, 1978; *What a Nightmare, Charlie Brown*, Random House, 1978; *It's Your First Kiss, Charlie Brown* (adapted from the television production; also see below), Random House, 1978.

Bon Voyage, Charlie Brown, and Don't Come Back! (adapted from the film production; also see below), Random House, 1980; *You're Not Elected, Charlie Brown*, Scholastic Book Services, 1980; *Life Is a Circus, Charlie Brown* (adapted from the television production; also see below), Random House, 1981; *She's a Good Skate, Charlie Brown* (adapted from the television production; also see below), Random House, 1981.

Published by Holt: *Go Fly a Kite, Charlie Brown* (also see below), 1960; *Peanuts Every Sunday* (also see below), 1961; *It's a Dog's Life, Charlie Brown* (also see below), 1962; *Snoopy Come Home* (also see below), 1962; *You Can't Win, Charlie Brown* (also see below), 1962; *You Can Do It, Charlie Brown* (also see below), 1963; *As You Like It, Charlie Brown* (also see below), 1964; *We're Right Behind You, Charlie Brown* (also see below), 1964.

There's a Vulture Outside, 1965; *Sunday's Fun Day, Charlie Brown* (also see below), 1965; *You Need Help, Charlie Brown* (also see below), 1965; *Snoopy and the Red Baron*, 1966; *The Unsinkable Charlie Brown* (also see below), 1966; *What's Wrong with Being Crabby?*, 1966; *Who's the Funny-Looking Kid with the Big Nose?*, 1966; *You're Something Else, Charlie Brown: A New Peanuts Book* (also see below), 1967; *It's a Long Way to Tipperary*, 1967; *You'll Flip, Charlie Brown* (also see below), 1967; *Peanuts Treasury* (American Library Association Notable Book), foreword by Johnny Hart, 1968; *You're You, Charlie Brown: A New Peanuts Book* (also see below), 1968; *A Boy Named Charlie Brown* (adapted from the film production; also see below), 1969; *You've Had It, Charlie Brown: A New Peanuts Book* (also see below), 1969; *Snoopy and His Sopwith Camel*, 1969.

Peanuts Classics, 1970; *Snoopy and "It Was a Dark and Stormy Night,"* 1970; *You're Out of Sight, Charlie Brown: A New Peanuts Book* (also see below), 1970; *You've Come a Long Way, Charlie Brown: A New Peanuts Book* (also see below), 1971; *"Ha Ha, Herman," Charlie Brown: A New Peanuts Book* (also see below), 1972; *Snoopy's Grand Slam*, 1972; *The "Snoopy, Come Home" Movie Book* (adapted from the film production; also see below), 1972; *Thompson Is in Trouble, Charlie Brown: A New Peanuts Book* (also see below), 1973; *You're the Guest of Honor, Charlie Brown: A New Peanuts Book* (also see below), 1973; *The Snoopy Festival*, 1974; *Win a Few, Lose a Few, Charlie Brown: A New Peanuts Book* (also see below), 1974.

Speak Softly, and Carry a Beagle: A New Peanuts Book (also see below), 1975; *Don't Hassle Me with Your Sighs, Chuck*, 1976; *"I Never Promised You an Apple Orchard": The Collected Writings of Snoopy, Being a Compendium of His Puns, Correspondence, Cautionary Tales, Witticisms, Titles Original and Borrowed, with Critical Commentary by His Friends, and, Published for the First Time in Its Entirety, the Novel "Toodle-oo, Caribou!," a Tale of the Frozen North*, 1976; *Always Stick Up for the Underbird: Cartoons from "Good Grief, More Peanuts!," and "Good Ol' Charlie Brown,"* 1977; *It's Great to Be a Superstar: Cartoons from "You're Out of Sight, Charlie Brown," and "You've Come a Long Way, Charlie Brown,"*

1977; *How Long, Great Pumpkin, How Long?: Cartoons from "You're the Guest of Honor, Charlie Brown," and "Win a Few, Lose a Few, Charlie Brown,"* 1977; *It's Hard Work Being Bitter: Cartoons from "Thompson Is in Trouble, Charlie Brown," and "You're the Guest of Honor, Charlie Brown,"* 1977; *There Goes the Shutout: Cartoons from "More Peanuts" and "Good Grief, More Peanuts!,"* 1977; *My Anxieties Have Anxieties: Cartoons from "You're You, Charlie Brown," and "You've Had It, Charlie Brown,"* 1977; *Sandlot Peanuts*, introduction by Joe Garagiola, 1977; *A Smile Makes a Lousy Umbrella: Cartoons from "You're Something Else, Charlie Brown," and "You're You, Charlie Brown,"* 1977; *Stop Snowing on My Secretary: Cartoons from "You've Come a Long Way, Charlie Brown," and "'Ha Ha, Herman,' Charlie Brown,"* 1977; *The Beagle Has Landed* (also see below), 1978; *Race for Your Life, Charlie Brown* (adapted from the television production; also see below), 1978; *Snoopy's Tennis Book: Featuring Snoopy at Wimbledon and Snoopy's Tournament Tips*, introduction by Billie Jean King, 1979; *And a Woodstock in a Birch Tree*, (also see below), 1979.

Here Comes the April Fool!, 1980; *Things I Learned After It Was Too Late (and Other Minor Truths)*, 1981; *Dr. Beagle and Mr. Hyde*, 1981. Also author of *Fly, You Stupid Kite, Fly, A Kiss on the Nose Turns Anger Aside, The Mad Punter Strikes Again, Thank Goodness for People, What Makes Musicians So Sarcastic?*, and *What Makes You Think You're So Happy?*.

Published by Fawcett: *Good Ol' Snoopy* (contains selections from *Snoopy*), 1958; *Wonderful World of Peanuts* (contains selections from *More Peanuts*), 1963; *Hey, Peanuts!* (contains selections from *More Peanuts*), 1963; *Good Grief, Charlie Brown!* (contains selections from *Good Grief, More Peanuts!*), 1963; *For the Love of Peanuts* (contains selections from *Good Grief, More Peanuts!*), 1963; *Fun with Peanuts* (contains selections from *Good Ol' Charlie Brown*), 1964; *Here Comes Charlie Brown* (contains selections from *Good Ol' Charlie Brown*), 1964.

Very Funny, Charlie Brown! (contains selections from *You're Out of Your Mind, Charlie Brown!*), 1965; *What Next, Charlie Brown?* (contains selections from *You're Out of Your Mind, Charlie Brown!*), 1965; *Here Comes Snoopy* (contains selections from *Snoopy*), 1966; *We're On Your Side, Charlie Brown* (contains selections from *But We Love You, Charlie Brown*), 1966; *You Are Too Much, Charlie Brown* (contains selections from *But We Love You, Charlie Brown*), 1966; *You're a Winner, Charlie Brown* (contains selections from *Go Fly a Kite, Charlie Brown*), 1967; *Let's Face It, Charlie Brown* (contains selections from *Go Fly a Kite, Charlie Brown*), 1967; *Who Do You Think You Are, Charlie Brown?* (contains selections from *Peanuts Every Sunday*), 1968; *You're My Hero, Charlie Brown* (contains selections from *Peanuts Every Sunday*), 1968; *This Is Your Life, Charlie Brown* (contains selections from *It's a Dog's Life, Charlie Brown*), 1968; *Slide, Charlie Brown, Slide* (contains selections from *It's a Dog's Life, Charlie Brown*), 1968; *All This and Snoopy, Too* (contains selections from *You Can't Win, Charlie Brown*), 1969; *Here's to You, Charlie Brown* (contains selections from *You Can't Win, Charlie Brown*), 1969; *Nobody's Perfect, Charlie Brown* (contains selections from *You Can Do It, Charlie Brown*), 1969; *You're a Brave Man, Charlie Brown* (contains selections from *You Can Do It, Charlie Brown*), 1969.

Peanuts for Everybody (contains selections from *We're Right Behind You, Charlie Brown*), 1970; *You've Done It Again, Charlie Brown* (contains selections from *We're Right Behind You, Charlie Brown*), 1970; *We Love You, Snoopy* (contains selections from *Snoopy, Come Home*), 1970; *It's for You, Snoopy* (contains selections from *Sunday's Fun Day, Charlie Brown*), 1971; *Have It Your Way, Charlie Brown* (contains selections from *Sunday's Fun Day, Charlie Brown*), 1971; *You're Not for Real, Snoopy* (contains selections from *You Need Help, Charlie Brown*), 1971; *You're a Pal, Snoopy* (contains selections from *You Need Help, Charlie Brown*), 1972; *What Now, Charlie Brown?* (contains selections from *The Unsinkable Charlie Brown*), 1972; *You're Something Special, Snoopy!* (contains selections from *The Unsinkable Charlie Brown*), 1972; *You've Got a Friend, Charlie Brown* (contains selections from *You'll Flip, Charlie Brown*), 1972; *Who Was That Dog I Saw You With, Charlie Brown?* (contains selections from *You're You, Charlie Brown*), 1973; *There's No One Like You, Snoopy* (contains selections from *You're You, Charlie Brown*), 1973.

It's All Yours, Snoopy (contains selections from *You've Come a Long Way, Charlie Brown*), 1975; *Peanuts Double,* Volume I, 1976, Volume II, 1978; *Watch Out, Charlie Brown* (contains selections from *You're Out of Sight, Charlie Brown*), 1977; *You' Got to Be You, Snoopy* (contains selections from *You've Come a Long Way, Charlie Brown*), 1978; *You're on Your Own, Snoopy* (contains selections from "*Ha Ha, Herman,*" *Charlie Brown*), 1978; *You Can't Win Them All, Charlie Brown* (contains selections from "*Ha Ha, Herman,*" *Charlie Brown*), 1978; *It's Your Turn, Snoopy* (contains selections from *You're the Guest of Honor, Charlie Brown*), 1978; *You Asked for It, Charlie Brown* (contains selections from *You're the Guest of Honor, Charlie Brown*), 1978; *It's Show Time, Snoopy* (contains selections from *Speak Softly, and Carry a Beagle*), 1978; *You've Got to Be Kidding, Snoopy,* 1978; *They're Playing Your Song, Charlie Brown,* 1978; *You're So Smart, Snoopy* (contains selections from *You're Out of Sight, Charlie Brown*), 1978; *Charlie Brown and Snoopy* (contains selections from *As You Like It, Charlie Brown*), 1978; *You're the Greatest, Charlie Brown* (contains selections from *As You Like It, Charlie Brown*), 1978; *Try It Again, Charlie Brown* (contains selections from *You're Something Else, Charlie Brown*), 1978; *Your Choice, Snoopy* (contains selections from *You're Something Else, Charlie Brown*), 1978; *Take It Easy, Charlie Brown* (contains selections from *You'll Flip, Charlie Brown*), 1978; *You've Got It Made, Snoopy* (contains selections from *You've Had It, Charlie Brown*), 1978; *Don't Give Up, Charlie Brown* (contains selections from *You've Had It, Charlie Brown*), 1978; *That's Life, Snoopy* (contains selections from *Thompson Is in Trouble, Charlie Brown*), 1978; *You've Come a Long Way, Snoopy* (contains selections from *Thompson Is in Trouble, Charlie Brown*), 1979; *Play Ball, Snoopy* (contains selections from *Win a Few, Lose a Few, Charlie Brown*), 1979; *Let's Hear It for Dinner, Snoopy,* 1979; *Keep Up the Good Work, Charlie Brown,* 1979; *Think Thinner, Snoopy,* 1979.

Stay with It, Snoopy (contains selections from *Summers Fly, Winters Walk,* Volume III), 1980; *Sing for Your Supper, Snoopy,* 1981; *Snoopy, Top Dog* (contains selections from *The Beagle Has Landed*), 1981; *You're Our Kind of Dog, Snoopy* (contains selections from *And a Woodstock in a Birch Tree*), 1981. Also author of *Love and Kisses, Snoopy.*

"Snoopy's Facts and Fun Book" series; published by Random House: *Snoopy's Facts and Fun Book about Boats,* 1979; . . . *about Houses,* 1979; . . . *about Planes,* 1979; . . . *about Seasons,* 1979; . . . *about Farms,* 1980; . . . *about Nature,* 1980; . . . *about Seashores,* 1980; . . . *about Trucks,* 1980.

Other books: *Peanuts Project Book,* Determined Productions, 1963; (with Kenneth F. Hall) *Two-by-Fours: A Sort of Serious Book about Small Children,* Warner Press, 1965; (contributor) Jeffrey H. Loria and others, *What's It All About, Charlie Brown?: Peanuts Kids Look at America Today,* Holt, 1968; (contributor)

Robert L. Short, *The Parables of Peanuts,* Harper, 1968; (with Lee Mendelson) *Charlie Brown and Charlie Schultz: In Celebration of the Twentieth Anniversary of Peanuts,* World Publishing, 1970; (author of foreword) Morrie Turner, *Nipper,* Westminster, 1970; (with Kathryn Wentzel Lumley) *Snoopy's Secret Code Book* (spelling and pronunciation guide), Holt, 1971; *The Charlie Brown Dictionary,* Random House, 1973; *Peanuts Jubilee: My Life and Art with Charlie Brown and Others,* Holt, 1975; *Charlie Brown's Super Book of Things to Do and Collect: Based on the Charles M. Schulz Characters,* Random House, 1975; *Charlie Brown's Super Book of Questions and Answers about All Kinds of Animals from Snails to People!,* Random House, 1976; *Charlie Brown's Second Super Book of Questions and Answers: About the Earth and Space from Plants to Planets!,* Random House, 1977; *Charlie Brown's Third Super Book of Questions and Answers: About All Kinds of Boats and Planes, Cars and Trains, and Other Things That Move!,* Random House, 1978; *Charlie Brown's Fourth Super Book of Questions and Answers: About All Kinds of People and How They Live!,* Random House, 1979; (with Mendelson) *Happy Birthday, Charlie Brown,* Random House, 1979; (with R. Smith Kiliper) *Charlie Brown, Snoopy and Me: And All the Other Peanuts Characters,* Doubleday, 1980; *Charlie Brown's Fifth Super Book of Questions and Answers: About All Kinds of Things and How They Work!,* Random House, 1981.

Teleplays—26-minute animated cartoons, produced for CBS-TV: "A Charlie Brown Christmas," December 9, 1965; "Charlie Brown's All-Stars," June 8, 1966; "It's the Great Pumpkin, Charlie Brown," October 27, 1966; "You're in Love, Charlie Brown," June 12, 1967; "He's Your Dog, Charlie Brown!," February 14, 1968; "It Was a Short Summer, Charlie Brown," September 27, 1969; "Play It Again, Charlie Brown," March 28, 1971; "It's the Easter Beagle, Charlie Brown," 1972; "You're Elected, Charlie Brown," October 29, 1972; "There's No Time for Love, Charlie Brown," March 11, 1973; "Race for Your Life, Charlie Brown," January, 1976; "It's Arbor Day, Charlie Brown," March 16, 1976; "It's Your First Kiss, Charlie Brown," 1978; "Life Is a Circus, Charlie Brown," 1981; "She's a Good Skate, Charlie Brown," 1981. Also writer of screenplays for feature-length animated films, "A Boy Named Charlie Brown," National General Pictures, 1969, "Snoopy, Come Home," National General Pictures, 1972, and "Bon Voyage, Charlie Brown, and Don't Come Back!," 1980.

Illustrator: Art Linkletter, *Kids Say the Darndest Things,* Prentice-Hall, 1957; Linkletter, *Kids Still Say the Darndest Things,* Geis, 1961; Bill Adler, compiler, *Dear President Johnson,* Morrow, 1964; Fritz Ridenour, editor, *I'm a Good Man, But . . . ,* Regal Books, 1969; June Dutton, *Peanuts Cookbook,* Determined Productions, 1969; Dutton, *Peanuts Lunch Bag Cookbook,* Determined Productions, 1970; *All I Want for Christmas Is . . . : Open Letters to Santa,* Hallmark, 1972; Evelyn Shaw, *The Snoopy Doghouse Cook Book,* Determined Productions, 1979; *Tubby Book Featuring Snoopy,* Simon & Schuster, 1980.

SIDELIGHTS: Charles "Sparky" Schulz maintains that the only thing he "really ever wanted to be was a cartoonist." A great admirer of Roy Crane, George Herriman, Al Capp, and Milt Caniff in his youth, he had a hard time selling his own comic strip at first; United Feature Syndicate finally bought it in 1950 and named it "Peanuts." "I was very upset with the title . . . and still am," recalls Schulz, who wanted to name the strip "Li'l Folks." "Peanuts" started in eight newspapers and brought a $90-a-month income; according to Schulz, "it took a long time to develop. . . . In fact, the next twenty years saw a basic evolution of the strip." According to the public, however, the strip was a success right from the beginning.

Schulz is the only cartoonist ever to have won the Reuben Award (the cartoonist's equivalent of the "Oscar," designed by and named after Rube Goldberg) twice, in 1955 and again in 1964. In a *Saturday Review* article entitled "The Not-So-Peanuts World of Charles M. Schulz," John Tebbel writes that in 1969 "the total income from the strip, including that of its twenty-one licensed subsidiaries, [had] been estimated at [up to] $50,000,000 a year," and that "Peanuts" has "audiences in more than 1,000 newspapers in the U.S. and Canada, and more than 100 others in forty-one foreign countries. Charlie Brown and his friends speak in twelve languages around the world."

"Peanuts" has in fact become the most popular comic strip of all time. As Lee Mendelson points out in his biography of Schulz, "Charlie Brown has become *the* symbol of mid century America . . . because [he is] a basic reflection of his time," the "Mr. Anxious" of the age. Richard R. Lingeman writes in the *New York Times* that the "Peanuts" children "precociously know that life can be lousy and their popularity from the late fifties on may be due to their reflecting a secret, self-doubting, self-questioning mood abroad in the nation: Charlie Brown is everybody's loser because everybody is a loser much of the time. 'Peanuts' offers a gentle philosophy of human relations, of stoically coping with existence, that is the underside of the preachments of those eupeptic middle-class yea-sayers from Norman Vincent Peale to 'How to Be Your Own Best Friend.'" Commenting on the universality of the appeal of Charlie Brown, the perpetual loser, Schulz says in *Peanuts Jubilee:* "Readers are generally sympathetic toward a lead character who is rather gentle, sometimes put upon, and not always the brightest person. Perhaps this is the kind of person who is easiest to love. Charlie Brown has to be the one who suffers because he is a caricature of the average person. Most of us are much more acquainted with losing than we are with winning. Winning is great, but it isn't funny."

Nonetheless, Schultz contends that there really is no specific "philosophy" behind the strip, and that his "chief purpose is to get the strips done in time to get down to the post office by five o'clock when it closes."

Unlike many cartoonists, Schulz does all the work for the strip himself because, as Tebbel says, "'Peanuts' is so much a projection of the Schulz personality that it is inconceivable that anyone else could do it. . . . In the hierarchy of immortal comic strips—'Blondie,' 'Little Orphan Annie,' 'Andy Gump,' 'L'il Abner,' 'Krazy Kat'—Schulz has created something unique, more successful than all the others, but paradoxically more fragile. Perhaps it is because the strip is so personal that it elicits an unprecedented identification and affection from its vast readership." Schulz draws material for the strip from his own childhood memories and from his experiences in raising five children. The popularity of the strip "cuts across every kind of classification," writes Tebbel, "for all kinds of special reasons. Schroeder, the Beethoven-loving character who is usually seen playing the piano when he isn't playing baseball, appeals to people who had never heard of Beethoven before. The little tyrant Lucy is seen by the small fry as a deliciously contrary girl. . . . Linus, with his security blanket, seems to speak to everyone who would like to have a blanket of his own in troubled times. And Snoopy, the beagle who has Van Goghs hanging in his doghouse and a World War I aviator's helmet on his head, is the kind of fantasy dog everyone would like to own."

Schulz added an extra dimension to Charlie Brown with his introduction to television in 1965, and his associates, Lee Mendelson and Bill Melendez, plan to produce a new special every

year. "Peanuts" subsidiaries, licensed by Schulz's Creative Associates, Inc., manufacture everything from clothing, toys, stationery, and cosmetics to furniture, lunch boxes, and Charlie Brown baseballs, and dozens of new applications for licenses roll in every day. Reprints of "Peanuts," handled by seven different publishers at last count, have passed the 90,000,000 mark; Tebbel notes that Charlie Brown and his friends have even "emerged as modern evangelists" in Robert L. Short's two books, *The Gospel According to Peanuts* and *The Parables of Peanuts*. The hit musical, "You're a Good Man, Charlie Brown," adapted by Clark Gesner from the comic strip, was first produced Off-Broadway at Theatre 80 St. Marks, March 7, 1967, and has since played all over the world; it was also on NBC-TV's Hallmark Hall of Fame, February 9, 1973. The book of the same title, including music, lyrics, and adaptation by Gesner, was published by Random House in 1967, and an original cast recording of the music from the play was released by M-G-M Records the same year. A documentary on Schulz, produced by Mendelson and Melendez, was broadcast by CBS-TV in 1969. The musical "Snoopy!!!," opened at the Little Fox Theatre in San Francisco, December 8, 1975.

Snoopy has been adopted by NASA as a promotional device, and, notes Tebbel, "Snoopy emblems are now worn by more than 800 members of the manned space flight team as rewards for outstanding work." As everyone knows, the ubiquitous beagle made international history as the official name of the LEM (Lunar Excursion Module) of the Apollo 10 manned flight to the moon in 1969. Great Pumpkin sightings are reported almost as often as UFO's, and Schroeder and his toy piano have been immortalized in the stained glass window of the Westminster Presbyterian Church in Buffalo, New York, along with Bach, Martin Luther, Duke Ellington, and Dr. Albert Schweitzer. And all because, as Tebbel concludes, "everyone sees something different, and something of himself, in Charlie Brown and his friends. He's everybody's boy."

AVOCATIONAL INTERESTS: Outdoor sports, especially ice hockey and golf.

CA INTERVIEW

CA interviewed Charles Schulz by phone March 13, 1981, at his home in Santa Rosa, California.

CA: You've become a tremendous success by doing something that you love doing. Are there ever times in spite of that when you still feel like Charlie Brown?

SCHULZ: I never said I felt like Charlie Brown. It's like any other job—you go to work every day and try to do the best you can. I always worry that perhaps I'll hit some kind of a slump and never get out of it. Yesterday I sat here all day and I really only came up with one pretty good idea, but then I started off this morning all right, and I'm always trying to make the strip better. But this whole business about my being like Charlie Brown, that's just talk.

CA: You've described the early interest in the funnies that you shared with your father, and you collected comic books at one time. Do you still have any of that early collection?

SCHULZ: No. I wish I did. I had the very first comic magazine which was ever published, and I can still remember the day I bought it. I was in downtown Saint Paul with my mother and I came across this copy of *Famous Funnies* and I was delighted; here was a whole magazine with sixty-four pages of color comics in it. I couldn't believe it. I had that magazine for years, and now I don't have the slightest idea what happened to it.

CA: Do you have current favorite comic strips?

SCHULZ: Not really. Once you've been in it for a long while, I suppose it's like any profession; there are still a few that I like very much, but I'd rather not say which fellows I prefer over the others.

CA: Do you still read a lot of them?

SCHULZ: I read the *San Francisco Chronicle* every morning—I read the entire comic page—and then I read the evening paper which is published in Santa Rosa. But there are several strips that I don't bother to read anymore; I just think that they're so poorly done that it's boring.

CA: Leo Rosten describes humor as the "affectionate communication of insight." Do you think that's a good definition?

SCHULZ: Yes, I guess so. I think you just have to see things the way you as an individual see them and hope that you have a unique approach. The comic strip medium, of course, is not one that gets the critical attention that other forms of literature do. We're way down on the totem pole as far as being considered sophisticated goes. Nobody ever reviews comic strips. I guess that's a good definition of humor. I think the Hyman Kaplan pieces are some of the greatest humor ever written.

CA: Over the thirty years of its life, "Peanuts" has become quite a big business. You do the strip single-handedly, I know. How many people do you have working in your offices?

SCHULZ: We have one full-time receptionist who answers the phone and talks to people and answers letters. We have a part-time girl who comes in usually in the afternoons and answers a lot of the general children's mail, and there's another lady who sometimes doubles as a secretary but really deals with the licensed products. She has to see everything that comes in and keep a record of what is submitted and check on its quality. If there is any doubt in her mind, she always asks me to step in her office and we look at it together. She has to keep records of all of these things. Then I have a businessman, an accountant who has a room in the studio and keeps track of all the financial aspects of what is going on, and now United Feature Syndicate has a man in our office here who also helps with the licensing.

CA: You've written a bit about your own children. Did they take an active interest in the strip as youngsters?

SCHULZ: They always liked the strip, and this was very important to me and very gratifying. I would have been quite disappointed if they had felt that it wasn't really worthwhile or it wasn't funny, or it was just silly or trite; but they always read all the books, and I guess the most flattering thing of all is that they would frequently ask for some of the originals themselves. If you were to visit them, you'd find that they have originals hanging on their walls. They were always asking for drawings for their friends, and they still do. This was very important to me.

CA: When they were very young, did you ever feel a great concern about their growing up in the affluence that your work had provided for them?

SCHULZ: I don't think about affluence as much as other people do. No. I never think of myself as being affluent.

CA: You get a tremendous amount of mail. Does the majority of it come from children or adults?

SCHULZ: We get a lot of mail from adults, but there's no doubt that the greater percentage comes from children. Of course, teachers have writing projects; they're always encouraging their classes to write, and they will frequently have these class projects where everybody has to write a letter to a so-called celebrity. Actually it's very annoying. There are a couple of other annoying aspects to the mail. One is that a lot of people write and don't include a legible return address, so you can't answer them. Some don't include a return address at all. Then others have no comprehension of the time element of mailing things; a student will write saying that he has a theme due Friday and has to write to somebody and would I respond right away, and I'll get the letter maybe a month after the theme was due. They just don't have any comprehension. I'm also astounded at the number of people who cannot spell the word *Snoopy*, who say, "*Snoppy* is my favorite character." How anyone can spell Snoopy S-n-o-p-p-y is beyond me. Yesterday I got a letter from a doctor who three times referred to *Snoppy*. One would hesitate to go to a doctor who can't spell Snoopy.

CA: How much of your mail comes from other countries?

SCHULZ: It's impossible to say how much, but we get a lot from Japan. Japanese children write very nice, neat, polite letters. I would say of all of the countries, if we had to name one we get the most mail from, it would be Japan. Japanese have liked the strip for twenty-five years. I think they admire things from the United States, and the strip has been very popular there.

CA: Do people ever send you their ideas for the strip?

SCHULZ: Not really, no. When I first started, it would happen a little bit, but apparently people know that I don't use them. One of the most peculiar things is the notion that when something becomes popular, it should then be used to educate. That, of course, is fatal; the quickest way to kill something would be suddenly to use it to educate. For example, if Peppermint Patty falls asleep in class, people write saying that we should do something to educate children to keep them from falling asleep in class. That of course, would immediately kill your whole idea. If you taught her how to stay awake, then you'd have to think of something else. People just have no comprehension of the difficulties of drawing a strip day after day, building up characters and themes and all of these things. It's very difficult and it's hard to sustain.

CA: There have been various attempts to interpret the strip from a theological or psychological point of view. How do you feel about this?

SCHULZ: Again, this is distorted. The only books that were written about the theological implications were written by Robert Short, and he was not really talking about what my strip was saying. What he was talking about was the ability to gather thoughts from all forms of literature than can lead to some sort of spiritual implications. Robert Short is quite a student of different forms of literature. He's very high on Kafka and Kierkegaard and Bonhoeffer. He realized that I had some things in there that other comic strips didn't have, so he wrote a thesis on the "Peanuts" strip. But he's the only one that's ever been given permission to do this. Since then we've had all sorts of people who have wanted to write a book about math or psychology or languages or anything you can think of, using the strip as the basis, but I always thought that we were very lucky to get away with it on the Robert Short books, and I didn't want to risk it on anything else. Besides, again, it could become very boring for people to see the strip being used for everything else by other people. I don't want other people using my strip that much, so we put a stop to that a long time ago.

CA: Have you ever sent a strip off and then wished that you had done it some other way?

SCHULZ: Not a particular script, but frequently something will work out very well and then you wish that you had been more careful with it from the beginning. One example would be Schroeder's playing the piano and another would be the Linus blanket thing. I think actually Charlie Brown was the first one to have a blanket. Then one thing led to another and I got some more ideas and I ended up giving the blanket to Linus. I think even the business with Schroeder playing the piano actually started with Charlie Brown singing a very light passage from Beethoven's Ninth Symphony, and that gave me the idea to use some more musical notes in the script, which I then gave to Schroeder. You don't always know how these things are going to work out; you might say you wish you had planned it a little more carefully, but you never know.

One of the good things, of course, about a comic strip is that it goes from day to day and you don't have to plan it like you would a novel—everything doesn't have to come out easily at the end. Yesterday's strip doesn't mean anything; the only thing that matters is the piece in the paper today.

CA: You've said too that you don't expect to please everybody every day.

SCHULZ: It would be fatal to try. It's wrong to worry about using something that may be directed too much to tennis players or baseball fans or musicians. I think people who are avid tennis players will appreciate it if you treat their sport with respect and authenticity. If a psychiatrist sees something in your comic strip which maybe only he understands, then he'll appreciate it all the more. But if you try to worry about whether everybody is going to understand it, you'll have a strip that is so bland that no one is going to care anything about it.

CA: Are you ever tempted to solve a problem for a "Peanuts" character, to make something too easy?

SCHULZ: It's always tempting and it is invariably a mistake. What is tempting, of course, is to attract attention by doing so. I could work up something that would be quite sensational if Charlie Brown was finally able to kick the footabll, and it would get a lot of attention that November, and I'm sure we'd get some write-ups in different newspapers and magazines. But it would be like blowing your savings account, spending all your money, and then you wouldn't have anything left; it would be a big mistake.

CA: In the early 1970s you began to read such writers as Joan Didion, John Cheever, and Joyce Carol Oates. Do you read a lot of current fiction?

SCHULZ: Yes. I read almost everything that comes out. I don't finish them all, but I find it almost impossible to go home in the evenings without stopping by at our local bookstore, somewhat like a man who can't go home without stopping by a bar for a drink. I go over to the bookstore almost every day and check to see what's come in that's new. I try to read a lot of the reviews to see what is coming out. I just finished reading *The Company of Women* by Mary Gordon last night. I read a lot, not for research or anything like that, but simply because I enjoy it. I know Joan Didion. I forced myself upon her down in Hollywood once—I went out where she lives and dropped in on her. We had a nice talk and since then I've seen her quite a bit. I like her very much. Another woman writer whom I like very much is Margaret Drabble. When I was over in London a few years ago I called her up and she and I had tea together in my hotel lobby. Since then we've kept up a very slight correspondence. I've also talked on the phone several times with Joanne Greenberg, who wrote *I Never Promised You a Rose Garden* and other things. I call her now and then and talk to her a little while. Someday I'd like to meet her and talk with her in person.

CA: For the TV specials, you audition many children to find voices for the cartoon characters. Is it difficult to make those choices?

SCHULZ: Almost impossible. The difficulty in working with the children is that they find it very hard to read the lines the way they are written. Now and then it will come out very well and we get a real good voice. There is a certain pattern to these children's voices. There are a lot of Charlie Brown voices and a lot of Linus voices. We discovered quite early on that Lucy voices tend to shriek and become annoying, which is why we don't have Lucy in the animated cartoons very much. But we've had some good Peppermint Patty voices, and the last girl that we had for Marcie was a real marvel, but she's growing up now and I think she's lost her voice.

CA: Are you still golfing?

SCHULZ: I've started in a little bit more. I quit almost totally for a long while, but the older you get, the more you miss being able to do things that you used to. I still get invited to play in the Bing Crosby Tournament each year and some other pro-ams, so I've kind of come out of retirement lately and have been practicing so that I can play better. I still play ice hockey a couple of times a week. Jeannie and I play a fair amount of tennis; she plays more than I do.

CA: Of all the awards you've won, is there one that has meant the most to you?

SCHULZ: I suppose the very first Reuben Award, which I won from the National Cartoonists' Society back in 1955, would have been the most exciting of all because I had only been drawing the strip for four or five years; I wanted so much to be accepted, I wanted it to be a good strip, it was my life's ambition, and then to be chosen totally out of the blue by these cartoonists themselves as the oustanding cartoonist of the year really was a tremendous thrill. I suppose that was the highlight. Winning that first Emmy, too, in 1966 for "A Charlie Brown Christmas" was very exciting.

CA: Is the Charles M. Schulz Award new this year?

SCHULZ: Yes. I didn't create it, United Feature Syndicate did. I think the judging is taking place now. There are several people on the panel and the drawings are being sent from person to person, so I should be getting them next week sometime, and then I imagine the announcement will be made after that.

CA: Do you get any personal appeals for advice or help from aspiring cartoonists?

SCHULZ: Now and then we do, which I find a little bit annoying, because I can't run a correspondence school. And I'm always a little mystified at people thinking that they can get opinions from others, that once you have something, you owe it to everyone else to give them advice. Plus the fact that your advice is really not necessary. If people really want to do something, they should just go ahead and do it; they don't have to be told whether or not they're good enough. If you have to be told, then maybe you shouldn't be doing it in the first place.

BIOGRAPHICAL/CRITICAL SOURCES—Books: Carmen Richards, *Minnesota Writers*, Denison, 1961; Robert L. Short, *The Gospel According to Peanuts*, John Knox, 1965; Charles M. Schulz, *Peanuts Treasury*, foreword by Johnny Hart, Holt, 1968; Short, *The Parables of Peanuts*, Harper, 1968; Theodore L. Gross, editor, *Representative Men*, Free Press, 1970; Lee Mendelson and Schulz, *Charlie Brown and Charlie Schulz: In Celebration of the Twentieth Anniversary of Peanuts*, World Publishing, 1970; Reinhold Reitberger and Wolfgang Fuchs, *Comics: Anatomy of a Mass Medium*, translated by Nadia Fowler, Studio Vista, 1972; Arthur Asa Berger, *The Comic-Stripped American*, Walker & Co., 1973; Schulz, *Peanuts Jubilee: My Life and Art with Charlie Brown and Others*, Holt, 1975; *Contemporary Literary Criticism*, Volume XII, Gale, 1980.

Periodicals: *Saturday Evening Post*, January 12, 1957, April 25, 1964; *Time*, March 3, 1957, April 9, 1965, January 5, 1970; *Look*, July 22, 1958; *Newsweek*, March 6, 1961, December 27, 1971; *Seventeen*, January, 1962; *New York Times Book Reivew*, March 12, 1967, December 7, 1975, October 26, 1980; *Village Voice*, March 16, 1967; *Life*, March 17, 1967; *New Yorker*, March 18, 1967; *New York Times Magazine*, April 16, 1967; *Redbook*, December, 1967; *Punch*, February 7, 1968; *Christian Science Monitor*, November 29, 1968, November 11, 1970; *Saturday Review*, April 12, 1969; *New York Times*, May 26, 1969, June 2, 1971; *Valuator*, spring, 1969; *U.S. Catholic*, July, 1969; *Business World*, December 20, 1969; *Washington Post*, April 4, 1970; *Booklist*, November 1, 1974; *New Republic*, December 7, 1974; *Publishers Weekly*, July 7, 1975; *Art in America*, March-April, 1976; *Times Literary Supplement*, December 3, 1976.

—*Interview by Jean W. Ross*

*   *   *

SCHWARTZ, Kessel 1920-

PERSONAL: Born March 19, 1920, in Kansas City, Mo.; son of Henry and Dora (Tanenbaum) Schwartz; married Barbara Lewin, April 3, 1947; children: Joseph David, Deborah Ann, Edward Stephen, Michael Henry. *Education:* University of Missouri, B.A., 1940, M.A., 1941; Columbia University, Ph.D., 1953. *Home:* 6400 Maynada, Coral Gables, Fla. 33146. *Office:* Department of Foreign Languages, University of Miami, Coral Gables, Fla. 33124.

CAREER: U.S. Department of State, Managua, Nicaragua, and Quito, Ecuador, director of cultural centers, 1946-48; Hofstra College (now University), Hempstead, N.Y., instructor in Spanish, 1949-50; Hamilton College, Clinton, N.Y., instructor in Spanish, 1950-51; Colby College, Waterford, Me., instructor in Spanish and Spanish literature, 1951-53; University of Vermont, Burlington, assistant professor of Romance languages, 1953-57; University of Arkansas, Fayetteville, professor of Spanish and chairman of department, 1957-62; University of Miami, Coral Gables, Fla., professor of modern languages, 1962—, chairman of department, 1962-64, 1974—. Visiting professor, University of North Carolina, 1966-67. *Military service:* U.S. Army, interpreter, 1942-46; became master sergeant. *Member:* Association Internacional de Hispanistas, Asociacion de Pensamiento Hispanico, Modern Lan-

guage Association of America, American Association of Teachers of Spanish and Portuguese, Phi Beta Kappa, Phi Sigma Iota, Pi Delta Phi, Sigma Delta Pi, Delta Phi Alpha, Omicron Delta Kappa. *Awards, honors:* Outstanding academic book award, American Association of College and Research Libraries, 1972, for *A New History of Spanish-American Fiction*.

WRITINGS: Contemporary Novel of Ecuador, University of Michigan Press, 1953; (with R. E. Chandler) *A New History of Spanish Literature*, Louisiana State University Press, 1961; (author of introduction and notes) Juan Goytisolo, *Fiestas*, Dell, 1964; (with Chandler) *A New Anthology of Spanish Literature*, two volumes, Louisiana State University Press, 1967; *Introduction to Modern Spanish Literature*, Twayne, 1968; *Vicente Aleixandre*, Twayne, 1969; *The Meaning of Existence in Contemporary Hispanic Literature*, University of Miami Press, 1970; *Juan Goytisolo*, Twayne, 1970; *A New History of Spanish-American Fiction*, two volumes, University of Miami Press, 1972. Contributor of chapters to several books on Spanish and Spanish-American literature, including *The Cry of Home*, University of Tennessee Press, 1972, and *New Critical Approaches*, Bilingual Press, 1981. Contrributor to *Arete Encyclopedia*, *Reader's Encyclopedia*, and *Encyclopedia of World Literature: Twentieth Century*. Contributor of over 200 articles and reviews to *Hispania*, *Symposium*, *Modern Drama*, *Journal of Spanish Studies*, *Twentieth Century*, and other scholarly publications. Associate editor, *Hispania*, beginning 1966; member of editorial advisory board, *Anales de la Novela de Posguerra* and *Forum*.

WORK IN PROGRESS: Continuing work on Goytisolo and Aleixandre.

SIDELIGHTS: Kessel Schwartz told *CA:* "In almost all of my writings, although I strive to maintain scholarly objectivity, I attempt . . . to associate various aspects of literature (which for me represents life itself) with the psychological, sociological, and political imperatives of our century. . . . I believe that one's duty to one's fellow man transcends incidental aesthetic anomalies, for, sooner or later, all writers need a spiritual regeneration."

*   *   *

SCHWARTZ, Richard D(erecktor) 1925-

PERSONAL: Born April 26, 1925, in Newark, N.J.; son of Selig and Tillie (Derecktor) Schwartz; married Emilie Z. Rosenbaum, 1946; children: David, Margaret Jane, Deborah Frances. *Education:* Yale University, B.A., 1947, Ph.D., 1952. *Home:* 15 Clarmar Rd., Fayetteville, N.Y. 13066. *Office:* College of Law, Syracuse University, Syracuse, N.Y. 13210.

CAREER: Institute of Human Relations, New Haven, Conn., research fellow in behavioral science, 1951-54; Yale University, New Haven, 1954-61, began as instructor, became assistant professor of sociology, assistant professor of sociology and law, 1959-61; Northwestern University, Evanston, Ill., associate professor, 1961-64, professor of sociology, 1964-71; State University of New York at Buffalo, professor of sociology and law, 1971-72, dean and provost, Faculty of Law and Jurisprudence, 1971-76; Syracuse University, Syracuse, N.Y., professor of sociology and Ernest I. White Professor of Law, 1977—. Consultant to American Bar Association and National Science Foundation. Member of Orange (Conn.) Board of Education, 1954-61. *Member:* American Sociological Association, Law and Society Association (trustee; president, 1973-76), Phi Beta Kappa. *Awards, honors:* Bishop Mathew Simpson Award, Northwestern University, 1970; Robert Jackson Award, Canisius College; L.L.D., American International College, 1977.

WRITINGS: (Contributor) Behavior Theory and Social Science, Yale University Press, 1955; (contributor) Criminal Law: Problems for Decision in the Promulgation, Invocation, and Administration of a Law of Crimes, Free Press of Glencoe, 1962; (contributor) Unobtrusive Measures, Rand McNally, 1966; (editor with J. H. Slolnick) Society and the Legal Order, Basic Books, 1970; (contributor) Criminal Law: Theory and Practice, Free Press, 1974. Contributor to New York Times Magazine, legal and sociological journals. Editor-in-chief, Law and Society Review, 1965-68.

WORK IN PROGRESS: An evaluation of legal service delivery; a study of legal services corporations, completion expected in 1980.

*   *   *

SCOBIE, James R(alston)   1929-1981

PERSONAL: Born June 16, 1929, in Valparaiso, Chile; died June 4, 1981, in Del Mar, Calif.; son of Jordan Ralston (an educator and banker) and Freda (Johnson) Scobie; married Patricia Beauchamp, November 1, 1957 (died, 1965); married Ingrid Ellen Winther (a historian), June 14, 1967; children: (first marriage) William Ralston, Clare Beauchamp; (second marriage) Kirsten Winther, Bruce Robert. Education: Princeton University, A.B., 1950; Harvard University, M.A., 1951, Ph.D., 1954. Home address: R.F.D. Box P-9, Del Mar, Calif. 92014. Office: Department of History, University of California, San Diego, La Jolla, Calif. 92093.

CAREER: University of California, Berkeley, instructor, 1957-59, assistant professor of history, 1960-64; Indiana University at Bloomington, associate professor, 1964-65, professor of history, 1965-77, director of Latin American studies, 1965-68, chairman of history department, 1970-74; University of California, San Diego, La Jolla, professor of history, 1977-81. Pan American Institute of Geography and History, U.S. national alternate, beginning 1968, representative, 1973-78. Visiting scholar of Latin American studies, Columbia University, 1962-63, and Institute for Advanced Study, Princeton University, 1974-75. Military service: U.S. Army, 1954-57; became first lieutenant. Member: American Historical Association, Conference on Latin American History (chairman, 1978-79), Latin American Studies Association, Academia Nacional de la Historia (Argentina; corresponding member), Pacific Coast Council on Latin American Studies, World Affairs Council of Northern California, Phi Beta Kappa. Awards, honors: Social Science Research Council faculty fellowship, 1959-60 and 1968-69; Organization of American States scholarship, 1959-60; Guggenheim fellowship, 1967-68; National Endowment for the Humanities research grant, 1974-76.

WRITINGS: (Editor with Palmira Bollo Cabrios) Correspondencia Mitre-Elizalde, University of Buenos Aires Press, 1960; Disolucion de un triunvirato, Seminario de Historia Argentina, 1960; Argentina: A City and a Nation, Oxford University Press, 1964, 2nd edition, 1971; Revolution on the Pampas: A Social History of Argentina Wheat, 1860-1910 (monograph), University of Texas Press, 1964; (editor and author of introduction with Dale Morgan) Three Years in California: William Perkins' Journal of Life at Sonora, 1849-52, University of California Press, 1964; La lucha por la consolidacion de la nacionalidad argentina, 1852-1862, Hachette, 1964; Buenos Aires: From Plaza to Suburb, 1870-1910, Oxford University Press, 1974. Contributing editor, Handbook of Latin American Studies, 1966-81; member of board of editors, Hispanic American History Review, 1966-72 and 1979-81; advisory editor, Latin American Research Review, 1967-69 and 1980-81.

WORK IN PROGRESS: A Tale of Three Argentine Provincial Cities: The Social History of Corrientes, Salta, and Mendoza, 1850-1910.

OBITUARIES: New York Times, June 11, 1981.

*   *   *

SCORTIA, Thomas N(icholas)   1926-
(Artur R. Kurz, Gerald McDow, Scott Nichols)

PERSONAL: Born August 29, 1926, in Alton, Ill.; son of Thomas Nicholas and Estella Lee (Byerley) Scortia; married Irene Baron, 1960 (divorced, 1968); adopted, Nicholas Joakim Julin, 1978. Education: Attended Michigan State College of Agriculture and Applied Science (now Michigan State University), 1944; Washington University, A.B., 1949, additional study, 1950. Home: 9213 Warbler Pl., Los Angeles, Calif. 90069.

CAREER: Union Starch and Refining Co., Granite City, Ill., senior chemist, 1954-57; Chromalloy-American Corp., Propellex Chemical Division, Edwardsville, Ill., director of research and development, 1957-60; Celanese Corp., Amcel Propulsion Division, Ashville, N.C., group leader, 1960-61; United Aircraft Corp., United Technology Center, Sunnyvale, Calif., assistant branch manager, 1961-70; free-lance writer, 1970—. President, Gebo Productions, Inc., 1978—. Frequent speaker at professional conferences. Military service: U.S. Army, Infantry, 1944-46; Chemical Corps, 1951-53. Member: American Institute of Aeronautics and Astronautics, Science Fiction Writers of America, Authors Guild, Authors League of America, Writers Guild West, Sigma Xi.

WRITINGS: What Mad Oracle, Regency, 1961; Artery of Fire, Doubleday, 1972; (editor) Strange Bedfellows, Random House, 1972; (editor with C. Quinn Yarbo) Two Views of Wonder, Ballantine, 1973; (with Frank M. Robinson) The Glass Inferno, Doubleday, 1974; Earthwreck, Fawcett, 1974; (with Robinson) The Prometheus Crisis, Doubleday, 1976; (editor with G. Zebrowski) Human Machines, Vintage, 1976; (with Robinson) The Nightmare Factor, Doubleday, 1978; (with Robinson) The Gold Crew, Warner Publications, 1979.

Collections: Caution! Inflammable! (short stories), Doubleday, 1976; The Best of Thomas N. Scortia, edited by Zebrowski, Doubleday, 1981. Also author of screenplays, "Endangered Species," 1976, and "Darker Than You Think," 1979. Contributor of numerous short stories and articles to popular magazines, and many professional papers to Journal of American Chemical Society.

WORK IN PROGRESS: A novel, Complexion of the Heart; a novel series, "April Harvest"; a play, "Little Boxes"; with Gene Roddenberry, a teleplay from the novel by Robert A. Heinlein, "The Puppet Masters," for Marble Arch Productions; with Roddenberry, a television pilot, 'Breakthrough," for Marble Arch Productions; a screenplay adapted from the novel, "The Prometheus Crisis," for Chelsea Pictures.

SIDELIGHTS: Thomas N. Scortia told CA: "I had been writing and publishing as a hobby since 1954 when the collapse of the aerospace industry [in 1970] forced me to a change of career. Since, in the parlance of the day, I was 'overqualified' for most jobs, I decided to gamble on devoting my full time to writing. I have had no cause to regret that decision. The last eight years have been the most exciting and creative of my life.

"I generally work on several projects at once, using a double 'floppy disk' Horizon II computer with terminal outlets in every room of my Los Angeles home and my research assistant's office, rewriting repeatedly on terminal until a high speed printer delivers final proof-read copy. I follow an irregular schedule, but much prefer to work late at night.

"My writing interests range from short stories and novels through screen and stage plays. I enjoy writing both the highly commercial suspense novel and the more thoughtfully-crafted general novel. My previous scientific career has given me a solid basis for many of my commercially successful novels based on the dangers of present day technology."

MEDIA ADAPTATIONS: The Glass Inferno was made into a movie entitled "The Towering Inferno" by Twentieth Century-Fox in 1974; *The Gold Crew* was purchased by Heritage Productions in 1979; *The Prometheus Crisis* was purchased by Chelsea Pictures.

*   *   *

SCOTT, Herbert   1931-

PERSONAL: Born February 8, 1931, in Norman, Okla.; son of Herbert Hicks (an educator) and Betty (an educator; maiden name, Pickard) Scott; married Virginia Corbin, August 24, 1950 (divorced June 29, 1972); married Shirley Stephens Clay (a professor), October 6, 1972; children: (first marriage) Herbert A., Megan, Rannah, Erin, Kyla; (second marriage) Wallace, Brian (stepchildren). *Education:* Fresno State College (now California State University, Fresno), B.A., 1964; University of Iowa, M.F.A., 1966; also attended University of Oklahoma, Lake Forest College, College of Sequoias, and Fresno City College. *Home:* 2620 Outlook, Kalamazoo, Mich. 49003. *Office:* Department of English, Western Michigan University, Kalamazoo, Mich. 49008.

CAREER: Worked at Safeway Stores in various California cities, 1953-64, began as clerk, became produce manager; Southeast Missouri State College (now University), Cape Girardeau, instructor in English, 1966-68; Western Michigan University, Kalamazoo, assistant professor, 1968-72, associate professor, 1972-79, professor of English, 1979—. Creative writing coordinator for Michigan Council for the Arts, 1971-74; poet-in-residence on the American Wind Symphony's Tour, 1976, 1977, and 1978. Founder and chairperson of Michigan Youth Arts Festival Creative Writing Awards; member of Michigan Cultural Activities Board. Has given poetry readings at colleges and universities. *Military service:* U.S. Naval Reserve, 1948-54. *Member:* American Association of University Professors, Poetry Society of America, Michigan Council of Teachers of English. *Awards, honors:* National Endowment for the Humanities fellowship, 1976 and 1980; poetry prize from *Quarterly West,* 1978; Contributors Prize from *Poetry Now,* 1978.

WRITINGS: Disguises (poems), University of Pittsburgh Press, 1974; *The Shoplifter's Handbook* (poems), Blue Mountain Press, 1974; *Groceries,* University of Pittsburgh Press, 1976; (editor with Hilberry and Tipton) *The Third Coast: Contemporary Michigan Poetry,* Wayne State University Press, 1976; *Dinosaurs,* Hofstadt, 1979.

Poetry has been represented in anthologies, including: *Michigan Signatures,* Quixote Press, 1969; *The Now Reader,* Scott, Foresman, 1969; *Poets Kalamazoo,* Westigan Review, 1970; *Down at the Santa Fe Depot: Twenty Fresno Poets,* Giligia, 1970; *Just What the Country Needs, Another Poetry Anthology,* Wadsworth, 1971; *Poems One Line and Longer,* Grossman, 1974; *What Is That Country Standing Inside You?,* Exploration Press, 1976; *A Geography of Poets,* Bantam, 1979; *Going for Coffee: North American Work Poems,* Harbour Publishing,

1980; *Poets Now: 80 for the 80's,* Poetry Now Press, 1982. Contributor of poems to literary magazines, including *Beloit Poetry Journal, Epoch, Harper's, Iowa Review, North American Review,* and *Southern Review.*

WORK IN PROGRESS: An American Childhood; Durations.

SIDELIGHTS: Reviewing *Disguises,* Herbert Scott's first book of poems, Carol Jane Bands writes in *Northwest Review* that his poetry "reveals not only a mature new voice, but an uncompromising mind. Scott has a knack for capturing personalities and characters in a few terse images, a knack some poets are satisfied to cultivate their entire careers. But Scott looks deeper—he is an ambitious poet in the finest sense, one who does not rest easy with success but must continually be pushing ahead. Instead of unwinding a poetic thread down the dark tunnel of experience he turns his poetry into a searchlight, a tool for exploring new depths and shadows."

Shenandoah's Conrad Hilberry also recognizes Scott's talent and writes in his review that the poems in *Groceries* "are populated by workers in the grocery store, by pensioners, widows, shoplifters, by the high heeled woman who leans her elbows on the cart, by the waitress at Aunt Hattie's across the street, by an armed robber, and, indirectly, by Scott himself. . . . The poems sketch these people, catching their language and the motion of their minds, precisely, matter-of-factly, neither condescending to them nor sentimentalizing them. Taken one by one, the poems are slight, but cumulatively they invite us to glimpse, under the direct, literal surface, the play of deeper hungers. The lines are frequently funny, yet the pervasive feeling is of emptiness, a poignant waiting or hoping. Though they are surrounded by food, the characters still are gnawed by appetites they cannot quite satisfy."

A color video-tape of Scott at work, at home, and reading some of his poetry was produced for the Michigan Poetry Series by Western Michigan University and the Michigan Council for the Arts. Recordings of his poetry have been produced and broadcast on the radio.

BIOGRAPHICAL/CRITICAL SOURCES: Choice, October, 1974; *Northwest Review,* summer, 1975; *Shenandoah,* spring, 1978.

*   *   *

SCOTT, John   1912-1976

PERSONAL: Original name, John Scott Nearing; born March 26, 1912, in Philadelphia, Pa.; died December 1, 1976, in Chicago, Ill.; son of Scott and Nellie (Seeds) Nearing; married Maria Dikareva (a teacher), June 15, 1934; children: Leigh Scott Schumann, Elena Scott Whiteside. *Education:* Attended University of Wisconsin, 1929-31, Magnitogorsk Metallurgical Institute, 1932-37, and Sorbonne, University of Paris, 1938-39. *Religion:* Protestant. *Home address:* P.O. Box 71, Ridgefield, Conn. 06877. *Office:* Time, Inc., Rockefeller Center, New York, N.Y. 10020.

CAREER: Worker in Siberian steel mills, 1932-37; Moscow correspondent, HAVAS (French news agency), 1937-40, and *London News Chronicle,* 1940; *Time,* New York, N.Y., Japan correspondent, 1941, contributing editor, 1942-43, Washington correspondent, 1943, war correspondent, 1943-48, Stockholm bureau chief, 1944-45, Central European bureau chief, 1945-48, special assistant to publisher, 1948-73; vice-president, Radio Free Europe-Radio Liberty, 1973-76. Visiting associate professor, Fletcher School of Law and Diplomacy, Tufts University, 1966-67. Radio and television commentator on foreign affairs; also broadcasted programs for Radio Free Europe and Voice of America. *Member:* Academy of Political Science, Council on Foreign Relations, Authors League, Overseas Press Club.

WRITINGS: Behind the Urals: An American Worker in Russia's City of Steel, Houghton, 1942, reprinted, Indiana University Press, 1973; *Duel for Europe,* Houghton, 1942; *Europe in Revolution,* Houghton, 1945; *Political Warfare,* John Day, 1955; *Democracy Is Not Enough,* Harcourt, 1960; *China: The Hungry Dragon,* Parents' Magazine Press, 1967; *Hunger: Man's Struggle to Feed Himself,* Parents' Magazine Press, 1969; *Divided They Stand: A Background Book on the Two Germanies,* Parents' Magazine Press, 1973.

Also author of numerous special reports for *Time,* Radio Free Europe-Radio Liberty, and other private and government organizations, including *East of Suez,* 1956, *The Soviet Empire,* 1959, *The New Europe,* 1961, *Crisis in Communist China,* 1962, *How Much Progress?,* 1963, *The Soviet World,* 1966, *Hunger: Must We Starve?,* 1966, *Peace in Asia,* 1968, *The Middle East at War,* 1970, *Detente through Soviet Eyes,* 1974, *The Pacific Community,* 1974, and *Millions Will Starve,* 1975.

SIDELIGHTS: In 1931, an unemployed former college student named John Scott decided to leave the United States in order to participate in one of the great social experiments of the twentieth century—the industrialization of the Soviet Union. After struggling with a year's worth of bureaucratic red tape (during which time he trained as a welder), the young man finally was allowed to set off for Russia and the job waiting for him at a construction camp located on the eastern slope of the Ural Mountains. For five years he worked twelve hours a day (followed by four hours of study) alongside Mongolian tribesmen and Russian peasants in a coke by-products factory, an experience he recalled in detail in *Behind the Urals.* Described by the *New York Times*'s Peter B. Flint as "a classic account of the brutal sacrifices imposed on Russian workers by Stalin's determination to industrialize the Soviet Union no matter what the cost in lives," Scott's book recounted the hardships he and his fellow workers endured—namely, crowded living quarters, a lack of food, supplies, and clothing, and appallingly unsafe conditions.

Scott remained in his job until Stalin's 1937 purge forced him out of Soviet industry. He then became a Moscow-based correspondent for French and British news services. In 1941, however, two weeks before Hitler ordered German troops to attack the Soviet Union, Scott was expelled from the country for "slandering" Soviet foreign policy and "inventing" reports of a rift between the two nations.

BIOGRAPHICAL/CRITICAL SOURCES: Time, October 8, 1956.

OBITUARIES: New York Times, December 3, 1976.†

*   *   *

SCOTT, John Anthony   1916-

PERSONAL: Born January 20, 1916, in London, England; became U.S. citizen, 1943; son of Philip (a dentist) and Nora (Mort de Bois) Scott; married Maria Malleville Haller (a teacher), August 27, 1940; children: Elizabeth (Mrs. Jean-Paul Jannot), John Wardlaw, Robert Alan. *Education:* Trinity College, Oxford, B.A. (first class honors), 1937, M.A., 1945; Columbia University, M.A., 1947, Ph.D., 1950. *Politics:* Independent. *Home:* 3902 Manhattan College Pkwy., New York, N.Y. 10471. *Office:* School of Law, Rutgers University, Newark, N.J. 07102.

CAREER: Columbia University, New York City, instructor in European history, 1946-48; Amherst College, Amherst, Mass., instructor in European history, 1948-51; Fieldston School, New

York City, instructor in United States history and chairperson of department, 1951-67; Rutgers University, School of Law, Newark, N.J., visiting professor of legal history, 1967—. Instructor at Seminar on American Culture, Cooperstown, N.Y., 1963. Instructor in folksong at seminars of teachers. Sometime ballad singer at Old Sturbridge Village. Civil rights movement organizer, 1956-63, aiding in organization of Prayer Pilgrimage to Washington, 1957, and two youth marches for integrated schools, 1958 and 1959; New York metropolitan coordinator for March on Washington for Equal Rights and Jobs, August, 1963. Director, Bronx Draft Information and Counselling Service, 1967-73. Consultant, National Humanities Faculty, 1970-80. *Military service:* U.S. Army, Armored Forces and Intelligence, 1942-45; became staff sergeant; received Field Citation.

MEMBER: American Historical Association, National Association of Independent Schools, Association for the Study of Negro Life and History, Authors Guild of Authors League of America, American Society for Legal History, Historians for Freedom of Information. *Awards, honors:* M.A. from Oxford University, 1945; Social Science Research Council fellow.

WRITINGS: Republican Ideas and the Liberal Tradition in France, Columbia University Press, 1951; *The Ballad of America: The History of the United States in Song and Story,* Bantam, 1966; *Settlers on the Eastern Shore, 1607-1750,* Knopf, 1967; *The Trumpet of a Prophecy: Revolutionary America, 1763-1783,* Knopf, 1969; *Teaching for a Change,* Bantam, 1973; *Fanny Kemble's America,* Crowell, 1973; *Hard Trials on My Way: Slavery and the Struggle against It, 1800-1860,* Knopf, 1974; *Woman against Slavery: The Life of Harriet Beecher Stowe,* Crowell, 1978.

Editor: *Introduction to Contemporary Civilization in the West,* Columbia University Press, 1946; Frances Anne Kemble, *Journal of a Residence on a Georgian Plantation in 1838-1839,* Knopf, 1961; *Living Documents in American History,* Washington Square Press, Volume I: *From Earliest Colonial Times to the Civil War,* 1964, Volume II: *From Reconstruction to the Outbreak of World War I,* 1968; (and translator and contributor) *The Defense of Gracchus Babeuf before the High Court of Vendome,* Gehenna Press, 1964, University of Massachusetts Press, 1967; Thomas More, *Utopia,* Washington Square Press, 1965; (and author of introduction) Frank Moore, compiler, *The Diary of the American Revolution, 1775-1781,* Washington Square Press, 1967; James M. McPherson, *Marching toward Freedom: The Negro in the Civil War, 1861-1865,* Knopf, 1968.

General editor, "The Living History Library" series, Knopf, 1965-76.

Also author of scripts and producer of recordings for Heirloom Records: "The New Deal through Its Songs and Ballads"; "Irish Immigration through Its Songs and Ballads"; "The Negro People through Their Songs and Ballads"; "New England Whaling through Its Songs and Ballads"; "New York City through Its Songs and Ballads"; "The Story of the Cowboy through His Songs and Ballads"; (and performer with Gene Bonyun and Bill Bonyun) "The American Revolution through Its Songs and Ballads"; (with Bill Bonyun) "The Civil War through Its Songs and Ballads." Contributor of articles to *Teaching and Learning, New York Folklore Quarterly, Activist, Journal of Negro History, Country Dancer, History Notes, Sing Out,* and to other folklore and education journals.

WORK IN PROGRESS: History of the Civil Rights Movement, 1954-68, for Crowell; *The Origins of Anglo-American Law;* second edition of *The Ballad of America.*

SIDELIGHTS: John Anthony Scott wrote *CA:* "I write for young people of all ages, from elementary school to the graduate level. Much of my writing has been inspired by students' questions, by the dozens of ideas thrown up by discussions with these students. Then I start collecting materials—books, letters, documents, songs, all the things that are the lifeblood of the historian's craft; and sooner or later a new book emerges.

"Writing I find both difficult and necessary. Necessary because an historian tries to contribute to historical truth, to add to what is known about people and life, or to make easily available the literary materials that are the historical heritage of the American public. Difficult, because writing is a way of investigating reality, a reality that is not always easy to understand. And then, again, writing is a craft that takes effort and patience to try and say what you mean, and to say it as briefly and as simply as possible."

AVOCATIONAL INTERESTS: Tennis, swimming, running, bicycle riding, cross-country skiing, hiking, canoeing, and travelling.

BIOGRAPHICAL/CRITICAL SOURCES: Time, June 1, 1962; *Best Sellers,* December 1, 1967, June 1, 1970; *New York Times Book Review,* February 25, 1968; *Library Journal,* June 15, 1970.

* * *

SEAGER, Ralph William 1911-

PERSONAL: Born November 3, 1911, in Geneva, N.Y.; son of William Thomas and Ellen (Nichols) Seager; married Ruth Lovejoy (a high school cafeteria manager), December 11, 1932; children: William, Douglas, Keith. *Education:* Attended University of California, Berkeley, 1950-51. *Religion:* Baptist. *Home and office:* 311 Keuka St., Penn Yan, N.Y. 14527.

CAREER: Poet. District manager and claims adjuster for insurance companies, Penn Yan, N.Y., 1932-37; physiotherapist for Bernarr MacFadden, Dansville, N.Y., 1937-38; clerk, U.S. Post Office, Penn Yan, 1938-67; Keuka College, Keuka Park, N.Y., 1960—, began as lecturer in creative verse, became professor emeritus, 1976—. Instructor at poetry workshops in Lakeside, Ohio, and East Dover, Vt. Director of poetry workshops at writers conferences, St. David's, Pa., 1958, 1963, Green Lake, Wis., 1963, at Judson College, Elgin, Ill., 1966, 1967, 1968, and 1969, East Dover, Vt., 1970, and at Aurora College. Lecturer at universities and high schools. *Military service:* U.S. Navy, 1944-45; served in South Pacific theater. *Member:* Poetry Society of America. *Awards, honors:* University of New Hampshire Writers' Conference, first prize in verse, 1954, second prize in nonfiction, 1956; Wake-Brook House award, 1958, for *Beyond the Green Gate;* D.Litt. from Keuka College, 1970.

WRITINGS—All poetry, except as otherwise noted: *Songs from a Willow Whistle,* Wake-Brook, 1956; *Beyond the Green Gate,* Wake-Brook, 1958; (with E. Merrill Root) *Writing Poetry* (nonfiction), Christian Authors' Guild, 1958; *Christmas Chimes in Rhyme,* Judson, 1962; *The Sound of an Echo* (prose), Wake-Brook, 1963; *Cup, Flagon, and Fountain,* Wake-Brook, 1965; *A Choice of Dreams,* Partridge, 1970; *Wheatfields and Vineyards,* Christian Herald, 1975; *Little Yates and the United States* (bicentennial history of Yates County), Tillman Press, 1976; *The Manager Mouse and Other Christmas Poems,* Judson, 1977, (editor) *Writings on the Wall* (prose and poetry), Tillman Press, 1979; *Sesquicentennial History of the First Baptist Church of Penn Yan* (history), Tillman Press, 1980.

Poetry has been represented in numerous anthologies. Poems have appeared in *Ladies' Home Journal, Saturday Evening*

Post, Good Housekeeping, McCall's, New York Times, New York Herald Tribune, and poetry journals.

WORK IN PROGRESS: Another book of verse.

SIDELIGHTS: Ralph William Seager told *CA:* "Man has inherited three essential 'thirsts': his thirst for environment, or whatever it is that makes him homesick; his thirst for companionship—he does not want to go it alone; his thirst to know who it is he means when he says 'Our Father.'" As for the poet's role in this world of "thirsts," Seager states: "The purpose of the poet is to share the common life with common man, but to share it uncommonly."

Seager's poetry has been broadcasted on Cairo radio in Egypt, on Armed Services Radio, and on various radio programs in the United States, including a reading by Basil Rathbone on NBC-Radio. There is a collection of Seager's manuscripts at Syracuse University.

AVOCATIONAL INTERESTS: Photography, music, nature.

BIOGRAPHICAL/CRITICAL SOURCES: Baptist Leader, November, 1961; *Lutheran Standard,* March 26, 1963; *Finger Lakes Chronicle,* October, 1965.

* * *

SEAGER, Robert II 1924-

PERSONAL: Born September 12, 1924, in Nanking, China; son of Warren Armstrong (an Episcopal clergyman and missionary) and Helen (Hales) Seager; married Caroline Parrish, August 14, 1945. *Education:* Attended The Citadel, 1942-43; U.S. Merchant Marine Academy, diploma, 1944; Rutgers University, B.A., 1948; Columbia University, M.A., 1949; Ohio State University, Ph.D., 1956; postdoctoral study at School of Advanced International Studies, Johns Hopkins University, 1956-57. *Politics:* Republican. *Religion:* Protestant Episcopal. *Home:* 543 Boonesboro Ave., Lexington, Ky. 40508. *Office:* Department of History, University of Kentucky, Lexington, Ky. 40506.

CAREER: Denison University, Granville, Ohio, 1949-61, began as instructor, became associate professor of American history; U.S. Naval Academy, Annapolis, Md., 1961-67, began as assistant professor, became associate professor of U.S. diplomatic and naval history; University of Maine, Orono, professor of American history and chairman of department, 1967-70; Washington College, Chestertown, Md., professor of American history and academic dean, 1970-72; University of Baltimore, Baltimore, Md., professor of American history and vice-president for academic affairs, 1972-77; University of Kentucky, Lexington, professor of American history, 1977—. *Military service:* U.S. Merchant Marine, 1944-46; served as deck officer. U.S. Naval Reserve, 1944-47; became lieutenant junior grade. *Member:* Organization of American Historians, U.S. Naval Institute, Society of Historians of American Foreign Relations, Southern Historical Association, Kentucky Historical Association.

AWARDS, HONORS: Koontz Prize for best article in *Pacific Historical Review* for 1959; Pulitzer Prize nomination in history, 1963, for *And Tyler Too; And Tyler Too* named one of hundred best books of 1963 by *New York Times Book Review;* U.S. Naval Institute Award of Merit, Navy League of the United States Award for Literary Achievement, North American Society for Oceanic History Lyman Book Award, and University of Kentucky Hallam Book Award, all 1978, all for *Alfred Thayer Mahan.*

WRITINGS: (Editor with W. M. Southgate) *Readings in Western Civilization,* Edwards Bros., 1958; *And Tyler Too: A Bi-*

ography of John and Julia Gardiner Tyler, McGraw, 1963; (editor with L. E. Decker) *America's Major Wars: Crusaders, Critics, and Scholars, 1775-1972*, two volumes, Addison-Wesley, 1973; (editor with D. D. Maguire) *Letters and Papers of Alfred Thayer Mahan*, three volumes, Naval Institute Press, 1975; *Alfred Thayer Mahan*, Naval Institute Press, 1977.

Contributor: William A. Williams, editor, *The Shaping of American Diplomacy*, Rand McNally, 1955; A. E. Campbell, editor, *Expansion and Imperialism*, Harper, 1970; Robert W. Love, Jr., editor, *Changing Interpretations and New Sources in Naval History*, Garland Publishing, 1980.

Editor, *The Papers of Henry Clay*, University Press of Kentucky, 1977—. Contributor to *Book of Knowledge Encyclopedia*, *Notable American Women, 1607-1950: A Biographical Dictionary*, and *Dictionary of Military Biography*. Contributor of articles and critical reviews to *American Historical Review*, *Journal of American History*, *New England Quarterly*, *Pacific Historical Review*, *Virginia Cavalcade*, *Washington Post*, and other publications.

WORK IN PROGRESS: Editing volumes seven and eight of *The Papers of Henry Clay*, for University Press of Kentucky; *Henry Clay and John Tyler: Compromise and Conscience in the Old South, 1800-1861*, for Louisiana State University Press.

SIDELIGHTS: Commenting on Robert Seager II's *And Tyler Too*, Ishbel Ross of the *New York Times Book Review* notes that the book "is essentially the history of two important families, a social narrative with a diversified cast of characters, fascinating in its accurate minutiae and strengthened on political issues with direct evidence from the Tyler and Gardiner correspondence." The *Christian Science Monitor*'s W. G. Andrews describes the biography as "clear, witty, and fair. [Seager] does not make Tyler admirable, though he gives him flesh, blood, and vitality. All this is done on a solid, scholarly foundation. . . . Most of [the author's] historical judgments are sound, though . . . outside the Tyler period, he treads less surely. . . . [But] this is picking at gnats. His accomplishments are real."

"If the most notable portions of Professor Seager's biography deal with matters political, by far the most entertaining concern the May-December romance of Tyler and Julia Gardiner," states Robert Cowley in his *Book Week* review of *And Tyler Too*. "At least half the book is devoted to the story of their years after the White House. . . . While all of this makes for interesting reading, it is something of a let-down after [the political] machinations [in Washington]. Even so, this is a good book, and it will doubtless serve as the standard biography of Tyler for many years to come. . . . One is relieved to find a scholar who has a respect for and a command of the English language—for Professor Seager writes with a refreshing clarity. He has succeeded in making John Tyler come alive."

AVOCATIONAL INTERESTS: Gardening, spectator sports.

BIOGRAPHICAL/CRITICAL SOURCES: Book Week, October 6, 1963; *New York Times Book Review*, October 13, 1963; *Best Sellers*, October 15, 1963; *Christian Science Monitor*, December 17, 1963.

*   *   *

SEARS, Donald A(lbert)   1923-

PERSONAL: Born May 25, 1923, in Portland, Me.; son of Albert J. (an engineer) and Doris (Robinson) Sears; married Madelyn Stover, September 22, 1945 (divorced, 1962); married Oretta Ferri (an attorney), January 3, 1963 (died, 1980); children: Jennifer A. Talbot, Jeanne R. Prince, Elizabeth Ellen,

Stephen Donald. *Education:* Bowdoin College, B.A. (magna cum laude), 1944; Harvard University, M.A., 1947, Ph.D., 1952. *Religion:* Congregational. *Office:* Department of Linguistics, California State University, Fullerton, Calif. 92634.

CAREER: Dartmouth College, Hanover, N.H., instructor in English, 1948-52; Upsala College, East Orange, N.J., 1952-62, began as assistant professor, became professor of English, associate director of development, 1961-62; Skidmore College, Saratoga Springs, N.Y., professor of English and chairman of department, 1962-64; American Council of Education, Washington, D.C., associate director of commission on plans and objectives for higher education, 1964-65; Howard University, Washington, D.C., professor of English, 1965-66; Ahmadu Bello University, Kano and Zaria, Northern Nigeria, professor of English, 1966-67; California State University, Fullerton, professor of English and linguistics, 1967—. Visiting professor, University of Massachusetts, 1957; professorial lecturer, Northern Center, University of Virginia, fall, 1964, and George Washington University, spring, 1965. University of Massachusetts, Humanities Center for a Liberal Education in an Industrial Society, staff member, 1955-59, director and clerk of corporation, 1961-63. Campus representative, Woodrow Wilson Foundation, 1959-62. Consultant in English, American Institute of Banking. *Military service:* U.S. Air Force, 1943-46 and 1950; served as chief instructor, Bombsight School, Lowry Air Force Base.

MEMBER: College English Association (president of Greater New York chapter, 1955-56; national director, 1957-60; executive director, 1962-70), Modern Language Association of America, Linguistics Society of America, American Association of Applied Linguistics, Milton Society, Malone Society, Maine Historical Society (honorary member), Phi Beta Kappa, Lotos Club (New York). *Awards, honors:* Lindback Foundation Award for distinguished teaching, 1961; Outstanding Professor Award, California State University, Fullerton, 1981.

WRITINGS: The Harbrace Guide to the Library and Research Paper, Harcourt, 1956, 2nd revised edition, 1973; (contributing editor) *College English: The First Year*, 3rd edition, Harcourt, 1960; (contributing editor) *Good Reading*, New American Library, 1960; (with Francis X. Connolly) *The Sentence in Context*, Harcourt, 1960; *The Discipline of English: A Guide to Literary Research*, Harcourt, 1963, revised edition, 1973; (contributor) *A Guide to Graduate Study*, 3rd edition, American Council on Education, 1965; *John Neal*, Twayne, 1978; (with Dwight Bolinger) *Aspects of Language*, 3rd edition, Harcourt, 1981; *Among the Maybes* (poems), Harian, 1982.

Editor of chapbooks of the College English Association. Contributing editor of texts of American Institute of Banking, including *Effective English* and *Bank Letters and Reports*. Contributor of poems and poetry translations to journals. Editor, *CEA Critic*, 1960-70.

SIDELIGHTS: Donald A. Sears comments: "It seems that I always write about language, either overtly in my more scholarly works or covertly in my poetry, which increasingly demands my primary attention. Even the poems that explore the subtle connections of landscape to human individuals find the bridge in language. While man works to control his setting, the setting is shaping the man, imperceptibly impinging its steadiness of place upon his restless mind and heart and will, until even the rhythms of his speech are a part of his nature and the Nature in which he lives.

"I suppose that in today's world that needs political statements to be made linguistically, I should add that I still use the word *man* to include *woman,* without whom, for me, there would be no poetry. For in that exploration of words that is poetic creation, my muse, as impeller and guide, is woman.''

*   *   *

SEBESTYEN, Gyorgy   1930-

PERSONAL: Born October 30, 1930, in Budapest, Hungary; son of Sandor and Rozsa (Fischer) Sebestyen; married; children: (previous marriage) Julia, Piroska, Anna. *Education:* University Eotvos Lorand, Budapest, Ph.D. (ethnology). *Religion:* Roman Catholic. *Home:* Ennsgasse 7, Vienna, Austria.

CAREER: Madach Theatre, Budapest, Hungary, lecturer, 1948-49; Hunnia Film Studio, Budapest, lecturer, 1949-50; *Szinhaz es Filmuveszet* (journal), Budapest, editor, 1950-52; *Magyar Nemzet* (newspaper), Budapest, cultural editor, 1952-55; *Magyar Hirado* (newspaper), Vienna, Austria, chief editor, 1957-61; currently chief editor of *Morgen* (quarterly), Vienna, and *Pannomia* (quarterly), Eisenstadt, Austria.

WRITINGS: (Editor) *Roppenj szikra* (lyric poetry anthology), Minsz (Budapest), 1948; (editor) *Orosz nepmesek* (folklore anthology), Ifjusagi-Konyv Kiado (Budapest), 1949; *Die Tueren schliessen sich* (novel; translation from the Hungarian of "Kilincs nelkueli ajtok"), translated by Lena Dur, Desch (Munich), 1957, translation by Peter White published as *Moment of Triumph,* Harcourt, 1958 (published in England as *The Doors Are Closing,* Angus & Robertson, 1958); *Der Mann im Sattel; oder, Ein langer Sonntag* (novel), Desch, 1961; *Die Schule der Verfuehrung* (novel), Desch, 1964; *Floetenspieler und Phantome* (guide book), Desch, 1965; *Lob der Venusbrust, und andere Leckereien,* Forum, 1966; *Anatomie eines Sieges* (essay), Zsolnay, 1967; *Beispiele,* Kremayr & Scheriau, 1967; *Thennberg; oder, Versuch einer Heimkehr* (novel), Desch, 1969.

Ungarn (essay), Schroll, 1970; *Die schoene Wienerin* (anthology), Desch, 1971; *Berengar und Berenice* (novel), Jugend & Volk (Vienna), 1971; *Agnes und Johanna* (play), Oesterreichische Verlagsanstalt (Vienna), 1972; *Der Faun im Park* (short story), Kremayr & Scheriau (Vienna), 1972; *Unterwegs im Burgenland* (essay), Roetzer (Eisenstadt), 1973; *Der Wiener Naschmarkt* (essay), Tusch (Vienna), 1974; *Das Leben als schoene Kunst* (essay), Desch, 1975; *Burgtheatergalerie* (essay), Tusch, 1976; *Parole Widerstand* (essay), Roetzer, 1977; *Burgenland, wo sich die Wege kreuzen* (essay), Roetzer, 1977; *Maria Theresia* (screenplay), Oesterreichischer Bundesverlag (Vienna), 1980; *Studien zur Literatur* (essay), Roetzer, 1980. Contributor of short stories to *Frankfurter Allgemeine Zeitung, Die Welt, Presse,* and other publications.

AVOCATIONAL INTERESTS: Cooking, women.

*   *   *

SELLS, Arthur Lytton   1895-

PERSONAL: Born May 28, 1895, in Birmingham, England; son of Arthur (a bank director) and Elizabeth (Whittaker) Sells; married Iris Robertson (a writer and lecturer), September 2, 1929; children: Christopher Cedric Lytton. *Education:* Sidney Sussex College, Cambridge, B.A., 1921, M.A., 1924; Sorbonne, University of Paris, Docteur de l'Universite de Paris, 1924. *Home:* Dunster House, The Avenue, Durham DH1 4DX, England.

CAREER: Cambridge University, Cambridge, England, lecturer in French, 1923-30; University of Durham, Durham, England, professor, 1930-49, on leave as professor at University of Padua, 1946-47; Indiana University at Bloomington, pro-

fessor, 1948-65, research professor, 1963-65, research professor emeritus, 1965—. Visiting professor at Harvard University, New York University, and University of Massachusetts—Amherst. Representative of British Council in Padua, Italy, 1946. *Member:* Modern Language Association of America, Dante Society of America, Athenaeum Club (London). *Awards, honors:* Laureat de l'Academie Francaise (Prix Bordin), 1925; Officier d'Academie, 1937.

WRITINGS: Les Sources francaises de Goldsmith, Champion, 1924, reprinted, Richard West, 1979; *The Early Life and Adventures of Jean Jacques Rousseau, 1712-1740,* Heffer, 1929; *Earth of the Tarentines* (novel), Muller, 1940; *The Italian Influence in English Poetry: From Chaucer to Southwell,* Indiana University Press, 1955, reprinted, Greenwood Press, 1971; *Animal Poetry in French and English Literature and the Greek Tradition,* Indiana University Press, 1955; *The Paradise of Travellers: The Italian Influence on Englishmen in the 17th Century,* Indiana University Press, 1964; *The Popular Revolutions of the Late Middle Ages,* Allen & Unwin, 1973; *Oliver Goldsmith: His Life and Works,* Barnes & Noble, 1974; *Lordship and Feudalism in the Middle Ages,* Allen & Unwin, 1976; *Thomas Gray: His Life and Works,* Allen & Unwin, 1980.

Translator: Andre Bonnard, *Greek Civilization,* Macmillan, Volume I, 1957, Volume II, 1959; Jean Lucas Dubreton, *Daily Life in Florence in the Time of the Medici,* Macmillan, 1961; (and editor) *The Memoirs of James II: His Campaigns as Duke of York, 1652-1660,* Indiana University Press, 1962. Contributor of articles and book reviews to journals.

AVOCATIONAL INTERESTS: Nature study.†

*   *   *

SEVERN, David
See UNWIN, David S(torr)

*   *   *

SHAFFER, Harry George   1919-

PERSONAL: Born August 28, 1919, in Vienna, Austria; son of Max and Toska (Infeld) Shaffer; married Juliet Martha Popper (a professor), August 11, 1960 (divorced May, 1975); children: Bernard Charles, Ronald Eric, Leonard Joseph, Tanya Elaine. *Education:* New York University, B.S. (cum laude), 1947, M.A., 1948, Ph.D., 1958. *Home:* 2606 Alabama St., Lawrence, Kan. *Office:* Department of Economics, University of Kansas, Lawrence, Kan. 66045.

CAREER: Concord College, Athens, W. Va., instructor in economics and business administration, 1948-49; University of Alabama, Tuscaloosa, instructor in economics, 1950-56; University of Kansas, Lawrence, 1956—, began as instructor, currently professor of economics and of Soviet and East European studies. Visiting professor of economics, Portland State College (now University), summer, 1963. Lawrence League for the Practice of Democracy, president, 1960-61, first vice-president, 1961—. *Military service:* U.S. Army, Military Intelligence, 1942-43. *Member:* American Economic Association, American Association for the Advancement of Slavic Studies, Association for Comparative Economics, American Association of University Professors, Beta Gamma Sigma. *Awards, honors:* New York University Founder's Day Award, 1959, for "consistent evidence of outstanding scholarship."

WRITINGS: (Editor) *The Soviet Economy: A Collection of Western and Soviet Views,* Appleton-Century-Crofts, 1963, revised edition, 1969; (editor) *The Soviet System in Theory and Practice: Selected Western and Soviet Views,* Appleton-Century-Crofts, 1965, 2nd edition, Pergamon, in press; (editor) *The Communist World: Marxist and Non-Marxist Views,* Appleton-Century-Crofts, 1967; (editor with Jan S. Prybyla) *From Underdevelopment to Affluence: Western, Soviet, and Chinese Views,* Appleton-Century-Crofts, 1968; *English-Language Periodic Publications on Communism: An Annotated Index,* Research Institute on Communist Affairs, Columbia University, 1971; *The U.S. Conquers the West,* Forum Press, 1974; *The Soviet Treatment of Jews,* Praeger, 1974; *Periodicals on the Socialist Countries and on Marxism: A New Annotated Index of English-Language Publications,* Praeger, 1977; *Soviet Agriculture: An Assessment of Its Contribution to Economic Development,* Praeger, 1977; *Women in the Two Germanies: A Comparison of a Socialist and a Non-Socialist Society,* Pergamon, 1981.

Contributor to *East Europe, Journal of Higher Education, Russian Review, Problems of Communism,* and various economics journals.

SIDELIGHTS: Harry G. Shaffer told *CA:* "Virtually all of my writings are on Communism; the majority, though not all of them, deal with the U.S.S.R. The Soviets classify Western social scientists who study the U.S.S.R. into three categories: (1) the scientific, by which they mean those who subscribe unquestioningly to Marxist-Leninist ideology; (2) the unscientific who are not Marxist-Leninists but who try to understand, approaching their subject with an open mind; and (3) the 'falsifiers,' who are those who always try to find fault but never give credit where credit is due, those, in other words, who take pictures of houses with cracks in them but never of new, near-perfect structures, who photograph women in Moscow shoveling snow or carrying heavy loads but never those who head scientific laboratories. I cannot lay claim to be classified in this sense as 'scientific'; but neither am I a 'falsifier.' I go out of my way to try to understand what they are doing, and I attempt with an open mind to see the achievements as well as the shortcomings of the Soviet system."

*   *   *

SHAGAN, Steve   1927-

PERSONAL: Born October 25, 1927, in New York, N.Y.; son of Barney (an owner of a pharmacy) and Ray (Anhalt) Shagan; married Elizabeth Leslie Florance, November 18, 1956; children: Robert. *Education:* Attended New York University. *Residence:* Los Angeles, Calif. *Agent:* Ron Mardigian (film) and Owen Laster (books), William Morris Agency, 151 El Camino Dr., Beverly Hills, Calif. 90212.

CAREER: Writer and producer; has worked as a salesman, film-printer, assistant theatre director, electrician, and advertising copywriter. Guest lecturer in screenwriting at University of Southern California. *Military service:* U.S. Coast Guard, 1944-48; served in Europe and Africa. *Member:* Writers Guild of America. *Awards, honors:* Best drama award from Writers Guild of America, 1973, for original screenplay "Save the Tiger"; nominated for Academy Award by Motion Picture Academy of Arts and Sciences, 1973, for screenplay "Save the Tiger," and 1976, for screenplay "Voyage of the Damned."

WRITINGS: Save the Tiger, Dial, 1973; *City of Angels,* Putnam, 1975; *The Formula,* Morrow, 1980. Author of screenplays "Save the Tiger," "City of Angels," and "The Formula," all based on his novels of the same titles; also author of screenplay "Voyage of the Damned."

SIDELIGHTS: Steve Shagan writes that he tries "to reflect the condition of the 'average' man in current American system—the lack of and need for sharper focus of national interest in the 'small' man in our society."

His first novel, *Save the Tiger,* revolves around Harry, a middle-aged, Los Angeles dress company executive whose firm is failing financially. Intertwined with Harry's present problems are memories of his life in the East thirty years ago. These memories, when juxtaposed with the modern-day realities of Los Angeles, give the novel a sense of nostalgia for an America which has been lost.

In Shagan's third novel, *The Formula,* Los Angeles detective Barney Caine finds the body of his murdered friend, the former chief of the Los Angeles police department. In seeking revenge, Caine discovers a complicated plot involving the oil companies who want to suppress a Nazi technological secret for making artificial gasoline. Eventually Caine realizes that those interested in keeping the formula out of the public domain will stop at nothing, and he begins to see the connection between this plot and the murder of his friend.

In his review of *The Formula, Los Angeles Times Book Review* critic Nick B. Williams writes: "What matters in a thriller is the thrills, and Shagan omits no details of the never-really-gentle art of murder. . . . [This book is] paced as swiftly as a cobra striking for the jugular, as sordidly as the hawking of a Hollywood Blvd. hooker, as factually perhaps as the expense account of any one-term Congressman."

The Formula has been published in French, Italian, Portugese, Chinese, German, Japanese, and Serbo-Croatian.

BIOGRAPHICAL/CRITICAL SOURCES: Los Angeles Times Book Review, September 23, 1979; *New York Times Book Review,* November 18, 1979, December 2, 1979; *New York Times,* December 19, 1980.

*   *   *

SHANNON, William V(incent)   1927-

PERSONAL: Born August 24, 1927, in Worcester, Mass.; son of Patrick Joseph (a carpenter) and Nora Agnes (McNamara) Shannon; married Elizabeth McNelly, August 5, 1961; children: Liam Anthony, Christopher Andrew, David Patrick. *Education:* Clark University, A.B., 1947; Harvard University, A.M., 1948. *Religion:* Roman Catholic.

CAREER: Free-lance writer in Washington, D.C., 1949-51; *New York Post,* New York, N.Y., Washington correspondent, 1951-57; columnist for *New York Post* and other newspapers, 1957-64; member of *New York Times* editorial board, 1964-77; United States ambassador to Ireland, 1977-81. Member of board of directors, American Irish Foundation. Trustee, Clark University. *Member:* National Press Club, Overseas Writers, Phi Beta Kappa, Cosmos Club (Washington, D.C.), Century Club (New York, N.Y.). *Awards, honors:* Page One Award, New York Newspaper Guild, 1951; Center for Study of Democratic Institutions fellow, 1961-62; Litt.D., Clark University, 1964; Edward J. Meeman Award, Scripps-Howard Foundation, 1968 and 1976, for conservation writings; Alicia Patterson Fund fellow, 1969-70; D.Litt., New Rochelle College, 1971; L.H.D., Boston University, 1976; LL.D., Sacred Heart University, Bridgeport, Conn., 1978; Gold Medal, American Irish Historical Society, 1979.

WRITINGS: (Contributor) Robert S. Allen, editor, *Our Sovereign State,* Vanguard, 1949; (with Allen) *The Truman Merry-Go-Round,* Vanguard, 1950; *The American Irish,* Macmillan, 1963, revised edition, 1974; *The Heir Apparent: Robert Kennedy and the Struggle for Power,* Macmillan, 1967; *They Could Not Trust the King: Nixon, Watergate and the American Peo-*

ple, Macmillan, 1974; (contributor) *Symbols and Aspirations, 1776-1976*, Cleveland Western Reserve Historical Society, 1976. Contributor to magazines.

WORK IN PROGRESS: A book, *The Way England Is Now*, for World Publishing.

SIDELIGHTS: The Heir Apparent: Robert Kennedy and the Struggle for Power was one of several books on Kennedy written during a turbulent pre-presidential election year. In a *New York Times* review, Eliot Fremont-Smith noted that "of the 22 books—by latest count—that have been or are being written about Robert Kennedy, *The Heir Apparent* is doubtless one of the most honest and balanced." Edwin Tetlow of the *Christian Science Monitor* judged it to be "a thoroughly professional assessment by one of the country's most knowledgeable and careful political commentators," while a reviewer for *Time* called the book "more compelling than its predecessors. Shannon is a native of Massachusetts, a Harvard graduate, an Irish Catholic and a liberal Democrat—the perfect candidate, it would seem, to write an admiring or even adoring book about Bobby. The surprise is that *The Heir Apparent* is often severely critical. But it is always dispassionate in its analysis and at times sympathetic."

On the other hand, Cabell Phillips of the *New York Times Book Review* observed: "Thoughtful, detailed, balanced, [*The Heir Apparent*] is written with the professional's understanding of politics and the political mentality. [But] only a computer, I suppose, could produce a totally objective biography. It is clear from this book that Mr. Shannon likes Robert Kennedy, that he has a certain controlled admiration for his capacities. Here and there, his control slips. . . . In the main however, . . . he looks at the whole man and his environment, reporting and evaluating what he sees as honestly as he can."

Concluded the *Washington Post Book World*'s V. S. Navasky: "[Shannon] is more enlightening on the milieu than the man. . . . [His] contribution has less to do with original illuminations about RFK-the-man than with sound, Times-depth sketches of state and local politics and politicians, and the contexts and environments in which he has had to operate, especially since the assassination of his brother. . . . Although one wishes Mr. Shannon's enterprise as a journalist matched his sense of balanced perspective as a historian, he has provided a service by assembling in one place an up-to-date, straight, uncondescending political biography."

BIOGRAPHICAL/CRITICAL SOURCES: New York Times, September 23, 1967; *Christian Science Monitor*, September 28, 1967; *Newsweek*, October 2, 1967; *Time*, October 6, 1967; *Washington Post Book World*, October 22, 1967; *New York Times Book Review*, October 29, 1967; *Commonweal*, February 2, 1968; *New Yorker*, February 4, 1974; *Best Sellers*, March 15, 1974.†

*   *   *

SHARPE, Lucretia
    See BURGESS, M(ichael) R(oy)

*   *   *

SHAW, Irene
    See ROBERTS, Irene

*   *   *

SHAW, Stanford Jay   1930-

PERSONAL: Born May 5, 1930, in St. Paul, Minn.; son of

Albert and Belle (Paymar) Shaw; married Ezel Kural; children: one daughter. *Education:* Stanford University, B.A., 1951, M.A., 1952; Princeton University, M.A., 1955, Ph.D., 1958; graduate study at University of Cairo, 1955-56, and University of Istanbul, 1956-57. *Home address:* P.O. Box 49753, Los Angeles, Calif. 90049. *Office:* Department of History, University of California, 405 Hilgard Ave., Los Angeles, Calif. 90024.

CAREER: Harvard University, Cambridge, Mass., research fellow, 1958-60, assistant professor of Turkish, 1960-65, associate professor of Turkish history, 1965-68; University of California, Los Angeles, professor of Turkish and Near Eastern history, 1968—. Visiting professor of history, University of Washington, 1970. Fellow, Royal Institute of International Affairs, 1962-67, and American Research Institute in Turkey, summer, 1968 and 1972. *Member:* Turkish Studies Association of North America, Middle East Institute, Middle East Studies Association, American Historical Association, Turkish Historical Society (honorary member). *Awards, honors:* Ford Foundation fellow, 1955-58; Guggenheim fellow, 1966-67; Social Science Research Council fellow, 1972; National Endowment for the Humanities research grant, 1972-73 and 1978-80.

WRITINGS: The Financial and Administrative Organization and Development of Ottoman Egypt, 1517-1798, Princeton University Press, 1962; (editor and translator) Ahmed Cezzar, *Ottoman Egypt in the Eighteenth Century*, Harvard University Press, 1962; *The Land Law of Ottoman Egypt, 960-1553*, [Berlin], 1962; (compiler) *List of Books in the Collection of the Reading Room, Center for Middle Eastern Studies*, Harvard University, 1962; (editor) H.A.R. Gibb, *Studies in the Civilization of Islam*, Beacon Press, 1962; (editor and translator) Husayn Afandi, *Ottoman Egypt in the Age of the French Revolution*, Harvard University Press, 1964; *The Budget of Ottoman Egypt*, Mouton, 1968; *Between Old and New: The Ottoman Empire under Sultan Selim III, 1789-1807*, Harvard University Press, 1971; *History of the Ottoman Empire and Modern Turkey* (History Book Club alternate selection), Cambridge University Press, Volume I: *Empire of the Gazis: The Rise and Decline of the Ottoman Empire, 1280-1808*, 1976, Volume II: (with wife, Ezel Kural Shaw) *Reform, Revolution and Republic: The Rise of Modern Turkey, 1808-1975*, 1977; (with Alessio Bombacci) *L'Impero Ottomano*, Utet (Turin), 1981. Also author of *Cairo's Archives and the History of Ottoman Egypt*, 1956. Contributor of articles to professional journals.

WORK IN PROGRESS: Islamic Society and the West in Nineteenth-Century Turkey, for Oxford University Press; *The Age of Abd ul-Hamid II: Crucible of Independence: Turkey at War, 1914-1923*.

*   *   *

SHEPHERD, George W., Jr.   1926-

PERSONAL: Born October 26, 1926, in Shanghai, China; married Shirley Brower, 1948; children: Mary Claire, Holland William, Sharon Anne, Harold Sargent. *Education:* Attended University of Michigan; University of London, Ph.D., 1952; Union Theological Seminary, post-graduate study. *Home:* 2370 South Franklin St., Denver, Colo. 80210. *Office:* Graduate School of International Studies, University of Denver, Denver, Colo.

CAREER: Technical assistant, African farmers' marketing organization, East Africa, 1952-53; American Committee on Africa, New York, N.Y., director, 1953-55; Brooklyn College (now Brooklyn College of the City University of New York), Brooklyn, N.Y., lecturer in political science, 1955-58; St. Olaf College, Northfield, Minn., acting chairman of department of political science and director of foreign service program, 1958-60; University of Denver, Social Science Foundation, Denver, Colo., assistant professor and research associate, 1961-65, Graduate School of International Studies, associate professor, 1965-68, professor of international studies, 1968—, director of Center of International Race Relations, 1968-74. Visiting professor, University of Minnesota, 1961. Chairman of International Relations Committee, United Church of Christ, 1967-72. *Member:* International Studies Association, Association of Concerned African Scholars (member of executive committee). *Awards, honors:* Anisfield-Wolf Award for contribution to race relations, 1956, for *They Wait in Darkness;* Rockefeller grant to study foreign policy of Ghana for Brookings Institution, 1961; United Nations fellowship, 1973.

WRITINGS: They Wait in Darkness, Day, 1955; *Politics of African Nationalism,* Praeger, 1962; *Nonaligned Black Africa,* Lexington Books, 1970; (editor) *Racial Influences in American Foreign Policy,* Basic Books, 1971; *Anti-Apartheid,* Greenwood Press, 1977. Also co-editor of *Global Human Rights,* 1981. Contributor to *Christian Century, New Republic,* and other magazines. Editor, *Africa Today,* 1965—.

WORK IN PROGRESS: Beyond Materialism: A Critique of Christian and Scientific Socialism; Third World Tribute; Indian Ocean Sketches; The Earth Mother; editing *Developing Human Rights.*

SIDELIGHTS: George W. Shepherd told *CA* that during "the past ten years [I] have been primarily concerned with race relations in Africa and the U.S. During the next ten I will expand my interests into problems of global rights and work with new mediums such as the novel, travelogues, scripts, and lectures on the issues of human rights, nuclear disaster, war and peace, ecology, and alternative life styles."

*   *   *

SHEPPERSON, Wilbur Stanley   1919-

PERSONAL: Born May 23, 1919, in Arbela, Mo.; son of Clinton Artis and Ruby (Dieterich) Shepperson; married Margaret Dietze, 1945; children: Stanley Carlyle, Tara Loraine. *Education:* Northeast Missouri State College (now University), B.S., 1941; Johns Hopkins University, graduate study, 1941-42; University of Denver, M.A., 1947; graduate study, University of London, 1948-49; Western Reserve University (now Case Western Reserve University), Ph.D., 1951. *Office:* Department of History, University of Nevada, Reno, Nev. 89507.

CAREER: Glenn L. Martin Aircraft Corp., Baltimore, Md., personnel consultant, 1941-42; Western State College of Colorado, Gunnison, instructor, 1947-48; U.S. Department of State, Washington, D.C., 1951; University of Nevada, Reno, 1951—, began as instructor, professor of history and chairman of department, 1963—. Visiting lecturer, University of Wales, 1954-55. *Military service:* U.S. Army Air Forces, 1942-46; became lieutenant. *Member:* American Historical Association, Society of Cymmrodorian (honorary fellow), Phi Alpha Theta (national councillor; national director). *Awards, honors:* Grants of $25,000 from various foundations for research purposes; Fulbright scholar, University of Liverpool, 1967-68.

WRITINGS: British Emigration to North America: Projects and Opinions in the Early Victorian Period, University of Minnesota Press, 1957; *Samuel Roberts: A Welsh Colonizer in Civil War Tennessee,* University of Tennessee Press, 1961; (con-

tributor) Fritiof Ander, editor, *In the Trek of Immigrants,* Augustana College Library, 1964; *Emigration and Disenchantment: Portraits of Englishmen Repatriated from the United States,* University of Oklahoma Press, 1965; *Retreat to Nevada: A Socialist Colony of World War I,* University of Nevada Press, 1966; *Restless Strangers: Nevada's Immigrants and Their Interpreters,* University of Nevada Press, 1970; *Questions from the Past,* University of Nevada Press, 1973; (editor) Anita Kunkler, *Hardscrabble: A Narrative of the California Hill Country,* University of Nevada Press, 1975. Also author of several pamphlets. Editor, "Nevada Studies in History and Political Science," 1960—. News editor, *Historian* (Phi Alpha Theta quarterly), 1951-53; editor, *Halcion: A Journal of the Humanities,* 1978—.

*   *   *

SHERLOCK, Philip Manderson   1902-

PERSONAL: Born February 25, 1902, in Jamaica, West Indies; son of Terence Manderson (a pastor) and Adina (Trotter) Sherlock; married Grace Marjorye Verity, December 2, 1942; children: John, Hilary, Christopher. *Education:* University of London (external student), B.A. (first class honors), 1925.

CAREER: University of the West Indies, Jamaica, director of adult education, 1947-60, pro-vice-chancellor, 1960-63, vice-chancellor, 1963-69. *Member:* Association of Caribbean Universities and Research Institutes (secretary general, 1969—), Author's Guild, National Liberal Club, West India Club. *Awards, honors:* Commander of the British Empire, 1957; L.L.D. from University of Leeds, 1958 and St. Andrews University, 1968; D.C.L. from University of New Brunswick, 1966 and Acadia University, 1966; Knight Commander of the British Empire, 1968.

WRITINGS: (Editor) *New Age Poetry Book,* Longmans, Green, 1932; *The Aborigines of Jamaica,* Institute of Jamaica, 1939; *Anansi: The Spider Man* (folk tales), Crowell, 1954; (with John Horace Parry) *A Short History of the West Indies,* St. Martin's, 1956, 3rd edition, 1971; *Caribbean Citizen,* Longmans, Green, 1957, 2nd edition, 1963; *Man in the Web and Other Folk Tales,* Longmans, Green, 1959.

West Indian Story, Longmans, Green, 1960, 3rd edition, 1971; *Three Finger Jack's Treasure,* Macmillan, 1962; *Jamaica Way,* Longmans, Green, 1962; *General Knowledge for Caribbean Schools,* Macmillan, 1964; (with Ridout) *Better English for Caribbean Schools,* Ginn, 1965; *Self Help English for Caribbean Schools,* Macmillan, 1965; *West Indian Folk Tales,* Oxford University Press, 1966; *Jamaica: A Junior History,* Collins, 1966; *The West Indies,* Walker & Co., 1966; *The Land and People of West Indies,* Lippincott, 1967; *This Is Jamaica,* Hodder & Stoughton, 1968; *Iguana's Trail: Crick Crack Stories from the Caribbean,* Crowell, 1969; *Belize,* Collins, 1969; *West Indian Nations: A New History,* St. Martin's, 1973; (with daughter, Hilary Sherlock) *Ears and Tails and Common Sense: More Stories from the Caribbean,* Crowell, 1974; *Shout for Freedom: A Tribute to Sam Sharpe,* Macmillan, 1976.†

*   *   *

SHERMAN, Joan
   See DERN, Erolie Pearl Gaddis

*   *   *

SHERWOOD, John (Herman Mulso)   1913-

PERSONAL: Born May 14, 1913, in Cheltenham, England;

son of Charles Edward and N. Claire (Flecker) Sherwood; married Joan Mary Yorke, 1952; children: Mary Claire. *Education:* Studied at Marlborough College, and at Oriel College, Oxford. *Religion:* Anglican Church. *Home:* 4 Surrenden Dering, Pluckley, Ashford, Kent TN27 0PR, England. *Agent:* A. P. Watt & Son, 26/28 Bedford Row, London WC1R 4HL, England.

CAREER: Freelance writer. Schoolmaster, 1935-39; executive and head of the French Language Service, British Broadcasting Corp., beginning 1945. *Military service:* British Army, Intelligence Corps, 1940-45; became major. *Member:* Crime Writers Association, Association of Broadcasting Staff, Royal Automobile Club, The Bushmen. *Awards, honors:* Radio documentary prize, Italia Prize Competition, 1961.

WRITINGS: Dr. Bruderstein Vanishes, Doubleday, 1949 (published in England as *The Disappearance of Dr. Bruderstein,* Hodder & Stoughton, 1949); *Ambush for Anatol,* Doubleday, 1952; *Mr. Blessington's Imperialist Plot,* Doubleday, 1951; *Two Died in Singapore,* Hodder & Stoughton, 1954; *Vote against Poison,* Hodder & Stoughton, 1956; *Undiplomatic Exit,* Doubleday, 1958; *The Sleuth and the Liar,* Doubleday, 1961 (published in England as *The Half Hunter,* Gollancz, 1961), reprinted, State Mutual Book, 1979; *No Golden Journey: A Biography of James Elroy Flecker,* Heinemann, 1973; *Honesty Will Get You Nowhere,* Gollancz, 1977; *Limericks of Lachasse,* Macmillan, 1978; *The Hour of the Hyenas,* Macmillan, 1979. Also author of scripts for British Broadcasting Corp.

WORK IN PROGRESS: Another thriller.†

*　　*　　*

SHERWOOD, Morgan B(ronson)　1929-

PERSONAL: Born October 22, 1929, in Anchorage, Alaska; son of Jay Robert (a railroad employee) and Agnes (Banner) Sherwood; married Jeanie Woods, June 7, 1963. *Education:* San Diego State College (now University), A.B., 1953; University of California, Berkeley, M.A., 1958, Ph.D., 1962. *Office:* Department of History, University of California, Davis, Calif. 95616.

CAREER: University of California, Berkeley, research historian in Washington, D.C., 1961-64; University of Cincinnati, Cincinnati, Ohio, assistant professor of history, 1964-65; University of California, Davis, assistant professor, 1965-69, associate professor, 1969-74, professor of history, 1974—. *Military service:* U.S. Army, 1953-54. *Member:* Organization of American Historians, Agricultural History Society, Society for the History of Technology, Western History Association.

WRITINGS: Exploration of Alaska, 1865-1900, Yale University Press, 1965; (editor with J. L. Penick, C. W. Pursell, and D. C. Swain) *The Politics of American Science,* Rand McNally, 1965, revised edition, MIT Press, 1972; (editor) *Alaska and Its History,* University of Washington Press, 1967; (contributor) M. Kranzberg and Pursell, editors, *Technology in Western Civilization,* Oxford University Press, 1967; (contributor) C. J. Schneer, editor, *Toward a History of Geology,* MIT Press, 1969; (editor) *The Cook Inlet Collection,* Alaska Northwest Publishers, 1974.

(Contributor) H. R. Lamar, editor, *The Reader's Encyclopedia of the American West,* Crowell, 1977; (contributor) *The Smithsonian Book of Invention,* Norton, 1978; (contributor) A. Shalkop, editor, *Exploration in Alaska,* Cook Inlet Historical Society, 1980; *Big Game in Alaska: A History of Wildlife and People,* Yale University Press, 1981. Contributor to profes-

sional journals. Editorial advisor to *Agricultural History, Pacific Historical Review,* and *Pacific Northwest Quarterly.*

WORK IN PROGRESS: Patent Nonsense in American Technology; Historiography of Alaska.

*　　*　　*

SHIFFERT, Edith (Marcombe)　1916-
(Edith Marion Marcombe)

PERSONAL: Born January 9, 1916, in Toronto, Ontario, Canada; daughter of John Benjamin (an engineer) and Annie Marie (Drew) Marcombe; married Steven R. Shiffert (a technical writer), March 15, 1940 (divorced, 1970). *Education:* Attended University of Washington, Seattle, 1956-62. *Religion:* Presently non-formal. *Office:* Department of English, Kyoto Seika College, Iwakura-Kino, Sakyo-ku, Kyoto, Japan 606.

CAREER: Doshisha University, Kyota, Japan, instructor in English, 1963-69; Kyoto Seika College, Kyoto, professor of English, 1969—. Lecturer at Kyoto University, 1966-68, 1975-77. Has read poetry on radio and television and at universities and bookstores.

WRITINGS: In an Open Woods (poetry), A. Swallow, 1961; *For a Return to Kona* (poetry), A. Swallow, 1964; *The Kyoto Years* (poetry), Kyoto Seika College Press (Japan), 1971; (translator and compiler with Yuki Sawa) *Anthology of Modern Japanese Poetry,* Tuttle, 1971; (translator with Sawa) *Chieko* (chapbook), Stinktree Press, 1973; (translator) Taeko Takaori, *When a Bird Rests and Other Tanka,* privately printed, 1974; *A Grasshopper* (poetry), White Pine Press, 1976; (translator with Sawa) *Haiku Master Buson,* Heian International Press, 1978; *New and Selected Poems,* White Pine Press, 1979; *A Way to Find Out* (poetry), Raiyu Press, 1979.

Contributor to anthologies, including: *Japan, Theme and Variations,* Tuttle, 1959; *The New York Times Book of Verse,* edited by T. Lask, Macmillan, 1970; *The Women Poets in English,* edited by A. Stanford, McGraw, 1972; *The Contemporary World Poets,* edited by D. Junkins, Harcourt, 1976; *For Rexroth,* edited by G. Gardner, The Ark, 1980. Contributor of poetry, translations, essays, and book reviews, to journals in the United States, Canada, Australia, and Japan.

SIDELIGHTS: Edith Shiffert was raised in western New York state and in Detroit, Mich. and has lived in California, Hawaii, Alaska, Washington state, and Kyoto, Japan. Half her adult life has been spent in remote mountain areas and half in large cities. She told *CA* that she "enjoys a quite life with friends, books, music, hiking, and travel, along with teaching and writing. [My] interests have centered around the Pacific area, its physical environment, history, anthropology, literatures, arts, religions, and changing patterns of life. [My] poetry is especially influenced by that of China and Japan as well as by their landscapes and daily life, and weathers. What [I have] most enjoyed teaching has been the poetry of Walt Whitman, Robert Frost, William Carlos Williams, and Theodore Roethke. The Asia poets from whom [I have] learned most have been Tu Fu, Han Shan, Milarepa, Buson, and Ry-kan."

*　　*　　*

SHILS, Edward B.　1915-

PERSONAL: Born May 29, 1915, in Philadelphia, Pa.; son of Benjamin (a manufacturer) and Dena (Berkowitz) Shils; married Shirley R. Seigle, July 31, 1942; children: Ronnie Lois, Nancy Ellen, Edward B., Jr. *Education:* University of Pennsylvania, B.S. in Economics, 1936, M.A., 1937, Ph.D., 1940.

Home: 335 South Woodbine Ave., Narberth, Pa. 19072. *Office:* Wharton Entrepreneurial Center, Wharton School, University of Pennsylvania, Philadelphia, Pa. 19104.

CAREER: Self-employed as governmental research consultant, 1937-42, as economist, personnel consultant, and management consultant, Philadelphia, Pa., 1946—; Temple University, Phialdelphia, professor of social science, 1948-55; University of Pennsylvania, Wharton School, Philadelphia, associate professor of industrial relations, 1956-68, professor of management and chairman of department, 1968-76, director of Wharton Entrepeneurial Center, 1973—. *Military service:* U.S. Army, Signal Corps, 1943-46; became lieutenant. *Member:* American Management Association, American Political Science Association, American Arbitration Association.

WRITINGS: Finance and Financial Administration of the School District of Philadelphia, Murrelle Publishing, 1941; *Automation and Industrial Relations,* Holt, 1963; (with C. Taylor Whittier) *Teachers, Administrators, and Collective Bargaining,* Crowell, 1968; (with others) *Industrial Peacemaker: George W. Taylor's Contributions to Collective Bargaining,* University of Pennsylvania Press, 1979. Contributor of articles to business and economics journals.

WORK IN PROGRESS: A political biography of a former mayor of one of America's great cities.

*   *   *

SHIRREFFS, Gordon D(onald) 1914-
(Gordon Donalds, Jackson Flynn, Stewart Gordon)

PERSONAL: Born January 15, 1914, in Chicago, Ill.; son of George and Rose (Warden) Shirreffs; married Alice Johanna Gutwein, February 8, 1941; children: Carole Alice, Brian Allen. *Education:* Attended Northwestern University, 1946-49; California State University, Northridge, B.A., 1967, M.A., 1973. *Home and office:* 17427 San Jose St., Granada Hills, Calif. 91344. *Agent:* Donald MacCampbell, Inc., 12 East 41st St., New York, N.Y. 10017.

CAREER: Union Tank Car Co., Chicago, Ill., clerk, 1935-40, 1946; Brown & Bigelow, Chicago, salesman, 1946-47; Shirreffs Gadgets and Toys, Chicago, owner, 1948-52; professional writer, 1952—. *Military service:* U.S. Army, 1940-45, 1948; became captain. *Member:* Authors Guild, Veterans of Foreign Wars, Disabled American Veterans, National Rifle Association, Western Writers of America. *Awards, honors:* Commonwealth Club of California Silver Medal Award, 1962, for *The Gray Sea Raiders.*

WRITINGS: Rio Bravo, Gold Medal Books, 1956; *Code of the Gun,* Crest Books, 1956; (under pseudonym Gordon Donalds) *Arizona Justice,* Avalon, 1956; *Range Rebel,* Pyramid Books, 1956; *Fort Vengeance,* Popular Library, 1957; (under pseudonym Stewart Gordon) *Gunswift,* Avalon, 1957; *Bugles on the Prairie,* Gold Medal Books, 1957; *Massacre Creek,* Popular Library, 1957; *Son of the Thunder People,* Westminster, 1957; (under pseudonym Gordon Donalds) *Top Gun,* Avalon, 1957; *Shadow Valley,* Popular Library, 1958; *Ambush on the Mesa,* Gold Medal Books, 1958; *Swiftwagon,* Westminster, 1958; *Last Train from Gun Hill,* Signet Books, 1958; *The Brave Rifles,* Gold Medal Books, 1959; *The Lonely Gun,* Avon, 1959; *Roanoke Raiders,* Westminster, 1959; *Fort Suicide,* Avon, 1959; *Trail's End,* Avalon, 1959; *Shadow of a Gunman,* Ace Books, 1959; *Renegade Lawman,* Avon, 1959.

Apache Butte, Ace Books, 1960; *They Met Danger,* Whitman, 1960; *The Mosquito Fleet,* Chilton, 1961; *The Rebel Trumpet,* Westminster, 1961; *The Proud Gun,* Avon, 1961; *Hangin'*

Pards, Ace Books, 1961; *Ride a Lone Trail,* Ace Books, 1961; *The Gray Sea Raiders,* Chilton, 1961; *Powder Boy of the Monitor,* Westminster, 1961; *The Valiant Bugles,* Signet Books, 1962; *Tumbleweed Trigger,* Ace Books, 1962; *The Haunted Treasure of the Espectros,* Chilton, 1962; *Voice of the Gun* (also see below), Ace Books, 1962; *Rio Desperado* (also see below), Ace Books, 1962; *Action Front!,* Westminster, 1962; *The Border Guidon,* Signet Books, 1962; *Mystery of Lost Canyon,* Chilton, 1963; *Slaughter at Broken Bow,* Avon, 1963; *The Cold Seas Beyond,* Westminster, 1963; *The Secret of the Spanish Desert,* Chilton, 1964; *Quicktrigger* (also see below), Ace Books, 1964; *Too Tough to Die,* Avon, 1964; *The Nevada Gun,* World Distributors, 1964; *The Hostile Beaches,* Westminster, 1964; *The Hidden Rider of Dark Mountain,* Ace Books, 1964; *Blood Justice,* Signet Books, 1964; *Gunslingers Three,* World Distributors, 1964; *Judas Gun,* Gold Medal Books, 1964; *Last Man Alive,* Avon, 1964; *Now He Is Legend,* Gold Medal Books, 1965; *The Lone Rifle,* Signet Books, 1965; *The Enemy Seas,* Westminster, 1965; *Barranca,* Signet Books, 1965; *Bolo Battalion,* Westminster, 1966; *Southwest Drifter,* Gold Medal Books, 1967; *Torpedoes Away,* Westminster, 1967; *The Godless Breed,* Gold Medal Books, 1968; *Five Graves to Boothill,* Avon, 1968, revised edition, 1970; *The Killer Sea,* Westminster, 1968; *Mystery of the Lost Cliffdwelling,* Prentice-Hall, 1968; *Showdown in Sonora,* Gold Medal Books, 1969.

Jack of Spades, Dell Books, 1970; *The Manhunter,* Gold Medal Books, 1970; *Brasada,* Dell Books, 1972; *Bowman's Kid,* Gold Medal Books, 1973; *Mystery of the Haunted Mine,* School Book Service, 1973; (under pseudonym Jackson Flynn) *Shootout,* Universal Publishing, 1974; *Renegade's Trail,* Gold Medal Books, 1974; *The Apache Hunter,* Gold Medal Books, 1976; *The Marauders,* Gold Medal Books, 1977; *Legend of the Damned,* Gold Medal Books, 1977; *Rio Diablo,* Ace Books, 1977; *Captain Cutlass,* Gold Medal Books, 1978; *Three from the West* (contains *Rio Desperado, Quicktrigger,* and *Voice of the Gun*), Ace Books, 1978.

Calgaich the Swordsman, Playboy Press, 1980; *The Untamed Breed,* Gold Medal Books, 1981. Contributor of over 150 short stories and novelettes to periodicals.

WORK IN PROGRESS: Two more novels which continue the "Southwestern Saga" series begun with *The Untamed Breed.*

SIDELIGHTS: Gordon D. Shirreffs's western novels have been published in Norway, Sweden, Denmark, Finland, Germany, France, Italy, Spain, England, Canada, and Australia. He told *CA:* "As a writer of the historical/saga type of novel, I like to walk the ground and view the scenes depicted in the novel. Some such areas which I covered thoroughly in a search for authenticity have been Sonora, Chihuahua, Durengo, and Baja California in Mexico; Scotland, England, and Rome for a 4th century A.D. novel *Calgaich the Swordsman;* four thousand miles by automobile through Utah, Wyoming, Colorado, West Texas, and New Mexico for background material essential to my 'Southwestern Saga' novel *The Untamed Breed.* . . . I like to feel that when I write of an area I have been there and know it well. I research many autobiographies, journals and contemporary accounts of the times involved in each novel. I believe that the land itself, the flora and fauna, are background characters in the novel. The weapons used, food and drink, types of housing, customs, etc., are thoroughly researched to give a full three-dimensional effect to the novel. I realize now, after twenty-eight years as a full time professional writer, that no story or novel is just quite what I wanted it to be, and that research is never quite complete. However, this serves to good purpose—it makes one strive just a little harder on the work in progress to achieve that will-o'-the-wisp goal.''

MEDIA ADAPTATIONS: Massacre Creek was filmed as "Galvanized Yankee" for "Playhouse 90" (television), *Rio Bravo* as "Oregon Passage" by Allied Artists, *Silent Reconing* as "The Lonesome Trail" by Lippert Productions, *Judas Gun* as "A Long Ride from Hell" by B.R.C. Productions, and *Blood Justice* by Jacques Bar Productions.

AVOCATIONAL INTERESTS: Arms collecting, model making, marksmanship (pistol, rifle, and bow), fishing, hunting, travel, Southwest legends, and sea lore.

*   *   *

SHORT, Ruth Gordon

PERSONAL: Born in New York, N.Y.; daughter of Samuel Louden and Elizabeth (Bourne) Gordon; married James J. Short (a physician), 1923 (died, 1970); children: Ellen Short Oblander, Beatrice Short Neall, J. Gordon, Carlyle Bryant. *Education:* Attended Washington Missionary College. *Religion:* Seventh-day Adventist. *Home:* 24 East Fountain Way, Fresno, Calif. 93704.

CAREER: Writer.

WRITINGS: Stories of the Reformation in England and Scotland, Review & Herald, 1944; *Stories of the Reformation in the Netherlands,* Review & Herald, 1948; *Meet Martin Luther,* Zondervan, 1959; *Martin Luther, the Man,* Good News Publishers, 1960; *Windows of Heaven,* Southern Publishing, 1960; *Affectionately Yours, John Wesley,* Southern Publishing, 1963; *Evenings with Famous Christians,* Review & Herald, 1964; *Into the Lion's Jaws: The Story of David Livingston,* Review & Herald, 1971; *George Whitefield, Trumpet of the Lord,* Review & Herald, 1979.

WORK IN PROGRESS: A biography of Sir Wilfred Grenfell.

SIDELIGHTS: Ruth Gordon Short spent 1960-61 in Korea, teaching conversational English.

*   *   *

SHULMAN, Irving   1913-

PERSONAL: Born May 21, 1913, in Brooklyn, N.Y.; son of Max and Sarah (Ress) Shulman; married Julia Grager, July 9, 1938; children: Joan. *Education:* Ohio University, A.B. (magna cum laude), 1937; Columbia University, A.M., 1938; University of California, Los Angeles, Ph.D., 1972; additional study at New York University, 1938-41, and George Washington University, 1941-43. *Office:* c/o William E. Stein, CPA, 9454 Wilshire Blvd., Suite 801, Beverly Hills, Calif. 90212.

CAREER: Employed with the U.S. Government, Washington, D.C., 1941-47, as statistician and information specialist with War Department, occupational analyst with Foreign Economic Administration, administrative assistant with Department of State; George Washington University, Washington, D.C., member of English faculty, 1943-47; University of California, Los Angeles, teaching assistant, English faculty, 1961-64; California State College at Los Angeles (now California State University, Los Angeles), assistant professor, English department, 1964-65. Screenwriter and novelist. *Member:* Modern Language Association of America, American Association of University Professors, Writers Guild of America West, Phi Epsilon Pi, Zeta Beta Tau, Alumni Association of Southern California (president, 1959-65).

WRITINGS: The Amboy Dukes, Doubleday, 1947, reprinted, Pocket Books, 1974; *Cry Tough,* Dial, 1949, reprinted, 1972; *The Big Brokers,* Dial, 1951; *The Square Trap,* Little, Brown,

1953, reprinted, Arno, 1976; (contributor) *Tales of Love and Fury,* Avon, 1953; *Children of the Dark,* Holt, 1955; *Good Deeds Must Be Punished,* Holt, 1955; *Calibre,* Popular Library, 1956; *The Velvet Knife,* Doubleday, 1959; *The Short End of the Stick* (also see below), Doubleday, 1960; (with Peggy Bristol) *The Roots of Fury,* Doubleday, 1961; *The Notorious Landlady* (novelization of screenplay of same title), Fawcett, 1962; *West Side Story* (novelization of play of same title), Pocket Books, 1961; *Harlow: An Intimate Biography,* Random House, 1964; *Valentino,* Trident, 1967; *The Short End of the Stick and Other Stories,* Pocket Books, 1968; *Jackie: The Exploitation of a First Lady,* Trident, 1970; *The Devil's Knee,* Trident, 1973; *Saturn's Child,* Saturday Review Press, 1976.

Screenplays: "City across the River" (based on Shulman's novel, *The Amboy Dukes;* also see above), Universal, 1949; "Journey into Light," Twentieth-Century Fox, 1951; "The Ring" (based on Shulman's novel, *The Square Trap;* also see above), United Artists, 1952; "Rebel without a Cause" (based on Shulman's novel, *Children of the Dark;* also see above), Warner Brothers, 1955; "Champ for a Day" (based on a story by William Fay), Republic, 1953; "College Confidential" (based on a story by Albert Zugsmith), Universal, 1960. Contributor of many short stories to popular magazines.

MEDIA ADAPTATIONS: Cry Tough was filmed by United Artist in 1959; *Harlow: An Intimate Biography* was filmed by Paramount in 1965; the film rights to *The Big Brokers* have been purchased.

AVOCATIONAL INTERESTS: Bonsai culture.

*   *   *

SIBLEY, Mulford Quickert   1912-

PERSONAL: Born June 14, 1912, in Marston, Mo.; son of William Austin (a physician) and Erna (Quickert) Sibley; married Marjorie Muriel Hedrick (a librarian), May 23, 1942; children: Muriel Katherine Sibley Welch, Martin Christopher Hedrick. *Education:* Central State College (now Central State University), Edmond, Okla., B.A., 1933; University of Oklahoma, M.A., 1934; University of Minnesota, Ph.D., 1938. *Politics:* Socialist. *Religion:* Quaker. *Home:* 2018 Fairmount, St. Paul, Minn. 55105. *Office:* Department of Political Science, University of Minnesota, Minneapolis, Minn. 55455.

CAREER: University of Illinois at Urbana-Champaign, 1938-48, began as instructor, became assistant professor of political science; University of Minnesota, Minneapolis, associate professor, 1948-57, professor of political science, 1958—. Visiting professor at Stanford University, 1957-58, Cornell University, 1962-63, State University of New York at Binghamton, 1967-68, and Duke University, 1977. Delegate to several Socialist Party conventions and chairman of Twin Cities Branch of Socialist Party, 1948-54; president, Twin Cities Co-ops Credit Union, 1957.

MEMBER: International Political Science Association, American Political Science Association (member of executive council, 1975-77), American Society for Psychical Research, American Association for Advancement of Science, Society for Social Responsibility in Science, American Studies Association, British Society for Psychical Research, War Resisters League, Fellowship of Reconciliation, Minnesota Civil Liberties Union (member of board of directors, 1969-76). *Awards, honors:* Franklin Roosevelt Prize, American Political Science Association, 1953, for *Conscription of Conscience* as "most significant study of relation of government to human welfare''; Rockefeller fellowship in political philosophy, 1959-60; distinguished teaching award, University of Minnesota.

WRITINGS: The Political Theories of Modern Pacifism, Pacifist Research Bureau, 1944, reprinted, Garland Publishing, 1972; (with P. E. Jacob) *Conscription of Conscience,* Cornell University Press, 1952; (contributor and editor) *Introduction to Social Science: Personality, Work, Community,* Lippincott, 1953, revised edition, 1961; *Unilateral Initiatives and Disarmament,* American Friends Service Committee, 1962; (and editor) *The Quiet Battle,* Doubleday, 1963; *Political Ideas and Ideologies,* Harper, 1970; *The Obligation to Disobey: Conscience and the Law,* Council of Religion and International Affairs, 1970; *Technology and Utopian Thought,* Burgess, 1971; *Life after Death?,* Dillon, 1975; *Nature and Civilization: Some Implications for Politics,* F. E. Peacock, 1977; (editor) *The Socialist Debate,* Lieber-Atherton, in press. Contributor to periodicals, including *Liberation, New Politics, New Republic,* and to professional journals. Member of board of editors, *Midwest Journal of Political Science,* 1955-58.

WORK IN PROGRESS: A book dealing with ghosts and evidence of out-of-the-body experiences.

SIDELIGHTS: Mulford Quickert Sibley wrote *CA:* ''I consider myself primarily a teacher, with writing as one mode of teaching—but not the most important one.'' *Avocational interests:* Psychical phenomena, religion, baking bread.†

* * *

SILL, Sterling Welling 1903-

PERSONAL: Born March 31, 1903, in Layton, Utah; son of Joseph A. (a school teacher) and Marietta (Welling) Sill; married Doris Mary Thornley, September 4, 1929; children: John Michael, David S., Carolyn (Mrs. Perry Fitzgerald). *Education:* Attended Utah State University, 1921-22, and University of Utah, 1926-27. *Religion:* Church of Jesus Christ of Latter-day Saints (Mormons). *Home:* 1264 Yale Ave., Salt Lake City, Utah 84105. *Office:* 50 East North Temple, No. 2043, Salt Lake City, Utah 84150.

CAREER: New York Life Insurance Co., Salt Lake City, Utah, agent, 1927-32, manager of Inter-Mountain Branch office, 1933-40, inspector of agencies, 1940-68. General authority for Church of Jesus Christ of Latter-day Saints, 1954.—. School teacher in Layton, Utah, 1927-29. Chartered life under-writer, 1934. Member of Layton City Council, 1928-32; member of board of regents of University of Utah, 1940-51; vice-president of *Deseret News,* 1952-62. *Member:* American College of Life Underwriters. *Awards, honors:* H.D.L. from University of Utah, 1953; Carnegie Hero Medal, 1959, for helping to save a drowning swimmer.

WRITINGS—All published by Bookcraft, except as indicated: *Leadership I,* 1958; *Leadership II,* 1960; *Glory of the Sun,* 1961; *The Upward Reach,* 1962; *Law of the Harvest,* 1963; *The Way of Success,* 1964; *What Doth It Profit,* 1964; *The Miracle of Personality,* 1966; *The Quest for Excellence,* 1967; *The Power of Believing,* 1968; *The Three Infinities,* 1969.

The Strength of Great Possessions, 1970; *Making the Most of Yourself,* 1971; *The Keys of the Kingdom,* 1972; *Principles, Promises, and Powers,* Deseret, 1973; *Christmas Sermons,* Deseret, 1973; *The Majesty of Books,* Deseret, 1974; *That Ye Might Have Life,* Deseret, 1974; *The Laws of Success,* Deseret, 1975; *Thy Kingdom Come,* Deseret, 1975; *This Nation under God,* 1976; *Wealth of Wisdom,* Deseret, 1977; *International Journal of Success,* National Institute of Financial Planning, 1978; *How to Personally Profit from the Laws of Success,*

National Institute of Financial Planning, 1978; *The Nine Lives of Sterling W. Sill,* Horizon, 1979; *This We Believe,* 1980.

WORK IN PROGRESS: Lessons from Great Lives, short biographies of famous people and lessons to be learned from each; *Poetry of Success,* poetry and literary lines from great poets and authors showing ways to success; *Meditations,* thoughts to ponder.

* * *

SILVERT, Kalman H(irsch) 1921-1976

PERSONAL: Born March 10, 1921, in Bryn Mawr, Pa.; died June 15, 1976, in New York, N.Y.; son of Henry Jacob (a furniture dealer) and Ida (Levine) Silvert; married Frieda Moskalik (a lecturer in sociology), July 24, 1942; children: Henry Morris, Benjamin Bela, Alexander Manuel. *Education:* University of Pennsylvania, B.A., 1942, M.A., 1947, Ph.D., 1948. *Politics:* Democrat. *Religion:* Jewish. *Home:* Hopson Rd., Norwich, Vt. *Office:* Ford Foundation, 320 East 43rd St., New York, N.Y. 10017.

CAREER: Tulane University, New Orleans, La., assistant professor, 1948-51, associate professor, 1951-56, professor of political science, 1956-60; Dartmouth College, Hanover, N.H., professor of government, 1960-67; New York University, New York, N.Y., professor of politics, 1967-76, director of Ibero-American Center, 1967-72. Visiting professor at University of Delaware, 1948, University of Buenos Aires, 1958, 1960-61, Harvard University, summer, 1964, Brandeis University, spring, 1967, and Boston University, 1973. Staff associate to director of studies of American Universities Field Staff, 1955-67; program adviser in social sciences to Ford Foundation, 1967-76. Consultant to Alliance for Progress.

MEMBER: Latin American Studies Association (founding president, 1965-67), Center for Inter-American Relations, Council on Foreign Relations. *Awards, honors:* Social Science Research Council grant for study in Guatemala, 1952-53; Middle American Research Institute fellowship, 1953; fellowships from Carnegie Corp., 1960-65, 1966-68 (through Brookings Institution); Faculdade Candido Mendes, Rio de Janeiro, Brazil, 1971.

WRITINGS: (With Leonard Reissman and Cliff Wing) *The New Orleans Registered Voter* (monograph), Tulane University, 1956; *A Study in Government: Guatemala,* Middle American Research Institute, Part I: *National and Local Government,* 1955, Part II: *The Constitutions of the State and Republic,* 1958; (with Frank Bonilla) *Education and the Social Meaning of Development: A Preliminary Statement,* American Universities Field Staff, 1961; *The Conflict Society: Reaction and Revolution in Latin America,* Hauser Press, 1961, revised edition, American Universities Field Staff, 1969; *Chile Yesterday and Today,* Holt, 1965; *La politica del desarrollo* (title means ''The Politics of Development''), Editorial Paidos, 1966; *Man's Power: A Biased Guide to Political Thought,* Viking, 1970; (with Reissman) *Education, Class, and Nation: The Experience of Chile and Venezuela,* Elsevier, 1976; (with Joel M. Jutkowitz) *Education, Values, and the Possibilities for Social Change in Chile,* Institute for the Study of Human Issues (Philadelphia), 1976; *The Reason for Democracy,* Viking, 1977; *Essays in Understanding Latin America,* Institute for the Study of Human Issues, 1977.

Editor and contributor: *Expectant Peoples: Nationalism and Development,* Random House, 1963, 2nd edition, Vintage, 1967; *Discussion at Bellagio: The Political Alternatives of Development,* American Universities Field Staff, 1964; *Churches und States: The Religious Institution and Modernization,* American Universities Field Staff, 1967; *The Social Reality of Scientific Myth,* American Universities Field Staff, 1969.

Contributor: *Integracion social en Guatemala* (title means "Social Integration in Guatemala"), Minis de Educacion, Volume III, 1955; R. N. Adams, editor, *Political Change in Guatemalan Indian Communities,* Middle American Research Institute, 1958; Herbert L. Matthews, editor, *The United States and Latin America,* American Assembly, 1959, revised edition, Prentice-Hall, 1963; William Manger, editor, *The Alliance for Progress: A Critical Appraisal,* Public Affairs Press, 1963; John J. Johnson, editor, *Continuity and Change in Latin America,* Stanford University Press, 1964; Werner Baer and Isaac Kerstenetsky, editors, *Inflation and Growth in Latin America,* Irwin, 1964; John D. Martx, editor, *The Dynamics of Change in Latin American Politics,* Prentice-Hall, 1965; W. H. Form and A. A. Blum, editors, *Industrial Relations and Social Change in Latin America,* University of Florida Press, 1965; Gene M. Lyons, editor, *America: Purpose and Power,* Quadrangle, 1965; Robert D. Thomasek, editor, *Latin American Politics: Twenty-Four Studies of the Contemporary Scene,* Doubleday, 1966; Peter G. Snow, editor, *Government and Politics in Latin America,* Holt, 1967; John Plank, editor, *Cuba and the United States,* Brookings Institution, 1967; Fredrick B. Pike, editor, *Latin American History: Select Problems,* Harcourt, 1969; Stanley R. Ross, editor, *Latin America in Transition: Problems in Training and Research,* State University of New York Press, 1970.

Author of reports for American Universities Field Staff, beginning 1955. Contributor to proceedings and annals, and *Encyclopaedia Britannica* and *International Encyclopaedia of the Social Sciences.* Contributor of about sixty articles and reviews to political science and social science journals, including *Social Change, American Journal of Sociology, International Journal, American Behavioral Scientist, Economic Development and Cultural Change,* and *Sociological Review Monograph.* Member of editorial advisory board of *Comparative Politics, American Behavioral Scientist, Transaction's* monograph series, and *Desarrollo Economico.* Consultant to *Encyclopaedia Britannica, World Book Encyclopedia,* and *Education and World Affairs.*

SIDELIGHTS: Kalman H. Silvert spent three years in Africa, and more than eight in Latin America, especially in Chile, Argentina, and Guatemala. He also did research in El Salvador, Mexico, Uruguay, Costa Rica, and Brazil.

OBITUARIES: New York Times, June 16, 1976; *Washington Post,* June 16, 1976.†

*   *   *

SIMON, Norma (Feldstein) 1927-

PERSONAL: Born December 24, 1927, in New York, N.Y.; daughter of Nathan Philip (a restaurant owner) and Winnie Bertha (Lepselter) Feldstein; married Edward Simon (in advertising and consumer research), June 7, 1951; children: Stephanie, Wendy (died, 1979), Jonathan. *Education:* Brooklyn College (now Brooklyn College of the City University of New York), B.A., 1947; Bank Street College of Education, certification in the education of young children, 1948, M.A., 1968; New School for Social Research, graduate study, 1948-50. *Home:* Old County Rd., South Wellfleet, Mass. 02663. *Agent:* Harriet Wasserman Literary Agency, Inc., 230 East 48th St., New York, N.Y. 10017.

CAREER: Frances I. duPont & Co. (broker), New York City, clerical worker, 1943-46; teacher at Vassar Summer Institute,

Poughkeepsie, N.Y., and for Department of Welfare, Brooklyn, N.Y., 1948-49, at Downtown Community School, New York City, 1949-52, and at Thomas School, Rowayton, Conn., 1952-53; Norwalk Community Cooperative Nursery School, Rowayton, founder, director, and teacher, 1953-54; teacher, Norwalk (Conn.) Public Schools, 1962-63; group therapist, Greater Bridgeport (Conn.) Child Guidance Center, 1965-67; special teacher, Mid-Fairfield (Conn.) Child Guidance Center, 1967-69. Consultant, Stamford (Conn.) Pre-School Program, 1965-69; consultant to School Division, Macmillan Publishing Co., Inc., 1968-70; consultant, Davidson Films, Inc., 1969-74, and Aesop Films, 1975; consultant in children's advertising, Dancer-Fitzgerald-Sample, Inc., 1969-79; Bank Street College of Education, consultant to Publications Division, 1967-74, and to Follow-Through Program, 1971-72. *Member:* Authors Guild, National Association for the Education of Young Children, Action for Children's Television, Bank Street College Alumni Association, Friends of Wellfleet Library, Delta Kappa Gamma (honorary member).

WRITINGS: Wet World, Lippincott, 1954; *Baby House,* Lippincott, 1955; *A Tree for Me,* Lippincott, 1956; *Up and Over the Hill,* Lippincott, 1957; *My Beach House,* Lippincott, 1958; *A Day at the County Fair,* Lippincott, 1959; *The Daddy Days,* Abelard, 1959; *Elly the Elephant,* St. Martin's, 1962; *Passover,* Crowell, 1965; *Hanukah,* Crowell, 1966; *Ruthie,* Meredith Corp., 1968; (contributor) Charlotte Winsor, editor, *Dimensions of Language Experience,* Agathon Press, 1975.

Published by Albert Whitman: *Benjy's Bird,* 1965; *What Do I Say?,* 1967; *See the First Star,* 1968; *What Do I Do?,* 1969; *How Do I Feel?,* 1970; *I Know What I Like,* 1971; *I Was So Mad,* 1974; *All Kinds of Families,* 1976; *Cuando me enojo,* 1976; *Why Am I Different?,* 1976; *We Remember Philip,* 1978; *I'm Busy, Too,* 1980; *Go Away, Warts,* 1980; *Nobody's Perfect, Not Even My Mother,* 1981.

Also author of books in two series on Jewish observances published by United Synagogue of America, *Happy Purim Night, The Purim Party, Rosh Hashanah, Yom Kippur, Our First Sukkah, My Simchat Torah Flag,* and *Happy Hanukah,* all 1959, and *Every Friday Night, My Family Seder,* and *Tu Bishvat,* all 1962. Materials development and skills editor, Bank Street/Macmillan Early Childhood Discovery Materials, 1968; associate skills editor, "Discoveries," Houghton, 1972.

SIDELIGHTS: Norma Simon told *CA:* "I have thought of my life's work as children more than writing. Writing books for children is one of the ways in which I can touch the lives of children I will never see. Children themselves have provided the material and inspiration for most of my books, and children reading my books often nod their heads in agreement as they recognize my mirror for their very own feelings, experiences and expressions.

"I've been particularly happy about the Spanish editions for three of my books as well as translations into Swedish, German and Danish of another, *All Kinds of Families.* A good number of my books have been made into film strips, providing still another way to reach children in schools and libraries. But, for myself, I still continue to reach out to children as my sources, and have been a volunteer in our local elementary school one day a week to make these close contacts with children.

"Children and parents seem to enjoy reading and rereading my books, finding new things to see and hear and talk about together and, hopefully, coming to a better understanding of each other."

SIMS, Edward H. 1923-

PERSONAL: Born May 29, 1923, in Orangeburg, S.C.; son of Hugo Sheridan and Jesse Lucile (Howell) Sims; married Martha Lurene Bass, 1960 (divorced); married Bente Christensen, 1969; children: (first marriage) Edward Howell, Jr., Robert Sheridan; (second marriage) Christian, Frederick. *Education:* Wofford College, A.B., 1943; Emory University, graduate study, 1946-47. *Religion:* Methodist. *Home:* 438 Partridge Circle, Sarasota, Fla. *Office address:* Box 532, Orangeburg, S.C. 29115.

CAREER: Times-Democrat, Orangeburg, S.C., managing editor, 1952—; Sims News Bureau, Washington, D.C., founder, 1947—; Editor's Copy Syndicate, Washington, D.C., bureau chief, 1951—, editor and publisher, 1953—; vice-president, Sims Publishing Co. U.S. consul, Munich, Germany, 1963—. *Military service:* U.S. Army Air Forces, three years; became first lieutenant; received six Air Medals as fighter pilot. *Member:* National Press Club (Washington, D.C.), White House Correspondents Association, American Legion, Veterans of Foreign Wars, Metropolitan Club (Washington, D.C.), Shriners, Masons, Rotary Club, Elks.

WRITINGS: American Aces, Harper, 1958; *Greatest Fighter Missions,* Harper, 1962; *The Greatest Aces,* Harper, 1968; *Fighter Tactics,* Harper, 1972. Contributor to magazines.

WORK IN PROGRESS: Missile Sub; Aces over the Oceans.

SIDELIGHTS: Edward H. Sims told *CA* that his view of the contemporary literary scene is "rather grim, not because of a lack of talent," he explained, "but because of the level of so much published. My effort has been to make the truth, as in air history, as exciting as fiction. And I still believe the truth, that is, nonfiction, is better, . . . more rewarding, and informative reading." Sims' books have been published in Germany, England, and several other countries.

* * *

SINGER, J(oel) David 1925-

PERSONAL: Born December 7, 1925, in Brooklyn, N.Y.; son of Morris L. (a businessman) and Anne (Newman) Singer; married Sara Eleanor Green, June 22, 1957; children: Kathryn Louise, Eleanor Anne. *Education:* Duke University, B.A., 1946; New York University, Ph.D., 1956. *Home:* 1042 South Maple Rd., Ann Arbor, Mich. *Office:* Department of Political Science, University of Michigan, Ann Arbor, Mich.

CAREER: Ken Classics Manufacturing Co., New York, N.Y., salesman, 1946-51; Vassar College, Poughkeepsie, N.Y., instructor, 1955-57; University of Michigan, Ann Arbor, visiting assistant professor of political science, 1958-60; U.S. Naval War College, Newport, R.I., resident consultant, 1960; University of Michigan, senior scientist, Mental Health Research Institute, 1960—, associate professor, 1964-65, professor of political science, 1965—, coordinator, world politics program, 1969-75. Visiting fellow, Harvard University, 1957-58; visiting professor, University of Oslo and Institute for Social Research, 1963-64, Carnegie Endowment for International Peace and Graduate Institute of International Studies (Geneva), 1967-68, ZUMA and University of Mannheim, 1976. Consultant to Institute for Defense Analyses, Bendix Systems Divison, Historical Evaluation and Research Organization, and several U.S. departments and agencies. *Military service:* U.S. Navy, 1943-46, 1951-53. *Member:* International Political Science Association, Peace Research Society (president, 1972-73), Amer-

ican Political Science Association. *Awards, honors:* Ford Foundation training grant, 1957-58; Phoenix Memorial Fund research grant, 1959; Fulbright Research Scholar, Institute of Social Research, Oslo, Norway, 1963-64; Carnegie research grant, 1963-67; National Science Foundation research grant, 1967-76, 1978-83; Guggenheim Foundation research grant, 1978-79.

WRITINGS: Financing International Organization: The United Nations Budget Process, Nijhoff, 1961; *Deterrence, Arms Control, and Disarmament: Toward a Synthesis in National Security Policy,* Ohio State University Press, 1962; (editor and contributor) *Human Behavior in International Politics: Contributions from the Social-Psychological Sciences,* Rand McNally, 1965; (editor and contributor) *Quantitative International Politics: Insights and Evidence,* Free Press, 1968; *A General Systems Taxonomy for Political Science* (monograph), General Learning Press, 1971; *Individual Values, National Interests, and Political Development in the International System* (monograph), Sage Publications, 1971; *The Scientific Study of Politics: An Approach to Foreign Policy Analysis* (monograph), General Learning Press, 1972; (with Melvin Small) *The Wages of War, 1816-1965: A Statistical Handbook,* Wiley, 1972; (with Susan Jones) *Beyond Conjecture in International Politics: Abstracts of Data-Based Research,* F. E. Peacock, 1972; (with Dorothy LaBarr) *The Study of International Politics: A Guide to Sources for the Student, Teacher, and Researcher,* Clio Books, 1976; *The Correlates of War I: Research Origins and Rationale,* Free Press, 1979; (with Michael Wallace) *To Auger Well: Early Warning Indicators in World Politics,* Sage Publications, 1979; *Explaining War,* Sage Publications, 1979; *The Correlates of War II: Testing Some Realpolitik Models,* Free Press, 1980; (with Small) *The Wages of War II: International and Civil War Data, 1816-1980,* Sage Publications, 1981.

Contributor: McClelland, editor, *Nuclear Weapons, Missiles, and Future War,* Chandler, 1960; Knorr and Verba, editors, *The International Yearbook of Political Behavior Research,* Free Press, 1965; Elton McNeil, editor, *The Nature of Human Conflict,* Prentice-Hall, 1965; Jacobson, editor, *American Foreign Policy,* Random House, 2nd edition (Singer was not associated with earlier edition), 1965; Lanyi and McWilliams, editors, *Crisis and Continuity in World Politics,* Random House, 1966, 2nd edition, 1972; Zawodny and Kruger, editors, *Man and International Relations,* [San Francisco], 1966; Falk and Mendlovitz, editors, *The Strategy of World Order,* Volume I, World Law Fund, 1966; Toma and Gyorgy, editors, *Basic Issues in International Relations,* Allyn & Bacon, 1967; Knorr and Rosenau, editors, *Contending Approaches to International Politics,* Princeton Unviersity Press, 1968; Snyder and Pruitt, editors, *Theory and Research on the Causes of War,* Prentice-Hall, 1969; Johnson and Singh, editors, *International Organization,* Dodd, 1969; Masannat and Abcarian, editors, *International Politics,* Scribner, 1969; Rosenau, editor, *International Politics and Foreign Policy,* Free Press, revised edition (Singer was not associated with earlier editions), 1969; Pfaltzgraff, editor, *Politics and the International System,* Lippincott, 1969, 2nd edition, 1972; McLellan and others, editors, *Theory and Practice of International Relations,* Prentice-Hall, 3rd edition (Singer was not associated with earlier editions), 1969; Rosenau, editor, *Linkage Politics: Essays in National and International Systems,* Free Press, 1969.

Garnett, editor, *Theories of Peace and Security,* Macmillan, 1970; Kessel, Seddig, and Cole, editors, *Micropolitics,* Holt, 1970; Edwards, editor, *Readings in International Political Analysis,* Holt, 1970; Friedman and others, editors, *Alliance in International Politics,* Allyn & Bacon, 1970; Beer, editor, *Alliances: Latent War Communities in the Contemporary World,*

Holt, 1970; Rosenbaum, editor, *Readings in International Political Behavior*, Prentice-Hall, 1970; Gadlin and Garskof, editors, *Social Issues in Modern Psychology: Readings*, Wadsworth, 1970; Lepawsky and others, editors, *The Search for World Order*, Appleton-Century-Crofts, 1971; Duchacek, editor, *Discord and Harmony*, Holt, 1972; Hahn, editor, *An Anthology of Articles on International Politics*, [Copenhagen], 1972; Rosenau, Davis, and East, editors, *The Analysis of International Politics*, Free Press, 1972; Russett, editor, *Peace, War, and Numbers*, Sage Publications, 1972; Kirkpatrick and Pettit, editors, *Social Psychology of Political Life*, Duxbury, 1973; Gary and Rizzo, editors, *Unity and Diversity: Essays in Honor of Ludwig von Bertalanffy*, Gordon & Breach Science Publishers, 1973; John Gilbert, editor, *American Foreign Policy: Prospects and Perspectives*, St. Martin's, 1974; Coplin and Kegley, editors, *Analyzing International Relations: A Multi-Method Introduction*, Praeger, 1975; Thomas Murray, editor, *Interdisciplinary Aspects of General Systems Theory*, Society for General Systems, 1975; Rosenau, editor, *In Search of Global Patterns*, Free Press, 1976; Bunge, Galtung, and Malitza, editors, *Mathematical Approaches to International Relations*, Romanian Academy of Social and Political Sciences, 1977; Israel Charny, editor, *Strategies against Violence*, Westview, 1978; de Conde, editor, *Dictionary of the History of American Foreign Policy*, Scribner, 1978; Kegley and McGowen, editors, *Challenges to America: U.S. Foreign Policy in the 1980's*, Sage Publications, 1979.

Deutsch, editor, *Methods of Political Behavior Research*, Free Press, 1981; Merritt and Russett, editors, *From National Development to Global Community*, Allen & Unwin, 1981. Also contributor to *Annals of American Academy of Political and Social Science*, 1970, and *Encyclopedia of the Social Sciences*. Contributor of more than eighty articles and reviews to political science journals, including *World Politics, Bulletin of the Atomic Scientists, Nation, Journal of Conflict Resolution, Behavioral Science*, and *International Journal*. Co-editor of special issue of *Journal of Conflict Resolution*, March, 1960. Member of editorial or advisory board of *Background on World Politics*, 1957-59, *Journal of Conflict Resolution*, 1959—, *Journal of Arms Control*, 1962-63, *Background: Journal of the International Studies Association*, 1962-66, *Journal of Peace Research*, 1964-72, *Trans-action*, 1966-72, *Journal of Politics*, 1968-75, *ABC: Political Science and Government*, 1968—, and *Political Science Review*, 1971—.

WORK IN PROGRESS: Several chapters for books and several articles for journals.

* * *

SINGH, Khushwant 1915-

PERSONAL: Born February 2, 1915, in Punjab, India; son of Sobha (a builder) and Veera (Bai) Singh; married; children: Rahul (son), Mala (daughter). *Education:* Government College, Lahore, India, B.A., 1934; Inner Temple, London, England, barrister-at-law, 1938; Kings College, London, LL.B., 1938. *Religion:* Sikh. *Home:* 1A, Janpath, New Delhi, India.

CAREER: Lawyer in practice before the high court, Lahore, India, 1940-47; Indian Government, press attache in Ottawa, Ontario, and London, England, 1947-52; UNESCO, Paris, France, mass communications staff member, 1954-56; Planning Commission, Delhi, India, editor, 1956-58; free-lance writer. Regular broadcaster at various times for Air India, British Broadcasting Corp., and Canadian Broadcasting Corp. Padma Bhushan, 1974; member of Parliament (upper house), 1980.

WRITINGS: The Mark of Vishnu, and Other Stories, Saturn Press, 1950; (editor with Peter Russell) *A Note on G. V. Desani's "All about H. Hatterr and Hali,"* Szeben, 1952; *The Sikhs*, Allen & Unwin, 1953; *Mano Majra*, Grove, 1956 (published in England as *Train to Pakistan*, Chatto & Windus, 1956), published as *Train to Pakistan*, Grove, 1961; *The Unending Trail*, privately printed, 1957; *The Voice of God, and Other Stories*, Jaico Publishing House (Bombay), 1957; (translator and author of introduction) *Adi-Granth, Jupji, the Sikh Prayer*, Royal India, Pakistan and Ceylon Society (London), c. 1958; *I Shall Not Hear the Nightingale*, Grove, 1959; *The Sikhs Today: Their Religion, History, Culture, Customs and Way of Life*, Orient Longmans, 1959, revised edition, 1964.

(Translator) Mirza Mohammad Hadi Ruswa, *The Courtesan of Lucknow*, Orient Longmans, 1961; *The Fall of the Kingdom of the Punjab*, Orient Longmans, 1962; Ranjit Singh, *Maharajah of the Punjab, 1780-1839*, Hillary, 1962; *A History of the Sikhs*, Princeton University Press, Volume I: *1469-1839*, 1963, Volume II: *1839-1964*, 1966; (editor with Jaya Thadani) *Land of the Five Rivers*, Jaico Publishing House, 1965; *Not Wanted in Pakistan*, Rajkamal Prakashan (Delhi), 1965; (with Suneet Vir Singh) *Homage to Guru Gobind Singh*, Jaico Publishing House, 1966, Orientalia, 1971; (with Satindra Singh) *Ghadar, 1915: India's First Armed Revolution*, R & K Publishing House (New Delhi), 1966; (editor) Sita Ram Kohli, *Sunset of the Sikh Empire*, Orient Longmans, 1967; *A Bride for the Sahib, and Other Stories*, Hind Pocket Books (Delhi), 1967; (translator) Rajindar Singh Bedi, *I Take This Woman*, Hind Pocket Books, 1967; (with Arun Joshi) *Shri Ram: A Biography*, Asia Publishing House, 1968; (translator) *Hymns of Guru Nanak*, Orient Longmans, 1969.

Khushwant Singh's India: A Mirror for Its Monsters and Monstrosities, edited by son, Rahul Singh, India Book House, 1970; (translator) Amrita Pritam, *Selected Poems*, Dialogue Calcutta Publications, 1970; *Black Jasmine* (short stories), Jaico Publishing House, 1971; (translator) S. Singh, *Dreams in Debris: A Collection of Punjabi Short Stories*, Jaico Publishing House, 1972; *Khushwant Singh's View of India: Lectures on India's People, Religions, History and Contemporary Affairs*, edited by Rahul Singh, India Book House, 1974; (editor with Qurratulain Hyder) *Stories from India*, Sterling Publishers (New Delhi), 1974; (editor) *Gurus, Godmen, and Good People*, Orient Longman, 1975; *Khushwant Singh on War and Peace in India, Pakistan and Bangladesh*, edited by daughter, Mala Dayal, Hind Pocket Books, 1976; *Good People, Bad People*, edited by Rahul Singh, Orient Paperbacks, 1977; *Indira Ghandi Returns*, Vision Books (New Delhi), 1979; *Iqbal's Dialogue with Allah*, Oxford University Press, 1980; *Editor's Page*, edited by Rahul Singh, India Book House, 1980.

Contributor to newspapers in India and to *Harper's, New York Times, Guardian, Observer*, and *Times Literary Supplement*. Editor, *Illustrated Weekly of India*, 1969-78, *National Herald*, 1978-79, and *Hindustani Times*, 1980—; chief editor, *New Delhi*, 1979-80.

SIDELIGHTS: Khushwant Singh, an Indian novelist, short story writer, historian, journalist, and editor, is best known in the Western world for his books *Train to Pakistan* and *I Shall Not Hear the Nightingale*. Each work, a blend of fiction and nonfiction, deals with various religious, moral, and sociopolitical conflicts of contemporary Indian life in a style critic Vasant Anant Shahane calls "traditional" and "episodic," with "many narrative elements of the tale." But in his attitude towards his subjects, Singh has proven himself to be a non-traditional Indian novelist, as both Phoebe Adams of the *Atlantic* and Santha Rama Rau of the *New York Times Book Review* point out.

"Khushwant Singh is unusual among the Indian novelists in this country in that his novels deal directly with violence," Adams states. "[He] is a businesslike writer, not given to frills or subtlety." Rama Rau agrees, adding: "Khushwant Singh is direct to the point of brutality, unsentimentally observant, and in his bold characterizations he is ready to explore the least appealing aspects of human nature and relationships. His humor—expertly integrated with an essentially sad and cynical story—is wild, broad, unsparing. Unlike most Indian novelists who exhibit either prudishness or a respectable reticence about sex, his love scenes—or rather, sex scenes—are startlingly explicit."

Train to Pakistan, widely regarded as Singh's masterpiece, uses the backdrop of the 1947 partition of Pakistan from India to examine religious unrest between Hindus and Muslims and its tragic effect on the love affair of a Sikh peasant and a Muslim girl. The novel, writes Shahane, is marked by "a well-thought-out structure, an artistically conceived plot, an absorbing narrative, and imaginatively realized characters," as well as "an unobtrusively symbolic framework, meaningful atmosphere and a powerful, unvarnished naturalistic mode of expression." In prose frequently described as "journalistic," Singh "projects with pitiless precision a picture of bestial horror," observes K. R. Srinivasa Iyengar in his book *Indian Writing in English*. "As a piece of fiction, *Train to Pakistan* is cleverly contrived, and the interior stitching and general colouring is beyond cavil. . . . It could not have been an easy novel to write. . . . Khushwant Singh, however, has succeeded through resolved limitation and rigorous selection in communicating to his readers a hint of the grossness, ghastliness and total insanity of the two-nation theory and the Partition tragedy." Shahane agrees that the book's "predominant quality . . . is its stark realism, its absolute fidelity to the truth of life, its trenchant exposition of one of the most moving, even tragic, events of contemporary Indian history. . . . [But it] is no mere realistic tract, nor is it a bare record of actual events. On the contrary, it is a creative rendering of the real, and it reaffirms the novelist's faith in man and renews artistically his avowed allegiance to the humanistic ideal."

I Shall Not Hear the Nightingale also explores the subject of conflict, this time from the perspective of two Indian families. Instead of religious conflict, however, the focus is on political conflict—namely, the question of loyalty to the British versus loyalty to the growing native independence movement. Iyengar notes that in this particular novel "Singh observes as with a microscope, and records his findings without any squeamishness; and his analysis of the complex of relationships within the family and in the wider world, and his unravelling of the tangle of conflicting loyalties, show both understanding and skill. Humour is blended with brutality, mere sentiment is eschewed, and the picture that emerges is arresting as well as amusing."

The *Saturday Review*'s Rosanne Archer, however, finds the novel only mildly interesting, citing the "one-dimensional characters, heavyhanded plotting, a flattened climax, and dollops of sex piled on irrelevantly" as failings that are somewhat redeemed by the author's "easy style" and "the charm and interest of [his] picture of the Punjab land and the Sikh people." On the other hand, Adams declares that "his major characters come to life, and their mistakes have the power to make the reader's conscience itch," while Margaret Parton of the *New York Herald Tribune Book Review* agrees that "Mr. Singh has breathed mordant life into the stock characters of Indian family life. . . . This book is, indeed, a tragedy about the lack of communication between human beings."

In some concluding remarks on Singh's work in general, Shahane writes: "Singh's stories, though masculine in spirit, do not belong to the world of sensation. They contain qualities which are associated with the essays of Addison and Steele, the perceptive comments on social and individual mores, a fine sense of humor, and a not-too-obtrusive moral intention. Though they lack the . . . surface graces of Addison's essays, they embody and encompass his delectable satirical art, his liveliness and humor. . . . [In short,] Khushwant Singh the typical Punjabi rustic has come to terms admirably with Khushwant Singh the highly educated, Westernized, cosmopolitan, cultured person. In this peculiar synthesis lies the extraordinary vigor and urbanity of his style, the down-to-earth worldliness, and the visionary gleam of his art as a creative writer of great passion and power."

AVOCATIONAL INTERESTS: Long walks, birds and trees, wine and women.

BIOGRAPHICAL/CRITICAL SOURCES: New York Times, February 19, 1956; *Springfield Republican*, March 11, 1956; *Commonweal*, March 23, 1956; *San Francisco Chronicle*, March 25, 1956; *New York Herald Tribune Book Review*, April 22, 1956, January 31, 1960; *Saturday Review*, December 12, 1959; *New York Times Book Review*, December 13, 1959; *Atlantic*, January, 1960; Vasant Anant Shahane, *Khushwant Singh*, Twayne, 1972; K. R. Srinivasa Iyengar, *Indian Writing in English*, Asia Publishing House, 1973; *Contemporary Literary Criticism*, Volume XI, Gale, 1979.

—Sketch by Deborah A. Straub

*   *   *

SINKANKAS, John   1915-

PERSONAL: Born May 15, 1915, in Paterson, N.J.; son of Joseph and Domicele (Klimas) Sinkankas; married Marjorie Jane McMichael, February 5, 1940; children: John William, George Martin, Sharon Jane (Mrs. David Tooley), Marjorie Ellen (Mrs. Michael Flood). *Education:* Paterson State Normal School (now William Paterson College of New Jersey), B.A., 1936; Gemological Institute of America, graduate gemologist; attended University of California, San Diego. *Politics:* Republican. *Religion:* Episcopalian. *Home:* 5372 Van Nuys Ct., San Diego, Calif. 92109.

CAREER: U.S. Navy, naval aviator, 1936-61, retiring as captain; *Lapidary Journal*, Del Mar, Calif., editor, 1961; San Diego State College (now University), San Diego, Calif., associate professor of mineralogy, 1963; University of California, San Diego, La Jolla, Scripps Institution of Oceanography, research associate in mineralogy, 1963-74; co-owner of Peri-Lithon Books. *Member:* Mineralogical Society of America (fellow), Authors Guild, Authors League of America, Mineralogical Association of Canada, Cosmos Club (Washington, D.C.). *Awards, honors: Desert* Magazine Southwest Literature Award, for Volume I of *Gemstones of North America*.

WRITINGS—All published by Van Nostrand, except as indicated: *Gem Cutting*, 1955, 2nd edition, 1962; *Gemstones of North America*, Volume I, 1959, Volume II, 1976; *Gemstones and Minerals—How and Where to Find Them*, 1961, 2nd edition published as *Prospecting for Gemstones and Minerals*, 1970; *Mineralogy for the Amateur*, 1964; *Mineralogy: A First Course*, 1966; *Van Nostrand's Standard Catalog of Gems*, 1968; (editor) Hellmuth Boegel, *The Studio Handbook of Minerals*, revised edition (Sinkankas was not associated with earlier edition), Viking, 1971; *Gemstone and Mineral Data Book*, Winchester Press, 1972; *Emeralds and Other Beryls*, Chilton,

1981. Contributor to *Encyclopedia of Science* and to numerous scientific and popular periodicals.

WORK IN PROGRESS: A Bibliography on Gems and Precious Stones.

SIDELIGHTS: John Sinkankas told *CA:* "I have always felt a compulsion to write, but only when providing information which is new or not commonly known, and always with the interests of the beginner-amateur-connoisseur of minerals and gemstones at heart. I refuse to write simply to have something published or to earn royalties. Too many works are now being written simply to 'cash-in' on fads, many such books, unfortunately, being written in the earth science fields of popular interests." If this practice continues, Sinkankas warns, "the public will be flooded with hastily prepared trivia, lavishly illustrated in color, and of little lasting value."

*   *   *

SINOR, Denis 1916-

PERSONAL: Born April 17, 1916, in Kolozsvar, Hungary. *Education:* Budapest University, teacher's degree, 1937; Cambridge University, M.A., 1948. *Office:* Goodbody Hall, Indiana University, Bloomington, Ind. 47405.

CAREER: Sorbonne, University of Paris, Paris, France, assistant, Institut des Hautes Etudes Chinoises, 1941-45; Centre National de la Recherche Scientifique, Paris, attache, 1946-48; Cambridge University, Cambridge, England, university lecturer, 1948-62; Indiana University at Bloomington, professor of Uralic and Altaic, and of history, 1963-75, distinguished professor, 1975—, chairman of department of Uralic and Altaic studies, 1963-81, director, Inner Asian and Uralic National Resource Center, 1963—, director of Asian Studies Research Institute, 1967-81. Secretary-general, Twenty-third International Congress of Orientalists, 1954. Scholar-in-residence, Rockefeller Foundation Study Center. *Military service:* Volunteer French Army, 1944-45. *Member:* Hungarian Academy of Sciences (honorary member), American Oriental Society (president, Midwest branch, 1968-70; national vice-president, 1975; national president, 1975-76), Association for Asian Studies, Linguistic Society of America, Historical Association, International Union of Orientalists (secretary, 1955-64), International Association of Hungarian Studies (vice-president, 1977—), Royal Asiatic Society (secretary, 1955-63), Association of British Orientalists (secretary, 1955-63), Societe Finno-ougrienne (corresponding member), Societe Asiatique, Deutsche Morgenlandische Gesellschaft, Societas Uralo-Altaica (vice-president, 1964—). *Awards, honors:* Research grants from American Council of Learned Societies, 1962, American Philosophical Society, 1963, U.S. Office of Education, 1964, 1965, and National Endowment for the Humanities, 1980-82; Guggenheim fellow, 1968-69, 1981-82; Dr. honoris causa, University of Szeged, 1971.

WRITINGS: (Editor and contributor) *Orientalism and History*, Heffer, 1954; *A Modern Hungarian-English Dictionary*, Heffer, 1957; *History of Hungary*, Praeger, 1959, reprinted, Greenwood Press, 1976; *Introduction a l'etude de l'Eurasie Centrale*, Harrassowitz, 1963; (editor) *Aspects of Altaic Civilizations*, Indiana University, 1963; (editor) *Studies in South, East, and Central Asia*, International Academy of Indian Culture, 1968; *Inner Asia: History, Civilization, Languages*, Indiana University, 1969, 2nd edition, 1971; (editor) *Modern Hungary*, Indiana University Press, 1977. Also author of *Inner Asia and Its Contacts with Medieval Europe*. Also editor of numerous proceedings and studies. Contributor of over two hundred articles, chapters, and reviews to books, encyclope-

dias, magazines, and journals. Editor, *Journal of Asian History;* general editor, "Speculum Historiale" reprint series, Cambridge (England), 1958-66; editor, "Uralic and Altaic" series, Indiana University; vice-chairman of editorial board, "History of the Civilizations of Central Asia" series, UNESCO.

WORK IN PROGRESS: Editing and contributing to *Cambridge History of Inner Asia*, for Cambridge University Press.

SIDELIGHTS: Denis Sinor told *CA:* "I am not a writer but a simple scholar who tries to understand some aspects of man's past. I do not apologize for not being creative because I believe that it is more deeply human to understand the lives of real people and peoples than to create beings that might never have lived. The writer of fiction, if good, is a genius. A good historian—which I have tried to be—creates nothing. His role is to understand what motivated others, how they lived, what were the factors that determined their lives, what were their hopes and why were they thwarted. The writer—if weary of his own life—might find solace in imaginary lives. The historian has no such escape. He must relive the sufferings and hardships of those whom, or whose society, he chose to study. For close to forty years I have tried to study the history of the 'barbarian.' It has not been an easy task and it resulted in many writings almost unreadable in their dryness. But, perhaps, here and there I managed to grasp and to convey to the reader an idea, a concept, a feeling not to be found elsewhere."

*   *   *

SKOU-HANSEN, Tage 1925-

PERSONAL: Born February 12, 1925, in Fredericia, Denmark; son of Johannes (a businessman) and Martha (Skou) Hansen; married Ellen Porsgaard, July 1, 1950; children: Jens, Gerd, Jakob. *Education:* University of Aarhus, M.A., 1950. *Home:* Bredkaer Tvaervej 31, Egaa 8250, Denmark.

CAREER: Free-lance writer, 1967—. *Heretica* (literary periodical), Copenhagen, Denmark, editor, 1952-53; Wivels Forlag (publisher), Copenhagen, literary adviser, 1952-53; Gyldendalske Boghandel Nordisk Forlag (publisher), Copenhagen, literary adviser, 1954-58; *Vindrosen* (literary periodical), Copenhagen, editor, 1954-58; Askov Folk High School, Vejen, Denmark, teacher, 1958-67. *Military service:* Danish Army, 1950-51. *Member:* Danish Film Foundation (member of board, 1970-72), Danish Author's Society (member of board, 1973), Danish State Art Foundation (member of board, 1974-77), Danish P.E.N. *Awards, honors:* Jeanne and Henri Nathansen's Memorial Scholarship, 1972; Critics' Prize, 1977, for *Den haarde frugt;* Danish Academy Prize, 1978; Booksellers' Golden Laurels Award, 1981, for *Over stregen.*

WRITINGS—Published by Gyldendal, except as indicated: *De nogne traeer*, 1957, translation by K. John published as *The Naked Trees*, J. Cape, 1959; *Dagstjernen*, 1962; (editor) *Den moderne roman*, Fremad, 1963; *Paa den anden side* (novel), 1965; *Hjemkomst* (novel), 1969; *Tredje halvleg* (novel), 1971; *Det midlertidige faellesskab* (criticism), 1972; *Tolvtemanden*, Broendums Forlag, 1972; *Medloeberen* (novel), 1973; *Den haarde frugt* (novel), 1977; *Nedtaelling* (play), 1978; *Over stregen* (novel), 1980.

WORK IN PROGRESS: A novel; a play.

*   *   *

SLEIGH, Barbara 1906-1982

PERSONAL: Born January 9, 1906, in Worcestershire, England; daughter of Bernard (an artist) and Stella (Phillp) Sleigh;

married David Davis (head of BBC "Children's Hour"), January 29, 1936; children: Anthony, Hilary (daughter), Fabia. *Education:* Studied at art school, 1922-25, and took art teachers training, 1925-28. *Religion:* Church of England. *Home:* 18 Mount Ave., London W.5, England. *Agent:* Harvey Unna and Stephen Durbridge, Ltd., 14 Beaumont Mews, Marylebone High St., London W1N 4HE, England.

CAREER: Smethwick High School, Staffordshire, England, art teacher, 1928-30; Goldsmiths' College, London, England, lecturer, 1930-33; British Broadcasting Corp., London, assistant on radio program, "Children's Hour," 1933-36; writer for children.

WRITINGS: Carbonel, Parrish, 1955, Bobbs-Merrill, 1958; *Patchwork Quilt,* Parrish, 1956; *Singing Wreath,* Parrish, 1957; *The Seven Days,* Parrish, 1958, Meredith, 1968; *The Kingdom of Carbonel,* Parrish, 1958, Bobbs-Merrill, 1960; *No One Must Know,* Collins, 1962, Bobbs-Merrill, 1963; *North of Nowhere,* Collins, 1964, Coward-McCann, 1966; *Jessamy,* Bobbs-Merrill, 1967; *Pen, Penny, Tuppence,* Hamish Hamilton, 1968; *The Snowball,* Brockhampton Press, 1969.

West of Widdershins, Collins, 1971; *The Smell of Privet* (adult autobiography), Hutchinson, 1971; *Stirabout Stories,* Bobbs-Merrill, 1972; *Ninety-Nine Dragons,* Brockhampton Press, 1974; *Funny Peculiar: An Anthology,* David & Charles, 1974; *Charlie Chumbles,* Hodder & Stoughton, 1977; *Grimblegraw and the Wuthering Witch,* Hodder & Stoughton, 1978; *Winged Magic,* Hodder & Stoughton, 1979. Author of radio plays, stories, and talks for children, for British Broadcasting Corp.

SIDELIGHTS: Barbara Sleigh told *CA:* "My own pleasure in story telling stems from the time when I was a small girl. My father, who among other artistic activities designed stained glass windows, would often use me as a model for an infant angel, or perhaps a young St. John the Baptist. To stop me fidgeting he would tell me tales which kept me riveted. I write stories in the hope that I may pass on some of this same delight to children today."

(Died February 13, 1982)

*   *   *

SMITH, Anna H(ester) 1912-

PERSONAL: Born April 30, 1912, in London, England; daughter of Johannes Jacobus (a professor) and Mabel Florence (Hardy) Smith. *Education:* University of Stellenbosch, M.A., 1933. *Home:* 103 Montevideo Ninth St., Killarney, Johannesburg 2193, South Africa. *Office:* Johannesburg Public Library, Market Square, Johannesburg 2001, South Africa.

CAREER: Stellenbosch University Library, Stellenbosch, Cape Province, South Africa, member of staff, 1934-38; Johannesburg Public Library, Johannesburg, South Africa, member of staff, 1938—, city librarian, 1960-75; Africana Museum, Johannesburg, director, 1960-75. Part-time lecturer in librarianship, University of the Witwatersrand, beginning 1958. *Member:* South African Library Association (fellow), Museums Association of Southern Africa, and other professional organizations. *Awards, honors:* Dr. of Laws from University of the Witwatersrand, 1974.

WRITINGS: (Compiler with Jan Ploeger) *Pictorial Atlas of the History of the Union of South Africa,* J. L. van Schaik (Pretoria, South Africa), 1949; (author of notes) *Claudius Water-Colours in the Africana Museum,* Africana Museum, 1952; (editor) *Pictorial History of Johannesburg,* Verry, 1956.

(Compiler) *Johannesburg Street Names,* Juta, 1971; *South Africa,* Abner Schram, 1971 (published in Amsterdam as *The Spread of Printing: Eastern Hemisphere, South Africa,* van

Gendt, 1971); (editor) *Africana Curiosities,* A. Donker, 1973; (editor) *Africana Byways,* A. Donker, 1976; (editor) *Sketches by Ida Mae Stone and Harry Clayton,* A. Donker, 1976; *Treasures of the Africana Museum,* Purnell, 1977; (editor) *Cape Views and Costumes,* Brenthurst Press, 1978.

Compiler of numerous museum and library catalogs, including: *Catalogue of Bantu, Khoisan and Malagasy in the Strange Collection of Africana,* Johannesburg Public Library, 1942, *The Language of Stamp Collecting,* Johannesburg Public Library, 1959, *Commemorative Medals of the Z.A.R.,* Africana Museum, 1958, and *Commemorative Medals of South African Interest in the Africana Museum,* 1979. Editor of quarterly, *Africana Notes and News,* 1960-75.

WORK IN PROGRESS: A biography of Charles Davidson Bell, completion expected about 1986; compilation of catalogue of South African botanical prints.

*   *   *

SMITH, Carmichael
See LINEBARGER, Paul M(yron) A(nthony)

*   *   *

SMITH, Cordwainer
See LINEBARGER, Paul M(yron) A(nthony)

*   *   *

SMITH, Elsdon C(oles) 1903-

PERSONAL: Born January 25, 1903, in Virginia, Ill.; son of George W. (a dentist) and Eva E. (Coles) Smith; married Clare I. Hutchins, December 23, 1933; children: Laurel G. Smith Miller (died July 3, 1962). *Education:* University of Illinois, B.S., 1925; Harvard University, LL.B., 1930. *Religion:* Protestant. *Home:* 8001 Lockwood Ave., Skokie, Ill. 60077.

CAREER: Lawyer; Follansbee, Shorey & Schupp, Chicago, Ill., associate and partner, 1933-48; Blumberg & Smith, Chicago, partner, 1949-58; Blumberg, Smith, Woff & Pennish, Chicago, partner, 1958-61; Pennish & Steel, Chicago, partner, 1961-63; Pennish, Smith, Jaffe & Geis, Chicago, partner, beginning 1963. Member of Chicago Law Institute. *Member:* American Bar Association, American Name Society (president, 1951-54, 1970), American Folklore Society, Modern Language Association of America, American Dialect Society, International Committee of Onomastic Sciences, Illinois Place-Name Survey, English Place-Name Society.

WRITINGS: Naming Your Baby, Chilton, 1943; *The Story of Our Names,* Harper, 1950; *Bibliography of Personal Names,* New York Public Library, 1952; *Dictionary of American Family Names,* Harper, 1956, revised and enlarged edition published as *New Dictionary of American Family Names,* 1973; *Treasury of Name Lore,* Harper, 1967; *American Surnames,* Chilton, 1969; *The Book of Smith,* Nellen Publishing Co., 1978. Contributor of articles to various periodicals. Review editor, *Names,* journal of American Name Society.

WORK IN PROGRESS: Research on personal names.

SIDELIGHTS: Elsdon C. Smith comments, "The concentrated study of personal names over a period of more than fifty years has given me an interesting and active life."

*   *   *

SMITH, Lacey Baldwin 1922-

PERSONAL: Born October 3, 1922, in Princeton, N.J.; son

of E. Baldwin and Ruth (Hall) Smith; married Jean E. Reeder (a university lecturer); children: MacAllister Baldwin, Dennison Baldwin, Katherine Chandler. *Education:* Bowdoin College, B.S., 1946; Princeton University, M.A., 1949, Ph.D., 1951. *Home:* 225 Laurel Ave., Wilmette, Ill. *Office:* Department of History, Northwestern University, Evanston, Ill. 60201.

CAREER: Princeton University, Princeton, N.J., instructor, 1951-53; Massachusetts Institute of Technology, Cambridge, assistant professor, 1953-55; Northwestern University, Evanston, Ill., associate professor, 1955-62, professor of history, 1962—. *Member:* American Historical Association, Conference on British Studies, Royal Historical Society, Royal Society of Literature. *Awards, honors:* Fulbright senior scholar, 1963-64; Guggenheim scholar, 1963-64; National Endowment for the Humanities senior fellow, 1973-74 and 1981-82; Chicago Foundation of Literature Award, 1976; D.Litt., Bowdoin College, 1977.

WRITINGS: Tudor Prelates and Politics, 1536-1558, Princeton University Press, 1953; *A Tudor Tragedy: The Life and Times of Catherine Howard,* Pantheon, 1961; (general editor and author of Volume II) *A History of England,* Heath, 1966, 3rd edition, 1976, Volume I: C. W. Hollister, *The Making of England: 55 B.C.-1399,* Volume II: *This Realm of England: 1399-1688,* Volume III: William B. Willcox, *The Age of Aristocracy: 1688-1830,* Volume IV: Walter L. Arnstein, *Britain Yesterday and Today: 1830 to the Present;* (with wife, Jean R. Smith) *World History in Outline,* Barron's, 1966, revised edition published as *Essentials of World History,* 1980; (with Leften Stavros Stavrianos) *India: A Culture in Perspective,* Allyn & Bacon, 1966; *The Elizabethan Epic,* J. Cape, 1966, published as *The Elizabethan World,* Houghton, 1967, illustrated edition published as *The Horizon Book of the Elizabethan World,* American Heritage Publishing Co., 1967; *Henry VIII: The Mask of Royalty,* Houghton, 1971; *Elizabeth Tudor: Portrait of a Queen,* Little, Brown, 1975; *Elizabeth I,* Forum Press, 1980; (editor with J. R. Smith) *The Past Speaks: Sources and Problems in English History to 1688,* Heath, 1981. Contributor to history journals.

WORK IN PROGRESS: Research on sixteenth-century English history.

SIDELIGHTS: In his book *Henry VIII: The Mask of Royalty,* Lacey Baldwin Smith examines the life of the noted English monarch from a somewhat different perspective than most other historians. As Thomas Lask explains in the *New York Times:* "Mr. Smith's aim is not to tell us what Henry did, but what kind of man it was who did it: what his values were, the nature of his thought and how these revealed themselves when combined with his character. He has worked from the inside of his mind, making clear the defense, the justifications, the rationale of his thinking and his acts."

The *New York Times Book Review*'s Lawrence Stone concurs with this assessment of the professor's intent, warning readers that *Henry VIII* "is not a traditional biography that tells a political narrative from the cradle to the grave, for it jumps about with studied disrespect for chronology. Nor is it a modern study in psychohistory on Eriksonian lines. . . . It is rather a neo-romantic essay on personality conveyed in a series of dazzling vignettes of the King in his later years, a probe into the mental set and the motivational drives of an elderly absolute monarch in the early 16th century."

Though the *Times Literary Supplement* critic feels that the reader who is unacquainted with Tudor history will have difficulty appreciating Smith's synthesis, most other reviewers admire his novel approach. The *Washington Post Book World*'s

John Kenyon, for instance, declares that *Henry VIII* "must be counted as one of the most perceptive chapter sketches we have of any ruler, and it makes a rich and satisfying book." Lask remarks that in examining Henry the man, Smith "has thrown open the age. . . . The author's arguments are so fine-grained and the illustrative material so fascinating in itself, and the writing so pithy and well turned, that no abstract can quite give the flavor of the text. . . . Henry is no hero to his author, who is sometimes bemused, sometimes cutting, always realistic. It's almost as if he were warning us that if we were contemplating setting up a king again, we ought to take a second look."

Peter S. Prescott of *Newsweek* praises Smith for daring to attempt "what other scholars usually avoid: he not only examines the age in its own terms, as any good historian must, he brings to his examination the knowledge of social structure and the perceptions of human nature that we have gained since Tudor times. Smith draws upon Max Weber, Erik Erikson and William James, but does so discreetly, as one must if the delicate balance of authority and speculation is to be preserved. The result, I think, is very exciting, a well-written book worth thinking on, a book that belongs to the history of ideas as well as of men." Stone agrees, stating that "Smith has succeeded better than any previous scholar in making this proud, suspicious monster of egotistical cruelty an intelligible and coherent personality. We can now understand him better, even if we cannot sympathize."

In short, concludes Kenyon, *Henry VIII* confirms that Lacey Baldwin Smith is far from being a run-of-the-mill historian. He is, says the reviewer, a "rare thing, a thoroughly equipped professional historian who can draw on all the sources at will, yet at the same time a writer of such distinction that he could have triumphed in any literary field. . . . Moreover, he shares with David Matthew, and with few other historians, the ability to convey the feel of life in another age, to define the nature of personal and political relationships based on social and moral assumptions very different from our own."

BIOGRAPHICAL/CRITICAL SOURCES: Washington Post Book World, November 7, 1971; *Times Literary Supplement,* November 12, 1971; *Newsweek,* November 22, 1971; *New York Times,* December 4, 1971; *Detroit News,* December 12, 1971; *New York Times Book Review,* December 19, 1971.

* * *

SMITH, Martin Cruz 1942-
   (Martin William Smith; pseudonyms: Nick Carter, Jake Logan, Martin Quinn, Simon Quinn)

PERSONAL: Original name, Martin William Smith; name legally changed in 1977; born November 3, 1942, in Reading, Pa.; son of John Calhoun (a musician) and Louise (an Indian rights leader; maiden name, Lopez) Smith; married Emily Arnold (a chef), June 15, 1968; children: Ellen Irish, Luisa Cruz, Samuel Kip. *Education:* University of Pennsylvania, B.A., 1964. *Agent:* Knox Burger Associates Ltd., 39½ Washington Sq. S., New York, N.Y. 10012.

CAREER: Writer. Worked for *Philadelphia Daily News,* 1965, and Magazine Management, 1966-69. *Member:* Authors Guild. *Awards, honors:* Edgar Award nomination, Mystery Writers of America, 1978, for *Nightwing.*

WRITINGS: Nightwing (suspense novel), Norton, 1977; *The Analog Bullet* (novel), Belmont-Tower, 1978; *Gorky Park* (novel; Book-of-the-Month Club selection), Random House, 1981.

Under name Martin William Smith: *The Indians Won* (novel), Belmont-Tower, 1970; *Gypsy in Amber* (mystery novel), Putnam, 1971; *Canto for a Gypsy* (mystery novel), Putnam, 1972; *The Human Factor* (novel), Dell, 1975.

Under pseudonym Jake Logan; all novels; all published by Playboy Press: *North to Dakota*, 1976; *Ride for Revenge*, 1977. Also author of several other novels under pseudonym Jake Logan.

Under pseudonym Martin Quinn: *Adventures of the Wilderness Family* (movie novelization), Ballantine, 1976.

Under pseudonym Simon Quinn; all novels; all published by Dell: *His Eminence, Death*, 1974; *Nuplex Red*, 1974; *The Midas Coffin*, 1975; *Last Rites for the Vulture*, 1975. Also author of *The Last Time I Saw Hell* and one other novel under pseudonym Simon Quinn.

Also author of other books under various pseudonyms, including Nick Carter.

WORK IN PROGRESS: A novel set in New Mexico.

SIDELIGHTS: In 1972, a struggling young writer named Martin William Smith approached his publisher, G. P. Putnam's Sons, with an idea for a different sort of mystery. Inspired by a *Newsweek* review of *The Face Finder*, a nonfiction book recounting the efforts of Soviet scientists to reconstruct faces from otherwise unidentifiable human remains, Smith outlined a plot involving a partnership between a Soviet detective and his American counterpart as they attempt to solve an unusual murder. (As the author later revealed in the *Washington Post*, his original inclination was to portray a sort of "Butch Cassidy and the Sundance Kid, but one [partner would be] Russian.") Putnam's liked Smith's proposal and agreed to pay him a $15,000 advance.

For the next five years, Smith eked out a living writing several dozen paperback novels, often under one of his various pseudonyms. ("I didn't want to be associated with those books," he told *Newsweek*'s Peter S. Prescott.) Whenever he had accumulated enough to live on for awhile, he did research for his murder mystery; in 1973, he even managed to make a two-week-long trip to Moscow ("the world's largest company town" is how he describes it), during which time he wandered through the city jotting down notes on how it looked and sketching scenes he hesitated to photograph. Later denied permission for a return visit, Smith instead spent hours pumping various Russian emigres and defectors for details about life in the Soviet Union "on everything from the quality of shoes . . . to whether a ranking policeman would have to be a member of the Communist Party," as Arthur Spiegelman of the *Chicago Tribune* notes. "I would write a scene and show it to one of my Russian friends," Smith recalls. "If he would say that some Russian must have told me that, then I knew it was OK."

By this time, Smith knew he no longer wanted to write a conventional thriller. "I suddenly realized that I had something," he commented in the *Washington Post*. "This [was] the book that [could] set me free." He abandoned the idea of a partnership between detectives, deciding instead to focus on the challenge of making the Soviet detective his hero. Putnam's, however, was less than enthusiastic about the change in plans, for they doubted that such a book would have much commercial appeal. Smith was urged to stick to more marketable plots—namely, those featuring an American hero.

The year 1977 proved to be a turning point of sorts for Smith; he not only bought back the rights to his novel from Putnam's (after a long and bitter battle) and changed his middle name from William to Cruz (his maternal grandmother's first name), he also received approximately a half million dollars when *Nightwing*, his vampire bat horror-thriller, became a surprise

success. The following period of financial security enabled Smith to put the finishing touches on his "simple detective story," which by now had grown into a 365-page novel. In 1980, he and his agent began negotiating with Random House and Ballantine for the publishing rights. Despite the lack of interest Putnam's had shown in his work, Smith was confident that his book would indeed be published—and at a price *he* would name. As he remarked to Prescott: "Every time I looked at the novel I decided to double the price. When I wrote the last line, I *knew*; I have never been so excited in my life, except for the birth of children, as when I wrote the last line of [that book]. Because I *knew* it was just right. I had this marvelous book and I was *damned* if I was going to sell it for anything less than a marvelous price. The words 'one million' seemed to come to mind." Before the end of the year, Smith *was* $1 million richer and Random House was preparing to gamble on an unusual 100,000-copy first printing of what soon would become one of the most talked-about books of 1981—*Gorky Park*.

The product of eight years of research and writing, *Gorky Park* chronicles the activities of homicide detective Arkady Renko as he investigates a bizarre murder. Three bullet-riddled bodies—two men and a woman—have been discovered frozen in the snow in Moscow's Gorky Park, their faces skinned and their fingertips cut off to hinder identification. Renko immediately realizes that this is no ordinary murder; his suspicions are confirmed when agents of the KGB arrive on the scene. But instead of taking over the investigation, the KGB suddenly insists that Renko handle the affair. From this point on, the main plot is complicated by an assortment of sub-plots and a large cast of characters, including a greedy American fur-dealer, a visiting New York City police detective who suspects one of the murder victims might be his politically radical brother, and a dissident Siberian girl with whom Renko falls in love. Before the end of the story, the detective has tracked the killer across two continents and has himself been stalked and harassed by the KGB, the CIA, the FBI, and the New York City police department.

As Spiegelman observes in his article, "First comment on *Gorky Park* has bordered on the ecstatic." Virtually every reviewer, even those who find fault with a few aspects of the book, describes it as a novel that "transcends the genre" in the tradition of such acknowledged masters as John Le Carre, Eric Ambler, Len Deighton, and Graham Greene. They praise its exceptionally vivid and authentic images of Moscow and the way of life in the Soviet Union, as well as its skillful depiction of characters who are not mere *types*, but *people*.

Peter Andrews's comments in the *New York Times Book Review* are typical. "Just when I was beginning to worry that the large-scale adventure novel might be suffering from a terminal case of the Folletts," he writes, "along comes *Gorky Park* . . . , a book that reminds you just how satisfying a smoothly turned thriller can be. Mr. Smith fulfills all of the requirements of the adventure novel and then transcends the genre. . . . *Gorky Park* is a police procedural of uncommon excellence." Margaret Cannon of *Maclean's* agrees that "on its surface, *Gorky Park* is a police procedural." But "at its heart," she says, "it's a novel of greed and betrayal in the best form of Le Carre or Graham Greene." The *Washington Post Book World*'s Peter Osnos also compares Smith to Le Carre. He writes: "*Gorky Park* is not at all a conventional thriller about Russians. It is to ordinary suspense stories what John Le Carre is to spy novels. The action is gritty, the plot complicated, the overriding quality is intelligence. You have to pay attention or you'll get hopelessly muddled. But staying with this book is easy enough since once one gets going, one doesn't want to stop."

One reason readers of *Gorky Park* find it difficult to stop, says Prescott of *Newsweek,* stems from Smith's ability to bring to life "the inside of a world that he, as an American, cannot have experienced." The *New Yorker* critic, too, finds Smith's portrait "astonishingly" real, with all "the texture and substance of reality," while Osnos declares that "more perhaps than any other recent work of American fiction, [*Gorky Park*] conveys a feeling for the Soviet Union, its capital, its moods and its people."

Smith's characterization is another feature of *Gorky Park* that critics single out for praise. Robert Lekachman of the *Nation,* for example, attributes the book's success to the fact that "Smith has invented some genuinely complicated individuals and placed them in challenging ethical predicaments. . . . [*Gorky Park*'s] characters will linger in memory for quite a while." Perhaps because he is the protagonist, Arkady Renko in particular seems to have impressed reviewers the most, though Osnos, among others, points out that Smith avoids making *any* of his characters into the "sinister stick figures" common in other novels about the Soviets. Stefan Kanfer of *Time,* for example, states that "despite his country of origin, Arkady is not the customary exotic beloved by lending-library readers." A slightly seedy but totally decent and competent man, Arkady is, according to Osnos, "a Russian-style Sam Spade, skilled yet vulnerable, solitary yet capable of love." The *New Republic*'s Tamar Jacoby regards the detective as an "unusual and winning . . . moral hero without a trace of righteousness, an enigmatic figure as alluring as the mystery he is trying to solve. . . . This is what makes *Gorky Park* so extraordinary among thrillers where the heroes are up against simple villains or enemy organizations. Smith sees to it that there is nothing easy or superior about the moral insight that Arkady earns."

While on the whole *Gorky Park* has met with a positive response from critics, it has also generated a few negative comments. Several reviewers, for example, do not think it is worthy of comparison to the work of authors who regularly "transcend the genre." Julian Symons, commenting in the *New York Review of Books,* insists its principal novelty lies in the fact that its hero is Russian and its setting is Moscow. "*Gorky Park* is much above the average thriller," he admits, "but almost equally far below the best of Ambler, Deighton, and Le Carre. Its outstanding virtue is the conviction with which the Moscow settings are rendered, and the assurance with which they are given to us in detail; its particular weaknesses are feeble characterization and an overindulgence in violence." Symons goes on to state that Arkady Renko emerges in the story as a "near-immortal hero" in the conventional role of "a good guy in a bad organization, with many people ready to deceive him, most hands against him," while some of the plot twists and "all-too-plentiful action" strike Symons as "outrageously improbable."

The "conventional" ending of *Gorky Park,* a bloody shootout on New York's Staten Island, also disappoints some critics. Richard J. Walton of the *Chicago Tribune Book World,* who otherwise feels the book is a "brilliant" work of "stunning originality," remarks in his review that "it is only when . . . the story comes to New York that [*Gorky Park*] begins to limp a little." Kanfer notes that "when the characters act for themselves, *Gorky Park* maintains its credibility and force. Only at the end, when the lines of Soviet intrigue are played out, does Smith allow action to rule character. In New York the story degenerates to shootout, and authenticity gives way to violence and the requisite antiromantic finale." Nevertheless, he adds, "it hardly matters. Beneath its contrivances, *Gorky Park* provides a rich social context and a knowledgeable portrait of Eastern Europe."

The *New York Times*'s Christopher Lehmann-Haupt, who criticizes what he calls the novel's "cliched international shoot-'em-up" ending, agrees that the ending "hardly matters," because we are still "under the spell of its beginning and middle. . . . For its first two-thirds . . . *Gorky Park* is superb. It is superb in its sense of mystery. . . . It is superb in its detective work. . . . It is superb in its pacing. . . . Most of all, it is superb in its evocation of the Moscow atmosphere."

Concludes Kanfer: "*Gorky Park* [is] the first thriller of the '80s with polish, wit and moral resonance. . . . This is no small achievement for any novel. For what is essentially an espionage tale, it is a signal for rejoicing. In Arkady Renko, the U.S.S.R. finally has an exportable sleuth. In Martin Cruz Smith, . . . the U.S. at last has a domestic Le Carre."

Despite such words of praise, Smith remains somewhat wary of success. "I always assume that there are angry gods," he told the *Washington Post,* "and that if you presume too much, they will take it all away." In the meantime, however, the man who once "bounced thirty-seven checks in a row" is enjoying the financial rewards of *Gorky Park;* he is especially looking forward to buying a house in the country so his children can have a dog as well as having enough time and money to write what he wants. Otherwise, he notes, success hasn't made that much of a difference in his life. "Before, I was treated as an idiot," Smith says. "Now, I'm treated as an idiot-savant."

BIOGRAPHICAL/CRITICAL SOURCES: New York Times, March 19, 1981; *Publishers Weekly,* March 20, 1981; *Chicago Tribune,* March 25, 1981; *Washington Post Book World,* March 29, 1981; *Time,* March 30, 1981; *Nation,* April 4, 1981; *New York Times Book Review,* April 5, 1981; *New Yorker,* April 6, 1981; *Newsweek,* April 6, 1981, May 25, 1981; *Business Week,* April 6, 1981; *Washington Post,* April 10, 1981; *Detroit News,* April 12, 1981; *Los Angeles Times Book Review,* April 19, 1981; *Chicago Tribune Book World,* April 19, 1981; *Maclean's,* May 4, 1981; *New Republic,* May 9, 1981; *People,* May 25, 1981; *Best Sellers,* June, 1981; *Times Literary Supplement,* June 5, 1981; *New York Review of Books,* June 11, 1981.†

—*Sketch by Deborah A. Straub*

*   *   *

SMITH, Martin William
See SMITH, Martin Cruz

*   *   *

SMITH, Morton   1915-

PERSONAL: Born May 28, 1915; son of Rupert Henry and Mary (Funk) Smith. *Education:* Harvard University, A.B., 1936, S.T.B., 1940, Th.D., 1957; Hebrew University, Jerusalem, Ph.D., 1948. *Office:* Department of History, Columbia University, New York, N.Y. 10027.

CAREER: Brown University, Providence, R.I., assistant professor of Biblical literature, 1950-56; Columbia University, New York, N.Y., assistant professor, 1957-60, associate professor, 1960-62, professor of history, 1962—. Visiting professor, Drew University, 1956-57. *Member:* American Academy of Arts and Sciences, American Academy for Jewish Research, Association of Ancient Historians, American Society of Papyrologists, American Numismatic Society, Society of Biblical Literature, Archaeological Institute of America, American Philological Association, American Society for the Study of Religion, Studiorum Novi Testamenti Societas. *Awards, honors:* Thayer fellow, American Schools of Oriental Research; Fulbright grant for postdoctoral work in Greece; Guggenheim fellowship; American Council of Learned Societies fellowship.

WRITINGS: Tannaitic Parallels to the Gospels, Society of Biblical Literature, 1951; *The Ancient Greeks,* Cornell University Press, 1960; (with M. Hadas) *Heroes and Gods: Spiritual Biographies in Antiquity,* Arno, 1963; *Palestinian Parties and Politics That Shaped the Old Testament,* Columbia University Press, 1971; *Clement of Alexandria and a Secret Gospel of Mark,* Harvard University Press, 1973; *The Secret Gospel: The Discovery and Interpretation of the Secret Gospel According to Mark,* Harper, 1973; (with Elias Bickerman) *The Ancient History of Western Civilization,* Harper, 1976; *Jesus the Magician,* Harper, 1978; *Hope and History: An Exploration,* Harper, 1980.

*   *   *

SMITH, Susy   1911-

PERSONAL: Born June 2, 1911, in Washington, D.C.; daughter of Merton M. and Elizabeth (Hardegen) Smith; married M. L. Smith (divorced). *Education:* Attended University of Texas, 1929-32, 1933-34, and University of Arizona, 1932-33. *Politics:* Independent Republican. *Religion:* Protestant. *Agent:* Donald R. MacCampbell, 12 East 41st St., New York, N.Y. 10017.

CAREER: Columnist for *Salt Lake Tribune* and *Deseret News,* Salt Lake City, Utah; free-lance writer. Had radio program on shopping information, Daytona Beach, Fla., 1960-62. Editor for Sherbourne Press, and lecturer. *Member:* International Platform Association, American Society for Psychical Research, Spiritual Frontiers Fellowship, Society for Psychical Research, Association for Research and Enlightenment, Authors' Guild, Chi Omega.

WRITINGS: (Editor) F.W.H. Myers, *Human Personality and Its Survival of Bodily Death,* University Books, 1961; *ESP,* Pyramid Publications, 1962; *World of the Strange,* Pyramid Publications, 1963; *The Mediumship of Mrs. Leonard,* University Books, 1963; *The Enigma of Out-of-Body Travel,* Garrett Publications, 1964; *ESP for the Millions,* Sherbourne, 1965; *A Supernatural Primer for the Millions,* Sherbourne, 1965; *Prominent American Ghosts,* World Publishing, 1966; *Haunted Houses for the Millions,* Sherbourne, 1966; *Stories of the Supernormal,* Pyramid Publications, 1966; *Talking Animals,* Arcone, 1967; *Adventures in the Supernormal,* Pyramid Publications, 1968; *Out-of-Body Experiences,* Dell, 1969; *Reincarnation,* Dell, 1969; *More ESP for the Millions,* Sherbourne, 1969.

Today's Witches, Prentice-Hall, 1970; *Ghosts around the House,* World Publications, 1970; *Widespread Psychic Wonders,* Ace Books, 1970; *Confessions of a Psychic,* Macmillan, 1971; *She Spoke to the Dead,* Award Books, 1972; *How to Develop Your ESP,* Putnam, 1972; *ESP and Hypnosis,* Macmillan, 1973; *The Book of James,* Putnam, 1974; *Life Is Forever: Evidence for Survival after Death,* Putnam, 1974; *Do We Live after Death?,* Manor, 1974; *The Power of the Mind,* Chilton, 1975; *The Conversion of a Psychic,* Doubleday, 1978.†

*   *   *

SMITH, Vernon Lomax   1927-

PERSONAL: Born January 1, 1927, in Wichita, Kan.; son of Vernon Chessman and Lulu Belle (Lomax) Smith; married Joyce Aline Harkleroad, 1950; married Carol L. Breckner,

1980; children: (first marriage) Deborah Aline, Eric Lomax, Torrie Diane. *Education:* Attended Friends University, 1944-45; California Institute of Technology, B.S., 1949; University of Kansas, M.A., 1951; Harvard University, Ph.D., 1955. *Religion:* Unitarian Universalist. *Office:* Department of Economics, University of Arizona, Tucson, Ariz. 85721.

CAREER: University of Kansas, Lawrence, instructor, 1950-52; Harvard University, Cambridge, Mass., research economist, 1954-55; Purdue University, West Lafayette, Ind., assistant professor, 1955-58, associate professor, 1958-61, professor of economics, 1961-67; Brown University, Providence, R.I., professor of economics, 1967-68; University of Massachusetts—Amherst, professor of economics, 1968-75; University of Arizona, Tucson, professor of economics, 1975—. Visiting professor, Stanford University, 1961-62. *Member:* American Economic Association. *Awards, honors:* Ford Foundation faculty research fellowship, 1957-58; Stanford University Center for Advanced Study in Behavioral Science fellow, 1972-73; Fairchild distinguished fellow, California Institute of Technology, 1973-74.

WRITINGS: Economics: An Analytic Approach, Irwin, 1957, 2nd edition, 1962; *Investment and Production,* Harvard University Press, 1961; (editor) *Economics of Natural and Environmental Resources,* Gordon & Breach, 1977; (editor) *Research in Experimental Economics,* Jai Press, 1978. Contributor to professional journals.

WORK IN PROGRESS: Group decision-making; experimental studies of competitive market behavior.

*   *   *

SNODGRASS, W(illiam) D(e Witt)   1926-
(S. S. Gardons)

PERSONAL: Born January 5, 1926, in Wilkinsburg, Pa.; son of Bruce De Witt (an accountant) and Jesse Helen (Murchie) Snodgrass; married Lila Jean Hank, June 6, 1946 (divorced December, 1953); married Janice Marie Ferguson Wilson, March 19, 1954 (divorced August, 1966); married Camille Rykowski, September 13, 1967 (divorced, 1978); children: (first marriage) Cynthia Jean; (second marriage) Kathy Ann Wilson (stepdaughter), Russell Bruce. *Education:* Attended Geneva College, 1943-44, 1946-47; University of Iowa, B.A., 1949, M.A., 1951, M.F.A., 1953. *Home:* R.D. 1, Erieville, N.Y. 13061.

CAREER: Worked as hotel clerk and hospital aide in Iowa; Cornell University, Ithaca, N.Y., instructor in English, 1955-57; University of Rochester, Rochester, N.Y., instructor, 1957-58; Wayne State University, Detroit, Mich., assistant professor of English, 1959-67; Syracuse University, Syracuse, N.Y., professor of English and speech, 1968-77; Old Dominion University, Norfolk, Va., visiting professor, 1978-79; University of Delaware, Newark, Del., distinguished visiting professor, 1979. Leader of poetry workshop, Morehead Writers' Conference, 1955, Antioch Writers' Conference, 1958, 1959, and Narrative Poetry Workshop, State University of New York at Binghamton, 1977. Lectures and gives poetry readings. *Military service:* U.S. Navy, 1944-46. *Member:* National Institute of Arts & Letters, Academy of American Poets (fellow). *Awards, honors:* Ingram Merrill Foundation Award, 1958; *Hudson Review* fellowship in poetry, 1958-59; Longview Foundation Literary Award, 1959; Poetry Society of America citation, 1960; National Institute of Arts and Letters grant, 1960; Pulitzer Prize for poetry, 1960, British Guinness Award, 1961, both for *Heart's Needle;* Yaddo resident award, 1960, 1961, 1965; Ford Foundation grant, 1963-64; Miles Poetry Award, 1966; National Endowment for the Arts grant, 1966-67; Guggenheim fellowship, 1972; Bicentennial medal from College of William and Mary, 1976; centennial medal from government of Romania, 1977.

WRITINGS: Heart's Needle (poetry), Knopf, 1959; (translator with Lore Segal) Christian Morgenstern, *Gallows Songs,* University of Michigan, 1967; *After Experience* (poetry), Harper, 1967; (under pseudonym S. S. Gardons) *Remains,* Perishable Press, 1970; *In Radical Pursuit* (critical essays), Harper, 1975; (translator) *Six Troubadour Songs,* Burning Deck Press, 1977; *The Fuehrer Bunker: A Cycle of Poems in Progress* (poetry; also see below), BOA Editions, 1977; (translator) *Traditional Hungarian Songs,* Charles Seluzicki, 1978; *If Birds Build with Your Hair* (poetry), Nadja Press, 1979; "The Fuehrer Bunker" (play; adaptation of book of poetry of the same title), first produced Off-Broadway at American Place Theatre, May 26, 1981.

Author of introduction: Tom Marotta, *For They Are My Friends,* Art Reflections, 1976; Barton Sutter, *Cedarhome* (poetry), BOA Editions, 1977; Rainer Maria Wilke, *The Roses and the Windows,* translated by A. Poulin, Graywolf, 1979; Michael Jennings, *The Hardeman County Poems* (based on photographs by Dorothea Lange), Heliographics, 1980.

Contributor: *From the Iowa Poetry Workshop,* Prairie Press, 1951; *Reading Modern Poetry,* Scott, 1955; *New Poets of England and America,* Meridian, 1957; *New World Writing,* New American Library, 1957; *Theodore Roethke: Essays on the Poetry,* University of Washington Press, 1965. Also translator, with Rosmarie Waldrop, of *Biedermann and the Firebugs,* by Max Frisch. Contributor to *The Syracuse Scholar* of translation of the four sonnets which are the basis of Vivaldi's "The Four Seasons." Contributor of poems, poetry translations (from the German and the Romanian), literary criticisms, essays, and reviews to magazines, journals, and newspapers.

WORK IN PROGRESS: A second volume in *The Fuehrer Bunker* cycle; two collections of song translations, one of songs by troubadours and Renaissance composers, the other of folk ballads; translations of the epitaphs from the Sapintza graveyard in Transylvania, Romania.

SIDELIGHTS: W. D. Snodgrass is often credited with being one of the founding members of the "confessional" school of poetry, even though he dislikes the term confessional and does not regard his work as such. Nevertheless, his Pulitzer Prize-winning first collection, *Heart's Needle,* has had a tremendous impact on that particular facet of contemporary poetry. The style was imitated and, in some cases, surpassed by other poets. This fact leads *Yale Review*'s Laurence Lieberman to comment that a later book, *After Experience,* reveals "an artist trapped in a style which . . . has reached a dead end," because the group style had taken a different direction than Snodgrass's own.

The combination of the traditional and the confessional in Snodgrass's writing prompts Thomas Lask of the *New York Times* to write, "In *Heart's Needle,* . . . Snodgrass spoke in a distinctive voice. It was one that was jaunty and assertive on the surface . . . but somber and hurt beneath. . . . It is one of the few books that successfully bridged the directness of contemporary free verse with the demands of the academy." Peter Porter echoes this opinion when he writes in *London Magazine:* "Snodgrass is a virtuoso, not just of versification but of his feelings. He sends them round the loops of self analysis with the same skill he uses to corset them into his poetry." The impact of Snodgrass's self-analytical approach is clearly felt in Stanley Moss's statement in the *New Republic* that the poet "has found a place for emotions felt, but previously left without words and out of consciousness. He has identified himself with exquisite suffering and guilt and with all those who barely manage to exist on the edge of life."

Regarding W. D. Snodgrass's translation (with Lore Segal) of Christian Morgenstern's *Gallows Songs,* Louise Bogan writes in *New Yorker:* "German . . . here takes on a demonic life of its own. . . . To translate Morgenstern is a very nearly impossible task, to which the present translators have faced up bravely and well." Even though some critics may not agree with Bogan—Hayden Carruth of *Poetry* calls the translation "dreadful"—*Books Abroad*'s Sidney Rosenfeld finds that in spite of its possible shortcomings, *Gallows Songs* opens "a door onto the world of Christian Morgenstern and impart[s] to the English reader some sense of the playfully profound genius that enlivens it."

Paul Gaston points out that Snodgrass's critical essays and translations help develop his talents and prevent him from reaching the complete dead end of Lieberman's prediction. "These endeavors," writes Gaston in his book *W. D Snodgrass,* "reveal a poet intent on carefully establishing his creative priorities and perfecting his language." He continues, "Snodgrass's criticism gives the impressions of a mind reaching beyond the pleasures of cleverness to the hard-won satisfactions of wisdom." And finally, "[His] work with translations . . . has encouraged the increasing linguistic, metrical, and structural diversity of his own work."

This diversity is apparent in Snodgrass's third volume of original poetry, *The Fuehrer Bunker,* which uses dramatic monologues to recreate what was said by the men and women who shared Hitler's bunker from April 1 to May 1, 1945. "In these poems," writes Gertrude M. White in *Odyssey: A Journal of the Humanities,* "we are overhearing people talking to themselves, each character speaking in a verse form expressive of his or her personality, revealing who and what they are with a dramatic power that carries conviction almost against our will."

Dictionary of Literary Biography writer Jeffrey Helterman remarks, "Snodgrass had been a poet concerned mostly with the problems of his own ego, but in *The Fuehrer Bunker* he has become what Keats would call a chameleon poet." Robert Peters, writing in the *American Book Review,* believes that the volume is "a rare example of ambitious, on-going verse sculpture. . . . It will be around for a long time to inspire writers who've come to realize the sad limitations of the locked-in, private, first person, obsessional poem."

Snodgrass told *CA* that "These Trees Stand . . . ," a poem which originally appeared in *Heart's Needle,* has been made into a volume "bound in exquisite leather in an edition of ten copies and two artist's proofs." The volume is illustrated with photographs by Robert Mahon. Several of Snodgrass's song translations have been performed by early music groups, including the Waverley Consort, Columbia Colleguim (New York), Persis Ensor (Boston), and the Antiqua Players (Pittsburgh).

AVOCATIONAL INTERESTS: Tennis, singing, playing guitar, lute, psaltery, and saz.

BIOGRAPHICAL/CRITICAL SOURCES: Kenyon Review, summer, 1959; *New Yorker,* October 24, 1959; *Poetry,* November, 1959, September, 1968; William White, compiler, *W. D. Snodgrass, a Bibliography,* Wayne State University Press, 1960; *Northwestern University Tri-Quarterly,* spring, 1960; Robert E. Spiller, editor, *A Time of Harvest,* Hill & Wang, 1962; *Literary Times,* April, 1965; *Detroit Free Press,* Sunday supplement, June 6, 1965; Edward Hungerford, editor, *Poets in Progress,* revised edition, Northwestern University Press,

1967; M. L. Rosenthal, *The New Poets*, Oxford University Press, 1967; Paul Carroll, *The Poem in Its Skin*, Follett, 1968; *New York Times*, March 30, 1968, June 3, 1981; *Book World*, April 14, 1968; *New York Times Book Review*, April 28, 1968; *New Republic*, June 15, 1968, February 15, 1975; *Shenandoah*, summer, 1968; *Yale Review*, autumn, 1968; *Nation*, September 16, 1968; *Observer Review*, December 15, 1968; Richard Howard, *Alone with America*, Atheneum, 1969; *London Magazine*, March, 1969; Jerome Mazzaro, editor, *Modern American Poetry: Essays in Criticism*, McKay, 1970; *Western Humanities Review*, winter, 1970; *Salmagundi*, spring, 1972, spring, 1973, summer, 1973; Robert Phillips, *The Confessional Poets*, Southern Illinois University Press, 1973; *Contemporary Literary Criticism*, Gale, Volume II, 1974, Volume VI, 1976, Volume X, 1979, Volume XVIII, 1981; *Massachusetts Review*, spring, 1975; *Southwest Review*, summer, 1975; *American Book Review*, December, 1977; *Papers on Language and Literature*, summer, 1977, fall, 1977; Paul Gaston, *W. D. Snodgrass*, Twayne, 1978; *Odyssey: A Journal of the Humanities*, April, 1979; *Dictionary of Literary Biography*, Volume V, Gale, 1980.

*   *   *

SNOW, Edward Rowe   1902-

PERSONAL: Born August 22, 1902, in Winthrop, Mass.; son of Edward Sumpter and Alice (Rowe) Snow; married Anna-Myrle Haegg, July 8, 1932; children: Dorothy Caroline. *Education:* Harvard University, B.A., 1932; Boston University, M.A., 1939. *Politics:* Republican. *Religion:* Congregationalist. *Home:* 550 Summer St., Marshfield, Mass. 02050. *Office: Patriot Ledger*, Temple St., Quincy, Mass. 02169.

CAREER: High school teacher in Winthrop, Mass., 1932-36; free-lance writer, 1946—. Daily columnist, *Patriot Ledger*, Quincy, Mass., 1957—. Lecturer in New England and eastern states; has made appearances on various radio and television programs, primarily in Boston, Mass. *Military service:* U.S. Air Force, 12th Bomber Command; wounded in 1942; became first lieutenant. *Member:* Explorers Club, Boston Marine Society. *Awards, honors:* Boys' Clubs of America Junior Book award, 1953, for *True Tales of Buried Treasure*.

WRITINGS—Published by Yankee Publishing, except as indicated: *Castle Island*, Andover Press, 1935; *The Islands of Boston Harbor*, Andover Press, 1935, revised edition published as *The Islands of Boston Harbor, 1630-1971*, Dodd, 1971; *The Story of Minot's Light*, 1940; *Historic Fort Warren*, 1941; *Sailing down Boston Bay*, 1941; *The Rise and Fall of the Boston Market*, 1942; *Great Storms and Famous Shipwrecks of the New England Coast*, 1943; *Pirates and Buccaneers of the Atlantic Coast*, 1944; *The Romance of Boston Bay*, 1944; *Winthrop by the Sea*, Boston Printing, 1945; *Famous New England Lighthouses*, 1945, published as *The Lighthouses of New England, 1716-1973*, Dodd, 1973; *Cruising the Massachusetts Coast*, 1945; *A Pilgrim Returns to Cape Cod*, 1946; *Searching for Treasure*, 1947; *South Shore to Cape Cod by Canoe*, 1948; *True Adventure Tales*, 1949.

Published by Dodd, except as indicated: *Mysteries and Adventures along the Atlantic Coast*, 1948, reprinted, Books for Libraries, 1969; *Exploring the Rim*, 1949; *Strange Tales from Nova Scotia to Cape Hatteras*, 1949; *Secrets of the North Atlantic Islands*, 1950; *A Century of the Boston Y.M.C.U.*, privately printed, 1951; *The Mayflower, Plymouth Rock and the Pilgrims*, 1951; *True Tales of Buried Treasure*, 1951, revised edition, 1960; *Forgotten Sea Tragedies*, 1952; *Great Gales and Dire Disasters*, 1952; *True Tales of Pirates and Their Gold*, 1953; *Amazing Sea Stories Never Told Before*,

1954; *Famous Lighthouses of America*, 1955; *Lighthouse Date Book*, 1956; *The Vengeful Sea*, 1956; *New England Sea Drama*, 1956; *Legends of the New England Coast*, 1957; *Great Sea Rescues, and Tales of Survival*, 1958; *Beacons of New England*, 1958; *Exploring Boston Bay*, 1959; *Piracy, Mutiny, and Murder*, 1959; *Down Massachusetts Bay*, 1959.

New England Sea Tragedies, 1960; *Nautical Engagement Calender*, 1960; *New England Coast in Maps and Stories*, 1961; *Mysterious Tales of the New England Coast*, 1961 (published in England as *Tales of the Atlantic Coast*, Redman, 1963); *Women of the Sea*, 1962; *True Tales of Terrible Shipwrecks*, 1963; *Unsolved Mysteries of Sea and Shore*, 1963; *The Fury of the Sea*, 1964; *Sea Mysteries and Adventures*, Redman, 1964; *Astounding Tales of the Sea*, 1965; *Tales of Sea and Shore*, 1966; *Incredible Mysteries and Legends of the Sea*, 1967; *Fantastic Folklore and Fact: New England Tales of Land and Sea*, 1968; *True Tales and Curious Legends: Dramatic Stories from the Yankee Past*, 1969.

Great Atlantic Adventures, 1970; *Ghosts, Gales and Gold*, 1972; *Supernatural Mysteries and Other Tales*, 1974; *The Romance of Casco Bay*, 1975; *Marine Mysteries and Dramatic Disasters of New England*, 1976; *Boston Bay Mysteries and Other Tales*, 1977; *Adventures, Blizzards, and Coastal Calamities*, 1978; *Tales of Terror and Tragedy*, 1979; *Sea Disasters and Inland Catastrophes*, 1980.

WORK IN PROGRESS: Romantic, Chronological, and Mysterious Boston.

BIOGRAPHICAL/CRITICAL SOURCES: Best Sellers, January 1, 1970.†

*   *   *

SOHN, David A.   1929-

PERSONAL: Born November 28, 1929, in Columbus, Ind.; son of Albert Edward and Margaret (Crittenden) Sohn; married Elizabeth Manning, October 15, 1954; children: Matthew, Elizabeth, Jennifer, Andrew. *Education:* Wabash College, A.B., 1950; Indiana University, A.M., 1952. *Office:* Board of Education, Illinois District 65, Cook County, Evanston, Ill. 60201.

CAREER: Teacher of English in public schools of Newtown, Conn., 1954-57, and Westport, Conn., 1957-60; Center for Programmed Instruction, New York City, coordinator of Carnegie reading project, 1960-61; Middlesex Junior High School, Darien, Conn., instructor in English, 1962-67; Fordham University, New York City, director of curriculum research for national film study project, 1967-68; School District 65, Evanston, Ill., curriculum consultant in language arts, 1968—. Assistant supervisor of study skills, Study Skills Office, Yale University, 1957-66; member of board of directors, Midwest Film Conference, 1968—, and Conference on Visual Literacy, 1971—. Consultant, Bantam Books, Inc., 1961-69, and Center for Teaching Professions, Northwestern University, 1971—. Associate producer of film ''The Light Fantastic Picture Show,'' 1974. *Member:* International Reading Association, National Council of Teachers of English (member of commission on composition and of committee on media study, 1974—), National Education Association, National Reading Conference, College Reading Association, New England Reading Association, Connecticut Education Association, Phi Delta Kappa.

WRITINGS: (Editor with Alexander Butman and Donald Reis and contributor) *Paperbacks in the Schools*, Bantam, 1963; (editor) *Great Tales of Horror by Poe*, Bantam, 1964; (editor with Alfred DeGrazia) *Programs, Teachers, and Machines*, Bantam, 1964; (editor with DeGrazia) *Revolution in Teaching:*

New Theory, Technology, and Curricula, Bantam, 1964; (with Hart Day Leavitt) *Stop, Look and Write!*, Bantam, 1964; (editor) *Ten Top Stories*, Bantam, 1964; (editor) *Peppermint: Prize Winning Student Writing from the Scholastic Writing Awards*, Scholastic Book Services, 1965; (editor) *Ten Modern American Short Stories*, Bantam, 1965; (editor with Leavitt) *The Writer's Eye*, Bantam, 1966; (with Ralph Staiger) *New Directions in Reading*, Bantam, 1967; (with Richard Tyre) *Frost: The Poet and His Poetry*, Holt, 1967, revised edition, 1969; *Film Study and the English Teacher*, Indiana University Audio-Visual Center, 1968; (editor with Melinda Stucker) *Film Study in the School: Grades Kindergarten through 8* (curriculum report), American Film Institute, 1968; *Pictures for Writing: A Visual Approach to Composition*, Bantam, 1969.

Film: The Creative Eye, Pflaum, 1970; *David Sohn's Film Notes on Selected Short Films*, Pflaum, 1975; (editor with Clifford Wood) *Coming Together: Love Poems*, Pflaum, 1975; (editor) *Good Looking: Film Studies, Short Films, and Filmmaking*, National Textbook Co., 1978.

"Learning Unit Series"; all published by Bantam: *How to Read, Study and Enjoy the Short Story*, 1963; *The Art of the Short Story*, 1963; (with Norman Fedde) *Improving Study Skills*, 1963; (with Nathan Lipofsky) *Focus on Youth: The Road to Maturity*, 1963; (with Lipofsky) *Youth and Challenge: Problems of Growing Up*, 1963; *Youth and Cars: Stimulating Reading*, 1963; (with Gordon Hall) *The Civil War: Perspectives*, 1963; (with Lipofsky) *Success in Reading: A Remedial Program*, 1964; (with Fedde) *Readings for the College-Bound Student: Backgrounds in Human Action in Science and Social Studies*, 1964; (with Fedde) *Readings for the College-Bound Student: Backgrounds in Literature*, 1964.

Also author of a film, "Autumn: Frost Country," Pyramid Films, 1969, a filmstrip, "Come to Your Senses: A Filmstrip Series on Observation," Scholastic, 1970, and a slide set, "Eye-Openers," 1973. Contributor to professional journals. *Media and Methods*, contributing editor, 1964-72, associate editor, 1972—; contributing editor, *K-8*, 1971-72.†

*   *   *

SOKEL, Walter H(erbert)   1917-

PERSONAL: Born December 17, 1917, in Vienna, Austria; son of Solomon and Rosa (Popper) Sokel; married Jacqueline Printz, September 24, 1961; children: Shari-Maria. *Education:* Attended University of Vienna, 1936-38; Rutgers University, B.A., 1941, M.A., 1944; Columbia University, Ph.D., 1953. *Home:* 220 Carrsbrook Dr., Charlottesville, Va. 22901. *Office:* Department of Germanic Languages, University of Virginia, Charlottesville, Va. 22901.

CAREER: Ohio State University, Columbus, instructor in German, 1946; Temple University, Philadelphia, Pa., instructor in German, 1947-53; Columbia University, New York, N.Y., instructor, 1953-56, assistant professor, 1956-60, associate professor of German, 1960-64; Stanford University, Stanford, Calif., professor of German, 1964-73; University of Virginia, Charlottesville, Commonwealth Professor of German, 1973—, Commonwealth Professor of German and English Literature, 1979—. Visiting professor, Harvard University, 1978-79. *Member:* American Comparative Literature Association, Modern Language Association of America (section chairman, 1962; member of executive council, 1979-82), Kafka Society (president, 1979—), American Academy of Arts and Sciences, American Association of Teachers of German, Phi Beta Kappa. *Awards, honors:* American Council of Learned Societies grant-in-aid, 1962; National Endowment for the Humanities senior

fellow, 1971-72; Alexander von Humboldt research prize fellow, 1982.

WRITINGS: The Writer in Extremis, Stanford University Press, 1959; (editor) *An Anthology of German Expressionist Drama*, Anchor Books, 1963; *Franz Kafka: Tragik und Ironie*, [Munich], 1964; *Franz Kafka*, Columbia University Press, 1966.

Contributor: P. Demetz, editor, *Brecht*, Prentice-Hall, 1962; O. Mann and W. Rothe, editors, *Deutsche Literature im 20. Jahrhundert*, Volume II, 5th revised edition, Francke, 1967; Rothe, editor, *Expressionismus als Literatur*, Francke, 1969; Reich-Ranicki, editor, *In Sachen Boell*, 3rd enlarged edition, Kiepenheuer & Witsch, 1970; V. Sander, editor, *Tragik und Tragoedie*, Wissenschaftliche Buchgesellschaft, 1971; R. Grimm, editor, *Deutsche Dramentheorien II*, Athenaeum Verlag, 1971; I. Solbrig and J. W. Storck, editors, *Rilke heute*, Suhrkamp, 1975; F. Kuna, editor, *On Kafka*, Paul Elek, 1976; A. Flores, editor, *The Problem of "The Judgment,"* Gordian, 1977; Flores, editor, *The Kafka Debate*, Gordian, 1977; C. David, editor, *Franz Kafka*, Vandenhoeck & Ruprecht, 1980; F. Baron, E. Dick, and W. R. Maurer, editors, *Rilke: The Alchemy of Alienation*, Regents Press of Kansas, 1980; J.P. Stern, editor, *The World of Franz Kafka*, Holt, 1980.

Member of editorial board, *Germanic Review*.

*   *   *

SOMERS, Paul
See WINTERTON, Paul

*   *   *

SORLEY WALKER, Kathrine

PERSONAL: Born in Aberdeen, Scotland; daughter of James (an editor and journalist) and Edith Jane (Robertson) Sorley Walker. *Education:* Attended Crouch End College, King's College, London, University of Besancon, and Trinity College of Music. *Religion:* Church of Scotland. *Home:* 60 Eaton Mews W., London SW1W 9ET, England.

CAREER: Geographical Magazine, London, England, editorial assistant, 1951-57; free-lance writer and editor. *Member:* Society of Authors, Critics' Circle (London).

WRITINGS: Brief for Ballet, Pitfield Press, 1947; *Beauty Is Built Anew* (verse), Maclellan, 1948; *Robert Helpmann* (monograph), Rockliff, 1958; (translator) *Haydn*, J. Calder, 1960; *The Heart's Variety* (verse), Mitre Press, 1960; (editor with Dorothy Gardiner) *Raymond Chandler Speaking*, Houghton, 1962; *Eyes on the Ballet*, Methuen, 1963, revised edition, John Day, 1965; *Joan of Arc*, J. Cape, 1965; *Eyes on Mime*, John Day, 1969; *Saladin: Sultan of the Holy Sword*, Dobson, 1971; *Dance and Its Creators*, John Day, 1972; (editor) D. V. Coton, *Writings on Dance, 1939-1969*, Dance Books, 1975; *Ballet for Boys and Girls*, Prentice-Hall, 1979; *Emotions and Atmosphere* (verse), Beacon Press, 1979; *The Royal Ballet: A Picture History*, Threshold Books, 1981; *De Basil's Ballets Russes*, Hutchinson, 1982. Also author of short stories and children's serial plays for BBC Scottish Radio.

London editor, *Dance Encyclopedia*, Simon & Schuster. Contributor to *Encyclopaedia Britannica*, *Encyclopedia of Dance and Ballet*, and *Enciclopedia dello Spettacolo*. Ballet critic, *Playgoer*, 1946-51, and *Daily Telegraph*, 1962—. Contributor to *Dancing Times*, *London Times*, *Stage*, *Lady*, *Theatre Notebook*, *Hemisphere*, *Dance Gazette*, *Dance and Dancers*, and other publications.

SIDELIGHTS: Kathrine Sorley Walker told *CA:* "I never envisaged any other career than that of a writer but intended it to be more diversified than it has turned out to be. My great interest in ballet led me into the field of dance criticism and most of my published writing has been specialized. I would still like to reach out into other fields—fiction, adult or juvenile, and drama." *Avocational interests:* Theater; history, particularly Europe in the seventeenth and eighteenth centuries; geography, natural history, and botany, particularly in reference to Australia.

*   *   *

SOUTHWORTH, John Van Duyn   1904-

PERSONAL: Born June 5, 1904, in Syracuse, N.Y.; son of Edward Franklin (a publisher) and Gertrude (a writer; maiden name, Van Duyn) Southworth; married Martha Barnard Collins, November 25, 1925 (died January, 1968); married Alice Keegan Barber, December 21, 1968 (died August, 1973); children: (first marriage) Joan Barnard (Mrs. Warren R. Sedlacek), Edward F. II, John Van Duyn, Jr. *Education:* Harvard University, B.A., 1926; Columbia University, M.A., 1936. *Politics:* Republican. *Religion:* Episcopalian. *Office:* 2135 First Ave. S., St. Petersburg, Fla. 33712.

CAREER: Iroquois Publishing Co., Inc., Syracuse, N.Y., editor, 1926-35; Birch-Wathen School, New York City, instructor in history, 1936-38; YMCA Evening High School, New York City, teacher of social studies, 1937-38; Brunswick School, Greenwich, Conn., head of history department, 1938-43, associate headmaster, 1941-43; Hockaday Junior College, Dallas, Tex., dean and head of history department, 1943-45; Iroquois Publishing Co., Inc., editor and vice-president, 1945-50, president, 1950-60. Nalkyrie Press, St. Petersburg, Fla., associate editor, 1975-76, editor-in-chief, 1976—. Member of board of directors, Gulf Beaches Public Libraries, 1976—. *Military service:* Texas State Guard, 1943-45. *Member:* U.S. Naval Institute, Navy League of United States (president of Syracuse council, 1958), Harvard Club of Syracuse (president, 1955-57), University Club of Syracuse, Phi Delta Kappa, Kappa Delta Pi, Syracuse Camera Club (president, 1963-65), Falcon Club (Harvard).

WRITINGS: How to Study, Iroquois, 1947; *The Iroquois Time Line for All History,* Iroquois, 1947; *Our Own United States,* Iroquois, 1948; *The American History Time Line and Date Chart,* Iroquois, 1951; *The Story of the World,* Pocket Books, 1954; *The World Civilization Time Line,* Iroquois, 1958; (with Ernest L. Thurston) *Our Homeland and the World,* Iroquois, 1958, revised edition (with Lawrence O. Haaby), C. E. Merrill, 1964; *The Pirate from Rome* (novel), Crown, 1965; *War at Sea,* four volumes, Twayne, 1968-72; *The Age of Steam,* Twayne, 1970; *Monarch and Conspirators: The Wives and Woes of Henry VIII,* Crown, 1973; *American History in Verse,* illustrated by Ronald D. Reams, Valkyrie Press, 1976; *Old World History in Verse,* Valkyrie Press, 1977.

With mother, Gertrude Van Duyn Southworth; all published by Iroquois, except as indicated: *What the Old World Gave the New,* 1924; *Old World History,* two volumes, 1929; *American History,* three volumes, 1930; *The Story of Long Ago,* 1934; *The Story of the Middle Ages,* 1934; *America's Old World Background,* 1934; *The Thirteen American Colonies,* 1935; *Early Days in America,* 1935; *The American Way,* 1942; *What about Communism?,* 1949; *Early Days in the New World,* 1950; *Long Ago in the Old World,* 1950, revised edition (with Vincent Cassidy), C. E. Merrill, 1963; *The Story of Our America,* 1951; *Heroes of Our America,* 1952.

Also author of film and radio scripts for "Cavalcade of America," "Meet the Composers," and other programs; author of regular feature, "History in Verse" in *Grit,* 1960-62. Contributor to *Encyclopedia Americana* and *Britannica Junior.*

WORK IN PROGRESS: The Blue Fleet and the Gray, for Twayne; *Crusade!,* a novel; *Morning Star,* novel; *The Naked Man,* a biography of Alcibiades.

AVOCATIONAL INTERESTS: Photography, oil painting.†

*   *   *

SPACHE, George D(aniel)   1909-

PERSONAL: Born February 22, 1909, in New York, N.Y.; son of Daniel William and Mary (Ratz) Spache; married Olga Yolanda Santoro, April 2, 1938; married second wife, Evelyn Bispham (an educator and writer), October 29, 1967; children: (first marriage) Jacqueline Spache Myers, Pamela, Jennifer. *Education:* New York University, B.S. in Ed., 1933, M.A., 1934, Ph.D., 1937. *Religion:* Methodist. *Office:* Reading Laboratory and Clinic, University of Florida, Gainesville, Fla.

CAREER: Teacher and school psychologist, New York City, 1930-36; school psychologist, Chappaqua, N.Y., 1944-48; New York University, New York City, instructor in department of educational psychology, 1944-48; Rutgers University, New Brunswick, N.J., instructor, Department of Educational Psychology, 1948-49; University of Florida, Gainesville, professor of education and head of reading laboratory and clinic, 1950-69, professor emeritus, 1969—. President of Spache Educational Consultants, Inc. Consultant, Educational Developmental Laboratories, St. Louis, Mo., 1956—, and Eli Lilly Foundation, Indianapolis, Ind., 1957—. *Member:* International Reading Association (member of board of directors, 1955-59; president, 1958), American Psychological Association (fellow), National Association for Remedial Teachers (president, 1954), National Reading Conference (president, 1951-63), Reading Research Services (president, 1962-63), National Council of Teachers of English, National Conference on Research in English, American Educational Research Association. *Awards, honors:* Apollo Award from American Optometric Association.

WRITINGS: Resources in Teaching Reading, privately printed, 1955; (with Paul C. Berg) *The Art of Efficient Reading,* Macmillan, 1956, 3rd edition, 1978; (with Lalia Boone) *Handwriting Elements,* Books 1-8, Colonial Press, 1957; *Good Reading for Poor Readers,* Garrard, 1958, 9th edition, 1974; (with Berg) *Faster Reading for Business,* Crowell, 1958; *Toward Better Reading,* Garrard, 1963; *Reading in the Elementary School,* Allyn & Bacon, 1964, 2nd edition (with wife, Evelyn B. Spache), Allyn & Bacon, 1969, 4th edition, 1977; (with E. Goldstein) *Go,* American Book Co., 1965; (editor) *Reading Disabilities and Perception,* International Reading Association, 1969; *Good Reading for the Disadvantaged Reader: Multi-Ethnic Resources,* Garrard, 1970, 2nd edition, 1975; *The Teaching of Reading,* Phi Delta Kappa, 1972; *Diagnosing and Correcting Reading Disabilities,* Allyn & Bacon, 1976, 2nd edition, 1980; *Investigating the Issues of Reading Disabilities,* Allyn & Bacon, 1976, revised edition, 1980.

Contributor: *Education in a Free World,* American Council on Education, 1955; Oscar S. Causey, editor, *The Reading Teacher's Reader,* Ronald, 1958; *Partners in Education,* University of Pennsylvania Press, 1958; *Evaluation of Reading* (monograph), University of Chicago Press, 1958; *The Positive Values in the American Educational System,* American Council on Education, 1958; Boone and James B. McMillan, *Communi-*

cative Arts, Books 9-11, Randall House, 1960; Berg, editor, *Reading Attitudes and Skills Needed for Our Times,* School of Education, University of South Carolina, 1960; M. Jerry Weiss, editor, *Reading in the Secondary Schools,* Odyssey, 1961.

Developed Binocular Reading Test, Keystone View Co., 1943, and Diagnostic Reading Scales, California Test Bureau, 1963. Contributor to yearbooks; also contributor of over one hundred articles to professional journals. Advisory editor, *Journal of Developmental Reading;* book review editor for *Reading Teacher.*

AVOCATIONAL INTERESTS: Golf, swimming.†

* * *

SPARTACUS, Tertius
   See BURGESS, M(ichael) R(oy)

* * *

SPEARS, Betty (Mary)   1918-

PERSONAL: Born January 16, 1918, in Clinton, Ind.; daughter of Archibald Douglas Spears and Mary (Zell) Spears Shumaker. *Education:* Attended Lindenwood College, 1934-35, and Indiana State Teachers College (now Indiana State University), 1937; Purdue University, B.S., 1940; Wellesley College, M.S., 1944; New York University, Ph.D., 1956. *Home:* 56 Van Meter Dr., Amherst, Mass. 01002. *Office:* Department of Sport Studies, University of Massachusetts, Amherst, Mass. 01003.

CAREER: Teacher or instructor at various high schools and colleges, 1940-52; Brooklyn College (now Brooklyn College of the City University of New York), Brooklyn, N.Y., substitute and assistant professor, 1952-60; Wellesley College, Wellesley, Mass., 1960-73, began as associate professor, became professor, head of physical education for women, 1971-73; University of Massachusetts—Amherst, professor of sports studies, 1973—. Conductor of clinics and lecturer on synchronized swimming. Consultant in health and physical education and sports studies field. *Member:* American Alliance for Health, Physical Education and Recreation and Dance, National Association for Physical Education of College Women (member of executive board of Eastern District Association, 1961-66; district president, 1965; national president, 1975-77), National Association for Physical Education in Higher Education, Women's National Aquatic Forum (member of executive committee, 1949-53, 1962-65; general chairman, 1952), North American Society for Sport History (president, 1981-83), Massachusetts Association for Health, Physical Education and Recreation. *Awards, honors:* Massachusetts Association for Health, Physical Education and Recreation Recognition Award, 1971.

WRITINGS: Beginning Synchronized Swimming, Burgess, 1950, 3rd edition published as *Fundamentals of Synchronized Swimming,* 1966; (contributor) *Physical Education for High School Students,* American Association for Health, Physical Education and Recreation, 1955; (with M. A. Gabrielsen and B. W. Gabrielsen) *Aquatics Handbook,* Prentice-Hall, 1960; (with Marlin Mackenzie) *Beginning Swimming,* Wadsworth, 1963; (contributor) *Aquatic Fun for Everyone,* Association Press, 1965; (with Aileene Lockhart) *Chronicle of American Physical Education,* W. C. Brown, 1972; (contributor) *Women's Athletics: Coping with Controversy,* American Association for Health, Physical Education and Recreation, 1974; (contributor) P. Graham and H. Veberhorst, editors, *The Modern Olympics,* Leisure Press, 1976; (with Richard Swanson) *The History of Sport and Physical Education in the United States,* W. C.

Brown, 1978; (contributor) C. A. Oglesby, editor, *Women and Sport: From Myth to Reality,* Lea & Febiger, 1978; (contributor) M. Glady Scott and M. J. Hoferek, editors, *Women as Leaders in Physical Education and Sport,* University of Iowa Press, 1979; (contributor) J. Segrave and D. Chu, editors, *Olympism,* Human Kinetics, 1981. Contributor to *Aquatics Guide, Fencing Guide,* and to recreation, physical education, and history journals. Editor, *Quest,* 1973-75.

AVOCATIONAL INTERESTS: Painting and hiking.

* * *

SPENCE, Clark C(hristian)   1923-

PERSONAL: Born May 25, 1923, in Great Falls, Mont.; son of Christian E. and Lela (Killion) Spence; married Mary Lee Nance, 1953; children: Thomas Christian, Ann Leslie. *Education:* University of Colorado, B.A., M.A.; University of Minnesota, Ph.D. *Home:* 1107 South Foley, Champaign, Ill. *Office:* Department of History, University of Illinois, Champaign, Ill.

CAREER: Carleton College, Northfield, Minn., history instructor, 1954-55; Pennsylvania State University, University Park, Pa., associate professor, 1955-60; University of California, Berkeley, Calif., lecturer, 1960-61; University of Illinois at Urbana-Champaign, associate professor, 1961-64, professor of history, 1964—. *Military service:* U.S. Army Air Forces, 1943-46; became sergeant. *Member:* Agricultural History Society, American Historical Association, Organization of American Historians, Western History Association (president, 1969-70), Phi Beta Kappa. *Awards, honors:* Fulbright scholar, United Kingdom, 1953-54; received A. J. Beveridge Awards, 1956; Agricultural History Society annual book award, 1959; Ford Faculty fellowship, 1963-64; Guggenheim fellow, 1969-70.

WRITINGS: British Investments and the American Mining Frontier, 1860-1901, Cornell University Press, 1958; *God Speed the Plow: The Coming of Steam Cultivation to Great Britain,* University of Illinois Press, 1960; *The Sinews of American Capitalism,* Hill & Wang, 1964; *The American West,* Crowell, 1966; *Mining Engineers and the American West,* Yale University Press, 1970; *Territorial Politics and Government in Montana, 1864-1889,* University of Illinois Press, 1975; *Montana: A Bicentennial History,* Norton, 1978; *The Rainmakers: American "Pluviculture" to World War II,* University of Nebraska Press, 1980.

* * *

SPENCER, Milton Harry   1926-

PERSONAL: Born March 25, 1926, in New York, N.Y.; married Roslyn N. Pernick, 1957; children: Darcy Lynn, Robin Carol, Cathy Hope. *Education:* Attended Queens College (now Queens College of the City University of New York), 1947-49; New York University, B.S., 1949, M.A., 1950; Cornell University, Ph.D., 1954. *Home:* 4543 Fairway Ridge, West Bloomfield, Mich. 48202. *Office:* School of Business Administration, Wayne State University, Detroit, Mich. 48202.

CAREER: Queens College of the City of New York (now Queens College of the City University of New York), Flushing, N.Y., instructor, 1949-52; Cornell University, Ithaca, N.Y., research assistant, 1952-54; Armour & Company, Chicago, Ill., economist, 1954; DePaul University, Chicago, assistant professor, 1954-55; Wayne State University, Detroit, Mich., associate professor, 1955-62, professor of business and economics, 1962—. Distinguished visiting lecturer at University of Chile, 1958, Valparaiso University, 1958, University of Buffalo (now State University of New York at Buffalo), 1959, Hebrew University, 1960, and University of Hawaii, 1966-67. Economic adviser to U.S. Department of State and to foreign governments. *Military service:* U.S. Army, 1943-45. *Member:* American Economic Association, National Association of Business Economists. *Awards, honors:* Certificates of distinguished service from U.S. and foreign government agencies; research grants from Wayne State University.

WRITINGS: Basic Economics, Prentice-Hall, 1951; *Economic Thought,* Norton, 1954; *Managerial Economics: Text, Problems and Short Cases,* Irwin, 1959, 4th edition, 1975; *Business and Economic Forecasting,* Irwin, 1961; *Contemporary Economics,* Worth Publishers, 1971, 4th edition, 1980; *Contemporary Macroeconomics,* Worth Publishers, 1975, 4th edition, 1980; *Contemporary Microeconomics,* Worth Publishers, 1975, 4th edition, 1980. Contributor to economics, business, and engineering journals.

WORK IN PROGRESS: Research in economic education and business policy.

SIDELIGHTS: Milton Spencer has traveled in Latin America, Europe, and the Middle East. *Avocational interests:* Literature, music.

*　　　*　　　*

SPINGARN, Lawrence Perreira 1917-

PERSONAL: Born July 11, 1917, in Jersey City, N.J.; son of Joseph and Ann (Birnbaum) Spingarn; married Sylvia Wainhouse, 1949. *Education:* Bowdoin College, B.S., 1940; University of Michigan, M.A., 1948; University of California, Los Angeles, additional study, 1949. *Home:* 13830 Erwin St., Van Nuys, Calif. *Office:* Los Angeles Valley College, 5800 Fulton Ave., Van Nuys, Calif. 91401.

CAREER: Library of Congress, Washington, D.C., special librarian, 1941-43; United Service Organizations, New York City, publicity, 1944-45; free-lance writing and work in own business, New York City and Los Angeles, Calif., 1945-59; Los Angeles Valley College, Van Nuys, Calif., teacher of English, 1959—. Editor, Perivale Press, 1968—. *Member:* Poetry Society of America, Poetry Society of London. *Awards, honors:* Bread Loaf fellowships, 1941 and 1942; McDowell resident fellowship, 1946; Huntington Hartford Foundation award of $500 in 1950, fellowships, 1955, 1956; Yaddo resident fellowship, 1958; received prize poem award, Poetry Society of America, 1975.

WRITINGS—All poetry, except as indicated: *Rococo Summer,* Dutton, 1947; *The Lost River,* Heinemann, 1951; *Letters from Exile,* Longmans, Green, 1961; *Madame Bidet, and Other Fixtures,* Perivale, 1968; *Freeway Problems and Others,* 1970; *The Blue Door and Other Stories* (fiction), Perivale, 1977; *The Dark Playground,* Perivale, 1979. Editor, *Poets West: An Anthology of Contemporary Poems from the Eleven Western States,* Perivale, 1976. Poetry anthologized in *Poetry Society of America Anthology,* 1946, *Poetry Awards,* 1949, *The Golden Year: Poetry Society of America,* 1960, and *New Yorker Book of Poems,* 1969. Short stories in *Best American Short Stories,* 1950-53, 1955, 1956, 1961. Contributor of poetry, fiction, essays, and general articles to magazines and newspapers, including *Harper's, Modern Age, New York Times, Poetry, Saturday Review, New Yorker, Southern Review, Kenyon Review;* contributor to professional journals in Canada, France, Great Britain, and West Indies, as well as in the United States. Founder and editor, *California Quarterly,* 1950-53; contributing editor, *Trace,* 1961-64.

WORK IN PROGRESS: A book of prose poems, *Moral Tales.*

SIDELIGHTS: Lawrence Spingarn told *CA,* "I have traveled extensively, but not exclusively, in countries of the mind."

*　　　*　　　*

SPIRO, Herbert J(ohn) 1924-

PERSONAL: Born September 7, 1924, in Hamburg, Germany; became a U.S. citizen; son of Albert John and Marianne (Stiefel) Spiro; married Elizabeth Petersen (an author), 1958; children: Peter, Alexander. *Education:* Harvard University, A.B. (summa cum laude), 1949, M.A., 1950, Ph.D., 1953. *Home:* 3418 Garfield St. N.W., Washington, D.C. 20007.

CAREER: U.S. War Department, Vienna, Austria, administrative assistant, 1945-46; Harvard University, Cambridge, Mass., teaching fellow, 1950-53, instructor, 1954-57, assistant professor of government, 1957-61; Amherst College, Amherst, Mass., associate professor of political science, 1961-65; chairman of Asian and African Studies Program of Amherst, Mt. Holyoke, and Smith Colleges and University of Massachusetts, 1964-65; University of Pennsylvania, Philadelphia, professor of political science, 1965-70; U.S. Department of State, Washington, D.C., member of policy planning staff, 1970-75, U.S. ambassador to Cameroon, Equatorial Guinea, 1975-76; Smithsonian Institution, Woodrow Wilson International Center for Scholars, Washington, D.C., fellow, 1977-79; Free University of Berlin, Berlin, Germany, professor of political science, 1980—. Visiting associate professor of political science, University of Chicago, 1961, and Stanford University, 1963. Visiting professor of international affairs, Woodrow Wilson School, Princeton University, 1966. U.S. Information Service lecturer in Japan, Thailand, India, Africa, Sweden, Austria, and Germany; lecturer at U.S. Army War College, Air University, Federal Executive Institute, and numerous other colleges, universities, and learned societies. Consultant to Japanese Constitutional Commission, and to British Commission on the Constitutional Future of the Federation of Rhodesia and Nyasaland, 1960. *Military service:* U.S. Army, 1943-45; became master sergeant; awarded Bronze Star with oak leaf cluster, Purple Heart.

MEMBER: African Studies Association, American Foreign Service Association, American Association of University Professors, American Political Science Association, American Society for Legal and Political Philosophy, International Political Science Association, Signet Society (Cambridge, Mass.), Phi Beta Kappa. *Awards, honors:* Bowdoin Prize, 1952; Fulbright fellowship, 1953-54; Rockefeller Foundation research fellowship, Harvard University, 1958-59; received Superior Honor Award, U.S. Department of State, 1959; Social Science Research Council faculty research fellowship, 1962 and 1967-68; National Science Foundation grants, 1966; M.A., University of Pennsylvania, 1971.

WRITINGS: (Co-author) *Governing Post-War Germany,* edited by Edward H. Litchfield, Cornell University Press, 1953; (co-author) *Patterns of Government: The Major Political Systems of Europe,* edited by S. H. Beer and A. B. Ulam, Random House, 1958, 2nd edition, 1962; *The Politics of German Codetermination,* Harvard University Press, 1958; (co-author) *Nomos I: Authority,* edited by C. J. Friedrich, Harvard University Press, 1958; *Government by Constitution: The Political Systems of Democracy,* Random House, 1959; (co-author) *Nomos III: Responsibility,* edited by C. J. Friedrich, Liberal Arts Press, 1960; *Politics in Africa: Prospects South of the Sahara,* Prentice-Hall, 1962; *Comparative Politics: A Comprehensive Approach,* Bobbs-Merrill, 1962; (co-author) *Five African States:*

Responses to Diversity, edited by Gwendolen M. Carter, Cornell University Press, 1963; (co-author and editor) *Africa: The Primacy of Politics,* Random House, 1966; *World Politics: The Global System,* Dorsey, 1966; (co-author and editor) *Patterns of African Development,* Prentice-Hall, 1967; (co-author) *Contemporary Political Analysis,* Free Press, 1967; (co-author) *Why Federations Fail,* New York University Press, 1968; *The Dialectic of Representation, 1619-1969,* University Press of Virginia, 1969; *Responsibility in Government: Theory and Practice,* Van Nostrand, 1969.

Politics as the Master Science: From Plato to Mao, Prentice-Hall, 1970; (co-author) *Nomos XIII: Privacy,* edited by Roland Pennock, Atherton Press, 1971; (co-author) *Between Sovereignty and Integration,* edited by Ghita Ionescu, Croom Helm, 1974; *A New Foreign Policy Consensus?,* Sage Publications, 1979. Also author of *Adversaries and the Truth: A Study of the Adversary System of the Common Law,* 1969. Author of fortnightly column, "Two Worlds," for Amherst, Mass. *Record,* 1963-66. Contributor to *International Encyclopedia of the Social Sciences* and *Encyclopaedia Britannica.* Also contributor of articles to professional journals.

WORK IN PROGRESS: Replication and Interdependence: The Unique Role of the United States in the World; From Bureaucratic Politics to Philosophy of History: The Theory of Replication.

*   *   *

SPIRO, Jack D. 1933-

PERSONAL: Born March 4, 1933, in New Orleans, La.; son of Harry and Rebecca (Cohen) Spiro; married Marilyn S. Loevy; children: Hillary Ann, David K. *Education:* Tulane University, B.A., 1953; Hebrew Union College-Jewish Institute of Religion, B.H.L., 1953, M.A., 1958, D.H.L., 1962. *Home:* 7 Bernard Rd., East Brunswick, N.J. 08816. *Office:* 222 Livingston Ave., New Brunswick, N.J. 08902.

CAREER: Temple Anshe Emeth, New Brunswick, N.J., rabbi, 1962—. *Military service:* U.S. Air Force, Chaplains Corps, 1958-61; became captain. *Member:* Academy of Religion and Mental Health, Central Conference of American Rabbis, B'nai B'rith, Phi Alpha Theta.

WRITINGS: (With Sylvan Schwartzman) *The Living Bible: A Topical Approach to the Jewish Scriptures,* Union of American Hebrew Congregations, 1962; *A Time to Mourn: Judaism and the Psychology of Bereavement,* Bloch Publishing, 1967; (editor) Albert Vorspan, *Jewish Values and Social Crisis: A Casebook for Social Action,* Union of American Hebrew Congregations, 1968; (with Abraham Sheingold) *Discussion Guide: Out of the Whirlwind,* Union of American Hebrew Congregations, 1968; (editor) Abraham Shumsky and Adaia Shumsky, *Hatznea Lechet: Walk Humbly,* Union of American Hebrew Congregations, 1971; (with John Shelby Spong) *Dialogue: In Search of Jewish-Christian Understanding,* Seabury, 1975. Contributor to religious periodicals.†

*   *   *

SPITZ, Lewis W(illiam) 1922-

PERSONAL: Born December 14, 1922, in Bertrand, Neb.; son of Lewis William and Pauline (Griebel) Spitz; married Edna Marie Huttenmaier, August 14, 1948; children: Stephen, Philip. *Education:* St. Paul's College, Concordia, Mo., 1940-42; Concordia College, A.B., 1944; Concordia Seminary, M.Div., 1947; University of Missouri, M.A., 1948; Harvard University, Ph.D., 1954; attended University of Chicago, summers,

1943-48. *Politics:* Republican. *Religion:* Lutheran. *Home:* 827 Lathrop Dr., Stanford, Calif. *Office:* History Department, Stanford University, Stanford, Calif.

CAREER: University of Missouri—Columbia, instructor, 1953-54, assistant professor, 1954-56, associate professor, 1957-60; Stanford University, Stanford, Calif., associate professor, 1960-64, professor of history, 1964—. Fulbright scholar, University of Vienna, 1952-53. Fulbright professor, Institute for European History, Mainz, Germany, 1960-61. *Member:* American Historical Association, American Society for Reformation Research (president), Renaissance Society of America (member of council), Luther-Gesellschaft, Concordia Historical Institute, Society for Religion in Higher Education, American Society of Church History. *Awards, honors:* Guggenheim fellow, 1956-57; Huntington Library fellow, 1959; American Council of Learned Societies fellow, 1960-61; Danforth Associates Award for Teaching, 1964-65.

WRITINGS: Conrad Celtis: The German Arch-Humanist, Harvard University Press, 1957; *Career of the Reformer IV,* Muhlenberg, 1960; (editor) *The Reformation—Material or Spiritual?,* Heath, 1962, 2nd edition, 1972; *The Religious Renaissance of the German Humanists,* Harvard University Press, 1963; (contributor) A. Huegli, editor, *Church and State under God,* Concordia, 1964; (editor with Richard Lyman) *Major Crises in Western Civilization,* two volumes, Harcourt, 1965; *Life in Two Worlds: William Sihler,* Concordia, 1966; *The Protestant Reformation,* Prentice-Hall, 1966; *The Renaissance and the Reformation Movements,* two volumes, Rand McNally, 1971; *The Northern Renaissance,* Prentice-Hall, 1972; (editor) *Reformation: Basic Interpretations,* Heath, 1972; (editor with Wenzel Lohff) *Discord, Dialogue, and Concord: Studies in the Lutheran Reformation's Formula of Concord,* Fortress, 1972. Member of board of editors, *Journal of Modern History* and *Archive for Reformation History.* Contributor to professional and religious journals.

WORK IN PROGRESS: The Protestant Reformation, 1517-1559, for Harper.

*   *   *

SPOTNITZ, Hyman 1908-

PERSONAL: Born 1908, in Boston, Mass; son of Eiser and Annie (Waxler) Spotnitz; married Miriam Berkman, 1934 (deceased, 1977), married Dorothy Weiss Harten, 1978; children: Henry Michael, Alan Jeffrey, William David. *Education:* Harvard University, B.A., 1929; Friedrich Wilhelms University, M.D., 1934; Columbia University, Med. Sc. D., 1939. *Home:* 1 West 64th St., New York, N.Y. 10023. *Office:* 41 Central Park W., New York, N.Y. 10023.

CAREER: Neurological Institute, New York City, began as research fellow, became research assistant, 1936-42; Columbia University, New York City, assistant in neurology, 1940-45; Vanderbilt Clinic, New York City, assistant neurologist, 1940-54; psychoanalyst and research psychiatrist, 1954—. Adjunct psychiatrist, Hospital for Joint Diseases, 1942-43; consultant psychiatrist, Jewish Board of Guardians, 1944-54.

MEMBER: American Association for the Advancement of Science (fellow), American Psychiatric Association (life fellow), American Orthopsychiatric Association (fellow), American Group Psychotherapy Association (fellow), New York Academy of Medicine (fellow), New York Academy of Sciences (fellow), American Medical Association, New York Neurological Society, Association for Research in Nervous and Mental Diseases, New York County Medical Society.

WRITINGS: *The Couch and the Circle,* Knopf, 1961; (co-author) *The Wandering Husband,* Prentice-Hall, 1964; *Modern Psychoanalysis of the Schizophrenic Patient,* Grune, 1969; (co-author) *How to Be Happy though Pregnant,* Coward, 1969; *Psychotherapy of Preoedipal Conditions,* Jason Aronson, 1976; (co-author) *Treatment of the Narcissistic Neuroses,* Manhattan Center for Modern Psychoanalytic Studies, 1976. Contributor of numerous chapters and scientific papers in professional books and journals. Consulting editor, *International Journal of Group Psychotherapy;* former consulting editor, *Psychoanalytic Review.*

*   *   *

SPROUT, Harold   1901-1980

PERSONAL: Born March 14, 1901, in Benzonia, Mich.; died December 12, 1980, in Princeton, N.J.; son of George Milton and Grace (Hance) Sprout; married Margaret A. Tuttle, 1924; children: Donald Francis, Elizabeth Sprout McGuire. *Education:* Oberlin College, A.B. and A.M., 1924; Western Reserve University (now Case Western Reserve University), additional study, 1925-26; University of Wisconsin, Ph.D., 1929. *Home:* 93 McCosh Circle, Princeton, N.J. *Office:* Corwin Hall, Princeton University, Princeton, N.J.

CAREER: Miami University, Oxford, Ohio, assistant professor, 1926-27; Stanford University, Stanford, Calif., assistant professor, 1929-31; Princeton University, Princeton, N.J., instructor, 1931-35, assistant professor, 1935-41, associate professor, 1941-45, professor of political science, 1945-69, Henry G. Bryant Professor of Geography and International Relations, 1952-69, professor emeritus, 1969-80, chairman of department of politics, 1949-52, Center of International Studies, faculty associate, 1962-69, research associate, beginning 1969. *Member:* American Geographical Society, American Political Science Association, American Association for the Advancement of Science, International Studies Association.

WRITINGS: *A War Atlas for Americans,* Simon & Schuster, 1944; *Man-Milieu Relationship Hypotheses in the Context of International Politics,* Center of International Studies, Princeton University, 1956; *The Context of Environmental Politics,* University Press of Kentucky, 1978.

With wife, Margaret Sprout: *The Rise of American Naval Power: Seventeen Seventy-Six to Nineteen Eighteen,* Princeton University Press, 1939, reprinted Naval Institute Press, 1980; *Toward a New Order of Sea Power,* Princeton University Press, 1940; *Foundations of National Power,* Princeton University Press, 1946, 2nd revised edition, 1951; *Foundations Of International Politics,* Van Nostrand, 1962; *The Ecological Perspective on Human Affairs,* Princeton University Press, 1965; *An Ecological Paradigm for the Study of International Politics,* Center of International Studies, Princeton University, 1968; *Toward a Politics of the Planet Earth,* Van Nostrand, 1971; *Multiple Vulnerabilities: The Context of Environmental Repair and Protection,* Center of International Studies, Princeton University, 1974; *The Context of Environmental Politics: Unfinished Business for America's Third Century,* University Press of Kentucky, 1978. Contributor to numerous journals in his field.

WORK IN PROGRESS: Further research and publication on national and international context of environmental repair and protection in collaboration with Margaret Sprout.

SIDELIGHTS: Harold Sprout once wrote to *CA:* "For nearly half a century—from 1924 until '69—I combined the reciprocal roles of college-university teaching with research and writing.

Since 1969, emeritus status has freed more time for writing and publication as the list of major publications indicates.

"I still work regularly at my specialty which has evolved into identification and assessment of the multiplicity of conditions, forces, and events that affect what public authorities undertake and what they leave undone to arrest progressive ruination of our earthly habitat by over-exploitation of natural resources (especially fossil fuels), resultant pollutions of air, water, and land, and accelerative disruption of fragile natural and societal systems. . . . I have found that a major incentive to scholarly research and writing in the academic milieu is the stimulus provided by one's students and professional peers."

OBITUARIES: *New York Times,* December 15, 1980.

*   *   *

SQUIRES, Radcliffe   1917-

PERSONAL: Born May 23, 1917, in Salt Lake City, Utah; son of Edward Frederick and Janet (McNeil) Squires; married Eileen Mulholland, 1945 (died, 1976). *Education:* University of Utah, B.A., 1940; University of Chicago, A.M., 1945; Harvard University, Ph.D., 1952. *Home:* 1225 Island Dr., Ann Arbor, Mich. *Office:* University of Michigan, 7616 Haven Hall, Ann Arbor, Mich.

CAREER: Dartmouth College, Dartmouth, N.H., instructor, 1945-48; Harvard University, Cambridge, Mass., fellow, 1948-52; University of Michigan, Ann Arbor, 1952—, began as instructor, professor of English, 1964—. Fulbright lecturer in American literature in Greece, 1959-60. *Military service:* U.S. Navy, 1941-44; became lieutenant. *Member:* Writers Guild, Poetry Society of America, P.E.N. *Awards, honors:* Young Poets Prize, *Voices* magazine, 1947.

WRITINGS: *Cornar,* Dorrance, 1940; *Where the Compass Spins,* Twayne, 1951; *The Loyalities of Robinson Jeffers,* University of Michigan Press, 1956; *The Major Themes of Robert Frost,* University of Michigan Press, 1963; *Frederic Prokosch,* Twayne, 1964; *Fingers of Hermes,* University of Michigan Press, 1965; *The Light under Islands,* University of Michigan Press, 1967; *Allen Tate: A Literary Biography,* Bobbs-Merrill, 1971; (editor) *Allen Tate and His Work,* University of Minnesota Press, 1972; *Waiting in the Bone: Poems,* Abattoir, 1973. Contributor to *Poetry, New Republic, Story, Paris Review, Sewanee Review,* and many other periodicals. Editor, *Chicago Review,* 1945-46 and *Michigan Quarterly Review,* 1971-76.

WORK IN PROGRESS: *A Dream of Rome; Gardens of the World.*

AVOCATIONAL INTERESTS: Gardening.

*   *   *

STACTON, David (Derek)   1925-1968
(Carse Boyd, Bud Clifton, David Dereksen)

PERSONAL: Born April 25, 1925, near Minden, Nev.; died January 19, 1968, in Fredensborg, Denmark; son of David and Dorothy (Green) Stacton; married. *Education:* Attended Stanford University, 1941-43; University of California, B.A., 1950; attended Stanford Radio and Television Institute, 1955. *Politics:* "Emphatically none." *Religion:* Episcopalian. *Residence:* Albuquerque, N.M.; and Copenhagen, Denmark. *Agent:* Malcolm Reiss, Paul R. Reynolds, Inc., 12 East 41st St., New York, N.Y. 10017.

CAREER: Writer. Glasgow Visiting Professor, Washington and Lee University, 1965-66. *Awards, honors:* Guggenheim fellow, 1960-61.

WRITINGS: A Ride on a Tiger (biography), Museum Press, 1954; *Dolores,* Faber, 1954; *A Fox Inside,* Faber, 1955; *The Self-Enchanted,* Faber, 1956; *Remember Me,* Faber, 1957; (under pseudonym Bud Clifton) *The Power Gods,* Eyre & Spottiswoode, 1958; (under pseudonym Bud Clifton) *D Is for Delinquent,* Ace Books, 1958; *On a Balcony,* Faber, 1958, London House, 1959; *Segaki,* Faber, 1958, Pantheon, 1959; *A Dancer in Darkness,* Faber, 1960, Pantheon, 1962; *A Signal Victory,* Faber, 1960, Pantheon, 1962; *The Judges of the Secret Court,* Pantheon, 1961; *Tom Fool,* Faber, 1962; (under pseudonym Carse Boyd) *Navarro,* Doubleday, 1962; (under pseudonym Carse Boyd) *Ride the Man Down,* John Long, 1962; *Old Acquaintance,* Faber, 1962, Putnam, 1964; *Sir William; or, A Lesson in Love,* Putnam, 1963; (under pseudonym David Dereksen) *The Crescent and the Cross: The Fall of Byzantium, May, 1543,* Putnam, 1964; *The World on the Last Day: The Sack of Constantinople by the Turks, May 29, 1543—Its Causes and Consequences* (nonfiction), Faber, 1965; *Kaliyuga; or, A Quarrel with the Gods,* Faber, 1965; *People of the Book,* Putnam, 1965; *The Bonapartes* (biography), Simon & Schuster, 1966; *Five Poems,* Limited Editions Unincorporated, 1977.

Work is represented in anthology, *O. Henry Prize Stories, 1964,* Doubleday, 1964. Contributor of short stories to *Contact, Town and Country, Virginia Quarterly Review,* and to British magazines.

WORK IN PROGRESS: Restless Sleep, a novel; a book about the nature of religious experience.

SIDELIGHTS: A historical and biographical novelist who examined some of the more unusual and unfamiliar people and events of the past, David Stacton never received the critical and popular acclaim many believed he deserved. According to Ronald Bryden of the *Spectator,* Stacton launched "a small revolution in historical fiction by rejecting its most cherished conventions." In what the reviewer termed an "intelligent" but "opinionated" and "rather scornful" manner, Stacton presented his readers with cynical and "astringent" observations of life in a style often described as elliptical. Though these qualities alienated quite a few critics, they impressed others as evidence of Stacton's imaginative brilliance and inventiveness. For example, a *Times Literary Supplement* reviewer once remarked: "Mr. Stacton is an original. He uses the historical background of his novels not to interpret the past or to bring distant times nearer but to study individuals who were far from typical of their own age and who would indeed at almost any point in history have been considered eccentric or insane." The *Saturday Review*'s Edmund Fuller agreed, pointing out that "the values that have shaped [Stacton's] style and thought are not those of the prevalent voices in American writing. . . . [He] writes from considerable cultural depth, with a concern for precision of diction."

Richard McLaughlin of the *Springfield Republican* felt that the typical Stacton work "is as much a conversation piece as it is an historical novel. . . . [Its] urbanity and flexibility of thought suggest the author has a gracefully balanced mind, which makes many of his contemporaries appear most commonplace. . . . [His characters] are all so wonderfully alive that one is convinced that David Stacton DID step back into their times and come away with an enchanting, richly rewarding entertainment. Also, he has such an unfailingly clear, precise grasp of the meaning of the words he uses that his prose is an unmixed joy to read."

On the other hand, some critics, such as the *New York Times Book Review*'s Martin Levin, described Stacton's style as "distractingly affected" and his characters as "somewhat bloodless, their individuality subordinated to the rhetoric." Even

Fuller noted that the author's "intensely epigrammatic" style and fondness for paradox gave his work "a certain decadence." The *Times Literary Supplement* reviewer commented on the "jagged and staccato" nature of Stacton's prose as well as on his "sometimes perverse" choice of words, while a colleague from the same publication observed that "his attitude towards his characters is presumptuous or condescending" and that "his self-satisfaction is in proportion to the density of his epigrams." The result, said this second reviewer, is a novel that "lapses too often into banality" written by a man who "seems to have the imaginative power to be a good novelist" but whose "heart is not in it."

Book Week's Richard Winston, however, did not view Stacton in quite the same way. He concluded: "The 18th-century spirit, clarity, coolness and rationality and delight in epigram and apothegm is perfectly mirrored in David Stacton's prose. . . . [He] has the wit, the power, the sharpness of insight and the fecundity of a major novelist. One can only hope that he will soon be recognized as such by his laggard contemporaries."

AVOCATIONAL INTERESTS: Travel.

BIOGRAPHICAL/CRITICAL SOURCES: Times Literary Supplement, February 28, 1958, November 14, 1958, June 2, 1961, April 8, 1960, October 21, 1965; *Springfield Republican,* August 30, 1959; *Time,* September 7, 1959, August 11, 1961, March 16, 1962, February 26, 1965; *Saturday Review,* September 26, 1959, October 5, 1963; *San Francisco Chronicle,* September 27, 1959, December 3, 1959, August 15, 1961, March 11, 1962; *New York Times Book Review,* October 4, 1959, August 13, 1961; *Booklist,* October 15, 1959; *New York Herald Tribune Book Review,* October 18, 1959; *Commonweal,* December 4, 1959; *Spectator,* April 1, 1960; *Christian Science Monitor,* August 3, 1961; *Chicago Sunday Tribune,* August 13, 1961, February 11, 1962, October 20, 1963; *New York Herald Tribune Books,* September 3, 1961, February 11, 1962; *Book Week,* October 13, 1963; *Atlantic,* February, 1965.

OBITUARIES: New York Times, January 24, 1968; *Time,* February 2, 1968; *Publishers Weekly,* February 12, 1968; *London Times,* February 21, 1968; *Antiquarian Bookman,* February 26, 1968; *Books Abroad,* spring, 1969.†

*   *   *

STAVRIANOS, Leften Stavros 1913-

PERSONAL: Born February 5, 1913, in Vancouver, British Columbia, Canada; naturalized U.S. citizen, 1940; son of Stavros and Margaret (Vernicos) Stavrianos; married Bertha Kelso (a psychologist), July 20, 1940; children: Peter, Marjorie. *Education:* University of British Columbia, B.A., 1933; Clark University, M.A., 1934, Ph.D., 1937. *Office:* Department of History, University of California, San Diego, La Jolla, Calif. 92093.

CAREER: Queen's University, Kingston, Ontario, lecturer in history, 1937-38; Smith College, Northampton, Mass., instructor, 1939-44, assistant professor of history, 1944-46; Northwestern University, Evanston, Ill., associate professor, 1946-56, professor of history, 1956-73, professor emeritus, 1973—; University of California, San Diego, La Jolla, adjunct professor of history, 1973—. *Wartime service:* Office of Strategic Services, 1944-45. *Member:* American Historical Association, National Education Association. *Awards, honors:* Royal Society of Canada traveling fellowship, 1938-39; Guggenheim fellowship, 1951-52; Ford faculty fellowship, 1953-54; grants from Carnegie Corp., 1958-67, for work in world history; Rockefeller Foundation fellowship, 1967-68; Center for Advanced Study in the Behavioral Sciences fellowship, 1972-73.

WRITINGS: *Balkan Federation: A History of the Movement toward Balkan Unity in Modern Times*, Smith College, 1944, reprinted, Archon Books, 1964; *Greece: American Dilemma and Opportunity*, Regnery, 1952; *The Ottoman Empire: Was It the Sick Man of Europe?*, Rinehart, 1957; *The Balkans since 1455*, Rinehart, 1959; (with others) *A Global History of Man*, Allyn & Bacon, 1962, revised edition published as *A Global History*, 1978; (co-editor) *Readings in World History*, Allyn & Bacon, 1962; *The Balkans, 1815-1914*, Holt, 1963; *The Soviet Union: A Culture Area in Perspective*, Allyn & Bacon, 1964; (with Loretta Kreider Andrews) *Sub-Saharan Africa: A Culture Area in Perspective*, Allyn & Bacon, 1964; (with George I. Blanksten) *Latin America: A Culture Area in Perspective*, Allyn & Bacon, 1964.

The World since 1500: A Global History (also see below), Prentice-Hall, 1966, 3rd edition, 1975; *The Middle East: A Culture Area in Perspective*, Allyn & Bacon, 1966; (editor) *The Epic of Modern Man: A Collection of Readings* (also see below), Prentice-Hall, 1966; (with Lacey Baldwin Smith) *India: A Culture Area in Perspective*, Allyn & Bacon, 1966; (with Roger R. Hackett) *China: A Culture Area in Perspective*, Allyn & Bacon, 1966; *The World to 1500: A Global History* (also see below), Prentice-Hall, 1970, 2nd edition, 1975; (editor) *The Epic of Man to 1500: A Collection of Readings* (also see below), Prentice-Hall, 1970; *The Epic of Man: A Collection of Readings* (includes selections from *The Epic of Modern Man* and *The Epic of Man to 1500*), Prentice-Hall, 1971; *Man's Past and Present: A Global History* (includes selections from *The World since 1500* and *The World to 1500*), Prentice-Hall, 1975; *The Promise of the Coming Dark Age*, W. H. Freeman, 1976; *Global Rift: The Third World Comes of Age*, Morrow, 1981. Contributor of articles to professional journals.

* * *

STEAD, Christian Karlson 1932-

PERSONAL: Surname rhymes with "head"; born October 17, 1932, in Auckland, New Zealand; son of James Walter (an accountant) and Olive (a music teacher; maiden name, Karlson) Stead; married Kathleen Elizabeth Roberts, January 8, 1955; children: Oliver William, Charlotte Mary, Margaret Hermione. *Education:* University of Auckland, B.A., 1953, M.A., 1955; University of Bristol, Ph.D., 1959. *Politics:* New Zealand Labour Party. *Religion:* None. *Home:* 37 Tohunga Cres., Auckland 1, New Zealand. *Office:* Department of English, Auckland University, Private Bag, Auckland, New Zealand.

CAREER: University of Auckland, Auckland, New Zealand, lecturer, 1959-61, senior lecturer, 1962-64, associate professor, 1964-68, professor of English, 1968—. Chairman of New Zealand Literary Fund Advisory Committee, 1972-75. *Awards, honors:* Katherine Mansfield Prize, 1960, for a short story; Nuffield travelling fellowship, 1965; Winn-Mansen Menton fellowship, 1972; Jessie McKay Award for Poetry, 1972; New Zealand Book Award for Poetry, 1975.

WRITINGS: *Whether the Will Is Free* (poems), Blackwood, 1964; *The New Poetic: Yeats to Eliot*, Hutchinson, 1964, 2nd edition, 1975, Harper, 1966; (editor) *World's Classics: New Zealand Short Stories*, 2nd series (Stead was not associated with earlier series), Oxford University Press, 1966, 3rd edition, 1975; *Smith's Dream* (novel), Longman, 1971; (editor) *Measure for Measure: A Casebook*, Macmillan, 1971, revised edition, 1973; *Crossing the Bar* (poems), Oxford University Press, 1972; *Quesada: Poems 1972-74*, The Shed (Auckland), 1975; *Walking Westward* (poems), The Shed, 1979; (editor) *Letters and Journals of Katherine Mansfield*, Allen Lane, 1977; *Five*

for the Symbol (short stories), Longman, 1981; (editor) *Collected Stories of Maurice Duggan*, Oxford University Press, 1981; *In the Glass Case: Essays on New Zealand Literature*, Oxford University Press, 1981; *Geographies* (poems), Oxford University Press, 1982.

WORK IN PROGRESS: A large book on Ezra Pound and modernism.

BIOGRAPHICAL/CRITICAL SOURCES: *Islands*, summer, 1972.

* * *

STEELE, Mary Q(uintard Govan) 1922-
(Wilson Gage)

PERSONAL: Born May 8, 1922, in Chattanooga, Tenn.; daughter of Gilbert Eaton (a librarian) and Christine (Noble) Govan; married William O. Steele (a writer), June 1, 1943; children: Mary Quintard, Jenifer Susan, Allerton William. *Education:* University of Chattanooga, B.S., 1943. *Politics:* Democrat. *Religion:* "Nominal" Episcopalian.

CAREER: Writer of children's books. *Awards, honors:* Aurianne Award of the American Library Association, 1966, for *Big Blue Island;* Newbery Honor Book award, 1969, for *Journey Outside;* American Library Association Notable Book award, 1976, for *Squash Pie*, 1977, for *Down in the Boon Docks*.

WRITINGS—Published by Greenwillow, except as indicated: *Journey Outside*, Viking, 1969; *The Living Year*, Viking, 1972; *The First of the Penguins*, Macmillan, 1974; (with husband, William O. Steele) *The Eye in the Forest*, Dutton, 1975; *Because of the Sand Witches There*, 1975; *The True Men*, 1976; *The Fifth Day*, 1978; *The Owl's Kiss*, 1978; *Wish, Come True*, 1979; *The Life (and Death) of Sarah Elizabeth Harwood*, 1980.

Under pseudonym Wilson Gage; published by World Publishing, except as indicated: *Secret of the Indian Mound*, 1958; *Secret of Crossbone Hill*, 1959; *Secret of Fiery Gorge*, 1960; *A Wild Goose Tale*, 1961; *Dan and the Miranda*, 1962; *Miss Osborne the Mop*, 1963; *Big Blue Island*, 1964; *Ghost of Five Owl Farm*, 1966; *Mike's Toads*, 1970; *Squash Pie*, Greenwillow, 1976; *Down in the Boon Docks*, Greenwillow, 1977. Contributor of articles to *Horn Book Magazine* and of book reviews to *Chattanooga Times*.

BIOGRAPHICAL/CRITICAL SOURCES: *New York Times Book Review*, October 12, 1969; *Times Literary Supplement*, October 30, 1970.

* * *

STEIN, Aaron Marc 1906-
(George Bagby, Hampton Stone)

PERSONAL: Born November 15, 1906, in New York, N.Y.; son of Max and Fannie (Blumberg) Stein. *Education:* Princeton University, A.B., 1927. *Home:* 1070 Park Ave., New York, N.Y. 10028.

CAREER: *New York Evening Post*, New York City, reporter, critic, and columnist, 1927-38; Time, Inc., New York City, an editor, 1938; U.S. Office of War Information, Washington, D.C., propaganda analyst, 1942-43; free-lance writer. *Military service:* U.S. Army, three years. *Member:* Princeton Club (New York), Nassau Club (Princeton, N.J.). *Awards, honors:* Grand Master Award, Mystery Writers of America, 1979, "for outstanding contribution to the craft of mystery writing."

WRITINGS—Published by Doubleday, except as indicated: *Spirals*, Covici, Friede, 1930; *Her Body Speaks*, Covici, Friede,

1931; *The Sun Is a Witness*, 1940; *Up to No Good*, 1941; *Only the Guilty*, 1942; *The Case of the Absent-Minded Professor*, 1943; *. . . And High Water*, 1946; *We Saw Him Die*, 1947; *Death Takes a Paying Guest*, 1947; *The Cradle and the Grave*, 1948; *The Second Burial*, 1949; *Days of Misfortune*, 1949; *Three—With Blood*, 1950; *Frightened Amazon*, 1950; *Shoot Me Dacent*, 1951; *Pistols for Two*, 1951; *Mask for Murder*, 1952; *The Dead Thing in the Pool*, 1952; *Death Meets 400 Rabbits*, 1953; *Moonmilk and Murder*, 1955; *Sitting Up Dead*, 1958; *Never Need an Enemy*, 1959.

Home and Murder, 1962; *Blood on the Stars*, 1964; *I Fear the Greeks*, 1966 (published in England as *Executioner's Rest*, R. Hale, 1967); *Deadly Delight*, 1967; *Snare Andalucian*, 1968 (published in England as *Faces of Death*, R. Hale, 1968); *Kill Is a Four-Letter Word*, 1968; *Alp Murder*, 1970; *The Finger*, 1973; *Lock and Key*, 1973; *Coffin Country*, 1976; *Lend Me Your Ears*, 1976; *Body Search*, 1977; *Nowhere?*, 1978; *Chill Factor*, 1978; *The Rolling Heads*, 1979; *One Dip Dead*, 1979; *The Cheating Butcher*, 1980; *A Nose for It*, 1980; *A Body for a Buddy*, in press.

Under pseudonym George Bagby; published by Doubleday, except as indicated: *Bachelor's Wife*, Covici, Friede, 1932; *Murder at the Piano*, Covici, Friede, 1935; *Ring around a Murder*, Covici, Friede, 1936; *Murder Half-Baked*, Covici, Friede, 1937; *Murder on the Nose*, 1938; *Bird Walking Weather: An Inspector Schmidt Story*, 1939; *The Corpse with the Purple Thighs*, 1939; *The Corpse Wore a Wig*, 1940; *Here Comes the Corpse*, 1941; *Red Is for Killing*, 1941; *Murder Calling "50": An Inspector Schmidt Story*, 1942; *Dead on Arrival*, 1946; *The Original Carcase*, 1946; *The Twin Killing*, 1947; *The Starting Gun*, 1948; *In Cold Blood*, 1948; *Drop Dead*, 1949; *Coffin Corner*, 1949.

Blood Will Tell, 1950; *Death Ain't Commercial*, 1951; *Scared to Death*, 1952; *The Corpse with Sticky Fingers*, 1952; *Give the Little Corpse a Great Big Hand*, 1953; *Dead Drunk*, 1953; *The Body in the Basket*, 1954; *A Dirty Way to Die*, 1955; *Dead Storage*, 1956; *Cop Killer*, 1956; *Dead Wrong*, 1957; *The Three-Time Losers*, 1958; *The Real Gone Goose*, 1959; *Evil Genius*, 1961; *Murder's Little Helper*, 1963; *Mysteriouser and Mysteriouser*, 1965 (published in England as *Murder in Wonderland*, Hammond, 1965); *Dirty Pool*, 1966 (published in England as *Bait for a Killer*, Hammond, 1967); *Corpse Candle*, 1967; *Another Day, Another Death*, 1968; *Honest, Reliable Corpse*, 1969.

Killer Boy Was Here, 1970; *Two in the Bush*, 1976; *My Dead Body*, 1976; *Innocent Bystander*, 1977; *The Tough Get Going*, 1977; *Better Dead*, 1978; *Guaranteed to Fade*, 1978; *I Could Have Died*, 1979; *Mugger's Day*, 1979; *Country and Fatal*, 1980; *A Question of Quarry*, 1981; *The Sitting Duck*, in press.

Under pseudonym Hampton Stone: "Inner Sanctum" mysteries, published by Simon & Schuster: *The Corpse in the Corner Saloon*, 1948; *The Girl with the Hole in Her Head*, 1949; *The Needle That Wouldn't Hold Still*, 1950; *The Murder That Wouldn't Stay Solved*, 1951; *The Corpse That Refused to Stay Dead*, 1952; *The Corpse Who Had Too Many Friends*, 1953; *The Man Who Had Too Much to Lose*, 1955; *The Strangler Who Couldn't Let Go*, 1956; *The Girl Who Kept Knocking Them Dead*, 1957; *The Man Who Was Three Jumps Ahead*, 1959; *The Man Who Looked Death in the Eye*, 1961; *The Babe with the Twistable Arm*, 1962; *The Real Serendipitous Kill*, 1964; *The Kid Was Last Seen Hanging Ten*, 1966; *The Funniest Killer in Town*, 1967; *The Corpse Was No Bargain at All*, 1968; *The Swinger Who Swung by the Neck*, 1970; *The Kid Who Came Home with a Corpse*, 1971.

WORK IN PROGRESS: Hangman's Row.

SIDELIGHTS: Aaron Marc Stein wrote *CA:* "With one hundred and seven published novels, two more on the presses scheduled for publication and what should be the one hundred and tenth now being written, I find myself regarded as a phenomenon. Since the first novel was written in [my] spare time in 1927 and 1928 and published in 1930 and I have never since been without a work in progress, it may not be as phenomenal as widely believed. There was, after all, Anthony Trollope who had forty-three published novels. I am depending for that figure on my memory. An only slightly older writer recently said: 'If the toothbrush is wet, I have brushed my teeth.' He might have been speaking for me. The Trollope novel number, therefore, may be in error but it won't be by more than a volume or two. Trollope had a government job. He did his writing from five in the morning till it was time for him to go into his office. He also found time for fox hunting. I also had my time as a spare-time writer but that was only till the close of 1938. Since then it has been full time on the novels. Each of the Trollope novels is at least six times the length of one of mine. It would, therefore, have to be more than two hundred and fifty published novels for me before I could begin to rival his output. The argument that he thought up only forty-three stories against my current score of one hundred and ten doesn't hold. He packed his books full of characters, incidents, plot and subplot. It must, then, be recognized that in each of his books he exceeded me by six times not only in wordage but in invention as well. At the most, therefore, I might be considered a latter-day Victorian.

"I do write rapidly. The rate is held down only by the speed at which I can type. I make no notes. I never outline. I do no research. I believe that what a novelist does is exploring the humanity of people. What he knows about people comes out of what he knows about himself and what he hears and sees around him. All of that comes to a novelist through the ordinary process of living. There is no research that can be done on it.

"The nearest thing to research that I have ever done for a novel has been with the purpose of establishing a setting that will be real for the reader. Apart from relatively brief intervals, I have lived all my life in New York City. The backgrounds for stories set there come automatically out of life experienced. When I am in some other place, I do the things I enjoy doing there and that includes walking the town. I am not looking at it with any idea of how I can use it. I am simply taking my pleasure of it. It becomes another piece of my life experience and, sooner or later, a story idea will come to me that will work best in that place.

"There is no time when a novelist is not working at some level or another. A novelist must be a congenital eavesdropper. His awareness is always at two levels—the ordinary awareness of experiences as they come to him and, keeping pace with it always, an objective watching of his reactions to the experience. These are the materials out of which he invents and they are best if they have not been sought. The researched experience is a distorted experience."

AVOCATIONAL INTERESTS: Archeology, painting.

BIOGRAPHICAL/CRITICAL SOURCES: New York Times Book Review, March 26, 1967, January 7, 1968, April 14, 1968, August 11, 1968, December 29, 1968, April 26, 1970, February 18, 1973, September 16, 1973, May 23, 1976, January 16, 1977, March 19, 1978, June 25, 1978; *Washington Post Book World*, September 8, 1968, April 18, 1976, November 21, 1976, September 25, 1977; *Los Angeles Times Book Review*, March 1, 1981.

STEPHENS, Henrietta Henkle 1909-
(Henrietta Buckmaster)

PERSONAL: Born in 1909, in Cleveland, Ohio; daughter of Rae D. (an editor) and Pearl (Wintermute) Henkle; married Peter John Stephens. Education: Educated in private schools in New York, N.Y. Politics: Liberal. Religion: Christian Science. Agent: Russell & Volkening, Inc., 551 Fifth Ave., New York, N.Y. 10017.

CAREER: Writer. Worked as editor at McFadden Publications, Harper's Bazaar, and Reader's Digest. Awards, honors: Ohioana Award in fiction, 1945, for Deep River; Guggenheim fellowship.

WRITINGS—All under pseudonym Henrietta Buckmaster: Tomorrow Is Another Day, R. D. Henkle, 1934; His End Was His Beginning, Henkle-Yewdale House, 1936; Let My People Go: The Story of the Underground Railroad and the Growth of the Abolition Movement, Harper, 1941 (published in England as Out of the House of Bondage: The Story of the Famous Underground Railroad of the American Negro Slaves, Gollancz, 1943); Deep River, Harcourt, 1944; Fire in the Heart, Harcourt, 1948; Bread from Heaven, Random House, 1952; And Walk in Love: A Novel Based on the Life of the Apostle Paul, Random House, 1956; All the Living: A Novel of One Year in the Life of William Shakespeare, Random House, 1962; Paul: A Man Who Changed the World (biography), McGraw, 1965; Freedom Bound, Macmillan, 1965; The Lion in the Stone (novel), Harcourt, 1968; The Walking Trip, Harcourt, 1972; Wait Until Evening, Harcourt, 1974.

Children's books; all under pseudonym Henrietta Buckmaster: Lucy and Loki, Scribner, 1958; Flight to Freedom: The Story of the Underground Railroad, Crowell, 1958; Walter Raleigh: Man of Two Worlds, Random House, 1964; The Seminole Wars, P. Collier, 1966; Women Who Shaped History, P. Collier, 1966; The Fighting Congressmen: Biographies of Black and White Congressmen in the Post-Civil War Period, Scholastic Book Service, 1974. Contributor of book reviews to numerous periodicals, including Saturday Review of Literature, Christian Science Monitor, and New York Sun.

SIDELIGHTS: A writer reviewing The Seminole Wars for Young Readers' Review acclaims Henrietta Henkle Stephens' "candor and frankness regarding the often degrading behavior of the American government and its agents" during this time in history. The critic continues: "Though some historians may object because certain perfidious deeds have not been included, the author's selection of incidents and details is quite sufficient to establish the pattern of behavior. . . . A young person will better be able to appreciate our accomplishments after reading such an honest account of our past, for he can then understand that despite the base, cruel, heartless actions we are capable of, we have adopted a different code of behavior."

Stephens once wrote CA: "I suppose what has prompted the writing of all my books was a concern for people. I was very young when I wrote Let My People Go, and each day became an extraordinary revelation of the horrors and injustices endured by the black people who were brought here as slaves, and, even more important, their unwillingness to accept bondage, and their own fight against it. Two novels, Deep River and Fire in the Heart, two nonfiction, Let My People Go and Freedom Bound, two children's books, Flight to Freedom and Women Who Shaped History, have dealt directly with what I learned of these remarkable struggles against indignity and human violation.

"Bread from Heaven dealt with another aspect of courage. It's a novel based on a young man I met—sixteen years of age—who had somehow survived eight concentration camps with a remarkable understanding of the qualities that permit survival.

"I found an unexpected theme running through my next three novels, And Walk in Love, All the Living, and The Lion in the Stone. The first is of Paul the Apostle, a spiritual genius, the second of Shakespeare, an imaginative genius, the third of a Secretary General of the United Nations, a moral genius. What distinguished them from other men? What gives them their special kind of courage and indestructability?"

Krishna Shah and Norman Muller have purchased film rights to The Lion in the Stone.

AVOCATIONAL INTERESTS: Theatre.

BIOGRAPHICAL/CRITICAL SOURCES: Young Readers' Review, April, 1966; Christian Science Monitor, May 5, 1966, June 6, 1968; Variety, August 19, 1970.†

*   *   *

STERN, Philip Van Doren 1900-
(Peter Storme)

PERSONAL: Born September 10, 1900, in Wyalusing, Pa.; son of I. U. and Anne (Van Doren) Stern; married Lillian Diamond, 1928; children: Marguerite Louise (Mrs. Allan Robinson). Education: Rutgers University, Litt.B., 1924. Home: 1212 Ben Franklin Dr., No. 706, Sarasota, Fla. 33577. Agent: Marie Rodell—Francis Collin Literary Agency, 156 East 52nd St., Suite 605, New York, N.Y. 10022.

CAREER: Free-lance writer and editor. Worked in advertising, 1924-26; worked as a designer for the publishing firms of Alfred A. Knopf and Simon & Schuster, part-time editor for Pocket Books; U.S. Office of War Information, editor and member of planning board, 1941-43, general manager of Editions for the Armed Services, 1943-45; Pocket Books, vice-president in charge of editorial work, 1945-46. Lecturer on Civil War history, New York University, 1961. Awards, honors: Litt.D. from Rutgers University, 1940 and Lincoln College, 1958; Fletcher Pratt Award of New York Civil War Round Table, 1958, for An End to Valor; Guggenheim fellowship, 1959-60; Huntington Library fellow, 1961.

WRITINGS: An Introduction to Typography, Harper, 1932; (under pseudonym Peter Storme) The Thing in the Brook (mystery), Simon & Schuster, 1937; The Man Who Killed Lincoln (Literary Guild selection), Random House, 1939, reprinted, World Publishing, 1965; (co-author, under pseudonym Peter Storme) How to Torture Your Friends, Simon & Schuster, 1941; The Drums of Morning, Doubleday, 1942; The Greatest Gift: A Christmas Tale, privately printed, 1943; Lola: A Love Story, Rinehart, 1949; Love Is the One with Wings, Farrar, Straus & Young, 1951; It's Always Too Late to Mend, Jarrolds, 1952; A Pictorial History of the Automobile, 1903-1953, Viking, 1953; Our Constitution Presented in Modern Everyday Language, Birk, 1953; "Tin Lizzie": The Story of the Fabulous Model T Ford, Simon & Schuster, 1955; An End to Valor: The Last Days of the Civil War, Houghton, 1958; They Were There: The Civil War in Action as Seen by Its Combat Artists, Crown, 1959; Secret Missions of the Civil War, Rand, McNally, 1959, reprinted, Greenwood Press, 1975; The Confederate Navy, Doubleday, 1962; Robert E. Lee: The Man and the Soldier, McGraw, 1963; When the Guns Roared: World Aspects of the American Civil War, Doubleday, 1965; (with wife, Lillian D. Stern) Beyond Paris: A Touring Guide to the French Provinces, Norton, 1967; (with L. Stern) Prehistoric Europe: From Stone

Age Man to the Early Greek, Norton, 1969; *Henry David Thoreau: Writer and Rebel,* Crowell, 1972; *Edgar Allan Poe: Visitor from the Night of Time,* Crowell, 1973; *The Beginnings of Art,* Four Winds Press, 1973.

Editor: (And author of the introduction) *The Selected Writings of Thomas de Quincey,* Random House, 1937; (and author of biographical essay) *The Life and Writings of Abraham Lincoln,* Random House, 1940; (and author of introduction) *The Pocket Reader,* Pocket Books, 1941; (and author of introduction) *The Midnight Reader,* Henry Holt, 1942; (and author of introduction) *The Pocket Companion,* Pocket Books, 1942; *The Pocket Book of America,* Pocket Books, 1942, revised edition, 1975; (and author of introduction) *The Pocket Book of Modern American Short Stories,* Blakiston, 1943, reprinted, Washington Square Press, 1963; *The Pocket Book of Adventure Stories,* Pocket Books, 1945; *The Portable Edgar Allan Poe,* Viking, 1945, reprinted, Penguin, 1977; (editor with Bernard Smith) *The Holiday Reader,* Simon & Schuster, 1947; (and author of introduction) *Travelers in Time,* Doubleday, 1947; (and author of introduction) *Great Ghost Stories,* Washington Square Press, 1947, reprinted, 1964; Arthur Machen, *Tales of Horror and the Supernatural,* Knopf, 1948; *The Pocket Week-End Book,* Pocket Books, 1949.

(And author of introduction and notes) John Esten Cooke, *Wearing of the Gray,* Indiana University Press, 1959; *Prologue to Sumter,* Indiana University Press, 1961; *Soldier Life in the Union and Confederate Armies,* Indiana University Press, 1961; *Civil War Christmas Album,* Hawthorn, 1961; Raphael Semmes, *The Confederate Raider Alabama,* Indiana University Press, 1962; Harriet Elizabeth Beecher Stowe, *The Annotated Uncle Tom's Cabin,* Bramhall House, 1964; Henry David Thoreau, *Walden: Or, Life in the Woods,* C. N. Potter, 1970.

Compiler: *The Breathless Moment: The World's Most Sensational News Photos,* Knopf, 1935; (and author of introduction) *The Moonlight Traveler: Great Tales of Fantasy and Imagination,* Doubleday, 1943; *Strange Beasts and Unnatural Monsters,* Fawcett, 1968; *The Other Side of the Clock: Stories Out of Time, Out of Place,* Van Nostrand, 1969.

Author of introduction: Ben Pitman, *The Assassination of President Lincoln, and the Trial of the Conspirators,* Funk, 1954; (and notes) James D. Bulloch, *Secret Service of the Confederate States in Europe,* two volumes, Yoseloff, 1959; (and chronology) Robert E. Lee, Jr., *My Father, General Lee,* Doubleday, 1960; Fitzhugh Lee, *General Lee,* Peter Smith, 1962.

SIDELIGHTS: The Man Who Killed Lincoln was dramatized and produced in New York City in 1940. *The Greatest Gift: A Christmas Tale* was the basis of the motion picture, "It's a Wonderful Life" was produced in 1946 by Liberty Films and Frank Capra; the original story was broadcast by Columbia Broadcasting System on Christmas Eve that year, and short waved throughout the world by the Department of State. Philip Van Doren Stern's books have been published in Australia and England, and in Spanish and Portuguese editions. *Avocational interests:* Photography, cars, and travel.

*   *   *

STEVENS, Clifford   1926-

PERSONAL: Born March 27, 1926, in Brattleboro, Vt.; son of Clarence Frederick and Agnes (Murray) Stevens. *Education:* Attended Creighton University, 1945-46, 1959-60, New Melleray Abbey Seminary, 1946-52, Conception Seminary, 1954-56, and St. Michael's College, 1972-73. *Home:* Tintern Monastery, Monastery Rd., Oakdale, Neb. 68761.

CAREER: Worked in a California shipyard one year before studying for the priesthood; ordained Roman Catholic priest in Omaha, Neb., 1956; parish priest in Omaha Diocese, 1956-61; U.S. Air Force, chaplain, stationed in California, in Alaska (as chaplain to men at remote radar sites), at Holloman Air Force Base, N.M., and in Itazuke, Japan, 1961-69; affiliated with Institute of Man and Science, Rensselaerville, N.Y., 1969; director, Theological Research Institute, Santa Fe, N.M., 1975-76; pastor, St. Francis Church, Neligh, Neb., 1976-81.

WRITINGS: Flame out of Dorset (historical novel), Doubleday, 1964; *Father Flanagan: Builder of Boys,* Kenedy, 1968; *Astro-Theology,* Divine Word Publications, 1969; *Portraits of Faith,* Our Sunday Visitor, 1975; *Man of Galilee,* Our Sunday Visitor, 1979; *Wild Dogs of Chong Do,* Our Sunday Visitor, 1979. Author of play, "Vitoria," produced at New Mexico State University, 1964. Contributor to *Catholic World, American Benedictine Review,* and other denominational publications. Executive editor, *Priest* magazine, 1968-69; editor and publisher, *Schema XIII* (journal for the priest in the modern world), 1969-71.

WORK IN PROGRESS: Celibacy and Sexuality: A New Summa Theologica; translations of minor works of St. Thomas Aquinas; *The Gothic Harvest,* a philosophical history from the end of the classical era to the scholastic period.

SIDELIGHTS: In a feature story in the *Anchorage News,* Clifford Stevens is quoted as saying that "my real purpose is to corner the market on green cheese," another way of stating that his career objective is to get into space. This aim was born of a ride with X15-pilot Robert M. White in an F104 in 1962. Later he co-authored an article, "An Astronaut's View of God," with White. Several other of his magazine articles have been on the aerospace-religious theme.

Stevens is currently in the process of realizing another dream, the establishment of Tintern Monastery, "a contemplative order of priests near Oakdale, Neb." According to the *Newsletter for Friends of Tintern* the "Tintern Monastery will be a cloistered monastic community of priests, dedicated solely and totally to a contemplative way of life. The four pillars of the life are solitude, psalmody, study, and eucharist, and the whole of the monastic life of Tintern will revolve around these four pillars."

The newsletter continues to explain: "The first community of Tintern monks will be composed of priests. When the community has been in existence for at least two years, candidates for the novitiate will be accepted, who must have completed at least two years of college or university studies. The community will support itself by working the land and by arts and crafts suitable to a monastic way of life. The present property is adequate to support a small monastic community of about thirty persons."

BIOGRAPHICAL/CRITICAL SOURCES: Anchorage Daily News, May 4, 1963; *El Paso Times,* February 16, 1964; *Aerospace Historian,* autumn, 1968; *Religious News Service,* December 30, 1969; *Newsletter for Friends of Tintern,* winter, 1981.

*   *   *

STEVENS, Clysle
   See WADE, John Stevens

*   *   *

STEWART, Ramona   1922-

PERSONAL: Born February 19, 1922, in San Francisco, Calif.;

daughter of James Oliver and Theresa (Waugh) Stewart. *Education:* Attended University of Southern California, 1938-41. *Agent:* International Creative Management, 40 West 57th St., New York, N.Y. 10019.

CAREER: Author.

WRITINGS: Desert Town, Morrow, 1945; *The Stars Abide,* Morrow, 1961; *The Surprise Party Complex,* Morrow, 1963; *Professor Descending,* Doubleday, 1964; *A Confidence in Magic,* Doubleday, 1965; *Kit Larkin,* Doubleday, 1966; *Casey,* Little, Brown, 1968; *The Possession of Joel Delaney,* Little, Brown, 1970; *The Apparition,* Little, Brown, 1972; *Age of Consent,* Dutton, 1975; *Seasons of the Heart,* Putnam, 1978; *Sixth Sense,* Delacorte, 1979; *The Nightmare Candidate,* Delacorte, 1980. Stories included in *Best Short Stories of 1950,* and *Two and Twenty,* St. Martin's, 1962.

MEDIA ADAPTATIONS: Ramona Stewart's novel *Desert Town* was filmed as "Desert Fury" by Paramount in 1946; *The Possession of Joel Delaney* was the basis for a movie of the same title, produced by Paramount in 1972.

BIOGRAPHICAL/CRITICAL SOURCES: Times Literary Supplement, June 22, 1967; *Publishers Weekly,* April 1, 1968; *New York Times,* October 16, 1970; *Chicago Tribune Book World,* June 8, 1980.

* * *

STIEBER, Jack 1919-

PERSONAL: Born March 27, 1919, in Hungary; son of Israel (a cantor) and Clara (Schechter) Stieber; married Carolyn Friedman (a professor), December 21, 1947; children: Allison, Joan. *Education:* City College (now City College of the City University of New York), B.S.S., 1940; University of Minnesota, M.A., 1948; Harvard University, Ph.D., 1956. *Home:* 231 Lexington Ave., East Lansing, Mich. 48823. *Office:* School of Labor and Industrial Relations, Michigan State University, East Lansing, Mich. 48823.

CAREER: U.S. Employment Service, Washington, D.C., labor market analyst, 1942; Office of the Housing Expediter, Washington, D.C., labor specialist, 1946-47; University of Minnesota, Minneapolis, instructor and research assistant, 1947-48; United Steelworkers of America, Congress of Industrial Organizations, Pittsburgh, Pa., research associate, 1948-50; National Security Resources Board, Washington, D.C., special assistant to Director of Manpower, 1950-51; Wage Stabilization Board, Washington, D.C., economist and executive assistant to labor members, 1951-52; Harvard University, Graduate School of Business Administration, Cambridge, Mass., research associate, 1954-56; Michigan State University, East Lansing, associate professor, 1956-59, professor of economics and director of School of Labor and Industrial Relations, 1959—. Guest professor, Royal College of Science and Technology, Scotland, 1959; executive secretary, President's Advisory Committee on Labor-Management Policy, 1962; research consultant, International Institute for Labour Studies, 1963-64. *Military service:* U.S. Army Air Forces, 1942-46; became captain. *Member:* American Economic Association, Industrial Relations Research Association (member of executive board, 1966-69; president-elect, 1983), American Association of University Professors, National Academy of Arbitrators.

WRITINGS: Ten Years of the Minnesota Labor Relations Act, University of Minnesota Press, 1949; (editor and contributor) *U.S. Industrial Relations: The Next Twenty Years,* Michigan State University Press, 1958; *The Steel Industry Wage Structure,* Harvard University Press, 1959; (contributor) Davey,

Kaltenborn, and Ruttenberg, editors, *New Dimensions in Collective Bargaining,* Harper, 1959; *Governing the UAW,* Wiley, 1962, revised edition, 1967; (editor) *Employment Problems of Automation and Advanced Technology: An International Perspective,* St. Martins, 1965; *Manpower Adjustments to Automation and Technological Change in Western Europe,* National Commission on Technology, Automation and Economic Progress, 1966; *Public Employee Unionism: Structure, Growth, Policy,* Brookings Institution, 1973; (co-editor) *Multinationals, Unions, and Labor Relations in Industrialized Countries,* Cornell University Press, 1973. Contributor to professional bulletins and journals.

* * *

STILLMAN, Myra Stephens 1915-

PERSONAL: Born March 7, 1915, in Albany, N.Y.; daughter of Frank William and Myra (deRouville) Stephens; married Nathan Stillman (a college professor), August 27, 1940; children: Robert, Michael. *Education:* New York College for Teachers (now State University of New York at Albany), A.B., 1936, M.A., 1937.

CAREER: Westfield State Farm, Bedford, N.Y., teacher, 1937; Albany County Welfare Department, Albany, N.Y., case worker, 1937-40; Poughkeepsie Day School, Poughkeepsie, N.Y., teacher, 1949-51. Member of Board of Education, Central School District, New Paltz, N.Y. *Member:* New Paltz Garden Club (member of board of directors).

WRITINGS—All with Beulah Tannenbaum; all published by McGraw: *Understanding Maps,* 1957, revised edition, 1969; *Understanding Time,* 1958; *Isaac Newton,* 1959; *Understanding Light,* 1960; *Understanding Food,* 1962; *Feeding the City,* 1971; *City Traffic,* 1972; *Understanding Sound,* 1973; *Clean Air,* 1973; *High Rises,* 1974.

WORK IN PROGRESS: Preparing elementary science text material.†

* * *

STONE, George Winchester, Jr. 1907-

PERSONAL: Born December 18, 1907, in Washington, D.C.; son of George Winchester (an architect) and Mary (Knight Bradford) Stone; married Hellen Elizabeth Dean, June 18, 1936; children: Katherine Moody, Anne Virginia, George Winchester III. *Education:* Dartmouth College, A.B., 1930; Harvard University, Ph.D., 1940. *Politics:* Democrat. *Religion:* Presbyterian. *Office:* Department of English, New York University, Washington Square, New York, N.Y.

CAREER: George Washington University, Washington, D.C., instructor, 1931-33, assistant professor, 1933-36, associate professor, 1936-41, professor of English, 1947-55; New York University, New York, N.Y., professor of English, 1955-74, professor emeritus, 1974—, dean of Graduate School of Arts and Sciences, 1964-71, dean of libraries, 1971-73. Visiting lecturer at Johns Hopkins University, summers, 1947-54; visiting professor at Washington State College (now Washington State University), 1952. Member, U.S. National Commission for UNESCO, 1959-62. *Military service:* U.S. Naval Reserve, 1942-46; became lieutenant commander. *Member:* International Federation for Modern Languages and Literatures (American vice-president, 1966-72), Modern Language Association of America (executive secretary, 1956-64; president, 1967), American Council of Learned Societies (member of board of directors, 1961—), American Association of Teachers of French, Century Association (New York), Cosmos Club

(Washington, D.C.). *Awards, honors:* Folger Library fellow; Guggenheim fellow, 1950-52, 1963; Fulbright fellow to England, 1963-64. Academic: Litt.D., Middlebury College, 1960; L.H.D., Hofstra University, 1963; L.L.D., George Washington University, 1967.

WRITINGS: The Journal of David Garrick, Modern Language Association of America, 1939, reprinted, Arden Library, 1979; (with W. K. Thompson) *A Naval Log,* Van Nostrand, 1945; *Issues, Problems and Approaches to the Teaching of English,* Holt, 1961; *The London Stage, 1747-1775,* three volumes, Southern Illinois University Press, 1963; (contributor) *On Stage and Off,* Washington State University Press, 1968; *British Dramatists from Dryden to Sheridan,* Houghton, 1969.

The Winchester Handbook, Frontier Press, 1973; *In Search of Restoration and Eighteenth-century Theatrical Biography,* University of California, 1976; (with George M. Kahrl) *David Garrick: A Critical Biography,* Illinois University Press, 1980. Contributor of articles on Garrick and Shakespeare to professional journals. Editor, *PMLA,* 1956-63.

SIDELIGHTS: Several of George Winchester Stone's books have been praised as being thorough and basic reference tools. For example, a critic for the *Times Literary Supplement* writes of *The London Stage, 1660-1800* that "those interested in the stage from the Restoration onwards will certainly have at their service a basic tool such as their predecessors may have dreamed of but never possessed. . . . Its author's meticulous scrutiny of the records has enabled him to reach conclusions and to make comments which could hardly have been thought of by any theatrical historian lacking his accumulated knowledge."

A *Choice* critic, reviewing another one of Stone's books, *David Garrick: A Critical Biography,* writes: "This major work on David Garrick by two scholars who probably know their subject better than anyone now living will be valuable not only to students of 18th century theater but to those interested generally in English life and letters during the actor-playwright's lifetime."

BIOGRAPHICAL/CRITICAL SOURCES: Times Literary Supplement, September 20, 1963; *New York Times Book Review,* December 8, 1963; *Choice,* September, 1980.†

*   *   *

STONE, Hampton
    See STEIN, Aaron Marc

*   *   *

STONE, Thomas H.
    See HARKNETT, Terry

*   *   *

STOREY, W(illiam) George   1923-

PERSONAL: Born April 23, 1923, in Sarnia, Ontario, Canada; son of Clifford Palmer and Avilla (Reynolds) Storey; married Elaine E. Curry, September 1, 1951; children: Elizabeth, Margaret, David, Joan, John, Paul, Clare. *Education:* Assumption College, University of Western Ontario, B.A., 1949, M.A., 1950; University of Notre Dame, M.M.S., 1954, D.M.S., 1959. *Home:* 1027 East Wayne, South Bend, Ind. 46617. *Office:* Department of Theology, University of Notre Dame, Notre Dame, Ind. 46556.

CAREER: Duquesne University, Pittsburgh, Pa., associate professor of medieval history and church history, beginning 1955;

currently affiliated with University of Notre Dame, Notre Dame, Ind. *Member:* North American Academy of Liturgy, American Humanist Association, Mediaeval Academy of America, American Society of Church History, Liturgical Conference, Catholic Interracial Council, American Association of University Professors.

WRITINGS: (Translator) *Introduction to Theology,* Fides, 1954; (translator) R. Hasseveldt, *The Church: A Divine Mystery,* Fides, 1954; *Morning Praise and Evensong: A Book of Common Prayer,* Fides, 1963; (editor) *Days of the Lord,* three volumes, B. Herder, 1965; (editor) *Morning Praise and Evensong: A Liturgy of the Hours in Musical Setting,* Fides, 1973; *Praise Him!,* Ave Maria Press, 1973; *Bless the Lord!,* Ave Maria Press, 1974; (with John Melloh) *Praise God in Song,* Gregorian Institute of America, 1979; *Lord Hear Our Prayer,* Ave Maria Press, 1978; *This Week with Christ,* Ave Maria Press, 1981.

WORK IN PROGRESS: Source Readings in the History of Christian Worship.

*   *   *

STORME, Peter
    See STERN, Philip Van Doren

*   *   *

STRASSER, Marland K(eith)   1915-

PERSONAL: Born October 25, 1915, in What Cheer, Iowa; son of Frank F. and Nina (Kirkpatrick) Strasser; married Roberta Ward, May 11, 1941; children: Norman Frank, Kenneth Ward. *Education:* University of California, B.A., 1938, M.A., 1939; New York University, Ed.D., 1950. *Office:* San Jose State University, San Jose, Calif. 95114.

CAREER: Teacher and business manager of public schools, Woodland, Calif., 1942-46; New York University, Center for Safety Education, New York City, research associate, 1946-48; Association of Casualty and Surety Cos., New York City, educational director and representative to San Francisco, 1948-59; San Jose State University, San Jose, Calif., professor of safety education, 1959—. Member of board of directors and executive committee, Santa Clara County Safety Council, 1959—. *Member:* American Driver and Traffic Safety Education Association, National Safety Council, American Academy of Safety Education (fellow), International Platform Association, California Driver Education Association (president, 1962-63), Phi Delta Kappa.

WRITINGS: (With John R. Eales, Cecil Zaun, and M. E. Mushlitz) *When You Take the Wheel,* Laidlaw Brothers, 1961; (with others) *Fundamentals of Safety Education,* Macmillan, 1964, 2nd edition, 1973; (with James Aaron) *The New Driver's Guide,* San Dale Press, 1965; (with Aaron) *Driver and Traffic Safety Education,* Macmillan, 1966, 2nd edition, 1977; (with Aaron and Eales) *Driver Education: Learning to Drive Defensively,* Laidlaw Brothers, 1969; (with Aaron) *Driving Task Instruction: Dual-Control, Simulation, and Multiple-Car,* Macmillan, 1974. Contributor of over a dozen articles on traffic safety and driver education to professional publications.†

*   *   *

STRAUS, Robert   1923-

PERSONAL: Born January 9, 1923, in New Haven, Conn.; son of Samuel Hirsh (a teacher) and Alma (Fleischner) Straus; married Ruth Elisabeth Dawson (a teacher), September 8, 1945;

children: Robert James, Carol Martin, Margaret Dawson (Mrs. Michael Binion), John William. *Education:* Yale University, B.A., 1943, M.A., 1945, Ph.D., 1947. *Religion:* Unitarian Universalist. *Home:* 511 Ridge Rd., Lexington, Ky. 40503. *Office:* Department of Behavioral Science, College of Medicine, University of Kentucky, Lexington, Ky. 40536.

CAREER: Yale University, New Haven, Conn., staff member, Center of Alcohol Studies, 1945-53, instructor in applied physiology, 1947-48, assistant professor, 1948-51, research associate, 1951-53; State University of New York Upstate Medical Center, Syracuse, assistant professor, 1953-55, associate professor of public health and preventive medicine, 1956; University of Kentucky, College of Medicine, Lexington, professor of medical sociology, 1956—, chairman of department of behavioral science, 1959—. Visiting fellow in sociology, Yale University, 1968-69; visiting professor, University of California, Berkeley, 1978. Staff director of Connecticut Governor's Commission on Health Resources, 1950-51; chairman of Cooperative (United States and Canada) Commission on the Study of Alcoholism, 1961-63, and of National Advisory Committee on Alcoholism, 1966-69. Consultant to National Institute of Mental Health, 1959-70, and to Addiction Research Center, National Institute on Drug Abuse, 1974-79. *Military service:* U.S. Army, 1943-44.

MEMBER: American Sociological Association (chairman of section on medical sociology, 1967-68), American Public Health Association (fellow), Institute of Medicine, National Academy of Sciences, Academy for Behavioral Medicine Research, Association of American Medical Colleges, Society for the Study of Social Problems, Society for Applied Anthropology, Society for Health and Human Values, Association for the Behavioral Sciences and Medical Education (president, 1974), Eastern Sociological Society, Southern Sociological Society, Phi Beta Kappa. *Awards, honors:* Scientific Achievement Award, Kentucky Medical Association, 1966; National Institute of Mental Health research fellow at Yale University, 1968-69; award for distinguished contribution to research, University of Kentucky Research Foundation, 1975.

WRITINGS: Medical Care for Seamen: The Development of Public Health Services in the United States, Yale University Press, 1950; (with Selden D. Bacon) *Alcoholism and Social Stability,* Hillhouse Press (New Haven), 1951; (with Bacon) *Drinking in College,* Yale University Press, 1953, reprinted, Greenwood Press, 1971; *Alcohol and Society* (monograph first published as entire issue of *Psychiatric Annals,* October, 1973), Insight Publishing, 1973; *Escape from Custody: A Study of Alcoholism and of Institutional Dependency as Reflected in the Life Record of a Homeless Man,* Harper, 1974.

Contributor: A. M. Rose, editor, *Mental Health and Mental Disorder,* Norton, 1955; Raymond G. McCarthy, editor, *Drinking and Intoxication,* Yale Center for Alcohol Studies and Free Press, 1959; David J. Pittman and Charles R. Snyder, editors, *Society, Culture and Drinking Patterns,* Wiley, 1962; S. P. Lucia, editor, *Alcohol and Civilization,* McGraw, 1963; M. T. Sussman, editor, *Sociology and Rehabilitation,* American Sociological Association, 1965; Robert K. Merton and Robert A. Nisbet, editors, *Contemporary Social Problems,* 2nd edition, Harcourt, 1966, 3rd edition, 1971, 4th edition, 1976; Thomas Weaver and Alvin Magid, editors, *Poverty: New Interdisciplinary Perspectives,* Chandler Publishing, 1969; George L. Maddox, editor, *The Domesticated Drug: Drinking among Collegians,* College & University Press, 1970; Basil Georgopoulos, editor, *Organization Research on Health Institutions,* Institute for Social Research, University of Michigan, 1972; Karl Schuessler and others, editors, *Social Policy and*

Sociology, Academic Press, 1975; W. J. Filstead and others editors, *Alcohol and Alcohol Problems: New Thinking and New Directions,* Ballinger Publishing, 1974; P. A. O'Gorman, S. Stringfield, and I. Smith, editors, *Defining Adolescent Alcohol Use,* National Council on Alcoholism, 1977; R. Elling and M. Sokolowska, editors, *Medical Sociologist at Work,* Transaction Books, 1978; E. G. Gallagher, editor, *The Doctor-Patient Relationship in the Changing Health Scene,* U.S. Government Printing Office, 1978; M. Blacker and D. R. Wekstein, editors, *Your Health after Sixty,* Dutton, 1979; E. S. Gomberg, H. R. White, and J. A. Carpenter, editors, *Alcohol Science and Society,* Journal of Studies on Alcohol, 1981; B. Kissen, editor, *Biology of Alcoholism,* Plenum, 1981.

Author or co-author of reports and special studies on public health, alcoholism, and medical education. Contributor of more than sixty articles to annals, yearbooks, and journals. Editor with John A. Clausen, *Medicine and Society,* Annals of the American Academy of Political and Social Science, March, 1963. Associate editor, *Quarterly Journal of Studies on Alcohol,* 1951—, and *Journal of Health and Human Behavior,* 1959-66; member of editorial board, University Press of Kentucky, 1968-72, and *Drugs in Health Care,* 1974-76; member of advisory board, *Research Advances in Alcohol and Drug Problems,* 1971—.

*   *   *

STROM, Leslie Winter
See WINTER, Leslie

*   *   *

STROMBERG, Roland N(elson)   1916-

PERSONAL: Born July 5, 1916, in Kansas City, Mo.; son of Clarence R. and Harriet (Ridgell) Stromberg; married June 10, 1939; wife's name Mary; children: Eric, Juliet. *Education:* University of Kansas City (now University of Missouri—Kansas City), B.A., 1939; American University, M.A., 1946; University of Maryland, Ph.D., 1952. *Office:* Department of History, University of Wisconsin—Milwaukee, Milwaukee, Wis. 53201.

CAREER: University of Maryland, College Park, 1952-66, began as assistant professor, became professor of history; Southern Illinois University at Carbondale, professor of history, 1966-67; University of Wisconsin—Milwaukee, professor of history, 1967—. Taught in Europe, 1952-55. Fellow, Woodrow Wilson International Center for Scholars, 1974, and Center for Twentieth Century Studies, 1980-81. Member of editorial board, Center for the Study of Armament and Disarmament, California State University, Los Angeles. *Member:* Society for Historians of American Foreign Relations, Society for History Education, American Historical Association. *Awards, honors:* Rockefeller Foundation fellow, 1957-58; University of Missouri—Kansas City Distinguished Alumnus Award, 1966; recipient of research grants from University of Maryland and University of Wisconsin.

WRITINGS: Religious Liberalism in Eighteenth Century England, Oxford University Press, 1954; (contributor) *American Civilization: History of the United States,* McGraw, 1957, 2nd edition published as *The United States: History of a Democracy,* 1960; (contributor) *The Shaping of American Diplomacy,* Rand McNally, 1957; (contributor) *Issues and Conflicts,* University of Kansas Press, 1959; (contributor) *World in Crisis,* Macmillan, 1962; *A History of Western Civilization,* Dorsey, 1963, revised edition, 1969; *Collective Security and American Foreign Policy,* Praeger, 1963; (contributor) Joel Larus, editor,

From Collective Security to Preventive Diplomacy, Wiley, 1965; (contributor) L. Finkelstein and M. Finkelstein, editors, *Collective Security,* Chandler, 1966; *An Intellectual History of Modern Europe,* Appleton-Century-Crofts, 1966, 2nd edition, Prentice-Hall, 1975, Chapters 7-14 published as *European Intellectual History since 1789,* 1975; (editor) *Realism, Naturalism, and Symbolism,* Harper, 1968; (with Paul K. Conkin) *The Heritage and Challenge of History,* Dodd, 1971; *Arnold J. Toynbee: Historian for an Age in Crisis,* Southern Illinois University Press, 1971; *After Everything: Western Intellectual History since 1945,* St. Martin's, 1975; *Europe in the Twentieth Century,* Prentice-Hall, 1980.

Contributor to *American Historical Review, Journal of the History of Ideas, Dalhousie Review, Midwest Quarterly, Psychoanalytic Review,* and other publications.

WORK IN PROGRESS: Redemption by War: The European Intellectuals and 1914, for University of Kansas.

*   *   *

STRUIK, Dirk Jan   1894-

PERSONAL: Born September 30, 1894, in Rotterdam, Netherlands; son of Hendrik Jan and Aartje (Schilperoort) Struik; married Saly Ruth Ramler; children: three daughters. *Education:* University of Leiden, Ph.D., 1922. *Home:* 52 Glendale Rd., Belmont, Mass. 02178. *Office:* Department of Mathematics, Massachusetts Institute of Technology, Cambridge, Mass.

CAREER: Technische Hoogeschool, Delft, Netherlands, assistant in mathematics department, 1917-24; Massachusetts Institute of Technology, Cambridge, 1926—, began as lecturer, professor of mathematics, 1940-60, professor emeritus, 1960—. Visiting professor, University of Puerto Rico, 1962, University of Utrecht, 1963-64, and University of Costa Rica, 1965. Lecturer in Netherlands, East and West Germany, Italy, U.S.S.R., Mexico, Puerto Rico, and United States. *Member:* International Academy of History of Science (corresponding member), American Academy of Arts and Sciences, American Mathematical Association, American Mathematical Society, Wiskundig Genootschap (Amsterdam), Royal Academy of Sciences (Amsterdam; corresponding member), Appalachian Mountain Club. *Awards, honors:* Profesor extraordinario, Universidad Nacional Mexico; Lobachevsky Award from University of Kazan.

WRITINGS: A Concise History of Mathematics, Dover, 1948, 3rd edition, 1967; *Yankee Science in the Making,* Little, Brown, 1948, 2nd edition, 1962; *Lectures in Classical Differential Geometry,* Addison-Wesley, 1950, 2nd edition, 1961; *Het Land van Stevin en Huygens,* Pegasus, 1958, 3rd edition, 1979; *Principal Works of Simon Stevin II,* [Amsterdam], 1958; (editor) *Economic and Philosophical Manuscripts of 1844 by Karl Marx,* International Publishers, 1964; *Liber desideratus,* Nieuwkoop, 1965; (editor) *A Source Book in Mathematics: 1200-1800,* Harvard University Press, 1969; *Birth of the Communist Manifesto,* International Publishers, 1971; *Tellen zonder en met cyfers,* Groningen, 1971. Editor, *Science and Society.*

SIDELIGHTS: Dirk Jan Struik's *A Concise History of Mathematics* has been translated into German, Polish, Hungarian, Chinese, Russian, Ukrainian, Czech, Japanese, Dutch, Spanish, Swedish, Italian and Danish.

STURTZEL, Howard A(llison)   1894-
(Paul Annixter)

PERSONAL: Born June 25, 1894, in Minneapolis, Minn.; son of Edward John and Carrie E. (Pirkiss) Sturtzel; married Jane Levington Comfort (a writer), February 18, 1920. *Education:* Attended Fargo College and North Dakota Agricultural College (now North Dakota State University). *Home:* 2581 Bonita Way, Laguna Beach, Calif. 92651. *Agent:* Janet Loranger, P.O. Box 113, West Redding, Conn. 06896.

CAREER: Writer since age of nineteen.

WRITINGS: Wilderness Ways, Penn, 1930; *Swiftwater,* Wyn, 1950; *Brought to Cover* (story collection), Wyn, 1951; *The Hunting Horn* (story collection), Hill & Wang, 1957; *Devil of the Woods* (story collection), Hill & Wang, 1958; *Pride of Lions* (story collection), Hill & Wang, 1960; (under pseudonym Paul Annixter) *Puck of the Dusk,* Scribner, 1970; (under pseudonym Paul Annixter) *The Best Nature Stories of Paul Annixter,* Lawrence Hill, 1974.

With wife, Janet Levington Sturtzel, under pseudonyms Paul Annixter and Jane Annixter; all published by Holiday House, except as indicated: *The Runner,* 1956; *Buffalo Chief,* 1958; *Horns of Plenty,* 1960; *Peace Comes to Castle Oak,* Longmans, Green, 1961; *The Phantom Stallion,* Golden Press, 1961; *Trouble at Paintrock,* Golden Press, 1962; *Windigo,* 1963; *Wagon Scout,* 1965; *The Cat That Clumped,* 1966; *The Great White,* 1966; *Vikan the Mighty,* 1969; *Ahmeek,* 1970; *White Shell Horse,* 1971; *Sea Otter,* 1972; *Trumpeter: The Story of a Swan,* 1973; *Wapootin,* Coward, 1976; *Monkeys and Apes,* F. Watts, 1976; *Brown Rats, Black Rats,* Prentice-Hall, 1977; *The Year of the She-Grizzly,* Coward, 1978; *The Last Monster,* Harcourt, 1980. Contributor of short stories to magazines.

SIDELIGHTS: "As a very young man," Howard A. Sturtzel told *CA,* "I took up a timber claim in northern Minnesota. It was while proving up on the land that I began writing, mostly nature stories about the animals and elements I was up against. Published more than five hundred short stories in the period prior to 1950, covering almost all American magazines from the *Saturday Evening Post* down to the pulps. In 1955, my wife and I began collaborating on nature novels for young people. . . . In the main our stories deal with some phase of human and animal interrelation, which offers to our minds a different and deeper sort of heart interest."

AVOCATIONAL INTERESTS: Reading, gardening, mountain climbing.

BIOGRAPHICAL/CRITICAL SOURCES: New York Times Book Review, May 9, 1965, January 22, 1967; *Book Week,* November 6, 1966, March 19, 1967; *Saturday Review,* September 19, 1970; *Christian Science Monitor,* February 27, 1971; *Spectator,* March, 1971; *Instructor,* May, 1974.

*   *   *

STURTZEL, Jane Levington   1903-
(Jane Annixter, Jane Levington Comfort)

PERSONAL: Born June 22, 1903, in Detroit, Mich.; daughter of Will Levington (a writer) and Ada Althea (Duffy) Comfort; married Howard Allison Sturtzel (a writer), February 18, 1920. *Education:* Attended schools in Detroit, Kingsville, Ontario, and Venice, Calif. *Home:* 2581 Bonita Way, Laguna Beach, Calif. 92651. *Agent:* Janet Loranger, P.O. Box 113, West Redding, Conn. 06896.

WRITINGS—Under name of Jane Levington Comfort: *From These Beginnings*, Dutton, 1937; *Time Out For Eternity*, Dutton, 1938.

With husband, Howard Allison Sturtzel, under pseudonyms Jane Annixter and Paul Annixter; all published by Holiday House, except as indicated: *The Runner*, 1956; *Buffalo Chief*, 1958; *Horns of Plenty*, 1960; *Peace Comes to Castle Oak*, Longmans, Green, 1961; *The Phantom Stallion*, Golden Press, 1961; *Trouble at Paintrock*, Golden Press, 1962; *Windigo*, 1963; *Wagon Scout*, 1965; *The Great White*, 1966; *The Cat That Clumped*, 1966; *Vikan the Mighty*, 1969; *Ahmeek*, 1970; *White Shell Horse*, 1971; *Sea Otter*, 1972; *Trumpeter: The Story of a Swan*, 1973; *Wapootin*, Coward, 1976; *Monkeys and Apes*, F. Watts, 1976; *Brown Rats, Black Rats*, Prentice-Hall, 1977; *The Year of the She-Grizzly*, Coward, 1978; *The Last Monster*, Harcourt, 1980. Contributor of short stories to periodicals.

SIDELIGHTS: Jane Levington Sturtzel told *CA*: "Writing began for me when I was nine, vacation time, when my father took me for a walk on the beach and talked about shells, stones, and stars, then asked me to write an essay for him! When my father ran out of spontaneous subjects for my daily essay, he set me to reading and 'reviewing' the classics in essay form—Thoreau, Emerson, Carlyle, and many others. For this 'cruel treatment' I am eternally grateful. The habit of written expression was deeply inculcated, along with the taste for reading.''

Speaking about her writing partnership with her husband, Sturtzel says that "for many years there were always two studies in our house and two careers going. Then about twenty-two years ago in a cabin in the San Bernardino Mountains my husband and I began to collaborate on nature novels for young people. The environment was perfect: our dooryard pitched thousands of feet to the floor of the Mojave Desert; our neighbors were deer, eagles, foxes and racoons. There at seventy-two hundred feet of altitude, well above the level of smog, traffic noise, telephones and similar evils, our work together has been done.''

AVOCATIONAL INTERESTS: Reading, gardening, mountain climbing.

BIOGRAPHICAL/CRITICAL SOURCES: *New York Times Book Review*, May 9, 1965, January 22, 1967; *Book Week*, November 6, 1966, March 19, 1967; *Saturday Review*, September 19, 1970; *Christian Science Monitor*, February 27, 1971; *Spectator*, March, 1971; *Instructor*, May, 1974.

*   *   *

STYAN, J(ohn) L(ouis)   1923-

PERSONAL: Born July 6, 1923, in London, England; married Constance W. M. Roberts, 1945; children: Leigh, Day, Kim, Valentina. *Education:* St. Catharine's College, Cambridge, M.A., 1948. *Home:* 1414 Ridge Ave., Evanston, Ill. 60201. *Office:* Department of English, Northwestern University, Evanston, Ill.

CAREER: The Grammar School, Falmouth, Cornwall, England, assistant master, 1948-50; University of Hull, Hull, England, staff tutor, 1950-63, senior staff tutor in literature and drama, 1963-66; University of Michigan, Ann Arbor, professor of English, 1966-74, chairman of department; University of Pittsburgh, Pittsburgh, Pa., Andrew W. Mellon Professor of English, 1974-77; Northwestern University, Evanston, Ill., Franklin Bliss Snyder Professor of English Literature, 1977—. Chairman, Yorkshire Rural Drama Committee, 1961-65; af-

filiated with B.B.C. and I.T.A. adult education committees, 1962-65; chairman, Shakespeare Globe Theatre Center, 1981. *Military service:* British Army, Royal Artillery, 1941-45; became lieutenant. *Member:* Modern Language Association of America (affiliated with executive committee of Division of Drama, 1981-85), Guild of Drama Adjudicators, British Drama League (chairman of York district, 1958-62), Association of Tutors in Adult Education (broadcasting liaison officer, 1961-65). *Awards, honors:* National Endowment for the Humanities research fellow, 1978-79.

WRITINGS—Published by Cambridge University Press, except as indicated: *The Elements of Drama*, 1960; *The Dark Comedy*, 1962, 2nd edition, 1968; *Television Drama in Contemporary Theatre*, Edward Arnold, 1962; *The Dramatic Experience*, 1965; *Shakespeare's Stagecraft*, 1967; *Chekhov in Performance: A Commentary on the Major Plays*, 1971; *The Challenge of the Theatre*, Dickenson Publishing Co., 1972; *Drama, Stage and Audience*, 1975; *The Shakespeare Revolution*, 1977; *Modern Drama in Theory and Practice*, three volumes, 1981; *Max Reinhardt*, 1982. Contributor to journals.

WORK IN PROGRESS: *All's Well That Ends Well*, for "Shakespeare in Performance'' series, Manchester University Press.

BIOGRAPHICAL/CRITICAL SOURCES: *Times Literary Supplement*, February 8, 1968; *Plays and Players*, August, 1971.

*   *   *

STYLES, (Frank) Showell   1908-
(Glyn Carr, S. Howell)

PERSONAL: Born March 14, 1908, in Four Oaks, Warwickshire, England; son of Frank (a banker) and Edith (Showell) Styles; married Jean Humphreys, 1954; children: Glynda Jane, Elisabeth Ann, David. *Education:* Attended Bishop Vesey's School in England. *Home:* Croesor, Merionethshire, North Wales, United Kingdom. *Agent:* Curtis Brown Ltd., 1 Craven Hill, London W2 3EW, England.

CAREER: Worked as a bank clerk, 1925-35; full-time writer, 1945—. Leader, British Lyngen Expedition, 1951, North Lyngen Expedition, 1952, Baudha Himalayan Expedition, 1954. *Military service:* Royal Navy, 1939-45, became lieutenant commander. *Member:* Royal Geographical Society, Detection Club, Midland Association of Mountaineers (president, 1959-60).

WRITINGS—Published by Selwyn & Blount, except as indicated: *Traitor's Mountain*, 1944, Macmillan, 1946; *Kidnap Castle*, 1947; *Hammer Island*, 1948; *Dark Hazard*, 1948; *The Rising of the Lark*, 1949; *Sir Devil*, 1949; *A Climber in Wales*, Cornish Brothers, 1949.

The Mountaineers Weekend Book, Seeley Service, 1951; *Path to Glory*, Faber, 1951; *Land from the Sea*, Faber, 1952; *Mr. Nelson's Ladies*, Faber, 1953; *Mountains of the Midnight Sun*, Hurst & Blackett, 1954; *The Frigate Captain*, Faber, 1954, Vanguard, 1956; *Introduction to Mountaineering*, Seeley Service, 1955; *The Moated Mountain*, Hurst & Blackett, 1955; *The Lost Glacier*, Hart-Davis, 1955, Vanguard, 1956; *Midshipman Quinn*, Faber, 1956, Vanguard, 1957; *His Was the Fire*, Faber, 1956; *Kami the Sherpa*, Brockhampton, 1956, published as *Sherpa Adventure*, Vanguard, 1959; *Tiger Patrol*, Collins, 1956; *The Trampers and Campers Weekend Book*, Seeley Service, 1957; *Tiger Patrol at Sea*, Collins, 1957; *How Mountains Are Climbed*, Routledge, 1958; *Introduction to Caravanning*, Seeley Service, 1958; *Tiger Patrol Presses On*, Collins, 1958; *The Admiral's Fancy*, Longmans, Green, 1958; *Getting to Know Mountains*, Newnes, 1958; *Quinn of the*

"Fury," Faber, 1958, Vanguard, 1961; *How Underground Britain Is Explored,* Routledge, 1958; *Shadow Buttress,* Faber, 1959; *Wolfe Commands You,* Faber, 1959; *The Lost Pothole,* Brockhampton, 1959; *The Battle of Cotton,* Constable, 1959.

Tiger Patrol Wins Through, Collins, 1960; *The Flying Ensign,* Faber, 1960; *Greencoats against Napoleon,* Vanguard, 1960; *Midshipman Quinn and Denise the Spy,* Vanguard, 1961; *Shop in the Mountain,* Vanguard, 1961; *Midshipman Quinn Wins Through,* Faber, 1961; *The Sea Officer,* Faber, 1961; *The Battle of Steam: Revolution in Britain,* Constable, 1961; *Gentleman Johnny,* Faber, 1962; *Byrd of the 95th,* Faber, 1962; *Look at Mountains,* Hamish Hamilton, 1962; *The Ladder of Snow,* Gollancz, 1962; *Greenhorn's Cruise,* Brockhampton, 1963, Van Nostrand, 1964; *H.M.S. Diamond Rock,* Faber, 1963; *A Necklace of Glaciers,* Gollancz, 1964; *The Camp in the Hills,* Benn, 1964; *Modern Mountaineering,* Faber, 1964; *Blue Remembered Hills,* Faber, 1965; *Thunder over Spain,* Vanguard, 1965; *Quinn at Trafalgar,* Vanguard, 1965; *Red for Adventure,* Brockhampton, 1965; *Mr. Fiddle,* Hamish Hamilton, 1965; *Number Two-Ninety,* Faber, 1965, published as *Confederate Raider,* Washburn, 1967; *Wolf Cub Island,* Brockhampton, 1965; *The Pass of Morning,* Washburn, 1966; *The Foundations of Climbing,* S. Paul, 1966; *Mr. Fiddle's Pig,* Hamish Hamilton, 1966; *The Arrow Book of Climbing,* Arrow Books, 1967; *Rock and Rope,* Faber, 1967; *Mallory of Everest,* Hamish Hamilton, 1967, Macmillan, 1968; *The Sea Cub,* Brockhampton, 1967; *Mr. Fiddle's Band,* Hamish Hamilton, 1967; *On Top of the World,* Hamish Hamilton, 1967, Macmillan, 1968; *Indestructible Jones,* Washburn, 1968; *The Climber's Bedside Book,* Faber, 1968; *Journey with a Secret,* Gollancz, 1968, Meredith, 1969; *Sea Road to Camperdown,* Faber, 1968; (compiler) *Men and Mountaineering: An Anthology of Writings by Climbers,* David White, 1968, Macmillan, 1969; *First Up Everest,* Macmillan, 1969; *A Case for Mr. Fiddle,* Hamish Hamilton, 1969; *Cubs of the Castle,* Brockhampton, 1969; *Jones's Private Navy,* Faber, 1969; *The Snowdon Rangers,* Faber, 1969.

The Forbidden Frontiers, Hamish Hamilton, 1970; *First on the Summits,* Gollancz, 1970; *A Tent on Top,* Gollancz, 1971; *Vincey Joe at Quiberon,* Faber, 1971; *Cubs on the Job,* Brockhampton, 1972; *Welsh Walks and Legends,* Jones, 1972, Mayflower, 1979; *Mystery of the Fleeing Girl,* Scholastic Publications, 1972; *The Mountains of North Wales,* Gollancz, 1973; *Marty's Mountain,* Brockhampton, 1973; *Admiral of England,* Faber, 1973; *Snowdon Range,* West Col Productions, 1973; *Glyder Range,* West Col Productions, 1974; *Welsh Tales for Children,* Gelert, 1974; *A Sword for Mr. Fitton,* Faber, 1975; *Legends of North Wales,* Gelert, 1975; *Backpacking: A Comprehensive Guide,* McKay, 1976; *Backpacking in the Alps and Pyrenees,* Gollancz, 1976; *Backpacking in Wales,* R. Hale, 1977; *Mr. Fitton's Commission,* Faber, 1977; *Llanberis Area Guide,* 3rd edition, Cicerone Press, 1978; *The Baltic Convoy,* Faber, 1979; *A Kiss for Captain Hardy,* Faber, 1979; *Walks in Gwynedd,* Jones, 1980; *Centurion Comes Home,* Faber, 1980.

Under pseudonym Glyn Carr; published by Bles, except as indicated: *Death on Milestone Buttress,* 1951; *Murder on the Matterhorn,* 1952, reprinted, Ulverscroft, 1968; *The Youth Hostel Murders,* 1952, reprinted, Chivers, 1980; *The Corpse in the Crevasse,* 1952; *Death under Snowdon,* 1954; *A Corpse at Camp Two,* 1955, reprinted, Ulverscroft, 1973; *Murder of an Owl,* 1956; *The Ice Axe Murders,* 1958; *Swing away Climber,* Washburn, 1959; *Holiday with Murder,* 1960; *Death Finds a Foothold,* 1961; *Lewker in Norway,* 1963; *Death of a Weirdy,* 1965; *Lewker in Tirol,* 1967; *Fat Man's Agony,* 1969.

SIDELIGHTS: About twenty of Showell Styles' books have been published by U.S. publishers. Several have also been

published in France, Norway, Germany, Holland, and Spain. *Avocational interests:* Mountaineering and music.

* * *

STYRON, William 1925-

PERSONAL: Born June 11, 1925, in Newport News, Va.; son of William Clark (a shipyard engineer) and Pauline (Abraham) Styron; married Rose Burgunder, May 4, 1953; children: Susanna, Paola, Thomas, Alexandra. *Education:* Attended Christchurch School, Middlesex County, Va., and Davidson College; Duke University, A.B., 1947; studied writing at New School for Social Research. *Politics:* Democrat. *Residence and office:* Roxbury, Conn.; and Vineyard Haven, Mass. (summer).

CAREER: Writer. McGraw-Hill Book Co. (publishers), New York, N.Y., associate editor, 1947. Honorary consultant in American Letters to the Library of Congress; fellow of Silliman College, Yale University. *Military service:* U.S. Marine Corps, World War II; became first lieutenant; recalled briefly in 1951. *Member:* National Institute of Arts and Letters, Signet Society of Harvard (honorary). *Awards, honors:* American Academy of Arts and Letters Prix de Rome, 1952, for *Lie Down in Darkness;* Pulitzer Prize, 1968, and Howells Medal of the American Academy of Arts and Letters, 1970, both for *The Confessions of Nat Turner;* American Book Award, National Book Critics Circle Award nominee, both 1980, both for *Sophie's Choice.*

WRITINGS: Lie Down in Darkness, Bobbs-Merrill, 1951; *The Long March,* Vintage, 1957; *Set This House on Fire,* Random House, 1960; *The Confessions of Nat Turner,* Random House, 1967; *In the Clap Shack* (three-act play; first produced in New Haven at Yale Repertory Theatre, December 15, 1972), Random House, 1973; *Sophie's Choice,* Random House, 1979. Editor of *Paris Review: Best Short Stories,* published by Dutton. Contributor to *Esquire, New York Review of Books,* and other publications.

SIDELIGHTS: William Styron's novels have brought him major literary awards, broad critical notice, and a reputation for raising controversial issues. In *The Confessions of Nat Turner* and *Sophie's Choice,* Styron writes about two victims of oppression: a slave and a concentration camp survivor. Although some critics question his approach, most praise Styron for probing into difficult subjects. Reviewers consider Styron's timing a positive factor in the success of these two books; *Sophie's Choice,* published during renewed concern about the Holocaust, and *The Confessions of Nat Turner,* published during the racially explosive late Sixties, both found large audiences. George Steiner comments in the *New Yorker:* "The crisis of civil rights, the new relationships to each other and to their own individual sensibilities that this crisis has forced on both whites and Negroes . . . give Mr. Styron's fable [*The Confessions of Nat Turner*] a special relevance."

Styron based *The Confessions of Nat Turner* on the transcript of testimony given by a slave, Nat Turner, who had led a brief revolt against slave owners in Virginia's Tidewater district. Styron considers his book a "meditation on history" rather than a strict retelling of events. He explains in a letter to the *Nation* that "in writing *The Confessions of Nat Turner* I at no time pretended that my narrative was an exact transcription of historical events; had perfect accuracy been my aim I would have written a work of history rather than a novel." Philip Rahv asserts that Styron's viewpoint is more valuable than a historical perspective. He writes in the *New York Review of Books:* "This narrative is something more than a novelistic counterpart of scholarly studies of slavery in America; it incarnates its theme, bringing home to us the monstrous reality of slavery in a psychodynamic manner that at the same time does not in the least neglect social or economic aspects.''

Styron's subjective approach draws ire from critics who feel that his portrait of Nat is based on white stereotypes. A *Negro Digest* critic takes particular issue with Styron's depiction of Nat's sexuality: ''In the name of fiction, Mr. Styron can do whatever he likes with History. When his interpretation, however, duplicates what is white America's favorite fantasy (*i.e.* every black male—especially the leader—is motivated by a latent(?) desire to sleep with the Great White Woman), he is obligated to explain (in the structure of the novel, of course) this coincidental duplication—or to be criticized accordingly. Since there is no such explanation in the technique of the novel and since it offers no vision or new perspective, but rather reaffirms an old stale, shameful fantasy (which is still quite salable) it is at best a good commercial novel.'' Albert Murray concurs in the *New Leader:* ''Alas, what Negroes will find in Styron's 'confessions' is much the same old failure of sensibility that plagues most other fiction about black people. That is to say, they will all find a Nat Turner whom many white people may accept at a safe distance, but hardly one with whom Negroes will easily identify.''

Other critics argue that Styron is entitled to give a personal interpretation of the story, whatever his views. Steiner asserts that Styron ''has every artistic right to make of his Nat Turner less an anatomy of the Negro mind than a fiction of complex relationships, of the relationship between a present-day white man of deep Southern roots and the Negro in today's whirlwind.'' Stylistically, Styron is often compared with William Faulkner, who shares his Southern white background and his interest in depicting Black characters. According to Philip Rahv, ''Styron has gained greatly from his ability to empathize with his Negro figures—with the protagonist, Nat, as well as with some of his followers—to live in them, as it were, in a way inconceivable even for Faulkner, Styron's prose-master. Whereas Faulkner's Negroes are still to some extent the white man's Negroes, Styron's are starkly themselves.''

Styron writes about human suffering in a more contemporary setting—post-World War II Brooklyn—in *Sophie's Choice.* Sophie is a beautiful Polish gentile who survived Auschwitz but lost two of her children and much of her self-esteem there. Her lover, Nathan (mad, brilliant, and Jewish) is haunted by the atrocities of the Holocaust, although he personally escaped them, and he torments Sophie with reminders. Stingo, a young writer who lives downstairs from Sophie and Nathan, narrates. According to Geoffrey Wolff of *Esquire,* ''Stingo is in the tradition of *The Great Gatsby*'s Nick Carraway. Like Nick, he bears witness to the passion of characters he chances upon and tries modestly to judge and pardon. Like Nick, he is a refugee from settled values—Virginia's Tidewater country—back from a great war to make his way in the great world.''

David Caute of the *New Statesman* hears additional voices. For him, the ''neo-Biblical cadences of Southern prose, of Wolfe and Faulkner, jostle with the cosmopolitan sensibility of an F. Scott Fitzgerald.'' Other critics agree that the influence of other writers sometimes muffles Styron's own voice. Jack Beatty writes in the *New Republic* that *Sophie's Choice* ''is written in an unvaryingly mannered style—High Southern— that draws constant spell-destroying attention to itself.'' The ''Southern style'' associated with Faulkner and Thomas Wolfe is characterized by elaborate, even Gothic descriptions, and although Styron is ''a novelist hard to categorise,'' he shows his allegiance to that style here and ''in all of [his] writing,'' according to Caute, with ''a tendency towards post-Wolfian

inflation, a reluctance to leave any noun uncaressed by an adjective.'' Paul Gray of *Time* agrees, noting that Styron ''often lets Stingo pile up adjectives in the manner of Thomas Wolfe: 'Brooklyn's greenly beautiful, homely, teeming, begrimed and incomprehensible vastness'. . . . True, Stingo is pictured as a beginning writer, heavily in debt to Faulkner, Wolfe and the Southern literary tradition, but Styron may preserve more redundant oratory than the effect of Stingo's youth strictly requires.''

Robert Towers, writing in the *New York Review of Books,* also faults Styron for verbosity. '''All my life, I have retained a strain of uncontrolled didacticism,' says Stingo at one point,'' Towers notes, ''and *Sophie's Choice* bears him out. The novel is made to drag along an enormous burden of commentary, ranging all the way from the meaning of the Holocaust, the ineluctable nature of evil, the corrosive effects of guilt, the horrors of slavery, and the frailty of goodness and hope to such topics as the misunderstanding of the South by Northern liberals, Southern manners as opposed to those of New York taxi drivers, and the existence of prejudice and cruelty in even the best of us.'' But Wolff defends Styron, observing that ''the book's narrative flow is suspenseful if languid, if sometimes even glacial,'' and that ''*Sophie's Choice* achieves an almost palpable evocation of its place and time—Poland before and during the war, Brooklyn and Coney Island immediately after.'' And Caute, despite his criticisms, contends that Styron's prose is ''marked also by clarity, honesty and accessibility.''

As evidence of Styron's narrative power, Gray asserts that he gives Sophie ''a core of individuality that elevates her role beyond that of a symbolic victim.'' Styron explains that his sympathy toward Sophie's character stems from personal experience. He modelled her after a woman he met when—like Stingo—he was an aspiring writer living in a Brooklyn rooming house. Inspiration for the story came, he tells Tony Schwartz in *Newsweek,* when one day ''I woke up with the remembrance of a girl I'd once known, Sophie. It was a very vivid half-dream, half-revelation, and all of a sudden I realized that hers was a story I had to tell.'' As in *Confessions,* Styron expanded on the original historical data when he wrote his story. ''The fact is,'' he relates, ''I didn't get to know [Sophie's prototype] very well and the story as it evolves in the book is made up. But what I realized is that it was necessary for me to write about Auschwitz. . . . It was the same sort of territory, modernized, that I explored in *The Confessions of Nat Turner.*''

In response to critics who question the validity of *Confessions* and *Sophie's Choice* on the grounds of Styron's personal background, Towers argues that ''it should not be necessary to defend the right of Styron—a non-Jew, a Southern Protestant in background—to this subject matter—any more than his right to assume, in the first person, the 'identity' of the leader of a slave rebellion in Virginia in 1831.'' Gray agrees. ''The question,'' he writes, ''is not whether Styron has a right to use alien experiences but whether his novel proves that he knows what he is writing about. In this instance, the overriding answer is yes.''

Manuscript collections of Styron's work are held by the Library of Congress, Washington, D.C., and Duke University, Durham, North Carolina.

CA INTERVIEW

CA interviewed William Styron by phone January 22, 1981, at his home in Roxbury, Connecticut.

CA: Writing Lie Down in Darkness *as a very young man, did you think a great deal about how it would be received?*

STYRON: I guess every young writer looks forward to the reception of his work with a sort of palpitating heart. He wants, like Byron, to wake up the day after his publication and find himself famous and rich and the object of a lot of attention. I would be dishonest if I said I wasn't hoping that it was received with great favor. I was happy to find that, in general, it *was* received with considerable favor.

CA: You said at least ten years ago that you basically dislike writing. Has it grown easier in any way?

STYRON: I have mixed feelings about my own attitude toward it now. On certain levels it is easier. The mechanics of writing have become simpler. The very fact that one writes so much allows one to write with a certain fluency that he did not have earlier on. On the larger level, however, I think it is just as difficult as it ever was, which is to say the deeper and more obdurate parts of the active writing are tough. Reconciling all the complexities of a work of fiction, or of any kind of narrative, is just as difficult as it ever was.

CA: You strive to perfect each sentence as you write. Is there much editorial changing after a book is finished?

STYRON: Very little. I happen to have an extremely good editor, Robert Loomis at Random House, who, throughout most of my career, has followed the work as it proceeds, as I write it. In other words, I've read enormous sections to Bob and he has offered very little criticism in the making of the book. When it gets to Random House, his criticisms are usually brief but very direct and to the point, and extremely valuable in every case. I almost always heed these criticisms although to be quite honest, they are never in any sense large or structural in terms of the overall scheme of the book.

CA: Andrew Fielding, in his article in Horizon *(June 1979), wrote "the density of [Styron's] prose seems almost symbolic of the density and complexity of the experience he is confronting." Is the achievement of this density a major part of your struggle in writing?*

STYRON: Yes, I think that one tries to achieve a density that is consonant with the complexity of the book. To write densely is, of course, not to write obscurely; it is to give body and weight to language and to the narrative. It's hard to achieve because it has to be balanced constantly with what I feel to be essentially a very important component of the work of fiction, *narrative drive.* It has to involve the reader in the narrative without slowing him down unduly through the density of the texture of the work itself. That is what one tries to do in a subtle way so that the forward momentum and the density go together and do not hinder or impede the story.

CA: Did your decision to settle away from the South have anything to do with your writing?

STYRON: Not really. I had no desire to live in the South, not because I was rejecting the South in any sense. The South had been my cradle; I had been nurtured there and educated there. It was and still remains a place about which I feel a great deal of emotion and affection. For me it was a rather practical thing. Had I had any friends or family who had continued to command my help and my loyalties, I might have stayed, but I did not have either. I was not rebelling against my father, who was living in Virginia, because we maintained an affectionate bond throughout his life, but there was just no need for me to stay down there. I wanted to taste the same challenges and pleasures that a young man from the Midwest or Far West wants. Just

as young Frenchmen want to go to Paris and young Englishmen want to go to London, I wanted to go to New York. The South was not a necessity for me as a locale, it did not command my immediate loyalty in that sense, so that's why I moved to the North.

CA: Much recent literary criticism seems to convey the impression that reading a book for pleasure—because it's a good, absorbing story and well told—is something one should hide in the bathroom to do. How much do you think readers and writers are affected by this sort of academic approach?

STYRON: I'm glad you asked that because it's a bothersome question and one that I react rather violently to. Academic criticism of the kind that is involved, among other things, in what they call postmodernism in literature, nouveau roman, and so on, I find very pernicious. And it's hard to describe my reaction because it's the kind of criticism that hails writers whom I rather admire—John Barth, Thomas Pynchon, and Donald Barthelme—as being writers it is worthwhile to read. But embodied in it is a parallel feeling that narrative fiction of the kind I and some other contemporaries write is completely declasse. It's a kind of parochialism which I find very pernicious because it's so exclusive; it's in effect saying that the narrative written in the traditional form is finished and that this other writing is the only thing worth reading. Plainly such a point of view does affect young and vulnerable readers and I find that really very bad news. I feel that the great thing about fiction as an art is that it is so mercurial, so fluid, so various. One should be able to read fiction in any mode, asking only that it be intelligent, exciting, poetic, or whatever words you wish to apply to it; but to define it so narrowly, to exclude the elements of character and narrative force, I find a very bad and almost deadly sign.

CA: Do you attempt to read all that's been written about your work?

STYRON: No, I don't. In fact, with my most recent work, *Sophie's Choice,* I really didn't read very many of the reviews at all, pro or con. I find it counterproductive.

CA: Do you think reviewers could do a better and fairer job?

STYRON: I suppose they could, but some reviewers are merely mediocre minds grappling often with things beyond them. Some reviewers are responsible and some are just plain vicious. The important thing is that it's very hard to destroy a good work, almost impossible. Therefore, although I've had my feelings hurt in the past by adverse criticism, I no longer really take it very seriously because the integrity and power of the work are bound to cause it to survive any amount of viciousness, and almost any good work is going to receive a certain amount of vicious treatment.

CA: The Confessions of Nat Turner (1967) won a Pulitzer Prize on the one hand and provoked on the other a body of adverse criticism that included an entire book. In the perspective of the intervening years, do you find any part of that criticism valid?

STYRON: Nothing at all of any major nature, no. A few details were picked up which were inevitable. They were small oversights in the factual field that I regretted myself having omitted, but so minor they're not even worth going into here. The major points of the attack I found totally indefensible, totally political, and totally immoral. I think the fact that the book has healthily survived those attacks is the ultimate indication of how irresponsible they were. I've been asked many times what my initial reaction was, and I've always had to respond that I was far less hurt than the nature of the attack logically might have led me to be. I simply knew from the very beginning that it was politically motivated and that the substance of the attack was based on practically nothing that could be proved. I had written not a work of historiography but a work of fiction, a work I hoped would be called literature. It was being judged entirely on tendentious and really racist themes. I also got a great deal of support from distinguished historians—C. Vann Woodward, Eugene Genovese, and others who were highly qualified and whose motives were beyond suspicion, even by most of the blacks—who simply came to my defense and said that the attacks on me were nonsense.

CA: You've spoken to audiences in this country and abroad. Do your audiences differ from country to country in interests and response?

STYRON: Yes. I don't speak a great deal, but I do selectively. I've gone to some places that interest me both here and abroad. I would say that one cannot speak in terms of relative merit about audiences here or abroad. But I would say also that somehow European audiences, especially in Eastern Europe, are almost magical in their fascination and attention. I've spoken, for instance, in Hungary and in Poland and in the Soviet Union. There, the passion and love they have, not so much for the speaker but for literature in general, are so intense as to be almost overwhelming. Here I think you feel a certain blase attitude. Often here I think you feel the audiences have come with a sort of ho-hum attitude, and you possibly don't count for a whole lot. On the other hand, I don't want to be too definitive when I say that, because I have had audiences here in the United States which plainly came out of affection and interest.

CA: In an August 1972 Esquire *article you expressed a distaste for politics. Have your feelings changed?*

STYRON: I certainly still feel that I would never want to get involved with politics. I think it's a rogue's game and therefore I wouldn't want to be in it. I have a peripheral interest in politics in that I enjoy watching the spectacle, like H. L. Mencken watching his three-ring circus, but I have no interest whatever in any involvement other than possibly to support every now and then as much as I can certain politicians I feel are doing a good job, such as our local congressman, Toby Moffett, here in Connecticut.

CA: Does your family play an active part in your work?

STYRON: Not really. They care, of course, about my work—I don't mean to sound as though there's any disaffection involved here. We have a very close-knit, devoted family, but in terms of the work itself, I don't feel that my family plays an integral part.

CA: Will you tell for those who haven't heard it the wonderful story of finishing a book in the early hours of the morning and how you celebrated that occasion?

STYRON: If I'm not mistaken, that was when I finished *Nat Turner.* I finished it around four or five in the morning. I can't remember the exact time of year, but it was in the cold months. I woke the kids up—they were all around six, seven, eight, nine years old—and put them on the mantlepiece, and I think we played some Mozart just to celebrate, and I broke open a

bottle of champagne. The kids all got some, and they got sort of woozy, too.

CA: Music is often present in your fiction. Does it play an important part in your life?

STYRON: Yes. I have an unprovable theory, but a strong theory, that most artists have to have a subsidiary art to support their own. Certain poets respond to visual art. For instance, E. E. Cummings was a very good painter and plainly derived a great deal of his talent from another aesthetic response. I know that there have been musicians who've been profoundly involved in literature, such as Berlioz. Music has been a very central fact of my life. I got it from both my mother and my father, who were not professional musicians but passionately devoted amateurs. I always had music in my life as a child and as I grew up. To this day I can't read a note, nor can I pick out a tune on the piano or guitar, but I respond intensely to music and I'm sure it has permeated my work—so much so that I can say with some confidence there would not be a writer by my name had there not existed Bach and Vivaldi and Mozart and Schumann and so on. It's intertwined in the rhythms of my work and my whole Weltanschauung and my whole understanding of the natural world. Without it I would not be a writer.

CA: Do you read any fiction by new writers?

STYRON: Occasionally, yes, when new writers come to my attention. But I probably read less than I should. Like a lot of writers, I tend to shy away from reading other fiction while I'm writing because there's a fear of being influenced by someone's writing style.

CA: Do you think a lot of good fiction is going to be written in the near future?

STYRON: It's going to have to if fiction is to survive as an art form. I'm rather optimistic because I do believe, in a way that I would not have believed even as recently as twenty years ago, that fiction is a very powerful and very widespread art form. I think the experience I've had with *Sophie's Choice* is a good example of what can happen when a work of fiction seizes a certain area of the popular imagination, and I'm not talking about just in this country but also abroad, where even in the Soviet Union it's going to be translated and apparently have a first edition of several hundred thousand copies. I'm saying this only because I believe it demonstrates a need for fiction, and if it does, then someone is going to have to come along and fill this need. When you have an art form that works, there will always be artists coming along to meet the demand, so I have high hopes for the future of fiction.

Fiction, when it really works, makes your hair stand on end and does all sorts of wonderful things to you. This is what the art of fiction still remains, the use of language in a way you hope will captivate the reader and make him see the way you see. Plainly, you can't be simpleminded. Narrative itself is a linear matter and you do hope that you're not going to sound like a Harold Robbins, that there is substance in your work. The great thing about fiction is that it's like a freight train—it can be loaded with all sorts of things. An important and essential thing is this narrative drive, this thing that causes the reader to become almost lost in the work. This to me is the sign of the power of narrative fiction, and nothing can supplant it.

BIOGRAPHICAL/CRITICAL SOURCES—Books: Malcolm Cowley, editor, *Writers at Work: The "Paris Review" Inter-*

views, First Series, Viking, 1958; Maxwell Geismar, *American Moderns,* Hill & Wang, 1958; Joseph J. Waldmeir, editor, *Recent American Fiction,* Michigan State University Press, 1963; Harry T. Moore, editor, *Contemporary American Novelists,* Southern Illinois University Press, 1964; Richard Kostelanetz, editor, *On Contemporary Literature,* Avon, 1964; Jonathan Baumbach, *The Landscape of Nightmare,* New York University Press, 1965; Walter Allen, *The Modern Novel,* Dutton, 1965; Louise Y. Gossett, *Violence in Recent Southern Fiction,* Duke University Press, 1965; Robert H. Fossum, *William Styron,* Eerdmans, 1968; Cooper R. Mackin, *William Styron,* Steck Vaughn, 1969; Richard Pearce, *William Styron* (Pamphlets on American Writers Series, No. 98), University of Minnesota Press, 1971; *Contemporary Literary Criticism,* Gale, Volume I, 1973, Volume III, 1975, Volume V, 1976, Volume XI, 1979, Volume XV, 1980; Melvin J. Friedman, *William Styron,* Bowling Green University, 1974; James L. West, *William Styron: A Descriptive Bibliography,* G. K. Hall, 1977.

Periodicals: *Harper's,* July, 1967; *New York Times,* August 5, 1967, October 3, 1967, May 29, 1979; *Book World,* October 1, 1967, October 8, 1967; *New York Times Book Review,* October 8, 1967, August 11, 1968, May 27, 1979; *Time,* October 13, 1967, June 11, 1979; *Nation,* October 16, 1967, April 22, 1968, July 7, 1979; *Newsweek,* October 16, 1967, May 28, 1979; *New York Review of Books,* October 26, 1967, September 12, 1968, July 19, 1979; *New Yorker,* November 25, 1967, June 18, 1979; *New Leader,* December 4, 1967; *Village Voice,* December 14, 1967; *Commonweal,* December 22, 1967; *Kenyon Review,* Volume XXX, number 1, 1968; *Partisan Review,* winter, 1968, summer, 1968; *Yale Review,* winter, 1968; *Negro Digest,* February, 1968; *Observer Review,* May 5, 1968; *Times Literary Supplement,* May 19, 1968, November 30, 1979; *American Dialog,* spring, 1968.

New Statesman, May 7, 1979; *Washington Post,* May 18, 1979; *Washington Post Book World,* May 20, 1979; *Chicago Tribune Book World,* May 27, 1979; *Detroit News,* June 24, 1979; *New Republic,* June 30, 1979; *Esquire,* July 3, 1979; *Spectator,* October 13, 1979.

—*Sketch by Elaine Guregian*

—*Interview by Jean W. Ross*

* * *

SUTTMEIER, Richard Peter 1942-

PERSONAL: Born January 3, 1942, in Richmond Hill, N.Y.; son of Christopher E. and Harriet (Klein) Suttmeier; married Merle Metcalfe (a teacher), February 22, 1963. *Education:* Dartmouth College, A.B., 1963; Indiana University, Ph.D., 1969. *Home address:* R.D. 1, Griffin Rd., Box 401, Clinton, N.Y. *Office:* Department of Political Science, Hamilton College, Clinton, N.Y. 13323.

CAREER: Chinese University of Hong Kong, Chung Chi College, Hong Kong, instructor in general education, 1963-65; National Aeronautics and Space Administration (NASA), Office of International Affairs, Washington, D.C., international affairs specialist, 1969-70; Hamilton College, Clinton, N.Y., assistant professor, 1970-76, associate professor of government, 1976—, chairman of department, 1978—. Visiting fellow at Technology and Development Institute, East-West Center, Honolulu, Hawaii, 1972-73; lecturer at University of Montreal, 1975. Adviser to National Academy of Science committee for scholarly communication with the People's Republic of China; member of chemistry delegation to the People's Republic of China sponsored by U.S. National Academy of Sci-

ence and by Science and Technology Association of the People's Republic of China, 1978. Consultant to U.S. Congress Office of Technology Assessment, U.S. Department of State, and to World Bank. *Member:* American Political Science Association, Association for Asian Studies, American Society for Public Administration (fellow; member of executive committee, section on international and comparative administration, 1974-76), American Association for the Advancement of Science, Society for the Social Studies of Science.

WRITINGS: (Contributor) Joseph R. Quinn, editor, *Medicine and Public Health in the People's Republic of China,* National Institutes of Health, 1972; *Research and Revolution: Science Policy and Societal Change in China,* Lexington Books, 1974; (contributor with Genevieve Dean) *Science and Technology in the People's Republic of China,* Organization for Economic Cooperation and Development (Paris), 1977; *Science, Technology and China's Drive for Modernization,* Hoover Institution, 1980; (contributor) Stuart Harris and Keichi Oshima, editors, *Australia and Japan: Nuclear Energy Issues in the Pacific,* Australia-Japan Economic Relations Research Project, 1980; (contributor) Richard Baum, editor, *China's Four Modernizations: The New Technological Revolution,* Westview, 1980; (contributor) Leo A. Orleans, editor, *Science in Contemporary China,* Stanford University Press, 1980; (contributor) Ronald Morse, editor, *The Politics of Japan's Energy Strategy,* Institute of East Asian Studies, University of California, Berkeley, 1981. Contributor to periodicals, including *Orbis, Asian Survey, Developing Economies, Science,* and *China Quarterly.*

WORK IN PROGRESS: Science and Technology as Instruments of Foreign Policy: The Case of U.S.-China Relations; a chapter on political participation in China for a book edited by Victor Falkenheim.

* * *

SWADOS, Harvey 1920-1972

PERSONAL: Surname pronounced *Sway-dos;* born October 28, 1920, in Buffalo, N.Y.; died December 11, 1972, in Holyoke, Mass., of an aneurysm; son of Aaron Meyer (a physician) and Rebecca (Bluestone) Swados; married Bette Beller, September 12, 1946; children: Marco, Felice, Robin (son). *Education:* University of Michigan, B.A., 1940. *Religion:* Jewish. *Agent:* Candida Donadio & Associates, Inc., 111 West 57th St., New York, N.Y. 10019.

CAREER: Writer. Worked as a riveter in an aircraft plant in Buffalo, N.Y., 1940-41, and in New York City, 1941-42; metal finisher, Ford Motor Co., Mahwah, N.J.; University of Iowa, Iowa City, visiting lecturer, 1956-57; Sarah Lawrence College, Bronxville, N.Y., member of literature faculty, 1958-60; San Francisco State College (now University), San Francisco, Calif., visiting professor, 1960-61; Sarah Lawrence College, member of literature faculty, 1962-70; University of Massachusetts—Amherst, member of literature faculty, 1970-72. Visiting lecturer or writer in residence at colleges and universities, including New York University, 1958, and Columbia University, 1965-66; National Book Awards judge, 1970; speech writer for Democratic vice-presidential candidate Sargent Shriver, 1972. *Military service:* U.S. Merchant Marine, 1942-45; served as radio officer. *Member:* Authors League, P.E.N. *Awards, honors: Hudson Review* fellowship, 1957; Sidney Hillman Award, 1958; Guggenheim fellowship, 1961; National Book Award nomination, 1963, for *The Will;* National Institute of Arts and Letters Award, 1965; National Endowment for the Arts grant, 1968.

WRITINGS: *Out Went the Candle* (novel), Viking, 1955; *On the Line* (stories), Atlantic-Little, Brown, 1957; *False Coin* (novel), Atlantic-Little, Brown, 1959; *Nights in the Gardens of Brooklyn* (stories), Atlantic-Little, Brown, 1961; (editor) *Years of Conscience: The Muckrakers*, Meridian, 1962; *A Radical's America* (essays), Atlantic-Little, Brown, 1962 (published in England as *A Radical at Large: American Essays*, Hart-Davis, 1968); *The Will* (novel), World Publishing, 1963; *A Story for Teddy, and Others*, Simon & Schuster, 1965; (editor) *The American Writers and the Great Depression*, Bobbs-Merrill, 1966; *Standing Fast* (novel), Doubleday, 1970; *Standing Up for the People: The Life and Work of Estes Kefauver*, Dutton, 1972; *Celebration*, Simon & Schuster, 1975, published as *Celebration: A Novel*, Dell, 1976. Contributor to anthologies, including *The Best Short Stories of 1938*. Contributor of stories and essays to periodicals, including *Partisan Review, Nation, Dissent, Saturday Review, Esquire, Saturday Evening Post*, and *New World Writing*.

WORK IN PROGRESS: An untitled novel.

SIDELIGHTS: A self-proclaimed socialist whose deepest sympathies were with the working-class victims of industrial society, Harvey Swados wrote that he considered himself "as 1) a novelist, 2) a short-story writer, with 3) an interest in social forces and ideas." Often called an heir to the social novelists of the 1930's, Swados, writes Charles Shapiro in *Contemporary American Novelists*, was "keenly aware of the social realities of today" and "well equipped to transform these realities into fiction." Joseph P. Fried of the *New York Times* explains: "Whether he was describing the agonizing boredom of work on the modern assembly line, the almost desperate groping for an unrealizable ideal, or the gradual fading of the dreams of youth, Mr. Swados often struck a familiar chord in the minds—and hearts—of his readers. Even those critics who found his prose flawed were often moved by a Swados work."

The stories in *On the Line* focus on the problems of the industrial laborer—problems which Swados had known from his own experience of working in the factory and had written about in numerous articles. Shapiro says of the book: "Not since Upton Sinclair's *The Jungle* have we had such a direct, steady look at the worker's world, one of dullness, continual pressures, and very little satisfaction." Calling the stories "reminiscent of the 'social protest' literature of the '30's," George Adelman of *Library Journal* concludes: "The writing is excellent and the characterization true to life, but everything is unmitigatedly tragic and without purpose." J. T. Farrell, however, notes in the *New Republic* that with "unmarred and unbroken" objectivity, Swados "conveys a sense of fate—the fate of those who work at de-sensitizing and psychologically-hurtful work in order that our prosperous society can maintain itself." C. S. Kilby of the *New York Herald Tribune Book Review* believes that the stories "give a better insight into the human side of mass production than any sociological study can do."

One important thematic concern of *False Coin* is the survival of the artist in modern society. "Given Swados's intelligence and seriousness," writes J. K. Hutchens in the *San Francisco Chronicle*, "something stirring should come out of this. Yet it does not. . . . The major theme seems constantly on the point of arriving, but somewhere along the way it is lost in diffusion and irrelevancies." But according to Granville Hicks in the *Saturday Review*, the novel "affirms not only that integrity is important but also that the artist cannot be free in our society, no matter what the beneficence of our rulers." Paul Engle comments in the *Chicago Sunday Tribune* that it is "a little terrifying to see how readily the subtle forces of 'togeth-

erness' can dominate the presumably independent artist." Hicks questions whether we shall ever see "the kind of revolution of which Swados [dreamed]" but asserts that "there can be no doubt that his vision of it . . . sharpened his insights into American life. He [was] a writer with a point of view, from which he [saw] much that we need to look at carefully. He [was] also a writer who [knew] how to clothe his vision, for the purposes of fiction, in flesh and blood."

Standing Fast—regarded by several critics as Swados's major work—follows a group of American radicals over a thirty-year period. In the beginning, they are all associated with a Trotskyite faction called the New Party, and the novel records their personal triumphs and failures against the historical backdrop of World War II, the Cold War, McCarthyism, and the assassination of President John F. Kennedy. Linda Comp notes in *Best Sellers* that the book "actually reads as a socio-historical account of a frustrated generation's socialist struggles against American capitalism and what it represents to them—war, depression, imperialism, and severe class differences. . . . [Yet,] Mr. Swados tells his story with genuine compassion for the radicals." In *Saturday Review*, Harding Lemay points out that though "it would be easy to fault Swados on nearly every aspect of fiction taught in the seminars . . . , his rare honesty finally wins us over completely." Other critics agree. Stephen Klaidman of the *Washington Post* says that "technically the book creaks like a machine with wooden gears. . . . [But] it has qualities that make it important and worthy despite its obvious failings, [and] first among these is compassionate honesty." John Leonard writes in the *New York Times* that despite its many technical flaws, *Standing Fast* "breaks the heart" because Swados "pays his way into the reader's credulity . . . with honesty. He was there, a witness, and he reports, unflinchingly. [The book] is written in defiance of the dominant attitude . . . of the last thirty years in American fiction. It is wholly without irony." Klaidman claims it is impossible not to feel that the characters are "real people experiencing genuine sadness, joy, triumph, failure—always failure—and moving on, giving way to another generation that will experience the same emotions under different conditions."

Swados finished *Celebration* shortly before he died, but it was not published until 1975, three years later. Described by several critics as ambitious and realistic, the novel portrays, through journal entries, six months in the life of Sam Lumen, an 89-year-old former radical caught between his establishment friends who want to name a building after him, and his grandson who wants an endorsement for his political group. According to R. Z. Sheppard in *Time*, the novel "has the virtues one cherished in Swados's fiction—decency, compassion, and gentle wit—[but it] suffers from what was always Swados's noble flaw as a novelist: a talent never quite up to the demands he put upon it." In the *Washington Post Book World*, Webster Schott echoes that assessment: "Swados seeks the bitterness of aging, the crookedness of achievement and the mysteries of personal and social change. . . . He reaches enough to engage us. But the themes are great ones calling for, I suppose, the gift of genius. Swados did not have that. He had compassion and skill." Nevertheless, *Newsweek's* Peter S. Prescott salutes Swados for trying to overcome "a nasty array of technical problems."

Dan Wakefield, however, believes the novel is successful. He writes in the *Atlantic* that Swados "was able to make that leap of imagination to the feelings and perceptions of advanced age. That was the kind of dangerous fictional feat he had often ventured, but he never so successfully achieved it as he did in this, his final *Celebration*." Other critics not only consider *Celebration* a success but also Swados's best novel. Thomas

LeClair offers this explanation in the *New York Times Book Review:* "The language of *Celebration* remains analytical, rather than presentational, and the journal form leads to technical weaknesses, but the novel has qualities that suggest Swados may have been moving toward a different kind of fiction. His concentration of social themes into metaphor, his attention to subtleties of character rather than ideology, and his creation of an ironic complexity are signs of an intensive fiction more like his best stories than *Standing Fast.* These qualities do not make *Celebration* a great novel, but they do combine with the perfect Swados persona—an educator and man of conscience—to demonstrate his considerable humane skills."

BIOGRAPHICAL/CRITICAL SOURCES: New York Herald Tribune Book Review, January 9, 1955, October 6, 1957; *Commonweal,* January 14, 1955, June 8, 1962; *Library Journal,* September 15, 1957; *New Republic,* October 14, 1957, November 16, 1963, March 22, 1975; *Kirkus Reviews,* November 1, 1959; *Saturday Review,* January 9, 1960, October 26, 1963, October 10, 1970; *New Yorker,* February 27, 1960; *Yale Review,* March, 1960; *New York Herald Tribune Lively Arts,* January 29, 1961; *Wilson Library Bulletin,* March, 1961; *Chicago Sunday Tribune,* March 5, 1961; *Sewanee Review,* Number 69, 1961; *Wisconsin Studies in Contemporary Literature,* winter, 1961; *New York Times Book Review,* April 8, 1962, August 30, 1969, September 13, 1970, March 9, 1975; *Book Week,* November 3, 1963; Harvey T. Moore, editor, *Contemporary American Novelists,* Southern Illinois University Press, 1964; *Critique,* spring, 1964; *Writer,* August, 1969; *New York Times,* September 15, 1970; *Washington Post Book World,* September 24, 1970, March 23, 1975; *Village Voice,* October 22, 1970; *Best Sellers,* November 1, 1970; *Commentary,* December, 1970; *Newsweek,* March 31, 1975; *Atlantic,* April, 1975; *Nation,* May 10, 1975; *Contemporary Literary Criticism,* Volume V, Gale, 1976.

OBITUARIES: New York Times, December 12, 1972; *Newsweek,* December 25, 1972; *Publishers Weekly,* January 15, 1973.†

—*Sketch by James G. Lesniak*

*   *   *

SWAIM, Alice Mackenzie 1911-

PERSONAL: Born June 5, 1911, in Aberdeen, Scotland; came to United States, 1928; naturalized, 1939; daughter of Donald Campbell (a professor at Princeton Theological Seminary) and Alice (Murray) Mackenzie; married William Thomas Swaim, Jr. (a minister and an administrator of Presbyterian Homes of Central Pennsylvania), December 27, 1932; children: Elizabeth Anne, Kathleen Mackenzie. *Education:* Attended Chatham College, 1928-30; Wilson College, A.B., 1932. *Religion:* Presbyterian. *Home:* 322 North 2nd St., Apt. 1606, Harrisburg, Pa. 17101.

CAREER: Poet. Poetry critic, National Writers Club, 1952-53; columnist for *Cornucopia,* 1953-55, *Evening Sentinel* (Carlisle, Pa.), 1956-70, and *Tejas,* 1968-70; book reviewer, American Poetry League, 1967-74; marketing editor, Poetry Society of New Hampshire; publicity director for Second World Congress of Poets, 1973. Judge of poetry contests. Consultant to Association for Poetry Therapy, 1970-74. *Member:* Poetry Society of America, National Federation of State Poetry Societies, American Poetry League (vice-president, 1964-67, 1967-70), Society of North American Poets, National Writers Club, Amateur Press Association; Centro Studi e Scambi (international executive committee, 1964), Pennsylvania Poetry Society (chapter vice-president, 1963), Poetry Society of New Hamp-

shire, Clan Mackenzie Organization, Dillsburg Fine Arts Club, Kimport Doll Talk Club.

AWARDS, HONORS: Anna Hempstead Branch Lyric Award, 1959; silver medal Esternaux award, 1959; Borestone Mountain Poetry Award, 1960; Henry Seidel Canby Award, 1962; $500 award for best book published by Pageant Press in 1960, for *Crickets Are Crying Autumn;* American Poetry League Award; named Poet-Laureate of the Sonnet, United Poets-Laureate International, 1963; medal of merit, Studie Scambi, Italy, 1965; prizes in Jesse Stuart Contest, 1970, and Clover International Contest, 1970; *Cycloflame* Award, 1971; American Heritage Award, John F. Kennedy Library for Minorities, 1974; grand prize, *World of Poetry* Contest, 1980; poetry awards from thirty other groups.

WRITINGS: Let the Deep Song Rise (poems), Blue River Press, 1952; *Up to the Stars* (poems), Allan Swallow, 1954; *Poetry Calendar* (poems), privately printed, 1956; *Sunshine in a Thimble* (poems), Telegraph Press, 1958; *Crickets Are Crying Autumn* (poems), Pageant Press, 1960; *The Gentle Dragon* (poems), Golden Quill, 1962; *Pennsylvania Profile,* privately printed, 1966; *Scented Honeysuckle Days,* privately printed, 1966; *Here on the Threshold,* privately printed, 1966; *Beyond a Dancing Star* (poems), privately printed, 1967; *Beyond My Catnip Garden* (poems), Golden Quill, 1970; *Celebration of Seasons,* Adams Press, 1978. Contributor of poems to anthologies, including *Anthology of Magazine Verse and Yearbook of American Poetry: 1980 Edition,* edited by Alan F. Pater, Monitor, 1980. Contributor of articles and over 6000 poems to more than 200 periodicals and newspapers, including *Reader's Digest, Pegasus, Al di La, Poet Lore, Voices International, Cycloflame,* and *Dalhousie Review.*

WORK IN PROGRESS: Unicorn and Thistle, a book of poems.

SIDELIGHTS: Alice Mackenzie Swaim writes: "I have always been interested and inspired by poetry and wrote occasional poems as a child; but [I] started writing seriously in 1947 when my health became poor, and I had to find an interest I could pursue quietly at home. Little did I suspect I would have poems translated into over a dozen languages, from French, German, [and] Portuguese to Hindu, Urdu, and Japanese—even Braille. [My] poems have been read on the radio here, in Europe and Africa, [and have also been] presented on WGAL-TV.

"At first poems are the result of inspiration—I tend to write from fifty to one hundred some weeks, then none for a month or so. While they must start with inspiration, they need polishing and perfecting at leisure, to be as fine as possible.

"I have several articles of advice to aspiring writers; but, briefly, I would suggest they read as widely as possible in all varieties of poetry books and magazines, and study and practice the techniques of poetry writing thoroughly—not merely write chopped-up prose under the guise of free verse. The true poet is inspired but needs to be at home in the media just as great musicians are. I think the current literary scene forgets to emphasize the beauty, music, and deep feeling of real poetry, at the same time [that it glorifies] ugliness, bad language, [and] clever gimmicks [that are] not necessarily poetic. A truly memorable poem . . . , though stark at times, [is free] from affected and artificial phrasing as much as from triteness.

"Poetry . . . has been an opening of many doors, not only of heightened awareness of life and literature, but of friendship, international understanding, [and] knowledge of the world of publishing and printing with its rewards and pitfalls. But best of all, [it is] an ongoing enrichment of life, not limited by retirement, ill health, isolation, or [any] other handicap."

AVOCATIONAL INTERESTS: Collecting foreign dolls (has more than four hundred), coin collecting, gardening, handicrafts, reading.

BIOGRAPHICAL/CRITICAL SOURCES: American Bard, fall, 1961; *Muse,* fall, 1961; *Wilson College Alumnae Bulletin,* winter, 1963; *Evening Sentinel* (Carlisle, Pa.), August 26, 1964; *Evening News* (Harrisburg, Pa.), June 24, 1971.

* * *

SWAIN, Su Zan (Noguchi) 1916-

PERSONAL: Born March 8, 1916, in Iliff, Colo.; daughter of Minosuke and Tomi (Ogawa) Noguchi; married Ralph Brownlee Swain (an entomologist; deceased); married William K. Firmage, 1968; children: (first marriage) Tom Alfred, Ralph Adrian. *Education:* University of Colorado, B.F.A. 1938. *Residence:* Great Barrington, Mass.; and Sun City Center, Fla. (winter).

CAREER: Free-lance illustrator. School Nature League, New York, N.Y., staff artist, 1938-40; American School, Managua, Nicaragua, substitute teacher, 1951-53. *Member:* American Association of University Women (chairman of art group, Summit, N.J., 1960-63), New York Entomological Society, John Burroughs Association, Art Association (Gulfport, Miss.), Summit Nature Club.

WRITINGS—Self-illustrated: *Insects in Their World,* Garden City, 1955; *Plants of Woodland and Wayside,* Garden City, 1958; *First Guide to Insects,* Doubleday, 1964.

Illustrator: Ralph Brownlee Swain, *The Insect Guide,* Doubleday, 1948; Dorothy Shuttlesworth, *Story of Rocks,* Garden City, 1956; Shuttlesworth, *Story of Spiders,* Garden City, 1959; *Nature Guide: Rocky Mountains,* Golden Press, 1964; *The Story of Ants,* Garden City, 1964; E. Klots, *Field Guide to Fresh Water Life,* Putnam, 1966; Shuttlesworth, *All Kinds of Bees,* Random House, 1967; Shuttlesworth, *Natural Partnership,* Doubleday, 1969. Contributor to *Merit Students Encyclopedia* and *Crowell-Colliers Encyclopedia.*

SIDELIGHTS: "I was always more of an illustrator than an author," Su Zan Swain told *CA.* "The neatness of every structure so well adapted to its particular life habits and fitting into its habitat brought me closer to Our Creator. I wanted to share the wonders with my readers who were not seeing what I was seeing through the microscope."

AVOCATIONAL INTERESTS: Travel (made a five-month round-the-world trip in 1965 and an eight-month trip in 1972), studying Spanish and Japanese, weaving, sewing, oil painting, conservation, Japanese Sumie, sculpture, and collecting records, especially classical music.

* * *

SWARTZ, Harry (Felix) 1911-
(Martin Moreno, H. Felix Valcoe)

PERSONAL: Born June 21, 1911, in Detroit, Mich.; son of Isaac and Anne (Srere) Swartz; married Eva Sutton, October 3, 1942; children: Mark Sutton. *Education:* University of Michigan, A.B., 1930, M.D., 1933; specialization in allergy at New York University Medical Center, 1936-38. *Home:* Apartado 752, Cuernavaca, Morelos, Mexico.

CAREER: Michael Reese Hospital, Chicago, Ill., intern, 1933-35; general practice of medicine in Detroit, Mich., 1935-36; private practice in allergy in New York, N.Y., 1938-71; *Investigacion Medica Internacional,* Mexico, editor-in-chief, 1974—. *Military service:* U.S. Army, Medical Corps, chief of allergy department at Tilton General Hospital, Fort Dix, N.J., 1942-46; became major.

MEMBER: American Academy of Allergy (fellow), American College of Allergists (fellow), American Association of Clinical Immunology and Allergy (fellow), American Association for the Advancement of Science, World Future Society, Royal Society of Health (fellow), Medical Society of the County of New York, Phi Beta Kappa, Phi Kappa Phi, Alpha Omega Alpha.

WRITINGS: Allergy: What It Is and What to Do about It, Rutgers University Press, 1949, 2nd revised and enlarged edition, Ungar, 1966; *Your Hay Fever and What to Do about It,* Funk, 1951, revised edition, Ungar, 1962; *The Allergic Child,* Coward, 1954; *Intelligent Layman's Medical Dictionary,* Ungar, 1955, enlarged edition published as *Layman's Medical Dictionary,* Ungar, 1963; *How to Master Your Allergy,* Nelson, 1961, published as *The Allergy Guide Book,* Ungar, 1966; *Your Body* (juvenile), Whitman Publishing, 1962; (editor) *Simplified Medical Dictionary,* Medical Economics, 1977; *Prescribers Handbook of Therapeutic Drugs,* Medical Economics, 1981.

Editor of health book series for the lay reader, published by Coward, 1952-53; translator from Spanish to English of biomedical material. Contributor of short stories, under pseudonym H. Felix Valcoe, and articles to medical journals and popular magazines. Scientific advisor, *Mundo Medico.*

WORK IN PROGRESS: The Mercy Chain of Children, a historical novel about Dr. Xavier Balmis; *The Two Masks of Dr. White,* under pseudonym Martin Moreno; an English-Spanish medical dictionary, for Saunders.

SIDELIGHTS: Harry Swartz writes: "To supplement a meager income from medical practice in the late thirties when the depression was still on, I began to write mystery shorts for *Detective Fiction Weekly,* one of the Munsey chain. I thought it wise to use a pseudonym, for surely no one could want to be a patient of a physician who writes murder stories. I did 600 typescript pages of a serious novel that I called *These the Roots.* The Whitlesey (?) House editor (a nice lady) called it vomit and not a novel. Then came the war (my war) and after that two more unpublished novels, and I got down to fact writing. In 1949, *Allergy: What It Is and What to Do about It* was published by Rutgers University Press. Earl Schenk Meyers was director and believed that even a university press ought to operate in the black. The book hit local best-seller lists for several weeks, was translated into a number of languages, [and] was taken over by Ungar who kept it alive until about 1979.

"After putting together or editing two specialized medical dictionaries, I am now at work on a real *obra* that will tax whatever lexicographic and writing skills I may have. This work is projected as a 40,000 English-entry medical dictionary, with the entries spelled out in Spanish for proper English pronunciation and definitions in Spanish. I have suggested a cassette for the English sounds not possible to spell out in Spanish, or a disk. No response [regarding] this suggestion from the publisher yet. I hate the International Phonetic Alphabet, and I know a great number of people who feel as I do. It is clumsy, strange and has to be looked up every time a symbol is run across. Surely nobody keeps such an artificial system in memory!

"Well, no Conan Doyle or Sammy Johnson, I keep on. Perhaps I may properly call myself an author, but a writer? I put words together as editorials, articles, monographs, press releases, promotional pieces and fall into a vacuum when I'm not doing it. I can guess at the underlying psychodynamics, but its their manifestation that keeps my motor running. Exploration of motivation can wait for another, a later, time.''

*   *   *

SWEENEY, James Johnson 1900-

PERSONAL: Born May 30, 1900, in Brooklyn, N.Y.; son of Patrick M. and Mary (Johnson) Sweeney; married Laura Harden, May 17, 1927; children: Ann (Mrs. Stephen B. Baxter), Sean, Siadhal, Tadhg, Ciannait Sweeney Tait. *Education:* Georgetown University, A.B., 1922; additional study at Jesus College, Cambridge, 1922-24, Sorbonne, University of Paris, 1925, and University of Siena, 1926. *Home:* 120 East End Ave., New York, N.Y. 10028.

CAREER: New York correspondent, *Chicago Evening Post,* 1931-32; director of Twentieth Century Painting and Sculpture exhibit, University of Chicago, 1933-34; New York University, New York City, lecturer, Institute of Fine Arts, 1935-40; Museum of Modern Art, New York City, director of painting and sculpture, 1945-46; Solomon R. Guggenheim Museum, New York City, director, 1952-60; Museum of Fine Arts of Houston, Houston, Tex., director, 1961-68, consulting director, 1968—. Resident scholar, University of Georgia, Athens, 1950-51. Lecturer in fine arts at Salzburg Seminar in American Studies, 1947-1948, and Harvard University, 1961; lecturer at other American universities and at museums in the United States and Canada. Director of art exhibitions, 1933-52, including African Negro Art exhibit at Museum of Modern Art, 1935, exhibitions of the work of Joan Miro, 1941, Alexander Calder, 1943, Alfred Stieglitz, 1947, and Picasso, 1949, all at Art Gallery of Toronto, Masterpieces of the Twentieth Century exhibit in Paris and London, 1952, Alexander Calder exhibit at Tate Gallery, London, 1962, and Twelve American Painters exhibit in Dublin, Ireland, 1963. Member of board of directors of Religious Art Center of America, American Academy in Rome, 1960, American Irish Foundation, and of art advisory committees at Bennington College, Phillips Academy at Andover, and numerous other institutions or organizations. Member of National Council on the Arts, 1965, and Arts Council, Dublin, 1966; member of advisory panel, Studio International, 1966—.

MEMBER: International Association of Art Critics (vice-president, 1948-57; president, 1957-63; director, 1964—), Edward MacDowell Association (director, 1942-62; president, 1955-62; counselor, 1963—), Federation Internationale du Film d'Art (president d'honneur, 1957—), Association of Art Museum Directors, Mediaeval Academy of America (member of council, 1966), Societe Europeenne de Culture, Royal Society of Arts, Patronato Mondiale del Libro (Padua, Italy), Royal Society of Antiquaries of Ireland (fellow), Yeats Association (honorary member); Century, Brook, Grolier, and Players Clubs (all New York); Cosmos Club (Washington, D.C.). *Awards, honors:* Chevalier, Legion d'Honneur, Paris, 1955; officer, Ordre des Arts et des Lettres, Paris, 1959; Art in America award, 1963. Academic: D.F.A. from Grinnell College, 1957, University of Michigan, 1960, University of Notre Dame, 1961, and University of Buffalo, 1962; L.H.D. from Rollins College, 1960, College of the Holy Cross, 1960, University of Miami, 1963, and Georgetown University, 1963; Arts D. from Ripon College, 1960; LL.D. from National University of Ireland.

WRITINGS: Plastic Redirections in XXth Century Painting, University of Chicago Press, 1934; (editor) *African Negro Art,* Museum of Modern Art, 1935, reprinted, Arno, 1966; *Joan Miro,* Museum of Modern Art, 1941, reprinted, Arno, 1969; *Alexander Calder,* Museum of Modern Art, 1943, 2nd edition,

1951, reprinted, Arno, 1969; (editor and author of introduction) *Three Young Rats,* Curt Valentin, 1944, 2nd edition, Museum of Modern Art, 1967; *Stuart Davis,* Museum of Modern Art, 1945; *Marc Chagall,* Museum of Modern Art, 1946, reprinted, Arno, 1969; *Henry Moore,* Museum of Modern Art, 1947; (author of introduction) *Hans Hartung,* D. Verlag (Munich), 1949; (with Paul Radin) *African Folk Tales and Sculpture,* Bollingen Foundation, 1952, 2nd edition, 1964; *Burri,* Obelisco (Rome), 1955; *The Miro Atmosphere,* Editorial Rog (Barcelona), 1959; (with Jose Luis Sert) *Antoni Gaudi,* Praeger, 1960; (author of introduction) *Afro,* [Rome], 1961; *Irish Illuminated Manuscripts,* Collins & World, 1965; *Photographs by Ugo Mulas,* New York Graphic Society, 1966; *Vision and Image: A Way of Seeing,* Simon & Schuster, 1968; *African Sculpture,* Princeton University Press, 1970; *Five American Sculptors,* Museum of Modern Art, 1971; *Contemporary Spanish Painters: Miro and After,* International Exhibitions Foundation, 1975.

Author of commentary for film "Henry Moore," 1948, and English commentary for film "Images Medievales," 1952; also author, with Richard de Rochemont, of commentary for film "The Road to the Olmec Head," 1963. Periodic contributor to *Irish Statesman,* 1924-32, and *New York Times,* 1929-33; also contributor to *Harper's Bazaar, Vogue, Kenyon Review, Poetry, Cahiers d'Art, House and Garden, Nation, Architectural Forum,* and other magazines in this country and abroad. Associate editor, *transition,* 1935-39; advisory editor, *Partisan Review,* 1948-63; director, *Burlington* (London), 1951-61; contributing critic, *New Republic,* 1952-53; member of comite internationale de redaction, *Quadrum* (Brussels), 1956—; member of comite de redaction, *Prisme des Arts* (Paris), 1956-59.†

*   *   *

SYME, (Neville) Ronald 1913-

PERSONAL: Born March 13, 1913, in Lancashire, England; son of David Godfrey and Ida Florence (Kerr) Syme; married Marama Amoa, February 12, 1960; children: Florence Tia te Pa Tua. *Education:* Attended school in England and New Zealand. *Politics:* Conservative. *Home:* Rarotonga, Cook Islands, South Pacific Ocean.

CAREER: British Merchant Service, cadet and officer, 1930-34, gunner, 1939-40; reporter and foreign correspondent, 1934-39; John Westhouse & Peter Lunn Ltd., London, England, assistant editor, 1946-48; British Road Federation, London, public relations officer, 1948-50; free-lance writer. *Military service:* British Army, Intelligence Corps, 1940-45; became major. *Member:* Authors Society (England). *Awards, honors:* Boys' Clubs of America medallist award, 1951, for *Bay of the North.*

WRITINGS—Nonfiction; published by Morrow, except as indicated: *Full Fathom Five,* Peter Lunn, 1946; *Hakluyt's Sea Stories,* Heinemann, 1948.

Bay of the North: The Story of Pierre Radisson, 1950, reprinted, 1967; *The Story of British Roads,* British Road Federation, 1951; *Cortes of Mexico,* 1951 (published in England as *Cortez: Conqueror of Mexico,* Hodder & Stoughton, 1952), reprinted, 1967; *Champlain of the St. Lawrence,* 1952; *Columbus: Finder of the New World,* 1952; *La Salle of the Mississippi,* 1952, reprinted, 1969; *The Story of Britain's Highways,* Pitman, 1952; *Magellan: First around the World,* 1953; *The Windward Islands,* Pitman, 1953; *John Smith of Virginia,* 1954, new edition, University of London Press, 1965; *The Story of New Zealand,* Pitman, 1954; *Henry Hudson,* 1955 (published in England as *Hudson of the Valley*, Hodder & Stoughton, 1955); *The Cook Islands*, Pitman, 1955; *Balboa: Finder of the Pacific*, 1956; *De Soto: Finder of the Mississippi*, 1957; *The Man Who Discovered the Amazon*, 1958; *Cartier: Finder of the St. Lawrence*, 1958; *On Foot to the Arctic: The Story of Samuel Hearne*, 1959 (published in England as *Trail to the North*, Hodder & Stoughton, 1959); *Vasco Da Gamma: Sailor towards the Sunrise*, 1959.

Captain Cook: Pacific Explorer, 1960; *Francis Drake: Sailor of the Unknown Seas*, 1961; *Walter Raleigh*, 1962; *The Young Nelson*, Parrish, 1962, Roy, 1963; *First Man to Cross America: The Story of Cabeza de Vaca*, 1962; *African Traveler: The Story of Mary Kingsley*, 1962; *Francisco Pizarro: Finder of Peru*, 1963; *Invaders and Invasions*, Batsford, 1964, Norton, 1965; *Nigerian Pioneer: The Story of Mary Slessor*, 1964; *Alexander Mackenzie: Canadian Explorer*, 1964; *Sir Henry Morgan: Buccaneer*, 1965; *Quesada of Colombia*, 1966; *William Penn: Founder of Pennsylvania*, 1966; *Francisco Coronado and the Seven Cities of Gold*, 1967; *Garibaldi: The Man Who Made a Nation*, 1967; *Bolivar: The Liberator*, 1968; *Captain John Paul Jones: America's Fighting Seaman*, 1968; *Amerigo Vespucci: Scientist and Sailor*, 1969; *Frontenac of New France*, 1969.

Benedict Arnold: Traitor to the Revolution, 1970; *Vancouver: Explorer of the Pacific Coast*, 1970; *Toussaint: The Black Liberator*, 1971; *The Travels of Captain Cook*, McGraw, 1971; *Zapata: Mexican Rebel*, 1971; *John Cabot and His Son Sebastian*, 1972; *Juarez: The Founder of Modern Mexico*, 1972; *Fur Trader of the North: The Story of Pierre de la Verendrye*, 1973; *Verrazano: Explorer of the Atlantic Coast*, 1973; *John Charles Fremont: The Last American Explorer*, 1974; *Marquette and Joliet: Voyagers on the Mississippi*, 1974; *Isles of the Frigate Bird* (autobiographical), M. Joseph, 1975; *Geronimo: The Fighting Apache*, 1975; *Osceola: Seminole Leader*, 1976; *The Lagoon Is Lonely Now*, Millwood Press, 1978.

Fiction; published by Hodder & Stoughton, except as indicated: *That Must Be Julian*, Peter Lunn, 1947; *Julian's River War*, Heinemann, 1949; *Ben of the Barrier*, Evans Brothers, 1949; *I, Mungo Park*, Burke Publishing, 1951; *I, Captain Anson: My Voyage around the World*, Burke Publishing, 1952; *The Settlers of Carriacou*, 1953; *I, Gordon of Khartoum*, Burke Publishing, 1953; *Gipsy Michael*, 1954; *They Came to an Island*, 1955; *Isle of Revolt*, 1956; *Ice Fighter*, 1956; *The Amateur Company*, 1957; *The Great Canoe*, 1957; *The Forest Fighters*, 1958; *River of No Return*, 1958; *The Spaniards Came at Dawn*, 1959; *Trail to the North*, 1959; *Thunder Knoll*, 1960; *The Mountainy Men*, 1961; *Coast of Danger*, 1961; *Nose-Cap Astray*, 1962; *Two Passengers for Spanish Fork*, 1963; *Switch Points as Kamlin*, 1964; *The Dunes and the Diamonds*, 1964; *The Missing Witness*, 1965; *The Saving of the Fair East Wind*, Dent, 1967.

SIDELIGHTS: Ronald Syme writes: "My native country is Ireland, where every second fellow you meet is a natural storyteller, an amateur historian, a musician . . . and invariably an individualist. It was only natural that I followed suit, particularly as there was a splendid library in our eighteenth-century home where I read with delight numerous volumes that any modern child psychiatrist would unhesitatingly describe as totally unfit for youthful minds.

"Kipling wrote of 'the cat that walked by itself in the wild, wet woods,' so my inherited streak of independence caused me to do the same. I had no wish to spend my life working in the unchanging company of others in a totally conformist community. I wanted to get out on my own and be on my own.

Writing seemed to be the handiest magic carpet in order to achieve my aim.

"When I took myself off from Europe thirty years ago to live on a (then) remote South Sea island, my friends and family regarded me as an impossible eccentric. But the leprechaun I always envisage as an invisible but friendly counsellor on my shoulder warned me that tough times were coming to the Western technological world. So I settled down on that remote island, married a shrewd and lovely Polynesian girl who had never heard of shampoos and/or conditioners but had a mass of glowing black hair that reached to her knees, and wrote books. Life was quiet but pleasant and the environment was superb. Social and/or financial pressures did not exist and neither did any form of commercial advertising. One acquired a sensation of being able to relax, have endless time to think and dream, and no need to live behind locked doors and burglar alarms.

"Six mornings a week, I sit on my verandah overlooking a subtropical garden of flowers and distant mountains. While drinking a strong mug of tea, I turn over in my mind the part of the story I will be writing on that particular day. After breakfast, I start work at nine a.m. and go right through until twelve noon. If the story has been running well, another thousand words of manuscript are generally completed by then. During the afternoons, I usually take myself off to fish on the nearby reef and review in my mind what I have written that morning. If a sudden weakness or *non sequitur* occurs to me, I correct my pages in the evening. If all has gone well, I never touch them again until the next morning.

"The thought has never occurred to me as to what I may/may not achieve by my writing. I was utterly content with the pleasure of being able to move in and out of the lives of others for a brief time while I was recreating their invariably remarkable careers. By the time I grew weary of them, or perhaps their spirits of me, the book was completed and I was already thinking of some other possible character.. Once a book of mine is off the printing presses, I have lost all interest in it and remain interested merely in the royalties accruing to me. But in the South Pacific where I live, money takes second place to one's enjoyment of the natural things of life, which is probably the main reason why I live there.

"Surviving friends of mine [back in Europe] write wistful letters to say how much they long to be away from it all and out in the South Pacific where smog, pollution, drugs and violence are unknown. Consequently I have a greater affection for that leprechaun than ever. Being of pure Irish origin, however, he has never cautioned me to take myself or my work more seriously and to play a more competitive role in the highly commercialised and tough world of authorship today. If ever he did so, I'd tell him to shut up. Authorship has provided me with a good and carefree life in my own unambitious way. I would dearly love to share one day the magnificent epitaph carved on Robert Louis Stevenson's grave in Samoa: 'Under the wide and starry sky,/ Dig the grave and let me lie./ Glad did I live and glad did I die,/ And I laid me down with a will./ This be the verse you carve for me: "Here he lies where he longed to be./ Home is the sailor, home from the sea,/ And the hunter home from the hill." ' "

BIOGRAPHICAL/CRITICAL SOURCES: May Hill Arbuthnot, *Children and Books*, 3rd edition, Scott, Foresman, 1964; *The Children's Bookshelf*, Bantam, 1965; *Books for Children, 1960-1965*, American Library Association, 1966; *New York Times Book Review*, March 16, 1969; Ronald Syme, *Isles of the Frigate Bird* (autobiographical), M. Joseph, 1975.

SYRKIN, Marie 1899-

PERSONAL: Born March 22, 1899, in Bern, Switzerland; came to United States, 1907; naturalized U.S. citizen, 1915; daughter of Nachman and Batya (Osnos) Syrkin; married Charles Reznikoff (a writer), May 27, 1930 (died, 1976); children: David Bodansky. *Education:* Cornell University, B.A., 1920, M.A., 1922. *Politics:* Socialist Zionist. *Religion:* Jewish. *Agent:* Curtis Brown Ltd., 575 Madison Ave., New York, N.Y. 10022. *Home:* 1008 Second St., Apt. 201, Santa Monica, Calif. 90403.

CAREER: Teacher of English in New York City high schools, 1925-50; Brandeis University, Waltham, Mass., 1950—, began as associate professor, professor of English, professor emerita, 1966–. Editor, Herzl Press, beginning 1971. *Member:* World Zionist Movement (member of executive board, 1965-69), Labor Zionist Movement of the United States (honorary president, 1965-70), American Association of University Professors, American Professors for Peace in the Middle East. *Awards, honors:* Hayim Greenberg Prize for *Way of Valor;* Twenty-fifth Anniversary of Israel Award, 1973; Myrtle Wreath, Hadassah, 1976.

WRITINGS: The Communists and the Arab Problem (pamphlet), League for Labor Palestine, c. 1936; *Why a Jewish Commonwealth?,* Political and Education Committee of Hadassah, c. 1944; *Your School, Your Children: A Teacher Looks at What's Wrong with Our Schools,* L. B. Fischer, 1944; *Blessed Is the Match: The Story of Jewish Resistance,* Knopf, 1947, reprinted, Jewish Publication Society, 1977; *Way of Valor: A Biography of Golda Myerson,* Sharon Books, 1955; *Nachman Syrkin, Socialist Zionist: A Biographical Memoir,* Herzl, 1961; *Golda Meir: Woman with a Cause,* Putnam, 1963, revised edition published as *Golda Meir: Israel's Leader,* 1969; (editor and author of introduction) *Hayim Greenberg Anthology,* Wayne State University Press, 1968; (editor) Golda Meir, *A Land of Our Own: An Oral Autobiography,* Putnam, 1973 (published in England as *Golda Meir Speaks Out,* Weidenfeld & Nicolson, 1973); *Gleanings: A Diary in Verse,* Rhythms Press, 1979; *The State of the Jews* (collection of previously published essays), New Republic Books, 1980. Also translator of poetry for anthologies. Contributor to periodicals, including *Nation, Midstream, Commentary, Dissent, Saturday Review, New York Times Magazine,* and *New Republic.* Editor, *Jewish Frontier,* 1950-72; member of editorial board, *Midstream.*

SIDELIGHTS: A journalist, editor, poet, and teacher, Marie Syrkin has been an ardent Zionist since childhood, when her father, Nachman Syrkin, helped establish the Labor Zionist movement. In *The State of the Jews,* Syrkin describes many facets of the Jewish experience from the 1930s to the present. Commenting on the book in the *Washington Post Book World,* Elie Weisel says that Syrkin's reporting "reflects a rare journalistic talent. Certain passages are astonishing. She describes the fall of the old city of Jerusalem in a style in which emotion and precision are beautifully balanced. Her interviews with Jewish children, still living in that hell, will appall you. To talk with a child of five or six who has seen dead bodies, dead bodies without end, who has seen *death,* one has to know what tone to adopt—and Marie Syrkin knew."

Julius Weinberg writes in *Commentary* that despite the range of topics in the book, the essays "are dominated by two principal concerns: the survival and security of the state of Israel, and the welfare of the Jewish people in the United States and elsewhere." Weinberg believes that the pieces "concerning the nature of the Zionist enterprise and Israel's relationship to its Arab neighbors provide an effective antidote to the lies currently gaining strength in the assembly halls of the United Nations, among Western leaders, and, unhappily, in some segments of the American Jewish community." Weinberg also claims that Syrkin's "responses to Hannah Arendt, Arnold Toynbee, I. F. Stone, and Vanessa Redgrave . . . are extremely well done; their scholarship is sound and their passion bracing."

BIOGRAPHICAL/CRITICAL SOURCES: New York Herald Tribune Weekly Book Review, August 31, 1947; *New York Times,* September 21, 1947; *Christian Science Monitor,* January 10, 1964; *New York Times Book Review,* January 26, 1964; *Commentary,* July, 1964, September, 1969, November, 1980; *Washington Post Book World,* August 3, 1980.

T

TAE-YONG, Ro
See RUTT, Richard

* * *

TALAMANTES, Florence Williams 1931-

PERSONAL: Born August 15, 1931, in Alliance, Ohio; daughter of Ernest Martin and Addie (Smith) Williams; married Eduardo Talamantes, March, 1970. *Education:* Mt. Union College, B.A., 1954; University of Cincinnati, M.A., 1956, Ph.D., 1961; graduate study at Indiana University, 1957-58. *Residence:* San Diego, Calif. *Office:* Department of Spanish, San Diego State University, San Diego, Calif. 92182.

CAREER: Teacher of Spanish and English in Windham, Ohio, 1954-55, and in Cincinnati, Ohio, 1956-57; Lake Forest College, Lake Forest, Ill., assistant professor of Spanish, 1961-62; San Diego State University, San Diego, Calif., assistant professor, 1962-67, associate professor of Spanish, 1967—. *Member:* Modern Language Association of America, American Association of Teachers of Spanish and Portuguese, American Federation of Teachers, National Organization for Women, Alpha Mu Gamma, Sigma Delta Pi. *Awards, honors:* San Diego State University faculty research grant, 1974.

WRITINGS: (Editor and author of introduction) Jose Maria de Pereda, *Don Gonzalo Gonzalez de la Gonzalera,* Costa-Amic (Mexico City), 1972; *Alfonsina Storni: Argentina's Feminist Poet,* San Marcos Press, 1975; (editor and translator) *Alfonsina Storni: Poemas de Amor* (Spanish text with English translation), Costa-Amic (Mexico City), 1977; (editor and author of introduction) *Jose Maria de Pereda: Selections from Sotileza and Penas Arriba,* University Press of America, 1978; (editor and translator) *Ramon Sender: Selecciones de Poesia Lirica y Aforistica* (Spanish text with English translation), El sol de California, 1979. Contributor of articles and book reviews to periodicals, including *Virginia Woolf Quarterly, Mosaic,* and *Polish Review. Virginia Woolf Quarterly,* member of editorial board, 1972-74, acting editor, 1973, co-editor, 1975—.

WORK IN PROGRESS: Research on Hispanic elements in the works of Joseph Conrad, in collaboration with Suzanne Henig.

* * *

TAYLOR, Joe Gray 1920-

PERSONAL: Born February 14, 1920, in Mason, Tenn.; son of Basil Gray (a carpenter) and Lennie Fee (Shinault) Taylor; married Helen Eva Friday, April 18, 1945; children: Joe Gray, Jr., Harriette Eva, Edward Coleman. *Education:* Memphis State University, B.S., 1947; Louisiana State University, M.A., 1948, Ph.D., 1951. *Politics:* Democrat. *Religion:* Presbyterian. *Home:* 712 Contour, Lake Charles, La. 70605. *Office:* Department of History, McNeese State University, Ryan St., Lake Charles, La. 70609.

CAREER: Teacher in one-room public school in Corona, Tenn., 1939-41; Nicholls Junior College (now Nicholls State University), Thibodaux, La., instructor, 1950-52, assistant professor, 1952-53, associate professor of history, 1958-63; Air University, Research Studies Institute, Maxwell Air Force Base, Ala., instructor, 1953-54, assistant professor of military history, 1954-57; Southeastern Louisiana University, Hammond, assistant professor of social science, 1957-58; McNeese State University, Lake Charles, La., professor of history, 1963—, chairman of department, 1968—. Instructor at Memphis State College (now Memphis State University), summer, 1947. *Military service:* U.S. Army Air Forces, bombardier-navigator, 1942-45; became first lieutenant; received Distinguished Flying Cross, Air Medal, three battle stars.

MEMBER: Organization of American Historians, American Association for State and Local History, Southern Historical Association, Red River Valley Historical Association, Louisiana Historical Association (president, 1967), Phi Kappa Phi, Phi Alpha Theta.

WRITINGS: Development of Night Air Operations, 1941-1952, Montgomery, 1953; *Close Air Support in the War against Japan,* Montgomery, 1954; *Pre-Invasion Air Bombardment: Pacific Theater, 1942-1943,* Montgomery, 1954; *Air Interdiction in China,* Montgomery, 1956; *Air Supply in the Burma Campaigns,* Montgomery, 1957; *Freedom versus Tyranny,* privately printed, 1962; *Negro Slavery in Louisiana,* Louisiana Historical Association, 1963; *Louisiana: A Student's Guide to Localized History,* Teachers College Press, 1966; (with others) *Rivers and Bayous of Louisiana,* Louisiana Education Research Association, 1968; *Louisiana Reconstructed: 1863-1877,* Louisiana State University Press, 1974; *Louisiana: A Bicentennial History,* Norton, 1976; (editor) George Hepworth, *The Whip, the Hoe, and the Sword,* Louisiana State University Press, 1979; (contributor) Robert R. MacDonald, John Randolph, and Edward F. Haas, editors, *Louisiana's Black Heritage,* Louisiana State Museum, 1980; (contributor) Otto Olsen, editor, *The Reconstruction and Redemption of the South: An Assess-*

ment, Louisiana State University Press, 1980; *Eating, Drinking, and Visiting in the South: A Short History,* Louisiana State University Press, 1982. Contributor to professional journals. Editor, *McNeese Review,* 1965-67; member of editorial board, *Journal of Southern History,* 1976-80.

WORK IN PROGRESS: A History of McNeese State University.

AVOCATIONAL INTERESTS: Fishing, hunting, bridge, gardening.

* * *

TEMPLE, Paul
    See DURBRIDGE, Francis (Henry)
    and McCONNELL, James Douglas Rutherford

* * *

TERRY, William
    See HARKNETT, Terry

* * *

TETHER, (Cynthia) Graham 1950-

PERSONAL: Born September 14, 1950, in White Plains, N.Y.; daughter of Willard L. (an investment counselor) and Doris A. (a public health nurse and teacher; maiden name, Bouton) Tether. *Education:* Mount Holyoke College, B.A. (with distinction) and teaching certificate, 1972; New York University, graduate study, 1974; Columbia University, M.B.A., 1980. *Religion:* Protestant. *Home:* 11 DeWitt Ave., Bronxville, N.Y. 10708. *Office:* Data Processing Division Headquarters, International Business Machines Corp., 1133 Westchester Ave., White Plains, N.Y. 10604.

CAREER: Citibank, New York City, research assistant, 1971; News Election Service, New York City, assistant to payroll manager, 1972; free-lance writer, 1972-73; Harper & Row Publishers, Inc., New York City, editorial assistant in trade department, 1974-78; International Business Machines Corp., financial analyst, 1980—. Assistant concertmistress for All New York State Orchestra; violinist in chamber ensembles. *Member:* Daughters of the American Revolution. *Awards, honors:* Lincoln Center award for instrumental music, 1968; first prize from Society of Children's Book Writers, 1973.

*WRITINGS—*For children: *Fudge Dream Supreme,* J. Philip O'Hara, 1975; *The Hair Book,* Random House, 1979; *Skunk and Possum,* Houghton, 1979. Contributor to national magazines, including *My Weekly Reader* and *Golden Magazines.*

WORK IN PROGRESS: A book for children, *Danny Dunce.*

* * *

THALER, M. N.
    See KERNER, Fred

* * *

THAMES, C. H.
    See MARLOWE, Stephen

* * *

THAYER, Jane
    See WOOLLEY, Catherine

THOMAS, Heather Smith 1944-

PERSONAL: Born February 13, 1944, in Kenosha, Wis.; daughter of Don Ian (a minister) and Betty (Moser) Smith; married Lynn Thomas (a rancher), March 5, 1966; children: Michael, Andrea. *Education:* University of Puget Sound, B.A., 1966. *Politics:* Republican. *Religion:* Methodist. *Address:* Box 215, Salmon, Idaho 83467.

CAREER: Rancher in Salmon, Idaho, 1967—. *Member:* Salmon River Trail Ride Association (secretary, 1974-81).

WRITINGS: A Horse in Your Life: A Guide for the New Owner, A. S. Barnes, 1966; *Your Horse and You,* A. S. Barnes, 1970; *Horses: Their Breeding, Care, and Training,* A. S. Barnes, 1974; *Horses: A Golden Exploring Earth Book,* Western Publishing, 1976; *The Wild Horse Controversy,* A. S. Barnes, 1979. Contributor to *Horse and Horseman, Horseman, Horse of Course, Western Livestock Reporter, Quarter Horse Digest, Cattleman, American Horseman,* and other horse and farm periodicals.

WORK IN PROGRESS: A book of ranch stories dealing with livestock anecdotes; a book on the coyote controversy and the issue over predator control; a novel dealing with competitive long-distance riding.

SIDELIGHTS: ''Animals have always been my great love,'' Heather Smith Thomas told *CA,* ''and I continue to learn all about them that I can. My philosophy in writing is to share with readers—especially those who are also interested in horses or livestock—things that I have learned and experienced, which might make their own care or training of animals easier. I have a great interest in veterinary medicine (I almost became a veterinarian but went into ranching instead), and much of my writing deals with putting good medical information into terms that the layman can easily understand; I consider myself a sort of 'bridge' between the veterinary profession and the horse or livestock owner.

''During the last six years I have also been writing on several controversial environmental issues, trying to help clarify these. I've done a great deal of research on the wild horse issue, writing many articles, and a book, *The Wild Horse Controversy,* which takes an in-depth look at the history of feral horses and burros in the West, and the development of public land-use problems and controversies in which these animals have played a role. The book is now being hailed as the most complete and authoritative work on the wild horse issue. At present I am doing research on the coyote, for a book on the coyote controversy—the issue over predator control. Most of these very emotional issues are quite complex, and often very misunderstood because they cannot be simply broken down into black-and-white. I firmly feel that if people can become aware of the background and facts in these issues, they will be better able to understand the complexities, the reasons behind opposing views, and perhaps come to a broader understanding of the issue. This is what must happen before some of these issues can be resolved. If I can dig out the history, the facts, the complexities, and put them in a form people will enjoy reading, I feel I have perhaps helped to be part of the solution instead of part of the problem.''

* * *

THOMAS, J(ames) D(avid) 1910-

PERSONAL: Born July 20, 1910, in Holliday, Tex.; son of William Albert (in clerical work) and Angie Belle (Wisdom)

Thomas; married Mary Katherine Payne, February 22, 1931; children: Deborah Gayle Thomas Fish (deceased), Hannah Belle (Mrs. Dwayne Kissick), John Paul. *Education:* Attended University of Texas, 1926-28; Abilene Christian College (now University), A.B., 1943; Southern Methodist University, M.A., 1944; University of Chicago, Ph.D., 1957. *Home:* 1334 Ruswood, Abilene, Tex. 79601. *Office address:* Abilene Christian University Station, Box 7768, Abilene, Tex. 79699.

CAREER: Clergyman of Church of Christ, 1937—; City of Lubbock, Lubbock, Tex., assistant city manager, 1939-42; minister in Chicago, Ill., 1945-49; Abilene Christian University, Abilene, Tex., associate professor, 1949-57, professor of Bible, 1957—, head of department, 1970-79, lectureship director, 1952-70. Elder of University Church of Christ, Abilene, 1955—. Lecturer in Japan, Korea, Taiwan, Hong Kong, and the Philippines, 1958. Publisher, owner, manager, and editor of Biblical Research Press, Abilene, Tex., 1958—. President of corporation board of *Restoration Quarterly,* beginning 1974. *Awards, honors:* Century Book Award, Family Book Club, 1966, for *Facts and Faith,* Volume I; Christian journalism award, *Twentieth Century Christian,* 1966; named outstanding educator by *Twentieth Century Christian,* 1981.

WRITINGS—Published by Biblical Research Press: *We Be Brethren,* 1958; *Evolution and Antiquity,* 1961; *Facts and Faith,* Volume I, 1966, Volume II, 1980; *The Spirit and Spirituality,* 1967, revised edition, 1981; *Self Study Guide to Galatians and Romans,* 1971; *Self Study Guide to Corinthians,* 1972; *Heaven's Window,* 1975; *What Lack We Yet,* 1977; *The Biblical Doctrine of Grace,* 1979; *Divorce and Remarriage,* 1980. Editor, "Great Preachers of Today" and "20th-Century Sermons" series for Biblical Research Press; editor, "Sermons for Today" series, 1981—. Contributor to *Journal of Biblical Literature.* Member of editorial board, *Restoration Quarterly,* 1957-74; staff writer for *Gospel Advocate* and *Twentieth Century Christian.*

WORK IN PROGRESS: The Roots of Morality.

SIDELIGHTS: J. D. Thomas told *CA* that his motivation "is to teach Christians, primarily, so that they in turn may teach others. The time is short and the need is great. The masses do not have the intellectual grasp they should have on the basic issues and the meanings in life. Writing should be done as a contribution to the education of humanity in matters spiritual, for these are the important matters."

His first book, *We Be Brethren,* was written to help solve a problem of interpretation that had developed among his colleagues, and since he had had business experience, he decided to publish it himself. This launched his publishing career, which now includes seventy-five titles. Several of his books have been translated into other languages.

*   *   *

THORELLI, Hans B(irger)   1921-

PERSONAL: Born September 18, 1921, in Newark, N.J.; son of Hans W. R. (an executive) and Hetty Thorelli; married Sarah V. Scott, May 14, 1948; children: Irene Margareta, Thomas Harold. *Education:* University of Stockholm, M.A., 1944, LL.B., 1945, Ph.D., 1954; Northwestern University, graduate study, 1946-47. *Office:* Graduate School of Business, Indiana University, Bloomington, Ind. 47401.

CAREER: United Nations Secretariat, New York, N.Y., consultant, 1952; Industrial Council for Social and Economic Studies, Stockholm, Sweden, executive director, 1953-56; consultant to Marketing Services Division, General Electric Co.,

1956-59; University of Chicago, Chicago, Ill., professor of business administration, 1959-64; Indiana University at Bloomington, professor of business administration, 1964-72, E. W. Kelley Professor of Business Administration, 1972—, chairman of marketing department, 1966-69. Visiting professor, Stanford University, 1962, Institut pour l'Etude des Methodes de Direction de l'Enterprise, 1964-65, University of South Africa, 1967, 1973, and London Graduate School of Business Studies, 1969-70. Conductor of field survey of Latin American operations for Sears, Roebuck & Co., 1962. Member of consumer advisory committee, Federal Energy Office, 1973—; consultant to various corporations, including LaSalle Steel, Tower Oil, and Monsanto.

MEMBER: American Economic Association, American Marketing Association (vice-president of public policy, 1972-73), Academy of Management, Association for Consumer Research, Royal Academy of Engineering Sciences (Sweden; fellow). *Awards, honors:* Honorary docent, University of Stockholm, 1954; Ford Foundation faculty research fellowship, 1963; Consumer Research Institute research grant, 1970; Midwest Universities Consortium for International Affairs research grant, 1973; Rockefeller Foundation research scholar, 1980; Fahlbeck Foundation Medal, University of Lund, for outstanding treatise in the field of political science.

WRITINGS: The Federal Antitrust Policy of the United States—Origination of an American Tradition, Johns Hopkins Press, 1955; (contributor) Wroe Alderson and S. J. Shapiro, editors, *Marketing and the Computer,* Prentice-Hall, 1963; (with Robert L. Graves) *International Operations Simulation, with Comments on Design and Use of Management Games,* Free Press of Glencoe, 1963; (contributor) Alderson and Reavis Cox, editors, *Theory in Marketing,* new edition (Thorelli was not associated with earlier editions), Irwin, 1964.

(Editor) *International Marketing Strategy,* Penguin, 1973, 2nd edition (with Helmut Becker), Pergamon, 1980; (with wife, Sarah Thorelli) *Consumer Information Handbook,* Praeger, 1974; (with Becker and J. Engledow) *The Information Seekers: An International Study of Consumer Information and Advertising Image,* Ballinger, 1975; (with S. Thorelli) *Consumer Information Systems and Consumer Policy,* Ballinger, 1977; (editor) *Strategy Plus Structure Equals Performance: The Strategic Planning Imperative,* Indiana University Press, 1977; (with G. D. Senbell) *Consumer Emancipation and Economic Development: The Case of Thailand,* Jai Press, in press.

Author of monographs and articles in English and Swedish on industrial marketing and economic, political, and administrative problems. Member of editorial board, *Journal of Marketing Research,* 1966-72, *Industrial Marketing Management,* 1971—, and *Journal of Consumer Research,* 1980—.

*   *   *

THORNE, Ian
See MAY, Julian

*   *   *

THORNE, Jean Wright
See MAY, Julian

*   *   *

THORP, Roderick Mayne, Jr.   1936-

PERSONAL: Born September 1, 1936, in New York, N.Y.; son of Roderick Mayne and Irene (Rehill) Thorp; children:

Roderick Mayne, III, Stephen Philip. *Education:* City College (now City College of the City University of New York), B.A., 1957. *Agent:* Raines & Raines, 475 Fifth Ave., New York, N.Y. 10017.

CAREER: Writer. Ramapo College, Mahwah, N.J., associate professor of literature, 1971-76. *Awards, honors:* Theodore Goodman Memorial Short Story Award, 1957.

WRITINGS: Into the Forest, Random House, 1961; *The Detective,* Dial, 1966; *Dionysus,* Coward, 1969; (editor with Robert Blake) *The Music of Their Laughter,* Harper, 1970; (with Blake) *Wives: An Investigation,* M. Evans, 1971; *Slaves,* M. Evans, 1972; *The Circle of Love,* Putnam, 1974; *Westfield,* Crown, 1977; *Nothing Lasts Forever,* Norton, 1979; *Jenny and Barnum,* Doubleday, 1981. Contributor to popular magazines.

SIDELIGHTS: Roderick Thorp's *The Detective* has sold over three million copies. A movie adaptation starring Frank Sinatra was released in 1968 by Twentieth Century-Fox.

BIOGRAPHICAL/CRITICAL SOURCES: Atlantic, July, 1966; *Newsweek,* July 4, 1966, June 9, 1969; *New York Times Book Review,* July 10, 1966, September 19, 1971; *National Observer,* June 30, 1969; *Books & Bookmen,* September, 1969; *Christian Science Monitor,* July 23, 1970; *Book World,* July 26, 1970; *Saturday Review,* August 15, 1970.

* * *

THUM, Marcella

PERSONAL: Born in St. Louis, Mo.; daughter of Frank and Louise (Holle) Thum. *Education:* Washington University, St. Louis, Mo., B.A., 1948; University of California, Berkeley, M.L.S., 1954; Webster College, M.A., 1977. *Politics:* Democrat. *Religion:* Protestant. *Home:* 6507 Gramond Dr., St. Louis, Mo. 63123. *Agent:* Lurton Blassingame, 60 East 42nd St., New York, N.Y. 10017.

CAREER: Advertising copywriter in St. Louis, Mo., 1948-49; U.S. Army, Public Information Office, civilian writer on Okinawa, 1949-50, with historical division in Heidelberg and Karlsruhe, Germany, 1951-53; U.S. Air Force, civilian librarian in Korea, at Scott Air Force Base, Ill., and at Schofield Barracks and Hickam Air Force Base, Hawaii, 1954-60; Affton Senior High School, Affton, Mo., school librarian, 1962-67; Meramec Community College, Kirkwood, Mo., reference librarian, 1968-79; Scott Air Force Base, Ill., AOS librarian, 1979—. *Member:* American Library Association, Missouri Writer's Guild, St. Louis Writer's Guild. *Awards, honors:* Dodd, Mead Librarian and Teacher Prize Competition award, 1964, for *Mystery at Crane's Landing;* "Edgar" award for best juvenile mystery, Mystery Writers of America, 1964, for *Mystery at Crane's Landing;* Missouri Writer's Guild award for best juvenile, 1966, for *Treasure of Crazy Quilt Farm;* American Library Association notable children's book award, 1975, for *Exploring Black America.*

WRITINGS: Mystery at Crane's Landing, Dodd, 1964; *Treasure of Crazy Quilt Farm,* Watts, 1965; *Anne of the Sandwich Islands,* Dodd, 1967; *Librarian with Wings,* Dodd, 1967; *Secret of the Sunken Treasure,* Dodd, 1969; (with sister Gladys Thum) *The Persuaders: Propaganda in War and Peace,* Atheneum, 1972; *Persuasion and Propaganda,* McDougal, Littel, 1973; *Fernwood,* Doubleday, 1973; *Exploring Black America,* Atheneum, 1975; *Abbey Court,* Doubleday, 1976; *Exploring Literary America,* Atheneum, 1979; *The White Rose,* Fawcett, 1980; (with Gladys Thum) *Exploring Military America,* Atheneum, 1981.

THURSTON, David B. 1918-

PERSONAL: Born September 20, 1918, in Mineola, Long Island, N.Y.; son of Henry (an artist and naturalist) and Fern (Goff) Thurston; married Evelyn Holthausen, April 14, 1944; children: Kent, Roy, Donna. *Education:* New York University, Bachelor of Aeronautical Engineering, 1940. *Religion:* Episcopalian. *Home:* 16 Jericho Dr., Old Lyme, Conn. 06371.

CAREER: Brewster Aeronautical Corp., New York City, design engineer and detailer, 1940-42; Grumman Aircraft Engineering Corp., Bethpage, N.Y., production and manufacturing engineer, 1942-55; Colonial Aircraft Corp., Sanford, Me., president, 1955-61; Thurston Erlandsen Corp., Sanford, president, 1961-66; Thurston Aircraft Corp., Sanford, president, 1966-71; Schweizer Aircraft Corp., Elmira, N.Y., engineering manager, 1972-76; Thurston Aeromarine Corp., Old Lyme, Conn., president, 1976—; International Aeromarine Corp., Sanford, Fla., founder, director, and engineering vice-president, 1979—. Instructor in engineering, New York University evening classes during World War II. Consultant to small manufacturing companies; consulting editor, McGraw-Hill Book Co., 1979—.

MEMBER: Institute of Aeronautics and Astronautics (associate fellow), Aviation/Space Writers Association, Aircraft Owners and Pilots Association, Seaplane Pilots Association, Experimental Aircraft Association, Delta Upsilon, Tau Beta Pi, Iota Alpha, Essex Yacht Club, Pettipaug Yacht Club, Frostbite Yacht Club. *Awards, honors:* Earl D. Osborn Award, Aviation/Space Writers Association, 1978, for *Design for Flying.*

WRITINGS: The Manual for the President of a Growing Company, Prentice-Hall, 1962; *Design for Flying,* McGraw, 1978; *Design for Safety,* McGraw, 1980; *Homebuilt Aircraft,* McGraw, 1981. Contributor of articles on aircraft design to periodicals, including *Vertical World* and *Aviation Magazine.*

SIDELIGHTS: David Thurston writes: "My writing is presently concerned with improving the safety level of general aviation aircraft through improved design and operating procedures. While there is very little sex in technical writing (and so sales are relatively small), the reward arises when someone writes to say my books have been helpful."

AVOCATIONAL INTERESTS: Ocean racing and cruising, skiing, flying.

* * *

TISCHLER, Hans 1915-

PERSONAL: Born January 18, 1915, in Vienna, Austria; son of Joachim and Grete (Spitz) Tischler; married Louise Hochdorf, July 27, 1938 (died, August 5, 1957); married Alice Bock, June 21, 1958; children: (first marriage) Judith Rae, Leonard Jordan; (second marriage) Mark Daniel, Laura Ruth. *Education:* New Vienna Conservatory, B.Mus., 1933; Vienna State Academy, M.Mus., 1936; University of Vienna, Ph.D., 1937; Yale University, Ph.D., 1942. *Home:* 711 East First St., Bloomington, Ind. 47401. *Office:* School of Music, Indiana University, Bloomington, Ind. 47405.

CAREER: Private teacher, Bridgeport, Conn., 1939-43; West Virginia Wesleyan College, Buckhannon, professor of music and head of department, 1945-47; Roosevelt University, Chicago, Ill., associate professor of music history and theory, 1947-65; Indiana University at Bloomington, professor of musicology, 1965—. Visiting professor, University of Chicago,

1956-57, and Tel Aviv University, 1972. *Military service:* U.S. Army, 1943-45. *Member:* International Musicology Society, American Musicology Society (member of council, 1960-66), International Society for Contemporary Music (founder, Chicago chapter, 1950, chairman, 1962-65), Association of American University Professors, Mediaeval Academy of America. *Awards, honors:* American Philosophical Society research grant, 1955, 1962, 1965; Chapelbrook Foundation grant, 1965, 1969; Guggenheim fellowship, 1964-65; American Council of Learned Societies grant, 1970; National Endowment for the Humanities grant, 1971, fellowship, 1975-76; received decoration from government of Uruguay.

WRITINGS: The Perceptive Music Listener, Prentice-Hall, 1955; *Practical Harmony,* Allyn & Bacon, 1964; *A Structural Analysis of Mozart's Piano Concertos,* Institute of Mediaeval Music, 1966; *A Medieval Motet Book,* Associated Music Publishers, 1973; (translator and editor) W. Apel, *History of Keyboard Music to 1700,* Indiana University Press, 1973; *The Montpellier Codex,* three volumes, A-R Editions, 1978; (with Samuel Rosenberg) *Chanter M'estuet: Songs of the Trouveres,* Indiana University Press, 1981; *The Earliest Motets: Complete Edition,* three volumes, Yale University Press, 1982; *The Parisian Two-Part Organa: Complete Edition,* three volumes, Pendragon Press, in press.

Contributor: *Music in the Middle Ages,* G. Reese, 1940; *Music in the Renaissance,* G. Reese, 1954; *Aspects of Medieval and Renaissance Music,* Norton, 1966; *Music in Europe and the United States,* E. Borroff, 1971. Contributor to *McGraw-Hill Encyclopedia of World Biography.* Contributor of reviews and about seventy musicological articles to professional journals in the United States and abroad.

WORK IN PROGRESS: The Earliest Motets: Their Style and Evolution; The Pre-Machaut Lais: Complete Edition.

AVOCATIONAL INTERESTS: Philosophy, history, literature, art, archeology.

*   *   *

TOCH, Henry 1923-

PERSONAL: Born August 15, 1923; son of L. and Alice (Muller) Toch; married Margit Schwarz (a social worker), April 3, 1957. *Education:* London School of Economics and Political Science, University of London, B.Com. (with second class honors), 1950. *Politics:* Labour Party. *Religion:* Jewish. *Home:* "Candida," 49 Hawkshead Lane, North Mymms, Hertfordshire, England. *Office:* City of London Polytechnic, Moorgate, London E.C.2, England.

CAREER: Tailor for various firms, London, England, 1939-44; British Inland Revenue, London, H.M. inspector of taxes, 1949-56; Hertfordshire County Council, St. Albans, England, teacher, 1956-57; City of London Polytechnic, London, senior lecturer, 1957—. Free-lance tax consultant. Examiner in economics, University of London, 1957-71; examiner in taxation, Association of Certified Accountants, 1961-70; district councillor, Weheyn-Hoffield District, 1973-76; member of Valuation Court, Hertfordshire, 1976—. Parliamentary Labour candidate, Poole, Dorsetshire, England, 1962, 1964, Rutland and Stamford, 1970, and southwest Norfolk, 1974. *Military service:* British Army, served in Italy and Germany, 1944-48; became sergeant; awarded Italy Star. *Member:* Association of Teachers in Technical Institutes, Josephine Butler Society (treasurer), Society of Authors.

WRITINGS: How to Pay Less Income Tax, Museum Press, 1959, 4th edition, 1973; *Tax Saving for the Business Man,*

Museum Press, 1961, 3rd edition, 1973; *British Political and Social Institutions,* Pitman, 1962; *Income Tax: Including Corporation Tax and Capital Gains Tax,* Macdonald & Evans, 1966, 11th edition, 1979; *How to Survive Inflation,* Pitman, 1971; *Economics for Professional Students,* Macdonald & Evans, 1977; *How to Pass Examinations in Taxation,* Cassell, 1979; *Cases in Income Tax Law,* Macdonald & Evans, 1981. Contributor of articles to *Journal of Business Law.*

SIDELIGHTS: Henry Toch told *CA:* "I regard myself as a teacher and write books for students. They are intended to help students and other teachers."

*   *   *

TODD, Alden 1918-

PERSONAL: Born January 12, 1918, in Washington, D.C.; son of Laurence and Constance (Leupp) Todd; married Jeannette Goldman, 1941; children: Paul, Philip. *Education:* Attended Princeton University, 1935-36; Swarthmore College, B.A., 1939. *Home and office:* 124 Howard Ter., Leonia, N.J. 07605.

CAREER: Friends School, Wilmington, Del., teacher, 1940-42; Federated Press, Washington, D.C., reporter, 1946-50, 1955; correspondent in Europe, 1950-51; reporter in Washington, D.C., 1952-54; free-lance writer, 1956-67; New York University, School of Continuing Education, New York City, adjunct assistant professor, 1966—; Deloitte Haskins & Sells, New York City, editor and publications director, 1968—. *Military service:* U.S. Army, 1943-46; served with 101st Airborne Division. *Member:* American Society of Journalists and Authors, Industrial Communication Council, Authors League of America. *Awards, honors:* Gavel Award, American Bar Association, 1965.

WRITINGS: Abandoned (History Book Club alternate selection), McGraw, 1961; *Justice on Trial: The Case of Louis D. Brandeis* (selection of Lawyers' Literary Club and Contemporary Affairs Society), McGraw, 1964; *A Spark Lighted in Portland,* McGraw, 1966; *Richard Montgomery: Rebel of 1775,* McKay, 1967; (with Dorothy B. Weisbord) *Favorite Subjects in Western Art,* Dutton, 1968; *Finding Facts Fast,* Morrow, 1972, new edition, Ten Speed Press, 1979. Contributor to magazines.

SIDELIGHTS: Alden Todd told *CA:* "I enjoy writing on a wide variety of subjects, particularly history, biography, and reference books, and explaining the seemingly complex in simple terms. I also enjoy editing and teaching, especially research techniques and fact-finding."

*   *   *

TOLAND, John (Willard) 1912-

PERSONAL: Born June 29, 1912, in La Crosse, Wis; son of Ralph (a concert singer) and Helen (Snow) Toland; married present wife, Toshiko Matsumura, March 12, 1960; children: (previous marriage) Diana, Marcia; (present marriage) Tamiko (daughter). *Education:* Williams College, B.A., 1936; attended Yale University, 1937. *Residence:* Danbury, Conn. *Agent:* Carl Brandt, Brandt & Brandt Literary Agents, Inc., 1501 Broadway, New York, N.Y. 10036.

CAREER: Professional writer. Advisor to the National Archives. *Military service:* U.S. Air Force, six years; became captain. *Member:* Overseas Press Club, Writers Guild, P.E.N. *Awards, honors:* Overseas Press Club award for best book on foreign affairs, 1961, for *But Not in Shame,* 1967, for *The Last*

100 Days, 1970, for *The Rising Sun,* 1976, for *Adolf Hitler;* L.H.D., Williams College, 1968; Van Wyck Brooks Award for nonfiction, 1970, for *The Rising Sun;* Pulitzer Prize for nonfiction, 1970, for *The Rising Sun;* L.H.D., University of Alaska, 1977; National Society of Arts and Letters gold medal, 1977, for *Adolf Hitler;* Accademia del Mediterrano, 1978.

WRITINGS—All published by Random House, except as indicated: *Ships in the Sky,* Holt, 1957; *Battle: The Story of the Bulge,* 1959; *But Not in Shame,* 1961; *The Dillinger Days,* 1963; *The Flying Tigers* (juvenile), 1963; *The Last 100 Days,* 1966; *The Battle of the Bulge* (juvenile), 1966; *The Rising Sun: The Decline and Fall of the Japanese Empire, 1936-1945,* 1970; *Adolf Hitler,* Doubleday, 1976; *Hitler: The Pictorial Documentary of His Life,* Doubleday, 1978; *No Man's Land: The Story of 1918,* Doubleday, 1980; *Infamy: Pearl Harbor and Its Aftermath,* Doubleday, 1982. Contributor of articles and stories to *Look, Life, Reader's Digest, Saturday Evening Post,* and other magazines.

SIDELIGHTS: John "Toland's approach to history," writes Diana Loercher in the *Christian Science Monitor,* "is that of an investigative reporter." For each of his books, Toland interviews the actual participants in an historic event, sometimes several hundred of them, in order to get all sides of a story from those people who know it best. He relates these interviews as objectively as possible. "I believe it's my duty," he says, "to tell you everything and let you draw your own conclusions. I keep my opinions to a minimum."

Laurence Cotterell of the *London Times* writes of *No Man's Land: The Story of 1918,* "While describing in exhaustive detail the direction and course of battle, Toland displays remarkably little partisanship . . . [and] yet evokes all the intrinsic colour and passion of the situation, enabling the reader to form his or her own conclusions." In the *New York Times Book Review,* Richard M. Watt finds that the book is "written with the careful research that has characterized [the] author's previous books. . . . [It] is scrupuously accurate while at the same time absorbing and dramatic."

Other reviewers are critical of Toland's approach. *No Man's Land* is "essentially a story without any real attempt to analyse issues, reappraise evidence or reach conclusions," Brian Bond writes in the *Times Literary Supplement.* In a *Detroit News* article, Bernard A. Weisberger says *"No Man's Land* does not somehow carry the full, bitter taste of the war's exhaustion. . . . [Toland] seems to have relied on first-hand accounts by soldiers who still had some notion of the war as an adventure." And Micheal Kernan of the *Washington Post* believes "the smooth reading comes at a price: Very little background is given on the cause, beginning and early progress of the war. . . . Such omissions, however, are balanced by the nice bits of digging that Toland presents almost in passing."

Toland's research has resulted in the clearing up of historical inaccuracies and the unearthing of new information. In his Pulitzer Prize-winning *The Rising Sun,* for instance, Toland found that a simple misunderstanding during Japanese-American negotiations prior to World War II was one of the reasons Japan declared war. During these negotiations, the United States had demanded that the Japanese remove their troops from China. Although agreeable to a withdrawal from China, the Japanese assumed this demand included Manchuria, an area of China they wished to keep, and so refused to withdraw. In fact, the United States had meant to exclude Manchuria from its demand. If this point had been clarified, Japanese-American relations may have been normalized and the subsequent war averted. "In showing how just about all of the Japanese leaders in 1941 sincerely hoped to avoid war," F.X.J. Homer notes

in *Best Sellers,* "Toland makes it possible for us to recognize that Pearl Harbor was the result of failings on the part of American diplomacy as well as of Japanese aggression. . . . Toland adds a new dimension to orthodox military history in going beyond grand strategy to portray the human side of the conflict."

BIOGRAPHICAL/CRITICAL SOURCES: New York Herald Tribune Book Review, February 18, 1966; *Wall Street Journal,* February 28, 1966; *Christian Science Monitor,* March 3, 1966, October 27, 1976; *Newsweek,* March 7, 1966, December 28, 1970, September 20, 1976; *Saturday Review,* March 12, 1966, September 18, 1976; *Modern Age,* fall, 1966; *New York Times Book Review,* November 29, 1970, September 26, 1976, November 12, 1980; *New York Times,* December 7, 1970; *Time,* December 7, 1970, December 6, 1976; *Book World,* January 3, 1971, August 29, 1976; *Best Sellers,* February 1, 1971; *Yale Review,* June, 1971; *American Historical Review,* February, 1972; *Times Literary Supplement,* September 1, 1972, February 6, 1981; *Village Voice,* November 15, 1976; *New Republic,* November 20, 1976; *Progressive,* February, 1977; *National Review,* April 29, 1977; *New York Review of Books,* May 26, 1977; *North American Review,* summer, 1977; *Virginia Quarterly Review,* summer, 1977; *Books & Bookmen,* July, 1977; *Chicago Tribune Book World,* September 28, 1980; *Detroit News,* October 19, 1980; *Washington Post,* October 27, 1980; *London Times,* December 11, 1980; *Los Angeles Times,* December 28, 1980.

*   *   *

TOLEGIAN, Aram   1909-

PERSONAL: Born September 4, 1909, in Fresno, Calif.; son of Manuel and Haiganoush (Tafralian) Tolegian; married Margaret Gevorkian, 1941; children: Lenore, Eugene, David. *Education:* University of California, Los Angeles, A.B., 1936; University of Southern California, M.A., 1940, Ph.D., 1960. *Religion:* Armenian Church. *Home:* 1820 South Atlantic Blvd., Monterey Park, Calif. 91754.

CAREER: High school teacher in Los Angeles, Calif., 1941-53; *Victory* magazine, Los Angeles, editor, 1950-53; East Los Angeles College, Los Angeles, professor of English, 1953-57, assistant dean and acting dean, 1957-64; Los Angeles Metropolitan College, Los Angeles, dean of evening division, 1964-68; East Los Angeles College, dean, 1966-68. Assistant professor of English, California State College at Los Angeles (now California State University, Los Angeles), 1955, 1957, 1959, 1961; lecturer in department of comparative literature, University of Southern California, 1955-57; head of Supplementary Education Planning Center and administrative coordinator, Superintendent's Office, Los Angeles City Schools, 1966-68; professor of education, Pepperdine University, 1972-73. Lecturer on poetry. Chairman of Human Relations Council, Los Angeles City Board of Education. *Member:* National Association for Armenian Studies and Research, Central Educational Council of the Armenian Schools of California, California Junior College Association, Rotary International.

WRITINGS: David of Sassoun: Armenian Folk Epic, Twayne, 1961; (editor and translator) *Armenian Poetry Old and New: A Bilingual Anthology,* Wayne State University Press, 1979.

WORK IN PROGRESS: Sketches from My Childhood, an autobiographical account of "the lives of the inhabitants of the San Joaquin Valley during the second decade of our century."

SIDELIGHTS: Aram Tolegian told CA: "A lifetime of interest in the study and writing of poetry brought me to an earlier than usual retirement so that I could devote much of my time to writing and translating. After five years of effort, *Armenian Poetry Old and New: A Bilingual Anthology* is the result. Over the years I had prepared myself for the task of translation by independent study of the Armenian language, and by occasionally translating for publication. In 1961, after the publication of my book length *David of Sassoun: Armenian Folk Epic,* I embarked on translating from a variety of authors, having felt for some time that my competency in the Armenian language now could give me the confidence I was working toward. Differences in the style of the poets and differences in the style of literary periods no longer seemed to overpower me. Of course, I traveled again and again to Armenia, met there with scholars and poets and secured the standard editions of some sixty poets. To the question why do I translate, I can only answer that once I have discovered something beautiful in the poetry of one language, I would like to share that beauty with others in the translated language.''

* * *

TRAVIS, Gerry
    See TRIMBLE, Louis P(reston)

* * *

TREECE, Henry   1912-1966

PERSONAL: Born 1912, in Wednesbury, Staffordshire, England; died June 10, 1966, in Barton-on-Humber, Lincolnshire, England; son of Richard and Mary (Mason) Treece; married Mary Woodman, 1939; children: Jennifer Elisabeth, Gareth Richard. *Education:* University of Birmingham, B.A., 1933, diploma in education, 1934; University of Santander, diploma, 1933. *Politics:* Conservative. *Religion:* Anglican. *Home and office:* East Acridge House, Barton-on-Humber, Lincolnshire, England. *Agent:* John Johnson, 51-54 Goschen Bldgs., 12-13 Henrietta St., London WC2E 8LF, England; and Ann Elmo, 52 Vanderbilt Ave., New York, N.Y. 10017.

CAREER: Officer at a Home Office School for delinquents in Leicestershire, England, 1933-34; Cleobury Mortimer College, Cleobury Mortimer, Shropshire, England, English master, 1934-35; Tynemouth School, Tynemouth, Northumberland, England, English master, 1935-39; Barton-on-Humber Grammar School, Barton-on-Humber, Lincolnshire, England, English master, 1939-59; full-time writer, 1959-66. Made numerous appearances on British radio and television, 1948-66; lectured in the United States, 1950-51. *Military service:* Royal Air Force, Bomber Command, 1941-46; served as intelligence officer; became flight lieutenant. *Member:* Barton Drama Club (president, 1953), Barton Cricket Club (vice-president, 1950-66). *Awards, honors:* Art Council Play Prize, 1955.

WRITINGS—Historical novels: *The Dark Island,* Gollancz, 1952, Random House, 1953, 2nd edition, Bodley Head, 1958, reprinted, Chivers, 1976; *The Rebels,* Gollancz, 1953; *The Golden Strangers,* Bodley Head, 1956, Random House, 1957; *The Great Captains,* Random House, 1956; *Red Queen, White Queen,* Random House, 1958; *The Master of Badger's Hall,* Random House, 1959; *A Fighting Man,* Bodley Head, 1960; *Jason,* Random House, 1961; *Electra,* Bodley Head, 1963, published as *The Amber Princess,* Random House, 1963; *Oedipus,* Bodley Head, 1964, published as *The Eagle King,* Random House, 1965; *The Queen's Brooch,* Hamish Hamilton, 1966, Putnam, 1967; *The Green Man,* Putnam, 1966.

Juvenile historical novels: *Legions of the Eagle,* Criterion, 1954; *The Eagles Have Flown,* Criterion, 1954; *Hounds of the King,* Criterion, 1955; *The Road to Miklagard,* Criterion, 1957; *Men*

of the Hills, Bodley Head, 1957, Criterion, 1958; *Viking's Dawn,* Criterion, 1957; *The Children's Crusade,* Criterion, 1958; *The Return of Robinson Crusoe,* Hulton, 1958, published as *The Further Adventures of Robinson Crusoe,* Criterion, 1958; *Wickham and the Armada,* Hulton, 1959; *The Bombard,* Bodley Head, 1959; *Perilous Pilgrimage,* Criterion, 1959; *Ride into Danger,* Criterion, 1959; *Red Settlement,* Bodley Head, 1960; *Viking's Sunset,* Criterion, 1961; *The Golden One,* Criterion, 1961; *War Dog,* Farrar, Straus, 1962; *The Man with a Sword,* Bodley Head, 1962, Pantheon, 1964; *Horned Helmet,* Criterion, 1963; *The Burning of Njal,* Random House, 1963; *The Last of the Vikings,* Brockhampton Press, 1964, published as *The Last Viking,* Pantheon, 1966; *Splintered Sword,* Brockhampton Press, 1965, Duell, 1966; *The Bronze Sword,* Hamish Hamilton, 1965, published as part 2 of *Centurion* (see below); *Swords from the North,* Pantheon, 1967; *Westward to Vinland,* S. G. Phillips, 1967; *Vinland the Good,* Bodley Head, 1967; *Centurion* (in three parts), Meredith, 1967; *The Dream Time,* Brockhampton Press, 1967, Meredith, 1968; *The Windswept City: A Novel of the Trojan War,* Hamish Hamilton, 1967, Meredith, 1968; *The Invaders,* Crowell, 1972.

Historical nonfiction: *Castles and Kings,* Criterion, 1959; *The True Book about Castles,* Muller, 1960; *The Crusades,* Bodley Head, 1962, Random House, 1963, juvenile version published as *Know about the Crusades,* Blackie, 1963, Dufour, 1967; (with R. E. Oakeshott) *Fighting Men: How Men Have Fought through the Ages,* Brockhampton Press, 1963, Putnam, 1965.

Mysteries: *Desperate Journey,* Faber, 1954; *Ask for King Billy,* Faber, 1955; *Hunter Hunted,* Faber, 1957; *Don't Expect Any Mercy,* Faber, 1958; *The Jet Beads,* Brockhampton Press, 1961; *Killer in Dark Glasses,* Faber, 1965; *Bang, You're Dead!,* Faber, 1965.

Verse: *38 Poems,* Fortune, 1940; *Towards a Personal Armageddon,* Decker, 1941; *Invitation and Warning,* Faber, 1942; *The Black Seasons,* Faber, 1945; *Collected Poems,* Knopf, 1946; *The Haunted Garden,* Faber, 1947; *The Exiles,* Faber, 1952.

Editor of anthologies: (With J. F. Hendry) *The New Apocalypse,* Fortune, 1939; (with Hendry) *The White Horseman,* Routledge & Kegan Paul, 1941; (with Hendry) *The Crown and the Sickle,* Staples, 1943; (with Stefan Schimanski) *Wartime Harvest,* Staples, 1943; (with Schimanski) *Transformation,* Gollancz, 1943, Drummond, 1944-47; (with John Pudney) *Air Force Poetry,* Bodley Head, 1944; *Herbert Read: An Introduction to His Work by Many Hands,* Faber, 1944, reprinted, Kennikat, 1969; (with Schimanski) *Leaves in the Storm: A Book of Diaries,* Drummond, 1947, reprinted, Century Bookbindery, 1977; *The Selected Poems of Swinburne,* Crown Classics, 1948; (with Schimanski) *A Map of Hearts,* Drummond, 1949; (with Schimanski) *A New Romantic Anthology,* New Directions, 1949.

Other: *How I See Apocalypse* (criticism), Drummond, 1946, reprinted, AMS Press, 1977; *I Cannot Go Hunting Tomorrow* (short stories), Grey Walls Press, 1946; *Dylan Thomas, "Dog among the Fairies"* (criticism), Drummond, 1949, 2nd edition, Benn, 1956, reprinted, Folcroft, 1974; *Carnival King* (play), Faber, 1955. Author of an unpublished play, "Footsteps in the Sea," 1956; also author of radio plays and features. Contributor to *Manchester Guardian, New Yorker,* and other publications. Former editor of *Seven, Kingdom Come,* and *World Review.*

SIDELIGHTS: Henry Treece said that his interest in history stemmed from childhood when he was given only historical books—with lots of colorful pictures—from which he developed "a sense of the past." Later, he read some history at the university, and, although he taught English, he saw books in relation to their times, historically: Richard II, Macbeth, Lear. His favorite period was the Celtic one. An obituary writer for the *New York Times* called Treece "a severe trial to literary critics. They were practically unanimous in their concessions to his formidable learning in history, anthropology, and archeology. But they were often convinced that they were being led down a misty, spirit-ridden path in Mr. Treece's historical novels, in which the author was the only one able to make out the guideposts." A reviewer for the *New Yorker* agreed that Treece had been known, on occasion, to romanticize historical events in his books; as an example, the reviewer cites *The Crusades:* "[Treece] does very well with the novelish side of history with dress-up drama, and all sorts of rough, simple men travelling into strangeness, complication, and violence. He does less well with the dull but necessary stitching together of a year-by-year connected narrative. As a result, his history, while it makes for lively reading, is Treece's Crusades rather than *the* Crusades." However, as a critic for the *Times Literary Supplement* wrote: "To make a fresh work of art from the material of ancient tales, one needs perhaps to be free from the immediate toils of one's love for the original; and to have into the bargain literary tact about what may be attempted with a source work. . . . [Treece] showed with what confidence and skill he could use these sources he loved, elaborating their slender statements into fully dramatic or humorous scenes where he would; diminishing also, and altering to suit his book."

Henry Treece also came under occasional criticism for the vivid portrayals of violence in some of his works. In a review of *The Amber Princess,* a novelization of Euripedes' "Electra," Gerald Gottlieb said that Treece "has obviously ransacked the ancient myth-sources, both well known and obscure from Pindar to Hyginus. But this is erudition gone berserk, for it monotonously produces only the most lurid, revolting, and depraved of all the possible readings of the myths. . . . Violence must be piled upon violence, incest upon incest, murder upon bloody murder, with a zest that is guaranteed to leave even the most unsqueamish reader numb. . . . Some passages have a strong, rude beauty that is like a breath of Mycenaean Greece. More often, though, something that could have been beautiful—or at least effective—is soiled and brutalized." But the historical periods of which Treece wrote were indeed turbulent and violent times, and many critics lauded his ability to establish a realistic, if somewhat harsh, tone in his novels. As J. P. Wood wrote in a review of *Westward to Vinland:* "Treece wrote in the bold, bald way of the Norse sagas themselves. His characters are less individuals than figures of epic. Blood and storms, the fury of men and women and the sea, murder and savagery are the basic elements in this tale of one of the world's great adventures."

In 1938 Treece met J. F. Hendry, a Scottish philosopher and poet, with whom he founded a Romantic literary movement that became known as the "New Apocalypse." The movement, which attracted many contemporary poets, was noted for its stand against totalitarianism and asserted man's right to free expression. With the outbreak of World War II, and the subsequent enlistment of Treece and Hendry in the armed forces, the group gradually disbanded; but the radical (for that time) principles expounded by the "New Apocalypse" were to cause Treece to become a favorite target of British critics for many years. Nevertheless, his almost universally acknowledged abilities as a writer and storyteller, his poetic prose style, and the scholarship exhibited in his work established a large and enthusiastic following throughout the United States and Europe.

AVOCATIONAL INTERESTS: Listening to and playing the Flamenco guitar.

BIOGRAPHICAL/CRITICAL SOURCES: Best Sellers, April 15, 1963, November 15, 1964, January 1, 1966, August 15, 1966; *Times Literary Supplement,* April 19, 1963, November 28, 1963, April 21, 1966, May 25, 1967, November 30, 1967; *Atlantic,* May, 1963; *New Yorker,* May 4, 1963; *New York Times Book Review,* August 4, 1963, January 31, 1965, January 26, 1966, March 20, 1966, March 21, 1967; *Book World,* October 20, 1963, February 23, 1964, July 10, 1966, July 16, 1967, November 5, 1967; *Class World,* November, 1963; *New Statesman,* September 18, 1964; *Commonweal,* May 26, 1967, November 22, 1968; Margery Fisher, *Henry Treece,* Bodley Head, 1970; *Children's Literature Review,* Volume II, Gale, 1976.

OBITUARIES: New York Times, June 12, 1966; *Newsweek,* June 20, 1966; *Publishers Weekly,* June 27, 1966; *Books Abroad,* spring, 1967.†

*   *   *

TREVATHAN, Robert E. 1925-

PERSONAL: Born February 21, 1925, in Detroit, Mich.; son of Robert and Christine (Bishop) Trevathan; married Velma Ward Gage, 1974; children: (previous marriage) Evan, Alison Diane. *Education:* Trinity University, B.A., 1949. *Home:* 7235 South Janet, Lot 3, Oklahoma City, Okla. 73150.

CAREER: Teacher in the public schools in San Antonio, Tex., 1949-51; U.S. Air Force, teacher at dependents' school in Japan, 1951-52; International Milling Co., Detroit, Mich., sales clerk, 1952-53; U.S. Army, Finance Center, Indianapolis, Ind., accounting clerk, 1953-55; U.S. Air Force, Civilian Personnel Office, Tinker Air Force Base, Oklahoma City, Okla., position classifier, 1955-71, Air Force historian, 1971-80. *Military service:* U.S. Navy, 1943-46; served in Alaska and Australia, participated in invasion of Okinawa; received battle star. *Member:* Western Writers of America, Oklahoma Historical Society.

WRITINGS—All published by Arcadia House, except as indicated: *Dead in the Saddle,* 1959; *Stage to Laredo,* 1961; *Longhorns for Fort Sill,* Criterion, 1962; *Rawhide Trap,* 1962; *Badman's Roost,* Avon, 1963; *Comanche Interlude,* 1963; *The Hide Rustlers,* 1967; *Cannon River,* 1967; *Desert Campfires,* 1967; *Showdown at Ringold,* Avalon, 1968; *Longhorn Gold,* Avalon, 1969; *Ballanger,* Manor, 1974; *Tracking the Bar-J Gold,* Avalon, 1978; *Red River Angel,* Manor, 1979. Also author of *Scatterwheel Road* and *Slater's Quest.* Contributor to *Chronicles of Oklahoma;* contributor of western stories and articles to magazines.

BIOGRAPHICAL/CRITICAL SOURCES: Daily Oklahoman, April 6, 1962.

*   *   *

TREVELYAN, Raleigh 1923-

PERSONAL: Surname is pronounced "Trevillian"; born July 6, 1923, in Port Blair, Andaman Islands, India; son of Walter Raleigh Fetherstonhaugh Trevelyan (a colonel in the Indian Army) and Olive Beatrice (Frost) Trevelyan Ralston. *Education:* Attended Winchester College, Winchester, England, 1937-42. *Religion:* Church of England. *Home:* St. Cadix, St. Veep, Lostwithiel, Cornwall, England; and 18 Hertford St., London W1, England. *Agent:* A. M. Heath & Co. Ltd., 40-42 William IV St., London WC2N 4DD, England. *Office:* Jonathan Cape Ltd., 30 Bedford Square, London WC1B 3EL, England.

CAREER: Samuel Montagu (merchant bankers), London, England, trainee, 1947-48; William Collins Sons & Co. Ltd.

(publishers; now Collins & World), London, editor, 1948-58; Hutchinson & Co. Ltd. (publishers), London, editor and director of Arrow Books Ltd. and New Authors Ltd., 1958-61; Penguin Books Ltd. (publishers), Harmondsworth, Middlesex, England, editor, 1961-62; Michael Joseph Ltd. (publishers), London, editorial director, 1962-73; Hamish Hamilton Ltd. (publishers), London, director, 1973-80; Jonathan Cape Ltd. (publishers), London, literary advisor, 1980—. Member of United Kingdom Goodwill Mission to Virginia for the Jamestown Festival, 1957. *Military service:* British Army, Rifle Brigade, Infantry, 1942-46; served with Military Mission to Italian Army in Rome, 1944-46; became captain; mentioned in dispatches. *Member:* Anglo-Italian Society for the Protection of Animals (director), Travellers Club, Garrick Club. *Awards, honors:* John Florio Prize, Translators Association, for *The Outlaws.*

WRITINGS: The Fortress: A Diary of Anzio and After (Book Society recommendation), Collins, 1956, St. Martin's, 1957; *A Hermit Disclosed* (Book Society choice), Longmans, Green, 1960, St. Martin's, 1961; (translator) Giuliano Palladino, *Peace at Alamein*, Hodder & Stoughton, 1962; *The Big Tomato*, Longmans, Green, 1966; (editor) *Italian Short Stories*, Penguin, 1965; (editor) *Italian Writing Today*, Penguin, 1967; (translator from the Italian) Luigi Meneghello, *The Outlaws*, Morrow, 1967; *Princes under the Volcano*, Morrow, 1972; *The Shadow of Vesuvius*, M. Joseph, 1976; *A Pre-Raphaelite Circle*, Chatto & Windus, 1978; *Rome '44: The Battle for the Eternal City*, Secker & Warburg, 1981, Viking, 1982. Contributor of book reviews to periodicals, including *Sunday Times, Observer, Listener*, and *Times Literary Supplement;* contributor of articles on art to *Apollo* and *Connoisseur.*

WORK IN PROGRESS: A study of the conquest of Granada, for Folio and Secker & Warburg; a book on his childhood in India.

AVOCATIONAL INTERESTS: Travel, gardening, collecting, theatre.

*   *   *

TRIMBLE, Louis P(reston)   1917-
(Stuart Brock, Gerry Travis)

PERSONAL: Born March 2, 1917, in Seattle, Wash.; son of Charles Louis (an artist) and Rose Alys (an artist and writer; maiden name, Bouche) Trimble; married Renee Eddy, January 2, 1938 (died, 1951); married Jacquelyn Whitney (a librarian and author), November 21, 1952 (divorced, 1974); married R. Mary Todd (a teacher of English as a second language), October 2, 1974; children: (first marriage) Victoria Rosemary Trimble Beetz. *Education:* Eastern Washington State College (now University), B.A., 1950, Ed.M., 1953; graduate study, Mexico City College, 1951, and University of Washington, 1955, 1957. *Politics:* Independent. *Residence:* England. *Agent:* Scott Meredith Literary Agency, 845 Third Ave., New York, N.Y. 10022.

CAREER: Junior accountant in Topeka, Kan., 1941-42; manager of ranch in Bloomington, Calif., 1942-43; Hotel Spokane, Spokane, Wash., assistant accountant, 1943-44; owner of ranch in Naples, Idaho, 1944-49; high school English teacher in Bonners Ferry, Idaho, 1946-47; Eastern Washington State College (now University), Cheney, instructor in Spanish and English, 1950-54; University of Pennsylvania, Philadelphia, teaching fellow, 1955-56; University of Washington, Seattle, instructor, 1956-59, assistant professor, 1959-65, associate professor of humanities and social studies, beginning 1965; co-director of English instruction program, American International

Education and Training, Inc., Corte Madera, Calif. Free-lance writer, 1938—. Editor in Architects Division, Corps of Engineers, U.S. Army. *Member:* International Association of Teachers of English as a Foreign Language, Association of Teachers of English as a Second Language, Science Fiction Writers of America, Western Writers of America (member of executive board, 1963-64), Mexican Association of Teachers of English as a Second Language. *Awards, honors:* National Spanish honorary, 1956.

WRITINGS: Sports of the World, Golden West, 1938; *Fit to Kill*, Phoenix Press, 1941; *Tragedy in Turquoise*, Phoenix Press, 1942; *Date for Murder*, Phoenix Press, 1942; *Murder Trouble*, Phoenix Press, 1945; *Design for Dying*, Phoenix Press, 1945; *Give Up the Body*, Superior, 1946; *You Can't Kill a Corpse*, Phoenix Press, 1946; *Valley of Violence*, Macrae Smith, 1948; *The Case of the Blank Cartridge*, Phoenix Press, 1949.

Gunsmoke Justice, Macrae Smith, 1950; *Blonds Are Skin Deep*, Lion Books, 1951; *Gaptown Law*, Macrae Smith, 1951; *Fighting Cowman*, Popular Publications, 1952; *Bring Back Her Body*, Wyn, 1953; *Crossfire*, Avalon, 1953; *Bullets on Bunchgrass*, Avalon, 1954; *The Virgin Victim*, Mercury, 1956; *Stab in the Dark*, Wyn, 1956; *Nothing to Lose But My Life*, Wyn, 1957; *Mountain Ambush*, Avalon, 1958; *The Smell of Trouble*, Wyn, 1958; *Corpse without a Country*, Wyn, 1959; *Till Death Do Us Part*, Wyn, 1959; *Girl on a Slay Ride*, Avon, 1960; *Montana Gun*, Hillman, 1961; *The City Machine*, D.A.W. Books, 1972; *The Wandering Variables*, D.A.W. Books, 1972; *The Bodelan Way*, D.A.W. Books, 1974.

Published by Ace Books: *Obit Deferred*, 1959; *The Duchess of Skid Row*, 1960; *Love Me and Die*, 1960; *The Surfside Caper*, 1961; *Deadman's Canyon*, 1961; *Siege at High Meadows*, 1961; *Wild Horse Range*, 1963; *The Man from Colorado*, 1963; *The Dead and the Deadly*, 1963; *Trouble at Gunsight*, 1964; *The Desperate Deputy of Cougar Hill*, 1965; *Holdout in the Diablos*, 1965; *Showdown in the Cayuse*, 1966; *Standoff at Massacre Buttes*, 1967; *Marshall of Sangaree*, 1968; *Anthropol*, 1968; *West to the Pecos*, 1968; *Hostile Peaks*, 1969; *Trouble Valley*, 1970; *The Lonesome Mountain*, 1970; *The Noblest Experiment in the Galaxy*, 1970; (with Tom West) *Lobo of Lynx Valley* [by Tom West and] *The Ragbag Army* [by Louis Trimble], 1971; (with Jacquelyn Trimble) *Guardians of the Gate*, 1971.

Editor: *Criteria for Highway Benefit Analysis*, National Academy of Sciences, Volume I (interim report), 1964, Volumes I and II (final report), 1965, revised edition (with Robert G. Hennes), National Highway Research Board, 1966-67; *Incorporation of Shelter into Apartments and Office Buildings*, Office of Civil Defense, Department of the Army, 1965.

Under pseudonym Stuart Brock: *Just around the Coroner*, Morrow, 1948; *Death Is My Lover*, Morrow, 1948; *Double Cross Ranch*, Avalon, 1954; *Whispering Canyon*, Avalon, 1955; *Action at Boundary Peak*, Avalon, 1955; *Forbidden Range*, Avalon, 1956; *Killer's Choice*, Graphic Books, 1956; *Railtown Sheriff*, Avalon, 1957.

Under pseudonym Gerry Travis: *Tarnished Love*, Phoenix Press, 1942; *A Lovely Mask for Murder*, Mystery House, 1956; *The Big Bite*, Mystery House, 1957.

Contributor of about forty mystery, Western, sports, and juvenile stories to periodicals and newspapers, including *Toronto Star Weekly* and *Future Farmer.*

WORK IN PROGRESS: Science fiction novels; a Western novel; research on the rhetoric of scientific and technical English and its application to teaching English as a second or foreign language.

SIDELIGHTS: Louis P. Trimble writes to *CA:* "I am interested in improving the teaching of the specialized uses of language, especially English, in developing countries. I feel that in these countries not only the university students and the professional people need specialized language training so that they can 'join the developed countries,' but, especially, the young people who are training to be technicians must learn to read the languages of the technical manuals accompanying the technology that comes to their countries."

Trimble has a reading knowledge of Spanish, French, German, Hungarian, Latin, and Serbo-Croatian.

AVOCATIONAL INTERESTS: Golf, hiking, studying languages, traveling to collect story locales and information.

*   *   *

TROW, W(illiam) Clark   1894-

PERSONAL: Born December 11, 1894, in Northampton, Mass.; son of William A. and Pamela (Clark) Trow; married Louise Brownell, 1920; children: Donald Brownell, William Herbert. *Education:* Colgate University, A.B., 1915; Columbia University, M.A., 1919, Ph.D., 1924. *Home:* 931 Oakdale Road, Ann Arbor, Mich. 48105. *Office:* School of Education, University of Michigan, Ann Arbor, Mich. 48104.

CAREER: University of Rochester, Rochester, N.Y., assistant professor, 1919-22; University of Cincinnati, Cincinnati, Ohio, associate professor, 1923-25; University of Michigan, Ann Arbor, associate professor, 1926-31, professor of education and psychology, 1931-64, professor emeritus, 1964—. Visiting associate professor, Yale University, 1925-26. Member of U.S. Education Mission to Japan, 1946. *Military service:* U.S. Army, Medical Corps, 1918-19; became sergeant first class; U.S. Army Civil Affairs Training Program, Michigan director during World War II. *Member:* American Psychological Association (president of Division of Educational Psychology, 1952), National Society of College Teachers of Education (president, 1960), American Educational Research Association, Phi Beta Kappa, Phi Delta Kappa.

WRITINGS: Scientific Method in Education, Houghton, 1925; (translator from the German) Oskar Kupy, *The Religious Development of Adolescents,* Macmillan, 1928; *Educational Psychology,* Houghton, 1931, second edition, 1950, reprinted, Greenwood Press, 1970; (editor) *Character Education in Soviet Russia,* Ann Arbor Press, 1934; *Introduction to Educational Psychology,* Houghton, 1937; *Psychology in Teaching and Learning,* Houghton, 1960; *Teacher and Technology: New Designs for Learning,* Appleton 1963; *Learning Process* (with filmstrips), National Education Association, 1963; *Paths to Educational Reform,* Educational Technology Publications, 1971; *Psychological Foundations of Educational Technology,* Educational Technology Publications, 1976. Also author of *Gulliver's Visit to Walden III: A Report on Values in Education,* 1976; contributor to McGraw's "Junior Citizenship" series, 1940. Contributor to professional journals. Editor, *Journal of Educational Psychology,* 1954-57; member of editorial board, *Psychology in the Schools,* 1964—.†

*   *   *

TUBBS, Stewart L(ee)   1943-

PERSONAL: Born September 6, 1943, in Cleveland, Ohio; son of Edwin B. (an accountant) and Mary (Baker) Tubbs; married Gail Sheahan, August 21, 1965; children: Brian Christian. *Education:* Bowling Green University, B.S.Ed., 1965, M.A., 1966; University of Kansas, Ph.D., 1969. *Residence:* Flint, Mich. *Office:* Department of Industrial Administration, General Motors Institute, 1200 West Third Ave., Flint, Mich. 48502.

CAREER: University of Kansas, Lawrence, assistant director of Extension, 1968-69; General Motors Institute, Flint, Mich., assistant professor, 1969-70, associate professor, 1970-74, professor of communication, 1974-80, head of management and organizational behavior, 1980—. Vice-president of Systems Development Institute; president of Miller Road Farms Association, 1975; consultant to General Motors Corp. *Member:* International Communication Association, Academy of Management, Speech Communication Association, Central States Speech Association, Michigan Speech Association. *Awards, honors:* Fellow, Harvard University Business School, 1980.

WRITINGS: (Editor) *New Directions in Communication,* International Communication Association, 1972; (with Sylvia Moss) *Human Communication: An Interpersonal Perspective,* Random House, 1974, 3rd edition, 1980; (with John Baird) *The Open Person: Self-Disclosure and Personal Growth,* C. E. Merrill, 1976; (with Moss) *Interpersonal Communication,* Random House, 1978, 2nd edition, 1981; *A Systems Approach to Small Group Interaction,* Addison-Wesley, 1978; (with Robert M. Carter) *Shared Experiences in Human Communication,* Hayden, 1978. Contributor to *Journal of Communication, Today's Education, Journal of Personality and Social Psychology, Speech Monographs, Kansas Speech Journal, Ohio Speech Journal,* and *Michigan Speech Journal.*

WORK IN PROGRESS: A new edition of *Human Communication,* for Random House, and of *A Systems Approach to Small Group Interaction,* for Addison-Wesley.

*   *   *

TUNNARD, Christopher   1910-1979

PERSONAL: Born July 7, 1910, in Victoria, British Columbia, Canada; came to America, 1939; naturalized U.S. citizen, 1949; died February 13, 1979, in New Haven, Conn., of cancer; son of Christopher Coney and Madeline (Kingscote) Tunnard; married Lydia Evans, June 9, 1945; children: Christopher. *Education:* Attended Victoria College, University of British Columbia, 1927-28, and Westminster Technical Institute; College of the Royal Horticultural Society, diploma, 1930. *Home:* 251 East Rock Rd., New Haven, Conn. 06511. *Office:* School of Architecture and Design, Yale University, New Haven, Conn. 06520.

CAREER: Draftsman-designer in London, England, 1930-31; P. S. Cane (site planners), London, designer, 1932-34; in private practice as designer and site planner in Surrey, England, 1934-37, and in London, 1937-39; Harvard University, Cambridge, Mass., lecturer in landscape architecture and regional planning, 1939-42, Wheelwright Fellow in Architecture, 1943-44; Yale University, New Haven, Conn., assistant professor, 1945-48, associate professor, 1948-61, professor of city planning, 1961-75, emeritus professor of city planning, 1975-79, director of graduate program in city planning, 1950-60, chairman of department, 1966-69, director of city planning studies, 1969-70. Visiting lecturer at Massachusetts Institute of Technology, School of Planning and Architecture, 1948-49, North Carolina State College (now North Carolina State University at Raleigh), 1950-51, University of Winnipeg, 1958, Clemson College (now Clemson University), 1958, and Harvard University, 1960-61; visiting critic, University of Minnesota, 1953. Chairman of town planning committee of Modern Architectural Research Society, London, 1938-39, and of New Haven City

Planning Commission, 1960; member of Connecticut State Site Selection Committee for the United Nations, 1947, and U.S. Advisory Council on Historic Preservation, 1967-69. *Military service:* Served with Royal Canadian Engineers, 1942-43. *Member:* Institute of Landscape Architects (honorary secretary, 1939), American Institute of Planners, American Institute of Architects, Century Association (New York City), Yale Club, Elizabethan Club.

AWARDS, HONORS: Special award for landscape design, Paris Exposition, 1937; Bronze medal, Federated Garden Clubs of Connecticut, 1949; Guggenheim fellow, 1950; Fulbright fellow, 1956; M.A., Yale University, 1962; honorary doctorate, Union College, 1964, and University of Victoria, 1970; National Book Award, 1964, for *Man-Made America.*

WRITINGS: Gardens in the Modern Landscape, Architectural Press, 1938; *The City of Man,* Scribner, 1953, 2nd edition, 1970; (editor with J. Pearce) *City Planning at Yale,* Department of Architecture, Yale University, 1954; (with Henry Hope Reed) *American Skyline,* Houghton, 1955; (with Boris Pushkarev) *Man-Made America: Chaos or Control?,* Yale University Press, 1963; *The Modern American City,* Van Nostrand, 1968; *Planning for Future Leisure: Sydney, 2000,* Faculty of Architecture, University of New South Wales, 1971; *A World with a View: An Inquiry into the Nature of Scenic Values,* Yale University Press, 1978. Contributor to various periodicals.

SIDELIGHTS: Christopher Tunnard is credited with having developed a new concept of city planning, that of thinking in terms of "regional cities" sometimes hundreds of miles long, instead of in terms of metropolitan areas. Thus he saw one "linear city" stretching from Portland, Maine, to Norfolk, Virginia, some 600 miles, comprising nearly one-fifth of the national population. From the aesthetic standpoint, he considered the lack of art in the urban environment one of our most serious social problems and was concerned over the destruction of the American landscape.

BIOGRAPHICAL/CRITICAL SOURCES: New York Times Book Review, April 21, 1963; *Architectural Forum,* June, 1963; *New York Times,* June 19, 1978.

OBITUARIES: New York Times, February 15, 1979.†

*   *   *

TURNBULL, Patrick Edward Xenophon 1908-

PERSONAL: Born March 17, 1908, in Barberton, Transvaal, South Africa; son of Hugh Xenophon and Ethel Mary (Webb) Turnbull; married Elsa Gryffydh-Jones, January 4, 1951; children: Dominic Xenophon, Giles Patrick. *Education:* Attended Bedford School and Royal Military College, Sandhurst, England. *Politics:* Conservative. *Religion:* Anglo-Catholic. *Address:* Number Two Pond Cottages, Chilton, Near Didcot, Oxfordshire OX11 0PG, England. *Agent:* Laurence Pollinger Ltd., 18 Maddox St., London W1R 0EU, England.

CAREER: British Army, 1928-31, 1939-56, retired as lieutenant colonel; spent 1933-39 in Morocco and Algeria; free-lance writer, 1956—. Served with Royal Sussex Regiment in India, 1928-31, with British Expeditionary Force in France, 1940, and with Infantry in Burma campaigns; held post-war assignments in Lebanon, Cyprus, and as assistant military attache in Salonica, Greece, 1951-56. *Awards, honors*—Military: Military Cross; mentioned in dispatches.

WRITINGS: Red Walls (novel), Hurst & Blackett, 1935; *Dusty Shoes* (novel), Hurst & Blackett, 1936; *Black Barbary* (travel), Hurst & Blackett, 1938; *Sahara Unveiled* (travel), Hurst & Blackett, 1940; *The Forgotten Battalion* (novel), Hurst &

Blackett, 1947; *The Last of Men* (novel), Hutchinson, 1960; *The Hotter Winds* (memoirs), Hutchinson, 1960; *A Phantom Called Glory* (historical novel), Hutchinson, 1961; *Wingless Eagle* (historical novel), Hutchinson, 1962; *The Foreign Legion: A History of the Foreign Legion,* Heinemann, 1964; *One Bullet for the General,* Holt, 1967, new edition, Remploy, 1979; *Death Is Our Playmate,* Pan Books, 1971; *La Porte des Indes,* Fleuve, 1971; *Napoleon's Second Empress,* M. Joseph, 1971, Walker, 1972; *Provence,* Batsford, 1972, published as *Discovering Provence,* 1973; *Eugenie of the French,* M. Joseph, 1974; *Clive of India,* Bailey Brothers & Swinfen, 1975; *Warren Hastings,* New English Library, 1975; *Gordon of Khartoum,* Bailey Brothers & Swinfen, 1975; *Corsica,* Batsford, 1976; *Dead for a Dead Thing,* New English Library, 1976; *Dunkirk: Anatomy of Disaster,* Holmes & Meier, 1978; *Search for Livingstone,* Macdonald Educational, 1978; *The Spanish Civil War: 1936-1939,* Osprey, 1978; *Battle of the Box,* Ian Allan, 1979; *Dordogne,* Batsford, 1979; *The Shadow of a Flying Bird,* R. Hale, 1979; *Some Scarred Slope,* R. Hale, 1981.

Also author of *Un Fortin a That Ninh,* 1966. Author of record script "Napoleon: General, Consul, and Emperor," 1963. Writer of monthly column on general events in south of France, 1957-61; correspondent critic, *Opera,* for Nice and Monte Carlo seasons, 1958-61. Contributor of articles and short stories to British, French, Scandinavian, Dutch, and American periodicals, including *Woman's Mirror, Cosmopolitan, History Today, Miroir de l'Histoire, Ici Paris, War Monthly,* and *British History Illustrated.*

WORK IN PROGRESS: A novel about the war in the Pacific, circa 1943; translating several of his books for French editions.

SIDELIGHTS: Patrick Turnbull holds an official interpretership in French, speaks Spanish and Italian, and knows some Urdu. During the years between the two world wars, he went into the Moroccan Sahara and spent considerable time with a Foreign Legion cavalry squadron in the desert post of Bou Malem; hence, his writing interest in the Foreign Legion. Turnbull considers Irwin Shaw's *The Young Lions* the best book to come out of World War II. As for other things American, he recalls a mint julep as one of the most pleasant drinks he has ever tasted.

AVOCATIONAL INTERESTS: Opera, horseback riding, mountain scenery, modern painting.

BIOGRAPHICAL/CRITICAL SOURCES: Books and Bookmen, September, 1960; *Oxford Times,* March 27, 1981.

*   *   *

TURNER, (Henry) Arlin 1909-1980

PERSONAL: Born November 25, 1909, in Abilene, Tex.; died April 24, 1980, in Austin, Tex.; son of John Henry (a farmer) and Verna Lee (Hatchell) Turner; married Thelma Elizabeth Sherrill (a language teacher), August 7, 1937; children: Arline Elizabeth (Mrs. Richard W. Fonda), Jack Sherrill, Richard Arlin. *Education:* West Texas State College (now University), B.A., 1927; University of Texas, M.A., 1930, Ph.D., 1934. *Home:* 1115 Woodburn Rd., Durham, N.C. 27705.

CAREER: University of Texas, Main University (now University of Texas at Austin), instructor in English, 1934-36; Louisiana State University, Baton Rouge, instructor, 1936-37, assistant professor, 1937-46, associate professor, 1946-49, professor of English, 1949-53; Duke University, Durham, N.C., professor of English, 1953-79, James B. Duke Professor of English, 1974-79, professor emeritus, 1979-80, chairman of department, 1958-64. Visiting professor at University of Montreal, 1951, University of Bombay, 1964, and Southwest Texas University, 1980; Fulbright lecturer at University of Western Australia, 1952, and University of Hull, 1966-67; summer instructor at other colleges and universities in United States, 1934-64. *Military service:* U.S. Naval Reserve, 1942-46; became lieutenant commander; received Secretary of the Navy Citation.

MEMBER: Modern Language Association of America (secretary-treasurer, American Literature Group, 1950-53; chairman, American Literature Section, 1966-67), American Studies Association, College English Association, National Council of Teachers of English (director, 1961-66), Society of American Historians, American Association of University Professors, American Council of Learned Socities (associate, 1956-66), South Central Modern Language Association, South Atlantic Modern Language Association, Southern Historical Association, Phi Beta Kappa. *Awards, honors:* Guggenheim fellow, 1947-48, 1959-60; Charles S. Sydnor Prize of Southern Historical Association, 1956 and 1957, for best book on southern history, *George W. Cable: A Biography;* National Endowment for the Humanities senior fellow, 1973-74; Huntington Library-National Endowment for the Humanities fellow, 1977.

WRITINGS: (Editor) *Hawthorne as Editor,* Louisiana State University Press, 1941, reprinted, Folcroft, 1976; *George W. Cable: A Biography,* Duke University Press, 1956; (editor) George W. Cable, *The Negro Question: A Selection of Writings on Civil Rights in the South,* Anchor Books, 1958; (editor) Nathaniel Hawthorne, *The Blithedale Romance,* Norton, 1958; (editor) *Creoles and Cajuns: Stories of Old Louisiana,* Anchor Books, 1959.

Mark Twain and George W. Cable: The Record of a Literary Friendship, Michigan State University Press, 1960; (editor) *Southern Stories,* Rinehart, 1960; *Nathaniel Hawthorne: An Introduction and Interpretation,* Barnes & Noble, 1961; (editor) *Chita: A Memory of Last Island,* University of North Carolina, 1969; (editor) *Miss Ravenel's Conversion from Sucession to Loyalty,* Merrill, 1969; (editor) *The Silent South,* Patterson Smith, 1969; (editor) *The Merrill Studies in "The Scarlet Letter,"* Merrill, 1970; (contributor) *The Chief Glory of Every People,* University of Southern Illinois, 1973; *The Comic Imagination in American Literature,* Rutgers University, 1973.

Nathaniel Hawthorne: A Biography, Oxford University Press, 1980; (editor) *Critical Essays on George Washington Cable,* G. K. Hall, 1980; *Toward A New American Literary History,* Duke University Press, 1980. Also contributor to *The Teacher and American Literature,* 1965. Contributor of essays to *Saturday Review* and other literary journals. *American Literature,* managing editor, 1954-63, editor, 1969-79; member of editorial board, *South Atlantic Quarterly,* beginning 1956.

BIOGRAPHICAL/CRITICAL SOURCES: Times Literary Supplement, June 12, 1981.

OBITUARIES: New York Times, April 30, 1980.†

U

UBBELOHDE, Carl (William, Jr.) 1924-

PERSONAL: Born November 4, 1924, in Waldo, Wis.; son of Carl William and Carrie (Stratton) Ubbelohde; married Mary Jean Tipler, 1952; children: Mary Susan, Carrie Ellan, Libby Jean, Katherine Johanna. *Education:* University of Wisconsin, B.S., 1948, M.A., 1950, Ph.D., 1954. *Home:* 2577 Overlook Rd., No. 5, Cleveland Heights, Ohio 44106. *Office:* Department of History, Case Western Reserve University, Cleveland, Ohio 44106.

CAREER: University of Colorado, Boulder, instructor, 1954-56, assistant professor, 1956-59, associate professor of history, 1959-65; Case Western Reserve University, Cleveland, Ohio, associate professor, 1965-68, professor, 1968-75, Henry Eldridge Bourne Professor of History, 1975—, acting chairman, 1968-69, chairman of department, 1973-76, 1980—. Visiting lecturer, University of Wisconsin, summer, 1961; visiting professor, University of Texas, 1964, University of Vermont, summer, 1966, summer, 1967, University of Pennsylvania, summer, 1968, Ohio State University, summer, 1969, University of Delaware, summer, 1970, and Texas Tech University, spring, 1980; Norman F. Furniss Lecturer in History, Colorado State University, 1976. *Military service:* U.S. Army, 1943-45; awarded Purple Heart. *Member:* Organization of American Historians, American Historical Association, American Association of University Professors, National Trust for Historic Preservation, American Association for State and Local History, Ohio Academy of History (chairman of American Bicentennial committee, 1973-78), Ohio Historical Society, Western Reserve Historical Society, Phi Beta Kappa (honorary member). *Awards, honors:* Genevieve Gorst Herfurth Award, University of Wisconsin, 1955; distinguished teacher award, University of Colorado, 1963; Carl Frederick Wittke Distinguished Teacher Award, Case Western Reserve University, 1967, 1973; teaching award, Adelbert College Student Council, 1967; award of merit, American Association for State and Local History, 1968.

WRITINGS: (Compiler with Lillian Krueger and P. H. Boeger) *Index to the Wisconsin Magazine of History,* State Historical Society of Wisconsin, 1955; (with R. G. Athearn) *Centennial Colorado,* Chambers, 1959; *The Vice-Admiralty Courts and the American Revolution,* University of North Carolina Press, 1960; (editor) *A Colorado Reader,* Pruett, 1962, revised edition, 1964; *Colorado: A Student's Guide to Localized History,* Bureau of Publications, Teachers College, Columbia University, 1965; *A Colorado History,* Pruett, 1965, 4th edition (with Maxine Benson and Duane A. Smith), 1976; (with Clifford L. Lord) *Clio's Servant: The State Historical Society of Wisconsin,* State Historical Society of Wisconsin, 1967; *The American Colonies and the British Empire,* Crowell, 1968, 2nd edition, AHM Publishing, 1975; (editor) *Contemporary Colorado,* University of Colorado Press, 1968.

(Editor and author of introduction) Herbert Freidenwald, *The Declaration of Independence,* Da Capa Press, 1974; (compiler with John Cary) *Guide to Sources on the American Revolution Located in Ohio Libraries,* Ohio Historical Society, 1977; (contributor) George G. Suggs, Jr., editor, *Perspectives on the American Revolution: A Bicentennial Contribution,* Southern Illinois University Press, 1977. Contributor to *Encyclopedia Americana, Dictionary of American History, Collier's Encyclopedia,* and *Encyclopedia of American History.* Contributor to professional journals. Book review editor, *Montana: The Magazine of Western History,* 1960-61.

* * *

UCHIDA, Yoshiko 1921-

PERSONAL: Surname is pronounced ''Oo-*chee*-dah''; born November 24, 1921, in Alameda, Calif.; daughter of Dwight Takashi (a businessman) and Iku (Umegaki) Uchida. *Education:* University of California, Berkeley, A.B. (cum laude), 1942; Smith College, M.Ed., 1944. *Politics:* Democrat. *Religion:* Protestant. *Residence:* Berkeley, Calif.

CAREER: Elementary school teacher in Japanese relocation center in Utah, beginning 1942; Frankford Friends' School, Philadelphia, Pa., teacher, 1944-45; membership secretary, Institute of Pacific Relations, 1946-47; secretary, United Student Christian Council, 1947-52; full-time writer, 1952-57; University of California, Berkeley, secretary, 1957-62; full-time writer, 1962—. *Awards, honors:* Ford Foundation research fellow in Japan, 1952; Children's Spring Book Festival honor award, *New York Herald Tribune,* 1955, for *The Magic Listening Cap;* Notable Book Award, American Library Association, 1972, for *Journey to Topaz;* medal for best juvenile book by a California author, Commonwealth Club of California, 1972, for *Samurai of Gold Hill;* Award of Merit, California Association of Teachers of English, 1973; citation, Contra Costa chapter of Japanese American Citizens League, 1976, for outstanding contribution to the cultural development of society; Morris S. Rosenblatt Award, Utah State Historical Society, 1981, for article, ''Topaz, City of Dust.''

WRITINGS: *The Dancing Kettle and Other Japanese Folk Tales,* Harcourt, 1949; *We Do Not Work Alone: Kanjiro Kawai,* Folk Art Society (Japan), 1953; (self-illustrated) *The Magic Listening Cap—More Folk Tales from Japan,* Harcourt, 1955; (self-illustrated) *The Full Circle* (junior high school study book), Friendship, 1957; *Takao and Grandfather's Sword,* Harcourt, 1958; *The Promised Year,* Harcourt, 1959; *Mik and the Prowler,* Harcourt, 1960; (translator of English portions) Soetsu Yanagi, editor, *Shoji Hamada,* Asahi Shimbun Publishing, 1961; *Makoto the Smallest Boy,* Crowell, 1970; *Journey Home,* Atheneum, 1978; *A Jar of Dreams,* Atheneum, 1981; *Desert Exile: The Uprooting of a Japanese-American Family,* University of Washington Press, 1982.

Published by Scribner: *New Friends for Susan,* 1951; *Rokubei and the Thousand Rice Bowls,* 1962; *The Forever Christmas Tree,* 1963; *Sumi's Prize,* 1964; *The Sea of Gold, and Other Tales from Japan,* 1965; *Sumi's Special Happening,* 1966; *In-Between Miya,* 1967; *Hisako's Mysteries,* 1969; *Sumi and the Goat and the Tokyo Express,* 1969; *Journey to Topaz,* 1971; *Samurai of Gold Hill,* 1972; *The Birthday Visitor,* 1975; *The Rooster Who Understood Japanese,* 1976.

Contributor of short stories for juveniles: *Scribner Anthology for Young People,* Scribner, 1976; *Sense,* Scott, Foresman, 1977; *Image,* Scott, Foresman, 1977; *Question and Form in Literature,* Scott, Foresman, 1979; *The Abracadabras,* Addison-Wesley, 1981.

Author of regular column, "Letter from San Francisco," in *Craft Horizons,* 1958-61. Contributor to exhibit catalogue of Oakland Museum, 1976. Contributor of adult stories and articles to newspapers and periodicals, including *Woman's Day, Gourmet, Utah Historical Quarterly, Far East,* and *California Monthly.*

SIDELIGHTS: Yoshiko Uchida writes to *CA:* "Through my books I hope to give young Asian Americans a sense of their past and to reinforce their self-esteem and self-knowledge. At the same time, I want to dispel the stereotypic image still held by many non-Asians about the Japanese and write about them as real people. I hope to convey the strength of spirit and the sense of hope and purpose I have observed in many first-generation Japanese. Beyond that, I write to celebrate our common humanity, for the basic elements of humanity are present in all our strivings."

Uchida's books have been translated into German and Dutch.

AVOCATIONAL INTERESTS: Fine arts, folk crafts.

BIOGRAPHICAL/CRITICAL SOURCES: *Young Readers' Review,* January, 1967; *Children's Book World,* November 5, 1967.

* * *

UDRY, Janice May 1928-

PERSONAL: Surname is pronounced *Yoo*-dri; born June 14, 1928, in Jacksonville, Ill.; daughter of Harold and Louise (Southwell) May; married Richard Udry (a teacher), August, 1950; children: Leslie, Susan. *Education:* Northwestern University, B.S., 1950. *Residence:* Chapel Hill, N.C.

CAREER: Free-lance writer. *Awards, honors:* Caldecott Award, 1956, for *A Tree Is Nice.*

WRITINGS—Published by Albert Whitman, except as indicated: *A Tree Is Nice,* Harper, 1956; *Theodore's Parents,* Lothrop, 1958; *Moon-Jumpers,* Harper, 1959; *Danny's Pig,* Lothrop, 1960; *Alfred,* 1960; *Let's Be Enemies,* Harper, 1961; *Is*

Susan Here?, Abelard, 1962; *The Mean Mouse, and Other Mean Stories,* Harper 1962; *The End of the Line,* 1962; *Betsy-Back-In-Bed,* 1963; *Next Door to Laura Linda,* 1965; *What Mary Jo Shared,* 1966; *If You're a Bear,* 1967; *Mary Ann's Mud Day,* Harper, 1967; *What Mary Jo Wanted,* 1968; *Glenda,* Harper, 1969; *The Sunflower Garden,* Harvey House, 1969; *Emily's Autumn,* 1969; *Mary Jo's Grandmother* (Junior Literary Guild selection), 1970; *Angie,* Harper, 1971; *How I Faded Away,* 1975; *Oh, No! Cat!,* Coward, 1976; *Thump and Plunk,* Harper, 1981.

SIDELIGHTS: "I love to read," Janice May Udry told *CA.* "Someone has said that not all readers are writers, but all writers are readers. I believe this is true. And a lot of reading in childhood often leads to a life time of writing. I love good books for children today as much as I did when I was a child. I probably appreciate them more now since I have been a writer of books for children for twenty-five years. A good book for children will not bore an adult."

BIOGRAPHICAL/CRITICAL SOURCES: Lee Bennett Hopkins, *Books Are by People,* Citation Press, 1969.

* * *

UNCLE GUS
See REY, H(ans) A(ugusto)

* * *

UNDERWOOD, Michael
See EVELYN, (John) Michael

* * *

UNGER, Merrill F. 1909-

PERSONAL: Born July 16, 1909, in Baltimore, Md.; son of Conrad H. and Catherine (Leistner) Unger; married September 9, 1949; wife's name, Elsie Aileen (died, 1967); married Pearl Catherine Stoffers, June 9, 1968; children: (first marriage) Clark Conrad, Shelley Aileen. *Education:* Johns Hopkins University, A.B., 1930, Ph.D., 1947; attended Southern Baptist Theological Seminary, 1932-33, and Nyack Missionary College, 1934; Dallas Theological Seminary, Th.M., 1943, Th.D., 1945. *Home and office:* 194 Inverness Rd., Severna Park, Md. 21146.

CAREER: Pastor of West Ferry Church, Buffalo, N.Y., 1934-40, Winnetka Church, Dallas, Tex., 1943-44, and Bible Presbyterian Church, Baltimore, Md., 1945-47; Gordon College, Boston, Mass., assistant professor of Greek, 1947-48; Dallas Theological Seminary, Dallas, Tex., professor and chairman of department of Old Testament, 1948-67, professor emeritus, 1967—. Lecturer, Gordon Divinity School, 1947-48. *Member:* American Schools of Oriental Research. *Awards, honors:* Cited as "theological author of quarter-century" by Zondervan Publishing House, 1956, for *Introductory Guide to the Old Testament* and *Archaeology and the Old Testament.*

WRITINGS: *Introductory Guide to the Old Testament,* Zondervan, 1952, reprinted, 1964; *Biblical Demonology: A Study of the Spiritual Forces behind the Present World Unrest,* Van Kampen Press, 1952, 7th edition, 1967; *The Baptizing Work of the Holy Spirit,* Scripture Press, 1953; *Pathways to Power,* Zondervan, 1953; *Archaeology and the Old Testament,* Zondervan, 1954; *Great Neglected Bible Prophecies,* Scripture Press, 1955; *Principles of Expository Preaching,* Zondervan, 1955, reprinted, 1973; *The God-filled Life,* Zondervan, 1956; *Bible Dictionary* (based on *The People's Bible Encyclopedia* edited by C. R. Barnes) Moody, 1957, 3rd revised edition published as *Unger's Bible Dictionary*, 1963; *The Dead Sea Scrolls and Other Amazing Discoveries*, Zondervan, 1957; *Starlit Paths*, Dunham, 1958; *Stop Existing and Start Living*, Eerdmans, 1959.

Archaeology and the New Testament, Zondervan, 1962; *Zechariah* (Bible commentary), Zondervan, 1963; *Unger's Bible Handbook: An Essential Guide to Understanding the Bible* (also see below), Moody, 1966; *Demons in the World Today: A Study of Occultism in the Light of God's Word*, Tyndale, 1971; *The Haunting of Bishop Pike: A Christian View of the Other Side*, Tyndale, 1971; *New Testament Teaching on Tongues*, Kregel, 1971; *Beyond the Crystal Ball*, Moody, 1973; *The Baptism and Gifts of the Holy Spirit*, Moody, 1974; *Unger's Guide to the Bible*, Tyndale, 1975; (with Zola Levitt) *God Is Waiting to Meet You*, Moody, 1975, published as *God, Where Are You?*, 1977; *The Parallel New Testament and Unger's Bible Handbook*, Iversen-Norman Associates, 1975; *What Demons Can Do to Saints*, Moody, 1977; (editor with William White, Jr.) *Nelson's Expository Dictionary of the Old Testament*, Thomas Nelson, 1980; *Israel and the Aramaens of Damascus*, Baker Book, 1980; *Unger's Bible Commentary: Genesis-Song of Solomon*, Moody, 1981.

*   *   *

UNNERSTAD, Edith Totterman   1900-

PERSONAL: Born July 28, 1900, in Helsinki, Finland; daughter of Axel A. and Ingeborg (Boman) Totterman; married Arvid B. Unnerstad (a civil engineer and managing director), January 8, 1924; children: Madeleine. *Education:* Studied at Detthow College, and at art school in Stockholm, Sweden. *Home:* Burevagen 12, Djursholm, Sweden.

CAREER: Writer of children's books, 1932—, novels, 1933—. *Member:* Swedish Authors Association, Swedish Childrens Authors Association, Authors Guild (United States). *Awards, honors:* Childrens Book Prize, 1949; Nils Holgersson Award, 1957; Swedish Government fellowships, 1956, 1959, 1966.

WRITINGS—Juveniles; published by Raben & Sjogren, except as indicated: *Uffe reser jorden runt*, Natur och Kultur, 1932; *Hoppentott i Vanliga skogen*, Natur och Kultur, 1938; *Muck*, Natur och Kultur, 1939; *Tummelunsarna i Vanliga skogen*, Natur & Kultur, 1939; *Pikku-Lotta*, Fahlcrantz & Gumaelius, 1941; *Kastrullresan*, 1949, reprinted 1964, translation published as *The Saucepan Journey*, Macmillan, 1951; *Nu seglar Pip-Larssons*, 1950, reprinted, 1971, translation by Lilian Seaton published as *The Pip-Larssons Go Sailing*, M. Joseph, 1963, and as *The Peep-Larssons Go Sailing*, Macmillan, 1966; *Ankhasten*, 1950; *Pysen*, 1952, translation published as *Pysen*, Macmillan, 1955, translation by Seaton published as *The Urchin*, M. Joseph, 1964, Penguin, 1967; *Pip-Larssons Lilla O*, 1955, translation published as *Little O*, Macmillan, 1957; *Farmorsresan*, 1956, translation published as *The Spettecake Holiday*, Macmillan, 1958; *Kattorna fran Sommaron*, 1957, translation by Holger Lundbergh published as *The Cats from Summer Island*, Macmillan, 1963; *Lasseman spelar*, 1958, translation by Gunvor Edwards published as *Larry Makes Music*, Norton, 1967; *Bollarulla*, 1958, published as *Bollarulla: sju sagor fran Soederasen*, 1968; *Mormorsresan*, 1959, translation published as *A Journey with Grandmother*, Macmillan, 1960.

Englandsresan, 1960, translation published as *Journey to England*, Macmillan, 1961; *Toppen och jag pa torpet*, 1962, translation by Seaton published as *Toppen and I at the Croft*, M. Joseph, 1966; *Boken om Pip-Larssons*, 1962; *Vi tankte ga till skogen*, 1964, translation published as *The Ditch Picnic*,

Norton, 1964 (published in England as *The Picnic*, Oliver, 1964); *Little O's Naughty Day*, translation from original Swedish manuscript by M. Turner, Burke Publishing, 1965; *Sagor vid dammen*, 1965; *Tva sma fnissor*, 1966, translation published as *Two Little Gigglers*, Norton, 1967; *Twilight Tales*, translation from original Swedish manuscript by Seaton, M. Joseph, 1967; *Kasperssons far till landet*, 1969; *Trollen i Tassuvaara*, Ahlen & Akerlund, 1969, translation by Seaton published as *A House for Spinner's Grandmother*, M. Joseph, 1970; *Mickie*, Four Winds Press, 1971; *Cherry Tree Party*, translation from original Swedish manuscript by P. Crampton, Dent, 1978.

Novels, except as indicated: *Garden vid Rodbergsgatan*, Wahlstrom & Widstrand, 1935; *Boken om Alarik Barck*, Bonniers, 1936; *Susann*, Natur och Kultur, 1943; *Bricken*, Natur och Kultur, 1945; *Sara och Lejonkringla*, Natur och Kultur, 1946; *Snackhuset*, Norstedt & Soner, 1949; *Ensam hemma med Johnny*, Norstedt & Soner, 1951; *Leksaksekon* (poetry), Norstedt & Soner, 1952; *Bockhornsgrand*, Norstedt & Soner, 1954; *Jag alskade Clarinda*, Norstedt & Soner, 1957. Also author of scripts for radio, television, and motion pictures.

*   *   *

UNWIN, David S(torr)   1918-
(David Severn)

PERSONAL: Born December 3, 1918, in London, England; son of Sir Stanley (the publisher) and Alice Mary (Storr) Unwin; married Periwinkle Herbert, July 31, 1945; children: Phyllida Mary and Richard Corydon (twins). *Education:* Attended schools in England and Germany. *Politics:* Liberal. *Home:* 33B Chalcot Square, London NW1, England. *Office:* George Allen & Unwin Ltd., 40 Museum St., London WC1 1LU, England.

CAREER: League of Nations Secretariat, Geneva, Switzerland, editorial assistant, 1938-39; Allen & Unwin Ltd. (publishers), London, England, art editor, 1940-43. Publisher's reader for Allen & Unwin and other firms. *Member:* Authors Society, P.E.N., Screenwriters Guild. *Awards, honors:* Authors Club First Novel Award, 1955, for *The Governor's Wife*.

WRITINGS—Adult novels: *The Governor's Wife*, M. Joseph, 1954, Dutton, 1955; *A View of the Heath*, M. Joseph, 1956.

Juvenile books; under pseudonym David Severn; published by Bodley Head, except as indicated: *Rick Afire!*, John Lane, 1942, Houghton, 1946; *A Cabin for Crusoe*, John Lane, 1943; *Wagon for Five*, John Lane, 1944, Houghton, 1947; *A Hermit in the Hills*, John Lane, 1945; *Forest Holiday*, John Lane, 1946; *Ponies and Poachers*, John Lane, 1947; *Bill Badger and the Pine Martens*, 1947; *Wily Fox and the Baby Show*, 1947; *The Cruise of the Maiden Castle*, 1948, Macmillan (New York), 1949; *Bill Badger and the Bathing Pool*, 1948; *Wily Fox and the Christmas Party*, 1948; *Treasure for Three*, 1949, Macmillan (New York), 1950; *Dream Gold*, 1949, Viking, 1952.

Wily Fox and the Missing Fireworks, 1950; *Bill Badger and the Buried Treasure*, 1950; *My Foreign Correspondent through Africa*, Meiklejohn, 1951; *Crazy Castle*, 1951, Macmillan (New York), 1952; *Burglars and Bandicoots*, 1952, Macmillan (New York), 1953; *Drumbeats!*, 1953; (with Geoffrey Higham) *Bill Badger Omnibus*, John Lane, 1954; *Blaze of Broadfurror Farm*, 1955; *Walnut Tree Meadow*, 1955; *The Green-Eyed Gryphon*, Hamish Hamilton, 1958; *The Future Took Us*, 1958; *Foxy-Boy*, 1959, published as *The Wild Valley*, Dutton, 1963; *Three at Sea*, 1959.

Jeff Dickson: Cowhand, J. Cape, 1963; *Clouds over the Alberhorn*, Hamish Hamilton, 1963; *The Girl in the Grove*, Allen

& Unwin, 1974, Harper, 1975; *The Wishing Bone*, Allen & Unwin, 1977.

WORK IN PROGRESS: Fifty Years with Father, a memoir.

SIDELIGHTS: J. D. Finn writes in *Commonweal* that David Unwin's *The Governor's Wife* "reveals a writer who is sure in his craft. [Unwin] plunges us into the action and maintains it at an ever-increasing pace, sketches characters economically, and evokes an almost palpable atmosphere with his description. And his novel has the elementary virtue without which other virtues are as straw: it is interesting." In the *New Statesman and Nation*, John Raymond claims that "if the book fails as a novel, it is because it is too full of meat, too crammed and episodic. . . . [But] the book succeeds through its vigorous and uncompromising reporting—an imaginative reporting that reminds me of Disraeli's *Sybil*."

David Unwin told *CA:* "I write, very largely, from personal experience and tend to dovetail my fictional plots into known topography, climate, [and] local conditions. . . . My books for children, which I began to write in my early twenties, are for the most part conceived out of a love for the English countryside. Many are set in specific locations: Cornwall, Wales, the New Forest. Some are straightforward holiday adventure stories; others are not—and I am perhaps happiest when, as often happens, my tales edge over into fantasy."

BIOGRAPHICAL/CRITICAL SOURCES: New Statesman and Nation, July 31, 1954; *New York Herald Tribune Book Review*, April 10, 1955; *New York Times*, April 17, 1955; *Commonweal*, June 3, 1955.

*　　*　　*

URQUHART, Fred(erick Burrows) 1912-

PERSONAL: Born July 12, 1912, in Edinburgh, Scotland; son of Frederick Burrows and Agnes (Harrower) Urquhart. *Education:* Attended village and secondary schools in Scotland. *Home:* Spring Garden Cottage, Fairwarp, Uckfield, Sussex TN22 3BG, England. *Agent:* Anthony Sheil Associates Ltd., 2-3 Morwell St., London WC1B 3AR, England.

CAREER: Left school at fifteen and worked in a bookshop, Edinburgh, Scotland, 1927-34; free-lance writer; reader for literary agency in London, England, 1947-51, and for Metro-Goldwyn-Mayer, 1951-54; Cassell & Co. Ltd., London, reader, 1951-74. London scout for Walt Disney Productions, 1959-60; reader for J. M. Dent & Sons Ltd,. 1967-71. *Awards, honors:* Tom Gallon Award, Society of Authors, 1951-52, for story, "The Ploughing Match"; Arts Council of Great Britain grants, 1966 and 1978; Scottish Arts Council grant, 1975.

WRITINGS: Time Will Knit (novel), Duckworth, 1938, Penguin (New York), 1943; *I Fell for a Sailor, and Other Stories*, Duckworth, 1940; *The Clouds Are Big with Mercy: Short Stories*, William Maclellan, 1946; *Selected Stories*, Maurice Fridberg, 1946; *The Last G.I. Bride Wore Tartan: A Novella and Some Short Stories*, Serif Books, 1947; *The Ferret Was Abraham's Daughter*, Methuen, 1949; *The Year of the Short Corn, and Other Stories*, Methuen, 1949; *The Last Sister, and Other Stories*, Methuen, 1950; *Jezebel's Dust*, Methuen, 1951; *The Laundry Girl and the Pole: Selected Stories*, Arco Publications, 1955; (author of text) Kenneth Scowen, *Scotland in Color*, Viking, 1961; *The Collected Stories of Fred Urquhart*, Hart-Davis, Volume I: *The Dying Stallion*, 1967, Volume II: *The Ploughing Match*, 1968; (with William Freeman) *Everyman's Dictionary of Fictional Characters*, 3rd edition (Urquhart was not associated with previous editions), Dent, 1973, published

as *Dictionary of Fictional Characters*, Writer, Inc., 1974; *Palace of Green Days* (novel), Quartet Books, 1979; *Proud Lady in a Cage, and Other Stories*, Paul Harris, 1980; *A Diver in China Seas, and Other Stories*, Quartet Books, 1980.

Editor: (With Maurice Lindsay) *No Scottish Twilight: New Scottish Short Stories*, William Maclellan, 1947; *W.S.C.: A Cartoon Biography* (of Winston Churchill), Cassell, 1955; *Scottish Short Stories*, 3rd revised edition, Faber, 1957; *Great True War Adventures*, Arco, 1957; *Men at War: The Best War Stories of All Time*, Arco, 1957; *The Cassell Miscellany (1848-1958)*, Cassell, 1958; *Great True Escape Stories*, Arco, 1958; (with Giles Gordon) *Modern Scottish Short Stories*, Hamish Hamilton, 1978; *The Book of Horses*, Morrow, 1981.

Contributor: Edward J. H. O'Brien, editor, *Best Stories of 1938*, Houghton, 1938; Cyril Connolly, editor, *Horizon Stories*, Faber, 1945; Whit Burnett and Hallie Burnett, editors, *Story: The Fiction of the Forties*, Dutton, 1950; Derek Hudson, editor, *Modern English Short Stories*, Oxford University Press, 1956; John Pudney, editor, *Pick of Today's Short Stories*, Volume XI, Putnam, 1960; J. M. Reid, editor, *Scottish Short Stories*, Oxford University Press, 1963; Michael Rheta Martin, editor, *The Language of Love*, Bantam, 1964; James Turner, editor, *Thy Neighbor's Wife*, Cassell, 1964; Turner, editor, *The Fourth Ghost Book*, Barrie & Rockliff, 1965; Turner, editor, *Unlikely Ghosts*, Taplinger, 1969; J. F. Hendry, editor, *Penguin Book of Scottish Short Stories*, Penguin, 1970; Denys Val Baker, editor, *Stories of Country Life*, Kimber, 1975; Gordon, editor, *Prevailing Spirits*, Hamish Hamilton, 1976; Baker, editor, *Stories of the Night*, Kimber, 1976; Baker, editor, *My Favourite Story*, Kimber, 1977; Baker, editor, *Stories of Horror and Suspense*, Kimber, 1978; Baker, editor, *Stories of the Occult*, Kimber, 1978; James Hale, editor, *The Midnight Ghost Book*, Barrie & Jenkins, 1978; John Laurie, editor, *My Favourite Stories of Scotland*, Lutterworth, 1978; Ronald Blythe, editor, *My Favourite Village Stories*, Lutterworth, 1979; Baker, editor, *Stories of the Supernatural*, Kimber, 1979; Baker, editor, *Stories of Fear*, Kimber, 1980. Contributor of one hundred short stories to periodicals, including *London Magazine, London Mercury, Adelphi, Horizon, Life and Letters, Spectator, New Statesman, Story*, and *Harper's*. Book reviewer for periodicals and newspapers, including *Time and Tide, Books of the Month, Sunday Telegraph*, and *Oxford Mail*.

WORK IN PROGRESS: A novel; short stories.

SIDELIGHTS: In *Spectator*, Frank Rudman calls Fred Urquhart "one of our most distinguished writers of the short story. . . . He writes fine Scots dialect as well as supple English, and knows Scottish history down to its minutest detail." Francis King says in *Spectator* that Urquhart "writes so simply and so effortlessly that it is easy to underrate him." Comparing *Palace of Green Days* to Urquhart's first novel, *Time Will Knit*, King sees "the same benign enjoyment of human nature in all its inequalities and oddnesses."

Urquhart's short stories have been read on radio and have been translated into several European languages.

BIOGRAPHICAL/CRITICAL SOURCES: Listener, December 14, 1967; *Spectator*, December 15, 1967, May 24, 1968, August 18, 1979, September 13, 1980; *Blackwood's Magazine*, February, 1968, March, 1980; *Punch*, June 5, 1968; Maurice Lindsay, *History of Scottish Literature*, R. Hale, 1977; *Observer*, July 29, 1979; *Guardian*, July 24, 1980, August 21, 1980; *Financial Times*, August 23, 1980; *Times Literary Supplement*, September 19, 1980.

V

VAHANIAN, Gabriel (Antoine) 1927-

PERSONAL: Born January 24, 1927, in Marseilles, France; son of Mesrop and Perouse (Tateossian) Vahanian; married Barbara Swanger, December 22, 1962; children: Paul-Michel, Noelle. *Education:* University of Grenoble, B.A., 1945; Sorbonne, University of Paris, diplome de l'Ecole des Hautes Etudes, 1948; Faculte de Theologie Protestante de Paris, B.D., 1949; Princeton Theological Seminary, Th.M., 1950, Th.D., 1958; received degree of Docteur en theologie, 1978. *Office:* Department of Religion, Syracuse University, Syracuse, N.Y. 13210.

CAREER: Princeton University, Princeton, N.J., instructor, 1955-58; Syracuse University, Syracuse, N.Y., assistant professor, 1958-62, associate professor, 1962-67, Eliphalet Remington Professor, 1967-73, Jeanette K. Watson Professor of Religion, 1973—, director of graduate studies in religion, 1967-75. Visiting professor, Universite des Sciences Humaines de Strasbourg, 1972-73, 1975-76, 1979-80, and University of Toronto, summer, 1978. Syracuse University, member of curriculum committee, College of Liberal Arts, 1966-68, member of committee on instruction, University Senate. *Military service:* French Army, Chasseurs Alpins, 1950-51; became sergeant. *Member:* American Association of University Professors, Societe des Professeurs Francais en Amerique, American Academy of Religion (member of board of directors; chairman of Section on Religion and the Arts, 1968-71), Hazen Society for Theological Discussion, Phi Eta Sigma. *Awards, honors:* American Council of Learned Societies fellow, 1964-65; Society for the Arts, Religion, and Contemporary Culture fellow, 1968; American Theological Society fellow, 1972; Officier, Ordre des Palmes Academiques.

WRITINGS: (Translator and author of introduction and bibliography) Karl Barth, *The Faith of the Church,* edited by Jean-Louis Leuba, Meridian, 1958; *The Death of God,* Braziller, 1961; *Wait without Idols,* Braziller, 1964; (contributor) Erich Dinkler, editor, *Zeit und Geschichte: Dankesgabe an Rudolf Bultmann zum 80 Geburtstag,* [Tuebingen], 1964; *No Other God,* Braziller, 1966; (author of introduction) Rosemary Ruether, *The Church against Itself,* Herder & Herder, 1967; (author of introduction) Jacques Durandeaux, *Living Questions to Dead Gods,* Sheed, 1968; *La condition de Dieu,* Editions du Seuil (Paris), 1970; *God and Utopia,* Seabury, 1977. Contributor to numerous anthologies. Contributor of articles, reviews, and poems to periodicals.

VALCOE, H. Felix
See SWARTZ, Harry (Felix)

*   *   *

VALDES, Mario J. 1934-

PERSONAL: Born January 28, 1934, in Chicago, Ill.; son of Mario (a businessman) and Juanita (San Martin) Valdes; married Maria Elena Diaz Barriga, August 13, 1955; children: Mario Teotimo, Michael Jordi. *Education:* University of Illinois, B.A., 1957, M.A., 1959, Ph.D., 1962. *Home:* 80 Dale Ave., Toronto, Ontario, Canada. *Office:* Centre for Comparative Literature, University of Toronto, Toronto, Ontario, Canada.

CAREER: University of Michigan, Ann Arbor, instructor in Spanish, 1962-63; University of Toronto, Toronto, Ontario, assistant professor, 1963-66, associate professor, 1966-70, professor of comparative and Spanish literature, 1970—, director of Centre for Comparative Literature, 1978—. Visiting professor, Columbia University, 1967, Transylvania College (now University), 1968, Odense University, Denmark, 1972; head of department of Spanish, Italian and Portuguese, University of Illinois at Chicago Circle, 1976-78. Has appeared on radio programs concerned with Borges, Cervantes, and contemporary Spanish poets on "Ideas" series, Canadian Broadcasting Corp. *Member:* International Comparative Literature Association (member of executive bureau, 1980-83), Canadian Comparative Literature Association (president, 1981-83), Canadian Association of Hispanists, Modern Language Association of America.

WRITINGS: Death in the Literature of Unamuno, University of Illinois Press, 1964, 2nd edition, 1966; (editor and author of introduction) Miguel de Unamuno y Jugo, *Niebla,* Prentice-Hall, 1969; *An Unamuno Source Book,* University of Toronto Press, 1973; (editor) *San Manuel Bueno Martir,* Catedra (Madrid), 1978; *Interpretation of Narrative,* University of Toronto Press, 1978; *Shadows in the Dark: Phenomenological Study of the Novel,* University of Toronto Press, 1981. Contributor to *Hispanofila, New Literary History,* and *University of Toronto Quarterly.* Editor, *Revista Canadiense de Estudios Hispanicos,* 1976—; member of editorial board, *Canadian Revue of Comparative Literature* and *Cuadernos de Comunicacion* (Mexico).

WORK IN PROGRESS: History of Narrative Form in Spanish Literature.

SIDELIGHTS: Mario J. Valdes writes to *CA:* "I believe that the only valid function for the literary critic is that of fellow discussant of the literary text. The literary text being the inexhaustable source for the reader, each reader will tend to find his own interests reflected in the text and is therefore in need of dialogue with others about the text if he is to recognize the inherent creative tension of reading. These views on criticism are derived in part from reader reception theory and in part from the phenomenological hermeneutics of Paul Ricoeur.

"I started writing as a literary critic almost twenty years ago under the fallacious assumption that as an academic I was a privileged reader who would enlighten my readers with my insight and scholarship. The more I reflected on this assumption the more questionable it became. I realized that the insight into texts always came because of the actual or implicit presence of the other person I was addressing about the text. The scholarship would follow as I attempted to convince myself and my discussant of the validity of our findings. At times the other was my implied reader, at other moments a friend and colleague, but most often it was my students. Consequently my theory is primarily based on my teaching experience. The latest challenge as a writer has been to undertake a revision of literary history."

AVOCATIONAL INTERESTS: Travel (visits Spain and Mexico in alternate years).

*   *   *

van den HAAG, Ernest 1914-

PERSONAL: Born September 15, 1914, in The Hague, Netherlands; came to United States in 1940; naturalized citizen in 1947; son of Max (an attorney) and Flora van den Haag. *Education:* Attended University of Naples, University of Florence, and Sorbonne, University of Paris, 1938-40; State University of Iowa, M.A., 1942; New York University, Ph.D., 1952. *Home:* 118 West 79th St., New York, N.Y. 10024.

CAREER: Practicing psychoanalyst. New York University, New York City, adjunct professor of social philosophy, 1946—; New School for Social Research, New York City, lecturer in sociology and psychology, 1946—. Visiting professor of criminal justice, State University of New York at Albany; visiting distinguished service professor at Queens College of the City University of New York; visiting distinguished scholar, Heritage Foundation. Lecturer at City College of the City University of New York, Brooklyn College of the City University of New York, Columbia University, Yale University, Harvard University, and other universities. National Endowment for the Humanities senior fellow, 1973. *Member:* American Sociological Association (fellow), Royal Economic Society (fellow), New York Academy of Sciences. *Awards, honors:* Guggenheim fellowship, 1967.

WRITINGS: Education as an Industry, Augustus Kelley, 1956, reprinted, 1972; (with Ralph Gilbert Ross) *The Fabric of Society,* Harcourt, 1957; (with Ross) *Passion and Social Constraint,* Stein & Day, 1963; *Symbols and Civilization,* Harcourt, 1963; *The Jewish Mystique,* Stein & Day, 1969, revised edition, 1977; *Political Violence and Civil Disobedience,* Harper, 1972; *Punishing Criminals: Concerning a Very Old and Painful Question,* Basic Books, 1975; *Capitalism: Sources of Hostility,* Heritage Foundation, 1979. Also author with Robert Martinson, *Crime Deterrence and Offender Career,* 1975.

Contributor: David White and Bernard Rosenberg, editors, *Mass Culture,* Free Press, 1957; Sidney Hook, editor, *Psychoanalysis: Scientific Method and Philosophy,* New York University

Press, 1959; *The American Scholar Reader,* Atheneum, 1960; Hook, editor, *Religious Experience and Truth,* New York University Press, 1961; Norman Jacobs, editor, *Culture for the Millions,* Van Nostrand, 1961; H. Ruitenbeek, editor, *Psychoanalysis and the Social Sciences,* Dutton, 1962; Hook, editor, *History and Philosophy,* New York University Press, 1963; John Chandos, editor, *To Deprave and Corrupt,* Association Press, 1963; Ruitenbeek, editor, *Varieties of Modern Social Theory,* Dutton, 1963. Also contributor of more than forty articles to *Harper's, Commonweal, Partisan Review, Modern Age, National Review, Commentary,* and other magazines and sociology journals in the United States, England, France and Italy.

*   *   *

VANDIVERT, Rita (Andre) 1905-

PERSONAL: Born December 1, 1905, in London, England; came to United States, 1946; naturalized U.S. citizen, 1950; daughter of Frank and Alice Frederica (Matthes) Andre; married William Vandivert (a photographer), June 7, 1940; children: Susan. *Education:* London School of Economics and Political Science, Regent Street Polytechnic School of Commerce, Inter. B. Comm., 1924. *Home:* Lindsell House, Sheep St., Charlbury, Oxford OX7 3RR, England.

CAREER: R.K.O. Radio Pictures, London, England, secretary and translator, three years; Time, Inc., *March of Time,* London, editorial assistant, 1935-41; British Information Services, New York City, film editor, 1942-44; Time, Inc., war correspondent in England, France, and Germany, 1944-46; Magnum Photos, Inc., New York City, president, 1947-48; freelance writer and researcher, 1948—.

WRITINGS: Common Wild Animals and Their Young, Dell, 1957; *The Porcupine Known as J.R.,* Dodd, 1959; *Young Russia,* Dodd, 1960; *Barnaby,* Dodd, 1963; *Chicken as You Like It,* Rand McNally, 1968; *Favorite Wild Animals of North America,* Scholastic Book Services, 1974; *Understanding Animals as Pets,* Warne, 1975; *Favorite Pets: How to Choose and Care for Them,* Scholastic Book Services, 1977; (advisory editor) *The Pet Encyclopedia,* Varsity (Nashville, Tenn.), 1981. Contributor to *Saturday Evening Post.*

AVOCATIONAL INTERESTS: Her family, good cooking, animals, and travel.

*   *   *

Van FOSSEN, Richard W(aight) 1927-

PERSONAL: Born July 17, 1927, in Washington, D.C.; son of John Raymond and Josephine (Waight) Van Fossen; married Ann Ione Fryer, 1955; children: David Phelps, Rachael Ione. *Education:* Duke University, A.B., 1949, A.M., 1951; Harvard University, Ph.D., 1958. *Religion:* Anglican. *Home:* 482 Country Club Crescent, Mississauga, Ontario, Canada. *Office:* Erindale College, University of Toronto, Mississauga, Ontario, Canada.

CAREER: Clemson College (now University), Clemson, S.C., instructor, 1950-52; Duke University, Durham, N.C., instructor, 1956-59; Cornell College, Mt. Vernon, Iowa, assistant professor, 1959-62, associate professor, 1962-68, professor of English, 1968-70; University of Toronto, Erindale College, Mississauga, Ontario, professor of English, 1970—, associate chairman of department, 1977-79, associate dean of humanities, 1979—, vice-principal, 1980—. *Military service:* U.S. Navy, 1945-46. *Member:* Modern Language Association of America (chairman of bibliographical evidence section, 1963-

64; chairman of advisory committee, 1965-66; chairman of election committee, 1971), Shakespeare Association of America (trustee, 1979-82; chairman of program advisory committee, 1981), Canadian Society for Renaissance Studies, Renaissance Society of America, Mississauga Symphonic Association (member of governing board, 1979—), Phi Beta Kappa. *Awards, honors:* Folger Library fellow; Newberry Library-ACM Seminar in the Humanities faculty fellow, 1965-66.

WRITINGS: (Editor) Thomas Heywood, *A Woman Killed with Kindness,* Harvard University Press, 1961; (editor) Christopher Marlowe, *The Jew of Malta,* University of Nebraska Press, 1964; (editor with W. Blissett and J. Patrick) *A Celebration of Ben Jonson,* University of Toronto Press, 1973; (editor) Chapman, Marston, and Jonson, *Eastward Ho,* Johns Hopkins Press, 1979. Contributor of articles and reviews to scholarly periodicals. Editor, *Renaissance and Reformation,* 1977—.

WORK IN PROGRESS: Ben Jonson and the Idea of the Theatre.

* * *

VANNIER, Maryhelen 1915-

PERSONAL: Born June 18, 1915, in Decatur, Ill.; daughter of W. H. and Maud (Rockwood) Vannier. *Education:* James Millikin University (now Millikin University), B.A., 1938; Columbia University, M.A., 1942; New York University, Ed.D., 1948. *Home:* 7006 Stefani Dr., Dallas, Tex. *Office:* Department of Physical Education, Southern Methodist University, Box 353, Dallas, Tex. 75275.

CAREER: Wellesley High School, Wellesley, Mass., director of department of health and physical education for girls, 1944-45; St. Lawrence University, Canton, N.Y., assistant professor and director of women's division of health, physical education and recreation, 1945-46; Drake University, Des Moines, Iowa, associate professor and director of women's division of health, physical education and recreation, 1946-48; University of Maryland, College Park, visiting lecturer, 1949-50; Southern Methodist University, Dallas, Tex., director, women's department of health, physical education and recreation, 1950—. Delegate, International Congress for Physical Education Teachers of Girls and Women, 1949 and 1958, and National Conference on Reference in Therapeutic Recreation. Member, President Eisenhower's Advisory Youth Council, 1960; member, advisory committee of board of trustees, St. Mark's Private School for Boys, Dallas. *Member:* American Academy of Physical Education (fellow), American Camping Association (member of board of directors), Soroptomist Club for Crippled Children of Dallas (member of board of directors, 1959—), Texas Recreation Society (member of state certification committee). *Awards, honors:* Distinguished alumni award, Millikin University, 1962; resident fellow, Council of Humanities, Southern Methodist University, 1962-63.

WRITINGS—All published by Saunders, except as indicated: *Teaching Physical Education in Elementary Schools,* 1954, 6th edition (with David L. Gallahue), 1978; *Methods and Materials in Recreation Leadership,* 1956, 3rd edition, Lea & Febiger, 1977; *Teaching Physical Education in Secondary Schools,* 1957, 5th edition, 1978; (with Hally B. Poindexter) *Individual and Team Sports for Girls and Women,* 1960, 4th edition, 1976; (contributor) *Youth in the Modern World,* American Association of Health, Physical Education and Recreation, 1962; *Teaching Health in Elementary Schools,* Harper, 1963, 2nd edition, Lea & Febiger, 1974; *A Physical Education Handbook for College Women,* 1964, 2nd edition, 1968; *A Better Figure for You through Easy Exercise and Diet,* Association Press,

1965, 2nd edition, 1973; *Body Conditioning: Figure and Weight Control,* Association Press, 1965; *Physical Activities for the Handicapped,* Prentice-Hall, 1977; *Physical Activities for Young Children,* Allyn & Bacon, 1979. Also author, *Recreation in the Modern Community.* Editor, "Physical Activities" series, for Saunders. Contributor to professional journals.

WORK IN PROGRESS: A book on leisure as a cultural opportunity.

SIDELIGHTS: Maryhelen Vannier has traveled to Europe fourteen times and around the world three times.

* * *

Van RIPER, Guernsey, Jr. 1909-

PERSONAL: Born July 5, 1909, in Indianapolis, Ind.; son of Guernsey (an advertising executive) and Edith (Longley) Van Riper; married Betty Cline, November 14, 1981. *Education:* DePauw University, A.B., 1930; Harvard University, M.B.A., 1932. *Home address:* P.O. Box 671, Carmel, Ind. 46032.

CAREER: Sidener & Van Riper, Indianapolis, Ind., advertising copywriter, 1933-39; Bobbs-Merrill Co., Inc. (publishers), Indianapolis, book editor, 1940-50; free-lance writer, 1950—. *Member:* Authors League of America, Phi Beta Kappa.

WRITINGS—Juveniles; all published by Bobbs-Merrill: *Lou Gehrig, Boy of the Sand Lots,* 1949; *Will Rogers, Young Cowboy,* 1951; *Knute Rockne, Young Athlete,* 1952; *Babe Ruth, Baseball Boy,* 1954; *Jim Thorpe, Indian Athlete,* 1956; *Richard Byrd, Boy Who Braved the Unknown,* 1959, published as *Richard Byrd, Boy of the South Pole,* 1963.

All published by Garrard: *Yea, Coach!: Three Great Football Coaches,* 1966; *The Game of Basketball,* 1968; *World Series Highlights: Four Famous Contests,* 1970; *The Mighty Macs: Three Famous Baseball Managers,* 1972; *Behind the Plate: Three Great Catchers,* 1973; (contributor) Bennett Wayne, editor, *Football Replays: Great Coaches, Games, and Players,* 1973; (contributor) Wayne, editor, *Big League Pitchers and Catchers,* 1974; *Golfing Greats: Two Top Pros,* 1975.

WORK IN PROGRESS: Research on subjects for "Childhood of Famous Americans" series.

* * *

van ZELLER, Claud 1905-
(Hubert van Zeller; pseudonyms: Brother Choleric, Hugh Venning)

PERSONAL: Born April 3, 1905, in Suez, Egypt; son of Francis (government official) and Monique (van de Velde) van Zeller. *Residence:* Downside Abbey, Bath, England.

CAREER: Became Benedictine monk, Downside Abbey, Bath, England, 1924; ordained to priesthood, 1930; religious name, Hubert van Zeller. Chief work is preaching and giving retreats in England and America.

WRITINGS—All under name Hubert van Zeller, except as indicated; published by Burns, Oats & Washbourne, except as indicated: *Prophets and Princes,* 1936; *Watch and Pray,* 1937; *Lord God* (book of prayers), 1937, 2nd edition, 1958; *Sackcloth and Ashes,* 1937; *Isaias: Man of Ideals,* 1938; *Liturgical Asides,* 1939; *Daniel: Man of Desires,* 1940, Newman, 1951; *From Creation to Christman,* 1943; *Famine of the Spirit,* 1949, revised edition, Templegate, 1964; *Moments of Light,* 1949; *Praying While You Work,* 1953.

Published by Sheed: *We Die Standing Up,* 1948; *We Live with Our Eyes Open,* 1949; *We Work While the Light Lasts,* 1951;

We Sing While There's Voice Left, 1951; *Willingly to School*, 1952; *Downside By and Large*, 1954; *The Outspoken Ones*, 1955; *The Gospel Priesthood*, 1956; *The Inner Search*, 1957; *The Holy Rule*, 1958; *Approach to Penance*, 1958; *Approach to Prayer*, 1958; *Approach to Christian Sculpture*, 1959; *Approach to Monasticism*, 1960; *Approach to the Crucified*, 1961; *Approach to Calvary*, 1961.

Published by Templegate: *The Choice of God*, 1956, reprinted, 1973; *The Yoke of Divine Love*, 1957; *The Way of the Cross*, 1958; *The Benedictine Idea*, 1959; *A Book of Private Prayer*, 1960; *Moments of Light*, 1963; *Ideas for Prayer*, 1965; *To Help the Mourner*, 1967; *More Ideas for Prayer*, 1967; *The Other Kingdom: A Book of Comfort*, 1969; *The Current of Spirituality*, 1970; *Leave Your Life Alone*, 1972; *A Book of Beginnings*, 1975; *Letters to a Soul*, 1976.

Others: *Jeremias: Man of Tears*, Sands, 1942; *Ezechiel: Man of Signs*, Sands, 1944; *Kaleidoscope*, Sands, 1947; (under pseudonym Hugh Venning) *The End: A Projection, Not a Prophecy*, Desmond & Stapleton, 1948; *Old Testament Stories*, Newman, 1949; *Family Case Book*, Collins, 1951; *We Die Standing Up*, Image, 1961; *The Benedictine Nun: Her Story and Aim*, Helicon, 1965; *One Foot in the Cradle* (autobiography), Holt, 1965; *First Person Singular*, J. Murray, 1970; *To Be in Christ*, S.P.C.K., 1979. Also author of *Giving to God* and *Come Lord*.

"In Other Words" series, published by Templegate: *Death in Other Words*, 1963; *Our Lady . . .*, 1963; *Prayer . . .*, 1963; *Sanctity . . .*, 1963; *The Psalms . . .*, 1964; *Suffering . . .*, 1964; *The Will of God . . .*, 1964; *The Gospel . . .*, 1965; *The Mass . . .*, 1965.

Cartoons; under pseudonym Brother Choleric; published by Sheed, except as indicated: *Cracks in the Cloister*, 1954; *Further Cracks in Fabulous Cloisters*, 1957; *Last Cracks in Legendary Cloisters*, 1961; *Posthumous Cracks in the Cloisters*, 1962; *Cracks in the Clouds*, St. Augustine's Press, 1976.

WORK IN PROGRESS: Old Testament in Other Words; Church History in Other Words; Originals Don't Fade; You Don't Have to Read It; Stories Short, Tall, and Partly True.

SIDELIGHTS: Hubert van Zeller's sculpture has been exhibited privately in England and publicly in America. *Avocational interests:* Sculpturing.

*   *   *

van ZELLER, Hubert
    See van ZELLER, Claud

*   *   *

VATIKIOTIS, P(anayiotis) J(erasimos) 1928-

PERSONAL: Born February 5, 1928, in Jerusalem, Palestine (now Israel); son of Jerassimos Y. (a civil servant) and Paraskevi (Meimarachi) Vatikiotis; married Patricia Mumford, March 22, 1956; children: Michael, Helen, Daphne. *Education:* American University in Cairo, B.A., 1948; Louisiana State University, M.A., 1951; Johns Hopkins University, Ph.D., 1954. *Office:* Department of Economic and Political Studies, School of Oriental and African Studies, University of London, London WC1E 7HP, England.

CAREER: American University in Cairo, Cairo, Egypt, instructor in social sciences, 1948-49; Johns Hopkins University, School of Advanced International Studies, Washington, D.C., instructor in Arabic, 1952-53; Indiana University at Bloomington, 1953-65, began as instructor, became professor of gov-

ernment; University of London, School of Oriental and African Studies, London, England, lecturer, 1964-65, professor of politics, 1965—. *Military service:* U.S. Army, 1954-56. *Awards, honors:* Guggenheim fellow, 1961-62.

WRITINGS: The Fatimid Theory of State, Orientalia Publications (Pakistan), 1957; (contributor) P. W. Thayer, editor, *Tensions in the Middle East*, Johns Hopkins Press, 1958.

The Egyptian Army in Politics, Indiana University Press, 1961; (contributor) Roy Macridis, editor, *Foreign Policy in World Politics*, 2nd revised edition (Vatikiotis was not associated with earlier edition), Prentice-Hall, 1962; (contributor) Jesse Harris Proctor, editor, *Islam and International Relations*, Praeger, 1965; *Politics and the Military in Jordon: A Study of the Arab Legion, 1921-57*, Praeger, 1967; (contributor) Peter Holt, *Political and Social Change in Modern Egypt*, Oxford University Press, 1968; (editor) *Egypt since the Revolution*, Praeger, 1968; *The Modern History of Egypt*, Praeger, 1969, 2nd edition published as *The History of Egypt from Mohammed Ali to Sadat*, Johns Hopkins Press, 1980.

Conflict in the Middle East, Allen & Unwin, 1971; *Revolution in the Middle East and Other Case Studies*, Rowman & Littlefield, 1972; (contributor) Paul Hammond and Sidney Alexander, editors, *Political Dynamics in the Middle East*, Elsevier (Netherlands), 1972; (contributor) Alvin Cottrell & James Theberge, editors, *The Western Mediterranean: Its Political, Economic, and Strategic Importance*, Praeger, 1973; (contributor) Ivo Lederer and Wayne Vucinich, editors, *The Soviet Union and the Middle East: Post World War II Era*, Hoover Institution, 1974; *Greece: A Political Essay*, Sage Publications, 1975; (contributor) Abraham L. Udovitch, editor, *The Middle East: Oil, Conflict and Hope*, Lexington Books, 1976; *Nasser and His Generation*, St. Martin's, 1978.

WORK IN PROGRESS: Islam and the Nation-State; John Metaxas of Greece, 1936-41.

SIDELIGHTS: P. J. Vatikiotis told *CA:* "I prefer writing essays to books, partly because I am too skeptical to seek final solutions. Another kind of writing I attempt in my spare time is short sketches on life amid Middle East foreign communities. These may be published someday under the title, *Mixed Upbringing.*" He speaks Greek, Arabic (three dialects fluently), French, and some Italian.

*   *   *

VAUGHAN WILLIAMS, Ursula Wood   1911-
    (Ursula Wood)

PERSONAL: Born March 15, 1911, in Valletta, Malta; daughter of Sir Robert Ferguson (an army officer) and Beryl (Penton) Lock; married Michael Forrester Wood (an army officer), May 24, 1933 (died, 1942); married Ralph Vaughan Williams (a composer), Feburary 7, 1953 (died, 1958). *Education:* Attended private schools in England and Brussels, Belgium. *Home:* 69 Gloucester Crescent, London N.W.1, England.

CAREER: Writer and lyricist. Royal Academy of Music, fellow, 1974, member of governing body; trustee, National Folk Music Library, Butterworth Trust, and British Music Information Centre; member of committee, Musicians Benevolent Fund. *Awards, honors:* Fellow, Royal College of Music, 1976.

WRITINGS: (Editor with Imogen Holst) Ralph Vaughan Williams and Gustav Holst, *Heirs and Rebels: Letters Written to Each Other and Occasional Writings on Music*, Oxford University Press, 1959, reprinted, Greenwood Press, 1980; (editor with Holst) *A Yacre of Land: Sixteen Folk-songs from the*

Manuscript Collection of Ralph Vaughan Williams, Oxford University Press, 1961; (author of preface) R. Vaughan Williams, *National Music and Other Essays,* Oxford University Press, 1963; *R.V.W.: A Biography of Ralph Vaughan Williams,* Oxford University Press, 1964; *Metamorphoses* (novel), Duckworth, 1966; *Set to Partners* (novel), Duckworth, 1968; (with John Lunn) *A Picture Biography of Ralph Vaughan Williams,* Oxford University Press, 1971.

Author of lyrics for musical compositons: (Under name Ursula Wood) R. Vaughan Williams, *The Sons of Light: A Cantata for Chorus and Orchestra,* Oxford University Press, 1951; R. Vaughan Williams, *Four Last Songs: For Medium Voice and Piano,* Oxford University Press, 1960; Charles Camillieri, *Melita* (opera), Novello, 1968; Malcolm Williamson, *The Brilliant and the Dark: An Operatic Sequence,* Weinberger, 1969; Williamson, *The Icy Mirror,* Weinberger, 1972; Williamson, *Ode to Music,* Weinberger, 1972; Phyllis Tate, *Compassion,* Oxford University Press, 1979; Elizabeth Lutyens, *Variations,* Oxford University Press, 1979. Also author of lyrics for "The Sofa," music by Elizabeth Maconchy, 1959, "David and Bathsheba," music by David Barlow, 1969, "Serenade," music by Anthony Scott, 1972, "Stars and Shadows," music by Brian Hughes, 1976, "Aspects," music by Roger Steptoe, 1978, "King of Maledon," music by Steptoe, 1979, "The Looking Glass," music by Steptoe, 1980, and "The Inheritor," music by Steptoe, 1980.

Under name Ursula Wood: *No Other Choice* (verse), Basil Blackwell, 1941; *Fall of Leaf* (verse), Basil Blackwell, 1943; (translator) Engel Lund, *A Second Book of Folk Songs,* C. Fischer, 1947; *Need for Speech* (verse), Basil Blackwell, 1948; *Wandering Pilgrimage* (verse), Hand & Flower Press, 1952; *Silence and Music* (verse), Essential Books, 1959.

AVOCATIONAL INTERESTS: The theatre and travel.

* * *

VEATCH, Henry Babcock   1911-

PERSONAL: Born September 26, 1911, in Evansville, Ind.; son of Henry Babcock (a building contractor) and Daisy (Flower) Veatch; married Mary Jane Wilson, June 24, 1939; children: Jane Sessions, Elizabeth Wilson Flower. *Education:* Harvard University, A.B., 1932, M.A., 1933, Ph.D., 1936; Heidelberg University, additional study, 1933-35. *Politics:* Democrat. *Religion:* Episcopalian. *Home:* 1001 Wilson Blvd., Apt. 307, Arlington, Va. 22209. *Office:* Department of Philosophy, Georgetown University, Washington, D.C. 20007.

CAREER: Indiana University at Bloomington, instructor, 1937-41, assistant professor, 1941-48, associate professor, 1948-51, professor of philosophy, 1951-61, Distinguished Service Professor, 1961-65; Northwestern University, Evanston, Ill., professor of philosophy, 1965-73, John Evans Professor, 1969-73; Georgetown University, Washington, D.C., professor of philosophy, 1973—, chairman of department, 1973-76. Visiting professor at Haverford College, 1957, University of Minnesota, 1961, Northwestern University, 1964-65, Colby College, 1979, and University of St. Thomas, 1981. *Member:* American Philosophical Association (president of western division, 1970-71), Metaphysical Society of America (president, 1960-61), American Catholic Philosophical Association (vice-president, 1978-79; president, 1979-80), American Association of University Professors (former chapter president), Guild of Scholars, Phi Gamma Delta, Phi Beta Kappa, Cosmos Club. *Awards, honors:* Ford Foundation faculty fellowship, 1952-53; Frederick Backman Lieber Award, Indiana University, 1954; Aquinas Medal, American Catholic Philosophical Association, 1971; Bunn Award, Georgetown University, 1979.

WRITINGS: Intentional Logic, Yale University Press, 1952, reprinted, Archon Books, 1970; *Realism and Nominalism Revisited,* Marquette University Press, 1954; (with Francis H. Parker) *Logic as a Human Instrument,* Harper, 1958; *Rational Man,* Indiana University, 1962; (translator) Mikel Dufrenne, *Language and Philosophy,* Greenwood Press, 1963; *Two Logics: The Conflict between Classical and Neo-Analytical Philosophy,* Northwestern University Press, 1969; *For an Ontology of Morals: A Critique of Contemporary Ethical Theory,* Northwestern University Press, 1971; *Aristotle: A Contemporary Appreciation,* Indiana University Press, 1974. Contributor to professional journals. Editorial consultant, *American Journal of Jurisprudence,* 1971, *Listening,* 1973—, and *American Philosophical Quarterly,* 1978—.

* * *

VENNING, Hugh
See van ZELLER, Claud

* * *

VERNEY, Michael P(almer)   1923-

PERSONAL: Born February 17, 1923, in Gloucester, England; son of John Palmer Setters (an electrical engineer) and Dorothy (Davis) Verney; married Dora Reader, November 20, 1948; children: Stephen Palmer, Michael Lee. *Education:* Attended Crypt School, Gloucester, England, 1933-40. *Home:* Hillsborough, 36 The Parkway, Rustington, Sussex BN16 2BU, England.

CAREER: River Severn Catchment Board, Stratford-upon-Avon, England, civil engineer, 1947-50; West Sussex River Board, Chichester, England, civil engineer, 1950-65; Sussex River Authority, Brighton, England, civil engineer, 1965-81. Inventor. Marine craft consultant. *Military service:* British Army, Royal Engineers, 1944-47. *Member:* Institution of Civil Engineers (London), Steamboat Association of Great Britain, Arun Yacht Club.

WRITINGS: Amateur Boat Building, J. Murray, 1948, 2nd edition published as *Complete Amateur Boat Building in Wood, Glass Fibre, and Metal,* 1959, 3rd edition published as *Complete Amateur Boat Building,* International Marine Publishing Co., 1979; *Practical Conversions and Yacht Repairs,* J. Murray, 1951; *Lifeboat into Yacht,* Yachting Monthly, 1953; *Building Chine Boats,* Yachting Monthly, 1960; *Yacht Repairs and Conversions,* J. Murray, 1961; *Boat Maintenance* (self-illustrated), Kaye & Ward, 1970; *Boat Repairs and Conversions,* J. Murray, 1972, revised edition, 1977; *The Care and Repair of Hulls,* Granada, 1979. Contributor of 150 articles to *Sunday Times* (London), *Look & Learn, Light Steam Power,* and boating magazines, 1944-71.

SIDELIGHTS: When Michael P. Verney built his first boat at the age of sixteen, he found there were no suitable instruction books available. To help rectify this he began writing boat construction manuals, many of which have become standard textbooks for amateurs and professionals alike. Verney told *CA:* "I have always taken great pains to compose each sentence with a minimum of words—while instilling confidence, adding a little jest, describing all possible pitfalls, and cramming in every hint and idea known to me—in a style which would be easy to read and understand. I take a great interest in choosing words carefully to make them equally well understood in all English-speaking countries.

"Nowadays, the book market is flooded with titles on boating subjects, and bookshops cannot stock them all. New enthusiasts are appearing all the time, but if a book is not on the shelves they may never get to hear about it, which is galling to the author. It takes me at least two years to write a new book or to modernize one of my earlier ones. I receive numerous complimentary letters from readers, especially in America, and this is most gratifying."

AVOCATIONAL INTERESTS: Photography, music, sailing, model-building, steam power, do-it-yourself hobbies.

*   *   *

VERNOR, D.
See CASEWIT, Curtis (Werner)

*   *   *

VOORHIS, H(orace) Jerry 1901-

PERSONAL: Born April 6, 1901, in Ottawa, Kan.; son of Charles B. (a businessman) and Ella Ward (Smith) Voorhis; married Louise Livingston, November 27, 1924; children: Alice Nell Voorhis Hansen, Charles Brown, Jerry Livingston. *Education:* Yale University, B.A., 1923; Claremont Colleges (now Claremont Graduate School), M.A., 1928. *Politics:* Democrat. *Religion:* Episcopalian. *Home:* 633 West Bonita Ave., Claremont, Calif. 91711. *Office:* 114 North Indian Hill Blvd., Claremont, Calif. 91711.

CAREER: Winchester Repeating Arms Co., New Haven, Conn., laborer, 1923; New York, New Haven & Hartford Railroad, New Haven, freight handler, 1923; Young Men's Christian Association, traveling representative in Germany, 1923-24; Ford Motor Co., Charlotte, N.C., laborer, 1925; Allendale Farm School, Lake Villa, Ill., teacher, 1925-26; Episcopal Home for Orphan Boys, Laramie, Wyo., director, 1926-27; Voorhis School for Boys, San Dimas, Calif., headmaster, 1928-38; U.S. House of Representatives, Washington, D.C., Congressman from Twelfth District of California, 1937-47; Cooperative League of U.S.A., Chicago, Ill., executive director 1947-65, president, 1965-67. Special lecturer, Pomona College, 1930-35. Group Health Association of America, Washington, D.C., secretary, 1947-71, member of executive board, 1971—; president, Board for International Cooperative Training, Madison, Wis., 1961-67.

MEMBER: United World Federalists, National Catholic Rural Life Conference, Adult Education Association, Pomona Valley Council of Churches, Phi Beta Kappa, Phi Delta Kappa. *Awards, honors:* LL.D. from St. Francis Xavier University, Antigonish, Nova Scotia, 1952, and from Claremont Graduate School, 1979.

WRITINGS: Morale of Democracy, Greystone, 1941; *Out of Debt, Out of Danger,* Devin-Adair, 1943; *Beyond Victory,* Farrar, Straus, 1944; *Confessions of a Congressman,* Doubleday, 1947; *The Christian in Politics,* Association Press, 1951; *American Cooperatives,* Harper, 1961; *The Strange Case of Richard Milhous Nixon,* Eriksson, 1972; *Cooperative Enterprise: The Little People's Chance in a World of Bigness,* Interstate, 1975; *The Life and Times of Aurelius Lyman Voorhis,* Vantage, 1976; *Confessions of Faith,* Vantage, 1978. Author of monthly column, "The Human Side of the Market Place," for Cooperative News Service; contributor of articles on cooperatives to encyclopedias.

W

WADDINGTON, C(onrad) H(al)   1905-1975

PERSONAL: Born November 8, 1905, in Evesham, England; died September 26, 1975, in Edinburgh, Scotland; son of Hal (a tea planter in India) and Mary Ellen (Warner) Waddington; married Cecil Elizabeth Lascelles, 1926; married second wife Margaret Justin Blanco White (an architect and town planner), 1936; children: (first marriage) Cecil Jacob; (second marriage) Caroline, Margaret Dusa. *Education:* Sidney Sussex College, Cambridge, B.A., 1927, Sc.D., 1938. *Home:* 15 Blacket Pl., Edinburgh, Scotland. *Office:* Institute of Animal Genetics, University of Edinburgh, West Mains Rd., Edinburgh, Scotland.

CAREER: Cambridge University, Cambridge, England, lecturer in zoology and embryologist at Strangeways Research Laboratory, 1933-45, fellow of Christ's College, 1934-45; University of Edinburgh, Edinburgh, Scotland, Buchanan Professor of Animal Genetics, beginning 1947. Honorary director of animal genetics unit of Agricultural Research Council; honorary director of epigenetics group of Medical Research Council; vice-president of International Biological Program. *Military service:* Royal Air Force, officer in charge of Operational Research Section, Coastal Command, 1944-45.

MEMBER: International Union of Biological Sciences (president), Royal Society of London (fellow), Royal Society of Edinburgh (fellow), American Academy of Arts and Sciences (foreign member), World Academy of Arts and Sciences (fellow), Athenaeum Club (London). *Awards, honors:* Rockefeller Foundation traveling fellow, 1932, 1938; Albert Brachet Prize for embryology, Royal Academy of Belgium, 1936; commander, Order of the British Empire, 1958; D.Sc., University of Montreal, 1958.

WRITINGS: How Animals Develop, Norton, 1935, revised edition, Harper, 1962; *An Introduction to Modern Genetics,* Norton, 1939; *Organisers and Genes,* Cambridge University Press, 1940; *The Scientific Attitude,* Penguin, 1941, new edition, Hutchinson, 1968; (editor) *Science and Ethics,* Allen & Unwin, 1942; *The Epigenetics of Birds,* Cambridge University Press, 1952; (editor with E.C.R. Reeve) *Quantitative Inheritance,* H.M.S.O., 1952; *Principles of Embryology,* Allen & Unwin, 1956; *The Strategy of the Genes,* Allen & Unwin, 1957; (editor) *Biological Organisation,* Pergamon, 1959; *The Ethical Animal,* Atheneum, 1960; *The Nature of Life,* Atheneum, 1961; *New Patterns in Genetics and Development,* Columbia University Press, 1962; *Biology for the Modern World,* Barnes & Noble,

1962; *Principles of Development and Differentiation,* Macmillan, 1966; (editor) *Towards a Theoretical Biology: An International Union of Biological Sciences Symposium,* Edinburgh University Press, Volume I: *Prolegomena,* 1968, Volume II: *Sketches,* 1969, Volume III: *Drafts,* 1970, Volume IV: *Essays,* 1972; *Behind Appearance: A Study of the Relations between Painting and the Natural Sciences in This Century,* Edinburgh University Press, 1969, Massachusetts Institute of Technology Press, 1970; *Biology, Purpose, and Ethics,* Clark University Press, 1971; *Biology and the History of the Future,* Edinburgh University Press, 1972; *Operation Research in World War II: Operational Research against the U-Boat,* Elek, 1973, British Book Centre, 1974; *The Evolution of an Evolutionist,* Cornell University Press, 1975; *Evolution and Consciousness: Human Systems in Transition,* Addison-Wesley, 1977; *Tools for Thought: How to Understand and Apply the Latest Scientific Techniques of Problem Solving,* Basic Books, 1977; *The Man-Made Future,* St. Martin's, 1978. Contributor of more than two hundred articles to scientific and popular journals.

SIDELIGHTS: Waddington's books have been translated into Russian, Spanish, Dutch, Japanese, and Swedish. *Avocational interests:* Painting.

OBITUARIES: New York Times, September 29, 1975; *AB Bookman's Weekly,* December 1, 1975.†

*   *   *

WADE, John Stevens   1927-
(Clysle Stevens)

PERSONAL: Original name Clysle Stevens; name legally changed; born December 8, 1927, in Smithfield, Me.; son of Earl Wade and Leanora May (Witham) Stevens; married Stella Rachel Taschlicky, June 13, 1954; children: Juanita, John Stevens. *Education:* Connecticut State Teachers College (now Central Connecticut State College), B.S., 1953. *Address:* P.O. Box 14, Mt. Vernon, Me. 04352.

CAREER: Poet, painter, and gold prospector. Former hotel manager. Editor and founder, *Northeast Literary Magazine,* 1963-64, and *Dimension,* 1964-66. *Military service:* U.S. Army, 1945-47.

WRITINGS—Poetry, except as indicated: (Under name Clysle Stevens) *Loose Stones: First Poems,* E. R. Hitchcock, 1954; *Climbs of Uncertainty,* New Athenaeum Press, 1961; (with John Judson) *Two from Where It Snows,* Northeast Chapbook

Series, 1964; *Drowning in The Dark,* The Group (Netherlands), 1965; *Small World* (literary cartoons), The Group, 1966; (translator from the Dutch and Flemish) *Poems from the Lowlands,* Small Pond, 1967; *Gallery,* Poet & Printer (London), 1969.

The Cats in the Colosseum, Crossing Press, 1973; *Well Water and Daisies,* Juniper Press, 1974; *Each to His Own Ground,* Juniper Press, 1976; (translator from the Dutch) *Waterland: A Gathering from Holland,* Holmgangers, 1977; *Some of My Best Friends Are Trees,* Sparrow, 1978; *Homecoming,* Icarus, 1979; *Up North,* Juniper Press, 1980.

Contributor to anthologies: *31 New American Poets,* Hill & Wang, 1969; *Man: In the Poetic Mode,* McDougal, Littell, 1970; *It's Only a Movie,* Prentice-Hall, 1971; *An Anthology of Contemporary Poetry,* Peace & Pieces Press, 1972; *The Search for Self,* McDougal, Littell, 1973; *Relating to Others,* Scholastic Book Services, 1977; *Nova: Anthology of Literary Types,* Prentice-Hall, 1979; *Always Begin Where You Are,* McGraw, 1980. Also contributor to numerous other anthologies. Contributor to more than 350 magazines, reviews, and journals.

SIDELIGHTS: John Stevens Wade told *CA:* "I wrote very bad poetry for years, and I was well into my thirties before I could produce work that I didn't want to destroy (my first book of poems was privately printed and privately burned). When I look back on the sea of sonnets, villanelles, sestinas, etc. that I wrote in my search for control, my head spins and my thoughts turn to happier moments. I was a long time learning that my poems must seek their own forms. Now with that agony behind me, and hopefully many new poems ahead, I can only assess my situation by admitting that I am no success story in terms of worldly goods. But I am a man who is happy with his life. I am doing the one thing I like best: I am making things."

Wade's poetry has been translated into Arabic, Flemish, French, and Italian.

AVOCATIONAL INTERESTS: Travel (including visits to Western European nations).

*   *   *

WAGENKNECHT, Edward (Charles) 1900-
(Julian Forrest)

PERSONAL: Born March 28, 1900, in Chicago, Ill.; son of Henry Ernest and Mary (Erichsen) Wagenknecht; married Dorothy Arnold, 1932; children: Robert, David, Walter. *Education:* University of Chicago, Ph.B., 1923, M.A., 1924; University of Washington, Seattle, Ph.D., 1932. *Home:* 233 Otis St., West Newton, Mass. 02165. *Agent:* Barbara Rhodes Literary Agency, 140 West End Ave., New York, N.Y. 10023.

CAREER: University of Chicago, Chicago, Ill., assistant, 1923-25; University of Washington, Seattle, 1925-43, began as associate, became associate professor; Illinois Institute of Technology, Chicago, associate professor, 1943-47; Boston University, Boston, Mass., professor of English, 1947-65, professor emeritus, 1965—. Literary editor, *Seattle Post-Intelligencer,* 1935-40, and *News-Tribune,* Waltham, Mass., 1966-79. Instructor in extension division, Harvard University, 1965-72.

WRITINGS: Lillian Gish: An Interpretation (pamphlet), University of Washington Book Store, 1927; *Values in Literature,* University of Washington Book Store, 1928, revised edition, 1935; *Geraldine Farrar: An Authorized Record of Her Career,* University of Washington Book Store, 1929; *Utopia Americana,* University of Washington Book Store, 1929; *The Man Charles Dickens: A Victorian Portrait,* Houghton, 1929, re-

vised edition, University of Oklahoma Press, 1966; *A Guide to Bernard Shaw,* Appleton, 1929; *Jenny Lind,* Houghton, 1931; *Mark Twain: The Man and His Work,* Yale University Press, 1935, revised edition, University of Oklahoma Press, 1961; *Cavalcade of the English Novel,* Holt, 1943, 2nd edition, 1954; *Cavalcade of the American Novel,* Holt, 1952; *A Preface to Literature,* Holt, 1954; *The Unknown Longfellow,* Boston University Press, 1954; *Longfellow: A Full-Length Portrait,* Longmans, Green, 1955; *The Seven Worlds of Theodore Roosevelt,* Longmans, Green, 1958.

Nathaniel Hawthorne: Man and Writer, Oxford University Press, 1961; *Washington Irving: Moderation Displayed,* Oxford University Press, 1962; *The Movies in the Age of Innocence,* University of Oklahoma Press, 1962; *Edgar Allan Poe: The Man Behind the Legend,* Oxford University Press, 1963; *Chicago,* University of Oklahoma Press, 1964; *Seven Daughters of the Theater,* University of Oklahoma Press, 1964; *Harriet Beecher Stowe: The Known and the Unknown,* Oxford University Press, 1965; *Dickens and the Scandalmongers,* University of Oklahoma Press, 1965; (contributor) R. E. Langford and W. E. Taylor, editors, *The Twenties: Poetry and Prose,* Everett/Edwards, 1966; *Henry Wadsworth Longfellow: Portrait of an American Humanist,* Oxford University Press, 1966; *Merely Players,* University of Oklahoma Press, 1966; (under pseudonym Julian Forrest) *Nine Before Fotherighay: A Novel about Mary Queen of Scots,* Bles, 1966; *As Far As Yesterday: Memories and Reflections,* University of Oklahoma Press, 1968; *The Personality of Chaucer,* University of Oklahoma Press, 1968; (under pseudonym Julian Forrest) *The Glory of the Lilies: A Novel about Joan of Arc,* Bles, 1969.

William Dean Howells: The Friendly Eye, Oxford University Press, 1970; *The Personality of Milton,* University of Oklahoma Press, 1970; *James Russell Lowell: Portrait of a Many-sided Man,* Oxford University Press, 1971; *Ambassadors for Christ,* Oxford University Press, 1972; *The Personality of Shakespeare,* University of Oklahoma Press, 1972; *Ralph Waldo Emerson: Portrait of a Balanced Soul,* Oxford University Press, 1974; (with Anthony Slide) *The Films of D. W. Griffith,* Crown, 1975; *A Pictorial History of New England,* Crown, 1976; *Eve and Henry James: Portraits of Women and Girls in His Fiction,* University of Oklahoma Press, 1978; (with Slide) *Fifty Great American Silent Films, 1912-1920: A Pictorial Survey,* Dover, 1980; *Henry David Thoreau: What Manner of Man?,* University of Massachusetts Press, 1981.

Editor: (With others) *The College Survey of English Literature,* Harcourt, 1942; *Six Novels of the Supernatural,* Viking, 1944; *The Fireside Book of Christmas Stories,* Bobbs-Merrill, 1945; *The Story of Jesus in the World's Literature,* Creative Age Press, 1946; *When I Was a Child,* Dutton, 1946; *The Fireside Book of Ghost Stories,* Bobbs-Merrill, 1947; *Abraham Lincoln: His Life, Work, and Character,* Creative Age Press, 1947; *The Fireside Book of Romance,* Bobbs-Merrill, 1948; *Joan of Arc: An Anthology of History and Literature,* Creative Age Press, 1948; *A Fireside Book of Yuletide Tales,* Bobbs-Merrill, 1948; *Murder by Gaslight,* Prentice-Hall, 1949; *The Collected Tales of Walter de la Mare,* Knopf, 1949; *An Introduction to Dickens,* Scott, Foresman, 1952; *Mrs. Longfellow: Selected Letters and Journals,* Longmans, Green, 1956; *Chaucer: Modern Essays in Criticism,* Oxford University Press, 1960; *Stories of Christ and Christmas,* McKay, 1963; *John Greenleaf Whittier, The Supernaturalism of New England,* University of Oklahoma Press, 1969; *Marilyn Monroe: A Composite View,* Chilton, 1969; *The Notorious Jumping Frog and Other Stories by Mark Twain,* Limited Editions Club, 1970; Walter de la Mare, *Eight Tales,* Arkham, 1971; *The Letters of James Branch Cabell,* University of Oklahoma Press, 1975; *The Stories and Fables of Ambrose*

Bierce, Stemmer House, 1977; *Washington Irving's Tales of the Supernatural*, Stemmer House, 1981.

Wrote introductions to Charles Dickens, Mark Twain, and James Branch Cabell classics re-issued by Limited Editions Club, Modern Library, Harcourt, and Washington Square, and to the Reilly & Lee edition of *The Wizard of Oz*, by L. Frank Baum, 1956, *The Art, Humor, and Humility of Mark Twain*, by Minnie M. Brashear and Robert M. Rodney, 1959, and to six of the Harper "Perennial Classics," 1965. Book reviewer since 1920's for several major publications; featured reviewer for *Chicago Sunday Tribune Magazine of Books*, 1944-63. Editor, Boston University's *Studies in English*, 1955-58.

WORK IN PROGRESS: Theodore Roosevelt's America: American Profile, 1900-1909; Gamaliel Bradford; The Novels of Henry James.

SIDELIGHTS: Edward Wagenknecht told *CA:* "I made up my mind to be a writer when I read *The Wizard of Oz* at the age of six. However, I still faced the necessity of earning a living, and since most human activities held no interest for me my choice was virtually limited to teaching and the ministry. I started with the latter. I loved preaching but disliked everything else a minister has to do; consequently, though I continued supply preaching for many years, I gradually found myself drawn into teaching. This was half-accident, half-choice; if the 'breaks' had occurred in the ministry rather than, as they did, in teaching, I might have chosen otherwise.

"My specialty as a writer is the psychograph or character portrait, which I learned from Gamaliel Bradford, who; in turn, had been inspired by Sainte-Beuve. Bradford furnished an introduction to my first book of consequence, *The Man Charles Dickens: A Victorian Portrait*, and in fact placed it with Houghton Mifflin Co. I use the psychographic method in all my books which deal with individuals, but as my list shows, I have also done, and am doing, other things."

*   *   *

WAGNER, Harvey M.   1931-

PERSONAL: Born November 20, 1931, in San Francisco, Calif.; married Ruth G. Glesby, June 26, 1954; children: Caroline Beth, Julie Lynne. *Education:* Stanford University, B.S., 1953, M.S., 1954; Massachusetts Institute of Technology, Ph.D., 1960; additional study at University of California, Los Angeles, summers, 1950 and 1951, Oxford University, summer, 1952, and King's College, Cambridge, 1954-55. *Home:* 3010 Devon Rd., Durham, N.C. 27707. *Office:* School of Business Administration, University of North Carolina at Chapel Hill, 012A Carroll Hall, Chapel Hill, N.C. 27514.

CAREER: Massachusetts Institute of Technology, School of Industrial Management, Cambridge, instructor, 1955-57; Stanford University, Graduate School of Business, Stanford, Calif., assistant professor, 1957-60, associate professor, 1960-63, professor of management science and statistics, 1963-67, director of doctoral studies, 1964-66, director of research, 1966-67; Yale University, School of Organization and Management, New Haven, Conn., professor of management science and operations research, 1967-76; University of North Carolina at Chapel Hill, School of Business Adminsitration, professor of management science and business policy, 1976—, dean, 1976-78. Visiting professor, Massachusetts Institute of Technology, spring, 1974, and Harvard University, spring, 1974, winter, 1974-75; Arthur Andersen Chair in Management Science, Katholieke Universiteit Leuven (Belgium), 1980. Member of governing board, Computer Research Center for Economics

and Management Science, National Bureau of Economic Research, 1970-76; member of panel on applied mathematics, operations research, statistics, and computer science, National Science Foundation Graduate Fellowship Program, 1970-72; member of Selection Committee, Special Grant Program in Economics and Anthropology, U.S. Office of Education, 1971-73; member of board of visitors, Graduate School of Business Administration, Duke University, 1974-77; member of review panel, READ Project, U.S. Department of Energy, 1978-79. North Carolina Symphony Board, president, 1977-79, vice-president of marketing, 1980—; member of North Carolina Governor's Commission on Governmental Productivity, 1978—; member of panel, North Carol...ia Governor's Business Awards in the Arts and Humanities, 1980. Consultant, RAND Corp., 1953-78, McKinsey & Co., 1960—, and Electric Power Research Institute, 1979—; member of advisory committee on basic research, U.S. Army Research Office, 1971-74; member of advisory committees, International Institute for Applied Systems Analysis, National Science Foundation, 1975—.

MEMBER: American Statistical Association (fellow), Institute of Management Sciences (president of North California chapter, 1961-62; American chairman of international meeting in Tokyo, 1963; member of council, 1969-71; national president, 1973), Operations Research Society of America (chairman of education committee, 1963-64; chairman of Western section, 1965; member of council, 1972-75; member of operations research journal advisory board, 1978—), Phi Beta Kappa. *Awards, honors:* Marshall scholarship, British government, 1954-55; research grants from Western Management Science Institute, 1960-62, 1962-65, and National Science Foundation, 1962-64, 1964-73; National Science Foundation travel grant, 1963; Ford Foundation faculty research fellow, 1963-64; Office of Naval Research grant, 1973—; Office of Army Research grant, 1974-77; Lanchester Prize, Operations Research Society of America, 1969; Maynard Book of the Year Award, American Institute of Industrial Engineers, 1970; Doctor Honoris Causa, Katholieke Universiteit Leuven, 1980.

WRITINGS: Statistical Management of Inventory Systems, Wiley, 1962; (with John Haldi) *Simulated Economic Models*, Irwin, 1963; (editor with C. Bonini and R. Jaedicke) *Management Controls: New Directions in Basic Research*, McGraw, 1964; *Principles of Operations Research with Applications to Managerial Decisions*, Prentice-Hall, 1969, 2nd edition, 1975; *Principles of Management Science with Applications to Executive Decisions*, Prentice-Hall, 1970, 2nd edition, 1975. Also author, with R. Ehrhardt, of a book in "Progress in Operations Research" series, North-Holland, 1981.

Contributor: Churchman and Verhulst, editors, *Management Science: Models and Techniques*, Pergamon, 1960; (with A. E. Story) Muth and Thompson, editors, *Industrial Scheduling*, Prentice-Hall, 1963; K. Koontz, editor, *Toward a Unified Theory of Management*, McGraw, 1964; (with T. M. Whitin) A. F. Veinott, editor, *Mathematical Studies in Management Science*, Macmillan, 1965; Alexis and Wilson, editors, *Organizational Decision Making*, Prentice-Hall, 1967; *Science, Technology, and the Modern Navy*, Office of Naval Research, 1976; (with R. Ehrhardt and C. R. Schultz) L. B. Schwarz, editor, *Multi-Level Production Inventory Systems: Theory and Practice*, North-Holland, 1981. Also contributor to *Theory of Inventory Management*, by T. M. Whitin.

Author or co-author of technical reports published by Stanford Computation Center, Stanford University, and RAND Corp. Contributor to *Implementation of Computer Based Decision Aids*, the proceedings of the Center for Information Systems Research Conference. Contributor of numerous articles and reviews to professional journals, including *Management Science, Operations Research, American Economic Review, Journal of Industrial Engineering,* and *Harvard Business Review.* Associate editor, *Journal of American Statistical Association,* 1963-69; departmental editor, *Journal of the Institute of Management Science,* 1969-72, and *Naval Research Logistics Quarterly,* 1977—; advisory editor, *Operations Research Letters,* 1980—.

* * *

WAKEFIELD, Jean L.
   See LAIRD, Jean E(louise)

* * *

WALKER, Ira
   See WALKER, Irma Ruth (Roden)

* * *

WALKER, Irma Ruth (Roden) 1921-
   (Andrea Harris, Ira Walker)

PERSONAL: Born August 2, 1921, in Cincinnati, Ohio; daughter of Earl M. (a musician) and Edith (Nethery) Roden; married George St. Clair Walker, June 1, 1941; children: Sharon June. *Education:* Attended schools in Cincinnati, Ohio. *Religion:* Protestant. *Home:* 2013 Vista Lane, Petaluma, Calif. 94952. *Agent:* Curtis Brown Ltd., 575 Madison Ave., New York, N.Y. 10022.

CAREER: Free-lance writer. *Member:* Mystery Writers of America, Science Fiction Writers of America, California Writers Club.

WRITINGS: (Under pseudonym Ira Walker) *Someone's Stolen Nellie Grey,* Abelard, 1963; (under pseudonym Ira Walker) *The Man in the Driver's Seat,* Abelard, 1964; (under pseudonym Ira Walker) *The Murdoch Legacy,* Bobbs-Merrill, 1975, published under name Irma Walker, Ballantine, 1978; (under pseudonym Ira Walker) *The Lucifer Wine,* Bobbs-Merrill, 1977, published under name Irma Walker, Ballantine, 1979; *The Maunaloa Curse,* Bobbs-Merrill, 1979; (under pseudonym Andrea Harris) *Windfall,* Playboy Press, 1979; *Inherit the Earth,* Atheneum, 1981; *A Celebration of Murder,* Raven Press, 1982; *An Affair of Convenience,* Ballantine, 1982.

WORK IN PROGRESS: A Fresh Start, for Ballantine; *Other Passions; Other Loves,* for Dell; *Portal to E'ewere,* a science fiction novel for Atheneum.

SIDELIGHTS: Someone's Stolen Nellie Grey was Irma Ruth Walker's first attempt at professional writing, and she found a publisher for it immediately. Married to a former member of the U.S. Air Force, she has lived in the Philippines and Hawaii and has traveled throughout the Orient.

* * *

WALKER, John 1906-

PERSONAL: Born December 24, 1906, in Pittsburgh, Pa.; son of Hay and Rebekah (Friend) Walker; married Lady Margaret Gwendolen Mary Drummond, February 3, 1937; children: Gillian Elizabeth Mary, John Anthony Drummond. *Education:* Harvard University, A.B., 1930. *Religion:* Roman Catholic. *Address:* 4th Floor, 1729 H St. N.W., Washington, D.C. 20006.

CAREER: American Academy in Rome, Rome, Italy, associate in charge of department of fine arts, 1935-39; National Gallery

of Art, Washington, D.C., chief curator, 1939-56, director, 1956-69. Trustee of American Academy in Rome, A. W. Mellon Educational and Charitable Trust, Wallace Foundation, National Trust for Historic Preservation, and American Federation of Art. *Member:* Century Association, Phi Beta Kappa, The Brook (New York), Chevy Chase Club. *Awards, honors:* D.F.A. from Tufts University, 1958, Brown University, 1959, Washington and Jefferson University, 1960, and La Salle College, 1962; Litt.D. from University of Notre Dame, 1959, Catholic University of America, 1964, New York University, 1965, Maryland Institute, 1966, and Georgetown University, 1966.

WRITINGS: (With Amey Aldrich) *A Guide to Villas and Gardens in Italy,* American Academy in Rome, 1938; (with Macgill James) *Great American Paintings from Smibert to Bellows,* Oxford University Press, 1943; (with Huntington Cairns) *Masterpieces of Painting from the National Gallery of Art,* Random House, 1944; *Paintings from America,* Penguin, 1951; *Great Paintings from the National Gallery of Art,* Macmillan, 1952; *The National Gallery of Art,* Abrams, 1956, revised edition, 1979; *Bellini and Titian at Farrara,* Phaidon, 1957.

(Editor with Cairns) *Treasures from the National Gallery of Art,* Abrams, 1964; (with Cairns) *Pageant of Painting,* Abrams, 1966; (author of foreword) *Fifteenth Century Engravings of Northern Europe,* National Gallery of Art, 1967; (with Charles L. Mee) *Lorenzo De Medici and the Renaissance,* American Heritage Publishing, 1969; *Self-Portrait with Donors: Confessions of a Art Collector,* Little, Brown, 1974; *Joseph Mallord William Turner,* Abrams, 1976; *Constable,* Abrams, 1979; (editor) *The Armand Hammer Collection: Five Centuries of Masterpieces,* Abrams, 1980.

Also author of *Paintings Other Than French in the Chester Dole Collection,* National Gallery of Art. Also author of forewords or introductions to numerous books, including: *The Civil War: A Centennial Exhibition of Eyewitness Drawings; Eighteenth and Nineteenth Century Paintings and Sculpture of the French School in the Chester Dale Collection; Painting and Sculpture from the Samuel H. Kress Collections; Paintings from the Albright-Knox Art Gallery.*

BIOGRAPHICAL/CRITICAL SOURCES: American Scholar, summer, 1965.†

* * *

WALKER, Kathrine Sorley
   See SORLEY WALKER, Kathrine

* * *

WALLACE, Ronald (William) 1945-

PERSONAL: Born February 18, 1945, in Cedar Rapids, Iowa; son of William Edward (a professor of law) and Loretta (Kamprath) Wallace; married Margaret McCreight, August 3, 1968; children: Molly Elizabeth, Emily Katherine. *Education:* College of Wooster, B.A., 1967; University of Michigan, M.A., 1968, Ph.D., 1971. *Home:* 2220 Chamberlain Ave., Madison, Wis. 53705. *Office:* Department of English, University of Wisconsin, Madison, Wis. 53706.

CAREER: University of Wisconsin—Madison, assistant professor, 1972-75, associate professor of English and director of creative writing, 1975—. *Member:* Associated Writing Programs. *Awards, honors:* Avery Hopwood Award, 1970, for poetry; American Council of Learned Societies fellowship, 1975-76, 1981; Poetry Book Award, Council for Wisconsin Writers,

1977, for *Installing the Bees;* Wisconsin Arts Board fellowship, 1979, 1980.

WRITINGS: Henry James and the Comic Form (nonfiction), University of Michigan Press, 1975; *Cucumbers* (poetry chapbook), Pendle Hill, 1977; *Installing the Bees* (poems), Chowder Chapbooks, 1977; *The Facts of Life* (poetry chapbook), Mary Phillips, 1979; *The Last Laugh: Form and Affirmation in the Contemporary American Comic Novel* (nonfiction), University of Missouri Press, 1979; *Plums, Stones, Kisses and Hooks* (poems), University of Missouri Press, 1981. Contributor of poems, articles, and reviews to *New Yorker, North American Review, Poetry Northwest, Iowa Review, New York Quarterly, Prairie Schooner, Perspective, Essays in Literature*, and other periodicals.

WORK IN PROGRESS: Mortality Is Fatal: Humor in American Poetry; Tunes for Bears to Dance To, a book of poems.

AVOCATIONAL INTERESTS: Gardening, bicycling, camping, piano, fishing, child's play.

*   *   *

WALLICH, Henry C(hristopher)   1914-

PERSONAL: Born June 10, 1914, in Berlin, Germany; son of Paul and Hildegard J. (Rehrmann) Wallich; married Mable Inness Brown, December 2, 1950; children: Christine Inness, Anna Hildegard, Paul Inness. *Education:* Attended Oxford University, 1932-33; Harvard University, M.A., 1941, Ph.D., 1944. *Home:* 1300 Ranleigh Rd., McLean, Va. 22101. *Office:* Board of Governors of the Federal Reserve System, Constitution Ave. and 20th St. N.W., Washington, D.C. 20551.

CAREER: Worked in export business in Argentina, 1933-35; Chemical Bank and Trust Co., New York City, member of staff in foreign and security analysis departments, 1935; Hackney, Hopkinson & Sutphen, New York City, security analyst, 1936-40; Federal Reserve Bank of New York, member of foreign research division staff, 1941-51, chief, 1946-51; Yale University, New Haven, Conn., professor of economics 1951-70, Seymour H. Knox Professor of Economics, 1970-74; U.S. Government, Federal Reserve System, Washington, D.C., member of board of governors, 1974—. Assistant to Secretary of Treasury, Washington, D.C., 1958-59; member of President's Council of Economic Advisers, 1959-61. Consultant to various government agencies, foreign central banks, and foreign governments. *Member:* American Economic Association, American Finance Association, Harvard Club (New York), University Club (Washington, D.C.).

WRITINGS: Monetary Problems of an Export Economy, Harvard University Press, 1950, reprinted, Arno, 1978; (with John H. Adler) *Public Finance in a Developing Country: El Salvador, a Case Study*, Harvard University Press, 1951, reprinted, Greenwood Press, 1968; *The Financial System of Portugal*, Economic Cooperation Administration, 1951; (with Robert Triffin) *Monetary and Banking Legislation of the Dominican Republic*, Federal Reserve Bank of New York, 1953; *Mainsprings of the German Revival*, Yale University Press, 1955, reprinted, Greenwood Press, 1976; *The Cost of Freedom: A New Look at Capitalism*, Harper, 1960; (with Henry G. Manne) *The Modern Corporation and Social Responsibility*, American Enterprise Institute for Public Policy Research, 1972; (editor and author of introduction) Hermann Wallich and Paul Wallich, *Zwei Generationen im Deutschen Bunkwesen*, (memoirs), Fritz Knapp Verlag, 1978.

Contributor: Seymour Harris, editor, *Economic Problems of Latin America*, McGraw, 1944; Harris, editor, *Economic Re-*

construction, McGraw, 1946; *Essays in Honor of John H. Williams*, Macmillan, 1951; A. N. Agarwala and S. P. Singh, *The Economics of Underdevelopment*, Oxford University Press, 1956; *The Federal Reserve System*, Harper, 1960; Howard S. Ellis, editor, *Economic Development for Latin America*, Macmillan, 1961; Herbert Prochnow, editor, *The Federal Reserve System*, Harper, 1960; Harris, editor, *The Dollar in Crisis*, Harcourt, 1961; Neil H. Jacoby, editor, *United States Monetary Policy*, 2nd edition (Wallich was not associated with earlier edition), Praeger, 1964; *Ten Economic Studies in the Tradition of Irving Fisher*, Wiley, 1967; Prochnow, editor, *The Five Year Outlook for Interest Rates*, Rand McNally, 1968.

C. P. Kindelberger and A. Schonfield, editors, *North American and Western European Economic Policies*, Macmillan, 1971; Victor Zarnowitz, editor, *The Business Cycle Today*, National Bureau of Economic Research, 1972; *Rethinking the Practice of Management*, Praeger, 1973; *Politica Economica en Centro y Periferia*, Fondo de Cultura Economica, 1976; Peter L. Bernstein, editor, *The Theory and Practice of Bond Portfolio Management*, Institutional Investor Books, 1976; Hugh Patrick and Henry Rosovsky, editors, *Asia's New Giant: How the Japanese Economy Works*, Brookings Institution, 1976; *The Bicentennial of American-German Relations*, Konrad Adenauer Stiftung, 1976; Edward I. Altman and Arnold W. Sametz, editors, *Financial Crises: Institutions and Markets in a Fragile Environment*, Wiley, 1977; Bela Balassa and Richard Nelson, editors, *Economic Progress, Private Values, and Public Policy*, North-Holland Publishing, 1977; Ronald L. Teigen, editor, *Readings in Money, National Income, and Stabilization Policy*, 4th edition, Irwin, 1978; *Zeitschrift fuer das gesamte Kreditwesen*, Fritz Knapp Verlag, 1978; Benjamin M. Friedman, editor, *New Challenges to the Role of Profit*, Lexington Books, 1978; Rudiger Dornbusch and Jacob A. Frenkel, editors, *International Economic Policy: Theory and Evidence*, Johns Hopkins Press, 1979.

Columnist, *Newsweek*, 1965-74. Contributor to business and academic journals, magazines, and newspapers in the United States, Europe, Cuba, Mexico, Costa Rica, Colombia, Brazil, and India. Editorial writer, *Washington Post*, 1961-64.

*   *   *

WALSH, Chad   1914-

PERSONAL: Born May 10, 1914, in South Boston, Va.; son of William Ernest and Katie (Wrenn) Walsh; married Eva May Tuttle, September 18, 1938; children: Damaris Wrenn McGuire, Madeline Walsh Hamblin, Sarah-Lindsay Walsh Parente, Alison Elise. *Education:* Attended Marion Junior College, 1934-36; University of Virginia, A.B., 1938; University of Michigan, A.M., 1939, Ph.D., 1943. *Politics:* Democrat. *Address:* c/o Beloit College, Beloit, Wis. 53511; and R.R.1 Box 74-12, Lake Iroquois, Richmond, Vt. 05477 (summer).

CAREER: Ordained priest of Episcopal Church, 1949; U.S. Army Signal Corps, Arlington, Va., research analyst, 1943-45; Beloit College, Beloit, Wis., 1945-77, began as assistant professor, became professor of English, chairman of department, and writer-in-residence. Fulbright lecturer, Turku, Finland, 1957-58, and Rome, Italy, 1962; visiting professor, Wellesley College, 1958-59, Juniata College, 1977-78, Calvin College, 1979, and Roanoke College, 1979. *Member:* International Association of University Professors of English, Phi Beta Kappa, Raven Society (University of Virginia). *Awards, honors:* Hopwood Award (playwriting), 1939; "Spirit" Medal, Catholic Poetry Society of America, 1964; Council for Wisconsin Writers First Award, 1965, for *The Psalm of Christ* and

The Unknowing Dance, and 1970, for *The End of Nature*; Society of Midland Authors Golden Anniversary Poetry Award, 1965, for *The Unknowing Dance,* and 1970, for *The End of Nature*; Yaddo resident, 1966 and 1970; Order of the White Rose of Finland, 1968.

WRITINGS: Stop Looking and Listen: An Invitation to the Christian Life, Harper, 1947; *C. S. Lewis: Apostle to the Skeptics,* Macmillan, 1949; *The Factual Dark* (poetry), Decker, 1949; *Early Christians of the Twenty-first Century,* Harper, 1950, reprinted, Greenwood Press, 1972; *Knock and Enter,* Morehouse, 1953; *Campus Gods on Trial,* Macmillan, 1953, revised edition, 1962; (with Eric Montizambert) *Faith and Behavior: Christian Answers to Moral Problems,* Morehouse, 1954; *Eden Two-Way* (poetry), Harper, 1954; *Behold the Glory,* Harper, 1956; *Nellie and Her Flying Crocodile,* Harper, 1956.

The Rough Years, Morehouse, 1960; (with wife, Eva Walsh) *Why Go to Church?,* Association Press, 1962; *Doors into Poetry,* Prentice-Hall, 1962, revised edition, 1970; *From Utopia to Nightmare,* Harper, 1962; *The Psalm of Christ* (poetry), Westminster, 1963; *The Unknowing Dance* (poetry), Abelard, 1964; (editor) *Today's Poets* (anthology), Scribner, 1964, revised edition, 1972; (editor) *Garlands for Christmas* (anthology), Macmillan, 1965; *The Honey and the Gall,* Macmillan, 1967; *The End of Nature,* Swallow Press, 1969; *God at Large,* Seabury, 1971; (editor with E. Walsh) *Twice Ten: An Introduction to Poetry,* Wiley, 1976; *The Literary Legacy of C. S. Lewis,* Harcourt, 1979; *A Rich Feast: Encountering the Bible from Genesis to Revelation,* Harper, 1981; *Hang Me Up My Begging Bowl* (poetry), Swallow (Ohio), 1981; (editor) *The Visionary Christian,* Macmillan, 1981.

Contributor of poems, articles, and book reviews to *Poetry, Saturday Review, Atlantic Monthly, Experiment, Epoch, New Republic, Sewanee Review,* and other journals and newspapers. Founder, with Robert Glauber, of *Beloit Poetry Journal,* 1950.

WORK IN PROGRESS: A long-range book project, *The Theology of the Arts;* a long sequence of religious sonnets.

SIDELIGHTS: Chad Walsh told *CA:* "I sometimes wonder why I have written so many books. Perhaps a neurotic compulsion. If I go long without writing, I feel as though some essential vitamin is lacking in my spiritual diet. On another level, it is a word game, but a serious game however playful the results may sometimes seem. It is easier to say how I first began to write. That was in the fourth grade, when the teacher told us to write a poem about autumn. This word game excited me, and when the teacher singled my poem out for praise, I was launched on my career as a poet. Later on I also began to explore the possibilities of prose.

"I suppose I hope to speak to readers through my books; I assume that they and I have our ordinary humanity in common, and that what interests me ought to interest them. In my books on religion there is the attempt to share what I believe. In my poetry I am offering whatever beauty I have been able to make incarnate in words.

"Most of the advice I could give aspiring authors is obvious enough. They must develop a thick skin and healthy ego, and a fanatical determination to stick to the writing, no matter how many discouragements come their way. It is very important that they not be at the mercy of their inner moods. Poor writing can be done while feeling inspired, and good writing can be done while feeling uninspired.

"It seems to me that for more than twenty years American poetry has gone very far in the direction of free forms and a preoccupation with the revelations of the troubled psyche—confessional poetry. I am glad to see that stricter forms are making a modest comeback, and that the newest poets seem less eager to share psychoanalytic secrets with their public.

"As for myself, I am always swinging back and forth between free forms and very strict ones. If there is one dominant theme running through my poetry I suppose it is the relation between human and divine love—but that is a job for the literary critics to figure out, not the poet, whose job is simply to write."

Some of Walsh's poetry has been translated into Italian. *The Rough Years* has been published in German, while *Stop Looking and Listen* has appeared in Norwegian.

BIOGRAPHICAL/CRITICAL SOURCES: Milwaukee Journal, March 6, 1960; *Book World,* August 17, 1969; *Christian Century,* September 17, 1969, January 13, 1971, April 7, 1971; *New York Times Book Review,* July 8, 1979.

*   *   *

WALTERS, John Beauchamp   1906-

PERSONAL: Born November 7, 1906, in Hastings, England; son of George Ernest (a clergyman) and Esther Grace (Beauchamp) Walters; married Leighla Joan Malyneux, August 22, 1932; children: David, Christopher. *Education:* Attended King's College, London, 1928-30. *Home:* Edificio Alca, Apt. A-5, El Botanico, Puerto de la Cruz, Tenerife, Canary Islands.

CAREER: Ran away to sea and served with British Merchant Navy, 1921-24; *London Daily Mirror,* London, England, reporter, 1930-36, special correspondent in New York, N.Y., 1936-54, chief foreign correspondent, 1954-58; Longacre Press, London, general manager and director, 1958-62; Waterlow & Sons Ltd., London, publications adviser, 1962-63. *Member:* Authors Club, Press Club, Buddhist Society, Pali Text Society (all London); Buddhist Publications Society (Ceylon).

WRITINGS: Will America Fight?, Hutchinson, 1940; *Light in the Window,* Kinsey, 1943; *Mind Unshaken: A Modern Introduction to Buddhism,* Rider & Co., 1961, 2nd edition, 1971; *The Essence of Buddhism,* Crowell, 1962; *Prince Philip's Tour of South America,* Waterlow, 1962; *Splendours and Scandal: The Reign of Beau Nash,* Jarrolds, 1968; *Aldershot Review,* Jarrolds, 1970; *The Royal Griffin: Frederick, Prince of Wales,* Jarrolds, 1972.

*   *   *

WALVOORD, John F(lipse)   1910-

PERSONAL: Born May 1, 1910, in Sheboygan, Wis,; son of John Garrett and Mary (Flipse) Walvoord; married Geraldine Lundgren, June 28, 1939; children: John Edward, James Randall, Timothy Peter, Paul David. *Education:* Wheaton College, Wheaton, Ill., A.B., 1931; Dallas Theological Seminary, Th.B., 1934, Th.M., 1934, Th.D., 1936; Texas Christian University, A.M., 1945. *Home:* 1302 El Patio Dr., Dallas, Tex. 75218. *Office:* Dallas Theological Seminary, 3909 Swiss Ave., Dallas, Tex. 75204.

CAREER: Minister, Independent Fundamental Churches of America. Dallas Theological Seminary, Dallas, Tex., registrar, 1935-45, associate professor, 1936-52, professor of systematic theology, 1952—, assistant to the president, 1945-52, president, 1952—. Chairman of the board of Scripture Press Publications and Bible Fellowships, Inc. *Member:* Evangelical Theological Society (president, 1954). *Awards, honors:* D.D., Wheaton College, Wheaton, Ill., 1960.

WRITINGS: The Doctrine of the Holy Spirit: A Study in Pneumatology, Dallas Theological Seminary, 1943, revised edition published as *The Holy Spirit: A Comprehensive Study of the Person and Work of the Holy Spirit*, Van Kampen Press, 1954, 3rd edition, Dunham, 1958; *The Return of the Lord*, Dunham, 1955; *The Thessalonian Epistles*, Dunham, 1956; *The Rapture Question*, Dunham, 1957; (editor) *Inspiration and Interpretation*, Eerdmans, 1957; *The Millennial Kingdom*, Dunham, 1959.

To Live Is Christ: An Exposition of the Epistle of Paul to the Philippians, Dunham, 1961; *Israel in Prophecy*, Zondervan, 1962; (editor) *Truth for Today: "Bibliotheca Sacra" Reader, Commemorating Thirty Years of Publication by Dallas Theological Seminary, 1934-1963*, Moody, 1963; *The Church in Prophecy*, Zondervan, 1964; *The Revelation of Jesus Christ: A Commentary*, Moody, 1966; *The Nations in Prophecy*, Zondervan, 1967; *Jesus Christ Our Lord*, Moody, 1969; *Daniel, the Key to Prophetic Revelation: A Commentary*, Moody, 1971; *Philippians: Joy and Peace*, Moody, 1971; *The Holy Spirit at Work Today*, Moody, 1973; (with Lewis S. Chafer) *Major Bible Themes: Fifty-two Vital Doctrines of the Scriptures Simplified and Explained*, revised edition (Walvoord was not associated with previous edition), Zondervan, 1974; (with John E. Walvoord) *Armageddon, Oil and the Middle East Crisis: What the Bible Says about the Future of the Middle East and the End of Western Civilization*, Zondervan, 1974; *Matthew: Thy Kingdom Come*, Moody, 1974; *The Blessed Hope and the Tribulation: A Biblical and Historical Study of Posttribulationism*, Zondervan, 1976; *The Thessalonian Epistles: A Study Guide Commentary*, Zondervan, 1976. Also author of *Prophetic Trilogy*, three volumes, Zondervan. Contributor to books on prophecy and to religious magazines. Editor, *Seminary Bulletin*, 1940-53, and *Bibliotheca Sacra*, 1952—.

SIDELIGHTS: John F. Walvoord told *CA* that his original aim in life was to be a foreign missionary, but in the course of events he became instead a faculty member of Dallas Theological Seminary and later its president. He has watched the school grow from less than 100 students to a current enrollment of 1,300, which makes it one of the largest theological schools in the world.

AVOCATIONAL INTERESTS: Travel (has visited all forty-eight contiguous states, as well as Hawaii, Australia, New Zealand, South America, Europe, and the Middle East).

*   *   *

WANNAMAKER, Bruce
  See MONCURE, Jane Belk

*   *   *

WARD, Barbara
  See JACKSON, Barbara (Ward)

*   *   *

WARD, Jonas
  See GARFIELD, Brian (Wynne)

*   *   *

WASIOLEK, Edward 1924-

PERSONAL: Born April 27, 1924, in Camden, N.J.; son of Ignacy and Mary (Szczesniewska) Wasiolek; married Emma Jones Thomson (a professor), 1948; children: Mark Allan, Karen Lee, Eric Wade. *Education:* Rutgers University, A.B., 1949; Harvard University, A.M., 1950, Ph.D., 1955; University of Bordeaux, certificate, 1951. *Home:* Butterfield Lane, Floss-

moor, Ill. 60422. *Office:* Department of Slavic Languages, University of Chicago, Chicago, Ill. 60637.

CAREER: Ohio Wesleyan University, Delaware, instructor in English, 1954-55; University of Chicago, Chicago, Ill., assistant professor of English, 1955-60, associate professor of English and Russian, 1960-64, professor of Russian and comparative literature, 1964-69, Distinguished Service Professor of Russian and Comparative Literature, 1969—, chairman of department of comparative literature, beginning 1965, chairman of department of Slavic languages and literature, 1971-77. Visiting professor of Slavic and comparative literature, Harvard University, 1966-67. *Military service:* U.S. Navy, 1943-46. *Member:* Phi Beta Kappa. *Awards, honors:* Quantrell Prize for excellence in undergraduate teaching, University of Chicago, 1962; Laing Press Prize, 1972.

WRITINGS: (With Raymond Bauer) *Nine Soviet Portraits*, Wiley, 1955; *Dostoevsky: The Major Fiction*, M.I.T. Press, 1964; *The Gambler with Paulina Juslova's Diary*, University of Chicago Press, 1972; *Tolstoy's Major Fiction*, University of Chicago Press, 1978.

Editor; published by University of Chicago Press, except as indicated: *"Crime and Punishment" and the Critics*, Wadsworth, 1961; *"The Brothers Karamazov" and the Critics*, Wadsworth, 1967; (and translator) Fyodor Dostoevsky, *The Notebooks for "Crime and Punishment,"* 1967; (and author of introduction) Dostoevsky, *The Notebooks for "The Idiot,"* 1967; (and author of introduction) Dostoevsky, *The Notebooks for "The Possessed,"* 1968; (and author of introduction) Dostoevsky, *The Notebooks for "A Raw Youth,"* 1969; (and translator) Dostoevsky, *The Notebooks for "The Brothers Karamazov,"* 1971. Contributor of numerous articles to *Saturday Review, Modern Age, Modern Philology, College English*, and other journals.

SIDELIGHTS: One of Edward Wasiolek's most critically acclaimed works has been the translated editions of the notebooks kept by Dostoevsky during the writing of his five major novels. Although the notebooks were originally published in the Soviet Union during the 1930's, Wasiolek's editions are the first in English. In his review of *The Notebooks for "Crime and Punishment,"* Ernest J. Simmons states: "These notebooks are extraordinarily interesting. They are also wholly necessary to any study of the complicated development and functioning of Dostoevsky's art."

Wasiolek told *CA* that his chief literary interests are "contemporary critical theory, and the Russian and American novel." He is "linguistically competent" in Russian, French, and Polish.

AVOCATIONAL INTERESTS: Swimming, tennis, boating, fishing, and skiing.

BIOGRAPHICAL/CRITICAL SOURCES: New York Times Book Review, May 7, 1967, February 18, 1968, July 16, 1978; *Commentary*, February, 1968; *Harper's*, October, 1969; *New York Times*, April 14, 1978.

*   *   *

WASSERFALL, Adel 1918-
  (Adel Pryor)

PERSONAL: Born December 2, 1918, in Norway; daughter of Aage Wilhelm and Dagny (Rasmusen) Moller; married Edward W(illiam) Pryor, 1943; married second husband, Aubrey Lionel Wasserfall, June 30, 1966. *Education:* Attended Cape Technical College, 1937. *Religion:* Baptist. *Home:* 8 Iona St., Milnerton 7405, Cape Province, South Africa.

CAREER: English governess, Copenhagen, Denmark, 1936; shorthand-typist, Cape Town, South Africa, 1938-43; doctor's receptionist, 1965-66. Chairman, Interdenominational Children's Services, Crippled Children's Home, 1946-54.

WRITINGS—Under name Adel Pryor, except as indicated; published by Zondervan, except as indicated: *Tangled Paths,* 1959; *Clouded Glass,* 1961; *Hidden Fire,* 1962; *Out of the Night,* 1963; *Hearts in Conflict,* 1964; *Forgotten Yesterday,* 1966; *Valley of Desire,* 1967; *Sound of the Sea,* 1968; *Free of a Dream,* 1969; *Her Secret Fear,* 1971; *A Norwegian Romance,* Pickering & Inglis, 1976; (under name Adel Wasserfall) *All Is Not Gold,* Sunday School Centre (Capetown, South Africa), 1979.

AVOCATIONAL INTERESTS: Psychology, character-study, reading, and foreign missions.

*   *   *

WASSERSTROM, Richard Alan   1936-

PERSONAL: Born January 9, 1936, in New York, N.Y.; son of Alfred Howard and Gertrude (Kopp) Wasserstrom; married Phyllis Ann Levin, 1957; children: Sara E., Jeffrey N., William L., Harold L. *Education:* Amherst College, B.A., 1957; University of Michigan, M.A., 1958, law student, 1957-59, Ph.D., 1960; Stanford University, LL.B., 1960. *Home:* 538 Escalona Dr., Santa Cruz, Calif. 95060. *Office:* Kresge College, University of California, Santa Cruz, Calif. 95064.

CAREER: Stanford University, Stanford, Calif., assistant professor of philosophy and law, 1960-62, assistant professor of law, 1962-63, associate professor (on leave), 1963-64; attorney for Civil Rights Division, U.S. Department of Justice, 1963-64; Tuskegee Institute, Tuskegee Institute, Ala., dean of College of Arts and Sciences, 1964-67; University of California, Los Angeles, professor of law and philosophy, 1967-79; University of California, Santa Cruz, professor of philosophy, 1979—. *Member:* American Association of University Professors, Association for Social and Legal Philosophy, Council for Philosophical Studies, California Council for Humanities in Public Policy, California Council for the Humanities (chairman).

WRITINGS: The Judicial Decision, Stanford University Press, 1961; (editor) *War and Morality,* Wadsworth, 1970; (editor) *Morality and the Law,* Wadsworth, 1971; (editor) *Today's Moral Problems,* Macmillan, 1975, 2nd edition, 1979; *Philosophy and Social Issues: Five Studies,* University of Notre Dame Press, 1980. Contributor of articles to professional journals.

*   *   *

WATSON, Alan D(ouglas)   1942-

PERSONAL: Born May 3, 1942, in Rocky Mount, N.C.; son of Joseph Winstead and Helen (Richardson) Watson; married Margaret Bunn, August 29, 1964; children: Katherine, Jennifer, Westray. *Education:* Duke University, B.A., 1964; East Carolina University, M.A., 1966; University of South Carolina, Ph.D., 1971. *Residence:* Wilmington, N.C. *Office:* Department of History, University of North Carolina at Wilmington, 601 South College Rd., Wilmington, N.C. 28403.

CAREER: University of North Carolina at Wilmington, associate professor of history, 1971—. State of North Carolina Department of Cultural Resources, Raleigh, member of advisory editorial committee for North Carolina Bicentennial, 1974—, member of advisory editorial committee of Division of Archives and History, 1975-80. *Member:* Organization of American Historians, Southern Historical Association, Historical Society of North Carolina, North Carolina Literary and Historical Association (vice-president, 1975-76, 1978-79), Association of Historians in Eastern North Carolina (secretary, 1975-76), Lower Cape Fear Historical Society (member of board of directors, 1975-78). *Awards, honors:* North Carolina Society of Sons of the American Revolution Award, 1975 and 1976, for best article relating to the American Revolution.

WRITINGS: Society in Colonial North Carolina, North Carolina Division of Archives and History, 1975; (contributor) William S. Powell, editor, *Dictionary of North Carolina Biography,* Volume I, University of North Carolina Press, 1979; (contributor) David C. Roller and Robert W. Twyman, editors, *Encyclopedia of Southern History,* Louisiana State University Press, 1979; (contributor) Larry E. Tise and Jeffrey J. Crow, editors, *The Study and Writing of North Carolina History,* North Carolina Division of Archives and History, 1979; *Burke County: A Brief History,* North Carolina Division of Archives and History, 1979; *Edgecombe County: A Brief History,* North Carolina Division of Archives and History, 1979; *Money and Monetary Problems in Early North Carolina,* North Carolina Division of Archives and History, 1980. Contributor of articles to periodicals, including *North Carolina Historical Review, South Carolina Historical Magazine, South Atlantic Quarterly, The State, William and Mary Quarterly, Journal of Negro History, Mississippi Quarterly,* and *Southern Studies.* Editor, *Lower Cape Fear Historical Bulletin,* 1975-77.

WORK IN PROGRESS: A Disparate People: Essays Concerning the Economic and Social History of Colonial North Carolinians.

SIDELIGHTS: Alan D. Watson writes: "Raised in a family atmosphere which stressed the importance of reading and an appreciation of genealogy and history, and living in proximity to land owned over two centuries ago by my forebears, I quickly developed a keen awareness of the past. Collegiate educational opportunities and the approaching bicentennial of the American Revolution further stimulated my interest in history.

"History, to me, is a most fascinating discipline. It is all-encompassing, embracing every conceivable emotion and subject. It is as broad (or as narrow) as the imagination of the writer. It can attempt the exactness of science; it can approach the subjectivity of philosophy. It can serve as a vehicle for change; it can be used to defend the status quo.

"On the whole, mine is a descriptive history, conservative and appreciative of the past. I would like to enjoy history and be entertained by it. At the same time I would extend the use and appreciation of history to others for their various applications of it. And that is crucial, for so few people care for the past and recognize the values to be derived from it."

*   *   *

WATT, W(illiam) Montgomery   1909-

PERSONAL: Born March 14, 1909, in Ceres, Fife, Scotland; son of Andrew and Mary (Burns) Watt; married Jean MacDonald Donaldson, 1943; children: Ann, Andrew, Mary, Jean, Glenys. *Education:* University of Edinburgh, M.A., 1930, Ph.D., 1944; Balliol College, Oxford, B.A., 1932, M.A., 1936, B.Litt., 1933; University of Jena, graduate study, summer, 1934. *Religion:* Scottish Episcopalian Church. *Home:* The Neuk, Dalkeith, Midlothian, Scotland.

CAREER: University of Edinburgh, Edinburgh, Scotland, assistant lecturer in moral philosophy, 1934-38; Anglican Bishopric of Jerusalem, Jerusalem, Palestine (now Israel), chaplain and researcher, 1943-46; University of Edinburgh, lecturer in ancient philosophy, 1946-47, reader in Arabic, 1947-64, professor of Arabic and Islamic studies, 1964-79. *Member:* Iona Community. *Awards, honors:* D.D., University of Aberdeen, 1966; Levidella Vida Medal, University of California, Los Angeles, 1981.

WRITINGS: Freewill and Predestination in Early Islam, Luzac, 1949; *The Faith and Practice of al-Ghazali,* Allen & Unwin, 1953; *Muhammad at Mecca,* Oxford University Press, 1953; *Muhammad at Medina,* Oxford University Press, 1956; *The Reality of God,* S.P.C.K., 1957; *The Cure for Human Troubles,* S.P.C.K., 1959.

(Translator) Eutychius of Alexandria, *The Book of the Demonstration,* [Louvain], 1960; *Muhammad, Prophet and Statesman,* Oxford University Press, 1961; *Islam and the Integration of Society,* Routledge & Kegan Paul, 1961; *Islamic Philosophy and Theology,* Quadrangle, 1962; *Muslim Intellectual: A Study of al-Ghazali,* Aldine, 1963; *Truth in the Religions,* Adine, 1963; *Islamic Spain,* Quadrangle, 1965; *A Companion to the Qur'an,* Allen & Unwin, 1967; *What Is Islam?,* Longmans, Green, 1968; *Islamic Political Thought,* Edinburgh University Press, 1968; *Islamic Revelation and the Modern World,* Edinburgh University Press, 1970; *Bell's Introduction to the Qur'an,* Edinburgh University Press, 1970; *The Influence of Islam on Medieval Europe,* Edinburgh University Press, 1972; *The Formative Period of Islamic Thought,* Edinburgh University Press, 1973; *The Majesty that Was Islam,* Sidgwick & Jackson, 1974; *Thoughts on Muslim-Christian Dialogue,* Hamdard Islamicus (Karachi), 1978; *Der Islam,* Volume I, Kohlhammer, 1980. Contributor to professional journals.

WORK IN PROGRESS: Volumes II and III of *Der Islam* for Kohlhammer; *The Career of Muhammad as Recorded in the Qur'an;* a general study on the nature of religious truth, with special reference to Islam and Christianity.

SIDELIGHTS: W. Montgomery Watt told *CA* that he is "keen to see a more general understanding of the importance of religious symbols for nations and for mankind as a whole, but I want this to be combined with the realization that the main struggle is not between religion and no-religion but between true religion and demonic religion."

Watt's books have been translated into French, German, Spanish, Russian, Arabic, Persian, Turkish, and Japanese.

*   *   *

WAUGH, Auberon (Alexander)   1939-

PERSONAL: Born November 17, 1939, in Dulverton, Somerset, England; son of Evelyn (a novelist) and Laura (Herbert) Waugh; married Teresa Onslow (a translator), July 1, 1961; children: Margaret Sophia Laura, Alexander Evelyn Michael, Daisy Louisa Dominica, Nathaniel Thomas Biafra. *Education:* Attended Christ Church, Oxford, 1959-60. *Politics:* "Antipolitical conservative." *Religion:* Roman Catholic. *Home:* Combe Florey House, Taunton, Somerset TA4 3JD, England. *Agent:* Harold Matson Co., Inc., 22 East 40th St., New York, N.Y. 10016. *Office: Private Eye,* 34 Greek St., London W1, England.

CAREER: Daily Telegraph, London, England, editorial writer, 1960-63; *Catholic Herald,* London, columnist, 1963-64; International Publishing Corp. (newspaper chain), London, columnist, 1963-67; *Spectator,* London, political correspondent, 1967-70; *Private Eye,* London, political correspondent and literary editor, 1970—. Columnist for London newspapers and periodicals, *News of the World,* 1969-70, *Sun,* 1969-70, *Times,*

1970, and *New Statesman,* 1973-75; chief fiction reviewer, *Spectator,* 1970-73, 1976—, *Evening Standard,* 1973-80, *Daily Mail,* 1981—, and *Sunday Telegraph,* 1981—. *Military service:* British Army, Royal Horse Guards, 1958-59. *Member:* P.E.N., National Union of Journalists, Society of Authors, Beefsteak Club (London). *Awards, honors:* Columnist of the Year Award, Independent Television, 1978; recipient of two British Press Critic of the Year Awards.

WRITINGS: The Foxglove Saga (novel), Chapman & Hall, 1960, Simon & Schuster, 1961; *Path of Dalliance* (novel), Chapman & Hall, 1963, Simon & Schuster, 1964; *Who Are the Violets Now?* (novel), Chapman & Hall, 1965, Simon & Schuster, 1966; *Consider the Lilies* (novel), M. Joseph, 1968, Little, Brown, 1969; (with Suzanne Cronje) *Biafra: Britain's Shame* (nonfiction), M. Joseph, 1969; *A Bed of Flowers; or, As You Like It* (novel), M. Joseph, 1972; *Country Topics* (essays previously published in *Evening Standard),* M. Joseph, 1974; *Four Crowded Years* (diaries), Deutsch, 1976; *In the Lion's Den* (essays previously published in *New Statesman),* M. Joseph, 1978; *The Last Word: An Eyewitness Account of the Trial of Jeremy Thorpe* (nonfiction), Little, Brown, 1980; *Auberon Waugh's Yearbook,* Pan Books, 1981. Contributor of articles and book reviews to *Times* (London), *New Statesman, Evening Standard* (London), *Esquire, New York Times, Le Monde, Spectator, Catholic Herald, Books and Bookmen, L'Express, Time,* and other British newspapers and periodicals.

SIDELIGHTS: The son of the late English novelist Evelyn Waugh, Auberon Waugh has established himself as a political journalist, essayist, critic, and novelist in his own right. A witty satirist, he has "a polished style and a nice talent for verbal mayhem," writes Granville Hicks in the *Saturday Review.* Dorothy Rea says in the *Washington Post Book World* that "Auberon Waugh, political journalist, can do just about anything, [but] the fictioneering [Auberon] is even better." Both his fiction and nonfiction works have received much critical attention and have frequently been compared—sometimes to his discredit—to his father's works.

When Auberon's first book, *The Foxglove Saga,* appeared in America and England, "he was called 'a born writer,'" notes Gene Baro in the *New York Times Book Review.* A *Kirkus Review* critic calls the work "a comic novel very much in the style of [the author's] father's earlier books"—an assessment that is shared by several other critics. Edward Weeks writes in the *Atlantic* that the novel "at its best" reminds him of *Decline and Fall* by Evelyn Waugh, and John Moran of *Library Journal* sees "the same sort of savage wit which distinguished [Evelyn's] *Scoop, Black Mischief,* [and] *Vile Bodies.* . . . The author has a sharp eye for the ironies which spring from the contrast between appearance and reality in human characters and institutions." Honor Tracy states in the *New Republic* that the book "has many good things in it which do not so much derive from Mr. Evelyn Waugh as belong to him entirely. They are genuine chips off the old block. There is, in the better parts, the same rueful awareness of contradiction and confusion, the wry eye for human frightfulness, the savagery, the gorgeous fun."

Yet, a *Time* critic considers the resemblance somewhat of a mixed blessing: "Auberon has his father's . . . hilarious sense of incongruity. But his father's titled ghosts seem oddly dated in Welfare State England. Moreover, there is something lacking—the figure of the innocent but virtuous hero . . . whose reasoned view gave a special cutting edge to the elder Waugh's comedy." *Saturday Review's* Aileen Pippett believes that the resemblance ultimately compromises the book's success: "This would be tremendous if it were new, if it did not lead to the suspicion that what we are being shown is merely a young man commendably following in father's footsteps. . . . [However,] *The Foxglove Saga* is patently derivative. It is an excellent copy, but it lacks surprise.'' Nevertheless, Nigel Dennis claims in the *New York Times Book Review* that ''almost all British satirists of today are sons of Evelyn Waugh to some degree'' and concludes: ''*The Foxglove Saga* shows that Waugh's own son has been quite unable to bypass the peculiar tone and talent of his formidable progenitor. Here is everything one expects from a Waugh novel. . . . And had it not all been done by the father, what honor would not be due to the son?''

Some critics also compare Auberon's second book, *Path of Dalliance,* to works by his father, whereas others regard it as a mature work with its own merit. Calling the book a feeble performance ''after the hard corruscation and ingenuity of *The Foxglove Saga,*'' Bernard Bergonzi says in the *New Statesman* that ''most damagingly, it directly invites comparison with the elder Waugh's early work: there is more to a single paragraph of the Oxford scenes in *Decline and Fall* than in the whole of Auberon's undergraduate section.'' But a *Times Literary Supplement* reviewer points out that ''echoing though as it does both *Decline and Fall* and *Brideshead Revisited,* [the book] also demonstrates a very assured and mature talent in its own right.'' Gene Baro claims Auberon ''is able to phrase some idiocies so close to the truth of things that one does a double take.'' Moreover, Harold Hobson notes in the *Christian Science Monitor* that Waugh ''dazzles with the brilliance of his scorn, and his picture of his own generation is at once a monstrous travesty and a true statement. In any case, it is wonderfully drawn.''

Of *Who Are the Violets Now?,* William Gavin writes in *America:* ''It has seemed to me that in recent years we have been labeling as satire any book that was both opinionated and nasty. It is reassuring to come across the real thing, in all its classic, biting, malicious glory.'' Gavin insists that though Auberon is occasionally inconsistent in tone, ''he is so very good that the only satirist with whom he can be compared shares his last name.'' In the *New York Times Book Review,* however, Frank Littler states that ''this Waugh simply doesn't understand the London he is supposed to be writing about.'' Littler adds that the book's ''narrative manner and dialogue are often a generation and a half out of date.''

Auberon Waugh told *CA* that he gave up writing novels in 1973 to protest the British free public library system that cuts down on bookstore sales; he intends to resume writing fiction ''as soon as the economic climate is more favorable to English novelists.'' Such a move has been commended by John Betjeman of *Books and Bookmen* as being ''sound and practical.'' Meanwhile, Waugh continues to produce marketable nonfiction that is generally praised and occasionally compared to his father's work. *Country Topics,* writes Betjeman, ''reads as though it is easily written. Easily read writing like this is difficult and takes time.'' Arthur Marshall of the *New Statesman* considers the articles of *In the Lion's Den* ''beautifully written, highly stimulating, frequently hilarious, and marvelously irreverent. . . . Nothing and nobody is safe for very long.'' Thomas Thompson says in the *Los Angeles Times Book Review* that *The Last Word* ''makes the reader keep checking the title page to see if Lewis Carroll and Gilbert & Sullivan didn't drop down as ghostwriters.'' And *Spectator's* Christopher Booker believes the diary entries in *Four Crowded Years* ''read astonishingly like a perfect parody of those of Waugh Senior. . . . Both father and son are malicious—often grossly unfair—[and] display little respect for most of the traditional Christian virtues which they are supposed to uphold. On the other hand, their strengths are also similar—they are both incredibly funny, and

they mock much of the mad, sad world in which we live in a way that it desperately needs to be mocked.''

BIOGRAPHICAL/CRITICAL SOURCES: Times Literary Supplement, October 21, 1960, November 1, 1963, October 21, 1965; *Kirkus Review,* May 15, 1961; *Time,* July 21, 1961; *New York Times Book Review,* July 23, 1961, July 19, 1964, May 29, 1966; *Saturday Review,* August 5, 1961, January 4, 1969; *New Republic,* August 7, 1961; *Atlantic,* September, 1961; *New Yorker,* September 2, 1961; *Commonweal,* November 17, 1961; *New Statesman,* November 1, 1963, September 22, 1978; *Christian Science Monitor,* July 23, 1964; *America,* May 14, 1966; *Washington Post Book World,* April 6, 1969; *Spectator,* November 29, 1969, December 11, 1976, September 23, 1978; *Books and Bookmen,* April, 1972, May, 1974; *Contemporary Literary Criticism,* Volume VII, Gale, 1977; *Economist,* February 23, 1980; *New York Times,* October 27, 1980; *Los Angeles Times Book Review,* November 9, 1980; *Washington Post,* November 15, 1980.

—Sketch by James G. Lesniak

*   *   *

WEBB, Jean Francis (III)   1910-
(Ethel Hamill, Roberta Morrison)

PERSONAL: Born October 1, 1910, in White Plains, N.Y.; son of Jean Francis, Jr. (an electrical engineer) and Ethel (Morrison) Webb; married Nancy Bukeley (a writer and public relations worker), May 27, 1936; children: Jean F. IV, Rodman B., Morrison DeSoto, Alexander Henderson. *Education:* Amherst College, B.A., 1931. *Politics:* Republican. *Religion:* Episcopalian. *Home:* 242 East 72nd St., Apt. 16A, New York, N.Y. 10021. *Agent:* Patricia Schartle, McIntosh & Otis, 475 Fifth Ave., New York, N.Y. 10017.

CAREER: Author of mystery, historical, romance, adventure, and children's novels. Held various ''bread and butter'' jobs, 1931-34. Teacher of adult courses in professional writing, University of Hawaii, 1940; guest lecturer at Columbia University and Amherst College. President, Lewisboro School League, 1947-48; secretary of trustees, South Salem (N.Y.) Library, 1946-71. *Member:* Mystery Writers of America (member of board of directors, 1976—), Sons of the Revolution, Phi Delta Theta (alumni chapter president, 1960-64). *Awards, honors:* New York Herald Tribune honor book award, 1962, for *Kaiulani: Crown Princess of Hawaii.*

WRITINGS: Love They Must (novel), Ives Washburn, 1933; *Forty Brothers* (short stories), Collegiate Press, 1934; *No Match for Murder,* Macmillan, 1942; (with wife, Nancy Webb) *Golden Feathers,* Bouregy, 1954; (with N. Webb) *The Hawaiian Islands from Monarchy to Democracy,* Viking, 1956, revised edition, 1963; (with N. Webb) *Kaiulani: Crown Princess of Hawaii,* Viking, 1962; (with N. Webb) *Will Shakespeare and His America,* Viking, 1964; *The Craigshaw Curse,* Meredith, 1968; *Roses from a Haunted Garden,* McKay, 1971; *Somewhere Within This House,* McKay, 1973; *The Bride of Cairngore,* McKay, 1974; *Is This Coffin Taken?,* Zebra Books, 1978. Also author of *Carnavaron's Castle,* 1969.

Under pseudonym Ethel Hamill; published by Avalon, except as indicated: *Reveille for Romance,* Arcadia House, 1946; *Challenge to Love,* Arcadia House, 1946; *Honeymoon in Honolulu,* 1950; *Tower in the Forest,* 1951; *Nurse on Horseback,* 1952; *The Dancing Mermaid,* 1952; *Bluegrass Doctor,* 1953; *The Minister's Daughter,* 1953; *Gloria and the Bullfighter,* 1954; *A Nurse Comes Home,* 1954; *Runaway Nurse,* 1955; *A Nurse for Galleon Key,* 1957; *The Golden Image,* 1959; *Aloha*

Nurse, 1961; *Sudden Love,* 1962; *The Nurse from Hawaii,* 1964.

Under pseudonym Roberta Morrison: *Tree of Evil,* Paperback Library, 1966.

Adapter of more than nine hundred motion picture scripts for magazine use and for books. Also author, with N. Webb, of daily radio program "Chick Carter, Boy Detective," 1944-45. Contributor of more than three hundred short stories, novelettes, and articles to *Cosmopolitan, Liberty, Collier's, Argosy, Writer's Digest, Show,* and other publications. Editor of various single-issue magazines for Dell.

SIDELIGHTS: Jean Francis Webb's stories have been translated into Spanish and Danish; four of his books have been published in Australia, five in England, and one in Argentina. He and his wife are collectors of Hawaiiana and have an extensive library. In his youth Webb worked briefly on the professional stage, and the theater is still one of his interests.

*   *   *

WEBB, Lucas
See BURGESS, M(ichael) R(oy)

*   *   *

WEINTRAUB, Sidney 1914-

PERSONAL: Born April 28, 1914, in New York, N.Y.; son of Aaron Isaac and Martha (Fisch) Weintraub; married Sheila Ellen Tarlow, August 25, 1940; children: E. Roy, Arthur Neil. *Education:* New York University, B.C.S., 1935, Ph.D., 1941; London School of Economics, graduate study, 1938-39. *Home:* 429 Montgomery Ave., Haverford, Pa. 19041. *Office:* McNeil Building, University of Pennsylvania, Philadelphia, Pa. 19104.

CAREER: St. John's University, Brooklyn, Jamaica, N.Y., instructor, 1939-42; U.S. Treasury Department, Washington, D.C., economist, 1942; Federal Reserve Bank, New York, N.Y., economist and editor, 1942-43; St. John's University, professor, 1946-50; University of Pennsylvania, Philadelphia, professor of economics, 1950—, chairman of department, 1960-61, chairman of graduate group in general economics, 1958-61, 1964-65. Distinguished Kennedy Professor, University of the South, fall, 1981, and Williams College, spring, 1982; lecturer at New School for Social Research, University of Minnesota, University of Hawaii, and University of Western Australia; frequent lecturer in the United States and abroad. Consultant to U.S. Treasury Department, U.S. State Department, Federal Communications Commission, Federal Power Commission, University of Waterloo, University of Puerto Rico, National Council for Applied Economic Research (New Delhi), and U.S. Forest Service. *Military service:* U.S. Army, 1943-45; served in European Theater. *Member:* American Economic Association, Econometric Society, Royal Economic Society, American Association of University Professors, Beta Gamma Sigma (honorary member), Faculty Club (University of Pennsylvania), Springfield Country Club. *Awards, honors:* Ford Foundation research fellowship, 1956-57.

WRITINGS: Price Theory, Pitman, 1949; *Income and Employment Analysis,* Pitman, 1951; *An Approach to the Theory of Income Distribution,* Chilton, 1958; *Stumpage Prices and Appraisal Policies,* U.S. Forest Service, 1958; *A General Theory of the Price Level, Output, Income Distribution, and Economic Growth,* Chilton, 1959; *Classical Keynesianism, Monetary Theory and the Price Level,* Chilton, 1961; *Wage Theory and Policy,* Chilton, 1963; *Intermediate Price Theory,* Chilton, 1964; *Growth without Inflation in India,* National Council for

Applied Economic Research (New Delhi), 1965; *A Keynesian Theory of Employment Growth and Income Distribution,* Chilton, 1966; *Keynes and the Monetarists,* Rutgers University Press, 1973; (editor) *Income Inequality,* American Academy of Political Science, 1973; (editor) *Modern Economic Thought,* University of Pennsylvania Press, 1977; *Capitalism's Inflation and Unemployment Crises,* Addison-Wesley, 1978; *Keynes, Keynesians, and Monetarists,* University of Pennsylvania Press, 1978; *Our Stagflation Malaise,* Greenwood Press, 1981. Columnist, *New Leader;* contributing columnist, *Philadelphia Evening Bulletin* and *New York Times.* Contributor to professional and popular journals in the United States and abroad. Co-editor, *Post Keynesian Economics,* 1978—; editor, *Puerto Rico Economic Quarterly,* 1979—.

WORK IN PROGRESS: Articles and monographs on economic analysis.

*   *   *

WEISS, Harvey 1922-

PERSONAL: Born April 10, 1922, in New York, N.Y.; son of Louis and Bertha (Stern) Weiss; married Miriam Schlein, 1954 (divorced); married Margaret I. McKinnickinnick, 1981; children: (first marriage) Elizabeth, John. *Education:* Attended New York University, 1939-40, University of Missouri, 1940-41, Arts Students League, and Rutgers University; studied sculpture in Paris. *Home:* 42 Maple Lane, Greens Farms, Conn. 06436. *Office:* Department of Art, Adelphi University, Garden City, N.Y. 11530.

CAREER: Worked as production manager for advertising firms, then became free-lance writer, illustrator, and sculptor; currently assistant professor of art, Adelphi University, Garden City, N.Y. His sculptures have been exhibited in one-man shows at Paul Rosenberg & Co., Fairfield University, and Silvermine Guild, and in group shows at Sculpture Center, Sculptors Guild, and Albright Knox Gallery; his work is represented in the permanent collections of Nelson Rockefeller, Joseph Hirshhorn, Kranert Museum, and others. *Military service:* U.S. Air Force. *Member:* Authors Guild, Sculptors Guild (president, 1970-73), Silvermine Guild. *Awards, honors:* Three books, *A Gondola for Fun, Paul's Horse, Herman,* and *Pencil, Pen, and Brush,* were selected as *New York Herald Tribune* Honor Books; Ford Foundation purchase award, 1960 and 1961; National Institute of Arts and Letters grant, 1970.

WRITINGS—Self-illustrated youth books: *Clay, Wood, and Wires: A How-to-Do-It Book of Sculpture,* W. R. Scott, 1956; *Twenty-Four and Stanley,* Putnam, 1956; *A Gondola for Fun,* Putnam, 1957; *Paul's Horse, Herman,* Putnam, 1958; *Paper, Ink, and Roller: Print-Making for Beginners,* W. R. Scott, 1958 (published in England as *The Young Printmaker: Printing with Paper, Ink and Roller,* Kaye & Ward, 1969); *The Sooner Hound,* Putnam, 1960; *The Expeditions of Willis Partridge,* Abelard, 1960, published as *The Adventures of Willis Partridge,* Young Readers Press, 1966; *Pencil, Pen, and Brush: Drawing for Beginners,* W. R. Scott, 1961; *How to Ooze, and Other Ways of Travelling,* Abelard, 1961; *Horse in No Hurry,* Putnam, 1961; *Sticks, Spools, and Feathers,* W. R. Scott, 1962; *My Closet Full of Hats,* Abelard, 1962; *Ceramics: From Clay to Kiln,* W. R. Scott, 1964; *Paint, Brush, and Palette,* W. R. Scott, 1966; *Sailing Small Boats,* W. R. Scott, 1967 (published in England as *Better Sailing,* edited by John Chamier, Kaye & Ward, 1969); *The Big Cleanup,* Abelard, 1967; *Rocks and Gemstones,* Crowell, 1967; *How to Be a Hero,* Parents Magazine Press, 1968; *Motors and Engines and How They Work,* Crowell, 1969.

Collage and Construction, Young Scott Books, 1970; *The Gadget Book,* Crowell, 1971; *Lens and Shutter: An Introduction to Photography,* Young Scott Books, 1971; *How to Make Your Own Movies: An Introduction to Filmmaking,* Young Scott Books, 1973; *Ship Models and How to Build Them,* Crowell, 1973; *How to Make Your Own Books,* Crowell, 1974; *Model Cars and Trucks and How to Build Them,* Crowell, 1974; *Model Airplanes and How to Build Them,* Crowell, 1975; *Carving: How to Carve Wood and Stone,* Addison-Wesley, 1976; *Games and Puzzles You Can Make Yourself,* Crowell, 1976; *How to Run a Railroad: Everything You Need to Know about Model Trains,* Crowell, 1977; *What Holds It Together?,* Atlantic-Little, Brown, 1977; *Working with Cardboard and Paper,* Addison-Wesley, 1977; *Model Buildings and How to Make Them,* Crowell, 1979; *How to Be an Inventor,* Crowell, 1980; *Hammer and Saw,* Crowell, 1981; *Machines at Work,* Crowell, 1982.

Illustrator: Joan Lexau, *Olaf Reads,* Dial, 1961; David Cornel DeJong, *The Happy Birthday Egg,* Atlantic-Little, Brown, 1962; Miriam Schlein, *The Pile of Junk,* Abelard, 1962; Robert Froman, *Rubber Bands, Baseballs and Doughnuts,* Crowell, 1972; David A. Adler, *3D, 2D, 1D,* Crowell, 1975.

BIOGRAPHICAL/CRITICAL SOURCES: Contemporary American Painting and Sculpture, University of Illinois Press, 1961.

*   *   *

WEISS, Leonard W(inchell) 1925-

PERSONAL: Born November 1, 1925, in Eugene, Ore.; son of Henry Leonard and Dorothy (Winchell) Weiss; married Elyse Crouse, 1956; children: Martha, Judith, Janet, Jo Katherine. *Education:* Northwestern University, B.S., 1945; graduate study at London School of Economics, 1949-50, and University of Wisconsin, 1951-52; Columbia University, Ph.D., 1954. *Office:* Department of Economics, University of Wisconsin—Madison, Madison, Wis. 53706.

CAREER: Wayne University (now Wayne State University), Detroit, Mich., instructor, 1950-51, 1952-55; San Jose State College (now University), San Jose, Calif., associate professor, 1955-60, 1961-62; University of Minnesota, Minneapolis, visiting associate professor, 1960-61; University of Wisconsin—Madison, 1962—, began as associate professor, currently professor of economics. *Military service:* U.S. Navy, 1943-47; became ensign. *Member:* American Economic Association.

WRITINGS: Economics and American Industry, Wiley, 1961; *Case Studies in American Industry,* Wiley, 1966, 3rd edition, 1980; *Economics and Society,* Wiley, 1975, 2nd edition, 1981; (with Allyn Strickland) *Regulation: A Case Approach,* McGraw, 1976, 2nd edition, 1982; (editor with M. Klass) *Case Studies in Regulation: Revolution and Reform,* Little, Brown, 1981. Contributor to professional journals.

WORK IN PROGRESS: Research on industrial concentration, non-advertising selling costs, dominant firms, auctions, union wage efforts, and conglomerate mergers.

*   *   *

WELCH, Pauline
See BODENHAM, Hilda Morris

*   *   *

WELLMAN, Manly Wade 1903-

PERSONAL: Born May 21, 1903, in Kamundongo, Angola;

son of Frederick Creighton (a medical officer and scientist) and Lydia (Isely) Wellman (American citizens); married Frances Obrist, June 14, 1930; children: Wade. *Education:* Municipal University of Wichita (now Wichita State University), A.B., 1926; Columbia University, B.Litt., 1927. *Politics:* Democrat. *Religion:* Episcopalian. *Home and office address:* P.O. Box 744, Chapel Hill, N.C. *Agent:* Blassingame, McCauley & Wood, 60 East 42nd St., New York, N.Y. 10017.

CAREER: Worked as reporter, book and motion picture reviewer, feature writer on various Kansas newspapers, 1927-34; free-lance writer, 1934—. Instructor in creative writing at Elon College, 1962-69, and University of North Carolina, 1964-71. *Awards, honors:* Ellery Queen Award, 1946; Mystery Writers of America Edgar Allan Poe Award for best non-fiction study of crime, 1955; Association for State and Local History award of merit, 1973; Lovecraft Award, 1975; North Carolina Award for Literature, 1978.

WRITINGS—Novels: Find My Killer, Farrar, Straus, 1948; *Fort Sun Dance: Candle of the Wicked,* Putnam, 1960; *Not at These Hands,* Putnam, 1961.

American history books: *Giant in Gray,* Scribner, 1949; *Dead and Gone,* University of North Carolina Press, 1954; *Rebel Boast,* Holt, 1955; *Fastest on the River,* Holt, 1957; (with Elizabeth Amis Blanchard) *The Life and Times of Sir Archie,* University of North Carolina Press, 1958; *The County of Warren,* University of North Carolina Press, 1959; *They Took Their Stand,* Putnam, 1959; (with Frances Wellman) *The Rebel Songster,* Heritage House, 1959; *Harpers Ferry: Prize of War,* McNally & Loftin, 1960; (with Robert F. Cope) *The County of Gaston,* Heritage House, 1961; *The County of Moore,* Moore County Historical Association, 1962; *Winston-Salem in History, Part I: The Founders,* Blair, 1966; *The Kingdom of Madison,* University of North Carolina Press, 1973.

Science fiction; published by Avalon, except as indicated: *Twice in Time,* 1957; *Giants From Eternity,* 1959; *The Dark Destroyers,* 1959; *Island in the Sky,* 1961; *Who Fears the Devil?,* Arkham, 1963; *Worse Things Waiting,* Carcosa, 1973.

Novels for young readers; published by I. Washburn, except as indicated: *The Sleuth Patrol,* Thomas Nelson, 1947; *The Mystery of Lost Valley,* Thomas Nelson, 1948; *The Haunts of Drowning Creek,* Thomas Nelson, 1951; *Wild Dogs of Drowning Creek,* Holiday House, 1952; *The Last Mammoth,* Holiday House, 1953; *Gray Riders,* Aladdin, 1954; *Rebel Mail Runner,* Holiday House, 1954; *Flag on the Levee,* 1955; *To Unknown Lands,* Holiday House, 1956; *Young Squire Morgan,* 1956; *Lights on Skeleton Ridge,* 1957; *The Ghost Battalion,* 1958; *Ride, Rebels!,* 1959; *Appomattox Road,* 1960; *Third String Center,* 1960; *Rifles at Ramsour's Mill,* 1961; *Battle for King's Mountain,* 1962; *Clash on the Catawba,* 1962; *The South Fork Rangers,* 1963; *The Master of Scare Hollow,* 1964; *The Specter of Bear Paw Gap,* 1966; *Battle at Bear Paw Gap,* 1967; *Carolina Pirate,* 1968; *Brave Horse,* Colonial Williamsburg, 1968; *Mountain Feud,* 1969; *Napoleon of the West,* 1970; *Fast Break Five,* 1971. Also author of stories in twelve anthologies; contributor of more than five hundred stories and articles, mostly on fantasy, mystery, and historical adventure, to national magazines.

SIDELIGHTS: Manly W. Wellman was six when his parents returned to America. "Both my father and mother were published authors of fiction. My oldest brother, Paul I. Wellman, is an author of substantial reputation. . . . My second brother, Frederick L. Wellman, a plant pathologist, has contributed importantly to the literature of his particular scientific calling. My son, Wade, has seen several of his poems published. But none of this possible advantage in heritage and environment must suggest an easy royal road to publication. Getting into print was a formidable task, and today I find it as hard to write as I ever did, however more sensibly and skillfully I may work.

"Though born abroad, I am from old American stock, and my soul's roots are deeply driven into the rock of whatever may be said to constitute America. I do not think I represent a particular school or preach a particular cult, unless I might be called a minor and modest figure among Southern regionalists."

AVOCATIONAL INTERESTS: American history, American folklore, sports, and travel.

* * *

WELSH, Alexander 1933-

PERSONAL: Born April 29, 1933, in Albany, N.Y.; married Katharine C. Tower, 1956; three children. *Education:* Harvard University, A.B., 1954, A.M., 1957, Ph.D., 1961. *Office:* Department of English, University of California, Los Angeles, Los Angeles, Calif. 90024.

CAREER: Yale University, New Haven, Conn., instructor, 1960-63, assistant professor, 1963-66, associate professor of English, 1966-67; University of Pittsburgh, Pittsburgh, Pa., professor of English, 1967-72; University of California, Los Angeles, professor of English, 1972—. *Military service:* U.S. Army, 1954-56. *Member:* Modern Language Association of America, Phi Beta Kappa. *Awards, honors:* Guggenheim fellow, 1969-70; National Endowment for the Humanities fellow, 1977.

WRITINGS: The Hero of the Waverley Novels, Yale University Press, 1963; (editor) Sir Walter Scott, *Old Mortality,* Houghton, 1966; (editor) *Thackeray: A Collection of Critical Essays,* Prentice-Hall, 1968; *The City of Dickens,* Oxford University Press, 1971; *Reflections on the Hero as Quixote,* Princeton University Press, 1981. Contributor to periodicals, including *New Republic* and *Yale Review.*

WORK IN PROGRESS: A study of blackmail and the novels of George Eliot.

* * *

WENGER, J(ohn) C(hristian) 1910-

PERSONAL: Born December 25, 1910, in Honey Brook, Pa.; son of A. Martin and Martha (Rock) Wenger; married Ruth D. Detweiler (a nurse), 1937; children: Daniel M., John Paul, Mary Lois, Elisabeth A. *Education:* Goshen College, B.A., 1934; University of Zurich, Th.D., 1938; University of Michigan, M.A., 1942. *Home:* 1300 Greencroft Dr., Goshen, Ind. *Office:* Goshen Biblical Seminary, 3003 Benham, Elkhart, Ind. 46517.

CAREER: Ordained minister in Mennonite Church, 1944, bishop, 1951. Goshen College, Goshen, Ind., professor of Bible, 1938-70; Goshen Biblical Seminary, Elkhart, Ind., professor of theology, 1946—. Member, Mennonite Board of Education, 1935-39; Mennonite Publication Board, member, 1945-71, president, 1950-53. Moderator, Mennonite General Conference, 1957-59. *Member:* American Society of Church History, American Society for Reformation Research, American Theological Society, Evangelical Theological Society, Mennonite Historical Society (president, 1962-73), Mennonitischer Geschichtsverein (Germany).

WRITINGS—All published by Herald Press, except as indicated: *History of the Mennonites of the Franconia Conference,*

Franconia Mennonite Historical Society, 1937; *Glimpses of Mennonite History and Doctrine,* 1940, 3rd edition, 1959; *Christ: The Redeemer and Judge,* 1942; *The Doctrines of the Mennonites,* 1950; *Separated unto God,* 1951; *Introduction to Theology,* 1954; *Even unto Death: The Heroic Witness of the Sixteenth-Century Anabaptists,* John Knox, 1961; *The Mennonites in Indiana and Michigan,* 1961; *Bless the Lord, O My Soul,* 1964; *Dealing Redemptively,* 1965; *God's Word Written,* 1966; *Mennonite Church in America,* 1967; *Christian Faith: A Concise, Nondenominational History of the Christian Faith,* 1971; *Our Christ-Centered Faith,* 1973; *Disciples of Jesus,* 1977; *How Mennonites Came to Be,* 1977; *The Way of Peace,* 1977; *The Way to a New Life,* 1977; *Why Mennonites Believe,* 1977; *The Book We Call the Bible,* 1980; *A Faith to Live By,* 1980; *The Family of Faith,* 1981.

Editor; all published by Herald Press, except as indicated: *The Complete Writings of Menno Simons,* 1956; *Mennonite Handbook, Indiana-Michigan Mennonite Conference,* 1956; *A. D. Wenger: 1867-1935,* Park View Press, 1961; *They Met God,* 1964; *Conrad Grebel's Programmatic Letters,* 1970; *A Cloud of Witnesses,* 1981.

Member of translation committee, *New International Bible,* 1978. Contributor to *Encyclopaedia Britannica* and *Encyclopedia Americana.*

SIDELIGHTS: Discussing his work on the committee to translate the Bible, J. C. Wenger told *CA:* "I can now empathize with [Martin] Luther [when he said] 'It is good for me that I have undertaken to translate the Bible, for otherwise I might have died with the fond persuasion that I was learned.'"

* * *

WERNER, K.
See CASEWIT, Curtis (Werner)

* * *

WEST, Ward
See BORLAND, Harold Glen

* * *

WESTBERG, Granger E(llsworth) 1913-

PERSONAL: Born July 11, 1913, in Chicago, Ill.; son of John and Alma (Ahlstrom) Westberg; married Helen Johnson, June 20, 1939; children: Jane, John, Joan, Jill. *Education:* Attended George Williams College, 1931-32; Augustana College and Theological Seminary (now Augustana College), A.B., 1935, B.D., 1939; University of Chicago, graduate study. *Home:* 4737 Florence Ave., Downers Grove, Ill. 60515. *Office:* Wholistic Health Centers, Inc., 137 South Garfield, Hinsdale, Ill. 60521.

CAREER: Ordained to ministry of Lutheran church, 1939; St. John's Lutheran Church, Bloomington, Ill., pastor, 1939-44; Augustana Lutheran Hospital, Chicago, Ill., chaplain, 1944-52; University of Chicago, Chicago, associate professor of religion and medicine, 1952-64, chaplain to University's hospitals, 1952-56; dean, Institute of Religion, Texas Medical Center, Houston, 1964-67; Wittenberg University, Hamma School of Theology, Springfield, Ohio, professor and director of continuing education, 1967-72; University of Illinois at the Medical Center, Chicago, clinical professor of preventive medicine and community health, beginning 1973; currently founder and director of Wholistic Health Centers, Inc., Hinsdale, Ill. First lecturer on medicine and religion in Australia and New

Zealand. *Member:* Academy of Religion and Mental Health. *Awards, honors:* D.D., Augustana College, 1955.

WRITINGS: Nurse, Pastor and Patient, Augustana Book Concern, 1955; *Premarital Counseling,* National Council of Churches, 1958; *Minister and Doctor Meet,* Harper, 1961; *Good Grief: A Constructive Approach to the Problem of Loss,* Fortress, 1962; (with Edgar Draper) *Community Health Concerns and the Clergyman,* C. C Thomas, 1965; (editor) *Theological Roots of Wholistic Health Care,* Wholistic Health Centers, Inc., 1979. Contributor to theological and medical journals. Member of editorial board, *Pastoral Psychology* and *Dialogue.*

WORK IN PROGRESS: The development of twenty-five Wholistic Health Centers in churches, universities, and hospitals.

*   *   *

WESTBROOK, Perry D(ickie)   1916-

PERSONAL: Born January 23, 1916, in Brooklyn, N.Y.; son of Francis Abeken and Madeleine (Dickie) Westbrook; married Myrtle Moyer, 1939 (divorced, 1960); married Arlen Runzler, 1961; children: (first marriage) Anne, Emily, Paul; (second marriage) Tempa, Joyce (both adopted). *Education:* Columbia College, A.B., 1937; Columbia University, M.A., 1938, Ph.D., 1951. *Home address:* R.D. 1, Voorheesville, N.Y. 12186. *Office:* Department of English, State University of New York, Albany, N.Y. 12222.

CAREER: University of Kansas, Lawrence, instructor in English, 1938-41; Georgia Institute of Technology, Atlanta, instructor in English, 1941-43; University of Maine at Orono, instructor in English, 1943-44; Orono High School, Orono, head of English department, 1944-45; State University of New York at Albany, professor of English, 1945—. Fulbright lecturer, Kerela University, India, 1962-63. *Member:* Modern Language Association of America, Phi Beta Kappa. *Awards, honors:* Guggenheim fellowship, 1953-54; Eugene Saxton fellowship, 1955.

WRITINGS: Acres of Flint: Literature of Rural New England, 1870-1900, Scarecrow, 1951; *Biography of an Island,* Yoseloff, 1958; *The Greatness of Man: An Essay on Dostoyevsky and Whitman,* Yoseloff, 1961, revised edition, 1973; (with Anne Westbrook) *Trail Horses and Trail Riding,* A. S. Barnes, 1963; *Mary Ellen Chase,* Twayne, 1965; *Mary Wilkins Freeman,* College & University Press, 1967; (editor) Mary Wilkins Freeman, *Pembroke,* College & University Press, 1971; *John Burroughs,* Twayne, 1974; *William Bradford,* Twayne, 1978; *Free Will and Determinism in American Literature,* Fairleigh Dickinson University Press, 1979.

Mystery novels: *Happy Deathday,* Phoenix Press, 1947; *The Red Herring Murder,* Phoenix Press, 1949; *Infra Blood,* Phoenix Press, 1950; *It Boils Down to Murder,* Arcadia House, 1953; *The Sting of Death,* Arcadia House, 1955. Contributor, Jac Tharpe, editor, *Frost Centennial Essays,* University Press of Mississippi, 1975, 1976, and *Mystery Writers' Handbook,* Harper, 1956. Editor, *Seacoast and Upland: A New England Anthology,* A. S. Barnes, 1972. Contributor to professional journals.

WORK IN PROGRESS: A book on New England towns in fact and fiction; editing, with wife Arlen Westbrook, an anthology of New England women writers.

SIDELIGHTS: Perry D. Westbrook told *CA:* "I am a teacher first and a writer second, an arrangement that I find very satisfactory in that it frees my writing from economic and other pressures. Moreover, I definitely do not regard my writing as merely an adjunct to my teaching. Though I may write on so-

called scholarly subjects, my aim has always been to write for a wide audience of educated persons, not solely for specialists."

AVOCATIONAL INTERESTS: Farming and fishing.

*   *   *

WEZEMAN, Frederick Hartog   1915-

PERSONAL: Born May 1, 1915, in Oak Park, Ill.; son of Paul Henry (a medical doctor) and Jacoba (Hartog) Wezeman; married Marjorie Vaughn, August 11, 1960; children: Christine, Peter. *Education:* Lewis Institute (Chicago, Ill.), B.S., 1937; Chicago Teachers College, M.E., 1940; University of Chicago, B.L.S., 1946. *Religion:* Methodist. *Home:* 114 Mt. Vernon Dr., Iowa City, Iowa 52240. *Office:* Library Science School, University of Iowa, Iowa City, Iowa 52240.

CAREER: Racine Public Library, Racine, Wis., director, 1947-53; Oak Park Public Library, Oak Park, Ill., director, 1953-55; University of Minnesota, Library School, Minneapolis, associate professor of library science, 1955-66; University of Iowa, Library Science School, Iowa City, director, beginning 1966. Has made numerous library surveys in Minnesota, Iowa, Montana, Wisconsin, Oklahoma, and Michigan; has planned and moderated conferences, institutes, and meetings. Member of executive board, University of Minnesota; chairman of personnel committee, Wesley Foundation. *Military service:* U.S. Naval Reserve, 1940-42; became specialist second class. *Member:* American Library Association (life member), Canadian Library Association (life member), American Association of University Professors, American Civil Liberties Union, Minnesota Library Association, Iowa Library Association, Minneapolis Public Library Friends (president, 1963-64).

WRITINGS: (Contributor) Alfred Stefferud, editor, *Wonderful World of Books,* Houghton, 1953; *Extension of Library Service in the Birmingham-Bloomfield Area of Michigan: A Survey,* Baldwin Public Library, 1962; *Sioux City Public Library, Sioux City, Iowa: A Survey of the Public Library,* Sioux City Public Library, 1963; (with Raymond H. Shove, Blanche E. Moen, and Harold G. Russell) *The Use of Books and Libraries,* 10th edition, University of Minnesota Press, 1963; *Duluth Public Library, Duluth, Minnesota: A Study of the Duluth Public Library,* Duluth Public Library, 1966; *Sheldon Public Library, Sheldon, Iowa,* Sheldon Public Library, 1966; *A Study of Branch Libraries: Lincoln City Libraries, Lincoln, Nebraska,* Lincoln Public Library, 1967. Contributor of articles and reviews to professional journals.

BIOGRAPHICAL/CRITICAL SOURCES: New York Times, November 11, 1962.

*   *   *

WHITCOMB, Helen Hafemann

PERSONAL: Born in Oradell, N.J.; daughter of Frank E. (a jeweler) and Elizabeth (Buedinger) Hafemann; married John P. Whitcomb (a teacher), July 16, 1950; children: Claire, Jonathan. *Education:* Ursinus College, A.B., 1946; studied at Eastman Business School, 1946-47, and Columbia University, 1947-50. *Religion:* Protestant. *Home:* 111 Timber Dr., Berkeley Heights, N.J. 07922.

CAREER: Chain Store Age, New York City, assistant editor in beauty field, druggist editions, 1947-51; McGraw-Hill Book Co., Inc., Gregg Publishing Division, New York City, managing editor of *Today's Secretary* (magazine), 1951-55; co-editor of weekly newspaper, *The Dispatch,* Herald Publications; free-lance writer and editor. *Member:* American Association of University Women.

WRITINGS: (With husband, John P. Whitcomb) *Strictly for Secretaries,* Whittlesey House, 1957, 2nd edition, 1965; (with Rosalind Lang) *Charm: The Career Girl's Guide to Business and Personal Success,* McGraw, 1964, 3rd edition published as *Today's Woman,* 1976; (with Lang) *A Portfolio of Activities for Charm* (workbook), McGraw, 1964, revised edition, 1971; (with Lang) *Manual for Charm* (teaching guide), McGraw, 1965, revised edition, 1971; (with Lang) *Charm for the Modern Woman* (textbook, activity guide, exercise booklet, and hair styling booklet), McGraw, 1967; (with Lang) *Manual and Key for Charm for the Modern Woman* (teaching guide), McGraw, 1967; (with Laura Cochran) *Charm for Miss Teen,* McGraw, 1969; (with Cochran) *Teacher's Manual and Key for Charm for Miss Teen,* McGraw, 1969.

(With Cochran) *The Modern Ms.,* McGraw, 1975; (with Cochran) *Teacher's Manual and Key for "The Modern Ms.,"* McGraw, 1975; (with Lang) *A Portfolio of Activities for "Today's Woman,"* McGraw, 1976; (with Lang) *Instructor's Manual and Key for "Today's Woman,"* McGraw, 1976.

WORK IN PROGRESS: With Audrey DeMuth, *Moving up in the Business World,* for McGraw.

SIDELIGHTS: Helen Hafemann Whitcomb told *CA:* "Imparting information in a lively manner has always given me a great deal of satisfaction. I envision the reader as someone who would rather do something else at the moment and my task as attracting her (or even him occasionally) to read and contemplate the ideas we want to get across." Whitcomb's book *Charm* has been translated into French and Spanish.

AVOCATIONAL INTERESTS: Reading, theater, travel, tennis.

*   *   *

WHITE, James Dillon
See WHITE, Stanley

*   *   *

WHITE, James F(loyd)   1932-

PERSONAL: Born January 23, 1932, in Boston, Mass.; son of Edwin Turner (an electrical engineer) and Madeline (Rinker) White; married Marilyn Atkinson, August 23, 1959; children: Louise, Robert, Ellen, Laura, Martin. *Education:* Harvard University, A.B., 1953; Union Theological Seminary, New York, N.Y., B.D., 1956; graduate study at Cambridge University, 1956-57; Duke University, Ph.D., 1960. *Politics:* Independent. *Religion:* United Methodist. *Home:* 2940 Fondren Dr., Dallas, Tex. 75205. *Office:* Perkins School of Theology, Southern Methodist University, Dallas, Tex. 75275.

CAREER: Ordained minister of United Methodist Church, California-Nevada Conference; Ohio Wesleyan University, Delaware, instructor in religion, 1959-61; Methodist Theological School, Delaware, instructor in church history, 1960-61; Southern Methodist University, Perkins School of Theology, Dallas, Tex., assistant professor, 1961-65, associate professor, 1965-71, professor of Christian worship, 1971—. *Member:* North American Academy of Liturgy (president, 1978), National Trust for Historic Preservation. *Awards, honors:* Danforth fellow, 1953-59; Fulbright scholar, 1956-57.

WRITINGS: The Cambridge Movement: The Ecclesiologists and the Gothic Revival, Cambridge University Press, 1962; (contributor) Stuart Henry, editor, *A Miscellany of American Christianity,* Duke University Press, 1963; (co-author) *The*

Celebration of the Gospel, Abingdon, 1964; *Protestant Worship and Church Architecture,* Oxford University Press, 1964; *Architecture at SMU,* Southern Methodist University Press, 1966; *The Worldliness of Worship,* Oxford University Press, 1967; *New Forms of Worship,* Abingdon, 1971; *Christian Worship in Transition,* Abingdon, 1976; *Introduction to Christian Worship,* Abingdon, 1980. Also author of *Sacraments as God's Self Giving.* Contributor to religious journals. Former editor, *Union Seminary Quarterly Review.*

AVOCATIONAL INTERESTS: Travel, hiking, music, nature.

BIOGRAPHICAL/CRITICAL SOURCES: Dallas Morning News, October 31, 1962; *Dallas Times-Herald,* July 31, 1963; *Encounter,* summer, 1967.

*   *   *

WHITE, Stanley   1913-
(Felix Krull, Peto, James Peto, James Dillon White)

PERSONAL: Born August 8, 1913, in London, England; son of Ernest Bentley (a civil servant) and Annie May (Rutterford) White; married Olive Joan Coppen, December 4, 1948; children: Anthony Dillon, Christopher Dillon, Jeremy Dillon. *Politics:* Liberal humanist. *Religion:* Christian. *Home:* Watchfield, St. Mary's Rd., Leatherhead, Surrey, England.

CAREER: Standard Life Assurance Co., London, England, regional agency manager, beginning 1930; free-lance writer. *Military service:* Royal Artillery; became captain. *Member:* National Book League, P.E.N., Army and Navy Club, Gresham Club.

WRITINGS—Under pseudonym James Dillon White, except as indicated: *Heartbreak Camp,* Quality Press, 1949; *The Tall Ship,* Heinemann, 1958, reprinted, Remploy, 1979; (under pseudonym Felix Krull) *The Village Pub Murders,* Ward, Lock, 1962; (under pseudonym James Peto) *Iscariot,* Jarrolds, 1962; *Young Mr. Kelso,* W. H. Allen, 1963; *Fair Wind to Malibar,* Merrimack Book Service, 1978; *Talking with a Child: What to Say after "Hello" What's Your Name, How Old Are You, Where Do You Go to School, When's Your Birthday, Well That's Nice,* Macmillan, 1978; *Tulsa Catholics,* Carlton Press, 1978; *The Brandenburg Affair,* Merrimack Book Service, 1979.

Published by Heinemann: *The Edge of the Forest,* 1952; *The Spoletta Story,* 1952; *A Stranger in Town,* 1953; *The Quiet River,* 1953; *The Maggie,* 1954; *Flamingo Lake,* 1954; *Genevieve,* 1955; *Night on the Bare Mountain,* 1957; *Born to Star* (biography), 1957.

Published by Hutchinson: *Brave Captain Kelso,* 1959; *Captain of Marine,* 1960; *The Princess of Persia,* 1961; *The Hound of Heaven,* 1966; *Commodore Kelso,* 1967; *Summer Has Gone,* 1967; *Sweet Evil,* 1968; *Kelso of the Paragon,* 1969; *The Furzedown Comet,* 1970; *Lords of Human Kind,* 1971; *The Running Lions,* 1972; *A Wind in the Rigging,* 1973; *The Leipzig Affair,* 1974; *A Spread of Sail,* 1975; *The Salzburg Affair,* 1977.

Also author, with Lindsay Galloway, of film script "Fire over Greece," and of a radio adaptation of *The Quiet River.* Reviewer of light fiction for *Smith's Trade News;* author of weekly column, "Inspectors' Table," *Post Magazine* and *Insurance Monitor.*

WORK IN PROGRESS: A novel, *The Sassenach.*

BIOGRAPHICAL/CRITICAL SOURCES: Books and Bookmen, April, 1971.†

WHITEHILL, Walter Muir   1905-1978

PERSONAL: Born September 28, 1905, in Cambridge, Mass.; died March 5, 1978; son of Walter Muir (an Episcopal clergyman) and Florence Marion (Williams) Whitehill; married Jane Revere Coolidge, June 5, 1930; children: Jane C. (Mrs. William Rotch), Diana (Mrs. C. Christopher Laing). *Education:* Harvard University, A.B., 1926, A.M., 1929; University of London, Ph.D., 1934. *Religion:* Episcopalian. *Home:* 44 Andover St., North Andover, Mass. 01845.

CAREER: Did research in medieval history in Europe, 1930-36; Peabody Museum of Salem, Salem, Mass., assistant director, 1936-42; Boston Athenaeum, Boston, Mass., director and librarian, 1946-73. Harvard University, Cambridge, Mass., member of faculty of Peabody Museum of Archaeology and Ethnology, 1951-72, Allston Burr Senior Tutor in Lowell House, 1952-56, lecturer in history, 1956-57, Lowell Institute lecturer, 1958. Trustee of Museum of Fine Arts (Boston), Peabody Museum of Salem, Museum of Navajo Ceremonial Art, Fruitlands Museum, Eleutherian Mills Hagley Foundation, and Marlboro College. Director of Athenaeum of Philadelphia and of University Press of Virginia; member of Massachusetts Historical Commission; president of Thomas Jefferson Memorial Foundation, Merrimack Valley Textile Museum, and Historic Boston, Inc.; honorary vice-president of Virginia Historical Society and of Naval Historical Foundation, Washington, D.C. *Military service:* U.S. Naval Reserve, active duty, 1942-46; commander (retired).

MEMBER: American Academy of Arts and Sciences (librarian), American Antiquarian Society (member of council), Hispanic Society of America, Massachusetts Historical Society (recording secretary), Colonial Society of Massachusetts, Phi Beta Kappa (president of Harvard chapter, 1959-61); Somerset Club, Tavern Club, and Odd Volumes Club (all Boston); Century Association (New York), Army and Navy Club (Washington). *Awards, honors:* D.Litt., University of New Brunswick, 1959; LL.D., Washington and Jefferson College, 1959; L.H.D., Northeastern University, 1961, University of Delaware, 1967, Merrimack College, 1968, University of Massachusetts, 1971, College of William and Mary, 1974; D. Humanities, Suffolk University, 1970; D.C.L., Marlboro College, 1975.

WRITINGS: Spanish Romanesque Architecture of the Eleventh Century, Oxford University Press, 1941, reprinted, 1968; *The East India Marine Society and the Peabody Museum of Salem,* Peabody Museum of Salem, 1949; (with Ernest J. King) *Fleet Admiral King: A Naval Record,* Norton, 1952; *Boston Public Library: A Centenary History,* Harvard University Press, 1956; *Boston: A Topographical History,* Harvard University Press, 1959, 2nd edition, 1968; *Independent Historical Societies,* Boston Athenaeum, 1962; (with Katharine Knowles) *Boston: Portrait of a City,* Barre, 1964; (with Knowles) *Cambridge,* Barre, 1965; *The Arts in Early American History,* University of North Carolina Press, 1965; *Boston in the Age of John F. Kennedy,* University of Oklahoma Press, 1966; *Dumbarton Oaks,* Harvard University Press, 1967; *Cabinet of Curiosities: Five Episodes in the Evolution of American Museums,* University Press of Virginia, 1967; *Analecta Biographica,* Greene, 1969; *Museum of Fine Arts Boston: A Centennial History,* two volumes, Harvard University Press, 1970; *Boston Statues,* Barre, 1970; (editor with Sinclair H. Hutchings) *Boston Prints and Printmakers,* University Press of Virginia, 1973; (author of introduction) *Paul Revere's Boston,* New York Geographical Society, 1975; (editor with others) *Boston Furniture of the*

Eighteenth Century, University Press of Virginia, 1975; (author of commentary) *Boston: Distinguished Buildings and Sites within the City and Orbit as Engraved on Wood by Rudolph Ruzicka,* Godine, 1975; (with Norman Kotker) *Massachusetts: A Pictorial History,* Scribner, 1976; (with Frederick Nichols) *Palladio in America,* Electa, 1976; (author of text) Nancy Sirkis, *Massachusetts: From the Berkshires to the Cape,* Viking, 1977.

Contributor to historical journals. Founding editor of *American Neptune: A Quarterly Journal of Maritime History,* 1941, and member of editorial board, beginning 1941; editor, Colonial Society of Massachusetts, beginning 1946; member of editorial board, *New England Quarterly.*

AVOCATIONAL INTERESTS: Historic preservation.

BIOGRAPHICAL/CRITICAL SOURCES: Walter Muir Whitehill: A Record Compiled by His Friends, [Minot, Mass.], 1958; *Bulletin of Bibliography and Magazine Notes,* July-September, 1973.

OBITUARIES: Time, March 20, 1978.†

*   *   *

WHITNEY, Eleanor Noss   1938-

PERSONAL: Born October 5, 1938, in Plainfield, N.J.; daughter of Henry (a dean, New York University) and Edith (Tyler) Noss; married William R. Whitney III (a teacher), August 9, 1960 (divorced March 21, 1974); children: Lynn, William Russell IV, Kara Lee. *Education:* Radcliffe College, A.B., 1960; Washington University, St. Louis, Mo., Ph.D., 1970. *Politics:* Independent. *Religion:* Agnostic. *Office:* Florida State University, Tallahassee, Fla. 32306.

WRITINGS: A Mah Jong Handbook: How to Play, Score, and Win the Modern Game, Tuttle, 1963; (with Eva M. Hamilton) *Understanding Nutrition,* West Publishing, 1977, 2nd edition, 1981; (with Hamilton) *Nutrition: Concepts and Controversies,* West Publishing, 1979, 2nd edition, 1982; *Understanding Nutrition and Diet Therapy,* West Publishing, 1982.

WORK IN PROGRESS: Translation of a German diary, written during the early 1940's by a refugee from what is now Poland; and an introduction to health, for West Publishing.

*   *   *

WILDER, Stephen
See MARLOWE, Stephen

*   *   *

WILLAN, Anne   1938-

PERSONAL: Born January 26, 1938, in Newcastle, England; naturalized U.S. citizen, 1973; daughter of William (a lawyer) and Joyce (Todd) Willan; married Mark Cherniavsky (a banker), July 9, 1966; children: Simon, Emma. *Education:* Cambridge University, M.A., 1959; attended cookery schools in London and Paris, 1960-64. *Office:* Ecole de Cuisine La Varenne, 34 Rue St. Dominique, Paris 75007, France.

CAREER: Gourmet, New York, N.Y., member of editorial staff, 1965-66; *Washington Star,* Washington, D.C., food editor, 1966-68; cookery editor and consultant, 1969-74; Ecole de Cuisine La Varenne, Paris, France, founder and president, 1975—. *Awards, honors:* Tastemaker Award, 1977, for *Great Cooks and Their Recipes,* and 1980, for *La Varenne's Basic French Cookery.*

WRITINGS: Entertaining Menus, Coward, 1974, published as *Entertaining: Complete Menus for All Occasions,* Batsford,

1980, David & Charles, 1981; *Great Cooks and Their Recipes: From Taillevent to Escoffier,* McGraw, 1977; *The Observer French Cookery School,* Macdonald, 1980; *La Varenne's Basic French Cookery,* H. P. Books, 1980; *French Regional Cooking,* Morrow, 1981; *La Varenne's Paris Kitchen,* Morrow, 1981; *La Varenne French Cookery Course,* Morrow, 1982. Editor-in-chief of "Grand Diplome Cooking Course," Grolier, 1970-73.

*   *   *

WILLGOOSE, Carl E(dward) 1916-

PERSONAL: Born August 29, 1916, in Needham, Mass.; son of Samuel and Cora (Wood) Willgoose; married Ruth Terrell, May 25, 1946; children: Tom, Richard, Laura, James. *Education:* Boston University, B.S. in Ed., 1939, Ed.M., 1940; Syracuse University, Ed.D., 1951. *Politics:* Republican. *Religion:* Methodist. *Home:* Endicott St., Wolfeboro, N.H. *Office:* School of Education, Boston University, Boston, Mass. 02215.

CAREER: Director of health and physical education, North Reading, Mass., 1940-41; director of health and physical education, Andover, Mass., 1941-42; Syracuse University, Syracuse, N.Y., chairman, department of physical education, 1946-51; Oswego State Teachers College (now State University of New York College at Oswego), professor of health and physical education, 1951-58; Temple University, Philadelphia, Pa., professor of education, 1958-60; Boston University, Boston, Mass., associate professor, 1960-64, professor of education, 1964—. *Military service:* U.S. Army Air Forces, Air Transport Command, 1942-46. U.S. Air Force Reserve, 1946—; currently lieutenant colonel. *Member:* American Association for Health, Physical Education and Recreation (fellow; vice-president, 1964-66), American Public Health Association (fellow), American College of Sports Medicine (fellow), American School Health Association (fellow), Association for the Advancement of Health Education.

WRITINGS: (Co-author) *Selected Team Sports for Men,* Saunders, 1952; *Health Education in the Elementary School,* Saunders, 1959, 5th edition, 1979; *Evaluation in Health Education and Physical Education,* McGraw, 1961; (with Charles A. Bucher) *The Foundations of Health,* Appleton, 1967, 2nd edition, 1976; *The Curriculum in Physical Education,* Prentice-Hall, 1969, 3rd edition, 1979; *Health Teaching in Secondary Schools,* Saunders, 1972, 3rd edition, 1982; *Environmental Health: Commitment for Survival,* Saunders, 1979. Contributor of about sixty articles to health and education journals. Associate editor of *Research Quarterly.*

WORK IN PROGRESS: Sixth edition of *Health Education in the Elementary School.*

*   *   *

WILLIAMS, Aubrey L(ake) 1922-

PERSONAL: Born September 25, 1922, in Jacksonville, Fla.; son of Aubrey Lake and Marguerite (Butler) Williams; children: Michael, Christopher, Katharine, Mary Margaret, Rachel, Donald. *Education:* Louisiana State University, B.A., 1947; Yale University, M.A., 1948, Ph.D., 1952. *Home:* 608 Northeast Fifth Ave., Gainesville, Fla. *Office:* English Department, University of Florida, Gainesville, Fla.

CAREER: Yale University, New Haven, Connecticut, 1950-58, began as instructor, assistant professor, 1955-58; University of Florida, Gainesville, associate professor, 1958-60; Rice University, Houston, Tex., professor, 1960-61; University of

Florida, Gainesville, professor of English, 1961—. *Military service:* U.S. Army, Field Artillery, 1943-46; became first lieutenant. *Member:* Modern Language Association of America. *Awards, honors:* Fulbright and Guggenheim fellow, 1956-57; American Council of Learned Societies grants, 1971, 1974.

WRITINGS: Pope's Dunciad, Louisiana State University Press, 1955; (editor with E. Audra) Alexander Pope, *Pastoral Poetry and An Essay on Criticism,* Yale University Press, 1961; (editor with others) *All These to Teach,* University of Florida Press, 1965; (editor) *Poetry and Prose of Alexander Pope,* Houghton, 1969; (editor with Louis Martz) *The Author in His Work: Essays on a Problem in Criticism,* Yale University Press, 1978; *An Approach to Congreve,* Yale University Press, 1979.

Contributor: John Butt, editor, *The Poems of Alexander Pope,* Yale University Press, 1963; Carroll Camden, editor, *Restoration and Eighteenth-Century Literature,* University of Toronto Press, 1963; Maynard Mack, editor, *Essential Articles for the Study of Alexander Pope,* Archon Books, 1964; Bertrand A. Goldgar, editor, *Literary Criticism of Alexander Pope,* University of Nebraska Press, 1965; Robert McHenry, editor, *The Rape of the Lock,* Bobbs-Merrill, 1968; Mack and Ian Gregor, editors, *Imagined World: Essays on Some English Novels and Novelists,* Methuen, 1968; G. S. Rousseau, editor, *Twentieth Century Interpretations of "The Rape of the Lock,"* Prentice-Hall, 1969; Frank Brady, John Palmer, and Martin Price, editors, *Literary Theory and Structure,* Yale University Press, 1973; Donald Kay, editor, *A Provision of Human Nature: Essays on Fielding and Others,* University of Alabama Press, 1977. Contributor of articles and reviews to numerous professional journals. Member of editorial board, *Studies in English Literature,* 1961—, *PMLA,* 1965-66, *Scholia Satyrica,* 1974—, and *South Atlantic Bulletin,* 1977—.

WORK IN PROGRESS: Restoration drama.

AVOCATIONAL INTERESTS: Game fishing, gardening.

*   *   *

WILLIAMS, John A(lfred) 1925-
(J. Dennis Gregory)

PERSONAL: Born December 5, 1925, in Jackson, Miss.; son of John Henry (a laborer) and Ola Mae Williams; married Carolyn Clopton, 1947 (divorced); married Lorrain Isaac, October 5, 1965; children: (first marriage) Gregory D., Dennis A.; (second marriage) Adam J. *Education:* Syracuse University, A.B., 1950, graduate study, 1950-51. *Residence:* Teaneck, N.J.

CAREER: Writer. Public relations man with Doug Johnson Associates, Syracuse, N.Y., 1952-54, and later with Arthur P. Jacobs Co.; Columbia Broadcasting System (CBS), Hollywood, Calif. and New York City, staff member for radio and television special events programs, 1954-55; Comet Press Books, New York City, publicity director, 1955-56; *Negro Market Newsletter,* New York City, publisher and editor, 1956-57; Abelard-Schuman Ltd., New York City, assistant to the publisher, 1957-58; American Committee on Africa, New York City, director of information, 1958; European correspondent for *Ebony* and *Jet* (magazines), New York City, 1958-59; Station WOV, New York, special events announcer, 1959; *Newsweek,* New York City, correspondent in Africa, 1964-65. Lecturer in writing, City College of the City University of New York, 1968; lecturer in Afro-American literature, College of the Virgin Islands, summer, 1968; guest writer at Sarah Lawrence College, Bronxville, N.Y.; regents lecturer, University of California, Santa Barbara, 1972; distinguished professor of

English, La Guardia Community College, 1973-74; visiting professor, University of Hawaii, summer, 1974, and Boston University, 1978-79; professor of English, Rutgers University, 1979—. Interviewer, "Newsfront" program, National Educational Television, 1968; has given lectures or readings at more than twenty major colleges and universities in the United States. *Military service:* U.S. Naval Reserve, pharmacist's mate, active duty, 1943-46; served in the Pacific. *Member:* Authors Guild, Authors League of America, New York State Council on the Arts (member of board of directors), Rabinowitz Foundation (member of board of directors). *Awards, honors:* Award from National Institute of Arts and Letters, 1962; centennial medal for outstanding achievement from Syracuse University, 1970; LL.D. from Southeastern Massachusetts University, 1978.

WRITINGS—Novels: *The Angry Ones*, Ace Books, 1960, published as *One for New York*, Chatham Bookseller, 1975; *Night Song*, Farrar, Straus, 1961; *Sissie*, Farrar, Straus, 1963 (published in England as *Journey Out of Anger*, Eyre & Spottiswoode, 1965); *The Man Who Cried I Am*, Little, Brown, 1967; *Sons of Darkness, Sons of Light: A Novel of Some Probability*, Little, Brown, 1969; *Captain Blackman*, Doubleday, 1972; *Mothersill and the Foxes*, Doubleday, 1975; *The Junior Bachelor Society*, Doubleday, 1976; *!Click Song*, Houghton, 1982.

Nonfiction: *Africa: Her History, Lands, and People*, Cooper Square, 1962, 3rd edition, 1969; (under pseudonym J. Dennis Gregory; with Harry J. Anslinger) *The Protectors: The Heroic Story of the Narcotics Agents, Citizens and Officials in Their Unending, Unsung Battles against Organized Crime in America and Abroad*, Farrar, Straus, 1964; *This is My Country Too*, New American Library, 1965; *The Most Native of Sons: A Biography of Richard Wright*, Doubleday, 1970; *The King God Didn't Save: Reflections on the Life and Death of Martin Luther King, Jr.*, Coward, 1970; *Flashbacks: A Twenty-Year Diary of Article Writing*, Doubleday, 1973; (author of introduction) *Romare Bearden*, Abrams, 1973; *Minorities in the City*, Harper, 1975.

Editor: *The Angry Black* (anthology), Lancer Books, 1962, 2nd edition published as *Beyond the Angry Black*, Cooper Square, 1966; (with Charles F. Harris) *Amistad I*, Knopf, 1970; (with Harris) *Amistad II*, Knopf, 1971.

Work is represented in anthologies, including: *Harlem: A Community in Transition*, Citadel, 1964; *Best Short Stories of Negro Writers*, Little, Brown, 1967; *Black on Black*, Macmillan, 1968; *Thirty-four by Schwartze Lieb*, Barmier & Nickel, 1968; *How We Live*, Macmillan, 1968; *Dark Symphony*, Free Press, 1968; *Nat Turner: Ten Black Writers Respond*, edited by John Henrik Clarke, Beacon Press, 1968; *The Now Reader*, Scott, Foresman, 1969; *The New Black Poetry*, International, 1969; *Black Literature in America*, Crowell, 1970; *The Black Novelist*, C. E. Merrill, 1970; *Black Identity*, Holt, 1970; *A Native Sons Reader*, Lippincott, 1970; *The New Lively Rhetoric*, Holt, 1970; *Brothers and Sisters*, Macmillan, 1970; *Nineteen Necromancers from Now*, Doubleday, 1970; *Black Insights*, Ginn, 1971; *The Immigrant Experience*, Dial, 1971; *Cavalcade*, Houghton, 1971; *Racism*, Crowell, 1971; *An Introduction to Poetry*, St. Martin's, 1972; *Different Drummers*, Random House, 1973.

Author and narrator of scripts "The History of the Negro People: Omwale—The Child Returns Home" (Nigeria), 1965, and author, narrator, and co-producer of "The Creative Person: Henry Roth" (Spain), 1966, both for National Educational Television. Has worked for about fifteen American newspapers as writer of special assignments, stringer, or contributor. Contributor of more than thirty stories and articles to magazines, including *Negro Digest, Yardbird, Holiday, Saturday Review,*

Ebony, and *New York.* Member of editorial board of *Audience,* 1970-72; contributing editor of *American Journal,* 1972—.

SIDELIGHTS: In 1961, John A. Williams was awarded a grant to the American Academy in Rome on the basis of his work in *Night Song,* but the grant was rescinded by the awarding panel. Williams felt that this happened because he was black and because of rumors that he was about to marry a white woman, which he later did. He has said: "The plain, unspoken fact is that the Negro is superfluous in American society as it is now constructed. Society must undergo a restructuring to make a place for him, or it will be called upon to get rid of him."

Some critics of Williams's earlier novels refer to him as an angry man whose anger is intertwined with a bitter-sweet trace of hope. Doris Grumbach, a *Critic* reviewer, believes both *Night Song* and *Sissie* are "angry and raw and full of violent scenes." Williams "writes with . . . rage and passion and sympathy," states *Library Journal* reviewer Eric Moon. Reviewing *The Man Who Cried I Am,* Moon remarks that Williams handles this novel "with superb skill and disciplined fury. . . . This seething, angry book is more than a fine novel; it is an important document of its time."

In *The Angry Ones, Night Song,* and *Sissie,* Williams writes about black men living in a white society. Steve Hill, the main character in *The Angry Ones,* spends a year working for a dishonest publisher; the bulk of the novel concerns his frustration resulting from the experience. *Night Song* takes place in the world of jazz where saxophonist Richie "Eagle" Stokes is near death and trying to come to terms with his past. The approaching death of Sissie Joplin in *Sissie* forces the main characters to examine their lives and their relationships to each other.

Whereas anger plays a part in Williams's first three novels, it plays an even larger role in the next three, each of which revolve around white exploitation and black survival. In each of these novels, Williams includes a complicated conspiracy: *The Man Who Cried I Am* contains the King Alfred Plan, which is a plan to exterminate the black race; *Sons of Darkness, Sons of Light* revolves around the eruption of a racial war in America; and *Captain Blackman* spans the history of the black soldier from the Revolutionary War to Vietnam and ends with a plot to have mulattoes pass as whites and take over the nuclear defense system of the United States.

Reviewing Williams's later novels, some critics share *Nation* reviewer Gil Muller's conviction that "Williams has been exploring the myths and realities of the black experience for more than two decades, and . . . [now] he deserves a reevaluation. . . . Recently Williams has been withholding the hecatomb that readers have come to expect of his endings, although the violence, or potential for it, is still there." Muller believes that "Williams is essentially the only novelist who has attempted to investigate how all of black America fits into the national jigsaw puzzle."

Mothersill and the Foxes is the story of Odell Mothersill, who is successful and in his mid-forties, looking back on his past in an effort to discover why he cannot establish a satisfying relationship with a woman. A *Publishers Weekly* reviewer calls the novel an "upbeat portrait [which] catches the bitterness and the hope of growing up black in postwar America." In *The Junior Bachelor Society,* Williams reveals the individual histories of a group of middle-aged ex-high school athletes who gather to celebrate the seventieth birthday of their coach. Williams interweaves these lives with those of several others, prompting a *New Yorker* critic to write: "Mr. Williams appears to have wanted to close the gap in literature about the black middle class single-handed. And he very nearly succeeds.''

Huel D. Perkins, writing in *Black World*, concludes: ''Williams is never as effective when he is nice, gentle, soft as he is when he is brutal, intense, basic. . . . Experience shapes the writer, and Williams has drained from his experiences every drop and distilled it into words for readers.''

MEDIA ADAPTATIONS: The Junior Bachelor Society *was filmed for television as* ''Sophisticated Gents,'' *1981.*

AVOCATIONAL INTERESTS: Travel (has visited Belgium, Cameroon, the Caribbean, Congo, Cyprus, Denmark, Egypt, Ethiopia, France, Germany, Ghana, Great Britain, Greece, Israel, Italy, Mexico, the Netherlands, Nigeria, Portugal, Senegal, Spain, the Sudan, Sweden).

CA INTERVIEW

CA interviewed John A. Williams by phone April 1, 1981, at his home in Teaneck, New Jersey.

CA: You started writing in the Pacific during World War II. Did you want to write earlier?

WILLIAMS: I'm not sure whether I did or not. I wanted to read a great deal earlier and since I draw a relationship between reading and writing, I suppose somewhere in the inner recesses of my psyche, I probably wanted to write earlier.

CA: Were your parents in any way influential in your becoming a writer?

WILLIAMS: No, only later as characters around whom you measure other people who would be characters in your books. But direct encouragement, no.

CA: Your parents, who were then living in Syracuse, New York, traveled to Jackson, Mississippi, for your birth, then back to Syracuse, where you grew up. Was Jackson the original home of both your parents?

WILLIAMS: Jackson was my mother's original home; my father's original home was upstate New York. My mother left Mississippi to go to work in Syracuse and there met my father. I was the first-born, at which point I guess it was still pretty ritualistic to go back home to have your first child. That's what happened.

CA: Did you feel any sense of Southern heritage or influence growing up?

WILLIAMS: Never.

CA: Early in your career you worked as a foreign correspondent for Ebony, Jet, Newsweek, *and* Holiday. *Did you enjoy that work?*

WILLIAMS: I liked the way *I* did it, which was being loosely a correspondent with press credentials and cable cards and so on, but without the rather rigid stipulations that apply to people these days. I traveled and I sent in pieces and I wrote what I thought was worthy. It was interesting. I think if I had come to it a bit younger I would have loved it a great deal, but at the time I was doing it, I was in my late thirties.

CA: Your work as a correspondent led to your being asked to write what turned out to be This Is My Country Too, *didn't it?*

WILLIAMS: Yes, as a matter of fact, that was an assignment for *Holiday*, to do essentially what John Steinbeck had done with his *Travels with Charley*. When I had finished the trip, we decided that I should sit down and do a book and let them select the parts they wanted to run in the magazine.

CA: In the travel and writing, were you often consciously aware of the structure of Steinbeck's book?

WILLIAMS: I had read it and had consciously gone many of the same routes that he went, particularly on U.S. Route 1 up around the northern part of the United States, fairly close to the Canadian border.

CA: Walker Percy said, ''It is the very absence of a tradition that makes for great originals like Faulkner and O'Connor and Poe.'' Other people, of course, have made similar observations. How do you think this applies to black writers?

WILLIAMS: I think with black writers particularly there has been a very solid tradition which most people have never recognized. I think it goes back to something Milton discussed in his *Arcopagitica* in 1644, that books, being ''not absolutely dead things . . . may chance to spring up armed men''—that is, to fight injustice. And if good literature is forged in the fires of injustice, as Joyce and a few other writers have said, then that tradition seems to me to be very solid, not only for black writers but for all writers. I personally believe that books should do things, they should make people want to do things. I would have to say that, in my judgment, Faulkner, Poe, and O'Connor were very much in touch with tradition.

CA: What are your current feelings about the teaching of black literature as a separate course in colleges and universities?

WILLIAMS: I've always felt it was a mistake because it perpetuates the fragmentation of American literature that we've always had to contend with. Very early on in the game, I said and wrote that I was opposed to it. When I have occasion to do what is called Afro-American literature, it actually turns out to be comparative American literature because I take one black and one white writer who have lived and worked in the same time periods, beginning with, say, Phillis Wheatley and Philip Freneau, and come all the way through up to the contemporary period. That's not at all difficult to do, and I don't understand why more people have not done it.

CA: You share with many other people a concern about the amount of money publishers spend on blockbusters to the neglect of many deserving writers. This of course has affected black writers. Do you think it would be even worse without the presence of the few black editors who are working for large publishers?

WILLIAMS: I know at the moment of only one, and back in the 1960s I think there must have been about ten around town. One just left a major publishing house about three weeks ago. The only one that I know of now is Toni Morrison.

CA: Some people, including Toni Morrison, think small independent publishers may be the great hope for minority fiction. Have you considered getting involved in such a venture?

WILLIAMS: I would not go into book publishing unless there was a solid arrangement in terms of enough dough to take a few losses and bounce back. If I went into publishing, it would be in journalism. Years ago I wrote, edited, and published a newsletter, and I'm inclined to consider doing that in a very special way again. I'm compiling some material, formats, and so on. I'm not sure that I'll do it, but it strikes me as something that needs to be done, particularly in the area that I'm thinking about.

CA: What hope do you think there is for more publication for all minority writers?

WILLIAMS: Individual minority groups have to come up with their own funding to do their own books, or at least come together in a combine, and put up the dough to do some round-robin publishing—say, for three months of the year do black books, for the next three months do Chicano books, and so on. There has to be some balance. I no longer have the faith that the publishing establishment, as it now is, is going to be at all conscientious about doing books by minority authors.

CA: Have you had much contact with the black writers in South Africa?

WILLIAMS: No. Back during the early 1960s, I knew several African writers, but the only guy I know now is Ezekiel Mphah-lele, who's back there. I last saw him when he was teaching at the University of Pennsylvania. That's very strange because he vanished and then I heard he had returned to South Africa to teach on some kind of sabbatical and was scheduled to come back to the States, but the South Africans wouldn't let him go. Then I read in Joseph Lelyveld's piece that he had chosen to stay there. I still don't know which is the truth.

CA: What do you enjoy reading?

WILLIAMS: I guess that I'm reading more nonfiction than fiction these days. I find a great deal of the fiction not, to my mind, calculated to make me want to explode with different emotions—anger or sympathy or compassion—but just there. Most of the writings are exercises, and that may be precisely what the author wants to do or what the publisher wants him or her to do. But I prefer work that makes me want to think or move, to do something.

CA: Have you enjoyed the teaching you've done?

WILLIAMS: Yes, I've enjoyed it and I'm still enjoying it. I can see problems in the entire educational system, and I think they're becoming intensified. There doesn't seem to me to be as much dedication in the field as there was when I first started teaching around thirteen years ago, and probably not as much as when I was a kid, and I had on occasion some very good teachers.

CA: Why do you think that's true?

WILLIAMS: It's bureaucracy. Everyone wants to make teachers responsible to him, to her, to it—school boards, presidents, deans, provosts, parents. And teachers don't seem to be able to say, "We want to be the way we were in the 1930s. We want respect. We think we can do the job if you'll let us do it, if we don't have to spend eighty percent of the time filling out papers and worrying about getting fired."

CA: What about the students? Do you think they're worse than they were ten years ago, twenty years ago?

WILLIAMS: In many ways, yes, but I don't think that's their fault. I think that society has fed young people a bill of goods. For example, not every student who is in college should be in college, but there is something in the system that says you cannot move up an inch unless you have been to college, so everybody goes. Now everybody is starting to find out that this is not quite as automatic as it seemed to be. Somebody pulled the plug so things are not so completely wired up anymore.

CA: Has the teaching helped in any way with the writing?

WILLIAMS: Yes. You get lots of good characters there, lots of conflicts with colleagues, lots of situations. Everything is a microcosm of how the world functions, whether you're in school, whether you're a journalist, or whatever. You find the same types and the same situations and very often you have to try to bring to bear on those situations the same solutions.

CA: Do you get good, lively, intelligent audiences for the lectures you give?

WILLIAMS: Sometimes yes, sometimes no. I'm not really into that as much as I once was or even wanted to be because it's part of literary show biz. I think you have to decide whether you want to be a writer or an entertainer. I maybe do five or six a year, and that's about it. I am going off to England to do some things at the end of this month for three or four days. I'll be at the University of Kent at Canterbury and the University of Nottingham and maybe the University of East Anglia.

CA: You got an LL.D. degree in 1978 from Southeastern Massachusetts University. Was it an honorary degree?

WILLIAMS: Yes.

CA: When you're out trout fishing, are you thinking about the writing?

WILLIAMS: No, I guess I'm just wondering why they're not biting any better than they are. I'm basically a mountain man— I prefer the mountains to the beaches—and it really clears my head just not doing anything except holding that pole and maybe a drink, and looking at the reflection of the tree line in the water.

CA: Would you like to talk about the new novel?

WILLIAMS: I can say that it's a very big novel for me; it's right now almost seven hundred pages. My editor and I are working very well on it. I like the house. Houghton Mifflin is not one of those houses that allowed itself to be purchased by a conglomerate, and I like that.

CA: Are there any other future plans or ideas you'd like to talk about?

WILLIAMS: I've got another novel that I've finished, kind of a lightweight novel. I've done a full-length play which I'm having so many strange reactions to, I don't know what I'm going to do with it. I don't want to convert it to a novel. I've got another novel that I started some years ago that's about a quarter of the way through. I guess I was anticipating that people like Naipaul and John Updike would be writing about African in fiction, and I wanted to do this. I started it some years ago and just never got around to finishing it. I've got lots of stuff to finish up. Then I've got a big nonfiction book that I've been dreaming up for about ten years that I have half a room full of notes for, and I've already started on that, but I want to go back and take another look at it and see where it is.

BIOGRAPHICAL/CRITICAL SOURCES: Library Journal, November 1, 1961, September 15, 1967; *Critic*, April, 1963;

Publishers Weekly, November 11, 1974; *Black World*, June, 1975; *Contemporary Literary Criticism*, Gale, Volume V, 1976, Volume XIII, 1980; *Prairie Schooner*, spring, 1976; *New York Times Book Review*, July 11, 1976; *New Yorker*, August 16, 1976; *Nation*, September 18, 1976; *Dictionary of Literary Biography*, Volume II: *American Novelists since World War II*, Gale, 1978.

—*Interview by Jean W. Ross*

*   *   *

WILLIAMS, Oscar 1900-1964

PERSONAL: Born December, 1900, in Brooklyn, N.Y.; died October 10, 1964; married Gene Derwood (died, 1954); children: Strephon (son). *Education:* Attended schools in Brooklyn, N.Y. *Religion:* Episcopalian. *Home and office:* 35 Water St., New York, N.Y.

CAREER: Worked in various advertising agencies, 1921-37. Poet, editor, critic; presented lectures and poetry readings at numerous universities; was poetry leader at three university writers' conferences; taught summer sessions at New York University; gave formal reading of own poetry at Library of Congress, 1958. *Member:* University Club (New York). *Awards, honors:* Yale Series of Younger Poets Award, 1921, for *The Golden Darkness*.

WRITINGS—Poetry: *The Golden Darkness*, Yale University Press, 1921, reprinted, AMS Press, 1971; *The Man Coming toward You*, Oxford University Press, 1940; *That's All That Matters*, Creative Age, 1944; *Selected Poems*, Scribner, 1947, October House, 1964.

Recordings: "The Poems of Oscar Williams, Read by the Poet," Gryphon Records; (editor) "An Album of Modern Poetry," Library of Congress, 1961.

Editor and anthologist: "New Poems Series," 1940-44; *The War Poets*, Day, 1945; *A Little Treasury of Great Poetry: English and American*, Scribner, 1947, reprinted, 1966; *Little Treasury of Modern Poetry*, Scribner, 1950, 3rd edition, 1970; *Little Treasury of American Poetry*, Scribner, 1952; *The Golden Treasury*, New American Library, 1953; *Pocket Book of Modern Verse*, Washington Square, 1954, 3rd edition (revised by Human J. Sobiloff), 1972; *New Pocket Anthology of American Poetry*, World, 1955, published as *An Anthology of American Verse from Colonial Days to the Present*, World, 1966, new edition (revised by Sobiloff), Pocket Books, 1972; *The Silver Treasury of Light Verse*, New American Library, 1957; (with Edwin Honig) *The Mentor Book of Major American Poets*, Mentor, 1962; *The Mentor Book of Major British Poets*, Mentor, 1963; *Immortal Poems of the English Language*, Washington Square, 1964; *Master Poems of the English Language*, Trident, 1966; (with Honig) *The Major Metaphysical Poets of the Seventeenth Century*, Washington Square, 1968. General editor, "Little Treasury" poetry series. Contributor to *Atlantic Monthly, Harper's, Harper's Bazaar, Saturday Review, Southern Review, Nation, New Republic*. Editor, *Rhythmus*, 1923; former poetry editor, *Forum*.

SIDELIGHTS: Oscar Williams was one of the best-known poetry anthologists of his time. His anthologies have sold millions of copies in both hardcover and paperback, and are used as textbooks in over 100 American colleges and universities.

Williams published his first book of poetry in 1921 as part of the "Yale Younger Poets" series. Shortly thereafter, he lost interest in poetry and began working in the advertising field where he held a number of prominent positions over the following 16 years. In 1937, he suddenly realized that writing poetry was what he had always wanted to do and immediately quit his advertising job and resumed writing.

His wife Gene Derwood, also a poet, had a collection of her poems published posthumously in 1955.

BIOGRAPHICAL/CRITICAL SOURCES: Time, April 29, 1940; *Nation*, May 4, 1940; *Poetry*, July, 1940, December, 1945; *New York Herald Tribune Book Review*, October 14, 1945; *Atlantic Monthly*, October, 1947; *Saturday Review*, February 13, 1965; *New York Times Book Review*, February 21, 1965; *Times Literary Supplement*, March 11, 1965.

OBITUARIES: New York Times, October 11, 1964; *Newsweek*, October 26, 1964; *Publishers Weekly*, October 26, 1964.†

*   *   *

WILLIAMSON, J. Peter 1929-

PERSONAL: Born December 8, 1929, in Toronto, Ontario, Canada; son of John D. and Marie (Peterkin) Williamson; married Sybil Benton, 1957; children: Anne, Sarah, Julia. *Education:* University of Toronto, B.A., 1952; Harvard University, M.B.A., 1954, LL.B., 1957, D.B.A., 1961. *Home:* 22 Rip Rd., Hanover, N.H. 03755. *Office:* Amos Tuck School, Dartmouth College, Hanover, N.H. 03755.

CAREER: Harvard University, Business School, Boston, Mass., assistant professor of business administration, 1957-61; Dartmouth College, Amos Tuck School, Hanover, N.H., associate professor, 1961-64, 1965-66, professor of business administration, 1966—. Visiting associate professor of law, University of Toronto, 1964-65.

WRITINGS: Securities Regulation in Canada, University of Toronto Press, 1960, supplement, Queen's Printer (Ontario), 1966; (with R. W. Austin) *Law in Business Administration*, Allyn & Bacon, 1962; *Contracts: Business and Law Cases*, Prentice-Hall, 1963; *Taxation of United States Private Investments in Canada*, Canadian Tax Foundation, 1963; (with R. L. Shurter) *Written Communication in Business*, 2nd edition (Williamson not associated with earlier edition), McGraw, 1964; (with Shurter and Wayne Broehl, Jr.) *Business Research and Report Writing*, McGraw, 1965; (with J. Taylor and Samuel Martin) *Business Finance*, McGraw (Canada), 1966; *Federal Taxation: Notes and Cases*, Scott, Foresman, 1968; *Investments: New Analytic Techniques*, Praeger, 1971; *Performance Measurement and Investment Objectives for Educational Endowment Funds*, Common Fund, 1972; (with Richard M. Ennis) *Spending Policy for Educational Endowments*, Common Fund, 1976; *Funds for the Future*, Twentieth Century Fund, 1975.

WORK IN PROGRESS: A text on fixed income investing; research on educational endowment funds, mutual funds, and bond portfolio management.

*   *   *

WILLIAMSON, William Bedford 1918-

PERSONAL: Born January 27, 1918, in Amsterdam, N.Y.; son of William Barlow and Agnes Hope (Cooper) Williamson; married Blanche Gray Heinbach, 1941; children: David Bedford, Ruth Anne. *Education:* Temple University, B.S., 1940, S.T.B., 1942, Ed.D., 1966; Lutheran Theological Seminary at Philadelphia, S.T.M., 1945; Lehigh University, M.A., 1950. *Home:* Timberlake Apartment, 406B, 2401 Stanbridge St., Norristown, Pa. 19401. *Office:* Department of Philosophy and Religion, Ursinus College, Collegeville, Pa. 19426.

CAREER: Methodist minister in Philadelphia, Pa., 1938-47; Lehigh University, Bethlehem, Pa., assistant professor, 1948-52; rector of Episcopal churches in Catasauqua, Pa., Honesdale, Pa., Williamsport, Pa., and Philadelphia, 1948-60; West Chester State College, West Chester, Pa., assistant professor of social science, 1960-61; Harcum Junior College, Bryn Mawr, Pa., professor, 1961-62; Cheyney State College, Cheyney, Pa., associate professor, 1962-66, professor of philosophy and social science, 1966-68; Ursinus College, Collegeville, Pa., professor of philosophy and chairman of department of philosophy and religion, 1968—. Visiting professor, Temple University, 1964-70. Rector, Church of the Atonement, Philadelphia, 1960-73; associate rector, St. Timothy's Church, Philadelphia, 1973—; chairman of hospital clergy, Council of Churches; member of National Conference of Christians and Jews. Member of board, Visiting Nurses Association. *Military service:* U.S. Army, 1945-47; served in European and Asiatic theaters as transport chaplain.

MEMBER: American Philosophical Association, National Education Association, Military Chaplains Association, Anglican Society, American Legion, Royal Overseas League, Welsh Society of Philadelphia, Society of the Sons of St. George, Pi Gamma Mu, Phi Alpha Theta. *Awards, honors:* D.D., National University (Washington, D.C.), 1953; Episcopal fellow in the philosophy of theology, Oxford University, 1964.

WRITINGS: *A Handbook for Episcopalians,* Morehouse, 1961; *Personal Devotions for Pastors,* Westminster, 1961; *Language Concepts in Christian Education,* Westminster, 1970; *Oneness,* CSS Publishing, 1973; *Discourses from the Upper Room,* CSS Publishing, 1973; *The Living Church,* CSS Publishing, 1974; *Decisions in Philosophy of Religion,* C. E. Merrill, 1976; *Ian T. Ramsey,* Word, 1981. Also author of *Decision Procedures in Ethics,* 1978. Contributor to religious, educational, and philosophical journals.

WORK IN PROGRESS: Two books, *Ethical Decisions in Health Care* and *Decisions in Philosophy.*

AVOCATIONAL INTERESTS: Vocal and instrumental music, both as "auditor and participator."

*　　*　　*

WILSON, Dorothy Clarke   1904-

PERSONAL: Born May 9, 1904, in Gardiner, Me.; daughter of Lewis H. (a minister) and Flora (Cross) Clarke; married Elwin L. Wilson (a minister), August 31, 1925; children: Joan, Harold E. *Education:* Bates College, Lewiston, Me., A.B., 1925. *Politics:* Democrat. *Religion:* Methodist. *Home:* 114 Forest Ave., Orono, Me.

CAREER: Taught course on writing religious drama at workshops in Mexico City, Mexico and Alexandria, Egypt, 1959, 1960; lecturer in England and Scotland, 1960. Trustee, Bates College. *Member:* American Association of University Women, Phi Beta Kappa. *Awards, honors:* Litt.D., Bates College, 1947; Westminster award for religious fiction, 1949, for *Prince of Egypt;* named Woman of Distinction, Alpha Delta Kappa, 1971; New England United Methodist award for excellence in social justice actions, 1975; distinguished achievement award, University of Maine at Augusta, 1977.

WRITINGS: *Twelve Months of Drama for the Average Church* (plays), Walter H. Baker, 1934; *The Brother,* Westminster, 1944; *The Herdsman,* Westminster, 1946; *Prince of Egypt,* Westminster, 1949; *House of Earth,* Westminster, 1952; *Jezebel,* McGraw, 1955; *The Gifts,* McGraw, 1957; *The Journey* (juvenile), Abingdon, 1962; *The Three Gifts* (juvenile), Abing-

don, 1963; *The Big-Little World of Doc Pritham,* McGraw, 1971; *Twelve Who Cared* (autobiography), Christian Herald Books, 1977.

Biographies; published by McGraw, except as indicated: *Dr. Ida: The Story of Ida Scudder of Vellore,* 1959; *Take My Hands: The Story of Dr. Mary Verghese,* 1963; *Ten Fingers for God* (*Reader's Digest* Condensed Book), 1965; *Handicap Race: The Inspiring Story of Roger Arnett,* 1967; *Palace of Healing,* 1968; *Lone Woman: The Story of Elizabeth Blackwell—the World's First Woman Doctor* (*Reader's Digest* Condensed Book), Little, Brown, 1970; *Hilary: The Brave World of Hilary Pole,* 1973; *Bright Eyes: The Story of Susette la Flesche, an Omaha Indian,* 1974; *Stranger and Traveler,* Little, Brown, 1975; *Granny Brand: Her Story,* Christian Herald Books, 1976; *Lincoln's Mothers: A Story of Nancy and Sally Lincoln,* Doubleday, 1981. Also author of *Fly with Me to India,* 1954, and of approximately seventy religious plays. Contributor of articles, short stories, and plays to religious publications.

SIDELIGHTS: Dorothy Clarke Wilson told *CA:* "My chief purpose in writing is to inspire people with lessons from courageous and constructive Christian lives, also to instill in readers the impulse to engage in humanitarian action.

"Many of my books, especially the biographies, have gone into foreign editions. . . . One, *Take My Hands,* the story of Mary Verghese, a paraplegic Indian doctor, has gone into more than a dozen languages, including Chinese, Indonesian, Arabic, and Hindu. The faith and courage of this disabled woman seem to have had universal appeal."

BIOGRAPHICAL/CRITICAL SOURCES: *Boston Post Magazine,* March 27, 1949; *Portland Sunday Telegram,* October 30, 1949; *Presbyterian Life,* November 12, 1949; *Wilson Library Bulletin,* June, 1951; *Lewiston Journal Magazine,* January 10, 1953, October 17, 1959; *Christian Science Monitor,* March 4, 1955; *Best Sellers,* November 1, 1967; *New York Times Book Review,* June 14, 1970.

*　　*　　*

WILSON, Hazel (Hutchins)   1898-

PERSONAL: Born April 8, 1898, in Portland, Me.; daughter of Fred Linwood (a real estate broker) and Emma (Jones) Hutchins; married William Jerome Wilson, September 16, 1930 (died, 1963); children: Jerome Linwood. *Education:* Bates College, A.B., 1919; Simmons College, B.S., 1920. *Politics:* Independent. *Religion:* Congregationalist. *Home:* 4912 Berkley St., Washington, D.C. 20016. *Agent:* McIntosh & Otis, Inc., 475 Fifth Ave., New York, N.Y. 10017.

CAREER: High school librarian, Portland, Me., 1920-23; Northeast Missouri State Teachers College (now Northeast Missouri State University), Kirksville, librarian, 1923-26; American library, Paris, France, head of circulation department, 1926-28; Bradford Academy, Bradford, Mass., librarian, 1928-29; supervisor of school libraries, Denver, Colo., 1929-30; George Washington University, Washington, D.C., lecturer, 1956-67. Has taught courses in writing for children. Frequent lecturer at book fairs and Parent-Teacher Association meetings. Has done some radio and television work. Consultant to foreign students. *Member:* American Newspaper Women's Club, Children's Book Guild of Washington, D.C. (president, 1955-56, 1970-71), Women in Communication. *Awards, honors:* Ohioana Award, for *Island Summer;* Boys' Clubs of America Junior Book Award, for *Thad Owen;* New York Herald Spring Book Festival Honor Book Award, for *Herbert;* Edison Award, 1955, for *His Indian Brother;* M.A., Bates College,

1959; Cumberland County (Maine) award, 1960, for "literary achievement."

WRITINGS: *The Red Dory,* Little, Brown, 1939, 2nd edition, 1959; *The Owen Boys* (Catholic Book Club selection), Abingdon, 1947; *Island Summer,* Abingdon, 1949; *Thad Owen,* Abingdon, 1950; *Herbert,* Knopf, 1950; *Herbert Again,* Knopf, 1951; *The Story of Lafayette,* Grosset, 1952; *The Story of Anthony Wayne,* Grosset, 1953; *More Fun With Herbert,* Knopf, 1954; *His Indian Brother,* Abingdon, 1955, reprinted, Houghton, 1970; *The Little Marquise: Madame Lafayette* (Junior Literary Guild selection), Knopf, 1957; *The Surprise of Their Lives* (Junior Literary Guild selection), Knopf, 1957; *Tall Ships,* Little, Brown, 1958; *Jerry's Charge Account* (Junior Literary Guild selection), Little, Brown, 1960; *Herbert's Homework,* Knopf, 1960; *The Seine: River of Paris,* Garrard, 1961; *The Last Queen of Hawaii,* Knopf, 1963; *Herbert's Space Trip,* Knopf, 1965; *The Years Between: Washington at Home at Mount Vernon, 1783-1789,* Knopf, 1969; *Herbert's Stilts,* Knopf, 1972. Book reviewer, *Childhood Education,* 1960-61, *Sunday Star,* Washington, D.C., 1963-69, *Parents' Magazine,* 1969-72.

WORK IN PROGRESS: Two books.

SIDELIGHTS: Hazel Wilson told *CA:* "I am optimistic about the future of the book. Children will not entirely desert reading for TV if there is motivation by both parents and teachers. Children read books they like over and over. . . . I think it is important to amuse children as well as to teach them. When they find books are a form of recreation even a reluctant reader will keep on reading."

*   *   *

WILSON, Monica Hunter   1908-

PERSONAL: Born January 3, 1908, in Lovedale, South Africa; daughter of David Alexander and Jessie (Macgregor) Hunter; married Godfrey Wilson, 1935 (died, 1944); children: Francis Aylmer Hunter, Timothy Dover. *Education:* Cambridge University, M.A., and Ph.D. *Religion:* Anglican Church. *Home:* Hunterstoun, Hogsback, Cape Province, South Africa 5705.

CAREER: Field work in Pondoland, South Africa, 1931, 1932, 1934, and Nyakyusa, Tanganyika, and Ngonde, Tanganyika, 1935-38, 1955; lecturer and warden of women, University College of Fort Hare, South Africa, 1944-46; Rhodes University, Grahamstown, South Africa, professor of social anthropology, 1947-51; University of Cape Town, Rondebosch, South Africa, professor of social anthropology, 1951-73. Frazer Lecturer, 1959; Scott Holland Lecturer, Cambridge University, 1969; corresponding member, School of Oriental and African Studies, University of London, 1969.

MEMBER: Royal Anthropological Institute, American Anthropological Association, Association of Social Anthropologists, Royal Society of South Africa (member of council, 1957-58, 1961-63), Royal Commonwealth Society (London), British Academy (corresponding fellow). *Awards, honors:* International African Institute research fellow, 1935-38; Carnegie Travel grant, 1950; Rivers Memorial Medal, 1952; Simon Biesheuvel Medal, 1965; Cambridge University, Girton College, fellow, 1968, Helen Cam fellow, 1974-75; D.Litt., Rhodes University, 1970, University of Witwatersrand, 1981; Center for Advanced Study in the Behavorial Sciences fellow, 1971-72; honorary doctorate, University of York, 1971.

WRITINGS: *Reaction to Conquest,* Oxford University Press, 1936, 2nd edition, 1961; (with husband, Godfrey Wilson) *The Analysis of Social Change,* Cambridge University Press, 1945,

reprinted, 1969; *Good Company,* Oxford University Press, 1951; (with others) *Social Structure,* Shuter & Shooter, 1952; (with others) *Land Tenure,* Shuter & Shooter, 1952; *Rituals of Kinship Among the Nyakyusa,* Oxford University Press, 1956; *Peoples of the Nyasa-Tanganyika Corridor,* University of Cape Town, 1958; *Communal Rituals of the Nyakyusa,* Oxford University Press, 1959; *Divine Kings and the "Breath of Men,"* Cambridge University Press, 1959; (with Archie Mafeje) *Langa, a Study of Social Groups in an African Township,* Oxford University Press, 1963; (editor with Leonard Thompson) *The Oxford History of South Africa,* Oxford University Press, Volume I: *To 1870,* 1969, Volume II: *1870-1966,* 1971; *Religion and the Transformation of Society: A Study in Social Change in Africa,* Cambridge University Press, 1971; *For Men and Elders,* International African Institute, 1977, Holmes & Meier, 1978; (contributor) *Freedom for My People,* Rex Collings, 1981. Contributor to anthropological journals.

WORK IN PROGRESS: *Comparative Study of African Ritual; Studies in South African History.*

AVOCATIONAL INTERESTS: Gardening.

*   *   *

WILSON, Samuel, Jr.   1911-

PERSONAL: Born August 6, 1911, in New Orleans, La.; son of Samuel (a businessman) and Stella (Poupeney) Wilson; married Ellen Elizabeth Latrobe, October 20, 1951. *Education:* Tulane University, B.Arch., 1931. *Home:* 1121 Washington Ave., New Orleans, La. 70130. *Office:* Koch & Wilson, Architects, 1100 Jackson Ave., New Orleans, La. 70130.

CAREER: Office of Moise H. Goldstein, New Orleans, La., draftsman, 1930-33; Historic American Buildings Survey in Louisiana, New Orleans, researcher, 1934-35; Richard Koch, Architect, New Orleans, architect, 1935-42, associate, 1945-55; Koch & Wilson, Architects, New Orleans, partner, 1955-70, 1971—. Lecturer on Louisiana architecture at Tulane University, 1945—; visiting lecturer at Cornell University, Columbia University, University of Illinois, and other universities, organizations, societies, and museums; presented television series, "New Orleans Houses," 1953. Member of board of curators, Louisiana State Museum, 1953-56. Member of board of Vieux Carrer Property Owners and Associates, 1953-68, Maison Hospitaliere, 1963—, Friends of the Cabildo, 1964—, and New Orleans Area Council of Boy Scouts of America, 1972. Adviser to General Services Administration and to board of Historic Natchez Foundation. *Military service:* U.S. Coast Guard Reserve, active duty, 1942-45.

MEMBER: American Institute of Architects (fellow; chairman of joint committee on architectural archives, 1957-60; chairman of committee on historic buildings, 1960; state preservation coordinator, 1968-77), Association for Preservation Technology, National Trust for Historic Preservation, Society of Architectural Historians (former member of board; member of bicentennial commission, 1971—), National Council of Architectural Registration Boards, Friends of Cast Iron Architecture, Louisiana Landmarks Society (member of board, 1950—; president, 1950-56), Louisiana Historical Society (member of editorial board; member of executive council, 1970—), Louisiana Historical Association, Louisiana Architects Association, Mississippi Historical Society, Friends of the Archives of Louisiana, Genealogical Research Society of New Orleans, Historic Natchez Foundation, Garden District Association, Jefferson Parish Historical Society, Boston Club.

AWARDS, HONORS: Edward Langley scholarship of American Institute of Architects, 1938, for travel and study in Europe;

Silver Beaver Award of Boy Scouts of America, 1939; received citation for significant achievement in historic preservation in the United States from National Trust for Historic Preservation, 1968; received citation for excellence in community architecture from American Institute of Architects, 1969; Award of Excellence of New Orleans Chamber of Commerce for restorations, 1972, and for urban design landscaping, 1973; Louisiana Council for Music and the Performing Business and Arts Award, 1974; award of merit from American Association of State and Local History, 1977; Harnett T. Kane Preservation Award, Louisiana Landmarks Society, 1977; Terry-Parkerson Award from Garden District Association, 1979; Preservation Award, Foundation for Historical Louisiana, 1979; named Preservationist of the Year by Louisiana Preservation Alliance, 1979.

WRITINGS: (Editor and author of introduction and notes) Benjamin Henry Boneral Latrobe, *Impressions Respecting New Orleans: Diary and Sketches, 1818-1820,* Columbia University Press, 1951; (with Garland Taylor and Leonard V. Huber) *Louisiana Purchase,* Louisiana Landmarks Society, 1953; (chairman of guide book committee) *A Guide to Architecture of New Orleans, 1699-1959,* Reinhold, for Louisiana Landmarks Society, 1959; (with Huber) *The St. Louis Cemeteries of New Orleans,* St. Louis Cathedral, 1963; (with Huber) *Baroness Pontalba's Buildings, Their Site and the Remarkable Woman Who Built Them,* Louisiana Landmarks Society, 1964, 2nd edition, 1966; (with Huber) *The Basilica on Jackson Square and Predecessors, Dedicated to St. Louis, King of France, 1717-1965,* [New Orleans], 1965, 3rd edition, 1969; *Bienville's New Orleans: A French Colonial Capital, 1718-1768,* Friends of the Cabildo, 1968; *The Vieux Carre, New Orleans: Its Plan, Its Growth, Its Architecture* (historic district demonstration study), Bureau of Governmental Research (New Orleans), 1968; (with Huber) *The Cabildo on Jackson Square,* Friends of the Cabildo, 1970, revised edition, 1973; (author with Bernard Lemann of text in Volume I and author with others of text in Volume II) *New Orleans Architecture,* Pelican, for Friends of the Cabildo, Volume I: *The Lower Garden District,* 1971, Volume II: *The American Sector,* 1972; (author of introduction) *The Autobiography of James Gallier, Architect* (reprint of 1864 edition), Da Capo Press, 1973; (with Huber) *The Presbytere on Jackson Square,* Friends of the Cabildo, 1981.

Contributor: McDermott, editor, *Frenchmen and French Ways in the Mississippi Valley,* University of Illinois, 1969; *Spain and Her Rivals on the Gulf Coast,* University of West Florida, 1971; McDermott, editor, *The Spanish in the Mississippi Valley, 1762-1804,* University of Illinois Press, 1974; Roulhac Toledano and others, editors, *New Orleans Architecture,* Pelican, 1974; Samuel Proctor, editor, *Eighteenth-Century Florida and Its Borderlands,* University of Florida, 1975; *Green Fields: Two Hundred Years of Louisiana Sugar,* Center for Louisiana Studies, University of Southwestern Louisiana, 1980; Charles L. Dufour, editor, *Women Who Cared,* Christian Woman's Exchange, 1980; *Old and New Architecture: Design Relationship,* Preservation Press, 1980; *Amerika, Amerika,* Hoffman und Campe, 1980.

Contributor to other historical symposia. Author or co-author of booklets on historical sites and architecture of New Orleans. Contributor to *Proceedings* of U.S. Naval Institute, *Magazine of Art, Antiques,* and other journals; reviewer for *Louisiana History, Journal of the Society of Architectural Historians, Historical Quarterly, Times Picayune,* and other periodicals. Member of editorial board, Louisiana Historical Society, 1974.

WIND, Herbert Warren 1916-

PERSONAL: Born August 11, 1916, in Brockton, Mass.; son of Max Eisen and Dora Wind. *Education:* Yale University, B.A., 1937; Cambridge University, M.A., 1939. *Home:* 301 East 66th St., New York, N.Y. *Office: New Yorker,* 25 East 43rd St., New York, N.Y. 10036.

CAREER: Member of staff of *New Yorker* magazine, 1947-54, 1960—, and *Sports Illustrated* magazine, 1954-60. *Military service:* U.S. Army Air Forces, 1942-46; became captain. *Member:* Yale Club (New York), Royal and Ancient Golf Club (St. Andrews, Scotland).

WRITINGS: The Story of American Golf, Farrar, Straus, 1948, 3rd edition, Knopf, 1975; (with Gene Sarazen) *Thirty Years of Championship Golf,* Prentice-Hall, 1950; (editor) *The Complete Golfer,* Simon & Schuster, 1954; (editor) *Tips from the Top,* Prentice-Hall, Volume I, 1955, Volume II, 1956; (with Ben Hogan) *The Modern Fundamentals of Golf,* A. S. Barnes, 1957; (co-editor) *Great Stories from the World of Sport,* Simon & Schuster, 1958; *On the Tour with Harry Sprague,* Simon & Schuster, 1960; *The Gilded Age of Sport,* Simon & Schuster, 1961; (editor) *The Realm of Sport,* Simon & Schuster, 1966; (with Jack Nicklaus) *The Greatest Game of All,* Simon & Schuster, 1969; *Herbert Warren Wind's Golf Book,* Simon & Schuster, 1971; *The World of P. G. Wodehouse,* Praeger, 1971; *Game, Set, and Match: The Tennis Boom of the 1960's and 70's,* Dutton, 1979.

*   *   *

WINDERS, Gertrude Hecker

PERSONAL: Born in Indianapolis, Ind.; daughter of Edward J. (a printer and writer) and Harriet L. (Humann) Hecker; married C. Garrison Winders (a sporting goods dealer); children: Barbara (Mrs. Richard H. Wich). *Education:* Butler University, A.B. *Home:* 1000 Beardsley St., Elkhart, Ind. 46514.

CAREER: Writer, lecturer. Speaker at Columbia University Scholastic Press Association Convention, New York, N.Y., 1956, 1962, Ohio State Convention of School Librarians, 1960, and *Indianapolis News* Book Fair, 1960, 1961. Creative writing teacher under auspices of American Association of University Women, 1951-60; teacher of creative writing, Indiana University—Purdue University at Indianapolis, 1970-75. Consultant, Indiana University Writers' Conference, 1960-75. *Member:* Pi Beta Phi, Phi Kappa Phi, Indianapolis Story-a-Month Club, National Society of Daughters of 1812.

WRITINGS—All published by Bobbs-Merrill, except as indicated: *James Fenimore Cooper: Leatherstocking Boy,* 1951; *Jim Bowie: Boy with a Hunting Knife,* 1953; *Ethan Allen: Green Mountain Boy,* 1954; *Jim Bridger: Mountain Boy,* 1955; *Jeb Stuart: Boy in the Saddle,* 1959; *Sam Colt and His Gun* (Junior Literary Guild selection), John Day, 1959; *Browning: World's Greatest Gunmaker,* John Day, 1961; *Horace Greeley: Newspaperman,* John Day, 1962; *Robert Goddard: Father of Rocketry,* John Day, 1963; *George M. Cohan: Boy Theater Genius,* 1968; *Harriet Tubman: Freedom Girl,* 1969; *Irvington Then and Now,* Irvington Historical Society, 1970. Contributor of short stories to popular magazines.

SIDELIGHTS: Commenting on the writing of her book on Harriet Tubman, Gertrude Hecker Winders told *CA:* "*Harriet Tubman: Freedom Girl* is my only book whose subject I did not choose. At the insistence of my publishers . . . I wrote the book, though reluctantly. I had once lived in the South for a year and was determined to be fair to Southerners in the painful and confused period preceding the Civil War. This attitude, I felt, would meet with general disapproval. Besides, there were enough recent books on Harriet Tubman.

"These I avoided in preparation for my book. I studied the one written in her lifetime which, realizing her sense of drama, I mentally edited. In writing biography all sources other than somebody else's biography on your subject are better material. No matter how objective an author thinks he is, he produces a character drawn through his impressions. You want to trust your own.

"I made a quick trip to New York to see the Tubman Collection in a Harlem library. Though the collection reinforced my growing realization of the importance of Harriet Tubman, I found little relating to her childhood. Old photographs taken in her adult years were fascinating and thought-provoking. One of several pleasant surprises in my research was correspondence with a niece of Harriet Tubman who remembered her Aunt Hattie. . . . But I was not happy with the published book. I had to write it too hurriedly; it was published too quickly. That its publishers were pleased gave me no reassurance.

"To my surprise, Science Research Associates, Inc., chose my *Harriet Tubman* to recommend to schools. The *Christian Science Monitor* included [it] in a list chosen from a survey of 'What Books Children Like' with the observation, 'White girls identify with Harriet Tubman.' Black children tell me they like the book. Their mothers read it, too. Black leaders have praised it. From reviewers it has received more serious attention than usually given a book written for children. Harriet keeps on surprising me, proving as popular for reprint as my dashing heroes Jim Bowie and Jeb Stuart. Sometimes publishers guess right."

*   *   *

WINDHAM, Donald 1920-

PERSONAL: Born July 2, 1920, in Atlanta, Ga.; son of Fred and Louise (Donaldson) Windham. *Education:* Attended schools in Atlanta, Ga. *Home:* 230 Central Park S., New York, N.Y. 10019.

CAREER: Dance Index magazine, New York, N.Y., editor, 1943-45; free-lance writer. *Awards, honors:* Guggenheim fellowship in creative writing, 1960.

WRITINGS: (With Tennessee Williams) *You Touched Me* (play; produced on Broadway, 1945), Samuel French, 1947; *The Dog Star* (novel), Doubleday, 1950; *The Hero Continues* (novel), Crowell, 1960; *The Warm Country* (short stories), Scribner, 1962; *Emblems of Conduct* (autobiography of childhood), Scribner, 1964; *Two People* (novel), Coward, 1965; (editor) *E. M. Forster's Letters to Donald Windham*, Sandy Campbell, 1975; (editor) *Tennessee Williams' Letters to Donald Windham*, Holt, 1977; *Tanaquil* (novel), Holt, 1977; *Stone in the Hourglass* (novel), Sandy Campbell, 1981.

*   *   *

WINTER, Leslie 1940-
(Leslie Winter Strom)

PERSONAL: Born April 22, 1940, in Lowell, Mass.; daughter of Solomon B. and Josephine (Loeb) Winter; married Harold Strom, 1958 (divorced, 1973); children: Carl. *Education:* Attended Columbia University and Temple University. *Agent:* Roberta Pryor, International Creative Management, 40 West 57th St., New York, N.Y. 10019.

WRITINGS: (Under name Leslie Winter Strom) *A Weed in the Garden*, Knopf, 1961; *Long Shots*, Delacorte, 1980.

WORK IN PROGRESS: A novel, *A Story of the Sixties.*

SIDELIGHTS: Leslie Winter told *CA:* "Mine has been a weird, cyclical life as a writer. My first book, *A Weed in the Garden*, a story of life's futility as seen through the eyes of an eighteen year old boy, was published when I was twenty-one. In the ensuing years, I raised a son and wrote (over and over again) two major novels, the first of which is . . . entitled *Long Shots*. I consider *Long Shots* to be the most important book I shall ever write, because it embraces the adult themes with which my mind and heart have been most preoccupied. I also believe that it is the most significant, personal statement I can make as a woman.

"My next book (still being revised) is one I have plodded over for years. I originally conceived of it as a satire, but that didn't work. It is now a serious novel (i.e. tragic) entitled *A Story of the Sixties*, set in Italy, although its three major characters are American. I think of this work as a kind of nightmarish fairy tale."

BIOGRAPHICAL/CRITICAL SOURCES: New York Times, July 17, 1961.

*   *   *

WINTERTON, Paul 1908-
(Roger Bax, Andrew Garve, Paul Somers)

PERSONAL: Born February 12, 1908, in Leicester, England; son of Ernest (a journalist and Member of Parliament) Winterton. *Education:* London School of Economics and Political Science, London, B.Sc., 1928. *Address:* c/o Curtis Brown Ltd., 1 Craven Hill, London W2 3EP, England.

CAREER: Economist, London, England, member of staff, 1929-33; *News Chronicle*, London, 1933-46, reporter, leader writer, and foreign correspondent, including assignment in Moscow, 1942-45; free-lance writer, 1946—. *Member:* Society of Authors, P.E.N., Crime Writers Association (founding member and first joint secretary), Detection Club, Mystery Writers of America.

WRITINGS: Russia: With Open Eyes, Lawrence & Wishart, 1937; *Mending Minds: The Truth about Our Mental Hospitals*, Davies, 1938; *Report on Russia*, Cresset, 1945; *Inquest on an Ally*, Cresset, 1948. Also author of *A Student in Russia*, 1931.

Suspense novels under pseudonym Roger Bax: *Death beneath Jerusalem*, Nelson, 1938; *Red Escapade*, Skeffington, 1941; *Disposing of Henry*, Harper, 1947; *The Trouble with Murder*, Harper, 1948 (published in England as *Blueprint for Murder*, Hutchinson, 1948); *Two If by Sea*, Harper, 1949 (published in England as *Came the Dawn*, Hutchinson, 1949); *A Grave Case of Murder*, Harper, 1951.

Suspense novels under pseudonym Andrew Garve: published by Harper, except as indicated: *No Tears for Hilda*, 1950, reprinted, Garland Publishing, 1970; *Fontego's Folly*, 1950 (published in England as *No Mask for Murder*, Collins, 1950); *Murder through the Looking Glass*, 1951 (published in England as *Murder in Moscow*, Collins, 1951); *By-Line for Murder*, 1951 (published in England as *A Press of Suspects*, Collins, 1951); *A Hole in the Ground*, 1952; *The Cuckoo Line Affair*, 1953; *Death and the Sky Above*, Collins, 1953, Harper, 1954; *The Riddle of Samson*, 1954; *The End of the Track*, 1956; *The Megstone Plot*, 1956; *The Narrow Search*, 1957; *The Galloway Case*, 1958; *A Hero for Leanda*, 1959; *The Far Sands*, 1960; *The Golden Deed*, 1960; *The House of Soldiers*, 1961; *The*

Prisoner's Friend, 1962; *The Sea Monks*, 1963; *Frame-Up*, 1964; *The Ashes of Loda*, 1965; *Hide and Go Seek*, 1966 (published in England as *Murderer's Fen*, Collins, 1966); *A Very Quiet Place*, 1967; *The Long Short Cut*, 1968; *The Ascent of D-13*, 1968; *Boomerang*, Collins, 1969, published as *Boomerang: An Australian Escapade*, Harper, 1970; *The Late Bill Smith*, 1971; *The Case of Robert Quarry*, 1972; *The Lester Affair*, 1974 (published in England as *The File on Lester*, Collins, 1974); *Home to Roost*, Crowell, 1976; *Counterstroke*, Crowell, 1978.

Suspense novels under pseudonym Paul Somers: *Beginner's Luck*, Harper, 1958; *Operation Piracy*, Collins, 1958, Harper, 1959; *The Shivering Mountain*, Harper, 1959; *The Broken Jigsaw*, Harper, 1961.

SIDELIGHTS: Paul Winterton's stories have been widely translated and have been broadcast and televised in Great Britain and the United States. Several of his works have been filmed, including *The Megstone Plot*, which became Paramount's "A Touch of Larceny." *Avocational interests:* Sailing, travel.†

*   *   *

WISE, William 1923-

PERSONAL: Born July 21, 1923, in New York, N.Y. *Education:* Yale University, B.A., 1948. *Agent:* Curtis Brown, Ltd., 575 Madison Ave., New York, N.Y. 10022.

CAREER: Free-lance writer.

WRITINGS—Juvenile, except as indicated: *Jonathan Blake*, Knopf, 1956; *Silversmith of Old New York: Myer Myers*, Farrar, Straus, and Jewish Publication Society, 1958.

Albert Einstein: Citizen of the World, Farrar, Straus, and Jewish Publication Society, 1960; *The House with the Red Roof*, Putnam, 1961; *The Cowboy Surprise*, Putnam, 1961; *Alexander Hamilton*, Putnam, 1963; *The Story of Mulberry Bend*, Dutton, 1963; *In the Time of the Dinosaurs*, Putnam, 1964; *Detective Pinkerton and Mr. Lincoln*, Dutton, 1964; *The Two Reigns of Tutankhamen*, Putnam, 1964; *The World of Giant Mammals*, Putnam, 1965; *The Spy and General Washington*, Dutton, 1965; *Franklin D. Roosevelt*, Putnam, 1967; *Monsters of Today and Yesterday*, Putnam, 1967; *When the Saboteurs Came*, Dutton, 1967; *Sir Howard, the Coward*, Putnam, 1967; *Killer Smog* (adult nonfiction), Rand McNally, 1968; *Monsters of the Ancient Seas*, Putnam, 1968; *Aaron Burr*, Putnam, 1968; *Booker T. Washington*, Putnam, 1968; *Secret Mission to the Philippines*, Dutton, 1969; *Nanette: The Hungry Pelican*, Rand McNally, 1969; *Giant Birds and Monsters of the Air* (Junior Literary Guild selection), Putnam, 1969; *The Terrible Trumpet*, Norton, 1969; *The Amazing Animals of Latin America*, Putnam, 1969.

The Amazing Animals of Australia (Junior Literary Guild selection), Putnam, 1970; *The Lazy Young Duke of Dundee*, Rand McNally, 1970; *Fresh as a Daisy, Neat as a Pin*, Parents' Magazine Press, 1970; *From Scrolls to Satellites*, Parents' Magazine Press, 1970; *Giant Snakes and Other Amazing Reptiles*, Putnam, 1970; *Charles A. Lindbergh: Aviation Pioneer*, Putnam, 1970; *Monsters of the Middle Ages*, Putnam, 1971; *Amazing Animals of North America*, Putnam, 1971; *Fresh, Canned, and Frozen*, Parents' Magazine Press, 1971; *All on a Summer's Day*, Pantheon, 1971; *Off We Go!*, Parents' Magazine Press, 1972; *Cities, Old and New*, Parents' Magazine Press, 1973; *Leaders, Laws, and Citizens*, Parents' Magazine Press, 1973; *The Strange World of Sea Mammals*, Putnam, 1973; *Monsters of the Deep*, Putnam, 1975; *American Freedom and the Bill of Rights*, Parents' Magazine Press, 1975; *Mas-*

sacre at Mountain Meadows (adult nonfiction), Crowell, 1976; *Monsters of North America*, Putnam, 1978; *Animal Rescue*, Putnam, 1978; *Monsters from Outer Space?*, Putnam, 1978.

Monster Myths of Ancient Greece, Putnam, 1981; *The Amazon Factor* (adult mystery), Harlequin, 1981. Also author of "Raven House" mysteries for Harlequin, 1980-82. Author of television scripts; contributor of fiction to *Harper's*, *Yale Review*, and other periodicals, and of reviews to *New York Times* and *Saturday Review*.

*   *   *

WOETZEL, Robert K(urt) 1930-

PERSONAL: Born December 5, 1930, in Shanghai, China; son of Kurt E(mil) and Eva (Gumprich) Woetzel; married Sheila Barry (annulled); children: Jonathan, Damian. *Education:* The Hague Academy of International Law, certificate, 1951; Columbia University, A.B., 1952; Oxford University, Ph.D., 1958; Bonn University, J.S.D., 1959. *Politics:* Democrat. *Religion:* Roman Catholic. *Home:* Harlaxton House, 286 Central St., Auburndale-Newton, Mass. 02166. *Office address:* Box 12, Foundation for the Establishment of an International Criminal Court, Auburndale-Newton, Mass. 02166; and Department of Politics and Law, Boston College, Chestnut Hill, Mass. 02167.

CAREER: U.S. House of Representatives, Washington, D.C., legislative assistant, 1956; Fordham University, New York City, assistant professor, 1959-60, adjunct associate professor, 1960-63; New York University, New York City, associate professor of international law, 1960-63; Center for the Study of Democratic Institutions, Santa Barbara, Calif., staff member, 1964-66; Boston College, Chestnut Hill, Mass., professor of politics and law, 1966—; Foundation for the Establishment of an International Criminal Court, Auburndale-Newton, Mass., president, 1970—. Visiting professor at Seminary of the Immaculate Conception, 1961-62, Old Mission Theological Seminary, 1964-65, University of Southern California Law School, 1970-71, Immaculate Heart College, 1972-73, Northeastern University, 1974—, and Harvard University, 1980—. U.S. director of International Institute of Space Law, 1960-63; president of International Criminal Law Commission and Humanitarian Law and Human Rights Conference, 1970—; United Nations affiliate, 1970—; Danforth associate, 1970—. Consultant to Carnegie Endowment of International Peace, 1960-61, and to National Aeronautics and Space Administration (NASA) Jet Propulsion Laboratory, 1965-66. *Military service:* U.S. Army, 1954-56.

MEMBER: American Society of International Law, American Political Science Association, American Institute of Aeronautics and Astronautics, American Academy of Political and Social Sciences, American Civil Liberties Union. *Awards, honors:* American Council of Learned Societies grant; Ford Fund for Public Affairs research grant; Einstein Prize; Stokes Prize; Henry fellow; Humboldt fellow; Curtis Gold Medal; Distinguished International Criminal Law Award.

WRITINGS: The Nuremberg Trials in International Law, Praeger, 1960, 2nd edition, 1962; *Die internationale Kontrolle der hoeheren Luftschichten und des Weltraums* (title means "The International Control of Space"), Asgard Verlag, 1960; *The Philosophy of Freedom*, Oceana, 1966; (editor with Julius Stone) *Toward a Feasible International Criminal Court*, World Peace Through Law Center (Geneva), 1970. Also author of *Une philosophie de la liberte*, 1969. Contributor to law reviews, international relations publications, magazines and newspapers.

WORK IN PROGRESS: A booklet, *Code of Offenses against Peace and Security of Mankind.*

SIDELIGHTS: Robert K. Woetzel speaks (in order of proficiency) German, Chinese, Spanish, French, and Japanese. *Avocational interests:* Hiking, concerts, ballet, opera, art galleries, old churches.

* * *

WOHLGELERNTER, Maurice 1921-

PERSONAL: Born February 13, 1921, in Poland; son of Jacob Isaac (a rabbi) and Deborah (Yagoda) Wohlgelernter; married Esther Feinerman (a teacher), February 1, 1948; children: Debra, Elli, Beth. *Education:* Yeshiva University, B.A., 1941, Rabbi, 1944; Columbia University, M.A., 1946, Ph.D., 1961. *Home:* 181 East 73rd St., New York, N.Y. 10021.

CAREER: Bernard M. Baruch College of the City University of New York, New York, N.Y., professor of English, 1972—. Visiting professor, Yeshiva University, 1955-70, City College (now City College of the City University of New York), summers, 1962-65, Bar-Ilan University, Israel, New School for Social Research, 1966-68, and Manhattanville College. Panelist on television programs, "Minorities in American Literature," WYNC-TV, and "The American Novel: Voice of Minorities," WNBC, 1965. *Member:* Modern Language Association of America, National Council of Teachers of English, American Association of University Professors, James Joyce Society, American Council of Irish Studies.

WRITINGS: Israel Zangwill: A Study, Columbia University Press, 1964; *Israel Zangwill: Selected Bibliography,* Jewish Book Council of America, 1964; (author of introduction) Israel Zangwill, *The King of Schnorrers,* Dover, 1965; *Frank O'Connor: An Introduction,* Columbia University Press, 1977; (editor) *History, Religion, and Spiritual Democracy,* Columbia University Press, 1980. Contributor to *Journal of Modern Literature, History of Ideas Newsletter, Midstream,* and *Congress Bi-Weekly.* Also contributing editor of *Tradition.*

WORK IN PROGRESS: A book, *Joseph Wood Krutch: Skeptical Humanist,* and a novel.

SIDELIGHTS: Maurice Wohlgelernter told *CA:* "Having paid my dues to academe, I decided to venture into the world of fiction. For there is, obviously, more to life than chasing footnotes, however significant, or reviewing books, however important. One must, at long last, seek to review also the human condition beyond the classroom. Hence, in addition to another critical study, I am presently engaged in writing three novellae—actually variations on a single theme—a theme best summed up in Hawthorne's trenchant comment that 'in this republican country, amid fluctuating waves of our social life, somebody is always at the drowning point.' It is to those 'at the drowning point' that I now direct my immediate attention."

BIOGRAPHICAL/CRITICAL SOURCES: New York Times, May 1, 1977, June 24, 1977.

* * *

WOLFBEIN, Seymour L(ouis) 1915-

PERSONAL: Born November 8, 1915, in Brooklyn, N.Y.; son of Samuel and Fanny (Katz) Wolfbein; married Mae Lachterman (a counselor), March 1, 1941; children: Susan Lois (Mrs. William Morris), Deeva Irene (Mrs. Robert Garel). *Education:* Brooklyn College (now Brooklyn College of the City University of New York), B.A., 1936; Columbia University, M.A., 1937, Ph.D., 1941. *Home:* 6305 Crathie Lane, Washington,

D.C. 20016. *Office:* School of Business Administration, Temple University, Philadelphia, Pa. 19103.

CAREER: U.S. Department of Labor, Washington, D.C., 1942-1967, chief of Manpower and Employment, Bureau of Labor Statistics, 1950-59, deputy assistant secretary of labor, 1959-62, director of Office of Manpower, Automation and Training, 1962-65, economic advisor to secretary of labor, 1965-67; American University, Washington, D.C., adjunct professor of economics, 1947-67; Temple University, Philadelphia, Pa., professor of economics, 1967-78, professor of business administration and economics, 1978—, dean of School of Business Administration, 1967-78. Visiting professor of education, University of Michigan, 1950-70; Salzburg Seminar in American studies, Austria, lecturer, 1965, dean of faculty, 1972; lecturer in the Far East, Greece, and Asia, for the Bureau of Cultural Affairs, U.S. Department of State, and International Communications Agency, 1970—. Vice-president, World Trade Council. Representative to International Association of Gerontology, Italy, 1957, Sweden, 1963; delegate to International Labor Office, Geneva, 1959-64, Organization for Economic Cooperation and Development, Paris, Lisbon, Venice, 1961-63, 1965, 1967, 1971, United Nations Industrial Development Organization, Athens, 1967. Member of advisory board to U.S. Secretary of Commerce, 1969-70; member of Commission on Human Resources, National Academy of Sciences, 1977-80; member of advisory committee, National Science Foundation, 1977—; member of board of directors, Lincoln Bank, Philadelphia, Pa. Consultant and lecturer at many insurance firms and industrial companies. *Military service:* U.S. Army, 1944-45. *Member:* American Association for the Advancement of Science (fellow), American Statistical Association (fellow), American Personnel and Guidance Association (trustee), Washington Statistical Society (president, 1957-59). *Awards, honors:* Distinguished Service Award, U.S. Department of Labor, 1954, 1961; Alumni Award of Honor, Brooklyn College (now Brooklyn College of the City University of New York), 1954; Eminent Career Award, National Vocational Guidance Association, 1970.

WRITINGS: Decline of a Cotton Textile City, Columbia University Press, 1944; (with H. Goldstein) *The World of Work,* Science Research Associates, 1951; *Employment and Unemployment in the United States,* Science Research Associates, 1964; *Employment, Unemployment and Public Policy,* Random House, 1966; *Education and Training for Full Employment,* Columbia University Press, 1968; *Occupational Information,* Random House, 1969; *Emerging Sectors of Collective Bargaining,* edited by D. H. Marks, General Learning Corp., 1970; *Work in American Society,* Scott, Foresman, 1971; (editor) *Manpower Policy: Perspectives and Prospects,* Temple University Press, 1973; (editor) *Labor Market Information for Youths,* Temple University Press, 1975; (editor) *Men in the Preretirement Years,* Temple University Press, 1977; *Establishment Reporting in the United States,* National Commission on Employment and Unemployment, 1979. Contributor to statistical, labor, and personnel guidance journals.

* * *

WOLFE, Gene (Rodman) 1931-

PERSONAL: Born May 7, 1931, in Brooklyn, N.Y.; son of Roy Emerson (a salesman) and Mary Olivia (Ayres) Wolfe; married Rosemary Frances Dietsch, November 3, 1956; children: Roy II, Madeleine, Therese, Matthew. *Education:* Attended Texas A & M University, 1949, 1952; University of Houston, B.S.M.E., 1956. *Religion:* Roman Catholic. *Home address:* P.O. Box 69, Barrington, Ill. 60010. *Agent:* Virginia Kidd, Box 278, Milford, Pa. 18337.

CAREER: Project engineer with Procter & Gamble, 1956-72; *Plant Engineering Magazine,* Barrington, Ill., senior editor, 1972— . *Military service:* U.S. Army, 1952-54; received Combat Infantry badge. *Member:* Science Fiction Writers of America, Authors Guild, P.E.N., World S.F., Science Fiction Poetry Association (president), American Institute of Plant Engineers, American Society of Business Press Editors. *Awards, honors:* Nebula Award from Science Fiction Writers of America, 1973, for "The Death of Doctor Island"; Chicago Foundation for Literature award, 1977, for *Peace;* Rhysling Award, 1978, for poem "The Computer Iterates the Greater Trumps"; Illinois Arts Council award, 1981, for short story "In Looking-Glass Castle"; World Fantasy Award, 1981, for *The Shadow of the Torturer.*

WRITINGS: Operation ARES, Berkley Publishing, 1970; *The Fifth Head of Cereberus,* Scribner's, 1972; *Peace,* Harper, 1975; (with Ursula K. LeGuin and James Tiptree, Jr.) *The New Atlantis, and Other Novellas of Science Fiction,* edited by Robert Silverberg, Hawthorn, 1975; *The Devil in a Forest* (juvenile), Follett, 1976; *The Island of Doctor Death and Other Stories and Other Stories,* Pocket Books, 1980; *Gene Wolfe's Book of Days,* Doubleday, 1981.

"The Book of the New Sun": *The Shadow of the Torturer,* Simon & Schuster, 1980; *The Claw of the Conciliator,* Simon & Schuster, 1981; *The Sword of the Lictor,* Simon & Schuster, 1982.

Work appears in anthologies, including: *Best SF: 70,* edited by Harry Harrison and Brian Aldiss, Putnam, 1970; *Nebula Award Stories 9,* edited by Kate Wilhelm, Harper, 1974; *The Best SF of the Year #3,* edited by Terry Carr, Ballantine, 1974; *Best SF: 73,* edited by Harrison and Aldiss, Berkley Publishing, 1974. Contributor of short stories to *Omni, New Yorker, Isaac Asimov's Science Fiction Magazine,* and other publications.

WORK IN PROGRESS: The remaining volumes of "The Book of the New Sun"; *The Castle of the Otter.*

SIDELIGHTS: Gene Wolfe's "The Book of the New Sun," a proposed tetralogy of which the first three volumes have been published, has earned him sudden stature in the science fiction field. Thomas D. Clareson, writing in *The Dictionary of Literary Biography,* judges *The Shadow of the Torturer,* the first volume of the tetralogy, "a rich tapestry rivaling any imaginary world portrayed in contemporary science fiction" and "one of the high accomplishments of modern science fiction." Thomas M. Disch writes in the *Washington Post Book World* that the tetralogy, although not yet completed, "already seems assured of classic status within the subgenre of science fantasy." "By the time the fourth volume appears," Algis Budrys states in the *Chicago Sun-Times,* "[Wolfe] will have become unchallengable in a reputation as one of SF's most potent names."

The tetralogy is set in a future Earth society reminiscent of medieval Europe but possessed of advanced technology. Severian, an apprentice torturer, is exiled from his city for aiding the suicide of a girl he loves in order that she may avoid further torture. Once exiled, he journeys from town to town with a stolen jewel, the Claw, which is capable of great healing powers. Severian must learn to use its powers correctly.

Critics have especially admired Wolfe's realistic presentation of his imaginary society. Writing in the *London Tribune,* Martin Hillman states: "In the evocation of the world, and the unsettling technologies, creatures, and behavioural rules within

it, [*The Shadow of the Torturer*] is streets ahead of most tales featuring sword-bearing heroes." Tom Hutchinson of the *London Times* believes that "Wolfe is not only deft at creating a whole and strange new world . . . he also, disturbingly, makes us understand a different way of thinking."

Writing in the *Magazine of Fantasy and Science Fiction,* Budrys calls "The Book of the New Sun" "the most promising long-term project currently underway in SF. . . . You will be missing a major—a seminal—event in the development of SF if you don't allow yourself the pleasure of reading [*The Shadow of the Torturer* and *The Claw of the Conciliator*]." Budrys goes even further in his praise. Speaking of *The Claw of the Conciliator,* he writes: "As a piece of literature, this work is simply overwhelming. Severian is a character realized in a depth and to a breadth we have never seen in SF before. . . . What we're talking about are attributes that are world-class as *prose,* not 'just' as SF."

Clareson concludes that Wolfe is "a major figure whose stories and novels must be considered among the most important science fiction published in the 1970s. He will undoubtedly become increasingly significant in the 1980s because he skillfully uses the materials of science fiction and fantasy to explore the themes which dominate contemporary fiction."

In a letter to *CA,* Wolfe states: "The books and stories I write are what are usually called escapist, in the pejorative sense. They do not teach the reader how to build a barbecue, or get a better job, or even how to murder his mother and escape detection. I have never understood what was wrong with escape. If I were in prison, or aboard a sinking vessel, I would escape if I could. I would try to escape from East Germany or the U.S.S.R., if I were unfortunate enough to find myself in one of those places. My work is intended to make life—however briefly —more tolerable for my readers, and to give them the feeling that change is possible, that the world need not always be as it is now, that their circumstances may be radically changed at any time, by their own act or God's."

BIOGRAPHICAL/CRITICAL SOURCES: Magazine of Fantasy and Science Fiction, April, 1971, May, 1978, June, 1981; *Times Literary Supplement,* May 18, 1973; *Booklist,* July 1, 1975; *New York Times Book Review,* July 13, 1975, September 12, 1976; *Science Fiction Review,* August, 1975, May, 1977, November, 1981; *Algol,* winter, 1976; *Chicago Tribune Book World,* June 8, 1980, June 14, 1981; *Chicago Sun-Times,* June 8, 1980; *Daily Iowan,* October 15, 1980; *The Dictionary of Literary Biography,* Volume VIII: *Twentieth Century American Science Fiction Writers,* Gale, 1981; *Washington Post Book World,* March 22, 1981, July 26, 1981; *Best Sellers,* April, 1981; *London Times,* April 2, 1981; *London Tribune,* April 24, 1981.

*   *   *

WOOD, Dorothy Adkins   1912-1975
(Dorothy C. Adkins)

PERSONAL: Born April 6, 1912, in Atlanta, Ohio; died December 19, 1975; daughter of George Hoadley and Pearl (James) Adkins; married David L. Wood, 1959. *Education:* Ohio State University, B.Sc. in Education, 1931, Ph.D., 1937. *Home:* 122 West Second Ave., Plain City, Ohio 43064. *Office:* 2633 Neil Ave., Columbus, Ohio 43204.

CAREER: University of Chicago, Chicago, Ill., assistant examiner, Board of Examinations, 1936-38, research associate in psychology, 1938-40; U.S. Social Security Board, Washington, D.C., chief of research and test construction unit, 1940-

44; U.S. Civil Service Commission, Washington, D.C., chief of social science testing, 1944-46, policy consultant to examination division, 1946-48, chief of test development section, 1948; University of North Carolina at Chapel Hill, professor of psychology, 1948-66, chairman of department, 1950-59; University of Hawaii, Honolulu, professor of educational psychology and researcher, 1966-74; affiliated with Consulting and Publishing, Inc., Columbus, Ohio, 1974-75. Part-time supervisor, North Carolina Merit System Council, 1956-58; member of cooperative research advisory committee, U.S. Office of Education, periodically, beginning 1958.

MEMBER: American Psychological Association (fellow; recording secretary, 1949-52; member of board of directors, 1956-58), Psychometric Society (president, 1949-50), North Carolina Psychological Association (president, 1951-52), Southeastern Psychological Association (secretary-treasurer, 1964-67), Scholaris, Pi Mu Epsilon, Gamma Psi Kappa, Pi Lambda Theta, Sigma Xi.

WRITINGS—Under name Dorothy C. Adkins: (With others) *Construction and Analysis of Achievement Tests,* U.S. Government Printing Office, 1948; (contributor) E. F. Lindquist, editor, *Educational Measurement,* American Council on Education, 1951; (with Samuel B. Lyerly) *Factor Analysis of Reasoning Tests,* University of North Carolina Press, 1952; *Test Construction: Development and Interpretation of Achievement Tests,* C. E. Merrill, 1960, 2nd edition, 1974; *Louis Leon Thurstone,* Educational Testing Services, 1962; *Statistics: An Introduction for Students in the Behavioral Sciences,* C. E. Merrill, 1964, 2nd edition, 1974; (with Hannah Herman) *Hawaii Head Start Evaluation, 1968-69,* University of Hawaii, 1970; (with Bonnie Balliff) *Motivation Curriculum: A Curriculum Module Designed to Promote Motivation for School Achievement,* University of Hawaii, 1971.

Contributor of articles and reviews to professional journals. *Psychometrika,* assistant managing editor, 1937-50, managing editor, 1950-56, member of editorial board, 1956-72; *Educational and Psychological Measurement,* associate editor, 1940-52, member of board of cooperating editors, beginning 1953; editorial consultant, *Public Personnel Review,* 1955-58.†

* * *

WOOD, Ursula
See VAUGHAN WILLIAMS, Ursula Wood

* * *

WOODBERRY, Joan (Merle) 1921-

PERSONAL: Born February 10, 1921, in Narrabri, New South Wales, Australia; daughter of Robert (an engineer) and Merle (Cain) Woodberry. *Education:* University of Sydney, B.A., 1942, Diploma in Education, 1943; University of Melbourne, B.Ed., 1960. *Home:* 657 Nelson Rd., Mount Nelson, Tasmania, Australia 7007.

CAREER: Teacher and librarian in New South Wales, Australia, 1946-52; British Council, London, England, bursar, 1953-58; Teachers' College, Launceston, Tasmania, Australia, lecturer, 1959-60; Teachers' College, Hobart, Tasmania, warden, lecturer in charge of academic subjects, 1962—. Writer for children. *Member:* Australian Federation of University Women, Australian Society of Authors, Fellowship of Australian Writers, Australian Journalists Association. *Awards, honors:* Australian Children's Book of the Year Award, 1962, for *Rafferty Rides a Winner.*

WRITINGS: Rafferty Takes to Fishing, Parrish, 1958; *Floodtide for Rafferty,* Parrish, 1959; *Rafferty Rides a Winner,* Parrish, 1961; *Rafferty Makes a Landfall,* Parrish, 1962; (with R. Yglesias and others) *Pleasure in English,* Longmans, Green, Book I, 1964, Book II, 1965; *Come Back Peter,* Rigby, 1968, Crowell, 1972; *Ash Tuesday,* Macmillan, 1969; *Little Black Swan,* Macmillan, 1970; *The Cider Duck,* Macmillan (Australia), 1969; *A Garland of Gannets,* Thomas Nelson (Australia), 1970; *Andrew Bent and the Freedom of the Press in Van Diemen's Land,* Fullers Bookshop, 1972; *Historic Hobart Sketchbook,* Rigby, 1976. Contributor to *English in Australia* and *Tasmanian Journal of Education.*

WORK IN PROGRESS: Children's fiction, *My Friend Rafferty* and *All in the Summer Weather.*

AVOCATIONAL INTERESTS: Water-color painting, gardening.

BIOGRAPHICAL/CRITICAL SOURCES: Times Literary Supplement, October 16, 1969, April 4, 1970.†

* * *

WOOLLEY, Catherine   1904-
(Jane Thayer)

PERSONAL: Born August 11, 1904, in Chicago, Ill.; daughter of Edward Mott (an author) and Anna L. (Thayer) Woolley. *Education:* University of California, Los Angeles, A.B. *Politics:* Democrat. *Religion:* Protestant. *Home:* Higgins Hollow Rd., Truro, Mass. 02666.

CAREER: American Radiator Co., New York City, advertising copywriter, 1927-30; free-lance writer, New York City, 1930-33; American Radiator & Standard Corp., New York City, copywriter, publicity, and house organ editor, 1933-40; *Architectural Record,* New York City, desk editor, 1940-42; *Society of Automotive Engineers Journal,* New York City, production editor, 1942-43; National Association of Manufacturers, New York City, public relations writer, 1943-47. Member of Passaic Redevelopment Agency, 1952-53, and of Passaic Board of Education, 1953-56; teacher of juvenile writing, Cape Cod Writers' Conference, 1965, 1966; conductor of workshop in juvenile writing, Truro Center for the Arts, 1977. Trustee, Truro Public Libraries, 1974—; member of board of directors, Day Nursery of Passaic. *Member:* Authors League of America, League of Women Voters (president, Passaic league, 1950-53), Kenilworth Society, Volunteers for A.I.M., Friends of Truro Libraries, Truro Historical Society. *Awards, honors:* New Jersey Association of Teachers of English, New Jersey children's book writer of 1964, for *Quiet on Account of Dinosaur.*

WRITINGS—All published by Morrow, except as indicated: *I Like Trains,* Harper, 1944, revised edition, 1965; *Two Hundred Pennies,* 1947; *Ginnie and Geneva,* 1948; *David's Railroad,* 1949; *Schoolroom Zoo,* 1950; *Railroad Cowboy,* 1951; *Ginnie Joins In,* 1951; *David's Hundred Dollars,* 1952; *Lunch for Lennie,* 1952; *The Little Car That Wanted a Garage,* Grosset, 1952; *The Animal Train and Other Stories,* 1953; *Holiday on Wheels,* 1953; *Ginnie and the New Girl,* 1954; *Ellie's Problem Dog,* 1955; *A Room for Cathy,* 1956; *Ginnie and the Mystery House,* 1957; *Miss Cathy Leonard,* 1958; *David's Campaign Buttons,* 1959; *Ginnie and the Mystery Doll,* 1960; *Cathy Leonard Calling,* 1961; *Look Alive, Libby!,* 1962; *Ginnie and Her Juniors,* 1963; *Cathy's Little Sister,* 1964; *Libby Looks for a Spy,* 1965; *The Shiny Red Rubber Boots,* 1965; *Ginnie and the Cooking Contest,* 1966; *Ginnie and the Wedding Bells,* 1967; *Chris in Trouble,* 1968; *Ginnie and the Mystery Cat,* 1969;*

Libby's Uninvited Guest, 1970; *Cathy and the Beautiful People,* 1971; *Cathy Uncovers a Secret,* 1972; *Ginnie and the Mystery Light,* 1973; *Libby Shadows a Lady,* 1974; *Ginnie and Geneva Cookbook,* 1975.

Under pseudonym Jane Thayer; all published by Morrow, except as indicated: *The Horse with the Easter Bonnet,* 1953; *The Popcorn Dragon,* 1953; *Where's Andy?,* 1954; *Mrs. Perrywinkle's Pets,* 1955; *Sandy and the Seventeen Balloons,* 1955; *The Chicken in the Tunnel,* 1956; *The Outside Cat,* 1957; *Charley and the New Car,* 1957; *Andy Wouldn't Talk,* 1958; *The Puppy Who Wanted a Boy,* 1958; *Funny Stories to Read Aloud,* Grosset, 1958; *The Second-Story Giraffe,* 1959; *Little Monkey,* 1959.

Andy and His Fine Friends, 1960; *The Pussy Who Went to the Moon,* 1960; *A Little Dog Called Kitty,* 1961; *The Blueberry Pie Elf,* 1961; *Andy's Square-Blue Animal,* 1962; *Gus Was a Friendly Ghost,* 1962; *A Drink for Little Red Diker,* 1963; *Andy and the Runaway Horse,* 1963; *Quiet on Account of Dinosaur,* 1964; *Emerald Enjoyed the Moonlight,* 1964; *Bunny in the Honeysuckle Patch,* 1965; *The Part-Time Dog,* 1965; *The Lighthearted Wolf,* 1966; *What's a Ghost Going to Do?,* 1966; *Rockets Don't Go to Chicago, Andy,* 1967; *A Contrary Little Quail,* 1968; *Little Mr. Greenthumb,* 1968; *Andy and Mr. Cunningham,* 1969; *Curious, Furious Chipmunk,* 1969.

I'm Not a Cat, Said Emerald, 1970; *Gus Was a Christmas Ghost,* 1970; *Mr. Turtle's Magic Glasses,* 1971; *Timothy and Madam Mouse,* 1971; *Gus and the Baby Ghost,* 1972; *The Little House,* 1972; *Andy and the Wild Worm,* 1973; *Gus Was a Mexican Ghost,* 1974; *I Don't Believe in Elves,* 1975; *The Mouse on the Fourteenth Floor,* 1977; *Gus Was a Gorgeous Ghost,* 1978; *Where Is Squirrel?,* 1979; *Applebaums Have a Robot,* 1980; *Clever Raccoon,* 1980. Contributor to juvenile anthologies, school readers, and juvenile magazines.

*   *   *

WOUK, Herman 1915-

PERSONAL: Surname is pronounced *woke;* born May 27, 1915, in New York, N.Y.; son of Abraham Isaac (an industrialist in the power laundry field who started as an immigrant laundry laborer at $3 a week) and Esther (Levine) Wouk; married Betty Sarah Brown, December 9, 1945; children: Abraham Isaac (deceased), Nathaniel, Joseph. *Education:* Columbia University, B.A. (with honors), 1934. *Religion:* Jewish. *Agent:* BSW Literary Agency, 3255 N St. N.W., Washington, D.C. 20007.

CAREER: Gagman for radio comedians, New York, N.Y., 1934-35; scriptwriter for the late Fred Allen, 1936-41; U.S. Treasury Department, "dollar-a-year-man," writing and producing radio plays to promote war bond sales, 1941; self-employed writer, 1946—. Visiting professor, Yeshiva University, 1953-57; scholar-in-residence, Aspen Institute of Humanistic Studies, 1973-74. Trustee, College of the Virgin Islands, 1962-69; member of board of directors, Washington National Symphony, 1969-71, and Kennedy Center Productions, 1974-75. *Military service:* U.S. Navy, 1942-46; served in Pacific aboard two destroyer-minesweepers, U.S.S. *Zane* and U.S.S. *Southard;* became lieutenant; awarded four campaign stars and Presidential Unit Citation. *Member:* Authors Guild, Authors League of America, P.E.N., Dramatists Guild, Reserve Officers Association of the United States, Writers Guild of America East, Century Club (New York City), Bohemian Club (San Francisco); Cosmos Club, Metropolitan Club (both Washington, D.C.).

AWARDS, HONORS: Richard H. Fox Prize, 1934; Pulitzer Prize in fiction, 1952, for *The Caine Mutiny: A Novel of World War II;* Columbia University Medal of Excellence, 1952; L.H.D., Yeshiva University, 1955; LL.D., Clark University, 1960; Litt.D., American International University, 1979; Alexander Hamilton Medal, Columbia College Alumni Association, 1980; American Book Award nomination, 1981, for *War and Remembrance;* Ralph Waldo Emerson Award, International Platform Association, 1981.

WRITINGS: Aurora Dawn; or The True History of Andrew Reale, Containing a Faithful Account of the Great Riot, Together with the Complete Texts of Michael Wilde's Oration and Father Stanfield's Sermon (novel; Book-of-the-Month Club selection), Simon & Schuster, 1947; *The City Boy: The Adventures of Herbie Bookbinder and His Cousin, Cliff* (novel; Reader's Digest Condensed Book Club selection; Family Book Club selection; Book-of-the-Month Club alternate selection), Simon & Schuster, 1948, published as *The City Boy,* Doubleday, 1952, published as *City Boy: The Adventures of Herbie Bookbinder,* Doubleday, 1969; *The Caine Mutiny: A Novel of World War II* (Reader's Digest Condensed Book Club selection; Literary Guild alternate selection), Doubleday, 1951, reprinted, Franklin Library, 1977, published as *The Caine Mutiny,* Dell, 1966; *Marjorie Morningstar* (novel; Reader's Digest Condensed Book Club selection; Book-of-the-Month Club selection), Doubleday, 1955, reprinted, Pocket Books, 1977; *This Is My God* (nonfiction; Reader's Digest Condensed Book Club selection; Book-of-the-Month Club alternate selection), Doubleday, 1959, published as *This Is My God: The Jewish Way of Life,* 1970, revised edition, Collins, 1973; *Youngblood Hawke* (novel; Reader's Digest Condensed Book Club selection; Book-of-the-Month Club selection), Doubleday, 1962; *Don't Stop the Carnival* (novel; Book-of-the-Month Club selection), Doubleday, 1965; *The "Lomokome" Papers,* Pocket Books, 1968; *The Winds of War* (novel; Literary Guild selection; Reader's Digest Condensed Book Club selection), Little, Brown, 1971; *War and Remembrance* (novel; sequel to *The Winds of War;* Literary Guild selection; Reader's Digest Condensed Book Club selection), Little, Brown, 1978.

Plays: *The Traitor* (two-act; first produced on Broadway at Forty-Eighth Street Theater, April 4, 1949), Samuel French, 1949; *The Caine Mutiny Court-Martial* (two-act; based on his novel *The Caine Mutiny;* first produced in Santa Barbara, Calif., 1953; produced on Broadway at Plymouth Theater, January 20, 1954), Doubleday, 1954, reprinted, Pocket Books, 1974; *Slattery's Hurricane* (screenplay; produced by Twentieth Century-Fox, 1949), Permabooks, 1956; *Nature's Way* (two-act comedy; first produced on Broadway at Coronet Theater, October 15, 1957), Doubleday, 1958, reprinted, Samuel French, 1977. Also author of screenplay "The Winds of War," ABC-TV.

SIDELIGHTS: An American novelist and playwright of Russian-Jewish heritage, Herman Wouk received the 1952 Pulitzer Prize in fiction for *The Caine Mutiny: A Novel of World War II* and has since published several other best-sellers, including *The Winds of War* and *War and Remembrance.* The *Atlantic's* Edward Weeks calls him a compelling narrator "who uses large canvases and who, without much fuss for style or symbolism, drives his story ahead with an infectious belief in the people he is writing about." According to a reviewer for *Time,* Wouk's chief significance is that "he spearheads a mutiny against the literary stereotypes of rebellion—against three decades of U.S. fiction dominated by skeptical criticism, sexual emancipation, social protest, and psychoanalytic sermonizing." He remains, writes Pearl K. Bell in *Commentary,* "an unembarrassed believer in such 'discredited' forms of commitment as valor, gallantry, leadership, patriotism." Because of the reaffirmation of traditional values in his works, Wouk has enjoyed wide readership but has also been accused by some critics of pandering to popular prejudice.

Wouk began writing fiction in 1943 while on sea duty in the Pacific, and he later used his Navy experience aboard the U.S.S. *Zane* and U.S.S. *Southard* as background for his third novel, *The Caine Mutiny* (which is not autobiographical). The book is not concerned with battles at sea but with adherence to appointive authority. The conflict centers around Lieutenant Commander Philip Francis Queeg, who, according to W. J. Stuckey in *The Pulitzer Prize Novels,* "manifests a professional incompetence that will probably remain unparalleled in or out of fiction." When it appears that Queeg is too terrified to issue the necessary orders to save the ship during a typhoon, Lieutenant Maryk, the ship's executive officer, is persuaded by Lieutenant Keefer and his followers to seize control. Maryk is subsequently tried but is acquitted through the efforts of Lieutenant Barney Greenwald, an adept trial lawyer. Ironically, at a party celebrating Maryk's acquittal, Greenwald tells Maryk that it is he, Maryk, (and not Queeg) who is morally guilty, for he deserted a military system that had, despite its flaws, protected America from foreign fascists.

Several critics consider Wouk's treatment of the military affair insightful and carefully constructed. Harry Gilroy, for example, writes in the *New York Times* that Wouk "has a profound understanding of what Navy men should be, and against some who fell short of the mark he has fired a deadly broadside." Edmund Fuller points out in his *Man in Modern Fiction* that the book's ability "to view the problem within the inescapable military premise without oversimplifying it" distinguishes *The Caine Mutiny* from other World War II novels. Discussing the justification of the mutiny in his *In My Opinion,* Orville Prescott says that it is "the crux of [the novel, and] Mr. Wouk develops it extremely well, with racy wit and genial humor, with lively pace and much ingenuity of incident and with unexpected subtlety." Similarly, a reviewer for the *Times Literary Supplement* concludes: "So convincingly has Mr. Wouk created his officers, so subtly has he contrived the series of incidents that culminate in the final drama, that, given both the characters and the situations, the climax is perfectly acceptable."

W. J. Stuckey, however, sees the climax as "the unwarranted whitewash" of Queeg: "Throughout three-fourths of the novel, Captain Queeg is a thoroughly incompetent and badly frightened man. However, toward the close of the book Wouk springs a wholly unprepared-for surprise: Queeg, he tells us, is not really the incompetent everyone thinks him; he is the victim of ambitious and cowardly subordinates. . . . While it is easy to understand the reason for Lieutenant Greenwald's emotional defense of the United States Navy, it is difficult to see why he—an intelligent trial lawyer, we are told—defends an incompetent American ship's captain who had not served in the Atlantic and who, if he had encountered Nazi warships, would have fled in terror. Greenwald's only defense of Queeg is that he was a member of the regular navy. It would make as much sense to defend a doctor guilty of malpractice on the grounds that he engaged in a humane calling. . . . The war in Europe and Hitler's treatment of the Jews had nothing to do with Queeg's or Maryk's innocence or guilt."

Eric Bentley finds the same weakness in *The Caine Mutiny Court Martial,* Wouk's play based on the court martial sequence of the novel. Discussing the theme that the important thing is not to save a particular ship but to preserve the authority of commanders, Bentley writes in *The New Republic:* "There is a good point here, and there must surely be a good play in it—a play that would show up the sentimentality of our prej-

udice against commanders and in favor of mutineers. If, however, Mr. Wouk wanted to write such a play, he chose the wrong story and told it in the wrong way, for we spend three quarters of the evening hoping that Queeg—the commander—will be found insane and the mutineers vindicated. When, in the very last scene, Mr. Wouk explains that this is not the right way to take the story, it is too late. We don't believe him. At best we say that he is preaching at us a notion that ought to have been dramatized. And no amount of shock technique—not even the reiterated image of Jews melted down for soap—can conceal the flaw."

Marjorie Morningstar, Wouk's fourth novel, also focuses on rebellion but in a civilian context. The book traces the life of a beautiful, intelligent girl who renounces the values and authority of her hard-working Jewish parents only to end up, years later, affirming them as a suburban matron and community servant. E. W. Foell notes in the *Christian Science Monitor* that Wouk "has not flinched at what he sees in his characters' thoughts, [but] many of his readers are likely to." A *Time* critic writes that, indeed, "Wouk [sets] teeth on edge by advocating chastity before marriage, suggesting that real happiness for a woman is found in a home and children, cheering loud and long for the American middle class and blasting Bohemia and Bohemians. Wouk is a Sinclair Lewis in reverse." Reviewing the book in the *New York Times,* Maxwell Geismar believes that "here as in *The Caine Mutiny* [the conflict] is settled by a final bow to the red-tape of a bureaucracy or to the properties of a social class, under the impression that these are among the eternal verities. *Marjorie Morningstar* is very good reading indeed. But to this reviewer at least the values of true culture are as remote from its polished orbit as are, at base, the impulses of real life."

Leslie A. Fiedler, however, sees the most popular novel of 1955 as untraditional in one regard. In *Love and Death in the American Novel,* Fiedler calls *Marjorie Morningstar* "the first fictional celebration of the mid-twentieth-century detente between the Jews and middle-class America." He explains: "In the high literature of Europe and, more slowly, in that of the United States, gentile and Jew have joined forces to portray the Jewish character as a figure representing man's fate in . . . an age of rootlessness, alienation, and terror, in which the exiled condition so long thought peculiar to the Jew comes to seem the common human lot. This is neither a cheery nor a reassuring view. . . . Wouk [suggests] a counterview: the contention that the Jew was never (or is, at least, no longer) the rootless dissenter, the stranger which legend has made him, but rather the very paragon of the happy citizen at home, loyal, chaste, thrifty, pious, and moderately successful—in short, . . . Marjorie Morningstar."

After *Marjorie Morningstar,* Wouk interrupted his career as a novelist to write a short, clear account of the Jewish faith from a personal viewpoint—something he had been thinking of doing for years. Dedicated to the memory of his grandfather, Mendel Leib Levine, a rabbi from Minsk, *This Is My God* was published in 1959 and became a best-seller. Then, with *Youngblood Hawke* and *Don't Stop the Carnival,* Wouk returned to writing fiction, but he also began work on a second ambition: a panoramic novel of World War II.

Wouk first considered doing a global war novel in 1944, according to *Time*'s Timothy Foote. Later, *The Caine Mutiny* "threatened to sprawl in that direction," notes Foote, "with more home-front material and a subplot in Europe. Wisely, Wouk cut it back and waited." Having begun reading standard histories in 1962, Wouk moved to Washington two years later to utilize the National Archives and Library of Congress, as well as to interview surviving military leaders. His quest for information also led him to England, France, Italy, Germany, Poland, Czechoslovakia, Israel, Iran, and the Soviet Union. Due to the scope of his task, Wouk ended up writing not one but two novels: *The Winds of War* and a sequel, *War and Remembrance*. "Since both have been best sellers, it is likely that more Americans have learned about, or remembered, the war through Wouk's account than from any other single source in the last decade," claims Michael Mandelbaum in *Political Science Quarterly*.

Generally praised by critics for their depth and accuracy of detail, the two books may be described as the history of the Second World War seen through the eyes of an American family and their immediate friends and contacts. *The Winds of War* takes Commander Victor "Pug" Henry and his family from the invasion of Poland to the attack on Pearl Harbor, and *War and Remembrance* details their experiences from Pearl Harbor to Hiroshima. Over the course of the war, Henry serves as a special presidential envoy; meets Hitler, Stalin, Churchill, and Mussolini; is in Hawaii the day after the attack on Pearl Harbor; is present at the summit meetings off Nova Scotia in 1940 and in Teheran in 1943; is in London during the Battle of Britain; accompanies the Harriman-Beaverbrook mission to Moscow in 1941; participates in the battles of Midway, Guadalcanal, and Leyte Gulf; tours the Russian front in 1944; and even comes in contact with people working on the Manhattan project. What he fails to witness, members of his family see: the invasion of Poland, the war in North Africa, the fall of Singapore, and the horrors of Auschwitz.

In reviewing the two books, critics often point out that this technique of depicting the effects of war on ordinary people (some of whom rub shoulders with the high and mighty) is a familiar one. Timothy Foote, among others, suggests that Wouk's opus is reminiscent of *War and Peace*—though not of the same quality—and that Wouk's aim is "nothing less than to do for the middle-class American vision of World War II pretty much what Tolstoy did for the Battle of Borodino." More often, however, reviewers like Granville Hicks of the *New York Times Book Review* cite the resemblance between "Pug" Henry and Upton Sinclair's Lanny Budd: "Like Lanny, Pug becomes a kind of secret Presidential agent. In this role, he turns up at most of the places where history is being made."

Several critics charge that the technique results in characterization that is purely functional. Though Hicks admits that Wouk has "the gift of compelling narrative," he feels that the characters in *The Winds of War*, "even Pug Henry, are never living human beings. Although [Wouk] tries to give these men and women some semblance of reality by involving them in more or less complicated love affairs, they remain essentially observers and reporters." Similarly, Pearl K. Bell, reviewing *War and Remembrance* in *Commentary*, describes the characters as "not merely trivial but offensively so. Time and again, Wouk the student of history writes a brilliantly evocative account of battle—he has mastered every maneuver, knows exactly how submarines, aircraft carriers, battleships, destroyers, dive bombers work, how the vast machinery of war was deployed during a particular operation—only to return with a dismaying thump to his super-Lanny Budd hero, Captain (eventually Admiral) Victor (Pug) Henry." Foote is willing "to forgive Henry, and the author, the narrative necessities that shoot [Henry] hither and yon and miraculously equip him with the Russian and German necessary to do his work for Wouk, F.D.R., and the reader. [But] not so the other Henrys. The wife who would worry about getting her hair done on the day of Armageddon, a wayward daughter caught up in the sleazy radio industry in New York, two naval-officer sons, all are

conventional appurtenances, without the emotional or dynastic depth to support a drama on the scale of World War II."

Nevertheless, Michael Mandelbaum asserts that Wouk's aim was to create something not purely fictional and that his "hybrid literary genre" of historical romance "turns out to be singularly appropriate." Other critics agree. Reviewing *The Winds of War* in the *Midwest Quarterly*, Richard R. Bolton writes: "Critics who have castigated the book for failing in various ways as a *novel* have seemingly overlooked the author's description of it as a romance. That form is older, and adheres to rather different standards, than the novel. Much criticism directed at the book's emphasis of incident and plot over deep character development, or its unfashionably detailed descriptions of people's appearances, becomes immaterial if one accepts Wouk's idea of what *The Winds of War* is—a historical romance, with a didactic purpose. That purpose is to dramatize the author's ideas about his themes—how the 'curse' emerged, how we might constructively understand it, and how 'men of good will' have been involved with it."

A major theme of the two books, according to Mandelbaum, "centers on the German question. Why did the Germans do it? Why did they cause so much trouble? Why, especially, did they behave in such brutal, aggressive fashion? These questions arise again and again, and Wouk has different characters give different answers—[geopolitical, political, cultural, historical]. Together they make for a symposium on the central puzzle of the twentieth century." Mandelbaum suggests that at the heart of the German question is the fate of the Jews under the Third Reich, the description of which "gives the two books their enduring message, a message that neither plain fiction nor standard history could convey as forcefully. It is not, [however,] the only, nor perhaps the primary, message that the author intends."

Wouk widens the scope of the story by presenting a German perspective on the war through excerpts of General Armin von Roon's *World Empire Lost,* an imaginary treatise based on actual writings of German generals. Bolton claims that von Roon's views, "and (in places) Henry's 'later' comments on them, jolt the reader out of enough preconceptions to make him more receptive to Wouk's own explanations of why things turned out as they did, or (more important) *how* they might have been made to turn out better." Bolton surmises that, according to Wouk, World War II was a "natural" disaster in that it arose from fallible human nature: "Human cruelty, of which war is the most massive and spectacular manifestation, occurs not because most people are cruel, but because most people are weak or lazy, or too wishful to perceive in time what truly cruel people like the Nazis are about. . . . Given that fallibility, World War II, and possibly other wars since, probably could not have been avoided." But, he continues, "given also the availability of enough men with the training and virtues of Victor Henry—the truly 'best' in Wouk's view, those who do not lack conviction—that war, and possibly others since, could have been ameliorated, at least. It was not ameliorated, because democratic societies, notably ours, have little stomach for the unpleasant facts that are a military professional's daily fare."

Thus, Bolton discerns a thematic relation to *The Caine Mutiny:* "Captain Henry can be seen as the fulfillment and justification of Lt. Barney Greenwald's unexpected and much discussed encomium to Regular Navy officers in the post-trial scene of *The Caine Mutiny*. Greenwald pays his tributes not so much to the *Caine*'s fallen captain as to what-Queeg-could-have-been . . .—the selfless and dedicated guardian of a reckless and unappreciative nation's safety. In Henry, Wouk presents a man who really *is* what Queeg could only try, pretend, or fail to be, the 'compleat' and admirable United States Navy officer.'' Pearl K. Bell believes that Wouk's traditionalist support of the military career man will strike many ''as at best naive, at worst absurdly out of touch with the Catch-22 lunacy of all war, including the war against Hitler. [However,] it is precisely to confute such facile and ahistorical cynicism that Wouk devotes so large and sober a part of his novel to the Final Solution and the ideological poison that overwhelmed the German people during Hitler's twelve years of power.''

In Wouk's eyes, men like Victor Henry, writes Bolton, have instincts and habits that ''predispose them to be builders and preservers. . . . 'Constructive' rather than creative, they build things that are not particularly original, but are for Wouk the cement of civilization—families, homes, churches, firms, and especially, professional reputations. What repels Capt. Henry first about Nazi racism is that it destroys these things, and judges men on factors other than their accomplishments. Only after learning of the *Einsatzgruppen*'s atrocities does he react to Nazi racism with more visceral rage.'' Referring to the one-word Hebrew epigraph of *The Winds of War,* ''Remember!,'' Bolton concludes: ''Part of remembering, in Wouk's sense, would be to emulate Victor Henry and to listen, early and attentively, to those men who live in his tradition. If we do not, the author suggests, . . . it becomes too easy to look away, to make excuses while the massacres begin, while terrorism becomes pardonable.''

MEDIA ADAPTATIONS: The Caine Mutiny has been translated into more than a dozen languages and was filmed by Columbia in 1954, starring Humphrey Bogart as Captain Queeg. A television adaptation of *The Caine Mutiny Court Martial,* with Barry Sullivan, Lloyd Nolan, and Frank Lovejoy, aired on ''Ford Star Jubilee'' in 1955. *The City Boy* was made into a motion picture by Columbia in 1950, and Warner Bros. filmed *Marjorie Morningstar* and *Youngblood Hawke* in 1958 and 1964, respectively.

AVOCATIONAL INTERESTS: Judaic scholarship, Zionist studies, travel (especially in Israel).

CA INTERVIEW

CA interviewed Herman Wouk in April, 1981.

CA: In addition to the 1952 Pulitzer Prize for fiction for The Caine Mutiny, *you've won other awards—for military performance as well as writing—and several honorary degrees. Is there one honor that has meant more to you than the others?*

WOUK: I was very moved by the Alexander Hamilton Medal, which I received in November 1980.

[The Alexander Hamilton Medal is awarded annually by the Columbia College Alumni Association of Columbia University to a living alumnus or a present or former member of the faculty ''for recognition of distinguished service and accomplishment in any field of human endeavor.'']

CA: You began your writing career as a gagman for radio comedians and worked for Fred Allen for five years. Did you think much during that time about writing fiction?

WOUK: During my Fred Allen years my aspiration was, quite naturally, to write Broadway farces—an ambition I briefly realized much later in my career, with the not very successful play *Nature's Way,* produced by Alfred de Liagre in 1957. I gave no thought whatever to writing fiction. During my four years at sea in World War II, I wrote several comedies to while away the time. One of them, *Aurora Dawn,* I transformed into my first novel. Intensive reading of novels at sea, especially the classics, gave me the idea of trying to write books.

CA: In an enthusiastic Commonweal *(June 29, 1962) review of* Youngblood Hawke, *William James Smith wrote, ''Herman Wouk is the only living nineteenth century novelist.'' You have yourself spoken and written about the opposite trend in contemporary literature, the experimental literary current you have chosen to swim against. Why do you think this trend has enjoyed such continued critical favor? Do you foresee its diminishing in the near future?*

WOUK: The modernist tradition in the novel reached its height very early in Joyce, Proust, Virginia Woolf, and Kafka, who themselves swam against the stream of the prevailing criticism. The modernists broadened and enriched our literature, and there is no going back to ''the nineteenth century'' as such. But serious younger writers seem to be returning to narrative, which modernism set aside, and which is at the heart of classic novel writing.

CA: Do you ever have the urge to return to writing comedy in any form?

WOUK: My novel *Don't Stop the Carnival* (1965) is a return to comedy. There are decided comic elements in my present work in progress; and also, of course, in *Marjorie Morningstar* and *The Caine Mutiny.*

CA: World War II and the Holocaust were major factors in the shaping of your literary consciousness. Do you think the books and television productions arising from recent renewed interest in the Holocaust have generally conveyed much of its reality?

WOUK: It is very early to judge these matters. The massacre of the European Jews by the German government in the 1940s is perhaps the most staggering event in human history. The world has yet to come to grips with it. In my sixteen-year labor of *The Winds of War* and *War and Remembrance,* my aim was only to show the thing as it happened, in a frame of global war. Historians, artists, thinkers, and politicians will be grappling with this gigantic horror for centuries, and meantime the main task is to ensure that it is never forgotten. Certainly that is why I wrote my books.

CA: Those sixteen years of research and writing included visits to major World War II sites and a quick course in Russian. What were the biggest research problems? What kind of feeling did you have after the long project was finished?

WOUK: The major research problem was *time;* the sense that I had taken on a task that might easily consume a long human life and yet remain undone. Planning the time and the labor so that I would live to complete the books was the besetting problem. When I finished, I was numb with gratitude to God because I had lasted the course.

The time problem was so oppressive because of the scope of the undertaking. I had committed myself to creating a historical framework for the human drama, which would measure up to the requirements of serious historians, and yet would correlate all the important war theaters as a single complex ongoing reality; somewhat as Franklin Roosevelt and Hitler must have regarded the situation, each from his own perspective. Or to put it another way, I wanted the reader to see the global war with the eye of God, in a way not possible at the time even to those world leaders, because of the fog of war.

There was no way to do this except with massive research, together with much travel and interviewing. In the end I gathered a World War II reference library of nearly two thousand volumes, and I visited nine countries, including the month in the Soviet Union and two long visits to Auschwitz. The book collection I have since donated to Columbia University's Butler Library, where I have deposited most of my papers over the years.

CA: So far there is a very small body of literature—even if we include movies and television productions—arising from the Vietnam War. Do you have any ideas on why this is true and whether the literature will increase?

WOUK: I, too, am puzzled by the small amount of art arising as yet from the Vietnam War. Some of it has been splendid. The film "The Deer Hunter" I consider one of the triumphs of the American cinema. There will be more and more art about that strange and important war, as time lends perspective to it.

CA: You sold your house in Saint Thomas in the mid-1960s and moved to Washington, D.C. Do you work better or more easily in a city environment?

WOUK: Working in a city is definitely harder. I moved to Washington in 1964 because of its research resources for *The Winds of War* and *War and Remembrance*. In 1972 I acquired a country home in Middleburg, Virginia, about an hour from Washington, and I wrote most of *War and Remembrance* there.

CA: Do you still do a lot of revision?

WOUK: I write in longhand. I get the words down on impulse and refine as I go in draft after draft. According to my wife—who is my agent and also types my early drafts—I revise and refine to tremendous excess. "You can't leave a clean page alone." She may well be right. I keep trying to modify this long-standing tendency, but I revised some chapters in *War and Remembrance* ten or fifteen times. I, too, call that excessive.

CA: You've expressed some interest in the preservation of endangered animal species. Are you actively involved in this cause?

WOUK: Mrs. Wouk and I actively support the wildlife preservation movement, but are not officers or committee members.

CA: How much of your personal and professional stability would you attribute to the strong family bonds that have marked your life?

WOUK: All of it. The work I have done and am doing is the product of a very strictly ordered and retired existence, which is a joy instead of a burden because of my pleasure in my family.

BIOGRAPHICAL/CRITICAL SOURCES—Periodicals: *Saturday Review of Literature,* April 19, 1947, August 21, 1948, March 31, 1951; *New York Herald Tribune Weekly Book Review,* April 20, 1947, August 29, 1948; *New York Times,* April 20, 1947, August 29, 1948, March 18, 1951, September 4, 1955, September 27, 1959; *Chicago Sunday Tribune,* March 18, 1951; *New York Herald Tribune Book Review,* March 18, 1951, September 4, 1955, May 20, 1962; *Time,* April 9, 1951,

September 5, 1955, May 18, 1962, March 5, 1965, November 22, 1971, October 16, 1978; *Atlantic,* August, 1951, October, 1955, December, 1971; *New York Times Book Review,* September 16, 1951, May 20, 1962, November 14, 1971, November 12, 1978; *Times Literary Supplement,* November 9, 1951; *Vogue,* February 15, 1952; *Partisan Review,* Volume XX, 1953; *Saturday Review,* February 6, 1954, September 3, 1955, September 26, 1959, May 19, 1962, November 27, 1971; *New Republic,* February 15, 1954, September 3, 1955, June 11, 1962, October 14, 1978.

Christian Science Monitor, September 1, 1955, September 24, 1959, May 24, 1962, October 23, 1978; *Antioch Review,* Volume XVI, 1956; *College English,* Volume XVII, 1956; *Life,* June, 1962, November 19, 1971; *Book Week,* March 7, 1965; *Newsweek,* March 8, 1965, November 29, 1971, October 9, 1978; *Critic,* August, 1965; *New York,* August 30, 1971; *Chicago Tribune Book World,* November 14, 1971; *Economist,* November 20, 1971; *Publishers Weekly,* February 7, 1972; *Midwest Quarterly,* July, 1975; *Washington Post Book World,* October 8, 1978; *Commentary,* December, 1978.

Books: Orville Prescott, *In My Opinion,* Bobbs-Merrill, 1952; Eric Bentley, *The Dramatic Event: An American Chronicle,* Horizon Press, 1954; Edmund Fuller, *Man in Modern Fiction: Some Minority Opinions on Contemporary American Writing,* Random House, 1958; Maxwell Geismar, *American Moderns from Rebellion to Conformity,* Hill & Wang, 1958; Leslie A. Fiedler, *Love and Death in the American Novel,* Stein & Day, 1966; Stanley Edgar Hyman, *Standards: A Chronicle of Books for Our Time,* Horizon Press, 1966; W. J. Stuckey, *The Pulitzer Prize Novels,* University of Oklahoma Press, 1966; *Contemporary Literary Criticism,* Gale, Volume I, 1973, Volume IX, 1978.

—*Sketch by James G. Lesniak*

—*Interview by Jean W. Ross*

*   *   *

WRIGHT, Esmond 1915-

PERSONAL: Born November 5, 1915, in Newcastle-on-Tyne, England; son of Esmond and Isabella (Gray) Wright; married Olive Adamson, 1945. *Education:* University of Durham, England, B.A., 1937, M.A., 1948; University of Virginia, M.A., 1940. *Home:* 31 Tavistock Sq., London WC1H 9E2, England. *Agent:* Curtis Brown Ltd., 1 Craven Hill, London W2 3EW, England. *Office:* University of London, Senate House, London W.C.1, England.

CAREER: University of Glasgow, Glasgow, Scotland, lecturer, 1946-51, senior lecturer, 1951-57, professor of modern history, 1957-67; member of Parliament, Pollok division of Glasgow, 1967-70; University of London, London, England, professor of American history and director of Institute of U.S. Studies, 1971—. Visiting lecturer in United States, 1948, 1952, 1961, 1963, 1968, 1973, and 1976. *Military service:* British Army, Intelligence, 1941-46; became colonel; served in Middle East. *Awards, honors:* Rockefeller fellow, Yale University, 1961.

WRITINGS: Short History of Our Own Times, 1919-1950, F. Watts, 1951; *Washington and the American Revolution,* English Universities Press, 1957; *Fabric of Freedom: 1763-1800,* Hill & Wang, 1961, revised edition, 1978; *The World Today,* Grant, 1961, 4th edition, McGraw, 1979; (editor with Kenneth Stampp) *Illustrated World History,* McGraw, 1964; *Benjamin Franklin and American Independence,* English Universities Press, 1966; *The Causes and Consequences of the American Revo-*

lution, Quadrangle Books, 1966; *A Time for Courage,* Dutton, 1971; (editor) *A Tug of Loyalties,* Athlone Press, 1975; (editor) *Red, White, and True Blue,* A.M.S. Press, 1977; (with Alasdair Nicolson) *Europe Today,* McGraw, 1979. Contributor to professional journals.

WORK IN PROGRESS: Benjamin Franklin.

SIDELIGHTS: Esmond Wright appears regularly on British Broadcasting Corp. programs.

*   *   *

WRIGHT, John S(herman) 1920-

PERSONAL: Born May 2, 1920, in Casselton, N.D.; son of John C. (a businessman) and Elizabeth (Sherman) Wright; married Jacqueline J. Goldsmith, April 2, 1955; children: John Kenneth, Anne Elizabeth. *Education:* University of North Dakota, Ph.B., 1942; University of Southern California, M.B.A., 1949; Ohio State University, Ph.D., 1954. *Politics:* Republican. *Religion:* Presbyterian. *Home:* 4021 Menlo Dr., Doraville, Ga. 30340. *Office:* Department of Marketing, Georgia State University, University Plaza, Atlanta, Ga. 30303.

CAREER: Montana State University, Missoula, instructor, 1949-51, associate professor, 1951-56, professor of marketing, 1956-60; San Diego State College (now San Diego State University), San Diego, Calif., associate professor of marketing, 1952-56; Northwestern University, Evanston, Ill., visiting professor, 1960-61, associate professor of advertising, 1961-64; University of Illinois at Chicago Circle, professor of marketing, 1965-67; United States International University, Graduate School of Business Administration, San Diego, dean, 1967-69; Georgia State University, Atlanta, professor of marketing, 1969—, chairman of department, 1969-74. Consultant to business firms and trade associations. *Military service:* U.S. Army, 1942-46; became first lieutenant. *Member:* American Marketing Association, American Academy of Advertising, Phi Beta Kappa, Beta Gamma Sigma.

WRITINGS: (With W. S. Peters) *Tourist Travel and Expenditures in Montana,* Montana State Highway Commission, 1959; (with Leo Knowlton) *A Survey of Mail-Order Buying Habits in Missoula County,* Bureau of Business and Economic Research, Montana State University, 1961; (editor) *Modern Marketing Concepts,* Lenox, Inc., 1962; (with D. S. Warner) *Advertising,* McGraw, 1962, 5th edition (with Willis Winter and Sheri Zeigler), 1982; (editor with Warner) *Speaking of Advertising,* McGraw, 1963; (editor with J. L. Goldstrucker) *New Ideas for Successful Marketing,* American Marketing Association, 1966; (editor with Parks B. Dimsdale) *Pioneers in Marketing,* College of Business Administration, Georgia State University, 1974; (editor with John E. Mertes) *Advertising's Role in Society,* West Publishing, 1974; (with Carl M. Larson and Robert Weigand) *Basic Retailing,* Prentice-Hall, 1976, 2nd edition, 1982. Contributor of articles to marketing and advertising publications.

WORK IN PROGRESS: Sales Promotion's Role in the Marketing Process; Marketing Communications: Principles and Cases.

*   *   *

WRIGHT, Ronald (William Vernon) Selby 1908-

PERSONAL: Born June 12, 1908, in Scotland; son of Vernon Oswald and Anna Gilberta (Selby) Wright. *Education:* Edinburgh University, M.A., 1933. *Home:* Queen's House, Moray Pl., Edinburgh EH3 6BX, Scotland.

CAREER: St. Giles's Cathedral, Edinburgh, Scotland, reader, 1929-36; Glasgow Cathedral, Glasgow, Scotland, assistant minister, 1936; The Canongate, Kirk of the Holyroodhouse, Edinburgh, minister, 1936-77. Warden, Canongate Boys' Club, 1927-78; president, Scottish Association of Boys' Clubs, 1947—. Chaplain of Edinburgh Castle, 1936—, to the Queen in Scotland, 1961—, and to the Queen's bodyguard in Scotland; honorary chaplain to Her Majesty's Forces. Justice of the Peace, Edinburgh, 1963—; former chairman, Edinburgh and Leith Old People's Welfare Council; former director and chaplain, Queensbury House. Moderator of the Presbytery of Edinburgh, 1963, and of the Church of Scotland, 1972-73. Frequent special and visiting preacher at various schools and universities. Radio padre for the British Broadcasting Corp. and the British Army, 1942-47. *Military service:* British Army, chaplains' department, 1938-47. *Member:* Royal Society of Edinburgh (fellow), Athenaeum Club (London), New Club (Edinburgh). *Awards, honors:* D.D., Edinburgh University, 1956; chaplain, Order of St. John of Jerusalem; Commander of the Royal Victorian Order, 1968.

WRITINGS: (With A. W. Loos) *Asking Why,* Oxford University Press, 1939; *Daily Prayer,* Oxford University Press, 1942; *The Average Man,* Longmans, 1942; *The Greater Victory,* Longmans, 1943; *Let's Ask the Padre,* Oliver & Boyd, 1943; *The Padre Presents,* Oliver & Boyd, 1944; *Small Talks,* Longmans, 1945; *The Order of Divine Service,* Oliver & Boyd, 1947; *Whatever the Years,* Epworth, 1947; *What Worries Me,* Epworth, 1950; *Great Men,* Epworth, 1951; *Our Club,* Oliver & Boyd, 1954; *They Looked unto Him,* Layman, 1954; *The Beloved Captain,* Geoffrey Bles, 1956; *The Kirk in the Canongate,* Oliver & Boyd, 1956; *The Selfsame Miracles,* Layman, 1957; *Roses in December,* Blackwood, 1960; *The Morning Service on the Lord's Day,* Blackwood, 1961; *The Seven Words from the Cross,* Blackwood, 1965; *A Guide to the Canongate,* Oliver & Boyd, 1965; (contributor) *The Statistical Account of Scotland: Edinburgh Volume,* 1966; *Take Up God's Armour,* Oxford University Press, 1967; *In Christ We Are All One,* Blackwood, 1972; *Seven Sevens,* Scottish Academic Press, 1977; *Another Home* (autobiography), Blackwood, 1980.

Editor and contributor: *Asking Them Questions—First Series,* Oxford University Press, 1936; *I Attack,* Allenson, 1937; *Asking Them Questions—Second Series,* Oxford University Press, 1938; Studdert-Kennedy, *Why Aren't All the Best Chaps Christians?,* Hodder & Stoughton, 1939; *Front Line Religion,* Hodder & Stoughton, 1941; *Soldiers Also Asked,* Oxford University Press, 1943; *Asking Them Questions—Third Series,* Oxford University Press, 1950; *Asking Them Questions—A Selection,* Oxford University Press, 1953; (with R. A. Knox and L. Menzies) *St. Margaret Queen of Scotland and Her Chapel,* [Edinburgh], 1957; (with T. F. Torrance) *A Manual of Church Doctrine,* Oxford University Press, 1960; *Fathers of the Kirk,* Oxford University Press, 1960; *Asking Them Questions—New Series,* Oxford University Press, Part I, 1972, Part II, 1973. Contributor to theological and other journals and to encyclopedias. Editor, *Scottish Forces Magazine,* 1941-77.

WORK IN PROGRESS: A book on confirmation for use in schools.

AVOCATIONAL INTERESTS: The history of old Edinburgh, hut camping.

*   *   *

WRONE, David R(ogers) 1933-

PERSONAL: Born May 15, 1933, in Clinton, Ill.; son of Harold (a merchant) and Esther (a teacher; maiden name, Matthews)

Wrone; married Elaine Ethel Alley (a lecturer in sociology), August 25, 1964; children: Elizabeth Maliha, David Alley. *Education:* University of Illinois, B.A., 1959, M.A., 1960, Ph.D., 1964. *Home:* 1518 Blackberry Lane, Stevens Point, Wis. 54481. *Office:* Department of History, University of Wisconsin, Stevens Point, Wis. 54481.

CAREER: University of Wisconsin—Stevens Point, assistant professor, 1964-68, associate professor, 1968-75, professor of history, 1975—. Director of Nancy McElroy Davis History Fund. *Military service:* U.S. Army, 1954-55. *Member:* American Historical Association, Organization of American Historians, Society of American Hegelians, State Historical Society of Wisconsin, Illinois Historical Society.

WRITINGS: (Contributor) Clyde C. Walton, editor, *An Illinois Reader,* Northern Illinois University Press, 1970; (co-editor) *Who's the Savage?: A Documentary History of the Mistreatment of the Native North Americans,* Fawcett, 1973, revised edition, Robert E. Krieger, 1982; *The Assassination of John Fitzgerald Kennedy: An Annotated Bibliography,* State Historical Society of Wisconsin, 1973; (editor) *Weisberg v. General Services,* Volume I: *Freedom of Information Act and Po-litical Assassinations,* University of Wisconsin—Stevens Point Press, 1975; (co-editor) *The Assassination of John F. Kennedy: A Comprehensive Historical and Legal Bibliography, 1963-1979,* Greenwood Press, 1980.

Contributor to *Papers,* published by Abraham Lincoln Association. Contributor to journals, including *Journal of Ethnic Studies, Journalism Quarterly, Journal of the Illinois State Historical Society, Wisconsin Magazine of History, Illinois Libraries,* and *Civil War Times Illustrated.*

WORK IN PROGRESS: A book of essays on war and peace; a book on the history of objective idealism.

*   *   *

WYNNE, Brian
  See GARFIELD, Brian (Wynne)

*   *   *

WYNNE, Frank
  See GARFIELD, Brian (Wynne)

Y

YADIN, Yigael 1917-

PERSONAL: Original surname, Sukenik; name legally changed; born March 21, 1917, in Jerusalem, Israel; son of Eleazar (an archaeologist) and Chassia (Feinsod) Sukenik; married Carmella Ruppin, December 22, 1941; children: Orly and Littal (daughters). *Education:* Hebrew University, Jerusalem, M.A., 1946, Ph.D., 1955. *Religion:* Jewish. *Home:* 47 Ramban Rd., Jerusalem, Israel. *Office:* Hebrew University, Jerusalem, Israel.

CAREER: Served in Haganah (underground Jewish defense corps that later became Israel Defense Forces), 1932-48, instructor in small arms, 1937, instructor in officer training school, 1940-41, adjutant to chief of staff, 1941-45, chief of planning department, 1945-47, chief of operations, 1947-48; Israel Defense Forces, chief of operations, 1948-49, chief of general staff, 1949-52, became lieutenant general; Hebrew University, Jerusalem, Israel, lecturer, 1955-59, associate professor, 1959-63, professor of archaeology, 1963—; Government of Israel, Jerusalem, deputy prime minister and member of Knesset, 1977-81. Director of archaeological expeditions to Megiddo and Hazor, 1955-58, to caves near Dead Sea, 1960-61, and to Masada, 1963-65. Chairman of Democratic Movement for Change Party, 1977-81. *Member:* Israel Academy of Science and Humanities, British Academy (corresponding fellow), French Academy (corresponding fellow). *Awards, honors:* Israel Prize in Jewish Studies, 1956, for *Megilat milkheinet bneior, birnei hoshekh;* honorary degrees from Brandeis University, 1959, and Hebrew Union College, 1963.

WRITINGS: New Light on the Dead Sea Scrolls (lecture), American Israel Society, 1954; (editor and author of introduction) *Megilat milkheinet bneior, birnei hoshekh,* Bialik Institute (Jerusalem), 1955, translation by Batya Rabin and Chaim Rabin published as *The Scroll of the War of the Sons of Light against the Sons of Darkness,* Oxford University Press, 1962; (translator and transcriber with Nahman Avigad) *A Genesis Apocryphon: A Scroll from the Wilderness of Judea,* Magnes Press, 1956; *The Message of the Scrolls,* Simon & Schuster, 1957; *Hazor,* Volume I, Magnes Press, 1958, Volume II: (with Yohanan Aharoni, Ruth Amiran, and Trude Dothan) *An Account of the Second Season of Excavations, 1956,* Magnes Press, 1960, Volumes III-IV: (with others) *An Account of the Third and Fourth Seasons of Excavations, 1957-58,* Oxford University Press, 1965; (editor with Abe Harman) *Israel,* introduction by David Ben-Gurion, Doubleday, 1958; (editor

with Chaim Rabin) *Aspects of the Dead Sea Scrolls,* Oxford University Press, 1958, 2nd edition, Magnes Press, 1965.

Military and Archaeological Aspects of the Conquest of Canaan in the Book of Joshua, Department for Education and Culture in the Diaspora of the Jewish Agency, 1960, 3rd edition, Hahevra Leheker Hamikra, 1965; (with Yoshinori Maeda and John Kenneth Galbraith) *The Past Speaks to the Present, Television for Teaching,* [and] *The Language of Economics* (the first by Yadin, the second by Maeda, the third by Galbraith), Granada TV Network (Manchester), 1962; *Torat ha-milhamah be-artsot ha-mikra,* International Publishing, 1963, translation by Moshe Pearlman published as *The Art of Warfare in Biblical Lands in the Light of Archaeological Study,* two volumes, McGraw, 1963; *The Finds from the Bar Kokhba Period in the Cave of Letters,* Israel Exploration Society, 1963; (author of introductions and commentary) *The Ben Sira Scroll from Masada,* Israel Exploration Society (Jerusalem), 1965; *The Excavation of Masada, 1963-64, Preliminary Report,* Israel Exploration Society, 1965; (translator) William Foxwell Albright, *Ha-Arkhe'ologyah shel erets yisrae* (translation of *The Archaeology of Palestine*), Am-Oved, 1965; *Metsadah,* Ma'ariv & Shikmona, 1966, translation by Pearlman published as *Masada: Herod's Fortress and the Zealots' Last Stand,* Random House, 1966; *The Story of Masada,* adapted for young readers by Gerald Gottlieb, Random House, 1969; *Tefillin from Qumran,* Israel Exploration Society, 1969.

Bar-Kokhba: The Rediscovery of the Legendary Hero of the Second Jewish Revolt against Rome, Random House, 1971; *Hazor: With a Chapter on Israelite Meggido* (Schweich lectures), Oxford University Press for British Academy, 1972; *Hazor: The Rediscovery of a Great Citadel of the Bible,* Random House, 1975; (editor) *Jerusalem Revealed: Archaeology in the Holy City, 1968-1974,* translation by R. Grafman, Israel Exploration Society, 1976; *Megillah ha Gimiqdush* (title means "The Temple Scroll"), three volumes, Israel Exploration Society, 1978; *Hazor: The Head of All Those Kingdoms, Joshua 11:10, with a Chapter on Israelite Meggido,* State Mutual Book, 1979.

WORK IN PROGRESS: The Cave of Letters, Volume II.

SIDELIGHTS: Yigael Yadin is "virtually a household name" in Israel, writes Morton Kondracke in the *New Republic.* Military chief of staff in Israel's 1948 war of independence and more recently deputy prime minister of Israel, Yadin has seldom been out of the public eye. But he is best known as an archaeologist "in a country where," according to Naomi Shepherd in the *New Statesman*, "archaeology is a modern religion." Following in the footsteps of his father, Eleazar Sukenik, the archaeologist who is credited with identifying the Dead Sea Scrolls, Yigael Yadin has built an international reputation for himself in the same field. Yadin managed to acquire for Israel four of the Dead Sea Scrolls, and several of his books are transliterations and/or explications of them. The expedition he led at Hazor has, Yadin claims, confirmed the Biblical narrative of the Book of Joshua, and his exploration at Masada—the fortress where, in 73 A.D., a group of Jewish defenders, besieged for three years by Roman attackers, preferred suicide to surrender—produced a text identical to that of a Dead Sea Scroll found at Qumran. His discovery of the letters of Simon Bar Kokhba, the Jewish insurgent chief who led the last revolt against the Romans in 132-135 A.D., provided the first confirmation of Bar Kokhba's existence.

Yigael Yadin wrote *CA:* "I find it the greatest challenge to tell the intelligent layman of my scientific discoveries—not to 'talk down' or 'up,' not to impress him with my knowledge, but rather with my finding—and make him understand. . . . That is the reward!"

BIOGRAPHICAL/CRITICAL SOURCES: Times Literary Supplement, February 27, 1964; *New York Times*, September 28, 1966; Shane Miller, *Desert Fighter: The Story of General Yigael Yadin and the Dead Sea Scrolls*, Hawthorn, 1967; Gray Poole and Lynn Poole, *Men Who Dig up History*, Dodd, 1968; *Best Sellers*, May 1, 1969; *New York Times Book Review*, July 16, 1969; Morris Rosenblum, *Heroes of Israel*, Fleet Press, 1972; *New Statesman*, June 11, 1976; *Newsweek*, June 14, 1976; *Time*, January 24, 1977; *New Republic*, February 26, 1977.

*   *   *

YATES, Elizabeth   1905-

PERSONAL: Born December 6, 1905, in Buffalo, N.Y.; daughter of Harry and Mary (Duffy) Yates; married William McGreal, November 6, 1929 (died December, 1963). *Education:* Attended schools in Buffalo, N.Y. and Mamaroneck, N.Y. *Home and office:* 381 Old Street Rd., Peterborough, N.H. 03458.

CAREER: Writer, lecturer. Staff member at writers conferences at University of New Hampshire, University of Connecticut, and Indiana University, 1956—; instructor at Christian Writers and Editors conferences, Green Lake, Wis., 1962—. *Member:* Delta Kappa Gamma. *Awards, honors: New York Herald Tribune* Spring Book Festival juvenile award, 1943, for *Patterns on the Wall;* John Newbery Medal, 1951, and William Allen White Children's Book Award, 1953, both for *Amos Fortune, Free Man;* Boys' Clubs of America Gold Medal, 1953, for *A Place for Peter;* Jane Addams Children's Book Award from U.S. section of Women's International League for Peace and Freedom, 1955, for *Rainbow 'round the World;* Sara Josepha Hale Award, 1970. Litt.D. from Aurora College, 1965, Eastern Baptist College, 1966, University of New Hampshire, 1967, Ripon College, 1970, New England College, 1972, Rivier College, 1978, and Franklin Pierce College, 1981.

WRITINGS: High Holiday, A. & C. Black, 1938; *Gathered Grace*, Heffer, 1938; *Hans and Frieda*, Thomas Nelson, 1939; *Climbing Higher*, A. & C. Black, 1939, Knopf, 1940; *Haven for the Brave*, Knopf, 1941; *Under the Little Fir*, Coward, 1942; *Around the Year in Iceland*, Heath, 1942; *Patterns on the Wall*, Knopf, 1943; *Mountain Born*, Coward, 1943; *Wind of Spring*, Coward, 1945; *Nearby*, Coward, 1947; *Once in the Year*, Coward, 1947; *The Young Traveller in the U.S.A.*, Phoenix House, 1948; *Beloved Bondage*, Coward, 1948.

Amos Fortune, Free Man, Aladdin, 1950; *Guardian Heart*, Coward, 1950; *Children of the Bible*, Aladdin, 1950; *Brave Interval*, Coward, 1952; *David Livingstone*, Row, Peterson & Co., 1952; *A Place for Peter*, Coward, 1953; *Hue and Cry*, Coward, 1953; *Your Prayers and Mine*, Houghton, 1954; *Rainbow 'round the World*, Bobbs-Merrill, 1954; *Prudence Crandall, Woman of Courage*, Aladdin, 1955; *The Carey Girl*, Coward, 1956; *Pebble in a Pool: The Widening Circles of Dorothy Canfield Fisher's Life*, Dutton, 1958; *The Lighted Heart*, Dutton, 1960; *The Next Fine Day*, John Day, 1962; *Someday You'll Write*, Dutton, 1962; *Sam's Secret Journal*, Friendship, 1964; *Carolina's Courage*, Dutton, 1964 (published in England as *Carolina and the Indian Doll*, Methuen, 1965); *Howard Thurman: Portrait of a Practical Dreamer*, John Day, 1964; *Up the Golden Stair*, Dutton, 1966; *Is There a Doctor in the Barn?*, Dutton, 1966; *With Pipe, Paddle and Song*, Dutton, 1968; *New Hampshire*, Coward, 1969; *On That Night*, Dutton, 1969; *Sara Whitcher's Story*, Dutton, 1971; *Lady from Vermont*, Stephen Greene, 1971; *Skeezer, Dog with a Mission*, Harvey House, 1972; *The Road through Sandwich Notch*, Stephen Greene, 1972; *We, the People*, Countryman Press, 1974; *A Book of Hours*, Vineyard Books, 1976; *Call It Zest*, Stephen Greene, 1977; *The Seventh One*, Walker & Co., 1978; *My Diary-My World*, Westminster, 1981; *Silver Lining*, Phoenix Publishing, 1981.

Editor and adapter: Enys Tregarthen, *Piskey Folk*, John Day, 1940; Tregarthen, *The Doll Who Came Alive*, John Day, 1942; *Joseph*, Knopf, 1947; Tregarthen, *The White Ring*, Harcourt, 1949; *The Christmas Story*, Knopf, 1949; George MacDonald, *Sir Gibbie*, Dutton, 1963. Contributor of articles, essays, and reviews to magazines and journals.

SIDELIGHTS: Elizabeth Yates told *CA:* "I'm a born recycler, for my desire is to use things in the most practical way. . . . Much of my early life was spent on my father's large productive farm. The rotation of crops, the rhythm of the seasons, the necessary hard work, together with the inter-relationships of animals and the land, were all meaningful. Everything had a purpose and deserved respect, and in the year's orderly procedure there was much beauty to be found.

"A deep and ever deepening conviction of the enduring nature of good has been my mainstay. Looking for it in people and in situations has given me that upon which I can build. As a person, I want to put myself on the side of good, no matter how small my service, and so make my life count in the sum total."

*   *   *

YORK, Carol Beach   1928-

PERSONAL: Born January 21, 1928, in Chicago, Ill.; daughter of Harold and Mary (Cantwell) Beach; married Richard Marten York, 1947 (divorced, 1969); children: Diana Carol. *Education:* Attended Thornton Junior College. *Residence:* Chicago, Ill.

CAREER: Author.

WRITINGS: Sparrow Lake, Coward, 1962; (with Mary Beach) *One Summer*, Coward, 1963; *Where Love Begins*, Coward, 1963; *The Doll in the Bake Shop*, F. Watts, 1965; *Ghost of the Isherwoods*, F. Watts, 1966; *Miss Know It All*, F. Watts, 1966; *Until We Fall in Love Again*, F. Watts, 1967; *The Christmas Dolls*, F. Watts, 1967; *The Blue Umbrella*, F. Watts, 1968; *The Good Day Mice*, F. Watts, 1968; *The Mystery of the Diamond Cat*, F. Watts, 1969; *Good Charlotte*, F. Watts, 1969.

The Ten O'Clock Club, F. Watts, 1970; *Nothing Ever Happens Here*, Hawthorn, 1970; *Mystery at Dark Wood*, F. Watts, 1972; *Miss Know It All Returns*, F. Watts, 1972; *Dead Man's Cat*, Thomas Nelson, 1972; *The Tree House Mystery*, Coward, 1973; *Mystery of the Spider Doll*, F. Watts, 1973; *Takers and Returners*, Thomas Nelson, 1973; *The Midnight Ghost*, Coward, 1973; *I Will Make You Disappear*, Thomas Nelson, 1974; *The Witch Lady Mystery*, Thomas Nelson, 1976; *Beware of This Shop*, Thomas Nelson, 1977; *Revenge of the Dolls*, Thomas Nelson, 1979; *When Midnight Comes*, Thomas Nelson, 1979.

Remember Me When I Am Dead, Elsevier-Dutton, 1980; *Stray Dog*, Beaufort Books, 1981; *The Look-Alike Girl*, Beaufort Books, 1981.

Published by Troll Associates, 1980: *Casey Jones; Febold Feboldson: The Fit-it Farmer; Johnny Appleseed; Mike Fink; Old Stormalong: The Seafaring Sailor; Sam Patch: The Big Time Jumper; Washington Irving's Ichabod Crane and the Headless Horseman; Washington Irving's Rip Van Winkle.*

Also author of short stories and nonfiction for women's and children's magazines.

SIDELIGHTS: Carol Beach York told *CA:* "I began to write when I was about seven years old. I wrote poems and short stories in spiral notebooks that sold (then) for ten cents apiece. My mother was my only reader.

"When I was in my twenties I began to write and submit short stories for women's and children's magazines, and then to write books for children. I enjoy 'elaborating' more than one can in short stories, so once I started on books I never went back to short stories. I love typing 'Chapter One' at the head of a page.

"*Where Love Begins* is based on a real true experience from my high school days, when, like the girls in the story, my girlfriend and I fell in love with two trapeze performers at a circus. *Until We Fall in Love Again* is also based largely on experiences from my own teenage years.

"Lately I have been writing mostly mysteries. They are fun to write. It is fun to decide exactly how many clues to give the reader without giving the final conclusion away."

*　　*　　*

YOUNG, Alan   1930-

PERSONAL: Born September 30, 1930, in Manchester, England; son of John (an electrical engineer) and Elsie (Armstrong) Young; married Renee Briscoe (a teacher), July 27, 1957; children: Jenny, Jonathan. *Education:* Sheffield City College, certificate in education, 1952; University of Manchester, B.A. (with honors), 1955, M.A., 1958, Ph.D., 1974. *Politics:* None. *Religion:* None. *Home:* 'Brook House," 5 Brook Lane, Timperley, Altrincham, Cheshire WA15 6RL, England. *Office:* Department of Arts Education, Manchester Polytechnic, Manchester, England.

CAREER: English and philosophy teacher in schools in Manchester, England, 1956-62; Didsbury College of Education, Manchester, principal lecturer in English studies, 1962-75, head of arts, 1975-78; Manchester Polytechnic, Manchester, head of arts education, 1978-82. Has lectured for Extra-Mural Department, University of Manchester, and has conducted radio braodcasts on literature and the arts for British Broadcasting Corp.

WRITINGS: (Contributor) Arthur Pollard and Ralph Willett, editors, *Webster's New World Companion to English and American Literature*, World Publishing, 1973; (editor) Edgell

Rickword, *Essays and Opinions: 1921-1931*, Dufour, 1974; (editor) *Literature in Society: Edgell Rickward's Essays and Opinions, 1931-1978*, Humanities Press, 1978; (contributor) Peter Jones and Michael Schmidt, editors, *British Poetry since 1970: A Critical Survey*, Carcanet, 1980; *Dada and After: Extremist Modernism and English Literature*, Humanities Press, 1981; (with Alan Munton) *Seven Writers of the English Left: A Bibliography of Literature and Politics 1916-1980*, Garland Publishing, 1981. Contributor to literary journals, including *Poetry Nation, Critical Quarterly, English in Education, Times Literary Supplement,* and *Tarasque.*

WORK IN PROGRESS: Contributing to a volume of *Dictionary of Literary Biography* on British poets from Thomas Hardy to World War II, for Gale.

AVOCATIONAL INTERESTS: Mozart, Manchester United Association Football Club, cricket.

*　　*　　*

YOUNG, J(ames) Harvey   1915-

PERSONAL: Born September 8, 1915, in Brooklyn, N.Y.; son of W. Harvey and Blanche (De Bra) Young; married Myrna Goode, 1940; children: Harvey Galen, James Walter. *Education:* Knox College, A.B., 1937; University of Illinois, A.M., 1938, Ph.D., 1941. *Home:* 272 Heaton Park Dr., Decatur, Ga. *Office:* Department of History, Emory University, Atlanta, Ga. 30322.

CAREER: Emory University, Atlanta, Ga., 1941—, began as instructor, professor of history, 1941-80, Candler Professor of American Social History, 1980—, chairman of department, 1958-66. Visiting professor, Columbia University, 1949-50. *Military service:* U.S. Army, 1943-45. *Member:* Various historical associations, Phi Beta Kappa, Phi Kappa Phi, Omicron Delta Kappa, Sigma Xi.

WRITINGS: The Toadstool Millionaires, Princeton University Press, 1961; (co-editor) *Truth, Myth, and Symbol*, Prentice-Hall, 1962; (contributor) Paul Talalay, editor, *Drugs in Our Society*, Johns Hopkins Press, 1964; *The Medical Messiahs*, Princeton University Press, 1967; *Quacksabler*, Lempp Verlag, 1972; *American Self-Dosage Medicines*, Coronado Press, 1974. Contributor of articles on social, intellectual, and medical history to journals.

WORK IN PROGRESS: A book on the history of food and drug regulation in America.

*　　*　　*

YOUNG, Philip   1918-

PERSONAL: Born May 26, 1918, in Boston, Mass.; son of Roswell Philip (a businessman) and Katharine (Pratt) Young; married Carolyn Anderson, February 12, 1944 (died, February 24, 1967); married Katherine Garner, November, 1968; children: (first marriage) Jeffrey Anderson; (second marriage) Rosalie. *Education:* Amherst College, B.A., 1940; graduate study at Harvard University, 1940-41; University of Iowa, Ph.D., 1948. *Politics:* Independent. *Home:* 525 West Park Ave., State College, Pa. 16801. *Agent:* Robert Lescher, 155 East 71st St., New York, N.Y. 10021. *Office:* 136 South Burrowes, Pennsylvania State University, University Park, Pa. 16802.

CAREER: New York University, New York, N.Y., 1948-53, began as instructor, became assistant professor of English; Kansas State University, Manhattan, associate professor of English, 1953-59; Pennsylvania State University, University Park, professor of American literature, 1959-66, research professor of English and fellow in the Institute for Arts and Humanistic Studies, 1966—. Visiting professor at University of Minnesota, 1955-56; U.S. Department of State specialist in India, 1957; Fulbright lecturer in France and Italy, 1962-63. *Military service:* U.S. Army, 1942-46; served in European theater; became first lieutenant; received Air Medal, three battle stars. *Member:* Modern Language Association of America, P.E.N. *Awards, honors:* American Council of Learned Societies scholar, 1950-51; D.H.L., Westminster College, 1971; American Revolution Round Table Award, 1978, for *Revolutionary Ladies*.

WRITINGS: Ernest Hemingway, Rinehart, 1952, revised edition published as *Ernest Hemingway: A Reconsideration*, Pennsylvania State University Press, 1966; (editor and author of introduction) Nathaniel Hawthorne, *The House of the Seven Gables*, Rinehart, 1957, revised edition, 1970; *Ernest Hemingway* (pamphlet), University of Minnesota Press, 1959; (editor) Herman Melville, *Typee*, Cassell, 1967; (editor with William White) *By-Line: Ernest Hemingway*, Collins, 1968; (with Charles W. Mann) *The Hemingway Manuscripts: An Inventory*, Pennsylvania State University Press, 1969; *Three Bags Full: Essays in American Fiction*, Harcourt, 1972; (editor) Ernest Hemingway, *The Nick Adams Stories*, Scribner, 1972; (editor with Stanley Weintraub) *Directions in Literary Criticism*, Pennsylvania State University Press, 1973; *Revolutionary Ladies*, Knopf, 1977.

Contributor: Robert P. Weeks, editor, *Hemingway: A Collection of Critical Essays*, Prentice-Hall, 1962; Bernard S. Oldsey and Arthur O. Lewis, Jr., editors, *Visions and Revisions in Modern American Literary Criticism*, Dutton, 1962; Carlos Baker, editor, *Ernest Hemingway: Critiques of Four Major Novels*, Scribner, 1962; James E. Miller, Jr. and Bernice Slote, editors, *Dimensions of the Short Story: A Critical Anthology*, Dodd, 1964; William Van O'Connor, editor, *Seven Modern American Novelists: An Introduction*, University of Minnesota Press, 1964; David Madden, editor, *Tough Guy Writers of the Thirties*, Southern Illinois University Press, 1968; R. Astro

and J. Nenson, editors, *Hemingway in Our Time*, Oregon State University Press, 1974; Jackson Benson, editor, *The Short Stories of Ernest Hemingway: Critical Essays*, Duke University Press, 1975; Myron Simon and Harvey Gross, editors, *Teacher and Critic: Essays by and about Austin Warren*, Plantin Press, 1976. Also contributor to other collections of criticism.

Contributor of articles on three American writers to *Dictionary of World Literature in Twentieth Century*, and of articles on Hemingway to *Collier's Encyclopedia, Reader's Encyclopedia of American Literature, Encyclopaedia Britannica*, and *Encyclopedia Americana;* contributor of articles on more than seventy authors to *Encyclopedia International*, 1963. Contributor of articles and reviews to periodicals, including *Sewanee Review, Kenyon Review, Southern Review, American Literature*, and *Atlantic*.

WORK IN PROGRESS: Dark Lady of the Republic.

SIDELIGHTS: Philip Young's *Ernest Hemingway* has been published in England and in German and Spanish translations; his pamphlet on the same writer has appeared in many translations, including Korean, Hindi, Arabic, Pushtu, Polish, Marathi, and French. Tagged as "the Hemingway man," Young told *CA:* "I think as well of my 'mythic studies' of Rip Van Winkle and Pocahontas, collected in *Three Bags Full* and many times reprinted. Indeed I am an admirer of . . . *Revolutionary Ladies*, though I have very little company."

BIOGRAPHICAL/CRITICAL SOURCES: Books Abroad, spring, 1967; *Times Literary Supplement*, March 7, 1968; *Listener*, March 14, 1968; *New York Times Book Review*, March 14, 1972; *Book World*, March 19, 1972; *Dialogue*, number 1, 1973.

*   *   *

YU-HO, Tseng
  See ECKE, Betty Tseng Yu-ho

Z

ZALL, Paul M. 1922-

PERSONAL: Born August 3, 1922, in Lowell, Mass.; son of Nathan and Bertha (Rubin) Zall; married Elisabeth Weisz, June 28, 1948; children: Jonathan, Andrew, Barnaby. *Education:* Swarthmore College, B.A., 1948; Harvard University, A.M., 1951, Ph.D., 1952. *Home:* 1911 Leman St., South Pasadena, Calif. *Office:* Department of English, California State University, 5151 State College Dr., Los Angeles, Calif. 90032.

CAREER: Cornell University, Ithaca, N.Y., instructor, 1952-55; University of Oregon, Eugene, instructor, 1955-56; Boeing Airplane Co., Seattle, Wash., technical research editor, 1956-57; California State University, Los Angeles, associate professor, 1957-63, professor of English, 1963—. Instructor, University of Washington, 1956-57. *Military service:* U.S. Air Force, Ordnance. *Member:* Modern Language Association of America, Renaissance Council of Southern California. *Awards, honors:* American Philosophical Society grant, 1964-68; John Carter Brown Library fellow, 1968.

WRITINGS: Elements of Technical Report Writing, Harper, 1962; (editor) *A Hundred Merry Tales*, University of Nebraska Press, 1963; *Literary Criticism of William Wordsworth*, University of Nebraska Press, 1966; (editor) *Simple Cobler of Aggawam*, University of Nebraska Press, 1969; (editor) *A Nest of Ninnies*, University of Nebraska Press, 1970; *Peter Pindar's Poems*, University of South Carolina Press, 1972; (editor) *Comical Spirit of Seventy-six*, Huntington Library, 1976; (editor) *Franklin's Autobiography: Genetic Text*, University of Tennessee Press, 1981; *Ben Franklin Laughing*, University of California Press, 1981. Contributor of over fifty articles on the English Romantic period to journals; also contributor of articles to technical journals in connection with technical research editing.

WORK IN PROGRESS: Anecdotes of Abe Lincoln.

*   *   *

ZANDERBERGEN, George
See MAY, Julian

*   *   *

ZEISEL, Hans 1905-

PERSONAL: Born December 1, 1905, in Kaaden, Czechoslovakia; son of Otto and Elsa (Frank) Zeisel; married Eva Striker (an industrial designer), 1938; children: Jean, John. *Education:* University of Vienna, Austria, Dr.Jur., 1927, Dr. Political Science, 1928. *Home:* 5825 South Dorchester, Chicago, Ill. 60637. *Office:* Law School, University of Chicago, Chicago, Ill. 60637.

CAREER: Marketing research consultant, Bata Shoe Co., Czechoslovakia, 1935, and Benton & Bowles, 1941; consultant, Bureau of Applied Social Research, 1942; Rutgers University, New Brunswick, N.J., instructor in economics and statistics, 1943; McCann-Erickson, Inc. (advertising agency), New York City, director of research and development, 1943-49; Tea Council of United States, New York City, director of research, 1949-53; University of Chicago, Chicago, Ill., professor of law and sociology, 1953-76, professor emeritus, 1976—. Instructor, Columbia University and New School for Social Research, 1951. Consultant to U.S. War Department, 1940-43, American Bar Foundation, Austrian Ministry of Justice, Police Foundation, and Rand Corp.; vice-president of research, Vera Institute of Justice, 1972-76. *Member:* American Statistical Association, American Sociological Society, American Association for Public Opinion Research, Market Research Council (former president). *Awards, honors:* American Association for Public Opinion Research award, 1964; National Science Foundation fellow, District Court of Chicago, 1972-73.

WRITINGS: (With Marie Jahoda and Paul F. Lazarfeld) *Die Arbeitslosen von Marienthal*, Hirzel, 1933, translation by the authors and others published as *Marienthal: The Sociography of an Unemployed Community*, Aldine-Atherton, 1971; *Say It with Figures*, Harper, 1947, 5th edition, 1968; (with Bernard Buchholz and Harry Kalven, Jr.) *Delay in the Court*, Little, Brown, 1959; (with Kalven) *The American Jury*, Little, Brown, 1966; *Some Data on Juror Attitudes Towards Capital Punishment*, University of Chicago Law School, 1968; (with Lucy N. Freidman) *First Annual Research Report on Supported Employment*, Vera Institute of Justice, 1973.

AVOCATIONAL INTERESTS: Shakespeare studies.

*   *   *

ZELDIS, Chayym 1927-

PERSONAL: Born October 7, 1927, in Buffalo, N.Y.; married Nina Zonenshine, 1974; children: (first marriage) David, Yona; (second marriage) Hope, Jodi. *Education:* Attended University of Michigan, 1945-47, and New School for Social Research, 1958-61. *Office:* Women's American ORT, 1250 Broadway, New York, N.Y. 10001.

CAREER: Writer and public relations man; currently affiliated with Women's American ORT, New York, N.Y. *Awards, honors:* Avery Hopwood Award in Poetry, University of Michigan, 1945; John Day Novel Award, New School for Social Research, 1958.

WRITINGS: Streams in the Wilderness, Yoseloff, 1962; (contributor) *American Scene: New Voices,* edited by Don Wolfe, Lyle Stuart, 1963; *Seek Haven* (verse), Reconstructionist Press, 1968; (editor) *May My Words Feed Others* (anthology), A. S. Barnes, 1968; *Golgotha* (novel), Avon, 1974; *Brothers* (novel), Random House, 1976; *The Marriage Bed* (novel), Putnam, 1978; *The Brothel* (novel), Putnam, 1979. Short stories have appeared in *New Campus Writing 3,* Grove, 1959, and *New Voices 4,* Hendricks House, 1960. Translator of books and articles from Hebrew. Contributor of poetry and fiction to literary magazines.

WORK IN PROGRESS: Three novels, *The Cuckold, Agreement with Zotoz,* and *The Healer.*

SIDELIGHTS: Chayym Zeldis spent nine years in Israel living in various agricultural settlements.

*   *   *

ZERNOV, Nicolas (Michael)   1898-1980

PERSONAL: Born October 9, 1898, in Moscow, Russia; died August 25, 1980; son of Michael and Sophia (Kesler) Zernov; married Militza Lavrov, 1927. *Education:* Moscow University, medical student, 1917; University of Belgrade, B.A. in Theology, 1925; Oxford University, D.Phil., 1932, M.A., 1947, D.D., 1967. *Religion:* Russian Orthodox. *Home:* 4A Northmoor Rd., Oxford OX2 6UP, England.

CAREER: General secretary, Russian Student Christian Movement Outside Russia, 1925-35; secretary, Fellowship of St. Albans and St. Sergius, 1935-47; Oxford University, Oxford, England, Spalding Lecturer in Eastern Orthodox Culture, 1947-66. Principal of Catholicate College, South India, 1953-54; visiting professor at Drew University, 1956, University of Iowa, and Duke University. Vice-president of Fellowship of St. Albans and St. Sergius; warden of St. Gregory and St. Macrina House, Oxford University. *Member:* Royal Society of Literature (fellow).

WRITINGS: Moscow, the Third Rome, Macmillan, 1937, reprinted, AMS Press, 1971; *St. Sergius, Builder of Russia,* Macmillan, 1939; *The Church of the Eastern Christians,* S.P.C.K., 1942, Macmillan, 1944; *Three Russian Prophets: Khomiakov, Dostoevsky, Soloviev,* S.C.M. Press, 1944, 3rd edition, Academic International, 1973; *The Russians and Their Church,* Macmillan, 1945, 3rd edition, S.P.C.K., 1964; (editor) *Manual of Eastern Orthodox Prayers,* Macmillan, 1945.

The Reintegration of the Church: A Study of Intercommunion, S.C.M. Press, 1952, Seabury, 1953; *Vselenskaia tserkov i russkoe pravoslavie,* Y.M.C.A. Press (Paris), 1952; *Ruslands kirke og nordens kirke,* [Copenhagen], 1954; *The Christian East: The Eastern Orthodox Church and Indian Christianity,* S.P.C.K. (Delhi), 1956; *Eastern Christendom: A Study of the Origins and Development of the Eastern Orthodox Church,* Putnam, 1961; *Orthodox Encounter: The Christian East and the Ecumenical Movement,* James Clarke, 1961; *Il Christianismo orientale Milano,* Il Saggiatore, 1962; *Christianismo orientale Madrid,* Ed. Guadarrama, 1962; *The Russian Religious Renaissance of the Twentieth Century,* Darton, Longman & Todd,

1963, Harper, 1964; (editor) Aleksei Khomiakov, *The Church Is One,* Fellowship of St. Alban and St. Sergius, 1968.

Na Perelome (about three generations of a Moscow family), Y.M.C.A. Press, 1970; *Za Rubegtom* (chronicle of the Zernov family), Y.M.C.A. Press, 1972; *Russian Emigre Authors: A Biographical Index and Bibliography of Their Works on Theology, Religious Philosophy, Church History and Orthodox Culture, 1921-1972,* G. K. Hall, 1973; (editor with James Pain) Sergius Bulgakov, *A Bulgakov Anthology: From Marxism to Christian Orthodoxy,* Westminster, 1976. Contributor of articles and book reviews to professional journals.†

*   *   *

ZOLLA, Elemire   1926-

PERSONAL: Born July 9, 1926, in Turin, Italy; son of Venanzio (a painter) and Blanche (a pianist; maiden name, Smith) Zolla. *Education:* University of Turin, Doctor in Jurisprudence, 1954. *Home:* Via Merulana 183, 00185 Rome, Italy. *Office:* Department of English and American Literature, University of Rome, Via Magenta 2, 00185 Rome, Italy.

CAREER: Tempo Presente (magazine), Rome, Italy, literary critic, 1956-59; University of Rome, Rome, 1959-67, began as lecturer, became professor of American literature; University of Catania, Catania, Italy, professor of English literature and chairman of department of American literature, 1967-70; University of Genoa, Genoa, Italy, professor of Germanic philology, chairman of department of American literature, and director of Institute of Foreign Languages, 1970-74; University of Rome, professor of American literature and chairman of department, 1974—. Secretary-general, Instituto Accademico di Roma, 1967-68; lecturer in the United States under auspices of U.S. Department of State, 1968; member of American Commission for Cultural Exchange with Italy, Italian Ministry of Foreign Affairs, 1968; director of Istituto Ticinese di Alti Studi (summer institute in symbology and archaeology), Lugano, Switzerland, 1969-73. *Awards, honors:* Premio Strega, opera prima, 1956, for *Minuetto all'inferno;* Premio Crotone, 1959, for *Eclissi dell'intellettuale.*

WRITINGS: Minuetto all'inferno (novel), Einaudi (Turin), 1956; *Eclissi dell'intellettuale* (essay), Bompiani (Milan), 1956, 5th edition, 1965, translation by Raymond Rosenthal published as *The Eclipse of the Intellectual* (also see below), Funk, 1969; *Cecilia; o, La Disattenzione* (novel), Garzanti, 1961; *Volgarita e dolore* (essay), Bompiani, 1962, 3rd edition, 1966, English translation included in *The Eclipse of the Intellectual; Le origini del trascendentalismo* (essay), Edizioni di Storia e Letteratura (Rome), 1963; *Storia del fantasticare* (essay), Bompiani, 1964; (translator into Spanish) Herman Melville, *Clarel,* Einaudi, 1965; *I Letterati e lo sciamano* (essay on the Indian in American literature), Bompiani, 1968, translation by Rosenthal published as *The Writer and the Shaman: Morphology of the American Indian,* Harcourt, 1973; *Le potenze dell'anima* (essay), Bompiani, 1968; *Che cos'e la tradizione?* (essay), Bompiani, 1971; *La meraviglie della natura: Introduzione all'alchimia,* Bompiani, 1973; *Language and Cosmogony,* Golgonooza Press, 1974; *The Uses of Imagination and the Decline of the West,* Golgonooza Press, 1978; *Archetypes,* Allen & Unwin, 1980; *The Androgyne: The Creative Tension of Male and Female,* Crossroads Books, 1981.

Editor: (With Alberto Moravia) *I Moralisti moderni* (anthology), Garzanti (Milan), 1959; *La Psicanalisi* (anthology), Garzanti, 1960; Emily Dickinson, *Selected Poems and Letters,* U. Mursia (Milan), 1961; *Antologia di Sade,* Longnesi, 1962; *I Mistici* (anthology), Garzanti, 1963, revised edition published in four volumes, Rizzoli, 1978-81; *Novencento Americano,* three volumes, Lucarini, 1980-81. Also editor of *L'esotismo nella letteratura americana,* Volume I, La Nuova Italia, Volume II, Lucarini. Editor of "Paramita" series, Rizzoli, 1981—. *Conoscenza Religiosa* (religious and literary studies quarterly), founder and director, 1969—, editor of special issues, 1970—.

Contributor: Rosenthal, editor, *McLuhan: Pro and Con,* Funk, 1968; T.M.P. Mahadevan, editor, *Spiritual Perspectives,* Heinemann (New Delhi), 1975; Yusuf Ibish and Ileana Marculescu, editors, *Contemplation and Action in World Religions,* University of Washington Press, 1978; T. A. Riese, editor, *Vistas of a Continent,* Anglistische Forschungen, 1979. Contributor to *Enciclopedia del Novecento,* 1981. Contributor to special issues of *Conoscenza Religiosa* and to other periodicals, including *Lo Spettatore Italiano, Il Pensiero Critico, Tempo Presente, Questioni, Nuovi Argomenti, Corriere della Sera* (Milan), and *La Nacion* (Buenos Aires).

SIDELIGHTS: A *Times Literary Supplement* critic calls Elemire Zolla "a thinker who must be watched. . . . His deep, polymathic probing of the terms of human existence makes it sensible to compare him with Simone Weil, while some of his conclusions about ultimate mysteries—expressed in signs, symbols and sacraments, the sense of which we have lost—will make us think of the later T. S. Eliot or the *Anathemata* of David Jones. . . . Far from being a romantic . . . , he writes in the spirit of a poet and artist in rebellion against a delirium of that negation which, according to Aquinas, was a definition of evil."

The Eclipse of the Intellectual is a study of twentieth-century philosophy and art against the background of technology and the blinding plea of human progress. Elaine Bender of *Library Journal* calls the book "a fascinating criticism by a man who seems to be able to generalize in spite of the fragmentation of our culture." Roger Shattuck writes in the *New York Review of Books* that Zolla "is concerned not so much with the avant-garde as with the modern. . . . His material is only slightly unfamiliar; Croce, Ortega, and Walter Benjamin have furnished him with some of his most important concepts. [But] beneath lies a slow-burning Catholicism that finally gives a passionate tone to his case against a culture produced by the trauma of the machine." Though Shattuck admits that Zolla "writes with power," he believes that Zolla "all too often deals in stereotypes and finally convinces me that he is in closer touch with the printed record of our lives than with those lives themselves. . . . I hear a man resolutely defending an intellectual position that he knows he will not be able to hold long in the face of forces to which he, more than most, is sensitive."

The Writer and the Shaman is a study of how American literature, in its images of the Indian, reflects the means by which a people and a culture have been destroyed on behalf of the idea of progress. A. H. DeRosier claims in *American Academy of Political and Social Science Annals* that this is the first "synthesis of the ideas that made possible a program of genocide that lasted for centuries." In the *Hudson Review,* Guy Davenport says that Zolla is "commendably thorough and searching: this book deserves the adjective *authoritative*. It will assume the status of *the* survey of the American Indian in our literature, and many theses will be generated from its ideas, pro and contra."

BIOGRAPHICAL/CRITICAL SOURCES: La Fiera Literaria, June 17, 1956, November 15, 1969, March 16, 1961; *Paragone,* XII, 1959, VIII, 1961; *Vitae Pensiers,* January, 1969; *Library Journal,* January 1, 1969; *New York Times Book Review,* August 10, 1969; *New York Review of Books,* March 12, 1970; *La Nacion,* April 2, 1971; *Settanta,* April 3, 1971; *Esquire,* May, 1971, May, 1974; *Times Literary Supplement,* October 29, 1971; *Choice,* March, 1974; *Hudson Review,* spring, 1974; *American Academy of Political and Social Science Annals,* July, 1974.